W9-DDE-007

The Sporting News

BASEBALL REGISTER

2000 EDITION

Editors/Baseball Register
BRENDAN ROBERTS
DAVID WALTON

Contributing Editor/Baseball Register
JOHN DUXBURY

The Sporting News

Efrem Zimbalist III, President and Chief Executive Officer, Times Mirror Magazines; **James H. Nuckols,** President, The Sporting News; **Francis X. Farrell,** Senior Vice President, Publisher; **John D. Rawlings,** Senior Vice President, Editorial Director; **John Kastberg,** Vice President, General Manager; **Kathy Kinkeade,** Vice President, Operations; **Steve Meyerhoff,** Executive Editor; **Joe Hoppel,** Senior Editor; **Ron Smith,** Senior Editor; **Craig Carter,** Statistical Editor; **Marilyn Kasal,** Production Director; **Terry Shea,** Database Analyst; **Michael Bruner,** Prepress Director; **Michael Behrens,** Art Director, Special Projects; **Christen Webster,** Production Artist; **Dan Fitzgerald, Joe Klaas, Chris Paul** and **Josh Smith,** Editorial Assistants.

A Times Mirror
Company

Major league and minor league statistics compiled by STATS, Inc., Skokie, Ill.

Copyright ©2000 by The Sporting News, a division of Times Mirror Magazines, Inc.,
10176 Corporate Square Drive, Suite 200, St. Louis, MO 63132-2924. All rights reserved. Printed in the U.S.A.

ISBN: 0-89204-629-5

10 9 8 7 6 5 4 3 2 1

CONTENTS

EXPLANATION OF FOOTNOTES AND ABBREVIATIONS

Note for statistical comparisons: Player strikes forced the cancellation of games in the 1972 season (10 days missed), the 1981 season (50 days missed), the 1994 season (52 days missed) and the 1995 season (18 games missed).

Positions are listed in descending order of games played; because of limited space, pinch-hitter and pinch-runner are listed in the regular-season section only if a player did not play a defensive position.

*   Led league. For fielding statistics, the player led the league at the position shown.

•   Tied for league lead. For fielding statistics, the player tied for the league lead at the position shown.

†   Led league, but number indicated is total figure for two or more positions. Actual league-leading figure for a position is mentioned in "Statistical Notes" section.

‡   Tied for league lead, but number indicated is total figure for two or more positions. Actual league-tying figure for a position is mentioned in "Statistical Notes" section.

§   Led or tied for league lead, but total figure is divided between two different teams. Actual league-leading or league-tying figure is mentioned in "Statistical Notes" section.

■   Indicates a player's movement from one major league organization to another major league organization or to an independent minor league organization.

. . . Statistic unavailable, inapplicable, unofficial or mathematically impossible to calculate.

—   Manager statistic inapplicable.

LEAGUES: Aa., Am. Assoc.—American Association. **A.L.**—American. **App., Appal.**—Appalachian. **Ar., Ariz.**—Arizona. **Cal., Calif.**—California. **Car., Caro.**—Carolina. **CRL**—Cocoa Rookie. **DSL**—Dominican Summer. **East.**—Eastern. **Evan.**—Evangeline. **Fla. St., Florida St.,** **FSL**—Florida State. **GCL**—Gulf Coast. **GSL**—Gulf States. **In.-Am.**—Inter-American. **Int'l.**—International. **J.P., Jap. Pac., Jp. Pac.**—Japan Pacific. **Jp. Cen., Jp. Cn.**—Japan Central. **Mex.**—Mexican. **Mex. Cen.**—Mexican Center. **Mid., Midw.**—Midwest. **Miss.-O.V.**—Mississippi-Ohio Valley. **N.C. St.**—North Carolina State. **N.L.**—National. **North.**—Northern. **N'west**—Northwest. **NYP, NY-Penn**—New York-Pennsylvania. **Pac. Coast, PCL**—Pacific Coast. **Pio.**—Pioneer. **S. Atl., SAL**—South Atlantic. **Soph.**—Sophomore. **Sou., South.**—Southern. **Taiw.**—Taiwan. **Tex.**—Texas. **W. Car., W. Caro.**—Western Carolinas.

TEAMS: Aguas.—Aguascalientes. **Alb./Colon.**—Albany/Colonie. **Ariz.**—Arizona. **Ariz. D-backs**—Arizona League Diamondbacks. **Belling.**—Bellingham. **Birm.**—Birmingham. **Brevard Co.**—Brevard County. **Cant./Akr.**—Canton/Akron. **Ced. Rap.**—Cedar Rapids. **Cent. Ore.**—Central Oregon. **Central Vall.**—Central Valley. **Char., Charl.**—Charleston. **Chatt.**—Chattanooga. **Chiba Lot.**—Chiba Lotte. **Ciu. Juarez**—Ciudad Juarez. **Colo. Spr., Colo. Springs**—Colorado Springs. **Dall./Fort W.**—Dallas/Fort Worth. **Day. Beach.**—Daytona Beach. **Dm., Dom.**—Dominican. **Dom. B. Jays**—Dominican Blue Jays. **Elizabeth.**—Elizabethton. **Estadio Quis.**—Estadio Quisqueya. **Eve.**—Everett. **Fort Lauder.**—Fort Lauderdale. **Fukuoka**—Fukuoka Daiei. **GC**—Gulf Coast. **GC Astros-Or.**—Gulf Coast Astros-Orange. **GC Royals-Bl.**—Gulf Coast Royals-Blue. **GC Whi. Sox**—Gulf Coast White Sox. **Grays Har.**—Grays Harbor. **Greens.**—Greensboro. **Greenw.**—Greenwood. **Guana.**—Guanajuato. **H.P.-Thomas.**—High Point-Thomasville. **Hunting.**—Huntington. **Jacksonv.**—Jacksonville. **Johns. City**—Johnson City. **Kane Co.**—Kane County. **Lake Charl.**—Lake Charles. **Matt.**—Mattoon. **M.C., Mex. City**—Mexico City. **Med. Hat.**—Medicine Hat. **Monc.**—Monclova. **Niag. F., Niag. Falls**—Niagara Falls. **Okla. City**—Oklahoma City. **Pan. City**—Panama City. **Phoe.**—Phoenix. **Pomp. Beach**—Pompano Beach. **Pres. Lions**—President Lions. **Prin. Will., Prin. William**—Prince William. **Ral./Dur.**—Raleigh/Durham. **Rancho Cuca.**—Rancho Cucamonga. **Rocky Mount.**—Rocky Mountain. **Salt.**—Saltillo. **San. Dom., San. Domingo**—Santo Domingo. **San Bern.**—San Bernardino. **San Fran.**—San Francisco. **Schen.**—Schenectady. **Scran./W.B.**—Scranton/Wilkes-Barre. **S.C.**—South Carolina. **S.F. de Mac.**—San Francisco de Macoris. **San Luis Pot.**—San Luis Potosi. **S. Oregon**—Southern Oregon. **Spartan.**—Spartanburg. **St. Cath., St. Cathar.**—St. Catharines. **St. Peters.**—St. Petersburg. **States.**—Statesville. **Stock.**—Stockton. **T.-C.**—Tri-Cities. **Vanc.**—Vancouver. **Vent. Co.**—Ventura County. **W. Mich.**—West Michigan. **Win.-Salem, Winst.-Salem**—Winston-Salem. **Wis. Rap., Wis. Rapids**—Wisconsin Rapids. **W.P. Beach**—West Palm Beach. **W.Va.**—West Virginia. **Yuc.**—Yucatan.

STATISTICS: A—assists. **AB**—at-bats. **Avg.**—average. **BB**—bases on balls. **CG**—complete games. **E**—errors. **ER**—earned runs. **ERA**—earned-run average. **G**—games. **GIDP**—grounded into double plays. **GS**—games started. **H**—hits. **HR**—home runs. **IP**—innings pitched. **L**—losses. **Pct.**—winning percentage. **PO**—putouts. **Pos.**—position. **R**—runs. **RBI**—runs batted in. **SB**—stolen bases. **ShO**—shutouts. **SO**—strikeouts. **Sv.**—saves. **W**—wins. **2B**—doubles. **3B**—triples.

PLAYERS

ABBOTT, JEFF — OF — WHITE SOX

PERSONAL: Born August 17, 1972, in Atlanta. ... 6-2/200. ... Bats right, throws left. ... Full name: Jeffrey William Abbott.
HIGH SCHOOL: Dunwoody (Ga.).
COLLEGE: Kentucky.
TRANSACTIONS/CAREER NOTES: Selected by Chicago White Sox organization in 32nd round of free-agent draft (June 3, 1993); did not sign. ... Selected by White Sox organization in fourth round of free-agent draft (June 2, 1994). ... On Charlotte disabled list (May 30-June 28 and August 1-10, 1999).

									BATTING						FIELDING		
Year	Team (League)	Pos.	G	AB	R	H	2B	3B	HR	RBI	Avg.	BB	SO	SB	PO	A	E	Avg.
1994—	Sarasota (GCL)	OF	4	15	4	7	1	0	1	3	.467	4	0	2	4	0	0	1.000
—	Hickory (SAL)	OF	63	224	47	88	16	6	6	48	.393	38	33	2	106	0	2	.981
1995—	Prince Will. (Caro.)	OF	70	264	41	92	16	0	4	47	.348	26	25	7	88	3	4	.958
—	Birmingham (Sou.)	OF	55	197	25	63	11	1	3	28	.320	19	20	1	55	1	2	.966
1996—	Nashville (A.A.)	OF-DH	113	440	64	143	27	1	14	60	.325	32	50	12	186	5	2	.990
1997—	Nashville (A.A.)	OF-DH	118	465	*88	152	35	3	11	63	.327	41	52	12	237	6	0	*1.000
—	Chicago (A.L.)	OF-DH	19	38	8	10	1	0	1	2	.263	0	6	0	15	0	0	1.000
1998—	Chicago (A.L.)	OF-DH	89	244	33	68	14	1	12	41	.279	9	28	3	132	0	4	.971
1999—	Chicago (A.L.)	OF	17	57	5	9	0	0	2	6	.158	5	12	1	25	0	1	.962
—	Charlotte (I.L.)	OF	67	277	42	88	24	1	9	37	.318	16	27	2	136	4	3	.979
Major League totals (3 years)			125	339	46	87	15	1	15	49	.257	14	46	4	172	0	5	.972

ABBOTT, JIM — P

PERSONAL: Born September 19, 1967, in Flint, Mich. ... 6-3/210. ... Throws left, bats left. ... Full name: James Anthony Abbott.
HIGH SCHOOL: Flint (Mich.) Central.
COLLEGE: Michigan.
TRANSACTIONS/CAREER NOTES: Selected by Toronto Blue Jays organization in 36th round of free-agent draft (June 3, 1985); did not sign. ... Selected by California Angels organization in first round (eighth pick overall) of free-agent draft (June 1, 1988). ... On disabled list (July 12-August 8, 1992). ... Traded by Angels to New York Yankees for 1B J.T. Snow, P Jerry Nielsen and P Russ Springer (December 6, 1992). ... On disabled list (June 10-25, 1993). ... Granted free agency (December 23, 1994). ... Signed by Chicago White Sox (April 8, 1995). ... Traded by White Sox with P Tim Fortugno to Angels for P Andrew Lorraine, P Bill Simas, P John Snyder and OF McKay Christensen (July 27, 1995). ... Granted free agency (October 31, 1995). ... Re-signed by Angels (January 9, 1996). ... Released by Angels (March 31, 1997). ... Signed by White Sox organization (May 27, 1998). ... Granted free agency (November 5, 1998). ... Signed by Milwaukee Brewers (January 27, 1999). ... Released by Brewers (July 23, 1999).
HONORS: Named Golden Spikes Award winner by USA Baseball (1987). ... Named lefthanded pitcher on THE SPORTING NEWS college All-America team (1988). ... Named lefthanded pitcher on THE SPORTING NEWS A.L. All-Star team (1991).
STATISTICAL NOTES: Tied for A.L. lead with four balks in 1991. ... Pitched 4-0 no-hit victory against Cleveland (September 4, 1993).
MISCELLANEOUS: Member of 1988 U.S. Olympic baseball team.

Year	League	W	L	Pct.	ERA	G	GS	CG	ShO	Sv.	IP	H	R	ER	BB	SO
1989—	California (A.L.)	12	12	.500	3.92	29	29	4	2	0	181 1/3	190	95	79	74	115
1990—	California (A.L.)	10	14	.417	4.51	33	33	4	1	0	211 2/3	*246	116	106	72	105
1991—	California (A.L.)	18	11	.621	2.89	34	34	5	1	0	243	222	85	78	73	158
1992—	California (A.L.)	7	15	.318	2.77	29	29	7	0	0	211	208	73	65	68	130
1993—	New York (A.L.)■	11	14	.440	4.37	32	32	4	1	0	214	221	115	104	73	95
1994—	New York (A.L.)	9	8	.529	4.55	24	24	2	0	0	160 1/3	167	88	81	64	90
1995—	Chicago (A.L.)■	6	4	.600	3.36	17	17	3	0	0	112 1/3	116	50	42	35	45
—	California (A.L.)	5	4	.556	4.15	13	13	1	1	0	84 2/3	93	43	39	29	41
1996—	California (A.L.)	2	*18	.100	7.48	27	23	1	0	0	142	171	128	118	78	58
—	Vancouver (PCL)	0	2	.000	3.41	4	4	1	0	0	29	16	12	11	20	20
1997—							Out of organized baseball.									
1998—	Hickory (SAL)■	0	0	...	2.25	1	1	0	0	0	4	3	1	1	2	2
—	Winston-Salem (Caro.)	2	1	.667	5.40	4	4	0	0	0	21 2/3	17	13	13	7	13
—	Birmingham (Sou.)	2	3	.400	5.40	8	8	0	0	0	41 2/3	53	33	25	21	35
—	Calgary (PCL)	2	2	.500	2.61	5	5	1	0	0	31	31	9	9	9	20
—	Chicago (A.L.)	5	0	1.000	4.55	5	5	0	0	0	31 2/3	35	16	16	12	14
1999—	Milwaukee (N.L.)■	2	8	.200	6.91	20	15	0	0	0	82	110	71	63	42	37
A.L. totals (9 years)		85	100	.459	4.12	243	239	31	6	0	1592	1669	809	728	578	851
N.L. totals (1 year)		2	8	.200	6.91	20	15	0	0	0	82	110	71	63	42	37
Major League totals (10 years)		87	108	.446	4.25	263	254	31	6	0	1674	1779	880	791	620	888

ABBOTT, KURT — IF

PERSONAL: Born June 2, 1969, in Zanesville, Ohio. ... 6-0/198. ... Bats right, throws right. ... Full name: Kurt Thomas Abbott.
HIGH SCHOOL: Dixie Hollins (St. Petersburg, Fla.).
JUNIOR COLLEGE: St. Petersburg (Fla.) Junior College.
TRANSACTIONS/CAREER NOTES: Selected by Oakland Athletics organization in 15th round of free-agent draft (June 5, 1989). ... On Modesto disabled list (May 26-June 6, 1991). ... Traded by A's to Florida Marlins for OF Kerwin Moore (December 20, 1993). ... On Florida disabled list (April 19-May 6, 1995); included rehabilitation assignment to Charlotte (April 30-May 6). ... On Florida disabled list (May 6-21, 1996); included rehabilitation assignment to Charlotte (May 16-20). ... Traded by Marlins to A's for P Eric Ludwick (December 19, 1997). ... On Oakland disabled list (March 22-April 16, 1998); included rehabilitation assignment to Edmonton (April 7-16). ... Traded by A's to Colorado Rockies for a player to be named later and cash (June 9, 1998); A's acquired P Ara Petrosian to complete deal (June 16, 1998). ... On disabled list (May 23-June 7 and July 23-August 7, 1999). ... Granted free agency (November 1, 1999).
STATISTICAL NOTES: Led Arizona League shortstops with .922 fielding percentage in 1989. ... Led Southern League shortstops with 87 double plays in 1992. ... Career major league grand slams: 3.
MISCELLANEOUS: Holds Florida Marlins all-time record for most triples (19).

Year	Team (League)	Pos.	G	AB	R	H	2B	3B	HR	RBI	Avg.	BB	SO	SB	PO	A	E	Avg.
1989—	Arizona A's (Ariz.)	SS-2B-3B	36	155	27	42	5	3	0	25	.271	8	40	0	59	90	10	†.937
—	S. Oregon (N'west)	SS	5	10	2	1	0	0	0	1	.100	0	3	1	6	7	1	.929
1990—	Madison (Midw.)	SS-2B-3B	104	362	38	84	18	0	0	28	.232	47	74	21	180	268	40	.918
1991—	Modesto (Calif.)	SS	58	216	36	55	8	2	3	25	.255	29	55	6	78	130	9	.959
—	Huntsville (Sou.)	SS	53	182	18	46	6	1	0	11	.253	17	39	6	89	164	13	.951
1992—	Huntsville (Sou.)	SS	124	452	64	115	14	5	9	52	.254	31	75	16	196	342	29	*.949
—	Tacoma (PCL)	SS	11	39	2	6	1	0	0	1	.154	4	9	1	21	32	4	.930
1993—	Tacoma (PCL)	SS-DH	133	480	75	153	36	11	12	79	.319	33	123	19	*210	367	30	.951
—	Oakland (A.L.)	OF-SS-2B	20	61	11	15	1	0	3	9	.246	3	20	2	36	13	2	.961
1994—	Florida (N.L.)■	SS	101	345	41	86	17	3	9	33	.249	16	98	3	162	260	15	.966
1995—	Charlotte (I.L.)	SS	5	18	3	5	0	0	1	3	.278	1	3	1	5	15	2	.909
—	Florida (N.L.)	SS	120	420	60	107	18	7	17	60	.255	36	110	4	149	290	19	.959
1996—	Florida (N.L.)	SS-3B-2B	109	320	37	81	18	7	8	33	.253	22	99	3	123	205	12	.965
—	Charlotte (I.L.)	SS-2B-3B	18	69	20	26	10	1	5	11	.377	7	18	2	31	60	2	.978
1997—	Florida (N.L.)	2-O-S-3-DH	94	252	35	69	18	2	6	30	.274	14	68	3	126	136	8	.970
1998—	Edmonton (PCL)■	SS-DH	7	25	5	10	2	0	2	4	.400	6	8	0	9	13	4	.846
—	Oakland (A.L.)	S-O-DH-3	35	123	17	33	7	1	2	9	.268	10	34	2	46	70	11	.913
—	Colorado (N.L.)■	O-2-S-3-DH	42	71	9	18	6	0	3	15	.254	2	19	0	32	24	1	.982
1999—	Colorado (N.L.)	2-1-O-S	96	286	41	78	17	2	8	41	.273	16	69	3	188	151	4	.988
American League totals (2 years)			55	184	28	48	8	1	5	18	.261	13	54	4	82	83	13	.927
National League totals (6 years)			562	1694	223	439	94	21	51	212	.259	106	463	16	780	1066	59	.969
Major League totals (7 years)			617	1878	251	487	102	22	56	230	.259	119	517	20	862	1149	72	.965

DIVISION SERIES RECORD

Year	Team (League)	Pos.	G	AB	R	H	2B	3B	HR	RBI	Avg.	BB	SO	SB	PO	A	E	Avg.
1997—	Florida (N.L.)	2B-PH	3	8	0	2	0	0	0	0	.250	0	0	0	3	6	0	1.000

CHAMPIONSHIP SERIES RECORD

Year	Team (League)	Pos.	G	AB	R	H	2B	3B	HR	RBI	Avg.	BB	SO	SB	PO	A	E	Avg.
1997—	Florida (N.L.)	2B	2	8	0	3	1	0	0	0	.375	0	2	0	4	1	0	1.000

NOTES: Member of World Series championship team (1997).

WORLD SERIES RECORD

Year	Team (League)	Pos.	G	AB	R	H	2B	3B	HR	RBI	Avg.	BB	SO	SB	PO	A	E	Avg.
1997—	Florida (N.L.)	DH-PH	3	3	0	0	0	0	0	0	.000	0	1	0	...	...	...	

ABBOTT, PAUL   P   MARINERS

PERSONAL: Born September 15, 1967, in Van Nuys, Calif. ... 6-3/195. ... Throws right, bats right. ... Full name: Paul David Abbott.

HIGH SCHOOL: Sunny Hills (Fullerton, Calif.).

TRANSACTIONS/CAREER NOTES: Selected by Minnesota Twins organization in third round of free-agent draft (June 3, 1985). ... On Minnesota disabled list (March 28-June 5 and August 14-September 1, 1992). ... Released by Twins (March 2, 1993). ... Signed by Charlotte, Cleveland Indians organization (March 27, 1993). ... On Charlotte disabled list (April 8-May 6, 1993). ... Granted free agency (October 15, 1993). ... Signed by Omaha, Kansas City Royals organization (November 21, 1993). ... On disabled list (March 18-May 25 and June 16-30, 1994). ... Released by Omaha (June 30, 1994). ... Signed by Iowa, Chicago Cubs organization (March 17, 1995). ... Granted free agency (October 16, 1995). ... Signed by San Diego Padres organization (November 29, 1995). ... Granted free agency (October 15, 1996). ... Signed by Seattle Mariners organization (January 10, 1997). ... On Tacoma disabled list (May 23-July 14, 1997). ... On Orlando disabled list (April 2-August 21, 1998); included rehabilitation assignment to Arizona League Mariners (August 19-21). ... Released by Mariners (December 14, 1998). ... Re-signed by Mariners (January 21, 1999). ... On New Haven disabled list (April 9-June 12, 1999).

STATISTICAL NOTES: Pitched 3-0 no-hit victory against Palm Springs (June 26, 1988, seven innings).

Year	League	W	L	Pct.	ERA	G	GS	CG	ShO	Sv.	IP	H	R	ER	BB	SO
1985—	Elizabethton (Appl.)	1	5	.167	6.94	10	10	1	0	0	35	33	32	27	32	34
1986—	Kenosha (Midw.)	6	10	.375	4.50	25	15	1	0	0	98	102	62	49	73	73
1987—	Kenosha (Midw.)	13	6	.684	3.65	26	25	1	0	0	145 1/3	102	76	59	103	138
1988—	Visalia (Calif.)	11	9	.550	4.18	28	•28	4	2	0	172 1/3	141	95	80	*143	*205
1989—	Orlando (Sou.)	9	3	.750	4.37	17	17	1	0	0	90 2/3	71	48	44	48	102
1990—	Portland (PCL)	5	14	.263	4.56	23	23	4	1	0	128 1/3	110	75	65	82	129
—	Minnesota (A.L.)	0	5	.000	5.97	7	7	0	0	0	34 2/3	37	24	23	28	25
1991—	Portland (PCL)	2	3	.400	3.89	8	8	1	1	0	44	36	19	19	28	40
—	Minnesota (A.L.)	3	1	.750	4.75	15	3	0	0	0	47 1/3	38	27	25	36	43
1992—	Portland (PCL)	4	1	.800	2.33	7	7	0	0	0	46 1/3	30	13	12	31	46
—	Minnesota (A.L.)	0	0	...	3.27	6	0	0	0	0	11	12	4	4	5	13
1993—	Canton/Akron (East.)■	4	5	.444	4.06	13	12	1	0	0	75 1/3	72	34	34	28	86
—	Cleveland (A.L.)	0	1	.000	6.38	5	5	0	0	0	18 1/3	19	15	13	11	7
—	Charlotte (I.L.)	0	1	.000	6.63	4	4	0	0	0	19	25	16	14	7	12
1994—	Omaha (A.A.)■	4	1	.800	4.87	15	10	0	0	0	57 1/3	57	32	31	45	48
1995—	Iowa (A.A.)■	7	7	.500	3.67	46	11	0	0	0	115 1/3	104	50	47	64	*127
1996—	Las Vegas (PCL)■	4	2	.667	4.18	28	0	0	0	7	28	27	14	13	12	37
1997—	Tacoma (PCL)■	8	4	.667	4.13	17	14	3	0	0	93 2/3	80	48	43	29	117
—	Ariz. Mariners (Ariz.)	0	0	...	0.93	3	3	0	0	0	9 2/3	0	2	1	7	13
1998—	Ariz. Mariners (Ariz.)	0	0	...	0.00	1	0	0	0	0	3	1	0	0	0	6
—	Tacoma (PCL)	1	0	1.000	1.20	3	3	0	0	0	15	9	2	2	5	20
—	Seattle (A.L.)	3	1	.750	4.01	4	4	0	0	0	24 2/3	24	11	11	10	22
1999—	Tacoma (PCL)	1	1	.500	6.43	2	2	0	0	0	14	21	11	10	4	10
—	Seattle (A.L.)	6	2	.750	3.10	25	7	0	0	0	72 2/3	50	31	25	32	68
Major League totals (6 years)		12	10	.545	4.36	62	26	0	0	0	208 2/3	180	112	101	122	178

ABREU, BOBBY — OF — PHILLIES

PERSONAL: Born March 11, 1974, in Aragua, Venezuela. ... 6-0/197. ... Bats left, throws right. ... Full name: Bob Kelly Abreu. ... Name pronounced uh-BRAY-yew.

TRANSACTIONS/CAREER NOTES: Signed as non-drafted free agent by Houston Astros organization (August 21, 1990). ... On Houston disabled list (May 25-July 1, 1997); included rehabilitation assignments to Jackson (June 23-26) and New Orleans (June 27-July 1). ... Selected by Tampa Bay Devil Rays in first round (sixth pick overall) of expansion draft (November 18, 1997). ... Traded by Devil Rays to Philadelphia Phillies for SS Kevin Stocker (November 18, 1997).

STATISTICAL NOTES: Led Gulf Coast League outfielders with 11 assists in 1991. ... Led Texas League with .530 slugging percentage in 1994. ... Led Pacific Coast League outfielders with 18 assists in 1995. ... Led Pacific Coast League in caught stealing with 18 in 1996. ... Career major league grand slams: 1.

Year Team (League)	Pos.	G	AB	R	H	2B	3B	HR	RBI	Avg.	BB	SO	SB	PO	A	E	Avg.
										BATTING					FIELDING		
1991—GC Astros (GCL)	OF-SS	56	183	21	55	7	3	0	20	.301	17	27	10	70	†13	5	.943
1992—Asheville (SAL)	OF	135	480	81	140	21	4	8	48	.292	63	79	15	167	15	11	.943
1993—Osceola (FSL)	OF	129	474	62	134	21	17	5	55	.283	51	90	10	179	18	8	.961
1994—Jackson (Texas)	OF	118	400	61	121	25	9	16	73	.303	42	81	12	113	3	4	.967
1995—Tucson (PCL)	OF-2B	114	415	72	126	24	*17	10	75	.304	67	120	16	207	†18	7	.970
1996—Tucson (PCL)	OF-DH	132	484	86	138	14	*16	13	68	.285	83	111	24	202	15	7	.969
—Houston (N.L.)	OF	15	22	1	5	1	0	0	1	.227	2	3	0	6	0	0	1.000
1997—Houston (N.L.)	OF	59	188	22	47	10	2	3	26	.250	21	48	7	84	4	2	.978
—Jackson (Texas)	OF	3	12	2	2	1	0	0	0	.167	1	5	0	1	0	0	1.000
—New Orleans (A.A.)	OF	47	194	25	52	9	4	2	22	.268	21	49	7	99	4	1	.990
1998—Philadelphia (N.L.)■	OF	151	497	68	155	29	6	17	74	.312	84	133	19	272	17	8	.973
1999—Philadelphia (N.L.)	OF-DH	152	546	118	183	35	•11	20	93	.335	109	113	27	260	8	3	.989
Major League totals (4 years)		377	1253	209	390	75	19	40	194	.311	216	297	53	622	29	13	.980

DIVISION SERIES RECORD

Year Team (League)	Pos.	G	AB	R	H	2B	3B	HR	RBI	Avg.	BB	SO	SB	PO	A	E	Avg.
										BATTING					FIELDING		
1997—Houston (N.L.)	PH	3	3	0	1	0	0	0	0	.333	0	2	1	...	...	...	...

ABREU, WINSTON — P — BRAVES

PERSONAL: Born April 5, 1977, in Cotui, Dominican Republic. ... 6-2/155. ... Throws right, bats right.

TRANSACTIONS/CAREER NOTES: Signed as non-drafted free agent by Atlanta Braves organization (July 2, 1993). ... On disabled list (April 21, 1997-entire season).

Year League	W	L	Pct.	ERA	G	GS	CG	ShO	Sv.	IP	H	R	ER	BB	SO
1994—GC Braves (GCL)	0	*8	.000	4.08	13	11	0	0	0	57 1/3	57	35	26	24	53
1995—Danville (Appl.)	6	3	.667	2.31	13	13	1	0	0	74	54	29	19	13	90
1996—Macon (SAL)	4	3	.571	3.00	12	12	0	0	0	60	51	29	20	25	60
1997—							Did not play.								
1998—Eugene (N.W.)	0	4	.000	6.35	17	10	0	0	0	45 1/3	39	36	32	31	52
1999—Macon (SAL)	7	2	.778	1.69	14	14	0	0	0	69 1/3	41	17	13	26	95
—Myrtle Beach (Caro.)	3	2	.600	3.28	13	12	0	0	0	68 2/3	53	26	25	41	76

ACEVEDO, JUAN — P — BREWERS

PERSONAL: Born May 5, 1970, in Juarez, Mexico. ... 6-2/220. ... Throws right, bats right. ... Full name: Juan Carlos Acevedo. ... Name pronounced ah-sah-VAY-doh.

HIGH SCHOOL: Dundee-Crown (Carpentersville, Ill.).

JUNIOR COLLEGE: Parkland College (Ill.).

TRANSACTIONS/CAREER NOTES: Selected by Colorado Rockies organization in 14th round of free-agent draft (June 1, 1992). ... Traded by Rockies with P Arnold Gooch to New York Mets for P Bret Saberhagen and a player to be named later (July 31, 1995); Rockies acquired P David Swanson to complete deal (August 4, 1995). ... On New York disabled list (March 26-May 9, 1996); included rehabilitation assignment to Norfolk (April 10-May 9). ... Traded by Mets to St. Louis Cardinals for P Rigo Beltran (March 29, 1998). ... On St. Louis disabled list (July 18-August 16, 1998); included rehabilitation assignment to Memphis (August 6-16). ... Traded by Cardinals with two players to be named later to Milwaukee Brewers for 2B Fernando Vina (December 20, 1999).

HONORS: Named Eastern League Pitcher of the Year (1994).

STATISTICAL NOTES: Tied for Eastern League lead with four balks in 1994. ... Tied for International League lead with four balks in 1997.

Year League	W	L	Pct.	ERA	G	GS	CG	ShO	Sv.	IP	H	R	ER	BB	SO
1992—Bend (N.W.)	0	0	...	13.50	1	0	0	0	0	2	4	3	3	1	3
—Visalia (Calif.)	3	4	.429	5.43	12	12	1	0	0	64 2/3	75	46	39	33	37
1993—Central Valley (Calif.)	9	8	.529	4.40	27	20	1	0	0	118 2/3	119	68	58	58	107
1994—New Haven (East.)	*17	6	.739	*2.37	26	26	5	2	0	174 2/3	142	56	46	38	161
1995—Colorado (N.L.)	4	6	.400	6.44	17	11	0	0	0	65 2/3	82	53	47	20	40
—Colorado Springs (PCL)	1	1	.500	6.14	3	3	0	0	0	14 2/3	18	11	10	7	7
—Norfolk (I.L.)■	0	0	...	0.00	2	2	0	0	0	3	0	0	0	1	2
1996—Norfolk (I.L.)	4	8	.333	5.96	19	19	2	1	0	102 2/3	116	70	68	53	83
1997—Norfolk (I.L.)	6	6	.500	3.86	18	18	1	0	0	116 2/3	111	55	50	34	99
—New York (N.L.)	3	1	.750	3.59	25	2	0	0	0	47 2/3	52	24	19	22	33
1998—St. Louis (N.L.)■	8	3	.727	2.56	50	9	0	0	15	98 1/3	83	30	28	29	56
—Memphis (PCL)	0	0	...	0.00	2	2	0	0	0	8 2/3	5	0	0	1	6
1999—St. Louis (N.L.)	6	8	.429	5.89	50	12	0	0	4	102 1/3	115	71	67	48	52
Major League totals (4 years)	21	18	.538	4.61	142	34	0	0	19	314	332	178	161	119	181

ADAMS, TERRY   P   DODGERS

PERSONAL: Born March 6, 1973, in Mobile, Ala. ... 6-3/205. ... Throws right, bats right. ... Full name: Terry Wayne Adams.
HIGH SCHOOL: Montgomery (Semmes, Ala.).
TRANSACTIONS/CAREER NOTES: Selected by Chicago Cubs organization in fourth round of free-agent draft (June 3, 1991). ... On disabled list (June 21-September 21, 1993). ... On Chicago disabled list (March 26-May 8 and June 19-July 4, 1999); included rehabilitation assignments to West Tenn (April 30-May 4) and Iowa (May 6-8). ... Traded by Cubs with P Chad Ricketts and a player to be named later to Los Angeles Dodgers for P Ismael Valdes and 2B Eric Young (December 12, 1999); Dodgers acquired P Brian Stephenson to complete deal (December 16, 1999).

Year League	W	L	Pct.	ERA	G	GS	CG	ShO	Sv.	IP	H	R	ER	BB	SO
1991— Huntington (Appl.)	0	*9	.000	5.77	14	13	0	0	0	57²/₃	67	*56	37	62	52
1992— Peoria (Midw.)	7	12	.368	4.41	25	25	3	1	0	157	144	95	77	86	96
1993— Daytona (FSL)	3	5	.375	4.97	13	13	0	0	0	70²/₃	78	47	39	43	35
1994— Daytona (FSL)	9	10	.474	4.38	39	7	0	0	7	84¹/₃	87	47	41	46	64
1995— Orlando (Sou.)	2	3	.400	1.43	37	0	0	0	19	37²/₃	23	9	6	16	26
— Iowa (A.A.)	0	0	...	0.00	7	0	0	0	5	6¹/₃	3	0	0	2	10
— Chicago (N.L.)	1	1	.500	6.50	18	0	0	0	1	18	22	15	13	10	15
1996— Chicago (N.L.)	3	6	.333	2.94	69	0	0	0	4	101	84	36	33	49	78
1997— Chicago (N.L.)	2	9	.182	4.62	74	0	0	0	18	74	91	43	38	40	64
1998— Chicago (N.L.)	7	7	.500	4.33	63	0	0	0	1	72²/₃	72	39	35	41	73
— Iowa (PCL)	0	0	...	0.00	3	0	0	0	0	4	1	1	0	3	5
1999— West Tenn (Sou.)	0	0	...	16.88	2	1	0	0	0	2²/₃	5	6	5	2	2
— Chicago (N.L.)	6	3	.667	4.02	52	0	0	0	13	65	60	33	29	28	57
Major League totals (5 years)	19	26	.422	4.03	276	0	0	0	37	330²/₃	329	166	148	168	287

AGBAYANI, BENNY   OF   METS

PERSONAL: Born December 28, 1971, in Honolulu, Hawaii. ... 5-11/225. ... Bats right, throws right. ... Full name: Benny Peter Agbayani Jr.
HIGH SCHOOL: St. Louis (Honolulu).
COLLEGE: Oregon Tech, then Hawaii Pacific.
TRANSACTIONS/CAREER NOTES: Selected by California Angels organization in 25th round of free-agent draft (June 1, 1992); did not sign. ... Selected by New York Mets organization in 30th round of free-agent draft (June 3, 1993). ... On Norfolk disabled list (May 10-June 6, 1998).
STATISTICAL NOTES: Tied for International League lead in caught stealing with 14 in 1997.

Year Team (League)	Pos.	G	AB	R	H	2B	3B	HR	RBI	Avg.	BB	SO	SB	PO	A	E	Avg.
							BATTING								FIELDING		
1993— Pittsfield (NY-P)	OF	51	167	26	42	6	3	2	22	.251	20	43	7	62	1	2	.969
1994— St. Lucie (FSL)	OF	119	411	72	115	13	5	5	63	.280	58	67	8	143	6	1	.993
1995— Binghamton (East.)	OF	88	295	38	81	11	2	1	26	.275	39	51	12	100	3	3	.972
— St. Lucie (FSL)	OF	44	155	24	48	9	3	2	29	.310	26	27	8	37	1	2	.950
1996— Binghamton (East.)	OF	21	53	7	9	1	0	2	8	.170	11	13	1	19	1	1	.952
— Norfolk (I.L.)	OF-1B	99	331	43	92	13	9	7	56	.278	30	57	14	172	8	2	.989
1997— Norfolk (I.L.)	OF	127	468	90	145	24	2	11	51	.310	67	106	29	207	12	5	.978
1998— Norfolk (I.L.)	OF-1B	90	322	43	91	20	5	11	53	.283	50	58	16	151	4	4	.975
— New York (N.L.)	OF	11	15	1	2	0	0	0	0	.133	1	5	0	6	0	0	1.000
1999— Norfolk (I.L.)	OF-1B-DH	28	101	21	36	8	1	8	32	.356	16	19	5	113	6	2	.983
— New York (N.L.)	OF-DH	101	276	42	79	18	3	14	42	.286	32	60	6	121	2	2	.984
Major League totals (2 years)		112	291	43	81	18	3	14	42	.278	33	65	6	127	2	2	.985

DIVISION SERIES RECORD

Year Team (League)	Pos.	G	AB	R	H	2B	3B	HR	RBI	Avg.	BB	SO	SB	PO	A	E	Avg.
							BATTING								FIELDING		
1999— New York (N.L.)	OF-PH	4	10	1	3	1	0	0	1	.300	0	3	0	5	0	0	1.000

CHAMPIONSHIP SERIES RECORD

Year Team (League)	Pos.	G	AB	R	H	2B	3B	HR	RBI	Avg.	BB	SO	SB	PO	A	E	Avg.
							BATTING								FIELDING		
1999— New York (N.L.)	OF-PH	4	7	2	1	0	0	0	0	.143	4	2	1	4	0	0	1.000

AGUILERA, RICK   P   CUBS

PERSONAL: Born December 31, 1961, in San Gabriel, Calif. ... 6-5/210. ... Throws right, bats right. ... Full name: Richard Warren Aguilera. ... Name pronounced AG-yuh-LAIR-uh.
HIGH SCHOOL: Edgewood (West Covina, Calif.).
COLLEGE: Brigham Young.
TRANSACTIONS/CAREER NOTES: Selected by St. Louis Cardinals organization in 37th round of free-agent draft (June 3, 1980); did not sign. ... Selected by New York Mets organization in third round of free-agent draft (June 6, 1983). ... On New York disabled list (September 3-15, 1985). ... On New York disabled list (May 23-August 24, 1987); included rehabilitation assignment to Tidewater (August 10-24). ... On New York disabled list (April 19-June 19 and July 12-September 7, 1988); included rehabilitation assignments to St. Lucie (June 7-14) and Tidewater (June 15-19). ... Traded by Mets with P David West and three players to be named later to Minnesota Twins for P Frank Viola (July 31, 1989); Portland, Twins organization, acquired P Kevin Tapani and P Tim Drummond (August 1, 1989), and Twins acquired P Jack Savage to complete deal (October 16, 1989). ... Traded by Twins to Boston Red Sox for P Frank Rodriguez and a player to be named later (July 6, 1995); Twins acquired OF J.J. Johnson to complete deal (October 11, 1995). ... Granted free agency (October 31, 1995). ... Signed by Twins (December 11, 1995). ... On Minnesota disabled list (March 24-June 11 and September 7, 1996-remainder of season); included rehabilitation assignment to Fort Myers (May 31-June 11). ... Traded by Twins with P Scott Downs to Chicago Cubs for P Kyle Lohse and P Jason Ryan (May 21, 1999). ... On Chicago disabled list (August 1-25, 1999).
MISCELLANEOUS: Holds Minnesota Twins all-time records for most saves (254) and most games pitched (490). ... Made an out in only appearance as pinch hitter with New York (1989).

Year League	W	L	Pct.	ERA	G	GS	CG	ShO	Sv.	IP	H	R	ER	BB	SO
1983—Little Falls (NY-P)	5	6	.455	3.72	16	15	4	•2	0	104	*109	55	43	26	84
1984—Lynchburg (Caro.)	8	3	.727	2.34	13	13	6	•3	0	88 1/3	72	29	23	28	101
—Jackson (Texas)	4	4	.500	4.57	11	11	2	1	0	67	68	37	34	19	71
1985—Tidewater (I.L.)	6	4	.600	2.51	11	11	2	1	0	79	64	24	22	17	55
—New York (N.L.)	10	7	.588	3.24	21	19	2	0	0	122 1/3	118	49	44	37	74
1986—New York (N.L.)	10	7	.588	3.88	28	20	2	0	0	141 2/3	145	70	61	36	104
1987—New York (N.L.)	11	3	.786	3.60	18	17	1	0	0	115	124	53	46	33	77
—Tidewater (I.L.)	1	1	.500	0.69	3	3	0	0	0	13	8	2	1	1	10
1988—New York (N.L.)	0	4	.000	6.93	11	3	0	0	0	24 2/3	29	20	19	10	16
—St. Lucie (FSL)	0	0	...	1.29	2	2	0	0	0	7	8	1	1	1	5
—Tidewater (I.L.)	0	0	...	1.50	1	1	0	0	0	6	6	1	1	1	4
1989—New York (N.L.)	6	6	.500	2.34	36	0	0	0	7	69 1/3	59	19	18	21	80
—Minnesota (A.L.)■	3	5	.375	3.21	11	11	3	0	0	75 2/3	71	32	27	17	57
1990—Minnesota (A.L.)	5	3	.625	2.76	56	0	0	0	32	65 1/3	55	27	20	19	61
1991—Minnesota (A.L.)	4	5	.444	2.35	63	0	0	0	42	69	44	20	18	30	61
1992—Minnesota (A.L.)	2	6	.250	2.84	64	0	0	0	41	66 2/3	60	28	21	17	52
1993—Minnesota (A.L.)	4	3	.571	3.11	65	0	0	0	34	72 1/3	60	25	25	14	59
1994—Minnesota (A.L.)	1	4	.200	3.63	44	0	0	0	23	44 2/3	57	23	18	10	46
1995—Minnesota (A.L.)	1	1	.500	2.52	22	0	0	0	12	25	20	7	7	6	29
—Boston (A.L.)■	2	2	.500	2.67	30	0	0	0	20	30 1/3	26	9	9	7	23
1996—Fort Myers (FSL)■	2	0	1.000	3.75	2	2	0	0	0	12	13	5	5	1	12
—Minnesota (A.L.)	8	6	.571	5.42	19	19	2	0	0	111 1/3	124	69	67	27	83
1997—Minnesota (A.L.)	5	4	.556	3.82	61	0	0	0	26	68 1/3	65	29	29	22	68
1998—Minnesota (A.L.)	4	9	.308	4.24	68	0	0	0	38	74 1/3	75	35	35	15	57
1999—Minnesota (A.L.)	3	1	.750	1.27	17	0	0	0	6	21 1/3	10	3	3	2	13
—Chicago (N.L.)■	6	3	.667	3.69	44	0	0	0	8	46 1/3	44	22	19	10	32
A.L. totals (11 years)	42	49	.462	3.47	520	30	5	0	274	724 1/3	667	307	279	186	609
N.L. totals (6 years)	43	30	.589	3.59	158	59	5	0	15	519 1/3	519	233	207	147	383
Major League totals (15 years)	85	79	.518	3.52	678	89	10	0	289	1243 2/3	1186	540	486	333	992

DIVISION SERIES RECORD

Year League	W	L	Pct.	ERA	G	GS	CG	ShO	Sv.	IP	H	R	ER	BB	SO
1995—Boston (A.L.)	0	0	...	13.50	1	0	0	0	0	2/3	3	1	1	0	1

CHAMPIONSHIP SERIES RECORD

Year League	W	L	Pct.	ERA	G	GS	CG	ShO	Sv.	IP	H	R	ER	BB	SO
1986—New York (N.L.)	0	0	...	0.00	2	0	0	0	0	5	2	1	0	2	2
1988—New York (N.L.)	0	0	...	1.29	3	0	0	0	0	7	3	1	1	2	4
1991—Minnesota (A.L.)	0	0	...	0.00	3	0	0	0	3	3 1/3	1	0	0	0	3
Champ. series totals (3 years)	0	0	...	0.59	8	0	0	0	3	15 1/3	6	2	1	4	9

WORLD SERIES RECORD

NOTES: Flied out in only appearance as pinch hitter (1991). ... Member of World Series championship team (1986 and 1991).

Year League	W	L	Pct.	ERA	G	GS	CG	ShO	Sv.	IP	H	R	ER	BB	SO
1986—New York (N.L.)	1	0	1.000	12.00	2	0	0	0	0	3	8	4	4	1	4
1991—Minnesota (A.L.)	1	1	.500	1.80	4	0	0	0	2	5	6	1	1	1	3
World Series totals (2 years)	2	1	.667	5.63	6	0	0	0	2	8	14	5	5	2	7

ALL-STAR GAME RECORD

Year League	W	L	Pct.	ERA	GS	CG	ShO	Sv.	IP	H	R	ER	BB	SO
1991—American	0	0	...	0.00	0	0	0	0	1 1/3	2	0	0	0	3
1992—American	0	0	...	13.50	0	0	0	0	2/3	1	1	1	0	0
1993—American	0	0	...	0.00	0	0	0	0	1	2	0	0	0	2
All-Star Game totals (3 years)	0	0	...	3.00	0	0	0	0	3	5	1	1	0	5

ALDRED, SCOTT   P   PHILLIES

PERSONAL: Born June 12, 1968, in Flint, Mich. ... 6-4/220. ... Throws left, bats left. ... Full name: Scott Phillip Aldred.

HIGH SCHOOL: Hill McCloy (Montrose, Mich.).

TRANSACTIONS/CAREER NOTES: Selected by Detroit Tigers organization in 16th round of free-agent draft (June 2, 1986). ... Selected by Colorado Rockies in first round (15th pick overall) of expansion draft (November 17, 1992). ... Claimed on waivers by Montreal Expos (April 29, 1993). ... On Montreal disabled list (May 15-September 11, 1993). ... Released by Expos (September 11, 1993). ... Missed entire 1994 season with injury. ... Signed by Detroit Tigers organization (February 19, 1995). ... Claimed on waivers by Minnesota Twins (May 28, 1996). ... On Salt Lake disabled list (August 7-September 19, 1997). ... Granted free agency (October 8, 1997). ... Signed by Tampa Bay Devil Rays (December 19, 1997). ... Traded by Devil Rays to Philadelphia Phillies (July 23, 1999), completing deal in which Phillies traded P Marty Barnett to Devil Rays for a player to be named later (July 20, 1999).

Year League	W	L	Pct.	ERA	G	GS	CG	ShO	Sv.	IP	H	R	ER	BB	SO
1987—Fayetteville (SAL)	4	9	.308	3.60	21	20	0	0	0	110	101	56	44	69	91
1988—Lakeland (FSL)	8	7	.533	3.56	25	25	1	1	0	131 1/3	122	61	52	72	102
1989—London (East.)	10	6	.625	3.84	20	20	3	1	0	122	98	55	52	59	97
1990—Toledo (I.L.)	6	15	.286	4.90	29	*29	2	0	0	158	145	93	86	81	133
—Detroit (A.L.)	1	2	.333	3.77	4	3	0	0	0	14 1/3	13	6	6	10	7
1991—Toledo (I.L.)	8	8	.500	3.92	22	20	2	0	1	135 1/3	127	65	59	72	95
—Detroit (A.L.)	2	4	.333	5.18	11	11	1	0	0	57 1/3	58	37	33	30	35
1992—Detroit (A.L.)	3	8	.273	6.78	16	13	0	0	0	65	80	51	49	33	34
—Toledo (I.L.)	4	6	.400	5.13	16	13	3	0	0	86	92	57	49	47	81
1993—Colorado (N.L.)■	0	0	...	10.80	5	0	0	0	0	6 2/3	10	10	8	9	5
—Montreal (N.L.)■	1	0	1.000	6.75	3	0	0	0	0	5 1/3	9	4	4	1	4
1994—							Did not play.								
1995—Lakeland (FSL)■	4	2	.667	3.19	13	7	0	0	2	67 2/3	57	25	24	19	64
—Jacksonville (Sou.)	1	0	1.000	0.00	2	2	0	0	0	12	9	0	0	1	11

Year League	W	L	Pct.	ERA	G	GS	CG	ShO	Sv.	IP	H	R	ER	BB	SO
1996— Detroit (A.L.)	0	4	.000	9.35	11	8	0	0	0	43 1/3	60	52	45	26	36
— Minnesota (A.L.)■	6	5	.545	5.09	25	17	0	0	0	122	134	73	69	42	75
1997— Minnesota (A.L.)	2	10	.167	7.68	17	15	0	0	0	77 1/3	102	66	66	28	33
— Salt Lake (PCL)	3	3	.500	7.03	7	7	0	0	0	39 2/3	56	39	31	16	23
1998— Durham (I.L.)■	2	4	.333	5.35	7	7	0	0	0	35 1/3	44	26	21	14	19
— Tampa Bay (A.L.)	0	0	...	3.73	48	0	0	0	0	31 1/3	33	13	13	12	21
1999— Tampa Bay (A.L.)	3	2	.600	5.18	37	0	0	0	0	24 1/3	26	15	14	14	22
— Philadelphia (N.L.)■	1	1	.500	3.90	29	0	0	0	1	32 1/3	33	15	14	15	19
A.L. totals (7 years)	17	35	.327	6.10	169	67	1	0	0	435	506	313	295	195	263
N.L. totals (2 years)	2	1	.667	5.28	37	0	0	0	1	44 1/3	52	29	26	25	28
Major League totals (8 years)	19	36	.345	6.03	206	67	1	0	1	479 1/3	558	342	321	220	291

ALEXANDER, CHAD   OF   MARINERS

PERSONAL: Born May 22, 1974, in Norfolk, Va. ... 6-1/195. ... Bats right, throws right. ... Full name: Chad Daniel Alexander.
HIGH SCHOOL: Lufkin (Texas).
COLLEGE: Texas A&M.
TRANSACTIONS/CAREER NOTES: Selected by Cincinnati Reds organization in second round of free-agent draft (June 1, 1992); did not sign. ... Selected by Houston Astros organization in third round of free-agent draft (June 1, 1995). ... On Jackson disabled list (May 3-17, 1999). ... Selected by Seattle Mariners from Astros organization in Rule 5 major league draft (December 13, 1999).

Year Team (League)	Pos.	G	AB	R	H	2B	3B	HR	RBI	Avg.	BB	SO	SB	PO	A	E	Avg.
1995— Auburn (NY-P)	OF	71	278	45	81	15	5	5	43	.291	25	37	7	129	8	5	.965
— Quad City (Midw.)	OF	2	7	2	2	0	0	0	1	.286	0	0	0	3	0	0	1.000
1996— Quad City (Midw.)	OF	118	435	68	115	25	4	13	69	.264	57	108	16	176	6	8	.958
1997— Kissimmee (FSL)	OF	129	469	67	127	31	6	4	46	.271	56	91	11	231	8	2	.992
1998— Jackson (Texas)	OF	128	416	77	119	33	2	13	45	.286	71	80	6	197	18	5	.977
— New Orleans (PCL)	OF	2	5	1	2	0	0	0	2	.400	0	2	0	3	0	0	1.000
1999— Jackson (Texas)		84	317	42	98	27	3	9	44	.309	34	58	9	168	3	2	.988
— New Orleans (PCL)		28	96	7	23	5	0	2	8	.240	6	22	0	64	2	1	.985

ALEXANDER, MANNY   IF   RED SOX

PERSONAL: Born March 20, 1971, in San Pedro de Macoris, Dominican Republic. ... 5-10/180. ... Bats right, throws right. ... Full name: Manuel DeJesus Alexander.
TRANSACTIONS/CAREER NOTES: Signed as non-drafted free agent by Baltimore Orioles organization (February 4, 1988). ... On disabled list (April 26-July 23, 1990). ... On Rochester disabled list (May 9-19 and June 9-17, 1993). ... On Baltimore disabled list (March 25-May 2, 1995). ... Traded by Orioles with IF Scott McLain to New York Mets for P Hector Ramirez (March 22, 1997). ... On New York disabled list (June 13-July 10 and August 1-11, 1997). ... Traded by Mets to Chicago Cubs (August 14, 1997), as part of deal in which Mets traded OF Lance Johnson and two players to be named later to Cubs for OF Brian McRae, P Mel Rojas and P Turk Wendell (August 8, 1997); Mets traded P Mark Clark to Cubs to complete deal (August 11, 1997). ... Traded by Cubs to Boston Red Sox for OF Damon Buford (December 10, 1999).
STATISTICAL NOTES: Led Appalachian League shortstops with 349 total chances in 1989. ... Led Carolina League shortstops with 651 total chances and 93 double plays in 1991.

Year Team (League)	Pos.	G	AB	R	H	2B	3B	HR	RBI	Avg.	BB	SO	SB	PO	A	E	Avg.
1988—						Dominican Summer League statistics unavailable.											
1989— Bluefield (Appl.)	SS	65	*274	49	*85	13	2	2	34	.310	20	49	19	*140	177	*32	.908
1990— Wausau (Midw.)	SS	44	152	16	27	3	1	0	11	.178	12	41	8	66	99	11	.938
1991— Hagerstown (East.)	SS	3	9	3	3	1	0	0	2	.333	1	3	0	5	4	0	1.000
— Frederick (Caro.)	SS	134	548	•81	*143	17	3	3	42	.261	44	68	47	*226	*393	32	*.951
1992— Hagerstown (East.)	SS	127	499	69	129	23	8	2	41	.259	25	62	43	216	253	36	.929
— Rochester (I.L.)	SS	6	24	3	7	1	0	0	3	.292	1	3	2	12	25	1	.974
— Baltimore (A.L.)	SS	4	5	1	1	0	0	0	0	.200	0	3	0	3	3	0	1.000
1993— Rochester (I.L.)	SS	120	471	55	115	23	8	6	51	.244	22	60	19	184	335	18	*.966
— Baltimore (A.L.)	PR-DH	3	0	1	0	0	0	0	0	...	0	0	0	...	...	...	...
1994— Rochester (I.L.)	SS-2B	111	426	63	106	23	6	6	39	.249	16	67	30	219	291	33	.939
1995— Baltimore (A.L.)	2-S-3-DH	94	242	35	57	9	1	3	23	.236	20	30	11	139	170	10	.969
1996— Baltimore (A.L.)	S-2-3-O-DH-P	54	68	6	7	0	0	0	4	.103	3	27	3	26	47	5	.936
1997— New York (N.L.)	2B-SS-3B	54	149	26	37	9	3	2	15	.248	9	38	11	59	130	4	.979
— St. Lucie (FSL)	SS	1	4	0	1	0	0	0	0	.250	0	1	0	1	4	0	1.000
— Chicago (N.L.)■	SS-2B	33	99	11	29	3	1	1	7	.293	8	16	2	38	91	7	.949
1998— Chicago (N.L.)	S-2-3-DH-O	108	264	34	60	10	1	5	25	.227	18	66	4	89	140	7	.970
1999— Chicago (N.L.)	S-3-2-O	90	177	17	48	11	2	0	15	.271	10	38	4	56	88	7	.954
American League totals (4 years)		155	315	43	65	9	1	3	27	.206	23	60	14	168	220	15	.963
National League totals (3 years)		285	689	88	174	33	7	8	62	.253	45	158	21	242	449	25	.965
Major League totals (7 years)		440	1004	131	239	42	8	11	89	.238	68	218	35	410	669	40	.964

DIVISION SERIES RECORD

Year Team (League)	Pos.	G	AB	R	H	2B	3B	HR	RBI	Avg.	BB	SO	SB	PO	A	E	Avg.
1996— Baltimore (A.L.)	DH-PR	3	0	2	0	0	0	0	0	...	0	0	0	...	...	...	...
1998— Chicago (N.L.)	SS-PH	2	5	0	0	0	0	0	0	.000	0	1	0	2	2	0	1.000
Division series totals (2 years)		5	5	2	0	0	0	0	0	.000	0	1	0	2	2	0	1.000

RECORD AS PITCHER

Year League	W	L	Pct.	ERA	G	GS	CG	ShO	Sv.	IP	H	R	ER	BB	SO
1996— Baltimore (A.L.)	0	0	...	67.50	1	0	0	0	0	2/3	1	5	5	4	0

ALFONSECA, ANTONIO   P   MARLINS

PERSONAL: Born April 16, 1972, in La Romana, Dominican Republic. ... 6-5/235. ... Throws right, bats right.
TRANSACTIONS/CAREER NOTES: Signed as non-drafted free agent by Montreal Expos organization (July 3, 1989). ... Selected by Edmonton, Florida Marlins organization, from Harrisburg, Expos organization in Rule 5 minor league draft (December 13, 1993). ... On Portland disabled list (May 15-June 15, 1995). On Charlotte disabled list (July 12-September 3, 1996). ... On disabled list (May 14-31, 1998).

Year League	W	L	Pct.	ERA	G	GS	CG	ShO	Sv.	IP	H	R	ER	BB	SO
1990— DSL Expos (DSL)	3	5	.375	3.60	13	13	1	0	0	60	60	29	24	32	19
1991— Gulf Coast Expos (GCL)	3	3	.500	3.88	11	10	0	0	0	51	46	33	22	25	38
1992— Gulf Coast Expos (GCL)	3	4	.429	3.68	12	10	1	1	0	66	55	31	27	35	62
1993— Jamestown (NY-P)	2	2	.500	6.15	15	4	0	0	1	33 2/3	31	26	23	22	29
1994— Kane County (Midw.)■	6	5	.545	4.07	32	9	0	0	0	86 1/3	78	41	39	21	74
1995— Portland (East.)	9	3	.750	3.64	19	17	1	0	0	96 1/3	81	43	39	42	75
1996— Charlotte (I.L.)	4	4	.500	5.53	14	13	0	0	1	71 2/3	86	47	44	22	51
1997— Charlotte (I.L.)	7	2	.778	4.32	46	0	0	0	7	58 1/3	58	34	28	20	45
— Florida (N.L.)	1	3	.250	4.91	17	0	0	0	0	25 2/3	36	16	14	10	19
1998— Florida (N.L.)	4	6	.400	4.08	58	0	0	0	8	70 2/3	75	36	32	33	46
1999— Florida (N.L.)	4	5	.444	3.24	73	0	0	0	21	77 2/3	79	28	28	29	46
Major League totals (3 years)	9	14	.391	3.83	148	0	0	0	29	174	190	80	74	72	111

DIVISION SERIES RECORD

Year League	W	L	Pct.	ERA	G	GS	CG	ShO	Sv.	IP	H	R	ER	BB	SO
1997— Florida (N.L.)							Did not play.								

CHAMPIONSHIP SERIES RECORD

Year League	W	L	Pct.	ERA	G	GS	CG	ShO	Sv.	IP	H	R	ER	BB	SO
1997— Florida (N.L.)							Did not play.								

WORLD SERIES RECORD

NOTES: Member of World Series championship team (1997).

Year League	W	L	Pct.	ERA	G	GS	CG	ShO	Sv.	IP	H	R	ER	BB	SO
1997— Florida (N.L.)	0	0	...	0.00	3	0	0	0	0	6 1/3	6	0	0	1	5

ALFONZO, EDGARDO   2B   METS

PERSONAL: Born November 8, 1973, in St. Teresa, Venezuela. ... 5-11/187. ... Bats right, throws right. ... Full name: Edgardo Antonio Alfonzo. ... Brother of Roberto Alfonzo, second baseman in New York Mets organization (1993-94).
HIGH SCHOOL: Cecilio Acosto (Venezuela).
TRANSACTIONS/CAREER NOTES: Signed as non-drafted free agent by New York Mets organization (February 19, 1991). ... On disabled list (August 11, 1995-remainder of season; and May 4-19, 1998).
RECORDS: Shares major league single-game records for most runs scored—6 (August 30, 1999); and most double plays by second baseman—4 (May 14, 1997).
HONORS: Named second baseman on THE SPORTING NEWS N.L. All-Star team (1999). ... Named second baseman on THE SPORTING NEWS N.L. Silver Slugger team (1999).
STATISTICAL NOTES: Led New York-Pennsylvania League shortstops with 389 total chances and 39 double plays in 1992. ... Had 20-game hitting streak (June 10-July 10, 1997). ... Hit three home runs in one game (August 30, 1999). ... Collected six hits in one game (August 30, 1999). ... Career major league grand slams: 1.

Year Team (League)	Pos.	G	AB	R	H	2B	3B	HR	RBI	Avg.	BB	SO	SB	PO	A	E	Avg.
1991— GC Mets (GCL)	2B-SS-3B	54	175	29	58	8	4	0	27	.331	34	12	6	99	108	9	.958
1992— St. Lucie (FSL)	2B	4	5	0	0	0	0	0	0	.000	0	0	0	1	3	0	1.000
— Pittsfield (NY-P)	SS	74	*298	44	*106	13	5	1	44	*.356	18	31	7	*126	*237	*26	.933
1993— St. Lucie (FSL)	SS	128	494	75	145	18	3	11	86	.294	57	51	26	183	425	29	.954
1994— Binghamton (East.)	SS-2B-1B	127	498	89	146	34	2	15	75	.293	64	55	14	206	408	27	.958
1995— New York (N.L.)	3B-2B-SS	101	335	26	93	13	5	4	41	.278	12	37	1	81	171	7	.973
1996— New York (N.L.)	2B-3B-SS	123	368	36	96	15	2	4	40	.261	25	56	2	146	246	11	.973
1997— New York (N.L.)	3B-SS-2B	151	518	84	163	27	2	10	72	.315	63	56	11	98	290	12	.970
1998— New York (N.L.)	3B-SS	144	557	94	155	28	2	17	78	.278	65	77	8	117	248	9	.976
1999— New York (N.L.)	2B	158	628	123	191	41	1	27	108	.304	85	85	9	298	409	5	*.993
Major League totals (5 years)		677	2406	363	698	124	12	62	339	.290	250	311	31	740	1364	44	.980

DIVISION SERIES RECORD

RECORDS: Shares N.L. single-series record for most runs scored—6 (1999). ... Shares single-game records for most home runs—2; most grand slams—1; and most runs batted in—5 (October 5, 1999). ... Shares single-inning record for most runs batted in—4 (October 5, 1999, ninth inning).

Year Team (League)	Pos.	G	AB	R	H	2B	3B	HR	RBI	Avg.	BB	SO	SB	PO	A	E	Avg.
1999— New York (N.L.)	2B	4	16	6	4	1	0	3	6	.250	3	2	0	5	11	0	1.000

CHAMPIONSHIP SERIES RECORD

Year Team (League)	Pos.	G	AB	R	H	2B	3B	HR	RBI	Avg.	BB	SO	SB	PO	A	E	Avg.
1999— New York (N.L.)	2B	6	27	2	6	4	0	0	1	.222	1	9	0	15	18	1	.971

ALICEA, LUIS   2B   RANGERS

PERSONAL: Born July 29, 1965, in Santurce, Puerto Rico. ... 5-9/176. ... Bats both, throws right. ... Full name: Luis Rene Alicea. ... Brother of Ed Alicea, minor league infielder with Atlanta Braves (1988-93), Colorado Rockies (1993) and New York Mets (1995).. ... Name pronounced AH-la-SAY-uh.
HIGH SCHOOL: Liceo Castro (Rio Piedras, Puerto Rico).
COLLEGE: Florida State.

TRANSACTIONS/CAREER NOTES: Selected by St. Louis Cardinals organization in first round (23rd pick overall) of free-agent draft (June 2, 1986). ... On St. Petersburg disabled list (April 6-June 4, 1990). ... On Louisville disabled list (April 25-May 25, 1991). ... On St. Louis disabled list (June 1-July 6, 1992); included rehabilitation assignment to Louisville (July 2-6). ... Traded by Cardinals to Boston Red Sox for P Nate Minchey and OF Jeff McNeely (December 7, 1994). ... Claimed on waivers by Cardinals (March 19, 1996). ... Granted free agency (October 31, 1996). ... Signed by Anaheim Angels organization (January 20, 1997). ... Granted free agency (October 30, 1997). ... Signed by Texas Rangers (December 9, 1997). ... Granted free agency (October 28, 1999). ... Re-signed by Rangers (December 7, 1999).

HONORS: Named second baseman on THE SPORTING NEWS college All-America team (1986).

STATISTICAL NOTES: Switch-hit home runs in one game (July 28, 1995). ... Led A.L. second basemen with 699 total chances and 103 double plays in 1995. ... Career major league grand slams: 1.

Year Team (League)	Pos.	G	AB	R	H	2B	3B	HR	RBI	Avg.	BB	SO	SB	PO	A	E	Avg.
1986—Erie (NY-P)	2B	47	163	40	46	6	1	3	18	.282	37	20	27	94	163	12	.955
—Arkansas (Texas)	2B-SS	25	68	8	16	3	0	0	3	.235	5	11	0	39	63	4	.962
1987—Arkansas (Texas)	2B	101	337	57	91	14	3	4	47	.270	49	28	13	184	251	11	*.975
—Louisville (A.A.)	2B	29	105	18	32	10	2	2	20	.305	9	9	4	69	81	4	.974
1988—Louisville (A.A.)	2B-SS-OF	49	191	21	53	11	6	1	21	.277	11	21	8	116	165	0	1.000
—St. Louis (N.L.)	2B	93	297	20	63	10	4	1	24	.212	25	32	1	206	240	14	.970
1989—Louisville (A.A.)	2B	124	412	53	102	20	3	8	48	.248	59	55	13	240	310	16	.972
1990—St. Petersburg (FSL)	2B	29	95	14	22	1	4	0	12	.232	20	14	9	20	23	0	1.000
—Arkansas (Texas)	2B	14	49	11	14	3	1	0	4	.286	7	8	2	24	34	4	.935
—Louisville (A.A.)	3B	25	92	10	32	6	3	0	10	.348	5	12	0	14	39	6	.898
1991—Louisville (A.A.)	2B	31	112	26	44	6	3	4	16	.393	14	8	5	68	95	5	.970
—St. Louis (N.L.)	2B-3B-SS	56	68	5	13	3	0	0	0	.191	8	19	0	19	23	0	1.000
1992—Louisville (A.A.)	2B-SS	20	71	11	20	8	0	0	6	.282	16	6	0	44	52	4	.960
—St. Louis (N.L.)	2B-SS	85	265	26	65	9	11	2	32	.245	27	40	2	136	233	7	.981
1993—St. Louis (N.L.)	2B-OF-3B	115	362	50	101	19	3	3	46	.279	47	54	11	210	281	11	.978
1994—St. Louis (N.L.)	2B-OF	88	205	32	57	12	5	5	29	.278	30	38	4	126	149	4	.986
1995—Boston (A.L.)■	2B	132	419	64	113	20	3	6	44	.270	63	61	13	254	429	16	.977
1996—St. Louis (N.L.)■	2B	129	380	54	98	26	3	5	42	.258	52	78	11	241	288	*24	.957
1997—Anaheim (A.L.)■	2B-3B-DH	128	388	59	98	16	7	5	37	.253	69	65	22	223	287	12	.977
1998—Texas (A.L.)■	2-3-DH-O	101	259	51	71	15	3	6	33	.274	37	40	4	97	143	9	.964
1999—Texas (A.L.)	2B-3B-DH-OF	68	164	33	33	10	0	3	17	.201	28	32	2	66	100	5	.971
American League totals (4 years)		429	1230	207	315	61	13	20	131	.256	197	198	41	640	959	42	.974
National League totals (6 years)		566	1577	187	397	79	26	16	173	.252	189	261	29	938	1214	60	.973
Major League totals (10 years)		995	2807	394	712	140	39	36	304	.254	386	459	70	1578	2173	102	.974

DIVISION SERIES RECORD

Year Team (League)	Pos.	G	AB	R	H	2B	3B	HR	RBI	Avg.	BB	SO	SB	PO	A	E	Avg.
1995—Boston (A.L.)	2B	3	10	1	6	1	0	1	1	.600	2	2	1	6	11	1	.944
1996—St. Louis (N.L.)	2B	3	11	1	2	2	0	0	0	.182	1	4	0	2	5	1	.875
1998—Texas (A.L.)	PH-DH	1	1	0	0	0	0	0	0	.000	0	0	0	...	...	...	...
1999—Texas (A.L.)								Did not play.									
Division series totals (3 years)		7	22	2	8	3	0	1	1	.364	3	6	1	8	16	2	.923

CHAMPIONSHIP SERIES RECORD

Year Team (League)	Pos.	G	AB	R	H	2B	3B	HR	RBI	Avg.	BB	SO	SB	PO	A	E	Avg.
1996—St. Louis (N.L.)	2B-PH	5	8	0	0	0	0	0	0	.000	2	1	0	5	7	1	.923

ALLEN, CHAD — OF — TWINS

PERSONAL: Born February 6, 1975, in Dallas. ... 6-1/195. ... Bats right, throws right. ... Full name: John Chad Allen.
HIGH SCHOOL: Duncanville (Texas).
COLLEGE: Texas A&M.
TRANSACTIONS/CAREER NOTES: Selected by Cincinnati Reds organization in 38th round of free-agent draft (June 3, 1993); did not sign. ... Selected by Minnesota Twins organization in fourth round of free-agent draft (June 4, 1996).
MISCELLANEOUS: Member of 1996 U.S. Olympic baseball team.

Year Team (League)	Pos.	G	AB	R	H	2B	3B	HR	RBI	Avg.	BB	SO	SB	PO	A	E	Avg.
1996—Fort Wayne (Midw.)	OF	7	21	2	9	0	0	0	2	.429	3	2	1	4	1	0	1.000
1997—Fort Myers (FSL)	OF	105	401	66	124	18	4	3	45	.309	40	51	27	206	10	5	.977
—New Britain (East.)	OF	30	115	20	29	9	1	4	18	.252	9	21	2	35	1	1	.973
1998—New Britain (East.)	OF	137	504	70	132	31	7	8	82	.262	51	78	21	185	11	4	.980
1999—Minnesota (A.L.)	OF-DH	137	481	69	133	21	3	10	46	.277	37	89	14	267	9	7	.975
Major League totals (1 year)		137	481	69	133	21	3	10	46	.277	37	89	14	267	9	7	.975

ALLENSWORTH, JERMAINE — OF — RED SOX

PERSONAL: Born January 11, 1972, in Anderson, Ind. ... 6-0/190. ... Bats right, throws right. ... Full name: Jermaine LaMont Allensworth.
HIGH SCHOOL: Madison Heights (Anderson, Ind.).
COLLEGE: Purdue.
TRANSACTIONS/CAREER NOTES: Selected by Pittsburgh Pirates organization in supplemental round ("sandwich pick" between first and second round, 34th pick overall) of free-agent draft (June 3, 1993); pick received as part of compensation for Houston Astros signing Type A free-agent P Doug Drabek. ... On Pittsburgh disabled list (May 16-June 22, 1997); included rehabilitation assignment to Calgary (June 18-22). ... Traded by Pirates to Kansas City Royals for P Manuel Bernal (June 27, 1998). ... Traded by Royals to New York Mets for a player to be named later (August 10, 1998); Royals received cash to complete deal (September 3, 1998). ... Traded by Mets to Boston Red Sox for OF Jon Nunnally (November 12, 1999).
STATISTICAL NOTES: Career major league grand slams: 1.

Year	Team (League)	Pos.	G	AB	R	H	2B	3B	HR	RBI	Avg.	BB	SO	SB	PO	A	E	Avg.
1993—	Welland (NY-P)..........	OF	67	263	44	81	16	4	1	32	.308	24	38	18	140	2	3	.979
1994—	Carolina (Sou.)	OF	118	452	63	109	26	8	1	34	.241	39	79	16	245	5	6	.977
1995—	Carolina (Sou.)	OF	56	219	37	59	14	2	1	14	.269	25	34	13	131	3	2	.985
—	Calgary (PCL)............	OF	51	190	46	60	13	4	3	11	.316	13	30	13	90	2	1	.989
1996—	Calgary (PCL)............	OF-DH	95	352	77	116	23	6	8	43	.330	39	61	25	196	4	6	.971
—	Pittsburgh (N.L.)	OF	61	229	32	60	9	3	4	31	.262	23	50	11	139	4	3	.979
1997—	Pittsburgh (N.L.)	OF	108	369	55	94	18	2	3	43	.255	44	79	14	189	5	4	.980
—	Calgary (PCL)............	OF	5	20	5	8	3	1	0	1	.400	2	4	1	8	0	0	1.000
1998—	Pittsburgh (N.L.)	OF	69	233	30	72	13	3	3	24	.309	17	43	8	145	4	3	.980
—	Kansas City (A.L.)■...	OF	30	73	15	15	5	0	0	3	.205	9	17	7	54	0	1	.982
—	New York (N.L.)■........	OF	34	54	9	11	2	0	2	4	.204	2	16	0	22	0	0	1.000
1999—	New York (N.L.)........	OF	40	73	14	16	2	0	3	9	.219	9	23	2	47	1	0	1.000
—	Norfolk (I.L.)............	OF-DH	81	273	44	72	20	5	5	20	.264	36	39	10	155	3	4	.975
American League totals (1 year)			30	73	15	15	5	0	0	3	.205	9	17	7	54	0	1	.982
National League totals (4 years)			312	958	140	253	44	8	15	111	.264	95	211	35	542	14	10	.982
Major League totals (4 years)			342	1031	155	268	49	8	15	114	.260	104	228	42	596	14	11	.982

ALMANZA, ARMANDO   P   MARLINS

PERSONAL: Born October 26, 1972, in El Paso, Texas. ... 6-3/205. ... Throws left, bats left.
HIGH SCHOOL: Belair (El Paso, Texas).
JUNIOR COLLEGE: New Mexico Junior College.
TRANSACTIONS/CAREER NOTES: Selected by St. Louis Cardinals organization in 21st round of free-agent draft (June 3, 1993). ... On Madison disabled list (April 8, 1994-entire season). ... On Memphis disabled list (July 10-21, 1998). ... Traded by Cardinals with P Braden Looper and SS Pablo Ozuna to Florida Marlins for SS Edgar Renteria (December 14, 1998). ... On Calgary disabled list (May 10-June 2, 1999).
STATISTICAL NOTES: Tied for Arizona League lead with 14 wild pitches in 1993.

Year	League	W	L	Pct.	ERA	G	GS	CG	ShO	Sv.	IP	H	R	ER	BB	SO
1993—	Ariz. Cardinals (Ariz.)	4	1	.800	3.21	20	4	0	0	0	42	38	19	15	14	56
—	Johnson City (Appl.)	1	1	.500	4.15	3	3	0	0	0	4¹/₃	6	2	2	3	4
1994—	Madison (Midw.)							Did not play.								
1995—	Savannah (SAL)	3	9	.250	3.92	20	20	0	0	0	108	108	62	47	40	72
1996—	Peoria (Midw.)	8	6	.571	2.76	52	1	0	0	0	62	50	27	19	32	67
1997—	Prince William (Caro.)	2	3	.400	1.67	•58	0	0	0	*36	64²/₃	38	18	12	32	83
1998—	Arkansas (Texas)................	4	1	.800	3.31	28	0	0	0	8	32²/₃	27	13	12	18	46
—	Memphis (PCL)	3	1	.750	3.03	31	0	0	0	1	35²/₃	35	18	12	19	45
1999—	Calgary (PCL)■................	2	2	.500	10.90	15	0	0	0	0	17¹/₃	29	27	21	18	20
—	Portland (East.)	0	1	.000	3.97	10	0	0	0	3	11¹/₃	5	5	5	4	20
—	Florida (N.L.)................	0	1	.000	1.72	14	0	0	0	0	15²/₃	8	4	3	9	20
Major League totals (1 year)		0	1	.000	1.72	14	0	0	0	0	15²/₃	8	4	3	9	20

ALMANZAR, CARLOS   P   PADRES

PERSONAL: Born November 6, 1973, in Santiago, Dominican Republic. ... 6-2/200. ... Throws right, bats right. ... Full name: Carlos Manuel Almanzar.
TRANSACTIONS/CAREER NOTES: Signed as non-drafted free agent by Toronto Blue Jays organization (December 10, 1990). ... On Knoxville disabled list (May 27-June 3, 1997). ... Traded by Blue Jays with P Woody Williams and OF Peter Tucci to San Diego Padres for P Joey Hamilton (December 13, 1998). ... On San Diego disabled list (April 24-May 27, 1999); included rehabilitation assignment to Las Vegas (May 22-27).

Year	League	W	L	Pct.	ERA	G	GS	CG	ShO	Sv.	IP	H	R	ER	BB	SO
1991—	Dom. Blue Jays (DSL)........	3	1	.750	2.83	6	6	1	0	0	35	36	17	11	11	20
1992—	Dom. Blue Jays (DSL)........	10	0	1.000	2.01	13	11	2	1	1	67	45	26	15	31	60
1993—	Dom. Blue Jays (DSL)........	5	2	.714	3.38	16	9	0	0	2	69¹/₃	60	35	26	32	59
1994—	Medicine Hat (Pio.)	7	4	.636	2.87	14	14	0	0	0	84²/₃	82	38	27	19	77
1995—	Knoxville (Sou.)................	3	12	.200	3.99	35	19	0	0	2	126¹/₃	144	77	56	32	93
1996—	Knoxville (Sou.)................	7	8	.467	4.85	54	0	0	0	9	94²/₃	106	58	51	33	105
1997—	Knoxville (Sou.)................	1	1	.500	4.91	21	0	0	0	8	25²/₃	30	14	14	5	25
—	Syracuse (I.L.)................	5	1	.833	1.41	32	0	0	0	3	51	30	9	8	8	47
—	Toronto (A.L.)................	0	1	.000	2.70	4	0	0	0	0	3¹/₃	1	1	1	1	4
1998—	Toronto (A.L.)................	2	2	.500	5.34	25	0	0	0	0	28²/₃	34	18	17	8	20
—	Syracuse (I.L.)................	3	6	.333	2.31	30	0	0	0	10	50²/₃	44	21	13	13	53
1999—	San Diego (N.L.)■	0	0	...	7.47	28	0	0	0	0	37¹/₃	48	32	31	15	30
—	Las Vegas (PCL)	1	3	.250	9.53	11	3	0	0	0	22²/₃	32	25	24	8	18
A.L. totals (2 years)		2	3	.400	5.06	29	0	0	0	0	32	35	19	18	9	24
N.L. totals (1 year)		0	0	...	7.47	28	0	0	0	0	37¹/₃	48	32	31	15	30
Major League totals (3 years)		2	3	.400	6.36	57	0	0	0	0	69¹/₃	83	51	49	24	54

ALMONTE, HECTOR   P   MARLINS

PERSONAL: Born October 17, 1975, in Santo Domingo, Dominican Republic. ... 6-2/190. ... Throws right, bats right. ... Full name: Hector Radhames Almonte.
HIGH SCHOOL: Liceo Jose Marti (Santo Domingo, Dominican Republic).
TRANSACTIONS/CAREER NOTES: Signed as non-drafted free agent by Florida Marlins organization (February 9, 1993).

Year	League	W	L	Pct.	ERA	G	GS	CG	ShO	Sv.	IP	H	R	ER	BB	SO
1993—	Dom. Marlins (DSL)..........	1	6	.143	4.79	13	7	1	0	1	56¹/₃	59	39	30	29	20
1994—	Dom. Marlins (DSL)..........	3	5	.375	4.34	20	4	0	0	0	58	68	40	28	26	26
1995—	Dom. Marlins (DSL)..........	1	2	.333	4.26	20	1	0	0	9	31²/₃	28	17	15	11	27
1996—	Dom. Marlins (DSL)..........	0	0	...	0.00	2	0	0	0	0	1²/₃	0	0	0	1	2

Year League	W	L	Pct.	ERA	G	GS	CG	ShO	Sv.	IP	H	R	ER	BB	SO
1997— GC Marlins (GCL)...............	2	0	1.000	0.76	8	0	0	0	3	23 2/3	12	3	2	6	25
— Kane County (Midw.)..........	0	1	.000	3.86	8	1	0	0	1	14	11	6	6	6	10
1998— Kane County (Midw.)..........	1	5	.167	3.95	43	0	0	0	21	43 1/3	51	22	19	19	51
1999— Portland (East.).................	1	4	.200	2.84	47	0	0	0	23	44 1/3	42	14	14	26	42
—Florida (N.L.)......................	0	2	.000	4.20	15	0	0	0	0	15	20	7	7	6	8
Major League totals (1 year)........	0	2	.000	4.20	15	0	0	0	0	15	20	7	7	6	8

ALOMAR, ROBERTO   2B   INDIANS

PERSONAL: Born February 5, 1968, in Ponce, Puerto Rico. ... 6-0/185. ... Bats both, throws right. ... Full name: Roberto Velazquez Alomar. ... Son of Sandy Alomar Sr., major league infielder with six teams (1964-78) and coach, Chicago Cubs; and brother of Sandy Alomar Jr., catcher, Cleveland Indians.

TRANSACTIONS/CAREER NOTES: Signed as non-drafted free agent by San Diego Padres organization (February 16, 1985). ... Traded by Padres with OF Joe Carter to Toronto Blue Jays for 1B Fred McGriff and SS Tony Fernandez (December 5, 1990). ... On suspended list (May 23-24, 1995). ... Granted free agency (October 30, 1995). ... Signed by Baltimore Orioles (December 21, 1995). ... On suspended list (April 1-7, 1997). ... On disabled list (July 30-August 26, 1997; and July 19-August 4, 1998). ... Granted free agency (October 26, 1998). ... Signed by Cleveland Indians (December 1, 1998).

RECORDS: Holds major league single-season record for most runs by switch-hitter—138 (1999). ... Holds A.L. career record for most consecutive errorless games by second baseman—104 (June 21, 1994 through July 3, 1995). ... Holds A.L. single-season record for fewest double plays by second baseman (150 or more games)—66 (1992). ... Shares A.L. single-season records for most games with switch-hit home runs—2 (1996); and fewest errors by second baseman (150 or more games)—5 (1992).

HONORS: Won A.L. Gold Glove at second base (1991-96, 1998 and 1999). ... Named second baseman on THE SPORTING NEWS A.L. All-Star team (1992, 1996, 1998 and 1999). ... Named second baseman on THE SPORTING NEWS A.L. Silver Slugger team (1992, 1996 and 1999).

STATISTICAL NOTES: Led South Atlantic League second basemen with 35 errors in 1985. ... Led Texas League shortstops with 167 putouts and 34 errors in 1987. ... Led N.L. with 17 sacrifice hits in 1989. ... Led N.L. second basemen with 17 errors in 1990. ... Switch-hit home runs in one game four times (May 10, 1991; May 3, 1995; July 25 and August 14, 1996). ... Had 22-game hitting streak (May 12-June 8, 1996). ... Hit three home runs in one game (April 26, 1997). ... Led A.L. with 13 sacrifice flies in 1999. ... Career major league grand slams: 5.

MISCELLANEOUS: Holds Toronto Blue Jays all-time record for highest career batting average (.307).

Year Team (League)	Pos.	G	AB	R	H	2B	3B	HR	RBI	Avg.	BB	SO	SB	PO	A	E	Avg.
1985— Char., S.C. (SAL)	2B-SS	*137	*546	89	160	14	3	0	54	.293	61	73	36	298	339	†36	.947
1986— Reno (Calif.)	2B	90	356	53	123	16	4	4	49	*.346	32	38	14	198	265	18	.963
1987— Wichita (Texas)	SS-2B	130	536	88	171	41	4	12	68	.319	49	74	43	†188	309	†36	.932
1988— Las Vegas (PCL)	2B	9	37	5	10	1	0	2	14	.270	1	4	3	22	29	1	.981
—San Diego (N.L.)	2B	143	545	84	145	24	6	9	41	.266	47	83	24	319	459	16	.980
1989— San Diego (N.L.)	2B	158	623	82	184	27	1	7	56	.295	53	76	42	341	472	*28	.967
1990— San Diego (N.L.)	2B-SS	147	586	80	168	27	5	6	60	.287	48	72	24	316	404	†19	.974
1991— Toronto (A.L.)■.........	2B	161	637	88	188	41	11	9	69	.295	57	86	53	333	447	15	.981
1992— Toronto (A.L.).........	2B-DH	152	571	105	177	27	8	8	76	.310	87	52	49	287	378	5	.993
1993— Toronto (A.L.).........	2B	153	589	109	192	35	6	17	93	.326	80	67	55	254	439	14	.980
1994— Toronto (A.L.).........	2B	107	392	78	120	25	4	8	38	.306	51	41	19	176	275	4	.991
1995— Toronto (A.L.).........	2B	130	517	71	155	24	7	13	66	.300	47	45	30	*272	267	4	*.993
1996— Baltimore (A.L.)■......	2B-DH	153	588	132	193	43	4	22	94	.328	90	65	17	279	445	11	.985
1997— Baltimore (A.L.)........	2B-DH	112	412	64	137	23	2	14	60	.333	40	43	9	202	301	6	.988
1998— Baltimore (A.L.)........	2B-DH	147	588	86	166	36	1	14	56	.282	59	70	18	251	*449	11	.985
1999— Cleveland (A.L.)■.......	2B-DH	159	563	*138	182	40	3	24	120	.323	99	96	37	270	466	6	*.992
American League totals (9 years)		1274	4857	871	1510	294	46	129	672	.311	610	565	287	2324	3467	76	.987
National League totals (3 years)		448	1754	246	497	78	12	22	157	.283	148	231	90	976	1335	63	.973
Major League totals (12 years)		1722	6611	1117	2007	372	58	151	829	.304	758	796	377	3300	4802	139	.983

DIVISION SERIES RECORD

RECORDS: Shares career record for most doubles—6. ... Shares single-series record for most doubles—4 (1999).

Year Team (League)	Pos.	G	AB	R	H	2B	3B	HR	RBI	Avg.	BB	SO	SB	PO	A	E	Avg.
1996— Baltimore (A.L.)..........	2B	4	17	2	5	0	0	1	4	.294	2	3	0	10	6	0	1.000
1997— Baltimore (A.L.)..........	2B-PH	4	10	1	3	2	0	0	2	.300	1	1	0	3	6	0	1.000
1999— Cleveland (A.L.)..........	2B	5	19	4	7	4	0	0	3	.368	2	3	2	13	14	1	.964
Division series totals (3 years)		13	46	7	15	6	0	1	9	.326	5	7	2	26	26	1	.981

CHAMPIONSHIP SERIES RECORD

RECORDS: Shares career record for most times grounded into double play—5.

NOTES: Named Most Valuable Player (1992).

Year Team (League)	Pos.	G	AB	R	H	2B	3B	HR	RBI	Avg.	BB	SO	SB	PO	A	E	Avg.
1991— Toronto (A.L.)............	2B	5	19	3	9	0	0	0	4	.474	2	3	2	14	9	0	1.000
1992— Toronto (A.L.)............	2B	6	26	4	11	1	0	2	4	.423	2	1	5	16	15	0	1.000
1993— Toronto (A.L.)............	2B	6	24	3	7	1	0	0	4	.292	4	3	4	14	19	0	1.000
1996— Baltimore (A.L.)........	2B	5	23	2	5	2	0	0	1	.217	0	4	0	15	26	2	.953
1997— Baltimore (A.L.)........	2B	6	22	2	4	0	0	1	2	.182	7	3	0	10	17	2	.931
Championship series totals (5 years)		28	114	14	36	4	0	3	15	.316	15	14	11	69	86	4	.975

WORLD SERIES RECORD

RECORDS: Shares record for most at-bats in one inning—2 (October 20, 1993, eighth inning).

NOTES: Member of World Series championship team (1992 and 1993).

Year Team (League)	Pos.	G	AB	R	H	2B	3B	HR	RBI	Avg.	BB	SO	SB	PO	A	E	Avg.
1992— Toronto (A.L.)............	2B	6	24	3	5	1	0	0	0	.208	3	3	3	5	12	0	1.000
1993— Toronto (A.L.)............	2B	6	25	5	12	2	1	0	6	.480	2	3	4	9	21	2	.938
World Series totals (2 years)		12	49	8	17	3	1	0	6	.347	5	6	7	14	33	2	.959

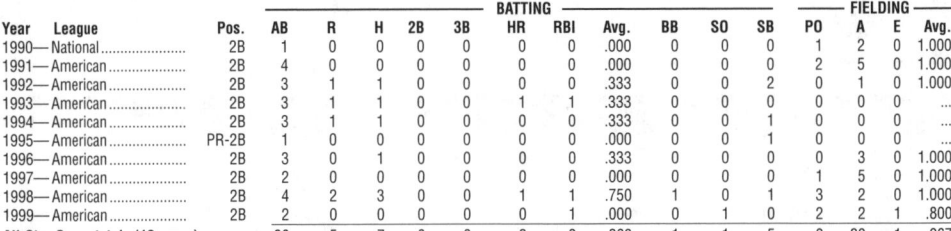

ALL-STAR GAME RECORD

RECORDS: Shares single-game record for most stolen bases—2 (July 14, 1992).
NOTES: Named Most Valuable Player (1998).

A

Year	League	Pos.	AB	R	H	2B	3B	HR	RBI	Avg.	BB	SO	SB	PO	A	E	Avg.
1990— National		2B	1	0	0	0	0	0	0	.000	0	0	0	1	2	0	1.000
1991— American		2B	4	0	0	0	0	0	0	.000	0	0	0	2	5	0	1.000
1992— American		2B	3	1	1	0	0	0	0	.333	0	0	2	0	1	0	1.000
1993— American		2B	3	1	1	0	0	1	1	.333	0	0	0	0	0	0	...
1994— American		2B	3	1	1	0	0	0	0	.333	0	0	1	0	0	0	...
1995— American		PR-2B	1	0	0	0	0	0	0	.000	0	0	1	0	0	0	...
1996— American		2B	3	0	1	0	0	0	0	.333	0	0	0	0	3	0	1.000
1997— American		2B	2	0	0	0	0	0	0	.000	0	0	0	1	5	0	1.000
1998— American		2B	4	2	3	0	0	1	1	.750	1	0	1	3	2	0	1.000
1999— American		2B	2	0	0	0	0	0	1	.000	0	1	0	2	2	1	.800
All-Star Game totals (10 years)			26	5	7	0	0	2	3	.269	1	1	5	9	20	1	.967

ALOMAR, SANDY   C   INDIANS

PERSONAL: Born June 18, 1966, in Salinas, Puerto Rico. ... 6-5/215. ... Bats right, throws right. ... Full name: Santos Velazquez Alomar Jr. ... Son of Sandy Alomar Sr., major league infielder with six teams (1964-78) and coach, Chicago Cubs; and brother of Roberto Alomar, second baseman, Cleveland Indians.
HIGH SCHOOL: Luis Munoz Rivera (Salinas, Puerto Rico).
TRANSACTIONS/CAREER NOTES: Signed as non-drafted free agent by San Diego Padres organization (October 21, 1983). ... Traded by Padres with OF Chris James and 3B Carlos Baerga to Cleveland Indians for OF Joe Carter (December 6, 1989). ... On Cleveland disabled list (May 15-June 17 and July 29, 1991-remainder of season); included rehabilitation assignments to Colorado Springs (June 8-17 and August 9-12). ... On disabled list (May 2-18, 1992). ... On suspended list (July 29-August 2, 1992). ... On Cleveland disabled list (May 1-August 7, 1993); included rehabilitation assignment to Charlotte, S.C. (July 22-August 7). ... On disabled list (April 24-May 11, 1994). ... On Cleveland disabled list (April 19-June 29, 1995); included rehabilitation assignment to Canton/Akron (June 22-29). ... On Cleveland disabled list (May 11-September 6, 1999); included rehabilitation assignments to Akron (July 5-19 and September 3-6) and Buffalo (August 10-27).
RECORDS: Shares major league single-game record for most doubles—4 (June 6, 1997).
HONORS: Named Minor League co-Player of the Year by THE SPORTING NEWS (1988). ... Named Pacific Coast League Player of the Year (1988-89). ... Named Minor League Player of the Year by THE SPORTING NEWS (1989). ... Named A.L. Rookie Player of the Year by THE SPORTING NEWS (1990). ... Won A.L. Gold Glove at catcher (1990). ... Named A.L. Rookie of the Year by Baseball Writers' Association of America (1990).
STATISTICAL NOTES: Led Northwest League catchers with .985 fielding percentage and 421 putouts in 1984. ... Led Pacific Coast League catchers with 14 errors in 1988. ... Led Pacific Coast League catchers with 573 putouts in 1988 and 702 in 1989. ... Led Pacific Coast League catchers with 633 total chances in 1988 and 761 in 1989. ... Had 30-game hitting streak (May 25-July 6, 1997). ... Career major league grand slams: 2.
MISCELLANEOUS: Batted as switch hitter (1984-86).

Year	Team (League)	Pos.	G	AB	R	H	2B	3B	HR	RBI	Avg.	BB	SO	SB	PO	A	E	Avg.
1984— Spokane (N.W.)		C-1B	59	219	13	47	5	0	0	21	.215	13	20	3	†465	51	8	†.985
1985— Char., S.C. (SAL)		C-OF	100	352	38	73	7	0	3	43	.207	31	30	3	779	75	18	.979
1986— Beaumont (Texas)		C	100	346	36	83	15	1	4	27	.240	15	35	2	505	60	*18	.969
1987— Wichita (Texas)		C	103	375	50	115	19	1	8	65	.307	21	37	1	*606	50	*15	.978
1988— Las Vegas (PCL)		C-OF	93	337	59	100	9	5	16	71	.297	28	35	1	†574	46	†14	.978
— San Diego (N.L.)		PH	1	1	0	0	0	0	0	0	.000	0	1	0	...	...	...	...
1989— Las Vegas (PCL)		C-OF	131	*523	88	160	33	8	13	101	.306	42	58	3	†706	47	12	.984
— San Diego (N.L.)		C	7	19	1	4	1	0	1	6	.211	3	3	0	33	1	0	1.000
1990— Cleveland (A.L.)■		C	132	445	60	129	26	2	9	66	.290	25	46	4	686	46	*14	.981
1991— Cleveland (A.L.)		C-DH	51	184	10	40	9	0	0	7	.217	8	24	0	280	19	4	.987
— Colo. Springs (PCL)		C	12	35	5	14	2	0	1	10	.400	5	0	0	5	0	1	.833
1992— Cleveland (A.L.)		C-DH	89	299	22	75	16	0	2	26	.251	13	32	3	477	39	2	.996
1993— Cleveland (A.L.)		C	64	215	24	58	7	1	6	32	.270	11	28	3	342	25	6	.984
— Charlotte (I.L.)		C	12	44	8	16	5	0	1	8	.364	5	8	0	20	1	0	1.000
1994— Cleveland (A.L.)		C	80	292	44	84	15	1	14	43	.288	25	31	8	453	41	2	.996
1995— Canton/Akron (East.)		C-DH	6	15	3	6	1	0	0	1	.400	1	1	0	23	0	1	.958
— Cleveland (A.L.)		C	66	203	32	61	6	0	10	35	.300	7	26	3	364	22	2	.995
1996— Cleveland (A.L.)		C-1B	127	418	53	110	23	0	11	50	.263	19	42	1	724	48	9	.988
1997— Cleveland (A.L.)		C-DH	125	451	63	146	37	0	21	83	.324	19	48	0	743	40	*12	.985
1998— Cleveland (A.L.)		C-DH	117	409	45	96	26	2	6	44	.235	18	45	0	712	42	6	.992
1999— Cleveland (A.L.)		C-DH	37	137	19	42	13	0	6	25	.307	4	23	0	257	10	7	.974
— Akron (East.)		DH-C	10	29	8	9	0	0	1	6	.310	3	2	1	12	1	1	.929
— Buffalo (I.L.)		C-DH	10	33	9	9	2	1	2	10	.273	6	3	0	35	0	3	.921
American League totals (10 years)			888	3053	372	841	178	6	85	411	.275	149	345	22	5038	332	64	.988
National League totals (2 years)			8	20	1	4	1	0	1	6	.200	3	4	0	33	1	0	1.000
Major League totals (12 years)			896	3073	373	845	179	6	86	417	.275	152	349	22	5071	333	64	.988

DIVISION SERIES RECORD

RECORDS: Shares career record for most games—21.

Year	Team (League)	Pos.	G	AB	R	H	2B	3B	HR	RBI	Avg.	BB	SO	SB	PO	A	E	Avg.
1995— Cleveland (A.L.)		C	3	11	1	2	1	0	0	1	.182	0	1	0	22	1	0	1.000
1996— Cleveland (A.L.)		C	4	16	0	2	0	0	0	3	.125	0	2	0	40	4	1	.978
1997— Cleveland (A.L.)		C	5	19	4	6	1	0	2	5	.316	0	2	0	28	1	1	.967
1998— Cleveland (A.L.)		C	4	13	2	3	3	0	0	2	.231	1	4	0	29	0	1	.967
1999— Cleveland (A.L.)		C	5	14	1	2	0	0	0	1	.143	2	6	0	33	1	1	.971
Division series totals (5 years)			21	73	8	15	5	0	2	12	.205	3	15	0	152	7	4	.975

CHAMPIONSHIP SERIES RECORD

						BATTING									FIELDING		
Year	Team (League)	Pos.	G	AB	R	H	2B	3B	HR	RBI	Avg.	BB	SO	SB	PO	A	E	Avg.
1995— Cleveland (A.L.).........		C	5	15	0	4	1	1	0	1	.267	1	1	0	30	3	1	.971
1997— Cleveland (A.L.).........		C	6	24	3	3	0	0	1	4	.125	1	3	0	49	1	0	1.000
1998— Cleveland (A.L.).........		C	5	16	1	1	0	0	0	0	.063	0	2	0	29	1	2	.938
Championship series totals (3 years)			16	55	4	8	1	1	1	5	.145	2	6	0	108	5	3	.974

WORLD SERIES RECORD

						BATTING									FIELDING		
Year	Team (League)	Pos.	G	AB	R	H	2B	3B	HR	RBI	Avg.	BB	SO	SB	PO	A	E	Avg.
1995— Cleveland (A.L.).........		C	5	15	0	3	2	0	0	1	.200	0	2	0	28	0	0	1.000
1997— Cleveland (A.L.).........		C	7	30	5	11	1	0	2	10	.367	2	3	0	49	3	0	1.000
World Series totals (2 years)			12	45	5	14	3	0	2	11	.311	2	5	0	77	3	0	1.000

ALL-STAR GAME RECORD

NOTES: Named Most Valuable Player (1997).

					BATTING								FIELDING		
Year	League	Pos.	AB	R	H	2B	3B	HR	RBI	Avg.	BB	SO	SB	PO	A	E	Avg.
1990— American....................		C	3	1	2	0	0	0	0	.667	0	0	0	3	0	0	1.000
1991— American....................		C	2	0	0	0	0	0	0	.000	0	0	0	2	0	0	1.000
1992— American....................		C	3	0	1	0	0	0	0	.333	0	0	0	3	0	0	1.000
1996— American....................		PH-C	2	0	0	0	0	0	0	.000	0	0	0	1	0	0	1.000
1997— American....................		C	1	1	1	0	0	1	2	1.000	0	0	0	4	0	0	1.000
1998— American....................		C	1	0	1	0	0	0	1	1.000	0	0	0	5	0	0	1.000
All-Star Game totals (6 years)			12	2	5	0	0	1	3	.417	0	0	0	18	0	0	1.000

ALOU, MOISES   OF   ASTROS

PERSONAL: Born July 3, 1966, in Atlanta. ... 6-3/195. ... Bats right, throws right. ... Full name: Moises Rojas Alou. ... Son of Felipe Alou, manager, Montreal Expos; nephew of Jesus Alou, major league outfielder with four teams (1963-75 and 1978-79); nephew of Matty Alou, major league outfielder with six teams (1960-74); and cousin of Mel Rojas, major league pitcher with five teams (1990-99). ... Name pronounced moy-SEZZ ah-LOO.

HIGH SCHOOL: C.E.E. (Santo Domingo, Dominican Republic).

JUNIOR COLLEGE: Canada College (Calif.).

TRANSACTIONS/CAREER NOTES: Selected by Pittsburgh Pirates organization in first round (second pick overall) of free-agent draft (January 14, 1986). ... Traded by Pirates organization to Montreal Expos (August 16, 1990), completing deal in which Expos traded P Zane Smith to Pirates for P Scott Ruskin, SS Willie Greene and a player to be named later (August 8, 1990). ... On Montreal disabled list (March 19, 1991-entire season; July 7-27, 1992; September 18, 1993-remainder of season; August 18-September 5, 1995 and September 11, 1995-remainder of season). ... On disabled list (July 8-23, 1996). ... On suspended list (August 23-27, 1996). ... Granted free agency (December 7, 1996). ... Signed by Florida Marlins (December 12, 1996). ... Traded by Marlins to Houston Astros for P Oscar Henriquez, P Manuel Barrios and a player to be named later (November 11, 1997); Marlins acquired P Mark Johnson to complete deal (December 16, 1997). ... On disabled list (April 3, 1999-entire season).

HONORS: Named outfielder on THE SPORTING NEWS N.L. All-Star team (1994 and 1998). ... Named outfielder on THE SPORTING NEWS N.L. Silver Slugger team (1994 and 1998).

STATISTICAL NOTES: Led American Association outfielders with seven double plays in 1990. ... Career major league grand slams: 2.

						BATTING									FIELDING		
Year	Team (League)	Pos.	G	AB	R	H	2B	3B	HR	RBI	Avg.	BB	SO	SB	PO	A	E	Avg.
1986— Watertown (NY-P)......		OF	69	254	30	60	9	*8	6	35	.236	22	72	14	134	6	7	.952
1987— Macon (SAL).............		OF	4	8	1	1	0	0	0	0	.125	2	4	0	6	0	0	1.000
— Watertown (NY-P)......		OF	39	117	20	25	6	2	4	8	.214	16	36	6	43	1	2	.957
1988— Augusta (SAL)...........		OF	105	358	58	112	23	5	7	62	.313	51	84	24	220	10	9	.962
1989— Salem (Caro.)............		OF	86	321	50	97	29	2	14	53	.302	35	69	12	166	12	10	.947
— Harrisburg (East.)......		OF	54	205	36	60	5	2	3	19	.293	17	38	8	89	1	2	.978
1990— Harrisburg (East.)......		OF	36	132	19	39	12	2	3	22	.295	16	21	7	93	2	1	.990
— Buffalo (A.A.)............		OF	75	271	38	74	4	6	5	31	.273	30	43	9	169	10	8	.957
— Pittsburgh (N.L.)		OF	2	5	0	1	0	0	0	0	.200	0	0	0	3	0	0	1.000
— Indianapolis (A.A.)■...		OF	15	55	6	12	1	0	0	6	.218	3	7	4	27	2	0	1.000
— Montreal (N.L.)		OF	14	15	4	3	0	1	0	0	.200	0	3	0	6	1	0	1.000
1991— Montreal (N.L.)..........								Did not play.										
1992— Montreal (N.L.)..........		OF	115	341	53	96	28	2	9	56	.282	25	46	16	170	6	4	.978
1993— Montreal (N.L.)..........		OF	136	482	70	138	29	6	18	85	.286	38	53	17	254	11	4	.985
1994— Montreal (N.L.)..........		OF	107	422	81	143	31	5	22	78	.339	42	63	7	201	4	3	.986
1995— Montreal (N.L.)..........		OF	93	344	48	94	22	0	14	58	.273	29	56	4	147	5	3	.981
1996— Montreal (N.L.)..........		OF	143	540	87	152	28	2	21	96	.281	49	83	9	259	8	3	.989
1997— Florida (N.L.)■..........		OF	150	538	88	157	29	5	23	115	.292	70	85	9	248	4	3	.988
1998— Houston (N.L.)■........		OF-DH	159	584	104	182	34	5	38	124	.312	84	87	11	232	11	5	.980
1999— Houston (N.L.)..........								Did not play.										
Major League totals (8 years)			919	3271	535	966	201	26	145	612	.295	337	476	73	1520	50	25	.984

DIVISION SERIES RECORD

						BATTING									FIELDING		
Year	Team (League)	Pos.	G	AB	R	H	2B	3B	HR	RBI	Avg.	BB	SO	SB	PO	A	E	Avg.
1997— Florida (N.L.).............		OF	3	14	1	3	1	0	0	1	.214	0	3	0	5	0	0	1.000
1998— Houston (N.L.)		OF	4	16	0	3	0	0	0	0	.188	0	2	0	4	0	0	1.000
Division series totals (2 years)			7	30	1	6	1	0	0	1	.200	0	5	0	9	0	0	1.000

CHAMPIONSHIP SERIES RECORD

						BATTING									FIELDING		
Year	Team (League)	Pos.	G	AB	R	H	2B	3B	HR	RBI	Avg.	BB	SO	SB	PO	A	E	Avg.
1997— Florida (N.L.).............		OF-PH	5	15	0	1	1	0	0	5	.067	1	3	0	3	0	0	1.000

WORLD SERIES RECORD

Year Team (League)	Pos.	G	AB	R	H	2B	3B	HR	RBI	Avg.	BB	SO	SB	PO	A	E	Avg.
1997— Florida (N.L.)	OF	7	28	6	9	2	0	3	9	.321	3	6	1	11	0	0	1.000

ALL-STAR GAME RECORD

Year League	Pos.	AB	R	H	2B	3B	HR	RBI	Avg.	BB	SO	SB	PO	A	E	Avg.
1994— National	OF	1	0	1	1	0	0	1	1.000	0	0	0	0	0		...
1997— National	OF	2	0	1	0	0	0	0	.500	0	0	0	1	0	0	1.000
1998— National	OF	3	1	1	0	0	0	0	.333	0	2	0	0	0		...
All-Star Game totals (3 years)		6	1	3	1	0	0	1	.500	0	2	0	1	0	0	1.000

ALVAREZ, GABE   3B   TIGERS

PERSONAL: Born March 6, 1974, in Navojoa, Sonora, Mexico. ... 6-1/205. ... Bats right, throws right. ... Full name: Gabriel De Jesus Alvarez.
HIGH SCHOOL: Bishop Amat (La Puente, Calif.).
COLLEGE: Southern California.
TRANSACTIONS/CAREER NOTES: Selected by San Diego Padres organization in second round of free-agent draft (June 1, 1995). ... Selected by Arizona Diamondbacks in first round (fifth pick overall) of expansion draft (November 18, 1997). ... Traded by Diamondbacks with 3B Joe Randa and P Matt Drews to Detroit Tigers for 3B Travis Fryman (November 18, 1997).
STATISTICAL NOTES: Led Southern League third basemen with 32 errors in 1997. ... Led Southern League in grounding into double plays with 21 in 1997. ... Career major league grand slams: 1.

Year Team (League)	Pos.	G	AB	R	H	2B	3B	HR	RBI	Avg.	BB	SO	SB	PO	A	E	Avg.
1995— Rancho Cuca. (Calif.)	SS-3B	59	212	41	73	17	2	6	36	.344	29	30	1	52	132	22	.893
— Memphis (Sou.)	2B-SS	2	9	0	5	1	0	0	4	.556	1	1	0	6	1	.857
1996— Memphis (Sou.)	3B-SS	104	368	58	91	23	1	8	40	.247	64	87	2	62	161	31	.878
1997— Mobile (Sou.)	3B-SS	114	427	71	128	28	2	14	78	.300	51	64	1	70	209	†33	.894
1998— Toledo (I.L.)■	3B	67	249	37	68	15	1	20	58	.273	30	60	3	38	142	15	.923
— Detroit (A.L.)	3B-DH	58	199	16	46	11	0	5	29	.231	18	65	1	38	93	19	.873
1999— Toledo (I.L.)	3-O-DH-S	110	410	70	117	24	0	21	67	.285	57	80	1	87	165	26	.906
— Detroit (A.L.)	DH-OF-3B	22	53	5	11	3	0	2	4	.208	3	9	0	3	1	0	1.000
Major League totals (2 years)		80	252	21	57	14	0	7	33	.226	21	74	1	41	94	19	.877

ALVAREZ, JUAN   P   ANGELS

PERSONAL: Born August 9, 1973, in Coral Gables, Fla. ... 6-0/175. ... Throws left, bats left. ... Full name: Juan M. Alvarez.
HIGH SCHOOL: Coral Gables (Fla.).
COLLEGE: St. Thomas.
TRANSACTIONS/CAREER NOTES: Signed as non-drafted free agent by California Angels organization (July 25, 1995). ... Angels franchise renamed Anaheim Angels for 1997 season.

Year League	W	L	Pct.	ERA	G	GS	CG	ShO	Sv.	IP	H	R	ER	BB	SO
1995— Boise (N.W.)	0	0	...	0.77	9	0	0	0	0	11 2/3	12	1	1	2	11
1996— Cedar Rapids (Midw.)	1	2	.333	3.40	40	0	0	0	3	53	50	25	20	30	53
1997— Lake Elsinore (Calif.)	4	2	.667	1.40	27	0	0	0	3	51 1/3	33	9	8	13	46
— Midland (Texas)	4	1	.800	8.27	24	0	0	0	0	37	63	42	34	22	27
1998— Midland (Texas)	3	4	.429	4.30	40	0	0	0	12	46	40	26	22	21	41
— Vancouver (PCL)	1	1	.500	5.02	18	0	0	0	0	14 1/3	14	9	8	8	12
1999— Erie (East.)	1	2	.333	2.05	23	0	0	0	4	30 2/3	20	14	7	6	22
— Edmonton (PCL)	0	3	.000	3.49	27	0	0	0	0	28 1/3	30	13	11	8	25
— Anaheim (A.L.)	0	1	.000	3.00	8	0	0	0	0	3	1	1	1	4	4
Major League totals (1 year)	0	1	.000	3.00	8	0	0	0	0	3	1	1	1	4	4

ALVAREZ, WILSON   P   DEVIL RAYS

PERSONAL: Born March 24, 1970, in Maracaibo, Venezuela. ... 6-1/235. ... Throws left, bats left. ... Full name: Wilson Eduardo Alvarez.
TRANSACTIONS/CAREER NOTES: Signed as non-drafted free agent by Texas Rangers organization (September 23, 1986). ... Traded by Rangers with IF Scott Fletcher and OF Sammy Sosa to Chicago White Sox for OF Harold Baines and IF Fred Manrique (July 29, 1989). ... Traded by White Sox with P Danny Darwin and P Roberto Hernandez to San Francisco Giants for SS Michael Caruso, OF Brian Manning, P Lorenzo Barcelo, P Keith Foulke, P Bobby Howry and P Ken Vining (July 31, 1997). ... Granted free agency (November 1, 1997). ... Signed by Tampa Bay Devil Rays (December 3, 1997). ... On Tampa Bay disabled list (May 21-July 6, 1998); included rehabilitation assignments to Gulf Coast Devil Rays (June 26-29), St. Petersburg (June 30-July 4) and Durham (July 5-6). ... On disabled list (April 12-29 and July 24-August 8, 1999).
RECORDS: Shares major league single-inning record for most strikeouts—4 (July 21, 1997, seventh inning).
STATISTICAL NOTES: Tied for Gulf Coast League lead with six home runs allowed in 1987. ... Pitched 7-0 no-hit victory for Chicago against Baltimore (August 11, 1991).

Year League	W	L	Pct.	ERA	G	GS	CG	ShO	Sv.	IP	H	R	ER	BB	SO
1987— Gastonia (SAL)	1	5	.167	6.47	8	6	0	0	0	32	39	24	23	23	19
— GC Rangers (GCL)	2	5	.286	5.24	10	10	0	0	0	44 2/3	41	29	26	21	46
1988— Gastonia (SAL)	4	11	.267	2.98	23	23	1	0	0	127	113	63	42	49	134
— Oklahoma City (A.A.)	1	1	.500	3.78	5	3	0	0	0	16 2/3	17	8	7	6	9
1989— Charlotte (FSL)	7	4	.636	2.11	13	13	3	2	0	81	68	29	19	21	51
— Tulsa (Texas)	2	2	.500	2.06	7	7	1	1	0	48	40	14	11	16	29
— Texas (A.L.)	0	1	.000	...	1	1	0	0	0	3	3	3	2	1	0
— Birmingham (Sou.)■	2	1	.667	3.03	6	6	0	0	0	35 2/3	32	12	12	16	18

Year League	W	L	Pct.	ERA	G	GS	CG	ShO	Sv.	IP	H	R	ER	BB	SO
1990— Birmingham (Sou.)	5	1	.833	4.27	7	7	1	0	0	46 1/3	44	24	22	25	36
—Vancouver (PCL)	7	7	.500	6.00	17	15	1	0	0	75	91	54	50	51	35
1991— Birmingham (Sou.)	10	6	.625	1.83	23	23	3	2	0	152 1/3	109	46	31	74	165
—Chicago (A.L.)	3	2	.600	3.51	10	9	2	1	0	56 1/3	47	26	22	29	32
1992— Chicago (A.L.)	5	3	.625	5.20	34	9	0	0	1	100 1/3	103	64	58	65	66
1993— Chicago (A.L.)	15	8	.652	2.95	31	31	1	1	0	207 2/3	168	78	68	*122	155
—Nashville (A.A.)	0	1	.000	2.84	1	1	0	0	0	6 1/3	7	7	2	2	8
1994— Chicago (A.L.)	12	8	.600	3.45	24	24	2	1	0	161 2/3	147	72	62	62	108
1995— Chicago (A.L.)	8	11	.421	4.32	29	29	3	0	0	175	171	96	84	93	118
1996— Chicago (A.L.)	15	10	.600	4.22	35	35	0	0	0	217 1/3	216	106	102	97	181
1997— Chicago (A.L.)	9	8	.529	3.03	22	22	2	1	0	145 2/3	126	61	49	55	110
—San Francisco (N.L.)■	4	3	.571	4.48	11	11	0	0	0	66 1/3	54	36	33	36	69
1998— Tampa Bay (A.L.)■	6	14	.300	4.73	25	25	0	0	0	142 2/3	130	78	75	68	107
—GC Devil Rays (GCL)	0	0	...	0.00	1	1	0	0	0	3	2	0	0	1	4
—St. Petersburg (FSL)	0	1	.000	27.00	1	1	0	0	0	1 2/3	5	5	5	2	2
—Durham (I.L.)	0	0	...	3.86	1	1	0	0	0	4 2/3	4	2	2	2	6
1999— Tampa Bay (A.L.)	9	9	.500	4.22	28	28	1	0	0	160	159	92	75	79	128
A.L. totals (10 years)	82	74	.526	3.94	239	213	11	4	1	1366 2/3	1270	676	598	672	1005
N.L. totals (1 year)	4	3	.571	4.48	11	11	0	0	0	66 1/3	54	36	33	36	69
Major League totals (10 years)	86	77	.528	3.96	250	224	11	4	1	1433	1324	712	631	708	1074

DIVISION SERIES RECORD

Year League	W	L	Pct.	ERA	G	GS	CG	ShO	Sv.	IP	H	R	ER	BB	SO
1997— San Francisco (N.L.)	0	1	.000	6.00	1	1	0	0	0	6	6	4	4	4	4

CHAMPIONSHIP SERIES RECORD

Year League	W	L	Pct.	ERA	G	GS	CG	ShO	Sv.	IP	H	R	ER	BB	SO
1993— Chicago (A.L.)	1	0	1.000	1.00	1	1	1	0	0	9	7	1	1	2	6

ALL-STAR GAME RECORD

Year League	W	L	Pct.	ERA	GS	CG	ShO	Sv.	IP	H	R	ER	BB	SO
1994— American	0	0	...	0.00	0	0	0	0	1	0	0	0	0	0

AMARAL, RICH — OF — ORIOLES

PERSONAL: Born April 1, 1962, in Visalia, Calif. ... 6-0/175. ... Bats right, throws right. ... Full name: Richard Louis Amaral. ... Name pronounced AM-ar-all.

HIGH SCHOOL: Estancia (Costa Mesa, Calif.).

JUNIOR COLLEGE: Orange Coast College (Calif.).

COLLEGE: UCLA.

TRANSACTIONS/CAREER NOTES: Selected by Chicago Cubs organization in second round of free-agent draft (June 6, 1983). ... Selected by Chicago White Sox organization from Cubs organization in Rule 5 minor league draft (December 6, 1988). ... Granted free agency (October 15, 1990). ... Signed by Seattle Mariners organization (November 25, 1990). ... On Seattle disabled list (May 29-July 17, 1991); included rehabilitation assignment to Calgary (July 11-17). ... On disabled list (August 1-16, 1993). ... On disabled list (March 28-April 14 and September 9, 1998-remainder of season). ... Granted free agency (October 26, 1998). ... Signed by Baltimore Orioles (December 21, 1998).

HONORS: Named second baseman on THE SPORTING NEWS college All-America team (1983).

STATISTICAL NOTES: Tied for New York-Pennsylvania League lead in double plays by second baseman with 39 in 1984. ... Tied for Carolina League lead in errors by second baseman with 25 in 1985. ... Led Pacific Coast League with .433 on-base percentage in 1991.

Year Team (League)	Pos.	G	AB	R	H	2B	3B	HR	RBI	Avg.	BB	SO	SB	PO	A	E	Avg.
1983— Geneva (NY-P)	2B-3B-SS	67	269	63	68	17	3	1	24	.253	45	47	22	135	205	14	.960
1984— Quad Cities (Midw.)	2B-SS	34	119	21	25	1	0	0	7	.210	24	29	12	62	73	6	.957
1985— Win.-Salem (Caro.)	2B-3B	124	428	62	116	15	5	3	36	.271	59	68	26	228	318	‡27	.953
1986— Pittsfield (East.)	2B	114	355	43	89	12	0	0	24	.251	39	65	25	228	266	14	.972
1987— Pittsfield (East.)	2B-1B	104	315	45	80	8	5	0	28	.254	43	50	28	242	274	18	.966
1988— Pittsfield (East.)	2-3-1-S-O	122	422	66	117	15	4	4	47	.277	56	53	54	288	262	19	.967
1989— Birmingham (Sou.)■	2B-SS-3B	122	432	*90	123	15	6	4	48	.285	88	66	57	198	256	23	.952
1990— Vancouver (PCL)	S-3-2-O-1	130	462	87	139	*39	5	4	56	.301	88	68	20	154	260	15	.965
1991— Calgary (PCL)	SS-2B	86	347	79	120	26	2	3	36	*.346	53	37	30	148	284	15	.966
—Seattle (A.L.)	2-3-S-DH-1	14	16	2	1	0	0	0	0	.063	1	5	0	13	16	2	.935
1992— Calgary (PCL)	SS-2B-OF	106	403	79	128	21	8	0	21	.318	67	69	*53	192	329	22	.959
—Seattle (A.L.)	S-3-O-1-2	35	100	9	24	3	0	1	7	.240	5	16	4	33	68	3	.971
1993— Seattle (A.L.)	2-3-S-D-1	110	373	53	108	24	1	1	44	.290	33	54	19	180	270	10	.978
1994— Seattle (A.L.)	2-O-S-D-1	77	228	37	60	10	2	4	18	.263	24	28	5	107	118	15	.938
—Calgary (PCL)	2B-OF	13	56	13	18	7	0	0	12	.321	4	6	2	28	35	3	.955
1995— Seattle (A.L.)	OF-DH	90	238	45	67	14	2	2	19	.282	21	33	21	121	6	1	.992
1996— Seattle (A.L.)	0-2-1-D-3	118	312	69	91	11	3	1	29	.292	47	55	25	195	24	0	1.000
1997— Seattle (A.L.)	0-1-2-D-3-S	89	190	34	54	5	0	1	21	.284	10	34	12	103	29	3	.978
1998— Seattle (A.L.)	0-2-1-D-3	73	134	25	37	6	0	1	4	.276	13	24	11	90	14	0	1.000
1999— Baltimore (A.L.)■	0-D-1-2-3	91	137	21	38	8	1	0	11	.277	15	20	9	70	2	0	1.000
Major League totals (9 years)		697	1728	295	480	81	9	11	153	.278	169	269	106	912	547	34	.977

DIVISION SERIES RECORD

Year Team (League)	Pos.	G	AB	R	H	2B	3B	HR	RBI	Avg.	BB	SO	SB	PO	A	E	Avg.
1995— Seattle (A.L.)						Did not play.											
1997— Seattle (A.L.)	1B-PH	2	4	2	2	0	0	0	0	.500	0	1	0	7	2	0	1.000

CHAMPIONSHIP SERIES RECORD

Year Team (League)	Pos.	G	AB	R	H	2B	3B	HR	RBI	Avg.	BB	SO	SB	PO	A	E	Avg.
1995— Seattle (A.L.)	PH	2	2	0	0	0	0	0	0	.000	0	1	0	...	...	...	...

AMBROSE, JOHN   P   CARDINALS

A

PERSONAL: Born November 1, 1974, in Evansville, Ind. ... 6-5/180. ... Throws right, bats right. ... Full name: John M. Ambrose.
HIGH SCHOOL: Evansville (Ind.) Memorial.
JUNIOR COLLEGE: John A. Logan College (Ill.).
TRANSACTIONS/CAREER NOTES: Selected by Chicago White Sox organization in second round of free-agent draft (June 3, 1994); pick received from Colorado Rockies as part of compensation for signing Type A free-agent OF Ellis Burks. ... On restricted list (April 9-September 6, 1996). ... Traded by White Sox to St. Louis Cardinals for P Sean Lowe (February 9, 1999).
STATISTICAL NOTES: Tied for Carolina League lead with five balks in 1997.

Year League	W	L	Pct.	ERA	G	GS	CG	ShO	Sv.	IP	H	R	ER	BB	SO
1994— GC White Sox (GCL)	1	2	.333	3.66	11	10	0	0	0	46²/₃	34	21	19	24	43
— Hickory (SAL)....................	1	1	.500	7.11	3	1	0	0	1	12²/₃	16	11	10	6	7
1995— Hickory (SAL)..................	4	8	.333	3.95	14	14	0	0	0	73	65	41	32	35	49
— South Bend (Midw.)	1	1	.500	5.40	3	3	1	0	0	16²/₃	18	13	10	10	15
1996—							Did not play.								
1997— Winston-Salem (Caro.).......	8	13	.381	5.47	27	27	1	1	0	149²/₃	136	102	*91	*117	137
1998— Birmingham (Sou.)...........	9	12	.429	5.18	31	22	0	0	0	140²/₃	156	90	81	69	103
1999— Arkansas (Texas)■............	4	12	.250	4.72	34	16	0	0	9	106²/₃	108	65	56	68	78

ANDERSON, BRADY   OF   ORIOLES

PERSONAL: Born January 18, 1964, in Silver Spring, Md. ... 6-1/202. ... Bats left, throws left. ... Full name: Brady Kevin Anderson.
HIGH SCHOOL: Carlsbad (Calif.).
COLLEGE: UC Irvine.
TRANSACTIONS/CAREER NOTES: Selected by Boston Red Sox organization in 10th round of free-agent draft (June 3, 1985). ... Traded by Red Sox with P Curt Schilling to Baltimore Orioles for P Mike Boddicker (July 29, 1988). ... On Baltimore disabled list (June 8-July 20, 1990); included rehabilitation assignments to Hagerstown (July 5-12) and Frederick (July 13-17). ... On Baltimore disabled list (May 28-June 14, 1991; and June 23-July 8, 1993). ... Granted free agency (October 27, 1997). ... Re-signed by Orioles (December 7, 1997). ... On disabled list (April 20-May 8, 1998).
RECORDS: Holds major league single-season record for most home runs leading off game—12 (1996). ... Shares major league single-inning record for most times hit by pitch—2 (May 23, 1999, first inning).
STATISTICAL NOTES: Led A.L. outfielders with six double plays in 1992. ... Led A.L. in being hit by pitch with 22 in 1996, 19 in 1997 and 24 in 1999. ... Career major league grand slams: 3.

Year Team (League)	Pos.	G	AB	R	H	2B	3B	HR	RBI	Avg.	BB	SO	SB	PO	A	E	Avg.
1985— Elmira (NY-P)	OF	71	215	36	55	7	•6	5	21	.256	*67	32	13	119	5	3	.976
1986— Winter Haven (FSL).......	OF	126	417	86	133	19	11	4	87	.319	*107	47	44	280	5	1	*.997
1987— New Britain (East.)	OF	52	170	30	50	4	3	6	35	.294	45	24	7	127	2	2	.985
— Pawtucket (I.L.).........	OF	23	79	18	30	4	0	2	8	.380	16	8	2	48	1	0	1.000
1988— Boston (A.L.)..............	OF	41	148	14	34	5	3	0	12	.230	15	35	4	87	3	1	.989
— Pawtucket (I.L.).........	OF	49	167	27	48	6	1	4	19	.287	26	33	8	115	4	2	.983
— Baltimore (A.L.)■.......	OF	53	177	17	35	8	1	1	9	.198	8	40	6	156	1	3	.981
1989— Baltimore (A.L.).........	OF-DH	94	266	44	55	12	2	4	16	.207	43	45	16	191	3	3	.985
— Rochester (I.L.)........	OF	21	70	14	14	1	2	1	8	.200	12	13	2	1	0	0	1.000
1990— Baltimore (A.L.).........	OF-DH	89	234	24	54	5	2	3	24	.231	31	46	15	149	3	2	.987
— Hagerstown (East.)......	OF	9	34	8	13	0	2	1	5	.382	5	5	2	8	1	0	1.000
— Frederick (Caro.)......	OF	2	7	2	3	1	0	0	3	.429	1	1	0	1	0	0	1.000
1991— Baltimore (A.L.).........	OF-DH	113	256	40	59	12	3	2	27	.230	38	44	12	150	3	3	.981
— Rochester (I.L.)........	OF	7	26	5	10	3	0	0	2	.385	7	4	4	19	1	0	1.000
1992— Baltimore (A.L.).........	OF	159	623	100	169	28	10	21	80	.271	98	98	53	382	10	8	.980
1993— Baltimore (A.L.).........	OF-DH	142	560	87	147	36	8	13	66	.263	82	99	24	296	7	2	.993
1994— Baltimore (A.L.).........	OF	111	453	78	119	25	5	12	48	.263	57	75	31	247	4	1	.996
1995— Baltimore (A.L.).........	OF	143	554	108	145	33	10	16	64	.262	87	111	26	268	1	3	.989
1996— Baltimore (A.L.).........	OF-DH	149	579	117	172	37	5	50	110	.297	76	106	21	341	10	3	.992
1997— Baltimore (A.L.).........	OF-DH	151	590	97	170	39	7	18	73	.288	84	105	18	276	2	3	.989
1998— Baltimore (A.L.).........	OF-DH	133	479	84	113	28	3	18	51	.236	75	78	21	269	1	4	.985
1999— Baltimore (A.L.).........	OF-DH	150	564	109	159	28	5	24	81	.282	96	105	36	308	3	1	.997
Major League totals (12 years)		1528	5483	919	1431	296	64	182	661	.261	790	987	283	3120	51	37	.988

DIVISION SERIES RECORD

NOTES: Hit home run in first at-bat (October 1, 1996).

Year Team (League)	Pos.	G	AB	R	H	2B	3B	HR	RBI	Avg.	BB	SO	SB	PO	A	E	Avg.
1996— Baltimore (A.L.).........	OF	4	17	3	5	0	0	2	4	.294	2	3	0	7	0	0	1.000
1997— Baltimore (A.L.).........	OF	4	17	3	6	1	0	1	4	.353	1	4	1	6	0	0	1.000
Division series totals (2 years)		8	34	6	11	1	0	3	8	.324	3	7	1	13	0	0	1.000

CHAMPIONSHIP SERIES RECORD

Year Team (League)	Pos.	G	AB	R	H	2B	3B	HR	RBI	Avg.	BB	SO	SB	PO	A	E	Avg.
1996— Baltimore (A.L.).........	OF	5	21	5	4	1	0	1	1	.190	3	5	0	8	0	0	1.000
1997— Baltimore (A.L.).........	OF	6	25	5	9	2	0	2	3	.360	4	4	2	13	0	1	.929
Championship series totals (2 years)		11	46	10	13	3	0	3	4	.283	7	9	2	21	0	1	.955

ALL-STAR GAME RECORD

Year League	Pos.	AB	R	H	2B	3B	HR	RBI	Avg.	BB	SO	SB	PO	A	E	Avg.
1992— American	OF	3	0	0	0	0	0	0	.000	0	0	0	1	0	0	1.000
1996— American	OF	2	0	0	0	0	0	0	.000	0	0	0	0	0	0	...
1997— American	OF	4	0	2	1	0	0	0	.500	0	0	0	1	0	0	1.000
All-Star Game totals (3 years)		9	0	2	1	0	0	0	.222	0	0	0	2	0	0	1.000

ANDERSON, BRIAN   P   DIAMONDBACKS

A

PERSONAL: Born April 26, 1972, in Geneva, Ohio. ... 6-1/190. ... Throws left, bats both. ... Full name: Brian James Anderson.
HIGH SCHOOL: Geneva (Ohio).
COLLEGE: Wright State.
TRANSACTIONS/CAREER NOTES: Selected by California Angels organization in first round (third pick overall) of free-agent draft (June 3, 1993). ... On California disabled list (May 7-June 7, 1994); included rehabilitation assignment to Lake Elsinore (May 27-June 7). ... On California disabled list (May 6-June 20, 1995); included rehabilitation assignment to Lake Elsinore (June 4-20). ... Traded by Angels to Cleveland Indians for P Jason Grimsley and P Pep Harris (February 15, 1996). ... On Cleveland disabled list (July 5-August 12, 1997); included rehabilitation assignment to Buffalo (August 3-13). ... Selected by Arizona Diamondbacks in first round (second pick overall) of expansion draft (November 18, 1997).
RECORDS: Shares major league single-inning record for most home runs allowed—4 (September 5, 1995, second inning).
HONORS: Named A.L. Rookie Pitcher of the Year by THE SPORTING NEWS (1994).
STATISTICAL NOTES: Tied for A.L. lead with five balks in 1994 and three in 1995. ... Tied for American Association lead with three balks in 1996. ... Led N.L. with six balks and tied for lead with 39 home runs allowed in 1998.
MISCELLANEOUS: Shares Arizona Diamondbacks all-time record for most shutouts (2). ... Scored one run in three appearances as pinch runner (1998). ... Scored a run in only appearance as pinch runner (1999).

Year League	W	L	Pct.	ERA	G	GS	CG	ShO	Sv.	IP	H	R	ER	BB	SO
1993—Midland (Texas)	0	1	.000	3.38	2	2	0	0	0	10 2/3	16	5	4	0	9
—Vancouver (PCL)	0	1	.000	12.38	2	2	0	0	0	8	13	12	11	6	2
—California (A.L.)	0	0	...	3.97	4	1	0	0	0	11 1/3	11	5	5	2	4
1994—California (A.L.)	7	5	.583	5.22	18	18	0	0	0	101 2/3	120	63	59	27	47
—Lake Elsinore (Calif.)	0	1	.000	3.00	2	2	0	0	0	12	6	4	4	0	9
1995—California (A.L.)	6	8	.429	5.87	18	17	1	0	0	99 2/3	110	66	65	30	45
—Lake Elsinore (Calif.)	1	1	.500	1.93	3	3	0	0	0	14	10	3	3	1	13
1996—Buffalo (A.A.)■	11	5	.688	3.59	19	19	2	0	0	128	125	57	51	28	85
—Cleveland (A.L.)	3	1	.750	4.91	10	9	0	0	0	51 1/3	58	29	28	14	21
1997—Buffalo (A.A.)	7	1	.875	3.05	15	15	1	1	0	85 2/3	78	33	29	15	60
—Cleveland (A.L.)	4	2	.667	4.69	8	8	0	0	0	48	55	28	25	11	22
1998—Arizona (N.L.)■	12	13	.480	4.33	32	32	2	1	0	208	221	109	100	24	95
1999—Arizona (N.L.)	8	2	.800	4.57	31	19	2	1	1	130	144	69	66	28	75
—Tucson (PCL)	0	1	.000	5.40	2	2	0	0	0	6 2/3	9	5	4	1	8
A.L. totals (5 years)	20	16	.556	5.25	58	53	1	0	0	312	354	191	182	84	139
N.L. totals (2 years)	20	15	.571	4.42	63	51	4	2	1	338	365	178	166	52	170
Major League totals (7 years)	40	31	.563	4.82	121	104	5	2	1	650	719	369	348	136	309

DIVISION SERIES RECORD

Year League	W	L	Pct.	ERA	G	GS	CG	ShO	Sv.	IP	H	R	ER	BB	SO
1999—Arizona (N.L.)	0	0	...	2.57	1	1	0	0	0	7	7	2	2	0	4

CHAMPIONSHIP SERIES RECORD

Year League	W	L	Pct.	ERA	G	GS	CG	ShO	Sv.	IP	H	R	ER	BB	SO
1997—Cleveland (A.L.)	1	0	1.000	1.42	3	0	0	0	0	6 1/3	1	1	1	3	7

WORLD SERIES RECORD

Year League	W	L	Pct.	ERA	G	GS	CG	ShO	Sv.	IP	H	R	ER	BB	SO
1997—Cleveland (A.L.)	0	0	...	2.45	3	0	0	0	1	3 2/3	2	1	1	0	2

ANDERSON, GARRET   OF   ANGELS

PERSONAL: Born June 30, 1972, in Los Angeles. ... 6-3/220. ... Bats left, throws left. ... Full name: Garret Joseph Anderson.
HIGH SCHOOL: John F. Kennedy (Granada Hills, Calif.).
TRANSACTIONS/CAREER NOTES: Selected by California Angels organization in fourth round of free-agent draft (June 4, 1990). ... Angels franchise renamed Anaheim Angels for 1997 season.
HONORS: Named A.L. Rookie Player of the Year by THE SPORTING NEWS (1995).
STATISTICAL NOTES: Collected six hits in one game (September 27, 1996). ... Had 28-game hitting streak (June 28-July 31, 1998). ... Had 16-game hitting streak (July 6-25, 1999). ... Had 17-game hitting streak (August 30-September 17, 1999). ... Career major league grand slams: 3.

Year Team (League)	Pos.	G	AB	R	H	2B	3B	HR	RBI	Avg.	BB	SO	SB	PO	A	E	Avg.
1990—Ariz. Angels (Ariz.)	OF	32	127	5	27	2	0	0	14	.213	2	24	3	53	2	2	.965
—Boise (N.W.)	OF	25	83	11	21	3	1	1	8	.253	4	18	0	38	0	2	.950
1991—Quad City (Midw.)	OF	105	392	40	102	22	2	2	42	.260	20	89	5	158	7	10	.943
1992—Palm Springs (Calif.)	OF	81	322	46	104	15	2	1	62	.323	21	61	1	137	4	6	.959
—Midland (Texas)	OF	39	146	16	40	5	0	2	19	.274	9	30	2	62	6	1	.986
1993—Vancouver (PCL)	OF-1B	124	467	57	137	34	4	4	71	.293	31	95	3	198	13	2	.991
1994—Vancouver (PCL)	OF-DH-1B	123	505	75	162	42	6	12	102	.321	28	93	3	196	10	2	.990
—California (A.L.)	OF	5	13	0	5	0	0	0	1	.385	0	2	0	10	0	0	1.000
1995—California (A.L.)	OF-DH	106	374	50	120	19	1	16	69	.321	19	65	6	213	7	5	.978
—Vancouver (PCL)	OF-DH	14	61	9	19	7	0	0	12	.311	5	14	0	22	0	1	.957
1996—California (A.L.)	OF-DH	150	607	79	173	33	2	12	72	.285	27	84	7	316	5	7	.979
1997—Anaheim (A.L.)	OF-DH	154	624	76	189	36	3	8	92	.303	30	70	10	343	14	3	.992
1998—Anaheim (A.L.)	OF	156	622	62	183	41	7	15	79	.294	29	80	8	326	11	6	.983
1999—Anaheim (A.L.)	OF-DH	157	620	88	188	36	2	21	80	.303	34	81	3	*406	7	3	.993
Major League totals (6 years)		728	2860	355	858	165	15	72	393	.300	139	382	34	1614	44	24	.986

ANDERSON, JIMMY   P   PIRATES

PERSONAL: Born January 22, 1976, in Portsmouth, Va. ... 6-1/207. ... Throws left, bats left. ... Full name: James Drew Anderson Jr.
HIGH SCHOOL: Western Branch (Chesapeake, Va.).

TRANSACTIONS/CAREER NOTES: Selected by Pittsburgh Pirates organization in ninth round of free-agent draft (June 2, 1994). ... On disabled list (July 5-12, 1998).

Year	League	W	L	Pct.	ERA	G	GS	CG	ShO	Sv.	IP	H	R	ER	BB	SO
1994—	GC Pirates (GCL)	5	1	.833	1.60	10	10	0	0	0	56 1/3	35	21	10	27	66
1995—	Augusta (SAL)	4	2	.667	1.53	14	14	0	0	0	76 2/3	51	15	13	31	75
	— Lynchburg (Caro.)	1	5	.167	4.13	10	9	0	0	0	52 1/3	56	29	24	21	32
1996—	Lynchburg (Caro.)	5	3	.625	1.93	11	11	1	1	0	65 1/3	51	25	14	21	56
	— Carolina (Sou.)	8	5	.615	3.34	17	16	0	0	0	97	92	40	36	44	79
1997—	Carolina (Sou.)	2	1	.667	1.46	4	4	0	0	0	24 2/3	16	6	4	9	23
	— Calgary (PCL)	7	6	.538	5.68	21	21	0	0	0	103	124	78	65	64	71
1998—	Nashville (PCL)	9	10	.474	5.02	35	17	0	0	0	123 2/3	144	87	69	72	63
1999—	Nashville (PCL)	11	2	*.846	3.84	21	21	1	0	0	133 2/3	153	67	57	41	93
	— Pittsburgh (N.L.)	2	1	.667	3.99	13	4	0	0	0	29 1/3	25	15	13	16	13
Major League totals (1 year)		2	1	.667	3.99	13	4	0	0	0	29 1/3	25	15	13	16	13

ANDERSON, MARLON — 2B — PHILLIES

PERSONAL: Born January 6, 1974, in Montgomery, Ala. ... 5-11/198. ... Bats left, throws right. ... Full name: Marlon Ordell Anderson.
HIGH SCHOOL: Prattville (Ala.).
COLLEGE: South Alabama.
TRANSACTIONS/CAREER NOTES: Selected by Philadelphia Phillies organization in second round of free-agent draft (June 1, 1995); choice received from St. Louis Cardinals as part of compensation for Cardinals signing Type A free-agent P Danny Jackson.
STATISTICAL NOTES: Led New York-Pennsylvania League second basemen with 398 total chances and 67 double plays in 1995. ... Led Eastern League with 748 total chances in 1997. ... Hit home run in first major league at-bat (September 8, 1998). ... Led International League second basemen with 681 total chances in 1998.

							BATTING								FIELDING		
Year	Team (League)	Pos.	G	AB	R	H	2B	3B	HR	RBI	Avg.	BB	SO	SB	PO	A	E	Avg.
1995—	Batavia (NY-P)	2B	74	*312	52	92	13	4	3	40	.295	15	20	22	*153	*231	14	*.965
1996—	Clearwater (FSL)	2B	60	257	37	70	10	3	2	22	.272	14	18	26	142	221	16	.958
	— Reading (East.)	2B	75	314	38	86	14	3	3	28	.274	26	44	17	166	239	18	.957
1997—	Reading (East.)	2B	137	*553	88	147	18	6	10	62	.266	42	77	27	*323	*396	*29	.961
1998—	Scranton/W.B. (I.L.)	2B	136	575	104	*176	32	*14	16	86	.306	28	77	24	262	391	*28	.959
	— Philadelphia (N.L.)	2B	17	43	4	14	3	0	1	4	.326	1	6	2	14	30	1	.978
1999—	Philadelphia (N.L.)	2B	129	452	48	114	26	4	5	54	.252	24	61	13	234	284	11	.979
Major League totals (2 years)			146	495	52	128	29	4	6	58	.259	25	67	15	248	314	12	.979

ANDERSON, MATT — P — TIGERS

PERSONAL: Born August 17, 1976, in Louisville, Ky. ... 6-4/200. ... Throws right, bats right. ... Full name: Matthew Jason Anderson.
HIGH SCHOOL: St. Xavier (Louisville, Ky.).
COLLEGE: Rice.
TRANSACTIONS/CAREER NOTES: Selected by Detroit Tigers organization in first round (first pick overall) of free-agent draft (June 3, 1997).

Year	League	W	L	Pct.	ERA	G	GS	CG	ShO	Sv.	IP	H	R	ER	BB	SO
1998—	Lakeland (FSL)	1	0	1.000	0.69	17	0	0	0	3	26	18	4	2	8	34
	— Jacksonville (Sou.)	1	0	1.000	0.60	13	0	0	0	10	15	7	1	1	5	11
	— Detroit (A.L.)	5	1	.833	3.27	42	0	0	0	0	44	38	16	16	31	44
1999—	Detroit (A.L.)	2	1	.667	5.68	37	0	0	0	0	38	33	27	24	35	32
	— Toledo (I.L.)	0	4	.000	6.39	24	4	0	0	5	38	32	27	27	31	35
Major League totals (2 years)		7	2	.778	4.39	79	0	0	0	0	82	71	43	40	66	76

ANDREWS, CLAYTON — P — BLUE JAYS

PERSONAL: Born May 15, 1978, in Dunedin, Fla. ... 6-0/180. ... Throws left, bats right. ... Full name: Clayton John Andrews.
HIGH SCHOOL: Seminole (Largo, Fla.).
TRANSACTIONS/CAREER NOTES: Selected by Toronto Blue Jays organization in third round of free-agent draft (June 4, 1996); pick received as compensation for Florida Marlins signing Type B free agent Devon White.
HONORS: Named South Atlantic League Most Valuable Pitcher (1998).

Year	League	W	L	Pct.	ERA	G	GS	CG	ShO	Sv.	IP	H	R	ER	BB	SO
1996—	Medicine Hat (Pio.)	2	4	.333	7.36	8	4	0	0	0	25 2/3	37	23	21	10	14
1997—	Hagerstown (SAL)	7	7	.500	4.55	28	15	0	0	0	114 2/3	120	70	58	47	112
1998—	Hagerstown (SAL)	10	7	.588	*2.28	27	26	2	1	0	162	112	59	41	46	193
1999—	Knoxville (Sou.)	10	8	.556	3.93	25	25	0	0	0	132 2/3	143	85	58	69	93
	— Syracuse (I.L.)	0	1	.000	7.80	3	3	0	0	0	15	10	14	13	13	9

ANDREWS, SHANE — 3B — CUBS

PERSONAL: Born August 28, 1971, in Dallas. ... 6-1/220. ... Bats right, throws right. ... Full name: Darrell Shane Andrews.
HIGH SCHOOL: Carlsbad (N.M.) Senior.
TRANSACTIONS/CAREER NOTES: Selected by Montreal Expos organization in first round (11th pick overall) of free-agent draft (June 4, 1990). ... On disabled list (August 3-11, 1993). ... On Montreal disabled list (May 1, 1997-remainder of season); included rehabilitation assignments to Ottawa (May 14-18) and West Palm Beach (July 26-August 10). ... On Montreal disabled list (May 11-June 1, 1999); included rehabilitation assignment to Ottawa (May 30-June 1). ... Released by Expos (September 7, 1999). ... Signed by Chicago Cubs (September 10, 1999).
STATISTICAL NOTES: Led South Atlantic League third basemen with 98 putouts in 1992. ... Led International League third basemen with 436 total chances in 1994. ... Career major league grand slams: 3.

Year Team (League)	Pos.	G	AB	R	H	2B	3B	HR	RBI	Avg.	BB	SO	SB	PO	A	E	Avg.
1990— GC Expos (GCL)	3B	56	190	31	46	7	1	3	24	.242	29	46	11	42	105	17	.896
1991— Sumter (SAL)	3B	105	356	46	74	16	7	11	49	.208	65	132	5	71	205	29	.905
1992— Albany (SAL)	3B-1B	136	453	76	104	18	1	*25	87	.230	*107	*174	8	†125	212	26	.928
1993— Harrisburg (East.).......	3B-SS	124	442	77	115	29	2	18	70	.260	64	118	10	74	217	23	.927
1994— Ottawa (I.L.)	3B-DH	137	460	79	117	25	2	16	85	.254	80	126	6	84	*320	*32	.927
1995— Montreal (N.L.)..........	3B-1B	84	220	27	47	10	1	8	31	.214	17	68	1	182	97	7	.976
1996— Montreal (N.L.)..........	3B	127	375	43	85	15	2	19	64	.227	35	119	3	64	256	15	.955
1997— Montreal (N.L.)..........	3B	18	64	10	13	3	0	4	9	.203	3	20	0	11	40	6	.895
— Ottawa (I.L.)................	3B	3	12	3	3	0	0	1	1	.250	1	0	0	2	4	0	1.000
— W.P. Beach (FSL)........	DH-3B	5	17	2	3	2	0	1	5	.176	2	7	0	2	9	1	.917
1998— Montreal (N.L.)..........	3B	150	492	48	117	30	1	25	69	.238	58	137	1	95	322	20	.954
1999— Montreal (N.L.)..........	3B-1B-DH	98	281	28	51	8	0	11	37	.181	43	88	1	159	134	14	.954
— Ottawa (I.L.)................	3B	2	8	1	2	0	0	1	4	.250	0	2	0	1	2	0	1.000
— Chicago (N.L.)■........	3B-1B	19	67	13	17	4	0	5	14	.254	7	21	0	8	34	2	.955
Major League totals (5 years)		496	1499	169	330	70	4	72	224	.220	163	453	6	519	883	64	.956

ANKIEL, RICK — P — CARDINALS

PERSONAL: Born July 19, 1979, in Fort Pierce, Fla. ... 6-1/210. ... Throws left, bats left. ... Full name: Richard Alexander Ankiel.
HIGH SCHOOL: Port St. Lucie (Fla.).
TRANSACTIONS/CAREER NOTES: Selected by St. Louis Cardinals organization in second round of free-agent draft (June 3, 1997).
HONORS: Named Carolina League Pitcher of the Year (1998). ... Named Minor League Player of the Year by THE SPORTING NEWS (1999).

Year League	W	L	Pct.	ERA	G	GS	CG	ShO	Sv.	IP	H	R	ER	BB	SO
1998— Peoria (Midw.)..................	3	0	1.000	2.06	7	7	0	0	0	35	15	8	8	12	41
— Prince William (Caro.)........	9	6	.600	2.79	21	21	1	0	0	126	91	46	39	38	181
1999— Arkansas (Texas).............	6	0	1.000	0.91	8	8	1	1	0	49 1/3	25	6	5	16	75
— Memphis (PCL).................	7	3	.700	3.16	16	16	0	0	0	88 1/3	73	37	31	46	119
— St. Louis (N.L.)..................	0	1	.000	3.27	9	5	0	0	1	33	26	12	12	14	39
Major League totals (1 year)........	0	1	.000	3.27	9	5	0	0	1	33	26	12	12	14	39

APPIER, KEVIN — P — ATHLETICS

PERSONAL: Born December 6, 1967, in Lancaster, Calif. ... 6-2/200. ... Throws right, bats right. ... Full name: Robert Kevin Appier. ... Name pronounced APE-ee-er.
HIGH SCHOOL: Antelope Valley (Lancaster, Calif.).
JUNIOR COLLEGE: Antelope Valley College (Calif.).
COLLEGE: Fresno State.
TRANSACTIONS/CAREER NOTES: Selected by Kansas City Royals organization in first round (ninth pick overall) of free-agent draft (June 2, 1987). ... On disabled list (July 26-August 12, 1995). ... On Kansas City disabled list (March 20-September 1, 1998); included rehabilitation assignments to Gulf Coast Royals (July 16-21), Lansing (July 22-26), Wichita (July 27-30) and Omaha (July 31-August 27). ... Traded by Royals to Oakland Athletics for P Blake Stein, P Jeff D'Amico, and P Brad Rigby (July 31, 1999).
RECORDS: Shares major league record for most strikeouts in one inning—4 (September 3, 1996, fourth inning).
HONORS: Named A.L. Rookie Pitcher of the Year by THE SPORTING NEWS (1990).
STATISTICAL NOTES: Pitched 4-0 one-hit, complete-game victory for Kansas City against Detroit (July 7, 1990). ... Pitched 1-0 one-hit, complete-game loss against Texas (July 27, 1993). ... Tied for A.L. lead with 14 wild pitches in 1997.
MISCELLANEOUS: Holds Kansas City Royals all-time record for strikeouts (1,451).

Year League	W	L	Pct.	ERA	G	GS	CG	ShO	Sv.	IP	H	R	ER	BB	SO
1987— Eugene (N.W.)....................	5	2	.714	3.04	15	•15	0	0	0	77	81	43	26	29	72
1988— Baseball City (FSL)............	10	9	.526	2.75	24	24	1	0	0	147 1/3	134	58	45	39	112
— Memphis (Sou.).................	2	0	1.000	1.83	3	3	0	0	0	19 2/3	11	5	4	7	18
1989— Omaha (A.A.).....................	8	8	.500	3.95	22	22	3	2	0	139	141	70	61	42	109
— Kansas City (A.L.)............	1	4	.200	9.14	6	5	0	0	0	21 2/3	34	22	22	12	10
1990— Omaha (A.A.).....................	2	0	1.000	1.50	3	3	0	0	0	18	15	3	3	3	17
— Kansas City (A.L.)............	12	8	.600	2.76	32	24	3	3	0	185 2/3	179	67	57	54	127
1991— Kansas City (A.L.)............	13	10	.565	3.42	34	31	6	3	0	207 2/3	205	97	79	61	158
1992— Kansas City (A.L.)............	15	8	.652	2.46	30	30	3	0	0	208 1/3	167	59	57	68	150
1993— Kansas City (A.L.)............	18	8	.692	*2.56	34	34	5	1	0	238 2/3	183	74	68	81	186
1994— Kansas City (A.L.)............	7	6	.538	3.83	23	23	1	0	0	155	137	68	66	63	145
1995— Kansas City (A.L.)............	15	10	.600	3.89	31	31	4	1	0	201 1/3	163	90	87	80	185
1996— Kansas City (A.L.)............	14	11	.560	3.62	32	32	5	1	0	211 1/3	192	87	85	75	207
1997— Kansas City (A.L.)............	9	13	.409	3.40	34	34	4	1	0	235 2/3	215	96	89	74	196
1998— Gulf Coast Royals (GCL)	0	1	.000	2.70	1	1	0	0	0	3 1/3	3	3	1	1	2
— Lansing (Midw.)................	0	0	...	2.25	1	1	0	0	0	4	4	1	1	0	5
— Wichita (Texas)	0	1	.000	6.00	1	1	0	0	0	6	8	4	4	2	1
— Omaha (PCL)...................	3	2	.600	7.03	6	6	0	0	0	32	41	25	25	12	22
— Kansas City (A.L.)	1	2	.333	7.80	3	3	0	0	0	15	21	13	13	5	9
1999— Kansas City (A.L.)............	9	9	.500	4.87	22	22	1	0	0	140 1/3	153	81	76	51	78
— Oakland (A.L.)■...............	7	5	.583	5.77	12	12	0	0	0	68 2/3	77	50	44	33	53
Major League totals (11 years)	121	94	.563	3.54	293	281	32	10	0	1889 1/3	1726	804	743	657	1504

ALL-STAR GAME RECORD

Year League	W	L	Pct.	ERA	GS	CG	ShO	Sv.	IP	H	R	ER	BB	SO
1995— American	0	0	...	0.00	0	0	0	0	2	0	0	0	0	1

ARACENA, JUAN — P — ORIOLES

PERSONAL: Born December 17, 1976, in La Vega, Dominican Republic. ... 6-0/190. ... Throws right, bats right.

TRANSACTIONS/CAREER NOTES: Signed as non-drafted free agent by Cleveland Indians organization (April 15, 1994). ... Traded by Indians with a player to be named later to Baltimore Orioles for DH Harold Baines (August 27, 1999); Orioles acquired P Jimmy Hamilton to complete deal (August 31, 1999).

Year	League	W	L	Pct.	ERA	G	GS	CG	ShO	Sv.	IP	H	R	ER	BB	SO
1994—	Dom. Indians (DSL)	4	1	.800	2.23	25	1	0	0	9	40 1/3	42	19	10	26	26
1995—	Dom. Indians (DSL)	6	2	.750	2.06	24	3	0	0	5	56 2/3	39	19	13	18	31
1996—	Burlington (Appl.)	3	4	.429	5.48	13	5	0	0	0	42 2/3	61	38	26	7	28
1997—	Burlington (Appl.)	1	4	.200	4.89	19	0	0	0	2	38 2/3	45	32	21	16	31
1998—	Watertown (NY-P)	1	4	.200	2.84	18	0	0	0	6	25 1/3	21	8	8	7	22
—	Columbus (SAL)	0	1	.000	13.50	5	0	0	0	0	6 2/3	15	10	10	6	4
1999—	Columbus (SAL)	2	0	1.000	3.28	32	0	0	0	18	35 2/3	32	13	13	3	30
—	Kinston (Caro.)	1	1	.500	2.57	5	0	0	0	0	7	7	2	2	1	7
—	Frederick (Caro.)■	0	0	...	0.00	2	0	0	0	0	2	2	1	0	0	0

ARDOIN, DANNY — C — ATHLETICS

PERSONAL: Born July 8, 1974, in Mamou, La. ... 6-0/218. ... Bats right, throws right. ... Full name: Daniel Wayne Ardoin.

HIGH SCHOOL: Sacred Heart (Ville Platte, La.).

COLLEGE: McNeese State.

TRANSACTIONS/CAREER NOTES: Selected by Oakland Athletics organization in fifth round of free-agent draft (June 1, 1995). ... On disabled list (July 27-August 4, 1998).

STATISTICAL NOTES: Led Northwest League catchers with 477 total chances in 1995. ... Led Pacific Coast League catchers with nine double plays in 1999.

Year	Team (League)	Pos.	G	AB	R	H	2B	3B	HR	RBI	Avg.	BB	SO	SB	PO	A	E	Avg.
1995—	S. Oregon (N.W.)	C	58	175	28	41	9	1	2	23	.234	31	50	2	*402	*61	*14	.971
1996—	Modesto (Calif.)	C-3B-1B	91	317	55	83	13	3	6	34	.262	47	81	5	577	62	21	.968
1997—	Visalia (Calif.)	C-1B-3B-OF	43	145	16	34	7	1	3	19	.234	21	39	0	331	38	5	.987
—	Huntsville (Sou.)	C-3B	57	208	26	48	10	1	4	23	.231	17	38	2	302	45	10	.972
1998—	Huntsville (Sou.)	C-OF-1B	109	363	67	90	21	0	16	62	.248	62	87	8	560	87	12	.982
1999—	Vancouver (PCL)	C-DH-3B-1B	109	336	53	85	13	2	8	46	.253	50	78	3	538	76	10	.984

ARIAS, ALEX — SS — PHILLIES

PERSONAL: Born November 20, 1967, in New York. ... 6-3/202. ... Bats right, throws right. ... Full name: Alejandro Arias. ... Name pronounced air-REE-ahs.

HIGH SCHOOL: George Washington (New York).

TRANSACTIONS/CAREER NOTES: Selected by Chicago Cubs organization in third round of free-agent draft (June 2, 1987). ... Traded by Cubs with 3B Gary Scott to Florida Marlins for P Greg Hibbard (November 17, 1992). ... On disabled list (June 14-July 2, 1997). ... Released by Marlins (December 12, 1997). ... Signed by Philadelphia Phillies (December 26, 1997).

STATISTICAL NOTES: Led Midwest League shortstops with 655 total chances and 83 double plays in 1989. ... Led Southern League shortstops with 583 total chances and 81 double plays in 1991.

Year	Team (League)	Pos.	G	AB	R	H	2B	3B	HR	RBI	Avg.	BB	SO	SB	PO	A	E	Avg.
1987—	Wytheville (Appl.)	SS-3B	61	233	41	69	7	0	0	24	.296	27	29	16	77	141	16	.932
1988—	Char., W.Va. (SAL)	SS-3B-2B	127	472	57	122	12	1	0	33	.258	54	44	41	184	396	32	.948
1989—	Peoria (Midw.)	SS	*136	506	74	140	10	*11	2	64	.277	49	67	31	*210	*408	37	.944
1990—	Charlotte (Sou.)	SS	119	419	55	103	16	3	4	38	.246	42	53	12	171	284	*42	.915
1991—	Charlotte (Sou.)	SS	134	488	69	134	26	4	4	47	.275	47	42	23	*203	*351	29	*.950
1992—	Iowa (A.A.)	SS-3B	106	409	52	114	23	3	5	40	.279	44	27	14	183	290	14	.971
—	Chicago (N.L.)	SS	32	99	14	29	6	0	0	7	.293	11	13	0	43	74	4	.967
1993—	Florida (N.L.)■	2B-3B-SS	96	249	27	67	5	1	2	20	.269	27	18	1	94	144	6	.975
1994—	Florida (N.L.)	SS-3B	59	113	4	27	5	0	0	15	.239	9	19	0	37	51	2	.978
1995—	Florida (N.L.)	SS-3B-2B	94	216	22	58	9	2	3	26	.269	22	20	1	57	127	9	.953
1996—	Florida (N.L.)	3-S-1-2	100	224	27	62	11	2	3	26	.277	17	28	2	48	127	7	.962
1997—	Florida (N.L.)	3BSS	74	93	13	23	2	0	1	11	.247	12	12	0	26	38	2	.970
1998—	Philadelphia (N.L.)■	SS-3B-2B	56	133	17	39	8	0	1	16	.293	13	18	2	43	88	2	.985
1999—	Philadelphia (N.L.)	SS-3B-2B	118	347	43	105	20	1	4	48	.303	36	31	2	120	208	4	.988
Major League totals (8 years)			629	1474	167	410	66	6	14	169	.278	147	159	8	468	857	36	.974

DIVISION SERIES RECORD

Year	Team (League)	Pos.	G	AB	R	H	2B	3B	HR	RBI	Avg.	BB	SO	SB	PO	A	E	Avg.
1997—	Florida (N.L.)	PH	1	1	0	1	0	0	0	1	1.000	0	0	0	...	...	...	...

CHAMPIONSHIP SERIES RECORD

Year	Team (League)	Pos.	G	AB	R	H	2B	3B	HR	RBI	Avg.	BB	SO	SB	PO	A	E	Avg.
1997—	Florida (N.L.)	3B-PH	3	1	0	1	0	0	0	0	1.000	0	0	0	0	0	0	...

WORLD SERIES RECORD

NOTES: Member of World Series championship team (1997).

Year	Team (League)	Pos.	G	AB	R	H	2B	3B	HR	RBI	Avg.	BB	SO	SB	PO	A	E	Avg.
1997—	Florida (N.L.)	3B-PR	2	1	1	0	0	0	0	0	.000	0	0	0	0	0	0	...

ARIAS, GEORGE   3B

PERSONAL: Born March 12, 1972, in Tucson, Ariz. ... 5-11/190. ... Bats right, throws right. ... Full name: George Alberto Arias.
HIGH SCHOOL: Pueblo (Tucson, Ariz.).
JUNIOR COLLEGE: Pima Community College (Ariz.).
COLLEGE: Arizona.
TRANSACTIONS/CAREER NOTES: Selected by California Angels organization in seventh round of free-agent draft (June 3, 1993). ... Angels franchise renamed Anaheim Angels for 1997 season. ... Traded by Angels to San Diego Padres (August 19, 1997), completing deal in which Padres traded OF Rickey Henderson to Angels for P Ryan Hancock, P Stevenson Agosto and a player to be named later (August 13, 1997). ... On San Diego disabled list (April 8-May 7, 1999); included rehabilitation assignments to Las Vegas (April 27-May 6) and Rancho Cucamonga (May 7). ... Granted free agency (October 15, 1999).
STATISTICAL NOTES: Led California League third basemen with 467 total chances and 27 double plays in 1994. ... Led Pacific Coast League third basemen with 99 putouts in 1997.

Year Team (League)	Pos.	G	AB	R	H	2B	3B	HR	RBI	Avg.	BB	SO	SB	PO	A	E	Avg.
1993—Cedar Rap. (Midw.)....	3B-SS	74	253	31	55	13	3	9	41	.217	31	65	6	59	159	23	.905
1994—Lake Elsinore (Calif.)..	3B	•134	514	89	144	28	3	23	80	.280	58	111	6	*122	*313	*32	.931
1995—Midland (Texas).........	3B-SS	134	520	91	145	19	10	30	104	.279	63	119	3	128	300	29	.937
1996—California (A.L.).........	3B-DH	84	252	19	60	8	1	6	28	.238	16	50	2	50	190	10	.960
—Vancouver (PCL)........	3B	59	243	49	82	24	0	9	55	.337	20	38	2	50	135	6	.969
1997—Vancouver (PCL)........	3B-SS-DH	105	401	71	112	28	3	11	60	.279	39	51	3	96	213	14	.957
—Anaheim (A.L.)..........	DH-3B	3	6	1	2	0	0	0	1	.333	0	0	0	0	3	0	1.000
—Las Vegas (PCL)■	3B-DH	10	30	4	10	4	1	1	5	.333	3	8	0	§6	15	2	.913
—San Diego (N.L.)........	3B	11	22	2	5	1	0	0	2	.227	0	1	0	4	12	1	.941
1998—Las Vegas (PCL)........	3B-DH-1B	114	435	73	134	33	4	36	*119	.308	37	108	0	98	234	17	.951
—San Diego (N.L.)........	3B-1B	20	36	4	7	1	1	1	4	.194	3	16	0	9	23	2	.941
1999—San Diego (N.L.)........	3B	55	164	20	40	8	0	7	20	.244	6	54	0	35	93	8	.941
—Las Vegas (PCL)........	3B-DH	26	95	30	27	7	2	10	30	.284	17	28	1	20	37	3	.950
—Rancho Cuca. (Calif.).	3B-DH	7	21	1	4	2	0	1	4	.190	2	9	0	1	3	1	.800
American League totals (2 years)		87	258	20	62	8	1	6	29	.240	16	50	2	50	193	10	.960
National League totals (3 years)		86	222	26	52	10	1	8	26	.234	9	71	0	48	128	11	.941
Major League totals (4 years)		173	480	46	114	18	2	14	55	.238	25	121	2	98	321	21	.952

DIVISION SERIES RECORD

Year Team (League)	Pos.	G	AB	R	H	2B	3B	HR	RBI	Avg.	BB	SO	SB	PO	A	E	Avg.
1998—San Diego (N.L.)	PH	1	1	0	0	0	0	0	0	.000	0	1	0	...	...	...	...

CHAMPIONSHIP SERIES RECORD

Year Team (League)	Pos.	G	AB	R	H	2B	3B	HR	RBI	Avg.	BB	SO	SB	PO	A	E	Avg.
1998—San Diego (N.L.)								Did not play.									

WORLD SERIES RECORD

Year Team (League)	Pos.	G	AB	R	H	2B	3B	HR	RBI	Avg.	BB	SO	SB	PO	A	E	Avg.
1998—San Diego (N.L.)								Did not play.									

ARMAS JR., TONY   P   EXPOS

PERSONAL: Born April 29, 1978, in Puerto Piritu, Venezuela. ... 6-4/205. ... Throws right, bats right. ... Full name: Antonio Jose Armas Jr. ... Son of Tony Armas, outfielder with four major league teams (1976-89).
TRANSACTIONS/CAREER NOTES: Signed as non-drafted free agent by New York Yankees organization (August 16, 1994). ... Traded by Yankees with a player to be named later to Boston Red Sox for C Mike Stanley and SS Randy Brown (August 13, 1997); Red Sox acquired P Jim Mecir to complete deal (September 29, 1997). ... Traded by Red Sox to Montreal Expos (December 18, 1997), completing deal in which Red Sox traded P Carl Pavano and a player to be named later for P Pedro Martinez (November 18, 1997).

Year League	W	L	Pct.	ERA	G	GS	CG	ShO	Sv.	IP	H	R	ER	BB	SO
1995—Gulf Coast Yankees (GCL)..	0	1	.000	0.64	5	4	0	0	0	14	12	9	1	6	13
1996—Oneonta (NY-P).................	1	1	.500	5.74	3	3	0	0	0	$15\frac{2}{3}$	14	12	10	11	14
—Gulf Coast Yankees (GCL)..	4	1	.800	3.15	8	7	0	0	1	$45\frac{2}{3}$	41	18	16	13	45
1997—Greensboro (SAL).............	5	2	.714	1.05	9	9	2	1	0	$51\frac{2}{3}$	36	13	6	13	64
—Tampa (FSL)......................	3	1	.750	3.33	9	9	0	0	0	46	43	23	17	16	26
—Sarasota (FSL)■	2	1	.667	6.62	3	3	0	0	0	$17\frac{2}{3}$	18	13	13	12	9
1998—Jupiter (FSL)■..................	12	8	.600	2.88	27	27	1	1	0	$153\frac{1}{3}$	140	63	49	59	136
1999—Harrisburg (East.).............	9	7	.563	2.89	24	24	2	1	0	$149\frac{2}{3}$	123	62	48	55	106
—Montreal (N.L.)..................	0	1	.000	1.50	1	1	0	0	0	6	8	4	1	2	2
Major League totals (1 year)........	0	1	.000	1.50	1	1	0	0	0	6	8	4	1	2	2

ARNOLD, JAMIE   P   DODGERS

PERSONAL: Born March 24, 1974, in Dearborn, Mich. ... 6-2/188. ... Throws right, bats right. ... Full name: James Lee Arnold.
HIGH SCHOOL: Osceola (Kissimmee, Fla.).
TRANSACTIONS/CAREER NOTES: Selected by Atlanta Braves organization in first-round (21st pick overall) of free-agent draft (June 1, 1992). ... Granted free agency (October 16, 1998). ... Signed by Los Angeles Dodgers organization (January 6, 1999).

Year League	W	L	Pct.	ERA	G	GS	CG	ShO	Sv.	IP	H	R	ER	BB	SO
1992—Gulf Coast Braves (GCL)	0	1	.000	4.05	7	5	0	0	0	20	16	12	9	6	22
1993—Macon (SAL)	8	9	.471	3.12	27	27	1	0	0	164 1/3	142	67	57	56	124
1994—Durham (Caro.)	7	7	.500	4.66	25	25	0	0	0	145	144	96	75	79	91
1995—Greenville (Sou.)	1	5	.167	6.35	10	10	0	0	0	56 2/3	76	42	40	25	19
—Durham (Caro.)	4	8	.333	3.94	15	14	1	0	0	80	86	42	35	21	44
1996—Greenville (Sou.)	7	7	.500	4.92	23	23	2	0	0	128	149	79	70	44	64
1997—Gulf Coast Braves (GCL)	1	0	1.000	2.84	5	5	0	0	0	19	13	6	6	6	21
—Durham (Caro.)	2	2	.500	5.92	5	5	0	0	0	24 1/3	25	21	16	13	21
—Greenville (Sou.)	0	1	.000	11.57	1	1	0	0	0	4 2/3	10	6	6	2	3
1998—Greenville (Sou.)	1	4	.200	4.43	32	6	0	0	1	83 1/3	93	51	41	46	48
—Richmond (I.L.)	1	0	1.000	9.58	9	2	0	0	1	20 2/3	30	22	22	17	10
1999—Albuquerque (PCL)■	0	2	.000	5.59	7	2	0	0	0	19 1/3	28	14	12	7	13
—Los Angeles (N.L.)	2	4	.333	5.48	36	3	0	0	1	69	81	50	42	34	26
Major League totals (1 year)	2	4	.333	5.48	36	3	0	0	1	69	81	50	42	34	26

ARROJO, ROLANDO   P   ROCKIES

PERSONAL: Born July 18, 1968, in Havana, Cuba. ... 6-4/220. ... Throws right, bats right. ... Full name: Luis Rolando Arrojo.

TRANSACTIONS/CAREER NOTES: Signed as non-drafted free agent by Tampa Bay Devil Rays organization (April 21, 1997). ... On disabled list (September 21, 1998-remainder of season). ... On Tampa Bay disabled list (May 25-July 15, 1999); included rehabilitation assignment to St. Petersburg (July 2-15). ... Traded by Devil Rays with IF Aaron Ledesma to Colorado Rockies for 3B Vinny Castilla (December 13, 1999).

HONORS: Named A.L. Rookie Pitcher of the Year by THE SPORTING NEWS (1998).

STATISTICAL NOTES: Led A.L. with 19 hit batsmen in 1998.

MISCELLANEOUS: Member of Cuban national baseball team (1986-96). ... Holds Tampa Bay Devil Rays all-time records for most wins (21), innings pitched (342 2/3) and strikeouts (259). ... Shares Tampa Bay Devil Rays all-time record for most shutouts (2).

Year League	W	L	Pct.	ERA	G	GS	CG	ShO	Sv.	IP	H	R	ER	BB	SO
1997—St. Petersburg (FSL)	5	6	.455	3.43	16	16	4	1	0	89 1/3	73	40	34	13	73
1998—Tampa Bay (A.L.)	14	12	.538	3.56	32	32	2	2	0	202	195	84	80	65	152
1999—Tampa Bay (A.L.)	7	12	.368	5.18	24	24	2	0	0	140 2/3	162	84	81	60	107
—St. Petersburg (FSL)	0	1	.000	4.50	2	2	0	0	0	10	11	6	5	1	10
Major League totals (2 years)	21	24	.467	4.23	56	56	4	2	0	342 2/3	357	168	161	125	259

ALL-STAR GAME RECORD

Year League	W	L	Pct.	ERA	GS	CG	ShO	Sv.	IP	H	R	ER	BB	SO
1998—American	0	0	...	0.00	0	0	0	0	1	2	0	0	0	1

ARROYO, BRONSON   P   PIRATES

PERSONAL: Born February 24, 1977, in Key West, Fla. ... 6-5/180. ... Throws right, bats right. ... Full name: Bronson Anthony Arroyo.

HIGH SCHOOL: Hernando (Fla.).

TRANSACTIONS/CAREER NOTES: Selected by Pittsburgh Pirates organization in third round of free-agent draft (June 1, 1995). ... On suspended list (May 29-June 1, 1996). ... On Carolina disabled list (May 18-June 7 and June 18-July 4, 1998).

Year League	W	L	Pct.	ERA	G	GS	CG	ShO	Sv.	IP	H	R	ER	BB	SO
1995—Bradenton Pirates (GCL)	5	4	.556	4.26	13	9	0	0	0	61 1/3	72	39	29	9	48
1996—Augusta (SAL)	8	6	.571	3.52	26	26	0	0	0	135 2/3	123	64	53	36	107
1997—Lynchburg (Caro.)	•12	4	.750	3.31	24	24	3	1	0	160 1/3	154	69	59	33	121
1998—Carolina (Sou.)	9	8	.529	5.46	23	22	1	0	0	127	158	91	77	51	90
1999—Altoona (East.)	•15	4	.789	3.65	25	25	2	1	0	153	167	73	62	58	100
—Nashville (PCL)	0	2	.000	10.38	3	3	0	0	0	13	22	15	15	10	11

ASHBY, ANDY   P   PHILLIES

PERSONAL: Born July 11, 1967, in Kansas City, Mo. ... 6-1/202. ... Throws right, bats right. ... Full name: Andrew Jason Ashby.

HIGH SCHOOL: Park Hill (Kansas City, Mo.).

JUNIOR COLLEGE: Crowder College (Mo.).

TRANSACTIONS/CAREER NOTES: Signed as non-drafted free agent by Philadelphia Phillies organization (May 4, 1986). ... On Spartanburg disabled list (April 7-July 10, 1988). ... On Spartanburg disabled list (April 6-26, 1989). ... On Philadelphia disabled list (April 27-August 11, 1992); included rehabilitation assignments to Scranton/Wilkes-Barre (July 8-August 2 and August 6-10). ... Selected by Colorado Rockies in first round (25th pick overall) of expansion draft (November 17, 1992). ... Traded by Rockies to San Diego Padres (July 27, 1993), completing deal in which Padres traded P Bruce Hurst and P Greg W. Harris to Rockies for C Brad Ausmus, P Doug Bochtler and a player to be named later (July 26, 1993). ... On disabled list (June 6-22, June 29-July 15 and July 27-September 1, 1996; May 20-June 15, 1997; and June 7-24, 1998). ... Traded by Padres to Phillies for P Carlton Loewer, P Steve Montgomery and P Adam Eaton (November 10, 1999).

RECORDS: Shares major league record by striking out side on nine pitches (June 15, 1991, fourth inning).

MISCELLANEOUS: Had sacrifice hit in only appearance as pinch hitter (1996). ... Appeared in one game as pinch runner (1997).

Year League	W	L	Pct.	ERA	G	GS	CG	ShO	Sv.	IP	H	R	ER	BB	SO
1986—Bend (N.W.)	1	2	.333	4.95	16	6	0	0	2	60	56	40	33	34	45
1987—Spartanburg (SAL)	4	6	.400	5.60	13	13	1	0	0	64 1/3	73	45	40	38	52
—Utica (NY-P)	3	7	.300	4.05	13	13	0	0	0	60	56	38	27	36	51
1988—Spartanburg (SAL)	1	1	.500	2.70	3	3	0	0	0	16 2/3	13	7	5	7	16
—Batavia (NY-P)	3	1	.750	1.61	6	6	2	1	0	44 2/3	25	11	8	16	32
1989—Spartanburg (SAL)	5	9	.357	2.87	17	17	3	1	0	106 2/3	95	48	34	49	100
—Clearwater (FSL)	1	4	.200	1.24	6	6	2	1	0	43 2/3	28	9	6	21	44
1990—Reading (East.)	10	7	.588	3.42	23	23	4	1	0	139 2/3	134	65	53	48	94
1991—Scranton/W.B. (I.L.)	11	11	.500	3.46	26	26	•6	•3	0	161 1/3	144	78	62	60	113
—Philadelphia (N.L.)	1	5	.167	6.00	8	8	0	0	0	42	41	28	28	19	26
1992—Philadelphia (N.L.)	1	3	.250	7.54	10	8	0	0	0	37	42	31	31	21	24
—Scranton/W.B. (I.L.)	0	3	.000	3.00	7	7	1	0	0	33	23	13	11	14	18

Year League	W	L	Pct.	ERA	G	GS	CG	ShO	Sv.	IP	H	R	ER	BB	SO
1993—Colorado (N.L.)■	0	4	.000	8.50	20	9	0	0	1	54	89	54	51	32	33
—Colorado Springs (PCL)	4	2	.667	4.10	7	6	1	0	0	41 2/3	45	25	19	12	35
—San Diego (N.L.)■	3	6	.333	5.48	12	12	0	0	0	69	79	46	42	24	44
1994—San Diego (N.L.)	6	11	.353	3.40	24	24	4	0	0	164 1/3	145	75	62	43	121
1995—San Diego (N.L.)	12	10	.545	2.94	31	•31	2	2	0	192 2/3	180	79	63	62	150
1996—San Diego (N.L.)	9	5	.643	3.23	24	24	1	0	0	150 2/3	147	60	54	34	85
1997—San Diego (N.L.)	9	11	.450	4.13	30	30	2	0	0	200 2/3	207	108	92	49	144
1998—San Diego (N.L.)	17	9	.654	3.34	33	33	5	1	0	226 2/3	223	90	84	58	151
1999—San Diego (N.L.)	14	10	.583	3.80	31	31	4	•3	0	206	204	95	87	54	132
Major League totals (9 years)	72	74	.493	3.98	223	210	18	6	1	1343	1357	666	594	396	910

DIVISION SERIES RECORD

Year League	W	L	Pct.	ERA	G	GS	CG	ShO	Sv.	IP	H	R	ER	BB	SO
1996—San Diego (N.L.)	0	0	...	6.75	1	1	0	0	0	5 1/3	7	4	4	1	5
1998—San Diego (N.L.)	0	0	...	6.75	1	1	0	0	0	4	6	3	3	1	4
Division series totals (2 years)	0	0	...	6.75	2	2	0	0	0	9 1/3	13	7	7	2	9

CHAMPIONSHIP SERIES RECORD

Year League	W	L	Pct.	ERA	G	GS	CG	ShO	Sv.	IP	H	R	ER	BB	SO
1998—San Diego (N.L.)	0	0	...	2.08	2	2	0	0	0	13	14	3	3	2	5

WORLD SERIES RECORD

Year League	W	L	Pct.	ERA	G	GS	CG	ShO	Sv.	IP	H	R	ER	BB	SO
1998—San Diego (N.L.)	0	1	.000	13.50	1	1	0	0	0	2 2/3	10	7	4	1	1

ALL-STAR GAME RECORD

Year League	W	L	Pct.	ERA	GS	CG	ShO	Sv.	IP	H	R	ER	BB	SO
1998—National	0	0	...	9.00	0	0	0	0	1	1	1	1	1	0
1999—National	0	0	...	0.00	0	0	0	0	1/3	0	0	0	0	0
All-Star Game totals (2 years)	0	0	...	6.75	0	0	0	0	1 1/3	1	1	1	1	0

ASSENMACHER, PAUL   P

PERSONAL: Born December 10, 1960, in Allen Park, Mich. ... 6-3/210. ... Throws left, bats left. ... Full name: Paul Andre Assenmacher. ... Name pronounced AHSS-en-MAHK-ur.

HIGH SCHOOL: Aquinas (Southgate, Mich.).

COLLEGE: Aquinas, Mich. (degree in business administration).

TRANSACTIONS/CAREER NOTES: Signed as non-drafted free agent by Atlanta Braves organization (July 10, 1983). ... On Atlanta disabled list (April 29-May 9, 1987 and August 10-25, 1988). ... Traded by Braves organization to Chicago Cubs for two players to be named later (August 24, 1989); Braves acquired C Kelly Mann and P Pat Gomez to complete deal (September 1, 1989). ... On disabled list (May 19-June 4, 1992). ... Traded by Cubs to New York Yankees as part of a three-way deal in which Yankees sent P John Habyan to Kansas City Royals and Royals sent OF Tuffy Rhodes to Cubs (July 30, 1993). ... Traded by Yankees to Chicago White Sox for P Brian Boehringer (March 21, 1994). ... Granted free agency (October 24, 1994). ... Signed by Cleveland Indians (April 10, 1995). ... Granted free agency (November 3, 1997). ... Re-signed by Indians (November 12, 1997). ... Granted free agency (November 4, 1999).

RECORDS: Shares major league record for most strikeouts in one inning—4 (August 22, 1989, fifth inning).

Year League	W	L	Pct.	ERA	G	GS	CG	ShO	Sv.	IP	H	R	ER	BB	SO
1983—Gulf Coast Braves (GCL)	1	0	1.000	2.21	10	3	1	1	2	36 2/3	35	14	9	4	44
1984—Durham (Caro.)	6	11	.353	4.28	26	24	3	1	0	147 1/3	153	78	70	52	147
1985—Durham (Caro.)	3	2	.600	3.29	14	0	0	0	1	38 1/3	38	16	14	13	36
—Greenville (Sou.)	6	0	1.000	2.56	29	0	0	0	4	52 2/3	46	15	15	11	59
1986—Atlanta (N.L.)	7	3	.700	2.50	61	0	0	0	7	68 1/3	61	23	19	26	56
1987—Atlanta (N.L.)	1	1	.500	5.10	52	0	0	0	2	54 2/3	58	41	31	24	39
—Richmond (I.L.)	1	2	.333	3.65	4	4	0	0	0	24 2/3	30	11	10	8	21
1988—Atlanta (N.L.)	8	7	.533	3.06	64	0	0	0	5	79 1/3	72	28	27	32	71
1989—Atlanta (N.L.)	1	3	.250	3.59	49	0	0	0	0	57 2/3	55	26	23	16	64
—Chicago (N.L.)■	2	1	.667	5.21	14	0	0	0	0	19	19	11	11	12	15
1990—Chicago (N.L.)	7	2	.778	2.80	74	1	0	0	10	103	90	33	32	36	95
1991—Chicago (N.L.)	7	8	.467	3.24	75	0	0	0	15	102 2/3	85	41	37	31	117
1992—Chicago (N.L.)	4	4	.500	4.10	70	0	0	0	8	68	72	32	31	26	67
1993—Chicago (N.L.)	2	1	.667	3.49	46	0	0	0	0	38 2/3	44	15	15	13	34
—New York (A.L.)■	2	2	.500	3.12	26	0	0	0	0	17 1/3	10	6	6	9	11
1994—Chicago (A.L.)	1	2	.333	3.55	44	0	0	0	1	33	26	13	13	13	29
1995—Cleveland (A.L.)■	6	2	.750	2.82	47	0	0	0	0	38 1/3	32	13	12	12	40
1996—Cleveland (A.L.)	4	2	.667	3.09	63	0	0	0	1	46 2/3	46	18	16	14	44
1997—Cleveland (A.L.)	5	0	1.000	2.94	75	0	0	0	4	49	43	17	16	15	53
1998—Cleveland (A.L.)	2	5	.286	3.26	69	0	0	0	3	47	54	22	17	19	43
1999—Cleveland (A.L.)	2	1	.667	8.18	55	0	0	0	0	33	50	32	30	17	29
A.L. totals (7 years)	22	14	.611	3.75	379	0	0	0	9	264 1/3	261	121	110	99	249
N.L. totals (8 years)	39	30	.565	3.44	505	1	0	0	47	591 1/3	556	250	226	216	558
Major League totals (14 years)	61	44	.581	3.53	884	1	0	0	56	855 2/3	817	371	336	315	807

DIVISION SERIES RECORD

RECORDS: Shares career record for most games by pitcher—14.

Year League	W	L	Pct.	ERA	G	GS	CG	ShO	Sv.	IP	H	R	ER	BB	SO
1995—Cleveland (A.L.)	0	0	...	0.00	3	0	0	0	0	1 2/3	0	0	0	0	3
1996—Cleveland (A.L.)	1	0	1.000	0.00	3	0	0	0	0	1 2/3	0	0	0	2	2
1997—Cleveland (A.L.)	0	0	...	5.40	4	0	0	0	0	3 1/3	2	2	2	2	2
1998—Cleveland (A.L.)	0	0	...	0.00	3	0	0	0	0	1	2	0	0	0	2
1999—Cleveland (A.L.)	0	0	...	27.00	1	0	0	0	0	1	5	3	3	0	0
Division series totals (5 years)	1	0	1.000	5.19	14	0	0	0	0	8 2/3	9	5	5	4	9

CHAMPIONSHIP SERIES RECORD

Year	League	W	L	Pct.	ERA	G	GS	CG	ShO	Sv.	IP	H	R	ER	BB	SO
1989— Chicago (N.L.)		0	0	...	13.50	2	0	0	0	0	²/₃	3	1	1	0	0
1995— Cleveland (A.L.)		0	0	...	0.00	3	0	0	0	0	1¹/₃	0	0	0	1	2
1997— Cleveland (A.L.)		1	0	1.000	9.00	5	0	0	0	0	2	5	2	2	1	3
1998— Cleveland (A.L.)		0	0	...	0.00	3	0	0	0	0	2	0	0	0	0	3
Champ. series totals (4 years)		**1**	**0**	**1.000**	**4.50**	**13**	**0**	**0**	**0**	**0**	**6**	**8**	**3**	**3**	**2**	**8**

WORLD SERIES RECORD

Year	League	W	L	Pct.	ERA	G	GS	CG	ShO	Sv.	IP	H	R	ER	BB	SO
1995— Cleveland (A.L.)		0	0	...	6.75	4	0	0	0	0	1¹/₃	1	2	1	3	3
1997— Cleveland (A.L.)		0	0	...	0.00	5	0	0	0	0	4	5	0	0	0	6
World Series totals (2 years)		**0**	**0**	**...**	**1.69**	**9**	**0**	**0**	**0**	**0**	**5¹/₃**	**6**	**2**	**1**	**3**	**9**

ASTACIO, PEDRO   P   ROCKIES

PERSONAL: Born November 28, 1969, in Hato Mayor, Dominican Republic. ... 6-2/208. ... Throws right, bats right. ... Full name: Pedro Julio Astacio. ... Name pronounced ah-STA-see-oh.

HIGH SCHOOL: Pilar Rondon (Dominican Republic).

TRANSACTIONS/CAREER NOTES: Signed as non-drafted free agent by Los Angeles Dodgers organization (November 21, 1987). ... On Albuquerque disabled list (April 26-May 21, 1992). ... Traded by Dodgers to Colorado Rockies for 2B Eric Young (August 19, 1997).

STATISTICAL NOTES: Led N.L. with nine balks in 1993. ... Led N.L. with 17 hit batsmen and tied for lead with 39 home runs allowed in 1998. ... Led N.L. with 38 home runs allowed in 1999.

MISCELLANEOUS: Holds Colorado Rockies all-time record for most strikeouts (431). ... Struck out in both appearances as pinch hitter and appeared in one game as pinch runner (1999).

Year	League	W	L	Pct.	ERA	G	GS	CG	ShO	Sv.	IP	H	R	ER	BB	SO
1989— Gulf Coast Dodgers (GCL)..		7	3	.700	3.17	12	12	1	•1	0	76²/₃	77	30	27	12	52
1990— Vero Beach (FSL)		1	5	.167	6.32	8	8	0	0	0	47	54	39	33	23	41
— Yakima (N.W.)		2	0	1.000	1.74	3	3	0	0	0	20²/₃	9	8	4	4	22
— Bakersfield (Calif.)		5	2	.714	2.77	10	7	1	0	0	52	46	22	16	15	34
1991— Vero Beach (FSL)		5	3	.625	1.67	9	9	3	1	0	59¹/₃	44	19	11	8	45
— San Antonio (Tex.-La.)		4	11	.267	4.78	19	19	2	1	0	113	142	67	60	39	62
1992— Albuquerque (PCL)		6	6	.500	5.47	24	15	1	0	0	98²/₃	115	68	60	44	66
— Los Angeles (N.L.)		5	5	.500	1.98	11	11	4	4	0	82	80	23	18	20	43
1993— Los Angeles (N.L.)		14	9	.609	3.57	31	31	3	2	0	186¹/₃	165	80	74	68	122
1994— Los Angeles (N.L.)		6	8	.429	4.29	23	23	3	1	0	149	142	77	71	47	108
1995— Los Angeles (N.L.)		7	8	.467	4.24	48	11	1	1	0	104	103	53	49	29	80
1996— Los Angeles (N.L.)		9	8	.529	3.44	35	32	0	0	0	211²/₃	207	86	81	67	130
1997— Los Angeles (N.L.)		7	9	.438	4.10	26	24	2	1	0	153²/₃	151	75	70	47	115
— Colorado (N.L.)■		5	1	.833	4.25	7	7	0	0	0	48²/₃	49	23	23	14	51
1998— Colorado (N.L.)		13	14	.481	6.23	35	34	0	0	0	209¹/₃	245	*160	*145	74	170
1999— Colorado (N.L.)		17	11	.607	5.04	34	34	7	0	0	232	258	140	130	75	210
Major League totals (8 years)		**83**	**73**	**.532**	**4.32**	**250**	**207**	**20**	**9**	**0**	**1376²/₃**	**1400**	**717**	**661**	**441**	**1029**

DIVISION SERIES RECORD

Year	League	W	L	Pct.	ERA	G	GS	CG	ShO	Sv.	IP	H	R	ER	BB	SO
1995— Los Angeles (N.L.)		0	0	...	0.00	3	0	0	0	0	3¹/₃	1	0	0	0	5
1996— Los Angeles (N.L.)		0	0	...	0.00	1	0	0	0	0	1²/₃	0	0	0	0	1
Division series totals (2 years)		**0**	**0**	**...**	**0.00**	**4**	**0**	**0**	**0**	**0**	**5**	**1**	**0**	**0**	**0**	**6**

AURILIA, RICH   SS   GIANTS

PERSONAL: Born September 2, 1971, in Brooklyn, N.Y. ... 6-1/185. ... Bats right, throws right. ... Full name: Richard Santo Aurilia. ... Name pronounced uh-REEL-yuh.

HIGH SCHOOL: Xaverian (Brooklyn, N.Y.).

COLLEGE: St. John's.

TRANSACTIONS/CAREER NOTES: Selected by Texas Rangers organization in 24th round of free-agent draft (June 1, 1992). ... On disabled list (April 9-16, 1993). ... Traded by Rangers with IF/OF Desi Wilson to San Francisco Giants for P John Burkett (December 24, 1994). ... On San Francisco disabled list (September 24, 1996-remainder of season). ... On disabled list (July 4-20, 1998).

STATISTICAL NOTES: Led Texas League shortstops with 635 total chances and tied for lead with 82 double plays in 1994. ... Career major league grand slams: 1.

Year	Team (League)	Pos.	G	AB	R	H	2B	3B	HR	RBI	Avg.	BB	SO	SB	PO	A	E	Avg.
							BATTING								FIELDING			
1992— Butte (Pio.)		SS	59	202	37	68	11	3	3	30	.337	42	18	13	78	154	14	*.943
1993— Charlotte (FSL)		SS	122	440	80	136	16	5	5	56	.309	75	57	15	200	445	24	.964
1994— Tulsa (Texas)		SS	129	458	67	107	18	6	12	57	.234	53	74	10	*237	374	24	*.962
1995— Shreveport (Texas)■..		SS	64	226	29	74	17	1	4	42	.327	27	26	10	122	237	14	.962
— Phoenix (PCL)		SS	71	258	42	72	12	0	5	34	.279	35	29	2	104	246	9	.975
— San Francisco (N.L.) ..		SS	9	19	4	9	3	0	2	4	.474	1	2	1	8	16	0	1.000
1996— Phoenix (PCL)		SS-2B	7	30	9	13	7	0	0	4	.433	2	3	1	10	25	1	.972
— San Francisco (N.L.) ..		SS-2B	105	318	27	76	7	1	3	26	.239	25	52	4	142	246	10	.975
1997— San Francisco (N.L.) ..		SS	46	102	16	28	8	0	5	19	.275	8	15	1	47	91	3	.979
— Phoenix (PCL)		SS	8	34	9	10	2	0	1	5	.294	5	4	2	14	22	0	1.000
1998— San Francisco (N.L.) ..		SS	122	413	54	110	27	2	9	49	.266	31	62	3	154	313	10	.979
1999— San Francisco (N.L.) ..		SS	152	558	68	157	23	1	22	80	.281	43	71	2	218	411	*28	.957
Major League totals (5 years)			**434**	**1410**	**169**	**380**	**68**	**4**	**41**	**178**	**.270**	**108**	**202**	**11**	**569**	**1077**	**51**	**.970**

AUSMUS, BRAD   C   TIGERS

PERSONAL: Born April 14, 1969, in New Haven, Conn. ... 5-11/195. ... Bats right, throws right. ... Full name: Bradley David Ausmus.
HIGH SCHOOL: Cheshire (Conn.).
COLLEGE: Dartmouth (degree in government).
TRANSACTIONS/CAREER NOTES: Selected by New York Yankees organization in 47th round of free-agent draft (June 2, 1987). ... Selected by Colorado Rockies in third round (54th pick overall) of expansion draft (November 17, 1992). ... Traded by Rockies with P Doug Bochtler and a player to be named later to San Diego Padres for P Bruce Hurst and P Greg W. Harris (July 26, 1993); Padres acquired P Andy Ashby to complete deal (July 27, 1993). ... Traded by Padres with SS Andujar Cedeno and P Russ Spear to Detroit Tigers for C John Flaherty and SS Chris Gomez (June 18, 1996). ... On Detroit suspended list (September 4-5, 1996). ... Traded by Tigers with P Jose Lima, P C.J. Nitkowski, P Trever Miller and IF Daryle Ward to Houston Astros for OF Brian L. Hunter, IF Orlando Miller, P Doug Brocail, P Todd Jones and cash (December 10, 1996). ... Traded by Astros with P C.J. Nitkowski to Tigers for C Paul Bako, P Dean Crow, P Mark Persails, P Brian Powell, and 3B Carlos Villalobos (January 14, 1999).
STATISTICAL NOTES: Led Gulf Coast League catchers with 434 total chances in 1988. ... Led International League catchers with 666 putouts and 738 total chances in 1992. ... Led N.L. catchers with 683 putouts and 749 total chances in 1994. ... Led N.L. catchers with 14 double plays in 1995. ... Tied for N.L. lead in assists by catcher with 63 in 1995. ... Career major league grand slams: 1.

						BATTING								FIELDING			
Year Team (League)	Pos.	G	AB	R	H	2B	3B	HR	RBI	Avg.	BB	SO	SB	PO	A	E	Avg.
1988— Oneonta (NY-P)	C	2	4	0	1	0	0	0	0	.250	0	2	0	0	0	0	...
— Sarasota (FSL)	C	43	133	22	34	2	0	0	15	.256	11	25	5	*378	*47	9	.979
1989— Oneonta (NY-P)	C-3B	52	165	29	43	6	0	1	18	.261	22	28	6	401	43	7	.984
1990— Prince Will. (Caro.)	C	107	364	46	86	12	2	0	27	.236	32	73	2	662	84	5	*.993
1991— Prince Will. (Caro.)	C	63	230	28	70	14	3	2	30	.304	24	37	17	419	54	5	.990
— Alb./Colonie (East.)	C	67	229	36	61	9	2	1	29	.266	27	36	14	470	56	4	.992
1992— Alb./Colonie (East.)	C	5	18	0	3	0	1	0	1	.167	2	3	2	30	2	1	.970
— Columbus (I.L.)	C-OF	111	364	48	88	14	3	2	35	.242	40	56	19	†666	63	9	.988
1993— Colo. Spr. (PCL)■	C-DH-OF	76	241	31	65	10	4	2	33	.270	27	41	10	393	57	6	.987
— San Diego (N.L.)■	C	49	160	18	41	8	1	5	12	.256	6	28	2	272	34	8	.975
1994— San Diego (N.L.)	C-1B	101	327	45	82	12	1	7	24	.251	30	63	5	†686	59	7	.991
1995— San Diego (N.L.)	C-1B	103	328	44	96	16	4	5	34	.293	31	56	16	656	‡63	6	.992
1996— San Diego (N.L.)	C	50	149	16	27	4	0	1	13	.181	13	27	1	300	22	6	.982
— Detroit (A.L.)■	C	75	226	30	56	12	0	4	22	.248	26	45	3	452	35	4	.992
1997— Houston (N.L.)	C	130	425	45	113	25	1	4	44	.266	38	78	14	807	73	7	.992
1998— Houston (N.L.)	C	128	412	62	111	10	4	6	45	.269	53	60	10	850	58	7	.992
1999— Detroit (A.L.)■	C	127	458	62	126	25	6	9	54	.275	51	71	12	754	56	2	*.998
American League totals (2 years)		202	684	92	182	37	6	13	76	.266	77	116	15	1206	91	6	.995
National League totals (6 years)		561	1801	230	470	75	11	28	172	.261	171	312	48	3571	309	41	.990
Major League totals (7 years)		763	2485	322	652	112	17	41	248	.262	248	428	63	4777	400	47	.991

DIVISION SERIES RECORD

						BATTING								FIELDING			
Year Team (League)	Pos.	G	AB	R	H	2B	3B	HR	RBI	Avg.	BB	SO	SB	PO	A	E	Avg.
1997— Houston (N.L.)	C	2	5	1	2	1	0	0	2	.400	0	1	0	13	0	0	1.000
1998— Houston (N.L.)	C	4	9	0	2	0	0	0	0	.222	0	4	0	28	1	0	1.000
Division series totals (2 years)		6	14	1	4	1	0	0	2	.286	0	5	0	41	1	0	1.000

ALL-STAR GAME RECORD

					BATTING								FIELDING			
Year League	Pos.	AB	R	H	2B	3B	HR	RBI	Avg.	BB	SO	SB	PO	A	E	Avg.
1999— American	C	1	0	0	0	0	0	0	.000	0	0	0	2	1	0	1.000

AVEN, BRUCE   OF   PIRATES

PERSONAL: Born March 4, 1972, in Orange, Texas. ... 5-9/180. ... Bats right, throws right. ... Full name: David Bruce Aven.
HIGH SCHOOL: West Orange-Stark (Orange, Texas).
COLLEGE: Lamar.
TRANSACTIONS/CAREER NOTES: Selected by Cleveland Indians organization in 30th round of free-agent draft (June 2, 1994). ... On Buffalo disabled list (April 9-17, April 23-May 23 and May 27, 1998-remainder of season). ... Claimed on waivers by Florida Marlins (October 20, 1998). ... Traded by Marlins to Pittsburgh Pirates for OF Brant Brown (December 13, 1999).
STATISTICAL NOTES: Led Eastern League outfielders with 289 total chances in 1996. ... Tied for American Association lead in being hit by pitch with 11 in 1997. ... Career major league grand slams: 2.

						BATTING								FIELDING			
Year Team (League)	Pos.	G	AB	R	H	2B	3B	HR	RBI	Avg.	BB	SO	SB	PO	A	E	Avg.
1994— Watertown (NY-P)	OF	61	220	49	73	14	5	5	33	.332	20	45	12	88	6	1	.989
1995— Kinston (Caro.)	OF	130	479	70	125	23	5	23	69	.261	41	109	15	158	11	3	.983
1996— Canton/Akron (East.)	OF	131	481	91	143	31	4	23	79	.297	43	101	22	280	3	6	.979
— Buffalo (A.A.)	OF	3	9	5	6	0	0	1	2	.667	1	1	0	7	0	0	1.000
1997— Buffalo (A.A.)	OF-DH	121	432	69	124	27	3	17	77	.287	50	99	10	219	3	2	.991
— Cleveland (A.L.)	OF	13	19	4	4	1	0	0	2	.211	1	5	0	15	1	0	1.000
1998— Buffalo (I.L.)	DH	5	15	4	3	1	0	1	1	.200	6	5	3	0	0	0	...
1999— Florida (N.L.)■	OF-DH	137	381	57	110	19	2	12	70	.289	44	82	3	181	4	3	.984
American League totals (1 year)		13	19	4	4	1	0	0	2	.211	1	5	0	15	1	0	1.000
National League totals (1 year)		137	381	57	110	19	2	12	70	.289	44	82	3	181	4	3	.984
Major League totals (2 years)		150	400	61	114	20	2	12	72	.285	45	87	3	196	5	3	.985

A

PERSONAL: Born April 14, 1970, in Trenton, Mich. ... 6-4/205. ... Throws left, bats left. ... Full name: Steven Thomas Avery. ... Son of Ken Avery, minor league pitcher (1962-63).

HIGH SCHOOL: John F. Kennedy (Taylor, Mich.).

TRANSACTIONS/CAREER NOTES: Selected by Atlanta Braves organization in first round (third pick overall) of free-agent draft (June 1, 1988). ... On Atlanta disabled list (July 13-September 2, 1996); included rehabilitation assignment to Greenville (August 12-18). ... Granted free agency (October 31, 1996). ... Signed by Boston Red Sox (January 22, 1997). ... On Boston disabled list (May 4-July 5, 1997); included rehabilitation assignments to Sarasota (June 12-25) and Gulf Coast Red Sox (June 25-July 5). ... Granted free agency (October 28, 1998). ... Signed by Cincinnati Reds (December 21, 1998). ... On disabled list (July 24, 1999-remainder of season). ... Granted free agency (October 29, 1999).

HONORS: Named lefthanded pitcher on THE SPORTING NEWS N.L. All-Star team (1993).

MISCELLANEOUS: Received base on balls in only appearance as pinch hitter and appeared in one game as pinch runner (1991). ... Appeared in one game as pinch runner with Boston (1997). ... Scored two runs in five appearances as pinch runner with Boston (1998).

Year League	W	L	Pct.	ERA	G	GS	CG	ShO	Sv.	IP	H	R	ER	BB	SO
1988—Pulaski (Appl.)	7	1	.875	1.50	10	10	3	•2	0	66	38	16	11	19	80
1989—Durham (Caro.)	6	4	.600	1.45	13	13	3	1	0	86 2/3	59	22	14	20	90
— Greenville (Sou.)	6	3	.667	2.77	13	13	1	0	0	84 1/3	68	32	26	34	75
1990—Richmond (I.L.)	5	5	.500	3.39	13	13	3	0	0	82 1/3	85	35	31	21	69
— Atlanta (N.L.)	3	11	.214	5.64	21	20	1	1	0	99	121	79	62	45	75
1991—Atlanta (N.L.)	18	8	.692	3.38	35	35	3	1	0	210 1/3	189	89	79	65	137
1992—Atlanta (N.L.)	11	11	.500	3.20	35	•35	2	2	0	233 2/3	216	95	83	71	129
1993—Atlanta (N.L.)	18	6	.750	2.94	35	35	3	1	0	223 1/3	216	81	73	43	125
1994—Atlanta (N.L.)	8	3	.727	4.04	24	24	1	0	0	151 2/3	127	71	68	55	122
1995—Atlanta (N.L.)	7	13	.350	4.67	29	29	3	1	0	173 1/3	165	92	90	52	141
1996—Atlanta (N.L.)	7	10	.412	4.47	24	23	1	0	0	131	146	70	65	40	86
— Greenville (Sou.)	0	0	...	0.00	1	1	0	0	0	2/3	0	0	0	0	0
1997—Boston (A.L.)■	6	7	.462	6.42	22	18	0	0	0	96 2/3	127	76	69	49	51
— Sarasota (FSL)	0	0	...	0.00	1	1	0	0	0	3	2	0	0	1	3
— GC Red Sox (GCL)	0	0	...	1.50	1	1	0	0	0	6	5	3	1	0	8
— Pawtucket (I.L.)	1	0	1.000	0.00	1	1	0	0	0	5	1	0	0	3	1
1998—Boston (A.L.)	10	7	.588	5.02	34	23	0	0	0	123 2/3	128	74	69	64	57
— Pawtucket (I.L.)	0	2	.000	5.56	3	3	0	0	0	11 1/3	9	9	7	9	6
1999—Cincinnati (N.L.)■	6	7	.462	5.16	19	19	0	0	0	96	75	62	55	78	51
A.L. totals (2 years)	16	14	.533	5.64	56	41	0	0	0	220 1/3	255	150	138	113	108
N.L. totals (8 years)	78	69	.531	3.93	222	220	14	6	0	1318 1/3	1255	639	575	449	866
Major League totals (10 years)	94	83	.531	4.17	278	261	14	6	0	1538 2/3	1510	789	713	562	974

DIVISION SERIES RECORD

Year League	W	L	Pct.	ERA	G	GS	CG	ShO	Sv.	IP	H	R	ER	BB	SO
1995—Atlanta (N.L.)	0	0	...	13.50	1	0	0	0	0	2/3	1	1	1	0	1

CHAMPIONSHIP SERIES RECORD

RECORDS: Holds career record for most consecutive scoreless innings—22 1/3 (1991-92). ... Holds single-series record for most consecutive scoreless innings—16 1/3 (1991).

NOTES: Named Most Valuable Player (1991).

Year League	W	L	Pct.	ERA	G	GS	CG	ShO	Sv.	IP	H	R	ER	BB	SO
1991—Atlanta (N.L.)	2	0	1.000	0.00	2	2	0	0	0	16 1/3	9	0	0	4	17
1992—Atlanta (N.L.)	1	1	.500	9.00	3	2	0	0	0	8	13	8	8	2	3
1993—Atlanta (N.L.)	0	0	...	2.77	2	2	0	0	0	13	9	5	4	6	10
1995—Atlanta (N.L.)	1	0	1.000	0.00	2	1	0	0	0	6	2	0	0	4	6
1996—Atlanta (N.L.)	0	0	...	0.00	2	0	0	0	0	2	2	0	0	1	1
Champ. series totals (5 years)	4	1	.800	2.38	11	7	0	0	0	45 1/3	35	13	12	17	37

WORLD SERIES RECORD

NOTES: Member of World Series championship team (1995).

Year League	W	L	Pct.	ERA	G	GS	CG	ShO	Sv.	IP	H	R	ER	BB	SO
1991—Atlanta (N.L.)	0	0	...	3.46	2	2	0	0	0	13	10	6	5	1	8
1992—Atlanta (N.L.)	0	1	.000	3.75	2	2	0	0	0	12	11	5	5	3	11
1995—Atlanta (N.L.)	1	0	1.000	1.50	1	1	0	0	0	6	3	1	1	5	3
1996—Atlanta (N.L.)	0	1	.000	13.50	1	0	0	0	0	2/3	1	2	1	4	0
World Series totals (4 years)	1	2	.333	3.41	6	5	0	0	0	31 2/3	25	14	12	13	22

ALL-STAR GAME RECORD

Year League	W	L	Pct.	ERA	GS	CG	ShO	Sv.	IP	H	R	ER	BB	SO
1993—National	0	0	...	0.00	0	0	0	0	1	1	3	0	1	1

PERSONAL: Born July 8, 1969, in Ventura, Calif. ... 6-3/210. ... Throws right, bats right. ... Full name: Robert Joseph Ayala. ... Name pronounced eye-YAH-luh.

HIGH SCHOOL: Rio Mesa (Oxnard, Calif.).

TRANSACTIONS/CAREER NOTES: Signed as non-drafted free agent by Cincinnati Reds organization (June 27, 1988). ... Traded by Reds with C Dan Wilson to Seattle Mariners for P Erik Hanson and 2B Bret Boone (November 2, 1993). ... On Seattle disabled list (April 23-June 20, 1996); included rehabilitation assignments to Port City (June 6-8) and Tacoma (June 16-20). ... Traded by Mariners to Montreal Expos for P Jimmy Turman (April 2, 1999). ... Released by Expos (August 27, 1999). ... Signed by Chicago Cubs (September 3, 1999). ... Granted free agency (November 1, 1999). ... Signed by Minnesota Twins organization (January 14, 2000).

Year	League	W	L	Pct.	ERA	G	GS	CG	ShO	Sv.	IP	H	R	ER	BB	SO
1988—Gulf Coast Reds (GCL)		0	4	.000	3.82	20	0	0	0	3	33	34	23	14	12	24
1989—Greensboro (SAL)		5	8	.385	4.10	22	19	1	0	0	105 1/3	97	73	48	50	70
1990—Cedar Rapids (Midw.)		3	2	.600	3.38	18	7	3	1	1	53 1/3	40	24	20	18	59
—Charleston, W.Va. (SAL)		6	1	.857	2.43	21	4	2	1	2	74	48	23	20	21	73
1991—Chattanooga (Sou.)		3	1	.750	4.67	39	8	1	0	4	90 2/3	79	52	47	58	92
1992—Chattanooga (Sou.)		12	6	.667	3.54	27	27	3	3	0	162 2/3	152	75	64	58	154
—Cincinnati (N.L.)		2	1	.667	4.34	5	5	0	0	0	29	33	15	14	13	23
1993—Indianapolis (A.A.)		0	2	.000	5.67	5	5	0	0	0	27	36	19	17	12	19
—Cincinnati (N.L.)		7	10	.412	5.60	43	9	0	0	3	98	106	72	61	45	65
1994—Seattle (A.L.)■		4	3	.571	2.86	46	0	0	0	18	56 2/3	42	25	18	26	76
1995—Seattle (A.L.)		6	5	.545	4.44	63	0	0	0	19	71	73	42	35	30	77
1996—Seattle (A.L.)		6	3	.667	5.88	50	0	0	0	3	67 1/3	65	45	44	25	61
—Port City (Sou.)		0	0	...	0.00	2	1	0	0	0	1 2/3	0	0	0	1	2
—Tacoma (PCL)		0	0	...	0.00	1	1	0	0	0	1	0	0	0	1	1
1997—Seattle (A.L.)		10	5	.667	3.82	71	0	0	0	8	96 2/3	91	45	41	41	92
1998—Seattle (A.L.)		1	10	.091	7.29	62	0	0	0	8	75 1/3	100	66	61	26	68
1999—Montreal (N.L.)■		1	6	.143	3.68	53	0	0	0	0	66	60	36	27	34	64
—Chicago (N.L.)■		0	1	.000	2.81	13	0	0	0	0	16	11	7	5	5	15
A.L. totals (5 years)		27	26	.509	4.88	292	0	0	0	56	367	371	223	199	148	374
N.L. totals (3 years)		10	18	.357	4.61	114	14	0	0	3	209	210	130	107	97	167
Major League totals (8 years)		37	44	.457	4.78	406	14	0	0	59	576	581	353	306	245	541

DIVISION SERIES RECORD

Year	League	W	L	Pct.	ERA	G	GS	CG	ShO	Sv.	IP	H	R	ER	BB	SO
1995—Seattle (A.L.)		0	0	...	54.00	2	0	0	0	0	2/3	6	4	4	1	0
1997—Seattle (A.L.)		0	0	...	40.50	1	0	0	0	0	1 1/3	4	6	6	3	2
Division series totals (2 years)		0	0	...	45.00	3	0	0	0	0	2	10	10	10	4	2

CHAMPIONSHIP SERIES RECORD

Year	League	W	L	Pct.	ERA	G	GS	CG	ShO	Sv.	IP	H	R	ER	BB	SO
1995—Seattle (A.L.)		0	0	...	2.45	2	0	0	0	0	3 2/3	3	1	1	3	3

AYBAR, MANNY   P   ROCKIES

PERSONAL: Born November 28, 1969, in Bani, Dominican Republic. ... 6-2/208. ... Throws right, bats right. ... Full name: Manuel Antonio Aybar. ... Name pronounced I-bar.

TRANSACTIONS/CAREER NOTES: Signed as non-drafted free agent by St. Louis Cardinals organization (October 21, 1991). ... Traded by Cardinals with P Jose Jimenez, P Rick Croushore and IF Brent Butler to Colorado Rockies for P Darryl Kile, P Dave Veres and P Luther Hackman (November 16, 1999).

MISCELLANEOUS: Appeared in two games as pinch runner (1999).

Year	League	W	L	Pct.	ERA	G	GS	CG	ShO	Sv.	IP	H	R	ER	BB	SO
1992—Dominican Cardinals (DSL)		1	0	1.000	0.00	55	0	0	0	0	3	1	0	0	3	1
1993—Dominican Cardinals (DSL)		4	4	.500	3.15	13	11	1	0	0	71 1/3	54	33	25	33	66
1994—Arizona Cardinals (Ariz.)		6	1	.857	2.12	13	13	1	0	0	72 1/3	69	25	17	9	79
1995—Savannah (SAL)		3	8	.273	3.04	18	18	2	1	0	112 2/3	82	46	38	36	99
—St. Petersburg (FSL)		2	5	.286	3.35	9	9	0	0	0	48 1/3	42	27	18	16	43
1996—Arkansas (Texas)		8	6	.571	3.05	20	20	0	0	0	121	120	53	41	34	83
—Louisville (A.A.)		2	2	.500	3.23	5	5	0	0	0	30 2/3	26	12	11	7	25
1997—Louisville (A.A.)		5	8	.385	3.48	22	22	3	•2	0	137	131	60	53	45	114
—St. Louis (N.L.)		2	4	.333	4.24	12	12	0	0	0	68	66	33	32	29	41
1998—St. Louis (N.L.)		6	6	.500	5.98	20	14	0	0	0	81 1/3	90	58	54	42	57
—Memphis (PCL)		10	0	1.000	2.60	13	13	0	0	0	83	62	24	24	17	63
1999—St. Louis (N.L.)		4	5	.444	5.47	65	1	0	0	3	97	104	67	59	36	74
Major League totals (3 years)		12	15	.444	5.30	97	27	0	0	3	246 1/3	260	158	145	107	172

RECORD AS POSITION PLAYER

Year	Team (League)	Pos.	G	AB	R	H	2B	3B	HR	RBI	Avg.	BB	SO	SB	PO	A	E	Avg.
					BATTING										FIELDING			
1992—Dom. Cardinals (DSL)		IF	55	153	18	31	5	0	1	11	.203	10	27	2	53	131	19	.906

BAERGA, CARLOS   2B/3B

PERSONAL: Born November 4, 1968, in San Juan, Puerto Rico. ... 5-11/215. ... Bats both, throws right. ... Full name: Carlos Obed Ortiz Baerga. ... Name pronounced by-AIR-guh.

HIGH SCHOOL: Barbara Ann Rooshart (Rio Piedras, Puerto Rico).

TRANSACTIONS/CAREER NOTES: Signed as non-drafted free agent by San Diego Padres organization (November 4, 1985). ... Traded by Padres organization with C Sandy Alomar and OF Chris James to Cleveland Indians for OF Joe Carter (December 6, 1989). ... Traded by Indians with IF Alvaro Espinoza to New York Mets for IF Jose Vizcaino and IF Jeff Kent (July 29, 1996). ... Granted free agency (October 26, 1998). ... Signed by St. Louis Cardinals (January 27, 1999). ... Released by Cardinals (March 17, 1999). ... Signed by Cincinnati Reds organization (March 23, 1999). ... Released by Reds (June 4, 1999). ... Signed by San Diego Padres organization (June 6, 1999). ... Traded by Padres to Indians for cash (August 16, 1999). ... Granted free agency (October 29, 1999).

RECORDS: Holds major league record for switch-hitting home runs in one inning (April 8, 1993, seventh inning). ... Shares major league single-inning record for most home runs—2 (April 8, 1993, seventh inning).

HONORS: Named second baseman on THE SPORTING NEWS A.L. All-Star team (1993 and 1995). ... Named second baseman on THE SPORTING NEWS A.L. Silver Slugger team (1993-94).

STATISTICAL NOTES: Led South Atlantic League second basemen with 29 errors in 1987. ... Led Texas League shortstops with 61 double plays in 1988. ... Led Pacific Coast League third basemen with 380 total chances in 1989. ... Led A.L. second basemen with 138 double plays in 1992. ... Led A.L. second basemen with 894 total chances in 1992 and 809 in 1993. ... Collected six hits in one game (April 11, 1992). ... Switch-hit home runs in one game (April 8, 1993). ... Hit three home runs in one game (June 17, 1993). ... Career major league grand slams: 1.

Year	Team (League)	Pos.	G	AB	R	H	2B	3B	HR	RBI	Avg.	BB	SO	SB	PO	A	E	Avg.
1986— Char., S.C. (SAL)	2B-SS	111	378	57	102	14	4	7	41	.270	26	60	6	202	245	27	.943
1987— Char., S.C. (SAL)	2B-SS	134	515	83	157	23	•9	7	50	.305	38	107	26	253	341	†36	.943
1988— Wichita (Texas)	SS-2B	122	444	67	121	28	1	12	65	.273	31	83	4	221	325	33	.943
1989— Las Vegas (PCL)	3B	132	520	63	143	28	2	10	74	.275	30	98	6	*92	256	*32	.916
1990— Cleveland (A.L.)■.......	3B-SS-2B	108	312	46	81	17	2	7	47	.260	16	57	0	79	164	17	.935
— Colo. Springs (PCL) ...	3B	12	50	11	19	2	1	1	11	.380	5	4	1	18	31	4	.925
1991— Cleveland (A.L.)..........	3B-2B-SS	158	593	80	171	28	2	11	69	.288	48	74	3	217	421	27	.959
1992— Cleveland (A.L.)..........	2B-DH	161	657	92	205	32	1	20	105	.312	35	76	10	*400	*475	19	.979
1993— Cleveland (A.L.)..........	2B-DH	154	624	105	200	28	6	21	114	.321	34	68	15	*347	*445	17	.979
1994— Cleveland (A.L.)..........	2B-DH	103	442	81	139	32	2	19	80	.314	10	45	8	205	335	*15	.973
1995— Cleveland (A.L.)..........	2B-DH	135	557	87	175	28	2	15	90	.314	35	31	11	231	*444	19	.973
1996— Cleveland (A.L.)..........	2B	100	424	54	113	25	0	10	55	.267	16	25	1	191	308	15	.971
— New York (N.L.)■......	1B-3B-2B	26	83	5	16	3	0	2	11	.193	5	2	0	103	12	4	.966
1997— New York (N.L.)..........	2B	133	467	53	131	25	1	9	52	.281	20	54	2	244	371	14	.978
1998— New York (N.L.)..........	2B	147	511	46	136	27	1	7	53	.266	24	55	0	289	340	9	.986
1999— Indianapolis (I.L.)■...3B-2B-1B-DH	52	221	32	64	10	0	3	27	.290	10	18	2	106	126	6	.975
— Las Vegas (PCL)■	3B-2B	21	91	15	26	7	0	2	9	.286	9	5	0	16	41	5	.919
— San Diego (N.L.) 2B-3B-1B-DH	33	80	6	20	1	0	2	5	.250	6	14	1	21	30	2	.962
— Cleveland (A.L.)■......	3B-2B-DH	22	57	4	13	0	0	1	5	.228	4	10	1	13	28	1	.976
American League totals (8 years)		941	3666	549	1097	190	15	104	565	.299	198	386	49	1683	2620	130	.971
National League totals (4 years)		339	1141	110	303	56	2	20	121	.266	55	125	3	657	753	29	.980
Major League totals (10 years)		1280	4807	659	1400	246	17	124	686	.291	253	511	52	2340	3373	159	.973

DIVISION SERIES RECORD

| | | | | | | | | | | | BATTING | | | | | FIELDING | | |
Year	Team (League)	Pos.	G	AB	R	H	2B	3B	HR	RBI	Avg.	BB	SO	SB	PO	A	E	Avg.
1995— Cleveland (A.L.)..........	2B	3	14	2	4	1	0	0	1	.286	0	1	0	8	5	1	.929

CHAMPIONSHIP SERIES RECORD

| | | | | | | | | | | | BATTING | | | | | FIELDING | | |
Year	Team (League)	Pos.	G	AB	R	H	2B	3B	HR	RBI	Avg.	BB	SO	SB	PO	A	E	Avg.
1995— Cleveland (A.L.)..........	2B	6	25	3	10	0	0	1	4	.400	2	3	0	12	22	0	1.000

WORLD SERIES RECORD

| | | | | | | | | | | | BATTING | | | | | FIELDING | | |
Year	Team (League)	Pos.	G	AB	R	H	2B	3B	HR	RBI	Avg.	BB	SO	SB	PO	A	E	Avg.
1995— Cleveland (A.L.)..........	2B	6	26	1	5	2	0	0	4	.192	1	1	0	15	24	1	.975

ALL-STAR GAME RECORD

| | | | | | | | | | | BATTING | | | | FIELDING | | |
Year	League	Pos.	AB	R	H	2B	3B	HR	RBI	Avg.	BB	SO	SB	PO	A	E	Avg.
1992— American	2B	1	1	1	1	0	0	1	1.000	0	0	0	1	2	0	1.000
1993— American	2B	2	1	0	0	0	0	0	.000	0	1	0	1	0	1.000
1995— American	2B	3	1	3	1	0	0	1	1.000	0	0	0	1	2	0	1.000
All-Star Game totals (3 years)		6	3	4	2	0	0	1	.667	0	1	0	2	5	0	1.000

BAEZ, DANYS — P — INDIANS

PERSONAL: Born September 10, 1977, in Pinar del Rio, Cuba. ... 6-4/225. ... Throws right, bats right.
TRANSACTIONS/CAREER NOTES: Signed as non-drafted free agent by Cleveland Indians organization (November 6, 1999).

BAGWELL, JEFF — 1B — ASTROS

PERSONAL: Born May 27, 1968, in Boston. ... 6-0/195. ... Bats right, throws right. ... Full name: Jeffrey Robert Bagwell.
HIGH SCHOOL: Xavier (Middletown, Conn.).
COLLEGE: Hartford.
TRANSACTIONS/CAREER NOTES: Selected by Boston Red Sox organization in fourth round of free-agent draft (June 5, 1989). ... Traded by Red Sox to Houston Astros for P Larry Andersen (August 31, 1990). ... On Houston disabled list (July 31-September 1, 1995); included rehabilitation assignment to Jackson (August 28-September 1). ... On disabled list (May 13-28, 1998).
RECORDS: Shares major league single-season record for most times hitting three or more home runs in a game—2 (1999). ... Shares major league single-game records for most doubles—4 (June 14, 1996); and most bases on balls—6 (August 20, 1999, 16 innings). ... Shares major league single-inning record for most home runs—2 (June 24, 1994, sixth inning). ... Shares N.L. career record for most major league ballparks, one or more home runs (since 1900)—22.
HONORS: Named Eastern League Most Valuable Player (1990). ... Named N.L. Rookie Player of the Year by THE SPORTING NEWS (1991). ... Named N.L. Rookie of the Year by Baseball Writers' Association of America (1991). ... Named Major League Player of the Year by THE SPORTING NEWS (1994). ... Named first baseman on THE SPORTING NEWS N.L. All-Star team (1994, 1996, 1997 and 1999). ... Won N.L. Gold Glove at first base (1994). ... Named first baseman on THE SPORTING NEWS N.L. Silver Slugger team (1994, 1997 and 1999). ... Named N.L. Most Valuable Player by Baseball Writers' Association of America (1994).
STATISTICAL NOTES: Led Eastern League with 220 total bases and 12 intentional bases on balls received in 1990. ... Led N.L. in being hit by pitch with 13 in 1991. ... Led N.L. with 13 sacrifice flies in 1992. ... Hit three home runs in one game (June 24, 1994; and April 21 and June 9, 1999). ... Led N.L. with .750 slugging percentage in 1994. ... Led N.L. first basemen with 120 assists in 1994. ... Tied for N.L. lead in errors by first basemen with nine and double plays by first basemen with 94 in 1994. ... Career major league grand slams: 2.
MISCELLANEOUS: Holds Houston Astros all-time record for most home runs (263), runs batted in (961) and highest career batting average (.304).

Year	Team (League)	Pos.	G	AB	R	H	2B	3B	HR	RBI	Avg.	BB	SO	SB	PO	A	E	Avg.
								BATTING								FIELDING		
1989—	GC Red Sox (GCL)	3B-2B	5	19	3	6	1	0	0	3	.316	3	0	0	2	12	2	.875
	—Winter Haven (FSL)....	3B-2B-1B	64	210	27	65	13	2	2	19	.310	22	25	1	53	109	12	.931
1990—	New Britain (East.)	3B	136	481	63	*160	•34	7	4	61	.333	73	57	5	93	267	34	.914
1991—	Houston (N.L.)■.......	1B	156	554	79	163	26	4	15	82	.294	75	116	7	1270	106	12	.991
1992—	Houston (N.L.)	1B	•162	586	87	160	34	6	18	96	.273	84	97	10	1334	133	7	.995
1993—	Houston (N.L.)	1B	142	535	76	171	37	4	20	88	.320	62	73	13	1200	113	9	.993
1994—	Houston (N.L.)	1B-OF	110	400	*104	147	32	2	39	*116	.368	65	65	15	923	†121	‡9	.991
1995—	Houston (N.L.)	1B	114	448	88	130	29	0	21	87	.290	79	102	12	1004	*129	7	.994
	—Jackson (Texas)	1B-DH	4	12	0	2	0	0	0	0	.167	3	2	0	24	6	0	1.000
1996—	Houston (N.L.)	1B	*162	568	111	179	*48	2	31	120	.315	135	114	21	1336	*136	*16	.989
1997—	Houston (N.L.)	1B-DH	•162	566	109	162	40	2	43	135	.286	127	122	31	1404	*137	11	.993
1998—	Houston (N.L.)	1B	147	540	124	164	33	1	34	111	.304	109	90	19	1239	128	7	.995
1999—	Houston (N.L.)	1B-DH	•162	562	*143	171	35	0	42	126	.304	*149	127	30	1336	106	8	.994
Major League totals (9 years)			1317	4759	921	1447	314	21	263	961	.304	885	906	158	11046	1109	86	.993

DIVISION SERIES RECORD

Year	Team (League)	Pos.	G	AB	R	H	2B	3B	HR	RBI	Avg.	BB	SO	SB	PO	A	E	Avg.
								BATTING								FIELDING		
1997—	Houston (N.L.)	1B	3	12	0	1	0	0	0	0	.083	1	5	0	17	6	2	.920
1998—	Houston (N.L.)	1B	4	14	0	2	0	0	0	4	.143	1	6	0	31	4	0	1.000
1999—	Houston (N.L.)	1B	4	13	3	2	0	0	0	0	.154	5	4	0	36	3	0	1.000
Division series totals (3 years)			11	39	3	5	0	0	0	4	.128	7	15	0	84	13	2	.980

ALL-STAR GAME RECORD

Year	League	Pos.	AB	R	H	2B	3B	HR	RBI	Avg.	BB	SO	SB	PO	A	E	Avg.
							BATTING								FIELDING		
1994—	National	PH-1B	4	1	2	0	0	0	0	.500	0	1	0	3	2	0	1.000
1996—	National	1B	2	0	0	0	0	0	0	.000	0	1	0	5	0	0	1.000
1997—	National	1B	3	0	0	0	0	0	0	.000	0	1	0	8	1	0	1.000
1999—	National	DH	3	0	1	0	0	0	0	.333	0	2	0	0	0	0	...
All-Star Game totals (4 years)			12	1	3	0	0	0	0	.250	0	4	0	16	3	0	1.000

BAINES, HAROLD — DH — ORIOLES

PERSONAL: Born March 15, 1959, in St. Michaels, Md. ... 6-2/195. ... Bats left, throws left. ... Full name: Harold Douglas Baines.

HIGH SCHOOL: St. Michaels (Easton, Md.).

TRANSACTIONS/CAREER NOTES: Selected by Chicago White Sox organization in first round (first pick overall) of free-agent draft (June 7, 1977). ... On disabled list (April 7-May 8, 1987). ... Traded by White Sox with IF Fred Manrique to Texas Rangers for SS Scott Fletcher, OF Sammy Sosa and P Wilson Alvarez (July 29, 1989). ... Traded by Rangers to Oakland Athletics for two players to be named later (August 29, 1990); Rangers acquired P Joe Bitker and P Scott Chiamparino to complete deal (September 4, 1990). ... Granted free agency (October 27, 1992); accepted arbitration. ... Traded by A's to Baltimore Orioles for P Bobby Chouinard and P Allen Plaster (January 14, 1993). ... On Baltimore disabled list (May 5-27, 1993); included rehabilitation assignment to Bowie (May 25-27). ... Granted free agency (November 1, 1993). ... Re-signed by Orioles (December 2, 1993). ... Granted free agency (October 20, 1994). ... Re-signed by Orioles (December 23, 1994). ... Granted free agency (November 6, 1995). ... Signed by White Sox (December 11, 1995). ... Granted free agency (November 18, 1996). ... Re-signed by White Sox (January 10, 1997). ... Re-signed by White Sox (January 10, 1997). ... Traded by White Sox to Orioles for a player to be named later (July 29, 1997); White Sox acquired SS Juan Bautista to complete deal (August 18, 1997). ... Granted free agency (October 29, 1997). ... Re-signed by Orioles (December 19, 1997). ... On disabled list (July 11-August 4, 1998). ... Traded by Orioles to Cleveland Indians for P Juan Aracena and a player to named later (August 27, 1999); Orioles acquired P Jimmy Hamilton to complete deal (August 31, 1999). ... Granted free agency (October 29, 1999). ... Signed by Orioles (December 9, 1999).

RECORDS: Shares major league single-game record for most plate appearances—12 (May 8, finished May 9, 1984, 25 innings). ... Shares A.L. record for longest errorless game by outfielder—25 innings (May 8, finished May 9, 1984). ... Shares A.L. single-game record for most innings by outfielder—25 (May 8, finished May 9, 1984).

HONORS: Named outfielder on THE SPORTING NEWS A.L. All-Star team (1985). ... Named designated hitter on THE SPORTING NEWS A.L. All-Star team (1988-89). ... Named designated hitter on THE SPORTING NEWS A.L. Silver Slugger team (1989).

STATISTICAL NOTES: Tied for American Association lead in double plays by outfielder with four in 1979. ... Hit three home runs in one game (July 7, 1982; September 17, 1984 and May 7, 1991). ... Led A.L. with 22 game-winning RBIs in 1983. ... Led A.L. with .541 slugging percentage in 1984. ... Career major league grand slams: 13.

Year	Team (League)	Pos.	G	AB	R	H	2B	3B	HR	RBI	Avg.	BB	SO	SB	PO	A	E	Avg.
								BATTING								FIELDING		
1977—	Appleton (Midw.).........	OF	69	222	37	58	11	2	5	29	.261	36	62	2	94	10	7	.937
1978—	Knoxville (Sou.).........	OF-1B	137	502	70	138	16	6	13	72	.275	43	91	3	291	22	13	.960
1979—	Iowa (A.A.)	OF	125	466	87	139	25	8	22	87	.298	33	80	5	222	•16	11	.956
1980—	Chicago (A.L.)■.........	OF-DH	141	491	55	125	23	6	13	49	.255	19	65	2	229	6	9	.963
1981—	Chicago (A.L.)	OF-DH	82	280	42	80	11	7	10	41	.286	12	41	6	120	10	2	.985
1982—	Chicago (A.L.)	OF	161	608	89	165	29	8	25	105	.271	49	95	10	326	10	7	.980
1983—	Chicago (A.L.)	OF	156	596	76	167	33	2	20	99	.280	49	85	7	312	10	9	.973
1984—	Chicago (A.L.)	OF	147	569	72	173	28	10	29	94	.304	54	75	1	307	8	6	.981
1985—	Chicago (A.L.)	OF-DH	160	640	86	198	29	3	22	113	.309	42	89	1	318	8	2	.994
1986—	Chicago (A.L.)	OF-DH	145	570	72	169	29	2	21	88	.296	38	89	2	295	15	5	.984
1987—	Chicago (A.L.)	DH-OF	132	505	59	148	26	4	20	93	.293	46	82	0	13	0	0	1.000
1988—	Chicago (A.L.)	DH-OF	158	599	55	166	39	1	13	81	.277	67	109	0	14	1	2	.882
1989—	Chicago (A.L.)	DH-OF	70	333	55	107	20	1	13	56	.321	60	52	0	52	0	1	.981
	—Texas (A.L.)■............	DH-OF	46	172	18	49	9	0	3	16	.285	13	27	0	2	0	1	.667
1990—	Texas (A.L.)	DH	103	321	41	93	10	1	13	44	.290	47	63	0	...	...	...	...
	—Oakland (A.L.)■........	DH-OF	32	94	11	25	5	0	3	21	.266	20	17	0	5	0	1	.833
1991—	Oakland (A.L.)	DH-OF	141	488	76	144	25	1	20	90	.295	72	67	0	11	1	1	.923
1992—	Oakland (A.L.)	DH-OF	140	478	58	121	18	0	16	76	.253	59	61	1	27	0	1	.964
1993—	Baltimore (A.L.)■......	DH	118	416	64	130	22	0	20	78	.313	57	52	0	...	...	...	...
	—Bowie (East.)	DH	2	6	0	0	0	0	0	0	.000	1	1	0	...	...	...	...

Year	Team (League)	Pos.	G	AB	R	H	2B	3B	HR	RBI	Avg.	BB	SO	SB	PO	A	E	Avg.
								BATTING								FIELDING		
1994—Baltimore (A.L.).........		DH	94	326	44	96	12	1	16	54	.294	30	49	0	...	...	...	...
1995—Baltimore (A.L.).........		DH	127	385	60	115	19	1	24	63	.299	70	45	0	...	...	...	...
1996—Chicago (A.L.)■........		DH	143	495	80	154	29	0	22	95	.311	73	62	3	...	...	...	...
1997—Chicago (A.L.)..........		DH-OF	93	318	40	97	18	0	12	52	.305	41	47	0	0	0	0	...
—Baltimore (A.L.)■.......		DH	44	134	15	39	5	0	4	15	.291	14	15	0	...	...	...	...
1998—Baltimore (A.L.).........		DH	104	293	40	88	17	0	9	57	.300	32	40	0	...	...	...	...
1999—Baltimore (A.L.)■.......		DH	107	345	40	111	16	1	24	81	.322	43	38	1	0	0	0	...
—Cleveland (A.L.)■........		DH	28	85	5	23	2	0	1	22	.271	11	10	0	0	0	0	...
Major League totals (20 years)			2672	9541	1270	2783	474	49	373	1583	.292	1018	1375	34	2031	69	47	.978

B

NOTES: Hit home run in first at-bat (October 2, 1997).

DIVISION SERIES RECORD

Year	Team (League)	Pos.	G	AB	R	H	2B	3B	HR	RBI	Avg.	BB	SO	SB	PO	A	E	Avg.
								BATTING								FIELDING		
1997—Baltimore (A.L.)..........		DH-PH	2	5	2	2	0	0	1	1	.400	1	0	0	...	...	...	...
1999—Cleveland (A.L.)..........		DH	4	14	1	5	0	0	1	4	.357	2	1	0	...	...	...	...
Division series totals (2 years)			6	19	3	7	0	0	2	5	.368	3	1	0	...	...	...	...

CHAMPIONSHIP SERIES RECORD

Year	Team (League)	Pos.	G	AB	R	H	2B	3B	HR	RBI	Avg.	BB	SO	SB	PO	A	E	Avg.
								BATTING								FIELDING		
1983—Chicago (A.L.)		OF	4	16	0	2	0	0	0	0	.125	1	3	0	5	1	0	1.000
1990—Oakland (A.L.)		DH	4	14	2	5	1	0	0	3	.357	2	1	1	...	...	...	...
1992—Oakland (A.L.)		DH	6	25	6	11	2	0	1	4	.440	0	3	0	...	...	...	...
1997—Baltimore (A.L.)..........		DH	6	17	1	6	0	0	1	2	.353	2	1	0	...	...	...	...
Championship series totals (4 years)			20	72	9	24	3	0	2	9	.333	5	8	1	5	1	0	1.000

WORLD SERIES RECORD

Year	Team (League)	Pos.	G	AB	R	H	2B	3B	HR	RBI	Avg.	BB	SO	SB	PO	A	E	Avg.
								BATTING								FIELDING		
1990—Oakland (A.L.)		DH-PH	3	7	1	1	0	0	1	2	.143	1	2	0	...	...	...	...

ALL-STAR GAME RECORD

Year	League	Pos.	AB	R	H	2B	3B	HR	RBI	Avg.	BB	SO	SB	PO	A	E	Avg.
						BATTING									FIELDING		
1985— American		PH	1	0	1	0	0	0	0	1.000	0	0	0	...	...	...	...
1986— American		PH	1	0	0	0	0	0	0	.000	0	0	0	...	...	...	...
1987— American		PH	1	0	0	0	0	0	0	.000	0	0	0	...	...	...	...
1989— American		DH	3	1	1	0	0	0	1	.333	0	1	0	...	...	...	...
1991— American		PH-DH	1	0	0	0	0	0	1	.000	0	0	0	...	...	...	...
1999— American		PH-DH	1	0	1	0	0	0	0	1.000	0	0	0	...	...	...	...
All-Star Game totals (6 years)			8	1	3	0	0	0	2	.375	0	1	0	...	...	...	...

BAKO, PAUL   C   ASTROS

PERSONAL: Born June 20, 1972, in Lafayette, La. ... 6-2/205. ... Bats left, throws right. ... Full name: Gabor Paul Bako.
HIGH SCHOOL: Lafayette (La.).
COLLEGE: Southwestern Louisiana.
TRANSACTIONS/CAREER NOTES: Selected by Cincinnati Reds organization in fifth round of free-agent draft (June 3, 1993). ... Traded by Reds with P Donne Wall to Detroit Tigers for OF Melvin Nieves (November 11, 1997). ... Traded by Tigers with P Dean Crow, P Mark Persails, P Brian Powell and 3B Carlos Villalobos to Houston Astros for C Brad Ausmus and P C.J. Nitkowski (January 14, 1999).
STATISTICAL NOTES: Tied for Carolina League lead with 15 passed balls in 1995. ... Led Southern League catchers with 791 total chances in 1996. ... Tied for American Association lead in double plays with 10 and passed balls with nine by a catcher in 1997.

Year	Team (League)	Pos.	G	AB	R	H	2B	3B	HR	RBI	Avg.	BB	SO	SB	PO	A	E	Avg.
								BATTING								FIELDING		
1993—Billings (Pio.)		C-1B	57	194	34	61	11	0	4	30	.314	22	37	5	323	45	6	.984
1994—Win.-Salem (Caro.)		C	90	289	29	59	9	1	3	26	.204	35	81	2	570	73	15	.977
1995—Win.-Salem (Caro.)		C	82	249	29	71	11	2	7	27	.285	42	66	3	478	49	6	.989
1996—Chattanooga (Sou.)		C	110	360	53	106	27	0	8	48	.294	48	93	1	*694	*84	13	.984
1997—Indianapolis (A.A.)......		C	104	321	34	78	14	1	8	43	.243	34	81	0	622	64	6	.991
1998—Toledo (I.L.)■.............		C	13	48	5	14	3	1	1	6	.292	1	13	0	75	5	1	.988
—Detroit (A.L.)		C	96	305	23	83	12	1	3	30	.272	23	82	1	493	45	6	.989
1999—New Orleans (PCL)■..		C	12	47	2	9	3	1	1	4	.191	1	11	0	58	4	1	.984
—Houston (N.L.)		C	73	215	16	55	14	1	2	17	.256	26	57	1	461	35	6	.988
American League totals (1 year)			96	305	23	83	12	1	3	30	.272	23	82	1	493	45	6	.989
National League totals (1 year)			73	215	16	55	14	1	2	17	.256	26	57	1	461	35	6	.988
Major League totals (2 years)			169	520	39	138	26	2	5	47	.265	49	139	2	954	80	12	.989

BALDWIN, JAMES   P   WHITE SOX

PERSONAL: Born July 15, 1971, in Southern Pines, N.C. ... 6-3/235. ... Throws right, bats right. ... Full name: James Baldwin Jr.
HIGH SCHOOL: Pinecrest (Southern Pines, N.C.).
TRANSACTIONS/CAREER NOTES: Selected by Chicago White Sox organization in fourth round of free-agent draft (June 4, 1990). ... On disabled list (August 3-19, 1994).
HONORS: Named A.L. Rookie Pitcher of the Year by THE SPORTING NEWS (1996).
STATISTICAL NOTES: Led American Association with 27 home runs allowed and tied for lead with three balks in 1995.. ... Tied for American Association lead with three balks in 1995. ... Tied for A.L. lead with 14 wild pitches and three balks in 1997.

Year	League	W	L	Pct.	ERA	G	GS	CG	ShO	Sv.	IP	H	R	ER	BB	SO
1990—	GC White Sox (GCL)	1	6	.143	4.10	9	7	0	0	0	37 1/3	32	29	17	18	32
1991—	GC White Sox (GCL)	3	1	.750	2.12	6	6	0	0	0	34	16	8	8	16	48
—	Utica (NY-P)	1	4	.200	5.30	7	7	1	0	0	37 1/3	40	26	22	27	23
1992—	South Bend (Midw.)	9	5	.643	2.42	21	21	1	1	0	137 2/3	118	53	37	45	137
—	Sarasota (FSL)	1	2	.333	2.87	6	6	1	0	0	37 2/3	31	13	12	7	39
1993—	Birmingham (Sou.)	8	5	.615	*2.25	17	17	•4	0	0	120	94	48	30	43	107
—	Nashville (A.A.)	5	4	.556	2.61	10	10	1	0	0	69	43	21	20	36	61
1994—	Nashville (A.A.)	12	6	.667	3.72	26	26	2	0	0	162	144	75	67	83	*156
1995—	Chicago (A.L.)	0	1	.000	12.89	6	4	0	0	0	14 2/3	32	22	21	9	10
—	Nashville (A.A.)	5	9	.357	5.85	18	18	0	0	0	95 1/3	120	76	62	44	89
1996—	Nashville (A.A.)	1	1	.500	0.64	2	2	1	0	0	14	5	1	1	4	15
—	Chicago (A.L.)	11	6	.647	4.42	28	28	0	0	0	169	168	88	83	57	127
1997—	Chicago (A.L.)	12	•15	.444	5.26	32	32	1	0	0	200	205	128	117	83	140
1998—	Chicago (A.L.)	13	6	.684	5.32	37	24	1	0	0	159	176	103	94	60	108
1999—	Chicago (A.L.)	12	13	.480	5.10	35	33	1	0	0	199 1/3	219	119	113	81	123
Major League totals (5 years)		48	41	.539	5.19	138	121	3	0	0	742	800	460	428	290	508

BALE, JOHN — P — BLUE JAYS

PERSONAL: Born May 22, 1974, in Cheverly, Md. ... 6-4/205. ... Throws left, bats left. ... Full name: John R. Bale.
HIGH SCHOOL: Crestview (Fla.).
JUNIOR COLLEGE: Jefferson Davis Community College (Ala.).
COLLEGE: Southern Mississippi.
TRANSACTIONS/CAREER NOTES: Selected by St. Louis Cardinals organization in 12th round of free-agent draft (June 2, 1994); did not sign. ... Selected by Toronto Blue Jays organization in fifth round of free-agent draft (June 4, 1996).

Year	League	W	L	Pct.	ERA	G	GS	CG	ShO	Sv.	IP	H	R	ER	BB	SO
1996—	St. Catharines (NY-P)	3	2	.600	4.86	8	8	0	0	0	33 1/3	39	21	18	11	35
1997—	Hagerstown (SAL)	7	7	.500	4.30	25	25	0	0	0	140 1/3	130	83	67	63	155
1998—	Dunedin (FSL)	4	5	.444	4.64	24	9	0	0	4	66	68	39	34	23	78
—	Knoxville (Sou.)	0	0	...	6.75	3	0	0	0	0	1 1/3	1	1	1	0	0
1999—	Knoxville (Sou.)	2	2	.500	3.75	33	4	0	0	1	62 1/3	64	32	26	16	91
—	Syracuse (I.L.)	0	3	.000	3.97	6	4	0	0	0	22 2/3	16	14	10	10	10
—	Toronto (A.L.)	0	0	...	13.50	1	0	0	0	0	2	2	3	3	2	4
Major League totals (1 year)		0	0	...	13.50	1	0	0	0	0	2	2	3	3	2	4

BANKS, BRIAN — C/1B — BREWERS

PERSONAL: Born September 28, 1970, in Mesa, Ariz. ... 6-3/208. ... Bats both, throws right. ... Full name: Brian Glen Banks.
HIGH SCHOOL: Mountain View (Mesa, Ariz.).
COLLEGE: Brigham Young.
TRANSACTIONS/CAREER NOTES: Selected by Milwaukee Brewers organization in second round of free-agent draft (June 3, 1993); pick received as part of compensation for Seattle Mariners signing Type A free-agent P Chris Bosio.
STATISTICAL NOTES: Tied for Midwest League lead in double plays by outfielder with four in 1994. ... Career major league grand slams: 1.

							BATTING							FIELDING		
Year	Team (League)	Pos.	G	AB	R	H	2B	3B	HR	RBI	Avg.	BB	SO	SB	PO	A	E	Avg.
1993—Helena (Pio.)		OF	12	48	8	19	1	1	2	8	.396	11	8	1	25	0	1	.962
—Beloit (Midw.)		OF	38	147	21	36	5	1	4	19	.245	7	34	1	47	2	1	.980
1994—Beloit (Midw.)		OF-1B-3B	65	237	41	71	13	1	9	47	.300	29	40	11	123	5	2	.985
—Stockton (Calif.)		OF	67	246	29	58	9	1	4	28	.236	38	46	3	108	5	4	.966
1995—El Paso (Texas)		OF-1B-3B	128	441	81	136	*39	10	12	78	.308	*81	113	9	245	11	10	.962
1996—New Orleans (A.A.)		OF-3B-DH-C	137	487	71	132	29	7	16	64	.271	66	105	17	256	18	8	.972
—Milwaukee (A.L.)		OF-1B	4	7	2	4	2	0	1	2	.571	1	2	0	15	1	0	1.000
1997—Tucson (PCL)		OF-C-DH	98	378	53	112	26	3	10	63	.296	35	83	7	194	13	3	.986
—Milwaukee (A.L.)		OF-1B-DH-3B	28	68	9	14	1	0	1	8	.206	6	17	0	30	7	2	.949
1998—Louisville (I.L.)		O-DH-C-1-3	85	299	58	87	18	1	21	66	.291	52	72	14	244	33	6	.979
—Milwaukee (A.L.)		C-1B-3B-OF	24	24	3	7	2	0	1	5	.292	4	7	0	12	1	1	.929
1999—Milwaukee (N.L.)		1B-C-OF	105	219	34	53	7	1	5	22	.242	25	59	6	370	34	5	.988
—Louisville (I.L.)		1B-OF-C	6	24	3	5	2	1	1	6	.208	2	5	0	29	1	1	.968
American League totals (2 years)			32	75	11	18	3	0	2	10	.240	7	19	0	45	8	2	.964
National League totals (2 years)			129	243	37	60	9	1	6	27	.247	29	66	6	382	35	6	.986
Major League totals (4 years)			161	318	48	78	12	1	8	37	.245	36	85	6	427	43	8	.983

BARAJAS, ROD — C — DIAMONDBACKS

PERSONAL: Born September 5, 1975, in Ontario, Calif. ... 6-2/220. ... Bats right, throws right. ... Full name: Rodrigo Richard Barajas.
HIGH SCHOOL: Sante Fe Springs (Calif.).
JUNIOR COLLEGE: Cerritos.
TRANSACTIONS/CAREER NOTES: Signed as non-drafted free agent by Arizona Diamondbacks organization (January 23, 1996). ... Loaned to Oakland Athletics organization (April 5-June 16, 1996).
STATISTICAL NOTES: Led Pioneer League catchers with .992 fielding percentage in 1996. ... Led Texas League catchers with 787 putouts, 95 assists, 14 errors and 896 total chances in 1999.

							BATTING							FIELDING		
Year	Team (League)	Pos.	G	AB	R	H	2B	3B	HR	RBI	Avg.	BB	SO	SB	PO	A	E	Avg.
1996—Visalia (Calif.)■		C	27	74	6	12	3	0	0	8	.162	7	21	0	83	14	0	1.000
—Lethbridge (Pio.)■		C-1B	51	175	47	59	9	3	10	50	.337	12	24	2	301	43	5	†.986
1997—High Desert (Calif.)		C-1B	57	199	24	53	11	0	7	30	.266	8	41	0	374	38	3	.993
1998—High Desert (Calif.)		C	113	442	67	134	26	0	23	81	.303	25	81	1	749	85	14	.983
1999—El Paso (Texas)		C-DH-1B	127	510	77	162	41	2	14	95	.318	24	73	2	†827	†97	†14	.985
—Arizona (N.L.)		C	5	16	3	4	1	0	1	3	.250	1	1	0	30	1	0	1.000
Major League totals (1 year)			5	16	3	4	1	0	1	3	.250	1	1	0	30	1	0	1.000

BARBER, BRIAN   P   INDIANS

PERSONAL: Born March 4, 1973, in Hamilton, Ohio. ... 6-1/190. ... Throws right, bats right. ... Full name: Brian Scott Barber.
HIGH SCHOOL: Dr. Phillips (Orlando).
TRANSACTIONS/CAREER NOTES: Selected by St. Louis Cardinals organization in first round (22nd pick overall) of free-agent draft (June 3, 1991); pick received as part of compensation for New York Mets signing Type B free-agent OF Vince Coleman. ... On Louisville disabled list (April 21-May 14, 1994; May 21-June 15 and August 1-September 9, 1996). ... On Louisville suspended list (July 6-8, 1995). ... On St. Louis disabled list (March 23-May 29, 1997); including rehabilitation assignments to Prince William (May 2-7) and Arkansas (May 12-22). ... Granted free agency (December 21, 1997). ... Signed by Kansas City Royals organization (January 5, 1998). ... Granted free agency (October 4, 1999). ... Signed by Cleveland Indians organization (December 3, 1999).

Year League	W	L	Pct.	ERA	G	GS	CG	ShO	Sv.	IP	H	R	ER	BB	SO
1991—Johnson City (Appl.)	4	6	.400	5.40	14	13	0	0	0	73 1/3	62	48	44	38	84
1992—Springfield (Midw.)	3	4	.429	3.73	8	8	0	0	0	50 2/3	39	21	21	24	56
—St. Petersburg (FSL)	5	5	.500	3.26	19	19	1	0	0	113 1/3	99	51	41	46	102
1993—Arkansas (Texas)	9	8	.529	4.02	24	24	1	0	0	143 1/3	154	70	64	56	126
—Louisville (A.A.)■	0	1	.000	4.76	1	1	0	0	0	5 2/3	4	3	3	4	5
1994—Louisville (A.A.)	4	7	.364	5.38	19	18	0	0	1	85 1/3	79	58	51	46	95
—Arkansas (Texas)	1	3	.250	3.25	6	6	0	0	0	36	31	15	13	16	54
1995—Louisville (A.A.)	6	5	.545	4.70	20	19	0	0	0	107 1/3	105	67	56	40	94
—St. Louis (N.L.)	2	1	.667	5.22	9	4	0	0	0	29 1/3	31	17	17	16	27
1996—Louisville (A.A.)	0	6	.000	5.62	11	11	1	0	0	49 2/3	49	37	31	26	33
—St. Louis (N.L.)	0	0	...	15.00	1	1	0	0	0	3	4	5	5	6	1
1997—Prince William (Caro.)........	1	1	.500	4.09	2	2	0	0	0	11	10	5	5	5	13
—Arkansas (Texas)	0	1	.000	10.47	3	3	0	0	0	16 1/3	28	19	19	5	15
—Louisville (A.A.)	4	8	.333	6.90	18	18	0	0	0	92 2/3	111	80	71	44	74
1998—Omaha (PCL)■	8	4	.667	3.75	22	22	2	1	0	136 2/3	114	63	57	53	100
—Kansas City (A.L.)	2	4	.333	6.00	8	8	0	0	0	42	45	28	28	13	24
1999—Kansas City (A.L.)	1	3	.250	9.64	8	3	0	0	1	18 2/3	31	20	20	10	7
—Omaha (PCL)	9	5	.643	4.56	19	19	2	1	0	120 1/3	128	68	61	29	75
A.L. totals (2 years)	3	7	.300	7.12	16	11	0	0	1	60 2/3	76	48	48	23	31
N.L. totals (2 years)	2	1	.667	6.12	10	5	0	0	0	32 1/3	35	22	22	22	28
Major League totals (4 years)	5	8	.385	6.77	26	16	0	0	1	93	111	70	70	45	59

BARCELO, LORENZO   P   WHITE SOX

PERSONAL: Born August 10, 1977, in San Pedro de Macoris, Dominican Republic. ... 6-4/220. ... Throws right, bats right. ... Full name: Lorenzo A. Barcelo.
HIGH SCHOOL: Sanatonio (San Pedro de Macoris, Dominican Republic).
TRANSACTIONS/CAREER NOTES: Signed as non-drafted free agent by San Francisco Giants organization (May 23, 1994). ... Traded by Giants with SS Mike Caruso, OF Brian Manning, P Keith Foulke, P Bob Howry and P Ken Vining by Giants to Chicago White Sox for P Wilson Alvarez, P Danny Darwin and P Roberto Hernandez (July 31, 1997). ... On Birmingham disabled list (April 2, 1998-entire season); included rehabilitation assignment to Arizona League White Sox (June 29-July 9). ... On Birmingham disabled list (April 8-August 13, 1999); included rehabilitation assignment to Burlington (August 11-13).
STATISTICAL NOTES: Led Midwest League with 16 home runs allowed in 1996.

Year League	W	L	Pct.	ERA	G	GS	CG	ShO	Sv.	IP	H	R	ER	BB	SO
1995—Bellingham (N.W.)	3	2	.600	3.45	12	11	0	0	0	47	43	23	18	19	34
1996—Bellingham (N.W.)	12	10	.545	3.54	26	26	1	0	0	152 2/3	138	70	60	46	139
1997—San Jose (Calif.)	5	4	.556	3.94	16	16	1	1	0	89	91	45	39	30	89
—Shreveport (Texas)	2	0	1.000	4.02	5	5	0	0	0	31 1/3	30	19	14	8	20
—Birmingham (Sou.)■	2	1	.667	4.86	6	6	0	0	0	33 1/3	36	20	18	9	29
1998—Ariz. White Sox (Ariz.)........	0	1	.000	1.50	3	3	0	0	0	6	6	1	1	0	9
1999—Ariz. White Sox (Ariz.)........	2	1	.667	1.69	9	9	0	0	0	42 2/3	36	14	8	6	57
—Burlington (Midw.)	1	0	1.000	3.60	1	1	0	0	0	5	3	2	2	0	6
—Birmingham (Sou.)	0	1	.000	3.60	4	4	0	0	0	20	14	8	8	6	14

BARKER, GLEN   OF   ASTROS

PERSONAL: Born May 10, 1971, in Albany, N.Y. ... 5-10/180. ... Bats right, throws right. ... Full name: Glen F. Barker.
HIGH SCHOOL: Albany (N.Y.).
COLLEGE: The College of St. Rose (N.Y.).
TRANSACTIONS/CAREER NOTES: Selected by Detroit Tigers organization in 11th round of free-agent draft (June 3, 1993). ... Selected by Houston Astros from Tigers organization in Rule 5 major league draft (December 14, 1998). ... On disabled list (August 24-September 8, 1999).
STATISTICAL NOTES: Led Southern League outfielders in total chances with 323 in 1998.

Year Team (League)	Pos.	G	AB	R	H	2B	3B	HR	RBI	Avg.	BB	SO	SB	PO	A	E	Avg.
						BATTING									FIELDING		
1993—Niagara Falls (NY-P)...	OF	72	253	49	55	11	4	5	23	.217	24	71	*37	148	3	1	*.993
1994—Fayetteville (SAL)	OF	74	267	38	61	13	5	1	30	.228	33	79	41	144	6	3	.980
—Lakeland (FSL)	OF	28	104	10	19	5	1	2	6	.183	4	34	5	71	4	2	.974
1995—Jacksonville (Sou.)......	OF	133	507	74	121	26	4	10	49	.239	33	*143	39	284	9	8	.973
1996—Jacksonville (Sou.)......	OF	43	120	9	19	2	1	0	8	.158	8	36	6	91	2	2	.979
—Fayetteville (SAL)	OF	37	132	23	38	1	0	1	9	.288	16	34	20	91	3	1	.989
—Toledo (I.L.)................	OF	24	80	13	20	2	1	0	2	.250	9	25	6	51	3	1	.982
1997—Toledo (I.L.)................	OF	21	47	9	9	1	0	1	3	.191	5	15	6	24	1	0	1.000
—Lakeland (FSL)	OF	13	57	9	18	4	0	1	11	.316	4	17	7	34	0	0	1.000
—Jacksonville (Sou.)......	OF	69	257	47	72	8	4	6	29	.280	29	72	17	154	6	2	.988
1998—Jacksonville (Sou.)......	OF	110	453	95	127	29	6	6	54	.280	57	120	31	*307	16	0	*1.000
1999—Houston (N.L.)■........	OF-DH	81	73	23	21	2	0	1	11	.288	11	19	17	50	2	1	.981
Major League totals (1 year)		81	73	23	21	2	0	1	11	.288	11	19	17	50	2	1	.981

DIVISION SERIES RECORD

Year Team (League)	Pos.	G	AB	R	H	2B	3B	HR	RBI	Avg.	BB	SO	SB	PO	A	E	Avg.
						BATTING									FIELDING		
1999—Houston (N.L.)	OF-PR	2	3	1	0	0	0	0	0	.000	0	2	1	1	0	0	1.000

BARKER, KEVIN   1B   BREWERS

PERSONAL: Born July 26, 1975, in Bristol, Va. ... 6-3/205. ... Bats right, throws right. ... Full name: Kevin S. Barker.
HIGH SCHOOL: Virginia (Bristol, Va.).
COLLEGE: Virginia Tech.
TRANSACTIONS/CAREER NOTES: Selected by Milwaukee Brewers organization in third round of free-agent draft (June 4, 1996).

Year Team (League)	Pos.	G	AB	R	H	2B	3B	HR	RBI	Avg.	BB	SO	SB	PO	A	E	Avg.
1996— Ogden (Pio.)	1B	71	281	61	89	19	4	9	56	.317	46	54	0	572	*44	11	.982
1997— El Paso (Texas)	1B	65	238	37	66	15	6	10	63	.277	28	40	3	455	30	9	.982
— Stockton (Calif.)	1B	70	267	47	81	20	5	13	45	.303	25	60	4	476	31	6	.988
1998— El Paso (Texas)	1B	20	85	14	26	6	0	5	14	.306	3	21	2	198	16	1	.995
— Louisville (I.L.)	1B-OF	124	463	59	128	26	4	23	96	.276	36	97	2	957	*73	9	.991
1999— Louisville (I.L.)	1B-OF	121	442	89	123	27	5	23	87	.278	59	94	2	1036	88	10	.991
— Milwaukee (N.L.)	1B	38	117	13	33	3	0	3	23	.282	9	19	1	254	18	1	.996
Major League totals (1 year)		38	117	13	33	3	0	3	23	.282	9	19	1	254	18	1	.996

BARKER, RICHIE   P   CUBS

PERSONAL: Born October 29, 1972, in Revere, Mass. ... 6-2/220. ... Throws right, bats right. ... Full name: Richard Frank Barker.
HIGH SCHOOL: Malden (Mass.).
JUNIOR COLLEGE: Quinsigamond Community College (Mass.).
TRANSACTIONS/CAREER NOTES: Selected by Chicago Cubs organization in 37th round of free-agent draft (June 2, 1994).

Year League	W	L	Pct.	ERA	G	GS	CG	ShO	Sv.	IP	H	R	ER	BB	SO
1994— Huntington (Appl.)	2	4	.333	5.95	17	0	0	0	0	39 1/3	36	35	26	25	22
1995— Rockford (Midw.)	2	0	1.000	3.71	32	0	0	0	1	43 2/3	45	20	18	20	23
1996— Daytona (FSL)	4	0	1.000	5.67	17	0	0	0	0	27	34	23	17	18	14
— Rockford (Midw.)	1	1	.500	5.18	19	0	0	0	1	33	42	24	19	15	23
1997— Daytona (FSL)	2	1	.667	3.35	29	1	0	0	1	51	49	27	19	15	38
— Orlando (Sou.)	0	1	.000	3.30	19	0	0	0	2	30	25	17	11	7	19
1998— West Tenn (Sou.)	2	5	.286	2.68	*51	0	0	0	16	53 2/3	51	22	16	17	23
— Iowa (PCL)	3	1	.750	4.84	16	0	0	0	0	22 1/3	31	14	12	5	21
1999— Iowa (PCL)	4	4	.500	4.26	55	2	0	0	7	74	72	37	35	30	52
— Chicago (N.L.)	0	0	...	7.20	5	0	0	0	0	5	6	4	4	4	3
Major League totals (1 year)	0	0	...	7.20	5	0	0	0	0	5	6	4	4	4	3

BARNES, LARRY   1B   ANGELS

PERSONAL: Born July 23, 1974, in Bakersfield, Calif. ... 6-1/195. ... Bats left, throws left. ... Full name: Larry Richard Barnes Jr.
HIGH SCHOOL: Bakersfield (Calif.).
JUNIOR COLLEGE: Bakersfield (Calif.) College.
COLLEGE: Fresno State.
TRANSACTIONS/CAREER NOTES: Selected by Florida Marlins organization in 69th round of free-agent draft (June 3, 1993); did not sign. ... Signed as non-drafted free agent by California Angels organization (June 6, 1995). ... Angels franchise renamed Anaheim Angels for 1997 season. ... On Erie disabled list (September 1, 1999-remainder of season).
HONORS: Named Midwest League Most Valuable Player (1996).
STATISTICAL NOTES: Led Arizona League first basemen with 49 double plays in 1995. ... Led Midwest League with 282 total bases and .577 slugging percentage in 1996. ... Tied for Midwest League lead with 80 assists by first baseman in 1996. ... Led California League first basemen with .993 fielding percentage in 1997. ... Led Eastern League with 16 sacrifice flies and seven intentional bases on balls received in 1999.

Year Team (League)	Pos.	G	AB	R	H	2B	3B	HR	RBI	Avg.	BB	SO	SB	PO	A	E	Avg.
1995— Ariz. Angels (Ariz.)	1B	•56	197	•42	61	8	3	3	•37	.310	27	42	12	*494	19	7	.987
1996— Cedar Rap. (Midw.)	1B-DH-OF-C	131	489	84	155	•36	5	*27	*112	.317	58	101	9	1062	‡81	11	.990
1997— Lake Elsinore (Calif.)	1B-OF	115	446	68	128	32	2	13	71	.287	43	84	3	1048	87	8	†.993
1998— Lake Elsinore (Calif.)	1B	51	183	32	45	11	2	7	33	.246	22	49	2	451	17	6	.987
— Midland (Texas)	1B-DH-OF	69	245	29	67	16	4	6	35	.273	28	54	4	534	37	7	.988
1999— Erie (East.)	1B-DH	130	497	73	142	25	9	20	100	.286	49	99	14	1047	87	9	.992

BARRETT, MICHAEL   3B/C   EXPOS

PERSONAL: Born October 22, 1976, in Atlanta. ... 6-2/200. ... Bats right, throws right. ... Full name: Michael P. Barrett.
HIGH SCHOOL: Pace Academy (Atlanta).
TRANSACTIONS/CAREER NOTES: Selected by Montreal Expos organization in first round (28th pick overall) of free-agent draft (June 1, 1995). ... On Montreal disabled list (June 24-July 11, 1999); included rehabilitation assignment to Ottawa (July 9-10).

Year Team (League)	Pos.	G	AB	R	H	2B	3B	HR	RBI	Avg.	BB	SO	SB	PO	A	E	Avg.
1995— GC Expos (GCL)	SS-3B	50	183	22	57	13	4	0	19	.311	15	19	7	65	143	25	.893
— Vermont (NY-P)	SS	3	10	0	1	0	0	0	1	.100	1	1	0	1	3	0	1.000
1996— Delmarva (SAL)	C-DH-3B	129	474	57	113	29	4	4	62	.238	18	42	5	607	74	15	.978
1997— W.P. Beach (FSL)	C-DH	119	423	52	120	30	0	8	61	.284	36	49	7	629	78	13	.982
1998— Harrisburg (East.)	C-3B-DH	120	453	78	145	32	2	19	87	.320	27	43	7	517	113	12	.981
— Montreal (N.L.)	C-3B	8	23	3	7	2	0	1	2	.304	3	6	0	22	9	3	.912
1999— Montreal (N.L.)	3B-C-SS	126	433	50	127	32	3	8	52	.293	32	39	0	374	130	14	.973
— Ottawa (I.L.)	3B	2	7	1	3	0	0	0	2	.429	1	0	0	0	4	1	.800
Major League totals (2 years)		134	456	56	134	34	3	9	54	.294	35	45	0	396	139	17	.969

B

BARRIOS, MANUEL P PHILLIES

PERSONAL: Born September 21, 1974, in Cabecea, Panama. ... 6-0/185. ... Throws right, bats right. ... Full name: Manuel Antonio Barrios.
TRANSACTIONS/CAREER NOTES: Signed as non-drafted free agent by Houston Astros organization (March 2, 1993). ... On suspended list (September 4-8, 1996). ... Traded by Astros with P Oscar Henriquez and a player to be named later to Florida Marlins for OF Moises Alou (November 11, 1997); Marlins acquired P Mark Johnson to complete deal (December 16, 1997). ... Traded by Marlins with OF Gary Sheffield, 3B Bobby Bonilla, C Charles Johnson and OF Jim Eisenreich to Los Angeles Dodgers for C Mike Piazza and 3B Todd Zeile (May 15, 1998). ... Claimed on waivers by Florida Marlins (August 10, 1998). ... Traded by Marlins to Cincinnati Reds for C Guillermo Garcia (December 2, 1998). ... Claimed on waivers by Philadelphia Phillies (October 22, 1999).

Year League	W	L	Pct.	ERA	G	GS	CG	ShO	Sv.	IP	H	R	ER	BB	SO
1993—Dom. Astros (DSL)	6	1	.857	4.64	13	12	2	0	0	77²/₃	77	57	40	23	59
1994—Quad City (Midw.)	0	6	.000	5.95	43	0	0	0	4	65	73	44	43	23	63
1995—Quad City (Midw.)	1	5	.167	2.25	50	0	0	0	23	52	44	16	13	17	55
1996—Jackson (Texas)	6	4	.600	2.37	60	0	0	0	23	68¹/₃	60	29	18	29	69
1997—New Orleans (A.A.)	4	8	.333	3.27	57	0	0	0	0	82²/₃	70	32	30	34	77
—Houston (N.L.)	0	0	...	12.00	2	0	0	0	0	3	6	4	4	3	3
1998—Charlotte (I.L.)■	2	0	1.000	3.70	18	1	0	0	0	24¹/₃	19	10	10	9	22
—Florida (N.L.)	0	0	...	3.38	2	0	0	0	0	2²/₃	4	1	1	2	1
—Albuquerque (PCL)■	1	3	.250	6.00	20	2	0	0	0	36	47	25	24	15	33
—Los Angeles (N.L.)	0	0	...	0.00	1	0	0	0	0	1	0	0	0	2	0
1999—Indianapolis (I.L.)■	2	7	.222	5.28	49	8	0	0	0	90¹/₃	94	60	53	35	73
Major League totals (2 years)	0	0	...	6.75	5	0	0	0	0	6²/₃	10	5	5	7	4

BARRY, JEFF OF

PERSONAL: Born September 22, 1968, in Medford, Ore. ... 6-1/204. ... Bats both, throws right. ... Full name: Jeffrey Finis Barry.
HIGH SCHOOL: Medford (Ore.).
COLLEGE: San Diego State.
TRANSACTIONS/CAREER NOTES: Selected by Montreal Expos organization in fourth round of free-agent draft (June 4, 1990). ... On disabled list (September 5-20, 1991). ... Traded by Expos organization to New York Mets organization for P Blaine Beatty (December 9, 1991). ... On St. Lucie disabled list (April 16-September 18, 1992). ... On disabled list (June 2-20, 1994). ... On suspended list (August 14-15, 1994). ... On Binghamton disabled list (August 26-September 5, 1995). ... Traded by Mets to San Diego Padres for P Pedro A. Martinez (December 15, 1995). ... Granted free agency (October 15, 1996). ... Signed by Colorado Rockies organization (January 8, 1997). ... Granted free agency (October 15, 1998). ... Re-signed by Rockies organization (December 18, 1998). ... Released by Rockies (December 20, 1999).
STATISTICAL NOTES: Tied for Eastern League lead with nine sacrifice flies in 1995. ... Tied for Pacific Coast League lead with three double plays by outfielder in 1998.

Year Team (League)	Pos.	G	AB	R	H	2B	3B	HR	RBI	Avg.	BB	SO	SB	PO	A	E	Avg.
1990—Jamestown (NY-P)	OF	70	263	40	76	18	1	5	38	.289	22	35	20	88	8	5	.950
1991—W.P. Beach (FSL)	OF	116	437	48	92	16	3	4	31	.211	34	68	20	200	14	7	.968
1992—St. Lucie (FSL)■	DH	3	9	0	3	2	0	0	1	.333	0	0	0	...	...	...	...
—GC Mets (GCL)	DH	8	23	5	4	1	0	0	2	.174	6	2	2	...	...	...	...
1993—St. Lucie (FSL)	OF	114	420	68	108	17	5	4	50	.257	49	37	17	167	12	1	.994
1994—Binghamton (East.)	OF	110	388	48	118	24	3	9	69	.304	35	62	10	144	6	5	.968
1995—Norfolk (I.L.)	1B	12	41	3	9	2	0	0	6	.220	3	6	0	117	9	2	.984
—Binghamton (East.)	OF-DH-1B	80	290	49	78	17	6	11	53	.269	31	61	4	129	6	0	1.000
—New York (N.L.)	OF	15	15	2	2	1	0	0	0	.133	1	8	0	2	0	0	1.000
1996—Memphis (Sou.)■	3B-OF-1B-2B	91	226	29	55	7	0	3	25	.243	29	48	3	90	81	13	.929
—Las Vegas (PCL)	OF	4	12	1	1	0	0	0	0	.083	3	0	0	12	0	1	.923
1997—New Haven (East.)■	OF-1B-DH	40	146	21	32	4	0	5	12	.219	4	34	3	122	11	6	.957
—Colo. Springs (PCL)	OF-DH	81	273	46	82	13	3	13	70	.300	30	45	5	130	11	0	1.000
1998—Colo. Springs (PCL)	O-DH-3-P-1	100	349	55	91	19	6	8	55	.261	46	52	5	190	14	9	.958
—Colorado (N.L.)	OF	15	34	4	6	1	0	0	2	.176	2	11	0	20	1	0	1.000
1999—Colo. Springs (PCL)	OF-3B	64	185	36	63	15	0	10	27	.341	19	31	6	90	15	0	1.000
—Colorado (N.L.)	OF	74	168	19	45	16	0	5	26	.268	19	29	0	90	4	0	1.000
Major League totals (3 years)		104	217	25	53	18	0	5	28	.244	22	48	0	112	5	0	1.000

RECORD AS PITCHER

Year League	W	L	Pct.	ERA	G	GS	CG	ShO	Sv.	IP	H	R	ER	BB	SO
1998—Colorado Springs (PCL)	0	0	...	0.00	1	0	0	0	1	1	3	1	0	0	1

BARTEE, KIMERA OF REDS

PERSONAL: Born July 21, 1972, in Omaha, Neb. ... 6-0/200. ... Bats right, throws right. ... Full name: Kimera Anotchi Bartee.
HIGH SCHOOL: Central (Omaha, Neb.).
COLLEGE: Creighton.
TRANSACTIONS/CAREER NOTES: Selected by Baltimore Orioles organization in 14th round of free-agent draft (June 3, 1993). ... On Bowie disabled list (June 8-August 8, 1995). ... Traded by Orioles to Minnesota Twins (September 18, 1995), completing deal in which Orioles acquired P Scott Erickson from Twins for P Scott Klingenbeck and a player to be named later (July 7, 1995). ... Selected by Orioles from Twins organization in Rule 5 major league draft (December 4, 1995). ... Claimed on waivers by Detroit Tigers (March 13, 1996). ... Traded by Tigers to Cincinnati Reds for a player to be named later or cash (December 12, 1999).
STATISTICAL NOTES: Led International League outfielders with 341 total chances in 1997.
MISCELLANEOUS: Batted as switch-hitter (1993-98).

Year Team (League)	Pos.	G	AB	R	H	2B	3B	HR	RBI	Avg.	BB	SO	SB	PO	A	E	Avg.
1993—Bluefield (Appl.)	OF	66	264	59	65	15	2	4	37	.246	44	66	*27	124	5	4	.970
1994—Frederick (Caro.)	OF	130	514	97	150	22	4	10	57	.292	56	117	44	*304	7	6	.981

Year	Team (League)	Pos.	G	AB	R	H	2B	3B	HR	RBI	Avg.	BB	SO	SB	PO	A	E	Avg.
1995—	GC Orioles (GCL)........	OF	5	21	5	5	0	0	1	3	.238	3	2	1	15	0	0	1.000
—	Bowie (East.)	OF	53	218	45	62	9	1	3	19	.284	23	45	22	155	4	6	.964
—	Rochester (I.L.)	OF	15	52	5	8	2	1	0	3	.154	0	16	0	37	2	0	1.000
1996—	Detroit (A.L.)■............	OF-DH	110	217	32	55	6	1	1	14	.253	17	77	20	217	1	2	.991
1997—	Toledo (I.L.)...............	OF	136	501	67	109	13	7	3	33	.218	52	*154	*33	*336	4	1	.997
—	Detroit (A.L.)	OF-DH	12	5	4	1	0	0	0	0	.200	2	2	3	3	0	0	1.000
1998—	Detroit (A.L.)	OF-DH	57	98	20	19	5	1	3	15	.194	6	35	9	51	3	2	.964
—	Toledo (I.L.)...............	OF-DH	51	215	24	53	10	0	2	13	.247	16	42	6	124	6	0	1.000
1999—	Toledo (I.L.)...............	OF	104	416	64	119	13	8	12	43	.286	38	76	21	239	5	1	*.996
—	Detroit (A.L.)	OF-DH	41	77	11	15	1	3	0	3	.195	9	20	3	67	0	1	.985
Major League totals (4 years)			220	397	67	90	12	5	4	32	.227	34	134	35	338	4	5	.986

BATISTA, MIGUEL — P — EXPOS

B

PERSONAL: Born February 19, 1971, in Santo Domingo, Dominican Republic. ... 6-2/195. ... Throws right, bats right. ... Full name: Miguel Jerez Decartes Batista.

HIGH SCHOOL: Nuevo Horizondes (San Pedro de Macoris, Dominican Republic).

TRANSACTIONS/CAREER NOTES: Signed as non-drafted free agent by Montreal Expos organization (February 29, 1988). ... Selected by Pittsburgh Pirates organization from Expos organization in Rule 5 major league draft (December 9, 1991). ... Returned to Expos organization (April 23, 1992). ... On disabled list (April 14-30 and May 7, 1994-remainder of season). ... Released by Expos (November 18, 1994). ... Signed by Florida Marlins organization (December 9, 1994). ... Claimed on waivers by Chicago Cubs (December 17, 1996). ... Traded by Cubs to Expos for OF Henry Rodriguez (December 12, 1997). ... On Montreal disabled list (July 16-August 10, 1999); included rehabilitation assignment to Ottawa (July 30-August 8).

Year	League	W	L	Pct.	ERA	G	GS	CG	ShO	Sv.	IP	H	R	ER	BB	SO
1988—	....						*Dominican Summer League statistics unavailable.*									
1989—	Dom. Expos (DSL)	1	7	.125	4.24	13	11	0	0	0	68	56	46	32	50	60
1990—	GC Expos (GCL)	4	3	.571	2.06	9	6	0	0	0	39 1/3	33	16	9	17	21
—	Rockford (Midw.)	0	1	.000	8.76	3	2	0	0	0	12 1/3	16	13	12	5	7
1991—	Rockford (Midw.)	11	5	.688	4.04	23	23	2	1	0	133 2/3	126	74	60	57	90
1992—	Pittsburgh (N.L.)■	0	0	...	9.00	1	0	0	0	0	2	4	2	2	3	1
—	W.P. Beach (FSL)■...........	7	7	.500	3.79	24	24	1	0	0	135 1/3	130	69	57	54	92
1993—	Harrisburg (East.)	13	5	.722	4.34	26	26	0	0	0	141	139	79	68	86	91
1994—	Harrisburg (East.)	0	1	.000	2.38	3	3	0	0	0	11 1/3	8	3	3	9	5
1995—	Charlotte (I.L.)■...............	6	12	.333	4.80	34	18	0	0	0	116 1/3	118	79	62	60	58
1996—	Charlotte (I.L.)	4	3	.571	5.38	47	2	0	0	4	77	93	57	46	39	56
—	Florida (N.L.)	0	0	...	5.56	9	0	0	0	0	11 1/3	9	8	7	7	6
1997—	Iowa (A.A.)■	9	4	.692	4.20	31	14	2	•2	0	122	117	60	57	38	95
—	Chicago (N.L.)	0	5	.000	5.70	11	6	0	0	0	36 1/3	36	24	23	24	27
1998—	Montreal (N.L.)■...............	3	5	.375	3.80	56	13	0	0	0	135	141	66	57	65	92
1999—	Ottawa (I.L.)	0	1	.000	2.25	3	3	0	0	0	8	3	2	2	4	7
—	Montreal (N.L.)	8	7	.533	4.88	39	17	2	1	1	134 2/3	146	88	73	58	95
Major League totals (5 years).......		11	17	.393	4.57	116	36	2	1	1	319 1/3	336	188	162	157	221

BATISTA, TONY — SS — BLUE JAYS

PERSONAL: Born December 9, 1973, in Puerto Plata, Dominican Republic. ... 6-0/185. ... Bats right, throws right. ... Full name: Leocadio Francisco Batista.

TRANSACTIONS/CAREER NOTES: Signed as non-drafted free agent by Oakland Athletics organization (February 8, 1991). ... On Tacoma disabled list (July 29, 1993-remainder of season). ... On Oakland disabled list (August 27-September 12, 1997); included rehabilitation assignment to Edmonton (September 11-12). ... Selected by Arizona Diamondbacks in first round (27th pick overall) of expansion draft (November 18, 1997). ... Traded by Diamondbacks with P John Frascatore to Toronto Blue Jays for P Dan Plesac (June 12, 1999).

STATISTICAL NOTES: Led California League shortstops with .950 fielding percentage in 1994. ... Had 17-game hitting streak (July 30-August 16, 1999). ... Career major league grand slams: 1.

Year	Team (League)	Pos.	G	AB	R	H	2B	3B	HR	RBI	Avg.	BB	SO	SB	PO	A	E	Avg.
1992—	Ariz. Athletics (Ariz.) ..	2B-SS-OF	45	167	32	41	6	2	0	22	.246	15	29	1	67	124	8	.960
1993—	Ariz. Athletics (Ariz.) ..	3B-2B-SS	24	104	21	34	6	2	2	17	.327	6	14	6	34	54	3	.967
—	Tacoma (PCL)	OF	4	12	1	2	1	0	0	1	.167	1	4	0	6	9	0	1.000
1994—	Modesto (Calif.)	SS-2B	119	466	91	131	26	3	17	68	.281	54	108	7	182	372	30	†.949
1995—	Huntsville (Sou.)	SS-2B	120	419	55	107	23	1	16	61	.255	29	98	7	168	371	29	.949
1996—	Edmonton (PCL)	SS	57	205	33	66	17	4	8	40	.322	15	30	2	75	213	8	.973
—	Oakland (A.L.)	2-3-DH-S	74	238	38	71	10	2	6	25	.298	19	49	7	96	191	5	.983
1997—	Oakland (A.L.)	S-3-DH-2	68	188	22	38	10	1	4	18	.202	14	31	2	96	174	8	.971
—	Edmonton (PCL)	SS-DH	33	124	25	39	10	1	3	21	.315	17	18	2	40	78	6	.952
1998—	Arizona (N.L.)■............	2B-SS-3B	106	293	46	80	16	1	18	41	.273	18	52	1	123	205	6	.982
1999—	Arizona (N.L.)	SS	44	144	16	37	5	0	5	21	.257	16	17	2	60	130	4	.979
—	Toronto (A.L.)■...........	SS	98	375	61	107	25	1	26	79	.285	22	79	2	165	308	12	.975
American League totals (3 years)			240	801	121	216	45	4	36	122	.270	55	159	11	357	673	25	.976
National League totals (2 years)			150	437	62	117	21	1	23	62	.268	34	69	3	183	335	10	.981
Major League totals (4 years)			390	1238	183	333	66	5	59	184	.269	89	228	14	540	1008	35	.978

BATTLE, HOWARD — 3B

PERSONAL: Born March 25, 1972, in Biloxi, Miss. ... 6-0/197. ... Bats right, throws right. ... Full name: Howard Dion Battle.

HIGH SCHOOL: Mercy Cross (Biloxi, Miss.).

TRANSACTIONS/CAREER NOTES: Selected by Toronto Blue Jays organization in fourth round of free-agent draft (June 4, 1990). ... Traded by Blue Jays with P Ricardo Jordan to Philadelphia Phillies for P Paul Quantrill (December 6, 1995). ... Claimed on waivers by Los Angeles Dodgers (September 30, 1996). ... Granted free agency (October 15, 1997). ... Signed by Chicago White Sox organization (January 27, 1998). ... On Birmingham disabled list (April 7-23, 1998). ... Released by White Sox (June 7, 1998). ... Signed by Atlanta Braves organization (June 9, 1998). ... Contract sold by Braves to Hanshin Tigers of Japan Central League (January 12, 2000).

STATISTICAL NOTES: Led Southern League third basemen with 436 total chances in 1993.

Year Team (League)	Pos.	G	AB	R	H	2B	3B	HR	RBI	Avg.	BB	SO	SB	PO	A	E	Avg.
1990— Medicine Hat (Pio.)	3B	61	233	25	62	17	1	5	32	.266	15	38	5	25	92	*34	.775
1991— Myrtle Beach (SAL)	3B	138	520	82	145	33	4	20	87	.279	48	87	15	86	184	29	.903
1992— Dunedin (FSL)	3B	*136	520	76	132	27	3	17	85	.254	49	89	6	58	292	33	.914
1993— Knoxville (Sou.)	3B	141	521	66	145	21	5	7	70	.278	45	94	12	88	*319	*29	.933
1994— Syracuse (I.L.)	3B-DH	139	517	72	143	26	8	14	75	.277	40	82	26	90	258	28	.926
1995— Syracuse (I.L.)	3B-SS-DH	118	443	43	111	17	4	8	48	.251	39	73	10	82	281	33	.917
— Toronto (A.L.)	3B-DH	9	15	3	3	0	0	0	0	.200	4	8	1	1	6	0	1.000
1996— Scranton/W.B. (I.L.)■	3B-SS-1B	115	391	37	89	24	1	8	44	.228	21	53	3	101	216	22	.935
— Philadelphia (N.L.)	3B	5	5	0	0	0	0	0	0	.000	0	2	0	0	0	0	...
1997— Albuq. (PCL)■ 3-DH-S-O-P-1		1	139	14	33	3	2	3	16	.237	6	23	1	31	52	9	.902
— San Antonio (Texas) ...	1B-DH-3B	16	33	2	8	1	0	0	1	.242	0	7	0	46	3	0	1.000
1998— Birm. (Sou.)■	DH-3B-1B	12	39	6	7	4	0	1	5	.179	4	7	0	18	3	1	.955
— Greenville (Sou.)■	3-S-DH-2	79	291	41	96	27	2	10	50	.330	35	51	3	47	138	14	.930
1999— Richmond (I.L.)	3-DH-1-2	121	454	80	129	29	1	24	74	.284	33	66	2	65	119	12	.939
— Atlanta (N.L.)	3B	15	17	2	6	0	0	1	5	.353	2	3	0	2	4	0	1.000
American League totals (1 year)		9	15	3	3	0	0	0	0	.200	4	8	1	1	6	0	1.000
National League totals (2 years)		20	22	2	6	0	0	1	5	.273	2	5	0	2	4	0	1.000
Major League totals (3 years)		29	37	5	9	0	0	1	5	.243	6	13	1	3	10	0	1.000

DIVISION SERIES RECORD

Year Team (League)	Pos.	G	AB	R	H	2B	3B	HR	RBI	Avg.	BB	SO	SB	PO	A	E	Avg.
1999— Atlanta (N.L.)	PH	1	1	0	0	0	0	0	0	.000	0	0	0	...	...	...	...

CHAMPIONSHIP SERIES RECORD

Year Team (League)	Pos.	G	AB	R	H	2B	3B	HR	RBI	Avg.	BB	SO	SB	PO	A	E	Avg.
1999— Atlanta (N.L.)	PH-1B-PR	3	2	0	0	0	0	0	0	.000	0	2	1	0	0	0	...

WORLD SERIES RECORD

Year Team (League)	Pos.	G	AB	R	H	2B	3B	HR	RBI	Avg.	BB	SO	SB	PO	A	E	Avg.
1999— Atlanta (N.L.)	PH	1	0	0	0	0	0	0	0	...	0	0	0	...	...	...	...

RECORD AS PITCHER

Year League	W	L	Pct.	ERA	G	GS	CG	ShO	Sv.	IP	H	R	ER	BB	SO
1997— Albuquerque (PCL)	0	0	...	0.00	1	0	0	0	0	$\frac{1}{3}$	1	0	0	0	1

BAUTISTA, DANNY • OF • MARLINS

PERSONAL: Born May 24, 1972, in Santo Domingo, Dominican Republic. ... 5-11/170. ... Bats right, throws right. ... Full name: Daniel Bautista. ... Stepson of Jesus de la Rosa, outfielder with Houston Astros (1974). ... Name pronounced bough-TEES-tuh.

TRANSACTIONS/CAREER NOTES: Signed as non-drafted free agent by Detroit Tigers organization (June 24, 1989). ... On disabled list (May 24-July 10, 1991). ... On Toledo disabled list (June 8-July 31, 1994). ... Traded by Tigers to Atlanta Braves for OF Anton French (May 31, 1996). ... On Atlanta disabled list (June 28, 1996-remainder of season). ... On Atlanta disabled list (March 23-April 23, 1997); included rehabilitation assignment to Richmond (April 18-23). ... On Atlanta disabled list (April 17-May 7 and August 25-September 17, 1998); included rehabilitation assignment to Greenville (May 5-7). ... Released by Braves (April 2, 1999). ... Signed by Florida Marlins organization (April 8, 1999). ... On Calgary disabled list (June 1-8, 1999).

RECORDS: Shares major league single-game record for most strikeouts (nine-inning game)—5 (May 28, 1995).

Year Team (League)	Pos.	G	AB	R	H	2B	3B	HR	RBI	Avg.	BB	SO	SB	PO	A	E	Avg.
1989—							Dominican Summer League statistics unavailable.										
1990— Bristol (Appl.)	OF	27	95	9	26	3	0	2	12	.274	8	21	2	43	2	0	1.000
1991— Fayetteville (SAL)	OF	69	234	21	45	6	4	1	30	.192	21	65	7	137	6	4	.973
1992— Fayetteville (SAL)	OF	121	453	59	122	22	0	5	52	.269	29	76	18	210	17	6	.974
1993— London (East.)	OF-DH	117	424	55	121	21	1	6	48	.285	32	69	28	256	13	3	.989
— Detroit (A.L.)	OF-DH	17	61	6	19	3	0	1	9	.311	1	10	3	38	2	0	1.000
1994— Detroit (A.L.)	OF	31	99	12	23	4	1	4	15	.232	3	18	1	66	0	0	1.000
— Toledo (I.L.)	OF	27	98	7	25	7	0	2	14	.255	6	23	2	54	1	1	.982
1995— Detroit (A.L.)	OF	89	271	28	55	9	0	7	27	.203	12	68	4	164	3	2	.988
— Toledo (I.L.)	OF	18	58	6	14	3	0	0	4	.241	1	10	1	32	1	2	.943
1996— Detroit (A.L.)	OF-DH	25	64	12	16	2	0	2	8	.250	9	15	1	38	0	1	.974
— Atlanta (N.L.)■	OF	17	20	1	3	0	0	0	1	.150	2	5	0	10	0	0	1.000
1997— Richmond (I.L.)	OF-DH	46	170	28	48	10	3	2	28	.282	19	30	1	104	4	0	1.000
— Atlanta (N.L.)	OF	64	103	14	25	3	2	3	9	.243	5	24	2	59	1	1	.984
1998— Atlanta (N.L.)	OF-DH	82	144	17	36	11	0	3	17	.250	7	21	1	47	0	2	.959
— Greenville (Sou.)	OF	2	6	1	2	0	0	1	2	.333	1	1	0	6	0	0	1.000
1999— Calgary (PCL)■	OF-DH	38	135	25	43	8	1	8	28	.319	11	18	3	90	5	3	.969
— Florida (N.L.)	OF	70	205	32	59	10	1	5	24	.288	4	30	3	140	3	3	.979
American League totals (4 years)		162	495	58	113	18	1	14	59	.228	25	111	9	306	5	3	.990
National League totals (4 years)		233	472	64	123	24	3	11	51	.261	18	80	6	256	4	6	.977
Major League totals (7 years)		395	967	122	236	42	4	25	110	.244	43	191	15	562	9	9	.984

DIVISION SERIES RECORD

							BATTING							FIELDING		
Year Team (League)	Pos.	G	AB	R	H	2B	3B	HR	RBI	Avg.	BB	SO	SB	PO	A	E	Avg.
1997—Atlanta (N.L.)..............	OF	3	3	0	1	0	0	0	2	.333	0	1	0	0	0	0	
1998—Atlanta (N.L.)..............	OF	2	2	0	1	1	0	0	0	.500	0	0	0	2	0	0	1.000
Division series totals (2 years)		5	5	0	2	1	0	0	2	.400	0	1	0	2	0	0	1.000

CHAMPIONSHIP SERIES RECORD

							BATTING							FIELDING		
Year Team (League)	Pos.	G	AB	R	H	2B	3B	HR	RBI	Avg.	BB	SO	SB	PO	A	E	Avg.
1997—Atlanta (N.L.)..............	OF	2	4	0	1	0	0	0	0	.250	0	0	0	4	0	0	1.000
1998—Atlanta (N.L.)..............	PR-OF	5	5	0	0	0	0	0	0	.000	0	1	0	2	0	1	.667
Championship series totals (2 years)		7	9	0	1	0	0	0	0	.111	0	1	0	6	0	1	.857

BECK, ROD   P   RED SOX   B

PERSONAL: Born August 3, 1968, in Burbank, Calif. ... 6-1/235. ... Throws right, bats right. ... Full name: Rodney Roy Beck.
HIGH SCHOOL: Grant (Van Nuys, Calif.).
TRANSACTIONS/CAREER NOTES: Selected by Oakland Athletics organization in 13th round of free-agent draft (June 2, 1986). ... Traded by A's organization to San Francisco Giants organization for P Charlie Corbell (March 23, 1988). ... On disabled list (April 6-30, 1994). ... Granted free agency (October 27, 1997). ... Signed by Chicago Cubs (January 15, 1998). ... On Chicago disabled list (May 17-July 21, 1999); included rehabilitation assignment to Iowa (July 17-21). ... Traded by Cubs to Boston Red Sox for P Mark Guthrie and a player to named later (August 31, 1999); Cubs acquired 3B Cole Liniak to complete deal (September 1, 1999).
MISCELLANEOUS: Holds San Francisco Giants franchise all-time record for most saves (199).

Year League	W	L	Pct.	ERA	G	GS	CG	ShO	Sv.	IP	H	R	ER	BB	SO
1986—Medford (N.W.)	1	3	.250	5.23	13	6	0	0	1	32 2/3	47	25	19	11	21
1987—Medford (N.W.)	5	8	.385	5.18	17	12	2	0	0	92	106	74	53	26	69
1988—Clinton (Midw.)■	12	7	.632	3.00	28	23	5	1	0	177	177	68	59	27	123
1989—San Jose (Calif.)................	11	2	*.846	2.40	13	13	4	0	0	97 1/3	91	29	26	26	88
—Shreveport (Texas)...........	7	3	.700	3.55	16	14	4	1	0	99	108	45	39	16	74
1990—Shreveport (Texas)............	10	3	.769	2.23	14	14	2	1	0	93	85	26	23	17	71
—Phoenix (PCL)	4	7	.364	4.93	12	12	2	0	0	76 2/3	100	51	42	18	43
1991—Phoenix (PCL)	4	3	.571	2.02	23	5	3	0	6	71 1/3	56	18	16	13	35
—San Francisco (N.L.)	1	1	.500	3.78	31	0	0	0	1	52 1/3	53	22	22	13	38
1992—San Francisco (N.L.)	3	3	.500	1.76	65	0	0	0	17	92	62	20	18	15	87
1993—San Francisco (N.L.)	3	1	.750	2.16	76	0	0	0	48	79 1/3	57	20	19	13	86
1994—San Francisco (N.L.)	2	4	.333	2.77	48	0	0	0	28	48 2/3	49	17	15	13	39
1995—San Francisco (N.L.)	5	6	.455	4.45	60	0	0	0	33	58 2/3	60	31	29	21	42
1996—San Francisco (N.L.)	0	9	.000	3.34	63	0	0	0	35	62	56	23	23	10	48
1997—San Francisco (N.L.)	7	4	.636	3.47	73	0	0	0	37	70	67	31	27	8	53
1998—Chicago (N.L.)■■	3	4	.429	3.02	*81	0	0	0	51	80 1/3	86	33	27	20	81
1999—Chicago (N.L.)	2	4	.333	7.80	31	0	0	0	7	30	41	26	26	13	13
—Iowa (PCL)	0	0	...	0.00	2	0	0	0	0	2	1	0	0	0	2
—Boston (A.L.)■	0	1	.000	1.93	12	0	0	0	3	14	9	3	3	5	12
A.L. totals (1 year)	0	1	.000	1.93	12	0	0	0	3	14	9	3	3	5	12
N.L. totals (9 years)	26	36	.419	3.23	528	0	0	0	257	573 1/3	531	223	206	126	487
Major League totals (9 years).......	26	37	.413	3.20	540	0	0	0	260	587 1/3	540	226	209	131	499

DIVISION SERIES RECORD

Year League	W	L	Pct.	ERA	G	GS	CG	ShO	Sv.	IP	H	R	ER	BB	SO
1997—San Francisco (N.L.)	0	0	...	0.00	1	0	0	0	0	1 1/3	1	0	0	0	1
1998—Chicago (N.L.)	0	0	...	16.20	1	0	0	0	0	1 2/3	5	3	3	2	1
1999—Boston (A.L.)	0	0	...	0.00	2	0	0	0	0	2	2	0	0	0	2
Division series totals (3 years)	0	0	...	5.40	4	0	0	0	0	5	8	3	3	2	4

CHAMPIONSHIP SERIES RECORD

Year League	W	L	Pct.	ERA	G	GS	CG	ShO	Sv.	IP	H	R	ER	BB	SO
1999—Boston (A.L.).....................	0	1	.000	27.00	2	0	0	0	0	2/3	2	2	2	0	1

ALL-STAR GAME RECORD

Year League	W	L	Pct.	ERA	GS	CG	ShO	Sv.	IP	H	R	ER	BB	SO
1993—National	0	0	...	9.00	0	0	0	0	1	2	1	1	0	1
1994—National	0	0	...	0.00	0	0	0	0	1 2/3	1	0	0	0	1
1997—National							Did not play.							
All-Star Game totals (2 years)	0	0	...	3.38	0	0	0	0	2 2/3	3	1	1	0	2

BECKER, RICH   OF   ATHLETICS

PERSONAL: Born February 1, 1972, in Aurora, Ill. ... 5-10/193. ... Bats left, throws left. ... Full name: Richard Goodhard Becker.
HIGH SCHOOL: Aurora (Ill.) West.
TRANSACTIONS/CAREER NOTES: Selected by Minnesota Twins organization in third round of free-agent draft (June 4, 1990). ... On Minnesota disabled list (September 13, 1993-remainder of season and April 29-May 17, 1994). ... Traded by Twins to New York Mets for OF Alex Ochoa (December 12, 1997). ... Claimed on waivers by Baltimore Orioles (June 16, 1998). ... Released by Orioles (December 9, 1998). ... Signed by Milwaukee Brewers (January 11, 1999). ... Traded by Brewers to Oakland Athletics for a player to be named later (August 17, 1999); Brewers acquired P Carl Dale to complete deal (August 20, 1999). ... Granted free agency (December 21, 1999). ... Re-signed by Athletics (December 29, 1999).
STATISTICAL NOTES: Led Appalachian League with .448 on-base percentage in 1990. ... Led Midwest League with 215 total bases in 1991. ... Led California League outfielders with 355 total chances in 1992. ... Led A.L. outfielders in double plays with five in 1995 and nine in 1996. ... Led A.L. outfielders with 412 total chances in 1996.

Year	Team (League)	Pos.	G	AB	R	H	2B	3B	HR	RBI	Avg.	BB	SO	SB	PO	A	E	Avg.
								BATTING								FIELDING		
1990—	Elizabethton (Appl.)....	OF	56	194	54	56	5	1	6	24	.289	*53	54	18	87	2	9	.908
1991—	Kenosha (Midw.)........	OF	130	494	100	132	*38	3	13	53	.267	72	108	19	270	19	11	.963
1992—	Visalia (Calif.)...........	OF	*136	506	*118	160	37	2	15	82	.316	*114	122	29	*332	17	6	.983
1993—	Nashville (Sou.)........	OF	138	516	•93	148	25	7	15	66	.287	94	117	29	303	5	6	.981
—	Minnesota (A.L.)......	OF	3	7	3	2	2	0	0	0	.286	5	4	1	7	0	1	.875
1994—	Minnesota (A.L.)........	OF-DH	28	98	12	26	3	0	1	8	.265	13	25	6	87	2	1	.989
—	Salt Lake (PCL)........	OF	71	282	64	89	21	3	2	38	.316	40	56	7	189	8	3	.985
1995—	Salt Lake (PCL)........	OF	36	123	26	38	7	0	6	28	.309	26	24	6	108	5	1	.991
—	Minnesota (A.L.)......	OF	106	392	45	93	15	1	2	33	.237	34	95	8	275	12	4	.986
1996—	Minnesota (A.L.)........	OF	148	525	92	153	31	4	12	71	.291	68	118	19	*391	18	3	.993
1997—	Minnesota (A.L.)........	OF	132	443	61	117	22	3	10	45	.264	62	130	17	319	5	5	.985
1998—	New York (N.L.)■.....	OF	49	100	15	19	4	2	3	10	.190	21	42	3	56	4	1	.984
—	Baltimore (A.L.)■.....	OF-DH	79	113	22	23	1	0	3	11	.204	22	34	2	59	1	1	.984
1999—	Milwaukee (N.L.)■.....	OF-DH	89	139	15	35	5	2	5	16	.252	33	38	5	62	3	2	.970
—	Oakland (A.L.)■.....	OF-DH	40	125	21	33	3	0	1	10	.264	25	43	3	66	4	1	.986
American League totals (7 years)			536	1703	256	447	77	8	29	178	.262	229	449	56	1204	42	16	.987
National League totals (2 years)			138	239	30	54	9	4	8	26	.226	54	80	8	118	7	3	.977
Major League totals (7 years)			674	1942	286	501	86	12	37	204	.258	283	529	64	1322	49	19	.986

BECKETT, JOSH — P — MARLINS

PERSONAL: Born May 15, 1980, in Spring, Texas. ... 6-4/190. ... Throws right, bats right.
HIGH SCHOOL: Spring (Texas).
TRANSACTIONS/CAREER NOTES: Selected by Florida Marlins organization in first round (second pick overall) of free-agent draft (June 2, 1999).

Year	League	W	L	Pct.	ERA	G	GS	CG	ShO	Sv.	IP	H	R	ER	BB	SO
1999—									Did not play.							

BEIRNE, KEVIN — P — WHITE SOX

PERSONAL: Born January 1, 1974, in Houston. ... 6-4/210. ... Throws right, bats left. ... Full name: Kevin P. Beirne. ... Son of Jim Beirne, wide receiver/tight end with Houston Oilers (1968-73, 1975 and 1976) and San Diego Chargers (1974).
HIGH SCHOOL: McCollough (The Woodlands, Texas).
COLLEGE: Texas A&M.
TRANSACTIONS/CAREER NOTES: Selected by Cincinnati Reds organization in 43rd round of free-agent draft (June 2, 1992); did not sign. ... Selected by Chicago White Sox organization in 11th round of free-agent draft (June 1, 1995). ... On Charlotte disabled list (May 6-14 and August 6, 1999-remainder of season).

Year	League	W	L	Pct.	ERA	G	GS	CG	ShO	Sv.	IP	H	R	ER	BB	SO
1995—	GC White Sox (GCL)	0	0	...	2.45	2	0	0	0	2	3²/₃	2	2	1	1	3
—	Bristol (Appl.)...................	1	0	1.000	0.00	9	0	0	0	2	9	4	0	0	4	12
—	Hickory (SAL).................	0	0	...	4.50	3	0	0	0	1	4	7	2	2	0	4
1996—	South Bend (Midw.).........	4	11	.267	4.15	26	25	1	0	0	145¹/₃	153	85	67	60	110
1997—	Winston-Salem (Caro.).......	4	4	.500	3.05	13	13	1	0	0	82²/₃	66	38	28	28	75
—	Birmingham (Sou.)............	6	4	.600	4.92	13	12	0	0	0	75	76	51	41	41	49
1998—	Birmingham (Sou.).............	13	9	.591	3.44	26	26	2	1	0	167¹/₃	142	77	64	87	153
—	Calgary (PCL)...................	0	0	...	4.50	2	2	0	0	0	8	12	5	4	4	6
1999—	Charlotte (I.L.)...................	5	5	.500	5.42	20	20	0	0	0	113	134	75	68	36	63

BELCHER, TIM — P — ANGELS

PERSONAL: Born October 19, 1961, in Sparta, Ohio. ... 6-3/235. ... Throws right, bats right. ... Full name: Timothy Wayne Belcher.
HIGH SCHOOL: Highland (Sparta, Ohio).
COLLEGE: Mt. Vernon (Ohio) Nazarene.
TRANSACTIONS/CAREER NOTES: Selected by Minnesota Twins organization in first round (first pick overall) of free-agent draft (June 6, 1983); did not sign. ... Selected by New York Yankees organization in secondary phase of free-agent draft (January 17, 1984); did not sign. ... Selected by Oakland Athletics organization in player compensation pool draft (February 8, 1984); A's received compensation for Baltimore Orioles signing Type A free-agent P Tom Underwood (February 7, 1984). ... On disabled list (April 10-May 4 and May 5-July 23, 1986). ... Traded by A's to Los Angeles Dodgers (September 3, 1987), completing deal in which Dodgers traded P Rick Honeycutt to A's for a player to be named later (August 29, 1987). ... On disabled list (August 17, 1990-remainder of season). ... Traded by Dodgers with P John Wetteland to Cincinnati Reds for OF Eric Davis and P Kip Gross (November 27, 1991). ... Traded by Reds to Chicago White Sox for P Johnny Ruffin and P Jeff Pierce (July 31, 1993). ... Granted free agency (October 26, 1993). ... Signed by Detroit Tigers (February 7, 1994). ... Granted free agency (October 20, 1994). ... Signed by Reds organization (May 3, 1995). ... Traded by Reds to Seattle Mariners for P Roger Salkeld (May 15, 1995). ... Granted free agency (October 31, 1995). ... Signed by Kansas City Royals (January 31, 1996). ... Granted free agency (October 26, 1998). ... Signed by Anaheim Angels (December 23, 1998). ... On disabled list (June 27-August 7, 1999).
HONORS: Named righthanded pitcher on THE SPORTING NEWS college All-America team (1983). ... Named N.L. Rookie Pitcher of the Year by THE SPORTING NEWS (1988).
STATISTICAL NOTES: Pitched 6-0 one-hit, complete-game victory against Pittsburgh (July 21, 1990). ... Pitched 4-0 one-hit, complete-game victory for Cincinnati against Atlanta (May 26, 1993). ... Led A.L. with 37 home runs allowed in 1998.

Year	League	W	L	Pct.	ERA	G	GS	CG	ShO	Sv.	IP	H	R	ER	BB	SO
1984—	Madison (Midw.)	9	4	.692	3.57	16	16	3	1	0	98¹/₃	80	45	39	48	111
—	Albany/Colonie (East.)	3	4	.429	3.33	10	10	2	0	0	54	37	30	20	41	40
1985—	Huntsville (Sou.)	11	10	.524	4.69	29	26	3	1	0	149²/₃	145	99	78	99	90
1986—	Huntsville (Sou.)	2	5	.286	6.57	9	9	0	0	0	37	50	28	27	22	25
1987—	Tacoma (PCL)	9	11	.450	4.42	29	28	2	1	0	163	143	89	80	*133	136
—	Los Angeles (N.L.)■	4	2	.667	2.38	6	5	0	0	0	34	30	11	9	7	23
1988—	Los Angeles (N.L.)	12	6	.667	2.91	36	27	4	1	4	179²/₃	143	65	58	51	152
1989—	Los Angeles (N.L.)	15	12	.556	2.82	39	30	•10	*8	1	230	182	81	72	80	200
1990—	Los Angeles (N.L.)	9	9	.500	4.00	24	24	5	2	0	153	136	76	68	48	102

Year League	W	L	Pct.	ERA	G	GS	CG	ShO	Sv.	IP	H	R	ER	BB	SO
1991— Los Angeles (N.L.)	10	9	.526	2.62	33	33	2	1	0	209 1/3	189	76	61	75	156
1992— Cincinnati (N.L.)■	15	14	.517	3.91	35	34	2	1	0	227 2/3	201	*104	*99	80	149
1993— Cincinnati (N.L.)	9	6	.600	4.47	22	22	4	2	0	137	134	72	68	47	101
— Chicago (A.L.)■	3	5	.375	4.40	12	11	1	1	0	71 2/3	64	36	35	27	34
1994— Detroit (A.L.)■	7	*15	.318	5.89	25	•25	3	0	0	162	192	*124	106	78	76
1995— Indianapolis (A.A.)■	0	0	...	1.80	2	2	0	0	0	10	6	2	2	1	8
— Seattle (A.L.)■	10	12	.455	4.52	28	28	1	0	0	179 1/3	188	101	90	88	96
1996— Kansas City (A.L.)■	15	11	.577	3.92	35	35	4	1	0	238 2/3	262	117	104	68	113
1997— Kansas City (A.L.)	13	12	.520	5.02	32	32	3	1	0	213 1/3	242	128	119	70	113
1998— Kansas City (A.L.)	14	14	.500	4.27	34	34	2	0	0	234	247	127	111	73	130
1999— Anaheim (A.L.)■	6	8	.429	6.73	24	24	0	0	0	132 1/3	168	104	99	46	52
A.L. totals (7 years)	68	77	.469	4.85	190	189	14	3	0	1231 1/3	1363	737	664	450	614
N.L. totals (7 years)	74	58	.561	3.34	195	175	27	15	5	1170 2/3	1015	485	435	388	883
Major League totals (13 years)	142	135	.513	4.12	385	364	41	18	5	2402	2378	1222	1099	838	1497

B

DIVISION SERIES RECORD

Year League	W	L	Pct.	ERA	G	GS	CG	ShO	Sv.	IP	H	R	ER	BB	SO
1995— Seattle (A.L.)	0	1	.000	6.23	2	0	0	0	0	4 1/3	4	3	3	5	0

CHAMPIONSHIP SERIES RECORD

Year League	W	L	Pct.	ERA	G	GS	CG	ShO	Sv.	IP	H	R	ER	BB	SO
1988— Los Angeles (N.L.)	2	0	1.000	4.11	2	2	0	0	0	15 1/3	12	7	7	4	16
1993— Chicago (A.L.)	1	0	1.000	2.45	1	0	0	0	0	3 2/3	3	1	1	3	1
1995— Seattle (A.L.)	0	1	.000	6.35	1	1	0	0	0	5 2/3	9	4	4	2	1
Champ. series totals (3 years)	3	1	.750	4.38	4	3	0	0	0	24 2/3	24	12	12	9	18

WORLD SERIES RECORD

NOTES: Member of World Series championship team (1988).

Year League	W	L	Pct.	ERA	G	GS	CG	ShO	Sv.	IP	H	R	ER	BB	SO
1988— Los Angeles (N.L.)	1	0	1.000	6.23	2	2	0	0	0	8 2/3	10	7	6	6	10

BELINDA, STAN　　　　P　　　　ROCKIES

PERSONAL: Born August 6, 1966, in Huntingdon, Pa. ... 6-3/215. ... Throws right, bats right. ... Full name: Stanley Peter Belinda.
HIGH SCHOOL: State College (Pa.) Area.
JUNIOR COLLEGE: Allegany Community College (Md.).
TRANSACTIONS/CAREER NOTES: Selected by Pittsburgh Pirates organization in 10th round of free-agent draft (June 2, 1986). ... On Gulf Coast Pirates disabled list (June 21-30, 1986). ... Traded by Pirates to Kansas City Royals for P Jon Lieber and P Dan Miceli (July 31, 1993). ... Granted free agency (December 23, 1994). ... Signed by Boston Red Sox (April 9, 1995). ... On Boston disabled list (April 21-May 6, 1995); included rehabilitation assignment to Sarasota (May 4-5). ... On Boston disabled list (March 19-April 6, May 30-July 26 and August 20, 1996-remainder of season); included rehabilitation assignments to Sarasota (June 6-9) and Pawtucket (July 14-25). ... Granted free agency (October 14, 1996). ... Signed by Cincinnati Reds (December 21, 1996). ... On disabled list (June 3-July 9 and August 11, 1998-remainder of season). ... On Cincinnati disabled list (March 24-June 25, 1999); included rehabilitation assignment to Indianapolis (June 3-24). ... Traded by Reds with OF Jeffrey Hammonds to Colorado Rockies for OF Dante Bichette and cash (October 30, 1999).

Year League	W	L	Pct.	ERA	G	GS	CG	ShO	Sv.	IP	H	R	ER	BB	SO
1986— Watertown (NY-P)	0	0	...	3.38	5	0	0	0	2	8	5	3	3	2	5
— GC Pirates (GCL)	3	2	.600	2.66	17	0	0	0	7	20 1/3	23	12	6	2	17
1987— Macon (SAL)	6	4	.600	2.09	50	0	0	0	16	82	59	26	19	27	75
1988— Salem (Caro.)	6	4	.600	2.76	53	0	0	0	14	71 2/3	54	33	22	32	63
1989— Harrisburg (East.)	1	4	.200	2.33	32	0	0	0	13	38 2/3	32	13	10	25	33
— Buffalo (A.A.)	2	2	.500	0.95	19	0	0	0	9	28 1/3	13	5	3	13	28
— Pittsburgh (N.L.)	0	1	.000	6.10	8	0	0	0	0	10 1/3	13	8	7	2	10
1990— Buffalo (A.A.)	3	1	.750	1.90	15	0	0	0	5	23 2/3	20	8	5	8	25
— Pittsburgh (N.L.)	3	4	.429	3.55	55	0	0	0	8	58 1/3	48	23	23	29	55
1991— Pittsburgh (N.L.)	7	5	.583	3.45	60	0	0	0	16	78 1/3	50	30	30	35	71
1992— Pittsburgh (N.L.)	6	4	.600	3.15	59	0	0	0	18	71 1/3	58	26	25	29	57
1993— Pittsburgh (N.L.)	3	1	.750	3.61	40	0	0	0	19	42 1/3	35	18	17	11	30
— Kansas City (A.L.)■	1	1	.500	4.28	23	0	0	0	0	27 1/3	30	13	13	6	25
1994— Kansas City (A.L.)	2	2	.500	5.14	37	0	0	0	1	49	47	36	28	24	37
1995— Sarasota (FSL)■	0	0	...	4.50	1	1	0	0	0	2	2	1	1	0	2
— Boston (A.L.)	8	1	.889	3.10	63	0	0	0	10	69 2/3	51	25	24	28	57
1996— Boston (A.L.)	2	1	.667	6.59	31	0	0	0	2	28 2/3	31	22	21	20	18
— Sarasota (FSL)	0	1	.000	45.00	1	1	0	0	0	1	6	5	5	1	1
— Pawtucket (I.L.)	1	0	1.000	0.00	6	0	0	0	0	7 2/3	2	2	0	2	7
1997— Cincinnati (N.L.)■	1	5	.167	3.71	84	0	0	0	1	99 1/3	84	42	41	33	114
1998— Cincinnati (N.L.)	4	8	.333	3.23	40	0	0	0	1	61 1/3	46	23	22	28	57
1999— Indianapolis (I.L.)	2	0	1.000	2.38	10	0	0	0	0	11 1/3	7	3	3	6	10
— Cincinnati (N.L.)	3	1	.750	5.27	29	0	0	0	2	42 2/3	42	26	25	18	40
A.L. totals (4 years)	13	5	.722	4.43	154	0	0	0	13	174 2/3	159	96	86	78	137
N.L. totals (8 years)	27	29	.482	3.69	375	0	0	0	65	464	376	196	190	185	434
Major League totals (11 years)	40	34	.541	3.89	529	0	0	0	78	638 2/3	535	292	276	263	571

DIVISION SERIES RECORD

Year League	W	L	Pct.	ERA	G	GS	CG	ShO	Sv.	IP	H	R	ER	BB	SO
1995— Boston (A.L.)	0	0	...	0.00	1	0	0	0	0	1/3	0	0	0	0	0

CHAMPIONSHIP SERIES RECORD

Year League	W	L	Pct.	ERA	G	GS	CG	ShO	Sv.	IP	H	R	ER	BB	SO
1990— Pittsburgh (N.L.)	0	0	...	2.45	3	0	0	0	0	3 2/3	3	1	1	0	4
1991— Pittsburgh (N.L.)	1	0	1.000	0.00	3	0	0	0	0	5	0	0	0	3	4
1992— Pittsburgh (N.L.)	0	0	...	0.00	2	0	0	0	0	1 2/3	2	0	0	1	2
Champ. series totals (3 years)	1	0	1.000	0.87	8	0	0	0	0	10 1/3	5	1	1	4	10

BELITZ, TODD   P   DEVIL RAYS

PERSONAL: Born October 23, 1975, in Des Moines, Iowa. ... 6-3/200. ... Throws left, bats left. ... Full name: Todd S. Belitz.
HIGH SCHOOL: Edison (Huntington Beach, Calif.).
COLLEGE: Washington State.
TRANSACTIONS/CAREER NOTES: Selected by Kansas City Royals organization in eighth round of free-agent draft (June 2, 1994); did not sign. ... Selected by Tampa Bay Devil Rays organization in fourth round of free-agent draft (June 3, 1997).

Year League	W	L	Pct.	ERA	G	GS	CG	ShO	Sv.	IP	H	R	ER	BB	SO
1997—Hudson Valley (NY-P)	4	5	.444	3.53	15	15	0	0	0	74	65	41	29	18	78
1998—Charleston, S.C. (SAL)	6	4	.600	2.42	21	21	0	0	0	130	99	44	35	48	123
—St. Petersburg (FSL)	2	2	.500	5.04	7	7	0	0	0	44 2/3	39	28	25	14	40
1999—Orlando (Sou.)	9	9	.500	5.77	28	•28	0	0	0	160 2/3	169	*114	*103	65	118

BELL, DAVID   IF   MARINERS

PERSONAL: Born September 14, 1972, in Cincinnati. ... 5-10/175. ... Bats right, throws right. ... Full name: David Michael Bell. ... Son of Buddy Bell, major league third baseman with four teams (1972-89) and manager, Colorado Rockies; brother of Mike Bell, minor league infielder (1993-99); and grandson of Gus Bell, major league outfielder with four teams (1950-64).
HIGH SCHOOL: Moeller (Cincinnati).
TRANSACTIONS/CAREER NOTES: Selected by Cleveland Indians organization in seventh round of free-agent draft (June 4, 1990). ... Traded by Indians with C Pepe McNeal and P Rick Heiserman to St. Louis Cardinals for P Ken Hill (July 27, 1995). ... On St. Louis disabled list (April 29-June 30, 1997); included rehabilitation assignments to Arkansas (June 10-19) and Louisville (June 20-26). ... Claimed on waivers by Indians (April 14, 1998). ... Traded by Indians to Seattle Mariners for 2B Joey Cora (August 31, 1998).
STATISTICAL NOTES: Led South Atlantic League in grounding into double plays with 22 in 1991. ... Led South Atlantic League third basemen with 389 total chances in 1991. ... Led Eastern League third basemen with 32 double plays in 1993. ... Led International League third basemen with .950 fielding percentage in 1994. ... Led A.L. second baseman with 313 putouts and 118 double plays in 1999.

Year Team (League)	Pos.	G	AB	R	H	2B	3B	HR	RBI	Avg.	BB	SO	SB	PO	A	E	Avg.
1990—GC Indians (GCL)	3B	30	111	18	29	5	1	0	13	.261	10	8	1	29	50	7	.919
—Burlington (Appl.)	3B	12	42	4	7	1	0		2	.167	2	5	2	8	27	3	.921
1991—Columbus (SAL)	3B	136	491	47	113	24	1	5	63	.230	37	50	3	90	*268	31	.920
1992—Kinston (Caro.)	3B	123	464	52	117	17	2	6	47	.252	54	66	2	83	264	20	.946
1993—Cant./Akron (East.)	3B-2B-SS	129	483	69	141	20	2	9	60	.292	43	54	3	117	283	21	.950
1994—Charlotte (I.L.)	3B-SS-2B	134	481	66	141	17	4	18	88	.293	41	54	2	109	326	20	†.956
1995—Buffalo (A.A.)	3B-SS-2B	70	254	34	69	11	1	8	34	.272	22	37	0	46	172	11	.952
—Cleveland (A.L.)	3B	2	2	0	0	0	0	0	0	.000	0	0	0	0	2	0	1.000
—Louisville (A.A.)	2B	18	76	9	21	3	1	1	9	.276	2	10	4	39	54	1	.989
—St. Louis (N.L.)	2B-3B	39	144	13	36	7	2	2	19	.250	4	25	1	77	108	7	.964
1996—St. Louis (N.L.)	3B-2B-SS	62	145	12	31	6	0	1	9	.214	10	22	1	45	113	5	.969
—Louisville (A.A.)	2B-3B-SS	42	136	9	24	5	1	0	7	.176	7	15	1	66	114	5	.973
1997—St. Louis (N.L.)	3B-2B-SS	66	142	9	30	7	2	1	12	.211	10	28	1	55	95	8	.949
—Arkansas (Texas)	3B-2B	9	32	3	7	2	0	1	3	.219	2	2	1	3	15	1	.947
—Louisville (A.A.)	2B-3B-DH-SS	6	22	3	5	0	0	1	4	.227	0	6	0	6	10	1	.941
1998—St. Louis (N.L.)	3B-2B	4	9	0	2	1	0	0	0	.222	0	3	0	1	4	0	1.000
—Cleveland (A.L.)	2-3-1-S	107	340	37	89	21	2	10	41	.262	22	54	0	201	306	9	.983
—Seattle (A.L.)	2B-1B-3B-OF	21	80	11	26	8	0	0	8	.325	5	8	0	61	46	1	.991
1999—Seattle (A.L.)	2B-1B-SS	157	597	92	160	31	2	21	78	.268	58	90	7	†329	427	17	.978
American League totals (3 years)		287	1019	140	275	60	4	31	127	.270	85	152	7	591	781	27	.981
National League totals (4 years)		171	440	34	99	21	4	4	40	.225	24	78	3	178	320	20	.961
Major League totals (5 years)		458	1459	174	374	81	8	35	167	.256	109	230	10	769	1101	47	.975

BELL, DEREK   OF   METS

PERSONAL: Born December 11, 1968, in Tampa. ... 6-2/215. ... Bats right, throws right. ... Full name: Derek Nathaniel Bell.
HIGH SCHOOL: King (Tampa).
TRANSACTIONS/CAREER NOTES: Selected by Toronto Blue Jays organization in second round of free-agent draft (June 2, 1987). ... On Knoxville disabled list (July 30, 1988-remainder of season; June 13-21 and July 2-12, 1990). ... On Toronto disabled list (April 9-May 8, 1992); included rehabilitation assignment to Dunedin (April 27-May 4). ... Traded by Blue Jays with OF Stoney Briggs to San Diego Padres for OF Darrin Jackson (March 30, 1993). ... On suspended list (July 9-12, 1993 and July 9-17, 1994). ... Traded by Padres with OF Phil Plantier, P Pedro Martinez, P Doug Brocail, IF Craig Shipley and SS Ricky Gutierrez to Houston Astros for 3B Ken Caminiti, OF Steve Finley, SS Andujar Cedeno, 1B Robert Petagine, P Brian Williams and a player to be named later (December 28, 1994); Padres acquired P Sean Fesh to complete deal (May 1, 1995). ... On Houston disabled list (May 14-June 13, 1997); included rehabilitation assignment to New Orleans (June 6-13). ... On disabled list (August 17-September 1, 1999). ... Traded by Astros with P Mike Hampton to New York Mets for OF Roger Cedeno, P Octavio Dotel and P Kyle Kessel (December 23, 1999).
HONORS: Named International League Most Valuable Player (1991).
STATISTICAL NOTES: Led International League with 243 total bases in 1991. ... Led International League outfielders with seven double plays in 1991. ... Tied for N.L. lead with 10 sacrifice flies in 1998. ... Career major league grand slams: 1.

Year Team (League)	Pos.	G	AB	R	H	2B	3B	HR	RBI	Avg.	BB	SO	SB	PO	A	E	Avg.
1987—St. Catharines (NY-P)	OF	74	273	46	72	11	3	10	42	.264	18	60	12	126	6	2	.985
1988—Knoxville (Sou.)	OF	14	52	5	13	3	1	0	4	.250	1	14	2	18	2	2	.909
—Myrtle Beach (SAL)	OF	91	352	55	121	29	5	12	60	*.344	15	67	18	148	12	10	.941
1989—Knoxville (Sou.)	OF	136	513	72	124	22	6	16	75	.242	26	92	15	216	12	9	.962
1990—Syracuse (I.L.)	OF	109	402	57	105	13	5	7	56	.261	23	75	21	220	9	5	.979
1991—Syracuse (I.L.)	OF	119	457	*89	*158	22	•12	13	*93	*.346	57	69	27	278	*15	*16	.948
—Toronto (A.L.)	OF	18	28	5	4	0	0	0	1	.143	6	5	3	16	0	2	.889
1992—Toronto (A.L.)	OF-DH	61	161	23	39	6	3	2	15	.242	15	34	7	105	4	0	1.000
—Dunedin (FSL)	OF	7	25	7	6	2	0	0	4	.240	4	4	3	13	0	2	.867

Year Team (League)	Pos.	G	AB	R	H	2B	3B	HR	RBI	Avg.	BB	SO	SB	PO	A	E	Avg.
						BATTING								FIELDING			
1993—San Diego (N.L.)■	OF-3B	150	542	73	142	19	1	21	72	.262	23	122	26	334	37	17	.956
1994—San Diego (N.L.)	OF	108	434	54	135	20	0	14	54	.311	29	88	24	247	3	10	.962
1995—Houston (N.L.)■	OF	112	452	63	151	21	2	8	86	.334	33	71	27	201	10	8	.963
1996—Houston (N.L.)	OF	158	627	84	165	40	3	17	113	.263	40	123	29	283	16	7	.977
1997—Houston (N.L.)	OF-DH	129	493	67	136	29	3	15	71	.276	40	94	15	226	5	8	.967
—New Orleans (A.A.).....	OF	5	13	0	2	0	0	0	1	.154	1	1	1	10	0	0	1.000
1998—Houston (N.L.)	OF	156	630	111	198	41	2	22	108	.314	51	126	13	281	8	8	.973
1999—Houston (N.L.)	OF	128	509	61	120	22	0	12	66	.236	50	129	18	192	4	3	.985
American League totals (2 years)		79	189	28	43	6	3	2	16	.228	21	39	10	121	4	2	.984
National League totals (7 years)		941	3687	513	1047	192	11	109	570	.284	266	753	152	1764	83	61	.968
Major League totals (9 years)		1020	3876	541	1090	198	14	111	586	.281	287	792	162	1885	87	63	.969

DIVISION SERIES RECORD

Year Team (League)	Pos.	G	AB	R	H	2B	3B	HR	RBI	Avg.	BB	SO	SB	PO	A	E	Avg.
						BATTING								FIELDING			
1997—Houston (N.L.)	OF	3	13	0	0	0	0	0	0	.000	0	3	0	3	0	0	1.000
1998—Houston (N.L.)	OF	4	16	1	2	0	0	1	1	.125	0	7	0	5	0	0	1.000
1999—Houston (N.L.)	OF-PH	2	3	0	1	0	0	0	0	.333	0	0	0	1	0	0	1.000
Division series totals (3 years)		9	32	1	3	0	0	1	1	.094	0	10	0	9	0	0	1.000

CHAMPIONSHIP SERIES RECORD

Year Team (League)	Pos.	G	AB	R	H	2B	3B	HR	RBI	Avg.	BB	SO	SB	PO	A	E	Avg.
						BATTING								FIELDING			
1992—Toronto (A.L.).............	PR-OF	2	0	1	0	0	0	0	0	...	1	0	0	1	0	0	1.000

WORLD SERIES RECORD

NOTES: Member of World Series championship team (1992).

Year Team (League)	Pos.	G	AB	R	H	2B	3B	HR	RBI	Avg.	BB	SO	SB	PO	A	E	Avg.
						BATTING								FIELDING			
1992—Toronto (A.L.).............	PH	2	1	1	0	0	0	0	0	.000	1	0	0	...	...	...	...

BELL, JAY — 2B — DIAMONDBACKS

PERSONAL: Born December 11, 1965, in Eglin AFB, Fla. ... 6-0/182. ... Bats right, throws right. ... Full name: Jay Stuart Bell.

HIGH SCHOOL: Tate (Gonzalez, Fla.).

TRANSACTIONS/CAREER NOTES: Selected by Minnesota Twins organization in first round (eighth pick overall) of free-agent draft (June 4, 1984). ... Traded by Twins with P Curt Wardle, OF Jim Weaver and a player to be named later to Cleveland Indians for P Bert Blyleven (August 1, 1985); Indians organization acquired P Rich Yett to complete deal (September 17, 1985). ... Traded by Indians to Pittsburgh Pirates for SS Felix Fermin (March 25, 1989). ... Traded by Pirates with 1B/3B Jeff King to Kansas City Royals for 3B Joe Randa, P Jeff Granger, P Jeff Martin and P Jeff Wallace (December 13, 1996). ... Granted free agency (November 4, 1997). ... Signed by Arizona Diamondbacks (November 17, 1997).

HONORS: Named shortstop on THE SPORTING NEWS N.L. All-Star team (1993). ... Won N.L. Gold Glove at shortstop (1993). ... Named shortstop on THE SPORTING NEWS N.L. Silver Slugger team (1993).

STATISTICAL NOTES: Led Appalachian League shortstops with 352 total chances and 43 double plays in 1984. ... Led California League shortstops with 84 double plays in 1985. ... Hit home run in first major league at-bat on first pitch (September 29, 1986). ... Led Eastern League shortstops with 613 total chances in 1986. ... Led American Association shortstops with 198 putouts, 322 assists, 30 errors and 550 total chances in 1987. ... Led N.L. with 39 sacrifice hits in 1990 and 30 in 1991. ... Had 22-game hitting streak (August 24-September 17, 1992). ... Led N.L. shortstops with 741 total chances in 1990, 754 in 1991, 816 in 1992, 794 in 1993 and 547 in 1994... ... Led N.L. shortstops with 94 double plays in 1992. ... Led N.L. second basemen with 22 errors in 1999. ... Career major league grand slams: 5.

MISCELLANEOUS: Holds Arizona Diamondbacks all-time records for most runs (211) and home runs (58).

Year Team (League)	Pos.	G	AB	R	H	2B	3B	HR	RBI	Avg.	BB	SO	SB	PO	A	E	Avg.
						BATTING								FIELDING			
1984—Elizabethton (Appl.).....	SS	66	245	43	54	12	1	6	30	.220	42	50	4	*109	*218	25	.929
1985—Visalia (Calif.)	SS	106	376	56	106	16	6	9	59	.282	41	73	10	176	330	53	.905
—Waterbury (East.)■....	SS	29	114	13	34	11	2	1	14	.298	9	16	3	41	79	6	.952
1986—Waterbury (East.)	SS	138	494	86	137	28	4	7	74	.277	87	65	10	197	*371	*45	.927
—Cleveland (A.L.)	2B-DH	5	14	3	5	2	0	1	4	.357	2	3	0	1	6	2	.778
1987—Buffalo (A.A.)■	SS-2B	110	362	71	94	15	4	17	60	.260	70	84	6	†201	†325	†30	.946
—Cleveland (A.L.)	SS	38	125	14	27	9	1	2	13	.216	8	31	2	67	93	9	.947
1988—Cleveland (A.L.)	SS-DH	73	211	23	46	5	1	2	21	.218	21	53	4	103	170	10	.965
—Colo. Springs (PCL) ...	SS	49	181	35	50	12	2	7	24	.276	26	27	3	87	171	18	.935
1989—Pittsburgh (N.L.)■	SS	78	271	33	70	13	3	2	27	.258	19	47	5	109	197	10	.968
—Buffalo (A.A.)	SS-3B	86	298	49	85	15	3	10	54	.285	38	55	12	110	223	16	.954
1990—Pittsburgh (N.L.)	SS	159	583	93	148	28	7	7	52	.254	65	109	10	*260	459	22	.970
1991—Pittsburgh (N.L.)	SS	157	608	96	164	32	8	16	67	.270	52	99	10	239	*491	*24	.968
1992—Pittsburgh (N.L.)	SS	159	632	87	167	36	6	9	55	.264	55	103	7	*268	*526	22	.973
1993—Pittsburgh (N.L.)	SS	154	604	102	187	32	9	9	51	.310	77	122	16	*256	*527	11	*.986
1994—Pittsburgh (N.L.)	SS	110	424	68	117	35	4	9	45	.276	49	82	2	152	*380	15	.973
1995—Pittsburgh (N.L.)	SS-3B	138	530	79	139	28	4	13	55	.262	55	110	2	206	415	14	.978
1996—Pittsburgh (N.L.)	SS	151	527	65	132	29	3	13	71	.250	54	108	6	215	*478	10	*.986
1997—Kansas City (A.L.)■	SS-3B	153	573	89	167	28	3	21	92	.291	71	101	10	229	450	10	.985
1998—Arizona (N.L.)■	SS-2B	155	549	79	138	29	5	20	67	.251	81	129	3	224	437	19	.972
1999—Arizona (N.L.)	2B-DH-SS	151	589	132	170	32	6	38	112	.289	82	132	7	320	340	†22	.968
American League totals (4 years)		269	923	129	245	44	5	26	130	.265	102	188	16	400	719	31	.973
National League totals (10 years)		1412	5317	834	1432	294	55	136	602	.269	589	1041	68	2249	4250	169	.975
Major League totals (14 years)		1681	6240	963	1677	338	60	162	732	.269	691	1229	84	2649	4969	200	.974

– 43 –

DIVISION SERIES RECORD

				BATTING												FIELDING			
Year	Team (League)	Pos.	G	AB	R	H	2B	3B	HR	RBI	Avg.	BB	SO	SB		PO	A	E	Avg.
1999— Arizona (N.L.)............		2B	4	14	3	4	1	0	0	3	.286	1	0	0		8	11	1	.950

CHAMPIONSHIP SERIES RECORD

RECORDS: Shares single-series record for most singles—9 (1991).

				BATTING												FIELDING			
Year	Team (League)	Pos.	G	AB	R	H	2B	3B	HR	RBI	Avg.	BB	SO	SB		PO	A	E	Avg.
1990— Pittsburgh (N.L.)		SS	6	20	3	5	1	0	1	1	.250	4	3	0		4	22	1	.963
1991— Pittsburgh (N.L.)		SS	7	29	2	12	2	0	1	1	.414	0	10	0		13	19	1	.970
1992— Pittsburgh (N.L.)		SS	7	29	3	5	2	0	1	4	.172	3	4	0		6	8	1	.933
Championship series totals (3 years)			20	78	8	22	5	0	3	6	.282	7	17	0		23	49	3	.960

ALL-STAR GAME RECORD

			BATTING										FIELDING			
Year	League	Pos.	AB	R	H	2B	3B	HR	RBI	Avg.	BB	SO	SB	PO	A	E	Avg.
1993— National		2B	1	0	0	0	0	0	0	.000	0	0	0	1	1	0	1.000
1999— National		2B	1	0	0	0	0	0	0	.000	1	1	0	0	1	0	1.000
All-Star Game totals (2 years)			2	0	0	0	0	0	0	.000	1	1	0	1	2	0	1.000

BELL, ROB　　　　　　　　　　P　　　　　　　　　　REDS

PERSONAL: Born January 17, 1977, in Newburgh, N.Y. ... 6-5/226. ... Throws right, bats right. ... Full name: Robert Allen Bell.
HIGH SCHOOL: Marlboro (N.Y.) Central.
TRANSACTIONS/CAREER NOTES: Selected by Atlanta Braves organization in third round of free-agent draft (June 1, 1995). ... Traded by Braves with OF Michael Tucker and P Denny Neagle to Cincinnati Reds for 2B Bret Boone and P Mike Remlinger (November 10, 1998). ... On Chattanooga disabled list (April 20-July 20, 1999).

Year	League	W	L	Pct.	ERA	G	GS	CG	ShO	Sv.	IP	H	R	ER	BB	SO
1995— Gulf Coast Braves (GCL)		1	6	.143	6.88	10	8	0	0	0	34	38	29	26	14	33
1996— Eugene (N.W.)		5	6	.455	5.11	16	•16	0	0	0	81	89	49	46	29	74
1997— Macon (SAL)		•14	7	.667	3.68	27	27	1	0	0	146 2/3	144	72	60	41	140
1998— Danville (Caro.)		7	9	.438	3.28	28	28	2	0	0	*178 1/3	169	79	65	46	*197
1999— Chattanooga (Sou.)■........		3	6	.333	3.13	12	12	2	1	0	72	75	30	25	17	68
— Gulf Coast Reds (GCL).......		0	0	...	1.13	2	2	0	0	0	8	3	1	1	0	11

BELLE, ALBERT　　　　　　　　　　OF　　　　　　　　　　ORIOLES

PERSONAL: Born August 25, 1966, in Shreveport, La. ... 6-2/210. ... Bats right, throws right. ... Full name: Albert Jojuan Belle. ... Formerly known as Joey Belle.
HIGH SCHOOL: Huntington (Shreveport, La.).
COLLEGE: Louisiana State.
TRANSACTIONS/CAREER NOTES: Selected by Cleveland Indians organization in second round of free-agent draft (June 2, 1987). ... On suspended list (July 12-18, 1991; August 4-8, 1992; June 4-7, 1993; August 1-7, 1994; and June 21-22, 1996). ... Granted free agency (October 28, 1996). ... Signed by Chicago White Sox (November 19, 1996). ... Granted free agency (October 27, 1998). ... Signed by Baltimore Orioles (December 1, 1998).
RECORDS: Shares major league records for fewest double plays by outfielder (150 or more games)—0 (1996 and 1997); and most home runs in two consecutive games—5 (September 18 [2] and 19 [3], 1995). ... Shares major league single-game record for most doubles—4 (August 24, 1999; and September 23, 1999). ... Shares A.L. single-season record for fewest errors by outfielder who led league in errors—8 (1998).
HONORS: Named outfielder on THE SPORTING NEWS A.L. All-Star team (1993-96 and 1998). ... Named outfielder on THE SPORTING NEWS A.L. Silver Slugger team (1993-96 and 1998). ... Named Major League Player of the Year by THE SPORTING NEWS (1995).
STATISTICAL NOTES: Hit three home runs in one game (September 4, 1992; September 19, 1995; and July 25, 1999). ... Led A.L. with 14 sacrifice flies in 1993. ... Led A.L. outfielders with seven double plays in 1993. ... Led A.L. in total bases with 294 in 1994 and 377 in 1995. ... Led A.L. with .690 slugging percentage in 1995. ... Led A.L. in grounding into double plays with 24 in 1995. ... Had 21-game hitting streak (April 27-May 21, 1996). ... Had 27-game hitting streak (May 3-June 1, 1997). ... Led A.L. in grounding into double plays with 26 in 1997. ... Led A.L. with 399 total bases, 15 sacrifice flies and .655 slugging percentage in 1998. ... Had 15-game hitting streak (September 1-17, 1999). ... Career major league grand slams: 11.
MISCELLANEOUS: Holds Cleveland Indians all-time record for most home runs (242).

				BATTING											FIELDING			
Year	Team (League)	Pos.	G	AB	R	H	2B	3B	HR	RBI	Avg.	BB	SO	SB	PO	A	E	Avg.
1987— Kinston (Caro.)............		OF	10	37	5	12	2	0	3	9	.324	8	16	0	5	0	0	1.000
1988— Kinston (Caro.)............		OF	41	153	21	46	16	0	8	39	.301	18	45	2	43	5	5	.906
— Waterloo (Midw.)		OF	9	28	2	7	1	0	1	2	.250	1	9	0	11	1	0	1.000
1989— Canton/Akron (East.)..		OF	89	312	48	88	20	0	20	69	.282	32	82	8	136	4	3	.979
— Cleveland (A.L.)..........		OF-DH	62	218	22	49	8	4	7	37	.225	12	55	2	92	3	2	.979
1990— Cleveland (A.L.)..........		DH-OF	9	23	1	4	0	0	1	3	.174	1	6	0	0	0	0	...
— Colo. Springs (PCL) ...		OF	24	96	16	33	3	1	5	19	.344	5	16	4	31	0	2	.939
— Canton/Akron (East.)..		DH	9	32	4	8	1	0	0	3	.250	3	7	0				...
1991— Cleveland (A.L.)..........		OF-DH	123	461	60	130	31	2	28	95	.282	25	99	3	170	8	•9	.952
— Colo. Springs (PCL) ...		OF	16	61	9	20	3	2	2	16	.328	2	8	1	19	1	1	.952
1992— Cleveland (A.L.)..........		DH-OF	153	585	81	152	23	1	34	112	.260	52	128	8	94	1	3	.969
1993— Cleveland (A.L.)..........		OF-DH	159	594	93	172	36	3	38	*129	.290	76	96	23	338	16	5	.986
1994— Cleveland (A.L.)..........		OF-DH	106	412	90	147	35	2	36	101	.357	58	71	9	205	8	6	.973
1995— Cleveland (A.L.)..........		OF-DH	143	546	•121	173	•52	1	*50	•126	.317	73	80	5	304	7	6	.981
1996— Cleveland (A.L.)..........		OF-DH	158	602	124	187	38	3	48	*148	.311	99	87	11	309	11	0	.970
1997— Chicago (A.L.)■..........		OF-DH	161	634	90	174	45	1	30	116	.274	53	105	4	351	11	10	.972
1998— Chicago (A.L.)............		OF-DH	163	609	113	200	48	2	49	152	.328	81	84	6	316	11	8	.976
1999— Baltimore (A.L.)■........		OF-DH	161	610	108	181	36	1	37	117	.297	101	82	17	252	•17	4	.985
Major League totals (11 years)			1398	5294	903	1569	352	20	358	1136	.296	631	893	88	2431	83	63	.976

DIVISION SERIES RECORD

							BATTING								FIELDING			
Year	Team (League)	Pos.	G	AB	R	H	2B	3B	HR	RBI	Avg.	BB	SO	SB	PO	A	E	Avg.
1995— Cleveland (A.L.).........		OF	3	11	3	3	1	0	1	3	.273	4	3	0	7	0	1	.875
1996— Cleveland (A.L.).........		OF	4	15	2	3	0	0	2	6	.200	4	2	1	11	1	0	1.000
Division series totals (2 years)			7	26	5	6	1	0	3	9	.231	8	5	1	18	1	1	.950

CHAMPIONSHIP SERIES RECORD

							BATTING								FIELDING			
Year	Team (League)	Pos.	G	AB	R	H	2B	3B	HR	RBI	Avg.	BB	SO	SB	PO	A	E	Avg.
1995— Cleveland (A.L.).........		OF	5	18	1	4	1	0	1	1	.222	3	5	0	4	0	2	.667

WORLD SERIES RECORD

							BATTING								FIELDING			
Year	Team (League)	Pos.	G	AB	R	H	2B	3B	HR	RBI	Avg.	BB	SO	SB	PO	A	E	Avg.
1995— Cleveland (A.L.).........		OF	6	17	4	4	0	0	2	4	.235	7	5	0	10	0	1	.909

ALL-STAR GAME RECORD

						BATTING								FIELDING			
Year	League	Pos.	AB	R	H	2B	3B	HR	RBI	Avg.	BB	SO	SB	PO	A	E	Avg.
1993— American		PH-DH	1	2	1	0	0	0	1	1.000	1	0	0	...	...	...	...
1994— American		OF	2	0	0	0	0	0	0	.000	0	0	0	1	0	0	1.000
1995— American		OF	3	0	0	0	0	0	0	.000	0	1	0	1	0	0	1.000
1996— American		OF	4	0	0	0	0	0	0	.000	0	3	0	1	0	0	1.000
1997— American							Did not play.										
All-Star Game totals (4 years)			10	2	1	0	0	0	1	.100	1	4	0	3	0	0	1.000

BELLIARD, RON   2B   BREWERS

PERSONAL: Born July 4, 1976, in Bronx, N.Y. ... 5-8/180. ... Bats right, throws right. ... Full name: Ronald Belliard. ... Name pronounced BELL-ee-ard.
HIGH SCHOOL: Central (Miami).
TRANSACTIONS/CAREER NOTES: Selected by Milwaukee Brewers organization in eighth round of free-agent draft (June 2, 1994).
STATISTICAL NOTES: Led Midwest League second basemen with 25 errors in 1995. ... Led Pacific Coast League second basemen with 229 putouts, 358 assists, 24 errors and 611 total chances and tied for league lead with 92 double plays in 1997. ... Led International League second basemen with 401 assists and 98 double plays in 1998.

							BATTING								FIELDING			
Year	Team (League)	Pos.	G	AB	R	H	2B	3B	HR	RBI	Avg.	BB	SO	SB	PO	A	E	Avg.
1994— Ariz. Brewers (Ariz.) ...		2B-3B-SS	39	143	32	42	7	3	0	27	.294	14	25	7	54	119	12	.935
1995— Beloit (Midw.).............		2B-3B	130	461	76	137	28	5	13	76	.297	36	67	16	221	346	†26	.956
1996— El Paso (Texas)...........		2B-DH	109	416	73	116	20	8	3	57	.279	60	51	26	246	314	16	.972
1997— Tucson (PCL)		2B-SS	118	443	80	125	35	4	4	55	.282	61	69	10	†233	†369	†26	.959
1998— Louisville (I.L.)............		2B-SS	133	507	*114	163	36	7	14	73	.321	69	77	33	231	†408	14	.979
— Milwaukee (N.L.)........		2B	8	5	1	1	0	0	0	0	.200	0	0	0	0	0	0	...
1999— Louisville (I.L.)...........		2B	29	108	14	26	4	0	1	8	.241	14	13	12	51	66	3	.975
— Milwaukee (N.L.)........		2B-3B-SS	124	457	60	135	29	4	8	58	.295	64	59	4	250	333	13	.978
Major League totals (2 years)			132	462	61	136	29	4	8	58	.294	64	59	4	250	333	13	.978

BELLINGER, CLAY   IF   YANKEES

PERSONAL: Born November 18, 1968, in Oneonta, N.Y. ... 6-3/195. ... Bats right, throws right. ... Full name: Clayton Daniel Bellinger.
HIGH SCHOOL: Oneonta (N.Y.).
COLLEGE: Rollins.
TRANSACTIONS/CAREER NOTES: Selected by San Francisco Giants organization in second round of free-agent draft (June 5, 1989). ... Granted free agency (October 16, 1995). ... Signed by Baltimore Orioles organization (November 22, 1995). ... Granted free agency (October 15, 1996). ... Signed by New York Yankees organization (November 4, 1996).

							BATTING								FIELDING			
Year	Team (League)	Pos.	G	AB	R	H	2B	3B	HR	RBI	Avg.	BB	SO	SB	PO	A	E	Avg.
1989— Everett (N.W.).............		SS	51	185	29	37	8	1	4	16	.200	19	47	3	57	110	24	.874
1990— Clinton (Midw.)		SS-3B	109	383	52	83	17	4	10	48	.217	27	102	13	144	229	29	.928
1991— San Jose (Calif.)		SS	105	368	65	95	29	2	8	62	.258	53	88	13	157	297	32	.934
1992— Shreveport (Texas)		SS	126	433	45	90	18	3	13	50	.208	36	82	7	183	346	*41	.928
1993— Phoenix (PCL)		3B-SS-1B	122	407	50	104	20	3	6	49	.256	38	81	7	123	272	28	.934
1994— Phoenix (PCL)		O-S-1-3-2-C	106	337	48	90	15	1	7	50	.267	18	56	6	248	140	8	.980
1995— Phoenix (PCL)		S-3-O-2-1-C	97	277	34	76	16	1	2	32	.274	27	52	3	116	145	8	.970
1996— Rochester (I.L.)■..		SS-1B-2B	125	459	68	138	34	4	15	78	.301	33	90	8	445	228	22	.968
1997— Columbus (I.L.)■.........		3-O-S-1-2	111	416	55	114	31	3	12	59	.274	34	74	10	187	137	15	.956
1998— Columbus (I.L.)...........		1-S-3-2-O-C	115	397	35	89	20	2	9	40	.224	35	79	6	342	185	14	.974
1999— New York (A.L.).........		3-1-D-O-2-S	32	45	12	9	2	0	1	2	.200	1	10	1	23	18	0	1.000
— Columbus (I.L.)		3-S-O-2-1	40	141	19	33	10	1	2	14	.234	13	32	6	68	89	2	.987
Major League totals (1 year)			32	45	12	9	2	0	1	2	.200	1	10	1	23	18	0	1.000

DIVISION SERIES RECORD

							BATTING								FIELDING			
Year	Team (League)	Pos.	G	AB	R	H	2B	3B	HR	RBI	Avg.	BB	SO	SB	PO	A	E	Avg.
1999— New York (A.L.).........		PR-DH	1	0	0	0	0	0	0	0	...	0	0	0	...	...	...	...

CHAMPIONSHIP SERIES RECORD

							BATTING								FIELDING			
Year	Team (League)	Pos.	G	AB	R	H	2B	3B	HR	RBI	Avg.	BB	SO	SB	PO	A	E	Avg.
1999— New York (A.L.).........		PH-SS-PR-DH	3	1	0	0	0	0	0	0	.000	0	1	0	0	1	0	1.000

WORLD SERIES RECORD

NOTES: Member of World Series championship team (1999).

Year Team (League)	Pos.	G	AB	R	H	2B	3B	HR	RBI	Avg.	BB	SO	SB	PO	A	E	Avg.
1999— New York (A.L.)								Did not play.									

RECORD AS PITCHER

Year League	W	L	Pct.	ERA	G	GS	CG	ShO	Sv.	IP	H	R	ER	BB	SO
1994— Phoenix (PCL)	0	0	...	9.00	2	0	0	0	0	2	6	2	2	0	0
1998— Columbus (I.L.)	0	0	...	0.00	1	0	0	0	0	$1/3$	1	0	0	1	0

BELTRAN, CARLOS   OF   ROYALS

B

PERSONAL: Born April 24, 1977, in Manati, Puerto Rico. ... 6-1/190. ... Bats both, throws right. ... Full name: Carlos Ivan Beltran.
HIGH SCHOOL: Fernando Callejas (Manati, Puerto Rico).
TRANSACTIONS/CAREER NOTES: Selected by Kansas City Royals organization in second round of free-agent draft (June 1, 1995).
HONORS: Named A.L. Rookie Player of the Year by THE SPORTING NEWS (1999). ... Named A.L. Rookie of the Year by Baseball Writers' Association of America (1999).
STATISTICAL NOTES: Led A.L. outfielders with 423 total chances in 1999.

Year Team (League)	Pos.	G	AB	R	H	2B	3B	HR	RBI	Avg.	BB	SO	SB	PO	A	E	Avg.
1995— GC Royals (GCL)	OF	52	180	29	50	9	0	0	23	.278	13	30	5	79	6	2	.977
1996— Lansing (Midw.)	OF	11	42	3	6	2	0	0	0	.143	1	11	1	28	2	2	.938
— Spokane (N.W.)	OF	59	215	29	58	8	3	7	29	.270	31	65	10	99	6	7	.938
1997— Wilmington (Caro.)	OF	120	419	57	96	15	4	11	46	.229	46	96	17	236	7	8	.968
1998— Wilmington (Caro.)	OF	52	192	32	53	14	0	5	32	.276	25	39	11	109	4	2	.983
— Wichita (Texas)	OF	47	182	50	64	13	3	14	44	.352	23	30	7	93	2	4	.960
— Kansas City (A.L.)	OF	14	58	12	16	5	3	0	7	.276	3	12	3	44	0	1	.978
1999— Kansas City (A.L.)	OF-DH	156	663	112	194	27	7	22	108	.293	46	123	27	395	16	*12	.972
Major League totals (2 years)		170	721	124	210	32	10	22	115	.291	49	135	30	439	16	13	.972

BELTRAN, RIGO   P   ROCKIES

PERSONAL: Born November 13, 1969, in Tijuana, Mexico. ... 5-11/185. ... Throws left, bats left. ... Full name: Rigoberto Beltran.
HIGH SCHOOL: Point Lomas (San Diego).
COLLEGE: Wyoming.
TRANSACTIONS/CAREER NOTES: Selected by St. Louis Cardinals organization in 26th round of free-agent draft (June 3, 1991). ... Traded by Cardinals to New York Mets for P Juan Acevedo (March 29, 1998). ... Traded by Mets with OF Brian McRae and OF Thomas Johnson to Colorado Rockies for OF Darryl Hamilton and P Chuck McElroy (July 31, 1999).
STATISTICAL NOTES: Led New York-Pennsylvania League with 12 balks in 1991. ... Led American Association with 18 wild pitches in 1994.
MISCELLANEOUS: Grounded out in only appearance as pinch hitter with Colorado (1999).

Year League	W	L	Pct.	ERA	G	GS	CG	ShO	Sv.	IP	H	R	ER	BB	SO
1991— Hamilton (NY-P)	5	2	.714	2.63	21	4	0	0	0	48	41	17	14	19	69
1992— Savannah (SAL)	6	1	.857	2.17	13	13	2	1	0	83	38	20	20	40	106
— St. Petersburg (FSL)	0	0	...	0.00	2	2	0	0	0	8	6	0	0	2	3
1993— Arkansas (Texas)	5	5	.500	3.25	18	16	0	0	0	$88^2/3$	74	39	32	38	82
1994— Arkansas (Texas)	4	0	1.000	0.64	4	4	1	1	0	28	12	2	2	3	21
— Louisville (A.A.)	11	11	.500	5.07	23	23	1	0	0	$138^1/3$	147	82	78	68	87
1995— Louisville (A.A.)	8	9	.471	5.21	24	24	0	0	0	$129^2/3$	156	81	75	34	92
1996— Louisville (A.A.)	8	6	.571	4.35	38	16	3	1	0	$130^1/3$	132	67	63	24	132
1997— Louisville (A.A.)	5	2	.714	2.32	9	8	1	0	0	$54^1/3$	45	17	14	21	46
— St. Louis (N.L.)	1	2	.333	3.48	35	4	0	0	1	$54^1/3$	47	25	21	17	50
1998— Norfolk (I.L.)■	6	5	.545	4.29	36	11	0	0	1	$94^1/3$	104	51	45	40	98
— New York (N.L.)	0	0	...	3.38	7	0	0	0	0	8	6	3	3	4	5
1999— Norfolk (I.L.)	2	1	.667	1.61	21	0	0	0	0	$22^1/3$	16	5	4	12	27
— New York (N.L.)	1	1	.500	3.48	21	0	0	0	0	31	30	15	12	12	35
— Colo. Springs (PCL)■	1	0	1.000	2.25	6	0	0	0	0	8	12	3	2	5	12
— Colorado (N.L.)	0	0	...	7.36	12	0	0	0	0	11	20	9	9	7	15
Major League totals (3 years)	2	3	.400	3.88	75	4	0	0	1	$104^1/3$	103	52	45	40	105

BELTRE, ADRIAN   3B   DODGERS

PERSONAL: Born April 7, 1979, in Santo Domingo, Dominican Republic. ... 5-11/170. ... Bats right, throws right. ... Name pronounced bell-TREE.
HIGH SCHOOL: Liceo Maximo Gomez (Santo Domingo, Dominican Republic).
TRANSACTIONS/CAREER NOTES: Signed as non-drafted free agent by Los Angeles Dodgers (July 7, 1994). ... On San Bernardino disabled list (June 25-July 2, 1996). ... On Albuquerque disabled list (April 23-May 1 and May 12-19, 1998).
HONORS: Named Florida State League Most Valuable Player (1997).
STATISTICAL NOTES: Led Florida State League with .561 slugging percentage and 12 intentional bases on balls in 1997. ... Led Florida State League third basemen with 26 double plays in 1997.

Year Team (League)	Pos.	G	AB	R	H	2B	3B	HR	RBI	Avg.	BB	SO	SB	PO	A	E	Avg.
1995— Dom. Dodgers (DSL) .	3B	62	218	56	67	15	3	8	40	.307	54	26	2	187	31	19	.920
1996— Savannah (SAL)	3B-2B	68	244	48	75	14	3	16	59	.307	35	46	4	55	143	19	.912
— San Bern. (Calif.)	3B-DH	63	238	40	62	13	1	10	40	.261	19	44	3	32	110	7	.953
1997— Vero Beach (FSL)	3B-OF	123	435	95	138	24	2	*26	*104	.317	67	66	25	83	231	37	.895
1998— San Antonio (Texas) ...	3B-DH	64	246	49	79	21	2	13	56	.321	39	37	20	41	130	17	.910
— Los Angeles (N.L.)	3B-SS	77	195	18	42	9	0	7	22	.215	14	37	3	32	131	13	.926
1999— Los Angeles (N.L.)	3B	152	538	84	148	27	5	15	67	.275	61	105	18	121	274	•29	.932
Major League totals (2 years)		229	733	102	190	36	5	22	89	.259	75	142	21	153	405	42	.930

PERSONAL: Born January 20, 1970, in Bluefields, Nicaragua. ... 5-9/185. ... Bats left, throws left. ... Full name: Marvin Larry Benard.
HIGH SCHOOL: Bell (Bell Gardens, Calif.).
JUNIOR COLLEGE: Los Angeles Harbor College.
COLLEGE: Lewis-Clark State (Idaho).
TRANSACTIONS/CAREER NOTES: Selected by Philadelphia Phillies organization in 20th round of free-agent draft (June 4, 1990); did not sign. ... Selected by San Francisco Giants organization in 50th round of free-agent draft (June 1, 1992). ... On Clinton disabled list (April 17-28, 1993).
STATISTICAL NOTES: Tied for Texas League lead in grounding into double plays with 15 in 1994. ... Led Texas League outfielders with five double plays in 1994.

								BATTING						FIELDING		
Year Team (League)	Pos.	G	AB	R	H	2B	3B	HR	RBI	Avg.	BB	SO	SB	PO	A	E	Avg.
1992—Everett (N.W.)............	OF	64	161	31	38	10	2	1	17	.236	24	39	17	90	8	3	.970
1993—Clinton (Midw.)	OF	112	349	84	105	14	2	5	50	.301	56	66	42	179	10	5	.974
1994—Shreveport (Texas).....	OF	125	454	66	143	32	3	4	48	.315	31	58	24	259	17	*12	.958
1995—Phoenix (PCL)............	OF-DH	111	378	70	115	14	6	6	32	.304	50	66	10	183	5	8	.959
—San Francisco (N.L.)..	OF	13	34	5	13	2	0	1	4	.382	1	7	1	19	0	0	1.000
1996—Phoenix (PCL)............	OF	4	19	2	7	0	0	0	4	.368	2	2	1	10	0	0	1.000
—San Francisco (N.L.)..	OF	135	488	89	121	17	4	5	27	.248	59	84	25	309	7	5	.984
1997—San Francisco (N.L.)..	OF-DH	84	114	13	26	4	0	1	13	.228	13	29	3	27	2	1	.967
—Phoenix (PCL)............	OF	17	60	14	20	5	0	0	5	.333	11	9	4	26	2	1	.966
1998—San Francisco (N.L.)..	OF-DH	121	286	41	92	21	1	3	36	.322	34	39	11	109	1	2	.982
1999—San Francisco (N.L.)..	OF	149	562	100	163	36	5	16	64	.290	55	97	27	323	5	4	.988
Major League totals (5 years)		502	1484	248	415	80	10	26	144	.280	162	256	67	787	15	12	.985

DIVISION SERIES RECORD

								BATTING						FIELDING		
Year Team (League)	Pos.	G	AB	R	H	2B	3B	HR	RBI	Avg.	BB	SO	SB	PO	A	E	Avg.
1997—San Francisco (N.L.)..	PH	2	2	0	0	0	0	0	0	.000	0	1	0	...	...	...	...

PERSONAL: Born January 21, 1972, in Evansville, Ind. ... 6-5/235. ... Throws right, bats right. ... Full name: Alan Paul Benes. ... Brother of Andy Benes, pitcher, St. Louis Cardinals; and brother of Adam Benes, pitcher, St. Louis Cardinals organization. ... Name pronounced BEN-ess.
HIGH SCHOOL: Lake Forest (Ill.).
COLLEGE: Creighton.
TRANSACTIONS/CAREER NOTES: Selected by San Diego Padres organization in 49th round of free-agent draft (June 4, 1990); did not sign. ... Selected by St. Louis Cardinals organization in first round (16th pick overall) of free-agent draft (June 3, 1993). ... On Louisville disabled list (May 3-August 9, 1995). ... On disabled list (July 31, 1997-remainder of season; and March 22, 1998-entire season). ... On St. Louis disabled list (March 26-September 5, 1999); included rehabilitation assignments to Arkansas (August 5-10 and August 26-30), Potomac (August 11-15 and August 31-September 3) and Memphis (August 16-25 and September 4-5).
HONORS: Named N.L. Rookie Pitcher of the Year by THE SPORTING NEWS (1996).

Year League	W	L	Pct.	ERA	G	GS	CG	ShO	Sv.	IP	H	R	ER	BB	SO
1993—Glens Falls (NY-P)	0	4	.000	3.65	7	7	0	0	0	37	39	20	15	14	29
1994—Savannah (SAL)	2	0	1.000	1.48	4	4	0	0	0	24 1/3	21	5	4	7	24
—St. Petersburg (FSL)	7	1	.875	1.61	11	11	0	0	0	78 1/3	55	18	14	15	69
—Arkansas (Texas).............	7	2	.778	2.98	13	13	1	0	0	87 2/3	58	38	29	26	75
—Louisville (A.A.)...............	1	0	1.000	2.93	2	2	1	0	0	15 1/3	10	5	5	4	16
1995—Louisville (A.A.)...............	4	2	.667	2.41	11	11	2	1	0	56	37	16	15	14	54
—St. Louis (N.L.)...............	1	2	.333	8.44	3	3	0	0	0	16	24	15	15	4	20
1996—St. Louis (N.L.)...............	13	10	.565	4.90	34	32	3	1	0	191	192	120	104	87	131
1997—St. Louis (N.L.)...............	9	9	.500	2.89	23	23	2	0	0	161 2/3	128	60	52	68	160
1998—St. Louis (N.L.)...............							Did not play.								
1999—Arkansas (Texas)	0	0	...	6.23	2	2	0	0	0	4 1/3	6	3	3	1	0
—Potomac (Caro.)...............	0	0	...	1.80	2	2	0	0	0	5	1	1	1	4	2
—Memphis (PCL)	0	1	.000	3.18	3	3	0	0	0	5 2/3	8	3	2	2	3
—St. Louis (N.L.)...............	0	0	...	0.00	2	0	0	0	0	2	2	0	0	0	2
Major League totals (4 years)	23	21	.523	4.15	62	58	5	1	0	370 2/3	346	195	171	159	313

CHAMPIONSHIP SERIES RECORD

Year League	W	L	Pct.	ERA	G	GS	CG	ShO	Sv.	IP	H	R	ER	BB	SO
1996—St. Louis (N.L.).................	0	1	.000	2.84	2	1	0	0	0	6 1/3	3	2	2	3	5

PERSONAL: Born August 20, 1967, in Evansville, Ind. ... 6-6/245. ... Throws right, bats right. ... Full name: Andrew Charles Benes. ... Brother of Alan Benes, pitcher, St. Louis Cardinals; and brother of Adam Benes, pitcher, Cardinals organization. ... Name pronounced BEN-ess.
HIGH SCHOOL: Central (Evansville, Ind.).
COLLEGE: Evansville.
TRANSACTIONS/CAREER NOTES: Selected by San Diego Padres organization in first round (first pick overall) of free-agent draft (June 1, 1988). ... On suspended list (September 28, 1993-remainder of season). ... Traded by Padres with a player to be named later to Seattle Mariners for P Ron Villone and OF Marc Newfield (July 31, 1995); Mariners acquired P Greg Keagle to complete deal (September 16, 1995). ... Granted free agency (October 31, 1995). ... Signed by St. Louis Cardinals (December 23, 1995). ... On disabled list (March 23-April 28, 1997); included rehabilitation assignments to Prince William (April 11), Louisville (April 16) and Arkansas (April 22). ... Granted free agency (October 29, 1997). ... Signed by Arizona Diamondbacks (February 3, 1998). ... Granted free agency (October 29, 1999). ... Signed by Cardinals (January 7, 2000).
RECORDS: Holds major league single-season record for fewest hits allowed for leader in most hits allowed—230 (1992).
HONORS: Named N.L. Rookie Pitcher of the Year by THE SPORTING NEWS (1989). ... Named Texas League Pitcher of the Year (1989).

STATISTICAL NOTES: Tied for N.L. lead with five balks in 1990. ... Pitched 7-0 one-hit, complete-game victory against New York (July 3, 1994).
MISCELLANEOUS: Holds San Diego Padres all-time record for most strikeouts (1,036). ... Member of 1988 U.S. Olympic baseball team (1988). ... Made an out in only appearance as pinch hitter (1998). ... Holds Arizona Diamondbacks all-time record for most wins (27) and innings pitched (429 $^2/_3$).

Year League	W	L	Pct.	ERA	G	GS	CG	ShO	Sv.	IP	H	R	ER	BB	SO
1989— Wichita (Texas)	8	4	.667	2.16	16	16	5	*3	0	108 $^1/_3$	79	32	26	39	115
— Las Vegas (PCL)	2	1	.667	8.10	5	5	0	0	0	26 $^2/_3$	41	29	24	12	29
— San Diego (N.L.)	6	3	.667	3.51	10	10	0	0	0	66 $^2/_3$	51	28	26	31	66
1990— San Diego (N.L.)	10	11	.476	3.60	32	31	2	0	0	192 $^1/_3$	177	87	77	69	140
1991— San Diego (N.L.)	15	11	.577	3.03	33	33	4	1	0	223	194	76	75	59	167
1992— San Diego (N.L.)	13	14	.481	3.35	34	34	2	2	0	231 $^1/_3$	*230	90	86	61	169
1993— San Diego (N.L.)	15	15	.500	3.78	34	34	4	2	0	230 $^2/_3$	200	111	97	86	179
1994— San Diego (N.L.)	6	*14	.300	3.86	25	25	2	2	0	172 $^1/_3$	155	82	74	51	*189
1995— San Diego (N.L.)	4	7	.364	4.17	19	19	1	1	0	118 $^2/_3$	121	65	55	45	126
— Seattle (A.L.)■	7	2	.778	5.86	12	12	0	0	0	63	72	42	41	33	45
1996— St. Louis (N.L.)■	18	10	.643	3.83	36	34	3	1	1	230 $^1/_3$	215	107	98	77	160
1997— Prince William (Caro.)	0	0	...	0.00	1	1	0	0	0	5	3	1	0	1	9
— Louisville (A.A.)	0	0	...	1.80	1	1	0	0	0	5	3	1	1	1	5
— Arkansas (Texas)	1	0	1.000	1.29	1	1	0	0	0	7	2	1	1	2	6
— St. Louis (N.L.)	10	7	.588	3.10	26	26	0	0	0	177	149	64	61	61	175
1998— Arizona (N.L.)■	14	13	.519	3.97	34	34	1	0	0	231 $^1/_3$	221	111	102	74	164
1999— Arizona (N.L.)	13	12	.520	4.81	33	32	0	0	0	198 $^1/_3$	216	117	106	82	141
A.L. totals (1 year)	7	2	.778	5.86	12	12	0	0	0	63	72	42	41	33	45
N.L. totals (11 years)	124	117	.515	3.72	316	312	19	9	1	2072	1929	938	857	696	1676
Major League totals (11 years)	131	119	.524	3.79	328	324	19	9	1	2135	2001	980	898	729	1721

DIVISION SERIES RECORD

Year League	W	L	Pct.	ERA	G	GS	CG	ShO	Sv.	IP	H	R	ER	BB	SO
1995— Seattle (A.L.)	0	0	...	5.40	2	2	0	0	0	11 $^2/_3$	10	7	7	9	8
1996— St. Louis (N.L.)	0	0	...	5.14	1	1	0	0	0	7	6	4	4	1	9
Division series totals (2 years)	0	0	...	5.30	3	3	0	0	0	18 $^2/_3$	16	11	11	10	17

CHAMPIONSHIP SERIES RECORD

RECORDS: Shares N.L. single-series record for most hits allowed—19 (1996).

Year League	W	L	Pct.	ERA	G	GS	CG	ShO	Sv.	IP	H	R	ER	BB	SO
1995— Seattle (A.L.)	0	1	.000	23.14	1	1	0	0	0	2 $^1/_3$	6	6	6	2	3
1996— St. Louis (N.L.)	0	0	...	5.28	3	2	0	0	0	15 $^1/_3$	19	9	9	3	9
Champ. series totals (2 years)	0	1	.000	7.64	4	3	0	0	0	17 $^2/_3$	25	15	15	5	12

ALL-STAR GAME RECORD

Year League	W	L	Pct.	ERA	GS	CG	ShO	Sv.	IP	H	R	ER	BB	SO
1993— National	0	0	...	4.50	0	0	0	0	2	2	1	1	0	2

BENITEZ, ARMANDO   P   METS

PERSONAL: Born November 3, 1972, in Ramon Santana, Dominican Republic. ... 6-4/229. ... Throws right, bats right.
TRANSACTIONS/CAREER NOTES: Signed as non-drafted free agent by Baltimore Orioles organization (April 1, 1990). ... On Baltimore disabled list (April 20-August 26, 1996); included rehabilitation assignments to Bowie (May 17-19) and Gulf Coast Orioles (August 13-26). ... On suspended list (May 20-28, 1998). ... Traded by Orioles to New York Mets for C Charles Johnson (December 1, 1998).

Year League	W	L	Pct.	ERA	G	GS	CG	ShO	Sv.	IP	H	R	ER	BB	SO
1990—					Dominican Summer League statistics unavailable.										
1991— Gulf Coast Orioles (GCL)	3	2	.600	2.72	14	3	0	0	0	36 $^1/_3$	35	16	11	11	33
1992— Bluefield (Appl.)	1	2	.333	4.31	25	0	0	0	5	31 $^1/_3$	35	31	15	23	37
1993— Albany (SAL)	5	1	.833	1.52	40	0	0	0	14	53 $^1/_3$	31	10	9	19	83
— Frederick (Caro.)	3	0	1.000	0.66	12	0	0	0	4	13 $^2/_3$	7	1	1	4	29
1994— Bowie (East.)	8	4	.667	3.14	53	0	0	0	16	71 $^2/_3$	41	29	25	39	106
— Baltimore (A.L.)	0	0	...	0.90	3	0	0	0	0	10	8	1	1	4	14
1995— Baltimore (A.L.)	1	5	.167	5.66	44	0	0	0	2	47 $^2/_3$	37	33	30	37	56
— Rochester (I.L.)	2	2	.500	1.25	17	0	0	0	8	21 $^2/_3$	10	4	3	7	37
1996— Baltimore (A.L.)	1	0	1.000	3.77	18	0	0	0	4	14 $^1/_3$	7	6	6	6	20
— Gulf Coast Orioles (GCL)	1	0	1.000	0.00	1	0	0	0	0	2	1	0	0	0	5
— Bowie (East.)	0	0	...	4.50	4	4	0	0	0	6	7	3	3	0	8
— Rochester (I.L.)	0	0	...	2.25	2	0	0	0	0	4	3	1	1	1	5
1997— Baltimore (A.L.)	4	5	.444	2.45	71	0	0	0	9	73 $^1/_3$	49	22	20	43	106
1998— Baltimore (A.L.)	5	6	.455	3.82	71	0	0	0	22	68 $^1/_3$	48	29	29	39	87
1999— New York (N.L.)■	4	3	.571	1.85	77	0	0	0	22	78	40	17	16	41	128
A.L. totals (5 years)	11	16	.407	3.62	207	0	0	0	37	213 $^2/_3$	149	91	86	129	283
N.L. totals (1 year)	4	3	.571	1.85	77	0	0	0	22	78	40	17	16	41	128
Major League totals (6 years)	15	19	.441	3.15	284	0	0	0	59	291 $^2/_3$	189	108	102	170	411

DIVISION SERIES RECORD

Year League	W	L	Pct.	ERA	G	GS	CG	ShO	Sv.	IP	H	R	ER	BB	SO
1996— Baltimore (A.L.)	2	0	1.000	2.25	3	0	0	0	0	4	1	1	1	2	6
1997— Baltimore (A.L.)	0	0	...	3.00	3	0	0	0	0	3	3	1	1	2	4
1999— New York (N.L.)	0	0	...	0.00	2	0	0	0	0	2 $^1/_3$	2	0	0	1	2
Division series totals (3 years)	2	0	1.000	1.93	8	0	0	0	0	9 $^1/_3$	6	2	2	5	12

CHAMPIONSHIP SERIES RECORD

Year League	W	L	Pct.	ERA	G	GS	CG	ShO	Sv.	IP	H	R	ER	BB	SO
1996— Baltimore (A.L.)	0	0	...	7.71	3	0	0	0	1	2 $^1/_3$	3	2	2	4	2
1997— Baltimore (A.L.)	0	2	.000	12.00	4	0	0	0	0	3	3	4	4	4	6
1999— New York (N.L.)	0	0	...	1.35	5	0	0	0	1	6 $^2/_3$	3	1	1	2	9
Champ. series totals (3 years)	0	2	.000	5.25	12	0	0	0	2	12	9	7	7	10	17

BENJAMIN, MIKE   IF   PIRATES

PERSONAL: Born November 22, 1965, in Euclid, Ohio. ... 6-0/172. ... Bats right, throws right. ... Full name: Michael Paul Benjamin.
HIGH SCHOOL: Bellflower (Calif.).
JUNIOR COLLEGE: Cerritos College (Calif.).
COLLEGE: Arizona State.
TRANSACTIONS/CAREER NOTES: Selected by Minnesota Twins organization in seventh round of free-agent draft (January 9, 1985); did not sign. ... Selected by San Francisco Giants organization in third round of free-agent draft (June 2, 1987). ... On San Francisco disabled list (March 31-June 5, 1992); included rehabilitation assignment to Phoenix (April 20-May 10). ... On San Francisco disabled list (July 8-August 6, 1993); included rehabilitation assignment to San Jose (August 4-6). ... Traded by Giants to Philadelphia Phillies for P Jeff Juden and OF/1B Tommy Eason (October 6, 1995). ... On Philadelphia disabled list (March 23-April 26 and July 20, 1996-remainder of season); included rehabilitation assignments to Clearwater (April 8-17) and Scranton/Wilkes-Barre (April 21-26). ... Granted free agency (October 8, 1996). ... Signed by Boston Red Sox organization (January 31, 1997). ... Granted free agency (October 27, 1997). ... Re-signed by Red Sox (November 21, 1997). ... Granted free agency (October 26, 1998). ... Signed by Pittsburgh Pirates (November 17, 1998). ... On disabled list (July 24-August 11, 1999).
RECORDS: Holds modern major league record for most hits in three consecutive games—14 (June 11 [4], 13 [4] and 14 [6], 1995).
STATISTICAL NOTES: Led Pacific Coast League shortstops with 626 total chances in 1990. ... Collected six hits in one game (June 14, 1995).

| | | | | | | | BATTING | | | | | | | FIELDING | | |
Year Team (League)	Pos.	G	AB	R	H	2B	3B	HR	RBI	Avg.	BB	SO	SB	PO	A	E	Avg.
1987— Fresno (Calif.)............	SS	64	212	25	51	6	4	6	24	.241	24	71	6	89	188	21	.930
1988— Shreveport (Texas).....	SS	89	309	48	73	19	5	6	37	.236	22	63	14	134	248	11	.972
— Phoenix (PCL)............	SS	37	106	13	18	4	1	0	6	.170	13	32	2	41	74	4	.966
1989— Phoenix (PCL)............	SS-2B	113	363	44	94	17	6	3	36	.259	18	82	10	149	332	15	.970
— San Francisco (N.L.) ..	SS	14	6	6	1	0	0	0	0	.167	0	1	0	4	4	0	1.000
1990— Phoenix (PCL)............	SS	118	419	61	105	21	7	5	39	.251	25	89	13	*216	*386	24	.962
— San Francisco (N.L.) ..	SS	22	56	7	12	3	1	2	3	.214	3	10	1	29	53	1	.988
1991— San Francisco (N.L.) ..	SS-3B	54	106	12	13	3	0	2	8	.123	7	26	3	64	123	3	.984
— Phoenix (PCL)............	SS	64	226	34	46	13	2	6	31	.204	20	67	3	109	252	9	.976
1992— San Francisco (N.L.) ..	SS-3B	40	75	4	13	2	1	1	3	.173	4	15	1	34	71	1	.991
— Phoenix (PCL)............	SS	31	108	15	33	10	2	0	17	.306	3	18	4	51	92	2	.986
1993— San Francisco (N.L.) ..	SS-2B-3B	63	146	22	29	7	0	4	16	.199	9	23	0	74	133	5	.976
— San Jose (Calif.)........	SS-2B	2	8	1	0	0	0	0	0	.000	1	0	0	1	5	0	1.000
1994— San Francisco (N.L.) ..	3B-2B-SS	38	62	9	16	5	1	1	9	.258	5	16	5	33	70	3	.972
1995— San Francisco (N.L.) ..	3B-SS-2B	68	186	19	41	6	0	3	12	.220	8	51	11	51	121	4	.977
1996— Clearwater (FSL)■.....	SS	8	23	3	4	1	0	0	4	.174	3	4	1	9	20	2	.935
— Scranton/W.B. (I.L.) ..	SS	4	13	2	5	2	0	0	4	.385	3	0	0	3	12	0	1.000
— Philadelphia (N.L.)......	SS-2B	35	103	13	23	5	1	4	13	.223	12	21	3	38	87	6	.954
1997— Pawtucket (I.L.)■........	S-D-3-2	33	105	12	26	4	1	4	12	.248	8	20	4	46	86	5	.964
— Boston (A.L.)..............3-S-2-1-D-P	49	116	12	27	9	1	0	7	.233	4	27	2	50	81	6	.956
1998— Boston (A.L.)............2-S-3-1-DH	124	349	46	95	23	0	4	39	.272	15	73	3	233	275	3	.994
1999— Pittsburgh (N.L.)■.....	SS-2B-3B	110	368	42	91	26	7	1	37	.247	20	90	10	162	334	8	.984
American League totals (2 years)		173	465	58	122	32	1	4	46	.262	19	100	5	283	356	9	.986
National League totals (9 years)		444	1108	134	239	57	11	18	101	.216	68	253	34	489	996	31	.980
Major League totals (11 years)		617	1573	192	361	89	12	22	147	.229	87	353	39	772	1352	40	.982

DIVISION SERIES RECORD

| | | | | | | | BATTING | | | | | | | FIELDING | | |
Year Team (League)	Pos.	G	AB	R	H	2B	3B	HR	RBI	Avg.	BB	SO	SB	PO	A	E	Avg.
1998— Boston (A.L.)..............	2B-1B	4	11	1	1	0	0	0	0	.091	1	3	0	13	9	0	1.000

RECORD AS PITCHER

Year League	W	L	Pct.	ERA	G	GS	CG	ShO	Sv.	IP	H	R	ER	BB	SO
1997— Boston (A.L.)....................	0	0	...	0.00	1	0	0	0	0	1	0	0	0	0	0

BENNETT, GARY   C   PHILLIES

PERSONAL: Born April 17, 1972, in Waukegan, Ill. ... 6-0/208. ... Bats right, throws right. ... Full name: Gary David Bennett Jr.
HIGH SCHOOL: Waukegan East (Ill.).
TRANSACTIONS/CAREER NOTES: Selected by Philadelphia Phillies organization in 11th round of free-agent draft (June 4, 1990). ... On Clearwater disabled list (September 5-15, 1993). ... Granted free agency (October 8, 1996). ... Signed by Boston Red Sox organization (February 10, 1997). ... Granted free agency (October 15, 1997). ... Signed by Phillies organization (December 27, 1997).
STATISTICAL NOTES: Led Eastern League with 22 passed balls in 1994. ... Led Eastern League catchers with 13 double plays in 1995.

| | | | | | | | BATTING | | | | | | | FIELDING | | |
Year Team (League)	Pos.	G	AB	R	H	2B	3B	HR	RBI	Avg.	BB	SO	SB	PO	A	E	Avg.
1990— Martinsville (Appl.).....	C	16	52	3	14	2	1	0	10	.269	4	15	0	80	3	3	.965
1991— Martinsville (Appl.).....	C	41	136	15	32	7	0	1	16	.235	17	26	0	291	34	2	.994
1992— Batavia (NY-P)............	C	47	146	22	30	2	0	0	12	.205	15	27	2	292	42	2	*.994
1993— Spartanburg (SAL).....	C	42	126	18	32	4	1	0	15	.254	12	22	0	199	35	2	.992
— Clearwater (FSL)	C	17	55	5	18	0	0	1	6	.327	3	10	0	70	12	0	1.000
1994— Clearwater (FSL)	C	19	55	6	13	3	0	0	10	.236	8	6	0	101	10	1	.991
— Reading (East.)..........	C	63	208	13	48	9	0	3	22	.231	14	26	0	376	64	2	.995
1995— Reading (East.)..........	C-DH	86	271	27	64	11	0	4	40	.236	22	36	0	551	65	4	.994
— Scranton/W.B. (I.L.) ...	C	7	20	1	3	0	0	0	1	.150	2	2	0	38	4	0	1.000
— Philadelphia (N.L.)......	PH	1	1	0	0	0	0	0	0	.000	0	1	0	...	...	...	...
1996— Scranton/W.B. (I.L.) ...	C	91	286	37	71	15	1	8	37	.248	24	43	1	517	61	7	.988
— Philadelphia (N.L.)......	C	6	16	0	4	0	0	0	1	.250	2	6	0	35	5	0	1.000
1997— Pawtucket (I.L.)■........	C-1B	71	224	16	48	7	1	4	22	.214	18	39	1	528	36	8	.986
1998— Scranton/W.B. (I.L.)■.	C-DH-1B	86	282	33	72	18	0	10	40	.255	25	41	0	425	35	1	.998
— Philadelphia (N.L.)......	C	9	31	4	9	0	0	0	3	.290	5	5	0	50	2	0	1.000
1999— Philadelphia (N.L.)......	C	36	88	7	24	4	0	1	21	.273	4	11	0	129	6	4	.971
Major League totals (4 years)		52	136	11	37	4	0	1	25	.272	11	23	0	214	13	4	.983

BENNETT, JOEL   P

PERSONAL: Born January 31, 1970, in Binghamton, N.Y. ... 6-1/160. ... Throws right, bats right. ... Full name: Joel Todd Bennett.
HIGH SCHOOL: Windsor (N.Y.) Central.
COLLEGE: East Stroudsburg (Pa.).
TRANSACTIONS/CAREER NOTES: Selected by Boston Red Sox organization in 21st round of free-agent draft (June 3, 1991). ... On disabled list (July 8-August 3, 1995). ... Released by Red Sox (May 6, 1996). ... Signed by Baltimore Orioles organization (July 27, 1996). ... Released by Orioles (July 27, 1998). ... Signed by Philadelphia Phillies organization (July 30, 1998). ... Granted free agency (October 15, 1998). ... Re-signed by Phillies organization (November 5, 1998). ... Granted free agency (October 6, 1999).
STATISTICAL NOTES: Tied for Carolina League lead with six intentional bases on balls issued in 1993.

Year League	W	L	Pct.	ERA	G	GS	CG	ShO	Sv.	IP	H	R	ER	BB	SO
1991—GC Red Sox (GCL)	0	0	...	1.80	2	2	0	0	0	10	6	2	2	4	8
—Elmira (NY-P)	5	3	.625	2.44	13	12	1	1	0	81	60	29	22	30	75
1992—Winter Haven (FSL)	7	11	.389	4.23	26	26	4	0	0	161 2/3	161	*86	*76	55	154
1993—Lynchburg (Caro.)	7	•12	.368	3.83	29	*29	3	1	0	*181	151	93	77	67	*221
1994—New Britain (East.)	11	7	.611	4.06	23	23	1	1	0	130 2/3	119	65	59	56	130
—Pawtucket (I.L.)	1	3	.250	6.86	4	4	0	0	0	21	19	16	16	12	24
1995—Pawtucket (I.L.)	2	4	.333	5.84	20	13	0	0	0	77	91	57	50	45	50
1996—Trenton (East.)	1	0	1.000	8.31	3	0	0	0	0	4 1/3	3	4	4	2	8
—Bowie (East.)■	2	3	.400	3.29	10	8	0	0	0	54 2/3	36	21	20	17	48
1997—Bowie (East.)	6	8	.429	3.18	44	10	0	0	4	113 1/3	89	45	40	40	146
1998—Rochester (I.L.)	10	0	1.000	3.64	18	15	1	0	0	101 1/3	99	46	41	37	99
—Baltimore (A.L.)	0	0	...	4.50	2	0	0	0	0	2	2	1	1	3	0
—Scranton/W.B. (I.L.)■	1	2	.333	5.29	8	7	0	0	0	47 2/3	51	29	28	25	35
1999—Scranton/W.B. (I.L.)	10	4	.714	4.61	20	20	1	1	0	127	134	71	65	47	125
—Philadelphia (N.L.)	2	1	.667	9.00	5	3	0	0	0	17	26	17	17	7	13
A.L. totals (1 year)	0	0	...	4.50	2	0	0	0	0	2	2	1	1	3	0
N.L. totals (1 year)	2	1	.667	9.00	5	3	0	0	0	17	26	17	17	7	13
Major League totals (2 years)	2	1	.667	8.53	7	3	0	0	0	19	28	18	18	10	13

BENNETT, SHAYNE   P   EXPOS

PERSONAL: Born April 10, 1972, in Adelaide, Australia. ... 6-5/220. ... Throws right, bats right. ... Full name: Shayne Anthony Bennett.
JUNIOR COLLEGE: DuPage (Ill.) Junior College.
TRANSACTIONS/CAREER NOTES: Selected by Boston Red Sox organization in 25th round of free-agent draft (June 2, 1993). ... Traded by Red Sox with P Rheal Cormier and 1B Ryan McGuire to Montreal Expos for SS Wil Cordero and P Bryan Eversgerd (January 10, 1996).

Year League	W	L	Pct.	ERA	G	GS	CG	ShO	Sv.	IP	H	R	ER	BB	SO
1993—GC Red Sox (GCL)	0	0	...	1.29	2	1	0	0	1	7	2	1	1	1	4
—Fort Lauderdale (FSL)	1	2	.333	1.72	23	0	0	0	6	31 1/3	26	8	6	11	23
1994—Sarasota (FSL)	1	6	.143	4.47	15	8	0	0	3	48 1/3	46	31	24	27	28
1995—Sarasota (FSL)	2	5	.286	2.56	52	0	0	0	24	59 2/3	50	23	17	21	69
—Trenton (East.)	0	1	.000	5.06	10	0	0	0	3	10 2/3	16	6	6	3	6
1996—Harrisburg (East.)■	8	8	.500	2.53	53	0	0	0	12	92 2/3	83	32	26	35	89
1997—Harrisburg (East.)	4	2	.667	4.40	23	1	0	0	2	47	47	28	23	20	38
—Ottawa (I.L.)	1	2	.333	1.57	25	0	0	0	14	34 1/3	23	8	6	21	29
—Montreal (N.L.)	0	1	.000	3.18	16	0	0	0	0	22 2/3	21	9	8	9	8
1998—Montreal (N.L.)	5	5	.500	5.50	62	0	0	0	1	91 2/3	97	61	56	45	59
1999—Ottawa (I.L.)	3	9	.250	5.04	38	8	0	0	8	89 1/3	96	53	50	37	70
—Montreal (N.L.)	0	1	.000	14.29	5	1	0	0	0	11 1/3	24	18	18	3	4
Major League totals (3 years)	5	7	.417	5.87	83	1	0	0	1	125 2/3	142	88	82	57	71

BENOIT, JOAQUIN   P   RANGERS

PERSONAL: Born July 26, 1979, in Santiago, Dominican Republic. ... 6-3/205. ... Throws right, bats right. ... Full name: Joaquin A. Benoit.
TRANSACTIONS/CAREER NOTES: Signed as non-drafted free agent by Texas Rangers organization (May 20, 1996).

Year League	W	L	Pct.	ERA	G	GS	CG	ShO	Sv.	IP	H	R	ER	BB	SO
1996—Dom. Rangers (DSL)	6	5	.545	2.28	14	13	2	1	0	75	63	26	19	23	63
1997—GC Rangers (GCL)	3	3	.500	2.05	10	10	1	0	0	44	40	14	10	11	38
1998—Savannah (SAL)	4	3	.571	3.83	15	1	0	0	0	80	79	41	34	18	68
1999—Charlotte (FSL)	7	4	.636	5.31	22	22	0	0	0	105	117	67	62	50	83

BENSON, KRIS   P   PIRATES

PERSONAL: Born November 7, 1974, in Kennesaw, Ga. ... 6-4/188. ... Throws right, bats right. ... Full name: Kristen James Benson.
HIGH SCHOOL: Spayberry (Marietta, Ga.).
COLLEGE: Clemson.
TRANSACTIONS/CAREER NOTES: Selected by Pittsburgh Pirates organization in first round (first pick overall) of free-agent draft (June 2, 1996).
STATISTICAL NOTES: Tied for N.L. lead in double plays by a pitcher with six in 1999.
MISCELLANEOUS: Member of 1996 U.S. Olympic baseball team.

Year League	W	L	Pct.	ERA	G	GS	CG	ShO	Sv.	IP	H	R	ER	BB	SO
1997—Lynchburg (Caro.)	5	2	.714	2.58	10	10	0	0	0	59 1/3	49	20	17	13	72
—Carolina (Sou.)	3	5	.375	4.98	14	14	0	0	0	68 2/3	81	49	38	32	66
1998—Nashville (PCL)	8	10	.444	5.37	28	28	1	1	0	156	162	102	93	50	129
1999—Pittsburgh (N.L.)	11	14	.440	4.07	31	31	2	0	0	196 2/3	184	105	89	83	139
Major League totals (1 year)	11	14	.440	4.07	31	31	2	0	0	196 2/3	184	105	89	83	139

B

PERSONAL: Born May 26, 1971, in Cambridge, Mass. ... 6-4/189. ... Throws right, bats right. ... Full name: Jason Phillip Bere. ... Name pronounced burr-AY.
HIGH SCHOOL: Wilmington (Mass.).
JUNIOR COLLEGE: Middlesex Community College (Mass.).
TRANSACTIONS/CAREER NOTES: Selected by Chicago White Sox organization in 36th round of free-agent draft (June 4, 1990). ... On Chicago disabled list (August 5-20, 1995); included rehabilitation assignment to South Bend (August 13-18). ... On Chicago disabled list (April 22-September 3 and September 14, 1996-remainder of season); included rehabilitation assignments to Nashville (May 14-19 and August 27-28), Gulf Coast White Sox (August 5-10), Hickory (August 10-16) and Birmingham (August 16-27). ... On Chicago disabled list (March 31-August 19, 1997); included rehabilitation assignments to Gulf Coast White Sox (July 2-7), Hickory (July 12), Birmingham (July 17-22) and Nashville (July 29-August 14). ... Released by White Sox (July 16, 1998). ... Signed by Cincinnati Reds organization (July 21, 1998). ... On Cincinnati disabled list (June 16-August 4, 1999); included rehabilitation assignment to Indianapolis (July 11-August 4). ... Released by Reds (August 4, 1999). ... Signed by Milwaukee Brewers organization (August 13, 1999). ... Granted free agency (November 1, 1999). ... Re-signed by Brewers (November 19, 1999).

Year — League	W	L	Pct.	ERA	G	GS	CG	ShO	Sv.	IP	H	R	ER	BB	SO
1990— GC White Sox (GCL)	0	4	.000	2.37	16	2	0	0	1	38	26	19	10	19	41
1991— South Bend (Midw.)	9	12	.429	2.87	27	27	2	1	0	163	116	66	52	*100	158
1992— Sarasota (FSL)	7	2	.778	2.41	18	18	1	1	0	116	84	35	31	34	106
— Birmingham (Sou.).............	4	4	.500	3.00	8	8	4	2	0	54	44	22	18	20	45
— Vancouver (PCL)	0	0	...	0.00	1	0	0	0	0	1	2	0	0	0	2
1993— Nashville (A.A.)	5	1	.833	2.37	8	8	0	0	0	49 1/3	36	19	13	25	52
— Chicago (A.L.)	12	5	.706	3.47	24	24	1	0	0	142 2/3	109	60	55	81	129
1994— Chicago (A.L.)	12	2	*.857	3.81	24	24	0	0	0	141 2/3	119	65	60	80	127
1995— Chicago (A.L.)	8	•15	.348	7.19	27	27	1	0	0	137 2/3	151	120	110	106	110
— Nashville (A.A.)	1	0	1.000	3.38	1	1	0	0	0	5 1/3	6	2	2	2	7
1996— Chicago (A.L.)	0	1	.000	10.26	5	5	0	0	0	16 2/3	26	19	19	18	19
— Nashville (A.A.)	0	0	...	1.42	3	3	0	0	0	12 2/3	9	2	2	4	15
— GC White Sox (GCL)	0	1	.000	6.00	1	1	0	0	0	3	3	2	2	1	3
— Hickory (SAL)...................	1	0	1.000	0.00	1	1	0	0	0	5	3	0	0	0	5
— Birmingham (Sou.).............	0	0	...	4.15	1	1	0	0	0	4 1/3	4	2	2	4	5
1997— GC White Sox (GCL)	0	0	...	0.00	2	2	0	0	0	5	2	0	0	0	5
— Hickory (SAL)	0	0	...	6.00	1	1	0	0	0	3	4	2	2	0	2
— Birmingham (Sou.).............	1	0	.000	7.71	2	2	0	0	0	7	8	7	6	2	7
— Nashville (A.A.)	1	1	.500	5.59	4	4	0	0	0	19 1/3	23	13	12	7	13
— Chicago (A.L.)	4	2	.667	4.71	6	6	0	0	0	28 2/3	20	15	15	17	21
1998— Chicago (A.L.)	3	7	.300	6.45	18	15	0	0	0	83 2/3	98	71	60	58	53
— Cincinnati (N.L.)■............	3	2	.600	4.12	9	7	0	0	0	43 2/3	39	20	20	20	31
1999— Cincinnati (N.L.)	3	0	1.000	6.85	12	10	0	0	0	43 1/3	56	37	33	40	28
— Indianapolis (I.L.)	0	2	.000	10.19	5	4	0	0	0	17 2/3	25	20	20	19	8
— Louisville (I.L.)■.................	2	1	.667	2.08	5	5	0	0	0	26	21	8	6	8	27
— Milwaukee (N.L.).................	2	0	1.000	4.63	5	4	0	0	0	23 1/3	23	15	12	10	19
A.L. totals (6 years)	39	32	.549	5.21	104	101	2	0	0	551	523	350	319	360	459
N.L. totals (2 years)	8	2	.800	5.30	26	21	0	0	0	110 1/3	118	72	65	70	78
Major League totals (7 years).......	47	34	.580	5.23	130	122	2	0	0	661 1/3	641	422	384	430	537

CHAMPIONSHIP SERIES RECORD

Year — League	W	L	Pct.	ERA	G	GS	CG	ShO	Sv.	IP	H	R	ER	BB	SO
1993— Chicago (A.L.)	0	0	...	11.57	1	1	0	0	0	2 1/3	5	3	3	2	3

ALL-STAR GAME RECORD

Year — League	W	L	Pct.	ERA	GS	CG	ShO	Sv.	IP	H	R	ER	BB	SO
1994— American	0	1	.000	...	0	0	0	0	2	1	1	0	0	

PERSONAL: Born September 3, 1970, in Roseville, Calif. ... 5-11/185. ... Bats right, throws right. ... Full name: David Scott Berg.
HIGH SCHOOL: Roseville (Calif.).
JUNIOR COLLEGE: Sacramento City College.
COLLEGE: Miami (Fla.).
TRANSACTIONS/CAREER NOTES: Selected by California Angels organization in 32nd round of free-agent draft (June 4, 1990); did not sign. ... Selected by Florida Marlins organization in 38th round of free-agent draft (June 3, 1993).
STATISTICAL NOTES: Led New York-Penn League third basemen with 158 assists in 1993. ... Led Midwest League third basemen with .948 fielding percentage in 1994.

Year — Team (League)	Pos.	G	AB	R	H	2B	3B	HR	RBI	Avg.	BB	SO	SB	PO	A	E	Avg.
1993— Elmira (NY-P)	3B-2B-OF	75	281	37	74	13	1	4	28	.263	34	37	7	55	†193	20	.925
1994— Kane County (Midw.)..	3B-2B	121	437	80	117	27	8	9	53	.268	54	80	8	73	236	17	†.948
1995— Brevard County (FSL).	SS-3B-2B	114	382	71	114	18	1	3	39	.298	68	61	9	157	348	26	.951
1996— Portland (East.)	SS-3B	109	414	64	125	28	5	9	73	.302	42	60	17	143	358	26	.951
1997— Charlotte (I.L.)	SS-2B-3B	117	424	76	125	26	6	9	47	.295	55	71	16	136	324	22	.954
1998— Florida (N.L.)	2B-3B-SS	81	182	18	57	11	0	2	21	.313	26	46	3	90	130	7	.969
1999— Florida (N.L.)	S-2-3-0	109	304	42	87	18	1	3	25	.286	27	59	2	103	195	8	.974
Major League totals (2 years)		190	486	60	144	29	1	5	46	.296	53	105	5	193	325	15	.972

PERSONAL: Born November 9, 1977, in Greenfield, Mass. ... 6-0/185. ... Bats left, throws right. ... Full name: Peter F. Bergeron.
HIGH SCHOOL: Greenfield (Mass.).

TRANSACTIONS/CAREER NOTES: Selected by Los Angeles Dodgers organization in fourth round of free-agent draft (June 4, 1996). ... Traded by Dodgers with 2B Wilton Guerrero, P Ted Lilly and 1B Jonathan Tucker to Montreal Expos for P Carlos Perez, SS Mark Grudzielanek and OF Hiram Bocachica (July 31, 1998).
STATISTICAL NOTES: Led Texas League outfielders with five double plays in 1998.

Year Team (League)	Pos.	G	AB	R	H	2B	3B	HR	RBI	Avg.	BB	SO	SB	PO	A	E	Avg.
1996—Yakima (N.W.)	OF	61	232	36	59	5	3	5	21	.254	28	59	13	99	3	1	*.990
1997—Savannah (SAL)	OF	131	492	89	138	18	5	5	36	.280	67	110	32	240	8	4	.984
—San Bern. (Calif.)	OF	2	8	1	2	0	0	0	1	.250	0	2	2	5	1	0	1.000
1998—San Antonio (Texas)	OF	109	416	81	132	17	8	8	54	.317	61	69	33	228	17	2	*.992
—Harrisburg (East.)■	OF	34	134	22	33	8	4	0	9	.246	17	26	8	67	5	0	1.000
1999—Harrisburg (East.)	OF-DH	42	162	29	53	14	2	4	18	.327	24	29	9	72	1	1	.986
—Ottawa (I.L.)	OF-DH	58	194	36	61	12	3	3	20	.314	23	40	14	64	8	2	.973
—Montreal (N.L.)	OF	16	45	12	11	2	0	0	1	.244	9	5	0	27	2	1	.967
Major League totals (1 year)		16	45	12	11	2	0	0	1	.244	9	5	0	27	2	1	.967

B

BERGMAN, SEAN — P — TWINS

PERSONAL: Born April 11, 1970, in Joliet, Ill. ... 6-4/225. ... Throws right, bats right. ... Full name: Sean Frederick Bergman.
HIGH SCHOOL: Joliet (Ill.) Catholic Academy.
COLLEGE: Southern Illinois-Carbondale.
TRANSACTIONS/CAREER NOTES: Selected by Detroit Tigers organization in fourth round of free-agent draft (June 3, 1991). ... On Detroit disabled list (June 26-July 17, 1995); included rehabilitation assignment to Toledo (July 10-17). ... Traded by Tigers with P Cade Gaspar and OF Todd Steverson to San Diego Padres for P Richie Lewis, OF Melvin Nieves and C Raul Casanova (March 22, 1996). ... Traded by Padres to Houston Astros for OF James Mouton (January 14, 1998). ... On Houston disabled list (June 27-August 6, 1999); included rehabilitation assignment to New Orleans (July 25-August 1). ... Released by Astros (August 31, 1999). ... Signed by Atlanta Braves (September 5, 1999). ... Claimed on waivers by Minnesota Twins (October 12, 1999).
MISCELLANEOUS: Fouled out in only appearance as pinch hitter and appeared in one game as pinch runner (1996).

Year League	W	L	Pct.	ERA	G	GS	CG	ShO	Sv.	IP	H	R	ER	BB	SO
1991—Niagara Falls (NY-P)	5	7	.417	4.46	15	15	0	0	0	84²/₃	87	57	42	42	77
1992—Lakeland (FSL)	5	2	.714	2.49	13	13	0	0	0	83	61	28	23	14	67
—London (East.)	4	7	.364	4.28	14	14	1	0	0	88¹/₃	85	52	42	45	59
1993—Toledo (I.L.)	8	9	.471	4.38	19	19	3	0	0	117	124	62	57	53	91
—Detroit (A.L.)	1	4	.200	5.67	9	6	1	0	0	39²/₃	47	29	25	23	19
1994—Toledo (I.L.)	11	8	.579	3.72	25	25	2	0	0	154²/₃	147	77	64	53	145
—Detroit (A.L.)	2	1	.667	5.60	3	3	0	0	0	17²/₃	22	11	11	7	12
1995—Detroit (A.L.)	7	10	.412	5.12	28	28	1	1	0	135¹/₃	169	95	77	67	86
—Toledo (I.L.)	0	1	.000	6.00	1	1	0	0	0	3	4	2	2	0	4
1996—San Diego (N.L.)■	6	8	.429	4.37	14	14	0	0	0	113¹/₃	119	63	55	33	85
1997—San Diego (N.L.)	2	4	.333	6.09	44	9	0	0	0	99	126	72	67	38	74
1998—Houston (N.L.)■	12	9	.571	3.72	31	27	1	0	0	172	183	81	71	42	100
1999—Houston (N.L.)	4	6	.400	5.36	19	16	2	1	0	99	130	60	59	26	38
—New Orleans (PCL)	0	1	.000	9.95	3	1	0	0	0	6¹/₃	9	8	7	2	2
—Atlanta (N.L.)■	1	0	1.000	2.84	6	0	0	0	0	6¹/₃	5	2	2	3	6
A.L. totals (3 years)	10	15	.400	5.28	40	37	2	1	0	192²/₃	238	135	113	97	117
N.L. totals (4 years)	25	27	.481	4.67	141	66	3	1	0	489²/₃	563	278	254	142	303
Major League totals (7 years)	35	42	.455	4.84	181	103	5	2	0	682¹/₃	801	413	367	239	420

DIVISION SERIES RECORD

Year League	W	L	Pct.	ERA	G	GS	CG	ShO	Sv.	IP	H	R	ER	BB	SO
1998—Houston (N.L.)								Did not play.							

BERKMAN, LANCE — OF — ASTROS

PERSONAL: Born February 10, 1976, in Waco, Texas. ... 6-1/205. ... Bats both, throws left. ... Full name: William Lance Berkman.
HIGH SCHOOL: Canyon (New Braunfels, Texas).
COLLEGE: Rice.
TRANSACTIONS/CAREER NOTES: Selected by Houston Astros organization in first round (16th pick overall) of free-agent draft (June 3, 1997). ... On New Orleans disabled list (April 13-May 14, 1999).
HONORS: Named first baseman on THE SPORTING NEWS college All-America first team (1997).
STATISTICAL NOTES: Led Texas League with 10 intentional bases on balls in 1998.

Year Team (League)	Pos.	G	AB	R	H	2B	3B	HR	RBI	Avg.	BB	SO	SB	PO	A	E	Avg.
1997—Kissimmee (FSL)	OF-DH	53	184	31	54	10	0	12	35	.293	37	38	2	70	2	0	1.000
1998—Jackson (Texas)	OF-DH	122	425	82	130	34	0	24	89	.306	85	82	6	183	9	4	.980
—New Orleans (PCL)	OF	17	59	14	16	4	0	6	13	.271	12	16	0	30	0	0	1.000
1999—New Orleans (PCL)	OF-1B-DH	64	226	42	73	20	0	8	49	.323	39	47	7	135	6	4	.972
—Houston (N.L.)	OF-1B	34	93	10	22	2	0	4	15	.237	12	21	5	43	0	2	.956
Major League totals (1 year)		34	93	10	22	2	0	4	15	.237	12	21	5	43	0	2	.956

BERROA, GERONIMO — OF/DH

PERSONAL: Born March 18, 1965, in Santo Domingo, Dominican Republic. ... 6-0/210. ... Bats right, throws right. ... Full name: Geronimo Emiliano Berroa. ... Name pronounced her-ON-i-mo bur-OH-uh.
TRANSACTIONS/CAREER NOTES: Signed as non-drafted free agent by Toronto Blue Jays organization (September 4, 1983). ... Selected by Atlanta Braves from Blue Jays organization in Rule 5 major league draft (December 5, 1988). ... Released by Braves (February 1, 1991). ... Signed by Calgary, Seattle Mariners organization (February 27, 1991). ... Contract sold by Mariners organization to Colorado Springs,

Cleveland Indians organization (March 28, 1991). ... Granted free agency (October 15, 1991). ... Signed by Nashville, Cincinnati Reds organization (October 31, 1991). ... Released by Reds (November 20, 1992). ... Signed by Florida Marlins (December 9, 1992). ... Granted free agency (October 15, 1993). ... Signed by Oakland Athletics organization (January 20, 1994). ... On disabled list (August 2, 1994-remainder of season). ... Traded by A's to Baltimore Orioles for P Jimmy Haynes and a player to be named later (June 27, 1997); A's acquired P Mark Seaver to complete deal (September 2, 1997). ... Granted free agency (December 21, 1997). ... Signed by Cleveland Indians (January 29, 1998). ... On Cleveland disabled list (May 3-June 3, 1998). ... Traded by Indians to Detroit Tigers for P Tim Worrell and OF Dave Roberts (June 24, 1998). ... Granted free agency (October 23, 1998). ... Signed by Blue Jays organization (December 14, 1998). ... On Toronto disabled list (May 2-June 15 and June 29-August 30, 1999); included rehabilitation assignments to Syracuse (May 20-27 and June 5-13) and Dunedin (August 25-30). ... Released by Blue Jays (August 30, 1999).

RECORDS: Shares major league single-season record for most games with three home runs—2 (1996).

STATISTICAL NOTES: Led Southern League with 297 total bases in 1987. ... Led International League in being hit by pitch with 10 and tied for lead in sacrifice flies with eight in 1988. ... Led International League in grounding into double plays with 17 in 1990. ... Hit three home runs in one game (May 22 and August 12, 1996). ... Career major league grand slams: 2.

							BATTING								FIELDING		
Year	Team (League)	Pos.	G	AB	R	H	2B	3B	HR	RBI	Avg.	BB	SO	SB	PO	A	E	Avg.
1984—GC Blue Jays (GCL)....		OF-1B	62	235	31	59	16	1	3	34	.251	12	34	2	104	2	5	.955
1985—Kinston (Caro.)..........		OF	19	43	4	8	0	0	1	4	.186	4	10	0	13	1	1	.933
—Medicine Hat (Pio.)		OF	54	201	39	69	*22	2	6	45	.343	18	40	7	58	3	3	.953
—Florence (SAL)..........		OF	19	66	7	21	2	0	3	20	.318	6	13	0	24	0	2	.923
1986—Ventura (Calif.)		OF	128	459	76	137	22	5	21	73	.298	38	92	12	194	9	14	.935
—Knoxville (Sou.)..........		OF	1	4	0	0	0	0	0	0	.000	0	1	0	2	0	0	1.000
1987—Knoxville (Sou.)..........		OF	134	523	87	150	33	3	36	108	.287	46	104	2	236	6	•15	.942
1988—Syracuse (I.L.)..........		OF	131	470	55	122	•29	1	8	64	.260	38	88	7	243	12	5	.981
1989—Atlanta (N.L.)■..........		OF	81	136	7	36	4	0	2	9	.265	7	32	0	67	1	2	.971
1990—Richmond (I.L.)..........		OF	135	499	56	134	17	2	12	80	.269	34	89	4	200	10	7	.968
—Atlanta (N.L.)..............		OF	7	4	0	0	0	0	0	0	.000	1	1	0	1	0	0	1.000
1991—Colo. Spr. (PCL)■		OF	125	478	81	154	31	7	18	91	.322	35	88	2	151	14	5	.971
1992—Nashville (A.A.)■		OF	112	461	73	151	33	2	22	88	.328	32	69	8	194	16	5	.977
—Cincinnati (N.L.)		OF	13	15	2	4	1	0	0	0	.267	2	1	0	2	1	0	1.000
1993—Edmonton (PCL)■		OF-1B	90	327	46	107	33	4	16	68	.327	36	71	1	210	10	7	.969
—Florida (N.L.)		OF	14	34	3	4	1	0	0	0	.118	2	7	0	9	1	2	.833
1994—Oakland (A.L.)■	DH-OF-1B	96	340	55	104	18	2	13	65	.306	41	62	7	131	5	1	.993
1995—Oakland (A.L.)		DH-OF	141	546	87	152	22	3	22	88	.278	63	98	7	129	5	4	.971
1996—Oakland (A.L.)		DH-OF	153	586	101	170	32	1	36	106	.290	47	122	0	91	6	2	.980
1997—Oakland (A.L.)		OF-DH	73	261	40	81	12	0	16	42	.310	36	58	3	71	1	1	.986
—Baltimore (A.L.).......		DH-OF	83	300	48	78	13	0	10	48	.260	40	62	1	70	1	3	.959
1998—Cleveland (A.L.)■......		OF-DH	20	65	6	13	3	1	0	3	.200	7	17	1	27	1	0	1.000
—Detroit (A.L.)■		DH-OF	52	126	17	30	4	1	1	10	.238	17	27	0	4	0	0	1.000
1999—Toronto (A.L.)■..........		DH-OF	22	62	11	12	3	0	1	6	.194	9	15	0	4	0	0	1.000
—Syracuse (I.L.)..........		DH-OF	10	33	7	9	0	0	3	8	.273	8	5	0	15	1	1	.941
—Dunedin (FSL)		OF-DH	4	5	1	1	1	0	0	2	.200	2	1	0	1	0	1	.500
American League totals (6 years)			640	2286	365	640	107	8	99	368	.280	260	461	19	527	19	11	.980
National League totals (4 years)			115	189	12	44	6	0	2	9	.233	12	41	0	79	3	4	.953
Major League totals (10 years)			755	2475	377	684	113	8	101	377	.276	272	502	19	606	22	15	.977

DIVISION SERIES RECORD

							BATTING								FIELDING		
Year	Team (League)	Pos.	G	AB	R	H	2B	3B	HR	RBI	Avg.	BB	SO	SB	PO	A	E	Avg.
1997—Baltimore (A.L.)..........		DH-OF	4	13	4	5	1	0	2	2	.385	2	2	0	0	0	0	...

CHAMPIONSHIP SERIES RECORD

							BATTING								FIELDING		
Year	Team (League)	Pos.	G	AB	R	H	2B	3B	HR	RBI	Avg.	BB	SO	SB	PO	A	E	Avg.
1997—Baltimore (A.L.)..........		OF-DH	6	21	1	6	2	0	0	3	.286	0	3	0	9	0	0	1.000

BERRY, SEAN   1B/3B   BREWERS

PERSONAL: Born March 22, 1966, in Santa Monica, Calif. ... 5-11/200. ... Bats right, throws right. ... Full name: Sean Robert Berry.

HIGH SCHOOL: West Torrance (Torrance, Calif.).

COLLEGE: UCLA.

TRANSACTIONS/CAREER NOTES: Selected by Boston Red Sox organization in fourth round of free-agent draft (June 4, 1984); did not sign. ... Selected by Kansas City Royals organization in secondary phase of free-agent draft (January 14, 1986). ... On disabled list (April 16-May 3, 1987). ... Traded by Royals with P Archie Corbin to Montreal Expos for P Bill Sampen and P Chris Haney (August 29, 1992). ... Traded by Expos to Houston Astros for P Dave Veres and C Raul Chavez (December 20, 1995). ... On Houston disabled list (April 7-22 and August 23-September 7, 1997); including rehabilitation assignment to New Orleans (April 18-22). ... Granted free agency (December 21, 1997). ... Re-signed by Astros (January 13, 1998). ... Granted free agency (October 26, 1998). ... Signed by Milwaukee Brewers (December 10, 1998).

STATISTICAL NOTES: Led Northwest League third basemen with 11 double plays in 1986. ... Career major league grand slams: 3.

							BATTING								FIELDING		
Year	Team (League)	Pos.	G	AB	R	H	2B	3B	HR	RBI	Avg.	BB	SO	SB	PO	A	E	Avg.
1986—Eugene (N.W.)		3B	65	238	53	76	20	2	5	44	.319	44	72	10	*63	96	21	.883
1987—Fort Myers (FSL)		3B	66	205	26	52	7	2	2	30	.254	46	65	5	39	101	23	.859
1988—Baseball City (FSL).....	3B-SS-OF	94	304	34	71	6	4	4	30	.234	31	62	24	84	161	28	.897
1989—Baseball City (FSL).....	3-0-2-S	116	399	67	106	19	7	4	44	.266	44	68	37	100	199	24	.926
1990—Memphis (Sou.)..........		3B	135	487	73	142	25	4	14	77	.292	44	89	18	79	238	27	.922
—Kansas City (A.L.)		3B	8	23	2	5	1	1	0	4	.217	2	5	0	7	10	1	.944
1991—Omaha (A.A.)..........	3B-SS-2B	103	368	62	97	21	9	11	54	.264	48	70	8	75	206	20	.934
—Kansas City (A.L.)		3B	31	60	5	8	3	0	0	1	.133	5	23	0	13	52	2	.970
1992—Omaha (A.A.)............		3B	122	439	61	126	22	2	21	77	.287	39	87	6	86	239	21	*.939
—Montreal (N.L.)■......		3B	24	57	5	19	1	0	1	4	.333	1	11	2	10	19	4	.879
1993—Montreal (N.L.)..........		3B	122	299	50	78	15	2	14	49	.261	41	70	12	66	153	15	.936
1994—Montreal (N.L.)..........		3B	103	320	43	89	19	2	11	41	.278	32	50	14	66	147	14	.938

B

Year	Team (League)	Pos.	G	AB	R	H	2B	3B	HR	RBI	Avg.	BB	SO	SB	PO	A	E	Avg.
1995—Montreal (N.L.)..........		3B-1B	103	314	38	100	22	1	14	55	.318	25	53	3	76	165	12	.953
1996—Houston (N.L.)■......		3B	132	431	55	121	38	1	17	95	.281	23	58	12	67	194	22	.922
1997—New Orleans (A.A.).....		3B	3	9	1	3	0	0	0	0	.333	3	3	0	0	6	0	1.000
—Houston (N.L.)..........		3B-DH	96	301	37	77	24	1	8	43	.256	25	53	1	47	140	16	.921
1998—Houston (N.L.).........		3B-DH	102	299	48	94	17	1	13	52	.314	31	50	3	55	150	10	.953
1999—Milwaukee (N.L.)■.....		1B	106	259	26	59	11	1	2	23	.228	17	50	0	438	27	5	.989
American League totals (2 years)			39	83	7	13	4	1	0	5	.157	7	28	0	20	62	3	.965
National League totals (8 years)			788	2280	302	637	147	9	80	362	.279	195	395	47	825	995	98	.949
Major League totals (10 years)			827	2363	309	650	151	10	80	367	.275	202	423	47	845	1057	101	.950

DIVISION SERIES RECORD

Year	Team (League)	Pos.	G	AB	R	H	2B	3B	HR	RBI	Avg.	BB	SO	SB	PO	A	E	Avg.
1997—Houston (N.L.)..........		PH	1	1	0	0	0	0	0	0	.000	0	0	0	0	0	0	
1998—Houston (N.L.)..........		3B	1	2	0	0	0	0	0	0	.000	0	1	0	0	2	1	.667
Division series totals (2 years)			2	3	0	0	0	0	0	0	.000	0	1	0	0	2	1	.667

BICHETTE, DANTE — OF — REDS

PERSONAL: Born November 18, 1963, in West Palm Beach, Fla. ... 6-3/238. ... Bats right, throws right. ... Full name: Alphonse Dante Bichette. ... Name pronounced bih-SHETT.
HIGH SCHOOL: Jupiter (Fla.).
JUNIOR COLLEGE: Palm Beach Community College (Fla.).
TRANSACTIONS/CAREER NOTES: Selected by California Angels organization in 17th round of free-agent draft (June 4, 1984). ... Traded by Angels to Milwaukee Brewers for DH Dave Parker (March 14, 1991). ... Traded by Brewers to Colorado Rockies for OF Kevin Reimer (November 17, 1992). ... Traded by Rockies with cash to Cincinnati Reds for OF Jeffrey Hammonds and P Stan Belinda (October 30, 1999).
HONORS: Named outfielder on THE SPORTING NEWS N.L. All-Star team (1995). ... Named outfielder on THE SPORTING NEWS N.L. Silver Slugger team (1995).
STATISTICAL NOTES: Led A.L. outfielders with seven double plays in 1991. ... Led N.L. outfielders with four double plays in 1994. ... Led N.L. with .620 slugging percentage and 359 total bases in 1995. ... Had 23-game hitting streak (May 22-June 18, 1995). ... Tied for N.L. lead with 10 sacrifice flies in 1996. ... Hit for the cycle (June 10, 1998). ... Tied for N.L. lead with six double plays by outfielder in 1998. ... Tied for N.L. lead with 10 sacrifice flies in 1999. ... Career major league grand slams: 7.
MISCELLANEOUS: Holds Colorado Rockies all-time records for most runs (665), hits (1,278), doubles (270) and runs batted in (826).

Year	Team (League)	Pos.	G	AB	R	H	2B	3B	HR	RBI	Avg.	BB	SO	SB	PO	A	E	Avg.
1984—Salem (N.W.)............		OF-1B-3B	64	250	27	58	9	2	4	30	.232	6	53	6	224	24	11	.958
1985—Quad Cities (Midw.).....		1B-OF-C	137	547	58	145	28	4	11	78	.265	25	89	25	300	21	15	.955
1986—Palm Springs (Calif.)...		OF-3B	68	290	39	79	15	0	10	73	.272	21	53	2	78	68	11	.930
—Midland (Texas)........		OF-3B	62	243	43	69	16	2	12	36	.284	18	50	3	131	30	11	.936
1987—Edmonton (PCL)........		OF-3B	92	360	54	108	20	3	13	50	.300	26	68	3	169	21	9	.955
1988—Edmonton (PCL)........		OF	132	509	64	136	29	•10	14	81	.267	25	78	7	218	*22	*15	.941
—California (A.L.).........		OF	21	46	1	12	2	0	0	8	.261	0	7	0	44	2	1	.979
1989—California (A.L.)........		OF-DH	48	138	13	29	7	0	3	15	.210	6	24	3	95	6	1	.990
—Edmonton (PCL)........		OF	61	226	39	55	11	2	11	40	.243	24	39	4	92	9	1	.990
1990—California (A.L.)........		OF	109	349	40	89	15	1	15	53	.255	16	79	5	183	12	7	.965
1991—Milwaukee (A.L.)■....		OF-3B	134	445	53	106	18	3	15	59	.238	22	107	14	270	14	7	.976
1992—Milwaukee (A.L.).......		OF-DH	112	387	37	111	27	2	5	41	.287	16	74	18	188	6	2	.990
1993—Colorado (N.L.)■.......		OF	141	538	93	167	43	5	21	89	.310	28	99	14	308	14	9	.973
1994—Colorado (N.L.)........		OF	*116	*484	74	147	33	2	27	95	.304	19	70	21	211	10	2	.991
1995—Colorado (N.L.)........		OF	139	579	102	•197	38	2	*40	*128	.340	22	96	13	208	9	3	.986
1996—Colorado (N.L.)........		OF	159	633	114	198	39	3	31	141	.313	45	105	31	255	5	9	.967
1997—Colorado (N.L.)........		OF-DH	151	561	81	173	31	2	26	118	.308	30	90	6	225	4	3	.987
1998—Colorado (N.L.)........		OF-DH	161	662	97	*219	48	2	22	122	.331	28	76	14	289	14	11	.965
1999—Colorado (N.L.)........		OF-DH	151	593	104	177	38	2	34	133	.298	54	84	6	238	17	13	.951
American League totals (5 years)			424	1365	144	347	69	6	38	176	.254	60	291	40	780	40	18	.979
National League totals (7 years)			1018	4050	665	1278	270	18	201	826	.316	226	620	105	1734	73	50	.973
Major League totals (12 years)			1442	5415	809	1625	339	24	239	1002	.300	286	911	145	2514	113	68	.975

DIVISION SERIES RECORD

RECORDS: Shares N.L. career record for most doubles—3. ... Shares N.L. single-series record for most runs scored—6 (1995).

Year	Team (League)	Pos.	G	AB	R	H	2B	3B	HR	RBI	Avg.	BB	SO	SB	PO	A	E	Avg.
1995—Colorado (N.L.)..........		OF	4	17	6	10	3	0	1	3	.588	1	3	0	9	0	0	1.000

ALL-STAR GAME RECORD

Year	League	Pos.	AB	R	H	2B	3B	HR	RBI	Avg.	BB	SO	SB	PO	A	E	Avg.
1994—National....................		PH	1	0	1	0	0	0	0	1.000	0	0	0	...	...	...	...
1995—National....................		OF	1	0	0	0	0	0	0	.000	0	1	0	2	0	0	1.000
1996—National....................		OF	3	1	1	1	0	0	0	.333	0	1	0	0	0	0	...
1998—National....................		OF	2	0	0	0	0	0	0	.000	0	1	0	1	0	0	1.000
All-Star Game totals (4 years)			7	1	2	1	0	0	0	.286	0	3	0	3	0	0	1.000

BIERBROLDT, NICK — P — DIAMONDBACKS

PERSONAL: Born May 16, 1978, in Tarzana, Calif. ... 6-5/190. ... Throws left, bats left. ... Full name: Nicholas Raymond Bierbroldt.
HIGH SCHOOL: Millikan (Long Beach, Calif.).
TRANSACTIONS/CAREER NOTES: Selected by Arizona Diamondbacks organization in first round (30th pick overall) of free-agent draft (June 4, 1996).

Year	League	W	L	Pct.	ERA	G	GS	CG	ShO	Sv.	IP	H	R	ER	BB	SO
1996— Ariz. D'backs (Ariz.)		1	1	.500	1.66	8	8	0	0	0	38	25	9	7	13	46
— Lethbridge (Pio.)		2	0	1.000	0.50	3	3	0	0	0	18	12	4	1	5	23
1997— South Bend (Midw.)		2	4	.333	4.04	15	15	0	0	0	75²/₃	77	43	34	37	64
1998— High Desert (Calif.)		8	7	.533	3.40	24	23	1	0	0	129²/₃	122	66	49	64	88
1999— El Paso (Texas)		5	6	.455	4.62	14	14	2	1	0	76	78	45	39	37	55
— Tucson (PCL)		1	4	.200	7.27	11	11	0	0	0	43¹/₃	57	42	35	30	43

BIGGIO, CRAIG   2B   ASTROS

PERSONAL: Born December 14, 1965, in Smithtown, N.Y. ... 5-11/180. ... Bats right, throws right. ... Full name: Craig Alan Biggio. ... Name pronounced BEE-jee-oh.
HIGH SCHOOL: Kings Park (N.Y.).
COLLEGE: Seton Hall.
TRANSACTIONS/CAREER NOTES: Selected by Houston Astros organization in first round (22nd pick overall) of free-agent draft (June 2, 1987). ... Granted free agency (October 31, 1995). ... Re-signed by Astros (December 14, 1995).
RECORDS: Shares N.L. record for most years leading league in games by second baseman—7.
HONORS: Named catcher on THE SPORTING NEWS college All-America team (1987). ... Named catcher on THE SPORTING NEWS N.L. Silver Slugger team (1989). ... Named second baseman on THE SPORTING NEWS N.L. All-Star team (1994-95 and 1997-98). ... Won N.L. Gold Glove at second base (1994-97). ... Named second baseman on THE SPORTING NEWS N.L. Silver Slugger team (1994-95 and 1997-98).
STATISTICAL NOTES: Led N.L. catchers with 889 putouts, 963 total chances and 13 passed balls in 1991. ... Led N.L. in being hit by pitch with 22 in 1995, 27 in 1996 and 34 in 1997. ... Led N.L. second basemen in total chances with 728 in 1995, 811 in 1996 and 863 in 1997. ... Led N.L. second basemen with 359 putouts, 430 assists, 801 total chances and 117 double plays in 1999. ... Career major league grand slams: 2.
MISCELLANEOUS: Holds Houston Astros all-time record for most runs (1,120) and most doubles (389).

							BATTING								FIELDING		
Year	Team (League)	Pos.	G	AB	R	H	2B	3B	HR	RBI	Avg.	BB	SO	SB	PO	A	E	Avg.
1987— Asheville (SAL)		C-OF	64	216	59	81	17	2	9	49	.375	39	33	31	378	46	2	.995
1988— Tucson (PCL)		C-OF	77	281	60	90	21	4	3	41	.320	40	39	19	318	33	6	.983
— Houston (N.L.)		C	50	123	14	26	6	1	3	5	.211	7	29	6	292	28	3	.991
1989— Houston (N.L.)		C-OF	134	443	64	114	21	2	13	60	.257	49	64	21	742	56	9	.989
1990— Houston (N.L.)		C-OF	150	555	53	153	24	2	4	42	.276	53	79	25	657	60	13	.982
1991— Houston (N.L.)		C-2B-OF	149	546	79	161	23	4	4	46	.295	53	71	19	†894	73	11	.989
1992— Houston (N.L.)		2B	•162	613	96	170	32	3	6	39	.277	94	95	38	*344	413	12	.984
1993— Houston (N.L.)		2B	155	610	98	175	41	5	21	64	.287	77	93	15	306	*447	14	.982
1994— Houston (N.L.)		2B	114	437	88	139	*44	5	6	56	.318	62	58	*39	•225	*338	7	.988
1995— Houston (N.L.)		2B	141	553	*123	167	30	2	22	77	.302	80	85	33	299	*419	10	.986
1996— Houston (N.L.)		2B	•162	605	113	174	24	4	15	75	.288	75	72	25	*361	*440	10	.988
1997— Houston (N.L.)		2B-DH	•162	619	*146	191	37	8	22	81	.309	84	107	47	*341	*504	18	.979
1998— Houston (N.L.)		2B-DH	160	646	123	210	*51	2	20	88	.325	64	113	50	318	431	15	.980
1999— Houston (N.L.)		2B-OF-DH	160	639	123	188	*56	0	16	73	.294	88	107	28	†365	†431	12	.985
Major League totals (12 years)			1699	6389	1120	1868	389	38	152	706	.292	786	973	346	5144	3640	134	.985

DIVISION SERIES RECORD

							BATTING								FIELDING		
Year	Team (League)	Pos.	G	AB	R	H	2B	3B	HR	RBI	Avg.	BB	SO	SB	PO	A	E	Avg.
1997— Houston (N.L.)		2B	3	12	0	1	0	0	0	0	.083	1	0	0	4	8	1	.923
1998— Houston (N.L.)		2B	4	11	3	2	1	0	0	1	.182	4	4	0	9	10	1	.950
1999— Houston (N.L.)		2B	4	19	1	2	0	0	0	0	.105	1	5	0	14	10	0	1.000
Division series totals (3 years)			11	42	4	5	1	0	0	1	.119	6	9	0	27	28	2	.965

ALL-STAR GAME RECORD

					BATTING							FIELDING		
Year	League	Pos.	AB	R	H	2B	3B	HR	RBI	Avg.	BB	SO	SB	PO	A	E	Avg.
1991— National		C	1	0	0	0	0	0	0	.000	0	0	0	2	0	1	.667
1992— National		2B	2	0	0	0	0	0	0	.000	0	0	0	0	2	0	1.000
1994— National		2B	1	1	0	0	0	0	0	.000	0	0	0	2	1	0	1.000
1995— National		2B	2	1	1	0	0	1	1	.500	0	0	0	2	1	0	1.000
1996— National		2B	3	0	0	0	0	0	1	.000	0	1	0	1	1	0	1.000
1997— National		2B	3	0	0	0	0	0	0	.000	0	1	0	4	0	0	1.000
1998— National		2B	3	0	0	0	0	0	0	.000	0	3	0	2	4	0	1.000
All-Star Game totals (7 years)			15	2	1	0	0	1	2	.067	0	5	0	9	13	1	.957

BILLINGSLEY, BRENT   P   EXPOS

PERSONAL: Born April 19, 1975, in Downey, Calif. ... 6-2/200. ... Throws left, bats left. ... Full name: Brent Aaron Billingsley.
HIGH SCHOOL: Chino (Calif.).
COLLEGE: East Carolina, then Cal State Fullerton.
TRANSACTIONS/CAREER NOTES: Selected by Florida Marlins organization in fifth round of free-agent draft (June 2, 1996). ... On Calgary disabled list (July 16-30, 1999). ... Claimed on waivers by Montreal Expos (November 18, 1999).
STATISTICAL NOTES: Tied for Eastern League lead with 24 home runs allowed in 1998.

Year	League	W	L	Pct.	ERA	G	GS	CG	ShO	Sv.	IP	H	R	ER	BB	SO
1996— Utica (NY-P)		4	5	.444	4.01	15	•15	0	0	0	89²/₃	83	46	40	28	82
1997— Kane County (Midw.)		14	7	.667	3.01	26	26	3	1	0	170²/₃	146	67	57	50	175
1998— Portland (East.)		6	13	.316	3.74	28	28	0	0	0	171	172	90	71	70	*183
1999— Calgary (PCL)		2	9	.182	5.55	21	21	0	0	0	116²/₃	133	81	72	48	79
— Florida (N.L.)		0	0	...	16.43	8	0	0	0	0	7²/₃	11	14	14	10	3
Major League totals (1 year)		0	0	...	16.43	8	0	0	0	0	7²/₃	11	14	14	10	3

BLAIR, WILLIE P TIGERS

PERSONAL: Born December 18, 1965, in Paintsville, Ky. ... 6-1/185. ... Throws right, bats right. ... Full name: William Allen Blair.
HIGH SCHOOL: Johnson Central (Paintsville, Ky.).
COLLEGE: Morehead State.
TRANSACTIONS/CAREER NOTES: Selected by Toronto Blue Jays organization in 11th round of free-agent draft (June 2, 1986). ... Traded by Blue Jays to Cleveland Indians for P Alex Sanchez (November 6, 1990). ... Traded by Indians with C Eddie Taubensee to Houston Astros for OF Kenny Lofton and IF Dave Rohde (December 10, 1991). ... Selected by Colorado Rockies in first round (21st pick overall) of expansion draft (November 17, 1992). ... Granted free agency (December 20, 1994). ... Signed by Las Vegas, San Diego Padres organization (April 10, 1995). ... Granted free agency (December 21, 1995). ... Re-signed by Padres (December 27, 1995). ... Traded by Padres with C Brian Johnson to Detroit Tigers for P Joey Eischen and P Cam Smith (December 17, 1996). ... On disabled list (May 5-June 3, 1997); included rehabilitation assignment to West Michigan (May 23-June 3). ... Granted free agency (October 27, 1997). ... Signed by Arizona Diamondbacks (December 6, 1997). ... Traded by Diamondbacks with C Jorge Fabregas and a player to be named later to New York Mets for OF Bernard Gilkey, P Nelson Figueroa and cash (July 31, 1998); Mets received cash to complete deal (September 3, 1998). ... Traded by Mets to Tigers for 3B Joe Randa (December 4, 1998).
STATISTICAL NOTES: Combined with starter Pat Hentgen and Enrique Burgos in 2-1 no-hit victory for Dunedin against Osceola (May 10, 1988).

Year League	W	L	Pct.	ERA	G	GS	CG	ShO	Sv.	IP	H	R	ER	BB	SO
1986—St. Catharines (NY-P)	5	0	1.000	1.68	21	0	0	0	*12	53 2/3	32	10	10	20	55
1987—Dunedin (FSL)	2	9	.182	4.43	50	0	0	0	13	85 1/3	99	51	42	29	72
1988—Dunedin (FSL)	2	0	1.000	2.70	4	0	0	0	0	6 2/3	5	2	2	4	5
—Knoxville (Sou.)	5	5	.500	3.62	34	9	0	0	3	102	94	49	41	35	76
1989—Syracuse (I.L.)	5	6	.455	3.97	19	17	3	1	0	106 2/3	94	55	47	38	76
1990—Toronto (A.L.)	3	5	.375	4.06	27	6	0	0	0	68 2/3	66	33	31	28	43
—Syracuse (I.L.)	0	2	.000	4.74	3	3	1	0	0	19	20	13	10	8	6
1991—Colorado Springs (PCL)■..	9	6	.600	4.99	26	15	0	0	4	113 2/3	130	74	63	30	57
—Cleveland (A.L.)	2	3	.400	6.75	11	5	0	0	0	36	58	27	27	10	13
1992—Tucson (PCL)■	4	4	.500	2.39	21	2	1	0	2	52 2/3	50	20	14	12	35
—Houston (N.L.)	5	7	.417	4.00	29	8	0	0	0	78 2/3	74	47	35	25	48
1993—Colorado (N.L.)■	6	10	.375	4.75	46	18	1	0	0	146	184	90	77	42	84
1994—Colorado (N.L.)	0	5	.000	5.79	47	1	0	0	3	77 2/3	98	57	50	39	68
1995—San Diego (N.L.)■	7	5	.583	4.34	40	12	0	0	0	114	112	60	55	45	83
1996—San Diego (N.L.)	2	6	.250	4.60	60	0	0	0	1	88	80	52	45	29	67
1997—Detroit (A.L.)■	16	8	.667	4.17	29	27	2	0	0	175	186	85	81	46	90
—West Michigan (Midw.)	0	0	...	0.00	1	1	0	0	0	5	1	0	0	0	7
—Toledo (I.L.)	0	0	...	0.00	1	1	0	0	0	7	1	1	0	2	4
1998—Arizona (N.L.)■	4	15	.211	5.34	23	23	0	0	0	146 2/3	165	91	87	51	71
—New York (N.L.)■	1	1	.500	3.14	11	2	0	0	0	28 2/3	23	10	10	10	21
1999—Detroit (A.L.)■	3	11	.214	6.85	39	16	0	0	0	134	169	107	102	44	82
A.L. totals (4 years)	24	27	.471	5.24	106	54	2	0	0	413 2/3	479	252	241	128	228
N.L. totals (6 years)	25	49	.338	4.75	256	64	1	0	4	679 2/3	736	407	359	241	442
Major League totals (10 years)	49	76	.392	4.94	362	118	3	0	4	1093 1/3	1215	659	600	369	670

DIVISION SERIES RECORD

Year League	W	L	Pct.	ERA	G	GS	CG	ShO	Sv.	IP	H	R	ER	BB	SO
1996—San Diego (N.L.)	0	0	...	0.00	1	0	0	0	0	2	1	0	0	2	3

BLAKE, CASEY 3B BLUE JAYS

PERSONAL: Born August 23, 1973, in Des Moines, Iowa. ... 6-2/200. ... Bats right, throws right. ... Full name: William Casey Blake.
HIGH SCHOOL: Indianola (Iowa).
COLLEGE: Wichita State.
TRANSACTIONS/CAREER NOTES: Selected by Philadelphia Phillies organization in 11th round of free-agent draft (June 1, 1992); did not sign. ... Selected by New York Yankees organization in 45th round of free-agent draft (June 1, 1995); did not sign. ... Selected by Toronto Blue Jays organization in seventh round of free-agent draft (June 4, 1996).
STATISTICAL NOTES: Led Florida State League third basemen with 98 putouts and 39 errors in 1997. ... Led International League third basemen with .967 fielding percentage in 1999. ... Tied for International League lead with 94 putouts by third basemen in 1999.

Year Team (League)	Pos.	G	AB	R	H	2B	3B	HR	RBI	Avg.	BB	SO	SB	PO	A	E	Avg.
1996—Hagerstown (SAL)	3B-1B-OF	48	172	29	43	13	1	2	18	.250	11	40	5	33	83	12	.906
1997—Dunedin (FSL)	3B-SS	129	449	56	107	21	0	7	39	.238	48	91	19	†98	235	†39	.895
1998—Dunedin (FSL)	3B	88	340	62	119	28	3	11	65	*.350	30	81	9	64	183	16	.939
—Knoxville (Sou.)	3B	45	172	41	64	15	4	7	38	.372	22	25	10	27	89	11	.913
1999—Syracuse (I.L.)	3B-DH-SS	110	387	69	95	16	2	22	75	.245	61	82	9	‡94	169	10	†.963
—Toronto (A.L.)	3B	14	39	6	10	2	0	1	1	.256	2	7	0	12	23	0	1.000
—St. Cath. (NY-P)	3B	1	3	0	2	0	0	0	0	.667	1	0	0	1	3	0	1.000
Major League totals (1 year)		14	39	6	10	2	0	1	1	.256	2	7	0	12	23	0	1.000

BLANCO, HENRY C BREWERS

PERSONAL: Born August 29, 1971, in Caracas, Venezuela. ... 5-11/190. ... Bats right, throws right. ... Full name: Henry Ramon Blanco.
HIGH SCHOOL: Antonio Jose de Sucre (Venezuela).
TRANSACTIONS/CAREER NOTES: Signed as non-drafted free agent by Los Angeles Dodgers organization (November 12, 1989). ... On disabled list (June 16-25, 1993). ... On Los Angeles disabled list (March 22-July 29, 1998); included rehabilitation assignment to San Bernardino (May 19-27). ... Granted free agency (October 15, 1998). ... Signed by Colorado Rockies organization (December 18, 1998). ... Traded by Rockies with P Jamey Wright to Milwaukee Brewers as part of three-way deal in which Rockies received 3B Jeff Cirillo, P Scott Karl and cash from Brewers, Oakland Athletics received P Justin Miller and cash from Rockies and Brewers received P Jimmy Haynes from Athletics (December 13, 1999).

STATISTICAL NOTES: Led Pioneer League third basemen with .947 fielding percentage and 10 double plays in 1991. ... Led California League third basemen with 345 total chances and 34 double plays in 1992. ... Led Texas League third basemen with .944 fielding percentage, 92 putouts and 270 total chances in 1993. ... Led Texas League catchers with 13 errors and 17 passed balls in 1996. ... Led Pacific Coast League catchers with 64 assists and 11 double plays in 1997.

Year	Team (League)	Pos.	G	AB	R	H	2B	3B	HR	RBI	Avg.	BB	SO	SB	PO	A	E	Avg.
1990—GC Dodgers (GCL)		3B	60	178	23	39	8	0	1	19	.219	26	41	7	*48	129	11	.941
1991—Vero Beach (FSL)		3B-SS	5	7	0	1	0	0	0	0	.143	2	0	0	6	4	0	1.000
—Great Falls (Pio.)		3B-1B	62	216	35	55	7	1	5	28	.255	27	39	3	93	99	8	†.960
1992—Bakersfield (Calif.)......		3B	124	401	42	94	21	2	5	52	.234	51	91	10	*95	*236	14	*.959
1993—San Antonio (Texas)...		3B-1B-SS	117	374	33	73	19	1	10	42	.195	29	80	3	†150	169	16	†.952
1994—San Antonio (Texas)...		3B-1B-P	*132	405	36	93	23	2	6	38	.230	53	67	6	77	178	21	.924
1995—San Antonio (Texas)...		3B-C	88	302	37	77	18	4	12	48	.255	29	52	1	81	210	11	.964
—Albuquerque (PCL).....		3B-1B-OF	29	97	11	22	4	1	2	13	.227	10	23	0	115	47	2	.988
1996—San Antonio (Texas)...		C-3B	92	307	39	82	14	1	5	40	.267	28	38	2	532	65	†13	.979
—Albuquerque (PCL).....		C	2	6	1	1	0	0	0	0	.167	0	3	0	11	1	0	1.000
1997—Albuquerque (PCL)...C-1B-DH-OF			91	294	38	92	20	1	6	47	.313	37	63	7	607	†68	3	.996
—Los Angeles (N.L.)		1B-3B	3	5	1	2	0	0	1	1	.400	0	1	0	5	0	0	1.000
1998—San Bern. (Calif.)........		C-DH	7	19	5	6	1	0	2	3	.316	4	6	1	17	3	0	1.000
—Albuquerque (PCL).....		C-DH	48	134	19	36	11	0	4	23	.269	22	27	2	243	20	4	.985
1999—Colo. Spr. (PCL)■......		C	15	57	8	19	4	0	3	12	.333	1	12	0	87	12	1	.990
—Colorado (N.L.)........		C-OF	88	263	30	61	12	3	6	28	.232	34	38	1	562	56	5	.992
Major League totals (2 years)			91	268	31	63	12	3	7	29	.235	34	39	1	567	58	5	.992

RECORD AS PITCHER

Year	League	W	L	Pct.	ERA	G	GS	CG	ShO	Sv.	IP	H	R	ER	BB	SO
1994—San Antonio (Texas)..........		0	0	...	9.00	1	0	0	0	0	1	3	1	1	0	1

BLANK, MATT   P   EXPOS

PERSONAL: Born April 5, 1976, in Texarkana, Texas. ... 6-2/195. ... Throws left, bats left. ... Full name: Clarence Matt Blank.
COLLEGE: Texas A&M.
TRANSACTIONS/CAREER NOTES: Selected by Montreal Expos organization in 11th round of free-agent draft (June 3, 1997).

Year	League	W	L	Pct.	ERA	G	GS	CG	ShO	Sv.	IP	H	R	ER	BB	SO
1997—Vermont (NY-P)	6	4	.600	*1.69	16	15	2	0	0	95 2/3	74	26	18	14	84	
1998—Cape Fear (SAL)	9	2	.818	2.61	21	21	2	2	0	134 2/3	121	45	39	24	114	
—Jupiter (FSL)	5	1	.833	2.34	8	6	0	0	0	42 1/3	33	14	11	10	26	
1999—Jupiter (FSL)	9	5	.643	2.40	14	14	3	1	0	90	64	26	24	19	66	
—Harrisburg (East.)	6	3	.667	3.92	15	14	0	0	0	85	94	41	37	26	42	

BLAUSER, JEFF   SS

PERSONAL: Born November 8, 1965, in Los Gatos, Calif. ... 6-1/190. ... Bats right, throws right. ... Full name: Jeffrey Michael Blauser. ... Name pronounced BLAU-zer.
HIGH SCHOOL: Placer (Sacramento).
COLLEGE: Sacramento City College.
TRANSACTIONS/CAREER NOTES: Selected by St. Louis Cardinals organization in first round (eighth pick overall) of free-agent draft (January 17, 1984); did not sign. ... Selected by Atlanta Braves organization in secondary phase of free-agent draft (June 4, 1984). ... On disabled list (May 14-30, 1990; May 2-20, 1994; and April 14-May 4 and July 16-September 1, 1996). ... Granted free agency (October 15, 1994). ... Re-signed by Braves (April 12, 1995). ... Granted free agency (November 2, 1997). ... Signed by Chicago Cubs (December 9, 1997). ... On disabled list (August 25-September 9, 1998). ... Granted free agency (October 29, 1999).
HONORS: Named shortstop on THE SPORTING NEWS N.L. All-Star team (1997). ... Named shortstop on THE SPORTING NEWS N.L. Silver Slugger team (1997).
STATISTICAL NOTES: Led Carolina League shortstops with 506 total chances in 1986. ... Hit three home runs in one game (July 12, 1992). ... Led N.L. in being hit by pitch with 16 in 1993. ... Career major league grand slams: 4.

Year	Team (League)	Pos.	G	AB	R	H	2B	3B	HR	RBI	Avg.	BB	SO	SB	PO	A	E	Avg.
1984—Pulaski (Appl.)..........		SS	62	217	41	54	6	1	3	24	.249	38	47	14	61	162	24	.903
1985—Sumter (SAL)		SS	125	422	74	99	19	0	5	49	.235	82	94	36	150	306	35	.929
1986—Durham (Caro.)		SS	123	447	94	128	27	3	13	52	.286	81	92	36	167	*314	25	*.951
1987—Richmond (I.L.)		SS-2B	33	113	11	20	1	0	1	12	.177	11	24	3	56	106	9	.947
—Atlanta (N.L.).............		SS	51	165	11	40	6	3	2	15	.242	18	34	7	65	166	9	.963
—Greenville (Sou.)		SS	72	265	35	66	13	3	4	32	.249	34	49	5	101	225	8	.976
1988—Richmond (I.L.).........		SS	69	271	40	77	19	1	5	23	.284	19	53	6	93	156	15	.943
—Atlanta (N.L.).............		2B-SS	18	67	7	16	3	1	2	7	.239	2	11	0	35	59	4	.959
1989—Atlanta (N.L.)...........		3-2-S-O	142	456	63	123	24	2	12	46	.270	38	101	5	137	254	21	.949
1990—Atlanta (N.L.)...........		S-2-3-O	115	386	46	104	24	3	8	39	.269	35	70	3	169	288	16	.966
1991—Atlanta (N.L.)...........		SS-2B-3B	129	352	49	91	14	3	11	54	.259	54	59	5	136	219	17	.954
1992—Atlanta (N.L.)...........		SS-2B-3B	123	343	61	90	19	3	14	46	.262	46	82	5	119	225	14	.961
1993—Atlanta (N.L.)...........		SS	161	597	110	182	29	2	15	73	.305	85	109	16	189	426	19	.970
1994—Atlanta (N.L.)...........		SS	96	380	56	98	21	4	6	45	.258	38	64	1	126	290	15	.970
1995—Atlanta (N.L.)...........		SS	115	431	60	91	16	2	12	31	.211	57	107	8	151	337	15	.970
1996—Atlanta (N.L.)...........		SS	83	265	48	65	14	1	10	35	.245	40	54	6	83	206	23	.926
1997—Atlanta (N.L.)...........		SS-DH	151	519	90	160	31	4	17	70	.308	70	101	5	204	372	16	.973
1998—Chicago (N.L.)■........		SS	119	361	49	79	11	3	4	26	.219	60	93	2	129	255	14	.965
1999—Chicago (N.L.)...........		2-S-3-O	104	200	41	48	5	2	9	26	.240	26	52	2	70	94	7	.959
Major League totals (13 years)			1407	4522	691	1187	217	33	122	513	.262	569	937	65	1613	3191	188	.962

DIVISION SERIES RECORD

Year	Team (League)	Pos.	G	AB	R	H	2B	3B	HR	RBI	Avg.	BB	SO	SB	PO	A	E	Avg.
1995—Atlanta (N.L.)		SS	3	6	0	0	0	0	0	0	.000	1	3	0	5	11	1	.941
1996—Atlanta (N.L.)		SS	3	9	0	1	0	0	0	0	.111	1	3	0	0	7	0	1.000
1997—Atlanta (N.L.)		SS	3	10	2	3	0	0	1	4	.300	2	2	0	2	10	0	1.000
1998—Chicago (N.L.)		PH	2	2	0	0	0	0	0	0	.000	0	1	0	...	...	...	...
Division series totals (4 years)			11	27	2	4	0	0	1	4	.148	4	9	0	7	28	1	.972

CHAMPIONSHIP SERIES RECORD

RECORDS: Shares single-series record for most times hit by pitch—2 (1996).

Year	Team (League)	Pos.	G	AB	R	H	2B	3B	HR	RBI	Avg.	BB	SO	SB	PO	A	E	Avg.
1991—Atlanta (N.L.)		SS-PH	2	2	0	0	0	0	0	0	.000	0	0	0	0	1	1	.500
1992—Atlanta (N.L.)		SS	7	24	3	5	0	1	1	4	.208	3	2	0	7	15	2	.917
1993—Atlanta (N.L.)		SS	6	25	5	7	1	0	2	4	.280	4	7	0	6	14	0	1.000
1995—Atlanta (N.L.)		SS	1	4	0	0	0	0	0	0	.000	1	2	0	4	6	0	1.000
1996—Atlanta (N.L.)		SS	7	17	5	3	0	1	0	2	.176	6	6	0	5	9	1	.933
1997—Atlanta (N.L.)		SS	6	20	5	6	0	0	1	1	.300	3	6	0	6	19	1	.962
Championship series totals (6 years)			29	92	18	21	1	2	4	11	.228	17	23	0	28	64	5	.948

WORLD SERIES RECORD

NOTES: Member of World Series championship team (1995); inactive due to injury.

Year	Team (League)	Pos.	G	AB	R	H	2B	3B	HR	RBI	Avg.	BB	SO	SB	PO	A	E	Avg.
1991—Atlanta (N.L.)		SS-PH	5	6	0	1	0	0	0	0	.167	1	1	0	3	3	0	1.000
1992—Atlanta (N.L.)		SS	6	24	2	6	0	0	0	0	.250	1	9	2	7	22	0	1.000
1995—Atlanta (N.L.)									Did not play.									
1996—Atlanta (N.L.)		SS	6	18	2	3	1	0	0	1	.167	1	4	0	9	15	1	.960
World Series totals (3 years)			17	48	4	10	1	0	0	1	.208	3	14	2	19	40	1	.983

ALL-STAR GAME RECORD

Year	League	Pos.	AB	R	H	2B	3B	HR	RBI	Avg.	BB	SO	SB	PO	A	E	Avg.
1993—National		SS	1	0	0	0	0	0	0	.000	0	1	0	1	2	1	.750
1997—National		SS	2	0	1	0	0	0	0	.500	0	0	0	1	1	0	1.000
All-Star Game totals (2 years)			3	0	1	0	0	0	0	.333	0	1	0	2	3	1	.833

BLOWERS, MIKE   3B/1B

PERSONAL: Born April 24, 1965, in Wurzburg, West Germany. ... 6-2/210. ... Bats right, throws right. ... Full name: Michael Roy Blowers.
HIGH SCHOOL: Bethel (Wash.).
JUNIOR COLLEGE: Tacoma (Wash.) Community College.
COLLEGE: Washington.
TRANSACTIONS/CAREER NOTES: Selected by Seattle Mariners organization in eighth round of free-agent draft (January 17, 1984); did not sign. ... Selected by San Francisco Giants organization in secondary phase of free-agent draft (June 4, 1984); did not sign. ... Selected by Baltimore Orioles organization in secondary phase of free-agent draft (January 9, 1985); did not sign. ... Selected by Montreal Expos organization in 10th round of free-agent draft (June 2, 1986). ... Traded by Expos to New York Yankees (August 31, 1989), completing deal in which Yankees traded P John Candelaria to Expos for a player to be named later (August 29, 1989). ... Traded by Yankees to Mariners for a player to be named later and cash (May 17, 1991); Yankees acquired P Jim Blueberg to complete deal (June 22, 1991). ... Traded by Mariners to Los Angeles Dodgers for 2B Miguel Cairo and 3B Willis Otanez (November 29, 1995). ... On disabled list (July 18, 1996-remainder of season). ... Granted free agency (October 15, 1996). ... Signed by Mariners organization (January 24, 1997). ... Granted free agency (October 28, 1997). ... Signed by Oakland Athletics (December 16, 1997). ... Granted free agency (October 23, 1998). ... Signed by Mariners organization (August 28, 1999). ... Granted free agency (November 5, 1999).
RECORDS: Shares major league single-month record for most grand slams—3 (August 1995). ... Shares A.L. single-game record for most errors by third baseman—4 (May 3, 1990).
STATISTICAL NOTES: Led Florida State League third basemen with .944 fielding percentage and 27 double plays in 1987. ... Led Southern League third basemen with 125 putouts and 27 double plays in 1988. ... Led American Association third basemen with .930 fielding percentage in 1989. ... Hit for the cycle (May 18, 1998). ... Career major league grand slams: 7.

Year	Team (League)	Pos.	G	AB	R	H	2B	3B	HR	RBI	Avg.	BB	SO	SB	PO	A	E	Avg.
1986—Jamestown (NY-P)		SS-3B	32	95	13	24	9	2	1	6	.253	17	18	3	48	73	16	.883
—GC Expos (GCL)		SS	31	115	14	25	3	1	2	17	.217	15	25	2	50	84	15	.899
1987—W.P. Beach (FSL)		3B-SS-1B	136	491	68	124	30	3	16	71	.253	48	118	4	75	239	18	†.946
1988—Jacksonville (Sou.)		3B-SS-2B	137	460	58	115	20	6	15	60	.250	68	114	6	†125	241	34	.915
1989—Indianapolis (A.A.)		3B-SS	131	461	49	123	29	6	14	56	.267	41	109	3	91	214	23	†.930
—New York (A.L.)■		3B	13	38	2	10	0	0	0	3	.263	3	13	0	9	14	4	.852
1990—New York (A.L.)		3B-DH	48	144	16	27	4	0	5	21	.188	12	50	1	26	63	10	.899
—Columbus (I.L.)		3B-1B-2B	62	230	30	78	20	6	6	50	.339	29	40	3	64	89	8	.950
1991—New York (A.L.)		3B	15	35	3	7	0	0	1	1	.200	4	3	0	4	16	3	.870
—Calgary (PCL)■		3B-SS-1B	90	329	56	95	20	2	9	59	.289	40	74	3	56	163	19	.920
1992—Calgary (PCL)		3B-1B-OF	83	300	56	95	28	2	9	67	.317	50	64	2	99	87	5	.974
—Seattle (A.L.)		3B-1B	31	73	7	14	3	0	1	2	.192	6	20	0	28	44	1	.986
1993—Seattle (A.L.)		3-D-O-1-C	127	379	55	106	23	3	15	57	.280	44	98	1	70	225	15	.952
1994—Seattle (A.L.)		3B-1B-DH-OF	85	270	37	78	13	0	9	49	.289	25	60	2	142	109	9	.965
1995—Seattle (A.L.)		3B-1B-OF	134	439	59	113	24	1	23	96	.257	53	128	2	116	174	16	.948
1996—Los Angeles (N.L.)■		3B-1B-SS	92	317	31	84	19	2	6	38	.265	37	77	0	76	122	9	.957
1997—Seattle (A.L.)■		1B-3B-OF-DH	68	150	22	44	5	0	5	20	.293	21	33	0	271	35	4	.987
1998—Oakland (A.L.)■		3B-1B-DH	129	409	56	97	24	2	11	71	.237	39	116	1	113	174	19	.938
1999—Tacoma (PCL)■		1B	3	13	1	3	1	0	0	2	.231	0	4	0	21	0	0	1.000
—Seattle (A.L.)		1B-3B-DH	19	46	2	11	1	0	2	7	.239	4	12	0	74	11	1	.988
American League totals (10 years)			669	1983	259	507	97	6	72	327	.256	211	533	7	853	865	82	.954
National League totals (1 year)			92	317	31	84	19	2	6	38	.265	37	77	0	76	122	9	.957
Major League totals (11 years)			761	2300	290	591	116	8	78	365	.257	248	610	7	929	987	91	.955

DIVISION SERIES RECORD

Year	Team (League)	Pos.	G	AB	R	H	2B	3B	HR	RBI	Avg.	BB	SO	SB	PO	A	E	Avg.
1995—Seattle (A.L.)		3B-1B	5	18	0	3	0	0	0	1	.167	3	7	0	2	6	0	1.000
1997—Seattle (A.L.)		3B	3	5	0	1	0	0	0	0	.200	0	3	0	1	2	0	1.000
Division series totals (2 years)			8	23	0	4	0	0	0	1	.174	3	10	0	3	8	0	1.000

CHAMPIONSHIP SERIES RECORD

NOTES: Hit home run in first at-bat (October 10, 1995).

Year	Team (League)	Pos.	G	AB	R	H	2B	3B	HR	RBI	Avg.	BB	SO	SB	PO	A	E	Avg.
1995—Seattle (A.L.)		3B	6	18	1	4	0	0	1	2	.222	0	4	0	5	9	0	1.000

BLUM, GEOFF　　　　SS　　　　EXPOS　　B

PERSONAL: Born April 26, 1973, in Redwood City, Calif. ... 6-3/195. ... Bats both, throws right. ... Full name: Geoffery E. Blum.
HIGH SCHOOL: Chino (Calif.).
COLLEGE: California.
TRANSACTIONS/CAREER NOTES: Selected by Montreal Expos organization in seventh round of free-agent draft (June 2, 1994). ... On Ottawa disabled list (May 21-June 15, 1999).

Year	Team (League)	Pos.	G	AB	R	H	2B	3B	HR	RBI	Avg.	BB	SO	SB	PO	A	E	Avg.
1994—Vermont (NY-P)		SS	63	241	48	83	15	1	3	38	.344	33	21	5	87	185	15	.948
1995—W.P. Beach (FSL)		2B-SS-3B	125	457	54	120	20	2	1	62	.263	34	61	6	166	298	18	.963
1996—Harrisburg (East.)		2-S-1-OF	120	396	47	95	22	2	1	41	.240	59	51	6	259	281	9	.984
1997—Ottawa (I.L.)		2B-SS-3B	118	407	59	101	21	2	3	35	.248	52	73	14	223	305	17	.969
1998—Ottawa (I.L.)		2B	8	23	1	4	0	0	0	1	.174	3	6	0	18	12	0	1.000
—GC Expos (GCL)		2B	5	18	0	3	1	1	0	1	.167	1	4	0	4	12	0	1.000
—Jupiter (FSL)		2B-3B-SS	17	58	13	16	6	0	0	5	.276	13	14	1	31	51	2	.976
—Harrisburg (East.)		SS-3B-2B-1B	39	139	25	43	12	3	6	21	.309	17	24	2	48	94	2	.986
1999—Ottawa (I.L.)		S-1-2-3-DH	77	268	43	71	14	1	10	37	.265	37	39	6	154	179	12	.965
—Montreal (N.L.)		SS-2B	45	133	21	32	7	2	8	18	.241	17	25	1	47	84	10	.929
Major League totals (1 year)			45	133	21	32	7	2	8	18	.241	17	25	1	47	84	10	.929

BOCACHICA, HIRAM　　　　2B　　　　DODGERS

PERSONAL: Born March 4, 1976, in Ponce, Puerto Rico. ... 5-11/165. ... Bats right, throws right. ... Full name: Hiram Colon Bocachica.
HIGH SCHOOL: Rexville (Bayamon, Puerto Rico).
TRANSACTIONS/CAREER NOTES: Selected by Montreal Expos organization in first round (21st pick overall) of free-agent draft (June 2, 1994). ... On West Palm Beach disabled list (May 16-July 12, 1996). ... On Harrisburg suspended list (June 15-18, 1997). ... On Harrisburg disabled list (June 18-25, 1997). ... Traded by Expos with P Carlos Perez and SS Mark Grudzielanek to Los Angeles Dodgers for 2B Wilton Guerrero, P Ted Lilly, OF Peter Bergeron and 1B Jonathan Tucker (July 31, 1998).
STATISTICAL NOTES: Led South Atlantic League shortstops with 58 errors in 1995. ... Led Texas League in being hit by pitch with 13 in 1999. ... Tied for Texas League lead with 77 double plays by second basemen in 1999.

Year	Team (League)	Pos.	G	AB	R	H	2B	3B	HR	RBI	Avg.	BB	SO	SB	PO	A	E	Avg.
1994—GC Expos (GCL)		SS	43	168	31	47	9	0	5	16	.280	15	42	11	72	126	*23	.896
1995—Albany (SAL)		SS-2B	96	380	65	108	20	10	2	30	.284	52	78	47	165	265	†58	.881
1996—W.P. Beach (FSL)		DH-SS	71	267	50	90	17	5	2	26	.337	34	47	21	37	83	24	.833
—GC Expos (GCL)		DH	9	32	11	8	3	0	0	2	.250	5	3	2	...	...	...	...
1997—Harrisburg (East.)		SS-2B-DH	119	443	82	123	19	3	11	35	.278	41	98	29	135	186	32	.909
1998—Harrisburg (East.)		OF-DH	80	296	39	78	18	4	4	27	.264	21	61	20	171	4	10	.946
—Ottawa (I.L.)		OF	12	41	5	8	3	1	0	5	.195	6	14	2	23	1	0	1.000
—Albuquerque (PCL)■		OF	26	101	16	24	7	1	4	16	.238	13	24	5	80	2	2	.976
1999—San Antonio (Texas)		2B-DH	123	477	84	139	22	10	11	60	.291	60	71	30	227	313	*31	.946

BOCHTLER, DOUG　　　　P

PERSONAL: Born July 5, 1970, in West Palm Beach, Fla. ... 6-3/200. ... Throws right, bats right. ... Full name: Douglas Eugene Bochtler. ... Name pronounced BOCK-ler.
HIGH SCHOOL: John I. Leonard (Lake Worth, Fla.).
JUNIOR COLLEGE: Indian River Community College (Fla.).
TRANSACTIONS/CAREER NOTES: Selected by Montreal Expos organization in ninth round of free-agent draft (June 5, 1989). ... On disabled list (June 18-September 6, 1992). ... Selected by Colorado Rockies in second round (32nd pick overall) of expansion draft (November 17, 1992). ... On Colorado Springs disabled list (April 18-26, 1993). ... Traded by Rockies with C Brad Ausmus and a player to be named later to San Diego Padres for P Bruce Hurst and P Greg W. Harris (July 26, 1993); Padres acquired P Andy Ashby to complete deal (July 27, 1993). On disabled list (June 16-24 and August 24, 1994-remainder of season). ... On disabled list (July 2-17, 1997). ... Traded by Padres with IF Jorge Velandia to Oakland Athletics for P Don Wengert and IF David Newhan (November 26, 1997). ... Traded by A's to Detroit Tigers for cash (March 25, 1998). ... Claimed on waivers by Los Angeles Dodgers (October 6, 1998). ... Released by Dodgers (January 11, 1999). ... Signed by Toronto Blue Jays organization (April 1, 1999). ... Traded by Blue Jays to Dodgers for cash (May 19, 1999). ... On Albuquerque disabled list (September 3, 1999-remainder of season). ... Granted free agency (October 4, 1999).

Year	League	W	L	Pct.	ERA	G	GS	CG	ShO	Sv.	IP	H	R	ER	BB	SO
1989—Gulf Coast Expos (GCL)		2	2	.500	3.21	9	9	1	0	0	47 2/3	46	22	17	20	45
1990—Rockford (Midw.)		9	12	.429	3.50	25	25	1	1	0	139	142	82	54	54	109
1991—West Palm Beach (FSL)		•12	9	.571	2.92	26	24	7	2	0	160 1/3	148	63	52	55	109
1992—Harrisburg (East.)		6	5	.545	2.32	13	13	2	1	0	77 2/3	50	25	20	36	89

Year	League	W	L	Pct.	ERA	G	GS	CG	ShO	Sv.	IP	H	R	ER	BB	SO
1993— Colo. Springs (PCL)■		1	4	.200	6.93	12	11	0	0	0	50²/₃	71	41	39	26	38
— Central Valley (Calif.)		3	1	.750	3.40	8	8	0	0	0	47²/₃	40	23	18	28	43
— Las Vegas (PCL)■		0	5	.000	5.22	7	7	1	0	0	39²/₃	52	26	23	11	30
1994— Las Vegas (PCL)		3	7	.300	5.20	22	20	2	1	0	100¹/₃	116	67	58	48	86
1995— Las Vegas (PCL)		2	3	.400	4.25	18	2	0	0	1	36	31	18	17	26	32
— San Diego (N.L.)		4	4	.500	3.57	34	0	0	0	1	45¹/₃	38	18	18	19	45
1996— San Diego (N.L.)		2	4	.333	3.02	63	0	0	0	3	65²/₃	45	25	22	39	68
1997— San Diego (N.L.)		3	6	.333	4.77	54	0	0	0	2	60¹/₃	51	35	32	50	46
1998— Detroit (A.L.)■		0	2	.000	6.15	51	0	0	0	0	67¹/₃	73	48	46	42	45
1999— Syracuse (I.L.)■		4	0	1.000	2.63	14	0	0	0	0	27¹/₃	18	9	8	10	28
— Los Angeles (N.L.)		0	0	...	5.54	12	0	0	0	0	13	11	8	8	6	7
— Albuquerque (PCL)		3	4	.429	3.18	18	0	0	0	3	22²/₃	16	9	8	11	25
A.L. totals (1 year)		0	2	.000	6.15	51	0	0	0	0	67¹/₃	73	48	46	42	45
N.L. totals (4 years)		9	14	.391	3.91	163	0	0	0	6	184¹/₃	145	86	80	114	166
Major League totals (5 years)		9	16	.360	4.51	214	0	0	0	6	251²/₃	218	134	126	156	211

DIVISION SERIES RECORD

Year	League	W	L	Pct.	ERA	G	GS	CG	ShO	Sv.	IP	H	R	ER	BB	SO
1996— San Diego (N.L.)		0	1	.000	27.00	1	0	0	0	0	¹/₃	0	1	1	3	0

BOEHRINGER, BRIAN   P   PADRES

PERSONAL: Born January 8, 1970, in St. Louis. ... 6-2/190. ... Throws right, bats both. ... Full name: Brian Edward Boehringer. ... Name pronounced BO-ring-er.
HIGH SCHOOL: Northwest (House Springs, Mo.).
JUNIOR COLLEGE: St. Louis Community College at Meramec.
COLLEGE: UNLV.
TRANSACTIONS/CAREER NOTES: Selected by Houston Astros organization in 10th round of free-agent draft (June 4, 1990); did not sign. ... Selected by Chicago White Sox organization in fourth round of free-agent draft (June 3, 1991). ... On Utica disabled list (June 29-August 25, 1991). ... On disabled list (June 24-August 25, 1992). ... Traded by White Sox to New York Yankees for P Paul Assenmacher (March 21, 1994). ... On New York disabled list (May 27-August 19, 1997; included rehabilitation assignments to Gulf Coast Yankees (August 10-12) and Tampa (August 13-19). ... Selected by Tampa Bay Devil Rays in second round (30th pick overall) of expansion draft (November 18, 1997). ... Traded by Devil Rays with SS Andy Sheets to San Diego Padres for C John Flaherty (November 18, 1997). ... On San Diego disabled list (August 14, 1999-remainder of season).
STATISTICAL NOTES: Tied for Eastern League lead with four balks in 1994. ... Led International League with 11 hit batsmen in 1996.

Year	League	W	L	Pct.	ERA	G	GS	CG	ShO	Sv.	IP	H	R	ER	BB	SO
1991— GC White Sox (GCL)		1	1	.500	6.57	5	1	0	0	0	12¹/₃	14	9	9	5	10
— Utica (NY-P)		1	1	.500	2.37	4	4	0	0	0	19	14	8	5	8	19
1992— South Bend (Midw.)		6	7	.462	4.38	15	15	2	0	0	86¹/₃	87	52	42	40	59
1993— Sarasota (FSL)		10	4	.714	2.80	18	17	3	0	0	119	103	47	37	51	92
— Birmingham (Sou.)		2	1	.667	3.54	7	7	1	0	0	40²/₃	41	20	16	14	29
1994— Alb./Colonie (East.)■		10	11	.476	3.62	27	27	5	1	0	171²/₃	165	85	69	57	145
1995— New York (A.L.)		0	3	.000	13.75	7	3	0	0	0	17²/₃	24	27	27	22	10
— Columbus (I.L.)		8	6	.571	2.77	17	17	3	0	0	104	101	39	32	31	58
1996— Columbus (I.L.)		11	7	.611	4.00	25	25	3	1	0	153	155	79	68	56	132
— New York (A.L.)		2	4	.333	5.44	15	3	0	0	0	46¹/₃	46	28	28	21	37
1997— New York (A.L.)		3	2	.600	2.63	34	0	0	0	0	48	39	16	14	32	53
— GC Yankees (GCL)		0	0	...	0.00	1	1	0	0	0	2	1	0	0	0	2
— Tampa (FSL)		0	1	.000	5.00	3	3	0	0	0	9	9	5	5	5	8
1998— San Diego (N.L.)■		5	2	.714	4.36	56	1	0	0	0	76¹/₃	75	38	37	45	67
1999— San Diego (N.L.)		6	5	.545	3.24	33	11	0	0	0	94¹/₃	97	38	34	35	64
A.L. totals (3 years)		5	9	.357	5.54	56	6	0	0	0	112	109	71	69	75	100
N.L. totals (2 years)		11	7	.611	3.74	89	12	0	0	0	170²/₃	172	76	71	80	131
Major League totals (5 years)		16	16	.500	4.46	145	18	0	0	0	282²/₃	281	147	140	155	231

DIVISION SERIES RECORD

Year	League	W	L	Pct.	ERA	G	GS	CG	ShO	Sv.	IP	H	R	ER	BB	SO
1996— New York (A.L.)		1	0	1.000	6.75	2	0	0	0	0	1¹/₃	3	2	1	2	0
1997— New York (A.L.)		0	0	...	0.00	1	0	0	0	0	1²/₃	1	0	0	1	2
1998— San Diego (N.L.)								Did not play.								
Division series totals (2 years)		1	0	1.000	3.00	3	0	0	0	0	3	4	2	1	3	2

CHAMPIONSHIP SERIES RECORD

Year	League	W	L	Pct.	ERA	G	GS	CG	ShO	Sv.	IP	H	R	ER	BB	SO
1998— San Diego (N.L.)		0	0	...	0.00	3	0	0	0	0	3	3	0	0	1	1

WORLD SERIES RECORD

NOTES: Member of World Series championship team (1996).

Year	League	W	L	Pct.	ERA	G	GS	CG	ShO	Sv.	IP	H	R	ER	BB	SO
1996— New York (A.L.)		0	0	...	5.40	2	0	0	0	0	5	5	5	3	0	5
1998— San Diego (N.L.)		0	0	...	9.00	2	0	0	0	0	2	4	2	2	2	3
World Series totals (2 years)		0	0	...	6.43	4	0	0	0	0	7	9	7	5	2	8

BOGAR, TIM   IF   ASTROS

PERSONAL: Born October 28, 1966, in Indianapolis. ... 6-2/198. ... Bats right, throws right. ... Full name: Timothy Paul Bogar.
HIGH SCHOOL: Buffalo Grove (Ill.).
COLLEGE: Eastern Illinois.
TRANSACTIONS/CAREER NOTES: Selected by New York Mets organization in eighth round of free-agent draft (June 2, 1987). ... On disabled list (June 14, 1990-remainder of season). ... On disabled list (August 16-September 1, 1993). ... On New York disabled list (May 6-June 9, 1994); included rehabilitation assignment to Norfolk (June 4-9). ... Traded by Mets to Houston Astros for IF Luis Lopez (March 31, 1997). ... On disabled list (September 5, 1997-remainder of season). ... Granted free agency (October 23, 1998). ... Re-signed by Astros (December 7, 1998).
MISCELLANEOUS: Played all nine positions in one game for Tidewater (September 4, 1991).

Year Team (League)	Pos.	G	AB	R	H	2B	3B	HR	RBI	Avg.	BB	SO	SB	PO	A	E	Avg.
1987—Little Falls (NY-P)	SS-2B	58	205	31	48	9	0	0	23	.234	18	39	2	79	194	24	.919
1988—Columbia (SAL)	2B-SS	45	142	19	40	4	2	3	21	.282	22	29	5	89	120	8	.963
—St. Lucie (FSL)	2B-SS-3B	76	236	34	65	7	1	2	30	.275	34	57	9	141	214	19	.949
1989—Jackson (Texas)	SS	112	406	44	108	13	5	4	45	.266	41	57	8	185	351	29	.949
1990—Tidewater (I.L.)	SS	33	117	10	19	2	0	0	4	.162	8	22	1	57	89	10	.936
1991—Williamsport (East.)	3B-2B-1B-SS	63	243	33	61	12	2	2	25	.251	20	44	13	100	137	8	.967
—Tidewater (I.L.)	S-2-3-C-1-O-P	65	218	23	56	11	0	1	23	.257	20	35	1	111	183	11	.964
1992—Tidewater (I.L.)	2-S-3-P-1	129	481	54	134	32	1	5	38	.279	14	65	7	211	327	15	.973
1993—New York (N.L.)	SS-3B-2B	78	205	19	50	13	0	3	25	.244	14	29	0	105	217	9	.973
1994—New York (N.L.)	3-1-S-2-O	50	52	5	8	0	0	2	5	.154	4	11	1	77	38	1	.991
—Norfolk (I.L.)	3B-2B	5	19	0	2	0	0	0	1	.105	1	4	0	5	11	0	1.000
1995—New York (N.L.)	S-3-1-2-O	78	145	17	42	7	0	1	21	.290	9	25	1	82	100	6	.968
1996—New York (N.L.)	1B-3B-SS-2B	91	89	17	19	4	0	0	6	.213	8	20	1	104	61	1	.994
1997—Houston (N.L.)■	SS-3B-1B	97	241	30	60	14	4	4	30	.249	24	42	4	110	229	6	.983
1998—Houston (N.L.)	SS-2B-3B-DH	79	156	12	24	4	1	1	8	.154	9	36	2	63	147	3	.986
1999—Houston (N.L.)	SS-3B-2B	107	309	44	74	16	2	4	31	.239	38	52	3	130	277	9	.978
Major League totals (7 years)		580	1197	144	277	58	7	15	126	.231	106	215	12	671	1069	35	.980

DIVISION SERIES RECORD

Year Team (League)	Pos.	G	AB	R	H	2B	3B	HR	RBI	Avg.	BB	SO	SB	PO	A	E	Avg.
1999—Houston (N.L.)	PH-SS	2	4	0	3	1	0	0	1	.750	1	0	0	4	4	0	1.000

RECORD AS PITCHER

Year League	W	L	Pct.	ERA	G	GS	CG	ShO	Sv.	IP	H	R	ER	BB	SO
1991—Tidewater (I.L.)	0	0	...	27.00	1	0	0	0	0	$\frac{1}{3}$	0	1	1	0	1
1992—Tidewater (I.L.)	0	0	...	12.00	3	0	0	0	0	3	4	4	4	3	1

BOGGS, WADE   3B

PERSONAL: Born June 15, 1958, in Omaha, Neb. ... 6-2/197. ... Bats left, throws right. ... Full name: Wade Anthony Boggs.
HIGH SCHOOL: H.B. Plant (Tampa).
JUNIOR COLLEGE: Hillsborough Community College (Fla.).
TRANSACTIONS/CAREER NOTES: Selected by Boston Red Sox organization in seventh round of free-agent draft (June 8, 1976). ... On disabled list (April 20-May 2, 1979). ... Granted free agency (October 26, 1992). ... Signed by New York Yankees (December 15, 1992). ... Granted free agency (November 1, 1995). ... Re-signed by Yankees (December 5, 1995). ... Granted free agency (November 1, 1997). ... Signed by Tampa Bay Devil Rays (December 9, 1997). ... On disabled list (April 18-May 8, 1998; and May 6-21 and September 3, 1999-remainder of season). ... Announced retirement (November 11, 1999).
RECORDS: Shares major league single-season records for most games with at least one hit—135 (1985); and fewest double plays by third baseman (150 or more games)—17 (1988). ... Holds A.L. records for most consecutive seasons with 200 or more hits—7 (1983-89); and most seasons and consecutive seasons leading league in intentional bases on balls received—6 (1987-92). ... Holds A.L. single-season record for most singles—187 (1985). ... Holds A.L. rookie-season record for highest batting average (100 or more games)—.349 (1982). ... Shares A.L. single-season record for fewest putouts by third baseman for leader—121 (1986); and fewest double plays by third baseman (150 or more games)—17 (1988).
HONORS: Named third baseman on THE SPORTING NEWS A.L. All-Star team (1983, 1985-88, 1991 and 1994). ... Named third baseman on THE SPORTING NEWS A.L. Silver Slugger team (1983, 1986-89, 1991 and 1993-94). ... Won A.L. Gold Glove at third base (1994-95).
STATISTICAL NOTES: Led Eastern League third basemen with .953 fielding percentage in 1979. ... Led International League with .3353 batting average in 1981. ... Led A.L. with .449 on-base percentage in 1983, .450 in 1985, .453 in 1986, .461 in 1987, .476 in 1988 and .430 in 1989. ... Led A.L. third basemen with 30 double plays in 1984, 37 in 1987, 29 in 1989 and 29 in 1993. ... Had 28-game hitting streak (June 24-July 26, 1985). ... Led A.L. third basemen with 486 total chances in 1985. ... Had 20-game hitting streak (August 29-September 18, 1986). ... Had 25-game hitting streak (May 28-June 24, 1987). ... Led A.L. with 19 intentional bases on balls received in 1987, 1989, 1990 and 1992, with 25 in 1991 and tied for lead with 18 in 1988. ... Led A.L. in grounding into double plays with 23 in 1988. ... Led A.L. third basemen with .981 fielding percentage in 1995. ... Career major league grand slams: 4.

Year Team (League)	Pos.	G	AB	R	H	2B	3B	HR	RBI	Avg.	BB	SO	SB	PO	A	E	Avg.
1976—Elmira (NY-P)	3B	57	179	29	47	6	0	0	15	.263	29	15	2	36	75	16	.874
1977—Win.-Salem (Car.)	3B-2B-SS	117	422	67	140	13	1	2	55	.332	65	22	8	145	223	27	.932
1978—Bristol (East.)	3B-SS-2B-OF	109	354	63	110	14	2	1	32	.311	53	25	1	62	107	7	.960
1979—Bristol (East.)	3B-SS-2B	113	406	56	132	17	2	0	41	.325	66	21	11	94	213	15	†.953
1980—Pawtucket (I.L.)	3B-1B	129	418	51	128	21	0	1	45	.306	64	25	3	108	156	12	.957
1981—Pawtucket (I.L.)	3B-1B	137	498	67	*167	*41	3	5	60	*.335	89	41	4	359	238	26	.958
1982—Boston (A.L.)	1B-3B-DH-OF	104	338	51	118	14	1	5	44	.349	35	21	1	489	168	8	.988
1983—Boston (A.L.)	3B	153	582	100	210	44	7	5	74	*.361	92	36	3	118	368	*27	.947
1984—Boston (A.L.)	3B-DH	158	625	109	203	31	4	6	55	.325	89	44	3	141	330	•20	.959
1985—Boston (A.L.)	3B	161	653	107	*240	42	3	8	78	*.368	96	61	2	134	335	17	.965
1986—Boston (A.L.)	3B	149	580	107	207	47	2	8	71	*.357	*105	44	0	*121	267	19	.953
1987—Boston (A.L.)	3B-1B-DH	147	551	108	200	40	6	24	89	*.363	105	48	1	112	277	14	.965
1988—Boston (A.L.)	3B-DH	155	584	*128	214	*45	6	5	58	*.366	*125	34	2	*122	250	11	.971
1989—Boston (A.L.)	3B-DH	156	621	•113	205	*51	7	3	54	.330	107	51	2	*123	264	17	.958
1990—Boston (A.L.)	3B-DH	155	619	89	187	44	5	6	63	.302	87	68	0	108	241	20	.946
1991—Boston (A.L.)	3B	144	546	93	181	42	2	8	51	.332	89	32	1	89	276	12	.968
1992—Boston (A.L.)	3B-DH	143	514	62	133	22	4	7	50	.259	74	31	1	70	229	15	.952
1993—New York (A.L.)■	3B-DH	143	560	83	169	26	1	2	59	.302	74	49	0	75	*311	12	†.970
1994—New York (A.L.)	3B-1B	97	366	61	125	19	1	11	55	.342	61	29	2	66	218	10	.966
1995—New York (A.L.)	3B-1B	126	460	76	149	22	4	5	63	.324	74	50	1	114	198	5	†.984
1996—New York (A.L.)	3B-DH	132	501	80	156	29	2	2	41	.311	67	32	1	62	201	7	.974
1997—New York (A.L.)	3B-DH-P	104	353	55	103	23	1	4	28	.292	48	38	0	42	140	4	.978
1998—Tampa Bay (A.L.)■	3B-DH	123	435	51	122	23	4	7	52	.280	46	54	3	52	131	5	.973
1999—Tampa Bay (A.L.)	3B-DH-1B-P	90	292	40	88	14	1	2	29	.301	38	23	1	77	100	9	.952
Major League totals (18 years)		2440	9180	1513	3010	578	61	118	1014	.328	1412	745	24	2115	4304	232	.965

DIVISION SERIES RECORD

Year Team (League)	Pos.	G	AB	R	H	2B	3B	HR	RBI	Avg.	BB	SO	SB	PO	A	E	Avg.
1995— New York (A.L.)..........	3B	4	19	4	5	2	0	1	3	.263	3	5	0	4	8	0	1.000
1996— New York (A.L.)..........	3B	3	12	0	1	1	0	0	0	.083	0	2	0	2	1	0	1.000
1997— New York (A.L.)..........	3B-PH	3	7	1	3	0	0	0	2	.429	0	0	0	0	1	0	1.000
Division series totals (3 years)		10	38	5	9	3	0	1	5	.237	3	7	0	6	10	0	1.000

CHAMPIONSHIP SERIES RECORD

RECORDS: Shares single-series record for most sacrifice flies—2 (1988).

Year Team (League)	Pos.	G	AB	R	H	2B	3B	HR	RBI	Avg.	BB	SO	SB	PO	A	E	Avg.
1986— Boston (A.L.).............	3B	7	30	3	7	1	1	0	2	.233	4	1	0	7	13	2	.909
1988— Boston (A.L.).............	3B	4	13	2	5	0	0	0	3	.385	3	4	0	6	6	0	1.000
1990— Boston (A.L.).............	3B	4	16	1	7	1	0	1	1	.438	0	3	0	6	10	0	1.000
1996— New York (A.L.)..........	3B	3	15	1	2	0	0	0	0	.133	1	3	0	2	11	0	1.000
Championship series totals (4 years)		18	74	7	21	2	1	1	6	.284	8	11	0	21	40	2	.968

WORLD SERIES RECORD

NOTES: Member of World Series championship team (1996).

Year Team (League)	Pos.	G	AB	R	H	2B	3B	HR	RBI	Avg.	BB	SO	SB	PO	A	E	Avg.
1986— Boston (A.L.).............	3B	7	31	3	9	3	0	0	3	.290	4	2	0	4	15	0	1.000
1996— New York (A.L.)..........	3B-PH	4	11	0	3	1	0	0	2	.273	1	0	0	0	0	0	...
World Series totals (2 years)		11	42	3	12	4	0	0	5	.286	5	2	0	4	15	0	1.000

ALL-STAR GAME RECORD

Year League	Pos.	AB	R	H	2B	3B	HR	RBI	Avg.	BB	SO	SB	PO	A	E	Avg.
1985— American	3B	0	0	0	0	0	0	0	...	1	0	0	0	0	0	...
1986— American	3B	3	0	1	0	0	0	0	.333	1	0	0	0	1	0	1.000
1987— American	3B	3	0	0	0	0	0	0	.000	0	0	0	0	3	0	1.000
1988— American	3B	3	0	1	0	0	0	0	.333	0	0	0	1	1	0	1.000
1989— American	3B	3	1	1	0	0	1	1	.333	0	0	0	1	1	0	1.000
1990— American	3B	2	0	2	0	0	0	0	1.000	1	0	0	0	4	0	1.000
1991— American	3B	2	1	1	0	0	0	0	.500	1	0	0	1	2	0	1.000
1992— American	3B	3	1	1	0	0	0	0	.333	0	1	0	1	0	0	1.000
1993— American	3B	1	0	0	0	0	0	0	.000	1	0	0	1	0	0	1.000
1994— American	3B	3	1	1	0	0	0	0	.333	0	2	0	0	2	0	1.000
1995— American	3B	2	0	1	0	0	0	0	.500	0	0	0	0	1	0	1.000
1996— American	3B	3	0	0	0	0	0	0	.000	0	0	0	1	2	0	1.000
All-Star Game totals (12 years)		28	4	9	0	0	1	1	.321	5	3	0	5	17	0	1.000

RECORD AS PITCHER

Year League	W	L	Pct.	ERA	G	GS	CG	ShO	Sv.	IP	H	R	ER	BB	SO
1997— New York (A.L.)...............	0	0	...	0.00	1	0	0	0	0	1	0	0	0	1	1
1999— Tampa Bay (A.L.)............	0	0	...	6.75	1	0	0	0	0	1 1/3	3	1	1	0	1
Major League totals (2 years).......	0	0	...	3.86	2	0	0	0	0	2 1/3	3	1	1	1	2

BOHANON, BRIAN   P   ROCKIES

PERSONAL: Born August 1, 1968, in Denton, Texas. ... 6-2/240. ... Throws left, bats left. ... Full name: Brian Edward Bohanon Jr.
HIGH SCHOOL: North Shore (Houston).
TRANSACTIONS/CAREER NOTES: Selected by Texas Rangers organization in first round (19th pick overall) of free-agent draft (June 2, 1987). ... On disabled list (April 17, 1988-remainder of season). ... On Charlotte disabled list (April 7-May 2, 1989). ... On Texas disabled list (April 7-July 1, 1991; included rehabilitation assignments to Charlotte (June 1-10), Tulsa (June 10-23) and Oklahoma City (June 23-30). ... On Texas disabled list (April 28-May 13, 1992). ... On Texas disabled list (June 9-30, 1993); included rehabilitation assignment to Oklahoma City (June 21-30). ... Granted free agency (December 23, 1994). ... Signed by Detroit Tigers organization (March 6, 1995). ... Released by Tigers (October 13, 1995). ... Signed by Toronto Blue Jays organization (February 20, 1996). ... Granted free agency (October 3, 1996). ... Signed by New York Mets organization (December 18, 1996). ... Traded by Mets to Los Angeles Dodgers for P Greg McMichael and cash (July 10, 1998). ... Granted free agency (October 27, 1998). ... Signed by Colorado Rockies (November 9, 1998).
MISCELLANEOUS: Singled and struck out once in two appearances as pinch hitter (1997). ... Grounded out in only appearance as pinch hitter (1999).

Year League	W	L	Pct.	ERA	G	GS	CG	ShO	Sv.	IP	H	R	ER	BB	SO
1987— Gulf Coast Rangers (GCL)..	0	2	.000	4.71	5	4	0	0	0	21	15	13	11	5	21
1988— Charlotte (FSL).................	0	1	.000	5.40	2	2	0	0	0	6 2/3	6	4	4	5	9
1989— Charlotte (FSL).................	0	3	.000	1.81	11	7	0	0	1	54 2/3	40	16	11	20	33
— Tulsa (Texas)..................	5	0	1.000	2.20	11	11	1	1	0	73 2/3	59	20	18	27	44
1990— Texas (A.L.)....................	0	3	.000	6.62	11	6	0	0	0	34	40	30	25	18	15
— Oklahoma City (A.A.).........	1	2	.333	3.66	14	4	0	0	1	32	35	16	13	8	22
1991— Charlotte (FSL)................	1	0	1.000	3.86	2	2	0	0	0	11 2/3	6	5	5	4	7
— Tulsa (Texas)..................	0	1	.000	2.31	2	2	0	0	0	11 2/3	9	8	3	11	6
— Oklahoma City (A.A.).........	0	4	.000	2.91	7	7	0	0	0	46 1/3	49	19	15	15	37
— Texas (A.L.)....................	4	3	.571	4.84	11	11	1	0	0	61 1/3	66	35	33	23	34
1992— Oklahoma City (A.A.)........	4	2	.667	2.73	9	9	3	0	0	56	53	21	17	15	24
— Texas (A.L.)....................	1	1	.500	6.31	18	7	0	0	0	45 2/3	57	38	32	25	29
— Tulsa (Texas)..................	2	1	.667	1.27	6	6	1	0	0	28 1/3	25	7	4	9	25
1993— Texas (A.L.)....................	4	4	.500	4.76	36	8	0	0	0	92 2/3	107	54	49	46	45
— Oklahoma City (A.A.).........	0	1	.000	6.43	2	2	0	0	0	7	7	6	5	3	7
1994— Oklahoma City (A.A.)........	5	10	.333	4.12	15	15	2	1	0	98 1/3	106	56	45	33	88
— Texas (A.L.)....................	2	4	.500	7.23	11	5	0	0	0	37 1/3	51	31	30	8	26
1995— Detroit (A.L.)■.................	1	1	.500	5.54	52	10	0	0	1	105 2/3	121	68	65	41	63
1996— Toronto (A.L.)■■...............	0	1	.000	7.77	20	0	0	0	1	22	27	19	19	19	17
— Syracuse (I.L.)................	4	3	.571	3.86	31	0	0	0	0	58 1/3	56	29	25	17	38

Year League	W	L	Pct.	ERA	G	GS	CG	ShO	Sv.	IP	H	R	ER	BB	SO
1997— Norfolk (I.L.)■	9	3	.750	2.63	15	14	4	2	0	96	88	37	28	32	84
— New York (N.L.)	6	4	.600	3.82	19	14	0	0	0	94 1/3	95	49	40	34	66
1998— New York (N.L.)	2	4	.333	3.15	25	4	0	0	0	54 1/3	47	21	19	21	39
— Los Angeles (N.L.)■	5	7	.417	2.40	14	14	2	0	0	97 1/3	74	35	26	36	72
1999— Colorado (N.L.)■	12	12	.500	6.20	33	33	3	1	0	197 1/3	236	146	136	92	120
A.L. totals (7 years)	12	15	.444	5.71	159	47	1	0	2	398 2/3	469	275	253	180	229
N.L. totals (3 years)	25	27	.481	4.49	91	65	5	1	0	443 1/3	452	251	221	183	297
Major League totals (10 years)	37	42	.468	5.07	250	112	6	1	2	842	921	526	474	363	526

BONDS, BARRY — OF — GIANTS

B

PERSONAL: Born July 24, 1964, in Riverside, Calif. ... 6-2/210. ... Bats left, throws left. ... Full name: Barry Lamar Bonds. ... Son of Bobby Bonds, outfielder with eight major league teams (1968-81) and coach with Cleveland Indians (1984-87) and San Francisco Giants (1993-96).

HIGH SCHOOL: Serra (San Mateo, Calif.).

COLLEGE: Arizona State.

TRANSACTIONS/CAREER NOTES: Selected by San Francisco Giants organization in second round of free-agent draft (June 7, 1982); did not sign. ... Selected by Pittsburgh Pirates organization in first round (sixth pick overall) of free-agent draft (June 3, 1985). ... On disabled list (June 15-July 4, 1992). ... Granted free agency (October 26, 1992). ... Signed by Giants (December 8, 1992). ... On suspended list (August 14-16, 1998). ... On disabled list (April 18-June 9, 1999).

RECORDS: Holds major league career record for most intentional bases on balls—298. ... Shares major league record for most seasons and consecutive seasons leading league in intentional bases on balls received—7 (1992-98). ... Shares major league single-season record for fewest assists by outfielder who led league in assists—14 (1990). ... Holds N.L. career record for most consecutive years leading league in bases on balls—4 (1994-97). ... Shares major league record for fewest double plays by outfielder (150 or more games)—0 (1997 and 1998). ... Shares N.L. single-season record for most consecutive times reached base safely—15 (August 31 [1], September 1 [5], 2 [4], 4, 5], 1998 [5 singles, 2 doubles, 2 home runs, 6 bases on balls]. ... Shares N.L. single-season record for fewest assists by outfielder (150 or more games)—2 (1993).

HONORS: Named outfielder on THE SPORTING NEWS college All-America team (1985). ... Named Major League Player of the Year by THE SPORTING NEWS (1990). ... Named N.L. Player of the Year by THE SPORTING NEWS (1990-91). ... Named outfielder on THE SPORTING NEWS N.L. All-Star team (1990-94 and 1996-97). ... Won N.L. Gold Glove as outfielder (1990-94 and 1996-98). ... Named outfielder on THE SPORTING NEWS N.L. Silver Slugger team (1990-94, 1996 and 1997). ... Named N.L. Most Valuable Player by Baseball Writers' Association of America (1990 and 1992-93).

STATISTICAL NOTES: Led N.L. with .565 slugging percentage in 1990, .624 in 1992 and .677 in 1993. ... Led N.L. with 32 intentional bases on balls received in 1992, 43 in 1993, 18 in 1994, 22 in 1995, 30 in 1996, 34 in 1997 and 29 in 1998. ... Led N.L. with .456 on-base percentage in 1992, .458 in 1993 and .431 in 1995. ... Led N.L. with 365 total bases in 1993. ... Hit three home runs in one game (August 2, 1994). ... Career major league grand slams: 8.

Year Team (League)	Pos.	G	AB	R	H	2B	3B	HR	RBI	Avg.	BB	SO	SB	PO	A	E	Avg.
1985— Prince Will. (Caro.)	OF	71	254	49	76	16	4	13	37	.299	37	52	15	202	4	5	.976
1986— Hawaii (PCL)	OF	44	148	30	46	7	2	7	37	.311	33	31	16	109	4	2	.983
— Pittsburgh (N.L.)	OF	113	413	72	92	26	3	16	48	.223	65	102	36	280	9	5	.983
1987— Pittsburgh (N.L.)	OF	150	551	99	144	34	9	25	59	.261	54	88	32	330	15	5	.986
1988— Pittsburgh (N.L.)	OF	144	538	97	152	30	5	24	58	.283	72	82	17	292	5	6	.980
1989— Pittsburgh (N.L.)	OF	159	580	96	144	34	6	19	58	.248	93	93	32	365	14	6	.984
1990— Pittsburgh (N.L.)	OF	151	519	104	156	32	3	33	114	.301	93	83	52	338	•14	6	.983
1991— Pittsburgh (N.L.)	OF	153	510	95	149	28	5	25	116	.292	107	73	43	321	13	3	.991
1992— Pittsburgh (N.L.)	OF	140	473	*109	147	36	5	34	103	.311	*127	69	39	310	4	3	.991
1993— San Fran. (N.L.)■	OF	159	539	129	181	38	4	*46	*123	.336	126	79	29	310	7	5	.984
1994— San Francisco (N.L.)	OF	112	391	89	122	18	1	37	81	.312	*74	43	29	198	10	3	.986
1995— San Francisco (N.L.)	OF	•144	506	109	149	30	7	33	104	.294	*120	83	31	279	12	6	.980
1996— San Francisco (N.L.)	OF	158	517	122	159	27	3	42	129	.308	*151	76	40	286	10	6	.980
1997— San Francisco (N.L.)	OF	159	532	123	155	26	5	40	101	.291	*145	87	37	289	10	5	.984
1998— San Francisco (N.L.)	OF	156	552	120	167	44	7	37	122	.303	130	92	28	301	2	5	.984
1999— San Francisco (N.L.)	OF-DH	102	355	91	93	20	2	34	83	.262	73	62	15	177	4	3	.984
Major League totals (14 years)		2000	6976	1455	2010	423	65	445	1299	.288	1430	1112	460	4076	129	67	.984

DIVISION SERIES RECORD

Year Team (League)	Pos.	G	AB	R	H	2B	3B	HR	RBI	Avg.	BB	SO	SB	PO	A	E	Avg.
1997— San Francisco (N.L.)	OF	3	12	0	3	2	0	0	2	.250	0	3	1	6	0	0	1.000

CHAMPIONSHIP SERIES RECORD

RECORDS: Shares single-inning record for most hits—2 (October 13, 1992, second inning).

Year Team (League)	Pos.	G	AB	R	H	2B	3B	HR	RBI	Avg.	BB	SO	SB	PO	A	E	Avg.
1990— Pittsburgh (N.L.)	OF	6	18	4	3	0	0	0	1	.167	6	5	2	13	0	0	1.000
1991— Pittsburgh (N.L.)	OF	7	27	1	4	1	0	0	0	.148	2	4	3	14	1	1	.938
1992— Pittsburgh (N.L.)	OF	7	23	5	6	1	0	1	2	.261	6	4	1	17	0	0	1.000
Championship series totals (3 years)		20	68	10	13	2	0	1	3	.191	14	13	6	44	1	1	.978

ALL-STAR GAME RECORD

Year League	Pos.	AB	R	H	2B	3B	HR	RBI	Avg.	BB	SO	SB	PO	A	E	Avg.
1990— National	OF	1	0	0	0	0	0	0	.000	1	0	0	2	0	0	1.000
1992— National	OF	3	1	1	1	0	0	0	.333	0	0	0	2	0	0	1.000
1993— National	OF	3	2	2	2	0	0	0	.667	0	0	0	1	0	0	1.000
1994— National	OF	3	0	0	0	0	0	1	.000	0	2	0	1	0	0	1.000
1995— National	OF	3	0	0	0	0	0	0	.000	0	1	0	0	0	0	...
1996— National	OF	3	0	1	0	0	0	0	.333	0	0	0	2	0	0	1.000
1997— National	OF	2	0	0	0	0	0	0	.000	1	1	1	2	0	0	1.000
1998— National	OF	2	1	1	0	0	1	3	.500	1	0	0	1	0	0	1.000
All-Star Game totals (8 years)		20	4	5	3	0	1	4	.250	3	4	1	11	0	0	1.000

PERSONAL: Born April 7, 1969, in Salinas, Puerto Rico. ... 6-0/202. ... Throws right, bats right. ... Full name: Ricardo Bones. ... Name pronounced BO-nuss.

HIGH SCHOOL: Guayama (Puerto Rico).

TRANSACTIONS/CAREER NOTES: Signed as non-drafted free agent by San Diego Padres organization (May 13, 1986). ... Traded by Padres with SS Jose Valentin and OF Matt Mieske to Milwaukee Brewers for 3B Gary Sheffield and P Geoff Kellogg (March 27, 1992). ... Traded by Brewers with a player to be named later to New York Yankees as compensation for injured status of OF/IF Pat Listach (August 29, 1996); Yankees acquired IF Gabby Martinez to complete deal (November 5, 1996). ... Granted free agency (October 25, 1996). ... Signed by Cincinnati Reds (December 10, 1996). ... Released by Reds (May 6, 1997). ... Signed by Brewers organization (May 12, 1997). ... Traded by Brewers to Kansas City Royals organization for cash (June 26, 1997). ... Granted free agency (November 5, 1997). ... Signed by Minnesota Twins organization (January 6, 1998). ... Released by Twins (May 22, 1998). ... Signed by Royals organization (May 26, 1998). ... Granted free agency (October 29, 1998). ... Signed by Baltimore Orioles (December 21, 1998). ... On disabled list (July 2-17, 1999). ... Released by Orioles (August 20, 1999). ... Signed by Florida Marlins organization (December 22, 1999).

STATISTICAL NOTES: Led Texas League with 22 home runs allowed in 1989.

MISCELLANEOUS: Appeared in one game as outfielder with no chances (1993). ... Appeared in one game as pinch runner with Kansas City (1997). ... Scored a run in only appearance as pinch runner (1999).

Year League	W	L	Pct.	ERA	G	GS	CG	ShO	Sv.	IP	H	R	ER	BB	SO
1986— Spokane (N.W.)	1	3	.250	5.59	18	9	0	0	0	58	63	44	36	29	46
1987— Charleston, S.C. (SAL)	12	5	.706	3.65	26	26	4	1	0	170 1/3	*183	81	69	45	130
1988— Riverside (Calif.)	15	6	.714	3.64	25	25	5	2	0	175 1/3	162	80	71	64	129
1989— Wichita (Texas)	10	9	.526	5.74	24	24	2	0	0	136 1/3	162	103	87	47	88
1990— Wichita (Texas)	6	4	.600	3.48	21	21	2	1	0	137	138	66	53	45	96
— Las Vegas (PCL)	2	1	.667	3.47	5	5	0	0	0	36 1/3	45	17	14	10	25
1991— Las Vegas (PCL)	8	6	.571	4.22	23	23	1	0	0	136 1/3	155	90	64	43	95
— San Diego (N.L.)	4	6	.400	4.83	11	11	0	0	0	54	57	33	29	18	31
1992— Milwaukee (A.L.)■	9	10	.474	4.57	31	28	0	0	0	163 1/3	169	90	83	48	65
1993— Milwaukee (A.L.)	11	11	.500	4.86	32	31	3	0	0	203 2/3	222	122	110	63	63
1994— Milwaukee (A.L.)	10	9	.526	3.43	24	24	4	1	0	170 2/3	166	76	65	45	57
1995— Milwaukee (A.L.)	10	12	.455	4.63	32	31	3	0	0	200 1/3	218	108	103	83	77
1996— Milwaukee (A.L.)	7	14	.333	5.83	32	23	0	0	0	145	170	104	94	62	59
— New York (A.L.)■	0	0	...	14.14	4	1	0	0	0	7	14	11	11	6	4
1997— Cincinnati (N.L.)	0	1	.000	10.19	9	2	0	0	0	17 2/3	31	22	20	11	8
— Tucson (PCL)■	5	0	1.000	2.79	8	7	0	0	0	42	40	18	13	8	22
— Kansas City (A.L.)■	4	7	.364	5.97	21	11	1	0	0	78 1/3	102	59	52	25	36
1998— Salt Lake (PCL)■	5	1	.833	3.42	8	8	0	0	0	47 1/3	41	20	18	19	41
— Omaha (PCL)■	1	2	.333	8.59	3	3	0	0	0	14 2/3	19	16	14	10	8
— Kansas City (A.L.)	2	2	.500	3.04	32	0	0	0	1	53 1/3	49	18	18	24	38
1999— Baltimore (A.L.)	0	3	.000	5.98	30	2	0	0	0	43 2/3	59	29	29	19	26
A.L. totals (8 years)	53	68	.438	4.77	238	151	11	1	1	1065 1/3	1169	617	565	375	425
N.L. totals (2 years)	4	7	.364	6.15	20	13	0	0	0	71 2/3	88	55	49	29	39
Major League totals (9 years)	57	75	.432	4.86	258	164	11	1	1	1137	1257	672	614	404	464

ALL-STAR GAME RECORD

Year League	W	L	Pct.	ERA	GS	CG	ShO	Sv.	IP	H	R	ER	BB	SO
1994— American							Did not play.							

PERSONAL: Born February 23, 1963, in New York. ... 6-3/240. ... Bats both, throws right. ... Full name: Roberto Martin Antonio Bonilla. ... Name pronounced bo-NEE-yah.

HIGH SCHOOL: Lehman (Bronx, N.Y.).

COLLEGE: New York Technical College.

TRANSACTIONS/CAREER NOTES: Signed as non-drafted free agent by Pittsburgh Pirates organization (July 11, 1981). ... On Pittsburgh disabled list (March 25-July 19, 1985). ... Selected by Chicago White Sox organization from Pirates organization in Rule 5 major league draft (December 10, 1985). ... Traded by White Sox to Pittsburgh Pirates for P Jose DeLeon (July 23, 1986). ... Granted free agency (October 28, 1991). ... Signed by New York Mets (December 2, 1991). ... On suspended list (July 27-28, 1992). ... On disabled list (April 3-19, 1992). ... Traded by Mets with a player to be named later to Baltimore Orioles for OF Alex Ochoa and OF Damon Buford (July 28, 1995); Orioles acquired P Jimmy Williams to complete deal (August 17, 1995). ... Granted free agency (November 18, 1996). ... Signed by Florida Marlins (November 22, 1996). ... On Florida disabled list (March 22-April 12, 1998). ... Traded by Marlins with OF Gary Sheffield, C Charles Johnson, OF Jim Eisenreich and P Manuel Barrios to Los Angeles Dodgers for C Mike Piazza and 3B Todd Zeile (May 15, 1998). ... On Los Angeles disabled list (June 18-July 3 and July 15-August 5, 1998). ... Traded by Dodgers to Mets for P Mel Rojas (November 11, 1998). ... On New York disabled list (May 11-31 and July 3-September 1, 1999); included rehabilitation assignment to Norfolk (August 27-September 1). ... Released by Mets (January 3, 1999).

RECORDS: Holds N.L. career record for most home runs by switch-hitter—237. ... Shares major league record for most doubles in one inning—2 (July 21, 1995, eighth inning). ... Shares A.L. single-season record for most sacrifice flies—17 (1996).

HONORS: Named third baseman on THE SPORTING NEWS N.L. All-Star team (1988). ... Named third baseman on THE SPORTING NEWS N.L. Silver Slugger team (1988). ... Named outfielder on THE SPORTING NEWS N.L. All-Star team (1990-91). ... Named outfielder on THE SPORTING NEWS N.L. Silver Slugger team (1990-91).

STATISTICAL NOTES: Led Eastern League outfielders with 15 errors in 1984. ... Switch-hit home runs in one game six times (July 3, 1987; April 6, 1988; April 23 and June 10, 1993; May 4, 1994; and May 12, 1995). ... Led N.L. third basemen with 489 total chances in 1988. ... Led N.L. third basemen with 35 errors in 1989. ... Led N.L. third basemen with 31 double plays in 1989. ... Led N.L. with 15 sacrifice flies in 1990. ... Had 20-game hitting streak (September 10-October 1, 1995). ... Led A.L. with 17 sacrifice flies in 1996. ... Career major league grand slams: 8.

					BATTING								FIELDING		
Year Team (League)	Pos.	G	AB	R	H	2B	3B	HR	RBI	Avg.	BB	SO	SB	PO	A	E	Avg.
1981— GC Pirates (GCL)	1B-C-3B	22	69	6	15	5	0	0	7	.217	7	17	2	124	23	5	.967
1982— GC Pirates (GCL)	1B	47	167	20	38	3	0	5	26	.228	11	20	2	318	36	*14	.962
1983— Alexandria (Caro.)	OF-1B	•136	504	88	129	19	7	11	59	.256	78	105	28	259	12	15	.948
1984— Nashua (East.)	OF-1B	136	484	74	128	19	5	11	71	.264	49	89	15	312	8	†15	.955
1985— Prince Will. (Caro.)	1B-3B	39	130	15	34	4	1	3	11	.262	16	29	1	180	9	2	.990
1986— Chicago (A.L.)■	OF-1B	75	234	27	63	10	2	2	26	.269	33	49	4	361	22	2	.995
— Pittsburgh (N.L.)■	OF-1B-3B	63	192	28	46	6	2	1	17	.240	29	39	4	90	16	3	.972

Year	Team (League)	Pos.	G	AB	R	H	2B	3B	HR	RBI	Avg.	BB	SO	SB	PO	A	E	Avg.
1987—	Pittsburgh (N.L.)	3B-OF-1B	141	466	58	140	33	3	15	77	.300	39	64	3	142	139	16	.946
1988—	Pittsburgh (N.L.)	3B	159	584	87	160	32	7	24	100	.274	85	82	3	121	*336	*32	.935
1989—	Pittsburgh (N.L.)	3B-1B-OF	•163	616	96	173	37	10	24	86	.281	76	93	8	190	334	†35	.937
1990—	Pittsburgh (N.L.)	OF-3B-1B	160	625	112	175	39	7	32	120	.280	45	103	4	315	35	15	.959
1991—	Pittsburgh (N.L.)	OF-3B-1B	157	577	102	174	*44	6	18	100	.302	90	67	2	247	144	15	.963
1992—	New York (N.L.)■	OF-1B	128	438	62	109	23	0	19	70	.249	66	73	4	277	9	4	.986
1993—	New York (N.L.)..........	OF-3B-1B	139	502	81	133	21	3	34	87	.265	72	96	3	238	112	17	.954
1994—	New York (N.L.)..........	3B	108	403	60	117	24	1	20	67	.290	55	101	1	78	215	*18	.942
1995—	New York (N.L.)	3B-OF-1B	80	317	49	103	25	4	18	53	.325	31	48	0	164	80	14	.946
—	Baltimore (A.L.)■	OF-3B	61	237	47	79	12	4	10	46	.333	23	31	0	80	48	5	.962
1996—	Baltimore (A.L.)..........	O-DH-1-3	159	595	107	171	27	5	28	116	.287	75	85	1	214	12	6	.974
1997—	Florida (N.L.)■	3B-DH-1B	153	562	77	167	39	3	17	96	.297	73	94	6	107	225	22	.938
1998—	Florida (N.L.)	3B	28	97	11	27	5	0	4	15	.278	12	22	0	18	41	5	.922
—	Los Angeles (N.L.)■..	3B-OF	72	236	28	56	6	1	7	30	.237	29	37	1	56	84	13	.915
1999—	New York (N.L.)■	OF-1B-DH	60	119	12	19	5	0	4	18	.160	19	16	0	59	4	2	.969
—	Norfolk (I.L.)	DH	3	13	1	3	0	0	0	1	.231	0	1	0	0	0	0	...
American League totals (3 years)			295	1066	181	313	49	11	40	188	.294	131	165	5	655	82	13	.983
National League totals (13 years)			1611	5734	863	1599	339	47	237	936	.279	721	935	39	2102	1774	211	.948
Major League totals (14 years)			1906	6800	1044	1912	388	58	277	1124	.281	852	1100	44	2757	1856	224	.954

DIVISION SERIES RECORD

Year	Team (League)	Pos.	G	AB	R	H	2B	3B	HR	RBI	Avg.	BB	SO	SB	PO	A	E	Avg.
1996—	Baltimore (A.L.).........	OF	4	15	4	3	0	0	2	5	.200	4	6	0	9	0	1	.900
1997—	Florida (N.L.).............	3B	3	12	1	4	0	0	1	3	.333	2	1	0	3	5	0	1.000
1999—	New York (N.L.).........	PH	2	1	1	0	0	0	0	0	.000	1	0	0	0	0	0	...
Division series totals (3 years)			9	28	6	7	0	0	3	8	.250	7	7	0	12	5	1	.944

CHAMPIONSHIP SERIES RECORD

RECORDS: Shares single-game record for most strikeouts—4 (October 10, 1996).

Year	Team (League)	Pos.	G	AB	R	H	2B	3B	HR	RBI	Avg.	BB	SO	SB	PO	A	E	Avg.
1990—	Pittsburgh (N.L.)	OF-3B	6	21	0	4	1	0	0	1	.190	3	1	0	4	5	1	.900
1991—	Pittsburgh (N.L.)	OF	7	23	2	7	2	0	0	1	.304	6	2	0	12	1	0	1.000
1996—	Baltimore (A.L.)..........	OF	5	20	1	1	0	0	1	2	.050	1	4	0	11	0	0	1.000
1997—	Florida (N.L.)	3B	6	23	3	6	1	0	0	4	.261	1	6	0	5	13	0	1.000
1999—	New York (N.L.)..........	PH	3	3	0	1	0	0	0	0	.333	0	2	0	0	0	0	...
Championship series totals (5 years)			27	90	6	19	4	0	1	8	.211	11	15	0	32	19	1	.981

WORLD SERIES RECORD

NOTES: Member of World Series championship team (1997).

Year	Team (League)	Pos.	G	AB	R	H	2B	3B	HR	RBI	Avg.	BB	SO	SB	PO	A	E	Avg.
1997—	Florida (N.L.)	3B	7	29	5	6	1	0	1	3	.207	3	5	0	3	20	2	.920

ALL-STAR GAME RECORD

Year	League	Pos.	AB	R	H	2B	3B	HR	RBI	Avg.	BB	SO	SB	PO	A	E	Avg.
1988—	National	3B	4	0	0	0	0	0	0	.000	0	0	0	0	2	0	1.000
1989—	National	PH-DH	2	0	2	0	0	0	0	1.000	0	0	0	...	...	...	...
1990—	National	1B	1	0	0	0	0	0	0	.000	0	0	0	1	0	0	1.000
1991—	National	DH	4	0	2	0	0	0	1	.500	0	1	0	...	...	...	...
1993—	National	OF	1	0	1	0	0	0	0	1.000	0	0	0	2	0	0	1.000
1995—	National	3B	1	0	0	0	0	0	0	.000	0	1	0	0	0	0	...
All-Star Game totals (6 years)			13	0	5	0	0	0	1	.385	0	2	0	3	2	0	1.000

BOONE, AARON   3B   REDS

PERSONAL: Born March 9, 1973, in La Mesa, Calif. ... 6-2/200. ... Bats right, throws right. ... Full name: Aaron John Boone. ... Son of Bob Boone, special assistant to the general manager, Cincinnati Reds, and catcher with three major league teams (1972-90); brother of Bret Boone, second baseman, San Diego Padres; grandson of Ray Boone, major league infielder with six teams (1948-60); and nephew of Rodney Boone, minor league catcher/outfielder (1972-75).

HIGH SCHOOL: Villa Park (Calif.).

COLLEGE: Southern California.

TRANSACTIONS/CAREER NOTES: Selected by California Angels organization in 43rd round of free-agent draft (June 3, 1991); did not sign. ... Selected by Cincinnati Reds organization in third round of free-agent draft (June 2, 1994).

STATISTICAL NOTES: Led Pioneer League third basemen with 46 putouts, 156 assists, 220 total chances and 13 double plays in 1994. ... Led Southern League third basemen with 101 putouts, 347 total chances and 28 double plays in 1996. ... Led American Association third basemen with 76 putouts, 241 assists, 336 total chances and 27 double plays in 1997. ... Career major league grand slams: 1.

Year	Team (League)	Pos.	G	AB	R	H	2B	3B	HR	RBI	Avg.	BB	SO	SB	PO	A	E	Avg.
1994—	Billings (Pio.)	3B-1B	67	256	48	70	15	5	7	55	.273	36	35	6	†60	†158	18	.924
1995—	Chattanooga (Sou.)....	3B	23	66	6	15	3	0	0	3	.227	5	12	2	14	28	6	.875
—	Win.-Salem (Car.).......	3B	108	395	61	103	19	1	14	50	.261	43	77	11	59	*272	21	*.940
1996—	Chattanooga (Sou.) ...	3B-SS-DH	136	*548	86	158	*44	7	17	95	.288	38	77	21	†123	257	22	.945
1997—	Indianapolis (A.A.)......	3B-SS-2B	131	476	79	138	30	4	22	75	.290	40	81	12	†112	†269	24	.941
—	Cincinnati (N.L.)	3B-2B	16	49	9	12	1	0	0	5	.245	2	5	1	11	22	3	.917
1998—	Cincinnati (N.L.)	3B-2B-SS	58	181	24	51	13	2	2	28	.282	15	36	6	37	97	8	.944
—	Indianapolis (I.L.)	3B-2B-SS	87	332	56	80	18	1	7	38	.241	31	71	17	72	243	19	.943
1999—	Cincinnati (N.L.)	3B-SS	139	472	56	132	26	5	14	72	.280	30	79	17	87	258	15	.958
—	Indianapolis (I.L.)	3B-2B-SS	11	41	6	14	2	1	0	7	.341	3	4	2	11	29	3	.930
Major League totals (3 years)			213	702	85	195	40	7	16	105	.278	47	120	24	135	377	26	.952

PERSONAL: Born April 6, 1969, in El Cajon, Calif. ... 5-10/180. ... Bats right, throws right. ... Full name: Bret Robert Boone. ... Son of Bob Boone, special assistant to the general manager, Cincinnati Reds and catcher with three major league teams (1972-90); brother of Aaron Boone, third baseman, Cincinnati Reds; grandson of Ray Boone, major league infielder with six teams (1948-60); and nephew of Rodney Boone, minor league catcher/outfielder (1972-75).

HIGH SCHOOL: El Dorado (Yorba Linda, Calif.).

COLLEGE: Southern California.

TRANSACTIONS/CAREER NOTES: Selected by Minnesota Twins organization in 28th round of free-agent draft (June 2, 1987); did not sign. ... Selected by Seattle Mariners organization in fifth round of free-agent draft (June 4, 1990). ... Traded by Mariners with P Erik Hanson to Cincinnati Reds for P Bobby Ayala and C Dan Wilson (November 2, 1993). ... On disabled list (April 1-16, 1996). ... Traded by Reds with P Mike Remlinger to Atlanta Braves for P Denny Neagle, OF Michael Tucker and P Rob Bell (November 10, 1998). ... Traded by Braves with OF/1B Ryan Klesko and P Jason Shiell to San Diego Padres for 2B Quilvio Veras, 1B Wally Joyner and OF Reggie Sanders (December 22, 1999).

RECORDS: Holds major league single-season record for highest fielding percentage by second baseman (100 or more games)—.997 (1997).

HONORS: Won N.L. Gold Glove at second base (1998).

STATISTICAL NOTES: Tied for Southern League lead in grounding into double plays with 21 in 1991. ... Led Southern League second basemen with 288 putouts in 1991. ... Led Pacific Coast League second basemen with 90 double plays in 1992. ... Led N.L. second basemen with 106 double plays in 1995. ... Hit three home runs in one game (September 20, 1998). ... Career major league grand slams: 1.

Year Team (League)	Pos.	G	AB	R	H	2B	3B	HR	RBI	Avg.	BB	SO	SB	PO	A	E	Avg.
1990— Peninsula (Caro.)	2B	74	255	42	68	13	2	8	38	.267	47	57	5	154	216	19	.951
1991— Jacksonville (Sou.).....	2B-3B	•139	475	64	121	18	1	19	75	.255	72	123	9	†300	369	21	.970
1992— Calgary (PCL)............	2B-SS	118	439	73	138	26	5	13	73	.314	60	88	17	268	366	10	.984
— Seattle (A.L.)............	2B-3B	33	129	15	25	4	0	4	15	.194	4	34	1	72	96	6	.966
1993— Calgary (PCL)............	2B	71	274	48	91	18	3	8	56	.332	28	58	3	146	180	8	.976
— Seattle (A.L.)............	2B-DH	76	271	31	68	12	2	12	38	.251	17	52	2	140	177	3	.991
1994— Cincinnati (N.L.)■.......	2B-3B	108	381	59	122	25	2	12	68	.320	24	74	3	191	269	12	.975
1995— Cincinnati (N.L.).........	2B	138	513	63	137	34	2	15	68	.267	41	84	5	*311	362	4	*.994
1996— Cincinnati (N.L.).........	2B	142	520	56	121	21	3	12	69	.233	31	100	3	315	381	6	*.991
1997— Cincinnati (N.L.).........	2B	139	443	40	99	25	1	7	46	.223	45	101	5	271	334	2	*.997
— Indianapolis (A.A.)......	2B	3	7	1	2	1	0	0	1	.286	2	2	1	6	10	0	1.000
1998— Cincinnati (N.L.).........	2B	157	583	76	155	38	1	24	95	.266	48	104	6	329	416	9	.988
1999— Atlanta (N.L.)■..........	2B	152	608	102	153	38	1	20	63	.252	47	112	14	270	424	13	.982
American League totals (2 years)		109	400	46	93	16	2	16	53	.233	21	86	3	212	273	9	.982
National League totals (6 years)		836	3048	396	787	181	10	90	409	.258	236	575	36	1687	2186	46	.988
Major League totals (8 years)		945	3448	442	880	197	12	106	462	.255	257	661	39	1899	2459	55	.988

DIVISION SERIES RECORD

RECORDS: Holds N.L. career record for highest batting average (20 or more at-bats)—.414. ... Shares N.L. single-game record for most at-bats—6 (October 8, 1999).

Year Team (League)	Pos.	G	AB	R	H	2B	3B	HR	RBI	Avg.	BB	SO	SB	PO	A	E	Avg.
1995— Cincinnati (N.L.)	2B	3	10	4	3	1	0	1	1	.300	1	3	1	7	5	0	1.000
1999— Atlanta (N.L.)..............	2B	4	19	3	9	1	0	0	1	.474	0	4	1	11	15	0	1.000
Division series totals (2 years)		7	29	7	12	2	0	1	2	.414	1	7	2	18	20	0	1.000

CHAMPIONSHIP SERIES RECORD

Year Team (League)	Pos.	G	AB	R	H	2B	3B	HR	RBI	Avg.	BB	SO	SB	PO	A	E	Avg.
1995— Cincinnati (N.L.)	2B	4	14	1	3	0	0	0	0	.214	1	2	0	9	13	0	1.000
1999— Atlanta (N.L.)..............	2B	6	22	2	4	1	0	0	1	.182	1	7	2	5	14	0	1.000
Championship series totals (2 years)		10	36	3	7	1	0	0	1	.194	2	9	2	14	27	0	1.000

WORLD SERIES RECORD

Year Team (League)	Pos.	G	AB	R	H	2B	3B	HR	RBI	Avg.	BB	SO	SB	PO	A	E	Avg.
1999— Atlanta (N.L.)..............	2B-PH	4	13	1	7	4	0	0	3	.538	1	3	0	4	9	0	1.000

ALL-STAR GAME RECORD

Year League	Pos.	AB	R	H	2B	3B	HR	RBI	Avg.	BB	SO	SB	PO	A	E	Avg.
1998— National....................							Did not play.									

PERSONAL: Born November 15, 1967, in Mao, Dominican Republic. ... 6-1/205. ... Throws left, bats left. ... Full name: Pedro Felix Borbon Jr. ... Son of Pedro Borbon, pitcher with four major league teams (1969-80). ... Name pronounced bor-BONE.

HIGH SCHOOL: DeWitt Clinton (Bronx, N.Y.).

JUNIOR COLLEGE: Ranger (Texas) Junior College.

TRANSACTIONS/CAREER NOTES: Selected by Milwaukee Brewers organization in 35th round of free-agent draft (June 3, 1985); did not sign. ... Selected by Los Angeles Dodgers organization in secondary phase of free-agent draft (January 14, 1986); did not sign. ... Signed as non-drafted free agent by Chicago White Sox organization (June 4, 1988). ... Released by White Sox organization (April 1, 1989). ... Signed by Atlanta Braves organization (August 25, 1989). ... On Atlanta disabled list (April 8-26 and August 23, 1996-remainder of season); included rehabilitation assignment to Greenville (April 23-26). ... On disabled list (March 30, 1997-entire season). ... On Atlanta disabled list (March 29, 1998-entire season); included rehabilitation assignments to Macon (June 4-7), Greenville (June 9-July 5 and July 9-14) and Richmond (July 16-August 31 and September 1-8). ... Granted free agency (October 1, 1998). ... Signed by Dodgers organization (December 29, 1998). ... Traded by Dodgers with OF Raul Mondesi to Toronto Blue Jays for OF Shawn Green and 2B Jorge Nunez (November 8, 1999).

STATISTICAL NOTES: Led Gulf Coast League with 14 balks in 1988.

Year League	W	L	Pct.	ERA	G	GS	CG	ShO	Sv.	IP	H	R	ER	BB	SO
1988— GC White Sox (GCL)	5	3	.625	2.41	16	11	1	1	1	74 2/3	52	28	20	17	67
1989—								Did not play.							
1990— Burlington (Midw.)■.........	11	3	.786	1.47	14	14	6	2	0	97 2/3	73	25	16	23	76
— Durham (Caro.)	4	5	.444	5.43	11	11	0	0	0	61 1/3	73	40	37	16	37
1991— Durham (Caro.)	4	3	.571	2.27	37	6	1	0	5	91	85	40	23	35	79
— Greenville (Sou.)	0	1	.000	2.79	4	4	0	0	0	29	23	12	9	10	22
1992— Greenville (Sou.)	8	2	.800	3.06	39	10	0	0	3	94	73	36	32	42	79
— Atlanta (N.L.)	0	1	.000	6.75	2	0	0	0	0	1 1/3	2	1	1	1	1
1993— Richmond (I.L.)	5	5	.500	4.23	52	0	0	0	1	76 2/3	71	40	36	42	95
— Atlanta (N.L.)	0	0	...	21.60	3	0	0	0	0	1 2/3	3	4	4	3	2
1994— Richmond (I.L.)	3	4	.429	2.79	59	0	0	0	4	80 2/3	66	29	25	41	82
1995— Atlanta (N.L.)	2	2	.500	3.09	41	0	0	0	2	32	29	12	11	17	33
1996— Atlanta (N.L.)	3	0	1.000	2.75	43	0	0	0	1	36	26	12	11	7	31
— Greenville (Sou.)	0	0	...	0.00	1	0	0	0	0	1	0	0	0	0	0
1997— Atlanta (N.L.)								Did not play.							
1998— Macon (SAL)	0	0	...	9.00	3	0	0	0	0	3	4	3	3	1	3
— Greenville (Sou.)	0	2	.000	4.74	16	0	0	0	0	19	21	14	10	14	10
— Richmond (I.L.)	0	1	.000	5.70	20	0	0	0	0	23 2/3	29	17	15	8	15
1999— Los Angeles (N.L.)■.......	4	3	.571	4.09	70	0	0	0	1	50 2/3	39	23	23	29	33
Major League totals (5 years).......	9	6	.600	3.70	159	0	0	0	4	121 2/3	99	52	50	57	100

DIVISION SERIES RECORD

Year League	W	L	Pct.	ERA	G	GS	CG	ShO	Sv.	IP	H	R	ER	BB	SO
1995— Atlanta (N.L.)	0	0	...	0.00	1	0	0	0	0	1	1	0	0	0	3

CHAMPIONSHIP SERIES RECORD

Year League	W	L	Pct.	ERA	G	GS	CG	ShO	Sv.	IP	H	R	ER	BB	SO
1995— Atlanta (N.L.)								Did not play.							

WORLD SERIES RECORD

NOTES: Member of World Series championship team (1995).

Year League	W	L	Pct.	ERA	G	GS	CG	ShO	Sv.	IP	H	R	ER	BB	SO
1995— Atlanta (N.L.)	0	0	...	0.00	1	0	0	0	1	1	0	0	0	0	2

BORDERS, PAT   C

PERSONAL: Born May 14, 1963, in Columbus, Ohio. ... 6-2/200. ... Bats right, throws right. ... Full name: Patrick Lance Borders. ... Brother of Todd Borders, minor league catcher (1988).

HIGH SCHOOL: Lake Wales (Fla.).

TRANSACTIONS/CAREER NOTES: Selected by Toronto Blue Jays organization in sixth round of free-agent draft (June 7, 1982). ... On Toronto disabled list (July 5-August 19, 1988); included rehabilitation assignment to Syracuse (July 30-August 19). ... Granted free agency (October 21, 1994). ... Signed by Kansas City Royals (April 10, 1995). ... Traded by Royals to Houston Astros for a player to be named later (August 12, 1995); Royals acquired P Rick Huisman to complete deal (August 17, 1995). ... On Houston suspended list (September 8-14, 1995). ... Granted free agency (November 6, 1995). ... Signed by St. Louis Cardinals organization (January 10, 1996). ... Traded by Cardinals to California Angels for P Ben VanRyn (June 15, 1996). ... Traded by Angels to Chicago White Sox for P Robert Ellis (July 27, 1996). ... Granted free agency (November 8, 1996). ... Signed by Cleveland Indians organization (December 13, 1996). ... Granted free agency (November 7, 1997). ... Re-signed by Indians organization (December 17, 1997). ... Granted free agency (November 3, 1998). ... Re-signed by Indians organization (February 26, 1999). ... Released by Indians (August 30, 1999). ... Signed by Blue Jays (August 31, 1999). ... Granted free agency (November 11, 1999).

STATISTICAL NOTES: Tied for Southern League lead with 16 passed balls in 1987. ... Led A.L. catchers with 880 total chances in 1992 and 962 in 1993. ... Led A.L. with nine passed balls in 1994. ... Career major league grand slams: 1.

							BATTING								FIELDING			
Year Team (League)	Pos.	G	AB	R	H	2B	3B	HR	RBI	Avg.	BB	SO	SB	PO	A	E	Avg.
1982— Medicine Hat (Pio.)	3B	61	217	30	66	12	2	5	33	.304	24	52	1	23	96	*25	.826
1983— Florence (SAL)	131	457	62	125	31	4	5	54	.274	46	116	4	70	233	*41	.881	
1984— Florence (SAL)	1B-3B-OF	131	467	69	129	32	5	12	85	.276	56	116	3	650	77	25	.967
1985— Kinston (Caro.)..........	1B	127	460	43	120	16	1	10	60	.261	45	116	6	854	42	*20	.978
1986— Florence (SAL)	C-OF	16	40	8	15	7	0	3	9	.375	2	9	0	22	1	0	1.000
— Knoxville (Sou.)..........	C-1B	12	34	3	12	1	0	2	5	.353	1	6	0	45	5	3	.943
— Kinston (Caro.)..........	C-1B-OF	49	174	24	57	10	0	6	26	.328	10	42	0	211	26	7	.971
1987— Dunedin (FSL)...........	1B	3	11	0	4	0	0	0	1	.364	0	3	0	21	1	0	1.000
— Knoxville (Sou.)..........	C-3B	94	349	44	102	14	1	11	51	.292	20	56	2	432	49	12	.976
1988— Toronto (A.L.)............C-DH-2B-3B	56	154	15	42	6	3	5	21	.273	3	24	0	205	19	7	.970	
— Syracuse (I.L.)...........	C	35	120	11	29	8	0	3	14	.242	16	22	0	202	17	2	.991
1989— Toronto (A.L.)	C-DH	94	241	22	62	11	1	3	29	.257	11	45	2	261	27	6	.980
1990— Toronto (A.L.)	C-DH	125	346	36	99	24	2	15	49	.286	18	57	0	515	46	4	.993
1991— Toronto (A.L.)	C	105	291	22	71	17	0	5	36	.244	11	45	0	505	48	4	.993
1992— Toronto (A.L.)	C	138	480	47	116	26	2	13	53	.242	33	75	1	784	*88	8	.991
1993— Toronto (A.L.)	C	138	488	38	124	30	0	9	55	.254	20	66	2	869	*80	*13	.986
1994— Toronto (A.L.)	C	85	295	24	73	13	1	3	26	.247	15	50	1	583	*60	8	.988
1995— Kansas City (A.L.)■.......	C-DH	52	143	14	33	8	1	4	13	.231	7	22	0	182	18	0	1.000
— Houston (N.L.)■.......	C	11	35	1	4	0	0	0	0	.114	2	7	0	70	5	1	.987
1996— St. Louis (N.L.)■.......	C-1B	26	69	3	22	3	0	0	4	.319	1	14	0	117	9	3	.977
— California (A.L.)■.......	C	19	57	6	13	3	0	2	8	.228	3	11	0	111	14	2	.984
— Chicago (A.L.)■.......	C-DH	31	94	6	26	1	0	3	6	.277	5	18	0	144	16	3	.982
1997— Cleveland (A.L.)■.......	C	55	159	17	47	7	1	4	15	.296	9	27	0	312	19	0	1.000
1998— Cleveland (A.L.)	C-3B	54	160	12	38	6	0	0	6	.238	10	40	0	283	20	8	.974
1999— Buffalo (I.L.)	C-DH	55	198	17	47	7	0	5	23	.237	12	31	0	316	25	5	.986
— Cleveland (A.L.)	C-3B	6	20	2	6	0	1	0	3	.300	0	3	0	32	1	2	.943
— Toronto (A.L.)■.......	DH-C	6	14	1	3	0	0	1	3	.214	1	2	0	7	2	0	1.000
American League totals (12 years)		964	2942	262	753	152	12	67	323	.256	146	485	6	4793	458	65	.988
National League totals (2 years)		37	104	4	26	3	0	0	4	.250	3	21	0	187	14	4	.980
Major League totals (12 years)		1001	3046	266	779	155	12	67	327	.256	149	506	6	4980	472	69	.988

CHAMPIONSHIP SERIES RECORD

Year	Team (League)	Pos.	G	AB	R	H	2B	3B	HR	RBI	Avg.	BB	SO	SB	PO	A	E	Avg.
1989— Toronto (A.L.).............		PH-C	1	1	0	1	0	0	0	1	1.000	0	0	0	1	0	0	1.000
1991— Toronto (A.L.).............		C	5	19	0	5	1	0	0	2	.263	0	0	0	38	4	2	.955
1992— Toronto (A.L.).............		C	6	22	3	7	0	0	1	3	.318	1	1	0	38	3	1	.976
1993— Toronto (A.L.).............		C	6	24	1	6	1	0	0	3	.250	0	6	1	41	4	0	1.000
Championship series totals (4 years)			18	66	4	19	2	0	1	9	.288	1	7	1	118	11	3	.977

WORLD SERIES RECORD

NOTES: Named Most Valuable Player (1992). ... Member of World Series championship team (1992 and 1993).

Year	Team (League)	Pos.	G	AB	R	H	2B	3B	HR	RBI	Avg.	BB	SO	SB	PO	A	E	Avg.
1992— Toronto (A.L.).............		C	6	20	2	9	3	0	1	3	.450	2	1	0	48	5	1	.981
1993— Toronto (A.L.).............		C	6	23	2	7	0	0	0	1	.304	2	1	0	50	2	1	.981
World Series totals (2 years)			12	43	4	16	3	0	1	4	.372	4	2	0	98	7	2	.981

BORDICK, MIKE — SS — ORIOLES

PERSONAL: Born July 21, 1965, in Marquette, Mich. ... 5-11/175. ... Bats right, throws right. ... Full name: Michael Todd Bordick.
HIGH SCHOOL: Hampden (Maine) Academy.
COLLEGE: Maine.
TRANSACTIONS/CAREER NOTES: Signed as non-drafted free agent by Oakland Athletics organization (July 10, 1986). ... On Tacoma disabled list (April 14-May 13, 1991). ... On Oakland disabled list (May 8-27, 1995); included rehabilitation assignment to Modesto (May 23-26). ... Granted free agency (December 7, 1996). ... Signed by Baltimore Orioles (December 13, 1996).
RECORDS: Shares major league career record for highest fielding percentage by shortstop (1,000 or more games)—.981.
STATISTICAL NOTES: Led Pacific Coast League shortstops with .972 fielding percentage and 82 double plays in 1990. ... Led A.L. shortstops with 280 putouts and tied for lead with 108 double plays in 1993. ... Led A.L. with 15 sacrifice hits in 1998. ... Led A.L. shortstops with 797 total chances and 132 double plays in 1999. ... Career major league grand slams: 1.

Year	Team (League)	Pos.	G	AB	R	H	2B	3B	HR	RBI	Avg.	BB	SO	SB	PO	A	E	Avg.
1986— Medford (N.W.)		SS	46	187	30	48	3	1	0	19	.257	40	21	6	68	143	18	.921
1987— Modesto (Calif.)		SS	133	497	73	133	17	0	3	75	.268	87	92	8	216	305	17	*.968
1988— Huntsville (Sou.)		2B-SS-3B	132	481	48	130	13	2	0	28	.270	87	50	7	260	406	24	.965
1989— Tacoma (PCL)		2B-SS-3B	136	487	55	117	17	1	1	43	.240	58	51	4	261	431	33	.954
1990— Oakland (A.L.)		3B-SS-2B	25	14	0	1	0	0	0	0	.071	1	4	0	9	8	0	1.000
— Tacoma (PCL)		SS-2B	111	348	49	79	16	1	2	30	.227	46	40	3	210	366	16	†.973
1991— Tacoma (PCL)		SS	26	81	15	22	4	1	2	14	.272	17	10	0	35	79	3	.974
— Oakland (A.L.)		SS-2B-3B	90	235	21	56	5	1	0	21	.238	14	37	3	146	213	11	.970
1992— Oakland (A.L.)		2B-SS	154	504	62	151	19	4	3	48	.300	40	59	12	311	449	16	.979
1993— Oakland (A.L.)		SS-2B	159	546	60	136	21	2	3	48	.249	60	58	10	†285	420	13	.982
1994— Oakland (A.L.)		SS-2B	114	391	38	99	18	4	2	37	.253	38	44	7	187	320	14	.973
1995— Oakland (A.L.)		SS-DH	126	428	46	113	13	0	8	44	.264	35	48	11	*245	338	10	.983
— Modesto (Calif.)		SS	1	2	0	0	0	0	0	0	.000	0	0	0	2	1	0	1.000
1996— Oakland (A.L.)		SS	155	525	46	126	18	4	5	54	.240	52	59	5	265	*476	16	.979
1997— Baltimore (A.L.)■......		SS	153	509	55	120	19	1	7	46	.236	33	66	0	224	424	13	.980
1998— Baltimore (A.L.)		SS	151	465	59	121	29	1	13	51	.260	39	65	6	236	*446	7	.990
1999— Baltimore (A.L.)		SS	160	631	93	175	35	7	10	77	.277	54	102	14	277	*511	9	*.989
Major League totals (10 years)			1287	4248	480	1098	177	24	51	426	.258	366	542	68	2185	3605	109	.982

DIVISION SERIES RECORD

Year	Team (League)	Pos.	G	AB	R	H	2B	3B	HR	RBI	Avg.	BB	SO	SB	PO	A	E	Avg.
1997— Baltimore (A.L.)		SS	4	10	4	4	1	0	0	4	.400	4	2	0	4	15	0	1.000

CHAMPIONSHIP SERIES RECORD

Year	Team (League)	Pos.	G	AB	R	H	2B	3B	HR	RBI	Avg.	BB	SO	SB	PO	A	E	Avg.
1990— Oakland (A.L.)											Did not play.							
1992— Oakland (A.L.)		SS-2B	6	19	1	1	0	0	0	0	.053	1	2	1	15	14	0	1.000
1997— Baltimore (A.L.)		SS	6	19	0	3	1	0	0	2	.158	0	6	0	5	14	0	1.000
Championship series totals (2 years)			12	38	1	4	1	0	0	2	.105	1	8	1	20	28	0	1.000

WORLD SERIES RECORD

Year	Team (League)	Pos.	G	AB	R	H	2B	3B	HR	RBI	Avg.	BB	SO	SB	PO	A	E	Avg.
1990— Oakland (A.L.)		SS-PR	3	0	0	0	0	0	0	0	...	0	0	0	0	2	0	1.000

BORKOWSKI, DAVE — P — TIGERS

PERSONAL: Born February 7, 1977, in Detroit. ... 6-1/200. ... Throws right, bats right. ... Full name: David Richard Borkowski.
HIGH SCHOOL: Sterling Heights (Mich.).
TRANSACTIONS/CAREER NOTES: Selected by Detroit Tigers organization in 11th round of free-agent draft (June 1, 1995).
STATISTICAL NOTES: Pitched 6-0 no-hit victory against Kane County (April 20, 1997). ... Led Southern League with 25 home runs allowed in 1998.

Year	League	W	L	Pct.	ERA	G	GS	CG	ShO	Sv.	IP	H	R	ER	BB	SO
1995— GC Tigers (GCL)		3	2	.600	2.96	10	10	1	0	0	51²/₃	45	24	17	8	36
— Lakeland (FSL)		1	0	1.000	0.00	1	1	0	0	0	5	2	0	0	1	3
1996— Fayetteville (SAL)		10	10	.500	3.33	27	27	5	0	0	178¹/₃	158	85	66	54	117

Year	League	W	L	Pct.	ERA	G	GS	CG	ShO	Sv.	IP	H	R	ER	BB	SO
1997— West Michigan (Midw.)		•15	3	•.833	3.46	25	25	4	2	0	164	143	79	63	31	104
1998— Jacksonville (Sou.).............		*16	7	.696	4.63	28	28	3	1	0	178²/₃	204	99	92	54	97
1999— Toledo (I.L.).......................		6	8	.429	3.50	19	19	3	0	0	126	119	59	49	43	94
— Detroit (A.L.).......................		2	6	.250	6.10	17	12	0	0	0	76²/₃	86	58	52	40	50
Major League totals (1 year)........		2	6	.250	6.10	17	12	0	0	0	76²/₃	86	58	52	40	50

BOTTALICO, RICKY   P   ROYALS

PERSONAL: Born August 26, 1969, in New Britain, Conn. ... 6-1/217. ... Throws right, bats left. ... Full name: Richard Paul Bottalico. ... Name pronounced ba-TAL-e-koh.

HIGH SCHOOL: South Catholic (Hartford, Conn.).

COLLEGE: Florida Southern, then Central Connecticut State.

TRANSACTIONS/CAREER NOTES: Signed as non-drafted free agent by Philadelphia Phillies organization (July 21, 1991). ... On Philadelphia disabled list (April 24-July 1, 1998); included rehabilitation assignment to Scranton/Wilkes-Barre (June 6-July 1). ... On suspended list (August 25-28, 1998). ... Traded by Phillies with P Garrett Stephenson to St. Louis Cardinals for OF Ron Gant, P Jeff Brantley and P Cliff Politte (November 19, 1998). ... Granted free agency (December 21, 1999). ... Signed by Kansas City Royals (January 14, 2000).

STATISTICAL NOTES: Pitched two innings, combining with starter Craig Holman (two innings), Gregory Brown (two innings) and Toby Borland (one inning) in seven-inning, 2-0 no-hit victory for Reading against New Britain (September 4, 1993, first game).

Year	League	W	L	Pct.	ERA	G	GS	CG	ShO	Sv.	IP	H	R	ER	BB	SO
1991— Martinsville (Appl.).............		3	2	.600	4.09	7	6	2	•1	0	33	32	20	15	13	38
— Spartanburg (SAL).............		2	0	1.000	0.00	2	2	0	0	0	15	4	0	0	2	11
1992— Spartanburg (SAL).............		5	10	.333	2.41	42	11	1	0	13	119²/₃	94	41	32	56	118
1993— Clearwater (FSL)		1	0	1.000	2.75	13	0	0	0	4	19²/₃	19	6	6	5	19
— Reading (East.).................		3	3	.500	2.25	49	0	0	0	20	72	63	22	18	26	65
1994— Scranton/W.B. (I.L.)		3	1	.750	8.87	19	0	0	0	3	22¹/₃	32	27	22	22	22
— Reading (East.).................		2	2	.500	2.53	38	0	0	0	22	42²/₃	29	13	12	10	51
— Philadelphia (N.L.)............		0	0	...	0.00	3	0	0	0	0	3	3	0	0	1	3
1995— Philadelphia (N.L.)............		5	3	.625	2.46	62	0	0	0	1	87²/₃	50	25	24	42	87
1996— Philadelphia (N.L.)............		4	5	.444	3.19	61	0	0	0	34	67²/₃	47	24	24	23	74
1997— Philadelphia (N.L.)............		2	5	.286	3.65	69	0	0	0	34	74	68	31	30	42	89
1998— Philadelphia (N.L.)............		1	5	.167	6.44	39	0	0	0	6	43¹/₃	54	31	31	25	27
— Scranton/W.B. (I.L.)		0	1	.000	2.92	10	5	0	0	1	12¹/₃	8	4	4	9	4
1999— St. Louis (N.L.)■		3	7	.300	4.91	68	0	0	0	20	73¹/₃	83	45	40	49	66
Major League totals (6 years).......		15	25	.375	3.84	302	0	0	0	95	349	305	156	149	182	346

ALL-STAR GAME RECORD

Year	League	W	L	Pct.	ERA	GS	CG	ShO	Sv.	IP	H	R	ER	BB	SO
1996— National.............................		0	0	...	0.00	0	0	0	0	1	0	0	0	0	1

BOTTENFIELD, KENT   P   CARDINALS

PERSONAL: Born November 14, 1968, in Portland, Ore. ... 6-3/240. ... Throws right, bats right. ... Full name: Kent Dennis Bottenfield. ... Twin brother of Keven Bottenfield, minor league catcher/infielder (1986-87).

HIGH SCHOOL: James Madison (Portland, Ore.).

TRANSACTIONS/CAREER NOTES: Selected by Montreal Expos organization in fourth round of free-agent draft (June 2, 1986). ... Traded by Expos to Colorado Rockies for P Butch Henry (July 16, 1993). ... On Colorado disabled list (March 25-May 9, 1994); included rehabilitation assignment to Colorado Springs (April 10-May 9). ... Granted free agency (June 27, 1994). ... Signed by Phoenix, San Francisco Giants organization (June 29, 1994). ... Released by Giants (November 8, 1994). ... Signed by Toledo, Detroit Tigers organization (April 3, 1995). ... Granted free agency (October 16, 1995). ... Signed by Iowa, Chicago Cubs organization (March 9, 1996). ... Granted free agency (December 21, 1997). ... Signed by St. Louis Cardinals (January 8, 1998).

Year	League	W	L	Pct.	ERA	G	GS	CG	ShO	Sv.	IP	H	R	ER	BB	SO
1986— Gulf Coast Expos (GCL)		5	6	.455	3.27	13	13	2	0	0	74¹/₃	73	•42	27	30	41
1987— Burlington (Midw.)		9	13	.409	4.53	27	27	6	3	0	161	175	98	81	42	103
1988— West Palm Beach (FSL)		10	8	.556	3.33	27	27	9	4	0	181	165	80	67	47	120
1989— Jacksonville (Sou.)..............		3	*17	.150	5.26	25	25	1	0	0	138²/₃	137	101	81	73	91
1990— Jacksonville (Sou.)..............		12	10	.545	3.41	29	28	2	1	0	169	158	72	64	67	121
1991— Indianapolis (A.A.)..............		8	15	.348	4.06	29	27	•5	2	0	166¹/₃	155	97	75	61	108
1992— Indianapolis (A.A.)..............		•12	8	.600	3.43	25	23	3	1	0	152¹/₃	139	64	58	58	111
— Montreal (N.L.).................		1	2	.333	2.23	10	4	0	0	1	32¹/₃	26	9	8	11	14
1993— Montreal (N.L.).................		2	5	.286	4.12	23	11	0	0	0	83	93	49	38	33	33
— Colorado (N.L.)■		3	5	.375	6.10	14	14	1	0	0	76²/₃	86	53	52	38	30
1994— Colorado Springs (PCL)		1	2	.333	4.94	5	4	1	0	0	31	35	19	17	11	17
— Colorado (N.L.)		3	1	.750	5.84	15	1	0	0	1	24²/₃	28	16	16	10	15
— Phoenix (PCL)■		2	1	.667	2.57	8	5	1	1	0	35	30	13	10	11	11
— San Francisco (N.L.)		0	0	...	10.80	1	0	0	0	0	1²/₃	5	2	2	0	0
1995— Toledo (I.L.)■		5	11	.313	4.54	27	19	2	1	1	136²/₃	148	80	69	55	68
1996— Iowa (A.A.)■		1	2	.333	2.19	28	0	0	0	18	24²/₃	19	9	6	8	14
— Chicago (N.L.)...................		3	5	.375	2.63	48	0	0	0	1	61²/₃	59	25	18	19	33
1997— Chicago (N.L.)		2	3	.400	3.86	64	0	0	0	2	84	82	39	36	35	74
1998— St. Louis (N.L.)■		4	6	.400	4.44	44	17	0	0	4	133²/₃	128	72	66	57	98
1999— St. Louis (N.L.)..................		18	7	.720	3.97	31	31	0	0	0	190¹/₃	197	91	84	89	124
Major League totals (7 years).......		36	34	.514	4.19	250	78	1	0	9	688	704	356	320	292	421

ALL-STAR GAME RECORD

Year	League	W	L	Pct.	ERA	GS	CG	ShO	Sv.	IP	H	R	ER	BB	SO
1999— National.............................		0	0	...	18.00	0	0	0	0	1	1	2	2	1	2

BOURNIGAL, RAFAEL 2B/SS

PERSONAL: Born May 12, 1966, in Azua, Dominican Republic. ... 5-11/175. ... Bats right, throws right. ... Full name: Rafael Antonio Bournigal.
HIGH SCHOOL: Domay (Dominican Republic).
JUNIOR COLLEGE: Canada College (Calif.).
COLLEGE: Florida State.
TRANSACTIONS/CAREER NOTES: Selected by Texas Rangers organization in 11th round of free-agent draft (January 9, 1985); did not sign. ... Selected by Baltimore Orioles organization in 10th round of free-agent draft (January 14, 1986); did not sign. ... Selected by Los Angeles Dodgers organization in 19th round of free-agent draft (June 2, 1987). ... On Albuquerque temporarily inactive list (April 22-30, 1994). ... Traded by Dodgers organization to Montreal Expos organization for P John Foster (June 9, 1995). ... On Ottawa disabled list (June 26-July 22, 1995). ... Granted free agency (October 16, 1995). ... Signed by Edmonton, Oakland Athletics organization (January 22, 1996). ... On disabled list (July 1-31, 1997); included rehabilitation assignment to Modesto (July 21-31). ... Released by Athletics (December 14, 1998). ... Signed by Pittsburgh Pirates organization (December 22, 1998). ... Released by Pirates (March 27, 1999). ... Signed by Rangers organization (March 30, 1999). ... Contract sold by Rangers to Seattle Mariners (April 27, 1999). ... Granted free agency (December 21, 1999).
STATISTICAL NOTES: Led Northwest League shortstops with .953 fielding percentage in 1988. ... Led Pacific Coast League shortstops with 636 total chances and 97 double plays in 1993.
MISCELLANEOUS: Served as player/coach with Vero Beach (1991).

| | | | | | | | BATTING | | | | | | | | FIELDING | | |
Year	Team (League)	Pos.	G	AB	R	H	2B	3B	HR	RBI	Avg.	BB	SO	SB	PO	A	E	Avg.
1987—	Great Falls (Pio.)	2B-SS	30	82	5	12	4	0	0	4	.146	3	7	0	49	47	4	.960
1988—	Salem (N.W.)	SS-2B-3B	70	275	54	86	10	1	0	25	.313	38	32	11	76	179	12	†.955
1989—	Vero Beach (FSL)	2B-SS	132	484	74	128	11	1	1	37	.264	33	21	18	219	378	15	.975
1990—	San Antonio (Texas)	SS-2B-3B	69	194	20	41	4	2	0	14	.211	8	25	2	99	136	6	.975
1991—	Vero Beach (FSL)	SS-3B	20	66	6	16	2	0	0	3	.242	1	3	2	29	56	1	.988
—	San Antonio (Texas)	3B-SS-2B	16	65	6	21	2	0	0	9	.323	2	7	2	28	43	0	1.000
—	Albuquerque (PCL)	SS-2B-3B	66	215	34	63	5	5	0	29	.293	14	13	4	100	188	9	.970
1992—	Albuquerque (PCL)	SS	122	395	47	128	18	1	0	34	.324	22	7	5	*201	369	9	*.984
—	Los Angeles (N.L.)	SS	10	20	1	3	1	0	0	0	.150	1	2	0	12	17	1	.967
1993—	Albuquerque (PCL)	SS	134	465	75	129	25	0	4	55	.277	29	18	3	196	*427	13	*.980
—	Los Angeles (N.L.)	SS-2B	8	18	0	9	1	0	0	3	.500	0	2	0	5	14	0	1.000
1994—	Albuquerque (PCL)	SS	61	208	29	69	8	0	1	22	.332	9	9	2	66	209	4	.986
—	Los Angeles (N.L.)	SS	40	116	2	26	3	1	0	11	.224	9	5	0	56	95	3	.981
1995—	Albuquerque (PCL)	SS	15	31	2	4	1	0	0	1	.129	1	2	0	7	32	2	.951
—	Ottawa (I.L.)■	SS-2B-3B	19	54	2	11	4	0	0	6	.204	2	4	0	15	51	1	.985
—	Harrisburg (East.)	SS	29	95	12	21	3	1	0	7	.221	11	8	1	27	64	3	.968
1996—	Oakland (A.L.)■	2B-SS	88	252	33	61	14	2	0	18	.242	16	19	4	128	208	2	.994
1997—	Oakland (A.L.)	SS-2B	79	222	29	62	9	0	1	20	.279	16	19	2	100	199	6	.980
—	Modesto (Calif.)	SS-DH	7	21	0	5	1	0	0	2	.238	3	2	0	5	7	0	1.000
1998—	Oakland (A.L.)	2B-SS-DH	85	209	23	47	11	0	1	19	.225	10	11	6	109	170	0	1.000
1999—	Oklahoma (PCL)■	2B-SS-DH-3B	17	56	16	21	6	0	3	14	.375	12	5	1	22	45	2	.971
—	Seattle (A.L.)	S-2-3-DH-O	55	95	16	26	5	0	2	14	.274	7	6	0	59	84	3	.979
American League totals (4 years)			307	778	101	196	39	2	4	71	.252	49	55	12	396	661	11	.990
National League totals (3 years)			58	154	3	38	5	1	0	14	.247	10	9	0	73	126	4	.980
Major League totals (7 years)			365	932	104	234	44	3	4	85	.251	59	64	12	469	787	15	.988

BOWERS, CEDRICK P DEVIL RAYS

PERSONAL: Born February 10, 1978, in Gainesville, Fla. ... 6-2/215. ... Throws left, bats right. ... Full name: Cedrick J. Bowers.
HIGH SCHOOL: Chiefland (Fla.).
TRANSACTIONS/CAREER NOTES: Selected by Tampa Bay Devil Rays organization in fourth round of free-agent draft (June 4, 1996).

Year	League	W	L	Pct.	ERA	G	GS	CG	ShO	Sv.	IP	H	R	ER	BB	SO
1996—	GC Devil Rays (GCL)	3	5	.375	5.37	13	•13	0	0	0	60 1/3	50	39	36	*39	85
1997—	Charleston, S.C. (SAL)	8	10	.444	3.21	28	28	0	0	0	157	119	74	56	78	164
1998—	St. Petersburg (FSL)	5	9	.357	4.38	28	26	0	0	0	150	144	89	73	80	156
1999—	Orlando (Sou.)	6	9	.400	5.98	27	27	1	0	0	125	125	94	83	76	138

BOWIE, MICAH P CUBS

PERSONAL: Born November 10, 1974, in Webster, Tex. ... 6-4/210. ... Throws left, bats left. ... Full name: Micah Andrew Bowie.
HIGH SCHOOL: Kingwood (Texas).
TRANSACTIONS/CAREER NOTES: Signed as non-drafted free agent by Atlanta Braves organization (July 15, 1993). ... On Durham disabled list (July 4, 1996-remainder of season). ... On Richmond disabled list (May 18-June 10, 1999). ... Traded by Braves with P Ruben Quevado and a minor league player to be named later to Chicago Cubs for P Terry Mulholland and SS Jose Hernandez (July 31, 1999); Cubs acquired P Joey Nation to complete deal (August 24, 1999).

Year	League	W	L	Pct.	ERA	G	GS	CG	ShO	Sv.	IP	H	R	ER	BB	SO
1994—	GC Braves (GCL)	0	3	.000	3.03	6	5	0	0	0	29 2/3	27	14	10	5	35
—	Danville (Appl.)	3	1	.750	3.58	7	5	0	0	0	32 2/3	28	16	13	13	38
1995—	Macon (SAL)	4	1	.800	2.28	5	5	0	0	0	27 2/3	9	8	7	11	36
—	Durham (Caro.)	4	11	.267	3.66	23	13	0	0	0	66 1/3	55	29	27	33	65
1996—	Durham (Caro.)	3	6	.333	3.66	14	13	0	0	0	66 1/3	55	29	27	33	65
1997—	Durham (Caro.)	2	2	.500	3.66	9	6	0	0	0	39 1/3	29	16	16	27	44
—	Greenville (Sou.)	3	2	.600	3.50	8	7	0	0	0	43 2/3	34	19	17	26	41
1998—	Greenville (Sou.)	11	6	.647	3.48	30	•29	1	0	0	163	132	73	63	64	160
1999—	Richmond (I.L.)	4	4	.500	2.96	13	13	0	0	0	73	65	24	24	14	82
—	Atlanta (N.L.)	0	1	.000	13.50	3	0	0	0	0	4	8	6	6	4	2
—	Chicago (N.L.)■	2	6	.250	9.96	11	11	0	0	0	47	73	54	52	30	39
Major League totals (1 year)		2	7	.222	10.24	14	11	0	0	0	51	81	60	58	34	41

BOYD, JASON   P   PIRATES

PERSONAL: Born February 23, 1973, in St. Clair, Ill. ... 6-3/173. ... Throws right, bats right. ... Full name: Jason Pernell Boyd.
HIGH SCHOOL: Edwardsville (Ill.).
JUNIOR COLLEGE: John A. Logan College (Ill.).
TRANSACTIONS/CAREER NOTES: Selected by Philadelphia Phillies organization in eighth round of free-agent draft (June 2, 1994). ... Selected by Arizona Diamondbacks in first round (23rd pick overall) of expansion draft (November 18, 1997). ... On disabled list (May 22, 1998-remainder of season). ... Traded by Diamondbacks to Pittsburgh Pirates (August 25, 1999), completing deal in which Pirates traded 2B Tony Womack to Diamondbacks for OF Paul Weichard and a player to named later (February 26, 1999).

Year	League	W	L	Pct.	ERA	G	GS	CG	ShO	Sv.	IP	H	R	ER	BB	SO
1994—	Martinsville (Appl.)	3	7	.300	4.17	14	13	1	0	0	69	65	46	32	32	45
1995—	Piedmont (SAL)	6	8	.429	3.58	26	24	1	0	0	151	151	77	60	44	129
1996—	Clearwater (FSL)	11	8	.579	3.90	26	26	2	0	0	161²/₃	160	75	70	49	120
1997—	Reading (East.)	10	6	.625	4.82	48	7	0	0	0	115²/₃	113	65	62	64	98
1998—	Tucson (PCL)■	2	2	.500	6.23	15	0	0	0	0	21²/₃	28	22	15	14	13
1999—	Tucson (PCL)	6	5	.545	4.52	44	0	0	0	5	75²/₃	76	42	38	27	60
—	Nashville (PCL)■	0	0	...	0.00	5	0	0	0	0	4²/₃	2	0	0	0	2
—	Pittsburgh (N.L.)	0	0	...	3.38	4	0	0	0	0	5¹/₃	5	2	2	2	4
Major League totals (1 year)		0	0	...	3.38	4	0	0	0	0	5¹/₃	5	2	2	2	4

BRADFORD, CHAD   P   WHITE SOX

PERSONAL: Born September 14, 1974, in Jackson, Miss. ... 6-5/205. ... Throws right, bats right. ... Full name: Chadwick L. Bradford.
HIGH SCHOOL: Byram (Jackson, Miss.).
JUNIOR COLLEGE: Hinds Community College (Miss.).
COLLEGE: Southern Mississippi.
TRANSACTIONS/CAREER NOTES: Selected by Chicago White Sox organization in 13th round of free-agent draft (June 4, 1996).

Year	League	W	L	Pct.	ERA	G	GS	CG	ShO	Sv.	IP	H	R	ER	BB	SO
1996—	Hickory (SAL)	0	2	.000	0.90	28	0	0	0	18	30	21	7	3	7	27
1997—	Winston-Salem (Caro.)	3	7	.300	3.95	46	0	0	0	15	54²/₃	51	30	24	25	43
1998—	Birmingham (Sou.)	1	1	.500	2.60	10	0	0	0	1	17¹/₃	13	6	5	8	14
—	Calgary (PCL)	4	1	.800	1.94	29	0	0	0	0	51	50	12	11	11	27
—	Chicago (A.L.)	2	1	.667	3.23	29	0	0	0	1	30²/₃	27	16	11	7	11
1999—	Charlotte (I.L.)	9	3	.750	1.94	47	0	0	0	5	74¹/₃	63	19	16	15	56
—	Chicago (A.L.)	0	0	...	19.64	3	0	0	0	0	3²/₃	9	8	8	5	0
Major League totals (2 years)		2	1	.667	4.98	32	0	0	0	1	34¹/₃	36	24	19	12	11

BRADLEY, MILTON   OF   EXPOS

PERSONAL: Born April 15, 1978, in Harbor City, Fla. ... 6-0/180. ... Bats both, throws right. ... Full name: Milton O. Bradley.
HIGH SCHOOL: Polytechnic (Long Beach, Calif.).
TRANSACTIONS/CAREER NOTES: Selected by Montreal Expos organization in second round of free-agent draft (June 4, 1996). ... On Harrisburg disabled list (June 14-25, 1999).

Year	Team (League)	Pos.	G	AB	R	H	2B	3B	HR	RBI	Avg.	BB	SO	SB	PO	A	E	Avg.
1996—	GC Expos (GCL)	OF	32	112	18	27	7	1	1	12	.241	13	15	7	54	2	3	.949
1997—	Vermont (NY-P)	OF	50	200	29	60	7	5	3	30	.300	17	34	7	113	3	4	.967
—	GC Expos (GCL)	OF	9	25	6	5	2	0	1	2	.200	4	4	2	15	0	1	.938
1998—	Cape Fear (SAL)	OF	75	281	54	85	21	4	6	50	.302	23	57	13	87	5	3	.968
—	Jupiter (FSL)	OF	67	261	55	75	14	1	5	34	.287	30	42	17	138	8	1	.993
1999—	Harrisburg (East.)	OF-DH	87	346	62	114	22	5	12	50	.329	33	61	14	166	3	5	.971

BRADLEY, RYAN   P   YANKEES

PERSONAL: Born October 26, 1975, in Covina, Calif. ... 6-4/226. ... Throws right, bats right. ... Full name: Ryan James Bradley.
HIGH SCHOOL: Ayala (Chino, Calif.).
COLLEGE: Arizona State.
TRANSACTIONS/CAREER NOTES: Selected by Kansas City Royals in 14th round of free-agent draft (June 2, 1994); did not sign. ... Selected by New York Yankees organization in supplemental round ("sandwich" pick between first and second round; 40th pick overall) of free-agent draft (June 3, 1997); pick received as compensation for Texas Rangers signing Type A free-agent P John Wetteland. ... On Columbus disabled list (July 3-15, 1999).
STATISTICAL NOTES: Pitched 8-0 no-hit victory for Tampa against Lakeland (June 22, 1998). ... Led International League with 23 wild pitches in 1999. ... Tied for International League lead with 28 home runs allowed in 1999.

Year	League	W	L	Pct.	ERA	G	GS	CG	ShO	Sv.	IP	H	R	ER	BB	SO
1997—	Oneonta (NY-P)	3	1	.750	1.35	14	0	0	0	1	26²/₃	22	5	4	5	22
1998—	Tampa (FSL)	7	4	.636	2.38	32	11	1	1	7	94²/₃	59	29	25	30	112
—	Norwich (East.)	2	0	1.000	1.44	3	3	1	1	0	25	8	4	4	8	25
—	Columbus (I.L.)	0	1	.000	6.19	3	3	0	0	0	16	15	13	11	13	12
—	New York (A.L.)	2	1	.667	5.68	5	1	0	0	0	12²/₃	12	9	8	9	13
1999—	Columbus (I.L.)	5	12	.294	6.21	29	24	1	0	0	145	163	112	100	73	118
Major League totals (1 year)		2	1	.667	5.68	5	1	0	0	0	12²/₃	12	9	8	9	13

BRAGG, DARREN — OF

PERSONAL: Born September 7, 1969, in Waterbury, Conn. ... 5-9/180. ... Bats left, throws right. ... Full name: Darren William Bragg.
HIGH SCHOOL: Taft (Watertown, Conn.).
COLLEGE: Georgia Tech.
TRANSACTIONS/CAREER NOTES: Selected by Seattle Mariners organization in 22nd round of free-agent draft (June 30, 1991). ... Traded by Mariners to Boston Red Sox for P Jamie Moyer (July 30, 1996). ... Granted free agency (December 21, 1998). ... Signed by St. Louis Cardinals (January 12, 1999). ... On disabled list (August 3, 1999-remainder of season). ... Released by Cardinals (December 16, 1999).
STATISTICAL NOTES: Led Carolina League in caught stealing with 19 in 1992. ... Led Pacific Coast League outfielders with 344 total chances and five double plays in 1994. ... Career major league grand slams: 2.

Year Team (League)	Pos.	G	AB	R	H	2B	3B	HR	RBI	Avg.	BB	SO	SB	PO	A	E	Avg.
1991— Peninsula (Caro.)	OF-2B	69	237	42	53	14	0	3	29	.224	66	72	21	167	9	4	.978
1992— Peninsula (Caro.)	OF	135	428	*83	117	29	5	9	58	.273	*105	76	44	262	11	4	.986
1993— Jacksonville (Sou.)	OF-P	131	451	74	119	26	3	11	46	.264	81	82	19	306	14	10	.970
1994— Calgary (PCL)	OF	126	500	112	175	33	6	17	85	.350	68	72	28	317	20	7	.980
— Seattle (A.L.)	DH-OF	8	19	4	3	1	0	0	2	.158	2	5	0	1	0	0	1.000
1995— Seattle (A.L.)	OF-DH	52	145	20	34	5	1	3	12	.234	18	37	9	83	7	1	.989
— Tacoma (PCL)	OF-DH	53	212	24	65	13	3	4	31	.307	23	39	10	115	7	4	.968
1996— Seattle (A.L.)	OF	69	195	36	53	12	1	7	25	.272	33	35	8	118	7	1	.992
— Tacoma (PCL)	OF	20	71	17	20	8	0	3	8	.282	14	14	1	32	2	0	1.000
— Boston (A.L.)■	OF	58	222	38	56	14	1	3	22	.252	36	39	6	136	5	2	.986
1997— Boston (A.L.)	OF-3B	153	513	65	132	35	2	9	57	.257	61	102	10	364	11	5	.987
1998— Boston (A.L.)	OF-DH	129	409	51	114	29	3	8	57	.279	42	99	5	218	6	1	*.996
1999— St. Louis (N.L.)■	OF	93	273	38	71	12	1	6	26	.260	44	67	3	155	7	3	.982
American League totals (5 years)		469	1503	214	392	96	8	30	175	.261	192	317	38	920	36	10	.990
National League totals (1 year)		93	273	38	71	12	1	6	26	.260	44	67	3	155	7	3	.982
Major League totals (6 years)		562	1776	252	463	108	9	36	201	.261	236	384	41	1075	43	13	.989

DIVISION SERIES RECORD

Year Team (League)	Pos.	G	AB	R	H	2B	3B	HR	RBI	Avg.	BB	SO	SB	PO	A	E	Avg.
1998— Boston (A.L.)	OF	3	12	0	1	0	0	0	0	.083	0	5	0	4	0	0	1.000

RECORD AS PITCHER

Year League	W	L	Pct.	ERA	G	GS	CG	ShO	Sv.	IP	H	R	ER	BB	SO
1993— Jacksonville (Sou.)	0	0	...	9.00	1	0	0	0	0	1	3	1	1	0	0

BRAMMER, J.D. — P — INDIANS

PERSONAL: Born January 30, 1975, in West Logan, W.Va. ... 6-4/235. ... Throws right, bats right. ... Full name: John D. Brammer.
HIGH SCHOOL: Logan (W.Va.).
COLLEGE: Stanford.
TRANSACTIONS/CAREER NOTES: Selected by Cleveland Indians organization in fourth round of free-agent draft (June 4, 1996). ... On Kinston disabled list (May 20-July 15, 1998).

Year League	W	L	Pct.	ERA	G	GS	CG	ShO	Sv.	IP	H	R	ER	BB	SO
1996— Watertown (NY-P)	5	0	1.000	3.55	17	0	0	0	1	38	27	22	15	28	49
1997— Columbia (SAL)	6	10	.375	7.02	28	23	0	0	1	116 2/3	132	102	*91	50	105
1998— Kinston (Caro.)	3	2	.600	1.33	15	0	0	0	2	27	15	6	4	8	33
— Akron (East.)	1	0	1.000	5.23	11	0	0	0	3	20 2/3	21	12	12	10	23
1999— Akron (East.)	3	2	.600	4.76	47	0	0	0	8	75 2/3	53	44	40	60	69

BRANTLEY, JEFF — P — PHILLIES

PERSONAL: Born September 5, 1963, in Florence, Ala. ... 5-10/197. ... Throws right, bats right. ... Full name: Jeffrey Hoke Brantley.
HIGH SCHOOL: W.A. Berry (Florence, Ala.).
COLLEGE: Mississippi State.
TRANSACTIONS/CAREER NOTES: Selected by Montreal Expos organization in 13th round of free-agent draft (June 4, 1984); did not sign. ... Selected by San Francisco Giants organization in sixth round of free-agent draft (June 3, 1985). ... Granted free agency (December 20, 1993). ... Signed by Cincinnati Reds (January 4, 1994). ... Granted free agency (October 17, 1994). ... Re-signed by Reds (October 28, 1994). ... On disabled list (March 19-April 6, 1996). ... On disabled list (March 27-April 15 and May 20, 1997-remainder of season). ... Traded by Reds to St. Louis Cardinals for 1B Dmitri Young (November 10, 1997). ... On St. Louis disabled list (March 23-April 9, 1998); included rehabilitation assignment to Arkansas (April 5-9). ... Traded by Cardinals with OF Ron Gant and P Cliff Politte to Philadelphia Phillies for P Ricky Bottalico and P Garrett Stephenson (November 19, 1998). ... On disabled list (April 29-May 16 and May 24, 1999-remainder of season). ... Granted free agency (November 1, 1999). ... Re-signed by Phillies (December 7, 1999).
STATISTICAL NOTES: Tied for Pacific Coast League lead with 11 hit batsmen in 1987.
MISCELLANEOUS: Appeared in one game as pinch runner with San Francisco (1989).

Year League	W	L	Pct.	ERA	G	GS	CG	ShO	Sv.	IP	H	R	ER	BB	SO
1985— Fresno (Calif.)	8	2	.800	3.33	14	13	3	0	0	94 2/3	83	39	35	37	85
1986— Shreveport (Texas)	8	10	.444	3.48	26	26	•8	3	0	165 2/3	139	78	64	68	125
1987— Shreveport (Texas)	0	1	.000	3.09	2	2	0	0	0	11 2/3	12	7	4	4	7
— Phoenix (PCL)	6	11	.353	4.65	29	28	2	0	0	170 1/3	187	110	88	82	111
1988— Phoenix (PCL)	9	5	.643	4.33	27	19	1	0	0	122 2/3	130	65	59	39	83
— San Francisco (N.L.)	0	1	.000	5.66	9	1	0	0	1	20 2/3	22	13	13	6	11
1989— San Francisco (N.L.)	7	1	.875	4.07	59	1	0	0	0	97 1/3	101	50	44	37	69
— Phoenix (PCL)	1	1	.500	1.26	7	0	0	0	3	14 1/3	6	2	2	6	20
1990— San Francisco (N.L.)	5	3	.625	1.56	55	0	0	0	19	86 2/3	77	18	15	33	61
1991— San Francisco (N.L.)	5	2	.714	2.45	67	0	0	0	15	95 1/3	78	27	26	52	81
1992— San Francisco (N.L.)	7	7	.500	2.95	56	4	0	0	7	91 2/3	67	32	30	45	86
1993— San Francisco (N.L.)	5	6	.455	4.28	53	12	0	0	0	113 2/3	112	60	54	46	76

Year League	W	L	Pct.	ERA	G	GS	CG	ShO	Sv.	IP	H	R	ER	BB	SO
1994—Cincinnati (N.L.)■	6	6	.500	2.48	50	0	0	0	15	65⅓	46	20	18	28	63
1995—Cincinnati (N.L.)	3	2	.600	2.82	56	0	0	0	28	70⅓	53	22	22	20	62
1996—Cincinnati (N.L.)	1	2	.333	2.41	66	0	0	0	•44	71	54	21	19	28	76
1997—Cincinnati (N.L.)	1	1	.500	3.86	13	0	0	0	1	11⅔	9	5	5	7	16
1998—Arkansas (Texas)■	0	0	...	0.00	2	0	0	0	0	1⅔	0	0	0	1	3
—St. Louis (N.L.)	0	5	.000	4.44	48	0	0	0	14	50⅔	40	26	25	18	48
1999—Philadelphia (N.L.)■	1	2	.333	5.19	10	0	0	0	5	8⅔	5	6	5	8	11
Major League totals (12 years)	41	38	.519	3.17	542	18	0	0	149	783	664	300	276	328	660

DIVISION SERIES RECORD

Year League	W	L	Pct.	ERA	G	GS	CG	ShO	Sv.	IP	H	R	ER	BB	SO
1995—Cincinnati (N.L.)	0	0	...	6.00	3	0	0	0	1	3	5	2	2	0	2

CHAMPIONSHIP SERIES RECORD

Year League	W	L	Pct.	ERA	G	GS	CG	ShO	Sv.	IP	H	R	ER	BB	SO
1989—San Francisco (N.L.)	0	0	...	0.00	3	0	0	0	0	5	1	0	0	2	3
1995—Cincinnati (N.L.)	0	0	...	0.00	2	0	0	0	0	2⅔	0	0	0	2	1
Champ. series totals (2 years)	0	0	...	0.00	5	0	0	0	0	7⅔	1	0	0	4	4

WORLD SERIES RECORD

Year League	W	L	Pct.	ERA	G	GS	CG	ShO	Sv.	IP	H	R	ER	BB	SO
1989—San Francisco (N.L.)	0	0	...	4.15	3	0	0	0	0	4⅓	5	2	2	3	1

ALL-STAR GAME RECORD

Year League	W	L	Pct.	ERA	GS	CG	ShO	Sv.	IP	H	R	ER	BB	SO
1990—National	0	1	.000	54.00	0	0	0	0	⅓	2	2	2	0	0

BRANYAN, RUSSELL — 3B — INDIANS

PERSONAL: Born December 19, 1975, in Warner Robins, Ga. ... 6-3/195. ... Bats left, throws right. ... Full name: Russell Oles Branyan.
HIGH SCHOOL: Stratford Academy (Warner Robins, Ga.).
TRANSACTIONS/CAREER NOTES: Selected by Cleveland Indians organization in seventh round of free-agent draft (June 2, 1994). ... On Akron disabled list (April 23-May 11 and May 16-August 15, 1998).
HONORS: Named Appalachian League Most Valuable Player (1996).
STATISTICAL NOTES: Led Appalachian League with .575 slugging percentage in 1996. ... Led Appalachian League third basemen with 24 double plays in 1996.

Year Team (League)	Pos.	G	AB	R	H	2B	3B	HR	RBI	Avg.	BB	SO	SB	PO	A	E	Avg.
1994—Burlington (Appl.)	3B	55	171	21	36	10	0	5	5	.211	25	64	4	32	88	21	.851
1995—Columbus (SAL)	3B	76	277	46	71	8	6	19	55	.256	27	120	1	34	120	26	.856
1996—Columbus (SAL)	3B-DH	130	482	102	129	20	4	*40	*106	.268	62	166	7	82	256	44	.885
1997—Kinston (Caro.)	3B-DH	83	297	59	86	26	2	27	75	.290	52	94	3	64	118	21	.897
—Akron (East.)	3B-DH	41	137	26	32	4	0	12	30	.234	28	56	0	31	98	11	.921
1998—Akron (East.)	3B-DH	43	163	35	48	11	3	16	46	.294	35	58	1	24	72	7	.932
—Cleveland (A.L.)	3B	1	4	0	0	0	0	0	0	.000	0	2	0	0	1	0	1.000
1999—Buffalo (I.L.)	3B-DH	109	395	51	82	11	1	30	67	.208	52	*187	8	63	205	23	.921
—Cleveland (A.L.)	3B-DH	11	38	4	8	2	0	1	6	.211	3	19	0	6	18	1	.960
Major League totals (2 years)		12	42	4	8	2	0	1	6	.190	3	21	0	6	19	1	.962

BREA, LESLI — P — METS

PERSONAL: Born October 12, 1978, in San Pedro de Macoris, Dominican Republic. ... 5-11/170. ... Throws right, bats right. ... Full name: Lesli Guillermo Brea.
HIGH SCHOOL: Santo Domingo (San Pedro de Macoris, Dominican Republic).
TRANSACTIONS/CAREER NOTES: Signed as non-drafted free agent by Seattle Mariners organization (January 20, 1996). ... Traded by Mariners to New York Mets for OF Butch Huskey (December 14, 1998).

Year League	W	L	Pct.	ERA	G	GS	CG	ShO	Sv.	IP	H	R	ER	BB	SO
1996—Arizona Mariners (Ariz.)	1	0	1.000	5.06	7	0	0	0	0	10⅔	7	10	6	6	12
1997—Lancaster (Calif.)	0	0	...	13.50	1	0	0	0	0	2	5	5	3	1	1
—Everett (N.W.)	2	4	.333	7.99	23	0	0	0	3	32⅓	34	29	29	29	49
1998—Wisconsin (Midw.)	3	4	.429	2.76	49	0	0	0	12	58⅔	47	26	18	40	86
1999—St. Lucie (FSL)■	1	7	.125	3.73	32	18	0	0	3	120⅔	95	64	50	68	136

BRESTER, JASON — P — PHILLIES

PERSONAL: Born December 7, 1976, in Lincoln, Neb. ... 6-3/190. ... Throws left, bats left. ... Full name: Jason Scott Brester.
HIGH SCHOOL: Burlington-Edison (Burlington, Wash.).
TRANSACTIONS/CAREER NOTES: Selected by San Francisco Giants organization in second round of free-agent draft (June 1, 1992). ... On Shreveport disabled list (April 2-May 4, 1998). ... Traded by Giants to Colorado Rockies (August 17, 1998), completing deal in which Rockies traded OF Ellis Burks to Giants for OF Darryl Hamilton, P Jim Stoops and a player to be named later (July 31, 1998). ... Claimed on waivers by Philadelphia Phillies (June 14, 1999).

Year League	W	L	Pct.	ERA	G	GS	CG	ShO	Sv.	IP	H	R	ER	BB	SO
1995—Bellingham (N.W.)	1	0	1.000	4.13	8	6	0	0	0	24	23	11	11	12	17
1996—Burlington (Midw.)	10	9	.526	3.96	27	27	0	0	0	157	139	78	69	64	143
1997—San Jose (Calif.)	9	9	.500	4.24	26	26	0	0	0	142⅓	164	80	67	52	172
1998—Shreveport (Texas)	2	8	.200	3.82	19	19	0	0	0	113	117	58	48	44	79
—New Haven (East.)■	2	0	1.000	1.59	5	4	0	0	0	22⅔	22	7	4	7	15
1999—Carolina (Sou.)	2	6	.250	5.76	11	11	0	0	0	59⅓	71	45	38	26	44
—Reading (East.)■	7	5	.583	3.76	16	16	3	0	1	105⅓	105	48	44	26	87

BREWER, BILLY   P

PERSONAL: Born April 15, 1968, in Fort Worth, Texas. ... 6-1/197. ... Throws left, bats left. ... Full name: William Robert Brewer.
HIGH SCHOOL: Spring Hill (Longview, Texas).
COLLEGE: Dallas Baptist.
TRANSACTIONS/CAREER NOTES: Selected by Cleveland Indians organization in 26th round of free-agent draft (June 5, 1989); did not sign. ... Selected by Montreal Expos organization in 28th round of free-agent draft (June 4, 1990). ... On disabled list (April 12-June 11, 1991). ... Selected by Kansas City Royals organization from Expos organization in Rule 5 major league draft (December 7, 1992). ... Traded by Royals to Los Angeles Dodgers for SS Jose Offerman (December 17, 1995). ... Traded by Dodgers to New York Yankees for P Mike Judd (June 22, 1996). ... Granted free agency (December 20, 1996). ... Signed by Cincinnati Reds organization (December 21, 1996). ... Released by Reds (March 10, 1997). ... Signed by Oakland Athletics organization (March 18, 1997). ... On Oakland disabled list (April 6-28, 1997); included rehabilitation assignments to Visalia (April 21-24) and Edmonton (April 25-28). ... Released by A's (May 22, 1997). ... Signed by Philadelphia Phillies organization (May 27, 1997). ... On Philadelphia disabled list (August 18, 1997-remainder of season). ... Released by Phillies (October 10, 1997). ... Re-signed by Phillies organization (December 15, 1997). ... On disabled list (April 9, 1998-remainder of season). ... Granted free agency (October 15, 1998). ... Re-signed by Phillies (December 7, 1998). ... Granted free agency (October 13, 1999).

Year	League	W	L	Pct.	ERA	G	GS	CG	ShO	Sv.	IP	H	R	ER	BB	SO
1990—	Jamestown (NY-P)	2	2	.500	2.93	11	2	0	0	1	27²/₃	23	10	9	13	37
1991—	Rockford (Midw.)	3	3	.500	1.98	29	0	0	0	5	41	32	12	9	25	43
1992—	West Palm Beach (FSL)	2	2	.500	1.73	28	0	0	0	8	36¹/₃	27	10	7	14	37
	— Harrisburg (East.)	2	0	1.000	5.01	20	0	0	0	0	23¹/₃	25	15	13	18	18
1993—	Kansas City (A.L.)■	2	2	.500	3.46	46	0	0	0	0	39	31	16	15	20	28
1994—	Kansas City (A.L.)	4	1	.800	2.56	50	0	0	0	3	38²/₃	28	11	11	16	25
1995—	Kansas City (A.L.)	2	4	.333	5.56	48	0	0	0	0	45¹/₃	54	28	28	20	31
	— Springfield (Midw.)	0	0	...	0.00	1	0	0	0	1	2	2	1	0	1	2
	— Omaha (A.A.)	0	0	...	0.00	6	0	0	0	0	7	1	0	0	7	5
1996—	Albuquerque (PCL)■	2	2	.500	3.13	31	0	0	0	2	31²/₃	28	13	11	22	33
	— New York (A.L.)■	1	0	1.000	9.53	4	0	0	0	0	5²/₃	7	6	6	8	8
	— Columbus (I.L.)	0	2	.000	7.20	13	4	0	0	0	25	27	21	20	19	27
1997—	Oakland (A.L.)■	0	0	...	13.50	3	0	0	0	0	2	4	3	3	2	1
	— Visalia (Calif.)	0	0	...	0.00	2	2	0	0	0	3	1	1	0	4	5
	— Edmonton (PCL)	0	0	...	5.63	7	1	0	0	1	8	8	5	5	6	11
	— Scranton/W.B. (I.L.)■	2	1	.667	3.00	11	0	0	0	1	9	10	7	3	5	9
	— Philadelphia (N.L.)	1	2	.333	3.27	25	0	0	0	0	22	15	8	8	11	16
1998—	Philadelphia (N.L.)	0	1	.000	108.00	2	0	0	0	0	¹/₃	3	4	4	2	0
1999—	Scranton/W.B. (I.L.)	6	1	.857	3.78	33	5	0	0	2	69	59	32	29	28	57
	— Philadelphia (N.L.)	1	1	.500	7.01	25	0	0	0	2	25²/₃	30	20	20	14	28
A.L. totals (5 years)		9	7	.563	4.34	151	0	0	0	3	130²/₃	124	64	63	66	93
N.L. totals (3 years)		2	4	.333	6.00	52	0	0	0	2	48	48	32	32	27	44
Major League totals (7 years)		11	11	.500	4.79	203	0	0	0	5	178²/₃	172	96	95	93	137

BRIGNAC, JUNIOR   OF   BRAVES

PERSONAL: Born February 15, 1978, in Sun Valley, Calif. ... 6-3/175. ... Bats right, throws right. ... Full name: James Michael Brignac.
HIGH SCHOOL: Grover Cleveland (Reseda, Calif.).
TRANSACTIONS/CAREER NOTES: Selected by Atlanta Braves organization in third round of free-agent draft (June 4, 1996).
STATISTICAL NOTES: Led Gulf Coast League shortstops with 39 errors in 1996.

											BATTING				FIELDING			
Year	Team (League)	Pos.	G	AB	R	H	2B	3B	HR	RBI	Avg.	BB	SO	SB	PO	A	E	Avg.
1996—	GC Braves (GCL)	2B-SS	53	191	15	37	7	0	0	8	.194	9	60	3	98	145	†39	.862
1997—	Danville (Appl.)	SS	59	225	47	55	10	0	4	25	.244	29	70	12	55	81	21	.866
1998—	Eugene (N.W.)	SS	70	270	36	63	13	1	3	29	.233	23	74	15	*108	175	*39	.879
1999—	Macon (SAL)	OF	69	268	35	80	18	3	7	38	.299	11	68	17	145	5	4	.974
	— Myrtle Beach (Caro.)	OF	64	254	32	58	7	2	7	35	.228	24	84	11	146	4	4	.974

BROCAIL, DOUG   P   TIGERS

PERSONAL: Born May 16, 1967, in Clearfield, Pa. ... 6-5/235. ... Throws right, bats left. ... Full name: Douglas Keith Brocail.
HIGH SCHOOL: Lamar (Colo.).
JUNIOR COLLEGE: Lamar (Colo.) Community College.
TRANSACTIONS/CAREER NOTES: Selected by San Diego Padres organization in first round (12th pick overall) of free-agent draft (January 14, 1986). ... On Las Vegas disabled list (May 5-12, 1993). ... On San Diego disabled list (April 2-June 28, 1994); included rehabilitation assignments to Wichita (May 26-June 3) and Las Vegas (June 3-23). ... Traded by Padres with OF Phil Plantier, OF Derek Bell, P Pedro Martinez, IF Craig Shipley and SS Ricky Gutierrez to Houston Astros for 3B Ken Caminiti, OF Steve Finley, SS Andujar Cedeno, 1B Robert Petagine, P Brian Williams and a player to be named later (December 28, 1994); Padres acquired P Sean Fesh to complete deal (May 1, 1995). ... On Houston disabled list (May 11-August 15, 1996); included rehabilitation assignments to Jackson (May 27-June 4) and Tucson (July 29-August 15). ... Traded by Astros with OF Brian L. Hunter, IF Orlando Miller, P Todd Jones and cash to Detroit Tigers for C Brad Ausmus, P Jose Lima, P C.J. Nitkowski, P Trever Miller and IF Daryle Ward (December 10, 1996). ... On suspended list (June 10-13, 1998). ... On disabled list (August 9-24, 1998).
MISCELLANEOUS: Appeared in six games as pinch runner with San Diego (1993). ... Appeared in two games as pinch runner with San Diego (1994). ... Appeared in one game as pinch runner with Houston (1995). ... Appeared in two games as pinch runner with Houston (1996).

Year	League	W	L	Pct.	ERA	G	GS	CG	ShO	Sv.	IP	H	R	ER	BB	SO
1986—	Spokane (N.W.)	5	4	.556	3.81	16	•15	0	0	0	85	85	52	36	53	77
1987—	Charleston, S.C. (SAL)	2	6	.250	4.09	19	18	0	0	0	92¹/₃	94	51	42	28	68
1988—	Charleston, S.C. (SAL)	8	6	.571	2.69	22	13	5	0	2	107	107	40	32	25	107
1989—	Wichita (Texas)	5	9	.357	5.21	23	22	1	1	0	134²/₃	158	88	78	50	95
1990—	Wichita (Texas)	2	2	.500	4.33	12	9	0	0	0	52	53	30	25	24	27
1991—	Wichita (Texas)	10	7	.588	3.87	34	16	3	•3	6	146¹/₃	147	77	63	43	108
1992—	Las Vegas (PCL)	10	10	.500	3.97	29	25	4	0	0	172¹/₃	187	82	76	63	103
	— San Diego (N.L.)	0	0	...	6.43	3	3	0	0	0	14	17	10	10	5	15

B

Year	League	W	L	Pct.	ERA	G	GS	CG	ShO	Sv.	IP	H	R	ER	BB	SO
1993— Las Vegas (PCL)		4	2	.667	3.68	10	8	0	0	1	51 1/3	51	26	21	14	32
— San Diego (N.L.)		4	13	.235	4.56	24	24	0	0	0	128 1/3	143	75	65	42	70
1994— Wichita (Texas)		0	0	...	0.00	2	0	0	0	0	4	3	1	0	1	2
— Las Vegas (PCL)		0	0	...	7.11	7	3	0	0	0	12 2/3	21	12	10	2	8
— San Diego (N.L.)		0	0	...	5.82	12	0	0	0	0	17	21	13	11	5	11
1995— Houston (N.L.)■		6	4	.600	4.19	36	7	0	0	1	77 1/3	87	40	36	22	39
— Tucson (PCL)		1	0	1.000	3.86	3	3	0	0	0	16 1/3	18	9	7	4	16
1996— Houston (N.L.)		1	5	.167	4.58	23	4	0	0	0	53	58	31	27	23	34
— Jackson (Texas)		0	0	...	0.00	2	2	0	0	0	4	1	0	0	1	5
— Tucson (PCL)		0	1	.000	7.36	5	1	0	0	0	7 1/3	12	6	6	1	4
1997— Detroit (A.L.)■		3	4	.429	3.23	61	4	0	0	2	78	74	31	28	36	60
1998— Detroit (A.L.)		5	2	.714	2.73	60	0	0	0	0	62 2/3	47	23	19	18	55
1999— Detroit (A.L.)		4	4	.500	2.52	70	0	0	0	2	82	60	23	23	25	78
A.L. totals (3 years)		12	10	.545	2.83	191	4	0	0	4	222 2/3	181	77	70	79	193
N.L. totals (5 years)		11	22	.333	4.63	98	38	0	0	1	289 2/3	326	169	149	97	169
Major League totals (8 years)		23	32	.418	3.85	289	42	0	0	5	512 1/3	507	246	219	176	362

BROCK, CHRIS — P — PHILLIES

PERSONAL: Born February 5, 1970, in Orlando. ... 6-0/185. ... Throws right, bats right. ... Full name: Terrence Christopher Brock.
HIGH SCHOOL: Lyman (Longwood, Fla.).
COLLEGE: Florida State.
TRANSACTIONS/CAREER NOTES: Selected by Atlanta Braves organization in 12th round of free-agent draft (June 1, 1992). ... On disabled list (July 26, 1995-remainder of season). ... Granted free agency (October 15, 1997). ... Signed by San Francisco Giants organization (December 20, 1997). ... On disabled list (July 24, 1999-remainder of season). ... Traded by Giants to Philadelphia Phillies for C Bobby Estalella (December 12, 1999).

Year	League	W	L	Pct.	ERA	G	GS	CG	ShO	Sv.	IP	H	R	ER	BB	SO
1992— Idaho Falls (Pio.)...............		6	4	.600	2.31	15	15	1	0	0	78	61	27	20	48	72
1993— Macon (SAL)		7	5	.583	2.70	14	14	1	0	0	80	61	37	24	33	92
— Durham (Caro.)		5	2	.714	2.51	12	12	1	0	0	79	63	28	22	35	67
1994— Greenville (Sou.)		7	6	.538	3.74	25	23	2	2	0	137 1/3	128	68	57	47	94
1995— Richmond (I.L.)...............		2	8	.200	5.40	22	9	0	0	0	60	68	37	36	27	43
1996— Richmond (I.L.)...............		10	11	.476	4.67	26	25	3	0	0	150 1/3	137	95	78	61	112
1997— Richmond (I.L.)...............		10	6	.625	3.34	20	19	0	0	0	118 2/3	97	50	44	51	83
— Atlanta (N.L.)		0	0	...	5.58	7	6	0	0	0	30 2/3	34	23	19	19	16
1998— Fresno (PCL)■		11	3	.786	3.29	17	17	2	0	0	115	111	47	42	33	112
— San Francisco (N.L.)		0	0	...	3.90	13	0	0	0	0	27 2/3	31	13	12	7	19
1999— San Francisco (N.L.)		6	8	.429	5.48	19	19	0	0	0	106 2/3	124	69	65	41	76
Major League totals (3 years)		6	8	.429	5.24	39	25	0	0	0	165	189	105	96	67	111

BROGNA, RICO — 1B — PHILLIES

PERSONAL: Born April 18, 1970, in Turners Falls, Mass. ... 6-2/203. ... Bats left, throws left. ... Full name: Rico Joseph Brogna. ... Name pronounced BRONE-yah.
HIGH SCHOOL: Watertown (Conn.).
TRANSACTIONS/CAREER NOTES: Selected by Detroit Tigers organization in first round (26th pick overall) of free-agent draft (June 1, 1988). ... On Toledo disabled list (May 25-June 2, 1991). ... Traded by Tigers to New York Mets for 1B Alan Zinter (March 31, 1994). ... On disabled list (June 20, 1996-remainder of season). ... Traded by Mets to Philadelphia Phillies for P Ricardo Jordan and P Toby Borland (November 27, 1996).
STATISTICAL NOTES: Led Eastern League first basemen with 1,261 total chances and 117 double plays in 1990. ... Tied for N.L. lead with 10 sacrifice flies in 1998. ... Career major league grand slams: 2.

Year	Team (League)	Pos.	G	AB	R	H	2B	3B	HR	RBI	Avg.	BB	SO	SB	PO	A	E	Avg.
1988— Bristol (Appl.)............		1B-OF	60	209	37	53	11	2	7	33	.254	25	42	3	319	26	6	.983
1989— Lakeland (FSL)............		1B	128	459	47	108	20	7	5	51	.235	38	82	2	1098	83	13	.989
1990— London (East.)		1B	137	488	70	128	21	3	*21	•77	.262	50	100	1	*1155	*93	13	.990
1991— Toledo (I.L.)...............		1B	41	132	13	29	6	1	2	13	.220	4	26	2	311	37	5	.986
— London (East.)		1B-OF	77	293	40	80	13	1	13	51	.273	25	59	0	368	46	6	.986
1992— Toledo (I.L.)...............		1B	121	387	45	101	19	4	10	58	.261	31	85	1	896	76	9	.991
— Detroit (A.L.)		1B-DH	9	26	3	5	1	0	1	3	.192	3	5	0	48	6	1	.982
1993— Toledo (I.L.)...............		1B-DH	129	483	55	132	30	3	11	59	.273	31	94	7	937	97	8	.992
1994— Norfolk (I.L.)■		1B	67	258	33	63	14	5	12	37	.244	15	62	1	583	47	3	.995
— New York (N.L.)........		1B	39	131	16	46	11	2	7	20	.351	6	29	1	307	28	1	.997
1995— New York (N.L.).........		1B	134	495	72	143	27	2	22	76	.289	39	111	0	1111	93	3	*.998
1996— New York (N.L.).........		1B	55	188	18	48	10	1	7	30	.255	19	50	0	440	31	2	.996
1997— Philadelphia (N.L.)■ ..		1B	148	543	68	137	36	1	20	81	.252	33	116	12	1053	119	7	.994
1998— Philadelphia (N.L.)......		1B	153	565	77	150	36	3	20	104	.265	49	125	7	1238	141	5	.996
1999— Philadelphia (N.L.)......		1B	157	619	90	172	29	4	24	102	.278	54	132	8	1240	123	7	.995
American League totals (1 year)			9	26	3	5	1	0	1	3	.192	3	5	0	48	6	1	.982
National League totals (6 years)			686	2541	341	696	149	13	100	413	.274	200	563	28	5389	535	25	.996
Major League totals (7 years)			695	2567	344	701	150	13	101	416	.273	203	568	28	5437	541	26	.996

BROHAWN, TROY — P — DIAMONDBACKS

PERSONAL: Born January 14, 1973, in Cambridge, Md. ... 6-1/190. ... Throws left, bats left. ... Full name: Michael Troy Brohawn.
HIGH SCHOOL: Cambridge South Dorchester (Cambridge, Md.).
COLLEGE: Nebraska.

TRANSACTIONS/CAREER NOTES: Selected by San Francisco Giants organization in fourth round of free-agent draft (June 2, 1994). ... Traded by Giants to Arizona Diamondbacks (December 21, 1998), completing trade in which Diamondbacks traded P Felix Rodriguez to Giants for future considerations (December 8, 1998). ... On Tucson disabled list (April 24-August 30, 1999). ... On Arizona disabled list (August 31, 1999-remainder of season).

Year League	W	L	Pct.	ERA	G	GS	CG	ShO	Sv.	IP	H	R	ER	BB	SO
1994— San Jose (Calif.)	0	2	.000	7.02	4	4	0	0	0	16 2/3	27	15	13	5	13
1995— San Jose (Calif.)	7	3	.700	1.65	11	10	0	0	0	65 1/3	45	14	12	20	57
1996— Shreveport (Texas)	9	10	.474	4.60	28	28	0	0	0	156 2/3	163	99	80	49	82
1997— Shreveport (Texas)	13	5	.722	*2.56	26	26	1	•1	0	169	148	57	48	64	98
1998— Fresno (PCL)	10	8	.556	5.25	30	19	0	0	0	121 2/3	144	75	71	36	87
1999— Tucson (PCL)■	1	0	1.000	3.29	3	2	0	0	0	13 2/3	22	8	5	3	12

B

BROSIUS, SCOTT — 3B — YANKEES

PERSONAL: Born August 15, 1966, in Hillsboro, Ore. ... 6-1/202. ... Bats right, throws right. ... Full name: Scott David Brosius. ... Name pronounced BRO-shus.

HIGH SCHOOL: Rex Putnam (Milwaukie, Ore.).

COLLEGE: Linfield College (Ore.).

TRANSACTIONS/CAREER NOTES: Selected by Oakland Athletics organization in 20th round of free-agent draft (June 2, 1987). ... On Tacoma disabled list (April 17-May 29, 1991). ... On Oakland disabled list (April 18-May 12, 1992); included rehabilitation assignment to Tacoma (May 6-12). ... On Oakland disabled list (July 13-August 3, 1992); included rehabilitation assignment to Tacoma (July 27-August 3). ... On Tacoma disabled list (July 28-August 5, 1993). ... On disabled list (June 8-26, 1994). ... On Oakland disabled list (May 5-June 25, 1996); included rehabilitation assignment to Edmonton (June 22-25). ... On Oakland disabled list (August 7-29, 1997); included rehabilitation assignment to Modesto (August 27-29). ... Traded by A's to New York Yankees (November 18, 1997), completing deal in which Yankees traded P Kenny Rogers and cash to A's for a player to be named later (November 7, 1997). ... Granted free agency (October 27, 1998). ... Re-signed by Yankees (November 10, 1998). ... On New York disabled list (April 14-29, 1999); included rehabilitation assignment to Tampa (April 27).

HONORS: Named third baseman on THE SPORTING NEWS A.L. All-Star team (1998). ... Won A.L. Gold Glove at third base (1999).

STATISTICAL NOTES: Led Northwest League with seven sacrifice flies in 1987. ... Led Southern League with 274 total bases in 1990. ... Tied for Pacific Coast League lead in double plays by third baseman with 24 in 1992. ... Career major league grand slams: 1.

							BATTING							FIELDING		
Year Team (League)	Pos.	G	AB	R	H	2B	3B	HR	RBI	Avg.	BB	SO	SB	PO	A	E	Avg.
1987— Medford (N.W.)	3-S-2-1-P	65	255	34	73	18	1	3	49	.286	26	36	5	123	148	38	.877
1988— Madison (Midw.)	SS-3B-OF-1B	132	504	82	153	28	2	9	58	.304	56	67	13	151	305	61	.882
1989— Huntsville (Sou.)	2B-3B-SS-1B	128	461	68	125	22	2	7	60	.271	58	62	4	225	316	34	.941
1990— Huntsville (Sou.)	SS-2B-3B	•142	547	94	*162	*39	2	23	88	.296	81	81	12	253	419	41	.942
— Tacoma (PCL)	2B	3	7	2	1	0	1	0	0	.143	1	3	0	3	5	0	1.000
1991— Tacoma (PCL)	3B-SS-2B	65	245	28	70	16	3	8	31	.286	18	29	4	49	168	14	.939
— Oakland (A.L.)	2B-OF-3B-DH	36	68	9	16	5	0	2	4	.235	3	11	3	31	16	0	1.000
1992— Oakland (A.L.)	0-3-1-DH-S	38	87	13	19	2	0	4	13	.218	3	13	3	68	15	1	.988
— Tacoma (PCL)	3B-OF	63	236	29	56	13	0	9	31	.237	23	44	8	50	167	10	.956
1993— Oakland (A.L.)	0-1-3-S-DH	70	213	26	53	10	1	6	25	.249	14	37	6	173	29	2	.990
— Tacoma (PCL)	3-0-2-1-S	56	209	38	62	13	2	8	41	.297	21	50	8	101	109	13	.942
1994— Oakland (A.L.)	3B-OF-1B	96	324	31	77	14	1	14	49	.238	24	57	2	82	157	13	.948
1995— Oakland (A.L.)	3-0-1-2-S-D	123	389	69	102	19	2	17	46	.262	41	67	4	208	121	15	.956
1996— Oakland (A.L.)	3B-1B-OF	114	428	73	130	25	0	22	71	.304	59	85	7	128	234	10	.973
— Edmonton (PCL)	3B	3	8	5	5	1	0	0	0	.625	3	1	0	0	4	2	.667
1997— Oakland (A.L.)	3B-SS-OF	129	479	59	97	20	1	11	41	.203	34	102	9	142	246	10	.975
— Modesto (Calif.)	3B	2	3	1	1	0	0	0	1	.333	1	0	0	1	1	1	.667
1998— New York (A.L.)■	3B-1B-OF	152	530	86	159	34	0	19	98	.300	52	97	11	114	294	22	.949
1999— New York (A.L.)	3B-DH	133	473	64	117	26	1	17	71	.247	39	74	9	87	239	13	*.962
— Tampa (FSL)	3B	1	3	0	1	0	0	0	0	.333	0	0	0	2	0	0	1.000
Major League totals (9 years)		891	2991	430	770	155	6	112	418	.257	269	543	54	1033	1351	86	.965

DIVISION SERIES RECORD

							BATTING							FIELDING		
Year Team (League)	Pos.	G	AB	R	H	2B	3B	HR	RBI	Avg.	BB	SO	SB	PO	A	E	Avg.
1998— New York (A.L.)	3B	3	10	1	4	0	0	1	3	.400	0	3	0	2	6	0	1.000
1999— New York (A.L.)	3B	3	10	0	1	1	0	0	1	.100	0	0	0	2	3	0	1.000
Division series totals (2 years)		6	20	1	5	1	0	1	4	.250	0	3	0	4	9	0	1.000

CHAMPIONSHIP SERIES RECORD

							BATTING							FIELDING		
Year Team (League)	Pos.	G	AB	R	H	2B	3B	HR	RBI	Avg.	BB	SO	SB	PO	A	E	Avg.
1998— New York (A.L.)	3B	6	20	2	6	1	0	1	6	.300	4	4	0	4	10	1	.933
1999— New York (A.L.)	3B	5	18	3	4	0	1	2	3	.222	1	4	0	5	4	0	1.000
Championship series totals (2 years)		11	38	5	10	1	1	3	9	.263	5	8	0	9	14	1	.958

WORLD SERIES RECORD

RECORDS: Shares record for most home runs in two consecutive innings—2 (October 20, 1998, seventh and eighth innings). ... Shares single-inning record for most at-bats—2 (October 17, 1998).

NOTES: Named Most Valuable Player (1998). ... Member of World Series championship team (1998 and 1999).

							BATTING							FIELDING		
Year Team (League)	Pos.	G	AB	R	H	2B	3B	HR	RBI	Avg.	BB	SO	SB	PO	A	E	Avg.
1998— New York (A.L.)	3B	4	17	3	8	0	0	2	6	.471	0	4	0	3	6	0	1.000
1999— New York (A.L.)	3B	4	16	2	6	1	0	0	1	.375	0	5	0	8	7	0	1.000
World Series totals (2 years)		8	33	5	14	1	0	2	7	.424	0	9	0	11	13	0	1.000

ALL-STAR GAME RECORD

					BATTING							FIELDING		
Year League	Pos.	AB	R	H	2B	3B	HR	RBI	Avg.	BB	SO	SB	PO	A	E	Avg.
1998— American	3B	2	1	1	0	0	0	0	.500	0	1	1	0	0	1	.000

Year	League	W	L	Pct.	ERA	G	GS	CG	ShO	Sv.	IP	H	R	ER	BB	SO
1987—Medford (N.W.)		0	0	...	0.00	1	0	0	0	0	2	0	0	0	0	1

BROWER, JIM — P — INDIANS

PERSONAL: Born December 29, 1972, in Edina, Minn. ... 6-2/205. ... Throws right, bats right. ... Full name: James Robert Brower.
HIGH SCHOOL: Minnetonka (Minn.).
COLLEGE: Minnesota.
TRANSACTIONS/CAREER NOTES: Selected by Texas Rangers organization in sixth round of free-agent draft (June 2, 1994). ... Released by Rangers organization (April 15, 1998). ... Signed by Cleveland Indians organization (April 18, 1998). ... Granted free agency (October 16, 1998). ... Re-signed by Indians organization (January 4, 1999).

Year	League	W	L	Pct.	ERA	G	GS	CG	ShO	Sv.	IP	H	R	ER	BB	SO
1994—Hudson Valley (NY-P)........		2	1	.667	3.20	4	4	1	0	0	19²/₃	14	10	7	6	15
—Charleston, S.C. (SAL)		7	3	.700	1.72	12	12	3	2	0	78²/₃	52	18	15	26	84
1995—Charlotte (FSL).................		7	10	.412	3.89	27	27	2	1	0	173²/₃	170	93	75	62	110
1996—Charlotte (FSL).................		9	8	.529	3.79	23	21	2	0	0	145	148	67	61	40	86
—Tulsa (Texas)		3	2	.600	3.78	5	5	1	1	0	33¹/₃	35	16	14	10	16
1997—Tulsa (Texas)		5	12	.294	5.21	23	23	1	0	0	140	156	99	81	42	103
—Oklahoma City (A.A.)		2	1	.667	7.23	4	3	0	0	0	18²/₃	30	17	15	8	7
1998—Akron (East.)■..................		13	5	.722	3.01	23	23	2	2	0	155²/₃	142	60	52	38	91
1999—Buffalo (I.L.)		11	11	.500	4.72	27	27	0	0	0	160	164	101	84	59	76
—Cleveland (A.L.)..................		3	1	.750	4.56	9	2	0	0	0	25²/₃	27	13	13	10	18
Major League totals (1 year)........		3	1	.750	4.56	9	2	0	0	0	25²/₃	27	13	13	10	18

BROWN, ADRIAN — OF — PIRATES

PERSONAL: Born February 7, 1974, in McComb, Miss. ... 6-0/185. ... Bats both, throws right. ... Full name: Adrian Demond Brown.
HIGH SCHOOL: McComb (Miss.).
TRANSACTIONS/CAREER NOTES: Selected by Pittsburgh Pirates organization in 48th round of free-agent draft (June 1, 1992).

Year	Team (League)	Pos.	G	AB	R	H	2B	3B	HR	RBI	Avg.	BB	SO	SB	PO	A	E	Avg.
1992—GC Pirates (GCL)........		OF-1B	39	121	11	31	2	2	0	12	.256	0	12	8	60	4	1	.985
1993—Lethbridge (Pio.)		OF	69	282	47	75	12	*9	3	27	.266	17	34	22	119	4	1	*.992
1994—Augusta (SAL).............		OF	79	308	41	80	17	1	1	18	.260	14	38	19	121	6	2	.984
1995—Lynchburg (Caro.)		OF	54	215	30	52	5	2	1	14	.242	12	20	11	110	6	2	.983
—Augusta (SAL)................		OF	76	287	64	86	15	4	4	31	.300	33	23	25	124	8	7	.950
1996—Lynchburg (Caro.)		OF	52	215	39	69	9	3	3	25	.321	14	24	18	99	4	2	.981
—Carolina (Sou.)		OF	84	341	48	101	11	3	3	25	.296	25	40	27	185	5	2	.990
1997—Carolina (Sou.)		OF	37	145	29	44	4	4	2	15	.303	18	12	9	63	2	3	.956
—Pittsburgh (N.L.)		OF	48	147	17	28	6	0	1	10	.190	13	18	8	74	3	1	.987
—Calgary (PCL)............		OF	62	248	53	79	10	1	1	19	.319	27	38	20	130	3	1	.993
1998—Nashville (PCL)		OF	85	311	58	90	12	5	3	27	.289	28	38	25	204	7	5	.977
—Pittsburgh (N.L.)		OF	41	152	20	43	4	1	0	5	.283	9	18	4	83	3	2	.977
1999—Pittsburgh (N.L.)		OF	116	226	34	61	5	2	4	17	.270	33	39	5	111	3	4	.966
—Nashville (PCL)		OF	17	56	10	18	3	1	0	4	.321	11	8	6	31	0	1	.969
Major League totals (3 years)			205	525	71	132	15	3	5	32	.251	55	75	17	268	9	7	.975

BROWN, BRANT — OF — MARLINS

PERSONAL: Born June 22, 1971, in Porterville, Calif. ... 6-3/220. ... Bats left, throws left. ... Full name: Brant Michael Brown.
HIGH SCHOOL: Monache (Porterville, Calif.).
COLLEGE: Fresno State.
TRANSACTIONS/CAREER NOTES: Selected by Chicago Cubs organization in third round of free-agent draft (June 1, 1992). ... On Daytona disabled list (April 10-25, 1993). ... On Iowa disabled list (July 22-August 11, 1996). ... On Chicago disabled list (June 26-July 25, 1998); included rehabilitation assignment to Iowa (July 22-25). ... Traded by Cubs to Pittsburgh Pirates for P Jon Lieber (December 14, 1998). ... Traded by Pirates to Florida Marlins for OF Bruce Aven (December 13, 1999).
STATISTICAL NOTES: Hit three home runs in one game (June 18, 1998).

Year	Team (League)	Pos.	G	AB	R	H	2B	3B	HR	RBI	Avg.	BB	SO	SB	PO	A	E	Avg.
1992— Peoria (Midw.)...........		1B	70	248	28	68	14	0	3	27	.274	24	49	3	582	39	6	.990
1993— Daytona (FSL)		1B	75	266	26	91	8	7	3	33	.342	11	38	8	643	55	5	.993
—Orlando (Sou.)		1B	28	111	17	35	11	3	4	23	.315	6	19	2	237	27	3	.989
1994— Orlando (Sou.)		1B-OF	127	470	54	127	30	6	5	37	.270	37	86	11	1031	80	12	.989
1995— Orlando (Sou.)		1B-OF-DH	121	446	67	121	27	4	6	53	.271	39	77	8	931	92	10	.990
1996— Iowa (A.A.)		1B	94	342	48	104	25	3	10	43	.304	19	65	6	762	66	8	.990
—Chicago (N.L.)		1B	29	69	11	21	1	0	5	9	.304	2	17	3	126	17	0	1.000
1997— Chicago (N.L.)		OF-1B	46	137	15	32	7	1	5	15	.234	7	28	2	121	7	2	.985
—Iowa (A.A.)		OF-1B-DH	71	256	51	77	19	3	16	51	.301	31	44	6	202	13	4	.982
1998— Chicago (N.L.)		OF-1B	124	347	56	101	17	7	14	48	.291	30	95	4	212	3	7	.968
—Iowa (PCL)		OF-1B	3	11	1	4	0	0	0	0	.364	0	6	0	5	0	0	1.000
1999— Pittsburgh (N.L.)■.....		OF-1B-DH	130	341	49	79	20	3	16	58	.232	22	114	3	187	7	3	.985
Major League totals (4 years)			329	894	131	233	45	11	40	130	.261	61	254	12	646	34	12	.983

DIVISION SERIES RECORD

Year	Team (League)	Pos.	G	AB	R	H	2B	3B	HR	RBI	Avg.	BB	SO	SB	PO	A	E	Avg.
1998—Chicago (N.L.)		PH	1	1	0	0	0	0	0	0	.000	0	0	0	...	...	...	...

B

BROWN, DEE — OF — ROYALS

PERSONAL: Born March 27, 1978, in Bronx, N.Y. ... 6-0/215. ... Bats left, throws right. ... Full name: Dermal Bram Brown.
HIGH SCHOOL: Marlboro (N.Y.) Central.
TRANSACTIONS/CAREER NOTES: Selected by Kansas City Royals organization in first round (14th pick overall) of free-agent draft (June 2, 1996).
HONORS: Named Northwest League Most Valuable Player in 1997.
STATISTICAL NOTES: Led Northwest League with 168 total bases and .564 slugging percentage in 1997. ... Tied for Carolina League lead with five intentional bases on balls received in 1998. ... Tied for Carolina League lead with six intentional bases on balls received in 1999.

Year	Team (League)	Pos.	G	AB	R	H	2B	3B	HR	RBI	Avg.	BB	SO	SB	PO	A	E	Avg.
1996—	GC Royals (GCL)	DH	7	20	1	1	1	0	0	1	.050	0	6	0	...	...	...	...
1997—	Spokane (N.W.)	OF	73	298	67	97	20	6	13	*73	.326	38	65	17	80	2	7	.921
1998—	Wilmington (Caro.)	OF	128	442	64	114	30	2	10	58	.258	53	115	26	124	5	13	.908
—	Kansas City (A.L.)	DH-OF	5	3	2	0	0	0	0	0	.000	0	1	0	1	0	0	1.000
1999—	Wilmington (Caro.)	OF-DH	61	221	49	68	10	2	13	46	.308	44	56	20	91	4	2	.979
—	Wichita (Texas)	OF	65	235	58	83	14	3	12	56	.353	35	41	10	110	4	5	.958
—	Kansas City (A.L.)	OF-DH	12	25	1	2	0	0	0	0	.080	2	7	0	12	1	1	.929
Major League totals (2 years)			17	28	3	2	0	0	0	0	.071	2	8	0	13	1	1	.933

BROWN, EMIL — OF — PIRATES

PERSONAL: Born December 29, 1974, in Chicago. ... 6-2/193. ... Bats right, throws right. ... Full name: Emil Quincy Brown.
HIGH SCHOOL: Harlan (Chicago).
JUNIOR COLLEGE: Indian River Community College (Fla.).
TRANSACTIONS/CAREER NOTES: Selected by Oakland Athletics organization in sixth round of free-agent draft (June 2, 1994). ... On Modesto disabled list (April 10-July 1, 1996). ... On Modesto suspended list (August 29-September 2, 1996). ... Selected by Pittsburgh Pirates organization from A's organization in Rule 5 major league draft (December 9, 1996). ... On Nashville disabled list (April 24-May 2, 1999).
STATISTICAL NOTES: Led Midwest League outfielders with four double plays in 1995.

Year	Team (League)	Pos.	G	AB	R	H	2B	3B	HR	RBI	Avg.	BB	SO	SB	PO	A	E	Avg.
1994—	Ariz. A's (Ariz.)	OF	32	86	13	19	1	1	3	12	.221	13	12	5	43	3	1	.979
1995—	W. Mich. (Midw.)	OF	124	459	63	115	17	3	3	67	.251	52	77	35	165	12	8	.957
1996—	Modesto (Calif.)	OF	57	211	50	64	10	1	10	47	.303	32	51	13	97	5	4	.962
—	Scottsdale (Ariz.)	OF	4	15	5	4	3	0	0	2	.267	3	2	1	3	1	0	1.000
1997—	Pittsburgh (N.L.)■	OF	66	95	16	17	2	1	2	6	.179	10	32	5	53	2	3	.948
1998—	Carolina (Sou.)	OF-DH	123	466	89	154	31	2	14	67	.330	50	71	24	199	10	6	.972
—	Pittsburgh (N.L.)	OF	13	39	2	10	1	0	0	3	.256	1	11	0	21	2	0	1.000
1999—	Nashville (PCL)	OF-DH	110	430	97	132	20	5	18	60	.307	35	80	16	173	10	*10	.948
—	Pittsburgh (N.L.)	OF	6	14	0	2	1	0	0	0	.143	0	3	0	8	0	0	1.000
Major League totals (3 years)			85	148	18	29	4	1	2	9	.196	11	46	5	82	4	3	.966

BROWN, JAMIE — P — INDIANS

PERSONAL: Born March 31, 1977, in Meridian, Miss. ... 6-2/205. ... Throws right, bats right. ... Full name: James Monroe Brown.
HIGH SCHOOL: West Lauderdale (Collinsville, Miss.).
JUNIOR COLLEGE: Okaloosa-Walton Community College (Fla.), then Meridian (Miss.) Community College.
TRANSACTIONS/CAREER NOTES: Selected by Cleveland Indians organization in 21st round of free-agent draft (June 4, 1996). ... On Akron disabled list (July 7-30, 1999).

Year	League	W	L	Pct.	ERA	G	GS	CG	ShO	Sv.	IP	H	R	ER	BB	SO
1997—	Watertown (NY-P)	10	2	.833	3.08	13	13	1	0	0	73	66	35	25	15	57
1998—	Kinston (Caro.)	11	9	.550	3.81	27	27	2	0	0	172²/₃	162	91	73	44	148
—	Akron (East.)	1	0	1.000	2.57	1	1	0	0	0	7	5	2	2	1	5
1999—	Akron (East.)	5	9	.357	4.57	23	23	1	0	0	138	140	72	70	39	98
—	Buffalo (I.L.)	1	0	1.000	5.40	1	0	0	0	0	5	8	4	3	1	2

BROWN, KEVIN — P — DODGERS

PERSONAL: Born March 14, 1965, in McIntyre, Ga. ... 6-4/200. ... Throws right, bats right. ... Full name: James Kevin Brown.
HIGH SCHOOL: Wilkinson County (Irwinton, Ga.).
COLLEGE: Georgia Tech.
TRANSACTIONS/CAREER NOTES: Selected by Texas Rangers organization in first round (fourth pick overall) of free-agent draft (June 2, 1986). ... On disabled list (August 14-29, 1990 and March 27-April 11, 1993). ... Granted free agency (October 15, 1994). ... Signed by Baltimore Orioles (April 9, 1995). ... On disabled list (June 23-July 17, 1995). ... Granted free agency (November 3, 1995). ... Signed by Florida Marlins (December 22, 1995). ... On disabled list (May 13-28, 1996). ... Traded by Marlins to San Diego Padres for P Rafael Medina, P Steve Hoff and 1B Derrek Lee (December 15, 1997). ... Granted free agency (October 26, 1998). ... Signed by Los Angeles Dodgers (December 12, 1998).
HONORS: Named righthanded pitcher on THE SPORTING NEWS college All-America team (1986). ... Named N.L. Pitcher of the Year by THE SPORTING NEWS (1998). ... Named righthanded pitcher on THE SPORTING NEWS N.L. All-Star team (1998).
STATISTICAL NOTES: Tied for A.L. lead with 13 hit batsmen in 1991. ... Tied for N.L. lead with 16 hit batsmen in 1996. ... Pitched 9-0 no-hit victory against San Francisco (June 10, 1997). ... Pitched 5-1 one-hit, complete-game victory against Los Angeles (July 16, 1997). ... Led N.L. with 14 hit batsmen in 1997. ... Pitched 4-0 one-hit, complete-game victory against Milwaukee (August 16, 1998). ... Led N.L. pitchers with 41 putouts and 93 total chances in 1999. ... Tied for N.L. lead in errors by a pitcher with six in 1999.
MISCELLANEOUS: Made an out in only appearance as pinch hitter (1990). ... Appeared in one game as pinch runner (1993). ... Appeared in two games as pinch runner (1996). ... Holds Florida Marlins all-time records for most shutouts (5) and complete games (11).

Year League	W	L	Pct.	ERA	G	GS	CG	ShO	Sv.	IP	H	R	ER	BB	SO
1986— GC Rangers (GCL).............	0	0	...	6.00	3	0	0	0	0	6	7	4	4	2	1
— Tulsa (Texas)....................	0	0	...	4.50	3	2	0	0	0	10	9	7	5	5	10
— Texas (A.L.)....................	1	0	1.000	3.60	1	1	0	0	0	5	6	2	2	0	4
1987— Tulsa (Texas)...................	1	4	.200	7.29	8	8	0	0	0	42	53	36	34	18	26
— Oklahoma City (A.A.).........	0	5	.000	10.73	5	5	0	0	0	24 1/3	32	32	29	17	9
— Charlotte (FSL)...............	0	2	.000	2.72	6	6	1	0	0	36 1/3	33	14	11	17	21
1988— Tulsa (Texas)..................	12	10	.545	3.51	26	26	5	0	0	174 1/3	174	94	68	61	118
— Texas (A.L.)....................	1	1	.500	4.24	4	4	1	0	0	23 1/3	33	15	11	8	12
1989— Texas (A.L.)....................	12	9	.571	3.35	28	28	7	0	0	191	167	81	71	70	104
1990— Texas (A.L.)....................	12	10	.545	3.60	26	26	6	2	0	180	175	84	72	60	88
1991— Texas (A.L.)....................	9	12	.429	4.40	33	33	0	0	0	210 2/3	233	116	103	90	96
1992— Texas (A.L.)....................	•21	11	.656	3.32	35	35	11	1	0	*265 2/3	*262	117	98	76	173
1993— Texas (A.L.)....................	15	12	.556	3.59	34	34	12	3	0	233	228	105	93	74	142
1994— Texas (A.L.)....................	7	9	.438	4.82	26	•25	3	0	0	170	*218	109	91	50	123
1995— Baltimore (A.L.)■..............	10	9	.526	3.60	26	26	3	1	0	172 1/3	155	73	69	48	117
1996— Florida (N.L.)■..............	17	11	.607	*1.89	32	32	5	*3	0	233	187	60	49	33	159
1997— Florida (N.L.).................	16	8	.667	2.69	33	33	6	2	0	237 1/3	214	77	71	66	205
1998— San Diego (N.L.)■	18	7	.720	2.38	36	•35	7	3	0	257	225	77	68	49	257
1999— Los Angeles (N.L.)■	18	9	.667	3.00	35	•35	5	1	0	252 1/3	210	99	84	59	221
A.L. totals (9 years)	88	73	.547	3.78	213	212	43	7	0	1451	1477	702	610	476	859
N.L. totals (4 years)	69	35	.663	2.50	136	135	23	9	0	979 2/3	836	313	272	207	842
Major League totals (13 years)	157	108	.592	3.27	349	347	66	16	0	2430 2/3	2313	1015	882	683	1701

DIVISION SERIES RECORD

RECORDS: Holds career record for most hit batsmen—3.

Year League	W	L	Pct.	ERA	G	GS	CG	ShO	Sv.	IP	H	R	ER	BB	SO
1997— Florida (N.L.)	0	0	...	1.29	1	1	0	0	0	7	4	1	1	0	5
1998— San Diego (N.L.)	1	0	1.000	0.61	2	2	0	0	0	14 2/3	5	1	1	7	21
Division series totals (2 years)	1	0	1.000	0.83	3	3	0	0	0	21 2/3	9	2	2	7	26

CHAMPIONSHIP SERIES RECORD

RECORDS: Shares single-game record for most hits allowed—11 (October 14, 1997).

Year League	W	L	Pct.	ERA	G	GS	CG	ShO	Sv.	IP	H	R	ER	BB	SO
1997— Florida (N.L.)	2	0	1.000	4.20	2	2	1	0	0	15	16	7	7	5	11
1998— San Diego (N.L.)	1	1	.500	2.61	2	1	1	1	0	10 1/3	5	3	3	4	12
Champ. series totals (2 years)	3	1	.750	3.55	4	3	2	1	0	25 1/3	21	10	10	9	23

WORLD SERIES RECORD

NOTES: Member of World Series championship team (1997).

Year League	W	L	Pct.	ERA	G	GS	CG	ShO	Sv.	IP	H	R	ER	BB	SO
1997— Florida (N.L.)	0	2	.000	8.18	2	2	0	0	0	11	15	10	10	5	6
1998— San Diego (N.L.)	0	1	.000	4.40	2	2	0	0	0	14 1/3	14	7	7	6	13
World Series totals (2 years)	0	3	.000	6.04	4	4	0	0	0	25 1/3	29	17	17	11	19

ALL-STAR GAME RECORD

Year League	W	L	Pct.	ERA	GS	CG	ShO	Sv.	IP	H	R	ER	BB	SO
1992— American	1	0	1.000	0.00	1	0	0	0	1	0	0	0	0	1
1996— National	0	0	...	0.00	0	0	0	0	1	0	0	0	0	0
1997— National	0	0	...	0.00	0	0	0	0	1	1	0	0	0	0
1998— National	0	0	...	0.00	0	0	0	0	2/3	0	0	0	0	1
All-Star Game totals (4 years)	1	0	1.000	0.00	1	0	0	0	3 2/3	1	0	0	0	2

BROWN, KEVIN   C   BLUE JAYS

PERSONAL: Born April 21, 1973, in Valparaiso, Ind. ... 6-2/215. ... Bats right, throws right. ... Full name: Kevin Lee Brown.

HIGH SCHOOL: Pike Central (Petersburg, Ind.).

COLLEGE: Southern Indiana.

TRANSACTIONS/CAREER NOTES: Selected by Texas Rangers organization in second round of free-agent draft (June 2, 1994). ... Traded by Rangers to Toronto Blue Jays for P Tim Crabtree (March 14, 1998). ... On Toronto disabled list (June 13-30, 1998); included rehabilitation assignment to Syracuse (June 28-30).

STATISTICAL NOTES: Led American Association catchers with .991 fielding percentage and tied for the league lead in double plays with 10 in 1997.

Year Team (League)	Pos.	G	AB	R	H	2B	3B	HR	RBI	Avg.	BB	SO	SB	PO	A	E	Avg.
1994— Hudson Valley (NY-P).	C	68	233	33	57	*19	1	6	32	.245	23	•86	0	316	34	7	.980
1995— Charlotte (FSL)...........	C-1B	107	355	48	94	25	1	11	57	.265	50	96	2	535	60	9	.985
— Oklahoma City (A.A.)..	C	3	10	1	4	1	0	0	0	.400	2	4	0	6	0	2	.750
1996— Tulsa (Texas)	C-DH-1B	128	460	77	121	27	1	26	86	.263	73	*150	0	594	69	13	.981
— Texas (A.L.)	C-DH	3	4	1	0	0	0	0	1	.000	2	2	0	11	1	0	1.000
1997— Oklahoma City (A.A.)..	C-1B-DH	116	403	56	97	18	2	19	50	.241	38	111	2	640	62	5	†.993
— Texas (A.L.)	C	4	5	1	2	0	0	1	1	.400	0	0	0	9	0	1	.900
1998— Toronto (A.L.)■..........	C	52	110	17	29	7	1	2	15	.264	9	31	0	261	19	2	.993
— Syracuse (I.L.)............	C	2	8	2	5	2	0	0	0	.625	0	2	0	7	1	0	1.000
1999— Syracuse (I.L.)...........	C-DH	88	295	39	76	18	2	13	51	.258	21	79	0	575	42	*13	.979
— Toronto (A.L.)............	C	2	9	1	4	2	0	0	1	.444	0	3	0	10	1	0	1.000
Major League totals (4 years)		61	128	20	35	9	1	3	18	.273	11	36	0	291	21	3	.990

BROWN, ROOSEVELT   OF   CUBS

PERSONAL: Born August 3, 1975, in Vicksburg, Miss. ... 5-11/195. ... Bats left, throws right. ... Full name: Roosevelt Lawayne Brown.
HIGH SCHOOL: Vicksburg (Miss.).
TRANSACTIONS/CAREER NOTES: Selected by Atlanta Braves organization in 20th round of free-agent draft (June 3, 1993). ... Traded by Braves to Florida Marlins for 3B Terry Pendleton (August 13, 1996). ... Selected by Chicago Cubs organization from Marlins organization in Rule 5 minor league draft (December 15, 1997).

Year	Team (League)	Pos.	G	AB	R	H	2B	3B	HR	RBI	Avg.	BB	SO	SB	PO	A	E	Avg.
1993—	GC Braves (GCL)	OF	26	80	4	9	1	2	0	5	.113	2	9	2	18	4	4	.846
1994—	Idaho Falls (Pio.)	OF	48	160	28	53	8	1	3	22	.331	17	15	8	63	3	1	.985
1995—	Eugene (N.W.)	OF	57	165	28	51	12	4	7	32	.309	13	30	6	45	3	8	.857
1996—	Macon (SAL)	OF	113	413	61	115	27	0	19	64	.278	33	60	21	154	6	12	.930
	— Kane Co. (Midw.)■	OF	11	40	1	6	2	0	0	3	.150	1	10	0	13	1	1	.933
1997—	Kane Co. (Midw.)	OF	61	211	29	50	7	1	4	30	.237	22	52	5	75	5	6	.930
	— Brevard Co. (FSL)	OF	33	114	8	28	7	1	1	12	.246	7	31	0	44	5	1	.980
1998—	Daytona (FSL)■	OF	68	244	49	84	15	5	9	43	.344	23	46	3	106	4	2	.982
	— West Tenn (Sou.)	OF	42	160	20	42	11	0	6	24	.263	13	30	3	61	4	3	.956
	— Iowa (PCL)	DH	1	3	0	1	1	0	0	2	.333	0	0	0	...	...	...	...
1999—	West Tenn (Sou.)	OF	34	125	12	37	12	0	3	12	.296	14	29	6	52	5	1	.983
	— Chicago (N.L.)	OF	33	64	6	14	6	1	1	10	.219	2	14	1	20	1	1	.955
	— Iowa (PCL)	OF-DH	74	268	50	96	25	2	22	79	.358	19	54	3	107	11	5	.959
Major League totals (1 year)			33	64	6	14	6	1	1	10	.219	2	14	1	20	1	1	.955

BROWNSON, MARK   P   PHILLIES

PERSONAL: Born June 17, 1975, in Lake Worth, Fla. ... 6-2/185. ... Throws right, bats left. ... Full name: Mark Phillip Brownson.
HIGH SCHOOL: Wellington (West Palm Beach, Fla.).
JUNIOR COLLEGE: Palm Beach Community College (Fla.).
TRANSACTIONS/CAREER NOTES: Selected by Colorado Rockies organization in 30th round of free-agent draft (June 3, 1993). ... On Colorado Springs disabled list (August 11-September 8, 1998; and August 21-September 9, 1999). ... Claimed on waivers by Philadelphia Phillies (November 18, 1999).
STATISTICAL NOTES: Led Eastern league with 14 hit batsmen in 1997. ... Pitched shutout in first major league game (July 21, 1998).

Year	League	W	L	Pct.	ERA	G	GS	CG	ShO	Sv.	IP	H	R	ER	BB	SO
1994—	Arizona Rockies (Ariz.)	4	1	.800	1.66	19	4	0	0	3	54 1/3	48	18	10	6	72
1995—	Asheville (SAL)	6	7	.462	4.01	23	12	0	0	1	98 2/3	106	52	44	29	94
	— New Haven (East.)	0	0	...	1.50	1	1	0	0	0	6	4	2	1	1	4
1996—	New Haven (East.)	8	13	.381	3.50	37	19	1	0	3	144	141	73	56	43	155
	— Salem (Caro.)	2	1	.667	4.02	9	1	0	0	1	15 2/3	16	8	7	10	9
1997—	New Haven (East.)	10	9	.526	4.19	29	29	2	0	0	184 2/3	172	101	86	55	170
1998—	Colorado Springs (PCL)	6	8	.429	5.34	21	21	3	0	0	124 2/3	131	85	74	37	82
	— Colorado (N.L.)	1	0	1.000	4.72	2	2	1	1	0	13 1/3	16	7	7	2	8
1999—	Colorado Springs (PCL)	6	6	.500	6.20	17	16	2	0	0	103	120	75	71	24	81
	— Colorado (N.L.)	0	2	.000	7.89	7	7	0	0	0	29 2/3	42	26	26	8	21
Major League totals (2 years)		1	2	.333	6.91	9	9	1	1	0	43	58	33	33	10	29

BRUMFIELD, JACOB   OF   BLUE JAYS

PERSONAL: Born May 27, 1965, in Bogalusa, La. ... 6-0/190. ... Bats right, throws right. ... Full name: Jacob Donnell Brumfield.
HIGH SCHOOL: Hammond (La.).
TRANSACTIONS/CAREER NOTES: Selected by Chicago Cubs organization in seventh round of free-agent draft (June 6, 1983). ... On disabled list (June 21, 1984-remainder of season). ... Released by Cubs organization (April 9, 1985). ... Signed by Kansas City Royals organization (August 16, 1986). ... Granted free agency (October 15, 1991). ... Signed by Cincinnati Reds organization (November 12, 1991). ... On Nashville disabled list (June 12-July 25, 1992). ... Traded by Reds to Pittsburgh Pirates for OF Danny Clyburn (October 13, 1994). ... On Pittsburgh disabled list (May 19-June 3, 1995); included rehabilitation assignment to Carolina (May 29-June 1). ... Traded by Pittsburgh Pirates to Toronto Blue Jays for 1B D.J. Boston (May 15, 1996). ... On disabled list (March 24-April 16, 1997); included rehabilitation assignment to Dunedin (April 7-16). ... Granted free agency (October 6, 1997). ... Re-signed by Blue Jays organization (January 5, 1998). ... Released by Blue Jays (March 24, 1998). ... Signed by Florida Marlins organization (April 15, 1998). ... On Charlotte disabled list (May 22-June 11, 1998). ... Granted free agency (October 15, 1998). ... Signed by Los Angeles Dodgers (March 5, 1999). ... Claimed on waivers by Blue Jays (May 7, 1999). ... Granted free agency (October 20, 1999). ... Re-signed by Blue Jays organization (December 7, 1999).
STATISTICAL NOTES: Led Florida State League with .429 on-base percentage in 1990. ... Led American Association in caught stealing with 16 in 1991.

Year	Team (League)	Pos.	G	AB	R	H	2B	3B	HR	RBI	Avg.	BB	SO	SB	PO	A	E	Avg.
1983—	Pikeville (Appl.)	OF	42	113	17	29	0	1	3	15	.257	25	34	8	34	3	5	.881
1984—	Pikeville (Appl.)					Did not play.												
1985—						Did not play.												
1986—	Fort Myers (FSL)■	SS	12	41	3	13	3	1	1	5	.317	2	11	0	18	16	8	.810
1987—	Fort Myers (FSL)	OF-3B	114	379	56	93	14	*10	6	34	.245	45	78	43	235	53	19	.938
	— Memphis (Sou.)	OF	9	39	7	13	3	2	1	6	.333	3	8	2	35	0	2	.946
1988—	Memphis (Sou.)	OF	128	433	70	98	15	5	6	48	.226	52	104	47	239	2	6	.976
1989—	Memphis (Sou.)	OF	104	346	43	79	14	2	1	25	.228	53	74	28	217	2	8	.965
1990—	Baseball City (FSL)	OF	109	372	66	125	24	3	0	40	*.336	60	44	47	186	*17	8	.962
	— Omaha (A.A.)	OF	24	77	10	25	6	1	2	11	.325	7	14	10	45	3	0	1.000
1991—	Omaha (A.A.)	OF	111	397	62	106	14	7	3	43	.267	33	64	*36	227	10	2	.992
1992—	Cincinnati (N.L.)■	OF	24	30	6	4	0	0	0	2	.133	2	4	6	20	1	0	1.000
	— Nashville (A.A.)	OF	56	208	32	59	10	3	5	19	.284	26	35	22	137	4	6	.959

Year Team (League)	Pos.	G	AB	R	H	2B	3B	HR	RBI	Avg.	BB	SO	SB	PO	A	E	Avg.
1993— Indianapolis (A.A.)......	OF	33	126	23	41	14	1	4	19	.325	6	14	11	74	4	4	.951
—Cincinnati (N.L.)........	OF-2B	103	272	40	73	17	3	6	23	.268	21	47	20	178	16	7	.965
1994—Cincinnati (N.L.)........	OF	68	122	36	38	10	2	4	11	.311	15	18	6	74	1	1	.987
1995—Pittsburgh (N.L.)■.....	OF	116	402	64	109	23	2	4	26	.271	37	71	22	241	8	8	.969
—Carolina (Sou.)..........	OF	3	12	2	5	0	0	2	2	.417	1	2	0	9	0	0	1.000
1996—Pittsburgh (N.L.)........	OF	29	80	11	20	9	0	2	8	.250	5	17	3	34	1	2	.946
—Toronto (A.L.)■.........	OF-DH	90	308	52	79	19	2	12	52	.256	24	58	12	159	8	3	.982
1997—Dunedin (FSL)...........	OF	6	25	2	4	0	0	0	2	.160	0	6	1	7	2	1	.900
—Toronto (A.L.)...........	OF-DH	58	174	22	36	5	1	2	20	.207	14	31	4	87	6	0	1.000
1998—Charlotte (I.L.)■........	OF	95	227	24	38	13	0	3	25	.167	34	41	7	107	6	5	.958
1999—Los Angeles (N.L.)■..	OF	18	17	4	5	0	1	0	1	.294	0	5	0	11	0	0	1.000
—Toronto (A.L.)■.........	OF-DH	62	170	25	40	8	3	2	19	.235	19	39	1	126	5	3	.978
American League totals (3 years)		210	652	99	155	32	6	16	91	.238	57	128	17	372	19	6	.985
National League totals (6 years)		358	923	161	249	59	8	16	71	.270	80	162	57	558	27	18	.970
Major League totals (7 years)		568	1575	260	404	91	14	32	162	.257	137	290	74	930	46	24	.976

BRUNETTE, JUSTIN   P   CARDINALS

PERSONAL: Born October 7, 1975, in Los Alamitos, Calif. ... 6-2/200. ... Throws left, bats left. ... Full name: Justin Thomas Brunette.
HIGH SCHOOL: Ocean View (Huntington Beach, Calif.).
COLLEGE: San Diego State.
TRANSACTIONS/CAREER NOTES: Selected by St. Louis Cardinals organization in 20th round of free-agent draft (June 3, 1997). ... On New Jersey disabled list (June 16, 1998-entire season).

Year League	W	L	Pct.	ERA	G	GS	CG	ShO	Sv.	IP	H	R	ER	BB	SO
1997— New Jersey (NY-P)............	1	0	1.000	7.94	6	0	0	0	0	5²/₃	13	6	5	0	6
1998— New Jersey (NY-P)............							Did not play.								
1999—Peoria (Midw.)...................	3	1	.750	1.81	38	0	0	0	2	44²/₃	34	9	9	16	44
—Arkansas (Texas)................	1	2	.333	1.96	18	0	0	0	0	18¹/₃	21	12	4	7	23

BRUNSON, WILL   P   ATHLETICS

PERSONAL: Born March 20, 1970, in Irving, Texas. ... 6-6/185. ... Throws left, bats left. ... Full name: William Donald Brunson.
HIGH SCHOOL: DeSoto (Texas).
COLLEGE: Southwest Texas State.
TRANSACTIONS/CAREER NOTES: Selected by Cincinnati Reds organization in 21st round of free-agent draft (June 1, 1992). ... Traded by Reds to Los Angeles Dodgers organization for P Ben VanRyn (December 16, 1994). ... Claimed on waivers by Detroit Tigers (September 6, 1998). ... Granted free agency (October 15, 1999). ... Signed by Oakland Athletics organization (November 23, 1999).

Year League	W	L	Pct.	ERA	G	GS	CG	ShO	Sv.	IP	H	R	ER	BB	SO
1992— Princeton (Appl.)................	5	5	.500	3.59	13	13	0	0	0	72²/₃	66	34	29	28	48
1993— Charleston, W.Va. (SAL).....	5	6	.455	3.93	37	15	0	0	0	123²/₃	119	68	54	50	103
1994— Winston-Salem (Caro.).......	12	7	.632	3.98	30	22	3	0	0	165	161	83	73	58	129
1995—San Bernardino (Calif.)■.....	10	0	1.000	2.05	13	13	0	0	0	83¹/₃	68	24	19	21	70
—San Antonio (Texas)...........	4	5	.444	4.95	14	14	0	0	0	80	105	46	44	22	44
1996—San Antonio (Texas)...........	3	1	.750	2.14	11	5	0	0	0	42	32	13	10	15	38
—Albuquerque (PCL).............	3	4	.429	4.47	9	9	1	0	0	54¹/₃	53	29	27	23	47
1997—Albuquerque (PCL).............	1	1	.500	6.49	27	0	0	0	0	26¹/₃	39	19	19	10	25
—San Antonio (Texas)...........	5	5	.500	3.47	17	11	2	•1	0	72²/₃	68	30	28	13	71
1998—Albuquerque (PCL).............	5	8	.385	4.65	34	15	1	0	2	120	135	69	62	40	100
—Los Angeles (N.L.).............	0	1	.000	11.57	2	0	0	0	0	2¹/₃	3	3	3	2	1
—Detroit (A.L.).....................	0	0	...	0.00	8	0	0	0	0	3	2	0	0	1	1
1999—Toledo (I.L.).....................	3	1	.750	4.53	38	1	0	0	3	47²/₃	45	28	24	17	41
—Detroit (A.L.).....................	1	0	1.000	6.00	17	0	0	0	0	12	18	9	8	6	9
A.L. totals (2 years)	1	0	1.000	4.80	25	0	0	0	0	15	20	9	8	7	10
N.L. totals (1 year)	0	1	.000	11.57	2	0	0	0	0	2¹/₃	3	3	3	2	1
Major League totals (2 years)	1	1	.500	5.71	27	0	0	0	0	17¹/₃	23	12	11	9	11

BUCHANAN, BRIAN   OF   TWINS

PERSONAL: Born July 21, 1973, in Miami. ... 6-4/230. ... Bats right, throws right. ... Full name: Brian James Buchanan.
HIGH SCHOOL: Fairfax (Va.).
COLLEGE: Virginia.
TRANSACTIONS/CAREER NOTES: Selected by New York Yankees organization in first round (24th pick overall) of free-agent draft (June 2, 1994). ... On disabled list (April 29, 1995-remainder of season). ... Traded by Yankees with P Eric Milton, P Danny Mota, SS Cristian Guzman and cash to Minnesota Twins for 2B Chuck Knoblauch (February 6, 1998). ... On Salt Lake disabled list (July 18-27 and July 29-August 9, 1999).
STATISTICAL NOTES: Tied for Pacific Coast League lead with three double plays by outfielder in 1998.

Year Team (League)	Pos.	G	AB	R	H	2B	3B	HR	RBI	Avg.	BB	SO	SB	PO	A	E	Avg.
1994— Oneonta (NY-P).........	OF	50	177	28	40	9	2	4	26	.226	24	53	5	87	2	0	1.000
1995— Greensboro (SAL)......	OF	23	96	19	29	3	0	3	12	.302	9	17	7	31	1	1	.970
1996—Tampa (FSL)...............	OF	131	526	65	137	22	4	10	58	.260	37	108	23	178	11	6	.969
1997— Norwich (East.)..........	OF	116	470	75	145	25	2	10	69	.309	32	85	11	192	11	8	.962
—Columbus (I.L.)..........	OF	18	61	8	17	1	0	4	7	.279	4	11	2	17	1	1	.947
1998—Salt Lake (PCL)■.......	OF	133	500	74	139	29	3	17	82	.278	36	90	14	244	6	8	.969
1999—Salt Lake (PCL)	OF-DH	107	391	67	116	24	1	10	60	.297	28	85	11	184	9	4	.980

PERSONAL: Born December 12, 1970, in Berea, Ohio. ... 6-3/210. ... Throws right, bats right. ... Full name: Michael J. Buddie.
HIGH SCHOOL: St. Ignatius (Cleveland).
COLLEGE: Wake Forest.
TRANSACTIONS/CAREER NOTES: Selected by New York Yankees organization in fourth round of free-agent draft (June 1, 1992).

Year League	W	L	Pct.	ERA	G	GS	CG	ShO	Sv.	IP	H	R	ER	BB	SO
1992—Oneonta (NY-P)	1	4	.200	3.88	13	13	1	0	0	67 1/3	69	36	29	34	87
1993—Greensboro (SAL)	13	10	.565	4.87	27	26	0	0	0	155 1/3	138	104	84	89	143
1994—Tampa (FSL)	12	5	.706	4.01	25	24	2	0	0	150 1/3	143	75	67	66	113
1995—Norwich (East.)	10	12	.455	4.81	29	27	2	0	1	149 2/3	155	*102	80	81	106
1996—Norwich (East.)	7	•12	.368	4.45	29	26	4	0	0	159 2/3	176	101	79	71	103
1997—Norwich (East.)	0	0	...	0.00	1	0	0	0	0	1	0	0	0	0	3
—Columbus (I.L.)	6	6	.500	2.64	53	0	0	0	13	75	85	24	22	25	67
1998—New York (A.L.)	4	1	.800	5.62	24	2	0	0	0	41 2/3	46	29	26	13	20
—Columbus (I.L.)	5	0	1.000	2.74	26	0	0	0	4	42 2/3	35	15	13	15	30
1999—Columbus (I.L.)	9	2	.818	2.86	49	2	0	0	0	78 2/3	80	30	25	22	68
—New York (A.L.)	0	0	...	4.50	2	0	0	0	0	2	3	1	1	0	1
Major League totals (2 years)	4	1	.800	5.56	26	2	0	0	0	43 2/3	49	30	27	13	21

PERSONAL: Born June 12, 1970, in Baltimore. ... 5-10/180. ... Bats right, throws right. ... Full name: Damon Jackson Buford. ... Son of Don Buford, outfielder with Chicago White Sox (1963-67) and Baltimore Orioles (1968); and brother of Don Buford Jr., minor league infielder (1987-89).
HIGH SCHOOL: Birmingham (Calif.).
COLLEGE: Southern California.
TRANSACTIONS/CAREER NOTES: Selected by Baltimore Orioles organization in 10th round of free-agent draft (June 4, 1990). ... Traded by Orioles with OF Alex Ochoa to New York Mets for 3B/OF Bobby Bonilla and a player to be named later (July 28, 1995); Orioles acquired P Jimmy Williams to complete deal (August 17, 1995). ... Traded by Mets to Texas Rangers for OF Terrell Lowery (January 25, 1996). ... Traded by Rangers with C Jim Leyritz to Boston Red Sox for P Aaron Sele, P Mark Brandenburg and C Bill Haselman (November 6, 1997). ... On disabled list (May 18-June 3 and August 27-September 11, 1998; and August 5-23, 1999). ... Traded by Red Sox to Chicago Cubs for IF Manny Alexander (December 11, 1999).
STATISTICAL NOTES: Led Eastern League outfielders with 279 total chances in 1992. ... Led International League outfielders with 347 total chances in 1994. ... Career major league grand slams: 3.

Year Team (League)	Pos.	G	AB	R	H	2B	3B	HR	RBI	Avg.	BB	SO	SB	PO	A	E	Avg.
1990—Wausau (Midw.)	OF	41	160	31	48	7	2	1	14	.300	21	32	15	89	2	2	.978
1991—Frederick (Caro.)	OF	133	505	71	138	25	6	8	54	.273	51	92	50	293	7	5	.984
1992—Hagerstown (East.)	OF	101	373	53	89	17	3	1	30	.239	42	62	41	*264	13	2	.993
—Rochester (I.L.)	OF	45	155	29	44	10	2	1	12	.284	14	23	23	100	1	3	.971
1993—Rochester (I.L.)	OF	27	116	24	33	6	1	1	4	.284	7	16	10	73	3	3	.962
—Baltimore (A.L.)	OF-DH	53	79	18	18	5	0	2	9	.228	9	19	2	61	2	1	.984
1994—Baltimore (A.L.)	DH-OF	4	2	2	1	0	0	0	0	.500	0	1	0	0	0	0	...
—Rochester (I.L.)	OF-DH	111	452	*89	122	21	4	16	66	.270	35	81	31	*339	4	4	.988
1995—Baltimore (A.L.)	OF	24	32	6	2	0	0	0	2	.063	6	7	3	40	0	0	1.000
—Rochester (I.L.)	OF	46	188	40	58	12	3	4	18	.309	17	26	17	115	2	2	.983
—New York (N.L.)■	OF	44	136	24	32	5	0	4	12	.235	19	28	7	67	2	2	.972
1996—Texas (A.L.)■	OF-DH	90	145	30	41	9	0	6	20	.283	15	34	8	93	3	0	1.000
1997—Texas (A.L.)	OF-DH	122	366	49	82	18	0	8	39	.224	30	83	18	282	7	3	.990
1998—Boston (A.L.)■	O-DH-2-3	86	216	37	61	14	4	10	42	.282	22	43	5	134	4	0	1.000
1999—Boston (A.L.)	OF-DH	91	297	39	72	15	2	6	38	.242	21	74	9	189	6	3	.985
American League totals (7 years)		470	1137	181	277	61	6	32	150	.244	103	261	45	799	22	7	.992
National League totals (1 year)		44	136	24	32	5	0	4	12	.235	19	28	7	67	2	2	.972
Major League totals (7 years)		514	1273	205	309	66	6	36	162	.243	122	289	52	866	24	9	.990

DIVISION SERIES RECORD

Year Team (League)	Pos.	G	AB	R	H	2B	3B	HR	RBI	Avg.	BB	SO	SB	PO	A	E	Avg.
1996—Texas (A.L.)	PR	2	0	0	0	0	0	0	0	...	0	0	0	0	0	0	...
1998—Boston (A.L.)	PR-OF-PH-DH	3	1	2	0	0	0	0	0	.000	0	0	0	1	0	0	1.000
1999—Boston (A.L.)	OF	1	3	0	0	0	0	0	0	.000	0	1	0	3	0	0	1.000
Division series totals (3 years)		6	4	2	0	0	0	0	0	.000	0	1	0	4	0	0	1.000

CHAMPIONSHIP SERIES RECORD

Year Team (League)	Pos.	G	AB	R	H	2B	3B	HR	RBI	Avg.	BB	SO	SB	PO	A	E	Avg.
1999—Boston (A.L.)	PR-OF-PH	4	5	1	2	0	0	0	0	.400	0	2	1	4	0	0	1.000

PERSONAL: Born August 13, 1964, in Louisville, Ky. ... 6-3/215. ... Bats right, throws right. ... Full name: Jay Campbell Buhner. ... Brother of Shawn Buhner, infielder, Seattle Mariners organization. ... Name pronounced BYOO-ner.
HIGH SCHOOL: Clear Creek (League City, Texas).
JUNIOR COLLEGE: McLennan Community College (Texas).
TRANSACTIONS/CAREER NOTES: Selected by Atlanta Braves organization in ninth round of free-agent draft (June 6, 1983); did not sign. ... Selected by Pittsburgh Pirates organization in secondary phase of free-agent draft (January 17, 1984). ... Traded by Pirates organization with IF Dale Berra and P Alfonso Pulido to New York Yankees for OF Steve Kemp, IF Tim Foli and cash (December 20, 1984). ... On disabled list

(April 11-July 28, 1986). ... Traded by Yankees with P Rich Balabon and a player to be named later to Seattle Mariners for DH Ken Phelps (July 21, 1988); Mariners acquired P Troy Evers to complete deal (October 12, 1988). ... On Seattle disabled list (June 29-August 19, 1989); included rehabilitation assignment to Calgary (August 16-19). ... On Seattle disabled list (March 31-June 1, 1990); included rehabilitation assignment to Calgary (May 18-June 1). ... On Seattle disabled list (June 17-August 23, 1990). ... Granted free agency (October 28, 1994). ... Re-signed by Mariners (December 21, 1994). ... On disabled list (June 6-22, 1995). ... On Seattle disabled list (April 7-June 11 and September 8, 1998-remainder of season); included rehabilitation assignment to Tacoma (June 9-11). ... On disabled list (May 19-July 15, 1999). ... On suspended list (August 25-28, 1999). ... Granted free agency (November 11, 1999). ... Re-signed by Mariners (December 6, 1999).

RECORDS: Shares major league records for most strikeouts in two consecutive nine-inning games—8 (August 23-24, 1990); and most strikeouts in three consecutive nine-inning games—10 (August 23-25, 1990).

HONORS: Won A.L. Gold Glove as outfielder (1996).

STATISTICAL NOTES: Tied for International League lead in double plays by outfielder with six in 1987. ... Hit for the cycle (June 23, 1993). ... Career major league grand slams: 8.

Year Team (League)	Pos.	G	AB	R	H	2B	3B	HR	RBI	Avg.	BB	SO	SB	PO	A	E	Avg.
1984—Watertown (NY-P)	OF	65	229	43	74	16	3	9	•58	.323	42	58	3	106	8	1	.991
1985—Fort Laud. (FSL)■	OF	117	409	65	121	18	10	11	76	.296	65	76	6	235	12	7	.972
1986—Fort Laud. (FSL)	OF	36	139	24	42	9	1	7	31	.302	15	30	1	84	7	3	.968
1987—Columbus (I.L.)	OF	134	502	83	140	23	1	*31	85	.279	55	124	4	275	*20	6	.980
—New York (A.L.)	OF	7	22	0	5	2	0	0	1	.227	1	6	0	11	1	0	1.000
1988—Columbus (I.L.)	OF	38	129	26	33	5	0	8	18	.256	19	33	1	83	3	1	.989
—New York (A.L.)	OF	25	69	8	13	0	0	3	13	.188	3	25	0	52	2	2	.964
—Seattle (A.L.)■	OF	60	192	28	43	13	1	10	25	.224	25	68	1	134	7	1	.993
1989—Calgary (PCL)	OF	56	196	43	61	12	1	11	45	.311	44	56	4	97	8	2	.981
—Seattle (A.L.)	OF	58	204	27	56	15	1	9	33	.275	19	55	1	106	6	4	.966
1990—Calgary (PCL)	OF	13	34	6	7	1	0	2	5	.206	7	11	0	14	1	0	1.000
—Seattle (A.L.)	OF-DH	51	163	16	45	12	0	7	33	.276	17	50	2	55	1	2	.966
1991—Seattle (A.L.)	OF	137	406	64	99	14	4	27	77	.244	53	117	0	244	15	5	.981
1992—Seattle (A.L.)	OF	152	543	69	132	16	3	25	79	.243	71	146	0	314	14	2	.994
1993—Seattle (A.L.)	OF-DH	158	563	91	153	28	3	27	98	.272	100	144	2	263	8	6	.978
1994—Seattle (A.L.)	OF-DH	101	358	74	100	23	4	21	68	.279	66	63	0	178	11	2	.990
1995—Seattle (A.L.)	OF-DH	126	470	86	123	23	0	40	121	.262	60	120	0	180	5	2	.989
1996—Seattle (A.L.)	OF-DH	150	564	107	153	29	0	44	138	.271	84	*159	0	251	9	3	.989
1997—Seattle (A.L.)	OF-DH	157	540	104	131	18	2	40	109	.243	119	*175	0	295	5	1	*.997
1998—Seattle (A.L.)	OF-DH	72	244	33	59	7	1	15	45	.242	38	71	0	127	5	2	.985
—Tacoma (PCL)	DH-OF	2	4	2	2	2	0	0	2	.500	2	2	0	0	0	0	...
1999—Seattle (A.L.)	OF-1B	87	266	37	59	11	0	14	38	.222	69	100	0	136	7	1	.993
Major League totals (13 years)		1341	4604	744	1171	211	19	282	878	.254	725	1299	6	2346	96	33	.987

DIVISION SERIES RECORD

Year Team (League)	Pos.	G	AB	R	H	2B	3B	HR	RBI	Avg.	BB	SO	SB	PO	A	E	Avg.
1995—Seattle (A.L.)	OF	5	24	2	11	1	0	1	3	.458	2	4	0	11	1	0	1.000
1997—Seattle (A.L.)	OF	4	13	2	3	0	0	2	2	.231	3	6	0	5	1	0	1.000
Division series totals (2 years)		9	37	4	14	1	0	3	5	.378	5	10	0	16	2	0	1.000

CHAMPIONSHIP SERIES RECORD

RECORDS: Shares A.L. single-series record for most strikeouts—8 (1995).

Year Team (League)	Pos.	G	AB	R	H	2B	3B	HR	RBI	Avg.	BB	SO	SB	PO	A	E	Avg.
1995—Seattle (A.L.)	OF	6	23	5	7	2	0	3	5	.304	2	8	0	15	0	1	.938

ALL-STAR GAME RECORD

Year League	Pos.	AB	R	H	2B	3B	HR	RBI	Avg.	BB	SO	SB	PO	A	E	Avg.
1996—American	OF	2	0	0	0	0	0	0	.000	0	0	0	1	0	0	1.000

BULLINGER, KIRK P

PERSONAL: Born October 28, 1969, in New Orleans. ... 6-2/170. ... Throws right, bats right. ... Full name: Kirk Matthew Bullinger. ... Brother of Jim Bullinger, pitcher with three major league teams (1992-99).

HIGH SCHOOL: Archbishop Rummel (Metairie, La.).

COLLEGE: Southeastern Louisiana.

TRANSACTIONS/CAREER NOTES: Selected by St. Louis Cardinals in 32nd round of free-agent draft (June 1, 1992). ... Traded by Cardinals organization with OF DaRond Stovall and P Bryan Eversgerd to Montreal Expos organization for P Ken Hill (April 5, 1995). ... On Ottawa disabled list (April 9-July 3, 1998); included rehabilitation assignment to Gulf Coast Expos (June 26-July 3). ... Granted free agency (October 15, 1998). ... Signed by Boston Red Sox organization (December 14, 1998). ... On Pawtucket disabled list (August 6-18, 1999). ... Granted free agency (October 4, 1999).

Year League	W	L	Pct.	ERA	G	GS	CG	ShO	Sv.	IP	H	R	ER	BB	SO
1992—Hamilton (NY-P)	2	2	.500	1.11	35	0	0	0	2	48 2/3	24	7	6	15	61
1993—Springfield (Midw.)	1	3	.250	2.28	50	0	0	0	*33	51 1/3	26	19	13	21	72
1994—St. Petersburg (FSL)	2	0	1.000	1.17	39	0	0	0	6	53 2/3	37	16	7	20	50
1995—Harrisburg (East.)■	5	3	.625	2.42	56	0	0	0	7	67	61	22	18	25	42
1996—Ottawa (I.L.)	2	1	.667	3.52	10	0	0	0	0	15 1/3	10	6	6	9	9
—Harrisburg (East.)	3	4	.429	1.97	47	0	0	0	22	45 2/3	46	16	10	18	29
1997—Harrisburg (East.)	3	0	1.000	2.67	21	0	0	0	6	27	22	9	8	6	21
—West Palm Beach (FSL)	2	0	1.000	0.00	2	0	0	0	0	3 2/3	3	0	0	0	7
—Ottawa (I.L.)	3	4	.429	1.71	22	0	0	0	5	31 2/3	17	7	6	10	15
1998—Gulf Coast Expos (GCL)	0	0	...	0.00	2	2	0	0	0	4	2	0	0	0	7
—Jupiter (FSL)	0	0	...	5.40	8	0	0	0	0	10	9	7	6	2	12
—Ottawa (I.L.)	0	0	...	1.06	13	0	0	0	3	17	16	2	2	6	7
—Montreal (N.L.)	1	0	1.000	9.00	8	0	0	0	0	7	14	8	7	0	2

Year	League	W	L	Pct.	ERA	G	GS	CG	ShO	Sv.	IP	H	R	ER	BB	SO
1999— Trenton (East.)■		1	1	.500	0.53	17	0	0	0	10	17	6	2	1	5	16
— Pawtucket (I.L.)		0	2	.000	2.39	35	0	0	0	15	37²/₃	37	14	10	13	27
— Boston (A.L.)		0	0	...	4.50	4	0	0	0	0	2	2	1	1	2	0
A.L. totals (1 year)		0	0	...	4.50	4	0	0	0	0	2	2	1	1	2	0
N.L. totals (1 year)		1	0	1.000	9.00	8	0	0	0	0	7	14	8	7	0	2
Major League totals (2 years)		1	0	1.000	8.00	12	0	0	0	0	9	16	9	8	2	2

BUNCH, MELVIN   P

PERSONAL: Born November 4, 1971, in Texarkana, Texas. ... 6-1/170. ... Throws right, bats right. ... Full name: Melvin Lynn Bunch Jr.
HIGH SCHOOL: Liberty Eylau (Texarkana, Texas).
JUNIOR COLLEGE: Texarkana (Texas) Community College.
TRANSACTIONS/CAREER NOTES: Selected by Kansas City Royals organization in 15th round of free-agent draft (June 1, 1992). ... On disabled list (May 9-July 25, 1994). ... Traded by Royals to Montreal Expos for OF Yamil Benitez (January 28, 1997). ... On Ottawa disabled list (July 10-24, 1998). ... Granted free agency (October 15, 1998). ... Signed by Seattle Mariners organization (April 21, 1999). ... Released by Mariners (December 6, 1999).
STATISTICAL NOTES: Led American Association with 32 home runs allowed in 1996.

Year	League	W	L	Pct.	ERA	G	GS	CG	ShO	Sv.	IP	H	R	ER	BB	SO
1992— Gulf Coast Royals (GCL)		2	1	.667	1.50	5	4	0	0	0	24	11	6	4	3	26
— Eugene (N.W.)		5	3	.625	2.78	10	10	0	0	0	64²/₃	62	23	20	13	69
1993— Rockford (Midw.)		6	4	.600	2.12	19	11	1	0	4	85	79	24	20	18	71
— Wilmington (Caro.)		5	3	.625	2.33	10	10	1	0	0	65²/₃	52	22	17	14	54
1994— Wilmington (Caro.)		5	3	.625	3.39	15	12	0	0	0	61	52	30	23	15	62
1995— Kansas City (A.L.)		1	3	.250	5.63	13	5	0	0	0	40	42	25	25	14	19
— Omaha (A.A.)		1	7	.125	4.57	12	11	1	0	0	65	63	37	33	20	50
1996— Omaha (A.A.)		8	9	.471	6.07	33	27	0	0	0	146²/₃	181	106	99	59	94
1997— Harrisburg (East.)■		3	3	.500	4.20	9	9	0	0	0	49¹/₃	45	27	23	22	50
— Ottawa (I.L.)		4	4	.500	6.35	16	14	0	0	0	78	102	63	55	45	58
1998— Ottawa (I.L.)		6	6	.500	4.59	25	19	0	0	0	104	101	58	53	48	99
1999— Tacoma (PCL)■		10	2	.833	*3.10	21	19	1	1	0	125	112	53	43	40	117
— Seattle (A.L.)		0	0	...	11.70	5	1	0	0	0	10	20	13	13	7	4
Major League totals (2 years)		1	3	.250	6.84	18	6	0	0	0	50	62	38	38	21	23

BURBA, DAVE   P   INDIANS

PERSONAL: Born July 7, 1966, in Dayton, Ohio. ... 6-4/240. ... Throws right, bats right. ... Full name: David Allen Burba. ... Nephew of Ray Hathaway, pitcher with Brooklyn Dodgers (1945).
HIGH SCHOOL: Kenton Ridge (Springfield, Ohio).
COLLEGE: Ohio State.
TRANSACTIONS/CAREER NOTES: Selected by Seattle Mariners organization in second round of free-agent draft (June 2, 1987). ... Traded by Mariners with P Bill Swift and P Mike Jackson to San Francisco Giants for OF Kevin Mitchell and P Mike Remlinger (December 11, 1991). ... Traded by Giants with OF Darren Lewis and P Mark Portugal to Cincinnati Reds for OF Deion Sanders, P John Roper, P Ricky Pickett, P Scott Service and IF Dave McCarty (July 21, 1995). ... On disabled list (August 7-27, 1997). ... Traded by Reds to Cleveland Indians for 1B Sean Casey (March 30, 1998).

Year	League	W	L	Pct.	ERA	G	GS	CG	ShO	Sv.	IP	H	R	ER	BB	SO
1987— Bellingham (N.W.)		3	1	.750	1.93	5	5	0	0	0	23¹/₃	20	10	5	3	24
— Salinas (Calif.)		1	6	.143	4.61	9	9	0	0	0	54²/₃	53	31	28	29	46
1988— San Bernardino (Calif.)		5	7	.417	2.68	20	20	0	0	0	114	106	41	34	54	102
1989— Williamsport (East.)		11	7	.611	3.16	25	25	5	1	0	156²/₃	138	69	55	55	89
1990— Calgary (PCL)		10	6	.625	4.67	31	18	1	0	2	113²/₃	124	64	59	45	47
— Seattle (A.L.)		0	0	...	4.50	6	0	0	0	0	8	8	6	4	2	4
1991— Calgary (PCL)		6	4	.600	3.53	23	9	0	0	4	71¹/₃	82	35	28	27	42
— Seattle (A.L.)		2	2	.500	3.68	22	2	0	0	1	36²/₃	34	16	15	14	16
1992— San Francisco (N.L.)■		2	7	.222	4.97	23	11	0	0	0	70²/₃	80	43	39	31	47
— Phoenix (PCL)		5	5	.500	4.72	13	13	0	0	0	74¹/₃	86	40	39	24	44
1993— San Francisco (N.L.)		10	3	.769	4.25	54	5	0	0	0	95¹/₃	95	49	45	37	88
1994— San Francisco (N.L.)		3	6	.333	4.38	57	0	0	0	0	74	59	39	36	45	84
1995— San Francisco (N.L.)		4	2	.667	4.98	37	0	0	0	0	43¹/₃	38	26	24	25	46
— Cincinnati (N.L.)■		6	2	.750	3.27	15	9	1	1	0	63¹/₃	52	24	23	26	50
1996— Cincinnati (N.L.)		11	13	.458	3.83	34	33	0	0	0	195	179	96	83	97	148
1997— Cincinnati (N.L.)		11	10	.524	4.72	30	27	2	0	0	160	157	88	84	73	131
1998— Cleveland (A.L.)■		15	10	.600	4.11	32	31	0	0	0	203²/₃	210	100	93	69	132
1999— Cleveland (A.L.)		15	9	.625	4.25	34	34	1	0	0	220	211	113	104	96	174
A.L. totals (4 years)		32	21	.604	4.15	94	67	1	0	1	468¹/₃	463	235	216	181	326
N.L. totals (6 years)		47	43	.522	4.28	250	85	3	1	0	701²/₃	660	365	334	334	594
Major League totals (10 years)		79	64	.552	4.23	344	152	4	1	1	1170	1123	600	550	515	920

DIVISION SERIES RECORD

Year	League	W	L	Pct.	ERA	G	GS	CG	ShO	Sv.	IP	H	R	ER	BB	SO
1995— Cincinnati (N.L.)		1	0	1.000	0.00	1	0	0	0	0	1	2	0	0	1	0
1998— Cleveland (A.L.)		1	0	1.000	5.06	1	0	0	0	0	5¹/₃	4	3	3	2	4
1999— Cleveland (A.L.)		0	0	...	0.00	1	1	0	0	0	4	1	0	0	1	0
Division series totals (3 years)		2	0	1.000	2.61	3	1	0	0	0	10¹/₃	7	3	3	4	4

CHAMPIONSHIP SERIES RECORD

Year	League	W	L	Pct.	ERA	G	GS	CG	ShO	Sv.	IP	H	R	ER	BB	SO
1995— Cincinnati (N.L.)		0	0	...	0.00	2	0	0	0	0	3²/₃	3	0	0	4	0
1998— Cleveland (A.L.)		1	0	1.000	3.00	3	0	0	0	0	6	3	4	2	5	8
Champ. series totals (2 years)		1	0	1.000	1.86	5	0	0	0	0	9²/₃	6	4	2	9	8

PERSONAL: Born November 28, 1964, in New Brighton, Pa. ... 6-3/215. ... Throws right, bats right. ... Full name: John David Burkett. ... Name pronounced bur-KETT.
HIGH SCHOOL: Beaver (Pa.).
TRANSACTIONS/CAREER NOTES: Selected by San Francisco Giants organization in sixth round of free-agent draft (June 6, 1983). ... Traded by Giants to Texas Rangers for IF Rich Aurilia and OF Desi Wilson (December 22, 1994). ... Granted free agency (April 7, 1995). ... Signed by Florida Marlins (April 9, 1995). ... Traded by Marlins to Texas Rangers for P Ryan Dempster and a player to be named later (August 8, 1996); Marlins acquired P Rick Helling to complete deal (September 3, 1996). ... On Texas disabled list (August 6-31, 1997); included rehabilitation assignment to Oklahoma City (August 26). ... On Texas disabled list (April 21-May 9, 1999); included rehabilitation assignment to Tulsa (May 1-9). ... Granted free agency (November 1, 1999). ... Signed by Tampa Bay Devil Rays organization (January 17, 2000).
STATISTICAL NOTES: Led N.L. 10 hit batsmen in 1991.
MISCELLANEOUS: Had sacrifice hit in only appearance as pinch hitter (1995).

Year League	W	L	Pct.	ERA	G	GS	CG	ShO	Sv.	IP	H	R	ER	BB	SO
1983— Great Falls (Pio.)	2	6	.250	6.26	13	9	0	0	0	50 1/3	73	44	35	30	38
1984— Clinton (Midw.)	7	6	.538	4.33	20	20	2	0	0	126 2/3	128	81	61	38	83
1985— Fresno (Calif.)	7	4	.636	2.87	20	20	1	1	0	109 2/3	98	43	35	46	72
1986— Fresno (Calif.)	0	3	.000	5.47	4	4	0	0	0	24 2/3	34	19	15	8	14
— Shreveport (Texas)	10	6	.625	2.66	22	21	4	2	0	128 2/3	99	46	38	42	73
1987— Shreveport (Texas)	•14	8	.636	3.34	27	27	6	1	0	*177 2/3	181	75	66	53	126
— San Francisco (N.L.)	0	0	...	4.50	3	0	0	0	0	6	7	4	3	3	5
1988— Phoenix (PCL)	5	11	.313	5.21	21	21	0	0	0	114	141	79	66	49	74
— Shreveport (Texas)	5	1	.833	2.13	7	7	2	1	0	50 2/3	33	15	12	18	34
1989— Phoenix (PCL)	10	11	.476	5.05	28	•28	2	1	0	167 2/3	197	111	94	59	105
1990— Phoenix (PCL)	2	1	.667	2.74	3	3	2	1	0	23	18	8	7	3	9
— San Francisco (N.L.)	14	7	.667	3.79	33	32	2	0	1	204	201	92	86	61	118
1991— San Francisco (N.L.)	12	11	.522	4.18	36	34	3	1	0	206 2/3	223	103	96	60	131
1992— San Francisco (N.L.)	13	9	.591	3.84	32	32	3	1	0	189 2/3	194	96	81	45	107
1993— San Francisco (N.L.)	•22	7	.759	3.65	34	34	2	1	0	231 2/3	224	100	94	40	145
1994— San Francisco (N.L.)	6	8	.429	3.62	25	25	0	0	0	159 1/3	176	72	64	36	85
1995— Florida (N.L.)■	14	14	.500	4.30	30	30	4	0	0	188 1/3	208	95	90	57	126
1996— Florida (N.L.)	6	10	.375	4.32	24	24	1	0	0	154	154	84	74	42	108
— Texas (A.L.)■	5	2	.714	4.06	10	10	1	1	0	68 2/3	75	33	31	16	47
1997— Texas (A.L.)	9	12	.429	4.56	30	30	2	0	0	189 1/3	240	106	96	30	139
— Oklahoma City (A.A.)	1	0	1.000	3.60	1	1	0	0	0	5	6	2	2	2	3
1998— Texas (A.L.)	9	13	.409	5.68	32	32	0	0	0	195	230	131	*123	46	131
1999— Texas (A.L.)	9	8	.529	5.62	30	25	0	0	0	147 1/3	184	95	92	46	96
— Tulsa (Texas)	0	1	.000	2.70	2	2	0	0	0	6 2/3	7	5	2	3	3
A.L. totals (4 years)	32	35	.478	5.13	102	97	3	1	0	600 1/3	729	365	342	138	413
N.L. totals (8 years)	87	66	.569	3.95	217	211	15	3	1	1339 2/3	1387	646	588	344	825
Major League totals (11 years)	119	101	.541	4.31	319	308	18	4	1	1940	2116	1011	930	482	1238

DIVISION SERIES RECORD

Year League	W	L	Pct.	ERA	G	GS	CG	ShO	Sv.	IP	H	R	ER	BB	SO
1996— Texas (A.L.)	1	0	1.000	2.00	1	1	1	0	0	9	10	2	2	1	7
1998— Texas (A.L.)					Did not play.										
1999— Texas (A.L.)					Did not play.										

ALL-STAR GAME RECORD

Year League	W	L	Pct.	ERA	GS	CG	ShO	Sv.	IP	H	R	ER	BB	SO
1993— National	0	1	.000	40.50	0	0	0	0	2/3	4	3	3	0	1

PERSONAL: Born September 11, 1964, in Vicksburg, Miss. ... 6-2/205. ... Bats right, throws right. ... Full name: Ellis Rena Burks.
HIGH SCHOOL: Everman (Texas).
JUNIOR COLLEGE: Ranger (Texas) Junior College.
TRANSACTIONS/CAREER NOTES: Selected by Boston Red Sox organization in first round (20th pick overall) of free-agent draft (January 11, 1983). ... On disabled list (March 26-April 12, 1988). ... On Boston disabled list (June 15-August 1, 1989); included rehabilitation assignment to Pawtucket (July 26-August 1). ... On disabled list (June 25, 1992-remainder of season). ... Granted free agency (December 19, 1992). ... Signed by Chicago White Sox (January 4, 1993). ... Granted free agency (October 27, 1993). ... Signed by Colorado Rockies (November 30, 1993). ... On Colorado disabled list (May 18-July 31, 1994); included rehabilitation assignment to Colorado Springs (July 18-20). ... On Colorado disabled list (April 17-May 5, 1995); included rehabilitation assignment to Colorado Springs (April 25-May 5). ... On disabled list (June 28-July 29, 1997). ... Traded by Rockies to San Francisco Giants for OF Darryl Hamilton, P James Stoops and a player to be named later (July 31, 1998); Rockies acquired P Jason Brester to complete deal (August 17, 1998). ... Granted free agency (November 2, 1998). ... Re-signed by Giants (November 13, 1998). ... On disabled list (June 9-26, 1999).
RECORDS: Shares major league single-inning record for most home runs—2 (August 27, 1990, fourth inning).
HONORS: Named outfielder on THE SPORTING NEWS A.L. All-Star team (1990). ... Named outfielder on THE SPORTING NEWS A.L. Silver Slugger team (1990). ... Won A.L. Gold Glove as outfielder (1990). ... Named outfielder on THE SPORTING NEWS N.L. All-Star team (1996). ... Named outfielder on THE SPORTING NEWS N.L. Silver Slugger team (1996).
STATISTICAL NOTES: Tied for Florida State League lead in double plays by outfielder with six in 1984. ... Led N.L. with 392 total bases and .639 slugging percentage in 1996. ... Career major league grand slams: 10.

Year Team (League)	Pos.	G	AB	R	H	2B	3B	HR	RBI	Avg.	BB	SO	SB	PO	A	E	Avg.
1983— Elmira (NY-P)	OF	53	174	30	42	9	0	2	23	.241	17	43	9	89	5	2	.979
1984— Winter Haven (FSL)	OF	112	375	52	96	15	4	6	43	.256	42	68	29	196	12	5	.977
1985— New Britain (East.)	OF	133	476	66	121	25	7	10	61	.254	42	85	17	306	9	8	.975
1986— New Britain (East.)	OF	124	462	70	126	20	3	14	55	.273	44	75	31	318	5	5	.985
1987— Pawtucket (I.L.)	OF	11	40	11	9	3	1	3	6	.225	7	7	1	25	0	0	1.000
— Boston (A.L.)	OF-DH	133	558	94	152	30	2	20	59	.272	41	98	27	320	15	4	.988

Year Team (League)	Pos.	G	AB	R	H	2B	3B	HR	RBI	Avg.	BB	SO	SB	PO	A	E	Avg.
1988—Boston (A.L.).............	OF-DH	144	540	93	159	37	5	18	92	.294	62	89	25	370	9	9	.977
1989—Boston (A.L.).............	OF-DH	97	399	73	121	19	6	12	61	.303	36	52	21	245	7	6	.977
—Pawtucket (I.L.).........	OF	5	21	4	3	1	0	0	0	.143	2	3	0	16	0	0	1.000
1990—Boston (A.L.).............	OF-DH	152	588	89	174	33	8	21	89	.296	48	82	9	324	7	2	.994
1991—Boston (A.L.).............	OF-DH	130	474	56	119	33	3	14	56	.251	39	81	6	283	2	2	.993
1992—Boston (A.L.).............	OF-DH	66	235	35	60	8	3	8	30	.255	25	48	5	120	3	2	.984
1993—Chicago (A.L.)■........	OF	146	499	75	137	24	4	17	74	.275	60	97	6	313	6	6	.982
1994—Colorado (N.L.)■........	OF	42	149	33	48	8	3	13	24	.322	16	39	3	79	2	3	.964
—Colo. Springs (PCL) ...	OF	2	8	4	4	1	0	1	2	.500	2	1	0	5	0	0	1.000
1995—Colo. Springs (PCL) ...	OF-DH	8	29	9	9	2	1	2	6	.310	4	8	0	16	0	0	1.000
—Colorado (N.L.)	OF	103	278	41	74	10	6	14	49	.266	39	72	7	158	3	5	.970
1996—Colorado (N.L.)	OF	156	613	*142	211	45	8	40	128	.344	61	114	32	279	6	5	.983
1997—Colorado (N.L.)	OF	119	424	91	123	19	2	32	82	.290	47	75	7	207	6	4	.982
1998—Colorado (N.L.)	OF	100	357	54	102	22	5	16	54	.286	39	80	3	187	5	5	.975
—San Fran. (N.L.)■........	OF	42	147	22	45	6	1	5	22	.306	19	31	8	89	1	1	.989
1999—San Francisco (N.L.) ..	OF-DH	120	390	73	110	19	0	31	96	.282	69	86	7	210	3	2	.991
American League totals (7 years)		868	3293	515	922	184	31	110	461	.280	311	547	99	1975	49	31	.985
National League totals (6 years)		682	2358	456	713	129	25	151	455	.302	290	497	67	1209	26	25	.980
Major League totals (13 years)		1550	5651	971	1635	313	56	261	916	.289	601	1044	166	3184	75	56	.983

DIVISION SERIES RECORD

Year Team (League)	Pos.	G	AB	R	H	2B	3B	HR	RBI	Avg.	BB	SO	SB	PO	A	E	Avg.
1995—Colorado (N.L.)	OF	2	6	1	2	1	0	0	2	.333	0	1	0	4	0	1	.800

CHAMPIONSHIP SERIES RECORD

Year Team (League)	Pos.	G	AB	R	H	2B	3B	HR	RBI	Avg.	BB	SO	SB	PO	A	E	Avg.
1988—Boston (A.L.).............	OF	4	17	2	4	1	0	0	1	.235	0	3	0	10	0	0	1.000
1990—Boston (A.L.)	OF	4	15	1	4	2	0	0	0	.267	1	1	1	9	1	0	1.000
1993—Chicago (A.L.)	OF	6	23	4	7	1	0	1	3	.304	3	5	0	15	0	0	1.000
Championship series totals (3 years)		14	55	7	15	4	0	1	4	.273	4	9	1	34	1	0	1.000

ALL-STAR GAME RECORD

NOTES: Named to A.L. All-Star team for 1990 game; replaced by Brook Jacoby due to injury.

Year League	Pos.	AB	R	H	2B	3B	HR	RBI	Avg.	BB	SO	SB	PO	A	E	Avg.
1990— American.....................		Selected, did not play—injured.														
1996— National	OF	2	0	1	0	1	0	0	.500	0	1	0	1	0	0	1.000

BURNETT, A.J. P MARLINS

PERSONAL: Born January 3, 1977, in North Little Rock, Ark. ... 6-5/205. ... Throws right, bats right. ... Full name: Allen James Burnett.
HIGH SCHOOL: Central Arkansas Christian (North Little Rock, Ark.).
TRANSACTIONS/CAREER NOTES: Selected by New York Mets organization in eighth round of free-agent draft (June 1, 1995). ... Traded by Mets with P Jesus Sanchez and OF Robert Stratton to Florida Marlins for P Al Leiter and 2B Ralph Milliard (February 6, 1998).
STATISTICAL NOTES: Tied for Appalachian League lead in wild pitches with 16 in 1996.

Year League	W	L	Pct.	ERA	G	GS	CG	ShO	Sv.	IP	H	R	ER	BB	SO
1995—Gulf Coast Mets (GCL) ..	2	3	.400	4.28	9	8	1	0	0	33²/₃	27	16	16	23	26
1996—Kingsport (Appalachian).....	4	0	1.000	3.88	12	12	0	0	0	58	31	26	25	54	68
1997—Gulf Coast Mets (GCL) ..	0	1	.000	3.18	3	2	0	0	0	11¹/₃	8	8	4	8	15
—Pittsfield (NY-P)	3	1	.750	4.70	20	9	0	0	0	44	28	26	23	35	48
1998—Kane County (Midw.)■...	10	4	.714	1.97	20	20	0	0	0	119	74	27	26	45	186
1999—Portland (East.)	6	12	.333	5.52	26	23	0	0	0	120²/₃	132	91	74	71	121
—Florida (N.L.)	4	2	.667	3.48	7	7	0	0	0	41¹/₃	37	23	16	25	33
Major League totals (1 year)........	4	2	.667	3.48	7	7	0	0	0	41¹/₃	37	23	16	25	33

BURNITZ, JEROMY OF BREWERS

PERSONAL: Born April 15, 1969, in Westminster, Calif. ... 6-0/205. ... Bats left, throws right. ... Full name: Jeromy Neal Burnitz.
HIGH SCHOOL: Conroe (Texas).
COLLEGE: Oklahoma State.
TRANSACTIONS/CAREER NOTES: Selected by Milwaukee Brewers organization in 24th round of free-agent draft (June 2, 1987); did not sign. ... Selected by New York Mets organization in first round (17th pick overall) of free-agent draft (June 4, 1990). ... On disabled list (August 23-September 18, 1992). ... On Norfolk suspended list (August 11-13, 1994). ... Traded by Mets with P Joe Roa to Cleveland Indians for P Paul Byrd, P Jerry DiPoto, P Dave Mlicki and a player to be named later (November 18, 1994); Mets acquired 2B Jesus Azuaje to complete deal (December 6, 1994). ... Traded by Indians to Milwaukee Brewers for 3B/1B Kevin Seitzer (August 31, 1996). ... On Milwaukee disabled list (July 18-August 20, 1999).
RECORDS: Shares A.L. record for most home runs by pinch hitter in consecutive at-bats—2 (August 2 and 3, 1997).
STATISTICAL NOTES: Led New York-Pennsylvania League with .444 on-base percentage and tied for lead with six intentional bases on balls received in 1990. ... Led American Association with .503 slugging percentage in 1995. ... Led American Association with eight intentional bases on balls received in 1995. ... Career major league grand slams: 5.

Year Team (League)	Pos.	G	AB	R	H	2B	3B	HR	RBI	Avg.	BB	SO	SB	PO	A	E	Avg.
1990—Pittsfield (NY-P)	OF	51	173	37	52	6	5	6	22	.301	45	39	12	79	2	0	1.000
—St. Lucie (FSL)	OF	11	32	6	5	1	0	0	3	.156	7	12	1	18	1	0	1.000

B

			BATTING											FIELDING			
Year Team (League)	Pos.	G	AB	R	H	2B	3B	HR	RBI	Avg.	BB	SO	SB	PO	A	E	Avg.
1991— Williamsport (East.) ...	OF	135	457	80	103	16	•10	*31	•85	.225	*104	127	31	237	13	•11	.958
1993— Norfolk (I.L.)	OF	65	255	33	58	15	3	8	44	.227	25	53	10	133	9	1	.993
— New York (N.L.).........	OF	86	263	49	64	10	6	13	38	.243	38	66	3	165	6	4	.977
1994— New York (N.L.).........	OF	45	143	26	34	4	0	3	15	.238	23	45	1	63	1	2	.970
— Norfolk (I.L.)	OF-DH	85	314	58	75	15	5	14	49	.239	49	82	18	170	13	4	.979
1995— Buffalo (A.A.)■	OF	128	443	72	126	26	7	19	*85	.284	50	83	13	241	12	5	.981
— Cleveland (A.L.).........	OF-DH	9	7	4	4	1	0	0	0	.571	0	0	0	10	0	0	1.000
1996— Cleveland (A.L.).........	OF-DH	71	128	30	36	10	0	7	26	.281	25	31	2	44	0	0	1.000
— Milwaukee (A.L.)■...	OF	23	72	8	17	4	0	2	14	.236	8	16	2	38	1	1	.975
1997— Milwaukee (A.L.)........	OF	153	494	85	139	37	8	27	85	.281	75	111	20	256	13	7	.975
1998— Milwaukee (N.L.)........	OF	161	609	92	160	28	1	38	125	.263	70	158	7	306	10	9	.972
1999— Milwaukee (N.L.)........	OF-DH	130	467	87	126	33	2	33	103	.270	91	124	7	262	8	5	.982
American League totals (3 years)		256	701	127	196	52	8	36	125	.280	108	158	24	348	14	8	.977
National League totals (4 years)		422	1482	254	384	75	9	87	281	.259	222	393	18	796	25	20	.976
Major League totals (7 years)		678	2183	381	580	127	17	123	406	.266	330	551	42	1144	39	28	.977

ALL-STAR GAME RECORD

			BATTING									FIELDING		
Year League	Pos.	AB	R	H	2B	3B	HR	RBI	Avg.	BB	SO	SB	PO	A	E	Avg.
1999— National	OF	2	1	1	1	0	0	0	.500	0	0	0	0	0	0	...

BURNSIDE, ADRIAN   P   REDS

PERSONAL: Born March 15, 1977, in Alice Springs, Australia. ... 6-3/168. ... Throws left, bats right. ... Full name: Adrian Mark Burnside.
TRANSACTIONS/CAREER NOTES: Signed as non-drafted free agent by Los Angeles Dodgers organization (July 12, 1995). ... On San Bernardino disabled list (April 22-May 7, 1999). ... Selected by Cincinnati Reds from Dodgers organization in Rule 5 major league draft (December 13, 1999).

Year League	W	L	Pct.	ERA	G	GS	CG	ShO	Sv.	IP	H	R	ER	BB	SO
1996— Great Falls (Pio.)	1	3	.250	6.80	14	5	0	0	0	41	44	35	31	38	33
1997— Yakima (N.W.)	6	3	.667	4.93	15	13	0	0	0	65²/₃	67	53	36	49	66
1998— San Bernardino (Calif.).......	1	10	.091	7.81	21	12	0	0	0	78¹/₃	97	79	68	48	65
— Yakima (N.W.)	1	4	.200	4.05	8	6	0	0	0	33¹/₃	27	21	15	30	34
1999— San Bernardino (Calif.).......	10	9	.526	4.17	26	22	0	0	0	131²/₃	124	69	61	55	129

BURRELL, PAT   1B   PHILLIES

PERSONAL: Born October 10, 1976, in Eureka Springs, Ark. ... 6-4/225. ... Bats right, throws right. ... Name pronounced BURL.
HIGH SCHOOL: Bellarmine Prep (San Jose, Calif.).
COLLEGE: Miami (Fla.).
TRANSACTIONS/CAREER NOTES: Selected by Boston Red Sox organization in 43rd round of free-agent draft (June 1, 1995); did not sign. ... Selected by Philadelphia Phillies organization in first round (first pick overall) of free-agent draft (June 2, 1998).

				BATTING									FIELDING		
Year Team (League)	Pos.	G	AB	R	H	2B	3B	HR	RBI	Avg.	BB	SO	SB	PO	A	E	Avg.
1998— Clearwater (FSL)	1B	37	132	29	40	7	1	7	30	.303	27	22	2	202	13	1	.995
1999— Reading (East.)............	1B-OF-DH	117	417	84	139	28	6	28	90	.333	79	103	3	715	56	12	.985
— Scranton/W.B. (I.L.) ...	1B-OF	10	33	4	5	0	0	1	4	.152	4	8	0	62	1	0	1.000

BUSBY, MIKE   P   BREWERS

PERSONAL: Born December 27, 1972, in Lomita, Calif. ... 6-4/210. ... Throws right, bats right. ... Full name: Michael James Busby.
HIGH SCHOOL: Banning (Wilmington, Calif.).
TRANSACTIONS/CAREER NOTES: Selected by St. Louis Cardinals organization in 14th round of free-agent draft (June 3, 1991). ... On Louisville disabled list (April 17-24, June 16-26, July 3-9, 1996 and April 3-June 10, 1997). ... On St. Louis disabled list (May 25-September 4, 1998); included rehabilitation assignment to Memphis (August 17-September 4). ... Granted free agency (October 15, 1999). ... Signed by Milwaukee Brewers organization (December 7, 1999).

Year League	W	L	Pct.	ERA	G	GS	CG	ShO	Sv.	IP	H	R	ER	BB	SO
1991— Arizona Cardinals (Ariz.)......	4	3	.571	3.51	11	11	0	0	0	59	67	35	23	29	71
1992— Savannah (SAL)	4	•13	.235	3.67	28	•28	1	0	0	149²/₃	145	96	61	67	84
1993— Savannah (SAL)	12	2	.857	2.44	23	21	1	1	0	143²/₃	116	49	39	31	125
1994— St. Petersburg (FSL)	6	•13	.316	4.45	26	26	1	0	0	151²/₃	166	82	75	49	89
1995— Arkansas (Texas)...............	7	6	.538	3.29	20	20	1	0	0	134	125	63	49	35	95
— Louisville (A.A.)..................	2	2	.500	3.29	6	6	1	0	0	38¹/₃	28	18	14	11	26
1996— St. Louis (N.L.)..................	0	1	.000	18.00	1	1	0	0	0	4	9	13	8	4	4
— Louisville (A.A.)..................	2	5	.286	6.38	14	14	0	0	0	72	89	57	51	44	53
1997— Louisville (A.A.)..................	4	8	.333	4.61	15	14	1	1	0	93²/₃	95	49	48	30	65
— St. Louis (N.L.)..................	0	2	.000	8.79	3	3	0	0	0	14¹/₃	24	14	14	4	6
1998— St. Louis (N.L.)..................	5	2	.714	4.50	26	2	0	0	0	46	45	23	23	15	33
— Memphis (PCL).................	0	0	...	3.38	7	2	0	0	0	8	5	3	3	2	5
1999— St. Louis (N.L.)..................	0	1	.000	7.13	15	0	0	0	0	17²/₃	21	15	14	14	7
— Memphis (PCL).................	3	4	.429	7.43	29	10	0	0	0	72²/₃	112	69	60	36	50
Major League totals (4 years).......	5	6	.455	6.48	45	6	0	0	0	82	99	65	59	37	50

BUSH, HOMER   2B   BLUE JAYS

PERSONAL: Born November 12, 1972, in East St. Louis, Ill. ... 5-10/180. ... Bats right, throws right. ... Full name: Homer Giles Bush.
HIGH SCHOOL: East St. Louis (Ill.).
COLLEGE: Southern Illinois-Edwardsville.
TRANSACTIONS/CAREER NOTES: Selected by San Diego Padres organization in seventh round of free-agent draft (June 3, 1991). ... On Rancho Cucamonga disabled list (April 27-May 4 and May 9-26, 1994). ... On disabled list (May 20, 1996-remainder of season). ... Traded by Padres with rights to P Hideki Irabu, OF Gordon Amerson and player to be named later to New York Yankees for OF Ruben Rivera, P Rafael Medina and cash (April 22, 1997); Yankees acquired OF Vernon Maxwell to complete deal (June 9, 1997). ... Traded by Yankees with P David Wells and P Graeme Lloyd to Toronto Blue Jays for P Roger Clemens (February 18, 1999). ... On Toronto disabled list (April 11-May 14, 1999); included rehabilitation assignment to Dunedin (May 9-14).

							BATTING								FIELDING		
Year Team (League)	Pos.	G	AB	R	H	2B	3B	HR	RBI	Avg.	BB	SO	SB	PO	A	E	Avg.
1991— Ariz. Padres (Ariz.)	3B	32	127	16	41	3	2	0	16	.323	4	33	11	25	60	10	.895
1992— Char., S.C. (SAL)	2B	108	367	37	86	10	5	0	18	.234	13	85	14	199	287	*34	.935
1993— Waterloo (Midw.)	2B	130	472	63	*152	19	3	5	51	.322	19	87	39	215	289	38	.930
1994— Rancho Cuca. (Calif.) .	2B	39	161	37	54	10	3	0	16	.335	9	29	9	69	102	7	.961
— Wichita (Texas)	2B	59	245	35	73	11	4	3	14	.298	10	39	20	101	135	8	.967
1995— Memphis (Sou.)	2B-DH	108	432	53	121	12	5	5	37	.280	15	83	34	235	268	16	.969
1996— Las Vegas (PCL)	2B-DH	32	116	24	42	11	1	2	3	.362	3	33	3	67	88	5	.969
1997— Las Vegas (PCL)	2B-DH	38	155	25	43	10	1	3	14	.277	7	40	5	73	103	4	.978
— Columbus (I.L.)■.......	2B	74	275	36	68	10	3	2	26	.247	25	56	12	153	253	9	.978
— New York (A.L.)	2B-DH	10	11	2	4	0	0	0	3	.364	0	0	0	8	13	2	.913
1998— New York (A.L.)	2-DH-3-S	45	71	17	27	3	0	1	5	.380	5	19	6	38	38	2	.974
1999— Toronto (A.L.)■..........	2B-SS	128	485	69	155	26	4	5	55	.320	21	82	32	246	404	16	.976
— Dunedin (FSL)	2B-DH	4	14	3	5	2	0	0	0	.357	1	1	1	7	7	0	1.000
Major League totals (3 years)		183	567	88	186	29	4	6	63	.328	26	101	38	292	455	20	.974

DIVISION SERIES RECORD

							BATTING								FIELDING		
Year Team (League)	Pos.	G	AB	R	H	2B	3B	HR	RBI	Avg.	BB	SO	SB	PO	A	E	Avg.
1998— New York (A.L.)	PR-DH	1	0	0	0	0	0	0	0	...	0	0	1	...	...	...	...

CHAMPIONSHIP SERIES RECORD

							BATTING								FIELDING		
Year Team (League)	Pos.	G	AB	R	H	2B	3B	HR	RBI	Avg.	BB	SO	SB	PO	A	E	Avg.
1998— New York (A.L.)	PR-DH	2	0	1	0	0	0	0	0	...	0	0	1	...	...	...	...

WORLD SERIES RECORD

NOTES: Member of World Series championship team (1998).

							BATTING								FIELDING		
Year Team (League)	Pos.	G	AB	R	H	2B	3B	HR	RBI	Avg.	BB	SO	SB	PO	A	E	Avg.
1998— New York (A.L.)	PR-DH	2	0	0	0	0	0	0	0	...	0	0	0	...	...	...	...

BUTLER, BRENT   IF   ROCKIES

PERSONAL: Born February 11, 1978, in Laurinburg, N.C. ... 6-0/180. ... Bats right, throws right. ... Full name: Justin Brent Butler.
HIGH SCHOOL: Scotland County (Laurinburg, N.C.).
TRANSACTIONS/CAREER NOTES: Selected by St. Louis Cardinals organization in third round of free-agent draft (June 2, 1996). ... On Prince William disabled list (June 21-June 28, 1998). ... Traded by Cardinals with P Jose Jimenez, P Manny Aybar and P Rick Croushore to Colorado Rockies for P Darryl Kile, P Dave Veres and P Luther Hackman (November 16, 1999).

							BATTING								FIELDING		
Year Team (League)	Pos.	G	AB	R	H	2B	3B	HR	RBI	Avg.	BB	SO	SB	PO	A	E	Avg.
1996— Johnson City (Appl.) ..	SS	62	248	45	85	21	1	8	50	.343	25	29	8	81	127	12	*.945
1997— Peoria (Midw.)	SS	129	480	81	147	37	2	15	71	.306	63	69	6	*220	345	35	.942
1998— Prince Will. (Caro.).....	S-3-DH-2	126	475	63	136	27	2	11	76	.286	39	74	3	152	349	29	.945
1999— Arkansas (Texas)......	SS-3B-2B	•139	528	68	142	21	1	13	54	.269	26	47	0	183	333	17	.968

BUTLER, RICH   OF   MARINERS

PERSONAL: Born May 1, 1973, in Toronto. ... 6-1/205. ... Bats left, throws right. ... Full name: Richard Dwight Butler. ... Brother of Rob Butler, outfielder with Toronto Blue Jays (1993-94 and 1999) and Philadelphia Phillies (1997).
HIGH SCHOOL: East York Collegiate (Toronto).
TRANSACTIONS/CAREER NOTES: Signed as non-drafted free agent by Toronto Blue Jays organization (September 24, 1990). ... On disabled list (April 4-August 17, 1996). ... Selected by Tampa Bay Devil Rays in first round (10th pick overall) of expansion draft (November 18, 1997). ... On Tampa Bay disabled list (May 10-June 16, 1998); included rehabilitation assignment to Durham (June 3-15). ... On Tampa Bay disabled list (March 29-April 16, 1999). ... On Durham disabled list (June 22-July 5, 1999). ... Granted free agency (October 15, 1999). ... Signed by Seattle Mariners organization (November 17, 1999).
STATISTICAL NOTES: Led International League with 281 total bases in 1997.

							BATTING								FIELDING		
Year Team (League)	Pos.	G	AB	R	H	2B	3B	HR	RBI	Avg.	BB	SO	SB	PO	A	E	Avg.
1991— GC Blue Jays (GCL)....	OF	59	213	30	56	•6	7	0	13	.263	17	45	10	104	2	1	*.991
1992— Myrtle Beach (SAL)....	OF	130	441	43	100	14	1	2	43	.227	37	90	11	186	4	8	.960
1993— Knoxville (Sou.)..........	OF	6	21	3	2	0	1	0	0	.095	3	5	0	11	0	0	1.000
— Dunedin (FSL)...........	OF	110	444	68	136	19	8	11	65	.306	48	64	11	157	7	2	.988
1994— Knoxville (Sou.)..........	OF	53	192	29	56	7	4	3	22	.292	19	31	7	96	0	3	.970
— Syracuse (I.L.)...........	OF	94	302	34	73	6	2	3	27	.242	22	66	8	219	4	3	.987

B

Year	Team (League)	Pos.	G	AB	R	H	2B	3B	HR	RBI	Avg.	BB	SO	SB	PO	A	E	Avg.
											BATTING				FIELDING			
1995—	Syracuse (I.L.)...........	OF	69	199	20	32	4	2	2	14	.161	9	45	2	101	9	4	.965
—	Knoxville (Sou.).........	OF	58	217	27	58	12	3	4	33	.267	25	41	11	106	5	3	.974
1996—	Dunedin (FSL)............	DH	10	28	1	2	0	0	0	0	.071	5	9	4	...	...	...	...
1997—	Syracuse (I.L.)...........	OF	•137	*537	*93	*161	30	9	24	87	.300	60	107	20	236	8	8	.968
—	Toronto (A.L.)............	OF	7	14	3	4	1	0	0	2	.286	2	3	0	5	0	0	1.000
1998—	Tampa Bay (A.L.)■.....	OF	72	217	25	49	3	3	7	20	.226	15	37	4	113	4	0	1.000
—	Durham (I.L.).............	OF	38	145	28	43	8	0	8	35	.297	22	24	6	60	1	3	.953
1999—	Tampa Bay (A.L.)........	OF-DH	90	332	52	96	28	2	10	63	.289	41	70	2	148	3	3	.981
—	Tampa Bay (A.L.)........	OF	7	20	2	3	1	0	0	3	.150	2	4	0	8	0	0	1.000
Major League totals (3 years)			86	251	30	56	5	3	7	22	.223	19	44	4	126	4	0	1.000

BUTLER, ROB   OF   B

PERSONAL: Born April 10, 1970, in East York, Ont. ... 5-11/185. ... Bats left, throws left. ... Full name: Robert Frank John Butler. ... Brother of Rich Butler, outfielder, Seattle Mariners.

HIGH SCHOOL: East York (Ont.) Collegiate.

TRANSACTIONS/CAREER NOTES: Signed as non-drafted free agent by Toronto Blue Jays organization (September 24, 1990). ... On disabled list (August 7, 1992-remainder of season). ... On Syracuse disabled list (May 12-28, 1993). ... On Toronto disabled list (June 23-September 1, 1993); included rehabilitation assignment to Syracuse (August 13-September 1). ... Traded by Blue Jays to Philadelphia Phillies for a player to be named later (December 5, 1994). ... On disabled list (May 3-9, 1996). ... On Philadelphia disabled list (April 30-May 22, 1997); including rehabilitation assignment to Scranton/Wilkes-Barre (May 20-22). ... Granted free agency (October 1, 1997). ... Signed by Houston Astros organization (December 22, 1997). ... On New Orleans disabled list (April 23-May 20, June 12-July 9 and September 2, 1998-remainder of season). ... Granted free agency (October 15, 1998). ... Signed by Blue Jays organization (December 23, 1998). ... On Toronto disabled list (July 20, 1999-remainder of season). ... Granted free agency (October 7, 1999).

HONORS: Named New York-Pennsylvania League Player of the Year (1991).

STATISTICAL NOTES: Led New York-Pennsylvania League with 152 total bases and five intentional bases on balls received in 1991.

MISCELLANEOUS: Member of Canadian Olympic Team (1988).

Year	Team (League)	Pos.	G	AB	R	H	2B	3B	HR	RBI	Avg.	BB	SO	SB	PO	A	E	Avg.
											BATTING				FIELDING			
1991—	St. Cath. (NY-P).........	OF	76	*311	71	*105	16	5	7	45	.338	20	21	33	147	8	3	.981
1992—	Dunedin (FSL)...........	OF	92	391	67	140	13	7	4	41	*.358	22	36	19	186	8	5	.975
1993—	Syracuse (I.L.)...........	OF	55	208	30	59	11	2	1	14	.284	15	29	7	93	1	1	.989
—	Toronto (A.L.)............	OF	17	48	8	13	4	0	0	2	.271	7	12	2	32	0	1	.970
1994—	Syracuse (I.L.)...........	OF-DH	25	95	16	25	6	1	1	11	.263	8	12	2	39	2	1	.976
—	Toronto (A.L.)............	OF-DH	41	74	13	13	0	1	0	5	.176	7	8	0	43	0	1	.977
1995—	Scranton/W.B. (I.L.) ...	OF-DH	92	327	46	98	16	4	3	35	.300	24	39	5	147	4	4	.974
1996—	Scranton/W.B. (I.L.) ...	OF-DH	91	298	39	76	15	8	4	34	.255	20	45	3	130	4	0	1.000
1997—	Scranton/W.B. (I.L.) ...	OF-DH	21	71	8	20	4	0	0	9	.282	1	9	0	23	1	0	1.000
—	Philadelphia (N.L.)......	OF	43	89	10	26	9	1	0	13	.292	5	8	1	33	3	0	1.000
1998—	New Orleans (PCL)■..	OF	70	223	21	61	11	1	1	29	.274	17	19	2	135	3	6	.958
1999—	Knoxville (Sou.)■.......	OF-DH	64	258	48	87	13	6	2	36	.337	19	21	4	111	7	3	.975
—	Toronto (A.L.)............	DH-OF	8	7	1	1	0	0	0	1	.143	0	0	0	1	0	0	1.000
American League totals (3 years)			66	129	22	27	4	1	0	8	.209	14	20	2	76	0	2	.974
National League totals (1 year)			43	89	10	26	9	1	0	13	.292	5	8	1	33	3	0	1.000
Major League totals (4 years)			109	218	32	53	13	2	0	21	.243	19	28	3	109	3	2	.982

CHAMPIONSHIP SERIES RECORD

Year	Team (League)	Pos.	G	AB	R	H	2B	3B	HR	RBI	Avg.	BB	SO	SB	PO	A	E	Avg.
											BATTING				FIELDING			
1993—	Toronto (A.L.)						Did not play.											

WORLD SERIES RECORD

NOTES: Member of World Series championship team (1993).

Year	Team (League)	Pos.	G	AB	R	H	2B	3B	HR	RBI	Avg.	BB	SO	SB	PO	A	E	Avg.
											BATTING				FIELDING			
1993—	Toronto (A.L.)............	PH	2	2	1	1	0	0	0	0	.500	0	0	0	...	...	...	...

BYRD, PAUL   P   PHILLIES

PERSONAL: Born December 3, 1970, in Louisville, Ky. ... 6-1/184. ... Throws right, bats right. ... Full name: Paul Gregory Byrd.

HIGH SCHOOL: St. Xavier (Louisville, Ky.).

COLLEGE: Louisiana State.

TRANSACTIONS/CAREER NOTES: Selected by Cincinnati Reds organization in 13th round of free-agent draft (June 1, 1988); did not sign. ... Selected by Cleveland Indians organization in fourth round of free-agent draft (June 3, 1991). ... On disabled list (August 12, 1992-remainder of season). ... On disabled list (May 23-July 24, 1993). ... Traded by Indians organization with P Dave Mlicki, P Jerry DiPoto and a player to be named later to New York Mets organization for OF Jeromy Burnitz and P Joe Roa (November 18, 1994); Mets acquired 2B Jesus Azuaje to complete deal (December 6, 1994). ... On Norfolk disabled list (June 1-19, 1995). ... On New York disabled list (March 22-June 9, 1996); included rehabilitation assignment to Norfolk (May 27-June 9). ... Traded by Mets with a player to be named later to Atlanta Braves for P Greg McMichael (November 25, 1996); Braves acquired P Andy Zwirchitz to complete deal (May 25, 1997). ... On Richmond disabled list (June 3-July 2, 1998). ... Claimed on waivers by Philadelphia Phillies (August 14, 1998).

STATISTICAL NOTES: Led Carolina League with seven balks in 1991. ... Led N.L. with 17 hit batsmen in 1999. ... Tied for N.L. lead in errors by a pitcher with six in 1999.

Year	League	W	L	Pct.	ERA	G	GS	CG	ShO	Sv.	IP	H	R	ER	BB	SO
1991—	Kinston (Caro.)..................	4	3	.571	3.16	14	11	0	0	0	62 2/3	40	27	22	36	62
1992—	Canton/Akron (East.)..........	14	6	.700	3.01	24	24	4	0	0	152 1/3	122	68	51	75	118
1993—	Charlotte (I.L.)....................	7	4	.636	3.89	14	14	1	1	0	81	80	43	35	30	54
—	Canton/Akron (East.)..........	0	0	...	3.60	2	1	0	0	0	10	7	4	4	3	8

Year League	W	L	Pct.	ERA	G	GS	CG	ShO	Sv.	IP	H	R	ER	BB	SO
1994—Canton/Akron (East.)..........	5	9	.357	3.81	21	20	4	1	0	139 1/3	135	70	59	52	106
—Charlotte (FSL)..................	2	2	.500	3.93	9	4	0	0	1	36 2/3	33	19	16	11	15
1995—Norfolk (I.L.)■	3	5	.375	2.79	22	10	1	0	6	87	71	29	27	21	61
—New York (N.L.)	2	0	1.000	2.05	17	0	0	0	0	22	18	6	5	7	26
1996—New York (N.L.)..............	1	2	.333	4.24	38	0	0	0	0	46 2/3	48	22	22	21	31
—Norfolk (I.L.)	2	0	1.000	3.52	5	0	0	0	1	7 2/3	4	3	3	4	8
1997—Atlanta (N.L.)■...............	4	4	.500	5.26	31	4	0	0	0	53	47	34	31	28	37
—Richmond (I.L.).................	2	1	.667	3.18	3	3	0	0	0	17	14	6	6	1	14
1998—Richmond (I.L.)..............	5	5	.500	3.69	17	17	2	0	0	102 1/3	92	44	42	36	84
—Atlanta (N.L.)..................	0	0	...	13.50	1	0	0	0	0	2	4	3	3	1	1
—Philadelphia (N.L.)■	5	2	.714	2.29	8	8	2	1	0	55	41	16	14	17	38
1999—Philadelphia (N.L.).............	15	11	.577	4.60	32	32	1	0	0	199 2/3	205	119	102	70	106
Major League totals (5 years).......	**27**	**19**	**.587**	**4.21**	**127**	**44**	**3**	**1**	**0**	**378 1/3**	**363**	**200**	**177**	**144**	**239**

ALL-STAR GAME RECORD

Year League	W	L	Pct.	ERA	GS	CG	ShO	Sv.	IP	H	R	ER	BB	SO
1999— National					Selected, did not play.									

BYRDAK, TIM — P — ROYALS

PERSONAL: Born October 31, 1973, in Oak Lawn, Ill. ... 5-11/180. ... Throws left, bats left. ... Full name: Timothy Christopher Byrdak. ... Name pronounced BIRD-ek.

HIGH SCHOOL: Oak Forest (Ill.).

JUNIOR COLLEGE: South Suburban College (Ill.).

COLLEGE: Rice.

TRANSACTIONS/CAREER NOTES: Selected by Kansas City Royals organization in fifth round of free-agent draft (June 2, 1994). ... On disabled list (June 27-August 19, 1996). ... On Omaha disabled list (April 3-June 9, 1997).

Year League	W	L	Pct.	ERA	G	GS	CG	ShO	Sv.	IP	H	R	ER	BB	SO
1994—Eugene (N.W.)	4	5	.444	3.07	15	15	0	0	0	73 1/3	60	33	25	20	77
1995—Wilmington (Caro.).............	11	5	.688	2.16	27	26	0	0	0	166 1/3	118	46	40	45	127
1996—Wichita (Texas)	5	7	.417	6.91	15	15	0	0	0	84 2/3	112	73	65	44	47
1997—Wilmington (Caro.).............	4	3	.571	3.51	22	2	0	0	3	41	34	17	16	12	47
1998—Wichita (Texas)	3	5	.375	4.15	34	0	0	0	2	52	58	29	24	28	37
—Omaha (PCL).....................	2	1	.667	2.45	26	0	0	0	1	36 2/3	31	13	10	20	32
—Kansas City (A.L.)	0	0	...	5.40	3	0	0	0	0	1 2/3	5	1	1	0	1
1999—Omaha (PCL)....................	3	1	.750	1.81	33	0	0	0	4	49 2/3	39	19	10	28	51
—Kansas City (A.L.)	0	3	.000	7.66	33	0	0	0	1	24 2/3	32	24	21	20	17
Major League totals (2 years).......	**0**	**3**	**.000**	**7.52**	**36**	**0**	**0**	**0**	**1**	**26 1/3**	**37**	**25**	**22**	**20**	**18**

CABRERA, JOLBERT — IF/OF — INDIANS

PERSONAL: Born December 8, 1972, in Cartagena, Colombia. ... 6-0/177. ... Bats right, throws right. ... Full name: Jolbert Alexis Cabrera. ... Brother of Orlando Cabrera, shortstop, Montreal Expos.

HIGH SCHOOL: Confenalco (Cartagena, Colombia).

TRANSACTIONS/CAREER NOTES: Signed as non-drafted free agent by Montreal Expos organization (July 3, 1990). ... Granted free agency (October 17, 1997). ... Signed by Cleveland Indians organization (January 19, 1998).

STATISTICAL NOTES: Led International League in caught stealing with 15 in 1998.

Year Team (League)	Pos.	G	AB	R	H	2B	3B	HR	RBI	Avg.	BB	SO	SB	PO	A	E	Avg.
							BATTING								FIELDING		
1990—Dom. Expos (DSL)	SS	29	115	31	36	3	2	0	12	.313	14	10	14	...	...	...	...
1991—Sumter (SAL)	SS	101	324	33	66	4	0	1	20	.204	19	62	10	141	256	28	.934
1992—Albany (SAL)	SS	118	377	44	86	9	2	0	23	.228	34	77	22	169	277	35	.927
1993—Burlington (Midw.)	SS	128	507	62	129	24	2	0	38	.254	39	93	31	•173	300	*36	.929
1994—W.P. Beach (FSL)........	SS	83	266	32	54	4	0	0	13	.203	14	48	7	136	228	26	.933
—San Bern. (Calif.)	SS	30	109	14	27	5	1	0	11	.248	14	24	2	51	82	7	.950
—Harrisburg (East.)......	SS	3	2	0	0	0	0	0	0	.000	0	1	0	0	1	0	1.000
1995—W.P. Beach (FSL).....	SS-2B-3B	103	357	62	102	23	2	1	25	.286	38	61	19	148	294	29	.938
—Harrisburg (East.)......	SS	9	35	4	10	2	0	0	1	.286	1	3	3	11	18	2	.935
1996—Harrisburg (East.).....	SS-OF-3B	107	354	40	85	18	2	3	29	.240	23	63	10	179	306	25	.951
1997—Harrisburg (East.).....	2B-SS-OF	48	171	28	43	9	0	2	11	.251	28	28	5	98	76	9	.951
—Ottawa (I.L.)..............3B-2B-SS-OF	68	191	28	54	10	4	0	12	.283	11	31	15	51	127	7	.962	
1998—Cleveland (A.L.)■........	SS	1	2	0	0	0	0	0	0	.000	0	1	0	2	2	0	1.000
—Buffalo (I.L.)...........	SS-OF-2B	129	494	94	157	24	1	10	45	.318	68	71	25	235	352	27	.956
1999—Cleveland (A.L.)........	OF-2B-DH	30	37	6	7	1	0	0	0	.189	1	8	3	26	4	1	.968
—Buffalo (I.L.)...............OF-SS-2B-3B	71	279	44	74	13	4	0	27	.265	26	43	20	153	82	6	.975	
Major League totals (2 years)		**31**	**39**	**6**	**7**	**1**	**0**	**0**	**0**	**.179**	**1**	**9**	**3**	**28**	**6**	**1**	**.971**

CABRERA, JOSE — P — ASTROS

PERSONAL: Born March 24, 1972, in Santiago, Dominican Republic. ... 6-0/180. ... Throws right, bats right. ... Full name: Jose Alberto Cabrera.

TRANSACTIONS/CAREER NOTES: Signed as non-drafted free agent by Cleveland Indians organization (October 12, 1990). ... On disabled list (May 11-28, 1993). ... On Canton disabled list (April 25-May 24, 1995). ... On Buffalo disabled list (April 4-13 and 17-25, 1997). ... Traded by Indians to Houston Astros for P Alvin Morman (May 10, 1997). ... On Houston disabled list (April 5, 1998-remainder of season); included rehabilitation assignment to New Orleans (July 4-20).

Year	League	W	L	Pct.	ERA	G	GS	CG	ShO	Sv.	IP	H	R	ER	BB	SO
1991—Dom. Indians (DSL)		6	4	.600	3.07	16	12	1	0	0	73 1/3	64	32	25	17	40
1992—Burlington (Appl.)		•8	3	.727	1.75	13	13	1	0	0	92 1/3	74	27	18	18	79
1993—Columbus (SAL)		11	6	.647	2.67	26	26	1	0	0	155 1/3	122	54	46	53	105
1994—Kinston (Caro.)		4	13	.235	4.44	24	24	0	0	0	133 2/3	134	84	66	43	110
1995—Canton/Akron (East.)		1	1	.500	1.02	4	3	0	0	0	17 2/3	7	2	2	8	19
—Bakersfield (Calif.)		2	2	.500	3.92	7	7	0	0	0	41 1/3	40	25	18	21	52
1996—Canton/Akron (East.)		4	3	.571	5.63	15	7	0	0	0	62 1/3	78	45	39	17	40
1997—Buffalo (A.A.)		3	0	1.000	1.20	5	0	0	0	0	15	8	2	2	7	11
—New Orleans (A.A.)■		2	2	.500	2.54	31	0	0	0	0	46	31	13	13	13	48
—Houston (N.L.)		0	0	...	1.17	12	0	0	0	0	15 1/3	6	2	2	6	18
1998—Houston (N.L.)		0	0	...	8.31	3	0	0	0	0	4 1/3	7	4	4	1	1
—New Orleans (PCL)		0	0	...	5.40	5	0	0	0	1	5	2	3	3	1	6
1999—New Orleans (PCL)		3	1	.750	2.82	31	0	0	0	7	51	34	18	16	12	41
—Houston (N.L.)		4	0	1.000	2.15	26	0	0	0	0	29 1/3	21	7	7	9	28
Major League totals (3 years)......		4	0	1.000	2.39	41	0	0	0	0	49	34	13	13	16	47

DIVISION SERIES RECORD

Year	League	W	L	Pct.	ERA	G	GS	CG	ShO	Sv.	IP	H	R	ER	BB	SO
1999—Houston (N.L.)		0	0	...	0.00	1	0	0	0	0	2	2	0	0	0	6

CABRERA, ORLANDO — SS — EXPOS

C

PERSONAL: Born November 2, 1974, in Cartagena, Columbia. ... 5-10/175. ... Bats right, throws right. ... Full name: Orlando Luis Cabrera. ... Brother of Jolbert Cabrera, infielder/outfielder, Cleveland Indians.

TRANSACTIONS/CAREER NOTES: Signed as non-drafted free agent by Montreal Expos organization (June 1, 1993). ... On disabled list (August 9, 1999-remainder of season).

Year	Team (League)	Pos.	G	AB	R	H	2B	3B	HR	RBI	Avg.	BB	SO	SB	PO	A	E	Avg.
1993—Dom. Expos (DSL)		IF	38	122	24	42	6	1	1	17	.344	18	11	14	86	76	3	.982
1994—GC Expos (GCL)		2B-SS-OF	22	73	13	23	4	1	0	11	.315	5	8	6	22	42	4	.941
1995—Vermont (NY-P)		2B-SS	65	248	37	70	12	5	3	33	.282	16	28	15	135	189	17	.950
1996—Delmarva (SAL)		SS-2B	134	512	86	129	28	4	14	65	.252	54	63	51	205	344	27	.953
1997—W.P. Beach (FSL)........		SS-DH-2B	69	279	56	77	19	2	5	26	.276	27	33	32	92	162	20	.927
—Harrisburg (East.)........		SS-2B	35	133	34	41	13	2	5	20	.308	15	18	7	57	83	5	.966
—Ottawa (I.L.)............		SS-2B	31	122	17	32	5	2	2	14	.262	7	16	8	45	94	3	.979
—Montreal (N.L.)..........		SS-2B	16	18	4	4	0	0	0	2	.222	1	3	1	11	15	1	.963
1998—Ottawa (I.L.)............		SS-2B	66	272	31	63	9	4	0	26	.232	28	27	19	122	190	12	.963
—Montreal (N.L.)..........		SS-2B	79	261	44	73	16	5	3	22	.280	18	27	6	122	196	7	.978
1999—Montreal (N.L.)..........		SS	104	382	48	97	23	5	8	39	.254	18	38	2	186	289	10	.979
Major League totals (3 years)			199	661	96	174	39	10	11	63	.263	37	68	9	319	500	18	.978

CAIRO, MIGUEL — 2B — DEVIL RAYS

PERSONAL: Born May 4, 1974, in Anaco, Venezuela. ... 6-1/160. ... Bats right, throws right. ... Full name: Miguel Jesus Cairo.

HIGH SCHOOL: Escuela Anaco (Anaco, Venezuela).

TRANSACTIONS/CAREER NOTES: Signed as non-drafted free agent by Los Angeles Dodgers organization (September 20, 1990). ... Traded by Dodgers with 3B Willis Otanez to Seattle Mariners for 3B Mike Blowers (November 29, 1995). ... Traded by Mariners with P Bill Risley to Toronto Blue Jays for P Edwin Hurtado and P Paul Menhart (December 18, 1995). ... Traded by Blue Jays to Chicago Cubs for P Jason Stevenson (November 20, 1996). ... Selected by Tampa Bay Devil Rays in first round (eighth pick overall) of expansion draft (November 18, 1997). ... On Tampa Bay disabled list (April 24-May 17 and July 26-August 11, 1999); included rehabilitation assignments to Orlando (May 14-17) and St. Petersburg (August 7-11).

STATISTICAL NOTES: Led California League in caught stealing with 23 in 1994. ... Led International League second basemen with 64 double plays in 1996. ... Led American Association in caught stealing with 15 in 1997.

MISCELLANEOUS: Holds Tampa Bay Devil Rays all-time record for most stolen bases (41).

Year	Team (League)	Pos.	G	AB	R	H	2B	3B	HR	RBI	Avg.	BB	SO	SB	PO	A	E	Avg.
1991—Dom. Dodgers (DSL) .		IF	57	203	16	45	5	1	0	17	.222	0	17	8	...	...	...	...
1992—Vero Beach (FSL)		2B-3B	36	125	7	28	0	0	0	7	.224	11	12	5	69	76	10	.935
—GC Dodgers (GCL)		SS-3B	21	76	10	23	5	2	0	9	.303	2	6	1	26	56	4	.953
1993—Vero Beach (FSL)		2B-SS-3B	90	346	50	109	10	1	1	23	.315	28	22	23	172	244	18	.959
1994—Bakersfield (Calif.)		2B-SS	133	533	76	155	23	4	2	48	.291	34	37	44	268	376	28	.958
1995—San Antonio (Texas) ...		2B-SS-DH	107	435	53	121	20	1	1	41	.278	26	31	33	210	316	23	.958
1996—Syracuse (I.L.)■		2B-3B-SS	120	465	71	129	14	4	3	48	.277	26	44	27	193	295	23	.955
—Toronto (A.L.)............		2B	9	27	5	6	2	0	0	1	.222	2	9	0	22	18	0	1.000
1997—Iowa (A.A.)■..............		2B-SS	135	*569	82	159	35	4	5	46	.279	24	54	*40	248	386	20	.969
—Chicago (N.L.)...........		2B-SS	16	29	7	7	1	0	0	1	.241	2	3	0	16	18	0	1.000
1998—Tampa Bay (A.L.)■.....		2B-DH	150	515	49	138	26	5	5	46	.268	24	44	19	278	426	16	.978
1999—Tampa Bay (A.L.)....		2B-DH	120	465	61	137	15	5	3	36	.295	24	46	22	251	377	9	.986
—Orlando (Sou.)		2B	3	13	1	5	2	0	0	1	.385	0	1	0	2	7	0	1.000
—St. Petersburg (FSL) ..		2B	3	13	2	5	0	0	0	0	.385	1	2	1	8	15	1	.958
American League totals (3 years)			279	1007	115	281	43	10	8	83	.279	50	99	41	551	824	25	.982
National League totals (1 year)			16	29	7	7	1	0	0	1	.241	2	3	0	16	18	0	1.000
Major League totals (4 years)			295	1036	122	288	44	10	8	84	.278	52	102	41	567	842	25	.983

PERSONAL: Born May 13, 1975, in Memphis, Tenn. ... 6-2/190. ... Throws right, bats right. ... Full name: Michael C. Callaway.
HIGH SCHOOL: Germantown (Tenn.).
COLLEGE: Mississippi.
TRANSACTIONS/CAREER NOTES: Selected by Tampa Bay Devil Rays organization in seventh round of free-agent draft (June 4, 1996). ... Loaned to Seattle Mariners organization (April 2-July 21, 1998). ... On Tampa Bay disabled list (June 19-July 6, 1999).
MISCELLANEOUS: Appeared in one game as pinch runner (1999).

Year League	W	L	Pct.	ERA	G	GS	CG	ShO	Sv.	IP	H	R	ER	BB	SO
1996—Butte (Pio.)	6	2	.750	3.71	16	11	0	0	0	63	70	37	26	25	57
1997—St. Petersburg (FSL)	11	7	.611	3.22	28	•28	3	0	0	170²/₃	162	74	61	39	109
1998—Orlando (Sou.)■	5	6	.455	4.42	18	17	0	0	0	89²/₃	103	56	44	44	57
—Durham (I.L.)■	5	3	.625	4.53	9	8	0	0	0	47²/₃	49	27	24	17	19
1999—Orlando (Sou.)	1	1	.500	4.50	2	2	0	0	0	10	15	6	5	2	7
—Durham (I.L.)	7	1	.875	4.20	15	15	0	0	0	81¹/₃	86	45	38	28	56
—Tampa Bay (A.L.)	1	2	.333	7.45	5	4	0	0	0	19¹/₃	30	20	16	14	11
Major League totals (1 year)	1	2	.333	7.45	5	4	0	0	0	19¹/₃	30	20	16	14	11

PERSONAL: Born January 8, 1973, in La Grange, Ga. ... 6-2/190. ... Bats right, throws right. ... Full name: Michael Terrance Cameron.
HIGH SCHOOL: La Grange (Ga.).
TRANSACTIONS/CAREER NOTES: Selected by Chicago White Sox organization in 18th round of free-agent draft (June 3, 1991). ... Traded by White Sox to Cincinnati Reds for 1B/3B Paul Konerko (November 11, 1998).
STATISTICAL NOTES: Tied for Carolina League lead in double plays by outfielder with four in 1994. ... Led Southern League with .600 slugging percentage and tied for lead in caught stealing with 15 in 1996. ... Led Southern League outfielders with 264 total chances in 1996.

Year Team (League)	Pos.	G	AB	R	H	2B	3B	HR	RBI	Avg.	BB	SO	SB	PO	A	E	Avg.
1991—GC White Sox (GCL)	OF	44	136	20	30	3	0	0	11	.221	17	29	13	55	3	3	.951
1992—Utica (NY-P)	OF	26	87	15	24	1	4	2	12	.276	11	26	3	60	3	0	1.000
—South Bend (Midw.)	OF	35	114	19	26	8	1	1	9	.228	10	37	2	67	0	3	.957
1993—South Bend (Midw.)	OF	122	411	52	98	14	5	0	30	.238	27	101	19	248	13	4	.985
1994—Prince Will. (Caro.)	OF	131	468	86	116	15	*17	6	48	.248	60	101	22	275	10	6	.979
1995—Birmingham (Sou.)	OF	107	350	64	87	20	5	11	60	.249	54	104	21	250	7	4	.985
—Chicago (A.L.)	OF	28	38	4	7	2	0	1	2	.184	3	15	0	33	1	0	1.000
1996—Birmingham (Sou.)	OF-DH	123	473	*120	142	34	12	28	77	.300	71	117	*39	*249	8	7	.973
—Chicago (A.L.)	OF-DH	11	11	1	1	0	0	0	0	.091	1	3	0	7	0	0	1.000
1997—Nashville (A.A.)	OF-DH	30	120	21	33	7	3	6	17	.275	18	31	4	63	3	1	.985
—Chicago (A.L.)	OF-DH	116	379	63	98	18	3	14	55	.259	55	105	23	334	5	5	.985
1998—Chicago (A.L.)	OF	141	396	53	83	16	5	8	43	.210	37	101	27	313	6	4	.988
1999—Cincinnati (N.L.)■	OF	146	542	93	139	34	9	21	66	.256	80	145	38	372	7	8	.979
American League totals (4 years)		296	824	121	189	36	8	23	100	.229	96	224	50	687	12	9	.987
National League totals (1 year)		146	542	93	139	34	9	21	66	.256	80	145	38	372	7	8	.979
Major League totals (5 years)		442	1366	214	328	70	17	44	166	.240	176	369	88	1059	19	17	.984

PERSONAL: Born April 21, 1963, in Hanford, Calif. ... 6-0/200. ... Bats both, throws right. ... Full name: Kenneth Gene Caminiti. ... Name pronounced CAM-uh-NET-ee.
HIGH SCHOOL: Leigh (San Jose, Calif.).
COLLEGE: San Jose State.
TRANSACTIONS/CAREER NOTES: Selected by Houston Astros organization in third round of free-agent draft (June 4, 1984). ... On disabled list (April 19-May 11, 1992). ... Traded by Astros with OF Steve Finley, SS Andujar Cedeno, 1B Robert Petagine, P Brian Williams and a player to be named later to San Diego Padres for OF Phil Plantier, OF Derek Bell, P Pedro Martinez, P Doug Brocail, IF Craig Shipley and SS Ricky Gutierrez (December 28, 1994); Padres acquired P Sean Fesh to complete deal (May 1, 1995). ... On disabled list (May 12-27, 1997; and May 2-23, 1998). ... Granted free agency (October 23, 1998). ... Signed by Astros (November 17, 1998). ... On Houston disabled list (May 22-August 16, 1999); included rehabilitation assignment to New Orleans (August 9-16).
RECORDS: Holds major league record for most consecutive games with switch-hit home runs—2 (September 16-17, 1995). ... Holds major league single-season record for most games with switch-hit home runs—4 (1996). ... Shares major league single-season record for most runs batted in by switch hitter—130 (1996). ... Holds N.L. career record for most games with switch-hit home runs—10. ... Holds N.L. record for most home runs by switch hitter in two consecutive seasons—66 (1995-96 and 1996-97).
HONORS: Named third baseman on THE SPORTING NEWS college All-America team (1984). ... Won N.L. Gold Glove at third base (1995-97). ... Named third baseman on THE SPORTING NEWS N.L. All-Star team (1996). ... Named third baseman on THE SPORTING NEWS N.L. Silver Slugger team (1996). ... Named N.L. Most Valuable Player by Baseball Writers' Association of America (1996).
STATISTICAL NOTES: Led Southern League third basemen with 34 double plays in 1986. ... Led Pacific Coast League third basemen with 382 total chances and 25 double plays in 1988. ... Switch-hit home runs in one game ten times (July 3, 1994; September 16, September 17 and September 19, 1995; August 1, August 21 and September 11, 1996; July 12, 1998; and August 20, 1999). ... Led N.L. third basemen with 424 total chances and 28 double plays in 1995. ... Tied for N.L. lead with 10 sacrifice flies in 1996. ... Hit three home runs in one game (July 12, 1998). ... Career major league grand slams: 5.

Year Team (League)	Pos.	G	AB	R	H	2B	3B	HR	RBI	Avg.	BB	SO	SB	PO	A	E	Avg.
1985—Osceola (FSL)	3B	126	468	83	133	26	9	4	73	.284	51	54	14	53	193	20	.925
1986—Columbus (Sou.)	3B	137	513	82	154	29	3	12	81	.300	56	79	5	105	*299	33	.924
1987—Columbus (Sou.)	3B	95	375	66	122	25	2	15	69	.325	25	58	11	55	205	21	.925
—Houston (N.L.)	3B	63	203	10	50	7	1	3	23	.246	12	44	0	50	98	8	.949
1988—Tucson (PCL)	3B	109	416	54	113	24	7	5	66	.272	29	54	13	*105	*250	27	.929
—Houston (N.L.)	3B	30	83	5	15	2	0	1	7	.181	5	18	0	12	43	3	.948

						BATTING									FIELDING		
Year Team (League)	Pos.	G	AB	R	H	2B	3B	HR	RBI	Avg.	BB	SO	SB	PO	A	E	Avg.
1989— Houston (N.L.)	3B	161	585	71	149	31	3	10	72	.255	51	93	4	126	335	22	.954
1990— Houston (N.L.)	3B	153	541	52	131	20	2	4	51	.242	48	97	9	118	243	21	.945
1991— Houston (N.L.)	3B	152	574	65	145	30	3	13	80	.253	46	85	4	129	293	23	.948
1992— Houston (N.L.)	3B	135	506	68	149	31	2	13	62	.294	44	68	10	102	210	11	.966
1993— Houston (N.L.)	3B	143	543	75	142	31	0	13	75	.262	49	88	8	123	264	24	.942
1994— Houston (N.L.)	3B	111	406	63	115	28	2	18	75	.283	43	71	4	79	200	9	.969
1995— San Diego (N.L.)■ ...	3B	143	526	74	159	33	0	26	94	.302	69	94	12	102	*295	*27	.936
1996— San Diego (N.L.)	3B	146	546	109	178	37	2	40	130	.326	78	99	11	103	310	20	.954
1997— San Diego (N.L.)	3B	137	486	92	141	28	0	26	90	.290	80	118	11	90	291	24	.941
1998— San Diego (N.L.)	3B	131	452	87	114	29	0	29	82	.252	71	108	6	77	207	*21	.931
1999— Houston (N.L.)■ ...	3B	78	273	45	78	11	1	13	56	.286	46	58	6	52	139	14	.932
— New Orleans (PCL).....	3B	6	20	6	7	4	0	0	3	.350	2	1	0	2	5	3	.700
Major League totals (13 years)		1583	5724	816	1566	318	16	209	897	.274	642	1041	85	1163	2928	227	.947

DIVISION SERIES RECORD

RECORDS: Holds N.L. career records for highest slugging average (20 or more at-bats)—.756; home runs—6; and runs batted in—11. ... Shares N.L. career record for most extra-base hits—6. ... Shares single-game record for most home runs—2 (October 5, 1996). ... Shares N.L. single-game record for most at-bats—6 (October 8, 1999).

						BATTING									FIELDING		
Year Team (League)	Pos.	G	AB	R	H	2B	3B	HR	RBI	Avg.	BB	SO	SB	PO	A	E	Avg.
1996— San Diego (N.L.)	3B	3	10	3	3	0	0	3	3	.300	3	5	0	0	5	3	.625
1998— San Diego (N.L.)	3B	4	14	2	2	0	0	0	0	.143	1	3	0	2	5	1	.875
1999— Houston (N.L.)	3B	4	17	3	8	0	0	3	8	.471	2	1	0	1	10	0	1.000
Division series totals (3 years)		11	41	8	13	0	0	6	11	.317	6	9	0	3	20	4	.852

CHAMPIONSHIP SERIES RECORD

RECORDS: Shares single-game record for most bases on balls received—4 (October 8, 1998).

						BATTING									FIELDING		
Year Team (League)	Pos.	G	AB	R	H	2B	3B	HR	RBI	Avg.	BB	SO	SB	PO	A	E	Avg.
1998— San Diego (N.L.)	3B	6	22	3	6	0	0	2	4	.273	5	4	0	5	10	0	1.000

WORLD SERIES RECORD

						BATTING									FIELDING		
Year Team (League)	Pos.	G	AB	R	H	2B	3B	HR	RBI	Avg.	BB	SO	SB	PO	A	E	Avg.
1998— San Diego (N.L.)	3B	4	14	1	2	1	0	0	1	.143	2	7	0	2	2	2	.667

ALL-STAR GAME RECORD

				BATTING									FIELDING		
Year League	Pos.	AB	R	H	2B	3B	HR	RBI	Avg.	BB	SO	SB	PO	A	E	Avg.
1994— National	3B	1	0	0	0	0	0	0	.000	0	0	0	0	0	0	...
1996— National	3B	2	1	1	0	0	1	1	.500	0	1	0	0	0	1	.000
1997— National	3B	2	0	0	0	0	0	0	.000	0	0	0	0	0	0	...
All-Star Game totals (3 years)		5	1	1	0	0	1	1	.200	0	1	0	0	0	1	.000

CAMMACK, ERIC — P — METS

PERSONAL: Born August 14, 1975, in Nederland, Texas. ... 6-1/180. ... Throws right, bats right. ... Full name: Eric Wade Cammack.
HIGH SCHOOL: Nederland (Texas).
COLLEGE: Lamar.
TRANSACTIONS/CAREER NOTES: Selected by New York Mets organization in 13th round of free-agent draft (June 3, 1997).

Year League	W	L	Pct.	ERA	G	GS	CG	ShO	Sv.	IP	H	R	ER	BB	SO
1997— Pittsfield (NY-P)	0	1	.000	0.86	23	0	0	0	8	31 1/3	9	4	3	14	32
1998— Capital City (SAL)..............	4	0	1.000	2.81	25	0	0	0	8	32	17	13	10	13	49
— St. Lucie (FSL)	3	2	.600	2.02	29	0	0	0	11	35 2/3	22	12	8	14	53
1999— Binghamton (East.)	4	2	.667	2.38	45	0	0	0	15	56 2/3	28	17	15	38	83
— Norfolk (I.L.)	0	0	...	3.12	9	0	0	0	4	8 2/3	7	3	3	1	17

CAMP, JARED — P — MARLINS

PERSONAL: Born May 4, 1975, in Huntington, W.Va. ... 6-2/195. ... Throws right, bats right. ... Full name: Jared Andrew Camp.
HIGH SCHOOL: Huntington East (Huntington, W.Va.).
JUNIOR COLLEGE: Indian River (Fla.).
TRANSACTIONS/CAREER NOTES: Selected by Milwaukee Brewers organization in fifth-round of free-agent draft (June 1, 1995). ... Traded by Brewers to Cleveland Indians (June 9, 1996), completing deal in which Indians traded C Jesse Levis to Brewers for P Scott Nate and a player to be named later (April 4, 1996). ... Selected by Minnesota Twins from Indians organization in Rule 5 major league draft (December 13, 1999). ... Traded by Twins to Florida Marlins for P Johan Santana and cash (December 13, 1999).

Year League	W	L	Pct.	ERA	G	GS	CG	ShO	Sv.	IP	H	R	ER	BB	SO
1995— Helena (Pio.)	1	4	.200	8.65	8	8	0	0	0	34 1/3	44	39	33	20	26
1996— Beloit (Midw.)...................	3	5	.375	5.43	11	11	0	0	0	53	56	42	32	39	47
— Watertown (NY-P)■	10	2	.833	1.69	15	•15	1	1	0	95 2/3	68	29	18	30	99
1997— Kinston (Caro.)	5	4	.556	3.79	13	12	0	0	0	73 2/3	57	36	31	20	64
— Akron (East.)	2	8	.200	6.19	12	12	1	0	0	64	79	49	44	26	39
1998— Akron (East.)	6	2	.750	3.78	18	16	0	0	0	85 2/3	84	37	36	31	42
1999— Kinston (Caro.)	3	2	.600	1.98	18	6	1	0	4	54 2/3	48	15	12	16	59
— Akron (East.)	1	2	.333	6.50	17	0	0	0	7	18	22	17	13	16	18
— Buffalo (I.L.)	0	0	...	0.84	10	0	0	0	1	10 2/3	4	2	1	13	14

CANCEL, ROBINSON   C   BREWERS

PERSONAL: Born May 4, 1976, in Lajas, Puerto Rico. ... 6-0/195. ... Bats right, throws right. ... Full name: Robinson Castro Cancel.
HIGH SCHOOL: Lajas (Puerto Rico).
TRANSACTIONS/CAREER NOTES: Selected by Milwaukee Brewers organization in 16th round of free-agent draft (June 2, 1994).

								BATTING						FIELDING			
Year	Team (League)	Pos.	G	AB	R	H	2B	3B	HR	RBI	Avg.	BB	SO	SB	PO	A	E	Avg.
1994—	Ariz. Brewers (Ariz.) ...	C	29	70	6	12	0	0	0	8	.171	9	19	0	98	13	5	.957
1995—	Helena (Pio.)	C	46	154	18	37	9	0	0	24	.240	9	20	8	349	53	9	.978
1996—	Beloit (Midw.)............	C	72	218	26	48	3	1	1	29	.220	14	31	13	483	81	12	.979
1997—	Beloit (Midw.)............	C	17	50	9	15	3	0	0	4	.300	7	9	0	111	15	1	.992
	— Stockton (Calif.)	C	64	211	25	59	11	0	1	16	.280	13	40	9	434	72	10	.981
1998—	Stockton (Calif.)	C	11	32	3	6	1	0	0	2	.188	4	8	2	67	16	1	.988
	— El Paso (Texas).............	C-1B-3B	58	158	17	51	10	0	1	30	.323	22	32	2	286	48	8	.977
1999—	Huntsville (Sou.)	C-DH-3B-OF	66	223	35	56	10	1	5	32	.251	23	38	8	299	52	9	.975
	— Louisville (I.L.).............	C	39	117	22	43	8	0	5	28	.368	14	28	6	210	25	2	.992
	— Milwaukee (N.L.)	C	15	44	5	8	2	0	0	5	.182	2	12	0	84	12	2	.980
Major League totals (1 year)			**15**	**44**	**5**	**8**	**2**	**0**	**0**	**5**	**.182**	**2**	**12**	**0**	**84**	**12**	**2**	**.980**

CANDIOTTI, TOM   P   ANGELS

C

PERSONAL: Born August 31, 1957, in Walnut Creek, Calif. ... 6-2/221. ... Throws right, bats right. ... Full name: Thomas Caesar Candiotti. ... Name pronounced KAN-dee-AH-tee.
HIGH SCHOOL: Concord (Calif.).
COLLEGE: St. Mary's, Calif. (degree in business administration, 1979).
TRANSACTIONS/CAREER NOTES: Signed as non-drafted free agent by Victoria, independent (July 17, 1979). ... Released by Victoria (January 4, 1980). ... Signed by Fort Myers, Kansas City Royals organization (January 5, 1980). ... On Jacksonville disabled list (June 7-26, 1980). ... Selected by Vancouver, Milwaukee Brewers organization, from Royals organization in Rule 5 minor league draft (December 9, 1980). ... On disabled list (April 10-May 12, 1981; and April 13, 1982-entire season). ... On Vancouver disabled list (May 30-June 15, 1984). ... On Milwaukee disabled list (August 2-September 1, 1984); included rehabilitation assignment to Beloit (August 24-31). ... Granted free agency (October 15, 1985). ... Signed by Cleveland Indians (December 12, 1985). ... On disabled list (August 4-19, 1988; July 2-17, 1989; and May 7-22, 1990). ... Traded by Indians with OF Turner Ward to Toronto Blue Jays for P Denis Boucher, OF Glenallen Hill, OF Mark Whiten and a player to be named later (June 27, 1991); Indians acquired cash to complete deal (October 15, 1991). ... Granted free agency (November 7, 1991). ... Signed by Los Angeles Dodgers (December 3, 1991). ... On disabled list (August 9-24, 1992). ... Granted free agency (November 3, 1995). ... Re-signed by Dodgers (December 15, 1995). ... On Los Angeles disabled list (July 20-August 13, 1996); included rehabilitation assignment to San Bernardino (August 7-13). ... Granted free agency (October 28, 1997). ... Signed by Oakland Athletics (December 9, 1997). ... Released by Athletics (June 16, 1999). ... Signed by Indians (June 29, 1999). ... Released by Indians (August 2, 1999). ... Signed by Anaheim Angels organization (January 24, 2000).
RECORDS: Shares modern N.L. record for most hit batsmen in nine-inning game—4 (September 13, 1997). ... Shares major league record for most hit batsmen in one inning—3 (September 13, 1997, first inning). ... Shares major league single-season record for fewest games lost for leader—15 (1992).
STATISTICAL NOTES: Pitched 2-0 one-hit, complete-game victory against New York (August 3, 1987).

Year League	W	L	Pct.	ERA	G	GS	CG	ShO	Sv.	IP	H	R	ER	BB	SO
1979— Victoria (N.W.)....................	5	1	.833	2.44	12	9	3	0	1	70	63	23	19	16	66
1980— Fort Myers (FSL)■	3	2	.600	2.25	7	5	3	0	0	44	32	16	11	9	31
— Jacksonville (Sou.)..........	7	8	.467	2.77	17	17	8	2	0	117	98	45	36	40	93
1981— El Paso (Texas)■	7	6	.538	2.80	21	14	6	1	0	119	137	51	37	27	68
1982— Vancouver (PCL)................						Did not play.									
1983— El Paso (Texas)................	1	0	1.000	2.92	7	0	0	0	2	24²/₃	23	10	8	7	18
— Vancouver (PCL)..............	6	4	.600	2.81	15	14	5	2	0	99¹/₃	87	35	31	16	61
— Milwaukee (A.L.).............	4	4	.500	3.23	10	8	2	1	0	55²/₃	62	21	20	16	21
1984— Vancouver (PCL)..............	8	4	.667	2.89	15	15	4	0	0	96²/₃	96	36	31	22	53
— Milwaukee (A.L.).............	2	2	.500	5.29	8	6	0	0	0	32¹/₃	38	21	19	10	23
— Beloit (Midw.)................	0	1	.000	2.70	2	2	0	0	0	10	12	5	3	5	12
1985— El Paso (Texas)................	1	0	1.000	2.76	4	4	2	1	0	29¹/₃	29	11	9	7	16
— Vancouver (PCL)..............	9	13	.409	3.94	24	24	7	0	0	150²/₃	178	83	66	36	97
1986— Cleveland (A.L.)■..............	16	12	.571	3.57	36	34	*17	3	0	252¹/₃	234	112	100	106	167
1987— Cleveland (A.L.)................	7	18	.280	4.78	32	32	7	2	0	201²/₃	193	132	107	93	111
1988— Cleveland (A.L.)................	14	8	.636	3.28	31	31	11	1	0	216²/₃	225	86	79	53	137
1989— Cleveland (A.L.)................	13	10	.565	3.10	31	31	4	0	0	206	188	80	71	55	124
1990— Cleveland (A.L.)................	15	11	.577	3.65	31	29	3	1	0	202	207	92	82	55	128
1991— Cleveland (A.L.)................	7	6	.538	2.24	15	15	3	0	0	108¹/₃	88	35	27	28	86
— Toronto (A.L.)■..............	6	7	.462	2.98	19	19	3	0	0	129²/₃	114	47	43	45	81
1992— Los Angeles (N.L.)■	11	•15	.423	3.00	32	30	6	2	0	203²/₃	177	78	68	63	152
1993— Los Angeles (N.L.)............	8	10	.444	3.12	33	32	2	0	0	213²/₃	192	86	74	71	155
1994— Los Angeles (N.L.)............	7	7	.500	4.12	23	22	5	0	0	153	149	77	70	54	102
1995— Los Angeles (N.L.)............	7	14	.333	3.50	30	30	1	1	0	190¹/₃	187	93	74	58	141
1996— Los Angeles (N.L.)............	9	11	.450	4.49	28	27	1	0	0	152¹/₃	172	91	76	43	79
— San Bernardino (Calif.).......	0	1	.000	5.00	2	2	0	0	0	9	11	6	5	4	10
1997— Los Angeles (N.L.)............	10	7	.588	3.60	41	18	0	0	0	135	128	60	54	40	89
1998— Oakland (A.L.)■................	11	•16	.407	4.84	33	33	3	0	0	201	222	124	108	63	98
1999— Oakland (A.L.)................	3	5	.375	6.35	11	11	0	0	0	56²/₃	67	46	40	23	30
— Cleveland (A.L.)■............	1	1	.500	11.05	7	2	0	0	0	14²/₃	19	18	18	7	11
A.L. totals (10 years).................	**99**	**100**	**.497**	**3.83**	**264**	**251**	**53**	**8**	**0**	**1677**	**1657**	**814**	**714**	**554**	**1017**
N.L. totals (6 years).....................	**52**	**64**	**.448**	**3.57**	**187**	**159**	**15**	**3**	**0**	**1048**	**1005**	**485**	**416**	**329**	**718**
Major League totals (16 years).....	**151**	**164**	**.479**	**3.73**	**451**	**410**	**68**	**11**	**0**	**2725**	**2662**	**1299**	**1130**	**883**	**1735**

DIVISION SERIES RECORD

Year League	W	L	Pct.	ERA	G	GS	CG	ShO	Sv.	IP	H	R	ER	BB	SO
1996— Los Angeles (N.L.)	0	0	...	0.00	1	0	0	0	0	2	0	0	0	0	1

CHAMPIONSHIP SERIES RECORD

Year League	W	L	Pct.	ERA	G	GS	CG	ShO	Sv.	IP	H	R	ER	BB	SO
1991— Toronto (A.L.)................	0	1	.000	8.22	2	2	0	0	0	7²/₃	17	9	7	2	5

CANGELOSI, JOHN   OF

PERSONAL: Born March 10, 1963, in Brooklyn, N.Y. ... 5-8/160. ... Bats both, throws left. ... Full name: John Anthony Cangelosi. ... Name pronounced KAN-juh-LO-see.

HIGH SCHOOL: Miami Springs (Fla.) Senior.

JUNIOR COLLEGE: Miami-Dade (North) Community College.

TRANSACTIONS/CAREER NOTES: Selected by Chicago White Sox organization in fourth round of free-agent draft (January 12, 1982). ... Loaned by White Sox organization with IF Manny Salinas to Mexico City Reds of Mexican League (March 4-June 1, 1985) as part of deal in which IF Nelson Barrera was purchased by White Sox. ... Traded by White Sox to Pittsburgh Pirates (March 30, 1987), completing deal in which Pirates traded P Jim Winn to White Sox for a player to be named later (March 27, 1987). ... On Pittsburgh disabled list (June 6-27, 1988); included rehabilitation assignment to Buffalo (June 20-27). ... Granted free agency (December 20, 1990). ... Signed by Vancouver, White Sox organization (April 7, 1991). ... Traded by White Sox to Milwaukee Brewers for SS Esteban Beltre (May 23, 1991). ... Granted free agency (October 15, 1991). ... Signed by Texas Rangers organization (November 7, 1991). ... Released by Rangers (July 19, 1992). ... Signed by Toledo, Detroit Tigers organization (July 28, 1992). ... Granted free agency (October 15, 1992). ... Re-signed by Toledo, Tigers organization (February 8, 1993). ... On disabled list (April 8-May 4, 1993). ... Granted free agency (October 15, 1993). ... Signed by New York Mets organization (November 17, 1993). ... On suspended list (June 15-18, 1994). ... Released by Mets (July 8, 1994). ... Signed by Tucson, Houston Astros organization (March 23, 1995). ... Granted free agency (November 2, 1995). ... Re-signed by Astros organization (December 7, 1995). ... On suspended list (August 16-19, 1996). ... Granted free agency (November 18, 1996). ... Signed by Florida Marlins (November 26, 1996). ... Granted free agency (September 29, 1998). ... Signed by White Sox organization (January 26, 1999). ... Released by White Sox (March 30, 1999). ... Signed by Colorado Rockies organization (September 1, 1999). ... Announced retirement (September 24, 1999).

STATISTICAL NOTES: Led Midwest League in caught stealing with 35 in 1983. ... Led International League in caught stealing with 18 in 1993.

Year Team (League)	Pos.	G	AB	R	H	2B	3B	HR	RBI	Avg.	BB	SO	SB	PO	A	E	Avg.
1982— Niagara Falls (NY-P)...	OF	•76	277	60	80	15	4	5	38	.289	•56	51	45	118	5	4	.969
1983— Appleton (Midw.).......	OF	128	439	87	124	12	4	1	48	.282	99	81	*87	262	10	6	.978
1984— Glens Falls (East.).....	OF	138	464	91	133	17	1	1	38	.287	*101	66	65	310	11	11	.967
1985— M.C. Reds (Mex.).......	OF	61	201	46	71	9	4	1	30	.353	50	19	17	127	7	6	.957
— Chicago (A.L.)	OF-DH	5	2	2	0	0	0	0	0	.000	0	1	0	1	0	0	1.000
— Buffalo (A.A.).............	OF	78	244	34	58	8	5	1	21	.238	46	32	14	148	9	2	.987
1986— Chicago (A.L.)	OF-DH	137	438	65	103	16	3	2	32	.235	71	61	50	276	7	9	.969
1987— Pittsburgh (N.L.)■......	OF	104	182	44	50	8	3	4	18	.275	46	33	21	74	3	3	.963
1988— Pittsburgh (N.L.).......	OF-P	75	118	18	30	4	1	0	8	.254	17	16	9	52	0	2	.963
— Buffalo (A.A.).............	OF	37	145	23	48	6	0	0	10	.331	19	19	14	89	3	0	1.000
1989— Pittsburgh (N.L.).......	OF	112	160	18	35	4	2	0	9	.219	35	20	11	71	1	2	.973
1990— Pittsburgh (N.L.).......	OF	58	76	13	15	2	0	0	1	.197	11	12	7	24	0	0	1.000
— Buffalo (A.A.).............	OF	24	89	17	31	2	2	0	7	.348	12	8	5	49	0	1	.980
1991— Vancouver (PCL)■.....	OF	30	102	15	25	1	0	0	10	.245	11	8	9	39	2	3	.932
— Denver (A.A.)■..........	OF-1B-P	83	303	69	89	8	3	3	25	.294	59	29	26	118	10	3	.977
1992— Texas (A.L.)■.............	OF-DH	73	85	12	16	2	0	1	6	.188	18	16	6	76	4	3	.964
— Toledo (I.L.)■.............	OF	27	74	9	20	3	0	0	6	.270	7	13	11	48	1	0	1.000
1993— Toledo (I.L.)..............	OF-P-DH	113	439	73	128	23	4	6	42	.292	56	59	39	252	5	7	.973
1994— New York (N.L.)■	OF	62	111	14	28	4	0	0	4	.252	19	20	5	64	5	0	1.000
1995— Tucson (PCL)■...........	OF	30	106	18	39	4	1	0	9	.368	19	11	11	67	2	1	.986
— Houston (N.L.)	OF-P	90	201	46	64	5	2	2	18	.318	48	42	21	92	4	5	.950
1996— Houston (N.L.)	OF	108	262	49	69	11	4	1	16	.263	44	41	17	113	5	3	.975
1997— Florida (N.L.)■............	OF-P	103	192	28	47	8	0	1	12	.245	19	33	5	84	1	0	1.000
1998— Florida (N.L.).............	OF-DH	104	171	19	43	8	0	1	10	.251	30	23	2	62	1	2	.969
1999— Colo. Spr. (PCL)■.......	OF-DH	29	109	22	36	7	0	1	13	.330	24	16	4	47	2	1	.980
— Colorado (N.L.)	OF	7	6	0	1	1	0	0	0	.167	0	4	0	1	0	0	1.000
American League totals (3 years)		215	525	79	119	18	3	3	38	.227	89	78	56	353	11	12	.968
National League totals (10 years)		823	1479	249	382	55	12	9	96	.258	269	244	98	637	20	17	.975
Major League totals (13 years)		1038	2004	328	501	73	15	12	134	.250	358	322	154	990	31	29	.972

DIVISION SERIES RECORD

Year Team (League)	Pos.	G	AB	R	H	2B	3B	HR	RBI	Avg.	BB	SO	SB	PO	A	E	Avg.
1997— Florida (N.L.).............	PH	1	1	0	0	0	0	0	0	.000	0	0	0	...	...	...	...

CHAMPIONSHIP SERIES RECORD

Year Team (League)	Pos.	G	AB	R	H	2B	3B	HR	RBI	Avg.	BB	SO	SB	PO	A	E	Avg.
1997— Florida (N.L.).............	PH-OF	3	5	0	1	0	0	0	0	.200	1	0	0	2	0	0	1.000

WORLD SERIES RECORD

NOTES: Member of World Series championship team (1997).

Year Team (League)	Pos.	G	AB	R	H	2B	3B	HR	RBI	Avg.	BB	SO	SB	PO	A	E	Avg.
1997— Florida (N.L.).............	PH	3	3	0	1	0	0	0	0	.333	0	2	0	...	...	...	...

RECORD AS PITCHER

Year League	W	L	Pct.	ERA	G	GS	CG	ShO	Sv.	IP	H	R	ER	BB	SO
1988— Pittsburgh (N.L.)	0	0	...	0.00	1	0	0	0	0	2	1	0	0	0	0
1991— Denver (A.A.)....................	0	0	...	2.45	2	0	0	0	0	3²/₃	3	1	1	2	1
1993— Toledo (I.L.)....................	0	0	...	81.00	1	0	0	0	0	²/₃	7	6	6	1	0
1995— Houston (N.L.)	0	0	...	0.00	1	0	0	0	0	1	0	0	0	1	0
1997— Florida (N.L.)	0	0	...	0.00	1	0	0	0	0	1	0	0	0	1	0
Major League totals (3 years)	0	0	...	0.00	3	0	0	0	0	4	1	0	0	2	0

CANIZARO, JAY   IF   GIANTS

PERSONAL: Born July 4, 1973, in Beaumont, Texas. ... 5-9/178. ... Bats right, throws right. ... Full name: Jason Kyle Canizaro.
HIGH SCHOOL: West Orange-Stark (Orange, Texas).
JUNIOR COLLEGE: Blinn College (Texas).
COLLEGE: Oklahoma State.
TRANSACTIONS/CAREER NOTES: Selected by San Francisco Giants organization in fourth round of free-agent draft (June 3, 1993). ... On Fresno disabled list (July 10-August 15, 1999).
STATISTICAL NOTES: Led Arizona League second basemen with 33 double plays in 1993. ... Led Texas League second basemen with 19 errors in 1995. ... Career major league grand slams: 1.

Year Team (League)	Pos.	G	AB	R	H	2B	3B	HR	RBI	Avg.	BB	SO	SB	PO	A	E	Avg.
1993—Ariz. Giants (Ariz.)......	2B-SS	49	180	34	47	10	•6	3	*41	.261	22	40	12	102	106	10	.954
1994—San Jose (Calif.).........	2-S-3-O	126	464	77	117	16	2	15	69	.252	46	98	12	262	362	30	.954
1995—Shreveport (Texas).....	2B-SS	126	440	83	129	25	7	12	60	.293	58	98	16	254	333	†23	.962
1996—Phoenix (PCL)..........	2-S-3-DH	102	363	50	95	21	2	7	64	.262	46	77	14	194	308	14	.973
—San Francisco (N.L.)..	2B-SS	43	120	11	24	4	1	2	8	.200	9	38	0	64	91	6	.963
1997—Phoenix (PCL)..........	2B-3B	23	81	12	16	7	0	2	12	.198	9	24	2	32	46	2	.975
—Shreveport (Texas).....	2-S-3-DH	50	176	36	45	9	0	11	38	.256	26	44	2	80	124	6	.971
1998—Shreveport (Texas)....	2B	83	281	47	63	7	1	12	32	.224	53	46	5	145	255	10	.976
—Fresno (PCL)............	2-DH-O-S	45	106	23	24	6	2	6	14	.226	17	23	0	49	64	2	.983
1999—Fresno (PCL)..........	2B-SS-3B	105	364	76	102	20	2	26	78	.280	49	79	16	184	268	15	.968
—San Francisco (N.L.)..	2B	12	18	5	8	2	0	1	9	.444	1	2	1	2	5	0	1.000
Major League totals (2 years)		55	138	16	32	6	1	3	17	.232	10	40	1	66	96	6	.964

CANSECO, JOSE   DH/OF   DEVIL RAYS

PERSONAL: Born July 2, 1964, in Havana, Cuba. ... 6-4/240. ... Bats right, throws right. ... Full name: Jose Canseco Jr. ... Identical twin brother of Ozzie Canseco, outfielder with Oakland Athletics (1990) and St. Louis Cardinals (1992). ... Name pronounced can-SAY-co.
HIGH SCHOOL: Miami Coral Park Senior.
TRANSACTIONS/CAREER NOTES: Selected by Oakland Athletics organization in 15th round of free-agent draft (June 7, 1982). ... On Huntsville disabled list (May 14-June 3, 1985). ... On Oakland disabled list (March 23-July 13, 1989); included rehabilitation assignments to Huntsville (May 6 and June 28-July 13). ... On disabled list (June 8-23, 1990 and July 1-16, 1992). ... Traded by A's to Texas Rangers for OF Ruben Sierra, P Jeff Russell, P Bobby Witt and cash (August 31, 1992). ... On disabled list (June 24, 1993-remainder of season). ... Traded by Rangers to Boston Red Sox for OF Otis Nixon and 3B Luis Ortiz (December 9, 1994). ... On Boston disabled list (May 15-June 20, 1995); included rehabilitation assignment to Pawtucket (June 18-20). ... Granted free agency (October 30, 1995). ... Re-signed by Red Sox (December 6, 1995). ... On Boston disabled list (April 24-May 9 and July 26-September 17, 1996); included rehabilitation assignment to Pawtucket (May 7-9). ... Traded by Red Sox to A's for P John Wasdin and cash (January 27, 1997). ... On disabled list (August 1-20 and August 27, 1997-remainder of season). ... Granted free agency (October 31, 1997). ... Signed by Toronto Blue Jays (February 4, 1998). ... Granted free agency (October 22, 1998). ... Signed by Tampa Bay Devil Rays (December 11, 1998). ... On disabled list (July 10-August 20, 1999).
RECORDS: Shares major league record for most strikeouts in two consecutive games—8 (July 14 [3] and 16 [5], 1997). ... Shares major league single-game record for most strikeouts (nine-inning game)—5 (July 16, 1997). ... Shares major league record for most consecutive bases on balls received—7 (August 4-5, 1992). ... Shares A.L. career record for most major league ballparks, one or more home runs (since 1900)—24.
HONORS: Named Minor League Player of the Year by THE SPORTING NEWS (1985). ... Named Southern League Most Valuable Player (1985). ... Named A.L. Rookie Player of the Year by THE SPORTING NEWS (1986). ... Named A.L. Rookie of the Year by Baseball Writers' Association of America (1986). ... Named A.L. Player of the Year by THE SPORTING NEWS (1988). ... Named outfielder on THE SPORTING NEWS A.L. All-Star team (1988 and 1990-91). ... Named outfielder on THE SPORTING NEWS A.L. Silver Slugger team (1988 and 1990-91). ... Named A.L. Most Valuable Player by Baseball Writers' Association of America (1988). ... Named designated hitter on THE SPORTING NEWS A.L. Silver Slugger team (1998).
STATISTICAL NOTES: Led California League outfielders with eight double plays in 1984. ... Hit three home runs in one game (July 3, 1988 and June 13, 1994). ... Led A.L. with .569 slugging percentage in 1988. ... Led A.L. in grounding into double plays with 20 in 1994. ... Career major league grand slams: 6.

Year Team (League)	Pos.	G	AB	R	H	2B	3B	HR	RBI	Avg.	BB	SO	SB	PO	A	E	Avg.
1982—Miami (FSL)...............	3B	6	9	0	1	0	0	0	0	.111	1	3	0	3	1	1	.800
—Idaho Falls (Pio.)........	3B-OF	28	57	13	15	3	0	2	7	.263	9	13	3	6	17	3	.885
1983—Madison (Midw.)........	OF	34	88	8	14	4	0	3	10	.159	10	36	2	23	2	1	.962
—Medford (N.W.)........	OF	59	197	34	53	15	2	11	40	.269	30	*78	6	46	5	5	.311
1984—Modesto (Calif.)	OF	116	410	61	113	21	2	15	73	.276	74	127	10	216	17	9	.963
1985—Huntsville (Sou.)	OF	58	211	47	67	10	2	25	80	.318	30	55	6	117	9	7	.947
—Tacoma (PCL)	OF	60	233	41	81	16	1	11	47	.348	40	66	5	81	7	2	.978
—Oakland (A.L.)	OF	29	96	16	29	3	0	5	13	.302	4	31	1	56	2	3	.951
1986—Oakland (A.L.)	OF-DH	157	600	85	144	29	1	33	117	.240	65	175	15	319	4	•14	.958
1987—Oakland (A.L.)	OF-DH	159	630	81	162	35	3	31	113	.257	50	157	15	263	12	7	.975
1988—Oakland (A.L.)	OF-DH	158	610	120	187	34	0	*42	*124	.307	78	128	40	304	11	7	.978
1989—Huntsville (Sou.)	OF	9	29	2	6	0	0	0	3	.207	5	11	1	9	0	0	1.000
—Oakland (A.L.)	OF-DH	65	227	40	61	9	1	17	57	.269	23	69	6	119	5	3	.976
1990—Oakland (A.L.)	OF-DH	131	481	83	132	14	2	37	101	.274	72	158	19	182	7	1	.995
1991—Oakland (A.L.)	OF-DH	154	572	115	152	32	1	•44	122	.266	78	152	26	245	5	•9	.965
1992—Oakland (A.L.)	OF-DH	97	366	66	90	11	0	22	72	.246	48	104	5	163	5	2	.988
—Texas (A.L.)■........	OF-DH	22	73	8	17	4	0	4	15	.233	15	24	1	32	0	1	.970
1993—Texas (A.L.)	OF-DH-P	60	231	30	59	14	1	10	46	.255	16	62	6	94	4	3	.970
1994—Texas (A.L.)	DH	111	429	88	121	19	2	31	90	.282	69	114	15	...	...	...	...
1995—Boston (A.L.)■.........	DH-OF	102	396	64	121	25	1	24	81	.306	42	93	4	1	0	0	1.000
—Pawtucket (I.L.).........	DH	2	6	1	1	0	0	0	1	.167	1	5	0	...	...	...	...
1996—Boston (A.L.).........	DH-OF	96	360	68	104	22	1	28	82	.289	63	82	3	17	1	0	1.000
—Pawtucket (I.L.).........	DH	2	5	0	1	0	0	0	0	.200	0	3	0	...	...	...	...
1997—Oakland (A.L.).........	DH-OF	108	388	56	91	19	0	23	74	.235	51	122	8	74	2	5	.938
1998—Toronto (A.L.)■........	DH-OF	151	583	98	138	26	0	46	107	.237	65	*159	29	117	4	5	.960
1999—Tampa Bay (A.L.)■.....	DH-OF	113	430	75	120	18	1	34	95	.279	58	135	3	7	1	0	1.000
Major League totals (15 years)		1713	6472	1093	1728	314	14	431	1309	.267	797	1765	196	1993	63	60	.972

DIVISION SERIES RECORD

Year Team (League)	Pos.	G	AB	R	H	2B	3B	HR	RBI	Avg.	BB	SO	SB	PO	A	E	Avg.
1995— Boston (A.L.)...............	DH-OF	3	13	0	0	0	0	0	0	.000	2	2	0	4	0	0	1.000

Header spanning: BATTING / FIELDING

CHAMPIONSHIP SERIES RECORD

Year Team (League)	Pos.	G	AB	R	H	2B	3B	HR	RBI	Avg.	BB	SO	SB	PO	A	E	Avg.
1988— Oakland (A.L.)............	OF	4	16	4	5	1	0	3	4	.313	1	2	1	6	0	0	1.000
1989— Oakland (A.L.)............	OF-PH	5	17	1	5	0	0	1	3	.294	3	7	0	6	1	1	.875
1990— Oakland (A.L.)............	OF	4	11	3	2	0	0	0	1	.182	5	5	2	14	0	0	1.000
Championship series totals (3 years)		13	44	8	12	1	0	4	8	.273	9	14	3	26	1	1	.964

WORLD SERIES RECORD

RECORDS: Shares single-game record for most grand slams—1 (October 15, 1988). ... Shares single-inning record for most runs batted in—4 (October 15, 1988, second inning).

NOTES: Hit home run in first at-bat (October 15, 1988). ... Member of World Series championship team (1989).

Year Team (League)	Pos.	G	AB	R	H	2B	3B	HR	RBI	Avg.	BB	SO	SB	PO	A	E	Avg.
1988— Oakland (A.L.)............	OF	5	19	1	1	0	0	1	5	.053	2	4	1	8	0	0	1.000
1989— Oakland (A.L.)............	OF	4	14	5	5	0	0	1	3	.357	4	3	1	6	0	0	1.000
1990— Oakland (A.L.)............	OF-PH-DH	4	12	1	1	0	0	1	2	.083	2	3	0	4	0	0	1.000
World Series totals (3 years)		13	45	7	7	0	0	3	10	.156	8	10	2	18	0	0	1.000

ALL-STAR GAME RECORD

Year League	Pos.	AB	R	H	2B	3B	HR	RBI	Avg.	BB	SO	SB	PO	A	E	Avg.
1986— American...................					Did not play.											
1988— American...................	OF	4	0	0	0	0	0	0	.000	0	1	0	3	0	0	1.000
1989— American...................					Selected, did not play—injured.											
1990— American...................	OF	4	0	0	0	0	0	0	.000	1	1	1	1	0	0	1.000
1992— American...................					Selected, did not play—injured.											
1999— American...................					Selected, did not play—injured.											
All-Star Game totals (2 years)		8	0	0	0	0	0	0	.000	1	2	1	4	0	0	1.000

RECORD AS PITCHER

Year League	W	L	Pct.	ERA	G	GS	CG	ShO	Sv.	IP	H	R	ER	BB	SO
1993— Texas (A.L.)...............	0	0	...	27.00	1	0	0	0	0	1	2	3	3	3	0

C

CARDONA, JAVIER — C — TIGERS

PERSONAL: Born September 15, 1975, in Santurce, Puerto Rico. ... 6-1/185. ... Bats right, throws right. ... Full name: Javier Peterson Cardona.

HIGH SCHOOL: Jose Alegria (Barrio Maguayo, Puerto Rico).

JUNIOR COLLEGE: Lake Land Community College (Ill.).

TRANSACTIONS/CAREER NOTES: Selected by Detroit Tigers organization in 19th round of free-agent draft (June 3, 1993); did not sign. ... Selected by Detroit Tigers organization in 23rd round of free-agent draft (June 4, 1994).

STATISTICAL NOTES: Led Southern League with .569 slugging percentage in 1999.

Year Team (League)	Pos.	G	AB	R	H	2B	3B	HR	RBI	Avg.	BB	SO	SB	PO	A	E	Avg.
1994— Jamestown (NY-P)	C	19	46	6	12	2	0	0	5	.261	7	9	0	89	17	4	.964
1995— Fayetteville (SAL)	C	51	165	18	34	8	0	3	19	.206	13	30	1	339	48	4	.990
1996— Fayetteville (SAL)	C	97	348	42	98	21	0	4	28	.282	28	53	1	677	112	15	.981
1997— Lakeland (FSL)	C	85	284	28	82	15	0	7	38	.289	25	51	1	498	75	12	.979
1998— Jacksonville (Sou.).....	C	46	163	31	54	16	1	4	40	.331	15	29	0	208	33	6	.976
— Toledo (I.L.)............	C	47	162	12	31	4	0	5	16	.191	9	32	0	262	31	5	.983
1999— Jacksonville (Sou.).....	C	108	418	84	129	31	0	*26	92	.309	46	69	4	565	58	11	.983

CARLSON, DAN — P

PERSONAL: Born January 26, 1970, in Portland, Ore. ... 6-0/200. ... Throws right, bats right. ... Full name: Daniel Scott Carlson.

HIGH SCHOOL: Reynolds (Troutdale, Ore.).

JUNIOR COLLEGE: Mt. Hood Community College (Ore.).

TRANSACTIONS/CAREER NOTES: Selected by San Francisco Giants organization in 33rd round of free-agent draft (June 5, 1989). ... On disabled list (May 14-21, 1995). ... On San Francisco disabled list (March 27-April 11, 1997); included rehabilitation assignment to Bakersfield (April 5-10). ... Selected by Tampa Bay Devil Rays in first round (28th pick overall) of expansion draft (November 18, 1997). ... On Durham disabled list (July 20-August 14, 1998). ... Granted free agency (October 15, 1998). ... Signed by Arizona Diamondbacks organization (December 17, 1998). ... Granted free agency (October 15, 1999).

STATISTICAL NOTES: Tied for Texas League lead with 15 home runs allowed in 1992.

Year League	W	L	Pct.	ERA	G	GS	CG	ShO	Sv.	IP	H	R	ER	BB	SO
1990— Everett (N.W.).................	2	6	.250	5.34	17	11	0	0	0	62 1/3	60	42	37	33	77
1991— Clinton (Midw.)	•16	7	.696	3.08	27	27	5	3	0	181 1/3	149	69	62	76	164
1992— Shreveport (Texas)............	*15	9	.625	3.19	27	•27	4	1	0	*186	166	85	66	60	*157
1993— Phoenix (PCL)...................	5	6	.455	6.56	13	12	0	0	0	70	79	54	51	32	48
— Shreveport (Texas)............	7	4	.636	2.24	15	15	2	1	0	100 1/3	86	30	25	26	81
1994— Phoenix (PCL)...................	*13	6	.684	4.64	31	22	0	0	1	151 1/3	173	80	78	55	117
1995— Phoenix (PCL)...................	9	5	.643	4.27	23	22	2	0	0	132 2/3	138	67	63	66	93
1996— Phoenix (PCL)...................	•13	6	.684	3.44	33	15	2	0	1	146 2/3	135	61	56	46	123
— San Francisco (N.L.)	1	0	1.000	2.70	5	0	0	0	0	10	13	6	3	2	4

Year League	W	L	Pct.	ERA	G	GS	CG	ShO	Sv.	IP	H	R	ER	BB	SO
1997—Bakersfield (Calif.).............	0	0	...	0.00	2	2	0	0	0	6	3	0	0	1	7
—Phoenix (PCL)................	13	3	*.813	3.88	29	14	0	0	3	109	102	53	47	36	108
—San Francisco (N.L.)	0	0	...	7.63	6	0	0	0	0	15 1/3	20	14	13	8	14
1998—Tampa Bay (A.L.)■.......	0	0	...	7.64	10	0	0	0	0	17 2/3	25	15	15	8	16
—Durham (I.L.).................	3	5	.375	6.35	19	11	0	0	0	68	87	52	48	28	59
1999—Tucson (PCL)■	4	9	.308	5.43	32	18	0	0	0	117 2/3	130	82	71	52	118
—Arizona (N.L.)	0	0	...	9.00	2	0	0	0	0	4	5	4	4	0	3
A.L. totals (1 year)	0	0	...	7.64	10	0	0	0	0	17 2/3	25	15	15	8	16
N.L. totals (3 years)	1	0	1.000	6.14	13	0	0	0	0	29 1/3	38	24	20	10	21
Major League totals (4 years).......	1	0	1.000	6.70	23	0	0	0	0	47	63	39	35	18	37

CARLYLE, BUDDY   P   PADRES

PERSONAL: Born December 21, 1977, in Omaha, Neb. ... 6-3/175. ... Throws right, bats left. ... Full name: Earl L. Carlyle.
HIGH SCHOOL: Bellevue (Neb.) East.
TRANSACTIONS/CAREER NOTES: Selected by Cincinnati Reds organization in second round of free-agent draft (June 4, 1996). ... Traded by Reds to San Diego Padres for P Marc Kroon (April 8, 1998).
STATISTICAL NOTES: Pitched 2-0 no-hit victory against Asheville (May 4, 1997, first game).

Year League	W	L	Pct.	ERA	G	GS	CG	ShO	Sv.	IP	H	R	ER	BB	SO
1996—Princeton (Appl.)	2	4	.333	4.66	10	9	1	0	0	46 1/3	47	33	24	16	42
1997—Charleston, W.Va. (SAL).....	•14	5	.737	2.77	23	23	4	1	0	143	130	51	44	27	111
1998—Chattanooga (Sou.)	0	1	.000	5.40	1	1	0	0	0	5	6	3	3	0	3
—Mobile (Sou.)■................	14	6	.700	3.38	27	27	2	1	0	183 2/3	179	77	69	46	97
1999—Las Vegas (PCL)	11	8	.579	4.89	25	25	0	0	0	160	180	99	87	42	138
—San Diego (N.L.)	1	3	.250	5.97	7	7	0	0	0	37 2/3	36	28	25	17	29
Major League totals (1 year)........	1	3	.250	5.97	7	7	0	0	0	37 2/3	36	28	25	17	29

CARMONA, RAFAEL   P

PERSONAL: Born October 2, 1972, in Rio Piedras, Puerto Rico. ... 6-2/185. ... Throws right, bats left.
HIGH SCHOOL: Juano Colon (Comerio, Puerto Rico).
JUNIOR COLLEGE: Indian Hills Community College (Iowa).
TRANSACTIONS/CAREER NOTES: Selected by Seattle Mariners organization in 13th round of free-agent draft (June 3, 1993). ... On Tacoma disabled list (April 30-June 8, 1997). ... On Seattle disabled list (March 22, 1998-entire season); included rehabilitation assignments to Lancaster (May 5-18) and Orlando (May 23-June 6). ... On Seattle disabled list (June 13-August 11, 1999); included rehabilitation assignment to Tacoma (July 23-August 11). ... Granted free agency (December 21, 1999).

Year League	W	L	Pct.	ERA	G	GS	CG	ShO	Sv.	IP	H	R	ER	BB	SO
1993—Bellingham (N.W.)	2	3	.400	3.79	23	0	0	0	2	35 2/3	33	19	15	14	30
1994—Riverside (Calif.)................	8	2	.800	2.81	50	0	0	0	21	67 1/3	48	22	21	19	63
1995—Port City (Sou.)	0	1	.000	1.80	15	0	0	0	4	15	11	5	3	3	17
—Seattle (A.L.)	2	4	.333	5.66	15	3	0	0	1	47 2/3	55	31	30	34	28
—Tacoma (PCL)	4	3	.571	5.06	8	8	1	1	0	48	52	29	27	19	37
1996—Tacoma (PCL)	0	0	...	1.42	4	1	0	0	0	6 1/3	5	1	1	5	9
—Seattle (A.L.)	8	3	.727	4.28	53	1	0	0	1	90 1/3	95	47	43	55	62
1997—Tacoma (PCL)	2	5	.286	3.79	32	5	0	0	4	59 1/3	52	31	25	35	56
—Seattle (A.L.)	0	0	...	3.18	4	0	0	0	0	5 2/3	3	3	2	2	6
1998—Lancaster (Calif.)	0	1	.000	6.23	4	4	0	0	0	13	12	10	9	5	11
—Orlando (Sou.)	0	3	.000	14.29	4	4	0	0	0	11 1/3	18	18	18	6	11
1999—Tacoma (PCL)	1	3	.250	3.53	27	0	0	0	2	43 1/3	39	18	17	20	38
—Seattle (A.L.)	1	0	1.000	7.94	9	0	0	0	0	11 1/3	18	11	10	9	0
Major League totals (4 years).......	11	7	.611	4.94	81	4	0	0	2	155	171	92	85	100	96

CARPENTER, CHRIS   P   BLUE JAYS

PERSONAL: Born April 27, 1975, in Exeter, N.H. ... 6-6/225. ... Throws right, bats right. ... Full name: Christopher John Carpenter.
HIGH SCHOOL: Trinity (Manchester, N.H.).
TRANSACTIONS/CAREER NOTES: Selected by Toronto Blue Jays organization in first round (15th pick overall) of free-agent draft (June 3, 1993). ... On Toronto disabled list (June 3-28, 1999); included rehabilitation assignment to St. Catharines (June 23-28).

Year League	W	L	Pct.	ERA	G	GS	CG	ShO	Sv.	IP	H	R	ER	BB	SO
1994—Medicine Hat (Pio.)	6	3	.667	2.76	15	15	0	0	0	84 2/3	76	40	26	39	80
1995—Dunedin (FSL)	3	5	.375	2.17	15	15	0	0	0	99 1/3	83	29	24	50	56
—Knoxville (Sou.).................	3	7	.300	5.18	12	12	0	0	0	64 1/3	71	47	37	31	53
1996—Knoxville (Sou.).................	7	9	.438	3.94	28	28	1	0	0	171 1/3	161	94	75	91	150
1997—Syracuse (I.L.)...................	4	9	.308	4.50	19	19	3	2	0	120	113	64	60	53	97
—Toronto (A.L.)	3	7	.300	5.09	14	13	1	1	0	81 1/3	108	55	46	37	55
1998—Toronto (A.L.)	12	7	.632	4.37	33	24	1	1	0	175	177	97	85	61	136
1999—Toronto (A.L.)	9	8	.529	4.38	24	24	4	1	0	150	177	81	73	48	106
—St. Catharines (NY-P)........	0	0	...	4.50	1	1	0	0	0	4	5	2	2	1	6
Major League totals (3 years).......	24	22	.522	4.52	71	61	6	3	0	406 1/3	462	233	204	146	297

CARRASCO, HECTOR   P   TWINS

PERSONAL: Born October 22, 1969, in San Pedro de Macoris, Dominican Republic. ... 6-2/220. ... Throws right, bats right. ... Full name: Hector Pacheco Pipo Carrasco. ... Name pronounced kuh-ROSS-ko.
HIGH SCHOOL: Liceo Mattias Mella (San Pedro de Macoris, Dominican Republic).

C

TRANSACTIONS/CAREER NOTES: Signed as non-drafted free agent by New York Mets organization (March 20, 1988). ... Released by Mets (January 6, 1992). ... Signed by Houston Astros organization (January 21, 1992). ... Traded by Astros organization with P Brian Griffiths to Florida Marlins organization for P Tom Edens (November 17, 1992). ... Traded by Marlins to Cincinnati Reds (September 10, 1993), completing deal in which Reds traded P Chris Hammond to Marlins for 3B Gary Scott and a player to be named later (March 27, 1993). ... On disabled list (May 12-June 1, 1994). ... Traded by Reds with P Scott Service to Kansas City Royals for OF Jon Nunnally and IF/OF Chris Stynes (July 15, 1997). ... Selected by Arizona Diamondbacks in second round (49th pick overall) of expansion draft (November 18, 1997). ... Claimed on waivers by Minnesota (April 3, 1998). ... On Minnesota disabled list (April 3-June 25, 1999); included rehabilitation assignments to Fort Myers (June 16-17) and Salt Lake (June 18-25).

Year League	W	L	Pct.	ERA	G	GS	CG	ShO	Sv.	IP	H	R	ER	BB	SO
1988— Gulf Coast Mets (GCL)	0	2	.000	4.17	14	2	0	0	0	36²/₃	37	29	17	13	21
1989— Kingsport (Appalachian).....	1	6	.143	5.74	12	10	0	0	0	53¹/₃	69	49	34	34	55
1990— Kingsport (Appalachian).....	0	0	...	4.05	3	1	0	0	0	6²/₃	8	3	3	1	5
1991— Pittsfield (NY-P)	0	1	.000	5.40	12	1	0	0	1	23¹/₃	25	17	14	21	20
1992— Asheville (SAL)■...............	5	5	.500	2.99	49	0	0	0	8	78¹/₃	66	30	26	47	67
1993— Kane County (Midw.)■.......	6	12	.333	4.11	28	*28	0	0	0	149	153	90	68	76	127
1994— Cincinnati (N.L.)■..............	5	6	.455	2.24	45	0	0	0	6	56¹/₃	42	17	14	30	41
1995— Cincinnati (N.L.)...............	2	7	.222	4.12	64	0	0	0	5	87¹/₃	86	45	40	46	64
1996— Cincinnati (N.L.)...............	4	3	.571	3.75	56	0	0	0	0	74¹/₃	58	37	31	45	59
— Indianapolis (A.A.)............	0	1	.000	2.14	13	2	0	0	0	21	18	7	5	13	17
1997— Indianapolis (A.A.)............	0	0	...	6.23	3	0	0	0	1	4¹/₃	5	3	3	3	4
— Cincinnati (N.L.)...............	1	2	.333	3.68	38	0	0	0	0	51¹/₃	51	25	21	25	46
— Kansas City (A.L.)■..........	1	6	.143	5.45	28	0	0	0	0	34²/₃	29	21	21	16	30
1998— Minnesota (A.L.)■............	4	2	.667	4.38	63	0	0	0	1	61²/₃	75	30	30	31	46
1999— Fort Myers (FSL)	0	0	...	4.50	1	1	0	0	0	2	2	1	1	1	1
— Salt Lake (PCL)	1	0	1.000	0.00	3	0	0	0	1	4¹/₃	3	0	0	1	3
— Minnesota (A.L.)...............	2	3	.400	4.96	39	0	0	0	1	49	48	29	27	18	35
A.L. totals (3 years)	7	11	.389	4.83	130	0	0	0	2	145¹/₃	152	80	78	65	111
N.L. totals (4 years)	12	18	.400	3.54	203	0	0	0	11	269¹/₃	237	124	106	146	210
Major League totals (6 years) ...	19	29	.396	3.99	333	0	0	0	13	414²/₃	389	204	184	211	321

CHAMPIONSHIP SERIES RECORD

Year League	W	L	Pct.	ERA	G	GS	CG	ShO	Sv.	IP	H	R	ER	BB	SO
1995— Cincinnati (N.L.)	0	0	...	0.00	1	0	0	0	0	1¹/₃	1	0	0	0	3

CARTER, LANCE — P — ROYALS

PERSONAL: Born December 18, 1974, in Bradenton, Fla. ... 6-1/190. ... Throws right, bats right. ... Full name: Lance David Carter.
HIGH SCHOOL: Manatee (Bradenton, Fla.).
JUNIOR COLLEGE: Manatee Community College (Fla.).
TRANSACTIONS/CAREER NOTES: Selected by Kansas City Royals organization in 21st round of free-agent draft (June 21, 1994). ... On disabled list (June 12, 1997-entire season).

Year League	W	L	Pct.	ERA	G	GS	CG	ShO	Sv.	IP	H	R	ER	BB	SO
1994— Eugene (N.W.)	1	0	1.000	5.47	8	7	0	0	0	26¹/₃	26	17	16	15	23
— Gulf Coast Royals (GCL)	3	0	1.000	0.29	5	5	0	0	0	31	19	1	1	3	36
1995— Springfield (Midw.)	9	5	.643	3.99	27	24	1	1	0	137²/₃	151	77	61	22	118
1996— Wilmington (Caro.)............	3	6	.333	6.34	16	12	0	0	0	65¹/₃	81	50	46	17	49
1997— Kingsport (Appalachian).....							Did not play.								
1998— Lansing (Midw.)	3	1	.750	0.67	15	2	0	0	2	40¹/₃	34	6	3	9	37
— Wilmington (Caro.)............	1	4	.200	3.29	28	1	0	0	5	52	50	21	19	14	61
1999— Wichita (Texas)	5	2	.714	0.78	44	0	0	0	13	69²/₃	49	10	6	27	77
— Kansas City (A.L.)	0	1	.000	5.06	6	0	0	0	0	5¹/₃	3	3	3	3	3
Major League totals (1 year)........	0	1	.000	5.06	6	0	0	0	0	5¹/₃	3	3	3	3	3

CARUSO, MIKE — SS — WHITE SOX

PERSONAL: Born May 27, 1977, in Queens, N.Y. ... 6-0/172. ... Bats left, throws right. ... Full name: Michael J. Caruso.
HIGH SCHOOL: Stoneman Douglas (Parkland, Fla.).
TRANSACTIONS/CAREER NOTES: Selected by San Francisco Giants organization in second round of free-agent draft (June 2, 1996). ... Traded by Giants with P Keith Foulke, P Lorenzo Barcelo, P Bobby Howry, P Ken Vining and OF Brian Manning to Chicago White Sox for P Danny Darwin, P Wilson Alvarez and P Roberto Hernandez (July 31, 1997).
STATISTICAL NOTES: Tied for A.L. lead in caught stealing with 14 in 1999.

							BATTING							FIELDING		
Year Team (League)	Pos.	G	AB	R	H	2B	3B	HR	RBI	Avg.	BB	SO	SB	PO	A	E	Avg.
1996— Bellingham (N.W.)	SS-3B	73	312	48	91	13	1	2	24	.292	16	23	24	107	231	40	.894
1997— San Jose (Calif.).........	SS-DH	108	441	76	147	24	11	2	50	.333	38	19	11	168	300	33	.934
— Win.-Salem (Car.)■......	SS-DH	28	119	12	27	3	2	0	14	.227	4	8	3	44	67	7	.941
1998— Chicago (A.L.)	SS	133	523	81	160	17	6	5	55	.306	14	38	22	216	378	*35	.944
1999— Chicago (A.L.)	SS-DH	136	529	60	132	11	4	2	35	.250	20	36	12	183	348	24	.957
Major League totals (2 years)		269	1052	141	292	28	10	7	90	.278	34	74	34	399	726	59	.950

CASEY, SEAN — 1B — REDS

PERSONAL: Born July 2, 1974, in Willingsboro, N.J. ... 6-4/226. ... Bats left, throws right. ... Full name: Sean Thomas Casey.
HIGH SCHOOL: Upper St. Clair (Pittsburgh).
COLLEGE: Richmond.
TRANSACTIONS/CAREER NOTES: Selected by Cleveland Indians organization in second round of free-agent draft (June 1, 1995). ... On disabled list (July 23-September 23, 1996). ... On Akron disabled list (April 4-June 8, 1997). ... Traded by Indians to Cincinnati Reds for

P Dave Burba (March 30, 1998). ... On Cincinnati disabled list (April 2-May 5, 1998); included rehabilitation assignment to Indianapolis (April 30-May 5).
RECORDS: Shares major league single-game record for most times reached base (nine-inning game)—7 (May 19, 1999).
STATISTICAL NOTES: Led Carolina League with .544 slugging percentage in 1996.

							BATTING								FIELDING		
Year	Team (League)	Pos.	G	AB	R	H	2B	3B	HR	RBI	Avg.	BB	SO	SB	PO	A	E	Avg.
1995— Watertown (NY-P)	1B	55	207	26	68	18	0	2	37	.329	18	21	3	510	24	8	.985
1996— Kinston (Caro.)..........	1B-DH	92	344	62	114	31	3	12	57	*.331	36	47	1	632	15	6	.991
1997— Akron (East.)..........	1B-DH	62	241	38	93	19	1	10	66	.386	23	34	0	405	22	5	.988
— Buffalo (A.A.).............	DH-1B	20	72	12	26	7	0	5	18	.361	9	11	0	17	1	0	1.000
1998— Cincinnati (N.L.)■	1B	96	302	44	82	21	1	7	52	.272	43	45	1	643	36	4	.994
— Indianapolis (I.L.)........	1B-DH	27	95	14	31	8	1	1	13	.326	14	10	0	205	10	2	.991
1999— Cincinnati (N.L.)........	1B-DH	151	594	103	197	42	3	25	99	.332	61	88	0	1189	55	6	.995
Major League totals (2 years)		247	896	147	279	63	4	32	151	.311	104	133	1	1832	91	10	.995

ALL-STAR GAME RECORD

						BATTING								FIELDING		
Year	League	Pos.	AB	R	H	2B	3B	HR	RBI	Avg.	BB	SO	SB	PO	A	E	Avg.
1999— National......................	1B	1	0	0	0	0	0	0	.000	0	0	0	4	0	0	1.000

CASIMIRO, CARLOS   2B   ORIOLES

C

PERSONAL: Born November 8, 1976, in San Pedro de Macoris, Dominican Republic ... 5-11/170. ... Bats right, throws right. ... Full name: Carlos Rafael Casimiro.
TRANSACTIONS/CAREER NOTES: Signed as non-drafted free agent by Baltimore Orioles organization (April 15, 1994).
STATISTICAL NOTES: Led Eastern League second basemen with 281 putouts and 631 total chances. ... Tied for Eastern League lead with 87 double plays by second baseman in 1999.

							BATTING								FIELDING		
Year	Team (League)	Pos.	G	AB	R	H	2B	3B	HR	RBI	Avg.	BB	SO	SB	PO	A	E	Avg.
1994— Dom. Orioles (DSL)....	IF	41	157	27	30	6	1	3	22	.191	28	41	14	64	76	19	.881
1995— GC Orioles (GCL)......	SS	32	107	14	27	4	2	2	11	.252	10	22	1	48	81	13	.908
1996— Bluefield (Appl.)	2B-3B	62	239	51	66	16	0	10	33	.276	20	52	22	103	131	13	.947
1997— Delmarva (SAL).........	2B	122	457	54	111	21	8	9	51	.243	26	108	20	204	287	21	.959
1998— Frederick (Caro.)	2B-3B-SS	131	478	44	113	23	9	15	61	.236	25	98	10	243	352	23	.963
1999— Bowie (East.)..............	2B-DH-3B	139	526	73	116	23	1	18	64	.221	39	101	7	†281	333	20	.968

CASTILLA, VINNY   3B   DEVIL RAYS

PERSONAL: Born July 4, 1967, in Oaxaca, Mexico. ... 6-1/205. ... Bats right, throws right. ... Full name: Vinicio Soria Castilla. ... Name pronounced kass-TEE-uh.
HIGH SCHOOL: Instituto Carlos Gracida (Oaxaca, Mexico).
TRANSACTIONS/CAREER NOTES: Signed as non-drafted free agent by Saltillo of Mexican League (1987). ... Contract sold by Saltillo to Atlanta Braves organization (March 19, 1990). ... Selected by Colorado Rockies in second round (40th pick overall) of expansion draft (November 17, 1992). ... On disabled list (May 20-June 4, 1993). ... Traded by Rockies to Tampa Bay Devil Rays for P Rolando Arrojo and IF Aaron Ledesma (December 13, 1999).
HONORS: Named third baseman on THE SPORTING NEWS N.L. All-Star team (1995 and 1997-98). ... Named third baseman on THE SPORTING NEWS N.L. Silver Slugger team (1995 and 1997-98).
STATISTICAL NOTES: Led International League shortstops with 550 total chances and 72 double plays in 1992. ... Led N.L. third basemen with 506 total chances and 43 double plays in 1996. ... Had 22-game hitting streak (August 9-September 1, 1997). ... Led N.L. third basemen with 41 double plays in 1997. ... Hit three home runs in one game (June 5, 1999). ... Career major league grand slams: 2.
MISCELLANEOUS: Holds Colorado Rockies all-time record for most home runs (203).

							BATTING								FIELDING		
Year	Team (League)	Pos.	G	AB	R	H	2B	3B	HR	RBI	Avg.	BB	SO	SB	PO	A	E	Avg.
1987— Saltillo (Mex.).............	3B	13	27	0	5	2	0	0	1	.185	0	5	0	10	31	1	.976
1988— Salt.-Monc. (Mex.)■ ..	SS	50	124	22	30	2	2	5	18	.242	8	29	1	53	105	13	.924
1989— Saltillo (Mex.)■.........	SS-3B	128	462	70	142	25	13	10	58	.307	33	70	11	224	427	34	.950
1990— Sumter (SAL)■...........	SS	93	339	47	91	15	2	9	53	.268	28	54	2	139	320	23	.952
— Greenville (Sou.)	SS	46	170	20	40	5	1	4	16	.235	13	23	4	71	167	7	.971
1991— Greenville (Sou.)	SS	66	259	34	70	17	3	7	44	.270	9	35	0	86	221	11	.965
— Richmond (I.L.)..........	SS	67	240	25	54	7	4	7	36	.225	14	32	1	93	208	12	.962
— Atlanta (N.L.).............	SS	12	5	1	1	0	0	0	0	.200	0	2	0	6	6	0	1.000
1992— Richmond (I.L.)..........	SS	127	449	49	113	29	1	7	44	.252	21	68	1	162	357	*31	.944
— Atlanta (N.L.).............	SS-3B	9	16	1	4	1	0	0	1	.250	1	4	0	2	12	1	.933
1993— Colorado (N.L.)■	SS	105	337	36	86	9	7	9	30	.255	13	45	2	141	282	11	.975
1994— Colorado (N.L.) SS-2B-3B-1B	52	130	16	43	11	1	3	18	.331	7	23	2	67	78	2	.986
— Colo. Springs (PCL) ...	3B-2B-SS	22	78	13	19	6	1	1	11	.244	7	11	0	20	60	3	.964
1995— Colorado (N.L.)	3B-SS	139	527	82	163	34	2	32	90	.309	30	87	2	86	264	15	.959
1996— Colorado (N.L.)	3B	160	629	97	191	34	0	40	113	.304	35	88	7	97	*389	20	.960
1997— Colorado (N.L.)	3B	159	612	94	186	25	2	40	113	.304	44	108	2	112	*323	21	.954
1998— Colorado (N.L.)	3B-SS	•162	645	108	206	28	4	46	144	.319	40	89	5	110	316	13	.970
1999— Colorado (N.L.)	3B	158	615	83	169	24	1	33	102	.275	53	75	2	96	298	19	.954
Major League totals (9 years)		956	3516	518	1049	166	17	203	611	.298	223	521	22	717	1968	102	.963

DIVISION SERIES RECORD

							BATTING								FIELDING		
Year	Team (League)	Pos.	G	AB	R	H	2B	3B	HR	RBI	Avg.	BB	SO	SB	PO	A	E	Avg.
1995— Colorado (N.L.)	3B	4	15	3	7	1	0	3	6	.467	0	1	0	3	13	1	.941

Year	League	Pos.	AB	R	H	2B	3B	HR	RBI	Avg.	BB	SO	SB	PO	A	E	Avg.
							BATTING								FIELDING		
1995—National		3B	2	0	0	0	0	0	0	.000	0	1	0	0	0	0	...
1998—National		3B	2	0	0	0	0	0	0	.000	0	0	0	0	2	0	1.000
All-Star Game totals (2 years)			4	0	0	0	0	0	0	.000	0	1	0	0	2	0	1.000

CASTILLO, ALBERTO — C — BLUE JAYS

PERSONAL: Born February 10, 1970, in San Juan de la Maguana, Dominican Republic. ... 6-0/185. ... Bats right, throws right. ... Full name: Alberto Terrero Castillo.
HIGH SCHOOL: Mercedes Maria Mateo (Dominican Republic).
TRANSACTIONS/CAREER NOTES: Signed as non-drafted free agent by New York Mets organization (April 15, 1987). ... On disabled list (July 3, 1992-remainder of season and June 1-July 13, 1994). ... On suspended list (August 27-29, 1994). ... Granted free agency (October 15, 1998). ... Signed by Philadelphia Phillies organization (November 5, 1998). ... Selected by St. Louis Cardinals from Phillies organization in Rule 5 major league draft (December 14, 1998). ... Traded by Cardinals with P Lance Painter and P Matt DeWitt to Toronto Blue Jays for P Pat Hentgen and P Paul Spoljaric (November 11, 1999).
STATISTICAL NOTES: Led International League catchers with 827 total chances and nine double plays in 1996.

Year	Team (League)	Pos.	G	AB	R	H	2B	3B	HR	RBI	Avg.	BB	SO	SB	PO	A	E	Avg.
								BATTING								FIELDING		
1987—Kingsport (Appal.)		C	7	9	1	1	0	0	0	0	.111	5	3	1	21	4	0	1.000
1988—GC Mets (GCL)		C	22	68	7	18	4	0	0	10	.265	4	4	2	126	13	1	.993
—Kingsport (Appal.)		C	24	75	7	22	3	0	1	14	.293	15	14	0	161	18	5	.973
1989—Kingsport (Appal.)		C-1B	27	74	15	19	4	0	3	12	.257	11	14	2	140	19	1	.994
—Pittsfield (NY-P)		C	34	123	13	29	8	0	1	13	.236	7	26	2	186	26	2	.991
—St. Lucie (FSL)			1	0	0	0	0	0	0	0	...	0	0	0	0	0	0	...
1990—Columbia (SAL)		C	30	103	8	24	4	3	1	14	.233	10	21	1	187	22	5	.977
—Pittsfield (NY-P)		C-OF-1B	58	187	19	41	8	1	4	24	.219	26	35	3	378	61	9	.980
1991—Columbia (SAL)		C	90	267	35	74	20	3	3	47	.277	43	44	6	*734	86	15	.982
1992—St. Lucie (FSL)		C	60	162	11	33	6	0	3	17	.204	16	37	0	317	40	12	.967
1993—St. Lucie (FSL)		C	105	333	37	86	21	0	5	42	.258	28	46	0	*604	80	12	.983
1994—Binghamton (East.)		C-1B	90	315	33	78	14	0	7	42	.248	41	46	1	643	54	6	.991
1995—Norfolk (I.L.)		C-DH	69	217	23	58	13	1	4	31	.267	26	32	2	469	44	7	.987
—New York (N.L.)		C	13	29	2	3	0	0	0	0	.103	3	9	1	66	9	2	.974
1996—New York (N.L.)		C	6	11	1	4	0	0	0	0	.364	0	4	0	23	0	0	1.000
—Norfolk (I.L.)		C	113	341	34	71	12	1	11	39	.208	39	67	2	*747	*72	8	.990
1997—New York (N.L.)		C	35	59	3	12	1	0	0	7	.203	9	16	0	142	8	2	.987
—Norfolk (I.L.)		C-OF	34	83	4	18	1	0	1	8	.217	17	16	1	197	16	7	.968
1998—New York (N.L.)		C-DH	38	83	13	17	4	0	2	7	.205	9	17	0	193	15	2	.990
—Norfolk (I.L.)		C-OF	21	49	4	9	2	0	1	6	.184	11	12	0	110	6	1	.991
1999—St. Louis (N.L.)■		C	93	255	21	67	8	0	4	31	.263	24	48	0	514	38	5	.991
Major League totals (5 years)			185	437	40	103	13	0	6	45	.236	45	94	1	938	70	11	.989

CASTILLO, CARLOS — P — WHITE SOX

PERSONAL: Born April 21, 1975, in Boston. ... 6-2/250. ... Throws right, bats right.
HIGH SCHOOL: Southwest (Miami).
TRANSACTIONS/CAREER NOTES: Selected by Chicago White Sox organization in third round of free-agent draft (June 2, 1994).
STATISTICAL NOTES: Tied for A.L. lead with three balks in 1998. ... Tied for International League lead with 28 home runs allowed in 1999.

Year	League	W	L	Pct.	ERA	G	GS	CG	ShO	Sv.	IP	H	R	ER	BB	SO
1994—GC White Sox (GCL)		4	3	.571	2.59	12	12	0	0	0	59	53	20	17	10	57
—Hickory (SAL)		2	0	1.000	0.00	3	1	0	0	0	12	3	0	0	2	17
1995—Hickory (SAL)		5	6	.455	3.73	14	12	2	0	1	79²/₃	85	42	33	18	67
1996—South Bend (Midw.)		9	9	.500	4.05	20	19	•5	0	0	133¹/₃	131	74	60	29	128
—Prince William (Caro.)		2	4	.333	3.95	6	6	•4	0	0	43¹/₃	45	22	19	4	30
1997—Chicago (A.L.)		2	1	.667	4.48	37	2	0	0	1	66¹/₃	68	35	33	33	43
—Nashville (A.A.)		0	0	...	1.50	4	0	0	0	3	6	4	1	1	0	4
1998—Chicago (A.L.)		6	4	.600	5.11	54	2	0	0	0	100¹/₃	94	61	57	35	64
—Calgary (PCL)		1	1	.500	9.00	2	2	0	0	0	8	12	8	8	4	4
1999—Charlotte (I.L.)		9	6	.600	5.15	20	20	*5	0	0	136¹/₃	150	88	78	30	105
—Chicago (A.L.)		2	2	.500	5.71	18	2	0	0	0	41	45	26	26	14	23
Major League totals (3 years)		10	7	.588	5.03	109	6	0	0	1	207²/₃	207	122	116	82	130

CASTILLO, LUIS — 2B — MARLINS

PERSONAL: Born September 12, 1975, in San Pedro de Macoris, Dominican Republic. ... 5-11/175. ... Bats both, throws right. ... Full name: Luis Antonio Donato Castillo.
HIGH SCHOOL: Colegio San Benito Abad (San Pedro de Macoris, Dominican Republic).
TRANSACTIONS/CAREER NOTES: Signed as non-drafted free agent by Florida Marlins organization (August 19, 1992). ... On Kane County disabled list (July 20-September 11, 1995). ... On Florida disabled list (May 7-22, 1997).
STATISTICAL NOTES: Led Gulf Coast League in caught stealing with 12 in 1994. ... Led Gulf Coast League second basemen with 142 putouts, 318 total chances, 40 double plays and .972 fielding percentage in 1994. ... Led Eastern League in caught stealing with 28 in 1996. ... Led Eastern League second basemen with 557 total chances and 87 double plays in 1996. ... Led International League in caught stealing with 15 in 1998. ... Had 22-game hitting streak (August 9-September 3, 1999).

Year	Team (League)	Pos.	G	AB	R	H	2B	3B	HR	RBI	Avg.	BB	SO	SB	PO	A	E	Avg.
1993—	Dom. Marlins (DSL)...	IF	69	266	48	75	7	1	4	31	.282	36	22	21	151	180	20	.943
1994—	GC Marlins (GCL).......	2B-SS	57	216	49	57	8	0	0	16	.264	37	36	31	†144	170	9	†.972
1995—	Kane Co. (Midw.)	2B	89	340	71	111	4	4	0	23	.326	55	50	41	193	241	17	.962
1996—	Portland (East.)	2B	109	420	83	133	15	7	1	35	.317	66	68	*51	217	*326	14	*.975
—	Florida (N.L.).............	2B	41	164	26	43	2	1	1	8	.262	14	46	17	99	118	3	.986
1997—	Florida (N.L.).............	2B	75	263	27	63	8	0	0	8	.240	27	53	16	129	177	9	.971
—	Charlotte (I.L.)...........	2B	37	130	25	46	5	0	0	5	.354	16	22	8	66	97	5	.970
1998—	Charlotte (I.L.)...........	2B	100	381	74	109	11	2	0	15	.286	75	68	41	232	281	16	.970
—	Florida (N.L.).............	2B	44	153	21	31	3	2	1	10	.203	22	33	3	117	113	7	.970
1999—	Florida (N.L.).............	2B	128	487	76	147	23	4	0	28	.302	67	85	50	257	343	15	.976
Major League totals (4 years)			288	1067	150	284	36	7	2	54	.266	130	217	86	602	751	34	.975

CASTRO, JUAN   IF   DODGERS

PERSONAL: Born June 20, 1972, in Los Mochis, Mexico. ... 5-10/187. ... Bats right, throws right.
HIGH SCHOOL: CBTIS 43 (Los Mochis, Mexico).
TRANSACTIONS/CAREER NOTES: Signed as non-drafted free agent by Los Angeles Dodgers organization (June 13, 1991). ... On Los Angeles disabled list (June 5-August 1, 1997).
STATISTICAL NOTES: Tied for Texas League lead in double plays by shortstop with 82 in 1994.

Year	Team (League)	Pos.	G	AB	R	H	2B	3B	HR	RBI	Avg.	BB	SO	SB	PO	A	E	Avg.
1991—	Great Falls (Pio.)	SS-2B	60	217	36	60	4	2	1	27	.276	33	31	7	90	155	21	.921
1992—	Bakersfield (Calif.)	SS	113	446	56	116	15	4	4	42	.260	37	64	14	180	309	38	.928
1993—	San Antonio (Texas)...	SS-2B	118	424	55	117	23	8	7	41	.276	30	40	12	169	314	28	.945
1994—	San Antonio (Texas)..	SS	123	445	55	128	25	4	4	44	.288	31	66	4	187	377	29	.951
1995—	Albuquerque (PCL).....	SS-2B	104	341	51	91	18	4	3	43	.267	20	42	4	152	344	14	.973
—	Los Angeles (N.L.)	3B-SS	11	4	0	1	0	0	0	0	.250	1	1	0	3	7	0	1.000
1996—	Albuquerque (PCL).....	3B-SS-2B	17	56	12	21	4	2	1	8	.375	6	7	1	17	33	2	.962
—	Los Angeles (N.L.)	S-3-2-O	70	132	16	26	5	3	0	5	.197	10	27	1	54	84	3	.979
1997—	Albuquerque (PCL).....	SS-2B	27	101	11	31	5	2	2	11	.307	4	20	1	33	83	9	.928
—	Los Angeles (N.L.)	SS-2B-3B	40	75	3	11	3	1	0	4	.147	7	20	0	36	65	1	.990
1998—	Los Angeles (N.L.)	SS-2B-3B	89	220	25	43	7	0	2	14	.195	15	37	0	95	182	10	.965
1999—	Albuquerque (PCL).....	S-3-2-DH	116	423	52	116	25	4	7	51	.274	34	70	2	126	286	19	.956
—	Los Angeles (N.L.)	2B-SS	2	1	0	0	0	0	0	0	.000	0	1	0	1	4	0	1.000
Major League totals (5 years)			212	432	44	81	15	4	2	23	.188	33	86	1	189	342	14	.974

DIVISION SERIES RECORD

Year	Team (League)	Pos.	G	AB	R	H	2B	3B	HR	RBI	Avg.	BB	SO	SB	PO	A	E	Avg.
1996—	Los Angeles (N.L.)	2B	2	5	0	1	1	0	0	1	.200	1	1	0	4	3	0	1.000

CASTRO, NELSON   SS   GIANTS

PERSONAL: Born June 4, 1976, in Monte Cristi, Dominican Republic. ... 5-10/190. ... Bats right, throws right. ... Full name: Nelson Daniel Castro.
TRANSACTIONS/CAREER NOTES: Signed as non-drafted free agent by California Angels organization (January 14, 1994). ... Angels franchise renamed Anaheim Angels for 1997 season. ... Claimed on waivers by San Francisco Giants (October 13, 1999).
STATISTICAL NOTES: Led Arizona League shortstops with 297 total chances and 32 double plays in 1997. ... Led Northwest League shortstops with 323 total chances in 1997. ... Led California League shortstops with 591 total chances and 71 double plays in 1998. ... Led California League shortstops with 74 double plays in 1999.

Year	Team (League)	Pos.	G	AB	R	H	2B	3B	HR	RBI	Avg.	BB	SO	SB	PO	A	E	Avg.
1995—	Ariz. Angels (Ariz.)	SS	55	190	34	37	1	2	0	22	.195	27	50	15	*106	*173	18	.939
1996—	Boise (N.W.)	PH	1	1	0	0	0	0	0	0	.000	0	0	0	...	...	...	...
—	Ariz. Angels (Ariz.)	SS	53	222	31	38	4	3	3	14	.171	32	42	25	75	164	14	.945
1997—	Boise (N.W.)	SS	69	293	74	86	16	1	7	37	.294	38	53	26	80	218	25	*.923
1998—	Lake Elsinore (Calif.)..	SS	131	470	73	110	16	7	4	41	.234	40	101	36	•185	*372	34	.942
1999—	Lake Elsinore (Calif.)..	SS	125	444	68	111	16	12	1	50	.250	36	75	*53	210	*370	23	*.962

CASTRO, RAMON   C   MARLINS

PERSONAL: Born March 1, 1976, in Vega Baja, Puerto Rico. ... 6-3/225. ... Bats right, throws right. ... Full name: Ramon A. Castro.
HIGH SCHOOL: Lino P. Rivera (Vega Baja, Puerto Rico).
TRANSACTIONS/CAREER NOTES: Selected by Houston Astros organization in first round (17th pick overall) of free-agent draft (June 2, 1994). ... On Jackson disabled list (April 27-May 15, 1998). ... Traded by Astros to Florida Marlins for P Jay Powell and C Scott Makarewicz (July 6, 1998).

Year	Team (League)	Pos.	G	AB	R	H	2B	3B	HR	RBI	Avg.	BB	SO	SB	PO	A	E	Avg.
1994—	GC Astros (GCL)	C	37	123	17	34	7	0	3	14	.276	17	14	5	210	24	4	.983
1995—	Kissimmee (FSL)........	C	36	120	6	25	5	0	0	8	.208	6	21	0	184	18	7	.967
—	Auburn (NY-P)..........	C	63	224	40	67	17	0	9	49	.299	24	27	0	297	46	2	.994
1996—	Quad City (Midw.)	C	96	314	38	78	15	0	7	43	.248	31	61	2	660	82	10	.987
1997—	Kissimmee (FSL)........	C	115	410	53	115	22	1	8	65	.280	53	73	1	630	88	6	*.992
1998—	Jackson (Texas).........	C	48	168	27	43	6	0	8	25	.256	13	31	0	329	40	10	.974
—	Portland (East.)■.......	C	31	88	9	22	3	0	3	11	.250	8	21	0	82	5	5	.946
1999—	Calgary (PCL).............	C-DH	97	349	43	90	22	0	15	61	.258	24	64	0	552	67	7	.989
—	Florida (N.L.).............	C	24	67	4	12	4	0	2	4	.179	10	14	0	105	17	1	.992
Major League totals (1 year)			24	67	4	12	4	0	2	4	.179	10	14	0	105	17	1	.992

CATALANOTTO, FRANK   IF   RANGERS

PERSONAL: Born April 27, 1974, in Smithtown, N.Y. ... 6-0/195. ... Bats left, throws right. ... Full name: Frank John Catalanotto.
HIGH SCHOOL: Smithtown (N.Y.) East.
TRANSACTIONS/CAREER NOTES: Selected by Detroit Tigers organization in 10th round of free-agent draft (June 1, 1992). ... Selected by Oakland Athletics from Tigers organization in Rule 5 major league draft (December 9, 1996). ... Returned to Tigers organization (March 21, 1997). ... On Toledo disabled list (June 18-25, 1998). ... Traded by Tigers with P Justin Thompson, P Francisco Cordero, OF Gabe Kapler, C Bill Haselman and P Alan Webb to Texas Rangers for OF Juan Gonzalez, P Danny Patterson and C Gregg Zaun (November 2, 1999).
STATISTICAL NOTES: Led Southern League second basemen with 681 total chances and 95 double plays in 1995. ... Led Southern League second basemen with 689 total chances and 99 double plays in 1996. ... Led International League second basemen with .984 fielding percentage in 1997.

							BATTING							FIELDING			
Year Team (League)	Pos.	G	AB	R	H	2B	3B	HR	RBI	Avg.	BB	SO	SB	PO	A	E	Avg.
1992— Bristol (Appl.)............	2B	21	50	6	10	2	0	0	4	.200	8	8	0	8	6	2	.875
1993— Bristol (Appl.)............	2B	55	199	37	61	9	5	3	22	.307	15	19	3	96	128	10	.957
1994— Fayetteville (SAL)	2B	119	458	72	149	24	8	3	56	.325	37	54	4	244	304	15	.973
1995— Jacksonville (Sou.).....	2B	134	491	66	111	19	5	8	48	.226	49	56	13	252	*411	18	*.974
1996— Jacksonville (Sou.).....	2B	132	497	105	148	34	6	17	67	.298	74	69	15	246	*421	•22	.968
1997— Toledo (I.L.)...............	2-3-O-DH	134	500	75	150	32	3	16	68	.300	47	80	12	168	351	18	†.966
— Detroit (A.L.)............	2B-DH	13	26	2	8	2	0	0	3	.308	3	7	0	7	9	0	1.000
1998— Detroit (A.L.)	2-DH-1-3	89	213	23	60	13	2	6	25	.282	12	39	3	162	51	3	.986
— Toledo (I.L.)...............	1B-2B-DH	28	105	20	35	6	3	4	28	.333	14	21	0	131	43	2	.989
1999— Detroit (A.L.)	1-2-3-DH	100	286	41	79	19	0	11	35	.276	15	49	3	252	98	5	.986
Major League totals (3 years)		202	525	66	147	34	2	17	63	.280	30	95	6	421	158	8	.986

CATHER, MIKE   P

PERSONAL: Born December 17, 1970, in San Diego. ... 6-2/195. ... Throws right, bats right. ... Full name: Michael Peter Cather.
HIGH SCHOOL: Folsom (Calif.).
COLLEGE: California Berkeley.
TRANSACTIONS/CAREER NOTES: Selected by Texas Rangers organization in 41st round of free-agent draft (June 3, 1993). ... Released by Rangers (June 14, 1995). ... Signed by Winnipeg, Northern League (July 4, 1995). ... Granted free agency following 1995 season. ... Signed by Atlanta Braves organization (February 9, 1996). ... On disabled list (May 30-June 12, 1996). ... On Atlanta disabled list (August 31, 1998-remainder of season). ... Granted free agency (October 15, 1999).

Year League	W	L	Pct.	ERA	G	GS	CG	ShO	Sv.	IP	H	R	ER	BB	SO
1993— Gulf Coast Rangers (GCL)..	1	1	.500	1.76	25	0	0	0	4	30²/₃	20	7	6	9	30
1994— Charlotte (FSL).................	8	6	.571	3.88	44	0	0	0	6	60¹/₃	56	33	26	40	53
1995— Tulsa (Texas)	0	2	.000	3.32	18	0	0	0	0	21²/₃	20	11	8	7	15
— Winnipeg (Nor.)■............	4	2	.667	1.45	45	0	0	0	8	31	18	6	5	12	35
1996— Greenville (Sou.)■	3	4	.429	3.70	53	0	0	0	5	87²/₃	89	42	36	29	61
1997— Greenville (Sou.)	5	2	.714	4.34	22	0	0	0	1	37¹/₃	37	18	18	7	29
— Richmond (I.L.)	0	0	...	1.73	13	0	0	0	3	26	17	6	5	9	22
— Atlanta (N.L.)....................	2	4	.333	2.39	35	0	0	0	0	37²/₃	23	12	10	19	29
1998— Atlanta (N.L.)....................	2	2	.500	3.92	36	0	0	0	0	41¹/₃	39	21	18	12	33
— Richmond (I.L.)....................	0	1	.000	5.87	11	0	0	0	0	15¹/₃	22	12	10	6	10
1999— Atlanta (N.L.)....................	1	0	1.000	10.13	4	0	0	0	0	2²/₃	5	3	3	1	0
— Richmond (I.L.)....................	2	7	.222	6.78	45	0	0	0	1	67²/₃	71	57	51	34	60
Major League totals (3 years)	5	6	.455	3.42	75	0	0	0	0	81²/₃	67	36	31	32	62

DIVISION SERIES RECORD

Year League	W	L	Pct.	ERA	G	GS	CG	ShO	Sv.	IP	H	R	ER	BB	SO
1997— Atlanta (N.L.).....................	0	0	...	0.00	1	0	0	0	0	2	0	0	0	1	2

CHAMPIONSHIP SERIES RECORD

Year League	W	L	Pct.	ERA	G	GS	CG	ShO	Sv.	IP	H	R	ER	BB	SO
1997— Atlanta (N.L.).....................	0	0	...	0.00	4	0	0	0	0	2²/₃	3	0	0	0	3

WORLD SERIES RECORD

Year League	W	L	Pct.	ERA	G	GS	CG	ShO	Sv.	IP	H	R	ER	BB	SO
1997— Atlanta (N.L.).....................							Did not play.								

CEDENO, DOMINGO   SS/2B   METS

PERSONAL: Born November 4, 1968, in La Romana, Dominican Republic. ... 6-0/170. ... Bats both, throws right.
TRANSACTIONS/CAREER NOTES: Signed as non-drafted free agent by Toronto Blue Jays organization (August 4, 1987). ... On disabled list (April 22-May 28, 1991). ... Traded by Blue Jays with P Tony Castillo to Chicago White Sox for P Luis Andujar and P Allen Halley (August 22, 1996). ... Granted free agency (December 20, 1996). ... Signed by Texas Rangers organization (January 15, 1997). ... On Texas disabled list (April 8-May 15, 1997); included rehabilitation assignment to Tulsa (May 3-15). ... Released by Rangers (December 11, 1998). ... Signed by Oakland Athletics organization (December 23, 1998). ... Released by Athletics (April 8, 1999). ... Signed by Seattle Mariners (April 11, 1999). ... Traded by Mariners to Philadelphia Phillies for IF Jose Flores (July 7, 1999). ... Released by Phillies (September 13, 1999). ... Signed by New York Mets organization (January 5, 2000).
STATISTICAL NOTES: Led Florida State League shortstops with 633 total chances and 74 double plays in 1990. ... Led Southern League with 12 sacrifice hits in 1991.

							BATTING							FIELDING			
Year Team (League)	Pos.	G	AB	R	H	2B	3B	HR	RBI	Avg.	BB	SO	SB	PO	A	E	Avg.
1988—							Dominican Summer League statistics unavailable.										
1989— Myrtle Beach (SAL)	SS	9	35	4	7	0	0	0	2	.200	3	12	1	12	20	7	.821
— Dunedin (FSL)	SS	9	28	3	6	0	1	0	1	.214	3	10	0	9	21	1	.968
— Medicine Hat (Pio.)	SS	53	194	28	45	6	4	1	20	.232	23	65	6	100	141	•25	.906

C

Year	Team (League)	Pos.	G	AB	R	H	2B	3B	HR	RBI	Avg.	BB	SO	SB	PO	A	E	Avg.
1990—	Dunedin (FSL)............	SS	124	493	64	109	12	10	7	61	.221	48	127	10	*215	*382	36	.943
1991—	Knoxville (Sou.).........	SS	100	336	39	75	7	6	1	26	.223	29	81	11	140	272	24	.945
1992—	Knoxville (Sou.).........	2B-SS	106	337	31	76	7	7	2	21	.226	18	88	8	189	254	28	.941
—	Syracuse (I.L.)...........	2B-SS	18	57	4	11	4	0	0	5	.193	3	14	0	36	43	0	1.000
1993—	Syracuse (I.L.)...........	SS-2B	103	382	58	104	16	10	2	28	.272	33	67	15	150	242	21	.949
—	Toronto (A.L.)............	SS-2B	15	46	5	8	0	0	0	7	.174	1	10	1	10	39	1	.980
1994—	Toronto (A.L.)............	2-S-3-OF	47	97	14	19	2	3	0	10	.196	10	31	1	40	64	8	.929
—	Syracuse (I.L.)...........	2-O-S-DH	22	80	11	23	5	1	1	9	.288	8	13	3	42	33	2	.974
1995—	Toronto (A.L.)............	SS-2B-3B	51	161	18	38	6	1	4	14	.236	10	35	0	85	132	3	.986
1996—	Toronto (A.L.)............	2B-3B-SS	77	282	44	79	10	2	2	17	.280	15	60	5	127	198	9	.973
—	Chicago (A.L.)■........	2B-SS-DH	12	19	2	3	2	0	0	3	.158	0	4	1	6	4	1	.909
1997—	Texas (A.L.)■..........	2-S-3-DH	113	365	49	103	19	6	4	36	.282	27	77	3	146	259	17	.960
—	Tulsa (Texas).............	SS	2	9	0	4	0	1	0	0	.444	0	3	0	3	9	1	.923
—	Okla. City (A.A.)........	2B	6	28	0	10	2	0	0	2	.357	0	6	0	13	20	0	1.000
1998—	Texas (A.L.)...............	SS-DH-2B	61	141	19	37	9	1	2	21	.262	10	32	2	41	79	6	.952
1999—	Seattle (A.L.)■..........	SS-2B-3B	21	42	4	9	2	0	2	8	.214	5	9	1	18	49	4	.944
—	Tacoma (PCL)...........	SS-2B	33	112	17	30	8	1	1	13	.268	7	36	1	45	71	6	.951
—	Philadelphia (N.L.)■..	SS-2B	32	66	5	10	4	0	1	5	.152	5	22	0	20	37	1	.983
American League totals (7 years)			397	1153	155	296	50	13	14	116	.257	78	258	14	473	824	49	.964
National League totals (1 year)			32	66	5	10	4	0	1	5	.152	5	22	0	20	37	1	.983
Major League totals (7 years)			429	1219	160	306	54	13	15	121	.251	83	280	14	493	861	50	.964

C

CEDENO, ROGER   OF   ASTROS

PERSONAL: Born August 16, 1974, in Valencia, Venezuela. ... 6-1/205. ... Bats both, throws right. ... Full name: Roger Leandro Cedeno.
TRANSACTIONS/CAREER NOTES: Signed as non-drafted free agent by Los Angeles Dodgers organization (March 28, 1991). ... On disabled list (June 27-July 14, 1994). ... On Los Angeles disabled list (March 25-April 17 and August 25, 1997-remainder of season); included rehabilitation assignment to Vero Beach (April 17-21). ... On Los Angeles disabled list (March 22-April 24, 1998); included rehabilitation assignment to Albuquerque (April 16-24). ... Traded by Dodgers with C Charles Johnson to New York Mets for C Todd Hundley and P Arnold Gooch (December 1, 1998). ... Traded by Mets with P Octavio Dotel and P Kyle Kessel to Houston Astros for P Mike Hampton and OF Derek Bell (December 23, 1999).
STATISTICAL NOTES: Tied for Pioneer League lead with three intentional bases on balls received in 1992. ... Led Texas League in caught stealing with 20 in 1993. ... Led Pacific Coast League in caught stealing with 18 in 1995.

Year	Team (League)	Pos.	G	AB	R	H	2B	3B	HR	RBI	Avg.	BB	SO	SB	PO	A	E	Avg.
1991—	Dom. Dodgers (DSL) .	OF	58	209	25	50	1	1	0	7	.239	0	0	26	...	...	...	...
1992—	Great Falls (Pio.)	OF	69	256	60	81	6	5	2	27	.316	51	53	*40	113	6	8	.937
1993—	San Antonio (Texas)...	OF	122	465	70	134	12	8	4	30	.288	45	90	28	213	6	9	.961
—	Albuquerque (PCL).....	OF	6	18	1	4	1	0	0	4	.222	3	3	0	12	0	1	.923
1994—	Albuquerque (PCL).....	OF	104	383	84	123	18	5	4	49	.321	51	57	30	194	7	8	.962
1995—	Albuquerque (PCL).....	OF-DH	99	367	67	112	19	9	2	44	.305	53	56	23	189	3	3	.985
—	Los Angeles (N.L.)	OF	40	42	4	10	2	0	0	3	.238	3	10	1	43	0	1	.977
1996—	Los Angeles (N.L.)	OF	86	211	26	52	11	1	2	18	.246	24	47	5	117	2	2	.983
—	Albuquerque (PCL).....	OF	33	125	16	28	2	3	1	10	.224	15	22	6	71	2	0	1.000
1997—	Los Angeles (N.L.)	OF	80	194	31	53	10	2	3	17	.273	25	44	9	148	1	2	.987
—	Albuquerque (PCL).....	OF	29	113	21	40	4	4	2	9	.354	22	16	5	53	1	2	.964
1998—	Vero Beach (FSL)	OF	6	21	5	9	0	1	1	6	.429	5	5	1	14	0	1	.933
—	Los Angeles (N.L.)	OF	105	240	33	58	11	1	2	17	.242	27	57	8	86	4	2	.978
1999—	New York (N.L.)■	OF-2B	155	453	90	142	23	4	4	36	.313	60	100	66	256	9	3	.989
Major League totals (5 years)			466	1140	184	315	57	8	11	91	.276	139	258	89	650	16	10	.985

DIVISION SERIES RECORD

Year	Team (League)	Pos.	G	AB	R	H	2B	3B	HR	RBI	Avg.	BB	SO	SB	PO	A	E	Avg.
1999—	New York (N.L.)..........	OF-PH	4	7	1	2	0	0	0	2	.286	1	1	1	4	0	0	1.000

CHAMPIONSHIP SERIES RECORD

Year	Team (League)	Pos.	G	AB	R	H	2B	3B	HR	RBI	Avg.	BB	SO	SB	PO	A	E	Avg.
1999—	New York (N.L.)..........	OF-PR	5	12	2	6	1	0	0	1	.500	0	1	2	12	0	0	1.000

CHACON, SHAWN   P   ROCKIES

PERSONAL: Born December 23, 1977, in Anchorage, Alaska. ... 6-3/212. ... Throws right, bats right. ... Full name: Shawn A. Chacon.
HIGH SCHOOL: Greeley (Colo.) Central.
TRANSACTIONS/CAREER NOTES: Selected by Colorado Rockies organization in third round of free-agent draft (June 4, 1996).

Year	League	W	L	Pct.	ERA	G	GS	CG	ShO	Sv.	IP	H	R	ER	BB	SO
1996—	Arizona Rockies (Ariz.).......	1	2	.333	*1.60	11	11	1	0	0	56 1/3	46	17	10	15	64
—	Portland (N.W.)	0	2	.000	6.86	4	4	0	0	0	19 2/3	24	18	15	9	17
1997—	Asheville (SAL).................	11	7	.611	3.89	28	27	1	0	0	162	155	80	70	63	149
1998—	Salem (Caro.)	0	4	.000	5.30	12	12	0	0	0	56	53	35	33	31	54
1999—	Salem (Caro.)	5	5	.500	4.13	12	12	0	0	0	72	69	44	33	34	66

CHARLTON, NORM   P   DEVIL RAYS

PERSONAL: Born January 6, 1963, in Fort Polk, La. ... 6-3/205. ... Throws left, bats both. ... Full name: Norman Wood Charlton III.
HIGH SCHOOL: James Madison (San Antonio).

COLLEGE: Rice (degrees in political science, religion and physical education, 1986).

TRANSACTIONS/CAREER NOTES: Selected by Montreal Expos organization in supplemental round ("sandwich pick" between first and second round, 28th pick overall) of free-agent draft (June 4, 1984); pick received as compensation for San Francisco Giants signing Type B free-agent 2B Manny Trillo. ... Traded by Expos with a player to be named later to Cincinnati Reds for IF Wayne Krenchicki (March 31, 1986); Reds acquired 2B Tim Barker to complete deal (April 2, 1986). ... On Cincinnati disabled list (April 6-June 26, 1987); included rehabilitation assignment to Nashville (June 9-26). ... On disabled list (May 26-June 11 and June 17-July 19, 1991). ... On suspended list (September 29 and October 4-6, 1991). ... Traded by Reds to Seattle Mariners for OF Kevin Mitchell (November 17, 1992). ... On suspended list (July 9-16, 1993). ... On disabled list (July 21-August 5 and August 8, 1993-remainder of season). ... Granted free agency (November 18, 1993). ... Signed by Philadelphia Phillies organization (February 3, 1994). ... On disabled list (March 31, 1994-entire season). ... Granted free agency (October 28, 1994). ... Re-signed by Phillies organization (December 22, 1994). ... Released by Phillies (July 10, 1995). ... Signed by Mariners (July 14, 1995). ... Granted free agency (November 7, 1997). ... Signed by Baltimore Orioles organization (December 15, 1997). ... Released by Orioles (July 28, 1998). ... Signed by Atlanta Braves organization (August 5, 1998). ... Granted free agency (October 27, 1998). ... Signed by Tampa Bay Devil Rays organization (January 20, 1999). ... On Durham disabled list (April 8-17, 1999). ... Granted free agency (November 2, 1999). ... Re-signed by Devil Rays organization (January 7, 2000).

STATISTICAL NOTES: Led American Association with 13 wild pitches in 1988.

MISCELLANEOUS: Appeared in one game as pinch runner (1990). ... Appeared in two games as pinch runner (1991).

Year League	W	L	Pct.	ERA	G	GS	CG	ShO	Sv.	IP	H	R	ER	BB	SO
1984— West Palm Beach (FSL)	1	4	.200	4.58	8	8	0	0	0	39 1/3	51	27	20	22	27
1985— West Palm Beach (FSL)	7	10	.412	4.57	24	23	5	2	0	128	135	79	65	79	71
1986— Vermont (East.)■	10	6	.625	2.83	22	22	6	1	0	136 2/3	109	55	43	74	96
1987— Nashville (A.A.)	2	8	.200	4.30	18	17	3	1	0	98 1/3	97	57	47	44	74
1988— Nashville (A.A.)	11	10	.524	3.02	27	27	8	1	0	182	149	69	61	56	*161
— Cincinnati (N.L.)	4	5	.444	3.96	10	10	0	0	0	61 1/3	60	27	27	20	39
1989— Cincinnati (N.L.)	8	3	.727	2.93	69	0	0	0	0	95 1/3	67	38	31	40	98
1990— Cincinnati (N.L.)	12	9	.571	2.74	56	16	1	1	2	154 1/3	131	53	47	70	117
1991— Cincinnati (N.L.)	3	5	.375	2.91	39	11	0	0	1	108 1/3	92	37	35	34	77
1992— Cincinnati (N.L.)	4	2	.667	2.99	64	0	0	0	26	81 1/3	79	39	27	26	90
1993— Seattle (A.L.)■	1	3	.250	2.34	34	0	0	0	18	34 2/3	22	12	9	17	48
1994— Philadelphia (N.L.)............						Did not play.									
1995— Philadelphia (N.L.)■	2	5	.286	7.36	25	0	0	0	0	22	23	19	18	15	12
— Seattle (A.L.)■	2	1	.667	1.51	30	0	0	0	14	47 2/3	23	12	8	16	58
1996— Seattle (A.L.)	4	7	.364	4.04	70	0	0	0	20	75 2/3	68	37	34	38	73
1997— Seattle (A.L.)	3	8	.273	7.27	71	0	0	0	14	69 1/3	89	59	56	47	55
1998— Baltimore (A.L.)■	2	1	.667	6.94	36	0	0	0	0	35	46	27	27	25	41
— Richmond (I.L.)■	0	0	...	0.00	2	0	0	0	0	2	2	0	0	0	1
— Atlanta (N.L.)	0	0	...	1.38	13	0	0	0	1	13	7	2	2	8	6
1999— Durham (I.L.)■	3	2	.600	3.69	18	0	0	0	1	31 2/3	27	13	13	10	29
— Tampa Bay (A.L.)................	2	3	.400	4.44	42	0	0	0	0	50 2/3	49	29	25	36	45
A.L. totals (6 years)	14	23	.378	4.57	283	0	0	0	66	313	297	176	159	179	320
N.L. totals (7 years)	33	29	.532	3.14	276	37	1	1	30	535 2/3	459	215	187	213	439
Major League totals (11 years)	47	52	.475	3.67	559	37	1	1	96	848 2/3	756	391	346	392	759

DIVISION SERIES RECORD

Year League	W	L	Pct.	ERA	G	GS	CG	ShO	Sv.	IP	H	R	ER	BB	SO
1995— Seattle (A.L.)	1	0	1.000	2.45	4	0	0	0	1	7 1/3	4	2	2	3	9
1997— Seattle (A.L.)	0	0	...	0.00	2	0	0	0	0	2 1/3	2	0	0	0	1
Division series totals (2 years)	1	0	1.000	1.86	6	0	0	0	1	9 2/3	6	2	2	3	10

CHAMPIONSHIP SERIES RECORD

Year League	W	L	Pct.	ERA	G	GS	CG	ShO	Sv.	IP	H	R	ER	BB	SO
1990— Cincinnati (N.L.)	1	1	.500	1.80	4	0	0	0	0	5	4	2	1	3	3
1995— Seattle (A.L.)	1	0	1.000	0.00	3	0	0	0	1	6	1	0	0	1	5
Champ. series totals (2 years)	2	1	.667	0.82	7	0	0	0	1	11	5	2	1	4	8

WORLD SERIES RECORD

NOTES: Member of World Series championship team (1990).

Year League	W	L	Pct.	ERA	G	GS	CG	ShO	Sv.	IP	H	R	ER	BB	SO
1990— Cincinnati (N.L.)	0	0	...	0.00	1	0	0	0	0	1	1	0	0	0	0

ALL-STAR GAME RECORD

Year League	W	L	Pct.	ERA	GS	CG	ShO	Sv.	IP	H	R	ER	BB	SO
1992— National	0	0	...	0.00	0	0	0	0	1	0	0	0	0	1

CHAVEZ, ERIC   3B   ATHLETICS

PERSONAL: Born December 7, 1977, in Los Angeles. ... 6-0/204. ... Bats left, throws right. ... Full name: Eric Cesar Chavez.

HIGH SCHOOL: Mount Carmel (San Diego).

TRANSACTIONS/CAREER NOTES: Selected by Oakland Athletics organization in first round (10th pick overall) of free-agent draft (June 2, 1996). ... On Oakland disabled list (August 21-September 19, 1999); included rehabilitation assignment to Vancouver (September 14-19).

STATISTICAL NOTES: Career major league grand slams: 1.

							BATTING								FIELDING		
Year Team (League)	Pos.	G	AB	R	H	2B	3B	HR	RBI	Avg.	BB	SO	SB	PO	A	E	Avg.
1997— Visalia (Calif.)	3B-DH	134	520	67	141	30	3	18	100	.271	37	91	13	84	268	*32	.917
1998— Huntsville (Sou.)	3B-DH	88	335	66	110	27	1	22	86	.328	42	61	12	54	146	14	.935
— Edmonton (PCL)	3B-DH	47	194	38	63	18	0	11	40	.325	12	32	2	34	66	7	.935
— Oakland (A.L.)	3B	16	45	6	14	4	1	0	6	.311	3	5	1	11	21	0	1.000
1999— Oakland (A.L.)	3B-DH-SS	115	356	47	88	21	2	13	50	.247	46	56	1	69	155	9	.961
Major League totals (2 years)		131	401	53	102	25	3	13	56	.254	49	61	2	80	176	9	.966

CHECO, ROBINSON   P   DODGERS

PERSONAL: Born September 9, 1971, in Santo Domingo, Dominican Republic. ... 6-1/185. ... Throws right, bats right. ... Full name: Robinson Perez Checo. ... Name pronounced CHAY-co.

TRANSACTIONS/CAREER NOTES: Signed as non-drafted free agent by California Angels organization (January 22, 1989). ... Released by Angels (March 5, 1990). ... Played for Hiroshima Toyo Carp organization of Japan Central League (1995 and 1996), including minor league seasons in Japan Western League (1992 and 1993). ... Played in China (1994). ... Rights obtained by Boston Red Sox from Carp (December 4, 1996). ... Signed by Red Sox (December 6, 1996). ... On Boston disabled list (March 21-May 13, 1997); including rehabilitation assignments to Sarasota (May 13-July 3), Pawtucket (July 4-26 and July 29-September 9) and Trenton (July 27-28). ... On Pawtucket disabled list (May 12-July 29, 1998). ... Granted free agency (December 21, 1998). ... Signed by Detroit Tigers organization (February 16, 1999). ... Traded by Tigers with P Apostol Garcia, P Rick Roberts and cash considerations to Los Angeles Dodgers for P Mel Rojas and P Dave Mlicki (April 16, 1999). ... On Los Angeles disabled list (July 29-September 12, 1999); included rehabilitation assignment to San Bernardino (August 19-September 7).

STATISTICAL NOTES: Tied for Pacific Coast League lead with four balks in 1999.

Year	League	W	L	Pct.	ERA	G	GS	CG	ShO	Sv.	IP	H	R	ER	BB	SO
1989—	Dom. Angels (DSL)					Dominican Summer League statistics unavailable.										
1995—	Hiroshima (Jap. Cen.)■	15	8	.652	2.74	28	17	10	3	0	193 2/3	143	64	59	98	166
1996—	Hiroshima (Jap. Cen.)	4	1	.800	4.80	9	9	3	1	0	50 2/3	52	31	27	24	36
1997—	Sarasota (FSL)■	1	4	.200	5.30	11	11	0	0	0	56	54	37	33	27	63
	— Trenton (East.)	1	0	1.000	2.35	1	1	0	0	0	7 2/3	6	3	2	1	9
	— Pawtucket (I.L.)	4	2	.667	3.42	9	9	2	1	0	55 1/3	41	22	21	16	56
	— Boston (A.L.)	1	1	.500	3.38	5	2	0	0	0	13 1/3	12	5	5	3	14
1998—	Pawtucket (I.L.)	6	2	.750	4.56	11	10	0	0	0	53 1/3	48	30	27	26	46
	— Boston (A.L.)	0	2	.000	9.39	2	2	0	0	0	7 2/3	11	8	8	5	5
	— GC Red Sox (GCL)	1	0	1.000	3.00	3	3	0	0	0	9	9	5	3	0	13
	— Sarasota (FSL)	0	1	1.000	9.00	1	1	0	0	0	2	3	2	2	1	4
1999—	Toledo (I.L.)■...................	0	0	...	0.00	2	1	0	0	0	5	2	0	0	1	6
	— Los Angeles (N.L.)■	2	2	.500	10.34	9	2	0	0	0	15 2/3	24	20	18	13	11
	— Albuquerque (PCL)	3	6	.333	4.33	16	15	0	0	0	79	68	40	38	39	98
	— San Bernardino (Calif.)	0	0	...	10.80	2	2	0	0	0	5	5	6	6	3	6
A.L. totals (2 years)		1	3	.250	5.57	7	4	0	0	0	21	23	13	13	8	19
N.L. totals (1 year)		2	2	.500	10.34	9	2	0	0	0	15 2/3	24	20	18	13	11
Major League totals (3 years)		3	5	.375	7.61	16	6	0	0	0	36 2/3	47	33	31	21	30

CHEN, BRUCE   P   BRAVES

PERSONAL: Born June 19, 1977, in Panama City, Panama. ... 6-1/180. ... Throws left, bats both. ... Full name: Bruce Kastulo Chen.
HIGH SCHOOL: Instituto Panamericano (Panama).
TRANSACTIONS/CAREER NOTES: Signed as non-drafted free agent by Atlanta Braves organization (July 1, 1993).
HONORS: Named Southern League Most Outstanding Pitcher (1998).

Year	League	W	L	Pct.	ERA	G	GS	CG	ShO	Sv.	IP	H	R	ER	BB	SO
1994—	Gulf Coast Braves (GCL)	1	4	.200	3.80	9	7	0	0	1	42 2/3	42	21	18	3	26
1995—	Danville (Appl.)..................	4	4	.500	3.97	14	13	1	0	0	70 1/3	78	42	31	19	56
1996—	Eugene (N.W.)	4	1	.800	2.27	11	8	0	0	0	35 2/3	23	13	9	14	55
1997—	Macon (SAL)	12	7	.632	3.51	28	28	1	1	0	146 1/3	120	67	57	44	182
1998—	Greenville (Sou.)	13	7	.650	3.29	24	23	1	0	0	139 1/3	106	57	51	48	164
	— Richmond (I.L.)	2	1	.667	1.88	4	4	0	0	0	24	17	5	5	19	29
	— Atlanta (N.L.)	2	0	1.000	3.98	4	4	0	0	0	20 1/3	23	9	9	9	17
1999—	Richmond (I.L.)	6	3	.667	3.81	14	14	0	0	0	78	73	36	33	26	90
	— Atlanta (N.L.)	2	2	.500	5.47	16	7	0	0	0	51	38	32	31	27	45
Major League totals (2 years)		4	2	.667	5.05	20	11	0	0	0	71 1/3	61	41	40	36	62

DIVISION SERIES RECORD

Year	League	W	L	Pct.	ERA	G	GS	CG	ShO	Sv.	IP	H	R	ER	BB	SO
1999—	Atlanta (N.L.)					Did not play.										

CHAMPIONSHIP SERIES RECORD

Year	League	W	L	Pct.	ERA	G	GS	CG	ShO	Sv.	IP	H	R	ER	BB	SO
1999—	Atlanta (N.L.)					Did not play.										

WORLD SERIES RECORD

Year	League	W	L	Pct.	ERA	G	GS	CG	ShO	Sv.	IP	H	R	ER	BB	SO
1999—	Atlanta (N.L.)					Did not play.										

CHIARAMONTE, GIUSEPPE   C   GIANTS

PERSONAL: Born February 19, 1976, in Santa Cruz, Calif. ... 6-0/200. ... Bats right, throws right. ... Full name: Giuseppe Cario Chiaramonte.
HIGH SCHOOL: Soquel (Calif.).
COLLEGE: Fresno State.
TRANSACTIONS/CAREER NOTES: Selected by San Francisco Giants organization in fifth round of free-agent draft (June 3, 1997).
STATISTICAL NOTES: Led California League with 12 sacrifice flies in 1998.

							BATTING							FIELDING			
Year	Team (League)	Pos.	G	AB	R	H	2B	3B	HR	RBI	Avg.	BB	SO	SB	PO	A	E	Avg.
1997—	San Jose (Calif.).........	C	64	223	29	51	11	1	12	44	.229	25	58	0	476	59	4	.993
1998—	San Jose (Calif.).........	C	129	502	87	137	33	3	22	87	.273	47	139	5	826	71	9	*.990
1999—	Shreveport (Texas).....	C	114	400	54	98	20	2	19	74	.245	40	88	4	550	40	8	.987

CHO, JIN HO   P   RED SOX

PERSONAL: Born August 16, 1975, in Jun Ju City, Korea. ... 6-3/220. ... Throws right, bats right.
COLLEGE: Won Kwang (South Korea).
TRANSACTIONS/CAREER NOTES: Signed as non-drafted free agent by Boston Red Sox organization (March 30, 1998).
MISCELLANEOUS: Member of 1996 South Korean Olympic team.

Year League	W	L	Pct.	ERA	G	GS	CG	ShO	Sv.	IP	H	R	ER	BB	SO
1998— Sarasota (FSL)	3	1	.750	3.09	5	5	0	0	0	32	33	14	11	5	30
— Trenton (East.)	5	2	.714	2.19	13	13	1	1	0	74	59	21	18	19	62
— Boston (A.L.)	0	3	.000	8.20	4	4	0	0	0	18²/₃	28	17	17	3	15
1999— Pawtucket (I.L.)	9	3	.750	3.45	17	17	4	0	0	109²/₃	99	46	42	29	80
— Boston (A.L.)	2	3	.400	5.72	9	7	0	0	0	39¹/₃	45	26	25	8	16
Major League totals (2 years)	2	6	.250	6.52	13	11	0	0	0	58	73	43	42	11	31

CHOUINARD, BOBBY   P   DIAMONDBACKS

PERSONAL: Born May 1, 1972, in Manilla, The Phillipines. ... 6-1/190. ... Throws right, bats right. ... Full name: Robert William Chouinard.
HIGH SCHOOL: Forest Grove (Ore.).
TRANSACTIONS/CAREER NOTES: Selected by Baltimore Orioles organization in fifth round of free-agent draft (June 4, 1990). ... Traded by Orioles with P Allen Plaster to Oakland Athletics organization for OF Harold Baines (January 14, 1993). ... Granted free agency (October 15, 1997). ... Signed by Milwaukee Brewers organization (October 31, 1997). ... Claimed on waivers by Arizona Diamondbacks (June 1, 1998). ... On Arizona disabled list (August 22-September 8, 1998); included rehabilitation assignment to Tucson (September 6-8). ... On Tucson disabled list (June 20-28, 1999).

Year League	W	L	Pct.	ERA	G	GS	CG	ShO	Sv.	IP	H	R	ER	BB	SO
1990— Bluefield (Appl.)	2	5	.286	3.70	10	10	2	1	0	56	61	34	23	14	30
1991— Kane County (Midw.)	2	4	.333	4.64	6	6	0	0	0	33	45	24	17	5	17
— Bluefield (Appl.)	5	1	.833	3.48	6	6	0	0	0	33²/₃	44	19	13	11	31
1992— Kane County (Midw.)	10	14	.417	*2.08	26	26	*9	•2	0	181²/₃	151	60	42	38	112
1993— Modesto (Calif.)■	8	10	.444	4.26	24	24	1	0	0	145²/₃	154	75	69	56	82
1994— Modesto (Calif.)	12	5	.706	2.59	29	20	0	0	3	145²/₃	147	53	42	32	74
1995— Huntsville (Sou.)	14	8	.636	3.62	29	*29	1	1	0	166²/₃	155	81	67	50	106
1996— Edmonton (PCL)	10	2	.833	2.77	15	15	0	0	0	84¹/₃	70	32	26	24	45
— Oakland (A.L.)	4	2	.667	6.10	13	11	0	0	0	59	75	41	40	32	32
1997— Edmonton (PCL)	6	6	.500	6.03	25	21	1	0	0	100	129	80	67	26	58
1998— Louisville (I.L.)■	2	1	.667	4.93	7	7	0	0	0	42	52	31	23	15	33
— Milwaukee (N.L.)	0	0	...	3.00	1	0	0	0	0	3	5	1	1	0	1
— Tucson (PCL)■	0	0	...	4.26	4	0	0	0	1	6¹/₃	6	3	3	0	6
— Arizona (N.L.)	0	2	.000	4.23	26	2	0	0	0	38¹/₃	41	23	18	11	26
1999— Tucson (PCL)	4	1	.800	4.06	12	9	0	0	0	62	70	33	28	13	63
— Arizona (N.L.)	5	2	.714	2.68	32	0	0	0	1	40¹/₃	31	16	12	12	23
A.L. totals (1 year)	4	2	.667	6.10	13	11	0	0	0	59	75	41	40	32	32
N.L. totals (2 years)	5	4	.556	3.42	59	2	0	0	1	81²/₃	77	40	31	23	50
Major League totals (3 years)	9	6	.600	4.54	72	13	0	0	1	140²/₃	152	81	71	55	82

DIVISION SERIES RECORD

Year League	W	L	Pct.	ERA	G	GS	CG	ShO	Sv.	IP	H	R	ER	BB	SO
1999— Arizona (N.L.)	0	0	...	4.50	2	0	0	0	0	2	3	1	1	0	1

CHRISTENSEN, McKAY   OF   WHITE SOX

PERSONAL: Born August 14, 1975, in Upland, Calif. ... 5-11/180. ... Bats left, throws left. ... Full name: McKay A. Christensen.
HIGH SCHOOL: Clovis West (Fresno, Calif.).
TRANSACTIONS/CAREER NOTES: Selected by California Angels organization in first round (sixth pick overall) of free-agent draft (June 2, 1994). ... Traded by Angels with P Andrew Lorraine, P Bill Simas and P John Snyder to Chicago White Sox for P Jim Abbott and P Tim Fortugno (July 27, 1995). ... On disabled list (April 10-28 and June 2-17, 1998). ... On Birmingham disabled list (July 13-August 1, 1999).
STATISTICAL NOTES: Tied for Carolina League lead with three double plays by outfielder in 1998.

						BATTING									FIELDING		
Year Team (League)	Pos.	G	AB	R	H	2B	3B	HR	RBI	Avg.	BB	SO	SB	PO	A	E	Avg.
1996— GC White Sox (GCL)	OF	35	133	17	35	7	5	1	16	.263	10	23	10	54	2	1	.982
— Hickory (SAL)	OF	6	11	0	0	0	0	0	0	.000	1	4	0	4	0	0	1.000
1997— Hickory (SAL)	OF	127	503	95	141	12	*12	5	47	.280	52	81	28	*280	5	9	.969
1998— Win.-Salem (Car.)	OF	95	361	69	103	17	6	4	32	.285	53	54	20	199	6	4	.981
1999— Chicago (A.L.)	OF	28	53	10	12	1	0	1	6	.226	4	7	2	50	0	3	.943
— Birmingham (Sou.)	OF	75	293	53	85	8	6	3	28	.290	31	46	18	190	2	2	.990
— Charlotte (I.L.)	OF	1	4	0	1	0	0	0	0	.250	0	0	1	2	0	0	1.000
Major League totals (1 year)		28	53	10	12	1	0	1	6	.226	4	7	2	50	0	3	.943

CHRISTENSON, RYAN   OF   ATHLETICS

PERSONAL: Born March 28, 1974, in Redlands, Calif. ... 6-0/191. ... Bats right, throws right. ... Full name: Ryan Alan Christenson.
HIGH SCHOOL: Apple Valley (Calif.).
COLLEGE: Pepperdine.
TRANSACTIONS/CAREER NOTES: Selected by Oakland Athletics organization in 10th round of free-agent draft (June 1, 1995).

Year	Team (League)	Pos.	G	AB	R	H	2B	3B	HR	RBI	Avg.	BB	SO	SB	PO	A	E	Avg.
1995—	S. Oregon (N'west).....	OF	49	158	14	30	4	1	1	16	.190	22	33	5	84	3	2	.978
1996—	S. Oregon (N'west).....	OF	36	136	31	39	11	0	5	21	.287	19	21	8	78	5	4	.954
	— W. Mich. (Midw.).....	OF-3B	33	122	21	38	2	2	2	18	.311	13	22	2	64	1	3	.956
1997—	Visalia (Calif.)............	OF	83	308	69	90	18	8	13	54	.292	70	72	20	164	4	3	.982
	— Huntsville (Sou.)........	OF	29	120	39	44	9	3	2	18	.367	24	23	5	81	1	1	.988
	— Edmonton (PCL)........	OF	16	49	12	14	2	2	2	5	.286	11	11	2	42	1	0	1.000
1998—	Edmonton (PCL)........	OF	22	88	17	23	6	1	1	7	.261	15	24	4	56	2	0	1.000
	— Oakland (A.L.)............	OF	117	370	56	95	22	2	5	40	.257	36	106	5	284	7	5	.983
1999—	Oakland (A.L.)..........	OF-DH	106	268	41	56	12	1	4	24	.209	38	58	7	213	3	7	.969
	— Vancouver (PCL)........	OF	33	128	30	44	8	1	1	16	.344	22	21	7	88	1	2	.978
Major League totals (2 years)			223	638	97	151	34	3	9	64	.237	74	164	12	497	10	12	.977

CHRISTIANSEN, JASON — P — PIRATES

PERSONAL: Born September 21, 1969, in Omaha, Neb. ... 6-5/241. ... Throws left, bats right. ... Full name: Jason Samuel Christiansen.
HIGH SCHOOL: Elkhorn (Neb.).
JUNIOR COLLEGE: Iowa Western College.
COLLEGE: Cameron (Okla.).
TRANSACTIONS/CAREER NOTES: Signed as non-drafted free agent by Pittsburgh Pirates organization (July 5, 1991). ... On Calgary disabled list (August 12-September 5, 1996). ... On Pittsburgh disabled list (March 31-June 19, 1997). ... On Pittsburgh disabled list (May 7-28; July 29-August 21 and August 24-September 23, 1999); included rehabilitation assignments to Altoona (May 22-28) and Nashville (August 16-21).

Year	League	W	L	Pct.	ERA	G	GS	CG	ShO	Sv.	IP	H	R	ER	BB	SO
1991—	Gulf Coast Pirates (GCL)....	1	0	1.000	0.00	6	0	0	0	1	8	4	0	0	1	8
	— Welland (NY-P)...............	0	1	.000	2.53	8	1	0	0	0	21 1/3	15	9	6	12	17
1992—	Augusta (SAL)..................	1	0	1.000	1.80	10	0	0	0	2	20	12	4	4	8	21
	— Salem (Caro.)..................	3	1	.750	3.24	38	0	0	0	2	50	47	20	18	22	59
1993—	Salem (Caro.)..................	1	1	.500	3.15	57	0	0	0	4	71 1/3	48	30	25	24	70
	— Carolina (Sou.)...............	0	0	...	0.00	2	0	0	0	0	2 2/3	3	0	0	1	2
1994—	Carolina (Sou.)...............	2	1	.667	2.09	28	0	0	0	2	38 2/3	30	10	9	14	43
	— Buffalo (A.A.)..................	3	1	.750	2.41	33	0	0	0	0	33 2/3	19	9	9	16	39
1995—	Pittsburgh (N.L.)............	1	3	.250	4.15	63	0	0	0	0	56 1/3	49	28	26	34	53
1996—	Calgary (PCL).................	1	0	1.000	3.27	2	2	0	0	0	11	9	4	4	1	10
	— Pittsburgh (N.L.)............	3	3	.500	6.70	33	0	0	0	0	44 1/3	56	34	33	19	38
1997—	Pittsburgh (N.L.)............	3	0	1.000	2.94	39	0	0	0	0	33 2/3	37	11	11	17	37
	— Carolina (Sou.)...............	0	1	.000	4.20	8	1	0	0	1	15	17	7	7	5	25
1998—	Pittsburgh (N.L.)............	3	3	.500	2.51	60	0	0	0	6	64 2/3	51	22	18	27	71
1999—	Pittsburgh (N.L.)............	2	3	.400	4.06	39	0	0	0	3	37 2/3	26	17	17	22	35
	— Altoona (East.)...............	0	0	...	0.00	2	1	0	0	0	3	1	0	0	1	2
	— Nashville (PCL)................	0	0	...	0.00	2	0	0	0	0	2	0	0	0	0	1
Major League totals (5 years).......		12	12	.500	3.99	234	0	0	0	9	236 2/3	219	112	105	119	234

CHRISTMAN, TIM — P — ROCKIES

PERSONAL: Born March 31, 1975, in Oneonta, N.Y. ... 6-0/195. ... Throws left, bats left. ... Full name: Timothy A. Christman.
HIGH SCHOOL: Oneonta (N.Y.).
COLLEGE: Siena.
TRANSACTIONS/CAREER NOTES: Selected by Colorado Rockies organization in 11th round of free-agent draft (June 4, 1996). ... On disabled list (April 10, 1998-entire season). ... On Salem disabled list (April 8-23, 1999).

Year	League	W	L	Pct.	ERA	G	GS	CG	ShO	Sv.	IP	H	R	ER	BB	SO
1996—	Portland (N.W.)................	1	2	.333	4.28	21	0	0	0	2	40	30	23	19	23	56
1997—	Asheville (SAL)................	7	3	.700	3.41	29	0	0	0	3	63 1/3	55	32	24	18	87
1998—								Did not play.								
1999—	Salem (Caro.)..................	1	2	.333	2.42	38	0	0	0	2	48 1/3	38	18	13	12	64

CIRILLO, JEFF — 3B — ROCKIES

PERSONAL: Born September 23, 1969, in Pasadena, Calif. ... 6-1/195. ... Bats right, throws right. ... Full name: Jeffrey Howard Cirillo.
HIGH SCHOOL: Providence (Burbank, Calif.).
COLLEGE: Southern California.
TRANSACTIONS/CAREER NOTES: Selected by Chicago Cubs organization in 37th round of free-agent draft (June 2, 1987); did not sign. ... Selected by Milwaukee Brewers organization in 11th round of free-agent draft (June 3, 1991). ... On New Orleans disabled list (July 22-August 6, 1993). ... Traded by Brewers with P Scott Karl and cash to Colorado Rockies as part of three-way deal in which Brewers received P Jamey Wright and C Henry Blanco from Rockies, Oakland Athletics received P Justin Miller and cash from Rockies and Brewers received P Jimmy Haynes from Athletics (December 13, 1999).
RECORDS: Shares N.L. single-season record for most double plays by third baseman—45 (1998).
STATISTICAL NOTES: Led Pioneer League in grounding into double plays with 11 in 1991. ... Led Pioneer League third basemen with 60 putouts, 104 assists and 179 total chances in 1991. ... Tied for Midwest League lead with six intentional bases on balls received in 1992. ... Led A.L. third basemen with 463 total chances and 29 double plays in 1997. ... Led N.L. in grounding into double plays with 26 in 1998. ... Led N.L. third basemen with 340 assists and 45 double plays in 1998. ... Led N.L. third basemen with 35 double plays in 1999. ... Career major league grand slams: 1.
MISCELLANEOUS: Holds Milwaukee Brewers all-time record for highest career batting average (.307).

Year	Team (League)	Pos.	G	AB	R	H	2B	3B	HR	RBI	Avg.	BB	SO	SB	PO	A	E	Avg.
1991—	Helena (Pio.)	3B-OF	•70	286	60	100	16	2	10	51	.350	31	28	3	†71	†104	15	.921
1992—	Stockton (Calif.)	3B	7	27	2	6	1	0	0	5	.222	2	0	0	7	10	0	1.000
	— Beloit (Midw.).............	3B-2B	126	444	65	135	27	3	9	71	.304	84	85	21	115	309	26	.942
1993—	El Paso (Texas)............	2B-3B	67	249	53	85	16	2	9	41	.341	26	37	2	83	142	9	.962
	— New Orleans (A.A.)	3-2-S-DH	58	215	31	63	13	2	3	32	.293	29	33	2	46	145	5	.974
1994—	New Orleans (A.A.)	3-2-DH-S	61	236	45	73	18	2	10	46	.309	28	39	4	67	139	8	.963
	— Milwaukee (A.L.)	3B-2B	39	126	17	30	9	0	3	12	.238	11	16	0	23	60	3	.965
1995—	Milwaukee (A.L.)	3-2-1-SS	125	328	57	91	19	4	9	39	.277	47	42	7	113	230	15	.958
1996—	Milwaukee (A.L.)	3-DH-1-2	158	566	101	184	46	5	15	83	.325	58	69	4	112	242	18	.952
1997—	Milwaukee (A.L.)	3B-DH	154	580	74	167	46	2	10	82	.288	60	74	4	•126	*320	17	.963
1998—	Milwaukee (N.L.)	3B-1B	156	604	97	194	31	1	14	68	.321	79	88	10	149	†353	11	.979
1999—	Milwaukee (N.L.)	3B	157	607	98	198	35	1	15	88	.326	75	83	7	*124	312	15	.967
	American League totals (4 years)		476	1600	249	472	120	11	37	216	.295	176	201	15	374	852	53	.959
	National League totals (2 years)		313	1211	195	392	66	2	29	156	.324	154	171	17	273	665	26	.973
	Major League totals (6 years)		789	2811	444	864	186	13	66	372	.307	330	372	32	647	1517	79	.965

ALL-STAR GAME RECORD

Year	League	Pos.	AB	R	H	2B	3B	HR	RBI	Avg.	BB	SO	SB	PO	A	E	Avg.
1997—	American	3B	1	0	0	0	0	0	0	.000	0	1	0	0	0	0	...

CLAPINSKI, CHRIS   IF   MARLINS

C

PERSONAL: Born August 20, 1971, in Buffalo, N.Y. ... 6-0/175. ... Bats both, throws right. ... Full name: Christopher Alan Clapinski. ... Name pronounced clap-in-SKEE.
HIGH SCHOOL: Palm Desert (Calif.).
COLLEGE: California.
TRANSACTIONS/CAREER NOTES: Signed as non-drafted free agent by Florida Marlins organization (June 10, 1992). ... Granted free agency (October 16, 1998). ... Re-signed by Marlins organization (December 21, 1998).
STATISTICAL NOTES: Led Gulf Coast League second basemen with 40 double plays and 333 total chances in 1992.

Year	Team (League)	Pos.	G	AB	R	H	2B	3B	HR	RBI	Avg.	BB	SO	SB	PO	A	E	Avg.
1992—	GC Marlins (GCL)	2B	59	212	36	51	8	1	1	15	.241	49	42	5	*156	*167	10	.970
1993—	Kane County (Midw.)..	2B-3B	82	214	22	45	12	1	0	27	.210	31	55	3	121	152	16	.945
1994—	Brev. County (FSL)	2B-3B-OF	65	157	33	45	12	3	1	13	.287	23	28	3	47	106	5	.968
1995—	Portland (East.)	3-2-S-1-O	87	208	32	49	9	3	4	30	.236	28	44	5	80	117	4	.980
1996—	Portland (East.)	SS	23	73	15	19	7	0	3	11	.260	13	13	3	29	68	2	.980
	— Charlotte (I.L.)............	S-3-2-O	105	362	74	103	20	1	10	39	.285	47	54	13	143	265	16	.962
1997—	Charlotte (I.L.)............	2-S-3-O	110	340	62	89	24	2	12	52	.262	48	64	14	148	234	12	.970
1998—	Charlotte (I.L.)............	O-3-S-2	100	312	53	84	18	1	9	35	.269	39	53	11	106	162	9	.968
	— Brev. County (FSL)	2B-SS-3B	5	14	1	1	0	1	0	4	.071	7	2	0	2	8	1	.909
1999—	Calgary (PCL)	3-S-O-2	81	267	51	86	21	6	8	35	.322	30	53	5	101	136	7	.971
	— Florida (N.L.) 3-S-O-2-DH		36	56	6	13	1	2	0	2	.232	9	12	1	17	23	3	.930
	Major League totals (1 year)		36	56	6	13	1	2	0	2	.232	9	12	1	17	23	3	.930

RECORD AS PITCHER

Year	League	W	L	Pct.	ERA	G	GS	CG	ShO	Sv.	IP	H	R	ER	BB	SO
1996—	Charlotte (I.L.)..................	0	0	...	4.50	1	0	0	0	0	2	1	1	1	0	2

CLARK, BRADY   OF   REDS

PERSONAL: Born April 18, 1973, in Portland, Ore. ... 6-2/195. ... Bats right, throws right. ... Full name: Brady William Clark.
HIGH SCHOOL: Sunset (Beaverton, Ore.).
COLLEGE: San Diego.
TRANSACTIONS/CAREER NOTES: Signed as non-drafted free agent by Cincinnati Reds organization (January 13, 1996). ... Released by Reds (April 10, 1996). ... Re-signed by Reds organization (February 15, 1997).
HONORS: Named Southern League Most Valuable Player (1999).
STATISTICAL NOTES: Led Midwest League outfielders with 278 total chances in 1997. ... Led Southern League with 261 total bases in 1999.

Year	Team (League)	Pos.	G	AB	R	H	2B	3B	HR	RBI	Avg.	BB	SO	SB	PO	A	E	Avg.
1997—	Burlington (Midw.)	OF	126	459	108	149	29	7	11	63	.325	76	71	31	*265	9	4	.986
1998—	Chattanooga (Sou.)	OF	64	222	41	60	13	1	2	16	.270	31	34	12	149	3	1	.993
1999—	Chattanooga (Sou.)	OF-3B	*138	506	103	165	37	4	17	75	.326	89	58	25	255	10	5	.981

CLARK, MARK   P   RANGERS

PERSONAL: Born May 12, 1968, in Bath, Ill. ... 6-5/235. ... Throws right, bats right. ... Full name: Mark Willard Clark.
HIGH SCHOOL: Balyki (Bath, Ill.).
JUNIOR COLLEGE: Lincoln Land Community College (Ill.).
TRANSACTIONS/CAREER NOTES: Selected by St. Louis Cardinals organization in ninth round of free-agent draft (June 1, 1988). ... On Arkansas disabled list (April 12-May 8, 1991). ... Traded by Cardinals with SS Juan Andujar to Cleveland Indians for OF Mark Whiten (March 31, 1993). ... On Cleveland disabled list (July 17-September 9, 1993 and July 21, 1994-remainder of season). ... Traded by Indians to New York Mets for P Reid Cornelius and OF Ryan Thompson (March 31, 1996). ... Traded by Mets to Chicago Cubs (August 11, 1997), as part of deal in which Mets traded OF Lance Johnson and two players to be named later to Cubs for OF Brian McRae, P Mel Rojas and P Turk Wendell (August 8, 1997); Mets traded IF Manny Alexander to Cubs to complete deal (August 14, 1997). ... Granted free agency (October 28, 1998). ... Signed by Texas Rangers (December 10, 1998). ... On Texas disabled list (June 20, 1999-remainder of season); included rehabilitation assignments to Savannah (August 29-31) and Charlotte (September 1-7).

Year	League	W	L	Pct.	ERA	G	GS	CG	ShO	Sv.	IP	H	R	ER	BB	SO
1988—Hamilton (NY-P)		6	7	.462	3.05	15	15	2	0	0	94 1/3	88	39	32	32	60
1989—Savannah (SAL)		•14	9	.609	2.44	27	27	4	2	0	173 2/3	143	61	47	52	132
1990—St. Petersburg (FSL)		3	2	.600	3.05	10	10	1	1	0	62	63	33	21	14	58
— Arkansas (Texas)		5	11	.313	3.82	19	19	*5	0	0	115 1/3	111	56	49	37	87
1991—Arkansas (Texas)		5	5	.500	4.00	15	15	4	1	0	92 1/3	99	50	41	30	76
— Louisville (A.A.)		3	2	.600	2.98	7	6	1	1	0	45 1/3	43	17	15	15	29
— St. Louis (N.L.)		1	1	.500	4.03	7	2	0	0	0	22 1/3	17	10	10	11	13
1992—Louisville (A.A.)		4	4	.500	2.80	9	9	4	*3	0	61	56	20	19	15	38
— St. Louis (N.L.)		3	10	.231	4.45	20	20	1	1	0	113 1/3	117	59	56	36	44
1993—Cleveland (A.L.)■		7	5	.583	4.28	26	15	1	0	0	109 1/3	119	55	52	25	57
— Charlotte (I.L.)		1	0	1.000	2.08	2	2	0	0	0	13	9	5	3	2	12
1994—Cleveland (A.L.)		11	3	.786	3.82	20	20	4	1	0	127 1/3	133	61	54	40	60
1995—Cleveland (A.L.)		9	7	.563	5.27	22	21	2	0	0	124 2/3	143	77	73	42	68
— Buffalo (A.A.)		4	0	1.000	3.57	5	5	0	0	0	35 1/3	39	14	14	10	17
1996—New York (N.L.)■		14	11	.560	3.43	32	32	2	0	0	212 1/3	217	98	81	48	142
1997—New York (N.L.)		8	7	.533	4.25	23	22	1	0	0	142	158	74	67	47	72
— Chicago (N.L.)■		6	1	.857	2.86	9	9	2	0	0	63	55	22	20	12	51
1998—Chicago (N.L.)		9	14	.391	4.84	33	33	2	1	0	213 2/3	236	116	115	48	161
1999—Texas (A.L.)■		3	7	.300	8.60	15	15	0	0	0	74 1/3	103	73	71	34	44
— Savannah (SAL)		0	0	...	0.00	1	1	0	0	0	4	2	0	0	1	1
— Charlotte (FSL)		0	0	...	1.29	2	2	0	0	0	7	5	1	1	1	2
A.L. totals (4 years)		30	22	.577	5.16	83	71	7	1	0	435 2/3	498	266	250	141	229
N.L. totals (5 years)		41	44	.482	4.10	124	118	8	2	0	766 2/3	800	379	349	202	483
Major League totals (9 years)		71	66	.518	4.48	207	189	15	3	0	1202 1/3	1298	645	599	343	712

DIVISION SERIES RECORD

Year	League	W	L	Pct.	ERA	G	GS	CG	ShO	Sv.	IP	H	R	ER	BB	SO
1998—Chicago (N.L.)		0	1	.000	3.00	1	1	0	0	0	6	7	4	2	1	4

CLARK, TONY — 1B — TIGERS

PERSONAL: Born June 15, 1972, in Newton, Kan. ... 6-7/245. ... Bats both, throws right. ... Full name: Anthony Christopher Clark.
HIGH SCHOOL: Valhalla (El Cajon, Calif.), then Christian (El Cajon, Calif.).
COLLEGE: Arizona (did not play baseball), then San Diego State.
TRANSACTIONS/CAREER NOTES: Selected by Detroit Tigers organization in first round (second pick overall) of free-agent draft (June 4, 1990). ... On Niagara Falls temporarily inactive list (June 17, 1991-remainder of season and August 17, 1992-remainder of season). ... On disabled list (August 24, 1993-remainder of season). ... On Detroit disabled list (May 26-June 10, 1999); included rehabilitation assignment to Toledo (June 8-10).
RECORDS: Holds A.L. single-season record for most games with switch-hit home runs—3 (1998).
STATISTICAL NOTES: Switch-hit home runs in one game six times (April 5, 1997; June 17, July 26 and August 1, 1998; and July 18 and July 25, 1999). ... Led A.L. first basemen with 1,533 total chances in 1997. ... Had 19-game hitting streak (July 10-August 1, 1999). ... Career major league grand slams: 1.

							BATTING								FIELDING		
Year	Team (League)	Pos.	G	AB	R	H	2B	3B	HR	RBI	Avg.	BB	SO	SB	PO	A	E	Avg.
1990—Bristol (Appl.)		OF	25	73	2	12	2	0	1	8	.164	6	28	0	23	3	0	1.000
1991—Niagara Falls (NY-P)						Did not play.												
1992—Niagara Falls (NY-P)		OF	27	85	12	26	9	0	5	17	.306	9	34	1	18	1	0	1.000
1993—Lakeland (FSL)		OF	36	117	14	31	4	1	1	22	.265	18	32	0	34	0	2	.944
1994—Trenton (East.)		DH-1B	107	394	50	110	25	0	21	86	.279	40	113	0	505	48	•13	.977
— Toledo (I.L.)		1B-DH	25	92	10	24	4	0	2	13	.261	12	25	2	144	12	0	1.000
1995—Toledo (I.L.)		1B-DH	110	405	50	98	17	2	14	63	.242	52	*129	0	615	51	*13	.981
— Detroit (A.L.)		1B	27	101	10	24	5	1	3	11	.238	8	30	0	253	18	4	.985
1996—Toledo (I.L.)		1B-DH	55	194	42	58	7	1	14	36	.299	31	58	1	400	28	3	.993
— Detroit (A.L.)		1B-DH	100	376	56	94	14	0	27	72	.250	29	127	0	766	54	6	.993
1997—Detroit (A.L.)		1B-DH	159	580	105	160	28	3	32	117	.276	93	144	1	*1423	100	10	.993
1998—Detroit (A.L.)		1B-DH	157	602	84	175	37	0	34	103	.291	63	128	3	1265	102	13	.991
1999—Detroit (A.L.)		1B-DH	143	536	74	150	29	0	31	99	.280	64	133	2	1126	85	10	.992
— Toledo (I.L.)		1B	1	3	0	0	0	0	0	0	.000	1	1	0	10	1	0	1.000
Major League totals (5 years)			586	2195	329	603	113	4	127	402	.275	257	562	6	4833	359	43	.992

CLARK, WILL — 1B — ORIOLES

PERSONAL: Born March 13, 1964, in New Orleans. ... 6-1/200. ... Bats left, throws left. ... Full name: William Nuschler Clark Jr.
HIGH SCHOOL: Jesuit (New Orleans).
COLLEGE: Mississippi State.
TRANSACTIONS/CAREER NOTES: Selected by Kansas City Royals organization in fourth round of free-agent draft (June 7, 1982); did not sign. ... Selected by San Francisco Giants organization in first round (second pick overall) of free-agent draft (June 3, 1985). ... On San Francisco disabled list (June 4-July 24, 1986); included rehabilitation assignment to Phoenix (July 7-24). ... On disabled list (August 26-September 10, 1993). ... Granted free agency (October 25, 1993). ... Signed by Texas Rangers (November 22, 1993). ... On Texas disabled list (June 8-23, June 30-July 15 and July 17-August 4, 1996); included rehabilitation assignment to Tulsa (August 1-4). ... On disabled list (March 28-April 18 and August 25, 1997-remainder of season). ... Granted free agency (November 5, 1998). ... Signed by Baltimore Orioles (December 7, 1998). ... On disabled list (April 19-May 25 and August 14, 1999-remainder of season).
HONORS: Named designated hitter on THE SPORTING NEWS college All-America team (1984). ... Named Golden Spikes Award winner by USA Baseball (1985). ... Named first baseman on THE SPORTING NEWS college All-America team (1985). ... Named first baseman on THE SPORTING NEWS N.L. All-Star team (1988-89 and 1991). ... Named first baseman on THE SPORTING NEWS N.L. Silver Slugger team (1989 and 1991). ... Won N.L. Gold Glove at first base (1991).

STATISTICAL NOTES: Led N.L. first basemen with 130 double plays in 1987, 126 in 1988, 118 in 1990, 115 in 1991 and 130 in 1992. ... Led N.L. with 27 intentional bases on balls received in 1988. ... Led N.L. first basemen with 1,608 total chances in 1988, 1,566 in 1989 and 1,587 in 1990. ... Led N.L. with .536 slugging percentage and tied for lead with 303 total bases in 1991. ... Led A.L. first basemen with 1,051 total chances in 1994. ... Had 16-game hitting streak (August 22-September 7, 1998). ... Career major league grand slams: 3.

MISCELLANEOUS: Member of 1984 U.S. Olympic baseball team. ... Hit home run in first minor league at-bat (June 21, 1985) and first major league at-bat (April 8, 1986); both were on the first swing.

Year Team (League)	Pos.	G	AB	R	H	2B	3B	HR	RBI	Avg.	BB	SO	SB	PO	A	E	Avg.
1985—Fresno (Calif.)............	1B-OF	65	217	41	67	14	0	10	48	.309	62	46	11	523	51	6	.990
1986—San Francisco (N.L.)	1B	111	408	66	117	27	2	11	41	.287	34	76	4	942	72	11	.989
—Phoenix (PCL)...........	DH	6	20	3	5	0	0	0	1	.250	4	2	1	...	...	...	...
1987—San Francisco (N.L.) ..	1B	150	529	89	163	29	5	35	91	.308	49	98	5	1253	103	13	.991
1988—San Francisco (N.L.) ..	1B	*162	575	102	162	31	6	29	*109	.282	*100	129	9	*1492	104	12	.993
1989—San Francisco (N.L.) ..	1B	159	588	•104	196	38	9	23	111	.333	74	103	8	*1445	111	10	.994
1990—San Francisco (N.L.) ..	1B	154	600	91	177	25	5	19	95	.295	62	97	8	*1456	119	12	.992
1991—San Francisco (N.L.) ..	1B	148	565	84	170	32	7	29	116	.301	51	91	4	1273	110	4	*.997
1992—San Francisco (N.L.) ..	1B	144	513	69	154	40	1	16	73	.300	73	82	12	1275	105	10	.993
1993—San Francisco (N.L.) ..	1B	132	491	82	139	27	2	14	73	.283	63	68	2	1078	88	14	.988
1994—Texas (A.L.)■............	1B-DH	110	389	73	128	24	2	13	80	.329	71	59	5	968	73	•10	.990
1995—Texas (A.L.)............	1B-DH	123	454	85	137	27	3	16	92	.302	68	50	0	1076	88	7	.994
1996—Texas (A.L.)............	1B	117	436	69	124	25	1	13	72	.284	64	67	2	956	73	4	.996
—Tulsa (Texas)............	1B	3	9	3	2	0	0	0	0	.222	2	0	0	21	3	0	1.000
1997—Texas (A.L.)............	1B-DH	110	393	56	128	29	1	12	51	.326	49	62	0	880	62	4	.996
1998—Texas (A.L.)............	1B-DH	149	554	98	169	41	1	23	102	.305	72	97	1	1079	73	13	.989
1999—Baltimore (A.L.)■......	1B-DH	77	251	40	76	15	0	10	29	.303	38	42	2	575	42	3	.995
American League totals (6 years)		686	2477	421	762	161	8	87	426	.308	362	377	10	5534	411	41	.993
National League totals (8 years)		1160	4269	687	1278	249	37	176	709	.299	506	744	52	10214	812	86	.992
Major League totals (14 years)		1846	6746	1108	2040	410	45	263	1135	.302	868	1121	62	15748	1223	127	.993

DIVISION SERIES RECORD

Year Team (League)	Pos.	G	AB	R	H	2B	3B	HR	RBI	Avg.	BB	SO	SB	PO	A	E	Avg.
1996—Texas (A.L.)...............	1B	4	16	1	2	0	0	0	0	.125	4	2	0	35	4	0	1.000
1998—Texas (A.L.)...............	1B	3	11	0	1	0	0	0	0	.091	1	2	0	21	2	0	1.000
Division series totals (2 years)		7	27	1	3	0	0	0	0	.111	5	4	0	56	6	0	1.000

CHAMPIONSHIP SERIES RECORD

RECORDS: Holds single-series record for most hits—13. ... Shares single-series record for most total bases—24 (1989). ... Holds single-game record for most runs batted in—6 (October 4, 1989). ... Shares single-series record for most runs—8 (1989). ... Shares single-game records for most runs—4; and most grand slams—1 (October 4, 1989). ... Shares single-inning record for most runs batted in—4 (October 4, 1989, fourth inning). ... Shares N.L. single-series record for most consecutive hits—5 (1989). ... Shares N.L. single-game record for most hits—4 (October 4, 1989).

NOTES: Named N.L. Championship Series Most Valuable Player (1989).

Year Team (League)	Pos.	G	AB	R	H	2B	3B	HR	RBI	Avg.	BB	SO	SB	PO	A	E	Avg.
1987—San Francisco (N.L.) ..	1B	7	25	3	9	2	0	1	3	.360	3	6	1	63	7	1	.986
1989—San Francisco (N.L.) ..	1B	5	20	8	13	3	1	2	8	.650	2	2	0	43	6	0	1.000
Championship series totals (2 years)		12	45	11	22	5	1	3	11	.489	5	8	1	106	13	1	.992

WORLD SERIES RECORD

Year Team (League)	Pos.	G	AB	R	H	2B	3B	HR	RBI	Avg.	BB	SO	SB	PO	A	E	Avg.
1989—San Francisco (N.L.) ..	1B	4	16	2	4	1	0	0	0	.250	1	3	0	40	2	0	1.000

ALL-STAR GAME RECORD

Year League	Pos.	AB	R	H	2B	3B	HR	RBI	Avg.	BB	SO	SB	PO	A	E	Avg.
1988—National....................	1B	2	0	0	0	0	0	0	.000	0	0	0	4	1	0	1.000
1989—National....................	1B	2	0	0	0	0	0	0	.000	0	1	0	5	0	0	1.000
1990—National....................	1B	3	0	1	0	0	0	0	.333	0	0	0	6	0	0	1.000
1991—National....................	1B	2	0	1	0	0	0	0	.500	1	0	0	2	0	0	1.000
1992—National....................	PH-1B	2	1	1	0	0	1	3	.500	0	1	0	1	0	0	1.000
1994—American..................	1B	2	0	2	0	0	0	0	1.000	0	0	1	7	0	0	1.000
All-Star Game totals (6 years)		13	1	5	0	0	1	3	.385	1	2	1	25	1	0	1.000

CLAYTON, ROYCE   SS   RANGERS

PERSONAL: Born January 2, 1970, in Burbank, Calif. ... 6-0/183. ... Bats right, throws right. ... Full name: Royce Spencer Clayton.

HIGH SCHOOL: St. Bernard (Playa del Ray, Calif.).

TRANSACTIONS/CAREER NOTES: Selected by San Francisco Giants organization in first round (15th pick overall) of free-agent draft (June 1, 1988); pick received as compensation for Cincinnati Reds signing Type B free-agent OF Eddie Milner. ... Traded by Giants with a player to be named later to St. Louis Cardinals for P Allen Watson, P Rich DeLucia and P Doug Creek (December 14, 1995); Cardinals acquired 2B Chris Wimmer to complete deal (January 16, 1996). ... On St. Louis disabled list (June 24-July 9, 1998). ... Traded by Cardinals with P Todd Stottlemyre to Texas Rangers for P Darren Oliver, 3B Fernando Tatis and a player to be named later (July 31, 1998); Cardinals acquired OF Mark Little to complete deal (August 9, 1998). ... Granted free agency (October 23, 1998). ... Re-signed by Rangers (December 2, 1998). ... On Texas disabled list (May 1-21, 1999); included rehabilitation assignment to Oklahoma (May 18-21).

STATISTICAL NOTES: Led Texas League shortstops with 80 double plays in 1991. ... Led N.L. shortstops with 103 double plays in 1993. ... Led N.L. shortstops with 654 total chances in 1995.

Year	Team (League)	Pos.	G	AB	R	H	2B	3B	HR	RBI	Avg.	BB	SO	SB	PO	A	E	Avg.
								BATTING								FIELDING		
1988—	Everett (N.W.)	SS	60	212	35	55	4	0	3	29	.259	27	54	10	75	166	35	.873
1989—	Clinton (Midw.)	SS	104	385	39	91	13	3	0	24	.236	39	101	28	182	332	31	.943
	— San Jose (Calif.)	SS	28	92	5	11	2	0	0	4	.120	13	27	10	53	71	8	.939
1990—	San Jose (Calif.)	SS	123	460	80	123	15	10	7	71	.267	68	98	33	*202	358	37	.938
1991—	Shreveport (Texas)	SS	126	485	84	136	22	8	5	68	.280	61	104	36	174	379	29	.950
	— San Francisco (N.L.)	SS	9	26	0	3	1	0	0	2	.115	1	6	0	16	6	3	.880
1992—	San Francisco (N.L.)	SS-3B	98	321	31	72	7	4	4	24	.224	26	63	8	142	257	11	.973
	— Phoenix (PCL)	SS	48	192	30	46	6	2	3	18	.240	17	25	15	81	150	7	.971
1993—	San Francisco (N.L.)	SS	153	549	54	155	21	5	6	70	.282	38	91	11	251	449	27	.963
1994—	San Francisco (N.L.)	SS	108	385	38	91	14	6	3	30	.236	30	74	23	177	330	14	.973
1995—	San Francisco (N.L.)	SS	138	509	56	124	29	3	5	58	.244	38	109	24	*223	•411	20	.969
1996—	St. Louis (N.L.)■	SS	129	491	64	136	20	4	6	35	.277	33	89	33	171	347	15	.972
1997—	St. Louis (N.L.)	SS	154	576	75	153	39	5	6	61	.266	33	109	30	228	*452	19	.973
1998—	St. Louis (N.L.)	SS	90	355	59	83	19	1	4	29	.234	40	51	19	140	286	13	.970
	— Texas (A.L.)■	SS	52	186	30	53	12	1	5	24	.285	13	32	5	88	152	7	.972
1999—	Texas (A.L.)	SS	133	465	69	134	21	5	14	52	.288	39	100	8	204	406	*25	.961
	— Oklahoma (PCL)	SS	2	7	1	1	0	0	0	1	.143	3	3	0	4	7	0	1.000
American League totals (2 years)			185	651	99	187	33	6	19	76	.287	52	132	13	292	558	32	.964
National League totals (8 years)			879	3212	377	817	150	28	37	309	.254	239	592	148	1348	2538	122	.970
Major League totals (9 years)			1064	3863	476	1004	183	34	56	385	.260	291	724	161	1640	3096	154	.969

DIVISION SERIES RECORD

Year	Team (League)	Pos.	G	AB	R	H	2B	3B	HR	RBI	Avg.	BB	SO	SB	PO	A	E	Avg.
								BATTING								FIELDING		
1996—	St. Louis (N.L.)	SS	2	6	1	2	0	0	0	0	.333	3	1	0	4	5	0	1.000
1998—	Texas (A.L.)	SS	3	9	0	2	0	0	0	0	.222	0	4	0	5	8	1	.929
1999—	Texas (A.L.)	SS	3	10	0	0	0	0	0	0	.000	0	1	0	4	10	0	1.000
Division series totals (3 years)			8	25	1	4	0	0	0	0	.160	3	6	0	13	23	1	.973

CHAMPIONSHIP SERIES RECORD

Year	Team (League)	Pos.	G	AB	R	H	2B	3B	HR	RBI	Avg.	BB	SO	SB	PO	A	E	Avg.
								BATTING								FIELDING		
1996—	St. Louis (N.L.)	SS	5	20	4	7	0	0	1	.350	1	4	1	5	16	2	.913

ALL-STAR GAME RECORD

Year	League	Pos.	AB	R	H	2B	3B	HR	RBI	Avg.	BB	SO	SB	PO	A	E	Avg.
						BATTING									FIELDING		
1997—	National	SS	1	0	0	0	0	0	0	.000	0	1	0	0	1	0	1.000

C

CLEMENS, ROGER   P   YANKEES

PERSONAL: Born August 4, 1962, in Dayton, Ohio. ... 6-4/230. ... Throws right, bats right. ... Full name: William Roger Clemens.

HIGH SCHOOL: Spring Woods (Houston).

JUNIOR COLLEGE: San Jacinto (North) College (Texas).

COLLEGE: Texas.

TRANSACTIONS/CAREER NOTES: Selected by New York Mets organization in 12th round of free-agent draft (June 8, 1981); did not sign. ... Selected by Boston Red Sox organization in first round (19th pick overall) of free-agent draft (June 6, 1983). ... On disabled list (July 8-August 3 and August 21, 1985-remainder of season). ... On suspended list (April 26-May 3, 1991). ... On Boston disabled list (June 19-July 16, 1993); included rehabilitation assignment to Pawtucket (July 11-16). ... On Boston disabled list (April 16-June 2, 1995); included rehabilitation assignments to Sarasota (May 25-28) and Pawtucket (May 28-June 2). ... Granted free agency (November 5, 1996). ... Signed by Toronto Blue Jays (December 13, 1996). ... Traded by Blue Jays to New York Yankees for P David Wells, P Graeme Lloyd and 2B Homer Bush (February 18, 1999). ... On disabled list (April 28-May 21, 1999).

RECORDS: Shares major league single-game record for most strikeouts (nine-inning game)—20 (April 29, 1986 and September 18, 1996). ... Shares major league record for most putouts by pitcher in one inning—3 (June 27, 1992, sixth inning). ... Holds A.L. record for most consecutive games won—20 (June 3, 1998-June 1, 1999). ... Shares A.L. record for most consecutive seasons with 200 or more strikeouts—7 (1986-92); most seasons with 200 or more strikeouts—10; and most consecutive seasons with 100 or more strikeouts—13 (1986-98). ... Shares A.L. single-game record for most consecutive strikeouts—8 (April 29, 1986).

HONORS: Named Major League Player of the Year by THE SPORTING NEWS (1986). ... Named A.L. Pitcher of the Year by THE SPORTING NEWS (1986, 1991, 1997 and 1998). ... Named righthanded pitcher on THE SPORTING NEWS A.L. All-Star team (1986-87, 1991 and 1997). ... Named A.L. Most Valuable Player by Baseball Writers' Association of America (1986). ... Named A.L. Cy Young Award winner by Baseball Writers' Association of America (1986, 1987, 1991, 1997 and 1998).

STATISTICAL NOTES: Struck out 15 batters in one game (August 21, 1984; July 9, 1988; August 15 and September 21, 1998). ... Struck out 20 batters in one game (April 29, 1986 and September 18, 1996). ... Struck out 16 batters in one game (May 9 and July 15, 1988 and July 12, 1997). ... Pitched 6-0 no-hit, complete-game victory against Cleveland (September 10, 1988). ... Led A.L. with 14 hit batsmen in 1995. ... Struck out 18 batters in one game (August 25, 1998).

MISCELLANEOUS: Singled in only appearance as pinch hitter (1996).

Year	League	W	L	Pct.	ERA	G	GS	CG	ShO	Sv.	IP	H	R	ER	BB	SO
1983—	Winter Haven (FSL)	3	1	.750	1.24	4	4	3	1	0	29	22	4	4	0	36
	— New Britain (East.)	4	1	.800	1.38	7	7	1	1	0	52	31	8	8	12	59
1984—	Pawtucket (I.L.)	2	3	.400	1.93	7	6	3	1	0	46 2/3	39	12	10	14	50
	— Boston (A.L.)	9	4	.692	4.32	21	20	5	1	0	133 1/3	146	67	64	29	126
1985—	Boston (A.L.)	7	5	.583	3.29	15	15	3	1	0	98 1/3	83	38	36	37	74
1986—	Boston (A.L.)	*24	4	*.857	*2.48	33	33	10	1	0	254	179	77	70	67	238
1987—	Boston (A.L.)	•20	9	.690	2.97	36	36	*18	*7	0	281 2/3	248	100	93	83	256
1988—	Boston (A.L.)	18	12	.600	2.93	35	35	•14	*8	0	264	217	93	86	62	*291
1989—	Boston (A.L.)	17	11	.607	3.13	35	35	8	3	0	253 1/3	215	101	88	93	230
1990—	Boston (A.L.)	21	6	.778	*1.93	31	31	7	•4	0	228 1/3	193	59	49	54	209
1991—	Boston (A.L.)	18	10	.643	*2.62	35	•35	13	*4	0	*271 1/3	219	93	79	65	*241
1992—	Boston (A.L.)	18	11	.621	*2.41	32	32	11	*5	0	246 2/3	203	80	66	62	208

Year League	W	L	Pct.	ERA	G	GS	CG	ShO	Sv.	IP	H	R	ER	BB	SO
1993—Boston (A.L.)....................	11	14	.440	4.46	29	29	2	1	0	191 2/3	175	99	95	67	160
—Pawtucket (I.L.)................	0	0	...	0.00	1	1	0	0	0	3 2/3	1	0	0	4	8
1994—Boston (A.L.)....................	9	7	.563	2.85	24	24	3	1	0	170 2/3	124	62	54	71	168
1995—Sarasota (FSL)	0	0	...	0.00	1	1	0	0	0	4	0	0	0	2	1
—Pawtucket (I.L.)................	0	0	...	0.00	1	1	0	0	0	5	1	0	0	3	5
—Boston (A.L.)....................	10	5	.667	4.18	23	23	0	0	0	140	141	70	65	60	132
1996—Boston (A.L.)....................	10	13	.435	3.63	34	34	6	2	0	242 2/3	216	106	98	106	*257
1997—Toronto (A.L.)■..............	*21	7	.750	*2.05	34	34	•9	•3	0	•264	204	65	60	68	*292
1998—Toronto (A.L.).................	•20	6	.769	*2.65	33	33	5	3	0	234 2/3	169	78	69	88	*271
1999—New York (A.L.)■..........	14	10	.583	4.60	30	30	1	1	0	187 2/3	185	101	96	90	163
Major League totals (16 years).....	247	134	.648	3.04	480	479	115	45	0	3462 1/3	2917	1289	1168	1102	3316

DIVISION SERIES RECORD

Year League	W	L	Pct.	ERA	G	GS	CG	ShO	Sv.	IP	H	R	ER	BB	SO
1995—Boston (A.L.).................	0	0	...	3.86	1	1	0	0	0	7	5	3	3	1	5
1999—New York (A.L.).............	1	0	1.000	0.00	1	1	0	0	0	7	3	0	0	2	2
Division series totals (2 years).....	1	0	1.000	1.93	2	2	0	0	0	14	8	3	3	3	7

CHAMPIONSHIP SERIES RECORD

RECORDS: Holds single-series record for most hits allowed—22 (1986). ... Shares single-series record for most earned runs allowed—11 (1986). ... Shares single-game records for most earned runs allowed—7 (October 7, 1986); and most consecutive strikeouts—4 (October 6, 1988). ... Holds A.L. single-series record for most innings pitched—22 2/3 (1986). ... Shares A.L. single-game record for most runs allowed—8 (October 7, 1986).

Year League	W	L	Pct.	ERA	G	GS	CG	ShO	Sv.	IP	H	R	ER	BB	SO
1986—Boston (A.L.)....................	1	1	.500	4.37	3	3	0	0	0	22 2/3	22	12	11	7	17
1988—Boston (A.L.)....................	0	0	...	3.86	1	1	0	0	0	7	6	3	3	0	8
1990—Boston (A.L.)....................	0	1	.000	3.52	2	2	0	0	0	7 2/3	7	3	3	5	4
1999—New York (A.L.).................	0	1	.000	22.50	1	1	0	0	0	2	6	5	5	2	2
Champ. series totals (4 years)......	1	3	.250	5.03	7	7	0	0	0	39 1/3	41	23	22	14	31

WORLD SERIES RECORD

NOTES: Member of World Series championship team (1999).

Year League	W	L	Pct.	ERA	G	GS	CG	ShO	Sv.	IP	H	R	ER	BB	SO
1986—Boston (A.L.)....................	0	0	...	3.18	2	2	0	0	0	11 1/3	9	5	4	6	11
1999—New York (A.L.).................	1	0	1.000	1.17	1	1	0	0	0	7 2/3	4	1	1	2	4
World Series totals (2 years)	1	0	1.000	2.37	3	3	0	0	0	19	13	6	5	8	15

ALL-STAR GAME RECORD

NOTES: Named Most Valuable Player (1986).

Year League	W	L	Pct.	ERA	GS	CG	ShO	Sv.	IP	H	R	ER	BB	SO
1986—American	1	0	1.000	0.00	1	0	0	0	3	0	0	0	0	2
1988—American	0	0	...	0.00	0	0	0	0	1	0	0	0	0	1
1990—American							Did not play.							
1991—American	0	0	...	9.00	0	0	0	0	1	1	1	1	0	0
1992—American	0	0	...	0.00	0	0	0	0	1	2	0	0	0	0
1997—American	0	0	...	0.00	0	0	0	0	1	1	0	0	0	1
1998—American	0	0	...	18.00	0	0	0	0	1	2	2	2	1	1
All-Star Game totals (6 years)	1	0	1.000	3.38	1	0	0	0	8	6	3	3	1	4

CLEMENT, MATT   P   PADRES

PERSONAL: Born August 12, 1974, in McCandless Township, Pa. ... 6-3/195. ... Throws right, bats right. ... Full name: Matthew Paul Clement.
HIGH SCHOOL: Butler (Pa.).
TRANSACTIONS/CAREER NOTES: Selected by San Diego Padres organization in third round of free-agent draft (June 3, 1993).
STATISTICAL NOTES: Led Pacific Coast League with 30 hit batsmen in 1998.

Year League	W	L	Pct.	ERA	G	GS	CG	ShO	Sv.	IP	H	R	ER	BB	SO
1994—Peoria (Ariz.)	•8	5	.615	4.43	13	13	0	0	0	67	65	38	33	17	76
—Spokane (N.W.)	1	1	.500	6.14	2	2	0	0	0	7 1/3	8	7	5	11	4
1995—Rancho Cuca. (Calif.)	3	4	.429	4.24	12	12	0	0	0	57 1/3	61	37	27	49	33
—Idaho Falls (Pio.)...............	6	3	.667	4.33	14	14	0	0	0	81	61	53	39	42	65
1996—Clinton (Midw.)	8	3	.727	2.80	16	16	1	•1	0	96 1/3	66	31	30	52	109
—Rancho Cuca. (Calif.)	4	5	.444	5.59	11	11	0	0	0	56 1/3	61	40	35	26	75
1997—Rancho Cuca. (Calif.)	6	3	.667	1.60	14	14	2	1	0	101	74	30	18	31	109
—Mobile (Sou.)	6	5	.545	2.56	13	13	1	1	0	88	83	37	25	32	92
1998—Las Vegas (PCL)	10	9	.526	3.98	27	27	1	0	0	171 2/3	157	94	76	85	160
—San Diego (N.L.)	2	0	1.000	4.61	4	2	0	0	0	13 2/3	15	8	7	7	13
1999—San Diego (N.L.)	10	12	.455	4.48	31	31	0	0	0	180 2/3	190	106	90	86	135
Major League totals (2 years).......	12	12	.500	4.49	35	33	0	0	0	194 1/3	205	114	97	93	148

CLEMENTE, EDGARD   OF   ROCKIES

PERSONAL: Born December 15, 1975, in Santurce, Puerto Rico. ... 5-11/188. ... Bats right, throws right. ... Full name: Edgard A. Velazquez Clemente. ... Nephew of Roberto Clemente, Hall of Fame outfielder with Pittsburgh Pirates (1955-72). ... Formerly known as Edgard Velazquez.
HIGH SCHOOL: Colegio Hostos (Guaynabo, Puerto Rico).
TRANSACTIONS/CAREER NOTES: Selected by Colorado Rockies organization in 10th round of free-agent draft (June 3, 1993).
STATISTICAL NOTES: Tied for South Atlantic League record in double plays by outfielder with five in 1994. ... Led Carolina League outfielders with 296 total chances in 1995. ... Led Pacific Coast League outfielders with five double plays in 1997. ... Tied for Pacific Coast League lead with three double plays by outfielder in 1998.

Year Team (League)	Pos.	G	AB	R	H	2B	3B	HR	RBI	Avg.	BB	SO	SB	PO	A	E	Avg.
										BATTING					FIELDING		
1993—Ariz. Rockies (Ariz.)....	OF	39	147	20	36	4	2	2	20	.245	16	35	7	70	3	6	.924
1994—Asheville (SAL)..........	OF	119	447	50	106	22	3	11	39	.237	23	120	9	219	15	•12	.951
1995—Salem (Caro.)............	OF	131	497	74	149	25	6	13	69	.300	40	102	7	273	•16	7	.976
1996—New Haven (East.)......	OF	132	486	72	141	29	4	19	62	.290	53	114	6	215	9	5	.978
1997—Colo. Springs (PCL) ...	OF-DH	120	438	70	123	24	10	17	73	.281	34	119	6	208	13	6	.974
1998—Colo. Springs (PCL) ...	OF-DH	135	493	79	124	21	7	22	82	.252	40	117	5	262	8	9	.968
—Colorado (N.L.)........	OF	11	17	2	6	0	1	0	2	.353	2	8	0	6	0	1	.857
1999—Colo. Springs (PCL)	OF-DH	75	276	46	84	24	1	17	60	.304	20	55	5	114	8	1	.992
—Colorado (N.L.)	OF	57	162	24	41	10	2	8	25	.253	7	46	0	101	2	3	.972
Major League totals (2 years)		68	179	26	47	10	3	8	27	.263	9	54	0	107	2	4	.965

CLINE, PAT — C — CUBS

PERSONAL: Born October 9, 1974, in Bradenton, Fla. ... 6-4/230. ... Bats right, throws right. ... Full name: James Patrick Cline.
HIGH SCHOOL: Manatee (Bradenton, Fla.).
TRANSACTIONS/CAREER NOTES: Selected by Chicago Cubs organization in sixth round of free-agent draft (June 3, 1993). ... On Gulf Coast Cubs disabled list (June 20-27, 1994). ... On Huntington disabled list (July 20, 1994-remainder of season).
STATISTICAL NOTES: Led Appalachian League with 17 passed balls in 1993. ... Tied for Midwest League lead with 18 passed balls in 1995. ... Led Florida State League catchers with 783 total chances in 1996. ... Led Pacific Coast League catchers with 867 total chances and 18 passed balls in 1998.

Year Team (League)	Pos.	G	AB	R	H	2B	3B	HR	RBI	Avg.	BB	SO	SB	PO	A	E	Avg.
										BATTING					FIELDING		
1993—Huntington (Appl.)	C	33	96	17	18	6	0	2	13	.188	17	28	0	174	10	5	.974
1994—GC Cubs (GCL)	C	3	3	0	0	0	0	0	0	.000	0	0	0	2	0	0	1.000
1995—Rockford (Midw.)	C	112	390	65	106	17	0	13	77	.272	58	93	6	549	64	17	.973
1996—Daytona (FSL)	C-DH	124	434	75	121	30	2	17	76	.279	54	79	10	*697	70	16	.980
1997—Orlando (Sou.)	C-DH	78	271	39	69	19	0	7	37	.255	27	78	2	416	35	5	.989
—Iowa (A.A.)	C	27	95	6	21	2	0	3	10	.221	10	24	0	188	11	2	.990
1998—Iowa (PCL)	C-DH-1B	122	424	52	119	22	2	13	60	.281	36	59	2	*806	50	11	.987
1999—Iowa (PCL)	C-DH-OF	98	290	27	66	20	1	6	42	.228	26	73	1	211	11	9	.961

CLONTZ, BRAD — P — DIAMONDBACKS

PERSONAL: Born April 25, 1971, in Stuart, Va. ... 6-1/203. ... Throws right, bats right. ... Full name: John Bradley Clontz.
HIGH SCHOOL: Patrick County (Stuart, Va.).
COLLEGE: Virginia Tech.
TRANSACTIONS/CAREER NOTES: Selected by Atlanta Braves organization in 10th round of free-agent draft (June 1, 1992). ... Released by Braves (March 30, 1998). ... Signed by Los Angeles Dodgers (April 9, 1998). ... Traded by Dodgers with P Hideo Nomo to New York Mets for P Dave Mlicki and P Greg McMichael (June 4, 1998). ... On New York disabled list (September 11, 1998-remainder of season). ... Granted free agency (October 15, 1998). ... Signed by Boston Red Sox organization (December 14, 1998). ... Released by Red Sox (April 6, 1999). ... Signed by Pittsburgh Pirates organization (April 8, 1999). ... Traded by Pirates to Arizona Diamondbacks for a player to be named later (December 13, 1999); Pirates acquired P Roberto Manzueta to complete deal (December 15, 1999).
HONORS: Named Southern League Outstanding Pitcher (1994).

Year League	W	L	Pct.	ERA	G	GS	CG	ShO	Sv.	IP	H	R	ER	BB	SO
1992—Pulaski (Appl.)..................	0	0	...	1.59	4	0	0	0	1	5 2/3	3	1	1	2	7
—Macon (SAL)	2	1	.667	3.91	17	0	0	0	2	23	19	14	10	10	18
1993—Durham (Caro.)	1	7	.125	2.75	51	0	0	0	10	75 1/3	69	32	23	26	79
1994—Greenville (Sou.)	1	2	.333	1.20	39	0	0	0	*27	45	32	13	6	10	49
—Richmond (I.L.)	0	0	...	2.10	24	0	0	0	11	25 2/3	19	6	6	9	21
1995—Atlanta (N.L.)	8	1	.889	3.65	59	0	0	0	4	69	71	29	28	22	55
1996—Atlanta (N.L.)	6	3	.667	5.69	*81	0	0	0	1	80 2/3	78	53	51	33	49
1997—Atlanta (N.L.)	5	1	.833	3.75	51	0	0	0	1	48	52	24	20	18	42
—Richmond (I.L.)	0	0	...	0.00	16	0	0	0	6	22	10	1	0	2	24
1998—Los Angeles (N.L.)■	2	0	1.000	5.66	18	0	0	0	0	20 2/3	15	13	13	10	14
—Albuquerque (PCL)	1	2	.333	7.71	6	0	0	0	0	7	11	10	6	5	12
—New York (N.L.)■	0	0	...	9.00	2	0	0	0	0	3	4	3	3	2	2
—Norfolk (I.L.)	2	4	.333	3.43	28	0	0	0	0	42	43	26	16	16	49
1999—Nashville (PCL)■	0	2	.000	3.50	12	0	0	0	7	18	12	8	7	6	23
—Pittsburgh (N.L.)	1	3	.250	2.74	56	0	0	0	2	49 1/3	49	21	15	24	40
Major League totals (5 years)	22	8	.733	4.32	267	0	0	0	8	270 2/3	269	143	130	109	202

DIVISION SERIES RECORD

Year League	W	L	Pct.	ERA	G	GS	CG	ShO	Sv.	IP	H	R	ER	BB	SO
1995—Atlanta (N.L.)	0	0	...	0.00	1	0	0	0	0	1 1/3	0	0	0	0	2
1996—Atlanta (N.L.)							Did not play.								

CHAMPIONSHIP SERIES RECORD

Year League	W	L	Pct.	ERA	G	GS	CG	ShO	Sv.	IP	H	R	ER	BB	SO
1995—Atlanta (N.L.)	0	0	...	0.00	1	0	0	0	0	1/3	1	0	0	0	0
1996—Atlanta (N.L.)	0	0	...	0.00	1	0	0	0	0	2/3	0	0	0	0	0
Champ. series totals (2 years)	0	0	...	0.00	2	0	0	0	0	1	1	0	0	0	0

WORLD SERIES RECORD

NOTES: Member of World Series championship team (1995).

Year League	W	L	Pct.	ERA	G	GS	CG	ShO	Sv.	IP	H	R	ER	BB	SO
1995—Atlanta (N.L.)	0	0	...	2.70	2	0	0	0	0	3 1/3	2	1	1	0	2
1996—Atlanta (N.L.)	0	0	...	0.00	3	0	0	0	0	1 2/3	1	0	0	2	2
World Series totals (2 years)	0	0	...	1.80	5	0	0	0	0	5	3	1	1	2	4

CLOUDE, KEN P MARINERS

PERSONAL: Born January 9, 1975, in Baltimore. ... 6-1/180. ... Throws right, bats right. ... Full name: Kenneth Brian Cloude.
HIGH SCHOOL: McDonogh (Owings Mills, Md.).
TRANSACTIONS/CAREER NOTES: Selected by Seattle Mariners organization in sixth round of free-agent draft (June 3, 1993).

Year League	W	L	Pct.	ERA	G	GS	CG	ShO	Sv.	IP	H	R	ER	BB	SO
1994— Arizona Mariners (Ariz.)	3	4	.429	2.06	12	7	0	0	0	52 1/3	36	22	12	19	61
1995— Wisconsin (Midw.)	9	8	.529	3.24	25	25	4	0	0	161	137	64	58	63	140
1996— Lancaster (Calif.)	15	4	.789	4.22	28	28	1	0	0	168 1/3	167	94	79	60	161
1997— Memphis (Sou.)	11	7	.611	3.87	22	22	3	•2	0	132 2/3	131	62	57	48	124
— Seattle (A.L.)	4	2	.667	5.12	10	9	0	0	0	51	41	32	29	26	46
1998— Seattle (A.L.)	8	10	.444	6.37	30	30	0	0	0	155 1/3	187	116	110	80	114
— Tacoma (PCL)	0	1	.000	6.75	1	1	0	0	0	4	4	3	3	1	4
1999— Tacoma (PCL)	5	1	.833	2.33	6	6	2	0	0	38 2/3	19	11	10	15	33
— Seattle (A.L.)	4	4	.500	7.96	31	6	0	0	1	72 1/3	106	67	64	46	35
Major League totals (3 years)	16	16	.500	6.56	71	45	0	0	1	278 2/3	334	215	203	152	195

CLYBURN, DANNY OF DEVIL RAYS

PERSONAL: Born April 6, 1974, in Lancaster, S.C. ... 6-0/220. ... Bats right, throws right. ... Full name: Danny Clyburn Jr.
HIGH SCHOOL: Lancaster (S.C.).
TRANSACTIONS/CAREER NOTES: Selected by Pittsburgh Pirates organization in second round of free-agent draft (June 1, 1992). ... On disabled list (April 7-17, 1994). ... Traded by Pirates to Cincinnati Reds for OF Jacob Brumfield (October 11, 1994). ... Traded by Reds with P Tony Nieto to Baltimore Orioles for P Brad Pennington (June 16, 1995). ... On Bowie disabled list (July 17-24, 1996). ... On Baltimore disabled list (March 19-June 16, 1998); included rehabilitation assignment to Rochester (May 28-June 15). ... Traded by Orioles with a player to be named later to Tampa Bay Devil Rays for P Jason Johnson (March 29, 1999); Devil Rays acquired SS Bolivar Volquez to complete deal (April 22, 1999).

C

							BATTING							FIELDING		
Year Team (League)	Pos.	G	AB	R	H	2B	3B	HR	RBI	Avg.	BB	SO	SB	PO	A	E	Avg.
1992— GC Pirates (GCL).......	OF	39	149	26	51	9	0	4	25	.342	5	20	7	41	0	3	.932
1993— Augusta (SAL)...........	OF	127	457	55	121	21	4	9	66	.265	37	97	5	156	9	7	.959
1994— Salem (Caro.)...........	OF-DH	118	461	57	126	19	0	22	90	.273	20	96	4	135	6	12	.922
1995— Win.-Salem (Car.)■....	OF-DH	59	227	27	59	10	2	11	41	.260	13	59	2	66	6	4	.947
— Frederick (Caro.).....	OF-DH	15	45	4	9	4	0	0	4	.200	4	18	1	13	0	1	.929
— High Desert (Calif.)....	OF-DH	45	160	20	45	3	1	12	37	.281	17	41	2	63	6	5	.932
1996— Bowie (East.).............	OF-DH	95	365	51	92	14	5	18	55	.252	17	88	4	103	4	12	.899
1997— Rochester (I.L.).........	OF-DH	•137	520	91	156	33	5	20	76	.300	53	107	14	241	5	*10	.961
— Baltimore (A.L.).........	OF	2	3	0	0	0	0	0	0	.000	0	2	0	0	0	0	...
1998— Rochester (I.L.)..........	OF-DH	84	322	58	92	21	1	14	54	.286	34	72	11	125	4	4	.970
— Baltimore (A.L.).........	OF-DH	11	25	6	7	0	0	1	3	.280	1	10	0	11	0	0	1.000
1999— Tampa Bay (A.L.)■.....	OF-DH	28	81	8	16	4	0	3	5	.198	7	21	0	39	3	0	1.000
— Durham (I.L.).............	OF-DH	82	303	38	71	11	1	9	33	.234	19	74	2	116	4	3	.976
Major League totals (3 years)		41	109	14	23	4	0	4	8	.211	8	33	0	50	3	0	1.000

COCO, PASQUAL P BLUE JAYS

PERSONAL: Born September 24, 1977, in Santo Domingo, Dominican Republic. ... 6-1/185. ... Throws right, bats right. ... Full name: Pasqual Reynoso Coco.
TRANSACTIONS/CAREER NOTES: Signed as non-drafted free agent by Toronto Blue Jays organization (August 10, 1994).
STATISTICAL NOTES: Pitched 3-1 no-hit loss for St. Catharines against Jamestown (August 16, 1998).

Year League	W	L	Pct.	ERA	G	GS	CG	ShO	Sv.	IP	H	R	ER	BB	SO
1995— Dom. Blue Jays (DSL)........	7	1	.875	2.78	11	11	0	0	0	58 1/3	51	30	18	36	38
1996— Dom. Blue Jays (DSL)........	7	2	.778	2.99	17	16	2	2	0	96 1/3	77	46	32	53	92
1997— St. Catharines (NY-P)........	1	4	.200	4.89	10	8	0	0	0	46	48	32	25	16	44
1998— St. Catharines (NY-P)	3	7	.300	3.20	15	15	1	0	0	81 2/3	62	52	29	32	84
1999— Hagerstown (SAL)..............	11	1	*.917	2.21	14	14	0	0	0	97 2/3	67	29	24	25	83
— Dunedin (FSL)..................	4	6	.400	5.28	13	13	2	0	0	75	79	52	44	33	44

COFFIE, IVANON IF ORIOLES

PERSONAL: Born May 16, 1977, in Curacao, Netherlands Antilles. ... 6-1/182. ... Bats left, throws right. ... Full name: Ivanon Angelino Coffie.
TRANSACTIONS/CAREER NOTES: Signed as non-drafted free agent by Baltimore Orioles organization (July 28, 1995).
STATISTICAL NOTES: Led Gulf Coast League shortstops with .941 fielding percentage in 1996.

							BATTING							FIELDING		
Year Team (League)	Pos.	G	AB	R	H	2B	3B	HR	RBI	Avg.	BB	SO	SB	PO	A	E	Avg.
1996— GC Orioles (GCL)........	SS-3B	56	193	29	42	8	4	0	20	.218	23	26	6	81	175	16	†.941
1997— Delmarva (SAL).........	SS-3B	90	305	41	84	14	5	3	48	.275	23	45	19	126	203	19	.945
1998— Frederick (Caro.)	3B-SS	130	473	62	121	19	2	16	75	.256	48	109	17	126	216	25	.932
1999— Bowie (East.).............	3B-SS	57	195	21	36	9	3	3	23	.185	20	46	2	39	90	8	.942
— Frederick (Caro.) .	3B-SS-DH	73	276	35	78	18	4	11	53	.283	28	62	7	51	139	20	.905

COGGIN, DAVE P PHILLIES

PERSONAL: Born October 30, 1976, in Covina, Calif. ... 6-4/205. ... Throws right, bats right. ... Full name: David Raymond Coggin.
HIGH SCHOOL: Upland (Calif.).

TRANSACTIONS/CAREER NOTES: Selected by Philadelphia Phillies organization in supplemental round ("sandwich pick" between first and second round, 30th pick overall) of free-agent draft (June 1, 1995). ... On Reading disabled list (April 20-May 26, 1998; May 14-June 4 and June 26, 1999-remainder of season).
STATISTICAL NOTES: Led Florida State League with 24 wild pitches in 1997.

Year League	W	L	Pct.	ERA	G	GS	CG	ShO	Sv.	IP	H	R	ER	BB	SO
1995—Martinsville (Appl.)	5	3	.625	3.00	11	11	0	0	0	48	45	25	16	31	37
1996—Piedmont (SAL)	9	12	.429	4.31	28	•28	3	3	0	169 1/3	156	87	*81	46	129
1997—Clearwater (FSL)	11	8	.579	4.70	27	27	3	2	0	155	160	96	81	86	110
1998—Reading (East.)	4	8	.333	4.14	20	20	0	0	0	108 2/3	106	58	50	62	65
1999—Reading (East.)	2	5	.286	7.50	9	9	0	0	0	42	55	37	35	20	21

COLANGELO, MIKE   OF   ANGELS

PERSONAL: Born October 22, 1976, in Teaneck, N.J. ... 6-1/185. ... Bats right, throws right. ... Full name: Michael G. Colangelo.
HIGH SCHOOL: C.D. Hylton (Woodbridge, Va.).
COLLEGE: George Mason.
TRANSACTIONS/CAREER NOTES: Selected by Anaheim Angels organization in 21st round of free-agent draft (June 3, 1997). ... On Anaheim disabled list (June 14, 1999-remainder of season).

							BATTING							FIELDING		
Year Team (League)	Pos.	G	AB	R	H	2B	3B	HR	RBI	Avg.	BB	SO	SB	PO	A	E	Avg.
1998—Cedar Rap. (Midw.)	OF	22	83	13	23	8	0	4	8	.277	12	16	5	14	0	1	.933
— Lake Elsinore (Calif.)	OF	36	145	33	55	11	3	5	21	.379	13	24	2	78	3	0	1.000
1999—Erie (East.)	OF-DH	28	109	24	37	10	3	1	13	.339	14	22	3	35	3	2	.950
— Edmonton (PCL)	OF	26	105	13	38	7	1	0	9	.362	13	18	2	29	3	2	.941
— Anaheim (A.L.)	OF	1	2	0	1	0	0	0	0	.500	1	0	0	1	1	0	1.000
Major League totals (1 year)		1	2	0	1	0	0	0	0	.500	1	0	0	1	1	0	1.000

COLBRUNN, GREG   1B   DIAMONDBACKS

PERSONAL: Born July 26, 1969, in Fontana, Calif. ... 6-0/205. ... Bats right, throws right. ... Full name: Gregory Joseph Colbrunn.
HIGH SCHOOL: Fontana (Calif.).
TRANSACTIONS/CAREER NOTES: Selected by Montreal Expos organization in sixth round of free-agent draft (June 2, 1987). ... On disabled list (April 10, 1991-entire season). ... On Indianapolis disabled list (April 9-May 5, 1992). ... On Montreal disabled list (August 2-18, 1992); included rehabilitation assignment to Indianapolis (August 13-18). ... On Montreal disabled list (April 5-21, 1993); included rehabilitation assignment to West Palm Beach (April 9-20). ... On Montreal disabled list (July 12, 1993-remainder of season); included rehabilitation assignment to Ottawa (July 27-August 2). ... Claimed on waivers by Florida Marlins (October 7, 1993). ... On Florida disabled list (April 9-May 27, and July 15-30, 1994); included rehabilitation assignments to Brevard County (June 12-18 and July 28-30) and Edmonton (May 18-27). ... On disabled list (July 24-August 8, 1996). ... Granted free agency (December 20, 1996). ... Signed by Minnesota Twins organization (January 24, 1997). ... Traded by Twins to Atlanta Braves for a player to be named later (August 14, 1997); Twins acquired OF Marc Lewis to complete deal (October 1, 1997). ... Granted free agency (October 23, 1997). ... Signed by Colorado Rockies organization (December 23, 1997). ... Traded by Rockies to Braves for P David Cortes, P Mike Porzio and a player to be named later (July 30, 1998); Rockies acquired P Anthony Briggs to complete deal (September 9, 1998). ... Granted free agency (October 23, 1998). ... Signed by Arizona Diamondbacks (November 17, 1998).
STATISTICAL NOTES: Had 21-game hitting streak (May 31-June 23, 1996). ... Career major league grand slams: 2.

							BATTING							FIELDING		
Year Team (League)	Pos.	G	AB	R	H	2B	3B	HR	RBI	Avg.	BB	SO	SB	PO	A	E	Avg.
1988—Rockford (Midw.)	C	115	417	55	111	18	2	7	46	.266	22	60	5	595	81	15	.978
1989—W.P. Beach (FSL)	C	59	228	20	54	8	0	0	25	.237	6	29	3	376	49	5	.988
— Jacksonville (Sou.)	C	55	178	21	49	11	1	3	18	.275	13	33	0	304	34	4	.988
1990—Jacksonville (Sou.)	C	125	458	57	138	29	1	13	76	.301	38	78	1	698	58	15	.981
1991—								Did not play.									
1992—Indianapolis (A.A.)	1B	57	216	32	66	19	1	11	48	.306	7	41	1	441	27	4	.992
— Montreal (N.L.)	1B	52	168	12	45	8	0	2	18	.268	6	34	3	363	29	3	.992
1993—W.P. Beach (FSL)	1B	8	31	6	12	2	1	1	5	.387	4	1	0	74	5	1	.988
— Montreal (N.L.)	1B	70	153	15	39	9	0	4	23	.255	6	33	4	372	27	2	.995
— Ottawa (I.L.)	1B	6	22	4	6	1	0	0	8	.273	1	2	1	50	1	0	1.000
1994—Florida (N.L.)■	1B	47	155	17	47	10	0	6	31	.303	9	27	1	304	26	4	.988
— Brevard County (FSL)	DH-1B	11	33	3	6	2	0	1	2	.545	1	0	0	16	1	1	.944
— Edmonton (PCL)	1B-DH	7	17	2	4	0	0	1	2	.235	0	1	0	28	1	1	.967
1995—Florida (N.L.)	1B	138	528	70	146	22	1	23	89	.277	22	69	11	1066	90	5	.996
1996—Florida (N.L.)	1B	141	511	60	146	26	2	16	69	.286	25	76	4	1169	101	6	.995
1997—Minnesota (A.L.)■	1B-DH	70	217	24	61	14	0	5	26	.281	8	38	1	475	35	6	.988
— Atlanta (N.L.)■	1B-DH	28	54	3	15	3	0	2	9	.278	2	11	0	54	6	1	.984
1998—Colorado (N.L.)■ 1B-OF-DH-C	62	122	12	38	8	2	2	13	.311	8	23	3	222	21	2	.992
— Atlanta (N.L.)■	1B-OF	28	44	6	13	3	0	1	10	.295	2	11	1	57	4	0	1.000
1999—Arizona (N.L.)■	1B-DH-3B	67	135	20	44	5	3	5	24	.326	12	23	1	203	19	1	.996
American League totals (1 year)		70	217	24	61	14	0	5	26	.281	8	38	1	475	35	6	.988
National League totals (8 years)		633	1870	215	533	94	8	61	286	.285	92	307	28	3810	323	24	.994
Major League totals (8 years)		703	2087	239	594	108	8	66	312	.285	100	345	29	4285	358	30	.994

DIVISION SERIES RECORD

							BATTING							FIELDING		
Year Team (League)	Pos.	G	AB	R	H	2B	3B	HR	RBI	Avg.	BB	SO	SB	PO	A	E	Avg.
1997—Atlanta (N.L.)	PH	1	1	0	1	0	0	0	2	1.000	0	0	0	...	...	...	...
1998—Atlanta (N.L.)	PH	2	2	0	0	0	0	0	0	.000	0	0	0	...	...	...	...
1999—Arizona (N.L.)	1B	2	5	1	2	1	0	1	2	.400	2	2	0	17	0	0	1.000
Division series totals (3 years)		5	8	1	3	1	0	1	4	.375	2	2	0	17	0	0	1.000

Year Team (League)	Pos.	G	AB	R	H	2B	3B	HR	RBI	Avg.	BB	SO	SB	PO	A	E	Avg.
1997—Atlanta (N.L.).............	PH	3	3	0	2	0	0	0	0	.667	0	0	0	...	...	...	...
1998—Atlanta (N.L.).............	PH	6	6	0	2	0	0	0	0	.333	0	2	0	...	...	...	...
Championship series totals (2 years)		9	9	0	4	0	0	0	0	.444	0	2	0	0	0	0	...

COLEMAN, MICHAEL — OF — RED SOX

PERSONAL: Born August 16, 1975, in Nashville, Tenn. ... 5-11/215. ... Bats right, throws right. ... Full name: Michael D. Coleman.
HIGH SCHOOL: Stratford (Nashville, Tenn.).
TRANSACTIONS/CAREER NOTES: Selected by Boston Red Sox organization in 18th round of free-agent draft (June 2, 1994). ... On Pawtucket disabled list (May 9-June 11, 1998; and April 8-27 and July 3-10, 1999).

Year Team (League)	Pos.	G	AB	R	H	2B	3B	HR	RBI	Avg.	BB	SO	SB	PO	A	E	Avg.
1994—GC Red Sox (GCL)	OF	25	95	15	26	6	1	3	15	.274	10	20	5	32	0	0	1.000
—Fort Myers (GCL)	OF	25	95	15	26	6	1	3	15	.274	10	20	5	32	0	0	1.000
—Utica (NY-P)	OF	23	65	16	11	2	0	1	3	.169	14	21	11	35	2	2	.949
1995—Michigan (Midw.)	OF	112	422	70	113	16	2	11	61	.268	40	93	29	251	5	5	.981
1996—Sarasota (FSL)	OF	110	407	54	100	20	5	1	36	.246	38	86	24	261	9	2	*.993
1997—Trenton (East.)	OF-DH	102	385	56	116	17	8	14	58	.301	41	89	20	259	6	5	.981
—Pawtucket (I.L.)..........	OF	28	113	27	36	9	2	7	19	.319	12	27	4	53	2	4	.932
—Boston (A.L.).............	OF	8	24	2	4	1	0	0	2	.167	0	11	1	16	0	1	.941
1998—Pawtucket (I.L.)..........	OF-DH	93	340	47	86	13	0	14	37	.253	27	92	12	173	9	4	.978
1999—Pawtucket (I.L.)..........	OF-DH	115	467	95	125	29	2	30	74	.268	51	128	14	299	2	6	.980
—Boston (A.L.).............	OF	2	5	1	1	0	0	0	0	.200	1	0	0	0	0	0	...
Major League totals (2 years)		10	29	3	5	1	0	0	2	.172	1	11	1	16	0	1	.941

COLLIER, LOU — IF — BREWERS

PERSONAL: Born August 21, 1973, in Chicago. ... 5-10/182. ... Bats right, throws right. ... Full name: Louis Keith Collier.
HIGH SCHOOL: Vocational (Chicago).
JUNIOR COLLEGE: Kishwaukee Junior College (Ill.), then Triton Community College (Ill.).
TRANSACTIONS/CAREER NOTES: Selected by Pittsburgh Pirates organization in 31st round of free-agent draft (June 1, 1992). ... On Pittsburgh disabled list (May 22-June 7, 1998); included rehabilitation assignment to Lynchburg (June 3-7). ... Claimed on waivers by Milwaukee Brewers (December 18, 1998).

Year Team (League)	Pos.	G	AB	R	H	2B	3B	HR	RBI	Avg.	BB	SO	SB	PO	A	E	Avg.
1993—Welland (NY-P)..........	SS	50	201	35	61	6	2	1	19	.303	12	31	8	74	138	27	.887
1994—Augusta (SAL)...........	SS	85	318	48	89	17	4	7	40	.280	25	53	32	106	262	34	.915
—Salem (Caro.)............	SS	43	158	25	42	4	1	6	16	.266	15	29	5	65	129	11	.946
1995—Lynchburg (Caro.)	SS	114	399	68	110	19	3	4	38	.276	51	60	31	156	361	35	.937
1996—Carolina (Sou.)	SS-DH	119	443	76	124	20	3	3	49	.280	48	73	29	189	310	30	.943
1997—Calgary (PCL)...........	SS-2B-DH	112	397	65	131	31	5	1	48	.330	37	47	12	187	315	34	.937
—Pittsburgh (N.L.)	SS	18	37	3	5	0	0	0	3	.135	1	11	1	9	36	0	1.000
1998—Pittsburgh (N.L.)	SS	110	334	30	82	13	6	2	34	.246	31	70	2	148	287	18	.960
—Lynchburg (Caro.)	SS	5	18	4	3	2	0	0	0	.167	2	0	2	5	16	4	.840
1999—Milwaukee (N.L.)■....SS-OF-3B-2B		74	135	18	35	9	0	2	21	.259	14	32	3	42	56	5	.951
—Louisville (I.L.)	3B-SS-OF	27	91	25	35	10	0	4	11	.385	15	14	6	17	59	3	.962
Major League totals (3 years)		202	506	51	122	22	6	4	58	.241	46	113	6	199	379	23	.962

COLON, BARTOLO — P — INDIANS

PERSONAL: Born May 24, 1975, in Altamira, Dominican Republic. ... 6-0/225. ... Throws right, bats right.
TRANSACTIONS/CAREER NOTES: Signed as non-drafted free agent by Cleveland Indians organization (June 26, 1993). ... On Canton/Akron disabled list (May 30-July 24, 1996).
HONORS: Named Carolina League Pitcher of the Year (1995).
STATISTICAL NOTES: Pitched 4-0 no-hit victory against New Orleans (June 20, 1997).

Year League	W	L	Pct.	ERA	G	GS	CG	ShO	Sv.	IP	H	R	ER	BB	SO
1993—Santiago (DSL)..................	6	1	.857	2.59	11	10	2	1	1	66	44	24	19	33	48
1994—Burlington (Appl.).............	7	4	.636	3.14	12	12	0	0	0	66	46	32	23	44	84
1995—Kinston (Caro.).............	13	3	*.813	1.96	21	21	0	0	0	128 2/3	91	31	28	39	*152
1996—Canton/Akron (East.).........	2	2	.500	1.74	13	12	0	0	0	62	44	17	12	25	56
—Buffalo (A.A.)................	0	0	...	6.00	8	0	0	0	0	15	16	10	10	8	19
1997—Cleveland (A.L.)................	4	7	.364	5.65	19	17	1	0	0	94	107	66	59	45	66
—Buffalo (A.A.)................	7	1	.875	2.22	10	10	1	1	0	56 2/3	45	15	14	23	54
1998—Cleveland (A.L.)................	14	9	.609	3.71	31	31	6	2	0	204	205	91	84	79	158
1999—Cleveland (A.L.)................	18	5	.783	3.95	32	32	1	1	0	205	185	97	90	76	161
Major League totals (3 years)	36	21	.632	4.17	82	80	8	3	0	503	497	254	233	200	385

DIVISION SERIES RECORD

Year League	W	L	Pct.	ERA	G	GS	CG	ShO	Sv.	IP	H	R	ER	BB	SO
1997—Cleveland (A.L.)................							Did not play.								
1998—Cleveland (A.L.)................	0	0	...	1.59	1	1	0	0	0	5 2/3	5	1	1	4	3
1999—Cleveland (A.L.)................	0	1	.000	9.00	2	2	0	0	0	9	11	9	9	4	12
Division series totals (2 years)	0	1	.000	6.14	3	3	0	0	0	14 2/3	16	10	10	8	15

CHAMPIONSHIP SERIES RECORD

Year League	W	L	Pct.	ERA	G	GS	CG	ShO	Sv.	IP	H	R	ER	BB	SO
1997— Cleveland (A.L.)................								Did not play.							
1998— Cleveland (A.L.)................	1	0	1.000	1.00	1	1	1	0	0	9	4	1	1	4	3

WORLD SERIES RECORD

Year League	W	L	Pct.	ERA	G	GS	CG	ShO	Sv.	IP	H	R	ER	BB	SO
1997— Cleveland (A.L.)................								Did not play.							

ALL-STAR GAME RECORD

Year League	W	L	Pct.	ERA	GS	CG	ShO	Sv.	IP	H	R	ER	BB	SO
1998— American....................	1	0	1.000	27.00	0	0	0	0	1	2	3	3	1	1

CONE, DAVID   P   YANKEES

C

PERSONAL: Born January 2, 1963, in Kansas City, Mo. ... 6-1/190. ... Throws right, bats left. ... Full name: David Brian Cone.

HIGH SCHOOL: Rockhurst (Kansas City, Mo.).

TRANSACTIONS/CAREER NOTES: Selected by Kansas City Royals organization in third round of free-agent draft (June 8, 1981). ... On disabled list (April 8, 1983-entire season). ... Traded by Royals with C Chris Jelic to New York Mets for C Ed Hearn, P Rick Anderson and P Mauro Gozzo (March 27, 1987). ... On New York disabled list (May 28-August 14, 1987); included rehabilitation assignment to Tidewater (July 30-August 14). ... Traded by Mets to Toronto Blue Jays for IF Jeff Kent and a player to be named later (August 27, 1992); Mets acquired OF Ryan Thompson to complete deal (September 1, 1992). ... Granted free agency (October 30, 1992). ... Signed by Royals (December 8, 1992). ... Traded by Royals to Blue Jays for P David Sinnes, IF Chris Stynes and IF Tony Medrano (April 6, 1995). ... Traded by Blue Jays to New York Yankees for P Marty Janzen, P Jason Jarvis and P Mike Gordon (July 28, 1995). ... Granted free agency (November 3, 1995). ... Re-signed by Yankees (December 21, 1995). ... On New York disabled list (May 3-September 2, 1996); included rehabilitation assignment to Norwich (August 21-September 1). ... On disabled list (August 18-September 20, 1997). ... Granted free agency (November 5, 1998). ... Re-signed by Yankees (November 11, 1998). ... Granted free agency (November 3, 1999). ... Re-signed by Yankees (December 7, 1999).

RECORDS: Shares major league record for striking out side on nine pitches (August 30, 1991, seventh inning).

HONORS: Named righthanded pitcher on THE SPORTING NEWS A.L. All-Star team (1994). ... Named A.L. Cy Young Award winner by Baseball Writers' Association of America (1994).

STATISTICAL NOTES: Led Southern League with 27 wild pitches in 1984. ... Pitched 6-0 one-hit, complete-game victory against San Diego (August 29, 1988). ... Tied for N.L. lead with 10 balks in 1988. ... Pitched 1-0 one-hit, complete-game victory against St. Louis (September 20, 1991). ... Struck out 19 batters in one game (October 6, 1991). ... Pitched 4-0 one-hit, complete-game victory against California (May 22, 1994). ... Led A.L. with 229 1/3 innings pitched in 1995. ... Struck out 16 batters in one game (June 23, 1997). ... Tied for A.L. lead with 14 wild pitches in 1997. ... Pitched 6-0 perfect game against Montreal (July 18, 1999).

MISCELLANEOUS: Singled in only appearance as pinch hitter (1990).

Year League	W	L	Pct.	ERA	G	GS	CG	ShO	Sv.	IP	H	R	ER	BB	SO
1981— GC Royals-Blue (GCL)........	6	4	.600	2.55	14	12	0	0	0	67	52	24	19	33	45
1982— Charleston, S.C. (SAL).......	9	2	.818	2.06	16	16	1	1	0	104 2/3	84	38	24	47	87
— Fort Myers (FSL)..............	7	1	.875	2.12	10	9	6	1	0	72 1/3	56	21	17	25	57
1983— Jacksonville (Sou.)...........								Did not play.							
1984— Memphis (Sou.)	8	12	.400	4.28	29	29	9	1	0	178 2/3	162	103	85	114	110
1985— Omaha (A.A.)...................	9	15	.375	4.65	28	27	5	1	0	158 2/3	157	90	82	*93	115
1986— Omaha (A.A.)...................	8	4	.667	2.79	39	2	2	0	14	71	60	23	22	25	63
— Kansas City (A.L.)	0	0	...	5.56	11	0	0	0	0	22 2/3	29	14	14	13	21
1987— New York (N.L.)■.............	5	6	.455	3.71	21	13	1	0	1	99 1/3	87	46	41	44	68
— Tidewater (I.L.)..............	0	1	.000	5.73	3	3	0	0	0	11	10	8	7	6	7
1988— New York (N.L.)...............	20	3	*.870	2.22	35	28	8	4	0	231 1/3	178	67	57	80	213
1989— New York (N.L.)...............	14	8	.636	3.52	34	33	7	2	0	219 2/3	183	92	86	74	190
1990— New York (N.L.)...............	14	10	.583	3.23	31	30	6	2	0	211 2/3	177	84	76	65	*233
1991— New York (N.L.)...............	14	14	.500	3.29	34	34	5	2	0	232 2/3	204	95	85	73	*241
1992— New York (N.L.)...............	13	7	.650	2.88	27	27	7	•5	0	196 2/3	162	75	63	*82	214
— Toronto (A.L.)■..............	4	3	.571	2.55	8	7	0	0	0	53	39	16	15	29	47
1993— Kansas City (A.L.)■■.........	11	14	.440	3.33	34	34	6	1	0	254	205	102	94	114	191
1994— Kansas City (A.L.).............	16	5	.762	2.94	23	23	4	3	0	171 2/3	130	60	56	54	132
1995— Toronto (A.L.)■..............	9	6	.600	3.38	17	17	5	2	0	130 1/3	113	53	49	41	102
— New York (A.L.)■...........	9	2	.818	3.82	13	13	1	0	0	§99	82	42	42	47	89
1996— New York (A.L.)...............	7	2	.778	2.88	11	11	1	0	0	72	50	25	23	34	71
— Norwich (East.).............	0	0	...	0.90	2	2	0	0	0	10	9	3	1	1	13
1997— New York (A.L.)...............	12	6	.667	2.82	29	29	1	0	0	195	155	67	61	86	222
1998— New York (A.L.)...............	•20	7	.741	3.55	31	31	3	0	0	207 2/3	186	89	82	59	209
1999— New York (A.L.)...............	12	9	.571	3.44	31	31	1	1	0	193 1/3	164	84	74	90	177
A.L. totals (9 years)	100	54	.649	3.28	208	196	22	7	0	1398 2/3	1153	552	510	567	1261
N.L. totals (6 years)	80	48	.625	3.08	182	165	34	15	1	1191 1/3	991	459	408	418	1159
Major League totals (14 years)	180	102	.638	3.19	390	361	56	22	1	2590	2144	1011	918	985	2420

DIVISION SERIES RECORD

RECORDS: Shares A.L. career record for most games started—5.

Year League	W	L	Pct.	ERA	G	GS	CG	ShO	Sv.	IP	H	R	ER	BB	SO
1995— New York (A.L.)...............	1	0	1.000	4.60	2	2	0	0	0	15 2/3	15	8	8	9	14
1996— New York (A.L.)...............	0	1	.000	9.00	2	1	0	0	0	6	8	6	6	2	8
1997— New York (A.L.)...............	0	0	...	16.20	1	1	0	0	0	3 1/3	7	6	6	2	2
1998— New York (A.L.)...............	1	0	1.000	0.00	1	1	0	0	0	5 2/3	2	0	0	1	6
1999— New York (A.L.)...............								Did not play.							
Division series totals (4 years)	2	1	.667	5.87	6	5	0	0	0	30 2/3	32	20	20	14	30

CHAMPIONSHIP SERIES RECORD

Year League	W	L	Pct.	ERA	G	GS	CG	ShO	Sv.	IP	H	R	ER	BB	SO
1988— New York (N.L.)..............	1	1	.500	4.50	3	2	1	0	0	12	10	6	6	5	9
1992— Toronto (A.L.)................	1	1	.500	3.00	2	2	0	0	0	12	11	7	4	5	9
1996— New York (A.L.)...............	0	0	...	3.00	1	1	0	0	0	6	5	2	2	5	5
1998— New York (A.L.)...............	1	0	1.000	4.15	2	2	0	0	0	13	12	6	6	6	13
1999— New York (A.L.)...............	1	0	1.000	2.57	1	1	0	0	0	7	7	2	2	3	9
Champ. series totals (5 years)	4	2	.667	3.60	9	8	1	0	0	50	45	23	20	24	45

NOTES: Member of World Series championship team (1992, 1996, 1998 and 1999).

Year	League	W	L	Pct.	ERA	G	GS	CG	ShO	Sv.	IP	H	R	ER	BB	SO
1992—	Toronto (A.L.)	0	0	...	3.48	2	2	0	0	0	10 1/3	9	5	4	8	8
1996—	New York (A.L.)	1	0	1.000	1.50	1	1	0	0	0	6	4	1	1	4	3
1998—	New York (A.L.)	0	0	...	3.00	1	1	0	0	0	6	2	3	2	3	4
1999—	New York (A.L.)	1	0	1.000	0.00	1	1	0	0	0	7	1	0	0	5	4
World Series totals (4 years)		**2**	**0**	**1.000**	**2.15**	**5**	**5**	**0**	**0**	**0**	**29 1/3**	**16**	**9**	**7**	**20**	**19**

ALL-STAR GAME RECORD

Year	League	W	L	Pct.	ERA	GS	CG	ShO	Sv.	IP	H	R	ER	BB	SO
1988—	National	0	0	...	0.00	0	0	0	0	1	0	0	0	0	1
1992—	National	0	0	...	0.00	0	0	0	0	1	0	0	0	0	1
1994—	American	0	0	...	13.50	0	0	0	0	2	4	3	3	0	3
1997—	American	0	0	...	0.00	0	0	0	0	1	0	0	0	2	0
1999—	American	0	0	...	4.50	0	0	0	0	2	4	1	1	1	3
All-Star Game totals (5 years)		**0**	**0**	**...**	**5.14**	**0**	**0**	**0**	**0**	**7**	**8**	**4**	**4**	**3**	**8**

CONINE, JEFF   1B/OF   ORIOLES

C

PERSONAL: Born June 27, 1966, in Tacoma, Wash. ... 6-1/220. ... Bats right, throws right. ... Full name: Jeffrey Guy Conine.

HIGH SCHOOL: Eisenhower (Rialto, Calif.).

COLLEGE: UCLA.

TRANSACTIONS/CAREER NOTES: Selected by Kansas City Royals organization in 58th round of free-agent draft (June 2, 1987). ... On disabled list (June 28, 1991-remainder of season). ... Selected by Florida Marlins in first round (22nd pick overall) of expansion draft (November 17, 1992). ... Traded by Marlins to Royals for P Blaine Mull (November 20, 1997). ... On Kansas City disabled list (March 25-May 5 and July 27-August 19, 1998); included rehabilitation assignment to Omaha (August 17-19). ... Traded by Royals to Baltimore Orioles for P Chris Fussell (April 2, 1999). ... Granted free agency (November 5, 1999). ... Re-signed by Orioles (December 15, 1999).

RECORDS: Shares major league rookie-season record for most games—162 (1993).

HONORS: Named Southern League Most Valuable Player (1990).

STATISTICAL NOTES: Led Southern League first basemen with 1,164 putouts, 95 assists, 22 errors, 1,281 total chances and 108 double plays in 1990. ... Led N.L. with 12 sacrifice flies in 1995. ... Career major league grand slams: 3.

MISCELLANEOUS: Holds Florida Marlins all-time records for most hits (737), runs batted in (422), doubles (122) and highest career batting average (.291).

							BATTING								FIELDING		
Year	Team (League)	Pos.	G	AB	R	H	2B	3B	HR	RBI	Avg.	BB	SO	SB	PO	A	E	Avg.
1988—	Baseball City (FSL)	1B-3B	118	415	63	113	23	9	10	59	.272	46	77	26	661	51	22	.970
1989—	Baseball City (FSL)	1B	113	425	68	116	12	7	14	60	.273	40	91	32	830	65	18	.980
1990—	Memphis (Sou.)	1B-3B	137	487	89	156	37	8	15	95	.320	94	88	21	†1164	†95	†22	.983
—	Kansas City (A.L.)	1B	9	20	3	5	2	0	0	2	.250	2	5	0	39	4	1	.977
1991—	Omaha (A.A.)	1B-OF	51	171	23	44	9	1	3	15	.257	26	39	0	392	41	7	.984
1992—	Omaha (A.A.)	1B-OF	110	397	69	120	24	5	20	72	.302	54	67	4	845	60	6	.993
—	Kansas City (A.L.)	OF-1B	28	91	10	23	5	2	0	9	.253	8	23	0	75	3	0	1.000
1993—	Florida (N.L.)■	OF-1B	*162	595	75	174	24	3	12	79	.292	52	135	2	403	25	2	.995
1994—	Florida (N.L.)	OF-1B	115	451	60	144	27	6	18	82	.319	40	92	1	408	24	6	.986
1995—	Florida (N.L.)	OF-1B	133	483	72	146	26	2	25	105	.302	66	94	2	292	18	6	.981
1996—	Florida (N.L.)	OF-1B	157	597	84	175	32	2	26	95	.293	62	121	1	478	48	8	.985
1997—	Florida (N.L.)	1B-OF	151	405	46	98	13	1	17	61	.242	57	89	2	897	104	8	.992
1998—	Kansas City (A.L.)■	OF-1B-DH	93	309	30	79	26	0	8	43	.256	26	68	3	235	7	1	.996
—	Omaha (PCL)	DH-OF	2	9	0	0	0	0	0	0	.000	0	3	0	2	0	0	1.000
1999—	Baltimore (A.L.)■	1-DH-O-3	139	444	54	129	31	1	13	75	.291	30	40	0	848	53	7	.992
American League totals (4 years)			269	864	97	236	64	3	21	129	.273	66	136	3	1197	67	9	.993
National League totals (5 years)			718	2531	337	737	122	14	98	422	.291	277	531	8	2478	219	30	.989
Major League totals (9 years)			987	3395	434	973	186	17	119	551	.287	343	667	11	3675	286	39	.990

DIVISION SERIES RECORD

							BATTING								FIELDING		
Year	Team (League)	Pos.	G	AB	R	H	2B	3B	HR	RBI	Avg.	BB	SO	SB	PO	A	E	Avg.
1997—	Florida (N.L.)	1B	3	11	3	4	1	0	0	0	.364	1	0	0	24	3	1	.964

CHAMPIONSHIP SERIES RECORD

							BATTING								FIELDING		
Year	Team (League)	Pos.	G	AB	R	H	2B	3B	HR	RBI	Avg.	BB	SO	SB	PO	A	E	Avg.
1997—	Florida (N.L.)	1B	6	18	1	2	0	0	0	1	.111	1	4	0	34	5	0	1.000

WORLD SERIES RECORD

NOTES: Member of World Series championship team (1997).

							BATTING								FIELDING		
Year	Team (League)	Pos.	G	AB	R	H	2B	3B	HR	RBI	Avg.	BB	SO	SB	PO	A	E	Avg.
1997—	Florida (N.L.)	1B-PH	6	13	1	3	0	0	0	2	.231	0	0	0	30	2	0	1.000

ALL-STAR GAME RECORD

NOTES: Hit home run in first at-bat (July 11, 1995). ... Named Most Valuable Player (1995).

						BATTING							FIELDING		
Year	League	Pos.	AB	R	H	2B	3B	HR	RBI	Avg.	BB	SO	SB	PO	A	E	Avg.
1994—	National							Did not play.									
1995—	National	PH	1	1	1	0	0	1	1	1.000	0	0	0	...	...	...	...

CONTI, JASON — OF — DIAMONDBACKS

PERSONAL: Born January 27, 1975, in Pittsburgh. ... 5-11/180. ... Bats left, throws right. ... Full name: Stanley Jason Conti.
HIGH SCHOOL: Seneca Valley (Harmony, Pa.).
COLLEGE: Pittsburgh.
TRANSACTIONS/CAREER NOTES: Selected by Arizona Diamondbacks organization in 32nd round of free-agent draft (June 4, 1996). ... Loaned by Diamondbacks to Tulsa, Texas Rangers organization (April 1, 1998). ... Returned to Diamondbacks organization (September 14, 1998).
STATISTICAL NOTES: Tied for Midwest League lead in double plays by outfielder with six in 1997. ... Led Pacific Coast League outfielders with 303 total chances in 1999.

Year Team (League)	Pos.	G	AB	R	H	2B	3B	HR	RBI	Avg.	BB	SO	SB	PO	A	E	Avg.
1996— Lethbridge (Pio.)	OF	63	226	63	83	15	1	4	49	.367	30	29	30	80	5	4	.955
1997— South Bend (Midw.) ...	OF	117	458	78	142	22	10	3	43	.310	45	99	30	240	13	5	.981
— High Desert (Calif.)	OF	14	59	15	21	5	1	2	8	.356	10	12	1	27	2	5	.853
1998— Tulsa (Texas)■	OF	130	530	*125	167	31	12	15	67	.315	63	96	19	183	*20	5	.976
1999— Tucson (PCL)■	OF	133	520	100	151	23	8	9	57	.290	55	89	22	278	17	8	.974

COOK, DENNIS — P — METS

PERSONAL: Born October 4, 1962, in Lamarque, Texas. ... 6-3/190. ... Throws left, bats left. ... Full name: Dennis Bryan Cook.
HIGH SCHOOL: Dickinson (Texas).
JUNIOR COLLEGE: Angelina College (Texas).
COLLEGE: Texas.
TRANSACTIONS/CAREER NOTES: Selected by San Diego Padres organization in sixth round of free-agent draft (January 11, 1983); did not sign. ... Selected by San Francisco Giants organization in 18th round of free-agent draft (June 3, 1985). ... Traded by Giants with P Terry Mulholland and 3B Charlie Hayes to Philadelphia Phillies for P Steve Bedrosian and a player to be named later (June, 18, 1989); Giants organization acquired IF Rick Parker to complete deal (August 7, 1989). ... Traded by Phillies to Los Angeles Dodgers for C Darrin Fletcher (September 13, 1990). ... Traded by Dodgers with P Mike Christopher to Cleveland Indians for P Rudy Seanez (December 10, 1991). ... Granted free agency (October 15, 1993). ... Signed by Chicago White Sox organization (January 5, 1994). ... Claimed on waivers by Indians (October 17, 1994). ... Traded by Indians to Texas Rangers for SS Guillermo Mercedes (June 22, 1995). ... Granted free agency (October 29, 1996). ... Signed by Florida Marlins (December 10, 1996). ... On suspended list (July 4-5, 1997). ... Traded by Marlins to New York Mets for OF Fletcher Bates and P Scott Comer (December 18, 1997). ... Granted free agency (October 23, 1998). ... Re-signed by Mets (November 18, 1998).
HONORS: Named Texas League Pitcher of the Year (1987).
STATISTICAL NOTES: Led A.L. with five balks in 1992.
MISCELLANEOUS: Appeared in one game as pinch runner with Philadelphia (1989). ... Singled once and scored once in five games as pinch hitter and appeared in one game as pinch runner with Philadelphia (1990). ... Appeared in one game as pinch runner (1997). ... Singled twice, scored once and had an RBI in two games as pinch hitter (1997).

Year League	W	L	Pct.	ERA	G	GS	CG	ShO	Sv.	IP	H	R	ER	BB	SO
1985— Clinton (Midw.)	5	4	.556	3.36	13	13	1	0	0	83	73	35	31	27	40
1986— Fresno (Calif.)..................	12	7	.632	3.97	27	25	2	1	1	170	141	92	75	100	*173
1987— Shreveport (Texas)	9	2	.818	2.13	16	16	1	1	0	105 2/3	94	32	25	20	98
— Phoenix (PCL)	2	5	.286	5.23	12	11	1	0	0	62	72	45	36	26	24
1988— Phoenix (PCL)	11	9	.550	3.88	26	25	5	1	0	141 1/3	138	73	61	51	110
— San Francisco (N.L.)	2	1	.667	2.86	4	4	1	1	0	22	9	8	7	11	13
1989— Phoenix (PCL)	7	4	.636	3.12	12	12	3	1	0	78	73	29	27	19	85
— San Francisco (N.L.)	1	0	1.000	1.80	2	2	1	0	0	15	13	3	3	5	9
— Philadelphia (N.L.)■■	6	8	.429	3.99	21	16	1	1	0	106	97	56	47	33	58
1990— Philadelphia (N.L.)	8	3	.727	3.56	42	13	2	1	1	141 2/3	132	61	56	54	58
— Los Angeles (N.L.)■	1	1	.500	7.53	5	3	0	0	0	14 1/3	23	13	12	2	6
1991— Albuquerque (PCL)	7	3	.700	3.63	14	14	1	0	0	91 2/3	73	46	37	32	84
— Los Angeles (N.L.)	1	0	1.000	0.51	20	1	0	0	0	17 2/3	12	3	1	7	8
— San Antonio (Texas)	1	3	.250	2.49	7	7	1	0	0	50 2/3	43	20	14	10	45
1992— Cleveland (A.L.)■■	5	7	.417	3.82	32	25	1	0	0	158	156	79	67	50	96
1993— Cleveland (A.L.)	5	5	.500	5.67	25	6	0	0	0	54	62	36	34	16	34
— Charlotte (I.L.)	3	2	.600	5.06	12	6	0	0	0	42 2/3	46	26	24	6	40
1994— Chicago (A.L.)■■	3	1	.750	3.55	38	0	0	0	0	33	29	17	13	14	26
1995— Cleveland (A.L.)■	0	0	...	6.39	11	0	0	0	0	12 2/3	16	9	9	10	13
— Texas (A.L.)■	0	2	.000	4.00	35	1	0	0	2	45	47	23	20	16	40
1996— Texas (A.L.)	5	2	.714	4.09	60	0	0	0	0	70 1/3	53	34	32	35	64
1997— Florida (N.L.)	1	2	.333	3.90	59	0	0	0	0	62 1/3	64	28	27	28	63
1998— New York (N.L.)■	8	4	.667	2.38	73	0	0	0	1	68	60	21	18	27	79
1999— New York (N.L.)	10	5	.667	3.86	71	0	0	0	3	63	50	27	27	27	68
A.L. totals (5 years)	18	17	.514	4.22	201	32	1	0	2	373	363	198	175	141	273
N.L. totals (7 years)	38	24	.613	3.49	297	39	5	3	5	510	460	220	198	194	362
Major League totals (12 years)	56	41	.577	3.80	498	71	6	3	7	883	823	418	373	335	635

DIVISION SERIES RECORD

Year League	W	L	Pct.	ERA	G	GS	CG	ShO	Sv.	IP	H	R	ER	BB	SO
1996— Texas (A.L.)	0	0	...	0.00	2	0	0	0	0	1 1/3	0	0	0	1	0
1997— Florida (N.L.)	1	0	1.000	0.00	2	0	0	0	0	3	0	0	0	1	3
1999— New York (N.L.)	0	0	...	0.00	1	0	0	0	0	1 2/3	1	0	0	1	1
Division series totals (3 years)	1	0	1.000	0.00	5	0	0	0	0	6	1	0	0	3	4

CHAMPIONSHIP SERIES RECORD

Year League	W	L	Pct.	ERA	G	GS	CG	ShO	Sv.	IP	H	R	ER	BB	SO
1997— Florida (N.L.)	0	0	...	0.00	2	0	0	0	0	2 1/3	0	0	0	0	2
1999— New York (N.L.)	0	0	...	0.00	3	0	0	0	0	1 1/3	1	0	0	2	1
Champ. series totals (2 years)	0	0	...	0.00	5	0	0	0	0	3 2/3	1	0	0	2	3

WORLD SERIES RECORD

NOTES: Member of World Series championship team (1997).

Year League	W	L	Pct.	ERA	G	GS	CG	ShO	Sv.	IP	H	R	ER	BB	SO
1997— Florida (N.L.)	1	0	1.000	0.00	3	0	0	0	0	3 2/3	1	0	0	1	5

PERSONAL: Born September 7, 1969, in Van Nuys, Calif. ... 6-0/195. ... Bats right, throws right. ... Full name: Brent Adam Cookson.
HIGH SCHOOL: Santa Paula (Calif.).
COLLEGE: Long Beach State.
TRANSACTIONS/CAREER NOTES: Selected by Oakland Athletics organization in 15th round of free-agent draft (June 3, 1991). ... Signed as free agent by San Francisco Giants organization (February 1, 1992). ... On suspended list (June 6-July 29 and August 26-September 7, 1993). ... On Phoenix disabled list (July 2-14 and July 25-September 6, 1994). ... Traded by Giants organization to Kansas City Royals organization (June 25, 1995); completing deal in which Giants acquired P Enrique Burgos for a player to be named later (April 22, 1995). ... Claimed on waivers by Boston Red Sox (October 6, 1995). ... Traded by Red Sox organization to Baltimore Orioles organization for future considerations (August 2, 1996). ... Granted free agency (September 30, 1996). ... Signed by Texas Rangers organization (March 15, 1997). ... Released by Rangers (April 1, 1997). ... Signed by Arizona Diamondbacks organization (June 12, 1997). ... Loaned by Diamondbacks organization to Laredo, Mexican League (June 13-September 11, 1997). ... Granted free agency (October 15, 1997). ... Re-signed by Diamondbacks organization (January 5, 1998). ... On Tucson disabled list (May 13-June 22 and July 14, 1998-remainder of season). ... Granted free agency (October 15, 1998). ... Signed by Los Angeles Dodgers organization (January 21, 1999). ... On Albuquerque disabled list (July 7-August 11, 1999). ... Granted free agency (October 4, 1999).

							BATTING							FIELDING		
Year Team (League)	Pos.	G	AB	R	H	2B	3B	HR	RBI	Avg.	BB	SO	SB	PO	A	E	Avg.
1991—Arizona A's (Ariz.)	OF	1	1	0	0	0	0	0	0	.000	0	1	0	0	0	0	...
—S. Oregon (N'west)	OF	6	9	0	0	0	0	0	0	.000	0	7	0	6	0	1	.857
1992—Clinton (Midw.)■	OF	46	145	30	31	5	1	8	20	.214	22	48	9	65	5	2	.972
—San Jose (Calif.)	OF	68	255	44	74	8	4	12	49	.290	25	69	9	96	3	5	.952
1993—San Jose (Calif.)	OF	67	234	43	60	10	1	17	50	.256	43	73	14	90	4	3	.969
1994—Shreveport (Texas)	OF	62	207	32	67	21	3	11	41	.324	18	57	4	84	4	3	.967
—Phoenix (PCL)	OF	14	43	7	12	0	1	1	6	.279	5	14	0	20	1	0	1.000
1995—Phoenix (PCL)	OF-DH	68	210	38	63	9	3	15	46	.300	25	36	3	86	2	3	.967
—Omaha (A.A.)■	OF-DH	40	137	28	55	13	0	4	20	.401	17	24	0	56	3	0	1.000
—Kansas City (A.L.)	OF-DH	22	35	2	5	1	0	0	5	.143	2	7	1	14	0	0	1.000
1996—Pawtucket (I.L.)■	OF-DH	73	255	51	69	13	1	19	50	.271	24	72	2	73	4	0	1.000
—Rochester (I.L.)■	OF-DH	30	113	22	30	7	0	6	21	.265	9	20	2	44	0	0	1.000
1997—Laredo (Mexican)■	OF	28	93	17	28	3	1	8	16	.301	20	15	1	...	...	...	...
1998—Tucson (PCL)■	OF-DH	36	100	24	36	12	0	6	19	.360	18	26	0	50	0	0	1.000
1999—Albuquerque (PCL)■.	OF-DH	85	277	57	89	18	1	28	70	.321	38	56	7	169	4	2	.989
—Los Angeles (N.L.)	OF	3	5	0	1	0	0	0	0	.200	0	1	0	4	0	0	1.000
American League totals (1 year)		22	35	2	5	1	0	0	5	.143	2	7	1	14	0	0	1.000
National League totals (1 year)		3	5	0	1	0	0	0	0	.200	0	1	0	4	0	0	1.000
Major League totals (2 years)		25	40	2	6	1	0	0	5	.150	2	8	1	18	0	0	1.000

C

PERSONAL: Born November 18, 1966, in Chicago. ... 5-11/206. ... Bats right, throws right. ... Full name: Ronald Bryan Coomer.
HIGH SCHOOL: Lockport (Ill.) Township.
COLLEGE: Taft (Calif.) College.
TRANSACTIONS/CAREER NOTES: Selected by Oakland Athletics organization in 14th round of free-agent draft (June 2, 1987). ... Released by A's organization (August 1, 1990). ... Signed by Chicago White Sox organization (March 18, 1991). ... On disabled list (June 5-19, 1992). ... On Birmingham disabled list (June 12-21, 1993). ... Traded by White Sox organization to Los Angeles Dodgers organization for P Isidro Martinez (December 27, 1993). ... Traded by Dodgers with P Greg Hansell, P Jose Parra and a player to be named later to Minnesota Twins for P Kevin Tapani and P Mark Guthrie (July 31, 1995); Twins acquired OF Chris Latham to complete deal (October 30, 1995).
STATISTICAL NOTES: Led Southern League with eight sacrifice flies and tied for lead in grounding into double plays with 21 in 1991. ... Led Southern League third basemen with 94 putouts, 396 total chances, 24 double plays and tied for lead with 26 errors in 1991. ... Led Pacific Coast League with 293 total bases in 1994. ... Led Pacific Coast League third basemen with .952 fielding percentage, 399 total chances and 299 assists in 1994. ... Tied for A.L. lead in grounding into double plays with 22 in 1998. ... Career major league grand slams: 1.

							BATTING							FIELDING		
Year Team (League)	Pos.	G	AB	R	H	2B	3B	HR	RBI	Avg.	BB	SO	SB	PO	A	E	Avg.
1987—Medford (N.W.)	3B-1B	45	168	23	58	10	2	1	26	.345	19	22	1	54	78	11	.923
1988—Modesto (Calif.)	3B-1B	131	495	67	138	23	2	17	85	.279	60	88	2	78	105	16	.920
1989—Madison (Midw.)	3B-1B	61	216	28	69	15	0	4	28	.319	30	34	0	67	64	6	.956
1990—Huntsville (Sou.)	2B-1B-3B	66	194	22	43	7	0	3	27	.222	21	40	3	200	100	11	.965
1991—Birmingham (Sou.)■.	3B-1B	137	505	*81	129	27	5	13	76	.255	59	78	0	†113	278	‡26	.938
1992—Vancouver (PCL)	3B	86	262	29	62	10	0	9	40	.237	16	36	3	49	115	13	.927
1993—Birmingham (Sou.)	3B-1B	69	262	44	85	18	0	13	50	.324	15	43	1	43	106	11	.931
—Nashville (A.A.)	3B	59	211	34	66	19	0	13	51	.313	10	29	1	30	107	16	.895
1994—Albuquerque (PCL)■..	3B-DH-2B	127	535	89	181	34	6	22	*123	.338	26	62	4	81	†299	19	†.952
1995—Albuquerque (PCL)	3B-1B-DH	85	323	54	104	23	2	16	76	.322	18	28	5	335	93	9	.979
—Minnesota (A.L.)■	1-3-DH-O	37	101	15	26	3	1	5	19	.257	9	11	0	138	32	2	.988
1996—Minnesota (A.L.)	1-O-3-DH	95	233	34	69	12	1	12	41	.296	17	24	3	275	42	4	.988
1997—Minnesota (A.L.)	3-1-DH-O	140	523	63	156	30	2	13	85	.298	22	91	4	123	223	11	.969
1998—Minnesota (A.L.)	3-1-DH-O	137	529	54	146	22	1	15	72	.276	18	72	2	428	150	6	.990
1999—Minnesota (A.L.)	1-3-DH-O	127	467	53	123	25	1	16	65	.263	30	69	2	542	148	6	.991
Major League totals (5 years)		536	1853	219	520	92	6	61	282	.281	96	267	11	1506	595	29	.986

ALL-STAR GAME RECORD

					BATTING								FIELDING		
Year League	Pos.	AB	R	H	2B	3B	HR	RBI	Avg.	BB	SO	SB	PO	A	E	Avg.
1999—American	1B	1	0	0	0	0	0	0	.000	0	1	0	4	0	0	1.000

COOPER, BRIAN   P   ANGELS

PERSONAL: Born August 19, 1974, in North Hollywood, Calif. ... 6-1/185. ... Throws right, bats right. ... Full name: Brian John Cooper.
HIGH SCHOOL: Glendora (Calif.).
COLLEGE: Southern California.
TRANSACTIONS/CAREER NOTES: Selected by California Angels organization in fourth round of free-agent draft (June 1, 1995). ... Angels franchise renamed Anaheim Angels for 1997 season.
STATISTICAL NOTES: Led Texas League with 35 home runs allowed in 1998.

Year League	W	L	Pct.	ERA	G	GS	CG	ShO	Sv.	IP	H	R	ER	BB	SO
1995— Boise (N.W.)	3	2	.600	3.92	13	11	0	0	1	62	60	31	27	22	66
1996— Lake Elsinore (Calif.)	7	9	.438	4.21	26	23	1	1	0	162 1/3	177	100	76	39	155
1997— Lake Elsinore (Calif.)	7	3	.700	3.54	17	17	1	0	0	117	111	56	46	27	104
1998— Midland (Texas)	8	10	.444	7.13	32	24	5	0	1	161 2/3	215	138	128	59	141
1999— Erie (East.)	10	5	.667	3.30	22	22	*6	0	0	158	146	61	58	29	143
— Edmonton (PCL)	2	1	.667	3.77	5	5	0	0	0	31	30	17	13	10	32
— Anaheim (A.L.)	1	1	.500	4.88	5	5	0	0	0	27 2/3	23	15	15	18	15
Major League totals (1 year)	1	1	.500	4.88	5	5	0	0	0	27 2/3	23	15	15	18	15

COPPINGER, ROCKY   P   BREWERS

PERSONAL: Born March 19, 1974, in El Paso, Texas ... 6-5/240. ... Throws right, bats right. ... Full name: John Thomas Coppinger. ... Name pronounced COP-in-jer.
HIGH SCHOOL: Coronado (El Paso, Texas).
JUNIOR COLLEGE: Hill Junior College (Hillsboro, Texas).
TRANSACTIONS/CAREER NOTES: Selected by Baltimore Orioles in 17th round of free-agent draft (June 3, 1993). ... On Baltimore disabled list (March 31-April 15 and May 10, 1997-remainder of season); included rehabilitation assignments to Rochester (May 14-22), Gulf Coast Orioles (July 1-12) and Bowie (July 17-27). ... On Bowie disabled list (April 10-May 24, 1998). ... Traded by Orioles to Milwaukee Brewers for a player to be named later (July 17, 1999); Orioles acquired P Al Reyes to complete deal (July 21, 1999).

Year League	W	L	Pct.	ERA	G	GS	CG	ShO	Sv.	IP	H	R	ER	BB	SO
1994— Bluefield (Appl.)	4	3	.571	2.45	14	13	0	0	0	73 1/3	51	24	20	40	88
1995— Frederick (Caro.)	7	1	.875	1.57	11	11	2	1	0	68 2/3	46	16	12	24	91
— Bowie (East.)	6	2	.750	2.69	13	13	2	2	0	83 2/3	58	33	25	43	62
— Rochester (I.L.)	3	0	1.000	1.04	5	5	0	0	0	34 2/3	23	5	4	17	19
1996— Rochester (I.L.)	6	4	.600	4.19	12	12	0	0	0	73	65	36	34	39	81
— Baltimore (A.L.)	10	6	.625	5.18	23	22	0	0	0	125	126	76	72	60	104
1997— Baltimore (A.L.)	1	1	.500	6.30	5	4	0	0	0	20	21	14	14	16	22
— Rochester (I.L.)	1	2	.333	5.52	3	3	0	0	0	14 2/3	16	10	9	11	9
— Gulf Coast Orioles (GCL)	0	0	...	1.80	3	3	0	0	0	10	7	3	2	0	13
— Bowie (East.)	1	1	.500	4.80	3	3	0	0	0	15	15	9	8	3	15
1998— Bowie (East.)	2	2	.500	4.35	7	6	0	0	0	31	26	18	15	11	30
— Rochester (I.L.)	8	3	.727	3.50	14	13	1	0	0	87 1/3	80	38	34	43	64
— Baltimore (A.L.)	0	0	...	5.17	6	1	0	0	0	15 2/3	16	9	9	7	13
1999— Rochester (I.L.)	2	2	.500	3.66	5	5	0	0	0	32	28	13	13	12	37
— Baltimore (A.L.)	0	1	.000	8.31	11	2	0	0	0	21 2/3	25	21	20	19	17
— Milwaukee (N.L.)■	5	3	.625	3.68	29	0	0	0	0	36 2/3	35	16	15	23	39
A.L. totals (4 years)	11	8	.579	5.68	45	29	0	0	0	182 1/3	188	120	115	102	156
N.L. totals (1 year)	5	3	.625	3.68	29	0	0	0	0	36 2/3	35	16	15	23	39
Major League totals (4 years)	16	11	.593	5.34	74	29	0	0	0	219	223	136	130	125	195

DIVISION SERIES RECORD

Year League	W	L	Pct.	ERA	G	GS	CG	ShO	Sv.	IP	H	R	ER	BB	SO
1996— Baltimore (A.L.)							Did not play.								

CHAMPIONSHIP SERIES RECORD

Year League	W	L	Pct.	ERA	G	GS	CG	ShO	Sv.	IP	H	R	ER	BB	SO
1996— Baltimore (A.L.)	0	1	.000	8.44	1	1	0	0	0	5 1/3	6	5	5	1	3

COQUILLETTE, TRACE   2B   EXPOS

PERSONAL: Born June 4, 1974, in Carmicheal, Calif. ... 5-11/185. ... Bats right, throws right. ... Full name: Trace Robert Coquillette. ... Name pronounced COE-kill-ette.
HIGH SCHOOL: Casa Roble (Orangevale, Calif.).
JUNIOR COLLEGE: Sacramento City College.
TRANSACTIONS/CAREER NOTES: Selected by Montreal Expos organization in 10th round of free-agent draft (June 3, 1993). ... On West Palm Beach disabled list (June 2-August 1, 1996). ... On Ottawa disabled list (April 14-May 20 and July 3-10, 1999).
STATISTICAL NOTES: Led New York-Pennsylvania League second basemen with 366 total chances in 1994. ... Led International League with a .434 on-base percentage and in being hit by pitch with 24 in 1999.

Year Team (League)	Pos.	G	AB	R	H	2B	3B	HR	RBI	Avg.	BB	SO	SB	PO	A	E	Avg.
1993— GC Expos (GCL)	2B	44	159	27	40	4	3	2	11	.252	37	28	16	80	123	•12	.944
— W.P. Beach (FSL)	2B	6	18	2	5	3	0	0	3	.278	2	5	0	8	16	1	.960
1994— Burlington (Midw.)	2B	5	17	2	3	1	0	0	0	.176	1	4	1	6	14	1	.952
— Vermont (NY-P)	2B	70	252	54	77	11	5	9	52	.306	23	40	7	125	216	*25	.932
1995— Albany (SAL)	2B	128	458	67	123	27	4	3	57	.269	64	91	17	252	292	14	.975
1996— GC Expos (GCL)	2B-3B	7	25	4	4	1	0	0	0	.160	4	6	1	16	16	1	.970
— W.P. Beach (FSL)	2B-3B	72	266	39	67	17	4	1	27	.252	27	72	9	100	142	22	.917
1997— Harrisburg (East.)	2B-3B	81	293	46	76	17	3	10	51	.259	25	40	9	116	169	16	.947
— W.P. Beach (FSL)	2B-3B-OF	53	188	34	60	18	2	8	33	.319	27	27	8	90	111	7	.966

Year	Team (League)	Pos.	G	AB	R	H	2B	3B	HR	RBI	Avg.	BB	SO	SB	PO	A	E	Avg.
							BATTING									FIELDING		
1998—Harrisburg (East.)	2B-3B	49	187	40	62	10	0	9	23	.332	15	41	10	61	124	7	.964
—Ottawa (I.L.)	2B-3B-OF	74	252	30	64	14	0	7	40	.254	17	38	3	125	140	9	.967
1999—Ottawa (I.L.)	2-3-DH-1	98	334	56	109	32	3	14	55	.326	44	68	10	159	212	16	.959
—Montreal (N.L.)	3B-2B	17	49	2	13	3	0	0	4	.265	4	7	1	13	28	1	.976
Major League totals (1 year)		17	49	2	13	3	0	0	4	.265	4	7	1	13	28	1	.976

CORA, ALEX   SS   DODGERS

PERSONAL: Born October 18, 1975, in Caguas, Puerto Rico. ... 6-0/180. ... Bats left, throws right. ... Full name: Jose Alexander Cora. ... Brother of Joey Cora, second baseman with four major league teams (1987-98).
HIGH SCHOOL: Bautista (Caguas, Puerto Rico).
COLLEGE: Miami (Fla.).
TRANSACTIONS/CAREER NOTES: Selected by Los Angeles Dodgers organization in third round of free-agent draft (June 4, 1996). ... On Los Angeles disabled list (March 25-June 27, 1999); included rehabilitation assignment to Albuquerque (June 8-27).
STATISTICAL NOTES: Led Texas League shortstops with 629 total chances and 88 double plays in 1997.

Year	Team (League)	Pos.	G	AB	R	H	2B	3B	HR	RBI	Avg.	BB	SO	SB	PO	A	E	Avg.
							BATTING									FIELDING		
1996—Vero Beach (FSL)	SS-OF	61	214	26	55	5	4	0	26	.257	12	36	5	86	164	16	.940
1997—San Antonio (Texas)	SS	127	448	52	105	20	4	3	48	.234	25	60	12	*197	*412	20	*.968
1998—Albuquerque (PCL)	SS-2B	81	299	42	79	17	5	5	45	.264	15	38	10	126	270	18	.957
—Los Angeles (N.L.)	SS-2B	29	33	1	4	0	1	0	0	.121	2	8	0	26	29	2	.965
1999—Albuquerque (PCL)	SS-DH-2B	80	302	51	93	11	7	4	37	.308	12	37	9	134	234	12	.968
—Los Angeles (N.L.)	SS-2B	11	30	2	5	1	0	0	3	.167	0	4	0	13	20	2	.943
Major League totals (2 years)		40	63	3	9	1	1	0	3	.143	2	12	0	39	49	4	.957

C

CORBIN, ARCHIE   P

PERSONAL: Born December 30, 1967, in Beaumont, Texas. ... 6-4/230. ... Throws right, bats right. ... Full name: Archie Ray Corbin.
HIGH SCHOOL: Beaumont (Texas) Charlton Pellard.
TRANSACTIONS/CAREER NOTES: Selected by New York Mets organization in 16th round of free-agent draft (June 2, 1986). ... On disabled list (April 6-May 4, 1990). ... Traded by Mets organization to Kansas City Royals organization for 1B/OF Pat Tabler (August 31, 1990). ... On Memphis disabled list (April 13-21, 1992). ... Traded by Royals with 3B Sean Berry to Montreal Expos for P Bill Sampen and P Chris Haney (August 29, 1992). ... Traded by Expos to Milwaukee Brewers for a player to be named later (November 20, 1992); Expos received cash to complete deal. ... Contract sold by Brewers to Expos (February 5, 1993). ... On temporarily inactive list (July 13-August 2, 1993). ... Granted free agency (October 15, 1993). ... Signed by Buffalo, Pittsburgh Pirates organization (November 22, 1993). ... On disabled list (July 18-August 4, 1995). ... Granted free agency (October 16, 1995). ... Signed by Oakland A's organization (November 29, 1995). ... Released by A's (March 31, 1996). ... Signed by Rochester, Baltimore Orioles organization (May 7, 1996). ... On disabled list (April 17-May 3, 1997). ... Granted free agency (October 6, 1997). ... Signed by San Diego Padres (November 7, 1997). ... Released by Padres (May 6, 1998). ... Signed by Florida Marlins organization (May 11, 1998). ... On Charlotte disabled list (June 10-28, 1998). ... Granted free agency (October 15, 1998). ... Re-signed by Marlins (November 17, 1998). ... On Florida disabled list (May 16-June 1 and June 2-22, 1999). ... Granted free agency (October 7, 1999).
RECORDS: Shares major league single-inning record for most strikeouts—4 (April 28, 1999, seventh inning).

Year	League	W	L	Pct.	ERA	G	GS	CG	ShO	Sv.	IP	H	R	ER	BB	SO
1986—Kingsport (Appalachian)		1	1	.500	4.75	18	1	0	0	0	30 1/3	31	23	16	28	30
1987—Kingsport (Appalachian)		2	3	.400	6.31	6	6	0	0	0	25 2/3	24	21	18	26	17
1988—Kingsport (Appalachian)		7	2	.778	1.56	11	10	4	1	0	69 1/3	47	23	12	17	47
1989—Columbia (SAL)		9	9	.500	4.51	27	23	4	2	1	153 2/3	149	86	77	72	130
1990—St. Lucie (FSL)		7	8	.467	2.97	20	18	3	0	0	118	97	47	39	59	105
1991—Memphis (Sou.)■		8	8	.500	4.66	28	25	1	0	0	156 1/3	139	90	*81	90	166
—Kansas City (A.L.)		0	0		3.86	2	0	0	0	0	2 1/3	3	1	1	2	1
1992—Memphis (Sou.)		7	8	.467	4.73	27	20	2	0	0	112 1/3	115	64	59	73	100
—Harrisburg (East.)■		0	0		0.00	1	1	0	0	0	3	2	0	0	1	3
1993—Harrisburg (East.)		5	3	.625	3.68	42	2	0	0	4	73 1/3	43	31	30	59	91
1994—Buffalo (A.A.)■		0	0		4.76	14	1	0	0	0	22 2/3	14	13	12	18	23
1995—Calgary (PCL)		1	5	.167	8.56	47	1	0	0	1	61	76	63	58	55	54
1996—Reynoso (Mex.)■		0	0		9.31	9	0	0	0	0	9 2/3	10	10	10	7	13
—Rochester (I.L.)■		0	2	.000	4.74	20	5	0	0	1	43 2/3	44	25	23	25	47
—Baltimore (A.L.)		2	0	1.000	2.30	18	0	0	0	0	27 1/3	22	7	7	22	20
1997—Rochester (I.L.)		4	3	.571	4.00	43	1	0	0	5	69 2/3	47	32	31	62	66
1998—Las Vegas (PCL)■		0	0		27.00	6	0	0	0	0	4 1/3	7	16	13	13	3
—Charlotte (I.L.)■		2		.500	2.59	34	0	0	0	3	48 2/3	25	15	14	46	55
1999—Calgary (PCL)		0	1	.000	6.75	12	0	0	0	0	13 1/3	13	11	10	10	16
—Florida (N.L.)		0	1	.000	7.29	17	0	0	0	0	21	25	20	17	15	30
A.L. totals (2 years)		2	0	1.000	2.43	20	0	0	0	0	29 2/3	25	8	8	24	21
N.L. totals (1 year)		0	1	.000	7.29	17	0	0	0	0	21	25	20	17	15	30
Major League totals (3 years)		2	1	.667	4.44	37	0	0	0	0	50 2/3	50	28	25	39	51

CORDERO, FRANCISCO   P   RANGERS

PERSONAL: Born August 11, 1977, in Santo Domingo, Dominican Republic. ... 6-2/200. ... Throws right, bats right. ... Full name: Francisco Javier Cordero.
HIGH SCHOOL: Colegio Luz de Arroyo Hondo (Dominican Republic).
TRANSACTIONS/CAREER NOTES: Signed as non-drafted free agent by Detroit Tigers organization (June 18, 1994). ... On Jamestown disabled list (June 28, 1996-remainder of season). ... On Jacksonville disabled list (May 22-June 18 and June 26, 1998-remainder of season). ... Traded by Tigers with P Justin Thompson, OF Gabe Kapler, C Bill Haselman, 2B Frank Catalanotto and P Alan Webb to Texas Rangers for OF Juan Gonzalez, P Danny Patterson and C Gregg Zaun (November 2, 1999).
HONORS: Named Southern League Most Outstanding Pitcher (1999).

Year	League	W	L	Pct.	ERA	G	GS	CG	ShO	Sv.	IP	H	R	ER	BB	SO
1994— Dominican Tigers (DSL).....		4	3	.571	3.90	12	12	0	0	0	60	65	47	26	27	36
1995— Fayetteville (SAL)		0	3	.000	6.30	4	4	0	0	0	20	26	16	14	12	19
— Jamestown (NY-P)		4	7	.364	5.22	15	14	0	0	0	88	96	62	51	37	54
1996— Fayetteville (SAL)		0	0	...	2.57	2	1	0	0	0	7	2	2	2	6	7
— Jamestown (NY-P)		0	0	...	0.82	2	2	0	0	0	11	5	1	1	2	10
1997— West Michigan (Midw.)		6	1	.857	0.99	50	0	0	0	*35	54 1/3	36	13	6	15	67
1998— Jacksonville (Sou.).............		1	1	.500	4.86	17	0	0	0	8	16 2/3	19	12	9	9	18
— Lakeland (FSL)		0	0	...	0.00	1	0	0	0	0	16 2/3	1	0	0	0	0
1999— Jacksonville (Sou.).............		4	1	.800	1.38	47	0	0	0	*27	52 1/3	35	9	8	22	58
— Detroit (A.L.)...................		2	2	.500	3.32	20	0	0	0	0	19	19	7	7	18	19
Major League totals (1 year)........		2	2	.500	3.32	20	0	0	0	0	19	19	7	7	18	19

CORDERO, WIL   1B/OF   PIRATES

PERSONAL: Born October 3, 1971, in Mayaguez, Puerto Rico. ... 6-2/200. ... Bats right, throws right. ... Full name: Wilfredo Nieva Cordero. ... Name pronounced cor-DARE-oh.

HIGH SCHOOL: Centro de Servicios Education de Mayaguez (Puerto Rico).

TRANSACTIONS/CAREER NOTES: Signed as non-drafted free agent by Montreal Expos organization (May 24, 1988). ... On Indianapolis disabled list (August 1, 1991-remainder of season; and May 12-June 11 and July 7-20, 1992). ... Traded by Expos with P Bryan Eversgerd to Boston Red Sox for P Rheal Cormier, 1B Ryan McGuire and P Shayne Bennett (January 10, 1996). ... On Boston disabled list (May 21-August 12, 1996); included rehabilitation assignments to Gulf Coast Red Sox (July 23-27) and Pawtucket (July 27-August 6). ... Released by Red Sox (September 28, 1997). ... Signed by Chicago White Sox (March 23, 1998). ... Granted free agency (November 3, 1998). ... Signed by Cleveland Indians (February 3, 1999). ... On Cleveland disabled list (June 9-September 8, 1999); included rehabilitation assignment to Akron (September 3-8). ... Granted free agency (October 29, 1999). ... Signed by Pittsburgh Pirates (December 14, 1999).

HONORS: Named shortstop on THE SPORTING NEWS N.L. Silver Slugger team (1994).

STATISTICAL NOTES: Career major league grand slams: 2.

Year	Team (League)	Pos.	G	AB	R	H	2B	3B	HR	RBI	Avg.	BB	SO	SB	PO	A	E	Avg.
								BATTING							FIELDING			
1988— Jamestown (NY-P)		SS	52	190	18	49	3	0	2	22	.258	15	44	3	82	159	31	.886
1989— W.P. Beach (FSL).........		SS	78	289	37	80	12	2	6	29	.277	33	58	2	121	224	29	.922
— Jacksonville (Sou.).....		SS	39	121	9	26	6	1	3	17	.215	12	33	1	62	93	7	.957
1990— Jacksonville (Sou.).....		SS	131	444	63	104	18	4	7	40	.234	56	122	9	179	349	41	.928
1991— Indianapolis (A.A.)......		SS	98	360	48	94	16	4	11	52	.261	26	89	9	157	287	27	.943
1992— Indianapolis (A.A.)......		SS	52	204	32	64	11	1	6	27	.314	24	54	6	75	146	12	.948
— Montreal (N.L.)..........		SS-2B	45	126	17	38	4	1	2	8	.302	9	31	0	51	92	8	.947
1993— Montreal (N.L.)..........		SS-3B	138	475	56	118	32	2	10	58	.248	34	60	12	163	373	36	.937
1994— Montreal (N.L.)..........		SS	110	415	65	122	30	3	15	63	.294	41	62	16	124	316	22	.952
1995— Montreal (N.L.)..........		SS-OF	131	514	64	147	35	2	10	49	.286	36	88	9	168	281	22	.953
1996— Boston (A.L.)■..........		2B-DH-1B	59	198	29	57	14	0	3	37	.288	11	31	2	82	110	10	.950
— GC Red Sox (GCL)		DH-2B	3	10	1	3	0	0	1	3	.300	0	2	0	1	1	0	1.000
— Pawtucket (I.L.)...........		2B-DH	4	10	2	3	1	0	1	2	.300	2	3	0	2	6	0	1.000
1997— Boston (A.L.)...........		OF-DH-2B	140	570	82	160	26	3	18	72	.281	31	122	1	248	11	2	.992
1998— Birmingham (Sou.)■....		1B-DH	11	35	6	10	2	0	2	11	.286	7	3	0	81	9	1	.989
— Chicago (A.L.)		1B-OF	96	341	58	91	18	2	13	49	.267	22	66	2	713	66	7	.991
1999— Cleveland (A.L.)■.......		OF-DH	54	194	35	58	15	0	8	32	.299	15	37	2	51	0	1	.981
— Akron (East.)		OF-DH	3	11	2	4	2	0	0	0	.364	0	3	0	0	0	0	...
American League totals (4 years)			349	1303	204	366	73	5	42	190	.281	79	256	7	1094	187	20	.985
National League totals (4 years)			424	1530	202	425	101	8	37	178	.278	120	241	37	506	1062	88	.947
Major League totals (8 years)			773	2833	406	791	174	13	79	368	.279	199	497	44	1600	1249	108	.963

DIVISION SERIES RECORD

Year	Team (League)	Pos.	G	AB	R	H	2B	3B	HR	RBI	Avg.	BB	SO	SB	PO	A	E	Avg.
								BATTING							FIELDING			
1999— Cleveland (A.L.)..........		PH-DH-OF	3	9	3	5	0	0	1	2	.556	1	2	0	3	0	0	1.000

ALL-STAR GAME RECORD

Year	League	Pos.	AB	R	H	2B	3B	HR	RBI	Avg.	BB	SO	SB	PO	A	E	Avg.
						BATTING								FIELDING			
1994— National		SS	2	0	0	0	0	0	0	.000	0	0	0	1	1	0	1.000

CORDOVA, FRANCISCO   P   PIRATES

PERSONAL: Born April 26, 1972, in Veracruz, Mexico. ... 6-1/197. ... Throws right, bats right.

TRANSACTIONS/CAREER NOTES: Signed as non-drafted free agent by Pittsburgh Pirates organization (January 18, 1996). ... On Pittsburgh disabled list (April 11-May 19, 1999); included rehabilitation assignments to Nashville (April 28-29 and May 14-15) and Altoona (May 3-4 and May 8-13).

STATISTICAL NOTES: Pitched nine innings, combining with Ricardo Rincon (one inning) in 3-0 no-hit victory against Houston (July 12, 1997).

Year	League	W	L	Pct.	ERA	G	GS	CG	ShO	Sv.	IP	H	R	ER	BB	SO
1992— M.C. Red Devils (Mex.)		3	0	1.000	5.79	16	1	0	0	0	28	28	19	18	14	15
1993— M.C. Red Devils (Mex.)		9	2	.818	3.23	43	4	1	0	4	106	96	44	38	47	71
1994— M.C. Red Devils (Mex.)		15	4	.789	2.33	41	15	6	3	8	150 1/3	122	43	39	43	104
1995— M.C. Red Devils (Mex.)		13	0	*1.000	3.10	27	20	1	0	4	125	131	52	43	42	88
1996— Pittsburgh (N.L.)■............		4	7	.364	4.09	59	6	0	0	12	99	103	49	45	20	95
1997— Pittsburgh (N.L.)...............		11	8	.579	3.63	29	29	2	2	0	178 2/3	175	80	72	49	121
1998— Pittsburgh (N.L.)...............		13	14	.481	3.31	33	33	3	2	0	220 1/3	204	91	81	69	157
1999— Pittsburgh (N.L.)...............		8	10	.444	4.43	27	27	2	0	0	160 2/3	166	83	79	59	98
— Nashville (PCL)		2	0	1.000	0.75	2	2	0	0	0	12	10	2	1	1	7
— Altoona (East.)		1	1	.500	4.66	2	2	0	0	0	9 2/3	13	8	5	4	12
Major League totals (4 years).......		36	39	.480	3.78	148	95	7	4	12	658 2/3	648	303	277	197	471

PERSONAL: Born July 10, 1969, in Las Vegas. ... 6-0/206. ... Bats right, throws right. ... Full name: Martin Keevin Cordova.
HIGH SCHOOL: Bishop Gorman (Las Vegas).
JUNIOR COLLEGE: Orange Coast College (Calif.).
COLLEGE: UNLV.
TRANSACTIONS/CAREER NOTES: Selected by San Diego Padres organization in eighth round of free-agent draft (June 2, 1987); did not sign. ... Selected by Minnesota Twins organization in 10th round of free-agent draft (June 5, 1989). ... On Visalia disabled list (April 12-May 20, 1991). ... On Salt Lake disabled list (April 7-May 11, 1994). ... On Minnesota disabled list (April 11-May 26, 1997); included rehabilitation assignment to Salt Lake (May 20-26). ... On disabled list (April 27-May 12, 1998). ... Granted free agency (October 7, 1999). ... Signed by Boston Red Sox organization (January 19, 2000).
HONORS: Named California League Most Valuable Player (1992). ... Named A.L. Rookie of the Year by Baseball Writers' Association of America (1995).
STATISTICAL NOTES: Led California League with 302 total bases and .589 slugging percentage and tied for lead in grounding into double plays with 20 in 1992. ... Had 23-game hitting streak (June 5-29, 1996).

							BATTING								FIELDING		
Year Team (League)	Pos.	G	AB	R	H	2B	3B	HR	RBI	Avg.	BB	SO	SB	PO	A	E	Avg.
1989—Elizabethton (Appl.)....	OF-3B	38	148	32	42	2	3	8	29	.284	14	29	2	6	9	4	.789
1990—Kenosha (Midw.)........	OF	81	269	35	58	7	5	7	25	.216	28	73	6	87	5	5	.948
1991—Visalia (Calif.)..........	OF	71	189	31	40	6	1	7	19	.212	17	46	2	58	2	5	.923
1992—Visalia (Calif.)..........	OF	134	513	103	175	31	6	*28	*131	.341	76	99	13	173	10	3	.984
1993—Nashville (Sou.).........	OF	138	508	83	127	30	5	19	77	.250	64	*153	10	209	7	2	*.991
1994—Salt Lake (PCL)........	OF-DH	103	385	69	138	25	4	19	66	.358	39	63	17	187	13	8	.962
1995—Minnesota (A.L.)	OF	137	512	81	142	27	4	24	84	.277	52	111	20	345	12	5	.986
1996—Minnesota (A.L.)	OF	145	569	97	176	46	1	16	111	.309	53	96	11	328	9	3	.991
1997—Minnesota (A.L.)	OF-DH	103	378	44	93	18	4	15	51	.246	30	92	5	217	12	2	.991
—Salt Lake (PCL)........	DH-OF	6	24	5	9	4	0	1	4	.375	2	3	1	3	0	1	.750
1998—Minnesota (A.L.)	OF-DH	119	438	52	111	20	2	10	69	.253	50	103	3	257	5	6	.978
1999—Minnesota (A.L.)	DH-OF	124	425	62	121	28	3	14	70	.285	48	96	13	38	0	3	.927
Major League totals (5 years)		628	2322	336	643	139	14	79	385	.277	233	498	52	1185	38	19	.985

PERSONAL: Born April 23, 1967, in Moncton, New Brunswick. ... 5-10/187. ... Throws left, bats left. ... Full name: Rheal Paul Cormier. ... Name pronounced ree-AL COR-mee-AY.
HIGH SCHOOL: Polyvalente Louis J. Robichaud.
JUNIOR COLLEGE: Community College of Rhode Island.
TRANSACTIONS/CAREER NOTES: Selected by St. Louis Cardinals organization in sixth round of free-agent draft (June 6, 1988). ... On Louisville disabled list (April 10-29, 1991). ... On disabled list (August 12-September 7, 1993). ... On St. Louis disabled list (April 28-May 13 and May 21-August 3, 1994); included rehabilitation assignments to Arkansas (July 7-18) and Louisville (July 18-30). ... Traded by Cardinals with OF Mark Whiten to Boston Red Sox for 3B Scott Cooper, P Cory Bailey and a player to be named later (April 8, 1995). ... Traded by Red Sox with 1B Ryan McGuire and P Shayne Bennett to Montreal Expos for SS Wil Cordero and P Bryan Eversgerd (Jauary 10, 1996). ... On disabled list (August 26-September 10, 1996). ... Granted free agency (October 30, 1997). ... Signed by Cleveland Indians organization (December 18, 1997). ... On Buffalo disabled list (April 9-June 2, 1998). ... On Akron disabled list (June 18, 1998-remainder of season). ... Granted free agency (October 15, 1998). ... Signed by Red Sox organization (January 5, 1999). ... On suspended list (May 7-10, 1999).
MISCELLANEOUS: Member of 1988 Canadian Olympic baseball team.

Year League	W	L	Pct.	ERA	G	GS	CG	ShO	Sv.	IP	H	R	ER	BB	SO
1989—St. Petersburg (FSL) ...	12	7	.632	2.23	26	26	4	1	0	169²/₃	141	63	42	33	122
1990—Arkansas (Texas)...............	5	•12	.294	5.04	22	21	3	1	0	121¹/₃	133	81	68	30	102
—Louisville (A.A.)............	1	1	.500	2.25	4	4	0	0	0	24	18	8	6	3	9
1991—Louisville (A.A.)............	7	9	.438	4.23	21	21	3	*3	0	127²/₃	140	64	60	31	74
—St. Louis (N.L.)...............	4	5	.444	4.12	11	10	2	0	0	67²/₃	74	35	31	8	38
1992—Louisville (A.A.)............	0	1	.000	6.75	1	1	0	0	0	4	8	4	3	0	1
—St. Louis (N.L.)...............	10	10	.500	3.68	31	30	3	0	0	186	194	83	76	33	117
1993—St. Louis (N.L.)...............	7	6	.538	4.33	38	21	1	0	0	145¹/₃	163	80	70	27	75
1994—St. Louis (N.L.)...............	3	2	.600	5.45	7	7	0	0	0	39²/₃	40	24	24	7	26
—Arkansas (Texas).............	1	0	1.000	1.93	2	2	0	0	0	9¹/₃	9	2	2	0	11
—Louisville (A.A.)............	1	2	.333	4.50	3	3	1	0	0	22	21	11	11	8	13
1995—Boston (A.L.)■............	7	5	.583	4.07	48	12	0	0	0	115	131	60	52	31	69
1996—Montreal (N.L.)■............	7	10	.412	4.17	33	27	1	1	0	159²/₃	165	80	74	41	100
1997—Montreal (N.L.)............	0	1	.000	33.75	1	1	0	0	0	1¹/₃	4	5	5	1	0
1998—Akron (East.)■............	0	0	...	6.52	3	3	0	0	0	9²/₃	15	7	7	2	6
1999—Boston (A.L.)■............	2	0	1.000	3.69	60	0	0	0	0	63¹/₃	61	34	26	18	39
A.L. totals (2 years)	9	5	.643	3.94	108	12	0	0	0	178¹/₃	192	94	78	49	108
N.L. totals (6 years)	31	34	.477	4.20	121	96	7	1	0	599²/₃	640	307	280	117	356
Major League totals (8 years)	40	39	.506	4.14	229	108	7	1	0	778	832	401	358	166	464

DIVISION SERIES RECORD

Year League	W	L	Pct.	ERA	G	GS	CG	ShO	Sv.	IP	H	R	ER	BB	SO
1995—Boston (A.L.).....................	0	0	...	13.50	2	0	0	0	0	²/₃	2	1	1	1	2
1999—Boston (A.L.).....................	0	0	...	0.00	2	0	0	0	0	4	2	0	0	1	4
Division series totals (2 years)	0	0	...	1.93	4	0	0	0	0	4²/₃	4	1	1	2	6

CHAMPIONSHIP SERIES RECORD

Year League	W	L	Pct.	ERA	G	GS	CG	ShO	Sv.	IP	H	R	ER	BB	SO
1999—Boston (A.L.).....................	0	0	...	0.00	4	0	0	0	0	3²/₃	3	0	0	3	4

C

CORNELIUS, REID   P   MARLINS

PERSONAL: Born June 2, 1970, in Thomasville, Ala. ... 6-0/200. ... Throws right, bats right. ... Full name: Jonathan Reid Cornelius.
HIGH SCHOOL: Thomasville (Alabaster, Ala.).
TRANSACTIONS/CAREER NOTES: Selected by Montreal Expos organization in 11th round of free-agent draft (June 1, 1988). ... On West Palm Beach disabled list (May 27-August 2, 1990 and May 20-June 3, 1991). ... On Harrisburg disabled list (August 6, 1991-remainder of season and April 27-September 6, 1992). ... On disabled list (July 12-28, 1994). ... Traded by Expos to New York Mets for 1B/OF David Segui (June 8, 1995). ... Traded by Mets with OF Ryan Thompson to Cleveland Indians for P Mark Clark (March 31, 1996). ... On disabled list (April 16-28 and June 26-July 28, 1996). ... Granted free agency (October 15, 1996). ... Signed by Portland, Florida Marlins organization (March 31, 1997). ... Granted free agency (October 17, 1997). ... Signed by Arizona Diamondbacks organization (November 24, 1997). ... Traded by Diamondbacks to Marlins for a player to be named later (July 24, 1998); Diamondbacks acquired OF Walt White to complete deal (October 29, 1998). ... Granted free agency (October 16, 1998). ... Signed by Anaheim Angels organization (November 18, 1998). ... Released by Angels (March 20, 1999). ... Signed by Marlins organization (April 9, 1999).
STATISTICAL NOTES: Led Pacific Coast League pitchers with 19 putouts and 47 total chances in 1999.

Year	League	W	L	Pct.	ERA	G	GS	CG	ShO	Sv.	IP	H	R	ER	BB	SO
1989—	Rockford (Midw.)	5	6	.455	4.27	17	17	0	0	0	84 1/3	71	58	40	63	66
1990—	West Palm Beach (FSL)	2	3	.400	3.38	11	11	0	0	0	56	54	25	21	25	47
1991—	West Palm Beach (FSL)	8	3	.727	2.39	17	17	0	0	0	109 1/3	79	31	29	43	81
—	Harrisburg (East.)	2	1	.667	2.89	3	3	1	1	0	18 2/3	15	6	6	7	12
1992—	Harrisburg (East.)	1	0	1.000	3.13	4	4	0	0	0	23	11	8	8	8	17
1993—	Harrisburg (East.)	10	7	.588	4.17	27	27	1	0	0	157 2/3	146	95	73	82	119
1994—	Ottawa (I.L.)	9	8	.529	4.38	25	24	1	0	0	148	149	89	72	75	87
1995—	Montreal (N.L.)	0	0	...	8.00	8	0	0	0	0	9	11	8	8	5	4
—	Ottawa (I.L.)	1	1	.500	6.75	4	3	0	0	0	10 2/3	16	12	8	5	7
—	Norfolk (I.L.)■	7	0	1.000	0.90	10	10	1	0	0	70 1/3	57	10	7	19	43
—	New York (N.L.)	3	7	.300	5.15	10	10	0	0	0	57 2/3	64	36	33	25	35
1996—	Buffalo (A.A.)■	5	7	.417	5.60	20	18	0	0	0	90	101	64	56	49	62
1997—	Portland (East.)■	5	0	1.000	2.73	6	6	0	0	0	33	32	11	10	17	24
—	Charlotte (I.L.)	12	5	.706	5.10	22	22	1	0	0	130 2/3	134	82	74	43	80
1998—	Tucson (PCL)■	4	7	.364	5.94	19	16	0	0	0	94	108	70	62	26	65
—	Charlotte (I.L.)■	3	2	.600	4.01	8	8	1	1	0	49 1/3	50	25	22	13	31
1999—	Calgary (PCL)	10	6	.625	4.49	27	27	2	1	0	172 1/3	184	96	86	68	135
—	Florida (N.L.)	1	0	1.000	3.26	5	2	0	0	0	19 1/3	16	7	7	5	12
Major League totals (2 years)		**4**	**7**	**.364**	**5.02**	**23**	**12**	**0**	**0**	**0**	**86**	**91**	**51**	**48**	**35**	**51**

CORSI, JIM   P

PERSONAL: Born September 9, 1961, in Newton, Mass. ... 6-1/220. ... Throws right, bats right. ... Full name: James Bernard Corsi.
HIGH SCHOOL: Newton (Mass.) North.
COLLEGE: St. Leo (Fla.) College (bachelor of arts degree in management).
TRANSACTIONS/CAREER NOTES: Selected by New York Yankees organization in 25th round of free-agent draft (June 7, 1982). ... On Fort Lauderdale disabled list (April 8-May 11, 1983). ... Released by Yankees organization (April 3, 1984). ... Signed by Boston Red Sox organization (April 1, 1985). ... Released by Red Sox organization (January 31, 1986). ... Re-signed by Red Sox organization (April 5, 1986). ... Released by Red Sox organization (April 2, 1987). ... Signed by Oakland Athletics organization (April 12, 1987). ... On Oakland disabled list (March 29, 1990-entire season); included rehabilitation assignment to Tacoma (June 29-July 25). ... Granted free agency (December 20, 1990). ... Signed by Houston Astros organization (March 19, 1991). ... Released by Astros (November 18, 1991). ... Signed by A's organization (March 16, 1992). ... Selected by Florida Marlins in second round (49th pick overall) of expansion draft (November 17, 1992). ... On Florida disabled list (March 27-April 30 and July 6, 1993-remainder of season); included rehabilitation assignment to High Desert (April 20-30). ... On Florida disabled list (July 6, 1993-remainder of season). ... Granted free agency (October 15, 1993). ... Re-signed by Marlins organization (January 24, 1994). ... On Brevard County disabled list (April 11-July 5, 1994). ... Granted free agency (October 15, 1994). ... Signed by Edmonton, A's organization (January 20, 1995). ... On Oakland disabled list (June 22-August 8, 1995). ... On Oakland disabled list (April 28-May 18, 1996); included rehabilitation assignment to Modesto (May 17-18). ... Granted free agency (November 4, 1996). ... Signed by Red Sox organization (February 3, 1997). ... On Boston disabled list (June 2-July 1, 1997); included rehabilitation assignment to Gulf Coast Red Sox (June 23-30). ... Granted free agency (October 28, 1997). ... Re-signed by Red Sox (December 3, 1997). ... On Boston disabled list (July 18-August 6, 1998); included rehabilitation assignment to Pawtucket (August 3-6). ... Released by Red Sox (June 22, 1999). ... Signed by Baltimore Orioles organization (July 2, 1999). ... On Baltimore disabled list (August 25-September 9, 1999). ... Granted free agency (November 3, 1999).

Year	League	W	L	Pct.	ERA	G	GS	CG	ShO	Sv.	IP	H	R	ER	BB	SO
1982—	Oneonta (NY-P)	0	0	...	10.80	1	0	0	0	0	3 1/3	5	4	4	2	6
—	Paintsville (Appl.)	0	2	.000	2.90	8	4	0	0	0	31	32	11	10	13	20
1983—	Greensboro (SAL)	2	2	.500	4.09	12	7	1	0	1	50 2/3	59	37	23	33	37
—	Oneonta (NY-P)	3	6	.333	4.25	11	10	2	0	0	59 1/3	76	38	28	21	47
1984—	......						Out of organized baseball.									
1985—	Greensboro (SAL)■	5	8	.385	4.23	41	2	1	0	9	78 2/3	94	49	37	23	84
1986—	New Britain (East.)	2	3	.400	2.28	29	0	0	0	3	51 1/3	52	13	13	20	38
1987—	Modesto (Calif.)■	3	1	.750	3.60	19	0	0	0	6	30	23	16	12	10	45
—	Huntsville (Sou.)	8	1	.889	2.81	28	0	0	0	4	48	30	17	15	15	33
1988—	Tacoma (PCL)	2	5	.286	2.75	50	0	0	0	16	59	60	25	18	23	40
—	Oakland (A.L.)	0	1	.000	3.80	11	1	0	0	0	21 1/3	20	10	9	6	10
1989—	Tacoma (PCL)	2	3	.400	4.13	23	0	0	0	8	28 1/3	40	17	13	9	23
—	Oakland (A.L.)	1	2	.333	1.88	22	0	0	0	0	38 1/3	26	8	8	10	21
1990—	Tacoma (PCL)	0	0	...	1.50	5	0	0	0	0	6	9	2	1	1	3
1991—	Tucson (PCL)■	0	0	...	0.00	2	0	0	0	0	3	2	0	0	0	4
—	Houston (N.L.)	0	5	.000	3.71	47	0	0	0	0	77 2/3	76	37	32	23	53
1992—	Tacoma (PCL)■	0	0	...	1.23	26	0	0	0	12	29 1/3	22	8	4	10	21
—	Oakland (A.L.)	4	2	.667	1.43	32	0	0	0	0	44	44	12	7	18	19
1993—	High Desert (Calif.)■	0	1	.000	3.00	3	3	0	0	0	9	11	3	3	2	6
—	Florida (N.L.)	0	2	.000	6.64	15	0	0	0	0	20 1/3	28	15	15	10	17
1994—	Brevard County (FSL)	0	1	.000	1.64	6	0	0	0	0	11	8	3	2	0	11
—	Edmonton (PCL)	0	0	.000	4.50	15	0	0	0	0	22	29	15	11	10	15

C

Year	League	W	L	Pct.	ERA	G	GS	CG	ShO	Sv.	IP	H	R	ER	BB	SO
1995— Edmonton (PCL)■		0	0	...	0.00	3	0	0	0	3	3	0	0	0	1	3
— Oakland (A.L.)		2	4	.333	2.20	38	0	0	0	2	45	31	14	11	26	26
1996— Oakland (A.L.)		6	0	1.000	4.03	56	0	0	0	3	73 2/3	71	33	33	34	43
— Modesto (Calif.)		0	0	...	0.00	1	1	0	0	0	1	0	0	0	0	2
1997— Boston (A.L.)■		5	3	.625	3.43	52	0	0	0	2	57 2/3	56	26	22	21	40
— Pawtucket (I.L.)		0	0	...	0.00	2	0	0	0	1	2 1/3	2	0	0	1	3
— Gulf Coast Red Sox (GCL)		1	0	1.000	0.00	3	2	0	0	0	4	2	1	0	0	6
1998— Boston (A.L.)		3	2	.600	2.59	59	0	0	0	0	66	58	23	19	23	49
— Pawtucket (I.L.)		0	0	...	0.00	1	1	0	0	0	2	3	0	0	0	1
1999— Boston (A.L.)		1	2	.333	5.25	23	0	0	0	0	24	25	15	14	19	14
— Rochester (I.L.)■		0	0	...	3.48	10	0	0	0	2	10 1/3	12	4	4	3	7
— Baltimore (A.L.)		0	1	.000	2.70	13	0	0	0	0	13 1/3	15	4	4	1	8
A.L. totals (8 years)		22	17	.564	2.98	306	1	0	0	7	383 1/3	346	145	127	158	230
N.L. totals (2 years)		0	7	.000	4.32	62	0	0	0	0	98	104	52	47	33	60
Major League totals (10 years)		22	24	.478	3.25	368	1	0	0	7	481 1/3	450	197	174	191	290

DIVISION SERIES RECORD

Year	League	W	L	Pct.	ERA	G	GS	CG	ShO	Sv.	IP	H	R	ER	BB	SO
1998— Boston (A.L.)		0	0	...	0.00	2	0	0	0	0	3	1	0	0	1	2

CHAMPIONSHIP SERIES RECORD

Year	League	W	L	Pct.	ERA	G	GS	CG	ShO	Sv.	IP	H	R	ER	BB	SO
1992— Oakland (A.L.)		0	0	...	0.00	3	0	0	0	0	2	2	0	0	3	0

CORTES, DAVID   P   BRAVES   C

PERSONAL: Born October 15, 1973, in Mexicali, Mexico. ... 5-11/195. ... Throws right, bats right. ... Full name: David C. Cortes.

TRANSACTIONS/CAREER NOTES: Signed as non-drafted free agent by Atlanta Braves organization (July 13, 1996). ... On disabled list (June 4-July 5, 1998). ... Traded by Braves with P Mike Porzio to Colorado Rockies for 1B Greg Colbrunn (July 30, 1998). ... Traded by Rockies to Braves for a player to be named later (August 19, 1998); Rockies acquired P Anthony Briggs to complete deal (September 8, 1998). ... On Richmond disabled list (April 8-15, 1999).

Year	League	W	L	Pct.	ERA	G	GS	CG	ShO	Sv.	IP	H	R	ER	BB	SO
1996— Eugene (N.W.)		2	1	.667	0.73	15	0	0	0	4	24 2/3	13	2	2	6	33
1997— Macon (SAL)		3	0	1.000	0.57	27	0	0	0	15	31 1/3	16	3	2	4	32
— Durham (Caro.)		2	0	1.000	2.33	19	0	0	0	8	19 1/3	15	5	5	5	16
— Greenville (Sou.)		0	1	.000	1.80	3	0	0	0	0	5	4	1	1	1	7
1998— Richmond (I.L.)		3	3	.500	2.82	29	0	0	0	4	44 2/3	37	15	14	14	46
— Colo. Springs (PCL)■		1	0	1.000	7.71	6	0	0	0	0	7	14	6	6	2	5
1999— Richmond (I.L.)■		2	3	.400	3.35	47	0	0	0	22	45 2/3	50	19	17	14	42
— Atlanta (N.L.)		0	0	...	4.91	4	0	0	0	0	3 2/3	3	3	2	4	2
Major League totals (1 year)		0	0	...	4.91	4	0	0	0	0	3 2/3	3	3	2	4	2

COTA, HUMBERTO   C   PIRATES

PERSONAL: Born February 7, 1979, in San Luis Rio Colorado, Mexico. ... 6-0/175. ... Bats right, throws right. ... Full name: Humberto Figueroa Cota.

TRANSACTIONS/CAREER NOTES: Signed as non-drafted free agent by Atlanta Braves organization (December 22, 1995). ... Loaned by Braves organization to Mexico City Tigers (June 23-September 23, 1996). ... Released by Braves (January 27, 1997). ... Signed by Tampa Bay Devil Rays organization (May 22, 1997). ... Traded by Devil Rays with C Joe Oliver to Pittsburgh Pirates for OF Jose Guillen and P Jeff Sparks (July 23, 1999).

STATISTICAL NOTES: Tied for Gulf Coast League lead in double plays by catcher with four in 1997.

						BATTING							FIELDING		
Year	Team (League)	Pos.	G	AB	R	H	2B	3B	HR	RBI	Avg.	BB	SO	SB	PO	A	E	Avg.
1997— Hudson Valley (NY-P.)		C	3	9	0	2	0	0	0	0	.222	0	1	0	29	0	0	1.000
— GC Devil Rays (GCL)		C	44	133	14	32	6	1	2	20	.241	17	27	3	294	26	5	.985
1998— Princeton (Appl.)		C	67	245	48	76	13	4	15	61	.310	32	59	4	*382	48	•12	.973
1999— Char., S.C. (SAL)		C-1B	85	336	42	94	21	1	9	61	.280	20	51	1	443	61	7	.986
— Hickory (SAL)■		C	37	133	28	36	11	2	2	20	.271	21	20	3	235	22	2	.992

COUNSELL, CRAIG   2B   DODGERS

PERSONAL: Born August 21, 1970, in South Bend, Ind. ... 6-0/175. ... Bats left, throws right. ... Full name: Craig John Counsell. ... Son of John Counsell, outfielder in Minnesota Twins organization (1964-68).

HIGH SCHOOL: Whitefish Bay (Milwaukee).

COLLEGE: Notre Dame.

TRANSACTIONS/CAREER NOTES: Selected by Colorado Rockies organization in 11th round of free-agent draft (June 1, 1992). ... On disabled list (April 7-May 13, July 30-August 6 and August 7-27, 1994). ... On disabled list (May 1-July 15 and July 18-September 3, 1996). ... Traded by Rockies to Florida Marlins for P Mark Hutton (July 27, 1997). ... On disabled list (August 4, 1998-remainder of season). ... Traded by Marlins to Los Angeles Dodgers for a player to be named later (June 15, 1999); Marlins acquired P Ryan Moskau to complete deal (July 15, 1999).

STATISTICAL NOTES: Led California League shortstops with 621 total chances in 1993. ... Led Pacific Coast League shortstops with 598 total chances and 86 double plays in 1995. ... Career major league grand slams: 2.

						BATTING							FIELDING		
Year	Team (League)	Pos.	G	AB	R	H	2B	3B	HR	RBI	Avg.	BB	SO	SB	PO	A	E	Avg.
1992— Bend (N.W.)		2B-SS	18	61	11	15	6	1	0	8	.246	9	10	1	23	36	2	.967
1993— Central Valley (Calif.)		SS	131	471	79	132	26	3	5	59	.280	95	68	14	*233	353	35	.944
1994— New Haven (East.)		SS-2B	83	300	47	84	20	1	5	37	.280	37	32	4	122	242	27	.931

Year	Team (League)	Pos.	G	AB	R	H	2B	3B	HR	RBI	Avg.	BB	SO	SB	PO	A	E	Avg.
1995—	Colo. Springs (PCL) ...	SS	118	399	60	112	22	6	5	53	.281	34	47	10	182	386	30	.950
—	Colorado (N.L.)	SS	3	1	0	0	0	0	0	0	.000	1	0	0	1	1	0	1.000
1996—	Colo. Springs (PCL) ...	2B-3B-SS	25	75	17	18	3	0	2	10	.240	24	7	4	35	64	4	.961
1997—	Colo. Springs (PCL) ...	2B-SS	96	376	77	126	31	6	5	63	.335	45	38	12	213	260	9	.981
—	Colorado (N.L.)	PR	1	0	0	0	0	0	0	0	0	...	0	0	0	...	...	...	...
—	Florida (N.L.)■	2B	51	164	20	49	9	2	1	16	.299	18	17	1	124	149	3	.989
1998—	Florida (N.L.)	2B	107	335	43	84	19	5	4	40	.251	51	47	3	237	299	5	.991
1999—	Florida (N.L.)	2B	37	66	4	10	1	0	0	2	.152	5	10	0	20	29	1	.980
—	Los Angeles (N.L.)■ ..	2B-SS	50	108	20	28	6	0	0	9	.259	9	14	1	54	86	1	.993
Major League totals (4 years)			249	674	87	171	35	7	5	67	.254	84	88	5	436	564	10	.990

DIVISION SERIES RECORD

Year	Team (League)	Pos.	G	AB	R	H	2B	3B	HR	RBI	Avg.	BB	SO	SB	PO	A	E	Avg.
1997—	Florida (N.L.)	2B	3	5	0	2	1	0	0	1	.400	1	0	0	5	2	1	.875

CHAMPIONSHIP SERIES RECORD

Year	Team (League)	Pos.	G	AB	R	H	2B	3B	HR	RBI	Avg.	BB	SO	SB	PO	A	E	Avg.
1997—	Florida (N.L.)	2B-PH	5	14	0	6	0	0	0	2	.429	3	3	0	7	9	1	.941

WORLD SERIES RECORD

NOTES: Member of World Series championship team (1997).

Year	Team (League)	Pos.	G	AB	R	H	2B	3B	HR	RBI	Avg.	BB	SO	SB	PO	A	E	Avg.
1997—	Florida (N.L.)	2B	7	22	4	4	1	0	0	2	.182	6	5	1	18	15	1	.971

COX, DARRON   C

PERSONAL: Born November 21, 1967, in Oklahoma City. ... 6-1/215. ... Bats right, throws right. ... Full name: James Darron Cox.

HIGH SCHOOL: Mustang (Okla.).

COLLEGE: Oklahoma.

TRANSACTIONS/CAREER NOTES: Selected by Cincinnati Reds organization in fifth round of free-agent draft (June 5, 1989). ... On disabled list (June 24-July 22, 1993). ... Traded by Reds with P Larry Luebbers and P Mike Anderson to Chicago Cubs for P Chuck McElroy (December 10, 1993). ... Granted free agency (October 16, 1995). ... Signed by Richmond, Atlanta Braves organization (November 15, 1995). ... Granted free agency (October 15, 1996). ... Signed by Tampa Bay Devil Rays organization (February 21, 1997). ... Loaned by Devil Rays to Cubs organization (April 28-May 10, 1997). ... Loaned by Devil Rays to Mexico City Tigres, Mexican League (May 11-September 11, 1997). ... Granted free agency (October 15, 1998). ... Signed by Montreal Expos organization (January 13, 1999). ... On Montreal disabled list (June 27, 1999-remainder of season); included rehabilitation assignment to Ottawa (July 17-24). ... Granted free agency (October 15, 1999).

Year	Team (League)	Pos.	G	AB	R	H	2B	3B	HR	RBI	Avg.	BB	SO	SB	PO	A	E	Avg.
1989—	Billings (Pio.)	C	49	157	20	43	6	0	0	18	.274	21	34	11	192	24	4	.982
1990—	Char., W.Va. (SAL)......	C	103	367	53	93	11	3	1	44	.253	40	75	14	486	*89	10	.983
1991—	Cedar Rap. (Midw.)	C	21	60	12	16	4	0	0	4	.267	8	11	7	93	12	8	.929
—	Char., W.Va. (SAL)......	C	79	294	37	71	14	1	2	28	.241	24	39	8	500	73	2	.997
—	Chattanooga (Sou.)	C	13	38	2	7	1	0	0	3	.184	2	9	0	74	6	1	.988
1992—	Chattanooga (Sou.)	C	98	331	29	84	19	1	1	38	.254	15	63	8	654	*91	6	*.992
1993—	Chattanooga (Sou.)	C	89	300	35	65	9	5	3	26	.217	38	63	7	519	87	8	.987
1994—	Iowa (A.A.)■	C	99	301	35	80	15	1	3	26	.266	28	47	5	507	*76	6	.990
1995—	Iowa (A.A.)	C-DH	33	94	7	22	6	0	1	14	.234	8	21	0	187	18	3	.986
—	Orlando (Sou.)	C	33	102	8	29	5	0	4	15	.284	8	16	3	157	24	5	.973
1996—	Richmond (I.L.).......	C-1B-DH-P	55	168	19	40	9	0	3	20	.238	5	22	1	319	29	0	1.000
1997—	Orlando (Sou.)■	C	3	9	2	2	1	0	1	4	.222	1	1	0	20	4	0	1.000
—	M.C. Tigres (Mex.)■..	C	107	352	47	101	19	4	3	46	.287	34	42	1	...	...	...	...
1998—	Durham (I.L.)■ C-DH-1B-3B		84	278	45	84	16	1	9	35	.302	23	41	2	550	57	10	.984
1999—	Montreal (N.L.)■........	C	15	25	2	6	1	0	1	2	.240	0	5	0	48	4	2	.963
—	Ottawa (I.L.)	C	3	9	0	0	0	0	0	0	.000	1	2	0	17	2	0	1.000
Major League totals (1 year)			15	25	2	6	1	0	1	2	.240	0	5	0	48	4	2	.963

COX, STEVE   1B   DEVIL RAYS

PERSONAL: Born October 31, 1974, in Delano, Calif. ... 6-4/222. ... Bats left, throws left. ... Full name: Charles Steven Cox.

HIGH SCHOOL: Monache (Porterville, Calif.).

TRANSACTIONS/CAREER NOTES: Selected by Oakland Athletics organization in fifth round of free-agent draft (June 1, 1992). ... On disabled list (July 23, 1993-remainder of season). ... Selected by Tampa Bay Devil Rays in second round (46th pick overall) of expansion draft (November 18, 1997). ... On Durham disabled list (April 12-26, 1998).

HONORS: Named International League Most Valuable Player (1999).

STATISTICAL NOTES: Led California League with 10 sacrifice flies in 1995. ... Tied for Pacific Coast League lead with nine sacrifice flies in 1997. ... Led International League first basemen with 1,079 total chances in 1998. ... Led International League with 314 total bases, a .588 slugging percentage and 11 intentional bases on balls received in 1999. ... Led International League first basemen with 1,203 total chances and 121 double plays in 1999.

Year	Team (League)	Pos.	G	AB	R	H	2B	3B	HR	RBI	Avg.	BB	SO	SB	PO	A	E	Avg.
1992—	Scottsdale (Ariz.)........	1B	52	184	30	43	4	1	1	35	.234	27	51	2	407	28	11	.975
1993—	S. Oregon (N'west.).....	1B	15	57	10	18	4	1	2	16	.316	5	15	0	104	11	2	.983
1994—	W. Mich. (Mid.)	1B-OF	99	311	37	75	19	2	6	32	.241	41	95	2	727	49	10	.987
1995—	Modesto (Calif.)	1B	132	483	95	144	29	3	*30	*110	.298	84	88	5	991	77	17	.984
1996—	Huntsville (Sou.)	1B-DH	104	381	59	107	21	1	12	61	.281	51	65	2	909	72	15	.985

Year	Team (League)	Pos.	G	AB	R	H	2B	3B	HR	RBI	Avg.	BB	SO	SB	PO	A	E	Avg.
1997—Edmonton (PCL)		1B-DH	131	467	84	128	34	1	15	93	.274	*88	90	1	1043	70	*10	.991
1998—Durham (I.L.)■..........		1B-OF-DH	119	430	64	109	23	2	13	67	.253	56	100	3	*1011	62	7	.994
1999—Durham (I.L.).............		1B-DH	134	534	*107	*182	*49	4	25	*127	.341	67	74	3	*1125	73	5	.996
—Tampa Bay (A.L.).......		1B-OF	6	19	0	4	1	0	0	0	.211	0	2	0	20	1	0	1.000
Major League totals (1 year)			6	19	0	4	1	0	0	0	.211	0	2	0	20	1	0	1.000

CRABTREE, TIM — P — RANGERS

PERSONAL: Born October 13, 1969, in Jackson, Mich. ... 6-4/220. ... Throws right, bats right. ... Full name: Timothy Lyle Crabtree.
HIGH SCHOOL: Grass Lake (Mich.).
COLLEGE: Michigan State.
TRANSACTIONS/CAREER NOTES: Selected by Toronto Blue Jays organization in second round of free-agent draft (June 1, 1992). ... On disabled list (August 16-September 6, 1996). ... On Toronto disabled list (June 4-August 3, 1997); included rehabilitation assignments to St. Catherines (July 22-24) and Syracuse (July 27-August 4). ... Traded by Blue Jays to Texas Rangers for C Kevin Brown (March 14, 1998).

Year	League	W	L	Pct.	ERA	G	GS	CG	ShO	Sv.	IP	H	R	ER	BB	SO
1992—St. Catherines (NY-P)		6	3	.667	1.57	12	12	2	0	0	69	45	19	12	22	47
—Knoxville (Sou.)..................		0	2	.000	0.95	3	3	1	0	0	19	14	8	2	4	13
1993—Knoxville (Sou.).............		9	14	.391	4.08	27	27	2	2	0	158 2/3	178	93	72	59	67
1994—Syracuse (I.L.).................		2	6	.250	4.17	51	9	0	0	2	108	125	58	50	49	58
1995—Syracuse (I.L.).................		0	2	.000	5.40	26	0	0	0	5	31 2/3	38	25	19	12	22
—Toronto (A.L.).................		0	2	.000	3.09	31	0	0	0	0	32	30	16	11	13	21
1996—Toronto (A.L.)...............		5	3	.625	2.54	53	0	0	0	1	67 1/3	59	26	19	22	57
1997—Toronto (A.L.)...............		3	3	.500	7.08	37	0	0	0	2	40 2/3	65	32	32	17	26
—St. Catharines (NY-P)		0	0	...	3.00	2	1	0	0	0	3	3	2	1	0	3
—Syracuse (I.L.).................		0	0	...	9.82	3	0	0	0	1	3 2/3	7	4	4	1	3
1998—Texas (A.L.)■....................		6	1	.857	3.59	64	0	0	0	0	85 1/3	86	40	34	35	60
1999—Texas (A.L.)......................		5	1	.833	3.46	68	0	0	0	0	65	71	26	25	18	54
Major League totals (5 years)		19	10	.655	3.75	253	0	0	0	3	290 1/3	311	140	121	105	218

DIVISION SERIES RECORD

Year	League	W	L	Pct.	ERA	G	GS	CG	ShO	Sv.	IP	H	R	ER	BB	SO
1998—Texas (A.L.)		0	0	...	0.00	2	0	0	0	0	4	1	0	0	0	2
1999—Texas (A.L.)		0	0	...	5.40	2	0	0	0	0	1 2/3	1	2	1	1	1
Division series totals (2 years)		0	0	...	1.59	4	0	0	0	0	5 2/3	2	2	1	1	3

CRAWFORD, PAXTON — P — RED SOX

PERSONAL: Born August 4, 1977, in Little Rock, Ark. ... 6-3/205. ... Throws right, bats right. ... Full name: Paxton Keith Crawford.
HIGH SCHOOL: Carlsbad (N.M.).
TRANSACTIONS/CAREER NOTES: Selected by Boston Red Sox organization in ninth round of free-agent draft (June 1, 1995).

Year	League	W	L	Pct.	ERA	G	GS	CG	ShO	Sv.	IP	H	R	ER	BB	SO
1995—GC Red Sox (GCL)		2	4	.333	2.74	12	7	1	0	2	46	38	17	14	12	44
1996—Michigan (Midw.)...............		6	11	.353	3.58	22	22	1	0	0	128 1/3	120	62	51	42	105
1997—Sarasota (FSL)		4	8	.333	4.55	12	11	2	1	0	65 1/3	69	42	33	27	56
1998—Trenton (East.)		6	5	.545	4.17	22	20	1	0	0	108	104	53	50	39	82
1999—Trenton (East.)		7	8	.467	4.08	28	•28	1	1	0	163 1/3	151	81	74	59	111

CREDE, JOE — 3B — WHITE SOX

PERSONAL: Born April 26, 1978, in Jefferson City, Mo. ... 6-3/195. ... Bats right, throws right. ... Full name: Joseph Crede.
HIGH SCHOOL: Fatima (Westphalia, Mo.).
TRANSACTIONS/CAREER NOTES: Selected by Chicago White Sox organization in fifth round of free-agent draft (June 2, 1996). ... On Birmingham disabled list (July 2, 1999-remainder of season).
HONORS: Named Carolina League Most Valuable Player (1998).
STATISTICAL NOTES: Led Gulf Coast League third basemen with 175 total chances in 1996. ... Led Carolina League with 253 total bases and 11 sacrifice flies in 1998. ... Led Carolina League third basemen with 420 total chances in 1998.

Year	Team (League)	Pos.	G	AB	R	H	2B	3B	HR	RBI	Avg.	BB	SO	SB	PO	A	E	Avg.
1996—GC White Sox (GCL) ..		3B	56	221	30	66	17	1	4	32	.299	9	41	1	*42	*108	*25	.857
1997—Hickory (SAL)............		3B	113	402	45	109	25	0	5	62	.271	24	83	3	84	232	33	.905
1998—Win.-Salem (Car.).......		3B	*137	492	•92	155	32	3	20	*88	*.315	53	98	9	*100	*290	*30	.929
1999—Birmingham (Sou.).....		3B-DH	74	291	37	73	14	1	4	42	.251	22	47	2	68	133	20	.910

CREEK, DOUG — P

PERSONAL: Born March 1, 1969, in Winchester, Va. ... 6-0/210. ... Throws left, bats left. ... Full name: Paul Douglas Creek.
HIGH SCHOOL: Martinsburg (W.Va.).
COLLEGE: Georgia Tech.
TRANSACTIONS/CAREER NOTES: Selected by California Angels organization in fifth round of free-agent draft (June 4, 1990); did not sign. ... Selected by St. Louis Cardinals organization in seventh round of free-agent draft (June 3, 1991). ... On Arkansas disabled list (April 10-May 21, 1992; July 25-August 1, 1993; and June 25-July 10, 1994). ... Traded by Cardinals with P Allen Watson and P Rich DeLucia to San Francisco Giants for SS Royce Clayton and a player to be named later (December 14, 1995); Cardinals acquired 2B Chris Wimmer to complete deal (January 16, 1996). ... Contract purchased by Chicago White Sox (November 7, 1997). ... Contract sold by White Sox to Hanshin Tigers of Japan Pacific League (December 4, 1997). ... Signed by Chicago Cubs organization (January 29, 1999). ... Released by Cubs (September 13, 1999).
STATISTICAL NOTES: Tied for Pacific Coast League lead with 12 hit batsmen in 1999.

C

Year League	W	L	Pct.	ERA	G	GS	CG	ShO	Sv.	IP	H	R	ER	BB	SO
1991— Hamilton (NY-P)	3	2	.600	5.12	9	5	0	0	1	38²/₃	39	22	22	18	45
— Savannah (SAL)	2	1	.667	4.45	5	5	0	0	0	28¹/₃	24	14	14	17	32
1992— Springfield (Midw.)	4	1	.800	2.58	6	6	0	0	0	38¹/₃	32	11	11	13	43
— St. Petersburg (FSL)	5	4	.556	2.82	13	13	0	0	0	73¹/₃	57	31	23	37	63
1993— Louisville (A.A.).................	0	0	...	3.21	2	2	0	0	0	14	10	5	5	9	9
— Arkansas (Texas)...............	11	10	.524	4.02	25	25	1	1	0	147²/₃	142	75	66	48	128
1994— Louisville (A.A.).................	1	4	.200	8.54	7	7	0	0	0	26¹/₃	37	26	25	23	16
— Arkansas (Texas)...............	3	10	.231	4.40	17	17	1	0	0	92	96	54	45	36	65
1995— Louisville (A.A.).................	3	2	.600	3.23	26	0	0	0	0	30²/₃	20	12	11	21	29
— Arkansas (Texas)...............	4	2	.667	2.88	26	0	0	0	1	34¹/₃	24	12	11	16	50
— St. Louis (N.L.).................	0	0	...	0.00	6	0	0	0	0	6²/₃	2	0	0	3	10
1996— San Francisco (N.L.)■.......	0	2	.000	6.52	63	0	0	0	0	48¹/₃	45	41	35	32	38
1997— Phoenix (PCL)	8	6	.571	4.93	25	23	2	1	0	129²/₃	140	76	71	66	*137
— San Francisco (N.L.)	1	2	.333	6.75	3	3	0	0	0	13¹/₃	12	12	10	14	14
1998— Hanshin (Jap. Pac.)■........	0	4	.000	565	...	...	...	...	0	28²/₃	...	...	...	...	24
1999— Iowa (PCL)■...................	7	3	.700	3.79	25	20	0	0	1	130²/₃	116	66	55	62	140
— Chicago (N.L.)...................	0	0	...	10.50	3	0	0	0	0	6	6	7	7	8	6
Major League totals (4 years).......	1	4	.200	6.30	75	3	0	0	0	74¹/₃	65	60	52	57	68

CRESPO, FELIPE — IF/OF — GIANTS

PERSONAL: Born March 5, 1973, in Rio Piedras, Puerto Rico. ... 5-11/200. ... Bats both, throws right. ... Full name: Felipe Javier Clauso Crespo.

HIGH SCHOOL: Notre Dame (Caguas, Puerto Rico).

TRANSACTIONS/CAREER NOTES: Selected by Toronto Blue Jays organization in third round of free-agent draft (June 4, 1990). ... On disabled list (May 26-July 2, 1995). ... On Toronto disabled list (April 1-24, 1996); included rehabilitation assignment to Dunedin (April 12-24). ... Released by Blue Jays (March 17, 1999). ... Signed by San Francisco Giants organization (April 27, 1999). ... Granted free agency (October 15, 1999). ... Re-signed by Giants organization (October 29, 1999).

STATISTICAL NOTES: Led Southern League third basemen with 127 putouts and 42 errors in 1994. ... Led Pacific Coast League with a .616 slugging percentage and a .447 on-base percentage in 1999.

									BATTING					FIELDING		
Year Team (League)	Pos.	G	AB	R	H	2B	3B	HR	RBI	Avg.	BB	SO	SB	PO	A	E	Avg.
1991— Medicine Hat (Pio.)	2B	49	184	40	57	11	4	4	31	.310	25	31	6	*97	133	*23	.909
1992— Myrtle Beach (SAL)	2B-3B	81	263	43	74	14	3	1	29	.281	58	38	7	161	149	22	.934
1993— Dunedin (FSL)	2B	96	345	51	103	16	8	6	39	.299	47	40	18	198	269	25	.949
1994— Knoxville (Sou.).........	3B-2B	129	502	74	135	30	4	8	49	.269	57	95	20	†127	270	†42	.904
1995— Syracuse (I.L.)...........	2B-DH	88	347	56	102	20	5	13	41	.294	41	56	12	160	220	*25	.938
1996— Dunedin (FSL)	2B	9	34	3	11	1	0	2	6	.324	2	3	1	18	18	2	.947
— Toronto (A.L.).............	2B-3B-1B	22	49	6	9	4	0	0	4	.184	12	13	1	34	38	1	.986
— Syracuse (I.L.)............	2B-OF-3B-1B	98	355	53	100	25	0	8	58	.282	56	39	10	220	143	19	.950
1997— Toronto (A.L.)	3B-DH-2B	12	28	3	8	0	1	1	5	.286	2	4	0	9	9	1	.947
— Syracuse (I.L.)............	O-2-1-DH-3	80	290	53	75	12	0	12	26	.259	46	38	7	247	103	12	.967
1998— Toronto (A.L.)...........	O-2-DH-3-1	66	130	11	34	8	1	1	15	.262	15	27	4	67	17	4	.955
1999— Fresno (PCL)■..........	1-O-2-D-3-S	112	385	98	128	27	5	24	84	.332	78	73	17	620	77	13	.982
Major League totals (3 years)		100	207	20	51	12	2	2	24	.246	29	44	5	110	64	6	.967

CRESSEND, JACK — P — TWINS

PERSONAL: Born May 13, 1975, in New Orleans. ... 6-1/190. ... Throws right, bats right. ... Full name: John Baptiste Cressend III.

HIGH SCHOOL: Mandeville (La.).

COLLEGE: Tulane.

TRANSACTIONS/CAREER NOTES: Signed as non-drafted free agent by Boston Red Sox organization (July 24, 1996). ... Claimed on waivers by Minnesota Twins (April 22, 1999).

Year League	W	L	Pct.	ERA	G	GS	CG	ShO	Sv.	IP	H	R	ER	BB	SO
1996— Lowell (NY-P)	3	2	.600	2.36	9	8	0	0	0	45²/₃	37	15	12	17	57
1997— Sarasota (FSL)	8	11	.421	3.80	28	25	2	1	0	165²/₃	163	98	70	56	149
1998— Trenton (East.)	10	11	.476	4.34	29	•29	1	1	0	149¹/₃	168	86	72	55	130
1999— Trenton (East.)	1	0	1.000	7.20	3	3	0	0	0	15	19	12	12	7	11
— New Britain (East.)■	7	10	.412	4.34	25	24	2	2	0	145	152	79	70	50	125

CROMER, D.T. — 1B/OF — REDS

PERSONAL: Born March 19, 1971, in Lake City, S.C. ... 6-2/190. ... Bats left, throws left. ... Full name: David Thomas Cromer. ... Son of Roy Cromer, former scout with St. Louis Cardinals and minor league pitcher/second baseman (1960-63); brother of Brandon Cromer, minor league shortstop (1992-99); brother of Tripp Cromer, infielder, Houston Astros; and brother of Burke Cromer, pitcher in Atlanta Braves organization (1992-93).

HIGH SCHOOL: Lexington (S.C.).

COLLEGE: South Carolina.

TRANSACTIONS/CAREER NOTES: Selected by Oakland Athletics organization in 11th round of free-agent draft (June 1, 1992). ... Granted free agency (October 15, 1998). ... Signed by Cincinnati Reds organization (December 15, 1998).

HONORS: Named California League Most Valuable Player (1996).

STATISTICAL NOTES: Led California League with 316 total bases and .626 slugging percentage in 1996. ... Led Southern League first basemen with 1,167 putouts, 18 errors, 1,285 total chances and 129 double plays in 1997. ... Led Pacific Coast League first basemen with 1,015 putouts, 89 assists, 1,117 total chances and 113 double plays in 1998.

Year	Team (League)	Pos.	G	AB	R	H	2B	3B	HR	RBI	Avg.	BB	SO	SB	PO	A	E	Avg.
1992—	S. Oregon (N'west.)....	OF	50	168	17	35	7	0	4	26	.208	13	34	4	61	6	5	.931
1993—	Madison (Midw.)........	OF-1B-DH	98	321	37	84	20	4	4	41	.262	22	72	8	233	8	7	.972
1994—	W. Mich. (Mid.).........	OF-1B	102	349	50	89	20	5	10	58	.255	33	76	11	328	28	10	.973
1995—	Modesto (Calif.)	OF-1B	108	378	59	98	18	5	14	52	.259	36	66	5	160	16	8	.957
1996—	Modesto (Calif.)	1B-OF-DH	124	505	100	166	40	10	30	130	.329	32	67	20	549	67	14	.978
1997—	Huntsville (Sou.)	1B-DH-OF	134	545	100	*176	*40	6	15	121	.323	60	102	12 †1169		101	†18	.986
1998—	Edmonton (PCL)	1B-DH-OF	125	504	75	148	30	3	16	85	.294	32	93	12 †1018		†89	15	.987
1999—	Indianapolis (I.L.)■.....	OF-1B-DH	136	535	83	166	37	4	30	107	.310	44	98	4	507	38	9	.984

CROMER, TRIPP   SS   ASTROS

PERSONAL: Born November 21, 1967, in Lake City, S.C. ... 6-2/166. ... Bats right, throws right. ... Full name: Roy Bunyan Cromer III. ... Son of Roy Cromer, former scout with St. Louis Cardinals and minor league pitcher/second baseman (1960-63); brother of Brandon Cromer, minor league shortstop (1992-99); brother of D.T. Cromer, first baseman/outfielder, Cincinnati Reds organization; and brother of Burke Cromer, pitcher in Atlanta Braves organization (1992-93).

HIGH SCHOOL: Lake City (S.C.).

COLLEGE: South Carolina.

TRANSACTIONS/CAREER NOTES: Selected by St. Louis Cardinals organization in third round of free-agent draft (June 5, 1989). ... On Arkansas disabled list (May 14-26, 1992). ... On Louisville disabled list (April 30-May 28 and July 5-August 3, 1993). ... On disabled list (May 20-27, 1996). ... Claimed on waivers by Los Angeles Dodgers (October 10, 1996). ... On disabled list (July 31, 1997-remainder of season). ... On Los Angeles disabled list (March 12-July 17 and July 31-September 1, 1998); included rehabilitation assignment to Albuquerque (June 16-26 and July 9-17) and San Bernardino (August 27-September 1). ... On Los Angeles disabled list (July 5-September 1, 1999); included rehabilitation assignments to Albuquerque (July 21-27) and San Bernardino (August 27-September 1). ... Granted free agency (November 24, 1999). ... Signed by Houston Astros organization (December 21, 1999).

C

Year	Team (League)	Pos.	G	AB	R	H	2B	3B	HR	RBI	Avg.	BB	SO	SB	PO	A	E	Avg.
1989—	Hamilton (NY-P)	SS	35	137	18	36	6	3	0	6	.263	17	30	4	66	85	11	.932
1990—	St. Petersburg (FSL) ..	SS	121	408	53	88	12	5	5	38	.216	46	78	7	202	334	32	.944
1991—	St. Petersburg (FSL) ..	SS	43	137	11	28	3	1	0	10	.204	9	17	0	79	134	3	.986
—	Arkansas (Texas).......	SS	73	227	28	52	12	1	1	18	.229	15	37	0	117	198	10	.969
1992—	Arkansas (Texas).......	SS	110	339	30	81	16	6	7	29	.239	22	82	4	135	315	18	*.962
—	Louisville (A.A.).........	SS	6	25	5	5	1	1	1	7	.200	1	2	0	13	20	0	1.000
1993—	Louisville (A.A.).........	SS	85	309	39	85	8	4	11	33	.275	15	60	1	123	253	12	.969
—	St. Louis (N.L.)..........	SS	10	23	1	2	0	0	0	0	.087	1	6	0	13	18	3	.912
1994—	Louisville (A.A.).........	SS	124	419	53	115	23	9	9	50	.274	33	85	5	165	370	12	*.978
—	St. Louis (N.L.)..........	SS	2	0	1	0	0	0	0	0	...	0	0	0	0	0	1	.000
1995—	St. Louis (N.L.)..........	SS-2B	105	345	36	78	19	0	5	18	.226	14	66	0	126	292	17	.961
1996—	St. Louis (N.L.)..........	SS-2B	80	244	28	55	4	4	4	25	.225	22	47	3	124	238	5	.986
1997—	Albuquerque (PCL)■..	SS	43	140	25	45	8	6	5	24	.321	14	34	4	65	106	6	.966
—	Los Angeles (N.L.)	2B-SS-3B	28	86	8	25	3	0	4	20	.291	6	16	0	47	61	3	.973
1998—	Albuquerque (PCL).....	SS-DH	12	30	3	10	1	0	2	5	.333	1	5	0	3	17	1	.952
—	Los Angeles (N.L.)	PH	6	6	1	1	0	0	1	1	.167	0	2	0	...	...	...	...
—	San Bern. (Calif.).......	2B-DH	4	15	3	6	1	0	2	6	.400	0	2	0	2	8	0	1.000
1999—	Los Angeles (N.L.) 2-S-3-OF-1		33	52	5	10	0	0	2	8	.192	5	10	0	21	36	0	1.000
—	Albuquerque (PCL).....	2B-1B-SS	5	15	1	4	2	0	0	1	.267	1	3	0	17	11	0	1.000
—	San Bern. (Calif.).......	1-2-3-SS	4	18	3	9	3	0	1	8	.500	0	3	0	9	8	0	1.000
Major League totals (6 years)			184	512	52	116	22	0	12	47	.227	26	100	0	207	407	24	.962

CROUSHORE, RICK   P   ROCKIES

PERSONAL: Born August 7, 1970, in Lakehurst, N.J. ... 6-4/210. ... Throws right, bats right. ... Full name: Richard Steven Croushore.

HIGH SCHOOL: Mount Vernon (Texas).

JUNIOR COLLEGE: Hutchinson (Kan.) Community College.

COLLEGE: James Madison.

TRANSACTIONS/CAREER NOTES: Signed as non-drafted free agent by St. Louis Cardinals organization (June 12, 1993). ... On disabled list (April 6-June 19, 1995). ... On Memphis disabled list (April 15-22, 1999). ... Traded by Cardinals with P Jose Jimenez, P Manny Aybar and SS Brent Butler to Colorado Rockies for P Darryl Kile, P Dave Veres and P Luther Hackman (November 16, 1999).

Year	League	W	L	Pct.	ERA	G	GS	CG	ShO	Sv.	IP	H	R	ER	BB	SO
1993—	Glens Falls (NY-P)	4	1	.800	3.05	31	0	0	0	1	41 1/3	38	16	14	22	36
1994—	Madison (Midw.)	6	6	.500	4.10	•62	0	0	0	0	94 1/3	90	49	43	46	103
1995—	St. Petersburg (FSL)	6	4	.600	3.51	12	11	0	0	0	59	44	25	23	32	57
1996—	Arkansas (Texas)	5	10	.333	4.92	34	17	2	0	3	108	113	75	59	51	85
1997—	Arkansas (Texas)	7	5	.583	4.18	17	16	1	0	0	92 2/3	111	52	43	37	67
—	Louisville (A.A.)................	1	2	.333	2.47	14	6	0	0	1	43 2/3	37	14	12	13	41
1998—	Memphis (PCL).................	0	3	.000	4.71	23	0	0	0	2	28 2/3	21	16	15	9	40
—	St. Louis (N.L.).................	0	3	.000	4.97	41	0	0	0	8	54 1/3	44	31	30	29	47
1999—	Memphis (PCL).................	1	0	1.000	6.75	7	0	0	0	4	6 2/3	8	5	5	6	11
—	St. Louis (N.L.).................	3	7	.300	4.14	59	0	0	0	3	71 2/3	68	42	33	43	88
Major League totals (2 years)......		3	10	.231	4.50	100	0	0	0	11	126	112	73	63	72	135

CRUZ, DEIVI   SS   TIGERS

PERSONAL: Born November 6, 1975, in Nizao de Bani, Dominican Republic. ... 6-0/184. ... Bats right, throws right. ... Full name: Deivi Garcia Cruz.

HIGH SCHOOL: Liceo Aliro Paulino Nizao (Dominican Republic).

TRANSACTIONS/CAREER NOTES: Signed as non-drafted free agent by San Francisco Giants (April 23, 1993). ... Selected by Los Angeles Dodgers organization from Giants organization in Rule 5 major league draft (December 9, 1996). ... Traded by Dodgers with OF Juan Hernaiz to Detroit Tigers for 2B Jeff Berblinger (December 9, 1996). ... On Detroit disabled list (March 20-April 27, 1998); included rehabilitation assignments to Lakeland (April 21-23) and Toledo (April 24-27).
STATISTICAL NOTES: Led Northwest League third basemen with 47 putouts and .941 fielding percentage in 1995. ... Led Midwest League shortstops with 427 assists and .980 fielding percentage in 1996. ... Career major league grand slams: 1.

Year Team (League)	Pos.	G	AB	R	H	2B	3B	HR	RBI	Avg.	BB	SO	SB	PO	A	E	Avg.
1993— Arizona Giants (Ariz.) .	3B-SS-1B	28	82	8	28	3	0	0	15	.341	4	5	3	17	52	2	.972
1994— Arizona Giants (Ariz.) .	SS-3B	18	53	10	16	8	0	0	5	.302	5	3	0	11	37	1	.980
1995— Burlington (Midw.)	2B-3B-SS	16	58	2	8	1	0	1	9	.138	4	7	1	20	42	2	.969
— Bellingham (N.W.)	3B-2B	62	223	32	66	17	0	3	28	.296	19	21	6	†55	124	10	†.947
1996— Burlington (Midw.)	SS-3B	127	517	72	152	27	2	9	64	.294	35	49	12	159	†444	13	†.979
1997— Detroit (A.L.)■..........	SS	147	436	35	105	26	0	2	40	.241	14	55	3	192	420	13	.979
1998— Lakeland (FSL)	SS	2	9	0	0	0	0	0	1	.000	0	1	0	1	2	0	1.000
— Toledo (I.L.)..............	SS	2	9	1	1	1	0	0	2	.111	2	3	0	2	7	0	1.000
— Detroit (A.L.)..............	SS	135	454	52	118	22	3	5	45	.260	13	55	3	196	445	11	.983
1999— Detroit (A.L.)	SS	155	518	64	147	35	0	13	58	.284	12	57	1	230	453	12	.983
Major League totals (3 years)		437	1408	151	370	83	3	20	143	.263	39	167	7	618	1318	36	.982

CRUZ, IVAN — 1B — PIRATES

C

PERSONAL: Born May 3, 1968, in Fajardo, Puerto Rico. ... 6-2/219. ... Bats left, throws left. ... Full name: Luis Ivan Cruz.
HIGH SCHOOL: Colegio Santiago (Fajardo, Puerto Rico).
COLLEGE: Jacksonville.
TRANSACTIONS/CAREER NOTES: Selected by Detroit Tigers organization in 28th round of free-agent draft (June 5, 1989). ... Granted free agency (October 16, 1995). ... Signed by New York Yankees organization (November 27, 1996). ... Granted free agency (October 3, 1998). ... Signed by Pittsburgh Pirates organization (December 22, 1998). ... On Pittsburgh disabled list (July 4, 1999-remainder of season); included rehabilitation assignments to Altoona (July 23-25) and Nashville (July 26-August 9).
STATISTICAL NOTES: Tied for Florida State League lead in double plays by first baseman with 75 in 1990. ... Led Southern League with .564 slugging percentage in 1995. ... Tied for Southern League lead in intentional bases on balls received with 15 in 1995. ... Led International League first basemen with 1,127 total chances and 88 double plays in 1996.

Year Team (League)	Pos.	G	AB	R	H	2B	3B	HR	RBI	Avg.	BB	SO	SB	PO	A	E	Avg.
1989— Niagara Falls (NY-P) ...	1B	64	226	43	62	11	2	7	40	.274	27	29	2	439	30	5	.989
1990— Lakeland (FSL)	1B	118	414	61	118	23	2	11	73	.285	49	71	8	938	44	11	.989
1991— London (East.)	1B	121	443	46	110	21	0	9	47	.248	36	73	3	845	49	12	.987
— Toledo (I.L.)..............	1B	8	29	2	4	0	0	1	4	.138	2	12	0	70	7	0	1.000
1992— London (East.)	1B	134	*524	71	143	25	1	14	*104	.273	37	102	1	549	35	8	.986
1993— Toledo (I.L.)..............	1B	115	402	44	91	18	4	13	50	.226	30	85	1	268	27	2	.993
1994— Toledo (I.L.)..............	1B-DH	97	303	36	75	11	2	15	43	.248	28	83	1	411	37	6	.987
1995— Toledo (I.L.)..............	1B-DH	11	36	5	7	2	0	0	3	.194	6	9	0	89	6	3	.969
— Jacksonville (Sou.)......	1B-DH	108	397	65	112	17	1	*31	93	.282	60	94	0	795	60	7	.992
1996— Columbus (I.L.)■........	1B-DH	130	446	84	115	26	0	28	96	.258	48	99	2	*1028	*94	5	*.996
1997— Columbus (I.L.)	1B-DH	116	417	69	125	35	1	24	95	.300	65	78	4	974	83	8	.992
— New York (A.L.)..........	DH-1B-OF	11	20	0	5	1	0	0	3	.250	2	4	0	8	0	0	1.000
1998— Columbus (I.L.)	1B-DH-OF	56	204	34	54	10	0	13	36	.265	29	44	0	503	39	5	.991
— GC Yankees (GCL)......	1B-DH	5	10	2	6	3	0	1	5	.600	3	3	0	18	0	0	1.000
1999— Nashville (PCL)■.......	1B-DH	75	273	57	89	20	1	25	81	.326	21	56	0	571	37	4	.993
— Pittsburgh (N.L.)	1B-OF	5	10	3	4	0	0	1	2	.400	0	2	0	13	1	0	1.000
— Altoona (East.)	DH	3	13	1	2	1	0	0	3	.154	1	8	0	0	0	0	...
American League totals (1 year)		11	20	0	5	1	0	0	3	.250	2	4	0	8	0	0	1.000
National League totals (1 year)		5	10	3	4	0	0	1	2	.400	0	2	0	13	1	0	1.000
Major League totals (2 years)		16	30	3	9	1	0	1	5	.300	2	6	0	21	1	0	1.000

CRUZ, JACOB — OF — INDIANS

PERSONAL: Born January 28, 1973, in Oxnard, Calif. ... 6-0/179. ... Bats left, throws left.
HIGH SCHOOL: Channel Islands (Oxnard, Calif.).
COLLEGE: Arizona State.
TRANSACTIONS/CAREER NOTES: Selected by California Angels organization in 45th round of free-agent draft (June 3, 1991); did not sign. ... Selected by San Francisco Giants organization in supplemental round ("sandwich pick" between first and second round; 32nd pick overall) of free-agent draft (June 2, 1994); pick received as part of compensation for Texas Rangers signing Type A free agent 1B Will Clark. ... Traded by Giants with P Steve Reed to Cleveland Indians for P Jose Mesa, IF Shawon Dunston and P Alvin Morman (July 24, 1998). ... On Cleveland disabled list (March 30-April 29 and August 3, 1999-remainder of season); included rehabilitation assignment to Buffalo (April 18-29).
STATISTICAL NOTES: Led Pacific Coast League with 11 sacrifice flies in 1996. ... Led Pacific Coast League with .434 on-base percentage and tied for league lead with nine intentional bases on balls in 1997.

Year Team (League)	Pos.	G	AB	R	H	2B	3B	HR	RBI	Avg.	BB	SO	SB	PO	A	E	Avg.
1994— San Jose (Calif.).........	OF	31	118	14	29	7	0	0	12	.246	9	22	0	42	2	2	.957
1995— Shreveport (Texas).....	OF	127	458	88	136	33	1	13	77	.297	57	72	9	235	16	1	*.996
1996— Phoenix (PCL)	OF-DH	121	435	60	124	26	4	7	75	.285	62	77	5	249	11	3	.989
— San Francisco (N.L.) ..	OF	33	77	10	18	3	0	3	10	.234	12	24	0	41	1	1	.977
1997— Phoenix (PCL)	OF-DH	127	493	97	178	*45	3	12	95	*.361	64	64	18	239	*16	8	.970
— San Francisco (N.L.) ..	OF	16	25	3	4	1	0	0	3	.160	3	4	0	12	2	1	.933

Year	Team (League)	Pos.	G	AB	R	H	2B	3B	HR	RBI	Avg.	BB	SO	SB	PO	A	E	Avg.
1998—Fresno (PCL)		OF-DH	89	342	60	102	17	3	18	62	.298	46	57	12	152	5	6	.963
—San Francisco (N.L.)		PH	3	3	0	0	0	0	0	0	.000	0	2	0	0	0	0	...
—Buffalo (I.L.)■		OF	43	169	32	56	8	2	13	36	.331	13	26	2	70	5	4	.949
—Cleveland (A.L.)		PH	1	1	0	0	0	0	0	0	.000	0	1	0	0	0	0	...
1999—Buffalo (I.L.)		OF-DH	54	202	29	55	7	2	7	31	.272	21	39	4	77	5	4	.953
—Cleveland (A.L.)		OF-DH	32	88	14	29	5	1	3	17	.330	5	13	0	48	0	0	1.000
American League totals (2 years)			33	89	14	29	5	1	3	17	.326	5	14	0	48	0	0	1.000
National League totals (3 years)			52	105	13	22	4	0	3	13	.210	15	30	0	53	3	2	.966
Major League totals (4 years)			85	194	27	51	9	1	6	30	.263	20	44	0	101	3	2	.981

CRUZ, JOSE — OF — BLUE JAYS

PERSONAL: Born April 19, 1974, in Arroyo, Puerto Rico. ... 6-0/200. ... Bats both, throws right. ... Full name: Jose Cruz Jr. ... Son of Jose Cruz Sr., outfielder with three major league teams (1970-88); nephew of Hector Cruz, outfielder/third baseman with four major league teams (1973, 1975-82); and nephew of Tommy Cruz, outfielder with St. Louis Cardinals (1973), Chicago White Sox (1977) and Nippon Ham Fighters of Japan League (1980-85).

HIGH SCHOOL: Bellaire (Houston).

COLLEGE: Rice.

TRANSACTIONS/CAREER NOTES: Selected by Atlanta Braves organization in 15th round of free-agent draft (June 1, 1992); did not sign. ... Selected by Seattle Mariners organization in first round (third pick overall) of free-agent draft (June 1, 1995). ... Traded by Mariners to Toronto Blue Jays for P Mike Timlin and P Paul Spoljaric (July 31, 1997). ... On Toronto disabled list (June 24-July 9, 1999); included rehabilitation assignment to Syracuse (July 5-9).

STATISTICAL NOTES: Switch-hit home runs in one game (August 24, 1997). ... Had 18-game hitting streak (August 5-24, 1998).

C

Year	Team (League)	Pos.	G	AB	R	H	2B	3B	HR	RBI	Avg.	BB	SO	SB	PO	A	E	Avg.
1995—Everett (N.W.)		OF	3	11	6	5	0	0	0	2	.455	3	3	1	7	0	0	1.000
—Riverside (Calif.)		OF	35	144	34	37	7	1	7	29	.257	24	50	3	70	4	3	.961
1996—Lancaster (Calif.)		OF-DH	53	203	38	66	17	1	6	43	.325	39	33	7	62	7	1	.986
—Port City (Sou.)		OF-DH	47	181	39	51	10	2	3	31	.282	27	38	5	90	6	1	.990
—Tacoma (PCL)		OF	22	76	15	18	1	2	6	15	.237	18	12	1	36	4	0	1.000
1997—Tacoma (PCL)		OF-DH	50	190	33	51	16	2	6	30	.268	34	44	3	70	3	0	1.000
—Seattle (A.L.)		OF	49	183	28	49	12	1	12	34	.268	13	45	1	83	1	3	.966
—Toronto (A.L.)■		OF	55	212	31	49	7	0	14	34	.231	28	72	6	98	3	2	.981
1998—Toronto (A.L.)		OF	105	352	55	89	14	3	11	42	.253	57	99	11	247	7	4	.984
—Syracuse (I.L.)		OF	40	141	29	42	14	1	7	23	.298	32	32	8	99	7	1	.991
1999—Toronto (A.L.)		OF	106	349	63	84	19	3	14	45	.241	64	91	14	277	8	3	.990
—Syracuse (I.L.)		OF-DH	31	103	17	19	3	1	3	14	.184	28	20	5	75	2	0	1.000
Major League totals (3 years)			315	1096	177	271	52	7	51	155	.247	162	307	32	705	19	12	.984

CRUZ, NELSON — P — TIGERS

PERSONAL: Born September 13, 1972, in Puerta Plata, Dominican Republic. ... 6-1/185. ... Throws right, bats right. ... Cousin of Jose Roman, pitcher with Cleveland Indians (1984-86).

HIGH SCHOOL: Liceo Jose Castellanos (Puerto Plata, Dominican Republic).

TRANSACTIONS/CAREER NOTES: Signed as non-drafted free agent by Montreal Expos organization (July 5, 1989). ... Released by Expos organization (March 27, 1992). ... Signed by Chicago White Sox organization (December 10, 1994). ... Granted free agency (October 15, 1998). ... Signed by Detroit Tigers (November 19, 1998).

Year	League	W	L	Pct.	ERA	G	GS	CG	ShO	Sv.	IP	H	R	ER	BB	SO
1990—Dom. Expos (DSL)		9	2	.818	2.62	16	16	0	0	0	103	105	49	30	42	83
1991—Gulf Coast Expos (GCL)		2	4	.333	2.40	12	8	1	•1	0	48 2/3	40	18	13	19	34
1992—								Out of organized baseball.								
1993—								Out of organized baseball.								
1994—								Out of organized baseball.								
1995—Bristol (Appl.)■		0	0	...	9.00	1	0	0	0	0	1	2	1	1	0	0
—Hickory (SAL)		2	7	.222	2.70	44	0	0	0	9	66 2/3	65	31	20	15	68
—Prince William (Caro.)		2	1	.667	0.47	9	0	0	0	1	19 1/3	12	1	1	6	15
1996—Birmingham (Sou.)		6	6	.500	3.20	37	18	2	1	1	149	150	65	53	41	142
1997—Nashville (A.A.)		11	7	.611	5.11	21	20	1	0	0	123 1/3	139	75	70	31	93
—Chicago (A.L.)		0	2	.000	6.49	19	0	0	0	0	26 1/3	29	19	19	9	23
1998—Calgary (PCL)■		10	6	.625	5.33	35	18	2	1	0	126 2/3	159	85	75	40	101
1999—Toledo (I.L.)■		7	1	.875	2.73	10	10	4	•2	0	62 2/3	47	20	19	21	41
—Detroit (A.L.)		2	5	.286	5.67	29	6	0	0	0	66 2/3	74	44	42	23	46
Major League totals (2 years)		2	7	.222	5.90	48	6	0	0	0	93	103	63	61	32	69

CUMMINGS, MIDRE — OF — TWINS

PERSONAL: Born October 14, 1971, in St. Croix, Virgin Islands. ... 6-0/195. ... Bats left, throws right. ... Full name: Midre Almeric Cummings.

HIGH SCHOOL: Miami Edison Senior.

TRANSACTIONS/CAREER NOTES: Selected by Minnesota Twins organization in supplemental round ("sandwich pick" between first and second round, 29th pick overall) of free-agent draft (June 4, 1990); pick received as part of compensation for Boston Red Sox signing Type A free-agent P Jeff Reardon. ... Traded by Twins organization with P Denny Neagle to Pittsburgh Pirates organization for P John Smiley (March 17, 1992). ... On Buffalo disabled list (April 21-June 6, 1994). ... On Calgary disabled list (June 17-July 1, 1995). ... Claimed on waivers by Philadelphia (July 8, 1997). ... Released by Phillies (February 24, 1998). ... Signed by Cincinnati Reds organization (February 27, 1998). ... Claimed on waivers by Boston Red Sox (March 19, 1998). ... On disabled list (July 29-September 7, 1998). ... Released by Red Sox (March 30, 1999). ... Signed by Twins organization (May 14, 1999).

MISCELLANEOUS: Batted as switch-hitter (1990-92).

Year	Team (League)	Pos.	G	AB	R	H	2B	3B	HR	RBI	Avg.	BB	SO	SB	PO	A	E	Avg.
1990—GC Twins (GCL).........		OF	47	177	28	56	3	4	5	28	.316	13	32	14	73	2	6	.926
1991—Kenosha (Midw.)........		OF	106	382	59	123	20	4	4	54	*.322	22	66	28	166	6	•13	.930
1992—Salem (Caro.)■.........		OF	113	420	55	128	20	5	14	75	.305	35	67	23	151	10	6	.964
1993—Carolina (Sou.)..........		OF	63	237	33	70	17	2	6	26	.295	14	23	5	99	7	4	.964
—Buffalo (A.A.).............		OF	60	232	36	64	12	1	9	21	.276	22	45	5	90	1	2	.978
—Pittsburgh (N.L.).......		OF	13	36	5	4	1	0	0	3	.111	4	9	0	21	0	0	1.000
1994—Buffalo (A.A.).............		OF	49	183	23	57	12	4	2	22	.311	13	26	5	117	2	0	1.000
—Pittsburgh (N.L.).......		OF	24	86	11	21	4	0	1	12	.244	4	18	0	49	1	2	.962
1995—Pittsburgh (N.L.).......		OF	59	152	13	37	7	1	2	15	.243	13	30	1	79	2	1	.988
—Calgary (PCL)............		OF	45	159	19	44	9	1	1	16	.277	6	27	1	96	4	6	.943
1996—Calgary (PCL)............	OF-DH	97	368	60	112	24	3	8	55	.304	21	60	6	176	9	5	.974
—Pittsburgh (N.L.).......		OF	24	85	11	19	3	1	3	7	.224	0	16	0	49	0	1	.980
1997—Pittsburgh (N.L.).......		OF	52	106	11	20	6	2	3	8	.189	8	26	0	37	1	0	1.000
—Philadelphia (N.L.)■ ..		OF	63	208	24	63	16	4	1	23	.303	23	30	2	113	1	1	.991
1998—Boston (A.L.)■............	DH-OF	67	120	20	34	8	0	5	15	.283	17	19	3	16	0	1	.941
1999—New Britain (East.)■ ..		OF	24	93	28	35	7	0	2	15	.376	17	14	3	50	2	0	1.000
—Salt Lake (PCL)	OF-DH	69	261	50	84	19	4	13	68	.322	23	43	4	101	3	5	.954
—Minnesota (A.L.)	OF-DH	16	38	1	10	0	0	1	9	.263	3	7	2	5	0	0	1.000
American League totals (2 years)			83	158	21	44	8	0	6	24	.278	20	26	5	21	0	1	.955
National League totals (5 years)			235	673	75	164	37	8	10	68	.244	52	129	3	348	5	5	.986
Major League totals (7 years)			318	831	96	208	45	8	16	92	.250	72	155	8	369	5	6	.984

DIVISION SERIES RECORD

RECORDS: Shares A.L. career record for most games by pinch hitter—3.

Year	Team (League)	Pos.	G	AB	R	H	2B	3B	HR	RBI	Avg.	BB	SO	SB	PO	A	E	Avg.
1998—Boston (A.L.)...............	PH	3	3	0	0	0	0	0	0	.000	0	0	0	...	...	...	...

CUNNANE, WILL   P   PADRES

PERSONAL: Born April 24, 1974, in Suffern, N.Y. ... 6-2/175. ... Throws right, bats right. ... Full name: William Joseph Cunnane.

HIGH SCHOOL: Clarkstown North (New City, N.Y.).

TRANSACTIONS/CAREER NOTES: Signed as non-drafted free agent by Florida Marlins organization (August 18, 1992). ... On Portland disabled list (August 7-23, 1996). ... Selected by San Diego Padres organization from Marlins organization in Rule 5 major league draft (December 9, 1996). ... On San Diego disabled list (March 29-June 21, 1998); included rehabilitation assignment to Las Vegas (June 9-21).

MISCELLANEOUS: Appeared in one game as pinch runner (1997).

Year	League	W	L	Pct.	ERA	G	GS	CG	ShO	Sv.	IP	H	R	ER	BB	SO
1993—GC Marlins (GCL)	3	3	.500	2.70	16	9	0	0	0	66 2/3	75	32	20	8	64
1994—Kane County (Midw.)......	11	3	.786	*1.43	32	16	5	*4	1	138 2/3	110	27	22	23	106
1995—Portland (East.)	9	2	*.818	3.67	21	21	1	1	0	117 2/3	120	48	48	34	83
1996—Portland (East.)	10	12	.455	3.74	25	25	4	0	0	151 2/3	156	73	63	30	101
1997—San Diego (N.L.)■	6	3	.667	5.81	54	8	0	0	0	91 1/3	114	69	59	49	79
1998—Las Vegas (PCL)	1	2	.333	5.25	33	0	0	0	4	36	45	26	21	19	30
—San Diego (N.L.)	0	0	...	6.00	3	0	0	0	0	3	4	2	2	1	1
1999—Las Vegas (PCL)	2	1	.667	0.98	28	0	0	0	11	36 2/3	30	5	4	16	54
—San Diego (N.L.)	2	1	.667	5.23	24	0	0	0	0	31	34	19	18	12	22
Major League totals (3 years)	8	4	.667	5.67	81	8	0	0	0	125 1/3	152	90	79	62	102

CURTIS, CHAD   OF   RANGERS

PERSONAL: Born November 6, 1968, in Marion, Ind. ... 5-10/185. ... Bats right, throws right. ... Full name: Chad David Curtis.

HIGH SCHOOL: Benson (Ariz.) Union.

JUNIOR COLLEGE: Yavapai College (Ariz.), then Cochise County Community College (Ariz.).

COLLEGE: Grand Canyon (Ariz.).

TRANSACTIONS/CAREER NOTES: Selected by California Angels organization in 45th round of free-agent draft (June 5, 1989). ... On disabled list (June 5-20, 1991). ... On suspended list (June 8-12, 1993). ... Traded by Angels to Detroit Tigers for OF/3B Tony Phillips (April 12, 1995). ... Traded by Tigers to Los Angeles Dodgers for P Joey Eischen and P John Cummings (July 31, 1996). ... Granted free agency (October 15, 1996). ... Signed by Cleveland Indians (December 18, 1996). ... On Cleveland disabled list (May 14-June 9, 1997). ... Traded by Indians to New York Yankees for P David Weathers (June 9, 1997); on disabled list when acquired by Yankees and activated on June 11. ... Traded by Yankees to Texas Rangers for P Brandon Knight and P Sam Marsonek (December 13, 1999).

STATISTICAL NOTES: Led Midwest League with 223 total bases in 1990. ... Tied for A.L. lead in caught stealing with 24 in 1993. ... Led A.L. outfielders with 448 total chances and tied for lead with nine errors in 1993. ... Led A.L. outfielders with 345 total chances in 1994. ... Career major league grand slams: 1.

Year	Team (League)	Pos.	G	AB	R	H	2B	3B	HR	RBI	Avg.	BB	SO	SB	PO	A	E	Avg.
1989—Arizona Angels (Ariz.).	2B-OF	32	122	30	37	4	4	3	20	.303	14	20	17	62	58	6	.952
—Quad City (Midw.)	OF	23	78	7	19	3	0	2	11	.244	6	17	7	34	1	1	.972
1990—Quad City (Midw.)	2B-OF	135	*492	87	*151	28	1	14	65	.307	57	76	64	216	221	26	.944
1991—Edmonton (PCL)	3B-2B-OF	115	431	81	136	28	7	9	61	.316	51	56	46	124	220	25	.932
1992—California (A.L.)	OF-DH	139	441	59	114	16	2	10	46	.259	51	71	43	250	*16	6	.978
1993—California (A.L.)	OF-2B	152	583	94	166	25	3	6	59	.285	70	89	48	426	13	‡9	.980
1994—California (A.L.)	OF	114	453	67	116	23	4	11	50	.256	37	69	25	*332	9	4	.988
1995—Detroit (A.L.)■	OF	144	586	96	157	29	3	21	67	.268	70	93	27	362	5	3	.992
1996—Detroit (A.L.)	OF	104	400	65	105	20	1	10	37	.263	53	73	16	243	6	9	.965
—Los Angeles (N.L.)■ ..	OF	43	104	20	22	5	0	2	9	.212	17	15	2	62	2	1	.985

Year Team (League)	Pos.	G	AB	R	H	2B	3B	HR	RBI	Avg.	BB	SO	SB	PO	A	E	Avg.
1997— Cleveland (A.L.)■......	OF	22	29	8	6	1	0	3	5	.207	7	10	0	20	0	0	1.000
— Akron (East.)	OF	4	18	5	7	1	0	3	6	.389	0	3	0	5	2	0	1.000
— New York (A.L.)■......	OF	93	320	51	93	21	1	12	50	.291	36	49	12	168	6	4	.978
1998— New York (A.L.).........	OF-DH	151	456	79	111	21	1	10	56	.243	75	80	21	306	8	5	.984
1999— New York (A.L.).........	OF-DH	96	195	37	51	6	0	5	24	.262	43	35	8	98	2	1	.990
American League totals (8 years)		1015	3463	556	919	162	15	88	394	.265	442	569	200	2205	65	41	.982
National League totals (1 year)		43	104	20	22	5	0	2	9	.212	17	15	2	62	2	1	.985
Major League totals (8 years)		1058	3567	576	941	167	15	90	403	.264	459	584	202	2267	67	42	.982

DIVISION SERIES RECORD

Year Team (League)	Pos.	G	AB	R	H	2B	3B	HR	RBI	Avg.	BB	SO	SB	PO	A	E	Avg.
1996— Los Angeles (N.L.)	OF	1	2	0	0	0	0	0	0	.000	1	1	0	2	0	0	1.000
1997— New York (A.L.).........	OF-PR	4	6	0	1	0	0	0	0	.167	3	1	0	4	0	0	1.000
1998— New York (A.L.).........	OF	3	3	1	2	1	0	0	0	.667	1	1	1	3	0	0	1.000
1999— New York (A.L.).........	OF-PR	3	3	1	0	0	0	0	0	.000	0	0	0	0	0	0	...
Division series totals (4 years)		11	14	2	3	1	0	0	0	.214	5	3	1	9	0	0	1.000

CHAMPIONSHIP SERIES RECORD

Year Team (League)	Pos.	G	AB	R	H	2B	3B	HR	RBI	Avg.	BB	SO	SB	PO	A	E	Avg.
1998— New York (A.L.).........	OF	2	4	0	0	0	0	0	0	.000	1	2	0	1	0	0	1.000
1999— New York (A.L.).........	OF-PR-DH	3	6	1	0	0	0	0	0	.000	0	2	1	0	0	0	...
Championship series totals (2 years)		5	10	1	0	0	0	0	0	.000	1	4	1	1	0	0	1.000

WORLD SERIES RECORD

NOTES: Member of World Series championship team (1998 and 1999).

Year Team (League)	Pos.	G	AB	R	H	2B	3B	HR	RBI	Avg.	BB	SO	SB	PO	A	E	Avg.
1998— New York (A.L.)								Did not play.									
1999— New York (A.L.)..........	PR-OF-PH	3	6	3	2	0	0	2	2	.333	0	0	0	5	0	0	1.000

DAAL, OMAR P DIAMONDBACKS

C
D

PERSONAL: Born March 1, 1972, in Maracaibo, Venezuela. ... 6-3/185. ... Throws left, bats left. ... Full name: Omar Jose Cordaro Daal.
HIGH SCHOOL: Valencia (Venezuela) Superior.
TRANSACTIONS/CAREER NOTES: Signed as non-drafted free agent by Los Angeles Dodgers organization (August 24, 1990). ... Traded by Dodgers to Montreal Expos for P Rick Clelland (December 14, 1995). ... Claimed on waivers by Toronto Blue Jays (July 25, 1997). ... Selected by Arizona Diamondbacks in second round (31st pick overall) of expansion draft (November 18, 1997). ... On Arizona disabled list (June 22-July 11, 1998); included rehabilitation assignment to Tucson (July 9-11).
MISCELLANEOUS: Shares Arizona Diamondbacks all-time record for most shutouts (2).

Year League	W	L	Pct.	ERA	G	GS	CG	ShO	Sv.	IP	H	R	ER	BB	SO
1990— Dom. Dodgers (DSL)	3	6	.333	1.18	17	13	6	0	2	91²/₃	61	29	12	29	91
1991— Dom. Dodgers (DSL)	7	2	.778	1.16	13	13	0	0	0	93	30	17	12	32	81
1992— Albuquerque (PCL)...........	0	2	.000	7.84	12	0	0	0	0	10¹/₃	14	9	9	11	9
— San Antonio (Texas)..........	2	6	.250	5.02	35	5	0	0	5	57¹/₃	60	39	32	33	52
1993— Albuquerque (PCL)............	1	1	.500	3.38	6	0	0	0	2	5¹/₃	5	2	2	3	2
— Los Angeles (N.L.)	2	3	.400	5.09	47	0	0	0	0	35¹/₃	36	20	20	21	19
1994— Albuquerque (PCL)............	4	2	.667	5.19	11	5	0	0	1	34²/₃	38	20	20	16	28
— Los Angeles (N.L.)	0	0	...	3.29	24	0	0	0	0	13²/₃	12	5	5	5	9
1995— Albuquerque (PCL)............	2	3	.400	4.05	17	9	0	0	1	53¹/₃	56	28	24	26	46
— Los Angeles (N.L.)	4	0	1.000	7.20	28	0	0	0	0	20	29	16	16	15	11
1996— Montreal (N.L.)■................	4	5	.444	4.02	64	6	0	0	0	87¹/₃	74	40	39	37	82
1997— Montreal (N.L.)..................	1	2	.333	9.79	33	0	0	0	1	30¹/₃	48	35	33	15	16
— Ottawa (I.L.)......................	0	1	.000	5.63	2	2	0	0	0	8	10	6	5	1	9
— Toronto (A.L.)■..................	1	1	.500	4.00	9	3	0	0	0	27	34	13	12	6	28
1998— Arizona (N.L.)■................	8	12	.400	2.88	33	23	3	1	0	162²/₃	146	60	52	51	132
— Tucson (PCL)	0	0	...	3.00	1	1	0	0	0	3	3	2	1	1	4
1999— Arizona (N.L.)....................	16	9	.640	3.65	32	32	2	1	0	214²/₃	188	92	87	79	148
A.L. totals (1 year)	1	1	.500	4.00	9	3	0	0	0	27	34	13	12	6	28
N.L. totals (7 years)	35	31	.530	4.02	261	61	5	2	1	564	533	268	252	223	417
Major League totals (7 years).......	36	32	.529	4.02	270	64	5	2	1	591	567	281	264	229	445

DIVISION SERIES RECORD

Year League	W	L	Pct.	ERA	G	GS	CG	ShO	Sv.	IP	H	R	ER	BB	SO
1999— Arizona (N.L.).....................	0	1	.000	6.75	1	1	0	0	0	4	6	3	3	3	4

DALE, CARL P

PERSONAL: Born December 7, 1972, in Indianapolis. ... 6-2/215. ... Throws right, bats right. ... Full name: James Carl Dale.
HIGH SCHOOL: Cookeville (Tenn.).
COLLEGE: Winthrop (S.C.).
TRANSACTIONS/CAREER NOTES: Selected by St. Louis Cardinals organization in second round of free-agent draft (June 2, 1994). ... Traded by Cardinals with OF Allen Battle, P Bret Wagner and P Jay Witasick to Oakland Athletics for P Todd Stottlemyre (January 6, 1996). ... On temporarily inactive list (June 12-19, 1996). ... On Huntsville disabled list (April 29-June 24, 1998). ... On Vancouver disabled list (April 29-June 17, 1999). ... Traded by Athletics to Milwaukee Brewers (August 20, 1999), completing deal in which Brewers traded OF Rich Becker to Athletics for a player to be named later (August 17, 1999). ... Granted free agency (December 21, 1999).

Year League	W	L	Pct.	ERA	G	GS	CG	ShO	Sv.	IP	H	R	ER	BB	SO
1994— New Jersey (NY-P)	2	7	.222	4.56	15	•15	0	0	0	73	79	44	37	38	75
1995— Peoria (Midw.)	9	9	.500	2.94	24	24	2	1	0	143 2/3	124	66	47	62	104
1996— Modesto (Calif.)■	8	2	.800	4.28	26	24	0	0	0	128 1/3	124	79	61	72	102
1997— Huntsville (Sou.)	6	4	.600	5.38	20	16	0	0	0	85 1/3	95	61	51	43	57
1998— Huntsville (Sou.)	1	1	.500	4.61	3	3	0	0	0	13 2/3	13	7	7	8	10
— Modesto (Calif.)	1	2	.333	2.37	3	3	0	0	0	19	15	6	5	2	14
— Edmonton (PCL)	5	3	.625	4.08	11	11	1	1	0	64	64	31	29	26	41
1999— Vancouver (PCL)	4	3	.571	3.48	29	0	0	0	4	44	41	19	17	18	27
— Louisville (I.L.)■	0	1	.000	4.63	7	0	0	0	1	11 2/3	8	6	6	5	8
— Milwaukee (N.L.)	0	1	.000	20.25	4	0	0	0	0	4	8	9	9	6	4
Major League totals (1 year)	0	1	.000	20.25	4	0	0	0	0	4	8	9	9	6	4

DALESANDRO, MARK   C/3B

PERSONAL: Born May 14, 1968, in Chicago. ... 6-0/195. ... Bats right, throws right. ... Full name: Mark Anthony Dalesandro. ... Name pronounced DEE-uh-SAN-droh.
HIGH SCHOOL: St. Ignatius College Prep School (Chicago).
COLLEGE: Illinois.
TRANSACTIONS/CAREER NOTES: Selected by California Angels organization in 18th round of free-agent draft (June 4, 1990). ... Released by Angels (February 6, 1996). ... Signed by New York Yankees organization (February 12, 1996). ... Released by Yankees (April 4, 1996). ... Re-signed by Yankees organization (May 3, 1996). ... Granted free agency (October 15, 1996). ... Signed by Chicago Cubs organization (December 23, 1996). ... On Iowa disabled list (April 27-May 4, 1997). ... Granted free agency (October 17, 1997). ... Signed by Toronto Blue Jays organization (December 2, 1997). ... On Syracuse disabled list (July 22, 1999-remainder of season). ... Granted free agency (October 5, 1999).
STATISTICAL NOTES: Tied for California League lead in grounding into double plays with 20 in 1992.

								BATTING						FIELDING		
Year Team (League)	Pos.	G	AB	R	H	2B	3B	HR	RBI	Avg.	BB	SO	SB	PO	A	E	Avg.
1990— Boise (N'west)	OF-3B-1B	55	224	35	75	10	2	6	44	.335	18	42	6	37	23	6	.909
1991— Quad City (Midw.)	3B-1B	125	487	63	133	17	8	5	69	.273	34	58	1	198	186	25	.939
1992— Palm Springs (Calif.)	1B-3B	126	492	72	146	30	3	7	92	.297	33	50	6	594	114	15	.979
1993— Palm Springs (Calif.)	C-1B-DH	46	176	22	43	5	3	1	25	.244	15	20	3	271	42	7	.978
— Midland (Texas)	3-C-DH-1	57	235	33	69	9	0	2	36	.294	8	30	1	137	60	12	.943
— Vancouver (PCL)	3B	26	107	16	32	8	1	2	15	.299	6	13	1	19	59	7	.918
1994— Vancouver (PCL)	3-C-1-DH-O	51	199	29	63	9	1	1	31	.317	7	19	1	153	71	11	.953
— California (A.L.)	C-3B-OF	19	25	5	5	1	0	1	2	.200	2	4	0	19	5	1	.960
1995— California (A.L.)	C-DH-OF	11	10	1	1	1	0	0	0	.100	0	2	0	11	0	0	1.000
— Vancouver (PCL)	O-3-DH-C-1	34	123	16	41	13	1	1	18	.333	6	12	2	56	8	2	.970
1996— Columbus (I.L.)■	DH-3-C-O-2	78	255	34	72	29	4	2	38	.282	17	31	2	128	75	10	.953
1997— Iowa (A.A.)■	C-3-1-DH-O	115	405	48	106	14	0	8	48	.262	33	51	0	467	90	4	.993
1998— Toronto (A.L.)■	C-3B-1B-OF	32	67	8	20	5	0	2	14	.299	1	6	0	76	9	2	.977
— Syracuse (I.L.)	DH-3B-C-OF	45	164	25	44	9	1	10	30	.268	12	20	1	60	16	3	.962
1999— Toronto (A.L.)	C-DH-3B	16	27	3	5	0	0	0	1	.185	0	2	1	22	3	0	1.000
— Syracuse (I.L.)	OF-C-3B-DH	20	71	3	16	2	0	0	5	.225	1	7	1	32	5	0	1.000
Major League totals (4 years)		78	129	17	31	7	0	3	17	.240	3	14	1	128	17	3	.980

D'AMICO, JEFF   P   BREWERS

PERSONAL: Born December 27, 1975, in St. Petersburg, Fla. ... 6-7/250. ... Throws right, bats right. ... Full name: Jeffrey Charles D'Amico.
HIGH SCHOOL: Northeast (St. Petersburg, Fla.).
TRANSACTIONS/CAREER NOTES: Selected by Milwaukee Brewers organization in first round (23rd pick overall) of free-agent draft (June 3, 1993). ... On disabled list (June 24, 1994-entire season). ... On Milwaukee disabled list (July 28-September 2, 1997; and January 14, 1998-entire season). ... On Milwaukee disabled list (March 29-September 25, 1999); included rehabilitation assignments to Beloit (July 6-15), Huntsville (July 16-21) and Louisville (August 12-25).

Year League	W	L	Pct.	ERA	G	GS	CG	ShO	Sv.	IP	H	R	ER	BB	SO
1994— Arizona Brewers (Ariz.)							Did not play.								
1995— Beloit (Midw.)	13	3	*.813	2.39	21	20	3	1	0	132	102	40	35	31	119
1996— El Paso (Texas)	5	4	.556	3.19	13	13	3	0	0	96	89	42	34	13	76
— Milwaukee (A.L.)	6	6	.500	5.44	17	17	0	0	0	86	88	53	52	31	53
1997— Milwaukee (A.L.)	9	7	.563	4.71	23	23	1	1	0	135 2/3	139	81	71	43	94
— Beloit (Midw.)	0	0	...	0.00	1	1	0	0	0	3	0	0	0	1	7
1998— Milwaukee (A.L.)							Did not play.								
1999— Beloit (Midw.)	1	0	1.000	0.00	2	2	0	0	0	8	7	0	0	1	6
— Huntsville (Sou.)	0	0	...	36.00	1	1	0	0	0	2	6	8	8	1	2
— Louisville (I.L.)	0	0	...	13.50	1	1	0	0	0	3 1/3	6	5	5	2	1
— Milwaukee (N.L.)	0	0	...	0.00	1	0	0	0	0	1	1	0	0	0	1
A.L. totals (2 years)	15	13	.536	4.99	40	40	1	1	0	221 2/3	227	134	123	74	147
N.L. totals (1 year)	0	0	...	0.00	1	0	0	0	0	1	1	0	0	0	1
Major League totals (3 years)	15	13	.536	4.97	41	40	1	1	0	222 2/3	228	134	123	74	148

D'AMICO, JEFF   P   ROYALS

PERSONAL: Born November 9, 1974, in Inglewood, Calif. ... 6-3/200. ... Throws right, bats right. ... Full name: Jeffrey Michael D'Amico.
HIGH SCHOOL: Redmond (Wash.).
TRANSACTIONS/CAREER NOTES: Selected by Oakland Athletics organization in second round of free-agent draft (June 3, 1993). ... On West Michigan disabled list (April 22-September 19, 1994). ... On Huntsville disabled list (June 25-July 10, 1998); included rehabilitation assignment to Arizona Athletics (June 27-July 7). ... Traded by Athletics with P Blake Stein and P Brad Rigby to Kansas City Royals for P Kevin Appier (July 31, 1999).
STATISTICAL NOTES: Led Southern League with five balks in 1998.
MISCELLANEOUS: Played infield (1993-96).

Year	League	W	L	Pct.	ERA	G	GS	CG	ShO	Sv.	IP	H	R	ER	BB	SO
1996—Modesto (Calif.)		0	0	...	18.00	1	0	0	0	0	1	3	3	2	1	0
—Arizona Athletics (Ariz.)		3	0	1.000	1.42	8	0	0	0	0	19	14	3	3	2	15
1997—Modesto (Calif.)		7	3	.700	3.80	20	13	0	0	1	97	115	57	41	34	89
—Edmonton (PCL)		1	2	.333	8.22	10	7	0	0	1	30 2/3	42	29	28	6	19
1998—Huntsville (Sou.)		5	5	.500	7.67	24	8	0	0	0	61	77	57	52	34	46
—Arizona Athletics (Ariz.)		0	0	...	3.86	4	1	0	0	0	9 1/3	6	4	4	1	8
1999—Midland (Texas)		1	2	.333	4.96	32	0	0	0	3	45 1/3	53	31	25	16	38
—Vancouver (PCL)		2	2	.500	2.65	14	0	0	0	3	17	16	6	5	10	10
—Omaha (PCL)■		1	3	.250	4.34	12	0	0	0	2	18 2/3	29	13	9	3	12

RECORD AS POSITION PLAYER

Year	Team (League)	Pos.	G	AB	R	H	2B	3B	HR	RBI	Avg.	BB	SO	SB	PO	A	E	Avg.
1993—S. Oregon (N'west)		SS-3B	33	114	12	30	9	0	3	15	.263	9	25	2	43	67	14	.887
1994—W. Mich. (Mid.)		SS	9	36	5	10	3	0	0	3	.278	4	7	2	14	25	1	.975
1995—W. Mich. (Mid.)		SS-3B	125	434	56	98	24	1	7	55	.226	56	94	8	120	304	37	.920
1996—Modesto (California)		3-2-S	47	172	28	46	7	1	4	21	.267	19	31	3	36	101	19	.878

DAMON, JOHNNY — OF — ROYALS

PERSONAL: Born November 5, 1973, in Fort Riley, Kan. ... 6-2/190. ... Bats left, throws left. ... Full name: Johnny David Damon.
HIGH SCHOOL: Dr. Phillips (Orlando).
TRANSACTIONS/CAREER NOTES: Selected by Kansas City Royals organization in supplemental round ("sandwich pick" between first and second round, 35th pick overall) of free-agent draft (June 1, 1992); pick received as part of compensation for San Diego Padres signing Type A free-agent IF Kurt Stillwell. ... On suspended list (September 5-7, 1997).
HONORS: Named Texas League Player of the Year (1995).
STATISTICAL NOTES: Led Gulf Coast League with 109 total bases in 1992. ... Led Midwest League outfielders with five double plays in 1993. ... Led Texas League with .434 on-base percentage in 1995. ... Led Texas League with .534 slugging percentage in 1995. ... Led Texas League with 13 intentional bases on balls received in 1995. ... Had 16-game hitting streak (April 27-May 12, 1999). ... Career major league grand slams: 2.

Year	Team (League)	Pos.	G	AB	R	H	2B	3B	HR	RBI	Avg.	BB	SO	SB	PO	A	E	Avg.
1992—GC Royals (GCL)		OF	50	192	*58	67	12	*9	4	24	*.349	31	21	33	77	7	1	.988
—Baseball City (FSL)		OF	1	1	0	0	0	0	0	0	.000	0	0	0	0	0	0	...
1993—Rockford (Midw.)		OF	127	511	82	148	25	*13	5	50	.290	52	83	59	240	14	6	.977
1994—Wilmington (Caro.)		OF	119	472	96	149	25	13	6	75	.316	62	55	44	273	9	3	.989
1995—Wichita (Texas)		OF-DH	111	423	83	145	15	9	16	54	.343	67	35	26	296	11	5	.984
—Kansas City (A.L.)		OF	47	188	32	53	11	5	3	23	.282	12	22	7	110	0	1	.991
1996—Kansas City (A.L.)		OF-DH	145	517	61	140	22	5	6	50	.271	31	64	25	350	5	6	.983
1997—Kansas City (A.L.)		OF-DH	146	472	70	130	12	8	8	48	.275	42	70	16	322	5	4	.988
1998—Kansas City (A.L.)		OF	161	642	104	178	30	10	18	66	.277	58	84	26	372	10	4	.990
1999—Kansas City (A.L.)		OF-DH	145	583	101	179	39	9	14	77	.307	67	50	36	301	8	4	.987
Major League totals (5 years)			644	2402	368	680	114	37	49	264	.283	210	290	110	1455	28	19	.987

DANEKER, PAT — P — WHITE SOX

PERSONAL: Born January 14, 1976, in Williamsport, Pa. ... 6-3/195. ... Throws right, bats right. ... Full name: Patrick R. Daneker.
HIGH SCHOOL: Loyalsock Township (Williamsport, Pa.).
COLLEGE: Virginia.
TRANSACTIONS/CAREER NOTES: Selected by Chicago White Sox organization in fifth round of free agent draft (June 3, 1997).

Year	League	W	L	Pct.	ERA	G	GS	CG	ShO	Sv.	IP	H	R	ER	BB	SO
1997—Bristol (Appl.)		3	6	.333	6.50	12	12	0	0	0	63 2/3	83	55	46	20	53
1998—Hickory (SAL)		6	6	.500	3.15	17	17	2	0	0	117	115	50	41	16	95
—Winston-Salem (Caro.)		5	0	1.000	2.04	7	7	2	0	0	53	51	13	12	5	43
1999—Charlotte (I.L.)		4	4	.500	6.57	9	9	1	0	0	49 1/3	64	36	36	16	36
—Chicago (A.L.)		0	0	...	4.20	3	2	0	0	0	15	14	8	7	6	5
—Birmingham (Sou.)		6	8	.429	3.22	16	16	3	0	0	109	106	46	39	30	71
Major League totals (1 year)		0	0	...	4.20	3	2	0	0	0	15	14	8	7	6	5

DARENSBOURG, VIC — P — MARLINS

PERSONAL: Born November 13, 1970, in Los Angeles. ... 5-10/165. ... Throws left, bats left. ... Full name: Victor Anthony Darensbourg.
HIGH SCHOOL: Westchester (Los Angeles).
COLLEGE: Lewis and Clark College (Ore.).
TRANSACTIONS/CAREER NOTES: Signed as non-drafted free agent by Florida Marlins organization (June 11, 1992). ... On disabled list entire 1995 season. ... On Portland disabled list (April 4-15, 1996). ... On Charlotte disabled list (April 25-June 21 and July 29-September 6, 1997).

Year	League	W	L	Pct.	ERA	G	GS	CG	ShO	Sv.	IP	H	R	ER	BB	SO
1992—Gulf Coast Marlins (GCL)		2	1	.667	0.64	8	4	0	0	2	42	28	5	3	11	37
1993—Kane County (Midw.)		9	1	.900	2.14	46	0	0	0	16	71 1/3	58	17	17	28	89
—High Desert (Calif.)		0	0	...	0.00	1	0	0	0	0	1	0	0	0	0	1
1994—Portland (East.)		10	7	.588	3.81	35	21	1	1	4	149	146	76	63	60	103
1995—					Did not play.											
1996—Brevard County (FSL)		0	0	...	0.00	2	0	0	0	0	3	1	0	0	1	5
—Charlotte (I.L.)		1	5	.167	3.69	47	0	0	0	7	63 1/3	61	30	26	32	66
1997—Charlotte (I.L.)		4	2	.667	4.38	27	0	0	0	2	24 2/3	22	12	12	15	21
1998—Florida (N.L.)		0	7	.000	3.68	59	0	0	0	1	71	52	29	29	30	74
1999—Florida (N.L.)		0	1	.000	8.83	56	0	0	0	0	34 2/3	50	36	34	21	16
—Calgary (PCL)		0	0	...	4.63	9	0	0	0	1	11 2/3	13	6	6	0	12
Major League totals (2 years)		0	8	.000	5.37	115	0	0	0	1	105 2/3	102	65	63	51	90

D

DARR, MIKE — OF — PADRES

PERSONAL: Born March 21, 1976, in Corona, Calif. ... 6-3/205. ... Bats left, throws right. ... Full name: Michael Curtis Darr.
HIGH SCHOOL: Corona (Calif.).
TRANSACTIONS/CAREER NOTES: Selected by Detroit Tigers organization in second round of free-agent draft (June 2, 1994). ... On disabled list (April 4-May 28, 1996). ... Traded by Tigers with P Mike Skrmetta to San Diego Padres for 2B Jody Reed (March 22, 1997). ... On Las Vegas disabled list (April 25-May 7, 1999).

Year Team (League)	Pos.	G	AB	R	H	2B	3B	HR	RBI	Avg.	BB	SO	SB	PO	A	E	Avg.
1994— Bristol (Appl.)	OF	44	149	23	41	6	0	1	18	.275	23	22	4	59	4	4	.940
1995— Fayetteville (SAL)	OF	112	395	58	114	21	2	5	66	.289	58	88	5	123	15	9	.939
1996— Lakeland (FSL)	OF	85	311	26	77	14	7	0	38	.248	28	64	7	128	8	3	.978
1997— Ran. Cuca. (Calif.)■	OF	134	521	104	179	32	11	15	94	.344	57	90	23	176	12	8	.959
1998— Mobile (Sou.)	OF	132	523	105	162	41	4	6	90	.310	62	79	28	261	13	6	.979
1999— Las Vegas (PCL)	OF-DH	100	383	57	114	34	0	10	62	.298	50	103	10	172	11	2	.989
— San Diego (N.L.)	OF	25	48	6	13	1	0	2	3	.271	5	18	2	28	0	0	1.000
Major League totals (1 year)		25	48	6	13	1	0	2	3	.271	5	18	2	28	0	0	1.000

DAUBACH, BRIAN — 1B — RED SOX

PERSONAL: Born February 11, 1972, in Belleville, Ill. ... 6-1/201. ... Bats left, throws right. ... Full name: Brian Michael Daubach.
HIGH SCHOOL: Belleville (Ill.) West.
TRANSACTIONS/CAREER NOTES: Selected by New York Mets organization in 17th round of free-agent draft (June 4, 1990). ... Granted free agency (October 15, 1996). ... Signed by Florida Marlins organization (November 7, 1996). ... Granted free agency (October 17, 1997). ... Re-signed by Marlins organization (January 6, 1998). ... Released by Marlins (November 19, 1998). ... Signed by Boston Red Sox organization (December 18, 1998).
STATISTICAL NOTES: Tied for Appalachian League lead in intentional bases on balls received with five in 1991. ... Led Appalachian League first basemen with 623 total chances and 41 double plays in 1991. ... Tied for Florida State League lead in double plays by first basemen with 127 in 1994. ... Led Eastern League first basemen with 111 double plays and .992 fielding percentage and tied for lead with 98 assists in 1995. ... Led Eastern League first basemen with 115 assists in 1996. ... Led International League with 10 sacrifice flies in 1997. ... Led International League with 315 total bases, .634 slugging percentage and nine intentional bases on balls received and tied for lead in being hit by pitch with 15 in 1998.

Year Team (League)	Pos.	G	AB	R	H	2B	3B	HR	RBI	Avg.	BB	SO	SB	PO	A	E	Avg.
1990— GC Mets (GCL)	1B	45	152	26	41	8	4	1	19	.270	22	41	2	274	16	7	.976
— Charlotte (I.L.)	OF-1B	140	497	102	157	45	4	35	124	.316	80	114	9	262	28	3	.990
1991— Kingsport (Appl.)	1B	65	218	30	53	9	1	7	42	.243	33	64	1	*562	*52	9	.986
1992— Pittsfield (NY-P)	1B	72	260	26	63	15	2	2	40	.242	30	61	4	609	•44	12	.982
1993— Capital City (SAL)	1B-OF	102	379	50	106	19	3	7	72	.280	52	84	6	393	43	5	.989
1994— St. Lucie (FSL)	1B	129	450	52	123	30	2	6	74	.273	58	120	14	*1157	*115	12	.991
1995— Binghamton (East.)	1B-3B	135	469	61	115	25	2	10	72	.245	51	104	6	1137	98	10	†.992
— Norfolk (I.L.)	1B	2	7	0	0	0	0	0	0	.000	1	0	0	21	3	0	1.000
1996— Binghamton (East.)	1B-3B	122	436	80	129	24	1	22	76	.296	74	103	7	1108	†115	11	.991
— Norfolk (I.L.)	1B	17	54	7	11	2	0	0	6	.204	6	14	1	72	3	0	1.000
1997— Charlotte (I.L.)■	1B	136	461	66	128	40	2	21	93	.278	65	126	1	870	62	8	.991
1998— Charlotte (I.L.)	OF-1B	140	497	102	157	*45	4	*35	*124	.316	80	114	9	362	28	3	.992
— Florida (N.L.)	1B	10	15	0	3	1	0	0	3	.200	1	5	0	23	1	0	1.000
1999— Boston (A.L.)■	1-DH-O-3	110	381	61	112	33	3	21	73	.294	36	92	0	420	35	8	.983
— Pawtucket (I.L.)	DH-1B-OF	9	31	4	9	2	0	1	6	.290	6	8	0	31	2	1	.971
American League totals (1 year)		110	381	61	112	33	3	21	73	.294	36	92	0	420	35	8	.983
National League totals (1 year)		10	15	0	3	1	0	0	3	.200	1	5	0	23	1	0	1.000
Major League totals (2 years)		120	396	61	115	34	3	21	76	.290	37	97	0	443	36	8	.984

DIVISION SERIES RECORD

RECORDS: Holds single-game record for most at-bats with no hits—6 (October 10, 1999). ... Shares single-game record for most at-bats (nine-inning game)—6 (October 10, 1999).

Year Team (League)	Pos.	G	AB	R	H	2B	3B	HR	RBI	Avg.	BB	SO	SB	PO	A	E	Avg.
1999— Boston (A.L.)	DH-PH-1B	4	16	3	4	2	0	1	3	.250	0	7	0	1	0	0	1.000

CHAMPIONSHIP SERIES RECORD

Year Team (League)	Pos.	G	AB	R	H	2B	3B	HR	RBI	Avg.	BB	SO	SB	PO	A	E	Avg.
1999— Boston (A.L.)	DH-1B-PH	5	17	2	3	1	0	1	3	.176	1	4	0	0	0	0	...

DaVANON, JEFF — OF — ANGELS

PERSONAL: Born December 8, 1973, in San Diego. ... 6-0/185. ... Bats both, throws right. ... Full name: Jeffrey Graham DaVanon. ... Son of Jerry DaVanon, infielder with five major league teams (1969-77).
HIGH SCHOOL: Bellaire (Texas).
COLLEGE: San Diego State.
TRANSACTIONS/CAREER NOTES: Selected by Oakland Athletics organization in 26th round of free-agent draft (June 1, 1995). ... Traded by Athletics with P Elvin Nina and OF Nathan Haynes to Anaheim Angels for P Omar Olivares and 2B Randy Velarde (July 29, 1999).

Year Team (League)	Pos.	G	AB	R	H	2B	3B	HR	RBI	Avg.	BB	SO	SB	PO	A	E	Avg.
1995— S. Oregon (N'west)	OF	57	167	29	42	6	2	1	17	.251	34	49	6	47	4	8	.864
1996— W. Mich. (Mid.)	OF-1B-2B	89	289	43	70	13	4	2	33	.242	49	66	5	72	9	2	.976
1997— Visalia (Calif.)	OF	119	408	70	104	17	3	6	38	.255	81	101	23	166	*17	10	.948
1998— Modesto (Calif.)	OF	84	301	66	101	17	4	5	60	.336	59	69	33	112	7	13	.902

D

Year Team (League)	Pos.	G	AB	R	H	2B	3B	HR	RBI	Avg.	BB	SO	SB	PO	A	E	Avg.
					BATTING									FIELDING			
1999—Midland (Texas)..........	OF-DH	100	374	87	128	29	11	11	60	.342	53	68	18	162	8	7	.960
—Edmonton (PCL)■	OF-DH	34	132	35	43	8	3	6	19	.326	20	27	11	74	6	0	1.000
—Anaheim (A.L.)	OF-DH	7	20	4	4	0	1	1	4	.200	2	7	0	5	0	0	1.000
Major League totals (1 year)		7	20	4	4	0	1	1	4	.200	2	7	0	5	0	0	1.000

DAVENPORT, JOE — P — WHITE SOX

PERSONAL: Born March 24, 1976, in Chicago. ... 6-5/225. ... Throws right, bats right. ... Full name: Joseph Jonathan Davenport.
HIGH SCHOOL: Santana (Santee, Calif.).
TRANSACTIONS/CAREER NOTES: Selected by Toronto Blue Jays organization in 13th round of free-agent draft (June 2, 1994). ... Selected by Chicago White Sox organization from Blue Jays organization in Rule 5 minor league draft (December 15, 1997).

Year League	W	L	Pct.	ERA	G	GS	CG	ShO	Sv.	IP	H	R	ER	BB	SO
1994—GC Blue Jays (GCL)...........	0	0	...	3.27	7	1	0	0	0	11	12	5	4	7	2
1995—Hagerstown (SAL)..............	0	1	.000	6.11	13	0	0	0	0	17²/₃	22	19	12	13	13
—GC Blue Jays (GCL)...........	2	3	.400	5.66	15	10	1	0	1	55²/₃	67	47	35	30	29
1996—St. Catharines (NY-P)	2	4	.333	5.13	20	8	0	0	0	66²/₃	71	44	38	23	43
1997—Hagerstown (SAL)..............	4	6	.400	3.68	37	0	0	0	0	51¹/₃	43	26	21	24	43
1998—Winston-Salem (Caro.)■ ...	2	0	1.000	1.38	20	0	0	0	2	26	25	9	4	4	26
—Birmingham (Sou.)..............	3	2	.600	7.22	26	0	0	0	1	38²/₃	54	36	31	30	22
1999—Birmingham (Sou.)..............	3	5	.375	3.10	40	0	0	0	10	49¹/₃	43	26	17	19	24
—Chicago (A.L.)	0	0	...	0.00	3	0	0	0	0	1²/₃	1	0	0	2	0
—Charlotte (I.L.).....................	0	0	...	8.00	6	0	0	0	0	9	13	8	8	1	6
Major League totals (1 year)........	0	0	...	0.00	3	0	0	0	0	1²/₃	1	0	0	2	0

DAVEY, TOM — P — MARINERS

PERSONAL: Born September 11, 1973, in Garden City, Mich. ... 6-7/230. ... Throws right, bats right. ... Full name: Thomas Joseph Davey.
HIGH SCHOOL: Plymouth Salem (Canton, Mich.).
JUNIOR COLLEGE: Henry Ford Community College (Mich.).
TRANSACTIONS/CAREER NOTES: Selected by Toronto Blue Jays organization in fifth round of free-agent draft (June 2, 1994). ... Selected by Baltimore Orioles organization from Blue Jays organization in Rule 5 major league draft (December 9, 1996). ... Returned to Blue Jays organization (March 20, 1997). ... Traded by Blue Jays with P Steve Sinclair to Seattle Mariners for 1B David Segui (July 28, 1999).

Year League	W	L	Pct.	ERA	G	GS	CG	ShO	Sv.	IP	H	R	ER	BB	SO
1994—Medicine Hat (Pio.)	2	•8	.200	5.12	14	14	0	0	0	65	76	59	37	*59	35
1995—St. Catharines (NY-P)........	4	3	.571	3.32	7	7	0	0	0	38	27	19	14	21	29
—Hagerstown (SAL)..............	4	1	.800	3.38	8	8	0	0	0	37¹/₃	29	23	14	31	25
1996—Hagerstown (SAL)..............	10	9	.526	3.87	26	26	2	1	0	155²/₃	132	76	67	91	98
1997—Dunedin (FSL)..................	1	3	.250	4.31	7	6	0	0	0	39²/₃	44	21	19	15	36
—Knoxville (Sou.).................	6	7	.462	5.83	20	16	0	0	0	92²/₃	108	65	60	50	72
1998—Knoxville (Sou.).................	5	3	.625	3.87	48	9	0	0	16	76²/₃	70	35	33	52	78
1999—Toronto (A.L.)...................	1	1	.500	4.70	29	0	0	0	1	44	40	28	23	26	42
—Syracuse (I.L.)...................	1	2	.333	3.48	6	6	0	0	0	33²/₃	30	15	13	19	20
—Seattle (A.L.)■	1	0	1.000	4.71	16	0	0	0	0	21	22	13	11	14	17
Major League totals (1 year)........	2	1	.667	4.71	45	0	0	0	1	65	62	41	34	40	59

D

DAVIDSON, CLEATUS — 2B/SS — TWINS

PERSONAL: Born November 1, 1976, in Bartow, Fla. ... 5-10/170. ... Bats both, throws right. ... Full name: Cleatus Lavon Davidson.
HIGH SCHOOL: Lake Wales (Fla.).
TRANSACTIONS/CAREER NOTES: Selected by Minnesota Twins organization in second round of free-agent draft (June 2, 1994). ... On Minnesota disabled list (September 29, 1999-remainder of season).
STATISTICAL NOTES: Led Appalachian League shortstops with 33 double plays and 335 total chances in 1996. ... Led Midwest League second basemen with 271 putouts, 405 assists, 696 total chances and 98 double plays in 1997. ... Led Florida State League with 13 sacrifice hits in 1998. ... Led Florida State League second basemen with 320 putouts, 403 assists, 748 total chances and 98 double plays in 1998.

Year Team (League)	Pos.	G	AB	R	H	2B	3B	HR	RBI	Avg.	BB	SO	SB	PO	A	E	Avg.
					BATTING									FIELDING			
1994—GC Twins (GCL).........	SS-OF	24	85	8	15	1	0	0	5	.176	9	19	3	15	65	11	.879
1995—GC Twins (GCL).........	SS-2B	21	75	11	15	2	1	0	5	.200	10	17	8	38	74	7	.941
—Elizabethton (Appl.)....	SS	39	152	27	45	6	2	3	27	.296	11	31	10	54	113	22	.884
1996—Fort Wayne (Midw.).....	SS	59	203	20	36	8	3	0	30	.177	23	45	2	86	185	24	.919
—Elizabethton (Appl.)....	SS	95	248	•53	71	10	6	6	31	.286	39	45	17	*100	*200	*35	.896
1997—Fort Wayne (Midw.).....	2B-OF	124	478	80	122	16	8	6	52	.255	52	100	39	†272	†405	20	.971
1998—Fort Myers (FSL)........	2B-SS	130	527	97	127	12	7	2	45	.241	45	99	44	†325	†417	27	.965
1999—New Britain (East.)	2B-SS	127	491	88	120	16	10	2	40	.244	53	110	40	295	374	16	.977
—Minnesota (A.L.)	2B-SS-DH	12	22	3	3	0	0	0	3	.136	0	4	2	18	28	1	.979
Major League totals (1 year)		12	22	3	3	0	0	0	3	.136	0	4	2	18	28	1	.979

DAVIS, BEN — C — PADRES

PERSONAL: Born March 10, 1977, in Chester, Pa. ... 6-4/215. ... Bats both, throws right. ... Full name: Matthew Benjamin Davis.
HIGH SCHOOL: Malvern (Pa.) Prep.
TRANSACTIONS/CAREER NOTES: Selected by San Diego Padres organization in first round (second pick overall) of free-agent draft (June 3, 1995).
STATISTICAL NOTES: Led Southern League catchers with 1,002 total chances in 1998.

Year	Team (League)	Pos.	G	AB	R	H	2B	3B	HR	RBI	Avg.	BB	SO	SB	PO	A	E	Avg.
1995—Idaho Falls (Pio.)	C	52	197	36	55	8	3	5	46	.279	17	36	0	*362	44	6	.985
1996—Rancho Cuca. (Calif.)	C-DH	98	353	35	71	10	1	6	41	.201	31	89	1	642	51	9	.987
1997—Rancho Cuca. (Calif.)	C-DH-1B	122	474	67	132	30	1	17	76	.278	28	107	3	993	103	14	.987
1998—Mobile (Sou.)	C-DH	116	433	65	124	29	2	14	75	.286	42	60	4	*920	76	6	.994
—San Diego (N.L.)	C	1	1	0	0	0	0	0	0	.000	0	0	0	2	0	0	1.000
1999—Las Vegas (PCL)	C	58	201	27	62	18	1	7	44	.308	24	41	4	454	32	4	.992
—San Diego (N.L.)	C	76	266	29	65	14	1	5	30	.244	25	70	2	471	29	7	.986
Major League totals (2 years)		77	267	29	65	14	1	5	30	.243	25	70	2	473	29	7	.986

DAVIS, CHILI   DH

PERSONAL: Born January 17, 1960, in Kingston, Jamaica. ... 6-3/240. ... Bats both, throws right. ... Full name: Charles Theodore Davis.
HIGH SCHOOL: Dorsey (Los Angeles).
TRANSACTIONS/CAREER NOTES: Selected by San Francisco Giants organization in 11th round of free-agent draft (June 7, 1977). ... On Phoenix disabled list (August 19-28, 1981). ... Granted free agency (November 9, 1987). ... Signed by California Angels (December 1, 1987). ... On disabled list (July 17-August 9, 1990). ... Granted free agency (December 7, 1990). ... Signed by Minnesota Twins (January 29, 1991). ... Granted free agency (November 3, 1992). ... Signed by Angels (December 11, 1992). ... On disabled list (June 20-July 18, 1995). ... Traded by Angels to Kansas City Royals for P Mark Gubicza and P Mike Bovee (October 28, 1996). ... On disabled list (March 23-April 14, 1997). ... Granted free agency (October 29, 1997). ... Signed by New York Yankees (December 10, 1997). ... On New York disabled list (April 3-August 17, 1998); included rehabilitation assignment to Norwich (July 30-August 10) and Columbus (August 11-17). ... Released by Yankees (December 1, 1999).
STATISTICAL NOTES: Switch-hit home runs in one game 10 times (June 5, 1983; June 27 and September 15, 1987; July 30, 1988; July 1, 1989; October 2, 1992; May 11 and July 30, 1994; August 21, 1996; and June 7, 1997). ... Tied for A.L. lead with 10 sacrifice flies in 1988. ... Career major league grand slams: 8.
MISCELLANEOUS: Original nickname was Chili Bowl, which was prompted by a friend who saw Davis after he received a haircut in the sixth grade. The nickname was later shortened to Chili.

Year	Team (League)	Pos.	G	AB	R	H	2B	3B	HR	RBI	Avg.	BB	SO	SB	PO	A	E	Avg.
1978—Cedar Rapids (Midw.)	C-OF	124	424	63	119	18	5	16	73	.281	36	103	15	365	45	25	.943
1979—Fresno (Calif.)	OF-C	134	490	91	132	24	5	21	95	.269	80	91	30	339	43	20	.950
1980—Shreveport (Texas)	OF-C	129	442	50	130	30	4	12	67	.294	52	94	19	184	20	12	.944
1981—San Francisco (N.L.)	OF	8	15	1	2	0	0	0	0	.133	1	2	2	7	0	0	1.000
—Phoenix (PCL)	OF	88	334	76	117	16	6	19	75	.350	46	54	40	175	7	6	.968
1982—San Francisco (N.L.)	OF	154	641	86	167	27	6	19	76	.261	45	115	24	404	•16	12	.972
1983—San Francisco (N.L.)	OF	137	486	54	113	21	2	11	59	.233	55	108	10	357	7	9	.976
—Phoenix (PCL)	OF	10	44	12	13	2	0	2	9	.295	4	6	5	15	0	2	.882
1984—San Francisco (N.L.)	OF	137	499	87	157	21	6	21	81	.315	42	74	12	292	9	9	.971
1985—San Francisco (N.L.)	OF	136	481	53	130	25	2	13	56	.270	62	74	15	279	10	6	.980
1986—San Francisco (N.L.)	OF	153	526	71	146	28	3	13	70	.278	84	96	16	303	9	•9	.972
1987—San Francisco (N.L.)	OF	149	500	80	125	22	1	24	76	.250	72	109	16	265	6	7	.975
1988—California (A.L.)■	OF-DH	158	600	81	161	29	3	21	93	.268	56	118	9	299	10	*19	.942
1989—California (A.L.)	OF-DH	154	560	81	152	24	1	22	90	.271	61	109	3	270	5	6	.979
1990—California (A.L.)	DH-OF	113	412	58	109	17	1	12	58	.265	61	89	1	77	5	3	.965
1991—Minnesota (A.L.)■	DH-OF	153	534	84	148	34	1	29	93	.277	95	117	5	2	0	0	1.000
1992—Minnesota (A.L.)	DH-OF-1B	138	444	63	128	27	2	12	66	.288	73	76	4	6	0	0	1.000
1993—California (A.L.)■	DH-P	153	573	74	139	32	0	27	112	.243	71	135	4	0	0	0	
1994—California (A.L.)	DH-OF	108	392	72	122	18	1	26	84	.311	69	84	3	5	0	0	1.000
1995—California (A.L.)	DH	119	424	81	135	23	0	20	86	.318	89	79	3	...	...	...	...
1996—California (A.L.)	DH	145	530	73	155	24	0	28	95	.292	86	99	5	...	...	...	...
1997—Kansas City (A.L.)■	DH	140	477	71	133	20	0	30	90	.279	85	96	6	...	...	...	...
1998—New York (A.L.)■	DH	35	103	11	30	7	0	3	9	.291	14	18	0	...	...	...	...
—Norwich (East.)	DH	11	37	2	9	3	0	1	5	.243	9	7	0	...	...	...	...
—Columbus (I.L.)	DH	6	22	4	8	1	0	0	3	.364	4	3	0	...	...	...	...
1999—New York (A.L.)	DH	146	476	59	128	25	1	19	78	.269	73	100	4	...	...	...	...
American League totals (12 years)		1562	5525	808	1540	280	10	249	954	.279	833	1120	47	659	20	28	.960
National League totals (7 years)		874	3148	432	840	144	20	101	418	.267	361	578	95	1907	57	52	.974
Major League totals (19 years)		2436	8673	1240	2380	424	30	350	1372	.274	1194	1698	142	2566	77	80	.971

DIVISION SERIES RECORD

Year	Team (League)	Pos.	G	AB	R	H	2B	3B	HR	RBI	Avg.	BB	SO	SB	PO	A	E	Avg.
1998—New York (A.L.)	DH	2	6	0	1	0	0	0	0	.167	0	2	0	...	...	...	...
1999—New York (A.L.)	DH	1	3	0	1	0	0	0	0	.333	0	2	0	...	...	...	...
Division series totals (2 years)		3	9	0	2	0	0	0	0	.222	0	4	0	...	...	...	...

CHAMPIONSHIP SERIES RECORD

RECORDS: Shares A.L. single-series record for most strikeouts—8 (1991).

Year	Team (League)	Pos.	G	AB	R	H	2B	3B	HR	RBI	Avg.	BB	SO	SB	PO	A	E	Avg.
1987—San Francisco (N.L.)	OF	6	20	2	3	1	0	0	0	.150	1	4	0	11	1	1	.923
1991—Minnesota (A.L.)	DH	5	17	3	5	2	0	0	2	.294	5	8	1	...	...	...	...
1998—New York (A.L.)	PH-DH	5	14	2	4	1	0	1	5	.286	2	3	0	...	...	...	...
1999—New York (A.L.)	DH-PH	5	11	0	1	0	0	0	1	.091	3	4	0	...	...	...	...
Championship series totals (4 years)		21	62	7	13	4	0	1	8	.210	11	19	1	11	1	1	.923

WORLD SERIES RECORD

NOTES: Member of World Series championship team (1991, 1998 and 1999).

					BATTING									FIELDING		
Year	Team (League)	Pos.	G	AB	R	H	2B	3B	HR	RBI	Avg.	BB	SO	SB	PO	A	E	Avg.
1991—	Minnesota (A.L.)	DH-PH-OF	6	18	4	4	0	0	2	4	.222	2	3	0	1	0	0	1.000
1998—	New York (A.L.)	DH-PH	3	7	3	2	0	0	0	2	.286	3	2	0	...	...	...	...
1999—	New York (A.L.)	DH	1	4	0	0	0	0	0	0	.000	0	2	0	...	...	...	...
World Series totals (3 years)		10	29	7	6	0	0	2	6	.207	5	7	0	1	0	0	1.000

ALL-STAR GAME RECORD

			BATTING									FIELDING		
Year	League	Pos.	AB	R	H	2B	3B	HR	RBI	Avg.	BB	SO	SB	PO	A	E	Avg.
1984—	National	PH	1	0	0	0	0	0	0	.000	0	0	0	...	...	...	...
1986—	National	OF	1	0	0	0	0	0	0	.000	0	1	0	0	0	0	...
1994—	American	PH	1	0	0	0	0	0	0	.000	0	0	0	...	...	...	...
All-Star Game totals (3 years)		3	0	0	0	0	0	0	.000	0	1	0	0	0	0	...

RECORD AS PITCHER

|Year|League|W|L|Pct.|ERA|G|GS|CG|ShO|Sv.|IP|H|R|ER|BB|SO|
|1993—|California (A.L.)|0|0|...|0.00|1|0|0|0|0|2|0|0|0|0|0|

DAVIS, DOUG — P — RANGERS

PERSONAL: Born September 21, 1975, in Sacramento. ... 6-3/190. ... Throws left, bats right. ... Full name: Douglas P. Davis.
HIGH SCHOOL: Northgate (Walnut Creek, Calif.).
JUNIOR COLLEGE: City College of San Francisco.
TRANSACTIONS/CAREER NOTES: Selected by Texas Rangers organization in 10th round of free-agent draft (June 4, 1996).

Year	League	W	L	Pct.	ERA	G	GS	CG	ShO	Sv.	IP	H	R	ER	BB	SO
1996—	GC Rangers (GCL)	3	1	.750	1.90	8	7	0	0	0	42 2/3	28	13	9	26	49
1997—	GC Rangers (GCL)	3	1	.750	1.71	4	4	0	0	0	21	14	5	4	15	27
—	Charlotte (FSL)	5	3	.625	3.10	9	8	1	0	0	49 1/3	29	19	17	33	52
1998—	Charlotte (FSL)	11	7	.611	3.24	27	27	1	1	0	155 1/3	129	69	56	74	*173
1999—	Tulsa (Texas)	4	4	.500	2.42	12	12	1	0	0	74 1/3	65	26	20	25	79
—	Oklahoma (PCL)	7	0	1.000	3.00	13	11	0	0	0	78	77	27	26	31	74
—	Texas (A.L.)	0	0	...	33.75	2	0	0	0	0	2 2/3	12	10	10	0	3
Major League totals (1 year)	0	0	...	33.75	2	0	0	0	0	2 2/3	12	10	10	0	3

DAVIS, ERIC — OF — CARDINALS

PERSONAL: Born May 29, 1962, in Los Angeles. ... 6-3/185. ... Bats right, throws right. ... Full name: Eric Keith Davis.
HIGH SCHOOL: Fremont (Los Angeles).
TRANSACTIONS/CAREER NOTES: Selected by Cincinnati Reds organization in eighth round of free-agent draft (June 3, 1980). ... On Cincinnati disabled list (August 16-September 1, 1984; May 3-18, 1989; April 25-May 19, 1990; June 12-27 and July 31-August 26, 1991). ... Traded by Reds with P Kip Gross to Los Angeles Dodgers for P Tim Belcher and P John Wetteland (November 27, 1991). ... On disabled list (May 23-June 19 and August 2-25, 1992). ... Granted free agency (November 3, 1992). ... Re-signed by Dodgers (December 1, 1992). ... Traded by Dodgers to Detroit Tigers for a player to be named later (August 31, 1993); Dodgers acquired P John DeSilva to complete deal (September 7, 1993). ... Granted free agency (October 28, 1993). ... Re-signed by Tigers (November 1, 1993). ... On disabled list (May 23-July 19 and July 27, 1994-remainder of season). ... Granted free agency (October 20, 1994). ... On retired list (October 20, 1994-January 2, 1996). ... Signed by Reds organization (January 2, 1996). ... On disabled list (May 26-June 10, 1996). ... Granted free agency (October 28, 1996). ... Signed by Baltimore Orioles (December 19, 1996). ... On disabled list (May 26-September 15, 1997). ... Granted free agency (October 27, 1998). ... Signed by St. Louis Cardinals (November 19, 1998). ... On disabled list (June 28, 1999-remainder of season).
RECORDS: Shares major league record for most grand slams in two consecutive games—2 (May 4 and 5, 1996); and most strikeouts in two consecutive games—9 (April 24 [4] and 25 [5], 1987, 21 innings). ... Shares major league single-month record for most grand slams—3 (May 1987). ... Holds N.L. career record for highest stolen-base percentage (300 or more attempts)—.861. ... Shares major league record for most grand slams in two consecutive games—2 (August 13 and 14, 1991).
HONORS: Named outfielder on THE SPORTING NEWS N.L. All-Star team (1987 and 1989). ... Named outfielder on THE SPORTING NEWS N.L. Silver Slugger team (1987 and 1989). ... Won N.L. Gold Glove as outfielder (1987-89). ... Named N.L. Comeback Player of the Year by THE SPORTING NEWS (1996).
STATISTICAL NOTES: Hit three home runs in one game (September 10, 1986 and May 3, 1987). ... Led N.L. outfielders with 394 total chances in 1987. ... Led N.L. with 21 game-winning RBIs in 1988. ... Hit for the cycle (June 2, 1989). ... Had 30-game hitting streak (July 12-August 15, 1998). ... Career major league grand slams: 10.

					BATTING									FIELDING		
Year	Team (League)	Pos.	G	AB	R	H	2B	3B	HR	RBI	Avg.	BB	SO	SB	PO	A	E	Avg.
1980—	Eugene (N'west)	SS-2B-OF	33	73	12	16	1	0	1	11	.219	14	26	10	29	36	11	.855
1981—	Eugene (N'west)	OF	62	214	*67	69	10	4	11	39	.322	57	59	*40	94	11	4	.963
1982—	Cedar Rap. (Midw.)	OF	111	434	80	120	20	5	15	56	.276	51	103	53	239	9	9	.965
1983—	Waterbury (East.)	OF	89	293	56	85	13	1	15	43	.290	65	75	39	214	8	2	.991
—	Indianapolis (A.A.)	OF	19	77	18	23	4	0	7	19	.299	8	22	9	61	1	1	.984
1984—	Wichita (A.A.)	OF	52	194	42	61	9	5	14	34	.314	25	55	27	110	5	5	.958
—	Cincinnati (N.L.)	OF	57	174	33	39	10	1	10	30	.224	24	48	10	125	4	1	.992
1985—	Cincinnati (N.L.)	OF	56	122	26	30	3	3	8	18	.246	7	39	16	75	3	1	.987
—	Denver (A.A.)	OF	64	206	48	57	10	2	15	38	.277	29	67	35	94	5	3	.971
1986—	Cincinnati (N.L.)	OF	132	415	97	115	15	3	27	71	.277	68	100	80	274	2	7	.975
1987—	Cincinnati (N.L.)	OF	129	474	120	139	23	4	37	100	.293	84	134	50	*380	10	4	.990
1988—	Cincinnati (N.L.)	OF	135	472	81	129	18	3	26	93	.273	65	124	35	300	2	6	.981
1989—	Cincinnati (N.L.)	OF	131	462	74	130	14	2	34	101	.281	68	116	21	298	2	5	.984
1990—	Cincinnati (N.L.)	OF	127	453	84	118	26	2	24	86	.260	60	100	21	257	10	2	.993
1991—	Cincinnati (N.L.)	OF	89	285	39	67	10	0	11	33	.235	48	92	14	190	5	3	.985
1992—	Los Angeles (N.L.)■..	OF	76	267	21	61	8	1	5	32	.228	36	71	19	123	0	5	.961
1993—	Los Angeles (N.L.)	OF	108	376	57	88	17	0	14	53	.234	41	88	33	221	7	2	.991
—	Detroit (A.L.)■	OF-DH	23	75	14	19	1	1	6	15	.253	14	18	2	52	0	1	.981
1994—	Detroit (A.L.)	OF	37	120	19	22	4	0	3	13	.183	18	45	5	85	1	1	.989

– 141 –

Year	Team (League)	Pos.	G	AB	R	H	2B	3B	HR	RBI	Avg.	BB	SO	SB	PO	A	E	Avg.
1995—	....							Did not play-retired.											
1996—	Cincinnati (N.L.)■......	OF-1B	129	415	81	119	20	0	26	83	.287	70	121	23	279	3	3	.989
1997—	Baltimore (A.L.)■......	OF-DH	42	158	29	48	11	0	8	25	.304	14	47	6	39	0	1	.975
1998—	Baltimore (A.L.)........	OF-DH	131	452	81	148	29	1	28	89	.327	44	108	7	119	4	1	.992
1999—	St. Louis (N.L.)■	OF-DH	58	191	27	49	9	2	5	30	.257	30	49	5	93	4	0	1.000
American League totals (4 years)			233	805	143	237	45	2	45	142	.294	90	218	20	295	5	4	.987
National League totals (12 years)			1227	4106	740	1084	173	21	227	730	.264	601	1082	327	2615	53	39	.986
Major League totals (15 years)			1460	4911	883	1321	218	23	272	872	.269	691	1300	347	2910	58	43	.986

DIVISION SERIES RECORD

Year	Team (League)	Pos.	G	AB	R	H	2B	3B	HR	RBI	Avg.	BB	SO	SB	PO	A	E	Avg.
1997—	Baltimore (A.L.)..........	OF	3	9	0	2	0	0	0	2	.222	0	5	0	1	0	0	1.000

CHAMPIONSHIP SERIES RECORD

Year	Team (League)	Pos.	G	AB	R	H	2B	3B	HR	RBI	Avg.	BB	SO	SB	PO	A	E	Avg.
1990—	Cincinnati (N.L.).........	OF	6	23	2	4	1	0	0	2	.174	1	9	0	12	1	0	1.000
1997—	Baltimore (A.L.)..........	OF-DH	6	13	1	2	0	0	1	1	.154	1	3	0	3	0	0	1.000
Championship series totals (2 years)			12	36	3	6	1	0	1	3	.167	2	12	0	15	1	0	1.000

WORLD SERIES RECORD

NOTES: Hit home run in first at-bat (October 16, 1990). ... Member of World Series championship team (1990).

Year	Team (League)	Pos.	G	AB	R	H	2B	3B	HR	RBI	Avg.	BB	SO	SB	PO	A	E	Avg.
1990—	Cincinnati (N.L.).........	OF	4	14	3	4	0	0	1	5	.286	0	0	0	4	0	0	1.000

ALL-STAR GAME RECORD

Year	League	Pos.	AB	R	H	2B	3B	HR	RBI	Avg.	BB	SO	SB	PO	A	E	Avg.
1987—	National	OF	3	0	0	0	0	0	0	.000	0	1	0	1	0	0	1.000
1989—	National	OF	2	0	0	0	0	0	0	.000	1	0	1	1	0	0	1.000
All-Star Game totals (2 years)			5	0	0	0	0	0	0	.000	1	1	1	2	0	0	1.000

D

DAVIS, RUSS — 3B — GIANTS

PERSONAL: Born September 13, 1969, in Birmingham, Ala. ... 6-0/195. ... Bats right, throws right. ... Full name: Russell Stewart Davis.
HIGH SCHOOL: Hueytown (Ala.).
JUNIOR COLLEGE: Shelton State Junior College (Ala.).
TRANSACTIONS/CAREER NOTES: Selected by New York Yankees organization in 29th round of free-agent draft (June 1, 1988). ... On disabled list (July 13-August 1, 1993). ... On Columbus disabled list (April 7-15 and August 26, 1994-remainder of season). ... Traded by Yankees with P Sterling Hitchcock to Seattle Mariners for 1B Tino Martinez, P Jeff Nelson and P Jim Mecir (December 7, 1995). ... On disabled list (June 8, 1996-remainder of season; and August 25-September 26, 1997). ... Granted free agency (December 21, 1999). ... Signed by San Francisco Giants organization (January 24, 2000).
HONORS: Named Eastern League Most Valuable Player (1992).
STATISTICAL NOTES: Tied for New York-Pennsylvania League lead with 11 double plays by third baseman in 1989. ... Led Carolina League third basemen with 336 total chances and 18 double plays in 1990. ... Tied for Eastern League lead with .917 fielding percentage, 83 putouts, 205 assists, 26 errors and 314 total chances by third basemen in 1991. ... Led Eastern League with 237 total bases and .483 slugging percentage in 1992. ... Led International League third basemen with 25 errors in 1993. ... Led A.L. third basemen with 32 errors in 1998.

Year	Team (League)	Pos.	G	AB	R	H	2B	3B	HR	RBI	Avg.	BB	SO	SB	PO	A	E	Avg.
1988—	GC Yankees (GCL)......	2B-3B	58	213	33	49	11	3	2	30	.230	16	39	6	64	105	15	.918
1989—	Fort Laud. (FSL).......	3B-2B	48	147	8	27	5	1	2	22	.184	11	38	3	32	72	17	.860
—	Oneonta (NY-P).........	3B	65	236	33	68	7	5	7	42	.288	19	44	3	27	87	17	.870
1990—	Prince Will. (Caro.)......	3B	137	510	55	127	*37	3	16	71	.249	37	136	3	*68	*244	24	.929
1991—	Alb./Colonie (East.)	3B-2B	135	473	57	103	23	3	8	58	.218	50	102	3	‡83	‡206	‡26	‡.917
1992—	Alb./Colonie (East.)	3B	132	491	77	140	23	4	22	71	.285	49	93	3	78	185	23	.920
1993—	Columbus (I.L.).........	3B-SS	113	424	63	108	24	1	26	83	.255	40	118	1	85	245	†26	.927
1994—	Columbus (I.L.)	3B-DH-1B	117	416	76	115	30	2	25	69	.276	62	93	3	86	250	23	.936
—	New York (A.L.).........	3B	4	14	0	2	0	0	0	1	.143	0	4	0	2	6	0	1.000
1995—	Columbus (I.L.).........	3B-SS	20	76	12	19	4	1	2	15	.250	17	23	0	17	31	7	.873
—	New York (A.L.).........	3B-DH-1B	40	98	14	27	5	2	2	12	.276	10	26	0	16	45	2	.968
1996—	Seattle (A.L.)■.........	3B	51	167	24	39	9	0	5	18	.234	17	50	2	31	67	7	.933
1997—	Seattle (A.L.)	3B-DH	119	420	57	114	29	1	20	63	.271	27	100	6	56	219	18	.939
1998—	Seattle (A.L.)	3B-OF	141	502	68	130	30	1	20	82	.259	34	134	4	56	254	†34	.901
1999—	Seattle (A.L.)	3B-SS	124	432	55	106	17	1	21	59	.245	32	111	3	71	207	12	.959
Major League totals (6 years)			479	1633	218	418	90	5	68	235	.256	120	425	15	232	798	73	.934

DIVISION SERIES RECORD

Year	Team (League)	Pos.	G	AB	R	H	2B	3B	HR	RBI	Avg.	BB	SO	SB	PO	A	E	Avg.
1995—	New York (A.L.)..........	3B	2	5	0	1	0	0	0	0	.200	0	2	0	0	1	0	1.000

DAVIS, TOMMY — C/1B — ORIOLES

PERSONAL: Born May 21, 1973, in Mobile, Ala. ... 6-1/210. ... Bats right, throws right. ... Full name: Thomas James Davis Jr.
HIGH SCHOOL: Mary G. Montgomery (Semmes, Ala.).
COLLEGE: Southern Mississippi.

TRANSACTIONS/CAREER NOTES: Selected by Baltimore Orioles organization in second round of free-agent draft (June 2, 1994). ... On disabled list (April 22-May 8, 1997). ... On Bowie disabled list (June 3, 1998-remainder of season).
STATISTICAL NOTES: Led South Atlantic League outfielders with 83 putouts, 37 errors and 360 total chances in 1995. ... Led Eastern League first basemen with .995 fielding percentage, 1,158 putouts and 1,259 total chances in 1996.

| | | | | | | | BATTING | | | | | | | | FIELDING | | |
Year Team (League)	Pos.	G	AB	R	H	2B	3B	HR	RBI	Avg.	BB	SO	SB	PO	A	E	Avg.
1994—Albany (SAL)	3B	61	216	35	59	10	1	5	35	.273	18	52	2	40	102	16	.899
1995—Frederick (Caro.)	3B-OF	130	496	62	133	28	3	15	57	.268	41	105	7	†83	240	†37	.897
—Bowie (East.)	1B	9	32	5	10	3	0	3	10	.313	1	9	0	28	2	0	1.000
1996—Bowie (East.)	1B-OF	137	524	75	137	32	2	14	54	.261	41	113	5	†1158	95	6	†.995
1997—Rochester (I.L.)	1B	119	438	74	133	22	2	15	62	.304	43	90	6	875	72	6	*.994
1998—Bowie (East.)	C-1B	37	132	12	37	11	0	1	15	.280	13	27	0	206	10	5	.977
1999—Rochester (I.L.)	C-DH-1B-3B	110	413	49	106	18	0	11	56	.257	24	65	1	536	60	11	.982
—Baltimore (A.L.)	C-1B	5	6	0	1	0	0	0	0	.167	0	2	0	11	1	1	.923
Major League totals (1 year)		5	6	0	1	0	0	0	0	.167	0	2	0	11	1	1	.923

DAWKINS, TRAVIS   SS   REDS

PERSONAL: Born May 12, 1979, in Newberry, S.C. ... 6-1/180. ... Bats right, throws right. ... Full name: Travis Sentell Dawkins.
HIGH SCHOOL: Newberry (S.C.).
TRANSACTIONS/CAREER NOTES: Selected by Cincinnati Reds organization in second round of free-agent draft (June 3, 1997).
STATISTICAL NOTES: Led Pioneer League shortstops with 368 total chances in 1997.

| | | | | | | | BATTING | | | | | | | | FIELDING | | |
Year Team (League)	Pos.	G	AB	R	H	2B	3B	HR	RBI	Avg.	BB	SO	SB	PO	A	E	Avg.
1997—Billings (Pio.)	SS	70	253	47	61	5	0	4	37	.241	30	38	16	*118	*216	34	.908
1998—Burlington (Midw.)	SS	102	367	52	97	7	6	1	30	.264	37	60	37	149	298	36	.925
1999—Rockford (Midw.)	SS	76	305	56	83	10	6	8	32	.272	35	38	38	120	206	17	.950
—Chattanooga (Sou.)	SS	32	129	24	47	7	0	2	13	.364	14	17	15	52	89	3	.979
—Cincinnati (N.L.)	SS	7	7	1	1	0	0	0	0	.143	0	4	0	2	4	0	1.000
Major League totals (1 year)		7	7	1	1	0	0	0	0	.143	0	4	0	2	4	0	1.000

DE LA ROSA, TOMAS   SS   EXPOS

PERSONAL: Born January 28, 1978, in La Victoria, Dominican Republic. ... 5-10/165. ... Bats right, throws right.
HIGH SCHOOL: Licey Padre Garcia (La Victoria, Dominican Republic).
TRANSACTIONS/CAREER NOTES: Signed as non-drafted free agent by Montreal Expos organization (July 12, 1995).
STATISTICAL NOTES: Led Gulf Coast League shortstops with 301 total chances in 1996. ... Led Eastern League shortstops with 83 double plays in 1999.

| | | | | | | | BATTING | | | | | | | | FIELDING | | |
Year Team (League)	Pos.	G	AB	R	H	2B	3B	HR	RBI	Avg.	BB	SO	SB	PO	A	E	Avg.
1996—GC Expos (GCL)	SS	54	187	35	47	7	1	0	21	.251	22	25	8	86	*189	26	.914
—Vermont (NY-P)	SS	3	8	1	2	0	0	0	1	.250	0	3	0	1	4	1	.833
1997—W.P. Beach (FSL)	SS	4	9	1	2	0	0	0	0	.222	2	3	2	5	6	1	.917
—Vermont (NY-P)	SS	69	271	46	72	14	6	2	40	.266	32	47	19	85	201	21	.932
1998—Jupiter (FSL)	SS	117	390	56	98	22	1	3	43	.251	37	61	27	*208	382	30	.952
1999—Harrisburg (East.)	SS-DH	135	467	70	122	22	3	6	43	.261	42	64	28	219	381	34	.946

DE LOS SANTOS, LUIS   P   YANKEES

PERSONAL: Born November 1, 1977, in Santo Domingo, Dominican Republic. ... 6-2/187. ... Throws right, bats right.
TRANSACTIONS/CAREER NOTES: Signed as non-drafted free agent by New York Yankees organization (February 11, 1995). ... On Norwich disabled list (April 23-May 22, 1998). ... On Columbus disabled list (May 6-July 5 and August 5-September 14, 1999). ... On New York disabled list (September 16, 1999-remainder of season).
STATISTICAL NOTES: Pitched 4-0 no-hit victory against Batavia (July 28, 1996).

Year League	W	L	Pct.	ERA	G	GS	CG	ShO	Sv.	IP	H	R	ER	BB	SO
1995—Dom. Yankees (DSL)								Statistics unavailable.							
—Tampa (FSL)	0	0	...	0.00	2	0	0	0	0	5	5	2	0	2	6
1996—Oneonta (NY-P)	4	4	.500	3.72	10	10	3	2	0	58	44	28	24	21	62
—Greensboro (SAL)	4	1	.800	4.83	7	6	0	0	0	31²/₃	39	17	17	11	21
1997—Greensboro (SAL)	5	6	.455	3.05	14	14	1	0	0	88²/₃	91	45	30	13	62
—Tampa (FSL)	5	0	1.000	2.34	10	10	0	0	0	61²/₃	49	19	16	8	39
—Norwich (East.)	1	1	.500	2.52	4	4	0	0	0	25	23	9	7	7	15
1998—Norwich (East.)	2	6	.250	4.90	13	13	2	0	0	79	97	49	43	23	51
—Tampa (FSL)	4	2	.667	4.18	10	10	1	0	0	66²/₃	69	40	31	11	33
1999—Columbus (I.L.)	6	3	.667	4.77	12	12	0	0	0	66	81	42	35	24	45
—GC Yankees (GCL)	0	0	...	0.00	2	2	0	0	0	8	5	0	0	0	7

DE LOS SANTOS, VALERIO   P   BREWERS

PERSONAL: Born October 6, 1975, in Las Matas, Dominican Republic. ... 6-2/180. ... Throws left, bats left. ... Full name: Valerio Lorenzo De Los Santos.
TRANSACTIONS/CAREER NOTES: Signed as non-drafted free agent by Milwaukee Brewers organization (January 26, 1993). ... On El Paso disabled list (April 27-May 4, 1998). ... On Milwaukee disabled list (April 29-September 23, 1999).

Year League	W	L	Pct.	ERA	G	GS	CG	ShO	Sv.	IP	H	R	ER	BB	SO
1993— Dom. Brewers (DSL).........	1	7	.125	6.50	19	6	1	0	0	63 2/3	91	57	46	37	39
1994— Dom. Brewers (DSL).........	7	6	.538	3.69	17	•16	1	1	0	90 1/3	90	52	37	35	50
1995— Arizona Brewers (Ariz.) ...	4	6	.400	2.20	14	12	0	0	0	82	81	34	20	12	57
1996— Beloit (Midw.)...................	10	8	.556	3.55	33	23	5	1	4	164 2/3	164	83	65	59	137
1997— El Paso (Texas).................	6	10	.375	5.75	26	16	1	0	2	114 1/3	146	83	73	38	61
1998— El Paso (Texas).................	6	2	.750	3.91	42	4	0	0	10	66 2/3	81	34	29	25	62
— Milwaukee (N.L.)................	0	0	...	2.91	13	0	0	0	0	21 2/3	11	7	7	2	18
— Louisville (I.L.).................	0	0	...	3.60	5	0	0	0	0	5	4	2	2	0	0
1999— Milwaukee (N.L.)	0	1	.000	6.48	7	0	0	0	0	8 1/3	12	6	6	7	5
Major League totals (2 years).......	0	1	.000	3.90	20	0	0	0	0	30	23	13	13	9	23

DECKER, STEVE　　　　　C　　　　　ANGELS

PERSONAL: Born October 25, 1965, in Rock Island, Ill. ... 6-3/220. ... Bats right, throws right. ... Full name: Steven Michael Decker.
HIGH SCHOOL: Rock Island (Ill.).
COLLEGE: Lewis-Clark State College (Idaho).
TRANSACTIONS/CAREER NOTES: Selected by San Francisco Giants organization in 21st round of free-agent draft (June 1, 1988). ... Selected by Florida Marlins in second round (35th pick overall) of expansion draft (November 17, 1992). ... On disabled list (May 18, 1993-remainder of season). ... On disabled list (April 8-May 14, 1994). ... Granted free agency (October 16, 1995). ... Signed by San Francisco Giants (April 5, 1996). ... Contract sold to Colorado Rockies (August 21, 1996). ... Released by Rockies (March 26, 1997). ... Signed by Tacoma, Seattle Mariners organization (April 8, 1997). ... Released by Mariners (September 2, 1997). ... Signed by Pittsburgh Pirates (November 24, 1997). ... Released by Pirates (May 8, 1998). ... Signed by New York Mets (May 10, 1998). ... Granted free agency (October 15, 1998). ... Signed by Anaheim Angels organization (November 18, 1998). ... Granted free agency (October 13, 1999). ... Re-signed by Angels organization (November 4, 1999).
STATISTICAL NOTES: Led Pacific Coast League catchers with 626 putouts and 694 total chances in 1992.

Year Team (League)	Pos.	G	AB	R	H	2B	3B	HR	RBI	Avg.	BB	SO	SB	PO	A	E	Avg.
1988— Everett (N'west)..........	C	13	42	11	22	2	0	2	13	.524	7	5	0	37	3	2	.952
— San Jose (Calif.).........	C	47	175	31	56	9	0	4	34	.320	21	21	0	199	26	5	.978
1989— San Jose (Calif.).........	C-1B	64	225	27	65	12	0	3	46	.289	44	36	8	417	51	7	.985
— Shreveport (Texas).......	C-1B	44	142	19	46	8	0	1	18	.324	11	24	0	229	22	5	.980
1990— Shreveport (Texas).......	C	116	403	52	118	22	1	15	80	.293	40	64	3	650	71	10	.986
— San Francisco (N.L.) ..	C	15	54	5	16	2	0	3	8	.296	1	10	0	75	11	1	.989
1991— San Francisco (N.L.) ..	C	79	233	11	48	7	1	5	24	.206	16	44	0	385	41	7	.984
— Phoenix (PCL)............	C	31	111	20	28	5	1	6	14	.252	13	29	0	156	16	1	.994
1992— Phoenix (PCL)............	C-1B	125	450	50	127	22	2	8	74	.282	47	64	2	†650	65	5	.993
— San Francisco (N.L.) ..	C	15	43	3	7	1	0	0	1	.163	6	7	0	94	4	0	1.000
1993— Florida (N.L.)■..........	C	8	15	0	0	0	0	0	1	.000	3	3	0	28	2	1	.968
1994— Edmonton (PCL)	C-DH-1B	73	259	38	101	23	0	11	48	.390	27	24	0	295	34	8	.976
1995— Florida (N.L.)..........	C-1B	51	133	12	30	2	1	3	13	.226	19	22	1	299	24	5	.985
1996— San Fran. (N.L.)■......	C-1B-3B	57	122	16	28	1	0	1	12	.230	15	26	0	203	17	0	1.000
— Colo. Springs (PCL)■	C	7	25	4	10	1	0	0	3	.400	4	3	0	56	4	1	.984
— Colorado (N.L.)	C	10	25	8	8	2	0	1	8	.320	3	3	1	51	6	0	1.000
1997— Tacoma (PCL)■ C-3B-DH-1B		99	350	44	104	25	1	10	52	.297	22	37	0	400	68	6	.987
1998— Nashville (PCL)■........	C	18	62	5	8	3	0	2	4	.129	5	14	0	119	10	0	1.000
— Norfolk (I.L.)■ 1B-C-DH-3B		102	354	55	111	21	0	12	60	.314	54	49	0	726	60	9	.989
1999— Edmonton (PCL)■.......3B-1B-DH-C		64	225	51	64	19	2	15	51	.284	44	38	0	169	72	7	.972
— Anaheim (A.L.)	C-1B-DH	28	63	5	15	6	0	0	5	.238	13	9	0	103	8	1	.991
American League totals (1 year)		28	63	5	15	6	0	0	5	.238	13	9	0	103	8	1	.991
National League totals (6 years)		235	625	55	137	15	2	13	67	.219	63	115	2	1135	105	14	.989
Major League totals (7 years)		263	688	60	152	21	2	13	72	.221	76	124	2	1238	113	15	.989

DEHAAN, KORY　　　　　OF　　　　　PADRES

PERSONAL: Born July 16, 1976, in Pella, Iowa. ... 6-2/187. ... Bats left, throws right. ... Full name: Korwin Jay Dehaan.
HIGH SCHOOL: Pella (Iowa) Christian.
COLLEGE: Morningside College (Iowa).
TRANSACTIONS/CAREER NOTES: Selected by Pittsburgh Pirates organization in seventh round of free-agent draft (June 3, 1997). ... Selected by San Diego Padres from Pirates organization in Rule 5 major league draft (December 13, 1999).

Year Team (League)	Pos.	G	AB	R	H	2B	3B	HR	RBI	Avg.	BB	SO	SB	PO	A	E	Avg.
1997— Erie (NY-P)..........	OF	58	205	43	49	8	6	1	18	.239	38	43	14	105	0	1	.991
1998— Augusta (SAL)...........	OF	132	475	85	149	*39	8	8	75	.314	69	114	33	244	7	4	.984
1999— Lynchburg (Caro.)......	OF	78	295	55	96	19	5	7	42	.325	36	63	32	164	2	4	.976
— Altoona (East.)	OF	47	190	26	51	13	2	3	24	.268	11	46	14	88	1	1	.989

DeHART, RICK　　　　　P

PERSONAL: Born March 21, 1970, in Topeka, Kan. ... 6-1/190. ... Throws left, bats left. ... Full name: Richard Allen DeHart.
HIGH SCHOOL: Seaman (Topeka, Kan.).
COLLEGE: Washburn (Kan.).
TRANSACTIONS/CAREER NOTES: Signed as non-drafted free agent by Montreal Expos organization (March 24, 1992). ... Contract sold by Expos to Hiroshima Toyo Carp of the Japan Central League (June 11, 1999).

Year	League	W	L	Pct.	ERA	G	GS	CG	ShO	Sv.	IP	H	R	ER	BB	SO
1992—Albany (SAL)		9	6	.600	2.46	38	10	1	1	3	117	91	42	32	40	133
1993—San Bernardino (Calif.)		4	3	.571	3.04	9	9	0	0	0	53 1/3	56	26	18	25	44
—Harrisburg (East.)		2	4	.333	7.68	12	7	0	0	0	34	45	31	29	19	18
—West Palm Beach (FSL)		1	3	.250	3.00	7	7	1	1	0	42	42	14	14	17	33
1994—West Palm Beach (FSL)		9	7	.563	3.37	30	20	3	2	0	136 1/3	132	61	51	34	68
1995—Harrisburg (East.)		6	7	.462	4.84	35	12	0	0	0	93	94	62	50	39	64
1996—Harrisburg (East.)		1	2	.333	2.68	30	2	0	0	1	43 2/3	46	19	13	19	30
1997—Ottawa (I.L.)		0	4	.000	4.00	43	0	0	0	2	63	60	33	28	22	57
—Montreal (N.L.)		2	1	.667	5.52	23	0	0	0	0	29 1/3	33	21	18	14	29
1998—Montreal (N.L.)		0	0	...	4.82	26	0	0	0	1	28	34	22	15	13	14
—Ottawa (I.L.)		7	1	.875	3.23	38	0	0	0	4	53	46	19	19	17	48
1999—Ottawa (I.L.)		2	4	.333	4.78	15	2	0	0	0	26 1/3	33	19	14	11	22
—Montreal (N.L.)		0	0	...	21.60	3	0	0	0	0	1 2/3	6	4	4	3	1
—Hiroshima (Jp. Cen.)■		0	1	...	8.53	6	1	0	0	0	6 1/3	13	8	6	5	3
Major League totals (3 years)		2	1	.667	5.64	52	0	0	0	1	59	73	47	37	30	44

DeJEAN, MIKE   P   ROCKIES

PERSONAL: Born September 28, 1970, in Baton Rouge, La. ... 6-2/212. ... Throws right, bats right. ... Full name: Michael Dwain DeJean.
HIGH SCHOOL: Walker (La.).
JUNIOR COLLEGE: Mississippi Delta Community College.
COLLEGE: Livingston (La.).
TRANSACTIONS/CAREER NOTES: Selected by New York Yankees organization in 24th round of free-agent draft (June 1, 1992). ... On disabled list (June 4-July 21 and July 26, 1993-remainder of season). ... Traded by Yankees with a player to be named later to Colorado Rockies for C Joe Girardi (November 20, 1995); Rockies acquired P Steve Shoemaker to complete deal (December 6, 1995). ... On Colorado disabled list (July 18-August 8, 1997); included rehabilitation assignment to New Haven (July 30-August 8). ... On disabled list (September 2, 1998-remainder of season). ... On Colorado disabled list (August 14-September 1, 1999); included rehabilitation assignment to Colorado Springs (August 30-September 1).

Year	League	W	L	Pct.	ERA	G	GS	CG	ShO	Sv.	IP	H	R	ER	BB	SO
1992—Oneonta (NY-P)		0	0	...	0.44	20	0	0	0	16	20 2/3	12	3	1	3	20
1993—Greensboro (SAL)		2	3	.400	5.00	20	0	0	0	9	18	22	12	10	8	16
1994—Tampa (FSL)		0	2	.000	2.38	34	0	0	0	16	34	39	15	9	13	22
—Albany (East.)		0	2	.000	4.38	16	0	0	0	4	24 2/3	22	14	12	15	13
1995—Norwich (East.)		5	5	.500	2.99	59	0	0	0	20	78 1/3	58	29	26	34	57
1996—Colo. Springs (PCL)■		0	2	.000	5.13	30	0	0	0	1	40 1/3	52	24	23	21	31
—New Haven (East.)		0	0	...	3.22	16	0	0	0	11	22 1/3	20	9	8	8	12
1997—Colo. Springs (PCL)		0	1	.000	5.40	10	0	0	0	4	10	17	6	6	7	9
—Colorado (N.L.)		5	0	1.000	3.99	55	0	0	0	2	67 2/3	74	34	30	24	38
—New Haven (East.)		0	1	.000	6.00	2	0	0	0	0	3	3	2	2	2	2
1998—Colorado (N.L.)		3	1	.750	3.03	59	1	0	0	2	74 1/3	78	29	25	24	27
1999—Colorado (N.L.)		2	4	.333	8.41	56	0	0	0	0	61	83	61	57	32	31
—Colo. Springs (PCL)		0	0	...	0.00	1	0	0	0	0	1	1	0	0	0	0
Major League totals (3 years)		10	5	.667	4.97	170	1	0	0	4	203	235	124	112	80	96

DEL TORO, MIGUEL   P   GIANTS

PERSONAL: Born June 22, 1972, in Sonora, Mexico. ... 6-1/180. ... Throws right, bats right. ... Full name: Miguel Alfonso Del Toro.
HIGH SCHOOL: Cobash (San Ignacio, Mexico).
TRANSACTIONS/CAREER NOTES: Signed as non-drafted free agent by Pittsburgh Pirates organization (April 3, 1992). ... Granted free agency (October 16, 1998). ... Signed by San Francisco Giants organization (November 20, 1998).

Year	League	W	L	Pct.	ERA	G	GS	CG	ShO	Sv.	IP	H	R	ER	BB	SO
1992—Gulf Coast Pirates (GCL)		2	5	.286	3.43	10	1	1	0	1	60 1/3	64	30	23	21	42
1993—M.C. Red Devils (Mex.)		0	0	...	7.94	5	0	0	0	0	5 2/3	7	7	5	5	2
1994—M.C. Red Devils (Mex.)		0	0	...	6.97	12	0	0	0	0	10 1/3	14	8	8	8	8
1995—Reynosa (Mex.)		5	4	.556	2.25	37	0	0	0	16	68	54	23	17	43	49
1996—Reynosa (Mex.)		1	1	.500	4.11	32	0	0	0	7	46	45	27	21	36	29
1997—M.C. Red Devils (Mex.)		0	0	...	3.75	26	0	0	0	0	36	21	18	15	32	30
1998—M.C. Red Devils (Mex.)		9	4	.692	3.82	39	10	0	0	5	92	81	41	39	44	56
1999—San Francisco (N.L.)■		0	0	...	4.18	14	0	0	0	0	23 2/3	24	11	11	11	20
—Fresno (PCL)		4	2	.667	4.42	40	0	0	0	0	71 1/3	76	41	35	29	71
Major League totals (1 year)		0	0	...	4.18	14	0	0	0	0	23 2/3	24	11	11	11	20

DELGADO, CARLOS   1B   BLUE JAYS

PERSONAL: Born June 25, 1972, in Aguadilla, Puerto Rico. ... 6-3/225. ... Bats left, throws right. ... Full name: Carlos Juan Delgado.
HIGH SCHOOL: Jose de Diego (Aguadilla, Puerto Rico).
TRANSACTIONS/CAREER NOTES: Signed as non-drafted free agent by Toronto Blue Jays organization (October 9, 1988). ... On Toronto disabled list (March 15-April 24, 1998); included rehabilitation assignment to Dunedin (April 17-19) and Syracuse (April 20-24).
HONORS: Named Florida State League Most Valuable Player (1992). ... Named Southern League Most Valuable Player (1993). ... Named first baseman on THE SPORTING NEWS A.L. Silver Slugger team (1999).
STATISTICAL NOTES: Led New York-Pennsylvania League catchers with 540 total chances and six double plays in 1990. ... Led South Atlantic League with 29 passed balls in 1991. ... Led Florida State League with 281 total bases, .579 slugging percentage, .402 on-base percentage and 11 intentional bases on balls received in 1992. ... Led Florida State League catchers with 784 total chances in 1992. ... Led Southern League with .524 slugging percentage, .430 on-base percentage and 18 intentional bases on balls received in 1993. ... Led Southern League catchers with 800 total chances in 1993. ... Led International League with .610 slugging percentage in 1995. ... Led International League with seven intentional bases on balls received in 1995. ... Had 19-game hitting streak (May 21-June 9, 1998). ... Hit three home runs in one game (August 4, 1998 and August 6, 1999). ... Led A.L. first baseman with 134 double plays in 1999. ... Career major league grand slams: 5.

Year	Team (League)	Pos.	G	AB	R	H	2B	3B	HR	RBI	Avg.	BB	SO	SB	PO	A	E	Avg.
1989—St. Cath. (NY-P).........	C	31	89	9	16	5	0	0	11	.180	23	39	0	63	13	2	.974	
1990—St. Cath. (NY-P).........	C	67	228	30	64	13	0	6	39	.281	35	65	2	*471	*62	7	.987	
1991—Myrtle Beach (SAL)....	C	132	441	72	126	18	2	18	70	.286	75	97	9	679	*100	19	.976	
—Syracuse (I.L.)..........	C	1	3	0	0	0	0	0	0	.000	0	2	0	5	0	0	1.000	
1992—Dunedin (FSL).........	C	133	485	83	*157	•30	2	*30	*100	.324	59	91	2	*684	89	11	.986	
1993—Knoxville (Sou.).........	C	140	468	91	142	28	0	*25	*102	.303	*102	98	10	*683	*103	*14	.983	
—Toronto (A.L.).............	DH-C	2	0	0	0	0	0	0	0	.000	1	0	0	2	0	0	1.000	
1994—Toronto (A.L.).............	OF-C	43	130	17	28	2	0	9	24	.215	25	46	1	56	2	2	.967	
—Syracuse (I.L.).............	DH-C-1B	85	307	52	98	11	0	19	58	.319	42	58	1	235	25	7	.974	
1995—Toronto (A.L.).............	OF-DH-1B	37	91	7	15	3	0	3	11	.165	6	26	0	54	2	0	1.000	
—Syracuse (I.L.).............	1B-OF	91	333	59	106	23	4	22	74	.318	45	78	0	724	49	4	.995	
1996—Toronto (A.L.).............	DH-1B	138	488	68	132	28	2	25	92	.270	58	139	0	221	13	4	.983	
1997—Toronto (A.L.).............	1B-DH	153	519	79	136	42	3	30	91	.262	64	133	0	962	67	12	.988	
1998—Dunedin (FSL).............	DH-1B	4	16	4	5	1	0	2	7	.313	2	4	0	13	0	0	1.000	
—Syracuse (I.L.).............	1B	2	7	4	4	2	0	1	6	.571	2	0	0	22	2	0	1.000	
—Toronto (A.L.).............	1B-DH	142	530	94	155	43	1	38	115	.292	73	139	3	1165	87	10	.992	
1999—Toronto (A.L.).............	1B-DH	152	573	113	156	39	0	44	134	.272	86	141	1	*1306	84	*14	.990	
Major League totals (7 years)		667	2332	378	622	157	6	149	467	.267	313	624	5	3766	255	42	.990	

DELGADO, WILSON — SS/2B — GIANTS

PERSONAL: Born July 15, 1975, in San Cristobal, Dominican Republic. ... 5-11/160. ... Bats both, throws right. ... Full name: Wilson Duran Delgado.

TRANSACTIONS/CAREER NOTES: Signed as non-drafted free agent by Seattle Mariners organization (October 29, 1992). ... Traded by Mariners with P Shawn Estes to San Francisco Giants for P Salomon Torres (May 21, 1995).

STATISTICAL NOTES: Led Pacific Coast League shortstops with 197 putouts, 547 total chances and 86 double plays in 1997.

Year	Team (League)	Pos.	G	AB	R	H	2B	3B	HR	RBI	Avg.	BB	SO	SB	PO	A	E	Avg.
1993—Dom. Mariners (DSL).	IF	60	171	19	50	8	0	0	26	.292	34	25	5	96	148	16	.938	
1994—Ariz. Mariners (Ariz.)..	SS-2B	39	149	30	56	5	4	0	10	*.376	15	24	13	58	114	10	.945	
1995—Wisconsin (Midw.)....	SS	19	70	13	17	3	0	0	7	.243	3	15	3	29	65	6	.940	
—Burlington (Midw.)■..	SS	93	365	52	113	20	3	5	37	.310	32	57	9	127	285	19	.956	
1996—San Jose (Calif.).......	SS	121	462	59	124	19	6	2	54	.268	48	89	8	192	343	24	.957	
—Phoenix (PCL)........	SS	12	43	1	6	0	1	0	1	.140	3	7	0	30	47	2	.975	
—San Francisco (N.L.) ..	SS	6	22	3	8	0	0		2	.364	1	5	1	12	12	1	.960	
1997—San Francisco (N.L.) ..	2B-SS	8	7	1	1	1	0	0	0	.143	0	2	0	2	3	0	1.000	
—Phoenix (PCL)........	SS-2B	119	416	47	120	22	4	9	59	.288	24	70	9	†208	347	18	.969	
1998—Fresno (PCL).............	SS	127	512	87	142	22	2	12	63	.277	52	92	9	205	373	23	.962	
—San Francisco (N.L.) ..	SS	10	12	1	2	1	0	0	1	.167	1	3	0	3	6	0	1.000	
1999—Fresno (PCL).............	SS-DH-2B	57	213	28	64	10	3	1	33	.300	18	35	4	86	166	15	.944	
—San Francisco (N.L.) ..	SS-2B	35	71	7	18	2	1	0	3	.254	5	9	1	39	42	5	.942	
Major League totals (4 years)		59	112	12	29	4	1	0	6	.259	7	19	2	56	63	6	.952	

DELLAERO, JASON — SS — WHITE SOX

PERSONAL: Born December 17, 1976, in Mount Kisco, N.Y. ... 6-2/195. ... Bats both, throws right. ... Full name: Jason Christopher Dellaero.
HIGH SCHOOL: Brewster (N.Y.).
COLLEGE: South Florida.
TRANSACTIONS/CAREER NOTES: Selected by New York Mets organization in 17th round of free-agent draft (June 2, 1994); did not sign. ... Selected by Chicago White Sox organization in first round (15th pick overall) of free-agent draft (June 3, 1997).

Year	Team (League)	Pos.	G	AB	R	H	2B	3B	HR	RBI	Avg.	BB	SO	SB	PO	A	E	Avg.
1997—GC White Sox (GCL) ..	SS	5	15	1	3	2	0	0	1	.200	1	2	0	5	6	2	.846	
—Hickory (SAL).............	SS	55	191	37	53	10	3	6	29	.277	17	49	3	79	150	14	.942	
1998—Win.-Salem (Car.).......	SS	121	428	45	89	23	3	10	49	.208	25	147	12	183	306	*46	.914	
1999—Win.-Salem (Car.).......	SS	54	184	22	41	13	0	2	19	.223	18	59	9	89	170	19	.932	
—Birmingham (Sou.).....	SS-DH	81	272	40	73	13	3	10	44	.268	14	76	6	138	227	20	.948	
—Chicago (A.L.).............	SS	11	33	1	3	0	0	0	2	.091	1	13	0	16	28	4	.917	
Major League totals (1 year)		11	33	1	3	0	0	0	2	.091	1	13	0	16	28	4	.917	

DELLUCCI, DAVID — OF — DIAMONDBACKS

PERSONAL: Born October 31, 1973, in Baton Rouge, La. ... 5-10/180. ... Bats left, throws left. ... Full name: David Michael Dellucci. ... Name pronounced duh-LOO-chee.
HIGH SCHOOL: Catholic (Baton Rouge, La.).
COLLEGE: Mississippi.
TRANSACTIONS/CAREER NOTES: Selected by Baltimore Orioles organization in 10th round of free agent draft (June 1, 1995). ... Selected by Arizona Diamondbacks in second round (45th pick overall) of expansion draft (November 18, 1997). ... On disabled list (July 25, 1999-remainder of season).
MISCELLANEOUS: Holds Arizona Diamondbacks all-time record for most triples (13).

Year	Team (League)	Pos.	G	AB	R	H	2B	3B	HR	RBI	Avg.	BB	SO	SB	PO	A	E	Avg.
1995—Frederick (Caro.)	OF	28	96	16	27	3	0	1	10	.281	12	10	1	26	2	1	.966	
—Bluefield (Appl.)	OF	20	69	11	23	5	1	2	12	.333	6	7	3	11	0	2	.846	
1996—Frederick (Caro.)	OF	59	185	33	60	11	1	4	28	.324	38	34	5	100	4	3	.972	
—Bowie (East.)	OF	66	251	27	73	14	1	2	33	.291	28	56	2	134	5	3	.979	

Year	Team (League)	Pos.	G	AB	R	H	2B	3B	HR	RBI	Avg.	BB	SO	SB	PO	A	E	Avg.
									BATTING							FIELDING		
1997—Bowie (East.).............		OF-DH	107	385	71	126	29	3	20	55	.327	58	69	11	162	2	1	.994
—Baltimore (A.L.).............		OF-DH	17	27	3	6	1	0	1	3	.222	4	7	0	20	1	0	1.000
1998—Tucson (PCL)■		OF	17	72	17	22	4	3	1	11	.306	5	8	4	38	0	0	1.000
—Arizona (N.L.).............		OF	124	416	43	108	19	*12	5	51	.260	33	103	3	230	3	3	.987
1999—Arizona (N.L.).............		OF-DH	63	109	27	43	7	1	1	15	.394	11	24	2	37	1	0	1.000
American League totals (1 year)			17	27	3	6	1	0	1	3	.222	4	7	0	20	1	0	1.000
National League totals (2 years)			187	525	70	151	26	13	6	66	.288	44	127	5	267	4	3	.989
Major League totals (3 years)			204	552	73	157	27	13	7	69	.284	48	134	5	287	5	3	.990

DeLUCIA, RICH P

PERSONAL: Born October 7, 1964, in Reading, Pa. ... 6-0/190. ... Throws right, bats right. ... Full name: Richard Anthony DeLucia. ... Name pronounced duh-LOO-sha.
HIGH SCHOOL: Wyomissing (Pa.) Area.
COLLEGE: Tennessee.
TRANSACTIONS/CAREER NOTES: Selected by Toronto Blue Jays organization in 15th round of free-agent draft (June 3, 1985); did not sign. ... Selected by Seattle Mariners organization in sixth round of free-agent draft (June 2, 1986). ... On disabled list (April 10, 1987-remainder of season). ... On disabled list (May 31-July 2 and July 7, 1989-remainder of season). ... On Seattle disabled list (August 5-September 1, 1992); included rehabilitation assignment to Calgary (August 26-31). ... On Seattle disabled list (June 28-July 22, 1993); included rehabilitation assignment to Calgary (July 16-22). ... Released by Mariners (March 29, 1994). ... Signed by Cincinnati Reds organization (April 2, 1994). ... Granted free agency (October 15, 1994). ... Signed by Rochester, Baltimore Orioles organization (November 17, 1994). ... Selected by St. Louis Cardinals from Orioles organization in Rule 5 major league draft (December 5, 1994). ... Traded by Cardinals with P Allen Watson and P Doug Creek to San Francisco Giants for SS Royce Clayton and a player to be named later (December 14, 1995); Cardinals acquired 2B Chris Wimmer to complete deal (January 16, 1996). ... On San Francisco disabled list (March 25-May 2 and July 27-August 23, 1996); included rehabilitation assignments to San Jose (April 25-May 2 and August 18-23). ... Traded by Giants to Anaheim Angels for a player to be named later (April 14, 1997); Giants acquired P Travis Thurmond to complete deal (May 2, 1997). ... On Anaheim disabled list (July 15-September 2, 1997). ... Granted free agency (October 31, 1997). ... Re-signed by Angels (December 7, 1997). ... On suspended list (June 15-16, 1998). ... Released by Angels (March 30, 1999). ... Signed by Cleveland Indians organization (April 5, 1999). ... On Buffalo disabled list (August 4-13, 1999). ... Granted free agency (October 4, 1999).
STATISTICAL NOTES: Pitched seven-inning, 1-0 no-hit victory against Everett (July 17, 1986). ... Led A.L. with 31 home runs allowed in 1991.

Year	League	W	L	Pct.	ERA	G	GS	CG	ShO	Sv.	IP	H	R	ER	BB	SO
1986—Bellingham (N'west)...........	8	2	.800	*1.70	13	11	1	•1	0	74	44	20	14	24	69
1987—Salinas (Calif.).................	0	0	...	9.00	1	0	0	0	0	1	2	1	1	0	1
1988—San Bernardino (Calif.).......	7	8	.467	3.10	22	22	0	0	0	127 2/3	110	57	44	59	118
1989—Williamsport (East.)...........	3	4	.429	3.79	10	10	0	0	0	54 2/3	59	28	23	13	41
1990—San Bernardino (Calif.).......	4	1	.800	2.05	5	5	1	0	0	30 2/3	19	9	7	3	35
—Williamsport (East.)...........	6	6	.500	2.11	18	18	2	1	0	115	92	30	27	30	76
—Calgary (PCL).....................	2	2	.500	3.62	5	5	1	0	0	32 1/3	30	17	13	12	23
—Seattle (A.L.).....................	1	2	.333	2.00	5	5	1	0	0	36	30	9	8	9	20
1991—Seattle (A.L.).................	12	13	.480	5.09	32	31	0	0	0	182	176	107	103	78	98
1992—Seattle (A.L.).................	3	6	.333	5.49	30	11	0	0	1	83 2/3	100	55	51	35	66
—Calgary (PCL).....................	4	2	.667	2.45	8	5	2	1	1	40 1/3	32	11	11	14	38
1993—Seattle (A.L.).................	3	6	.333	4.64	30	1	0	0	0	42 2/3	46	24	22	23	48
—Calgary (PCL).....................	1	5	.167	5.73	8	7	0	0	1	44	45	30	28	20	38
1994—Indianapolis (A.A.)■	5	1	.833	2.30	36	0	0	0	19	43	22	12	11	24	52
—Cincinnati (N.L.).................	0	0	...	4.22	8	0	0	0	0	10 2/3	9	6	5	5	15
1995—St. Louis (N.L.)■..............	8	7	.533	3.39	56	1	0	0	0	82 1/3	63	38	31	36	76
1996—San Jose (Calif.)■.............	0	0	...	2.45	5	4	0	0	0	7 1/3	5	2	2	3	11
—San Francisco (N.L.)..........	3	6	.333	5.84	56	0	0	0	0	61 2/3	62	44	40	31	55
1997—San Francisco (N.L.)..........	0	0	...	10.80	3	0	0	0	0	1 2/3	6	3	2	0	2
—Anaheim (A.L.)■.................	6	4	.600	3.61	33	0	0	0	3	42 1/3	29	18	17	27	42
1998—Anaheim (A.L.).................	2	6	.250	4.27	61	0	0	0	3	71 2/3	56	36	34	46	73
1999—Buffalo (I.L.)■.................	2	3	.400	4.18	44	0	0	0	19	47 1/3	39	24	22	29	46
—Cleveland (A.L.).................	0	1	.000	6.75	6	0	0	0	0	9 1/3	13	7	7	9	7
A.L. totals (7 years)	27	38	.415	4.66	197	48	1	0	7	467 2/3	450	256	242	227	354
N.L. totals (4 years)	11	13	.458	4.49	123	1	0	0	0	156 1/3	140	91	78	72	148
Major League totals (10 years).....	38	51	.427	4.62	320	49	1	0	7	624	590	347	320	299	502

DEMPSTER, RYAN P MARLINS

PERSONAL: Born May 3, 1977, in Sachelt, B.C. ... 6-1/201. ... Throws right, bats right. ... Full name: Ryan Scott Dempster.
HIGH SCHOOL: Elphinstone (Gibsons, B.C.).
TRANSACTIONS/CAREER NOTES: Selected by Texas Rangers organization in third round of free-agent draft (June 1, 1995). ... Traded by Rangers with a player to be named later to Florida Marlins for P John Burkett (August 8, 1996); Marlins acquired P Rick Helling to complete deal (September 3, 1996).
MISCELLANEOUS: Appeared in one game as pinch runner (1999).

Year	League	W	L	Pct.	ERA	G	GS	CG	ShO	Sv.	IP	H	R	ER	BB	SO
1995—GC Rangers (GCL)..........	3	1	.750	2.36	8	6	1	0	0	34 1/3	34	21	9	17	37
—Hudson Valley (NY-P).........	1	0	1.000	3.18	1	1	0	0	0	5 2/3	7	2	2	1	6
1996—Charleston, S.C. (SAL).......	7	11	.389	3.30	23	23	2	0	0	144 1/3	120	71	53	58	141
—Kane County (Midw.)■●	2	1	.667	2.73	4	4	1	1	0	26 1/3	18	10	8	18	16
1997—Brevard County (FSL).......	10	9	.526	4.90	28	26	2	1	0	165 1/3	190	100	*90	46	131
1998—Portland (East.).................	4	3	.571	3.22	7	7	0	0	0	44 2/3	34	20	16	15	33
—Florida (N.L.).....................	1	5	.167	7.08	14	11	0	0	0	54 2/3	72	47	43	38	35
—Charlotte (I.L.)...................	3	1	.750	3.27	5	5	1	0	0	33	33	14	12	12	24
1999—Calgary (PCL)...................	1	1	.500	4.99	5	5	0	0	0	30 2/3	30	17	17	10	29
—Florida (N.L.).....................	7	8	.467	4.71	25	25	0	0	0	147	146	77	77	93	126
Major League totals (2 years).......	8	13	.381	5.36	39	36	0	0	0	201 2/3	218	124	120	131	161

D

DePAULA, SEAN   P   INDIANS

PERSONAL: Born November 7, 1973, in Newton, Mass. ... 6-4/215. ... Throws right, bats right.
HIGH SCHOOL: Pinkerton Academy (Derry, N.H.), then Cushing Academy (Ashburnham, Mass.).
COLLEGE: Wake Forest.
TRANSACTIONS/CAREER NOTES: Selected by Boston Red Sox organization in eighth round of free-agent draft (June 3, 1993); did not sign. ... Selected by Cleveland Indians organization in ninth round of free-agent draft (June 4, 1996).

Year League	W	L	Pct.	ERA	G	GS	CG	ShO	Sv.	IP	H	R	ER	BB	SO
1996—Burlington (Appl.)	4	2	.667	3.82	23	0	0	0	1	35 1/3	31	16	15	13	42
—Watertown (NY-P)	0	0	...	0.00	1	0	0	0	0	2	0	0	0	0	5
1997—Columbus (SAL)	4	5	.444	5.20	29	1	0	0	0	71	71	56	41	43	75
—Watertown (NY-P)	1	1	.500	2.84	9	0	0	0	0	19	21	6	6	8	17
1998—Kinston (Caro.)	3	2	.600	2.36	28	1	0	0	1	49 2/3	50	20	13	18	59
—Akron (East.)	1	1	.500	4.76	8	1	0	0	0	17	16	10	9	15	17
1999—Kinston (Caro.)	4	2	.667	2.28	23	0	0	0	7	51 1/3	36	17	13	17	75
—Akron (East.)	1	0	1.000	3.54	14	0	0	0	1	28	20	11	11	17	31
—Buffalo (I.L.)	0	0	...	0.00	5	0	0	0	2	5	0	0	0	3	7
—Cleveland (A.L.)	0	0	...	4.63	11	0	0	0	0	11 2/3	8	6	6	3	18
Major League totals (1 year)	0	0	...	4.63	11	0	0	0	0	11 2/3	8	6	6	3	18

DIVISION SERIES RECORD

Year League	W	L	Pct.	ERA	G	GS	CG	ShO	Sv.	IP	H	R	ER	BB	SO
1999—Cleveland (A.L.)	0	0	...	1.80	3	0	0	0	0	5	2	1	1	3	5

DeROSA, MARK   SS   BRAVES

PERSONAL: Born February 2, 1975, in Passaic, N.J. ... 6-1/190. ... Bats right, throws right. ... Full name: Mark Thomas DeRosa.
HIGH SCHOOL: Bergen Catholic (Oradell, N.J.).
JUNIOR COLLEGE: Pennsylvania.
TRANSACTIONS/CAREER NOTES: Selected by Atlanta Braves organization in seventh round of free-agent draft (June 4, 1996).

Year Team (League)	Pos.	G	AB	R	H	2B	3B	HR	RBI	Avg.	BB	SO	SB	PO	A	E	Avg.
1996—Eugene (N'west)	SS	70	255	43	66	13	1	2	28	.259	38	48	3	82	196	24	.921
1997—Durham (Caro.)	SS	92	346	51	93	11	3	8	37	.269	25	73	6	136	245	21	.948
1998—Greenville (Sou.)	SS	125	461	67	123	26	2	8	49	.267	60	57	7	195	338	20	*.964
—Atlanta (N.L.)	SS	5	3	2	1	0	0	0	0	.333	0	1	0	1	1	0	1.000
1999—Richmond (I.L.)	SS-DH	105	364	41	99	16	2	1	40	.272	21	49	7	139	249	20	.951
—Atlanta (N.L.)	SS	7	8	0	0	0	0	0	0	.000	0	2	0	2	2	0	1.000
Major League totals (2 years)		12	11	2	1	0	0	0	0	.091	0	3	0	3	3	0	1.000

DeSHIELDS, DELINO   2B   ORIOLES

PERSONAL: Born January 15, 1969, in Seaford, Del. ... 6-1/175. ... Bats left, throws right. ... Full name: Delino Lamont DeShields. ... Name pronounced duh-LINE-oh.
HIGH SCHOOL: Seaford (Del.).
COLLEGE: Villanova.
TRANSACTIONS/CAREER NOTES: Selected by Montreal Expos organization in first round (12th pick overall) of free-agent draft (June 2, 1987). ... On disabled list (June 16-July 12, 1990 and August 12-September 11, 1993). ... Traded by Expos to Los Angeles Dodgers for P Pedro J. Martinez (November 19, 1993). ... On disabled list (May 26-June 20, 1994). ... Granted free agency (October 29, 1996). ... Signed by St. Louis Cardinals (November 20, 1996). ... On St. Louis disabled list (July 5-August 10, 1998); included rehabilitation assignment to Arkansas (August 5-10). ... Granted free agency (October 23, 1998). ... Signed by Baltimore Orioles (December 7, 1998). ... On Baltimore disabled list (March 25-April 11, June 21-July 23 and October 1, 1999-remainder of season); included rehabilitation assignments to Bowie (April 9-11 and July 20-22), Delmarva (July 15-16) and Frederick (July 17-19).
RECORDS: Shares modern N.L. record for most hits in first major league game—4 (April 9, 1990). ... Shares major league single-game record for most strikeouts (nine-inning game)—5 (September 17, 1991, second game).
STATISTICAL NOTES: Led Gulf Coast League shortstops with 22 errors in 1987. ... Had 21-game hitting streak (June 28-July 21, 1993). ... Had 18-game hitting streak (May 30-June 20, 1998). ... Career major league grand slams: 1.

Year Team (League)	Pos.	G	AB	R	H	2B	3B	HR	RBI	Avg.	BB	SO	SB	PO	A	E	Avg.
1987—GC Expos (GCL)	SS-3B	31	111	17	24	5	2	1	4	.216	21	30	16	47	90	†22	.862
—Jamestown (NY-P)	SS	34	96	16	21	1	2	1	5	.219	24	28	14	25	57	21	.796
1988—Rockford (Midw.)	SS	129	460	97	116	26	6	12	46	.252	95	110	59	173	344	42	.925
1989—Jacksonville (Sou.)	SS	93	307	55	83	10	6	3	35	.270	76	80	37	127	218	34	.910
—Indianapolis (A.A.)	SS	47	181	29	47	8	4	2	14	.260	16	53	16	73	101	13	.930
1990—Montreal (N.L.)	2B	129	499	69	144	28	6	4	45	.289	66	96	42	236	371	12	.981
1991—Montreal (N.L.)	2B	151	563	83	134	15	4	10	51	.238	95	*151	56	285	405	*27	.962
1992—Montreal (N.L.)	2B	135	530	82	155	19	8	7	56	.292	54	108	46	251	360	15	.976
1993—Montreal (N.L.)	2B	123	481	75	142	17	7	2	29	.295	72	64	43	243	381	11	.983
1994—Los Angeles (N.L.)■..	2B-SS	89	320	51	80	11	3	2	33	.250	54	53	27	156	282	7	.984
1995—Los Angeles (N.L.)	2B	127	425	66	109	18	3	8	37	.256	63	83	39	204	330	•11	.980
1996—Los Angeles (N.L.)	2B	154	581	75	130	12	8	5	41	.224	53	124	48	274	400	17	.975
1997—St. Louis (N.L.)■	2B	150	572	92	169	26	*14	11	58	.295	55	72	55	272	398	19	.972
1998—St. Louis (N.L.)■	2B-1B	117	420	74	122	21	8	7	44	.290	56	61	26	247	273	9	.983
—Arkansas (Texas)	2B-DH	4	13	1	2	0	0	0	0	.154	2	6	0	6	5	0	1.000
1999—Bowie (East.)■	2B-DH	4	15	2	4	1	0	0	0	.267	3	2	0	5	5	0	1.000
—Baltimore (N.L.)	2B	96	330	46	87	11	2	6	34	.264	37	52	11	178	249	10	.977
—Delmarva (SAL)	2B	2	7	1	2	0	0	1	2	.286	1	1	0	4	5	0	1.000
—Frederick (Caro.)	2B	2	8	1	1	0	0	1	2	.125	0	1	0	5	5	0	1.000
American League totals (1 year)		96	330	46	87	11	2	6	34	.264	37	52	11	178	249	10	.977
National League totals (9 years)		1175	4391	667	1185	167	61	56	394	.270	568	812	382	2168	3200	128	.977
Major League totals (10 years)		1271	4721	713	1272	178	63	62	428	.269	605	864	393	2346	3449	138	.977

Year	Team (League)	Pos.	G	AB	R	H	2B	3B	HR	RBI	Avg.	BB	SO	SB	PO	A	E	Avg.
							BATTING									FIELDING		
1995—	Los Angeles (N.L.)	2B	3	12	1	3	0	0	0	0	.250	1	3	0	8	7	0	1.000
1996—	Los Angeles (N.L.)	2B	2	4	0	0	0	0	0	0	.000	0	1	0	3	2	0	1.000
Division series totals (2 years)			5	16	1	3	0	0	0	0	.188	1	4	0	11	9	0	1.000

DESSENS, ELMER   P   REDS

PERSONAL: Born January 13, 1972, in Hermosillo, Mexico. ... 6-0/187. ... Throws right, bats right. ... Full name: Elmer Dessens Jusaino. ... Name pronounced DAH-cenz.

HIGH SCHOOL: Carrera Technica (Hermosillo, Mexico).

TRANSACTIONS/CAREER NOTES: Signed as non-drafted free agent by Pittsburgh Pirates organization (January 27, 1993). ... Loaned by Pirates organization to Mexico City Red Devils of Mexican League for 1993 and 1994 seasons; returned to Pirates organization for 1995 season. ... Loaned by Pirates organization to Red Devils (May 7, 1996). ... Returned to Pirates organization (June 21, 1996). ... On Pittsburgh disabled list (July 31-September 10, 1996); included rehabilitation assignment to Carolina (August 16-September 10). ... Loaned by Pirates to Red Devils (March 27, 1997). ... Returned to Pirates (September 5, 1997). ... On Pittsburgh disabled list (April 8-24, 1998); included rehabilitation assignment to Nashville (April 21-24). ... Released by Pirates (March 31, 1999). ... Played in Japan (1999). ... Signed by Cincinnati Reds (December 15, 1999).

Year	League	W	L	Pct.	ERA	G	GS	CG	ShO	Sv.	IP	H	R	ER	BB	SO
1993—	M.C. Red Devils (Mex.)	3	1	.750	2.35	14	0	0	0	2	30²/₃	31	8	8	5	16
1994—	M.C. Red Devils (Mex.)	11	4	.733	2.04	37	15	4	1	3	127²/₃	121	37	29	32	51
1995—	Carolina (Sou.)■	*15	8	.652	*2.49	27	27	1	0	0	152	170	62	42	21	68
1996—	Calgary (PCL)	2	2	.500	3.15	6	6	0	0	0	34¹/₃	40	14	12	15	15
	—M.C. Red Devils (Mex.)■ ..	7	0	1.000	1.26	7	7	1	0	0	50	44	12	7	10	17
	—Pittsburgh (N.L.)■	0	2	.000	8.28	15	3	0	0	0	25	40	23	23	4	13
	—Carolina (Sou.)■	0	1	.000	5.40	5	1	0	0	0	11²/₃	15	8	7	4	7
1997—	M.C. Red Devils (Mex.)■ ...	•16	5	.762	3.56	26	25	3	1	0	159¹/₃	156	73	63	51	61
	—Pittsburgh (N.L.)	0	0	...	0.00	3	0	0	0	0	3¹/₃	2	0	0	0	2
1998—	Pittsburgh (N.L.)	2	6	.250	5.67	43	5	0	0	0	74²/₃	90	50	47	25	43
	—Nashville (PCL)	3	1	.750	3.30	6	5	0	0	0	30	32	12	11	6	13
1999—	Yomiuri (Jap. Cen.)■	0	1	.000	3.86	6	0	0	0	0	16¹/₃	24	7	7	4	6
Major League totals (3 years)		2	8	.200	6.12	61	8	0	0	0	103	132	73	70	29	58

DEWEY, JASON   C   ANGELS

D

PERSONAL: Born April 18, 1977, in Syracuse, N.Y. ... 6-1/190. ... Bats right, throws right. ... Full name: Jason M. Dewey.

HIGH SCHOOL: Brandon (Fla.).

JUNIOR COLLEGE: Indian River Community College (Fla.).

TRANSACTIONS/CAREER NOTES: Selected by California Angels organization in 26th round of free-agent draft (June 4, 1996). ... Angels franchise renamed Anaheim Angels for 1997 season.

STATISTICAL NOTES: Led California League with 30 passed balls in 1998.

Year	Team (League)	Pos.	G	AB	R	H	2B	3B	HR	RBI	Avg.	BB	SO	SB	PO	A	E	Avg.
							BATTING									FIELDING		
1997—	Boise (N'west)	C	68	272	55	88	17	2	13	64	.324	41	70	5	*483	36	5	.990
1998—	Lake Elsinore (Calif.) ..	C-OF	111	391	64	115	30	3	15	66	.294	66	118	8	599	62	13	.981
1999—	Erie (East.)	C	40	139	17	31	7	0	4	14	.223	17	50	0	277	28	6	.981
	—Lake Elsinore (Calif.) ..	C-DH	66	242	48	78	23	0	10	31	.322	30	62	0	443	45	8	.984

DeWITT, MATT   P   BLUE JAYS

PERSONAL: Born September 4, 1977, in San Bernardino, Calif. ... 6-3/210. ... Throws right, bats right. ... Full name: Matthew B. DeWitt.

HIGH SCHOOL: Valley (Las Vegas).

TRANSACTIONS/CAREER NOTES: Selected by St. Louis Cardinals organization in 10th round of free-agent draft (June 1, 1995). ... Traded by Cardinals with P Lance Painter and C Alberto Castillo to Toronto Blue Jays for P Pat Hentgen and P Paul Spoljaric (November 11, 1999).

STATISTICAL NOTES: Led Appalachian League pitchers with 17 home runs allowed in 1996.

Year	League	W	L	Pct.	ERA	G	GS	CG	ShO	Sv.	IP	H	R	ER	BB	SO
1995—	Johnson City (Appl.)	2	6	.250	7.04	13	12	0	0	0	62²/₃	84	56	*49	32	45
1996—	Johnson City (Appl.)	5	5	.500	5.42	14	*14	0	0	0	*79²/₃	66	53	48	26	58
1997—	Peoria (Midw.)	9	9	.500	4.09	27	•27	1	0	0	158¹/₃	152	84	72	57	121
1998—	Prince William (Caro.)	6	9	.400	3.64	24	24	1	0	0	148¹/₃	132	65	60	18	118
1999—	Arkansas (Texas)	9	8	.529	4.43	26	26	3	0	0	148¹/₃	153	87	73	59	107

DIAZ, ALEX   OF

PERSONAL: Born October 5, 1968, in Brooklyn, N.Y. ... 5-11/180. ... Bats both, throws right. ... Full name: Alexis Diaz. ... Son of Mario Caballero Diaz, minor league infielder (1959-64).

HIGH SCHOOL: Manuel Mendez Licihea (Puerto Rico).

TRANSACTIONS/CAREER NOTES: Signed as non-drafted free agent by New York Mets organization (August 24, 1986). ... Traded by Mets with OF Darren Reed to Montreal Expos for OF Terrel Hansen and P David Sommer (April 2, 1991). ... On suspended list (August 30, 1991-remainder of season). ... Traded by Expos organization to Milwaukee Brewers organization for IF George Canale (October 15, 1991). ... On Milwaukee disabled list (May 3-August 30, 1993); included rehabilitation assignment to New Orleans (August 13-30). ... Granted free agency (December 20, 1993). ... Re-signed by Brewers (December 21, 1993). ... On disabled list (July 31, 1994-remainder of season). ... Claimed on waivers by Seattle Mariners (October 14, 1994). ... On Seattle disabled list (June 5-August 4 and August 12-September 2, 1996); included rehabilitation assignments to Tacoma (July 15-August 4 and August 31-September 2). ... Granted free agency (October 8, 1996). ... Signed by Mets organization (November 19, 1996). ... Released by Mets organization (April 13, 1997). ... Signed by Texas Rangers organization (April 16, 1997). ... Granted free agency (October 15, 1997). ... Signed by San Francisco Giants organization (January 21, 1998). ... On Fresno disabled list (July 24-September 14, 1998). ... Released by Giants (September 14, 1998). ... Signed by Houston Astros organization (January 21, 1999). ... On disabled list (June 21-August 31, 1999). ... Released by Astros (August 31, 1999).

Year	Team (League)	Pos.	G	AB	R	H	2B	3B	HR	RBI	Avg.	BB	SO	SB	PO	A	E	Avg.
1987—	Kingsport (Appl.)........	SS	54	212	29	56	9	1	0	13	.264	16	31	*34	67	126	18	.915
—	Little Falls (NY-P)	SS	12	47	7	16	4	1	0	8	.340	2	3	2	13	22	4	.897
1988—	Columbia (SAL).........	SS	123	481	82	126	14	*11	0	37	.262	21	49	28	175	299	*72	.868
—	St. Lucie (FSL)	SS	3	6	2	0	0	0	0	1	.000	0	4	0	3	3	3	.667
1989—	St. Lucie (FSL)	SS-OF	102	416	54	106	11	10	1	33	.255	20	38	43	151	244	28	.934
—	Jackson (Texas)	2B	23	95	11	26	5	1	2	9	.274	3	11	3	25	65	3	.968
1990—	Tidewater (I.L.).........	OF-2B-SS	124	437	55	112	15	2	1	36	.256	30	39	23	196	101	11	.964
1991—	Indianapolis (A.A.)■..OF-SS-3B-2B		108	370	48	90	14	4	1	21	.243	27	46	17	207	45	8	.969
1992—	Denver (A.A.)■.........	OF-2B-SS	106	455	67	122	17	4	1	41	.268	24	36	42	240	43	7	.976
—	Milwaukee (A.L.)........	OF-DH	22	9	5	1	0	0	0	1	.111	0	0	3	10	0	0	1.000
1993—	Milwaukee (A.L.)........	OF-DH	32	69	9	22	2	0	0	1	.319	0	12	5	46	1	1	.979
—	New Orleans (A.A.).....	OF	16	55	8	16	2	0	0	5	.291	3	6	7	38	1	0	1.000
1994—	Milwaukee (A.L.)	OF-2B-DH	79	187	17	47	5	7	1	17	.251	10	19	5	138	11	2	.987
1995—	Seattle (A.L.)■..........	OF	103	270	44	67	14	0	3	27	.248	13	27	18	145	4	2	.987
—	Tacoma (PCL)	OF-DH	10	40	3	10	1	0	0	4	.250	2	5	1	15	1	0	1.000
1996—	Seattle (A.L.)	OF-DH	38	79	11	19	2	0	1	5	.241	2	8	6	55	1	1	.982
—	Tacoma (PCL)	OF-DH-3B	44	176	19	43	5	0	0	7	.244	7	20	5	76	5	2	.976
1997—	Norfolk (I.L.)■..........	OF	7	26	0	2	1	0	0	1	.077	2	3	0	10	2	1	.923
—	Okla. City (A.A.)■.......O-2-DH-P-S		1	426	65	122	25	2	12	49	.286	33	53	26	180	52	10	.959
—	Texas (A.L.)	OF-1B-DH	28	90	8	20	4	0	2	12	.222	5	13	1	54	3	1	.983
1998—	San Fran. (N.L.)■.......	OF	34	62	5	8	2	0	0	5	.129	0	15	1	28	2	0	1.000
—	Fresno (PCL)	OF-DH	11	39	2	7	0	0	0	2	.179	2	5	1	8	1	2	.818
1999—	Houston (N.L.)■.......	OF	30	50	3	11	2	0	1	7	.220	3	13	2	8	1	1	.900
American League totals (6 years)			302	704	94	176	27	7	7	63	.250	30	79	38	448	20	7	.985
National League totals (2 years)			64	112	8	19	4	0	1	12	.170	3	28	3	36	3	1	.975
Major League totals (8 years)			366	816	102	195	31	7	8	75	.239	33	107	41	484	23	8	.984

DIVISION SERIES RECORD

Year	Team (League)	Pos.	G	AB	R	H	2B	3B	HR	RBI	Avg.	BB	SO	SB	PO	A	E	Avg.
1995—	Seattle (A.L.)	OF-PH	2	3	0	1	0	0	0	0	.333	1	1	0	1	1	0	1.000

CHAMPIONSHIP SERIES RECORD

Year	Team (League)	Pos.	G	AB	R	H	2B	3B	HR	RBI	Avg.	BB	SO	SB	PO	A	E	Avg.
1995—	Seattle (A.L.)	PH-OF	4	7	0	3	1	0	0	0	.429	1	1	0	1	0	0	1.000

RECORD AS PITCHER

Year	Team (League)	W	L	Pct.	ERA	G	GS	CG	ShO	Sv.	IP	H	R	ER	BB	SO
1997—	Oklahoma City (A.A.)..........	0	0	...	0.00	1	0	0	0	0	1	0	1	0	3	1

DIAZ, EDWIN — 2B/SS — RANGERS

PERSONAL: Born January 15, 1975, in Vega Alta, Puerto Rico. ... 5-11/170. ... Bats right, throws right.
HIGH SCHOOL: Maestro Ladi (Puerto Rico).
TRANSACTIONS/CAREER NOTES: Selected by Texas Rangers organization in second round of free-agent draft (June 3, 1993); pick received as compensation for Chicago Cubs signing Type A free-agent P Jose Guzman. ... Selected by Arizona Diamondbacks in first round (11th pick overall) of expansion draft (November 18, 1997). ... On Arizona disabled list (September 7, 1999-remainder of season). ... Released by Diamondbacks (December 9, 1999). ... Signed by Texas Rangers organization (December 20, 1999).

Year	Team (League)	Pos.	G	AB	R	H	2B	3B	HR	RBI	Avg.	BB	SO	SB	PO	A	E	Avg.
1993—	GC Rangers (GCL)......	2B	43	154	27	47	10	5	1	23	.305	19	21	12	78	100	6	.967
1994—	Char., S.C. (SAL)		122	413	52	109	22	7	11	60	.264	22	107	11	204	303	31	.942
1995—	Charlotte (FSL)	2B-SS	115	450	48	128	26	5	8	56	.284	33	94	8	213	277	16	.968
1996—	Tulsa (Texas)		121	499	70	132	33	6	16	65	.265	25	122	8	238	322	19	.967
1997—	Oklahoma City (A.A.)..	2B-DH	20	73	6	8	3	1	1	4	.110	2	27	1	37	48	6	.934
—	Tulsa (Texas)	2B	105	440	65	121	31	1	15	46	.275	33	102	6	170	312	*19	.962
1998—	Arizona (N.L.)■.........	2B	3	7	0	0	0	0	0	0	.000	0	2	0	7	8	1	.938
—	Tucson (PCL)	2-3-S-DH	131	510	61	134	31	*12	2	49	.263	27	105	9	247	342	28	.955
1999—	Tucson (PCL)	2B-SS-DH	107	415	72	129	24	1	11	50	.311	17	77	6	181	282	20	.959
—	Arizona (N.L.)	2B-SS	4	5	2	2	2	0	0	1	.400	3	1	0	4	5	0	1.000
Major League totals (2 years)			7	12	2	2	2	0	0	1	.167	3	3	0	11	13	1	.960

DIAZ, EINAR — C — INDIANS

PERSONAL: Born December 28, 1972, in Chiniqui, Panama. ... 5-10/165. ... Bats right, throws right. ... Full name: Einar Antonio Diaz.
TRANSACTIONS/CAREER NOTES: Signed as non-drafted free agent by Cleveland Indians organization (October 5, 1990).
STATISTICAL NOTES: Led Appalachian League third basemen with 125 assists and .959 fielding percentage in 1992. ... Led Appalachian League catchers with 54 assists and nine errors in 1993. ... Led South Atlantic League in grounding into double plays with 18 in 1994. ... Led South Atlantic League catchers with 966 total chances, 845 putouts, 112 assists and tied for lead with eight double plays in 1994. ... Led Carolina League catchers with 107 assists and .992 fielding percentage in 1995. ... Led Eastern League catchers with 15 errors in 1996. ... Led American Association catchers with 18 errors in 1997. ... Led International League catchers with 873 total chances in 1998.

Year	Team (League)	Pos.	G	AB	R	H	2B	3B	HR	RBI	Avg.	BB	SO	SB	PO	A	E	Avg.
1991—	Dom. Indians (DSL) ...		62	239	35	67	6	3	1	29	.280	14	5	10				
1992—	Burlington (Appl.).......	3B-SS	52	178	19	37	3	0	1	14	.208	20	9	2	27	†137	7	†.959
1993—	Burlington (Appl.).......	C-3B	60	231	40	69	15	3	5	33	.299	8	7	7	315	†55	†10	.974
—	Columbus (SAL)........	C	1	5	0	0	0	0	0	0	.000	0	1	0	3	1	0	1.000

Year	Team (League)	Pos.	G	AB	R	H	2B	3B	HR	RBI	Avg.	BB	SO	SB	PO	A	E	Avg.
1994—Columbus (SAL)........		C-3B	120	491	67	137	23	2	16	71	.279	17	34	4	†848	†134	9	.991
1995—Kinston (Caro.)..........		C-3B-DH	104	373	46	98	21	0	6	43	.263	12	29	3	676	†111	7	†.991
1996—Cant./Akron (East.).......		C-3B	104	395	47	111	26	2	3	35	.281	12	22	3	765	88	†15	.983
—Cleveland (A.L.)........		C	4	1	0	0	0	0	0	0	.000	0	0	0	4	0	0	1.000
1997—Buffalo (A.A.).............		C-3B	109	336	40	86	18	2	3	31	.256	18	34	2	653	67	†19	.974
—Cleveland (A.L.)........		C	5	7	1	1	1	0	0	1	.143	0	2	0	18	3	1	.955
1998—Cleveland (A.L.)........		C	17	48	8	11	1	0	2	9	.229	3	2	0	101	9	3	.973
—Buffalo (I.L.)........		C	115	415	62	130	21	3	8	63	.313	21	33	3	*791	*70	*12	.986
1999—Cleveland (A.L.)........		C	119	392	43	110	21	1	3	32	.281	23	41	11	751	81	10	.988
Major League totals (4 years)			145	448	52	122	23	1	5	42	.272	26	45	11	874	93	14	.986

DIVISION SERIES RECORD

Year	Team (League)	Pos.	G	AB	R	H	2B	3B	HR	RBI	Avg.	BB	SO	SB	PO	A	E	Avg.
1998—Cleveland (A.L.)........									Did not play.									
1999—Cleveland (A.L.)..........		C-PH	2	1	0	0	0	0	0	0	.000	0	0	0	3	0	0	1.000

CHAMPIONSHIP SERIES RECORD

Year	Team (League)	Pos.	G	AB	R	H	2B	3B	HR	RBI	Avg.	BB	SO	SB	PO	A	E	Avg.
1998—Cleveland (A.L.).........		C	4	4	0	0	0	0	0	0	.000	0	1	0	13	3	0	1.000

DICKSON, JASON   P   ANGELS

PERSONAL: Born March 30, 1973, in London, Ont. ... 6-0/195. ... Throws right, bats left. ... Full name: Jason Royce Dickson.
HIGH SCHOOL: James M. Hill (Chatham, New Brunswick).
JUNIOR COLLEGE: Northeastern Oklahoma A&M.
TRANSACTIONS/CAREER NOTES: Selected by California Angels organization in sixth round of free-agent draft (June 2, 1994). ... Angels franchise renamed Anaheim Angels for 1997 season. ... On disabled list (April 4, 1999-entire season).
HONORS: Named A.L. Rookie Pitcher of the Year by THE SPORTING NEWS (1997).

Year	League	W	L	Pct.	ERA	G	GS	CG	ShO	Sv.	IP	H	R	ER	BB	SO
1994—Boise (N'west)..................		3	1	.750	3.86	9	7	0	0	1	44 1/3	40	22	19	18	37
1995—Cedar Rapids (Midw.).....		14	6	.700	2.86	25	25	*9	1	0	173	151	71	55	45	134
1996—Midland (Texas).............		5	2	.714	3.58	8	8	3	1	0	55 1/3	55	27	22	10	40
—Vancouver (PCL)...............		7	11	.389	3.80	18	18	*7	0	0	130 1/3	134	73	55	40	70
—California (A.L.).................		1	4	.200	4.57	7	7	0	0	0	43 1/3	52	22	22	18	20
1997—Anaheim (A.L.).................		13	9	.591	4.29	33	32	2	1	0	203 2/3	236	111	97	56	115
1998—Anaheim (A.L.).................		10	10	.500	6.05	27	18	0	0	0	122	147	89	82	41	61
—Vancouver (PCL)...............		2	1	.667	1.78	4	4	0	0	0	25 1/3	26	5	5	4	18
1999—Anaheim (A.L.)................								Did not play.								
Major League totals (3 years)......		24	23	.511	4.90	67	57	2	1	0	369	435	222	201	115	196

ALL-STAR GAME RECORD

Year	League	W	L	Pct.	ERA	GS	CG	ShO	Sv.	IP	H	R	ER	BB	SO
1997—American						Did not play.									

DIFELICE, MIKE   C   DEVIL RAYS

PERSONAL: Born May 28, 1969, in Philadelphia. ... 6-2/205. ... Bats right, throws right. ... Full name: Michael William Difelice. ... Name pronounced DEE-fah-lease.
HIGH SCHOOL: Bearden (Knoxville, Tenn.).
COLLEGE: Tennessee.
TRANSACTIONS/CAREER NOTES: Selected by St. Louis Cardinals organization in 11th round of free-agent draft (June 3, 1991). ... Selected by Tampa Bay Devil Rays in first round (20th pick overall) of expansion draft (November 18, 1997).
RECORDS: Shares major league single-season record for fewest double plays by catcher for leader—8 (1998).
STATISTICAL NOTES: Tied for N.L. lead in passed balls with 12 in 1997. ... Tied for A.L. lead in double plays by catcher with eight in 1998.

Year	Team (League)	Pos.	G	AB	R	H	2B	3B	HR	RBI	Avg.	BB	SO	SB	PO	A	E	Avg.
1991—Hamilton (NY-P).........		C	43	157	10	33	5	0	4	15	.210	9	40	1	297	40	9	.974
1992—Hamilton (NY-P).........		C-1B	18	58	11	20	3	0	2	9	.345	4	7	2	135	19	5	.969
—St. Pete. (FSL)...........		C	17	53	0	12	3	0	0	4	.226	3	11	0	73	11	2	.977
1993—Springfield (Midw.)		C	8	20	5	7	1	0	0	3	.350	2	3	0	52	9	0	1.000
—St. Pete. (FSL)...........		C	30	97	5	22	2	0	0	8	.227	11	13	1	165	23	7	.964
1994—Arkansas (Texas).......		C	71	200	19	50	11	2	2	15	.250	12	48	0	419	40	6	.987
1995—Arkansas (Texas)........		C	62	176	14	47	10	1	1	24	.267	23	29	0	327	48	6	.984
—Louisville (A.A.).........		C	21	63	8	17	4	0	0	3	.270	5	11	1	111	10	2	.984
1996—Louisville (A.A.).........		C	79	246	25	70	13	0	9	33	.285	20	43	0	455	48	8	.984
—St. Louis (N.L.)..........		C	4	7	0	2	1	0	0	2	.286	0	1	0	15	1	0	1.000
1997—Arkansas (Texas)........		C	1	3	0	1	1	0	0	0	.333	1	0	0	6	2	0	1.000
—St. Louis (N.L.)..........		C-1B	93	260	16	62	10	1	4	30	.238	19	61	1	587	64	6	.991
—Louisville (A.A.).........		C	1	4	1	1	0	0	1	1	.250	0	1	0	3	1	0	1.000
1998—Tampa Bay (A.L.)■.....		C	84	248	17	57	12	3	3	23	.230	15	56	0	483	52	4	.993
1999—Tampa Bay (A.L.)........		C	51	179	21	55	11	0	6	27	.307	8	23	0	344	28	5	.987
American League totals (2 years)			135	427	38	112	23	3	9	50	.262	23	79	0	827	80	9	.990
National League totals (2 years)			97	267	16	64	11	1	4	32	.240	19	62	1	602	65	6	.991
Major League totals (4 years)			232	694	54	176	34	4	13	82	.254	42	141	1	1429	145	15	.991

DINGMAN, CRAIG — P — YANKEES

PERSONAL: Born March 12, 1974, in Wichita, Kan. ... 6-4/195. ... Throws right, bats right. ... Full name: Craig Allen Dingman.
HIGH SCHOOL: North (Wichita, Kan.).
JUNIOR COLLEGE: Hutchinson (Kan.) Community College.
TRANSACTIONS/CAREER NOTES: Selected by New York Yankees organization in 36th round of free-agent draft (June 3, 1993). ... On disabled list (June 19, 1995-entire season).

Year League	W	L	Pct.	ERA	G	GS	CG	ShO	Sv.	IP	H	R	ER	BB	SO
1994—Gulf Coast Yankees (GCL) ..	0	5	.000	3.38	17	1	0	0	1	32	27	17	12	10	51
1995—							Did not play.								
1996—Oneonta (NY-P)	0	2	.000	2.04	20	0	0	0	9	35 1/3	17	11	8	9	52
1997—Greensboro (SAL)	2	0	1.000	1.91	30	0	0	0	19	33	19	7	7	12	41
—Tampa (FSL)	0	4	.000	5.24	19	0	0	0	6	22 1/3	15	14	13	14	26
1998—Tampa (FSL)	5	4	.556	2.93	50	0	0	0	7	70 2/3	48	29	23	39	95
1999—Norwich (East.)	8	6	.571	1.57	55	0	0	0	9	74 1/3	56	16	13	12	90

DIPOTO, JERRY — P — ROCKIES

PERSONAL: Born May 24, 1968, in Jersey City, N.J. ... 6-2/205. ... Throws right, bats right. ... Full name: Gerard Peter Dipoto III.
HIGH SCHOOL: Toms River (N.J.).
COLLEGE: Virginia Commonwealth.
TRANSACTIONS/CAREER NOTES: Selected by Cleveland Indians organization in third round of free-agent draft (June 5, 1989). ... On Cleveland disabled list (March 25-June 12, 1994); included rehabilitation assignment to Charlotte (May 10-June 8). ... Traded by Indians with P Paul Byrd, P Dave Mlicki and a player to be named later to New York Mets for OF Jeromy Burnitz and P Joe Roa (November 18, 1994); Mets acquired 2B Jesus Azuaje to complete deal (December 6, 1994). ... Traded by Mets to Colorado Rockies for P Armando Reynoso (November 27, 1996). ... Granted free agency (November 3, 1999). ... Re-signed by Rockies (November 17, 1999).
STATISTICAL NOTES: Led Eastern League with 15 wild pitches and tied for lead with three balks in 1991.

Year League	W	L	Pct.	ERA	G	GS	CG	ShO	Sv.	IP	H	R	ER	BB	SO
1989—Watertown (NY-P)	6	5	.545	3.61	14	14	1	0	0	87 1/3	75	42	35	39	98
1990—Kinston (Caro.)	11	4	.733	3.78	24	24	1	0	0	145 1/3	129	75	61	77	143
—Canton/Akron (East.)	1	0	1.000	2.57	3	2	0	0	0	14	11	5	4	4	12
1991—Canton/Akron (East.)	6	11	.353	3.81	28	26	2	0	0	156	143	83	66	74	97
1992—Colo. Springs (PCL)	9	9	.500	4.94	50	9	0	0	2	122	148	78	67	66	62
1993—Charlotte (I.L.)	6	3	.667	1.93	34	0	0	0	12	46 2/3	34	10	10	13	44
—Cleveland (A.L.)	4	4	.500	2.40	46	0	0	0	11	56 1/3	57	21	15	30	41
1994—Charlotte (I.L.)	3	2	.600	3.15	25	2	0	0	9	34 1/3	37	13	12	12	26
—Cleveland (A.L.)	0	0	...	8.04	7	0	0	0	0	15 2/3	26	14	14	10	9
1995—New York (N.L.)■	4	6	.400	3.78	58	0	0	0	2	78 2/3	77	41	33	29	49
1996—New York (N.L.)	7	2	.778	4.19	57	0	0	0	0	77 1/3	91	44	36	45	52
1997—Colorado (N.L.)■	5	3	.625	4.70	74	0	0	0	16	95 2/3	108	56	50	33	74
1998—Colorado (N.L.)	3	4	.429	3.53	68	0	0	0	19	71 1/3	61	31	28	25	49
1999—Colorado (N.L.)	4	5	.444	4.26	63	0	0	0	1	86 2/3	91	44	41	44	69
A.L. totals (2 years)	4	4	.500	3.63	53	0	0	0	11	72	83	35	29	40	50
N.L. totals (5 years)	23	20	.535	4.13	320	0	0	0	38	409 2/3	428	216	188	176	293
Major League totals (7 years)	27	24	.529	4.05	373	0	0	0	49	481 2/3	511	251	217	216	343

DiSARCINA, GARY — SS — ANGELS

PERSONAL: Born November 19, 1967, in Malden, Mass. ... 6-2/194. ... Bats right, throws right. ... Full name: Gary Thomas DiSarcina. ... Brother of Glenn DiSarcina, shortstop in Chicago White Sox organization (1991-96). ... Name pronounced DEE-sar-SEE-na.
HIGH SCHOOL: Billerica (Mass.) Memorial.
COLLEGE: Massachusetts.
TRANSACTIONS/CAREER NOTES: Selected by California Angels organization in sixth round of free-agent draft (June 1, 1988). ... On disabled list (August 27, 1993-remainder of season and August 4-September 17, 1995). ... Angels franchise renamed Anaheim Angels for 1997 season. ... On Anaheim disabled list (March 24-June 22, 1999); included rehabilitation assignments to Lake Elsinore (June 10-14) and Erie (June 15-22).
RECORDS: Holds A.L. single-season record for fewest putouts by shortstop (150 or more games)—212 (1996).
STATISTICAL NOTES: Led Pacific Coast League shortstops with .968 fielding percentage and 419 assists in 1991. ... Led A.L. shortstops with 761 total chances in 1992. ... Led A.L. shortstops with 103 double plays in 1998.

Year Team (League)	Pos.	G	AB	R	H	2B	3B	HR	RBI	Avg.	BB	SO	SB	PO	A	E	Avg.
1988—Bend (N'west)	SS	71	295	40	90	11	•5	2	39	.305	27	34	7	104	*237	27	.927
1989—Midland (Texas)	SS	126	441	65	126	18	7	4	54	.286	24	54	11	206	*411	30	*.954
—California (A.L.)	SS	2	0	0	0	0	0	0	0	...	0	0	0	0	0	0	...
1990—Edmonton (PCL)	SS	97	330	46	70	12	2	4	37	.212	25	46	5	165	289	24	.950
—California (A.L.)	SS-2B	18	57	8	8	1	1	0	0	.140	3	10	1	17	57	4	.949
1991—Edmonton (PCL)	SS-2B	119	390	61	121	21	4	4	58	.310	29	32	16	191	†425	20	†.969
—California (A.L.)	SS-2B-3B	18	57	5	12	2	0	0	3	.211	3	4	0	29	45	4	.949
1992—California (A.L.)	SS	157	518	48	128	19	0	3	42	.247	20	50	9	250	*486	•25	.967
1993—California (A.L.)	SS	126	416	44	99	20	1	3	45	.238	15	38	5	193	362	14	.975
1994—California (A.L.)	SS	112	389	53	101	14	2	3	33	.260	18	28	3	159	*358	9	.983
1995—California (A.L.)	SS	99	362	61	111	28	6	5	41	.307	20	25	7	146	275	6	.986
1996—California (A.L.)	SS	150	536	62	137	26	4	5	48	.256	21	36	2	212	460	20	.971
1997—Anaheim (A.L.)	SS	154	549	52	135	28	2	4	47	.246	17	29	7	227	421	15	.977
1998—Anaheim (A.L.)	SS	157	551	73	158	39	3	3	56	.287	21	51	11	253	437	14	.980
1999—Lake Elsinore (Calif.) ..	SS-DH	4	12	0	1	0	0	0	1	.083	1	0	1	5	1	1	.857
—Erie (East.)	SS	5	20	1	6	0	0	0	2	.300	0	4	0	5	12	0	1.000
—Anaheim (A.L.)	SS	81	271	32	62	7	1	1	29	.229	15	32	2	138	249	15	.963
Major League totals (11 years)		1074	3706	438	951	184	20	27	344	.257	153	303	47	1624	3150	126	.974

Year	League	Pos.	AB	R	H	2B	3B	HR	RBI	Avg.	BB	SO	SB	PO	A	E	Avg.
								BATTING								FIELDING	
1995—American		PR-SS	1	0	0	0	0	0	0	.000	0	0	0	0	0	0	...

DOSTER, DAVE — IF — PHILLIES

PERSONAL: Born October 8, 1970, in Fort Wayne, Ind. ... 5-10/181. ... Bats right, throws right. ... Full name: David Eric Doster.
HIGH SCHOOL: New Haven (Ind.).
COLLEGE: Indiana State.
TRANSACTIONS/CAREER NOTES: Selected by Philadelphia Phillies organization in 27th round of free-agent draft (June 3, 1993).
STATISTICAL NOTES: Led Florida State League second basemen with 743 total chances and 115 double plays in 1994. ... Led Eastern League with 254 total bases in 1995. ... Led Eastern League second basemen with 420 assists, 693 total chances and 91 double plays in 1995. ... Led International League with 10 sacrifice flies in 1998. ... Led International League third basemen with 283 assists and 389 total chances in 1998.

| | | | | | | | | BATTING | | | | | | | | FIELDING | |
Year	Team (League)	Pos.	G	AB	R	H	2B	3B	HR	RBI	Avg.	BB	SO	SB	PO	A	E	Avg.
1993—Spartanburg (SAL)		2B	60	223	34	61	15	0	3	20	.274	25	36	1	111	205	13	.960
—Clearwater (FSL)		2B-3B	9	28	4	10	3	1	0	2	.357	2	2	2	16	29	5	.900
1994—Clearwater (FSL)		2B	131	480	76	135	*42	4	13	74	.281	54	71	12	*278	*445	20	.973
1995—Reading (East.)		2B-OF	139	*551	84	146	39	3	21	79	.265	51	61	11	261	†420	12	.983
1996—Scranton/W.B. (I.L.)		2B	88	322	37	83	20	0	7	48	.258	26	54	7	197	203	6	.985
—Philadelphia (N.L.)		2B-3B	39	105	14	28	8	0	1	8	.267	7	21	0	52	57	3	.973
1997—Scranton/W.B. (I.L.)		2B-3B	108	410	70	129	32	2	16	79	.315	30	60	5	152	248	14	.966
1998—Scranton/W.B. (I.L.)		3B-2B-SS	*141	*579	79	160	38	4	16	84	.276	51	80	23	107	†312	20	.954
1999—Philadelphia (N.L.)		2B-3B-SS	99	97	9	19	2	0	3	10	.196	12	23	1	78	88	1	.994
Major League totals (2 years)			138	202	23	47	10	0	4	18	.233	19	44	1	130	145	4	.986

DOTEL, OCTAVIO — P — ASTROS

PERSONAL: Born November 25, 1975, in Santo Domingo, Dominican Republic. ... 6-0/175. ... Throws right, bats right. ... Full name: Octavio Eduardo Dotel. ... Brother of Angel Dotel, third baseman in Los Angeles Dodgers organization (1991-93).
HIGH SCHOOL: Liceo Eansino Afuera (Dominican Republic).
TRANSACTIONS/CAREER NOTES: Signed as non-drafted free agent by New York Mets organization (March 20, 1993). ... On disabled list (July 18-August 16, 1996). ... On Binghamton disabled list (June 3-24, 1997). ... On Norfolk disabled list (May 7-17, 1999). ... Traded by Mets with OF Roger Cedeno and P Kyle Kessel to Houston Astros for P Mike Hampton and OF Derek Bell (December 23, 1999).

D

Year	League	W	L	Pct.	ERA	G	GS	CG	ShO	Sv.	IP	H	R	ER	BB	SO
1993—Dom. Mets (DSL)		6	2	.750	4.10	...	11	0	0	0	59 1/3	46	30	27	38	48
1994—Dom. Mets (DSL)		5	0	1.000	4.32	15	14	1	0	0	81 1/3	84	53	39	31	95
1995—Gulf Coast Mets (GCL)		•7	4	.636	2.18	13	12	2	0	0	*74 1/3	48	23	18	17	*86
—St. Lucie (FSL)		1	0	1.000	5.63	3	0	0	0	8	8	10	5	5	4	9
1996—Columbia (SAL)		11	3	.786	3.59	22	19	0	0	0	115 1/3	89	49	46	49	142
1997—St. Lucie (FSL)		5	2	.714	2.52	9	8	1	1	0	50	44	18	14	23	39
—Binghamton (East.)		3	4	.429	5.98	12	12	0	0	0	55 2/3	66	50	37	38	40
—Gulf Coast Mets (GCL)		0	0	...	0.96	3	2	0	0	1	9 1/3	9	1	1	2	7
1998—Binghamton (East.)		4	2	.667	1.97	10	10	2	1	0	68 2/3	41	19	15	24	82
—Norfolk (I.L.)		8	6	.571	3.45	17	16	1	0	0	99	82	47	38	43	118
1999—Norfolk (I.L.)		5	2	.714	3.84	13	13	1	0	0	70 1/3	52	33	30	34	90
—New York (N.L.)		8	3	.727	5.38	19	14	0	0	0	85 1/3	69	52	51	49	85
Major League totals (1 year)		8	3	.727	5.38	19	14	0	0	0	85 1/3	69	52	51	49	85

DIVISION SERIES RECORD

Year	League	W	L	Pct.	ERA	G	GS	CG	ShO	Sv.	IP	H	R	ER	BB	SO
1999—New York (N.L.)		0	0	...	54.00	1	0	0	0	0	1/3	1	2	2	2	0

CHAMPIONSHIP SERIES RECORD

Year	League	W	L	Pct.	ERA	G	GS	CG	ShO	Sv.	IP	H	R	ER	BB	SO
1999—New York (N.L.)		1	0	1.000	3.00	1	0	0	0	0	3	4	1	1	2	5

DOUGHERTY, JIM — P — CARDINALS

PERSONAL: Born March 8, 1968, in Brentwood, N.Y. ... 6-0/210. ... Throws right, bats right. ... Full name: James E. Dougherty.
HIGH SCHOOL: Ross (Brentwood, N.Y.).
COLLEGE: North Carolina.
TRANSACTIONS/CAREER NOTES: Selected by Houston Astros organization in 26th round of free-agent draft (June 4, 1990). ... On disabled list (August 22, 1994-remainder of season). ... Released by Astros (January 9, 1997). ... Signed by New York Mets organization (March 11, 1997). ... Granted free agency (October 15, 1997). ... Signed by Oakland Athletics organization (December 5, 1997). ... Granted free agency (October 15, 1998). ... Signed by Pittsburgh Pirates organization (December 22, 1998). ... Granted free agency (October 4, 1999). ... Signed by St. Louis Cardinals organization (January 19, 2000).

Year	League	W	L	Pct.	ERA	G	GS	CG	ShO	Sv.	IP	H	R	ER	BB	SO
1991—Asheville (SAL)		3	1	.750	1.52	62	0	0	0	28	83	63	17	14	25	78
1992—Osceola (FSL)		5	2	.714	1.56	57	0	0	0	31	81	66	21	14	22	77
1993—Jackson (Texas)		2	2	.500	1.87	52	0	0	0	*36	53	39	15	11	21	55
1994—Tucson (PCL)		5	4	.556	4.12	55	0	0	0	*21	59	70	32	27	30	49
1995—Houston (N.L.)		8	4	.667	4.92	56	0	0	0	0	67 2/3	76	37	37	25	49
—Tucson (PCL)		1	0	1.000	3.27	8	0	0	0	1	11	11	4	4	5	12
1996—Tucson (PCL)		4	3	.571	3.50	46	0	0	0	1	61 2/3	65	35	24	27	53
—Houston (N.L.)		0	2	.000	9.00	12	0	0	0	0	13	14	14	13	11	6
1997—Norfolk (I.L.)■		10	1	*.909	1.45	49	0	0	0	4	62	45	11	10	43	59

Year League	W	L	Pct.	ERA	G	GS	CG	ShO	Sv.	IP	H	R	ER	BB	SO
1998— Oakland (A.L.)■	0	2	.000	8.25	9	0	0	0	0	12	17	11	11	7	3
— Edmonton (PCL)	2	1	.667	3.75	45	0	0	0	6	57 2/3	57	24	24	33	45
1999— Nashville (PCL)■	3	3	.500	5.43	53	0	0	0	10	59 2/3	69	38	36	27	55
— Pittsburgh (N.L.)	0	0	...	9.00	2	0	0	0	0	2	3	3	2	3	1
A.L. totals (1 year)	0	2	.000	8.25	9	0	0	0	0	12	17	11	11	7	3
N.L. totals (3 years)	8	6	.571	5.66	70	0	0	0	0	82 2/3	93	54	52	39	56
Major League totals (4 years)	8	8	.500	5.99	79	0	0	0	0	94 2/3	110	65	63	46	59

DOWNS, SCOTT   P   CUBS

PERSONAL: Born March 17, 1976, in Louisville, Ky. ... 6-2/190. ... Throws left, bats left. ... Full name: Scott Jeremy Downs.
HIGH SCHOOL: Pleasure Ridge Park (Louisville, Ky.).
COLLEGE: Kentucky.
TRANSACTIONS/CAREER NOTES: Selected by Chicago Cubs organization in third round of free-agent draft (June 3, 1997). ... Traded by Cubs to Minnesota Twins (November 3, 1998), completing deal in which Twins traded P Mike Morgan to Cubs for cash and a player to be named later (August 25, 1998). ... Traded by Twins with P Rick Aguilera to Cubs for P Kyle Lohse and P Jason Ryan (May 21, 1999).

Year League	W	L	Pct.	ERA	G	GS	CG	ShO	Sv.	IP	H	R	ER	BB	SO
1997— Williamsport (NY-P)	0	2	.000	2.74	5	5	0	0	0	23	15	11	7	7	28
— Rockford (Midw.)	3	0	1.000	1.25	5	5	0	0	0	36	17	5	5	8	43
1998— Daytona (FSL)	8	9	.471	3.90	27	27	2	0	0	161 2/3	179	83	70	55	117
1999— New Britain (East.)■	0	0	...	8.69	6	3	0	0	0	19 2/3	33	21	19	10	22
— Fort Myers (FSL)	0	1	.000	0.00	2	2	0	0	0	9 2/3	7	3	0	6	9
— Daytona (FSL)■	5	0	1.000	1.88	7	7	1	1	0	48	41	12	10	11	41
— West Tenn (Sou.)	8	1	.889	1.35	13	12	1	0	0	80	56	13	12	28	101

DRANSFELDT, KELLY   SS   RANGERS

PERSONAL: Born April 16, 1975, in Joliet, Ill. ... 6-2/195. ... Bats right, throws right. ... Full name: Kelly D. Dransfeldt.
HIGH SCHOOL: Morris (Ill.).
COLLEGE: Michigan.
TRANSACTIONS/CAREER NOTES: Selected by Texas Rangers organization in fourth round of free-agent draft (June 4, 1996). ... On Oklahoma disabled list (June 29-July 7, 1999).
STATISTICAL NOTES: Led New York-Pennsylvania League shortstops with 391 total chances in 1996. ... Led Florida State League shortstops with 227 putouts and 85 double plays in 1997.

Year Team (League)	Pos.	G	AB	R	H	2B	3B	HR	RBI	Avg.	BB	SO	SB	PO	A	E	Avg.
1996— Hudson Valley (NY-P).	SS	75	284	42	67	17	1	7	29	.236	27	76	13	*117	*253	*21	.946
1997— Charlotte (FSL)	SS-3B	135	466	64	106	20	7	6	58	.227	42	115	25	†227	369	36	.943
1998— Charlotte (FSL)	SS	67	245	46	79	17	0	18	76	.322	29	67	7	100	205	19	.941
— Tulsa (Texas)	SS	58	226	43	57	15	4	9	36	.252	18	79	8	81	184	14	.950
1999— Oklahoma (PCL).........	SS-2B-DH	102	359	55	85	21	2	10	44	.237	24	108	6	162	297	19	.960
— Texas (A.L.)	SS	16	53	3	10	1	0	1	5	.189	3	12	0	31	54	3	.966
Major League totals (1 year)		16	53	3	10	1	0	1	5	.189	3	12	0	31	54	3	.966

DREIFORT, DARREN   P   DODGERS

PERSONAL: Born May 3, 1972, in Wichita, Kan. ... 6-2/211. ... Throws right, bats right. ... Full name: Darren John Dreifort. ... Name pronounced DRY-fert.
HIGH SCHOOL: Wichita (Kan.) Heights.
COLLEGE: Wichita State.
TRANSACTIONS/CAREER NOTES: Selected by New York Mets organization in 11th round of free-agent draft (June 4, 1990); did not sign. ... Selected by Los Angeles Dodgers organization in first round (second pick overall) of free-agent draft (June 3, 1993). ... On San Antonio disabled list (July 7-28, 1994). ... On Albuquerque disabled list (August 27, 1994-remainder of season). ... On disabled list (April 23, 1995-entire season). ... On Los Angeles disabled list (March 25-May 16, 1996); included rehabilitation assignment to Albuquerque (April 18-May 15). ... On disabled list (May 12-June 17, 1997); included rehabilitation assignment to Albuquerque (June 11-17).
HONORS: Named righthanded pitcher on THE SPORTING NEWS college All-America team (1992-93). ... Named Golden Spikes Award winner by USA Baseball (1993).
STATISTICAL NOTES: Tied for N.L. lead with four balks in 1999.
MISCELLANEOUS: Member of 1992 U.S. Olympic baseball team. ... Singled with an RBI in one game as pinch hitter with Los Angeles (1994). ... Made an out in only appearance as pinch hitter with Los Angeles (1996). ... Received a base on balls in only appearance as pinch hitter (1998).

Year League	W	L	Pct.	ERA	G	GS	CG	ShO	Sv.	IP	H	R	ER	BB	SO
1994— Los Angeles (N.L.)	0	5	.000	6.21	27	0	0	0	6	29	45	21	20	15	22
— San Antonio (Texas)	3	1	.750	2.80	8	8	0	0	0	35 1/3	36	14	11	13	32
— Albuquerque (PCL)	1	0	1.000	5.68	1	1	0	0	0	6 1/3	8	4	4	3	3
1995— Los Angeles (N.L.)						Did not play.									
1996— Albuquerque (PCL)	5	6	.455	4.17	18	18	0	0	0	86 1/3	88	49	40	52	75
— Los Angeles (N.L.)	1	4	.200	4.94	19	0	0	0	0	23 2/3	23	13	13	12	24
1997— Los Angeles (N.L.)	5	2	.714	2.86	48	0	0	0	4	63	45	21	20	34	63
— Albuquerque (PCL)	0	0	...	1.59	2	2	0	0	0	5 2/3	2	1	1	1	3
1998— Los Angeles (N.L.)	8	12	.400	4.00	32	26	1	1	0	180	171	84	80	57	168
1999— Los Angeles (N.L.)	13	13	.500	4.79	30	29	1	1	0	178 2/3	177	105	95	76	140
Major League totals (5 years)	27	36	.429	4.33	156	55	2	2	10	474 1/3	461	244	228	194	417

DIVISION SERIES RECORD

Year League	W	L	Pct.	ERA	G	GS	CG	ShO	Sv.	IP	H	R	ER	BB	SO
1996— Los Angeles (N.L.)	0	0	...	0.00	1	0	0	0	0	2/3	0	0	0	0	0

DREW, J.D.　　　　　　　OF　　　　　　　CARDINALS

PERSONAL: Born November 20, 1975, in Valdosta, Ga. ... 6-1/195. ... Bats left, throws right. ... Full name: David Jonathan Drew. ... Brother of Tim Drew, pitcher, Cleveland Indians organization.
HIGH SCHOOL: Lowndes County (Hahira, Ga.).
COLLEGE: Florida State.
TRANSACTIONS/CAREER NOTES: Selected by San Francisco Giants organization in 20th round of free-agent draft (June 2, 1994); did not sign. ... Selected by Philadelphia Phillies organization in first round (second pick overall) of free-agent draft (June 3, 1997); did not sign. ... Selected by St. Louis Cardinals organization in first round (fifth pick overall) of free-agent draft (June 2, 1998). ... On Arkansas disabled list (July 21-August 6, 1998). ... On St. Louis disabled list (May 16-June 17, 1999); included rehabilitation assignment to Memphis (May 28-June 17).
HONORS: Named Golden Spikes Award winner by USA Baseball (1997). ... Named college Player of the Year by THE SPORTING NEWS (1997). ... Named outfielder on THE SPORTING NEWS college All-America team (1997).
STATISTICAL NOTES: Led N.L. outfielders with six double plays in 1999.

| | | | | | | | BATTING | | | | | | | | FIELDING | | |
Year Team (League)	Pos.	G	AB	R	H	2B	3B	HR	RBI	Avg.	BB	SO	SB	PO	A	E	Avg.
1997—St. Paul (Northern).....	OF	44	170	51	58	6	1	18	50	.341	30	40	5	...	...	...	...
1998—St. Paul (Northern).....	OF	30	114	27	44	11	2	9	33	.386	21	32	8	...	...	...	...
—Arkansas (Texas)■.....	OF	19	67	18	22	3	1	5	11	.328	13	15	2	46	2	1	.980
—Memphis (PCL).........	OF	26	79	15	25	8	1	2	13	.316	22	18	1	54	3	2	.966
—St. Louis (N.L.).........	OF	14	36	9	15	3	1	5	13	.417	4	10	0	19	1	0	1.000
1999—St. Louis (N.L.)..........	OF	104	368	72	89	16	6	13	39	.242	50	77	19	235	9	7	.972
—Memphis (PCL).........	OF	25	87	11	26	5	1	2	15	.299	8	20	6	44	2	0	1.000
Major League totals (2 years)		118	404	81	104	19	7	18	52	.257	54	87	19	254	10	7	.974

DuBOSE, ERIC　　　　　　　P　　　　　　　ATHLETICS

PERSONAL: Born May 15, 1976, in Bradenton, Fla. ... 6-3/215. ... Throws left, bats left. ... Full name: Eric Ladell DuBose.
HIGH SCHOOL: Patrician Academy (Butler, Ala.).
COLLEGE: Mississippi State.
TRANSACTIONS/CAREER NOTES: Selected by Oakland Athletics organization in first round (21st pick overall) of free-agent draft (June 3, 1997); pick received as compensation for Baltimore Orioles signing SS Mike Bordick. ... On Midland disabled list (June 18-July 23, 1999).

Year League	W	L	Pct.	ERA	G	GS	CG	ShO	Sv.	IP	H	R	ER	BB	SO
1997—Southern Oregon (N'west) .	1	0	1.000	0.00	3	1	0	0	0	10	5	0	0	6	15
—Visalia (Calif.)...................	1	3	.250	7.04	10	9	0	0	0	38⅓	43	37	30	28	39
1998—Visalia (Calif.)...................	6	1	.857	3.38	17	10	0	0	1	72	56	34	27	25	85
—Huntsville (Sou.)................	7	6	.538	2.70	14	14	1	1	0	83⅓	86	37	25	34	66
1999—Midland (Texas).................	4	2	.667	5.49	21	14	0	0	1	77	89	57	47	44	68

DUCEY, ROB　　　　　　　OF　　　　　　　PHILLIES

PERSONAL: Born May 24, 1965, in Toronto. ... 6-2/183. ... Bats left, throws right. ... Full name: Robert Thomas Ducey.
HIGH SCHOOL: Glenview Park (Toronto).
JUNIOR COLLEGE: Seminole Community College (Fla.).
TRANSACTIONS/CAREER NOTES: Signed as non-drafted free agent by Toronto Blue Jays organization (May 16, 1984). ... On Toronto disabled list (June 9-September 2, 1989); included rehabilitation assignments to Syracuse (July 5-14 and August 24-September 2). ... Traded by Blue Jays with C Greg Myers to California Angels for P Mark Eichhorn (July 30, 1992). ... Released by Angels (November 19, 1992). ... Signed by Texas Rangers organization (December 18, 1992). ... On Oklahoma City disabled list (April 21-May 16, 1993). ... Released by Rangers (October 14, 1994). ... Signed by Nippon Ham Fighters of Japan Pacific League prior to 1995 season. ... Signed by Seattle Mariners organization (January 22, 1997). ... On Seattle disabled list (August 3-21, 1997). ... On disabled list (March 27-April 20, 1998). ... Granted free agency (December 21, 1998). ... Signed by Philadelphia Phillies (December 21, 1998).
STATISTICAL NOTES: Tied for Southern League lead in double plays by outfielder with six in 1986. ... Tied for International League lead in double plays by outfielder with four in 1990.

| | | | | | | | BATTING | | | | | | | | FIELDING | | |
Year Team (League)	Pos.	G	AB	R	H	2B	3B	HR	RBI	Avg.	BB	SO	SB	PO	A	E	Avg.
1984—Medicine Hat (Pio.)....	OF-1B	63	235	49	71	10	3	12	49	.302	41	61	13	185	11	6	.970
1985—Florence (SAL)..........	OF-1B	134	529	78	133	22	2	13	86	.251	49	103	12	228	8	9	.963
1986—Ventura (Calif.).........	OF-1B	47	178	36	60	11	3	12	38	.337	21	24	17	97	3	2	.980
—Knoxville (Sou.).........	OF	88	344	49	106	22	3	11	58	.308	29	59	7	186	10	6	.970
1987—Syracuse (I.L.).........	OF	100	359	62	102	14	•10	10	60	.284	61	89	8	171	13	6	.968
—Toronto (A.L.)............	OF-DH	34	48	12	9	1	0	1	6	.188	8	10	2	31	0	0	1.000
1988—Syracuse (I.L.).........	OF	90	317	40	81	14	4	7	42	.256	43	81	7	233	6	4	.984
—Toronto (A.L.)............	OF-DH	27	54	15	17	4	1	0	6	.315	5	7	1	35	1	0	1.000
1989—Toronto (A.L.)............	OF-DH	41	76	5	16	4	0	0	7	.211	9	25	2	56	3	0	1.000
—Syracuse (I.L.).........	OF	10	29	0	3	0	1	0	3	.103	10	13	0	14	0	1	.933
1990—Syracuse (I.L.).........	OF	127	438	53	117	32	7	7	47	.267	60	87	13	262	13	13	.955
—Toronto (A.L.)............	OF	19	53	7	16	5	0	0	7	.302	7	15	1	37	0	0	1.000
1991—Syracuse (I.L.).........	OF	72	266	53	78	10	3	8	40	.293	51	58	5	120	1	0	1.000
—Toronto (A.L.)............	OF-DH	39	68	8	16	2	2	1	4	.235	6	26	2	32	1	4	.892
1992—Toronto (A.L.)............	OF-DH	23	21	3	1	1	0	0	0	.048	0	10	0	11	0	0	1.000
—California (A.L.)■.......	OF-DH	31	59	4	14	3	0	0	2	.237	5	12	2	32	2	2	.944
1993—Okla. City (A.A.)■.......	OF	105	389	68	118	17	•10	17	56	.303	46	97	17	244	8	7	.973
—Texas (A.L.).............	OF	27	85	15	24	6	3	2	9	.282	10	17	2	51	1	0	1.000
1994—Oklahoma City (A.A.)..	OF-DH	115	403	69	108	27	9	17	65	.268	75	91	9	221	9	4	.983
—Texas (A.L.).............	OF	11	29	1	5	1	0	0	1	.172	2	1	0	15	0	2	.882
1995—Nippon (Jp.Pac.)■.......		117	425	61	106	19	4	25	61	.249	54	103	7	...	...	...	...
1996—Nippon (Jp.Pac.)........	OF	120	427	68	105	17	5	26	59	.246	86	90	3	...	...	...	...

D

Year	Team (League)	Pos.	G	AB	R	H	2B	3B	HR	RBI	Avg.	BB	SO	SB	PO	A	E	Avg.
									BATTING							FIELDING		
1997—Tacoma (PCL)■		OF	23	74	8	24	8	0	0	11	.324	8	15	0	44	3	3	.940
—Seattle (A.L.)		OF	76	143	25	41	15	2	5	10	.287	6	31	3	66	3	1	.986
1998—Seattle (A.L.)		OF	97	217	30	52	18	2	5	23	.240	23	61	4	127	4	4	.970
1999—Philadelphia (N.L.)■		OF-DH	104	188	29	49	10	2	8	33	.261	38	57	2	89	1	0	1.000
American League totals (10 years)			425	853	125	211	60	10	14	75	.247	81	215	19	493	15	13	.975
National League totals (1 year)			104	188	29	49	10	2	8	33	.261	38	57	2	89	1	0	1.000
Major League totals (11 years)			529	1041	154	260	70	12	22	108	.250	119	272	21	582	16	13	.979

DIVISION SERIES RECORD

Year	Team (League)	Pos.	G	AB	R	H	2B	3B	HR	RBI	Avg.	BB	SO	SB	PO	A	E	Avg.
									BATTING							FIELDING		
1997—Seattle (A.L.)		PH-OF	2	4	0	2	0	0	0	1	.500	0	0	0	0	0	0	...

CHAMPIONSHIP SERIES RECORD

Year	Team (League)	Pos.	G	AB	R	H	2B	3B	HR	RBI	Avg.	BB	SO	SB	PO	A	E	Avg.
									BATTING							FIELDING		
1989—Toronto (A.L.)									Did not play.									
1991—Toronto (A.L.)		PR-OF	1	1	0	0	0	0	0	0	.000	0	0	0	0	0	0	...

DUNCAN, CARLOS　　3B/SS　　PHILLIES

PERSONAL: Born June 30, 1977, in San Pedro de Macoris, Dominican Republic. ... 6-1/185. ... Bats right, throws right. ... Full name: Jan Carlos Duncan. ... Brother of Mariano Duncan, infielder with five major league teams (1985-87 and 1989-97).
TRANSACTIONS/CAREER NOTES: Signed as non-drafted free agent by Philadelphia Phillies organization (November 12, 1994). ... On Piedmont disabled list (April 24-May 4 and July 22, 1999-remainder of season).

Year	Team (League)	Pos.	G	AB	R	H	2B	3B	HR	RBI	Avg.	BB	SO	SB	PO	A	E	Avg.
									BATTING							FIELDING		
1995—Dom. Phillies (DSL)		3B	51	182	27	42	7	4	0	25	.231	20	44	8	96	28	11	.919
1996—Dom. Phillies (DSL)		3B	61	227	44	59	8	1	7	35	.260	20	51	23	...	...	...	...
1997—Martinsville (Appl.)		SS	54	204	38	53	8	4	13	33	.260	14	62	11	74	157	29	.888
1998—Piedmont (SAL)		3B-SS	32	111	20	22	3	2	3	12	.198	15	47	8	22	81	17	.858
—Batavia (NY-P)		3B	71	276	55	73	23	4	5	43	.264	29	101	13	41	159	24	.893
1999—Piedmont (SAL)		3B-SS	73	276	41	60	15	3	11	40	.217	19	88	15	83	173	26	.908

DUNN, ADAM　　OF　　REDS

PERSONAL: Born November 9, 1979, in Houston. ... 6-6/235. ... Bats left, throws right. ... Full name: Adam Troy Dunn.
HIGH SCHOOL: New Caney (Texas).
COLLEGE: Texas.
TRANSACTIONS/CAREER NOTES: Selected by Cincinnati Reds organization in second round of free-agent draft (June 2, 1998).

Year	Team (League)	Pos.	G	AB	R	H	2B	3B	HR	RBI	Avg.	BB	SO	SB	PO	A	E	Avg.
									BATTING							FIELDING		
1998—Billings (Pio.)		OF	34	125	26	36	3	1	4	13	.288	22	33	4	35	2	6	.860
1999—Rockford (Midw.)		OF	93	313	62	96	16	2	11	44	.307	46	64	21	85	5	8	.918

DUNSTON, SHAWON　　OF/IF

PERSONAL: Born March 21, 1963, in Brooklyn, N.Y. ... 6-1/180. ... Bats right, throws right. ... Full name: Shawon Donnell Dunston.
HIGH SCHOOL: Thomas Jefferson (Brooklyn, N.Y.).
TRANSACTIONS/CAREER NOTES: Selected by Chicago Cubs organization in first round (first pick overall) of free-agent draft (June 7, 1982). ... On disabled list (May 31-June 10, 1983). ... On Chicago disabled list (June 16-August 21, 1987); included rehabilitation assignment to Iowa (August 14-21). ... On disabled list (May 5, 1992-remainder of season and March 27-September 1, 1993). ... On suspended list (September 8-12, 1995). ... Granted free agency (October 31, 1995). ... Signed by San Francisco Giants (January 9, 1996). ... On disabled list (April 24-May 13 and August 5-October 1, 1996). ... Traded by Cubs (November 18, 1996). ... Signed by Cubs (December 7, 1996). ... On Chicago disabled list (June 9-24, 1997). ... Traded by Cubs to Pittsburgh Pirates for a player to be named later (August 31, 1997). ... Granted free agency (October 28, 1997). ... Signed by Cleveland Indians (February 16, 1998). ... Traded by Indians with P Jose Mesa and P Alvin Morman to Giants for P Steve Reed and OF Jacob Cruz (July 23, 1998). ... Granted free agency (October 23, 1998). ... Signed by St. Louis Cardinals (February 16, 1999). ... On suspended list (June 17-20, 1999). ... On St. Louis disabled list (June 23-July 9, 1999). ... Traded by Cardinals to New York Mets for IF Craig Paquette (July 31, 1999). ... Granted free agency (October 29, 1999).
RECORDS: Shares modern major league single-game record for most triples—3 (July 28, 1990).
HONORS: Named shortstop on THE SPORTING NEWS N.L. All-Star team (1989).
STATISTICAL NOTES: Led N.L. shortstops with 817 total chances and tied for lead in double plays with 96 in 1986. ... Career major league grand slams: 3.

Year	Team (League)	Pos.	G	AB	R	H	2B	3B	HR	RBI	Avg.	BB	SO	SB	PO	A	E	Avg.
									BATTING							FIELDING		
1982—GC Cubs (GCL)		SS-3B	53	190	27	61	11	0	2	28	.321	11	22	32	61	129	24	.888
1983—Quad Cities (Midw.)		SS	117	455	65	141	17	8	4	62	.310	7	51	58	172	326	47	.914
1984—Midland (Texas)		SS	73	298	44	98	13	3	3	34	.329	11	38	11	164	203	32	.920
—Iowa (A.A.)		SS	61	210	25	49	11	1	7	27	.233	4	40	9	90	165	26	.907
1985—Chicago (N.L.)		SS	74	250	40	65	12	4	4	18	.260	19	42	11	144	248	17	.958
—Iowa (A.A.)		SS	73	272	24	73	9	6	2	28	.268	5	48	17	138	176	12	.963
1986—Chicago (N.L.)		SS	150	581	66	145	36	3	17	68	.250	21	114	13	*320	*465	*32	.961
1987—Chicago (N.L.)		SS	95	346	40	85	18	3	5	22	.246	10	68	12	160	271	14	.969
—Iowa (A.A.)		SS	5	19	1	8	1	0	0	2	.421	0	3	1	6	12	1	.947
1988—Chicago (N.L.)		SS	155	575	69	143	23	6	9	56	.249	16	108	30	*257	455	20	.973
1989—Chicago (N.L.)		SS	138	471	52	131	20	6	9	60	.278	30	86	19	213	379	17	.972
1990—Chicago (N.L.)		SS	146	545	73	143	22	8	17	66	.262	15	87	25	255	392	20	.970

Year	Team (League)	Pos.	G	AB	R	H	2B	3B	HR	RBI	Avg.	BB	SO	SB	PO	A	E	Avg.
1991—Chicago (N.L.).............		SS	142	492	59	128	22	7	12	50	.260	23	64	21	*261	383	21	.968
1992—Chicago (N.L.).............		SS	18	73	8	23	3	1	0	2	.315	3	13	2	28	42	1	.986
1993—Chicago (N.L.).............		SS	7	10	3	4	2	0	0	2	.400	0	1	0	5	0	0	1.000
1994—Chicago (N.L.).............		SS	88	331	38	92	19	0	11	35	.278	16	48	3	121	218	12	.966
1995—Chicago (N.L.).............		SS	127	477	58	141	30	6	14	69	.296	10	75	10	187	336	17	.969
1996—San Fran. (N.L.)■......		SS	82	287	27	86	12	2	5	25	.300	13	40	8	116	217	15	.957
1997—Chicago (N.L.)■......		SS-OF	114	419	57	119	18	4	9	41	.284	8	64	29	179	227	12	.971
— Pittsburgh (N.L.)■......		SS	18	71	14	28	4	1	5	16	.394	0	11	3	28	55	3	.965
1998—Cleveland (A.L.)■......2B-SS-OF-DH			62	156	26	37	11	3	3	12	.237	6	18	9	63	76	4	.972
— San Fran. (N.L.)■......		SS-OF-2B	36	51	10	9	2	0	3	8	.176	0	10	0	20	5	2	.926
1999—St. Louis (N.L.)■......O-1-S-3-DH			62	150	23	46	5	2	5	25	.307	2	23	6	78	23	2	.981
— New York (N.L.)■......		OF-3B	42	93	12	32	6	1	0	16	.344	0	16	4	44	2	1	.979
American League totals (1 year)			62	156	26	37	11	3	3	12	.237	6	18	9	63	76	4	.972
National League totals (15 years)			1494	5222	649	1420	254	54	125	579	.272	186	870	196	2416	3718	206	.968
Major League totals (15 years)			1556	5378	675	1457	265	57	128	591	.271	192	888	205	2479	3794	210	.968

DIVISION SERIES RECORD

Year	Team (League)	Pos.	G	AB	R	H	2B	3B	HR	RBI	Avg.	BB	SO	SB	PO	A	E	Avg.
1999—New York (N.L.)...........	OF-PH-PR		4	6	0	1	0	0	0	0	.167	0	1	0	7	0	0	1.000

CHAMPIONSHIP SERIES RECORD

Year	Team (League)	Pos.	G	AB	R	H	2B	3B	HR	RBI	Avg.	BB	SO	SB	PO	A	E	Avg.
1989—Chicago (N.L.).............		SS	5	19	2	6	0	0	0	0	.316	1	1	1	10	14	1	.960
1999—New York (N.L.).............		PH-OF	5	7	2	1	0	0	0	0	.143	0	2	1	0	0	0	...
Championship series totals (2 years)			10	26	4	7	0	0	0	0	.269	1	3	2	10	14	1	.960

ALL-STAR GAME RECORD

Year	League	Pos.	AB	R	H	2B	3B	HR	RBI	Avg.	BB	SO	SB	PO	A	E	Avg.
1988— National.....................								Did not play.									
1990— National.....................		SS	2	0	0	0	0	0	0	.000	0	0	0	0	0	0	...

DUNWOODY, TODD   OF   ROYALS

PERSONAL: Born April 11, 1975, in Lafayette, Ind. ... 6-1/195. ... Bats left, throws left. ... Full name: Todd Franklin Dunwoody.
HIGH SCHOOL: West Lafayette (Ind.) Harrison.
TRANSACTIONS/CAREER NOTES: Selected by Florida Marlins organization in seventh round of free-agent draft (June 3, 1993). ... On Charlotte disabled list (April 11-18, 1998). ... Traded by Marlins to Kansas City Royals for IF Sean McNally (December 15, 1999).
STATISTICAL NOTES: Led Eastern League with 267 total bases in 1996.

Year	Team (League)	Pos.	G	AB	R	H	2B	3B	HR	RBI	Avg.	BB	SO	SB	PO	A	E	Avg.
1993—GC Marlins (GCL).......	OF		31	109	13	21	2	2	0	7	.193	7	28	5	45	1	1	.979
1994—GC Marlins (GCL).......	OF		46	169	32	44	6	6	1	25	.260	21	28	11	91	1	1	.989
— Kane County (Midw.)..	OF		15	45	7	5	0	0	1	1	.111	5	17	-1	21	2	0	1.000
1995—Kane County (Midw.)..	OF		132	494	89	140	20	8	14	89	.283	52	105	39	284	6	5	.983
1996—Portland (East.).........	OF		138	*552	88	153	30	6	24	93	.277	45	*149	24	254	2	1	*.996
1997—Charlotte (I.L.).........	OF-DH		107	401	74	105	16	7	23	62	.262	39	129	25	231	5	2	.992
— Florida (N.L.).............	OF		19	50	7	13	2	2	2	7	.260	7	21	2	26	0	2	.929
1998—Charlotte (I.L.).........	OF		28	102	20	31	6	3	6	22	.304	12	28	4	76	2	1	.987
— Florida (N.L.).............	OF		116	434	53	109	27	7	5	28	.251	21	113	5	273	9	3	.989
1999—Florida (N.L.).............	OF		64	186	20	41	6	3	2	20	.220	12	41	3	102	3	2	.981
— Calgary (PCL).............	OF-DH		65	246	35	67	16	7	9	36	.272	10	56	7	159	10	4	.977
Major League totals (3 years)			199	670	80	163	35	12	9	55	.243	40	175	10	401	12	7	.983

DURAZO, ERUBIEL   1B   DIAMONDBACKS

PERSONAL: Born January 23, 1974, in Hermosillo, Mexico. ... 6-3/225. ... Bats left, throws left. ... Full name: Erubiel Cardenas Durazo.
HIGH SCHOOL: Amphitheater (Tucson, Ariz.).
JUNIOR COLLEGE: Pima Community College (Ariz.).
TRANSACTIONS/CAREER NOTES: Signed by Monterrey, Mexican League (1997). ... Contract sold by Monterrey to Arizona Diamondbacks organization (December 16, 1998).

Year	Team (League)	Pos.	G	AB	R	H	2B	3B	HR	RBI	Avg.	BB	SO	SB	PO	A	E	Avg.
1997—Monterrey (Mex.).......	1B-OF		110	358	47	101	21	10	8	61	.282	52	43	3	480	48	3	.994
1998—Monterrey (Mex.).......	OF-1B		119	420	84	147	32	2	19	98	.350	99	71	4	219	15	0	1.000
1999—El Paso (Texas)■.......	1B		64	226	53	91	18	3	14	55	.403	44	37	2	523	36	10	.982
— Tucson (PCL).............	1B-DH		30	118	27	48	7	0	10	28	.407	14	18	1	241	20	1	.996
— Arizona (N.L.).............	1B		52	155	31	51	4	2	11	30	.329	26	43	1	324	20	0	1.000
Major League totals (1 year)			52	155	31	51	4	2	11	30	.329	26	43	1	324	20	0	1.000

DIVISION SERIES RECORD

Year	Team (League)	Pos.	G	AB	R	H	2B	3B	HR	RBI	Avg.	BB	SO	SB	PO	A	E	Avg.
1999—Arizona (N.L.).............	1B		2	7	1	1	0	0	1	1	.143	1	0	0	15	1	0	1.000

DURBIN, CHAD   P   ROYALS

PERSONAL: Born December 3, 1977, in Spring Valley, Ill. ... 6-1/175. ... Throws right, bats right. ... Full name: Chad Griffin Durbin.
HIGH SCHOOL: Woodlawn (Shreveport, La.).
TRANSACTIONS/CAREER NOTES: Selected by Kansas City Royals organization in third round of free-agent draft (June 4, 1996).

Year League	W	L	Pct.	ERA	G	GS	CG	ShO	Sv.	IP	H	R	ER	BB	SO
1996— Gulf Coast Royals (GCL)	3	2	.600	4.26	11	8	1	1	0	44 1/3	34	22	21	25	43
1997— Lansing (Midw.)	5	8	.385	4.79	26	26	0	0	0	144 2/3	157	85	77	53	116
1998— Wilmington (Caro.)	10	7	.588	2.93	26	26	0	0	0	147 2/3	126	57	48	59	162
1999— Wichita (Texas)	8	10	.444	4.64	28	27	1	1	0	157	154	88	81	49	122
— Kansas City (A.L.)	0	0	...	0.00	1	0	0	0	0	2 1/3	1	0	0	1	3
Major League totals (1 year)	**0**	**0**	**...**	**0.00**	**1**	**0**	**0**	**0**	**0**	**2 1/3**	**1**	**0**	**0**	**1**	**3**

DURHAM, RAY   2B   WHITE SOX

PERSONAL: Born November 30, 1971, in Charlotte. ... 5-8/180. ... Bats both, throws right.
HIGH SCHOOL: Harding (Charlotte).
TRANSACTIONS/CAREER NOTES: Selected by Chicago White Sox organization in fifth round of free-agent draft (June 4, 1990). ... On Utica suspended list (April 1-May 22, 1992). ... On Sarasota disabled list (June 16-July 9, 1992).
RECORDS: Holds major league single-season record for fewest putouts by second baseman (150 or more games)—236 (1996).
STATISTICAL NOTES: Led Southern League in caught stealing with 25 in 1993. ... Led Southern League second basemen with 541 total chances in 1993. ... Led American Association with 261 total bases in 1994. ... Led American Association second basemen with 701 total chances and 92 double plays in 1994. ... Led A.L. second basemen with 738 total chances and 128 double plays in 1998. ... Career major league grand slams: 2.

Year Team (League)	Pos.	G	AB	R	H	2B	3B	HR	RBI	Avg.	BB	SO	SB	PO	A	E	Avg.
1990— GC White Sox (GCL) ..	2B-SS	35	116	18	32	3	3	0	13	.276	15	36	23	61	85	15	.907
1991— Utica (NY-P)	2B	39	142	29	36	2	7	0	17	.254	25	44	12	54	101	12	.928
— GC White Sox (GCL) ..	2B	6	23	3	7	1	0	0	4	.304	3	5	5	18	15	0	1.000
1992— Sarasota (FSL)	2B	57	202	37	55	6	3	0	7	.272	32	36	28	66	107	10	.945
— GC White Sox (GCL) ..	2B	5	13	3	7	2	0	0	2	.538	3	1	1	4	3	0	1.000
1993— Birmingham (Sou.)....	2B	137	528	83	143	22	*10	3	37	.271	42	100	39	227	284	*30	.945
1994— Nashville (A.A.)	2B	133	527	89	156	33	•12	16	66	.296	46	91	34	*254	*429	*19	*.973
1995— Chicago (A.L.)	2B-DH	125	471	68	121	27	6	7	51	.257	31	83	18	245	298	15	.973
1996— Chicago (A.L.)	2B-DH	156	557	79	153	33	5	10	65	.275	58	95	30	236	423	11	.984
1997— Chicago (A.L.)	2B-DH	155	634	106	172	27	5	11	53	.271	61	96	33	270	395	*18	.974
1998— Chicago (A.L.)	2B	158	635	126	181	35	8	19	67	.285	73	105	36	282	438	18	.976
1999— Chicago (A.L.)	2B-DH	153	612	109	181	30	8	13	60	.296	73	105	34	305	412	19	.974
Major League totals (5 years)		747	2909	488	808	152	32	60	296	.278	296	484	151	1338	1966	81	.976

ALL-STAR GAME RECORD

Year League	Pos.	AB	R	H	2B	3B	HR	RBI	Avg.	BB	SO	SB	PO	A	E	Avg.
1998— American	2B	1	1	1	0	0	0	1	1.000	0	0	0	0	0	0	...

DURRINGTON, TRENT   2B   ANGELS

PERSONAL: Born August 27, 1975, in Sydney, Australia. ... 5-10/188. ... Bats right, throws right. ... Full name: Trent John Durrington.
HIGH SCHOOL: The Southport School (Australia).
TRANSACTIONS/CAREER NOTES: Signed as non-drafted free agent by California Angels organization (April 22, 1994).

Year Team (League)	Pos.	G	AB	R	H	2B	3B	HR	RBI	Avg.	BB	SO	SB	PO	A	E	Avg.
1994— Ariz. Angels (Ariz.)	SS-2B	16	52	13	14	3	0	1	2	.269	11	16	5	18	31	5	.907
1995— Boise (N'west)	2B-SS	50	140	23	24	4	1	3	19	.171	17	35	2	70	119	8	.959
1996— Cedar Rap. (Midw.)	2B	25	76	12	19	1	0	0	4	.250	33	20	15	46	48	3	.969
— Boise (N'west)..........	2B-3B-SS	40	154	38	43	7	2	0	14	.279	31	32	24	87	122	12	.946
1997— Lake Elsinore (Calif.)..	2B-OF-3B	123	409	80	101	21	3	3	36	.247	51	90	52	222	311	17	.969
1998— Midland (Texas)...........	2-0-3-SS	112	351	62	79	10	1	1	30	.225	50	74	24	191	241	13	.971
1999— Erie (East.)	2B	107	396	84	114	26	1	3	34	.288	52	66	59	212	312	14	.974
— Anaheim (A.L.)	2B-DH	43	122	14	22	2	0	0	2	.180	9	28	4	73	98	6	.966
Major League totals (1 year)		43	122	14	22	2	0	0	2	.180	9	28	4	73	98	6	.966

DUVALL, MIKE   P   DEVIL RAYS

PERSONAL: Born October 11, 1974, in Warrenton, Va. ... 6-0/185. ... Throws left, bats right. ... Full name: Michael Alan Duvall.
HIGH SCHOOL: Fauquier (Warrenton, Va.).
JUNIOR COLLEGE: Potomac State College (W.Va.).
TRANSACTIONS/CAREER NOTES: Selected by Florida Marlins organization in 19th round of free-agent draft (June 1, 1995). ... Selected by Tampa Bay Devil Rays in second round (32nd pick overall) of expansion draft (November 18, 1997). ... On Durham disabled list (April 9-May 13, 1998). ... On Tampa Bay disabled list (June 9-July 6, 1999).

Year League	W	L	Pct.	ERA	G	GS	CG	ShO	Sv.	IP	H	R	ER	BB	SO
1995— Gulf Coast Marlins (GCL) ...	5	0	1.000	2.22	16	1	0	0	1	28 1/3	15	8	7	12	34
1996— Kane County (Midw.).........	4	1	.800	2.06	41	0	0	0	8	48	43	20	11	21	46
1997— Brevard County (FSL)........	1	0	1.000	0.73	11	0	0	0	6	12 1/3	7	1	1	3	9
— Portland (East.)	4	6	.400	1.84	45	0	0	0	18	68 1/3	63	20	14	20	49

Year	League	W	L	Pct.	ERA	G	GS	CG	ShO	Sv.	IP	H	R	ER	BB	SO
1998—St. Petersburg (FSL)■		0	0	...	2.70	2	0	0	0	0	3 1/3	4	1	1	2	3
	—Durham (I.L.)	5	3	.625	3.22	32	9	1	0	0	72 2/3	74	31	26	32	55
	—Tampa Bay (A.L.)	0	0	...	6.75	3	0	0	0	0	4	4	3	3	2	1
1999—Tampa Bay (A.L.)................		1	1	.500	4.05	40	0	0	0	0	40	46	21	18	27	18
	—Durham (I.L.)	2	2	.500	5.40	19	1	0	0	2	30	32	20	18	12	27
Major League totals (2 years).......		1	1	.500	4.30	43	0	0	0	0	44	50	24	21	29	19

DYE, JERMAINE   OF   ROYALS

PERSONAL: Born January 28, 1974, in Vacaville, Calif. ... 6-5/220. ... Bats right, throws right. ... Full name: Jermaine Trevell Dye.
HIGH SCHOOL: Will C. Wood (Vacaville, Calif.).
JUNIOR COLLEGE: Cosumnes River College (Calif.).
TRANSACTIONS/CAREER NOTES: Selected by Atlanta Braves organization in 17th round of free-agent draft (June 3, 1993). ... On disabled list (July 13-August 9, 1995). ... Traded by Braves with P Jamie Walker to Kansas City Royals for OF Michael Tucker and IF Keith Lockhart (March 27, 1997). ... On Kansas City disabled list (April 17-May 3, 1997); included rehabilitation assignment to Omaha (May 1-3). ... On Kansas City disabled list (July 10-August 13, 1997); included rehabilitation assignment to Omaha (July 27-August 13). ... On Kansas City disabled list (March 23-May 8 and September 1, 1998-remainder of season); included rehabilitation assignment to Omaha (April 21-May 8).
STATISTICAL NOTES: Led South Atlantic League outfielders with six double plays in 1994. ... Led A.L. outfielders with six double plays in 1999. ... Career major league grand slams: 1.
MISCELLANEOUS: Hit home run in first major league at-bat (May 17, 1996).

							BATTING								FIELDING		
Year	Team (League)	Pos.	G	AB	R	H	2B	3B	HR	RBI	Avg.	BB	SO	SB	PO	A	E	Avg.
1993— GC Braves (GCL)		OF-3B	31	124	17	43	14	0	0	27	.347	5	13	5	46	9	3	.948
	—Danville (Appl.)...........	OF	25	94	6	26	6	1	2	12	.277	8	10	19	51	1	2	.963
1994— Macon (SAL)		OF	135	506	73	151	*41	1	15	98	.298	33	82	19	263	*22	9	.969
1995— Greenville (Sou.)		OF	104	403	50	115	26	4	15	71	.285	27	74	4	234	*22	5	.981
1996— Richmond (I.L.).........		OF	36	142	25	33	7	1	6	19	.232	5	25	3	83	2	4	.955
	—Atlanta (N.L.)	OF	98	292	32	82	16	0	12	37	.281	8	67	1	150	2	8	.950
1997— Kansas City (A.L.)■ ..		OF	75	263	26	62	14	0	7	22	.236	17	51	2	164	7	6	.966
	—Omaha (A.A.).............	OF-DH	39	144	21	44	6	0	10	25	.306	9	25	0	41	2	0	1.000
1998— Omaha (PCL).............		OF-1B-DH	41	157	29	47	6	0	12	35	.299	19	29	7	119	4	1	.992
	—Kansas City (A.L.)	OF	60	214	24	50	5	1	5	23	.234	11	46	2	152	4	2	.987
1999— Kansas City (A.L.)		OF-DH	158	608	96	179	44	8	27	119	.294	58	119	2	362	•17	6	.984
American League totals (3 years)			293	1085	146	291	63	9	39	164	.268	86	216	6	678	28	14	.981
National League totals (1 year)			98	292	32	82	16	0	12	37	.281	8	67	1	150	2	8	.950
Major League totals (4 years)			391	1377	178	373	79	9	51	201	.271	94	283	7	828	30	22	.975

DIVISION SERIES RECORD

							BATTING								FIELDING		
Year	Team (League)	Pos.	G	AB	R	H	2B	3B	HR	RBI	Avg.	BB	SO	SB	PO	A	E	Avg.
1996— Atlanta (N.L.).............		OF	3	11	1	2	0	0	1	1	.182	0	6	1	11	1	0	1.000

CHAMPIONSHIP SERIES RECORD

RECORDS: Shares N.L. single-game record for most at-bats—6 (October 14, 1996).

							BATTING								FIELDING		
Year	Team (League)	Pos.	G	AB	R	H	2B	3B	HR	RBI	Avg.	BB	SO	SB	PO	A	E	Avg.
1996— Atlanta (N.L.).............		OF	7	28	2	6	1	0	0	4	.214	1	7	0	14	0	0	1.000

WORLD SERIES RECORD

							BATTING								FIELDING		
Year	Team (League)	Pos.	G	AB	R	H	2B	3B	HR	RBI	Avg.	BB	SO	SB	PO	A	E	Avg.
1996— Atlanta (N.L.).............		OF	5	17	0	2	0	0	0	1	.118	1	1	0	15	0	1	.938

DYKHOFF, RADHAMES   P   ORIOLES

PERSONAL: Born September 27, 1974, in Paradera, Aruba. ... 6-0/200. ... Throws left, bats left. ... Full name: Radhames Alviro Dykhoff. ... Name pronounced RAD-ham-es DIKE-off.
TRANSACTIONS/CAREER NOTES: Signed as non-drafted free agent by Baltimore Orioles organization (January 6, 1993).

Year	League	W	L	Pct.	ERA	G	GS	CG	ShO	Sv.	IP	H	R	ER	BB	SO
1993—Gulf Coast Orioles (GCL)....		1	2	.333	3.40	14	3	0	0	1	45	37	22	17	11	29
1994—Gulf Coast Orioles (GCL)....		3	6	.333	3.33	12	12	1	0	0	73	69	34	27	17	67
1995—High Desert (Calif.)..........		1	5	.167	5.02	34	2	0	0	3	80 2/3	95	68	45	44	88
1996—Frederick (Caro.)		2	6	.250	5.66	33	0	0	0	3	62	77	45	39	22	75
1997—Bowie (East.)		0	0	...	8.31	7	0	0	0	0	8 2/3	10	9	8	7	7
	—Delmarva (SAL).............	0	0	...	0.00	1	0	0	0	1	3	3	0	0	0	3
	—Frederick (Caro.)	3	3	.500	2.42	31	0	0	0	5	67	48	19	18	52	98
1998—Bowie (East.)		3	7	.300	4.71	38	8	0	0	1	93 2/3	83	51	49	52	98
	—Baltimore (A.L.).............	0	0	...	18.00	1	0	0	0	0	1	2	2	2	1	1
1999—Rochester (I.L.)		2	0	1.000	3.94	47	0	0	0	1	82 1/3	69	42	36	31	57
Major League totals (1 year)........		0	0	...	18.00	1	0	0	0	0	1	2	2	2	1	1

EASLEY, DAMION   2B   TIGERS

PERSONAL: Born November 11, 1969, in New York. ... 5-11/185. ... Bats right, throws right. ... Full name: Jacinto Damion Easley.
HIGH SCHOOL: Lakewood (Calif.).
JUNIOR COLLEGE: Long Beach (Calif.) City College.
COLLEGE: Long Beach State.

D
E

TRANSACTIONS/CAREER NOTES: Selected by California Angels organization in 30th round of free-agent draft (June 1, 1988). ... On disabled list (June 19-July 4 and July 28, 1993-remainder of season; and May 30-June 17, 1994). ... On California disabled list (April 1-May 10, 1996); included rehabilitation assignment to Vancouver (April 30-May 10). ... Traded by Angels to Detroit Tigers for P Greg Gohr (July 31, 1996).

RECORDS: Holds major league single-season record for fewest putouts by second baseman for leader—285 (1998). ... Holds major league single-game record for most times hit by pitch—3 (May 31, 1999).

HONORS: Named second baseman on THE SPORTING NEWS A.L. Silver Slugger team (1998).

STATISTICAL NOTES: Led A.L. second basemen with 285 putouts and .985 fielding percentage in 1998. ... Had 19-game hitting streaks (May 10-30 and July 3-23, 1998). ... Career major league grand slams: 1.

Year Team (League)	Pos.	G	AB	R	H	2B	3B	HR	RBI	Avg.	BB	SO	SB	PO	A	E	Avg.
1989— Bend (N'west)	2B	36	131	34	39	5	1	4	21	.298	25	21	9	49	89	22	.863
1990— Quad City (Midw.)	SS	103	365	59	100	19	3	10	56	.274	41	60	25	136	206	41	.893
1991— Midland (Texas).........	SS	127	452	73	115	24	5	6	57	.254	58	67	23	186	388	*47	.924
1992— Edmonton (PCL)	SS-3B	108	429	61	124	18	3	3	44	.289	31	44	26	152	342	30	.943
— California (A.L.)	3B-SS	47	151	14	39	5	0	1	12	.258	8	26	9	30	102	5	.964
1993— California (A.L.)	2B-3B-DH	73	230	33	72	13	2	2	22	.313	28	35	6	111	157	6	.978
1994— California (A.L.)	3B-2B	88	316	41	68	16	1	6	30	.215	29	48	4	122	179	7	.977
1995— California (A.L.)	2B-SS	114	357	35	77	14	2	4	35	.216	32	47	5	186	276	10	.979
1996— Vancouver (PCL)	SS-2B-3B	12	48	13	15	2	1	2	8	.313	9	6	4	20	26	2	.958
— Midland (Texas)	3B-SS	4	14	1	6	2	0	0	2	.429	0	0	1	5	12	1	.944
— California (A.L.)...S-2-3-DH-O		28	45	4	7	1	0	2	7	.156	6	12	0	23	39	3	.954
— Detroit (A.L.)■	2-S-3-DH	21	67	10	23	1	0	2	10	.343	4	13	3	22	47	3	.958
1997— Detroit (A.L.)	2B-SS-DH	151	527	97	139	37	3	22	72	.264	68	102	28	244	405	12	.982
1998— Detroit (A.L.)	2B-SS-DH	153	594	84	161	38	2	27	100	.271	39	112	15	†312	480	12	†.985
1999— Detroit (A.L.)	2B-SS	151	549	83	146	30	1	20	65	.266	51	124	11	318	445	8	.990
Major League totals (8 years)		826	2836	401	732	155	11	86	353	.258	265	519	81	1368	2130	66	.981

ALL-STAR GAME RECORD

Year League	Pos.	AB	R	H	2B	3B	HR	RBI	Avg.	BB	SO	SB	PO	A	E	Avg.
1998— American	PH	1	1	1	0	0	0	0	1.000	0	0	0	0	0	0	...

EBERT, DERRIN   P   BRAVES

PERSONAL: Born August 21, 1976, in Anaheim, Calif. ... 6-3/200. ... Throws left, bats right. ... Full name: Derrin Lee Ebert.

HIGH SCHOOL: Hesperia (Calif.).

JUNIOR COLLEGE: Victor Valley Community College (Calif.).

COLLEGE: Cal State Fullerton.

TRANSACTIONS/CAREER NOTES: Selected by Atlanta Braves organization in 18th round of free-agent draft (June 2, 1994).

STATISTICAL NOTES: Pitched 6-0 seven-inning no-hit victory against Gulf Coast Marlins (August 12, 1994).

Year League	W	L	Pct.	ERA	G	GS	CG	ShO	Sv.	IP	H	R	ER	BB	SO
1994— Gulf Coast Braves (GCL)	1	3	.250	2.93	10	7	1	1	0	43	40	18	14	8	25
1995— Macon (SAL)	*14	5	.737	3.31	28	28	0	0	0	*182	*184	87	67	46	124
1996— Durham (Caro.)	12	9	.571	4.00	27	27	2	0	0	166 1/3	189	102	74	37	99
1997— Greenville (Sou.)	11	8	.579	4.10	27	25	0	0	0	175 2/3	191	95	80	48	101
1998— Richmond (I.L.)	9	9	.500	4.51	29	29	0	0	0	163 2/3	195	94	82	49	88
1999— Atlanta (N.L.)	0	1	.000	5.63	5	0	0	0	1	8	9	5	5	5	4
— Richmond (I.L.)	8	7	.533	4.30	25	24	2	1	0	150 2/3	173	79	72	44	82
Major League totals (1 year)........	0	1	.000	5.63	5	0	0	0	1	8	9	5	5	5	4

ECHEVARRIA, ANGEL   OF   ROCKIES

PERSONAL: Born May 25, 1971, in Bridgeport, Conn. ... 6-3/226. ... Bats right, throws right. ... Full name: Angel Santos Echevarria.

HIGH SCHOOL: Bassick (Bridgeport, Conn.).

COLLEGE: Rutgers.

TRANSACTIONS/CAREER NOTES: Selected by Colorado Rockies organization in 17th round of free-agent draft (June 1, 1992). ... On Colorado disabled list (April 29-June 4 and July 29-August 16, 1997).

Year Team (League)	Pos.	G	AB	R	H	2B	3B	HR	RBI	Avg.	BB	SO	SB	PO	A	E	Avg.
1992— Bend (N'west)	OF	57	205	24	46	4	1	5	30	.224	19	54	8	65	7	0	1.000
1993— Central Valley (Calif.)..	OF	104	358	45	97	16	2	6	52	.271	44	74	6	141	8	6	.961
1994— Central Valley (Calif.)..	OF	50	192	25	58	8	1	6	35	.302	9	25	2	52	3	1	.982
— New Haven (East.).......	OF	58	205	25	52	6	0	6	32	.254	15	46	2	91	5	2	.980
1995— New Haven (East.).......	OF	124	453	78	136	30	1	21	*100	.300	56	93	8	202	*20	5	.978
1996— Colo. Springs (PCL) ...	OF-DH	110	415	67	140	19	2	16	74	.337	38	81	4	168	8	4	.978
— Colorado (N.L.)	OF	26	21	2	6	0	0	0	6	.286	2	5	0	1	0	0	1.000
1997— Colo. Springs (PCL) ... OF-DH-1B		77	295	59	95	24	0	13	80	.322	28	47	6	135	9	1	.993
— Colorado (N.L.)	OF	15	20	4	5	2	0	0	0	.250	2	5	0	4	1	0	1.000
1998— Colo. Springs (PCL) ... 1B-OF-DH		85	301	50	98	21	2	15	60	.326	14	47	0	408	28	7	.984
— Colorado (N.L.)	1B-OF	19	29	7	11	3	0	1	9	.379	2	3	0	23	2	0	1.000
1999— Colorado (N.L.)	OF-1B	102	191	28	56	7	0	11	35	.293	17	34	1	122	7	1	.992
Major League totals (4 years)		162	261	41	78	12	0	12	50	.299	23	47	1	150	10	1	.994

ECKSTEIN, DAVID   2B   RED SOX

PERSONAL: Born January 20, 1975, in Sanford, Fla. ... 5-8/165. ... Bats right, throws right. ... Full name: David Mark Eckstein.

HIGH SCHOOL: Seminole (Sanford, Fla.).

COLLEGE: Florida.
TRANSACTIONS/CAREER NOTES: Selected by Boston Red Sox organization in 19th round of free-agent draft (June 3, 1997).
STATISTICAL NOTES: Tied for New York-Pennsylvania League lead in sacrifice hits with eight in 1997. ... Led Florida State League in being hit by pitch with 22 in 1998. ... Led Florida State League second basemen in fielding percentage with .989 in 1998. ... Tied for Eastern League lead with 87 double plays by second baseman in 1999.

								BATTING							FIELDING		
Year	Team (League)	Pos.	G	AB	R	H	2B	3B	HR	RBI	Avg.	BB	SO	SB	PO	A	E	Avg.
1997— Lowell (NY-P)		2B	68	249	43	75	11	4	4	39	.301	33	29	21	139	166	9	*.971
1998— Sarasota (FSL)		2B-SS	135	503	99	154	29	4	3	58	.306	87	51	45	214	368	8	†.986
1999— Trenton (East.)		2B-DH	131	483	109	151	22	5	6	52	.313	89	48	32	232	359	9	.985

EDMONDS, JIM   OF   ANGELS

PERSONAL: Born June 27, 1970, in Fullerton, Calif. ... 6-1/212. ... Bats left, throws left. ... Full name: James Patrick Edmonds. ... Name pronounced ED-muns.
HIGH SCHOOL: Diamond Bar (Calif.).
TRANSACTIONS/CAREER NOTES: Selected by California Angels organization in seventh round of free-agent draft (June 1, 1988). ... On disabled list (June 19-September 2, 1989; April 10-May 7 and May 23, 1991-remainder of season). ... On Vancouver disabled list (June 29-July 19, 1993). ... On California disabled list (May 26-June 10 and June 12-July 18, 1996); included rehabilitation assignment to Lake Elsinore (July 13-18). ... Angels franchise renamed Anaheim Angels for 1997 season. ... On disabled list (August 1-16, 1997). ... On Anaheim disabled list (March 30-August 2, 1999): included rehabilitation assignment to Lake Elsinore (July 26-August 2).
HONORS: Named outfielder on THE SPORTING NEWS A.L. All-Star team (1995). ... Won A.L. Gold Glove as outfielder (1997-98).
STATISTICAL NOTES: Had 23-game hitting streak (June 4-29, 1995). ... Career major league grand slams: 1.

								BATTING							FIELDING		
Year	Team (League)	Pos.	G	AB	R	H	2B	3B	HR	RBI	Avg.	BB	SO	SB	PO	A	E	Avg.
1988— Bend (N'west)		OF	35	122	23	27	4	0	0	13	.221	20	44	4	59	1	1	.984
1989— Quad City (Midw.)		OF	31	92	11	24	4	0	1	4	.261	7	34	1	47	2	3	.942
1990— Palm Springs (Calif.)		OF	91	314	36	92	18	6	3	56	.293	27	75	5	199	9	10	.954
1991— Palm Springs (Calif.)		OF-1B-P	60	187	28	55	15	1	2	27	.294	40	57	2	97	6	0	1.000
1992— Midland (Texas)		OF	70	246	42	77	15	2	8	32	.313	41	83	3	139	6	5	.967
— Edmonton (PCL)		OF	50	194	37	58	15	2	6	36	.299	14	55	3	79	5	1	.988
1993— Vancouver (PCL)		OF	95	356	59	112	28	4	9	74	.315	41	81	6	167	4	3	.983
— California (A.L.)		OF	18	61	5	15	4	1	0	4	.246	2	16	0	47	4	1	.981
1994— California (A.L.)		OF-1B	94	289	35	79	13	1	5	37	.273	30	72	4	301	20	3	.991
1995— California (A.L.)		OF	141	558	120	162	30	4	33	107	.290	51	130	1	401	8	1	.998
1996— California (A.L.)		OF-DH	114	431	73	131	28	3	27	66	.304	46	101	4	280	6	1	.997
— Lake Elsinore (Calif.)		OF-DH	5	15	4	6	2	0	1	4	.400	1	1	0	5	0	0	1.000
1997— Anaheim (A.L.)		OF-1B-DH	133	502	82	146	27	0	26	80	.291	60	80	5	395	16	5	.988
1998— Anaheim (A.L.)		OF	154	599	115	184	42	1	25	91	.307	57	114	7	392	10	5	.988
1999— Lake Elsinore (Calif.)		DH	5	19	4	8	2	0	0	3	.421	4	2	2	0	0	0	...
— Anaheim (A.L.)		OF-DH-1B	55	204	34	51	17	2	5	23	.250	28	45	5	138	5	1	.993
Major League totals (7 years)			709	2644	464	768	161	12	121	408	.290	274	558	26	1954	69	17	.992

ALL-STAR GAME RECORD

						BATTING							FIELDING		
Year	League	Pos.	AB	R	H	2B	3B	HR	RBI	Avg.	BB	SO	SB	PO	A	E	Avg.
1995— American		PH-OF	1	0	0	0	0	0	0	.000	0	1	0	0	0	0	...

RECORD AS PITCHER

Year	League	W	L	Pct.	ERA	G	GS	CG	ShO	Sv.	IP	H	R	ER	BB	SO
1991— Palm Springs (Calif.)		0	0	...	0.00	1	0	0	0	0	2	1	0	0	3	2

EDMONDSON, BRIAN   P   MARLINS

PERSONAL: Born January 29, 1973, in Fontana, Calif. ... 6-2/175. ... Throws right, bats right. ... Full name: Brian Christopher Edmondson.
HIGH SCHOOL: Norte Vista (Riverside, Calif.).
TRANSACTIONS/CAREER NOTES: Selected by Detroit Tigers organization in third round of free-agent draft (June 3, 1991); pick received as part of compensation for Milwaukee Brewers signing Type B free-agent P Edwin Nunez. ... Claimed on waivers by New York Mets (April 24, 1995). ... Selected by Atlanta Braves from Mets organization in Rule 5 major league draft (December 15, 1997). ... Claimed on waivers by Florida Marlins (June 4, 1998).
STATISTICAL NOTES: Tied for Appalachian League lead with seven home runs allowed in 1991.

Year	League	W	L	Pct.	ERA	G	GS	CG	ShO	Sv.	IP	H	R	ER	BB	SO
1991— Bristol (Appl.)		4	4	.500	4.57	12	12	1	0	0	69	72	38	35	23	42
1992— Fayetteville (SAL)		10	6	.625	3.36	28	27	3	1	0	155 1/3	145	69	58	67	125
1993— Lakeland (FSL)		8	5	.615	2.99	19	19	1	0	0	114 1/3	115	44	38	43	64
— London (East.)		0	4	.000	6.26	5	5	1	0	0	23	30	23	16	13	17
1994— Trenton (East.)		11	9	.550	4.56	26	26	2	0	0	162	171	89	82	61	90
1995— Binghamton (East.)■		7	11	.389	4.76	23	22	2	1	0	134 1/3	150	82	71	59	69
1996— Binghamton (East.)		6	6	.500	4.25	39	13	1	0	0	114 1/3	130	69	54	38	83
1997— Binghamton (East.)		2	0	1.000	1.23	14	0	0	0	3	22	17	4	3	7	18
— Norfolk (I.L.)		4	3	.571	2.90	31	4	0	0	1	68 1/3	62	27	22	37	65
1998— Atlanta (N.L.)■		0	1	.000	4.32	10	0	0	0	0	16 2/3	14	10	8	8	8
— Florida (N.L.)■		4	3	.571	3.79	43	0	0	0	0	59 1/3	62	28	25	29	32
1999— Florida (N.L.)		5	8	.385	5.84	68	0	0	0	1	94	106	65	61	44	58
Major League totals (2 years)		9	12	.429	4.98	121	0	0	0	1	170	182	103	94	81	98

E

EILAND, DAVE   P   DEVIL RAYS

PERSONAL: Born July 5, 1966, in Dade City, Fla. ... 6-3/210. ... Throws right, bats right. ... Full name: David William Eiland. ... Name pronounced EYE-land.
HIGH SCHOOL: Zephyrhills (Fla.).
COLLEGE: South Florida, then Florida.
TRANSACTIONS/CAREER NOTES: Selected by New York Yankees organization in seventh round of free-agent draft (June 2, 1987). ... On New York disabled list (May 28-July 12, 1991); included rehabilitation assignment to Columbus (June 16-July 12). ... Released by Yankees (January 19, 1992). ... Signed by San Diego Padres organization (January 27, 1992). ... On San Diego disabled list (May 4-June 26, 1992); included rehabilitation assignment to Las Vegas (May 27-June 25). ... On San Diego disabled list (July 5-August 26, 1992); included rehabilitation assignment to Las Vegas (July 28-August 26). ... Granted free agency (December 7, 1992). ... Signed by Padres organization (February 28, 1993). ... Granted free agency (May 27, 1993). ... Signed by Cleveland Indians organization (May 29, 1993). ... Traded by Indians organization to Texas Rangers organization for P Gerald Alexander and P Allan Anderson (August 4, 1993). ... Granted free agency (October 15, 1993). ... Signed by Yankees organization (March 12, 1994). ... Granted free agency (October 3, 1995). ... Signed by St. Louis Cardinals organization (December 6, 1995). ... On Louisville temporarily inactive list (April 10-18, 1996). ... On Louisville disabled list (May 14-22 and June 3-15, 1996). ... Released by Cardinals (June 15, 1996). ... Signed by Yankees organization (June 18, 1996). ... Granted free agency (October 15, 1996). ... Re-signed by Yankees organization (December 23, 1996). ... On Columbus disabled list (May 14-25, 1997). ... Granted free agency (October 15, 1997). ... Signed by Tampa Bay Devil Rays (December 19, 1997). ... Granted free agency (October 15, 1998). ... Re-signed by Devil Rays (November 28, 1998). ... On Tampa Bay disabled list (June 8-23 and August 27-September 11, 1999); included rehabilitation assignment to Durham (September 6-8).
HONORS: Named International League Most Valuable Pitcher (1990).
STATISTICAL NOTES: Hit home run in first major league at-bat (April 10, 1992).

Year	League	W	L	Pct.	ERA	G	GS	CG	ShO	Sv.	IP	H	R	ER	BB	SO
1987—	Oneonta (NY-P)	4	0	1.000	1.84	5	5	0	0	0	29 1/3	20	6	6	3	16
	—Fort Lauderdale (FSL)	5	3	.625	1.88	8	8	4	1	0	62 1/3	57	17	13	8	28
1988—	Albany/Colonie (East.)	9	5	.643	2.56	18	18	•7	2	0	119 1/3	95	39	34	22	66
	—Columbus (I.L.)	1	1	.500	2.59	4	4	0	0	0	24 1/3	25	8	7	6	13
	—New York (A.L.)	0	0	...	6.39	3	3	0	0	0	12 2/3	15	9	9	4	7
1989—	Columbus (I.L.)	9	4	.692	3.76	18	18	2	0	0	103	107	47	43	21	45
	—New York (A.L.)	1	3	.250	5.77	6	6	0	0	0	34 1/3	44	25	22	13	11
1990—	Columbus (I.L.)	*16	5	.762	2.87	27	26	*11	•3	0	175 1/3	155	63	56	32	96
	—New York (A.L.)	2	1	.667	3.56	5	5	0	0	0	30 1/3	31	14	12	5	16
1991—	New York (A.L.)	2	5	.286	5.33	18	13	0	0	0	72 2/3	87	51	43	23	18
	—Columbus (I.L.)	6	1	.857	2.40	9	9	2	0	0	60	54	22	16	7	18
1992—	San Diego (N.L.)■	0	2	.000	5.67	7	7	0	0	0	27	33	21	17	5	10
	—Las Vegas (PCL)	4	5	.444	5.23	14	14	0	0	0	63 2/3	78	43	37	11	31
1993—	San Diego (N.L.)	0	3	.000	5.21	10	9	0	0	0	48 1/3	58	33	28	17	14
	—Charlotte (I.L.)■	1	3	.250	5.30	8	8	0	0	0	35 2/3	42	22	21	12	13
	—Oklahoma City (A.A.)■	3	1	.750	4.29	7	7	1	0	0	35 2/3	39	18	17	9	15
1994—	Columbus (I.L.)	9	6	.600	3.58	26	26	0	0	0	140 2/3	141	72	56	33	84
1995—	Columbus (I.L.)	8	7	.533	3.14	19	18	1	1	0	109	109	44	38	22	62
	—New York (A.L.)	1	1	.500	6.30	4	1	0	0	0	10	16	10	7	3	6
1996—	Louisville (A.A.)■	0	1	.000	5.55	8	6	0	0	0	24 1/3	27	17	15	8	17
	—Columbus (I.L.)	8	4	.667	2.92	15	15	3	0	0	92 1/3	77	37	30	13	76
1997—	Columbus (I.L.)	4	2	.667	6.64	13	11	0	0	0	62 1/3	80	47	46	14	43
	—Gulf Coast Yankees (GCL)	0	1	.000	9.00	2	1	0	0	0	7	12	8	7	0	5
	—Tampa (FSL)	1	0	1.000	3.75	3	3	0	0	0	12	11	5	5	0	11
1998—	Durham (I.L.)■	13	5	.722	2.99	28	28	2	1	0	171 2/3	177	70	57	27	112
	—Tampa Bay (A.L.)	0	1	.000	20.25	1	1	0	0	0	2 2/3	6	6	6	3	1
1999—	Columbus (I.L.)	5	3	.625	3.36	10	10	0	0	0	59	60	26	22	9	46
	—Tampa Bay (A.L.)	4	8	.333	5.60	21	15	0	0	0	80 1/3	98	59	50	27	53
A.L. totals (7 years)		10	19	.345	5.52	58	44	0	0	0	243	297	174	149	78	112
N.L. totals (2 years)		0	5	.000	5.38	17	16	0	0	0	75 1/3	91	54	45	22	24
Major League totals (9 years)		10	24	.294	5.48	75	60	0	0	0	318 1/3	388	228	194	100	136

EINERTSON, DARRELL   P   YANKEES

PERSONAL: Born September 4, 1972, in Rhinelander, Wis. ... 6-2/190. ... Throws right, bats right. ... Full name: Darrell Lee Einertson.
HIGH SCHOOL: Urbandale (Iowa).
JUNIOR COLLEGE: Indian Hills Community College (Iowa).
COLLEGE: Cameron, then Iowa Wesleyan.
TRANSACTIONS/CAREER NOTES: Selected by New York Yankees organization in 11th round of free-agent draft (June 1, 1995). ... On Norwich disabled list (May 22-August 31, 1998). ... On New York disabled list (August 31, 1998-remainder of season). ... On New York disabled list (March 26-July 19, 1999); included rehabilitation assignments to Gulf Coast Yankees (June 19-23), Tampa (June 25-30) and Norwich (July 1-18).

Year	League	W	L	Pct.	ERA	G	GS	CG	ShO	Sv.	IP	H	R	ER	BB	SO
1995—	Oneonta (NY-P)	0	4	.000	1.88	25	0	0	0	0	38 1/3	32	20	8	15	35
1996—	Greensboro (SAL)	3	9	.250	2.70	48	0	0	0	0	70	69	29	21	19	48
1997—	Tampa (FSL)	5	4	.556	2.15	45	0	0	0	6	71	63	24	17	19	55
1998—	Norwich (East.)	3	1	.750	1.02	17	0	0	0	0	35 1/3	23	7	4	10	33
1999—	Gulf Coast Yankees (GCL)	0	1	.000	0.00	1	0	0	0	0	2	3	3	0	1	4
	—Tampa (FSL)	0	0	...	1.93	2	1	0	0	0	4 2/3	1	1	1	1	3
	—Norwich (East.)	2	2	.500	4.97	21	0	0	0	0	29	39	23	16	10	16

ELARTON, SCOTT   P   ASTROS

PERSONAL: Born February 23, 1976, in Lamar, Colo. ... 6-7/240. ... Throws right, bats right. ... Full name: Vincent Scott Elarton.
HIGH SCHOOL: Lamar (Colo.).
TRANSACTIONS/CAREER NOTES: Selected by Houston Astros organization in first round (25th pick overall) of free-agent draft (June 2, 1994).
MISCELLANEOUS: Appeared in one game as outfielder with no chances (1999).

Year	League	W	L	Pct.	ERA	G	GS	CG	ShO	Sv.	IP	H	R	ER	BB	SO
1994— Gulf Coast Astros (GCL).....		4	0	1.000	0.00	5	5	0	0	0	28	9	0	0	5	28
— Quad City (Midw.)		4	1	.800	3.29	9	9	0	0	0	54²/₃	42	23	20	18	42
1995— Quad City (Midw.)		13	7	.650	4.45	26	26	0	0	0	149²/₃	149	86	74	71	112
1996— Kissimmee (FSL)..............		12	7	.632	2.92	27	27	3	1	0	172¹/₃	154	67	56	54	130
1997— Jackson (Texas)		7	4	.636	3.24	20	20	2	0	0	133¹/₃	103	57	48	47	141
— New Orleans (A.A.).............		4	4	.500	5.33	9	9	0	0	0	54	51	36	32	17	50
1998— New Orleans (PCL)...........		9	4	.692	4.01	14	14	2	1	0	92	71	42	41	41	100
— Houston (N.L.)		2	1	.667	3.32	28	2	0	0	2	57	40	21	21	20	56
1999— Houston (N.L.)		9	5	.643	3.48	42	15	0	0	1	124	111	55	48	43	121
Major League totals (2 years)		11	6	.647	3.43	70	17	0	0	3	181	151	76	69	63	177

DIVISION SERIES RECORD

Year	League	W	L	Pct.	ERA	G	GS	CG	ShO	Sv.	IP	H	R	ER	BB	SO
1998— Houston (N.L.)		0	1	.000	4.50	1	0	0	0	0	2	1	1	1	1	3
1999— Houston (N.L.)		0	0	...	3.86	2	0	0	0	0	2¹/₃	4	1	1	1	3
Division series totals (2 years)		0	1	.000	4.15	3	0	0	0	0	4¹/₃	5	2	2	2	6

ELDER, DAVID   P   RANGERS

PERSONAL: Born September 23, 1975, in Atlanta. ... 6-0/180. ... Throws right, bats right. ... Full name: David M. Elder.
HIGH SCHOOL: Booker T. Washington (Pensacola, Fla.).
COLLEGE: Georgia Tech.
TRANSACTIONS/CAREER NOTES: Selected by Texas Rangers organization in fourth round of free-agent draft (June 3, 1997). ... On Pulaski disabled list (April 7, 1998-entire season). ... On Charlotte disabled list (May 8-19, 1999).

Year	League	W	L	Pct.	ERA	G	GS	CG	ShO	Sv.	IP	H	R	ER	BB	SO
1997— Pulaski (Appl.)....................		2	2	.500	1.95	20	0	0	0	6	32¹/₃	18	8	7	12	57
1998— Pulaski (Appl.)....................								Did not play.								
1999— Charlotte (FSL)..................		4	2	.667	2.84	24	1	0	0	4	44¹/₃	33	15	14	25	42
— Tulsa (Texas)		1	0	1.000	8.10	3	0	0	0	0	6²/₃	8	7	6	6	7

ELDRED, CAL   P   WHITE SOX

PERSONAL: Born November 24, 1967, in Cedar Rapids, Iowa. ... 6-4/237. ... Throws right, bats right. ... Full name: Calvin John Eldred.
HIGH SCHOOL: Urbana (Iowa) Community.
COLLEGE: Iowa.
TRANSACTIONS/CAREER NOTES: Selected by Milwaukee Brewers organization in first round (17th pick overall) of free-agent draft (June 5, 1989). ... On disabled list (May 15, 1995-remainder of season). ... On Milwaukee disabled list (March 29-July 14, 1996); included rehabilitation assignment to New Orleans (June 10-July 9). ... On disabled list (July 26, 1998-remainder of season). ... On Milwaukee disabled list (March 29-April 20 and July 2-August 15, 1999); included rehabilitation assignments to Huntsville (April 8-17) and Louisville (April 18-20 and July 31-August 15). ... Traded by Brewers with SS Jose Valentin to Chicago White Sox for P Jaime Navarro and P John Snyder (January 12, 2000).
RECORDS: Shares N.L. single-inning record for most consecutive home runs allowed—3 (August 22, 1999, first inning).
HONORS: Named A.L. Rookie Pitcher of the Year by THE SPORTING NEWS (1992).
STATISTICAL NOTES: Led American Association with 12 hit batsmen in 1991.
MISCELLANEOUS: Appeared in one game as pinch runner (1998). ... Scored one run in three appearances as pinch runner (1999).

Year	League	W	L	Pct.	ERA	G	GS	CG	ShO	Sv.	IP	H	R	ER	BB	SO
1989— Beloit (Midw.).....................		2	1	.667	2.30	5	5	0	0	0	31¹/₃	23	10	8	11	32
1990— Stockton (Calif.)		4	2	.667	1.62	7	7	3	1	0	50	31	12	9	19	75
— El Paso (Texas)		5	4	.556	4.49	19	19	0	0	0	110¹/₃	126	61	55	47	93
1991— Denver (A.A.).....................		13	9	.591	3.75	29	*29	3	1	0	*185	161	82	77	84	*168
— Milwaukee (A.L.)		2	0	1.000	4.50	3	3	0	0	0	16	20	9	8	6	10
1992— Denver (A.A.).....................		10	6	.625	3.00	19	19	4	1	0	141	122	49	47	42	99
— Milwaukee (A.L.)		11	2	.846	1.79	14	14	2	1	0	100¹/₃	76	21	20	23	62
1993— Milwaukee (A.L.)		16	16	.500	4.01	36	•36	8	1	0	*258	232	120	115	91	180
1994— Milwaukee (A.L.)		11	11	.500	4.68	25	•25	6	0	0	179	158	96	93	84	98
1995— Milwaukee (A.L.)		1	1	.500	3.42	4	4	0	0	0	23²/₃	24	10	9	10	18
1996— New Orleans (A.A.)...........		2	2	.500	3.34	6	6	0	0	0	32¹/₃	24	12	12	17	30
— Milwaukee (A.L.)		4	4	.500	4.46	15	15	0	0	0	84²/₃	82	43	42	38	50
1997— Milwaukee (A.L.)		13	•15	.464	4.99	34	34	1	1	0	202	207	118	112	89	122
1998— Milwaukee (N.L.)		4	8	.333	4.80	23	23	0	0	0	133	157	82	71	61	86
1999— Huntsville (Sou.)		0	1	.000	7.50	2	2	1	0	0	12	13	10	10	3	10
— Louisville (I.L.)		0	1	.000	5.30	4	4	0	0	0	18²/₃	19	12	11	10	21
— Milwaukee (N.L.)		2	8	.200	7.79	20	15	0	0	0	82	101	75	71	46	60
A.L. totals (7 years)		58	49	.542	4.16	131	131	17	3	0	863²/₃	799	417	399	341	540
N.L. totals (2 years)		6	16	.273	5.94	43	38	0	0	0	215	258	157	142	107	146
Major League totals (9 years)		64	65	.496	4.51	174	169	17	3	0	1078²/₃	1057	574	541	448	686

EMBREE, ALAN   P   GIANTS

PERSONAL: Born January 23, 1970, in Vancouver, Wash. ... 6-2/190. ... Throws left, bats left. ... Full name: Alan Duane Embree.
HIGH SCHOOL: Prairie (Vancouver, Wash.).
TRANSACTIONS/CAREER NOTES: Selected by Cleveland Indians organization in fifth round of free-agent draft (June 5, 1989). ... On Cleveland disabled list (April 1-June 2 and June 2, 1993-remainder of season); included rehabilitation assignment to Canton/Akron (June 2-15). ... On Cleveland disabled list (August 1-September 7, 1996); included rehabilitation assignment to Buffalo (August 6-September 4). ... Traded by Indians with OF Kenny Lofton to Atlanta Braves for OF Marquis Grissom and OF Dave Justice (March 25, 1997). ... Traded by Braves to Arizona Diamondbacks for P Russ Springer (June 23, 1998). ... Traded by Diamondbacks to San Francisco Giants for OF Dante Powell (November 10, 1998).

E

Year League	W	L	Pct.	ERA	G	GS	CG	ShO	Sv.	IP	H	R	ER	BB	SO
1990— Burlington (Appl.)	4	4	.500	2.64	15	•15	0	0	0	81²/₃	87	36	24	30	58
1991— Columbus (SAL)	10	8	.556	3.59	27	26	3	1	0	155¹/₃	126	80	62	77	137
1992— Kinston (Caro.)	10	5	.667	3.30	15	15	1	0	0	101	89	48	37	32	115
— Canton/Akron (East.)	7	2	.778	2.28	12	12	0	0	0	79	61	24	20	28	56
— Cleveland (A.L.)	0	2	.000	7.00	4	4	0	0	0	18	19	14	14	8	12
1993— Canton/Akron (East.)	0	0	...	3.38	1	1	0	0	0	5¹/₃	3	2	2	3	4
1994— Canton/Akron (East.)	9	•16	.360	5.50	30	27	2	1	0	157	183	106	96	64	81
1995— Buffalo (A.A.)	3	4	.429	0.89	30	0	0	0	5	40²/₃	31	10	4	19	56
— Cleveland (A.L.)	3	2	.600	5.11	23	0	0	0	1	24²/₃	23	16	14	16	23
1996— Cleveland (A.L.)	1	1	.500	6.39	24	0	0	0	0	31	30	26	22	21	33
— Buffalo (A.A.)	4	1	.800	3.93	20	0	0	0	5	34¹/₃	26	16	15	14	46
1997— Atlanta (N.L.)■	3	1	.750	2.54	66	0	0	0	0	46	36	13	13	20	45
1998— Atlanta (N.L.)	1	0	1.000	4.34	20	0	0	0	0	18²/₃	23	14	9	10	19
— Arizona (N.L.)■	3	2	.600	4.11	35	0	0	0	1	35	33	18	16	13	24
1999— San Francisco (N.L.)■	3	2	.600	3.38	68	0	0	0	0	58²/₃	42	22	22	26	53
A.L. totals (3 years)	4	5	.444	6.11	51	4	0	0	1	73²/₃	72	56	50	45	68
N.L. totals (3 years)	10	5	.667	3.41	189	0	0	0	1	158¹/₃	134	67	60	69	141
Major League totals (6 years)	14	10	.583	4.27	240	4	0	0	2	232	206	123	110	114	209

DIVISION SERIES RECORD

Year League	W	L	Pct.	ERA	G	GS	CG	ShO	Sv.	IP	H	R	ER	BB	SO
1996— Cleveland (A.L.)	0	0	...	9.00	3	0	0	0	0	1	0	1	1	0	1

CHAMPIONSHIP SERIES RECORD

Year League	W	L	Pct.	ERA	G	GS	CG	ShO	Sv.	IP	H	R	ER	BB	SO
1995— Cleveland (A.L.)	0	0	...	0.00	1	0	0	0	0	¹/₃	0	0	0	0	1
1997— Atlanta (N.L.)	0	0	...	0.00	1	0	0	0	0	1	0	0	0	1	1
Champ. series totals (2 years)	0	0	...	0.00	2	0	0	0	0	1¹/₃	0	0	0	1	2

WORLD SERIES RECORD

Year League	W	L	Pct.	ERA	G	GS	CG	ShO	Sv.	IP	H	R	ER	BB	SO
1995— Cleveland (A.L.)	0	0	...	2.70	4	0	0	0	0	3¹/₃	2	1	1	2	2

ENCARNACION, JUAN   OF   TIGERS

PERSONAL: Born March 8, 1976, in Las Matas de Faran, Dominican Republic. ... 6-3/187. ... Bats right, throws right. ... Full name: Juan DeDios Encarnacion. ... Name pronounced en-car-nah-CION.
HIGH SCHOOL: Liceo Mercedes Maria Mateo (Las Matas de Faran, Dominican Republic).
TRANSACTIONS/CAREER NOTES: Signed as non-drafted free agent by Detroit Tigers organization (December 27, 1992). ... On Detroit disabled list (March 20-April 29, 1998); included rehabilitation assignment to Lakeland (April 24-29).
STATISTICAL NOTES: Led Southern League in being hit by pitch with 12 in 1997. ... Tied for International League lead in double plays by outfielder with three in 1998. ... Career major league grand slams: 1.

							BATTING							FIELDING			
Year Team (League)	Pos.	G	AB	R	H	2B	3B	HR	RBI	Avg.	BB	SO	SB	PO	A	E	Avg.
1993— Dom. Tigers (DSL)	OF	72	251	36	63	13	4	13	49	.251	15	65	6	110	13	17	.879
1994— Bristol (Appl.)	OF	54	197	16	49	7	1	4	31	.249	13	54	9	83	*9	3	.968
— Fayetteville (SAL)	OF	24	83	6	16	1	1	1	4	.193	8	36	1	22	1	2	.920
— Lakeland (FSL)	OF	3	6	1	2	0	0	0	0	.333	0	3	0	0	0	0	...
1995— Fayetteville (SAL)	OF	124	457	62	129	31	7	16	72	.282	30	113	30	143	10	7	.956
1996— Lakeland (FSL)	OF	131	499	54	120	31	2	15	58	.240	24	104	11	233	12	6	.976
1997— Jacksonville (Sou.)	OF-DH	131	493	91	159	31	4	26	90	.323	43	86	17	208	12	3	.987
— Detroit (A.L.)	OF	11	33	7	7	1	1	1	5	.212	3	12	3	22	0	0	1.000
1998— Lakeland (FSL)	OF	4	16	4	4	0	1	0	4	.250	2	4	4	7	1	0	1.000
— Toledo (I.L.)	OF-DH	92	356	55	102	17	3	8	41	.287	29	85	24	168	10	5	.973
— Detroit (A.L.)	OF-DH	40	164	30	54	9	4	7	21	.329	7	31	7	60	4	1	.985
1999— Detroit (A.L.)	OF	132	509	62	130	30	6	19	74	.255	14	113	33	264	10	9	.968
Major League totals (3 years)		183	706	95	191	40	11	27	100	.271	24	156	43	346	14	10	.973

ENCARNACION, MARIO   OF   ATHLETICS

PERSONAL: Born September 24, 1977, in Bani, Dominican Republic. ... 6-2/205. ... Bats right, throws right. ... Full name: Mario Gonzalez Encarnacion.
TRANSACTIONS/CAREER NOTES: Signed as non-drafted free agent by Oakland Athletics organization (July 11, 1994).

							BATTING							FIELDING			
Year Team (League)	Pos.	G	AB	R	H	2B	3B	HR	RBI	Avg.	BB	SO	SB	PO	A	E	Avg.
1995— Dom. Athletics (DSL)	OF	64	229	56	79	11	5	8	44	.345	40	36	17	112	9	7	.945
1996— W. Mich. (Mid.)	OF	118	401	55	92	14	3	7	43	.229	49	131	23	192	13	11	.949
1997— Modesto (Calif.)	OF	111	364	70	108	17	9	18	78	.297	42	121	14	145	7	12	.927
1998— Huntsville (Sou.)	OF	110	357	70	97	15	2	15	61	.272	60	123	11	181	8	6	.969
1999— Midland (Texas)	OF-DH	94	353	69	109	21	4	18	71	.309	47	86	9	126	6	9	.936
— Vancouver (PCL)	OF-DH	39	145	18	35	5	0	3	17	.241	6	44	5	91	6	4	.960

ENOCHS, CHRIS   P   ATHLETICS

PERSONAL: Born October 11, 1975, in Weirton, W.Va. ... 6-3/225. ... Throws right, bats right. ... Full name: Christopher Brian Enochs.
HIGH SCHOOL: Oak Glenn (New Cumberland, W.Va.).
COLLEGE: West Virginia.
TRANSACTIONS/CAREER NOTES: Selected by Oakland Athletics organization in first round (11th pick overall) of free-agent draft (June 3, 1997). ... On Midland disabled list (May 27-July 23, 1999).

Year	League	W	L	Pct.	ERA	G	GS	CG	ShO	Sv.	IP	H	R	ER	BB	SO
1997—Southern Oregon (N'west)		0	0	...	3.48	3	3	0	0	0	10 1/3	12	4	4	2	10
—Modesto (Calif.)		3	0	1.000	2.78	10	9	0	0	0	45 1/3	51	20	14	12	45
1998—Huntsville (Sou.)		9	10	.474	4.74	26	26	0	0	0	148	159	101	78	64	100
1999—Midland (Texas)		3	5	.375	10.00	13	11	0	0	0	45	69	57	50	34	33
—Visalia (Calif.)		0	0	...	4.91	4	4	0	0	0	18 1/3	24	10	10	10	19

ERDOS, TODD   P   YANKEES

PERSONAL: Born November 21, 1973, in Washington, Pa. ... 6-1/190. ... Throws right, bats right. ... Full name: Todd Michael Erdos. ... Name pronounced er-DOHS.
HIGH SCHOOL: Meadville (Pa.).
TRANSACTIONS/CAREER NOTES: Selected by San Diego Padres organization in ninth round of free-agent draft (June 1, 1992). ... On Arizona Padres disabled list (June 4, 1994-entire season). ... Selected by Arizona Diamondbacks in second round (41st pick overall) of expansion draft (November 18, 1997). ... Traded by Diamondbacks with P Marty Janzen to New York Yankees for IF Andy Fox (March 8, 1998). ... On Columbus disabled list (July 24, 1998-remainder of season).
STATISTICAL NOTES: Led Northwest League with 13 home runs allowed in 1993.

Year	League	W	L	Pct.	ERA	G	GS	CG	ShO	Sv.	IP	H	R	ER	BB	SO
1992—Arizona Padres (Ariz.)		3	4	.429	2.65	12	9	1	0	0	57 2/3	36	28	17	18	61
—Spokane (N'west)		1	0	1.000	0.69	2	2	0	0	0	13	9	2	1	5	11
1993—Spokane (N'west)		5	6	.455	3.19	16	15	0	0	0	90 1/3	73	39	32	•53	64
—Waterloo (Midw.)		1	9	.100	8.31	11	11	0	0	0	47 2/3	64	51	44	31	27
1994—Arizona Padres (Ariz.)								Did not play.								
1995—Idaho Falls (Pio.)		5	3	.625	3.48	32	0	0	0	0	41 1/3	34	19	16	30	48
1996—Rancho Cuca. (Calif.)		3	3	.500	3.74	55	0	0	0	17	67 1/3	63	33	28	37	82
1997—Mobile (Sou.)		1	4	.200	3.36	55	0	0	0	27	59	45	22	22	22	49
—San Diego (N.L.)		2	0	1.000	5.27	11	0	0	0	0	13 2/3	17	9	8	4	13
1998—Columbus (I.L.)■		3	2	.600	4.62	39	0	0	0	16	48 2/3	52	27	25	20	50
—New York (A.L.)		0	0	...	9.00	2	0	0	0	0	2	5	2	2	1	0
1999—Columbus (I.L.)		3	2	.600	6.56	27	8	0	0	0	59	70	47	43	25	53
—New York (A.L.)		0	0	...	3.86	4	0	0	0	0	7	5	4	3	4	4
A.L. totals (2 years)		0	0	...	5.00	6	0	0	0	0	9	10	6	5	5	4
N.L. totals (1 year)		2	0	1.000	5.27	11	0	0	0	0	13 2/3	17	9	8	4	13
Major League totals (3 years)		2	0	1.000	5.16	17	0	0	0	0	22 2/3	27	15	13	9	17

ERICKSON, SCOTT   P   ORIOLES

PERSONAL: Born February 2, 1968, in Long Beach, Calif. ... 6-4/230. ... Throws right, bats right. ... Full name: Scott Gavin Erickson.
HIGH SCHOOL: Homestead (Cupertino, Calif.).
JUNIOR COLLEGE: San Jose City College.
COLLEGE: Arizona.
TRANSACTIONS/CAREER NOTES: Selected by New York Mets organization in 36th round of free-agent draft (June 2, 1986); did not sign. ... Selected by Houston Astros organization in 34th round of free-agent draft (June 2, 1987); did not sign. ... Selected by Toronto Blue Jays organization in 44th round of free-agent draft (June 1, 1988); did not sign. ... Selected by Minnesota Twins organization in fourth round of free-agent draft (June 5, 1989). ... On disabled list (June 30-July 15, 1991; April 3-18, 1993 and May 15-31, 1994). ... Traded by Twins to Baltimore Orioles for P Scott Klingenbeck and a player to be named later (July 7, 1995); Twins acquired OF Kimera Bartee to complete deal (September 18, 1995).
RECORDS: Holds A.L. single-season record for fewest innings pitched for league leader—251 1/3 (1998).
STATISTICAL NOTES: Pitched 5-0 one-hit, complete-game victory against Boston (July 24, 1992, first game). ... Pitched 6-0 no-hit victory against Milwaukee (April 27, 1994). ... Tied for A.L. lead with nine hit batsmen in 1994. ... Led A.L. pitchers with 24 putouts and 68 total chances in 1999.

E

Year	League	W	L	Pct.	ERA	G	GS	CG	ShO	Sv.	IP	H	R	ER	BB	SO
1989—Visalia (Calif.)		3	4	.429	2.97	12	12	2	0	0	78 2/3	79	29	26	22	59
1990—Orlando (Sou.)		8	3	.727	3.03	15	15	3	1	0	101	75	38	34	24	69
—Minnesota (A.L.)		8	4	.667	2.87	19	17	1	0	0	113	108	49	36	51	53
1991—Minnesota (A.L.)		•20	8	.714	3.18	32	32	5	3	0	204	189	80	72	71	108
1992—Minnesota (A.L.)		13	12	.520	3.40	32	32	5	3	0	212	197	86	80	83	101
1993—Minnesota (A.L.)		8	*19	.296	5.19	34	34	1	0	0	218 2/3	*266	*138	126	71	116
1994—Minnesota (A.L.)		8	11	.421	5.44	23	23	2	1	0	144	173	95	87	59	104
1995—Minnesota (A.L.)		4	6	.400	5.95	15	15	0	0	0	87 2/3	102	61	58	32	45
—Baltimore (A.L.)■		9	4	.692	3.89	17	16	7	2	0	108 2/3	111	47	47	35	61
1996—Baltimore (A.L.)		13	12	.520	5.02	34	34	6	0	0	222 1/3	262	137	124	66	100
1997—Baltimore (A.L.)		16	7	.696	3.69	34	33	3	2	0	221 2/3	218	100	91	61	131
1998—Baltimore (A.L.)		16	13	.552	4.01	36	*36	*11	2	0	*251 1/3	*284	125	112	69	186
1999—Baltimore (A.L.)		15	12	.556	4.81	34	34	6	*3	0	230 1/3	244	127	123	*99	106
Major League totals (10 years)		130	108	.546	4.27	310	306	47	16	0	2013 2/3	2154	1045	956	697	1111

DIVISION SERIES RECORD

Year	League	W	L	Pct.	ERA	G	GS	CG	ShO	Sv.	IP	H	R	ER	BB	SO
1996—Baltimore (A.L.)		0	0	...	4.05	1	1	0	0	0	6 2/3	6	3	3	2	6
1997—Baltimore (A.L.)		1	0	1.000	4.05	1	1	0	0	0	6 2/3	7	3	3	2	6
Division series totals (2 years)		1	0	1.000	4.05	2	2	0	0	0	13 1/3	13	6	6	4	12

CHAMPIONSHIP SERIES RECORD

RECORDS: Shares A.L. record for most runs allowed in one inning—6 (October 13, 1996, third inning). ... Holds record for most home runs allowed in one inning—3 (October 13, 1996, third inning).

Year	League	W	L	Pct.	ERA	G	GS	CG	ShO	Sv.	IP	H	R	ER	BB	SO
1991—Minnesota (A.L.)		0	0	...	4.50	1	1	0	0	0	4	3	2	2	5	2
1996—Baltimore (A.L.)		0	1	.000	2.38	2	2	0	0	0	11 1/3	14	9	3	4	8
1997—Baltimore (A.L.)		1	0	1.000	4.26	2	2	0	0	0	12 2/3	15	7	6	1	6
Champ. series totals (3 years)		1	1	.500	3.54	5	5	0	0	0	28	32	18	11	10	16

NOTES: Member of World Series championship team (1991).

Year League	W	L	Pct.	ERA	G	GS	CG	ShO	Sv.	IP	H	R	ER	BB	SO
1991— Minnesota (A.L.)	0	0	...	5.06	2	2	0	0	0	$10^2/_3$	10	7	6	4	5

ERSTAD, DARIN OF ANGELS

PERSONAL: Born June 4, 1974, in Jamestown, N.D. ... 6-2/212. ... Bats left, throws left. ... Full name: Darin Charles Erstad.
HIGH SCHOOL: Jamestown (N.D.).
COLLEGE: Nebraska.
TRANSACTIONS/CAREER NOTES: Selected by New York Mets organization in 13th round of free-agent draft (June 1, 1992); did not sign. ... Selected by California Angels organization in first round (first pick overall) of free-agent draft (June 1, 1995). ... Angels franchise renamed Anaheim Angels for 1997 season. ... On disabled list (August 4-19, 1998; and August 11-26, 1999).
STATISTICAL NOTES: Had 15-game hitting streak (April 1-18, 1998). ... Career major league grand slams: 1.

							BATTING							FIELDING		
Year Team (League)	Pos.	G	AB	R	H	2B	3B	HR	RBI	Avg.	BB	SO	SB	PO	A	E	Avg.
1995— Arizona Angels (Ariz.)..	OF	4	18	2	10	1	0	0	1	.556	1	1	1	3	0	0	1.000
— Lake Elsinore (Calif.)..	OF	25	113	24	41	7	2	5	24	.363	6	22	3	65	2	1	.985
1996— Vancouver (PCL)	OF-1B-DH	85	351	63	107	22	5	6	41	.305	44	53	11	184	10	1	.995
— California (A.L.).........	OF	57	208	34	59	5	1	4	20	.284	17	29	3	121	2	3	.976
1997— Anaheim (A.L.)..........	1B-DH-OF	139	539	99	161	34	4	16	77	.299	51	86	23	1003	64	11	.990
1998— Anaheim (A.L.)	OF-1B-DH	133	537	84	159	39	3	19	82	.296	43	77	20	580	43	3	.995
1999— Anaheim (A.L.)	1B-OF-DH	142	585	84	148	22	5	13	53	.253	47	101	13	854	48	1	.999
Major League totals (4 years)		471	1869	301	527	100	13	52	232	.282	158	293	59	2558	157	18	.993

ALL-STAR GAME RECORD

						BATTING							FIELDING		
Year League	Pos.	AB	R	H	2B	3B	HR	RBI	Avg.	BB	SO	SB	PO	A	E	Avg.
1998— American..................	OF	2	1	0	0	0	0	0	.000	0	0	0	3	0	0	1.000

ESCOBAR, ALEX OF METS

PERSONAL: Born September 6, 1978, in Valencia, Venezuela. ... 6-1/180. ... Bats right, throws right. ... Full name: Alexander Jose Escobar.
HIGH SCHOOL: El Santuario (Valencia, Venezuela).
TRANSACTIONS/CAREER NOTES: Signed as non-drafted free agent by New York Mets organization (July 1, 1995). ... On St. Lucie disabled list (April 14-June 21 and July 8, 1999-remainder of season).

							BATTING							FIELDING		
Year Team (League)	Pos.	G	AB	R	H	2B	3B	HR	RBI	Avg.	BB	SO	SB	PO	A	E	Avg.
1996— GC Mets (GCL)	OF-SS	24	75	15	27	4	0	0	10	.360	4	9	0	42	2	3	.936
1997— Kingsport (Appl.)........	OF	10	36	6	7	3	0	0	3	.194	3	8	1	19	0	2	.905
— GC Mets (GCL)..........	OF	26	73	12	18	4	1	1	11	.247	10	17	0	26	2	1	.966
1998— Capital City (SAL).......	OF	112	416	90	129	23	5	27	91	.310	54	133	49	186	5	12	.941
1999— GC Mets (GCL)	DH-OF	2	8	1	3	2	0	1	1	.375	1	2	0	1	0	0	1.000
— St. Lucie (FSL)	OF	1	3	1	2	0	0	1	3	.667	1	1	1	2	0	0	1.000

ESCOBAR, KELVIM P BLUE JAYS

PERSONAL: Born April 11, 1976, in La Guaria, Venezuela. ... 6-1/195. ... Throws right, bats right. ... Full name: Kelvim Jose Bolivar Escobar.
TRANSACTIONS/CAREER NOTES: Signed as non-drafted free agent by Toronto Blue Jays organization (July 9, 1992). ... On Toronto disabled list (April 16-May 6, 1998); included rehabilitation assignment to Syracuse (May 2-6).

Year League	W	L	Pct.	ERA	G	GS	CG	ShO	Sv.	IP	H	R	ER	BB	SO
1993— Dom. Blue Jays (DSL)........	2	1	.667	4.13	8	7	0	0	0	$32^2/_3$	34	17	15	25	31
1994— GC Blue Jays (GCL)........	4	4	.500	2.35	11	10	1	0	1	65	56	23	17	18	64
1995— Dom. Blue Jays (DSL)........	0	1	.000	1.72	3	2	0	0	0	$15^2/_3$	14	3	3	5	20
— Medicine Hat (Pio.)	3	3	.500	5.71	14	14	1	•1	0	$69^1/_3$	66	47	44	33	75
1996— Dunedin (FSL)........	9	5	.643	2.69	18	18	1	0	0	$110^1/_3$	101	44	33	33	113
— Knoxville (Sou.)................	3	4	.429	5.33	10	10	0	0	0	54	61	36	32	24	44
1997— Knoxville (Sou.)................	2	1	.667	3.70	5	5	1	0	0	$24^1/_3$	20	13	10	16	31
— Dunedin (FSL)................	0	1	.000	3.75	3	2	0	0	0	12	16	9	5	3	16
— Toronto (A.L.)...................	3	2	.600	2.90	27	0	0	0	14	31	28	12	10	19	36
1998— Toronto (A.L.)................	7	3	.700	3.73	22	10	0	0	0	$79^2/_3$	72	37	33	35	72
— Syracuse (I.L.)................	2	2	.500	3.77	13	10	0	0	1	$59^2/_3$	51	26	25	24	64
1999— Toronto (A.L.)................	14	11	.560	5.69	33	30	1	0	0	174	203	118	110	81	129
Major League totals (3 years).......	24	16	.600	4.84	82	40	1	0	14	$284^2/_3$	303	167	153	135	237

ESPADA, JOSUE 2B/SS ATHLETICS

PERSONAL: Born August 30, 1975, in Santurce, Puerto Rico. ... 5-10/175. ... Bats right, throws right.
COLLEGE: University of Mobile (Ala.).
TRANSACTIONS/CAREER NOTES: Selected by Oakland Athletics in second round of 1996 draft (June 4, 1996). ... On disabled list (April 18-May 23 and June 11-July 18, 1998). ... Selected by Minnesota Twins from Athletics organization in Rule 5 major league draft (December 14, 1998). ... Returned to Athletics organization (April 1, 1999).

							BATTING							FIELDING		
Year Team (League)	Pos.	G	AB	R	H	2B	3B	HR	RBI	Avg.	BB	SO	SB	PO	A	E	Avg.
1996— S. Oregon (N'west.)....	SS	15	54	7	12	1	0	1	5	.222	5	10	0	19	29	2	.960
— W. Mich. (Midw.)........	SS	23	74	9	20	2	0	0	4	.270	13	11	3	19	56	6	.926
1997— Visalia (Calif.)	SS	118	445	90	122	7	3	3	39	.274	72	69	46	196	346	32	.944
1998— Huntsville (Sou.)	SS	51	161	29	41	7	1	1	22	.255	27	15	7	57	116	9	.951
1999— Midland (Texas).........	SS-2B	113	435	85	147	15	2	6	51	.338	62	51	22	176	282	35	.929
— Vancouver (PCL)	2B	6	26	2	8	1	0	0	0	.308	3	4	1	13	17	1	.968

E

ESTALELLA, BOBBY   C   GIANTS

PERSONAL: Born August 23, 1974, in Hialeah, Fla. ... 6-1/205. ... Bats right, throws right. ... Full name: Robert M. Estalella. ... Grandson of Bobby Estalella, outfielder with Washington Senators (1935-36, 1939 and 1942), St. Louis Browns (1941), and Philadelphia Athletics (1943-45 and 1949).
HIGH SCHOOL: Cooper City (Fla.).
JUNIOR COLLEGE: Miami-Dade (South) Community College.
TRANSACTIONS/CAREER NOTES: Selected by Philadelphia Phillies organization in 23rd round of free-agent draft (June 1, 1992). ... On Philadelphia disabled list (March 27-April 29, 1999); included rehabilitation assignments to Clearwater (April 9-17) and to Scranton/Wilkes-Barre (April 19-29). ... Traded by Phillies to San Francisco Giants for P Chris Brock (December 12, 1999).
STATISTICAL NOTES: Tied for South Atlantic League lead in double plays by catcher with eight in 1994. ... Led Florida State League catchers with 864 total chances in 1995. ... Led International League with 928 total chances and tied for league lead in double plays by catcher with nine in 1997. ... Hit three home runs in one game (September 4, 1997). ... Led International League catchers with 10 double plays in 1999. ... Career major league grand slams: 1.

							BATTING							FIELDING		
Year Team (League)	Pos.	G	AB	R	H	2B	3B	HR	RBI	Avg.	BB	SO	SB	PO	A	E	Avg.
1993—Martinsville (Appl.).....	C	35	122	14	36	11	0	3	19	.295	14	24	0	210	25	6	.975
—Clearwater (FSL)........	C	11	35	4	8	0	0	0	4	.229	2	3	0	47	8	0	1.000
1994—Spartanburg (SAL).....	C	86	299	34	65	19	1	9	41	.217	31	85	0	592	87	10	.985
—Clearwater (FSL)........	C	13	46	3	12	1	0	2	9	.261	3	17	0	92	5	1	.990
1995—Clearwater (FSL)........	C	117	404	61	105	24	1	15	58	.260	56	76	0	*771	82	11	.987
—Reading (East.)..........	C	10	34	5	8	1	0	2	9	.235	4	7	0	60	9	1	.986
1996—Reading (East.)..........	C	111	365	48	89	14	2	23	72	.244	67	104	2	775	84	14	.984
—Scranton/W.B. (I.L.) ...	C	11	36	7	9	3	0	3	8	.250	5	10	0	55	6	2	.968
—Philadelphia (N.L.)......	C	7	17	5	6	0	0	2	4	.353	1	6	1	24	1	0	1.000
1997—Scranton/W.B. (I.L.) ...	C-DH	123	433	63	101	32	0	16	65	.233	56	109	3	*844	71	13	.986
—Philadelphia (N.L.)......	C	13	29	9	10	1	0	4	9	.345	7	7	0	49	3	0	1.000
1998—Scranton/W.B. (I.L.) ...	C-DH	76	242	49	68	14	1	17	49	.281	66	49	0	469	25	5	.990
—Philadelphia (N.L.)......	C	47	165	16	31	6	1	8	20	.188	13	49	0	321	12	4	.988
1999—Clearwater (FSL)........	C-DH	8	26	3	11	3	0	1	8	.423	3	3	0	37	4	1	.976
—Scranton/W.B. (I.L.) ...	C-DH	110	386	58	89	23	2	15	62	.231	55	100	4	652	43	5	.993
—Philadelphia (N.L.)......	C	9	18	2	3	0	0	0	1	.167	4	7	0	38	2	1	.976
Major League totals (4 years)		76	229	32	50	7	1	14	34	.218	25	69	1	432	18	5	.989

ESTES, SHAWN   P   GIANTS

PERSONAL: Born February 18, 1973, in San Francisco. ... 6-2/192. ... Throws left, bats left. ... Full name: Aaron Shawn Estes.
HIGH SCHOOL: Douglas (Minden, Nev.).
TRANSACTIONS/CAREER NOTES: Selected by Seattle Mariners organization in first round (11th pick overall) of free-agent draft (June 3, 1991). ... On disabled list (August 19, 1993-remainder of season). ... On Appleton disabled list (April 8-July 19 and July 25-August 15, 1994). ... Traded by Mariners with IF Wilson Delgado to San Francisco Giants for P Salomon Torres (May 21, 1995). ... On disabled list (March 23-April 6, 1997). ... On San Francisco disabled list (July 11-September 4, 1998); included rehabilitation assignments to Bakersfield (August 26-29) and Fresno (August 30-September 4).
STATISTICAL NOTES: Tied for N.L. lead with 15 wild pitches in 1999.
MISCELLANEOUS: Appeared in four games as pinch runner with San Francisco (1996). ... Appeared in four games as pinch runner (1997). ... Scored two runs in two games as pinch runner with San Francisco (1998). ... Struck out in both appearances as pinch hitter and scored two runs in eight appearances as pinch runner (1999).

Year League	W	L	Pct.	ERA	G	GS	CG	ShO	Sv.	IP	H	R	ER	BB	SO
1991—Bellingham (N'west)...........	1	3	.250	6.88	9	9	0	0	0	34	27	33	26	55	35
1992—Bellingham (N'west)...........	3	3	.500	4.32	15	15	0	0	0	77	84	55	37	45	77
1993—Appleton (Midw.)...............	5	9	.357	7.24	19	18	0	0	0	83 1/3	108	85	67	52	65
1994—Appleton (Midw.)...............	0	2	.000	4.58	5	4	0	0	0	19 2/3	19	13	10	17	28
—Arizona Mariners (Ariz.)	0	3	.000	3.15	5	5	0	0	0	20	16	9	7	6	31
1995—Wisconsin (Midw.).............	0	0	...	0.90	2	2	0	0	0	10	5	1	1	5	11
—Burlington (Midw.)■.........	0	0	...	4.11	4	4	0	0	0	15 1/3	13	8	7	12	22
—San Jose (Calif.)................	5	2	.714	2.17	9	8	0	0	0	49 2/3	32	13	12	17	61
—Shreveport (Texas)	2	0	1.000	2.01	4	4	0	0	0	22 1/3	14	5	5	10	18
—San Francisco (N.L.)	0	3	.000	6.75	3	3	0	0	0	17 1/3	16	14	13	5	14
1996—Phoenix (PCL)...................	9	3	.750	3.43	18	18	0	0	0	110 1/3	92	43	42	38	95
—San Francisco (N.L.)	3	5	.375	3.60	11	11	0	0	0	70	63	30	28	39	60
1997—San Francisco (N.L.)	19	5	.792	3.18	32	32	3	2	0	201	162	80	71	*100	181
1998—San Francisco (N.L.)	7	12	.368	5.06	25	25	1	1	0	149 1/3	150	89	84	80	136
—Bakersfield (Calif.)..............	0	0	...	0.00	1	1	0	0	0	4 1/3	3	0	0	1	5
—Fresno (PCL).....................	1	0	1.000	1.80	1	1	0	0	0	5	3	1	1	3	6
1999—San Francisco (N.L.)	11	11	.500	4.92	32	32	1	1	0	203	209	121	111	112	159
Major League totals (5 years)......	40	36	.526	4.31	103	103	5	4	0	640 2/3	600	334	307	336	550

DIVISION SERIES RECORD

Year League	W	L	Pct.	ERA	G	GS	CG	ShO	Sv.	IP	H	R	ER	BB	SO
1997—San Francisco (N.L.)	0	0	...	15.00	1	1	0	0	0	3	5	5	5	4	3

ALL-STAR GAME RECORD

Year League	W	L	Pct.	ERA	GS	CG	ShO	Sv.	IP	H	R	ER	BB	SO
1997—National......................	0	1	.000	18.00	0	0	0	0	1	1	2	2	1	1

ESTRADA, HORACIO   P   BREWERS

PERSONAL: Born October 19, 1975, in San Joaquin, Venezuela. ... 6-0/160. ... Throws left, bats left. ... Full name: Horacio Jimenez Estrada.
HIGH SCHOOL: Domingo Segado (San Joaquin, Venezuela).

E

TRANSACTIONS/CAREER NOTES: Signed as non-drafted free agent by Milwaukee Brewers organization (July 3, 1992). ... On Louisville disabled list (May 28, 1998-remainder of season; and June 9-19, 1999).

Year	League	W	L	Pct.	ERA	G	GS	CG	ShO	Sv.	IP	H	R	ER	BB	SO
1993—	Dom. Brewers (DSL)..........	1	2	.333	4.41	22	3	0	0	0	51	39	33	25	37	60
1994—	Dom. Brewers (DSL)..........	3	4	.429	2.67	26	2	0	0	7	60 2/3	41	27	18	46	52
1995—	Arizona Brewers (Ariz.)	0	1	.000	3.71	8	1	0	0	2	17	13	9	7	8	21
—	Helena (Pio.)	1	2	.333	5.40	13	0	0	0	0	30	27	21	18	24	30
1996—	Beloit (Midw.).....................	2	1	.667	1.23	17	0	0	0	1	29 1/3	21	8	4	11	34
—	Stockton (Calif.)	1	3	.250	4.59	29	0	0	0	3	51	43	29	26	21	62
1997—	El Paso (Texas)..................	8	10	.444	4.74	29	23	1	0	1	153 2/3	174	93	81	70	127
1998—	El Paso (Texas)..................	5	0	1.000	4.53	8	8	0	0	0	49 2/3	50	27	25	21	37
—	Louisville (I.L.)	0	0	...	3.00	2	2	0	0	0	12	10	4	4	5	4
1999—	Louisville (I.L.)	6	6	.500	5.67	25	24	1	0	0	131 2/3	128	87	83	65	112
—	Milwaukee (N.L.)	0	0	...	7.36	4	0	0	0	0	7 1/3	10	6	6	4	5
Major League totals (1 year)........		0	0	...	7.36	4	0	0	0	0	7 1/3	10	6	6	4	5

ESTRELLA, LEO   P   BLUE JAYS

PERSONAL: Born February 20, 1975, in Puerto Plata, Dominican Republic. ... 6-1/185. ... Throws right, bats right. ... Full name: Leoncio Estrella.
HIGH SCHOOL: Liceo Padre Las Casas (Puerto Plata, Dominican Republic).
TRANSACTIONS/CAREER NOTES: Signed as non-drafted free agent by New York Mets organization (October 12, 1993). ... On Capital City disabled list (April 10-24, 1998). ... Traded by Mets to Toronto Blue Jays for IF/OF Tony Phillips (July 31, 1998).

Year	League	W	L	Pct.	ERA	G	GS	CG	ShO	Sv.	IP	H	R	ER	BB	SO
1994—	Dominican Mets (DSL).......	5	0	1.000	3.47	30	0	0	0	3	36 1/3	33	28	14	32	20
1995—	Dominican Mets (DSL).......	2	4	.333	5.44	12	8	0	0	0	43	61	37	26	13	32
1996—	Little Falls (NY-P)	6	3	.667	3.88	15	7	1	0	0	58	54	32	25	24	52
1997—	Pittsfield (NY-P)	7	6	.538	3.03	15	15	0	0	0	92	91	48	31	27	55
1998—	Columbia (SAL).................	10	8	.556	3.93	20	20	3	0	0	119	120	66	52	23	97
—	Hagerstown (SAL)■...........	1	3	.250	4.50	5	5	0	0	0	30	34	19	15	13	27
1999—	Dunedin (FSL)..................	14	7	.667	3.21	27	24	2	2	0	168	166	74	60	47	116

EUSEBIO, TONY   C   ASTROS

PERSONAL: Born April 27, 1967, in San Jose de Los Llames, Dominican Republic. ... 6-2/210. ... Bats right, throws right. ... Full name: Raul Antonio Eusebio. ... Name pronounced you-SAY-bee-o.
HIGH SCHOOL: San Rafael (Dominican Republic).
TRANSACTIONS/CAREER NOTES: Signed as non-drafted free agent by Houston Astros organization (May 30, 1985). ... On disabled list (August 5, 1990-remainder of season; April 16-23, 1992; and August 24, 1993-remainder of season). ... On Houston disabled list (May 8-June 17 and June 22-August 7, 1996); included rehabilitation assignments to Tucson (June 10-17 and July 29-August 7). ... On disabled list (July 30-August 15, 1999). ... Granted free agency (October 29, 1999). ... Re-signed by Astros (December 2, 1999).
STATISTICAL NOTES: Tied for Southern League lead in double plays by catcher with eight in 1989. ... Led Texas League catchers with .9963 fielding percentage and 12 double plays in 1992. ... Career major league grand slams: 2.

Year	Team (League)	Pos.	G	AB	R	H	2B	3B	HR	RBI	Avg.	BB	SO	SB	PO	A	E	Avg.
1985—	GC Astros (GCL)	C	1	1	0	0	0	0	0	0	.000	0	0	0	4	0	0	1.000
1985—	....					Dominican Summer League statistics unavailable.												
1986—	....					Dominican Summer League statistics unavailable.												
1987—	GC Astros (GCL)	C-1B	42	125	26	26	1	2	1	15	.208	18	19	8	204	24	4	.983
1988—	Osceola (FSL).............	C-OF	118	392	45	96	6	3	0	40	.245	40	69	19	611	66	8	.988
1989—	Columbus (Sou.)........	C	65	203	20	38	6	1	0	18	.187	38	47	7	355	46	7	.983
—	Osceola (FSL).............	C	52	175	22	50	6	3	0	30	.286	19	27	5	290	40	5	.985
1990—	Columbus (Sou.)........	C	92	318	36	90	18	0	4	37	.283	21	80	6	558	69	4	*.994
1991—	Jackson (Texas)..........	C	66	222	27	58	8	3	2	31	.261	25	54	3	424	48	7	.985
—	Tucson (PCL)	C	5	20	5	8	1	0	0	2	.400	3	3	1	40	1	0	1.000
—	Houston (N.L.)	C	10	19	4	2	1	0	0	0	.105	6	8	0	49	4	1	.981
1992—	Jackson (Texas)..........	C	94	339	33	104	9	3	5	44	.307	25	58	1	493	51	2	*.996
1993—	Tucson (PCL)	C	78	281	39	91	20	1	1	43	.324	22	40	1	450	46	3	.994
1994—	Houston (N.L.)	C	55	159	18	47	9	1	5	30	.296	8	33	0	263	24	2	.993
1995—	Houston (N.L.)	C	113	368	46	110	21	1	6	58	.299	31	59	0	645	49	5	.993
1996—	Houston (N.L.)	C	58	152	15	41	7	2	1	19	.270	18	20	0	255	24	1	.996
—	Tucson (PCL)	C-DH	15	53	8	22	4	0	0	14	.415	2	7	0	45	1	0	1.000
1997—	Houston (N.L.)	C	60	164	12	45	2	0	1	18	.274	19	27	0	297	16	4	.987
1998—	Houston (N.L.)	C	66	182	13	46	6	1	4	36	.253	18	31	1	352	19	3	.992
1999—	Houston (N.L.)	C	103	323	31	88	15	0	4	33	.272	40	67	0	652	37	4	.994
Major League totals (7 years)			465	1367	139	379	61	5	18	194	.277	140	245	1	2513	173	20	.993

DIVISION SERIES RECORD

Year	Team (League)	Pos.	G	AB	R	H	2B	3B	HR	RBI	Avg.	BB	SO	SB	PO	A	E	Avg.
1997—	Houston (N.L.)	C	1	3	1	2	0	0	0	0	.667	0	1	1	6	1	0	1.000
1998—	Houston (N.L.)	C	1	3	0	1	1	0	0	0	.333	0	2	0	6	0	0	1.000
1999—	Houston (N.L.)	C	4	15	2	4	0	0	1	3	.267	1	2	0	34	3	1	.974
Division series totals (3 years)			6	21	3	7	1	0	1	3	.333	1	5	1	46	4	1	.980

EVERETT, ADAM   SS   ASTROS

PERSONAL: Born February 2, 1977, in Austell, Ga. ... 6-0/156. ... Bats right, throws right.
HIGH SCHOOL: Harrison (Kennesaw, Ga.).
COLLEGE: North Carolina State, then South Carolina.

TRANSACTIONS/CAREER NOTES: Selected by Boston Red Sox organization in first round (12th pick overall) of free-agent draft (June 2, 1998). ... Traded by Red Sox with P Greg Miller to Houston Astros for OF Carl Everett (December 15, 1999).

Year Team (League)	Pos.	G	AB	R	H	2B	3B	HR	RBI	Avg.	BB	SO	SB	PO	A	E	Avg.
1998— Lowell (NY-P)	SS	21	71	11	21	6	2	0	9	.296	11	13	2	34	67	9	.918
1999— Trenton (East.)	SS	98	338	56	89	11	0	10	44	.263	41	64	21	150	273	18	.959

EVERETT, CARL — OF — RED SOX

PERSONAL: Born June 3, 1971, in Tampa. ... 6-0/190. ... Bats both, throws right. ... Full name: Carl Edward Everett.
HIGH SCHOOL: Hillsborough (Tampa).
TRANSACTIONS/CAREER NOTES: Selected by New York Yankees organization in first round (10th pick overall) of free-agent draft (June 4, 1990). ... On Fort Lauderdale disabled list (July 7-August 15, 1992). ... Selected by Florida Marlins in second round (27th pick overall) of expansion draft (November 17, 1992). ... On High Desert disabled list (April 8-13, 1993). ... On Florida disabled list (July 23-August 10, 1994). ... On Edmonton suspended list (August 29, 1994-remainder of season). ... Traded by Marlins to New York Mets for 2B Quilvio Veras (November 29, 1994). ... On disabled list (April 12-27, 1996). ... Traded by Mets to Houston Astros for P John Hudek (December 22, 1997). ... On disabled list (July 16-August 6, 1999). ... Traded by Astros to Boston Red Sox for SS Adam Everett and P Greg Miller (December 15, 1999).
STATISTICAL NOTES: Led South Atlantic League in being hit by pitch with 23 in 1991. ... Switch-hit home runs in one game three times (April 20, 1997, first game; April 24, 1998; and August 7, 1999). ... Career major league grand slams: 4.

Year Team (League)	Pos.	G	AB	R	H	2B	3B	HR	RBI	Avg.	BB	SO	SB	PO	A	E	Avg.
1990— GC Yankees (GCL)	OF	48	185	28	48	8	5	1	14	.259	15	38	15	64	5	5	.932
1991— Greensboro (SAL)	OF	123	468	96	127	18	0	4	40	.271	57	122	28	250	14	7	.974
1992— Fort Laud. (FSL)	OF	46	183	30	42	8	2	2	9	.230	12	40	11	111	5	3	.975
— Prince Will. (Caro.)	OF	6	22	7	7	0	0	4	9	.318	5	7	1	12	1	0	1.000
1993— High Desert (Calif.)■	OF	59	253	48	73	12	6	10	52	.289	22	73	24	124	6	2	.985
— Florida (N.L.)	OF	11	19	0	2	0	0	0	0	.105	1	9	1	6	0	1	.857
— Edmonton (PCL)	OF-DH	35	136	28	42	13	4	6	16	.309	19	45	12	69	12	2	.976
1994— Edmonton (PCL)	OF-DH	78	321	63	108	17	2	11	47	.336	19	65	16	167	11	2	.989
— Florida (N.L.)	OF	16	51	7	11	1	0	2	6	.216	3	15	4	28	2	0	1.000
1995— New York (N.L.)■	OF	79	289	48	75	13	1	12	54	.260	39	67	2	148	9	3	.981
— Norfolk (I.L.)	OF-DH-SS	67	260	52	78	16	4	6	35	.300	20	47	12	133	7	0	1.000
1996— New York (N.L.)	OF	101	192	29	46	8	1	1	16	.240	21	53	6	96	4	7	.935
1997— New York (N.L.)	OF	142	443	58	110	28	3	14	57	.248	32	102	17	226	8	7	.971
1998— Houston (N.L.)■	OF	133	467	72	138	34	4	15	76	.296	44	102	14	296	12	4	.987
1999— Houston (N.L.)	OF-DH	123	464	86	151	33	3	25	108	.325	50	94	27	256	11	6	.978
Major League totals (7 years)		605	1925	300	533	117	12	69	317	.277	190	442	71	1056	46	28	.975

DIVISION SERIES RECORD

Year Team (League)	Pos.	G	AB	R	H	2B	3B	HR	RBI	Avg.	BB	SO	SB	PO	A	E	Avg.
1998— Houston (N.L.)	OF-PH	4	13	1	2	0	0	0	0	.154	0	4	0	8	0	0	1.000
1999— Houston (N.L.)	OF	4	15	2	2	0	0	0	1	.133	2	8	1	8	0	0	1.000
Division series totals (2 years)		8	28	3	4	0	0	0	1	.143	2	12	1	16	0	0	1.000

EYRE, SCOTT — P — WHITE SOX

PERSONAL: Born May 30, 1972, in Inglewood, Calif. ... 6-1/200. ... Throws left, bats left. ... Full name: Scott Alan Eyre.
HIGH SCHOOL: Cyprus (Magna, Utah).
JUNIOR COLLEGE: College of Southern Idaho.
TRANSACTIONS/CAREER NOTES: Selected by Texas Rangers organization in ninth round of free-agent draft (June 3, 1991). ... Traded by Rangers organization to Chicago White Sox organization for SS Esteban Beltre (March 28, 1994). ... On disabled list (April 8-27, 1994). ... On Prince William disabled list (April 6-September 7, 1995). ... On Charlotte disabled list (June 2-13, 1999). ... On Chicago disabled list (August 31-September 26, 1999); included rehabilitation assignment to Charlotte (September 8-26).
HONORS: Named Southern League Most Outstanding Pitcher (1997).

Year League	W	L	Pct.	ERA	G	GS	CG	ShO	Sv.	IP	H	R	ER	BB	SO
1992— Butte (Pio.)	7	3	.700	2.90	15	14	2	1	0	80²/₃	71	30	26	39	94
1993— Charleston, S.C. (SAL)	11	7	.611	3.45	26	26	0	0	0	143²/₃	115	74	55	59	154
1994— South Bend (Midw.)■	8	4	.667	3.47	19	18	2	0	0	111²/₃	108	56	43	37	111
1995— GC White Sox (GCL)	0	2	.000	2.30	9	9	0	0	0	27¹/₃	16	7	7	12	40
1996— Birmingham (Sou.)	12	7	.632	4.38	27	27	0	0	0	158¹/₃	170	90	77	79	137
1997— Birmingham (Sou.)	•13	5	.722	3.84	22	22	0	0	0	126²/₃	110	61	54	55	127
— Chicago (A.L.)	4	4	.500	5.04	11	11	0	0	0	60²/₃	62	36	34	31	36
1998— Chicago (A.L.)	3	8	.273	5.38	33	17	0	0	0	107	114	78	64	64	73
1999— Charlotte (I.L.)	6	4	.600	3.82	12	11	0	0	0	68¹/₃	75	32	29	23	63
— Chicago (A.L.)	1	1	.500	7.56	21	0	0	0	0	25	38	22	21	15	17
Major League totals (3 years)	8	13	.381	5.56	65	28	0	0	0	192²/₃	214	136	119	110	126

FABREGAS, JORGE — C — ROYALS

PERSONAL: Born March 13, 1970, in Miami. ... 6-3/215. ... Bats left, throws right. ... Name pronounced FAB-ruh-gas.
HIGH SCHOOL: Christopher Columbus (Miami).
COLLEGE: Miami (Fla.).
TRANSACTIONS/CAREER NOTES: Selected by Cleveland Indians organization in 11th round of free-agent draft (June 1, 1988); did not sign. ... Selected by California Angels organization in supplemental round ("sandwich pick" between first and second round, 34th pick overall) of free-agent draft (June 3, 1991); pick received as part of compensation for Minnesota Twins signing Type A free-agent OF/DH Chili Davis. ...

E
F

On disabled list (April 12-May 4 and July 28-September 5, 1992). ... Angels franchise renamed Anaheim Angels for 1997 season. ... Traded by Angels with P Chuck McElroy to Chicago White Sox for OF Tony Phillips and C Chad Kreuter (May 18, 1997). ... Selected by Arizona Diamondbacks in first round (seventh pick overall) of expansion draft (November 18, 1997). ... On Arizona disabled list (May 31-June 30, 1998); included rehabilitation assignment to Tucson (June 22-30). ... Traded by Diamondbacks with P Willie Blair and cash considerations to New York Mets for OF Bernard Gilkey, P Nelson Figueroa and cash (July 31, 1998). ... Traded by Mets to Florida Marlins for P Oscar Henriquez (November 20, 1998). ... Released by Marlins (August 26, 1999). ... Signed by Atlanta Braves (August 31, 1999). ... Released by Braves (November 5, 1999). ... Signed by Kansas City Royals organization (January 12, 2000).

STATISTICAL NOTES: Led Texas League with 17 passed balls in 1993.

Year— Team (League)	Pos.	G	AB	R	H	2B	3B	HR	RBI	Avg.	BB	SO	SB	PO	A	E	Avg.
1992— Palm Springs (Calif.)..	C	70	258	35	73	13	0	0	40	.283	30	27	0	436	63	*17	.967
1993— Midland (Texas).........	C	113	409	63	118	26	3	6	56	.289	31	60	1	620	99	•11	.985
—Vancouver (PCL)	C	4	13	1	3	1	0	0	1	.231	1	3	0	30	3	0	1.000
1994—Vancouver (PCL)	C-DH	66	211	17	47	6	1	1	24	.223	12	25	1	365	41	4	.990
—California (A.L.)	C	43	127	12	36	3	0	0	16	.283	7	18	2	217	16	3	.987
1995—California (A.L.)	C	73	227	24	56	10	0	1	22	.247	17	28	0	391	36	6	.986
—Vancouver (PCL)	C	21	73	9	18	3	0	4	10	.247	9	12	0	112	12	4	.969
1996—California (A.L.)	C-DH	90	254	18	73	6	0	2	26	.287	17	27	0	502	46	6	.989
—Vancouver (PCL)	DH-C-1B	10	37	4	11	3	0	0	5	.297	4	4	0	27	2	0	1.000
1997—Anaheim (A.L.)	C	21	38	2	3	1	0	0	3	.079	3	3	0	81	5	1	.989
—Chicago (A.L.)■........	C-1B	100	322	31	90	10	1	7	48	.280	11	43	1	520	46	7	.988
1998—Arizona (N.L.)■.........	C	50	151	8	30	4	0	1	15	.199	13	26	0	228	30	1	.996
—Tucson (PCL)	C-DH	6	20	2	5	1	0	0	3	.250	3	1	0	28	3	0	1.000
—New York (N.L.)■	C	20	32	3	6	0	0	1	5	.188	1	6	0	62	6	2	.971
1999—Florida (N.L.)■.........	C	82	223	20	46	10	2	3	21	.206	26	27	0	404	52	5	.989
—Atlanta (N.L.)■	C-1B	6	8	0	0	0	0	0	0	.000	0	0	0	21	1	0	1.000
American League totals (4 years)		327	968	87	258	30	1	10	115	.267	55	119	3	1711	149	23	.988
National League totals (2 years)		158	414	31	82	14	2	5	41	.198	40	59	0	715	89	8	.990
Major League totals (6 years)		485	1382	118	340	44	3	15	156	.246	95	178	3	2426	238	31	.988

CHAMPIONSHIP SERIES RECORD

Year— Team (League)	Pos.	G	AB	R	H	2B	3B	HR	RBI	Avg.	BB	SO	SB	PO	A	E	Avg.
1999— Atlanta (N.L.)..............	PH	2	2	0	0	0	0	0	0	.000	0	1	0	...	...	...	...

WORLD SERIES RECORD

Year— Team (League)	Pos.	G	AB	R	H	2B	3B	HR	RBI	Avg.	BB	SO	SB	PO	A	E	Avg.
1999— Atlanta (N.L.)..............	PH	1	1	0	0	0	0	0	0	.000	0	1	0	0	0	0	...

FALKENBORG, BRIAN   P   ORIOLES

PERSONAL: Born January 18, 1978, in Newport Beach, Calif. ... 6-6/195. ... Throws right, bats right. ... Full name: Brian Thomas Falkenborg.
HIGH SCHOOL: Redmond (Wash.).
TRANSACTIONS/CAREER NOTES: Selected by Baltimore Orioles organization in second round of free-agent draft (June 4, 1996). ... On Bowie disabled list (June 14-August 16, 1999).

Year League	W	L	Pct.	ERA	G	GS	CG	ShO	Sv.	IP	H	R	ER	BB	SO
1996—Gulf Coast Orioles (GCL)....	0	3	.000	2.57	8	6	0	0	0	28	21	13	8	8	36
—High Desert (Calif.)............	0	0	...	0.00	1	0	0	0	0	1	1	0	0	0	1
1997—Delmarva (SAL)...................	7	9	.438	4.46	25	25	0	0	0	127	122	73	63	46	107
—Bowie (East.)....................	0	1	.000	16.20	1	1	0	0	0	1²/₃	3	3	3	3	0
1998—Frederick (Caro.)	5	5	.500	4.50	15	14	1	1	0	78	83	42	39	18	70
1999—Bowie (East.)....................	3	6	.333	3.78	16	16	0	0	0	83¹/₃	77	40	35	36	77
—Gulf Coast Orioles (GCL)....	1	0	1.000	2.00	3	2	0	0	0	9	6	2	2	3	11
—Baltimore (A.L.)..................	0	0	...	0.00	2	0	0	0	0	3	2	0	0	2	1
Major League totals (1 year)........	0	0	...	0.00	2	0	0	0	0	3	2	0	0	2	1

FALTEISEK, STEVE   P   INDIANS

PERSONAL: Born January 28, 1972, in Mineola, N.Y. ... 6-2/200. ... Throws right, bats right. ... Full name: Steven James Falteisek. ... Name pronounced FALT-e-seck.
HIGH SCHOOL: Memorial (Floral Park, N.Y.).
COLLEGE: South Alabama.
TRANSACTIONS/CAREER NOTES: Selected by Montreal Expos organization in 10th round of free-agent draft (June 1, 1992). ... Granted free agency (October 15, 1998). ... Signed by Milwaukee Brewers organization (November 5, 1998). ... Released by Brewers (September 5, 1999). ... Signed by Cleveland Indians organization (January 26, 2000).
MISCELLANEOUS: Scored a run in only appearance as pinch runner (1999).

Year League	W	L	Pct.	ERA	G	GS	CG	ShO	Sv.	IP	H	R	ER	BB	SO
1992—Jamestown (NY-P)	3	*8	.273	3.56	15	•15	2	0	0	*96	84	47	38	31	82
1993—Burlington (Midw.)	3	5	.375	5.90	14	14	0	0	0	76¹/₃	86	59	50	35	63
1994—West Palm Beach (FSL)	9	4	.692	2.54	27	24	0	0	0	159²/₃	144	72	45	49	91
1995—Harrisburg (East.).............	9	6	.600	2.95	25	25	•5	0	0	168	152	74	55	64	112
—Ottawa (I.L.)	2	0	1.000	1.17	3	3	1	1	0	23	17	4	3	5	18
1996—Harrisburg (East.).............	2	5	.286	6.36	12	12	0	0	0	58	75	45	41	25	26
—Ottawa (I.L.)	6	5	.545	3.81	17	17	1	0	0	115²/₃	111	60	49	48	62
1997—Ottawa (I.L.)	6	9	.400	3.96	22	22	1	0	0	125	135	67	55	54	56
—Montreal (N.L.)..................	0	0	...	3.38	5	0	0	0	0	8	8	4	3	3	2
1998—Ottawa (I.L.)	10	11	.476	5.46	34	22	1	0	0	161²/₃	186	110	98	59	83
1999—Louisville (I.L.)■	5	11	.313	6.84	42	4	0	0	0	76¹/₃	98	65	58	41	34
—Milwaukee (N.L.)	0	0	...	7.50	10	0	0	0	0	12	18	10	10	3	5
Major League totals (2 years)	0	0	...	5.85	15	0	0	0	0	20	26	14	13	6	7

FARNSWORTH, KYLE   P   CUBS

PERSONAL: Born April 14, 1976, in Wichita, Kan. ... 6-4/215. ... Throws right, bats right. ... Full name: Kyle Lynn Farnsworth.
HIGH SCHOOL: Milton (Alpharetta, Ga.).
JUNIOR COLLEGE: Abraham Baldwin College (Ga.).
TRANSACTIONS/CAREER NOTES: Selected by Chicago Cubs organization in 47th round of free-agent draft (June 2, 1994).

Year League	W	L	Pct.	ERA	G	GS	CG	ShO	Sv.	IP	H	R	ER	BB	SO
1995— Gulf Coast Cubs (GCL)	3	2	.600	0.87	16	0	0	0	1	31	22	8	3	11	18
1996— Rockford (Midw.)	9	6	.600	3.70	20	20	1	0	0	112	122	62	46	35	82
1997— Daytona (FSL)	10	10	.500	4.09	27	27	2	0	0	156 1/3	178	91	71	47	105
1998— West Tenn (Sou.)	8	2	.800	2.77	13	13	0	0	0	81 1/3	70	32	25	21	73
— Iowa (PCL)	5	9	.357	6.93	18	18	0	0	0	102 2/3	129	88	79	36	79
1999— Iowa (PCL)	2	2	.500	3.20	6	6	0	0	0	39 1/3	38	16	14	9	29
— Chicago (N.L.)	5	9	.357	5.05	27	21	1	1	0	130	140	80	73	52	70
Major League totals (1 year)	5	9	.357	5.05	27	21	1	1	0	130	140	80	73	52	70

FASANO, SAL   C   ROYALS

PERSONAL: Born August 10, 1971, in Chicago. ... 6-2/230. ... Bats right, throws right. ... Full name: Salvatore Frank Fasano.
HIGH SCHOOL: Hoffman Estates (Ill.).
COLLEGE: Evansville.
TRANSACTIONS/CAREER NOTES: Selected by Kansas City Royals organization in 37th round of free-agent draft (June 3, 1993). ... On Kansas City disabled list (April 20-May 9 and August 30, 1998-remainder of season); included rehabilitation assignment to Omaha (May 5-9). ... On Omaha disabled list (August 1-26, 1999).
STATISTICAL NOTES: Led Northwest League catchers with seven double plays in 1993. ... Led Pacific Coast League in being hit by pitch with 26 in 1999. ... Tied for Pacific Coast League lead with 12 errors by catcher in 1999.

						BATTING								FIELDING			
Year Team (League)	Pos.	G	AB	R	H	2B	3B	HR	RBI	Avg.	BB	SO	SB	PO	A	E	Avg.
1993— Eugene (N'west)	C	49	176	25	47	11	1	10	36	.267	19	49	4	276	38	1	.997
1994— Rockford (Midw.)	C-1B	97	345	61	97	16	1	25	81	.281	33	66	8	527	86	12	.981
— Wilmington (Caro.)	C-1B	23	90	15	29	7	0	7	32	.322	13	24	0	80	9	4	.957
1995— Wilmington (Caro.)	C-1B	23	88	12	20	2	1	2	7	.227	5	16	0	132	12	0	1.000
— Wichita (Texas)	C-1B	87	317	60	92	19	2	20	66	.290	27	61	3	589	64	14	.979
1996— Kansas City (A.L.)	C	51	143	20	29	2	0	6	19	.203	14	25	1	291	14	5	.984
— Omaha (A.A.)	C-1B-3B	29	104	12	24	4	0	4	15	.231	6	21	0	198	21	4	.982
1997— Omaha (A.A.)	C-DH	49	152	17	25	7	0	4	14	.164	12	53	0	296	34	4	.988
— Kansas City (A.L.)	C-DH	13	38	4	8	2	0	1	1	.211	1	12	0	53	3	1	.982
— Wichita (Texas)	C-1B	40	131	27	31	5	0	13	27	.237	20	35	0	232	21	4	.984
1998— Kansas City (A.L.)	C-1B-3B	74	216	21	49	10	0	8	31	.227	10	56	1	437	25	2	.996
— Omaha (PCL)	C	4	14	1	3	1	0	1	2	.214	1	4	0	26	1	0	1.000
1999— Omaha (PCL)	C-DH-1B	88	280	63	77	15	0	21	49	.275	42	69	4	582	51	‡12	.981
— Kansas City (A.L.)	C	23	60	11	14	2	0	5	16	.233	7	17	0	143	8	0	1.000
Major League totals (4 years)		161	457	56	100	16	0	20	67	.219	32	110	2	924	50	8	.992

FASSERO, JEFF   P   RED SOX

PERSONAL: Born January 5, 1963, in Springfield, Ill. ... 6-1/195. ... Throws left, bats left. ... Full name: Jeffrey Joseph Fassero. ... Name pronounced fuh-SAIR-oh.
HIGH SCHOOL: Griffin (Springfield, Ill.).
JUNIOR COLLEGE: Lincoln Land Community College (Ill.).
COLLEGE: Mississippi.
TRANSACTIONS/CAREER NOTES: Selected by St. Louis Cardinals organization in 22nd round of free-agent draft (June 4, 1984). ... Selected by Chicago White Sox organization from Cardinals organization in Rule 5 minor league draft (December 5, 1989). ... Released by White Sox organization (April 3, 1990). ... Signed by Cleveland Indians organization (April 9, 1990). ... Granted free agency (October 15, 1990). ... Signed by Indianapolis, Montreal Expos organization (January 3, 1991). ... On disabled list (July 24-August 11, 1994). ... Traded by Expos with P Alex Pacheco to Seattle Mariners for C Chris Widger, P Trey Moore and P Matt Wagner (October 29, 1996). ... On disabled list (March 22-April 12, 1998). ... Traded by Mariners to Texas Rangers for a player to named later (August 27, 1999); Mariners acquired OF Adrian Myers to complete deal (September 22, 1999). ... Granted free agency (October 28, 1999). ... Signed by Boston Red Sox (December 22, 1999).
STATISTICAL NOTES: Pitched 5-0 no-hit victory for Arkansas against Jackson (June 12, 1989).

Year League	W	L	Pct.	ERA	G	GS	CG	ShO	Sv.	IP	H	R	ER	BB	SO
1984— Johnson City (Appl.)	4	7	.364	4.59	13	11	2	0	1	66 2/3	65	42	34	39	59
1985— Springfield (Midw.)	4	8	.333	4.01	29	15	1	0	1	119	125	78	53	45	65
1986— St. Petersburg (FSL)	13	7	.650	2.45	26	•26	6	1	0	*176	156	63	48	56	112
1987— Arkansas (Texas)	10	7	.588	4.10	28	27	2	1	0	151 1/3	168	90	69	67	118
1988— Arkansas (Texas)	5	5	.500	3.58	70	1	0	0	17	78	94	48	31	41	72
1989— Louisville (A.A.)	3	10	.231	5.22	22	19	0	0	0	112	136	79	65	47	73
— Arkansas (Texas)	4	1	.800	1.64	6	6	2	1	0	44	32	11	8	12	38
1990— Canton/Akron (East.)■	5	4	.556	2.80	*61	0	0	0	6	64 1/3	66	24	20	24	61
1991— Indianapolis (A.A.)■	3	0	1.000	1.47	18	0	0	0	4	18 1/3	11	3	3	7	12
— Montreal (N.L.)	2	5	.286	2.44	51	0	0	0	8	55 1/3	39	17	15	17	42
1992— Montreal (N.L.)	8	7	.533	2.84	70	0	0	0	1	85 2/3	81	35	27	34	63
1993— Montreal (N.L.)	12	5	.706	2.29	56	15	1	0	1	149 2/3	119	50	38	54	140
1994— Montreal (N.L.)	8	6	.571	2.99	21	21	1	0	0	138 2/3	119	54	46	40	119
1995— Montreal (N.L.)	13	14	.481	4.33	30	30	1	0	0	189	207	102	91	74	164
1996— Montreal (N.L.)	15	11	.577	3.30	34	34	5	1	0	231 2/3	217	95	85	55	222

Year League	W	L	Pct.	ERA	G	GS	CG	ShO	Sv.	IP	H	R	ER	BB	SO
1997— Seattle (A.L.)■	16	9	.640	3.61	35	•35	2	1	0	234 1/3	226	108	94	84	189
1998— Seattle (A.L.)	13	12	.520	3.97	32	32	7	0	0	224 2/3	223	115	99	66	176
1999— Seattle (A.L.)	4	14	.222	7.38	30	24	0	0	0	139	188	123	114	73	101
— Texas (A.L.)■	1	0	1.000	5.71	7	3	0	0	0	17 1/3	20	12	11	10	13
A.L. totals (3 years)	34	35	.493	4.65	104	94	9	1	0	615 1/3	657	358	318	233	479
N.L. totals (6 years)	58	48	.547	3.20	262	100	8	1	10	850	782	353	302	274	750
Major League totals (9 years)	92	83	.526	3.81	366	194	17	2	10	1465 1/3	1439	711	620	507	1229

DIVISION SERIES RECORD

Year League	W	L	Pct.	ERA	G	GS	CG	ShO	Sv.	IP	H	R	ER	BB	SO
1997— Seattle (A.L.)	1	0	1.000	1.13	1	1	0	0	0	8	3	1	1	4	3
1999— Texas (A.L.)	0	0	...	9.00	1	0	0	0	0	1	2	1	1	1	1
Division series totals (2 years)	1	0	1.000	2.00	2	1	0	0	0	9	5	2	2	5	4

FEBLES, CARLOS   2B   ROYALS

PERSONAL: Born May 24, 1976, in El Seybo, Dominican Republic. ... 5-11/185. ... Bats right, throws right. ... Full name: Carlos Manuel Febles.
HIGH SCHOOL: Sagrado Corazon de Jesus (Dominican Republic).
TRANSACTIONS/CAREER NOTES: Signed as non-drafted free agent by Kansas City Royals (November 2, 1993). ... On disabled list (August 24-September 17, 1999).
STATISTICAL NOTES: Led Gulf Coast League second basemen with 230 total chances and 39 double plays in 1995. ... Led Carolina League with 590 total chances and 85 double plays in 1997. ... Led Texas League with .441 on-base percentage in 1998.

									BATTING					FIELDING			
Year Team (League)	Pos.	G	AB	R	H	2B	3B	HR	RBI	Avg.	BB	SO	SB	PO	A	E	Avg.
1994— Dom. Royals (DSL)	2B	56	184	38	61	9	3	2	37	.332	38	27	12	113	113	16	.934
1995— GC Royals (GCL)	2B	54	188	40	53	13	5	3	20	.282	26	30	16	*117	101	12	.948
1996— Lansing (Midw.)	2B-SS	102	363	84	107	23	5	5	43	.295	66	64	30	206	292	19	.963
1997— Wilmington (Caro.)	2B	122	438	78	104	27	6	3	29	.237	51	95	49	212	*355	*23	.961
1998— Wichita (Texas)	2B	126	432	110	141	28	9	14	52	.326	80	70	*51	248	334	19	.968
— Kansas City (A.L.)	2B	11	25	5	10	1	2	0	2	.400	4	7	2	16	18	0	1.000
1999— Kansas City (A.L.)	2B	123	453	71	116	22	9	10	53	.256	47	91	20	272	375	14	.979
Major League totals (2 years)		134	478	76	126	23	11	10	55	.264	51	98	22	288	393	14	.980

FELIZ, PEDRO   3B   GIANTS

PERSONAL: Born April 27, 1977, in Azua, Dominican Republic. ... 6-1/195. ... Bats right, throws right.
HIGH SCHOOL: Augustine de Chequer (Dominican Republic).
TRANSACTIONS/CAREER NOTES: Signed as non-drafted free agent by San Francisco Giants organization (February 7, 1994).
STATISTICAL NOTES: Led California League third basemen with 457 total chances and 39 double plays in 1997. ... Led Texas League third basemen with 21 double plays in 1998. ... Led Texas League in grounding into double plays with 18 in 1999. ... Led Texas League third baseman with 407 total chances in 1999.

									BATTING					FIELDING			
Year Team (League)	Pos.	G	AB	R	H	2B	3B	HR	RBI	Avg.	BB	SO	SB	PO	A	E	Avg.
1994— Arizona Giants (Ariz.)	3B	38	119	7	23	0	0	0	3	.193	2	20	2	19	82	5	.953
1995— Bellingham (N'west)	3B-1B	43	113	14	31	2	1	0	16	.274	7	33	1	30	37	2	.971
1996— Bellingham (N'west)	3B-1B	93	321	36	85	12	2	5	36	.265	18	65	5	66	186	17	.937
1997— Bakersfield (Calif.)	3B	135	515	59	140	25	4	14	56	.272	23	90	5	*112	*322	23	*.950
1998— Shreveport (Texas)	3B	100	364	39	96	23	2	12	50	.264	9	62	0	*71	204	22	*.926
— Fresno (PCL)	3B	3	7	1	3	1	0	1	3	.429	1	0	0	0	2	0	1.000
1999— Shreveport (Texas)	3B	131	491	52	124	24	6	13	77	.253	19	90	4	76	*304	27	.934

FERNANDEZ, ALEX   P   MARLINS

F

PERSONAL: Born August 13, 1969, in Miami Beach, Fla. ... 6-1/225. ... Throws right, bats right. ... Full name: Alexander Fernandez.
HIGH SCHOOL: Pace (Miami).
JUNIOR COLLEGE: Miami-Dade (South) Community College.
COLLEGE: Miami (Fla.).
TRANSACTIONS/CAREER NOTES: Selected by Milwaukee Brewers organization in first round (24th pick overall) of free-agent draft (June 1, 1988); did not sign. ... Selected by Chicago White Sox organization in first round (fourth pick overall) of free-agent draft (June 4, 1990). ... Granted free agency (December 7, 1996). ... Signed by Florida Marlins (December 9, 1996). ... On disabled list (March 21, 1998-entire season; and April 12-27, May 2-18 and September 7, 1999-remainder of season).
HONORS: Named Golden Spikes Award winner by USA Baseball (1990).
STATISTICAL NOTES: Pitched 7-0 one-hit, complete-game victory for Chicago against Milwaukee (May 4, 1992). ... Pitched 1-0 one-hit, complete-game victory against Chicago (April 10, 1997).
MISCELLANEOUS: Had a sacrifice hit in only appearance as pinch hitter (1997). ... Flied out in only appearance as pinch hitter (1999).

Year League	W	L	Pct.	ERA	G	GS	CG	ShO	Sv.	IP	H	R	ER	BB	SO
1990— GC White Sox (GCL)	1	0	1.000	3.60	2	2	0	0	0	10	11	4	4	1	16
— Sarasota (FSL)	1	1	.500	1.84	2	2	0	0	0	14 2/3	8	4	3	3	23
— Birmingham (Sou.)	3	0	1.000	1.08	4	4	0	0	0	25	20	7	3	6	27
— Chicago (A.L.)	5	5	.500	3.80	13	13	3	0	0	87 2/3	89	40	37	34	61
1991— Chicago (A.L.)	9	13	.409	4.51	34	32	2	0	0	191 2/3	186	100	96	88	145
1992— Chicago (A.L.)	8	11	.421	4.27	29	29	4	2	0	187 2/3	199	100	89	50	95
— Vancouver (PCL)	2	1	.667	0.94	4	3	2	1	0	28 2/3	15	8	3	6	27
1993— Chicago (A.L.)	18	9	.667	3.13	34	34	3	1	0	247 1/3	221	95	86	67	169
1994— Chicago (A.L.)	11	7	.611	3.86	24	24	4	3	0	170 1/3	163	83	73	50	122
1995— Chicago (A.L.)	12	8	.600	3.80	30	30	5	2	0	203 2/3	200	98	86	65	159

Year League	W	L	Pct.	ERA	G	GS	CG	ShO	Sv.	IP	H	R	ER	BB	SO
1996— Chicago (A.L.)	16	10	.615	3.45	35	35	6	1	0	258	248	110	99	72	200
1997— Florida (N.L.)■..................	17	12	.586	3.59	32	32	5	1	0	220²/₃	193	93	88	69	183
1998— Florida (N.L.)......................							Did not play.								
1999— Florida (N.L.)......................	7	8	.467	3.38	24	24	1	0	0	141	135	60	53	41	91
A.L. totals (7 years)	79	63	.556	3.78	199	197	27	9	0	1346¹/₃	1306	626	566	426	951
N.L. totals (2 years)	24	20	.545	3.51	56	56	6	1	0	361²/₃	328	153	141	110	274
Major League totals (9 years).......	103	83	.554	3.73	255	253	33	10	0	1708	1634	779	707	536	1225

DIVISION SERIES RECORD

Year League	W	L	Pct.	ERA	G	GS	CG	ShO	Sv.	IP	H	R	ER	BB	SO
1997— Florida (N.L.)......................	1	0	1.000	2.57	1	1	0	0	0	7	7	2	2	0	5

CHAMPIONSHIP SERIES RECORD

Year League	W	L	Pct.	ERA	G	GS	CG	ShO	Sv.	IP	H	R	ER	BB	SO
1993— Chicago (A.L.)	0	2	.000	1.80	2	2	0	0	0	15	15	6	3	6	10
1997— Florida (N.L.)......................	0	1	.000	16.88	1	1	0	0	0	2²/₃	6	5	5	1	3
Champ. series totals (2 years)	0	3	.000	4.08	3	3	0	0	0	17²/₃	21	11	8	7	13

WORLD SERIES RECORD

NOTES: Member of World Series championship team (1997); inactive due to injury.

Year League	W	L	Pct.	ERA	G	GS	CG	ShO	Sv.	IP	H	R	ER	BB	SO
1997— Florida (N.L.)......................							Did not play.								

FERNANDEZ, JOSE — 3B

PERSONAL: Born November 2, 1974, in La Vega, Dominican Republic. ... 6-0/220. ... Bats left, throws right. ... Full name: Jose Mayobanex Fernandez.
HIGH SCHOOL: Instituto Evangelico (Santo Domingo, Dominican Republic).
COLLEGE: Universidad Madre y Maestra (Santiago, Dominican Republic).
TRANSACTIONS/CAREER NOTES: Signed as non-drafted free agent by Montreal Expos organization (March 2, 1993). ... On Ottawa disabled list (September 1, 1998-remainder of season). ... Released by Expos (December 13, 1999).
STATISTICAL NOTES: Tied for International League lead with 94 putouts by third baseman in 1999. ... Led International League third basemen with 31 errors in 1999.

							BATTING							FIELDING		
Year Team (League)	Pos.	G	AB	R	H	2B	3B	HR	RBI	Avg.	BB	SO	SB	PO	A	E	Avg.
1993— Dom. Expos (DSL)	IF	65	251	40	80	8	1	10	49	.319	32	23	2	103	223	25	.929
1994— GC Expos (GCL)	3B-1B	45	172	27	40	8	0	5	23	.233	14	35	11	87	77	9	.948
— Ottawa (I.L.)	3B-1B	21	60	8	16	4	1	0	4	.267	5	14	3	35	18	5	.914
1995— Vermont (NY-P).........	3B	66	270	38	74	6	7	4	41	.274	13	51	29	48	157	21	.907
1996— Delmarva (SAL)........	3B	126	421	72	115	23	6	12	70	.273	50	76	23	*102	239	35	.907
1997— Harrisburg (East.).......	3B-1B	29	96	10	22	3	1	4	11	.229	11	28	2	41	31	6	.923
— W.P. Beach (FSL).......	3B-1B	97	350	49	108	21	3	9	58	.309	37	76	22	89	193	15	.949
1998— Harrisburg (East.).......	3B-1B	104	369	59	109	27	1	17	58	.295	36	73	16	119	167	22	.929
1999— Ottawa (I.L.)	3-1-DH-2	124	465	73	126	30	2	14	68	.271	31	136	14	‡185	229	†31	.930
— Montreal (N.L.)...........	3B	8	24	0	5	2	0	0	1	.208	1	7	0	7	9	2	.889
Major League totals (1 year)		8	24	0	5	2	0	0	1	.208	1	7	0	7	9	2	.889

FERNANDEZ, TONY — 3B/DH

PERSONAL: Born June 30, 1962, in San Pedro de Macoris, Dominican Republic. ... 6-2/195. ... Bats both, throws right. ... Full name: Octavio Antonio Castro Fernandez.
HIGH SCHOOL: Gasto Fernando de Ligne (San Pedro de Macoris, Dominican Republic).
TRANSACTIONS/CAREER NOTES: Signed as non-drafted free agent by Toronto Blue Jays organization (April 24, 1979). ... On Syracuse disabled list (August 10-27, 1981). ... On disabled list (April 8-May 2, 1989). ... Traded by Blue Jays with 1B Fred McGriff to San Diego Padres for OF Joe Carter and 2B Roberto Alomar (December 5, 1990). ... Traded by Padres to New York Mets for P Wally Whitehurst, OF D.J. Dozier and a player to be named later (October 26, 1992); Padres acquired C Raul Casanova from Mets to complete deal (December 7, 1992). ... Traded by Mets to Blue Jays for OF Darrin Jackson (June 11, 1993). ... Granted free agency (November 3, 1993). ... Signed by Cincinnati Reds organization (March 8, 1994). ... Granted free agency (October 13, 1994). ... Signed by New York Yankees (December 15, 1994). ... On disabled list (May 21-June 8, 1995). ... On disabled list (March 24, 1996-remainder of season). ... Granted free agency (November 18, 1996). ... Signed by Cleveland Indians (December 28, 1996). ... Granted free agency (October 30, 1997). ... Signed by Blue Jays (December 8, 1997). ... Granted free agency (November 5, 1999).
RECORDS: Shares major league record for most times caught stealing in one inning—2 (June 26, 1992, fifth inning). ... Holds A.L. career record for highest fielding percentage by shortstop (1,000 or more games)—.982. ... Holds A.L. single-season record for most games by shortstop—163 (1986). ... Shares A.L. single-season record for most games by switch hitter—163 (1986).
HONORS: Named shortstop on THE SPORTING NEWS A.L. All-Star team (1986). ... Won A.L. Gold Glove at shortstop (1986-89).
STATISTICAL NOTES: Led International League shortstops with 87 double plays in 1983. ... Led A.L. shortstops with 791 total chances in 1985 and 786 in 1990. ... Led N.L. third basemen with .991 fielding percentage in 1994. ... Hit for the cycle (September 3, 1995, 10 innings). ... Career major league grand slams: 2.
MISCELLANEOUS: Holds Toronto Blue Jays all-time record for most hits (1,565), doubles (287) and triples (72).

							BATTING							FIELDING		
Year Team (League)	Pos.	G	AB	R	H	2B	3B	HR	RBI	Avg.	BB	SO	SB	PO	A	E	Avg.
1980— Kinston (Caro.)..........	SS	62	187	28	52	6	2	0	12	.278	28	17	7	93	205	28	.914
1981— Kinston (Caro.)..........	SS	75	280	57	89	10	6	1	13	.318	49	20	15	121	227	19	.948
— Syracuse (I.L.)..........	SS	31	115	13	32	6	2	1	9	.278	7	15	9	69	80	3	.980
1982— Syracuse (I.L.)..........	SS	134	523	78	158	21	6	4	56	.302	42	31	22	*246	364	23	*.964
1983— Syracuse (I.L.)..........	SS	117	437	65	131	18	6	5	38	.300	57	27	35	*211	361	26	.957
— Toronto (A.L.)..........	SS-DH	15	34	5	9	1	1	0	2	.265	2	2	0	16	17	0	1.000
1984— Toronto (A.L.)..........	SS	26	94	12	24	1	0	0	6	.255	13	9	1	46	72	5	.959
— Toronto (A.L.)..........	SS-3B-DH	88	233	29	63	5	3	3	19	.270	17	15	5	119	195	9	.972

F

Year Team (League)	Pos.	G	AB	R	H	2B	3B	HR	RBI	Avg.	BB	SO	SB	PO	A	E	Avg.
								BATTING								**FIELDING**	
1985— Toronto (A.L.)............	SS	161	564	71	163	31	10	2	51	.289	43	41	13	283	*478	30	.962
1986— Toronto (A.L.)............	SS	*163	*687	91	213	33	9	10	65	.310	27	52	25	*294	445	13	*.983
1987— Toronto (A.L.)............	SS	146	578	90	186	29	8	5	67	.322	51	48	32	*270	396	14	.979
1988— Toronto (A.L.)............	SS	154	648	76	186	41	4	5	70	.287	45	65	15	247	470	14	.981
1989— Toronto (A.L.)............	SS	140	573	64	147	25	9	11	64	.257	29	51	22	260	475	6	*.992
1990— Toronto (A.L.)............	SS	161	635	84	175	27	*17	4	66	.276	71	70	26	*297	*480	9	.989
1991— San Diego (N.L.)■■	SS	145	558	81	152	27	5	4	38	.272	55	74	23	247	440	20	.972
1992— San Diego (N.L.)	SS	155	622	84	171	32	4	4	37	.275	56	62	20	240	405	11	.983
1993— New York (N.L.)■...	SS	48	173	20	39	5	2	1	14	.225	25	19	6	83	150	6	.975
— Toronto (A.L.)■...	SS	94	353	45	108	18	9	4	50	.306	31	26	15	196	260	7	.985
1994— Cincinnati (N.L.)■...	3B-SS-2B	104	366	50	102	18	6	8	50	.279	44	40	12	67	195	4	†.985
1995— New York (N.L.)■...	SS-2B	108	384	57	94	20	2	5	45	.245	42	40	6	148	283	10	.977
1996— New York (A.L.)							Did not play.										
1997— Cleveland (A.L.)■...	2B-SS-DH	120	409	55	117	21	1	11	44	.286	22	47	6	219	322	11	.980
1998— Toronto (A.L.)■...	2B-3B-DH	138	486	71	156	36	2	9	72	.321	45	53	13	160	296	13	.972
1999— Toronto (A.L.)	3B-DH-2B	142	485	73	159	41	0	6	75	.328	77	62	6	65	212	18	.939
American League totals (13 years)		1630	6069	811	1776	328	75	75	690	.293	502	572	184	2574	4329	154	.978
National League totals (4 years)		452	1719	235	464	82	17	17	139	.270	180	195	61	637	1190	41	.978
Major League totals (16 years)		2082	7788	1046	2240	410	92	92	829	.288	682	767	245	3211	5519	195	.978

DIVISION SERIES RECORD

Year Team (League)	Pos.	G	AB	R	H	2B	3B	HR	RBI	Avg.	BB	SO	SB	PO	A	E	Avg.
								BATTING								**FIELDING**	
1995— New York (A.L.).........	SS	5	21	0	5	2	0	0	0	.238	2	2	0	9	15	0	1.000
1997— Cleveland (A.L.)	2B-PH	4	11	0	2	1	0	0	4	.182	0	0	0	8	9	0	1.000
Division series totals (2 years)		9	32	0	7	3	0	0	4	.219	2	2	0	17	24	0	1.000

CHAMPIONSHIP SERIES RECORD

Year Team (League)	Pos.	G	AB	R	H	2B	3B	HR	RBI	Avg.	BB	SO	SB	PO	A	E	Avg.
								BATTING								**FIELDING**	
1985— Toronto (A.L.)............	SS	7	24	2	8	2	0	0	2	.333	1	2	0	11	15	2	.929
1989— Toronto (A.L.)............	SS	5	20	6	7	3	0	0	1	.350	1	2	5	9	15	0	1.000
1993— Toronto (A.L.)............	SS	6	22	1	7	0	0	0	1	.318	2	4	0	12	8	0	1.000
1997— Cleveland (A.L.)	2B-PH	5	14	1	5	1	0	1	2	.357	1	2	0	9	10	1	.950
Championship series totals (4 years)		23	80	10	27	6	0	1	6	.338	5	10	5	41	48	3	.967

WORLD SERIES RECORD

NOTES: Member of World Series championship team (1993).

Year Team (League)	Pos.	G	AB	R	H	2B	3B	HR	RBI	Avg.	BB	SO	SB	PO	A	E	Avg.
								BATTING								**FIELDING**	
1993— Toronto (A.L.)............	SS	6	21	2	7	1	0	0	9	.333	3	3	0	11	8	0	1.000
1997— Cleveland (A.L.).........	2B-PH	5	17	1	8	1	0	0	4	.471	0	1	0	9	14	2	.920
World Series totals (2 years)		11	38	3	15	2	0	0	13	.395	3	4	0	20	22	2	.955

ALL-STAR GAME RECORD

Year League	Pos.	AB	R	H	2B	3B	HR	RBI	Avg.	BB	SO	SB	PO	A	E	Avg.
						BATTING									**FIELDING**	
1986— American	SS	0	0	0	0	0	0	0	...	0	0	0	0	0	0	...
1987— American	SS	2	0	0	0	0	0	0	.000	0	0	0	1	3	0	1.000
1989— American	PR-SS	1	0	0	0	0	0	0	.000	0	0	0	2	2	0	1.000
1992— National	SS	2	1	1	0	0	0	0	.500	0	0	0	3	0	0	1.000
1999— American	3B	2	0	0	0	0	0	0	.000	0	1	0	0	2	0	1.000
All-Star Game totals (5 years)		7	1	1	0	0	0	0	.143	0	1	0	6	7	0	1.000

F

FETTERS, MIKE   P   DODGERS

PERSONAL: Born December 19, 1964, in Van Nuys, Calif. ... 6-4/226. ... Throws right, bats right. ... Full name: Michael Lee Fetters.
HIGH SCHOOL: Iolani (Honolulu, Hawaii).
COLLEGE: Pepperdine.
TRANSACTIONS/CAREER NOTES: Selected by Los Angeles Dodgers organization in 22nd round of free-agent draft (June 6, 1983); did not sign. ... Selected by California Angels organization in supplemental round ("sandwich pick" between first and second round, 27th pick overall) of free-agent draft (June 2, 1986); pick received as compensation for Baltimore Orioles signing Type A free-agent OF/IF Juan Beniquez. ... Traded by Angels with P Glenn Carter to Milwaukee Brewers for P Chuck Crim (December 10, 1991). ... On disabled list (May 3-19, 1992 and May 25-June 9, 1995). ... On Milwaukee disabled list (April 4-May 5, 1997; included rehabilitation assignment to Tucson (April 30-May 5). ... Traded by Brewers with P Ben McDonald and P Ron Villone to Cleveland Indians for OF Marquis Grissom and P Jeff Juden (December 8, 1997). ... Traded by Indians to Oakland Athletics for P Steve Karsay (December 8, 1997). ... On Oakland disabled list (April 6-26, 1998). ... Traded by A's to Anaheim Angels for a player to be named later and cash (August 10, 1998). ... Granted free agency (October 26, 1998). ... Signed by Baltimore Orioles organization (February 4, 1999). ... On Baltimore disabled list (June 7-September 1, 1999); included rehabilitation assignment to Rochester (August 23-31). ... Granted free agency (November 1, 1999). ... Signed by Dodgers organization (December 15, 1999).

Year League	W	L	Pct.	ERA	G	GS	CG	ShO	Sv.	IP	H	R	ER	BB	SO
1986— Salem (N'west)..................	4	2	.667	3.38	12	12	1	0	0	72	60	39	27	51	72
1987— Palm Springs (Calif.).........	9	7	.563	3.57	19	19	2	0	0	116	106	62	46	73	105
1988— Midland (Texas)..............	8	8	.500	5.92	20	20	2	0	0	114	116	78	75	67	101
— Edmonton (PCL)	2	0	1.000	1.93	2	2	1	0	0	14	8	3	3	10	11
1989— Edmonton (PCL)	12	8	.600	3.80	26	26	•6	2	0	168	160	80	71	72	*144
— California (A.L.).................	0	0	...	8.10	1	0	0	0	0	3 1/3	5	4	3	1	4
1990— Edmonton (PCL)	1	1	.500	0.99	5	5	1	1	0	27 1/3	22	9	3	13	26
— California (A.L.).................	1	1	.500	4.12	26	2	0	0	1	67 2/3	77	33	31	20	35

Year League	W	L	Pct.	ERA	G	GS	CG	ShO	Sv.	IP	H	R	ER	BB	SO
1991—Edmonton (PCL)	2	7	.222	4.87	11	11	1	0	0	61	65	39	33	26	43
—California (A.L.)	2	5	.286	4.84	19	4	0	0	0	44 2/3	53	29	24	28	24
1992—Milwaukee (A.L.)■	5	1	.833	1.87	50	0	0	0	2	62 2/3	38	15	13	24	43
1993—Milwaukee (A.L.)	3	3	.500	3.34	45	0	0	0	0	59 1/3	59	29	22	22	23
1994—Milwaukee (A.L.)	1	4	.200	2.54	42	0	0	0	17	46	41	16	13	27	31
1995—Milwaukee (A.L.)	0	3	.000	3.38	40	0	0	0	22	34 2/3	40	16	13	20	33
1996—Milwaukee (A.L.)	3	3	.500	3.38	61	0	0	0	32	61 1/3	65	28	23	26	53
1997—Milwaukee (A.L.)	1	5	.167	3.45	51	0	0	0	6	70 1/3	62	30	27	33	62
—Tucson (PCL)	0	0	...	10.80	2	0	0	0	0	1 2/3	1	2	2	1	0
1998—Oakland (A.L.)■	1	6	.143	3.99	48	0	0	0	5	47 1/3	48	26	21	21	34
—Anaheim (A.L.)■	1	2	.333	5.56	12	0	0	0	0	11 1/3	14	8	7	4	9
1999—Baltimore (A.L.)	1	0	1.000	5.81	27	0	0	0	0	31	35	23	20	22	22
—Rochester (I.L.)	0	0	...	0.00	4	0	0	0	0	3 2/3	0	0	0	2	6
Major League totals (11 years)	19	33	.365	3.62	422	6	0	0	85	539 2/3	537	257	217	248	373

FICK, ROBERT   C/1B   TIGERS

PERSONAL: Born March 15, 1974, in Torrance, Calif. ... 6-1/189. ... Bats left, throws right. ... Full name: Robert Charles John Fick. ... Brother of Chris Fick, former outfielder/first baseman in St. Louis Cardinals and Arizona Diamondacks organizations; and brother of Chuck Fick, St. Louis Cardinals scout and former catcher in Montreal Expos and Oakland Athletics organizations.

HIGH SCHOOL: Newbury Park (Calif.).

JUNIOR COLLEGE: Ventura (Calif.) College.

COLLEGE: Cal State Northridge.

TRANSACTIONS/CAREER NOTES: Selected by Oakland Athletics organization in 45th round of free-agent draft (June 1, 1992); did not sign. ... Selected by Detroit Tigers organization in 43rd round of free-agent draft (June 1, 1995); did not sign. ... Selected by Tigers organization in fifth round of free-agent draft (June 4, 1996). ... On Detroit disabled list (March 31-September 7, 1999); included rehabilitation assignments to Gulf Coast Tigers (August 18-20), West Michigan (August 21-23) and Toledo (August 24-September 6).

HONORS: Named Midwest League Most Valuable Player (1996).

STATISTICAL NOTES: Led Midwest League with 262 total bases and .566 slugging percentage in 1997. ... Career major league grand slams: 1.

							BATTING						FIELDING		
Year Team (League)	Pos.	G	AB	R	H	2B	3B	HR	RBI	Avg.	BB	SO	SB	PO	A	E	Avg.
1996—Jamestown (NY-P)	C	43	133	18	33	6	0	1	14	.248	12	25	3	155	13	3	.982
1997—W. Mich. (Mid.)	1B-C-3B	122	463	100	*158	*50	3	16	90	*.341	75	74	13	1043	68	12	.989
1998—Jacksonville (Sou.)	C-1B-OF	130	515	101	164	47	6	18	114	.318	71	83	8	540	45	9	.985
—Detroit (A.L.)	C-DH-1B	7	22	6	8	1	0	3	7	.364	2	7	1	27	1	1	.966
1999—GC Tigers (GCL)	DH-C-1B	3	9	2	3	1	0	0	2	.333	2	0	1	13	5	0	1.000
—W. Mich. (Mid.)	DH-C-1B	3	11	2	3	0	0	0	0	.273	2	0	1	18	3	2	.913
—Toledo (I.L.)	1B-C-DH-3B	14	48	11	15	0	1	2	8	.313	8	5	1	77	8	5	.944
—Detroit (A.L.)	DH-C	15	41	6	9	0	0	3	10	.220	7	6	1	24	1	0	1.000
Major League totals (2 years)		22	63	12	17	1	0	6	17	.270	9	13	2	51	2	1	.981

FIGGA, MIKE   C

PERSONAL: Born July 31, 1970, in Tampa. ... 6-0/200. ... Bats right, throws right. ... Full name: Michael Anthony Figga.

HIGH SCHOOL: Plant (Tampa).

JUNIOR COLLEGE: Central Florida Community College.

TRANSACTIONS/CAREER NOTES: Selected by New York Yankees organization in 44th round of free-agent draft (June 5, 1989). ... On disabled list (August 31, 1996-remainder of season). ... On Columbus disabled list (July 29-August 12, 1998). ... Claimed on waivers by Baltimore Orioles (June 3, 1999). ... Claimed on waivers by Tampa Bay Devil Rays (November 18, 1999). ... Granted free agency (December 21, 1999).

STATISTICAL NOTES: Led Gulf Coast League catchers with 296 total chances in 1990. ... Led International League catchers with 15 double plays in 1998.

							BATTING						FIELDING		
Year Team (League)	Pos.	G	AB	R	H	2B	3B	HR	RBI	Avg.	BB	SO	SB	PO	A	E	Avg.
1990—GC Yankees (GCL)	C	40	123	19	35	1	1	2	18	.285	17	33	4	*270	19	7	.976
1991—Prince Will. (Caro.)	C	55	174	15	34	6	0	3	17	.195	19	51	2	278	33	5	.984
1992—Fort Laud. (FSL)	C	80	249	12	44	13	0	1	15	.177	13	78	3	568	71	12	.982
—Prince Will. (Caro.)	C	3	10	0	2	1	0	0	0	.200	2	3	1	27	1	0	1.000
1993—San Bern. (Calif.)	C	83	308	48	82	17	1	25	71	.266	17	84	2	491	70	12	.979
—Alb./Colo. (East.)	C	6	22	3	5	0	0	0	2	.227	2	9	1	31	2	1	.971
1994—Tampa (FSL)	C	111	420	48	116	17	5	15	75	.276	22	94	2	703	79	10	.987
—Alb./Colo. (East.)	C	1	2	1	1	1	0	0	0	.500	0	1	0	5	0	0	1.000
1995—Norwich (East.)	C	109	399	59	108	22	4	13	61	.271	43	90	1	640	92	11	.985
—Columbus (I.L.)	C	8	25	2	7	1	0	1	3	.280	3	5	0	29	4	0	1.000
1996—Columbus (I.L.)	C	4	11	3	3	1	0	0	0	.273	1	3	0	17	2	0	1.000
1997—Columbus (I.L.)	C-DH	110	390	48	95	14	4	12	54	.244	18	104	3	706	62	11	.986
—New York (A.L.)	DH-C	2	4	0	0	0	0	0	0	.000	0	3	0	6	0	0	1.000
1998—Columbus (I.L.)	C-DH-1B	123	461	57	129	30	3	26	95	.280	35	109	2	733	63	10	.988
—New York (A.L.)	C	1	4	1	1	0	0	0	0	.250	0	1	0	3	1	0	1.000
1999—New York (A.L.)	C	2	0	0	0	0	0	0	0	...	0	0	0	3	0	0	1.000
—Baltimore (A.L.)■	C	41	86	12	19	4	0	1	5	.221	2	27	0	168	12	5	.973
Major League totals (3 years)		46	94	13	20	4	0	1	5	.213	2	31	0	180	13	5	.975

F

FIGUEROA, NELSON   P   DIAMONDBACKS

PERSONAL: Born May 18, 1974, in Brooklyn, N.Y. ... 6-1/155. ... Throws right, bats both. ... Full name: Nelson Walter Figueroa Jr.

HIGH SCHOOL: Abraham Lincoln (Brooklyn, N.Y.).

COLLEGE: Brandeis University (Mass.).

TRANSACTIONS/CAREER NOTES: Selected by New York Mets organization in 30th round of free-agent draft (June 1, 1995). ... Traded by Mets with OF Bernard Gilkey and cash to Arizona Diamondbacks for P Willie Blair, C Jorge Fabregas and cash considerations (July 31, 1998). ... On Tucson disabled list (June 12-23 and July 6-30, 1999).

HONORS: Named South Atlantic League Most Outstanding Pitcher (1996).

Year League	W	L	Pct.	ERA	G	GS	CG	ShO	Sv.	IP	H	R	ER	BB	SO
1995— Kingsport (Appalachian).....	7	3	.700	3.07	12	12	2	*2	0	76 1/3	57	31	26	22	79
1996— Columbia (SAL)■..............	14	7	.667	*2.04	26	25	*8	4	0	*185 1/3	119	55	42	58	*200
1997— Binghamton (East.)	5	11	.313	4.34	33	22	0	0	0	143	137	76	69	68	116
1998— Binghamton (East.)	12	3	.800	4.66	21	21	3	2	0	123 2/3	133	73	64	44	116
— Tucson (PCL)■	2	2	.500	3.70	7	7	0	0	0	41 1/3	46	22	17	16	29
1999— Tucson (PCL)	11	6	.647	3.94	24	21	1	1	0	128	128	59	56	41	106
— Ariz. D'backs (Ariz.)...........	0	1	.000	0.00	1	1	0	0	0	3	3	1	0	0	2

FINLEY, CHUCK   P   INDIANS

PERSONAL: Born November 26, 1962, in Monroe, La. ... 6-6/226. ... Throws left, bats left. ... Full name: Charles Edward Finley.
HIGH SCHOOL: West Monroe (La.).
COLLEGE: Northeast Louisiana.
TRANSACTIONS/CAREER NOTES: Selected by California Angels organization in 15th round of free-agent draft (June 4, 1984); did not sign. ... Selected by Angels organization in secondary phase of free-agent draft (January 9, 1985). ... On disabled list (August 22-September 15, 1989 and April 6-22, 1992). ... Granted free agency (November 7, 1995). ... Re-signed by Angels (January 4, 1996). ... Angels franchise renamed Anaheim Angels for 1997 season. ... On Anaheim disabled list (March 23-April 15 and August 20, 1997-remainder of season); included rehabilitation assignment to Lake Elsinore (April 5-10). ... Granted free agency (November 2, 1999). ... Signed by Cleveland Indians (December 16, 1999).
RECORDS: Shares major league single-inning record for most strikeouts—4 (May 12, 1999, third inning; and August 15, 1999, first inning).
HONORS: Named lefthanded pitcher on THE SPORTING NEWS A.L. All-Star team (1989-90).
STATISTICAL NOTES: Pitched 5-0 one-hit, complete-game victory against Boston (May 26, 1989). ... Struck out 15 batters in one game (June 24, 1989 and May 23, 1995). ... Led A.L. with 17 wild pitches in 1996 and 15 wild pitches in 1999.
MISCELLANEOUS: Holds Anaheim Angels franchise all-time records for most wins (165), innings pitched (2,675) and games pitched (436).

Year League	W	L	Pct.	ERA	G	GS	CG	ShO	Sv.	IP	H	R	ER	BB	SO
1985— Salem (N'west)..................	3	1	.750	4.66	18	0	0	0	5	29	34	21	15	10	32
1986— Quad Cities (Midw.)...........	1	0	1.000	0.00	10	0	0	0	6	12	4	0	0	3	16
— California (A.L.)................	3	1	.750	3.30	25	0	0	0	0	46 1/3	40	17	17	23	37
1987— California (A.L.)................	2	7	.222	4.67	35	3	0	0	0	90 2/3	102	54	47	43	63
1988— California (A.L.)................	9	15	.375	4.17	31	31	2	0	0	194 1/3	191	95	90	82	111
1989— California (A.L.)................	16	9	.640	2.57	29	29	9	1	0	199 2/3	171	64	57	82	156
1990— California (A.L.)................	18	9	.667	2.40	32	32	7	2	0	236	210	77	63	81	177
1991— California (A.L.)................	18	9	.667	3.80	34	34	4	2	0	227 1/3	205	102	96	101	171
1992— California (A.L.)................	7	12	.368	3.96	31	31	4	1	0	204 1/3	212	99	90	98	124
1993— California (A.L.)................	16	14	.533	3.15	35	35	*13	2	0	251 1/3	243	108	88	82	187
1994— California (A.L.)................	10	10	.500	4.32	25	•25	7	2	0	*183 1/3	178	95	88	71	148
1995— California (A.L.)................	15	12	.556	4.21	32	32	2	1	0	203	192	106	95	93	195
1996— California (A.L.)................	15	16	.484	4.16	35	35	4	1	0	238	241	124	110	94	215
1997— Lake Elsinore (Calif.)	0	0	...	2.00	2	2	0	0	0	9	5	3	2	4	12
— Anaheim (A.L.)...............	13	6	.684	4.23	25	25	3	1	0	164	152	79	77	65	155
1998— Anaheim (A.L.)...............	11	9	.550	3.39	34	34	1	1	0	223 1/3	210	97	84	109	212
1999— Anaheim (A.L.)...............	12	11	.522	4.43	33	33	1	0	0	213 1/3	197	117	105	94	200
Major League totals (14 years).....	165	140	.541	3.72	436	379	57	14	0	2675	2544	1234	1107	1118	2151

CHAMPIONSHIP SERIES RECORD

Year League	W	L	Pct.	ERA	G	GS	CG	ShO	Sv.	IP	H	R	ER	BB	SO
1986— California (A.L.)	0	0	...	0.00	3	0	0	0	0	2	1	0	0	0	1

ALL-STAR GAME RECORD

Year League	W	L	Pct.	ERA	GS	CG	ShO	Sv.	IP	H	R	ER	BB	SO
1989— American					Did not play.									
1990— American	0	0	...	0.00	0	0	0	0	1	0	0	0	1	1
1995— American					Did not play.									
1996— American	0	0	...	4.50	0	0	0	0	2	3	1	1	0	4
All-Star Game totals (2 years)	0	0	...	3.00	0	0	0	0	3	3	1	1	1	5

F

FINLEY, STEVE   OF   DIAMONDBACKS

PERSONAL: Born March 12, 1965, in Union City, Tenn. ... 6-2/180. ... Bats left, throws left. ... Full name: Steven Allen Finley.
HIGH SCHOOL: Paducah (Ky.) Tilghman.
COLLEGE: Southern Illinois (degree in physiology).
TRANSACTIONS/CAREER NOTES: Selected by Atlanta Braves organization in 11th round of free-agent draft (June 2, 1986); did not sign. ... Selected by Baltimore Orioles organization in 13th round of free-agent draft (June 2, 1987). ... On Baltimore disabled list (April 4-22, 1989). ... On Baltimore disabled list (July 29-September 1, 1989); included rehabilitation assignment to Hagerstown (August 21-23). ... Traded by Orioles with P Pete Harnisch and P Curt Schilling to Houston Astros for 1B Glenn Davis (January 10, 1991). ... On disabled list (April 25-May 14, 1993). ... On Houston disabled list (June 13-July 3, 1994); included rehabilitation assignment to Jackson (June 28-July 3). ... Traded by Astros with 3B Ken Caminiti, SS Andujar Cedeno, 1B Roberto Petagine, P Brian Williams and a player to be named later to San Diego Padres for OF Phil Plantier, OF Derek Bell, P Pedro Martinez, P Doug Brocail, IF Craig Shipley and SS Ricky Gutierrez (December 28, 1994); Padres acquired P Sean Fesh to complete deal (May 1, 1995). ... On San Diego disabled list (April 20-May 6, 1997); included rehabilitation assignment to Rancho Cucamonga (April 25-May 6). ... Granted free agency (October 26, 1998). ... Signed by Arizona Diamondbacks (December 18, 1998).
RECORDS: Shares major league single-season records for most games with three home runs—2 (1997); and fewest double plays by outfielder (150 or more games)—0 (1999).
HONORS: Won N.L. Gold Glove as outfielder (1995-96 and 1999).

STATISTICAL NOTES: Led International League outfielders with 315 total chances in 1988. ... Had 21-game hitting streak (June 20-July 14, 1996). ... Hit three home runs in one game (May 19 and June 23, 1997; and September 8, 1999). ... Tied for N.L. lead with six double plays by outfielder in 1998. ... Career major league grand slams: 7.

Year Team (League)	Pos.	G	AB	R	H	2B	3B	HR	RBI	Avg.	BB	SO	SB	PO	A	E	Avg.
1987— Newark (NY-P)	OF	54	222	40	65	13	2	3	33	.293	22	24	26	122	7	4	.970
— Hagerstown (Caro.)....	OF	15	65	9	22	3	2	1	5	.338	1	6	7	32	3	0	1.000
1988— Hagerstown (Caro.)....	OF	8	28	2	6	2	0	0	3	.214	4	3	4	17	0	0	1.000
— Charlotte (Sou.)........	OF	10	40	7	12	4	2	1	6	.300	4	3	2	14	0	1	1.000
— Rochester (I.L.)	OF	120	456	61	*143	19	7	5	54	*.314	28	55	20	*289	14	*12	.962
1989— Baltimore (A.L.).........	OF-DH	81	217	35	54	5	2	2	25	.249	15	30	17	144	1	2	.986
— Rochester (I.L.)	OF	7	25	2	4	0	0	0	2	.160	1	5	3	17	2	0	1.000
— Hagerstown (East.)......	OF	11	48	11	20	3	1	0	7	.417	4	3	4	35	2	3	.925
1990— Baltimore (A.L.).........	OF-DH	142	464	46	119	16	4	3	37	.256	32	53	22	298	4	7	.977
1991— Houston (N.L.)■........	OF	159	596	84	170	28	10	8	54	.285	42	65	34	323	13	5	.985
1992— Houston (N.L.)	OF	•162	607	84	177	29	13	5	55	.292	58	63	44	417	8	3	.993
1993— Houston (N.L.)	OF	142	545	69	145	15	*13	8	44	.266	28	65	19	329	12	4	.988
1994— Houston (N.L.)	OF	94	373	64	103	16	5	11	33	.276	28	52	13	214	9	4	.982
— Jackson (Texas)	OF-DH	5	13	3	4	0	0	0	0	.308	4	0	1	6	0	0	1.000
1995— San Diego (N.L.)■	OF	139	562	104	167	23	8	10	44	.297	59	62	36	291	8	7	.977
1996— San Diego (N.L.)	OF	161	655	126	195	45	9	30	95	.298	56	87	22	385	7	7	.982
1997— San Diego (N.L.)	OF	143	560	101	146	26	5	28	92	.261	43	92	15	338	10	4	.989
— Rancho Cuca. (Calif.) .	DH-OF	4	14	3	4	0	0	2	3	.286	3	2	1	0	0	0	...
— Mobile (Sou.)	DH	1	4	1	2	0	0	1	2	.500	1	2	0	...	...	...	...
1998— San Diego (N.L.)	OF	159	619	92	154	40	6	14	67	.249	45	103	12	351	12	7	.981
1999— Arizona (N.L.)■.........	OF-DH	156	590	100	156	32	10	34	103	.264	63	94	8	397	5	2	.995
American League totals (2 years)		223	681	81	173	21	6	5	62	.254	47	83	39	442	5	9	.980
National League totals (9 years)		1315	5107	824	1413	254	79	148	587	.277	422	683	203	3045	84	43	.986
Major League totals (11 years)		1538	5788	905	1586	275	85	153	649	.274	469	766	242	3487	89	52	.986

DIVISION SERIES RECORD

RECORDS: Shares N.L. single-game record for most runs batted in—5 (October 6, 1999).

Year Team (League)	Pos.	G	AB	R	H	2B	3B	HR	RBI	Avg.	BB	SO	SB	PO	A	E	Avg.
1996— San Diego (N.L.)	OF	3	12	0	1	0	0	0	1	.083	0	4	1	10	0	0	1.000
1998— San Diego (N.L.)	OF-PR	4	10	2	1	1	0	0	1	.100	1	4	0	6	0	0	1.000
1999— Arizona (N.L.)	OF	4	13	0	5	1	0	0	5	.385	3	1	0	10	0	0	1.000
Division series totals (3 years)		11	35	2	7	2	0	0	7	.200	4	9	1	26	0	0	1.000

CHAMPIONSHIP SERIES RECORD

Year Team (League)	Pos.	G	AB	R	H	2B	3B	HR	RBI	Avg.	BB	SO	SB	PO	A	E	Avg.
1998— San Diego (N.L.)	OF	6	21	3	7	1	0	0	2	.333	6	2	1	15	0	0	1.000

WORLD SERIES RECORD

Year Team (League)	Pos.	G	AB	R	H	2B	3B	HR	RBI	Avg.	BB	SO	SB	PO	A	E	Avg.
1998— San Diego (N.L.)	OF	3	12	0	1	1	0	0	0	.083	0	2	1	9	1	0	1.000

ALL-STAR GAME RECORD

Year League	Pos.	AB	R	H	2B	3B	HR	RBI	Avg.	BB	SO	SB	PO	A	E	Avg.
1997— National	OF	1	0	0	0	0	0	0	.000	0	1	0	1	0	0	1.000

FLAHERTY, JOHN   C   DEVIL RAYS

PERSONAL: Born October 21, 1967, in New York. ... 6-1/200. ... Bats right, throws right. ... Full name: John Timothy Flaherty.

HIGH SCHOOL: St. Joseph's Regional (Montvale, N.J.).

COLLEGE: George Washington.

TRANSACTIONS/CAREER NOTES: Selected by Boston Red Sox organization in 25th round of free-agent draft (June 1, 1988). ... Traded by Red Sox to Detroit Tigers for C Rich Rowland (April 1, 1994). ... Traded by Tigers with SS Chris Gomez to San Diego Padres for C Brad Ausmus, SS Andujar Cedeno and P Russ Spear (June 18, 1996). ... Traded by Padres to Tampa Bay Devil Rays for P Brian Boehringer and IF Andy Sheets (November 18, 1997). ... On Tampa Bay disabled list (May 26-June 20, 1998); included rehabilitation assignment to Durham (June 14-20).

STATISTICAL NOTES: Tied for Florida State League lead with 19 passed balls in 1989. ... Had 27-game hitting streak (June 21-July 27, 1996). ... Career major league grand slams: 1.

Year Team (League)	Pos.	G	AB	R	H	2B	3B	HR	RBI	Avg.	BB	SO	SB	PO	A	E	Avg.
1988— Elmira (NY-P)	C	46	162	17	38	3	0	3	16	.235	12	23	2	235	39	7	.975
1989— Winter Haven (FSL).......	C-1B	95	334	31	87	14	2	4	28	.260	20	44	1	369	60	9	.979
1990— Pawtucket (I.L.)..........	C-3B	99	317	35	72	18	0	4	32	.227	24	43	1	509	59	10	.983
— Lynchburg (Caro.)........	C	1	4	0	0	0	0	0	0	1.000	0	1	0	3	2	0	1.000
1991— New Britain (East.)	C	67	225	27	65	9	0	3	18	.289	31	22	0	337	46	9	.977
— Pawtucket (I.L.)...........	C	45	156	18	29	7	0	3	13	.186	15	14	0	270	18	•9	.970
1992— Boston (A.L.)..........	C	35	66	3	13	2	0	0	2	.197	3	7	0	102	7	2	.982
— Pawtucket (I.L.)..........	C	31	104	11	26	3	0	0	7	.250	5	8	0	158	17	4	.978
1993— Pawtucket (I.L.)..........	C	105	365	29	99	22	0	6	35	.271	26	41	0	626	78	10	.986
— Boston (A.L.)	C	13	25	3	3	2	0	0	2	.120	2	6	0	35	9	0	1.000
1994— Toledo (I.L.)■............	C-DH	44	151	20	39	10	2	7	17	.258	6	21	3	286	24	2	.994
— Detroit (A.L.)	C-DH	34	40	2	6	1	0	0	4	.150	1	11	0	78	9	0	1.000
1995— Detroit (A.L.)	C	112	354	39	86	22	1	11	40	.243	18	47	0	569	33	*11	.982

Year Team (League)	Pos.	G	AB	R	H	2B	3B	HR	RBI	Avg.	BB	SO	SB	PO	A	E	Avg.
						BATTING									FIELDING		
1996—Detroit (A.L.)	C	47	152	18	38	12	0	4	23	.250	8	25	1	243	13	5	.981
—San Diego (N.L.)■	C	72	264	22	80	12	0	9	41	.303	9	36	2	471	29	5	.990
1997—San Diego (N.L.)	C	129	439	38	120	21	1	9	46	.273	33	62	4	753	65	11	.987
1998—Tampa Bay (A.L.)■	C	91	304	21	63	11	0	3	24	.207	22	46	0	542	45	4	.993
—Durham (I.L.)	DH-C	6	23	1	3	1	0	0	2	.130	1	5	0	23	4	0	1.000
1999—Tampa Bay (A.L.)	C-DH	117	446	53	124	19	0	14	71	.278	19	64	0	726	*87	6	.993
American League totals (7 years)		449	1387	139	333	69	1	32	166	.240	73	206	1	2295	203	28	.989
National League totals (2 years)		201	703	60	200	33	1	18	87	.284	42	98	6	1224	94	16	.988
Major League totals (8 years)		650	2090	199	533	102	2	50	253	.255	115	304	7	3519	297	44	.989

DIVISION SERIES RECORD

Year Team (League)	Pos.	G	AB	R	H	2B	3B	HR	RBI	Avg.	BB	SO	SB	PO	A	E	Avg.
						BATTING									FIELDING		
1996—San Diego (N.L.)	C	2	4	0	0	0	0	0	0	.000	0	1	0	9	0	0	1.000

FLETCHER, DARRIN — C — BLUE JAYS

PERSONAL: Born October 3, 1966, in Elmhurst, Ill. ... 6-2/205. ... Bats left, throws right. ... Full name: Darrin Glen Fletcher. ... Son of Tom Fletcher, pitcher with Detroit Tigers (1962); and grandson of Glen Fletcher, pitcher in Philadelphia Phillies organization (1938-48).

HIGH SCHOOL: Oakwood (Ill.).

COLLEGE: Illinois.

TRANSACTIONS/CAREER NOTES: Selected by Los Angeles Dodgers organization in sixth round of free-agent draft (June 2, 1987). ... Traded by Dodgers to Philadelphia Phillies for P Dennis Cook (September 13, 1990). ... Traded by Phillies with cash to Montreal Expos for P Barry Jones (December 9, 1991). ... On Montreal disabled list (May 12-June 15, 1992); included rehabilitation assignment to Indianapolis (May 31-June 14). ... On disabled list (June 18-July 3, 1997). ... Granted free agency (October 27, 1997). ... Signed by Toronto Blue Jays (November 26, 1997). ... On disabled list (May 30-June 14, 1998). ... On Toronto disabled list (May 1-June 1, 1999); included rehabilitation assignment to Syracuse (May 24-27).

STATISTICAL NOTES: Tied for Texas League lead in double plays by catcher with nine in 1988. ... Led Pacific Coast League catchers with 787 total chances in 1990. ... Led N.L. with 12 sacrifice flies in 1994. ... Career major league grand slams: 3.

Year Team (League)	Pos.	G	AB	R	H	2B	3B	HR	RBI	Avg.	BB	SO	SB	PO	A	E	Avg.
						BATTING									FIELDING		
1987—Vero Beach (FSL)	C	43	124	13	33	7	0	0	15	.266	22	12	0	212	35	3	.988
1988—San Antonio (Texas)	C	89	279	19	58	8	0	1	20	.208	17	42	2	529	64	5	*.992
1989—Albuquerque (PCL)	C	100	315	34	86	16	1	5	44	.273	30	38	1	632	63	9	.987
—Los Angeles (N.L.)	C	5	8	1	4	0	0	1	2	.500	1	0	0	16	1	0	1.000
1990—Albuquerque (PCL)	C	105	350	58	102	23	1	13	65	.291	40	37	1	*715	64	8	.990
—Los Angeles (N.L.)	C	2	1	0	0	0	0	0	0	.000	0	1	0	0	0	0	...
—Philadelphia (N.L.)■	C	9	22	3	3	1	0	0	1	.136	1	5	0	30	3	0	1.000
1991—Scranton/W.B. (I.L.)	C-1B	90	306	39	87	13	1	8	50	.284	23	29	1	491	44	5	.991
—Philadelphia (N.L.)	C	46	136	5	31	8	0	1	12	.228	5	15	0	242	22	2	.992
1992—Montreal (N.L.)■	C	83	222	13	54	10	2	2	26	.243	14	28	0	360	33	2	.995
—Indianapolis (A.A.)	C	13	51	2	13	2	0	1	9	.255	2	10	0	65	7	1	.986
1993—Montreal (N.L.)	C	133	396	33	101	20	1	9	60	.255	34	40	0	620	41	8	.988
1994—Montreal (N.L.)	C	94	285	28	74	18	1	10	57	.260	25	23	0	479	20	2	.996
1995—Montreal (N.L.)	C	110	350	42	100	21	1	11	45	.286	32	23	0	613	44	4	.994
1996—Montreal (N.L.)	C	127	394	41	105	22	0	12	57	.266	27	42	0	721	30	6	.992
1997—Montreal (N.L.)	C	96	310	39	86	20	1	17	55	.277	17	35	1	606	26	4	.994
1998—Toronto (A.L.)■	C-DH	124	407	37	115	23	1	9	52	.283	25	39	0	832	51	8	.991
1999—Toronto (A.L.)	C	115	412	48	120	26	0	18	80	.291	26	47	0	638	42	2	.997
—Syracuse (I.L.)	C-DH	4	15	0	4	0	0	0	0	.267	1	1	0	18	5	0	1.000
American League totals (2 years)		239	819	85	235	49	1	27	132	.287	51	86	0	1470	93	10	.994
National League totals (9 years)		705	2124	205	558	120	6	63	315	.263	156	212	1	3687	220	28	.993
Major League totals (11 years)		944	2943	290	793	169	7	90	447	.269	207	298	1	5157	313	38	.993

ALL-STAR GAME RECORD

Year League	Pos.	AB	R	H	2B	3B	HR	RBI	Avg.	BB	SO	SB	PO	A	E	Avg.
				BATTING										FIELDING		
1994—National	C	0	0	0	0	0	0	0	...	0	0	0	3	0	0	1.000

FLORIE, BRYCE — P — RED SOX

PERSONAL: Born May 21, 1970, in Charleston, S.C. ... 5-11/192. ... Throws right, bats right. ... Full name: Bryce Bettencourt Florie.

HIGH SCHOOL: Hanahan (Charleston, S.C.).

COLLEGE: Trident Technical College (S.C.).

TRANSACTIONS/CAREER NOTES: Selected by San Diego Padres organization in fifth round of free-agent draft (June 1, 1988). ... Traded by Padres with P Ron Villone and OF Marc Newfield to Milwaukee Brewers for OF Greg Vaughn and a player to be named later (July 31, 1996); Padres acquired OF Gerald Parent to complete deal (September 16, 1996). ... On disabled list (August 31-September 8, 1997). ... Traded by Brewers with a player to be named later to Detroit Tigers for P Mike Myers, P Rick Greene and SS Santiago Perez (November 20, 1997). ... On Detroit disabled list (June 23-July 20, 1998); included rehabilitation assignment to Toledo (July 14-20). ... On Detroit disabled list (March 31-May 6, 1999); included rehabilitation assignment to Lakeland (May 1-6). ... Traded by Tigers to Boston Red Sox for P Mike Maroth (July 31, 1999).

STATISTICAL NOTES: Led Texas League with 25 wild pitches in 1993.

Year League	W	L	Pct.	ERA	G	GS	CG	ShO	Sv.	IP	H	R	ER	BB	SO
1988—Arizona Padres (Ariz.)	4	5	.444	7.98	11	6	0	0	0	38 1/3	52	44	34	22	29
1989—Spokane (N'west)	4	5	.444	7.08	14	14	0	0	0	61	79	•66	48	40	50
—Charleston, S.C. (SAL)	1	7	.125	6.95	12	12	0	0	0	44	54	47	34	42	22
1990—Waterloo (Midw.)	4	5	.444	4.39	14	14	1	0	0	65 2/3	60	37	32	37	38
1991—Waterloo (Midw.)	7	6	.538	3.92	23	23	2	0	0	133	119	66	58	79	90

Year League	W	L	Pct.	ERA	G	GS	CG	ShO	Sv.	IP	H	R	ER	BB	SO
1992— High Desert (Calif.)............	9	7	.563	4.12	26	24	0	0	0	137²/₃	99	79	63	*114	106
— Charleston, S.C. (SAL)	0	1	.000	1.80	1	1	0	0	0	5	5	3	1	0	5
1993— Wichita (Texas)	11	8	.579	3.96	27	•27	0	0	0	154²/₃	128	80	68	*100	133
1994— Las Vegas (PCL)	2	5	.286	5.15	50	0	0	0	1	71²/₃	76	47	41	47	67
— San Diego (N.L.)	0	0	...	0.96	9	0	0	0	0	9¹/₃	8	1	1	3	8
1995— San Diego (N.L.)	2	2	.500	3.01	47	0	0	0	1	68²/₃	49	30	23	38	68
1996— San Diego (N.L.)	2	2	.500	4.01	39	0	0	0	0	49¹/₃	45	24	22	27	51
— Milwaukee (A.L.)■..........	0	1	.000	6.63	15	0	0	0	0	19	20	16	14	13	12
1997— Milwaukee (A.L.)	4	4	.500	4.32	32	8	0	0	0	75	74	43	36	42	53
1998— Detroit (A.L.)■..............	8	9	.471	4.80	42	16	0	0	0	133	141	80	71	59	97
— Toledo (I.L.)......................	0	0	...	0.00	1	1	0	0	0	4	0	0	0	0	3
1999— Lakeland (FSL)	0	0	...	0.00	1	1	0	0	0	3	0	0	0	0	7
— Detroit (A.L.)	2	1	.667	4.56	27	3	0	0	0	51¹/₃	61	31	26	20	40
— Boston (A.L.)■..................	2	0	1.000	4.80	14	2	0	0	0	30	33	19	16	15	25
A.L. totals (4 years)	16	15	.516	4.76	130	29	0	0	0	308¹/₃	329	189	163	149	227
N.L. totals (3 years)	4	4	.500	3.25	95	0	0	0	1	127¹/₃	102	55	46	68	127
Major League totals (6 years).......	20	19	.513	4.32	225	29	0	0	1	435²/₃	431	244	209	217	354

DIVISION SERIES RECORD

Year League	W	L	Pct.	ERA	G	GS	CG	ShO	Sv.	IP	H	R	ER	BB	SO
1999— Boston (A.L.)......................							Did not play.								

CHAMPIONSHIP SERIES RECORD

Year League	W	L	Pct.	ERA	G	GS	CG	ShO	Sv.	IP	H	R	ER	BB	SO
1999— Boston (A.L.)......................							Did not play.								

FLOYD, CLIFF — OF — MARLINS

PERSONAL: Born December 5, 1972, in Chicago. ... 6-4/240. ... Bats left, throws right. ... Full name: Cornelius Clifford Floyd.
HIGH SCHOOL: Thornwood (South Holland, Ill.).
TRANSACTIONS/CAREER NOTES: Selected by Montreal Expos organization in first round (14th pick overall) of free-agent draft (June 3, 1991). ... On disabled list (May 16-September 11, 1995). ... Traded by Expos to Florida Marlins for OF Joe Orsulak and P Dustin Hermanson (March 26, 1997). ... On Florida disabled list (May 9-24 and June 21-September 1, 1997); included rehabilitation assignment to Charlotte (July 20-September 1). ... On Florida disabled list (March 30-April 27 and June 20-September 7, 1999); included rehabilitation assigment to Calgary (August 28-September 7).
HONORS: Named Minor League Player of the Year by THE SPORTING NEWS (1993). ... Named Eastern League Most Valuable Player (1993).
STATISTICAL NOTES: Led South Atlantic League with 261 total bases and nine intentional bases on balls received in 1992. ... Led Eastern League with .600 slugging percentage and 12 intentional bases on balls received in 1993.

							BATTING						FIELDING		
Year Team (League)	Pos.	G	AB	R	H	2B	3B	HR	RBI	Avg.	BB	SO	SB	PO	A	E	Avg.
1991— GC Expos (GCL)	1B	56	214	35	56	9	3	6	30	.262	19	37	13	451	27	*15	.970
1992— Albany (SAL)........	OF-1B	134	516	83	157	24	*16	16	*97	.304	45	75	32	423	29	17	.964
— W.P. Beach (FSL).......	OF	1	4	0	0	0	0	0	1	.000	0	1	0	2	0	0	1.000
1993— Harrisburg (East.)........	1B-OF	101	380	82	125	17	4	•26	*101	.329	54	71	31	564	27	19	.969
— Ottawa (I.L.)...........	1B	32	125	12	30	2	2	2	18	.240	16	34	2	272	23	5	.983
— Montreal (N.L.)...........	1B	10	31	3	7	0	0	1	2	.226	0	9	0	79	4	0	1.000
1994— Montreal (N.L.)...........	1B-OF	100	334	43	94	19	4	4	41	.281	24	63	10	565	42	6	.990
1995— Montreal (N.L.)...........	1B-OF	29	69	6	9	1	0	1	8	.130	7	22	3	146	12	3	.981
1996— Ottawa (I.L.)	OF-DH-3B	20	76	7	23	3	1	1	8	.303	7	20	2	38	1	2	.951
— Montreal (N.L.)...........	OF-1B	117	227	29	55	15	4	6	26	.242	30	52	7	109	2	5	.957
1997— Florida (N.L.)■..........	OF-1B	61	137	23	32	9	1	6	19	.234	24	33	6	96	5	3	.971
— Charlotte (I.L.)...........	OF-1B	39	131	27	48	10	0	9	33	.366	10	29	7	79	5	1	.988
1998— Florida (N.L.)...........	OF-DH	153	588	85	166	45	3	22	90	.282	47	112	27	251	10	7	.974
1999— Florida (N.L.)...........	OF-DH	69	251	37	76	19	1	11	49	.303	30	47	5	115	4	6	.952
— Calgary (PCL)...........	OF	9	31	6	12	1	0	3	8	.387	2	8	0	8	0	0	1.000
Major League totals (7 years)		539	1637	226	439	108	13	51	235	.268	162	338	58	1361	79	30	.980

DIVISION SERIES RECORD

							BATTING						FIELDING		
Year Team (League)	Pos.	G	AB	R	H	2B	3B	HR	RBI	Avg.	BB	SO	SB	PO	A	E	Avg.
1997— Florida (N.L.).............								Did not play.								

CHAMPIONSHIP SERIES RECORD

							BATTING						FIELDING		
Year Team (League)	Pos.	G	AB	R	H	2B	3B	HR	RBI	Avg.	BB	SO	SB	PO	A	E	Avg.
1997— Florida (N.L.).............								Did not play.								

WORLD SERIES RECORD

NOTES: Member of World Series championship team (1997).

							BATTING						FIELDING		
Year Team (League)	Pos.	G	AB	R	H	2B	3B	HR	RBI	Avg.	BB	SO	SB	PO	A	E	Avg.
1997— Florida (N.L.)	PH-DH	4	2	1	0	0	0	0	0	.000	1	1	0	...	...	...	...

FLURY, PATRICK — P — REDS

PERSONAL: Born March 14, 1973, in Reno, Nev. ... 6-1/220. ... Throws right, bats right. ... Full name: Patrick Shannon Flury.
HIGH SCHOOL: Edward C. Reed (Sparks, Nev.).
JUNIOR COLLEGE: College of Southern Idaho.
COLLEGE: UNLV.

F

TRANSACTIONS/CAREER NOTES: Selected by Kansas City Royals organization in seventh round of free-agent draft (June 3, 1993). ... Claimed on waivers by Boston Red Sox (April 29, 1998). ... Traded by Red Sox to Cincinnati Reds for OF Jon Nunnally (March 25, 1999).

Year League	W	L	Pct.	ERA	G	GS	CG	ShO	Sv.	IP	H	R	ER	BB	SO
1993— Eugene (N'west)	2	2	.500	3.27	27	0	0	0	7	33	25	15	12	22	34
1994— Rockford (Midw.)	1	3	.250	3.93	34	0	0	0	2	55	61	27	24	33	41
1995— Springfield (Midw.)	2	6	.250	4.31	34	0	0	0	1	54 1/3	65	32	26	24	35
— Wilmington (Caro.)	1	0	1.000	2.45	15	0	0	0	1	22	18	6	6	9	14
1996— Wilmington (Caro.)	7	2	.778	1.92	45	0	0	0	5	84 1/3	66	22	18	29	67
1997— Wichita (Texas)	8	3	.727	3.56	42	0	0	0	5	48	47	26	19	18	47
— Omaha (A.A.)	1	0	1.000	6.07	18	0	0	0	0	26 2/3	29	18	18	16	24
1998— Wichita (Texas)	1	1	.500	5.25	8	0	0	0	0	12	14	11	7	7	13
— Pawtucket (I.L.)■	0	0	...	5.73	17	0	0	0	0	22	23	15	14	16	22
— Trenton (East.)	0	0	...	1.74	26	0	0	0	16	31	24	6	6	11	37
1999— Chattanooga (Sou.)■	1	1	.500	2.87	43	0	0	0	15	53 1/3	36	20	17	31	69
— Indianapolis (I.L.)	1	1	.500	7.04	23	0	0	0	6	23	27	18	18	20	20

FONTENOT, JOE   P   MARLINS

PERSONAL: Born March 20, 1977, in Lafayette, La. ... 6-2/185. ... Throws right, bats right. ... Full name: Joseph D. Fontenot.
HIGH SCHOOL: Acadiana (Lafayette, La.).
TRANSACTIONS/CAREER NOTES: Selected by San Francisco Giants organization in first round (16th pick overall) of free-agent draft (June 1, 1995). ... Traded by Giants with P Mike Villano and P Mick Pageler to Florida Marlins for P Robb Nen (November 18, 1997). ... On Florida disabled list (July 3, 1998-remainder of season); included rehabilitation assignment to Charlotte (July 28-August 1). ... On Calgary disabled list (May 20-September 6, 1999). ... On Florida disabled list (September 7, 1999-remainder of season).
STATISTICAL NOTES: Led Texas League in hit batsmen with 12 in 1997.

Year League	W	L	Pct.	ERA	G	GS	CG	ShO	Sv.	IP	H	R	ER	BB	SO
1995— Bellingham (N'west)	0	3	.000	1.93	6	6	0	0	0	18 2/3	14	5	4	10	14
1996— San Jose (Calif.)	9	4	.692	4.44	26	23	0	0	0	144	137	87	71	74	124
1997— Shreveport (Texas)	10	11	.476	5.53	26	26	1	0	0	151 1/3	171	105	93	65	103
1998— Portland (East.)■	3	1	.750	3.08	7	7	0	0	0	38	37	16	13	13	31
— Florida (N.L.)	0	7	.000	6.33	8	8	0	0	0	42 2/3	56	34	30	20	24
— Charlotte (I.L.)	0	1	.000	12.00	1	1	0	0	0	3	4	4	4	2	0
1999— Calgary (PCL)	3	2	.600	5.11	8	8	1	1	0	44	52	26	25	19	18
Major League totals (1 year)	0	7	.000	6.33	8	8	0	0	0	42 2/3	56	34	30	20	24

FONVILLE, CHAD   SS/2B   RED SOX

PERSONAL: Born March 5, 1971, in Jacksonville, N.C. ... 5-6/155. ... Bats both, throws right. ... Full name: Chad Everette Fonville.
HIGH SCHOOL: White Oak (Jacksonville, N.C.).
JUNIOR COLLEGE: Louisburg (N.C.) College.
TRANSACTIONS/CAREER NOTES: Selected by San Francisco Giants organization in 11th round of free-agent draft (June 1, 1992). ... On disabled list (April 8-June 10, 1994). ... Selected by Montreal Expos from Giants organization in Rule 5 major league draft (December 5, 1994). ... Claimed on waivers by Los Angeles Dodgers (May 31, 1995). ... Traded by Dodgers to Chicago White Sox (September 2, 1997), completing trade in which White Sox traded OF Darren Lewis to Dodgers for a player to be named later (August 27, 1997). ... Claimed on waivers by Cleveland Indians (November 25, 1997). ... Released by Indians (March 9, 1998). ... Signed by Mets organization (March 14, 1998); contract later voided due to pre-existing injury (March 26, 1998). ... Signed by Colorado Rockies organization (June 22, 1998). ... Granted free agency (October 15, 1998). ... Signed by Boston Red Sox organization (February 4, 1999). ... On Pawtucket disabled list (August 16-September 1, 1999).
STATISTICAL NOTES: Led Northwest League second basemen with 131 putouts and tied for lead with 17 errors in 1992.

Year Team (League)	Pos.	G	AB	R	H	2B	3B	HR	RBI	Avg.	BB	SO	SB	PO	A	E	Avg.
							BATTING								FIELDING		
1992— Everett (N'west)	2B-SS	63	260	56	71	9	1	1	33	.273	31	39	36	†134	141	‡18	.939
1993— Clinton (Midw.)	SS-3B-2B	120	447	80	137	16	10	1	44	.306	40	48	52	167	319	36	.931
1994— San Jose (Calif.)	SS-2B-OF	68	283	58	87	9	6	0	26	.307	34	34	22	119	203	22	.936
1995— Montreal (N.L.)■	2B	14	12	2	4	0	0	0	0	.333	0	3	0	0	0	0	...
— Los Angeles (N.L.)■..	SS-2B-OF	88	308	41	85	6	1	0	16	.276	23	39	20	125	195	11	.967
1996— Los Angeles (N.L.)	OF-2B-SS-3B	103	201	34	41	4	1	0	13	.204	17	31	7	84	71	6	.963
— Albuquerque (PCL)	SS-2B-OF	25	96	17	23	1	0	0	5	.240	8	13	7	42	70	6	.949
1997— Los Angeles (N.L.)	2B	9	14	1	2	0	0	0	1	.143	2	3	0	5	5	1	.833
— Albuquerque (PCL)	OF-2B-SS	102	371	49	81	5	2	0	22	.218	30	39	23	173	149	15	.955
— Chicago (A.L.)■	OF-2B-SS-DH	9	9	1	1	0	0	0	1	.111	1	1	2	9	3	1	.923
1998— New Haven (East.)■.	OF-2B-DH	54	189	26	47	2	0	0	9	.249	23	24	16	67	33	3	.971
1999— Pawtucket (I.L.)■	2-S-O-3-DH	74	257	31	65	3	2	1	14	.253	20	31	6	102	104	16	.928
— Boston (A.L.)	2B	3	2	1	0	0	0	0	0	.000	2	0	1	6	3	1	.900
American League totals (2 years)		12	11	2	1	0	0	0	1	.091	3	1	3	15	6	2	.913
National League totals (3 years)		214	535	78	132	10	2	0	30	.247	42	76	27	209	271	18	.964
Major League totals (4 years)		226	546	80	133	10	2	0	31	.244	45	77	30	224	277	20	.962

DIVISION SERIES RECORD

Year Team (League)	Pos.	G	AB	R	H	2B	3B	HR	RBI	Avg.	BB	SO	SB	PO	A	E	Avg.
							BATTING								FIELDING		
1995— Los Angeles (N.L.)	SS	3	12	1	6	0	0	0	0	.500	0	1	0	1	7	1	.889

FORD, BEN   P   YANKEES

PERSONAL: Born August 15, 1975, in Cedar Rapids, Iowa. ... 6-7/200. ... Throws right, bats right. ... Full name: Benjamin Cooper Ford.
HIGH SCHOOL: George Washington (Cedar Rapids, Iowa).
JUNIOR COLLEGE: Indian Hills Community College (Iowa).

TRANSACTIONS/CAREER NOTES: Selected by New York Yankees organization in 20th round of free-agent draft (June 2, 1994). ... Selected by Arizona Diamondbacks in first round (17th pick overall) of expansion draft (November 18, 1997). ... Traded by Diamondbacks with C Izzy Molina to Yankees for P Darren Holmes and cash (March 30, 1999).

Year League	W	L	Pct.	ERA	G	GS	CG	ShO	Sv.	IP	H	R	ER	BB	SO
1994— Gulf Coast Yankees (GCL) ..	2	2	.500	2.38	18	0	0	0	3	34	27	13	9	8	31
1995— Oneonta (NY-P)	5	0	1.000	0.87	29	0	0	0	0	52	39	23	5	16	50
— Greensboro (SAL)	0	0	...	5.14	7	0	0	0	0	7	4	4	4	5	8
1996— Greensboro (SAL)	2	6	.250	4.26	43	0	0	0	2	82 1/3	75	48	39	33	84
1997— Tampa (FSL)	4	0	1.000	1.93	32	0	0	0	18	37 1/3	27	8	8	14	37
— Norwich (East.)	4	3	.571	4.22	28	0	0	0	1	42 2/3	35	28	20	19	38
1998— Tucson (PCL)■	2	5	.286	4.35	48	0	0	0	13	68 1/3	68	41	33	33	63
— Arizona (N.L.)	0	0	...	9.90	8	0	0	0	0	10	13	12	11	3	5
1999— Columbus (I.L.)■	6	3	.667	4.73	53	0	0	0	3	70 1/3	69	42	37	39	40
Major League totals (1 year)........	0	0	...	9.90	8	0	0	0	0	10	13	12	11	3	5

FORDYCE, BROOK   C   WHITE SOX

PERSONAL: Born May 7, 1970, in New London, Conn. ... 6-0/190. ... Bats right, throws right. ... Full name: Brook Alexander Fordyce. ... Name pronounced FOR-dice.

HIGH SCHOOL: St. Bernard (Uncasville, Conn.).

TRANSACTIONS/CAREER NOTES: Selected by New York Mets organization in third round of free-agent draft (June 5, 1989). ... On disabled list (June 19-July 2 and July 18-August 30, 1994). ... On suspended list (August 30-September 1, 1994). ... Claimed on waivers by Cleveland Indians (May 15, 1995). ... Granted free agency (October 16, 1995). ... Signed by Cincinnati Reds organization (December 7, 1995). ... On disabled list (July 16-August 5, 1997); included rehabilitation assignment to Indianapolis (July 21-August 5). ... On Cincinnati disabled list (July 13-August 12, 1998); included rehabilitation assignment to Indianapolis (August 4-12). ... Traded by Reds to Chicago White Sox for P Jake Meyer (March 25, 1999).

STATISTICAL NOTES: Led Appalachian League catchers with .991 fielding percentage in 1989. ... Led South Atlantic League in slugging percentage with .478 and tied for lead in grounding into double plays with 18 in 1990. ... Led South Atlantic League with 30 passed balls in 1990. ... Led Eastern League catchers with 795 total chances in 1992. ... Led International League catchers with 810 total chances and tied for lead in double plays by catcher with 11 in 1993.

							BATTING								FIELDING		
Year Team (League)	Pos.	G	AB	R	H	2B	3B	HR	RBI	Avg.	BB	SO	SB	PO	A	E	Avg.
1989— Kingsport (Appal.)	C-OF-3B	69	226	45	74	15	0	9	38	.327	30	26	10	311	28	4	†.988
1990— Columbia (SAL)	C	104	372	45	117	29	1	10	54	.315	39	42	4	574	63	15	.977
1991— St. Lucie (FSL)	C	115	406	42	97	19	3	7	55	.239	37	50	4	630	87	13	.982
1992— Binghamton (East.)	C	118	425	59	118	30	0	11	61	.278	37	78	1	*713	*79	3	*.996
1993— Norfolk (I.L.)	C	116	409	33	106	21	2	2	41	.259	26	62	2	*735	67	8	.990
1994— Norfolk (I.L.)	C-DH	66	229	26	60	13	3	3	32	.262	19	26	1	330	33	7	.981
1995— New York (N.L.)		4	2	1	1	1	0	0	0	.500	1	0	0	0	0	0	...
— Buffalo (A.A.)■	C	58	176	18	44	13	0	0	9	.250	14	20	1	306	18	3	.991
1996— Indianapolis (A.A.)■ ..	C-DH-1B	107	374	48	103	20	3	16	64	.275	25	56	2	620	49	4	*.994
— Cincinnati (N.L.)	C	4	7	0	2	1	0	0	1	.286	3	1	0	18	0	0	1.000
1997— Cincinnati (N.L.)	C-DH	47	96	7	20	5	0	1	8	.208	8	15	2	162	12	3	.983
— Indianapolis (A.A.)	C-DH	12	47	7	11	2	0	2	6	.234	5	6	1	73	8	0	1.000
1998— Cincinnati (N.L.)	C	57	146	8	37	9	0	3	14	.253	11	28	0	288	20	7	.978
— Indianapolis (I.L.)	C	6	24	4	6	1	0	2	3	.250	1	2	0	28	4	0	1.000
1999— Chicago (A.L.)■	C	105	333	36	99	25	1	9	49	.297	21	48	2	561	30	8	.987
American League totals (1 year)		105	333	36	99	25	1	9	49	.297	21	48	2	561	30	8	.987
National League totals (4 years)		112	251	16	60	16	0	4	23	.239	23	44	2	468	32	10	.980
Major League totals (5 years)		217	584	52	159	41	1	13	72	.272	44	92	4	1029	62	18	.984

FOSSAS, TONY   P   YANKEES

PERSONAL: Born September 23, 1957, in Havana, Cuba. ... 6-0/198. ... Throws left, bats left. ... Full name: Emilio Anthony Fossas.

HIGH SCHOOL: St. Mary's (Brookline, Mass.).

COLLEGE: South Florida.

TRANSACTIONS/CAREER NOTES: Selected by Minnesota Twins organization in ninth round of free-agent draft (June 6, 1978); did not sign. ... Selected by Texas Rangers organization in 12th round of free-agent draft (June 5, 1979). ... Released by Rangers organization (February 18, 1982). ... Signed by Chicago Cubs organization (March 11, 1982). ... Loaned by Cubs organization to Tabasco of Mexican League (March 15-April 7, 1982). ... Released by Cubs organization (April 7, 1982). ... Signed by Rangers organization (May 3, 1982). ... Granted free agency (October 15, 1985). ... Signed by California Angels organization (December 13, 1985). ... On disabled list (June 2, 1986-remainder of season). ... Granted free agency (October 15, 1987). ... Signed by Rangers organization (December 1, 1987). ... Granted free agency (October 15, 1988). ... Signed by Milwaukee Brewers organization (January 21, 1989). ... Released by Brewers organization (December 6, 1990). ... Signed by Boston Red Sox organization (January 23, 1991). ... Released by Red Sox (December 11, 1992). ... Re-signed by Red Sox organization (January 18, 1993). ... Granted free agency (December 20, 1993). ... Re-signed by Red Sox organization (January 20, 1994). ... Granted free agency (December 23, 1994). ... Signed by St. Louis Cardinals organization (April 11, 1995). ... Granted free agency (October 27, 1997). ... Signed by Seattle Mariners (December 16, 1997). ... Released by Mariners (June 10, 1998). ... Signed by Chicago Cubs organization (June 19, 1998). ... Released by Cubs (August 4, 1998). ... Signed by Texas Rangers (August 19, 1998). ... Granted free agency (October 19, 1998). ... Re-signed by Rangers organization (January 7, 1999). ... Released by Rangers (March 24, 1999). ... Signed by New York Yankees organization (March 25, 1999). ... Released by Yankees (April 1, 1999). ... Re-signed by Yankees organization (April 3, 1999). ... On Columbus disabled list (July 15-August 5, 1999).

Year League	W	L	Pct.	ERA	G	GS	CG	ShO	Sv.	IP	H	R	ER	BB	SO
1979— GC Rangers (GCL)	6	3	.667	3.00	10	9	1	0	0	60	54	28	20	26	49
— Tulsa (Texas)	1	1	.500	6.55	2	2	0	0	0	11	14	10	8	4	3
1980— Asheville (SAL)	8	2	.800	3.15	30	•27	8	2	2	*197	*187	84	69	69	140
1981— Tulsa (Texas)	5	6	.455	4.16	38	12	1	1	2	106	113	65	49	44	57
1982— Tabasco (Mex.)■	0	3	.000	5.56	3	3	0	0	0	11 1/3	15	14	7	10	6
— Burlington (Midw.)■	8	9	.471	3.08	25	18	10	1	0	146 1/3	121	63	50	33	115

Year League	W	L	Pct.	ERA	G	GS	CG	ShO	Sv.	IP	H	R	ER	BB	SO
1983— Tulsa (Texas)	8	7	.533	4.20	24	16	6	1	0	133	123	77	62	46	103
— Oklahoma City (A.A.)	1	2	.333	7.90	10	5	0	0	0	35⅓	55	33	31	12	23
1984— Tulsa (Texas)	0	1	.000	4.50	4	0	0	0	2	10	12	5	5	3	7
— Oklahoma City (A.A.)	5	9	.357	4.31	29	15	3	0	0	121	143	65	58	34	74
1985— Oklahoma City (A.A.)	7	6	.538	4.75	30	13	2	0	2	110	121	65	58	36	49
1986— Edmonton (PCL)■	3	3	.500	4.57	7	7	2	1	0	43⅓	53	23	22	12	15
1987— Edmonton (PCL)	6	8	.429	4.99	40	15	1	0	0	117⅓	152	76	65	29	54
1988— Oklahoma City (A.A.)■	3	0	1.000	2.84	52	0	0	0	4	66⅔	64	21	21	16	42
— Texas (A.L.)	0	0	...	4.76	5	0	0	0	0	5⅔	11	3	3	2	0
1989— Denver (A.A.)■	5	1	.833	2.04	24	1	0	0	0	35⅓	27	9	8	11	35
— Milwaukee (A.L.)	2	2	.500	3.54	51	0	0	0	1	61	57	27	24	22	42
1990— Milwaukee (A.L.)	2	3	.400	6.44	32	0	0	0	0	29⅓	44	23	21	10	24
— Denver (A.A.)	5	2	.714	1.51	25	0	0	0	4	35⅔	29	8	6	10	45
1991— Boston (A.L.)■	3	2	.600	3.47	64	0	0	0	1	57	49	27	22	28	29
1992— Boston (A.L.)	1	2	.333	2.43	60	0	0	0	2	29⅔	21	9	8	14	19
1993— Boston (A.L.)	1	1	.500	5.18	71	0	0	0	0	40	38	28	23	15	39
1994— Boston (A.L.)	2	0	1.000	4.76	44	0	0	0	1	34	35	18	18	15	31
— Pawtucket (I.L.)	2	0	1.000	0.00	11	0	0	0	0	9⅔	4	1	0	3	8
1995— St. Louis (N.L.)■	3	0	1.000	1.47	58	0	0	0	0	36⅔	28	6	6	10	40
1996— St. Louis (N.L.)	0	4	.000	2.68	65	0	0	0	2	47	43	19	14	21	36
1997— St. Louis (N.L.)	2	7	.222	3.83	71	0	0	0	0	51⅔	62	32	22	26	41
1998— Seattle (A.L.)■	0	3	.000	8.74	23	0	0	0	0	11⅓	19	11	11	6	10
— Iowa (PCL)■	0	0	...	3.60	10	0	0	0	0	5	10	4	2	2	2
— Chicago (N.L.)	0	0	...	9.00	8	0	0	0	0	4	8	4	4	6	6
— Oklahoma (PCL)■	0	1	.000	5.40	4	0	0	0	0	6⅔	6	4	4	4	3
— Texas (A.L.)	1	0	1.000	0.00	10	0	0	0	0	7⅓	3	0	0	4	7
1999— Columbus (I.L.)■	1	0	1.000	4.05	26	0	0	0	0	20	17	10	9	6	15
— New York (A.L.)	0	0	...	36.00	5	0	0	0	0	1	6	4	4	1	0
A.L. totals (9 years)	12	13	.480	4.36	365	0	0	0	5	276⅓	293	150	134	117	201
N.L. totals (4 years)	5	11	.313	2.97	202	0	0	0	2	139⅓	141	61	46	63	123
Major League totals (12 years)	17	24	.415	3.90	567	0	0	0	7	415⅔	434	211	180	180	324

DIVISION SERIES RECORD

Year League	W	L	Pct.	ERA	G	GS	CG	ShO	Sv.	IP	H	R	ER	BB	SO
1996— St. Louis (N.L.)							Did not play.								

CHAMPIONSHIP SERIES RECORD

Year League	W	L	Pct.	ERA	G	GS	CG	ShO	Sv.	IP	H	R	ER	BB	SO
1996— St. Louis (N.L.)	0	0	...	2.08	5	0	0	0	0	4⅓	1	1	1	4	1

FOSTER, KRIS   P   DODGERS

PERSONAL: Born June 30, 1974, in Riverdale, N.J. ... 6-1/200. ... Throws right, bats right. ... Full name: John Kristian Foster.
HIGH SCHOOL: Riverdale (Fort Myers, Fla.).
JUNIOR COLLEGE: Edison Community College (Fla.).
TRANSACTIONS/CAREER NOTES: Selected by Montreal Expos organization in 39th round of free-agent draft (June 1, 1992). ... Traded by Expos to Los Angeles Dodgers for SS Rafael Bournigal (June 10, 1995). ... On Albuquerque disabled list (April 8-20, 1999). ... Granted free agency (October 15, 1999). ... Re-signed by Dodgers (October 22, 1999).

Year League	W	L	Pct.	ERA	G	GS	CG	ShO	Sv.	IP	H	R	ER	BB	SO
1993— Gulf Coast Expos (GCL)	1	6	.143	3.43	17	3	0	0	1	44⅔	44	26	17	16	30
1994— Gulf Coast Expos (GCL)	4	2	.667	1.55	18	5	0	0	4	52⅓	34	21	9	32	65
1995— Yakima (N'west)■	2	3	.400	2.89	15	10	0	0	3	56	38	27	18	38	55
1996— San Bernardino (Calif.)	3	5	.375	3.86	30	8	0	0	2	81⅔	66	46	35	54	78
1997— Vero Beach (FSL)	6	3	.667	5.32	17	17	2	0	0	89⅔	97	69	53	44	77
1998— Vero Beach (FSL)	3	5	.375	6.79	24	6	0	0	1	53	59	45	40	27	52
1999— Vero Beach (FSL)	1	1	.500	1.76	8	0	0	0	0	15⅓	10	5	3	2	15
— San Antonio (Texas)	0	2	.000	3.59	33	0	0	0	4	52⅔	43	24	21	26	53

FOULKE, KEITH   P   WHITE SOX

PERSONAL: Born October 19, 1972, in San Diego. ... 6-0/200. ... Throws right, bats right. ... Full name: Keith Charles Foulke.
HIGH SCHOOL: Hargrove (Huffman, Texas).
JUNIOR COLLEGE: Galveston (Texas) College.
COLLEGE: Lewis-Clark State (Idaho).
TRANSACTIONS/CAREER NOTES: Selected by San Francisco Giants organization in ninth round of free-agent draft (June 2, 1994). ... Traded by Giants with SS Mike Caruso, OF Brian Manning, P Lorenzo Barcelo, P Bobby Howry and P Ken Vining to Chicago White Sox for P Wilson Alvarez, P Danny Darwin and P Roberto Hernandez (July 31, 1997). ... On disabled list (August 28, 1998-remainder of season).

Year League	W	L	Pct.	ERA	G	GS	CG	ShO	Sv.	IP	H	R	ER	BB	SO
1994— Everett (N'west)	2	0	1.000	0.93	4	4	0	0	0	19⅓	17	4	2	3	22
1995— San Jose (Calif.)	13	6	.684	3.50	28	26	2	1	0	177⅓	166	85	69	32	168
1996— Shreveport (Texas)	12	7	.632	*2.76	27	27	4	2	0	*182⅔	149	61	56	35	129
1997— Phoenix (PCL)	5	4	.556	4.50	12	12	0	0	0	76	79	38	38	15	54
— San Francisco (N.L.)	1	5	.167	8.26	11	8	0	0	0	44⅔	60	41	41	18	33
— Nashville (A.A.)■	0	0	...	5.79	1	1	0	0	0	4⅔	8	3	3	0	4
— Chicago (A.L.)	3	0	1.000	3.45	16	0	0	0	3	28⅔	28	11	11	5	21
1998— Chicago (A.L.)	3	2	.600	4.13	54	0	0	0	1	65⅓	51	31	30	20	57
1999— Chicago (A.L.)	3	3	.500	2.22	67	0	0	0	9	105⅓	72	28	26	21	123
A.L. totals (3 years)	9	5	.643	3.03	137	0	0	0	13	199⅓	151	70	67	46	201
N.L. totals (1 year)	1	5	.167	8.26	11	8	0	0	0	44⅔	60	41	41	18	33
Major League totals (3 years)	10	10	.500	3.98	148	8	0	0	13	244	211	111	108	64	234

PERSONAL: Born January 12, 1971, in Sacramento. ... 6-4/205. ... Bats left, throws right. ... Full name: Andrew Junipero Fox.
HIGH SCHOOL: Christian Brothers (Sacramento).
TRANSACTIONS/CAREER NOTES: Selected by New York Yankees organization in second round of free-agent draft (June 5, 1989). ... On disabled list (June 11-21, 1991; April 9-22, 1992 and June 10-August 1, 1993). ... On Columbus disabled list (August 5-19, 1997). ... Traded by Yankees to Arizona Diamondbacks for P Marty Janzen and P Todd Erdos (March 8, 1998). ... On disabled list (August 28-September 11, 1999).
STATISTICAL NOTES: Led Carolina League third basemen with 96 putouts in 1992. ... Led Eastern League third basemen with 30 errors in 1994. ... Led International League third basemen with 22 double plays in 1995.

Year	Team (League)	Pos.	G	AB	R	H	2B	3B	HR	RBI	Avg.	BB	SO	SB	PO	A	E	Avg.
1989—GC Yankees (GCL)......		3B	40	141	26	35	9	2	3	25	.248	31	29	6	37	78	10	.920
1990—Greensboro (SAL)......		3B	134	455	68	99	19	4	9	55	.218	92	132	26	93	238	*45	.880
1991—Prince Will. (Caro.)....		3B	126	417	60	96	22	2	10	46	.230	81	104	15	85	247	*29	.920
1992—Prince Will. (Caro.)....		3B-SS	125	473	75	113	18	3	7	42	.239	54	81	28	†97	304	27	.937
1993—Alb./Colonie (East.)		3B	65	236	44	65	16	1	3	24	.275	32	54	12	59	150	19	.917
1994—Alb./Colonie (East.)	3B-SS-2B		121	472	75	105	20	3	11	43	.222	62	102	22	110	261	†34	.916
1995—Norwich (East.)		SS	44	175	23	36	3	5	5	17	.206	19	36	8	77	127	9	.958
—Columbus (I.L.).........	3B-SS-OF-2B		82	302	61	105	16	6	9	37	.348	43	41	22	84	211	9	.970
1996—New York (A.L.).........	3-2-S-DH-O		113	189	26	37	4	0	3	13	.196	20	28	11	96	158	12	.955
1997—Columbus (I.L.).........	3-2-S-O-DH		95	318	66	87	11	4	6	33	.274	54	64	28	111	218	14	.959
—New York (A.L.).........	3-2-DH-S-O		22	31	13	7	1	0	0	1	.226	7	9	2	19	30	1	.980
1998—Arizona (N.L.).........	2B-OF-3B-1B		139	502	67	139	21	6	9	44	.277	43	97	14	307	175	8	.984
1999—Arizona (N.L.).............		SS-3B	99	274	34	70	12	2	6	33	.255	33	61	4	100	196	14	.955
American League totals (2 years)			135	220	39	44	5	0	3	14	.200	27	37	13	115	188	13	.959
National League totals (2 years)			238	776	101	209	33	8	15	77	.269	76	158	18	407	371	22	.973
Major League totals (4 years)			373	996	140	253	38	8	18	91	.254	103	195	31	522	559	35	.969

DIVISION SERIES RECORD

Year	Team (League)	Pos.	G	AB	R	H	2B	3B	HR	RBI	Avg.	BB	SO	SB	PO	A	E	Avg.
1996—New York (A.L.).........		DH-PR	2	0	0	0	0	0	0	0	...	0	0	0	...	...	...	...
1997—New York (A.L.).........		2B-PR	2	0	0	0	0	0	0	0	...	0	0	0	0	0	0	...
1999—Arizona (N.L.).............		SS	1	3	0	0	0	0	0	0	.000	0	1	0	1	2	1	.750
Division series totals (3 years)			5	3	0	0	0	0	0	0	.000	0	1	0	1	2	1	.750

CHAMPIONSHIP SERIES RECORD

Year	Team (League)	Pos.	G	AB	R	H	2B	3B	HR	RBI	Avg.	BB	SO	SB	PO	A	E	Avg.
1996—New York (A.L.).........		DH-PR	2	0	0	0	0	0	0	0	...	0	0	0	...	...	...	...

WORLD SERIES RECORD

NOTES: Member of World Series championship team (1996).

Year	Team (League)	Pos.	G	AB	R	H	2B	3B	HR	RBI	Avg.	BB	SO	SB	PO	A	E	Avg.
1996—New York (A.L.).........	2B-PR-3B		4	0	1	0	0	0	0	0	...	0	0	0	1	0	0	1.000

PERSONAL: Born September 3, 1970, in Coronado, Calif. ... 6-3/190. ... Throws right, bats right. ... Full name: Chad Douglas Fox.
HIGH SCHOOL: Westfield (Houston).
JUNIOR COLLEGE: Blinn College (Texas).
COLLEGE: Tarleton State (Texas).
TRANSACTIONS/CAREER NOTES: Selected by Cincinnati Reds organization in 23rd round of free-agent draft (June 1, 1992). ... Traded by Reds organization with a player to be named later to Atlanta Braves for OF Mike Kelly (January 9, 1996); Braves acquired P Ray King to complete deal (June 11, 1996). ... On disabled list (July 16-September 3, 1996). ... Traded by Braves to Milwaukee Brewers for OF Gerald Williams (December 11, 1997). ... On Milwaukee disabled list (May 11-June 30, 1998); included rehabilitation assignment to Beloit (June 25-July 1). ... On disabled list (April 21, 1999-remainder of season).
STATISTICAL NOTES: Led Carolina League with 20 wild pitches in 1994.

Year	League	W	L	Pct.	ERA	G	GS	CG	ShO	Sv.	IP	H	R	ER	BB	SO
1992—Princeton (Appl.)................		4	2	.667	4.74	15	8	0	0	0	49 1/3	55	43	26	34	37
1993—Charleston, W.Va. (SAL).....		9	12	.429	5.37	27	26	0	0	0	135 2/3	138	100	81	97	81
1994—Winston-Salem (Caro.).......		12	5	.706	3.86	25	25	1	0	0	156 1/3	121	77	67	*94	137
1995—Chattanooga (Sou.)...........		4	5	.444	5.06	20	17	0	0	0	80	76	49	45	52	56
1996—Richmond (I.L.)■..............		3	10	.231	4.72	18	18	1	0	0	93 1/3	91	57	49	49	87
1997—Richmond (I.L.)..................		1	0	1.000	3.70	13	0	0	0	0	24 1/3	24	10	10	14	25
—Atlanta (N.L.)...................		0	1	.000	3.29	30	0	0	0	0	27 1/3	24	12	10	16	28
1998—Milwaukee (N.L.)■............		1	4	.200	3.95	49	0	0	0	0	57	56	27	25	20	64
—Beloit (Midw.)...................		0	1	.000	4.50	2	1	0	0	0	2	1	1	1	0	3
1999—Milwaukee (N.L.).............		0	0	...	10.80	6	0	0	0	0	6 2/3	11	8	8	4	12
**Major League totals (3 years)....... **		1	5	.167	4.25	85	0	0	0	0	91	91	47	43	40	104

PERSONAL: Born September 17, 1960, in Brooklyn, N.Y. ... 5-10/185. ... Throws left, bats left. ... Full name: John Anthony Franco.
HIGH SCHOOL: Lafayette (Brooklyn, N.Y.).
COLLEGE: St. John's.

F

TRANSACTIONS/CAREER NOTES: Selected by Los Angeles Dodgers organization in fifth round of free-agent draft (June 8, 1981). ... Traded by Dodgers organization with P Brett Wise to Cincinnati Reds organization for IF Rafael Landestoy (May 9, 1983). ... Traded by Reds with OF Don Brown to New York Mets for P Randy Myers and P Kip Gross (December 6, 1989). ... On disabled list (June 30-August 1 and August 26, 1992-remainder of season; April 17-May 7 and August 3-26, 1993). ... Granted free agency (October 18, 1994). ... Re-signed by Mets (April 5, 1995). ... On New York disabled list (July 3-September 4, 1999); included rehabilitation assignment to Binghamton (September 3-4).

RECORDS: Holds N.L. career record for most saves—416.

HONORS: Named N.L. Fireman of the Year by THE SPORTING NEWS (1988, 1990 and 1994).

MISCELLANEOUS: Holds Cincinnati Reds all-time record for most saves (148). ... Holds New York Mets all-time record for most saves (268) and games pitched (485).

Year League	W	L	Pct.	ERA	G	GS	CG	ShO	Sv.	IP	H	R	ER	BB	SO
1981— Vero Beach (FSL)	7	4	.636	3.53	13	11	3	0	0	79	78	41	31	41	60
1982— Albuquerque (PCL)	1	2	.333	7.24	5	5	0	0	0	27 1/3	41	22	22	15	24
— San Antonio (Texas)	10	5	.667	4.96	17	17	3	0	0	105 1/3	137	70	58	46	76
1983— Albuquerque (PCL)	0	0	...	5.40	11	0	0	0	0	15	10	11	9	11	8
— Indianapolis (A.A.)■	6	10	.375	4.85	23	18	2	0	2	115	148	69	62	42	54
1984— Wichita (A.A.)	1	0	1.000	5.79	6	0	0	0	0	9 1/3	8	6	6	4	11
— Cincinnati (N.L.)	6	2	.750	2.61	54	0	0	0	4	79 1/3	74	28	23	36	55
1985— Cincinnati (N.L.)	12	3	.800	2.18	67	0	0	0	12	99	83	27	24	40	61
1986— Cincinnati (N.L.)	6	6	.500	2.94	74	0	0	0	29	101	90	40	33	44	84
1987— Cincinnati (N.L.)	8	5	.615	2.52	68	0	0	0	32	82	76	26	23	27	61
1988— Cincinnati (N.L.)	6	6	.500	1.57	70	0	0	0	*39	86	60	18	15	27	46
1989— Cincinnati (N.L.)	4	8	.333	3.12	60	0	0	0	32	80 2/3	77	35	28	36	60
1990— New York (N.L.)■	5	3	.625	2.53	55	0	0	0	*33	67 2/3	66	22	19	21	56
1991— New York (N.L.)	5	9	.357	2.93	52	0	0	0	30	55 1/3	61	27	18	18	45
1992— New York (N.L.)	6	2	.750	1.64	31	0	0	0	15	33	24	6	6	11	20
1993— New York (N.L.)	4	3	.571	5.20	35	0	0	0	10	36 1/3	46	24	21	19	29
1994— New York (N.L.)	1	4	.200	2.70	47	0	0	0	*30	50	47	20	15	19	42
1995— New York (N.L.)	5	3	.625	2.44	48	0	0	0	29	51 2/3	48	17	14	17	41
1996— New York (N.L.)	4	3	.571	1.83	51	0	0	0	28	54	54	15	11	21	48
1997— New York (N.L.)	5	3	.625	2.55	59	0	0	0	36	60	48	18	17	20	53
1998— New York (N.L.)	0	8	.000	3.62	61	0	0	0	38	64 2/3	66	28	26	29	59
1999— New York (N.L.)	0	2	.000	2.88	46	0	0	0	19	40 2/3	40	14	13	19	41
— Binghamton (East.)	0	0	...	0.00	1	1	0	0	0	1 1/3	0	0	0	0	1
Major League totals (16 years)	77	70	.524	2.64	878	0	0	0	416	1041 1/3	961	365	306	404	801

DIVISION SERIES RECORD

Year League	W	L	Pct.	ERA	G	GS	CG	ShO	Sv.	IP	H	R	ER	BB	SO
1999— New York (N.L.)	1	0	1.000	0.00	3	0	0	0	0	3 2/3	1	0	0	0	2

CHAMPIONSHIP SERIES RECORD

Year League	W	L	Pct.	ERA	G	GS	CG	ShO	Sv.	IP	H	R	ER	BB	SO
1999— New York (N.L.)	0	0	...	3.38	3	0	0	0	0	2 2/3	3	1	1	1	3

ALL-STAR GAME RECORD

Year League	W	L	Pct.	ERA	GS	CG	ShO	Sv.	IP	H	R	ER	BB	SO
1986— National				Did not play.										
1987— National	0	0	...	0.00	0	0	0	0	2/3	0	0	0	0	0
1989— National				Did not play.										
1990— National	0	0	...	0.00	0	0	0	0	1	0	0	0	0	0
1991— National				Did not play.										
All-Star Game totals (2 years)	0	0	...	0.00	0	0	0	0	1 2/3	0	0	0	0	0

FRANCO, JULIO 1B/DH

PERSONAL: Born August 23, 1961, in San Pedro de Macoris, Dominican Republic. ... 6-1/200. ... Bats right, throws right. ... Full name: Julio Cesar Franco.

HIGH SCHOOL: Divine Providence (San Pedro de Macoris, Dominican Republic).

TRANSACTIONS/CAREER NOTES: Signed as non-drafted free agent by Philadelphia Phillies organization (June 23, 1978). ... Traded by Phillies with 2B Manny Trillo, OF George Vukovich, P Jay Baller and C Jerry Willard to Cleveland Indians for OF Von Hayes (December 9, 1982). ... On disabled list (July 13-August 8, 1987). ... Traded by Indians to Texas Rangers for 1B Pete O'Brien, OF Oddibe McDowell and 2B Jerry Browne (December 6, 1988). ... On disabled list (March 28-April 19, May 4-June 1 and July 9, 1992-remainder of season). ... Granted free agency (October 27, 1993). ... Signed by Chicago White Sox (December 15, 1993). ... Granted free agency (October 21, 1994). ... Signed by Chiba Lotte Marines of Japan Pacific League (December 28, 1994). ... Signed as free agent by Indians (December 7, 1995). ... On disabled list (July 7-25 and August 4-30, 1996). ... Released by Indians (August 13, 1997). ... Signed by Milwaukee Brewers (August 13, 1997). ... Granted free agency (October 28, 1997). ... Played for Chiba Lotte Marines of Japan Pacific League (1998). ... Signed by Tampa Bay Devil Rays organization (February 19, 1999). ... Loaned to Mexico City Tigres, Mexican League (March 29-September 18, 1999). ... Granted free agency (October 13, 1999).

HONORS: Named Carolina League Most Valuable Player (1980). ... Named second baseman on THE SPORTING NEWS A.L. Silver Slugger team (1988-1991). ... Named second baseman on THE SPORTING NEWS A.L. All-Star team (1989-1991). ... Named designated hitter on THE SPORTING NEWS A.L. Silver Slugger team (1994).

STATISTICAL NOTES: Led Northwest League with 153 total bases in 1979. ... Led Northwest League shortstops with 45 double plays in 1979. ... Led Carolina League shortstops with 73 double plays in 1980. ... Led American Association shortstops with 42 errors in 1982. ... Led A.L. shortstops with 35 errors in 1985. ... Led A.L. in grounding into double plays with 28 in 1986 and 27 in 1989. ... Had 21-game hitting streak (May 11-June 3, 1988). ... Had 22-game hitting streak (July 3-27, 1988). ... Career major league grand slams: 6.

						BATTING							FIELDING		
Year Team (League)	Pos.	G	AB	R	H	2B	3B	HR	RBI	Avg.	BB	SO	SB	PO	A	E	Avg.
1978— Butte (Pio.)	SS	47	141	34	43	5	2	3	28	.305	17	30	4	37	52	25	.781
1979— Central Ore. (N'west)	SS	•71	299	57	*98	15	5	•10	45	.328	24	59	22	103	*256	31	.921
1980— Peninsula (Caro.)	SS	•140	*555	105	178	25	6	11	*99	.321	33	66	44	179	*412	42	.934
1981— Reading (East.)	SS	*139	*532	70	160	17	3	8	74	.301	52	60	27	246	437	30	.958
1982— Oklahoma City (A.A.)	SS-3B	120	463	80	139	19	5	21	66	.300	39	56	33	211	350	†42	.930
— Philadelphia (N.L.)	SS-3B	16	29	3	8	1	0	0	3	.276	2	4	0	8	25	0	1.000

Year	Team (League)	Pos.	G	AB	R	H	2B	3B	HR	RBI	Avg.	BB	SO	SB	PO	A	E	Avg.
1983—Cleveland (A.L.)■......	SS	149	560	68	153	24	8	8	80	.273	27	50	32	247	438	28	.961
1984—Cleveland (A.L.).........	SS-DH	160	*658	82	188	22	5	3	79	.286	43	68	19	280	481	*36	.955
1985—Cleveland (A.L.).........	SS-2B-DH	160	636	97	183	33	4	6	90	.288	54	74	13	252	437	†36	.950
1986—Cleveland (A.L.).........	SS-2B-DH	149	599	80	183	30	5	10	74	.306	32	66	10	248	413	19	.972
1987—Cleveland (A.L.).........	SS-2B-DH	128	495	86	158	24	3	8	52	.319	57	56	32	175	313	18	.964
1988—Cleveland (A.L.).........	2B-DH	152	613	88	186	23	6	10	54	.303	56	72	25	310	434	14	.982
1989—Texas (A.L.)■............	2B-DH	150	548	80	173	31	5	13	92	.316	66	69	21	256	386	13	.980
1990—Texas (A.L.).............	2B-DH	157	582	96	172	27	1	11	69	.296	82	83	31	310	444	•19	.975
1991—Texas (A.L.).............	2B	146	589	108	201	27	3	15	78	*.341	65	78	36	294	372	14	.979
1992—Texas (A.L.).............	DH-2B-OF	35	107	19	25	7	0	2	8	.234	15	17	1	21	17	3	.927
1993—Texas (A.L.).............	DH	144	532	85	154	31	3	14	84	.289	62	95	9	...	...	...	...
1994—Chicago (A.L.)■.........	DH-1B	112	433	72	138	19	2	20	98	.319	62	75	8	88	7	3	.969
1995—Chiba Lotte (Jp.Pc.)■	1B	127	474	60	145	25	3	10	58	.306	...	...	11	...	...	...	...
1996—Cleveland (A.L.)■.......	1B-DH	112	432	72	139	20	1	14	76	.322	61	82	8	852	77	9	.990
1997—Cleveland (A.L.)........	2B-DH-1B	78	289	46	82	13	1	3	25	.284	38	75	8	70	107	3	.983
—Milwaukee (A.L.)■.....	DH-1B	42	141	22	34	3	0	4	19	.241	31	41	7	108	11	1	.992
1998—Chiba Lotte (Jp.Pc.)■		131	487	78	141	27	2	18	77	.290	...	...	7	...	...	...	...
1999—M.C. Tigres (Mex.)■..		93	326	90	138	22	6	14	77	.423	80	44	...	...	...	...	...
—Tampa Bay (A.L.)■.....	1B	1	1	0	0	0	0	0	0	.000	0	1	0	2	0	0	1.000
American League totals (15 years)		1875	7215	1101	2169	334	47	141	978	.301	751	1002	260	3513	3937	216	.972
National League totals (1 year)		16	29	3	8	1	0	0	3	.276	2	4	0	8	25	0	1.000
Major League totals (16 years)		1891	7244	1104	2177	335	47	141	981	.301	753	1006	260	3521	3962	216	.972

DIVISION SERIES RECORD

Year	Team (League)	Pos.	G	AB	R	H	2B	3B	HR	RBI	Avg.	BB	SO	SB	PO	A	E	Avg.
1996—Cleveland (A.L.)..........	1B-DH	4	15	1	2	0	0	0	1	.133	1	6	0	18	1	0	1.000

NOTES: Named Most Valuable Player (1990).

ALL-STAR GAME RECORD

Year	League	Pos.	AB	R	H	2B	3B	HR	RBI	Avg.	BB	SO	SB	PO	A	E	Avg.
1989—American..................	2B	3	0	1	0	0	0	0	.333	0	0	0	1	1	0	1.000
1990—American..................	PH-2B	3	0	1	1	0	0	2	.333	0	0	0	1	0	0	1.000
1991—American..................							Did not play.									
All-Star Game totals (2 years)		6	0	2	1	0	0	2	.333	0	0	0	2	1	0	1.000

FRANCO, MATT   IF/OF   METS

PERSONAL: Born August 19, 1969, in Santa Monica, Calif. ... 6-1/210. ... Bats left, throws right. ... Full name: Matthew Neil Franco. ... Nephew of actor Kurt Russell.

HIGH SCHOOL: Westlake (Calif.).

TRANSACTIONS/CAREER NOTES: Selected by Chicago Cubs organization in seventh round of free-agent draft (June 2, 1987). ... On disabled list (May 6-13, 1994). ... Traded by Cubs to New York Mets organization for a player to be named later (April 8, 1996); Cubs acquired P Chris DeWitt to complete deal (June 11, 1996). ... On Norfolk disabled list (April 8-11, 1996). ... Granted free agency (October 15, 1996). ... Re-signed by Mets organization (November 21, 1996). ... On New York disabled list (June 29-July 14, 1998); included rehabilitation assignment to Norfolk (July 9-14).

RECORDS: Holds major league single-season record for most bases on balls by pinch hitter—20 (1999).

STATISTICAL NOTES: Led Midwest League in grounding into double plays with 19 in 1990.

Year	Team (League)	Pos.	G	AB	R	H	2B	3B	HR	RBI	Avg.	BB	SO	SB	PO	A	E	Avg.
1987—Wytheville (Appl.)	3B-1B-2B	62	202	25	50	10	1	1	21	.248	26	41	4	95	88	23	.888
1988—Wytheville (Appl.)	3B-1B	20	79	14	31	9	1	0	16	.392	7	5	0	31	24	6	.902
—Geneva (NY-P)	3B-1B	44	164	19	42	2	0	3	21	.256	19	13	2	190	43	14	.943
1989—Char., W.Va. (SAL)	3-1-O-S	109	377	42	102	16	1	5	48	.271	57	40	2	113	189	22	.932
—Peoria (Midw.)	3B	16	58	4	13	4	0	0	9	.224	5	5	0	11	32	6	.878
1990—Peoria (Midw.)	1B-3B	123	443	52	125	*33	2	6	65	.282	43	39	4	810	75	18	.980
1991—Win.-Salem (Caro.)	3B-1B-SS	104	307	47	66	12	1	4	41	.215	46	42	4	711	53	11	.986
1992—Charlotte (Sou.)	3B-1B-OF	108	343	35	97	18	3	2	31	.283	26	46	3	248	69	13	.961
1993—Orlando (Sou.)	1-3B	68	237	31	75	20	1	7	37	.316	29	30	3	444	40	4	.992
—Iowa (A.A.)	1-DH-O-2	62	199	24	58	17	4	5	29	.291	16	30	4	450	39	2	.996
1994—Iowa (A.A.)	1-DH-3-O	128	437	63	121	32	4	11	71	.277	52	66	3	976	81	7	.993
1995—Iowa (A.A.)	3-1-DH-C-P	121	455	51	128	28	5	6	58	.281	37	44	1	283	179	19	.960
—Chicago (N.L.)	2B-1B-3B	16	17	3	5	1	0	0	1	.294	0	4	0	2	2	0	1.000
1996—Norfolk (I.L.)■	3B-1B-DH	133	508	74	*164	*40	2	7	81	.323	36	55	5	383	167	22	.962
—New York (N.L.)	3B-1B	14	31	3	6	1	0	1	2	.194	1	5	0	15	12	3	.900
1997—Norfolk (I.L.)	OF-DH-1B-3B	7	26	5	7	2	0	0	0	.269	2	2	0	13	4	0	1.000
—New York (N.L.)	3-1-DH-O	112	163	21	45	5	0	5	21	.276	13	23	1	61	52	4	.966
1998—New York (N.L.)	3-O-1-DH	103	161	20	44	7	2	1	13	.273	23	26	0	84	23	1	.991
—Norfolk (I.L.)	3B-OF-1B	5	19	2	7	1	0	0	1	.368	3	1	2	16	4	2	.909
1999—New York (N.L.)	1-O-3-DH-P	122	132	18	31	5	0	4	21	.235	28	21	0	55	23	1	.987
Major League totals (5 years)		367	504	65	131	19	2	11	58	.260	65	79	1	217	112	9	.973

DIVISION SERIES RECORD

Year	Team (League)	Pos.	G	AB	R	H	2B	3B	HR	RBI	Avg.	BB	SO	SB	PO	A	E	Avg.
1999—New York (N.L.)..........	PH	1	0	0	0	0	0	0	0	...	1	0	0	0	0	0	...

F

Year	Team (League)	Pos.	G	AB	R	H	2B	3B	HR	RBI	Avg.	BB	SO	SB	PO	A	E	Avg.
						BATTING									FIELDING			
1999—New York (N.L.).........		PH	5	2	1	1	1	0	0	0	.500	1	0	0	0	0	0	...

RECORD AS PITCHER

Year	League	W	L	Pct.	ERA	G	GS	CG	ShO	Sv.	IP	H	R	ER	BB	SO
1993—Iowa (A.A.)		0	0	...	36.00	1	0	0	0	0	1	5	4	4	1	1
1995—Iowa (A.A.)		0	0	...	0.00	1	0	0	0	0	1	1	0	0	1	1
1999—New York (N.L.).................		0	0	...	13.50	2	0	0	0	0	1 1/3	3	2	2	3	2

FRANK, MIKE — OF — REDS

PERSONAL: Born January 14, 1975, in Pomona, Calif. ... 6-2/195. ... Bats left, throws left. ... Full name: Stephen Michael Frank.
HIGH SCHOOL: Escondido (Calif.).
COLLEGE: Santa Clara.
TRANSACTIONS/CAREER NOTES: Selected by Cincinnati Reds organization in seventh round of free-agent draft (June 3, 1997). ... On Cincinnati disabled list (July 27-August 25, 1998).
STATISTICAL NOTES: Tied for Pioneer League lead in intentional bases on balls received with five in 1997.

Year	Team (League)	Pos.	G	AB	R	H	2B	3B	HR	RBI	Avg.	BB	SO	SB	PO	A	E	Avg.
						BATTING									FIELDING			
1997—Billings (Pio.)		OF	69	266	62	100	22	6	10	62	.376	35	24	18	•118	*11	4	.970
1998—Chattanooga (Sou.)		OF	58	231	43	75	12	4	12	43	.325	19	28	5	127	3	2	.985
—Indianapolis (I.L.)		OF	22	88	8	30	4	0	0	13	.341	7	9	1	44	2	1	.979
—Cincinnati (N.L.)		OF	28	89	14	20	6	0	0	7	.225	7	12	0	60	1	0	1.000
1999—Indianapolis (I.L.).......		OF-DH	121	433	73	128	36	7	9	62	.296	36	55	10	220	10	1	.996
Major League totals (1 year)			28	89	14	20	6	0	0	7	.225	7	12	0	60	1	0	1.000

FRANKLIN, RYAN — P — MARINERS

PERSONAL: Born March 5, 1973, in Fort Smith, Ark. ... 6-3/185. ... Throws right, bats right. ... Full name: Ryan Ray Franklin.
HIGH SCHOOL: Spiro (Okla.).
JUNIOR COLLEGE: Seminole (Okla.) State College.
TRANSACTIONS/CAREER NOTES: Selected by Toronto Blue Jays organization in 25th round of free-agent draft (June 3, 1991); did not sign. ... Selected by Seattle Mariners organization in 23rd round of free-agent draft (June 1, 1992).
STATISTICAL NOTES: Led Southern League with 16 hit batsmen in 1996. ... Pitched 6-0 no-hit victory against Carolina (April 21, 1997, first game).

Year	League	W	L	Pct.	ERA	G	GS	CG	ShO	Sv.	IP	H	R	ER	BB	SO
1993—Bellingham (N'west)..........		5	3	.625	2.92	15	14	1	1	0	74	72	38	24	27	55
1994—Appleton (Midw.)..............		9	6	.600	3.13	18	18	5	1	0	118	105	60	41	23	102
—Riverside (Calif.)................		4	2	.667	3.06	8	8	1	1	0	61 2/3	61	26	21	8	35
—Calgary (PCL)...................		0	0	...	7.94	1	1	0	0	0	5 2/3	9	6	5	1	2
1995—Port City (Sou.)		6	10	.375	4.32	31	20	1	1	0	146	153	84	70	43	102
1996—Port City (Sou.)		6	12	.333	4.01	28	27	2	0	0	182	186	99	81	37	127
1997—Memphis (Sou.)		4	2	.667	3.03	11	8	2	•2	0	59 1/3	45	22	20	14	49
—Tacoma (PCL)		5	5	.500	4.18	14	14	0	0	0	90 1/3	97	48	42	24	59
1998—Tacoma (PCL)		5	6	.455	4.51	34	16	1	0	1	127 2/3	148	75	64	32	90
1999—Tacoma (PCL)		6	9	.400	4.71	29	19	2	1	2	135 2/3	142	81	71	33	94
—Seattle (A.L.)..................		0	0	...	4.76	6	0	0	0	0	11 1/3	10	6	6	8	6
Major League totals (1 year)........		0	0	...	4.76	6	0	0	0	0	11 1/3	10	6	6	8	6

FRANKLIN, WAYNE — P — ASTROS

PERSONAL: Born March 9, 1974, in Wilmington, Del. ... 6-2/195. ... Throws left, bats left. ... Full name: Gary Wayne Franklin Jr.
HIGH SCHOOL: Northeast (Md.).
COLLEGE: Maryland-Baltimore County.
TRANSACTIONS/CAREER NOTES: Selected by Los Angeles Dodgers organization in 36th round of free-agent draft (June 4, 1996). ... Selected by Houston Astros from Dodgers organization in Rule 5 minor league draft (December 14, 1998).

Year	League	W	L	Pct.	ERA	G	GS	CG	ShO	Sv.	IP	H	R	ER	BB	SO
1996—Yakima (N'west)		1	0	1.000	2.52	20	0	0	0	1	25	32	10	7	12	22
1997—Savannah (SAL)		5	3	.625	3.18	28	7	1	0	2	82	79	41	29	35	54
—San Bernardino (Calif.)..........		0	0	...	0.00	1	0	0	0	0	2	2	0	0	0	1
1998—Vero Beach (FSL)		9	3	.750	3.53	48	0	0	0	10	86 2/3	81	43	34	26	78
1999—Kissimmee (FSL)■.............		3	0	1.000	1.53	12	0	0	0	1	17 2/3	11	4	3	6	22
—Jackson (Texas)		3	1	.750	1.61	46	0	0	0	20	50 1/3	31	11	9	16	40

FRASCATORE, JOHN — P — BLUE JAYS

PERSONAL: Born February 4, 1970, in Queens, N.Y. ... 6-1/223. ... Throws right, bats right. ... Full name: John Vincent Frascatore. ... Name pronounced FRASS-kuh-TOR-ee.
HIGH SCHOOL: Oceanside (N.Y.).
COLLEGE: C.W. Post (N.Y.).
TRANSACTIONS/CAREER NOTES: Selected by St. Louis Cardinals organization in 24th round of free-agent draft (June 3, 1991). ... Traded by Cardinals to Arizona Diamondbacks for P Clint Sodowsky (March 30, 1999). ... Traded by Diamondbacks with SS Tony Batista to Toronto Blue Jays for P Dan Plesac (June 12, 1999).
RECORDS: Shares N.L. single-inning record for most consecutive home runs allowed—3 (August 26, 1998, ninth inning).

Year	League	W	L	Pct.	ERA	G	GS	CG	ShO	Sv.	IP	H	R	ER	BB	SO
1991—Hamilton (NY-P)		2	7	.222	9.20	30	1	0	0	1	30⅓	44	38	31	22	18
1992—Savannah (SAL)		5	7	.417	3.84	50	0	0	0	23	58⅔	49	32	25	29	56
1993—Springfield (Midw.)		7	12	.368	3.78	27	26	2	1	0	157⅓	157	84	66	33	126
1994—Arkansas (Texas)		7	3	.700	3.10	12	12	4	1	0	78⅓	76	37	27	15	63
—Louisville (A.A.)		8	3	.727	3.39	13	12	2	1	0	85	82	34	32	33	58
—St. Louis (N.L.)		0	1	.000	16.20	1	1	0	0	0	3⅓	7	6	6	2	2
1995—Louisville (A.A.)		2	8	.200	3.95	28	10	1	0	5	82	89	54	36	34	55
—St. Louis (N.L.)		1	1	.500	4.41	14	4	0	0	0	32⅔	39	19	16	16	21
1996—Louisville (A.A.)		6	13	.316	5.18	36	21	3	0	0	156⅓	180	106	90	42	95
1997—St. Louis (N.L.)		5	2	.714	2.47	59	0	0	0	0	80	74	25	22	33	58
1998—St. Louis (N.L.)		3	4	.429	4.14	69	0	0	0	0	95⅔	95	48	44	36	49
1999—Arizona (N.L.)■		1	4	.200	4.09	26	0	0	0	0	33	31	16	15	12	15
—Toronto (A.L.)■		7	1	.875	3.41	33	0	0	0	1	37	42	16	14	9	22
A.L. totals (1 year)		7	1	.875	3.41	33	0	0	0	1	37	42	16	14	9	22
N.L. totals (5 years)		10	12	.455	3.79	169	5	0	0	0	244⅔	246	114	103	99	145
Major League totals (5 years)		17	13	.567	3.74	202	5	0	0	1	281⅔	288	130	117	108	167

FRIAS, HANLEY · SS · DIAMONDBACKS

PERSONAL: Born December 5, 1973, in Villa Atiagracia, Dominican Republic. ... 6-0/165. ... Bats both, throws right. ... Full name: Hanley Acevedo Frias. ... Name pronounced FREE-us.

TRANSACTIONS/CAREER NOTES: Signed as non-drafted free agent by Texas Rangers organization (July 3, 1990). ... Selected by Arizona Diamondbacks in second round (51st pick overall) of expansion draft (November 18, 1997). ... On Arizona disabled list (March 20-July 14, 1998); included rehabilitation assignment to Tucson (June 9-July 8).

STATISTICAL NOTES: Tied for American Association lead in caught stealing with 15 in 1997. ... Led American Association shortstops with 623 total chances in 1997.

Year	Team (League)	Pos.	G	AB	R	H	2B	3B	HR	RBI	Avg.	BB	SO	SB	PO	A	E	Avg.
1991—																		
	Dominican Summer League statistics unavailable.																	
1992—GC Rangers (GCL)		2B-SS	58	205	37	50	9	2	0	28	.244	27	30	28	90	143	11	.955
1993—Char., S.C. (SAL)		2-O-S-3	132	473	61	109	20	4	4	37	.230	40	108	27	211	249	25	.948
1994—High Desert (Calif.)		SS	124	452	70	115	17	6	3	59	.254	41	74	37	169	*404	37	.939
1995—Charlotte (FSL)		SS	33	120	23	40	6	3	0	14	.333	15	11	8	45	106	11	.932
—Tulsa (Texas)		SS	93	360	44	101	18	4	0	27	.281	45	53	14	137	301	24	.948
1996—Tulsa (Texas)		SS	134	505	73	145	24	12	2	41	.287	30	73	9	197	*417	23	.964
1997—Okla. City (A.A.)		SS-DH	132	484	64	128	17	4	5	46	.264	56	72	35	*176	*414	33	.947
—Texas (A.L.)		SS-2B	14	26	4	5	1	0	0	1	.192	1	4	0	12	13	0	1.000
1998—Tucson (PCL)■		SS-3B-2B	63	253	32	73	10	4	1	21	.289	24	41	16	92	172	12	.957
—Arizona (N.L.)		2B-3B-SS	15	23	4	3	0	1	1	2	.130	0	5	0	9	10	0	1.000
1999—Arizona (N.L.)		SS-2B	69	150	27	41	3	2	1	16	.273	29	18	4	46	101	5	.967
—Tucson (PCL)		3B-2B-SS	23	80	15	24	3	0	0	6	.300	7	15	3	23	41	4	.941
American League totals (1 year)			14	26	4	5	1	0	0	1	.192	1	4	0	12	13	0	1.000
National League totals (2 years)			84	173	31	44	3	3	2	18	.254	29	23	4	55	111	5	.971
Major League totals (3 years)			98	199	35	49	4	3	2	19	.246	30	27	4	67	124	5	.974

DIVISION SERIES RECORD

Year	Team (League)	Pos.	G	AB	R	H	2B	3B	HR	RBI	Avg.	BB	SO	SB	PO	A	E	Avg.
1999—Arizona (N.L.)		SS	4	7	0	0	0	0	0	0	.000	0	3	0	4	1	0	1.000

FRYE, JEFF · 2B · RED SOX

PERSONAL: Born August 31, 1966, in Oakland. ... 5-9/170. ... Bats right, throws right. ... Full name: Jeffrey Dustin Frye.

HIGH SCHOOL: Panama (Okla.).

JUNIOR COLLEGE: Carl Albert (Poteau, Okla.).

COLLEGE: Southeastern State (Okla.).

TRANSACTIONS/CAREER NOTES: Selected by Texas Rangers organization in 30th round of free-agent draft (June 1, 1988). ... On Texas disabled list (March 27, 1993-entire season; June 9-24, 1994; and June 3-18 and June 21-July 6, 1995). ... Granted free agency (December 21, 1995). ... Re-signed by Rangers organization (March 25, 1996). ... Released by Rangers organization (June 5, 1996). ... Signed by Boston Red Sox (June 5, 1996). ... On disabled list (March 13, 1998-entire season). ... On Boston disabled list (June 16-September 1, 1999); included rehabilitation assignments to Gulf Coast Red Sox (July 31-August 9) and Pawtucket (August 10-18).

STATISTICAL NOTES: Led Pioneer League second basemen with 44 double plays in 1988. ... Tied for American Association lead in being hit by pitch with 11 in 1992.

Year	Team (League)	Pos.	G	AB	R	H	2B	3B	HR	RBI	Avg.	BB	SO	SB	PO	A	E	Avg.
1988—Butte (Pio.)		2B	54	185	47	53	7	1	0	14	.286	35	25	16	96	149	7	.972
1989—Gastonia (SAL)		2B	125	464	85	145	26	3	1	40	*.313	72	53	33	242	340	14	*.977
1990—Charlotte (FSL)		2B	131	503	77	137	16	7	0	50	.272	80	66	29	252	350	13	*.979
1991—Tulsa (Texas)		2B	131	503	92	152	32	11	4	41	.302	71	60	15	262	322	*26	.957
1992—Okla. City (A.A.)		2B	87	337	64	101	26	2	2	28	.300	51	39	11	212	248	7	.985
—Texas (A.L.)		2B	67	199	24	51	9	4	1	12	.256	16	27	1	120	196	7	.978
1993—Texas (A.L.)								Did not play.										
1994—Okla. City (A.A.)		2B	17	68	7	19	3	0	1	5	.279	6	7	2	28	44	1	.986
—Texas (A.L.)		2B-DH-3B	57	205	37	67	20	3	0	18	.327	29	23	6	90	136	4	.983
1995—Texas (A.L.)		2B	90	313	38	87	15	2	4	29	.278	24	45	3	173	248	11	.975
1996—Okla. City (A.A.)		2B-SS-OF-3B	49	181	25	43	10	0	1	18	.238	24	21	10	94	148	8	.968
—Boston (A.L.)■		2-O-S-DH	105	419	74	120	27	2	4	41	.286	54	57	18	211	317	9	.983
1997—Boston (A.L.)		2-3-O-D-S-1	127	404	56	126	36	2	3	51	.312	27	44	19	227	264	12	.976

F

Year Team (League)	Pos.	G	AB	R	H	2B	3B	HR	RBI	Avg.	BB	SO	SB	PO	A	E	Avg.
1998—Boston (A.L.)										Did not play.							
1999—Boston (A.L.)...........2B-3B-DH-SS		41	114	14	32	3	0	1	12	.281	14	11	2	52	71	4	.969
— GC Red Sox (GCL) 2B-DH		6	20	4	8	1	0	0	1	.400	2	2	0	3	12	0	1.000
— Pawtucket (I.L.)......... 2B		3	9	0	3	0	0	0	2	.333	2	1	0	1	11	0	1.000
Major League totals (6 years)		487	1654	243	483	110	10	13	163	.292	164	207	49	873	1232	47	.978

FRYMAN, TRAVIS — 3B — INDIANS

PERSONAL: Born March 25, 1969, in Lexington, Ky. ... 6-1/195. ... Bats right, throws right. ... Full name: David Travis Fryman.

HIGH SCHOOL: Tate (Gonzalez, Fla.).

TRANSACTIONS/CAREER NOTES: Selected by Detroit Tigers organization in supplemental round ("sandwich pick" between first and second round, 30th pick overall) of free-agent draft (June 2, 1987); pick received as compensation for Philadelphia Phillies signing Type A free-agent C Lance Parrish. ... Traded by Tigers to Arizona Diamondbacks for 3B Joe Randa, P Matt Drews and 3B Gabe Alvarez (November 18, 1997). ... Traded by Diamondbacks with P Tom Martin and cash to Cleveland Indians for 3B Matt Williams (December 1, 1997). ... On Cleveland disabled list (June 6-25 and July 4-September 2, 1999); included rehabilitation assignments to Akron (August 24-30) and Buffalo (August 31-September 2).

HONORS: Named shortstop on THE SPORTING NEWS A.L. All-Star team (1992). ... Named shortstop on THE SPORTING NEWS A.L. Silver Slugger team (1992). ... Named third baseman on THE SPORTING NEWS A.L. All-Star team (1993).

STATISTICAL NOTES: Led Appalachian League shortstops with 313 total chances in 1987. ... Hit for the cycle (July 28, 1993). ... Tied for A.L. lead with 13 sacrifice flies in 1994. ... Led A.L. third basemen with 313 total chances in 1994 and 337 in 1995. ... Led A.L. third basemen with 38 double plays in 1995. ... Led A.L. third basemen with 133 putouts and .979 fielding percentage in 1996. ... Career major league grand slams: 4.

Year Team (League)	Pos.	G	AB	R	H	2B	3B	HR	RBI	Avg.	BB	SO	SB	PO	A	E	Avg.
1987—Bristol (Appl.)............	SS	67	248	25	58	9	0	2	20	.234	22	39	6	*103	187	*23	.927
1988—Fayetteville (SAL)	SS-2B	123	411	44	96	17	4	0	47	.234	24	83	16	174	390	32	.946
1989—London (East.)	SS	118	426	52	113	*30	1	9	56	.265	19	78	5	192	346	*27	.952
1990—Toledo (I.L.)...............	SS	87	327	38	84	22	2	10	53	.257	17	59	4	128	277	26	.940
—Detroit (A.L.)	3B-SS-2B	66	232	32	69	11	1	9	27	.297	17	51	3	47	145	14	.932
1991—Detroit (A.L.).............	3B-SS	149	557	65	144	36	3	21	91	.259	40	149	12	153	354	23	.957
1992—Detroit (A.L.).............	SS-3B	161	*659	87	175	31	4	20	96	.266	45	144	8	220	489	22	.970
1993—Detroit (A.L.).............	SS-3B-DH	151	607	98	182	37	5	22	97	.300	77	128	9	169	382	23	.960
1994—Detroit (A.L.).............	3B	114	*464	66	122	34	5	18	85	.263	45	*128	2	78	*221	14	.955
1995—Detroit (A.L.).............	3B	144	567	79	156	21	5	15	81	.275	63	100	4	107	*337	14	.969
1996—Detroit (A.L.).............	3B-SS	157	616	90	165	32	3	22	100	.268	57	118	4	149	†354	10	†.981
1997—Detroit (A.L.).............	3B	154	595	90	163	27	3	22	102	.274	46	113	16	•126	312	10	*.978
1998—Cleveland (A.L.)■...	3B-SS-DH	146	557	74	160	33	2	28	96	.287	44	125	10	101	242	13	.963
1999—Cleveland (A.L.).............	3B	85	322	45	82	16	2	10	48	.255	25	57	2	41	146	6	.969
—Akron (East.)	DH-3B	4	12	4	3	0	0	1	4	.250	2	4	0	0	2	0	1.000
—Buffalo (I.L.)..............	3B-DH	3	11	1	2	0	0	1	2	.182	0	3	0	0	3	1	.750
Major League totals (10 years)		1327	5176	726	1418	278	33	187	823	.274	459	1113	70	1191	2982	149	.966

DIVISION SERIES RECORD

Year Team (League)	Pos.	G	AB	R	H	2B	3B	HR	RBI	Avg.	BB	SO	SB	PO	A	E	Avg.
1998—Cleveland (A.L.).........	3B	4	13	1	2	1	0	0	0	.154	3	4	1	5	8	0	1.000
1999—Cleveland (A.L.).........	3B	5	15	2	4	0	0	1	4	.267	3	2	1	0	10	0	1.000
Division series totals (2 years)		9	28	3	6	1	0	1	4	.214	6	6	2	5	18	0	1.000

CHAMPIONSHIP SERIES RECORD

Year Team (League)	Pos.	G	AB	R	H	2B	3B	HR	RBI	Avg.	BB	SO	SB	PO	A	E	Avg.
1998—Cleveland (A.L.).........	3B	6	23	2	4	0	0	0	0	.174	1	5	1	1	7	1	.889

ALL-STAR GAME RECORD

Year League	Pos.	AB	R	H	2B	3B	HR	RBI	Avg.	BB	SO	SB	PO	A	E	Avg.
1992—American	SS	1	1	1	0	0	0	1	1.000	1	0	0	0	3	0	1.000
1993—American	SS	1	0	0	0	0	0	0	.000	0	0	0	1	1	0	1.000
1994—American	PH	1	0	0	0	0	0	0	.000	0	0	0	...	...	...	...
1996—American	PH-3B	1	0	0	0	0	0	0	.000	0	1	0	0	1	0	1.000
All-Star Game totals (4 years)		4	1	1	0	0	0	1	.250	1	1	0	1	5	0	1.000

FUENTES, BRIAN — P — MARINERS

PERSONAL: Born August 9, 1975, in Merced, Calif. ... 6-4/220. ... Throws left, bats left. ... Full name: Brian Christopher Fuentes.

HIGH SCHOOL: Merced (Calif.).

JUNIOR COLLEGE: Merced (Calif.) Junior College.

TRANSACTIONS/CAREER NOTES: Selected by Seattle Mariners organization in 25th round of free-agent draft (June 1, 1995). ... On disabled list (April 2-20, 1998). ... On New Haven disabled list (June 9-August 22, 1999).

Year League	W	L	Pct.	ERA	G	GS	CG	ShO	Sv.	IP	H	R	ER	BB	SO
1996—Everett (N'west).................	0	1	.000	4.39	13	2	0	0	0	26 2/3	23	14	13	13	26
1997—Wisconsin (Midw.)............	6	7	.462	3.56	22	22	0	0	0	118 2/3	84	52	47	59	153
1998—Lancaster (Calif.)..............	7	7	.500	4.17	24	22	0	0	0	118 2/3	121	73	55	81	137
1999—New Haven (East.).............	3	3	.500	4.95	15	14	0	0	0	60	53	36	33	46	66

F

FULLMER, BRAD   1B   EXPOS

PERSONAL: Born January 17, 1975, in Chatsworth, Calif. ... 6-0/215. ... Bats left, throws right. ... Full name: Bradley Ryan Fullmer.
HIGH SCHOOL: Montclair Prep (Van Nuys, Calif.).
TRANSACTIONS/CAREER NOTES: Selected by Montreal Expos organization in second round of free-agent draft (June 3, 1993). ... On disabled list (June 20, 1994-entire season).
STATISTICAL NOTES: Hit home run in first major league at-bat (September 2, 1997). ... Had 16-game hitting streak (August 7-22, 1999). ... Career major league grand slams: 1.

								BATTING								FIELDING		
Year	Team (League)	Pos.	G	AB	R	H	2B	3B	HR	RBI	Avg.	BB	SO	SB	PO	A	E	Avg.
1994—	....							Did not play.										
1995—	Albany (SAL)	3B-1B	123	468	69	•151	38	4	8	67	.323	36	33	10	269	66	30	.918
1996—	W.P. Beach (FSL)........	OF-1B	102	380	52	115	29	1	5	63	.303	32	43	4	197	10	7	.967
	— Harrisburg (East.).......	OF-1B	24	98	11	27	4	1	4	14	.276	3	8	0	43	1	2	.957
1997—	Harrisburg (East.).......	1B-OF-DH	94	357	60	111	24	2	19	62	.311	30	25	6	538	41	6	.990
	— Ottawa (I.L.)	1B-DH-OF	24	91	13	27	7	0	3	17	.297	3	10	1	173	12	1	.995
	— Montreal (N.L.)...........	1B-OF	19	40	4	12	2	0	3	8	.300	2	7	0	50	7	2	.966
1998—	Montreal (N.L.)..........	1B	140	505	58	138	44	2	13	73	.273	39	70	6	1070	79	*17	.985
1999—	Montreal (N.L.)..........	1B	100	347	38	96	34	2	9	47	.277	22	35	2	700	41	7	.991
	— Ottawa (I.L.).............	1B-DH	39	142	31	45	9	0	11	32	.317	12	16	2	187	13	2	.990
Major League totals (3 years)			259	892	100	246	80	4	25	128	.276	63	112	8	1820	127	26	.987

FULTZ, AARON   P   GIANTS

PERSONAL: Born September 4, 1973, in Memphis, Tenn. ... 6-0/196. ... Throws left, bats left. ... Full name: Richard Aaron Fultz.
HIGH SCHOOL: Munford (Tenn.).
JUNIOR COLLEGE: North Florida Community College.
TRANSACTIONS/CAREER NOTES: Selected by San Francisco Giants organization in sixth round of free-agent draft (June 1, 1992). ... Traded by Giants with SS Andres Duncan and P Greg Brummett to Minnesota Twins for P Jim Deshaies (August 28, 1993). ... Released by Twins (April 1, 1996). ... Signed by Giants organization (April 4, 1996). ... Granted free agency (October 16, 1998). ... Re-signed by Giants organization (October 23, 1998).

Year	League	W	L	Pct.	ERA	G	GS	CG	ShO	Sv.	IP	H	R	ER	BB	SO
1992—	Arizona Giants (Ariz.)	3	2	.600	2.13	14	•14	0	0	0	67 2/3	51	24	16	33	72
1993—	Clinton (Midw.)	14	8	.636	3.41	26	25	2	1	0	148	132	63	56	64	144
	— Fort Wayne (Midw.)■.......	0	0	...	9.00	1	1	0	0	0	4	10	4	4	0	3
1994—	Fort Myers (FSL)	9	10	.474	4.33	28	28	3	0	0	168 1/3	193	95	*81	60	132
1995—	New Britain (East.)	0	2	.000	6.60	3	3	0	0	0	15	11	12	11	9	12
	— Fort Myers (FSL)	3	6	.333	3.25	21	21	2	2	0	122	115	52	44	41	127
1996—	San Jose (Calif.)■............	9	5	.643	3.96	36	12	0	0	1	104 2/3	101	52	46	54	103
1997—	Shreveport (Texas)	6	3	.667	2.83	49	0	0	0	1	70	65	30	22	19	60
1998—	Shreveport (Texas)	5	7	.417	3.77	54	0	0	0	15	62	58	40	26	29	61
	— Fresno (PCL)	0	0	...	5.06	10	0	0	0	0	16	22	10	9	2	13
1999—	Fresno (PCL)	9	8	.529	4.98	37	20	1	0	0	137 1/3	141	87	76	51	151

FUSSELL, CHRIS   P   ROYALS

PERSONAL: Born May 19, 1976, in Oregon, Ohio. ... 6-2/200. ... Throws right, bats right. ... Full name: Christopher Wren Fussell.
HIGH SCHOOL: Clay (Ohio).
TRANSACTIONS/CAREER NOTES: Selected by Baltimore Orioles organization in ninth round of free-agent draft (June 2, 1994). ... On disabled list (July 13, 1996-remainder of season). ... Traded by Orioles to Kansas City Royals for OF/1B Jeff Conine (April 2, 1999). ... On Omaha disabled list (July 21-29, 1999).

Year	League	W	L	Pct.	ERA	G	GS	CG	ShO	Sv.	IP	H	R	ER	BB	SO
1994—	Gulf Coast Orioles (GCL)....	2	3	.400	4.15	14	8	0	0	0	56 1/3	53	30	26	24	65
1995—	Bluefield (Appl.)	9	1	.900	2.19	12	12	1	1	0	65 2/3	37	18	16	32	98
1996—	Frederick (Caro.)	5	2	.714	2.81	15	14	1	1	0	86 1/3	71	36	27	44	94
1997—	Bowie (East.)	1	8	.111	7.11	19	18	0	0	0	82 1/3	102	71	65	58	71
	— Frederick (Caro.)	3	3	.500	3.96	9	9	1	1	0	50	42	23	22	31	54
1998—	Bowie (East.)	3	7	.300	4.26	18	18	0	0	0	93	87	54	44	52	84
	— Rochester (I.L.)	5	2	.714	3.99	10	10	0	0	0	58 2/3	50	30	26	28	51
	— Baltimore (A.L.)	0	1	.000	8.38	3	2	0	0	0	9 2/3	11	9	9	9	8
1999—	Omaha (PCL)■	10	3	.769	3.54	14	13	1	1	0	81 1/3	66	35	32	27	80
	— Kansas City (A.L.)	0	5	.000	7.39	17	8	0	0	2	56	72	51	46	36	37
Major League totals (2 years).......		0	6	.000	7.54	20	10	0	0	2	65 2/3	83	60	55	45	45

FYHRIE, MICHAEL   P   ANGELS

PERSONAL: Born December 9, 1969, in Westminster, Calif. ... 6-2/203. ... Throws right, bats right. ... Full name: Michael Edwin Fyhrie. ... Name pronounced Feery.
HIGH SCHOOL: Ocean View (Huntington Beach, Calif.).
COLLEGE: UCLA.
TRANSACTIONS/CAREER NOTES: Selected by Kansas City Royals organization in 12th round of free-agent draft (June 3, 1991). ... Traded by Royals to New York Mets for a player to be named later (March 23, 1996). ... Released by Mets (November 25, 1996). ... Re-signed by Mets organization (December 6, 1997). ... On Norfolk disabled list (August 2, 1998-remainder of season). ... Granted free agency (October 15, 1998). ... Signed by Anaheim Angels organization (November 18, 1998).
HONORS: Named International League Most Valuable Pitcher in 1996.

F

Year— League	W	L	Pct.	ERA	G	GS	CG	ShO	Sv.	IP	H	R	ER	BB	SO
1991— Eugene (N'west)	2	1	.667	2.52	21	0	0	0	5	39 1/3	42	17	11	19	45
1992— Baseball City (FSL)	7	13	.350	2.50	26	26	0	0	0	162	148	65	45	37	92
1993— Wilmington (Caro.)	3	2	.600	3.68	5	5	0	0	0	29 1/3	32	15	12	8	19
— Memphis (Sou.)	11	4	.733	3.56	22	22	3	0	0	131 1/3	143	59	52	59	59
1994— Omaha (A.A.)	6	5	.545	5.72	18	16	0	0	0	85	100	57	54	33	37
— Memphis (Sou.)	2	5	.286	3.22	11	11	0	0	0	67	67	29	24	17	38
1995— Wichita (Texas)	3	2	.600	3.04	17	9	0	0	1	74	76	31	25	23	41
— Omaha (A.A.)	3	4	.429	4.45	14	11	0	0	0	60 2/3	71	34	30	14	39
1996— Norfolk (I.L.)■	*15	6	.714	3.04	27	27	2	•2	0	169	150	61	57	33	103
— New York (N.L.)	0	1	.000	15.43	2	0	0	0	0	2 1/3	4	4	4	3	0
1998— Norfolk (I.L.)	3	7	.300	6.64	24	17	0	0	0	100 1/3	115	83	74	45	60
1999— Edmonton (PCL)■	9	5	.643	3.47	19	18	0	0	0	114	90	47	44	40	113
— Anaheim (A.L.)	0	4	.000	5.05	16	7	0	0	0	51 2/3	61	32	29	21	26
A.L. totals (1 year)	0	4	.000	5.05	16	7	0	0	0	51 2/3	61	32	29	21	26
N.L. totals (1 year)	0	1	.000	15.43	2	0	0	0	0	2 1/3	4	4	4	3	0
Major League totals (2 years)	0	5	.000	5.50	18	7	0	0	0	54	65	36	33	24	26

GAETTI, GARY — 3B

PERSONAL: Born August 19, 1958, in Centralia, Ill. ... 6-0/205. ... Bats right, throws right. ... Full name: Gary Joseph Gaetti. ... Name pronounced guy-ETT-ee.

HIGH SCHOOL: Centralia (Ill.).

JUNIOR COLLEGE: Lake Land College (Ill.).

COLLEGE: Northwest Missouri State.

TRANSACTIONS/CAREER NOTES: Selected by St. Louis Cardinals organization in fourth round of free-agent draft (January 10, 1978); did not sign. ... Selected by Chicago White Sox organization in secondary phase of free-agent draft (June 6, 1978); did not sign. ... Selected by Minnesota Twins organization in secondary phase of free-agent draft (June 5, 1979). ... Granted free agency (November 9, 1987). ... Re-signed by Twins (January 7, 1988). ... On disabled list (August 21-September 5, 1988 and August 26-September 13, 1989). ... Granted free agency (December 7, 1990). ... Signed by California Angels (January 23, 1991). ... Released by Angels (June 3, 1993). ... Signed by Kansas City Royals (June 19, 1993). ... Granted free agency (October 25, 1993). ... Re-signed by Royals organization (December 16, 1993). ... On disabled list (July 5-20, 1994). ... Granted free agency (October 28, 1994). ... Re-signed by Royals organization (December 20, 1994). ... Granted free agency (November 3, 1995). ... Signed by Cardinals (December 18, 1995). ... On disabled list (April 28-May 14, 1996). ... Granted free agency (October 27, 1997). ... Re-signed by Cardinals (December 6, 1997). ... Released by Cardinals (August 14, 1998). ... Signed by Chicago Cubs (August 19, 1998). ... Granted free agency (October 23, 1998). ... Re-signed by Cubs (December 7, 1998). ... Released by Cubs (October 15, 1999).

RECORDS: Shares major league rookie-season record for most sacrifice flies—13 (1982).

HONORS: Won A.L. Gold Glove at third base (1986-89). ... Named third baseman on THE SPORTING NEWS A.L. Silver Slugger team (1995).

STATISTICAL NOTES: Tied for Appalachian League lead in errors by third baseman with 18 in 1979. ... Led Midwest League third basemen with 492 total chances and 35 double plays in 1980. ... Led Southern League third basemen with 122 putouts, 281 assists, 32 errors and 435 total chances in 1981. ... Hit home run in first major-league at-bat (September 20, 1981). ... Led A.L. with 13 sacrifice flies in 1982. ... Led A.L. third basemen with 131 putouts in 1983, 142 in 1984 and 146 in 1985. ... Led A.L. third basemen with 46 double plays in 1983, 36 in 1986 and 1990 and 39 in 1991. ... Led A.L. third basemen with 496 total chances in 1984, 473 in 1986, 438 in 1990 and 481 in 1991. ... Led A.L. third basemen with 334 assists in both 1984 and 1986 and 318 in 1990. ... Tied for A.L. lead in errors by third basemen with 20 in 1984. ... Led A.L. in grounding into double plays with 25 in 1987. ... Led A.L. third basemen with .982 fielding percentage in 1994. ... Led N.L. third basemen in fielding percentage with .978 in 1997 and .983 in 1998. ... Career major league grand slams: 11.

								BATTING							FIELDING		
Year— Team (League)	Pos.	G	AB	R	H	2B	3B	HR	RBI	Avg.	BB	SO	SB	PO	A	E	Avg.
1979— Elizabethton (Appl.)	3B-SS	66	230	50	59	15	2	14	42	.257	43	40	6	70	134	‡21	.907
1980— Wisconsin (Midw.)	3B	138	503	77	134	27	3	*22	82	.266	67	120	24	*94	*363	•35	.929
1981— Orlando (Sou.)	3B	137	495	92	137	19	2	30	93	.277	58	105	15	†143	†283	†32	.930
— Minnesota (A.L.)	3B-DH	9	26	4	5	0	0	2	3	.192	0	6	0	5	17	0	1.000
1982— Minnesota (A.L.)	3B-SS-DH	145	508	59	117	25	4	25	84	.230	37	107	0	106	291	17	.959
1983— Minnesota (A.L.)	3B-SS-DH	157	584	81	143	30	3	21	78	.245	54	121	7	†131	361	17	.967
1984— Minnesota (A.L.)	3B-OF-SS	•162	588	55	154	29	4	5	65	.262	44	81	11	†163	†335	‡21	.960
1985— Minnesota (A.L.)	3B-OF-1B-DH	160	560	71	138	31	0	20	63	.246	37	89	13	†162	316	18	.964
1986— Minnesota (A.L.)	3B-SS-OF-2B	157	596	91	171	34	1	34	108	.287	52	108	14	120	†335	21	.956
1987— Minnesota (A.L.)	3B-DH	154	584	95	150	36	2	31	109	.257	37	92	10	•134	261	11	.973
1988— Minnesota (A.L.)	3B-DH-SS	133	468	66	141	29	2	28	88	.301	36	85	7	105	191	7	.977
1989— Minnesota (A.L.)	3B-DH-1B	130	498	63	125	11	4	19	75	.251	25	87	6	115	253	10	.974
1990— Minnesota (A.L.)	3B-SS	154	577	61	132	27	5	16	85	.229	36	101	6	125	†319	18	.961
1991— California (A.L.)■	3B	152	586	58	144	22	1	18	66	.246	33	104	5	111	*353	17	.965
1992— California (A.L.)	3B-1B-DH	130	456	41	103	13	2	12	48	.226	21	79	3	423	196	22	.966
1993— California (A.L.)	3B-1B-DH	20	50	3	9	2	0	0	4	.180	5	12	1	38	7	1	.978
— Kansas City (A.L.)■	3B-1B-DH	82	281	37	72	18	1	14	46	.256	16	75	0	147	146	6	.980
1994— Kansas City (A.L.)	3B-1B	90	327	53	94	15	3	12	57	.287	19	63	0	99	166	4	†.985
1995— Kansas City (A.L.)	3B-1B-DH	137	514	76	134	27	0	35	96	.261	47	91	3	182	228	16	.962
1996— St. Louis (N.L.)■	3B-1B	141	522	71	143	27	4	23	80	.274	35	97	2	148	231	10	.974
1997— St. Louis (N.L.)	3B-1B-P	148	502	63	126	24	1	17	69	.251	36	88	7	133	250	7	†.982
1998— St. Louis (N.L.)	3-1-P-2-0	91	306	39	81	23	1	11	43	.265	31	39	1	62	153	3	.986
— Chicago (N.L.)■	3B	37	128	21	41	11	0	8	27	.320	12	23	0	24	68	2	‡.979
1999— Chicago (N.L.)	3B-1B-P-SS	113	280	22	57	9	1	9	46	.204	21	51	0	74	147	9	.961
American League totals (15 years)		1972	7203	914	1832	349	32	292	1075	.254	499	1301	86	2166	3775	206	.966
National League totals (4 years)		530	1738	216	448	94	7	68	265	.258	135	298	10	441	849	31	.977
Major League totals (19 years)		2502	8941	1130	2280	443	39	360	1340	.255	634	1599	96	2607	4624	237	.968

DIVISION SERIES RECORD

								BATTING							FIELDING		
Year— Team (League)	Pos.	G	AB	R	H	2B	3B	HR	RBI	Avg.	BB	SO	SB	PO	A	E	Avg.
1996— St. Louis (N.L.)	3B	3	11	1	1	0	0	1	3	.091	0	3	0	1	3	0	1.000
1998— Chicago (N.L.)	3B	3	11	0	1	0	0	0	0	.091	0	4	0	2	6	1	.889
Division series totals (2 years)		6	22	1	2	0	0	1	3	.091	0	7	0	3	9	1	.923

F
G

RECORDS: Shares single-game record for most grand slams—1 (October 10, 1996). ... Shares single-inning record for most runs batted in—4 (October 10, 1996, seventh inning).
NOTES: Hit home run in first at-bat (October 7, 1987). ... Named Most Valuable Player (1987).

Year	Team (League)	Pos.	G	AB	R	H	2B	3B	HR	RBI	Avg.	BB	SO	SB	PO	A	E	Avg.
								BATTING								FIELDING		
1987—	Minnesota (A.L.)	3B	5	20	5	6	1	0	2	5	.300	1	3	0	8	7	0	1.000
1996—	St. Louis (N.L.)	3B	7	24	1	7	0	0	1	4	.292	1	5	0	4	12	0	1.000
Championship series totals (2 years)			**12**	**44**	**6**	**13**	**1**	**0**	**3**	**9**	**.295**	**2**	**8**	**0**	**12**	**19**	**0**	**1.000**

WORLD SERIES RECORD

RECORDS: Shares single-inning records for most at-bats—2; and most hits—2 (October 17, 1987, fourth inning).
NOTES: Member of World Series championship team (1987).

Year	Team (League)	Pos.	G	AB	R	H	2B	3B	HR	RBI	Avg.	BB	SO	SB	PO	A	E	Avg.
								BATTING								FIELDING		
1987—	Minnesota (A.L.)	3B	7	27	4	7	2	1	1	4	.259	2	5	2	6	15	0	1.000

ALL-STAR GAME RECORD

Year	League	Pos.	AB	R	H	2B	3B	HR	RBI	Avg.	BB	SO	SB	PO	A	E	Avg.
							BATTING								FIELDING		
1988—	American	PH	1	0	0	0	0	0	0	.000	0	0	0	...	...	...	...
1989—	American	3B	1	0	0	0	0	0	0	.000	0	1	0	1	0	0	1.000
All-Star Game totals (2 years)			**2**	**0**	**0**	**0**	**0**	**0**	**0**	**.000**	**0**	**1**	**0**	**1**	**0**	**0**	**1.000**

RECORD AS PITCHER

Year	League	W	L	Pct.	ERA	G	GS	CG	ShO	Sv.	IP	H	R	ER	BB	SO
1997—	St. Louis (N.L.)..................	0	0	...	0.00	1	0	0	0	0	1/3	1	0	0	0	0
1998—	St. Louis (N.L.)..................	0	0	...	0.00	1	0	0	0	0	1	2	0	0	0	0
1999—	Chicago (N.L.)..................	0	0	...	18.00	1	0	0	0	0	1	2	2	2	1	1
Major League totals (3 years)....		**0**	**0**	...	**7.71**	**3**	**0**	**0**	**0**	**0**	**2 1/3**	**5**	**2**	**2**	**1**	**1**

GAGNE, ERIC   P   DODGERS

PERSONAL: Born January 7, 1976, in Montreal. ... 6-2/195. ... Throws right, bats right. ... Full name: Eric Serge Gagne.
HIGH SCHOOL: Polyvalente Edouard Montpetit (Montreal).
TRANSACTIONS/CAREER NOTES: Signed as non-drafted free agent by Los Angeles Dodgers organization (July 26, 1995). ... On disabled list entire 1997 season.
HONORS: Named Texas League Pitcher of the Year (1999).

Year	League	W	L	Pct.	ERA	G	GS	CG	ShO	Sv.	IP	H	R	ER	BB	SO
1996—	Savannah (SAL)	7	6	.538	3.28	23	21	1	1	0	115 1/3	94	48	42	43	131
1997—								Did not play.								
1998—	Vero Beach (FSL)	9	7	.563	3.74	25	25	3	1	0	139 2/3	118	69	58	48	144
1999—	San Antonio (Texas).........	12	4	.750	*2.63	26	26	0	0	0	167 2/3	122	55	49	64	*185
	—Los Angeles (N.L.)	1	1	.500	2.10	5	5	0	0	0	30	18	8	7	15	30
Major League totals (1 year)........		**1**	**1**	**.500**	**2.10**	**5**	**5**	**0**	**0**	**0**	**30**	**18**	**8**	**7**	**15**	**30**

GAILLARD, EDDIE   P   REDS

PERSONAL: Born August 13, 1970, in Camden, N.J. ... 6-2/195. ... Throws right, bats right. ... Full name: Julian Edward Gaillard III. ... Namd pronounced GAY-lard.
HIGH SCHOOL: Forest Hills (West Palm Beach, Fla.).
JUNIOR COLLEGE: Palm Beach Community College (Fla.).
COLLEGE: Florida Southern.
TRANSACTIONS/CAREER NOTES: Selected by Detroit Tigers organization in 13th round of free-agent draft (June 3, 1993). ... Claimed on waivers by Tampa Bay Devil Rays (April 2, 1998). ... On Tampa Bay disabled list (May 21-August 24, 1998); included rehabilitation assignments to Gulf Coast Devil Rays (June 20-22 and August 21-24), St. Petersburg (June 23-25) and Durham (June 26-July 10). ... Claimed on waivers by Cincinnati Reds (November 24, 1999).

Year	League	W	L	Pct.	ERA	G	GS	CG	ShO	Sv.	IP	H	R	ER	BB	SO
1993—	Niagara Falls (NY-P)	1	2	.333	3.68	3	3	0	0	0	14 2/3	15	6	6	4	12
	—Fayetteville (SAL)	5	2	.714	4.09	11	11	0	0	0	61 2/3	64	30	28	20	41
1994—	Lakeland (FSL)	6	1	.857	2.84	30	9	0	0	2	92	82	37	29	29	51
1995—	Jacksonville (Sou.).............	0	1	1.000	5.63	8	0	0	0	0	8	11	5	5	5	4
	—Lakeland (FSL)	2	4	.333	1.31	43	0	0	0	25	55	48	13	8	18	51
1996—	Jacksonville (Sou.).............	9	6	.600	3.38	56	0	0	0	1	88	82	40	33	50	76
1997—	Toledo (I.L.)........................	1	4	.200	4.25	55	0	0	0	*28	53	52	27	25	24	54
	—Detroit (A.L.)	1	0	1.000	5.31	16	0	0	0	1	20 1/3	16	12	12	10	12
1998—	Tampa Bay (A.L.)■.............	0	0	...	5.87	6	0	0	0	0	7 2/3	4	5	5	3	5
	—GC Devil Rays (GCL)	0	0	...	0.00	2	2	0	0	0	4	0	0	0	1	5
	—St. Petersburg (FSL)	0	0	...	0.00	1	1	0	0	0	2	1	0	0	0	2
	—Durham (I.L.)	2	0	1.000	7.65	18	0	0	0	0	20	27	18	17	11	21
1999—	Durham (I.L.)......................	3	6	.333	2.89	59	0	0	0	26	62 1/3	67	30	20	23	67
	—Tampa Bay (A.L.)...............	1	0	1.000	2.08	8	0	0	0	0	8 2/3	12	9	2	4	7
Major League totals (3 years).......		**2**	**0**	**1.000**	**4.66**	**30**	**0**	**0**	**0**	**1**	**36 2/3**	**32**	**26**	**19**	**17**	**24**

GALARRAGA, ANDRES   1B   BRAVES

PERSONAL: Born June 18, 1961, in Caracas, Venezuela. ... 6-3/235. ... Bats right, throws right. ... Full name: Andres Jose Galarraga. ... Name pronounced GAHL-ah-RAH-guh.
HIGH SCHOOL: Enrique Felmi (Caracas, Venezuela).

G

TRANSACTIONS/CAREER NOTES: Signed as non-drafted free agent by Montreal Expos organization (January 19, 1979). ... On disabled list (July 10-August 19 and August 20-September 4, 1986; and May 26-July 4, 1991). ... Traded by Expos to St. Louis Cardinals for P Ken Hill (November 25, 1991). ... On St. Louis disabled list (April 8-May 22, 1992); included rehabilitation assignment to Louisville (May 13-22). ... Granted free agency (October 27, 1992). ... Signed by Colorado Rockies (November 16, 1992). ... On disabled list (May 10-27 and July 25-August 21, 1993). ... Granted free agency (October 25, 1993). ... Re-signed by Rockies (December 6, 1993). ... On disabled list (July 29, 1994-remainder of season). ... On suspended list (August 3-5, 1997). ... Granted free agency (October 27, 1997). ... Signed by Atlanta Braves (November 20, 1997). ... On suspended list (September 2-5, 1998). ... On Atlanta disabled list (April 3, 1999-entire season).

RECORDS: Shares major league single-inning record for most times hit by pitch—2 (July 12, 1996, seventh inning).

HONORS: Named Southern League Most Valuable Player (1984). ... Named first baseman on THE SPORTING NEWS N.L. Silver Slugger team (1988 and 1996). ... Won N.L. Gold Glove at first base (1989-90). ... Named N.L. Comeback Player of the Year by THE SPORTING NEWS (1993).

STATISTICAL NOTES: Led Southern League with 271 total bases, .508 slugging percentage and 10 intentional bases on balls received and tied for lead in being hit by pitch with nine in 1984. ... Led Southern League first basemen with 1,428 total chances and 130 double plays in 1984. ... Led N.L. in being hit by pitch with 10 in 1987 and tied for lead with 13 in 1989. ... Hit three home runs in one game (June 25, 1995). ... Collected six hits in one game (July 3, 1995). ... Led N.L. first basemen with 1,432 total chances and 129 double plays in 1995. ... Led N.L. first basemen with 1,528 putouts, 1,658 total chances and 154 double plays in 1996. ... Led N.L. first basemen with 1,590 total chances and 176 double plays in 1997. ... Had 15-game hitting streak (April 23-May 8, 1998). ... Career major league grand slams: 9.

| | | | | | | | | BATTING | | | | | | | FIELDING | | |
Year	Team (League)	Pos.	G	AB	R	H	2B	3B	HR	RBI	Avg.	BB	SO	SB	PO	A	E	Avg.
1979—W.P. Beach (FSL)........	1B	7	23	3	3	0	0	0	1	.130	2	11	0	2	1	0	1.000
—Calgary (Pio.)	1B-3B-C	42	112	14	24	3	1	4	16	.214	9	42	1	187	21	5	.977
1980—Calgary (Pio.)	1B-3B-C-OF	59	190	27	50	11	4	4	22	.263	7	55	3	287	52	21	.942
1981—Jamestown (NY-P)	C-1B-OF-3B	47	154	24	40	5	4	6	26	.260	15	44	0	154	15	0	1.000
1982—W.P. Beach (FSL)	1B-OF	105	338	39	95	20	2	14	51	.281	34	77	2	462	36	9	.982
1983—W.P. Beach (FSL)	1B-OF-3B	104	401	55	116	18	3	10	66	.289	33	68	7	861	77	13	.986
1984—Jacksonville (Sou.)....	1B	143	533	81	154	28	4	27	87	.289	59	122	2	*1302	*110	16	.989
1985—Indianapolis (A.A.)......	1B-OF	121	439	*75	118	15	8	25	87	.269	45	103	3	930	63	14	.986
—Montreal (N.L.).........	1B	24	75	9	14	1	0	2	4	.187	3	18	1	173	22	1	.995
1986—Montreal (N.L.).........	1B	105	321	39	87	13	0	10	42	.271	30	79	6	805	40	4	.995
1987—Montreal (N.L.).........	1B	147	551	72	168	40	3	13	90	.305	41	127	7	*1300	103	10	.993
1988—Montreal (N.L.).........	1B	157	609	99	*184	*42	8	29	92	.302	39	*153	13	1464	103	15	.991
1989—Montreal (N.L.).........	1B	152	572	76	147	30	1	23	85	.257	48	*158	12	1335	91	11	.992
1990—Montreal (N.L.).........	1B	155	599	65	148	29	0	20	87	.256	40	*169	10	1300	94	10	.993
1991—Montreal (N.L.).........	1B	107	375	34	82	13	2	9	33	.219	23	86	5	887	80	9	.991
1992—St. Louis (N.L.)■	1B	95	325	38	79	14	2	10	39	.243	11	69	5	777	62	8	.991
—Louisville (A.A.).........	1B	11	34	3	6	0	1	2	3	.176	0	8	1	61	7	2	.971
1993—Colorado (N.L.)■	1B	120	470	71	174	35	4	22	98	*.370	24	73	2	1018	103	11	.990
1994—Colorado (N.L.).........	1B	103	417	77	133	21	0	31	85	.319	19	93	8	953	65	8	.992
1995—Colorado (N.L.).........	1B	143	554	89	155	29	3	31	106	.280	32	*146	12	*1299	120	*13	.991
1996—Colorado (N.L.).........	1B-3B	159	626	119	190	39	3	*47	*150	.304	40	157	18	†1528	116	14	.992
1997—Colorado (N.L.).........	1B	154	600	120	191	31	3	41	*140	.318	54	141	15	*1458	117	*15	.991
1998—Atlanta (N.L.)■.........	1B-DH	153	555	103	169	27	1	44	121	.305	63	146	7	1218	81	11	.992
1999— Atlanta (N.L.)								Did not play.									
Major League totals (14 years)		1774	6629	1011	1921	364	30	332	1172	.290	467	1615	121	15515	1197	140	.992

DIVISION SERIES RECORD

| | | | | | | | | BATTING | | | | | | | FIELDING | | |
Year	Team (League)	Pos.	G	AB	R	H	2B	3B	HR	RBI	Avg.	BB	SO	SB	PO	A	E	Avg.
1995—Colorado (N.L.)	1B	4	18	1	5	1	0	0	2	.278	0	6	0	41	2	0	1.000
1998—Atlanta (N.L.).............	1B	3	12	1	3	0	0	0	0	.250	1	3	0	5	0	0	1.000
Division series totals (2 years)		7	30	2	8	1	0	0	2	.267	1	9	0	46	2	0	1.000

CHAMPIONSHIP SERIES RECORD

RECORDS: Shares single-inning record for most runs batted in—4 (October 11, 1998, seventh inning).

| | | | | | | | | BATTING | | | | | | | FIELDING | | |
Year	Team (League)	Pos.	G	AB	R	H	2B	3B	HR	RBI	Avg.	BB	SO	SB	PO	A	E	Avg.
1998—Atlanta (N.L.).............	1B	6	21	1	2	0	0	1	4	.095	6	6	0	63	11	4	.949

ALL-STAR GAME RECORD

| | | | | | | | BATTING | | | | | | | FIELDING | | |
Year	League	Pos.	AB	R	H	2B	3B	HR	RBI	Avg.	BB	SO	SB	PO	A	E	Avg.
1988—National......	1B	2	0	0	0	0	0	0	.000	0	1	0	6	0	0	1.000
1993—National......	1B	1	0	0	0	0	0	0	.000	0	0	0	0	0	0	...
1997—National......	PH-DH	1	0	0	0	0	0	0	.000	0	1	0	0	0	0	...
1998—National......	1B	2	0	0	0	0	0	0	.000	0	0	0	7	0	0	1.000
All-Star Game totals (4 years)		6	0	0	0	0	0	0	.000	0	2	0	13	0	0	1.000

G — GANT, RON · OF · PHILLIES

PERSONAL: Born March 2, 1965, in Victoria, Texas. ... 6-0/196. ... Bats right, throws right. ... Full name: Ronald Edwin Gant.

HIGH SCHOOL: Victoria (Texas).

TRANSACTIONS/CAREER NOTES: Selected by Atlanta Braves organization in fourth round of free-agent draft (June 6, 1983). ... On suspended list (July 31, 1991). ... Released by Braves (March 15, 1994). ... Signed by Cincinnati Reds (June 21, 1994). ... On disabled list (June 21, 1994-remainder of season). ... On suspended list (September 11-15, 1995). ... Granted free agency (October 30, 1995). ... Signed by St. Louis Cardinals (December 23, 1995). ... On disabled list (May 11-June 14, 1996). ... On disabled list (June 21-July 11, 1998). ... Traded by Cardinals with P Jeff Brantley and P Cliff Politte to Philadelphia Phillies for P Ricky Bottalico and P Garrett Stephenson (November 19, 1998).

HONORS: Named outfielder on THE SPORTING NEWS N.L. All-Star team (1991). ... Named outfielder on THE SPORTING NEWS N.L. Silver Slugger team (1991). ... Named N.L. Comeback Player of the Year by THE SPORTING NEWS (1991).

STATISTICAL NOTES: Led South Atlantic League second basemen with 75 double plays in 1984. ... Led Carolina League with 271 total bases in 1986. ... Led Southern League second basemen with 783 total chances and 108 double plays in 1987. ... Led N.L. second basemen with 26 errors in 1988. ... Career major league grand slams: 4.

Year	Team (League)	Pos.	G	AB	R	H	2B	3B	HR	RBI	Avg.	BB	SO	SB	PO	A	E	Avg.
1983—GC Braves (GCL).......		SS	56	193	32	45	2	2	1	14	.233	41	34	4	68	134	22	.902
1984—Anderson (SAL).........		2B	105	359	44	85	14	6	3	38	.237	29	65	13	248	263	31	.943
1985—Sumter (SAL)		2B-SS-OF	102	305	46	78	14	4	7	37	.256	33	59	19	160	200	10	.973
1986—Durham (Caro.)		2B	137	512	108	142	31	10	*26	102	.277	78	85	35	240	384	26	.960
1987—Greenville (Sou.)		2B	140	527	78	130	27	3	14	82	.247	59	91	24	*328	*434	21	*.973
—Atlanta (N.L.)............		2B	21	83	9	22	4	0	2	9	.265	1	11	4	45	59	3	.972
1988—Richmond (I.L.).........		2B	12	45	3	14	2	2	0	4	.311	2	10	1	22	23	5	.900
—Atlanta (N.L.)............		2B-3B	146	563	85	146	28	8	19	60	.259	46	118	19	316	417	†31	.959
1989—Atlanta (N.L.)............		3B-OF	75	260	26	46	8	3	9	25	.177	20	63	9	70	103	17	.911
—Sumter (SAL)		OF	12	39	13	15	4	1	1	5	.385	11	3	4	19	1	2	.909
—Richmond (I.L.).........		OF-3B	63	225	42	59	13	2	11	27	.262	29	42	6	111	14	5	.962
1990—Atlanta (N.L.)............		OF	152	575	107	174	34	3	32	84	.303	50	86	33	357	7	8	.978
1991—Atlanta (N.L.)............		OF	154	561	101	141	35	3	32	105	.251	71	104	34	338	7	6	.983
1992—Atlanta (N.L.)............		OF	153	544	74	141	22	6	17	80	.259	45	101	32	277	5	4	.986
1993—Atlanta (N.L.)............		OF	157	606	113	166	27	4	36	117	.274	67	117	26	271	5	*11	.962
1994—Cincinnati (N.L.)■......								Did not play.										
1995—Cincinnati (N.L.)		OF	119	410	79	113	19	4	29	84	.276	74	108	23	191	7	3	.985
1996—St. Louis (N.L.)■		OF	122	419	74	103	14	2	30	82	.246	73	98	13	216	4	5	.978
1997—St. Louis (N.L.)..........		OF-DH	139	502	68	115	21	4	17	62	.229	58	162	14	247	4	6	.977
1998—St. Louis (N.L.)..........		OF	121	383	60	92	17	1	26	67	.240	51	92	8	162	4	5	.971
1999—Philadelphia (N.L.)■ ..		OF-DH	138	516	107	134	27	5	17	77	.260	85	112	13	260	7	2	.993
Major League totals (12 years)			1497	5422	903	1393	256	43	266	856	.257	641	1172	228	2750	629	101	.971

DIVISION SERIES RECORD

Year	Team (League)	Pos.	G	AB	R	H	2B	3B	HR	RBI	Avg.	BB	SO	SB	PO	A	E	Avg.
1995—Cincinnati (N.L.)		OF	3	13	3	3	0	0	1	2	.231	0	3	0	8	1	0	1.000
1996—St. Louis (N.L.)		OF	3	10	3	4	1	0	1	4	.400	2	0	2	5	0	0	1.000
Division series totals (2 years)			6	23	6	7	1	0	2	6	.304	2	3	2	13	1	0	1.000

CHAMPIONSHIP SERIES RECORD

RECORDS: Shares single-game record for most grand slams—1 (October 7, 1992). ... Shares single-inning records for most runs batted in— 4 (October 7, 1992, fifth inning); and most stolen bases—2 (October 10, 1991, third inning). ... Holds N.L. career record for most strikeouts— 26. ... Holds N.L. single-series record for most stolen bases—7 (1991). ... Shares N.L. single-game record for most stolen bases—3 (October 10, 1991).

Year	Team (League)	Pos.	G	AB	R	H	2B	3B	HR	RBI	Avg.	BB	SO	SB	PO	A	E	Avg.
1991—Atlanta (N.L.)..............		OF	7	27	4	7	1	0	1	3	.259	2	4	7	15	2	0	1.000
1992—Atlanta (N.L.)..............		OF	7	22	5	4	0	0	2	6	.182	4	4	1	16	0	0	1.000
1993—Atlanta (N.L.)..............		OF	6	27	4	5	3	0	0	3	.185	2	9	0	10	1	1	.917
1995—Cincinnati (N.L.)..........		OF	4	16	1	3	0	0	0	1	.188	0	3	0	9	0	0	1.000
1996—St. Louis (N.L.)..........		OF	7	25	3	6	1	0	2	4	.240	2	6	0	12	0	0	1.000
Championship series totals (5 years)			31	117	17	25	5	0	5	17	.214	10	26	8	62	3	1	.985

WORLD SERIES RECORD

Year	Team (League)	Pos.	G	AB	R	H	2B	3B	HR	RBI	Avg.	BB	SO	SB	PO	A	E	Avg.
1991—Atlanta (N.L.)..............		OF	7	30	3	8	0	1	0	4	.267	2	3	1	19	0	0	1.000
1992—Atlanta (N.L.).............		OF-PR-PH	4	8	2	1	1	0	0	0	.125	1	2	2	3	1	0	1.000
World Series totals (2 years)			11	38	5	9	1	1	0	4	.237	3	5	3	22	1	0	1.000

ALL-STAR GAME RECORD

Year	League	Pos.	AB	R	H	2B	3B	HR	RBI	Avg.	BB	SO	SB	PO	A	E	Avg.
1992—National		PH-OF	2	0	0	0	0	0	0	.000	0	0	0	1	0	0	1.000
1995—National		DH	2	0	0	0	0	0	0	.000	0	1	0	...	...	...	...
All-Star Game totals (2 years)			4	0	0	0	0	0	0	.000	0	1	0	1	0	0	1.000

GARCES, RICHARD   P   RED SOX

PERSONAL: Born May 18, 1971, in Maracay, Venezuela. ... 6-0/215. ... Throws right, bats right. ... Full name: Richard Aron Garces Jr. ... Name pronounced gar-SESS.

HIGH SCHOOL: Jose Felix Rivas (Maracay, Venezuela).

COLLEGE: Venezuela Universidad.

TRANSACTIONS/CAREER NOTES: Signed as non-drafted free agent by Minnesota Twins organization (December 29, 1987). ... On Portland suspended list (May 17-September 16, 1991). ... On Portland disabled list (July 28, 1991-remainder of season). ... Granted free agency (October 15, 1994). ... Signed by Chicago Cubs organization (January 30, 1995). ... Claimed on waivers by Florida Marlins (August 9, 1995). ... Granted free agency (October 16, 1995). ... Signed by Boston Red Sox (April 25, 1996). ... On Boston disabled list (July 25-August 20 and August 24, 1996-remainder of season); included rehabilitation assignment to Pawtucket (August 9-20). ... On disabled list (March 27-April 27 and June 2-23, 1997); included rehabilitation assignments to Pawtucket (April 18-21, April 25-27 and June 12-23). ... On Boston disabled list (April 11-May 7, July 1-17 and August 3, 1998-remainder of season); included rehabilitation assignments to Pawtucket (April 21-May 7 and August 30-September 3) and Gulf Coast Red Sox (August 12-29). ... Released by Red Sox (November 23, 1998). ... Re-signed by Red Sox organization (January 26, 1999). ... On Pawtucket disabled list (April 8-22 and May 15-31, 1999).

Year	League	W	L	Pct.	ERA	G	GS	CG	ShO	Sv.	IP	H	R	ER	BB	SO
1988—Elizabethton (Appl.)...........		5	4	.556	2.29	17	3	1	0	5	59	51	22	15	27	69
1989—Kenosha (Midw.)...............		9	10	.474	3.41	24	24	4	1	0	142²/₃	117	70	54	62	84
1990—Visalia (Calif.)................		2	2	.500	1.81	47	0	0	0	*28	54²/₃	33	14	11	16	75
—Orlando (Sou.).................		2	1	.667	2.08	15	0	0	0	8	17¹/₃	17	4	4	14	22
—Minnesota (A.L.)		0	0	...	1.59	5	0	0	0	2	5²/₃	4	2	1	4	1

Year	League	W	L	Pct.	ERA	G	GS	CG	ShO	Sv.	IP	H	R	ER	BB	SO
1991—	Portland (PCL)	0	1	.000	4.85	10	0	0	0	3	13	10	7	7	8	13
—	Orlando (Sou.)	2	1	.667	3.31	10	0	0	0	0	16 1/3	12	6	6	14	17
1992—	Orlando (Sou.)	3	3	.500	4.54	58	0	0	0	13	73 1/3	76	46	37	39	72
1993—	Portland (PCL)	1	3	.250	8.33	35	7	0	0	0	54	70	55	50	64	48
—	Minnesota (A.L.)	0	0	...	0.00	3	0	0	0	0	4	4	2	0	2	3
1994—	Nashville (Sou.)................	4	5	.444	3.72	40	1	0	0	3	77 1/3	70	40	32	31	76
1995—	Iowa (A.A.)■	0	2	.000	2.86	23	0	0	0	7	28 1/3	25	10	9	8	36
—	Chicago (N.L.)	0	0	...	3.27	7	0	0	0	0	11	11	6	4	3	6
—	Florida (N.L.)■	0	2	.000	5.40	11	0	0	0	0	13 1/3	14	9	8	8	16
1996—	Pawtucket (I.L.)■	4	0	1.000	2.30	10	0	0	0	0	15 2/3	10	4	4	5	13
—	Boston (A.L.)....................	3	2	.600	4.91	37	0	0	0	0	44	42	26	24	33	55
1997—	Boston (A.L.)....................	0	1	.000	4.61	12	0	0	0	0	13 2/3	14	9	7	9	12
—	Pawtucket (I.L.).................	2	1	.667	1.45	26	0	0	0	5	31	24	5	5	13	42
1998—	Boston (A.L.)....................	1	1	.500	3.33	30	0	0	0	1	46	36	19	17	27	34
—	Pawtucket (I.L.).................	0	1	.000	5.40	7	0	0	0	3	8 1/3	6	5	5	2	10
—	GC Red Sox (GCL)	0	0	...	3.27	7	7	0	0	0	11	11	4	4	0	8
1999—	Pawtucket (I.L.).................	1	0	1.000	3.25	21	0	0	0	7	27 2/3	24	11	10	10	24
—	Boston (A.L.)....................	5	1	.833	1.55	30	0	0	0	2	40 2/3	25	9	7	18	33
A.L. totals (6 years)		9	5	.643	3.27	117	0	0	0	5	154	125	67	56	93	138
N.L. totals (1 year)		0	2	.000	4.44	18	0	0	0	0	24 1/3	25	15	12	11	22
Major League totals (7 years)......		9	7	.563	3.43	135	0	0	0	5	178 1/3	150	82	68	104	160

DIVISION SERIES RECORD

Year	League	W	L	Pct.	ERA	G	GS	CG	ShO	Sv.	IP	H	R	ER	BB	SO
1999—	Boston (A.L.)....................	1	0	1.000	3.86	2	0	0	0	0	2 1/3	2	1	1	3	2

CHAMPIONSHIP SERIES RECORD

Year	League	W	L	Pct.	ERA	G	GS	CG	ShO	Sv.	IP	H	R	ER	BB	SO
1999—	Boston (A.L.)....................	0	0	...	12.00	2	0	0	0	0	3	3	5	4	1	2

GARCIA, AMAURY · 2B · MARLINS

PERSONAL: Born May 20, 1975, in Santo Domingo, Dominican Republic. ... 5-10/160. ... Bats right, throws right. ... Full name: Amaury Miguel Garcia.

HIGH SCHOOL: Colegio Discipulos de Jesus (Santo Domingo, Dominican Republic).

TRANSACTIONS/CAREER NOTES: Signed as non-drafted free agent by Florida Marlins organization (December 4, 1992).

STATISTICAL NOTES: Led Eastern League second basemen with 669 total chances in 1998. ... Led Pacific Coast league second basemen with 90 double plays in 1999.

							BATTING						FIELDING			
Year	Team (League)	Pos.	G	AB	R	H	2B	3B	HR	RBI	Avg.	BB	SO	SB	PO	A	E	Avg.
1993—	Dom. Marlins (DSL) ...	IF	64	237	35	67	5	3	4	29	.283	31	41	9	129	112	19	.927
1994—	GC Marlins (GCL)	3B-2B-OF	58	208	46	65	9	3	0	25	.313	33	49	10	44	113	17	.902
1995—	Kane County (Midw.)..	3B-2B	26	58	19	14	4	1	1	5	.241	18	12	5	11	31	13	.764
—	Elmira (NY-P)	2B	62	231	40	63	7	3	0	17	.273	34	50	*41	128	178	18	.944
1996—	Kane County (Midw.)..	2B	106	395	65	104	19	7	6	36	.263	62	84	37	219	286	19	.964
1997—	Brev. County (FSL).....	2B	124	479	77	138	30	2	7	44	.288	49	97	45	246	329	16	.973
1998—	Portland (East.)..........	2B	137	544	79	147	19	6	13	62	.270	45	126	23	*287	355	*27	.960
1999—	Calgary (PCL)..........	2B	119	479	94	152	37	•9	17	53	.317	44	79	17	227	308	16	.971
—	Florida (N.L.).............	2B	10	24	6	6	0	1	2	2	.250	3	11	0	15	26	3	.932
Major League totals (1 year)			10	24	6	6	0	1	2	2	.250	3	11	0	15	26	3	.932

GARCIA, APOSTOL · P · DODGERS

PERSONAL: Born August 3, 1976, in Las Matas de Faran, Dominican Republic. ... 6-0/155. ... Throws right, bats right.

HIGH SCHOOL: Liceo Mercedes Maria Mateo (Las Matas de Faran, Dominican Republic).

TRANSACTIONS/CAREER NOTES: Signed as non-drafted free agent by Detroit Tigers organization (December 6, 1992). ... Traded by Tigers with P Robinson Checo and P Rick Roberts to Los Angeles Dodgers for P Mel Rojas and P Dave Mlicki (April 16, 1999).

MISCELLANEOUS: Played infield (1993-96).

Year	Team (League)	W	L	Pct.	ERA	G	GS	CG	ShO	Sv.	IP	H	R	ER	BB	SO
1997—	West Michigan (Midw.)......	7	2	.778	3.02	33	5	0	0	1	65 2/3	48	26	22	31	52
1998—	Lakeland (FSL)	5	8	.385	5.43	34	16	1	0	1	119 1/3	155	89	72	52	56
1999—	Jacksonville (Sou.)............	0	0	...	0.00	3	0	0	0	0	4 1/3	0	0	0	1	0
—	San Antonio (Texas)■	7	5	.583	3.36	32	11	0	0	1	101 2/3	110	57	38	45	50

RECORD AS POSITION PLAYER

							BATTING						FIELDING		
Year	Team (League)	Pos.	G	AB	R	H	2B	3B	HR	RBI	Avg.	BB	SO	SB	PO	A	E	Avg.
1993—	Dom. Tigers (DSL)	OF-IF	65	150	24	29	2	0	0	6	.193	15	32	14	107	26	13	.911
1994—	Bristol (Appal.)........	SS-2B	47	130	20	20	3	0	0	8	.154	18	35	18	68	107	9	.951
—	Lakeland (Fla. St.)......	SS	6	15	0	4	0	0	0	0	.267	0	3	1	3	10	2	.867
1995—	Jamestown (NYP)	SS-2B	60	200	25	47	8	3	0	21	.235	10	36	10	66	189	28	.901
1996—	Fayetteville (SAL)	SS-2B	74	242	33	47	7	1	2	17	.194	21	77	12	105	181	30	.905

GARCIA, CARLOS · 2B

PERSONAL: Born October 15, 1967, in Tachira, Venezuela. ... 6-1/197. ... Bats right, throws right. ... Full name: Carlos Jesus Garcia.

HIGH SCHOOL: Bolivar (Venezuela).

G

TRANSACTIONS/CAREER NOTES: Signed as non-drafted free agent by Pittsburgh Pirates organization (January 9, 1987). ... On disabled list (July 28-August 14, 1995). ... On Pittsburgh disabled list (May 2-17 and July 22-August 27, 1996); included rehabilitation assignment to Calgary (August 23-25). ... Traded by Pirates with OF Orlando Merced and P Dan Plesac to Toronto Blue Jays for P Jose Silva, P Jose Pett, IF Brandon Cromer and three players to be named later (November 14, 1996); Pirates acquired P Mike Halperin, IF Abraham Nunez and C/OF Craig Wilson to complete deal (December 11, 1996). ... Granted free agency (December 21, 1997). ... Signed by Cleveland Indians (January 6, 1998). ... Released by Indians (March 25, 1998). ... Signed by Anaheim Angels (March 30, 1998). ... On Anaheim disabled list (May 13-June 13, 1998); included rehabilitation assignment to Vancouver (May 17-June 5). ... Granted free agency (September 29, 1998). ... Signed by San Diego Padres organization (December 27, 1998). ... On Las Vegas disabled list (May 8-28 and August 8-20, 1999). ... Granted free agency (October 4, 1999).

STATISTICAL NOTES: Led N.L. second basemen with 80 double plays in 1994. ... Had 21-game hitting streak (June 5-27, 1995).

										BATTING				FIELDING			
Year Team (League)	Pos.	G	AB	R	H	2B	3B	HR	RBI	Avg.	BB	SO	SB	PO	A	E	Avg.
1987—Macon (SAL)	SS	110	373	44	95	14	3	3	38	.255	23	80	20	161	262	42	.910
1988—Augusta (SAL)	SS	73	269	32	78	13	2	1	45	.290	22	46	11	138	207	29	.922
—Salem (Caro.)	SS	62	236	21	65	9	3	1	28	.275	10	32	8	131	151	24	.922
1989—Salem (Caro.)	SS	81	304	45	86	12	4	7	49	.283	18	51	19	137	262	32	.926
—Harrisburg (East.)	SS	54	188	28	53	5	5	3	25	.282	8	36	6	84	131	7	.968
1990—Harrisburg (East.)	SS	65	242	36	67	11	2	5	25	.277	16	36	12	101	209	14	.957
—Buffalo (A.A.)	SS	63	197	23	52	10	0	5	18	.264	16	41	7	106	170	19	.936
—Pittsburgh (N.L.)	SS	4	4	1	2	0	0	0	0	.500	0	2	0	0	4	0	1.000
1991—Buffalo (A.A.)	SS	127	463	62	123	21	6	7	60	.266	33	78	30	*212	332	*31	.946
—Pittsburgh (N.L.)	SS-3B-2B	12	24	2	6	0	2	0	1	.250	1	8	0	11	18	1	.967
1992—Buffalo (A.A.)	SS-2B	113	426	73	129	28	9	13	70	.303	24	64	21	192	314	28	.948
—Pittsburgh (N.L.)	2B-SS	22	39	4	8	1	0	0	4	.205	0	9	0	25	35	2	.968
1993—Pittsburgh (N.L.)	2B-SS	141	546	77	147	25	5	12	47	.269	31	67	18	299	347	11	.983
1994—Pittsburgh (N.L.)	2B	98	412	49	114	15	2	6	28	.277	16	67	18	•225	315	12	.978
1995—Pittsburgh (N.L.)	2B-SS	104	367	41	108	24	2	6	50	.294	25	55	8	234	298	15	.973
1996—Pittsburgh (N.L.)	2B-SS-3B	101	390	66	111	18	4	6	44	.285	23	58	16	160	284	11	.976
—Calgary (PCL)	SS	2	6	0	2	0	1	0	0	.333	0	0	0	3	5	0	1.000
1997—Toronto (A.L.)■	2B-SS-3B	103	350	29	77	18	2	3	23	.220	15	60	11	171	256	10	.977
1998—Anaheim (A.L.)■	2B-SS-DH	19	35	4	5	1	0	0	0	.143	3	11	2	24	33	1	.983
—Vancouver (PCL)	SS-2B-DH	44	161	18	41	6	0	3	15	.255	8	22	2	78	103	10	.948
1999—San Diego (N.L.)■	3B-1B	6	11	1	2	0	0	0	0	.182	1	3	0	6	3	2	.818
—Las Vegas (PCL)	1-3-2-DH-S	78	274	36	77	19	0	3	28	.281	17	61	5	290	88	8	.979
American League totals (2 years)		122	385	33	82	19	2	3	23	.213	18	71	13	195	289	11	.978
National League totals (8 years)		488	1793	241	498	83	15	30	174	.278	97	269	60	960	1304	54	.977
Major League totals (10 years)		610	2178	274	580	102	17	33	197	.266	115	340	73	1155	1593	65	.977

CHAMPIONSHIP SERIES RECORD

										BATTING				FIELDING			
Year Team (League)	Pos.	G	AB	R	H	2B	3B	HR	RBI	Avg.	BB	SO	SB	PO	A	E	Avg.
1992—Pittsburgh (N.L.)	2B	1	1	0	0	0	0	0	0	.000	0	0	0	0	0	0	...

ALL-STAR GAME RECORD

								BATTING				FIELDING			
Year League	Pos.	AB	R	H	2B	3B	HR	RBI	Avg.	BB	SO	SB	PO	A	E	Avg.
1994—National	2B	2	0	1	0	0	0	0	.500	0	0	0	0	1	0	1.000

GARCIA, FREDDY   IF   BRAVES

PERSONAL: Born August 1, 1972, in La Romana, Dominican Republic. ... 6-2/224. ... Bats right, throws right. ... Full name: Freddy Adrian Garcia.

TRANSACTIONS/CAREER NOTES: Signed as non-drafted free agent by Toronto Blue Jays organization (May 16, 1991). ... Selected by Pittsburgh Pirates from Blue Jays organization in Rule 5 major league draft (December 5, 1994). ... On Nashville disabled list (August 19-31, 1999). ... Traded by Pirates to Atlanta Braves for P Greg Dukeman (September 8, 1999).

STATISTICAL NOTES: Led Pioneer League third basemen with 267 total chances and tied for lead in double plays with 18 in 1993. ... Led New York-Pennsylvania League third basemen with 257 total chances and 18 double plays in 1994. ... Tied for Carolina League lead with 12 sacrifice flies in 1996. ... Led Carolina League third basemen with 29 double plays in 1996.

										BATTING				FIELDING			
Year Team (League)	Pos.	G	AB	R	H	2B	3B	HR	RBI	Avg.	BB	SO	SB	PO	A	E	Avg.
1991—Villa Mella (DSL)	IF	53	154	28	39	4	1	1	19	.253	39	36	8	...	...	...	...
1992—Blue Jays East (DSL)	IF	70	249	56	73	13	2	12	62	.293	61	52	5	146	32	5	.973
1993—Medicine Hat (Pio.)	3B	72	264	47	63	8	2	11	42	.239	31	71	4	*63	*175	•29	.891
1994—St. Catharines (NY-P)	3B	73	260	46	74	10	2	*13	40	.285	33	57	1	63	*169	25	.903
1995—Pittsburgh (N.L.)■	OF-3B	42	57	5	8	1	1	0	1	.140	8	17	0	19	15	1	.971
1996—Lynchburg (Caro.)	3B-DH	129	474	79	145	*39	3	•21	86	.306	44	86	4	96	285	*35	.916
1997—Calgary (PCL)	3B-DH	35	121	21	29	6	0	5	17	.240	9	20	0	18	53	12	.855
—Pittsburgh (N.L.)	3B-1B	20	40	4	6	1	0	3	5	.150	2	17	0	21	9	3	.909
—Carolina (Sou.)	3B-1B-DH	73	282	47	82	17	4	19	57	.291	18	56	0	93	155	22	.919
1998—Pittsburgh (N.L.)	3B-1B	56	172	27	44	11	1	9	26	.256	18	45	0	53	104	8	.952
—Nashville (PCL)	3B-1B-DH-OF	88	326	52	88	24	4	22	55	.270	25	89	0	185	153	19	.947
1999—Pittsburgh (N.L.)	OF-3B-DH-1B	55	130	16	30	5	0	6	23	.231	4	41	0	44	14	2	.967
—Nashville (PCL)	3B-DH	4	9	0	0	0	0	0	0	.000	1	3	0	1	2	0	1.000
—Atlanta (N.L.)■	OF	2	2	1	1	0	0	1	1	.500	1	1	0	0	0	0	...
Major League totals (4 years)		175	401	53	89	18	2	19	56	.222	33	121	0	137	142	14	.952

GARCIA, FREDDY   P   MARINERS

PERSONAL: Born October 6, 1976, in Caracas, Venezuela. ... 6-4/235. ... Throws right, bats right.

TRANSACTIONS/CAREER NOTES: Signed as non-drafted free agent by Houston Astros organization (October 21, 1993). ... Traded by Astros with SS Carlos Guillen and a player to be named later to Seattle Mariners for P Randy Johnson (July 31, 1998); Mariners acquired P John Halama to complete deal (October 1, 1998).

G

STATISTICAL NOTES: Tied for A.L. lead with three balks in 1999.

MISCELLANEOUS: Struck out in only appearance as pinch hitter (1999).

Year League	W	L	Pct.	ERA	G	GS	CG	ShO	Sv.	IP	H	R	ER	BB	SO
1994— Dom. Astros (DSL)............	4	6	.400	5.29	16	15	0	0	0	85	80	61	50	38	68
1995— Gulf Coast Astros (GCL).....	6	3	.667	4.47	11	11	0	0	0	58 1/3	60	32	29	14	58
1996— Quad City (Midw.)	5	4	.556	3.12	13	13	0	0	0	60 2/3	57	27	21	27	50
1997— Kissimmee (FSL)................	10	8	.556	2.56	27	27	5	2	0	179	165	63	51	49	131
1998— Jackson (Texas)	6	7	.462	3.24	19	19	2	0	0	119 1/3	94	48	43	58	115
— New Orleans (PCL)............	1	0	1.000	3.14	2	2	0	0	0	14 1/3	14	5	5	1	13
— Tacoma (PCL)■	3	1	.750	3.86	5	5	0	0	0	32 2/3	30	14	14	13	30
1999— Seattle (A.L.)	17	8	.680	4.07	33	33	2	1	0	201 1/3	205	96	91	90	170
Major League totals (1 year)........	**17**	**8**	**.680**	**4.07**	**33**	**33**	**2**	**1**	**0**	**201 1/3**	**205**	**96**	**91**	**90**	**170**

GARCIA, GUILLERMO C/IF

PERSONAL: Born April 4, 1972, in Santiago, Dominican Republic. ... 6-3/215. ... Bats right, throws right. ... Full name: Guillermo Antonio Morel Garcia.

HIGH SCHOOL: Liceo Republica (Santiago, Dominican Republic).

TRANSACTIONS/CAREER NOTES: Signed as non-drafted free agent by New York Mets organization (November 20, 1989). ... Released by Mets (October 20, 1994). ... Signed by Cincinnati Reds organization (November 7, 1994). ... Traded by Reds to Florida Marlins for P Manuel Barrios (December 2, 1998). ... Contract sold by Marlins to Reds organization (April 20, 1999). ... On Indianapolis disabled list (August 19, 1999-remainder of season). ... Released by Reds (December 13, 1999).

STATISTICAL NOTES: Led South Atlantic League catchers with 36 passed balls in 1993. ... Led International League catchers with .990 fielding percentage in 1998.

						BATTING								FIELDING		
Year Team (League)	Pos.	G	AB	R	H	2B	3B	HR	RBI	Avg.	BB	SO	SB	PO	A	E	Avg.
1990— GC Mets (GCL)	2B-3B	42	136	9	25	1	2	0	6	.184	7	34	1	87	91	9	.952
1991— Kingsport (Appal.)........	SS-P	14	33	9	8	1	1	0	2	.242	4	4	0	4	8	4	.750
— Pittsfield (NY-P)	2B-SS	45	157	23	43	13	2	0	24	.274	15	38	4	120	120	5	.980
1992— Pittsfield (NY-P) 2B-C-1B-SS		73	272	36	54	11	1	2	26	.199	20	52	3	323	125	14	.970
1993— Capital City (SAL)	C-3B-2B	119	429	64	124	28	2	3	72	.289	49	60	10	650	115	19	.976
1994— St. Lucie (FSL) C-3B-1B-2B		55	203	22	48	9	1	1	23	.236	13	24	0	244	53	3	.990
1995— Win.-Salem (Car.)■....C-1B-3B-SS		78	245	26	58	10	2	3	29	.237	28	32	2	402	67	8	.983
1996— Indianapolis (A.A.).......	C-2B-1B	16	47	4	12	2	0	0	0	.255	2	6	0	66	19	5	.944
— Chattanooga (Sou.)...C-2B-1B-3B		60	203	25	64	12	0	6	36	.315	12	32	3	280	65	6	.983
1997— Chattanooga (Sou.)....C-2B-1B-SS		20	74	11	21	1	1	4	19	.284	8	13	0	95	19	1	.991
— Indianapolis (A.A.)........C-2B-3B-1B		55	151	16	36	2	0	10	20	.238	9	46	0	216	31	1	.996
1998— Indianapolis (I.L.).......	C-1B-3B	93	334	48	85	20	0	19	60	.254	22	81	0	581	70	6	†.991
— Cincinnati (N.L.).........	C	12	36	3	7	2	0	2	4	.194	2	13	0	74	6	1	.988
1999— Florida (N.L.)■...........	C	4	4	0	1	0	0	0	0	.250	0	2	0	5	0	0	1.000
— Chatt. (Sou.)■...........C-DH-1B-3B		10	42	11	13	3	3	1	7	.310	2	6	0	35	9	0	1.000
— Indianapolis (I.L.).......	C-1B-3B	65	233	30	67	9	0	10	28	.288	22	44	1	448	31	6	.988
Major League totals (2 years)		**16**	**40**	**3**	**8**	**2**	**0**	**2**	**4**	**.200**	**2**	**15**	**0**	**79**	**6**	**1**	**.988**

RECORD AS PITCHER

Year League	W	L	Pct.	ERA	G	GS	CG	ShO	Sv.	IP	H	R	ER	BB	SO
1991— Kingsport (Appal.)...............	0	0	...	0.00	2	0	0	0	0	2	1	0	0	0	3

GARCIA, JESSE SS/2B ORIOLES

PERSONAL: Born September 24, 1973, in Corpus Christi, Texas. ... 5-10/171. ... Bats right, throws right. ... Full name: Jesus Jesse Garcia Jr.

HIGH SCHOOL: Robstown (Texas).

JUNIOR COLLEGE: Lee College (Texas).

TRANSACTIONS/CAREER NOTES: Selected by Baltimore Orioles organization in 26th round of free-agent draft (June 3, 1993). ... On disabled list (June 19, 1994-remainder of season). ... Granted free agency (December 21, 1998). ... Re-signed by Orioles organization (December 21, 1998). ... On Rochester disabled list (May 25-July 18, 1999).

STATISTICAL NOTES: Led California League with 20 sacrifice hits in 1996. ... Led California League second basemen with 263 putouts, 409 assists, .968 fielding percentage, 694 total chances and 81 double plays in 1996; tied for lead in errors with 22. ... Led Eastern League with 24 sacrifice hits in 1997. ... Led Eastern League second basemen with .985 fielding percentage in 1997.

						BATTING								FIELDING		
Year Team (League)	Pos.	G	AB	R	H	2B	3B	HR	RBI	Avg.	BB	SO	SB	PO	A	E	Avg.
1993— GC Orioles (GCL)........	2B-SS-3B	48	156	20	37	4	0	0	16	.237	21	32	14	61	136	14	.934
1994— Bluefield (Appl.)									Did not play.								
1995— Frederick (Caro.)	2B	124	365	52	82	11	3	3	27	.225	49	75	5	283	275	28	.952
1996— High Desert (Calif.)......	2B-SS	137	459	94	122	21	5	10	66	.266	57	81	25	†263	†409	‡22	†.968
1997— Bowie (East.)..............	2B-SS-3B	*141	437	52	103	18	1	5	42	.236	38	71	7	290	377	13	†.981
1998— Bowie (East.)..............	2B-SS-OF	86	258	46	73	13	1	2	20	.283	34	37	12	133	196	9	.973
— Rochester (I.L.)	2B	44	160	20	47	6	4	0	18	.294	7	22	7	102	145	8	.969
1999— Baltimore (A.L.).........SS-2B-3B-DH		17	29	6	6	0	0	2	2	.207	2	3	0	16	22	0	1.000
— Rochester (I.L.)	SS-2B	62	220	25	56	10	2	2	23	.255	11	21	9	95	156	15	.944
Major League totals (1 year)		**17**	**29**	**6**	**6**	**0**	**0**	**2**	**2**	**.207**	**2**	**3**	**0**	**16**	**22**	**0**	**1.000**

GARCIA, JOSE P BREWERS

PERSONAL: Born April 29, 1978, in San Gabriel, Calif. ... 6-3/196. ... Throws right, bats right. ... Full name: Jose Antonio Garcia.

HIGH SCHOOL: Baldwin Park (Calif.).

TRANSACTIONS/CAREER NOTES: Selected by Milwaukee Brewers organization in second round of free-agent draft (June 4, 1996). ... On disabled list (April 8, 1999-entire season).

G

Year	League	W	L	Pct.	ERA	G	GS	CG	ShO	Sv.	IP	H	R	ER	BB	SO
1996—	Helena (Pio.)	0	0	...	16.20	2	0	0	0	0	1 $2/3$	1	3	3	3	2
1997—	Beloit (Midw.)	6	11	.353	4.00	27	26	2	0	0	155 $1/3$	145	89	69	70	126
1998—	Stockton (Calif.)	11	12	.478	3.67	28	•28	1	0	0	169 $1/3$	147	89	69	91	167
1999—	Huntsville (Sou.)								Did not play.							

GARCIA, KARIM   OF   TIGERS

PERSONAL: Born October 29, 1975, in Ciudad Obregon, Mexico. ... 6-0/172. ... Bats left, throws left. ... Full name: Gustavo Garcia.
HIGH SCHOOL: Preparatoria Abierta (Ciudad Obregon, Mexico).
TRANSACTIONS/CAREER NOTES: Signed as non-drafted free agent by Los Angeles Dodgers organization (July 16, 1992). ... On Los Angeles disabled list (September 1, 1997-remainder of season). ... Selected by Arizona Diamondbacks in first round (ninth pick overall) of expansion draft (November 18, 1997). ... Traded by Diamondbacks to Detroit Tigers for OF Luis Gonzalez (December 28, 1998).
HONORS: Named Minor League Player of the Year by THE SPORTING NEWS (1995).
STATISTICAL NOTES: Career major league grand slams: 1.

Year	Team (League)	Pos.	G	AB	R	H	2B	3B	HR	RBI	Avg.	BB	SO	SB	PO	A	E	Avg.
1993—	Bakersfield (Calif.)	OF	123	460	61	111	20	9	19	54	.241	37	109	5	193	12	*13	.940
1994—	Vero Beach (FSL)	OF	121	452	72	120	28	10	*21	84	.265	37	229	8	229	12	5	.980
1995—	Albuquerque (PCL)	OF-DH	124	474	88	151	26	10	20	•91	.319	38	102	12	185	7	*14	.932
	—Los Angeles (N.L.)	OF	13	20	1	4	0	0	0	0	.200	0	4	0	5	2	0	1.000
1996—	Albuquerque (PCL)	OF-DH	84	327	54	97	17	10	13	58	.297	29	67	6	148	4	13	.921
	—San Antonio (Texas)	OF	35	129	21	32	6	1	5	22	.248	9	38	1	60	6	2	.971
	—Los Angeles (N.L.)	OF	1	1	0	0	0	0	0	0	.000	0	1	0	0	0	0	...
1997—	Albuquerque (PCL)	OF-DH	71	262	53	80	17	6	20	66	.305	23	70	11	97	3	5	.952
	—Los Angeles (N.L.)	OF	15	39	5	5	0	0	1	8	.128	6	14	0	13	0	0	1.000
1998—	Arizona (N.L.)■	OF	113	333	39	74	10	8	9	43	.222	18	78	5	191	6	5	.975
	—Tucson (PCL)	OF	27	106	21	33	4	2	10	27	.311	15	24	5	67	1	3	.958
1999—	Detroit (A.L.)■	OF-DH	96	288	38	69	10	3	14	32	.240	20	67	2	152	7	7	.958
American League totals (1 year)			96	288	38	69	10	3	14	32	.240	20	67	2	152	7	7	.958
National League totals (4 years)			142	393	45	83	10	8	10	51	.211	24	97	5	209	8	5	.977
Major League totals (5 years)			238	681	83	152	20	11	24	83	.223	44	164	7	361	15	12	.969

GARCIA, LUIS   IF

PERSONAL: Born May 20, 1975, in San Francisco de Macoris, Dominican Republic. ... 6-0/175. ... Bats right, throws right. ... Full name: Luis Rafael Garcia.
HIGH SCHOOL: Liceo Salome Urenna (Dominican Republic).
TRANSACTIONS/CAREER NOTES: Signed as non-drafted free agent by Detroit Tigers organization (February 3, 1993). ... Released by Tigers (November 18, 1999).
STATISTICAL NOTES: Led Southern League shortstops with 676 total chances in 1996.

Year	Team (League)	Pos.	G	AB	R	H	2B	3B	HR	RBI	Avg.	BB	SO	SB	PO	A	E	Avg.
1993—	Bristol (Appl.)	2B-SS-3B	24	57	7	12	1	0	1	7	.211	3	11	3	33	55	5	.946
1994—	Jamestown (NY-P)	SS	67	239	21	47	8	2	1	19	.197	8	48	6	115	205	*27	.922
1995—	Lakeland (FSL)	SS-2B	102	361	39	101	10	4	2	35	.280	8	42	9	167	302	34	.932
	—Jacksonville (Sou.)	SS-3B	17	47	6	13	0	0	0	5	.277	1	8	2	19	46	5	.929
1996—	Jacksonville (Sou.)	SS	131	522	68	128	22	4	9	46	.245	12	90	15	*205	*435	*36	*.947
1997—	Jacksonville (Sou.)	SS	126	456	55	122	19	1	5	48	.268	10	59	3	176	370	30	.948
1998—	Toledo (I.L.)	SS-3B-2B	114	407	37	105	19	4	3	31	.258	8	59	3	158	292	23	.951
1999—	Detroit (A.L.)	SS-2B	8	9	0	1	1	0	0	0	.111	0	2	0	3	2	0	1.000
	—Toledo (I.L.)	SS-3B	89	308	30	32	19	1	3	34	.266	5	41	3	138	256	18	.962
Major League totals (1 year)			8	9	0	1	1	0	0	0	.111	0	2	0	3	2	0	1.000

GARCIA, MIKE   P   PIRATES

PERSONAL: Born May 11, 1968, in Riverside, Calif. ... 6-2/220. ... Throws right, bats right. ... Full name: Michael R. Garcia.
HIGH SCHOOL: Riverside North (Riverside, Calif.).
JUNIOR COLLEGE: Riverside (Calif.) Community College.
TRANSACTIONS/CAREER NOTES: Selected by Detroit Tigers organization in 55th round of free-agent draft (June 5, 1989). ... Released by Tigers (May 5, 1993). ... Signed by Rochester, Northern League (1993). ... Signed by Colorado Rockies organization (October 8, 1993). ... Released by Rockies (March 26, 1994). ... Signed by Tabasco, Mexican League (1994). ... Played in Taiwan (1996-98). ... Signed by Pittsburgh Pirates organization (December 23, 1998).

Year	League	W	L	Pct.	ERA	G	GS	CG	ShO	Sv.	IP	H	R	ER	BB	SO
1989—	Bristol (Appl.)	0	3	.000	4.60	8	0	0	0	0	15 $2/3$	17	9	8	4	13
	—Niagara Falls (NY-P)	5	1	.833	1.56	7	6	1	0	0	40 $1/3$	27	12	7	7	39
1990—	Fayetteville (SAL)	12	8	.600	2.55	28	28	6	2	0	*180 $1/3$	152	69	51	41	113
1991—	Lakeland (FSL)	6	8	.429	3.13	25	24	0	0	0	144	130	63	50	41	109
1992—	London (East.)	8	8	.500	3.89	27	20	1	1	0	136 $2/3$	149	69	59	35	92
1993—	London (East.)	8	4	.667	3.89	42	7	0	0	3	111	103	53	48	37	110
	—Rochester (North.)■	9	2	.818	2.94	16	16	1	0	0	95	89	36	31	27	*100
1994—	Tabasco (Mex.)■	3	5	.375	2.14	36	4	1	1	15	71 $1/3$	57	21	17	25	71
1995—	Tabasco (Mex.)	2	1	.667	1.94	26	2	1	0	14	46 $1/3$	36	10	10	6	30
1996—	Weichuan (Taiwan)■	4	5	.444	2.09	58	2	0	0	29	146 $1/3$	124	44	34	22	183
1997—	Weichuan (Taiwan)	7	4	.636	1.89	50	1	1	1	20	104 $2/3$	87	33	22	21	128
1998—	Weichuan (Taiwan)	6	7	.462	3.01	48	1	0	0	26	95 $2/3$	84	32	32	19	133
1999—	M.C. Red Devils (Mex.)■	0	0	...	0.75	12	0	0	0	8	12	5	1	1	3	20
	—Nashville (PCL)■	0	2	.000	3.95	23	0	0	0	2	27 $1/3$	24	12	12	10	35
	—Pittsburgh (N.L.)	1	0	1.000	1.29	7	0	0	0	0	7	2	1	1	3	9
Major League totals (1 year)		1	0	1.000	1.29	7	0	0	0	0	7	2	1	1	3	9

G

PERSONAL: Born July 23, 1973, in Whittier, Calif. ... 6-0/175. ... Bats right, throws right. ... Full name: Anthony Nomar Garciaparra.
HIGH SCHOOL: St. John Bosco (Bellflower, Calif.).
COLLEGE: Georgia Tech.
TRANSACTIONS/CAREER NOTES: Selected by Milwaukee Brewers organization in fifth round of free-agent draft (June 3, 1991); did not sign. ... Selected by Boston Red Sox organization in first round (12th pick overall) of free-agent draft (June 2, 1994). ... On Pawtucket disabled list (April 4-15 and April 19-July 11, 1996). ... On disabled list (May 9-28, 1998).
RECORDS: Shares major league single-game record for most grand slams—2 (May 10, 1999). ... Holds A.L. rookie-season record for most consecutive games batted safely—30 (1997).
HONORS: Named A.L. Rookie Player of the Year by THE SPORTING NEWS (1997). ... Named shortstop on THE SPORTING NEWS A.L. All-Star team (1997 and 1999). ... Named shortstop on THE SPORTING NEWS A.L. Silver Slugger team (1997). ... Named A.L. Rookie of the Year by Baseball Writers' Association of America (1997).
STATISTICAL NOTES: Led Eastern League shortstops with 624 total chances in 1994. ... Had 30-game hitting streak (July 26-August 29, 1997). ... Led A.L. shortstops in total chances with 720 and double plays with 113 in 1997. ... Had 16-game hitting streak (April 2-19, 1998). ... Had 24-game hitting streak (June 7-July 3, 1998). ... Had 16-game hitting streak (April 26-May 14, 1999). ... Hit three home runs in one game (May 10, 1999). ... Had 17-game hitting streak (June 13-July 2, 1999). ... Career major league grand slams: 3.
MISCELLANEOUS: Member of 1992 U.S. Olympic baseball team.

Year Team (League)	Pos.	G	AB	R	H	2B	3B	HR	RBI	Avg.	BB	SO	SB	PO	A	E	Avg.
1994—Sarasota (FSL)	SS	28	105	20	31	8	1	1	16	.295	10	6	5	42	72	3	.974
1995—Trenton (East.)	SS	125	513	77	137	20	8	8	47	.267	50	42	35	205	*396	23	.963
1996—Pawtucket (I.L.)	SS	43	172	40	59	15	2	16	46	.343	14	21	3	63	120	5	.973
—GC Red Sox (GCL)	SS	5	14	4	4	2	1	0	5	.286	1	0	0	7	12	1	.950
—Boston (A.L.)	SS-DH-2B	24	87	11	21	2	3	4	16	.241	4	14	5	37	51	1	.989
1997—Boston (A.L.)	SS	153	*684	122	*209	44	*11	30	98	.306	35	92	22	*249	450	21	.971
1998—Boston (A.L.)	SS	143	604	111	195	37	8	35	122	.323	33	62	12	228	402	25	.962
1999—Boston (A.L.)	SS	135	532	103	190	42	4	27	104	*.357	51	39	14	232	357	17	.972
Major League totals (4 years)		455	1907	347	615	125	26	96	340	.322	123	207	53	746	1260	64	.969

DIVISION SERIES RECORD

RECORDS: Holds career record for highest slugging average (20 or more at-bats)—1.037.

Year Team (League)	Pos.	G	AB	R	H	2B	3B	HR	RBI	Avg.	BB	SO	SB	PO	A	E	Avg.
1998—Boston (A.L.)	SS	4	15	4	5	1	0	3	11	.333	2	0	0	3	7	0	1.000
1999—Boston (A.L.)	SS	4	12	6	5	2	0	2	4	.417	3	3	0	5	11	0	1.000
Division series totals (2 years)		8	27	10	10	3	0	5	15	.370	5	3	0	8	18	0	1.000

CHAMPIONSHIP SERIES RECORD

Year Team (League)	Pos.	G	AB	R	H	2B	3B	HR	RBI	Avg.	BB	SO	SB	PO	A	E	Avg.
1999—Boston (A.L.)	SS	5	20	2	8	2	0	2	5	.400	2	2	1	7	13	4	.833

ALL-STAR GAME RECORD

Year League	Pos.	AB	R	H	2B	3B	HR	RBI	Avg.	BB	SO	SB	PO	A	E	Avg.
1997—American	SS	1	0	0	0	0	0	0	.000	0	0	0	1	0	0	1.000
1999—American	SS	2	0	0	0	0	0	0	.000	0	0	0	0	0	0	...
All-Star Game totals (2 years)		3	0	0	0	0	0	0	.000	0	0	0	1	0	0	1.000

PERSONAL: Born March 1, 1962, in Los Angeles. ... 6-1/220. ... Throws right, bats right. ... Full name: Mark Allan Gardner.
HIGH SCHOOL: Clovis (Calif.).
JUNIOR COLLEGE: Fresno (Calif.) City College.
COLLEGE: Fresno State.
TRANSACTIONS/CAREER NOTES: Selected by California Angels organization in sixth round of free-agent draft (January 11, 1983); did not sign. ... Selected by Cleveland Indians organization in 17th round of free-agent draft (June 4, 1984); did not sign. ... Selected by Montreal Expos organization in eighth round of free-agent draft (June 3, 1985). ... On disabled list (September 20, 1990-remainder of season). ... On Montreal disabled list (April 2-May 14, 1991); included rehabilitation assignment to Indianapolis (April 11-May 8). ... Traded by Expos with P Doug Piatt to Kansas City Royals for C Tim Spehr and P Jeff Shaw (December 9, 1992). ... On Kansas City disabled list (July 7-August 27, 1993); included rehabilitation assignment to Omaha (July 28-August 26). ... Released by Royals (December 8, 1993). ... Signed by Edmonton, Florida Marlins organization (January 6, 1994). ... On Florida disabled list (June 8-26, 1994); included rehabilitation assignment to Brevard County (June 18-22). ... Granted free agency (February 17, 1995). ... Re-signed by Marlins (April 7, 1995). ... Granted free agency (October 16, 1995). ... Re-signed by Marlins organization (December 8, 1995) ... Granted free agency (March 28, 1996). ... Signed by San Francisco Giants (March 29, 1996). ... On San Francisco disabled list (July 3-21, 1996); included rehabilitation assignment to San Jose (July 17-21). ... Granted free agency (October 23, 1998). ... Re-signed by Giants (November 9, 1998). ... On San Francisco disabled list (April 17-May 9, 1999); included rehabilitation assignment to San Jose (April 28-May 9).
RECORDS: Shares major league single-inning record for most hit batsmen—3 (August 15, 1992, first inning).
HONORS: Named American Association Pitcher of the Year (1989).
STATISTICAL NOTES: Led N.L. with nine hit batsmen in 1990. ... Pitched nine hitless innings against Los Angeles Dodgers, but gave up two hits in 10th inning and lost, 1-0, when reliever Jeff Fassero gave up game-winning hit in 10th (July 26, 1991).
MISCELLANEOUS: Struck out once in two appearances as pinch hitter for Montreal (1991). ... Had two sacrifice hits in three appearances as pinch hitter for San Francisco (1996).

Year League	W	L	Pct.	ERA	G	GS	CG	ShO	Sv.	IP	H	R	ER	BB	SO
1985—Jamestown (NY-P)	0	0	...	2.77	3	3	0	0	0	13	9	4	4	4	16
—W.P. Beach (FSL)	5	4	.556	2.37	10	9	4	0	0	60 2/3	54	24	16	18	44
1986—Jacksonville (Sou.)	10	11	.476	3.84	29	28	3	1	0	168 2/3	144	88	72	90	140

G

Year	League	W	L	Pct.	ERA	G	GS	CG	ShO	Sv.	IP	H	R	ER	BB	SO
1987— Indianapolis (A.A.)		3	3	.500	5.67	9	9	0	0	0	46	48	32	29	28	41
— Jacksonville (Sou.)		4	6	.400	4.19	17	17	1	0	0	101	101	50	47	42	78
1988— Jacksonville (Sou.)		6	3	.667	1.60	15	15	4	2	0	112 1/3	72	24	20	36	130
— Indianapolis (A.A.)		4	2	.667	2.77	13	13	3	1	0	84 1/3	65	30	26	32	71
1989— Indianapolis (A.A.)		12	4	*.750	2.37	24	23	4	2	0	163 1/3	122	51	43	59	*175
— Montreal (N.L.)		0	3	.000	5.13	7	4	0	0	0	26 1/3	26	16	15	11	21
1990— Montreal (N.L.)		7	9	.438	3.42	27	26	3	3	0	152 2/3	129	62	58	61	135
1991— Indianapolis (A.A.)		2	0	1.000	3.48	6	6	0	0	0	31	26	13	12	16	38
— Montreal (N.L.)		9	11	.450	3.85	27	27	0	0	0	168 1/3	139	78	72	75	107
1992— Montreal (N.L.)		12	10	.545	4.36	33	30	0	0	0	179 2/3	179	91	87	60	132
1993— Kansas City (A.L.)■		4	6	.400	6.19	17	16	0	0	0	91 2/3	92	65	63	36	54
— Omaha (A.A.)		4	2	.667	2.79	8	8	1	0	0	48 1/3	34	17	15	19	41
1994— Florida (N.L.)■		4	4	.500	4.87	20	14	0	0	0	92 1/3	97	53	50	30	57
— Edmonton (PCL)		1	0	1.000	0.00	1	1	0	0	0	6	4	0	0	1	11
— Brevard County (FSL)		1	0	1.000	0.00	1	1	0	0	0	5	1	0	0	1	3
1995— Florida (N.L.)		5	5	.500	4.49	39	11	1	1	1	102 1/3	109	60	51	43	87
1996— San Francisco (N.L.)■		12	7	.632	4.42	30	28	4	1	0	179 1/3	200	105	88	57	145
— San Jose (Calif.)		0	0	...	3.18	1	1	0	0	0	5 2/3	4	2	2	0	7
1997— San Francisco (N.L.)		12	9	.571	4.29	30	30	2	1	0	180 1/3	188	92	86	57	136
1998— San Francisco (N.L.)		13	6	.684	4.33	33	33	4	2	0	212	203	106	102	65	151
1999— San Francisco (N.L.)		5	11	.313	6.47	29	21	1	0	0	139	142	103	100	57	86
— San Jose (Calif.)		1	0	1.000	4.50	2	2	0	0	0	10	10	5	5	3	13
A.L. totals (1 year)		4	6	.400	6.19	17	16	0	0	0	91 2/3	92	65	63	36	54
N.L. totals (10 years)		79	75	.513	4.45	275	224	15	8	1	1432 1/3	1412	766	709	516	1057
Major League totals (11 years)		83	81	.506	4.56	292	240	15	8	1	1524	1504	831	772	552	1111

GATES, BRENT   2B

PERSONAL: Born March 14, 1970, in Grand Rapids, Mich. ... 6-1/190. ... Bats both, throws right. ... Full name: Brent Robert Gates.
HIGH SCHOOL: Grandville (Mich.).
COLLEGE: Minnesota.
TRANSACTIONS/CAREER NOTES: Selected by Oakland Athletics organization in first round (26th pick overall) of free-agent draft (June 3, 1991). ... On disabled list (April 10-May 5 and July 17, 1994-remainder of season). ... On disabled list (June 16, 1996-remainder of season). ... Released by A's (March 11, 1997). ... Signed by Seattle Mariners (March 16, 1997). ... Released by Mariners (December 15, 1997). ... Signed by Minnesota Twins organization (December 23, 1997). ... Granted free agency (September 30, 1998). ... Re-signed by Twins organization (December 15, 1998). ... Granted free agency (October 6, 1999).
STATISTICAL NOTES: Led California League second basemen with 735 total chances and 105 double plays in 1992. ... Career major league grand slams: 1.

							BATTING							FIELDING		
Year	Team (League)	Pos.	G	AB	R	H	2B	3B	HR	RBI	Avg.	BB	SO	SB	PO	A	E	Avg.
1991— S. Oregon (N'west)	SS-2B-3B	58	219	41	63	11	0	3	26	.288	30	33	8	77	177	15	.944
— Madison (Midw.)	SS-3B	4	12	4	4	2	0	0	1	.333	3	2	1	6	10	0	1.000
1992— Modesto (Calif.)	2B	133	505	94	162	39	2	10	88	.321	85	60	9	*293	*420	•22	.970
1993— Huntsville (Sou.)	2B	12	45	7	15	4	0	1	11	.333	7	9	0	32	28	0	1.000
— Tacoma (PCL)	2B	12	44	7	15	7	0	1	4	.341	4	6	2	27	36	1	.984
— Oakland (A.L.)	2B	139	535	64	155	29	2	7	69	.290	56	75	7	281	431	14	.981
1994— Oakland (A.L.)	2B-1B	64	233	29	66	11	1	2	24	.283	21	32	3	113	159	8	.971
1995— Oakland (A.L.)	2B-DH-1B	136	524	60	133	24	4	5	56	.254	46	84	3	241	428	12	.982
1996— Oakland (A.L.)	2B	64	247	26	65	19	2	2	30	.263	18	35	1	140	183	9	.973
1997— Seattle (A.L.)■	3-2-S-D-1-O	65	151	18	36	8	0	3	20	.238	14	21	0	26	82	5	.956
— Tacoma (PCL)	2B-SS	7	33	7	15	3	0	0	6	.455	4	2	0	10	12	4	.846
1998— Minnesota (A.L.)■	3-2-DH-1-S	107	333	31	83	15	0	3	42	.249	36	46	3	85	157	9	.964
1999— Minnesota (A.L.)	3-2-1-DH-S	110	306	40	78	13	2	3	38	.255	34	56	1	98	174	3	.989
Major League totals (7 years)		685	2329	268	616	119	11	25	279	.264	225	349	18	984	1614	60	.977

DIVISION SERIES RECORD

							BATTING							FIELDING		
Year	Team (League)	Pos.	G	AB	R	H	2B	3B	HR	RBI	Avg.	BB	SO	SB	PO	A	E	Avg.
1997— Seattle (A.L.)	3B-PH	2	4	0	0	0	0	0	0	.000	0	0	0	1	2	0	1.000

GIAMBI, JASON   1B   ATHLETICS

G

PERSONAL: Born January 8, 1971, in West Covina, Calif. ... 6-3/235. ... Bats left, throws right. ... Full name: Jason Gilbert Giambi. ... Brother of Jeremy Giambi, first basemen/outfielder, Kansas City Royals. ... Name pronounced GEE-om-bee.
HIGH SCHOOL: South Hills (West Covina, Calif.).
COLLEGE: Long Beach State.
TRANSACTIONS/CAREER NOTES: Selected by Milwaukee Brewers organization in 43rd round of free-agent draft (June 5, 1989); did not sign. ... Selected by Oakland Athletics organization in second round of free-agent draft (June 1, 1992). ... On disabled list (July 27-August 28, 1993). ... On Huntsville disabled list (April 7-14, 1994).
STATISTICAL NOTES: Had 25-game hitting streak (May 12-June 23, 1997). ... Had 17-game hitting streak (July 16-August 2, 1998). ... Had 16-game hitting streak (September 5-24, 1998). ... Had 19-game hitting streak (July 23-August 10, 1999). ... Career major league grand slams: 3.
MISCELLANEOUS: Member of 1992 U.S. Olympic baseball team.

							BATTING							FIELDING		
Year	Team (League)	Pos.	G	AB	R	H	2B	3B	HR	RBI	Avg.	BB	SO	SB	PO	A	E	Avg.
1992— S. Oregon (N'west)	3B	13	41	9	13	3	0	3	13	.317	9	6	1	5	20	1	.962
1993— Modesto (Calif.)	3B	89	313	72	91	16	2	12	60	.291	73	47	2	49	145	19	.911
1994— Huntsville (Sou.)	3B-1B	56	193	31	43	9	0	6	30	.223	27	31	0	111	77	11	.945
— Tacoma (PCL)	3B-SS	52	176	28	56	20	0	4	38	.318	25	32	1	39	110	8	.949

Year	Team (League)	Pos.	G	AB	R	H	2B	3B	HR	RBI	Avg.	BB	SO	SB	PO	A	E	Avg.
1995—	Edmonton (PCL)	3B-DH-1B	55	190	34	65	26	1	3	41	.342	34	26	0	38	98	9	.938
	—Oakland (A.L.)	3B-1B-DH	54	176	27	45	7	0	6	25	.256	28	31	2	194	55	4	.984
1996—	Oakland (A.L.)	1-O-3-DH	140	536	84	156	40	1	20	79	.291	51	95	0	478	117	11	.982
1997—	Oakland (A.L.)	OF-1-DH	142	519	66	152	41	2	20	81	.293	55	89	0	501	44	7	.987
1998—	Oakland (A.L.)	1B-DH	153	562	92	166	28	0	27	110	.295	81	102	2	1255	73	*14	.990
1999—	Oakland (A.L.)	1B-DH-3B	158	575	115	181	36	1	33	123	.315	105	106	1	1251	45	7	.995
	Major League totals (5 years)		647	2368	384	700	152	4	106	418	.296	320	423	5	3679	334	43	.989

GIAMBI, JEREMY — 1B/OF — ROYALS

PERSONAL: Born September 30, 1974, in San Jose, Calif. ... 6-0/200. ... Bats left, throws left. ... Full name: Jeremy Dean Giambi. ... Brother of Jason Giambi, first baseman, Oakland Athletics.
HIGH SCHOOL: South Hills (West Covina, Calif.).
COLLEGE: Cal State Fullerton.
TRANSACTIONS/CAREER NOTES: Selected by Kansas City Royals organization in sixth round of free-agent draft (June 4, 1996). ... On Omaha disabled list (July 12-August 2, 1998). ... On Kansas City disabled list (March 27-May 15, 1999); included rehabilitation assignment to Omaha (April 28-May 15).
HONORS: Led Northwest League with .440 on-base percentage in 1996. ... Led Pacific Coast League with .469 on-base percentage in 1998.

Year	Team (League)	Pos.	G	AB	R	H	2B	3B	HR	RBI	Avg.	BB	SO	SB	PO	A	E	Avg.
1996—	Spokane (N.W.)	OF	67	231	•58	63	17	0	6	39	.273	*61	32	22	97	3	*11	.901
1997—	Lansing (Midw.)	OF	31	116	33	39	11	1	5	21	.336	23	16	5	30	2	0	1.000
	—Wichita (Texas)	OF-1B	74	268	50	86	15	1	11	52	.321	44	47	4	117	2	3	.975
1998—	Omaha (PCL)	OF-1B	96	325	68	121	21	2	20	66	*.372	57	64	8	113	8	3	.976
	—Kansas City (A.L.)	OF-DH	18	58	6	13	4	0	2	8	.224	11	9	0	14	1	0	1.000
1999—	Kansas City (A.L.)	DH-1B-OF	90	288	34	82	13	1	3	34	.285	40	67	0	213	8	2	.991
	—Omaha (PCL)	OF-1B-DH	35	127	31	44	5	1	12	28	.346	31	30	1	156	9	2	.988
	Major League totals (2 years)		108	346	40	95	17	1	5	42	.275	51	76	0	227	9	2	.992

GIBBS, KEVIN — OF — DODGERS

PERSONAL: Born April 3, 1974, in Washington D.C. ... 6-2/185. ... Bats both, throws right. ... Full name: Kevin Casey Gibbs.
HIGH SCHOOL: St. John's (Washington, D.C.).
COLLEGE: Old Dominion.
TRANSACTIONS/CAREER NOTES: Selected by Los Angeles Dodgers in sixth round of free-agent draft (June 1, 1995). ... On disabled list (April 20-May 1 and July 19-26, 1997). ... On Albuquerque disabled list (April 10, 1998-remainder of season; and May 8-June 3, 1999). ... On Los Angeles disabled list (June 4, 1999-remainder of season).
STATISTICAL NOTES: Tied for Florida State League lead in caught stealing with 19 in 1996. ... Tied for Florida State League lead in double plays by outfielder with four in 1996.

Year	Team (League)	Pos.	G	AB	R	H	2B	3B	HR	RBI	Avg.	BB	SO	SB	PO	A	E	Avg.
1995—	Vero Beach (FSL)	OF	7	20	1	5	1	0	0	2	.250	0	0	1	12	0	0	1.000
	—San Bern. (Calif.)	OF	5	13	1	3	1	0	0	0	.231	0	2	1	5	0	0	1.000
	—Yakima (N.W.)	OF	52	182	36	57	6	4	1	18	.313	36	46	*38	71	1	2	.973
1996—	Vero Beach (FSL)	OF	118	423	69	114	9	*11	0	33	.270	65	80	*60	252	11	4	.985
1997—	San Antonio (Texas) ...	OF	101	358	89	120	21	6	2	34	.335	72	48	49	215	2	4	.982
1998—	Albuquerque (PCL)	OF	2	8	1	1	0	0	0	1	.125	2	1	0	4	0	0	1.000
1999—	Albuquerque (PCL)	OF-DH	11	21	4	6	3	0	0	1	.286	4	6	2	11	0	0	1.000

GIBSON, DERRICK — OF — ROCKIES

PERSONAL: Born February 5, 1975, in Winter Haven, Fla. ... 6-2/244. ... Bats right, throws right. ... Full name: Derrick Lamont Gibson.
HIGH SCHOOL: Haines City (Fla.).
TRANSACTIONS/CAREER NOTES: Selected by Colorado Rockies organization in 13th round of free-agent draft (June 3, 1993).
STATISTICAL NOTES: Tied for Pacific Coast League lead with three double plays by outfielder in 1998.

Year	Team (League)	Pos.	G	AB	R	H	2B	3B	HR	RBI	Avg.	BB	SO	SB	PO	A	E	Avg.
1993—	Ariz. Rockies (Ariz.)	OF	34	119	13	18	2	2	0	10	.151	5	55	3	22	1	5	.821
1994—	Bend (N.W.)	OF	73	284	47	75	19	5	•12	57	.264	29	*102	14	82	*10	9	.911
1995—	Asheville (SAL)	OF	135	506	91	148	16	10	•32	*115	.292	29	136	31	190	11	9	.957
1996—	New Haven (East.)	OF	122	449	58	115	21	4	15	62	.256	31	125	3	168	10	*13	.932
1997—	New Haven (East.)	OF-DH	119	461	91	146	24	2	23	75	.317	36	100	20	188	8	*11	.947
	—Colo. Springs (PCL) ...	OF-DH	21	78	14	33	7	0	3	12	.423	5	9	0	30	0	1	.968
1998—	Colo. Springs (PCL) ...	OF-DH	126	497	84	145	20	3	14	81	.292	35	110	14	211	11	*13	.945
	—Colorado (N.L.)	OF	7	21	4	9	1	0	0	2	.429	1	4	0	11	2	1	.929
1999—	Colo. Springs (PCL) ...	OF-DH	110	385	68	106	19	6	17	67	.275	30	82	12	171	5	8	.957
	—Colorado (N.L.)	OF	10	28	2	5	1	0	2	6	.179	0	7	0	15	2	1	.944
	Major League totals (2 years)		17	49	6	14	2	0	2	8	.286	1	11	0	26	4	2	.938

GILES, BRIAN — OF — PIRATES

PERSONAL: Born January 20, 1971, in El Cajon, Calif. ... 5-10/200. ... Bats left, throws left. ... Full name: Brian Stephen Giles. ... Brother of Marcus Giles, second baseman, Atlanta Braves organization. ... Name pronounced JYLES.
HIGH SCHOOL: Granite Hills (El Cajon, Calif.).

G

TRANSACTIONS/CAREER NOTES: Selected by Cleveland Indians organization in 17th round of free-agent draft (June 5, 1989). ... On Canton/Akron disabled list (May 15-July 7, 1992). ... On Cleveland disabled list (June 1-July 7, 1998); included rehabilitation assignment to Buffalo (June 23-July 7). ... Traded by Indians to Pittsburgh Pirates for P Ricardo Rincon (November 18, 1998).
STATISTICAL NOTES: Led International League with 10 intentional bases on balls received in 1994. ... Led International League outfielders with five double plays in 1994. ... Career major league grand slams: 2.

												BATTING					FIELDING	
Year	Team (League)	Pos.	G	AB	R	H	2B	3B	HR	RBI	Avg.	BB	SO	SB	PO	A	E	Avg.
1989— Burlington (Appl.).......		OF	36	129	18	40	7	0	0	20	.310	11	19	6	52	3	1	.982
1990— Watertown (NY-P)		OF	70	246	44	71	15	2	1	23	.289	48	23	11	108	8	1	.991
1991— Kinston (Caro.)...........		OF	125	394	71	122	14	0	4	47	.310	68	70	19	187	10	5	.975
1992— Canton/Akron (East.)..		OF	23	74	6	16	4	0	0	3	.216	10	10	3	45	0	0	1.000
— Kinston (Caro.)...........		OF	42	140	28	37	5	1	3	18	.264	30	21	3	74	3	1	.987
1993— Canton/Akron (East.)..		OF	123	425	64	139	17	6	6	64	.327	57	43	18	186	3	5	.974
1994— Charlotte (I.L.)...........		OF	128	434	74	136	18	3	16	58	.313	55	61	8	242	12	4	.984
1995— Buffalo (A.A.).............		OF-DH	123	413	67	128	18	•8	15	67	.310	54	40	7	248	4	5	.981
— Cleveland (A.L.).........		OF-DH	6	9	6	5	0	0	1	3	.556	0	1	0	2	1	0	1.000
1996— Buffalo (A.A.).............		OF	83	318	65	100	17	6	20	64	.314	42	29	1	132	5	2	.986
— Cleveland (A.L.).........		DH-OF	51	121	26	43	14	1	5	27	.355	19	13	3	26	0	0	1.000
1997— Cleveland (A.L.).........		OF-DH	130	377	62	101	15	3	17	61	.268	63	50	13	201	7	6	.972
1998— Cleveland (A.L.).........		OF-DH	112	350	56	94	19	0	16	66	.269	73	75	10	213	7	5	.978
— Buffalo (I.L.).............		DH-OF	13	46	5	11	2	0	2	7	.239	6	8	0	18	0	1	.947
1999— Pittsburgh (N.L.)■.....		OF-DH	141	521	109	164	33	3	39	115	.315	95	80	6	294	8	3	.990
American League totals (4 years)			299	857	150	243	48	4	39	157	.284	155	139	26	442	15	11	.976
National League totals (1 year)			141	521	109	164	33	3	39	115	.315	95	80	6	294	8	3	.990
Major League totals (5 years)			440	1378	259	407	81	7	78	272	.295	250	219	32	736	23	14	.982

DIVISION SERIES RECORD

												BATTING					FIELDING	
Year	Team (League)	Pos.	G	AB	R	H	2B	3B	HR	RBI	Avg.	BB	SO	SB	PO	A	E	Avg.
1996— Cleveland (A.L.)..........		PH	1	1	0	0	0	0	0	0	.000	0	1	0	...	...	...	...
1997— Cleveland (A.L.)..........		OF	3	7	0	1	0	0	0	0	.143	0	1	0	4	1	0	1.000
1998— Cleveland (A.L.)..........		OF-DH	3	10	1	2	1	0	0	0	.200	1	4	0	4	0	0	1.000
Division series totals (3 years)			7	18	1	3	1	0	0	0	.167	1	6	0	8	1	0	1.000

CHAMPIONSHIP SERIES RECORD

												BATTING					FIELDING	
Year	Team (League)	Pos.	G	AB	R	H	2B	3B	HR	RBI	Avg.	BB	SO	SB	PO	A	E	Avg.
1997— Cleveland (A.L.)..........		OF	6	16	1	3	3	0	0	0	.188	2	6	0	9	0	0	1.000
1998— Cleveland (A.L.)..........		OF-PH	4	12	0	1	0	0	0	0	.083	1	3	0	7	0	1	.875
Championship series totals (2 years)			10	28	1	4	3	0	0	0	.143	3	9	0	16	0	1	.941

WORLD SERIES RECORD

												BATTING					FIELDING	
Year	Team (League)	Pos.	G	AB	R	H	2B	3B	HR	RBI	Avg.	BB	SO	SB	PO	A	E	Avg.
1997— Cleveland (A.L.)..........		PH-OF	5	4	1	2	1	0	0	2	.500	4	1	0	2	0	0	1.000

GILKEY, BERNARD　　　　　OF　　　　　DIAMONDBACKS

PERSONAL: Born September 24, 1966, in St. Louis. ... 6-0/200. ... Bats right, throws right. ... Full name: Otis Bernard Gilkey.
HIGH SCHOOL: University City (Mo.).
TRANSACTIONS/CAREER NOTES: Signed as non-drafted free agent by St. Louis Cardinals organization (August 22, 1984). ... On disabled list (April 10-25, 1986 and May 29, 1987-remainder of season). ... On St. Louis disabled list (June 14-July 11, 1991 and April 29-May 14, 1993). ... On suspended list (July 8-9, 1994). ... Granted free agency (April 7, 1995). ... Re-signed by Cardinals (April 8, 1995). ... On St. Louis disabled list (June 28-July 17, 1995); included rehabilitation assignment to Louisville (July 15-17). ... Traded by Cardinals to New York Mets for P Eric Ludwick, P Erik Hiljus and OF Yudith Ozorio (January 22, 1996). ... On New York disabled list (April 27-May 12, 1998). ... Traded by Mets with P Nelson Figueroa and cash to Arizona Diamondbacks for P Willie Blair, C Jorge Fabregas and a player to be named later (July 31, 1998); Mets received cash to complete deal (September 3, 1998).
STATISTICAL NOTES: Led New York-Pennsylvania League outfielders with 185 total chances in 1985. ... Led Texas League in caught stealing with 22 in 1989. ... Led American Association in caught stealing with 33 in 1990. ... Led N.L. outfielders with 19 assists in 1993. ... Tied for N.L. lead in double plays by outfielder with four in 1995. ... Tied for N.L. lead with 12 sacrifice flies in 1997.

												BATTING					FIELDING	
Year	Team (League)	Pos.	G	AB	R	H	2B	3B	HR	RBI	Avg.	BB	SO	SB	PO	A	E	Avg.
1985— Erie (NY-P)		OF	•77	*294	57	60	9	1	7	27	.204	55	57	34	*164	*13	*8	.957
1986— Savannah (SAL)		OF	105	374	64	88	15	4	6	36	.235	84	57	32	220	7	5	.978
1987— Springfield (Midw.)		OF	46	162	30	37	5	0	0	9	.228	39	28	18	79	5	4	.955
1988— Springfield (Midw.)		OF	125	491	84	120	18	7	6	36	.244	65	54	54	165	10	6	.967
1989— Arkansas (Texas)........		OF	131	500	*104	139	25	3	6	57	.278	70	54	*53	236	*22	9	.966
1990— Louisville (A.A.)..........		OF	132	499	83	147	26	8	3	46	.295	*75	49	45	236	18	•11	.958
— St. Louis (N.L.)...........		OF	18	64	11	19	5	2	1	3	.297	8	5	6	47	2	2	.961
1991— St. Louis (N.L.)...........		OF	81	268	28	58	7	2	5	20	.216	39	33	14	164	6	1	.994
— Louisville (A.A.)...........		OF	11	41	5	6	2	0	0	2	.146	6	10	1	33	1	0	1.000
1992— St. Louis (N.L.)...........		OF	131	384	56	116	19	4	7	43	.302	39	52	18	217	9	5	.978
1993— St. Louis (N.L.)...........		OF-1B	137	557	99	170	40	5	16	70	.305	56	66	15	251	†20	8	.971
1994— St. Louis (N.L.)...........		OF	105	380	52	96	22	1	6	45	.253	39	65	15	168	9	3	.983
1995— St. Louis (N.L.)...........		OF	121	480	73	143	33	4	17	69	.298	42	70	12	206	10	3	.986
— Louisville (A.A.)...........		OF	2	6	3	2	1	0	1	1	.333	1	0	0	2	0	0	1.000
1996— New York (N.L.)■		OF	153	571	108	181	44	3	30	117	.317	73	125	17	309	*18	6	.982
1997— New York (N.L.)..........		OF-DH	145	518	85	129	31	1	18	78	.249	70	111	7	251	*17	3	.989
1998— New York (N.L.)..........		OF	82	264	33	60	15	0	4	28	.227	32	66	5	121	9	1	.992
— Arizona (N.L.)■..........		OF	29	101	8	25	0	0	1	5	.248	11	14	4	49	3	1	.981
1999— Arizona (N.L.)............		OF	94	204	28	60	16	1	8	39	.294	29	42	2	90	3	3	.969
Major League totals (10 years)			1096	3791	581	1057	232	23	113	517	.279	438	649	115	1873	106	36	.982

G

DIVISION SERIES RECORD

Year Team (League)	Pos.	G	AB	R	H	2B	3B	HR	RBI	Avg.	BB	SO	SB	PO	A	E	Avg.
1999— Arizona (N.L.)	OF	2	6	0	0	0	0	0	0	.000	0	0	0	5	0	0	1.000

GIOVANOLA, ED   IF

PERSONAL: Born March 4, 1969, in Los Gatos, Calif. ... 5-10/170. ... Bats left, throws right. ... Full name: Edward Thomas Giovanola.
HIGH SCHOOL: Bellarmine College Prepatory (San Jose, Calif.).
COLLEGE: Santa Clara.
TRANSACTIONS/CAREER NOTES: Selected by Atlanta Braves organization in seventh round of free-agent draft (June 4, 1990). ... On disabled list (May 29-June 5 and June 23-July 23, 1992). ... On Richmond disabled list (June 28-July 21, 1995). ... Claimed on waivers by San Diego Padres (October 13, 1997). ... Granted free agency (September 29, 1999).
STATISTICAL NOTES: Led International League with .417 on-base percentage in 1995.

Year Team (League)	Pos.	G	AB	R	H	2B	3B	HR	RBI	Avg.	BB	SO	SB	PO	A	E	Avg.
1990— Idaho Falls (Pio.)	2B	25	98	25	38	6	0	0	13	.388	17	9	6	32	72	2	.981
— Sumter (SAL)	2B	35	119	20	29	4	0	0	8	.244	34	17	8	61	125	3	.984
1991— Durham (Caro.)	3-S-2-0	101	299	50	76	9	0	6	27	.254	57	39	18	112	182	15	.951
1992— Greenville (Sou.)	3B	75	270	39	72	5	0	5	30	.267	29	40	4	35	168	18	.919
1993— Greenville (Sou.)	3B-2B	120	384	70	108	21	5	5	43	.281	84	49	6	94	281	14	.964
1994— Greenville (Sou.)	3B	25	84	13	20	6	1	4	16	.238	10	12	2	20	41	2	.968
— Richmond (I.L.)	3-S-2-0	98	344	48	97	16	2	6	30	.282	31	49	7	94	211	16	.950
1995— Richmond (I.L.)	SS-3B	99	321	45	103	18	2	4	36	.321	55	37	8	125	286	15	.965
— Atlanta (N.L.)	2B-3B-SS	13	14	2	1	0	0	0	0	.071	3	5	0	9	7	0	1.000
1996— Richmond (I.L.)	S-2-3-O-DH	62	210	29	62	15	1	3	16	.295	37	34	2	77	155	11	.955
— Atlanta (N.L.)	SS-3B-2B	43	82	10	19	2	0	0	7	.232	8	13	1	24	56	1	.988
1997— Richmond (I.L.)	3-S-O-DH	116	395	65	115	23	5	2	46	.291	64	56	2	87	227	16	.952
— Atlanta (N.L.)	3B-2B-SS	14	8	0	2	0	0	0	0	.250	2	1	0	0	6	0	1.000
1998— San Diego (N.L.)■	3B-2B-SS	92	139	19	32	3	3	1	9	.230	22	22	1	56	122	3	.983
— Las Vegas (PCL)	3B	4	15	4	5	0	0	0	1	.333	2	3	0	1	15	1	.941
1999— Las Vegas (PCL)	3B-SS-2B	36	106	23	30	6	1	2	10	.283	16	23	2	27	62	4	.957
— San Diego (N.L.)	3B-2B-SS-P	56	58	10	11	0	1	0	3	.190	9	8	2	36	47	2	.976
Major League totals (5 years)		218	301	41	65	5	4	1	19	.216	44	49	4	125	238	6	.984

DIVISION SERIES RECORD

Year Team (League)	Pos.	G	AB	R	H	2B	3B	HR	RBI	Avg.	BB	SO	SB	PO	A	E	Avg.
1998— San Diego (N.L.)								Did not play.									

CHAMPIONSHIP SERIES RECORD

Year Team (League)	Pos.	G	AB	R	H	2B	3B	HR	RBI	Avg.	BB	SO	SB	PO	A	E	Avg.
1998— San Diego (N.L.)								Did not play.									

WORLD SERIES RECORD

Year Team (League)	Pos.	G	AB	R	H	2B	3B	HR	RBI	Avg.	BB	SO	SB	PO	A	E	Avg.
1998— San Diego (N.L.)								Did not play.									

RECORD AS PITCHER

Year League	W	L	Pct.	ERA	G	GS	CG	ShO	Sv.	IP	H	R	ER	BB	SO
1999— San Diego (N.L.)	0	0	...	0.00	1	0	0	0	0	1 1/3	1	0	0	2	0

GIPSON, CHARLES   OF/IF   MARINERS

PERSONAL: Born December 16, 1972, in Orange, Calif. ... 6-2/180. ... Bats right, throws right. ... Full name: Charles Wells Gipson Jr.
HIGH SCHOOL: Loara (Anaheim, Calif.).
JUNIOR COLLEGE: Cypress (Calif.) College.
TRANSACTIONS/CAREER NOTES: Selected by Seattle Mariners organization in 63rd round of free-agent draft (June 3, 1991). ... On disabled list (May 4-19, 1993). ... On Seattle disabled list (July 11-September 1, 1999); included rehabilitation assignments to New Haven (August 14-21) and Everett (August 22-September 1).
STATISTICAL NOTES: Led Midwest League in being hit by pitch with 27 in 1993. ... Tied for Southern League lead in double plays by outfielder with four in 1995. ... Tied for Southern League lead in caught stealing with 15 in 1996.

Year Team (League)	Pos.	G	AB	R	H	2B	3B	HR	RBI	Avg.	BB	SO	SB	PO	A	E	Avg.
1992— Ariz. Mariners (Ariz.)	SS	39	124	30	29	2	0	0	14	.234	13	19	11	49	114	•23	.876
1993— Appleton (Midw.)	2B-OF-SS	109	348	53	89	13	1	0	20	.256	61	76	21	192	201	28	.933
1994— Riverside (Calif.)	OF	128	481	*102	141	12	3	1	41	.293	76	67	34	293	14	9	.972
1995— Port City (Sou.)	OF-2B	112	391	36	87	11	2	0	29	.223	30	66	10	235	19	6	.977
1996— Port City (Sou.)	OF-SS	119	407	54	109	12	3	1	30	.268	41	62	15	210	162	15	.961
1997— Memphis (Sou.)	SS-3B-2B-OF	88	320	56	79	9	4	1	28	.247	34	71	31	143	211	23	.939
— Tacoma (PCL)	3B-OF-2B-SS	11	35	5	11	2	0	0	5	.314	4	3	0	15	16	3	.912
1998— Seattle (A.L.)	OF-3B-DH	44	51	11	12	1	0	0	2	.235	5	9	2	40	5	2	.957
— Tacoma (PCL)	OF-SS-2B-3B	79	278	39	67	16	2	0	11	.241	27	50	14	142	88	11	.954
1999— Seattle (A.L.)	O-3-DH-2-S	55	80	16	18	5	2	0	9	.225	6	13	3	35	52	3	.967
— Tacoma (PCL)	S-O-3-2-DH	47	174	26	52	6	3	0	21	.299	14	24	18	76	65	4	.940
— New Haven (East.)	2-DH-3-S-O	5	18	2	0	0	0	0	0	.000	3	2	1	10	7	1	.944
— Everett (N.W.)	SS	1	2	0	1	0	1	0	1	.500	2	0	1	0	4	0	1.000
Major League totals (2 years)		99	131	27	30	6	2	0	11	.229	11	22	5	75	57	5	.964

G

PERSONAL: Born October 14, 1964, in Peoria, Ill. ... 5-11/200. ... Bats right, throws right. ... Full name: Joseph Elliott Girardi. ... Name pronounced jeh-RAR-dee.
HIGH SCHOOL: Spalding Institute (Peoria, Ill.).
COLLEGE: Northwestern (degree in industrial engineering, 1986).
TRANSACTIONS/CAREER NOTES: Selected by Chicago Cubs organization in fifth round of free-agent draft (June 2, 1986). ... On disabled list (August 27, 1986-remainder of season and August 7, 1988-remainder of season). ... On Chicago disabled list (April 17-August 6, 1991); included rehabilitation assignment to Iowa (July 23-August 6). ... Selected by Colorado Rockies in first round (19th pick overall) of expansion draft (November 17, 1992). ... On Colorado disabled list (June 5-August 11, 1993); included rehabilitation assignment to Colorado Springs (August 1-11). ... On disabled list (July 11-26, 1994). ... Traded by Rockies to New York Yankees for P Mike DeJean and a player to be named later (November 20, 1995); Rockies acquired P Steve Shoemaker to complete deal (December 6, 1995). ... Granted free agency (November 5, 1996). ... Re-signed by Yankees (December 3, 1996). ... Granted free agency (November 5, 1999). ... Signed by Cubs (December 15, 1999).
STATISTICAL NOTES: Led Carolina League catchers with 661 total chances and tied for lead with 17 passed balls in 1987. ... Led Eastern League catchers with .992 fielding percentage, 448 putouts, 76 assists and 528 total chances and tied for lead with five double plays in 1988. ... Tied for N.L. lead with 16 passed balls in 1990.

							BATTING							FIELDING			
Year	Team (League)	Pos.	G	AB	R	H	2B	3B	HR	RBI	Avg.	BB	SO	SB	PO	A	E	Avg.
1986— Peoria (Midw.)	C	68	230	36	71	13	1	3	28	.309	17	36	6	405	34	5	.989
1987— Win.-Salem (Car.)	C	99	364	51	102	9	8	8	46	.280	33	64	9	*569	*74	18	.973
1988— Pittsfield (East.)	C-OF	104	357	44	97	14	1	7	41	.272	29	51	7	†460	†76	6	†.989
1989— Chicago (N.L.)	C	59	157	15	39	10	0	1	14	.248	11	26	2	332	28	7	.981
— Iowa (A.A.)	C	32	110	12	27	4	2	2	11	.245	5	19	3	172	21	1	.995
1990— Chicago (N.L.)	C	133	419	36	113	24	2	1	38	.270	17	50	8	653	61	11	.985
1991— Chicago (N.L.)	C	21	47	3	9	2	0	0	6	.191	6	6	0	95	11	3	.972
— Iowa (A.A.)	C	12	36	3	8	1	0	0	4	.222	4	8	2	62	5	3	.957
1992— Chicago (N.L.)	C	91	270	19	73	3	1	1	12	.270	19	38	0	369	51	4	.991
1993— Colorado (N.L.)	C	86	310	35	90	14	5	3	31	.290	24	41	6	478	46	6	.989
— Colo. Springs (PCL)	C	8	31	6	15	1	1	1	6	.484	0	3	1	40	3	1	.977
1994— Colorado (N.L.)	C	93	330	47	91	9	4	4	34	.276	21	48	3	549	56	5	.992
1995— Colorado (N.L.)	C	125	462	63	121	17	2	8	55	.262	29	76	3	730	60	10	.988
1996— New York (A.L.)■	C-DH	124	422	55	124	22	3	2	45	.294	30	55	13	803	46	3	.996
1997— New York (A.L.)	C	112	398	38	105	23	1	1	50	.264	26	53	2	829	55	5	.994
1998— New York (A.L.)	C	78	254	31	70	11	4	3	31	.276	14	38	2	541	38	3	.995
1999— New York (A.L.)	C	65	209	23	50	16	1	2	27	.239	10	26	3	452	34	8	.984
American League totals (4 years)		379	1283	147	349	72	9	8	153	.272	80	172	20	2625	173	19	.993
National League totals (7 years)		608	1995	218	536	79	14	18	190	.269	127	285	22	3206	313	46	.987
Major League totals (11 years)		987	3278	365	885	151	23	26	343	.270	207	457	42	5831	486	65	.990

DIVISION SERIES RECORD

							BATTING							FIELDING			
Year	Team (League)	Pos.	G	AB	R	H	2B	3B	HR	RBI	Avg.	BB	SO	SB	PO	A	E	Avg.
1995— Colorado (N.L.)	C	4	16	0	2	0	0	0	0	.125	0	2	0	25	3	1	.966
1996— New York (A.L.)	C-PR	4	9	1	2	0	0	0	0	.222	4	1	0	28	1	...	1.000
1997— New York (A.L.)	C	5	15	2	2	0	0	0	0	.133	1	3	0	21	2	0	1.000
1998— New York (A.L.)	C	2	7	0	3	0	0	0	0	.429	0	1	0	19	1	0	1.000
1999— New York (A.L.)	C	2	6	0	0	0	0	0	0	.000	0	1	0	12	0	0	1.000
Division series totals (5 years)		17	53	3	9	0	0	0	0	.170	5	8	0	105	7	1	.991

CHAMPIONSHIP SERIES RECORD

							BATTING							FIELDING			
Year	Team (League)	Pos.	G	AB	R	H	2B	3B	HR	RBI	Avg.	BB	SO	SB	PO	A	E	Avg.
1989— Chicago (N.L.)	C	4	10	1	1	0	0	0	0	.100	1	2	0	20	0	0	1.000
1996— New York (A.L.)	C-PH	4	12	1	3	0	0	0	0	.250	1	3	0	22	0	0	1.000
1998— New York (A.L.)	C	3	8	2	2	0	0	0	0	.250	1	0	0	22	1	0	1.000
1999— New York (A.L.)	C	3	8	0	2	0	0	0	0	.250	0	2	0	20	1	0	1.000
Championship series totals (4 years)		14	38	4	8	0	1	0	0	.211	3	7	0	84	2	0	1.000

WORLD SERIES RECORD

NOTES: Member of World Series championship team (1996, 1998 and 1999).

							BATTING							FIELDING			
Year	Team (League)	Pos.	G	AB	R	H	2B	3B	HR	RBI	Avg.	BB	SO	SB	PO	A	E	Avg.
1996— New York (A.L.)	C	4	10	1	2	0	1	0	1	.200	1	2	0	23	4	0	1.000
1998— New York (A.L.)	C	2	6	0	0	0	0	0	0	.000	0	2	0	9	2	0	1.000
1999— New York (A.L.)	C	2	7	1	2	0	0	0	0	.286	0	1	0	9	2	0	1.000
World Series totals (3 years)		8	23	2	4	0	1	0	1	.174	1	5	0	41	8	0	1.000

G

PERSONAL: Born January 4, 1978, in Tacoma, Wash. ... 6-5/200. ... Throws right, bats right. ... Full name: Christopher Odell Gissell.
HIGH SCHOOL: Hudson's Bay (Vancouver, Wash.).
TRANSACTIONS/CAREER NOTES: Selected by Chicago Cubs organization in fourth round of free-draft (June 4, 1996). ... On West Tenn disabled list (July 29, 1999-remainder of season).

Year	League	W	L	Pct.	ERA	G	GS	CG	ShO	Sv.	IP	H	R	ER	BB	SO
1996— Gulf Coast Cubs (GCL)	4	2	.667	2.35	11	10	0	0	0	61 1/3	54	23	16	8	64
1997— Rockford (Midw.)	6	11	.353	4.45	26	24	3	1	0	143 2/3	155	89	71	62	105
1998— Rockford (Midw.)	3	0	1.000	0.80	5	5	0	0	0	33 2/3	27	8	3	15	23
— Daytona (FSL)	7	6	.538	4.17	22	21	1	0	0	136	149	80	63	38	123
— West Tenn (Sou.)	0	1	.000	13.50	1	1	0	0	0	4	5	7	6	4	4
1999— West Tenn (Sou.)	3	8	.273	5.99	20	18	0	0	0	97 2/3	121	76	65	62	57

GLANVILLE, DOUG   OF   PHILLIES

PERSONAL: Born August 25, 1970, in Hackensack, N.J. ... 6-2/172. ... Bats right, throws right. ... Full name: Douglas Metunwa Glanville.
HIGH SCHOOL: Teaneck (N.J.).
COLLEGE: Pennsylvania (degree in science and engineering).
TRANSACTIONS/CAREER NOTES: Selected by Chicago Cubs organization in first round (12th pick overall) of free-agent draft (June 3, 1991). ... Traded by Cubs to Philadelphia Phillies for 2B Mickey Morandini (December 23, 1997).
STATISTICAL NOTES: Led Carolina League outfielders with 312 total chances in 1992. ... Led Southern League in caught stealing with 20 in 1994. ... Led Southern League outfielders with 339 total chances in 1994. ... Had 18-game hitting streak (May 1-20, 1998). ... Had 17-game hitting streak (May 30-June 17, 1998).

| | | | | | | | | BATTING | | | | | | FIELDING | | |
Year Team (League)	Pos.	G	AB	R	H	2B	3B	HR	RBI	Avg.	BB	SO	SB	PO	A	E	Avg.
1991—Geneva (NY-P)	OF	36	152	29	46	8	0	2	12	.303	11	25	17	77	4	0	1.000
1992—Win.-Salem (Car.)	OF	120	485	72	125	18	4	4	36	.258	40	78	32	*293	12	7	.978
1993—Daytona (FSL)	OF	61	239	47	70	10	1	2	21	.293	28	24	18	123	11	7	.950
—Orlando (Sou.)	OF	73	296	42	78	14	4	9	40	.264	12	41	15	168	8	5	.972
1994—Orlando (Sou.)	OF	130	483	53	127	22	2	5	52	.263	24	49	26	*322	14	3	.991
1995—Iowa (A.A.)	OF-DH	112	419	48	113	16	2	4	37	.270	16	64	13	209	9	4	.982
1996—Iowa (A.A.)	OF-DH	90	373	53	115	23	3	3	34	.308	12	35	15	217	6	3	.987
—Chicago (N.L.)	OF	49	83	10	20	5	1	1	10	.241	3	11	2	35	1	1	.973
1997—Chicago (N.L.)	OF	146	474	79	142	22	5	4	35	.300	24	46	19	247	12	3	.989
1998—Philadelphia (N.L.)■	OF	158	*678	106	189	28	7	8	49	.279	42	89	23	360	14	2	.995
1999—Philadelphia (N.L.)	OF	150	628	101	204	38	6	11	73	.325	48	82	34	385	13	8	.980
Major League totals (4 years)		503	1863	296	555	93	19	24	167	.298	117	228	78	1027	40	14	.987

GLAUS, TROY   3B   ANGELS

PERSONAL: Born August 3, 1976, in Tarzana, Calif. ... 6-5/229. ... Bats right, throws right. ... Full name: Troy Edward Glaus. ... Name pronounced GLOSS.
HIGH SCHOOL: Carlsbad (Calif.).
COLLEGE: UCLA.
TRANSACTIONS/CAREER NOTES: Selected by San Diego Padres organization in second round of free-agent draft (June 2, 1994); did not sign. ... Selected by Anaheim Angels organization in first round (third pick overall) of free-agent draft (June 3, 1997).
MISCELLANEOUS: Member of 1996 U.S. Olympic baseball team.

| | | | | | | | | BATTING | | | | | | FIELDING | | |
Year Team (League)	Pos.	G	AB	R	H	2B	3B	HR	RBI	Avg.	BB	SO	SB	PO	A	E	Avg.
1998—Midland (Texas)	3B	50	188	51	58	11	2	19	51	.309	39	41	4	34	101	11	.925
—Vancouver (PCL)	3B	59	219	33	67	16	0	16	42	.306	21	55	3	46	131	13	.932
—Anaheim (A.L.)	3B	48	165	19	36	9	0	1	23	.218	15	51	1	27	85	7	.941
1999—Anaheim (A.L.)	3B-DH	154	551	85	132	29	0	29	79	.240	71	143	5	114	277	19	.954
Major League totals (2 years)		202	716	104	168	38	0	30	102	.235	86	194	6	141	362	26	.951

GLAVINE, TOM   P   BRAVES

PERSONAL: Born March 25, 1966, in Concord, Mass. ... 6-0/185. ... Throws left, bats left. ... Full name: Thomas Michael Glavine. ... Brother of Mike Glavine, first baseman, Atlanta Braves organization. ... Name pronounced GLAV-in.
HIGH SCHOOL: Billerica (Mass.).
TRANSACTIONS/CAREER NOTES: Selected by Atlanta Braves organization in second round of free-agent draft (June 4, 1984).
HONORS: Named N.L. Pitcher of the Year by The Sporting News (1991). ... Named lefthanded pitcher on The Sporting News N.L. All-Star team (1991-92 and 1998). ... Named pitcher on The Sporting News N.L. Silver Slugger team (1991, 1995, 1996 and 1998). ... Named N.L. Cy Young Award winner by Baseball Writers' Association of America (1991 and 1998).
STATISTICAL NOTES: Led Gulf Coast League with 12 wild pitches in 1984. ... Led N.L. pitchers with 59 assists in 1999. ... Tied for N.L. lead in double plays by a pitcher with six in 1999.
MISCELLANEOUS: Selected by Los Angeles Kings in fourth round (69th pick overall) of NHL entry draft (June 9, 1984). ... Appeared in eight games as pinch runner (1988). ... Appeared in one game as pinch runner (1989). ... Appeared in one game as pinch runner (1990). ... Received a base on balls and scored once in one game as pinch hitter and appeared in one game as pinch runner (1991). ... Singled and struck out in two appearances as pinch hitter (1992). ... Struck out in only appearance as pinch hitter (1994). ... Singled and struck out in three appearances as pinch hitter (1996). ... Had a sacrifice hit in only appearance as pinch hitter (1999).

Year League	W	L	Pct.	ERA	G	GS	CG	ShO	Sv.	IP	H	R	ER	BB	SO
1984—Gulf Coast Braves (GCL)	2	3	.400	3.34	8	7	0	0	0	32 1/3	29	17	12	13	34
1985—Sumter (SAL)	9	6	.600	*2.35	26	26	2	1	0	168 2/3	114	58	44	73	174
1986—Greenville (Sou.)	11	6	.647	3.41	22	22	2	1	0	145 1/3	129	62	55	70	114
—Richmond (I.L.)	1	5	.167	5.63	7	7	1	1	0	40	40	29	25	27	12
1987—Richmond (I.L.)	6	12	.333	3.35	22	22	4	1	0	150 1/3	142	70	56	56	91
—Atlanta (N.L.)	2	4	.333	5.54	9	9	0	0	0	50 1/3	55	34	31	33	20
1988—Atlanta (N.L.)	7	*17	.292	4.56	34	34	1	0	0	195 1/3	201	111	99	63	84
1989—Atlanta (N.L.)	14	8	.636	3.68	29	29	6	4	0	186	172	88	76	40	90
1990—Atlanta (N.L.)	10	12	.455	4.28	33	33	1	0	0	214 1/3	232	111	102	78	129
1991—Atlanta (N.L.)	•20	11	.645	2.55	34	34	•9	1	0	246 2/3	201	83	70	69	192
1992—Atlanta (N.L.)	•20	8	.714	2.76	33	33	7	•5	0	225	197	81	69	70	129
1993—Atlanta (N.L.)	•22	6	.786	3.20	36	•36	4	2	0	239 1/3	236	91	85	90	120
1994—Atlanta (N.L.)	13	9	.591	3.97	25	25	2	0	0	165 1/3	173	76	73	70	140
1995—Atlanta (N.L.)	16	7	.696	3.08	29	29	3	1	0	198 2/3	182	76	68	66	127
1996—Atlanta (N.L.)	15	10	.600	2.98	36	*36	1	0	0	235 1/3	222	91	78	85	181
1997—Atlanta (N.L.)	14	7	.667	2.96	33	33	5	2	0	240	197	86	79	79	152
1998—Atlanta (N.L.)	*20	6	.769	2.47	33	33	4	3	0	229 1/3	202	67	63	74	157
1999—Atlanta (N.L.)	14	11	.560	4.12	35	•35	2	0	0	234	*259	115	107	83	138
Major League totals (13 years)	187	116	.617	3.38	399	399	45	18	0	2659 2/3	2529	1110	1000	900	1659

G

DIVISION SERIES RECORD

RECORDS: Holds N.L. career record for most bases on balls allowed—13.

Year League	W	L	Pct.	ERA	G	GS	CG	ShO	Sv.	IP	H	R	ER	BB	SO
1995—Atlanta (N.L.)	0	0	...	2.57	1	1	0	0	0	7	5	3	2	1	3
1996—Atlanta (N.L.)	1	0	1.000	1.35	1	1	0	0	0	6 2/3	5	1	1	3	7
1997—Atlanta (N.L.)	1	0	1.000	4.50	1	1	0	0	0	6	5	3	3	5	4
1998—Atlanta (N.L.)	0	0	...	1.29	1	1	0	0	0	7	3	1	1	1	8
1999—Atlanta (N.L.)	0	0	...	3.00	1	1	0	0	0	6	5	2	2	3	6
Division series totals (5 years)	2	0	1.000	2.48	5	5	0	0	0	32 2/3	23	10	9	13	28

CHAMPIONSHIP SERIES RECORD

RECORDS: Holds career record for most losses—8; earned runs allowed—32; and hit batsmen—5. ... Holds single-inning records for most runs allowed—8 (October 13, 1992, second inning); and most earned runs allowed—7 (October 13, 1992, second inning). ... Shares career records for most games started—13; and hits allowed—81. ... Shares single-game record for most earned runs allowed—7 (October 13, 1992 and October 14, 1997). ... Shares single-inning record for most hits allowed—6 (October 13, 1992, second inning). ... Shares N.L. career record for most series with one team—8 (Atlanta, 1991-93 and 1995-99). ... Shares N.L. single-series record for most hit batsmen—2 (1992).

NOTES: Received a base on balls in only appearance as pinch hitter (1998).

Year League	W	L	Pct.	ERA	G	GS	CG	ShO	Sv.	IP	H	R	ER	BB	SO
1991—Atlanta (N.L.)	0	2	.000	3.21	2	2	0	0	0	14	12	5	5	6	11
1992—Atlanta (N.L.)	0	2	.000	12.27	2	2	0	0	0	7 1/3	13	11	10	3	2
1993—Atlanta (N.L.)	1	0	1.000	2.57	1	1	0	0	0	7	6	2	2	0	5
1995—Atlanta (N.L.)	0	0	...	1.29	1	1	0	0	0	7	7	1	1	2	5
1996—Atlanta (N.L.)	1	1	.500	2.08	2	2	0	0	0	13	10	3	3	0	9
1997—Atlanta (N.L.)	1	1	.500	5.40	2	2	0	0	0	13 1/3	13	8	8	11	9
1998—Atlanta (N.L.)	0	2	.000	2.31	2	2	0	0	0	11 2/3	13	6	3	9	8
1999—Atlanta (N.L.)	1	0	1.000	0.00	1	1	0	0	0	7	7	0	0	1	8
Champ. series totals (8 years)	4	8	.333	3.59	13	13	0	0	0	80 1/3	81	36	32	32	57

WORLD SERIES RECORD

RECORDS: Shares single-inning records for most bases on balls allowed—4 (October 24, 1991, sixth inning); and most consecutive bases on balls allowed—3 (October 24, 1991, sixth inning).

NOTES: Named Most Valuable Player (1995). ... Member of World Series championship team (1995).

Year League	W	L	Pct.	ERA	G	GS	CG	ShO	Sv.	IP	H	R	ER	BB	SO
1991—Atlanta (N.L.)	1	1	.500	2.70	2	2	1	0	0	13 1/3	8	6	4	7	8
1992—Atlanta (N.L.)	1	1	.500	1.59	2	2	2	0	0	17	10	3	3	4	8
1995—Atlanta (N.L.)	2	0	1.000	1.29	2	2	0	0	0	14	4	2	2	6	11
1996—Atlanta (N.L.)	0	1	.000	1.29	1	1	0	0	0	7	4	2	1	3	8
1999—Atlanta (N.L.)	0	0	...	5.14	1	1	0	0	0	7	7	5	4	0	3
World Series totals (5 years)	4	3	.571	2.16	8	8	3	0	0	58 1/3	33	18	14	20	38

ALL-STAR GAME RECORD

RECORDS: Holds single-game record for most hits allowed—9 (July 14, 1992). ... Holds single-inning record for most hits allowed—7 (July 14, 1992, first inning).

Year League	W	L	Pct.	ERA	GS	CG	ShO	Sv.	IP	H	R	ER	BB	SO
1991—National	0	0	...	0.00	1	0	0	0	2	1	0	0	1	3
1992—National	0	1	.000	27.00	1	0	0	0	1 2/3	9	5	5	0	2
1993—National						Did not play.								
1996—National	0	0	...	0.00	0	0	0	0	1	0	0	0	0	1
1997—National						Did not play.								
1998—National	0	0	...	27.00	0	0	0	0	1 1/3	5	4	4	3	0
All-Star Game totals (4 years)	0	1	.000	13.50	2	0	0	0	6	15	9	9	4	6

GLOVER, GARY — P — BLUE JAYS

PERSONAL: Born December 3, 1976, in Cleveland. ... 6-5/205. ... Throws right, bats right. ... Full name: John Gary Glover.

HIGH SCHOOL: Deland (Fla.).

TRANSACTIONS/CAREER NOTES: Selected by Toronto Blue Jays organization in 15th round of free-agent draft (June 2, 1994). ... On disabled list (August 10-September 8, 1994).

Year League	W	L	Pct.	ERA	G	GS	CG	ShO	Sv.	IP	H	R	ER	BB	SO
1994—GC Blue Jays (GCL)	0	0	...	47.25	2	0	0	0	0	1 1/3	4	8	7	4	2
1995—GC Blue Jays (GCL)	3	7	.300	4.91	12	10	2	0	0	62 1/3	62	48	34	26	46
1996—Medicine Hat (Pio.)	3	*12	.200	7.75	15	•15	*2	0	0	83 2/3	*119	*94	72	29	54
1997—Hagerstown (SAL)	6	*17	.261	3.73	28	28	3	0	0	173 2/3	165	94	72	58	155
1998—Knoxville (Sou.)	0	5	.000	6.75	8	8	0	0	0	37 1/3	41	36	28	28	14
—Dunedin (FSL)	7	6	.538	4.28	19	18	0	0	0	109 1/3	117	66	52	36	88
1999—Knoxville (Sou.)	8	2	.800	3.56	13	13	1	0	0	86	70	39	34	27	77
—Syracuse (I.L.)	4	6	.400	5.19	14	14	0	0	0	76 1/3	93	50	44	35	57
—Toronto (A.L.)	0	0	...	0.00	1	0	0	0	0	1	0	0	0	1	0
Major League totals (1 year)	0	0	...	0.00	1	0	0	0	0	1	0	0	0	1	0

GLYNN, RYAN — P — RANGERS

G

PERSONAL: Born November 1, 1974, in Portsmouth, Va. ... 6-3/195. ... Throws right, bats right. ... Full name: Ryan David Glynn.

HIGH SCHOOL: Churchland (Portsmouth, Va.).

COLLEGE: Virginia Military Institute.

TRANSACTIONS/CAREER NOTES: Selected by Texas Rangers organization in fourth round of free-agent draft (June 1, 1995).

Year League	W	L	Pct.	ERA	G	GS	CG	ShO	Sv.	IP	H	R	ER	BB	SO
1995—Hudson Valley (NY-P)	3	3	.500	4.70	9	8	0	0	0	44	56	27	23	16	21
1996—Charleston, S.C. (SAL)	8	7	.533	4.54	19	19	2	1	0	121	118	70	61	59	72
1997—Charlotte (FSL)	8	7	.533	4.97	23	22	5	1	1	134	148	81	74	44	96
—Tulsa (Texas)	1	1	.500	3.38	3	3	0	0	0	21 1/3	21	9	8	10	18
1998—Tulsa (Texas)	9	6	.600	3.44	26	24	4	1	0	157	140	66	60	64	111
1999—Oklahoma (PCL)	6	2	.750	3.39	16	16	2	1	0	90 1/3	81	46	34	36	55
—Texas (A.L.)	2	4	.333	7.24	13	10	0	0	0	54 2/3	71	46	44	35	39
Major League totals (1 year)	2	4	.333	7.24	13	10	0	0	0	54 2/3	71	46	44	35	39

GOMES, WAYNE P PHILLIES

PERSONAL: Born January 15, 1973, in Hampton, Va. ... 6-2/227. ... Throws right, bats right. ... Full name: Wayne Maurice Gomes.
HIGH SCHOOL: Phoebus (Hampton, Va.).
COLLEGE: Old Dominion.
TRANSACTIONS/CAREER NOTES: Selected by Philadelphia Phillies organization in first round (fourth pick overall) of free-agent draft (June 3, 1993). ... On disabled list (May 12-June 23, 1995).
STATISTICAL NOTES: Led Florida State League with 27 wild pitches in 1994. ... Tied for Eastern League lead with six balks in 1995.

Year League	W	L	Pct.	ERA	G	GS	CG	ShO	Sv.	IP	H	R	ER	BB	SO
1993— Batavia (NY-P)	1	0	1.000	1.23	5	0	0	0	0	7 1/3	1	1	1	8	11
— Clearwater (FSL)	0	0	...	1.17	9	0	0	0	4	7 2/3	4	1	1	9	13
1994— Clearwater (FSL)	6	8	.429	4.74	23	21	1	1	0	104 1/3	85	63	55	82	102
1995— Reading (East.)	7	4	.636	3.96	22	22	1	1	0	104 2/3	89	54	46	70	102
1996— Reading (East.)	0	4	.000	4.48	*67	0	0	0	24	64 1/3	53	35	32	48	79
1997— Scranton/W.B. (I.L.)	3	1	.750	2.37	26	0	0	0	7	38	31	11	10	24	36
— Philadelphia (N.L.)	5	1	.833	5.27	37	0	0	0	0	42 2/3	45	26	25	24	24
1998— Philadelphia (N.L.)	9	6	.600	4.24	71	0	0	0	1	93 1/3	94	48	44	35	86
1999— Philadelphia (N.L.)	5	5	.500	4.26	73	0	0	0	19	74	70	38	35	56	58
Major League totals (3 years)	19	12	.613	4.46	181	0	0	0	20	210	209	112	104	115	168

GOMEZ, CHRIS SS PADRES

PERSONAL: Born June 16, 1971, in Los Angeles. ... 6-1/195. ... Bats right, throws right. ... Full name: Christopher Cory Gomez.
HIGH SCHOOL: Lakewood (Calif.).
COLLEGE: Loyola Marymount, then Long Beach State.
TRANSACTIONS/CAREER NOTES: Selected by California Angels organization in 37th round of free-agent draft (June 5, 1989); did not sign. ... Selected by Detroit Tigers organization in third round of free-agent draft (June 1, 1992). ... Traded by Tigers with C John Flaherty to San Diego Padres for C Brad Ausmus, SS Andujar Cedeno and P Russ Spear (June 18, 1996). ... On San Diego disabled list (June 2-July 31, 1999); included rehabilitation assignment to Las Vegas (July 15-30).

Year Team (League)	Pos.	G	AB	R	H	2B	3B	HR	RBI	Avg.	BB	SO	SB	PO	A	E	Avg.
1992— London (East.)	SS	64	220	20	59	13	2	1	19	.268	20	34	1	100	174	14	.951
1993— Toledo (I.L.)	SS	87	277	29	68	12	2	0	20	.245	23	37	6	133	261	16	.961
— Detroit (A.L.)	SS-2B-DH	46	128	11	32	7	1	0	11	.250	9	17	2	69	118	5	.974
1994— Detroit (A.L.)	SS-2B	84	296	32	76	19	0	8	53	.257	33	64	5	140	210	8	.978
1995— Detroit (A.L.)	SS-2B-DH	123	431	49	96	20	2	11	50	.223	41	96	4	210	361	15	.974
1996— Detroit (A.L.)	SS	48	128	21	31	5	0	1	16	.242	18	20	1	77	114	6	.970
— San Diego (N.L.)■	SS	89	328	32	86	16	1	3	29	.262	39	64	2	124	261	13	.967
1997— San Diego (N.L.)	SS	150	522	62	132	19	2	5	54	.253	53	114	5	226	433	15	.978
1998— San Diego (N.L.)	SS	145	449	55	120	32	3	4	39	.267	51	87	1	180	397	12	*.980
1999— San Diego (N.L.)	SS	76	234	20	59	8	1	1	15	.252	27	49	1	101	195	12	.961
— Las Vegas (PCL)	SS	10	27	3	9	1	0	0	4	.333	2	6	0	8	20	2	.933
American League totals (4 years)		301	983	113	235	51	3	20	130	.239	101	197	12	496	803	34	.974
National League totals (4 years)		460	1533	169	397	75	7	13	137	.259	170	314	9	631	1286	52	.974
Major League totals (7 years)		761	2516	282	632	126	10	33	267	.251	271	511	21	1127	2089	86	.974

DIVISION SERIES RECORD

Year Team (League)	Pos.	G	AB	R	H	2B	3B	HR	RBI	Avg.	BB	SO	SB	PO	A	E	Avg.
1996— San Diego (N.L.)	SS	3	12	0	2	0	0	0	1	.167	0	4	0	8	5	0	1.000
1998— San Diego (N.L.)	SS	4	11	1	3	0	0	0	0	.273	4	1	0	6	9	1	.938
Division series totals (2 years)		7	23	1	5	0	0	0	1	.217	4	5	0	14	14	1	.966

CHAMPIONSHIP SERIES RECORD

Year Team (League)	Pos.	G	AB	R	H	2B	3B	HR	RBI	Avg.	BB	SO	SB	PO	A	E	Avg.
1998— San Diego (N.L.)	SS	6	20	2	3	1	0	0	0	.150	2	5	0	5	14	1	.950

WORLD SERIES RECORD

Year Team (League)	Pos.	G	AB	R	H	2B	3B	HR	RBI	Avg.	BB	SO	SB	PO	A	E	Avg.
1998— San Diego (N.L.)	SS	4	11	2	4	0	1	0	0	.364	1	1	0	5	9	0	1.000

GONZALEZ, ALEX SS BLUE JAYS

PERSONAL: Born April 8, 1973, in Miami. ... 6-0/200. ... Bats right, throws right. ... Full name: Alexander Scott Gonzalez.
HIGH SCHOOL: Miami Killian.
TRANSACTIONS/CAREER NOTES: Selected by Toronto Blue Jays organization in 14th round of free-agent draft (June 3, 1991). ... On Toronto disabled list (April 29-May 27, 1994); included rehabilitation assignment to Syracuse (May 14-27). ... On disabled list (August 13-September 14, 1997). ... On disabled list (May 17, 1999-remainder of season).
RECORDS: Shares major league single-game record for most strikeouts—6 (September 9, 1998, 13 innings). ... Shares A.L. record for most assists by shortstop (nine-inning game)—13 (1996).
STATISTICAL NOTES: Led Gulf Coast League shortstops with 247 total chances in 1991. ... Led Southern League with 253 total bases in 1993. ... Led Southern League shortstops with 682 total chances and 92 double plays in 1993. ... Led International League shortstops with 542 total chances in 1994. ... Led A.L. shortstops with 765 total chances and 122 double plays in 1996.

G

Year	Team (League)	Pos.	G	AB	R	H	2B	3B	HR	RBI	Avg.	BB	SO	SB	PO	A	E	Avg.
1991—GC Blue Jays (GCL)....		SS	53	191	29	40	5	4	0	10	.209	12	41	7	66	*160	21	.915
1992—Myrtle Beach (SAL)....		SS	134	535	83	145	22	9	10	62	.271	38	119	26	*248	*406	48	.932
1993—Knoxville (SAL)		SS	*142	561	*93	162	29	7	16	69	.289	39	110	38	*224	*428	30	*.956
1994—Toronto (A.L.)............		SS	15	53	7	8	3	1	0	1	.151	4	17	3	18	49	6	.918
—Syracuse (I.L.)..........		SS-DH	110	437	69	124	22	4	12	57	.284	53	92	23	*163	*348	*31	.943
1995—Toronto (A.L.)............		SS-3B-DH	111	367	51	89	19	4	10	42	.243	44	114	4	164	227	19	.954
1996—Toronto (A.L.)............		SS	147	527	64	124	30	5	14	64	.235	45	127	16	279	465	21	.973
1997—Toronto (A.L.)............		SS	126	426	46	102	23	2	12	35	.239	34	94	15	209	341	8	*.986
1998—Toronto (A.L.)............		SS	158	568	70	136	28	1	13	51	.239	28	121	21	259	427	17	.976
1999—Toronto (A.L.)............		SS-DH	38	154	22	45	13	0	2	12	.292	16	23	4	69	132	4	.980
Major League totals (6 years)			595	2095	260	504	116	13	51	205	.241	171	496	63	998	1641	75	.972

GONZALEZ, ALEX   SS   MARLINS

PERSONAL: Born February 15, 1977, in Cagua, Venezuela. ... 6-0/170. ... Bats right, throws right. ... Full name: Alexander Gonzalez.
HIGH SCHOOL: Liceo Ramon Bastidas (Venezuela).
TRANSACTIONS/CAREER NOTES: Signed as non-drafted free agent by Florida Marlins organization (April 18, 1994). ... On Kane County disabled list (April 5-August 17, 1996). ... On Portland disabled list (September 7, 1996-remainder of season).

Year	Team (League)	Pos.	G	AB	R	H	2B	3B	HR	RBI	Avg.	BB	SO	SB	PO	A	E	Avg.
1994—Dom. Marlins (DSL) ...		SS	54	239	30	54	7	3	3	31	.226	15	36	4	140	222	34	.914
1995—GC Marlins (GCL)		SS	53	187	30	55	7	4	2	30	.294	19	27	11	65	168	17	.932
—Brev. County (FSL)		SS	17	59	6	12	2	1	0	8	.203	1	14	1	26	51	8	.906
1996—Portland (East.)		SS	11	34	4	8	0	1	0	1	.235	2	10	0	17	38	7	.887
—Kane Co. (Midw.)		SS	4	10	2	2	0	0	0	0	.200	2	4	0	2	10	0	1.000
—GC Marlins (GCL)		SS	10	41	6	16	3	0	0	6	.390	2	4	1	14	30	5	.898
1997—Portland (East.)		SS	133	449	69	114	16	4	19	65	.254	27	83	4	192	423	*37	.943
1998—Charlotte (I.L.)............		SS	108	422	71	117	20	10	10	51	.277	28	80	4	161	322	20	.960
—Florida (N.L.).............		SS	25	86	11	13	2	0	3	7	.151	9	30	1	29	58	2	.978
1999—Florida (N.L.).............		SS	136	560	81	155	28	4	14	59	.277	15	113	3	237	339	27	.955
Major League totals (2 years)			161	646	92	168	30	8	17	66	.260	24	143	3	266	397	29	.958

ALL-STAR GAME RECORD

Year	League	Pos.	AB	R	H	2B	3B	HR	RBI	Avg.	BB	SO	SB	PO	A	E	Avg.
1999—National		PH-SS	1	0	0	0	0	0	0	.000	0	0	0	1	0	0	1.000

GONZALEZ, DICKY   P   METS

PERSONAL: Born October 21, 1978, in Bayamon, Puerto Rico. ... 5-11/170. ... Throws right, bats right. ... Full name: Dicky Angel Gonzalez.
HIGH SCHOOL: Puig (Puerto Rico).
TRANSACTIONS/CAREER NOTES: Selected by New York Mets organization in 16th round of free-agent draft (June 4, 1996).

Year	League	W	L	Pct.	ERA	G	GS	CG	ShO	Sv.	IP	H	R	ER	BB	SO
1996—Gulf Coast Mets (GCL)		4	2	.667	2.66	11	8	2	1	0	47 1/3	50	19	14	3	51
—Little Falls (NY-P)		1	0	1.000	1.80	1	1	0	0	0	5	4	2	1	0	7
1997—Capital City (SAL)		1	4	.200	4.94	10	7	1	0	0	47 1/3	50	28	26	15	49
—Little Falls (NY-P)		3	6	.333	4.36	12	12	1	0	0	66	70	38	32	10	76
1998—St. Lucie (FSL)		2	1	.667	3.09	8	8	0	0	0	46 2/3	46	22	16	13	23
—Capital City (SAL)		10	3	.769	3.31	18	18	1	0	0	111 1/3	104	57	41	14	107
1999—St. Lucie (FSL)		14	9	.609	2.83	25	25	3	0	0	168 2/3	156	66	53	30	143
—Norfolk (I.L.)		0	1	.000	2.70	1	1	0	0	0	6 2/3	5	2	2	1	3

GONZALEZ, JEREMI   P   CUBS

PERSONAL: Born January 8, 1975, in Maracaibo, Venezuela. ... 6-2/215. ... Throws right, bats right. ... Full name: Geremis Segundo Acosta Gonzalez.
HIGH SCHOOL: Colegro La Chinita (Maracaibo, Venezuela).
TRANSACTIONS/CAREER NOTES: Signed as non-drafted free agent by Chicago Cubs organization (October 21, 1991). ... On disabled list (July 6-August 10, 1996). ... On disabled list (July 25, 1998-remainder of season). ... On Chicago disabled list (April 1, 1999-entire season); included rehabilitation assignments to Dayton (April 16-22), West Tenn (April 26-May 8) and Iowa (May 12-18 and May 29-31).
STATISTICAL NOTES: Led Arizona League with 10 hit batsmen in 1992.
MISCELLANEOUS: Appeared in one game as pinch runner (1998).

Year	League	W	L	Pct.	ERA	G	GS	CG	ShO	Sv.	IP	H	R	ER	BB	SO
1992—Arizona Cubs (Ariz.)		0	5	.000	7.80	14	7	0	0	0	45	65	59	39	22	39
1993—Huntington (Appl.)		3	9	.250	6.25	12	12	1	0	0	67 2/3	82	59	47	38	42
1994—Peoria (Midw.)		1	7	.125	5.55	13	13	1	0	0	71 1/3	86	53	44	32	39
—Williamsport (NY-P)		4	6	.400	4.24	16	12	1	1	0	80 2/3	83	46	38	29	64
1995—Rockford (Midw.)		4	4	.500	5.10	12	12	1	0	0	65 1/3	63	43	37	28	36
—Daytona (FSL)		5	1	.833	1.22	19	2	0	0	4	44 1/3	34	15	6	13	30
1996—Orlando (Sou.)		6	3	.667	3.34	17	14	0	0	0	97	95	39	36	28	85
1997—Iowa (A.A.)		2	2	.500	3.48	10	10	1	1	0	62	47	27	24	21	58
—Chicago (N.L.)		11	9	.550	4.25	23	23	1	1	0	144	126	73	68	69	93
1998—Chicago (N.L.)		7	7	.500	5.32	20	20	1	1	0	110	124	72	65	41	70
1999—Daytona (FSL)		0	0	...	0.00	2	2	0	0	0	4 2/3	2	0	0	0	4
—West Tenn (Sou.)		0	0	...	1.74	3	3	0	0	0	10 1/3	7	2	2	9	12
—Iowa (PCL)		0	1	.000	4.50	3	3	0	0	0	10	10	8	5	6	10
Major League totals (2 years)		18	16	.529	4.71	43	43	2	2	0	254	250	145	133	110	163

G

PERSONAL: Born October 16, 1969, in Vega Baja, Puerto Rico. ... 6-3/220. ... Bats right, throws right. ... Full name: Juan Alberto Vazquez Gonzalez.

HIGH SCHOOL: Vega Baja (Puerto Rico).

TRANSACTIONS/CAREER NOTES: Signed as non-drafted free agent by Texas Rangers organization (May 30, 1986). ... On disabled list (April 27-June 17, 1988; March 30-April 26, 1991; April 16-June 1 and July 27-August 16, 1995; May 8-June 1, 1996; and March 24-May 2, 1997). ... Traded by Rangers with P Danny Patterson and C Gregg Zaun to Detroit Tigers for P Justin Thompson, P Francisco Cordero, OF Gabe Kapler, C Bill Haselman, 2B Frank Catalanotto and P Alan Webb (November 2, 1999).

RECORDS: Shares major league single-game record for most sacrifice flies—3 (July 3, 1999). ... Holds A.L. single-season record for most major league ballparks, one or more home runs—16 (1999).

HONORS: Named American Association Most Valuable Player (1990). ... Named outfielder on THE SPORTING NEWS A.L. Silver Slugger team (1992-93 and 1996-98). ... Named outfielder on THE SPORTING NEWS A.L. All-Star team (1993, 1996 and 1998). ... Named A.L. Most Valuable Player by Baseball Writers' Association of America (1996 and 1998).

STATISTICAL NOTES: Led Texas League with 254 total bases in 1989. ... Led American Association with 252 total bases in 1990. ... Hit three home runs in one game (June 7, 1992; August 28, 1993; and September 24, 1999). ... Led A.L. with .632 slugging percentage in 1993. ... Had 21-game hitting streaks (June 25-July 19 and August 8-31, 1996). ... Had 20-game hitting streak (August 20-September 9, 1998). ... Career major league grand slams: 7.

MISCELLANEOUS: Holds Texas Rangers all-time records for most runs (791), hits (1,421), doubles (282), home runs (340 and runs batted in (1,075).

Year Team (League)	Pos.	G	AB	R	H	2B	3B	HR	RBI	Avg.	BB	SO	SB	PO	A	E	Avg.
1986— GC Rangers (GCL)......	OF	60	*233	24	56	4	1	0	36	.240	21	57	7	89	6	•6	.941
1987— Gastonia (SAL).........	OF	127	509	69	135	21	2	14	74	.265	30	92	9	234	10	12	.953
1988— Charlotte (FSL)..........	OF	77	277	25	71	14	3	8	43	.256	25	64	5	139	5	4	.973
1989— Tulsa (Texas).............	OF	133	502	73	147	30	7	21	85	.293	31	98	1	292	15	9	.972
— Texas (A.L.)................	OF	24	60	6	9	3	0	1	7	.150	6	17	0	53	0	2	.964
1990— Okla. City (A.A.).........	OF	128	496	78	128	29	4	*29	*101	.258	32	109	2	220	7	8	.966
— Texas (A.L.)................	OF-DH	25	90	11	26	7	1	4	12	.289	2	18	0	33	0	0	1.000
1991— Texas (A.L.)................	OF-DH	142	545	78	144	34	1	27	102	.264	42	118	4	310	6	6	.981
1992— Texas (A.L.)................	OF-DH	155	584	77	152	24	2	*43	109	.260	35	143	0	379	9	10	.975
1993— Texas (A.L.)................	OF-DH	140	536	105	166	33	1	*46	118	.310	37	99	4	265	5	4	.985
1994— Texas (A.L.)................	OF	107	422	57	116	18	4	19	85	.275	30	66	6	223	9	2	.991
1995— Texas (A.L.)................	DH-OF	90	352	57	104	20	2	27	82	.295	17	66	0	6	1	0	1.000
1996— Texas (A.L.)................	OF-DH	134	541	89	170	33	2	47	144	.314	45	82	2	163	6	6	.988
1997— Texas (A.L.)................	DH-OF	133	533	87	158	24	3	42	131	.296	33	107	0	128	6	4	.971
1998— Texas (A.L.)................	OF-DH	154	606	110	193	*50	2	45	*157	.318	46	126	2	213	8	4	.982
1999— Texas (A.L.)................	OF-DH	144	562	114	183	36	1	39	128	.326	51	105	3	223	7	4	.983
Major League totals (11 years)		1248	4831	791	1421	282	19	340	1075	.294	344	947	21	1996	57	38	.982

DIVISION SERIES RECORD

RECORDS: Shares single-series record for most home runs—5 (1996). ... Shares single-game record for most home runs—2 (October 2, 1996).

NOTES: Shares postseason single-series record for most home runs—5 (1996).

Year Team (League)	Pos.	G	AB	R	H	2B	3B	HR	RBI	Avg.	BB	SO	SB	PO	A	E	Avg.
1996— Texas (A.L.)	OF	4	16	5	7	0	0	5	9	.438	4	2	0	8	0	0	1.000
1998— Texas (A.L.)	OF	3	12	1	1	1	0	0	0	.083	0	3	0	8	0	0	1.000
1999— Texas (A.L.)	OF	3	11	1	2	0	0	1	1	.182	1	3	0	5	0	0	1.000
Division series totals (3 years)		10	39	7	10	1	0	6	10	.256	5	8	0	21	0	0	1.000

ALL-STAR GAME RECORD

Year League	Pos.	AB	R	H	2B	3B	HR	RBI	Avg.	BB	SO	SB	PO	A	E	Avg.
1993— American	OF	1	0	0	0	0	0	0	.000	1	1	0	1	0	0	1.000
1998— American	OF	3	0	0	0	0	0	1	.000	0	1	0	0	0	0	...
All-Star Game totals (2 years)		4	0	0	0	0	0	1	.000	1	2	0	1	0	0	1.000

PERSONAL: Born May 25, 1976, in San Cristobal, Dominican Republic. ... 6-4/228. ... Throws right, bats right. ... Full name: Lariel Alfonso Gonzalez.

TRANSACTIONS/CAREER NOTES: Signed as non-drafted free agent by Colorado Rockies organization (May 19, 1993). ... On Colorado Springs disabled list (April 14-May 17, 1999). ... Traded by Rockies with P Bobby M. Jones to New York Mets for P Masato Yoshii (January 14, 2000).

STATISTICAL NOTES: Tied for Northwest League lead with five balks in 1995.

Year League	W	L	Pct.	ERA	G	GS	CG	ShO	Sv.	IP	H	R	ER	BB	SO
1993— Dom. Rockies (DSL)	0	4	.000	9.38	14	7	0	0	1	24	32	34	25	46	17
1994— Arizona Rockies (Ariz.)	3	2	.600	4.71	16	1	0	0	0	28 2/3	28	24	15	21	23
1995— Portland (N.W.)	3	4	.429	4.06	15	11	0	0	2	57 2/3	44	31	26	43	48
1996— Asheville (SAL)	1	1	.500	3.60	35	0	0	0	4	45	37	21	18	37	53
1997— Salem (Caro.)	5	0	1.000	2.53	44	0	0	0	8	57	42	19	16	23	79
1998— New Haven (East.)	0	4	.000	4.19	58	0	0	0	22	58	46	30	27	40	63
— Colorado (N.L.)	0	0	...	0.00	1	0	0	0	0	1	0	0	0	0	0
1999— Colo. Springs (PCL)	0	1	.000	10.13	11	0	0	0	0	13 1/3	18	16	15	12	9
— Carolina (Sou.)	2	1	.667	5.29	30	0	0	0	14	34	39	27	20	22	41
Major League totals (1 year)	0	0	...	0.00	1	0	0	0	0	1	0	0	0	0	0

G

GONZALEZ, LUIS   OF   DIAMONDBACKS

PERSONAL: Born September 2, 1967, in Tampa. ... 6-2/190. ... Bats left, throws right. ... Full name: Luis Emilio Gonzalez.
HIGH SCHOOL: Jefferson (Tampa).
COLLEGE: South Alabama.
TRANSACTIONS/CAREER NOTES: Selected by Houston Astros organization in fourth round of free-agent draft (June 1, 1988). ... On disabled list (May 26-July 5, 1989 and August 29-September 13, 1991). ... On Houston disabled list (July 21-August 5, 1992). ... Traded by Astros with C Scott Servais to Chicago Cubs for C Rick Wilkins (June 28, 1995). ... Granted free agency (December 7, 1996). ... Signed by Astros (December 19, 1996). ... Granted free agency (October 28, 1997). ... Signed by Detroit Tigers (December 9, 1997). ... Traded by Tigers to Arizona Diamondbacks for OF Karim Garcia (December 28, 1998).
STATISTICAL NOTES: Tied for Southern League lead with 12 sacrifice flies and nine intentional bases on balls received in 1990. ... Led N.L. with 10 sacrifice flies in 1993. ... Had 23-game hitting streak (May 26-June 20, 1997). ... Had 30-game hitting streak (April 11-May 18, 1999). ... Had 16-game hitting streak (August 16-September 1, 1999). ... Career major league grand slams: 1.
MISCELLANEOUS: Holds Arizona Diamondbacks all-time record for highest career batting average (.336).

| | | | | | | | BATTING | | | | | | | | FIELDING | | |
Year	Team (League)	Pos.	G	AB	R	H	2B	3B	HR	RBI	Avg.	BB	SO	SB	PO	A	E	Avg.
1988—	Asheville (SAL)..........	3B	31	115	13	29	7	1	2	14	.252	12	17	2	19	62	6	.931
—	Auburn (NY-P).........	3B-SS-1B	39	157	32	49	10	3	5	27	.312	12	19	2	37	83	13	.902
1989—	Osceola (FSL)..........	DH	86	287	46	82	16	7	6	38	.286	37	49	2	...	...	...	...
1990—	Columbus (Sou.)........	1B-3B	138	495	86	131	30	6	•24	89	.265	54	100	27	1039	88	23	.980
—	Houston (N.L.)	3B-1B	12	21	1	4	2	0	0	0	.190	2	5	0	22	10	0	1.000
1991—	Houston (N.L.)	OF	137	473	51	120	28	9	13	69	.254	40	101	10	294	6	5	.984
1992—	Houston (N.L.)	OF	122	387	40	94	19	3	10	55	.243	24	52	7	261	5	2	.993
—	Tucson (PCL)	OF	13	44	11	19	4	2	1	9	.432	5	7	4	26	0	1	.963
1993—	Houston (N.L.)	OF	154	540	82	162	34	3	15	72	.300	47	83	20	347	10	8	.978
1994—	Houston (N.L.)	OF	112	392	57	107	29	4	8	67	.273	49	57	15	228	5	2	.991
1995—	Houston (N.L.)	OF	56	209	35	54	10	4	6	35	.258	18	30	1	94	2	2	.980
—	Chicago (N.L.)■	OF	77	262	34	76	19	4	7	34	.290	39	33	5	172	5	4	.978
1996—	Chicago (N.L.)	OF-1B	146	483	70	131	30	4	15	79	.271	61	49	9	244	7	3	.988
1997—	Houston (N.L.)	OF-1B	152	550	78	142	31	2	10	68	.258	71	67	10	266	10	5	.982
1998—	Detroit (A.L.)■	OF-DH	154	547	84	146	35	5	23	71	.267	57	62	12	232	8	3	.988
1999—	Arizona (N.L.)■..........	OF-DH	153	614	112	*206	45	4	26	111	.336	66	63	9	271	10	5	.983
American League totals (1 year)			154	547	84	146	35	5	23	71	.267	57	62	12	232	8	3	.988
National League totals (9 years)			1121	3931	560	1096	247	37	110	590	.279	417	540	86	2199	70	36	.984
Major League totals (10 years)			1275	4478	644	1242	282	42	133	661	.277	474	602	98	2431	78	39	.985

DIVISION SERIES RECORD

| | | | | | | | BATTING | | | | | | | | FIELDING | | |
Year	Team (League)	Pos.	G	AB	R	H	2B	3B	HR	RBI	Avg.	BB	SO	SB	PO	A	E	Avg.
1997—	Houston (N.L.)	OF	3	12	0	4	0	0	0	0	.333	0	1	0	13	1	1	.933
1999—	Arizona (N.L.)	OF	4	10	3	2	1	0	1	2	.200	5	1	0	6	0	0	1.000
Division series totals (2 years)			7	22	3	6	1	0	1	2	.273	5	2	0	19	1	1	.952

ALL-STAR GAME RECORD

| | | | | | | BATTING | | | | | | | | FIELDING | | |
Year	League	Pos.	AB	R	H	2B	3B	HR	RBI	Avg.	BB	SO	SB	PO	A	E	Avg.
1999—	National......................	OF	2	0	1	1	0	0	0	.500	0	0	0	0	0	0	...

GONZALEZ, WIKI   C   PADRES

PERSONAL: Born May 17, 1974, in Aragua, Venezuela. ... 5-11/203. ... Bats right, throws right. ... Full name: Wiklenman Vicente Gonzalez.
TRANSACTIONS/CAREER NOTES: Signed as non-drafted free agent by Pittsburgh Pirates organization (February 12, 1992). ... Selected by San Diego Padres organization from Pirates organization in Rule 5 minor league draft (December 9, 1996). ... Granted free agency (October 16, 1998). ... Re-signed by Padres organization (October 23, 1998). ... On Mobile disabled list (May 24-June 6, 1999).

| | | | | | | | BATTING | | | | | | | | FIELDING | | |
Year	Team (League)	Pos.	G	AB	R	H	2B	3B	HR	RBI	Avg.	BB	SO	SB	PO	A	E	Avg.
1992—	Dom. Pirates (DSL)....	C	63	190	20	48	6	1	3	33	.253	22	12	4	244	42	9	.969
1993—	Dom. Pirates (DSL)....	C-IF	69	244	47	73	10	3	7	47	.299	40	15	24	506	48	8	.986
1994—	GC Pirates (GCL).....	C-1B	41	143	25	48	8	2	4	26	.336	13	13	2	259	37	12	.961
1995—	Augusta (SAL)..........	C	84	278	41	67	17	0	3	36	.241	26	32	5	345	43	6	.985
1996—	Augusta (SAL)..........	C	118	419	52	106	21	3	4	62	.253	58	41	4	810	115	*23	.976
1997—	Rancho Cuca. (Calif.)■	C	33	110	18	33	9	1	5	26	.300	7	25	1	117	17	2	.985
—	Mobile (Sou.)	C	47	143	15	39	7	1	4	25	.273	10	12	1	250	24	3	.989
1998—	Rancho Cuca. (Calif.) .	C	75	292	51	84	24	2	10	59	.288	26	54	0	346	56	3	.993
—	Mobile (Sou.)	C	22	67	20	26	9	0	4	26	.388	14	4	0	65	7	0	1.000
1999—	Mobile (Sou.)	C-DH	61	225	38	76	16	2	10	49	.338	29	28	0	329	43	7	.982
—	Las Vegas (PCL)	C-DH	24	92	13	25	6	0	6	12	.272	5	10	0	175	10	3	.984
—	San Diego (N.L.)	C	30	83	7	21	2	1	3	12	.253	1	8	0	109	15	1	.992
Major League totals (1 year)			30	83	7	21	2	1	3	12	.253	1	8	0	109	15	1	.992

GOODEN, DWIGHT   P   ASTROS

PERSONAL: Born November 16, 1964, in Tampa. ... 6-3/210. ... Throws right, bats right. ... Full name: Dwight Eugene Gooden. ... Uncle of Gary Sheffield, outfielder, Los Angeles Dodgers.
HIGH SCHOOL: Hillsborough (Tampa).
TRANSACTIONS/CAREER NOTES: Selected by New York Mets organization in first round (fifth pick overall) of free-agent draft (June 7, 1982). ... On New York disabled list (April 1-June 5, 1987); included rehabilitation assignment to Tidewater (May 12-17 and May 21-June 1). ... On disabled list (July 2-September 2, 1989; August 24, 1991-remainder of season and July 18-August 8, 1992). ... On suspended list (September

G

2-7, 1993). ... On New York disabled list (April 22-June 9, 1994); included rehabilitation assignments to Norfolk (May 30-June 4) and Binghamton (June 4-9). ... On suspended list (June 28, 1994-remainder of season). ... Granted free agency (October 24, 1994). ... On suspended list (November 4, 1994-entire 1995 season). ... Signed by New York Yankees (February 20, 1996). ... On New York disabled list (April 11-June 15, 1997); included rehabilitation assignment to Norwich (May 18-June 2). ... Granted free agency (November 1, 1997). ... Signed by Cleveland Indians (December 8, 1997). ... On Cleveland disabled list (March 22-May 20, 1998); included rehabilitation assignment to Buffalo (May 3-20). ... On Cleveland disabled list (August 3-31, 1999); included rehabilitation assignments to Akron (August 19-23) and Buffalo (August 24-31). ... Granted free agency (November 3, 1999). ... Signed by Houston Astros organization (January 6, 2000).

RECORDS: Holds major league rookie-season record for most strikeouts—276 (1984). ... Holds N.L. record for most strikeouts in three consecutive games—43 (September 7 [11], 12 [16] and 17 [16], 1984).

HONORS: Named Carolina League Pitcher of the Year (1983). ... Named N.L. Rookie Pitcher of the Year by THE SPORTING NEWS (1984). ... Named N.L. Rookie of the Year by Baseball Writers' Association of America (1984). ... Named N.L. Pitcher of the Year by THE SPORTING NEWS (1985). ... Named righthanded pitcher on THE SPORTING NEWS N.L. All-Star team (1985). ... Named N.L. Cy Young Award winner by Baseball Writers' Association of America (1985). ... Named pitcher on THE SPORTING NEWS N.L. Silver Slugger team (1992).

STATISTICAL NOTES: Pitched 10-0 one-hit, complete-game victory against Chicago (September 17, 1984). ... Struck out 16 batters in one game (September 12 and September 17, 1984; August 20, 1985). ... Tied for N.L. lead with seven balks in 1984. ... Struck out 15 batters in one game (May 11, 1990). ... Pitched 2-0 no-hit victory against Seattle (May 14, 1996).

MISCELLANEOUS: Appeared in one game as pinch runner (1990). ... Singled and made an out in two appearances as pinch hitter (1992). ... Tripled with an RBI in only appearance as pinch hitter (1993).

Year League	W	L	Pct.	ERA	G	GS	CG	ShO	Sv.	IP	H	R	ER	BB	SO
1982— Kingsport (Appl.)	5	4	.556	2.47	9	9	4	2	0	65 2/3	53	34	18	25	66
— Little Falls (NY-P)	0	1	.000	4.15	2	2	0	0	0	13	11	6	6	3	18
1983— Lynchburg (Caro.)	*19	4	.826	*2.50	27	27	10	*6	0	191	121	58	53	*112	*300
1984— New York (N.L.)	17	9	.654	2.60	31	31	7	3	0	218	161	72	63	73	*276
1985— New York (N.L.)	*24	4	.857	*1.53	35	35	*16	8	0	*276 2/3	198	51	47	69	*268
1986— New York (N.L.)	17	6	.739	2.84	33	33	12	2	0	250	197	92	79	80	200
1987— Tidewater (I.L.)	3	0	1.000	2.05	4	4	1	0	0	22	20	7	5	9	24
— Lynchburg (Caro.)	0	0	...	0.00	1	1	0	0	0	4	2	0	0	2	3
— New York (N.L.)	15	7	.682	3.21	25	25	7	3	0	179 2/3	162	68	64	53	148
1988— New York (N.L.)	18	9	.667	3.19	34	34	10	3	0	248 1/3	242	98	88	57	175
1989— New York (N.L.)	9	4	.692	2.89	19	17	0	0	1	118 1/3	93	42	38	47	101
1990— New York (N.L.)	19	7	.731	3.83	34	34	2	1	0	232 2/3	229	106	99	70	223
1991— New York (N.L.)	13	7	.650	3.60	27	27	3	1	0	190	185	80	76	56	150
1992— New York (N.L.)	10	13	.435	3.67	31	31	3	0	0	206	197	93	84	70	145
1993— New York (N.L.)	12	15	.444	3.45	29	29	7	2	0	208 2/3	188	89	80	61	149
1994— New York (N.L.)	3	4	.429	6.31	7	7	0	0	0	41 1/3	46	32	29	15	40
— Norfolk (I.L.)	0	0	...	0.00	1	1	0	0	0	3	0	0	0	1	4
— Binghamton (East.)	1	0	1.000	0.00	1	1	0	0	0	5	2	0	0	1	4
1995—							Out of organized baseball.								
1996— New York (A.L.)■	11	7	.611	5.01	29	29	1	1	0	170 2/3	169	101	95	88	126
1997— New York (A.L.)	9	5	.643	4.91	20	19	0	0	0	106 1/3	116	61	58	53	66
— Norwich (East.)	3	0	1.000	3.00	3	3	0	0	0	18	13	6	6	5	14
— Columbus (I.L.)	1	1	.500	3.75	2	2	0	0	0	12	7	5	5	4	10
1998— Buffalo (I.L.)■	1	2	.333	9.00	4	4	0	0	0	16	23	16	16	7	18
— Cleveland (A.L.)	8	6	.571	3.76	23	23	0	0	0	134	135	59	56	51	83
1999— Cleveland (A.L.)	3	4	.429	6.26	26	22	0	0	0	115	127	90	80	67	88
— Akron (East.)	0	0	...	3.00	1	1	0	0	0	3	3	2	1	1	2
— Buffalo (I.L.)	0	1	.000	2.45	1	1	0	0	0	3 2/3	6	1	1	3	3
A.L. totals (4 years)	31	22	.585	4.94	98	93	1	1	0	526	547	311	289	259	363
N.L. totals (11 years)	157	85	.649	3.10	305	303	67	23	1	2169 2/3	1898	823	747	651	1875
Major League totals (15 years)	188	107	.637	3.46	403	396	68	24	1	2695 2/3	2445	1134	1036	910	2238

DIVISION SERIES RECORD

Year League	W	L	Pct.	ERA	G	GS	CG	ShO	Sv.	IP	H	R	ER	BB	SO
1997— New York (A.L.)	0	0	...	1.59	1	1	0	0	0	5 2/3	5	1	1	3	5
1998— Cleveland (A.L.)	0	0	...	54.00	1	1	0	0	0	1/3	1	2	2	2	1
1999— Cleveland (A.L.)							Did not play.								
Division series totals (2 years)	0	0	...	4.50	2	2	0	0	0	6	6	3	3	5	6

CHAMPIONSHIP SERIES RECORD

RECORDS: Holds single-series record for most strikeouts—20 (1988). ... Shares N.L. single-game record for most innings pitched—10 (October 14, 1986).

Year League	W	L	Pct.	ERA	G	GS	CG	ShO	Sv.	IP	H	R	ER	BB	SO
1986— New York (N.L.)	0	1	.000	1.06	2	2	0	0	0	17	16	2	2	5	9
1988— New York (N.L.)	0	0	...	2.95	3	2	0	0	0	18 1/3	10	6	6	8	20
1998— Cleveland (A.L.)	0	1	.000	5.79	1	1	0	0	0	4 2/3	3	3	3	3	3
Champ. series totals (3 years)	0	2	.000	2.47	6	5	0	0	0	40	29	11	11	16	32

WORLD SERIES RECORD

NOTES: Member of World Series championship team (1986). ... Member of World Series championship team (1996); inactive.

Year League	W	L	Pct.	ERA	G	GS	CG	ShO	Sv.	IP	H	R	ER	BB	SO
1986— New York (N.L.)	0	2	.000	8.00	2	2	0	0	0	9	17	10	8	4	9

ALL-STAR GAME RECORD

RECORDS: Holds career record for most balks—2. ... Shares career record for most games lost—2.

Year League	W	L	Pct.	ERA	GS	CG	ShO	Sv.	IP	H	R	ER	BB	SO
1984— National	0	0	...	0.00	0	0	0	0	2	1	0	0	0	3
1985— National						Did not play.								
1986— National	0	1	.000	6.00	1	0	0	0	3	3	2	2	0	2
1988— National	0	1	.000	3.00	1	0	0	0	3	3	1	1	1	1
All-Star Game totals (3 years)	0	2	.000	3.38	2	0	0	0	8	7	3	3	1	6

G

GOODWIN, CURTIS   OF

PERSONAL: Born September 30, 1972, in Oakland. ... 5-11/180. ... Bats left, throws left. ... Full name: Curtis LaMar Goodwin.
HIGH SCHOOL: San Leandro (Calif.).
TRANSACTIONS/CAREER NOTES: Selected by Baltimore Orioles organization in 12th round of free-agent draft (June 3, 1991). ... On Baltimore disabled list (August 20-September 4, 1995). ... Traded by Orioles with OF Trovin Valdez to Cincinnati Reds for P David Wells (December 26, 1995). ... Traded by Reds to Colorado Rockies for P Mark Hutton (December 10, 1997). ... Claimed on waivers by Chicago Cubs (March 29, 1999). ... Claimed on waivers by Toronto Blue Jays (August 6, 1999). ... Announced retirement (August 12, 1999).
STATISTICAL NOTES: Led Midwest League outfielders with 327 total chances and seven double plays in 1992. ... Led Eastern League with 13 sacrifice hits in 1994. ... Led Eastern League outfielders with 323 total chances in 1994.

Year Team (League)	Pos.	G	AB	R	H	2B	3B	HR	RBI	Avg.	BB	SO	SB	PO	A	E	Avg.
1991— GC Orioles (GCL)	OF	48	151	32	39	5	0	0	9	.258	38	25	26	77	5	1	.988
1992— Kane County (Midw.)	OF	134	*542	85	153	7	5	1	42	.282	38	106	52	301	15	11	.966
1993— Frederick (Caro.)	OF	•138	*555	*98	•156	15	*10	2	42	.281	52	90	*61	271	9	7	.976
1994— Bowie (East.)	OF	*142	*597	*105	*171	18	8	2	37	.286	40	78	*59	*301	12	10	.969
1995— Rochester (I.L.)	OF	36	140	24	37	3	3	0	7	.264	12	15	17	81	1	3	.965
— Baltimore (A.L.)	OF-DH	87	289	40	76	11	3	1	24	.263	15	53	22	202	1	2	.990
1996— Indianapolis (A.A.)■	OF-DH	91	337	57	88	19	4	2	30	.261	54	67	*40	172	4	4	.978
— Cincinnati (N.L.)	OF	49	136	20	31	3	0	0	5	.228	19	34	15	64	0	2	.970
1997— Indianapolis (A.A.)	OF	30	116	14	32	4	1	1	7	.276	15	20	11	57	2	0	1.000
— Cincinnati (N.L.)	OF	85	265	27	67	11	0	1	12	.253	24	53	22	159	3	0	1.000
1998— Colorado (N.L.)■	OF	119	159	27	39	7	0	1	6	.245	16	40	5	118	1	2	.983
1999— Chicago (N.L.)■	OF	89	157	15	38	6	1	0	9	.242	13	38	2	115	3	2	.983
— Toronto (A.L.)	OF	2	8	0	0	0	0	0	0	.000	0	3	0	7	1	0	1.000
American League totals (2 years)		89	297	40	76	11	3	1	24	.256	15	56	22	209	2	2	.991
National League totals (4 years)		342	717	89	175	27	1	2	32	.244	72	165	44	456	7	6	.987
Major League totals (5 years)		431	1014	129	251	38	4	3	56	.248	87	221	66	665	9	8	.988

GOODWIN, TOM   OF   ROCKIES

PERSONAL: Born July 27, 1968, in Fresno, Calif. ... 6-1/175. ... Bats left, throws right. ... Full name: Thomas Jones Goodwin.
HIGH SCHOOL: Central (Fresno, Calif.).
COLLEGE: Fresno State.
TRANSACTIONS/CAREER NOTES: Selected by Pittsburgh Pirates organization in sixth round of free-agent draft (June 2, 1986); did not sign. ... Selected by Los Angeles Dodgers organization in first round (22nd pick overall) of free-agent draft (June 5, 1989). ... Claimed on waivers by Kansas City Royals (January 6, 1994). ... Traded by Royals to Texas Rangers for 3B Dean Palmer (July 25, 1997). ... On Texas disabled list (June 11-27 and June 28-August 6, 1999); included rehabilitation assignment to Charlotte (August 2-6). ... Granted free agency (October 28, 1999). ... Signed by Colorado Rockies (December 9, 1999).
HONORS: Named outfielder on THE SPORTING NEWS college All-America team (1989).
STATISTICAL NOTES: Tied for Pacific Coast League lead in caught stealing with 23 in 1991. ... Led American Association in caught stealing with 20 in 1994. ... Led A.L. in sacrifice hits with 14 in 1995 and 21 in 1996. ... Led A.L. in caught stealing with 22 in 1996 and 20 in 1998.
MISCELLANEOUS: Member of 1988 U.S. Olympic baseball team.

Year Team (League)	Pos.	G	AB	R	H	2B	3B	HR	RBI	Avg.	BB	SO	SB	PO	A	E	Avg.
1989— Great Falls (Pio.)	OF	63	240	*55	74	12	3	2	33	.308	28	30	*60	67	3	1	.986
1990— San Antonio (Texas)	OF	102	428	76	119	15	4	0	28	.278	38	72	*60	264	7	3	*.989
— Bakersfield (Calif.)	OF	32	134	24	39	6	2	0	13	.291	11	22	22	55	2	0	1.000
1991— Albuquerque (PCL)	OF	132	509	84	139	19	4	1	45	.273	59	83	48	284	6	3	.990
— Los Angeles (N.L.)	OF	16	7	3	1	0	0	0	0	.143	0	0	1	8	0	0	1.000
1992— Albuquerque (PCL)	OF	82	319	48	96	10	4	2	28	.301	37	47	27	184	5	1	.995
— Los Angeles (N.L.)	OF	57	73	15	17	1	1	0	3	.233	6	10	7	43	0	0	1.000
1993— Los Angeles (N.L.)	OF	30	17	6	5	1	0	0	1	.294	1	4	1	8	0	0	1.000
— Albuquerque (PCL)	OF	85	289	48	75	5	5	1	28	.260	30	51	21	145	1	2	.986
1994— Kansas City (A.L.)■	DH-OF	2	2	0	0	0	0	0	0	.000	0	1	0	1	0	0	1.000
— Omaha (A.A.)	OF	113	429	67	132	17	7	2	34	.308	23	60	*50	276	3	2	.993
1995— Kansas City (A.L.)	OF-DH	133	480	72	138	16	3	4	28	.288	38	72	50	292	6	3	.990
1996— Kansas City (A.L.)	OF-DH	143	524	80	148	14	4	1	35	.282	39	79	66	303	7	5	.984
1997— Kansas City (A.L.)	OF	97	367	51	100	13	4	2	22	.272	19	51	34	232	3	1	.996
— Texas (A.L.)■	OF	53	207	39	49	13	2	0	17	.237	25	37	16	138	3	2	.986
1998— Texas (A.L.)	OF-DH	154	520	102	151	13	3	2	33	.290	73	90	38	370	5	3	.992
1999— Texas (A.L.)	OF	109	405	63	105	12	6	3	33	.259	40	61	39	258	4	3	.989
— Charlotte (FSL)	OF	3	11	2	4	1	0	0	0	.364	1	4	0	8	0	0	1.000
American League totals (6 years)		691	2505	407	691	81	22	12	168	.276	234	391	243	1594	28	17	.990
National League totals (3 years)		103	97	24	23	2	1	0	4	.237	7	14	9	59	0	0	1.000
Major League totals (9 years)		794	2602	431	714	83	23	12	172	.274	241	405	252	1653	28	17	.990

DIVISION SERIES RECORD

Year Team (League)	Pos.	G	AB	R	H	2B	3B	HR	RBI	Avg.	BB	SO	SB	PO	A	E	Avg.
1998— Texas (A.L.)	OF	2	4	0	1	0	0	0	0	.250	0	1	0	1	0	0	1.000
1999— Texas (A.L.)	OF	3	7	0	1	0	0	0	0	.143	0	1	0	6	0	0	1.000
Division series totals (2 years)		5	11	0	2	0	0	0	0	.182	0	2	0	7	0	0	1.000

GORDON, TOM   P   RED SOX

PERSONAL: Born November 18, 1967, in Sebring, Fla. ... 5-9/190. ... Throws right, bats right. ... Full name: Thomas Gordon.
HIGH SCHOOL: Avon Park (Fla.).

G

TRANSACTIONS/CAREER NOTES: Selected by Kansas City Royals organization in sixth round of free-agent draft (June 2, 1986). ... On disabled list (August 12-September 1, 1992; and May 8-24, 1995). ... Granted free agency (October 30, 1995). ... Signed by Boston Red Sox (December 21, 1995). ... On Boston disabled list (April 18-May 10 and June 12-September 27, 1999); included rehabilitation assignments to Trenton (September 11-13) and Augusta (September 14-25).

HONORS: Named A.L. Rookie Pitcher of the Year by THE SPORTING NEWS (1989). ... Named A.L. Fireman of the Year by THE SPORTING NEWS (1998).

STATISTICAL NOTES: Tied for Northwest League lead with four balks in 1987.

MISCELLANEOUS: Appeared in one game as pinch runner (1991). ... Appeared in one game as pinch runner (1995).

Year	League	W	L	Pct.	ERA	G	GS	CG	ShO	Sv.	IP	H	R	ER	BB	SO
1986—	Gulf Coast Royals (GCL)	3	1	.750	1.02	9	7	2	1	0	44	31	12	5	23	47
	—Omaha (A.A.)....................	0	0	...	47.25	1	0	0	0	0	1 1/3	6	7	7	2	3
1987—	Eugene (N.W.)....................	•9	0	•1.000	2.86	15	13	0	0	1	72 1/3	48	33	23	47	91
	—Fort Myers (FSL)...............	1	0	1.000	2.63	3	3	0	0	0	13 2/3	5	4	4	17	11
1988—	Appleton (Midw.)................	7	5	.583	2.06	17	17	5	1	0	118	69	30	27	43	*172
	—Memphis (Sou.)...............	6	0	1.000	0.38	6	6	2	2	0	47 1/3	16	3	2	17	62
	—Omaha (A.A.)....................	3	0	1.000	1.33	3	3	0	0	0	20 1/3	11	3	3	15	29
	—Kansas City (A.L.)	0	2	.000	5.17	5	2	0	0	0	15 2/3	16	9	9	7	18
1989—	Kansas City (A.L.)	17	9	.654	3.64	49	16	1	1	1	163	122	67	66	86	153
1990—	Kansas City (A.L.)	12	11	.522	3.73	32	32	6	1	0	195 1/3	192	99	81	99	175
1991—	Kansas City (A.L.)	9	14	.391	3.87	45	14	1	0	1	158	129	76	68	87	167
1992—	Kansas City (A.L.)	6	10	.375	4.59	40	11	0	0	0	117 2/3	116	67	60	55	98
1993—	Kansas City (A.L.)	12	6	.667	3.58	48	14	2	0	1	155 2/3	125	65	62	77	143
1994—	Kansas City (A.L.)	11	7	.611	4.35	24	24	0	0	0	155 1/3	136	79	75	87	126
1995—	Kansas City (A.L.)	12	12	.500	4.43	31	31	2	0	0	189	204	110	93	89	119
1996—	Boston (A.L.)■...................	12	9	.571	5.59	34	34	4	1	0	215 2/3	249	143	*134	105	171
1997—	Boston (A.L.).....................	6	10	.375	3.74	42	25	2	1	11	182 1/3	155	85	76	78	159
1998—	Boston (A.L.).....................	7	4	.636	2.72	73	0	0	0	*46	79 1/3	55	24	24	25	78
1999—	Boston (A.L.).....................	0	2	.000	5.60	21	0	0	0	11	17 2/3	17	11	11	12	24
Major League totals (12 years)		**104**	**96**	**.520**	**4.15**	**444**	**203**	**18**	**4**	**71**	**1645**	**1516**	**835**	**759**	**807**	**1431**

DIVISION SERIES RECORD

Year	League	W	L	Pct.	ERA	G	GS	CG	ShO	Sv.	IP	H	R	ER	BB	SO
1998—	Boston (A.L.).....................	0	1	.000	9.00	2	0	0	0	0	3	4	3	3	4	1
1999—	Boston (A.L.).....................	0	0	...	4.50	2	0	0	0	0	2	1	1	1	1	3
Division series totals (2 years)		**0**	**1**	**.000**	**7.20**	**4**	**0**	**0**	**0**	**0**	**5**	**5**	**4**	**4**	**5**	**4**

CHAMPIONSHIP SERIES RECORD

Year	League	W	L	Pct.	ERA	G	GS	CG	ShO	Sv.	IP	H	R	ER	BB	SO
1999—	Boston (A.L.).....................	0	0	...	13.50	3	0	0	0	0	2	3	3	3	1	3

ALL-STAR GAME RECORD

Year	League	W	L	Pct.	ERA	GS	CG	ShO	Sv.	IP	H	R	ER	BB	SO
1998—	American	0	0	...	18.00	0	0	0	0	1	3	2	2	1	0

GRABOWSKI, JASON　　　3B　　　RANGERS

PERSONAL: Born May 24, 1976, in New Haven, Conn. ... 6-3/200. ... Bats left, throws right. ... Full name: Jason William Grabowski.
HIGH SCHOOL: The Morgan School (Clinton, Conn.).
COLLEGE: Connecticut.
TRANSACTIONS/CAREER NOTES: Selected by New York Yankees organization in 17th round of free-agent draft (June 2, 1994); did not sign. ... Selected by Texas Rangers organization in second round of free-agent draft (June 3, 1997).

							BATTING									FIELDING		
Year	Team (League)	Pos.	G	AB	R	H	2B	3B	HR	RBI	Avg.	BB	SO	SB	PO	A	E	Avg.
1997—	Pulaski (Appl.).............	C	50	174	36	51	14	0	4	24	.293	40	32	6	386	40	8	.982
1998—	Savannah (SAL)	C-1B	104	352	63	95	13	6	14	52	.270	57	93	16	573	50	6	.990
1999—	Charlotte (FSL)..........	3B-1B	123	434	68	136	31	6	12	87	.313	65	66	13	100	199	27	.917
	—Tulsa (Texas)		2	6	1	1	0	0	0	0	.167	2	2	0	0	0	0	...

GRACE, MARK　　　1B　　　CUBS

PERSONAL: Born June 28, 1964, in Winston-Salem, N.C. ... 6-2/200. ... Bats left, throws left. ... Full name: Mark Eugene Grace.
HIGH SCHOOL: Tustin (Calif.).
JUNIOR COLLEGE: Saddleback Community College (Calif.).
COLLEGE: San Diego State.
TRANSACTIONS/CAREER NOTES: Selected by Minnesota Twins organization in 15th round of free-agent draft (January 17, 1984); did not sign. ... Selected by Chicago Cubs organization in 24th round of free-agent draft (June 3, 1985). ... On disabled list (June 5-23, 1989). ... Granted free agency (October 15, 1994). ... Re-signed by Cubs (April 7, 1995). ... Granted free agency (November 3, 1995). ... Re-signed by Cubs (December 19, 1995). ... On disabled list (June 11-28, 1996; and April 4-19, 1997).
RECORDS: Holds major league single-season record for fewest double plays by first baseman (150 or more games)—82 (1998). ... Shares major league record for most assists by first baseman in one inning—3 (May 23, 1990, fourth inning). ... Holds N.L. single-season record for most assists by first baseman—180 (1990).
HONORS: Named Eastern League Most Valuable Player (1987). ... Named N.L. Rookie Player of the Year by THE SPORTING NEWS (1988). ... Won N.L. Gold Glove at first base (1992-93 and 1995-96).
STATISTICAL NOTES: Led Midwest League first basemen with 103 double plays in 1986. ... Led Eastern League with .545 slugging percentage in 1987. ... Led N.L. first basemen with 1,695 total chances in 1991, 1,725 in 1992 and 1,573 in 1993. ... Tied for N.L. lead in grounding into double plays with 25 in 1993. ... Led N.L. first basemen with 134 double plays in 1993. ... Hit for the cycle (May 9, 1993). ... Tied for N.L. lead with 10 sacrifice flies in 1999. ... Career major league grand slams: 1.

G

Year Team (League)	Pos.	G	AB	R	H	2B	3B	HR	RBI	Avg.	BB	SO	SB	PO	A	E	Avg.
1986—Peoria (Midw.)...........	1B-OF	126	465	81	159	30	4	15	95	*.342	60	28	6	1050	69	13	.989
1987—Pittsfield (East.).........	1B	123	453	81	151	29	8	17	*101	.333	48	24	5	1054	*96	6	*.995
1988—Iowa (A.A.)................	1B	21	67	11	17	4	0	0	14	.254	13	4	1	189	20	1	.995
—Chicago (N.L.)..........	1B	134	486	65	144	23	4	7	57	.296	60	43	3	1182	87	•17	.987
1989—Chicago (N.L.)..........	1B	142	510	74	160	28	3	13	79	.314	80	42	14	1230	126	6	.996
1990—Chicago (N.L.)..........	1B	157	589	72	182	32	1	9	82	.309	59	54	15	1324	*180	12	.992
1991—Chicago (N.L.)..........	1B	160	*619	87	169	28	5	8	58	.273	70	53	3	*1520	*167	8	.995
1992—Chicago (N.L.)..........	1B	158	603	72	185	37	5	9	79	.307	72	36	6	*1580	*141	4	.998
1993—Chicago (N.L.)..........	1B	155	594	86	193	39	4	14	98	.325	71	32	8	*1456	112	5	.997
1994—Chicago (N.L.)..........	1B	106	403	55	120	23	3	6	44	.298	48	41	0	925	78	7	.993
1995—Chicago (N.L.)..........	1B	143	552	97	180	*51	3	16	92	.326	65	46	6	1211	114	7	.995
1996—Chicago (N.L.)..........	1B	142	547	88	181	39	1	9	75	.331	62	41	2	1259	107	4	.997
1997—Chicago (N.L.)..........	1B	151	555	87	177	32	5	13	78	.319	88	45	2	1202	120	6	.995
1998—Chicago (N.L.)..........	1B	158	595	92	184	39	3	17	89	.309	93	56	4	1279	122	8	.994
1999—Chicago (N.L.)..........	1B	161	593	107	183	44	5	16	91	.309	83	44	3	1335	93	8	.994
Major League totals (12 years)		1767	6646	982	2058	415	42	137	922	.310	851	533	66	15503	1447	92	.995

DIVISION SERIES RECORD

Year Team (League)	Pos.	G	AB	R	H	2B	3B	HR	RBI	Avg.	BB	SO	SB	PO	A	E	Avg.
1998—Chicago (N.L.)...........	1B	3	12	0	1	0	0	0	1	.083	0	2	0	20	2	0	1.000

CHAMPIONSHIP SERIES RECORD

NOTES: Hit home run in first at-bat (October 4, 1989).

Year Team (League)	Pos.	G	AB	R	H	2B	3B	HR	RBI	Avg.	BB	SO	SB	PO	A	E	Avg.
1989—Chicago (N.L.)...........	1B	5	17	3	11	3	1	1	8	.647	4	1	1	44	3	0	1.000

ALL-STAR GAME RECORD

Year League	Pos.	AB	R	H	2B	3B	HR	RBI	Avg.	BB	SO	SB	PO	A	E	Avg.
1993—National	DH	3	0	0	0	0	0	0	.000	0	0	0	...	...	...	...
1995—National	1B	0	0	0	0	0	0	0	...	0	0	0	1	0	0	1.000
1997—National	1B	1	0	0	0	0	0	0	.000	0	0	0	1	0	0	1.000
All-Star Game totals (3 years)		4	0	0	0	0	0	0	.000	0	0	0	2	0	0	1.000

GRACE, MIKE   P

PERSONAL: Born June 20, 1970, in Joliet, Ill. ... 6-4/219. ... Throws right, bats right. ... Full name: Michael James Grace.
HIGH SCHOOL: Joliet (Ill.) Catholic.
COLLEGE: Bradley.
TRANSACTIONS/CAREER NOTES: Selected by Philadelphia Phillies organization in 10th round of free-agent draft (June 3, 1991). ... On disabled list (April 9-June 8, July 8-20 and July 27, 1992-remainder of season; April 8, 1993-entire season; April 7-June 14, 1994; and June 3, 1996-remainder of season). ... On Philadelphia disabled list (March 27-June 25, 1997); included rehabilitation assignments to Reading (May 28-June 14) and Scranton/Wilkes-Barre (June 14-25). ... Granted free agency (October 6, 1999).

Year League	W	L	Pct.	ERA	G	GS	CG	ShO	Sv.	IP	H	R	ER	BB	SO
1991—Batavia (NY-P)...................	1	2	.333	1.39	6	6	0	0	0	32 1/3	20	9	5	14	36
—Spartanburg (SAL)........	3	1	.750	1.89	6	6	0	0	0	33 1/3	24	7	7	9	23
1992—Spartanburg (SAL)	0	1	.000	4.94	6	6	0	0	0	27 1/3	25	16	15	8	21
1993—							Did not play.								
1994—Spartanburg (SAL)	5	5	.500	4.82	15	15	0	0	0	80 1/3	84	50	43	20	45
1995—Reading (East.)..................	13	6	.684	3.54	24	24	2	0	0	147 1/3	137	65	58	35	118
—Scranton/W.B. (I.L.)	2	0	1.000	1.59	2	2	1	0	0	17	17	3	3	2	13
—Philadelphia (N.L.)..........	1	1	.500	3.18	2	2	0	0	0	11 1/3	10	4	4	4	7
1996—Philadelphia (N.L.)..........	7	2	.778	3.49	12	12	1	1	0	80	72	33	31	16	49
1997—Reading (East.)..................	1	3	.250	5.75	4	4	0	0	0	20 1/3	28	17	13	6	10
—Scranton/W.B. (I.L.)	5	6	.455	4.56	12	12	4	0	0	75	84	43	38	27	55
—Philadelphia (N.L.)..........	3	2	.600	3.46	6	6	1	1	0	39	32	16	15	10	26
1998—Philadelphia (N.L.)..........	4	7	.364	5.48	21	15	0	0	0	90 1/3	116	61	55	30	46
—Scranton/W.B. (I.L.)	3	6	.333	5.04	11	10	2	0	0	75	92	44	42	18	39
1999—Philadelphia (N.L.)..........	1	4	.200	7.69	27	5	0	0	0	55	80	48	47	30	28
—Scranton/W.B. (I.L.)	2	2	.500	4.44	10	9	0	0	0	46 2/3	52	25	23	17	27
Major League totals (5 years)	16	16	.500	4.96	68	40	2	2	0	275 2/3	310	162	152	90	156

GRAFFANINO, TONY   2B/SS   DEVIL RAYS

PERSONAL: Born June 6, 1972, in Amityville, N.Y. ... 6-1/195. ... Bats right, throws right. ... Full name: Anthony Joseph Graffanino. ... Name pronounced GRAF-uh-NEE-noh.
HIGH SCHOOL: East Islip (Islip Terrace, N.Y.).
TRANSACTIONS/CAREER NOTES: Selected by Atlanta Braves organization in 10th round of free-agent draft (June 4, 1990). ... On disabled list (July 3, 1995-remainder of season). ... Released by Braves (April 2, 1999). ... Signed by Tampa Bay Devil Rays organization (April 9, 1999).
STATISTICAL NOTES: Led Pioneer League shortstops with 41 double plays in 1991. ... Led Carolina League second basemen with .968 fielding percentage in 1993. ... Led International League second basemen with 441 total chances in 1996.

Year Team (League)	Pos.	G	AB	R	H	2B	3B	HR	RBI	Avg.	BB	SO	SB	PO	A	E	Avg.
1990—Pulaski (Appl.)............	SS	42	131	23	27	5	1	0	11	.206	26	17	6	60	105	24	.873
1991—Idaho Falls (Pio.)........	SS	66	274	53	95	16	4	4	56	.347	27	37	19	112	187	*29	.912
1992—Macon (SAL)..............	2B	112	400	50	96	15	5	10	31	.240	50	84	9	178	239	17	.961

G

Year Team (League)	Pos.	G	AB	R	H	2B	3B	HR	RBI	Avg.	BB	SO	SB	PO	A	E	Avg.
1993— Durham (Caro.)	2B-DH-SS	123	459	78	126	30	5	15	69	.275	45	78	24	186	263	15	†.968
1994— Greenville (Sou.)	2B-DH	124	440	66	132	28	3	7	52	.300	50	53	29	254	326	14	.976
1995— Richmond (I.L.)	2B	50	179	20	34	6	0	4	17	.190	15	49	2	102	127	4	.983
1996— Richmond (I.L.)	2B	96	353	57	100	29	2	7	33	.283	34	72	11	*215	216	10	.977
— Atlanta (N.L.)	2B	22	46	7	8	1	1	0	2	.174	4	13	0	24	39	2	.969
1997— Atlanta (N.L.)	2-3-SS-1	104	186	33	48	9	1	8	20	.258	26	46	6	90	180	5	.982
1998— Atlanta (N.L.)	2B-SS-3B	105	289	32	61	14	1	5	22	.211	24	68	1	139	227	11	.971
1999— Durham (I.L.)■	2B-DH-3B	87	345	66	108	25	6	9	58	.313	37	46	16	182	233	1	.998
— Tampa Bay (A.L.)	2-SS-DH-3	39	130	20	41	9	4	2	19	.315	9	22	3	66	114	5	.973
American League totals (1 year)		39	130	20	41	9	4	2	19	.315	9	22	3	66	114	5	.973
National League totals (3 years)		231	521	72	117	24	3	13	44	.225	54	127	7	253	446	18	.975
Major League totals (4 years)		270	651	92	158	33	7	15	63	.243	63	149	10	319	560	23	.975

DIVISION SERIES RECORD

Year Team (League)	Pos.	G	AB	R	H	2B	3B	HR	RBI	Avg.	BB	SO	SB	PO	A	E	Avg.
1997— Atlanta (N.L.)	2B	3	3	0	0	0	0	0	0	.000	2	1	0	1	6	0	1.000
1998— Atlanta (N.L.)	PH	1	0	0	0	0	0	0	0	...	0	0	0				
Division series totals (2 years)		4	3	0	0	0	0	0	0	.000	2	1	0	1	6	0	1.000

CHAMPIONSHIP SERIES RECORD

Year Team (League)	Pos.	G	AB	R	H	2B	3B	HR	RBI	Avg.	BB	SO	SB	PO	A	E	Avg.
1997— Atlanta (N.L.)	2B	3	8	1	2	1	0	0	0	.250	0	3	0	4	2	0	1.000
1998— Atlanta (N.L.)	PH-2B	4	3	2	1	1	0	0	1	.333	2	1	0	2	5	0	1.000
Championship series totals (2 years)		7	11	3	3	2	0	0	1	.273	2	4	0	6	7	0	1.000

GRAHE, JOE   P

PERSONAL: Born August 14, 1967, in West Palm Beach, Fla. ... 6-0/200. ... Throws right, bats right. ... Full name: Joseph Milton Grahe. ... Name pronounced GRAY.

HIGH SCHOOL: Palm Beach Gardens (West Palm Beach, Fla.).

JUNIOR COLLEGE: Palm Beach Junior College (Fla.).

COLLEGE: Miami (Fla.).

TRANSACTIONS/CAREER NOTES: Selected by Milwaukee Brewers organization in 28th round of free-agent draft (June 2, 1986); did not sign. ... Selected by Oakland Athletics organization in fifth round of free-agent draft (June 1, 1988); did not sign. ... Selected by California Angels organization in second round of free-agent draft (June 5, 1989). ... On California disabled list (June 5-July 15, 1993); included rehabilitation assignment to Vancouver (July 2-15). ... Granted free agency (November 26, 1994). ... Signed by Colorado Rockies organization (December 15, 1994). ... On Colorado Springs disabled list (April 6-May 11, 1995). ... On Colorado disabled list (July 18-September 1, 1995). ... Released by Rockies (October 10, 1995). ... Signed by Ottawa, Montreal Expos organization (February 20, 1996). ... On disabled list (April 4-September 3, 1996). ... Granted free agency (October 15, 1996). ... Signed by Bangor, Northeast League (July 18, 1997). ... Signed by Nashua, Atlantic League (May 1998). ... Contract purchased by New York Yankees organization (July 14, 1998). ... Granted free agency (October 15, 1998). ... Signed by Philadelphia Phillies organization (February 2, 1999). ... Granted free agency (October 6, 1999).

Year League	W	L	Pct.	ERA	G	GS	CG	ShO	Sv.	IP	H	R	ER	BB	SO
1990— Midland (Texas)	7	5	.583	5.29	18	18	1	0	0	119	145	75	70	34	58
— Edmonton (PCL)	3	0	1.000	1.35	5	5	2	0	0	40	35	10	6	11	21
— California (A.L.)	3	4	.429	4.98	8	8	0	0	0	43 1/3	51	30	24	23	25
1991— Edmonton (PCL)	9	3	.750	4.01	14	14	3	1	0	94 1/3	121	55	42	30	55
— California (A.L.)	3	7	.300	4.81	18	10	1	0	0	73	84	43	39	33	40
1992— California (A.L.)	5	6	.455	3.52	46	7	0	0	21	94 2/3	85	37	37	39	39
— Edmonton (PCL)	1	0	1.000	3.20	3	3	0	0	0	19 2/3	18	7	7	5	12
1993— California (A.L.)	4	1	.800	2.86	45	0	0	0	11	56 2/3	54	22	18	25	31
— Vancouver (PCL)	1	1	.500	4.50	4	2	0	0	0	6	4	3	3	2	5
1994— California (A.L.)	2	5	.286	6.65	40	0	0	0	13	43 1/3	68	33	32	18	26
1995— Colo. Springs (PCL)■	1	1	.500	3.27	2	2	1	0	0	11	7	4	4	3	4
— Colorado (N.L.)	4	3	.571	5.08	17	9	0	0	0	56 2/3	69	42	32	27	27
1996— Ottawa (I.L.)■							Did not play.								
1997— Bangor (NEL)■	3	2	.600	2.54	7	5	1	1	2	28 1/3	25	13	8	8	19
1998— Nashua (Atl.)■	4	3	.571	2.44	10	10	3	0	0	66 1/3	49	23	18	21	43
— Columbus (I.L.)■	4	2	.667	4.53	12	5	1	0	0	43 2/3	42	23	22	11	22
1999— Reading (East.)■	0	0	...	0.90	7	0	0	0	4	10	7	3	1	2	12
— Scranton/W.B. (I.L.)	3	1	.750	3.00	23	4	0	0	10	36	38	15	12	15	25
— Philadelphia (N.L.)	1	4	.200	3.86	13	5	0	0	0	32 2/3	40	16	14	17	16
A.L. totals (5 years)	17	23	.425	4.34	157	25	1	0	45	311	342	165	150	138	161
N.L. totals (2 years)	5	7	.417	4.63	30	14	0	0	0	89 1/3	109	58	46	44	43
Major League totals (7 years)	22	30	.423	4.41	187	39	1	0	45	400 1/3	451	223	196	182	204

GRATEROL, BEIKER   P

PERSONAL: Born November 9, 1974, in Edo Lara, Venezuela. ... 6-2/165. ... Throws right, bats right.

TRANSACTIONS/CAREER NOTES: Signed as non-drafted free agent by Toronto Blue Jays organization (November 17, 1992). ... Traded by Blue Jays to Detroit Tigers for P Eric Ludwick (December 14, 1998). ... On Toledo disabled list (June 17-30 and July 23, 1999-remainder of season). ... Granted free agency (October 15, 1999).

Year League	W	L	Pct.	ERA	G	GS	CG	ShO	Sv.	IP	H	R	ER	BB	SO
1993— Dom. Blue Jays (DSL)	2	5	.286	3.95	13	13	1	0	0	70 2/3	59	39	31	29	40
1994— Dom. Blue Jays (DSL)	5	3	.625	4.41	16	11	0	0	1	65 1/3	72	40	32	32	49
1995— Dom. Blue Jays (DSL)	4	3	.571	3.99	23	6	0	0	10	65 1/3	61	33	29	23	69
1996— St. Catharines (NY-P)	9	1	.900	1.50	14	13	1	1	0	84	59	24	14	21	66

G

Year	League	W	L	Pct.	ERA	G	GS	CG	ShO	Sv.	IP	H	R	ER	BB	SO
1997—	Hagerstown (SAL)	1	0	1.000	0.00	4	0	0	0	2	11	7	1	0	3	12
—	Dunedin (FSL)	4	7	.364	4.22	17	10	1	0	1	81	86	46	38	26	54
—	Knoxville (Sou.)	2	1	.667	5.40	3	3	0	0	0	16 2/3	24	12	10	9	11
1998—	Knoxville (Sou.)	5	6	.455	5.24	12	12	0	0	0	67	76	46	39	22	52
—	Syracuse (I.L.)	9	2	.818	4.59	16	16	0	0	0	96	103	55	49	32	62
1999—	Toledo (I.L.)■	3	9	.250	5.83	17	15	0	0	0	78 2/3	89	55	51	38	47
—	Detroit (A.L.)	0	1	.000	15.75	1	1	0	0	0	4	4	7	7	4	2
Major League totals (1 year)		0	1	.000	15.75	1	1	0	0	0	4	4	7	7	4	2

GRAVES, DANNY — P — REDS

PERSONAL: Born August 7, 1973, in Saigon, Vietnam. ... 5-11/185. ... Throws right, bats right. ... Full name: Daniel Peter Graves.
HIGH SCHOOL: Brandon (Fla.).
COLLEGE: Miami (Fla.).
TRANSACTIONS/CAREER NOTES: Selected by Cleveland Indians organization in fourth round of free-agent draft (June 2, 1994). ... Traded by Indians with P Jim Crowell, P Scott Winchester and IF Damian Jackson to Cincinnati Reds for P John Smiley and IF Jeff Branson (July 31, 1997).
MISCELLANEOUS: Injured knee during 1994 College World Series and did not play professional baseball during 1994 season.

Year	League	W	L	Pct.	ERA	G	GS	CG	ShO	Sv.	IP	H	R	ER	BB	SO
1995—	Kinston (Caro.)	3	1	.750	0.82	38	0	0	0	21	44	30	11	4	12	46
—	Canton/Akron (East.)	1	0	1.000	0.00	17	0	0	0	10	23 1/3	10	1	0	2	11
—	Buffalo (A.A.)	0	0	...	3.00	3	0	0	0	0	3	5	4	1	1	2
1996—	Buffalo (A.A.)	4	3	.571	1.48	43	0	0	0	19	79	57	14	13	24	46
—	Cleveland (A.L.)	2	0	1.000	4.55	15	0	0	0	0	29 2/3	29	18	15	10	22
1997—	Buffalo (A.A.)	2	3	.400	4.19	19	3	0	0	2	43	45	21	20	11	21
—	Cleveland (A.L.)	0	0	...	4.76	5	0	0	0	0	11 1/3	15	8	6	9	4
—	Indianapolis (A.A.)■	1	0	1.000	3.09	11	0	0	0	5	11 2/3	7	4	4	5	5
—	Cincinnati (N.L.)	0	0	...	6.14	10	0	0	0	0	14 2/3	26	14	10	11	7
1998—	Indianapolis (I.L.)	1	0	1.000	1.93	13	0	0	0	0	14	15	3	3	3	11
—	Cincinnati (N.L.)	2	1	.667	3.32	62	0	0	0	8	81 1/3	76	31	30	28	44
1999—	Cincinnati (N.L.)	8	7	.533	3.08	75	0	0	0	27	111	90	42	38	49	69
A.L. totals (2 years)		2	0	1.000	4.61	20	0	0	0	0	41	44	26	21	19	26
N.L. totals (3 years)		10	8	.556	3.39	147	0	0	0	35	207	192	87	78	88	120
Major League totals (4 years)		12	8	.600	3.59	167	0	0	0	35	248	236	113	99	107	146

GREBECK, CRAIG — IF — BLUE JAYS

PERSONAL: Born December 29, 1964, in Johnstown, Pa. ... 5-7/155. ... Bats right, throws right. ... Full name: Craig Allen Grebeck. ... Brother of Brian Grebeck, infielder with California Angels and Houston Astros organizations (1990-97). ... Name pronounced GRAY-bek.
HIGH SCHOOL: Lakewood (Calif.).
COLLEGE: Cal State Dominguez Hills.
TRANSACTIONS/CAREER NOTES: Signed as non-drafted free agent by Chicago White Sox organization (August 13, 1986). ... On disabled list (August 9, 1992-remainder of season). ... On Chicago disabled list (May 21-June 30, 1994); included rehabilitation assignment at Nashville (June 23-30). ... Granted free agency (December 21, 1995). ... Signed by Florida Marlins organization (December 22, 1995). ... On disabled list (July 4-August 15, 1996). ... Granted free agency (October 31, 1996). ... Signed by Anaheim Angels (December 6, 1996). ... Granted free agency (October 9, 1997). ... Signed by Toronto Blue Jays organization (November 27, 1997). ... On Toronto disabled list (April 20-May 5, 1998). ... Granted free agency (October 23, 1998). ... Re-signed by Blue Jays (October 27, 1998). ... On Toronto disabled list (April 11-May 14 and August 5, 1999-remainder of season); included rehabilitation assignment to Syracuse (May 10-14).
STATISTICAL NOTES: Led Southern League in grounding into double plays with 15 in 1989. ... Career major league grand slams: 1.

Year	Team (League)	Pos.	G	AB	R	H	2B	3B	HR	RBI	Avg.	BB	SO	SB	PO	A	E	Avg.
1987—	Peninsula (Caro.)	SS-3B	104	378	63	106	22	3	15	67	.280	37	62	3	137	278	16	.963
1988—	Birmingham (Sou.)	2B	133	450	57	126	21	1	9	53	.280	65	72	5	238	368	19	.970
1989—	Birmingham (Sou.)	SS-3B-2B	•143	•533	85	*153	25	4	5	80	.287	63	77	14	234	364	28	.955
1990—	Chicago (A.L.)	3B-SS-2B	59	119	7	20	3	1	1	9	.168	8	24	0	36	98	3	.978
—	Vancouver (PCL)	SS-3B-2B	12	41	8	8	0	0	1	3	.195	6	7	1	28	26	1	.982
1991—	Chicago (A.L.)	3B-2B-SS	107	224	37	63	16	3	6	31	.281	38	40	1	104	183	10	.966
1992—	Chicago (A.L.)	SS-3B-OF	88	287	24	77	21	2	3	35	.268	30	34	0	112	283	8	.980
1993—	Chicago (A.L.)	SS-2B-3B	72	190	25	43	5	0	1	12	.226	26	26	1	91	185	5	.982
1994—	Chicago (A.L.)	2B-SS-3B	35	97	17	30	5	0	0	5	.309	12	5	0	44	65	2	.982
—	Nashville (A.A.)	SS	5	15	3	6	2	0	0	4	.400	1	2	0	5	12	1	.944
1995—	Chicago (A.L.)	SS-3B-2B	53	154	19	40	12	0	1	18	.260	21	23	0	76	127	7	.967
1996—	Florida (N.L.)■	2B-SS-3B	50	95	8	20	1	0	1	9	.211	4	14	0	67	66	2	.985
1997—	Anaheim (A.L.)■	2-S-3-O-DH	63	126	12	34	9	0	1	6	.270	18	11	0	68	88	2	.987
1998—	Toronto (A.L.)■	2B-SS-3B	102	301	33	77	17	2	2	27	.256	29	42	2	151	269	11	.974
—	Syracuse (I.L.)	2B	1	3	0	1	0	0	0	0	.333	0	0	0	2	6	0	1.000
1999—	Toronto (A.L.)	2B-DH-SS-3B	34	113	18	41	7	0	0	10	.363	15	13	0	42	45	5	.946
—	Syracuse (I.L.)	2B-SS	4	16	3	4	1	0	1	2	.250	1	1	0	9	10	2	.905
American League totals (9 years)			613	1611	192	425	95	8	15	153	.264	197	218	4	724	1343	53	.975
National League totals (1 year)			50	95	8	20	1	0	1	9	.211	4	14	0	67	66	2	.985
Major League totals (10 years)			663	1706	200	445	96	8	16	162	.261	201	232	4	791	1409	55	.976

CHAMPIONSHIP SERIES RECORD

Year	Team (League)	Pos.	G	AB	R	H	2B	3B	HR	RBI	Avg.	BB	SO	SB	PO	A	E	Avg.
1993—	Chicago (A.L.)	PH-3B	1	1	0	1	0	0	0	0	1.000	0	0	0	0	0	0	...

G

GREEN, CHAD — OF — BREWERS

PERSONAL: Born June 28, 1975, in Dunkirk, N.Y. ... 5-10/180. ... Bats both, throws right. ... Full name: Chad Elton Green.
HIGH SCHOOL: Mentor (Ohio).
COLLEGE: Kentucky.
TRANSACTIONS/CAREER NOTES: Selected by Kansas City Royals organization in ninth round of free-agent draft (June 3, 1993); did not sign. ... Selected by Milwaukee Brewers organization in first round (eighth pick overall) of free-agent draft (June 4, 1996). ... On Stockton disabled list (April 2-May 8 and June 24-July 18, 1998). ... On El Paso disabled list (July 27-August 10, 1998).
STATISTICAL NOTES: Led California League outfielders with 311 total chances in 1997.
MISCELLANEOUS: Member of 1996 U.S. Olympic baseball team.

										BATTING					FIELDING		
Year	Team (League)	Pos.	G	AB	R	H	2B	3B	HR	RBI	Avg.	BB	SO	SB	PO	A	E	Avg.
1996— Ogden (Pio.)		OF	21	81	22	29	4	1	3	8	.358	15	23	12	53	3	0	1.000
1997— Stockton (Calif.)		OF	127	513	78	128	26	14	2	43	.250	37	138	37	*291	11	9	.971
1998— Stockton (Calif.)		OF	40	151	30	52	13	2	0	17	.344	12	22	22	61	6	0	1.000
— El Paso (Texas)		PH	7	6	0	0	0	0	0	0	.000	1	3	0	0	0	0	...
1999— Huntsville (Sou.)		OF	116	422	56	104	22	3	10	46	.246	46	109	28	240	6	4	.984

GREEN, JASON — P — ASTROS

PERSONAL: Born June 5, 1975, in Port Hope, Ont. ... 6-1/205. ... Throws right, bats right. ... Full name: David Jason Green.
HIGH SCHOOL: District High School (Port Hope, Ont.).
JUNIOR COLLEGE: Chipola Junior College (Fla.).
TRANSACTIONS/CAREER NOTES: Selected by Houston Astros organization in 30th round of free-agent draft (June 3, 1993). ... On disabled list (July 1-September 11, 1996). ... On Jackson disabled list (May 1-28, 1999).

Year	League	W	L	Pct.	ERA	G	GS	CG	ShO	Sv.	IP	H	R	ER	BB	SO
1994— Gulf Coast Astros (GCL)		2	1	.667	2.74	18	0	0	0	1	23	16	11	7	16	12
1995— Auburn (NY-P)		8	2	.800	3.81	14	14	2	•1	0	82⅔	82	48	35	29	48
1996— Auburn (NY-P)		0	0	...	0.00	2	2	0	0	0	6	4	1	0	1	2
1997— Kissimmee (FSL)		0	3	.000	5.19	8	0	0	0	0	8⅔	11	12	5	10	3
— Quad City (Midw.)		7	12	.368	4.58	23	22	1	0	0	125⅔	126	79	64	53	96
1998— Kissimmee (FSL)		2	5	.286	3.34	51	3	0	0	14	67⅓	64	34	25	32	67
1999— Jackson (Texas)		3	3	.500	3.40	33	0	0	0	10	42⅓	41	20	16	20	50

GREEN, SCARBOROUGH — OF — RANGERS

PERSONAL: Born June 9, 1974, in Creve Coeur, Mo. ... 5-10/175. ... Bats right, throws right. ... Full name: Bertrum Scarborough Green.
HIGH SCHOOL: Lafayette (Ballwin, Mo.).
JUNIOR COLLEGE: St. Louis Community College at Meramec.
TRANSACTIONS/CAREER NOTES: Selected by St. Louis Cardinals organization in 10th round of free-agent draft (June 1, 1992). ... Claimed on waivers by Texas Rangers organization (September 8, 1998).
STATISTICAL NOTES: Tied for Texas League lead with four intentional bases on balls in 1997.

										BATTING					FIELDING		
Year	Team (League)	Pos.	G	AB	R	H	2B	3B	HR	RBI	Avg.	BB	SO	SB	PO	A	E	Avg.
1993— Ariz. Cardinals (Ariz.)		SS	33	95	16	21	3	1	0	11	.221	7	17	3	35	87	14	.897
1994— Johnson City (Appl.)		SS-OF	54	199	32	48	5	0	0	11	.241	25	61	22	58	140	22	.900
1995— Savannah (SAL)		SS	132	429	48	98	7	6	1	25	.228	55	101	26	*205	358	51	.917
1996— St. Petersburg (FSL)		OF	36	140	26	41	4	1	1	11	.293	21	22	13	90	4	2	.979
— Arkansas (Texas)		OF	92	300	45	60	6	3	3	24	.200	38	56	21	194	7	2	.990
1997— Arkansas (Texas)		OF	76	251	45	77	14	4	2	29	.307	36	48	11	170	8	1	.994
— Louisville (A.A.)		OF	52	209	26	53	11	2	3	13	.254	22	55	10	138	7	1	.993
— St. Louis (N.L.)		OF	20	31	5	3	0	0	0	1	.097	2	5	0	19	1	1	.952
1998— Memphis (PCL)		OF	26	81	11	16	5	0	0	2	.198	8	22	1	48	1	0	1.000
— Arkansas (Texas)		OF	18	75	16	27	2	1	2	9	.360	6	12	9	44	1	0	1.000
1999— Texas (A.L.)■		OF-DH	18	13	4	4	0	0	0	0	.308	1	2	0	6	0	0	1.000
— Oklahoma (PCL)		OF	104	359	68	89	16	6	3	29	.248	34	86	26	219	13	6	.975
American League totals (1 year)			18	13	4	4	0	0	0	0	.308	1	2	0	6	0	0	1.000
National League totals (1 year)			20	31	5	3	0	0	0	1	.097	2	5	0	19	1	1	.952
Major League totals (2 years)			38	44	9	7	0	0	0	1	.159	3	7	0	25	1	1	.963

G

GREEN, SHAWN — OF — DODGERS

PERSONAL: Born November 10, 1972, in Des Plaines, Ill. ... 6-4/200. ... Bats left, throws left. ... Full name: Shawn David Green.
HIGH SCHOOL: Tustin (Calif.).
TRANSACTIONS/CAREER NOTES: Selected by Toronto Blue Jays organization in first round (16th pick overall) of free-agent draft (June 3, 1991); pick received as compensation for San Francisco Giants signing Type A free-agent P Bud Black. ... On disabled list (June 30-July 23, 1992). ... On Knoxville disabled list (June 11-July 24, 1993). ... Traded by Blue Jays with 2B Jorge Nunez to Los Angeles Dodgers for OF Raul Mondesi and P Pedro Borbon (November 8, 1999).
HONORS: Won A.L. Gold Glove as outfielder (1999). ... Named outfielder on THE SPORTING NEWS A.L. All-Star team (1999). ... Named outfielder on THE SPORTING NEWS A.L. Silver Slugger team (1999).
STATISTICAL NOTES: Tied for Florida State League lead with eight sacrifice flies in 1992. ... Had 28-game hitting streak (June 29-July 31, 1999). ... Led A.L. with 361 total bases in 1999. ... Career major league grand slams: 2.

							BATTING							FIELDING		
Year	Team (League)	Pos.	G	AB	R	H	2B	3B	HR	RBI	Avg.	BB	SO	SB	PO	A	E	Avg.
1992—Dunedin (FSL)		OF	114	417	44	114	21	3	1	49	.273	28	66	22	182	3	5	.974
1993—Knoxville (Sou.)		OF	99	360	40	102	14	2	4	34	.283	26	72	4	172	3	8	.956
— Toronto (A.L.)		OF-DH	3	6	0	0	0	0	0	0	.000	0	1	0	1	0	0	1.000
1994—Syracuse (I.L.)		OF-DH	109	433	82	149	27	3	13	61	*.344	40	54	19	220	5	1	*.996
— Toronto (A.L.)		OF	14	33	1	3	1	0	0	1	.091	1	8	1	12	2	0	1.000
1995—Toronto (A.L.)		OF	121	379	52	109	31	4	15	54	.288	20	68	1	207	9	6	.973
1996—Toronto (A.L.)		OF-DH	132	422	52	118	32	3	11	45	.280	33	75	5	254	10	2	.992
1997—Toronto (A.L.)		OF-DH	135	429	57	123	22	4	16	53	.287	36	99	14	173	6	3	.984
1998—Toronto (A.L.)		OF	138	630	106	175	33	4	35	100	.278	50	142	35	311	14	7	.979
1999—Toronto (A.L.)		OF	153	614	134	190	*45	0	42	123	.309	66	117	20	340	5	1	.997
Major League totals (7 years)			716	2513	402	718	164	15	119	376	.286	206	510	76	1298	46	19	.986

ALL-STAR GAME RECORD

						BATTING								FIELDING		
Year	League	Pos.	AB	R	H	2B	3B	HR	RBI	Avg.	BB	SO	SB	PO	A	E	Avg.
1999— American		OF	1	0	1	0	0	0	0	1.000	0	0	0	0	0	0	...

GREEN, TYLER　　　　　P　　　　　ROYALS

PERSONAL: Born February 18, 1970, in Springfield, Ohio. ... 6-5/205. ... Throws right, bats right. ... Full name: Tyler Scott Green.
HIGH SCHOOL: Thomas Jefferson (Denver).
COLLEGE: Wichita State.
TRANSACTIONS/CAREER NOTES: Selected by Cincinnati Reds organization in third round of free-agent draft (June 1, 1988); did not sign. ... Selected by Philadelphia Phillies organization in first round (10th pick overall) of free-agent draft (June 3, 1991). ... On Clearwater disabled list (August 7, 1991-remainder of season). ... On Scranton/Wilkes-Barre disabled list (July 10, 1992-remainder of season and May 3-22, 1993). ... On disabled list (March 23, 1996-entire season). ... On Philadelphia disabled list (March 27-June 1, 1997); including rehabilitation assignment to Scranton/Wilkes-Barre (April 29-May 25). ... On disabled list (July 28-August 28, 1998). ... On Philadelphia disabled list (March 25-June 24, 1999); included rehabilitation assignment to Scranton/Wilkes-Barre (June 6-24). ... Granted free agency (October 15, 1999). ... Signed by Kansas City Royals (November 11, 1999).
STATISTICAL NOTES: Pitched 3-1 no-hit victory for Scranton/Wilkes-Barre against Ottawa (July 4, 1993, first game). ... Led International League with 12 hit batsmen in 1994.
MISCELLANEOUS: Appeared in one game as pinch runner (1995).

Year	League	W	L	Pct.	ERA	G	GS	CG	ShO	Sv.	IP	H	R	ER	BB	SO
1991— Batavia (NY-P)		1	0	1.000	1.20	3	3	0	0	0	15	7	2	2	6	19
— Clearwater (FSL)		2	0	1.000	1.38	2	2	0	0	0	13	3	2	2	8	20
1992— Reading (East.)		6	3	.667	1.88	12	12	0	0	0	62 1/3	46	16	13	20	67
— Scranton/W.B. (I.L.)		0	1	.000	6.10	2	2	0	0	0	10 1/3	7	7	7	12	15
1993— Philadelphia (N.L.)		0	0	...	7.36	3	2	0	0	0	7 1/3	16	9	6	5	7
— Scranton/W.B. (I.L.)		6	10	.375	3.95	28	14	4	0	0	118 1/3	102	62	52	43	87
1994— Scranton/W.B. (I.L.)		7	*16	.304	5.56	27	26	4	0	0	162	179	*110	*100	*77	95
1995— Philadelphia (N.L.)		8	9	.471	5.31	26	25	4	2	0	140 2/3	157	86	83	66	85
1996— Philadelphia (N.L.)								Did not play.								
1997— Scranton/W.B. (I.L.)		4	8	.333	6.10	12	12	3	0	0	72 1/3	80	54	49	29	40
— Philadelphia (N.L.)		4	4	.500	4.93	14	14	0	0	0	76 2/3	72	50	42	45	58
1998— Philadelphia (N.L.)		6	12	.333	5.03	27	27	0	0	0	159 1/3	142	97	89	85	113
1999— Scranton/W.B. (I.L.)		4	6	.400	7.69	19	7	1	0	0	50 1/3	78	47	43	24	31
Major League totals (4 years)		18	25	.419	5.16	70	68	4	2	0	384	387	242	220	201	263

ALL-STAR GAME RECORD

Year	League	W	L	Pct.	ERA	GS	CG	ShO	Sv.	IP	H	R	ER	BB	SO
1995— National		0	0	...	0.00	0	0	0	0	1	2	0	0	0	1

GREENE, CHARLIE　　　　　C

PERSONAL: Born January 23, 1971, in Miami. ... 6-2/190. ... Bats right, throws right. ... Full name: Charles Patrick Greene.
HIGH SCHOOL: Miami Killian.
JUNIOR COLLEGE: Miami-Dade (South) Community College.
TRANSACTIONS/CAREER NOTES: Selected by San Diego Padres organization in 19th round of free-agent draft (June 3, 1991). ... Selected by New York Mets organization from Padres organization in Rule 5 minor league draft (December 13, 1993). ... Claimed on waivers by Baltimore Orioles (September 11, 1997). ... Claimed on waivers by Milwaukee Brewers (December 5, 1998). ... Granted free agency (October 11, 1999).
STATISTICAL NOTES: Tied for Midwest League lead in double plays by catcher with 11 in 1993.

							BATTING							FIELDING		
Year	Team (League)	Pos.	G	AB	R	H	2B	3B	HR	RBI	Avg.	BB	SO	SB	PO	A	E	Avg.
1991—Ariz. Padres (Ariz.)		C-1B-3B	49	183	27	52	15	1	5	38	.284	16	26	6	334	30	3	.992
1992—Char., S.C. (SAL)		C-3B	98	298	22	55	9	1	1	24	.185	11	60	1	561	119	14	.980
1993—Waterloo (Midw.) C-1B-3B-SS			84	213	19	38	8	0	2	20	.178	13	33	0	460	96	16	.972
1994—St. Lucie (FSL)■		C	69	224	23	57	4	0	0	21	.254	9	31	0	380	65	13	.972
— Binghamton (East.)		C	30	106	13	18	4	0	0	2	.170	6	18	0	190	30	3	.987
1995—Binghamton (East.)		C	100	346	26	82	13	0	2	34	.237	15	47	2	670	54	4	*.995
— Norfolk (I.L.)		C	27	88	6	17	3	0	0	4	.193	3	28	0	157	25	0	1.000
1996—Binghamton (East.)		C	100	336	35	82	17	0	2	27	.244	17	52	2	550	75	3	.995
— New York (N.L.)		C	2	1	0	0	0	0	0	0	.000	0	0	0	1	0	0	1.000
1997—Norfolk (I.L.)		C	76	238	27	49	7	0	8	28	.206	9	54	1	475	49	8	.985
— Baltimore (A.L.)■		C	5	2	0	0	0	0	0	1	.000	0	1	0	4	0	0	1.000
1998—Rochester (I.L.)		C	77	250	23	53	10	0	4	28	.212	9	54	1	517	55	7	.988
— Baltimore (A.L.)		C	13	21	1	4	1	0	0	0	.190	0	8	0	58	4	0	1.000
1999—Louisville (I.L.)■		C	56	161	16	34	8	0	4	15	.211	7	26	0	306	27	2	.994
— Milwaukee (N.L.)		C	32	42	4	8	1	0	0	1	.190	5	11	0	104	8	1	.991
American League totals (2 years)			18	23	1	4	1	0	0	1	.174	0	9	0	62	4	0	1.000
National League totals (2 years)			34	43	4	8	1	0	0	1	.186	5	11	0	105	8	1	.991
Major League totals (4 years)			52	66	5	12	2	0	0	2	.182	5	20	0	167	12	1	.994

G

GREENE, RICK   P   TWINS

PERSONAL: Born January 2, 1971, in Fort Knox, Ky. ... 6-5/200. ... Throws right, bats right. ... Full name: Richard Douglas Greene Jr.
HIGH SCHOOL: Coral Gables (Fla.).
COLLEGE: Louisiana State.
TRANSACTIONS/CAREER NOTES: Selected by Detroit Tigers organization in first round (16th pick overall) of free-agent draft (June 1, 1992). ... Missed entire 1992 season due to injury. ... On disabled list (May 23-July 17, 1995). ... Traded by Tigers with P Mike Myers and SS Santiago Perez to Milwaukee Brewers for P Bryce Florie (November 20, 1997). ... Granted free agency (October 15, 1998). ... Signed by Cincinnati Reds organization (February 9, 1999). ... Granted free agency (October 12, 1999). ... Signed by Minnesota Twins organization (December 15, 1999).
MISCELLANEOUS: Member of 1992 U.S. Olympic baseball team.

Year	League	W	L	Pct.	ERA	G	GS	CG	ShO	Sv.	IP	H	R	ER	BB	SO
1992—								Did not play.								
1993—	Lakeland (FSL)	2	3	.400	6.20	26	0	0	0	2	40 2/3	57	28	28	16	32
—	London (East.)	2	2	.500	6.52	23	0	0	0	0	29	31	22	21	20	19
1994—	Trenton (East.)	1	1	.500	7.91	20	0	0	0	3	19 1/3	17	17	17	21	5
—	Lakeland (FSL)	0	4	.000	4.32	19	2	0	0	4	33 1/3	50	23	16	10	28
1995—	Jacksonville (Sou.)	6	2	.750	3.49	32	0	0	0	0	38 2/3	45	19	15	15	29
1996—	Jacksonville (Sou.)	2	7	.222	4.98	57	0	0	0	30	56	67	44	31	39	42
1997—	Toledo (I.L.)	6	8	.429	2.83	57	0	0	0	1	70	49	29	22	32	51
1998—	Louisville (I.L.)■	6	6	.500	3.51	58	0	0	0	18	66 2/3	73	31	26	33	44
1999—	Indianapolis (I.L.)■	5	7	.417	3.69	61	0	0	0	9	78	78	37	32	35	40
—	Cincinnati (N.L.)	0	0	...	4.76	1	0	0	0	0	5 2/3	7	4	3	1	3
Major League totals (1 year)		0	0	...	4.76	1	0	0	0	0	5 2/3	7	4	3	1	3

GREENE, TODD   OF/DH   ANGELS

PERSONAL: Born May 8, 1971, in Augusta, Ga. ... 5-10/208. ... Bats right, throws right. ... Full name: Todd Anthony Greene.
HIGH SCHOOL: Evans (Ga.).
COLLEGE: Georgia Southern.
TRANSACTIONS/CAREER NOTES: Selected by Atlanta Braves organization in 27th round of free-agent draft (June 5, 1989); did not sign. ... Selected by California Angels organization in 12th round of free-agent draft (June 3, 1993). ... On Vancouver disabled list (April 11-May 25, 1996). ... Angels franchise renamed Anaheim Angels for 1997 season. ... On Anaheim disabled list (August 20, 1997-remainder of season). ... On Anaheim disabled list (March 19-August 5, 1998); included rehabilitation assignments to Lake Elsinore (April 14-May 16, May 21 and May 27-31) and Vancouver (May 17-20, May 22-26, June 1-2 and July 17-August 5). ... On suspended list (May 13-16, 1999).
HONORS: Named California League Most Valuable Player (1994).
STATISTICAL NOTES: Led California League with 306 total bases, 12 intentional bases on balls received and .584 slugging percentage in 1994. ... Led California League catchers with 15 errors, 13 double plays and 44 passed balls in 1994. ... Career major league grand slams: 1.

								BATTING							FIELDING			
Year	Team (League)	Pos.	G	AB	R	H	2B	3B	HR	RBI	Avg.	BB	SO	SB	PO	A	E	Avg.
1993—	Boise (N.W.)	OF	•76	*305	55	82	15	3	*15	*71	.269	34	44	4	136	4	3	.979
1994—	Lake Elsinore (Calif.)	C-OF-1B	133	524	98	158	*39	2	*35	*124	.302	64	96	10	624	90	†15	.979
1995—	Midland (Texas)	C-DH-1B	82	318	59	104	19	1	26	57	.327	17	55	3	314	44	3	.992
—	Vancouver (PCL)	C-DH	43	168	28	42	3	1	4	14	.250	11	36	1	175	17	1	.995
1996—	Vancouver (PCL)	C-DH	60	223	27	68	18	0	5	33	.305	16	36	0	219	37	3	.988
—	California (A.L.)	C-DH	29	79	9	15	1	0	2	9	.190	4	11	2	119	19	0	1.000
1997—	Anaheim (A.L.)	C-DH	34	124	24	36	6	0	9	24	.290	7	25	2	153	7	0	1.000
—	Vancouver (PCL)	C-DH-1B-OF	64	260	51	92	22	0	25	75	.354	20	31	5	331	43	3	.992
1998—	Lake Elsinore (Calif.)	DH-1B	12	44	9	10	2	0	1	6	.227	4	7	1	9	1	2	.833
—	Vancouver (PCL)	DH-1B-C-OF	30	108	16	30	12	0	7	20	.278	12	17	1	97	7	1	.990
—	Anaheim (A.L.)	OF-DH-1B	29	71	3	18	4	0	1	7	.254	2	20	0	28	1	0	1.000
1999—	Anaheim (A.L.)	DH-OF-C	97	321	36	78	20	0	14	42	.243	12	63	1	91	8	2	.980
—	Edmonton (PCL)	OF-DH	19	74	10	18	6	0	5	14	.243	0	12	0	23	0	0	1.000
Major League totals (4 years)			189	595	72	147	31	0	26	82	.247	25	119	5	391	35	2	.995

G

GREENE, WILLIE   3B/OF   CUBS

PERSONAL: Born September 23, 1971, in Milledgeville, Ga. ... 5-11/192. ... Bats left, throws right. ... Full name: Willie Louis Greene.
HIGH SCHOOL: Jones County (Gray, Ga.).
TRANSACTIONS/CAREER NOTES: Selected by Pittsburgh Pirates organization in first round (18th pick overall) of free-agent draft (June 5, 1989). ... Traded by Pirates with P Scott Ruskin and a player to be named later to Montreal Expos for P Zane Smith (August 8, 1990); Expos acquired OF Moises Alou to complete deal (August 16, 1990). ... Traded by Expos with OF Dave Martinez and P Scott Ruskin to Cincinnati Reds for P John Wetteland and P Bill Risley (December 11, 1991). ... On Cincinnati disabled list (August 21, 1993-remainder of season). ... On Indianapolis disabled list (June 7-19, 1995). ... On disabled list (June 27-July 12, 1996). ... Traded by Reds to Baltimore Orioles for OF Jeffrey Hammonds (August 10, 1998). ... Granted free agency (December 21, 1998). ... Signed by Toronto Blue Jays (January 19, 1999). ... Granted free agency (October 15, 1999). ... Signed by Chicago Cubs (January 18, 2000).
STATISTICAL NOTES: Led Florida State League third basemen with 31 errors in 1991. ... Led Southern League third basemen with 24 double plays in 1992. ... Led American Association third basemen with 23 errors in 1993. ... Hit three home runs in one game (September 24, 1996). ... Career major league grand slams: 3.

								BATTING							FIELDING			
Year	Team (League)	Pos.	G	AB	R	H	2B	3B	HR	RBI	Avg.	BB	SO	SB	PO	A	E	Avg.
1989—	Princeton (Appl.)	SS	39	136	22	44	6	4	2	24	.324	9	29	4	33	69	19	.843
—	GC Pirates (GCL)	SS	23	86	17	24	3	3	5	11	.279	9	6	4	25	49	3	.961
1990—	Augusta (SAL)	SS-2B	86	291	59	75	12	4	11	47	.258	61	58	7	117	209	34	.906
—	Salem (Caro.)	SS	17	60	9	11	1	1	3	9	.183	7	18	0	22	43	2	.970
—	Rockford (Midw.)■	SS	11	35	4	14	3	0	0	2	.400	6	7	2	14	37	4	.927
1991—	W.P. Beach (FSL)	3B-SS	99	322	46	70	9	3	12	43	.217	50	93	10	72	184	†32	.889

Year	Team (League)	Pos.	G	AB	R	H	2B	3B	HR	RBI	Avg.	BB	SO	SB	PO	A	E	Avg.
1992—Cedar Rap. (Midw.)■.		3B	34	120	26	34	8	2	12	40	.283	18	27	3	13	60	8	.901
—Chattanooga (Sou.)....		3B	96	349	47	97	19	2	15	66	.278	46	90	9	*77	174	14	*.947
—Cincinnati (N.L.)......		3B	29	93	10	25	5	2	2	13	.269	10	23	0	15	40	3	.948
1993—Indianapolis (A.A.)......		3B-SS	98	341	62	91	19	0	22	58	.267	51	83	2	77	171	†23	.915
—Cincinnati (N.L.)........		SS-3B	15	50	7	8	1	1	2	5	.160	2	19	0	19	37	1	.982
1994—Cincinnati (N.L.)........		3B-OF	16	37	5	8	2	0	0	3	.216	6	14	0	2	21	1	.958
—Indianapolis (A.A.)......		3B-SS-DH	114	435	77	124	24	1	23	80	.285	56	88	8	93	249	17	.953
1995—Cincinnati (N.L.)........		3B	8	19	1	2	0	0	0	0	.105	3	7	0	1	13	0	1.000
—Indianapolis (A.A.).		3-S-DH-O	91	325	57	79	12	2	19	45	.243	38	67	3	60	160	12	.948
1996—Cincinnati (N.L.)		3-O-1-S-2	115	287	48	70	5	5	19	63	.244	36	88	0	57	149	16	.928
1997—Cincinnati (N.L.)		3-0-1-S	151	495	62	125	22	1	26	91	.253	78	111	6	176	175	17	.954
1998—Cincinnati (N.L.)		3-0-S-DH	111	356	57	96	18	1	14	49	.270	56	80	6	92	132	13	.945
—Baltimore (A.L.)■......		OF-DH	24	40	8	6	1	0	1	5	.150	13	10	1	15	1	1	.941
1999—Toronto (A.L.)■		DH-3B-OF	81	226	22	46	7	0	12	41	.204	20	56	0	7	7	1	.933
—Syracuse (I.L.)...........		OF	14	52	12	17	1	0	5	11	.327	6	14	0	24	2	0	1.000
American League totals (2 years)			105	266	30	52	8	0	13	46	.195	33	66	1	22	8	2	.938
National League totals (7 years)			445	1337	190	334	53	10	63	224	.250	191	342	12	362	567	51	.948
Major League totals (8 years)			550	1603	220	386	61	10	76	270	.241	224	408	13	384	575	53	.948

GREER, RUSTY   OF   RANGERS

PERSONAL: Born January 21, 1969, in Fort Rucker, Ala. ... 6-0/195. ... Bats left, throws left. ... Full name: Thurman Clyde Greer III.
HIGH SCHOOL: Albertville (Ala.).
COLLEGE: Montevallo (Ala.).
TRANSACTIONS/CAREER NOTES: Selected by Texas Rangers organization in 10th round of free-agent draft (June 4, 1990). ... On disabled list (July 31-August 22, 1992).
RECORDS: Shares major league record for fewest double plays by outfielder (150 or more games)—0 (1997 and 1998).
STATISTICAL NOTES: Led Florida State League with .395 on-base percentage in 1991. ... Career major league grand slams: 6.

Year	Team (League)	Pos.	G	AB	R	H	2B	3B	HR	RBI	Avg.	BB	SO	SB	PO	A	E	Avg.
1990—Butte (Pio.).................		OF	62	226	48	78	12	6	10	50	.345	41	23	9	84	5	*8	.918
1991—Charlotte (FSL)..........		OF-1B	111	388	52	114	25	1	5	48	.294	66	48	12	213	15	7	.970
—Tulsa (Texas).............		OF	20	64	12	19	3	2	3	12	.297	17	6	2	34	0	0	1.000
1992—Tulsa (Texas).............		1B-OF	106	359	47	96	22	4	5	37	.267	60	63	2	814	50	11	.987
1993—Tulsa (Texas).............		1B	129	474	76	138	25	6	15	59	.291	53	79	10	1055	93	8	.993
—Oklahoma City (A.A.)..		OF	8	27	6	6	2	0	1	4	.222	6	7	0	16	0	0	1.000
1994—Oklahoma City (A.A.)..		OF-DH-1B	31	111	18	35	12	1	3	13	.315	18	24	1	52	3	3	.948
—Texas (A.L.).............		OF-1B	80	277	36	87	16	1	10	46	.314	46	46	0	216	4	6	.973
1995—Texas (A.L.).............		OF-1B	131	417	58	113	21	2	13	61	.271	55	66	3	240	9	6	.976
1996—Texas (A.L.).............		OF-DH-1B	139	542	96	180	41	6	18	100	.332	62	86	9	304	6	5	.984
1997—Texas (A.L.).............		OF-DH	157	601	112	193	42	3	26	87	.321	83	87	9	318	9	*12	.965
1998—Texas (A.L.).............		OF	155	598	107	183	31	5	16	108	.306	80	93	2	304	6	3	.990
1999—Texas (A.L.).............		OF-DH	147	556	107	167	41	3	20	101	.300	96	67	2	286	3	5	.983
Major League totals (6 years)			809	2991	516	923	192	20	103	503	.309	422	445	25	1668	37	37	.979

DIVISION SERIES RECORD

Year	Team (League)	Pos.	G	AB	R	H	2B	3B	HR	RBI	Avg.	BB	SO	SB	PO	A	E	Avg.
1996—Texas (A.L.)...............		OF	4	16	2	2	0	0	0	0	.125	3	3	0	12	0	0	1.000
1998—Texas (A.L.)...............		OF	3	11	0	1	0	0	0	0	.091	1	2	0	4	1	0	1.000
1999—Texas (A.L.)...............		OF	3	9	0	1	0	0	0	0	.111	3	1	0	9	0	0	1.000
Division series totals (3 years)			10	36	2	4	0	0	0	0	.111	7	6	0	25	1	0	1.000

GREGG, KEVIN   P   ATHLETICS

PERSONAL: Born June 20, 1978, in Corvallis, Ore. ... 6-7/200. ... Throws right, bats right. ... Full name: Kevin Marschall Gregg.
HIGH SCHOOL: Corvallis (Ore.).
TRANSACTIONS/CAREER NOTES: Selected by Oakland Athletics organization in 15th round of free-agent draft (June 4, 1996).
STATISTICAL NOTES: Led California League pitchers with 26 wild pitches in 1997.

Year	League	W	L	Pct.	ERA	G	GS	CG	ShO	Sv.	IP	H	R	ER	BB	SO
1996—Arizona Angels (Ariz.)........		3	3	.500	3.10	11	9	0	0	0	40 2/3	30	14	14	21	48
1997—Visalia (Calif.)..................		6	8	.429	5.70	25	24	0	0	0	115 1/3	116	81	73	74	136
1998—Modesto (Calif.).............		8	7	.533	3.81	30	24	0	0	1	144	139	72	61	76	141
1999—Visalia (Calif.)..................		4	4	.500	3.80	13	11	1	1	1	64	60	34	27	23	48
—Midland (Texas).................		4	7	.364	3.74	16	16	2	0	0	91 1/3	75	45	38	31	66
—Vancouver (PCL)..............		1	0	1.000	3.60	1	1	0	0	0	5	6	2	2	2	4

G

GREISINGER, SETH   P   TIGERS

PERSONAL: Born July 29, 1975, in Kansas City, Kan. ... 6-3/200. ... Throws right, bats right. ... Full name: Seth Adam Greisinger.
HIGH SCHOOL: McLean (Va.).
COLLEGE: Virginia.
TRANSACTIONS/CAREER NOTES: Selected by Cleveland Indians organization in seventh round of free-agent draft (June 3, 1993); did not sign. ... Selected by Detroit Tigers organization in first round (sixth pick overall) of free-agent draft (June 4, 1996). ... On Detroit disabled list (March 26, 1999-entire season); included rehabilitation assignments to Lakeland (May 12-25) and Toledo (June 1-30).
STATISTICAL NOTES: Led Southern League in home runs allowed with 29 in 1997.
MISCELLANEOUS: Member of 1996 U.S. Olympic baseball team.

Year	League	W	L	Pct.	ERA	G	GS	CG	ShO	Sv.	IP	H	R	ER	BB	SO
1997—Jacksonville (Sou.)............		10	6	.625	5.20	28	*28	1	0	0	159 1/3	194	103	92	53	105
1998—Toledo (I.L.).....................		3	4	.429	2.91	10	10	0	0	0	58 2/3	50	21	19	22	37
—Detroit (A.L.).....................		6	9	.400	5.12	21	21	0	0	0	130	142	79	74	48	66
1999—Lakeland (FSL)..................		0	0	...	3.86	1	1	0	0	0	4 2/3	2	2	2	1	2
—Toledo (I.L.).....................		0	1	.000	5.87	2	2	0	0	0	7 2/3	9	5	5	3	4
Major League totals (1 year)........		6	9	.400	5.12	21	21	0	0	0	130	142	79	74	48	66

GRIEVE, BEN   OF   ATHLETICS

PERSONAL: Born May 4, 1976, in Arlington, Texas. ... 6-4/230. ... Bats left, throws right. ... Full name: Benjamin Grieve. ... Son of Tom Grieve, outfielder with four major league teams (1970-79); first father/son combination to be selected in first round of free-agent draft.
HIGH SCHOOL: James W. Martin (Arlington, Texas).
TRANSACTIONS/CAREER NOTES: Selected by Oakland Athletics organization in first round (second pick overall) of free-agent draft (June 2, 1994).
RECORDS: Shares major league record for fewest double plays by outfielder (150 or more games)—0 (1998).
HONORS: Named Minor League Player of the Year by THE SPORTING NEWS (1997). ... Named Southern League Most Valuable Player (1997). ... Named A.L. Rookie Player of the Year by THE SPORTING NEWS (1998). ... Named A.L. Rookie of the Year by Baseball Writers' Association of America (1998).
STATISTICAL NOTES: Tied for Northwest League lead with seven intentional bases on balls received in 1994. ... Led Southern League with .455 on-base percentage in 1997.

Year	Team (League)	Pos.	G	AB	R	H	2B	3B	HR	RBI	Avg.	BB	SO	SB	PO	A	E	Avg.
1994—S. Oregon (N'west).....		OF	72	252	44	83	13	0	7	50	.329	51	48	2	133	8	6	.959
1995—W. Mich. (Mid.)		OF	102	371	53	97	16	1	4	62	.261	60	75	11	125	6	8	.942
—Modesto (Calif.)		OF	28	107	17	28	5	0	2	14	.262	14	15	2	37	2	2	.951
1996—Modesto (Calif.)		OF-DH	72	281	61	100	20	1	11	51	.356	38	52	8	104	5	5	.956
—Huntsville (Sou.)		OF-DH	63	232	34	55	8	1	8	32	.237	35	53	0	79	2	4	.953
1997—Huntsville (Sou.)		OF-DH	100	372	100	122	29	2	24	108	.328	81	75	5	193	6	•8	.961
—Edmonton (PCL)		OF	27	108	27	46	11	1	7	28	.426	12	16	0	51	2	2	.964
—Oakland (A.L.)		OF	24	93	12	29	6	0	3	24	.312	13	25	0	39	1	0	1.000
1998—Oakland (A.L.)		OF-DH	155	583	94	168	41	2	18	89	.288	85	123	2	262	7	2	.993
1999—Oakland (A.L.)		OF-DH	148	486	80	129	21	0	28	86	.265	63	108	4	232	6	3	.988
Major League totals (3 years)			327	1162	186	326	68	2	49	199	.281	161	256	6	533	14	5	.991

ALL-STAR GAME RECORD

Year	League	Pos.	AB	R	H	2B	3B	HR	RBI	Avg.	BB	SO	SB	PO	A	E	Avg.
1998—American...................		PH	0	0	0	0	0	0	0	...	1	0	0	...	...	...	...

GRIFFEY JR., KEN   OF   MARINERS

PERSONAL: Born November 21, 1969, in Donora, Pa. ... 6-3/205. ... Bats left, throws left. ... Full name: George Kenneth Griffey Jr. ... Son of Ken Griffey Sr., hitting coach, Cincinnati Reds, and major league outfielder with four teams (1973-91); and brother of Craig Griffey, outfielder in Seattle Mariners and Cincinnati Reds organizations (1991-97).
HIGH SCHOOL: Moeller (Cincinnati).
TRANSACTIONS/CAREER NOTES: Selected by Seattle Mariners organization in first round (first pick overall) of free-agent draft (June 2, 1987). ... On San Bernardino disabled list (June 9-August 15, 1988). ... On disabled list (July 24-August 20, 1989; June 9-25, 1992; and June 20-July 13, 1996). ... On Seattle disabled list (May 27-August 15, 1995); included rehabilitation assignment to Tacoma (August 13-15).
RECORDS: Shares major league record for most consecutive games with one or more home runs—8 (July 20 through July 28, 1993). ... Holds A.L. single-season record for most major league ballparks, one or more home runs—16 (1998). ... Shares A.L. career record for most major league ballparks, one or more home runs (since 1900)—24.
HONORS: Won A.L. Gold Glove as outfielder (1990-99). ... Named outfielder on THE SPORTING NEWS A.L. All-Star team (1991, 1993-94 and 1996-99). ... Named outfielder on THE SPORTING NEWS A.L. Silver Slugger team (1991, 1993-94 and 1996-99). ... Named Major League Player of the Year by THE SPORTING NEWS (1997). ... Named A.L. Most Valuable Player by Baseball Writers' Association of America (1997).
STATISTICAL NOTES: Led A.L. outfielders with six double plays in 1989. ... Led A.L. with 359 total bases in 1993 and 393 in 1997. ... Hit three home runs in one game (May 24, 1996 and April 25, 1997). ... Led A.L. with 23 intentional bases on balls received in 1997. ... Led A.L. in slugging percentage with .646 in 1997. ... Led A.L. outfielders with 409 putouts and 425 total chances in 1998. ... Had 16-game hitting streak (May 10-28, 1999). ... Tied for A.L. lead with 17 intentional bases on balls received in 1999. ... Career major league grand slams: 12.
MISCELLANEOUS: Holds Seattle Mariners franchise all-time record for most runs (1,063), hits (1,742), home runs (398) and runs batted in (1,152).

Year	Team (League)	Pos.	G	AB	R	H	2B	3B	HR	RBI	Avg.	BB	SO	SB	PO	A	E	Avg.
1987—Bellingham (N.W.)		OF	54	182	43	57	9	1	14	40	.313	44	42	13	117	4	1	*.992
1988—San Bern. (Calif.)........		OF	58	219	50	74	13	3	11	42	.338	34	39	32	145	3	2	.987
—Vermont (East.)		OF	17	61	10	17	5	1	2	10	.279	5	12	4	40	2	1	.977
1989—Seattle (A.L.)		OF-DH	127	455	61	120	23	0	16	61	.264	44	83	16	302	12	•10	.969
1990—Seattle (A.L.)		OF	155	597	91	179	28	7	22	80	.300	63	81	16	330	8	7	.980
1991—Seattle (A.L.)		OF-DH	154	548	76	179	42	1	22	100	.327	71	82	18	360	15	4	.989
1992—Seattle (A.L.)		OF-DH	142	565	83	174	39	4	27	103	.308	44	67	10	359	8	1	.997
1993—Seattle (A.L.)	OF-DH-1B	156	582	113	180	38	3	45	109	.309	96	91	17	317	8	3	.991
1994—Seattle (A.L.)		OF-DH	111	433	94	140	24	4	*40	90	.323	56	73	11	225	12	4	.983
1995—Seattle (A.L.)		OF-DH	72	260	52	67	7	0	17	42	.258	52	53	4	190	5	2	.990
—Tacoma (PCL)		DH	1	3	0	0	0	0	0	0	.000	0	1	0	...	...	...	...
1996—Seattle (A.L.)		OF-DH	140	545	125	165	26	2	49	140	.303	78	104	16	375	10	4	.990
1997—Seattle (A.L.)		OF-DH	157	608	*125	185	34	3	*56	*147	.304	76	121	15	388	9	6	.985
1998—Seattle (A.L.)	OF-DH-1B	161	633	120	180	33	3	*56	146	.284	76	121	20	†409	11	5	.988
1999—Seattle (A.L.)		OF-DH	160	606	123	173	26	3	*48	134	.285	91	108	24	387	10	9	.978
Major League totals (11 years)			1535	5832	1063	1742	320	30	398	1152	.299	747	984	167	3642	108	55	.986

G

DIVISION SERIES RECORD

RECORDS: Holds single-series record for most runs scored—9 (1995). ... Shares single-game record for most home runs—2 (October 3, 1995). ... Shares single-series record for most home runs—5 (1996).
NOTES: Shares postseason single-series record for most home runs—5 (1995).

Year	Team (League)	Pos.	G	AB	R	H	2B	3B	HR	RBI	Avg.	BB	SO	SB	PO	A	E	Avg.
1995—Seattle (A.L.)		OF	5	23	9	9	0	0	5	7	.391	2	4	1	15	1	0	1.000
1997—Seattle (A.L.)		OF	4	15	0	2	0	0	0	2	.133	1	3	2	12	1	0	1.000
Division series totals (2 years)			9	38	9	11	0	0	5	9	.289	3	7	3	27	2	0	1.000

CHAMPIONSHIP SERIES RECORD

Year	Team (League)	Pos.	G	AB	R	H	2B	3B	HR	RBI	Avg.	BB	SO	SB	PO	A	E	Avg.
1995—Seattle (A.L.)		OF	6	21	2	7	2	0	1	2	.333	4	4	2	13	0	1	.929

ALL-STAR GAME RECORD

NOTES: Named Most Valuable Player (1992).

Year	League	Pos.	AB	R	H	2B	3B	HR	RBI	Avg.	BB	SO	SB	PO	A	E	Avg.
1990—American		OF	2	0	0	0	0	0	0	.000	1	0	0	2	0	0	1.000
1991—American		OF	3	0	2	0	0	0	0	.667	0	0	0	2	0	0	1.000
1992—American		OF	3	2	3	1	0	1	2	1.000	0	0	0	1	0	0	1.000
1993—American		OF	3	1	1	0	0	0	1	.333	0	1	0	2	0	0	1.000
1994—American		OF	3	0	2	1	0	0	1	.667	0	0	0	2	0	0	1.000
1995—American								Selected, did not play—injured.									
1996—American								Selected, did not play—injured.									
1997—American		OF	4	0	0	0	0	0	0	.000	0	2	0	0	0	0	...
1998—American		OF	3	1	2	0	0	0	1	.667	1	0	1	0	0	1	.000
1999—American		OF	2	0	0	0	0	0	0	.000	0	1	0	0	0	0	...
All-Star Game totals (8 years)			23	4	10	2	0	1	5	.435	2	4	1	9	0	1	.900

GRIMSLEY, JASON   P   YANKEES

PERSONAL: Born August 7, 1967, in Cleveland, Texas. ... 6-3/180. ... Throws right, bats right. ... Full name: Jason Alan Grimsley.
HIGH SCHOOL: Tarkington (Cleveland, Texas).
TRANSACTIONS/CAREER NOTES: Selected by Philadelphia Phillies organization in 10th round of free-agent draft (June 3, 1985). ... On Clearwater disabled list (April 8-May 10, 1988). ... On Philadelphia disabled list (June 6-August 22, 1991); included rehabilitation assignments to Scranton/Wilkes-Barre (June 15-30 and August 7-21). ... Traded by Phillies to Houston Astros for P Curt Schilling (April 2, 1992). ... On disabled list (May 14-June 14, 1992). ... Released by Astros (March 30, 1993). ... Signed by Cleveland Indians organization (April 7, 1993). ... On Charlotte disabled list (April 15-26, 1993). ... Traded by Indians with P Pep Harris to California Angels for P Brian Anderson (February 15, 1996). ... Granted free agency (October 8, 1996). ... Signed by Detroit Tigers organization (January 17, 1997). ... Released by Tigers (March 20, 1997). ... Signed by Milwaukee Brewers (April 3, 1997). ... Traded by Brewers to Kansas City Royals for P Jamie Brewington (July 29, 1997). ... Granted free agency (October 15, 1997). ... Signed by Indians organization (January 8, 1998). ... Granted free agency (October 15, 1998). ... Signed by New York Yankees organization (January 22, 1999). ... On suspended list (August 11-15, 1999).
STATISTICAL NOTES: Led New York-Pennsylvania League with 11 hit batsmen and 18 wild pitches in 1986. ... Pitched 3-0 no-hit victory for Reading against Harrisburg (May 3, 1989, first game). ... Led International League with 18 wild pitches in 1990. ... Tied for A.L. lead with 13 hit batsmen in 1996. ... Led Pacific Coast League with 20 wild pitches in 1997.
MISCELLANEOUS: Appeared in one game as pinch runner with Philadelphia (1990).

Year	League	W	L	Pct.	ERA	G	GS	CG	ShO	Sv.	IP	H	R	ER	BB	SO
1985—Bend (N.W.)		0	1	.000	13.50	6	1	0	0	0	11⅓	12	21	17	25	10
1986—Utica (NY-P)		1	•10	.091	6.40	14	14	3	0	0	64⅔	63	61	46	*77	46
1987—Spartanburg (SAL)		7	4	.636	3.16	23	9	3	0	0	88⅓	59	48	31	54	98
1988—Clearwater (FSL)		4	7	.364	3.73	16	15	2	0	0	101⅓	80	48	42	37	90
—Reading (East.)		1	3	.250	7.17	5	4	0	0	0	21⅓	20	19	17	13	14
1989—Reading (East.)		11	8	.579	2.98	26	26	8	2	0	172	121	65	57	*109	134
—Philadelphia (N.L.)		1	3	.250	5.89	4	4	0	0	0	18⅓	19	13	12	19	7
1990—Scranton/W.B. (I.L.)		8	5	.615	3.93	22	22	0	0	0	128⅓	111	68	56	78	99
—Philadelphia (N.L.)		3	2	.600	3.30	11	11	0	0	0	57⅓	47	21	21	43	41
1991—Philadelphia (N.L.)		1	7	.125	4.87	12	12	0	0	0	61	54	34	33	41	42
—Scranton/W.B. (I.L.)		2	3	.400	4.35	9	9	0	0	0	51⅔	48	28	25	37	43
1992—Tucson (PCL)■		8	7	.533	5.05	26	20	0	0	0	124⅔	152	79	70	55	90
1993—Charlotte (I.L.)		6	6	.500	3.39	28	19	3	1	0	135⅓	138	64	51	49	102
—Cleveland (A.L.)		3	4	.429	5.31	10	6	0	0	0	42⅓	52	26	25	20	27
1994—Charlotte (I.L.)		7	0	1.000	3.42	10	10	2	0	0	71	58	36	27	17	60
—Cleveland (A.L.)		5	2	.714	4.57	14	13	1	0	0	82⅔	91	47	42	34	59
1995—Cleveland (A.L.)		0	0	...	6.09	15	2	0	0	1	34	37	24	23	32	25
—Buffalo (A.A.)		5	3	.625	2.91	10	10	2	0	0	68	61	26	22	19	40
1996—Vancouver (PCL)■		2	0	1.000	1.20	2	2	1	0	0	15	8	2	2	3	11
—California (A.L.)		5	7	.417	6.84	35	20	2	1	0	130⅓	150	110	99	74	82
1997—Tucson (PCL)■		5	10	.333	5.70	36	10	0	0	4	85⅓	96	70	54	43	65
—Omaha (A.A.)■		1	5	.167	6.68	7	6	0	0	0	31	36	26	23	29	22
1998—Buffalo (I.L.)■		6	3	.667	3.76	52	0	0	0	0	88⅔	76	40	37	57	68
1999—New York (A.L.)■		7	2	.778	3.60	55	0	0	0	1	75	66	39	30	40	49
A.L. totals (5 years)		20	15	.571	5.41	129	41	3	1	2	364⅓	396	246	219	200	242
N.L. totals (3 years)		5	12	.294	4.35	27	27	0	0	0	136⅔	120	68	66	103	90
Major League totals (8 years)		25	27	.481	5.12	156	68	3	1	2	501	516	314	285	303	332

DIVISION SERIES RECORD

Year	League	W	L	Pct.	ERA	G	GS	CG	ShO	Sv.	IP	H	R	ER	BB	SO
1999—New York (A.L.)								Did not play.								

Year	League	W	L	Pct.	ERA	G	GS	CG	ShO	Sv.	IP	H	R	ER	BB	SO
1999— New York (A.L.)									Did not play.							

WORLD SERIES RECORD

NOTES: Member of World Series championship team (1999).

Year	League	W	L	Pct.	ERA	G	GS	CG	ShO	Sv.	IP	H	R	ER	BB	SO
1999— New York (A.L.)	0	0	...	0.00	1	0	0	0	0	2 1/3	2	0	0	2	0	

GRISSOM, MARQUIS   OF   BREWERS

PERSONAL: Born April 17, 1967, in Atlanta. ... 5-11/188. ... Bats right, throws right. ... Full name: Marquis Deon Grissom. ... Brother of Antonio Grissom, outfielder in Philadelphia Phillies (1990-91) and Montreal Expos organizations (1992-94). ... Name pronounced mar-KEESE.
HIGH SCHOOL: Lakeshore (College Park, Ga.).
COLLEGE: Florida A&M.
TRANSACTIONS/CAREER NOTES: Selected by Montreal Expos organization in third round of free-agent draft (June 1, 1988). ... On Montreal disabled list (May 29-June 30, 1990); included rehabilitation assignment to Indianapolis (June 25-30). ... Traded by Expos to Atlanta Braves for OF Roberto Kelly, OF Tony Tarasco and P Esteban Yan (April 6, 1995). ... Traded by Braves with OF Dave Justice to Cleveland Indians for OF Kenny Lofton and P Alan Embree (March 25, 1997). ... On disabled list (April 22-May 5, 1997). ... Traded by Indians with P Jeff Juden to Milwaukee Brewers for P Ben McDonald, P Mike Fetters and P Ron Villone (December 8, 1997).
HONORS: Won N.L. Gold Glove as outfielder (1993-96).
STATISTICAL NOTES: Led New York-Pennsylvania League with 146 total bases in 1988. ... Led N.L. outfielders with 333 total chances in 1994. ... Had 28-game hitting streak (July 25-August 24, 1996). ... Career major league grand slams: 3.

Year	Team (League)	Pos.	G	AB	R	H	2B	3B	HR	RBI	Avg.	BB	SO	SB	PO	A	E	Avg.
								BATTING								FIELDING		
1988— Jamestown (NY-P)	OF	74	*291	*69	94	14	7	8	39	.323	35	39	23	123	•11	3	.978	
1989— Jacksonville (Sou.)	OF	78	278	43	83	15	4	3	31	.299	24	31	24	141	7	3	.980	
— Indianapolis (A.A.)	OF	49	187	28	52	10	4	2	21	.278	14	23	16	106	5	0	1.000	
— Montreal (N.L.)	OF	26	74	16	19	2	0	1	2	.257	12	21	1	32	1	2	.943	
1990— Montreal (N.L.)	OF	98	288	42	74	14	2	3	29	.257	27	40	22	165	5	2	.988	
— Indianapolis (A.A.)	OF	5	22	3	4	0	0	2	3	.182	0	5	1	16	0	0	1.000	
1991— Montreal (N.L.)	OF	148	558	73	149	23	9	6	39	.267	34	89	*76	350	•15	6	.984	
1992— Montreal (N.L.)	OF	159	*653	99	180	39	6	14	66	.276	42	81	*78	401	7	7	.983	
1993— Montreal (N.L.)	OF	157	630	104	188	27	2	19	95	.298	52	76	53	416	8	7	.984	
1994— Montreal (N.L.)	OF	110	475	96	137	25	4	11	45	.288	41	66	36	*321	7	5	.985	
1995— Atlanta (N.L.)■	OF	139	551	80	142	23	3	12	42	.258	47	61	29	309	9	2	.994	
1996— Atlanta (N.L.)	OF	158	671	106	207	32	10	23	74	.308	41	73	28	338	10	1	.997	
1997— Cleveland (A.L.)	OF	144	558	74	146	27	6	12	66	.262	43	89	22	356	7	3	.992	
1998— Milwaukee (N.L.)■	OF	142	542	57	147	28	1	10	60	.271	24	78	13	317	8	3	.991	
1999— Milwaukee (N.L.)	OF	154	603	92	161	27	1	20	83	.267	49	109	24	374	1	5	.987	
American League totals (1 year)		144	558	74	146	27	6	12	66	.262	43	89	22	356	7	3	.992
National League totals (10 years)		1291	5045	765	1404	240	38	119	535	.278	369	694	360	3023	71	40	.987
Major League totals (11 years)		1435	5603	839	1550	267	44	131	601	.277	412	783	382	3379	78	43	.988

DIVISION SERIES RECORD

RECORDS: Holds single-game record for most hits—5 (October 7, 1995). ... Holds N.L. single-series record for most hits—11 (1995). ... Shares single-game records for most at-bats (nine-inning game)—6 (October 4, 1995); and most home runs—2 (October 4, 1995). ... Shares career record for most triples—1.

Year	Team (League)	Pos.	G	AB	R	H	2B	3B	HR	RBI	Avg.	BB	SO	SB	PO	A	E	Avg.
								BATTING								FIELDING		
1995— Atlanta (N.L.)	OF	4	21	5	11	2	0	3	4	.524	0	3	2	9	0	0	1.000	
1996— Atlanta (N.L.)	OF	3	12	2	1	0	0	0	0	.083	1	2	1	4	0	1	.800	
1997— Cleveland (A.L.)	OF	5	17	3	4	0	1	0	0	.235	1	2	0	14	0	0	1.000	
Division series totals (3 years)		12	50	10	16	2	1	3	4	.320	2	7	3	27	0	1	.964

CHAMPIONSHIP SERIES RECORD

RECORDS: Holds single-series record for most at-bats—35 (1996). ... Shares single-game record for most strikeouts—4 (October 11 [12 innings] and 15 [11 innings], 1997). ... Shares N.L. single-game record for most at-bats—6 (October 14 and 17, 1996).
NOTES: Named A.L. Championship Series Most Valuable Player (1997).

Year	Team (League)	Pos.	G	AB	R	H	2B	3B	HR	RBI	Avg.	BB	SO	SB	PO	A	E	Avg.
								BATTING								FIELDING		
1995— Atlanta (N.L.)	OF	4	19	2	5	0	1	0	0	.263	1	4	0	8	0	1	.889	
1996— Atlanta (N.L.)	OF	7	35	7	10	1	0	1	3	.286	0	8	2	17	0	1	.944	
1997— Cleveland (A.L.)	OF	6	23	2	6	0	0	1	4	.261	1	9	3	13	1	0	1.000	
Championship series totals (3 years)		17	77	11	21	1	1	2	7	.273	2	21	5	38	1	2	.951

WORLD SERIES RECORD

NOTES: Member of World Series championship team (1995).

Year	Team (League)	Pos.	G	AB	R	H	2B	3B	HR	RBI	Avg.	BB	SO	SB	PO	A	E	Avg.
								BATTING								FIELDING		
1995— Atlanta (N.L.)	OF	6	25	3	9	1	0	0	1	.360	1	3	3	13	0	0	1.000	
1996— Atlanta (N.L.)	OF	6	27	4	12	2	1	0	5	.444	1	2	1	7	0	1	.875	
1997— Cleveland (A.L.)	OF	7	25	5	9	1	0	0	2	.360	4	4	0	19	0	1	.950	
World Series totals (3 years)		19	77	12	30	4	1	0	8	.390	6	9	4	39	0	2	.951

ALL-STAR GAME RECORD

Year	League	Pos.	AB	R	H	2B	3B	HR	RBI	Avg.	BB	SO	SB	PO	A	E	Avg.
							BATTING								FIELDING		
1993— National	OF	3	0	0	0	0	0	0	.000	0	1	0	1	0	0	1.000	
1994— National	OF	1	1	1	0	0	1	1	1.000	1	0	0	2	1	0	1.000	
All-Star Game totals (2 years)		4	1	1	0	0	1	1	.250	1	1	0	3	1	0	1.000

G

GROOM, BUDDY — P — ORIOLES

PERSONAL: Born July 10, 1965, in Dallas. ... 6-2/207. ... Throws left, bats left. ... Full name: Wedsel Gary Groom Jr.
HIGH SCHOOL: Red Oak (Texas).
COLLEGE: Mary Hardin-Baylor (Texas).
TRANSACTIONS/CAREER NOTES: Selected by Chicago White Sox organization in 12th round of free-agent draft (June 2, 1987). ... Selected by Detroit Tigers organization from White Sox organization in Rule 5 minor league draft (December 3, 1990). ... Traded by Tigers to Florida Marlins for a player to be named later (August 7, 1995); Tigers acquired P Mike Myers to complete deal (August 9, 1995). ... Granted free agency (October 16, 1995). ... Signed by Oakland Athletics organization (November 27, 1995). ... Granted free agency (November 1, 1999). ... Signed by Baltimore Orioles (December 21, 1999).

Year League	W	L	Pct.	ERA	G	GS	CG	ShO	Sv.	IP	H	R	ER	BB	SO
1987— GC White Sox (GCL)	1	0	1.000	0.75	4	1	0	0	1	12	12	1	1	2	8
— Daytona Beach (FSL)	7	2	.778	3.59	11	10	2	0	0	67 2/3	60	30	27	33	29
1988— Tampa (FSL)	13	10	.565	2.54	27	27	8	0	0	*195	181	69	55	51	118
1989— Birmingham (Sou.)	13	8	.619	4.52	26	26	3	1	0	167 1/3	172	101	84	78	94
1990— Birmingham (Sou.)	6	8	.429	5.07	20	20	0	0	0	115 1/3	135	81	65	48	66
1991— Toledo (I.L.)■	2	5	.286	4.32	24	6	0	0	1	75	75	39	36	25	49
— London (East.)	7	1	.875	3.48	11	7	0	0	0	51 2/3	51	20	20	12	39
1992— Toledo (I.L.)	7	7	.500	2.80	16	16	1	0	0	109 1/3	102	41	34	23	71
— Detroit (A.L.)	0	5	.000	5.82	12	7	0	0	1	38 2/3	48	28	25	22	15
1993— Toledo (I.L.)	9	3	.750	2.74	16	15	0	0	0	102	98	34	31	30	78
— Detroit (A.L.)	0	2	.000	6.14	19	3	0	0	0	36 2/3	48	25	25	13	15
1994— Toledo (I.L.)	0	0	...	2.25	5	0	0	0	0	4	2	1	1	0	6
— Detroit (A.L.)	0	1	.000	3.94	40	0	0	0	1	32	31	14	14	13	27
1995— Detroit (A.L.)	1	3	.250	7.52	23	4	0	0	1	40 2/3	55	35	34	26	23
— Toledo (I.L.)	2	3	.400	1.91	6	5	1	0	0	33	31	14	7	4	24
— Florida (N.L.)■	1	2	.333	7.20	14	0	0	0	0	15	26	12	12	6	12
1996— Oakland (A.L.)■	5	0	1.000	3.84	72	1	0	0	2	77 1/3	85	37	33	34	57
1997— Oakland (A.L.)	2	2	.500	5.15	78	0	0	0	3	64 2/3	75	38	37	24	45
1998— Oakland (A.L.)	3	1	.750	4.24	75	0	0	0	0	57 1/3	62	30	27	20	36
1999— Oakland (A.L.)■	3	2	.600	5.09	•76	0	0	0	0	46	48	29	26	18	32
A.L. totals (8 years)	14	16	.467	5.06	395	15	0	0	8	393 1/3	452	236	221	170	250
N.L. totals (1 year)	1	2	.333	7.20	14	0	0	0	0	15	26	12	12	6	12
Major League totals (8 years)	15	18	.455	5.14	409	15	0	0	8	408 1/3	478	248	233	176	262

GROSS, KIP — P

PERSONAL: Born August 24, 1964, in Scottsbluff, Neb. ... 6-2/194. ... Throws right, bats right. ... Full name: Kip Lee Gross.
HIGH SCHOOL: Gering (Neb.).
COLLEGE: Murray State, then Nebraska.
TRANSACTIONS/CAREER NOTES: Selected by St. Louis Cardinals organization in third round of free-agent draft (January 9, 1985); did not sign. ... Selected by New York Mets organization in fourth round of free-agent draft (June 2, 1986). ... Traded by Mets organization with P Randy Myers to Cincinnati Reds for P John Franco and OF Don Brown (December 6, 1989). ... Traded by Reds with OF Eric Davis to Los Angeles Dodgers for P Tim Belcher and P John Wetteland (November 27, 1991). ... On Albuquerque disabled list (August 5-12, 1993). ... On Albuquerque temporarily inactive list (May 5-10, 1994). ... Released by Dodgers organization (May 10, 1994). ... Played for Nippon Ham Fighters of Japan Pacific League (1994-98). ... Signed by Boston Red Sox (January 5, 1999). ... On Boston disabled list (May 17-June 4, 1999); included rehabilitation assignment to Pawtucket (May 25-June 1). ... Granted free agency (October 4, 1999).

Year League	W	L	Pct.	ERA	G	GS	CG	ShO	Sv.	IP	H	R	ER	BB	SO
1987— Lynchburg (Caro.)	7	4	.636	2.72	16	15	2	0	0	89 1/3	92	37	27	22	39
1988— St. Lucie (FSL)	13	9	.591	2.62	28	27	7	3	0	178 1/3	153	72	52	53	124
1989— Jackson (Texas)	6	5	.545	2.49	16	16	4	0	0	112	96	47	31	13	60
— Tidewater (I.L.)	4	4	.500	3.97	12	12	0	0	0	70 1/3	72	33	31	17	39
1990— Nashville (A.A.)■	12	7	.632	3.33	40	11	2	1	3	127	113	54	47	47	62
— Cincinnati (N.L.)	0	0	...	4.26	5	0	0	0	0	6 1/3	6	3	3	2	3
1991— Nashville (A.A.)	5	3	.625	2.08	14	6	1	1	0	47 2/3	39	13	11	16	28
— Cincinnati (N.L.)	6	4	.600	3.47	29	9	1	0	0	85 2/3	93	43	33	40	40
1992— Albuquerque (PCL)■	6	5	.545	3.51	31	14	2	0	8	107 2/3	96	48	42	36	58
— Los Angeles (N.L.)	1	1	.500	4.18	16	1	0	0	0	23 2/3	32	14	11	10	14
1993— Albuquerque (PCL)	13	7	.650	4.05	59	7	0	0	13	124 1/3	115	58	56	41	96
— Los Angeles (N.L.)	0	0	...	0.60	10	0	0	0	0	15	13	1	1	4	12
1994— Albuquerque (PCL)	1	1	.500	5.06	10	0	0	0	1	16	14	9	9	6	11
— Nippon Ham (Jap. Pac.)	6	12	.333	4.29	25	...	...	...	0	149	...	...	71	56	62
1995— Nippon Ham (Jap. Pac.)	16	13	.552	3.04	31	...	...	...	0	231	...	...	78	59	114
1996— Nippon Ham (Jap. Pac.)	17	9	.654	3.62	28	...	...	...	0	193 2/3	...	...	78	53	79
1997— Nippon Ham (Jap. Pac.)	13	11	.542	3.63	33	...	...	...	0	233 1/3	...	...	94	69	98
1998— Nippon Ham (Jap. Pac.)	3	4	.429	3.96	7	7	1	0	0	36 1/3	30	18	16	15	11
1999— Boston (A.L.)■	0	2	.000	7.82	11	1	0	0	0	12 2/3	15	11	11	8	9
— Pawtucket (I.L.)	1	0	1.000	5.40	10	2	0	0	0	21 2/3	24	14	13	12	16
A.L. totals (1 year)	0	2	.000	7.82	11	1	0	0	0	12 2/3	15	11	11	8	9
N.L. totals (4 years)	7	5	.583	3.31	60	10	1	0	0	130 2/3	144	61	48	56	69
Major League totals (5 years)	7	7	.500	3.70	71	11	1	0	0	143 1/3	159	72	59	64	78

GRUDZIELANEK, MARK — SS — DODGERS

PERSONAL: Born June 30, 1970, in Milwaukee. ... 6-1/185. ... Bats right, throws right. ... Full name: Mark James Grudzielanek. ... Name pronounced gress-UH-lawn-ick.
HIGH SCHOOL: J.M. Hanks (El Paso, Texas).
JUNIOR COLLEGE: Trinidad (Colo.) State Junior College.

G

TRANSACTIONS/CAREER NOTES: Selected by New York Mets organization in 17th round of free-agent draft (June 5, 1989); did not sign. ... Selected by Montreal Expos organization in 11th round of free-agent draft (June 3, 1991). ... On disabled list (July 13-August 9, 1993 and May 12-19, 1994). ... Traded by Expos with P Carlos Perez and OF Hiram Bocachica to Los Angeles Dodgers for 2B Wilton Guerrero, P Ted Lilly, OF Peter Bergeron and 1B Jonathan Tucker (July 31, 1998). ... On Los Angeles disabled list (June 3-July 6, 1999); included rehabilitation assignment to San Bernadino (July 2-6).

RECORDS: Holds major league single-season record for fewest chances accepted by shortstop who led league in chances accepted—683 (1997). ... Shares major league single-season record for fewest putouts by shortstop (150 or more games)—180 (1996).

HONORS: Named Eastern League Most Valuable Player (1994).

STATISTICAL NOTES: Led Eastern League shortstops with .959 fielding percentage in 1994. ... Led N.L. shortstops with 715 total chances and 99 double plays in 1997. ... Led N.L. shortstops with 33 errors in 1998.

							BATTING								FIELDING			
Year	Team (League)	Pos.	G	AB	R	H	2B	3B	HR	RBI	Avg.	BB	SO	SB	PO	A	E	Avg.
1991— Jamestown (NY-P)		SS	72	275	44	72	9	3	2	32	.262	18	43	14	112	206	23	.933
1992— Rockford (Midw.)		SS	128	496	64	122	12	5	5	54	.246	22	59	25	173	290	41	.919
1993— W.P. Beach (FSL)	2B-SS-OF-3B	86	300	41	80	11	6	1	34	.267	14	42	17	105	135	13	.949
1994— Harrisburg (East.)		SS-3B	122	488	92	157	•37	3	11	66	.322	43	66	32	178	344	23	†.958
1995— Montreal (N.L.)		SS-3B-2B	78	269	27	66	12	2	1	20	.245	14	47	8	94	198	10	.967
— Ottawa (I.L.)		SS	49	181	26	54	9	1	1	22	.298	10	17	12	58	156	14	.939
1996— Montreal (N.L.)		SS	153	657	99	201	34	4	6	49	.306	26	83	33	180	453	27	.959
1997— Montreal (N.L.)		SS	156	*649	76	177	*54	3	4	51	.273	23	76	25	237	446	*32	.955
1998— Montreal (N.L.)		SS	105	396	51	109	15	1	8	41	.275	21	50	11	152	283	23	.950
— Los Angeles (N.L.)■		SS	51	193	11	51	6	0	2	21	.264	5	23	7	78	172	§10	.962
1999— Los Angeles (N.L.)		SS	123	488	72	159	23	5	7	46	.326	31	65	6	171	306	13	.973
— San Bern. (Calif.)		SS	4	16	2	4	0	0	0	0	.250	0	1	0	1	11	0	1.000
Major League totals (5 years)			666	2652	336	763	144	15	28	228	.288	120	344	90	912	1858	115	.960

ALL-STAR GAME RECORD

					BATTING							FIELDING			
Year	League	Pos.	AB	R	H	2B	3B	HR	RBI	Avg.	BB	SO	SB	PO	A	E	Avg.
1996— National	3B	1	0	0	0	0	0	0	.000	0	0	0	0	0	0	...

GUARDADO, EDDIE · P · TWINS

PERSONAL: Born October 2, 1970, in Stockton, Calif. ... 6-0/194. ... Throws left, bats right. ... Full name: Edward Adrian Guardado. ... Name pronounced gwar-DAH-doh.

HIGH SCHOOL: Franklin (Stockton, Calif.).

COLLEGE: San Joaquin Delta College (Calif.).

TRANSACTIONS/CAREER NOTES: Selected by Minnesota Twins organization in 21st round of free-agent draft (June 4, 1990). ... On Minnesota disabled list (May 22-June 28, 1999); included rehabilitation assignment to New Britain (June 22-28).

STATISTICAL NOTES: Pitched 5-0 no-hit victory against Pulaski (August 26, 1991).

Year	League	W	L	Pct.	ERA	G	GS	CG	ShO	Sv.	IP	H	R	ER	BB	SO
1991— Elizabethton (Appl.)		8	4	.667	1.86	14	13	3	•1	0	92	67	30	19	31	*106
1992— Kenosha (Midw.)		5	10	.333	4.37	18	18	2	1	0	101	106	57	49	30	103
— Visalia (Calif.)		7	0	1.000	1.64	7	7	1	1	0	49 1/3	47	13	9	10	39
1993— Nashville (Sou.)		4	0	1.000	1.24	10	10	2	2	0	65 1/3	53	10	9	10	57
— Minnesota (A.L.)		3	8	.273	6.18	19	16	0	0	0	94 2/3	123	68	65	36	46
1994— Salt Lake (PCL)		12	7	.632	4.83	24	24	2	0	0	151	171	90	81	51	87
— Minnesota (A.L.)		0	2	.000	8.47	4	4	0	0	0	17	26	16	16	4	8
1995— Minnesota (A.L.)		4	9	.308	5.12	51	5	0	0	2	91 1/3	99	54	52	45	71
1996— Minnesota (A.L.)		6	5	.545	5.25	•83	0	0	0	4	73 2/3	61	45	43	33	74
1997— Minnesota (A.L.)		0	4	.000	3.91	69	0	0	0	1	46	45	23	20	17	54
1998— Minnesota (A.L.)		3	1	.750	4.52	79	0	0	0	0	65 2/3	66	34	33	28	53
1999— Minnesota (A.L.)		2	5	.286	4.50	63	0	0	0	2	48	37	24	24	25	50
— New Britain (East.)		0	0	...	1.93	3	0	0	0	0	4 2/3	3	1	1	0	5
Major League totals (7 years)		18	34	.346	5.22	368	25	0	0	9	436 1/3	457	264	253	188	356

GUBANICH, CREIGHTON · C/IF

PERSONAL: Born March 27, 1972, in Belleville, N.J. ... 6-3/200. ... Bats right, throws right. ... Full name: Creighton Wade Gubanich.

HIGH SCHOOL: Phoenixville Area (Phoenixville, Pa.).

TRANSACTIONS/CAREER NOTES: Selected by Oakland Athletics organization in sixth round of free-agent draft (June 4, 1990). ... Traded by Athletics to Milwaukee Brewers for P Tony Phillips (June 19, 1997). ... Traded by Brewers to Colorado Rockies for SS Jeff Huson (August 5, 1997). ... Granted free agency (October 17, 1997). ... Signed by San Diego Padres organization (November 20, 1997). ... Granted free agency (October 16, 1998). ... Signed by Boston Red Sox organization (November 4, 1998). ... Granted free agency (October 15, 1999).

STATISTICAL NOTES: Career major league grand slams: 1.

							BATTING								FIELDING			
Year	Team (League)	Pos.	G	AB	R	H	2B	3B	HR	RBI	Avg.	BB	SO	SB	PO	A	E	Avg.
1991— S. Oregon (N'west.)		C-3B-1B	43	132	23	30	7	2	4	18	.227	19	33	0	197	30	9	.962
1992— Madison (Midw.)		C-1B-3B	121	404	46	100	19	3	9	55	.248	41	102	0	609	113	21	.972
1993— Madison (Midw.)		C-3B-1B	119	373	65	100	19	2	19	78	.268	63	105	3	547	120	11	.984
1994— Modesto (Calif.)		C-3B-1B	108	375	53	88	20	3	15	55	.235	54	102	5	543	80	7	.989
1995— Huntsville (Sou.)	C-1B-3B-OF	94	274	37	60	7	1	13	43	.219	48	82	1	435	79	7	.987
1996— Huntsville (Sou.)		C-1B-3B	62	217	40	60	19	0	9	43	.276	31	71	1	244	34	6	.979
— Edmonton (PCL)		C	34	117	14	29	7	1	4	19	.248	6	33	3	113	13	1	.992
1997— Edmonton (PCL)		C	43	145	23	48	13	0	7	34	.331	14	42	0	194	17	2	.991
— Tucson (PCL)■		C	24	85	13	29	5	0	5	17	.341	1	19	1	81	14	5	.950
— Colo. Spr. (PCL)■		C	14	47	4	9	1	0	3	6	.191	4	18	0	89	8	3	.970
1998— Las Vegas (PCL)■		C-1B-3B	86	292	48	85	22	0	19	70	.291	30	85	1	570	60	8	.987
1999— Pawtucket (I.L.)■		C-DH-1B	27	92	12	26	3	0	5	10	.283	6	23	0	136	14	4	.974
— Boston (A.L.)		C-DH-3B	18	47	4	13	2	1	1	11	.277	3	13	0	40	11	1	.981
Major League totals (1 year)			18	47	4	13	2	1	1	11	.277	3	13	0	40	11	1	.981

G

Year	League	W	L	Pct.	ERA	G	GS	CG	ShO	Sv.	IP	H	R	ER	BB	SO
1994—Modesto (Calif.)		0	0	...	0.00	1	0	0	0	0	1	1	0	0	0	0

GUERRERO, VLADIMIR — OF — EXPOS

PERSONAL: Born February 9, 1976, in Nizao Bani, Dominican Republican ... 6-3/205. ... Bats right, throws right. ... Full name: Vladimir Alvino Guerrero. ... Brother of Wilton Guerrero, second baseman, Montreal Expos.
TRANSACTIONS/CAREER NOTES: Signed as non-drafted free agent by Montreal Expos organization (March 1, 1993). ... On Montreal disabled list (March 30-May 2, June 5-21 and July 12-27, 1997); including rehabilitation assignment to West Palm Beach (April 29-May 2).
HONORS: Named Eastern League Most Valuable Player (1996). ... Named Minor League Player of the Year by THE SPORTING NEWS (1996). ... Named outfielder on THE SPORTING NEWS N.L. All-Star team (1999). ... Named outfielder on THE SPORTING NEWS N.L. Silver Slugger team (1999).
STATISTICAL NOTES: Tied for South Atlantic League lead in double plays by outfielder with four in 1995. ... Led Eastern League with .438 on-base percentage and 13 intentional bases on balls received in 1996. ... Had 31-game hitting streak (July 27-August 26, 1999).

							BATTING								FIELDING		
Year	Team (League)	Pos.	G	AB	R	H	2B	3B	HR	RBI	Avg.	BB	SO	SB	PO	A	E	Avg.
1993—Dom. Expos (DSL)		OF-IF-P	34	105	19	35	4	0	1	14	.333	8	13	4	75	7	5	.943
1994—Dom. Expos (DSL)		OF	25	92	34	39	11	0	12	35	.424	21	6	5	38	6	2	.957
—GC Expos (GCL)		OF	37	137	24	43	13	3	5	25	.314	11	18	0	64	9	1	.986
1995—Albany (SAL)		OF	110	421	77	140	21	10	16	63	*.333	30	45	12	207	15	11	.953
1996—W.P. Beach (FSL)........		OF	20	80	16	29	8	0	5	18	.363	3	10	2	28	5	3	.917
—Harrisburg (East.).......		OF	118	417	84	150	32	8	19	78	*.360	51	42	17	184	13	8	.961
—Montreal (N.L.)............		OF	9	27	2	5	0	0	1	1	.185	0	3	0	11	0	0	1.000
1997—W.P. Beach (FSL)........		OF	3	10	0	4	2	0	0	2	.400	1	0	1	4	1	0	1.000
—Montreal (N.L.)............		OF	90	325	44	98	22	2	11	40	.302	19	39	3	148	10	*12	.929
1998—Montreal (N.L.)..........		OF	159	623	108	202	37	7	38	109	.324	42	95	11	323	9	*17	.951
1999—Montreal (N.L.)..........		OF	160	610	102	193	37	5	42	131	.316	55	62	14	332	15	*19	.948
Major League totals (4 years)			418	1585	256	498	96	14	92	281	.314	116	199	28	814	34	48	.946

ALL-STAR GAME RECORD

						BATTING								FIELDING		
Year	League	Pos.	AB	R	H	2B	3B	HR	RBI	Avg.	BB	SO	SB	PO	A	E	Avg.
1999—National		OF	1	0	0	0	0	0	0	.000	0	0	0	1	0	0	1.000

RECORD AS PITCHER

Year	League	W	L	Pct.	ERA	G	GS	CG	ShO	Sv.	IP	H	R	ER	BB	SO
1993—Dom. Expos (DSL)		0	0	...	2.25	3	0	0	0	0	8	10	3	2	4	6

GUERRERO, WILTON — 2B — EXPOS

PERSONAL: Born October 24, 1974, in Don Gregorio, Dominican Republic. ... 6-0/175. ... Bats both, throws right. ... Brother of Vladimir Guerrero, outfielder, Montreal Expos.
HIGH SCHOOL: Escuela Primaria Don Gregorio (Dominican Republic).
TRANSACTIONS/CAREER NOTES: Signed as non-drafted free agent by Los Angeles Dodgers organization (October 8, 1991). ... On Albuquerque disabled list (June 26-July 5 and July 26-August 23, 1996). ... On suspended list (June 2-9, 1997). ... Traded by Dodgers with P Ted Lilly, OF Peter Bergeron and 1B Jonathan Tucker to Montreal Expos for P Carlos Perez, SS Mark Grudzielanek and OF Hiram Bocachica (July 31, 1998).
STATISTICAL NOTES: Led Florida State League in caught stealing with 20 in 1994. ... Led Texas League in caught stealing with 22 in 1995. ... Career major league grand slams: 1.

							BATTING								FIELDING		
Year	Team (League)	Pos.	G	AB	R	H	2B	3B	HR	RBI	Avg.	BB	SO	SB	PO	A	E	Avg.
1992—Dom. Dodgers (DSL) .		SS	61	225	52	87	7	4	0	38	.387	34	21	15	104	215	21	.938
1993—Great Falls (Pio.)		SS	66	256	44	76	5	1	0	21	.297	24	33	20	76	184	21	.925
—Dom. Dodgers (DSL) .		SS	8	31	6	11	0	1	0	4	.355	4	3	2	15	18	1	.971
1994—Vero Beach (FSL)		SS	110	402	55	118	11	4	1	32	.294	29	71	23	111	292	17	.960
1995—San Antonio (Texas)....		SS	95	382	53	133	13	6	0	26	*.348	26	63	21	121	263	19	.953
—Albuquerque (PCL).....		SS-OF	14	49	10	16	1	1	0	2	.327	1	7	2	13	39	9	.852
1996—Albuquerque (PCL).....		2B-SS	98	425	79	146	17	12	2	38	.344	26	48	26	183	306	19	.963
—Los Angeles (N.L.)		OF	5	2	1	0	0	0	0	0	.000	0	2	0	0	0	0	...
1997—Los Angeles (N.L.)......		2B-SS	111	357	39	104	10	9	4	32	.291	8	52	6	148	231	4	.990
—Albuquerque (PCL).....		SS-2B	10	45	9	18	0	1	0	5	.400	2	3	3	16	38	5	.915
1998—Los Angeles (N.L.)......		2B-SS-OF	64	180	21	51	4	3	0	7	.283	4	33	5	71	91	7	.959
—Albuquerque (PCL).....		2B-OF-DH	30	121	15	36	3	2	1	10	.298	9	12	11	55	49	1	.990
—Montreal (N.L.)■.......		2B	52	222	29	63	10	6	2	20	.284	10	30	3	103	130	6	.975
1999—Montreal (N.L.)..........		2B-OF-DH	132	315	42	92	15	7	2	31	.292	13	38	7	86	98	12	.939
Major League totals (4 years)			364	1076	132	310	39	25	8	90	.288	35	155	21	408	550	29	.971

G

GUEVARA, GIOMAR — 2B/SS — TIGERS

PERSONAL: Born October 23, 1972, in Miranda, Venezuela. ... 5-8/150. ... Bats both, throws right. ... Full name: Giomar Antonio Guevara.
TRANSACTIONS/CAREER NOTES: Signed as non-drafted free agent by Seattle Mariners organization (November 13, 1990). ... On disabled list (June 14-July 21, 1995). ... On Seattle disabled list (March 27-September 1, 1998); included rehabilitation assignments to Lancaster (July 18-August 10) and Orlando (August 14-September 1). ... On Tacoma disabled list (May 28-June 9 and June 30, 1999-remainder of season). ... Granted free agency (October 4, 1999). ... Signed by Detroit Tigers organization (December 20, 1999).

Year	Team (League)	Pos.	G	AB	R	H	2B	3B	HR	RBI	Avg.	BB	SO	SB	PO	A	E	Avg.
1991—	Dom. Mariners (DSL)						Dominican Summer League statistics unavailable.											
1992—	Dom. Mariners (DSL).	IF	45	163	30	51	13	4	1	24	.313	19	30	14	37	103	10	.933
1993—	Bellingham (N.W.)	SS	62	211	31	48	8	3	1	23	.227	34	46	4	83	172	16	.941
1994—	Appleton (Midw.)	SS-2B	110	385	57	116	23	3	8	46	.301	42	77	9	171	270	23	.950
	—Jacksonville (Sou.)	SS	7	20	2	4	2	0	1	3	.200	2	9	0	12	25	3	.925
1995—	Riverside (Calif.)	SS	83	292	53	71	12	3	2	34	.243	30	71	7	123	231	27	.929
1996—	Port City (Sou.)	SS-2B	119	414	60	110	18	2	2	41	.266	54	102	21	187	350	35	.939
1997—	Tacoma (PCL)	2B-SS	54	176	29	43	5	1	2	13	.244	5	39	3	102	129	11	.955
	—Memphis (Sou.)	SS	65	228	30	60	10	4	4	28	.263	20	42	5	80	217	13	.958
	—Seattle (A.L.)	DH-2B-SS	5	4	0	0	0	0	0	0	.000	0	2	1	2	6	1	.889
1998—	Lancaster (Calif.)	2B-SS-3B	19	61	15	15	4	0	0	3	.246	14	20	1	28	58	2	.977
	—Orlando (Sou.)	SS-2B	14	45	13	15	5	1	0	6	.333	8	11	0	19	45	5	.928
	—Seattle (A.L.)	2B-SS-DH	11	13	4	3	2	0	0	0	.231	4	4	0	8	13	0	1.000
1999—	Tacoma (PCL)	SS-2B	32	116	15	34	13	0	3	15	.293	12	22	0	56	87	4	.973
	—Seattle (A.L.)	SS	10	12	2	3	2	0	0	2	.250	0	2	0	6	14	3	.870
Major League totals (3 years)			26	29	6	6	4	0	0	2	.207	4	8	1	16	33	4	.925

GUILLEN, CARLOS — 2B — MARINERS

PERSONAL: Born September 30, 1975, in Maracay, Venezuela. ... 6-1/180. ... Bats both, throws right. ... Full name: Carlos Alfonso Guillen.

TRANSACTIONS/CAREER NOTES: Signed as non-drafted free agent by Houston Astros organization (September 19, 1992). ... On disabled list (June 1-September 12, 1994). ... On disabled list (May 21-September 11, 1996). ... Traded by Astros with P Freddy Garcia and a player to be named later to Seattle Mariners for P Randy Johnson (July 31, 1998); Mariners acquired P John Halama to complete deal (October 1, 1998). ... On disabled list (April 7, 1999-remainder of season).

Year	Team (League)	Pos.	G	AB	R	H	2B	3B	HR	RBI	Avg.	BB	SO	SB	PO	A	E	Avg.
1993—	Dom. Astros (DSL)	IF	18	56	12	14	4	2	0	8	.250	8	12	0	37	6	2	.956
1994—							Did not play.											
1995—	GC Astros (GCL)		30	105	17	31	4	2	2	15	.295	9	17	17	...	...	...	...
1996—	Quad City (Midw.)	SS	29	112	23	37	7	1	3	17	.330	16	25	13	47	71	9	.929
1997—	Jackson (Texas)	SS-DH	115	390	47	99	16	1	10	39	.254	38	78	6	169	313	35	.932
	—New Orleans (A.A.)	SS	3	13	3	4	1	0	0	0	.308	0	4	0	5	6	0	1.000
1998—	New Orleans (PCL)	SS	100	374	67	109	18	4	12	51	.291	31	61	3	145	287	26	.943
	—Tacoma (PCL)■	2B	24	92	8	21	1	1	1	4	.228	9	17	1	49	63	2	.982
	—Seattle (A.L.)	2B	10	39	9	13	1	1	0	5	.333	3	9	2	15	29	0	1.000
1999—	Seattle (A.L.)	SS-2B	5	19	2	3	0	1	0	1	.158	1	6	0	12	15	1	.964
Major League totals (2 years)			15	58	11	16	1	1	1	8	.276	4	15	2	27	44	1	.986

GUILLEN, JOSE — OF — DEVIL RAYS

PERSONAL: Born May 17, 1976, in San Cristobal, Dominican Republic. ... 5-11/195. ... Bats right, throws right. ... Full name: Jose Manuel Guillen.

TRANSACTIONS/CAREER NOTES: Signed as non-drafted free agent by Pittsburgh Pirates organization (August 19, 1992). ... Traded by Pirates with P Jeff Sparks to Tampa Bay Devil Rays for C Joe Oliver and C Humberto Cota (July 23, 1999). ... On Durham disabled list (July 23-30, 1999).

RECORDS: Shares major league single-inning record for most doubles—2 (May 16, 1999, fourth inning).

HONORS: Named Carolina League Most Valuable Player (1996).

STATISTICAL NOTES: Led Carolina League with 263 total bases and grounding into double plays with 16 in 1996. ... Led Carolina League outfielders with six double plays in 1996. ... Career major league grand slams: 1.

Year	Team (League)	Pos.	G	AB	R	H	2B	3B	HR	RBI	Avg.	BB	SO	SB	PO	A	E	Avg.
1993—	Dom. Pirates (DSL)	OF	63	234	39	53	3	4	11	41	.226	21	55	10	112	12	7	.947
1994—	GC Pirates (GCL)	OF	30	110	17	29	4	1	4	11	.264	7	15	2	59	5	2	.970
1995—	Erie (NY-P)	OF	66	258	41	81	17	1	*12	46	.314	10	44	1	107	10	13	.900
	—Augusta (SAL)	OF	10	34	6	8	1	1	2	6	.235	2	9	0	5	0	0	1.000
1996—	Lynchburg (Caro.)	OF-DH	136	*528	78	*170	30	0	•21	94	.322	20	73	24	224	16	*13	.949
1997—	Pittsburgh (N.L.)	OF	143	498	58	133	20	5	14	70	.267	17	88	1	226	9	9	.963
1998—	Pittsburgh (N.L.)	OF	153	573	60	153	38	2	14	84	.267	21	100	3	283	16	10	.968
1999—	Pittsburgh (N.L.)	OF	40	120	18	32	6	0	1	18	.267	10	21	1	58	1	3	.952
	—Nashville (PCL)	OF-DH	35	132	28	44	10	0	5	22	.333	8	21	0	57	5	4	.939
	—Durham (I.L.)■	OF	9	34	8	13	1	0	3	12	.382	7	7	0	19	1	0	1.000
	—Tampa Bay (A.L.)	OF	47	168	24	41	10	0	2	13	.244	10	36	0	80	5	3	.966
American League totals (1 year)			47	168	24	41	10	0	2	13	.244	10	36	0	80	5	3	.966
National League totals (3 years)			336	1191	136	318	64	7	29	172	.267	48	209	5	567	26	22	.964
Major League totals (3 years)			383	1359	160	359	74	7	31	185	.264	58	245	5	647	31	25	.964

GUILLEN, OZZIE — SS — BRAVES

PERSONAL: Born January 20, 1964, in Ocumare del Tuy, Miranda, Venezuela. ... 5-11/165. ... Bats left, throws right. ... Full name: Oswaldo Jose Barrios Guillen. ... Name pronounced GHEE-un.

TRANSACTIONS/CAREER NOTES: Signed as non-drafted free agent by San Diego Padres organization (December 17, 1980). ... Traded by Padres organization with P Tim Lollar, P Bill Long and 3B Luis Salazar to Chicago White Sox for P LaMarr Hoyt, P Kevin Kristan and P Todd Simmons (December 6, 1984). ... On disabled list (April 22, 1992-remainder of season). ... Granted free agency (October 31, 1997). ... Signed by Baltimore Orioles organization (January 29, 1998). ... Released by Orioles (May 1, 1998). ... Signed by Atlanta Braves (May 6, 1998). ... Granted free agency (November 2, 1998). ... Re-signed by Braves (December 2, 1998).

G

RECORDS: Holds major league single-season record for fewest bases on balls received (150 or more games)—10 (1996). ... Holds A.L. single-season record for fewest putouts by shortstop (150 or more games)—220 (1985).

HONORS: Named A.L. Rookie Player of the Year by THE SPORTING NEWS (1985). ... Named A.L. Rookie of the Year by Baseball Writers' Association of America (1985). ... Won A.L. Gold Glove at shortstop (1990).

STATISTICAL NOTES: Tied for California League lead with 14 sacrifice hits in 1982. ... Led Pacific Coast League shortstops with 362 assists and 549 total chances in 1984. ... Led A.L. shortstops with 760 total chances in 1987 and 863 in 1988. ... Led A.L. shortstops with 105 double plays in 1987. ... Career major league grand slams: 1.

MISCELLANEOUS: Batted as switch-hitter (1981-84).

							BATTING								FIELDING		
Year	Team (League)	Pos.	G	AB	R	H	2B	3B	HR	RBI	Avg.	BB	SO	SB	PO	A	E	Avg.
1981— GC Padres (GCL)	SS-2B	55	189	26	49	4	1	0	16	.259	13	24	8	105	135	15	.941
1982— Reno (Calif.)	SS	130	528	*103	*183	33	1	2	54	.347	16	53	25	*240	399	41	.940
1983— Beaumont (Texas)	SS	114	427	62	126	20	4	2	48	.295	15	29	7	185	327	*38	.931
1984— Las Vegas (PCL)	SS-2B	122	463	81	137	26	6	5	53	.296	13	40	9	172	†364	17	.969
1985— Chicago (A.L.)■	SS	150	491	71	134	21	9	1	33	.273	12	36	7	220	382	12	*.980
1986— Chicago (A.L.)	SS-DH	159	547	58	137	19	4	2	47	.250	12	52	8	261	459	22	.970
1987— Chicago (A.L.)	SS	149	560	64	156	22	7	2	51	.279	22	52	25	266	475	19	.975
1988— Chicago (A.L.)	SS	156	566	58	148	16	7	0	39	.261	25	40	25	273	*570	20	.977
1989— Chicago (A.L.)	SS	155	597	63	151	20	8	1	54	.253	15	48	36	272	512	22	.973
1990— Chicago (A.L.)	SS	160	516	61	144	21	4	1	58	.279	26	37	13	252	474	17	.977
1991— Chicago (A.L.)	SS	154	524	52	143	20	3	3	49	.273	11	38	21	249	439	21	.970
1992— Chicago (A.L.)	SS	12	40	5	8	4	0	0	7	.200	1	5	1	20	39	0	1.000
1993— Chicago (A.L.)	SS	134	457	44	128	23	4	4	50	.280	10	41	5	189	361	16	.972
1994— Chicago (A.L.)	SS	100	365	46	105	9	5	1	39	.288	14	35	5	139	237	16	.959
1995— Chicago (A.L.)	SS-DH	122	415	50	103	20	3	1	41	.248	13	25	6	167	319	12	.976
1996— Chicago (A.L.)	SS-OF	150	499	62	131	24	8	4	45	.263	10	27	6	222	348	11	.981
1997— Chicago (A.L.)	SS	142	490	59	120	21	6	4	52	.245	22	24	5	207	348	15	.974
1998— Baltimore (A.L.)■	SS-3B	12	16	2	1	0	0	0	0	.063	1	2	0	3	11	1	.933
— Atlanta (N.L.)■	SS-2B-1B-3B	83	264	35	73	15	1	1	22	.277	24	25	1	97	166	6	.978
1999— Atlanta (N.L.)	SS-3B-2B	92	232	21	56	16	0	1	20	.241	15	17	4	58	146	7	.967
American League totals (14 years)		1755	6083	695	1609	240	68	24	565	.265	194	462	163	2740	4974	204	.974
National League totals (2 years)		175	496	56	129	31	1	2	42	.260	39	42	5	155	312	13	.973
Major League totals (15 years)		1930	6579	751	1738	271	69	26	607	.264	233	504	168	2895	5286	217	.974

DIVISION SERIES RECORD

							BATTING								FIELDING		
Year	Team (League)	Pos.	G	AB	R	H	2B	3B	HR	RBI	Avg.	BB	SO	SB	PO	A	E	Avg.
1998— Atlanta (N.L.)	PH	1	1	0	0	0	0	0	0	.000	0	0	0	...	...	...	...
1999— Atlanta (N.L.)	PH	1	1	0	0	0	0	0	0	.000	0	0	0	0	0	0	...
Division series totals (2 years)		2	2	0	0	0	0	0	0	.000	0	0	0	0	0	0	...

CHAMPIONSHIP SERIES RECORD

							BATTING								FIELDING		
Year	Team (League)	Pos.	G	AB	R	H	2B	3B	HR	RBI	Avg.	BB	SO	SB	PO	A	E	Avg.
1993— Chicago (A.L.)	SS	6	22	4	6	1	0	0	2	.273	0	2	1	12	14	0	1.000
1998— Atlanta (N.L.)	PH-SS	4	12	1	5	0	0	0	1	.417	0	1	0	1	6	0	1.000
1999— Atlanta (N.L.)	PH-SS	3	3	0	1	0	0	0	1	.333	0	0	0	0	0	0	...
Championship series totals (3 years)		13	37	5	12	1	0	0	4	.324	0	3	1	13	20	0	1.000

WORLD SERIES RECORD

							BATTING								FIELDING		
Year	Team (League)	Pos.	G	AB	R	H	2B	3B	HR	RBI	Avg.	BB	SO	SB	PO	A	E	Avg.
1999— Atlanta (N.L.)	PH-SS-DH	3	5	0	0	0	0	0	0	.000	0	1	0	4	3	1	.875

ALL-STAR GAME RECORD

NOTES: Named to A.L. All-Star team; replaced by Kurt Stillwell due to injury (1988).

						BATTING							FIELDING		
Year	League	Pos.	AB	R	H	2B	3B	HR	RBI	Avg.	BB	SO	SB	PO	A	E	Avg.
1988— American						Selected, did not play—injured.										
1990— American	SS	2	0	0	0	0	0	0	.000	0	0	0	0	2	0	1.000
1991— American	SS	0	0	0	0	0	0	0	...	0	0	0	1	0	0	1.000
All-Star Game totals (2 years)		2	0	0	0	0	0	0	.000	0	0	0	1	2	0	1.000

GUNDERSON, ERIC   P

G

PERSONAL: Born March 29, 1966, in Portland, Ore. ... 6-0/190. ... Throws left, bats right. ... Full name: Eric Andrew Gunderson.

HIGH SCHOOL: Aloha (Portland, Ore.).

COLLEGE: Portland State.

TRANSACTIONS/CAREER NOTES: Selected by San Francisco Giants organization in second round of free-agent draft (June 2, 1987). ... Released by Giants (March 31, 1992). ... Signed by Seattle Mariners organization (April 10, 1992). ... On Jacksonville disabled list (April 10-17, 1992). ... On Seattle suspended list (September 30-October 4, 1992). ... Released by Mariners (April 29, 1993). ... Signed by New York Mets organization (June 10, 1993). ... Granted free agency (October 15, 1993). ... Signed by San Diego Padres organization (December 24, 1993). ... Released by Las Vegas (April 2, 1994). ... Signed by Mets organization (May 5, 1994). ... Claimed on waivers by Mariners (August 4, 1995). ... Claimed on waivers by Boston Red Sox (August 10, 1995). ... Granted free agency (October 7, 1996). ... Signed by Texas Rangers organization (January 24, 1997). ... On disabled list (August 26-September 7, 1997). ... On Texas disabled list (May 8, 1999-remainder of season); included rehabilitation assignment to Oklahoma (June 9-July 8). ... Released by Rangers (October 28, 1999).

STATISTICAL NOTES: Led California League with 17 hit batsmen in 1988.

Year League	W	L	Pct.	ERA	G	GS	CG	ShO	Sv.	IP	H	R	ER	BB	SO
1987—Everett (N.W.)	8	4	.667	2.46	15	•15	*5	•3	0	98²/₃	80	34	27	34	*99
1988—San Jose (Calif.)	12	5	.706	2.65	20	20	5	•4	0	149¹/₃	131	56	44	52	151
—Shreveport (Texas)	1	2	.333	5.15	7	6	0	0	0	36²/₃	45	25	21	13	28
1989—Shreveport (Texas)	8	2	*.800	2.72	11	11	2	1	0	72²/₃	68	24	22	23	61
—Phoenix (PCL)	2	4	.333	5.04	14	14	2	1	0	85²/₃	93	51	48	36	56
1990—San Francisco (N.L.)	1	2	.333	5.49	7	4	0	0	0	19²/₃	24	14	12	11	14
—Phoenix (PCL)	5	7	.417	8.23	16	16	0	0	0	82	137	87	75	46	41
—Shreveport (Texas)	2	2	.500	3.25	8	8	1	1	0	52²/₃	51	24	19	17	44
1991—San Francisco (N.L.)	0	0	...	5.40	2	0	0	0	1	3¹/₃	6	4	2	1	2
—Phoenix (PCL)	7	6	.538	6.14	40	14	0	0	3	107	153	85	73	44	53
1992—Jacksonville (Sou.)■	2	0	1.000	2.31	15	0	0	0	2	23¹/₃	18	10	6	7	23
—Calgary (PCL)	0	2	.000	6.02	27	1	0	0	5	52¹/₃	57	37	35	31	50
—Seattle (A.L.)	2	1	.667	8.68	9	0	0	0	0	9¹/₃	12	12	9	5	2
1993—Calgary (PCL)	0	1	.000	18.90	5	0	0	0	0	6²/₃	14	15	14	8	3
—Binghamton (East.)■	2	1	.667	5.24	20	1	0	0	1	22¹/₃	20	14	13	14	26
—Norfolk (I.L.)	3	2	.600	3.71	6	5	1	0	0	34	41	16	14	9	26
1994—St. Lucie (FSL)	1	0	1.000	0.00	3	0	0	0	1	4²/₃	4	0	0	0	6
—Norfolk (I.L.)	3	1	.750	3.68	19	2	1	1	1	36²/₃	25	16	15	17	31
—New York (N.L.)	0	0	...	0.00	14	0	0	0	0	9	5	0	0	4	4
1995—New York (N.L.)	1	1	.500	3.70	30	0	0	0	0	24¹/₃	25	10	10	8	19
—Boston (A.L.)■	2	1	.667	5.11	19	0	0	0	0	12¹/₃	13	7	7	9	9
1996—Pawtucket (I.L.)	2	1	.667	3.48	26	1	0	0	2	33²/₃	38	15	13	9	34
—Boston (A.L.)	0	1	.000	8.31	28	0	0	0	0	17¹/₃	21	17	16	8	7
1997—Texas (A.L.)■	2	1	.667	3.26	60	0	0	0	1	49²/₃	45	19	18	15	31
1998—Texas (A.L.)	0	3	.000	5.19	68	1	0	0	0	67²/₃	88	43	39	19	41
1999—Texas (A.L.)	0	0	...	7.20	11	0	0	0	0	10	20	8	8	2	6
—Oklahoma (PCL)	0	1	.000	8.10	5	0	0	0	1	6²/₃	11	6	6	1	3
A.L. totals (6 years)	6	7	.462	5.25	195	1	0	0	1	166¹/₃	199	106	97	58	96
N.L. totals (4 years)	2	3	.400	3.83	53	4	0	0	1	56¹/₃	60	28	24	24	39
Major League totals (9 years)	8	10	.444	4.89	248	5	0	0	2	222²/₃	259	134	121	82	135

GUTHRIE, MARK   P   CUBS

PERSONAL: Born September 22, 1965, in Buffalo. ... 6-4/215. ... Throws left, bats right. ... Full name: Mark Andrew Guthrie.
HIGH SCHOOL: Venice (Fla.).
COLLEGE: Louisiana State.
TRANSACTIONS/CAREER NOTES: Selected by St. Louis Cardinals organization in fourth round of free-agent draft (June 2, 1986); did not sign. ... Selected by Minnesota Twins organization in seventh round of free-agent draft (June 2, 1987). ... On disabled list (May 29, 1993-remainder of season). ... Traded by Twins with P Kevin Tapani to Los Angeles Dodgers for 1B/3B Ron Coomer, P Greg Hansell, P Jose Parra and a player to be named later (July 31, 1995); Twins acquired OF Chris Latham to complete deal (October 30, 1995). ... Granted free agency (October 29, 1996). ... Re-signed by Dodgers (November 6, 1996). ... Granted free agency (October 26, 1998). ... Signed by Boston Red Sox (December 19, 1998). ... On Boston disabled list (July 5-24, 1999); included rehabilitation assignment to Pawtucket (July 22-23). ... Traded by Red Sox with a player to named later to Chicago Cubs for P Rod Beck (August 31, 1999); Cubs acquired 3B Cole Liniak to complete deal (September 1, 1999).
MISCELLANEOUS: Appeared in one game as pinch runner (1991).

Year League	W	L	Pct.	ERA	G	GS	CG	ShO	Sv.	IP	H	R	ER	BB	SO
1987—Visalia (Calif.)	2	1	.667	4.50	4	1	0	0	0	12	10	7	6	5	9
1988—Visalia (Calif.)	12	9	.571	3.31	25	25	4	1	0	171¹/₃	169	81	63	86	182
1989—Orlando (Sou.)	8	3	.727	1.97	14	14	0	0	0	96	75	32	21	38	103
—Portland (PCL)	3	4	.429	3.65	7	7	1	0	0	44¹/₃	45	21	18	16	35
—Minnesota (A.L.)	2	4	.333	4.55	13	8	0	0	0	57¹/₃	66	32	29	21	38
1990—Minnesota (A.L.)	7	9	.438	3.79	24	21	3	1	0	144²/₃	154	65	61	39	101
—Portland (PCL)	1	3	.250	2.98	9	8	1	0	0	42¹/₃	47	19	14	12	39
1991—Minnesota (A.L.)	7	5	.583	4.32	41	12	0	0	2	98	116	52	47	41	72
1992—Minnesota (A.L.)	2	3	.400	2.88	54	0	0	0	5	75	59	27	24	23	76
1993—Minnesota (A.L.)	2	1	.667	4.71	22	0	0	0	0	21	20	11	11	16	15
1994—Minnesota (A.L.)	4	2	.667	6.14	50	2	0	0	1	51¹/₃	65	43	35	18	38
1995—Minnesota (A.L.)	5	3	.625	4.46	36	0	0	0	0	42¹/₃	47	22	21	16	48
—Los Angeles (N.L.)■	0	2	.000	3.66	24	0	0	0	0	19²/₃	19	11	8	9	19
1996—Los Angeles (N.L.)	2	3	.400	2.22	66	0	0	0	1	73	65	21	18	22	56
1997—Los Angeles (N.L.)	1	4	.200	5.32	62	0	0	0	1	69¹/₃	71	44	41	30	42
1998—Los Angeles (N.L.)	2	1	.667	3.50	53	0	0	0	0	54	56	26	21	24	45
1999—Boston (A.L.)■	1	1	.500	5.83	46	0	0	0	2	46¹/₃	50	32	30	20	36
—Pawtucket (I.L.)	0	0	...	0.00	1	1	0	0	0	1	0	0	0	0	1
—Chicago (N.L.)■	0	2	.000	3.65	11	0	0	0	0	12¹/₃	7	6	5	4	9
A.L. totals (8 years)	30	28	.517	4.33	286	43	3	1	10	536	577	284	258	194	424
N.L. totals (5 years)	5	12	.294	3.67	216	0	0	0	2	228¹/₃	218	108	93	89	171
Major League totals (11 years)	35	40	.467	4.13	502	43	3	1	12	764¹/₃	795	392	351	283	595

DIVISION SERIES RECORD

Year League	W	L	Pct.	ERA	G	GS	CG	ShO	Sv.	IP	H	R	ER	BB	SO
1995—Los Angeles (N.L.)	0	0	...	6.75	3	0	0	0	0	1¹/₃	2	1	1	1	1
1996—Los Angeles (N.L.)	0	0	...	0.00	1	0	0	0	0	¹/₃	0	0	0	1	1
Division series totals (2 years)	0	0	...	5.40	4	0	0	0	0	1²/₃	2	1	1	2	2

CHAMPIONSHIP SERIES RECORD

Year League	W	L	Pct.	ERA	G	GS	CG	ShO	Sv.	IP	H	R	ER	BB	SO
1991—Minnesota (A.L.)	1	0	1.000	0.00	2	0	0	0	0	2²/₃	0	0	0	0	0

WORLD SERIES RECORD

NOTES: Member of World Series championship team (1991).

Year League	W	L	Pct.	ERA	G	GS	CG	ShO	Sv.	IP	H	R	ER	BB	SO
1991—Minnesota (A.L.)	0	1	.000	2.25	4	0	0	0	0	4	3	1	1	4	3

G

GUTIERREZ, RICKY   SS   CUBS

PERSONAL: Born May 23, 1970, in Miami. ... 6-1/175. ... Bats right, throws right. ... Full name: Ricardo Gutierrez.
HIGH SCHOOL: American (Hialeah, Fla.).
TRANSACTIONS/CAREER NOTES: Selected by Baltimore Orioles organization in supplemental round ("sandwich pick" between first and second round, 28th pick overall) of free-agent draft (June 1, 1988); pick received as compensation for Orioles failing to sign 1987 No. 1 pick P Brad DuVall. ... Traded by Orioles to San Diego Padres (September 4, 1992), completing deal in which Padres traded P Craig Lefferts to Orioles for P Erik Schullstrom and a player to be named later (August 31, 1992). ... Traded by Padres with OF Phil Plantier, OF Derek Bell, P Pedro Martinez, P Doug Brocail and IF Craig Shipley to Houston Astros for 3B Ken Caminiti, OF Steve Finley, SS Andujar Cedeno, 1B Robert Petagine, P Brian Williams and a player to be named later (December 28, 1994); Padres acquired P Sean Fesh to complete deal (May 1, 1995). ... On disabled list (March 31-May 6, 1997); included rehabilitation assignment to New Orleans (April 29-May 6). ... On Houston disabled list (April 28-June 7 and July 10-August 9, 1999); included rehabilitation assignments to Jackson (June 3-7) and New Orleans (August 5-9). ... Granted free agency (October 28, 1999). ... Signed by Chicago Cubs (December 20, 1999).
STATISTICAL NOTES: Led Appalachian League shortstops with 309 total chances in 1988.

Year	Team (League)	Pos.	G	AB	R	H	2B	3B	HR	RBI	Avg.	BB	SO	SB	PO	A	E	Avg.
1988—	Bluefield (Appl.)	SS	62	208	35	51	8	2	2	19	.245	44	40	5	*100	175	34	.890
1989—	Frederick (Caro.)	SS	127	456	48	106	16	2	3	41	.232	39	89	15	190	372	34	*.943
1990—	Frederick (Caro.)	SS	112	425	54	117	16	4	1	46	.275	38	59	12	192	286	26	.948
—	Hagerstown (East.)	SS	20	64	4	15	0	1	0	6	.234	3	8	2	31	36	4	.944
1991—	Hagerstown (East.)	SS	84	292	47	69	6	4	0	30	.236	57	52	11	158	196	22	.941
—	Rochester (I.L.)	SS-3B	49	157	23	48	5	3	0	15	.306	24	27	4	61	129	8	.960
1992—	Rochester (I.L.)	2B-SS	125	431	54	109	9	3	0	41	.253	53	77	14	251	283	15	.973
—	Las Vegas (PCL)	SS	3	6	0	1	0	0	0	1	.167	1	3	0	1	8	0	1.000
1993—	Las Vegas (PCL)	2B-SS	5	24	4	10	4	0	0	4	.417	4	4	4	11	14	2	.926
—	San Diego (N.L.)	SS-2B-OF-3B	133	438	76	110	10	5	5	26	.251	50	97	4	194	305	14	.973
1994—	San Diego (N.L.)	SS-2B	90	275	27	66	11	2	1	28	.240	32	54	2	93	202	22	.931
1995—	Houston (N.L.)■	SS-3B	52	156	22	43	6	0	0	12	.276	10	33	5	64	108	8	.956
—	Tucson (PCL)	SS-DH	64	236	46	71	12	4	1	26	.301	28	28	9	91	167	6	.977
1996—	Houston (N.L.)	SS-3B-2B	89	218	28	62	8	1	1	15	.284	23	42	6	86	149	12	.951
1997—	New Orleans (A.A.)	SS	7	27	2	5	1	0	0	4	.185	2	4	0	12	21	1	.971
—	Houston (N.L.)	SS-3B-2B	102	303	33	79	14	4	3	34	.261	21	50	5	104	191	8	.974
1998—	Houston (N.L.)	SS	141	491	55	128	24	3	2	46	.261	54	84	13	215	404	15	.976
1999—	Houston (N.L.)	SS-3B	85	268	33	70	7	5	1	25	.261	37	45	2	102	203	9	.971
—	Jackson (Texas)	SS-DH	4	12	4	4	1	0	0	1	.333	4	3	0	2	5	0	1.000
—	New Orleans (PCL)	SS	4	14	0	3	0	0	0	1	.214	2	3	0	10	11	3	.875
Major League totals (7 years)			692	2149	274	558	80	20	13	186	.260	227	405	37	858	1562	88	.965

DIVISION SERIES RECORD

Year	Team (League)	Pos.	G	AB	R	H	2B	3B	HR	RBI	Avg.	BB	SO	SB	PO	A	E	Avg.
1997—	Houston (N.L.)	SS	3	8	0	1	0	0	0	0	.125	2	1	0	5	5	0	1.000
1998—	Houston (N.L.)	SS	4	10	1	3	0	0	0	0	.300	3	7	1	7	13	0	1.000
1999—	Houston (N.L.)	SS	3	10	0	0	0	0	0	0	.000	2	5	0	4	16	1	.952
Division series totals (3 years)			10	28	1	4	0	0	0	0	.143	7	13	1	16	34	1	.980

GUZMAN, CRISTIAN   SS   TWINS

PERSONAL: Born March 21, 1978, in Santo Domingo, Dominican Republic. ... 6-0/188. ... Bats both, throws right.
TRANSACTIONS/CAREER NOTES: Signed as non-drafted free agent by New York Yankees organization (August 24, 1994). ... Traded by Yankees with P Eric Milton, P Danny Mota, OF Brian Buchanan and cash to Minnesota Twins for 2B Chuck Knoblauch (February 6, 1998). ... On disabled list (May 27-June 11, 1999). ... On suspended list (September 10-13, 1999).
STATISTICAL NOTES: Led South Atlantic League shortstops with 68 double plays in 1997. ... Led Eastern League with 17 sacrifice hits in 1998. ... Led Eastern League shortstops with 95 double plays in 1998.

Year	Team (League)	Pos.	G	AB	R	H	2B	3B	HR	RBI	Avg.	BB	SO	SB	PO	A	E	Avg.
1995—	Dom. Yankees (DSL)..	SS	46	160	24	43	6	5	3	20	.269	12	23	11	159	29	13	.935
1996—	GC Yankees (GCL)	SS	42	170	37	50	8	2	1	21	.294	10	31	7	55	106	20	.890
1997—	Tampa (FSL)	SS	4	14	4	4	0	0	0	1	.286	1	1	0	6	10	2	.889
—	Greensboro (SAL)	SS	124	495	68	135	21	4	4	52	.273	17	105	23	173	364	37	.936
1998—	New Britain (East.)■..	SS	•140	566	68	157	29	5	1	40	.277	21	111	23	211	*426	*32	.952
1999—	Minnesota (A.L.)	SS	131	420	47	95	12	3	1	26	.226	22	90	9	196	363	24	.959
Major League totals (1 year)			131	420	47	95	12	3	1	26	.226	22	90	9	196	363	24	.959

GUZMAN, DOMINGO   P   PADRES

PERSONAL: Born April 5, 1975, in San Cristobal, Dominican Republic. ... 6-0/210. ... Throws right, bats right. ... Full name: Domingo Serrano Guzman.
TRANSACTIONS/CAREER NOTES: Signed as non-drafted free agent by San Diego Padres organization (June 15, 1993). ... On Clinton suspended list (May 15-18, 1997). ... On Rancho Cucamonga disabled list (April 2-May 26, 1998). ... On Mobile disabled list (August 7-27, 1998; and April 28-May 27, 1999).
STATISTICAL NOTES: Pitched 6-0 no-hit victory vs. Butte (August 15, 1996).

Year	League	W	L	Pct.	ERA	G	GS	CG	ShO	Sv.	IP	H	R	ER	BB	SO
1994—	Arizona Padres (Ariz.)	•8	4	.667	4.11	13	13	0	0	0	70	65	39	32	25	55
1995—	Idaho Falls (Pio.)	2	1	.667	6.66	27	0	0	0	•11	25 2/3	25	22	19	25	33
1996—	Idaho Falls (Pio.)	4	2	.667	4.13	15	10	1	•1	0	65 1/3	52	41	30	29	75
—	Clinton (Midw.)	0	5	.000	12.63	6	5	0	0	0	20 2/3	32	33	29	19	18

G

Year League	W	L	Pct.	ERA	G	GS	CG	ShO	Sv.	IP	H	R	ER	BB	SO
1997— Clinton (Midw.)	4	5	.444	3.19	12	12	5	0	0	79	66	36	28	25	91
— Rancho Cuca. (Calif.)	3	2	.600	5.45	6	6	0	0	0	38	42	23	23	16	39
1998— Rancho Cuca. (Calif.)	1	1	.500	3.74	4	4	0	0	0	21 2/3	22	11	9	6	16
— Mobile (Sou.)	5	2	.714	4.50	12	8	0	0	1	48	51	34	24	26	39
1999— Mobile (Sou.)	1	2	.333	5.47	41	0	0	0	6	51	60	33	31	25	38
— San Diego (N.L.)	0	1	.000	21.60	7	0	0	0	0	5	13	12	12	3	4
Major League totals (1 year)........	0	1	.000	21.60	7	0	0	0	0	5	13	12	12	3	4

GUZMAN, EDWARDS — 3B/C — GIANTS

PERSONAL: Born September 11, 1976, in Bayamon, Puerto Rico. ... 5-10/205. ... Bats left, throws right.
HIGH SCHOOL: Emilio Delgado (Corozal, Puerto Rico).
TRANSACTIONS/CAREER NOTES: Selected by San Francisco Giants organization in 50th round of free-agent draft (June 1, 1995). ... On Fresno disabled list (June 12-23, 1999).

Year Team (League)	Pos.	G	AB	R	H	2B	3B	HR	RBI	Avg.	BB	SO	SB	PO	A	E	Avg.
1996— San Jose (Calif.).........	3B-OF	106	367	41	99	19	5	4	40	.270	39	60	3	69	213	25	.919
1997— Shreveport (Texas).....	3B	118	380	52	108	15	4	3	42	.284	33	57	3	73	199	19	.935
1998— Fresno (PCL)	3B-C	102	325	50	99	17	0	9	48	.305	24	47	1	80	131	14	.938
1999— Fresno (PCL) 3B-C-1B-DH		90	358	48	98	13	0	7	48	.274	17	50	6	282	129	26	.941
— San Francisco (N.L.) ..	3B-C	14	15	0	0	0	0	0	0	.000	0	4	0	3	7	0	1.000
Major League totals (1 year)		14	15	0	0	0	0	0	0	.000	0	4	0	3	7	0	1.000

GUZMAN, ELPIDIO — OF — ANGELS

PERSONAL: Born February 24, 1979, in Santo Domingo, Dominican Republic. ... 6-0/165. ... Bats left, throws left.
HIGH SCHOOL: Carl Morgan (Santo Domingo, Dominican Republic).
TRANSACTIONS/CAREER NOTES: Signed as non-drafted free agent by California Angels organization (October 15, 1995). ... Angels franchise renamed Anaheim Angels for 1997 season.
STATISTICAL NOTES: Led Pioneer League outfielders with 147 total chances in 1998.

Year Team (League)	Pos.	G	AB	R	H	2B	3B	HR	RBI	Avg.	BB	SO	SB	PO	A	E	Avg.
1996— Dom. Angels (DSL)	OF	42	116	11	27	6	0	0	13	.233	19	17	11	76	2	6	.929
1997— Butte (Pio.)................	OF	17	43	12	13	2	1	3	13	.302	5	5	3	21	2	1	.958
1998— Butte (Pio.)................	OF	69	299	70	99	16	5	9	61	.331	24	44	40	*136	6	5	.966
1999— Cedar Rap. (Midw.)	OF	130	526	74	144	26	13	4	48	.274	41	84	52	256	9	13	.953

GUZMAN, GERALDO — P — DIAMONDBACKS

PERSONAL: Born November 28, 1973, in Teoares, Dominican Republic. ... 6-2/180. ... Throws right, bats right.
TRANSACTIONS/CAREER NOTES: Played in Taiwan. ... Signed as non-drafted free agent by Arizona Diamondbacks organization (November 12, 1999).

GUZMAN, JUAN — P — DEVIL RAYS

PERSONAL: Born October 28, 1966, in Santo Domingo, Dominican Republic. ... 5-11/195. ... Throws right, bats right. ... Full name: Juan Andres Correa Guzman.
HIGH SCHOOL: Liceo Las Americas (Dominican Republic).
TRANSACTIONS/CAREER NOTES: Signed as non-drafted free agent by Los Angeles Dodgers organization (March 16, 1985). ... Traded by Dodgers to Toronto Blue Jays organization for IF Mike Sharperson (September 22, 1987). ... On Toronto disabled list (August 4-29, 1992); included rehabilitation assignment to Syracuse (August 24-25). ... On Toronto disabled list (May 16-June 5 and August 10-29, 1995); included rehabilitation assignment to Syracuse (August 25-26). ... On Toronto disabled list (May 23-June 7, 1996; May 29-June 26 and July 16-September 28, 1997). ... Traded by Blue Jays to Baltimore Orioles for P Nerio Rodriguez and OF Shannon Carter (July 31, 1998). ... Traded by Orioles to Cincinnati Reds for P B.J. Ryan and P Jacobo Sequea (July 31, 1999). ... Granted free agency (October 29, 1999). ... Signed by Tampa Bay Devil Rays (January 7, 2000).
RECORDS: Holds A.L. single-season record for most wild pitches—26 (1993).
HONORS: Named A.L. Rookie Pitcher of the Year by THE SPORTING NEWS (1991).
STATISTICAL NOTES: Led Gulf Coast League with 15 wild pitches in 1985. ... Led Florida State League with 16 wild pitches in 1986. ... Led Southern League with 21 wild pitches in 1990. ... Led A.L. with 26 wild pitches in 1993 and tied for lead with 13 in 1994. ... Tied for A.L. lead with 16 losses in 1998.

Year League	W	L	Pct.	ERA	G	GS	CG	ShO	Sv.	IP	H	R	ER	BB	SO
1985— GC Dodgers (GCL)	5	1	.833	3.86	21	3	0	0	4	42	39	26	18	25	43
1986— Vero Beach (FSL)	10	9	.526	3.49	20	24	3	0	0	131 1/3	114	69	51	90	96
1987— Bakersfield (Calif.)	5	6	.455	4.75	22	21	0	0	0	110	106	71	58	84	113
1988— Knoxville (Sou.)■.............	4	5	.444	2.36	46	2	0	0	6	84	52	29	22	61	90
1989— Syracuse (I.L.).................	1	1	.500	3.98	14	0	0	0	0	20 1/3	13	9	9	30	28
— Knoxville (Sou.).................	1	4	.200	6.23	22	8	0	0	0	47 2/3	34	36	33	60	50
1990— Knoxville (Sou.)...............	11	9	.550	4.24	37	21	2	0	1	157	145	84	74	80	138
1991— Syracuse (I.L.).................	4	5	.444	4.03	12	11	0	0	0	67	46	39	30	42	67
— Toronto (A.L.)...................	10	3	.769	2.99	23	23	1	0	0	138 2/3	98	53	46	66	123
1992— Toronto (A.L.)...................	16	5	.762	2.64	28	28	1	0	0	180 2/3	135	56	53	72	165
— Syracuse (I.L.).................	0	0	...	6.00	1	1	0	0	0	3	6	2	2	1	3
1993— Toronto (A.L.)..................	14	3	*.824	3.99	33	33	2	1	0	221	211	107	98	110	194
1994— Toronto (A.L.)..................	12	11	.522	5.68	25	•25	2	0	0	147 1/3	165	102	93	76	124

G

Year League	W	L	Pct.	ERA	G	GS	CG	ShO	Sv.	IP	H	R	ER	BB	SO
1995—Toronto (A.L.)	4	14	.222	6.32	24	24	3	0	0	135 1/3	151	101	95	73	94
—Syracuse (I.L.)	0	0	...	0.00	1	1	0	0	0	5	1	0	0	3	5
1996—Toronto (A.L.)	11	8	.579	*2.93	27	27	4	1	0	187 2/3	158	68	61	53	165
1997—Toronto (A.L.)	3	6	.333	4.95	13	13	0	0	0	60	48	42	33	31	52
—Dunedin (FSL)	0	0	...	0.00	2	2	0	0	0	4	3	0	0	1	3
1998—Toronto (A.L.)	6	12	.333	4.41	22	22	2	0	0	145	133	83	71	65	113
—Baltimore (A.L.)■	4	§4	.500	4.23	11	11	0	0	0	66	60	34	31	33	55
1999—Baltimore (A.L.)	5	9	.357	4.18	21	21	1	1	0	122 2/3	124	63	57	65	95
—Cincinnati (N.L.)■	6	3	.667	3.03	12	12	1	0	0	77 1/3	70	33	26	21	60
A.L. totals (9 years)	85	75	.531	4.09	227	227	16	3	0	1404 1/3	1283	709	638	644	1180
N.L. totals (1 year)	6	3	.667	3.03	12	12	1	0	0	77 1/3	70	33	26	21	60
Major League totals (9 years)	91	78	.538	4.03	239	239	17	3	0	1481 2/3	1353	742	664	665	1240

CHAMPIONSHIP SERIES RECORD

RECORDS: Shares single-inning record for most wild pitches—2 (October 5, 1993, first inning).

Year League	W	L	Pct.	ERA	G	GS	CG	ShO	Sv.	IP	H	R	ER	BB	SO
1991—Toronto (A.L.)	1	0	1.000	3.18	1	1	0	0	0	5 2/3	4	2	2	4	2
1992—Toronto (A.L.)	2	0	1.000	2.08	2	2	0	0	0	13	12	3	3	5	11
1993—Toronto (A.L.)	2	0	1.000	2.08	2	2	0	0	0	13	8	4	3	9	9
Champ. series totals (3 years)	5	0	1.000	2.27	5	5	0	0	0	31 2/3	24	9	8	18	22

WORLD SERIES RECORD

NOTES: Member of World Series championship team (1992 and 1993).

Year League	W	L	Pct.	ERA	G	GS	CG	ShO	Sv.	IP	H	R	ER	BB	SO
1992—Toronto (A.L.)	0	0	...	1.13	1	1	0	0	0	8	8	2	1	1	7
1993—Toronto (A.L.)	0	1	.000	3.75	2	2	0	0	0	12	10	6	5	8	12
World Series totals (2 years)	0	1	.000	2.70	3	3	0	0	0	20	18	8	6	9	19

ALL-STAR GAME RECORD

Year League	W	L	Pct.	ERA	GS	CG	ShO	Sv.	IP	H	R	ER	BB	SO
1992—American	0	0	...	0.00	0	0	0	0	1	2	0	0	1	2

GUZMAN, JUAN   P   ORIOLES

PERSONAL: Born March 4, 1978, in San Pedro de Macoris, Dominican Republic ... 6-2/184. ... Throws right, bats right. ... Full name: Juan Ramon Guzman.
TRANSACTIONS/CAREER NOTES: Signed as non-drafted free agent by Baltimore Orioles organization (December 16, 1994).
MISCELLANEOUS: Played catcher (1995-97).

Year League	W	L	Pct.	ERA	G	GS	CG	ShO	Sv.	IP	H	R	ER	BB	SO
1998—Bluefield (Appl.)	1	2	.333	1.42	15	0	0	0	1	25 1/3	22	12	4	7	26
1999—Delmarva (SAL)	9	5	.643	3.55	29	18	0	0	3	124 1/3	124	51	49	44	134

RECORD AS POSITION PLAYER

							BATTING							FIELDING		
Year Team (League)	Pos.	G	AB	R	H	2B	3B	HR	RBI	Avg.	BB	SO	SB	PO	A	E	Avg.
1995—Dom. Orioles (DSL)	C-1B	37	120	12	24	6	0	0	12	.200	6	20	2	141	38	6	.974
1996—Dom. Orioles (DSL)	C	61	200	24	45	8	3	2	19	.225	14	31	5	298	44	2	.994
1997—GC. Orioles (GCL)	C	15	47	1	7	1	0	0	4	.149	1	18	8	79	15	1	.989

GWYNN, TONY   OF   PADRES

PERSONAL: Born May 9, 1960, in Los Angeles. ... 5-11/220. ... Bats left, throws left. ... Full name: Anthony Keith Gwynn. ... Brother of Chris Gwynn, major league outfielder with three teams (1987-96) and current scout, San Diego Padres.
HIGH SCHOOL: Long Beach (Calif.) Polytechnic.
COLLEGE: San Diego State.
TRANSACTIONS/CAREER NOTES: Selected by San Diego Padres organization in third round of free-agent draft (June 8, 1981). ... On San Diego disabled list (August 26-September 10, 1982). ... On San Diego disabled list (March 26-June 21, 1983); included rehabilitation to Las Vegas (May 31-June 20). ... On disabled list (May 8-29, 1988; July 2-August 6, 1996; and August 13-September 1, 1998). ... On disabled list (May 22-June 12 and June 20-July 19, 1999).
RECORDS: Holds N.L. career records for most years leading league in singles—7 (1984, 1986-87, 1989, 1994, 1995 and 1997); and most consecutive years batting .300 or over (50 or more games) since 1900—16. ... Holds N.L. single-season record for lowest batting average by leader—.313 (1988). ... Shares N.L. single-season record for most times collecting five or more hits in one game—4 (1993). ... Shares N.L. career record for most years leading league in batting average—8.
HONORS: Named Northwest League Most Valuable Player (1981). ... Named outfielder on THE SPORTING NEWS N.L. All-Star team (1984, 1986-87, 1989, 1994 and 1997). ... Named outfielder on THE SPORTING NEWS N.L. Silver Slugger team (1984, 1986-87, 1989, 1994-95 and 1997). ... Won N.L. Gold Glove as outfielder (1986-87 and 1989-91).
STATISTICAL NOTES: Had 25-game hitting streak (August 21-September 18, 1983). ... Led N.L. with .410 on-base percentage in 1984. ... Led N.L. outfielders with 360 total chances in 1986. ... Collected six hits in one game (August 4, 1993, 12 innings). ... Led N.L. in grounding into double plays with 20 in 1994. ... Had 20-game hitting streak (May 20-June 10, 1997). ... Tied for N.L. lead with 12 sacrifice flies in 1997. ... Had 16-game hitting streak (September 5-21, 1999). ... Career major league grand slams: 3.
MISCELLANEOUS: Holds San Diego Padres all-time records for most runs (1,361), hits (3,067), doubles (522), triples (84), highest career batting average (.339), most runs batted in (1,104) and most stolen bases (318). ... Selected by San Diego Clippers in 10th round (210th pick overall) of 1981 NBA draft (June 9, 1981).

							BATTING							FIELDING		
Year Team (League)	Pos.	G	AB	R	H	2B	3B	HR	RBI	Avg.	BB	SO	SB	PO	A	E	Avg.
1981—Walla Walla (N.W.)	OF	42	178	46	59	12	1	12	37	*.331	23	21	17	76	2	3	.963
—Amarillo (Texas)	OF	23	91	22	42	8	2	4	19	.462	5	7	5	41	1	0	1.000
1982—Hawaii (PCL)	OF	93	366	65	120	23	2	5	46	.328	18	18	14	208	11	4	.982
—San Diego (N.L.)	OF	54	190	33	55	12	2	1	17	.289	14	16	8	110	1	1	.991

Year	Team (League)	Pos.	G	AB	R	H	2B	3B	HR	RBI	Avg.	BB	SO	SB	PO	A	E	Avg.
1983—	Las Vegas (PCL)	OF	17	73	15	25	6	0	0	7	.342	6	5	3	23	2	3	.893
—	San Diego (N.L.)	OF	86	304	34	94	12	2	1	37	.309	23	21	7	163	9	1	.994
1984—	San Diego (N.L.)	OF	158	606	88	*213	21	10	5	71	*.351	59	23	33	345	11	4	.989
1985—	San Diego (N.L.)	OF	154	622	90	197	29	5	6	46	.317	45	33	14	337	14	4	.989
1986—	San Diego (N.L.)	OF	160	*642	•107	*211	33	7	14	59	.329	52	35	37	*337	19	4	.989
1987—	San Diego (N.L.)	OF	157	589	119	*218	36	13	7	54	*.370	82	35	56	298	13	6	.981
1988—	San Diego (N.L.)	OF	133	521	64	163	22	5	7	70	*.313	51	40	26	264	8	5	.982
1989—	San Diego (N.L.)	OF	158	604	82	*203	27	7	4	62	*.336	56	30	40	353	13	6	.984
1990—	San Diego (N.L.)	OF	141	573	79	177	29	10	4	72	.309	44	23	17	327	11	5	.985
1991—	San Diego (N.L.)	OF	134	530	69	168	27	11	4	62	.317	34	19	8	291	8	3	.990
1992—	San Diego (N.L.)	OF	128	520	77	165	27	3	6	41	.317	46	16	3	270	9	5	.982
1993—	San Diego (N.L.)	OF	122	489	70	175	41	3	7	59	.358	36	19	14	244	8	5	.981
1994—	San Diego (N.L.)	OF	110	419	79	*165	35	1	12	64	*.394	48	19	5	191	6	3	.985
1995—	San Diego (N.L.)	OF	135	535	82	•197	33	1	9	90	*.368	35	15	17	245	8	2	.992
1996—	San Diego (N.L.)	OF	116	451	67	159	27	2	3	50	*.353	39	17	11	182	2	2	.989
1997—	San Diego (N.L.)	OF-DH	149	592	97	*220	49	2	17	119	*.372	43	28	12	218	8	4	.983
1998—	San Diego (N.L.)	OF-DH	127	461	65	148	35	0	16	69	.321	35	18	3	142	5	1	.993
1999—	San Diego (N.L.)	OF-DH	111	411	59	139	27	0	10	62	.338	29	14	7	147	4	1	.993
Major League totals (18 years)			2333	9059	1361	3067	522	84	133	1104	.339	771	421	318	4464	157	62	.987

DIVISION SERIES RECORD

RECORDS: Shares N.L. career record for most doubles—3.

Year	Team (League)	Pos.	G	AB	R	H	2B	3B	HR	RBI	Avg.	BB	SO	SB	PO	A	E	Avg.
1996—	San Diego (N.L.)	OF	3	13	0	4	1	0	0	1	.308	0	2	1	2	0	0	1.000
1998—	San Diego (N.L.)	OF	4	15	1	3	2	0	0	2	.200	0	2	0	4	1	0	1.000
Division series totals (2 years)			7	28	1	7	3	0	0	3	.250	0	4	1	6	1	0	1.000

CHAMPIONSHIP SERIES RECORD

Year	Team (League)	Pos.	G	AB	R	H	2B	3B	HR	RBI	Avg.	BB	SO	SB	PO	A	E	Avg.
1984—	San Diego (N.L.)	OF	5	19	6	7	3	0	0	3	.368	1	2	0	9	0	0	1.000
1998—	San Diego (N.L.)	OF	6	26	1	6	1	0	0	2	.231	1	2	0	5	0	0	1.000
Championship series totals (2 years)			11	45	7	13	4	0	0	5	.289	2	4	0	14	0	0	1.000

WORLD SERIES RECORD

Year	Team (League)	Pos.	G	AB	R	H	2B	3B	HR	RBI	Avg.	BB	SO	SB	PO	A	E	Avg.
1984—	San Diego (N.L.)	OF	5	19	1	5	0	0	0	0	.263	3	2	1	12	1	1	.929
1998—	San Diego (N.L.)	OF	4	16	2	8	0	0	1	3	.500	1	0	0	6	0	0	1.000
World Series totals (2 years)			9	35	3	13	0	0	1	3	.371	4	2	1	18	1	1	.950

ALL-STAR GAME RECORD

RECORDS: Shares single-game record for most at-bats in nine-inning game—5 (July 12, 1994).
NOTES: Named to All-Star team for 1996 game; replaced by Henry Rodriguez due to injury.

Year	League	Pos.	AB	R	H	2B	3B	HR	RBI	Avg.	BB	SO	SB	PO	A	E	Avg.
1984—	National	OF	3	0	1	0	0	0	0	.333	0	0	0	0	0	0	...
1985—	National	OF	1	0	0	0	0	0	0	.000	0	0	0	1	0	0	1.000
1986—	National	OF	3	0	0	0	0	0	0	.000	0	0	0	1	0	0	1.000
1987—	National	PH	1	0	0	0	0	0	0	.000	0	0	0	...	...	...	...
1989—	National	OF	2	1	1	0	0	0	0	.500	1	1	1	2	0	0	1.000
1990—	National	PH	0	0	0	0	0	0	0	...	1	0	0	...	...	...	...
1991—	National	OF	4	1	2	0	0	0	0	.500	0	0	0	6	0	0	1.000
1992—	National	OF	2	0	0	0	0	0	0	.000	1	0	0	0	2	0	1.000
1993—	National	OF	1	0	0	0	0	0	0	.000	0	0	0	0	0	0	...
1994—	National	OF	5	2	2	1	0	0	2	.400	0	0	0	2	0	0	1.000
1995—	National	OF	2	0	0	0	0	0	0	.000	0	0	0	1	0	0	1.000
1996—	National						Selected, did not play—injured.										
1997—	National	DH	3	0	0	0	0	0	0	.000	0	0	0	0	0	0	...
1998—	National	OF	2	0	1	0	0	0	2	.500	0	0	0	0	0	0	...
1999—	National						Selected, did not play—injured.										
All-Star Game totals (13 years)			29	4	7	1	0	0	4	.241	3	1	1	13	2	0	1.000

HAAD, YAMID   C   PIRATES

PERSONAL: Born September 2, 1977, in Cartagena, Colombia. ... 6-2/204. ... Bats right, throws right. ... Full name: Yamid Salcedo Haad.
TRANSACTIONS/CAREER NOTES: Signed as non-drafted free agent by Pittsburgh Pirates organization (December 8, 1994).

Year	Team (League)	Pos.	G	AB	R	H	2B	3B	HR	RBI	Avg.	BB	SO	SB	PO	A	E	Avg.
1995—	Dom. Pirates (DSL)....	C	36	118	17	30	1	0	0	8	.254	9	17	1	265	31	6	.980
1996—	Dom. Pirates (DSL)....	C	56	205	29	66	9	0	5	28	.322	10	38	8	402	59	3	.994
1997—	Erie (NY-P)	C	43	155	27	45	7	3	1	19	.290	7	27	3	267	30	3	.990
1998—	Lynchburg (Caro.)	C	88	299	32	76	8	2	5	34	.254	13	54	1	593	77	12	.982
1999—	Lynchburg (Caro.) C-DH-1-O-3		59	209	31	53	11	1	5	33	.254	33	42	5	293	21	2	.994
—	Altoona (East.)	C	43	137	20	25	3	0	6	10	.182	19	32	7	272	37	10	.969
—	Pittsburgh (N.L.)	PH	1	1	0	0	0	0	0	0	.000	0	0	0	0	0	0	...
Major League totals (1 year)			1	1	0	0	0	0	0	0	.000	0	0	0	0	0	0	...

G
H

HAAS, CHRIS — 3B/1B — CARDINALS

PERSONAL: Born October 15, 1976, in Paducah, Ky. ... 6-1/205. ... Bats left, throws right. ... Full name: Christopher M. Haas.
HIGH SCHOOL: St. Mary's (Paducah, Ky.).
TRANSACTIONS/CAREER NOTES: Selected by St. Louis Cardinals organization in supplemental round ("sandwich pick" between first and second round, 29th pick overall) of free-agent draft (June 1, 1995); pick received as part of compensation for Philadelphia Phillies signing Type A free-agent 1B Gregg Jefferies. ... On Memphis disabled list (July 2-16, 1999).
STATISTICAL NOTES: Led Appalachian League third basemen with 187 total chances in 1995.

							BATTING								FIELDING		
Year Team (League)	Pos.	G	AB	R	H	2B	3B	HR	RBI	Avg.	BB	SO	SB	PO	A	E	Avg.
1995— Johnson City (Appl.) ..	3B	•67	242	43	65	15	3	7	50	.269	*52	93	1	51	*116	20	.893
1996— Peoria (Midw.)...........	3B	124	421	56	101	19	1	11	65	.240	64	169	3	75	241	42	.883
1997— Peoria (Midw.)...........	3B	36	115	23	36	11	0	5	22	.313	22	38	1	16	52	6	.919
— Prince Will. (Caro.).....	3B	100	361	58	86	10	2	14	54	.238	42	144	1	89	183	19	*.935
1998— Arkansas (Texas)........	3B-1B	132	445	75	122	27	4	20	83	.274	73	129	1	146	211	22	.942
1999— Memphis (PCL)..........	3B-1B-DH	114	397	63	91	19	2	18	73	.229	66	155	4	312	180	12	.976

HACKMAN, LUTHER — P — CARDINALS

PERSONAL: Born October 10, 1974, in Lawndale, Miss. ... 6-4/195. ... Throws right, bats right. ... Full name: Luther Gean Hackman.
HIGH SCHOOL: Columbus (Miss.).
TRANSACTIONS/CAREER NOTES: Selected by Colorado Rockies organization in sixth round of free-agent draft (June 2, 1994). ... On disabled list (June 1-July 10, 1996). ... Traded by Rockies with P Darryl Kile and P Dave Veres to St. Louis Cardinals for P Jose Jimenez, P Manny Aybar, P Rick Croushore and SS Brent Butler (November 16, 1999).

Year League	W	L	Pct.	ERA	G	GS	CG	ShO	Sv.	IP	H	R	ER	BB	SO
1994— Arizona Rockies (Ariz.).......	1	3	.250	2.10	12	12	0	0	0	55²/₃	50	21	13	16	63
1995— Asheville (SAL).................	11	11	.500	4.64	28	28	2	0	0	165	162	*95	*85	65	108
1996— Carolina (Sou.).................	5	7	.417	4.24	21	21	1	0	0	110¹/₃	93	60	52	69	83
1997— New Haven (East.).............	0	6	.000	7.82	10	10	0	0	0	50²/₃	58	49	44	34	34
— Salem (Caro.)....................	1	4	.200	5.80	15	15	2	0	0	80²/₃	99	60	52	37	59
1998— New Haven (East.).............	3	12	.200	5.44	28	23	1	0	0	139	169	•102	84	54	90
1999— Carolina (Sou.).................	4	3	.571	4.04	11	10	0	0	0	62¹/₃	53	33	28	28	50
— Colo. Springs (PCL)	7	6	.538	3.74	15	15	1	1	0	101	106	49	42	44	88
— Colorado (N.L.)................	1	2	.333	10.69	5	3	0	0	0	16	26	19	19	12	10
Major League totals (1 year)........	1	2	.333	10.69	5	3	0	0	0	16	26	19	19	12	10

HAIRSTON, JERRY — 2B/SS — ORIOLES

PERSONAL: Born May 29, 1976, in Des Moines, Iowa. ... 5-10/173. ... Bats right, throws right. ... Full name: Jerry W. Hairston Jr. ... Grandson of Sam Hairston, catcher with Chicago White Sox (1951) and Cincinnati and Indianapolis of Negro American League (1945-49); son of Jerry Hairston, outfielder with Chicago White Sox (1973-77 and 1981-89) and Pittsburgh Pirates (1977); nephew of John Hairston, catcher/outfielder with Chicago Cubs (1969); and nephew of Sam Hairston Jr., former minor league player in Chicago White Sox organization (1966 and 1969).
HIGH SCHOOL: Naperville (Ill.) North.
COLLEGE: Southern Illinois-Carbondale.
TRANSACTIONS/CAREER NOTES: Selected by Baltimore Orioles organization in 11th round of free-agent draft (June 3, 1997).
STATISTICAL NOTES: Tied for Appalachian League lead in caught stealing with nine in 1997.

							BATTING								FIELDING		
Year Team (League)	Pos.	G	AB	R	H	2B	3B	HR	RBI	Avg.	BB	SO	SB	PO	A	E	Avg.
1997— Bluefield (Appl.)	SS	59	221	44	73	13	4	2	36	.330	21	29	13	84	174	14	*.949
1998— Frederick (Caro.)	SS-2B	80	293	56	83	22	3	5	33	.283	28	32	13	116	281	24	.943
— Bowie (East.)	2B-SS	55	221	42	72	12	3	5	37	.326	20	25	6	109	135	5	.980
— Baltimore (A.L.)..........	2B	6	7	2	0	0	0	0	0	.000	0	1	0	4	2	2	.750
1999— Rochester (I.L.).........	2B-SS	107	413	65	120	24	5	7	48	.291	30	50	19	206	277	16	.968
— Baltimore (A.L.)..........	2B	50	175	26	47	12	1	4	17	.269	11	24	9	115	154	0	1.000
Major League totals (2 years)		56	182	28	47	12	1	4	17	.258	11	25	9	119	156	2	.993

HALAMA, JOHN — P — MARINERS

PERSONAL: Born February 22, 1972, in Brooklyn, N.Y. ... 6-5/200. ... Throws left, bats left. ... Full name: John Thadeuz Halama. ... Name pronounced ha-LA-ma.
HIGH SCHOOL: Bishop Ford (Brooklyn, N.Y.).
COLLEGE: St. Francis (N.Y.).
TRANSACTIONS/CAREER NOTES: Selected by Houston Astros organization in 23rd round of free-agent draft (June 3, 1994). ... On New Orleans disabled list (July 2-August 6, 1998). ... Traded by Astros to Seattle Mariners (October 1, 1998), completing deal in which Mariners traded P Randy Johnson to Astros for SS Carlos Guillen, P Freddy Garcia and a player to be named later (July 31, 1998).

Year League	W	L	Pct.	ERA	G	GS	CG	ShO	Sv.	IP	H	R	ER	BB	SO
1994— Auburn (NY-P)...................	4	1	.800	1.29	6	3	0	0	1	28	18	5	4	5	27
— Quad City (Midw.)	3	4	.429	4.56	9	9	1	1	0	51¹/₃	63	31	26	18	37
1995— Quad City (Midw.).............	1	2	.333	2.02	55	0	0	0	2	62¹/₃	48	16	14	22	56
1996— Jackson (Texas)	9	10	.474	3.21	27	27	0	0	0	162²/₃	151	77	58	59	110
1997— New Orleans (A.A.)...........	13	3	*.813	2.58	26	24	1	0	0	171	150	57	49	32	126
1998— Houston (N.L.)..............	1	1	.500	5.85	6	6	0	0	0	32¹/₃	37	21	21	13	21
— New Orleans (PCL).............	12	3	.800	3.20	17	17	4	1	0	121	118	48	43	16	86
1999— Seattle (A.L.)■	11	10	.524	4.22	38	24	1	1	0	179	193	88	84	56	105
A.L. totals (1 year)..................	11	10	.524	4.22	38	24	1	1	0	179	193	88	84	56	105
N.L. totals (1 year)..................	1	1	.500	5.85	6	6	0	0	0	32¹/₃	37	21	21	13	21
Major League totals (2 years).......	12	11	.522	4.47	44	30	1	1	0	211¹/₃	230	109	105	69	126

H

PERSONAL: Born May 14, 1977, in Denver. ... 6-6/225. ... Throws right, bats right. ... Full name: Harry Leroy Halladay III.
HIGH SCHOOL: Arvada (Colo.) West.
TRANSACTIONS/CAREER NOTES: Selected by Toronto Blue Jays organization in first round (17th pick overall) of free-agent draft (June 1, 1995). ... On Syracuse disabled list (May 15-June 17, 1998).
STATISTICAL NOTES: Pitched 2-1 one-hit, complete-game victory against Detroit (September 27, 1998).

Year League	W	L	Pct.	ERA	G	GS	CG	ShO	Sv.	IP	H	R	ER	BB	SO
1995— GC Blue Jays (GCL)	3	5	.375	3.40	10	8	0	0	0	50⅓	35	25	19	16	48
1996— Dunedin (FSL)	15	7	.682	2.73	27	27	2	•2	0	164⅔	158	75	50	46	109
1997— Knoxville (Sou.)	2	3	.400	5.40	7	7	0	0	0	36⅔	46	26	22	11	30
— Syracuse (I.L.)	7	10	.412	4.58	22	22	2	2	0	125⅔	132	74	64	53	64
1998— Syracuse (I.L.)	9	5	.643	3.79	21	21	1	1	0	116⅓	107	52	49	53	71
— Toronto (A.L.)	1	0	1.000	1.93	2	2	1	0	0	14	9	4	3	2	13
1999— Toronto (A.L.)	8	7	.533	3.92	36	18	1	1	1	149⅓	156	76	65	79	82
Major League totals (2 years)	9	7	.563	3.75	38	20	2	1	1	163⅓	165	80	68	81	95

PERSONAL: Born November 8, 1969, in La Plata, Md. ... 6-0/180. ... Bats right, throws right. ... Full name: Shane David Halter.
HIGH SCHOOL: Hooks (Texas).
JUNIOR COLLEGE: Seminole (Okla.) Junior College.
COLLEGE: Texas.
TRANSACTIONS/CAREER NOTES: Selected by Cincinnati Reds organization in 16th round of free-agent draft (June 4, 1990); did not sign. ... Selected by Kansas City Royals organization in fifth round of free-agent draft (June 3, 1991). ... Traded by Royals to New York Mets for OF Jonathan Guzman (March 23, 1999).
STATISTICAL NOTES: Led Midwest League shortstops with 64 double plays in 1992. ... Led American Association with 19 sacrifice hits in 1995. ... Led International League with 17 sacrifice hits and in caught stealing with 18 in 1999.

Year Team (League)	Pos.	G	AB	R	H	2B	3B	HR	RBI	Avg.	BB	SO	SB	PO	A	E	Avg.
1991— Eugene (N.W.)	SS	64	236	41	55	9	1	1	18	.233	49	60	12	*118	154	21	.928
1992— Appleton (Midw.)	SS	80	313	50	83	22	3	3	33	.265	41	54	21	150	227	16	.959
— Baseball City (FSL)	SS	44	117	11	28	1	0	1	14	.239	24	31	5	70	115	6	.969
1993— Wilmington (Caro.)	SS	54	211	44	63	8	5	5	32	.299	27	55	5	84	146	15	.939
— Memphis (Sou.)	SS	81	306	50	79	7	0	4	20	.258	30	74	4	142	229	16	.959
1994— Memphis (Sou.)	SS	129	494	61	111	23	1	6	35	.225	39	102	10	177	369	29	.950
1995— Omaha (A.A.)	SS-2B	124	392	42	90	19	3	8	39	.230	40	97	2	225	355	19	.968
1996— Omaha (A.A.)	O-3-S-2-P	93	299	43	77	24	0	3	33	.258	31	49	7	130	75	13	.940
— Charlotte (I.L.)	O-2-DH-3-1	16	41	3	12	1	0	0	4	.293	2	8	0	15	10	1	.962
1997— Omaha (A.A.)	3-OF-2-SS	14	49	10	13	1	1	2	9	.265	6	10	0	22	14	2	.947
— Kansas City (A.L.)	O-2-3-S-DH	74	123	16	34	5	1	2	10	.276	10	28	4	63	40	1	.990
1998— Kansas City (A.L.)	S-O-3-2-P-1	86	204	17	45	12	0	2	13	.221	12	38	2	91	177	10	.964
— Omaha (PCL)	S-1-2-3-OF	22	97	15	30	6	1	1	13	.309	6	15	4	64	46	3	.973
1999— Norfolk (I.L.)■	S-O-2-3-C	127	474	77	130	22	3	6	35	.274	60	90	19	187	239	20	.955
— New York (N.L.)	OF-SS	7	0	0	0	0	0	0	0	...	0	0	0	0	0	0	...
American League totals (2 years)		160	327	33	79	17	1	4	23	.242	22	66	6	154	217	11	.971
National League totals (1 year)		7	0	0	0	0	0	0	0	...	0	0	0	0	0	0	...
Major League totals (3 years)		167	327	33	79	17	1	4	23	.242	22	66	6	154	217	11	.971

RECORD AS PITCHER

Year Team (League)	W	L	Pct.	ERA	G	GS	CG	ShO	Sv.	IP	H	R	ER	BB	SO
1996— Omaha (Am. Assoc.)	0	0	...	9.00	1	0	0	0	0	1	2	1	1	1	0
1998— Kansas City (A.L.)	0	0	...	0.00	1	0	0	0	0	1	1	0	0	0	0

PERSONAL: Born December 3, 1964, in Baton Rouge, La. ... 6-1/192. ... Bats left, throws right. ... Full name: Darryl Quinn Hamilton.
HIGH SCHOOL: University (Baton Rouge, La.).
COLLEGE: Nicholls State (La.).
TRANSACTIONS/CAREER NOTES: Selected by Milwaukee Brewers organization in 11th round of free-agent draft (June 2, 1986). ... On disabled list (May 22-June 15, 1991; May 6-24, 1992; May 2-17, 1993; May 11-26 and June 10, 1994-remainder of season). ... Granted free agency (November 1, 1995). ... Signed by Texas Rangers (December 14, 1995). ... Granted free agency (November 18, 1996). ... Signed by San Francisco Giants (January 10, 1997). ... On San Francisco disabled list (April 18-May 8, 1997); included rehabilitation assignment to Phoenix (May 5-8, 1997). ... Traded by Giants with P James Stoops and a player to be named later to Colorado Rockies for OF Ellis Burks (July 31, 1998); Rockies acquired P Jason Brester to complete deal (August 17, 1998). ... Granted free agency (October 23, 1998). ... Re-signed by Rockies (November 9, 1998). ... Traded by Rockies with P Chuck McElroy to New York Mets for OF Brian McRae, P Rigo Beltran and OF Thomas Johnson (July 31, 1999).
RECORDS: Shares major league career record for highest fielding average by outfielder (1,000 or more games)—.995.
STATISTICAL NOTES: Led California League with nine intentional bases on balls received in 1987. ... Led N.L. outfielders with .997 fielding percentage in 1998. ... Led N.L. outfielders with 1.000 fielding percentage in 1999. ... Career major league grand slams: 3.

Year Team (League)	Pos.	G	AB	R	H	2B	3B	HR	RBI	Avg.	BB	SO	SB	PO	A	E	Avg.
1986— Helena (Pio.)	OF	65	248	*72	•97	12	•6	0	35	*.391	51	18	34	132	9	0	*1.000
1987— Stockton (Calif.)	OF	125	494	102	162	17	6	8	61	.328	74	59	42	221	8	1	*.996
1988— Denver (A.A.)	OF	72	277	55	90	11	4	0	32	.325	39	48	28	160	2	2	.988
— Milwaukee (A.L.)	OF-DH	44	103	14	19	4	0	1	11	.184	12	9	7	75	1	0	1.000
1989— Denver (A.A.)	OF	129	497	72	142	24	4	2	40	.286	42	58	20	263	11	0	*1.000

H

Year Team (League)	Pos.	G	AB	R	H	2B	3B	HR	RBI	Avg.	BB	SO	SB	PO	A	E	Avg.
1990—Milwaukee (A.L.)	OF-DH	89	156	27	46	5	0	1	18	.295	9	12	10	120	1	1	.992
1991—Milwaukee (A.L.)	OF	122	405	64	126	15	6	1	57	.311	33	38	16	234	3	1	.996
1992—Milwaukee (A.L.)	OF	128	470	67	140	19	7	5	62	.298	45	42	41	279	10	0	*1.000
1993—Milwaukee (A.L.)	OF-DH	135	520	74	161	21	1	9	48	.310	45	62	21	340	10	3	.992
1994—Milwaukee (A.L.)	OF-DH	36	141	23	37	10	1	1	13	.262	15	17	3	60	2	0	1.000
1995—Milwaukee (A.L.)	OF-DH	112	398	54	108	20	6	5	44	.271	47	35	11	262	4	3	.989
1996—Texas (A.L.)■............	OF	148	627	94	184	29	4	6	51	.293	54	66	15	387	2	0	•1.000
1997—San Fran. (N.L.)■.......	OF	125	460	78	124	23	3	5	43	.270	61	61	15	243	1	5	.980
— Phoenix (PCL)...........	OF	3	14	1	4	1	0	1	2	.286	0	2	0	6	0	0	1.000
1998—San Francisco (N.L.) ..	OF	97	367	65	108	19	2	1	26	.294	59	53	9	194	4	0	§1.000
— Colorado (N.L.)■	OF	51	194	30	65	9	1	5	25	.335	23	20	4	103	1	1	§.990
1999—Colorado (N.L.)	OF	91	337	63	102	11	3	4	24	.303	38	21	4	205	1	0	§1.000
— New York (N.L.)■	OF	55	168	19	57	8	1	5	21	.339	19	18	2	100	2	0	§1.000
American League totals (8 years)		814	2820	417	821	123	25	29	304	.291	260	281	124	1757	33	8	.996
National League totals (3 years)		419	1526	255	456	70	10	20	139	.299	200	173	34	845	9	6	.993
Major League totals (11 years)		1233	4346	672	1277	193	35	49	443	.294	460	454	158	2602	42	14	.995

DIVISION SERIES RECORD

Year Team (League)	Pos.	G	AB	R	H	2B	3B	HR	RBI	Avg.	BB	SO	SB	PO	A	E	Avg.
1996—Texas (A.L.)	OF	4	19	0	3	0	0	0	0	.158	0	2	0	16	1	0	1.000
1997—San Francisco (N.L.) ..	OF	2	5	1	0	0	0	0	0	.000	0	1	0	3	0	0	1.000
1999—New York (N.L.).........	OF-PH	4	8	0	1	0	0	0	2	.125	2	0	0	9	0	0	1.000
Division series totals (3 years)		10	32	1	4	0	0	0	2	.125	2	3	0	28	1	0	1.000

CHAMPIONSHIP SERIES RECORD

Year Team (League)	Pos.	G	AB	R	H	2B	3B	HR	RBI	Avg.	BB	SO	SB	PO	A	E	Avg.
1999—New York (N.L.).........	OF	5	17	0	6	1	0	0	2	.353	0	4	0	8	0	0	1.000

HAMILTON, JIMMY   P   ORIOLES

PERSONAL: Born August 1, 1975, in Harrisonburg, Va. ... 6-3/190. ... Throws left, bats left. ... Full name: James A. Hamilton.
HIGH SCHOOL: Turner Ashby (Dayton, Va.).
COLLEGE: Ferrum (Va.).
TRANSACTIONS/CAREER NOTES: Selected by Cleveland Indians organization in seventh round of free-agent draft (June 4, 1996). ... Traded by Indians to Baltimore Orioles (August 31, 1999), completing deal in which Orioles traded DH Harold Baines to Indians for P Juan Acarena and a player to named later (August 27, 1999).

Year League	W	L	Pct.	ERA	G	GS	CG	ShO	Sv.	IP	H	R	ER	BB	SO
1996—Burlington (Appl.).............	1	3	.250	4.00	10	10	0	0	0	45	45	22	20	16	50
1997—Columbus (SAL)...............	5	7	.417	4.46	22	22	0	0	0	123	123	68	61	66	137
1998—Kinston (Caro.).................	4	6	.400	2.75	44	0	0	0	4	75 1/3	61	25	23	21	83
1999—Akron (East.)	0	2	.000	3.73	25	0	0	0	2	31 1/3	19	14	13	24	27
— Buffalo (I.L.)......................	1	2	.333	5.18	26	0	0	0	0	24 1/3	24	22	14	27	25
— Rochester (I.L.)■..............	0	0	...	13.50	3	0	0	0	0	2	1	3	3	4	2

HAMILTON, JOEY   P   BLUE JAYS

PERSONAL: Born September 9, 1970, in Statesboro, Ga. ... 6-4/230. ... Throws right, bats right. ... Full name: Johns Joseph Hamilton.
HIGH SCHOOL: Statesboro (Ga.).
COLLEGE: Georgia Southern.
TRANSACTIONS/CAREER NOTES: Selected by Baltimore Orioles organization in 28th round of free-agent draft (June 1, 1988); did not sign. ... Selected by San Diego Padres organization in first round (eighth pick overall) of free-agent draft (June 3, 1991). ... On Rancho Cucamonga disabled list (April 5-20, 1993). ... On disabled list (April 24-May 17, 1997). ... Traded by Padres to Toronto Blue Jays for P Woody Williams, P Carlos Almanzar and OF Peter Tucci (December 13, 1998). ... On Toronto disabled list (April 14-May 24, 1999); included rehabilitation assignment to Syracuse (May 10-24).
HONORS: Named righthanded pitcher on THE SPORTING NEWS college All-America second team (1990).
MISCELLANEOUS: Made an out in only appearance as pinch hitter (1998).

Year League	W	L	Pct.	ERA	G	GS	CG	ShO	Sv.	IP	H	R	ER	BB	SO
1992—Charleston, S.C. (SAL)	2	2	.500	3.38	7	7	0	0	0	34 2/3	37	24	13	4	35
— High Desert (Calif.).............	4	3	.571	2.74	9	8	0	0	0	49 1/3	46	20	15	18	43
— Wichita (Texas)	3	0	1.000	2.86	6	6	0	0	0	34 2/3	33	12	11	11	26
1993—Rancho Cuca. (Calif.)	1	0	1.000	4.09	2	2	0	0	0	11	11	5	5	2	6
— Wichita (Texas)	4	9	.308	3.97	15	15	0	0	0	90 2/3	101	55	40	36	20
— Las Vegas (PCL)	3	2	.600	4.40	8	8	0	0	0	47	49	25	23	22	33
1994—Las Vegas (PCL)	3	5	.375	2.73	9	9	1	1	0	59 1/3	69	25	18	22	32
— San Diego (N.L.)	9	6	.600	2.98	16	16	1	1	0	108 2/3	98	40	36	29	61
1995—San Diego (N.L.)	6	9	.400	3.08	31	30	2	2	0	204 1/3	189	89	70	56	123
1996—San Diego (N.L.)	15	9	.625	4.17	34	33	3	1	0	211 2/3	206	100	98	83	184
1997—San Diego (N.L.)	12	7	.632	4.25	31	29	1	0	0	192 2/3	199	100	91	69	124
1998—San Diego (N.L.)	13	13	.500	4.27	34	34	0	0	0	217 1/3	220	113	103	*106	147
1999—Toronto (A.L.)■................	7	8	.467	6.52	22	18	0	0	0	98	118	73	71	39	56
— Syracuse (I.L.)...................	0	1	.000	5.11	3	3	0	0	0	12 1/3	15	8	7	5	9
A.L. totals (1 year)	7	8	.467	6.52	22	18	0	0	0	98	118	73	71	39	56
N.L. totals (5 years)	55	44	.556	3.83	146	142	7	4	0	934 2/3	912	442	398	343	639
Major League totals (6 years).......	62	52	.544	4.09	168	160	7	4	0	1032 2/3	1030	515	469	382	695

H

DIVISION SERIES RECORD

Year League	W	L	Pct.	ERA	G	GS	CG	ShO	Sv.	IP	H	R	ER	BB	SO
1996— San Diego (N.L.)	0	1	.000	4.50	1	1	0	0	0	6	5	3	3	0	6
1998— San Diego (N.L.)	0	0	...	0.00	2	0	0	0	0	3 1/3	1	0	0	2	3
Division series totals (2 years)	0	1	.000	2.89	3	1	0	0	0	9 1/3	6	3	3	2	9

CHAMPIONSHIP SERIES RECORD

Year League	W	L	Pct.	ERA	G	GS	CG	ShO	Sv.	IP	H	R	ER	BB	SO
1998— San Diego (N.L.)	0	1	.000	4.91	2	1	0	0	0	7 1/3	7	4	4	3	6

WORLD SERIES RECORD

Year League	W	L	Pct.	ERA	G	GS	CG	ShO	Sv.	IP	H	R	ER	BB	SO
1998— San Diego (N.L.)	0	0	...	0.00	1	0	0	0	0	1	0	0	0	1	1

HAMMONDS, JEFFREY   OF   ROCKIES

PERSONAL: Born March 5, 1971, in Scotch Plains, N.J. ... 6-0/195. ... Bats right, throws right. ... Full name: Jeffrey Bryan Hammonds. ... Brother of Reggie Hammonds, outfielder with Pittsburgh Pirates organization (1984-86).
HIGH SCHOOL: Scotch Plains (N.J.)-Fanwood.
COLLEGE: Stanford.
TRANSACTIONS/CAREER NOTES: Selected by Toronto Blue Jays organization in ninth round of free-agent draft (June 5, 1989); did not sign. ... Selected by Baltimore Orioles organization in first round (fourth pick overall) of free-agent draft (June 1, 1992). ... On Hagerstown temporarily inactive list (August 6-September 14, 1992). ... On Rochester disabled list (May 17-28, 1993). ... On Baltimore disabled list (August 8-September 1 and September 28, 1993-remainder of season); included rehabilitation assignment to Bowie (August 28-September 1). ... On Baltimore disabled list (May 4-June 16, 1994; July 18-September 3, 1995; and August 17-September 22, 1996). ... On Baltimore disabled list (June 3-July 11, 1998); included rehabilitation assignment to Bowie (July 9-11). ... Traded by Orioles to Cincinnati Reds for 3B/OF Willie Greene (August 10, 1998). ... Traded by Reds with P Stan Belinda to Colorado Rockies for OF Dante Bichette and cash (October 30, 1999).
HONORS: Named outfielder on THE SPORTING NEWS college All-America team (1990 and 1992).
STATISTICAL NOTES: Hit three home runs in one game (May 19, 1999). ... Career major league grand slams: 1.
MISCELLANEOUS: Member of 1992 U.S. Olympic baseball team.

							BATTING							FIELDING		
Year Team (League)	Pos.	G	AB	R	H	2B	3B	HR	RBI	Avg.	BB	SO	SB	PO	A	E	Avg.
1992— Hagerstown (East.)							Did not play.									
1993— Bowie (East.)	OF	24	92	13	26	3	0	3	10	.283	9	18	4	48	2	0	1.000
—Rochester (I.L.)	OF	36	151	25	47	9	1	5	23	.311	5	27	6	72	1	0	1.000
—Baltimore (A.L.)	OF-DH	33	105	10	32	8	0	3	19	.305	2	16	4	47	2	2	.961
1994— Baltimore (A.L.)	OF	68	250	45	74	18	2	8	31	.296	17	39	5	147	5	6	.962
1995— Baltimore (A.L.)	OF-DH	57	178	18	43	9	1	4	23	.242	9	30	4	88	1	1	.989
—Bowie (East.)	OF-DH	9	31	7	12	3	1	1	11	.387	10	7	3	12	0	1	.923
1996— Baltimore (A.L.)	OF-DH	71	248	38	56	10	1	9	27	.226	23	53	3	145	3	3	.980
—Rochester (I.L.)	OF-DH	34	125	24	34	4	2	3	19	.272	19	19	3	75	1	1	.987
1997— Baltimore (A.L.)	OF-DH	118	397	71	105	19	3	21	55	.264	32	73	15	240	4	5	.980
1998— Baltimore (A.L.)	OF-DH	63	171	36	46	12	1	6	28	.269	26	38	7	94	2	2	.980
—Bowie (East.)	OF	3	6	4	2	0	0	0	0	.333	2	2	3	3	0	0	1.000
—Cincinnati (N.L.)■.......	OF	26	86	14	26	4	1	0	11	.302	13	18	1	64	3	1	.985
1999— Cincinnati (N.L.)	OF	123	262	43	73	13	0	17	41	.279	27	64	3	157	5	0	1.000
American League totals (6 years)		410	1349	218	356	76	8	51	183	.264	109	249	38	761	17	19	.976
National League totals (2 years)		149	348	57	99	17	1	17	52	.284	40	82	4	221	8	1	.996
Major League totals (7 years)		559	1697	275	455	93	9	68	235	.268	149	331	42	982	25	20	.981

DIVISION SERIES RECORD

						BATTING							FIELDING		
Year Team (League)	Pos.	G	AB	R	H	2B	3B	HR	RBI	Avg.	BB	SO	SB	PO	A	E	Avg.
1997— Baltimore (A.L.)	OF-PR	4	10	3	1	1	0	0	2	.100	2	2	1	8	1	0	1.000

CHAMPIONSHIP SERIES RECORD

						BATTING							FIELDING		
Year Team (League)	Pos.	G	AB	R	H	2B	3B	HR	RBI	Avg.	BB	SO	SB	PO	A	E	Avg.
1997— Baltimore (A.L.)	PH-OF-PR	5	3	0	0	0	0	0	0	.000	1	2	1	2	0	0	1.000

HAMPTON, MIKE   P   METS

PERSONAL: Born September 9, 1972, in Brooksville, Fla. ... 5-10/180. ... Throws left, bats right. ... Full name: Michael William Hampton.
HIGH SCHOOL: Crystal River (Fla.).
TRANSACTIONS/CAREER NOTES: Selected by Seattle Mariners organization in sixth round of free-agent draft (June 4, 1990). ... Traded by Mariners with OF Mike Felder to Houston Astros for OF Eric Anthony (December 10, 1993). ... On disabled list (May 15-June 13, 1995; June 16-July 4, 1998). ... Traded by Astros with OF Derek Bell to New York Mets for OF Roger Cedeno, P Octavio Dotel and P Kyle Kessel (December 23, 1999).
HONORS: Named N.L. Pitcher of the Year by THE SPORTING NEWS (1999). ... Named lefthanded pitcher on THE SPORTING NEWS N.L. All-Star team (1999). ... Named pitcher on THE SPORTING NEWS N.L. Silver Slugger team (1999).
STATISTICAL NOTES: Led Arizona League with 10 wild pitches in 1990. ... Pitched 6-0 no-hit victory for San Bernardino against Visalia (May 31, 1991).
MISCELLANEOUS: Appeared in two games as pinch runner (1996).

Year League	W	L	Pct.	ERA	G	GS	CG	ShO	Sv.	IP	H	R	ER	BB	SO
1990— Arizona Mariners (Ariz.)	•7	2	.778	2.66	14	•13	0	0	0	64 1/3	52	32	19	40	59
1991— San Bernardino (Calif.)	1	7	.125	5.25	18	15	1	1	0	73 2/3	71	58	43	47	57
—Bellingham (N.W.)	5	2	.714	1.58	9	9	0	0	0	57	32	15	10	26	65
1992— San Bernardino (Calif.)	13	8	.619	3.12	25	25	6	•2	0	170	163	75	59	66	132
—Jacksonville (Sou.)	0	1	.000	4.35	2	2	0	0	0	10 1/3	13	5	5	1	6

H

Year League	W	L	Pct.	ERA	G	GS	CG	ShO	Sv.	IP	H	R	ER	BB	SO
1993—Seattle (A.L.)	1	3	.250	9.53	13	3	0	0	1	17	28	20	18	17	8
—Jacksonville (Sou.)	6	4	.600	3.71	15	14	1	0	0	87 1/3	71	43	36	33	84
1994—Houston (N.L.)■	2	1	.667	3.70	44	0	0	0	0	41 1/3	46	19	17	16	24
1995—Houston (N.L.)	9	8	.529	3.35	24	24	0	0	0	150 2/3	141	73	56	49	115
1996—Houston (N.L.)	10	10	.500	3.59	27	27	2	1	0	160 1/3	179	79	64	49	101
1997—Houston (N.L.)	15	10	.600	3.83	34	34	7	2	0	223	217	105	95	77	139
1998—Houston (N.L.)	11	7	.611	3.36	32	32	1	1	0	211 2/3	227	92	79	81	137
1999—Houston (N.L.)	*22	4	*.846	2.90	34	34	3	2	0	239	206	86	77	101	177
A.L. totals (1 year)	1	3	.250	9.53	13	3	0	0	1	17	28	20	18	17	8
N.L. totals (6 years)	69	40	.633	3.40	195	151	13	6	0	1026	1012	454	388	373	693
Major League totals (7 years)	70	43	.619	3.50	208	154	13	6	1	1043	1040	474	406	390	701

DIVISION SERIES RECORD

Year League	W	L	Pct.	ERA	G	GS	CG	ShO	Sv.	IP	H	R	ER	BB	SO
1997—Houston (N.L.)	0	1	.000	11.57	1	1	0	0	0	4 2/3	2	6	6	8	2
1998—Houston (N.L.)	0	0	...	1.50	1	1	0	0	0	6	2	1	1	1	2
1999—Houston (N.L.)	0	0	...	3.86	1	1	0	0	0	7	6	3	3	1	9
Division series totals (3 years)	0	1	.000	5.09	3	3	0	0	0	17 2/3	10	10	10	10	13

ALL-STAR GAME RECORD

Year League	W	L	Pct.	ERA	GS	CG	ShO	Sv.	IP	H	R	ER	BB	SO
1999—National	0	0	...	0.00	0	0	0	0	2/3	0	0	0	0	0

HANEY, CHRIS   P   INDIANS

PERSONAL: Born November 16, 1968, in Baltimore. ... 6-3/210. ... Throws left, bats left. ... Full name: Christopher Deane Haney. ... Son of Larry Haney, catcher with five major league teams (1966-70 and 1972-78), and coach, Milwaukee Brewers (1978-91).
HIGH SCHOOL: Orange County (Va.).
COLLEGE: UNC Charlotte.
TRANSACTIONS/CAREER NOTES: Selected by Milwaukee Brewers organization in 25th round of free-agent draft (June 2, 1987); did not sign. ... Selected by Montreal Expos organization in second round of free-agent draft (June 4, 1990). ... On Indianapolis disabled list (June 17-25, 1992). ... Traded by Expos with P Bill Sampen to Kansas City Royals for 3B Sean Berry and P Archie Corbin (August 29, 1992). ... On disabled list (July 13, 1995-remainder of season). ... On Kansas City disabled list (April 15-June 17 and June 27-September 3, 1997); included rehabilitation assignments to Omaha (May 31-June 13) and Wichita (August 25-29). ... On Kansas City disabled list (June 8-24, 1998); included rehabilitation assignment to Gulf Coast Royals (June 22). ... Contract sold by Royals to Chicago Cubs (September 12, 1998). ... Granted free agency (October 27, 1998). ... Signed by Los Angeles Dodgers organization (January 6, 1999). ... Released by Dodgers (April 1, 1999). ... Signed by Cleveland Indians organzation (April 6, 1999). ... On Buffalo disabled list (May 3-June 11, 1999). ... Granted free agency (October 28, 1999). ... Re-signed by Indians organization (January 8, 2000).
MISCELLANEOUS: Appeared in one game as pinch runner with Montreal (1992).

Year League	W	L	Pct.	ERA	G	GS	CG	ShO	Sv.	IP	H	R	ER	BB	SO
1990—Jamestown (NY-P)	3	0	1.000	0.96	6	5	0	0	1	28	17	3	3	10	26
—Rockford (Midw.)	2	4	.333	2.21	8	8	3	0	0	53	40	15	13	6	45
—Jacksonville (Sou.)	1	0	1.000	0.00	1	1	0	0	0	6	6	0	0	3	6
1991—Harrisburg (East.)	5	3	.625	2.16	12	12	3	0	0	83 1/3	65	21	20	31	68
—Montreal (N.L.)	3	7	.300	4.04	16	16	0	0	0	84 2/3	94	49	38	43	51
—Indianapolis (A.A.)	1	1	.500	4.35	2	2	0	0	0	10 1/3	14	10	5	6	8
1992—Montreal (N.L.)	2	3	.400	5.45	9	6	1	1	0	38	40	25	23	10	27
—Indianapolis (A.A.)	5	2	.714	5.14	15	15	0	0	0	84	88	50	48	42	61
—Kansas City (A.L.)■	2	3	.400	3.86	7	7	1	1	0	42	35	18	18	16	27
1993—Omaha (A.A.)	6	1	.857	2.27	8	7	2	0	0	47 2/3	43	13	12	14	32
—Kansas City (A.L.)	9	9	.500	6.02	23	23	1	1	0	124	141	87	83	53	65
1994—Kansas City (A.L.)	2	2	.500	7.31	6	6	0	0	0	28 1/3	36	25	23	11	18
—Omaha (A.A.)	8	7	.533	5.25	18	18	1	0	0	104 2/3	125	77	61	37	78
1995—Kansas City (A.L.)	3	4	.429	3.65	16	13	1	0	0	81 1/3	78	35	33	33	31
1996—Kansas City (A.L.)	10	14	.417	4.70	35	35	4	1	0	228	*267	136	119	51	115
1997—Kansas City (A.L.)	1	2	.333	4.38	8	3	0	0	0	24 2/3	29	16	12	5	16
—Omaha (A.A.)	1	0	1.000	3.79	4	3	0	0	0	19	16	12	8	6	7
—Wichita (Texas)	0	1	.000	2.70	2	2	0	0	0	6 2/3	5	3	2	0	2
1998—Kansas City (A.L.)	6	6	.500	7.03	33	12	0	0	0	97 1/3	125	78	76	36	51
—Gulf Coast Royals (GCL)	0	1	.000	0.00	1	1	0	0	0	2 1/3	2	2	0	0	1
—Chicago (N.L.)■	0	0	...	7.20	5	0	0	0	0	5	3	4	4	1	4
1999—Buffalo (I.L.)■	2	5	.286	3.22	13	10	0	0	0	58 2/3	50	25	21	22	37
—Cleveland (A.L.)	0	2	.000	4.69	13	4	0	0	0	40 1/3	43	22	21	16	22
A.L. totals (8 years)	33	42	.440	5.20	141	103	7	3	0	666	754	417	385	221	345
N.L. totals (3 years)	5	10	.333	4.58	30	22	1	1	0	127 2/3	137	78	65	54	82
Major League totals (9 years)	38	52	.422	5.10	171	125	8	4	0	793 2/3	891	495	450	275	427

HANSELL, GREG   P

PERSONAL: Born March 12, 1971, in Bellflower, Calif. ... 6-5/224. ... Throws right, bats right. ... Full name: Gregory Michael Hansell.
HIGH SCHOOL: John F. Kennedy (La Palma, Calif.).
TRANSACTIONS/CAREER NOTES: Selected by Boston Red Sox organization in 10th round of free-agent draft (June 5, 1989). ... Traded by Red Sox organization with OF Ed Perozo and a player to be named later to New York Mets organization for 1B Mike Marshall (July 27, 1990); Mets acquired C Paul Williams to complete deal (November 19, 1990). ... Traded by Mets organization with P Bob Ojeda to Los Angeles Dodgers organization for OF Hubie Brooks (December 15, 1990). ... On disabled list (June 19-July 8, 1993). ... Traded by Dodgers with 3B/1B Ron Coomer, P Jose Parra and a player to be named later to Minnesota Twins for P Kevin Tapani and P Mark Guthrie (July 31, 1995); Twins acquired OF Chris Latham to complete deal (October 30, 1995). ... Claimed on waivers by Red Sox (October 11, 1996). ... Released by Red Sox (March 26, 1997). ... Signed by Milwaukee Brewers organization (March 31, 1997). ... Granted free agency (October 15, 1997). ... Signed by Arizona Diamondbacks organization (December 18, 1997). ... Released by Diamondbacks (March 25, 1998). ... Signed by Oakland Athletics

H

organization (March 31, 1998). ... Traded by A's to Kansas City Royals (May 10, 1998), completing trade in which Royals traded C Mike Macfarlane to A's for OF Shane Mack and a player to be named later (April 8, 1998). ... Granted free agency (October 15, 1998). ... Signed by San Francisco Giants (December 4, 1998). ... Released by Giants (April 2, 1999). ... Signed by Pittsburgh Pirates organization (April 7, 1999). ... Contract sold by Pirates to Hanshin Tigers of Japan Central League (December 7, 1999).

STATISTICAL NOTES: Tied for Florida State League lead with 14 losses and 27 games started in 1990.

Year	League	W	L	Pct.	ERA	G	GS	CG	ShO	Sv.	IP	H	R	ER	BB	SO
1989—	GC Red Sox (GCL)	3	2	.600	2.53	10	8	0	0	2	57	51	23	16	23	44
1990—	Winter Haven (FSL)............	7	10	.412	3.59	21	21	2	1	0	115 1/3	95	63	46	64	79
	— St. Lucie (FSL)■...............	2	§4	.333	2.84	6	§6	0	0	0	38	34	22	12	15	16
1991—	Bakersfield (Calif.)■............	14	5	.737	2.87	25	25	0	0	0	150 2/3	142	56	48	42	132
1992—	San Antonio (Texas)............	6	4	.600	2.83	14	14	0	0	0	92 1/3	80	40	29	33	64
	— Albuquerque (PCL)............	1	5	.167	5.24	13	13	0	0	0	68 2/3	84	46	40	35	38
1993—	Albuquerque (PCL)............	5	10	.333	6.93	26	20	0	0	0	101 1/3	131	86	78	60	60
1994—	Albuquerque (PCL)............	10	2	*.833	2.99	47	6	0	0	8	123 1/3	109	44	41	31	101
1995—	Los Angeles (N.L.)............	0	1	.000	7.45	20	0	0	0	0	19 1/3	29	17	16	6	13
	— Albuquerque (PCL)............	1	1	.500	8.44	8	1	0	0	1	16	25	15	15	6	15
	— Salt Lake (PCL)■............	3	1	.750	5.01	7	5	0	0	0	32 1/3	39	20	18	4	17
1996—	Minnesota (A.L.)	3	0	1.000	5.69	50	0	0	0	3	74 1/3	83	48	47	31	46
1997—	Tucson (PCL)■.................	2	3	.400	4.64	40	9	0	0	2	87 1/3	99	52	45	27	76
	— Milwaukee (A.L.)............	0	0	...	9.64	3	0	0	0	0	4 2/3	5	5	5	1	5
1998—	Edmonton (PCL)■............	0	0	...	1.23	13	0	0	0	6	14 2/3	13	2	2	3	16
	— Omaha (PCL)■............	8	3	.727	3.00	46	0	0	0	7	69	63	25	23	15	59
1999—	Nashville (PCL)■............	3	3	.500	2.00	22	0	0	0	2	27	18	8	6	9	36
	— Pittsburgh (N.L.)	1	3	.250	3.89	33	0	0	0	0	39 1/3	42	20	17	11	34
A.L. totals (2 years)		3	0	1.000	5.92	53	0	0	0	3	79	88	53	52	32	51
N.L. totals (2 years)		1	4	.200	5.06	53	0	0	0	0	58 2/3	71	37	33	17	47
Major League totals (4 years)		4	4	.500	5.56	106	0	0	0	3	137 2/3	159	90	85	49	98

HANSEN, DAVE — 3B — DODGERS

PERSONAL: Born November 24, 1968, in Long Beach, Calif. ... 6-0/195. ... Bats left, throws right. ... Full name: David Andrew Hansen.
HIGH SCHOOL: Rowland (Long Beach, Calif.).
TRANSACTIONS/CAREER NOTES: Selected by Los Angeles Dodgers organization in second round of free-agent draft (June 2, 1986). ... On disabled list (May 9-28, 1994). ... Granted free agency (November 27, 1996). ... Signed by Chicago Cubs organization (January 22, 1997). ... Granted free agency (October 27, 1997). ... Signed by Hanshin Tigers of Japan Central League (November 7, 1997). ... Signed by Dodgers (January 11, 1999).
STATISTICAL NOTES: Led California League third basemen with 45 errors in 1987. ... Led Florida State League with 210 total bases and tied for lead with nine sacrifice flies in 1988. ... Led Florida State League third basemen with 383 total chances and 24 double plays in 1988. ... Led Pacific Coast League third basemen with .926 fielding percentage, 254 assists, 349 total chances and 25 double plays in 1990. ... Career major league grand slams: 1.

							BATTING								FIELDING		
Year	Team (League)	Pos.	G	AB	R	H	2B	3B	HR	RBI	Avg.	BB	SO	SB	PO	A	E	Avg.
1986—	Great Falls (Pio.)	OF-3B-C-2B	61	204	39	61	7	3	1	36	.299	27	28	9	54	10	7	.901
1987—	Bakersfield (Calif.)......	3B-OF	132	432	68	113	22	1	3	38	.262	65	61	4	79	198	†45	.860
1988—	Vero Beach (FSL)	3B	135	512	68	*149	•28	6	7	*81	.291	56	46	2	*102	*263	18	*.953
1989—	San Antonio (Texas) ...	3B	121	464	72	138	21	4	6	52	.297	50	44	3	*92	208	16	*.949
	— Albuquerque (PCL).....	3B	6	30	6	8	1	0	2	10	.267	2	3	0	3	8	3	.786
1990—	Albuquerque (PCL).....	3B-OF-SS	135	487	90	154	20	3	11	92	.316	*90	54	9	71	†255	26	†.926
	— Los Angeles (N.L.).....	3B	5	7	0	1	0	0	0	1	.143	0	0	0	0	1	1	.500
1991—	Albuquerque (PCL).....	3B-SS	68	254	42	77	11	1	5	40	.303	49	33	4	43	125	6	.966
	— Los Angeles (N.L.).....	3B-SS	53	56	3	15	4	0	1	5	.268	2	12	1	5	19	0	1.000
1992—	Los Angeles (N.L.)	3B	132	341	30	73	11	0	6	22	.214	34	49	0	61	183	8	*.968
1993—	Los Angeles (N.L.)	3B	84	105	13	38	3	0	4	30	.362	21	13	0	11	27	3	.927
1994—	Los Angeles (N.L.)	3B	40	44	3	15	3	0	0	5	.341	5	5	0	6	1	.857
1995—	Los Angeles (N.L.)	3B	100	181	19	52	10	0	1	14	.287	28	28	0	27	70	7	.933
1996—	Los Angeles (N.L.)	3B-1B	80	104	7	23	1	0	0	6	.221	11	22	0	60	23	1	.988
1997—	Chicago (N.L.)■........	3B-1B-2B	90	151	19	47	8	2	3	21	.311	31	32	1	45	47	7	.929
1998—	Hanshin (Jp. Cen.)■..	3B	121	400	42	101	13	1	11	55	.253	42	89	0				
1999—	Los Angeles (N.L.)■..	1-3-DH-O	100	107	14	27	8	1	2	17	.252	26	20	0	58	17	3	.962
Major League totals (9 years)			684	1096	108	291	48	3	17	121	.266	158	181	2	267	393	31	.955

DIVISION SERIES RECORD

							BATTING								FIELDING		
Year	Team (League)	Pos.	G	AB	R	H	2B	3B	HR	RBI	Avg.	BB	SO	SB	PO	A	E	Avg.
1995—	Los Angeles (N.L.)	PH	3	3	0	2	0	0	0	0	.667	0	0	0	...	...	...	
1996—	Los Angeles (N.L.)	PH-3B	2	2	0	0	0	0	0	0	.000	0	0	0	1	0	0	1.000
Division series totals (2 years)			5	5	0	2	0	0	0	0	.400	0	0	0	1	0	0	1.000

HANSEN, JED — 2B/SS — PADRES

PERSONAL: Born August 19, 1972, in Tacoma, Wash. ... 6-1/195. ... Bats right, throws right. ... Full name: Jed Ramon Hansen.
HIGH SCHOOL: Capital (Olympia, Wash.).
COLLEGE: Stanford.
TRANSACTIONS/CAREER NOTES: Selected by Cleveland Indians organization in 21st round of free-agent draft (June 3, 1991); did not sign. ... Selected by Kansas City Royals organization in second round of free-agent draft (June 2, 1994). ... Claimed on waivers by San Diego Padres (October 6, 1999). ... Released by Padres (December 13, 1999). ... Re-signed by Padres organization (January 17, 2000).
STATISTICAL NOTES: Led Northwest League second basemen with 337 total chances in 1994. ... Tied for American Association lead in errors by second baseman with 17 in 1997.

H

Year Team (League)	Pos.	G	AB	R	H	2B	3B	HR	RBI	Avg.	BB	SO	SB	PO	A	E	Avg.
1994— Eugene (N.W.)	2B	66	235	26	57	8	2	3	17	.243	24	56	6	*141	*189	7	*.979
1995— Springfield (Midw.)	2B	122	414	86	107	27	7	9	50	.258	78	73	44	220	*345	22	.963
1996— Wichita (Texas)	2B-OF	99	405	60	116	27	4	12	50	.286	29	72	14	196	276	10	.979
— Omaha (A.A.)..............	2B	29	99	14	23	4	0	3	9	.232	12	22	2	66	75	7	.953
1997— Omaha (A.A.)............	2-S-3-DH	114	380	43	102	20	2	11	44	.268	32	78	8	205	323	‡23	.958
— Kansas City (A.L.)	2B	34	94	11	29	6	1	1	14	.309	13	29	3	56	77	1	.993
1998— Kansas City (A.L.)	2B	4	3	0	0	0	0	0	0	.000	0	3	0	1	0	0	1.000
— Omaha (PCL).............	2B-SS-OF	127	417	63	116	19	7	16	56	.278	44	125	17	211	353	28	.953
1999— Omaha (PCL)	2B-SS-OF	54	175	35	48	8	5	7	22	.274	32	72	8	116	135	8	.969
— Kansas City (A.L.) 2-S-3-D-O-1		49	79	16	16	1	0	3	5	.203	10	32	0	57	67	1	.992
Major League totals (3 years)		87	176	27	45	7	1	4	19	.256	23	64	3	114	144	2	.992

HARIKKALA, TIM   P

PERSONAL: Born July 15, 1971, in West Palm Beach, Fla. ... 6-2/185. ... Throws right, bats right. ... Full name: Timothy Allan Harikkala. ... Name pronounced ha-RICK-a-la.
HIGH SCHOOL: Lake Worth Christian (Lantana, Fla.).
COLLEGE: Florida Atlantic.
TRANSACTIONS/CAREER NOTES: Selected by Seattle Mariners organization in 34th round of free-agent draft (June 1, 1992). ... Granted free agency (October 15, 1998). ... Signed by Boston Red Sox organization (December 14, 1998). ... On Pawtucket disabled list (July 13, 1999-remainder of season). ... Granted free agency (October 4, 1999).

Year League	W	L	Pct.	ERA	G	GS	CG	ShO	Sv.	IP	H	R	ER	BB	SO
1992— Bellingham (N.W.)	2	0	1.000	2.70	15	2	0	0	1	33 1/3	37	15	10	16	18
1993— Bellingham (N.W.)	1	0	1.000	1.13	4	0	0	0	0	8	3	1	1	2	12
— Appleton (Midw.)..............	3	3	.500	6.52	15	4	0	0	0	38 2/3	50	30	28	12	33
1994— Appleton (Midw.)................	8	3	.727	1.92	13	13	3	0	0	93 2/3	69	31	20	24	63
— Riverside (Calif.).............	4	0	1.000	0.62	4	4	0	0	0	29	16	6	2	10	30
— Jacksonville (Sou.)............	4	1	.800	3.98	9	9	0	0	0	54 1/3	70	30	24	19	22
1995— Seattle (A.L.)	0	0	...	16.20	1	0	0	0	0	3 1/3	7	6	6	1	1
— Tacoma (PCL)	5	12	.294	4.24	25	24	4	1	0	146 1/3	151	78	69	55	73
1996— Tacoma (PCL)	8	12	.400	4.83	27	27	1	1	0	158 1/3	204	98	85	48	115
— Seattle (A.L.)	0	1	.000	12.46	1	1	0	0	0	4 1/3	6	6	6	2	1
1997— Tacoma (PCL)	6	8	.429	6.43	21	21	0	0	0	113 1/3	160	93	81	50	86
— Memphis (Sou.)...............	3	1	.750	3.74	5	5	1	0	0	33 2/3	39	18	14	4	26
1998— Orlando (Sou.)	5	7	.417	4.53	15	15	3	•2	0	103 1/3	112	56	52	14	55
— Tacoma (PCL)	2	3	.400	4.89	18	4	1	1	1	57	74	32	31	13	44
1999— Pawtucket (I.L.)■...............	1	2	.333	5.40	14	1	0	0	0	30	44	19	18	7	19
— Boston (A.L.)..................	1	1	.500	6.23	7	0	0	0	0	13	15	9	9	6	7
Major League totals (3 years)	1	2	.333	9.15	9	1	0	0	0	20 2/3	26	21	21	9	9

HARNISCH, PETE   P   REDS

PERSONAL: Born September 23, 1966, in Commack, N.Y. ... 6-0/228. ... Throws right, bats right. ... Full name: Peter Thomas Harnisch.
HIGH SCHOOL: Commack (N.Y.).
COLLEGE: Fordham.
TRANSACTIONS/CAREER NOTES: Selected by Baltimore Orioles organization in supplemental round ("sandwich pick" between first and second round, 27th pick overall) of free-agent draft (June 2, 1987); pick received as compensation for Cleveland Indians signing Type A free-agent C Rick Dempsey. ... Traded by Orioles with P Curt Schilling and OF Steve Finley to Houston Astros for 1B Glenn Davis (January 10, 1991). ... On suspended list (July 7-9, 1992). ... On Houston disabled list (May 23-June 30, 1994); included rehabilitation assignment to Tucson (June 25-26). ... Traded by Astros to New York Mets for two players to be named later (November 28, 1994); Astros acquired P Andy Beckerman (December 6, 1994) and P Juan Castillo (April 12, 1995) to complete deal. ... Granted free agency (December 23, 1994). ... Re-signed by Mets (April 7, 1995). ... On disabled list (August 2, 1995-remainder of season). ... On New York disabled list (March 26-April 14, 1996); included rehabilitation assignment to St. Lucie (March 30-April 14). ... On New York suspended list (May 22-31, 1996). ... On New York disabled list (April 2-August 5, 1997); included rehabilitation assignments to Gulf Coast Mets (July 7-10), St. Lucie (July 11-19) and Norfolk (July 20-August 5). ... Traded by Mets to Milwaukee Brewers for OF Donny Moore (August 31, 1997). ... Granted free agency (October 27, 1997). ... Signed by Cincinnati Reds (January 21, 1998).
RECORDS: Shares major league record for striking out side on nine pitches (September 6, 1991, seventh inning). ... Shares N.L. record for most consecutive home runs allowed in one inning—4 (July 23, 1996, first inning).
STATISTICAL NOTES: Pitched 4-0 one-hit, complete-game victory against Chicago (July 10, 1993). ... Pitched 3-0 one-hit, complete-game victory against San Diego (September 17, 1993).
MISCELLANEOUS: Appeared in one game as pinch runner with Houston (1994). ... Appeared in one game as pinch runner with New York (1996).

Year League	W	L	Pct.	ERA	G	GS	CG	ShO	Sv.	IP	H	R	ER	BB	SO
1987— Bluefield (Appl.)	3	1	.750	2.56	9	9	0	0	0	52 2/3	38	19	15	26	64
— Hagerstown (Caro.)...........	1	2	.333	2.25	4	4	0	0	0	20	17	7	5	14	18
1988— Charlotte (Sou.).................	7	6	.538	2.58	20	20	4	2	0	132 1/3	113	55	38	52	141
— Rochester (I.L.).................	4	1	.800	2.16	7	7	3	2	0	58 1/3	44	16	14	14	43
— Baltimore (A.L.)...............	0	2	.000	5.54	2	2	0	0	0	13	13	8	8	9	10
1989— Baltimore (A.L.)...............	5	9	.357	4.62	18	17	2	0	0	103 1/3	97	55	53	64	70
— Rochester (I.L.).................	5	5	.500	2.58	12	12	3	1	0	87 1/3	60	27	25	35	59
1990— Baltimore (A.L.)...............	11	11	.500	4.34	31	31	3	0	0	188 2/3	189	96	91	86	122
1991— Houston (N.L.)■...............	12	9	.571	2.70	33	33	4	2	0	216 2/3	169	71	65	83	172
1992— Houston (N.L.).................	9	10	.474	3.70	34	34	0	0	0	206 2/3	182	92	85	64	164
1993— Houston (N.L.).................	16	9	.640	2.98	33	33	5	*4	0	217 2/3	171	84	72	79	185
1994— Houston (N.L.).................	8	5	.615	5.40	17	17	1	0	0	95	100	59	57	39	62
— Tucson (PCL)	0	0	...	0.00	1	1	0	0	0	5	2	0	0	1	1
1995— New York (N.L.)■	2	8	.200	3.68	18	18	0	0	0	110	111	55	45	24	82

H

Year League	W	L	Pct.	ERA	G	GS	CG	ShO	Sv.	IP	H	R	ER	BB	SO
1996— St. Lucie (FSL)	1	0	1.000	2.77	2	2	0	0	0	13	11	4	4	0	12
— New York (N.L.)	8	12	.400	4.21	31	31	2	1	0	194 2/3	195	103	91	61	114
1997— Gulf Coast Mets (GCL)	0	0	—	12.00	1	1	0	0	0	3	7	4	4	0	5
— St. Lucie (FSL)	1	0	1.000	3.00	2	2	0	0	0	12	5	5	4	4	7
— Norfolk (I.L.)	1	1	.500	5.40	3	3	0	0	0	16 2/3	16	12	10	10	16
— New York (N.L.)	0	1	.000	8.06	6	5	0	0	0	25 2/3	35	24	23	11	12
— Milwaukee (A.L.)■	1	1	.500	5.14	4	3	0	0	0	14	13	9	8	12	10
1998— Cincinnati (N.L.)■	14	7	.667	3.14	32	32	2	1	0	209	176	79	73	64	157
1999— Cincinnati (N.L.)	16	10	.615	3.68	33	33	2	2	0	198 1/3	190	86	81	57	120
A.L. totals (4 years)	17	23	.425	4.51	55	53	5	0	0	319	312	168	160	171	212
N.L. totals (9 years)	85	71	.545	3.62	237	236	16	10	0	1473 2/3	1329	653	592	482	1068
Major League totals (12 years).....	102	94	.520	3.78	292	289	21	10	0	1792 2/3	1641	821	752	653	1280

ALL-STAR GAME RECORD

Year League	W	L	Pct.	ERA	GS	CG	ShO	Sv.	IP	H	R	ER	BB	SO
1991— National............................	0	0	—	0.00	0	0	0	0	1	2	0	0	0	1

HARRIS, LENNY — IF/OF — DIAMONDBACKS

PERSONAL: Born October 28, 1964, in Miami. ... 5-10/220. ... Bats left, throws right. ... Full name: Leonard Anthony Harris.
HIGH SCHOOL: Jackson (Miami).
JUNIOR COLLEGE: Miami-Dade (North) Community College.
TRANSACTIONS/CAREER NOTES: Selected by Cincinnati Reds organization in fifth round of free-agent draft (June 6, 1983). ... Loaned by Reds organization to Glens Falls, Detroit Tigers organization (May 6-28, 1988). ... Traded by Reds with OF Kal Daniels to Los Angeles Dodgers for P Tim Leary and SS Mariano Duncan (July 18, 1989). ... Granted free agency (October 8, 1993). ... Signed by Reds (December 1, 1993). ... Granted free agency (October 31, 1996). ... Re-signed by Reds (November 13, 1996). ... Traded by Reds to New York Mets for P John Hudek (July 3, 1998). ... Granted free agency (October 27, 1998). ... Signed by Colorado Rockies (November 9, 1998). ... Traded by Rockies to Arizona Diamondbacks for IF Belvani Martinez (August 31, 1999).
STATISTICAL NOTES: Led Florida State League third basemen with 34 double plays in 1985. ... Led Eastern League third basemen with 116 putouts, 28 errors and 360 total chances in 1986. ... Led American Association in caught stealing with 22 in 1988. ... Led American Association second basemen with 23 errors in 1988. ... Career major league grand slams: 2.

						BATTING								FIELDING			
Year Team (League)	Pos.	G	AB	R	H	2B	3B	HR	RBI	Avg.	BB	SO	SB	PO	A	E	Avg.
1983— Billings (Pio.)	3B	56	224	37	63	8	1	1	26	.281	13	35	7	34	95	22	.854
1984— Cedar Rapids (Midw.) ...	3B	132	468	52	115	15	3	6	53	.246	42	59	31	111	204	*34	.903
1985— Tampa (FSL)..............	3B	132	499	66	129	11	8	3	51	.259	37	57	15	89	*277	*35	.913
1986— Vermont (East.).........	3B-SS	119	450	68	114	17	2	10	52	.253	29	38	36	†119	220	†28	.924
1987— Nashville (A.A.).........	SS-3B	120	403	45	100	12	3	2	31	.248	27	43	30	124	210	34	.908
1988— Nashville (A.A.)■......	2B-SS-3B	107	422	46	117	20	2	0	35	.277	22	36	*45	203	247	†25	.947
— Glens Falls (East.)■	2B	17	65	9	22	5	1	1	7	.338	9	6	6	40	49	5	.947
— Cincinnati (N.L.)■.....	3B-2B	16	43	7	16	1	0	0	8	.372	5	4	4	14	33	1	.979
1989— Cincinnati (N.L.)	2B-SS-3B	61	188	17	42	4	0	2	11	.223	9	20	10	92	134	13	.946
— Nashville (A.A.)	2B	8	34	6	9	2	0	3	6	.265	0	5	0	23	20	0	1.000
— Los Angeles (N.L.)■..	O-2-3-S	54	147	19	37	6	1	1	15	.252	11	13	4	55	34	2	.978
1990— Los Angeles (N.L.) ...	3-2-O-S	137	431	61	131	16	4	2	29	.304	29	31	15	140	205	11	.969
1991— Los Angeles (N.L.) ...	3-2-S-O	145	429	59	123	16	1	3	38	.287	37	32	12	125	250	20	.949
1992— Los Angeles (N.L.) ...	2-3-O-S	135	347	28	94	11	0	0	30	.271	24	24	19	199	248	27	.943
1993— Los Angeles (N.L.) ...	2-3-S-O	107	160	20	38	6	1	2	11	.238	15	15	3	61	99	3	.982
1994— Cincinnati (N.L.)■	3-1-O-2	66	100	13	31	3	1	0	14	.310	5	13	7	27	29	6	.903
1995— Cincinnati (N.L.)	3-1-O-2	101	197	32	41	8	3	2	16	.208	14	20	10	147	68	4	.982
1996— Cincinnati (N.L.)	O-3-1-2	125	302	33	86	17	2	5	32	.285	21	31	14	199	66	6	.978
1997— Cincinnati (N.L.)	O-2-3-1	120	238	32	65	13	1	3	20	.273	18	18	4	120	57	3	.983
1998— Cincinnati (N.L.)	OF-DH-P	57	122	12	36	8	0	0	10	.295	8	9	1	37	2	3	.929
— New York (N.L.)	O-3-2-1	75	168	18	39	7	0	6	17	.232	9	12	5	84	14	2	.980
1999— Colorado (N.L.)■......	2-O-DH-3	91	158	15	47	12	0	0	13	.297	6	6	1	60	53	9	.926
— Arizona (N.L.)■..........	3B-OF	19	29	2	11	1	0	1	7	.379	0	1	1	6	5	0	1.000
Major League totals (12 years)		1309	3059	368	837	129	14	27	279	.274	211	249	110	1366	1297	110	.960

DIVISION SERIES RECORD

						BATTING								FIELDING			
Year Team (League)	Pos.	G	AB	R	H	2B	3B	HR	RBI	Avg.	BB	SO	SB	PO	A	E	Avg.
1999— Arizona (N.L.).............	PH-3B	2	2	0	0	0	0	0	0	.000	0	0	0	0	0	0	...

CHAMPIONSHIP SERIES RECORD

						BATTING								FIELDING			
Year Team (League)	Pos.	G	AB	R	H	2B	3B	HR	RBI	Avg.	BB	SO	SB	PO	A	E	Avg.
1995— Cincinnati (N.L.)	PH	3	2	0	2	0	0	0	1	1.000	0	0	1	0	0	0	...

RECORD AS PITCHER

Year League	W	L	Pct.	ERA	G	GS	CG	ShO	Sv.	IP	H	R	ER	BB	SO
1998— Cincinnati (N.L.)	0	0	...	0.00	1	0	0	0	0	1	0	0	0	0	1

HARRIS, REGGIE — P

H

PERSONAL: Born August 12, 1968, in Waynesboro, Va. ... 6-2/217. ... Throws right, bats right. ... Full name: Reginald Allen Harris. ... Cousin of Dell Curry, guard, Toronto Raptors.
HIGH SCHOOL: Waynesboro (Va.).
TRANSACTIONS/CAREER NOTES: Selected by Boston Red Sox organization in first round (26th pick overall) of free-agent draft (June 2, 1987). ... Selected by Oakland Athletics from Red Sox organization in Rule 5 major league draft (December 4, 1989). ... On Oakland disabled list (March 29-July 3, 1990); included rehabilitation assignment to Huntsville (May 26-June 24). ... On Tacoma disabled list (June 17-August

4, 1991). ... Selected by Seattle Mariners from A's organization in Rule 5 major league draft (December 7, 1992). ... On Jacksonville disabled list (May 19-28, 1993). ... On Calgary temporarily inactive list (July 21-August 1, 1993). ... Granted free agency (October 15, 1993). ... Re-signed by Mariners (November 11, 1993). ... Granted free agency (October 3, 1994). ... Signed by Omaha, Kansas City Royals organization (February 4, 1995). ... On disabled list (April 6-18, 1995). ... Released by Royals organization (April 25, 1995). ... Signed by Weichuan, Taiwan League (1995). ... Signed by Colorado Rockies organization (February 14, 1996). ... Released by Rockies (March 26, 1996). ... Signed by Boston Red Sox organization (May 7, 1996). ... On Trenton disabled list (June 12-24, 1996). ... Released by Red Sox (December 5, 1996). ... Signed by Philadelphia Phillies organization (December 23, 1996). ... On suspended list (August 29-September 1, 1997). ... Granted free agency (October 7, 1997). ... Signed by Houston Astros organization (January 9, 1998). ... Granted free agency (October 16, 1998). ... Signed by Milwaukee Brewers organization (December 4, 1998). ... Granted free agency (October 15, 1999).

STATISTICAL NOTES: Led Pacific Coast League with 20 wild pitches in 1992.

Year	League	W	L	Pct.	ERA	G	GS	CG	ShO	Sv.	IP	H	R	ER	BB	SO
1987—Elmira (NY-P)		2	3	.400	5.01	9	8	1	1	0	46 2/3	50	29	26	22	25
1988—Lynchburg (Caro.)		1	8	.111	7.45	17	11	0	0	0	64	86	60	53	34	48
—Elmira (NY-P)		3	6	.333	5.30	10	10	0	0	0	54 1/3	56	37	32	28	46
1989—Winter Haven (FSL)		10	13	.435	3.99	29	26	1	0	0	153 1/3	144	81	68	77	85
1990—Huntsville (Sou.)■		0	2	.000	3.03	5	5	0	0	0	29 2/3	26	12	10	16	34
—Oakland (A.L.)		1	0	1.000	3.48	16	1	0	0	0	41 1/3	25	16	16	21	31
1991—Tacoma (PCL)		5	4	.556	4.99	16	15	0	0	0	83	83	55	46	58	72
—Oakland (A.L.)		0	0	...	12.00	2	0	0	0	0	3	5	4	4	3	2
1992—Tacoma (PCL)		6	*16	.273	5.71	29	•28	1	0	0	149 2/3	141	*108	*95	*117	111
1993—Jacksonville (Sou.)■		1	4	.200	4.78	9	8	0	0	0	37 2/3	33	24	20	22	30
—Calgary (PCL)		8	6	.571	5.20	17	15	1	0	0	88 1/3	74	55	51	61	75
1994—Calgary (PCL)		6	9	.400	8.12	20	18	0	0	0	98 2/3	137	99	89	51	73
1995—Omaha (A.A.)■		0	1	.000	18.00	2	0	0	0	0	2	5	4	4	1	2
—Weichuan (Taiwan)■		3	5	.375	3.00	9	...	...	...	0	63	53	...	...	47	32
1996—Trenton (East.)■		2	1	.667	1.46	33	0	0	0	17	37	17	6	6	19	43
—Boston (A.L.)		0	0	...	12.46	4	0	0	0	0	4 1/3	7	6	6	5	4
1997—Philadelphia (N.L.)■		1	3	.250	5.30	50	0	0	0	0	54 1/3	55	33	32	43	45
1998—New Orleans (PCL)■		2	3	.400	4.44	51	0	0	0	23	52 2/3	38	27	26	28	53
—Houston (N.L.)		0	0	...	6.00	6	0	0	0	0	6	6	4	4	2	2
1999—Louisville (I.L.)■		3	4	.429	4.72	41	0	0	0	16	40	43	21	21	20	45
—Milwaukee (N.L.)		0	0	...	3.00	8	0	0	0	0	12	8	4	4	7	11
A.L. totals (3 years)		1	0	1.000	4.81	22	1	0	0	0	48 2/3	37	26	26	29	37
N.L. totals (3 years)		1	3	.250	4.98	64	0	0	0	0	72 1/3	69	41	40	52	58
Major League totals (6 years)		2	3	.400	4.91	86	1	0	0	0	121	106	67	66	81	95

HARVILLE, CHAD   P   ATHLETICS

PERSONAL: Born September 16, 1976, in Selmer, Tenn. ... 5-9/180. ... Throws right, bats right. ... Full name: Chad Ashley Harville.
HIGH SCHOOL: Hardin County (Savannah, Tenn.).
COLLEGE: Memphis.
TRANSACTIONS/CAREER NOTES: Selected by Oakland Athletics organization in second round of free-agent draft (June 3, 1997).

Year	League	W	L	Pct.	ERA	G	GS	CG	ShO	Sv.	IP	H	R	ER	BB	SO
1997—S. Oregon (N'west)		1	0	1.000	0.00	3	0	0	0	0	5	3	0	0	3	6
—Visalia (Calif.)		0	0	...	5.79	14	0	0	0	0	18 2/3	25	14	12	13	24
1998—Visalia (Calif.)		4	3	.571	3.00	24	7	0	0	4	69	59	25	23	31	76
—Huntsville (Sou.)		0	0	...	2.45	12	0	0	0	8	14 2/3	6	4	4	13	24
1999—Midland (Texas)		2	0	1.000	2.01	17	0	0	0	7	22 1/3	13	6	5	9	35
—Vancouver (PCL)		1	0	1.000	1.75	22	0	0	0	11	25 2/3	24	5	5	11	36
—Oakland (A.L.)		0	2	.000	6.91	15	0	0	0	0	14 1/3	18	11	11	10	15
Major League totals (1 year)		0	2	.000	6.91	15	0	0	0	0	14 1/3	18	11	11	10	15

HASEGAWA, SHIGETOSHI   P   ANGELS

PERSONAL: Born August 1, 1968, in Kobe, Japan ... 5-11/178. ... Throws right, bats right. ... Name pronounced SHE-geh-TOE-she HAH-seh-GAH-wah.
COLLEGE: Ritsumeikan University (Kyoto, Japan).
TRANSACTIONS/CAREER NOTES: Played for Orix Blue Wave of Japan Pacific League (1991-96). ... Signed as non-drafted free agent by Anaheim Angels (January 9, 1997).

Year	League	W	L	Pct.	ERA	G	GS	CG	ShO	Sv.	IP	H	R	ER	BB	SO
1991—Orix (Jap. Pac.)		12	9	.571	3.55	28	25	11	3	1	185	184	76	73	50	111
1992—Orix (Jap. Pac.)		6	8	.429	3.27	24	19	4	0	1	143 1/3	138	60	52	51	86
1993—Orix (Jap. Pac.)		12	6	.667	2.71	23	22	9	3	0	159 2/3	146	61	48	48	86
1994—Orix (Jap. Pac.)		11	9	.550	3.11	25	22	8	3	1	156 1/3	169	61	54	46	86
1995—Orix (Jap. Pac.)		12	7	.632	2.89	24	23	9	4	0	171	167	62	55	51	91
1996—Orix (Jap. Pac.)		4	6	.400	5.34	18	16	2	0	1	87 2/3	109	60	52	40	55
1997—Anaheim (A.L.)■		3	7	.300	3.93	50	7	0	0	0	116 2/3	118	60	51	46	83
1998—Anaheim (A.L.)		8	3	.727	3.14	61	0	0	0	5	97 1/3	86	37	34	32	73
1999—Anaheim (A.L.)		4	6	.400	4.91	64	1	0	0	2	77	80	45	42	34	44
Major League totals (3 years)		15	16	.484	3.93	175	8	0	0	7	291	284	142	127	112	200

HASELMAN, BILL   C   RANGERS

PERSONAL: Born May 25, 1966, in Long Branch, N.J. ... 6-3/223. ... Bats right, throws right. ... Full name: William Joseph Haselman.
HIGH SCHOOL: Saratoga (Calif.).
COLLEGE: UCLA.
TRANSACTIONS/CAREER NOTES: Selected by Texas Rangers organization in first round (23rd pick overall) of free-agent draft (June 2, 1987); pick received as compensation for New York Yankees signing Type A free-agent OF Gary Ward. ... On Oklahoma City disabled list (March 28-

H

May 4, 1992). ... Claimed on waivers by Seattle Mariners (May 29, 1992). ... On suspended list (July 22-25, 1993). ... Granted free agency (October 15, 1994). ... Signed by Boston Red Sox (November 7, 1994). ... On disabled list (June 30-August 8, 1997); included rehabilitation assignment to Gulf Coast Red Sox (July 29-August 1) and Trenton (August 1-8). ... Traded by Red Sox with P Aaron Sele and P Mark Brandenburg to Rangers for C Jim Leyritz and OF Damon Buford (November 6, 1997). ... Granted free agency (October 23, 1998). ... Signed by Detroit Tigers (December 14, 1998). ... Traded by Tigers with P Justin Thompson, P Francisco Cordero, OF Gabe Kapler, 2B Frank Catalanotto and P Alan Webb to Rangers for OF Juan Gonzalez, P Danny Patterson and C Gregg Zaun (November 2, 1999).

RECORDS: Holds major league record for most chances accepted in consecutive nine-inning games—37 (April 29 and 30, 1996). ... Shares A.L. single-game record for most chances accepted by catcher (nine-inning game)—20 (September 18, 1996).

STATISTICAL NOTES: Led Texas League with 12 passed balls in 1989. ... Led Texas League catchers with 676 putouts, 90 assists, 20 errors, 786 total chances and 20 passed balls in 1990. ... Led American Association catchers with 673 putouts and 751 total chances in 1991. ... Tied for A.L. lead in passed balls with 17 in 1997. ... Career major league grand slams: 1.

						BATTING									FIELDING		
Year Team (League)	Pos.	G	AB	R	H	2B	3B	HR	RBI	Avg.	BB	SO	SB	PO	A	E	Avg.
1987—Gastonia (SAL)	C	61	235	35	72	13	1	8	33	.306	19	46	1	26	2	2	.933
1988—Charlotte (FSL)	C	122	453	56	111	17	2	10	54	.245	45	99	8	249	30	6	.979
1989—Tulsa (Texas)	C	107	352	38	95	17	2	7	36	.270	40	88	5	508	63	9	.984
1990—Tulsa (Texas)	C-1B-OF-3B	120	430	68	137	39	2	18	80	.319	43	96	3	†722	†93	†20	.976
—Texas (A.L.)	DH-C	7	13	0	2	0	0	0	3	.154	1	5	0	8	0	0	1.000
1991—Okla. City (A.A.)	C-OF-1B-3B	126	442	57	113	22	2	9	60	.256	61	89	10	†706	71	11	.986
1992—Okla. City (A.A.)	OF-C	17	58	8	14	5	0	1	9	.241	13	12	1	45	7	3	.945
—Calgary (PCL)■	C-OF	88	302	49	77	14	2	19	53	.255	41	89	3	227	23	6	.977
—Seattle (A.L.)	C-OF	8	19	1	5	0	0	0	0	.263	0	7	1	19	2	0	1.000
1993—Seattle (A.L.)	C-DH-OF	58	137	21	35	8	0	5	16	.255	12	19	2	236	17	2	.992
1994—Seattle (A.L.)	C-DH-OF	38	83	11	16	7	1	1	8	.193	3	11	1	157	6	3	.982
—Calgary (PCL)	C-DH-1B	44	163	44	54	10	0	15	46	.331	30	33	1	219	16	5	.979
1995—Boston (A.L.)■	C-DH-1B	64	152	22	37	6	1	5	23	.243	17	30	0	259	16	3	.989
1996—Boston (A.L.)	C-DH-1B	77	237	33	65	13	1	8	34	.274	19	52	4	507	33	3	.994
1997—Boston (A.L.)	C	67	212	22	50	15	0	6	26	.236	15	44	0	373	40	7	.983
—GC Red Sox (GCL)	DH	4	16	2	2	0	0	0	1	.125	0	1	1	0	0	0	...
—Trenton (East.)	C-DH	7	26	3	6	1	0	2	3	.231	2	2	0	30	2	0	1.000
1998—Texas (A.L.)■	C-DH	40	105	11	33	6	0	6	17	.314	3	17	0	176	8	1	.995
1999—Detroit (A.L.)■	C-DH	48	143	13	39	8	0	4	14	.273	10	26	2	231	13	1	.996
Major League totals (9 years)		407	1101	134	282	63	3	35	141	.256	80	211	9	1966	135	20	.991

DIVISION SERIES RECORD

						BATTING									FIELDING		
Year Team (League)	Pos.	G	AB	R	H	2B	3B	HR	RBI	Avg.	BB	SO	SB	PO	A	E	Avg.
1995—Boston (A.L.)	C	1	2	0	0	0	0	0	0	.000	0	0	0	6	0	0	1.000

HATTEBERG, SCOTT   C   RED SOX

PERSONAL: Born December 14, 1969, in Salem, Ore. ... 6-1/205. ... Bats left, throws right. ... Full name: Scott Allen Hatteberg. ... Name pronounced HAT-ee-berg.

HIGH SCHOOL: Eisenhower (Yakima, Wash.).

COLLEGE: Washington State.

TRANSACTIONS/CAREER NOTES: Selected by Philadelphia Phillies organization in 12th round of free-agent draft (June 1, 1988); did not sign. ... Selected by Boston Red Sox organization in supplemental round ("sandwich pick" between first and second round, 43rd pick overall) of free-agent draft (June 3, 1991); pick received as part of compensation for Kansas City signing Type A free-agent P Mike Boddicker. ... On disabled list (July 27-August 3, 1992). ... On Boston disabled list (April 15-May 7 and May 17-August 16, 1999); included rehabilitation assignments to Pawtucket (May 4-7 and August 3-13), Gulf Coast Red Sox (July 24-31) and Sarasota (August 1-2).

STATISTICAL NOTES: Tied for A.L. lead in double plays by catcher with 13 and passed balls with 17 in 1997. ... Career major league grand slams: 1.

						BATTING									FIELDING		
Year Team (League)	Pos.	G	AB	R	H	2B	3B	HR	RBI	Avg.	BB	SO	SB	PO	A	E	Avg.
1991—Winter Haven (FSL)	C	56	191	21	53	7	3	1	25	.277	22	22	1	261	35	5	.983
—Lynchburg (Caro.)	C	8	25	4	5	1	0	0	2	.200	7	6	0	35	2	0	1.000
1992—New Britain (East.)	C	103	297	28	69	13	2	1	30	.232	41	49	1	473	44	11	.979
1993—New Britain (East.)	C	68	227	35	63	10	2	7	28	.278	42	38	1	410	45	10	.978
—Pawtucket (I.L.)	C	18	53	6	10	0	0	1	2	.189	6	12	0	131	4	5	.964
1994—New Britain (East.)	C	20	68	6	18	4	1	1	9	.265	7	9	0	125	14	1	.993
—Pawtucket (I.L.)	C	78	238	26	56	14	0	7	19	.235	32	49	2	467	36	7	.986
1995—Pawtucket (I.L.)	C-DH	85	251	36	68	15	1	7	27	.271	40	39	2	446	45	•8	.984
—Boston (A.L.)	C	2	2	1	1	0	0	0	0	.500	0	0	0	4	0	0	1.000
1996—Pawtucket (I.L.)	C-DH	90	287	52	77	16	0	12	49	.268	58	66	1	566	42	6	.990
—Boston (A.L.)	C	10	11	3	2	1	0	0	0	.182	3	2	0	32	2	0	1.000
1997—Boston (A.L.)	C-DH	114	350	46	97	23	1	10	44	.277	40	70	0	574	46	11	.983
1998—Boston (A.L.)	C	112	359	46	99	23	1	12	43	.276	43	58	0	664	61	5	.993
1999—Boston (A.L.)	C-DH	30	80	12	22	5	0	1	11	.275	18	14	0	128	14	1	.993
—Pawtucket (I.L.)	C-DH	10	34	3	6	2	0	0	4	.176	4	6	0	47	4	0	1.000
—GC Red Sox (GCL)	C-DH	6	15	4	6	2	0	1	6	.400	7	1	0	37	4	0	1.000
—Sarasota (FSL)	C	1	1	0	1	0	0	0	1	1.000	0	0	0	3	1	0	1.000
Major League totals (5 years)		268	802	108	221	52	2	23	98	.276	104	144	0	1402	123	17	.989

DIVISION SERIES RECORD

						BATTING									FIELDING		
Year Team (League)	Pos.	G	AB	R	H	2B	3B	HR	RBI	Avg.	BB	SO	SB	PO	A	E	Avg.
1998—Boston (A.L.)	C	3	9	0	1	0	0	0	0	.111	3	1	0	20	0	0	1.000
1999—Boston (A.L.)	C	1	1	1	1	0	0	0	1	1.000	0	0	0	2	0	0	1.000
Division series totals (2 years)		4	10	1	2	0	0	0	1	.200	3	1	0	22	0	0	1.000

H

					BATTING								FIELDING		
Year	Team (League)	Pos.	G	AB	R	H	2B	3B	HR	RBI	Avg.	BB	SO	SB	PO	A	E	Avg.
1999—Boston (A.L.).............		PH-C	3	1	0	0	0	0	0	0	.000	0	1	0	0	0	0	...

HAWKINS, LaTROY — P — TWINS

PERSONAL: Born December 21, 1972, in Gary, Ind. ... 6-5/204. ... Throws right, bats right.
HIGH SCHOOL: West Side (Gary, Ind.).
TRANSACTIONS/CAREER NOTES: Selected by Minnesota Twins organization in seventh round of free-agent draft (June 3, 1991).
STATISTICAL NOTES: Tied for A.L. lead with three balks in 1997.

Year	League	W	L	Pct.	ERA	G	GS	CG	ShO	Sv.	IP	H	R	ER	BB	SO
1991—Gulf Coast Twins (GCL)......		4	3	.571	4.75	11	11	0	0	0	55	62	34	29	26	47
1992—Gulf Coast Twins (GCL)......		3	2	.600	3.22	6	6	1	0	0	36⅓	36	19	13	10	35
—Elizabethton (Appl.)............		0	1	.000	3.38	5	5	1	0	0	26⅔	21	12	10	11	36
1993—Fort Wayne (Midw.).........		•15	5	.750	*2.06	26	23	4	•3	0	157⅓	110	53	36	41	*179
1994—Fort Myers (FSL).............		4	0	1.000	2.33	6	6	1	1	0	38⅔	32	10	10	6	36
—Nashville (Sou.).................		9	2	*.818	2.33	11	11	1	0	0	73⅓	50	23	19	28	53
—Salt Lake (PCL).................		5	4	.556	4.08	12	12	1	0	0	81⅔	92	42	37	33	37
1995—Minnesota (A.L.).............		2	3	.400	8.67	6	6	1	0	0	27	39	29	26	12	9
—Salt Lake (PCL).................		9	7	.563	3.55	22	22	4	1	0	144⅓	150	63	57	40	74
1996—Minnesota (A.L.).............		1	1	.500	8.20	7	6	0	0	0	26⅓	42	24	24	9	24
—Salt Lake (PCL).................		9	8	.529	3.92	20	20	4	1	0	137⅔	138	66	60	31	99
1997—Salt Lake (PCL).............		9	4	.692	5.45	14	13	2	1	0	76	100	53	46	16	53
—Minnesota (A.L.)...............		6	12	.333	5.84	20	20	0	0	0	103⅓	134	71	67	47	58
1998—Minnesota (A.L.).............		7	14	.333	5.25	33	33	0	0	0	190⅓	227	126	111	61	105
1999—Minnesota (A.L.).............		10	14	.417	6.66	33	33	1	0	0	174⅓	238	*136	*129	60	103
Major League totals (5 years).......		**26**	**44**	**.371**	**6.16**	**99**	**98**	**2**	**0**	**0**	**521⅓**	**680**	**386**	**357**	**189**	**299**

HAYES, CHARLIE — 3B/1B — METS

PERSONAL: Born May 29, 1965, in Hattiesburg, Miss. ... 6-0/220. ... Bats right, throws right. ... Full name: Charles Dewayne Hayes.
HIGH SCHOOL: Forrest County Agricultural (Brooklyn, Miss.).
TRANSACTIONS/CAREER NOTES: Selected by San Francisco Giants organization in fourth round of free-agent draft (June 6, 1983). ... On disabled list (July 20, 1983-remainder of season). ... Traded by Giants with P Dennis Cook and P Terry Mulholland to Philadelphia Phillies for P Steve Bedrosian and a player to be named later (June 18, 1989); Giants organization acquired IF Rick Parker to complete deal (August 7, 1989). ... Traded by Phillies to New York Yankees (February 19, 1992), completing deal in which Yankees traded P Darrin Chapin to Phillies for a player to be named later (January 8, 1992). ... Selected by Colorado Rockies in first round (third pick overall) of expansion draft (November 17, 1992). ... On suspended list (August 10-13, 1993). ... Granted free agency (December 23, 1994). ... Signed by Phillies (April 6, 1995). ... Granted free agency (November 2, 1995). ... Signed by Pittsburgh Pirates (December 28, 1995). ... Traded by Pirates to Yankees for a player to be named later (August 30, 1996); Pirates acquired P Chris Corn to complete deal (August 31, 1996). ... Traded by Yankees with cash to Giants for OF Chris Singleton and P Alberto Castillo (November 11, 1997). ... On suspended list (July 28-30, 1998). ... On suspended list (April 20-24, 1999). ... On disabled list (July 2-21, 1999). ... Granted free agency (November 1, 1999). ... Signed by New York Mets organization (January 19, 2000).
STATISTICAL NOTES: Led Texas League third basemen with 27 double plays in 1986. ... Led Texas League third basemen with 334 total chances in 1987. ... Led Pacific Coast League in grounding into double plays with 19 in 1988. ... Led N.L. third basemen with 324 assists and tied for lead with 465 total chances in 1990. ... Tied for A.L. lead in double plays by third baseman with 29 in 1992. ... Tied for N.L. lead in grounding into double plays with 25 in 1993. ... Led N.L. in grounding into double plays with 23 in 1995. ... Career major league grand slams: 3.

						BATTING								FIELDING		
Year	Team (League)	Pos.	G	AB	R	H	2B	3B	HR	RBI	Avg.	BB	SO	SB	PO	A	E	Avg.
1983—Great Falls (Pio.)		3B-OF	34	111	9	29	4	2	0	9	.261	7	26	1	13	32	9	.833
1984—Clinton (Midw.)		3B	116	392	41	96	17	2	2	51	.245	34	110	4	68	216	28	.910
1985—Fresno (Calif.)		3B	131	467	73	132	17	2	4	68	.283	56	95	7	*100	233	18	*.949
1986—Shreveport (Texas).....		3B	121	434	52	107	23	2	5	45	.247	28	83	1	89	*259	25	.933
1987—Shreveport (Texas)....		3B	128	487	66	148	33	3	14	75	.304	26	76	5	*100	*212	22	*.934
1988—Phoenix (PCL).........		OF-3B	131	492	71	151	26	4	7	71	.307	34	91	4	206	100	23	.930
—San Francisco (N.L.) ..		OF-3B	7	11	0	1	0	0	0	0	.091	0	3	0	5	0	0	1.000
1989—Phoenix (PCL).........		3-0-1-S-2	61	229	25	65	15	1	7	27	.284	15	48	5	76	76	8	.950
—San Francisco (N.L.) ..		3B	3	5	0	1	0	0	0	0	.200	0	1	0	2	1	0	1.000
—Scranton/W.B. (I.L.)■		3B	7	27	4	11	3	1	1	3	.407	0	3	0	8	8	0	1.000
—Philadelphia (N.L.)......		3B	84	299	26	77	15	1	8	43	.258	11	49	3	49	173	22	.910
1990—Philadelphia (N.L.)......		3B-1B-2B	152	561	56	145	20	0	10	57	.258	28	91	4	151	†329	20	.960
1991—Philadelphia (N.L.)......		3B-SS	142	460	34	106	23	1	12	53	.230	16	75	3	88	240	15	.956
1992—New York (A.L.)■......		3B-1B	142	509	52	131	19	2	18	66	.257	28	100	3	125	249	13	.966
1993—Colorado (N.L.)		3B-SS	157	573	89	175	*45	2	25	98	.305	43	82	11	123	292	20	.954
1994—Colorado (N.L.)		3B	113	423	46	122	23	4	10	50	.288	36	71	3	72	216	17	.944
1995—Philadelphia (N.L.)		3B	141	529	58	146	30	3	11	85	.276	50	88	5	•104	264	14	.963
1996—Pittsburgh (N.L.)■......		3B	128	459	51	114	21	2	10	62	.248	36	78	6	66	275	18	.950
—New York (A.L.)■......		3B	20	67	7	19	3	0	2	13	.284	1	12	0	14	30	0	1.000
1997—New York (A.L.)		3B-DH	100	353	39	91	16	0	11	53	.258	40	66	3	67	169	13	.948
1998—San Fran. (N.L.)■.......		3B-1B-DH	111	329	39	94	8	0	12	62	.286	34	61	2	369	101	3	.994
1999—San Francisco (N.L.) ..		3-1-DH-O	95	264	33	54	9	1	6	48	.205	33	41	3	130	91	7	.969
American League totals (3 years)			262	929	98	241	38	2	31	132	.259	69	178	6	206	448	26	.962
National League totals (10 years)			1133	3913	432	1035	194	14	104	558	.265	287	640	40	1159	1982	136	.958
Major League totals (12 years)			1395	4842	530	1276	232	16	135	690	.264	356	818	46	1365	2430	162	.959

DIVISION SERIES RECORD

						BATTING								FIELDING		
Year	Team (League)	Pos.	G	AB	R	H	2B	3B	HR	RBI	Avg.	BB	SO	SB	PO	A	E	Avg.
1996—New York (A.L.)..........		3B-DH	3	5	0	1	0	0	0	1	.200	0	0	0	1	3	0	1.000
1997—New York (A.L.)..........		3B-2B	5	15	0	5	0	0	0	1	.333	0	2	0	3	9	3	.800
Division series totals (2 years)			8	20	0	6	0	0	0	2	.300	0	2	0	4	12	3	.842

H

Year	Team (League)	Pos.	G	AB	R	H	2B	3B	HR	RBI	Avg.	BB	SO	SB	PO	A	E	Avg.
											BATTING						FIELDING	
1996—	New York (A.L.)	PH-3B-DH	4	7	0	1	0	0	0	0	.143	2	2	0	0	3	0	1.000

WORLD SERIES RECORD

NOTES: Member of World Series championship team (1996).

Year	Team (League)	Pos.	G	AB	R	H	2B	3B	HR	RBI	Avg.	BB	SO	SB	PO	A	E	Avg.
											BATTING						FIELDING	
1996—	New York (A.L.)	3B-PH-1B	4	16	2	3	0	0	0	1	.188	1	5	0	3	6	0	1.000

HAYNES, JIMMY   P   BREWERS

PERSONAL: Born September 5, 1972, in La Grange, Ga. ... 6-4/203. ... Throws right, bats right. ... Full name: Jimmy Wayne Haynes.
HIGH SCHOOL: Troup (La Grange, Ga.).
TRANSACTIONS/CAREER NOTES: Selected by Baltimore Orioles organization in seventh round of free-agent draft (June 3, 1991). ... Traded by Orioles with a player to be named later to Oakland Athletics for OF Geronimo Berroa (June 27, 1997); A's acquired P Mark Seaver to complete deal (September 2, 1997). ... Traded by Athletics to Milwaukee Brewers as part of three-way deal in which Athletics received P Justin Miller and cash from Colorado Rockies, Brewers received P Jamey Wright and C Henry Blanco from Rockies and Rockies received 3B Jeff Cirillo, P Scott Karl and cash from Brewers (December 13, 1999).
STATISTICAL NOTES: Led A.L. pitchers with five errors in 1999.

Year	League	W	L	Pct.	ERA	G	GS	CG	ShO	Sv.	IP	H	R	ER	BB	SO
1991—	Gulf Coast Orioles (GCL)	3	2	.600	1.60	14	8	1	0	2	62	44	27	11	21	67
1992—	Kane County (Midw.)	7	11	.389	2.56	24	24	4	0	0	144	131	66	41	45	141
1993—	Frederick (Caro.)	12	8	.600	3.03	27	27	2	1	0	172 1/3	139	73	58	61	174
1994—	Bowie (East.)	13	8	.619	2.90	25	25	5	1	0	173 2/3	154	67	56	46	*177
—	Rochester (I.L.)	1	0	1.000	6.75	3	3	0	0	0	13 1/3	20	12	10	6	14
1995—	Rochester (I.L.)	•12	8	.600	3.29	26	25	3	1	0	167	162	77	61	49	*140
—	Baltimore (A.L.)	2	1	.667	2.25	4	3	0	0	0	24	11	6	6	12	22
1996—	Baltimore (A.L.)	3	6	.333	8.29	26	11	0	0	1	89	122	84	82	58	65
—	Rochester (I.L.)	1	1	.500	5.65	5	5	0	0	0	28 2/3	31	19	18	18	24
1997—	Rochester (I.L.)	5	4	.556	3.44	16	16	2	1	0	102	89	49	39	55	113
—	Edmonton (PCL)■	0	2	.000	4.85	5	5	0	0	0	29 2/3	36	22	16	11	24
—	Oakland (A.L.)	3	6	.333	4.42	13	13	0	0	0	73 1/3	74	38	36	40	65
1998—	Oakland (A.L.)	11	9	.550	5.09	33	33	1	1	0	194 1/3	229	124	110	88	134
1999—	Oakland (A.L.)	7	12	.368	6.34	30	25	0	0	0	142	158	112	100	80	93
Major League totals (5 years)		26	34	.433	5.75	106	85	1	1	1	522 2/3	594	364	334	278	379

HEAMS, SHANE   P   TIGERS

PERSONAL: Born September 29, 1975, in Toledo, Ohio. ... 6-1/175. ... Throws right, bats right. ... Full name: Shane Timothy Heams.
HIGH SCHOOL: Bedford (Temperance, Mich.).
COLLEGE: Illinois.
TRANSACTIONS/CAREER NOTES: Selected by Seattle Mariners organization in 41st round of free-agent draft (June 2, 1994). ... Announced retirement (March 24, 1998). ... Signed by Detroit Tigers organization (April 23, 1998).
MISCELLANEOUS: Played outfield (1995).

Year	League	W	L	Pct.	ERA	G	GS	CG	ShO	Sv.	IP	H	R	ER	BB	SO
1996—	Arizona Mariners (Ariz.)	1	1	.500	2.93	9	0	0	0	2	15 1/3	10	7	5	6	12
1997—	Arizona Mariners (Ariz.)	•6	2	*.750	1.70	21	0	0	0	2	37	30	20	7	22	42
1998—	Jamestown (NY-P)■	2	2	.500	3.99	24	0	0	0	6	47 1/3	43	27	21	16	73
1999—	West Michigan (Midw.)	5	4	.556	2.35	51	0	0	0	10	69	41	26	18	39	101

RECORD AS POSITION PLAYER

Year	Team (League)	Pos.	G	AB	R	H	2B	3B	HR	RBI	Avg.	BB	SO	SB	PO	A	E	Avg.
											BATTING						FIELDING	
1995—	Everett (N.W.)	OF	27	61	5	12	4	0	1	0	.197	3	28	2	13	4	2	.895

HEISERMAN, RICK   P   CARDINALS

PERSONAL: Born February 22, 1973, in Atlantic, Iowa. ... 6-7/225. ... Throws right, bats right. ... Full name: Richard Michael Heiserman.
HIGH SCHOOL: Millard South (Omaha, Neb.).
COLLEGE: Creighton.
TRANSACTIONS/CAREER NOTES: Selected by Cleveland Indians organization in third round of free-agent draft (June 2, 1994). ... Traded by Indians with C Pepe McNeal and IF David Bell to St. Louis Cardinals for P Ken Hill (July 27, 1995). ... On Memphis disabled list (June 11-20, 1998).

Year	League	W	L	Pct.	ERA	G	GS	CG	ShO	Sv.	IP	H	R	ER	BB	SO
1994—	Watertown (NY-P)	1	0	1.000	2.31	7	0	0	0	0	11 2/3	6	3	3	5	6
1995—	Kinston (Caro.)	9	3	.750	3.74	19	19	1	0	0	113	97	55	47	42	86
—	St. Petersburg (FSL)■	2	3	.400	5.46	6	5	0	0	0	28	28	18	17	11	18
1996—	St. Petersburg (FSL)	10	8	.556	3.24	26	26	1	1	0	155 1/3	168	68	56	41	104
1997—	Arkansas (Texas)	5	8	.385	4.17	34	20	1	•1	4	131 2/3	151	73	61	36	90
—	Louisville (A.A.)	0	0	...	4.50	1	0	0	0	0	2	2	1	1	1	0
1998—	Arkansas (Texas)	0	3	.000	4.96	18	0	0	0	9	16 1/3	20	11	9	5	9
—	Memphis (PCL)	2	3	.400	4.02	40	0	0	0	6	40 1/3	54	21	18	14	28
1999—	Memphis (PCL)	2	3	.400	5.11	52	0	0	0	20	61 2/3	67	37	35	21	57
—	St. Louis (N.L.)	0	0	...	8.31	3	0	0	0	0	4 1/3	8	4	4	4	4
Major League totals (1 year)		0	0	...	8.31	3	0	0	0	0	4 1/3	8	4	4	4	4

PERSONAL: Born December 15, 1970, in Devils Lake, N.D. ... 6-3/220. ... Throws right, bats right. ... Full name: Ricky Allen Helling.
HIGH SCHOOL: Lakota (Fargo, N.D.), then Shanley (N.D.).
JUNIOR COLLEGE: Kishwaukee College (Ill.).
COLLEGE: North Dakota, then Stanford.
TRANSACTIONS/CAREER NOTES: Selected by New York Mets organization in 50th round of free-agent draft (June 4, 1990); did not sign. ... Selected by Texas Rangers organization in first round (22nd pick overall) of free-agent draft (June 1, 1992). ... Traded by Rangers to Florida Marlins (September 3, 1996), completing deal in which Marlins traded P John Burkett to Rangers for P Ryan Dempster and a player to be named later (August 8, 1996). ... Traded by Marlins to Rangers for P Ed Vosberg (August 12, 1997).
STATISTICAL NOTES: Pitched 4-0 no-hit victory against Nashville (August 13, 1996). ... Led A.L. with 41 home runs allowed in 1999.
MISCELLANEOUS: Member of 1992 U.S. Olympic baseball team.

Year League	W	L	Pct.	ERA	G	GS	CG	ShO	Sv.	IP	H	R	ER	BB	SO
1992—Charlotte (FSL)	1	1	.500	2.29	3ˈ	3	0	0	0	19²/₃	13	5	5	4	20
1993—Tulsa (Texas)	12	8	.600	3.60	26	26	2	•2	0	177¹/₃	150	76	71	46	*188
—Oklahoma City (A.A.)	1	1	.500	1.64	2	2	1	0	0	11	5	3	2	3	17
1994—Texas (A.L.)	3	2	.600	5.88	9	9	1	1	0	52	62	34	34	18	25
—Oklahoma City (A.A.)	4	12	.250	5.78	20	20	2	0	0	132¹/₃	153	93	85	43	85
1995—Texas (A.L.)	0	2	.000	6.57	3	3	0	0	0	12¹/₃	17	11	9	8	5
—Oklahoma City (A.A.)	4	8	.333	5.33	20	20	3	0	0	109²/₃	132	73	65	41	80
1996—Texas (A.L.)	12	4	.750	2.96	23	22	2	1	0	140	124	54	46	38	157
—Florida (N.L.)■	1	2	.333	7.52	6	2	0	0	0	20¹/₃	23	17	17	9	16
1997—Texas (A.L.)	2	1	.667	1.95	5	4	0	0	0	27²/₃	14	6	6	7	26
—Florida (N.L.)	2	6	.250	4.38	31	8	0	0	0	76	61	38	37	48	53
—Texas (A.L.)■	3	3	.500	4.58	10	8	0	0	0	55	47	29	28	21	46
1998—Texas (A.L.)	•20	7	.741	4.41	33	33	4	2	0	216¹/₃	209	109	106	78	164
1999—Texas (A.L.)	13	11	.542	4.84	35	*35	3	0	0	219¹/₃	228	127	118	85	131
A.L. totals (6 years)	40	27	.597	4.88	96	90	8	3	0	575¹/₃	586	327	312	219	387
N.L. totals (2 years)	4	7	.364	3.73	36	12	0	0	0	103²/₃	75	44	43	55	79
Major League totals (6 years)	44	34	.564	4.71	132	102	8	3	0	679	661	371	355	274	466

DIVISION SERIES RECORD

Year League	W	L	Pct.	ERA	G	GS	CG	ShO	Sv.	IP	H	R	ER	BB	SO
1998—Texas (A.L.)	0	1	.000	4.50	1	1	0	0	0	6	8	3	3	1	9
1999—Texas (A.L.)	0	1	.000	2.84	1	1	0	0	0	6¹/₃	5	2	2	1	8
Division series totals (2 years)	0	2	.000	3.65	2	2	0	0	0	12¹/₃	13	5	5	2	17

PERSONAL: Born May 12, 1976, in Gastonia, N.C. ... 6-4/230. ... Bats right, throws right. ... Full name: Wesley Ray Helms.
HIGH SCHOOL: Ashbrook (Gastonia, N.C.).
TRANSACTIONS/CAREER NOTES: Selected by Atlanta Braves organization in 10th round of free-agent draft (June 2, 1994). ... On Atlanta disabled list (April 3-July 15 and September 5, 1999-remainder of season); included rehabilitation assignment to Gulf Coast Braves (June 22-July 11). ... On Greenville disabled list (August 15-September 4, 1999).
STATISTICAL NOTES: Led South Atlantic League third basemen with 25 double plays in 1995. ... Led International League third basemen with 24 double plays in 1998.

Year Team (League)	Pos.	G	AB	R	H	2B	3B	HR	RBI	Avg.	BB	SO	SB	PO	A	E	Avg.
1994—GC Braves (GCL)	3B	56	184	22	49	15	1	4	29	.266	22	36	6	•47	93	20	.875
1995—Macon (SAL)	3B	136	*539	89	149	32	1	11	85	.276	50	107	2	91	*269	40	.900
1996—Durham (Caro.)	3B	67	258	40	83	19	2	13	54	.322	12	51	1	40	133	15	.920
—Greenville (Sou.)	3B	64	231	24	59	13	2	4	22	.255	13	48	2	50	96	12	.924
1997—Richmond (I.L.)	3B	32	110	11	21	4	0	3	15	.191	10	34	1	18	65	9	.902
—Greenville (Sou.)	3B	86	314	50	93	14	1	11	44	.296	13	50	3	60	147	11	.950
1998—Richmond (I.L.)	3B-DH	125	451	56	124	27	1	13	75	.275	35	103	6	75	220	15	.952
—Atlanta (N.L.)	3B	7	13	2	4	1	0	1	2	.308	0	4	0	1	2	1	.750
1999—GC Braves (GCL)	DH-1B	9	33	1	15	2	0	0	10	.455	5	4	0	27	0	0	1.000
—Greenville (Sou.)	1B	30	113	15	34	6	0	8	26	.301	7	34	1	226	18	4	.984
Major League totals (1 year)		7	13	2	4	1	0	1	2	.308	0	4	0	1	2	1	.750

PERSONAL: Born August 20, 1973, in Knoxville, Tenn. ... 6-2/206. ... Bats left, throws left. ... Full name: Todd Lynn Helton.
HIGH SCHOOL: Knoxville (Tenn.) Central.
COLLEGE: Tennessee.
TRANSACTIONS/CAREER NOTES: Selected by San Diego Padres organization in second round of free-agent draft (June 1, 1992); did not sign. ... Selected by Colorado Rockies organization in first round (eighth pick overall) of free-agent draft (June 3, 1995). ... On New Haven disabled list (June 15-24, 1996).
HONORS: Named N.L. Rookie Player of the Year by THE SPORTING NEWS (1998).
STATISTICAL NOTES: Led N.L. first basemen with 156 double plays in 1998. ... Hit for the cycle (June 19, 1999). ... Led N.L. first baseman with 152 double plays in 1999.

Year Team (League)	Pos.	G	AB	R	H	2B	3B	HR	RBI	Avg.	BB	SO	SB	PO	A	E	Avg.
1995—Asheville (SAL)	1B-DH	54	201	24	51	11	1	1	15	.254	25	32	1	388	21	4	.990
1996—New Haven (East.)	1B-DH	93	319	46	106	24	2	7	51	.332	51	37	2	788	61	5	.994
—Colo. Springs (PCL)	1B-OF	21	71	13	25	4	1	2	13	.352	11	12	0	144	17	2	.988
1997—Colo. Springs (PCL)	1B-OF-DH	99	392	87	138	31	2	16	88	.352	61	68	3	622	64	9	.987
—Colorado (N.L.)	OF-1B	35	93	13	26	2	1	5	11	.280	8	11	0	84	12	0	1.000
1998—Colorado (N.L.)	1B	152	530	78	167	37	1	25	97	.315	53	54	3	1164	*146	7	.995
1999—Colorado (N.L.)	1B	159	578	114	185	39	5	35	113	.320	68	77	7	1243	103	9	.993
Major League totals (3 years)		346	1201	205	378	78	7	65	221	.315	129	142	10	2491	261	16	.994

H

PERSONAL: Born December 17, 1971, in Santa Clara, Calif. ... 6-2/200. ... Bats both, throws right. ... Full name: Bret Ryan Hemphill.
HIGH SCHOOL: Cupertino (Calif.).
COLLEGE: Cal State Fullerton.
TRANSACTIONS/CAREER NOTES: Selected by Houston Astros organization in 29th round of free-agent draft (June 4, 1990); did not sign. ... Selected by California Angels in 14th round of free-agent draft (June 2, 1994). ... Angels franchise renamed Anaheim Angels for 1997 season. ... On disabled list (June 12-29 and August 8, 1997-remainder of season; and April 2-June 4, 1998). ... On Edmonton disabled list (May 28-June 4, 1999).
STATISTICAL NOTES: Led Northwest League catchers with 534 putouts, 68 assists and 613 total chances and tied for lead in double plays with four in 1994. ... Led California League catchers with 989 total chances in 1996.

Year Team (League)	Pos.	G	AB	R	H	2B	3B	HR	RBI	Avg.	BB	SO	SB	PO	A	E	Avg.
1994— Boise (N.W.)	C-1B	71	252	44	74	16	1	3	36	.294	40	53	1	†548	†69	11	.982
1995— Cedar Rapids (Midw.)	C	72	234	36	59	11	1	8	28	.252	21	54	0	429	69	4	.992
— Lake Elsinore (Calif.)	C	45	146	12	29	7	0	1	17	.199	18	36	2	354	47	10	.976
1996— Lake Elsinore (Calif.)	C	108	399	64	105	21	3	17	64	.263	52	93	4	*879	*92	18	.982
1997— Midland (Texas)	C-DH	78	266	46	82	15	2	10	63	.308	47	56	0	425	48	7	.985
1998— Vancouver (PCL)	C-DH	47	155	16	39	10	2	4	12	.252	12	33	0	226	15	3	.988
1999— Edmonton (PCL)	C-1B	74	246	29	77	16	1	7	31	.313	31	58	1	384	47	3	.993
— Anaheim (A.L.)	C	12	21	3	3	0	0	0	2	.143	4	4	0	36	6	2	.955
Major League totals (1 year)		12	21	3	3	0	0	0	2	.143	4	4	0	36	6	2	.955

PERSONAL: Born December 25, 1958, in Chicago. ... 5-10/190. ... Bats right, throws left. ... Full name: Rickey Henley Henderson.
HIGH SCHOOL: Technical (Oakland).
TRANSACTIONS/CAREER NOTES: Selected by Oakland Athletics organization in fourth round of free-agent draft (June 8, 1976). ... Traded by A's with P Bert Bradley and cash to New York Yankees for OF Stan Javier, P Jose Rijo, P Eric Plunk and P Tim Birtsas (December 5, 1984). ... On New York disabled list (March 30-April 22, 1985); included rehabilitation assignment to Fort Lauderdale (April 19-22). ... On disabled list (June 5-29 and July 26-September 1, 1987). ... Traded by Yankees to A's for P Greg Cadaret, P Eric Plunk and OF Luis Polonia (June 21, 1989). ... Granted free agency (November 13, 1989). ... Re-signed by A's (November 28, 1989). ... On disabled list (April 12-27, 1991; May 28-June 17 and June 30-July 16, 1992). ... Traded by A's to Toronto Blue Jays for P Steve Karsay and a player to be named later (July 31, 1993); A's acquired OF Jose Herrera to complete deal (August 6, 1993). ... Granted free agency (October 29, 1993). ... Signed by A's (December 17, 1993). ... On disabled list (May 11-27, 1994). ... Granted free agency (October 30, 1995). ... Signed by San Diego Padres (December 29, 1995). ... On San Diego disabled list (May 9-24, 1997). ... Traded by Padres to Anaheim Angels for P Ryan Hancock, P Stevenson Agosto and a player to be named later (August 13, 1997); Padres acquired 3B George Arias to complete deal (August 19, 1997). ... Granted free agency (October 27, 1997). ... Signed by A's (January 22, 1998). ... Granted free agency (October 26, 1998). ... Signed by New York Mets (December 16, 1998). ... On disabled list (May 3-22, 1999).
RECORDS: Holds major league career records for most stolen bases—1,334; most times caught stealing—311; and most home runs leading off game—75. ... Holds major league single-season records for most stolen bases—130 (1982); and most times caught stealing—42 (1982). ... Holds major league record for most seasons leading league in stolen bases—12. ... Holds A.L. career records for most stolen bases—1,231; most home runs leading off game—69; and most times caught stealing—282. ... Holds A.L. records for most years with 50 or more stolen bases—12; and most consecutive years with 50 or more stolen bases—7 (1980-86). ... Shares A.L. single-season record for fewest times caught stealing (50 or more stolen bases)—8 (1993). ... Shares A.L. record for most stolen bases in two consecutive games—7 (July 3 [4], 15 innings, and 4 [3], 1983).
HONORS: Named outfielder on THE SPORTING NEWS A.L. All-Star team (1981, 1985 and 1990). ... Named outfielder on THE SPORTING NEWS A.L. Silver Slugger team (1981, 1985 and 1990). ... Won A.L. Gold Glove as outfielder (1981). ... Won THE SPORTING NEWS Silver Shoe Award (1982). ... Won THE SPORTING NEWS Golden Shoe Award (1983). ... Named A.L. Most Valuable Player by Baseball Writers' Association of America (1990). ... Named N.L. Comeback Player of the Year by THE SPORTING NEWS (1999).
STATISTICAL NOTES: Led California League in caught stealing with 22 in 1977. ... Led Eastern League in caught stealing with 28 in 1978. ... Led Eastern League outfielders with four double plays in 1978. ... Led A.L. in caught stealing with 26 in 1980, 22 in 1981, 42 in 1982, 19 in 1983 and tied for lead with 18 in 1986. ... Led A.L. outfielders with 341 total chances in 1981. ... Tied for A.L. lead in double plays by outfielder with five in 1988. ... Led A.L. with 77 stolen bases and 126 bases on balls in 1989. ... Tied for A.L. lead with 113 runs scored in 1989. ... Led A.L. with .439 on-base percentage in 1990. ... Career major league grand slams: 3.
MISCELLANEOUS: Holds Oakland Athletics franchise all-time records for most runs (1,270) and most stolen bases (867). ... Holds New York Yankees all-time record for most stolen bases (326).

Year Team (League)	Pos.	G	AB	R	H	2B	3B	HR	RBI	Avg.	BB	SO	SB	PO	A	E	Avg.
1976— Boise (N.W.)	OF	46	140	34	47	13	2	3	23	.336	33	32	29	99	3	*12	.895
1977— Modesto (Calif.)	OF	134	481	120	166	18	4	11	69	.345	104	67	*95	278	15	*20	.936
1978— Jersey City (East.)	OF	133	455	81	141	14	4	0	34	.310	83	67	*81	305	•15	7	.979
1979— Ogden (PCL)	OF	71	259	66	80	11	8	3	26	.309	53	41	44	149	6	6	.963
— Oakland (A.L.)	OF	89	351	49	96	13	3	1	26	.274	34	39	33	215	5	6	.973
1980— Oakland (A.L.)	OF-DH	158	591	111	179	22	4	9	53	.303	117	54	*100	407	15	7	.984
1981— Oakland (A.L.)	OF	108	423	*89	*135	18	7	6	35	.319	64	68	*56	*327	7	7	.979
1982— Oakland (A.L.)	OF-DH	149	536	119	143	24	4	10	51	.267	*116	94	*130	379	2	9	.977
1983— Oakland (A.L.)	OF-DH	145	513	105	150	25	7	9	48	.292	*103	80	*108	349	9	3	.992
1984— Oakland (A.L.)	OF	142	502	113	147	27	4	16	58	.293	86	81	*66	341	7	11	.969
1985— Fort Laud. (FSL)■	OF	3	6	5	1	0	1	0	3	.167	5	2	1	6	0	0	1.000
— New York (A.L.)	OF-DH	143	547	*146	172	28	5	24	72	.314	99	65	*80	439	7	9	.980
1986— New York (A.L.)	OF-DH	153	608	*130	160	31	5	28	74	.263	89	81	*87	426	4	6	.986
1987— New York (A.L.)	OF-DH	95	358	78	104	17	3	17	37	.291	80	52	41	189	3	4	.980
1988— New York (A.L.)	OF-DH	140	554	118	169	30	2	6	50	.305	82	54	*93	320	7	12	.965
1989— New York (A.L.)	OF	65	235	41	58	13	1	3	22	.247	56	29	25	144	5	1	.993
— Oakland (A.L.)■	OF-DH	85	306	§72	90	13	2	9	35	.294	§70	29	§52	191	3	3	.985
1990— Oakland (A.L.)	OF-DH	136	489	*119	159	33	3	28	61	.325	97	60	*65	289	5	5	.983
1991— Oakland (A.L.)	OF-DH	134	470	105	126	17	1	18	57	.268	98	73	*58	249	10	8	.970
1992— Oakland (A.L.)	OF-DH	117	396	77	112	18	3	15	46	.283	95	56	48	231	9	4	.984

H

							BATTING							FIELDING		
Year Team (League)	Pos.	G	AB	R	H	2B	3B	HR	RBI	Avg.	BB	SO	SB	PO	A	E	Avg.
1993—Oakland (A.L.)	OF-DH	90	318	77	104	19	1	17	47	.327	85	46	31	182	5	5	.974
—Toronto (A.L.)■........	OF	44	163	37	35	3	1	4	12	.215	35	19	22	76	1	2	.975
1994—Oakland (A.L.)	OF-DH	87	296	66	77	13	0	6	20	.260	72	45	22	166	4	4	.977
1995—Oakland (A.L.)	OF-DH	112	407	67	122	31	1	9	54	.300	72	66	32	162	5	2	.988
1996—San Diego (N.L.)■....	OF	148	465	110	112	17	2	9	29	.241	125	90	37	228	3	6	.975
1997—San Diego (N.L.)	OF-DH	88	288	63	79	11	0	6	27	.274	71	62	29	160	4	7	.959
—Anaheim (A.L.)■.......	DH-OF	32	115	21	21	3	0	2	7	.183	26	23	16	26	0	0	1.000
1998—Oakland (A.L.)■........	OF	152	542	101	128	16	1	14	57	.236	*118	114	*66	327	3	4	.988
1999—New York (N.L.)■.......	OF-DH	121	438	89	138	30	0	12	42	.315	82	82	37	168	0	2	.988
American League totals (19 years)		2376	8720	1841	2487	414	58	251	922	.285	1694	1238	1231	5435	114	112	.980
National League totals (3 years)		357	1191	262	329	58	2	27	98	.276	278	234	103	556	7	15	.974
Major League totals (21 years)		2733	9911	2103	2816	472	60	278	1020	.284	1972	1472	1334	5991	121	127	.980

DIVISION SERIES RECORD

RECORDS: Holds N.L. career record for most stolen bases—6.

							BATTING							FIELDING		
Year Team (League)	Pos.	G	AB	R	H	2B	3B	HR	RBI	Avg.	BB	SO	SB	PO	A	E	Avg.
1981—Oakland (A.L.)	OF	3	11	3	2	0	0	0	0	.182	2	0	2	8	0	0	1.000
1996—San Diego (N.L.)	OF	3	12	2	4	0	0	1	1	.333	2	3	0	4	0	0	1.000
1999—New York (N.L.)	OF	4	15	5	6	0	0	0	1	.400	3	1	6	7	1	0	1.000
Division series totals (3 years)		10	38	10	12	0	0	1	2	.316	7	4	8	19	1	0	1.000

CHAMPIONSHIP SERIES RECORD

RECORDS: Holds career record for most stolen bases—17. ... Holds single-series record for most stolen bases—8 (1989). ... Holds single-game record for most stolen bases—4 (October 4, 1989). ... Shares single inning records for most at-bats in—2; most hits in—2; most singles in—2 (October 6, 1990, ninth inning); and most stolen bases in—2 (October 4, 1989, fourth and seventh innings). ... Shares single-series record for most runs—8 (1989). ... Shares A.L. career record for most bases on balls received—17. ... Shares A.L. single-game record for most at-bats—6 (October 5, 1993).

NOTES: Named Most Valuable Player (1989).

							BATTING							FIELDING		
Year Team (League)	Pos.	G	AB	R	H	2B	3B	HR	RBI	Avg.	BB	SO	SB	PO	A	E	Avg.
1981—Oakland (A.L.)	OF	3	11	0	4	2	1	0	1	.364	1	2	2	6	0	1	.857
1989—Oakland (A.L.)	OF	5	15	8	6	1	1	2	5	.400	7	0	8	13	0	1	.929
1990—Oakland (A.L.)	OF	4	17	1	5	0	0	0	3	.294	1	2	2	10	0	0	1.000
1992—Oakland (A.L.)	OF	6	23	5	6	0	0	0	1	.261	4	4	2	15	0	3	.833
1993—Toronto (A.L.)	OF	6	25	4	3	2	0	0	0	.120	4	5	2	9	0	1	.900
1999—New York (N.L.)	OF	6	23	2	4	1	0	0	1	.174	0	5	1	7	2	1	.900
Championship series totals (6 years)		30	114	20	28	6	2	2	11	.246	17	18	17	60	2	7	.899

WORLD SERIES RECORD

RECORDS: Shares single-game record for most at-bats—6 (October 28, 1989).

NOTES: Member of World Series championship team (1989 and 1993).

							BATTING							FIELDING		
Year Team (League)	Pos.	G	AB	R	H	2B	3B	HR	RBI	Avg.	BB	SO	SB	PO	A	E	Avg.
1989—Oakland (A.L.)	OF	4	19	4	9	1	2	1	3	.474	2	2	3	9	0	0	1.000
1990—Oakland (A.L.)	OF	4	15	2	5	2	0	1	1	.333	2	3	4	12	1	0	1.000
1993—Toronto (A.L.)	OF	6	22	6	5	2	0	0	2	.227	5	2	1	8	0	0	1.000
World Series totals (3 years)		14	56	12	19	5	2	2	6	.339	10	8	7	29	1	0	1.000

ALL-STAR GAME RECORD

RECORDS: Shares single-game record for most singles—3 (July 13, 1982).

						BATTING							FIELDING		
Year League	Pos.	AB	R	H	2B	3B	HR	RBI	Avg.	BB	SO	SB	PO	A	E	Avg.
1980—American	OF	1	0	0	0	0	0	0	.000	0	1	0	0	0	0	...
1982—American	OF	4	1	3	0	0	0	0	.750	0	0	1	3	0	1	.750
1983—American	OF	1	0	0	0	0	0	1	.000	0	0	0	0	0	0	...
1984—American	OF	2	0	0	0	0	0	0	.000	0	0	0	0	0	0	...
1985—American	OF	3	1	1	0	0	0	0	.333	0	1	1	1	0	0	1.000
1986—American	OF	3	0	0	0	0	0	0	.000	0	1	0	2	0	0	1.000
1987—American	OF	3	0	1	0	0	0	0	.333	0	0	0	0	0	0	...
1988—American	OF	2	0	1	0	0	0	0	.500	1	0	0	1	0	0	1.000
1990—American	OF	3	0	0	0	0	0	0	.000	0	1	0	2	0	0	1.000
1991—American	OF	2	1	1	0	0	0	0	.500	0	0	0	0	0	0	...
All-Star Game totals (10 years)		24	3	7	0	0	0	1	.292	1	4	2	9	0	1	.900

HENLEY, BOB   C   EXPOS

PERSONAL: Born January 30, 1973, in Mobile, Ala. ... 6-2/205. ... Bats right, throws right. ... Full name: Robert Clifton Henley.

HIGH SCHOOL: Mobile County (Grand Bay, Ala.).

JUNIOR COLLEGE: Okaloosa-Walton Community College (Fla.).

TRANSACTIONS/CAREER NOTES: Selected by Montreal Expos organization in 26th round of free-agent draft (June 13, 1991). ... On disabled list (June 18-August 13, 1992). ... On disabled list (July 20-30 and July 31, 1997-remainder of season). ... On Montreal disabled list (March 30-May 5, 1998); included rehabilitation assignment to Jupiter (April 21-May 5). ... On Ottawa disabled list (May 27-June 19, 1998). ... On Monteal disabled list (March 31, 1999-entire season); included rehabilitation assignment to Gulf Coast Expos (July 3-4).

STATISTICAL NOTES: Led South Atlantic League catchers with nine double plays in 1995. ... Tied for Eastern League lead with 11 double plays by catcher in 1996.

H

Year	Team (League)	Pos.	G	AB	R	H	2B	3B	HR	RBI	Avg.	BB	SO	SB	PO	A	E	Avg.
									BATTING								FIELDING	
1992— GC Expos (GCL)........								Did not play.										
1993— Jamestown (NY-P).....		C	60	206	25	53	10	4	7	29	.257	20	60	0	143	36	4	.978
1994— Burlington (Midw.).....		C-1B	98	346	72	104	20	1	20	67	.301	49	91	1	322	64	11	.972
1995— Albany (SAL).............		C	102	335	45	94	20	1	3	46	.281	83	57	1	684	*111	•14	.983
1996— Harrisburg (East.).......		C	103	289	33	66	12	1	3	27	.228	70	78	1	565	*92	9	.986
1997— Harrisburg (East.).......		C-DH	79	280	41	85	19	0	12	49	.304	32	40	5	574	77	3	*.995
1998— Jupiter (FSL)		C-DH	13	50	10	17	3	0	2	14	.340	5	5	1	63	8	1	.986
— Ottawa (I.L.)		C-DH	37	126	13	31	6	1	4	20	.246	12	34	1	176	22	2	.990
— Montreal (N.L.)..........		C	41	115	16	35	8	1	3	18	.304	11	26	3	189	14	1	.995
1999— GC Expos (GCL)		DH-C	2	4	0	1	0	0	0	1	.250	1	1	0	3	0	1	.750
Major League totals (1 year)			41	115	16	35	8	1	3	18	.304	11	26	3	189	14	1	.995

HENRY, BUTCH   P   ROCKIES

PERSONAL: Born October 7, 1968, in El Paso, Texas. ... 6-1/205. ... Throws left, bats left. ... Full name: Floyd Bluford Henry III.
HIGH SCHOOL: Eastwood (El Paso, Texas).
TRANSACTIONS/CAREER NOTES: Selected by Cincinnati Reds organization in 15th round of free-agent draft (June 2, 1987). ... On disabled list (April 28, 1989-remainder of season). ... Traded by Reds with C Terry McGriff and P Keith Kaiser to Houston Astros (September 7, 1990), completing deal in which Astros traded 2B Bill Doran to Reds for three players to be named later (August 30, 1990). ... Selected by Colorado Rockies in second round (36th pick overall) of expansion draft (November 17, 1992). ... Traded by Rockies to Montreal Expos for P Kent Bottenfield (July 16, 1993). ... On disabled list (August 16, 1995-remainder of season). ... Claimed on waivers by Boston Red Sox (October 13, 1995). ... On disabled list (March 22, 1996-entire season). ... On Boston disabled list (May 5-June 23, 1997); included rehabilitation assignment to Sarasota (June 14-23). ... On Boston disabled list (March 14-April 14 and April 21, 1998-remainder of season); included rehabilitation assignment to Sarasota (April 8-10). ... Granted free agency (October 22, 1998). ... Signed by Seattle Mariners (December 22, 1998). ... On Seattle disabled list (April 30-September 3, 1999); included rehabilitation assignment to Tacoma (August 23-September 3). ... Granted free agency (October 4, 1999). ... Signed by Rockies organization (December 12, 1999).

Year	League	W	L	Pct.	ERA	G	GS	CG	ShO	Sv.	IP	H	R	ER	BB	SO
1987— Billings (Pio.)	4	0	1.000	4.63	9	5	0	0	1	35	37	21	18	12	38
1988— Cedar Rapids (Midw.)	16	2	*.889	2.26	27	27	1	1	0	187	144	59	47	56	163
1989— Chattanooga (Sou.)	1	3	.250	3.42	7	7	0	0	0	26 1/3	22	12	10	12	19
1990— Chattanooga (Sou.)	8	8	.500	4.21	24	22	2	0	0	143 1/3	151	74	67	58	95
1991— Tucson (PCL)■	10	11	.476	4.80	27	27	2	0	0	153 2/3	192	92	82	42	97
1992— Houston (N.L.)	6	9	.400	4.02	28	28	2	1	0	165 1/3	185	81	74	41	96
1993— Colorado (N.L.)■	2	8	.200	6.59	20	15	1	0	0	84 2/3	117	66	62	24	39
— Montreal (N.L.)■	1	1	.500	3.93	10	1	0	0	0	18 1/3	18	10	8	4	8
— Ottawa (I.L.)	3	1	.750	3.73	5	5	1	0	0	31 1/3	34	15	13	1	25
1994— Ottawa (I.L.)	2	0	1.000	0.00	2	2	1	1	0	14	11	0	0	2	11
— Montreal (N.L.)	8	3	.727	2.43	24	15	0	0	1	107 1/3	97	30	29	20	70
1995— Montreal (N.L.)	7	9	.438	2.84	21	21	1	1	0	126 2/3	133	47	40	28	60
1996— Boston (A.L.)■					Did not play.											
1997— Boston (A.L.)	7	3	.700	3.52	36	5	0	0	6	84 1/3	89	36	33	19	51
— Sarasota (FSL)	0	1	.000	5.40	2	2	0	0	0	8 1/3	8	5	5	0	7
1998— Sarasota (FSL)	0	1	.000	1.35	1	1	0	0	0	6 2/3	4	2	1	0	5
— Boston (A.L.)	0	0	...	4.00	2	2	0	0	0	9	8	4	4	3	6
1999— Seattle (A.L.)■	2	0	1.000	5.04	7	0	0	0	0	25	30	15	14	10	15
— Tacoma (PCL)	2	0	1.000	0.00	4	0	0	0	0	5	4	0	0	1	3
A.L. totals (3 years)	9	3	.750	3.88	45	11	0	0	6	118 1/3	127	55	51	32	72
N.L. totals (4 years)	24	30	.444	3.81	103	80	4	2	1	502 2/3	550	234	213	117	273
Major League totals (7 years)	33	33	.500	3.83	148	91	4	2	7	621	677	289	264	149	345

HENRY, DOUG   P   ASTROS

PERSONAL: Born December 10, 1963, in Sacramento. ... 6-4/205. ... Throws right, bats right. ... Full name: Richard Douglas Henry.
HIGH SCHOOL: Tennyson (Hayward, Calif.).
COLLEGE: Arizona State.
TRANSACTIONS/CAREER NOTES: Selected by New York Mets organization in 16th round of free-agent draft (June 7, 1982); did not sign. ... Selected by Milwaukee Brewers organization in eighth round of free-agent draft (June 3, 1985). ... On El Paso disabled list (April 5-June 5 and June 18-August 9, 1989). ... On Milwaukee disabled list (March 25-April 26, 1994); included rehabilitation assignments to El Paso (April 8-22) and New Orleans (April 22-26). ... Traded by Brewers to New York Mets for two players to be named later (November 30, 1994); Brewers acquired C Javier Gonzales (December 6, 1994) and IF Fernando Vina (December 22, 1994) to complete deal. ... Released by Mets (November 25, 1996). ... Signed by San Francisco Giants (January 9, 1997). ... Granted free agency (October 27, 1997). ... Signed by Houston Astros (November 26, 1997). ... On Houston disabled list (May 10-July 15, 1999); included rehabilitation assignments to New Orleans (July 4-12) and Jackson (July 13-15). ... Granted free agency (November 1, 1999). ... Re-signed by Astros (December 3, 1999).
STATISTICAL NOTES: Combined with Michael Ignasiak in 6-3 no-hit victory for Stockton against San Jose (April 15, 1990, first game).

Year	League	W	L	Pct.	ERA	G	GS	CG	ShO	Sv.	IP	H	R	ER	BB	SO
1986— Beloit (Midw.)...................	7	8	.467	4.65	27	24	4	1	1	143 1/3	153	95	74	56	115
1987— Beloit (Midw.)...................	8	9	.471	4.88	31	15	1	0	2	132 2/3	145	83	72	51	106
1988— Stockton (Calif.)...............	7	1	.875	1.78	23	1	1	0	7	70 2/3	46	19	14	31	71
— El Paso (Texas)...............	4	0	1.000	3.15	14	3	3	0	0	45 2/3	33	16	16	19	50
1989— Stockton (Calif.)...............	0	1	.000	0.00	4	3	0	0	0	11	9	4	0	3	9
— El Paso (Texas)...............	0	0	...	13.50	1	1	0	0	0	2	3	3	3	2	2
1990— Stockton (Calif.)...............	1	0	1.000	1.13	4	0	0	0	1	8	4	1	1	3	13
— El Paso (Texas)...............	1	0	1.000	2.93	15	0	0	0	9	30 2/3	31	13	10	11	25
— Denver (A.A.)...................	2	3	.400	4.44	27	0	0	0	8	50 2/3	46	26	25	27	54
1991— Denver (A.A.)...................	3	2	.600	2.18	32	0	0	0	14	57 2/3	47	16	14	20	47
— Milwaukee (A.L.)..............	2	1	.667	1.00	32	0	0	0	15	36	16	4	4	14	28
1992— Milwaukee (A.L.)..............	1	4	.200	4.02	68	0	0	0	29	65	64	34	29	24	52
1993— Milwaukee (A.L.)..............	4	4	.500	5.56	54	0	0	0	17	55	67	37	34	25	38
1994— Milwaukee (A.L.)..............	1	0	1.000	5.40	6	0	0	0	3	8 1/3	7	5	5	2	10
— New Orleans (A.A.)..........	1	0	1.000	1.84	10	0	0	0	3	14 2/3	5	3	3	10	10
— Milwaukee (A.L.)..............	2	3	.400	4.60	25	0	0	0	0	31 1/3	32	17	16	23	20

H

– 248 –

Year League	W	L	Pct.	ERA	G	GS	CG	ShO	Sv.	IP	H	R	ER	BB	SO
1995—New York (N.L.)■	3	6	.333	2.96	51	0	0	0	4	67	48	23	22	25	62
1996—New York (N.L.)	2	8	.200	4.68	58	0	0	0	9	75	82	48	39	36	58
1997—San Francisco (N.L.)■	4	5	.444	4.71	75	0	0	0	3	70 2/3	70	45	37	41	69
1998—Houston (N.L.)■	8	2	.800	3.04	59	0	0	0	2	71	55	25	24	35	59
1999—Houston (N.L.)	2	3	.400	4.65	35	0	0	0	2	40 2/3	45	24	21	24	36
—New Orleans (PCL)	0	0	...	4.50	3	3	0	0	0	4	4	2	2	3	3
—Jackson (Texas)	0	1	.000	4.50	2	1	0	0	0	2	2	1	1	1	3
A.L. totals (4 years)	9	12	.429	3.99	179	0	0	0	61	187 1/3	179	92	83	86	138
N.L. totals (5 years)	19	24	.442	3.97	278	0	0	0	20	324 1/3	300	165	143	161	284
Major League totals (9 years)	28	36	.438	3.98	457	0	0	0	81	511 2/3	479	257	226	247	422

DIVISION SERIES RECORD

Year League	W	L	Pct.	ERA	G	GS	CG	ShO	Sv.	IP	H	R	ER	BB	SO
1997—San Francisco (N.L.)	0	0	...	0.00	1	0	0	0	0	2	1	0	0	3	2
1998—Houston (N.L.)	0	0	...	5.40	2	0	0	0	0	1 2/3	2	1	1	0	1
1999—Houston (N.L.)	0	0	...	0.00	2	0	0	0	0	3 2/3	1	0	0	3	2
Division series totals (3 years)	0	0	...	1.23	5	0	0	0	0	7 1/3	4	1	1	6	5

HENTGEN, PAT   P   CARDINALS

PERSONAL: Born November 13, 1968, in Detroit. ... 6-2/195. ... Throws right, bats right. ... Full name: Patrick George Hentgen. ... Name pronounced HENT-ghen.

HIGH SCHOOL: Fraser (Mich.).

TRANSACTIONS/CAREER NOTES: Selected by Toronto Blue Jays organization in fifth round of free-agent draft (June 2, 1986). ... On Toronto disabled list (August 13-September 29, 1992); included rehabilitation assignment to Syracuse (September 1-8). ... Traded by Blue Jays with P Paul Spoljaric to St. Louis Cardinals for P Lance Painter, C Alberto Castillo and P Matt DeWitt (November 11, 1999).

HONORS: Named A.L. Pitcher of the Year by THE SPORTING NEWS (1996). ... Named righthanded pitcher on THE SPORTING NEWS A.L. All-Star team (1996). ... Named A.L. Cy Young Award winner by Baseball Writers' Association of America (1996).

STATISTICAL NOTES: Combined with relievers Willie Blair and Enrique Burgos in 2-1 no-hit victory against Osceola (May 10, 1988).

Year League	W	L	Pct.	ERA	G	GS	CG	ShO	Sv.	IP	H	R	ER	BB	SO
1986—St. Catharines (NY-P)	0	4	.000	4.50	13	11	0	0	1	40	38	27	20	30	30
1987—Myrtle Beach (SAL)	11	5	.688	2.35	32	*31	2	2	0	*188	145	62	49	60	131
1988—Dunedin (FSL)	3	12	.200	3.45	31	*30	0	0	0	151 1/3	139	80	58	65	125
1989—Dunedin (FSL)	9	8	.529	2.68	29	28	0	0	0	151 1/3	123	53	45	71	148
1990—Knoxville (Sou.)	9	5	.643	3.05	28	26	0	0	0	153 1/3	121	57	52	68	142
1991—Syracuse (I.L.)	8	9	.471	4.47	31	•28	1	0	0	171	146	91	85	*90	*155
—Toronto (A.L.)	0	0	...	2.45	3	1	0	0	0	7 1/3	5	2	2	3	3
1992—Toronto (A.L.)	5	2	.714	5.36	28	2	0	0	0	50 1/3	49	30	30	32	39
—Syracuse (I.L.)	1	2	.333	2.66	4	4	0	0	0	20 1/3	15	6	6	8	17
1993—Toronto (A.L.)	19	9	.679	3.87	34	32	3	0	0	216 1/3	215	103	93	74	122
1994—Toronto (A.L.)	13	8	.619	3.40	24	24	6	3	0	174 2/3	158	74	66	59	147
1995—Toronto (A.L.)	10	14	.417	5.11	30	30	2	0	0	200 2/3	*236	*129	*114	90	135
1996—Toronto (A.L.)	20	10	.667	3.22	35	35	*10	•3	0	*265 2/3	238	105	95	94	177
1997—Toronto (A.L.)	15	10	.600	3.68	35	•35	•9	•3	0	•264	253	116	108	71	160
1998—Toronto (A.L.)	12	11	.522	5.17	29	29	0	0	0	177 2/3	208	109	102	69	94
1999—Toronto (A.L.)	11	12	.478	4.79	34	34	1	0	0	199	225	115	106	65	118
Major League totals (9 years)	105	76	.580	4.14	252	222	31	9	0	1555 2/3	1587	783	716	557	995

CHAMPIONSHIP SERIES RECORD

Year League	W	L	Pct.	ERA	G	GS	CG	ShO	Sv.	IP	H	R	ER	BB	SO
1993—Toronto (A.L.)	0	1	.000	18.00	1	1	0	0	0	3	9	6	6	2	3

WORLD SERIES RECORD

NOTES: Member of World Series championship team (1993).

Year League	W	L	Pct.	ERA	G	GS	CG	ShO	Sv.	IP	H	R	ER	BB	SO
1993—Toronto (A.L.)	1	0	1.000	1.50	1	1	0	0	0	6	5	1	1	3	6

ALL-STAR GAME RECORD

Year League	W	L	Pct.	ERA	GS	CG	ShO	Sv.	IP	H	R	ER	BB	SO
1993—American						Did not play.								
1994—American	0	0	...	0.00	0	0	0	0	1	1	0	0	0	0
1997—American	0	0	...	0.00	0	0	0	0	1	0	0	0	0	0
All-Star Game totals (2 years)	0	0	...	0.00	0	0	0	0	2	1	0	0	0	0

HEREDIA, FELIX   P   CUBS

PERSONAL: Born June 18, 1976, in Barahona, Dominican Republic. ... 6-0/180. ... Throws left, bats left.

HIGH SCHOOL: Escuela Dominical (Barahona, Dominican Republic).

TRANSACTIONS/CAREER NOTES: Signed as non-drafted free agent by Florida Marlins organization (November 22, 1992). ... Traded by Marlins with P Steve Hoff to Chicago Cubs for 3B Kevin Orie, P Todd Noel and P Justin Speier (July 31, 1998).

Year League	W	L	Pct.	ERA	G	GS	CG	ShO	Sv.	IP	H	R	ER	BB	SO
1993—Gulf Coast Marlins (GCL)	5	1	.833	2.47	12	•12	0	0	0	62	50	18	17	11	53
1994—Kane County (Midw.)	4	5	.444	5.69	24	8	1	0	3	68	86	55	43	14	65
1995—Brevard County (FSL)	6	4	.600	3.57	34	8	0	0	1	95 2/3	101	52	38	36	76
1996—Portland (East.)	8	1	.889	1.50	55	0	0	0	5	60	48	11	10	15	42
—Florida (N.L.)	1	1	.500	4.32	21	0	0	0	0	16 2/3	21	8	8	10	10
1997—Florida (N.L.)	5	3	.625	4.29	56	0	0	0	0	56 2/3	53	30	27	30	54
1998—Florida (N.L.)	0	3	.000	5.49	41	2	0	0	2	41	38	30	25	32	38
—Chicago (N.L.)■	3	0	1.000	4.08	30	0	0	0	0	17 2/3	19	9	8	6	16
1999—Chicago (N.L.)	3	1	.750	4.85	69	0	0	0	1	52	56	35	28	25	50
Major League totals (4 years)	12	8	.600	4.70	217	2	0	0	3	184	187	112	96	103	168

H

DIVISION SERIES RECORD

Year	League	W	L	Pct.	ERA	G	GS	CG	ShO	Sv.	IP	H	R	ER	BB	SO
1997—	Florida (N.L.)							Did not play.								
1998—	Chicago (N.L.)	0	0	...	54.00	1	0	0	0	0	$^1/_3$	0	2	2	2	0

CHAMPIONSHIP SERIES RECORD

Year	League	W	L	Pct.	ERA	G	GS	CG	ShO	Sv.	IP	H	R	ER	BB	SO
1997—	Florida (N.L.)	0	0	...	5.40	2	0	0	0	0	$3^1/_3$	3	2	2	2	4

WORLD SERIES RECORD

NOTES: Member of World Series championship team (1997).

Year	League	W	L	Pct.	ERA	G	GS	CG	ShO	Sv.	IP	H	R	ER	BB	SO
1997—	Florida (N.L.)	0	0	...	0.00	4	0	0	0	0	$5^1/_3$	2	0	0	1	5

HEREDIA, GIL   P   ATHLETICS

PERSONAL: Born October 26, 1965, in Nogales, Ariz. ... 6-1/221. ... Throws right, bats right. ... Full name: Gilbert Heredia. ... Name pronounced err-AY-dee-uh.
HIGH SCHOOL: Nogales (Ariz.).
JUNIOR COLLEGE: Pima Community College (Ariz.).
COLLEGE: Arizona.
TRANSACTIONS/CAREER NOTES: Selected by Pittsburgh Pirates organization in first round (16th pick overall) of free-agent draft (January 17, 1984); did not sign. ... Selected by Baltimore Orioles organization in sixth round of free-agent draft (January 9, 1985); did not sign. ... Selected by San Francisco Giants organization in ninth round of free-agent draft (June 2, 1987). ... Loaned by Giants organization to San Luis Potosi of Mexican League (1989). ... Claimed on waivers by Montreal Expos (August 18, 1992). ... Granted free agency (December 21, 1995). ... Signed by Texas Rangers organization (January 5, 1996). ... Released by Rangers (November 13, 1996). ... Signed by Expos organization (January 13, 1997). ... Traded by Expos organization to Chicago Cubs organization for 2B Saul Bustos and OF David Jefferson (June 23, 1997). ... Granted free agency (October 15, 1997). ... Signed by Oakland Athletics organization (December 16, 1997).

Year	League	W	L	Pct.	ERA	G	GS	CG	ShO	Sv.	IP	H	R	ER	BB	SO
1987—	Everett (N.W.)	2	0	1.000	3.60	3	3	1	0	0	20	24	8	8	1	14
—	Fresno (Calif.)	5	3	.625	2.90	11	11	5	2	0	$80^2/_3$	62	28	26	23	60
1988—	San Jose (Calif.)	13	12	.520	3.49	27	27	9	0	0	*$206^1/_3$	•216	107	80	46	121
1989—	Shreveport (Texas)	1	0	1.000	2.55	7	2	1	0	0	$24^2/_3$	28	10	7	4	8
—	San Luis Potosi (Mex.)■...	14	9	.609	2.99	24	24	15	3	0	$180^2/_3$	183	73	60	35	125
1990—	Phoenix (PCL)■	9	7	.563	4.10	29	19	0	0	1	147	159	81	67	37	75
1991—	Phoenix (PCL)	9	11	.450	*2.82	33	15	•5	1	1	$140^1/_3$	155	60	44	28	75
—	San Francisco (N.L.)	0	2	.000	3.82	7	4	0	0	0	33	27	14	14	7	13
1992—	Phoenix (PCL)	5	5	.500	2.01	22	7	1	1	1	$80^2/_3$	83	30	18	13	37
—	San Francisco (N.L.)	2	3	.400	5.40	13	4	0	0	0	30	32	20	18	16	15
—	Indianapolis (A.A.)■	2	0	1.000	1.02	3	3	0	0	0	$17^2/_3$	18	2	2	3	10
—	Montreal (N.L.)	0	0	...	1.84	7	1	0	0	0	$14^2/_3$	12	3	3	4	7
1993—	Ottawa (I.L.)	8	4	.667	2.98	16	16	1	0	0	$102^2/_3$	97	46	34	26	66
—	Montreal (N.L.)	4	2	.667	3.92	20	9	1	0	2	$57^1/_3$	66	28	25	14	40
1994—	Montreal (N.L.)	6	3	.667	3.46	39	3	0	0	0	$75^1/_3$	85	34	29	13	62
1995—	Montreal (N.L.)	5	6	.455	4.31	40	18	0	0	1	119	137	60	57	21	74
1996—	Texas (A.L.)■	2	5	.286	5.89	44	0	0	0	0	$73^1/_3$	91	50	48	14	43
—	Oklahoma City (A.A.)	0	0	...	1.86	6	0	0	0	0	$9^2/_3$	11	3	2	0	4
1997—	Ottawa (I.L.)■	0	4	.000	4.70	28	0	0	0	0	44	50	29	23	9	41
—	Iowa (A.A.)■	4	2	.667	3.86	31	1	0	0	1	$46^2/_3$	54	22	20	9	30
1998—	Edmonton (PCL)■	10	8	.556	3.67	29	19	6	1	1	$144^2/_3$	154	69	59	18	99
—	Oakland (A.L.)	3	3	.500	2.74	8	6	0	0	0	$42^2/_3$	43	14	13	3	27
1999—	Oakland (A.L.)	13	8	.619	4.81	33	33	1	0	0	$200^1/_3$	228	119	107	34	117
A.L. totals (3 years)		18	16	.529	4.78	85	39	1	0	1	$316^1/_3$	362	183	168	51	187
N.L. totals (5 years)		17	16	.515	3.99	126	39	1	0	3	$329^1/_3$	359	159	146	75	211
Major League totals (8 years)		35	32	.522	4.38	211	78	2	0	4	$645^2/_3$	721	342	314	126	398

HERGES, MATT   P   DODGERS

PERSONAL: Born April 1, 1970, in Champaign, Ill. ... 6-0/200. ... Throws right, bats left. ... Full name: Matthew Tyler Herges.
HIGH SCHOOL: Centennial (Champaign, Ill.).
COLLEGE: Illinois State.
TRANSACTIONS/CAREER NOTES: Signed as non-drafted free agent by Los Angeles Dodgers organization (June 13, 1992). ... Granted free agency (October 15, 1998). ... Re-signed by Dodgers organization (January 6, 1999).

Year	League	W	L	Pct.	ERA	G	GS	CG	ShO	Sv.	IP	H	R	ER	BB	SO
1992—	Yakima (N.W.)	2	3	.400	3.22	27	0	0	0	9	$44^2/_3$	33	21	16	24	57
1993—	Bakersfield (Calif.)	2	6	.250	3.69	51	0	0	0	2	$90^1/_3$	70	49	37	56	84
1994—	Vero Beach (FSL)	8	9	.471	3.32	48	3	1	0	3	111	115	45	41	33	61
1995—	San Antonio (Texas)	0	3	.000	4.88	19	0	0	0	8	$27^2/_3$	34	16	15	16	18
—	San Bernardino (Calif.)	5	2	.714	3.66	22	2	0	0	1	$51^2/_3$	58	29	21	15	35
1996—	San Antonio (Texas)	3	2	.600	2.71	30	6	0	0	3	83	83	38	25	28	45
—	Albuquerque (PCL)	4	1	.800	2.60	10	4	2	1	0	$34^2/_3$	33	11	10	14	15
1997—	Albuquerque (PCL)	0	8	.000	8.89	31	12	0	0	0	85	120	92	84	46	61
—	San Antonio (Texas)	0	1	.000	8.80	4	3	0	0	0	$15^1/_3$	22	15	15	10	12
1998—	Albuquerque (PCL)	3	5	.375	5.71	34	8	0	0	0	$88^1/_3$	115	64	56	37	75
—	San Antonio (Texas)	0	0	...	0.00	3	0	0	0	0	6	3	0	0	2	3
1999—	Albuquerque (PCL)	8	3	.727	4.73	21	21	2	0	0	$131^1/_3$	135	82	69	47	88
—	Los Angeles (N.L.)	0	2	.000	4.07	17	0	0	0	0	$24^1/_3$	24	13	11	8	18
Major League totals (1 year)		0	2	.000	4.07	17	0	0	0	0	$24^1/_3$	24	13	11	8	18

– 250 –

HERMANSEN, CHAD — OF/IF — PIRATES

PERSONAL: Born September 10, 1977, in Salt Lake City. ... 6-2/185. ... Bats right, throws right. ... Full name: Chad B. Hermansen.
HIGH SCHOOL: Green Valley (Henderson, Nev.).
TRANSACTIONS/CAREER NOTES: Selected by Pittsburgh Pirates organization in first round (10th pick overall) of free-agent draft (June 1, 1995).
STATISTICAL NOTES: Tied for Southern League lead in errors by outfielder with eight in 1997.

Year	Team (League)	Pos.	G	AB	R	H	2B	3B	HR	RBI	Avg.	BB	SO	SB	PO	A	E	Avg.
1995—	GC Pirates (GCL)	SS	24	92	14	28	10	1	3	17	.304	9	19	0	20	56	10	.884
—	Erie (NY-P)	SS	44	165	30	45	8	3	6	25	.273	18	39	4	52	104	30	.839
1996—	Augusta (SAL)	SS-DH	62	226	41	57	11	3	14	41	.252	38	65	11	71	135	25	.892
—	Lynchburg (Caro.)	SS-DH	66	251	40	69	11	3	10	46	.275	29	56	5	75	168	28	.897
1997—	Carolina (Sou.)	O-S-2-DH	129	487	87	134	31	4	20	70	.275	69	*136	18	194	125	‡39	.891
1998—	Nashville (PCL)	OF-2B	126	458	81	118	26	5	28	78	.258	50	152	21	208	21	14	.942
1999—	Nashville (PCL)	OF-DH	125	496	89	134	27	3	32	97	.270	35	119	19	258	9	3	.989
—	Pittsburgh (N.L.)	OF	19	60	5	14	3	0	1	1	.233	7	19	2	29	0	0	1.000
Major League totals (1 year)			19	60	5	14	3	0	1	1	.233	7	19	2	29	0	0	1.000

HERMANSON, DUSTIN — P — EXPOS

PERSONAL: Born December 21, 1972, in Springfield, Ohio. ... 6-2/200. ... Throws right, bats right. ... Full name: Dustin Michael Hermanson.
HIGH SCHOOL: Kenton Ridge (Springfield, Ohio).
COLLEGE: Kent.
TRANSACTIONS/CAREER NOTES: Selected by Pittsburgh Pirates organization in 39th round of free-agent draft (June 3, 1991); did not sign. ... Selected by San Diego Padres organization in first round (third pick overall) of free-agent draft (June 2, 1994). ... Traded by Padres to Florida Marlins for 2B Quilvio Veras (November 21, 1996). ... Traded by Marlins with OF Joe Orsulak to Montreal Expos for OF/1B Cliff Floyd (March 26, 1997). ... On disabled list (May 15-30, 1998).
STATISTICAL NOTES: Hit home run in first major league at-bat (April 16, 1997).

Year	League	W	L	Pct.	ERA	G	GS	CG	ShO	Sv.	IP	H	R	ER	BB	SO
1994—	Wichita (Texas)	1	0	1.000	0.43	16	0	0	0	8	21	13	1	1	6	30
—	Las Vegas (PCL)	0	0		6.14	7	0	0	0	3	7⅓	6	5	5	5	6
1995—	Las Vegas (PCL)	0	1	.000	3.50	31	0	0	0	11	36	35	23	14	29	42
—	San Diego (N.L.)	3	1	.750	6.82	26	0	0	0	0	31⅔	35	26	24	22	19
1996—	Las Vegas (PCL)	1	4	.200	3.13	42	0	0	0	21	46	41	20	16	27	54
—	San Diego (N.L.)	1	0	1.000	8.56	8	0	0	0	0	13⅔	18	15	13	4	11
1997—	Montreal (N.L.)■	8	8	.500	3.69	32	28	1	1	0	158⅓	134	68	65	66	136
1998—	Montreal (N.L.)	14	11	.560	3.13	32	30	1	0	0	187	163	80	65	56	154
1999—	Montreal (N.L.)	9	14	.391	4.20	34	34	0	0	0	216⅓	225	110	101	69	145
Major League totals (5 years)		35	34	.507	3.97	132	92	2	1	0	607	575	299	268	217	465

HERNANDEZ, ALEX — OF — PIRATES

PERSONAL: Born May 28, 1977, in San Juan, Puerto Rico. ... 6-4/186. ... Bats left, throws left. ... Full name: Alexander Vargas Hernandez.
TRANSACTIONS/CAREER NOTES: Selected by Pittsburgh Pirates organization in fourth round of free-agent draft (June 1, 1995).

Year	Team (League)	Pos.	G	AB	R	H	2B	3B	HR	RBI	Avg.	BB	SO	SB	PO	A	E	Avg.
1995—	GC Pirates (GCL)	OF-1B	49	186	24	50	5	3	1	17	.269	17	33	4	148	7	5	.969
1996—	Erie (NY-P)	OF-1B	61	225	38	65	13	4	4	30	.289	20	47	7	305	19	7	.979
1997—	Lynchburg (Caro.)	OF	131	520	75	151	37	4	5	68	.290	27	140	13	212	*15	9	.962
1998—	Carolina (Sou.)	OF	115	452	62	117	22	7	8	48	.259	41	81	11	217	15	11	.955
1999—	Altoona (East.)	OF-DH-1B	126	475	76	122	26	3	15	63	.257	54	110	11	249	15	5	.981

HERNANDEZ, CARLOS — C — PADRES

PERSONAL: Born May 24, 1967, in San Felix, Bolivar, Venezuela. ... 5-11/215. ... Bats right, throws right. ... Full name: Carlos Alberto Hernandez.
HIGH SCHOOL: Escula Tecnica Industrial (San Felix, Bolivar, Venezuela).
TRANSACTIONS/CAREER NOTES: Signed as non-drafted free agent by Los Angeles Dodgers organization (October 10, 1984). ... On Albuquerque disabled list (May 27-June 20, 1990). ... On disabled list (April 4-22, 1994). ... On Los Angeles disabled list (May 17-June 14, 1996); included rehabilitation assignment to Albuquerque (June 5-14). ... Granted free agency (October 15, 1996). ... Signed by San Diego Padres organization (December 2, 1996). ... On San Diego disabled list (July 13-August 15, 1997); included rehabilitation assignments to Rancho Cucamonga (August 9-10) and Las Vegas (August 11-15). ... Granted free agency (October 31, 1997). ... Re-signed by Padres (November 12, 1997). ... Granted free agency (October 23, 1998). ... Re-signed by Padres (December 2, 1998). ... On San Diego disabled list (March 29, 1999-entire season).
STATISTICAL NOTES: Tied for Gulf Coast League lead in double plays by catcher with three in 1986. ... Led Texas League catchers with 737 total chances in 1989. ... Led Pacific Coast League catchers with 684 total chances in 1991.

Year	Team (League)	Pos.	G	AB	R	H	2B	3B	HR	RBI	Avg.	BB	SO	SB	PO	A	E	Avg.
1985—	GC Dodgers (GCL)	3B-1B	22	49	3	12	1	0	0	0	.245	3	8	0	48	16	2	.970
1986—	GC Dodgers (GCL)	C-3B	57	205	19	64	7	0	1	31	.312	5	18	1	217	36	10	.962
1987—	Bakersfield (Calif.)	C	48	162	22	37	6	1	3	22	.228	14	23	8	181	26	8	.963
1988—	Bakersfield (Calif.)	C	92	333	37	103	15	2	5	52	.309	16	39	3	480	88	14	.976
—	Albuquerque (PCL)	C	3	8	0	1	0	0	0	1	.125	0	0	0	11	0	1	.917
1989—	San Antonio (Texas)	C	99	370	37	111	16	3	8	41	.300	12	46	2	*629	*90	*18	.976
—	Albuquerque (PCL)	C	4	14	1	3	0	0	0	1	.214	2	1	0	23	3	3	.897

Year Team (League)	Pos.	G	AB	R	H	2B	3B	HR	RBI	Avg.	BB	SO	SB	PO	A	E	Avg.
1990— Albuquerque (PCL).....	C	52	143	11	45	8	1	0	16	.315	8	25	2	207	31	8	.967
— Los Angeles (N.L.)	C	10	20	2	4	1	0	0	1	.200	0	2	0	37	2	0	1.000
1991— Albuquerque (PCL).....	C	95	345	60	119	24	2	8	44	.345	24	36	5	*592	*77	*15	.978
— Los Angeles (N.L.)	C-3B	15	14	1	3	1	0	0	1	.214	0	5	1	24	4	1	.966
1992— Los Angeles (N.L.)	C	69	173	11	45	4	0	3	17	.260	11	21	0	295	37	7	.979
1993— Los Angeles (N.L.)	C	50	99	6	25	5	0	2	7	.253	2	11	0	181	15	7	.966
1994— Los Angeles (N.L.)	C	32	64	6	14	2	0	2	6	.219	1	14	0	104	13	0	1.000
1995— Los Angeles (N.L.)	C	45	94	3	14	1	0	2	8	.149	7	25	0	210	25	4	.983
1996— Los Angeles (N.L.)	C	13	14	1	4	0	0	0	0	.286	2	2	0	31	1	0	1.000
— Albuquerque (PCL)....C-DH-1B-3B		66	233	19	56	11	0	5	30	.240	11	49	5	331	38	9	.976
1997— San Diego (N.L.)■	C-1B	50	134	15	42	7	1	3	14	.313	3	27	0	239	29	3	.989
— Rancho Cuca. (Calif.) .	C	1	4	0	1	0	0	0	0	.250	0	1	0	11	1	0	1.000
— Las Vegas (PCL)	C	3	10	1	4	0	0	1	5	.400	1	3	0	15	2	0	1.000
1998— San Diego (N.L.)	C-1B	129	390	34	102	15	0	9	52	.262	16	54	2	795	53	7	.992
1999— San Diego (N.L.)						Did not play.											
Major League totals (9 years)		413	1002	79	253	36	1	21	106	.252	42	161	3	1916	179	29	.986

DIVISION SERIES RECORD

Year Team (League)	Pos.	G	AB	R	H	2B	3B	HR	RBI	Avg.	BB	SO	SB	PO	A	E	Avg.
1998— San Diego (N.L.)	C	4	12	0	5	0	0	0	0	.417	0	0	0	34	6	0	1.000

CHAMPIONSHIP SERIES RECORD

Year Team (League)	Pos.	G	AB	R	H	2B	3B	HR	RBI	Avg.	BB	SO	SB	PO	A	E	Avg.
1998— San Diego (N.L.)	C	6	18	2	6	1	0	0	0	.333	1	5	0	36	4	0	1.000

WORLD SERIES RECORD

Year Team (League)	Pos.	G	AB	R	H	2B	3B	HR	RBI	Avg.	BB	SO	SB	PO	A	E	Avg.
1998— San Diego (N.L.)	C-PH	4	10	0	2	0	0	0	0	.200	0	3	0	18	1	0	1.000

HERNANDEZ, CARLOS   SS/2B   ASTROS

PERSONAL: Born December 12, 1975, in Caracas, Venezuela. ... 5-9/175. ... Bats right, throws right. ... Full name: Carlos Eduardo Hernandez.
TRANSACTIONS/CAREER NOTES: Signed as non-drafted free agent by Houston Astros organization (July 2, 1992). ... On disabled list (August 1, 1997-remainder of season).
STATISTICAL NOTES: Tied for Midwest League lead in double plays by second baseman with 79 in 1996. ... Led Pacific Coast League second basemen with .983 fielding percentage in 1998.

Year Team (League)	Pos.	G	AB	R	H	2B	3B	HR	RBI	Avg.	BB	SO	SB	PO	A	E	Avg.
1993— Dom. Astros (DSL).....	IF	67	245	52	75	13	4	1	36	.306	27	29	36	181	134	21	.938
1994— GC Astros (GCL)	2B-SS	51	192	45	62	10	1	0	23	.323	19	22	25	89	149	8	.967
1995— Quad City (Midw.)	2B-SS	126	470	74	122	19	6	4	40	.260	39	68	*58	188	349	21	.962
1996— Quad City (Midw.)	2B-SS	112	456	67	123	15	7	5	49	.270	27	71	41	238	336	19	.968
1997— Jackson (Texas)	2B	91	363	62	106	12	1	4	33	.292	33	59	17	187	269	8	.983
1998— New Orleans (PCL)......	2B-SS	134	494	64	147	23	2	1	54	.298	21	81	29	249	359	13	†.979
1999— New Orleans (PCL)......	SS-2B	94	355	56	104	14	0	0	43	.293	27	65	22	145	292	15	.967
— Houston (N.L.)	2B-SS	16	14	4	2	0	0	0	1	.143	0	0	3	7	11	1	.947
Major League totals (1 year)		16	14	4	2	0	0	0	1	.143	0	0	3	7	11	1	.947

HERNANDEZ, JOSE   IF   BREWERS

PERSONAL: Born July 14, 1969, in Vega Alta, Puerto Rico. ... 6-1/180. ... Bats right, throws right. ... Full name: Jose Antonio Hernandez.
HIGH SCHOOL: Maestro Ladi (Vega Alta, Puerto Rico).
COLLEGE: Interamerican University (Puerto Rico).
TRANSACTIONS/CAREER NOTES: Signed as non-drafted free agent by Texas Rangers organization (January 13, 1987). ... Claimed on waivers by Cleveland Indians (April 3, 1992). ... Traded by Indians to Chicago Cubs for P Heathcliff Slocumb (June 1, 1993). ... Traded by Cubs with P Terry Mulholland to Atlanta Braves for P Micah Bowie, P Ruben Quevado and a minor league player to be named later (July 31, 1999); Cubs acquired P Joey Nation to complete deal (August 24, 1999). ... Granted free agency (November 5, 1999). ... Signed by Milwaukee Brewers (December 16, 1999).
STATISTICAL NOTES: Led Gulf Coast League third basemen with .950 fielding percentage, 47 putouts and 11 double plays in 1988. ... Led Florida State League shortstops with .959 fielding percentage in 1990. ... Career major league grand slams: 1.

Year Team (League)	Pos.	G	AB	R	H	2B	3B	HR	RBI	Avg.	BB	SO	SB	PO	A	E	Avg.
1987— GC Rangers (GCL)......	SS	24	52	5	9	1	1	0	2	.173	9	25	2	30	38	5	.932
1988— GC Rangers (GCL)......	3-2-S-1-0	55	162	19	26	7	1	1	13	.160	12	36	4	†68	115	8	†.958
1989— Gastonia (SAL)..........3B-SS-2B-OF		91	215	35	47	7	6	1	16	.219	33	67	9	101	169	17	.941
1990— Charlotte (FSL)..........	SS-OF	121	388	43	99	14	7	1	44	.255	50	122	11	192	372	25	†.958
1991— Tulsa (Texas)	SS	91	301	36	72	17	4	1	20	.239	26	75	4	151	300	15	*.968
— Oklahoma City (A.A.)..	SS	14	46	6	14	1	1	1	3	.304	4	10	0	32	43	3	.962
— Texas (A.L.)	SS-3B	45	98	8	18	2	1	0	4	.184	3	31	0	49	111	4	.976
1992— Cant./Akron (East.)■..	SS	130	404	56	103	16	4	3	46	.255	37	108	7	*226	320	*40	.932
— Cleveland (A.L.).........	SS	3	4	0	0	0	0	0	0	.000	0	2	0	3	3	1	.857
1993— Cant./Akron (East.).....	SS-3B	45	150	19	30	6	0	2	17	.200	10	39	9	75	135	7	.968
— Orlando (Sou.)■	SS	71	263	42	80	8	3	8	33	.304	20	60	8	136	205	14	.961
— Iowa (A.A.)	SS	6	24	3	6	1	0	0	3	.250	0	6	0	14	26	1	.976
1994— Chicago (N.L.)...........3B-SS-2B-OF		56	132	18	32	2	3	1	9	.242	8	29	2	46	86	4	.971

H

– 252 –

Year	Team (League)	Pos.	G	AB	R	H	2B	3B	HR	RBI	Avg.	BB	SO	SB	PO	A	E	Avg.
1995—	Chicago (N.L.)	SS-2B-3B	93	245	37	60	11	4	13	40	.245	13	69	1	113	189	9	.971
1996—	Chicago (N.L.)	SS-3B-2B-OF	131	331	52	80	14	1	10	41	.242	24	97	4	148	248	20	.952
1997—	Chicago (N.L.)	3-S-2-O-D-1	121	183	33	50	8	5	7	26	.273	14	42	2	79	91	8	.955
1998—	Chicago (N.L.)	3-O-S-1-2	149	488	76	124	23	7	23	75	.254	40	140	4	193	226	13	.970
1999—	Chicago (N.L.)	SS-OF-1B	99	342	57	93	12	2	15	43	.272	40	101	7	140	249	11	.973
—Atlanta (N.L.)■		SS-1B-OF	48	166	22	42	8	0	4	19	.253	12	44	4	54	114	6	.966
American League totals (2 years)			48	102	8	18	2	1	0	4	.176	3	33	0	52	114	5	.971
National League totals (6 years)			697	1887	295	481	78	22	73	253	.255	151	522	24	773	1203	71	.965
Major League totals (8 years)			745	1989	303	499	80	23	73	257	.251	154	555	24	825	1317	76	.966

DIVISION SERIES RECORD

Year	Team (League)	Pos.	G	AB	R	H	2B	3B	HR	RBI	Avg.	BB	SO	SB	PO	A	E	Avg.
1998—	Chicago (N.L.)	SS	2	7	1	2	0	0	0	0	.286	0	2	0	5	1	2	.750
1999—	Atlanta (N.L.)	SS	4	11	1	1	0	0	0	0	.091	1	3	1	6	9	1	.938
Division series totals (2 years)			6	18	2	3	0	0	0	0	.167	1	5	1	11	10	3	.875

CHAMPIONSHIP SERIES RECORD

Year	Team (League)	Pos.	G	AB	R	H	2B	3B	HR	RBI	Avg.	BB	SO	SB	PO	A	E	Avg.
1999—	Atlanta (N.L.)	PH	2	2	0	1	0	0	0	2	.500	0	1	0	...	...	...	...

WORLD SERIES RECORD

Year	Team (League)	Pos.	G	AB	R	H	2B	3B	HR	RBI	Avg.	BB	SO	SB	PO	A	E	Avg.
1999—	Atlanta (N.L.)	PH-SS-DH	2	5	0	1	1	0	0	2	.200	0	2	1	1	0	0	1.000

HERNANDEZ, LIVAN   P   GIANTS

PERSONAL: Born February 20, 1975, in Villa Clara, Cuba. ... 6-2/225. ... Throws right, bats right. ... Full name: Eisler Hernandez. ... Half-brother of Orlando Hernandez, pitcher, New York Yankees.
TRANSACTIONS/CAREER NOTES: Signed as non-drafted free agent by Florida Marlins orgaization (January 13, 1996). ... Traded by Marlins to San Francisco Giants for P Jason Grilli and P Nathan Bump (July 24, 1999).
STATISTICAL NOTES: Led International League with four balks in 1996.
MISCELLANEOUS: Member of Cuban national baseball team (1994-95). ... Struck out once in two appearances as pinch hitter (1998). ... Struck out in only appearance as pinch hitter with Giants (1999).

Year	League	W	L	Pct.	ERA	G	GS	CG	ShO	Sv.	IP	H	R	ER	BB	SO
1996—	Charlotte (I.L.)	2	4	.333	5.14	10	10	0	0	0	49	61	32	28	34	45
—Florida (N.L.)		0	0	...	0.00	1	0	0	0	0	3	3	0	0	2	2
1997—	Portland (East.)	0	0	...	2.25	1	1	0	0	0	4	2	1	1	7	2
—Charlotte (I.L.)		5	3	.625	3.98	14	14	0	0	0	81 1/3	76	39	36	38	58
—Florida (N.L.)		9	3	.750	3.18	17	17	0	0	0	96 1/3	81	39	34	38	72
1998—	Florida (N.L.)	10	12	.455	4.72	33	33	9	0	0	234 1/3	*265	133	123	104	162
1999—	Florida (N.L.)	5	9	.357	4.76	20	20	2	0	0	136	161	78	72	55	97
—San Francisco (N.L.)■		3	3	.500	4.38	10	10	0	0	0	63 2/3	66	32	31	21	47
Major League totals (4 years)		27	27	.500	4.39	81	80	11	0	0	533 1/3	576	282	260	220	380

DIVISION SERIES RECORD

Year	League	W	L	Pct.	ERA	G	GS	CG	ShO	Sv.	IP	H	R	ER	BB	SO
1997—	Florida (N.L.)	0	0	...	2.25	1	0	0	0	0	4	3	1	1	0	3

CHAMPIONSHIP SERIES RECORD

NOTES: Named N.L. Championship Series Most Valuable Player (1997).

Year	League	W	L	Pct.	ERA	G	GS	CG	ShO	Sv.	IP	H	R	ER	BB	SO
1997—	Florida (N.L.)	2	0	1.000	0.84	2	1	1	0	0	10 2/3	5	1	1	2	16

WORLD SERIES RECORD

NOTES: Named Most Valuable Player (1997). ... Member of World Series championship team (1997).

Year	League	W	L	Pct.	ERA	G	GS	CG	ShO	Sv.	IP	H	R	ER	BB	SO
1997—	Florida (N.L.)	2	0	1.000	5.27	2	2	0	0	0	13 2/3	15	9	8	10	7

HERNANDEZ, ORLANDO   P   YANKEES

PERSONAL: Born October 11, 1965, in Villa Clara, Cuba. ... 6-2/190. ... Throws right, bats right. ... Full name: Orlando P. Hernandez. ... Nickname: El Duque. ... Half-brother of Livan Hernandez, pitcher, San Francisco Giants.
TRANSACTIONS/CAREER NOTES: Signed as non-drafted free agent by New York Yankees (March 23, 1998).

Year	League	W	L	Pct.	ERA	G	GS	CG	ShO	Sv.	IP	H	R	ER	BB	SO
1998—	Tampa (FSL)	1	1	.500	1.00	2	2	0	0	0	9	3	2	1	3	15
—Columbus (I.L.)		6	0	1.000	3.83	7	7	0	0	0	42 1/3	41	19	18	17	59
—New York (A.L.)		12	4	.750	3.13	21	21	3	1	0	141	113	53	49	52	131
1999—	New York (A.L.)	17	9	.654	4.12	33	33	2	1	0	214 1/3	187	108	98	87	157
Major League totals (2 years)		29	13	.690	3.72	54	54	5	2	0	355 1/3	300	161	147	139	288

DIVISION SERIES RECORD

Year	League	W	L	Pct.	ERA	G	GS	CG	ShO	Sv.	IP	H	R	ER	BB	SO
1998—	New York (A.L.)							Did not play.								
1999—	New York (A.L.)	1	0	1.000	0.00	1	1	0	0	0	8	2	0	0	6	4

H

CHAMPIONSHIP SERIES RECORD

NOTES: Named A.L. Championship Series Most Valuable Player (1999).

Year League	W	L	Pct.	ERA	G	GS	CG	ShO	Sv.	IP	H	R	ER	BB	SO
1998— New York (A.L.)	1	0	1.000	0.00	1	1	0	0	0	7	3	0	0	2	6
1999— New York (A.L.)	1	0	1.000	1.80	2	2	0	0	0	15	12	4	3	6	13
Champ. series totals (2 years)	2	0	1.000	1.23	3	3	0	0	0	22	15	4	3	8	19

WORLD SERIES RECORD

NOTES: Member of World Series championship team (1998 and 1999).

Year League	W	L	Pct.	ERA	G	GS	CG	ShO	Sv.	IP	H	R	ER	BB	SO
1998— New York (A.L.)	1	0	1.000	1.29	1	1	0	0	0	7	6	1	1	3	7
1999— New York (A.L.)	1	0	1.000	1.29	1	1	0	0	0	7	1	1	1	2	10
World Series totals (2 years)	2	0	1.000	1.29	2	2	0	0	0	14	7	2	2	5	17

HERNANDEZ, RAMON   C   ATHLETICS

PERSONAL: Born May 20, 1976, in Caracas, Venezuela. ... 6-0/227. ... Bats right, throws right. ... Full name: Ramon Jose Marin Hernandez.
TRANSACTIONS/CAREER NOTES: Signed as non-drafted free agent by Oakland Athletics organization (February 18, 1994). ... On Oakland disabled list (July 26-August 27, 1999); included rehabilitation assignment to Vancouver (August 13-27).
HONORS: Named Arizona League Most Valuable Player (1995).
STATISTICAL NOTES: Led Arizona League catchers with a .982 fielding percentage in 1995. ... Led Midwest League catchers with 877 putouts and 981 totals chances and tied for lead with 20 errors in 1996. ... Led California League with .427 on-base percentage in 1997. ... Led California League catchers with 16 errors in 1997. ... Led Southern League in being hit by pitch with 19 in 1998.

								BATTING								FIELDING		
Year Team (League)	Pos.	G	AB	R	H	2B	3B	HR	RBI	Avg.	BB	SO	SB	PO	A	E	Avg.
1994— Dom. Athletics (DSL)	C	42	134	24	33	2	0	2	18	.246	18	10	1	182	28	2	.991
1995— Ariz. Athletics (Ariz.)	C-1B-3B	48	143	37	52	9	6	4	37	.364	39	16	6	358	61	12	†.972
1996— W. Mich. (Mid.)	C-DH-1B	123	447	62	114	26	2	12	68	.255	69	62	2	†917	85	‡20	.980
1997— Visalia (Calif.)	C-DH-1B	86	332	57	120	21	2	15	85	*.361	35	47	2	577	80	†16	.976
— Huntsville (Sou.)	C-DH-1B-3B	44	161	27	31	3	0	4	24	.193	18	23	0	274	27	1	.997
1998— Huntsville (Sou.)	DH-C-1B	127	479	83	142	24	1	15	98	.296	57	61	4	524	42	11	.981
1999— Vancouver (PCL)	C-DH-3B-1B	77	291	38	76	11	3	13	55	.261	23	37	1	339	40	5	.987
— Oakland (A.L.)	C	40	136	13	38	7	0	3	21	.279	18	11	1	274	19	6	.980
Major League totals (1 year)		40	136	13	38	7	0	3	21	.279	18	11	1	274	19	6	.980

HERNANDEZ, ROBERTO   P   DEVIL RAYS

PERSONAL: Born November 11, 1964, in Santurce, Puerto Rico. ... 6-4/235. ... Throws right, bats right. ... Full name: Roberto Manuel Hernandez.
HIGH SCHOOL: New Hampton (N.H.) Prep.
COLLEGE: South Carolina-Aiken.
TRANSACTIONS/CAREER NOTES: Selected by California Angels organization in first round (16th pick overall) of free-agent draft (June 2, 1986); pick received as compensation for Baltimore Orioles signing Type A free-agent OF/IF Juan Beniquez. ... On disabled list (May 6-21 and June 4-August 14, 1987). ... Traded by Angels with OF Mark Doran to Chicago White Sox organization for OF Mark Davis (August 2, 1989). ... On Vancouver disabled list (May 17-August 10, 1991). ... Traded by White Sox with P Wilson Alvarez and P Danny Darwin to San Francisco Giants for SS Mike Caruso, OF Brian Manning, P Lorenzo Barcelo, P Keith Foulke, P Bobby Howry and P Ken Vining (July 31, 1997). ... Granted free agency (October 30, 1997). ... Signed by Tampa Bay Devil Rays (November 18, 1997).
MISCELLANEOUS: Holds Tampa Bay Devil Rays all-time record for most games pitched (139) and saves (69).

Year League	W	L	Pct.	ERA	G	GS	CG	ShO	Sv.	IP	H	R	ER	BB	SO
1986— Salem (N.W.)	2	2	.500	4.58	10	10	0	0	0	55	57	37	28	42	38
1987— Quad City (Midw.)	2	3	.400	6.86	7	6	0	0	1	21	24	21	16	12	21
1988— Quad City (Midw.)	9	10	.474	3.17	24	24	6	1	0	164²/₃	157	70	58	48	114
— Midland (Texas)	0	2	.000	6.57	3	3	0	0	0	12¹/₃	16	13	9	8	7
1989— Midland (Texas)	2	7	.222	6.89	12	12	0	0	0	64	94	57	49	30	42
— Palm Springs (Calif.)	1	4	.200	4.64	7	7	0	0	0	42²/₃	49	27	22	16	33
— South Bend (Midw.)■	1	1	.500	3.33	4	4	0	0	0	24¹/₃	19	9	9	7	17
1990— Birmingham (Sou.)	8	5	.615	3.67	17	17	1	0	0	108	103	57	44	43	62
— Vancouver (PCL)	3	5	.375	2.84	11	11	3	1	0	79¹/₃	73	33	25	26	49
1991— Birmingham (Sou.)	2	1	.667	1.99	4	4	0	0	0	22²/₃	11	5	5	6	21
— Vancouver (PCL)	4	1	.800	3.22	7	7	0	0	0	44²/₃	41	17	16	23	40
— GC White Sox (GCL)	0	0	...	0.00	1	1	0	0	0	6	2	0	0	0	7
— Chicago (A.L.)	1	0	1.000	7.80	9	3	0	0	0	15	18	15	13	7	6
1992— Chicago (A.L.)	7	3	.700	1.65	43	0	0	0	12	71	45	15	13	20	68
— Vancouver (PCL)	3	3	.500	2.61	9	0	0	0	2	20²/₃	13	9	6	11	23
1993— Chicago (A.L.)	3	4	.429	2.29	70	0	0	0	38	78²/₃	66	21	20	20	71
1994— Chicago (A.L.)	4	4	.500	4.91	45	0	0	0	14	47²/₃	44	29	26	19	50
1995— Chicago (A.L.)	3	7	.300	3.92	60	0	0	0	32	59²/₃	63	30	26	28	84
1996— Chicago (A.L.)	6	5	.545	1.91	72	0	0	0	38	84²/₃	65	21	18	38	85
1997— Chicago (A.L.)	5	1	.833	2.44	46	0	0	0	27	48	38	15	13	24	47
— San Francisco (N.L.)■	5	2	.714	2.48	28	0	0	0	4	32²/₃	29	9	9	14	35
1998— Tampa Bay (A.L.)■	2	6	.250	4.04	67	0	0	0	26	71¹/₃	55	33	32	41	55
1999— Tampa Bay (A.L.)	2	3	.400	3.07	72	0	0	0	43	73¹/₃	68	27	25	33	69
A.L. totals (9 years)	33	33	.500	3.05	484	3	0	0	230	549¹/₃	462	206	186	230	535
N.L. totals (1 year)	5	2	.714	2.48	28	0	0	0	4	32²/₃	29	9	9	14	35
Major League totals (9 years)	38	35	.521	3.02	512	3	0	0	234	582	491	215	195	244	570

DIVISION SERIES RECORD

Year League	W	L	Pct.	ERA	G	GS	CG	ShO	Sv.	IP	H	R	ER	BB	SO
1997— San Francisco (N.L.)	0	1	.000	20.25	3	0	0	0	0	1¹/₃	5	3	3	3	1

H

Year League	W	L	Pct.	ERA	G	GS	CG	ShO	Sv.	IP	H	R	ER	BB	SO
1993— Chicago (A.L.)	0	0	...	0.00	4	0	0	0	1	4	4	0	0	0	1

ALL-STAR GAME RECORD

Year League	W	L	Pct.	ERA	GS	CG	ShO	Sv.	IP	H	R	ER	BB	SO
1996— American	0	0	...	0.00	0	0	0	0	1	1	0	0	0	0
1999— American	0	0	...	0.00	0	0	0	0	1	0	0	0	0	0
All-Star Game totals (2 years)	0	0	...	0.00	0	0	0	0	2	1	0	0	0	0

HERSHISER, OREL   P   DODGERS

PERSONAL: Born September 16, 1958, in Buffalo. ... 6-3/195. ... Throws right, bats right. ... Full name: Orel Leonard Hershiser IV. ... Brother of Gordie Hershiser, minor league pitcher (1987-88). ... Name pronounced her-SHY-zer.
HIGH SCHOOL: Cherry Hill (N.J.) East.
COLLEGE: Bowling Green State.
TRANSACTIONS/CAREER NOTES: Selected by Los Angeles Dodgers organization in 17th round of free-agent draft (June 5, 1979). ... On disabled list (April 27, 1990-remainder of season). ... On Los Angeles disabled list (March 31-May 29, 1991); included rehabilitation assignments to Bakersfield (May 8-13 and May 18-24), Albuquerque (May 13-18) and San Antonio (May 24-29). ... Granted free agency (November 1, 1991). ... Re-signed by Dodgers (December 3, 1991). ... Granted free agency (October 17, 1994). ... Signed by Cleveland Indians (April 8, 1995). ... On disabled list (June 22-July 7, 1995 and July 29-August 13, 1997). ... Granted free agency (October 29, 1997). ... Signed by San Francisco Giants (December 9, 1997). ... Granted free agency (November 2, 1998). ... Signed by Indians organization (February 20, 1999). ... Released by Indians (March 25, 1999). ... Signed by New York Mets (March 25, 1999). ... Granted free agency (November 1, 1999). ... Signed by Dodgers (December 17, 1999).
RECORDS: Holds major league single-season record for most consecutive scoreless innings—59 (August 30, sixth inning through September 28, 10th inning, 1988). ... Shares major league single-season record for fewest games lost for leader—15 (1992). ... Shares N.L. single-season record for fewest games lost by pitcher who led league in games lost—15 (1989 and 1992). ... Shares N.L. record for most shutouts in one month—5 (September 1988).
HONORS: Named Major League Player of the Year by THE SPORTING NEWS (1988). ... Named N.L. Pitcher of the Year by THE SPORTING NEWS (1988). ... Named righthanded pitcher on THE SPORTING NEWS N.L. All-Star team (1988). ... Won N.L. Gold Glove at pitcher (1988). ... Named N.L. Cy Young Award winner by Baseball Writers' Association of America (1988). ... Named pitcher on THE SPORTING NEWS N.L. Silver Slugger team (1993).
STATISTICAL NOTES: Pitched 2-0 one-hit, complete-game victory against San Diego (April 26, 1985). ... Pitched 6-0 one-hit, complete-game victory against Pittsburgh (July 23, 1985). ... Tied for N.L. lead with 19 sacrifice hits in 1988. ... Tied for N.L. lead with 13 intentional bases on balls issued in 1993.
MISCELLANEOUS: Had sacrifice hit in only appearance as pinch hitter (1988). ... Singled once in two appearances as pinch hitter (1992). ... Started one game at third base but was replaced before first plate appearance and never played in field (1993).

Year League	W	L	Pct.	ERA	G	GS	CG	ShO	Sv.	IP	H	R	ER	BB	SO
1979— Clinton (Midw.)	4	0	1.000	2.09	15	4	1	0	2	43	33	15	10	17	33
1980— San Antonio (Texas)..........	5	9	.357	3.55	49	3	1	0	14	109	120	59	43	59	75
1981— San Antonio (Texas)..........	7	6	.538	4.68	42	4	3	0	*15	102	94	54	53	50	95
1982— Albuquerque (PCL)...........	9	6	.600	3.71	47	7	2	0	4	123²/₃	121	73	51	63	93
1983— Albuquerque (PCL)...........	10	8	.556	4.09	49	10	6	0	16	134¹/₃	132	73	61	57	95
— Los Angeles (N.L.)	0	0	...	3.38	8	0	0	0	1	8	7	6	3	6	5
1984— Los Angeles (N.L.)	11	8	.579	2.66	45	20	8	•4	2	189²/₃	160	65	56	50	150
1985— Los Angeles (N.L.)	19	3	*.864	2.03	36	34	9	5	0	239²/₃	179	72	54	68	157
1986— Los Angeles (N.L.)	14	14	.500	3.85	35	35	8	1	0	231¹/₃	213	112	99	86	153
1987— Los Angeles (N.L.)	16	16	.500	3.06	37	35	10	1	1	*264²/₃	247	105	90	74	190
1988— Los Angeles (N.L.)	•23	8	.742	2.26	35	34	•15	*8	1	*267	208	73	67	73	178
1989— Los Angeles (N.L.)	15	•15	.500	2.31	35	33	8	4	0	*256²/₃	226	75	66	77	178
1990— Los Angeles (N.L.)	1	1	.500	4.26	4	4	0	0	0	25¹/₃	26	12	12	4	16
1991— Bakersfield (Calif.)	2	0	1.000	0.82	2	2	0	0	0	11	5	2	1	1	6
— Albuquerque (PCL)............	0	0	...	0.00	1	1	0	0	0	5	5	0	0	0	5
— San Antonio (Texas)	0	1	.000	2.57	1	1	0	0	0	7	11	3	2	1	5
— Los Angeles (N.L.)	7	2	.778	3.46	21	21	0	0	0	112	112	43	43	32	73
1992— Los Angeles (N.L.)	10	•15	.400	3.67	33	33	1	0	0	210²/₃	209	101	86	69	130
1993— Los Angeles (N.L.)	12	14	.462	3.59	33	33	5	1	0	215²/₃	201	106	86	72	141
1994— Los Angeles (N.L.)	6	6	.500	3.79	21	21	1	0	0	135¹/₃	146	67	57	42	72
1995— Cleveland (A.L.)■.............	16	6	.727	3.87	26	26	1	1	0	167¹/₃	151	76	72	51	111
1996— Cleveland (A.L.).................	15	9	.625	4.24	33	33	1	0	0	206	238	115	97	58	125
1997— Cleveland (A.L.).................	14	6	.700	4.47	32	32	1	0	0	195¹/₃	199	105	97	69	107
1998— San Francisco (N.L.)■	11	10	.524	4.41	34	34	0	0	0	202	200	105	99	85	126
1999— New York (N.L.)■.............	13	12	.520	4.58	32	32	0	0	0	179	175	92	91	77	89
A.L. totals (3 years)	45	21	.682	4.21	91	91	3	1	0	568²/₃	588	296	266	178	343
N.L. totals (14 years)	158	124	.560	3.22	409	369	65	24	5	2537	2309	1034	909	815	1658
Major League totals (17 years)	203	145	.583	3.41	500	460	68	25	5	3105²/₃	2897	1330	1175	993	2001

DIVISION SERIES RECORD

Year League	W	L	Pct.	ERA	G	GS	CG	ShO	Sv.	IP	H	R	ER	BB	SO
1995— Cleveland (A.L.).................	1	0	1.000	0.00	1	1	0	0	0	7¹/₃	3	0	0	2	7
1996— Cleveland (A.L.).................	0	0	...	5.40	1	1	0	0	0	5	7	4	3	3	3
1997— Cleveland (A.L.).................	0	0	...	3.97	2	2	0	0	0	11¹/₃	14	5	5	2	4
1999— New York (N.L.).................	0	0	...	0.00	1	0	0	0	0	1	0	0	0	0	1
Division series totals (4 years)	1	0	1.000	2.92	5	4	0	0	0	24²/₃	24	9	8	7	15

CHAMPIONSHIP SERIES RECORD

RECORDS: Holds career record for lowest earned-run average (30 or more innings)—1.52. ... Holds single-series record for most innings pitched—24²/₃ (1988). ... Holds N.L. single-game record for most hit batsmen—2 (October 12, 1988). ... Shares N.L. career record for most complete games—2. ... Shares N.L. single-series record for most hit batsmen—2 (1988).
NOTES: Named N.L. Championship Series Most Valuable Player (1988). ... Named A.L. Championship Series Most Valuable Player (1995).

H

Year League	W	L	Pct.	ERA	G	GS	CG	ShO	Sv.	IP	H	R	ER	BB	SO
1983— Los Angeles (N.L.)							Did not play.								
1985— Los Angeles (N.L.)	1	0	1.000	3.52	2	2	1	0	0	15 1/3	17	6	6	6	5
1988— Los Angeles (N.L.)	1	0	1.000	1.09	4	3	1	1	1	24 2/3	18	5	3	7	15
1995— Cleveland (A.L.)	2	0	1.000	1.29	2	2	0	0	0	14	9	3	2	3	15
1997— Cleveland (A.L.)	0	0	...	0.00	1	1	0	0	0	7	4	0	0	1	7
1999— New York (N.L.)	0	0	...	0.00	2	0	0	0	0	4 1/3	1	0	0	3	5
Champ. series totals (5 years)	4	0	1.000	1.52	11	8	2	1	1	65 1/3	49	14	11	20	47

WORLD SERIES RECORD

RECORDS: Shares single-game record for most earned runs allowed—7 (October 18, 1997).
NOTES: Named Most Valuable Player (1988). ... Member of World Series championship team (1988).

Year League	W	L	Pct.	ERA	G	GS	CG	ShO	Sv.	IP	H	R	ER	BB	SO
1988— Los Angeles (N.L.)	2	0	1.000	1.00	2	2	2	1	0	18	7	2	2	6	17
1995— Cleveland (A.L.)	1	1	.500	2.57	2	2	0	0	0	14	8	5	4	4	13
1997— Cleveland (A.L.)	0	2	.000	11.70	2	2	0	0	0	10	15	13	13	6	5
World Series totals (3 years)	3	3	.500	4.07	6	6	2	1	0	42	30	20	19	16	35

ALL-STAR GAME RECORD

Year League	W	L	Pct.	ERA	GS	CG	ShO	Sv.	IP	H	R	ER	BB	SO
1987— National	0	0	...	0.00	0	0	0	0	2	1	0	0	1	0
1988— National	0	0	...	0.00	0	0	0	0	1	0	0	0	0	0
1989— National							Did not play.							
All-Star Game totals (2 years)	0	0	...	0.00	0	0	0	0	3	1	0	0	1	0

HIDALGO, RICHARD   OF   ASTROS

PERSONAL: Born July 2, 1975, in Caracas, Venezuela. ... 6-3/190. ... Bats right, throws right. ... Full name: Richard Jose Hidalgo.
TRANSACTIONS/CAREER NOTES: Signed as non-drafted free agent by Houston Astros organization (July 2, 1991). ... On Houston disabled list (May 30-July 21, 1998); included rehabilitation assignment to New Orleans (July 11-21). ... On disabled list (August 9, 1999-remainder of season).
STATISTICAL NOTES: Led Texas League in grounding into double plays with 24 in 1996.

Year Team (League)	Pos.	G	AB	R	H	2B	3B	HR	RBI	Avg.	BB	SO	SB	PO	A	E	Avg.
1992— GC Astros (GCL)	OF	51	184	20	57	7	3	1	27	.310	13	27	14	67	6	0	1.000
1993— Asheville (SAL)..........	OF	111	403	49	109	23	3	10	55	.270	30	76	21	197	*30	6	.974
1994— Quad City (Midw.)	OF	124	476	68	139	*47	6	12	76	.292	23	80	12	202	*23	11	.953
1995— Jackson (Texas)	OF	133	489	59	130	28	6	14	59	.266	32	76	8	238	14	5	.981
1996— Jackson (Texas)	OF-DH	130	513	66	151	34	2	14	78	.294	29	55	11	302	14	6	.981
1997— New Orleans (A.A.).....	OF-DH	134	526	74	147	*37	5	11	78	.279	35	57	6	261	*15	9	.968
— Houston (N.L.)	OF	19	62	8	19	5	0	2	6	.306	4	18	1	28	0	0	1.000
1998— Houston (N.L.)	OF	74	211	31	64	15	0	7	35	.303	17	37	3	131	3	3	.978
— New Orleans (PCL).....	OF	10	24	0	4	2	0	0	1	.167	3	2	0	17	0	0	1.000
1999— Houston (N.L.)	OF	108	383	49	87	25	2	15	56	.227	56	73	8	214	15	2	.991
Major League totals (3 years)		201	656	88	170	45	2	24	97	.259	77	128	12	373	18	5	.987

DIVISION SERIES RECORD

Year Team (League)	Pos.	G	AB	R	H	2B	3B	HR	RBI	Avg.	BB	SO	SB	PO	A	E	Avg.
1997— Houston (N.L.)	OF	2	5	1	0	0	0	0	0	.000	1	2	0	5	0	0	1.000
1998— Houston (N.L.)	OF	1	4	0	1	0	0	0	0	.250	0	1	0	1	0	0	1.000
1999— Houston (N.L.)								Did not play.									
Division series totals (2 years)		3	9	1	1	0	0	0	0	.111	1	3	0	6	0	0	1.000

HIGGINSON, BOBBY   OF   TIGERS

PERSONAL: Born August 18, 1970, in Philadelphia. ... 5-11/195. ... Bats left, throws right. ... Full name: Robert Leigh Higginson.
HIGH SCHOOL: Frankford (Philadelphia).
COLLEGE: Temple.
TRANSACTIONS/CAREER NOTES: Selected by Detroit Tigers organization in 12th round of free-agent draft (June 1, 1992). ... On Detroit disabled list (May 11-June 7, 1996); included rehabilitation assignment to Toledo (June 4-7). ... On disabled list (June 15-26, 1997). ... On suspended list (September 26, 1997). ... On disabled list (July 24-August 24, 1999).
RECORDS: Shares major league record for most consecutive home runs—4 (June 30 [3], July 1 [1], 1997).
STATISTICAL NOTES: Hit three home runs in one game (June 30, 1997). ... Tied for A.L. lead in double plays by outfielder with five in 1997. ... Career major league grand slams: 4.

Year Team (League)	Pos.	G	AB	R	H	2B	3B	HR	RBI	Avg.	BB	SO	SB	PO	A	E	Avg.
1992— Niagara Falls (NY-P) ...	OF	70	232	35	68	17	4	2	37	.293	33	47	12	109	5	2	.983
1993— Lakeland (FSL)	OF	61	223	42	67	11	7	3	25	.300	40	31	8	88	7	2	.979
— London (East.)	OF	63	224	25	69	15	4	4	35	.308	19	37	3	100	11	2	.982
1994— Toledo (I.L.)	OF	137	476	81	131	28	3	23	67	.275	46	99	16	282	10	8	.973
1995— Detroit (A.L.)	OF-DH	131	410	61	92	17	5	14	43	.224	62	107	6	247	*13	4	.985
1996— Detroit (A.L.)	OF-DH	130	440	75	141	35	0	26	81	.320	65	66	6	227	9	9	.963
— Toledo (I.L.)	OF	3	13	4	4	0	1	0	1	.308	3	0	0	3	0	0	1.000
1997— Detroit (A.L.)	OF-DH	146	546	94	163	30	5	27	101	.299	70	85	12	287	*20	9	.972
1998— Detroit (A.L.)	OF-DH	157	612	92	174	37	4	25	85	.284	63	101	3	303	18	6	.982
1999— Detroit (A.L.)	OF-DH	107	377	51	90	18	0	12	46	.239	64	66	4	175	2	3	.983
Major League totals (5 years)		671	2385	373	660	137	14	104	356	.277	324	425	31	1239	62	31	.977

H

PERSONAL: Born December 25, 1972, in Panorama City, Calif. ... 6-5/230. ... Throws right, bats right. ... Full name: Erik Kristian Hiljus.
HIGH SCHOOL: Canyon (Anaheim).
TRANSACTIONS/CAREER NOTES: Selected by New York Mets organization in fourth round of free-agent draft (June 3, 1991). ... Traded by Mets with P Eric Ludwick and OF Yudith Ozono to St. Louis Cardinals for OF Bernard Gilkey (January 23, 1996). ... On disabled list (April 4-July 14, 1996). ... On disabled list (April 3-August 20, 1997). ... Released by Cardinals (August 20, 1997). ... Signed by Detroit Tigers organization (March 9, 1998). ... On Toledo disabled list (April 8-19, 1999).

Year League	W	L	Pct.	ERA	G	GS	CG	ShO	Sv.	IP	H	R	ER	BB	SO
1991— Gulf Coast Mets (GCL)	2	3	.400	4.26	9	9	1	•1	0	38	31	27	18	37	38
1992— Little Falls (NY-P)	3	6	.333	5.09	12	11	0	0	0	70²/₃	66	49	40	40	63
1993— Capital City (SAL)	7	10	.412	4.32	27	27	1	0	0	145²/₃	114	76	70	*111	157
1994— St. Lucie (FSL)	11	10	.524	3.98	26	26	3	1	0	160²/₃	159	85	71	*90	140
1995— St. Lucie (FSL)	8	4	.667	2.99	17	17	0	0	0	111¹/₃	85	46	37	50	98
— Binghamton (East.)	2	4	.333	5.86	10	10	0	0	0	55¹/₃	60	38	36	32	40
1996— Arkansas (Texas)■	3	5	.375	6.11	10	10	0	0	0	45²/₃	62	37	31	30	21
1997—							Did not play.								
1998— Jacksonville (Sou.)■	2	3	.400	3.70	42	0	0	0	2	65²/₃	49	31	27	35	85
1999— Lakeland (FSL)	0	0	...	2.25	3	0	0	0	0	4	4	1	1	0	9
— Jacksonville (Sou.)	1	0	1.000	1.04	10	0	0	0	0	17¹/₃	5	4	2	5	28
— Toledo (I.L.)	2	3	.400	4.40	33	0	0	0	5	59¹/₃	49	31	29	16	73
— Detroit (A.L.)	0	0	...	5.19	6	0	0	0	0	8²/₃	7	5	5	5	1
Major League totals (1 year)	0	0	...	5.19	6	0	0	0	0	8²/₃	7	5	5	5	1

PERSONAL: Born March 22, 1965, in Santa Cruz, Calif. ... 6-3/230. ... Bats right, throws right.
HIGH SCHOOL: Santa Cruz (Calif.).
TRANSACTIONS/CAREER NOTES: Selected by Toronto Blue Jays organization in ninth round of free-agent draft (June 6, 1983). ... On disabled list (July 6-21, 1990). ... Traded by Blue Jays with P Denis Boucher, OF Mark Whiten and a player to be named later to Cleveland Indians for P Tom Candiotti and OF Turner Ward (June 27, 1991); Indians acquired cash instead of player to complete deal (October 15, 1991). ... On Cleveland disabled list (September 8, 1991-remainder of season). ... On Cleveland disabled list (April 23-May 22, 1992); included rehabilitation assignment to Canton/Akron (May 18-22). ... Traded by Indians to Chicago Cubs for OF Candy Maldonado (August 19, 1993). ... Granted free agency (October 27, 1993). ... Re-signed by Cubs (November 24, 1993). ... Granted free agency (April 7, 1995). ... Signed by San Francisco Giants (April 9, 1995). ... On San Francisco disabled list (May 27-August 5, 1996); included rehabilitation assignment to Phoenix (July 29-August 5). ... Granted free agency (October 29, 1997). ... Signed by Seattle Mariners organization (January 8, 1998). ... Claimed on waivers by Cubs (July 6, 1998). ... Granted free agency (October 23, 1998). ... Re-signed by Cubs (December 7, 1998). ... On disabled list (May 8-23, 1999).
STATISTICAL NOTES: Led Southern League with 287 total bases and tied for lead with 13 sacrifice flies in 1986. ... Led International League with 279 total bases and .578 slugging percentage in 1989. ... Career major league grand slams: 4.

Year Team (League)	Pos.	G	AB	R	H	2B	3B	HR	RBI	Avg.	BB	SO	SB	PO	A	E	Avg.
1983— Medicine Hat (Pio.)	OF	46	133	34	63	3	4	6	27	.474	17	49	4	63	3	6	.917
1984— Florence (SAL)	OF	129	440	75	105	19	5	16	64	.239	63	*150	30	281	9	16	.948
1985— Kinston (Caro.)	OF	131	466	57	98	13	0	20	56	.210	57	*211	42	234	12	13	.950
1986— Knoxville (Sou.)	OF	141	*570	87	159	23	6	*31	96	.279	39	*153	18	230	9	*21	.919
1987— Syracuse (I.L.)	OF	*137	536	65	126	25	6	16	77	.235	25	*152	22	176	10	10	.949
1988— Syracuse (I.L.)	OF	51	172	21	40	7	0	4	19	.233	15	59	7	101	2	1	.990
— Knoxville (Sou.)	OF	79	269	37	71	13	2	12	38	.264	28	75	10	130	6	5	.965
1989— Syracuse (I.L.)	OF	125	483	*86	*155	31	*15	*21	72	.321	34	107	21	242	3	*7	.972
— Toronto (A.L.)	OF-DH	19	52	4	15	0	0	1	7	.288	3	12	2	27	0	1	.964
1990— Toronto (A.L.)	OF-DH	84	260	47	60	11	3	12	32	.231	18	62	8	115	4	2	.983
1991— Toronto (A.L.)	DH-OF	35	99	14	25	5	2	3	11	.253	7	24	2	29	0	1	.967
— Cleveland (A.L.)■	OF-DH	37	122	15	32	3	0	5	14	.262	16	30	4	89	0	2	.978
1992— Cleveland (A.L.)	OF-DH	102	369	38	89	16	1	18	49	.241	20	73	9	126	5	6	.956
— Canton/Akron (East.)	OF	3	9	1	1	1	0	0	1	.111	3	4	0	4	0	1	.800
1993— Cleveland (A.L.)	OF-DH	66	174	19	39	7	2	5	25	.224	11	50	7	62	1	4	.940
— Chicago (N.L.)■	OF	31	87	14	30	7	0	10	22	.345	6	21	3	42	2	2	.957
1994— Chicago (N.L.)	OF	89	269	48	80	12	1	10	38	.297	29	57	19	149	0	2	.987
1995— San Fran. (N.L.)■	OF	132	497	71	131	29	4	24	86	.264	39	98	25	226	10	10	.959
1996— San Francisco (N.L.)	OF	98	379	56	106	26	0	19	67	.280	33	95	6	160	6	7	.960
— Phoenix (PCL)	OF	5	17	4	6	1	0	2	2	.353	1	3	1	8	0	0	1.000
1997— San Francisco (N.L.)	OF-DH	128	398	47	104	28	4	11	64	.261	19	87	7	158	2	9	.947
1998— Seattle (A.L.)■	OF	74	259	37	75	20	2	12	33	.290	14	45	1	107	2	4	.965
— Chicago (N.L.)■	OF	48	131	26	46	5	0	8	23	.351	14	34	0	59	3	1	.984
1999— Chicago (N.L.)	OF-DH	99	253	43	76	9	1	20	55	.300	22	61	5	81	3	4	.955
American League totals (6 years)		417	1335	174	335	62	10	56	171	.251	89	296	33	555	12	20	.966
National League totals (7 years)		625	2014	305	573	116	10	102	355	.285	162	453	63	875	26	35	.963
Major League totals (11 years)		1042	3349	479	908	178	20	158	526	.271	251	749	96	1430	38	55	.964

DIVISION SERIES RECORD

						BATTING								FIELDING			
Year Team (League)	Pos.	G	AB	R	H	2B	3B	HR	RBI	Avg.	BB	SO	SB	PO	A	E	Avg.
1997— San Francisco (N.L.)	OF-PH	3	7	0	0	0	0	0	0	.000	2	2	0	2	0	0	1.000
1998— Chicago (N.L.)	OF	1	3	0	1	0	0	0	0	.333	1	2	1	3	0	0	1.000
Division series totals (2 years)		4	10	0	1	0	0	0	0	.100	3	4	1	5	0	0	1.000

H

PERSONAL: Born December 14, 1965, in Lynn, Mass. ... 6-2/215. ... Throws right, bats right. ... Full name: Kenneth Wade Hill.
HIGH SCHOOL: Classical (Lynn, Mass.).
COLLEGE: North Adams (Mass.) State.
TRANSACTIONS/CAREER NOTES: Signed as non-drafted free agent by Detroit Tigers organization (February 14, 1985). ... Traded by Tigers with a player to be named later to St. Louis Cardinals for C Mike Heath (August 10, 1986); Cardinals acquired 1B Mike Laga to complete deal (September 2, 1986). ... On St. Louis disabled list (March 26-May 9, 1988). ... On St. Louis disabled list (August 11-September 1, 1991); included rehabilitation assignment to Louisville (August 29-30). ... Traded by Cardinals to Montreal Expos for 1B Andres Galarraga (November 25, 1991). ... On Montreal disabled list (June 26-July 17, 1993); included rehabilitation assignment to Ottawa (July 12-15). ... Traded by Expos to Cardinals for P Brian Eversgerd, P Kirk Bullinger and OF Darond Stovall (April 5, 1995). ... Traded by Cardinals to Cleveland Indians for 3B/2B David Bell, P Rick Heiserman and C Pepe McNeal (July 27, 1995). ... Granted free agency (November 1, 1995). ... Signed by Texas Rangers (December 22, 1995). ... Traded by Rangers to Anaheim Angels for C Jim Leyritz and a player to be named later (July 29, 1997); Rangers acquired IF Rob Sasser to complete deal (October 31, 1997). ... On disabled list (May 1-24, 1997); included rehabilitation assignment to Tulsa (May 20-24). ... Granted free agency (November 7, 1997). ... Re-signed by Angels (November 15, 1997). ... On Anaheim disabled list (June 11-August 28, 1998); included rehabilitation assignments to Cedar Rapids (August 9-17) and Lake Elsinore (August 18-24). ... On disabled list (July 1-19 and August 15-September 1, 1999).
RECORDS: Shares N.L. single-season record for fewest games lost by pitcher who led league in games lost—15 (1989).
STATISTICAL NOTES: Pitched 6-0 one-hit, complete-game victory against New York (June 8, 1992). ... Led N.L. with 16 sacrifice hits in 1994. ... Pitched 11-0 one-hit, complete-game victory against Detroit (May 3, 1996). ... Led A.L. with four balks in 1996. ... Led A.L. with 95 bases on balls in 1997.
MISCELLANEOUS: Made an out in only appearance as pinch hitter with Montreal (1993). ... Had sacrifice hit in only appearance as pinch hitter (1994).

Year League	W	L	Pct.	ERA	G	GS	CG	ShO	Sv.	IP	H	R	ER	BB	SO
1985— Gastonia (SAL)	3	6	.333	4.96	15	12	0	0	0	69	60	51	38	57	48
1986— Gastonia (SAL)	9	5	.643	2.79	22	16	1	0	0	122²/₃	95	51	38	80	86
— Glens Falls (East.)	0	1	.000	5.14	1	1	0	0	0	7	4	4	4	6	4
— Arkansas (Texas)■	1	2	.333	4.50	3	3	1	0	0	18	18	10	9	7	9
1987— Arkansas (Texas)	3	5	.375	5.20	18	8	0	0	2	53²/₃	60	33	31	30	48
— St. Petersburg (FSL)	1	3	.250	4.17	18	4	0	0	2	41	38	19	19	17	32
1988— St. Louis (N.L.)	0	1	.000	5.14	4	1	0	0	0	14	16	9	8	6	6
— Arkansas (Texas)	9	9	.500	4.92	22	22	3	1	0	115¹/₃	129	76	63	50	107
1989— Louisville (A.A.)	0	2	.000	3.50	3	3	0	0	0	18	13	8	7	10	18
— St. Louis (N.L.)	7	•15	.318	3.80	33	33	2	1	0	196²/₃	186	92	83	*99	112
1990— St. Louis (N.L.)	5	6	.455	5.49	17	14	1	0	0	78²/₃	79	49	48	33	58
— Louisville (A.A.)	6	1	.857	1.79	12	12	2	1	0	85¹/₃	47	20	17	27	104
1991— St. Louis (N.L.)	11	10	.524	3.57	30	30	0	0	0	181¹/₃	147	76	72	67	121
— Louisville (A.A.)	0	0	...	0.00	1	1	0	0	0	1	0	0	0	0	2
1992— Montreal (N.L.)■	16	9	.640	2.68	33	33	3	3	0	218	187	76	65	75	150
1993— Montreal (N.L.)	9	7	.563	3.23	28	28	2	0	0	183²/₃	163	84	66	74	90
— Ottawa (I.L.)	0	0	...	0.00	1	1	0	0	0	4	1	0	0	1	0
1994— Montreal (N.L.)	•16	5	.762	3.32	23	23	2	1	0	154²/₃	145	61	57	44	85
1995— St. Louis (N.L.)■	6	7	.462	5.06	18	18	0	0	0	110¹/₃	125	71	62	45	50
— Cleveland (A.L.)■	4	1	.800	3.98	12	11	1	0	0	74²/₃	77	36	33	32	48
1996— Texas (A.L.)■	16	10	.615	3.63	35	35	7	•3	0	250²/₃	250	110	101	95	170
1997— Texas (A.L.)	5	8	.385	5.19	19	19	0	0	0	111	129	69	64	56	68
— Tulsa (Texas)	0	0	...	0.00	1	1	0	0	0	5	2	0	0	1	3
— Anaheim (A.L.)■	4	4	.500	3.65	12	12	1	0	0	79	65	34	32	§39	38
1998— Anaheim (A.L.)	9	6	.600	4.98	19	19	0	0	0	103	123	60	57	47	57
— Cedar Rapids (Midw.)	0	0	...	1.23	2	2	0	0	0	7¹/₃	7	1	1	1	6
— Lake Elsinore (Calif.)	0	0	...	6.75	1	1	0	0	0	4	5	4	3	5	2
1999— Anaheim (A.L.)	4	11	.267	4.77	26	22	0	0	0	128¹/₃	129	72	68	76	76
A.L. totals (5 years)	42	40	.512	4.28	123	118	9	3	0	746²/₃	773	381	355	345	457
N.L. totals (8 years)	70	60	.538	3.65	186	180	10	5	0	1137¹/₃	1048	518	461	443	672
Major League totals (12 years)	112	100	.528	3.90	309	298	19	8	0	1884	1821	899	816	788	1129

DIVISION SERIES RECORD

Year League	W	L	Pct.	ERA	G	GS	CG	ShO	Sv.	IP	H	R	ER	BB	SO
1995— Cleveland (A.L.)	1	0	1.000	0.00	1	0	0	0	0	1¹/₃	1	0	0	0	2
1996— Texas (A.L.)	0	0	...	4.50	1	1	0	0	0	6	5	3	3	3	1
Division series totals (2 years)	1	0	1.000	3.68	2	1	0	0	0	7¹/₃	6	3	3	3	3

CHAMPIONSHIP SERIES RECORD

Year League	W	L	Pct.	ERA	G	GS	CG	ShO	Sv.	IP	H	R	ER	BB	SO
1995— Cleveland (A.L.)	1	0	1.000	0.00	1	1	0	0	0	7	5	0	0	3	6

WORLD SERIES RECORD

Year League	W	L	Pct.	ERA	G	GS	CG	ShO	Sv.	IP	H	R	ER	BB	SO
1995— Cleveland (A.L.)	0	1	.000	4.26	2	1	0	0	0	6¹/₃	7	3	3	4	1

ALL-STAR GAME RECORD

Year League	W	L	Pct.	ERA	GS	CG	ShO	Sv.	IP	H	R	ER	BB	SO
1994— National	0	0	...	0.00	0	0	0	0	2	0	0	0	1	0

HILLENBRAND, SHEA   C

PERSONAL: Born July 27, 1975, in Mesa, Ariz. ... 6-1/200. ... Bats right, throws right. ... Full name: Shea Matthew Hillenbrand.
HIGH SCHOOL: Mountain View (Mesa, Ariz.).
JUNIOR COLLEGE: Mesa (Ariz.) Community College.

TRANSACTIONS/CAREER NOTES: Selected by Boston Red Sox organization in 10th round of free-agent draft (June 4, 1996). ... On Trenton disabled list (July 5-August 31, 1999). ... On Boston disabled list (August 31, 1999-remainder of season). ... Granted free agency (December 21, 1999).
STATISTICAL NOTES: Led New York-Penn League first beasmen with 17 errors in 1996. ... Led Midwest League with 272 total bases and .546 slugging percentage in 1998. ... Led Midwest League with 20 passed balls in 1998.

							BATTING							FIELDING		
Year	Team (League)	Pos.	G	AB	R	H	2B	3B	HR	RBI	Avg.	BB	SO	SB	PO	A	E	Avg.
1996— Lowell (NY-P)	1B-SS-3B	72	279	33	88	18	2	2	38	.315	18	32	4	440	57	†33	.938
1997— Michigan (Midw.)	1B-3B	64	224	28	65	13	3	3	39	.290	9	20	1	137	16	8	.950
— Sarasota (FSL)	1B-3B	57	220	25	65	12	0	2	28	.295	7	29	9	198	53	20	.926
1998— Michigan (Midw.)	C-1B-3B	129	498	80	174	33	4	19	93	.349	19	49	13	700	64	14	.982
1999— Trenton (East.)	C-DH	69	282	41	73	15	0	7	36	.259	14	27	6	337	41	5	.987

HINCH, A.J. C ATHLETICS

PERSONAL: Born May 15, 1974, in Waverly, Iowa. ... 6-1/207. ... Bats right, throws right. ... Full name: Andrew Jay Hinch.
HIGH SCHOOL: Midwest City (Okla.).
COLLEGE: Stanford.
TRANSACTIONS/CAREER NOTES: Selected by Chicago White Sox organization in second round of free-agent draft (June 2, 1992); did not sign. ... Selected by Minnesota Twins organization in third round of free-agent draft (June 1, 1995); did not sign. ... Selected by Oakland Athletics organization in third round of free-agent draft (June 4, 1996). ... On Modesto suspended list (June 7-9, 1997).
RECORDS: Shares major league single-season record for fewest double plays by catcher for leader—8 (1998).
STATISTICAL NOTES: Led California League catchers with .996 fielding percentage in 1997. ... Tied for A.L. lead in double plays by catcher with eight in 1998. ... Career major league grand slams: 1.
MISCELLANEOUS: Member of 1996 U.S. Olympic baseball team.

							BATTING							FIELDING		
Year	Team (League)	Pos.	G	AB	R	H	2B	3B	HR	RBI	Avg.	BB	SO	SB	PO	A	E	Avg.
1997— Modesto (Calif.)	C-DH-1B	95	333	70	103	25	3	20	73	.309	42	68	8	622	66	3	†.996
— Edmonton (PCL)	C-DH-OF	39	125	23	47	7	0	4	24	.376	20	13	2	201	7	3	.986
1998— Oakland (A.L.)	C	120	337	34	78	10	0	9	35	.231	30	89	3	602	47	•9	.986
1999— Oakland (A.L.)	C	76	205	26	44	4	1	7	24	.215	11	41	6	368	26	5	.987
— Vancouver (PCL)	C-DH	15	61	9	23	3	0	2	7	.377	3	12	1	83	3	1	.989
Major League totals (2 years)		196	542	60	122	14	1	16	59	.225	41	130	9	970	73	14	.987

HINCHLIFFE, BRETT P ANGELS

PERSONAL: Born July 21, 1974, in Detroit. ... 6-5/190. ... Throws right, bats right.
HIGH SCHOOL: Bishop Gallagher (Harper Woods, Mich.).
TRANSACTIONS/CAREER NOTES: Selected by Seattle Mariners organization in 16th round of free-agent draft (June 1, 1992). ... On suspended list (April 21-25, 1999). ... Released by Mariners (January 3, 2000). ... Signed by Anaheim Angels organization (January 19, 2000).
STATISTICAL NOTES: Pitched 12-0 no-hit victory against Cedar Rapids (June 28, 1994).

Year	League	W	L	Pct.	ERA	G	GS	CG	ShO	Sv.	IP	H	R	ER	BB	SO
1992— Arizona Mariners (Ariz.)	5	4	.556	2.31	*24	0	0	0	3	35	42	17	9	9	26
1993— Arizona Mariners (Ariz.)	0	4	.000	5.08	10	9	0	0	0	44 1/3	55	32	25	5	29
1994— Appleton (Midw.)	11	7	.611	3.21	27	27	3	1	0	173 2/3	140	79	62	50	160
1995— Riverside (Calif.)	3	8	.273	6.61	15	15	0	0	0	77 2/3	110	69	57	35	68
1996— Lancaster (Calif.)	11	10	.524	4.24	27	26	0	0	0	163 1/3	179	105	77	64	146
1997— Memphis (Sou.)	10	10	.500	4.45	24	24	*5	1	0	145 2/3	159	81	72	45	107
1998— Lancaster (Calif.)	1	1	.500	1.59	3	3	0	0	0	17	8	5	3	5	26
— Tacoma (PCL)	10	8	.556	4.00	25	25	2	1	0	159 2/3	132	80	71	88	100
1999— Seattle (A.L.)	0	4	.000	8.80	11	4	0	0	0	30 2/3	41	31	30	21	14
— Tacoma (PCL)	9	7	.563	5.15	21	21	3	0	0	131	141	78	75	44	107
Major League totals (1 year)	0	4	.000	8.80	11	4	0	0	0	30 2/3	41	31	30	21	14

HITCHCOCK, STERLING P PADRES

PERSONAL: Born April 29, 1971, in Fayetteville, N.C. ... 6-1/192. ... Throws left, bats left. ... Full name: Sterling Alex Hitchcock.
HIGH SCHOOL: Armwood (Seffner, Fla.).
TRANSACTIONS/CAREER NOTES: Selected by New York Yankees organization in ninth round of free-agent draft (June 5, 1989). ... On disabled list (June 26-August 14, 1991). ... On Columbus disabled list (May 23-July 21, 1993). ... Traded by Yankees with 3B Russ Davis to Seattle Mariners for 1B Tino Martinez, P Jeff Nelson and P Jim Mecir (December 7, 1995). ... Traded by Mariners to San Diego Padres for P Scott Sanders (December 6, 1996). ... On disabled list (June 6-July 3, 1997).
STATISTICAL NOTES: Pitched 1-0 no-hit victory against Sumter (July 16, 1990). ... Struck out 15 batters in one game (August 29, 1998). ... Tied for N.L. lead with 15 wild pitches in 1999.

Year	League	W	L	Pct.	ERA	G	GS	CG	ShO	Sv.	IP	H	R	ER	BB	SO
1989— Gulf Coast Yankees (GCL)	*9	1	.900	1.64	13	•13	0	0	0	76 2/3	48	16	14	27	*98
1990— Greensboro (SAL)	12	12	.500	2.91	27	27	6	*5	0	173 1/3	122	68	56	60	*171
1991— Prince William (Caro.)	7	7	.500	2.64	19	19	2	0	0	119 1/3	111	49	35	26	101
1992— Albany/Colonie (East.)	6	9	.400	2.58	24	24	2	0	0	146 2/3	116	51	42	42	*155
— New York (A.L.)	0	2	.000	8.31	3	3	0	0	0	13	23	12	12	6	6
1993— Columbus (I.L.)	3	5	.375	4.81	16	16	0	0	0	76 2/3	80	43	41	28	85
— New York (A.L.)	1	2	.333	4.65	6	6	0	0	0	31	32	18	16	14	26
1994— New York (A.L.)	4	1	.800	4.20	23	5	1	0	2	49 1/3	48	24	23	29	37
— Columbus (I.L.)	3	4	.429	4.32	10	9	1	0	0	50	53	30	24	18	47
— Albany/Colonie (East.)	1	0	1.000	1.80	1	1	0	0	0	5	4	1	1	0	7
1995— New York (A.L.)	11	10	.524	4.70	27	27	4	1	0	168 1/3	155	91	88	68	121
1996— Seattle (A.L.)■	13	9	.591	5.35	35	35	0	0	0	196 2/3	245	131	117	73	132

H

Year League	W	L	Pct.	ERA	G	GS	CG	ShO	Sv.	IP	H	R	ER	BB	SO
1997— San Diego (N.L.)■	10	11	.476	5.20	32	28	1	0	0	161	172	102	93	55	106
1998— San Diego (N.L.)	9	7	.563	3.93	39	27	2	1	1	176 1/3	169	83	77	48	158
1999— San Diego (N.L.)	12	14	.462	4.11	33	33	1	0	0	205 2/3	202	99	94	76	194
A.L. totals (5 years)	29	24	.547	5.03	94	76	5	1	2	458 1/3	503	276	256	190	322
N.L. totals (3 years)	31	32	.492	4.38	104	88	4	1	1	543	543	284	264	179	458
Major League totals (8 years)	60	56	.517	4.67	198	164	9	2	3	1001 1/3	1046	560	520	369	780

DIVISION SERIES RECORD

Year League	W	L	Pct.	ERA	G	GS	CG	ShO	Sv.	IP	H	R	ER	BB	SO
1995— New York (A.L.)	0	0	...	5.40	2	0	0	0	0	1 2/3	2	2	1	2	1
1998— San Diego (N.L.)	1	0	1.000	1.50	1	1	0	0	0	6	3	1	1	0	11
Division series totals (2 years)	1	0	1.000	2.35	3	1	0	0	0	7 2/3	5	3	2	2	12

CHAMPIONSHIP SERIES RECORD

RECORDS: Shares single-inning record for most wild pitches—2 (October 14, 1998, second inning).

NOTES: Named N.L. Championship Series Most Valuable Player (1998).

Year League	W	L	Pct.	ERA	G	GS	CG	ShO	Sv.	IP	H	R	ER	BB	SO
1998— San Diego (N.L.)	2	0	1.000	0.90	2	2	0	0	0	10	5	1	1	8	14

WORLD SERIES RECORD

Year League	W	L	Pct.	ERA	G	GS	CG	ShO	Sv.	IP	H	R	ER	BB	SO
1998— San Diego (N.L.)	0	0	...	1.50	1	1	0	0	0	6	7	2	1	1	7

HOCKING, DENNY   IF   TWINS

PERSONAL: Born April 2, 1970, in Torrance, Calif. ... 5-10/183. ... Bats both, throws right. ... Full name: Dennis Lee Hocking.

HIGH SCHOOL: West Torrance (Calif.).

COLLEGE: El Camino College (Calif.).

TRANSACTIONS/CAREER NOTES: Selected by Minnesota Twins organization in 52nd round of free-agent draft (June 5, 1989). ... On Nashville disabled list (April 8-29, 1993). ... On Minnesota disabled list (March 22-April 30, May 30-June 29 and July 31-September 8, 1996); included rehabilitation assignments to Salt Lake (April 4-30, June 21-29 and August 24-September 8).

STATISTICAL NOTES: Led California League shortstops with 721 total chances in 1992. ... Led Pacific Coast League shortstops with .966 fielding percentage and 390 assists in 1995. ... Career major league grand slams: 1.

							BATTING								FIELDING		
Year Team (League)	Pos.	G	AB	R	H	2B	3B	HR	RBI	Avg.	BB	SO	SB	PO	A	E	Avg.
1990— Elizabethton (Appl.)	SS-2B-3B	54	201	45	59	6	2	6	30	.294	40	26	14	77	179	20	.928
1991— Kenosha (Midw.)	SS	125	432	72	110	17	8	2	36	.255	77	69	22	193	308	42	.923
1992— Visalia (Calif.)	SS	135	*550	117	*182	34	9	7	81	.331	72	77	38	214	*469	38	.947
1993— Nashville (Sou.)	SS-DH-2B	107	409	54	109	9	4	8	50	.267	34	66	15	144	300	30	.937
— Minnesota (A.L.)	SS-2B	15	36	7	5	1	0	0	0	.139	6	8	1	19	23	1	.977
1994— Salt Lake (PCL)	SS	112	394	61	110	14	6	5	57	.279	28	57	13	143	342	26	.949
— Minnesota (A.L.)	SS	11	31	3	10	3	0	0	2	.323	0	4	2	11	27	0	1.000
1995— Salt Lake (PCL)	SS-DH-2B	117	397	51	112	24	2	8	75	.282	25	41	12	173	†393	20	†.966
— Minnesota (A.L.)	SS	9	25	4	5	0	2	0	3	.200	2	2	1	13	20	1	.971
1996— Minnesota (A.L.)	O-S-2-DH-1	49	127	16	25	6	0	1	10	.197	8	24	3	67	9	1	.987
— Salt Lake (PCL)	S-O-D-1-2-3	37	130	18	36	6	2	3	22	.277	10	17	2	51	69	3	.976
1997— Minnesota (A.L.)	S-3-O-2-D-1	115	253	28	65	12	4	2	25	.257	18	51	3	124	146	4	.985
1998— Minnesota (A.L.)	2-S-O-3-D-1	110	198	32	40	6	1	3	15	.202	16	44	2	118	102	4	.982
1999— Minnesota (A.L.)	S-2-O-3-1	136	386	47	103	18	2	7	41	.267	22	54	11	193	190	3	.992
Major League totals (7 years)		445	1056	137	253	46	9	13	96	.240	72	187	23	545	517	14	.987

HODGES, KEVIN   P   MARINERS

PERSONAL: Born June 24, 1973, in Houston. ... 6-4/200. ... Throws right, bats right. ... Full name: Kevin Jon Hodges.

HIGH SCHOOL: Klein Oak (Spring, Texas).

TRANSACTIONS/CAREER NOTES: Selected by Kansas City Royals organization in eighth round of free-agent draft (June 3, 1991). ... Granted free agency (October 17, 1997). ... Signed by Houston Astros organization (March 31, 1998). ... Traded by Astros to Seattle Mariners for OF Matt Mieske (June 20, 1999).

Year League	W	L	Pct.	ERA	G	GS	CG	ShO	Sv.	IP	H	R	ER	BB	SO
1991— Gulf Coast Royals (GCL)	1	2	.333	4.30	9	3	0	0	0	23	22	14	11	11	13
1992— Gulf Coast Royals (GCL)	5	3	.625	4.71	11	9	0	0	0	49 2/3	60	30	26	25	24
1993— Gulf Coast Royals (GCL)	7	2	.778	2.03	12	10	0	0	0	71	52	25	16	25	40
— Wilmington (Caro.)	1	1	.500	0.00	3	0	0	0	0	4 2/3	2	0	0	3	1
1994— Rockford (Midw.)	9	6	.600	3.38	24	17	2	1	3	114 1/3	96	53	43	35	83
1995— Wilmington (Caro.)	2	3	.400	4.53	12	10	0	0	0	53 2/3	53	31	27	25	27
1996— Lansing (Midw.)	1	2	.333	4.66	9	9	0	0	0	48 1/3	47	32	25	19	23
1997— Wilmington (Caro.)	8	11	.421	4.48	28	20	0	0	1	124 2/3	150	78	62	44	63
1998— Jackson (Texas)■	4	5	.444	3.61	29	15	0	0	0	107 1/3	108	55	43	38	70
1999— Jackson (Texas)	1	4	.200	2.94	8	8	0	0	0	49	48	22	16	16	21
— New Orleans (PCL)	1	3	.250	7.24	5	5	0	0	0	27 1/3	34	23	22	11	16
— Tacoma (PCL)■	3	3	.500	3.25	14	12	0	0	1	83	88	31	30	27	42

HOFFMAN, TREVOR   P   PADRES

PERSONAL: Born October 13, 1967, in Bellflower, Calif. ... 6-0/205. ... Throws right, bats right. ... Full name: Trevor William Hoffman. ... Brother of Glenn Hoffman, assistant coach, Los Angeles Dodgers; and infielder with Boston Red Sox (1980-87), Los Angeles Dodgers (1987) and California Angels (1989).

HIGH SCHOOL: Savanna (Anaheim).

JUNIOR COLLEGE: Cypress (Calif.) College.

COLLEGE: Arizona.

TRANSACTIONS/CAREER NOTES: Selected by Cincinnati Reds organization in 11th round of free-agent draft (June 5, 1989). ... Selected by Florida Marlins in first round (eighth pick overall) of expansion draft (November 17, 1992). ... Traded by Marlins with P Jose Martinez and P Andres Berumen to San Diego Padres for 3B Gary Sheffield and P Rich Rodriguez (June 24, 1993).

RECORDS: Shares N.L. single-season record for most saves—53 (1998).

HONORS: Named N.L. Fireman of the Year by THE SPORTING NEWS (1996 and 1998).

STATISTICAL NOTES: Tied for N.L. lead with 13 intentional bases on balls issued in 1993.

MISCELLANEOUS: Holds San Diego Padres all-time record for most games pitched (411) and saves (226).

Year League	W	L	Pct.	ERA	G	GS	CG	ShO	Sv.	IP	H	R	ER	BB	SO
1991— Cedar Rapids (Midw.)	1	1	.500	1.87	27	0	0	0	12	33 2/3	22	8	7	13	52
— Chattanooga (Sou.)	1	0	1.000	1.93	14	0	0	0	8	14	10	4	3	7	23
1992— Chattanooga (Sou.)	3	0	1.000	1.52	6	6	0	0	0	29 2/3	22	6	5	11	31
— Nashville (A.A.)	4	6	.400	4.27	42	5	0	0	6	65 1/3	57	32	31	32	63
1993— Florida (N.L.)■...............	2	2	.500	3.28	28	0	0	0	2	35 2/3	24	13	13	19	26
— San Diego (N.L.)■...........	2	4	.333	4.31	39	0	0	0	3	54 1/3	56	30	26	20	53
1994— San Diego (N.L.)	4	4	.500	2.57	47	0	0	0	20	56	39	16	16	20	68
1995— San Diego (N.L.)	7	4	.636	3.88	55	0	0	0	31	53 1/3	48	25	23	14	52
1996— San Diego (N.L.)	9	5	.643	2.25	70	0	0	0	42	88	50	23	22	31	111
1997— San Diego (N.L.)	6	4	.600	2.66	70	0	0	0	37	81 1/3	59	25	24	24	111
1998— San Diego (N.L.)	4	2	.667	1.48	66	0	0	0	*53	73	41	12	12	21	86
1999— San Diego (N.L.)	2	3	.400	2.14	64	0	0	0	40	67 1/3	48	23	16	15	73
Major League totals (7 years)	36	28	.563	2.69	439	0	0	0	228	509	365	167	152	164	580

DIVISION SERIES RECORD

Year League	W	L	Pct.	ERA	G	GS	CG	ShO	Sv.	IP	H	R	ER	BB	SO
1996— San Diego (N.L.)	0	1	.000	10.80	2	0	0	0	0	1 2/3	3	2	2	1	2
1998— San Diego (N.L.)	0	0	...	0.00	4	0	0	0	2	3	3	1	0	1	4
Division series totals (2 years)	0	1	.000	3.86	6	0	0	0	2	4 2/3	6	3	2	2	6

CHAMPIONSHIP SERIES RECORD

Year League	W	L	Pct.	ERA	G	GS	CG	ShO	Sv.	IP	H	R	ER	BB	SO
1998— San Diego (N.L.)	1	0	1.000	2.08	3	0	0	0	1	4 1/3	2	1	1	2	7

WORLD SERIES RECORD

Year League	W	L	Pct.	ERA	G	GS	CG	ShO	Sv.	IP	H	R	ER	BB	SO
1998— San Diego (N.L.)	0	1	.000	9.00	1	0	0	0	0	2	2	2	2	1	0

ALL-STAR GAME RECORD

Year League	W	L	Pct.	ERA	GS	CG	ShO	Sv.	IP	H	R	ER	BB	SO
1998— National	0	0	...	9.00	0	0	0	0	1	1	1	1	0	1
1999— National	0	0	...	0.00	0	0	0	0	1/3	0	0	0	0	1
All-Star Game totals (2 years)	0	0	...	6.75	0	0	0	0	1 1/3	1	1	1	0	2

RECORD AS POSITION PLAYER

Year Team (League)	Pos.	G	AB	R	H	2B	3B	HR	RBI	Avg.	BB	SO	SB	PO	A	E	Avg.
1989— Billings (Pioneer)........	SS	61	201	22	50	5	0	1	20	.249	19	40	1	*116	140	•25	.911
1990— Char., W.Va. (SAL)......	SS-3B	103	278	41	59	10	1	2	23	.212	38	53	3	114	209	30	.915

HOLBERT, RAY   IF   ROYALS

PERSONAL: Born September 25, 1970, in Torrance, Calif. ... 6-0/185. ... Bats right, throws right. ... Full name: Ray Arthur Holbert III. ... Brother of Aaron Holbert, minor league shortstop (1990-1999).

HIGH SCHOOL: David Starr Jordan (Long Beach, Calif.).

TRANSACTIONS/CAREER NOTES: Selected by San Diego Padres organization in third round of free-agent draft (June 1, 1988). ... On disabled list (July 7-28, 1992). ... On San Diego disabled list (July 30, 1995-remainder of season). ... Traded by Padres to Houston Astros for P Pedro A. Martinez (October 10, 1995). ... Granted free agency (October 15, 1996). ... Signed by Detroit Tigers organization (December 19, 1996). ... Granted free agency (October 15, 1997). ... Signed by Atlanta Braves organization (January 13, 1998). ... Released by Braves (May 13, 1998). ... Signed by Montreal Expos organization (May 18, 1998). ... Granted free agency (October 15, 1998). ... Signed by Kansas City Royals organization (December 17, 1998). ... On Omaha disabled list (May 8-July 4, 1999).

STATISTICAL NOTES: Led Arizona League shortstops with .927 fielding percentage and 132 assists in 1988. ... Led Midwest League shortstops with 642 total chances and 75 double plays in 1990. ... Led Texas League with nine sacrifice flies in 1993. ... Led Pacific Ccast League with 10 sacrifice hits in 1994. ... Led Pacific Coast League shortstops with 34 errors in 1994. ... Led International League shortstops with 183 putouts in 1997. ... Career major league grand slams: 1.

Year Team (League)	Pos.	G	AB	R	H	2B	3B	HR	RBI	Avg.	BB	SO	SB	PO	A	E	Avg.
1988— Ariz. Padres (Ariz.)	SS-3B	49	170	38	44	1	0	3	19	.259	38	32	20	59	†137	15	†.929
1989— Waterloo (Midw.)	SS-3B	117	354	37	55	7	1	0	20	.155	41	99	13	205	303	32	.941
1990— Waterloo (Midw.)	SS	133	411	51	84	10	1	3	39	.204	51	117	16	*233	*378	31	.952
1991— High Desert (Calif.)......	SS	122	386	76	102	14	2	4	51	.264	56	83	19	196	331	*37	.934
1992— Wichita (Texas)	SS	95	304	46	86	7	3	2	23	.283	42	68	26	150	217	17	.956
1993— Wichita (Texas)	SS	112	388	56	101	13	5	5	48	.260	54	87	30	155	267	30	.934
1994— Las Vegas (PCL)	SS-OF	118	426	68	128	21	5	8	52	.300	50	99	27	157	333	†34	.935
— San Diego (N.L.)	SS	5	5	1	1	0	0	0	0	.200	0	4	0	0	0	0	...
1995— San Diego (N.L.)	SS-2B-OF	63	73	11	13	2	1	2	5	.178	8	20	4	27	58	5	.944
— Las Vegas (PCL)	2B	9	26	3	3	1	0	0	3	.115	5	10	1	9	26	1	.972
1996— Tucson (PCL)■	SS	28	97	13	24	3	2	0	10	.247	7	19	4	37	65	9	.919
1997— Toledo (I.L.)■.............	SS-3B	109	372	43	90	18	7	7	37	.242	32	109	16	†187	302	25	.951

H

Year Team (League)	Pos.	G	AB	R	H	2B	3B	HR	RBI	Avg.	BB	SO	SB	PO	A	E	Avg.
1998— Richmond (I.L.)■	SS	1	1	1	0	0	0	0	0	.000	2	1	0	2	3	1	.833
—Atlanta (N.L.)	SS	8	15	2	2	0	0	0	1	.133	2	4	0	6	14	1	.952
—Ottawa (I.L.)■	SS-3B-2B	86	266	38	82	17	4	2	25	.308	29	66	10	133	207	11	.969
—Montreal (N.L.)	2B	2	5	0	0	0	0	0	0	.000	0	1	0	2	3	0	1.000
1999— Omaha (PCL)■	SS-2B	33	128	26	38	4	0	4	12	.297	12	35	13	51	72	4	.969
—GC Royals (GCL)	SS-DH	5	16	5	3	2	0	0	1	.188	1	4	1	7	7	0	1.000
—Kansas City (A.L.)	SS-2B-3B	34	100	14	28	3	0	0	5	.280	8	20	7	45	76	2	.984
American League totals (1 year)		34	100	14	28	3	0	0	5	.280	8	20	7	45	76	2	.984
National League totals (3 years)		78	98	14	16	2	1	2	6	.163	10	29	4	35	75	6	.948
Major League totals (4 years)		112	198	28	44	5	1	2	11	.222	18	49	11	80	151	8	.967

HOLLANDSWORTH, TODD — OF — DODGERS

PERSONAL: Born April 20, 1973, in Dayton, Ohio. ... 6-2/215. ... Bats left, throws left. ... Full name: Todd Mathew Hollandsworth.
HIGH SCHOOL: Newport (Bellevue, Wash.).
TRANSACTIONS/CAREER NOTES: Selected by Los Angeles Dodgers organization in third round of free-agent draft (June 3, 1991); pick received as part of compensation for Kansas City Royals signing Type B free-agent OF/DH Kirk Gibson. ... On Los Angeles disabled list (May 3-July 7 and August 9-September 12, 1995); included rehabilitation assignments to San Bernardino (June 6-7) and Albuquerque (June 27-July 7). ... On Los Angeles disabled list (August 2-16 and August 17-September 6, 1997); included rehabilitation assignment to San Bernardino (August 15-17). ... On disabled list (June 5, 1998-remainder of season). ... On Los Angeles disabled list (April 3-23 and June 4-19, 1999); included rehabilitation assignment to San Bernardino (April 20-23 and June 18-19).
HONORS: Named N.L. Rookie of the Year by Baseball Writers' Association of America (1996).

Year Team (League)	Pos.	G	AB	R	H	2B	3B	HR	RBI	Avg.	BB	SO	SB	PO	A	E	Avg.
1991— Yakima (N.W.)	OF	56	203	34	48	5	1	8	33	.236	27	57	11	106	1	7	.939
1992— Bakersfield (Calif.)......	OF	119	430	70	111	23	5	13	58	.258	50	113	27	230	8	6	.975
1993— San Antonio (Texas).....	OF	126	474	57	119	24	9	17	63	.251	29	101	24	246	13	12	.956
1994— Albuquerque (PCL).....	OF	132	505	80	144	31	5	19	91	.285	46	96	15	237	5	13	.949
1995— Los Angeles (N.L.).....	OF	41	103	16	24	2	0	5	13	.233	10	29	2	60	1	4	.938
—San Bern. (Calif.)........	OF	1	2	0	1	0	0	0	0	.500	0	1	0	0	0	0	...
—Albuquerque (PCL).....	OF	10	38	9	9	2	0	2	4	.237	6	8	1	19	3	0	1.000
1996— Los Angeles (N.L.).....	OF	149	478	64	139	26	4	12	59	.291	41	93	21	217	7	5	.978
1997— Los Angeles (N.L.).....	OF	106	296	39	73	20	2	4	31	.247	17	60	5	185	2	3	.984
—Albuquerque (PCL).....	OF	13	56	13	24	4	3	1	14	.429	4	4	2	32	1	0	1.000
—San Bern. (Calif.)........	OF	2	8	1	2	0	1	0	2	.250	1	2	0	2	1	0	1.000
1998— Los Angeles (N.L.).....	OF	55	175	23	47	6	4	3	20	.269	9	42	4	87	1	4	.957
1999— San Bern. (Calif.)........	OF	4	13	3	5	2	0	0	3	.385	2	4	0	3	1	0	1.000
—Los Angeles (N.L.)	OF-1B	92	261	39	74	12	2	9	32	.284	24	61	5	211	11	3	.987
Major League totals (5 years)		443	1313	181	357	66	12	33	155	.272	101	285	37	760	22	19	.976

DIVISION SERIES RECORD

RECORDS: Shares N.L. career record for most doubles—3.

Year Team (League)	Pos.	G	AB	R	H	2B	3B	HR	RBI	Avg.	BB	SO	SB	PO	A	E	Avg.
1995— Los Angeles (N.L.)	OF-PH	2	2	0	0	0	0	0	0	.000	0	0	0	0	0	0	...
1996— Los Angeles (N.L.)	OF	3	12	1	4	3	0	0	1	.333	0	3	0	4	0	0	1.000
Division series totals (2 years)		5	14	1	4	3	0	0	1	.286	0	3	0	4	0	0	1.000

HOLLINS, DAVE — 3B/1B — DEVIL RAYS

PERSONAL: Born May 25, 1966, in Orchard Park, NY. ... 6-1/232. ... Bats both, throws right. ... Full name: David Michael Hollins.
HIGH SCHOOL: Orchard Park (N.Y.).
COLLEGE: South Carolina.
TRANSACTIONS/CAREER NOTES: Selected by San Diego Padres organization in sixth round of free-agent draft (June 2, 1987). ... Selected by Philadelphia Phillies from Padres organization in Rule 5 major league draft (December 4, 1989). ... On Philadelphia disabled list (August 16-September 6, 1991); included rehabilitation assignment to Scranton/Wilkes-Barre (September 2-5). ... On suspended list (September 29-October 3, 1992). ... On disabled list (June 11-28, 1993). ... On Philadelphia disabled list (May 23-July 23 and July 25, 1994-remainder of season); included rehabilitation assignment to Scranton/Wilkes-Barre (July 16-23). ... On Philadelphia disabled list (June 12-27, 1995). ... Traded by Phillies to Boston Red Sox for OF Mark Whiten (July 24, 1995). ... On Boston disabled list (August 9, 1995-remainder of season). ... Granted free agency (December 21, 1995). ... Signed by Minnesota Twins (December 23, 1995). ... Traded by Twins to Seattle Mariners for a player to be named later (August 29, 1996); Twins acquired 1B David Arias to complete deal (September 13, 1996). ... Granted free agency (October 31, 1996). ... Signed by Anaheim Angels (November 20, 1996). ... On disabled list (August 10, 1998-remainder of season). ... Traded by Angels with cash to Toronto Blue Jays for SS Tomas Perez (March 30, 1999). ... On Toronto disabled list (April 18-May 21, 1999); included rehabilitation assignment to Syracuse (May 10-13). ... Released by Blue Jays (June 21, 1999). ... Signed by Chicago White Sox organization (July 1, 1999). ... Granted free agency (October 5, 1999). ... Signed by Tampa Bay Devil Rays organization (January 14, 2000).
STATISTICAL NOTES: Led Northwest League with seven intentional bases on balls received in 1987. ... Led Northwest League third basemen with 241 total chances in 1987. ... Led Texas League with 10 sacrifice flies in 1989. ... Led N.L. in being hit by pitch with 19 in 1992. ... Led A.L. third basemen with 29 errors in 1997. ... Career major league grand slams: 3.

Year Team (League)	Pos.	G	AB	R	H	2B	3B	HR	RBI	Avg.	BB	SO	SB	PO	A	E	Avg.
1987— Spokane (N.W.)	3B	75	278	52	86	14	4	2	44	.309	53	36	20	*59	*167	15	*.938
1988— Riverside (Calif.)........	3B-1B-SS	139	516	90	157	32	1	9	92	.304	82	67	13	102	248	29	.923
1989— Wichita (Texas)	3B	131	459	69	126	29	4	9	79	.275	63	88	8	77	209	25	.920
1990— Philadelphia (N.L.)■ ..	3B-1B	72	114	14	21	0	0	5	15	.184	10	28	0	27	37	4	.941
1991— Philadelphia (N.L.)......	3B-1B	56	151	18	45	10	2	6	21	.298	17	26	1	67	62	8	.942
—Scranton/W.B. (I.L.).....	3B-1B	72	229	37	61	11	6	8	35	.266	43	43	4	67	105	10	.945
1992— Philadelphia (N.L.)......	3B-1B	156	586	104	158	28	4	27	93	.270	76	110	9	120	253	18	.954

H

Year Team (League)	Pos.	G	AB	R	H	2B	3B	HR	RBI	Avg.	BB	SO	SB	PO	A	E	Avg.
1993— Philadelphia (N.L.).....	3B	143	543	104	148	30	4	18	93	.273	85	109	2	73	215	27	.914
1994— Philadelphia (N.L.).....	3B-OF	44	162	28	36	7	1	4	26	.222	23	32	1	39	48	11	.888
— Scranton/WB. (I.L.).....	OF	6	19	6	4	0	0	1	3	.211	5	4	0	12	1	2	.867
1995— Philadelphia (N.L.).....	1B	65	205	46	47	12	2	7	25	.229	53	38	1	532	30	7	.988
— Boston (A.L.)■........	DH-OF	5	13	2	2	0	0	0	1	.154	4	7	0	3	0	0	1.000
1996— Minnesota (A.L.)■	3B-DH-SS	121	422	71	102	26	0	13	53	.242	71	102	6	81	206	15	.950
— Seattle (A.L.)■........	3B-1B	28	94	17	33	3	0	3	25	.351	13	15	0	21	53	3	.961
1997— Anaheim (A.L.)■........	3B-1B	149	572	101	165	29	2	16	85	.288	62	124	16	208	249	†29	.940
1998— Anaheim (A.L.)	3B-1B-DH	101	363	60	88	16	2	11	39	.242	44	69	11	107	150	17	.938
1999— Toronto (A.L.)■........	DH	27	99	12	22	5	0	2	6	.222	5	22	0	0	0	0	...
— Syracuse (I.L.).......	DH	4	15	2	3	1	0	0	1	.200	1	5	0	0	0	0	...
— Charlotte (I.L.)■........	3B-1B-DH	63	199	49	63	18	0	8	33	.317	33	37	5	92	58	10	.938
American League totals (5 years)		431	1563	263	412	79	4	45	209	.264	199	339	33	420	658	64	.944
National League totals (6 years)		536	1761	314	455	87	13	67	273	.258	264	343	14	858	645	75	.952
Major League totals (10 years)		967	3324	577	867	166	17	112	482	.261	463	682	47	1278	1303	139	.949

CHAMPIONSHIP SERIES RECORD

Year Team (League)	Pos.	G	AB	R	H	2B	3B	HR	RBI	Avg.	BB	SO	SB	PO	A	E	Avg.
1993— Philadelphia (N.L.).....	3B	6	20	2	4	1	0	2	4	.200	5	4	1	5	4	0	1.000

WORLD SERIES RECORD

Year Team (League)	Pos.	G	AB	R	H	2B	3B	HR	RBI	Avg.	BB	SO	SB	PO	A	E	Avg.
1993— Philadelphia (N.L.).....	3B	6	23	5	6	1	0	0	2	.261	6	5	0	9	9	0	1.000

ALL-STAR GAME RECORD

Year League	Pos.	AB	R	H	2B	3B	HR	RBI	Avg.	BB	SO	SB	PO	A	E	Avg.
1993— National.....................	3B	1	0	1	1	0	0	0	1.000	0	0	0	1	0	0	1.000

HOLMES, DARREN　　　　P　　　　DIAMONDBACKS

PERSONAL: Born April 25, 1966, in Asheville, N.C. ... 6-0/202. ... Throws right, bats right. ... Full name: Darren Lee Holmes.
HIGH SCHOOL: T.C. Roberson (Asheville, N.C.).
TRANSACTIONS/CAREER NOTES: Selected by Los Angeles Dodgers organization in 16th round of free-agent draft (June 4, 1984). ... On disabled list (June 5, 1986-remainder of season). ... Loaned by Dodgers organization to San Luis Potosi of the Mexican League (1988). ... Traded by Dodgers to Milwaukee Brewers for C Bert Heffernan (December 20, 1990). ... On Milwaukee disabled list (July 3-18, 1991); included rehabilitation assignment to Beloit (July 13-18). ... Selected by Colorado Rockies in first round (fifth pick overall) of expansion draft (November 17, 1992). ... On Colorado disabled list (May 30-June 24 and July 21-August 11, 1994); included rehabilitation assignments to Asheville (June 14-19) and Colorado Springs (June 20). ... On disabled list (April 30-May 15, 1997). ... Granted free agency (October 27, 1997). ... Signed by New York Yankees (December 22, 1997). ... On New York disabled list (July 30-September 4, 1998); included rehabilitation assignment to Tampa (August 31-September 4). ... Traded by Yankees with cash to Arizona Diamondbacks for C Izzy Molina and P Ben Ford (March 30, 1999). ... On Arizona disabled list (June 24-July 15 and July 18-August 11, 1999); included rehabilitation assignments to Arizona League Diamondbacks (August 3-8) and Tucson (August 9-11).

Year League	W	L	Pct.	ERA	G	GS	CG	ShO	Sv.	IP	H	R	ER	BB	SO
1984— Great Falls (Pio.)	2	5	.286	6.65	18	6	1	0	0	44 2/3	53	41	33	30	29
1985— Vero Beach (FSL)	4	3	.571	3.11	33	0	0	0	2	63 2/3	57	31	22	35	46
1986— Vero Beach (FSL)	3	6	.333	2.92	11	10	0	0	0	64 2/3	55	30	21	39	59
1987— Vero Beach (FSL)	6	4	.600	4.52	19	19	1	0	0	99 2/3	111	60	50	53	46
1988— San Luis Potosi (Mex.)■....	9	9	.500	4.64	23	23	7	1	0	139 2/3	151	88	72	92	110
— Albuquerque (PCL)■.........	0	1	.000	5.06	2	1	0	0	0	5 1/3	6	3	3	1	1
1989— San Antonio (Texas)	5	8	.385	3.83	17	16	3	2	1	110 1/3	102	59	47	44	81
— Albuquerque (PCL)...........	1	4	.200	7.45	9	8	0	0	0	38 2/3	50	32	32	18	31
1990— Albuquerque (PCL)............	12	2	*.857	3.11	56	0	0	0	13	92 2/3	78	34	32	39	99
— Los Angeles (N.L.)	0	1	.000	5.19	14	0	0	0	0	17 1/3	15	10	10	11	19
1991— Denver (A.A.)■..............	0	0	...	9.00	1	0	0	0	0	1	1	1	1	2	2
— Milwaukee (A.L.)............	1	4	.200	4.72	40	0	0	0	3	76 1/3	90	43	40	27	59
— Beloit (Midw.).................	0	0	...	0.00	2	0	0	0	0	2	0	0	0	0	3
1992— Denver (A.A.)................	0	0	...	1.38	12	0	0	0	7	13	7	2	2	1	12
— Milwaukee (A.L.)............	4	4	.500	2.55	41	0	0	0	6	42 1/3	35	12	12	11	31
1993— Colorado (N.L.)	3	3	.500	4.05	62	0	0	0	25	66 2/3	56	31	30	20	60
— Colo. Springs (PCL)	1	0	1.000	0.00	3	2	0	0	0	8 2/3	1	1	0	1	9
1994— Colorado (N.L.)	0	3	.000	6.35	29	0	0	0	3	28 1/3	35	25	20	24	33
— Colo. Springs (PCL)	0	1	.000	8.22	4	2	0	0	0	7 2/3	11	7	7	3	12
— Asheville (SAL)................	0	0	...	0.00	2	1	0	0	0	3	1	0	0	0	7
1995— Colorado (N.L.)	6	1	.857	3.24	68	0	0	0	14	66 2/3	59	26	24	28	61
1996— Colorado (N.L.)	5	4	.556	3.97	62	0	0	0	1	77	78	41	34	28	73
1997— Colorado (N.L.)	9	2	.818	5.34	42	6	0	0	3	89 1/3	113	58	53	36	70
1998— New York (A.L.)■.............	0	3	.000	3.33	34	0	0	0	2	51 1/3	53	19	19	14	31
— Tampa (FSL)	0	1	.000	4.50	2	1	0	0	0	2	4	2	1	0	6
1999— Arizona (N.L.)■..............	4	3	.571	3.70	44	0	0	0	2	48 2/3	50	21	20	25	35
— Ariz. Diamondbacks (Ariz.).	0	0	...	0.00	2	2	0	0	0	2 2/3	1	0	0	0	4
— Tucson (PCL)	0	0	...	0.00	1	1	0	0	0	1	0	0	0	1	0
A.L. totals (3 years)	5	11	.313	3.76	115	0	0	0	11	170	178	74	71	52	121
N.L. totals (7 years)	27	17	.614	4.36	321	6	0	0	46	394	406	212	191	172	351
Major League totals (10 years)	32	28	.533	4.18	436	6	0	0	57	564	584	286	262	224	472

H

Year League	W	L	Pct.	ERA	G	GS	CG	ShO	Sv.	IP	H	R	ER	BB	SO
1995—Colorado (N.L.)	1	0	1.000	0.00	3	0	0	0	0	1 2/3	6	2	0	9	2
1998—New York (A.L.)							Did not play.								
1999—Arizona (N.L.)	0	0	...	27.00	1	0	0	0	0	1 1/3	1	4	4	3	0
Division series totals (2 years)	1	0	1.000	12.00	4	0	0	0	0	3	7	6	4	12	2

CHAMPIONSHIP SERIES RECORD

Year League	W	L	Pct.	ERA	G	GS	CG	ShO	Sv.	IP	H	R	ER	BB	SO
1998—New York (A.L.)							Did not play.								

WORLD SERIES RECORD

NOTES: Member of World Series championship team (1998).

Year League	W	L	Pct.	ERA	G	GS	CG	ShO	Sv.	IP	H	R	ER	BB	SO
1998—New York (A.L.)							Did not play.								

HOLT, CHRIS — P — ASTROS

PERSONAL: Born September 18, 1971, in Dallas. ... 6-4/205. ... Throws right, bats right. ... Full name: Christopher Michael Holt.
HIGH SCHOOL: Skyline (Dallas).
JUNIOR COLLEGE: Navarro College (Texas).
TRANSACTIONS/CAREER NOTES: Selected by Houston Astros organization in third round of free-agent draft (June 1, 1992). ... On Houston disabled list (March 30, 1998-entire season); included rehabilitation assignment to Kissimmee (April 25-26).

Year League	W	L	Pct.	ERA	G	GS	CG	ShO	Sv.	IP	H	R	ER	BB	SO
1992—Auburn (NY-P)...................	2	5	.286	4.45	14	14	0	0	0	83	75	48	41	24	81
1993—Quad City (Midw.)	11	10	.524	2.27	26	26	*10	•3	0	*186 1/3	162	70	47	54	176
1994—Jackson (Texas)	10	9	.526	3.45	26	25	5	•2	0	167	169	78	64	22	111
1995—Jackson (Texas)	2	2	.500	1.67	5	5	1	1	0	32 1/3	27	8	6	5	24
—Tucson (PCL)	5	8	.385	4.10	20	19	0	0	0	118 2/3	155	65	54	32	69
1996—Tucson (PCL)	9	6	.600	3.62	28	27	4	1	0	*186 1/3	208	87	75	38	137
—Houston (N.L.)	0	1	.000	5.79	4	0	0	0	0	4 2/3	5	3	3	3	0
1997—Houston (N.L.)	8	12	.400	3.52	33	32	0	0	0	209 2/3	211	98	82	61	95
1998—Kissimmee (FSL)...............	0	1	.000	9.00	1	1	0	0	0	4	6	4	4	4	1
1999—Houston (N.L.)	5	13	.278	4.66	32	26	0	0	1	164	193	92	85	57	115
Major League totals (3 years)	13	26	.333	4.04	69	58	0	0	1	378 1/3	409	193	170	121	210

DIVISION SERIES RECORD

Year League	W	L	Pct.	ERA	G	GS	CG	ShO	Sv.	IP	H	R	ER	BB	SO
1999—Houston (N.L.)	0	0	...	...	1	0	0	0	0		3	3	3	0	0

HOLTZ, MIKE — P — ANGELS

PERSONAL: Born October 10, 1972, in Arlington, Va. ... 5-9/188. ... Throws left, bats left. ... Full name: Michael James Holtz.
HIGH SCHOOL: Central Cambria (Ebensburg, Pa.).
COLLEGE: Clemson.
TRANSACTIONS/CAREER NOTES: Selected by California Angels organization in 17th round of free-agent draft (June 2, 1994). ... Angels franchise renamed Anaheim Angels for 1997 season. ... On suspended list (June 18-20, 1998). ... On Anaheim disabled list (August 25-September 10, 1999).

Year League	W	L	Pct.	ERA	G	GS	CG	ShO	Sv.	IP	H	R	ER	BB	SO
1994—Boise (N.W.)	0	0	...	0.51	22	0	0	0	11	35	22	4	2	11	59
1995—Lake Elsinore (Calif.)	4	4	.500	2.29	*56	0	0	0	3	82 2/3	70	26	21	23	101
1996—Midland (Texas)	1	2	.333	4.17	33	0	0	0	2	41	52	34	19	9	41
—California (A.L.)	3	3	.500	2.45	30	0	0	0	0	29 1/3	21	11	8	19	31
1997—Anaheim (A.L.)	3	4	.429	3.32	66	0	0	0	2	43 1/3	38	21	16	15	40
1998—Anaheim (A.L.)	2	2	.500	4.75	53	0	0	0	1	30 1/3	38	16	16	15	29
—Vancouver (PCL)	0	0	...	1.74	10	0	0	0	2	10 1/3	10	4	2	6	18
1999—Anaheim (A.L.)	2	3	.400	8.06	28	0	0	0	0	22 1/3	26	20	20	15	17
—Edmonton (PCL)	2	1	.667	2.30	20	0	0	0	1	27 1/3	20	7	7	11	39
Major League totals (4 years)	10	12	.455	4.31	177	0	0	0	3	125 1/3	123	68	60	64	117

HOUSTON, TYLER — C — BREWERS

PERSONAL: Born January 17, 1971, in Long Beach, Calif. ... 6-1/210. ... Bats left, throws right. ... Full name: Tyler Sam Houston.
HIGH SCHOOL: Valley (Las Vegas).
TRANSACTIONS/CAREER NOTES: Selected by Atlanta Braves organization in first round (second pick overall) of free-agent draft (June 5, 1989). ... On Greenville disabled list (June 25-July 5, 1993). ... Traded by Braves to Chicago Cubs for P Ismael Villegas (June 27, 1996). ... On disabled list (May 3-19, 1997); included rehabilitation assignment to Iowa (May 14-19, 1997). ... On Chicago disabled list (June 11-July 11, 1997); included rehabilitation assignment to Rockford (July 9-11). ... On suspended list (September 16, 1997). ... On disabled list (May 26-June 24, 1998). ... Traded by Cubs to Cleveland Indians for P Richard Negrette (August 31, 1999). ... Granted free agency (December 21, 1999). ... Signed by Milwaukee Brewers (January 17, 2000).
STATISTICAL NOTES: Led Pioneer League with 14 passed balls in 1989.

							BATTING						FIELDING		
Year Team (League)	Pos.	G	AB	R	H	2B	3B	HR	RBI	Avg.	BB	SO	SB	PO	A	E	Avg.
1989—Idaho Falls (Pio.)	C	50	176	30	43	11	0	4	24	.244	25	41	4	148	15	5	.970
1990—Sumter (SAL)	C	117	442	58	93	14	3	13	56	.210	49	101	6	498	55	*18	.968
1991—Macon (SAL)	C	107	351	41	81	16	3	8	47	.231	39	70	10	591	75	10	.985
1992—Durham (Caro.)	C-3B-1B	117	402	39	91	17	1	7	38	.226	20	89	5	493	65	15	.974
1993—Greenville (Sou.)	C-OF	84	262	27	73	14	1	5	33	.279	13	50	5	410	34	9	.980
—Richmond (I.L.)	C-DH	13	36	4	5	1	1	1	3	.139	1	8	0	69	2	3	.959

H

Year	Team (League)	Pos.	G	AB	R	H	2B	3B	HR	RBI	Avg.	BB	SO	SB	PO	A	E	Avg.
1994—	Richmond (I.L.).........1B-C-DH-OF		97	312	33	76	15	2	4	33	.244	16	44	3	619	54	7	.990
1995—	Richmond (I.L.).........1-C-O-3-DH		103	349	41	89	10	3	12	42	.255	18	62	3	579	69	11	.983
1996—	Atlanta (N.L.)........ 1B-OF-3B		33	27	3	6	2	1	1	8	.222	1	9	0	16	1	0	1.000
	—Chicago (N.L.)■........C-3B-2B-1B		46	115	18	39	7	0	2	19	.339	8	18	3	139	25	3	.982
1997—	Chicago (N.L.)........... C-3-1-2-S		72	196	15	51	10	0	2	28	.260	9	35	1	280	37	5	.984
	—Iowa (A.A.)............ 3B-DH-C		6	23	0	5	2	0	0	4	.217	0	2	0	6	9	2	.882
	—Rockford (Midw.)....... C-3B		2	6	1	3	1	0	0	1	.500	0	0	0	5	0	0	1.000
1998—	Chicago (N.L.)........... C-3B-1B		95	255	26	65	7	1	9	33	.255	13	53	2	451	36	5	.990
1999—	Chicago (N.L.)..........3B-C-1B-OF		100	249	26	58	9	1	9	27	.233	28	67	1	109	89	17	.921
	—Cleveland (A.L.)■....... 3B-C		13	27	2	4	1	0	1	3	.148	3	11	0	7	11	0	1.000
American League totals (1 year)			13	27	2	4	1	0	1	3	.148	3	11	0	7	11	0	1.000
National League totals (4 years)			346	842	88	219	35	3	23	115	.260	59	182	7	995	188	30	.975
Major League totals (4 years)			359	869	90	223	36	3	24	118	.257	62	193	7	1002	199	30	.976

DIVISION SERIES RECORD

Year	Team (League)	Pos.	G	AB	R	H	2B	3B	HR	RBI	Avg.	BB	SO	SB	PO	A	E	Avg.
1998—	Chicago (N.L.)............	C	3	6	1	1	0	0	1	1	.167	0	3	0	13	0	0	1.000
1999—	Cleveland (A.L.).........										Did not play.							

HOWARD, DAVID   IF/OF

PERSONAL: Born February 26, 1967, in Sarasota, Fla. ... 6-0/175. ... Bats both, throws right. ... Full name: David Wayne Howard. ... Son of Bruce Howard, pitcher with three major league teams (1963-68).

HIGH SCHOOL: Riverview (Sarasota, Fla.).

JUNIOR COLLEGE: Manatee Community College (Fla.).

TRANSACTIONS/CAREER NOTES: Selected by Kansas City Royals organization in 32nd round of free-agent draft (June 2, 1986). ... On disabled list (May 12-31 and July 23-August 9, 1989). ... On Kansas City disabled list (April 22-July 6, 1992); included rehabilitation assignments to Baseball City (June 16-20) and Omaha (June 20-July 5). ... On Kansas City disabled list (April 19-May 17, 1993); included rehabilitation assignment to Omaha (May 10-17). ... On Kansas City disabled list (June 7-August 10, 1993); included rehabilitation assignments to Omaha (July 15-23 and July 31-August 10). ... On disabled list (May 27-June 17, 1995; and August 14-September 1, 1997). ... Granted free agency (October 28, 1997). ... Signed by St. Louis Cardinals (December 4, 1997). ... On disabled list (May 24-June 8 and July 3, 1998-remainder of season). ... On St. Louis disabled list (April 4-19 and April 24-June 23, 1999); included rehabilitation assignment to Memphis (June 4-23). ... Granted free agency (October 28, 1999).

STATISTICAL NOTES: Led A.L. shortstops with .982 fielding percentage in 1996.

Year	Team (League)	Pos.	G	AB	R	H	2B	3B	HR	RBI	Avg.	BB	SO	SB	PO	A	E	Avg.
1987—	Fort Myers (FSL).......	SS	89	289	26	56	9	4	1	19	.194	30	68	11	123	273	28	.934
1988—	Appleton (Midw.)........	SS	110	368	48	82	9	4	1	22	.223	25	80	10	151	275	43	.908
1989—	Baseball City (FSL).....SS-OF-3B-2B		83	267	36	63	7	3	3	30	.236	23	44	12	141	225	18	.953
1990—	Memphis (Sou.)	SS-2B	116	384	41	96	10	4	5	44	.250	39	73	15	194	321	32	.941
1991—	Omaha (A.A.)...............	SS-2B	14	41	2	5	0	0	0	2	.122	7	11	1	30	43	3	.961
	—Kansas City (A.L.) S-2-3-O-DH		94	236	20	51	7	0	1	17	.216	16	45	3	129	248	12	.969
1992—	Kansas City (A.L.)	SS-OF	74	219	19	49	6	2	1	18	.224	15	43	3	124	204	8	.976
	—Baseball City (FSL)	SS	3	9	3	4	1	0	0	0	.444	2	0	0	3	7	1	.909
	—Omaha (A.A.)...............	SS	19	68	5	8	1	0	0	5	.118	3	8	1	25	52	8	.906
1993—	Kansas City (A.L.) 2B-SS-3B-OF		15	24	5	8	0	1	0	2	.333	2	5	1	17	28	3	.938
	—Omaha (A.A.)...............	SS	47	157	15	40	8	2	0	18	.255	7	20	3	76	137	8	.964
1994—	Kansas City (A.L.) 3-S-2-DH-P-O		46	83	9	19	4	0	1	13	.229	11	23	3	27	79	1	.991
1995—	Kansas City (A.L.) 2-S-O-DH-1		95	255	23	62	13	4	0	19	.243	24	41	6	167	195	29	.926
1996—	Kansas City (A.L.) S-2-1-DH-O		143	420	51	92	14	5	4	48	.219	40	74	5	210	411	11	†.983
1997—	Kansas City (A.L.) 2-O-S-3-DH		80	162	24	39	8	1	1	13	.241	10	31	2	96	109	7	.967
1998—	St. Louis (N.L.)■.......... 2B-SS-3B-OF		46	102	15	25	1	1	2	12	.245	12	22	0	53	82	2	.985
1999—	St. Louis (N.L.).......... S-1-2-0-3		52	82	3	17	4	0	1	6	.207	7	27	0	59	41	1	.990
	—Memphis (PCL) 2B-SS-DH-OF		8	19	3	5	0	0	0	2	.263	1	6	2	12	11	0	1.000
American League totals (7 years)			547	1399	151	320	52	13	8	130	.229	118	262	23	770	1274	71	.966
National League totals (2 years)			98	184	18	42	5	1	3	18	.228	19	49	0	112	123	3	.987
Major League totals (9 years)			645	1583	169	362	57	14	11	148	.229	137	311	23	882	1397	74	.969

RECORD AS PITCHER

Year	League	W	L	Pct.	ERA	G	GS	CG	ShO	Sv.	IP	H	R	ER	BB	SO
1994—	Kansas City (A.L.)	0	0	...	4.50	1	0	0	0	0	2	2	1	1	5	0

HOWARD, THOMAS   OF   CARDINALS

PERSONAL: Born December 11, 1964, in Middletown, Ohio. ... 6-2/205. ... Bats both, throws right. ... Full name: Thomas Sylvester Howard.

HIGH SCHOOL: Valley View (Germantown, Ohio).

COLLEGE: Ball State.

TRANSACTIONS/CAREER NOTES: Selected by San Diego Padres organization in first round (11th pick overall) of free-agent draft (June 2, 1986). ... On disabled list (June 5-July 17, 1989). ... Traded by Padres to Cleveland Indians for SS Jason Hardtke and a player to be named later (April 14, 1992); Padres acquired C Christopher Maffett to complete deal (July 10, 1992). ... Traded by Indians to Cincinnati Reds (August 20, 1993), completing deal in which Reds traded 1B Randy Milligan to Indians for a player to be named later (August 17, 1993). ... On Cincinnati disabled list (March 23-April 20, 1996); included rehabilitation assignments to Chattanooga (April 11-19) and Indianapolis (April 19-20). ... Released by Reds (November 18, 1996). ... Signed by Houston Astros (December 4, 1996). ... Granted free agency (October 28, 1997). ... Signed by Los Angeles Dodgers organization (January 7, 1998). ... Released by Dodgers (June 29, 1998). ... Signed by St. Louis Cardinals organization (December 31, 1998). ... Granted free agency (November 4, 1999). ... Re-signed by Cardinals (December 22, 1999).

HONORS: Named outfielder on The Sporting News college All-America team (1986).

H

Year	Team (League)	Pos.	G	AB	R	H	2B	3B	HR	RBI	Avg.	BB	SO	SB	PO	A	E	Avg.
1986—	Spokane (N.W.)	OF	13	55	16	23	3	3	2	17	.418	3	9	2	24	3	0	1.000
—	Reno (Calif.)	OF	61	223	35	57	7	3	10	39	.256	34	49	10	104	5	6	.948
1987—	Wichita (Texas)	OF	113	401	72	133	27	4	14	60	.332	36	72	26	226	6	6	.975
1988—	Wichita (Texas)	OF	29	103	15	31	9	2	0	16	.301	13	14	6	51	2	2	.964
—	Las Vegas (PCL)	OF	44	167	29	42	9	1	0	15	.251	12	31	3	74	3	2	.975
1989—	Las Vegas (PCL)	OF	80	303	45	91	18	3	3	31	.300	30	56	22	178	7	2	.989
1990—	Las Vegas (PCL)	OF	89	341	58	112	26	8	5	51	.328	44	63	27	159	6	2	.988
—	San Diego (N.L.)	OF	20	44	4	12	2	0	0	0	.273	0	11	0	19	0	1	.950
1991—	San Diego (N.L.)	OF	106	281	30	70	12	3	4	22	.249	24	57	10	182	4	1	.995
—	Las Vegas (PCL)	OF	25	94	22	29	3	1	2	16	.309	10	16	11	54	2	2	.966
1992—	San Diego (N.L.)	PH	5	3	1	1	0	0	0	0	.333	0	0	0	...	...	...	...
—	Cleveland (A.L.)■....	OF-DH	117	358	36	99	15	2	2	32	.277	17	60	15	185	5	2	.990
1993—	Cleveland (A.L.).........	OF-DH	74	178	26	42	7	0	3	23	.236	12	42	5	81	3	2	.977
—	Cincinnati (N.L.)■....	OF	38	141	22	39	8	3	4	13	.277	12	21	5	73	4	1	.987
1994—	Cincinnati (N.L.)	OF	83	178	24	47	11	0	5	24	.264	10	30	4	80	2	3	.965
1995—	Cincinnati (N.L.)	OF	113	281	42	85	15	2	3	26	.302	20	37	17	127	2	2	.985
1996—	Cincinnati (N.L.)	OF	121	360	50	88	19	10	6	42	.244	17	51	6	160	7	3	.982
—	Chattanooga (Sou.).....	OF-DH	8	30	4	10	1	0	1	2	.333	2	7	1	8	0	0	1.000
—	Indianapolis (A.A.)......	OF	1	6	2	2	0	0	1	2	.333	0	0	0	3	0	0	1.000
1997—	Houston (N.L.)	OF	107	255	24	63	16	1	3	22	.247	26	48	1	107	5	0	1.000
1998—	Los Angeles (N.L.)■..	OF-DH	47	76	9	14	4	0	2	4	.184	3	15	1	33	2	0	1.000
1999—	Memphis (PCL)■.......	OF	35	119	24	43	10	2	2	21	.361	13	21	1	54	2	1	.982
—	St. Louis (N.L.).........	OF-DH	98	195	16	57	10	0	6	28	.292	17	26	1	77	0	1	.987
American League totals (2 years)			191	536	62	141	22	2	5	55	.263	29	102	20	266	8	4	.986
National League totals (10 years)			738	1814	222	476	97	19	33	181	.262	129	296	45	858	26	12	.987
Major League totals (10 years)			929	2350	284	617	119	21	38	236	.263	158	398	65	1124	34	16	.986

DIVISION SERIES RECORD

Year	Team (League)	Pos.	G	AB	R	H	2B	3B	HR	RBI	Avg.	BB	SO	SB	PO	A	E	Avg.
1995—	Cincinnati (N.L.)	OF	3	10	0	1	1	0	0	0	.100	0	2	0	5	0	0	1.000
1997—	Houston (N.L.)	PH	2	1	0	0	0	0	0	0	.000	1	1	0	0	0	0	...
Division series totals (2 years)			5	11	0	1	1	0	0	0	.091	1	3	0	5	0	0	1.000

CHAMPIONSHIP SERIES RECORD

Year	Team (League)	Pos.	G	AB	R	H	2B	3B	HR	RBI	Avg.	BB	SO	SB	PO	A	E	Avg.
1995—	Cincinnati (N.L.)	PH-OF	4	8	0	2	1	0	0	1	.250	2	0	0	2	0	0	1.000

HOWELL, JACK — 3B

PERSONAL: Born August 18, 1961, in Tucson, Ariz. ... 6-0/190. ... Bats left, throws right. ... Full name: Jack Robert Howell.
HIGH SCHOOL: Palo Verde (Tucson, Ariz.).
JUNIOR COLLEGE: Pima Community College (Ariz.).
COLLEGE: Arizona.
TRANSACTIONS/CAREER NOTES: Signed as non-drafted free agent by California Angels organization (August 6, 1983). ... On Edmonton disabled list (June 21-July 7, 1985). ... On California disabled list (May 23-June 9, 1990 and May 5-28, 1991). ... Traded by Angels to San Diego Padres for OF Shawn Abner (July 30, 1991). ... Granted free agency (October 28, 1991). ... Signed by Yakult Swallows of Japan Central League (December 8, 1991). ... Signed by Yomiuri Giants of Japan Central League (December 7, 1994). ... Signed by Angels organization (December 5, 1995). ... On California disabled list (June 14-July 19, 1996); included rehabilitation assignment to Lake Elsinore (July 13-19). ... Granted free agency (November 18, 1996). ... Re-signed by Angels organization (December 20, 1996). ... Angels franchise renamed Anaheim Angels for 1997 season. ... Granted free agency (October 30, 1997). ... Signed by Houston Astros (December 9, 1997). ... On disabled list (May 20, 1998-remainder of season). ... On Houston disabled list (May 25-June 24 and July 18, 1999-remainder of season); included rehabilitation assignment to Jackson (June 21-24). ... Granted free agency (November 10, 1999).
HONORS: Named Most Valuable Player of Japan Central League (1992).
STATISTICAL NOTES: Led California League third basemen with .943 fielding percentage, 259 assists, 368 total chances and 23 double plays in 1984. ... Led A.L. third basemen with .974 fielding percentage, 322 assists and 428 total chances in 1989. ... Career major league grand slams: 1.

Year	Team (League)	Pos.	G	AB	R	H	2B	3B	HR	RBI	Avg.	BB	SO	SB	PO	A	E	Avg.
1983—	Salem (N.W.)	3B-2B	21	76	23	30	2	5	3	12	.395	17	11	26	19	32	11	.823
1984—	Redwood (Calif.)	3B-1B	135	451	62	111	21	5	5	64	.246	44	95	12	96	†260	21	†.944
1985—	Edmonton (PCL)	3B-SS	79	284	55	106	22	3	13	48	.373	52	57	3	67	130	12	.943
—	California (A.L.)	3B	43	137	19	27	4	0	5	18	.197	16	33	1	33	75	8	.931
1986—	Edmonton (PCL)	3B	44	156	39	56	17	3	3	28	.359	38	29	1	28	84	8	.933
—	California (A.L.)	3B-DH-OF	63	151	26	41	14	2	4	21	.272	19	28	2	38	57	2	.979
1987—	California (A.L.)	OF-3B-DH	138	449	64	110	18	5	23	64	.245	57	118	4	185	95	7	.976
1988—	California (A.L.)	3B-OF	154	500	59	127	32	2	16	63	.254	46	130	2	97	249	17	.953
1989—	California (A.L.)	3B-OF	144	474	56	108	19	4	20	52	.228	52	125	0	97	†322	11	†.974
1990—	California (A.L.)	3B-SS-1B	105	316	35	72	19	1	8	33	.228	46	61	3	76	196	18	.938
—	Edmonton (PCL)	3B-1B	20	75	14	25	7	1	2	15	.333	7	13	3	22	33	1	.982
1991—	California (A.L.) 2-0-1-3-DH		32	81	11	17	2	0	2	7	.210	11	11	1	53	55	2	.982
—	San Diego (N.L.)	3B	58	160	24	33	3	1	6	16	.206	18	33	0	33	98	2	.985
1992—	Yakult (Jap. Cen.)■...	3B	113	387	67	128	21	1	*38	87	*.331	41	86	3	...	...	...	...
1993—	Yakult (Jap. Cen.).......	IF	121	396	72	117	15	1	28	88	.295	86	83	3	...	...	...	...
1994—	Yakult (Jap. Cen.).......	IF	109	363	54	91	14	0	20	56	.251	62	74	4	...	...	...	...
1995—	Yomiuri (Jap. Cen.)■.	IF	66	219	35	61	10	0	14	41	.279	37	66	1	...	...	...	...
1996—	California (A.L.)■....3B-DH-1B-2B	66	126	20	34	4	1	8	21	.270	10	30	0	28	44	9	.889
—	Lake Elsinore (Calif.)..	3B-DH	4	12	2	2	1	0	1	3	.167	3	4	0	3	8	1	.917
1997—	Anaheim (A.L.)	3B-DH-1B	77	174	25	45	7	0	14	34	.259	13	36	1	58	33	3	.968

H

Year	Team (League)	Pos.	G	AB	R	H	2B	3B	HR	RBI	Avg.	BB	SO	SB	PO	A	E	Avg.
							BATTING									FIELDING		
1998—Houston (N.L.)■	1B-3B	24	38	4	11	5	0	1	7	.289	4	12	0	64	11	0	1.000
1999—Houston (N.L.)	1B-3B-DH	37	33	2	7	2	0	1	1	.212	8	9	0	10	5	0	1.000
—Jackson (Texas)	1B	3	8	2	3	1	0	2	3	.375	0	2	0	20	2	0	1.000
American League totals (9 years)		822	2408	315	581	119	15	100	313	.241	270	572	14	665	1126	77	.959
National League totals (3 years)		119	231	30	51	10	1	8	24	.221	30	54	0	107	114	2	.991
Major League totals (11 years)		941	2639	345	632	129	16	108	337	.239	300	626	14	772	1240	79	.962

CHAMPIONSHIP SERIES RECORD

Year	Team (League)	Pos.	G	AB	R	H	2B	3B	HR	RBI	Avg.	BB	SO	SB	PO	A	E	Avg.
							BATTING									FIELDING		
1986—California (A.L.)	PH	2	1	0	0	0	0	0	0	.000	1	1	0	...	...	...	

HOWRY, BOBBY   P   WHITE SOX

PERSONAL: Born August 4, 1973, in Phoenix. ... 6-5/220. ... Throws right, bats left. ... Full name: Bobby Dean Howry.
HIGH SCHOOL: Deer Valley (Phoenix).
JUNIOR COLLEGE: Yavapai College (Ariz.).
COLLEGE: McNeese State.
TRANSACTIONS/CAREER NOTES: Selected by San Francisco Giants organization in fifth round of free-agent draft (June 2, 1994). ... Traded by Giants with SS Mike Caruso, OF Brian Manning, P Keith Foulke, P Lorenzo Barcelo and P Ken Vining to Chicago White Sox for P Wilson Alvarez, P Danny Darwin and P Roberto Hernandez (July 31, 1997).

Year	League	W	L	Pct.	ERA	G	GS	CG	ShO	Sv.	IP	H	R	ER	BB	SO
1994—Everett (N.W.).....................	0	4	.000	4.74	5	5	0	0	0	19	29	15	10	10	16
—Clinton (Midw.)	1	3	.250	4.20	9	8	0	0	0	49 1/3	61	29	23	16	22
1995—San Jose (Calif.)................	12	10	.545	3.54	27	25	1	0	0	165 1/3	171	79	65	54	107
1996—Shreveport (Texas)............	12	10	.545	4.65	27	27	0	0	0	156 2/3	163	90	81	56	57
1997—Shreveport (Texas)............	6	3	.667	4.91	48	0	0	0	*22	55	58	35	30	21	43
—Birmingham (Sou.)■	0	0	...	2.84	12	0	0	0	0	12 2/3	16	4	4	3	3
1998—Calgary (PCL)..................	1	2	.333	3.41	23	0	0	0	5	31 2/3	25	12	12	10	22
—Chicago (A.L.)..................	0	3	.000	3.15	44	0	0	0	9	54 1/3	37	20	19	19	51
1999—Chicago (A.L.)..................	5	3	.625	3.59	69	0	0	0	28	67 2/3	58	34	27	38	80
Major League totals (2 years).......	5	6	.455	3.39	113	0	0	0	37	122	95	54	46	57	131

HUBBARD, TRENIDAD   OF   BRAVES

PERSONAL: Born May 11, 1966, in Chicago. ... 5-9/185. ... Bats right, throws right. ... Full name: Trenidad Aviel Hubbard. ... Cousin of Joe Cribbs, running back with Buffalo Bills (1980-83 and 1985).
HIGH SCHOOL: South Shore (Chicago).
COLLEGE: Southern (La.).
TRANSACTIONS/CAREER NOTES: Selected by Houston Astros organization in 12th round of free-agent draft (June 2, 1986). ... Granted free agency (October 15, 1992). ... Signed by Colorado Rockies organization (October 30, 1992). ... On disabled list (June 15-24, 1993). ... Granted free agency (October 15, 1993). ... Re-signed by Rockies organization (December 3, 1993). ... Granted free agency (October 15, 1994). ... Re-signed by Colorado Springs, Rockies organization (November 14, 1994). ... Claimed on waivers by San Francisco Giants (August 21, 1996). ... On San Francisco disabled list (September 13, 1996-remainder of season). ... Traded by Giants to Cleveland Indians for P Joe Roa (December 16, 1996), completing deal in which Indians traded IF Jeff Kent, IF Jose Vizcaino, P Julian Tavarez and a player to be named later to Giants for 3B Matt Williams and a player to be named later (November 13, 1996). ... Granted free agency (October 8, 1997). ... Signed by Los Angeles Dodgers (December 3, 1997). ... On Los Angeles disabled list (May 14-June 22, 1998); included rehabilitation assignment to Albuquerque (June 9-22). ... Granted free agency (January 18, 2000). ... Signed by Atlanta Braves organization (January 20, 2000).
STATISTICAL NOTES: Led Texas League second basemen with 296 putouts, 653 total chances and 81 double plays in 1991. ... Tied for Pacific Coast League lead in caught stealing with 18 in 1993. ... Led Pacific Coast League with .416 on-base percentage in 1995.
MISCELLANEOUS: Batted lefthanded on occasion though not a switch hitter (1986-91).

Year	Team (League)	Pos.	G	AB	R	H	2B	3B	HR	RBI	Avg.	BB	SO	SB	PO	A	E	Avg.
							BATTING									FIELDING		
1986—Auburn (NY-P)............	2B-OF	70	242	42	75	12	1	1	32	.310	28	42	35	131	110	18	.931
1987—Asheville (SAL)............	2-O-C-3-P	101	284	39	67	8	1	1	35	.236	28	42	28	124	108	14	.943
1988—Osceola (FSL).............	2-C-O-3-1	130	446	68	116	15	11	3	65	.260	61	72	44	261	150	12	.972
1989—Columbus (Sou.).........	2B-C-OF-3B	104	348	55	92	7	8	3	37	.264	43	53	28	321	122	15	.967
—Tucson (PCL)	OF-3B-C	21	50	3	11	2	0	0	2	.220	1	10	3	20	9	1	.967
1990—Columbus (Sou.).........	2B-OF-C-3B	95	335	39	84	14	4	4	35	.251	32	51	17	216	116	11	.968
—Tucson (PCL)	2B-3B-C	12	27	5	6	2	2	0	2	.222	3	6	1	20	22	3	.933
1991—Jackson (Texas)........	2B-OF-1B-P	126	455	78	135	21	3	2	41	.297	65	81	39	†299	338	21	.968
—Tucson (PCL)	2B	2	4	0	0	0	0	0	0	.000	0	0	0	1	2	0	1.000
1992—Tucson (PCL)	2B-3B	115	420	69	130	16	4	2	33	.310	45	68	34	238	353	18	.970
1993—Colo. Spr. (PCL)■......	O-2-3-D-S	117	439	83	138	24	8	7	56	.314	47	57	33	208	29	6	.975
1994—Colo. Springs (PCL) ...	OF	79	320	78	116	22	5	8	38	.363	44	40	28	183	5	7	.964
—Colorado (N.L.)	OF	18	25	3	7	1	1	1	3	.280	3	4	0	4	0	0	1.000
1995—Colo. Springs (PCL) ...	OF	123	480	*102	163	29	7	12	66	.340	61	69	*37	285	11	6	.980
—Colorado (N.L.)	OF	24	58	13	18	4	0	3	9	.310	8	6	2	16	1	0	1.000
1996—Colorado (N.L.)	OF	45	60	12	13	5	1	1	12	.217	9	22	2	32	0	0	1.000
—Colo. Springs (PCL) ...	O-2-3-C	50	188	41	59	15	5	6	16	.314	28	14	6	89	55	4	.973
—San Fran. (N.L.)■......	OF	10	29	3	6	0	1	1	2	.207	2	5	0	19	1	0	1.000
1997—Buffalo (A.A.)■	OF-3B-DH	103	375	71	117	22	1	16	60	.312	57	52	26	236	2	2	.992
—Cleveland (A.L.)..........	OF	7	12	3	3	1	0	0	0	.250	1	3	1	3	0	0	1.000
1998—Los Angeles (N.L.)■...	OF-3B	94	208	29	62	9	1	7	18	.298	18	46	9	110	3	1	.991
—Albuquerque (PCL).....	OF-DH	11	30	6	9	0	0	3	5	.300	5	5	2	13	1	0	1.000
1999—Albuquerque (PCL).....	OF-DH	32	123	24	41	8	2	5	24	.333	16	27	16	72	2	2	.974
—Los Angeles (N.L.)	OF-C-2B	82	105	23	33	5	0	1	13	.314	13	24	4	50	1	1	.981
American League totals (1 year)		7	12	3	3	1	0	0	0	.250	1	3	1	3	0	0	1.000
National League totals (5 years)		273	485	83	139	24	4	14	57	.287	53	107	17	231	6	2	.992
Major League totals (6 years)		280	497	86	142	25	4	14	57	.286	54	110	19	234	6	2	.992

H

DIVISION SERIES RECORD

Year Team (League)	Pos.	G	AB	R	H	2B	3B	HR	RBI	Avg.	BB	SO	SB	PO	A	E	Avg.
					BATTING									FIELDING			
1995— Colorado (N.L.)	PH	3	2	0	0	0	0	0	0	.000	0	0	0	...	...	...	...

RECORD AS PITCHER

Year League	W	L	Pct.	ERA	G	GS	CG	ShO	Sv.	IP	H	R	ER	BB	SO
1987— Asheville (SAL)..................	0	0	...	0.00	1	0	0	0	0	1	1	0	0	1	0
1991— Jackson (Texas)	0	0	...	0.00	1	0	0	0	0	1	0	0	0	2	0

HUDEK, JOHN   P   CARDINALS

PERSONAL: Born August 8, 1966, in Tampa. ... 6-1/205. ... Throws right, bats both. ... Full name: John Raymond Hudek. ... Name pronounced HOO-dek.
HIGH SCHOOL: H.B. Plant (Tampa).
COLLEGE: Florida Southern.
TRANSACTIONS/CAREER NOTES: Selected by Texas Rangers organization in 30th round of free-agent draft (June 3, 1985); did not sign. ... Selected by Chicago White Sox organization in 10th round of free-agent draft (June 1, 1988). ... Selected by Detroit Tigers from White Sox organization in Rule 5 minor league draft (December 7, 1992). ... On Toledo disabled list (April 8-28 and June 17-July 1, 1993). ... Claimed on waivers by Houston Astros (July 29, 1993). ... On disabled list (June 26, 1995-remainder of season). ... On Houston disabled list (March 22-July 15, 1996); included rehabilitation assignments to Kissimmee (June 21-30) and Tucson (June 30-July 15). ... Traded by Astros to New York Mets for OF Carl Everett (December 22, 1997). ... Traded by Mets to Cincinnati Reds for OF/IF Lenny Harris (July 3, 1998). ... Traded by Reds to Atlanta Braves for P Mark Wohlers and cash (April 16, 1999). ... On Atlanta disabled list (May 15-June 28, 1999); included rehabilitation assignment to Richmond (May 31-June 27). ... Released by Braves (July 30, 1999). ... Signed by Toronto Blue Jays organization (July 31, 1999). ... Released by Blue Jays (October 20, 1999). ... Signed by St. Louis Cardinals organization (January 19, 2000).
STATISTICAL NOTES: Combined with starter Jose Ventura and Chris Howard in 4-1 no-hit victory against Charlotte (April 18, 1991).

Year League	W	L	Pct.	ERA	G	GS	CG	ShO	Sv.	IP	H	R	ER	BB	SO
1988— South Bend (Midw.)	7	2	.778	1.98	26	0	0	0	8	54 2/3	45	19	12	21	35
1989— Sarasota (FSL)	1	3	.250	1.67	27	0	0	0	15	43	22	10	8	13	39
— Birmingham (Sou.).............	1	1	.500	4.24	18	0	0	0	11	17	14	8	8	9	10
1990— Birmingham (Sou.).............	6	6	.500	4.58	42	10	0	0	4	92 1/3	84	59	47	52	67
1991— Birmingham (Sou.).............	5	10	.333	3.84	51	0	0	0	13	65 2/3	58	39	28	28	49
1992— Birmingham (Sou.).............	0	1	.000	2.31	5	0	0	0	1	11 2/3	9	4	3	11	9
— Vancouver (PCL)	8	1	.889	3.16	39	3	1	1	2	85 1/3	69	36	30	45	61
1993— Toledo (I.L.)■....................	1	3	.250	5.82	16	5	0	0	0	38 2/3	44	26	25	22	32
— Tucson (PCL)■	3	1	.750	3.79	13	1	0	0	0	19	17	11	8	11	18
1994— Tucson (PCL)	0	0	...	4.91	6	0	0	0	2	7 1/3	3	4	4	3	14
— Houston (N.L.)	0	2	.000	2.97	42	0	0	0	16	39 1/3	24	14	13	18	39
1995— Houston (N.L.)	2	2	.500	5.40	19	0	0	0	7	20	19	12	12	5	29
1996— Kissimmee (FSL)..............	0	0	...	0.00	2	1	0	0	0	3	2	0	0	2	3
— Tucson (PCL)	1	0	1.000	3.10	17	2	0	0	4	20 1/3	17	8	7	8	26
— Houston (N.L.)	2	0	1.000	2.81	16	0	0	0	2	16	12	5	5	5	14
1997— Houston (N.L.)	1	3	.250	5.98	40	0	0	0	4	40 2/3	38	27	27	33	36
— New Orleans (A.A.)............	0	0	...	0.44	19	0	0	0	7	20 2/3	3	1	1	3	26
1998— New York (N.L.)■.............	1	4	.200	4.00	28	0	0	0	0	27	23	13	12	19	28
— Cincinnati (N.L.)■..............	4	2	.667	2.43	30	0	0	0	0	37	27	14	10	28	40
1999— Cincinnati (N.L.)	0	1	.000	27.00	2	0	0	0	0	1	4	3	3	3	0
— Atlanta (N.L.)■..................	0	1	.000	6.48	15	0	0	0	0	16 2/3	21	14	12	11	18
— Richmond (I.L.)	0	0	...	6.35	12	0	0	0	0	11 1/3	14	8	8	5	17
— Syracuse (I.L.)■	0	2	.000	5.50	12	0	0	0	1	18	17	12	11	8	15
— Toronto (A.L.)	0	0	...	12.27	3	0	0	0	0	3 2/3	8	5	5	1	2
A.L. totals (1 year)	0	0	...	12.27	3	0	0	0	0	3 2/3	8	5	5	1	2
N.L. totals (6 years)	10	15	.400	4.28	191	0	0	0	29	197 2/3	168	102	94	122	204
Major League totals (6 years)	10	15	.400	4.43	194	0	0	0	29	201 1/3	176	107	99	123	206

ALL-STAR GAME RECORD

Year League	W	L	Pct.	ERA	GS	CG	ShO	Sv.	IP	H	R	ER	BB	SO
1994— National	0	0	...	27.00	0	0	0	0	2/3	1	2	2	1	1

HUDSON, TIM   P   ATHLETICS

PERSONAL: Born July 14, 1975, in Columbus, Ga. ... 6-0/160. ... Throws right, bats right. ... Full name: Timothy Adam Hudson.
HIGH SCHOOL: Glenwood (Phenix City, Ala.).
COLLEGE: Auburn.
TRANSACTIONS/CAREER NOTES: Selected by Oakland Athletics organization in sixth-round of free-agent draft (June 3, 1997).
HONORS: Named A.L. Rookie Pitcher of the Year by The Sporting News (1999).
MISCELLANEOUS: Appeared in three games as pinch runner (1999).

Year League	W	L	Pct.	ERA	G	GS	CG	ShO	Sv.	IP	H	R	ER	BB	SO
1997— S. Oregon (N'west.)...........	3	1	.750	2.51	8	4	0	0	0	28 2/3	12	8	8	15	37
1998— Modesto (Calif.)	4	0	1.000	1.67	8	5	0	0	0	37 2/3	19	10	7	18	48
— Huntsville (Sou.)	10	9	.526	4.54	22	22	2	0	0	134 2/3	136	84	68	71	104
1999— Midland (Texas)	3	0	1.000	0.50	3	3	0	0	0	18	9	1	1	3	18
— Vancouver (PCL)	4	0	1.000	2.20	8	8	0	0	0	49	38	16	12	21	61
— Oakland (A.L.)	11	2	.846	3.23	21	21	1	0	0	136 1/3	121	56	49	62	132
Major League totals (1 year)........	11	2	.846	3.23	21	21	1	0	0	136 1/3	121	56	49	62	132

HUGHES, BOBBY   C   BREWERS

PERSONAL: Born April 10, 1971, in Burbank, Calif. ... 6-4/229. ... Bats right, throws right. ... Full name: Robert E. Hughes.
HIGH SCHOOL: Notre Dame (Sherman Oaks, Calif.).

H

COLLEGE: Loyola Marymount, then Southern California.

TRANSACTIONS/CAREER NOTES: Selected by Detroit Tigers organization in 47th round of free-agent draft (June 3, 1991); did not sign. ... Selected by Milwaukee Brewers organization in second round of free-agent draft (June 1, 1992). ... On disabled list (April 3-11 and May 4-20, 1997). ... On Milwaukee disabled list (July 25-August 20 and August 24, 1999-remainder of season); included rehabilitation assignment to Louisville (August 9-20).

STATISTICAL NOTES: Led Midwest League catchers with 17 errors in 1993. ... Led Pacific Coast League catchers with 12 errors in 1997.

Year Team (League)	Pos.	G	AB	R	H	2B	3B	HR	RBI	Avg.	BB	SO	SB	PO	A	E	Avg.
										BATTING						FIELDING	
1992— Helena (Pio.)	OF-C	11	40	5	7	1	1	0	6	.175	4	14	0	64	9	1	.986
1993— Beloit (Midw.).............	C-1B	98	321	42	89	11	3	17	56	.277	23	76	1	573	67	†18	.973
1994— Stockton (Calif.)	C-1B-3B	95	322	54	81	24	3	11	53	.252	33	83	2	517	63	8	.986
— El Paso (Texas)	C	12	36	3	10	4	1	0	12	.278	5	7	0	52	8	1	.984
1995— Stockton (Calif.)	C-DH-1B	52	179	22	42	9	2	8	31	.235	17	41	2	252	50	4	.987
— El Paso (Texas)	C	51	173	11	46	12	0	7	27	.266	12	30	0	299	29	8	.976
1996— New Orleans (A.A.).....C-DH-1B-3B		37	125	11	25	5	0	4	15	.200	4	31	1	176	27	5	.976
— El Paso (Texas)	C-DH	67	237	43	72	18	1	15	39	.304	30	40	3	250	32	6	.979
1997— Tucson (PCL)	C-DH-3B	89	290	43	90	29	2	7	51	.310	24	46	0	455	48	†12	.977
1998— Milwaukee (N.L.)......	C-OF	85	218	28	50	7	2	9	29	.229	16	54	1	398	29	2	.995
1999— Milwaukee (N.L.)	C-DH	48	101	10	26	2	0	3	8	.257	5	28	0	149	15	2	.988
— Louisville (I.L.)	C	10	32	5	6	2	0	1	2	.188	2	7	0	41	2	0	1.000
Major League totals (2 years)		133	319	38	76	9	2	12	37	.238	21	82	1	547	44	4	.993

HUNDLEY, TODD   C   DODGERS

PERSONAL: Born May 27, 1969, in Martinsville, Va. ... 5-11/199. ... Bats both, throws right. ... Full name: Todd Randolph Hundley. ... Son of Randy Hundley, catcher with four major league teams (1964-77).

HIGH SCHOOL: William Fremd (Palatine, Ill.).

COLLEGE: William Rainey Harper College (Ill.).

TRANSACTIONS/CAREER NOTES: Selected by New York Mets organization in second round of free-agent draft (June 2, 1987); pick received as compensation for Baltimore Orioles signing Type B free-agent 3B/1B Ray Knight. ... On Tidewater disabled list (June 29-July 6, 1991). ... On disabled list (July 23, 1995-remainder of season). ... On New York disabled list (March 21-July 11 and August 28-September 12, 1998); included rehabilitation assignments to St. Lucie (June 24-July 6 and July 9), Gulf Coast Mets (July 7-8) and Norfolk (July 10-11 and August 31-September 8). ... Traded by Mets with P Arnold Gooch to Los Angeles Dodgers for C Charles Johnson and OF Roger Cedeno (December 1, 1998). ... On suspended list (July 22-24, 1999).

RECORDS: Holds major league single-season record for most home runs by catcher—41 (1996). ... Holds N.L. single-season record for most strikeouts by switch hitter—146 (1996).

STATISTICAL NOTES: Led South Atlantic League in intentional bases on balls received with 10 and in grounding into double plays with 20 in 1989. ... Led South Atlantic League catchers with 826 putouts and 930 total chances in 1989. ... Tied for International League lead in errors by catcher with nine and double plays with 12 in 1991. ... Switch-hit home runs in one game five times (June 18, 1994; May 18; June 10, 1996; May 5 and July 20, 1997). ... Career major league grand slams: 5.

Year Team (League)	Pos.	G	AB	R	H	2B	3B	HR	RBI	Avg.	BB	SO	SB	PO	A	E	Avg.
										BATTING						FIELDING	
1987— Little Falls (NY-P)	C	34	103	12	15	4	0	1	10	.146	12	27	0	181	25	7	.967
1988— Little Falls (NY-P)	C	52	176	23	33	8	0	2	18	.188	16	31	1	345	54	8	.980
— St. Lucie (FSL)	C	1	1	0	0	0	0	0	0	.000	2	1	0	4	0	1	.800
1989— Columbia (SAL).........	C-OF	125	439	67	118	23	4	11	66	.269	54	67	6	†829	91	13	.986
1990— Jackson (Texas)	C-3B	81	279	27	74	12	2	1	35	.265	34	44	5	474	63	9	.984
— New York (N.L.).........	C	36	67	8	14	6	0	0	2	.209	6	18	0	162	8	2	.988
1991— Tidewater (I.L.).........	C-1B	125	454	62	124	24	4	14	66	.273	51	95	1	585	63	‡9	.986
— New York (N.L.).........	C	21	60	5	8	0	1	1	7	.133	6	14	0	85	11	0	1.000
1992— New York (N.L.).........	C	123	358	32	75	17	0	7	32	.209	19	76	3	700	48	3	.996
1993— New York (N.L.).........	C	130	417	40	95	17	2	11	53	.228	23	62	1	592	63	8	.988
1994— New York (N.L.).........	C	91	291	45	69	10	1	16	42	.237	25	73	2	448	28	5	.990
1995— New York (N.L.).........	C	90	275	39	77	11	0	15	51	.280	42	64	1	488	29	7	.987
1996— New York (N.L.).........	C	153	540	85	140	32	1	41	112	.259	79	146	1	911	72	8	.992
1997— New York (N.L.).........	C-DH	132	417	78	114	21	2	30	86	.273	83	116	2	678	54	10	.987
1998— St. Lucie (FSL)	OF-DH	12	42	4	9	2	0	1	6	.214	12	8	0	17	1	2	.900
— GC Mets (GCL)	OF	1	2	0	0	0	0	0	0	.000	2	1	0	2	0	0	1.000
— Norfolk (I.L.)	OF-DH-C	10	30	9	13	1	0	4	15	.433	14	10	0	22	2	1	.960
— New York (N.L.).........	OF-C	53	124	8	20	4	0	3	12	.161	16	55	1	60	4	5	.928
1999— Los Angeles (N.L.)■..	C	115	376	49	78	14	0	24	55	.207	44	113	3	681	51	*16	.979
Major League totals (10 years)		944	2925	389	690	132	7	148	452	.236	343	737	14	4805	368	64	.988

ALL-STAR GAME RECORD

Year League	Pos.	AB	R	H	2B	3B	HR	RBI	Avg.	BB	SO	SB	PO	A	E	Avg.
							BATTING								FIELDING	
1996— National	C	1	0	0	0	0	0	0	.000	0	0	0	1	0	0	1.000
1997— National							Did not play.									

HUNTER, BRIAN   OF   MARINERS

PERSONAL: Born March 5, 1971, in Portland, Ore. ... 6-3/180. ... Bats right, throws right. ... Full name: Brian Lee Hunter.

HIGH SCHOOL: Fort Vancouver (Vancouver, Wash.).

TRANSACTIONS/CAREER NOTES: Selected by Houston Astros organization in second round of free-agent draft (June 5, 1989); pick received as part of compensation for Texas Rangers signing Type A free-agent P Nolan Ryan. ... On Houston disabled list (July 5-23, 1995); included rehabilitation assignment to Jackson (July 21-23). ... On Houston disabled list (June 29-July 27, 1996); included rehabilitation assignment to Tucson (July 23-27). ... Traded by Astros with IF Orlando Miller, P Doug Brocail, P Todd Jones and cash to Detroit Tigers for C Brad Ausmus, P Jose Lima, P C.J. Nitkowski, P Trever Miller and IF Daryle Ward (December 10, 1996). ... Traded by Tigers to Seattle Mariners for two play-

H

ers to be named later (April 29, 1999); Tigers acquired P Andrew Vanhekken (June 27, 1999) and OF Jerry Amador (August 26, 1999) to complete deal. ... On Seattle disabled list (July 12-27, 1999).
RECORDS: Holds major league record for most at-bats with no hits in doubleheader (more than 18 innings)—13 (June 20, 1998, 26 innings). ... Shares major league single season record for fewest double plays by outfielder (150 or more games)—0 (1997).
STATISTICAL NOTES: Tied for American Association lead with 249 total bases in 1997. ... Led A.L. in caught stealing with 18 in 1997. ... Led A.L. outfielders with 420 total chances in 1997. ... Led A.L. with 44 stolen bases in 1999. ... Career major league grand slams: 1.

| | | | | | | | BATTING | | | | | | | | FIELDING | | |
Year	Team (League)	Pos.	G	AB	R	H	2B	3B	HR	RBI	Avg.	BB	SO	SB	PO	A	E	Avg.
1989—	GC Astros (GCL)	OF	51	206	15	35	2	0	0	13	.170	7	42	12	95	4	2	.980
1990—	Asheville (SAL)...........	OF	127	444	84	111	14	6	0	16	.250	60	72	45	219	13	11	.955
1991—	Osceola (FSL)...........	OF	118	392	51	94	15	3	1	30	.240	45	75	32	250	7	9	.966
1992—	Osceola (FSL)...........	OF	131	489	62	146	18	9	1	62	.299	31	76	39	295	10	9	.971
1993—	Jackson (Texas)	OF-DH	133	523	84	154	22	5	10	52	.294	34	85	*35	276	9	*14	.953
1994—	Tucson (PCL)	OF-DH	128	513	*113	*191	28	9	10	51	*.372	52	52	*49	244	14	5	.981
—	Houston (N.L.)..........	OF	6	24	2	6	1	0	0	0	.250	1	6	2	14	1	1	.938
1995—	Tucson (PCL)	OF	38	155	28	51	5	1	1	16	.329	17	13	11	91	1	0	1.000
—	Houston (N.L.)..........	OF	78	321	52	97	14	5	2	28	.302	21	52	24	182	8	9	.955
—	Jackson (Texas)	OF	2	6	1	3	0	0	0	0	.500	1	0	0	5	0	0	1.000
1996—	Houston (N.L.)..........	OF	132	526	74	145	27	2	5	35	.276	17	92	35	279	11	•12	.960
—	Tucson (PCL)	OF	3	14	3	5	0	1	0	1	.357	0	2	3	8	0	0	1.000
1997—	Detroit (A.L.).■..........	OF	•162	658	112	177	29	7	4	45	.269	66	121	*74	*408	8	4	.990
1998—	Detroit (A.L.).............	OF	142	595	67	151	29	3	4	36	.254	36	94	42	386	11	5	.988
1999—	Detroit (A.L.).............	OF	18	55	8	13	2	1	0	0	.236	5	11	0	49	1	0	1.000
—	Seattle (A.L.).■..........	OF	121	484	71	112	11	5	4	34	.231	32	80	§44	252	14	4	.985
American League totals (3 years)			443	1792	258	453	71	16	12	115	.253	139	306	160	1095	34	13	.989
National League totals (3 years)			216	871	128	248	42	7	7	63	.285	39	150	61	475	20	22	.957
Major League totals (6 years)			659	2663	386	701	113	23	19	178	.263	178	456	221	1570	54	35	.979

HUNTER, BRIAN   1B   BRAVES

PERSONAL: Born March 4, 1968, in El Toro, Calif. ... 6-0/225. ... Bats right, throws left. ... Full name: Brian Ronald Hunter.
HIGH SCHOOL: Paramount (Calif.).
JUNIOR COLLEGE: Cerritos College (Calif.).
TRANSACTIONS/CAREER NOTES: Selected by Atlanta Braves organization in eighth round of free-agent draft (June 2, 1987). ... On Atlanta disabled list (April 18-May 18, 1993). ... Traded by Braves to Pittsburgh Pirates for a player to be named later (November 17, 1993); Braves acquired SS Jose Delgado to complete deal (June 6, 1994). ... Traded by Pirates to Cincinnati Reds for a player to be named later (July 27, 1994); Pirates acquired OF Micah Franklin to complete deal (October 13, 1994). ... On Cincinnati disabled list (June 19-July 24 and August 14-September 1, 1995); included rehabilitation assignment to Indianapolis (August 22-31). ... Released by Reds (March 8, 1996). ... Signed by Seattle Mariners (May 4, 1996). ... Granted free agency (October 8, 1996). ... Signed by Reds organization (January 14, 1997). ... Granted free agency (October 15, 1997). ... Signed by St. Louis Cardinals (March 30, 1998). ... Released by Cardinals (August 2, 1998). ... Signed by Chicago White Sox organization (August 14, 1998). ... On Calgary disabled list (August 25-September 2, 1998). ... Granted free agency (October 15, 1998). ... Signed by Braves organization (February 23, 1999). ... Granted free agency (November 9, 1999). ... Re-signed by Braves organization (December 7, 1999).
STATISTICAL NOTES: Led Appalachian League first basemen with 43 double plays in 1987. ... Led Midwest League first basemen with 21 errors in 1988. ... Tied for Southern League lead with nine sacrifice flies in 1989. ... Career major league grand slams: 2.

| | | | | | | | BATTING | | | | | | | | FIELDING | | |
Year	Team (League)	Pos.	G	AB	R	H	2B	3B	HR	RBI	Avg.	BB	SO	SB	PO	A	E	Avg.
1987—	Pulaski (Appl.)...........	1B-OF	65	251	38	58	10	2	8	30	.231	18	47	3	498	29	11	.980
1988—	Burlington (Midw.)	1B-OF	117	417	58	108	17	0	•22	71	.259	45	90	7	987	69	†22	.980
—	Durham (Caro.).........	OF-1B	13	49	13	17	3	0	3	9	.347	7	8	2	52	6	0	1.000
1989—	Greenville (Sou.)	OF-1B	124	451	57	114	19	2	19	82	.253	33	62	5	248	15	4	.985
1990—	Richmond (I.L.)..........	OF-1B	43	137	13	27	4	0	5	16	.197	18	37	2	126	5	3	.978
—	Greenville (Sou.)	OF-1B	88	320	45	77	13	1	14	55	.241	43	62	6	189	19	8	.963
1991—	Richmond (I.L.)..........	OF	48	181	28	47	7	0	10	30	.260	11	24	3	121	4	4	.969
—	Atlanta (N.L.)...........	1B-OF	97	271	32	68	16	1	12	50	.251	17	48	0	624	46	8	.988
1992—	Atlanta (N.L.)...........	1B-OF	102	238	34	57	13	2	14	41	.239	21	50	1	542	50	4	.993
1993—	Atlanta (N.L.)...........	1B-OF	37	80	4	11	3	1	0	8	.138	2	15	0	168	13	1	.995
—	Richmond (I.L.)..........	1B-OF	30	99	16	24	7	0	6	26	.242	10	21	4	174	15	0	1.000
1994—	Pittsburgh (N.L.).■.....	1B-OF	76	233	28	53	15	1	11	47	.227	15	55	0	496	37	5	.991
—	Cincinnati (N.L.).■......	OF-1B	9	23	6	7	1	0	4	10	.304	2	1	0	20	1	0	1.000
1995—	Cincinnati (N.L.)	OF	40	79	9	17	6	0	1	9	.215	11	21	2	171	13	3	.984
—	Indianapolis (A.A.)......	OF-1B	9	36	7	13	5	0	4	11	.361	6	11	0	42	2	1	.978
1996—	Tacoma (PCL).■.........	OF-1B-DH	25	92	19	32	6	1	7	24	.348	9	11	1	45	5	1	.980
—	Seattle (A.L.).............	OF-1B	75	198	21	53	10	0	7	28	.268	15	43	0	280	10	5	.983
1997—	Indianapolis (A.A.)	1B-OF-DH	139	506	74	142	36	4	21	85	.281	42	76	9	734	56	9	.989
1998—	St. Louis (N.L.).■........	OF-1B-DH	62	112	11	23	9	1	4	13	.205	7	23	1	66	3	3	.958
—	Calgary (PCL).■.........	OF-1B	11	31	1	3	1	0	0	6	.097	2	9	0	26	2	0	1.000
1999—	Atlanta (N.L.)...........	1B-OF	114	181	28	45	12	1	6	30	.249	31	40	0	435	36	4	.992
American League totals (1 year)			75	198	21	53	10	0	7	28	.268	15	43	0	280	10	5	.983
National League totals (7 years)			537	1217	152	281	75	7	52	208	.231	106	253	4	2522	199	28	.990
Major League totals (8 years)			612	1415	173	334	85	7	59	236	.236	121	296	4	2802	209	33	.989

DIVISION SERIES RECORD

| | | | | | | | BATTING | | | | | | | | FIELDING | | |
Year	Team (League)	Pos.	G	AB	R	H	2B	3B	HR	RBI	Avg.	BB	SO	SB	PO	A	E	Avg.
1999—	Atlanta (N.L.).............	1B	3	4	0	0	0	0	0	0	.000	1	3	0	11	1	0	1.000

H

CHAMPIONSHIP SERIES RECORD

Year	Team (League)	Pos.	G	AB	R	H	2B	3B	HR	RBI	Avg.	BB	SO	SB	PO	A	E	Avg.
							BATTING									FIELDING		
1991—Atlanta (N.L.)	1B	5	18	2	6	2	0	1	4	.333	0	2	0	30	4	0	1.000
1992—Atlanta (N.L.)	1B-PH	3	5	1	1	0	0	0	0	.200	0	1	0	7	0	0	1.000
1999—Atlanta (N.L.)	1B-PH	6	10	1	1	0	0	0	2	.100	5	2	1	31	2	1	.971
Championship series totals (3 years)		14	33	4	8	2	0	1	6	.242	5	5	1	68	6	1	.987

WORLD SERIES RECORD

RECORDS: Shares single-inning record for most errors by first baseman—2 (October 23, 1999, eighth inning).

Year	Team (League)	Pos.	G	AB	R	H	2B	3B	HR	RBI	Avg.	BB	SO	SB	PO	A	E	Avg.
							BATTING									FIELDING		
1991—Atlanta (N.L.)	OF-1B-PH	7	21	2	4	1	0	1	3	.190	0	2	0	6	1	0	1.000
1992—Atlanta (N.L.)	1B-PH-PR	4	5	0	1	0	0	0	2	.200	0	1	0	14	1	0	1.000
1999—Atlanta (N.L.)	1B	2	4	0	1	0	0	0	0	.250	0	1	0	9	2	2	.846
World Series totals (3 years)		13	30	2	6	1	0	1	5	.200	0	4	0	29	4	2	.943

HUNTER, TORII   OF   TWINS

PERSONAL: Born July 18, 1975, in Pine Bluff, Ark. ... 6-2/205. ... Bats right, throws right. ... Full name: Torii Kedar Hunter. ... Name pronounced TORE-ee.

HIGH SCHOOL: Pine Bluff (Ark.).

TRANSACTIONS/CAREER NOTES: Selected by Minnesota Twins organization in first round (20th pick overall) of free-agent draft (June 3, 1993); pick recieved as part of compensation for Cincinnati Reds signing Type A free-agent P John Smiley. ... On New Britain disabled list (April 4-May 10, 1996). ... On Salt Lake disabled list (July 28-August 11, 1998).

STATISTICAL NOTES: Led Florida State League outfielders with seven double plays in 1995. ... Tied for Eastern League lead for double plays by an outfielder with four in 1997. ... Career major league grand slams: 1.

Year	Team (League)	Pos.	G	AB	R	H	2B	3B	HR	RBI	Avg.	BB	SO	SB	PO	A	E	Avg.
							BATTING									FIELDING		
1993—GC Twins (GCL)	OF	28	100	6	19	3	0	0	8	.190	4	23	4	50	1	•6	.895
1994—Fort Wayne (Midw.)	OF	91	335	57	98	17	1	10	50	.293	25	80	8	224	12	7	.971
1995—Fort Myers (FSL)	OF	113	391	64	96	15	2	7	36	.246	38	77	7	242	15	7	.973
1996—New Britain (East.)	OF	99	342	49	90	20	3	7	33	.263	28	60	7	207	11	4	.982
—Fort Myers (FSL)	OF	4	16	1	3	0	0	0	1	.188	2	5	1	9	0	0	1.000
1997—New Britain (East.)	OF-DH	127	471	57	109	22	2	8	56	.231	47	94	8	252	7	7	.974
—Minnesota (A.L.)	PR	1	0	0	0	0	0	0	0	...	0	0	0	...	...	...	...
1998—New Britain (East.)	OF	82	308	42	87	24	3	6	32	.282	19	64	11	168	8	2	.989
—Minnesota (A.L.)	OF	6	17	0	4	1	0	0	2	.235	2	6	0	8	0	0	1.000
—Salt Lake (PCL)	OF-DH	26	92	15	31	7	0	4	20	.337	1	13	2	55	1	2	.966
1999—Minnesota (A.L.)	OF	135	384	52	98	17	2	9	35	.255	26	72	10	284	7	1	.997
Major League totals (3 years)		142	401	52	102	18	2	9	37	.254	28	78	10	292	7	1	.997

HUSKEY, BUTCH   OF/1B

PERSONAL: Born November 10, 1971, in Anadarko, Okla. ... 6-3/244. ... Bats right, throws right. ... Full name: Robert Leon Huskey.

HIGH SCHOOL: Eisenhower (Lawton, Okla.).

TRANSACTIONS/CAREER NOTES: Selected by New York Mets organization in seventh round of free-agent draft (June 5, 1989). ... On New York disabled list (August 3-September 1, 1998); included rehabilitation assignment to Norfolk (August 21-23). ... Traded by Mets to Seattle Mariners for P Lesli Brea (December 14, 1998). ... Traded by Mariners to Boston Red Sox for P Robert Ramsay (July 26, 1999). ... Granted free agency (December 21, 1999).

HONORS: Named International League Most Valuable Player (1995).

STATISTICAL NOTES: Led Gulf Coast League third basemen with 50 putouts and 23 errors in 1989. ... Led Appalachian League third basemen with 217 total chances and tied for lead with 11 double plays in 1990. ... Led South Atlantic League with 256 total bases in 1991. ... Led South Atlantic League third basemen with 21 double plays in 1991. ... Led Florida State League third basemen with 456 total chances and 28 double plays in 1992. ... Led Eastern League third basemen with 101 putouts, 297 assists, 34 errors and 432 total chances in 1993. ... Led International League third basemen with 31 double plays in 1994. ... Had 20-game hitting streak (August 22-September 13, 1997). ... Career major league grand slams: 2.

Year	Team (League)	Pos.	G	AB	R	H	2B	3B	HR	RBI	Avg.	BB	SO	SB	PO	A	E	Avg.
							BATTING									FIELDING		
1989—GC Mets (GCL)	3B-1B	54	190	27	50	14	2	6	34	.263	14	36	4	†73	106	†23	.886
1990—Kingsport (Appal.)	3B	*72	*279	39	75	13	0	14	53	.269	24	74	7	45	*150	*22	.899
1991—Columbia (SAL)	3B	134	492	88	141	27	5	*26	*99	.287	54	89	22	*102	218	31	.912
1992—St. Lucie (FSL)	3B	134	493	65	125	17	1	18	75	.254	33	74	7	*108	*310	*38	.917
1993—Binghamton (East.)	3B-SS-DH	*139	*526	72	132	23	1	25	98	.251	48	102	11	†101	†297	†34	.921
—New York (N.L.)	3B	13	41	2	6	1	0	0	3	.146	1	13	0	9	27	3	.923
1994—Norfolk (I.L.)	3B-DH	127	474	59	108	23	3	10	57	.228	37	88	16	*95	297	25	.940
1995—Norfolk (I.L.)	3-0-1-DH	109	394	66	112	18	1	*28	87	.284	39	88	8	248	132	13	.967
—New York (N.L.)	3B-OF	28	90	8	17	1	0	3	11	.189	10	16	1	16	60	6	.927
1996—New York (N.L.)	1B-OF-3B	118	414	43	115	16	2	15	60	.278	27	77	1	638	54	15	.979
1997—New York (N.L.)	O-1-3-DH	142	471	61	135	26	2	24	81	.287	25	84	8	377	38	15	.965
1998—New York (N.L.)	OF-DH	113	369	43	93	18	0	13	59	.252	26	66	7	166	8	4	.978
—Norfolk (I.L.)	DH	2	8	0	2	0	0	0	3	.250	0	1	0	0	0	0	...
1999—Seattle (A.L.)■	OF-1B-DH-3B	74	262	44	76	9	0	15	49	.290	27	45	3	177	4	1	.995
—Boston (A.L.)	DH-OF-3B	45	124	18	33	6	0	7	28	.266	7	20	0	5	2	0	1.000
American League totals (1 year)		119	386	62	109	15	0	22	77	.282	34	65	3	182	6	1	.995
National League totals (5 years)		414	1385	157	366	62	4	55	214	.264	89	256	17	1206	187	43	.970
Major League totals (6 years)		533	1771	219	475	77	4	77	291	.268	123	321	20	1388	193	44	.973

H

DIVISION SERIES RECORD

								BATTING							FIELDING		
Year	Team (League)	Pos.	G	AB	R	H	2B	3B	HR	RBI	Avg.	BB	SO	SB	PO	A	E	Avg.
1999— Boston (A.L.)..............		DH	2	5	0	1	0	0	0	0	.200	0	1	0	0	0	0	...

CHAMPIONSHIP SERIES RECORD

								BATTING							FIELDING		
Year	Team (League)	Pos.	G	AB	R	H	2B	3B	HR	RBI	Avg.	BB	SO	SB	PO	A	E	Avg.
1999— Boston (A.L.)..............		PH-DH	4	5	1	1	1	0	0	0	.200	1	1	0	0	0	0	...

HUSON, JEFF IF CUBS

PERSONAL: Born August 15, 1964, in Scottsdale, Ariz. ... 6-1/180. ... Bats left, throws right. ... Full name: Jeffrey Kent Huson. ... Name pronounced HYOO-son.

HIGH SCHOOL: Mingus Union (Cottonwood, Ariz.).

JUNIOR COLLEGE: Glendale (Ariz.) Community College.

COLLEGE: Wyoming.

TRANSACTIONS/CAREER NOTES: Signed as non-drafted free agent by Montreal Expos organization (August 18, 1985). ... Traded by Expos to Texas Rangers for P Drew Hall (April 2, 1990). ... On Texas disabled list (August 8-31, 1991); included rehabilitation assignment to Oklahoma City (August 29-31). ... On Texas disabled list (March 27-May 27, June 5-July 15, and July 24-August 23, 1993); included rehabilitation assignment to Oklahoma City (May 24-27, July 10-15 and July 31-August 19). ... On Texas disabled list (March 25-June 6, 1994); included rehabilitation assignment to Oklahoma City (May 17-June 5). ... Released by Rangers (November 30, 1994). ... Signed by Rochester, Baltimore Orioles organization (December 31, 1994). ... On Baltimore disabled list (May 18-July 15, 1996); including rehabilitation assignment to Frederick (June 27-July 15). ... Released by Orioles (August 13, 1996). ... Signed by Colorado Springs, Colorado Rockies organization (August 19, 1996). ... Traded by Rockies to Milwaukee Brewers for a player to be named later (April 23, 1997). ... Granted free agency (October 28, 1997). ... Signed by Rockies organization (November 18, 1997). ... Selected by Seattle Mariners from Rockies organization in Rule 5 major league draft (December 15, 1997). ... Released by Mariners (July 8, 1998). ... Signed by Arizona Diamondbacks organization (August 7, 1998). ... Granted free agency (October 15, 1998). ... Signed by Anaheim Angels organization (November 18, 1998). ... Granted free agency (November 1, 1999). ... Signed by Chicago Cubs organization (January 14, 2000).

							BATTING							FIELDING		
Year	Team (League)	Pos.	G	AB	R	H	2B	3B	HR	RBI	Avg.	BB	SO	SB	PO	A	E	Avg.
1986— Burlington (Midw.)	SS-3B-2B	133	457	85	132	19	1	16	72	.289	76	68	32	183	324	37	.932
— Jacksonville (Sou.)	3B	1	4	0	0	0	0	0	0	.000	0	0	0	0	1	0	1.000
1987— W.P. Beach (FSL)........	SS-OF-2B	131	455	54	130	15	4	1	53	.286	50	30	33	234	347	34	.945
1988— Jacksonville (Sou.).....SS-2B-OF-3B	128	471	72	117	18	1	0	34	.248	59	45	*56	217	285	26	.951
— Montreal (N.L.)............	SS-2B-3B-OF	20	42	7	13	2	0	0	3	.310	4	3	2	18	41	4	.937
1989— Indianapolis (A.A.)	SS-OF-2B	102	378	70	115	17	4	3	35	.304	50	26	30	172	214	17	.958
— Montreal (N.L.)............	SS-2B-3B	32	74	1	12	5	0	0	2	.162	6	6	3	40	65	8	.929
1990— Texas (A.L.)■............	SS-3B-2B	145	396	57	95	12	2	0	28	.240	46	54	12	183	304	19	.962
1991— Texas (A.L.)............	SS-2B-3B	119	268	36	57	8	3	2	26	.213	39	32	8	143	269	15	.965
— Okla. City (A.A.)........	SS	2	6	0	3	1	0	0	2	.500	0	1	0	5	3	0	1.000
1992— Texas (A.L.)............	S-2-O-DH	123	318	49	83	14	3	4	24	.261	41	43	18	178	250	9	.979
1993— Okla. City (A.A.)........3B-SS-2B-OF	24	76	11	22	5	0	1	10	.289	13	10	1	39	52	3	.968
— Texas (A.L.)............SS-2B-DH-3B	23	45	3	6	1	1	0	2	.133	0	10	0	25	42	6	.918
1994— Okla. City (A.A.)........2-3-0-DH-S	83	302	47	91	20	2	1	27	.301	30	32	18	140	165	7	.978
1995— Rochester (I.L.)■........	SS-2B	60	223	28	56	9	0	3	21	.251	26	29	16	110	203	7	.978
— Baltimore (A.L.)........3B-2B-DH-SS	66	161	24	40	4	2	1	19	.248	15	20	5	59	89	1	.993
1996— Baltimore (A.L.)	2B-3B-OF	17	28	5	9	1	0	0	2	.321	1	3	0	20	17	1	.974
— Rochester (I.L.)	OF	2	8	0	2	0	0	0	1	.250	0	2	0	4	0	0	1.000
— Frederick (Caro.)	OF	4	16	4	7	2	0	1	1	.438	2	0	0	6	0	0	1.000
— Bowie (East.)	OF-3B	3	13	3	5	2	0	0	0	.385	1	0	0	4	4	0	1.000
— Colo. Spr. (PCL)■......	2B-SS	14	61	10	18	4	0	0	8	.295	3	1	6	36	42	1	.987
1997— Colo. Springs (PCL) ...	3B-2B	9	20	3	7	3	0	1	5	.350	2	2	0	5	8	0	1.000
— Milwaukee (A.L.)■........2-1-0-DH-3	84	143	12	29	3	0	0	11	.203	5	15	3	109	52	1	.994
1998— Seattle (A.L.)■..........2-3-1-DH-S-O	31	49	8	8	1	0	1	4	.163	5	6	1	31	14	2	.957
— Tucson (PCL)■............	SS-2B-3B-OF	27	82	7	25	4	1	1	12	.305	5	14	0	39	54	6	.939
1999— Anaheim (A.L.)■..........2-S-3-1-D-O	97	225	21	59	7	1	0	18	.262	16	27	10	104	147	5	.980
American League totals (9 years)		705	1633	215	386	51	12	8	134	.236	168	210	57	852	1184	59	.972
National League totals (2 years)		52	116	8	25	7	0	0	5	.216	10	9	5	58	106	12	.932
Major League totals (11 years)		757	1749	223	411	58	12	8	139	.235	178	219	62	910	1290	71	.969

HUTCHINS, NORM OF ANGELS

PERSONAL: Born November 20, 1975, in White Plains, N.Y. ... 5-11/198. ... Bats both, throws left. ... Full name: Norman Elliot Hutchins.

HIGH SCHOOL: Lincoln (N.Y.).

TRANSACTIONS/CAREER NOTES: Selected by California Angels organization in second round of free-agent draft (June 2, 1994). ... Angels franchise renamed Anaheim Angels for 1997 season. ... On Midland disabled list (May 15-June 28, 1998).

STATISTICAL NOTES: Tied for Pacific Coast League lead in caught stealing with 17 in 1999.

							BATTING							FIELDING		
Year	Team (League)	Pos.	G	AB	R	H	2B	3B	HR	RBI	Avg.	BB	SO	SB	PO	A	E	Avg.
1994— Mesa Angels (Ariz.).....	OF	43	136	8	26	4	1	0	7	.191	3	44	5	70	0	6	.921
1995— Mesa Angels (Ariz.).....	OF	14	59	9	16	1	1	0	7	.271	4	10	8	17	0	2	.895
— Boise (N.W.)	OF	45	176	34	44	6	2	2	11	.250	15	44	10	92	3	2	.979
1996— Cedar Rap. (Midw.)	OF	126	466	59	105	13	16	2	52	.225	28	110	22	*303	2	14	.956
1997— Lake Elsinore (Calif.) ..	OF	132	564	82	163	31	12	15	69	.289	23	147	39	266	9	•13	.955
1998— Midland (Texas)..........	OF-DH	89	394	74	123	20	10	10	50	.312	14	84	32	191	4	8	.961
— Vancouver (PCL)	OF	7	29	4	6	0	0	1	3	.207	2	9	1	12	0	0	1.000
1999— Edmonton (PCL)	OF	126	521	80	130	27	6	7	51	.250	40	127	25	*294	2	5	.983

HUTCHINSON, CHAD — P — CARDINALS

PERSONAL: Born February 21, 1977, in Del Mar, Calif. ... 6-5/230. ... Throws right, bats right. ... Son of Lloyd Hutchinson, outfielder in Philadelphia Phillies organization (1969-72).
HIGH SCHOOL: Torrey Pines (Encinitas, Calif.).
COLLEGE: Stanford.
TRANSACTIONS/CAREER NOTES: Selected by Atlanta Braves organization in first round (26th overall) of free-agent draft (June 1, 1995); did not sign. ... Selected by St. Louis Cardinals organization in second round of free-agent draft (June 2, 1998).
STATISTICAL NOTES: Led Texas League with 20 wild pitches in 1999.

Year League	W	L	Pct.	ERA	G	GS	CG	ShO	Sv.	IP	H	R	ER	BB	SO
1998— New Jersey (NY-P)	0	1	.000	3.52	3	3	0	0	0	15 1/3	15	7	6	4	20
— Prince William (Caro.)	2	0	1.000	2.79	5	5	0	0	0	29	20	12	9	11	31
1999— Arkansas (Texas)	7	11	.389	4.72	25	25	0	0	0	141	127	79	74	*85	150
— Memphis (PCL)	2	0	1.000	2.19	2	2	0	0	0	12 1/3	4	3	3	8	16

HYERS, TIM — 1B

PERSONAL: Born October 3, 1971, in Atlanta. ... 6-1/195. ... Bats left, throws left. ... Full name: Timothy James Hyers.
HIGH SCHOOL: Newton County (Covington, Ga.).
TRANSACTIONS/CAREER NOTES: Selected by Toronto Blue Jays organization in supplemental round ("sandwich pick" between second and third round) of free-agent draft (June 4, 1990); pick received as compensation for Detroit Tigers signing Type C free-agent OF Lloyd Moseby. ... Selected by San Diego Padres from Blue Jays organization in Rule 5 major league draft (December 13, 1993). ... On San Diego disabled list (June 22-August 10, 1994); included rehabilitation assignment to Las Vegas (July 26-August 10). ... Traded by Padres to Detroit Tigers for a player to be named later (November 14, 1995). ... Granted free agency (October 15, 1997). ... Signed by Arizona Diamondbacks organization (January 21, 1998). ... On Tucson disabled list (April 15-22, 1998). ... Released by Diamondbacks (April 22, 1998). ... Re-signed by Diamondbacks organization (April 30, 1998). ... Released by Diamondbacks (May 19, 1998). ... Signed by Florida Marlins organization (May 22, 1998). ... Granted free agency (October 4, 1999).
STATISTICAL NOTES: Led Pioneer League first basemen with 565 total chances in 1990. ... Led Florida State League first basemen with 1,260 total chances in 1992. ... Led Southern League first basemen with 1,330 total chances and 105 double plays in 1993.

Year Team (League)	Pos.	G	AB	R	H	2B	3B	HR	RBI	Avg.	BB	SO	SB	PO	A	E	Avg.
1990— Medicine Hat (Pio.)	1B	61	224	29	49	7	2	2	19	.219	29	22	4	*516	38	*11	.981
1991— Myrtle Beach (SAL)	1B	132	398	31	81	8	0	3	37	.204	27	52	6	915	84	14	.986
1992— Dunedin (FSL)	1B	124	464	54	114	24	3	8	59	.246	41	54	2	*1149	102	9	.993
1993— Knoxville (Sou.)	1B	140	487	72	149	26	3	3	61	.306	53	51	12	*1209	*116	5	*.996
1994— San Diego (N.L.)■	1B-OF	52	118	13	30	3	0	0	7	.254	9	15	3	258	23	4	.986
— Las Vegas (PCL)	OF-1B	14	47	4	12	1	0	1	5	.255	4	4	0	27	2	0	1.000
1995— San Diego (N.L.)	1B	6	5	0	0	0	0	0	0	.000	0	1	0	1	1	0	1.000
— Las Vegas (PCL)	1B-OF	82	259	46	75	12	1	1	23	.290	24	33	0	490	25	3	.994
1996— Toledo (I.L.)■	1B-C-DH	117	437	55	113	17	6	7	59	.259	40	57	7	821	69	5	.994
— Detroit (A.L.)	1B-DH-OF	17	26	1	2	1	0	0	0	.077	4	5	0	33	1	0	1.000
1997— Toledo (I.L.)	1-O-DH-3	121	424	61	116	22	3	12	55	.274	41	65	1	892	95	11	.989
1998— Tucson (PCL)■	OF-1B-P	19	27	7	6	1	0	1	5	.222	5	5	1	11	0	0	1.000
— Charlotte (I.L.)■	1B-OF-DH	85	300	50	84	22	2	7	52	.280	27	41	0	397	26	2	.995
1999— Florida (N.L.)	OF-1B-DH	58	81	8	18	4	1	2	12	.222	14	11	0	86	3	0	1.000
— Calgary (PCL)	OF-DH-1B	51	179	25	48	12	0	4	20	.268	14	22	1	191	9	1	.995
American League totals (1 year)		17	26	1	2	1	0	0	0	.077	4	5	0	33	1	0	1.000
National League totals (3 years)		116	204	21	48	7	1	2	19	.235	23	27	3	345	27	4	.989
Major League totals (4 years)		133	230	22	50	8	1	2	19	.217	27	32	3	378	28	4	.990

RECORD AS PITCHER

Year League	W	L	Pct.	ERA	G	GS	CG	ShO	Sv.	IP	H	R	ER	BB	SO
1998— Tucson (PCL)	1	0	1.000	9.00	1	0	0	0	0	1	2	1	1	2	1

IBANEZ, RAUL — OF — MARINERS

PERSONAL: Born June 2, 1972, in Manhattan, N.Y. ... 6-2/200. ... Bats left, throws right. ... Full name: Raul Javier Ibanez.
HIGH SCHOOL: Sunset (Miami).
JUNIOR COLLEGE: Miami-Dade (South) Community College.
TRANSACTIONS/CAREER NOTES: Selected by Seattle Mariners organization in 36th round of free-agent draft (June 1, 1992). ... On disabled list (June 4-July 16, 1994). ... On Seattle disabled list (March 30-June 29, 1998); included rehabilitation assignment to Tacoma (May 30-June 28). ... On Tacoma disabled list (July 7-14, 1998). ... On Seattle disabled list (May 18-June 3, 1999); included rehabilitation assignment to Tacoma (May 26-June 3).
STATISTICAL NOTES: Led California League with .612 slugging percentage in 1995. ... Led California League with 25 passed balls in 1995. ... Career major league grand slams: 1.

Year Team (League)	Pos.	G	AB	R	H	2B	3B	HR	RBI	Avg.	BB	SO	SB	PO	A	E	Avg.
1992— Ariz. Mariners (Ariz.)	1B-C-OF	33	120	25	37	8	2	1	16	.308	9	18	1	51	3	4	.931
1993— Appleton (Midw.)	1B-C-OF	52	157	26	43	9	0	5	21	.274	24	31	0	98	2	2	.980
— Bellingham (N.W.)	C	43	134	16	38	5	2	0	15	.284	21	23	0	137	15	1	.993
1994— Appleton (Midw.)	C-1B-OF	91	327	55	102	30	3	7	59	.312	32	37	10	304	28	10	.971
1995— Riverside (Calif.)	C-1B	95	361	59	120	23	9	20	108	.332	41	49	4	465	54	12	.977
1996— Tacoma (PCL)	OF-1B-DH	111	405	59	115	20	3	11	47	.284	44	56	7	201	12	11	.951
— Port City (Sou.)	OF-DH-C-1B	19	76	12	28	8	1	1	13	.368	8	7	3	36	2	4	.905
— Seattle (A.L.)	DH	4	5	0	0	0	0	0	0	.000	0	1	0	0	0	0	...
1997— Tacoma (PCL)	OF	111	438	84	133	30	5	15	84	.304	32	75	7	192	12	5	.976
— Seattle (A.L.)	OF-DH	11	26	3	4	0	1	1	4	.154	0	6	0	9	0	0	1.000
1998— Tacoma (PCL)	OF-DH	52	190	24	41	8	1	6	25	.216	24	47	1	78	2	1	.988
— Seattle (A.L.)	OF-1B-DH	37	98	12	25	7	1	2	12	.255	5	22	0	105	7	1	.991
1999— Seattle (A.L.)	OF-1B-DH-C	87	209	23	54	7	0	9	27	.258	17	32	5	234	8	3	.988
— Tacoma (PCL)	OF-DH-1B	8	31	6	11	1	0	3	5	.355	1	7	1	13	0	0	1.000
Major League totals (4 years)		139	338	38	83	14	2	12	43	.246	22	61	5	348	15	4	.989

IRABU, HIDEKI   P   EXPOS

PERSONAL: Born May 5, 1969, in Hyogo, Japan. ... 6-4/240. ... Throws right, bats right.

TRANSACTIONS/CAREER NOTES: Rights acquired by San Diego Padres from Chiba Lotte Marines of Japan Pacific League (January 13, 1997). ... Rights traded by Padres with 2B Homer Bush, OF Gordon Amerson and a player to be named later to New York Yankees for OF Ruben Rivera, P Rafael Medina and cash (April 22, 1997); Padres traded OF Vernon Maxwell to Yankees to complete deal (June 9, 1997). ... Signed by Yankees (May 29, 1997). ... Traded by Yankees to Montreal Expos for P Jake Westbrook and two players to be named (December 22, 1999).

STATISTICAL NOTES: Tied for A.L. lead with three balks in 1997.

Year League	W	L	Pct.	ERA	G	GS	CG	ShO	Sv.	IP	H	R	ER	BB	SO
1988— Lotte Orions (Jap. Pac.)	2	5	.286	3.89	14	6	...	...	1	39 1/3	30	19	17	15	21
1989— Lotte Orions (Jap. Pac.)	0	2	.000	3.53	33	2	...	...	9	51	37	20	20	27	50
1990— Lotte Orions (Jap. Pac.)	8	5	.615	3.78	34	7	...	...	0	123 2/3	110	56	52	72	102
1991— Lotte Orions (Jap. Pac.)	3	8	.273	6.88	24	14	...	...	0	100 2/3	110	78	77	70	78
1992— Chiba Lotte (Jap. Pac.)■	0	5	.000	3.86	28	4	...	...	0	77	38	33	33	37	55
1993— Chiba Lotte (Jap. Pac.)	8	7	.533	3.10	32	8	...	...	1	142 1/3	125	59	49	58	160
1994— Chiba Lotte (Jap. Pac.)	*15	10	.600	3.04	27	20	...	...	0	207 1/3	170	77	70	94	239
1995— Chiba Lotte (Jap. Pac.)	11	11	.500	*2.53	28	18	...	...	0	203	158	70	57	72	239
1996— Chiba Lotte (Jap. Pac.)	12	6	.667	*2.40	23	20	3	...	0	157 1/3	108	57	42	59	167
1997— Tampa (FSL)■	1	0	1.000	0.00	2	2	0	0	0	9	4	0	0	0	12
— Norwich (East.)	1	1	.500	4.50	2	2	0	0	0	10	13	5	5	0	9
— Columbus (I.L.)	2	0	1.000	1.67	4	4	1	1	0	27	19	7	5	5	28
— New York (A.L.)	5	4	.556	7.09	13	9	0	0	0	53 1/3	69	47	42	20	56
1998— New York (A.L.)	13	9	.591	4.06	29	28	2	1	0	173	148	79	78	76	126
1999— New York (A.L.)	11	7	.611	4.84	32	27	2	1	0	169 1/3	180	98	91	46	133
Major League totals (3 years)	29	20	.592	4.80	74	64	4	2	0	395 2/3	397	224	211	142	315

DIVISION SERIES RECORD

Year League	W	L	Pct.	ERA	G	GS	CG	ShO	Sv.	IP	H	R	ER	BB	SO
1998— New York (A.L.)							Did not play.								
1999— New York (A.L.)							Did not play.								

CHAMPIONSHIP SERIES RECORD

Year League	W	L	Pct.	ERA	G	GS	CG	ShO	Sv.	IP	H	R	ER	BB	SO
1998— New York (A.L.)							Did not play.								
1999— New York (A.L.)	0	0	...	13.50	1	0	0	0	0	4 2/3	13	8	7	0	3

WORLD SERIES RECORD

NOTES: Member of World Series championship team (1998 and 1999); did not play.

Year League	W	L	Pct.	ERA	G	GS	CG	ShO	Sv.	IP	H	R	ER	BB	SO
1998— New York (A.L.)							Did not play.								
1999— New York (A.L.)							Did not play.								

IRELAND, ERIC   P   ASTROS

PERSONAL: Born March 11, 1977, in Granada Hills, Calif. ... 6-1/170. ... Throws right, bats right. ... Full name: Eric Wayne Ireland.

HIGH SCHOOL: Robert A. Millikan (Long Beach, Calif.).

TRANSACTIONS/CAREER NOTES: Selected by Houston Astros organization in second round of free-agent draft (June 1, 1995).

STATISTICAL NOTES: Pitched 5-0 no-hit victory for Kissimmee against St. Petersburg (June 23, 1999). ... Tied for Florida State League lead in putouts with 15 and total chances by pitcher with 47 and led Florida State League pitchers with eight errors in 1999.

Year League	W	L	Pct.	ERA	G	GS	CG	ShO	Sv.	IP	H	R	ER	BB	SO
1996— Gulf Coast Astros (GCL)	3	4	.429	4.70	12	11	0	0	0	53 2/3	54	33	28	23	43
1997— Auburn (NY-P)	5	7	.417	3.70	16	16	2	0	0	*107	*111	55	44	21	79
1998— Quad City (Midw.)	14	9	.609	2.88	29	•28	•6	•2	0	*206	172	80	66	71	191
1999— Kissimmee (FSL)	10	7	.588	*2.06	24	24	•5	2	0	*170 1/3	145	59	39	30	133
— Jackson (Texas)	0	1	.000	4.30	3	3	0	0	0	14 2/3	19	9	7	2	15

ISRINGHAUSEN, JASON   P   ATHLETICS

PERSONAL: Born September 7, 1972, in Brighton, Ill. ... 6-3/210. ... Throws right, bats right. ... Full name: Jason Derik Isringhausen. ... Name pronounced IS-ring-how-zin.

HIGH SCHOOL: Southwestern (Brighton, Ill.).

JUNIOR COLLEGE: Lewis & Clark Community College (Ill.).

TRANSACTIONS/CAREER NOTES: Selected by New York Mets organization in 44th round of free-agent draft (June 3, 1991). ... On disabled list (August 13-September 1, 1996). ... On disabled list (March 24-August 27, 1997); included rehabilitation assignment to Norfolk (April 6-11 and August 22-27), Gulf Coast Mets (August 6-11) and St. Lucie (August 11-22). ... On disabled list (March 21, 1998-entire season). ... Traded by Mets with P Greg McMichael to Oakland Athletics for P Billy Taylor (July 31, 1999).

HONORS: Named International League Most Valuable Pitcher (1995).

Year League	W	L	Pct.	ERA	G	GS	CG	ShO	Sv.	IP	H	R	ER	BB	SO
1992— Gulf Coast Mets (GCL)	2	4	.333	4.34	6	6	0	0	0	29	26	19	14	17	25
— Kingsport (Appalachian)	4	1	.800	3.25	7	6	1	1	0	36	32	22	13	12	24
1993— Pittsfield (NY-P)	7	4	.636	3.29	15	15	2	0	0	90 1/3	68	45	33	28	*104
1994— St. Lucie (FSL)	6	4	.600	2.23	14	14	•6	•3	0	101	76	31	25	27	59
— Binghamton (East.)	5	1	.556	3.02	14	14	2	0	0	92 1/3	78	35	31	23	69
1995— Binghamton (East.)	2	1	.667	2.85	6	6	1	0	0	41	26	15	13	12	59
— Norfolk (I.L.)	9	1	*.900	1.55	12	12	3	*3	0	87	64	17	15	24	75
— New York (N.L.)	9	2	.818	2.81	14	14	1	0	0	93	88	29	29	31	55
1996— New York (N.L.)	6	14	.300	4.77	27	27	2	1	0	171 2/3	190	103	91	73	114

Year League	W	L	Pct.	ERA	G	GS	CG	ShO	Sv.	IP	H	R	ER	BB	SO
1997—Norfolk (I.L.)	0	2	.000	4.05	3	3	0	0	0	20	20	10	9	8	17
—Gulf Coast Mets (GCL)	1	0	1.000	1.93	1	0	0	0	0	4 2/3	2	1	1	1	7
—St. Lucie (FSL)	1	0	1.000	0.00	2	2	0	0	0	12	8	1	0	5	15
—New York (N.L.)	2	2	.500	7.58	6	6	0	0	0	29 2/3	40	27	25	22	25
1998—New York (N.L.)................							Did not play.								
1999—Norfolk (I.L.)	3	1	.750	2.29	12	8	0	0	0	51	33	18	13	20	51
—New York (N.L.)	1	3	.250	6.41	13	5	0	0	1	39 1/3	43	29	28	22	31
—Oakland (A.L.)■................	0	1	.000	2.13	20	0	0	0	8	25 1/3	21	6	6	12	20
A.L. totals (1 year)	0	1	.000	2.13	20	0	0	0	8	25 1/3	21	6	6	12	20
N.L. totals (4 years)	18	21	.462	4.67	60	52	3	1	1	333 2/3	361	188	173	148	225
Major League totals (4 years)	18	22	.450	4.49	80	52	3	1	9	359	382	194	179	160	245

JACKSON, DAMIAN — SS — PADRES

PERSONAL: Born August 6, 1973, in Los Angeles. ... 5-11/185. ... Bats right, throws right. ... Full name: Damian Jacques Jackson.
HIGH SCHOOL: Ygnacio Valley (Concord, Calif.).
JUNIOR COLLEGE: Laney (Calif.).
TRANSACTIONS/CAREER NOTES: Selected by Cleveland Indians organization in 44th round of free-agent draft (June 3, 1991). ... Traded by Indians with P Danny Graves, P Jim Crowell and P Scott Winchester to Cincinnati Reds for P John Smiley and IF Jeff Branson (July 31, 1997). ... Traded by Reds with OF Reggie Sanders and P Josh Harris to San Diego Padres for OF Greg Vaughn and OF/1B Mark Sweeney (February 2, 1999).
STATISTICAL NOTES: Led Appalachian League shortstops with 342 total chances and 45 double plays in 1992. ... Led Eastern League shortstops with 241 putouts, 446 assists, 54 errors, 741 total chances and 85 double plays in 1994. ... Led Eastern League in caught stealing with 22 in 1995. ... Tied for Eastern League lead in double plays by shortstop with 80 in 1995. ... Led American Association shortstops with 635 total chances and 84 double plays in 1996. ... Led International League shortstops with 227 putouts, 434 assists, 44 errors, 705 total chances and 101 double plays in 1998.

							BATTING							FIELDING		
Year Team (League)	Pos.	G	AB	R	H	2B	3B	HR	RBI	Avg.	BB	SO	SB	PO	A	E	Avg.
1992—Burlington (Appl.).......	SS	62	226	32	56	12	1	0	23	.248	32	31	29	*102	*217	23	.933
1993—Columbus (SAL).........	SS	108	350	70	94	19	3	6	45	.269	41	61	26	191	324	52	.908
1994—Canton/Akron (East.)..	SS-OF	138	531	85	143	29	5	5	60	.269	60	121	37	†241	†446	†54	.927
1995—Canton/Akron (East.)..	SS	131	484	67	120	20	2	3	34	.248	65	103	40	*220	337	*36	.939
1996—Buffalo (A.A.).............	SS	133	452	77	116	15	1	12	49	.257	48	78	24	*203	*403	29	.954
—Cleveland (A.L.)............	SS	5	10	2	3	2	0	0	1	.300	1	4	0	3	13	0	1.000
1997—Buffalo (A.A.).............	SS-2B-OF	73	266	51	78	12	0	4	13	.293	37	45	20	128	246	23	.942
—Cleveland (A.L.)............	SS-2B	8	9	2	1	0	0	0	0	.111	0	1	1	7	7	0	1.000
—Indianapolis (A.A.)■.....	2B-SS	19	71	12	19	6	1	0	7	.268	10	17	4	36	55	5	.948
—Cincinnati (N.L.)	SS-2B	12	27	6	6	2	1	1	2	.222	4	7	1	12	21	1	.971
1998—Indianapolis (I.L.).......	SS-OF	131	517	102	135	36	10	6	49	.261	62	125	25	†230	†435	†44	.938
—Cincinnati (N.L.)	SS-OF	13	38	4	12	5	0	0	7	.316	4	2	2	20	21	1	.976
1999—San Diego (N.L.)■.....	SS-2B-OF	133	388	56	87	20	2	9	39	.224	53	105	34	174	303	26	.948
American League totals (2 years)		13	19	4	4	2	0	0	1	.211	1	5	1	10	20	0	1.000
National League totals (3 years)		158	453	66	105	27	3	10	48	.232	63	116	37	206	345	28	.952
Major League totals (4 years)		171	472	70	109	29	3	10	49	.231	64	121	38	216	365	28	.954

JACKSON, DARRIN — OF

PERSONAL: Born August 22, 1963, in Los Angeles. ... 6-0/191. ... Bats right, throws right. ... Full name: Darrin Jay Jackson.
HIGH SCHOOL: Culver City (Calif.).
TRANSACTIONS/CAREER NOTES: Selected by Chicago Cubs organization in second round of free-agent draft (June 8, 1981). ... Traded by Cubs with P Calvin Schiraldi and a player to be named later to San Diego Padres for OF Marvell Wynne and IF Luis Salazar (August 30, 1989); Padres acquired 1B Phil Stephenson to complete deal (September 5, 1989). ... Traded by Padres to Toronto Blue Jays for OF Derek Bell and OF Stoney Briggs (March 30, 1993). ... Traded by Blue Jays to New York Mets for SS Tony Fernandez (June 11, 1993). ... On New York disabled list (July 19-September 1, 1993). ... Granted free agency (December 20, 1993). ... Signed by Chicago White Sox organization (December 28, 1993). ... Granted free agency (October 15, 1994). ... Played with Seibu Lions of Japan Pacific League (1995-96). ... Signed by San Francisco Giants organization (December 20, 1996). ... Released by Giants (March 31, 1997). ... Signed by Minnesota Twins organization (April 24, 1997). ... Traded by Twins to Milwaukee Brewers for a player to be named later (August 30, 1997); Twins acquired P Mick Fieldbinder to complete deal (September 4, 1997). ... Granted free agency (October 27, 1997). ... Re-signed by Brewers (December 6, 1997). ... On disabled list (March 23-April 7, 1998). ... Granted free agency (October 22, 1998). ... Signed by White Sox organization (January 26, 1999). ... On Chicago disabled list (July 27-August 13, 1999). ... Granted free agency (November 5, 1999). ... Announced retirement (December 2, 1999).
STATISTICAL NOTES: Led Gulf Coast League outfielders with 127 total chances in 1981. ... Tied for Texas League lead in double plays by outfielder with six in 1984. ... Tied for American Association lead in double plays by outfielder with six in 1987. ... Led N.L. in grounding into double plays with 21 in 1992. ... Led N.L. outfielders with 455 total chances and nine double plays in 1992. ... Career major league grand slams: 4.

							BATTING							FIELDING		
Year Team (League)	Pos.	G	AB	R	H	2B	3B	HR	RBI	Avg.	BB	SO	SB	PO	A	E	Avg.
1981—GC Cubs (GCL)..........	OF	62	210	29	39	5	0	1	15	.186	28	53	18	*121	5	1	.992
1982—Quad Cities (Midw.)....	OF	132	529	86	146	23	5	5	48	.276	47	106	58	266	9	8	.972
1983—Salinas (Calif.)..........	OF	129	509	70	126	18	5	6	54	.248	38	111	36	237	15	13	.951
1984—Midland (Texas).........	OF	132	496	63	134	18	2	15	54	.270	49	102	13	286	*19	8	.974
1985—Iowa (A.A.)	OF	10	40	0	7	2	1	0	1	.175	3	10	1	19	0	0	1.000
—Pittsfield (East.)..........	OF	91	325	38	82	10	1	3	30	.252	34	64	8	221	5	0	1.000
—Chicago (N.L.)..........	OF	5	11	0	1	0	0	0	0	.091	0	3	0	7	0	0	1.000
1986—Pittsfield (East.).........	OF	137	•520	82	139	28	2	15	64	.267	43	115	42	320	*16	7	.980
1987—Iowa (A.A.)	OF	132	474	81	130	32	5	23	81	.274	26	110	13	290	15	6	.981
—Chicago (N.L.)..........	OF	7	5	2	4	1	0	0	0	.800	0	0	0	1	0	0	1.000
1988—Chicago (N.L.)	OF	100	188	29	50	11	3	6	20	.266	5	28	4	116	1	2	.983

Year	Team (League)	Pos.	G	AB	R	H	2B	3B	HR	RBI	Avg.	BB	SO	SB	PO	A	E	Avg.
															BATTING			FIELDING
1989— Chicago (N.L.)	OF	45	83	7	19	4	0	1	8	.229	6	17	1	61	3	2	.970
—Iowa (A.A.)	OF	30	120	18	31	4	1	7	17	.258	7	22	4	66	12	0	1.000
—San Diego (N.L.)■	OF	25	87	10	18	3	0	3	12	.207	7	17	0	60	2	3	.954
1990— San Diego (N.L.)	OF	58	113	10	29	3	0	3	9	.257	5	24	3	63	1	1	.985
—Las Vegas (PCL)	OF	29	98	14	27	4	0	5	15	.276	9	21	3	61	4	0	1.000
1991— San Diego (N.L.)	OF-P	122	359	51	94	12	1	21	49	.262	27	66	5	243	2	2	.992
1992— San Diego (N.L.)	OF	155	587	72	146	23	5	17	70	.249	26	106	14	436	*18	2	.996
1993— Toronto (A.L.)■	OF	46	176	15	38	8	0	5	19	.216	8	53	0	86	2	1	.989
—New York (N.L.)■	OF	31	87	4	17	1	0	1	7	.195	2	22	0	51	4	0	1.000
1994— Chicago (A.L.)■	OF	104	369	43	115	17	3	10	51	.312	27	56	7	223	2	1	.996
1995— Seibu (Jap. Pac.)■		128	506	66	146	28	3	20	68	.289	34	104	9	...	...	...	...
1996— Seibu (Jap. Pac.)		126	489	42	130	21	3	19	64	.266	30	70	10	...	...	...	...
1997— Salt Lake (PCL)■	OF-DH	19	80	14	24	3	3	1	12	.300	5	17	3	26	2	0	1.000
—Minnesota (A.L.)	OF	49	130	19	33	2	1	3	21	.254	4	21	2	93	4	1	.990
—Milwaukee (A.L.)■	OF	26	81	7	22	7	0	2	15	.272	2	10	2	55	2	0	1.000
1998— Milwaukee (N.L.)	OF-DH	114	204	20	49	13	1	4	20	.240	9	37	1	106	3	2	.982
1999— Chicago (A.L.)■	OF-DH	73	149	22	41	9	1	4	16	.275	3	20	4	103	2	3	.972
American League totals (4 years)		298	905	106	249	43	5	24	122	.275	44	160	15	560	12	6	.990
National League totals (9 years)		662	1724	205	427	71	10	56	195	.248	87	320	28	1144	34	14	.988
Major League totals (12 years)		960	2629	311	676	114	15	80	317	.257	131	480	43	1704	46	20	.989

RECORD AS PITCHER

Year	League	W	L	Pct.	ERA	G	GS	CG	ShO	Sv.	IP	H	R	ER	BB	SO
1991— San Diego (N.L.)		0	0	...	9.00	1	0	0	0	0	2	3	2	2	2	0

JACKSON, MIKE P PHILLIES

PERSONAL: Born December 22, 1964, in Houston. ... 6-2/225. ... Throws right, bats right. ... Full name: Michael Ray Jackson.
HIGH SCHOOL: Forest Brook (Houston).
JUNIOR COLLEGE: Hill Junior College (Texas).
TRANSACTIONS/CAREER NOTES: Selected by Philadelphia Phillies organization in 29th round of free-agent draft (June 6, 1983); did not sign. ... Selected by Phillies organization in secondary phase of free-agent draft (January 17, 1984). ... On Philadelphia disabled list (August 6-21, 1987). ... Traded by Phillies organization with OF Glenn Wilson and OF Dave Brundage to Seattle Mariners for OF Phil Bradley and P Tim Fortugno (December 9, 1987). ... Traded by Mariners with P Bill Swift and P Dave Burba to San Francisco Giants for OF Kevin Mitchell and P Mike Remlinger (December 11, 1991). ... On disabled list (July 24-August 9, 1993; June 17-July 2 and July 7, 1994-remainder of season). ... Granted free agency (October 17, 1994). ... Signed by Cincinnati Reds (April 8, 1995). ... On Cincinnati disabled list (April 20-June 5, 1995); included rehabilitation assignments to Chattanooga (May 21-30) and Indianapolis (May 30-June 5). ... Granted free agency (November 3, 1995). ... Signed by Mariners (February 2, 1996). ... Granted free agency (October 30, 1996). ... Signed by Cleveland Indians (December 12, 1996). ... Granted free agency (October 28, 1999). ... Signed by Phillies (December 7, 1999).
STATISTICAL NOTES: Led Carolina League with seven balks in 1985. ... Tied for N.L. lead with eight balks in 1987. ... Tied for A.L. lead with three balks in 1998.
MISCELLANEOUS: Holds Seattle Mariners all-time record for most games pitched (335).

Year	League	W	L	Pct.	ERA	G	GS	CG	ShO	Sv.	IP	H	R	ER	BB	SO
1984— Spartanburg (SAL)	7	2	.778	2.68	14	0	0	0	0	80 2/3	53	35	24	50	77	
1985— Peninsula (Caro.)	7	9	.438	4.60	31	18	0	0	1	125 1/3	127	71	64	53	96	
1986— Reading (East.)	2	3	.400	1.66	30	0	0	0	6	43 1/3	25	9	8	22	42	
—Portland (PCL)	3	1	.750	3.18	17	0	0	0	3	22 2/3	18	8	8	13	23	
—Philadelphia (N.L.)	0	0	...	3.38	9	0	0	0	0	13 1/3	12	5	5	4	3	
1987— Philadelphia (N.L.)	3	10	.231	4.20	55	7	0	0	1	109 1/3	88	55	51	56	93	
—Maine (I.L.)	1	0	1.000	0.82	2	2	0	0	0	11	9	2	1	5	13	
1988— Seattle (A.L.)■	6	5	.545	2.63	62	0	0	0	4	99 1/3	74	37	29	43	76	
1989— Seattle (A.L.)	4	6	.400	3.17	65	0	0	0	7	99 1/3	81	43	35	54	94	
1990— Seattle (A.L.)	5	7	.417	4.54	63	0	0	0	3	77 1/3	64	42	39	44	69	
1991— Seattle (A.L.)	7	7	.500	3.25	72	0	0	0	14	88 2/3	64	35	32	34	74	
1992— San Francisco (N.L.)■	6	6	.500	3.73	67	0	0	0	2	82	76	35	34	33	80	
1993— San Francisco (N.L.)	6	6	.500	3.03	*81	0	0	0	1	77 1/3	58	28	26	24	70	
1994— San Francisco (N.L.)	3	2	.600	1.49	36	0	0	0	4	42 1/3	23	8	7	11	51	
1995— Chattanooga (Sou.)■	0	0	...	0.00	3	2	0	0	0	3	2	0	0	0	2	
—Indianapolis (A.A.)	0	0	...	0.00	2	1	0	0	0	2	0	0	0	0	1	
—Cincinnati (N.L.)	6	1	.857	2.39	40	0	0	0	2	49	38	13	13	19	41	
1996— Seattle (A.L.)■	1	1	.500	3.63	73	0	0	0	6	72	61	32	29	24	70	
1997— Cleveland (A.L.)■	2	5	.286	3.24	71	0	0	0	15	75	59	33	27	29	74	
1998— Cleveland (A.L.)	1	1	.500	1.55	69	0	0	0	40	64	43	11	11	13	55	
1999— Cleveland (A.L.)	3	4	.429	4.06	72	0	0	0	39	68 2/3	60	32	31	26	55	
A.L. totals (8 years)	29	36	.446	3.25	547	0	0	0	128	644 1/3	506	265	233	267	567	
N.L. totals (6 years)	24	25	.490	3.28	288	7	0	0	10	373 1/3	295	144	136	147	338	
Major League totals (14 years)	53	61	.465	3.26	835	7	0	0	138	1017 2/3	801	409	369	414	905	

DIVISION SERIES RECORD

NOTES: Shares A.L. single-series record for most saves—3.

Year	League	W	L	Pct.	ERA	G	GS	CG	ShO	Sv.	IP	H	R	ER	BB	SO
1995— Cincinnati (N.L.)	0	0	...	0.00	3	0	0	0	0	3 2/3	4	0	0	0	1	
1997— Cleveland (A.L.)	1	0	1.000	0.00	4	0	0	0	0	4 1/3	3	0	0	1	5	
1998— Cleveland (A.L.)	0	0	...	4.50	3	0	0	0	3	4	3	2	2	1	1	
1999— Cleveland (A.L.)	0	0	...	4.50	2	0	0	0	0	2	2	1	1	1	1	
Division series totals (4 years)	1	0	1.000	1.93	12	0	0	0	3	14	12	3	3	3	8	

CHAMPIONSHIP SERIES RECORD

Year League	W	L	Pct.	ERA	G	GS	CG	ShO	Sv.	IP	H	R	ER	BB	SO
1995— Cincinnati (N.L.)	0	1	.000	23.14	3	0	0	0	0	2 1/3	5	6	6	4	1
1997— Cleveland (A.L.).................	0	0	...	0.00	5	0	0	0	0	4 1/3	1	0	0	1	7
1998— Cleveland (A.L.).................	0	0	...	0.00	1	0	0	0	1	1	0	0	0	0	2
Champ. series totals (3 years)	0	1	.000	7.04	9	0	0	0	1	7 2/3	6	6	6	5	10

WORLD SERIES RECORD

Year League	W	L	Pct.	ERA	G	GS	CG	ShO	Sv.	IP	H	R	ER	BB	SO
1997— Cleveland (A.L.)..............	0	0	...	1.93	4	0	0	0	0	4 2/3	5	1	1	3	4

JACKSON, RYAN   1B/OF   DEVIL RAYS

PERSONAL: Born November 11, 1971, in Sarasota, Fla. ... 6-3/185. ... Bats left, throws left. ... Full name: Ryan Dewitte Jackson.
HIGH SCHOOL: Cardinal Mooney (Sarasota, Fla.).
COLLEGE: Duke.
TRANSACTIONS/CAREER NOTES: Selected by Florida Marlins organization in seventh round of free-agent draft (June 2, 1994). ... On Kane County disabled list (April 5-August 1, 1996). ... On Portland disabled list (August 1-26, 1996). ... Claimed on waivers by Seattle Mariners (April 2, 1999). ... Released by Mariners (November 18, 1999). ... Signed by Tampa Bay Devil Rays organization (January 14, 2000).
STATISTICAL NOTES: Career major league grand slams: 1.

						BATTING							FIELDING		
Year Team (League)	Pos.	G	AB	R	H	2B	3B	HR	RBI	Avg.	BB	SO	SB	PO	A	E	Avg.
1994— Elmira (NY-P)	OF-1B	72	276	46	80	18	1	6	41	.290	22	40	4	176	15	7	.965
1995— Kane County (Midw.)..	OF-1B	132	471	78	138	*39	6	10	82	.293	67	74	13	571	32	7	.989
1996— Brevard Co. (FSL).......	1B	6	26	4	8	2	0	1	4	.308	1	7	1	28	2	2	.938
— GC Marlins (GCL).......	1B-OF	8	26	5	9	0	0	0	7	.346	1	3	2	35	3	0	1.000
1997— Portland (East.).......	OF-1B	134	491	87	153	28	4	26	98	.312	51	85	2	227	9	5	.979
1998— Florida (N.L.).............	1B-OF-DH	111	260	26	65	15	1	5	31	.250	20	73	1	341	21	10	.973
— Charlotte (I.L.)...........	1B-OF	13	50	5	19	4	0	2	11	.380	4	14	2	57	6	0	1.000
1999— Tacoma (PCL)■	1B-DH-OF	105	409	57	126	25	2	8	62	.308	36	64	12	714	56	9	.988
— Seattle (A.L.)..............	1B-OF	32	68	4	16	3	0	0	10	.235	6	19	3	167	11	2	.989
American League totals (1 year)		32	68	4	16	3	0	0	10	.235	6	19	3	167	11	2	.989
National League totals (1 year)		111	260	26	65	15	1	5	31	.250	20	73	1	341	21	10	.973
Major League totals (2 years)		143	328	30	81	18	1	5	41	.247	26	92	4	508	32	12	.978

JAHA, JOHN   DH/1B   ATHLETICS

PERSONAL: Born May 27, 1966, in Portland, Ore. ... 6-1/217. ... Bats right, throws right. ... Full name: John Emil Jaha. ... Name pronounced JAH-ha.
HIGH SCHOOL: David Douglas (Portland, Ore.).
TRANSACTIONS/CAREER NOTES: Selected by Milwaukee Brewers organization in 14th round of free-agent draft (June 4, 1984). ... On disabled list (April 6-August 1, 1990 and May 21-June 6, 1995). ... On Milwaukee disabled list (June 24-July 27, 1995); included rehabilitation assignments to Beloit (July 16-20) and New Orleans (July 20-27). ... On disabled list (June 3, 1997-remainder of season). ... On Milwaukee disabled list (August 4 and August 16-September 1, 1998); included rehabilitation assignment to Beloit (June 4-8). ... Granted free agency (October 26, 1998). ... Signed by Oakland Athletics organization (February 17, 1999).
HONORS: Named Texas League Most Valuable Player (1991). ... Named A.L. Comeback Player of the Year by The Sporting News (1999).
STATISTICAL NOTES: Led Northwest League with 144 total bases and tied for lead with four intentional bases on balls received in 1986. ... Led Texas League with 301 total bases, .619 slugging percentage and .438 on-base percentage in 1991. ... Led Texas League first basemen with 81 assists in 1991. ... Career major league grand slams: 7.

						BATTING							FIELDING		
Year Team (League)	Pos.	G	AB	R	H	2B	3B	HR	RBI	Avg.	BB	SO	SB	PO	A	E	Avg.
1985— Helena (Pio.)	3B	24	68	13	18	3	0	2	14	.265	14	23	4	9	32	1	.976
1986— Tri-Cities (N.W.).........	1B-3B	•73	258	65	82	13	2	*15	67	.318	*70	75	9	352	101	18	.962
1987— Beloit (Midw.)............	3B-1B-SS	122	376	68	101	22	0	7	47	.269	102	86	10	493	113	18	.971
1988— Stockton (Calif.)	1B	99	302	58	77	14	6	8	54	.255	69	85	10	793	60	5	*.994
1989— Stockton (Calif.)	1B-3B	140	479	83	140	26	5	25	91	.292	*112	115	8	1081	62	8	.993
1990— Stockton (Calif.)	DH	26	84	12	22	5	0	4	19	.262	18	25	0	...	...	...	...
1991— El Paso (Texas)..........	1B-3B	130	486	*121	167	38	3	*30	*134	.344	78	101	12	883	†87	10	.990
1992— Denver (A.A.).............	1B	79	274	61	88	18	2	18	69	.321	50	60	6	654	50	7	.990
— Milwaukee (A.L.)........	1B-DH-OF	47	133	17	30	3	1	2	10	.226	12	30	10	286	22	0	1.000
1993— Milwaukee (A.L.)........	1B-3B-2B	153	515	78	136	21	0	19	70	.264	51	109	13	1187	128	10	.992
1994— Milwaukee (A.L.)........	1B-DH	84	291	45	70	14	0	12	39	.241	32	75	3	660	47	8	.989
— New Orleans (A.A.).....	1B-DH	18	62	8	25	7	1	2	16	.403	12	8	2	122	14	1	.993
1995— Milwaukee (A.L.).........	1B-DH	88	316	59	99	20	2	20	65	.313	36	66	2	649	60	2	.997
— Beloit (Midw.)...........	DH	1	4	1	0	0	0	0	0	.000	0	1	0	0	0	0	...
— New Orleans (A.A.).....	DH-1B	3	10	2	4	1	0	1	3	.400	2	1	0	9	2	0	1.000
1996— Milwaukee (A.L.)........	1B-DH	148	543	108	163	28	1	34	118	.300	85	118	3	676	58	6	.992
1997— Milwaukee (A.L.)........	1B-DH	46	162	25	40	7	0	11	26	.247	25	40	1	220	14	2	.992
1998— Milwaukee (N.L.)........	1B-DH	73	216	29	45	6	1	7	38	.208	49	66	1	441	23	3	.994
— Beloit (Midw.)...........	DH	2	4	1	0	0	0	0	0	.000	2	2	0	...	...	...	...
1999— Oakland (A.L.)■	DH-1B	142	457	93	126	23	0	35	111	.276	101	129	2	42	4	0	1.000
American League totals (7 years)		708	2417	425	664	116	4	133	439	.275	342	567	34	3720	333	28	.993
National League totals (1 year)		73	216	29	45	6	1	7	38	.208	49	66	1	441	23	3	.994
Major League totals (8 years)		781	2633	454	709	122	5	140	477	.269	391	633	35	4161	356	31	.993

ALL-STAR GAME RECORD

				BATTING									FIELDING	
Year League	Pos.	AB	R	H	2B	3B	HR	RBI	Avg.	BB	SO	SB	PO	A	E	Avg.
1999— American	PH-DH	1	0	0	0	0	0	0	.000	0	1	0	0	0	0	...

JARVIS, KEVIN   P

PERSONAL: Born August 1, 1969, in Lexington, Ky. ... 6-2/200. ... Throws right, bats left. ... Full name: Kevin Thomas Jarvis.
HIGH SCHOOL: Tates Creek (Lexington, Ky.).
COLLEGE: Wake Forest.
TRANSACTIONS/CAREER NOTES: Selected by Cincinnati Reds organization in 21st round of free-agent draft (June 3, 1991). ... Claimed on waivers by Detroit Tigers (May 2, 1997). ... Claimed on waivers by Minnesota Twins (May 9, 1997). ... Claimed on waivers by Tigers (June 17, 1997). ... On Detroit disabled list (June 25-July 14, 1997); included rehabilitation assignment to Toledo (July 4-14). ... Released by Tigers (December 12, 1997). ... Signed by Chunichi Dragons of the Japan Central League (January 23, 1998). ... Signed by Reds organization (August 27, 1998). ... Released by Reds (September 9, 1998). ... Signed by Oakland Athletics organization (January 4, 1999). ... On Oakland disabled list (April 19-June 4, 1999); included rehabilitation assignment to Modesto (May 28-June 4). ... Granted free agency (October 8, 1999).

Year	League	W	L	Pct.	ERA	G	GS	CG	ShO	Sv.	IP	H	R	ER	BB	SO
1991—	Princeton (Appl.)	5	6	.455	2.42	13	13	4	•1	0	85²/₃	73	34	23	29	79
1992—	Cedar Rapids (Midw.)	0	0	...	0.00	1	0	0	0	0	1	1	0	0	0	0
	— Charleston, W.Va. (SAL)	6	8	.429	3.11	28	18	2	1	0	133	123	59	46	37	131
1993—	Winston-Salem (Caro.)	8	7	.533	3.41	21	20	2	1	0	145	133	68	55	48	101
	— Chattanooga (Sou.)	3	1	.750	1.69	7	3	2	0	0	37¹/₃	26	7	7	11	18
1994—	Cincinnati (N.L.)	1	1	.500	7.13	6	3	0	0	0	17²/₃	22	14	14	5	10
	— Indianapolis (A.A.)	10	2	•.833	3.54	21	20	2	0	0	132¹/₃	136	55	52	34	90
1995—	Indianapolis (A.A.)	4	2	.667	4.45	10	10	2	1	0	60²/₃	62	33	30	18	37
	— Cincinnati (N.L.)	3	4	.429	5.70	19	11	1	1	0	79	91	56	50	32	33
1996—	Indianapolis (A.A.)	4	3	.571	5.06	8	8	0	0	0	42²/₃	45	27	24	12	32
	— Cincinnati (N.L.)	8	9	.471	5.98	24	20	2	1	0	120¹/₃	152	93	80	43	63
1997—	Cincinnati (N.L.)	0	1	.000	10.13	9	0	0	0	1	13¹/₃	21	16	15	7	12
	— Toledo (I.L.)	0	1	.000	6.75	2	2	0	0	0	8	7	6	6	4	5
	— Minnesota (A.L.)■	0	0	...	12.46	6	2	0	0	0	13	23	18	18	8	9
	— Detroit (A.L.)■	0	3	.000	5.40	17	3	0	0	0	41²/₃	55	28	25	14	27
1998—	Chunichi (Jap. Cen.)■	1	2	.333	4.41	4	...	...	...	...	16¹/₃	16	18	...	5	7
	— Indianapolis (I.L.)	1	0	1.000	9.00	2	2	0	0	0	7	10	7	7	1	5
1999—	Vancouver (PCL)■	10	2	.833	3.41	17	16	2	1	0	103	110	47	39	26	64
	— Oakland (A.L.)	0	1	.000	11.57	4	1	0	0	0	14	28	19	18	6	11
	— Modesto (Calif.)	0	0	...	1.29	2	2	0	0	0	7	4	1	1	1	10
A.L. totals (2 years)		0	4	.000	8.00	27	6	0	0	0	68²/₃	106	65	61	28	47
N.L. totals (4 years)		12	15	.444	6.21	58	34	3	2	1	230¹/₃	286	179	159	87	118
Major League totals (5 years)		12	19	.387	6.62	85	40	3	2	1	299	392	244	220	115	165

JAVIER, STAN   OF   MARINERS

PERSONAL: Born January 9, 1964, in San Francisco de Macoris, Dominican Republic. ... 6-0/202. ... Bats both, throws right. ... Full name: Stanley Julian Javier. ... Son of Julian Javier, infielder with St. Louis Cardinals (1960-71) and Cincinnati Reds (1972). ... Name pronounced HA-vee-AIR.
HIGH SCHOOL: La Altagracia (San Francisco de Macoris, Dominican Republic).
TRANSACTIONS/CAREER NOTES: Signed as non-drafted free agent by St. Louis Cardinals organization (March 26, 1981). ... Traded by Cardinals organization with SS Bobby Meacham to New York Yankees organization for OF Bob Helsom, P Marty Mason and P Steve Fincher (December 14, 1982). ... Traded by Yankees organization with P Jay Howell, P Jose Rijo, P Eric Plunk and P Tim Birtsas to Oakland Athletics for OF Rickey Henderson, P Bert Bradley and cash (December 5, 1984). ... On Oakland disabled list (August 3-September 1, 1987); included rehabilitation assignment to Tacoma (August 20-September 1). ... On disabled list (August 18-September 2, 1988 and July 7-24, 1989). ... Traded by A's to Los Angeles Dodgers for 2B Willie Randolph (May 13, 1990). ... Traded by Dodgers to Philadelphia Phillies for P Steve Searcy and a player to be named later (July 2, 1992). ... Dodgers acquired IF Julio Peguero to complete deal (July 28, 1992). ... Granted free agency (October 27, 1992). ... Signed by California Angels organization (January 15, 1993). ... Granted free agency (October 29, 1993). ... Signed by A's (December 7, 1993). ... Granted free agency (November 2, 1995). ... Signed by San Francisco Giants (December 8, 1995). ... On San Francisco disabled list (April 13-29 and July 17, 1996-remainder of season); included rehabilitation assignment to San Jose (April 26-29). ... On restricted list (April 13-18, 1997). ... Granted free agency (October 28, 1997). ... Re-signed by Giants (November 26, 1997). ... Traded by Giants to Houston Astros for P Joe Messman (August 31, 1999). ... Granted free agency (October 28, 1999). ... Signed by Seattle Mariners (December 20, 1999).
STATISTICAL NOTES: Led A.L. outfielders with 1.000 fielding percentage in 1995.

							BATTING								FIELDING		
Year	Team (League)	Pos.	G	AB	R	H	2B	3B	HR	RBI	Avg.	BB	SO	SB	PO	A	E	Avg.
1981—	Johnson City (Appl.)	OF	53	144	30	36	5	4	3	19	.250	40	33	2	53	2	3	.948
1982—	Johnson City (Appl.)	OF	57	185	45	51	3	•4	8	36	.276	42	55	11	94	8	4	.962
1983—	Greensboro (SAL)■	OF	129	489	109	152	*34	6	12	77	.311	75	95	33	250	10	15	.945
1984—	New York (A.L.)	OF	7	7	1	1	0	0	0	0	.143	0	1	0	3	0	0	1.000
	— Nashville (Sou.)	OF	76	262	40	76	17	4	7	38	.290	39	57	17	202	4	7	.967
	— Columbus (I.L.)	OF	32	99	12	22	3	1	0	7	.222	12	26	1	77	4	2	.976
1985—	Huntsville (Sou.)■	OF	140	486	105	138	22	8	9	64	.284	*112	92	61	363	8	7	.981
1986—	Tacoma (PCL)	OF-1B	69	248	50	81	16	2	4	51	.327	47	46	18	172	9	6	.968
	— Oakland (A.L.)	OF-DH	59	114	13	23	8	0	0	8	.202	16	27	8	118	1	0	1.000
1987—	Oakland (A.L.)	OF-1B-DH	81	151	22	28	3	1	2	9	.185	19	33	3	149	5	3	.981
	— Tacoma (PCL)	OF-1B	15	51	6	11	2	0	0	2	.216	4	12	3	26	0	2	.929
1988—	Oakland (A.L.)	OF-DH	125	397	49	102	13	3	2	35	.257	32	63	20	274	7	5	.983
1989—	Oakland (A.L.)	OF-2B-1B	112	310	42	77	12	3	1	28	.248	31	45	12	221	8	2	.991
1990—	Oakland (A.L.)	OF-DH	19	33	4	8	0	2	0	3	.242	3	6	0	19	0	0	1.000
	— Los Angeles (N.L.)■	OF	104	276	56	84	9	4	3	24	.304	37	44	15	204	2	0	1.000
1991—	Los Angeles (N.L.)	OF-1B	121	176	21	36	5	3	1	11	.205	16	36	7	90	4	3	.969
1992—	Los Angeles (N.L.)	OF	56	58	6	11	3	0	1	5	.190	6	11	1	17	0	0	1.000
	— Philadelphia (N.L.)■	OF	74	276	36	72	14	1	0	24	.261	31	43	17	212	7	3	.986
1993—	California (A.L.)■	OF-1B-2B-DH	92	237	33	69	10	4	3	28	.291	27	33	12	167	4	4	.977
1994—	Oakland (A.L.)■	OF-1B-3B	109	419	75	114	23	0	10	44	.272	49	76	24	274	4	4	.986
1995—	Oakland (A.L.)	OF-3B	130	442	81	123	20	2	8	56	.278	49	63	36	332	3	0	†1.000
1996—	San Fran. (N.L.)■	OF	71	274	44	74	25	0	2	22	.270	25	51	14	180	2	3	.984
	— San Jose (Calif.)	OF-DH	3	5	1	2	0	0	0	1	.400	1	1	0	1	0	0	1.000

Year Team (League)	Pos.	G	AB	R	H	2B	3B	HR	RBI	Avg.	BB	SO	SB	PO	A	E	Avg.
1997—San Francisco (N.L.) ..	OF-1B	142	440	69	126	16	4	8	50	.286	56	70	25	279	2	7	.976
1998—San Francisco (N.L.) ..	OF	135	417	63	121	13	5	4	49	.290	65	63	21	217	0	3	.986
1999—San Francisco (N.L.) ..	OF-DH	112	333	49	92	15	1	3	30	.276	29	55	13	158	4	4	.976
—Houston (N.L.).■	OF	20	64	12	21	4	1	0	4	.328	9	8	3	31	1	0	1.000
American League totals (9 years)		734	2110	320	545	89	15	26	211	.258	226	347	115	1557	32	18	.989
National League totals (7 years)		835	2314	356	637	104	19	22	219	.275	274	381	116	1388	22	23	.984
Major League totals (15 years)		1569	4424	676	1182	193	34	48	430	.267	500	728	231	2945	54	41	.987

DIVISION SERIES RECORD

Year Team (League)	Pos.	G	AB	R	H	2B	3B	HR	RBI	Avg.	BB	SO	SB	PO	A	E	Avg.
1997—San Francisco (N.L.) ..	OF	3	12	2	5	1	0	0	1	.417	0	2	1	11	0	0	1.000
1999—Houston (N.L.)	PH-OF	4	11	1	3	0	0	0	0	.273	1	1	0	4	0	0	1.000
Division series totals (2 years)		7	23	3	8	1	0	0	1	.348	1	3	1	15	0	0	1.000

CHAMPIONSHIP SERIES RECORD

Year Team (League)	Pos.	G	AB	R	H	2B	3B	HR	RBI	Avg.	BB	SO	SB	PO	A	E	Avg.
1988—Oakland (A.L.)	OF-PR	2	4	0	2	0	0	0	1	.500	1	0	0	5	0	0	1.000
1989—Oakland (A.L.)	OF	1	2	0	0	0	0	0	0	.000	0	1	0	1	0	0	1.000
Championship series totals (2 years)		3	6	0	2	0	0	0	1	.333	1	1	0	6	0	0	1.000

WORLD SERIES RECORD

NOTES: Member of World Series championship team (1989).

Year Team (League)	Pos.	G	AB	R	H	2B	3B	HR	RBI	Avg.	BB	SO	SB	PO	A	E	Avg.
1988—Oakland (A.L.)	PR-OF	3	4	0	2	0	0	0	2	.500	0	1	0	1	0	0	1.000
1989—Oakland (A.L.)	OF	1	0	0	0	0	0	0	0	...	0	0	0	0	0	0	...
World Series totals (2 years)		4	4	0	2	0	0	0	2	.500	0	1	0	1	0	0	1.000

JEFFERIES, GREGG   OF   TIGERS

PERSONAL: Born August 1, 1967, in Burlingame, Calif. ... 5-10/185. ... Bats both, throws right. ... Full name: Gregory Scott Jefferies.

HIGH SCHOOL: Serra (San Mateo, Calif.).

TRANSACTIONS/CAREER NOTES: Selected by New York Mets organization in first round (20th pick overall) of free-agent draft (June 3, 1985). ... On disabled list (April 27-May 13, 1991). ... Traded by Mets with OF Kevin McReynolds and 2B Keith Miller to Kansas City Royals for P Bret Saberhagen and IF Bill Pecota (December 11, 1991). ... Traded by Royals with OF Ed Gerald to St. Louis Cardinals for OF Felix Jose and IF/OF Craig Wilson (February 12, 1993). ... Granted free agency (October 18, 1994). ... Signed by Philadelphia Phillies (December 14, 1994). ... On disabled list (June 17-July 2, 1995). ... On Philadelphia disabled list (April 5-June 4, 1996); included rehabilitation assignment to Scranton/Wilkes-Barre (May 30-June 4). ... On disabled list (August 18-September 2, 1997). ... Traded by Phillies to Anaheim Angels for a player to be named later (August 28, 1998); Phillies acquired P Doug Nickle to complete deal (September 9, 1998). ... Granted free agency (October 26, 1998). ... Signed by Detroit Tigers (December 28, 1998). ... On Detroit disabled list (June 21-July 6, August 3-20 and August 22-September 6, 1999); included rehabilitation assignment to Toledo (July 2-6).

HONORS: Named Appalachian League Player of the Year (1985). ... Named Carolina League Most Valuable Player (1986). ... Named Texas League Most Valuable Player (1987).

STATISTICAL NOTES: Led Carolina League with .549 slugging percentage in 1986. ... Led Texas League with 18 intentional bases on balls received in 1987. ... Tied for International League lead with 10 intentional bases on balls received in 1988. ... Led International League third basemen with 240 assists in 1988. ... Led A.L. third basemen with 26 errors in 1992. ... Tied for N.L. lead with 94 double plays by first basemen in 1994 ... Hit for the cycle (August 25, 1995). ... Had 15-game hitting streak (August 20-September 5, 1998). ... Career major league grand slams: 2.

Year Team (League)	Pos.	G	AB	R	H	2B	3B	HR	RBI	Avg.	BB	SO	SB	PO	A	E	Avg.
1985—Kingsport (Appal.)......	SS-2B	47	166	27	57	18	2	3	29	.343	14	16	21	78	130	21	.908
—Columbia (SAL).........	2B-SS	20	64	7	18	2	2	1	12	.281	4	4	7	28	26	2	.964
1986—Columbia (SAL).........	SS	25	112	29	38	6	1	5	24	.339	9	10	13	36	83	7	.944
—Lynchburg (Caro.).......	SS	95	390	66	138	25	9	11	80	*.354	33	29	43	138	273	20	.954
—Jackson (Texas).......	SS-3B	5	19	1	8	1	1	0	7	.421	2	2	1	7	9	1	.941
1987—Jackson (Texas).......	SS-3B	134	510	81	187	*48	5	20	101	.367	49	43	26	167	388	35	.941
—New York (N.L.).........	PH	6	6	0	3	1	0	0	2	.500	0	0	0	...	...	...	...
1988—Tidewater (I.L.)........3B-SS-2B-OF	132	504	62	142	28	4	7	61	.282	32	35	32	110	†330	27	.942
—New York (N.L.)........	3B-2B	29	109	19	35	8	2	6	17	.321	8	10	5	33	46	2	.975
1989—New York (N.L.)........	2B-3B	141	508	72	131	28	2	12	56	.258	39	46	21	242	280	14	.974
1990—New York (N.L.)........	2B-3B	153	604	96	171	*40	3	15	68	.283	46	40	11	242	341	16	.973
1991—New York (N.L.)........	2B-3B	136	486	59	132	19	2	9	62	.272	47	38	26	170	271	17	.963
1992—Kansas City (A.L.).■ ..	3B-DH-2B	152	604	66	172	36	3	10	75	.285	43	29	19	96	304	†26	.939
1993—St. Louis (N.L.).■	1B-2B	142	544	89	186	24	3	16	83	.342	62	32	46	1281	77	9	.993
1994—St. Louis (N.L.).........	1B	103	397	52	129	27	1	12	55	.325	45	26	12	889	53	7	.993
1995—Philadelphia (N.L.).■ ..	1B-OF	114	480	69	147	31	2	11	56	.306	35	26	9	579	36	3	.995
1996—Philadelphia (N.L.)......	1B-OF	104	404	59	118	17	3	7	51	.292	36	21	20	522	39	1	.998
—Scranton/W.B. (I.L.).....	1B-DH	4	17	1	2	0	1	0	0	.118	1	3	0	22	3	1	.962
1997—Philadelphia (N.L.)......	OF	130	476	68	122	25	3	11	48	.256	53	27	12	211	5	3	.986
1998—Philadelphia (N.L.)......	OF	125	483	65	142	22	3	8	48	.294	29	27	11	168	7	1	.994
—Anaheim (A.L.)........	OF-1B	19	72	7	25	6	0	1	10	.347	0	5	1	48	2	0	1.000
1999—Detroit (A.L.).■ DH-1B-2B-OF	70	205	22	41	8	0	6	18	.200	13	11	3	21	5	0	1.000
—Toledo (I.L.)...............	DH	2	8	0	2	0	0	0	0	.250	0	2	0	...	...	...	...
American League totals (3 years)		241	881	95	238	50	3	17	103	.270	56	45	23	165	311	26	.948
National League totals (11 years)		1183	4497	648	1316	242	24	107	546	.293	400	293	173	4337	1155	73	.987
Major League totals (13 years)		1424	5378	743	1554	292	27	124	649	.289	456	338	196	4502	1466	99	.984

Year Team (League)	Pos.	G	AB	R	H	2B	3B	HR	RBI	Avg.	BB	SO	SB	PO	A	E	Avg.
1988— New York (N.L.)..........	3B	7	27	2	9	2	0	0	1	.333	4	0	0	5	8	1	.929

ALL-STAR GAME RECORD

Year League	Pos.	AB	R	H	2B	3B	HR	RBI	Avg.	BB	SO	SB	PO	A	E	Avg.
1993— National	PH-DH	1	0	0	0	0	0	0	.000	0	1	0	...	...	...	...
1994— National	1B	1	2	1	1	0	0	0	1.000	0	0	0	6	0	0	1.000
All-Star Game totals (2 years)		2	2	1	1	0	0	0	.500	0	1	0	6	0	0	1.000

J

JEFFERSON, REGGIE — DH/1B

PERSONAL: Born September 25, 1968, in Tallahassee, Fla. ... 6-4/215. ... Bats left, throws left. ... Full name: Reginald Jirod Jefferson.

HIGH SCHOOL: Lincoln (Tallahassee, Fla.).

TRANSACTIONS/CAREER NOTES: Selected by Cincinnati Reds organization in third round of free-agent draft (June 2, 1986). ... On disabled list (May 25, 1990-remainder of season). ... Traded by Reds to Cleveland Indians for 1B Tim Costo (June 14, 1991). ... On Cleveland disabled list (June 24-July 1, 1991); included rehabilitation assignment to Canton/Akron (June 25-July 1). ... On Cleveland disabled list (March 28-July 4, 1992); included rehabilitation assignment to Colorado Springs (June 15-July 4). ... On Colorado Springs suspended list (September 6-9, 1992). ... Traded by Indians with SS Felix Fermin and cash to Seattle Mariners for SS Omar Vizquel (December 20, 1993). ... On disabled list (May 21-June 10, 1994). ... Granted free agency (March 11, 1995). ... Signed by Boston Red Sox (April 9, 1995). ... On disabled list (July 10-September 19, 1995). ... On Boston disabled list (July 15, 1998-remainder of season); included rehabilitation assignments to Gulf Coast Red Sox (August 10) and Sarasota (August 11-12 and August 29-September 1). ... On Boston disabled list (April 1-16, 1999); included rehabilitation assignments to Sarasota (April 10-13) and Pawtucket (April 14-16). ... Granted free agency (November 4, 1999).

STATISTICAL NOTES: Led Gulf Coast League first basemen with 624 total chances in 1986. ... Had 22-game hitting streak (July 13-August 8, 1997). ... Career major league grand slams: 2.

MISCELLANEOUS: Batted as switch hitter (1986 and 1989-May 1994).

Year Team (League)	Pos.	G	AB	R	H	2B	3B	HR	RBI	Avg.	BB	SO	SB	PO	A	E	Avg.
1986— GC Reds (GCL)..........	1B	59	208	28	54	4	•5	3	33	.260	24	40	10	*581	*36	7	.989
1987— Billings (Pio.)	1B	8	22	10	8	1	0	1	9	.364	4	2	1	21	1	0	1.000
— Cedar Rapids (Midw.)	1B	15	54	9	12	5	0	3	11	.222	1	12	1	120	11	1	.992
1988— Cedar Rapids (Midw.)	1B	135	517	76	149	26	2	18	*90	.288	40	89	2	1084	91	13	.989
1989— Chattanooga (Sou.)....	1B	135	487	66	140	19	3	17	80	.287	43	73	2	1004	79	16	.985
1990— Nashville (A.A.)	1B	37	126	24	34	11	2	5	23	.270	14	30	1	314	20	4	.988
1991— Nashville (A.A.)	1B	28	103	15	33	3	1	3	20	.320	10	22	3	196	13	2	.991
— Cincinnati (N.L.)	1B	5	7	1	1	0	0	1	1	.143	1	2	0	14	1	0	1.000
— Cleveland (A.L.)■..........	1B	26	101	10	20	3	0	2	12	.198	3	22	0	252	24	2	.993
— Canton/Akron (East.)..	1B	6	25	2	7	1	0	0	4	.280	1	5	0	46	3	0	1.000
— Colo. Springs (PCL) ...	1B	39	136	29	42	11	0	3	21	.309	16	28	0	289	25	3	.991
1992— Colo. Springs (PCL) ...	1B	57	218	49	68	11	4	11	44	.312	29	50	1	363	34	5	.988
— Cleveland (A.L.)..........	1B-DH	24	89	8	30	6	2	1	6	.337	1	17	0	129	12	1	.993
1993— Cleveland (A.L.)..........	DH-1B	113	366	35	91	11	2	10	34	.249	28	78	1	112	10	3	.976
1994— Seattle (A.L.)■..........	DH-1B-OF	63	162	24	53	11	0	8	32	.327	17	32	0	95	10	2	.981
1995— Boston (A.L.)■..........	DH-1B-OF	46	121	21	35	8	0	5	26	.289	9	24	0	28	4	0	1.000
1996— Boston (A.L.)..........	DH-OF-1B	122	386	67	134	30	4	19	74	.347	25	89	0	178	17	3	.985
1997— Boston (A.L.)..........	DH-1B	136	489	74	156	33	1	13	67	.319	24	93	1	74	5	2	.975
1998— Boston (A.L.)..........	DH-1B	62	196	24	60	16	1	8	31	.306	21	40	0	37	4	2	.953
— GC Red Sox (GCL)	DH	1	4	0	0	0	0	0	0	.000	0	1	0	...	...	...	...
— Sarasota (FSL)	DH	4	14	2	5	0	0	0	2	.357	1	3	0	...	...	...	...
1999— Sarasota (FSL)	1B	3	14	4	6	2	0	1	2	.429	1	2	0	30	4	0	1.000
— Pawtucket (I.L.)..........	1B-DH	3	10	1	0	0	0	0	0	.000	2	3	0	18	1	0	1.000
— Boston (A.L.)	DH-1B	83	206	21	57	13	1	5	17	.277	17	55	0	8	1	0	1.000
American League totals (9 years)		675	2116	284	636	131	11	71	299	.301	145	450	2	913	87	15	.985
National League totals (1 year)		5	7	1	1	0	0	1	1	.143	1	2	0	14	1	0	1.000
Major League totals (9 years)		680	2123	285	637	131	11	72	300	.300	146	452	2	927	88	15	.985

DIVISION SERIES RECORD

Year Team (League)	Pos.	G	AB	R	H	2B	3B	HR	RBI	Avg.	BB	SO	SB	PO	A	E	Avg.
1995— Boston (A.L.)..........	DH	1	4	1	1	0	0	0	0	.250	0	1	0	...	...	...	...
1999— Boston (A.L.)								Did not play.									

CHAMPIONSHIP SERIES RECORD

Year Team (League)	Pos.	G	AB	R	H	2B	3B	HR	RBI	Avg.	BB	SO	SB	PO	A	E	Avg.
1999— Boston (A.L.)								Did not play.									

JENKINS, GEOFF — OF — BREWERS

PERSONAL: Born July 21, 1974, in Olympia, Wash. ... 6-1/204. ... Bats left, throws right. ... Full name: Geoffrey Scott Jenkins.

HIGH SCHOOL: Cordova Senior (Rancho Cordova, Calif.).

COLLEGE: Southern California.

TRANSACTIONS/CAREER NOTES: Selected by Milwaukee Brewers organization in first round (ninth pick overall) of free-agent draft (June 1, 1995). ... On El Paso disabled list (May 8-July 23, 1996). ... On disabled list (July 4-August 11, 1997).

Year	Team (League)	Pos.	G	AB	R	H	2B	3B	HR	RBI	Avg.	BB	SO	SB	PO	A	E	Avg.
1995—	Helena (Pio.)		7	28	2	9	0	1	0	9	.321	3	11	0	15	1	0	1.000
	—Stockton (Calif.)	OF	13	47	13	12	2	0	3	12	.255	10	12	2	14	3	2	.895
	—El Paso (Texas)	OF	22	79	12	22	4	2	1	13	.278	8	23	3	41	1	7	.857
1996—	El Paso (Texas)..........	DH	22	77	17	22	5	4	1	11	.286	12	21	1	...	...	...	...
	—Stockton (Calif.)	DH-OF	37	138	27	48	8	4	3	25	.348	20	32	3	2	0	0	1.000
1997—	Tucson (PCL)	OF-SS	93	347	44	82	24	3	10	56	.236	33	87	0	115	7	5	.961
1998—	Louisville (I.L.)	OF	55	215	38	71	10	4	7	52	.330	14	39	1	90	3	2	.979
	—Milwaukee (N.L.)	OF	84	262	33	60	12	1	9	28	.229	20	61	1	115	6	4	.968
1999—	Milwaukee (N.L.)	OF	135	447	70	140	43	3	21	82	.313	35	87	5	250	14	7	.974
Major League totals (2 years)			219	709	103	200	55	4	30	110	.282	55	148	6	365	20	11	.972

JENNINGS, ROBIN   OF   TWINS

PERSONAL: Born April 11, 1972, in Republic of Singapore. ... 6-2/210. ... Bats left, throws left. ... Full name: Robin Christopher Jennings.
HIGH SCHOOL: Annandale (Va.).
JUNIOR COLLEGE: Manatee Community College (Fla.).
TRANSACTIONS/CAREER NOTES: Selected by Baltimore Orioles organization in 30th round of free-agent draft (June 4, 1990); did not sign. ... Selected by Chicago Cubs organization in 33rd round of free-agent draft (June 3, 1991). ... On Iowa disabled list (May 31-June 11 and August 10-20, 1996). ... On Chicago disabled list (March 22-June 8, 1998); included rehabilitation assignments to West Tenn (June 1-3) and Iowa (June 4-8). ... On Chicago disabled list (April 1-June 21, 1999); included rehabilitation assignments to West Tenn (May 25-June 8) and Iowa (June 9-21). ... Granted free agency (October 15, 1999). ... Signed by Minnesota Twins organization (November 30, 1999).
STATISTICAL NOTES: Tied for New York-Pennsylvania League lead in double plays by outfielder with two in 1992. ... Led Midwest League outfielders with 20 assists in 1993.

Year	Team (League)	Pos.	G	AB	R	H	2B	3B	HR	RBI	Avg.	BB	SO	SB	PO	A	E	Avg.
1992—	Geneva (NY-P)...........	OF	72	275	39	82	12	2	7	47	.298	20	43	10	96	*9	4	.963
1993—	Peoria (Midw.)...........	OF-1B	132	474	64	146	29	5	3	65	.308	46	73	11	219	†31	7	.973
1994—	Daytona (FSL)	OF	128	476	54	133	24	5	8	60	.279	45	54	2	165	8	8	.956
1995—	Orlando (Sou.)	OF	132	490	71	145	27	7	17	79	.296	44	61	7	242	15	10	.963
1996—	Iowa (A.A.)	OF-DH	86	331	53	94	15	6	18	56	.284	32	53	2	156	5	3	.982
	—Chicago (N.L.)	OF	31	58	7	13	5	0	0	4	.224	3	9	1	19	2	0	1.000
1997—	Iowa (A.A.)	OF-DH	126	464	67	128	25	5	20	71	.276	56	73	5	197	10	3	.986
	—Chicago (N.L.)	OF	9	18	1	3	1	0	0	2	.167	0	2	0	5	0	0	1.000
1998—	West Tenn (Sou.)	OF	2	6	0	0	0	0	0	0	.000	0	2	0	1	0	0	1.000
	—Iowa (PCL)	OF-1B	81	298	57	74	23	2	16	62	.248	33	49	4	129	5	5	.964
1999—	West Tenn (Sou.)	OF	13	53	11	17	3	0	5	17	.321	5	7	1	18	1	0	1.000
	—Iowa (PCL)	OF-DH-1B	67	259	47	80	20	5	9	43	.309	25	34	6	126	7	3	.978
	—Chicago (N.L.)...........		5	5	0	1	0	0	0	0	.200	0	2	0	0	0	0	...
Major League totals (3 years)			45	81	8	17	6	0	0	6	.210	3	13	1	24	2	0	1.000

JENSEN, MARCUS   C   TWINS

PERSONAL: Born December 14, 1972, in Oakland. ... 6-4/204. ... Bats both, throws right. ... Full name: Marcus C. Jensen.
HIGH SCHOOL: Skyline (Oakland).
TRANSACTIONS/CAREER NOTES: Selected by San Francisco Giants organization in supplemental round ("sandwich pick" between first and second round, 33rd pick overall) of free-agent draft (June 4, 1990); pick received as part of compensation for San Diego Padres signing Type A free-agent P Craig Lefferts. ... On disabled list (June 1-14, 1993). ... Traded by Giants to Detroit Tigers for C Brian Johnson (July 16, 1997). ... Granted free agency (July 22, 1997). ... Re-signed by Tigers (July 26, 1997). ... Released by Tigers (March 25, 1998). ... Signed by Milwaukee Brewers organization (April 5, 1998). ... On Louisville disabled list (April 9-21, 1998). ... Released by Brewers (September 29, 1998). ... Signed by St. Louis Cardinals organization (January 13, 1999). ... Granted free agency (October 15, 1999). ... Signed by Minnesota Twins organization (January 4, 2000).
STATISTICAL NOTES: Tied for Arizona League lead with three intentional bases on balls received in 1991. ... Led California League catchers with 722 total chances in 1994. ... Led Texas League catchers with 546 total chances in 1995.

Year	Team (League)	Pos.	G	AB	R	H	2B	3B	HR	RBI	Avg.	BB	SO	SB	PO	A	E	Avg.
1990—	Everett (N.W.)............	C	51	171	21	29	3	0	2	12	.170	24	60	0	191	27	3	.986
1991—	Arizona Giants (Ariz.) .	C-1B	48	155	28	44	8	3	2	30	.284	34	22	4	226	29	7	.973
1992—	Clinton (Midw.)	C-1B	86	264	35	62	14	0	4	33	.235	54	87	4	493	68	10	.982
1993—	Clinton (Midw.)	C	104	324	53	85	24	2	11	56	.262	66	98	1	641	73	7	.990
1994—	San Jose (Calif.)........	C-DH	118	418	66	101	18	0	7	47	.242	61	100	1	*627	86	9	.988
1995—	Shreveport (Texas)	C-DH	95	321	55	91	22	8	4	45	.283	41	68	0	*471	70	5	.991
1996—	Phoenix (PCL)	C-DH	120	405	41	107	22	4	5	53	.264	44	95	1	568	65	8	.988
	—San Francisco (N.L.) ..	C	9	19	4	4	1	0	0	4	.211	8	7	0	37	5	2	.955
1997—	San Francisco (N.L.) ..	C	30	74	5	11	2	0	1	3	.149	7	23	0	106	10	2	.983
	—Toledo (I.L.)■..........	C-DH	24	80	5	14	5	0	0	9	.175	9	25	0	149	6	1	.994
	—Detroit (A.L.)	C	8	11	1	2	0	0	0	1	.182	1	5	0	26	1	1	.964
1998—	Louisville (I.L.)■	C-1B	74	230	29	52	13	0	10	33	.226	33	64	0	444	34	3	.994
	—Milwaukee (N.L.)	C	2	2	0	0	0	0	0	0	.000	0	2	0	1	0	0	1.000
1999—	Memphis (PCL)■.......	C-DH	72	237	38	69	19	4	8	44	.291	30	59	0	380	32	2	.995
	—St. Louis (N.L.)..........	C	16	34	5	8	5	0	1	1	.235	6	12	0	71	9	1	.988
American League totals (1 year)			8	11	1	2	0	0	0	1	.182	1	5	0	26	1	1	.964
National League totals (4 years)			57	129	14	23	8	0	2	8	.178	21	44	0	215	24	5	.980
Major League totals (4 years)			65	140	15	25	8	0	2	9	.179	22	49	0	241	25	6	.978

JENSEN, RYAN   P   GIANTS

PERSONAL: Born September 17, 1975, in Salt Lake City, Utah. ... 6-0/205. ... Throws right, bats right. ... Full name: Larry Ryan Jensen.
HIGH SCHOOL: Cottonwood (Salt Lake City, Utah).
COLLEGE: Southern Utah.
TRANSACTIONS/CAREER NOTES: Selected by San Francisco Giants organization in eighth round of free-agent draft (June 4, 1996). ... On Fresno disabled list (June 21-30, 1999).
STATISTICAL NOTES: Tied for Northwest League lead in home runs allowed with 10 in 1997.

Year	League	W	L	Pct.	ERA	G	GS	CG	ShO	Sv.	IP	H	R	ER	BB	SO
1996—	Bellingham (N.W.)	2	4	.333	4.98	13	11	0	0	0	47	35	30	26	38	31
1997—	Bakersfield (Calif.)	0	0	...	13.50	1	1	0	0	0	1 1/3	3	2	2	0	2
	— Salem-Kaizer (N.W.)	7	3	.700	5.15	16	•16	0	0	0	80 1/3	87	55	46	32	67
1998—	Bakersfield (Calif.)	11	12	.478	3.37	29	27	0	0	0	168 1/3	162	89	63	61	164
	— Fresno (PCL)	0	0	...	4.76	2	1	0	0	0	5 2/3	4	5	3	4	6
1999—	Fresno (PCL)	11	10	.524	5.12	27	27	0	0	0	156 1/3	160	96	89	68	150

JETER, DEREK   SS   YANKEES

PERSONAL: Born June 26, 1974, in Pequannock, N.J. ... 6-3/195. ... Bats right, throws right. ... Full name: Derek Sanderson Jeter.
HIGH SCHOOL: Central (Kalamazoo, Mich.).
COLLEGE: Michigan.
TRANSACTIONS/CAREER NOTES: Selected by New York Yankees organization in first round (sixth pick overall) of free-agent draft (June 1, 1992). ... On New York disabled list (June 3-19, 1998); included rehabilitation assignment to Columbus (June 18-19).
HONORS: Named Minor League Player of the Year by THE SPORTING NEWS (1994). ... Named A.L. Rookie Player of the Year by THE SPORTING NEWS (1996). ... Named A.L. Rookie of the Year by Baseball Writers' Association of America (1996).
STATISTICAL NOTES: Had 15-game hitting streak (May 2-20, 1998). ... Had 16-game hitting streak (May 4-22, 1999).

							BATTING							FIELDING		
Year	Team (League)	Pos.	G	AB	R	H	2B	3B	HR	RBI	Avg.	BB	SO	SB	PO	A	E	Avg.
1992—	GC Yankees (GCL)	SS	47	173	19	35	10	0	3	25	.202	19	36	2	67	132	12	.943
	— Greensboro (SAL)	SS	11	37	4	9	0	0	1	4	.243	7	16	0	14	25	9	.813
1993—	Greensboro (SAL)	SS	128	515	85	152	14	11	5	71	.295	56	95	18	158	292	56	.889
1994—	Tampa (FSL)	SS	69	292	61	96	13	8	0	39	.329	23	30	28	93	204	12	.961
	— Alb./Colonie (East.)	SS	34	122	17	46	7	2	2	13	.377	15	16	12	42	105	6	.961
	— Columbus (I.L.)	SS	35	126	25	44	7	1	3	16	.349	20	15	10	54	93	7	.955
1995—	Columbus (I.L.)	SS	123	486	*96	154	27	9	2	45	.317	61	56	20	189	394	*29	.953
	— New York (A.L.)	SS	15	48	5	12	4	1	0	7	.250	3	11	0	17	34	2	.962
1996—	New York (A.L.)	SS	157	582	104	183	25	6	10	78	.314	48	102	14	244	444	22	.969
1997—	New York (A.L.)	SS	159	654	116	190	31	7	10	70	.291	74	125	23	243	*457	18	.975
1998—	New York (A.L.)	SS	149	626	*127	203	25	8	19	84	.324	57	119	30	223	393	9	.986
	— Columbus (I.L.)	SS	1	5	2	2	2	0	0	0	.400	0	2	0	4	3	1	.875
1999—	New York (A.L.)	SS	158	627	134	*219	37	9	24	102	.349	91	116	19	230	391	14	.978
Major League totals (5 years)			638	2537	486	807	122	31	63	341	.318	273	473	86	957	1719	65	.976

DIVISION SERIES RECORD

							BATTING							FIELDING		
Year	Team (League)	Pos.	G	AB	R	H	2B	3B	HR	RBI	Avg.	BB	SO	SB	PO	A	E	Avg.
1996—	New York (A.L.)	SS	4	17	2	7	1	0	0	1	.412	0	2	0	8	10	2	.900
1997—	New York (A.L.)	SS	5	21	6	7	1	0	2	2	.333	3	5	1	12	15	0	1.000
1998—	New York (A.L.)	SS	3	9	0	1	0	0	0	0	.111	2	2	0	4	5	0	1.000
1999—	New York (A.L.)	SS	3	11	3	5	1	1	0	0	.455	2	3	0	5	10	0	1.000
Division series totals (4 years)			15	58	11	20	3	1	2	3	.345	7	12	1	29	40	2	.972

CHAMPIONSHIP SERIES RECORD

							BATTING							FIELDING		
Year	Team (League)	Pos.	G	AB	R	H	2B	3B	HR	RBI	Avg.	BB	SO	SB	PO	A	E	Avg.
1996—	New York (A.L.)	SS	5	24	5	10	2	0	1	1	.417	0	5	2	6	13	0	1.000
1998—	New York (A.L.)	SS	6	25	3	5	1	1	0	2	.200	2	5	3	9	13	0	1.000
1999—	New York (A.L.)	SS	5	20	3	7	1	0	1	3	.350	2	3	0	10	10	2	.909
Championship series totals (3 years)			16	69	11	22	4	1	2	6	.319	4	13	5	25	36	2	.968

WORLD SERIES RECORD
NOTES: Member of World Series championship team (1996, 1998 and 1999).

							BATTING							FIELDING		
Year	Team (League)	Pos.	G	AB	R	H	2B	3B	HR	RBI	Avg.	BB	SO	SB	PO	A	E	Avg.
1996—	New York (A.L.)	SS	6	20	5	5	0	0	0	1	.250	4	6	1	15	22	2	.949
1998—	New York (A.L.)	SS	4	17	4	6	0	0	0	1	.353	3	3	0	7	8	0	1.000
1999—	New York (A.L.)	SS	4	17	4	6	1	0	0	1	.353	1	3	3	6	15	0	1.000
World Series totals (3 years)			14	54	13	17	1	0	0	3	.315	8	12	4	28	45	2	.973

ALL-STAR GAME RECORD

						BATTING							FIELDING		
Year	League	Pos.	AB	R	H	2B	3B	HR	RBI	Avg.	BB	SO	SB	PO	A	E	Avg.
1998—	American	SS	1	0	0	0	0	0	0	.000	0	1	0	0	2	0	1.000
1999—	American	SS	1	0	0	0	0	0	0	.000	0	1	0	1	0	0	1.000
All-Star Game totals (2 years)			2	0	0	0	0	0	0	.000	0	2	0	1	2	0	1.000

JIMENEZ, D'ANGELO   SS   YANKEES

PERSONAL: Born December 21, 1977, in Santo Domingo, Dominican Republic. ... 6-0/160. ... Bats right, throws right.
TRANSACTIONS/CAREER NOTES: Signed as non-drafted free agent by New York Yankees organization (August 1, 1994). ... On Columbus disabled list (August 6-19, 1999).
STATISTICAL NOTES: Led Gulf Coast League shortstops with 289 total chances in 1995. ... Led South Atlantic League shortstops with 640 total chances in 1996. ... Led International League shortstops with 188 putouts in 1999.

											BATTING				FIELDING			
Year	Team (League)	Pos.	G	AB	R	H	2B	3B	HR	RBI	Avg.	BB	SO	SB	PO	A	E	Avg.
1995—GC Yankees (GCL).....		SS	57	214	41	60	14	*8	2	28	.280	23	31	6	*95	*173	21	.927
1996—Greensboro (SAL)......		SS	138	*537	68	131	25	5	6	48	.244	56	113	15	190	*400	*50	.922
1997—Columbus (A.A.)........		SS	2	7	1	1	0	0	0	1	.143	0	1	0	2	8	2	.833
—Tampa (FSL)........		SS	94	352	52	99	14	6	6	48	.281	50	50	8	147	283	21	.953
1998—Norwich (East.).........		SS	40	152	21	41	6	2	2	21	.270	25	26	5	62	119	12	.938
—Columbus (I.L.).........		SS-2B	91	344	55	88	19	4	8	51	.256	46	67	6	150	302	26	.946
1999—Columbus (I.L.).......		SS-3B-2B	126	526	97	172	32	5	15	88	.327	59	75	26	†202	372	26	.957
—New York (A.L.).........		3B-2B	7	20	3	8	2	0	0	4	.400	3	4	0	3	9	0	1.000
Major League totals (1 year)			7	20	3	8	2	0	0	4	.400	3	4	0	3	9	0	1.000

JIMENEZ, JOSE   P   ROCKIES

PERSONAL: Born July 7, 1973, in San Pedro de Macoris, Dominican Republic. ... 6-3/190. ... Throws right, bats right.
TRANSACTIONS/CAREER NOTES: Signed as non-drafted free agent by St. Louis Cardinals organization (October 21, 1991). ... Traded by Cardinals with P Manny Aybar, P Rick Croushore and SS Brent Butler to Colorado Rockies for P Darryl Kile, P Dave Veres and P Luther Hackman (November 16, 1999).
HONORS: Named Texas League Pitcher of the Year (1998).
STATISTICAL NOTES: Pitched 6-0 no-hit victory for Arkansas against Shreveport (August 27, 1998). ... Pitched 1-0 no-hit victory against Arizona (June 25, 1999).
MISCELLANEOUS: Scored one run in two appearances as pinch runner (1999).

Year	League	W	L	Pct.	ERA	G	GS	CG	ShO	Sv.	IP	H	R	ER	BB	SO
1992—Dom. Cardinals (DSL)........		3	2	.600	6.10	18	2	0	0	0	48 2/3	68	43	33	23	21
1993—Dom. Cardinals (DSL)........		3	5	.375	3.51	12	12	0	0	0	56 1/3	61	47	22	35	30
1994—Dom. Cardinals (DSL)........		3	9	.250	2.77	19	9	0	0	3	68 1/3	54	43	21	30	54
1995—Johnson City (Appl.)		5	7	.417	3.49	14	•14	1	1	0	*90 1/3	81	48	35	25	85
1996—Peoria (Midw.)........		12	9	.571	2.92	28	27	3	1	0	172 1/3	158	75	56	53	129
1997—Prince William (Caro.)........		9	7	.563	3.09	24	24	2	0	0	145 2/3	128	73	50	42	81
1998—Arkansas (Texas)........		15	6	.714	3.11	26	26	1	1	0	179 2/3	156	71	62	68	88
—St. Louis (N.L.).................		3	0	1.000	2.95	4	3	0	0	0	21 1/3	22	8	7	8	12
1999—St. Louis (N.L.)..................		5	14	.263	5.85	29	28	2	2	0	163	173	114	106	71	113
—Memphis (PCL).................		2	2	.500	3.04	4	4	0	0	0	26 2/3	30	10	9	9	18
Major League totals (2 years)......		8	14	.364	5.52	33	31	2	2	0	184 1/3	195	122	113	79	125

JOHNS, DOUG   P

PERSONAL: Born December 19, 1967, in South Bend, Ind. ... 6-2/195. ... Throws left, bats right. ... Full name: Douglas Alan Johns.
HIGH SCHOOL: Nova (Fort Lauderdale, Fla.).
COLLEGE: Virginia.
TRANSACTIONS/CAREER NOTES: Selected by Oakland Athletics organization in 16th round of free-agent draft (June 4, 1990). ... Claimed on waivers by Kansas City Royals (March 14, 1997). ... Released by Royals (May 29, 1997). ... Signed by Baltimore Orioles (June 30, 1997). ... Granted free agency (October 15, 1997). ... Re-signed by Orioles (January 9, 1998). ... Played in Europe during 1998 season. ... On Baltimore disabled list (May 3-18, 1998). ... Granted free agency (December 21, 1999).
STATISTICAL NOTES: Pitched 3-0 no-hit victory against Burlington (July 17, 1991).
MISCELLANEOUS: Appeared in two games as pinch runner (1996).

Year	League	W	L	Pct.	ERA	G	GS	CG	ShO	Sv.	IP	H	R	ER	BB	SO
1990—Arizona Athletics (Ariz.)......		3	1	.750	1.84	8	7	1	0	0	44	36	17	9	9	38
—Southern Oregon (N.W.).....		0	2	.000	5.73	6	2	0	0	1	11	13	9	7	11	9
1991—Madison (Midw.)...............		12	6	.667	3.23	38	14	1	1	2	128 1/3	108	59	46	54	104
1992—Reno (Calif.).....................		13	10	.565	3.26	27	26	4	1	0	*179 1/3	194	98	65	64	101
—Huntsville (Sou.)		0	0	...	3.94	3	1	0	0	0	16	21	11	7	5	4
1993—Huntsville (Sou.)		7	5	.583	2.97	40	6	0	0	1	91	82	41	30	31	56
1994—Huntsville (Sou.)		3	0	1.000	1.20	9	0	0	0	0	15	16	2	2	12	9
—Tacoma (PCL)		9	8	.529	2.89	22	19	2	1	0	134	114	55	43	48	65
1995—Edmonton (PCL)		9	5	.643	3.41	23	21	0	0	0	132	148	55	50	43	70
—Oakland (A.L.)		5	3	.625	4.61	11	9	1	1	0	54 2/3	44	32	28	26	25
1996—Oakland (A.L.)		6	12	.333	5.98	42	23	1	0	1	158	187	112	105	69	71
1997—Omaha (A.A.)■		1	5	.167	7.56	9	6	1	0	0	41 2/3	58	36	35	11	24
—Rochester (I.L.)■...........		3	1	.750	3.74	9	8	2	1	0	55 1/3	57	25	23	13	42
1998—Rochester (I.L.)...............		0	1	.000	1.69	2	2	0	0	0	10 2/3	7	3	2	6	4
—Baltimore (A.L.)............		3	3	.500	4.57	31	10	0	0	1	86 2/3	108	46	44	32	34
1999—Baltimore (A.L.)...............		6	4	.600	4.47	32	5	0	0	0	86 2/3	81	45	43	25	50
—Rochester (I.L.)................		1	1	.500	4.85	6	6	1	0	0	29 2/3	34	20	16	6	18
Major League totals (4 years).......		20	22	.476	5.13	116	47	2	1	2	386	420	235	220	152	180

JOHNSON, BRIAN   C   ROYALS

PERSONAL: Born January 8, 1968, in Oakland. ... 6-2/210. ... Bats right, throws right. ... Full name: Brian David Johnson.
HIGH SCHOOL: Skyline (Oakland).
COLLEGE: Stanford.

J

TRANSACTIONS/CAREER NOTES: Selected by Montreal Expos organization in 36th round of free-agent draft (June 2, 1986); did not sign. ... Selected by New York Yankees organization in 16th round of free-agent draft (June 5, 1989). ... Selected by Las Vegas, San Diego Padres organization from Albany/Colonie, Yankees organization, in Rule 5 minor league draft (December 9, 1991). ... On disabled list (April 22-May 16, 1992). ... Traded by Padres with P Willie Blair to Detroit Tigers for P Joey Eischen and P Cam Smith (December 17, 1996). ... Traded by Tigers to San Francisco Giants for C Marcus Jensen (July 16, 1997). ... On San Francisco disabled list (May 4-21 and July 22-August 7, 1998); included rehabilitation assignment to Fresno (July 31-August 7). ... Granted free agency (December 21, 1998). ... Signed by Cincinnati Reds (January 11, 1999). ... On Cincinnati disabled list (June 14-August 1, 1999); included rehabilitation assignment to Indianapolis (July 23-30). ... Released by Reds (October 8, 1999). ... Signed by Kansas City Royals (December 14, 1999).

STATISTICAL NOTES: Led South Atlantic League catchers with 752 putouts and 844 total chances in 1990. ... Led Florida State League catchers with 654 putouts in 1991. ... Career major league grand slams: 3.

							BATTING								FIELDING		
Year	Team (League)	Pos.	G	AB	R	H	2B	3B	HR	RBI	Avg.	BB	SO	SB	PO	A	E	Avg.
1989— GC Yankees (GCL)		C	17	61	7	22	1	1	0	8	.361	4	5	0	84	14	1	.990
1990— Greensboro (SAL)		C-3B-1B	137	496	58	118	15	0	7	51	.238	57	65	4	†773	91	13	.985
1991— Alb./Colonie (East.)		C-1B	2	8	0	0	0	0	0	0	.000	0	2	0	10	2	0	1.000
— Fort Laud. (FSL)		C-1B-3B	113	394	35	94	19	0	1	44	.239	34	67	4	†738	65	13	.984
1992— Wichita (Texas)■		C-3B	75	245	30	71	20	0	3	26	.290	22	32	3	472	40	3	.994
1993— Las Vegas (PCL)		C-3B-DH-OF	115	416	58	141	35	6	10	71	.339	41	53	0	513	67	9	.985
1994— San Diego (N.L.)		C-1B	36	93	7	23	4	1	3	16	.247	5	21	0	185	15	0	1.000
— Las Vegas (PCL)		C-DH	15	51	6	11	1	0	2	9	.216	8	6	0	61	5	0	1.000
1995— San Diego (N.L.)		C-1B	68	207	20	52	9	0	3	29	.251	11	39	0	403	32	4	.991
1996— San Diego (N.L.)		C-1B-3B	82	243	18	66	13	1	8	35	.272	4	36	0	456	21	5	.990
1997— Detroit (A.L.)■		C-DH	45	139	13	33	6	1	2	18	.237	5	19	1	217	9	3	.987
— Toledo (I.L.)		C-DH	7	21	0	3	2	0	0	1	.143	0	2	0	38	4	0	1.000
— San Fran. (N.L.)■		C-1B	56	179	19	50	7	2	11	27	.279	14	26	0	352	24	2	.995
1998— San Francisco (N.L.)		C-OF	99	308	34	73	8	1	13	34	.237	28	67	0	591	33	4	.994
— Fresno (PCL)		OF	5	19	4	6	1	0	2	3	.316	1	5	0	10	0	0	1.000
1999— Cincinnati (N.L.)■		C	45	117	12	27	7	0	5	18	.231	9	31	0	201	11	1	.995
— Indianapolis (I.L.)		C	6	19	2	4	3	0	0	4	.211	1	3	0	22	2	0	1.000
American League totals (1 year)			45	139	13	33	6	1	2	18	.237	5	19	1	217	9	3	.987
National League totals (6 years)			386	1147	110	291	48	5	43	159	.254	71	220	0	2188	136	16	.993
Major League totals (6 years)			431	1286	123	324	54	6	45	177	.252	76	239	1	2405	145	19	.993

DIVISION SERIES RECORD

							BATTING								FIELDING		
Year	Team (League)	Pos.	G	AB	R	H	2B	3B	HR	RBI	Avg.	BB	SO	SB	PO	A	E	Avg.
1996— San Diego (N.L.)		C	2	8	2	3	1	0	0	0	.375	0	1	0	15	3	0	1.000
1997— San Francisco (N.L.)		C	3	10	2	1	0	0	1	1	.100	1	4	0	18	0	0	1.000
Division series totals (2 years)			5	18	4	4	1	0	1	1	.222	1	5	0	33	3	0	1.000

JOHNSON, CHARLES   C   ORIOLES

PERSONAL: Born July 20, 1971, in Fort Pierce, Fla. ... 6-2/220. ... Bats right, throws right. ... Full name: Charles Edward Johnson Jr. ... Nephew of Fred McGriff, first baseman, Tampa Bay Devil Rays.

HIGH SCHOOL: Westwood (Fort Pierce, Fla.).

COLLEGE: Miami (Fla.).

TRANSACTIONS/CAREER NOTES: Selected by Montreal Expos organization in first round (10th pick overall) of free-agent draft (June 5, 1989); did not sign. ... Selected by Florida Marlins organization in first round (28th pick overall) of free-agent draft (June 1, 1992). ... On Florida disabled list (August 9-September 1, 1995); included rehabilitation assignment to Portland (August 30-September 1). ... On disabled list (July 28-September 1, 1996). ... Traded by Marlins with OF Gary Sheffield, 3B Bobby Bonilla, OF Jim Eisenreich and P Manuel Barrios to Los Angeles Dodgers for C Mike Piazza and 3B Todd Zeile (May 15, 1998). ... Traded by Dodgers with OF Roger Cedeno to New York Mets for C Todd Hundley and P Arnold Gooch; then traded by Mets to Baltimore Orioles for P Armando Benitez (December 1, 1998).

RECORDS: Holds major league career records for most consecutive errorless games by catcher—159 (June 24, 1996-September 28, 1997); and most consecutive chances accepted by catcher without an error—1,294 (June 23, 1996-September 28, 1997). ... Holds major league single-season records for most consecutive errorless games by catcher—123 (April 1 through September 28, 1997); and most chances accepted without an error by catcher—973 (April 1 through September 28, 1997). ... Shares major league single-season records for highest fielding average by catcher (100 or more games)—1.000 (1997); and fewest errors (100 or more games)—0 (1997).

HONORS: Named catcher on THE SPORTING NEWS college All-America team (1992). ... Won N.L. Gold Glove at catcher (1995-98).

STATISTICAL NOTES: Led Midwest League with 230 total bases in 1993. ... Led Midwest League catchers with 1,004 total chances in 1993. ... Led N.L. catchers with 12 double plays in 1996. ... Led A.L. catchers with 14 double plays in 1999.

MISCELLANEOUS: Member of 1992 U.S. Olympic baseball team.

							BATTING								FIELDING		
Year	Team (League)	Pos.	G	AB	R	H	2B	3B	HR	RBI	Avg.	BB	SO	SB	PO	A	E	Avg.
1993— Kane County (Midw.)		C	135	488	74	134	29	5	19	*94	.275	62	111	9	*852	*140	12	.988
1994— Portland (East.)		C-DH	132	443	64	117	29	1	*28	80	.264	*74	97	4	713	*84	7	.991
— Florida (N.L.)		C	4	11	5	5	1	0	1	4	.455	1	4	0	18	2	0	1.000
1995— Florida (N.L.)		C	97	315	40	79	15	1	11	39	.251	46	71	0	641	•63	6	.992
— Portland (East.)		C	2	7	0	0	0	0	0	0	.000	1	3	0	21	2	1	.958
1996— Florida (N.L.)		C	120	386	34	84	13	1	13	37	.218	40	91	1	751	70	4	*.995
1997— Florida (N.L.)		C	124	416	43	104	26	1	19	63	.250	60	109	0	901	73	0	*1.000
1998— Florida (N.L.)		C	31	113	13	25	5	0	7	23	.221	16	30	0	193	10	2	.990
— Los Angeles (N.L.)■		C	102	346	31	75	13	0	12	35	.217	29	99	0	715	50	6	.992
1999— Baltimore (A.L.)■		C	135	426	58	107	19	1	16	54	.251	55	107	0	770	66	5	.994
American League totals (1 year)			135	426	58	107	19	1	16	54	.251	55	107	0	770	66	5	.994
National League totals (5 years)			478	1587	166	372	73	3	63	201	.234	192	404	1	3219	268	18	.995
Major League totals (6 years)			613	2013	224	479	92	4	79	255	.238	247	511	1	3989	334	23	.995

DIVISION SERIES RECORD

					BATTING									FIELDING		
Year	Team (League)	Pos.	G	AB	R	H	2B	3B	HR	RBI	Avg.	BB	SO	SB	PO	A	E	Avg.
1997—Florida (N.L.)		C	3	8	5	2	1	0	1	2	.250	3	2	0	21	3	0	1.000

CHAMPIONSHIP SERIES RECORD

					BATTING									FIELDING		
Year	Team (League)	Pos.	G	AB	R	H	2B	3B	HR	RBI	Avg.	BB	SO	SB	PO	A	E	Avg.
1997—Florida (N.L.)		C	6	17	1	2	2	0	0	5	.118	3	8	0	52	3	2	.965

WORLD SERIES RECORD

NOTES: Member of World Series championship team (1997).

					BATTING									FIELDING		
Year	Team (League)	Pos.	G	AB	R	H	2B	3B	HR	RBI	Avg.	BB	SO	SB	PO	A	E	Avg.
1997—Florida (N.L.)		C	7	28	4	10	0	0	1	3	.357	1	6	0	49	2	0	1.000

ALL-STAR GAME RECORD

				BATTING									FIELDING		
Year	League	Pos.	AB	R	H	2B	3B	HR	RBI	Avg.	BB	SO	SB	PO	A	E	Avg.
1997—National		C	1	0	0	0	0	0	0	.000	0	1	0	2	0	0	1.000

JOHNSON, JASON   P   ORIOLES

PERSONAL: Born October 27, 1973, in Santa Barbara, Calif. ... 6-6/235. ... Throws right, bats right. ... Full name: Jason Michael Johnson.
HIGH SCHOOL: Conner (Hebron, Ky.).
TRANSACTIONS/CAREER NOTES: Signed as non-drafted free agent by Pittsburgh Pirates organization (July 21, 1992). ... Selected by Tampa Bay Devil Rays in first round (14th pick overall) of expansion draft (November 18, 1997). ... On Tampa Bay disabled list (July 4, 1998-remainder of season). ... Traded by Devil Rays to Baltimore Orioles for OF Danny Clyburn and a player to be named later (March 29, 1999); Devil Rays acquired SS Bolivar Voquez to complete deal (April 22, 1999).

Year	League	W	L	Pct.	ERA	G	GS	CG	ShO	Sv.	IP	H	R	ER	BB	SO
1992—Gulf Coast Pirates (GCL)		2	0	1.000	3.68	5	0	0	0	0	7 1/3	6	3	3	6	3
1993—Gulf Coast Pirates (GCL)		1	4	.200	2.33	9	9	0	0	0	54	48	22	14	14	39
—Welland (NY-P)		1	5	.167	4.63	6	6	1	0	0	35	33	24	18	9	19
1994—Augusta (SAL)		2	12	.143	4.03	20	19	1	0	0	102 2/3	119	67	46	32	69
1995—Augusta (SAL)		3	5	.375	4.36	11	11	1	0	0	53 2/3	57	32	26	17	42
—Lynchburg (Caro.)		1	2	.333	2.05	5	4	0	0	0	22	23	6	5	5	9
1996—Lynchburg (Caro.)		1	4	.200	6.50	15	5	0	0	0	44 1/3	56	37	32	12	27
—Augusta (SAL)		4	4	.500	3.11	14	14	1	1	0	84	82	40	29	25	83
1997—Lynchburg (Caro.)		8	4	.667	3.71	17	17	0	0	0	99 1/3	98	43	41	30	92
—Carolina (Sou.)		3	3	.500	4.08	9	9	1	0	0	57 1/3	56	31	26	16	63
—Pittsburgh (N.L.)		0	0	...	6.00	3	0	0	0	0	6	10	4	4	1	3
1998—Durham (I.L.)■		1	0	1.000	2.92	2	2	0	0	0	12 1/3	6	4	4	2	14
—Tampa Bay (A.L.)		2	5	.286	5.70	13	13	0	0	0	60	74	38	38	27	36
1999—Rochester (I.L.)■		4	2	.667	3.65	8	8	0	0	0	44 1/3	35	19	18	27	47
—Baltimore (A.L.)		8	7	.533	5.46	22	21	0	0	0	115 1/3	120	74	70	55	71
A.L. totals (2 years)		10	12	.455	5.54	35	34	0	0	0	175 1/3	194	112	108	82	107
N.L. totals (1 year)		0	0	...	6.00	3	0	0	0	0	6	10	4	4	1	3
Major League totals (3 years)		10	12	.455	5.56	38	34	0	0	0	181 1/3	204	116	112	83	110

JOHNSON, JONATHAN   P   RANGERS

PERSONAL: Born July 16, 1974, in LaGrange, Ga. ... 6-0/180. ... Throws right, bats right. ... Full name: Jonathan Kent Johnson.
HIGH SCHOOL: Forest (Ocala, Fla.).
COLLEGE: Florida State.
TRANSACTIONS/CAREER NOTES: Selected by Texas Rangers organization in first round (seventh pick overall) of free-agent draft (June 1, 1995). ... On Oklahoma disabled list (May 1-17, 1998; and May 13-July 5, 1999).

Year	League	W	L	Pct.	ERA	G	GS	CG	ShO	Sv.	IP	H	R	ER	BB	SO
1995—Charlotte (FSL)		1	5	.167	2.70	8	7	1	0	0	43 1/3	34	14	13	16	25
1996—Tulsa (Texas)		*13	10	.565	3.56	26	25	*6	0	0	174 1/3	176	86	69	41	97
—Oklahoma City (A.A.)		1	0	1.000	0.00	1	1	1	1	0	9	2	0	0	1	6
1997—Oklahoma City (A.A.)		1	8	.111	7.29	13	12	1	0	1	58	83	54	47	29	33
—Tulsa (Texas)		5	4	.556	3.52	10	10	4	0	0	71 2/3	70	35	28	15	47
1998—Oklahoma (PCL)		6	6	.500	4.90	19	18	1	0	1	112	109	66	61	32	94
—Charlotte (FSL)		0	2	.000	4.63	3	3	0	0	0	11 2/3	10	6	6	4	11
—Texas (A.L.)		0	0	...	8.31	1	1	0	0	0	4 1/3	5	4	4	5	3
1999—Oklahoma (PCL)		8	4	.667	6.25	21	8	0	0	2	67 2/3	91	53	47	23	38
—Gulf Coast Rangers (GCL)..		0	0	...	1.80	1	1	0	0	0	5	3	1	1	0	5
—Tulsa (Texas)		0	0	...	9.53	1	1	0	0	0	5 2/3	12	6	6	0	4
—Texas (A.L.)		0	0	...	15.00	1	0	0	0	0	3	9	5	5	2	3
Major League totals (2 years)		0	0	...	11.05	2	1	0	0	0	7 1/3	14	9	9	7	6

JOHNSON, LANCE   OF   INDIANS

PERSONAL: Born July 6, 1963, in Lincoln Heights, Ohio. ... 5-11/165. ... Bats left, throws left. ... Full name: Kenneth Lance Johnson.
HIGH SCHOOL: Princeton (Cincinnati).
JUNIOR COLLEGE: Triton College (Ill.).
COLLEGE: South Alabama.

TRANSACTIONS/CAREER NOTES: Selected by Pittsburgh Pirates organization in 30th round of free-agent draft (June 8, 1981); did not sign. ... Selected by Seattle Mariners organization in 31st round of free-agent draft (June 7, 1982); did not sign. ... Selected by St. Louis Cardinals organization in sixth round of free-agent draft (June 4, 1984). ... Traded by Cardinals with P Rick Horton and cash to Chicago White Sox for P Jose DeLeon (February 9, 1988). ... Granted free agency (November 8, 1995). ... Signed by New York Mets (December 14, 1995). ... On New York disabled list (May 2-June 16, 1997). ... Traded by Mets with two players to be named later to Chicago Cubs for OF Brian McRae, P Mel Rojas and P Turk Wendell (August 8, 1997); Cubs acquired P Mark Clark (August 11) and IF Manny Alexander (August 14) to complete deal. ... On disabled list (April 28-July 13, 1998). ... On Chicago disabled list (June 10-August 21, 1999). ... Released by Cubs (October 6, 1999). ... Signed by Cleveland Indians organization (January 13, 2000).

RECORDS: Holds major league record for most consecutive years leading league in triples—4 (1991-94). ... Shares A.L. single-game record for most triples—3 (September 23, 1995).

HONORS: Named American Association Most Valuable Player (1987).

STATISTICAL NOTES: Led New York-Pennsylvania League outfielders with 201 total chances in 1984. ... Led Texas League in caught stealing with 15 in 1986. ... Led American Association outfielders with 333 total chances in 1987. ... Led Pacific Coast League outfielders with five double plays in 1988. ... Led Pacific Coast League outfielders with 273 total chances in 1989. ... Led Pacific Coast League in caught stealing with 18 in 1989. ... Led A.L. in caught stealing with 22 in 1990. ... Led N.L. outfielders with 412 total chances in 1996. ... Had 25-game hitting streak (July 16-August 11, 1992). ... Collected six hits in one game (September 23, 1995). ... Career major league grand slams: 1.

							BATTING							FIELDING		
Year Team (League)	Pos.	G	AB	R	H	2B	3B	HR	RBI	Avg.	BB	SO	SB	PO	A	E	Avg.
1984—Erie (NY-P)	OF	71	283	*63	*96	7	5	1	28	.339	45	20	29	*188	5	8	.960
1985—St. Petersburg (FSL)	OF	129	497	68	134	17	10	2	55	.270	58	39	33	338	16	5	.986
1986—Arkansas (Texas)	OF	127	445	82	128	24	6	2	33	.288	59	57	*49	262	11	7	.975
1987—Louisville (A.A.)	OF	116	477	89	159	21	11	5	50	.333	49	45	42	*319	6	•8	.976
—St. Louis (N.L.)	OF	33	59	4	13	2	1	0	7	.220	4	6	6	27	0	2	.931
1988—Chicago (A.L.)■	OF-DH	33	124	11	23	4	1	0	6	.185	6	11	6	63	1	2	.970
—Vancouver (PCL)	OF	100	411	71	126	12	6	2	36	.307	42	52	49	262	9	5	.982
1989—Vancouver (PCL)	OF	106	408	69	124	11	7	0	28	.304	46	36	33	*261	7	5	.982
—Chicago (A.L.)	OF-DH	50	180	28	54	8	2	0	16	.300	17	24	16	113	0	2	.983
1990—Chicago (A.L.)	OF-DH	151	541	76	154	18	9	1	51	.285	33	45	36	353	5	10	.973
1991—Chicago (A.L.)	OF	159	588	72	161	14	•13	0	49	.274	26	58	26	425	11	2	.995
1992—Chicago (A.L.)	OF	157	567	67	158	15	*12	3	47	.279	34	33	41	433	11	6	.987
1993—Chicago (A.L.)	OF	147	540	75	168	18	*14	0	47	.311	36	33	35	*427	7	•9	.980
1994—Chicago (A.L.)	OF-DH	106	412	56	114	11	*14	3	54	.277	26	23	26	317	1	0	*1.000
1995—Chicago (A.L.)	OF-DH	142	*607	98	*186	18	12	10	57	.306	32	31	40	338	8	3	.991
1996—New York (N.L.)■	OF	160	*682	117	*227	31	*21	9	69	.333	33	40	50	*391	9	•12	.971
1997—New York (N.L.)	OF	72	265	43	82	10	6	1	24	.309	33	21	15	152	4	4	.975
—Chicago (N.L.)■	OF-DH	39	145	17	44	6	2	4	15	.303	9	10	5	79	0	3	.963
1998—Chicago (N.L.)	OF	85	304	51	85	8	4	2	21	.280	26	22	10	154	5	4	.975
1999—Chicago (N.L.)	OF	95	335	46	87	11	6	1	21	.260	37	20	13	235	6	3	.988
American League totals (8 years)		945	3559	483	1018	106	77	17	327	.286	210	258	226	2469	44	34	.987
National League totals (5 years)		484	1790	278	538	68	40	17	157	.301	142	119	99	1038	24	28	.974
Major League totals (13 years)		1429	5349	761	1556	174	117	34	484	.291	352	377	325	3507	68	62	.983

DIVISION SERIES RECORD

							BATTING							FIELDING		
Year Team (League)	Pos.	G	AB	R	H	2B	3B	HR	RBI	Avg.	BB	SO	SB	PO	A	E	Avg.
1998—Chicago (N.L.)	OF	3	12	0	2	0	0	0	1	.167	0	1	0	10	0	0	1.000

CHAMPIONSHIP SERIES RECORD

							BATTING							FIELDING		
Year Team (League)	Pos.	G	AB	R	H	2B	3B	HR	RBI	Avg.	BB	SO	SB	PO	A	E	Avg.
1987—St. Louis (N.L.)	PR	1	0	1	0	0	0	0	0	...	0	0	1	...	...	...	...
1993—Chicago (A.L.)	OF	6	23	2	5	1	1	1	6	.217	2	1	1	15	0	0	1.000
Championship series totals (2 years)		7	23	3	5	1	1	1	6	.217	2	1	2	15	0	0	1.000

WORLD SERIES RECORD

							BATTING							FIELDING		
Year Team (League)	Pos.	G	AB	R	H	2B	3B	HR	RBI	Avg.	BB	SO	SB	PO	A	E	Avg.
1987—St. Louis (N.L.)	PR	1	0	0	0	0	0	0	0	...	0	0	1	...	...	...	...

ALL-STAR GAME RECORD

					BATTING							FIELDING		
Year League	Pos.	AB	R	H	2B	3B	HR	RBI	Avg.	BB	SO	SB	PO	A	E	Avg.
1996—National	OF	4	1	3	1	0	0	0	.750	0	0	1	5	0	0	1.000

JOHNSON, MARK   P   TIGERS

PERSONAL: Born May 2, 1975, in Dayton, Ohio. ... 6-3/226. ... Throws right, bats right. ... Full name: Mark J. Johnson.

HIGH SCHOOL: Springboro (Ohio).

COLLEGE: Hawaii.

TRANSACTIONS/CAREER NOTES: Selected by Houston Astros organization in first round (19th pick overall) of free-agent draft (June 4, 1996). ... Traded by Astros to Florida Marlins (December 16, 1997), completing deal in which Marlins traded OF Moises Alou to Astros for P Oscar Henriquez, P Manuel Barrios and a player to be named later (November 11, 1997). ... Traded by Marlins with P Ed Yarnall and P Todd Noel to New York Yankees for 3B Mike Lowell (February 1, 1999). ... Selected by Detroit Tigers from Yankees organization in Rule 5 major league draft (December 13, 1999).

Year League	W	L	Pct.	ERA	G	GS	CG	ShO	Sv.	IP	H	R	ER	BB	SO
1997—Kissimmee (FSL)	8	9	.471	3.07	26	26	3	1	0	155 1/3	150	67	53	39	127
1998—Portland (East.)■	5	•14	.263	4.62	26	26	2	0	0	142 1/3	147	89	73	60	120
1999—Norwich (East.)	9	3	.750	3.68	16	15	0	0	0	88	88	51	36	39	52
—Gulf Coast Yankees (GCL)	0	3	.000	8.18	3	2	0	0	0	11	15	11	10	5	10
—Tampa (FSL)	1	0	1.000	1.50	1	1	0	0	0	6	4	1	1	1	6

JOHNSON, MARK   C   WHITE SOX

PERSONAL: Born September 12, 1975, in Wheatridge, Colo. ... 6-0/185. ... Bats left, throws right. ... Full name: Mark Landon Johnson.
HIGH SCHOOL: Warner Robins (Ga.).
TRANSACTIONS/CAREER NOTES: Selected by Chicago White Sox organization in first round (26th pick overall) of free-agent draft (June 2, 1994).
STATISTICAL NOTES: Led Carolina League with .420 on-base percentage in 1997. ... Led Carolina League catchers with 1000 total chances and tied for league lead with eight double plays in 1997. ... Led Southern League with .443 on-base percentage in 1998.

								BATTING							FIELDING		
Year	Team (League)	Pos.	G	AB	R	H	2B	3B	HR	RBI	Avg.	BB	SO	SB	PO	A	E	Avg.
1994— GC White Sox (GCL) ..		C	32	87	10	21	5	0	0	14	.241	14	15	1	182	22	3	.986
1995— Hickory (SAL)............		C	107	319	31	58	9	0	2	17	.182	59	52	3	*681	67	11	.986
1996— South Bend (Midw.) ...		C	67	214	29	55	14	3	2	27	.257	39	25	3	408	37	9	.980
— Prince Will. (Caro.)...		C	18	58	9	14	3	0	0	3	.241	13	6	0	112	8	1	.992
1997— Win.-Salem (Car.)......		C	120	375	59	95	27	4	4	46	.253	*106	85	4	*899	90	11	*.989
1998— Birmingham (Sou.).....		C-1B	117	382	68	108	11	3	9	59	.283	*105	72	0	723	65	8	.990
— Chicago (A.L.)...........		C	7	23	2	2	0	2	0	1	.087	1	8	0	36	2	0	1.000
1999— Chicago (A.L.)		C-DH	73	207	27	47	11	0	4	16	.227	36	58	3	413	33	3	.993
Major League totals (2 years)			80	230	29	49	11	2	4	17	.213	37	66	3	449	35	3	.994

JOHNSON, MIKE   P   EXPOS

PERSONAL: Born October 3, 1975, in Edmonton. ... 6-2/170. ... Throws right, bats left. ... Full name: Michael Keith Johnson.
HIGH SCHOOL: Salisbury Composite (Edmonton).
TRANSACTIONS/CAREER NOTES: Selected by Toronto Blue Jays organization in 17th round of free-agent draft (June 3, 1993). ... Selected by San Francisco Giants organization from Blue Jays organization in Rule 5 major league draft (December 9, 1996). ... Traded by Giants to Baltimore Orioles for cash considerations (December 9, 1996). ... Traded by Orioles to Montreal Expos for a player to be named later (July 31, 1997); Orioles acquired P Everett Stull to complete deal (October 31, 1997).
STATISTICAL NOTES: Led International League pitchers with six errors in 1999.

Year	League	W	L	Pct.	ERA	G	GS	CG	ShO	Sv.	IP	H	R	ER	BB	SO
1993— GC Blue Jays (GCL)...........		0	2	.000	4.87	16	1	0	0	1	44 1/3	51	40	24	22	31
1994— Medicine Hat (Pio.)		1	3	.250	4.46	9	9	0	0	0	36 1/3	48	31	18	22	8
1995— GC Blue Jays (GCL)...........		0	2	.000	7.20	3	3	0	0	0	15	20	15	12	8	13
— Medicine Hat (Pio.)		4	1	.800	3.86	19	0	0	0	3	49	46	26	21	25	32
1996— Hagerstown (SAL)..............		11	8	.579	3.15	29	23	5	3	0	162 2/3	157	74	57	39	155
1997— Baltimore (A.L.)■..............		0	1	.000	7.94	14	5	0	0	0	39 2/3	52	36	35	16	29
— Montreal (N.L.)■..............		2	5	.286	5.94	11	11	0	0	0	50	54	34	33	21	28
1998— Harrisburg (East.)..............		3	2	.600	6.95	7	7	0	0	0	33 2/3	35	27	26	10	38
— Ottawa (I.L.).....................		4	9	.308	4.29	18	18	1	0	0	109	105	63	52	38	88
— Montreal (N.L.).................		0	2	.000	14.73	2	2	0	0	0	7 1/3	16	12	12	2	4
1999— Ottawa (I.L.).....................		6	12	.333	5.38	28	27	0	0	0	147 1/3	174	105	88	63	120
— Montreal (N.L.).................		0	0		8.64	3	1	0	0	0	8 1/3	12	8	8	7	6
A.L. totals (1 year)		0	1	.000	7.94	14	5	0	0	2	39 2/3	52	36	35	16	29
N.L. totals (3 years)		2	7	.222	7.26	16	14	0	0	0	65 2/3	82	54	53	30	38
Major League totals (3 years)		2	8	.200	7.52	30	19	0	0	2	105 1/3	134	90	88	46	67

JOHNSON, NICK   1B   YANKEES

PERSONAL: Born September 19, 1978, in Sacramento. ... 6-3/195. ... Bats left, throws left. ... Full name: Nicholas Robert Johnson.
HIGH SCHOOL: McClatchy (Sacramento).
TRANSACTIONS/CAREER NOTES: Selected by New York Yankees organization in third round of free-agent draft (June 4, 1996).
STATISTICAL NOTES: Led Gulf Coast League with .422 on-base percentage in 1996. ... Led South Atlantic League first basemen with 99 double plays in 1997. ... Led Florida State League with .466 on-base percentage in 1998. ... Led Eastern League with a .525 on-base percentage and in being hit by pitch with 37 in 1999.

								BATTING							FIELDING		
Year	Team (League)	Pos.	G	AB	R	H	2B	3B	HR	RBI	Avg.	BB	SO	SB	PO	A	E	Avg.
1996— GC Yankees (GCL)......		1B	47	157	31	45	11	1	2	.287		30	35	0	314	19	3	.991
1997— Greensboro (SAL)......		1B	127	433	77	118	23	1	16	75	.273	76	99	16	*1176	59	16	.987
1998— Tampa (FSL)..........		1B	92	303	69	96	14	1	17	58	.317	68	76	1	785	58	12	.986
1999— Norwich (East.)		1B	132	420	*114	145	33	5	14	87	*.345	*123	88	8	1070	85	*20	.983

JOHNSON, RANDY   P   DIAMONDBACKS

PERSONAL: Born September 10, 1963, in Walnut Creek, Calif. ... 6-10/230. ... Throws left, bats right. ... Full name: Randall David Johnson.
HIGH SCHOOL: Livermore (Calif.).
COLLEGE: Southern California.
TRANSACTIONS/CAREER NOTES: Selected by Atlanta Braves organization in third round of free-agent draft (June 7, 1982); did not sign. ... Selected by Montreal Expos organization in second round of free-agent draft (June 3, 1985). ... Traded by Expos with P Brian Holman and P Gene Harris to Seattle Mariners for P Mark Langston and a player to be named later (May 25, 1989); Expos acquired P Mike Campbell to complete deal (July 31, 1989). ... On disabled list (June 11-27, 1992). ... On Seattle disabled list (May 15-August 6 and August 27, 1996-remainder of season); included rehabilitation assignment to Everett (August 3-6). ... On suspended list (April 24-27, 1998). ... Traded by Mariners to Houston Astros for SS Carlos Guillen, P Freddy Garcia and a player to be named later (July 31, 1998); Mariners acquired P John Halama to complete deal (October 1, 1998). ... Granted free agency (October 28, 1998). ... Signed by Arizona Diamondbacks (December 10, 1998).
RECORDS: Shares major league single-game record for most strikeouts by lefthander—19 (June 24 and August 8, 1997). ... Holds N.L. single-season record for most games with 10 or more strikeouts—23 (1999). ... Shares A.L. record for most strikeouts in two consecutive games—

32 (August 8 [19] and 15 [13], 1997, 17 innings). ... Shares N.L. record for most strikeouts in three consecutive games—43 (June 25 [14] and 30 [17] and July 5 [12], 1999).

HONORS: Named A.L. Pitcher of the Year by THE SPORTING NEWS (1995). ... Named lefthanded pitcher on THE SPORTING NEWS A.L. All-Star team (1995 and 1997). ... Named A.L. Cy Young Award winner by Baseball Writers' Association of America (1995). ... Named N.L. Cy Young Award winner by Baseball Writers' Association of America (1999).

STATISTICAL NOTES: Led American Association with 20 balks in 1988. ... Pitched 2-0 no-hit victory against Detroit (June 2, 1990). ... Pitched 4-0 one-hit, complete-game victory against Oakland (August 14, 1991). ... Struck out 15 batters in one game (September 16, 1992; June 14 and September 16, 1993; June 4 and August 11, 1994; June 24 and September 23, 1995; May 28 and June 8, 1997; April 10, May 24 and July 11, 1998; and April 10, 1999). ... Struck out 18 batters in one game (September 27, 1992). ... Led A.L. with 18 hit batsmen in 1992 and 16 in 1993. ... Pitched 7-0 one-hit, complete-game victory against Oakland (May 16, 1993). ... Struck out 16 batters in one game (July 15, 1995; July 18, 1997; and August 28, 1998). ... Struck out 19 batters in one game (June 24 and August 8, 1997). ... Pitched 3-0 one-hit, complete-game victory against Minnesota (July 16, 1998). ... Struck out 17 batters in one game (June 30, 1999).

MISCELLANEOUS: Holds Seattle Mariners franchise all-time records for most wins (130), lowest earned-run average (3.42), most innings pitched (1,838 1/3), most strikeouts (2,162) and most shutouts (19). ... Appeared in one game as outfielder with no chances (1993). ... Shares Arizona Diamondbacks all-time record for most shutouts (2). ... Holds Arizona Diamondbacks all-time records for most strikeouts (364) and lowest earned-run average (2.48).

Year League	W	L	Pct.	ERA	G	GS	CG	ShO	Sv.	IP	H	R	ER	BB	SO
1985— Jamestown (NY-P)	0	3	.000	5.93	8	8	0	0	0	27 1/3	29	22	18	24	21
1986— West Palm Beach (FSL)	8	7	.533	3.16	26	•26	2	1	0	119 2/3	89	49	42	*94	133
1987— Jacksonville (Sou.)	11	8	.579	3.73	25	24	0	0	0	140	100	63	58	128	*163
1988— Indianapolis (A.A.)	8	7	.533	3.26	20	19	0	0	0	113 1/3	85	52	41	72	111
— Montreal (N.L.)	3	0	1.000	2.42	4	4	1	0	0	26	23	8	7	7	25
1989— Montreal (N.L.)	0	4	.000	6.67	7	6	0	0	0	29 2/3	29	25	22	26	26
— Indianapolis (A.A.)	1	1	.500	2.00	3	3	0	0	0	18	13	5	4	9	17
— Seattle (A.L.)■	7	9	.438	4.40	22	22	2	0	0	131	118	75	64	70	104
1990— Seattle (A.L.)	14	11	.560	3.65	33	33	5	2	0	219 2/3	174	103	89	*120	194
1991— Seattle (A.L.)	13	10	.565	3.98	33	33	2	1	0	201 1/3	151	96	89	*152	228
1992— Seattle (A.L.)	12	14	.462	3.77	31	31	6	2	0	210 1/3	154	104	88	*144	*241
1993— Seattle (A.L.)	19	8	.704	3.24	35	34	10	3	1	255 1/3	185	97	92	99	*308
1994— Seattle (A.L.)	13	6	.684	3.19	23	23	*9	*4	0	172	132	65	61	72	*204
1995— Seattle (A.L.)	18	2	*.900	*2.48	30	30	6	3	0	214 1/3	159	65	59	65	*294
1996— Seattle (A.L.)	5	0	1.000	3.67	14	8	0	0	1	61 1/3	48	27	25	25	85
— Everett (N.W.)	0	0	...	0.00	1	1	0	0	0	2	0	0	0	0	5
1997— Seattle (A.L.)	20	4	*.833	2.28	30	29	5	2	0	213	147	60	54	77	291
1998— Seattle (A.L.)	9	10	.474	4.33	23	23	6	2	0	160	146	90	77	60	213
— Houston (N.L.)■	10	1	.909	1.28	11	11	4	4	0	84 1/3	57	12	12	26	116
1999— Arizona (N.L.)■	17	9	.654	*2.48	35	•35	*12	2	0	*271 2/3	207	86	75	70	*364
A.L. totals (10 years)	130	74	.637	3.42	274	266	51	19	2	1838 1/3	1414	782	698	884	2162
N.L. totals (4 years)	30	14	.682	2.54	57	56	17	6	0	411 2/3	316	131	116	129	531
Major League totals (12 years)	160	88	.645	3.26	331	322	68	25	2	2250	1730	913	814	1013	2693

DIVISION SERIES RECORD

RECORDS: Holds career records for most losses—5; innings pitched—45 1/3; and strikeouts—60. ... Holds single-game record for most strikeouts—13 (October 5, 1997). ... Holds A.L. career record for most strikeouts—32.

Year League	W	L	Pct.	ERA	G	GS	CG	ShO	Sv.	IP	H	R	ER	BB	SO
1995— Seattle (A.L.)	2	0	1.000	2.70	2	1	0	0	0	10	5	3	3	6	16
1997— Seattle (A.L.)	0	2	.000	5.54	2	2	1	0	0	13	14	8	8	6	16
1998— Houston (N.L.)	0	2	.000	1.93	2	2	0	0	0	14	12	4	3	2	17
1999— Arizona (N.L.)	0	1	.000	7.56	1	1	0	0	0	8 1/3	8	7	7	3	11
Division series totals (4 years)	2	5	.286	4.17	7	6	1	0	0	45 1/3	39	22	21	17	60

CHAMPIONSHIP SERIES RECORD

Year League	W	L	Pct.	ERA	G	GS	CG	ShO	Sv.	IP	H	R	ER	BB	SO
1995— Seattle (A.L.)	0	1	.000	2.35	2	2	0	0	0	15 1/3	12	6	4	2	13

ALL-STAR GAME RECORD

Year League	W	L	Pct.	ERA	GS	CG	ShO	Sv.	IP	H	R	ER	BB	SO
1990— American						Did not play.								
1993— American	0	0	...	0.00	0	0	0	0	2	0	0	0	0	1
1994— American	0	0	...	9.00	0	0	0	0	1	2	1	1	0	0
1995— American	0	0	...	0.00	1	0	0	0	2	0	0	0	1	3
1997— American	0	0	...	0.00	0	0	0	0	2	0	0	0	1	2
1999— National	0	0	...	0.00	0	0	0	0	1	0	0	0	0	1
All-Star Game totals (5 years)	0	0	...	1.13	2	0	0	0	8	2	1	1	2	7

JOHNSON, RUSS   IF   ASTROS

PERSONAL: Born February 22, 1973, in Baton Rouge, La. ... 5-10/180. ... Bats right, throws right. ... Full name: William Russell Johnson.

HIGH SCHOOL: Denham Springs (La.).

COLLEGE: Louisiana State.

TRANSACTIONS/CAREER NOTES: Selected by Houston Astros organization in supplemental round ("sandwich pick" between first and second round, 30th pick overall) of free-agent draft (June 2, 1994); pick received as part of compensation for San Francisco Giants signing Type A free-agent P Mark Portugal.

STATISTICAL NOTES: Led Texas League shortstops with 664 total chances and 87 double plays in 1995. ... Led Pacific Coast League third basemen with .962 fielding percentage in 1998.

						BATTING								FIELDING		
Year Team (League)	Pos.	G	AB	R	H	2B	3B	HR	RBI	Avg.	BB	SO	SB	PO	A	E	Avg.
1995— Jackson (Texas)	SS	132	475	65	118	16	2	9	53	.248	50	60	10	182	383	13	.978
1996— Jackson (Texas)	SS	132	496	86	154	24	5	15	74	.310	56	50	9	219	411	34	.949
1997— New Orleans (A.A.)	3B-SS-DH	122	445	72	123	16	6	4	49	.276	66	78	7	86	269	21	.944
— Houston (N.L.)	3B-2B	21	60	7	18	1	0	2	9	.300	6	14	1	13	24	1	.974

Year	Team (League)	Pos.	G	AB	R	H	2B	3B	HR	RBI	Avg.	BB	SO	SB	PO	A	E	Avg.
1998—New Orleans (PCL)		3-2-S-DH	122	453	*95	140	28	2	7	52	.309	*90	64	11	76	235	11	†.966
—Houston (N.L.)		3B-2B	8	13	2	3	1	0	0	0	.231	1	5	1	3	9	0	1.000
1999—New Orleans (PCL)		2B-SS-OF	22	77	17	27	6	0	1	12	.351	16	13	1	32	60	3	.968
—Houston (N.L.)		3B-2B-SS	83	156	24	44	10	0	5	23	.282	20	31	2	33	88	7	.945
Major League totals (3 years)			112	229	33	65	12	0	7	32	.284	27	50	4	49	121	8	.955

DIVISION SERIES RECORD

Year	Team (League)	Pos.	G	AB	R	H	2B	3B	HR	RBI	Avg.	BB	SO	SB	PO	A	E	Avg.
1997—Houston (N.L.)		PH	1	1	0	0	0	0	0	0	.000	0	1	0	...	...	...	...
1999—Houston (N.L.)		PH	2	1	0	1	1	0	0	0	1.000	1	0	0	0	0	0	...
Division series totals (2 years)			3	2	0	1	1	0	0	0	.500	1	1	0	0	0	0	...

JOHNSTONE, JOHN — P — GIANTS — J

PERSONAL: Born November 25, 1968, in Liverpool, N.Y. ... 6-3/210. ... Throws right, bats right. ... Full name: John William Johnstone.
HIGH SCHOOL: Bishop Ludden (Syracuse, N.Y.).
JUNIOR COLLEGE: Onondaga Community College (N.Y.).
TRANSACTIONS/CAREER NOTES: Selected by New York Mets organization in 20th round of free-agent draft (June 2, 1987). ... On disabled list (June 24-July 7, 1992). ... Selected by Florida Marlins in second round (31st pick overall) of expansion draft (November 17, 1992). ... On disabled list (May 8, 1995-remainder of season). ... Granted free agency (December 21, 1995). ... Signed by Houston Astros organization (December 28, 1995). ... Granted free agency (September 30, 1996). ... Signed by San Francisco Giants organization (December 17, 1996). ... Claimed on waivers by Oakland Athletics (August 7, 1997). ... Granted free agency (August 31, 1997). ... Signed by Giants organization (September 1, 1997).

Year	League	W	L	Pct.	ERA	G	GS	CG	ShO	Sv.	IP	H	R	ER	BB	SO
1987—Kingsport (Appalachian)		1	1	.500	7.45	17	1	0	0	0	29	42	28	24	20	21
1988—Gulf Coast Mets (GCL)		3	4	.429	2.68	12	12	3	0	0	74	65	29	22	25	57
1989—Pittsfield (NY-P)		*11	2	.846	2.77	15	15	2	1	0	104	101	47	32	28	60
1990—St. Lucie (FSL)		*15	6	.714	2.24	25	25	*9	3	0	172 2/3	145	53	43	60	120
1991—Williamsport (East.)		7	9	.438	3.97	27	•27	2	0	0	165 1/3	159	94	73	79	100
1992—Binghamton (East.)		7	7	.500	3.74	24	24	2	0	0	149 1/3	132	66	62	36	121
1993—Edmonton (PCL)■		4	*15	.211	5.18	30	21	1	0	4	144 1/3	167	95	83	59	126
—Florida (N.L.)		0	2	.000	5.91	7	0	0	0	0	10 2/3	16	8	7	7	5
1994—Edmonton (PCL)		5	3	.625	4.46	29	0	0	0	4	42 1/3	46	23	21	9	43
—Florida (N.L.)		1	2	.333	5.91	17	0	0	0	0	21 1/3	23	20	14	16	23
1995—Florida (N.L.)		0	0	...	3.86	4	0	0	0	0	4 2/3	7	2	2	2	3
1996—Tucson (PCL)■		3	3	.500	3.42	45	1	0	0	5	55 1/3	59	27	21	22	70
—Houston (N.L.)		1	0	1.000	5.54	9	0	0	0	0	13	17	8	8	5	5
1997—Phoenix (PCL)■		0	3	.000	4.03	38	0	0	0	*24	38	34	17	17	15	30
—San Francisco (N.L.)		0	0	...	3.38	13	0	0	0	0	18 2/3	15	7	7	7	15
—Oakland (A.L.)■		0	0	...	2.84	5	0	0	0	0	6 1/3	7	2	2	7	4
1998—San Francisco (N.L.)		6	5	.545	3.07	70	0	0	0	0	88	72	32	30	38	86
1999—San Francisco (N.L.)		4	6	.400	2.60	62	0	0	0	3	65 2/3	48	24	19	20	56
Major League totals (7 years)		12	15	.444	3.53	182	0	0	0	3	222	198	101	87	95	193

JONES, ANDRUW — OF — BRAVES

PERSONAL: Born April 23, 1977, in Willemstad, Curacao. ... 6-1/210. ... Bats right, throws right. ... Full name: Andruw Rudolf Jones.
HIGH SCHOOL: St. Paulus (Willemstad, Curacao).
TRANSACTIONS/CAREER NOTES: Signed as non-drafted free agent by Atlanta Braves organization (July 1, 1993).
RECORDS: Holds N.L. single-season record for fewest singles (150 or more games)—55 (1997).
HONORS: Named South Atlantic League Most Valuable Player (1995). ... Won N.L. Gold Glove as outfielder (1998 and 1999).
STATISTICAL NOTES: Led South Atlantic League with nine sacrifice flies in 1995. ... Led South Atlantic League outfielders with 246 total chances and tied for lead with four double plays in 1995. ... Led N.L. outfielders with 435 total chances and tied for lead with six double plays in 1998. ... Led N.L. outfielders with 515 total chances in 1999. ... Career major league grand slams: 1.

Year	Team (League)	Pos.	G	AB	R	H	2B	3B	HR	RBI	Avg.	BB	SO	SB	PO	A	E	Avg.
1994—GC Braves (GCL)		OF	27	95	22	21	5	1	2	10	.221	16	19	5	90	0	3	.968
—Danville (Appl.)		OF	36	143	20	48	9	2	1	16	.336	9	25	16	81	3	2	.977
1995—Macon (SAL)		OF	•139	537	*104	149	41	5	25	100	.277	70	122	*56	*332	10	4	.988
1996—Durham (Caro.)		OF	66	243	65	76	14	3	17	43	.313	42	54	16	174	9	7	.963
—Greenville (Sou.)		OF	38	157	39	58	10	1	12	37	.369	17	34	12	129	7	1	.993
—Richmond (I.L.)		OF	12	45	11	17	3	1	5	12	.378	1	9	2	34	1	1	.972
—Atlanta (N.L.)		OF	31	106	11	23	7	1	5	13	.217	7	29	3	73	4	2	.975
1997—Atlanta (N.L.)		OF	153	399	60	92	18	1	18	70	.231	56	107	20	287	14	7	.977
1998—Atlanta (N.L.)		OF	159	582	89	158	33	8	31	90	.271	40	129	27	*413	•20	2	.995
1999—Atlanta (N.L.)		OF	•162	592	97	163	35	5	26	84	.275	76	103	24	*492	13	10	.981
Major League totals (4 years)			505	1679	257	436	93	15	80	257	.260	179	368	74	1265	51	21	.984

DIVISION SERIES RECORD

RECORDS: Holds record for most at-bats without a hit—14.

Year	Team (League)	Pos.	G	AB	R	H	2B	3B	HR	RBI	Avg.	BB	SO	SB	PO	A	E	Avg.
1996—Atlanta (N.L.)		OF-PR	3	0	0	0	0	0	0	0	...	1	0	0	2	0	0	1.000
1997—Atlanta (N.L.)		OF	3	5	1	0	0	0	0	1	.000	1	1	0	10	0	0	1.000
1998—Atlanta (N.L.)		OF	3	9	2	0	0	0	0	1	.000	3	2	2	8	0	0	1.000
1999—Atlanta (N.L.)		OF	4	18	1	4	1	0	0	2	.222	1	3	0	12	0	0	1.000
Division series totals (4 years)			13	32	4	4	1	0	0	4	.125	6	6	2	32	0	0	1.000

CHAMPIONSHIP SERIES RECORD

Year Team (League)	Pos.	G	AB	R	H	2B	3B	HR	RBI	Avg.	BB	SO	SB	PO	A	E	Avg.
1996— Atlanta (N.L.).............	OF-PR-PH	5	9	3	2	0	0	1	3	.222	3	2	0	5	0	0	1.000
1997— Atlanta (N.L.).............	OF-PH	5	9	0	4	0	0	0	1	.444	1	1	0	12	1	0	1.000
1998— Atlanta (N.L.).............	OF	6	22	3	6	0	0	1	2	.273	1	4	1	15	0	0	1.000
1999— Atlanta (N.L.).............	OF	6	23	5	5	0	0	0	1	.217	4	3	0	17	0	0	1.000
Championship series totals (4 years)		22	63	11	17	0	0	2	7	.270	9	10	1	49	1	0	1.000

WORLD SERIES RECORD

RECORDS: Shares record for most home runs in two consecutive innings—2 (October 20, 1996, second and third innings). ... Shares single-inning record for most putouts by outfielder—3 (October 24, 1999, seventh inning).

NOTES: Hit home runs in first two at-bats (October 20, 1996, second and third innings).

Year Team (League)	Pos.	G	AB	R	H	2B	3B	HR	RBI	Avg.	BB	SO	SB	PO	A	E	Avg.
1996— Atlanta (N.L.).............	OF	6	20	4	8	1	0	2	6	.400	3	6	1	7	1	0	1.000
1999— Atlanta (N.L.).............	OF	4	13	1	1	0	0	0	0	.077	1	3	0	10	0	0	1.000
World Series totals (2 years)		10	33	5	9	1	0	2	6	.273	4	9	1	17	1	0	1.000

JONES, BOBBY J.   P   METS

PERSONAL: Born February 10, 1970, in Fresno, Calif. ... 6-4/225. ... Throws right, bats right. ... Full name: Robert Joseph Jones.
HIGH SCHOOL: Fresno (Calif.).
COLLEGE: Fresno State.
TRANSACTIONS/CAREER NOTES: Selected by New York Mets organization in supplemental round ("sandwich pick" between first and second round, 36th pick overall) of free-agent draft (June 3, 1991); pick received as part of compensation for Los Angeles Dodgers signing Type A free-agent OF Darryl Strawberry. ... On New York disabled list (May 24-September 10, 1999); included rehabilitation assignments to Binghamton (August 7-17 and September 5-10) and Norfolk (August 18-25).
HONORS: Named Eastern League Pitcher of the Year (1992).
STATISTICAL NOTES: Led International League with 11 hit batsmen in 1993. ... Led N.L. with 18 sacrifice hits in 1995.

Year League	W	L	Pct.	ERA	G	GS	CG	ShO	Sv.	IP	H	R	ER	BB	SO
1991— Columbia (SAL)................	3	1	.750	1.85	5	5	0	0	0	24 1/3	20	5	5	3	35
1992— Binghamton (East.)	12	4	.750	*1.88	24	24	4	*4	0	158	118	40	33	43	143
1993— Norfolk (I.L.)	12	10	.545	3.63	24	24	6	*3	0	166	149	72	67	32	126
— New York (N.L.).■............	2	4	.333	3.65	9	9	0	0	0	61 2/3	61	35	25	22	35
1994— New York (N.L.)	12	7	.632	3.15	24	24	1	1	0	160	157	75	56	56	80
1995— New York (N.L.)	10	10	.500	4.19	30	30	3	1	0	195 2/3	209	107	91	53	127
1996— New York (N.L.)	12	8	.600	4.42	31	31	3	1	0	195 2/3	219	102	96	46	116
1997— New York (N.L.)	15	9	.625	3.63	30	30	2	1	0	193 1/3	177	88	78	63	125
1998— New York (N.L.)	9	9	.500	4.05	30	30	0	0	0	195 1/3	192	94	88	53	115
1999— New York (N.L.)	3	3	.500	5.61	12	9	0	0	0	59 1/3	69	37	37	11	31
— Binghamton (East.)	1	2	.333	3.86	3	3	0	0	0	11 2/3	11	5	5	5	12
— Norfolk (I.L.)	2	0	1.000	2.45	2	2	0	0	0	11	11	3	3	3	8
Major League totals (7 years)	63	50	.558	4.00	166	163	9	4	0	1061	1084	538	471	304	629

DIVISION SERIES RECORD

Year League	W	L	Pct.	ERA	G	GS	CG	ShO	Sv.	IP	H	R	ER	BB	SO
1999— New York (N.L.).................							Did not play.								

CHAMPIONSHIP SERIES RECORD

Year League	W	L	Pct.	ERA	G	GS	CG	ShO	Sv.	IP	H	R	ER	BB	SO
1999— New York (N.L.).................							Did not play.								

ALL-STAR GAME RECORD

Year League	W	L	Pct.	ERA	GS	CG	ShO	Sv.	IP	H	R	ER	BB	SO
1997— National	0	0	...	0.00	0	0	0	0	1	1	0	0	0	2

JONES, BOBBY M.   P   METS

PERSONAL: Born April 11, 1972, in Orange, N.J. ... 6-0/178. ... Throws left, bats right. ... Full name: Robert Mitchell Jones.
HIGH SCHOOL: Rutherford (N.J.).
JUNIOR COLLEGE: Chipola Junior College (Fla.).
TRANSACTIONS/CAREER NOTES: Selected by Milwaukee Brewers organization in 44th round of free-agent draft (June 3, 1991). ... Selected by Colorado Rockies organization from Brewers organization in Rule 5 minor league draft (December 5, 1994). ... Traded by Rockies with P Lariel Gonzalez to New York Mets for P Masato Yoshii (January 21, 2000).
STATISTICAL NOTES: Tied for Pacific Coast League lead with 12 hit batsmen in 1997.

Year League	W	L	Pct.	ERA	G	GS	CG	ShO	Sv.	IP	H	R	ER	BB	SO
1992— Helena (Pio.)	5	4	.556	4.36	14	13	1	0	0	76 1/3	93	51	37	23	53
1993— Beloit (Midw.)..................	10	10	.500	4.11	25	25	4	0	0	144 2/3	159	82	66	65	115
1994— Stockton (Calif.)	6	12	.333	4.21	26	26	2	0	0	147 2/3	131	90	69	64	147
1995— New Haven (East.).■......	5	2	.714	2.58	27	8	0	0	3	73 1/3	61	27	21	36	70
— Colo. Springs (PCL)	1	2	.333	7.30	11	8	0	0	0	40 2/3	50	38	33	33	48
1996— Colo. Springs (PCL)	2	8	.200	4.97	57	0	0	0	3	88 2/3	88	54	49	63	78
1997— Colo. Springs (PCL)	7	11	.389	5.14	25	21	0	0	0	133	135	89	76	71	104
— Colorado (N.L.)	1	1	.500	8.38	4	4	0	0	0	19 1/3	30	18	18	12	5
1998— Colorado (N.L.)	7	8	.467	5.22	35	20	1	0	0	141 1/3	153	87	82	66	109
1999— Colorado (N.L.)	6	10	.375	6.33	30	20	0	0	0	112 1/3	132	91	79	77	74
— Colo. Springs (PCL)	2	1	.667	5.40	3	3	0	0	0	16 2/3	17	13	10	15	14
Major League totals (3 years)	14	19	.424	5.90	69	44	1	0	0	273	315	196	179	155	188

PERSONAL: Born April 24, 1972, in De Land, Fla. ... 6-4/210. ... Bats both, throws right. ... Full name: Larry Wayne Jones.

HIGH SCHOOL: The Bolles School (Jacksonville).

TRANSACTIONS/CAREER NOTES: Selected by Atlanta Braves organization in first round (first pick overall) of free-agent draft (June 4, 1990). ... On Atlanta disabled list (March 20, 1994-entire season). ... On disabled list (March 22-April 6, 1996).

RECORDS: Holds major league single-season records for fewest putouts by third baseman (150 or more games)—77 (1997); and fewest chances accepted by third baseman (150 or more games)—318. ... Holds N.L. record for most home runs by switch hitter in two consecutive seasons—79 (1998-99). ... Holds N.L. single-season records for most home runs by switch hitter—45 (1999); most home runs hit at home by switch hitter—25 (1999); highest slugging average by switch hitter—.633 (1999); most bases on balls by switch-hitter—126 (1999); fewest putouts by third baseman (150 or more games)—77 (1997); fewest assists by third baseman (150 or more games)—237 (1999); and fewest chances by third baseman (150 or more games)—318 (1997).. ... Shares major league single-season record for most extra-base hits by switch-hitter—87 (1999). ... Shares N.L. single-season record for fewest double plays by third baseman (150 or more games)—10 (1999).

HONORS: Named N.L. Rookie Player of the Year by THE SPORTING NEWS (1995). ... Named N.L. Most Valuable Player by Baseball Writers' Association of America (1999). ... Named third baseman on THE SPORTING NEWS N.L. All-Star team (1999). ... Named third baseman on THE SPORTING NEWS N.L. Silver Slugger team (1999).

STATISTICAL NOTES: Led South Atlantic League with 10 sacrifice flies in 1991. ... Led South Atlantic League shortstops with 692 total chances and 71 double plays in 1991. ... Led International League with 268 total bases in 1993. ... Led International League shortstops with 619 total chances in 1993. ... Switch-hit home runs in one game three times (May 1, August 1 and September 21, 1999). ... Career major league grand slams: 4.

Year	Team (League)	Pos.	G	AB	R	H	2B	3B	HR	RBI	Avg.	BB	SO	SB	PO	A	E	Avg.
1990—	GC Braves (GCL)	SS	44	140	20	32	1	1	1	18	.229	14	25	5	64	140	18	.919
1991—	Macon (SAL)	SS	136	473	*104	154	24	11	15	98	.326	69	70	40	*217	*419	56	.919
1992—	Durham (Caro.)	SS	70	264	43	73	22	1	4	31	.277	31	34	10	106	200	14	.956
—	Greenville (Sou.)	SS	67	266	43	92	17	11	9	42	.346	11	32	14	92	218	18	.945
1993—	Richmond (I.L.)	SS	139	536	*97	*174	31	*12	13	89	.325	57	70	23	195	381	*43	.931
—	Atlanta (N.L.)	SS	8	3	2	2	1	0	0	0	.667	1	1	0	1	1	0	1.000
1994—	Atlanta (N.L.)							Did not play.										
1995—	Atlanta (N.L.)	3B-OF	140	524	87	139	22	3	23	86	.265	73	99	8	103	255	25	.935
1996—	Atlanta (N.L.)	3B-SS-OF	157	598	114	185	32	5	30	110	.309	87	88	14	103	288	17	.958
1997—	Atlanta (N.L.)	3B-OF	157	597	100	176	41	3	21	111	.295	76	88	20	83	241	15	.956
1998—	Atlanta (N.L.)	3B	160	601	123	188	29	5	34	107	.313	96	93	16	105	290	12	.971
1999—	Atlanta (N.L.)	3B-SS	157	567	116	181	41	1	45	110	.319	126	94	25	88	237	17	.950
Major League totals (6 years)			779	2890	542	871	166	17	153	524	.301	459	463	83	483	1312	86	.954

DIVISION SERIES RECORD

RECORDS: Holds career record for most bases on balls—17. ... Shares single-game record for most home runs—2 (October 3, 1995). ... Holds N.L. career records for most at-bats—58; runs—13; hits—18; and total bases—32. ... Holds N.L. career record for most games—17; and extra-base hits—6.

Year	Team (League)	Pos.	G	AB	R	H	2B	3B	HR	RBI	Avg.	BB	SO	SB	PO	A	E	Avg.
1995—	Atlanta (N.L.)	3B	4	18	4	7	2	0	2	4	.389	2	2	0	3	4	0	1.000
1996—	Atlanta (N.L.)	3B	3	9	2	2	0	0	1	2	.222	3	4	1	1	3	0	1.000
1997—	Atlanta (N.L.)	3B	3	8	3	4	0	0	1	2	.500	3	2	1	2	3	1	.833
1998—	Atlanta (N.L.)	3B	3	10	2	2	0	0	0	1	.200	4	3	0	2	2	0	1.000
1999—	Atlanta (N.L.)	3B	4	13	2	3	0	0	0	1	.231	5	2	0	3	4	1	.875
Division series totals (5 years)			17	58	13	18	2	0	4	10	.310	17	13	2	11	16	2	.931

CHAMPIONSHIP SERIES RECORD

RECORDS: Holds N.L. career record for most runs scored—19. ... Shares single-series record for most singles—9 (1996). ... Shares single-game record for most singles—4 (October 9, 1996).

Year	Team (League)	Pos.	G	AB	R	H	2B	3B	HR	RBI	Avg.	BB	SO	SB	PO	A	E	Avg.
1995—	Atlanta (N.L.)	3B	4	16	3	7	0	0	1	3	.438	3	1	1	4	13	0	1.000
1996—	Atlanta (N.L.)	3B	7	25	6	11	2	0	0	4	.440	3	1	1	5	7	1	.923
1997—	Atlanta (N.L.)	3B	6	24	5	7	1	0	2	4	.292	2	3	0	1	8	0	1.000
1998—	Atlanta (N.L.)	3B	6	24	2	5	1	0	0	1	.208	4	5	0	1	12	0	1.000
1999—	Atlanta (N.L.)	3B	6	19	3	5	2	0	0	1	.263	9	7	3	5	8	2	.867
Championship series totals (5 years)			29	108	19	35	6	0	3	13	.324	21	17	5	16	48	3	.955

WORLD SERIES RECORD

NOTES: Member of World Series championship team (1995).

Year	Team (League)	Pos.	G	AB	R	H	2B	3B	HR	RBI	Avg.	BB	SO	SB	PO	A	E	Avg.
1995—	Atlanta (N.L.)	3B	6	21	3	6	3	0	0	1	.286	4	3	0	6	12	1	.947
1996—	Atlanta (N.L.)	3B-SS	6	21	3	6	3	0	0	3	.286	4	2	0	4	7	0	1.000
1999—	Atlanta (N.L.)	3B	4	13	2	3	0	0	1	2	.231	4	2	0	1	5	0	1.000
World Series totals (3 years)			16	55	8	15	6	0	1	6	.273	12	7	0	11	24	1	.972

ALL-STAR GAME RECORD

Year	League	Pos.	AB	R	H	2B	3B	HR	RBI	Avg.	BB	SO	SB	PO	A	E	Avg.
1996—	National	3B	2	1	1	0	0	0	0	.500	0	0	0	1	1	0	1.000
1997—	National	3B	1	0	0	0	0	0	0	.000	0	0	0	0	1	0	1.000
1998—	National	3B	2	1	0	0	0	0	0	.000	1	0	0	0	0	0	...
All-Star Game totals (3 years)			5	2	1	0	0	0	0	.200	1	0	0	1	2	0	1.000

PERSONAL: Born June 24, 1957, in Covina, Calif. ... 6-2/224. ... Throws right, bats right. ... Full name: Douglas Reid Jones.
HIGH SCHOOL: Lebanon (Ind.).
JUNIOR COLLEGE: Central Arizona College.
COLLEGE: Butler.
TRANSACTIONS/CAREER NOTES: Selected by Milwaukee Brewers organization in third round of free-agent draft (January 10, 1978). ... On disabled list (June 20-July 12, 1978). ... On Vancouver disabled list (April 11-September 1, 1983 and April 25-May 30, 1984). ... Granted free agency (October 15, 1984). ... Signed by Waterbury, Cleveland Indians organization (April 3, 1985). ... Granted free agency (December 20, 1991). ... Signed by Houston Astros organization (January 24, 1992). ... Traded by Astros with P Jeff Juden to Philadelphia Phillies for P Mitch Williams (December 2, 1993). ... Granted free agency (October 15, 1994). ... Signed by Baltimore Orioles (April 8, 1995). ... Granted free agency (November 3, 1995). ... Signed by Chicago Cubs (December 28, 1995). ... Released by Cubs (June 15, 1996). ... Signed by New Orleans, Brewers organization (June 28, 1996). ... Granted free agency (November 6, 1996). ... Re-signed by Brewers (December 7, 1996). ... On disabled list (July 16-August 3, 1997). ... Granted free agency (October 27, 1997). ... Re-signed by Brewers (November 18, 1997). ... Traded by Brewers to Indians for P Eric Plunk (July 23, 1998). ... Granted free agency (October 29, 1998). ... Signed by Oakland Athletics (January 11, 1999).
HONORS: Named N.L. co-Fireman of the Year by The Sporting News (1992).
MISCELLANEOUS: Holds Cleveland Indians all-time record for most saves (129).

Year League	W	L	Pct.	ERA	G	GS	CG	ShO	Sv.	IP	H	R	ER	BB	SO
1978— Newark (NY-P)	2	4	.333	5.21	15	3	1	0	2	38	49	30	22	15	27
1979— Burlington (Midw.)	10	10	.500	*1.75	28	20	*16	•3	0	*190	144	63	37	73	115
1980— Stockton (Calif.)	6	2	.750	2.84	11	11	5	1	0	76	63	32	24	31	54
—Vancouver (PCL)	3	2	.600	3.23	8	8	1	1	0	53	52	19	19	15	28
—Holyoke (East.)	5	3	.625	2.90	8	8	4	2	0	62	57	23	20	26	39
1981— El Paso (Texas)	5	7	.417	5.80	15	15	3	1	0	90	121	67	58	28	62
—Vancouver (PCL)	5	3	.625	3.04	11	10	2	0	0	80	79	29	27	22	38
1982— Milwaukee (A.L.)	0	0	...	10.13	4	0	0	0	0	2 2/3	5	3	3	1	1
—Vancouver (PCL)	5	8	.385	2.97	23	9	4	0	2	106	109	48	35	31	60
1983— Vancouver (PCL)	0	1	.000	10.29	3	1	0	0	0	7	10	8	8	5	4
1984— Vancouver (PCL)	1	0	1.000	10.13	3	0	0	0	0	8	9	9	9	3	2
—El Paso (Texas)	6	8	.429	4.28	16	16	7	0	0	109 1/3	120	61	52	35	62
1985— Waterbury (East.)■	9	4	.692	3.65	39	1	0	0	7	116	123	59	47	36	113
1986— Maine (I.L.)	5	6	.455	*2.09	43	3	0	0	9	116 1/3	105	35	27	27	98
—Cleveland (A.L.)	1	0	1.000	2.50	11	0	0	0	1	18	18	5	5	6	12
1987— Cleveland (A.L.)	6	5	.545	3.15	49	0	0	0	8	91 1/3	101	45	32	24	87
—Buffalo (A.A.)	5	2	.714	2.04	23	0	0	0	7	61 2/3	49	18	14	12	61
1988— Cleveland (A.L.)	3	4	.429	2.27	51	0	0	0	37	83 1/3	69	26	21	16	72
1989— Cleveland (A.L.)	7	10	.412	2.34	59	0	0	0	32	80 2/3	76	25	21	13	65
1990— Cleveland (A.L.)	5	5	.500	2.56	66	0	0	0	43	84 1/3	66	26	24	22	55
1991— Cleveland (A.L.)	4	8	.333	5.54	36	4	0	0	7	63 1/3	87	42	39	17	48
—Colo. Springs (PCL)	2	2	.500	3.28	17	2	1	1	7	35 2/3	30	14	13	5	29
1992— Houston (N.L.)■	11	8	.579	1.85	80	0	0	0	36	111 2/3	96	29	23	17	93
1993— Houston (N.L.)	4	10	.286	4.54	71	0	0	0	26	85 1/3	102	46	43	21	66
1994— Philadelphia (N.L.)■	2	4	.333	2.17	47	0	0	0	27	54	55	14	13	6	38
1995— Baltimore (A.L.)■	0	4	.000	5.01	52	0	0	0	22	46 2/3	55	30	26	16	42
1996— Chicago (N.L.)■	2	2	.500	5.01	28	0	0	0	2	32 1/3	41	20	18	7	26
—New Orleans (A.A.)■	0	3	.000	3.75	13	0	0	0	6	24	28	10	10	6	17
—Milwaukee (A.L.)	5	0	1.000	3.41	24	0	0	0	1	31 2/3	31	13	12	13	34
1997— Milwaukee (A.L.)■	6	6	.500	2.02	75	0	0	0	36	80 1/3	62	20	18	9	82
1998— Milwaukee (N.L.)	3	4	.429	5.17	46	0	0	0	12	54	65	32	31	11	43
—Cleveland (A.L.)■	1	2	.333	3.45	23	0	0	0	1	31 1/3	34	12	12	6	28
1999— Oakland (A.L.)■	5	5	.500	3.55	70	0	0	0	10	104	106	43	41	24	63
A.L. totals (12 years)	43	49	.467	3.19	520	4	0	0	198	717 2/3	710	290	254	167	589
N.L. totals (5 years)	22	28	.440	3.42	272	0	0	0	103	337 1/3	359	141	128	62	266
Major League totals (15 years)	65	77	.458	3.26	792	4	0	0	301	1055	1069	431	382	229	855

DIVISION SERIES RECORD

Year League	W	L	Pct.	ERA	G	GS	CG	ShO	Sv.	IP	H	R	ER	BB	SO
1998— Cleveland (A.L.)	0	0	...	6.75	1	0	0	0	0	2 2/3	3	2	2	1	1

CHAMPIONSHIP SERIES RECORD

Year League	W	L	Pct.	ERA	G	GS	CG	ShO	Sv.	IP	H	R	ER	BB	SO
1998— Cleveland (A.L.)							Did not play.								

ALL-STAR GAME RECORD

Year League	W	L	Pct.	ERA	GS	CG	ShO	Sv.	IP	H	R	ER	BB	SO
1988— American	0	0	...	0.00	0	0	0	0	2/3	0	0	0	0	1
1989— American	0	0	...	0.00	0	0	0	1	1 1/3	1	0	0	0	0
1990— American							Did not play.							
1992— National	0	0	...	27.00	0	0	0	0	1	4	3	3	0	2
1994— National	1	0	1.000	0.00	0	0	0	0	1	2	0	0	0	2
All-Star Game totals (4 years)	1	0	1.000	6.75	0	0	0	1	4	7	3	3	0	5

PERSONAL: Born April 25, 1975, in San Diego. ... 5-10/176. ... Bats left, throws left. ... Full name: Jacque Dewayne Jones.
HIGH SCHOOL: San Diego High.
COLLEGE: Southern California.
TRANSACTIONS/CAREER NOTES: Selected by Minnesota Twins organization in second round of free-agent draft (June 2, 1996).
MISCELLANEOUS: Member of 1996 U.S. Olympic baseball team.

Year	Team (League)	Pos.	G	AB	R	H	2B	3B	HR	RBI	Avg.	BB	SO	SB	PO	A	E	Avg.
1996— Fort Myers (FSL)........		OF	1	3	0	2	1	0	0	1	.667	0	0	0	0	0	0	
1997— Fort Myers (FSL)........		OF	131	539	84	*160	33	6	15	82	.297	33	110	24	313	8	7	.979
1998— New Britain (East.)		OF-DH	134	518	78	155	39	3	21	85	.299	37	134	18	288	12	10	.968
1999— Salt Lake (PCL)		OF	52	198	32	59	13	2	4	26	.298	9	36	9	150	2	2	.987
— Minnesota (A.L.)		OF	95	322	54	93	24	2	9	44	.289	17	63	3	231	9	5	.980
Major League totals (1 year)			95	322	54	93	24	2	9	44	.289	17	63	3	231	9	5	.980

JONES, TERRY   OF   YANKEES

PERSONAL: Born February 15, 1971, in Birmingham, Ala. ... 5-10/165. ... Bats both, throws right. ... Full name: Terry Lee Jones.
HIGH SCHOOL: Pinson Valley (Pinson, Ala.).
JUNIOR COLLEGE: Wallace State Community College (Ala.).
COLLEGE: North Alabama.
TRANSACTIONS/CAREER NOTES: Selected by Colorado Rockies organization in 40th round of free-agent draft (June 3, 1993). ... Traded by Rockies with a player to be named later to Montreal Expos for P Dave Veres and a player to be named later (December 10, 1997). ... On Ottawa disabled list (April 21-May 7, 1999). ... Granted free agency (October 4, 1999). ... Signed by Los Angeles Dodgers organization (October 28, 1999). ... Traded by Dodgers to New York Yankees for a player to be named later (January 6, 2000).
STATISTICAL NOTES: Led California League outfielders with 342 total chances and tied for lead with four double plays in 1994. ... Led Pacific Coast League outfielders with 311 total chances in 1996.

Year	Team (League)	Pos.	G	AB	R	H	2B	3B	HR	RBI	Avg.	BB	SO	SB	PO	A	E	Avg.
1993— Bend (N.W.)................		OF	33	138	21	40	5	4	0	18	.290	12	19	16	57	7	1	.985
— Central Valley (Calif.)..		OF	21	73	16	21	1	0	0	7	.288	10	15	5	36	2	1	.974
1994— Central Valley (Calif.)..		OF	129	*536	94	157	20	1	2	34	.293	42	85	44	*312	*16	14	.959
1995— New Haven (East.)......		OF	124	472	78	127	12	1	1	26	.269	39	104	*51	264	18	*10	.966
1996— Colo. Springs (PCL) ...		OF	128	497	75	143	7	4	0	33	.288	37	80	26	281	14	*16	.949
— Colorado (N.L.)		OF	12	10	6	3	0	0	0	1	.300	0	3	0	5	0	0	1.000
1997— Colo. Springs (PCL) ...		OF	92	363	70	98	14	4	1	25	.270	25	49	*36	139	11	1	.993
1998— Ottawa (I.L.)■..........		OF	81	278	36	66	3	4	0	21	.237	32	48	35	193	5	4	.980
— Montreal (N.L.)..........		OF	60	212	30	46	7	2	1	15	.217	21	46	16	161	4	2	.988
1999— Ottawa (I.L.)..........		OF-DH	88	332	49	87	17	2	0	23	.262	24	66	30	172	9	3	.984
— Montreal (N.L.)..........		OF	17	63	4	17	1	1	0	3	.270	3	14	1	47	2	0	1.000
Major League totals (3 years)			89	285	40	66	8	3	1	19	.232	24	63	17	213	6	2	.991

JONES, TODD   P   TIGERS

PERSONAL: Born April 24, 1968, in Marietta, Ga. ... 6-3/230. ... Throws right, bats left. ... Full name: Todd Barton Jones.
HIGH SCHOOL: Osborne (Ga.).
COLLEGE: Jacksonville (Ala.) State.
TRANSACTIONS/CAREER NOTES: Selected by New York Mets organization in 41st round of free-agent draft (June 2, 1986); did not sign. ... Selected by Houston Astros organization in supplemental round ("sandwich pick" between first and second round, 27th pick overall) of free-agent draft (June 5, 1989); pick received as part of compensation for Texas Rangers signing Type A free-agent P Nolan Ryan. ... On suspended list (September 14-16, 1993). ... On Houston disabled list (July 19-August 12 and August 18-September 12, 1996); included rehabilitation assignment to Tucson (August 9-12). ... Traded by Astros with OF Brian Hunter, IF Orlando Miller, P Doug Brocail and cash to Detroit Tigers for C Brad Ausmus, P Jose Lima, P C.J. Nitkowski, P Trever Miller and IF Daryle Ward (December 10, 1996).

Year	League	W	L	Pct.	ERA	G	GS	CG	ShO	Sv.	IP	H	R	ER	BB	SO
1989— Auburn (NY-P)...................		2	3	.400	5.44	11	9	1	0	0	49²/₃	47	39	30	42	71
1990— Osceola (FSL)...................		12	10	.545	3.51	27	•27	1	0	0	151¹/₃	124	81	59	*109	106
1991— Osceola (FSL)...................		4	4	.500	4.35	14	14	0	0	0	72¹/₃	69	38	35	35	51
— Jackson (Texas)		4	3	.571	4.88	10	10	0	0	0	55¹/₃	51	37	30	39	37
1992— Jackson (Texas)		3	7	.300	3.14	*61	0	0	0	25	66	52	28	23	44	60
— Tucson (PCL)		0	1	.000	4.50	3	0	0	0	0	4	1	2	2	10	4
1993— Tucson (PCL)		4	2	.667	4.44	41	0	0	0	12	48²/₃	49	26	24	31	45
— Houston (N.L.)		1	2	.333	3.13	27	0	0	0	2	37¹/₃	28	14	13	15	25
1994— Houston (N.L.)		5	2	.714	2.72	48	0	0	0	5	72²/₃	52	23	22	26	63
1995— Houston (N.L.)		6	5	.545	3.07	68	0	0	0	15	99²/₃	89	38	34	52	96
1996— Houston (N.L.)		6	3	.667	4.40	51	0	0	0	17	57¹/₃	61	30	28	32	44
— Tucson (PCL)		0	0	...	0.00	1	0	0	0	0	2	1	1	0	2	0
1997— Detroit (A.L.)■		5	4	.556	3.09	68	0	0	0	31	70	60	29	24	35	70
1998— Detroit (A.L.)		1	4	.200	4.97	65	0	0	0	28	63¹/₃	58	38	35	36	57
1999— Detroit (A.L.)		4	4	.500	3.80	65	0	0	0	30	66¹/₃	64	30	28	35	64
A.L. totals (3 years)		10	12	.455	3.92	198	0	0	0	89	199²/₃	182	97	87	106	191
N.L. totals (4 years)		18	12	.600	3.27	194	0	0	0	39	267	230	105	97	125	228
Major League totals (7 years)		28	24	.538	3.55	392	0	0	0	128	466²/₃	412	202	184	231	419

JORDAN, BRIAN   OF   BRAVES

PERSONAL: Born March 29, 1967, in Baltimore. ... 6-1/206. ... Bats right, throws right. ... Full name: Brian O'Neal Jordan.
HIGH SCHOOL: Milford (Baltimore).
COLLEGE: Richmond.
TRANSACTIONS/CAREER NOTES: Selected by Cleveland Indians organization in 20th round of free-agent draft (June 3, 1985); did not sign. ... Selected by St. Louis Cardinals organization in supplemental round ("sandwich pick" between first and second round, 30th pick overall) of free-agent draft (June 1, 1988); pick received as part of compensation for New York Yankees signing Type A free-agent 1B/OF Jack Clark. ... On disabled list (May 1-8 and June 3-10, 1991). ... On temporarily inactive list (July 3, 1991-remainder of season). ... On St. Louis disabled list (May 23-June 22, 1992); included rehabilitation assignment to Louisville (June 10-22). ... On Louisville disabled list (June 7-14, 1993). ...

On disabled list (July 10, 1994-remainder of season; and March 31-April 15, 1996). ... On St. Louis disabled list (May 6-June 13, June 26-August 10 and August 25, 1997-remainder of season); included rehabilitation assignment to Louisville (June 5-13). ... Granted free agency (October 22, 1998). ... Signed by Atlanta Braves (November 23, 1998).

STATISTICAL NOTES: Tied for N.L. lead with six double plays by outfielder in 1998. ... Career major league grand slams: 3.

Year Team (League)	Pos.	G	AB	R	H	2B	3B	HR	RBI	Avg.	BB	SO	SB	PO	A	E	Avg.
1988—Hamilton (NY-P).........	OF	19	71	12	22	3	1	4	12	.310	6	15	3	32	1	1	.971
1989—St. Petersburg (FSL)..	OF	11	43	7	15	4	1	2	11	.349	0	8	0	22	2	0	1.000
1990—Arkansas (Texas)........	OF	16	50	4	8	1	0	0	0	.160	0	11	0	28	0	2	.933
—St. Petersburg (FSL)..	OF	9	30	3	5	0	1	0	1	.167	2	11	0	23	0	0	1.000
1991—Louisville (A.A.).........	OF	61	212	35	56	11	4	4	24	.264	17	41	10	144	3	2	.987
1992—Louisville (A.A.).........	OF	43	155	23	45	3	1	4	16	.290	8	21	13	89	3	1	.989
—St. Louis (N.L.)..........	OF	55	193	17	40	9	4	5	22	.207	10	48	7	101	4	1	.991
1993—St. Louis (N.L.)..........	OF	67	223	33	69	10	6	10	44	.309	12	35	6	140	4	4	.973
—Louisville (A.A.).........	OF	38	144	24	54	13	2	5	35	.375	16	17	9	75	2	0	1.000
1994—St. Louis (N.L.)..........	OF-1B	53	178	14	46	8	2	5	15	.258	16	40	4	105	6	1	.991
1995—St. Louis (N.L.)..........	OF	131	490	83	145	20	4	22	81	.296	22	79	24	267	4	1	.996
1996—St. Louis (N.L.)..........	OF-1B	140	513	82	159	36	1	17	104	.310	29	84	22	310	9	2	.994
1997—St. Louis (N.L.)..........	OF	47	145	17	34	5	0	0	10	.234	10	21	6	82	2	0	1.000
—Louisville (A.A.).........	OF-DH	6	20	1	3	0	0	0	2	.150	1	2	0	6	0	0	1.000
1998—St. Louis (N.L.)..........	OF-DH-3B	150	564	100	178	34	7	25	91	.316	40	66	17	284	12	9	.970
1999—Atlanta (N.L.)■..........	OF	153	576	100	163	28	4	23	115	.283	51	81	13	295	9	3	.990
Major League totals (8 years)		796	2882	446	834	150	28	107	482	.289	190	454	99	1584	50	21	.987

DIVISION SERIES RECORD

RECORDS: Shares N.L. single-game record for most runs batted in—5 (October 8, 1999). ... Shares single-inning record for most at-bats—2 (October 9, 1999, sixth inning).

Year Team (League)	Pos.	G	AB	R	H	2B	3B	HR	RBI	Avg.	BB	SO	SB	PO	A	E	Avg.
1996—St. Louis (N.L.)..........	OF	3	12	4	4	0	0	1	3	.333	1	3	1	5	0	0	1.000
1999—Atlanta (N.L.).............	OF	4	17	2	8	1	0	1	7	.471	1	2	0	12	1	0	1.000
Division series totals (2 years)		7	29	6	12	1	0	2	10	.414	2	5	1	17	1	0	1.000

CHAMPIONSHIP SERIES RECORD

Year Team (League)	Pos.	G	AB	R	H	2B	3B	HR	RBI	Avg.	BB	SO	SB	PO	A	E	Avg.
1996—St. Louis (N.L.)..........	OF	7	25	3	6	1	1	1	2	.240	2	3	0	13	0	0	1.000
1999—Atlanta (N.L.).............	OF	6	25	3	5	0	0	2	5	.200	3	5	0	17	0	0	1.000
Championship series totals (2 years)		13	50	6	11	1	1	3	7	.220	5	8	0	30	0	0	1.000

WORLD SERIES RECORD

Year Team (League)	Pos.	G	AB	R	H	2B	3B	HR	RBI	Avg.	BB	SO	SB	PO	A	E	Avg.
1999—Atlanta (N.L.).............	OF	4	13	1	1	0	0	0	1	.077	4	2	0	8	0	1	.889

ALL-STAR GAME RECORD

Year League	Pos.	AB	R	H	2B	3B	HR	RBI	Avg.	BB	SO	SB	PO	A	E	Avg.
1999—National	OF	1	0	1	0	0	0	0	1.000	1	0	0	0	0	0	...

RECORD AS FOOTBALL PLAYER

TRANSACTIONS/CAREER NOTES: Selected by Buffalo Bills in seventh round (173rd pick overall) of 1989 NFL draft. ... Signed by Bills (July 17, 1989). ... Claimed on waivers by Atlanta Falcons (September 5, 1989). ... On injured reserve with ankle injury (September 9-October 22, 1989). ... On developmental squad (October 23-December 2, 1989). ... Granted free agency (February 1, 1992).

PRO STATISTICS: 1989—Recovered two fumbles. 1990—Recovered one fumble. 1991—Credited with two safeties and recovered one fumble.

MISCELLANEOUS: Played safety. ... Named alternate for 1992 Pro Bowl.

Year Team	G	INTERCEPTIONS				SACKS	PUNT RETURNS				KICKOFF RETURNS				TOTAL		
		No.	Yds.	Avg.	TD	No.	No.	Yds.	Avg.	TD	No.	Yds.	Avg.	TD	TD	Pts.	Fum.
1989—Atlanta NFL.................	4	0	0	...	0	0.0	4	34	8.5	0	3	27	9.0	0	0	0	1
1990—Atlanta NFL.................	16	3	14	4.7	0	0.0	2	19	9.5	0	0	0	...	0	0	0	0
1991—Atlanta NFL.................	16	2	3	1.5	0	4.0	14	116	8.3	0	5	100	20.0	0	0	4	0
Pro totals (3 years)	36	5	17	3.4	0	4.0	20	169	8.5	0	8	127	15.9	0	0	4	1

JORDAN, KEVIN — IF — PHILLIES

PERSONAL: Born October 9, 1969, in San Francisco. ... 6-1/201. ... Bats right, throws right. ... Full name: Kevin Wayne Jordan.

HIGH SCHOOL: Lowell (San Francisco).

JUNIOR COLLEGE: Canada College (Calif.).

COLLEGE: Nebraska.

TRANSACTIONS/CAREER NOTES: Selected by Los Angeles Dodgers organization in 10th round of free-agent draft (June 5, 1989); did not sign. ... Selected by New York Yankees organization in 20th round of free-agent draft (June 4, 1990). ... Traded by Yankees with P Bobby Munoz and P Ryan Karp to Philadelphia Phillies for P Terry Mulholland and a player to be named later (February 9, 1994); Yankees acquired P Jeff Patterson to complete deal (November 8, 1994). ... On disabled list (May 1-June 20, 1994; and June 17, 1996-remainder of season).

STATISTICAL NOTES: Led Eastern League with 234 total bases in 1993. ... Led Eastern League second basemen with 93 double plays in 1993.

Year Team (League)	Pos.	G	AB	R	H	2B	3B	HR	RBI	Avg.	BB	SO	SB	PO	A	E	Avg.
1990—Oneonta (NY-P).........	2B	73	276	47	92	13	•7	4	54	.333	23	31	19	131	158	8	.973
1991—Fort Lauderdale (FSL)....	2B-1B	121	448	61	122	25	5	4	53	.272	37	66	14	182	306	16	.968
1992—Prince William (Caro.)	2B-3B	112	438	67	136	29	8	8	63	.311	27	54	6	192	288	20	.960
1993—Alb./Colonie (East.)	2B	135	513	87	145	*33	4	16	87	.283	41	53	8	261	359	21	.967

Year	Team (League)	Pos.	G	AB	R	H	2B	3B	HR	RBI	Avg.	BB	SO	SB	PO	A	E	Avg.
1994—Scran./W.B. (I.L.)■	2B-3B-DH	81	314	44	91	22	1	12	57	.290	29	28	0	160	237	16	.961
1995—Scranton/W.B. (I.L.).....	2B-DH	106	410	61	127	29	4	5	60	.310	28	36	3	217	279	12	.976
—Philadelphia (N.L.).....	2B-3B	24	54	6	10	1	0	2	6	.185	2	9	0	29	35	1	.985
1996—Philadelphia (N.L.).....	1B-2B-3B	43	131	15	37	10	0	3	12	.282	5	20	2	243	27	0	1.000
1997—Scranton/W.B. (I.L.)......1B-3B	3B-2B-1B	7	30	5	9	2	2	0	2	.300	2	6	2	23	18	1	.976
—Philadelphia (N.L.)......1B-3B-2B-DH	84	177	19	47	8	0	6	30	.266	3	26	0	157	31	6	.969
1998—Philadelphia (N.L.).....	1-2-DH-3	112	250	23	69	13	0	2	27	.276	8	30	0	195	77	4	.986
1999—Philadelphia (N.L.).....	3B-2B-1B	120	347	36	99	17	3	4	51	.285	24	34	0	151	164	10	.969
Major League totals (5 years)		383	959	99	262	49	3	17	126	.273	42	119	2	775	334	21	.981

JOSEPH, KEVIN   P   GIANTS

J

PERSONAL: Born August 1, 1976, in Camp Hill, Pa. ... 6-4/200. ... Throws right, bats right. ... Full name: Kevin John Joseph.
HIGH SCHOOL: Trinity Christian (Addison, Texas).
COLLEGE: Rice.
TRANSACTIONS/CAREER NOTES: Selected by San Francisco Giants organization in sixth round of free-agent draft (June 3, 1997).

Year	League	W	L	Pct.	ERA	G	GS	CG	ShO	Sv.	IP	H	R	ER	BB	SO
1997—Salem-Kaizer (N.W.)..........	3	5	.375	5.40	17	6	0	0	1	45	44	35	27	26	45
1998—Bakersfield (Calif.).............	0	4	.000	8.14	6	6	0	0	0	21	35	26	19	20	17
—Salem-Kaizer (N.W.)..........	1	1	.500	4.36	23	0	0	0	0	43 1/3	36	25	21	27	37
1999—San Jose (Calif.).............	1	2	.333	2.35	20	0	0	0	2	30 2/3	17	9	8	13	30
—Shreveport (Texas).............	0	2	.000	1.42	7	0	0	0	0	12 2/3	8	4	2	5	16

JOYNER, WALLY   1B   BRAVES

PERSONAL: Born June 16, 1962, in Atlanta. ... 6-2/200. ... Bats left, throws left. ... Full name: Wallace Keith Joyner.
HIGH SCHOOL: Redan (Stone Mountain, Ga.).
COLLEGE: Brigham Young.
TRANSACTIONS/CAREER NOTES: Selected by California Angels organization in third round of free-agent draft (June 6, 1983); pick received as compensation for New York Yankees signing free-agent DH Don Baylor. ... On disabled list (July 12, 1990-remainder of season). ... Granted free agency (October 28, 1991). ... Signed by Kansas City Royals (December 9, 1991). ... On disabled list (June 26-July 14, 1994). ... Traded by Royals with P Aaron Dorlarque to San Diego Padres for 2B/OF Bip Roberts and P Bryan Wolff (December 21, 1995). ... On San Diego disabled list (June 3-July 11, 1996); included rehabilitation assignment to Rancho Cucamonga (July 7-11). ... On San Diego disabled list (April 28-May 13, 1997); included rehabilitation assignment to Las Vegas (May 8-12). ... On San Diego disabled list (May 17-June 25, 1999); included rehabilitation assignment to Las Vegas (June 18-25). ... Traded by Padres with 2B Quilvio Veras and OF Reggie Sanders to Atlanta Braves for OF/1B Ryan Klesko, 2B Bret Boone and P Jason Shiell (December 22, 1999).
RECORDS: Shares major league record for most home runs in month of October—4 (1987).
STATISTICAL NOTES: Tied for Eastern League lead with eight intentional bases on balls received in 1984. ... Led Pacific Coast League first basemen with 1,229 total chances and 121 double plays in 1985. ... Led A.L. with 12 sacrifice flies in 1986. ... Hit three home runs in one game (October 3, 1987). ... Led A.L. first basemen with 1,520 total chances in 1988 and 1,441 in 1991. ... Led A.L. first basemen with 148 double plays in 1988 and 138 in 1992. ... Career major league grand slams: 6.

Year	Team (League)	Pos.	G	AB	R	H	2B	3B	HR	RBI	Avg.	BB	SO	SB	PO	A	E	Avg.
1983—Peoria (Midw.)............	1B	54	192	25	63	16	2	3	33	.328	19	25	1	480	45	6	.989
1984—Waterbury (East.).......	1B-OF	134	467	81	148	24	7	12	72	.317	67	60	0	906	86	9	.991
1985—Edmonton (PCL)	1B	126	477	68	135	29	5	12	73	.283	60	64	2	*1107	*107	•15	.988
1986—California (A.L.)	1B	154	593	82	172	27	3	22	100	.290	57	58	5	1222	139	15	.989
1987—California (A.L.)	1B	149	564	100	161	33	1	34	117	.285	72	64	8	1276	92	10	.993
1988—California (A.L.)	1B	158	597	81	176	31	2	13	85	.295	55	51	8	*1369	*143	8	.995
1989—California (A.L.)	1B	159	593	78	167	30	2	16	79	.282	46	58	3	*1487	99	4	*.997
1990—California (A.L.)	1B	83	310	35	83	15	0	8	41	.268	41	34	2	727	62	4	.995
1991—California (A.L.)	1B	143	551	79	166	34	3	21	96	.301	52	66	2	*1335	98	8	.994
1992—Kansas City (A.L.)■ ...	1B-DH	149	572	66	154	36	2	9	66	.269	55	50	11	1236	137	10	.993
1993—Kansas City (A.L.) ...	1B	141	497	83	145	36	3	15	65	.292	66	67	5	1116	145	7	.994
1994—Kansas City (A.L.) ...	1B-DH	97	363	52	113	20	3	8	57	.311	47	43	3	777	64	8	.991
1995—Kansas City (A.L.) ...	1B-DH	131	465	69	144	28	0	12	83	.310	69	65	3	1111	118	3	*.998
1996—San Diego (N.L.)■ ...	1B	121	433	59	120	29	1	8	65	.277	69	71	5	1059	89	3	*.997
—Rancho Cuca. (Calif.) .	1B	3	10	1	3	1	0	0	2	.300	1	1	0	14	2	0	1.000
1997—San Diego (N.L.)	1B	135	455	59	149	29	2	13	83	.327	51	51	3	1027	89	4	*.996
—Las Vegas (PCL)	1B	3	8	1	2	0	0	0	1	.250	0	1	0	16	1	0	1.000
1998—San Diego (N.L.)	1B	131	439	58	131	30	1	12	80	.298	51	44	1	985	81	7	.993
1999—San Diego (N.L.)	1B-DH	110	323	34	80	14	2	5	43	.248	58	54	0	731	66	4	.995
—Las Vegas (PCL)	1B	6	17	4	4	0	0	0	2	.235	3	2	0	38	2	0	1.000
American League totals (10 years)		1364	5105	725	1481	290	19	158	789	.290	560	556	50	11656	1097	77	.994
National League totals (4 years)		497	1650	210	480	102	6	38	271	.291	229	220	9	3802	325	18	.996
Major League totals (14 years)		1861	6755	935	1961	392	25	196	1060	.290	789	776	59	15458	1422	95	.994

DIVISION SERIES RECORD

Year	Team (League)	Pos.	G	AB	R	H	2B	3B	HR	RBI	Avg.	BB	SO	SB	PO	A	E	Avg.
1996—San Diego (N.L.)	1B	3	9	0	1	0	0	0	0	.111	0	2	0	12	2	0	1.000
1998—San Diego (N.L.)	1B	4	6	1	1	0	0	1	2	.167	1	2	0	19	1	1	.952
Division series totals (2 years)		7	15	1	2	0	0	1	2	.133	1	4	0	31	3	1	.971

CHAMPIONSHIP SERIES RECORD

						BATTING								FIELDING		
Year	Team (League)	Pos.	G	AB	R	H	2B	3B	HR	RBI	Avg.	BB	SO	SB	PO	A	E	Avg.
1986— California (A.L.)		1B	3	11	3	5	2	0	1	2	.455	2	0	0	24	1	0	1.000
1998— San Diego (N.L.)		1B	6	16	3	5	0	0	0	2	.313	4	3	0	45	6	0	1.000
Championship series totals (2 years)			9	27	6	10	2	0	1	4	.370	6	3	0	69	7	0	1.000

WORLD SERIES RECORD

						BATTING								FIELDING		
Year	Team (League)	Pos.	G	AB	R	H	2B	3B	HR	RBI	Avg.	BB	SO	SB	PO	A	E	Avg.
1998— San Diego (N.L.)		1B	3	8	0	0	0	0	0	0	.000	3	1	0	22	0	0	1.000

ALL-STAR GAME RECORD

				BATTING								FIELDING		
Year	League	Pos.	AB	R	H	2B	3B	HR	RBI	Avg.	BB	SO	SB	PO	A	E	Avg.
1986— American		1B	1	0	0	0	0	0	0	.000	0	0	0	3	1	0	1.000

JUDD, MIKE   P   DODGERS

PERSONAL: Born June 30, 1975, in San Diego. ... 6-1/217. ... Throws right, bats right. ... Full name: Michael Galen Judd.
HIGH SCHOOL: Helix (La Mesa, Calif.).
JUNIOR COLLEGE: Grossmont College (San Diego).
TRANSACTIONS/CAREER NOTES: Selected by New York Yankees organization in ninth round of free-agent draft (June 1, 1995). ... Traded by Yankees to Los Angeles Dodgers for P Billy Brewer (June 22, 1996).

Year	League	W	L	Pct.	ERA	G	GS	CG	ShO	Sv.	IP	H	R	ER	BB	SO
1995— Gulf Coast Yankees (GCL) ..		1	1	.500	1.11	21	0	0	0	8	32 $\frac{1}{3}$	18	5	4	6	30
— Greensboro (SAL)		0	0	...	0.00	1	0	0	0	0	2 $\frac{2}{3}$	2	0	0	0	1
1996— Greensboro (SAL)		2	2	.500	3.81	29	0	0	0	10	28 $\frac{1}{3}$	22	14	12	8	36
— Savannah (SAL)■.............		4	2	.667	2.44	15	8	1	0	3	55 $\frac{1}{3}$	40	21	15	15	62
1997— Vero Beach (FSL)		6	5	.545	3.53	14	14	1	0	0	86 $\frac{2}{3}$	67	37	34	39	104
— San Antonio (Texas)..........		4	2	.667	2.73	12	12	0	0	0	79	69	27	24	33	65
— Los Angeles (N.L.)		0	0	...	0.00	1	0	0	0	0	2 $\frac{2}{3}$	4	0	0	0	4
1998— Albuquerque (PCL)		5	7	.417	4.56	17	17	3	1	0	94 $\frac{2}{3}$	98	62	48	44	77
— Los Angeles (N.L.)		0	0	...	15.09	7	0	0	0	0	11 $\frac{1}{3}$	19	19	19	9	14
1999— Albuquerque (PCL)		8	7	.533	6.67	21	21	1	0	0	110 $\frac{2}{3}$	132	90	82	47	122
— Los Angeles (N.L.)		3	1	.750	5.46	7	4	0	0	0	28	30	17	17	12	22
Major League totals (3 years)		3	1	.750	7.71	15	4	0	0	0	42	53	36	36	21	40

JUDEN, JEFF   P   YANKEES

PERSONAL: Born January 19, 1971, in Salem, Mass. ... 6-8/265. ... Throws right, bats both. ... Full name: Jeffrey Daniel Juden. ... Cousin of Daniel Juden, right winger in Tampa Bay Lightning organization (1994-97). ... Name pronounced JOO-den.
HIGH SCHOOL: Salem (Mass.).
TRANSACTIONS/CAREER NOTES: Selected by Houston Astros organization in first round (12th pick overall) of free-agent draft (June 5, 1989). ... On disabled list (June 14-21, 1992). ... Traded by Astros with P Doug Jones to Philadelphia Phillies for P Mitch Williams (December 2, 1993). ... On Scranton/Wilkes-Barre disabled list (June 22-July 24 and July 25, 1994-remainder of season). ... Traded by Phillies with OF/1B Tommy Eason to San Francisco Giants for IF Mike Benjamin (October 6, 1995). ... Claimed on waivers by Montreal Expos (July 11, 1996). ... On Montreal suspended list (September 4-7, 1996). ... Traded by Expos to Cleveland Indians for P Steve Kline (July 31, 1997). ... Traded by Indians with OF Marquis Grissom to Milwaukee Brewers for P Ben McDonald, P Mike Fetters and P Ron Villone (December 8, 1997). ... Claimed on waivers by Anaheim Angels (August 7, 1998). ... Released by Angels (November 16, 1998). ... Signed by New York Yankees organization (February 5, 1999). ... On Columbus disabled list (July 23-August 7, 1999).
STATISTICAL NOTES: Led Pacific Coast League with seven balks in 1992. ... Led International League with 17 hit batsmen in 1999. ... Career major league grand slams: 1.

Year	League	W	L	Pct.	ERA	G	GS	CG	ShO	Sv.	IP	H	R	ER	BB	SO
1989— Sarasota (FSL)		1	4	.200	3.40	9	8	0	0	0	39 $\frac{2}{3}$	33	21	15	17	49
1990— Osceola (FSL)		10	1	*.909	2.27	15	15	2	1	0	91	72	37	23	42	85
— Columbus (Sou.)		1	3	.250	5.37	11	11	0	0	0	52	55	36	31	42	40
1991— Jackson (Texas)		6	3	.667	3.10	16	16	0	0	0	95 $\frac{2}{3}$	84	43	33	44	75
— Tucson (PCL)		3	2	.600	3.18	10	10	0	0	0	56 $\frac{2}{3}$	56	28	20	25	51
— Houston (N.L.)		0	2	.000	6.00	4	3	0	0	0	18	19	14	12	7	11
1992— Tucson (PCL)		9	10	.474	4.04	26	26	0	0	0	147	149	84	66	71	120
1993— Tucson (PCL)		11	6	.647	4.63	27	27	0	0	0	169	174	102	87	*76	156
— Houston (N.L.)		0	1	.000	5.40	2	0	0	0	0	5	4	3	3	4	7
1994— Philadelphia (N.L.)■		1	4	.200	6.18	6	5	0	0	0	27 $\frac{2}{3}$	29	25	19	12	22
— Scranton/W.B. (I.L.)		2	2	.500	8.53	6	6	0	0	0	25 $\frac{1}{3}$	30	28	24	19	28
1995— Scranton/W.B. (I.L.)		6	4	.600	4.10	14	13	0	0	0	83 $\frac{1}{3}$	73	43	38	33	65
— Philadelphia (N.L.)		2	4	.333	4.02	13	10	1	0	0	62 $\frac{2}{3}$	53	31	28	31	47
1996— San Fran. (N.L.)■		4	0	1.000	4.10	36	0	0	0	0	41 $\frac{2}{3}$	39	23	19	20	35
— Montreal (N.L.)■		1	0	1.000	2.20	22	0	0	0	0	32 $\frac{2}{3}$	22	12	8	14	26
1997— Montreal (N.L.)		11	5	.688	4.22	22	22	3	0	0	130	125	64	61	57	107
— Cleveland (A.L.)■		0	1	.000	5.46	8	5	0	0	0	31 $\frac{1}{3}$	32	21	19	15	29
1998— Milwaukee (N.L.)■		7	11	.389	5.53	24	24	2	0	0	138 $\frac{1}{3}$	149	91	85	66	109
— Anaheim (A.L.)■		1	3	.250	6.75	8	6	0	0	0	40	33	32	30	18	39
1999— Columbus (I.L.)■		11	12	.478	5.56	27	26	4	1	0	*176 $\frac{1}{3}$	164	124	109	76	*151
— New York (A.L.)		0	1	.000	1.59	2	1	0	0	0	5 $\frac{2}{3}$	5	9	1	3	9
A.L. totals (3 years)		1	5	.167	5.84	18	12	0	0	0	77	70	62	50	36	77
N.L. totals (7 years)		26	27	.491	4.64	129	64	6	0	0	456	440	263	235	211	364
Major League totals (8 years)		27	32	.458	4.81	147	76	6	0	0	533	510	325	285	247	441

Year	League	W	L	Pct.	ERA	G	GS	CG	ShO	Sv.	IP	H	R	ER	BB	SO
					DIVISION SERIES RECORD											
1997— Cleveland (A.L.)									Did not play.							

Year	League	W	L	Pct.	ERA	G	GS	CG	ShO	Sv.	IP	H	R	ER	BB	SO
					CHAMPIONSHIP SERIES RECORD											
1997— Cleveland (A.L.)		0	0	...	0.00	3	0	0	0	0	1	2	0	0	2	2

Year	League	W	L	Pct.	ERA	G	GS	CG	ShO	Sv.	IP	H	R	ER	BB	SO
					WORLD SERIES RECORD											
1997— Cleveland (A.L.)		0	0	...	4.50	2	0	0	0	0	2	2	1	1	2	0

JUSTICE, DAVID   OF/DH   INDIANS

J

PERSONAL: Born April 14, 1966, in Cincinnati. ... 6-3/200. ... Bats left, throws left. ... Full name: David Christopher Justice.
HIGH SCHOOL: Covington (Ky.) Latin.
COLLEGE: Thomas More College (Ky.).
TRANSACTIONS/CAREER NOTES: Selected by Atlanta Braves organization in fourth round of free-agent draft (June 3, 1985). ... On Atlanta disabled list (June 27-August 20, 1991); included rehabilitation assignment to Macon (August 16-20). ... On disabled list (April 12-27, 1992; June 2-17, 1995 and May 16, 1996-remainder of season). ... Traded by Braves with OF Marquis Grissom to Cleveland Indians for OF Kenny Lofton and P Alan Embree (March 25, 1997). ... On disabled list (June 24-July 10, 1997).
RECORDS: Holds major league single-season record for fewest errors by outfielder who led league in errors—8 (1992).
HONORS: Named N.L. Rookie Player of the Year by THE SPORTING NEWS (1990). ... Named N.L. Rookie of the Year by Baseball Writers' Association of America (1990). ... Named outfielder on THE SPORTING NEWS N.L. All-Star team (1993). ... Named outfielder on THE SPORTING NEWS N.L. Silver Slugger team (1993). ... Named outfielder on THE SPORTING NEWS A.L. Silver Slugger team (1997). ... Named A.L. Comeback Player of the Year by THE SPORTING NEWS (1997). ... Named outfielder on THE SPORTING NEWS A.L. All-Star team (1997).
STATISTICAL NOTES: Tied for Appalachian League lead with five sacrifice flies in 1985. ... Career major league grand slams: 4.

Year Team (League)	Pos.	G	AB	R	H	2B	3B	HR	RBI	Avg.	BB	SO	SB	PO	A	E	Avg.
1985— Pulaski (Appl.)	OF	66	204	39	50	8	0	•10	46	.245	40	30	0	86	2	4	.957
1986— Sumter (SAL)	OF	61	220	48	66	16	0	10	61	.300	48	28	10	124	7	4	.970
— Durham (Caro.)	OF-1B	67	229	47	64	9	1	12	44	.279	46	24	2	163	5	1	.994
1987— Greenville (Sou.)	OF	93	348	38	79	12	4	6	40	.227	53	48	3	199	4	8	.962
1988— Richmond (I.L.)	OF	70	227	27	46	9	1	8	28	.203	39	55	4	136	5	4	.972
— Greenville (Sou.)	OF	58	198	34	55	13	1	9	37	.278	37	41	6	100	3	5	.954
1989— Richmond (I.L.)	OF-1B	115	391	47	102	24	3	12	58	.261	59	66	12	220	15	6	.975
— Atlanta (N.L.)	OF	16	51	7	12	3	0	1	3	.235	3	9	2	24	0	0	1.000
1990— Richmond (I.L.)	OF-1B	12	45	7	16	5	1	2	7	.356	7	6	0	23	4	2	.931
— Atlanta (N.L.)	1B-OF	127	439	76	124	23	2	28	78	.282	64	92	11	604	42	14	.979
1991— Atlanta (N.L.)	OF	109	396	67	109	25	1	21	87	.275	65	81	8	204	9	7	.968
— Macon (SAL)	OF	3	10	2	2	0	0	2	5	.200	2	1	0	1	0	0	1.000
1992— Atlanta (N.L.)	OF	144	484	78	124	19	5	21	72	.256	79	85	2	313	8	*8	.976
1993— Atlanta (N.L.)	OF	157	585	90	158	15	4	40	120	.270	78	90	3	323	9	5	.985
1994— Atlanta (N.L.)	OF	104	352	61	110	16	2	19	59	.313	69	45	2	192	6	*11	.947
1995— Atlanta (N.L.)	OF	120	411	73	104	17	2	24	78	.253	73	68	4	233	8	4	.984
1996— Atlanta (N.L.)	OF	40	140	23	45	9	0	6	25	.321	21	22	1	88	3	0	1.000
1997— Cleveland (A.L.)■	OF-DH	139	495	84	163	31	1	33	101	.329	80	79	3	120	3	2	.984
1998— Cleveland (A.L.)	DH-OF	146	540	94	151	39	2	21	88	.280	76	98	9	37	0	0	1.000
1999— Cleveland (A.L.)	OF-DH	133	429	75	123	18	0	21	88	.287	94	90	1	161	7	4	.977
American League totals (3 years)		418	1464	253	437	88	3	75	277	.298	250	267	13	318	10	6	.982
National League totals (8 years)		817	2858	475	786	127	16	160	522	.275	452	492	33	1981	85	49	.977
Major League totals (11 years)		1235	4322	728	1223	215	19	235	799	.283	702	759	46	2299	95	55	.978

DIVISION SERIES RECORD

RECORDS: Shares career record for most doubles—6. ... Shares single-series record for most doubles—4 (1998).

Year Team (League)	Pos.	G	AB	R	H	2B	3B	HR	RBI	Avg.	BB	SO	SB	PO	A	E	Avg.
1995— Atlanta (N.L.)	OF	4	13	2	3	0	0	0	0	.231	5	2	0	6	0	1	.857
1997— Cleveland (A.L.)	DH	5	19	3	5	2	0	1	2	.263	2	3	0	0	0	0	...
1998— Cleveland (A.L.)	DH-OF	4	16	2	5	4	0	1	6	.313	0	1	0	5	1	0	1.000
1999— Cleveland (A.L.)	OF	3	8	0	0	0	0	0	1	.000	2	2	0	7	2	0	1.000
Division series totals (4 years)		16	56	7	13	6	0	2	9	.232	9	8	0	18	3	1	.955

CHAMPIONSHIP SERIES RECORD

Year Team (League)	Pos.	G	AB	R	H	2B	3B	HR	RBI	Avg.	BB	SO	SB	PO	A	E	Avg.
1991— Atlanta (N.L.)	OF	7	25	4	5	1	0	1	2	.200	3	7	0	17	0	1	.944
1992— Atlanta (N.L.)	OF	7	25	5	7	1	0	2	6	.280	6	2	0	19	3	0	1.000
1993— Atlanta (N.L.)	OF	6	21	2	3	1	0	0	4	.143	3	3	0	14	0	1	.933
1995— Atlanta (N.L.)	OF	3	11	1	3	0	0	0	1	.273	2	1	0	0	0	0	...
1997— Cleveland (A.L.)	DH	6	21	3	7	1	0	0	0	.333	2	4	0	...	...	...	...
1998— Cleveland (A.L.)	OF-DH-PH	6	19	2	3	0	0	1	2	.158	3	3	0	3	0	0	1.000
Championship series totals (6 years)		35	122	17	28	4	0	4	15	.230	19	20	0	53	3	2	.966

WORLD SERIES RECORD

NOTES: Member of World Series championship team (1995).

Year Team (League)	Pos.	G	AB	R	H	2B	3B	HR	RBI	Avg.	BB	SO	SB	PO	A	E	Avg.
1991— Atlanta (N.L.)	OF	7	27	5	7	0	0	2	6	.259	5	5	2	21	1	1	.957
1992— Atlanta (N.L.)	OF	6	19	4	3	0	0	1	3	.158	6	5	1	15	0	1	.938
1995— Atlanta (N.L.)	OF	6	20	3	5	1	0	1	5	.250	5	1	0	16	0	0	1.000
1997— Cleveland (A.L.)	OF-DH	7	27	4	5	0	0	0	4	.185	6	8	0	9	0	0	1.000
World Series totals (4 years)		26	93	16	20	1	0	4	18	.215	22	19	3	61	1	2	.969

Year League	Pos.	AB	R	H	2B	3B	HR	RBI	Avg.	BB	SO	SB	PO	A	E	Avg.
1993— National	OF	3	0	1	0	0	0	0	.333	0	0	0	1	0	1	.500
1994— National	OF	2	0	0	0	0	0	0	.000	0	0	0	1	0	0	1.000
1997— American..................							Selected, did not play—injured.										
All-Star Game totals (2 years)		**5**	**0**	**1**	**0**	**0**	**0**	**0**	**.200**	**0**	**0**	**0**	**2**	**0**	**1**	**.667**

KALINOWSKI, JOSH   P   ROCKIES

PERSONAL: Born December 12, 1976, in Pasco, Wash. ... 6-2/186. ... Throws left, bats left. ... Full name: Joshua D. Kalinowski.
HIGH SCHOOL: Natrona County (Casper, Wyoming).
JUNIOR COLLEGE: Indian Hills Community College (Iowa).
TRANSACTIONS/CAREER NOTES: Selected by Colorado Rockies organization in 37th round of free-agent draft (June 1, 1995); did not sign. ... Selected by Colorado Rockies organization in 33rd round of free-agent draft (June 4, 1996). ... On Salem disabled list (May 2-9, 1999).
HONORS: Named Carolina League Pitcher of the Year (1999).
STATISTICAL NOTES: Pitches 5-0 no-hit victory for Asheville against Charleston, S.C. (August 26, 1998). ... Led Carolina League pitchers with 34 assists in 1999.

Year League	W	L	Pct.	ERA	G	GS	CG	ShO	Sv.	IP	H	R	ER	BB	SO
1997— Portland (N.W.)	0	1	.000	2.41	6	6	0	0	0	18 2/3	15	6	5	10	27
1998— Asheville (SAL).................	12	10	.545	3.92	28	28	3	1	0	172 1/3	159	93	75	65	*215
1999— Salem (Caro.)	11	6	.647	*2.11	27	27	1	0	0	162 1/3	119	47	38	71	*176

KAMIENIECKI, SCOTT   P   INDIANS

PERSONAL: Born April 19, 1964, in Mt. Clemens, Mich. ... 6-0/200. ... Throws right, bats right. ... Full name: Scott Andrew Kamieniecki. ... Name pronounced KAM-ah-NIK-ee.
HIGH SCHOOL: Redford St. Mary's (Detroit).
COLLEGE: Michigan (degree in physical education).
TRANSACTIONS/CAREER NOTES: Selected by Detroit Tigers organization in second round of free-agent draft (June 7, 1982); did not sign. ... Selected by Milwaukee Brewers organization in 23rd round of free-agent draft (June 3, 1985); did not sign. ... Selected by New York Yankees organization in 14th round of free-agent draft (June 2, 1986). ... On New York disabled list (August 3, 1991-remainder of season). ... On New York disabled list (April 2-29, 1992); included rehabilitation assignments to Fort Lauderdale (April 9-17) and Columbus (April 17-29). ... On New York disabled list (May 6-July 15, 1995); included rehabilitation assignments to Tampa (July 5-10) and Columbus (July 10-12). ... On New York disabled list (March 27-April 24 and July 31, 1996-remainder of season); included rehabilitation assignment to Tampa (April 6-24). ... On Columbus disabled list (June 20-July 31, 1996). ... Granted free agency (December 20, 1996). ... Signed by Baltimore Orioles organization (January 22, 1997). ... Granted free agency (October 30, 1997). ... Re-signed by Orioles (December 5, 1997). ... On Baltimore disabled list (April 25-May 12, May 23-July 25 and August 23, 1998-remainder of season); included rehabilitation assignment to Bowie (July 9-25). ... On Baltimore disabled list (March 25-May 8, 1999); included rehabilitation assignments to Bowie (April 25-29) and Frederick (April 30-May 3). ... Granted free agency (November 2, 1999). ... Signed by Cleveland Indians (December 3, 1999).

Year League	W	L	Pct.	ERA	G	GS	CG	ShO	Sv.	IP	H	R	ER	BB	SO
1987— Alb./Colonie (East.)	1	3	.250	5.35	10	7	0	0	0	37	41	25	22	33	19
— Prince William (Caro.)	9	5	.643	4.17	19	19	1	0	0	112 1/3	91	61	52	78	84
1988— Prince William (Caro.)	6	7	.462	4.40	15	15	•7	2	0	100 1/3	115	62	49	50	72
— Fort Lauderdale (FSL)	3	6	.333	3.62	12	11	1	1	0	77	71	36	31	40	51
1989— Alb./Colonie (East.)	10	9	.526	3.70	24	23	6	3	1	151	142	67	62	57	*140
1990— Alb./Colonie (East.)	10	9	.526	3.20	22	21	3	1	0	132	113	55	47	61	99
1991— Columbus (I.L.)	6	3	.667	2.36	11	11	3	1	0	76 1/3	61	25	20	20	58
— New York (A.L.)	4	4	.500	3.90	9	9	0	0	0	55 1/3	54	24	24	22	34
1992— Fort Lauderdale (FSL)	1	0	1.000	1.29	1	1	1	0	0	7	8	1	1	0	3
— Columbus (I.L.)	1	0	1.000	0.69	2	2	0	0	0	13	6	1	1	4	12
— New York (A.L.)	6	14	.300	4.36	28	28	4	0	0	188	193	100	91	74	88
1993— New York (A.L.)	10	7	.588	4.08	30	20	2	0	1	154 1/3	163	73	70	59	72
— Columbus (I.L.)	1	0	1.000	1.50	1	1	0	0	0	6	5	1	1	0	4
1994— New York (A.L.)	8	6	.571	3.76	22	16	1	0	0	117 1/3	115	53	49	59	71
1995— New York (A.L.)	7	6	.538	4.01	17	16	1	0	0	89 2/3	83	43	40	49	43
— Tampa (FSL)......................	1	0	1.000	1.80	1	1	0	0	0	5	6	2	1	1	2
— Columbus (I.L.)	1	0	1.000	0.00	1	1	0	0	0	6 2/3	2	0	0	1	10
1996— Tampa (FSL)......................	2	1	.667	1.17	3	3	1	0	0	23	20	6	3	4	17
— New York (A.L.)	1	2	.333	11.12	7	5	0	0	0	22 2/3	36	30	28	19	15
— Columbus (I.L.)	2	1	.667	5.64	5	5	2	0	0	30 1/3	33	21	19	8	27
1997— Baltimore (A.L.)■.............	10	6	.625	4.01	30	30	0	0	0	179 1/3	179	83	80	67	109
1998— Baltimore (A.L.)	2	6	.250	6.75	12	11	0	0	0	54 2/3	67	41	41	26	25
— Bowie (East.)	1	0	1.000	4.76	3	3	0	0	0	11 1/3	13	6	6	2	5
1999— Bowie (East.)	0	1	.000	3.60	1	1	0	0	0	5	6	2	2	0	1
— Frederick (Caro.)	0	0	...	0.00	1	1	0	0	0	4	0	0	0	1	3
— Baltimore (A.L.)	2	4	.333	4.95	43	3	0	0	2	56 1/3	52	32	31	29	39
— Rochester (I.L.)	1	2	.333	5.09	4	4	0	0	0	23	23	13	13	6	14
Major League totals (9 years)	**50**	**55**	**.476**	**4.45**	**198**	**138**	**8**	**0**	**3**	**917 2/3**	**942**	**479**	**454**	**404**	**496**

DIVISION SERIES RECORD

Year League	W	L	Pct.	ERA	G	GS	CG	ShO	Sv.	IP	H	R	ER	BB	SO
1995— New York (A.L.)	0	0	...	7.20	1	1	0	0	0	5	9	5	4	4	4
1997— Baltimore (A.L.)							Did not play.									

CHAMPIONSHIP SERIES RECORD

Year League	W	L	Pct.	ERA	G	GS	CG	ShO	Sv.	IP	H	R	ER	BB	SO
1997— Baltimore (A.L.)	1	0	1.000	0.00	2	1	0	0	0	8	4	0	0	2	5

J
K

PERSONAL: Born August 31, 1975, in Hollywood, Calif. ... 6-2/208. ... Bats right, throws right. ... Full name: Gabriel Stefan Kapler.
JUNIOR COLLEGE: Moorpark (Calif.) College.
TRANSACTIONS/CAREER NOTES: Selected by Detroit Tigers organization in 57th round of free-agent draft (June 1, 1995). ... Traded by Tigers with P Justin Thompson, P Francisco Cordero, C Bill Haselman, 2B Frank Catalanotto and P Alan Webb to Texas Rangers for OF Juan Gonzalez, P Danny Patterson and C Gregg Zaun (November 2, 1999).
HONORS: Named Minor League Player of the Year by THE SPORTING NEWS (1998). ... Named Southern League Most Valuable Player (1998).
STATISTICAL NOTES: Led South Atlantic League with 280 total bases in 1996. ... Led Florida State League with 262 total bases in 1997. ... Led Southern League with 319 total bases and 11 sacrifice flies in 1998.

							BATTING							FIELDING		
Year Team (League)	Pos.	G	AB	R	H	2B	3B	HR	RBI	Avg.	BB	SO	SB	PO	A	E	Avg.
1995—Jamestown (NY-P)	OF	63	236	38	68	19	4	4	34	.288	23	37	1	103	9	9	.926
1996—Fayetteville (SAL)	OF-3B	138	524	81	*157	*45	0	26	99	.300	62	73	14	195	14	7	.968
1997—Lakeland (FSL)	OF	137	519	87	153	*40	6	19	87	.295	54	68	8	252	14	6	.978
1998—Jacksonville (Sou.)......	OF-1B	139	547	*113	*176	*47	6	*28	*146	.322	66	93	6	294	12	5	.984
— Detroit (A.L.).............	OF-DH	7	25	3	5	0	1	0	0	.200	1	4	2	9	0	0	1.000
1999—Detroit (A.L.)	OF-DH	130	416	60	102	22	4	18	49	.245	42	74	11	302	4	6	.981
— Toledo (I.L.)...............	OF	14	54	11	17	6	2	3	14	.315	9	10	0	33	0	0	1.000
Major League totals (2 years)		137	441	63	107	22	5	18	49	.243	43	78	13	311	4	6	.981

PERSONAL: Born June 28, 1967, in Berwick, Pa. ... 6-4/220. ... Throws right, bats right. ... Full name: Matthew Dean Karchner.
HIGH SCHOOL: Berwick (Pa.).
COLLEGE: Bloomsburg (Pa.).
TRANSACTIONS/CAREER NOTES: Selected by Kansas City Royals organization in eighth round of free-agent draft (June 5, 1989). ... On disabled list (August 1-8, 1991). ... Selected by Montreal Expos from Royals organization in Rule 5 major league draft (December 9, 1991). ... Returned to Royals (April 4, 1992). ... On disabled list (September 2-18, 1992; and May 10, 1993-remainder of season). ... Selected by Chicago White Sox organization from Royals organization, in Rule 5 minor league draft (December 13, 1993). ... On Chicago disabled list (August 11-September 1, 1996); included rehabilitation assignment to Nashville (August 30-September 1). ... On Chicago disabled list (May 7-23 and June 24-July 9, 1998). ... Traded by White Sox to Chicago Cubs for P Jon Garland (July 29, 1998). ... On Chicago disabled list (April 26-June 24 and July 17, 1999-remainder of season); included rehabilitation assignment to Iowa (May 30-June 7 and June 18-23).

Year League	W	L	Pct.	ERA	G	GS	CG	ShO	Sv.	IP	H	R	ER	BB	SO
1989—Eugene (N.W.)	1	1	.500	3.90	8	5	0	0	0	30	30	19	13	8	25
1990—Appleton (Midw.)...........	2	7	.222	4.82	27	11	1	0	0	71	70	42	38	31	58
1991—Baseball City (FSL)............	6	3	.667	1.97	38	0	0	0	5	73	49	28	16	25	65
1992—Memphis (Sou.)............	8	8	.500	4.47	33	18	2	0	1	141	161	83	70	35	88
1993—Memphis (Sou.)............	3	2	.600	4.20	6	5	0	0	0	30	34	16	14	4	14
1994—Birmingham (Sou.)■	5	2	.714	1.26	39	0	0	0	6	43	36	10	6	14	29
—Nashville (A.A.)............	4	2	.667	1.37	17	0	0	0	2	26 1/3	18	5	4	7	19
1995—Nashville (A.A.)............	3	3	.500	1.45	28	0	0	0	9	37 1/3	39	7	6	10	29
—Chicago (A.L.)............	4	2	.667	1.69	31	0	0	0	0	32	33	8	6	12	24
1996—Chicago (A.L.)............	7	4	.636	5.76	50	0	0	0	1	59 1/3	61	42	38	41	46
—Nashville (A.A.)............	0	0	...	0.00	1	0	0	0	0	2/3	0	0	0	0	0
1997—Nashville (A.A.)............	2	1	.667	1.93	13	0	0	0	3	18 2/3	12	5	4	6	11
—Chicago (A.L.)............	3	1	.750	2.91	52	0	0	0	15	52 2/3	50	18	17	26	30
1998—Chicago (A.L.)............	2	4	.333	5.15	32	0	0	0	11	36 2/3	33	21	21	19	30
—Chicago (N.L.)■............	3	1	.750	5.14	29	0	0	0	0	28	30	18	16	14	22
1999—Chicago (N.L.)............	1	0	1.000	2.50	16	0	0	0	0	18	16	5	5	9	9
—Iowa (PCL)............	0	0	...	6.35	5	1	0	0	0	5 2/3	6	4	4	1	6
A.L. totals (4 years)	16	11	.593	4.08	165	0	0	0	27	180 2/3	177	89	82	98	130
N.L. totals (2 years)	4	1	.800	4.11	45	0	0	0	0	46	46	23	21	23	31
Major League totals (5 years).......	20	12	.625	4.08	210	0	0	0	27	226 2/3	223	112	103	121	161

DIVISION SERIES RECORD

Year League	W	L	Pct.	ERA	G	GS	CG	ShO	Sv.	IP	H	R	ER	BB	SO
1998—Chicago (N.L.)	0	0	...	13.50	1	0	0	0	0	2/3	1	1	1	0	1

PERSONAL: Born August 9, 1971, in Riverside, Calif. ... 6-2/209. ... Throws left, bats left. ... Full name: Randall Scott Karl.
HIGH SCHOOL: Carlsbad (Calif.).
COLLEGE: Hawaii.
TRANSACTIONS/CAREER NOTES: Selected by Milwaukee Brewers organization in sixth round of free-agent draft (June 1, 1992). ... On New Orleans disabled list (April 27-May 31, 1994). ... Traded by Brewers with 3B Jeff Cirillo and cash to Colorado Rockies as part of three-way deal in which Brewers received P Jamey Wright and C Henry Blanco from Rockies, Oakland Athletics received P Justin Miller and cash from Rockies and Brewers received P Jimmy Haynes from Athletics (December 13, 1999).
STATISTICAL NOTES: Tied for Texas League lead with seven balks in 1993.
MISCELLANEOUS: Appeared in one game as pinch runner (1998).

Year League	W	L	Pct.	ERA	G	GS	CG	ShO	Sv.	IP	H	R	ER	BB	SO
1992—Helena (Pio.)	7	0	•1.000	*1.46	9	9	1	1	0	61 2/3	54	13	10	16	57
1993—El Paso (Texas)..................	13	8	.619	2.45	27	•27	•4	•2	0	*180	172	67	49	35	95
1994—New Orleans (A.A.)............	5	5	.500	3.84	15	13	2	0	0	89	92	38	38	33	54
—El Paso (Texas)................	5	1	.833	2.96	8	8	3	0	0	54 2/3	44	21	18	15	51
1995—New Orleans (A.A.)............	3	4	.429	3.30	8	6	1	1	0	46 1/3	47	18	17	12	29
—Milwaukee (A.L.)............	6	7	.462	4.14	25	18	1	0	0	124	141	65	57	50	59
1996—Milwaukee (A.L.)	13	9	.591	4.86	32	32	3	1	0	207 1/3	220	124	112	72	121

Year League	W	L	Pct.	ERA	G	GS	CG	ShO	Sv.	IP	H	R	ER	BB	SO
1997— Milwaukee (A.L.)	10	13	.435	4.47	32	32	1	0	0	193 1/3	212	103	96	67	119
1998— Milwaukee (N.L.)	10	11	.476	4.40	33	33	0	0	0	192 1/3	219	104	94	66	102
1999— Milwaukee (N.L.)	11	11	.500	4.78	33	33	0	0	0	197 2/3	246	121	105	69	74
A.L. totals (3 years)	29	29	.500	4.55	89	82	5	1	0	524 2/3	573	292	265	189	299
N.L. totals (2 years)	21	22	.488	4.59	66	66	0	0	0	390	465	225	199	135	176
Major League totals (5 years)	50	51	.495	4.57	155	148	5	1	0	914 2/3	1038	517	464	324	475

KARROS, ERIC   1B   DODGERS

PERSONAL: Born November 4, 1967, in Hackensack, N.J. ... 6-4/226. ... Bats right, throws right. ... Full name: Eric Peter Karros. ... Name pronounced CARE-ose.
HIGH SCHOOL: Patrick Henry (San Diego).
COLLEGE: UCLA.
TRANSACTIONS/CAREER NOTES: Selected by Los Angeles Dodgers organization in sixth round of free-agent draft (June 1, 1988). ... On Los Angeles disabled list (March 29-April 24, 1998); included rehabilitation assignment to San Bernardino (April 19-25).
HONORS: Named N.L. Rookie Player of the Year by THE SPORTING NEWS (1992). ... Named N.L. Rookie of the Year by Baseball Writers' Association of America (1992). ... Named first baseman on THE SPORTING NEWS N.L. All-Star team (1995). ... Named first baseman on THE SPORTING NEWS N.L. Silver Slugger team (1995).
STATISTICAL NOTES: Tied for Pioneer League lead in errors by first baseman with 14 in 1988. ... Led California League first basemen with 1,232 putouts, 110 assists and 1,358 total chances in 1989. ... Led Texas League with 282 total bases in 1990. ... Led Texas League first basemen with 1,337 total chances and 129 double plays in 1990. ... Led Pacific Coast League with 269 total bases in 1991. ... Tied for Pacific Coast League lead with eight intentional bases on balls received in 1991. ... Led Pacific Coast League first basemen with 1,095 putouts, 109 assists and 1,215 total chances in 1991. ... Led N.L. in grounding into double plays with 27 in 1996. ... Career major league grand slams: 1.

							BATTING						FIELDING		
Year Team (League)	Pos.	G	AB	R	H	2B	3B	HR	RBI	Avg.	BB	SO	SB	PO	A	E	Avg.
1988— Great Falls (Pio.)	1B-3B	66	268	68	98	12	1	12	55	.366	32	35	8	516	31	‡19	.966
1989— Bakersfield (Calif.)	1B-3B	*142	545	86	*165	*40	1	15	86	.303	63	99	18	†1238	†113	19	.986
1990— San Antonio (Texas)	1B	•131	509	91	*179	*45	2	18	78	.352	57	79	8	*1223	*106	8	*.994
1991— Albuquerque (PCL)	1B-3B	132	488	88	154	33	8	22	101	.316	58	80	3	†1095	†109	11	.991
— Los Angeles (N.L.)	1B	14	14	0	1	1	0	0	1	.071	1	6	0	33	2	0	1.000
1992— Los Angeles (N.L.)	1B	149	545	63	140	30	1	20	88	.257	37	103	2	1211	126	9	.993
1993— Los Angeles (N.L.)	1B	158	619	74	153	27	2	23	80	.247	34	82	0	1335	*147	12	.992
1994— Los Angeles (N.L.)	1B	111	406	51	108	21	1	14	46	.266	29	53	2	896	118	•9	.991
1995— Los Angeles (N.L.)	1B	143	551	83	164	29	3	32	105	.298	61	115	4	1234	109	7	.995
1996— Los Angeles (N.L.)	1B	154	608	84	158	29	1	34	111	.260	53	121	8	1314	121	15	.990
1997— Los Angeles (N.L.)	1B	•162	628	86	167	28	0	31	104	.266	61	116	15	1317	121	11	.992
1998— San Bern. (Calif.)	1B	4	15	3	4	1	0	0	1	.267	0	2	0	32	2	0	1.000
— Los Angeles (N.L.)	1B-DH	139	507	59	150	20	1	23	87	.296	47	93	7	1150	110	0	1.000
1999— Los Angeles (N.L.)	1B	153	578	74	176	40	0	34	112	.304	53	119	8	1291	*126	13	.991
Major League totals (9 years)		1183	4456	574	1217	225	9	211	734	.273	376	808	46	9781	980	88	.992

DIVISION SERIES RECORD
RECORDS: Shares single-game record for most home runs—2 (October 4, 1995).

							BATTING						FIELDING		
Year Team (League)	Pos.	G	AB	R	H	2B	3B	HR	RBI	Avg.	BB	SO	SB	PO	A	E	Avg.
1995— Los Angeles (N.L.)	1B	3	12	3	6	1	0	2	4	.500	1	0	0	14	0	0	1.000
1996— Los Angeles (N.L.)	1B	3	9	0	0	0	0	0	0	.000	2	3	0	28	2	0	1.000
Division series totals (2 years)		6	21	3	6	1	0	2	4	.286	3	3	0	42	2	0	1.000

KARSAY, STEVE   P   INDIANS

PERSONAL: Born March 24, 1972, in Flushing, N.Y. ... 6-3/205. ... Throws right, bats right. ... Full name: Stefan Andrew Karsay. ... Name pronounced CAR-say.
HIGH SCHOOL: Christ the King (Queens, N.Y.).
TRANSACTIONS/CAREER NOTES: Selected by Toronto Blue Jays organization in first round (22nd pick overall) of free-agent draft (June 4, 1990). ... On Knoxville disabled list (July 3-16, 1993). ... Traded by Blue Jays with a player to be named later to Oakland Athletics for OF Rickey Henderson (July 31, 1993); A's acquired OF Jose Herrera to complete deal (August 6, 1993). ... On disabled list (April 26, 1994-remainder of season and April 24, 1995-entire season; and August 6, 1997-remainder of season). ... Traded by A's to Cleveland Indians for P Mike Fetters (December 8, 1997). ... On Buffalo disabled list (May 14-25 and June 12-July 15, 1998). ... On Cleveland disabled list (July 2-26 and August 25-September 22, 1999).
MISCELLANEOUS: Appeared in one game as pinch runner (1997).

Year League	W	L	Pct.	ERA	G	GS	CG	ShO	Sv.	IP	H	R	ER	BB	SO
1990— St. Catharines (NY-P)	1	1	.500	0.79	5	5	0	0	0	22 2/3	11	4	2	12	25
1991— Myrtle Beach (SAL)	4	9	.308	3.58	20	20	1	0	0	110 2/3	96	58	44	48	100
1992— Dunedin (FSL)	6	3	.667	2.73	16	16	3	2	0	85 2/3	56	32	26	29	87
1993— Knoxville (Sou.)	8	4	.667	3.38	19	18	1	0	0	104	98	42	39	32	100
— Huntsville (Sou.)■	0	0	...	5.14	2	2	0	0	0	14	13	8	8	3	22
— Oakland (A.L.)	3	3	.500	4.04	8	8	0	0	0	49	49	23	22	16	33
1994— Oakland (A.L.)	1	1	.500	2.57	4	4	1	0	0	28	26	8	8	8	15
1995— Oakland (A.L.)							Did not play.								
1996— Modesto (Calif.)	0	1	.000	2.65	14	14	0	0	0	34	35	16	10	1	31
1997— Oakland (A.L.)	3	12	.200	5.77	24	24	0	0	0	132 2/3	166	92	85	47	92
1998— Buffalo (I.L.)■	6	4	.600	3.76	16	14	0	0	0	79	89	39	33	15	63
— Cleveland (A.L.)	0	2	.000	5.92	11	1	0	0	0	24 1/3	31	16	16	6	13
1999— Cleveland (A.L.)	10	2	.833	2.97	50	3	0	0	1	78 2/3	71	29	26	30	68
Major League totals (5 years)	17	20	.459	4.52	97	40	1	0	1	312 2/3	343	168	157	107	221

DIVISION SERIES RECORD
Year League	W	L	Pct.	ERA	G	GS	CG	ShO	Sv.	IP	H	R	ER	BB	SO
1999— Cleveland (A.L.)	0	0	...	9.00	2	0	0	0	0	3	5	3	3	1	3

KELLER, KRIS — P — TIGERS

PERSONAL: Born March 1, 1978, in Williamsport, Pa. ... 6-2/225. ... Throws right, bats right. ... Full name: Kristopher Shane Keller.
HIGH SCHOOL: Fletcher (Neptune Beach, Fla.).
TRANSACTIONS/CAREER NOTES: Selected by Detroit Tigers organization in fourth round of free-agent draft (June 4, 1996).

Year	League	W	L	Pct.	ERA	G	GS	CG	ShO	Sv.	IP	H	R	ER	BB	SO
1996—	Gulf Coast Tigers (GCL)	1	1	.500	2.38	8	6	0	0	0	34	23	12	9	21	23
1997—	Jamestown (NY-P)	0	2	.000	8.67	16	0	0	0	0	27	37	33	26	20	18
1998—	Jamestown (NY-P)	1	3	.250	3.27	27	0	0	0	8	33	29	12	12	16	41
1999—	West Michigan (Midw.)	5	3	.625	2.92	49	0	0	0	8	77	63	28	25	36	87

KELLY, MIKE — OF — METS

PERSONAL: Born June 2, 1970, in Los Angeles. ... 6-4/195. ... Bats right, throws right. ... Full name: Michael Raymond Kelly.
HIGH SCHOOL: Los Alamitos (Calif.).
COLLEGE: Arizona State.
TRANSACTIONS/CAREER NOTES: Selected by New York Mets organization in 24th round of free-agent draft (June 1, 1988); did not sign. ... Selected by Atlanta Braves organization in first round (second pick overall) of free-agent draft (June 3, 1991). ... Traded by Braves to Cincinnati Reds for P Chad Fox and a player to be named later (January 9, 1996); Braves acquired P Ray King to complete deal (June 11, 1996). ... Traded by Reds to Tampa Bay Devil Rays for a player to be named later (November 11, 1997); Reds acquired 1B Dmitri Young to complete deal (November 18). ... On Tampa Bay disabled list (April 1-21, 1998); included rehabilitation assignment to Durham (April 16-21). ... Released by Devil Rays (March 31, 1999). ... Signed by Colorado Rockies organization (April 2, 1999). ... Granted free agency (October 4, 1999). ... Signed by Mets organization (December 2, 1999).
HONORS: Named College Player of the Year by THE SPORTING NEWS (1990). ... Named outfielder on THE SPORTING NEWS college All-America team (1990). ... Named Golden Spikes Award winner by USA Baseball (1991).

Year	Team (League)	Pos.	G	AB	R	H	2B	3B	HR	RBI	Avg.	BB	SO	SB	PO	A	E	Avg.
1991—	Durham (Caro.)	OF	35	124	29	31	6	1	6	17	.250	19	47	6	4	0	0	1.000
1992—	Greenville (Sou.)	OF	133	471	83	108	18	4	25	71	.229	65	*162	22	244	7	3	.988
1993—	Richmond (I.L.)	OF	123	424	63	103	13	1	19	58	.243	36	109	11	270	6	2	*.993
1994—	Atlanta (N.L.)	OF	30	77	14	21	10	1	2	9	.273	2	17	0	25	0	1	.962
	—Richmond (I.L.)	OF-DH	81	313	46	82	14	4	15	45	.262	32	96	9	181	5	1	.995
1995—	Richmond (I.L.)	OF	15	45	5	13	1	0	2	8	.289	5	17	0	24	0	0	1.000
	—Atlanta (N.L.)	OF	97	137	26	26	6	1	3	17	.190	11	49	7	63	0	4	.940
1996—	Cincinnati (N.L.)■.....	OF	19	49	5	9	4	0	1	7	.184	9	11	4	34	1	1	.972
	—Indianapolis (A.A.)......	OF-DH	88	292	43	61	10	1	8	30	.209	30	80	13	132	2	4	.971
1997—	Chattanooga (Sou.)	OF	15	60	14	21	7	0	3	12	.350	3	16	3	32	2	0	1.000
	—Indianapolis (A.A.)......	OF	27	92	28	32	8	0	7	18	.348	23	23	7	51	1	2	.963
	—Cincinnati (N.L.).....	OF-DH	73	140	27	41	13	2	6	19	.293	10	30	6	88	2	2	.978
1998—	Tampa Bay (A.L.)■.....	OF-DH	106	279	39	67	11	2	10	33	.240	22	80	13	137	4	0	1.000
	—Durham (I.L.)	OF	4	12	2	1	0	0	0	0	.083	4	5	0	12	0	1	.923
1999—	Colorado (N.L.)■.....	OF	2	2	0	1	1	0	0	1	.500	0	0	0	0	0	0	...
	—Colo. Springs (PCL) ...	OF-DH	114	394	69	109	27	3	9	50	.277	57	93	10	188	10	5	.975
American League totals (1 year)			106	279	39	67	11	2	10	33	.240	22	80	13	137	4	0	1.000
National League totals (5 years)			221	405	72	98	34	4	12	53	.242	32	107	17	210	3	8	.964
Major League totals (6 years)			327	684	111	165	45	6	22	86	.241	54	187	30	347	7	8	.978

KELLY, PAT — 2B — ANGELS

PERSONAL: Born October 14, 1967, in Philadelphia. ... 6-0/182. ... Bats right, throws right. ... Full name: Patrick Franklin Kelly.
HIGH SCHOOL: Catashuqua (Pa.).
COLLEGE: West Chester (Pa.).
TRANSACTIONS/CAREER NOTES: Selected by New York Yankees organization in ninth round of free-agent draft (June 1, 1988). ... On New York disabled list (April 21-May 7, 1992); included rehabilitation assignment to Albany/Colonie (May 5-7). ... On New York disabled list (June 22-July 7, 1994); included rehabilitation assignment to Albany/Colonie (July 6-7). ... On New York disabled list (May 27-July 7, 1995); included rehabilitation assignments to Gulf Coast Yankees (July 3-4) and Tampa (July 4-7). ... On New York disabled list (March 27-July 26, August 12 and August 23-September 7, 1996); included rehabilitation assignments to Gulf Coast Yankees (July 1-5), Tampa (July 5-8 and July 11-16), Columbus (July 16-26) and Norwich (August 8-12). ... On New York disabled list (May 10-June 3 and August 17-September 1, 1997); included rehabilitation assignment to Columbus (May 21-June 2, 1997). ... Granted free agency (November 7, 1997). ... Signed by Toronto Blue Jays organization (November 27, 1997). ... Contract sold by Blue Jays to St. Louis Cardinals (July 16, 1998). ... Granted free agency (October 26, 1998). ... Re-signed by Cardinals organization (December 7, 1998). ... Released by Cardinals (April 7, 1999). ... Signed by Blue Jays (April 15, 1999). ... Released by Blue Jays (June 9, 1999). ... Signed by Anaheim Angels organization (January 7, 2000).
STATISTICAL NOTES: Led Carolina League second basemen with 76 double plays and tied for lead with 641 total chances in 1989. ... Led Eastern League second basemen with 667 total chances and 97 double plays in 1990. ... Led A.L. with 14 sacrifice hits in 1994.

Year	Team (League)	Pos.	G	AB	R	H	2B	3B	HR	RBI	Avg.	BB	SO	SB	PO	A	E	Avg.
1988—	Oneonta (NY-P)	2B-SS	71	280	49	92	11	6	2	34	.329	15	45	25	124	207	16	.954
1989—	Prince Will. (Caro.).....	2B	124	436	61	116	21	*7	3	45	.266	32	79	31	244	*372	25	.961
1990—	Alb./Colonie (East.)	2B	126	418	67	113	19	6	8	44	.270	37	79	31	*266	*381	*20	.970
1991—	Columbus (I.L.)	2B	31	116	27	39	9	2	3	19	.336	9	16	8	53	97	4	.974
	—New York (A.L.)	3B-2B	96	298	35	72	12	4	3	23	.242	15	52	12	78	204	18	.940
1992—	New York (A.L.)	2B-DH	106	318	38	72	22	2	7	27	.226	25	72	8	203	296	11	.978
	—Alb./Colonie (East.)	2B	2	6	1	0	0	0	0	0	.000	2	4	0	4	8	0	1.000
1993—	New York (A.L.)	2B	127	406	49	111	24	1	7	51	.273	24	68	14	245	369	14	.978
1994—	New York (A.L.)	2B	93	286	35	80	21	2	3	41	.280	19	51	6	180	258	10	.978
	—Alb./Colonie (East.)	2B	1	4	1	1	0	0	0	0	.250	0	1	1	2	2	0	1.000
1995—	New York (A.L.)	2B-DH	89	270	32	64	12	1	4	29	.237	23	65	8	161	255	7	.983
	—GC Yankees (GCL)......	2B	1	2	2	0	0	0	0	1	.000	1	0	0	3	3	0	1.000
	—Tampa (FSL)...............	2B	3	17	0	4	1	0	0	2	.235	0	1	0	8	14	0	1.000

– 301 –

Year	Team (League)	Pos.	G	AB	R	H	2B	3B	HR	RBI	Avg.	BB	SO	SB	PO	A	E	Avg.
1996—	GC Yankees (GCL)......	2B-DH	5	17	7	6	2	0	1	1	.353	3	2	3	5	5	0	1.000
	— Tampa (FSL).........	2B	6	22	6	6	0	0	1	2	.273	1	7	0	15	9	2	.923
	— Columbus (I.L.).........	2B	8	37	6	14	1	1	2	7	.378	2	11	3	19	19	0	1.000
	— New York (A.L.).........	2B-DH	13	21	4	3	0	0	0	2	.143	2	9	0	8	24	1	.970
	— Norwich (East.).........	2B	4	17	3	5	2	1	0	0	.294	0	2	1	7	13	1	.952
1997—	New York (A.L.).........	2B-DH	67	120	25	29	6	1	2	10	.242	14	37	8	63	92	3	.981
	— Columbus (I.L.).........	2B	11	44	8	15	4	0	2	6	.341	4	6	1	15	39	0	1.000
1998—	Syracuse (I.L.)■	2B-DH	80	291	58	82	22	3	17	39	.282	39	60	18	133	211	8	.977
	— St. Louis (N.L.)■	2B-OF-SS	53	153	18	33	5	0	4	14	.216	13	48	5	79	109	7	.964
1999—	Toronto (A.L.)■......	2B-DH	37	116	17	31	7	0	6	20	.267	10	23	0	60	92	6	.962
American League totals (8 years)			628	1835	235	462	104	11	32	203	.252	132	377	56	998	1590	70	.974
National League totals (1 year)			53	153	18	33	5	0	4	14	.216	13	48	5	79	109	7	.964
Major League totals (9 years)			681	1988	253	495	109	11	36	217	.249	145	425	61	1077	1699	77	.973

DIVISION SERIES RECORD

Year	Team (League)	Pos.	G	AB	R	H	2B	3B	HR	RBI	Avg.	BB	SO	SB	PO	A	E	Avg.
1995—	New York (A.L.)..........	2B-PR	5	3	3	0	0	0	0	1	.000	1	3	0	2	4	0	1.000

KELLY, ROBERTO — OF — YANKEES

K

PERSONAL: Born October 1, 1964, in Panama City, Panama. ... 6-2/198. ... Bats right, throws right. ... Full name: Roberto Conrado Kelly.

HIGH SCHOOL: Panama City (Panama).

COLLEGE: Jose Dolores Moscote College (Panama).

TRANSACTIONS/CAREER NOTES: Signed as non-drafted free agent by New York Yankees organization (February 21, 1982). ... On disabled list (July 10-August 23, 1986). ... On New York disabled list (June 29-September 1, 1988; May 26-June 12, 1989; and July 6-August 13, 1991). ... Traded by Yankees to Cincinnati Reds for OF Paul O'Neill and 1B Joe DeBerry (November 3, 1992). ... On disabled list (July 14, 1993-remainder of season). ... Traded by Reds with P Roger Etheridge to Atlanta Braves for OF Deion Sanders (May 29, 1994). ... Traded by Braves with OF Tony Tarasco and P Esteban Yan to Montreal Expos for OF Marquis Grissom (April 6, 1995). ... Traded by Expos with P Joey Eischen to Los Angeles Dodgers for OF Henry Rodriguez and IF Jeff Treadway (May 23, 1995). ... Granted free agency (November 6, 1995). ... Signed by Minnesota Twins (January 29, 1996). ... On disabled list (June 27-July 12, 1996). ... On Minnesota disabled list (March 24-April 16, 1997); included rehabilitation assignment to Fort Myers (April 11-16). ... Traded by Twins to Seattle Mariners for two players to be named later (August 20, 1997); Twins acquired P Joe Mays and P Jeromy Palki to complete deal (October 9, 1997). ... Granted free agency (October 31, 1997). ... Signed by Texas Rangers (December 9, 1997). ... On disabled list (April 27-June 6, 1998). ... Granted free agency (October 28, 1999). ... Signed by Yankees organization (January 26, 2000).

RECORDS: Holds major league single-season record for most times reaching base on catcher's interference—8 (1992). ... Shares major league single-season record for fewest double plays by outfielder (150 or more games)—0 (1990).

STATISTICAL NOTES: Led International League outfielders with 345 total chances in 1987. ... Led A.L. outfielders with 430 total chances in 1990. ... Career major league grand slams: 2.

MISCELLANEOUS: Batted as switch hitter (1985).

Year	Team (League)	Pos.	G	AB	R	H	2B	3B	HR	RBI	Avg.	BB	SO	SB	PO	A	E	Avg.
1982—	GC Yankees (GCL)......	SS-OF	31	86	13	17	1	1	1	18	.198	10	18	3	47	79	19	.869
1983—	Oneonta (NY-P).........	OF-3B	48	167	17	36	1	2	2	17	.216	12	20	12	70	3	5	.936
	— Greensboro (SAL).........	OF-SS	20	49	6	13	0	0	0	3	.265	3	5	3	30	2	0	1.000
1984—	Greensboro (SAL).........	OF-1B	111	361	68	86	13	2	1	26	.238	57	49	42	228	5	4	.983
1985—	Fort Lauderdale (FSL).........	OF	114	417	86	103	4	*13	3	38	.247	58	70	49	187	1	1	.995
1986—	Alb./Colonie (East.)	OF	86	299	42	87	11	4	2	43	.291	29	63	10	206	8	7	.968
1987—	Columbus (I.L.).........	OF	118	471	77	131	19	8	13	62	.278	33	116	*51	*331	4	10	.971
	— New York (A.L.).........	OF-DH	23	52	12	14	3	0	1	7	.269	5	15	9	42	0	2	.955
1988—	New York (A.L.).........	OF-DH	38	77	9	19	4	1	1	7	.247	3	15	5	70	1	1	.986
	— Columbus (I.L.).........	OF	30	120	25	40	8	1	3	16	.333	6	29	11	51	1	0	1.000
1989—	New York (A.L.).........	OF	137	441	65	133	18	3	9	48	.302	41	89	35	353	9	6	.984
1990—	New York (A.L.).........	OF	*162	641	85	183	32	4	15	61	.285	33	148	42	420	5	5	.988
1991—	New York (A.L.).........	OF	126	486	68	130	22	2	20	69	.267	45	77	32	268	4	8	.986
1992—	New York (A.L.).........	OF	152	580	81	158	31	2	10	66	.272	41	96	28	389	8	7	.983
1993—	Cincinnati (N.L.)■	OF	78	320	44	102	17	3	9	35	.319	17	43	21	198	3	1	.995
1994—	Cincinnati (N.L.).........	OF	47	179	29	54	8	0	3	21	.302	11	35	9	118	2	1	.992
	— Atlanta (N.L.)■......	OF	63	255	44	73	15	3	6	24	.286	24	36	10	128	3	2	.985
1995—	Montreal (N.L.)■......	OF	24	95	11	26	4	0	1	9	.274	7	14	4	42	1	0	1.000
	— Los Angeles (N.L.)■..	OF	112	409	47	114	19	2	6	48	.279	15	65	15	183	2	6	.969
1996—	Minnesota (A.L.).........	OF-DH	98	322	41	104	17	4	6	47	.323	23	53	10	203	4	2	.990
1997—	Fort Myers (FSL).........	OF	4	11	2	4	0	0	1	3	.364	4	1	0	6	0	0	1.000
	— Minnesota (A.L.).........	OF-DH	75	247	39	71	19	2	5	37	.287	17	50	7	101	1	0	1.000
	— Seattle (A.L.)■.........	OF-DH	30	121	19	36	7	0	7	22	.298	5	17	2	53	1	0	1.000
1998—	Texas (A.L.)■	OF-DH	75	257	48	83	7	3	16	46	.323	8	46	0	155	5	4	.976
1999—	Texas (A.L.).........	OF	87	290	41	87	17	1	8	37	.300	21	57	6	155	4	3	.981
American League totals (10 years)			1003	3514	508	1018	177	22	98	447	.290	242	663	176	2209	46	34	.985
National League totals (3 years)			324	1258	175	369	63	8	25	137	.293	74	193	59	669	11	10	.986
Major League totals (13 years)			1327	4772	683	1387	240	30	123	584	.291	316	856	235	2878	57	44	.985

DIVISION SERIES RECORD

Year	Team (League)	Pos.	G	AB	R	H	2B	3B	HR	RBI	Avg.	BB	SO	SB	PO	A	E	Avg.
1995—	Los Angeles (N.L.)	OF	3	11	0	4	0	0	0	0	.364	1	0	0	8	0	1	.889
1997—	Seattle (A.L.)..............	OF-PH	4	13	1	4	3	0	0	1	.308	0	3	0	4	0	0	1.000
1998—	Texas (A.L.)..............	OF	2	7	0	1	1	0	0	0	.143	0	2	0	3	0	0	1.000
1999—	Texas (A.L.)................	OF	1	3	0	1	0	0	0	0	.333	0	2	0	1	0	0	1.000
Division series totals (4 years)			10	34	1	10	4	0	0	1	.294	1	7	0	16	0	1	.941

ALL-STAR GAME RECORD

Year	League	Pos.	AB	R	H	2B	3B	HR	RBI	Avg.	BB	SO	SB	PO	A	E	Avg.
								BATTING							FIELDING		
1992— American		OF	2	0	1	1	0	0	2	.500	0	1	0	1	0	0	1.000
1993— National		OF	1	0	0	0	0	0	0	.000	0	1	0	0	1	0	1.000
All-Star Game totals (2 years)			3	0	1	1	0	0	2	.333	0	2	0	1	1	0	1.000

KENDALL, JASON — C — PIRATES

K

PERSONAL: Born June 26, 1974, in San Diego. ... 6-0/195. ... Bats right, throws right. ... Full name: Jason Daniel Kendall. ... Son of Fred Kendall, former coach, Detroit Tigers; and catcher/first baseman with three major league teams (1969-80).
HIGH SCHOOL: Torrance (Calif.).
TRANSACTIONS/CAREER NOTES: Selected by Pittsburgh Pirates organization in first round (23rd pick overall) of free-agent draft (June 1, 1992). ... On suspended list (July 21-23, 1998). ... On disabled list (July 5, 1999-remainder of season).
HONORS: Named Southern League Most Valuable Player (1995). ... Named N.L. Rookie Player of the Year by THE SPORTING NEWS (1996).
STATISTICAL NOTES: Led Gulf Coast League with 13 passed balls in 1992. ... Led Southern League with .414 on-base percentage in 1995. ... Led Southern League catchers with 754 total chances in 1995. ... Led N.L. catchers with 20 double plays in 1997. ... Led N.L. in being hit by pitch with 31 in 1998. ... Led N.L. catchers with 1,082 total chances in 1998. ... Had 16-game hitting streak (May 20-June 7, 1999). ... Led N.L. catchers with 13 double plays in 1999.

								BATTING							FIELDING		
Year	Team (League)	Pos.	G	AB	R	H	2B	3B	HR	RBI	Avg.	BB	SO	SB	PO	A	E	Avg.
1992— GC Pirates (GCL)		C	33	111	7	29	2	0	0	10	.261	8	9	2	182	36	5	.978
1993— Augusta (SAL)		C	102	366	43	101	17	4	1	40	.276	22	30	8	472	65	20	.964
1994— Salem (Caro.)		C	101	371	68	118	19	2	7	66	.318	47	21	14	409	33	9	.980
— Carolina (Sou.)		C	13	47	6	11	2	0	0	6	.234	2	3	0	54	9	2	.969
1995— Carolina (Sou.)		C	117	429	87	140	26	1	8	71	.326	56	22	10	*692	54	8	.989
1996— Pittsburgh (N.L.)		C	130	414	54	124	23	5	3	42	.300	35	30	5	797	71	*18	.980
1997— Pittsburgh (N.L.)		C	144	486	71	143	36	4	8	49	.294	49	53	18	952	*103	11	.990
1998— Pittsburgh (N.L.)		C	149	535	95	175	36	3	12	75	.327	51	51	26	*1015	58	9	.992
1999— Pittsburgh (N.L.)		C	78	280	61	93	20	3	8	41	.332	38	32	22	505	48	7	.988
Major League totals (4 years)			501	1715	281	535	115	15	31	207	.312	173	166	71	3269	280	45	.987

ALL-STAR GAME RECORD

								BATTING							FIELDING		
Year	League	Pos.	AB	R	H	2B	3B	HR	RBI	Avg.	BB	SO	SB	PO	A	E	Avg.
1996— National		C	0	0	0	0	0	0	0	...	0	0	0	0	0	0	...
1998— National		PH	1	0	1	0	0	0	0	1.000	0	0	0	...	...	...	...
All-Star Game totals (2 years)			1	0	1	0	0	0	0	1.000	0	0	0	0	0	0	...

KENNEDY, ADAM — 2B/SS — CARDINALS

PERSONAL: Born January 10, 1976, in Riverside, Calif. ... 6-2/180. ... Bats left, throws right. ... Full name: Adam Thomas Kennedy.
HIGH SCHOOL: J.W. North (Riverside, Calif.).
COLLEGE: Cal State Northridge.
TRANSACTIONS/CAREER NOTES: Selected by St. Louis Cardinals organization in first round (20th pick overall) of free-agent draft (June 3, 1997). ... On Memphis disabled list (June 9-19, 1999).

								BATTING							FIELDING		
Year	Team (League)	Pos.	G	AB	R	H	2B	3B	HR	RBI	Avg.	BB	SO	SB	PO	A	E	Avg.
1997— New Jersey (NY-P)		SS	29	114	20	39	6	3	0	19	.342	13	10	9	41	96	7	.951
— Prince William (Caro.)		SS	35	154	24	48	9	3	1	27	.312	6	17	4	63	92	10	.939
1998— Prince William (Caro.)		2B-SS	17	69	9	18	6	0	0	7	.261	5	12	5	26	49	5	.938
— Arkansas (Texas)		SS-2B	52	205	35	57	11	2	6	24	.278	8	21	6	91	143	15	.940
— Memphis (PCL)		SS-2B	74	305	36	93	22	7	4	41	.305	12	42	15	128	225	10	.972
1999— Memphis (PCL)		2-S-O-3-DH	91	367	69	120	22	4	10	63	.327	29	36	20	160	206	18	.953
— St. Louis (N.L.)		2B	33	102	12	26	10	1	1	16	.255	3	8	0	68	64	4	.971
Major League totals (1 year)			33	102	12	26	10	1	1	16	.255	3	8	0	68	64	4	.971

KENT, JEFF — 2B — GIANTS

PERSONAL: Born March 7, 1968, in Bellflower, Calif. ... 6-1/205. ... Bats right, throws right. ... Full name: Jeffrey Franklin Kent.
HIGH SCHOOL: Edison (Huntington Beach, Calif.).
COLLEGE: California.
TRANSACTIONS/CAREER NOTES: Selected by Toronto Blue Jays organization in 20th round of free-agent draft (June 5, 1989). ... Traded by Blue Jays with a player to be named later to New York Mets for P David Cone (August 27, 1992); Mets acquired OF Ryan Thompson to complete deal (September 1, 1992). ... On disabled list (July 6-21, 1995). ... Traded by New York Mets with IF Jose Vizcaino to Cleveland Indians for 2B Carlos Baerga and IF Alvaro Espinoza (July 29, 1996). ... Traded by Indians with IF Jose Vizcaino, P Julian Tavarez and a player to be named later to San Francisco Giants for 3B Matt Williams and a player to be named later (November 13, 1996); Indians traded P Joe Roa to Giants for OF Trenidad Hubbard to complete deal (December 16, 1996). ... On suspended list (August 22-25, 1997). ... On disabled list (June 10-July 10, 1998; and August 3-21, 1999).
STATISTICAL NOTES: Led Florida State League second basemen with 680 total chances and 83 double plays in 1990. ... Led Southern League second basemen with 673 total chances and 96 double plays in 1991. ... Led N.L. second basemen in errors with 18 in 1993 and 20 in 1998. ... Tied for N.L. lead with 10 sacrifice flies in 1998. ... Hit for the cycle (May 3, 1999). ... Career major league grand slams: 8.

Year	Team (League)	Pos.	G	AB	R	H	2B	3B	HR	RBI	Avg.	BB	SO	SB	PO	A	E	Avg.
1989— St. Catharines (NY-P) .	SS-3B	73	268	34	60	14	1	*13	37	.224	33	81	5	103	178	29	.906
1990— Dunedin (FSL)	2B	132	447	72	124	32	2	16	60	.277	53	98	17	*261	*404	15	.978
1991— Knoxville (Sou.)........	2B	•139	445	68	114	*34	1	2	61	.256	80	104	25	249	*395	*29	.957
1992— Toronto (A.L.)...........	3B-2B-1B	65	192	36	46	13	1	8	35	.240	20	47	2	62	112	11	.941
— New York (N.L.)■	2B-SS-3B	37	113	16	27	8	1	3	15	.239	7	29	0	62	93	3	.981
1993— New York (N.L.).........	2B-3B-SS	140	496	65	134	24	0	21	80	.270	30	88	4	261	341	†22	.965
1994— New York (N.L.).........	2B	107	415	53	121	24	5	14	68	.292	23	84	1	222	337	•14	.976
1995— New York (N.L.).........	2B	125	472	65	131	22	3	20	65	.278	29	89	3	245	354	10	.984
1996— New York (N.L.).........	3B	89	335	45	97	20	1	9	39	.290	21	56	4	75	184	21	.925
— Cleveland (A.L.)■.....1B-2B-3B-DH		39	102	16	27	7	0	3	16	.265	10	22	2	125	46	1	.994
1997— San Fran. (N.L.).........	2B-1B	155	580	90	145	38	2	29	121	.250	48	133	11	405	429	16	.981
1998— San Francisco (N.L.) ..	2B-1B	137	526	94	156	37	3	31	128	.297	48	110	9	279	404	†20	.972
1999— San Francisco (N.L.) ..	2B-1B	98	511	86	148	40	2	23	101	.290	61	112	13	286	326	10	.984
American League totals (2 years)		104	294	52	73	20	1	11	51	.248	30	69	4	187	158	12	.966
National League totals (8 years)		928	3448	514	959	213	17	150	617	.278	267	701	45	1835	2468	116	.974
Major League totals (8 years)		1032	3742	566	1032	233	18	161	668	.276	297	770	49	2022	2626	128	.973

DIVISION SERIES RECORD

RECORDS: Shares single-game record for most home runs—2 (October 3, 1997).

Year	Team (League)	Pos.	G	AB	R	H	2B	3B	HR	RBI	Avg.	BB	SO	SB	PO	A	E	Avg.
1996— Cleveland (A.L.)..........2B-1B-PR-3B		4	8	2	1	1	0	0	0	.125	0	0	0	3	3	0	1.000
1997— San Francisco (N.L.) ..	2B-1B	3	10	2	3	0	0	2	2	.300	2	1	0	19	7	0	1.000
Division series totals (2 years)		7	18	4	4	1	0	2	2	.222	2	1	0	22	10	0	1.000

ALL-STAR GAME RECORD

| | | | | BATTING | | | | | | | | FIELDING | | |
Year	League	Pos.	AB	R	H	2B	3B	HR	RBI	Avg.	BB	SO	SB	PO	A	E	Avg.
1999— National	2B	1	0	0	0	0	0	0	.000	1	0	0	1	2	0	1.000

KIDA, MASAO   P   TIGERS

PERSONAL: Born September 12, 1968, in Tokyo, Japan. ... 6-2/210. ... Throws right, bats right.

TRANSACTIONS/CAREER NOTES: Played with Yomiuri Giants (1989-97) and Orix Blue Wave (1998) of Japan League. ... Signed as non-drafted free agent by Detroit Tigers (December 16, 1998). ... On Detroit disabled list (June 30-July 28, 1999); included rehabilitation assignment to Toledo (July 14-28).

Year	League	W	L	Pct.	ERA	G	GS	CG	ShO	Sv.	IP	H	R	ER	BB	SO
1988— Miami (FSL)■.................		7	17	.292	3.99	27	27	9	1	0	162 1/3	199	88	72	62	100
1989— Yomiuri (Jap. Cen.)■........		2	1	.667	4.62	8	4	1	0	0	37	41	19	19	14	26
1990— Yomiuri (Jap. Cen.)		12	8	.600	2.71	32	17	13	1	7	182 2/3	130	56	55	51	182
1991— Yomiuri (Jap. Cen.)		4	7	.364	6.44	19	5	2	0	1	50 1/3	51	41	36	31	44
1992— Yomiuri (Jap. Cen.)		3	6	.333	4.53	29	11	2	1	0	93 1/3	103	48	47	35	87
1993— Yomiuri (Jap. Cen.)		7	7	.500	3.35	35	17	1	1	2	131 2/3	129	50	49	40	97
1994— Yomiuri (Jap. Cen.)		6	8	.429	4.93	28	13	1	0	1	87 2/3	86	52	48	37	61
1995— Yomiuri (Jap. Cen.)		7	9	.438	3.40	40	12	2	0	1	121 2/3	117	49	46	31	97
1996— Yomiuri (Jap. Cen.)		7	9	.438	3.78	33	16	3	2	2	123 2/3	121	53	52	34	99
1997— Yomiuri (Jap. Cen.)		2	2	.500	1.99	39	0	0	0	7	49 2/3	47	13	11	22	53
1998— Orix (Jap. Pac.)■.............		4	7	.364	4.62	36	13	1	0	16	97 1/3	97	54	50	36	74
1999— Detroit (A.L.)■...............		1	0	1.000	6.26	49	0	0	0	1	64 2/3	73	48	45	30	50
— Toledo (I.L.)......................		0	0	...	3.18	3	0	0	0	0	5 2/3	6	2	2	1	4
Major League totals (1 year)........		1	0	1.000	6.26	49	0	0	0	1	64 2/3	73	48	45	30	50

KILE, DARRYL   P   CARDINALS

PERSONAL: Born December 2, 1968, in Garden Grove, Calif. ... 6-5/212. ... Throws right, bats right. ... Full name: Darryl Andrew Kile.

HIGH SCHOOL: Norco Senior (Calif.).

JUNIOR COLLEGE: Chaffey College (Calif.).

TRANSACTIONS/CAREER NOTES: Selected by Houston Astros organization in 30th round of free-agent draft (June 2, 1987). ... On Tucson disabled list (June 25-July 5, 1992). ... Granted free agency (October 28, 1997). ... Signed by Colorado Rockies (December 4, 1997). ... Traded by Rockies with P Dave Veres and P Luther Hackman to St. Louis Cardinals for P Jose Jimenez, P Manny Aybar, P Rick Croushore and SS Brent Butler (November 16, 1999).

RECORDS: Shares modern N.L. record for most hit batsmen (nine-inning game)—4 (June 2, 1996).

STATISTICAL NOTES: Led N.L. with 15 hit batsmen in 1993. ... Pitched 7-1 no-hit victory against New York (September 8, 1993). ... Tied for N.L. lead with 10 wild pitches in 1994. ... Tied for N.L. lead with 16 hit batsmen in 1996.

MISCELLANEOUS: Appeared in two games as pinch runner (1996). ... Had one sacrifice hit in two appearances as pinch hitter and appeared in one game as pinch runner (1998).

Year	League	W	L	Pct.	ERA	G	GS	CG	ShO	Sv.	IP	H	R	ER	BB	SO
1988— Gulf Coast Astros (GCL).....		5	3	.625	3.17	12	12	0	0	0	59 2/3	48	34	21	33	54
1989— Columbus (Sou.)...............		11	6	.647	2.58	20	20	6	•2	0	125 2/3	74	47	36	68	108
— Tucson (PCL)		2	1	.667	5.96	6	6	1	1	0	25 2/3	33	20	17	13	18
1990— Tucson (PCL)		5	10	.333	6.64	26	23	1	0	0	123 1/3	147	97	91	68	77
1991— Houston (N.L.)		7	11	.389	3.69	37	22	0	0	0	153 2/3	144	81	63	84	100
1992— Houston (N.L.)		5	10	.333	3.95	22	22	2	0	0	125 1/3	124	61	55	63	90
— Tucson (PCL)		4	1	.800	3.99	9	9	0	0	0	56 1/3	50	31	25	32	43
1993— Houston (N.L.)		15	8	.652	3.51	32	26	4	2	0	171 2/3	152	73	67	69	141
1994— Houston (N.L.)		9	6	.600	4.57	24	24	0	0	0	147 2/3	153	84	75	*82	105
1995— Houston (N.L.)		4	12	.250	4.96	25	21	0	0	0	127	114	81	70	73	113
— Tucson (PCL)		2	1	.667	8.51	4	4	0	0	0	24 1/3	29	23	23	12	15

Year League	W	L	Pct.	ERA	G	GS	CG	ShO	Sv.	IP	H	R	ER	BB	SO
1996— Houston (N.L.)	12	11	.522	4.19	35	33	4	0	0	219	233	113	102	97	219
1997— Houston (N.L.)	19	7	.731	2.57	34	34	6	4	0	255²/₃	208	87	73	94	205
1998— Colorado (N.L.)■	13	*17	.433	5.20	36	•35	4	1	0	230¹/₃	257	141	133	96	158
1999— Colorado (N.L.)	8	13	.381	6.61	32	32	1	0	0	190²/₃	225	*150	*140	109	116
Major League totals (9 years)......	92	95	.492	4.32	277	249	21	7	0	1621	1610	871	778	767	1247

DIVISION SERIES RECORD

Year League	W	L	Pct.	ERA	G	GS	CG	ShO	Sv.	IP	H	R	ER	BB	SO
1997— Houston (N.L.)	0	1	.000	2.57	1	1	0	0	0	7	2	2	2	2	4

ALL-STAR GAME RECORD

Year League	W	L	Pct.	ERA	GS	CG	ShO	Sv.	IP	H	R	ER	BB	SO
1993— National						Did not play.								
1997— National						Did not play.								

KIM, BYUNG-HYUN — P — DIAMONDBACKS

PERSONAL: Born January 21, 1979, in Kwangsan-ku Songjunsdon, Korea. ... 5-11/176. ... Throws right, bats right.
HIGH SCHOOL: Kwang-ju (Korea).
MISCELLANEOUS: Member of Korean National team (1997-98).
TRANSACTIONS/CAREER NOTES: Signed as non-drafted free agent by Arizona Diamondbacks organization (February 19, 1999).

Year League	W	L	Pct.	ERA	G	GS	CG	ShO	Sv.	IP	H	R	ER	BB	SO
1999— El Paso (Texas)...................	2	0	1.000	2.11	10	0	0	0	0	21¹/₃	6	5	5	9	32
— Tucson (PCL)	4	0	1.000	2.40	11	3	0	0	1	30	21	9	8	15	40
— Arizona (N.L.)	1	2	.333	4.61	25	0	0	0	1	27¹/₃	20	15	14	20	31
— Ariz. D'backs (Ariz.)...........	0	0	...	0.00	1	1	0	0	0	2	1	0	0	1	2
Major League totals (1 year)........	1	2	.333	4.61	25	0	0	0	1	27¹/₃	20	15	14	20	31

KING, CESAR — C — RANGERS

PERSONAL: Born February 28, 1978, in LaRomana, Dominican Republic. ... 6-0/215. ... Bats right, throws right.
TRANSACTIONS/CAREER NOTES: Signed as non-drafted free agent by Texas Rangers organization (September 4, 1994). ... On Tulsa disabled list (August 1-30, 1998; and May 13-20, 1999).
STATISTICAL NOTES: Led Florida State League catchers with 10 double plays in 1997. ... Led Texas League catchers with 12 double plays and 18 passed balls in 1998. ... Led Texas League catchers with 17 passed balls in 1999.

Year Team (League)	Pos.	G	AB	R	H	2B	3B	HR	RBI	Avg.	BB	SO	SB	PO	A	E	Avg.
1995— Dom. Rangers (DSL)..	C	54	182	33	55	9	0	3	22	.302	22	34	3	277	43	11	.967
1996— Char., S.C. (SAL)........	C	84	276	35	69	10	1	7	28	.250	21	58	8	399	71	14	.971
1997— Charlotte (FSL)........	C-DH-3B	91	307	51	91	14	4	6	37	.296	35	58	8	553	84	10	.985
— Tulsa (Texas)	C-DH	14	45	6	16	1	0	1	8	.356	5	3	0	85	8	3	.969
1998— Tulsa (Texas)	C-DH	90	316	40	70	16	2	3	39	.222	30	68	1	585	73	8	.988
1999— Tulsa (Texas)	C-DH	95	321	41	73	19	2	11	45	.227	32	70	2	614	75	12	.983

KING, CURTIS — P — INDIANS

PERSONAL: Born October 25, 1970, in Norristown, Pa. ... 6-5/205. ... Throws right, bats right. ... Full name: Curtis Albert King.
HIGH SCHOOL: Plymouth-Whitemarsh (Plymouth Meeting, Pa.).
COLLEGE: Philadelphia Textile.
TRANSACTIONS/CAREER NOTES: Selected by St. Louis Cardinals organization in fifth round of free-agent draft (June 2, 1994). ... On Memphis disabled list (April 28-May 6 and May 13-June 12, 1999). ... On St. Louis disabled list (June 21-September 1, 1999); included rehabilitation assignment to Memphis (August 3-September 1). ... Signed by Cleveland Indians organization (January 26, 2000).

Year League	W	L	Pct.	ERA	G	GS	CG	ShO	Sv.	IP	H	R	ER	BB	SO
1994— New Jersey (NY-P)............	1	0	1.000	2.61	5	4	0	0	0	20²/₃	19	7	6	11	14
— Savannah (SAL)	4	1	.800	1.87	8	8	2	2	0	53	37	14	11	9	40
1995— St. Petersburg (FSL)	7	8	.467	2.58	28	21	3	0	0	136	117	49	39	49	65
1996— Arkansas (Texas)...............	0	1	.000	19.80	5	0	0	0	1	5	15	12	11	6	5
— St. Petersburg (FSL)	3	3	.500	2.75	48	0	0	0	30	55²/₃	41	20	17	24	27
1997— Arkansas (Texas)...............	2	3	.400	4.46	32	0	0	0	16	36¹/₃	38	19	18	10	29
— Louisville (A.A.)	2	1	.667	2.05	16	0	0	0	3	22	19	5	5	6	9
— St. Louis (N.L.)	4	2	.667	2.76	30	0	0	0	0	29¹/₃	38	14	9	11	13
1998— Memphis (PCL)..................	0	1	.000	2.10	27	0	0	0	12	25²/₃	31	6	6	6	23
— St. Louis (N.L.)	2	0	1.000	3.53	36	0	0	0	2	51	50	20	20	20	28
1999— Memphis (PCL)..................	2	2	.500	2.61	27	3	0	0	7	31	21	13	9	10	25
— St. Louis (N.L.)..................	0	0	...	18.00	2	0	0	0	0	1	3	2	2	0	1
Major League totals (3 years).......	6	2	.750	3.43	68	0	0	0	2	81¹/₃	91	36	31	31	42

KING, JEFF — 1B

PERSONAL: Born December 26, 1964, in Marion, Ind. ... 6-1/188. ... Bats right, throws right. ... Full name: Jeffrey Wayne King. ... Son of Jack King, minor league catcher (1954-55).
HIGH SCHOOL: Rampart (Colorado Springs, Colo.).
COLLEGE: Arkansas.
TRANSACTIONS/CAREER NOTES: Selected by Chicago Cubs organization in 23rd round of free-agent draft (June 6, 1983); did not sign. ... Selected by Pittsburgh Pirates organization in first round (first pick overall) of free-agent draft (June 2, 1986). ... On Pittsburgh disabled list (May 5-31, 1991); included rehabilitation assignment to Buffalo (May 25-31). ... On Pittsburgh disabled list (June 13-October 7, 1991);

K

included rehabilitation assignment to Buffalo (August 28-September 6). ... On disabled list (May 25-June 9, 1994 and June 16-July 1, 1995). ... Traded by Pirates with SS Jay Bell to Kansas City Royals for 3B Joe Randa, P Jeff Granger, P Jeff Martin and P Jeff Wallace (December 13, 1996). ... On disabled list (August 16-September 1, 1998; and April 19-May 9, 1999). ... Announced retirement (May 24, 1999).

RECORDS: Shares major league single-inning record for most home runs—2 (August 8, 1995, second inning and April 30, 1996, fourth inning).

HONORS: Named College Player of the Year by THE SPORTING NEWS (1986). ... Named third baseman on THE SPORTING NEWS college All-America team (1986).

STATISTICAL NOTES: Led Carolina League with .565 slugging percentage in 1987. ... Led N.L. third basemen with 353 assists and 475 total chances in 1993. ... Led N.L. third basemen with 27 double plays in 1994. ... Led A.L. first basemen in double plays with 135 in 1997. ... Career major league grand slams: 8.

Year Team (League)	Pos.	G	AB	R	H	2B	3B	HR	RBI	Avg.	BB	SO	SB	PO	A	E	Avg.
1986— Prince William (Caro.)	3B	37	132	18	31	4	1	6	20	.235	19	34	1	25	50	8	.904
1987— Salem (Caro.)	1B-3B	90	310	68	86	9	1	26	71	.277	61	88	6	572	106	13	.981
— Harrisburg (East.)	1B	26	100	12	24	7	0	2	25	.240	4	27	0	107	10	1	.992
1988— Harrisburg (East.)	3B	117	411	49	105	21	1	14	66	.255	46	87	5	97	208	24	.927
1989— Buffalo (A.A.)	1B-3B	51	169	26	43	5	2	6	29	.254	57	60	11	213	61	8	.972
— Pittsburgh (N.L.)	1B-3B-2B-SS	75	215	31	42	13	3	5	19	.195	20	34	4	403	59	4	.991
1990— Pittsburgh (N.L.)	3B-1B	127	371	46	91	17	1	14	53	.245	21	50	3	61	215	18	.939
1991— Pittsburgh (N.L.)	3B	33	109	16	26	1	1	4	18	.239	14	15	3	15	62	2	.975
— Buffalo (A.A.)	3B	9	18	3	4	1	1	0	2	.222	6	3	1	2	8	1	.909
1992— Pittsburgh (N.L.)	3-2-1-S-O	130	480	56	111	21	2	14	65	.231	27	56	4	368	234	12	.980
— Buffalo (A.A.)	3B-1B-2B	7	29	6	10	2	0	2	5	.345	2	2	1	21	12	0	1.000
1993— Pittsburgh (N.L.)	3B-SS-2B	158	611	82	180	35	3	9	98	.295	59	54	8	108	†362	18	.963
1994— Pittsburgh (N.L.)	3B-2B	94	339	36	89	23	0	5	42	.263	30	38	3	61	198	13	.952
1995— Pittsburgh (N.L.)	3B-1B-2B-SS	122	445	61	118	27	2	18	87	.265	55	63	7	352	206	17	.970
1996— Pittsburgh (N.L.)	1B-2B-3B	155	591	91	160	36	4	30	111	.271	70	95	15	896	252	11	.991
1997— Kansas City (A.L.)■	1B-DH	155	543	84	129	30	1	28	112	.238	89	96	16	1217	*147	5	*.996
1998— Kansas City (A.L.)	1B-DH-3B	131	486	83	128	17	1	24	93	.263	42	73	10	935	91	5	.995
1999— Kansas City (A.L.)	1B-DH	21	72	14	17	2	0	3	11	.236	15	10	2	188	15	2	.990
American League totals (3 years)		307	1101	181	274	49	2	55	216	.249	146	179	28	2340	253	12	.995
National League totals (8 years)		894	3161	419	817	173	16	99	493	.258	296	405	47	2264	1588	95	.976
Major League totals (11 years)		1201	4262	600	1091	222	18	154	709	.256	442	584	75	4604	1841	107	.984

CHAMPIONSHIP SERIES RECORD

Year Team (League)	Pos.	G	AB	R	H	2B	3B	HR	RBI	Avg.	BB	SO	SB	PO	A	E	Avg.
1990— Pittsburgh (N.L.)	3B-PH	5	10	0	1	0	0	0	0	.100	1	5	0	1	4	0	1.000
1992— Pittsburgh (N.L.)	3B	7	29	4	7	4	0	0	2	.241	0	1	0	11	19	1	.968
Championship series totals (2 years)		12	39	4	8	4	0	0	2	.205	1	6	0	12	23	1	.972

KING, RAY   P   CUBS

PERSONAL: Born January 15, 1974, in Chicago. ... 6-1/230. ... Throws left, bats left. ... Full name: Raymond Keith King.
HIGH SCHOOL: Ripley (Tenn.).
COLLEGE: Lambuth (Tenn.).
TRANSACTIONS/CAREER NOTES: Selected by Cincinnati Red organization in eighth round of free-agent draft (June 1, 1995). ... Loaned by Reds organization to Atlanta Braves organization (March 22-June 11, 1996). ... Traded by Reds to Braves (June 11, 1996), completing deal in which Braves traded OF Mike Kelly to Reds for P Chad Fox and a player to be named later (January 9, 1996). ... Traded by Braves to Chicago Cubs for P Jon Ratliff (January 20, 1998).

Year League	W	L	Pct.	ERA	G	GS	CG	ShO	Sv.	IP	H	R	ER	BB	SO
1995— Billings (Pio.)	3	0	1.000	1.67	28	0	0	0	5	43	31	11	8	15	43
1996— Macon (SAL)■	3	5	.375	2.80	18	10	1	0	0	70²/₃	63	34	22	20	63
— Durham (Caro.)	3	6	.333	4.46	14	14	2	0	0	82²/₃	104	54	41	15	52
1997— Greenville (Sou.)	5	5	.500	6.85	12	9	0	0	0	65²/₃	85	53	50	24	42
— Durham (Caro.)	6	9	.400	5.40	24	6	0	0	3	71²/₃	89	54	43	26	60
1998— West Tenn (Sou.)■	1	2	.333	2.43	25	0	0	0	3	29²/₃	23	9	8	10	26
— Iowa (PCL)	1	3	.250	5.01	37	0	0	0	2	32¹/₃	36	20	18	15	26
1999— Iowa (PCL)	4	4	.500	1.88	37	0	0	0	2	43	31	11	9	22	41
— Chicago (N.L.)	0	0	...	5.91	10	0	0	0	0	10²/₃	11	8	7	10	5
Major League totals (1 year)	0	0	...	5.91	10	0	0	0	0	10²/₃	11	8	7	10	5

KINGSALE, GENE   OF   ORIOLES

PERSONAL: Born August 20, 1976, in Oranjestad, Aruba. ... 6-3/194. ... Bats both, throws right. ... Full name: Eugene Humphrey Kingsale.
HIGH SCHOOL: John F. Kennedy Technical School (Oranjestad, Aruba).
TRANSACTIONS/CAREER NOTES: Signed as non-drafted free agent by Baltimore Orioles organization (June 19, 1993). ... On Frederick disabled list (May 29-August 31, 1996). ... On Bowie disabled list (April 8-August 8, 1997).
STATISTICAL NOTES: Tied for Gulf Coast League lead in double plays by outfielder with two in 1994.

Year Team (League)	Pos.	G	AB	R	H	2B	3B	HR	RBI	Avg.	BB	SO	SB	PO	A	E	Avg.
1994— GC Orioles (GCL)	OF-2B	50	168	26	52	2	3	0	9	.310	18	24	15	100	2	3	.971
1995— Bluefield (Appl.)	OF	47	171	45	54	11	2	0	16	.316	27	31	20	95	3	*11	.899
1996— Frederick (Caro.)	OF	49	166	26	45	6	4	0	9	.271	19	32	23	100	1	4	.962
— Baltimore (A.L.)	OF	3	0	0	0	0	0	0	0	...	0	0	0	2	0	0	1.000
1997— Bowie (East.)	OF	13	46	8	19	6	0	0	4	.413	5	4	5	23	0	1	.958
— GC Orioles (GCL)	OF	6	17	2	5	0	0	0	0	.294	2	2	1	16	0	1	.941
1998— Bowie (East.)	OF	111	427	69	112	11	5	1	34	.262	48	79	29	279	9	6	.980
— Rochester (I.L.)	OF-DH	18	55	3	12	1	1	0	2	.218	4	8	3	38	2	0	1.000
— Baltimore (A.L.)	OF-DH	11	2	1	0	0	0	0	0	.000	0	1	0	2	0	0	1.000

Year	Team (League)	Pos.	G	AB	R	H	2B	3B	HR	RBI	Avg.	BB	SO	SB	PO	A	E	Avg.
1999— Bowie (East.)..............		OF	67	268	43	63	11	4	3	23	.235	33	46	13	173	2	4	.978
— Rochester (I.L.).............		OF	48	191	31	59	9	0	2	20	.309	13	23	10	118	1	3	.975
— Baltimore (A.L.).........		OF-DH	28	85	9	21	2	0	0	7	.247	5	13	1	48	1	1	.980
Major League totals (3 years)			42	87	10	21	2	0	0	7	.241	5	14	1	52	1	1	.981

KINKADE, MIKE 3B METS

PERSONAL: Born May 6, 1973, in Livonia, Mich. ... 6-1/210. ... Bats right, throws right. ... Full name: Michael A. Kinkade.
HIGH SCHOOL: Tigard (Ore.).
COLLEGE: Washington State.
TRANSACTIONS/CAREER NOTES: Selected by Milwaukee Brewers organization in ninth round of free-agent draft (June 1, 1995). ... On Louisville disabled list (April 20-May 14, 1998). ... Traded by Brewers to New York Mets for P Bill Pulsipher (July 31, 1998).
HONORS: Named Texas League Player of the Year (1997).
STATISTICAL NOTES: Led Texas League with .455 on-base percentage and tied for league lead with 275 total bases in 1997.

Year	Team (League)	Pos.	G	AB	R	H	2B	3B	HR	RBI	Avg.	BB	SO	SB	PO	A	E	Avg.
1995— Helena (Pio.)	3B-1B-C		69	266	76	94	19	1	4	39	.353	43	38	26	291	79	10	.974
1996— Beloit (Midw.).............	3B-C-1B		135	499	105	151	33	4	15	100	.303	47	69	23	148	310	39	.922
1997— El Paso (Texas)...........	3B-DH		125	468	•112	*180	35	12	12	*109	*.385	52	66	17	*79	249	*60	.845
1998— Louisville (I.L.)	3B-1B-DH		80	291	57	90	24	6	7	46	.309	36	52	10	183	120	15	.953
— Norfolk (I.L.)■.........	3B-1B		30	125	12	35	5	0	1	18	.280	3	24	6	32	61	5	.949
— New York (N.L.)..........	3B		3	2	2	0	0	0	0	0	.000	0	0	0	0	0	0	...
1999— New York (N.L.)...........	OF-3B-C-1B		28	46	3	9	2	1	2	6	.196	3	9	1	18	2	0	1.000
— Norfolk (I.L.)	3-C-1-O-DH		84	312	53	96	20	2	7	49	.308	21	31	7	209	88	10	.967
Major League totals (2 years)			31	48	5	9	2	1	2	6	.188	3	9	1	18	2	0	1.000

DIVISION SERIES RECORD

Year	Team (League)	Pos.	G	AB	R	H	2B	3B	HR	RBI	Avg.	BB	SO	SB	PO	A	E	Avg.
1999— New York (N.L.)								Did not play.										

CHAMPIONSHIP SERIES RECORD

Year	Team (League)	Pos.	G	AB	R	H	2B	3B	HR	RBI	Avg.	BB	SO	SB	PO	A	E	Avg.
1999— New York (N.L.)								Did not play.										

KINNEY, MATT P TWINS

PERSONAL: Born December 16, 1976, in Bangor, Maine. ... 6-4/200. ... Throws right, bats right. ... Full name: Matthew John Kinney.
HIGH SCHOOL: Bangor (Maine).
TRANSACTIONS/CAREER NOTES: Selected by Boston Red Sox organization in sixth round of free-agent draft (June 1, 1995). ... Traded by Red Sox with P Joe Thomas and P John Barnes to Minnesota Twins for P Greg Swindell and 1B Orlando Merced (July 31, 1998). ... On New Britain disabled list (June 7-August 16, 1999).
STATISTICAL NOTES: Led Florida State League with 93 bases on balls and 25 wild pitches in 1998.

Year	League	W	L	Pct.	ERA	G	GS	CG	ShO	Sv.	IP	H	R	ER	BB	SO
1995— Gulf Coast Red Sox (GCL)..		1	3	.250	2.93	8	2	0	0	2	27 2/3	29	13	9	10	11
1996— Lowell (NY-P)..................		3	9	.250	2.68	15	•15	0	0	0	87 1/3	68	51	26	44	72
1997— Michigan (Midw.)		8	5	.615	3.53	22	22	2	1	0	117 1/3	93	59	46	78	123
1998— Sarasota (FSL)		9	6	.600	4.01	22	20	2	1	1	121 1/3	109	70	54	*75	96
— Fort Myers (FSL)■.............		3	2	.600	3.13	7	7	0	0	0	37 1/3	31	18	13	§18	39
1999— New Britain (East.)		4	7	.364	7.12	14	13	0	0	0	60 2/3	69	54	48	36	50
— Gulf Coast Twins (GCL)......		0	1	.000	4.76	3	3	0	0	0	5 2/3	6	4	3	3	8

KLASSEN, DANNY SS/2B DIAMONDBACKS

PERSONAL: Born September 22, 1975, in Learington, Ont. ... 6-0/175. ... Bats right, throws right. ... Full name: Daniel Victor Klassen.
HIGH SCHOOL: John Carroll (Fort Pierce, Fla.).
TRANSACTIONS/CAREER NOTES: Selected by Milwaukee Brewers organization in second round of free-agent draft (June 3, 1993). ... On disabled list (April 7-June 23, 1995 and April 11-22, 1996). ... Selected by Arizona Diamondbacks in second round (37th pick overall) of expansion draft (November 18, 1997). ... On Tucson disabled list (August 13-September 8, 1998; and June 11-August 26, 1999).
STATISTICAL NOTES: Tied for Arizona League lead in intentional bases on balls received with three in 1994.

Year	Team (League)	Pos.	G	AB	R	H	2B	3B	HR	RBI	Avg.	BB	SO	SB	PO	A	E	Avg.
1993— Ariz. Brewers (Ariz.) ...	SS		38	117	26	26	5	0	2	20	.222	24	28	14	45	97	12	.922
— Helena (Pio.)	SS		18	45	8	9	1	0	0	3	.200	7	11	2	25	42	7	.905
1994— Beloit (Midw.).............	SS		133	458	61	119	20	3	6	54	.260	58	123	28	177	328	40	.927
1995— Beloit (Midw.).............	SS-3B		59	218	27	60	15	2	2	25	.275	16	43	12	73	133	18	.920
1996— Stockton (Calif.)........	SS		118	432	58	116	22	4	2	46	.269	34	77	14	186	373	*33	.944
1997— El Paso (Texas)..........	SS		135	519	112	172	30	6	14	81	.331	48	104	16	177	399	*50	.920
1998— Tucson (PCL)■..........	SS-2B		73	281	47	82	25	2	10	47	.292	19	54	6	128	202	8	.976
— Arizona (N.L.)..............	2B		29	108	12	21	2	1	3	8	.194	9	33	1	60	74	5	.964
1999— Tucson (PCL)	SS-DH-2B		64	245	38	66	16	3	6	33	.269	20	51	5	87	193	9	.969
— Ariz. D'backs (Ariz.)....	SS		6	17	2	4	1	0	0	1	.235	1	4	0	4	21	1	.962
— Arizona (N.L.)	PH		1	1	0	1	0	0	0	0	1.000	0	0	0	0	0	0	...
Major League totals (2 years)			30	109	12	22	2	1	3	8	.202	9	33	1	60	74	5	.964

K

PERSONAL: Born June 12, 1971, in Westminster, Calif. ... 6-3/220. ... Bats left, throws left. ... Full name: Ryan Anthony Klesko.
HIGH SCHOOL: Westminster (Calif.).
TRANSACTIONS/CAREER NOTES: Selected by Atlanta Braves organization in fifth round of free-agent draft (June 5, 1989). ... On Atlanta disabled list (May 3-18, 1995); included rehabilitation assignment to Greenville (May 13-17). ... Traded by Braves with 2B Bret Boone and P Jason Shiell to San Diego Padres for 2B Quilvio Veras, 1B Wally Joyner and OF Reggie Sanders (December 22, 1999).
HONORS: Named Southern League Most Valuable Player (1991).
STATISTICAL NOTES: Career major league grand slams: 6.

Year	Team (League)	Pos.	G	AB	R	H	2B	3B	HR	RBI	Avg.	BB	SO	SB	PO	A	E	Avg.
1989—	GC Braves (GCL)	DH	17	57	14	23	5	4	1	16	.404	6	6	4	...	...	...	...
—	Sumter (SAL)	1B	25	90	17	26	6	0	1	12	.289	11	14	1	173	11	4	.979
1990—	Sumter (SAL)	1B	63	231	41	85	15	1	10	38	.368	31	30	13	575	43	14	.978
—	Durham (Caro.)	1B	77	292	40	80	16	1	7	47	.274	32	53	10	490	34	13	.976
1991—	Greenville (Sou.)	1B	126	419	64	122	22	3	14	67	.291	75	60	14	1043	57	*17	.985
1992—	Richmond (I.L.)	1B	123	418	63	105	22	2	17	59	.251	41	72	3	947	51	*11	.989
—	Atlanta (N.L.)	1B	13	14	0	0	0	0	0	1	.000	0	5	0	25	0	0	1.000
1993—	Richmond (I.L.)	1B-OF	98	343	59	94	14	2	22	74	.274	47	69	4	587	45	12	.981
—	Atlanta (N.L.)	1B-OF	22	17	3	6	1	0	2	5	.353	3	4	0	8	0	0	1.000
1994—	Atlanta (N.L.)	OF-1B	92	245	42	68	13	3	17	47	.278	26	48	1	89	3	7	.929
1995—	Atlanta (N.L.)	OF-1B	107	329	48	102	25	2	23	70	.310	47	72	5	131	4	8	.944
—	Greenville (Sou.)	DH-OF	4	13	1	3	0	0	1	4	.231	2	1	0	2	0	0	1.000
1996—	Atlanta (N.L.)	OF-1B	153	528	90	149	21	4	34	93	.282	68	129	6	204	8	5	.977
1997—	Atlanta (N.L.)	OF-1B	143	467	67	122	23	6	24	84	.261	48	130	4	245	6	6	.977
1998—	Atlanta (N.L.)	OF-1B	129	427	69	117	29	1	18	70	.274	56	66	5	195	13	2	.990
1999—	Atlanta (N.L.)	1B-OF-DH	133	404	55	120	28	2	21	80	.297	53	69	5	554	32	6	.990
Major League totals (8 years)			792	2431	374	684	140	18	139	450	.281	301	523	26	1451	66	34	.978

DIVISION SERIES RECORD

RECORDS: Shares career record for most grand slams—1 (September 30, 1998). ... Shares single-inning record for most runs batted in—4 (September 30, 1998). ... Holds N.L. career record for most strikeouts—16. ... Shares N.L. career record for most games—17.

Year	Team (League)	Pos.	G	AB	R	H	2B	3B	HR	RBI	Avg.	BB	SO	SB	PO	A	E	Avg.
1995—	Atlanta (N.L.)	OF	4	15	5	7	1	0	0	1	.467	0	3	0	3	0	0	1.000
1996—	Atlanta (N.L.)	OF	3	8	1	1	0	0	1	1	.125	3	4	1	2	0	1	.667
1997—	Atlanta (N.L.)	OF	3	8	2	2	1	0	1	1	.250	0	2	0	3	0	1	.750
1998—	Atlanta (N.L.)	OF	3	11	1	3	0	0	1	4	.273	0	3	0	5	0	0	1.000
1999—	Atlanta (N.L.)	1B-PH	4	12	3	4	0	0	0	1	.333	1	4	0	22	2	0	1.000
Division series totals (5 years)			17	54	12	17	2	0	3	8	.315	4	16	1	35	2	2	.949

CHAMPIONSHIP SERIES RECORD

Year	Team (League)	Pos.	G	AB	R	H	2B	3B	HR	RBI	Avg.	BB	SO	SB	PO	A	E	Avg.
1995—	Atlanta (N.L.)	OF-PH	4	7	0	0	0	0	0	0	.000	3	4	0	1	0	0	1.000
1996—	Atlanta (N.L.)	OF	6	16	1	4	0	0	1	3	.250	2	6	0	13	0	0	1.000
1997—	Atlanta (N.L.)	OF	5	17	2	4	0	0	2	4	.235	2	3	0	5	0	0	1.000
1998—	Atlanta (N.L.)	OF-PH	5	12	2	1	0	0	0	1	.083	6	3	0	3	0	1	.750
1999—	Atlanta (N.L.)	1B-PH	4	8	1	1	0	0	1	1	.125	2	1	0	27	2	2	.935
Championship series totals (5 years)			24	60	6	10	0	0	4	9	.167	15	17	0	49	2	3	.944

WORLD SERIES RECORD

NOTES: Member of World Series championship team (1995).

Year	Team (League)	Pos.	G	AB	R	H	2B	3B	HR	RBI	Avg.	BB	SO	SB	PO	A	E	Avg.
1995—	Atlanta (N.L.)	OF-DH	6	16	4	5	0	0	3	4	.313	3	4	0	1	0	0	1.000
1996—	Atlanta (N.L.)	DH-OF-1B-PH	5	10	2	1	0	0	0	1	.100	3	4	0	1	0	1	.500
1999—	Atlanta (N.L.)	1B-PH	4	12	0	2	0	0	0	0	.167	0	1	0	21	0	0	1.000
World Series totals (3 years)			15	38	6	8	0	0	3	5	.211	6	9	0	23	0	1	.958

PERSONAL: Born August 22, 1972, in Sunbury, Pa. ... 6-1/215. ... Throws left, bats both. ... Full name: Steven James Kline.
HIGH SCHOOL: Lewisburg (Pa.).
COLLEGE: West Virginia.
TRANSACTIONS/CAREER NOTES: Selected by Cleveland Indians organization in eighth round of free-agent draft (June 3, 1993). ... On disabled list (May 23-August 5, 1995). ... On temporarily inactive list (April 5-20, 1996). ... Traded by Indians to Montreal Expos for P Jeff Juden (July 31, 1997). ... On disabled list (April 11-27, 1999).
STATISTICAL NOTES: Led N.L. pitchers with 41 putouts in 1999.

Year	League	W	L	Pct.	ERA	G	GS	CG	ShO	Sv.	IP	H	R	ER	BB	SO
1993—	Burlington (Appl.)	1	1	.500	4.91	2	1	0	0	0	7 1/3	11	4	4	2	4
—	Watertown (NY-P)	5	4	.556	3.19	13	13	2	1	0	79	77	36	28	12	45
1994—	Columbus (SAL)	*18	5	.783	3.01	28	•28	2	1	0	*185 2/3	175	67	62	36	*174
1995—	Canton/Akron (East.)	2	3	.400	2.42	14	14	0	0	0	89 1/3	86	34	24	30	45
1996—	Canton/Akron (East.)	8	12	.400	5.46	25	24	0	0	0	146 2/3	168	98	89	55	107
1997—	Cleveland (A.L.)	3	1	.750	5.81	20	1	0	0	0	26 1/3	42	19	17	13	17
—	Buffalo (A.A.)	3	3	.500	4.03	20	4	0	0	1	51 1/3	53	26	23	13	41
—	Montreal (N.L.)■	1	3	.250	6.15	26	0	0	0	0	26 1/3	31	18	18	10	20

Year League	W	L	Pct.	ERA	G	GS	CG	ShO	Sv.	IP	H	R	ER	BB	SO
1998—Ottawa (I.L.)	0	0	...	0.00	2	0	0	0	0	$2^2/_3$	1	0	0	0	1
—Montreal (N.L.)	3	6	.333	2.76	78	0	0	0	1	$71^2/_3$	62	25	22	41	76
1999—Montreal (N.L.)	7	4	.636	3.75	*82	0	0	0	0	$69^2/_3$	56	32	29	33	69
A.L. totals (1 year)	3	1	.750	5.81	20	1	0	0	0	$26^1/_3$	42	19	17	13	17
N.L. totals (3 years)	11	13	.458	3.70	186	0	0	0	1	$167^2/_3$	149	75	69	84	165
Major League totals (3 years)	14	14	.500	3.99	206	1	0	0	1	194	191	94	86	97	182

KNOBLAUCH, CHUCK　　　　2B　　　　YANKEES

PERSONAL: Born July 7, 1968, in Houston. ... 5-9/170. ... Bats right, throws right. ... Full name: Edward Charles Knoblauch. ... Son of Ray Knoblauch, minor league pitcher (1947-56); and nephew of Ed Knoblauch, minor league outfielder (1938-42 and 1947-55). ... Name pronounced NOB-lock.

HIGH SCHOOL: Bellaire (Houston).

COLLEGE: Texas A&M.

TRANSACTIONS/CAREER NOTES: Selected by Philadelphia Phillies organization in 18th round of free-agent draft (June 2, 1986); did not sign. ... Selected by Minnesota Twins organization in first round (25th pick overall) of free-agent draft (June 5, 1989). ... Traded by Twins to New York Yankees for P Eric Milton, P Danny Mota, OF Brian Buchanan, SS Cristian Guzman and cash (February 6, 1998).

HONORS: Named A.L. Rookie Player of the Year by THE SPORTING NEWS (1991). ... Named A.L. Rookie of the Year by Baseball Writers' Association of America (1991). ... Named second baseman on THE SPORTING NEWS A.L. All-Star team (1994 and 1997). ... Named second baseman on THE SPORTING NEWS A.L. Silver Slugger team (1995 and 1997). ... Won A.L. Gold Glove at second base (1997).

STATISTICAL NOTES: Had 20-game hitting streak (September 2-25, 1991). ... Led A.L. second basemen with 424 assists, 101 double plays and 718 total chances in 1997. ... Led A.L. in being hit by pitch with 18 in 1998. ... Career major league grand slams: 3.

MISCELLANEOUS: Holds Minnesota Twins all-time record for most stolen bases (276).

Year Team (League)	Pos.	G	AB	R	H	2B	3B	HR	RBI	Avg.	BB	SO	SB	PO	A	E	Avg.
1989—Kenosha (Midw.)	SS	51	196	29	56	13	1	2	19	.286	32	23	9	60	124	21	.898
—Visalia (Calif.)	SS	18	77	20	28	10	0	0	21	.364	6	11	4	23	52	10	.882
1990—Orlando (Sou.)	2B	118	432	74	125	23	6	2	53	.289	63	31	23	275	300	20	.966
1991—Minnesota (A.L.)	2B	151	565	78	159	24	6	1	50	.281	59	40	25	249	460	18	.975
1992—Minnesota (A.L.)	2B-DH-SS	155	600	104	178	19	6	2	56	.297	88	60	34	306	415	6	.992
1993—Minnesota (A.L.)	2B-SS-OF	153	602	82	167	27	4	2	41	.277	65	44	29	302	431	9	.988
1994—Minnesota (A.L.)	2B-SS	109	445	85	139	*45	3	5	51	.312	41	56	35	191	285	3	.994
1995—Minnesota (A.L.)	2B-SS	136	538	107	179	34	8	11	63	.333	78	95	46	254	400	10	.985
1996—Minnesota (A.L.)	2B-DH	153	578	140	197	35	*14	13	72	.341	98	74	45	271	390	8	*.988
1997—Minnesota (A.L.)	2B-DH-SS	156	611	117	178	26	10	9	58	.291	84	84	62	285	†428	12	.983
1998—New York (A.L.)■	2B-DH	150	603	117	160	25	4	17	64	.265	76	70	31	275	408	13	.981
1999—New York (A.L.)	2B	150	603	120	176	36	4	18	68	.292	83	57	28	254	425	*26	.963
Major League totals (9 years)		1313	5145	950	1533	271	59	78	523	.298	672	580	335	2387	3642	105	.983

DIVISION SERIES RECORD

Year Team (League)	Pos.	G	AB	R	H	2B	3B	HR	RBI	Avg.	BB	SO	SB	PO	A	E	Avg.
1998—New York (A.L.)	2B	3	11	0	1	0	0	0	0	.091	0	4	0	4	10	1	.933
1999—New York (A.L.)	2B	3	12	1	2	0	0	0	0	.167	1	3	0	2	11	1	.929
Division series totals (2 years)		6	23	1	3	0	0	0	0	.130	1	7	0	6	21	2	.931

CHAMPIONSHIP SERIES RECORD

Year Team (League)	Pos.	G	AB	R	H	2B	3B	HR	RBI	Avg.	BB	SO	SB	PO	A	E	Avg.
1991—Minnesota (A.L.)	2B	5	20	5	7	2	0	0	3	.350	3	3	2	8	14	0	1.000
1998—New York (A.L.)	2B	6	25	4	5	1	0	0	0	.200	4	2	0	9	17	0	1.000
1999—New York (A.L.)	2B	5	18	3	6	1	0	0	1	.333	3	0	1	8	10	1	.947
Championship series totals (3 years)		16	63	12	18	4	0	0	4	.286	10	5	3	25	41	1	.985

WORLD SERIES RECORD

NOTES: Member of World Series championship team (1991, 1998 and 1999).

Year Team (League)	Pos.	G	AB	R	H	2B	3B	HR	RBI	Avg.	BB	SO	SB	PO	A	E	Avg.
1991—Minnesota (A.L.)	2B	7	26	3	8	1	0	0	2	.308	4	2	4	15	14	1	.967
1998—New York (A.L.)	2B	4	16	3	6	0	0	1	3	.375	3	2	1	7	10	1	.944
1999—New York (A.L.)	2B	4	16	5	5	1	0	1	3	.313	1	3	1	10	10	0	1.000
World Series totals (3 years)		15	58	11	19	2	0	2	8	.328	8	7	6	32	34	2	.971

ALL-STAR GAME RECORD

Year League	Pos.	AB	R	H	2B	3B	HR	RBI	Avg.	BB	SO	SB	PO	A	E	Avg.
1992—American	PH-2B	1	0	0	0	0	0	0	.000	1	0	0	0	0	0	...
1994—American	2B	3	1	0	0	0	0	0	.000	0	2	0	1	2	0	1.000
1996—American	2B	1	0	1	0	0	0	0	1.000	0	0	0	3	1	0	1.000
1997—American	2B	0	0	0	0	0	0	0	...	0	0	0	1	1	0	1.000
All-Star Game totals (4 years)		5	1	1	0	0	0	0	.200	1	2	0	5	4	0	1.000

KNORR, RANDY　　　　C　　　　PIRATES

PERSONAL: Born November 12, 1968, in San Gabriel, Calif. ... 6-2/215. ... Bats right, throws right. ... Full name: Randy Duane Knorr. ... Name pronounced NOR.

HIGH SCHOOL: Baldwin Park (Calif.).

TRANSACTIONS/CAREER NOTES: Selected by Toronto Blue Jays organization in 10th round of free-agent draft (June 2, 1986). ... On disabled list (June 24-July 4, 1986 and May 10, 1989-remainder of season). ... On Syracuse disabled list (May 11-23, 1992). ... On Toronto disabled list (August 20-September 30, 1992). ... On Toronto disabled list (July 1-August 11, 1995); included rehabilitation assignment to Syracuse (July 21-August 9). ... Traded by Blue Jays to Houston Astros for cash (May 17, 1996). ... Granted free agency (December 20, 1996). ... Re-signed by Astros organization (December 23, 1996). ... On Houston disabled list (August 29-September 6, 1997); included rehabilitation assignment to New Orleans (August 29-September 6). ... Granted free agency (October 14, 1997). ... Signed by Florida Marlins organization (December 22, 1997). ... On Charlotte disabled list (April 24-May 22, 1998). ... Granted free agency (September 29, 1998). ... Signed by Astros organization (January 21, 1999). ... Granted free agency (October 20, 1999). ... Signed by Pittsburgh Pirates organization (December 20, 1999).

STATISTICAL NOTES: Led South Atlantic League catchers with 960 total chances and 25 passed balls in 1988.

Year	Team (League)	Pos.	G	AB	R	H	2B	3B	HR	RBI	Avg.	BB	SO	SB	PO	A	E	Avg.
1986—	Medicine Hat (Pio.)	1B	55	215	21	58	13	0	4	52	.270	17	53	0	451	29	10	.980
1987—	Myrtle Beach (SAL)	C-1B-2B	46	129	17	34	4	0	6	21	.264	6	46	0	95	7	1	.990
—	Medicine Hat (Pio.) ...	C	26	106	21	31	7	0	10	24	.292	5	26	0	70	5	4	.949
1988—	Myrtle Beach (SAL)	C	117	364	43	85	13	0	9	42	.234	41	91	0	*870	75	15	.984
1989—	Dunedin (FSL)	C	33	122	13	32	6	0	6	23	.262	6	21	0	186	20	2	.990
1990—	Knoxville (Sou.)	C	116	392	51	108	12	1	13	64	.276	31	83	0	599	72	15	.978
1991—	Knoxville (Sou.)	C-1B	24	74	7	13	4	0	0	4	.176	10	18	2	136	16	2	.987
—	Syracuse (I.L.)..........	C	91	342	29	89	20	0	5	44	.260	23	58	1	477	49	7	.987
—	Toronto (A.L.)..........	C	3	1	0	0	0	0	0	0	.000	1	1	0	6	1	0	1.000
1992—	Syracuse (I.L.)..........	C	61	228	27	62	13	1	11	27	.272	17	38	1	220	22	3	.988
—	Toronto (A.L.)..........	C	8	19	1	5	0	0	1	2	.263	1	5	0	33	3	0	1.000
1993—	Toronto (A.L.)..........	C	39	101	11	25	3	2	4	20	.248	9	29	0	168	20	0	1.000
1994—	Toronto (A.L.)..........	C	40	124	20	30	2	0	7	19	.242	10	35	0	247	21	2	.993
1995—	Toronto (A.L.)..........	C	45	132	18	28	8	0	3	16	.212	11	28	0	243	22	8	.971
—	Syracuse (I.L.)..........	C-DH	18	67	6	18	5	1	1	6	.269	5	14	0	129	14	3	.979
1996—	Syracuse (I.L.)..........	C-DH	12	36	1	10	5	0	0	5	.278	5	8	0	53	2	0	1.000
—	Houston (N.L.)■	C	37	87	7	17	5	0	1	7	.195	5	18	0	204	14	0	1.000
1997—	New Orleans (A.A.).....	C	72	244	22	58	10	0	5	27	.238	22	38	0	502	54	9	.984
—	Houston (N.L.)	C-1B	4	8	1	3	0	0	1	1	.375	0	2	0	19	3	0	1.000
1998—	Charlotte (I.L.)■	C-DH	68	201	30	66	15	0	7	39	.328	34	41	1	349	25	9	.977
—	Florida (N.L.)	C	15	49	4	10	4	1	2	11	.204	1	10	0	82	7	1	.989
1999—	New Orleans (PCL)■..C-1B-DH-OF		77	270	33	95	22	1	11	41	.352	20	41	0	437	40	7	.986
—	Houston (N.L.)	C	30	30	2	5	1	0	0	0	.167	1	8	0	54	3	0	1.000
American League totals (5 years)			135	377	50	88	13	2	15	57	.233	32	98	0	697	67	10	.987
National League totals (4 years)			69	174	14	35	10	1	4	19	.201	7	38	0	359	27	1	.997
Major League totals (9 years)			204	551	64	123	23	3	19	76	.223	39	136	0	1056	94	11	.991

CHAMPIONSHIP SERIES RECORD

Year	Team (League)	Pos.	G	AB	R	H	2B	3B	HR	RBI	Avg.	BB	SO	SB	PO	A	E	Avg.
1992—	Toronto (A.L.)								Did not play.									
1993—	Toronto (A.L.)								Did not play.									

WORLD SERIES RECORD

NOTES: Member of World Series championship team (1992 and 1993).

Year	Team (League)	Pos.	G	AB	R	H	2B	3B	HR	RBI	Avg.	BB	SO	SB	PO	A	E	Avg.
1992—	Toronto (A.L.)								Did not play.									
1993—	Toronto (A.L.)	C	1	0	0	0	0	0	0	0	...	0	0	0	3	0	0	1.000

KOCH, BILLY — P — BLUE JAYS

PERSONAL: Born December 14, 1974, in Rockville Center, N.Y. ... 6-3/205. ... Throws right, bats right. ... Full name: William Christopher Koch.
HIGH SCHOOL: West Babylon (N.Y.).
COLLEGE: Clemson.
TRANSACTIONS/CAREER NOTES: Selected by Toronto Blue Jays organization in first round (fourth pick overall) of free-agent draft (June 4, 1996). ... On disabled list (April 14, 1997-remainder of season).
RECORDS: Holds A.L. rookie-season record for most saves—31 (1999).
MISCELLANEOUS: Member of 1996 U.S. Olympic baseball team.

Year	League	W	L	Pct.	ERA	G	GS	CG	ShO	Sv.	IP	H	R	ER	BB	SO
1997—	Dunedin (FSL)...................	0	1	.000	2.49	3	3	0	0	0	21²/₃	27	10	6	3	20
1998—	Dunedin (FSL)...................	•14	7	.667	3.75	25	25	0	0	0	124²/₃	120	65	52	41	108
—	Syracuse (I.L.)..................	0	1	.000	14.29	2	2	0	0	0	5²/₃	9	9	9	5	9
1999—	Syracuse (I.L.)..................	3	0	1.000	3.86	5	5	0	0	0	25²/₃	27	11	11	10	22
—	Toronto (A.L.)..................	0	5	.000	3.39	56	0	0	0	31	63²/₃	55	26	24	30	57
Major League totals (1 year)........		0	5	.000	3.39	56	0	0	0	31	63²/₃	55	26	24	30	57

KOLB, BRANDON — P — PADRES

PERSONAL: Born November 20, 1973, in Oakland. ... 6-1/190. ... Throws right, bats right. ... Full name: Brandon Charles Kolb.
HIGH SCHOOL: Danville (Calif.).
COLLEGE: Texas Tech.
TRANSACTIONS/CAREER NOTES: Selected by San Diego Padres organization in fourth round of free-agent draft (June 1, 1995). ... On Las Vegas disabled list (July 27-August 20, 1999).

Year	League	W	L	Pct.	ERA	G	GS	CG	ShO	Sv.	IP	H	R	ER	BB	SO
1995—	Idaho Falls (Pio.)...............	2	3	.400	7.04	9	8	0	0	0	38¹/₃	42	33	30	29	21
—	Arizona Padres (Ariz.)	1	1	.500	1.17	4	4	1	•1	0	23	13	10	3	13	21

Year	League	W	L	Pct.	ERA	G	GS	CG	ShO	Sv.	IP	H	R	ER	BB	SO
1996—Clinton (Midw.)		*16	9	.640	3.42	27	27	3	0	0	181 1/3	170	84	69	76	138
1997—Rancho Cuca. (Calif.)		3	2	.600	3.00	10	10	0	0	0	63	60	29	21	22	49
1998—Mobile (Sou.)		4	3	.571	4.50	21	6	0	0	1	62	46	33	31	40	58
—Rancho Cuca. (Calif.)		0	2	.000	3.05	4	4	0	0	0	20 2/3	14	8	7	18	16
1999—Mobile (Sou.)		0	2	.000	0.79	7	0	0	0	2	11 1/3	8	4	1	4	14
—Las Vegas (PCL)		2	1	.667	3.94	42	0	0	0	4	61 2/3	72	36	27	29	63

KOLB, DANNY   P   RANGERS

PERSONAL: Born March 29, 1975, in Sterling, Ill. ... 6-4/215. ... Throws right, bats right. ... Full name: Daniel Lee Kolb. ... Cousin of Gary Kolb, outfielder with four major league teams (1960-69).
HIGH SCHOOL: Walnut (Ill.).
JUNIOR COLLEGE: Sauk Valley Community College (Ill.).
TRANSACTIONS/CAREER NOTES: Selected by Minnesota Twins organization in 17th round of free-agent draft (June 3, 1993); did not sign. ... Selected by Texas Rangers organization in sixth round of free-agent draft (June 3, 1995). ... On Texas disabled list (October 3, 1999-remainder of season).
STATISTICAL NOTES: Pitched six-inning, 3-0 no-hit victory against Columbus (June 12, 1996). ... Tied for Appalachian League lead with 22 hit batsmen in 1996.

Year	League	W	L	Pct.	ERA	G	GS	CG	ShO	Sv.	IP	H	R	ER	BB	SO
1995—Gulf Coast Twins (GCL)......		1	7	.125	2.21	12	11	0	0	0	53	38	22	13	28	46
1996—Charleston, S.C. (SAL)		8	6	.571	2.57	20	20	4	2	0	126	80	50	36	60	127
—Charlotte (FSL)		2	2	.500	4.26	6	6	0	0	0	38	38	18	18	14	28
—Tulsa (Texas)		1	0	1.000	0.77	2	2	0	0	0	11 2/3	5	1	1	8	7
1997—Charlotte (FSL)		4	10	.286	4.87	24	23	3	0	0	133	146	91	72	62	83
—Tulsa (Texas)		0	2	.000	4.76	2	2	0	0	0	11 1/3	7	7	6	11	6
1998—Tulsa (Texas)		12	11	.522	4.82	28	28	2	0	0	162 1/3	187	104	87	76	83
—Oklahoma (PCL)		0	0	...	0.00	1	0	0	0	0	1	1	0	0	1	0
1999—Tulsa (Texas)		1	2	.333	2.79	7	7	1	1	0	38 2/3	38	16	12	18	32
—Oklahoma (PCL)		5	3	.625	5.10	11	8	0	0	0	60	74	35	34	27	21
—Texas (A.L.)		2	1	.667	4.65	16	0	0	0	0	31	33	18	16	15	15
Major League totals (1 year)........		2	1	.667	4.65	16	0	0	0	0	31	33	18	16	15	15

KONERKO, PAUL   1B/3B   WHITE SOX

PERSONAL: Born March 5, 1976, in Providence, R.I. ... 6-3/211. ... Bats right, throws right. ... Full name: Paul Henry Konerko.
HIGH SCHOOL: Chaparral (Scottsdale, Ariz.).
TRANSACTIONS/CAREER NOTES: Selected by Los Angeles Dodgers organization in first round (13th pick overall) of free-agent draft (June 2, 1994). ... Traded by Dodgers with P Dennis Reyes to Cincinnati Reds for P Jeff Shaw (July 4, 1998). ... Traded by Reds to Chicago White Sox for OF Mike Cameron (November 11, 1998).
HONORS: Named Pacific Coast League Most Valuable Player (1997).
STATISTICAL NOTES: Led Northwest League with seven sacrifice flies in 1994. ... Led Pacific Coast League with 300 total bases and .621 slugging percentage in 1997. ... Career major league grand slams: 1.

Year	Team (League)	Pos.	G	AB	R	H	2B	3B	HR	RBI	Avg.	BB	SO	SB	PO	A	E	Avg.
1994—Yakima (N.W.)		C-DH	67	257	25	74	15	2	6	*58	.288	36	52	1	271	33	5	.984
1995—San Bern. (Calif.)........		C-DH	118	448	7	124	21	1	19	77	.277	59	88	3	676	68	11	.985
1996—San Antonio (Texas)...		1B-DH	133	470	78	141	23	2	29	86	.300	72	85	1	1114	92	14	.989
—Albuquerque (PCL)......		1B	4	14	2	6	0	0	1	2	.429	1	2	0	30	0	0	1.000
1997—Albuquerque (PCL)......		3-1-DH-2	130	483	97	156	31	1	*37	*127	.323	64	61	2	257	216	24	.952
—Los Angeles (N.L.)		1B-3B	6	7	0	1	0	0	0	0	.143	1	2	0	3	0	0	1.000
1998—Los Angeles (N.L.)...1B-3B-OF-DH			49	144	14	31	1	0	4	16	.215	10	30	1	187	30	2	.991
—Albuquerque (PCL)......		OF-1B-3B	24	87	16	33	10	0	6	26	.379	11	12	0	61	3	3	.955
—Cincinnati (N.L.)■.......		3B-1B-OF	26	73	7	16	3	0	3	13	.219	6	10	0	48	24	0	1.000
—Indianapolis (I.L.)........		3B	39	150	25	49	8	0	8	39	.327	19	18	1	21	68	4	.957
1999—Chicago (A.L.)■....		1B-DH-3B	142	513	71	151	31	4	24	81	.294	45	68	1	740	58	4	.995
American League totals (1 year)			142	513	71	151	31	4	24	81	.294	45	68	1	740	58	4	.995
National League totals (2 years)			81	224	21	48	4	0	7	29	.214	17	42	0	238	54	2	.993
Major League totals (3 years)			223	737	92	199	35	4	31	110	.270	62	110	1	978	112	6	.995

KOSKIE, COREY   3B/OF   TWINS

PERSONAL: Born June 28, 1973, in Anola, Man. ... 6-3/217. ... Bats left, throws right. ... Full name: Cordel Leonard Koskie.
HIGH SCHOOL: Springfield Collegiate (Oakbank, Man.).
JUNIOR COLLEGE: Des Moines (Iowa) Area Community College.
COLLEGE: Manitoba, then Kwantlen (B.C.).
TRANSACTIONS/CAREER NOTES: Selected by Minnesota Twins organization in 26th round of free-agent draft (June 2, 1994). ... On Fort Myers disabled list (May 10-28 and June 25-July 4, 1996).
STATISTICAL NOTES: Tied for Eastern League lead with 10 intentional bases on balls in 1997. ... Career major league grand slams: 1.

Year	Team (League)	Pos.	G	AB	R	H	2B	3B	HR	RBI	Avg.	BB	SO	SB	PO	A	E	Avg.
1994—Elizabethton (Appl.)....		3B	34	107	13	25	2	1	3	10	.234	18	27	0	23	84	8	.930
1995—Fort Wayne (Midw.).....		3B	123	462	64	143	37	5	8	78	.310	38	79	2	80	244	36	.900
1996—Fort Myers (FSL)		3B	95	338	43	88	19	4	9	55	.260	40	76	1	62	176	19	.926
1997—New Britain (East.)		3B-DH	131	437	88	125	26	6	23	79	.286	90	106	9	72	234	22	.933
1998—Salt Lake (PCL)		3B-DH	135	505	91	152	32	5	26	105	.301	51	104	15	83	250	23	.935
—Minnesota (A.L.)		3B	11	29	2	4	0	0	1	2	.138	2	10	0	6	10	1	.941
1999—Minnesota (A.L.)		3B-OF-DH	117	342	42	106	21	0	11	58	.310	40	72	4	58	143	8	.962
Major League totals (2 years)			128	371	44	110	21	0	12	60	.296	42	82	4	64	153	9	.960

KOTSAY, MARK — OF — MARLINS

PERSONAL: Born December 2, 1975, in Whittier, Calif. ... 6-0/190. ... Bats left, throws left. ... Full name: Mark Steven Kotsay.
HIGH SCHOOL: Santa Fe Springs (Calif.).
COLLEGE: Cal State Fullerton.
TRANSACTIONS/CAREER NOTES: Selected by Florida Marlins organization in first round (ninth pick overall) of free-agent draft (June 4, 1996).
HONORS: Named Golden Spikes Award winner by USA Baseball (1995). ... Named Most Outstanding Player of College World Series (1995).
STATISTICAL NOTES: Tied for Eastern League lead in double plays by outfielder with four in 1997. ... Tied for N.L. lead with 20 assists by outfielder in 1998. ... Led N.L. outfielders with 19 assists in 1999. ... Career major league grand slams: 1.
MISCELLANEOUS: Member of 1996 U.S. Olympic baseball team.

										BATTING					FIELDING		
Year	Team (League)	Pos.	G	AB	R	H	2B	3B	HR	RBI	Avg.	BB	SO	SB	PO	A	E	Avg.
1996— Kane County (Midw.)..		OF	17	60	16	17	5	0	2	8	.283	16	8	3	37	2	0	1.000
1997— Portland (East.)		OF-DH	114	438	*103	134	27	2	20	77	.306	75	65	17	230	12	2	*.992
— Florida (N.L.)		OF	14	52	5	10	1	1	0	4	.192	4	7	3	31	2	0	1.000
1998— Florida (N.L.)		OF-1B	154	578	72	161	25	7	11	68	.279	34	61	10	350	‡21	6	.984
1999— Florida (N.L.)		OF-1B	148	495	57	134	23	9	8	50	.271	29	50	7	349	†27	5	.987
Major League totals (3 years)			316	1125	134	305	49	17	19	122	.271	67	118	20	730	50	11	.986

KREUTER, CHAD — C — DODGERS

PERSONAL: Born August 26, 1964, in Greenbrae, Calif. ... 6-2/200. ... Bats both, throws right. ... Full name: Chad Michael Kreuter. ... Name pronounced CREW-ter.
HIGH SCHOOL: Redwood (Calif.).
COLLEGE: Pepperdine.
TRANSACTIONS/CAREER NOTES: Selected by Texas Rangers organization in fifth round of free-agent draft (June 3, 1985). ... Granted free agency (October 15, 1991). ... Signed by Toledo, Detroit Tigers organization (January 2, 1992). ... Granted free agency (December 23, 1994). ... Signed by Seattle Mariners (April 8, 1995). ... On Seattle disabled list (June 19-July 6, 1995). ... On Tacoma disabled list (August 4-25, 1995). ... Granted free agency (October 16, 1995). ... Signed by Chicago White Sox organization (December 11, 1995). ... On disabled list (July 20, 1996-remainder of season). ... Granted free agency (October 14, 1996). ... Re-signed by White Sox organization (January 29, 1997). ... Traded by White Sox with OF Tony Phillips to Anaheim Angels for P Chuck McElroy and C Jorge Fabregas (May 18, 1997). ... Granted free agency (November 7, 1997). ... Signed by White Sox (December 10, 1997). ... Traded by White Sox to Angels for cash considerations (September 18, 1998). ... Granted free agency (October 26, 1998). ... Signed by Kansas City Royals (December 15, 1998). ... Granted free agency (October 29, 1999). ... Signed by Los Angeles Dodgers organization (January 20, 2000).
RECORDS: Shares major league single-game record for most sacrifice flies—3 (July 30, 1994). ... Shares major league record for most hits in one inning in first major league game—2 (September 14, 1988, fifth inning).
STATISTICAL NOTES: Led Carolina League catchers with 21 errors and 17 double plays and tied for lead with 113 assists in 1986. ... Tied for Texas League lead in double plays by catcher with nine in 1988. ... Led A.L. with 21 passed balls in 1989. ... Switch-hit home runs in one game (September 7, 1993). ... Career major league grand slams: 1.
MISCELLANEOUS: Batted righthanded only (1985 and 1990).

										BATTING					FIELDING		
Year	Team (League)	Pos.	G	AB	R	H	2B	3B	HR	RBI	Avg.	BB	SO	SB	PO	A	E	Avg.
1985— Burlington (Midw.)		C	69	199	25	53	9	0	4	26	.266	38	48	3	349	34	8	.980
1986— Salem (Caro.)		C-OF-3B	125	387	55	85	21	2	6	49	.220	67	82	5	613	†115	†21	.972
1987— Charlotte (FSL)		C-OF-3B	85	281	36	61	18	1	9	40	.217	31	32	1	380	54	8	.982
1988— Tulsa (Texas)		C	108	358	46	95	24	6	3	51	.265	55	66	2	603	71	•13	.981
— Texas (A.L.)		C	16	51	3	14	2	1	1	5	.275	7	13	0	93	8	1	.990
1989— Texas (A.L.)		C	87	158	16	24	3	0	5	9	.152	27	40	0	453	26	4	.992
— Oklahoma City (A.A.)..		C	26	87	10	22	3	0	4	6	.253	13	11	1	146	14	2	.988
1990— Texas (A.L.)		C	22	22	2	1	1	0	0	2	.045	8	9	0	39	4	1	.977
— Oklahoma City (A.A.)..		C	92	291	41	65	17	1	7	35	.223	52	80	0	559	64	10	.984
1991— Texas (A.L.)		C	3	4	0	0	0	0	0	0	.000	0	1	0	5	0	0	1.000
— Oklahoma City (A.A.)..		C	24	70	14	19	6	0	1	12	.271	18	16	2	146	23	7	.960
— Tulsa (Texas)		C	42	128	23	30	5	1	2	10	.234	29	23	1	269	27	4	.987
1992— Detroit (A.L.)■		C-DH	67	190	22	48	9	0	2	16	.253	20	38	0	271	22	5	.983
1993— Detroit (A.L.)		C-DH-1B	119	374	59	107	23	3	15	51	.286	49	92	2	522	70	7	.988
1994— Detroit (A.L.)		C-1B-OF	65	170	17	38	8	0	1	19	.224	28	36	0	280	22	4	.987
1995— Seattle (A.L.)■		C	26	75	12	17	5	0	1	8	.227	5	22	0	151	12	4	.976
— Tacoma (PCL)		C-DH	15	48	6	14	5	0	1	11	.292	8	11	0	70	10	1	.988
1996— Chicago (A.L.)■		C-1B-DH	46	114	14	25	8	0	3	18	.219	13	29	0	182	12	2	.990
1997— Chicago (A.L.)		C-1B	19	37	6	8	2	1	1	3	.216	8	9	0	59	4	2	.969
— Anaheim (A.L.)■		C-DH	70	160	19	51	7	1	4	18	.234	21	57	0	431	29	3	.994
1998— Chicago (A.L.)■		C	93	245	26	62	9	1	2	33	.253	32	45	1	424	35	7	.985
— Anaheim (A.L.)■		C	3	7	1	1	1	0	0	0	.143	1	4	0	14	1	2	.882
1999— Kansas City (A.L.)■ ...		C-DH	107	324	31	73	15	0	5	35	.225	34	65	0	460	44	3	.994
Major League totals (12 years)			743	1989	228	469	93	7	40	217	.236	253	460	3	3384	289	45	.988

KUBENKA, JEFF — P — DIAMONDBACKS

PERSONAL: Born August 24, 1974, in Weimer, Texas. ... 6-1/191. ... Throws left, bats right. ... Full name: Jeffrey S. Kubenka.
HIGH SCHOOL: Schulenburg (Texas).
COLLEGE: St. Mary's (Texas).
TRANSACTIONS/CAREER NOTES: Selected by Los Angeles Dodgers organization in 38th round of free-agent draft (June 4, 1996). ... On Albuquerque disabled list (May 6-July 9, 1998). ... Claimed on waivers by Arizona Diamondbacks (September 20, 1999).

Year	League	W	L	Pct.	ERA	G	GS	CG	ShO	Sv.	IP	H	R	ER	BB	SO
1996— Yakima (N.W.)		5	1	.833	2.51	28	0	0	0	*14	32 1/3	20	11	9	10	61
1997— San Bernardino (Calif.).......		5	1	.833	0.92	34	0	0	0	19	39	24	4	4	11	62
— San Antonio (Texas)		3	0	1.000	0.70	19	0	0	0	4	25 2/3	10	2	2	6	38
— Albuquerque (PCL)		0	2	.000	8.59	8	0	0	0	2	7 1/3	11	9	7	2	10

Year League	W	L	Pct.	ERA	G	GS	CG	ShO	Sv.	IP	H	R	ER	BB	SO
1998— Albuquerque (PCL)............	2	5	.286	2.45	28	0	0	0	9	40 1/3	32	11	11	12	40
— San Antonio (Texas)	0	0	...	7.00	9	0	0	0	0	9	10	11	7	7	10
— Los Angeles (N.L.)	1	0	1.000	0.96	6	0	0	0	0	9 1/3	4	1	1	8	10
1999— Albuquerque (PCL)............	4	4	.500	3.22	51	0	0	0	11	67	62	33	24	23	63
— Los Angeles (N.L.)	0	1	.000	11.74	6	0	0	0	0	7 2/3	13	12	10	4	2
Major League totals (2 years)......	1	1	.500	5.82	12	0	0	0	0	17	17	13	11	12	12

KUBINSKI, TIM   P   ATHLETICS

PERSONAL: Born January 20, 1972, in Pullman, Wash. ... 6-4/205. ... Throws left, bats left. ... Full name: Timothy Mark Kubinski.
HIGH SCHOOL: San Luis Obispo (Calif.).
COLLEGE: UCLA.
TRANSACTIONS/CAREER NOTES: Selected by Oakland Athletics organization in seventh round of free-agent draft (June 3, 1993).
STATISTICAL NOTES: Led Midwest League with 10 balks in 1994.

Year League	W	L	Pct.	ERA	G	GS	CG	ShO	Sv.	IP	H	R	ER	BB	SO
1993— Arizona Athletics (Ariz.)......	0	1	.000	6.00	1	1	0	0	0	3	5	2	2	0	3
— Southern Oregon (N.W.)......	5	5	.500	2.83	12	12	1	0	0	70	67	36	22	18	51
1994— West Michigan (Midw.)	14	6	.700	3.63	30	23	1	0	0	158 2/3	168	82	64	36	126
1995— Modesto (Calif.)	6	10	.375	4.95	25	17	0	0	2	109	126	73	60	24	83
— Edmonton (PCL)	1	2	.333	4.78	6	5	0	0	0	32	34	18	17	10	12
1996— Huntsville (Sou.)	8	7	.533	2.38	43	3	0	0	3	102	84	41	27	36	78
— Edmonton (PCL)	0	0	...	0.00	1	0	0	0	0	1	1	0	0	1	0
1997— Edmonton (PCL)	4	4	.500	4.50	47	0	0	0	7	76	64	39	38	34	53
— Oakland (A.L.)	0	0	...	5.68	11	0	0	0	0	12 2/3	12	9	8	6	10
1998— Edmonton (PCL)	6	5	.545	4.56	57	1	0	0	2	75	77	40	38	22	54
1999— Vancouver (PCL)	5	3	.625	3.44	46	1	0	0	6	73 1/3	70	30	28	27	56
— Oakland (A.L.)	0	0	...	5.84	14	0	0	0	0	12 1/3	14	8	8	5	7
Major League totals (2 years)......	0	0	...	5.76	25	0	0	0	0	25	26	17	16	11	17

KUSIEWICZ, MIKE   P   TWINS

PERSONAL: Born November 1, 1976, in Montreal. ... 6-2/190. ... Throws left, bats right. ... Full name: Michael Edward Kusiewicz.
HIGH SCHOOL: St. Pius X (Nepean, Ont.).
TRANSACTIONS/CAREER NOTES: Selected by Colorado Rockies organization in eighth round of free-agent draft (June 2, 1994). ... On Carolina disabled list (April 8, 1999-entire season); included rehabilitation assignment to Arizona League Rockies (August 15-September 10). ... Claimed on waivers by Minnesota Twins (November 18, 1999).
STATISTICAL NOTES: Led Eastern League with 16 hit batsmen in 1998.

Year League	W	L	Pct.	ERA	G	GS	CG	ShO	Sv.	IP	H	R	ER	BB	SO
1995— Asheville (SAL)..................	8	4	.667	*2.06	21	21	0	0	0	122 1/3	92	40	28	34	103
— Salem (Caro.)	0	0	...	1.50	1	1	0	0	0	6	7	1	1	0	7
1996— New Haven (East.)..............	2	4	.333	3.30	14	14	0	0	0	76 1/3	83	38	28	27	64
— Salem (Caro.)	0	1	.000	5.09	5	3	0	0	1	23	19	15	13	12	18
1997— New Haven (East.)..............	2	4	.333	6.35	10	4	0	0	0	28 1/3	41	28	20	10	11
— Salem (Caro.)	8	6	.571	2.52	19	18	1	1	0	117 2/3	99	44	33	32	107
1998— New Haven (East.)..............	14	7	.667	2.32	27	26	2	0	0	178 2/3	161	59	46	35	151
1999— Arizona Rockies (Ariz.).......	1	3	.250	5.47	6	6	0	0	0	24 2/3	26	16	15	9	27

LAKER, TIM   C   PIRATES

PERSONAL: Born November 27, 1969, in Encino, Calif. ... 6-3/200. ... Bats right, throws right. ... Full name: Timothy John Laker.
HIGH SCHOOL: Simi Valley (Calif.).
JUNIOR COLLEGE: Oxnard (Calif.) College.
TRANSACTIONS/CAREER NOTES: Selected by Kansas City Royals organization in 49th round of free-agent draft (June 2, 1987); did not sign. ... Selected by Montreal Expos organization in sixth round of free-agent draft (June 1, 1988). ... On Ottawa disabled list (April 30-May 14, 1993). ... On disabled list (March 29, 1996-entire season). ... Claimed on waivers by Baltimore Orioles (March 25, 1997). ... On Rochester disabled list (June 5-16, 1997). ... Granted free agency (October 15, 1997). ... Signed by Tampa Bay Devil Rays (December 19, 1997). ... Released by Devil Rays (June 26, 1998). ... Signed by Pittsburgh Pirates organization (July 9, 1998). ... Released by Pirates (December 18, 1998). ... Signed by Los Angeles Dodgers organization (January 6, 1999). ... Traded by Dodgers to Pirates for a player to be named later (March 26, 1999). ... Granted free agency (October 14, 1999). ... Re-signed by Pirates organization (December 20, 1999).
STATISTICAL NOTES: Led New York-Pennsylvania League with 16 passed balls in 1989. ... Led Midwest League catchers with 125 assists, 18 errors and 944 total chances in 1990. ... Tied for International League lead in errors by catcher with 11 in 1993. ... Led International League with 20 passed balls in 1994. ... Tied for Pacific Coast League lead with 12 errors by catcher in 1999.

					BATTING								FIELDING		
Year Team (League)	Pos.	G	AB	R	H	2B	3B	HR	RBI	Avg.	BB	SO	SB	PO	A	E	Avg.
1988— Jamestown (NY-P)	C-OF	47	152	14	34	9	0	0	17	.224	8	30	2	236	22	2	.992
1989— Rockford (Midw.)	C	14	48	4	11	1	1	0	4	.229	3	6	1	91	6	4	.960
— Jamestown (NY-P)	C	58	216	25	48	9	1	2	24	.222	16	40	8	437	61	8	.984
1990— Rockford (Midw.)	C-OF	120	425	46	94	18	3	7	57	.221	32	83	7	802	†125	†18	.981
— W.P. Beach (FSL)........	C	2	3	0	0	0	0	0	0	.000	0	1	0	2	0	0	1.000
1991— Harrisburg (East.).......	C	11	35	4	10	1	0	1	5	.286	2	5	0	67	4	3	.959
— W.P. Beach (FSL)........	C	100	333	35	77	15	2	5	33	.231	22	51	10	560	87	*14	.979
1992— Harrisburg (East.).......	C	117	409	55	99	19	3	15	68	.242	39	89	3	630	62	*14	.980
— Montreal (N.L.)..........	C	28	46	8	10	3	0	0	4	.217	2	14	1	102	8	1	.991
1993— Montreal (N.L.)..........	C	43	86	3	17	2	1	0	7	.198	2	16	2	136	18	2	.987
— Ottawa (I.L.)	C-1B	56	204	26	47	10	0	4	23	.230	21	41	3	341	37	‡11	.972
1994— Ottawa (I.L.)	C-DH	118	424	68	131	32	2	12	71	.309	47	96	11	643	*89	•11	.985

Year Team (League)	Pos.	G	AB	R	H	2B	3B	HR	RBI	Avg.	BB	SO	SB	PO	A	E	Avg.
1995—Montreal (N.L.)..........	C	64	141	17	33	8	1	3	20	.234	14	38	0	265	27	7	.977
1996—Montreal (N.L.)..........						Did not play.											
1997—Rochester (I.L.)■......	DH-C	79	290	45	75	11	1	11	37	.259	34	49	1	283	17	6	.980
—Baltimore (A.L.)..........	C	7	14	0	0	0	0	0	1	.000	2	9	0	28	0	1	.966
1998—Durham (I.L.)■.......	C-DH	40	134	36	32	7	0	11	26	.239	28	32	1	197	19	2	.991
—Tampa Bay (A.L.).......	C-DH	3	5	1	1	0	0	0	0	.200	1	1	0	5	0	0	1.000
—Nashville (PCL)■.......	C-1B-DH	44	152	30	54	16	1	11	34	.355	21	26	1	277	26	4	.987
—Pittsburgh (N.L.)........	1B-C	14	24	2	9	1	0	1	2	.375	1	3	0	35	1	0	1.000
1999—Nashville (PCL)	C-1B-DH-3B	112	405	48	109	29	3	12	65	.269	29	68	3	726	69	‡15	.981
—Pittsburgh (N.L.)	C	6	9	0	3	0	0	0	0	.333	0	2	0	9	0	0	1.000
American League totals (2 years)		10	19	1	1	0	0	0	1	.053	3	10	0	33	0	1	.971
National League totals (5 years)		155	306	30	72	14	2	4	33	.235	19	73	3	547	54	10	.984
Major League totals (6 years)		165	325	31	73	14	2	4	34	.225	22	83	3	580	54	11	.983

LAMB, DAVID   SS/2B   DEVIL RAYS

PERSONAL: Born June 6, 1975, in West Hills, Cailf. ... 6-2/165. ... Bats both, throws right. ... Full name: David Christian Lamb.
HIGH SCHOOL: Newbury Park (Calif.).
TRANSACTIONS/CAREER NOTES: Selected by Baltimore Orioles organization in second round of free-agent draft (June 3, 1993). ... Selected by Tampa Bay Devil Rays from Orioles organization in Rule 5 major league draft (December 14, 1998). ... On Tampa Bay disabled list (August 14-September 1, 1999); included rehabilitation assignment to Durham (August 24-31).

Year Team (League)	Pos.	G	AB	R	H	2B	3B	HR	RBI	Avg.	BB	SO	SB	PO	A	E	Avg.
1993—GC Orioles (GCL)........	SS	16	56	4	10	1	0	0	6	.179	10	8	2	16	22	3	.927
1994—Albany (SAL).............	SS	92	308	37	74	9	2	0	29	.240	32	40	4	118	230	22	.941
1995—Bowie (East.).............	SS	1	4	0	1	0	0	0	1	.250	0	1	0	1	3	1	.800
—Frederick (Caro.)	SS-2B	124	436	39	97	14	2	2	34	.222	38	81	6	151	348	24	.954
1996—High Desert (Calif.)......	SS	116	460	63	118	24	3	3	55	.257	50	68	5	202	356	18	.969
1997—Frederick (Caro.)	2B-SS-3B	70	249	30	65	21	1	2	39	.261	25	32	3	119	183	9	.971
—Bowie (East.).............	SS-3B-2B	73	269	46	89	20	2	4	38	.331	34	35	0	81	159	11	.956
1998—Bowie (East.).............	SS	66	241	29	73	10	1	2	25	.303	27	33	1	73	171	14	.946
—Rochester (I.L.).........	SS-3B-2B	48	178	24	53	7	1	1	16	.298	17	25	1	69	116	7	.964
1999—Tampa Bay (A.L.)■■.......	SS-2B-DH	55	124	18	28	5	1	1	13	.226	10	18	0	58	100	9	.946
—Durham (I.L.)	SS-2B	7	30	7	7	3	0	0	7	.233	2	4	0	13	23	3	.923
Major League totals (1 year)		55	124	18	28	5	1	1	13	.226	10	18	0	58	100	9	.946

LAMB, MIKE   3B   RANGERS

PERSONAL: Born August 9, 1975, in West Covina, Calif. ... 6-1/185. ... Bats left, throws right. ... Full name: Michael Robert Lamb.
HIGH SCHOOL: Bishop Amat (La Puente, Calif.).
COLLEGE: Cal State Fullerton.
TRANSACTIONS/CAREER NOTES: Selected by Texas Rangers organization in seventh round of free-agent draft (June 3, 1997).
STATISTICAL NOTES: Led Florida State League third basemen with 98 putouts, 304 assists, 432 total chances, 19 double plays and .931 fielding percentage in 1998.

Year Team (League)	Pos.	G	AB	R	H	2B	3B	HR	RBI	Avg.	BB	SO	SB	PO	A	E	Avg.
1997—Pulaski (Appl.)............	3B	60	233	59	78	19	3	9	47	.335	31	18	7	38	118	25	.862
1998—Charlotte (FSL)...........	3B-1B	135	536	83	162	35	3	9	93	.302	45	63	18	†124	†305	31	†.933
1999—Tulsa (Texas).............	3B-C	137	*544	98	*176	*51	5	21	100	.324	53	65	4	90	284	28	.930
—Oklahoma (PCL)........	3B	2	2	0	1	0	0	0	0	.500	1	0	0	0	0	0	...

LAMBER, JUSTIN   P   ROYALS

PERSONAL: Born May 22, 1976, in Ridgewood, N.J. ... 6-0/210. ... Throws left, bats right. ... Full name: Justin Daniel Lamber.
HIGH SCHOOL: Hackensack (N.J.).
COLLEGE: Richmond.
TRANSACTIONS/CAREER NOTES: Selected by Kansas City Royals organization in 17th round of free-agent draft (June 3, 1997). ... On Wilmington disabled list (July 4-14, 1999).

Year League	W	L	Pct.	ERA	G	GS	CG	ShO	Sv.	IP	H	R	ER	BB	SO
1997—Spokane (N.W.)	1	1	.500	4.28	25	0	0	0	4	27⅓	24	14	13	20	40
1998—Wilmington (Caro.)............	2	2	.500	3.38	32	0	0	0	2	53⅓	43	21	20	29	68
1999—Wilmington (Caro.)............	5	3	.625	3.67	39	2	0	0	6	68⅔	68	29	28	33	67

LAMPKIN, TOM   C   MARINERS

PERSONAL: Born March 4, 1964, in Cincinnati. ... 5-11/195. ... Bats left, throws right. ... Full name: Thomas Michael Lampkin.
HIGH SCHOOL: Blanchet (Seattle).
JUNIOR COLLEGE: Edmonds College (Wash.).
COLLEGE: Portland.
TRANSACTIONS/CAREER NOTES: Selected by Cleveland Indians organization in 11th round of free-agent draft (June 2, 1986). ... On disabled list (July 6, 1989-remainder of season). ... Traded by Indians to San Diego Padres for OF Alex Cole (July 11, 1990). ... Traded by Padres to Milwaukee Brewers for cash (March 25, 1993). ... Granted free agency (December 20, 1993). ... Signed by San Francisco Giants organization (January 5, 1994). ... On San Francisco disabled list (March 31-April 24 and August 26, 1996-remainder of season); included rehabilitation assignment to San Jose (April 22-24). ... Traded by Giants to St. Louis Cardinals for a player to be named later or cash (December 19, 1996); Giants acquired P Rene Arocha to complete deal (February 12, 1997). ... Granted free agency (October 23, 1998). ... Signed by Seattle Mariners (December 14, 1998).

L

STATISTICAL NOTES: Led Pacific Coast League catchers with 11 double plays in 1992. ... Led Pacific Coast League catchers with 595 putouts in 1994.

Year	Team (League)	Pos.	G	AB	R	H	2B	3B	HR	RBI	Avg.	BB	SO	SB	PO	A	E	Avg.
								BATTING								FIELDING		
1986— Batavia (NY-P)	C	63	190	24	49	5	1	1	20	.258	31	14	4	323	36	8	.978
1987— Waterloo (Midw.)	C	118	398	49	106	19	2	7	55	.266	34	41	5	689	*100	15	.981
1988— Williamsport (East.) ...	C	80	263	38	71	10	0	3	23	.270	25	20	1	431	60	9	.982
— Colo. Springs (PCL) ...	C	34	107	14	30	5	0	0	7	.280	9	2	0	171	28	5	.975
— Cleveland (A.L.)	C	4	4	0	0	0	0	0	0	.000	1	0	0	3	0	0	1.000
1989— Colo. Springs (PCL) ...	C	63	209	26	67	10	3	4	32	.321	10	18	4	305	21	8	.976
1990— Colo. Springs (PCL) ...	C-2B	69	199	32	44	7	5	1	18	.221	19	19	7	312	36	12	.967
— San Diego (N.L.)■..	C	26	63	4	14	0	1	1	4	.222	4	9	0	91	10	3	.971
— Las Vegas (PCL)	C	1	2	0	1	0	0	0	0	.500	0	1	0	3	0	0	1.000
1991— San Diego (N.L.)	C	38	58	4	11	3	1	0	3	.190	3	9	0	49	5	0	1.000
— Las Vegas (PCL)	C-1B-OF	45	164	25	52	11	1	2	29	.317	10	19	2	211	26	6	.975
1992— Las Vegas (PCL)	C	108	340	45	104	17	4	3	48	.306	53	27	15	506	*64	12	.979
— San Diego (N.L.)	C-OF	9	17	3	4	0	0	0	0	.235	6	1	2	30	3	0	1.000
1993— New Orleans (A.A.)■..	C-OF	25	80	18	26	5	0	2	10	.325	18	4	5	152	12	3	.982
— Milwaukee (A.L.)	C-OF-DH	73	162	22	32	8	0	4	25	.198	20	26	7	242	24	6	.978
1994— Phoenix (PCL)■........	C-DH-OF	118	453	76	136	32	8	8	70	.300	42	49	8	†595	59	10	.985
1995— San Francisco (N.L.) ..	C-OF	65	76	8	21	2	0	1	9	.276	9	8	2	62	5	0	1.000
1996— San Jose (Calif.)........	C	2	7	2	2	0	1	0	2	.286	1	2	0	10	1	0	1.000
— San Francisco (N.L.) ..	C	66	177	26	41	8	0	6	29	.232	20	22	1	342	27	3	.992
1997— St. Louis (N.L.)■	C	108	229	28	56	8	1	7	22	.245	28	30	2	413	37	5	.989
1998— St. Louis (N.L.)...........	C-OF-1B	93	216	25	50	12	1	6	28	.231	24	32	3	337	19	5	.986
1999— Seattle (A.L.)■...........	C-DH-OF	76	206	29	60	11	2	9	34	.291	13	32	1	292	27	5	.985
American League totals (3 years)		153	372	51	92	19	2	13	59	.247	34	58	8	537	51	11	.982
National League totals (7 years)		405	836	98	197	33	4	21	95	.236	94	111	10	1324	106	16	.989
Major League totals (10 years)		558	1208	149	289	52	6	34	154	.239	128	169	18	1861	157	27	.987

LANGSTON, MARK   P   INDIANS

L

PERSONAL: Born August 20, 1960, in San Diego. ... 6-2/185. ... Throws left, bats right. ... Full name: Mark Edward Langston.

HIGH SCHOOL: Buchser (Santa Clara, Calif.).

COLLEGE: San Jose State.

TRANSACTIONS/CAREER NOTES: Selected by Chicago Cubs organization in 15th round of free-agent draft (June 6, 1978); did not sign. ... Selected by Seattle Mariners organization in third round of free-agent draft (June 8, 1981); pick received as compensation for Texas Rangers signing free-agent Bill Stein. ... On disabled list (June 7-July 22, 1985). ... Traded by Mariners with a player to be named later to Montreal Expos for P Randy Johnson, P Brian Holman and P Gene Harris (May 25, 1989); Expos acquired P Mike Campbell to complete deal (July 31, 1989). ... Granted free agency (November 13, 1989). ... Signed by California Angels (December 1, 1989). ... On disabled list (April 10-May 11, 1994). ... On California disabled list (May 6-31, July 12-28, and August 10, 1996-remainder of season); included rehabilitation assignment to Lake Elsinore (May 26-31). ... Angels franchise renamed Anaheim Angels for 1997 season. ... On disabled list (May 20-August 20 and August 21, 1997-remainder of season). ... Granted free agency (October 28, 1997). ... Signed by San Diego Padres organization (January 7, 1998). ... On disabled list (April 15-May 23 and August 23-September 8, 1998). ... Granted free agency (November 2, 1998). ... Re-signed by Padres organization (December 7, 1998). ... Released by Padres (March 31, 1999). ... Signed by Cleveland Indians organization (April 4, 1999). ... On Cleveland disabled list (May 25-June 17 and August 18-September 10, 1999); included rehabilitation assignment to Buffalo (May 30-June 17). ... Granted free agency (November 1, 1999). ... Re-signed by Indians organization (December 7, 1999).

RECORDS: Holds major league single-season record for fewest assists by pitcher who led league in assists—42 (1990).

HONORS: Named A.L. Rookie Pitcher of the Year by THE SPORTING NEWS (1984). ... Won A.L. Gold Glove at pitcher (1987-88 and 1991-95).

STATISTICAL NOTES: Pitched seven innings, combining with Mike Witt (two innings) in 1-0 no-hit victory against Seattle (April 11, 1990). ... Struck out 15 batters in one game (June 25, 1986). ... Struck out 16 batters in one game (May 10, 1988). ... Pitched 3-0 one-hit, complete-game victory against Texas (September 24, 1988).

MISCELLANEOUS: Scored in only appearance as pinch runner and struck out twice in two appearances as designated hitter (1992). ... Had a sacrifice hit in only appearance as pinch hitter.

Year	League	W	L	Pct.	ERA	G	GS	CG	ShO	Sv.	IP	H	R	ER	BB	SO
1981— Bellingham (N.W.)	7	3	.700	3.39	13	13	5	1	0	85	81	37	32	46	97
1982— Bakersfield (Calif.).............	12	7	.632	2.54	26	26	7	3	0	177 1/3	143	71	50	102	161
1983— Chattanooga (Sou.)..........	14	9	.609	3.59	28	28	10	0	0	198	187	104	79	102	142
1984— Seattle (A.L.)	17	10	.630	3.40	35	33	5	2	0	225	188	99	85	118	204
1985— Seattle (A.L.)	7	14	.333	5.47	24	24	2	0	0	126 2/3	122	85	77	91	72
1986— Seattle (A.L.)	12	14	.462	4.85	37	36	9	0	0	239 1/3	234	142	129	123	245
1987— Seattle (A.L.)	19	13	.594	3.84	35	35	14	3	0	272	242	132	116	114	262
1988— Seattle (A.L.)	15	11	.577	3.34	35	35	9	3	0	261 1/3	222	108	97	110	235
1989— Seattle (A.L.)	4	5	.444	3.56	10	10	2	1	0	73 1/3	60	30	29	19	60
— Montreal (N.L.)■..............	12	9	.571	2.39	24	24	6	4	0	176 2/3	138	57	47	93	175
1990— California (A.L.)■...............	10	17	.370	4.40	33	33	5	1	0	223	215	120	109	104	195
1991— California (A.L.)	19	8	.704	3.00	34	34	7	0	0	246 1/3	190	89	82	96	183
1992— California (A.L.)	13	14	.481	3.66	32	32	9	2	0	229	206	103	93	74	174
1993— California (A.L.)	16	11	.593	3.20	35	35	7	0	0	256 1/3	220	100	91	85	196
1994— California (A.L.)	7	8	.467	4.68	18	18	2	1	0	119 1/3	121	67	62	54	109
1995— California (A.L.)	15	7	.682	4.63	31	31	2	0	0	200 1/3	212	109	103	64	142
1996— California (A.L.)	6	5	.545	4.82	18	18	2	0	0	123 1/3	116	68	66	45	83
— Lake Elsinore (Calif.)	0	0	...	0.00	1	1	0	0	0	4	3	0	0	0	5
1997— Anaheim (A.L.)	2	4	.333	5.85	9	9	0	0	0	47 2/3	61	34	31	29	30
— Lake Elsinore (Calif.)	0	2	.000	3.21	3	3	0	0	0	14	11	7	5	2	10
1998— San Diego (N.L.)■	4	6	.400	5.86	22	16	0	0	0	81 1/3	107	55	53	41	56
1999— Buffalo (I.L.)■..................	0	1	.000	3.86	4	4	0	0	0	18 2/3	16	9	8	8	11
— Cleveland (A.L.)	1	2	.333	5.25	25	5	0	0	0	61 2/3	69	40	36	29	43
A.L. totals (15 years)	163	143	.533	4.01	411	388	75	14	0	2704 2/3	2478	1326	1206	1155	2233
N.L. totals (2 years)	16	15	.516	3.49	46	40	6	4	0	258	245	112	100	134	231
Major League totals (16 years)	179	158	.531	3.97	457	428	81	18	0	2962 2/3	2723	1438	1306	1289	2464

DIVISION SERIES RECORD

Year League	W	L	Pct.	ERA	G	GS	CG	ShO	Sv.	IP	H	R	ER	BB	SO
1998— San Diego (N.L.)							Did not play.								
1999—Cleveland (A.L.)							Did not play.								

CHAMPIONSHIP SERIES RECORD

Year League	W	L	Pct.	ERA	G	GS	CG	ShO	Sv.	IP	H	R	ER	BB	SO
1998— San Diego (N.L.)	0	0	...	0.00	3	0	0	0	0	1 1/3	1	0	0	0	1

WORLD SERIES RECORD

Year League	W	L	Pct.	ERA	G	GS	CG	ShO	Sv.	IP	H	R	ER	BB	SO
1998— San Diego (N.L.)	0	0	...	40.50	1	0	0	0	0	2/3	1	3	3	3	0

ALL-STAR GAME RECORD

Year League	W	L	Pct.	ERA	GS	CG	ShO	Sv.	IP	H	R	ER	BB	SO
1987— American	0	0	...	0.00	0	0	0	0	2	0	0	0	0	3
1991— American							Did not play.							
1992— American	0	0	...	9.00	0	0	0	0	1	2	1	1	0	1
1993— American	0	0	...	9.00	1	0	0	0	2	3	2	2	1	2
All-Star Game totals (3 years)	0	0	...	5.40	1	0	0	0	5	5	3	3	1	6

LANKFORD, RAY — OF — CARDINALS

PERSONAL: Born June 5, 1967, in Modesto, Calif. ... 5-11/200. ... Bats left, throws left. ... Full name: Raymond Lewis Lankford. ... Nephew of Carl Nichols, catcher with Baltimore Orioles (1986-88) and Houston Astros (1989-91).
HIGH SCHOOL: Grace Davis (Modesto, Calif.).
JUNIOR COLLEGE: Modesto (Calif.) Junior College.
TRANSACTIONS/CAREER NOTES: Selected by Chicago Cubs organization in third round of free-agent draft (January 14, 1986); did not sign. ... Selected by St. Louis Cardinals organization in third round of free-agent draft (June 2, 1987). ... On disabled list (June 24-July 9, 1993). ... On St. Louis disabled list (March 27-April 22, 1997); included rehabilitation assignment to Prince William (April 14-22). ... On disabled list (March 26-April 24, 1999).
RECORDS: Shares major league single-season record for fewest double plays by outfielder (150 or more games)—0 (1992).
HONORS: Named Texas League Most Valuable Player (1989).
STATISTICAL NOTES: Led Appalachian League outfielders with 155 total chances in 1987. ... Led Appalachian League in caught stealing with 11 in 1987. ... Led Midwest League with 242 total bases in 1988. ... Led Texas League outfielders with 387 total chances in 1989. ... Led American Association outfielders with 352 total chances in 1990. ... Tied for American Association lead with nine intentional bases on balls received in 1990. ... Hit for the cycle (September 15, 1991). ... Led N.L. in caught stealing with 24 in 1992. ... Career major league grand slams: 5.

Year Team (League)	Pos.	G	AB	R	H	2B	3B	HR	RBI	Avg.	BB	SO	SB	PO	A	E	Avg.
1987— Johnson City (Appl.) ..	OF	66	253	45	78	17	4	3	32	.308	19	43	14	*143	7	5	.968
1988— Springfield (Midw.)	OF	135	532	90	151	26	*16	11	66	.284	60	92	33	284	5	7	.976
1989— Arkansas (Texas).........	OF	*134	498	98	*158	28	*12	11	98	.317	65	57	38	*367	9	11	.972
1990— Louisville (A.A.).........	OF	132	473	61	123	25	8	10	72	.260	72	81	30	*333	8	•11	.969
— St. Louis (N.L.)...........	OF	39	126	12	36	10	1	3	12	.286	13	27	8	92	1	1	.989
1991— St. Louis (N.L.)...........	OF	151	566	83	142	23	*15	9	69	.251	41	114	44	367	7	6	.984
1992— St. Louis (N.L.)...........	OF	153	598	87	175	40	6	20	86	.293	72	*147	42	*438	5	2	.996
1993— St. Louis (N.L.)...........	OF	127	407	64	97	17	3	7	45	.238	81	111	14	312	6	7	.978
1994— St. Louis (N.L.)...........	OF	109	416	89	111	25	5	19	57	.267	58	113	11	260	5	6	.978
1995— St. Louis (N.L.)...........	OF	132	483	81	134	35	2	25	82	.277	63	110	24	300	7	3	.990
1996— St. Louis (N.L.)...........	OF	149	545	100	150	36	8	21	86	.275	79	133	35	356	9	1	*.997
1997— Prince Will. (Caro.).....	DH-OF	4	13	3	4	1	0	0	4	.308	4	5	1	6	0	0	1.000
— St. Louis (N.L.)...........	OF	133	465	94	137	36	3	31	98	.295	95	125	21	293	4	9	.971
1998— St. Louis (N.L.)...........	OF-DH	154	533	94	156	37	1	31	105	.293	86	151	26	338	7	5	.986
1999— St. Louis (N.L.)...........	OF-DH	122	422	77	129	32	1	15	63	.306	49	110	14	214	6	3	.987
Major League totals (10 years)		1269	4561	781	1267	291	45	181	703	.278	637	1141	239	2970	57	43	.986

DIVISION SERIES RECORD

Year Team (League)	Pos.	G	AB	R	H	2B	3B	HR	RBI	Avg.	BB	SO	SB	PO	A	E	Avg.
1996— St. Louis (N.L.)..........	OF-PH	1	2	1	1	0	0	0	0	.500	1	0	0	4	0	0	1.000

CHAMPIONSHIP SERIES RECORD

Year Team (League)	Pos.	G	AB	R	H	2B	3B	HR	RBI	Avg.	BB	SO	SB	PO	A	E	Avg.
1996— St. Louis (N.L.)..........	OF-PH	5	13	1	0	0	0	0	1	.000	1	4	0	7	0	0	1.000

ALL-STAR GAME RECORD

Year League	Pos.	AB	R	H	2B	3B	HR	RBI	Avg.	BB	SO	SB	PO	A	E	Avg.
1997— National	OF	2	0	0	0	0	0	0	.000	1	1	0	0	0	0	...

LANSING, MIKE — 2B — ROCKIES

PERSONAL: Born April 3, 1968, in Rawlins, Wyo. ... 6-0/195. ... Bats right, throws right. ... Full name: Michael Thomas Lansing.
HIGH SCHOOL: Natrona County (Casper, Wyo.).
COLLEGE: Wichita State.
TRANSACTIONS/CAREER NOTES: Selected by Baltimore Orioles organization in ninth round of free-agent draft (June 5, 1989); did not sign. ... Selected by Miami Miracle, independent, in sixth round of free-agent draft (June 4, 1990). ... On disabled list (April 29-May 9, 1991). ... Contract sold by Miami to Montreal Expos organization (September 18, 1991). ... On disabled list (May 31-June 15, 1995). ... Traded by Expos

to Colorado Rockies for P Jake Westbrook, P John Nicholson and OF Mark Hamlin (November 18, 1997). ... On disabled list (May 21, 1999-remainder of season).

RECORDS: Shares major league single-inning record for most home runs—2 (May 7, 1997, sixth inning).

STATISTICAL NOTES: Led Eastern League shortstops with 76 double plays in 1992. ... Hit three home runs in one game (September 22, 1998). ... Career major league grand slams: 2.

Year	Team (League)	Pos.	G	AB	R	H	2B	3B	HR	RBI	Avg.	BB	SO	SB	PO	A	E	Avg.
1990—Miami (FSL)		SS	61	207	20	50	5	2	2	11	.242	29	35	15	104	166	10	.964
1991—Miami (FSL)		SS-2B	104	384	54	110	20	7	6	55	.286	40	75	29	148	273	27	.940
1992—Harrisburg (East.)■ ...		SS	128	483	66	135	20	6	6	54	.280	52	64	46	189	*373	20	*.966
1993—Montreal (N.L.)		3B-SS-2B	141	491	64	141	29	1	3	45	.287	46	56	23	136	336	24	.952
1994—Montreal (N.L.)..........		2B-3B-SS	106	394	44	105	21	2	5	35	.266	30	37	12	164	283	10	.978
1995—Montreal (N.L.)..........		2B-SS	127	467	47	119	30	2	10	62	.255	28	65	27	306	373	6	.991
1996—Montreal (N.L.)..........		2B-SS	159	641	99	183	40	2	11	53	.285	44	85	23	349	395	11	.985
1997—Montreal (N.L.)..........		2B	144	572	86	161	45	2	20	70	.281	45	92	11	279	395	9	.987
1998—Colorado (N.L.)■		2B-3B	153	584	73	161	39	2	12	66	.276	39	88	10	345	425	10	.987
1999—Colorado (N.L.)		2B	35	145	24	45	9	0	4	15	.310	7	22	2	91	98	2	.990
Major League totals (7 years)			865	3294	437	915	213	11	65	346	.278	239	445	108	1670	2305	72	.982

LARA, NELSON   P   MARLINS

PERSONAL: Born July 15, 1978, in Santo Domingo, Dominican Republic. ... 6-4/185. ... Throws right, bats right. ... Full name: Nelson Rafael Lara.

HIGH SCHOOL: Colegio San Jose (Santo Domingo, Dominican Republic).

TRANSACTIONS/CAREER NOTES: Signed as non-drafted free agent by Florida Marlins organization (September 15, 1994).

Year	League	W	L	Pct.	ERA	G	GS	CG	ShO	Sv.	IP	H	R	ER	BB	SO
1995—Dom. Marlins (DSL)		0	3	.000	8.10	5	5	0	0	0	20	26	24	18	17	8
—Gulf Coast Marlins (GCL) ...		1	1	.500	3.74	11	0	0	0	1	21²/₃	21	13	9	11	9
1996—Gulf Coast Marlins (GCL) ...		1	2	.333	5.59	7	0	0	0	0	9²/₃	6	11	6	12	3
1997—Kane County (Midw.)..........		1	2	.333	3.99	29	0	0	0	3	38¹/₃	37	20	17	14	43
1998—Brevard County (FSL).........		2	5	.286	9.42	19	4	0	0	0	28²/₃	27	36	30	33	32
—Kane County (Midw.).........		2	2	.500	6.14	10	4	0	0	0	29¹/₃	29	23	20	23	21
1999—Kane County (Midw.)..........		3	2	.600	6.06	46	0	0	0	10	52	50	38	35	47	45

LARKIN, BARRY   SS   REDS

PERSONAL: Born April 28, 1964, in Cincinnati. ... 6-0/185. ... Bats right, throws right. ... Full name: Barry Louis Larkin. ... Brother of Steve Larkin, outfielder/first baseman, Baltimore Orioles organization; and cousin of Nathan Davis, defensive tackle with Atlanta Falcons (1997).

HIGH SCHOOL: Moeller (Cincinnati).

COLLEGE: Michigan.

TRANSACTIONS/CAREER NOTES: Selected by Cincinnati Reds organization in second round of free-agent draft (June 7, 1982); did not sign. ... Selected by Reds organization in first round (fourth pick overall) of free-agent draft (June 3, 1985). ... On disabled list (April 13-May 2, 1987). ... On Cincinnati disabled list (July 11-September 1, 1989); included rehabilitation assignment to Nashville (August 27-September 1). ... On disabled list (May 18-June 4, 1991; April 19-May 8, 1992; and August 5, 1993-remainder of season). ... On disabled list (June 17-August 2 and September 1, 1997-remainder of season; and March 12-April 7, 1998).

RECORDS: Holds major league single-season record for fewest putouts by shortstop for leader—230 (1996). ... Shares major league record for most home runs in two consecutive games—5 (June 27 [2] and 28 [3], 1991).

HONORS: Named shortstop on THE SPORTING NEWS college All-America team (1985). ... Named American Association Most Valuable Player (1986). ... Named shortstop on THE SPORTING NEWS N.L. All-Star team (1988-92, 1994-96, 1998 and 1999). ... Named shortstop on THE SPORTING NEWS N.L. Silver Slugger team (1988-92, 1995-96, 1998 and 1999). ... Won N.L. Gold Glove at shortstop (1994-96). ... Named N.L. Most Valuable Player by Baseball Writers' Association of America (1995).

STATISTICAL NOTES: Led American Association with .525 slugging percentage in 1986. ... Had 21-game hitting streak (September 10-October 2, 1988). ... Tied for N.L. lead in double plays by shortstop with 86 in 1990. ... Hit three home runs in one game (June 28, 1991). ... Had 16-game hitting streak (June 20-July 6, 1999).

MISCELLANEOUS: Member of 1984 U.S. Olympic baseball team.

Year	Team (League)	Pos.	G	AB	R	H	2B	3B	HR	RBI	Avg.	BB	SO	SB	PO	A	E	Avg.
1985—Vermont (East.).........		SS	72	255	42	68	13	2	1	31	.267	23	21	12	110	166	17	.942
1986—Denver (A.A.).........		SS-2B	103	413	67	136	31	10	10	51	.329	31	43	19	172	287	18	.962
—Cincinnati (N.L.)		SS-2B	41	159	27	45	4	3	3	19	.283	9	21	8	51	125	4	.978
1987—Cincinnati (N.L.)		SS	125	439	64	107	16	2	12	43	.244	36	52	21	168	358	19	.965
1988—Cincinnati (N.L.)		SS	151	588	91	174	32	5	12	56	.296	41	24	40	231	470	•29	.960
1989—Cincinnati (N.L.)		SS	97	325	47	111	14	4	4	36	.342	20	23	10	142	267	10	.976
—Nashville (A.A.)		SS	2	5	2	5	1	0	0	0	1.000	0	0	0	1	3	0	1.000
1990—Cincinnati (N.L.)		SS	158	614	85	185	25	6	7	67	.301	49	49	30	254	*469	17	.977
1991—Cincinnati (N.L.)		SS	123	464	88	140	27	4	20	69	.302	55	64	24	226	372	15	.976
1992—Cincinnati (N.L.)		SS	140	533	76	162	32	6	12	78	.304	63	58	15	233	408	11	.983
1993—Cincinnati (N.L.)		SS	100	384	57	121	20	3	8	51	.315	51	33	14	159	281	16	.965
1994—Cincinnati (N.L.)		SS	110	427	78	119	23	5	9	52	.279	64	58	26	*178	312	10	.980
1995—Cincinnati (N.L.)		SS	131	496	98	158	29	6	15	66	.319	61	49	51	192	341	11	.980
1996—Cincinnati (N.L.)		SS	152	517	117	154	32	4	33	89	.298	96	52	36	*230	426	17	.975
1997—Cincinnati (N.L.)		SS-DH	73	224	34	71	17	3	4	20	.317	47	24	14	77	171	5	.980
1998—Cincinnati (N.L.)		SS	145	538	93	166	34	10	17	72	.309	79	69	26	207	361	12	.979
1999—Cincinnati (N.L.)		SS	161	583	108	171	30	4	12	75	.293	93	57	30	220	401	14	.978
Major League totals (14 years)			1707	6291	1063	1884	335	65	168	793	.299	764	633	345	2568	4762	190	.975

L

DIVISION SERIES RECORD

							BATTING								FIELDING		
Year Team (League)	Pos.	G	AB	R	H	2B	3B	HR	RBI	Avg.	BB	SO	SB	PO	A	E	Avg.
1995— Cincinnati (N.L.)	SS	3	13	2	5	0	0	0	1	.385	1	2	4	3	8	0	1.000

CHAMPIONSHIP SERIES RECORD

							BATTING								FIELDING		
Year Team (League)	Pos.	G	AB	R	H	2B	3B	HR	RBI	Avg.	BB	SO	SB	PO	A	E	Avg.
1990— Cincinnati (N.L.)	SS	6	23	5	6	2	0	0	1	.261	3	1	3	21	15	1	.973
1995— Cincinnati (N.L.)	SS	4	18	1	7	2	1	0	0	.389	1	1	1	10	15	1	.962
Championship series totals (2 years)		10	41	6	13	4	1	0	1	.317	4	2	4	31	30	2	.968

WORLD SERIES RECORD

RECORDS: Shares single-inning record for most at-bats—2 (October 19, 1990, third inning).
NOTES: Member of World Series championship team (1990).

							BATTING								FIELDING		
Year Team (League)	Pos.	G	AB	R	H	2B	3B	HR	RBI	Avg.	BB	SO	SB	PO	A	E	Avg.
1990— Cincinnati (N.L.)	SS	4	17	3	6	1	1	0	1	.353	2	0	0	1	14	0	1.000

ALL-STAR GAME RECORD

						BATTING								FIELDING		
Year League	Pos.	AB	R	H	2B	3B	HR	RBI	Avg.	BB	SO	SB	PO	A	E	Avg.
1988— National	SS	2	0	0	0	0	0	0	.000	0	1	0	0	1	0	1.000
1989— National						Did not play.										
1990— National	PR-SS	0	0	0	0	0	0	0		0	0	1	1	2	0	1.000
1991— National	SS	1	0	0	0	0	0	0	.000	0	0	0	0	1	0	1.000
1993— National	SS	2	0	0	0	0	0	1	.000	0	1	0	2	1	0	1.000
1994— National					Selected, did not play—injured.											
1995— National	SS	3	0	0	0	0	0	0	.000	0	0	0	2	3	0	1.000
1996— National	SS	3	1	1	0	0	0	0	.333	0	0	0	0	2	0	1.000
1997— National					Selected, did not play—injured.											
1999— National	SS	3	0	1	0	0	0	1	.333	0	1	0	1	1	0	1.000
All-Star Game totals (7 years)		14	1	2	0	0	0	2	.143	0	3	1	6	12	0	1.000

L

LARSON, BRANDON   3B   REDS

PERSONAL: Born May 24, 1976, in San Antonio, Texas. ... 6-0/210. ... Bats right, throws right. ... Full name: Brandon John Larson.
HIGH SCHOOL: Holmes (San Antonio, Texas).
JUNIOR COLLEGE: Blinn College (Texas).
COLLEGE: Louisiana State.
TRANSACTIONS/CAREER NOTES: Selected by Pittsburgh Pirates organization in 46th round of free-agent draft (June 2, 1994); did not sign. ... Selected by Pittsburgh Pirates organization in 38th round of free-agent draft (June 1, 1995); did not sign. ... Selected by San Francisco Giants organization in 44th round of free-agent draft (June 4, 1996); did not sign. ... Selected by Cincinnati Reds organization in first round (14th pick overall) of free-agent draft (June 3, 1997). ... On Chattanooga disabled list (July 3-18, 1999).

							BATTING								FIELDING		
Year Team (League)	Pos.	G	AB	R	H	2B	3B	HR	RBI	Avg.	BB	SO	SB	PO	A	E	Avg.
1997— Chattanooga (Sou.)	SS	11	41	4	11	5	1	0	6	.268	1	10	0	19	22	5	.891
1998— Burlington (Midw.)	3B	18	68	5	15	3	0	2	9	.221	4	16	2	10	52	0	1.000
1999— Rockford (Midw.)	3B	69	250	38	75	18	1	13	52	.300	25	67	12	33	153	18	.912
— Chattanooga (Sou.)	3B	43	172	28	49	10	0	12	42	.285	10	51	4	22	93	15	.885

LaRUE, JASON   C   REDS

PERSONAL: Born March 19, 1974, in Houston. ... 5-11/200. ... Bats right, throws right. ... Full name: Michael Jason LaRue.
HIGH SCHOOL: Spring Valley (Spring Branch, Tex.).
COLLEGE: Dallas Baptist.
TRANSACTIONS/CAREER NOTES: Selected by Cincinnati Reds organization in fifth round of free-agent draft (June 1, 1995). ... On disabled list (June 30-September 13, 1996).
STATISTICAL NOTES: Tied for Pioneer League lead in being hit by pitch with 12 in 1995. ... Led Pioneer League catchers with seven double plays in 1995. ... Led Southern League with .617 slugging percentage in 1998. ... Tied for Southern League lead with 21 passed balls in 1998.

							BATTING								FIELDING		
Year Team (League)	Pos.	G	AB	R	H	2B	3B	HR	RBI	Avg.	BB	SO	SB	PO	A	E	Avg.
1995— Billings (Pio.)	C	58	183	35	50	8	1	5	31	.273	16	28	3	346	46	8	.980
1996— Char., W.Va. (SAL)......	C-1B	37	123	17	26	8	0	2	14	.211	11	28	3	234	48	6	.979
1997— Char., W.Va. (SAL)......C-1B-3B-OF		132	473	78	149	*50	3	8	81	.315	47	90	14	711	84	19	.977
1998— Chattanooga (Sou.)....	C-3B-1B	105	386	71	141	39	8	14	82	*.365	40	60	4	546	90	10	.985
— Indianapolis (I.L.).......	C	15	51	5	12	4	0	0	5	.235	4	8	0	83	11	0	1.000
1999— Indianapolis (I.L.).......	C-DH	70	263	42	66	12	2	12	37	.251	15	52	0	384	45	7	.984
— Cincinnati (N.L.)	C	36	90	12	19	7	0	3	10	.211	11	32	4	179	15	2	.990
Major League totals (1 year)		36	90	12	19	7	0	3	10	.211	11	32	4	179	15	2	.990

LATHAM, CHRIS   OF   ROCKIES

PERSONAL: Born May 26, 1973, in Coeur d'Alene, Idaho. ... 6-0/198. ... Bats both, throws right. ... Full name: Christopher Joseph Latham.
HIGH SCHOOL: Basic Technical (Las Vegas).
TRANSACTIONS/CAREER NOTES: Selected by Los Angeles Dodgers organization in 11th round of free-agent draft (June 3, 1991). ... Traded by Dodgers organization to Minnesota Twins (October 30, 1995), completing deal in which Twins traded P Mark Guthrie and P Kevin Tapani

to Dodgers for 1B/3B Ron Coomer, P Greg Hansell, P Jose Parra and a player to be named later (July 31, 1995). ... On disabled list (August 30-September 9, 1996). ... Traded by Twins to Colorado Rockies for P Scott Randall (December 7, 1999).

STATISTICAL NOTES: Led Northwest League with 148 total bases and 20 caught stealing in 1994. ... Tied for Northwest League lead with seven intentional bases on balls received in 1994. ... Led Northwest League outfielders with 154 total chances in 1994. ... Led Pacific Coast League lead in caught stealing with 19 in 1997.

							BATTING								FIELDING		
Year Team (League)	Pos.	G	AB	R	H	2B	3B	HR	RBI	Avg.	BB	SO	SB	PO	A	E	Avg.
1991— GC Dodgers (GCL)	2B	43	109	17	26	2	1	0	11	.239	16	45	14	47	63	10	.917
1992— Great Falls (Pio.)	2B	17	37	8	12	2	0	0	3	.324	8	8	1	17	24	6	.872
— GC Dodgers (GCL)	2B-SS-3B	14	48	4	11	2	0	0	2	.229	5	17	2	26	14	1	.976
1993— Yakima (N.W.)	OF	54	192	46	50	2	*6	4	17	.260	39	53	25	83	5	6	.936
— Bakersfield (Calif.)	OF	6	27	1	5	1	0	0	3	.185	4	5	2	12	0	1	.923
1994— Bakersfield (Calif.)	OF	52	191	29	41	5	2	2	15	.215	28	49	28	88	4	7	.929
— Yakima (N.W.)	OF	71	288	*69	*98	19	*8	5	32	*.340	55	66	33	*144	6	4	.974
1995— Vero Beach (FSL)	OF	71	259	53	74	13	4	6	39	.286	56	54	42	125	5	7	.949
— San Antonio (Texas) ...	OF	58	214	38	64	14	5	9	37	.299	33	59	11	135	2	4	.972
— Albuquerque (PCL)	OF	5	18	2	3	0	1	0	3	.167	1	4	1	7	0	0	1.000
1996— Salt Lake (PCL)■	OF-DH	115	376	59	103	16	6	9	50	.274	36	91	26	235	9	9	.964
1997— Minnesota (A.L.)	OF	15	22	4	4	1	0	0	1	.182	0	8	0	11	0	1	.917
1998— Salt Lake (PCL)	OF-DH	97	377	81	122	21	4	11	51	.324	56	99	29	201	8	9	.959
— Minnesota (A.L.)	OF	34	94	14	15	1	0	1	5	.160	13	36	4	69	1	2	.972
1999— Minnesota (A.L.)	OF	14	22	1	2	0	0	0	3	.091	0	13	0	13	0	0	1.000
— Salt Lake (PCL)	OF	94	382	93	123	24	8	15	51	.322	54	95	18	262	9	6	.978
Major League totals (3 years)		63	138	19	21	2	0	1	9	.152	13	57	4	93	1	3	.969

LAWRENCE, JOE — 3B — BLUE JAYS

PERSONAL: Born February 13, 1977, in Lake Charles, La. ... 6-2/200. ... Bats right, throws right. ... Full name: Joseph D. Lawrence.
HIGH SCHOOL: Barbe (Lake Charles, La.).
TRANSACTIONS/CAREER NOTES: Selected by Toronto Blue Jays organization in first round (16th pick overall) of free-agent draft (June 4, 1996); pick received as compensation for Baltimore Orioles signing Type A free-agent 2B Roberto Alomar. ... On Knoxville disabled list (June 30, 1999-remainder of season).

							BATTING								FIELDING		
Year Team (League)	Pos.	G	AB	R	H	2B	3B	HR	RBI	Avg.	BB	SO	SB	PO	A	E	Avg.
1996— St. Cath. (NY-P)	SS-3B	29	98	23	22	7	2	0	11	.224	14	17	1	31	67	11	.899
1997— Hagerstown (SAL)	SS	116	446	63	102	24	1	8	38	.229	49	107	10	134	278	33	.926
1998— Dunedin (FSL)	SS-3B	125	454	102	140	31	6	11	44	.308	*105	88	15	163	345	48	.914
1999— Knoxville (Sou.)	3B-DH-SS	70	250	52	66	16	2	7	24	.264	56	48	7	30	114	14	.911

LAWTON, MATT — OF — TWINS

PERSONAL: Born November 3, 1971, in Gulfport, Miss. ... 5-10/186. ... Bats left, throws right. ... Full name: Matthew Lawton III.
HIGH SCHOOL: Harrison Central (Gulfport, Miss.).
JUNIOR COLLEGE: Gulf Coast Community College (Fla.).
TRANSACTIONS/CAREER NOTES: Selected by Minnesota Twins organization in 12th round of free-agent draft (June 3, 1991). ... On Minnesota disabled list (June 9-July 18, 1999); included rehabilitation assignments to Fort Myers (July 12-16) and Gulf Coast Twins (July 17-18).
STATISTICAL NOTES: Led Florida State League with .407 on-base percentage in 1994. ... Career major league grand slams: 3.

							BATTING								FIELDING		
Year Team (League)	Pos.	G	AB	R	H	2B	3B	HR	RBI	Avg.	BB	SO	SB	PO	A	E	Avg.
1992— GC Twins (GCL)..........	2B	53	173	39	45	8	3	2	26	.260	27	27	20	129	142	12	.958
1993— Fort Wayne (Midw.).....	OF	111	340	50	97	21	3	9	38	.285	65	42	23	65	6	3	.959
1994— Fort Myers (FSL)	OF	122	446	79	134	30	1	7	51	.300	80	64	42	188	13	6	.971
1995— New Britain (East.)	OF-DH	114	412	75	111	19	5	13	54	.269	56	70	26	221	12	2	*.991
— Minnesota (A.L.)	OF-DH	21	60	11	19	4	1	1	12	.317	7	11	1	34	1	1	.972
1996— Minnesota (A.L.)	OF-DH	79	252	34	65	7	1	6	42	.258	28	28	4	196	4	3	.985
— Salt Lake (PCL)	OF-DH	53	212	40	63	16	1	7	33	.297	26	34	2	88	0	6	.936
1997— Minnesota (A.L.)	OF	142	460	74	114	29	3	14	60	.248	76	81	7	278	9	7	.976
1998— Minnesota (A.L.)	OF	152	557	91	155	36	6	21	77	.278	86	64	16	398	12	4	.990
1999— Minnesota (A.L.)	OF-DH	118	406	58	105	18	0	7	54	.259	57	42	26	213	3	4	.982
— Fort Myers (FSL)	OF	4	14	3	8	1	0	0	2	.571	3	1	1	8	0	0	1.000
— GC Twins (GCL)..........	OF	1	4	0	1	0	0	0	1	.250	0	2	0	1	0	0	1.000
Major League totals (5 years)		512	1735	268	458	94	11	49	245	.264	254	226	54	1119	29	19	.984

LAXTON, BRETT — P — ATHLETICS

PERSONAL: Born October 5, 1973, in Stafford, N.J. ... 6-2/210. ... Throws right, bats left. ... Full name: Brett William Laxton. ... Son of Bill Laxton, pitcher with five major league teams (1970-71, 1974 and 1976-77).
HIGH SCHOOL: Audobon (N.J.).
COLLEGE: Louisiana State.
TRANSACTIONS/CAREER NOTES: Selected by San Diego Padres organization in fourth round of free-agent draft (June 1, 1992); did not sign. ... Selected by Oakland Athletics organization in 24th round of free-agent draft (June 4, 1996).

Year League	W	L	Pct.	ERA	G	GS	CG	ShO	Sv.	IP	H	R	ER	BB	SO
1996— Southern Oregon (N.W.).....	0	5	.000	7.71	13	8	0	0	0	32 2/3	39	34	28	26	38
1997— Visalia (Calif.)	11	5	.688	2.99	29	22	0	0	0	138 2/3	141	62	46	50	121
1998— Huntsville (Sou.)	11	4	.733	3.40	21	21	0	0	0	129 2/3	109	64	49	79	82
— Edmonton (PCL)	2	4	.333	6.60	8	8	0	0	0	46 1/3	45	35	34	24	21
1999— Vancouver (PCL)	13	8	.619	3.46	25	25	3	1	0	161 1/3	158	68	62	49	112
— Oakland (A.L.)	0	1	.000	7.45	3	2	0	0	0	9 2/3	12	12	8	7	9
Major League totals (1 year)........	0	1	.000	7.45	3	2	0	0	0	9 2/3	12	12	8	7	9

PERSONAL: Born June 7, 1977, in Arroyo, Puerto Rico. ... 6-6/205. ... Bats right, throws right. ... Full name: Juan Arturo LeBron. ... Son of Juan LeBron, infielder/outfielder/catcher in Pittsburgh Pirates organization (1970-75).
HIGH SCHOOL: Carmen Huyke (Puerto Rico).
TRANSACTIONS/CAREER NOTES: Selected by Kansas City Royals organization in first round (19th pick overall) of free-agent draft (June 1, 1995). ... Traded by Royals to New York Mets for 3B/2B Joe Randa (December 10, 1998). ... On St. Lucie disabled list (April 8, 1999-entire season).
STATISTICAL NOTES: Led Gulf Coast League in grounding into double plays with nine in 1996.

										BATTING					FIELDING		
Year Team (League)	Pos.	G	AB	R	H	2B	3B	HR	RBI	Avg.	BB	SO	SB	PO	A	E	Avg.
1995—GC Royals (GCL)	OF	47	147	17	26	5	2	2	13	.177	10	38	0	54	0	5	.915
1996—GC Royals (GCL)	OF	58	215	19	62	9	2	3	30	.288	6	34	1	52	2	2	.964
1997—Lansing (Midw.)	OF	35	113	12	24	7	0	3	20	.212	0	32	0	45	2	2	.959
—Spokane (N.W.)	OF	69	288	49	88	*27	1	7	45	.306	17	74	8	104	9	8	.934
1998—Lansing (Midw.)	OF	121	442	70	111	26	9	17	84	.251	57	129	18	184	10	8	.960
1999—St. Lucie (FSL)■							Did not play.										

PERSONAL: Born November 22, 1973, in Ponce, Puerto Rico. ... 6-1/160. ... Bats left, throws left. ... Full name: Ricardo Alberto Ledee. ... Name pronounced le-DAY.
HIGH SCHOOL: Colonel Nuestra Sonora de Valvanera (Coano, Puerto Rico).
TRANSACTIONS/CAREER NOTES: Selected by New York Yankees organization in 16th round of free-agent draft (June 3, 1990). ... On Tampa disabled list (April 6-May 27, 1996). ... On Columbus disabled list (May 5-16 and May 22-August 4, 1997; and May 25-June 3, 1999).
STATISTICAL NOTES: Career major league grand slams: 1.

										BATTING					FIELDING		
Year Team (League)	Pos.	G	AB	R	H	2B	3B	HR	RBI	Avg.	BB	SO	SB	PO	A	E	Avg.
1990—GC Yankees (GCL)	OF	19	37	5	4	2	0	0	1	.108	6	18	2	18	1	0	1.000
1991—GC Yankees (GCL)	OF	47	165	22	44	6	2	0	18	.267	22	40	3	79	6	6	.934
1992—GC Yankees (GCL)	OF	52	179	25	41	9	2	2	23	.229	24	47	1	62	4	2	.971
1993—Oneonta (NY-P)	OF	52	192	32	49	7	6	8	20	.255	25	46	7	91	6	3	.970
1994—Greensboro (SAL)	OF	134	484	87	121	23	9	22	71	.250	91	126	10	170	10	5	.973
1995—Greensboro (SAL)	OF	89	335	65	90	16	6	14	49	.269	51	66	10	160	7	3	.982
1996—Norwich (East.)	OF	39	137	27	50	11	1	8	37	.365	16	25	2	48	2	1	.980
—Columbus (I.L.)	OF	96	358	79	101	22	6	21	64	.282	44	95	6	97	3	5	.952
1997—Columbus (I.L.)	OF-DH	43	170	38	52	12	1	10	39	.306	21	49	4	56	0	2	.966
—GC Yankees (GCL)	DH-OF	7	21	3	7	1	0	0	2	.333	2	4	0	1	0	0	1.000
1998—Columbus (I.L.)	OF-DH	96	360	70	102	21	1	19	41	.283	54	108	7	132	1	4	.971
—New York (A.L.)	OF	42	79	13	19	5	2	1	12	.241	7	29	3	47	4	1	.981
1999—New York (A.L.)	OF-DH	88	250	45	69	13	5	9	40	.276	28	73	4	143	3	9	.942
—Columbus (I.L.)	OF	30	115	18	29	7	1	4	15	.252	17	29	4	59	2	3	.953
Major League totals (2 years)		130	329	58	88	18	7	10	52	.267	35	102	7	190	7	10	.952

DIVISION SERIES RECORD

										BATTING					FIELDING		
Year Team (League)	Pos.	G	AB	R	H	2B	3B	HR	RBI	Avg.	BB	SO	SB	PO	A	E	Avg.
1998— New York (A.L.)							Did not play.										
1999— New York (A.L.)	OF	3	11	1	3	2	0	0	2	.273	1	5	0	6	0	0	1.000

CHAMPIONSHIP SERIES RECORD

RECORDS: Shares single-game record for most grand slams—1 (October 17, 1999). ... Shares single-inning record for most runs batted in— 4 (October 17, 1999, ninth inning).

										BATTING					FIELDING		
Year Team (League)	Pos.	G	AB	R	H	2B	3B	HR	RBI	Avg.	BB	SO	SB	PO	A	E	Avg.
1998— New York (A.L.)	PH-OF-PR-DH	3	5	0	0	0	0	0	0	.000	0	0	0	3	0	0	1.000
1999— New York (A.L.)	OF-PH-DH	3	8	2	2	0	0	1	4	.250	1	4	0	3	0	1	.750
Championship series totals (2 years)		6	13	2	2	0	0	1	4	.154	1	4	0	6	0	1	.857

WORLD SERIES RECORD

NOTES: Member of World Series championship team (1998 and 1999).

										BATTING					FIELDING		
Year Team (League)	Pos.	G	AB	R	H	2B	3B	HR	RBI	Avg.	BB	SO	SB	PO	A	E	Avg.
1998— New York (A.L.)	OF-PH	4	10	1	6	3	0	0	4	.600	2	1	0	8	0	0	1.000
1999— New York (A.L.)	OF	3	10	0	2	1	0	0	1	.200	1	4	0	1	0	0	1.000
World Series totals (2 years)		7	20	1	8	4	0	0	5	.400	3	5	0	9	0	0	1.000

PERSONAL: Born June 3, 1971, in Union City, Calif. ... 6-2/210. ... Bats right, throws right. ... Full name: Aaron David Ledesma.
HIGH SCHOOL: James Logan (Union City, Calif.).
JUNIOR COLLEGE: Chabot College (Calif.).
TRANSACTIONS/CAREER NOTES: Selected by New York Mets organization in second round of free-agent draft (June 4, 1990). ... On disabled list (April 13-May 24, 1991 and July 19, 1993-remainder of season). ... On suspended list (July 29-31, 1994). ... Traded by Mets to California Angels for OF Kevin Flora (January 18, 1996). ... Granted free agency (October 15, 1996). ... Signed by Rochester, Baltimore Orioles organization (January 17, 1997). ... Selected by Tampa Bay Devil Rays in third round (62nd pick overall) of expansion draft (November 18, 1997). ... On Tampa Bay disabled list (April 4-May 12, 1999; included rehabilitation assignments to St. Petersburg (May 7-10) and Durham (May 11-12). ... Traded by Devil Rays with P Rolando Arrojo to Colorado Rockies for 3B Vinny Castilla (December 13, 1999).

STATISTICAL NOTES: Led Florida State League shortstops with 641 total chances and 79 double plays in 1992. ... Led International League shortstops with 68 double plays in 1994. ... Led Pacific Coast League in grounding into double plays with 18 in 1996.

Year	Team (League)	Pos.	G	AB	R	H	2B	3B	HR	RBI	Avg.	BB	SO	SB	PO	A	E	Avg.
1990—	Kingsport (Appal.)	SS	66	243	50	81	11	1	5	38	.333	30	28	27	78	*170	24	.912
1991—	Columbia (SAL)	SS	33	115	19	39	8	0	1	14	.339	8	16	3	44	64	10	.915
1992—	St. Lucie (FSL)	SS	134	456	51	120	17	2	2	50	.263	46	66	20	185	*411	45	.930
1993—	Binghamton (East.)	SS	66	206	23	55	12	0	5	22	.267	14	43	2	36	65	10	.910
1994—	Norfolk (I.L.)	SS-DH	119	431	49	118	20	1	3	57	.274	28	41	18	157	347	26	*.951
1995—	Norfolk (I.L.)	3B-1B-SS	56	201	26	60	12	1	0	28	.299	10	22	6	73	94	10	.944
—	New York (I.L.)	3B-1B-SS	21	33	4	8	0	0	0	3	.242	6	7	0	5	12	2	.895
1996—	Vancouver (PCL)■..	SS-DH-3B	109	440	60	134	27	4	1	51	.305	32	59	2	150	261	20	.954
1997—	Rochester (I.L.)■.....	SS-DH-1B	85	326	40	106	26	1	3	43	.325	35	48	12	121	185	13	.959
—	Baltimore (A.L.)	2B-3B-1B-SS	43	88	24	31	5	1	2	11	.352	13	9	1	68	52	3	.976
1998—	Tampa Bay (A.L.)■..S-2-3-DH-1		95	299	30	97	16	3	0	29	.324	9	51	9	151	227	12	.969
1999—	St. Petersburg (FSL) ..	3B-SS	2	7	0	1	1	0	0	0	.143	1	1	0	3	4	1	.875
—	Durham (I.L.)	2B-SS	2	10	0	1	0	0	0	0	.100	0	1	0	7	10	1	.944
—	Tampa Bay (A.L.)......S-3-2-1-DH		93	294	32	78	15	0	0	30	.265	14	35	1	164	225	10	.975
American League totals (3 years)			231	681	86	206	36	4	2	70	.302	36	95	11	383	504	25	.973
National League totals (1 year)			21	33	4	8	0	0	0	3	.242	6	7	0	5	12	2	.895
Major League totals (4 years)			252	714	90	214	36	4	2	73	.300	42	102	11	388	516	27	.971

LEE, CARLOS — OF — WHITE SOX

PERSONAL: Born June 20, 1976, in Aguadulce, Panama. ... 6-2/220. ... Bats right, throws right. ... Full name: Carlos Noriel Lee.
TRANSACTIONS/CAREER NOTES: Signed as non-drafted free agent by Chicago White Sox organization (February 8, 1994).
STATISTICAL NOTES: Led Southern League in grounding into double plays with 32 in 1998. ... Hit home run in first major league at-bat (May 7, 1999). ... Had 15-game hitting streak (August 23-September 6, 1999). ... Career major league grand slams: 2.

Year	Team (League)	Pos.	G	AB	R	H	2B	3B	HR	RBI	Avg.	BB	SO	SB	PO	A	E	Avg.
1994—	Sarasota (GCL)	3B	29	56	6	7	1	0	0	1	.125	4	8	0	18	29	2	.959
1995—	Hickory (SAL)	3B	63	218	18	54	9	1	4	30	.248	8	34	1	30	76	19	.848
—	Bristol (Appl.)	3B-1B	*67	*269	43	*93	17	1	7	45	.346	8	34	17	84	107	18	.914
1996—	Hickory (SAL)	3B-1B	119	480	65	150	23	6	8	70	.313	23	50	18	149	235	32	.923
1997—	Win.-Salem (Car.)	3B-DH	*139	*546	81	*173	*50	4	17	82	.317	36	65	11	*93	233	34	.906
1998—	Birmingham (Sou.)	3B-DH	138	*549	77	166	33	2	21	106	.302	39	55	11	*99	223	*35	.902
1999—	Charlotte (I.L.).........3B-OF-1B-DH		25	94	16	33	5	0	4	20	.351	8	14	2	56	22	4	.951
—	Chicago (A.L.)	OF-DH-1B	127	492	66	144	32	2	16	84	.293	13	72	4	225	7	5	.979
Major League totals (1 year)			127	492	66	144	32	2	16	84	.293	13	72	4	225	7	5	.979

LEE, COREY — P — RANGERS

PERSONAL: Born December 26, 1974, in Raleigh, N.C. ... 6-2/185. ... Throws left, bats both. ... Full name: Corey W. Lee.
HIGH SCHOOL: Clayton (N.C.).
COLLEGE: North Carolina State.
TRANSACTIONS/CAREER NOTES: Selected by Texas Rangers organization in supplemental round ("sandwich pick" between first and second round, 32nd pick overall) of free-agent draft (June 2, 1996); pick received as compensation for New York Yankees signing Type A free-agent P Kenny Rogers.

Year	League	W	L	Pct.	ERA	G	GS	CG	ShO	Sv.	IP	H	R	ER	BB	SO
1996—	Hudson Valley (NY-P)........	1	4	.200	3.29	9	9	0	0	0	54²/₃	42	24	20	21	59
1997—	Charlotte (FSL)	*15	5	.750	3.47	23	23	6	2	0	160²/₃	132	66	62	60	147
1998—	Tulsa (Texas)	10	9	.526	4.51	26	25	1	0	0	143²/₃	105	81	72	102	132
1999—	Tulsa (Texas)	8	5	.615	4.44	22	22	0	0	0	127²/₃	132	76	63	44	121
—	Oklahoma (PCL)................	3	0	1.000	2.03	4	4	0	0	0	26²/₃	21	6	6	8	25
—	Texas (A.L.)	0	1	.000	27.00	1	0	0	0	0	1	2	3	3	1	0
Major League totals (1 year)........		0	1	.000	27.00	1	0	0	0	0	1	2	3	3	1	0

LEE, DAVID — P — ROCKIES

PERSONAL: Born March 12, 1973, in Pittsburgh. ... 6-1/202. ... Throws right, bats right. ... Full name: David Emmer Lee.
HIGH SCHOOL: Langley (Pittsburgh, Pa.).
JUNIOR COLLEGE: Community College of Allegheny County-North Campus (Pa.).
COLLEGE: Mercyhurst College (Pa.).
TRANSACTIONS/CAREER NOTES: Selected by Colorado Rockies organization in 23rd round of free-agent draft (June 1, 1995).

Year	League	W	L	Pct.	ERA	G	GS	CG	ShO	Sv.	IP	H	R	ER	BB	SO
1996—	Portland (N.W.)	5	1	.833	0.78	17	0	0	0	7	23	13	3	2	16	24
—	Salem (Caro.)	0	2	.000	2.25	8	0	0	0	1	12	14	6	3	6	10
1997—	Asheville (SAL).................	4	8	.333	4.08	51	0	0	0	22	53	61	30	24	23	59
1998—	Salem (Caro.)	3	5	.375	3.77	54	0	0	0	25	57¹/₃	57	26	24	15	54
1999—	Carolina (Sou.)	0	0	...	1.04	16	0	0	0	10	17¹/₃	8	3	2	3	16
—	Colorado (N.L.)	3	2	.600	3.67	36	0	0	0	0	49	43	21	20	29	38
—	Colo. Springs (PCL)	0	0	...	0.00	6	0	0	0	3	5²/₃	0	0	0	1	7
Major League totals (1 year)........		3	2	.600	3.67	36	0	0	0	0	49	43	21	20	29	38

LEE, DERREK   1B   MARLINS

PERSONAL: Born September 6, 1975, in Sacramento. ... 6-5/225. ... Bats right, throws right. ... Full name: Derrek Leon Lee. ... Son of Leon Lee, infielder in St. Louis Cardinals organization (1969-71) and Lotte Orions (1978-82), Taiyo Whales (1983-85) and Yakult Swallows (1986-87) of Japan League; and nephew of Leron Lee, outfielder with four major league teams (1969-1976) and Lotte Orions (1977-87) of Japan League.

HIGH SCHOOL: El Camino (Sacramento).

TRANSACTIONS/CAREER NOTES: Selected by San Diego Padres in first round (14th pick overall) of free-agent draft (June 2, 1994). ... Traded by Padres with P Rafael Medina and P Steve Hoff to Florida Marlins for P Kevin Brown (December 15, 1997).

RECORDS: Shares major league single-inning record for most assists by first baseman—3 (June 2, 1999, second inning).

HONORS: Named Southern League Most Valuable Player (1996).

STATISTICAL NOTES: Led Southern League with 285 total bases in 1996. ... Led Southern League first basemen 1,121 putouts in 1996. ... Led Pacific Coast League first basemen with 1,189 total chances and 108 double plays in 1997. ... Career major league grand slams: 2.

								BATTING							FIELDING		
Year	Team (League)	Pos.	G	AB	R	H	2B	3B	HR	RBI	Avg.	BB	SO	SB	PO	A	E	Avg.
1993—	Ariz. Padres (Ariz.)	1B	15	52	11	17	1	1	2	5	.327	6	7	4	115	14	2	.985
—	Rancho Cuca. (Calif.) .	1B-DH	20	73	13	20	5	1	1	10	.274	10	20	0	115	6	5	.960
1994—	Rancho Cuca. (Calif.) .	DH-1B	126	442	66	118	19	2	8	53	.267	42	95	18	289	27	4	.988
1995—	Rancho Cuca. (Calif.) .	1B	128	502	82	151	25	2	23	95	.301	49	130	14	970	86	*18	.983
—	Memphis (Sou.)	1B	2	9	0	1	0	0	0	1	.111	0	2	0	16	3	0	1.000
1996—	Memphis (Sou.)	1B-DH-3B	134	500	98	140	39	2	34	*104	.280	65	*170	13	†1121	77	11	.991
1997—	Las Vegas (PCL)	1B	125	472	86	153	29	2	13	64	.324	60	116	17	*1069	*111	9	*.992
—	San Diego (N.L.)	1B	22	54	9	14	3	0	1	4	.259	9	24	0	131	13	0	1.000
1998—	Florida (N.L.)■..........	1B	141	454	62	106	29	1	17	74	.233	47	120	5	950	114	8	.993
1999—	Florida (N.L.)	1B	70	218	21	45	9	1	5	20	.206	17	70	2	463	47	3	.994
—	Calgary (PCL)	1B-DH	89	339	60	96	20	1	19	73	.283	30	90	3	718	68	14	.983
Major League totals (3 years)			233	726	92	165	41	2	23	98	.227	73	214	7	1544	174	11	.994

LEE, SANG   P   RED SOX

PERSONAL: Born March 11, 1971, in Seoul, Korea. ... 6-1/190. ... Throws left, bats left. ... Full name: Sang-Hoon Lee.

COLLEGE: Korea University.

TRANSACTIONS/CAREER NOTES: Signed as non-drafted free agent by Boston Red Sox organization (December 23, 1999).

Year	League	W	L	Pct.	ERA	G	GS	CG	ShO	Sv.	IP	H	R	ER	BB	SO
1998—	Chunichi (Jap. Cen.)...........	1	0	1.000	4.68	11	1	0	0	0	32²/₃	32	17	17	12	33
1999—	Chunichi (Jap. Cen.)...........	6	5	.545	2.84	36	11	2	0	3	95	75	30	30	30	65

LEE, TRAVIS   OF   DIAMONDBACKS

PERSONAL: Born May 26, 1975, in San Diego. ... 6-3/210. ... Bats left, throws left. ... Full name: Travis Reynolds Lee.

HIGH SCHOOL: Olympia (Wash.).

COLLEGE: San Diego State.

TRANSACTIONS/CAREER NOTES: Selected by Minnesota Twins organization in first round (second pick overall) of free-agent draft (June 4, 1996). ... Granted free agency (June 19, 1996). ... Signed by Arizona Diamondbacks organization (October 15, 1996). ... Loaned by Diamondbacks organization to Tucson, Milwaukee Brewers organization (June 5, 1997). ... Returned to Diamondbacks (March 30, 1998). ... On disabled list (July 25-August 9, 1998; and August 16-September 9, 1999).

HONORS: Named Golden Spikes Award winner by USA Baseball (1996).

STATISTICAL NOTES: Led N.L. first basemen with .997 fielding percentage in 1999. ... Career major league grand slams: 2.

MISCELLANEOUS: Member of 1996 U.S. Olympic baseball team.

								BATTING							FIELDING		
Year	Team (League)	Pos.	G	AB	R	H	2B	3B	HR	RBI	Avg.	BB	SO	SB	PO	A	E	Avg.
1997—	High Desert (Calif.)......	1B-DH	61	226	63	82	18	1	18	63	.363	47	36	5	553	67	1	.998
—	Tucson (PCL)■	1B-DH-OF	59	227	42	68	16	2	14	46	.300	31	46	2	382	32	3	.993
1998—	Arizona (N.L.)■..........	1B	146	562	71	151	20	2	22	72	.269	67	123	8	1269	100	3	.998
1999—	Arizona (N.L.)	1B-OF	120	375	57	89	16	2	9	50	.237	58	50	17	805	62	3	†.997
Major League totals (2 years)			266	937	128	240	36	4	31	122	.256	125	173	25	2074	162	6	.997

LEITER, AL   P   METS

PERSONAL: Born October 23, 1965, in Toms River, N.J. ... 6-3/220. ... Throws left, bats left. ... Full name: Alois Terry Leiter. ... Brother of Mark Leiter, pitcher with seven major league teams (1990-99); and brother of Kurt Leiter, minor league pitcher (1982-84 and 1986). ... Name pronounced LIE-ter.

HIGH SCHOOL: Central Regional (Bayville, N.J.).

TRANSACTIONS/CAREER NOTES: Selected by New York Yankees organization in second round of free-agent draft (June 4, 1984). ... On New York disabled list (June 22-July 26, 1988); included rehabilitation assignment to Columbus (July 17-25). ... Traded by Yankees to Toronto Blue Jays for OF Jesse Barfield (April 30, 1989). ... On Toronto disabled list (May 11, 1989-remainder of season); included rehabilitation assignment to Dunedin (August 12-29). ... On Syracuse disabled list (May 20-June 13, 1990). ... On Toronto disabled list (April 27, 1991-remainder of season); included rehabilitation assignments to Dunedin (May 20-28 and July 19-August 7). ... On disabled list (April 24-May 9, 1993 and June 9-24, 1994). ... Granted free agency (November 6, 1995). ... Signed by Florida Marlins (December 14, 1995). ... On disabled list (May 1-20 and August 13-29, 1997). ... Traded by Marlins with 2B Ralph Milliard to New York Mets for P Jesus Sanchez, P A.J. Burnett and OF Robert Stratton (February 6, 1998). ... On disabled list (June 27-July 18, 1998).

HONORS: Named lefthanded pitcher on THE SPORTING NEWS N.L. All-Star team (1996).

STATISTICAL NOTES: Tied for A.L. lead with five balks in 1994. ... Led A.L. with 14 wild pitches in 1995. ... Pitched 11-0 no-hit victory against Colorado (May 11, 1996). ... Struck out 15 batters in one game (August 1, 1999).

Year League	W	L	Pct.	ERA	G	GS	CG	ShO	Sv.	IP	H	R	ER	BB	SO
1984— Oneonta (NY-P)	3	2	.600	3.63	10	10	0	0	0	57	52	32	23	26	48
1985— Oneonta (NY-P)	3	2	.600	2.37	6	6	2	0	0	38	27	14	10	25	34
— Fort Lauderdale (FSL)	1	6	.143	6.48	17	17	1	0	0	82	87	70	59	57	44
1986— Fort Lauderdale (FSL)	4	8	.333	4.05	22	21	1	1	0	117 2/3	96	64	53	90	101
1987— Columbus (I.L.)	1	4	.200	6.17	5	5	0	0	0	23 1/3	21	18	16	15	23
— Alb./Colonie (East.)	3	3	.500	3.35	15	14	2	0	0	78	64	34	29	37	71
— New York (A.L.)	2	2	.500	6.35	4	4	0	0	0	22 2/3	24	16	16	15	28
1988— New York (A.L.)	4	4	.500	3.92	14	14	0	0	0	57 1/3	49	27	25	33	60
— Columbus (I.L.)	0	2	.000	3.46	4	4	0	0	0	13	5	7	5	14	12
1989— New York (A.L.)	1	2	.333	6.07	4	4	0	0	0	26 2/3	23	20	18	21	22
— Toronto (A.L.)■	0	0	...	4.05	1	1	0	0	0	6 2/3	9	3	3	2	4
— Dunedin (FSL)	0	2	.000	5.63	3	3	0	0	0	8	11	5	5	5	4
1990— Dunedin (FSL)	0	0	...	2.63	6	6	0	0	0	24	18	8	7	12	14
— Syracuse (I.L.)	3	8	.273	4.62	15	14	1	1	0	78	59	43	40	68	69
— Toronto (A.L.)	0	0	...	0.00	4	0	0	0	0	6 1/3	1	0	0	2	5
1991— Toronto (A.L.)	0	0	...	27.00	3	0	0	0	0	1 2/3	3	5	5	5	1
— Dunedin (FSL)	0	0	...	1.86	4	3	0	0	0	9 2/3	5	2	2	7	5
1992— Syracuse (I.L.)	8	9	.471	3.86	27	27	2	0	0	163 1/3	159	82	70	64	108
— Toronto (A.L.)	0	0	...	9.00	1	0	0	0	0	1	1	1	1	2	0
1993— Toronto (A.L.)	9	6	.600	4.11	34	12	1	1	2	105	93	52	48	56	66
1994— Toronto (A.L.)	6	7	.462	5.08	20	20	1	0	0	111 2/3	125	68	63	65	100
1995— Toronto (A.L.)	11	11	.500	3.64	28	28	2	1	0	183	162	80	74	*108	153
1996— Florida (N.L.)■	16	12	.571	2.93	33	33	2	1	0	215 1/3	153	74	70	*119	200
1997— Florida (N.L.)	11	9	.550	4.34	27	27	0	0	0	151 1/3	133	78	73	91	132
1998— New York (N.L.)■	17	6	.739	2.47	28	28	4	2	0	193	151	55	53	71	174
1999— New York (N.L.)	13	12	.520	4.23	32	32	1	1	0	213	209	107	100	93	162
A.L. totals (9 years)	33	32	.508	4.36	113	83	4	2	2	522	490	272	253	309	439
N.L. totals (4 years)	57	39	.594	3.45	120	120	7	4	0	772 2/3	646	314	296	374	668
Major League totals (13 years)	90	71	.559	3.82	233	203	11	6	2	1294 2/3	1136	586	549	683	1107

DIVISION SERIES RECORD

Year League	W	L	Pct.	ERA	G	GS	CG	ShO	Sv.	IP	H	R	ER	BB	SO
1997— Florida (N.L.)	0	0	...	9.00	1	1	0	0	0	4	7	4	4	3	3
1999— New York (N.L.)	0	0	...	3.52	1	1	0	0	0	7 2/3	3	3	3	3	4
Division series totals (2 years)	0	0	...	5.40	2	2	0	0	0	11 2/3	10	7	7	6	7

CHAMPIONSHIP SERIES RECORD

Year League	W	L	Pct.	ERA	G	GS	CG	ShO	Sv.	IP	H	R	ER	BB	SO
1993— Toronto (A.L.)	0	0	...	3.38	2	0	0	0	0	2 2/3	4	1	1	2	2
1997— Florida (N.L.)	0	1	.000	4.32	2	1	0	0	0	8 1/3	13	4	4	2	6
1999— New York (N.L.)	0	1	.000	6.43	2	2	0	0	0	7	5	6	5	4	5
Champ. series totals (3 years)	0	2	.000	5.00	6	3	0	0	0	18	22	11	10	8	13

WORLD SERIES RECORD

RECORDS: Shares single-inning record for most bases on balls allowed—4 (October 21, 1997, fourth inning).
NOTES: Member of World Series championship team (1993 and 1997).

Year League	W	L	Pct.	ERA	G	GS	CG	ShO	Sv.	IP	H	R	ER	BB	SO
1993— Toronto (A.L.)	1	0	1.000	7.71	3	0	0	0	0	7	12	6	6	2	5
1997— Florida (N.L.)	0	0	...	5.06	2	2	0	0	0	10 2/3	10	9	6	10	10
World Series totals (2 years)	1	0	1.000	6.11	5	2	0	0	0	17 2/3	22	15	12	12	15

ALL-STAR GAME RECORD

Year League	W	L	Pct.	ERA	GS	CG	ShO	Sv.	IP	H	R	ER	BB	SO
1996— National	0	0	...	0.00	0	0	0	0	1/3	0	0	0	0	0

LEITER, MARK   P

PERSONAL: Born April 13, 1963, in Joliet, Ill. ... 6-3/220. ... Throws right, bats right. ... Full name: Mark Edward Leiter. ... Brother of Al Leiter, pitcher, New York Mets; and brother of Kurt Leiter, minor league pitcher (1982-84 and 1986). ... Name pronounced LIE-ter.
HIGH SCHOOL: Central Regional (Bayville, N.J.).
JUNIOR COLLEGE: Connors State College (Okla.).
COLLEGE: Ramapo College of New Jersey.
TRANSACTIONS/CAREER NOTES: Selected by Baltimore Orioles organization in fourth round of free-agent draft (January 11, 1983). ... On disabled list (April 10, 1986-entire season; April 10, 1987-entire season; and April 10-June 13, 1988). ... Released by Orioles organization (June 13, 1988). ... Signed by Fort Lauderdale, New York Yankees organization (September 29, 1988). ... Traded by Yankees to Detroit Tigers for IF Torey Lovullo (March 19, 1991). ... On Detroit disabled list (June 6-23, 1991; July 24-August 24, 1992; and August 4-September 1, 1993). ... Released by Tigers (March 15, 1994). ... Signed by California Angels (March 21, 1994). ... Granted free agency (December 23, 1994). ... Signed by Phoenix, San Francisco Giants organization (April 10, 1995). ... Traded by Giants to Montreal Expos for P Tim Scott and P Kirk Rueter (July 30, 1996). ... Granted free agency (November 5, 1996). ... Signed by Philadelphia Phillies (December 12, 1996). ... On disabled list (June 21-July 5, 1997). ... Traded by Phillies to Seattle Mariners for P Paul Spoljaric (November 9, 1998). ... On Seattle disabled list (March 26-April 28 and May 2, 1999-remainder of season); included rehabilitation assignment in Tacoma (April 14-17). ... Granted free agency (November 5, 1999).
STATISTICAL NOTES: Tied for A.L. lead with nine hit batsmen in 1994. ... Led N.L. with 17 hit batsmen in 1995 and tied for lead with 16 in 1996. ... Led N.L. with 37 home runs allowed in 1996.

Year League	W	L	Pct.	ERA	G	GS	CG	ShO	Sv.	IP	H	R	ER	BB	SO
1983— Bluefield (Appl.)	2	1	.667	2.70	6	6	2	0	0	36 2/3	33	17	11	13	35
— Hagerstown (Caro.)	1	5	.167	7.25	8	8	0	0	0	36	42	31	29	28	18
1984— Hagerstown (Caro.)	8	•13	.381	5.62	27	24	5	1	0	139 1/3	132	96	87	*108	105
1985— Hagerstown (Caro.)	2	8	.200	3.46	34	6	1	0	8	83 1/3	77	44	32	29	82
— Charlotte (Sou.)	0	1	.000	1.42	5	0	0	0	1	6 1/3	3	1	1	2	8

Year League	W	L	Pct.	ERA	G	GS	CG	ShO	Sv.	IP	H	R	ER	BB	SO
1986— Charlotte (Sou.)							Did not play.								
1987— Charlotte (Sou.)							Did not play.								
1988— Charlotte (Sou.)							Did not play.								
1989— Fort Lauderdale (FSL)■	2	2	.500	1.53	6	4	1	0	1	35 1/3	27	9	6	5	22
— Columbus (I.L.)	9	6	.600	5.00	22	12	0	0	0	90	102	50	50	34	70
1990— Columbus (I.L.)	9	4	.692	3.60	30	14	2	1	1	122 2/3	114	56	49	27	115
— New York (A.L.)	1	1	.500	6.84	8	3	0	0	0	26 1/3	33	20	20	9	21
1991— Toledo (I.L.)■	1	0	1.000	0.00	5	0	0	0	1	6 2/3	6	0	0	3	7
— Detroit (A.L.)	9	7	.563	4.21	38	15	1	0	1	134 2/3	125	66	63	50	103
1992— Detroit (A.L.)	8	5	.615	4.18	35	14	1	0	0	112	116	57	52	43	75
1993— Detroit (A.L.)	6	6	.500	4.72	27	13	1	0	0	106 2/3	111	61	56	44	70
1994— California (A.L.)■	4	7	.364	4.72	40	7	0	0	2	95 1/3	99	56	50	35	71
1995— San Francisco (N.L.)■	10	12	.455	3.82	30	29	7	1	0	195 2/3	185	91	83	55	129
1996— San Francisco (N.L.)	4	10	.286	5.19	23	22	1	0	0	135 1/3	151	93	78	50	118
— Montreal (N.L.)■	4	2	.667	4.39	12	12	1	0	0	69 2/3	68	35	34	19	46
1997— Philadelphia (N.L.)■	10	*17	.370	5.67	31	31	3	0	0	182 2/3	216	*132	*115	64	148
1998— Philadelphia (N.L.)	7	5	.583	3.55	69	0	0	0	23	88 2/3	67	36	35	47	84
1999— Tacoma (PCL)■	0	0	...	4.50	1	1	0	0	0	2	2	1	1	0	3
— Seattle (A.L.)	0	0	...	6.75	2	0	0	0	0	1 1/3	2	1	1	0	1
A.L. totals (6 years)	28	26	.519	4.57	150	52	3	0	3	476 1/3	486	261	242	181	341
N.L. totals (4 years)	35	46	.432	4.62	165	94	12	1	23	672	687	387	345	235	525
Major League totals (10 years)	63	72	.467	4.60	315	146	15	1	26	1148 1/3	1173	648	587	416	866

LEIUS, SCOTT 3B/SS

PERSONAL: Born September 24, 1965, in Yonkers, N.Y. ... 6-3/208. ... Bats right, throws right. ... Full name: Scott Thomas Leius. ... Name pronounced LAY-us.

HIGH SCHOOL: Mamaroneck (N.Y.).

COLLEGE: Concordia College (N.Y.).

TRANSACTIONS/CAREER NOTES: Selected by Minnesota Twins organization in 13th round of free-agent draft (June 2, 1986). ... On disabled list (August 3, 1989-remainder of season and April 22, 1993-remainder of season). ... Granted free agency (October 10, 1995). ... Signed by Cleveland Indians (March 31, 1996). ... On Cleveland disabled list (June 7-27, 1996); included rehabilitation assignment to Buffalo (June 13-27). ... Granted free agency (September 30, 1996). ... Signed by Boston Red Sox organization (February 8, 1997). ... Released by Red Sox (March 29, 1997). ... Signed by Chicago White Sox organization (May 20, 1997). ... Granted free agency (October 15, 1997). ... Signed by Kansas City Royals organization (March 9, 1998). ... On Kansas City disabled list (August 14-September 4, 1998); included rehabilitation assignment to Omaha (August 31-September 4). ... Granted free agency (October 28, 1998). ... Re-signed by Royals organization (December 17, 1998). ... On disabled list (July 4, 1999-remainder of season). ... Granted free agency (October 29, 1999).

STATISTICAL NOTES: Led Appalachian League shortstops with 174 assists and 33 double plays in 1986. ... Led Midwest League shortstops with 74 double plays in 1987.

			BATTING											FIELDING			
Year Team (League)	Pos.	G	AB	R	H	2B	3B	HR	RBI	Avg.	BB	SO	SB	PO	A	E	Avg.
1986— Elizabethton (Appl.)	SS-3B	61	237	37	66	14	1	4	23	.278	26	45	5	67	†176	18	.931
1987— Kenosha (Midw.)	SS	126	414	65	99	16	4	8	51	.239	50	88	6	183	331	31	.943
1988— Visalia (Calif.)	SS	93	308	44	73	14	4	3	46	.237	42	50	3	154	234	15	.963
1989— Orlando (Sou.)	SS	99	346	49	105	22	2	4	45	*.303	38	74	3	148	257	22	.948
1990— Portland (PCL)	SS-2B	103	352	34	81	13	5	2	23	.230	35	66	5	155	323	18	.964
— Minnesota (A.L.)	SS-3B	14	25	4	6	1	0	1	4	.240	2	2	0	20	25	0	1.000
1991— Minnesota (A.L.)	3B-SS-OF	109	199	35	57	7	2	5	20	.286	30	35	5	56	129	7	.964
1992— Minnesota (A.L.)	3B-SS	129	409	50	102	18	2	2	35	.249	34	61	6	63	261	15	.956
1993— Minnesota (A.L.)	SS	10	18	4	3	0	0	0	2	.167	2	4	0	10	26	2	.947
1994— Minnesota (A.L.)	3B-SS	97	350	57	86	16	1	14	49	.246	37	58	2	63	185	8	.969
1995— Minnesota (A.L.)	3B-SS-DH	117	372	51	92	16	5	4	45	.247	49	54	2	60	187	14	.946
1996— Cleveland (A.L.)■	3B-1B-2B-DH	27	43	3	6	4	0	1	3	.140	2	8	0	45	16	1	.984
— Buffalo (A.A.)	1-DH-2-3-O	35	123	22	33	3	1	4	17	.268	12	16	0	110	36	7	.954
1997— Nashville (A.A.)■	3B-DH-1B	30	104	15	25	2	0	7	17	.240	11	6	0	57	27	5	.944
1998— Omaha (PCL)■	3B-DH-2B-SS	71	258	40	77	10	0	15	46	.298	17	30	7	37	110	11	.930
— Kansas City (A.L.)	3B-SS-DH	17	46	2	8	0	0	0	4	.174	1	6	0	8	19	4	.871
1999— Kansas City (A.L.)	1-3-DH-S-2	37	74	8	15	1	0	1	10	.203	4	8	1	68	20	2	.978
Major League totals (9 years)		557	1536	214	375	63	10	28	172	.244	161	236	16	393	868	53	.960

CHAMPIONSHIP SERIES RECORD

			BATTING											FIELDING			
Year Team (League)	Pos.	G	AB	R	H	2B	3B	HR	RBI	Avg.	BB	SO	SB	PO	A	E	Avg.
1991— Minnesota (A.L.)	3B-PH	3	4	0	0	0	0	0	0	.000	1	1	0	1	4	0	1.000

WORLD SERIES RECORD

NOTES: Member of World Series championship team (1991).

			BATTING											FIELDING			
Year Team (League)	Pos.	G	AB	R	H	2B	3B	HR	RBI	Avg.	BB	SO	SB	PO	A	E	Avg.
1991— Minnesota (A.L.)	3B-PH-SS	7	14	2	5	0	0	1	2	.357	1	2	0	5	8	1	.929

LENNON, PATRICK OF

PERSONAL: Born April 27, 1968, in Whiteville, N.C. ... 6-2/230. ... Bats right, throws right. ... Full name: Patrick Orlando Lennon.

HIGH SCHOOL: Whiteville (N.C.).

TRANSACTIONS/CAREER NOTES: Selected by Seattle Mariners organization in first round (eighth pick overall) of free-agent draft (June 2, 1986). ... On Calgary disabled list (May 18, 1992-remainder of season). ... Granted free agency (October 15, 1992). ... Signed by Colorado

Rockies (October 29, 1992). ... Released by Colorado Springs, Rockies organization (April 2, 1993). ... Signed by Torreon of Mexican League (1993). ... Signed by Canton/Akron, Cleveland Indians organization (July 19, 1993). ... Granted free agency (October 15, 1993). ... Signed by New Britain, Boston Red Sox organization (March 7, 1994). ... On disabled list (August 4-12, 1994). ... Released by Red Sox organization (July 20, 1995). ... Signed by Salt Lake, Minnesota Twins organization (July 22, 1995). ... Granted free agency (October 16, 1995). ... Signed by Kansas City Royals (March 31, 1996). ... Released by Royals (April 29, 1996). ... Signed by Edmonton, Oakland Athletics organization (June 1, 1996). ... On Edmonton disabled list (September 10-18, 1996). ... On Oakland disabled list (August 20-September 12, 1997); included rehabilitation assignments to Modesto (August 28-September 3) and Edmonton (Septmeber 3-12). ... Released by A's (December 15, 1997). ... Signed by Anaheim Angels organization (January 30, 1998). ... Released by Angels (March 11, 1998). ... Signed by Toronto Blue Jays organization (March 25, 1998). ... Released by Blue Jays (February 9, 1999). ... Re-signed by Blue Jays organization (February 28, 1999). ... Released by Blue Jays (June 9, 1999). ... Signed by Detroit Tigers organization (June 10, 1999). ... Granted free agency (October 15, 1999).

STATISTICAL NOTES: Led Midwest League third basemen with 39 errors in 1987.

| | | | | | | | BATTING | | | | | | | | FIELDING | | |
Year Team (League)	Pos.	G	AB	R	H	2B	3B	HR	RBI	Avg.	BB	SO	SB	PO	A	E	Avg.
1986— Bellingham (N.W.)	SS-3B	51	169	35	41	5	2	3	27	.243	36	50	8	57	90	27	.845
1987— Wausau (Midw.)	3B-SS	98	319	54	80	21	3	7	34	.251	45	82	25	73	190	†40	.868
1988— Vermont (East.)	3B	95	321	44	83	9	3	9	40	.259	21	87	15	81	143	*28	.889
1989— Williamsport (East.)	OF-3B	66	248	32	65	14	2	3	31	.262	23	53	7	67	20	14	.861
1990— San Bern. (Calif.)	3B-OF	44	163	29	47	6	2	8	30	.288	15	51	6	29	40	7	.908
— Williamsport (East.)	OF-3B	49	167	24	49	6	4	5	22	.293	10	37	10	62	40	10	.911
1991— Calgary (PCL)	OF-3B	112	416	75	137	29	5	15	74	.329	46	68	12	114	3	6	.951
— Seattle (A.L.)	DH-OF	9	8	2	1	1	0	0	1	.125	3	1	0	2	0	0	1.000
1992— Seattle (A.L.)	1B	1	2	0	0	0	0	0	0	.000	0	0	0	5	0	0	1.000
— Calgary (PCL)	OF-3B	13	48	8	17	3	0	1	9	.354	6	10	4	12	0	1	.923
1993— Torreon (Mex.)■	OF	27	97	18	34	5	0	5	15	.351	11	31	0	27	1	0	1.000
— Cant./Akron (East.)■	OF-1B	45	152	24	39	7	1	4	23	.257	30	45	4	45	3	4	.923
1994— New Britain (East.)■	OF-DH-1B	114	429	80	140	30	5	17	67	.326	48	96	13	189	12	3	.985
1995— Pawtucket (I.L.)	OF-DH	40	128	20	35	6	2	3	20	.273	16	42	6	54	4	3	.951
— Trenton (East.)	OF-DH	27	98	19	39	7	0	1	8	.398	14	22	7	32	2	3	.919
— Salt Lake (PCL)■	DH-OF	34	115	26	46	15	0	6	29	.400	12	29	2	10	0	0	1.000
1996— Kansas City (A.L.)■	OF-DH	14	30	5	7	3	0	0	1	.233	7	10	0	18	0	1	.947
— Edmonton (PCL)■	OF-DH	68	251	37	82	16	2	12	42	.327	28	82	3	57	5	4	.939
1997— Edmonton (PCL)	DH-OF	39	134	28	46	7	0	9	35	.343	22	34	0	13	1	0	1.000
— Oakland (A.L.)	OF-DH	56	116	14	34	6	1	1	14	.293	15	35	0	55	0	3	.948
— Modesto (Calif.)	DH-OF	5	16	3	3	1	0	1	4	.188	3	5	0	2	0	0	1.000
1998— Syracuse (I.L.)■	OF-DH	126	438	87	127	22	4	27	95	.290	*87	121	12	132	11	8	.947
— Toronto (A.L.)	OF	2	4	1	2	2	0	0	0	.500	0	1	0	3	0	0	1.000
1999— Syracuse (I.L.)	OF-DH	37	134	26	45	5	0	9	33	.336	22	40	3	39	2	0	1.000
— Toronto (A.L.)	OF	9	29	3	6	2	0	1	6	.207	2	12	0	23	1	0	1.000
— Toledo (I.L.)■	OF-DH	74	280	49	74	16	1	21	50	.264	33	66	1	68	3	3	.959
Major League totals (6 years)		91	189	25	50	14	1	2	22	.265	27	59	0	106	1	4	.964

LESKANIC, CURTIS   P   BREWERS

PERSONAL: Born April 2, 1968, in Homestead, Pa. ... 6-0/186. ... Throws right, bats right. ... Full name: Curtis John Leskanic. ... Name pronounced lees-CAN-ik.

HIGH SCHOOL: Steel Valley (Munhall, Pa.).

COLLEGE: Louisiana State.

TRANSACTIONS/CAREER NOTES: Selected by Cleveland Indians organization in eighth round of free-agent draft (June 5, 1989). ... On disabled list (April 23-June 25, 1990). ... Traded by Indians organization with P Oscar Munoz to Minnesota Twins organization for 1B Paul Sorrento (March 28, 1992). ... Selected by Colorado Rockies in third round (66th pick overall) of expansion draft (November 17, 1992). ... Loaned by Rockies organization to Wichita, Padres organization (April 7-May 20, 1993). ... On Colorado disabled list (May 30-June 28, 1996); included rehabilitation assignment to Colorado Springs (June 22-27). ... On Colorado disabled list (March 23-April 12, 1997); included rehabilitation assignment to Salem (April 6-8). ... Traded by Rockies to Milwaukee Brewers for P Mike Myers (November 17, 1999).

MISCELLANEOUS: Had a sacrifice hit in only appearance as pinch hitter (1998). ... Holds Colorado Rockies all-time record for most games pitched (356).

Year League	W	L	Pct.	ERA	G	GS	CG	ShO	Sv.	IP	H	R	ER	BB	SO
1990— Kinston (Caro.)	6	5	.545	3.68	14	14	2	0	0	73 1/3	61	34	30	30	71
1991— Kinston (Caro.)	•15	8	.652	2.79	28	28	0	0	0	174 1/3	143	63	54	91	*163
1992— Orlando (Sou.)■	9	11	.450	4.30	26	23	3	0	0	152 2/3	158	84	73	64	126
— Portland (PCL)	1	2	.333	9.98	5	3	0	0	0	15 1/3	16	17	17	8	14
1993— Wichita (Texas)■	3	2	.600	3.45	7	7	0	0	0	44 1/3	37	20	17	17	42
— Colo. Springs (PCL)■	4	3	.571	4.47	9	7	1	1	0	44 1/3	39	24	22	26	38
— Colorado (N.L.)	1	5	.167	5.37	18	8	0	0	0	57	59	40	34	27	30
1994— Colo. Springs (PCL)	5	7	.417	3.31	21	21	2	0	0	130 1/3	129	60	48	54	98
— Colorado (N.L.)	1	1	.500	5.64	8	3	0	0	0	22 1/3	27	14	14	10	17
1995— Colorado (N.L.)	6	3	.667	3.40	*76	0	0	0	10	98	83	38	37	33	107
1996— Colorado (N.L.)	7	5	.583	6.23	70	0	0	0	6	73 2/3	82	51	51	38	76
— Colo. Springs (PCL)	0	0	...	3.00	3	0	0	0	0	3	5	1	1	1	2
1997— Salem (Caro.)	0	0	...	3.86	2	1	0	0	0	2 1/3	5	2	1	1	3
— Colorado (N.L.)	4	0	1.000	5.55	55	0	0	0	2	58 1/3	59	36	36	24	53
— Colo. Springs (PCL)	0	0	...	3.79	10	3	0	0	2	19	11	9	8	18	20
1998— Colorado (N.L.)	6	4	.600	4.40	66	0	0	0	2	75 2/3	75	37	37	40	55
1999— Colorado (N.L.)	6	2	.750	5.08	63	0	0	0	0	85	87	54	48	49	77
Major League totals (7 years)	31	20	.608	4.92	356	11	0	0	20	470	472	270	257	221	415

DIVISION SERIES RECORD

Year League	W	L	Pct.	ERA	G	GS	CG	ShO	Sv.	IP	H	R	ER	BB	SO
1995— Colorado (N.L.)	0	1	.000	6.00	3	0	0	0	0	3	3	2	2	0	4

LEVINE, AL   P   ANGELS

PERSONAL: Born May 22, 1968, in Park Ridge, Ill. ... 6-3/198. ... Throws right, bats right. ... Full name: Alan Brian Levine.
HIGH SCHOOL: Hoffman Estates (Ill.).
JUNIOR COLLEGE: Harper Junior College (Ill.).
COLLEGE: Southern Illinois-Carbondale.
TRANSACTIONS/CAREER NOTES: Selected by Chicago White Sox in 11th round of free-agent draft (June 3, 1991). ... Traded by White Sox with P Larry Thomas to Texas Rangers for SS Benji Gil (December 19, 1997). ... Claimed on waivers by Anaheim Angels (April 2, 1999).

Year League	W	L	Pct.	ERA	G	GS	CG	ShO	Sv.	IP	H	R	ER	BB	SO
1991— Utica (NY-P)	6	4	.600	3.18	16	12	2	1	1	85	75	45	30	26	83
1992— South Bend (Midw.)	9	5	.643	2.81	23	23	2	0	0	156 2/3	151	67	49	36	131
— Sarasota (FSL)	0	2	.000	4.02	3	2	0	0	0	15 2/3	17	11	7	5	11
1993— Sarasota (FSL)	11	8	.579	3.68	27	26	5	1	0	161 1/3	169	87	66	50	*129
1994— Birmingham (Sou.)	5	9	.357	3.31	18	18	1	0	0	114 1/3	117	50	42	44	94
— Nashville (A.A.)	0	2	.000	7.88	8	4	0	0	0	24	34	23	21	11	24
1995— Nashville (A.A.)	0	2	.000	5.14	3	3	0	0	0	14	20	10	8	7	14
— Birmingham (Sou.)	4	3	.571	2.34	43	1	0	0	7	73	61	22	19	25	68
1996— Nashville (A.A.)	4	5	.444	3.65	43	0	0	0	12	61 2/3	58	27	25	24	45
— Chicago (A.L.)	0	1	.000	5.40	16	0	0	0	0	18 1/3	22	14	11	7	12
1997— Chicago (A.L.)	2	2	.500	6.91	25	0	0	0	0	27 1/3	35	22	21	16	22
— Nashville (A.A.)	1	1	.500	7.13	26	0	0	0	2	35 1/3	58	32	28	11	29
1998— Oklahoma (PCL)■	1	3	.250	4.72	12	7	0	0	1	53 1/3	51	33	28	17	30
— Texas (A.L.)	0	1	.000	4.50	30	0	0	0	0	58	68	30	29	16	19
1999— Anaheim (A.L.)■	1	1	.500	3.39	50	1	0	0	0	85	76	40	32	29	37
Major League totals (4 years)	**3**	**5**	**.375**	**4.44**	**121**	**1**	**0**	**0**	**0**	**188 2/3**	**201**	**106**	**93**	**68**	**90**

LEVIS, JESSE   C   INDIANS

PERSONAL: Born April 14, 1968, in Philadelphia. ... 5-9/200. ... Bats left, throws right.
HIGH SCHOOL: Northeast (Philadelphia).
COLLEGE: North Carolina.
TRANSACTIONS/CAREER NOTES: Selected by Philadelphia Phillies organization in 36th round of free-agent draft (June 2, 1986); did not sign. ... Selected by Cleveland Indians organization in fourth round of free-agent draft (June 5, 1989). ... Traded by Indians to Milwaukee Brewers for P Scott Nate and a player to be named later (April 4, 1996); Indians acquired P Jared Camp to complete deal (June 9, 1996). ... On disabled list (May 8, 1998-remainder of season). ... Released by Brewers (September 29, 1998). ... Signed by Tampa Bay Devil Rays organization (December 18, 1998). ... On Durham disabled list (April 8-May 8, 1999). ... Released by Devil Rays (July 28, 1999). ... Signed by Indians (July 30, 1999). ... Granted free agency (October 4, 1999). ... Re-signed by Indians organization (January 13, 2000).
STATISTICAL NOTES: Led Eastern League catchers with 733 total chances in 1991.

						BATTING								FIELDING		
Year Team (League)	Pos.	G	AB	R	H	2B	3B	HR	RBI	Avg.	BB	SO	SB	PO	A	E	Avg.
1989— Burlington (Appl.)	C	27	93	11	32	4	0	4	16	.344	10	7	1	189	27	2	.991
— Kinston (Caro.)	C	27	87	11	26	6	0	2	11	.299	12	15	1	95	17	2	.982
— Colo. Springs (PCL)	PH	1	1	0	0	0	0	0	0	.000	0	0	0	...	...	...	...
1990— Kinston (Caro.)	C	107	382	63	113	18	3	7	64	.296	64	42	4	517	63	5	.991
1991— Canton/Akron (East.)	C	115	382	31	101	17	3	6	45	.264	40	36	2	*644	*77	12	.984
1992— Colo. Springs (PCL)	C	87	253	39	92	20	1	6	44	.364	37	25	1	375	47	4	.991
— Cleveland (A.L.)	C-DH	28	43	2	12	4	0	1	3	.279	0	5	0	59	5	1	.985
1993— Charlotte (I.L.)	C	47	129	10	32	6	1	2	20	.248	15	12	0	266	22	4	.986
— Cleveland (A.L.)	C	31	63	7	11	2	0	0	4	.175	2	10	0	109	7	1	.991
1994— Charlotte (I.L.)	C-DH	111	375	55	107	20	0	10	59	.285	55	39	2	452	34	4	.992
— Cleveland (A.L.)	PH	1	1	0	1	0	0	0	0	1.000	0	0	0	...	...	...	...
1995— Buffalo (A.A.)	C-DH	66	196	26	61	16	0	4	20	.311	32	11	0	338	20	2	.994
— Cleveland (A.L.)	C	12	18	1	6	2	0	0	3	.333	1	0	0	33	5	0	1.000
1996— Milwaukee (A.L.)■	C-DH	104	233	27	55	6	1	1	21	.236	38	15	0	373	26	1	*.998
1997— Milwaukee (A.L.)	C-DH	99	200	19	57	7	0	1	19	.285	24	17	1	296	19	2	.994
1998— Milwaukee (N.L.)	C	22	37	4	13	0	0	0	4	.351	7	6	1	83	2	0	1.000
1999— Durham (I.L.)■	C-DH	27	94	20	31	5	0	1	8	.330	15	9	0	142	9	0	1.000
— Orlando (Sou.)	C-DH	13	48	6	19	7	0	1	11	.396	6	4	0	52	4	1	.982
— Cleveland (A.L.)	C	10	26	0	4	0	0	0	3	.154	1	6	0	53	3	0	1.000
American League totals (7 years)		**285**	**584**	**56**	**146**	**21**	**1**	**3**	**53**	**.250**	**66**	**53**	**1**	**923**	**65**	**5**	**.995**
National League totals (1 year)		**22**	**37**	**4**	**13**	**0**	**0**	**0**	**4**	**.351**	**7**	**6**	**1**	**83**	**2**	**0**	**1.000**
Major League totals (8 years)		**307**	**621**	**60**	**159**	**21**	**1**	**3**	**57**	**.256**	**73**	**59**	**2**	**1006**	**67**	**5**	**.995**

LEVRAULT, ALLEN   P   BREWERS

PERSONAL: Born August 15, 1977, in Fall River, Mass. ... 6-3/230. ... Throws right, bats right. ... Full name: Allen Harry Levrault.
HIGH SCHOOL: Westport (Mass.).
JUNIOR COLLEGE: Community College of Rhode Island.
TRANSACTIONS/CAREER NOTES: Selected by Milwaukee Brewers organization in 13th round of free-agent draft (June 4, 1996). ... On Huntsville disabled list (June 20-July 10 and August 1-17, 1999).
STATISTICAL NOTES: Led Midwest League with 12 balks in 1997.

Year League	W	L	Pct.	ERA	G	GS	CG	ShO	Sv.	IP	H	R	ER	BB	SO
1996— Helena (Pio.)	4	3	.571	5.32	18	11	0	0	1	71	70	43	42	22	68
1997— Beloit (Midw.)	3	10	.231	5.28	24	24	1	0	0	131 1/3	141	89	77	40	112
1998— Stockton (Calif.)	9	3	.750	2.87	16	15	*4	•1	0	97 1/3	76	33	31	27	86
— El Paso (Texas)	1	5	.167	5.89	11	11	0	0	0	62 2/3	77	51	41	17	46
1999— Huntsville (Sou.)	9	2	*.818	3.43	16	16	2	1	0	99 2/3	77	44	38	33	82
— Louisville (I.L.)	1	3	.250	8.65	9	5	0	0	0	34 1/3	48	37	33	16	33

PERSONAL: Born August 28, 1967, in Berkeley, Calif. ... 6-0/190. ... Bats right, throws right. ... Full name: Darren Joel Lewis.
HIGH SCHOOL: Moreau (Hayward, Calif.).
JUNIOR COLLEGE: Chabot College (Calif.).
COLLEGE: California.
TRANSACTIONS/CAREER NOTES: Selected by Los Angeles Dodgers organization in sixth round of free-agent draft (January 14, 1986); did not sign. ... Selected by Toronto Blue Jays organization in 45th round of free-agent draft (June 2, 1987); did not sign. ... Selected by Oakland Athletics organization in 18th round of free-agent draft (June 1, 1988). ... Traded by A's with a player to be named later to San Francisco Giants for IF Ernest Riles (December 4, 1990); Giants acquired P Pedro Pena to complete deal (December 17, 1990). ... On disabled list (August 20-September 4, 1993). ... Traded by Giants with P Mark Portugal and P Dave Burba to Cincinnati Reds for OF Deion Sanders, P John Roper, P Ricky Pickett, P Scott Service and IF Dave McCarty (July 21, 1995). ... Released by Reds (December 1, 1995). ... Signed by Chicago White Sox (December 14, 1995). ... Traded by White Sox to Los Angeles Dodgers for a player to be named later (August 27, 1997); White Sox acquired IF Chad Fonville to complete deal (September 2, 1997). ... Granted free agency (October 27, 1997). ... Signed by Boston Red Sox (December 23, 1997). ... Granted free agency (November 3, 1998). ... Re-signed by Red Sox (November 5, 1998).
RECORDS: Holds major league records for most consecutive errorless games by outfielder—392 (August 21, 1990-June 29, 1994); and most consecutive chances accepted without an error by outfielder—938 (August 21, 1990-June 29, 1994). ... Shares major league career record for highest fielding average by outfielder (1,000 or more games)—.995. ... Shares major league record for fewest double plays by outfielder (150 or more games)—0 (1998). ... Holds N.L. records for most consecutive errorless games by outfielder—369 (July 13, 1991-June 29, 1994); and most consecutive chances accepted without an error by outfielder—905 (July 13, 1991-June 29, 1994).
HONORS: Won N.L. Gold Glove as outfielder (1994).
STATISTICAL NOTES: Led California League outfielders with 324 total chances in 1989. ... Career major league grand slams: 1.

Year	Team (League)	Pos.	G	AB	R	H	2B	3B	HR	RBI	Avg.	BB	SO	SB	PO	A	E	Avg.
									BATTING							FIELDING		
1988—Ariz. Athletics (Ariz.) ..	OF	5	15	8	5	3	0	0	4	.333	6	5	4	15	1	0	1.000
—Madison (Midw.)	OF-2B	60	199	38	49	4	1	0	11	.246	46	37	31	195	3	4	.980
1989—Modesto (Calif.)	OF	129	503	74	150	23	5	4	39	.298	59	84	27	*311	8	5	.985
—Huntsville (Sou.)	OF	9	31	7	10	1	1	1	7	.323	2	6	0	16	0	0	1.000
1990—Huntsville (Sou.)	OF	71	284	52	84	11	3	3	23	.296	36	28	21	186	6	0	1.000
—Tacoma (PCL)	OF	60	247	32	72	5	2	2	26	.291	16	35	16	132	9	2	.986
—Oakland (A.L.)	OF-DH	25	35	4	8	0	0	0	1	.229	7	4	2	33	0	0	1.000
1991—Phoenix (PCL)■	OF	81	315	63	107	12	10	2	52	.340	41	36	32	243	5	2	.992
—San Francisco (N.L.) ..	OF	72	222	41	55	5	3	1	15	.248	36	30	13	159	2	0	1.000
1992—San Francisco (N.L.) ..	OF	100	320	38	74	8	1	1	18	.231	29	46	28	225	3	0	1.000
—Phoenix (PCL)	OF	42	158	22	36	5	2	0	6	.228	11	15	9	93	2	0	1.000
1993—San Francisco (N.L.) ..	OF	136	522	84	132	17	7	2	48	.253	30	40	46	344	4	0	•1.000
1994—San Francisco (N.L.) ..	OF	114	451	70	116	15	•9	4	29	.257	53	50	30	279	5	2	.993
1995—San Francisco (N.L.) ..	OF	74	309	47	78	10	3	1	16	.252	17	37	21	200	2	1	.995
—Cincinnati (N.L.)■	OF	58	163	19	40	3	0	0	8	.245	17	20	11	121	3	1	.992
1996—Chicago (A.L.)■	OF	141	337	55	77	12	2	4	53	.228	45	40	21	287	0	3	.990
1997—Chicago (A.L.)	OF-DH	81	77	15	18	1	0	0	5	.234	11	14	11	90	1	0	1.000
—Los Angeles (N.L.)■	OF	26	77	7	23	3	1	1	10	.299	6	17	3	49	1	1	.980
1998—Boston (A.L.)■■	OF-DH	155	585	95	157	25	3	8	63	.268	70	94	29	382	6	3	.992
1999—Boston (A.L.)	OF-DH	135	470	63	113	14	6	2	40	.240	45	52	16	309	4	2	.994
American League totals (5 years)		537	1504	232	373	52	11	14	162	.248	178	204	79	1101	11	8	.993
National League totals (6 years)		580	2064	306	518	61	24	10	144	.251	188	240	152	1377	20	5	.996
Major League totals (10 years)		1117	3568	538	891	113	35	24	306	.250	366	444	231	2478	31	13	.995

DIVISION SERIES RECORD

Year	Team (League)	Pos.	G	AB	R	H	2B	3B	HR	RBI	Avg.	BB	SO	SB	PO	A	E	Avg.
									BATTING							FIELDING		
1995—Cincinnati (N.L.)	OF-PH	3	3	0	0	0	0	0	0	.000	0	1	0	3	0	0	1.000
1998—Boston (A.L.)	OF	4	14	4	5	2	0	0	0	.357	1	3	1	10	0	0	1.000
1999—Boston (A.L.)	OF	4	16	5	6	1	0	0	2	.375	0	2	1	7	0	0	1.000
Division series totals (3 years)		11	33	9	11	3	0	0	2	.333	1	6	2	20	0	0	1.000

CHAMPIONSHIP SERIES RECORD

Year	Team (League)	Pos.	G	AB	R	H	2B	3B	HR	RBI	Avg.	BB	SO	SB	PO	A	E	Avg.
									BATTING							FIELDING		
1995—Cincinnati (N.L.)	OF-PR	2	1	0	0	0	0	0	0	.000	0	0	0	2	0	0	1.000
1999—Boston (A.L.)	OF	5	17	2	2	1	0	0	1	.118	1	3	1	7	0	1	.875
Championship series totals (2 years)		7	18	2	2	1	0	0	1	.111	1	3	1	9	0	1	.900

L

PERSONAL: Born November 30, 1969, in Hamilton, Ohio. ... 6-1/195. ... Bats right, throws right. ... Full name: Mark David Lewis.
HIGH SCHOOL: Hamilton (Ohio).
TRANSACTIONS/CAREER NOTES: Selected by Cleveland Indians organization in first round (second pick overall) of free-agent draft (June 1, 1988). ... On Kinston disabled list (May 29-June 20, 1989). ... Traded by Indians to Cincinnati Reds for IF Tim Costo (December 14, 1994). ... Traded by Reds to Detroit Tigers (November 16, 1995), completing deal in which Reds acquired P David Wells for P C.J. Nitkowski, P David Tuttle and a player to be named later (July 31, 1995). ... Traded by Tigers to San Francisco Giants for 1B Jesus Ibarra (December 16, 1996). ... On disabled list (March 31-April 12, 1997). ... Granted free agency (December 21, 1997). ... Signed by Philadelphia Phillies (December 23, 1997). ... Granted free agency (October 26, 1998). ... Signed by Cincinnati Reds (December 23, 1998). ... Granted free agency (October 29, 1999). ... Re-signed by Reds (November 16, 1999).
STATISTICAL NOTES: Tied for A.L. lead in errors by shortstop with 25 in 1992. ... Tied for International League lead in grounding into double plays with 19 in 1993. ... Led International League shortstops with 81 double plays in 1993. ... Career major league grand slams: 1.

Year	Team (League)	Pos.	G	AB	R	H	2B	3B	HR	RBI	Avg.	BB	SO	SB	PO	A	E	Avg.
1988—Burlington (Appl.).......	SS	61	227	39	60	13	1	7	43	.264	25	44	14	70	*177	23	.915
1989—Kinston (Caro.).........	SS	93	349	50	94	16	3	1	32	.269	34	50	17	130	244	32	.921
—Cant./Akron (East.)....	SS	7	25	4	5	1	0	0	1	.200	1	3	0	15	28	2	.956
1990—Cant./Akron (East.).....	SS	102	390	55	106	19	3	1	60	.272	23	49	8	152	286	31	.934
—Colo. Springs (PCL) ...	SS	34	124	16	38	8	1	1	21	.306	9	13	2	52	84	11	.925
1991—Colo. Springs (PCL) ...	SS-2B-3B	46	179	29	50	10	3	2	31	.279	18	23	3	65	135	10	.952
—Cleveland (A.L.).........	2B-SS	84	314	29	83	15	1	0	30	.264	15	45	2	129	231	9	.976
1992—Cleveland (A.L.).........	SS-3B	122	413	44	109	21	0	5	30	.264	25	69	4	184	336	‡26	.952
1993—Charlotte (I.L.)..........	SS	126	507	93	144	30	4	17	67	.284	34	76	9	168	*403	23	.961
—Cleveland (A.L.)..........	SS	14	52	6	13	2	0	1	5	.250	0	7	3	22	31	2	.964
1994—Cleveland (A.L.).........	SS-3B-2B	20	73	6	15	5	0	1	8	.205	2	13	1	17	40	6	.905
—Charlotte (I.L.)..........	SS-2B-3B	86	328	56	85	16	1	8	34	.259	35	48	2	117	199	12	.963
1995—Cincinnati (N.L.)■......	3B-2B-SS	81	171	25	58	13	1	3	30	.339	21	33	0	19	107	4	.969
1996—Detroit (A.L.)■........	2B-DH	145	545	69	147	30	3	11	55	.270	42	109	6	264	413	9	.987
1997—San Fran. (N.L.)■......	3B-2B-DH	118	341	50	91	14	6	10	42	.267	23	62	3	74	157	14	.943
1998—Philadelphia (N.L.)■..	2B	142	518	52	129	21	2	9	54	.249	48	111	3	276	437	16	.978
1999—Cincinnati (N.L.)■......	3B-2B	88	173	18	44	16	0	6	28	.254	7	24	0	21	55	6	.927
American League totals (5 years)		385	1397	154	367	73	4	18	128	.263	84	243	16	616	1051	52	.970
National League totals (4 years)		429	1203	145	322	64	9	28	154	.268	99	230	6	390	756	40	.966
Major League totals (9 years)		814	2600	299	689	137	13	46	282	.265	183	473	22	1006	1807	92	.968

DIVISION SERIES RECORD

Year	Team (League)	Pos.	G	AB	R	H	2B	3B	HR	RBI	Avg.	BB	SO	SB	PO	A	E	Avg.
1995—Cincinnati (N.L.)	3B-PH	2	2	2	1	0	0	1	5	.500	1	0	0	0	0	1	.000
1997—San Francisco (N.L.) ..	2B	1	5	0	3	0	0	0	1	.600	0	0	0	1	3	0	1.000
Division series totals (2 years)		3	7	2	4	0	0	1	6	.571	1	0	0	1	3	1	.800

CHAMPIONSHIP SERIES RECORD

Year	Team (League)	Pos.	G	AB	R	H	2B	3B	HR	RBI	Avg.	BB	SO	SB	PO	A	E	Avg.
1995—Cincinnati (N.L.)	3B	2	4	0	1	0	0	0	0	.250	1	1	0	2	3	0	1.000

LEYRITZ, JIM · C/1B · YANKEES

PERSONAL: Born December 27, 1963, in Lakewood, Ohio. ... 5-11/220. ... Bats right, throws right. ... Full name: James Joseph Leyritz. ... Name pronounced LAY-rits.
HIGH SCHOOL: Turpin (Cincinnati).
JUNIOR COLLEGE: Middle Georgia College.
COLLEGE: Kentucky.
TRANSACTIONS/CAREER NOTES: Signed as non-drafted free agent by New York Yankees organization (August 24, 1985). ... Traded by Yankees to Anaheim Angels for two players to be named later (December 5, 1996); Yankees acquired 3B Ryan Kane and P Jeremy Blevins to complete deal (December 9, 1996). ... Traded by Angels with a player to be named later to Texas Rangers for P Ken Hill (July 29, 1997); Rangers acquired IF Rob Sasser to complete deal (October 31, 1997). ... Traded by Rangers with OF Damon Buford to Boston Red Sox for P Aaron Sele, P Mark Brandenburg and C Bill Haselman (November 6, 1997). ... Traded by Red Sox with OF Ethan Faggett to San Diego Padres for P Carlos Reyes, P Dario Veras and C Mandy Romero (June 21, 1998). ... On San Diego disabled list (June 23-July 30, 1999); included rehabilitation assignments to Rancho Cucamonga (July 27-28) and Las Vegas (July 29-30). ... Traded by Padres to Yankees for P Geraldo Padua (July 31, 1999).
STATISTICAL NOTES: Led Florida State League with 25 passed balls in 1987. ... Tied for Eastern League lead in being hit by pitch with nine in 1989. ... Career major league grand slams: 2.

Year	Team (League)	Pos.	G	AB	R	H	2B	3B	HR	RBI	Avg.	BB	SO	SB	PO	A	E	Avg.
1986—Oneonta (NY-P)	C	23	91	12	33	3	1	4	15	.363	5	10	1	170	21	2	.990
—Fort Laud. (FSL)	C	12	34	3	10	1	1	0	1	.294	4	5	0	32	8	1	.976
1987—Fort Laud. (FSL)	C	102	374	48	115	22	0	6	51	.307	38	54	2	458	*76	13	.976
1988—Alb./Colonie (East.)	C-3B-1B	112	382	40	92	18	3	5	56	.241	43	62	3	418	73	6	.988
1989—Alb./Colonie (East.)	C-OF-3B	114	375	53	118	18	2	10	66	*.315	65	51	2	421	41	3	.994
1990—Columbus (I.L.)	3-2-1-O-C	59	204	36	59	11	1	8	32	.289	37	33	4	75	96	13	.929
—New York (A.L.)	3B-OF-C	92	303	28	78	13	1	5	25	.257	27	51	2	117	107	13	.945
1991—New York (A.L.)	3B-C-1B-DH	32	77	8	14	3	0	0	4	.182	13	15	0	38	21	3	.952
—Columbus (I.L.)	C-3B-SS-2B	79	270	50	72	24	1	11	48	.267	38	50	1	209	48	5	.981
1992—New York (A.L.)	D-C-O-3-1-2	63	144	17	37	6	0	7	26	.257	14	22	0	96	15	1	.991
1993—New York (A.L.)	1B-OF-DH-C	95	259	43	80	14	0	14	53	.309	37	59	0	333	15	2	.994
1994—New York (A.L.)	C-DH-1B	75	249	47	66	12	0	17	58	.265	35	61	0	282	15	0	1.000
1995—New York (A.L.)	C-DH-1B	77	264	37	71	12	0	7	37	.269	37	73	1	417	24	3	.993
1996—New York (A.L.)	C-D-3-1-O-2	88	265	23	70	10	0	7	40	.264	30	68	2	387	31	6	.986
1997—Anaheim (A.L.)■	C-1B-DH	84	294	47	81	7	0	11	50	.276	37	56	1	440	45	2	.996
—Texas (A.L.)■	C-DH-1B	37	85	11	24	4	0	0	14	.282	23	22	1	116	7	1	.992
1998—Boston (A.L.)■	DH-C-1B	52	129	17	37	6	0	8	24	.287	21	34	0	13	0	0	1.000
—San Diego (N.L.)■ ...	C-1B-3B-OF	62	143	17	38	10	0	4	18	.266	21	40	0	276	19	3	.990
1999—San Diego (N.L.)	C-1B-3B	50	134	17	32	5	0	8	21	.239	15	37	0	266	23	3	.990
—Rancho Cuca. (Calif.) .	DH	1	4	0	0	0	0	0	0	.000	0	1	0	0	0	0	...
—Las Vegas (PCL)	1B	2	8	0	0	0	0	0	0	.000	0	5	0	17	1	0	1.000
—New York (A.L.)■	DH-1B-C-3B	31	66	8	15	4	1	0	5	.227	13	17	0	62	10	2	.973
American League totals (10 years)		726	2135	286	573	91	2	76	336	.268	287	478	7	2301	290	33	.987
National League totals (2 years)		112	277	34	70	15	0	12	39	.253	36	77	0	542	42	6	.990
Major League totals (10 years)		838	2412	320	643	106	2	88	375	.267	323	555	7	2843	332	39	.988

DIVISION SERIES RECORD

RECORDS: Shares A.L. career record for most games by pinch hitter—3.

Year Team (League)	Pos.	G	AB	R	H	2B	3B	HR	RBI	Avg.	BB	SO	SB	PO	A	E	Avg.
1995— New York (A.L.).........	C-PH	2	7	1	1	0	0	1	2	.143	0	1	0	13	0	0	1.000
1996— New York (A.L.).........	C-DH	2	3	0	0	0	0	0	1	.000	0	1	0	4	0	0	1.000
1998— San Diego (N.L.)	1B-C-PH	4	10	3	4	0	0	3	5	.400	0	2	0	34	0	0	1.000
1999— New York (A.L.).........	PH-DH	2	2	0	0	0	0	0	1	.000	1	0	0	0	0	0	...
Division series totals (4 years)		10	22	4	5	0	0	4	9	.227	1	4	0	51	0	0	1.000

CHAMPIONSHIP SERIES RECORD

Year Team (League)	Pos.	G	AB	R	H	2B	3B	HR	RBI	Avg.	BB	SO	SB	PO	A	E	Avg.
1996— New York (A.L.).........	C-OF-PH	3	8	1	2	0	0	1	2	.250	1	4	0	11	2	0	1.000
1998— San Diego (N.L.)	PH-1B-C	5	12	1	2	0	0	1	4	.167	0	2	0	24	1	0	1.000
1999— New York (A.L.)							Did not play.										
Championship series totals (2 years)		8	20	2	4	0	0	2	6	.200	1	6	0	35	3	0	1.000

WORLD SERIES RECORD

NOTES: Member of World Series championship team (1996 and 1999).

Year Team (League)	Pos.	G	AB	R	H	2B	3B	HR	RBI	Avg.	BB	SO	SB	PO	A	E	Avg.
1996— New York (A.L.).........	C-PH	4	8	1	3	0	0	1	3	.375	4	2	1	15	0	0	1.000
1998— San Diego (N.L.) DH-PH-1B-C		4	10	0	0	0	0	0	0	.000	1	4	0	19	0	0	1.000
1999— New York (A.L.).........	PH-DH	2	1	1	1	0	0	1	2	1.000	1	0	0	0	0	0	...
World Series totals (3 years)		10	19	2	4	0	0	2	5	.211	6	6	1	34	0	0	1.000

LIDLE, CORY   P   DEVIL RAYS

PERSONAL: Born March 22, 1972, in Hollywood, Calif. ... 5-11/180. ... Throws right, bats right. ... Full name: Cory Fulton Lidle. ... Twin brother of Kevin Lidle, catcher, San Diego Padres organization.
HIGH SCHOOL: South Hills (Covina, Calif.).
TRANSACTIONS/CAREER NOTES: Signed as non-drafted free agent by Minnesota Twins organization (August 25, 1990). ... Released by Twins (April 1, 1993). ... Signed by Pocatello, Pioneer League (May 28, 1993). ... Contract sold by Pocatello to Milwaukee Brewers organization (September 17, 1993). ... Traded by Brewers to New York Mets for C Kelly Stinnett (January 17, 1996). ... Selected by Arizona Diamondbacks in first round (13th pick overall) of expansion draft (November 18, 1997). ... On Arizona disabled list (March 31, 1998-entire season); included rehabilitation assignments to High Desert (April 20-28) and Tucson (September 3-7). ... Claimed on waivers by Tampa Bay Devil Rays (October 7, 1998). ... On Tampa Bay disabled list (March 23-September 18, 1999); included rehabilitation assignments to St. Petersburg (August 20-28) and Durham (August 29-September 18).

Year League	W	L	Pct.	ERA	G	GS	CG	ShO	Sv.	IP	H	R	ER	BB	SO
1991— Gulf Coast Twins (GCL)......	1	1	.500	5.79	4	0	0	0	0	4 2/3	5	3	3	0	5
1992— Elizabethton (Appl.)............	2	1	.667	3.71	19	2	0	0	6	43 2/3	40	29	18	21	32
1993— Pocatello (Pio.)■..............	•8	4	.667	4.13	17	16	3	0	1	106 2/3	104	59	49	54	91
1994— Stockton (Calif.)■.............	1	2	.333	4.43	25	1	0	0	4	42 2/3	60	32	21	13	38
— Beloit (Midw.)..................	3	4	.429	2.61	13	9	1	1	0	69	65	24	20	11	62
1995— El Paso (Texas)..................	5	4	.556	3.36	45	9	0	0	2	109 2/3	126	52	41	36	78
1996— Binghamton (East.)■.........	14	10	.583	3.31	27	27	•6	1	0	*190 1/3	186	78	70	49	141
1997— Norfolk (I.L.)....................	4	2	.667	3.64	7	7	1	0	0	42	46	20	17	10	34
— New York (N.L.).................	7	2	.778	3.53	54	2	0	0	2	81 2/3	86	38	32	20	54
1998— High Desert (Calif.)■.........	0	0	...	0.00	1	1	0	0	0	2 2/3	2	1	0	2	6
— Tucson (PCL)...................	0	0	...	0.00	1	1	0	0	0	4 2/3	2	0	0	2	2
1999— St. Petersburg (FSL)■.......	0	0	...	0.00	2	2	0	0	0	5	2	0	0	2	4
— Durham (I.L.)...................	0	0	...	4.76	3	2	0	0	0	5 2/3	9	3	3	1	6
— Tampa Bay (A.L.)................	1	0	1.000	7.20	5	1	0	0	0	5	8	4	4	2	4
A.L. totals (1 year)	1	0	1.000	7.20	5	1	0	0	0	5	8	4	4	2	4
N.L. totals (1 year)	7	2	.778	3.53	54	2	0	0	2	81 2/3	86	38	32	20	54
Major League totals (2 years)	8	2	.800	3.74	59	3	0	0	2	86 2/3	94	42	36	22	58

LIEBER, JON   P   CUBS

PERSONAL: Born April 2, 1970, in Council Bluffs, Iowa. ... 6-3/225. ... Throws right, bats left. ... Full name: Jonathan Ray Lieber. ... Name pronounced LEE-ber.
HIGH SCHOOL: Abraham Lincoln (Council Bluffs, Iowa.).
JUNIOR COLLEGE: Iowa Western Community College-Council Bluffs.
COLLEGE: South Alabama.
TRANSACTIONS/CAREER NOTES: Selected by Chicago Cubs organization in ninth round of free-agent draft (June 3, 1991); did not sign. ... Selected by Kansas City Royals organization in second round of free-agent draft (June 1, 1992); pick received as part of compensation for New York Yankees signing Type A free-agent OF Danny Tartabull. ... Traded by Royals with P Dan Miceli to Pittsburgh Pirates for P Stan Belinda (July 31, 1993). ... On disabled list (August 21-September 15, 1998). ... Traded by Pirates to Cubs for OF Brant Brown (December 14, 1998). ... On disabled list (April 21-May 8, 1999).

Year League	W	L	Pct.	ERA	G	GS	CG	ShO	Sv.	IP	H	R	ER	BB	SO
1992— Eugene (N.W.)	3	0	1.000	1.16	5	5	0	0	0	31	26	6	4	2	23
— Baseball City (FSL)............	3	3	.500	4.65	7	6	0	0	0	31	45	20	16	8	19
1993— Wilmington (Caro.)............	9	3	.750	2.67	17	16	2	0	0	114 2/3	125	47	34	9	89
— Memphis (Sou.).................	2	1	.667	6.86	4	4	0	0	0	21	32	16	16	6	17
— Carolina (Sou.)■................	4	2	.667	3.97	6	6	0	0	0	34	39	15	15	10	28
1994— Carolina (Sou.)................	2	0	1.000	1.29	3	3	1	1	0	21	13	4	3	2	21
— Buffalo (A.A.)...................	1	1	.500	1.69	3	3	0	0	0	21 1/3	16	4	4	1	21
— Pittsburgh (N.L.)	6	7	.462	3.73	17	17	1	0	0	108 2/3	116	62	45	25	71

Year	League	W	L	Pct.	ERA	G	GS	CG	ShO	Sv.	IP	H	R	ER	BB	SO
1995—Pittsburgh (N.L.)		4	7	.364	6.32	21	12	0	0	0	72 2/3	103	56	51	14	45
—Calgary (PCL)		1	5	.167	7.01	14	14	0	0	0	77	122	69	60	19	34
1996—Pittsburgh (N.L.)		9	5	.643	3.99	51	15	0	0	1	142	156	70	63	28	94
1997—Pittsburgh (N.L.)		11	14	.440	4.49	33	32	1	0	0	188 1/3	193	102	94	51	160
1998—Pittsburgh (N.L.)		8	14	.364	4.11	29	28	2	0	1	171	182	93	78	40	138
1999—Chicago (N.L.)■		10	11	.476	4.07	31	31	3	1	0	203 1/3	226	107	92	46	186
Major League totals (6 years)		48	58	.453	4.30	182	135	7	1	2	886	976	490	423	204	694

LIEBERTHAL, MIKE   C   PHILLIES

PERSONAL: Born January 18, 1972, in Glendale, Calif. ... 6-0/190. ... Bats right, throws right. ... Full name: Michael Scott Lieberthal. ... Name pronounced LEE-ber-thal.

HIGH SCHOOL: Westlake (Westlake Village, Calif.).

TRANSACTIONS/CAREER NOTES: Selected by Philadelphia Phillies organization in first round (third pick overall) of free-agent draft (June 4, 1990). ... On Scranton/Wilkes-Barre disabled list (August 31, 1992-remainder of season). ... On disabled list (August 22, 1996-remainder of season; and July 24-September 2, 1998).

HONORS: Won N.L. Gold Glove at catcher (1999).

STATISTICAL NOTES: Tied for N.L. lead with 12 passed balls in 1997. ... Tied for N.L. lead with 11 passed balls in 1999. ... Career major league grand slams: 2.

							BATTING							FIELDING			
Year	Team (League)	Pos.	G	AB	R	H	2B	3B	HR	RBI	Avg.	BB	SO	SB	PO	A	E	Avg.
1990—Martinsville (Appl.)		C	49	184	26	42	9	0	4	22	.228	11	40	2	421	*52	5	*.990
1991—Spartanburg (SAL)		C	72	243	34	74	17	0	0	31	.305	23	25	1	565	68	10	.984
—Clearwater (FSL)		C	16	52	7	15	2	0	0	7	.288	3	12	0	128	9	1	.993
1992—Reading (East.)		C	86	309	30	88	16	1	2	37	.285	19	26	4	524	48	7	.988
—Scranton/W.B. (I.L.)		C	16	45	4	9	1	0	0	4	.200	2	5	0	86	6	1	.989
1993—Scranton/W.B. (I.L.)		C	112	382	35	100	17	0	7	40	.262	24	32	2	659	75	•11	.985
1994—Scranton/W.B. (I.L.)		C-DH	84	296	23	69	16	0	1	32	.233	21	29	1	472	50	9	.983
—Philadelphia (N.L.)		C	24	79	6	21	3	1	1	5	.266	3	5	0	122	4	4	.969
1995—Philadelphia (N.L.)		C	16	47	1	12	2	0	0	4	.255	5	5	0	95	10	1	.991
—Scranton/W.B. (I.L.)		C-DH-3B	85	278	44	78	20	2	6	42	.281	44	26	1	503	46	5	.991
1996—Philadelphia (N.L.)		C	50	166	21	42	8	0	7	23	.253	10	30	0	284	20	3	.990
1997—Philadelphia (N.L.)		C-DH	134	455	59	112	27	1	20	77	.246	44	76	3	934	73	12	.988
1998—Philadelphia (N.L.)		C	86	313	39	80	15	3	8	45	.256	17	44	2	607	41	8	.988
1999—Philadelphia (N.L.)		C	145	510	84	153	33	1	31	96	.300	44	86	0	881	*62	3	*.997
Major League totals (6 years)			455	1570	210	420	88	6	67	250	.268	123	246	5	2923	210	31	.990

ALL-STAR GAME RECORD

					BATTING							FIELDING			
Year	League	Pos.	AB	R	H	2B	3B	HR	RBI	Avg.	BB	SO	SB	PO	A	E	Avg.
1999—National		C	1	0	0	0	0	0	0	.000	0	0	0	1	0	0	1.000

LIEFER, JEFF   1B/OF   WHITE SOX

PERSONAL: Born August 17, 1974, in Fontana, Calif. ... 6-3/195. ... Bats left, throws right. ... Full name: Jeffery David Liefer.

HIGH SCHOOL: Upland (Calif.).

COLLEGE: Long Beach State.

TRANSACTIONS/CAREER NOTES: Selected by Cleveland Indians organization in sixth round of free-agent draft (June 1, 1992); did not sign. ... Selected by Chicago White Sox organization in first round (25th pick overall) of free-agent draft (June 1, 1995). ... On Charlotte disabled list (August 30, 1999-remainder of season).

							BATTING							FIELDING			
Year	Team (League)	Pos.	G	AB	R	H	2B	3B	HR	RBI	Avg.	BB	SO	SB	PO	A	E	Avg.
1996—South Bend (Midw.)		DH-3B	74	277	60	90	14	0	15	58	.325	30	62	6	31	62	23	.802
—Prince Will. (Caro.)		DH	37	147	17	33	6	0	1	13	.224	11	27	0	0	0	0	...
1997—Birmingham (Sou.)		OF-DH	119	474	67	113	24	9	15	71	.238	38	115	2	166	2	•8	.955
1998—Birmingham (Sou.)		1B-DH-OF	127	471	84	137	33	6	21	89	.291	60	125	1	763	60	11	.987
—Calgary (PCL)		OF-DH-1B	8	31	3	8	3	0	1	10	.258	2	12	0	26	3	0	1.000
1999—Chicago (A.L.)		OF-1B-DH	45	113	8	28	7	1	0	14	.248	8	28	2	124	12	0	1.000
—Charlotte (I.L.)		1B-OF-3B	46	171	36	58	17	1	9	34	.339	21	26	2	226	24	3	.988
Major League totals (1 year)			45	113	8	28	7	1	0	14	.248	8	28	2	124	12	0	1.000

LIGTENBERG, KERRY   P   BRAVES

PERSONAL: Born May 11, 1971, in Rapid City, S.D. ... 6-2/215. ... Throws right, bats right. ... Full name: Kerry Dale Ligtenberg. ... Name pronounced Light-en-berg.

HIGH SCHOOL: Park (Cottage Grove, Minn.).

COLLEGE: Minnesota-Morris, then Minnesota.

TRANSACTIONS/CAREER NOTES: Signed by Minneapolis, North Central League (1994). ... Contract sold by Minneapolis to Seattle Mariners organization (March 28, 1995). ... Released by Mariners (April 2, 1995). ... Signed by Minneapolis, Prairie League (1995). ... Contract sold by Minneapolis to Atlanta Braves organization (January 27, 1996). ... On disabled list (April 3, 1999-entire season).

Year	League	W	L	Pct.	ERA	G	GS	CG	ShO	Sv.	IP	H	R	ER	BB	SO
1994—Minneapolis (NCL)		5	5	.500	3.31	19	19	2	...	0	114 1/3	103	47	42	44	94
1995—Minneapolis (Prairie)		11	2	.846	2.73	17	15	4	...	0	108 2/3	101	41	33	26	100
1996—Durham (Caro.)■		7	4	.636	2.41	49	0	0	0	20	59 2/3	58	20	16	16	76
1997—Greenville (Sou.)		3	1	.750	2.04	31	0	0	0	16	35 1/3	20	8	8	14	43
—Richmond (I.L.)		0	3	.000	4.32	14	0	0	0	1	25	21	13	12	2	35
—Atlanta (N.L.)		1	0	1.000	3.00	15	0	0	0	1	15	12	5	5	4	19
1998—Atlanta (N.L.)		3	2	.600	2.71	75	0	0	0	30	73	51	24	22	24	79
1999—Atlanta (N.L.)									Did not play.							
Major League totals (2 years)		4	2	.667	2.76	90	0	0	0	31	88	63	29	27	28	98

DIVISION SERIES RECORD

Year League	W	L	Pct.	ERA	G	GS	CG	ShO	Sv.	IP	H	R	ER	BB	SO
1998—Atlanta (N.L.)	0	0	...	0.00	3	0	0	0	0	3 1/3	1	0	0	5	3

CHAMPIONSHIP SERIES RECORD

Year League	W	L	Pct.	ERA	G	GS	CG	ShO	Sv.	IP	H	R	ER	BB	SO
1997—Atlanta (N.L.)	0	0	...	0.00	2	0	0	0	0	3	1	0	0	0	4
1998—Atlanta (N.L.)	0	1	.000	7.36	4	0	0	0	0	3 2/3	3	3	3	2	5
Champ. series totals (2 years)	0	1	.000	4.05	6	0	0	0	0	6 2/3	4	3	3	2	9

LILLY, TED   P   EXPOS

PERSONAL: Born January 4, 1976, in Lameta, Calif. ... 6-0/185. ... Throws left, bats left. ... Full name: Theodore R. Lilly.
HIGH SCHOOL: Yosemite (Oakhurst, Calif.).
JUNIOR COLLEGE: Fresno (Calif.) City College.
TRANSACTIONS/CAREER NOTES: Selected by Los Angeles Dodgers in 23rd round of free-agent draft (June 4, 1996). ... Traded by Dodgers with 2B Wilton Guerrero, OF Peter Bergeron and 1B Jonathan Tucker to Montreal Expos for P Carlos Perez, SS Mark Grudzielanek and IF Hiram Bocachica (July 31, 1998). ... On Ottawa disabled list (June 21, 1999-remainder of season).
HONORS: Named California League Pitcher of the Year (1997).
STATISTICAL NOTES: Pitched 8-0 no-hit victory against Lake Elsinore (May 10, 1997).

Year League	W	L	Pct.	ERA	G	GS	CG	ShO	Sv.	IP	H	R	ER	BB	SO
1996—Yakima (N.W.)	4	0	1.000	0.84	13	8	0	0	0	53 2/3	25	9	5	14	75
1997—San Bernardino (Calif.)	7	8	.467	*2.81	23	21	2	1	0	134 2/3	116	52	42	32	158
1998—San Antonio (Texas)	8	4	.667	3.30	17	17	0	0	0	111 2/3	114	50	41	37	96
—Albuquerque (PCL)	1	3	.250	4.94	5	5	0	0	0	31	39	20	17	9	25
—Ottawa (I.L.)■	2	2	.500	4.85	7	7	0	0	0	39	45	28	21	19	49
1999—Ottawa (I.L.)	8	5	.615	3.84	16	16	0	0	0	89	81	40	38	23	78
—Montreal (N.L.)	0	1	.000	7.61	9	3	0	0	0	23 2/3	30	20	20	9	28
Major League totals (1 year)	0	1	.000	7.61	9	3	0	0	0	23 2/3	30	20	20	9	28

LIMA, JOSE   P   ASTROS

L

PERSONAL: Born September 30, 1972, in Santiago, Dominican Republic. ... 6-2/205. ... Throws right, bats right. ... Full name: Jose D. Lima. ... Name pronounced LEE-mah.
HIGH SCHOOL: Escuela Primaria Las Charcas (Santiago, Dominican Replublic).
TRANSACTIONS/CAREER NOTES: Signed as non-drafted free agent by Detroit Tigers organization (July 5, 1989). ... Traded by Tigers with C Brad Ausmus, P C.J. Nitkowski, P Trever Miller and IF Daryle Ward to Houston Astros for OF Brian Hunter, IF Orlando Miller, P Doug Brocail, P Todd Jones and cash (December 10, 1996).
RECORDS: Shares N.L. single-inning record for most consecutive home runs allowed—3 (September 17, 1999, fourth inning).
HONORS: Named righthanded pitcher on THE SPORTING NEWS N.L. All-Star team (1999).
STATISTICAL NOTES: Led Florida State League with 14 home runs allowed in 1992. ... Led Eastern League with 13 balks in 1993. ... Pitched 3-0 no-hit victory for Toledo against Pawtucket (August 17, 1994).
MISCELLANEOUS: Appeared in one game as third baseman with no chances (1999).

Year League	W	L	Pct.	ERA	G	GS	CG	ShO	Sv.	IP	H	R	ER	BB	SO
1990—Bristol (Appl.)	3	8	.273	5.02	14	12	1	0	1	75 1/3	89	49	42	22	64
1991—Lakeland (FSL)	0	1	.000	10.38	4	1	0	0	0	8 2/3	16	10	10	2	5
—Fayetteville (SAL)	1	3	.250	4.97	18	7	0	0	0	58	53	38	32	25	60
1992—Lakeland (FSL)	5	11	.313	3.16	25	25	5	2	0	151	132	57	53	21	137
1993—London (East.)	8	•13	.381	4.07	27	27	2	0	0	177	160	96	80	59	138
1994—Toledo (I.L.)	7	9	.438	3.60	23	22	3	2	0	142 1/3	124	70	57	48	117
—Detroit (A.L.)	0	1	.000	13.50	3	1	0	0	0	6 2/3	11	10	10	3	7
1995—Lakeland (FSL)	3	1	.750	2.57	4	4	0	0	0	21	23	11	6	0	20
—Toledo (I.L.)	5	3	.625	3.01	11	11	1	0	0	74 2/3	69	26	25	14	40
—Detroit (A.L.)	3	9	.250	6.11	15	15	0	0	0	73 2/3	85	52	50	18	37
1996—Toledo (I.L.)	5	4	.556	6.78	12	12	0	0	0	69	93	53	52	12	57
—Detroit (A.L.)	5	6	.455	5.70	39	4	0	0	3	72 2/3	87	48	46	22	59
1997—Houston (N.L.)■	1	6	.143	5.28	52	1	0	0	2	75	79	45	44	16	63
1998—Houston (N.L.)	16	8	.667	3.70	33	33	3	1	0	233 1/3	229	100	96	32	169
1999—Houston (N.L.)	21	10	.677	3.58	35	•35	3	0	0	246 1/3	256	108	98	44	187
A.L. totals (3 years)	8	16	.333	6.24	57	20	0	0	3	153	183	110	106	43	103
N.L. totals (3 years)	38	24	.613	3.86	120	69	6	1	2	554 2/3	564	253	238	92	419
Major League totals (6 years)	46	40	.535	4.37	177	89	6	1	5	707 2/3	747	363	344	135	522

DIVISION SERIES RECORD

Year League	W	L	Pct.	ERA	G	GS	CG	ShO	Sv.	IP	H	R	ER	BB	SO
1997—Houston (N.L.)	0	0	...	0.00	1	0	0	0	0	1	0	0	0	1	1
1998—Houston (N.L.)							Did not play.								
1999—Houston (N.L.)	0	1	.000	5.40	1	1	0	0	0	6 2/3	9	4	4	2	4
Division series totals (2 years)	0	1	.000	4.70	2	1	0	0	0	7 2/3	9	4	4	3	5

ALL-STAR GAME RECORD

Year League	W	L	Pct.	ERA	GS	CG	ShO	Sv.	IP	H	R	ER	BB	SO
1999—National	0	0	...	0.00	0	0	0	0	1	1	0	0	0	0

LINCOLN, MIKE   P   TWINS

PERSONAL: Born April 10, 1975, in Carmichael, Calif. ... 6-2/211. ... Throws right, bats right. ... Full name: Michael George Lincoln.
HIGH SCHOOL: Casa Roble (Orangevale, Calif.).

JUNIOR COLLEGE: American River College (Calif.).
COLLEGE: Tennessee.
TRANSACTIONS/CAREER NOTES: Selected by Minnesota Twins organization in 13th round of free-agent draft (June 4, 1996).

Year League	W	L	Pct.	ERA	G	GS	CG	ShO	Sv.	IP	H	R	ER	BB	SO
1996— Fort Myers (FSL)	5	2	.714	4.07	12	11	0	0	0	59²/₃	64	31	27	25	24
1997— Fort Myers (FSL)	13	4	.765	2.28	20	20	1	1	0	134	130	41	34	25	75
1998— New Britain (East.)	*15	7	.682	3.22	26	26	1	0	0	173¹/₃	180	80	62	35	109
1999— Minnesota (A.L.)	3	10	.231	6.84	18	15	0	0	0	76¹/₃	102	59	58	26	27
— Salt Lake (PCL)	5	2	.714	7.78	9	9	0	0	0	59	82	52	51	21	39
Major League totals (1 year)	3	10	.231	6.84	18	15	0	0	0	76¹/₃	102	59	58	26	27

LINEBRINK, SCOTT — P — GIANTS

PERSONAL: Born August 4, 1976, in Austin, Texas. ... 6-3/185. ... Throws right, bats right. ... Full name: Scott Cameron Linebrink.
HIGH SCHOOL: McNeil (Austin, Texas).
COLLEGE: Concordia, then Southwest Texas State.
TRANSACTIONS/CAREER NOTES: Selected by San Francisco Giants organization in second round of free-agent draft (June 3, 1997). ... On Shreveport disabled list (April 8-July 17, 1999).

Year League	W	L	Pct.	ERA	G	GS	CG	ShO	Sv.	IP	H	R	ER	BB	SO
1997— San Jose (Calif.)	2	1	.667	3.18	6	6	0	0	0	28¹/₃	29	11	10	10	40
— Salem-Kaizer (N.W.)	0	0	...	4.50	3	3	0	0	0	10	7	5	5	6	6
1998— Shreveport (Texas)	10	8	.556	5.02	21	21	0	0	0	113	101	66	63	58	128
1999— Shreveport (Texas)	1	8	.111	6.44	10	10	0	0	0	43¹/₃	48	31	31	14	33

LINIAK, COLE — 3B — CUBS

PERSONAL: Born August 23, 1976, in Encinitas, Calif. ... 6-1/190. ... Bats right, throws right. ... Full name: Cole Edward Liniak.
HIGH SCHOOL: San Dieguito (Encinitas, Calif.).
TRANSACTIONS/CAREER NOTES: Selected by Boston Red Sox organization in seventh round of free-agent draft (June 1, 1995). ... On Pawtucket disabled list (May 24-June 17, 1999). ... Traded by Red Sox to Chicago Cubs (September 1, 1999), completing deal in which Cubs traded P Rod Beck to Red Sox for P Mark Guthrie and a player to named later (August 31, 1999).
STATISTICAL NOTES: Led Midwest League third basemen with .967 fielding percentage in 1996.

							BATTING								FIELDING		
Year— Team (League)	Pos.	G	AB	R	H	2B	3B	HR	RBI	Avg.	BB	SO	SB	PO	A	E	Avg.
1995— GC Red Sox (GCL)	3B	23	79	9	21	7	0	1	8	.266	4	8	2	21	53	2	.974
1996— Michigan (Midw.)	3B-2B	121	437	65	115	26	2	3	46	.263	59	59	7	79	248	11	†.967
1997— Sarasota (FSL)	3B	64	217	32	73	16	0	6	42	.336	22	31	1	38	116	18	.895
— Trenton (East.)	3B	53	200	20	56	11	0	2	18	.280	17	29	0	35	82	9	.929
1998— Pawtucket (I.L.)	3B	112	429	65	112	31	1	17	59	.261	39	71	4	86	192	18	.939
— GC Red Sox (GCL)	DH	2	8	1	0	0	0	0	0	.000	0	1	0	...	...	...	...
1999— Pawtucket (I.L.)	3B-DH	95	348	55	92	25	0	12	42	.264	40	57	0	66	156	14	.941
— Chicago (N.L.)■	3B	12	29	3	7	2	0	0	2	.241	1	4	0	8	8	0	1.000
Major League totals (1 year)		12	29	3	7	2	0	0	2	.241	1	4	0	8	8	0	1.000

LINTON, DOUG — P

PERSONAL: Born September 2, 1965, in Santa Ana, Calif. ... 6-1/190. ... Throws right, bats right. ... Full name: Douglas Warren Linton.
HIGH SCHOOL: Canyon (Anaheim, Calif.).
COLLEGE: UC Irvine.
TRANSACTIONS/CAREER NOTES: Selected by Toronto Blue Jays organization in 43rd round of free-agent draft (June 2, 1986). ... On disabled list (April 30-May 24 and July 29-September 2, 1987). ... On Knoxville disabled list (April 7-July 21, 1988). ... On disabled list (April 7-July 21, 1989). ... Claimed on waivers by California Angels (June 17, 1993). ... Released by Angels (September 14, 1993). ... Signed by New York Mets organization (December 17, 1993). ... On Norfolk suspended list (July 21-29, 1994). ... Granted free agency (October 15, 1994). ... Signed by Kansas City Royals organization (April 25, 1995). ... Granted free agency (October 11, 1995). ... Re-signed by Royals organization (October 22, 1995). ... Released by Royals (March 4, 1997). ... Signed by New York Yankees organization (January 26, 1998). ... Released by Yankees (March 14, 1998). ... Signed by Minnesota Twins organizaiton (May 26, 1998). ... Granted free agency (October 16, 1998). ... Signed by Baltimore Orioles organization (December 17, 1998). ... Released by Orioles (December 7, 1999).
STATISTICAL NOTES: Led International League with 21 home runs allowed and tied for lead with 10 hit batsmen in 1991.

Year League	W	L	Pct.	ERA	G	GS	CG	ShO	Sv.	IP	H	R	ER	BB	SO
1987— Myrtle Beach (SAL)	14	2	.875	*1.55	20	19	2	0	1	122	94	34	21	25	155
— Knoxville (Sou.)	0	0	...	9.00	1	1	0	0	0	3	5	3	3	1	1
1988— Dunedin (FSL)	2	1	.667	1.63	12	0	0	0	2	27²/₃	19	5	5	9	28
1989— Dunedin (FSL)	1	2	.333	2.96	9	1	0	0	2	27¹/₃	27	12	9	9	35
— Knoxville (Sou.)	5	4	.556	2.60	14	13	3	•2	0	90	68	28	26	23	93
1990— Syracuse (I.L.)	10	10	.500	3.40	26	26	8	•3	0	*177¹/₃	174	77	67	67	113
1991— Syracuse (I.L.)	10	12	.455	5.01	30	26	3	1	0	161²/₃	181	108	90	56	93
1992— Syracuse (I.L.)	12	10	.545	3.74	25	25	7	1	0	170²/₃	176	83	71	70	126
— Toronto (A.L.)	1	3	.250	8.63	8	3	0	0	0	24	31	23	23	17	16
1993— Syracuse (I.L.)	2	6	.250	5.32	13	7	0	0	0	47¹/₃	48	29	28	14	42
— Toronto (A.L.)	0	1	.000	6.55	4	1	0	0	0	11	11	8	8	9	4
— California (A.L.)■	2	0	1.000	7.71	19	0	0	0	0	25²/₃	35	22	22	14	19
1994— Norfolk (I.L.)■	2	1	.667	2.00	3	3	0	0	0	18	11	6	4	1	15
— New York (N.L.)	6	2	.750	4.47	32	3	0	0	0	50¹/₃	74	27	25	20	29
1995— Kansas City (A.L.)■	0	1	.000	7.25	7	2	0	0	0	22¹/₃	22	21	18	10	13
— Omaha (A.A.)	7	7	.500	4.40	18	18	2	1	0	108¹/₃	129	60	53	24	85
1996— Omaha (A.A.)	1	1	.500	4.76	4	4	0	0	0	22²/₃	26	13	12	7	14
— Kansas City (A.L.)	7	9	.438	5.02	21	18	0	0	0	104	111	65	58	26	87
1997—									Did not play.						

Year League	W	L	Pct.	ERA	G	GS	CG	ShO	Sv.	IP	H	R	ER	BB	SO
1998—Salt Lake (PCL)■	4	4	.500	5.99	18	14	0	0	0	79 2/3	106	57	53	14	60
1999—Rochester (I.L.)■	7	5	.583	3.65	18	18	1	0	0	118 1/3	120	58	48	27	97
—Baltimore (A.L.)	1	4	.200	5.95	14	8	0	0	0	59	69	41	39	25	31
A.L. totals (5 years)	11	18	.379	6.15	73	32	0	0	0	246	279	180	168	101	170
N.L. totals (1 year)	6	2	.750	4.47	32	3	0	0	0	50 1/3	74	27	25	20	29
Major League totals (6 years)	17	20	.459	5.86	105	35	0	0	0	296 1/3	353	207	193	121	199

LIRA, FELIPE   P

PERSONAL: Born April 26, 1972, in Miranda, Venezuela. ... 6-0/170. ... Throws right, bats right. ... Full name: Antonio Felipe Lira.
HIGH SCHOOL: Rafael O. Figueroa (Venezuela).
TRANSACTIONS/CAREER NOTES: Signed as non-drafted free agent by Detroit Tigers organization (February 20, 1990). ... On Lakeland disabled list (April 10-June 10, 1991). ... Traded by Tigers with P Omar Olivares to Seattle Mariners for P Scott Sanders, P Dean Crow and 3B Carlos Villalobos (July 18, 1997). ... Granted free agency (October 15, 1998). ... Signed by Tigers organization (November 24, 1998). ... Granted free agency (October 15, 1999).
STATISTICAL NOTES: Pitched seven-inning, 4-0 no-hit victory against Columbus (May 4, 1994). ... Led International League with 16 wild pitches in 1994.

Year League	W	L	Pct.	ERA	G	GS	CG	ShO	Sv.	IP	H	R	ER	BB	SO
1990—Bristol (Appl.)	5	5	.500	2.41	13	10	2	1	1	78 1/3	70	26	21	16	71
—Lakeland (FSL)	0	0	...	5.40	1	0	0	0	0	1 2/3	3	1	1	3	4
1991—Fayetteville (SAL)	5	5	.500	4.66	15	13	0	0	1	73 1/3	79	43	38	19	56
1992—Lakeland (FSL)	11	5	.688	2.39	32	8	2	1	1	109	95	36	29	16	84
1993—London (East.)	10	4	.714	3.38	22	22	2	0	0	152	157	63	57	39	122
—Toledo (I.L.)	1	2	.333	4.60	5	5	0	0	0	31 1/3	32	18	16	11	23
1994—Toledo (I.L.)	7	12	.368	4.70	26	26	1	1	0	151 1/3	171	91	79	45	110
1995—Detroit (A.L.)	9	13	.409	4.31	37	22	0	0	1	146 1/3	151	74	70	56	89
1996—Detroit (A.L.)	6	14	.300	5.22	32	32	3	2	0	194 2/3	204	123	113	66	113
1997—Detroit (A.L.)	5	7	.417	5.77	20	15	1	1	0	92	101	61	59	45	64
—Seattle (A.L.)■	0	4	.000	9.16	8	3	0	0	0	18 2/3	31	21	19	10	9
—Everett (N.W.)	1	0	1.000	3.60	1	1	0	0	0	5	6	3	2	2	9
—Tacoma (PCL)	2	0	1.000	3.43	3	3	0	0	0	21	21	8	8	5	17
1998—Tacoma (PCL)	6	8	.429	4.26	20	20	2	1	0	129	142	69	61	42	88
—Seattle (A.L.)	1	0	1.000	4.60	7	0	0	0	0	15 2/3	22	10	8	5	16
1999—Detroit (A.L.)■	0	0	...	10.80	2	0	0	0	0	3 1/3	7	5	4	2	3
—Toledo (I.L.)	2	11	.154	6.71	30	17	0	0	1	114	163	97	85	35	70
Major League totals (5 years)	21	38	.356	5.22	106	72	4	3	1	470 2/3	516	294	273	184	294

LLOYD, GRAEME   P   EXPOS

PERSONAL: Born April 9, 1967, in Geelong, Victoria, Australia. ... 6-7/234. ... Throws left, bats left. ... Full name: Graeme John Lloyd. ... Name pronounced GRAM.
HIGH SCHOOL: Geelong Technical School (Victoria, Australia).
COLLEGE: Geelong Tech.
TRANSACTIONS/CAREER NOTES: Signed as non-drafted free agent by Toronto Blue Jays organization (January 26, 1988). ... On Myrtle Beach disabled list (June 29-September 1, 1989). ... Selected by Philadelphia Phillies from Blue Jays organization in Rule 5 major league draft (December 7, 1992). ... Traded by Phillies to Milwaukee Brewers for P John Trisler (December 8, 1992). ... On disabled list (August 20-September 4, 1993 and July 25-September 10, 1995). ... On suspended list (September 5-9, 1993). ... Traded by Brewers with OF Pat Listach to New York Yankees for OF Gerald Williams and P Bob Wickman (August 23, 1996). ... On disabled list (April 22-May 8, 1998). ... On suspended list (May 25-27, 1998). ... Traded by Yankees with P David Wells and 2B Homer Bush to Toronto Blue Jays for P Roger Clemens (February 18, 1999). ... Granted free agency (October 29, 1999). ... Signed by Montreal Expos (December 20, 1999).

Year League	W	L	Pct.	ERA	G	GS	CG	ShO	Sv.	IP	H	R	ER	BB	SO
1988—Myrtle Beach (SAL)	3	2	.600	3.62	41	0	0	0	2	59 2/3	71	33	24	30	43
1989—Dunedin (FSL)	0	0	...	10.13	2	0	0	0	0	2 2/3	6	3	3	1	0
—Myrtle Beach (SAL)	0	0	...	5.40	1	1	0	0	0	5	5	4	3	0	3
1990—Myrtle Beach (SAL)	5	2	.714	2.72	19	6	0	0	6	49 2/3	51	20	15	16	42
1991—Dunedin (FSL)	2	5	.286	2.24	50	0	0	0	24	60 1/3	54	17	15	25	39
—Knoxville (Sou.)	0	0	...	0.00	2	0	0	0	0	1 2/3	1	0	0	1	2
1992—Knoxville (Sou.)	4	8	.333	1.96	49	7	1	0	14	92	79	30	20	25	65
1993—Milwaukee (A.L.)■	3	4	.429	2.83	55	0	0	0	0	63 2/3	64	24	20	13	31
1994—Milwaukee (A.L.)	2	3	.400	5.17	43	0	0	0	3	47	49	28	27	15	31
1995—Milwaukee (A.L.)	0	5	.000	4.50	33	0	0	0	4	32	28	16	16	8	13
1996—Milwaukee (A.L.)	2	4	.333	2.82	52	0	0	0	0	51	49	19	16	17	24
—New York (A.L.)■	0	2	.000	17.47	13	0	0	0	0	5 2/3	12	11	11	5	6
1997—New York (A.L.)	1	1	.500	3.31	46	0	0	0	1	49	55	24	18	20	26
1998—New York (A.L.)	3	0	1.000	1.67	50	0	0	0	0	37 2/3	26	10	7	6	20
1999—Toronto (A.L.)■	5	3	.625	3.63	74	0	0	0	3	72	68	36	29	23	47
Major League totals (7 years)	16	22	.421	3.62	366	0	0	0	11	358	351	168	144	107	198

DIVISION SERIES RECORD

Year League	W	L	Pct.	ERA	G	GS	CG	ShO	Sv.	IP	H	R	ER	BB	SO
1996—New York (A.L.)	0	0	...	0.00	2	0	0	0	0	1	1	0	0	0	0
1997—New York (A.L.)	0	0	...	0.00	2	0	0	0	0	1 1/3	0	0	0	0	1
1998—New York (A.L.)	0	0	...	0.00	1	0	0	0	0	1/3	0	0	0	0	0
Division series totals (3 years)	0	0	...	0.00	5	0	0	0	0	2 2/3	1	0	0	0	1

CHAMPIONSHIP SERIES RECORD

Year League	W	L	Pct.	ERA	G	GS	CG	ShO	Sv.	IP	H	R	ER	BB	SO
1996—New York (A.L.)	0	0	...	0.00	2	0	0	0	0	1 2/3	0	0	0	0	1
1998—New York (A.L.)	0	0	...	0.00	1	0	0	0	0	2/3	1	0	0	0	0
Champ. series totals (2 years)	0	0	...	0.00	3	0	0	0	0	2 1/3	1	0	0	0	1

NOTES: Member of World Series championship team (1996 and 1998).

Year League	W	L	Pct.	ERA	G	GS	CG	ShO	Sv.	IP	H	R	ER	BB	SO
1996— New York (A.L.)	1	0	1.000	0.00	4	0	0	0	0	2⅔	0	0	0	0	4
1998— New York (A.L.)	0	0	...	0.00	1	0	0	0	0	⅓	0	0	0	0	0
World Series totals (2 years)	1	0	1.000	0.00	5	0	0	0	0	3	0	0	0	0	4

LOAIZA, ESTEBAN — P — RANGERS

PERSONAL: Born December 31, 1971, in Tijuana, Mexico. ... 6-3/210. ... Throws right, bats right. ... Full name: Esteban Antonio Veyna Loaiza. ... Name pronounced low-EYE-zah.

HIGH SCHOOL: Mar Vista (Imperial Beach, Calif.).

TRANSACTIONS/CAREER NOTES: Signed as non-drafted free agent by Pittsburgh Pirates organization (March 21, 1991). ... Loaned by Pirates organization to Mexico City Red Devils of the Mexican League (May 7, 1993). ... Returned to Pirates organization (May 28, 1993). ... On disabled list (April 7-28 and July 7-14, 1994). ... Loaned to Red Devils of the Mexican League (June 19, 1996). ... Returned to Pirates organization (August 14, 1996). ... Traded by Pirates to Texas Rangers for P Todd Van Poppel and 2B Warren Morris (July 17, 1998). ... On Texas disabled list (May 12-July 5, 1999); included rehabilitation assignment to Oklahoma City (June 26-July 5).

MISCELLANEOUS: Made an out in only appearance as pinch hitter (1995). ... Had a sacrifice hit in only appearance as pinch hitter (1996).

Year League	W	L	Pct.	ERA	G	GS	CG	ShO	Sv.	IP	H	R	ER	BB	SO
1991— Gulf Coast Pirates (GCL)	5	1	.833	2.26	11	11	1	•1	0	51⅔	48	17	13	14	41
1992— Augusta (SAL)	10	8	.556	3.89	26	25	3	0	0	143⅓	134	72	62	60	123
1993— Salem (Caro.)	6	7	.462	3.39	17	17	3	0	0	109	113	53	41	30	61
— M.C. Red Devils (Mex.)■	1	1	.500	5.18	4	3	0	0	0	24⅓	32	18	14	4	15
— Carolina (Sou.)■	2	1	.667	3.77	7	7	1	0	0	43	39	18	18	12	40
1994— Carolina (Sou.)	10	5	.667	3.79	24	24	3	0	0	154⅓	169	69	65	30	115
1995— Pittsburgh (N.L.)	8	9	.471	5.16	32	•31	1	0	0	172⅔	205	*115	*99	55	85
1996— Calgary (PCL)	3	4	.429	4.02	12	11	1	1	0	69⅓	61	34	31	25	38
— M.C. Red Devils (Mex.)■	2	0	1.000	2.43	5	5	0	0	0	33⅓	28	12	9	14	16
— Pittsburgh (N.L.)■	2	3	.400	4.96	10	10	1	1	0	52⅔	65	32	29	19	32
1997— Pittsburgh (N.L.)	11	11	.500	4.13	33	32	1	0	0	196⅓	214	99	90	56	122
1998— Pittsburgh (N.L.)	6	5	.545	4.52	21	14	0	0	0	91⅔	96	50	46	30	53
— Texas (A.L.)■	3	6	.333	5.90	14	14	1	0	0	79⅓	103	57	52	22	55
1999— Texas (A.L.)	9	5	.643	4.56	30	15	0	0	0	120⅓	128	65	61	40	77
— Oklahoma (PCL)	0	0	...	0.00	2	2	0	0	0	4⅓	3	0	0	3	6
A.L. totals (2 years)	12	11	.522	5.09	44	29	1	0	0	199⅔	231	122	113	62	132
N.L. totals (4 years)	27	28	.491	4.63	96	87	3	1	0	513⅓	580	296	264	160	292
Major League totals (5 years)	39	39	.500	4.76	140	116	4	1	0	713	811	418	377	222	424

Year League	W	L	Pct.	ERA	G	GS	CG	ShO	Sv.	IP	H	R	ER	BB	SO
1998— Texas (A.L.)							Did not play.								
1999— Texas (A.L.)	0	1	.000	3.86	1	1	0	0	0	7	5	3	3	1	4

LOCKHART, KEITH — 2B — BRAVES

PERSONAL: Born November 10, 1964, in Whittier, Calif. ... 5-10/170. ... Bats left, throws right. ... Full name: Keith Virgil Lockhart.

HIGH SCHOOL: Northview (Covina, Calif.).

JUNIOR COLLEGE: Mount San Antonio (Texas) Junior College.

COLLEGE: Oral Roberts.

TRANSACTIONS/CAREER NOTES: Selected by Cincinnati Reds organization in 11th round of free-agent draft (June 2, 1986). ... Contract sold by Reds organization to Tacoma, Oakland Athletics organization (February 4, 1992). ... Granted free agency (October 15, 1992). ... Signed by St. Louis Cardinals organization (December 12, 1992). ... Granted free agency (October 15, 1993). ... Signed by San Diego Padres organization (January 7, 1994). ... Granted free agency (October 15, 1994). ... Signed by Omaha, Kansas City Royals organization (November 14, 1994). ... Traded by Royals with OF Michael Tucker to Atlanta Braves for OF Jermaine Dye and P Jamie Walker (March 27, 1997). ... On disabled list (August 6-22, 1997).

STATISTICAL NOTES: Led Midwest League third basemen with 33 double plays in 1987. ... Led Southern League with 11 sacrifice flies in 1988. ... Led American Association second basemen with 631 total chances in 1989. ... Career major league grand slams: 1.

Year Team (League)	Pos.	G	AB	R	H	2B	3B	HR	RBI	Avg.	BB	SO	SB	PO	A	E	Avg.
1986— Billings (Pio.)	2B-3B	53	202	51	70	11	3	7	31	.347	35	22	4	81	150	17	.931
— Cedar Rapids (Midw.)	2B-3B	13	42	4	8	2	0	0	1	.190	6	6	1	17	15	0	1.000
1987— Cedar Rapids (Midw.)	3B-2B	*140	511	101	160	37	5	23	84	.313	86	70	20	85	292	28	.931
1988— Chattanooga (Sou.)	3B-2B	139	515	74	137	27	3	12	67	.266	61	59	7	102	323	36	.922
1989— Nashville (A.A.)	2B	131	479	77	128	21	6	14	58	.267	61	41	4	*279	*335	17	.973
1990— Nashville (A.A.)	2B-3B-OF	126	431	48	112	25	4	9	63	.260	51	74	8	173	248	5	.979
1991— Nashville (A.A.)	3B-2B-OF	116	411	53	107	25	3	8	36	.260	24	64	3	153	241	13	.968
1992— Tacoma (PCL)■	2B-3B-SS	107	363	44	101	25	3	5	37	.278	29	21	5	199	239	11	.976
1993— Louisville (A.A.)■	3B-2B-OF-1B	132	467	66	140	24	3	13	68	.300	60	43	3	157	239	12	.971
1994— San Diego (N.L.)■	3B-2B-SS-OF	27	43	4	9	0	0	2	6	.209	4	10	1	10	21	1	.969
— Las Vegas (PCL)	O-S-2-3-P-C	89	331	61	106	15	5	7	43	.320	26	37	3	143	113	10	.962
1995— Omaha (A.A.)■	3B-DH	44	148	24	56	7	1	5	19	.378	16	10	1	31	72	8	.928
— Kansas City (A.L.)	2B-3B-DH	94	274	41	88	19	3	6	33	.321	14	21	8	111	178	8	.973
1996— Kansas City (A.L.)	2B-3B-DH	138	433	49	118	33	3	7	55	.273	30	40	11	137	281	13	.970
1997— Atlanta (N.L.)■	2B-3B-DH	96	147	25	41	5	3	6	32	.279	14	17	0	24	48	3	.960
1998— Atlanta (N.L.)	2B-DH-3B	109	366	50	94	21	0	9	37	.257	29	37	2	130	250	6	.984
1999— Atlanta (N.L.)	2B-3B-DH	108	161	20	42	3	1	1	21	.261	19	21	3	27	64	1	.989
American League totals (2 years)		232	707	90	206	52	6	13	88	.291	44	61	19	248	459	21	.971
National League totals (4 years)		340	717	99	186	29	4	18	96	.259	66	85	6	191	383	11	.981
Major League totals (6 years)		572	1424	189	392	81	10	31	184	.275	110	146	25	439	842	32	.976

DIVISION SERIES RECORD

						BATTING									FIELDING		
Year Team (League)	Pos.	G	AB	R	H	2B	3B	HR	RBI	Avg.	BB	SO	SB	PO	A	E	Avg.
1997—Atlanta (N.L.).............	2B	2	6	0	0	0	0	0	0	.000	0	1	0	1	8	1	.900
1998—Atlanta (N.L.).............	2B	3	12	2	4	0	0	0	0	.333	1	0	0	9	9	0	1.000
1999—Atlanta (N.L.).............	PH-2B	3	1	0	0	0	0	0	0	.000	0	1	0	0	0	0	...
Division series totals (3 years)		8	19	2	4	0	0	0	0	.211	1	2	0	10	17	1	.964

CHAMPIONSHIP SERIES RECORD

						BATTING									FIELDING		
Year Team (League)	Pos.	G	AB	R	H	2B	3B	HR	RBI	Avg.	BB	SO	SB	PO	A	E	Avg.
1997—Atlanta (N.L.).............	2B-PH	5	16	4	8	1	1	0	3	.500	1	1	0	14	5	0	1.000
1998—Atlanta (N.L.).............	2B-PH	6	17	2	4	1	1	0	0	.235	0	4	0	5	12	0	1.000
1999—Atlanta (N.L.).............	PH-2B	3	5	0	2	0	1	0	1	.400	0	2	0	1	3	0	1.000
Championship series totals (3 years)		14	38	6	14	2	3	0	4	.368	1	7	0	20	20	0	1.000

WORLD SERIES RECORD

						BATTING									FIELDING		
Year Team (League)	Pos.	G	AB	R	H	2B	3B	HR	RBI	Avg.	BB	SO	SB	PO	A	E	Avg.
1999—Atlanta (N.L.).............	PH-2B-DH	4	7	1	1	0	0	0	0	.143	2	0	0	1	2	0	1.000

RECORD AS PITCHER

Year League	W	L	Pct.	ERA	G	GS	CG	ShO	Sv.	IP	H	R	ER	BB	SO
1994—Las Vegas (PCL)	0	0	...	0.00	1	1	0	0	0	1	0	0	0	0	0

LoDUCA, PAUL · C · DODGERS

PERSONAL: Born April 12, 1972, in Brooklyn, N.Y. ... 5-10/185. ... Bats right, throws right. ... Full name: Paul Anthony LoDuca.
HIGH SCHOOL: Apollo (Phoenix).
JUNIOR COLLEGE: Glendale (Ariz.) Community College.
COLLEGE: Arizona State.
TRANSACTIONS/CAREER NOTES: Selected by Los Angeles Dodgers organization in 25th round of free-agent draft (June 3, 1993). ... On Albuquerque disabled list (June 4-July 20, 1999).
STATISTICAL NOTES: Led Florida State League with .400 on-base percentage in 1996. ... Led Florida State League catchers with 17 errors in 1996. ... Led Texas League catchers with .990 fielding percentage, 84 assists and 667 total chances in 1997. ... Led Pacific Coast League in grounding into double plays with 20 in 1998.

						BATTING									FIELDING		
Year Team (League)	Pos.	G	AB	R	H	2B	3B	HR	RBI	Avg.	BB	SO	SB	PO	A	E	Avg.
1993—Vero Beach (FSL)	C	39	134	17	42	6	0	0	13	.313	13	22	0	209	26	2	.992
1994—Bakersfield (Calif.)	1B-C	123	455	65	144	32	1	6	68	.316	52	49	16	657	59	5	.993
1995—San Antonio (Texas) ...	C-1B-3B	61	199	27	49	8	0	1	8	.246	26	25	5	353	43	11	.973
1996—Vero Beach (FSL)	C-1B-3B	124	439	54	134	22	0	3	66	.305	70	38	8	747	116	†18	.980
1997—San Antonio (Texas) ...	C-1B	105	385	63	126	28	2	7	69	.327	46	27	16	636	†91	7	†.990
1998—Albuquerque (PCL)......	C-1B-3B	126	451	66	144	30	3	8	58	.319	59	40	19	742	92	17	.980
—Los Angeles (N.L.)	C	6	14	2	4	1	0	0	1	.286	0	1	0	18	2	0	1.000
1999—Los Angeles (N.L.)	C	36	95	11	22	1	0	3	11	.232	10	9	1	178	21	2	.990
—Albuquerque (PCL).....	C-DH-1B	26	76	17	28	9	0	1	8	.368	10	1	1	162	15	4	.978
Major League totals (2 years)		42	109	13	26	2	0	3	12	.239	10	10	1	196	23	2	.991

LOEWER, CARLTON · P · PADRES

PERSONAL: Born September 24, 1973, in Lafayette, La. ... 6-6/211. ... Throws right, bats right. ... Full name: Carlton Edward Loewer.
HIGH SCHOOL: St. Edmund (Eunice, La.).
COLLEGE: Mississippi State.
TRANSACTIONS/CAREER NOTES: Selected by Toronto Blue Jays organization in seventh round of free-agent draft (June 3, 1991); did not sign. ... Selected by Philadelphia Phillies organization in first round (23rd pick overall) of free-agent draft (June 2, 1994). ... On Philadelphia disabled list (June 6-September 6, 1999); included rehabilitation assignments to Gulf Coast League Phillies (August 26-30) and Clearwater (August 31-September 6). ... Traded by Phillies with P Steve Montgomery and P Adam Eaton to San Diego Padres for P Andy Ashby (November 10, 1999).
STATISTICAL NOTES: Led Eastern League with 24 home runs allowed in 1996.

Year League	W	L	Pct.	ERA	G	GS	CG	ShO	Sv.	IP	H	R	ER	BB	SO
1995—Clearwater (FSL)	7	5	.583	3.30	20	20	1	0	0	114²/₃	124	59	42	36	83
—Reading (East.)..................	4	1	.800	2.16	8	8	0	0	0	50	42	17	12	31	35
1996—Reading (East.).................	7	10	.412	5.26	27	27	3	1	0	171	*191	115	100	57	119
1997—Scranton/W.B. (I.L.)	5	13	.278	4.60	29	*29	4	0	0	184	*198	*120	94	50	152
1998—Scranton/W.B. (I.L.)	7	3	.700	2.87	12	12	*5	•2	0	94	89	34	30	22	69
—Philadelphia (N.L.)............	7	8	.467	6.09	21	21	1	0	0	122²/₃	154	86	83	39	58
1999—Philadelphia (N.L.).............	2	6	.250	5.12	20	13	2	1	0	89²/₃	100	54	51	26	48
—Gulf Coast Phillies (GCL)....	0	0	...	0.00	1	1	0	0	0	2	2	0	0	0	2
—Clearwater (FSL)	0	2	.000	7.71	3	3	0	0	0	7	10	6	6	1	5
Major League totals (2 years)	9	14	.391	5.68	41	34	3	1	0	212¹/₃	254	140	134	65	106

LOFTON, KENNY · OF · INDIANS

PERSONAL: Born May 31, 1967, in East Chicago, Ind. ... 6-0/180. ... Bats left, throws left. ... Full name: Kenneth Lofton.
HIGH SCHOOL: Washington (East Chicago, Ind.).
COLLEGE: Arizona.

TRANSACTIONS/CAREER NOTES: Selected by Houston Astros organization in 17th round of free-agent draft (June 1, 1988). ... Traded by Astros with IF Dave Rohde to Cleveland Indians for P Willie Blair and C Eddie Taubensee (December 10, 1991). ... On disabled list (July 17-August 1, 1995). ... Traded by Indians with P Alan Embree to Atlanta Braves for OF Marquis Grissom and OF Dave Justice (March 25, 1997). ... On disabled list (June 18-July 5 and July 6-28, 1997). ... Granted free agency (October 28, 1997). ... Signed by Indians (December 8, 1997). ... On disabled list (July 28-August 14 and August 17-September 1, 1999).

RECORDS: Holds A.L. rookie-season record for most stolen bases—66 (1992). ... Shares A.L. single-season record for fewest errors by outfielder who led league in errors—8 (1998).

HONORS: Won A.L. Gold Glove as outfielder (1993-96).

STATISTICAL NOTES: Tied for Pacific Coast League lead in caught stealing with 23 in 1991. ... Led Pacific Coast League outfielders with 344 total chances in 1991. ... Led N.L. in caught stealing with 20 in 1997. ... Career major league grand slams: 1.

MISCELLANEOUS: Holds Cleveland Indians all-time record for most stolen bases (404).

							BATTING								FIELDING		
Year Team (League)	Pos.	G	AB	R	H	2B	3B	HR	RBI	Avg.	BB	SO	SB	PO	A	E	Avg.
1988—Auburn (NY-P)	OF	48	187	23	40	6	1	1	14	.214	19	51	26	94	5	4	.961
1989—Auburn (NY-P)	OF	34	110	21	29	3	1	0	8	.264	14	30	26	37	4	8	.837
—Asheville (SAL)	OF	22	82	14	27	2	0	1	9	.329	12	10	14	38	1	2	.951
1990—Osceola (FSL)	OF	124	481	98	*159	15	5	2	35	.331	61	77	62	246	13	7	.974
1991—Tucson (PCL)	OF	130	*545	93	*168	19	*17	2	50	.308	52	95	40	*308	*27	9	.974
—Houston (N.L.)	OF	20	74	9	15	1	0	0	0	.203	5	19	2	41	1	1	.977
1992—Cleveland (A.L.)■	OF	148	576	96	164	15	8	5	42	.285	68	54	*66	420	14	8	.982
1993—Cleveland (A.L.)	OF	148	569	116	185	28	8	1	42	.325	81	83	*70	402	11	•9	.979
1994—Cleveland (A.L.)	OF	112	459	105	*160	32	9	12	57	.349	52	56	*60	276	•13	2	.993
1995—Cleveland (A.L.)	OF-DH	118	481	93	149	22	*13	7	53	.310	40	49	*54	248	•11	8	.970
1996—Cleveland (A.L.)	OF	154	*662	132	210	35	4	14	67	.317	61	82	*75	376	13	10	.975
1997—Atlanta (N.L.)■	OF	122	493	90	164	20	6	5	48	.333	64	83	27	290	5	5	.983
1998—Cleveland (A.L.)■	OF	154	600	101	169	31	6	12	64	.282	87	80	54	339	*19	8	.978
1999—Cleveland (A.L.)	OF-DH	120	465	110	140	28	6	7	39	.301	79	84	25	255	11	3	.989
American League totals (7 years)		954	3812	753	1177	191	54	58	364	.309	468	488	404	2316	92	48	.980
National League totals (2 years)		142	567	99	179	21	6	5	48	.316	69	102	29	331	6	6	.983
Major League totals (9 years)		1096	4379	852	1356	212	60	63	412	.310	537	590	433	2647	98	54	.981

DIVISION SERIES RECORD

							BATTING								FIELDING		
Year Team (League)	Pos.	G	AB	R	H	2B	3B	HR	RBI	Avg.	BB	SO	SB	PO	A	E	Avg.
1995—Cleveland (A.L.)	OF	3	13	1	2	0	0	0	0	.154	1	3	0	9	0	2	.818
1996—Cleveland (A.L.)	OF	4	18	3	3	0	0	0	1	.167	2	3	5	10	0	0	1.000
1997—Atlanta (N.L.)	OF	3	13	2	2	1	0	0	0	.154	1	2	0	6	1	0	1.000
1998—Cleveland (A.L.)	OF	4	16	5	6	1	0	2	4	.375	1	1	2	10	0	0	1.000
1999—Cleveland (A.L.)	OF	5	16	5	2	1	0	0	1	.125	5	6	2	14	0	1	.933
Division series totals (5 years)		19	76	16	15	3	0	2	6	.197	10	15	9	49	1	3	.943

CHAMPIONSHIP SERIES RECORD

							BATTING								FIELDING		
Year Team (League)	Pos.	G	AB	R	H	2B	3B	HR	RBI	Avg.	BB	SO	SB	PO	A	E	Avg.
1995—Cleveland (A.L.)	OF	6	24	4	11	0	2	0	3	.458	4	6	5	15	0	0	1.000
1997—Atlanta (N.L.)	OF	6	27	3	5	0	1	0	1	.185	1	7	1	9	1	2	.833
1998—Cleveland (A.L.)	OF	6	27	2	5	1	0	1	3	.185	1	7	1	8	0	1	.889
Championship series totals (3 years)		18	78	9	21	1	3	1	7	.269	6	20	7	32	1	3	.917

WORLD SERIES RECORD

RECORDS: Shares single-inning record for most stolen bases—2 (October 21, 1995).

							BATTING								FIELDING		
Year Team (League)	Pos.	G	AB	R	H	2B	3B	HR	RBI	Avg.	BB	SO	SB	PO	A	E	Avg.
1995—Cleveland (A.L.)	OF	6	25	6	5	0	0	0	0	.200	3	1	6	12	0	0	1.000

ALL-STAR GAME RECORD

RECORDS: Shares single-game record for most stolen bases—2 (July 9, 1996).

					BATTING							FIELDING		
Year League	Pos.	AB	R	H	2B	3B	HR	RBI	Avg.	BB	SO	SB	PO	A	E	Avg.
1994—American	OF	2	0	1	0	0	0	2	.500	0	1	1	1	0	0	1.000
1995—American	OF	3	0	0	0	0	0	0	.000	0	1	0	0	0	0	...
1996—American	OF	3	0	2	0	0	0	0	.667	0	0	2	0	0	0	...
1997—National						Selected, did not play—injured.										
1998—American	OF	3	0	1	0	0	0	0	.333	1	0	1	2	0	0	1.000
1999—American	OF	3	1	1	0	0	0	0	.333	0	1	1	0	0	0	...
All-Star Game totals (5 years)		14	1	5	0	0	0	2	.357	1	3	5	3	0	0	1.000

LOISELLE, RICH　　　　　P　　　　　PIRATES

PERSONAL: Born January 12, 1972, in Neenah, Wis. ... 6-5/253. ... Throws right, bats right. ... Full name: Richard Frank Loiselle.

HIGH SCHOOL: Lawton (Okla.).

JUNIOR COLLEGE: Odessa (Texas) College.

TRANSACTIONS/CAREER NOTES: Selected by San Diego Padres organization in 38th round of free-agent draft (June 3, 1991). ... Traded by Padres with P Jeff Tabaka to Houston Astros for OF Phil Plantier (July 19, 1995). ... On Tucson disabled list (August 2, 1995-remainder of season). ... Traded by Astros to Pittsburgh Pirates for P Danny Darwin (July 23, 1996). ... On Pittsburgh disabled list (July 20-August 17, 1998); included rehabilitation assignment to Nashville (August 7-16). ... On disabled list (May 8, 1999-remainder of season).

Year League	W	L	Pct.	ERA	G	GS	CG	ShO	Sv.	IP	H	R	ER	BB	SO
1991— Arizona Padres (Ariz.)	2	3	.400	3.52	12	12	0	0	0	61 1/3	72	40	24	26	47
1992— Charleston (A.A.)	4	8	.333	3.71	19	19	2	2	0	97	93	51	40	42	64
1993— Waterloo (Midw.)	1	5	.167	3.94	14	10	1	1	0	59 1/3	55	28	26	29	47
— Rancho Cuca. (Calif.)	5	8	.385	5.77	14	14	1	0	0	82 2/3	109	64	53	34	53
1994— Rancho Cuca. (Calif.)	9	10	.474	3.96	27	27	0	0	0	156 2/3	160	83	69	76	120
1995— Memphis (Sou.)	6	3	.667	3.55	13	13	1	0	0	78 2/3	82	46	31	33	48
— Las Vegas (PCL)	2	2	.500	7.24	8	7	1	1	0	27 1/3	36	27	22	9	16
— Tucson (PCL)■	0	0	...	2.61	2	1	0	0	0	10 1/3	8	4	3	4	4
1996— Jackson (Texas)	7	4	.636	3.47	16	16	2	0	0	98 2/3	107	46	38	27	65
— Tucson (PCL)	2	2	.500	2.43	5	5	1	1	0	33 1/3	28	20	9	11	31
— Calgary (PCL)■	2	2	.500	4.09	8	8	0	0	0	50 2/3	64	28	23	16	41
— Pittsburgh (N.L.)	1	0	1.000	3.05	5	3	0	0	0	20 2/3	22	8	7	8	9
1997— Pittsburgh (N.L.)	1	5	.167	3.10	72	0	0	0	29	72 2/3	76	29	25	24	66
1998— Pittsburgh (N.L.)	2	7	.222	3.44	54	0	0	0	19	55	56	26	21	36	48
— Nashville (PCL)	0	0	...	0.00	4	0	0	0	2	5	3	0	0	0	6
1999— Pittsburgh (N.L.)	3	2	.600	5.28	13	0	0	0	0	15 1/3	16	9	9	9	14
Major League totals (4 years)	**7**	**14**	**.333**	**3.41**	**144**	**3**	**0**	**0**	**48**	**163 2/3**	**170**	**72**	**62**	**77**	**137**

LOMASNEY, STEVE — C — RED SOX

PERSONAL: Born August 29, 1977, in Melrose, Mass. ... 6-0/195. ... Bats right, throws right. ... Full name: Steven James Lomasney.
HIGH SCHOOL: Peabody (Mass.).
TRANSACTIONS/CAREER NOTES: Selected by Boston Red Sox organization in fifth round of free-agent draft (June 1, 1995). ... On Sarasota disabled list (April 8-17 and June 10-21, 1999).
STATISTICAL NOTES: Led New York-Pennsylvania League catchers with 21 passed balls in 1996.

							BATTING							FIELDING		
Year Team (League)	Pos.	G	AB	R	H	2B	3B	HR	RBI	Avg.	BB	SO	SB	PO	A	E	Avg.
1995— GC Red Sox (GCL)	C	29	92	10	15	6	0	0	7	.163	8	16	2	146	29	5	.972
1996— Lowell (NY-P)	C	59	173	26	24	10	0	4	21	.139	42	63	2	402	47	9	.980
1997— Michigan (Midw.)	C	102	324	50	89	27	3	12	51	.275	32	98	3	623	83	12	.983
1998— Sarasota (FSL)	C-1B	122	443	74	106	22	1	22	63	.239	59	145	13	590	79	13	.981
1999— Sarasota (FSL)	C-DH-1B	55	189	35	51	10	0	8	28	.270	26	57	5	284	46	9	.973
— Trenton (East.)	C-DH	47	151	24	37	6	0	12	31	.245	31	44	7	355	33	12	.970
— Boston (A.L.)	C	1	2	0	0	0	0	0	0	.000	0	2	0	7	2	0	1.000
Major League totals (1 year)		**1**	**2**	**0**	**0**	**0**	**0**	**0**	**0**	**.000**	**0**	**2**	**0**	**7**	**2**	**0**	**1.000**

LOMBARD, GEORGE — OF — BRAVES

PERSONAL: Born September 14, 1975, in Atlanta. ... 6-0/202. ... Bats left, throws right. ... Full name: George Paul Lombard.
HIGH SCHOOL: Lovett (Atlanta).
TRANSACTIONS/CAREER NOTES: Selected by Atlanta Braves organization in second round of free-agent draft (June 2, 1994). ... On disabled list (August 16, 1996-remainder of season). ... On Richmond disabled list (May 29-June 22 and July 2-August 11, 1999).
STATISTICAL NOTES: Tied for South Atlantic League lead in caught stealing with 13 in 1995. ... Led Carolina League outfielders with 284 total chances in 1997. ... Led Southern League with 10 intentional bases on balls in 1998.

							BATTING							FIELDING		
Year Team (League)	Pos.	G	AB	R	H	2B	3B	HR	RBI	Avg.	BB	SO	SB	PO	A	E	Avg.
1994— GC Braves (GCL)	OF	40	129	10	18	2	0	0	5	.140	14	47	10	33	1	2	.944
1995— Eugene (N.W.)	OF	68	262	38	66	5	3	5	19	.252	23	91	35	71	5	3	.962
— Macon (SAL)	OF	49	180	32	37	6	1	3	16	.206	27	44	16	44	2	2	.958
1996— Macon (SAL)	OF-DH	116	444	76	109	16	8	15	51	.245	36	122	24	229	2	7	.971
1997— Durham (Caro.)	OF-DH	131	462	65	122	25	7	14	72	.264	66	145	35	*270	5	9	.968
1998— Greenville (Sou.)	OF	122	422	84	130	25	4	22	65	.308	71	140	35	170	8	10	.947
— Atlanta (N.L.)	OF	6	6	2	2	0	0	1	1	.333	0	1	1	2	0	0	1.000
1999— Richmond (I.L.)	OF-DH	74	233	25	48	11	3	7	29	.206	35	98	21	108	3	3	.974
— Atlanta (N.L.)	OF	6	6	1	2	0	0	0	0	.333	1	2	2	4	0	0	1.000
Major League totals (2 years)		**12**	**12**	**3**	**4**	**0**	**0**	**1**	**1**	**.333**	**1**	**3**	**3**	**6**	**0**	**0**	**1.000**

LONG, TERRENCE — OF — ATHLETICS

PERSONAL: Born February 29, 1976, in Montgomery, Ala. ... 6-1/190. ... Bats left, throws left. ... Full name: Terrence Deon Long.
HIGH SCHOOL: Stanhope Elmore (Millbrook, Ala.).
TRANSACTIONS/CAREER NOTES: Selected by New York Mets organization in first round (20th pick overall) of free-agent draft (June 2, 1994); pick received as compensation for Baltimore Orioles signing Type A free-agent P Sid Fernandez. ... On disabled list (May 15-27, 1996). ... Traded by Mets with P Leo Vasquez to Oakland Athletics for P Kenny Rogers (July 23, 1999).

							BATTING							FIELDING		
Year Team (League)	Pos.	G	AB	R	H	2B	3B	HR	RBI	Avg.	BB	SO	SB	PO	A	E	Avg.
1994— Kingsport (Appal.)	OF-1B	60	215	39	50	9	2	12	39	.233	32	52	9	237	5	5	.980
1995— Capital City (SAL)	OF	55	178	27	35	1	2	2	13	.197	28	43	8	69	5	5	.937
— Pittsfield (NY-P)	OF	51	187	24	48	9	4	4	31	.257	18	36	11	111	3	1	*.991
1996— Columbia (SAL)	OF-DH	123	473	66	136	26	9	12	78	.288	36	120	32	246	8	5	.981
1997— St. Lucie (FSL)	OF-DH	126	470	52	118	29	7	8	61	.251	40	102	24	235	7	7	.972
1998— Binghamton (East.)	OF-DH	130	455	69	135	20	*10	16	58	.297	62	105	23	218	9	10	.958
1999— Norfolk (I.L.)	OF	78	304	41	99	20	4	7	47	.326	23	41	14	192	8	4	.980
— New York (N.L.)		3	3	0	0	0	0	0	0	.000	0	2	0	0	0	0	...
— Vancouver (PCL)■....	OF-DH	40	154	16	38	6	2	2	21	.247	10	29	7	95	3	4	.961
Major League totals (1 year)		**3**	**3**	**0**	**0**	**0**	**0**	**0**	**0**	**.000**	**0**	**2**	**0**	**0**	**0**	**0**	**...**

L

LOOPER, BRADEN   P   MARLINS

PERSONAL: Born October 28, 1974, in Weatherford, Okla. ... 6-5/225. ... Throws right, bats right. ... Full name: Braden LaVern Looper. ... Name pronounced BRAY-dun.
HIGH SCHOOL: Mangum (Okla.).
COLLEGE: Wichita State.
TRANSACTIONS/CAREER NOTES: Selected by St. Louis Cardinals organization in first round (third pick overall) of free-agent draft (June 2, 1996). ... On Memphis disabled list (May 6-June 21, 1998). ... Traded by Cardinals with P Armando Almanza and SS Pablo Ozuna to Florida Marlins for SS Edgar Renteria (December 14, 1998).
MISCELLANEOUS: Member of 1996 U.S. Olympic baseball team.

Year League	W	L	Pct.	ERA	G	GS	CG	ShO	Sv.	IP	H	R	ER	BB	SO
1997—Prince William (Caro.)	3	6	.333	4.48	12	12	0	0	0	64 1/3	71	38	32	25	58
—Arkansas (Texas)	1	4	.200	5.91	19	0	0	0	5	21 1/3	24	14	14	7	20
1998—St. Louis (N.L.)	0	1	.000	5.40	4	0	0	0	0	3 1/3	5	4	2	1	4
—Memphis (PCL)	2	3	.400	3.10	40	0	0	0	20	40 2/3	43	16	14	13	43
1999—Florida (N.L.)■	3	3	.500	3.80	72	0	0	0	0	83	96	43	35	31	50
Major League totals (2 years)	3	4	.429	3.86	76	0	0	0	0	86 1/3	101	47	37	32	54

LOPEZ, ALBIE   P   DEVIL RAYS

PERSONAL: Born August 18, 1971, in Mesa, Ariz. ... 6-2/185. ... Throws right, bats right. ... Full name: Albert Anthony Lopez.
HIGH SCHOOL: Westwood (Mesa, Ariz.).
JUNIOR COLLEGE: Mesa (Ariz.) Community College.
TRANSACTIONS/CAREER NOTES: Selected by San Francisco Giants organization in 46th round of free-agent draft (June 5, 1989); did not sign. ... Selected by Seattle Mariners organization in 19th round of free-agent draft (June 4, 1990); did not sign. ... Selected by Cleveland Indians organization in 20th round of free-agent draft (June 3, 1991). ... On Cleveland disabled list (July 2-28 and August 13-September 1, 1997). ... Selected by Tampa Bay Devil Rays in second round (48th pick overall) of expansion draft (November 18, 1997). ... On Tampa Bay disabled list (August 1-26, 1998); included rehabilitation assignments to Durham (August 15-18) and St. Petersburg (August 25-26). ... On Tampa Bay disabled list (May 12-June 20, 1999); included rehabilitation assignment to St. Petersburg (June 14-20).
STATISTICAL NOTES: Led American Association with 10 hit batsmen and tied for lead with three balks in 1996.
MISCELLANEOUS: Holds Tampa Bay Devils Rays all-time record for lowest earned-run average (3.51).

Year League	W	L	Pct.	ERA	G	GS	CG	ShO	Sv.	IP	H	R	ER	BB	SO
1991—Burlington (Appl.)	4	5	.444	3.44	13	13	0	0	0	73 1/3	61	33	28	23	81
1992—Columbus (SAL)	7	2	.778	2.88	16	16	1	0	0	97	80	41	31	33	117
—Kinston (Caro.)	5	2	.714	3.52	10	10	1	1	0	64	56	28	25	26	44
1993—Canton/Akron (East.)	9	4	.692	3.11	16	16	2	0	0	110	79	44	38	47	80
—Cleveland (A.L.)	3	1	.750	5.98	9	9	0	0	0	49 2/3	49	34	33	32	25
—Charlotte (I.L.)	1	0	1.000	2.25	3	2	0	0	0	12	8	3	3	2	7
1994—Charlotte (I.L.)	13	3	.813	3.94	22	22	3	0	0	144	136	68	63	42	105
—Cleveland (A.L.)	1	2	.333	4.24	4	4	1	1	0	17	20	11	8	6	18
1995—Buffalo (A.A.)	5	10	.333	4.44	18	18	1	1	0	101 1/3	101	57	50	51	82
—Cleveland (A.L.)	0	0	...	3.13	6	2	0	0	0	23	17	8	8	7	22
1996—Buffalo (A.A.)	10	2	.833	3.87	17	17	2	0	0	104 2/3	90	54	45	40	89
—Cleveland (A.L.)	5	4	.556	6.39	13	10	0	0	0	62	80	47	44	22	45
1997—Cleveland (A.L.)	3	7	.300	6.93	37	6	0	0	0	76 2/3	101	61	59	40	63
—Buffalo (A.A.)	1	0	1.000	0.00	7	0	0	0	1	11 1/3	6	0	0	2	13
—Akron (East.)	0	0	...	0.00	1	0	0	0	0	1	2	0	0	0	2
1998—Tampa Bay (A.L.)■	7	4	.636	2.60	54	0	0	0	1	79 2/3	73	31	23	32	62
—Durham (I.L.)	0	0	...	0.00	2	0	0	0	0	3	4	0	0	1	2
—St. Petersburg (FSL)	0	1	.000	18.00	1	1	0	0	0	1	2	2	2	0	1
1999—Tampa Bay (A.L.)	3	2	.600	4.64	51	0	0	0	1	64	66	40	33	24	37
—St. Petersburg (FSL)	0	0	...	5.40	2	1	0	0	0	3 1/3	7	5	2	0	3
Major League totals (7 years)	22	20	.524	5.03	174	31	1	1	2	372	406	232	208	163	272

LOPEZ, JAVY   C   BRAVES

PERSONAL: Born November 5, 1970, in Ponce, Puerto Rico. ... 6-3/200. ... Bats right, throws right. ... Full name: Javier Torres Lopez.
HIGH SCHOOL: Academia Cristo Rey (Urb la Ramble Ponce, Puerto Rico).
TRANSACTIONS/CAREER NOTES: Signed as non-drafted free agent by Atlanta Braves organization (November 6, 1987). ... On Greenville disabled list (July 18-August 2, 1992). ... On disabled list (July 6-22, 1997; and June 21-July 15 and July 25, 1999-remainder of season).
HONORS: Named Southern League Most Valuable Player (1992).
STATISTICAL NOTES: Led Midwest League catchers with 11 double plays and 31 passed balls in 1990. ... Led Carolina League catchers with 701 total chances and 14 double plays in 1991. ... Led Southern League catchers with 763 total chances and 19 double plays in 1992. ... Led International League catchers with 15 passed balls in 1993. ... Tied for N.L. lead with 10 passed balls in 1994. ... Career major league grand slams: 2.

Year Team (League)	Pos.	G	AB	R	H	2B	3B	HR	RBI	Avg.	BB	SO	SB	PO	A	E	Avg.
							BATTING								FIELDING		
1988—GC Braves (GCL)	C	31	94	8	18	4	0	1	9	.191	3	19	1	131	30	7	.958
1989—Pulaski (Appl.)	C	51	153	27	40	8	1	3	27	.261	5	35	3	264	26	5	.983
1990—Burlington (Midw.)	C	116	422	48	112	17	3	11	55	.265	14	84	0	724	79	11	.986
1991—Durham (Caro.)	C	113	384	43	94	14	2	11	51	.245	25	88	10	*610	85	6	.991
1992—Greenville (Sou.)	C	115	442	63	142	28	3	16	60	.321	24	47	7	*680	75	8	.990
—Atlanta (N.L.)	C	9	16	3	6	2	0	0	2	.375	0	1	0	28	2	0	1.000
1993—Richmond (I.L.)	C-DH	100	380	56	116	23	2	17	74	.305	12	53	1	718	70	10	.987
—Atlanta (N.L.)	C	8	16	1	6	1	1	1	2	.375	0	2	0	37	2	1	.975
1994—Atlanta (N.L.)	C	80	277	27	68	9	0	13	35	.245	17	61	0	559	35	3	.995
1995—Atlanta (N.L.)	C	100	333	37	105	11	4	14	51	.315	14	57	0	625	50	8	.988

Year	Team (League)	Pos.	G	AB	R	H	2B	3B	HR	RBI	Avg.	BB	SO	SB	PO	A	E	Avg.
1996—Atlanta (N.L.)		C	138	489	56	138	19	1	23	69	.282	28	84	1	993	*81	6	.994
1997—Atlanta (N.L.)		C	123	414	52	122	28	1	23	68	.295	40	82	1	792	56	6	.993
1998—Atlanta (N.L.)		C-DH	133	489	73	139	21	1	34	106	.284	30	85	5	978	68	5	*.995
1999—Atlanta (N.L.)		C-DH	65	246	34	78	18	1	11	45	.317	20	41	0	413	29	4	.991
Major League totals (8 years)			656	2280	283	662	109	9	119	378	.290	149	413	7	4425	323	33	.993

DIVISION SERIES RECORD

Year	Team (League)	Pos.	G	AB	R	H	2B	3B	HR	RBI	Avg.	BB	SO	SB	PO	A	E	Avg.
1995—Atlanta (N.L.)		C	3	9	0	4	0	0	0	3	.444	0	3	0	22	3	0	1.000
1996—Atlanta (N.L.)		C	2	7	1	2	0	0	1	1	.286	1	...	1	21	1	1	.957
1997—Atlanta (N.L.)		C	2	7	3	2	2	0	0	1	.286	2	1	0	18	0	0	1.000
1998—Atlanta (N.L.)		C	2	7	1	2	0	0	1	1	.286	1	1	0	20	3	0	1.000
Division series totals (4 years)			9	30	5	10	2	0	2	6	.333	4	5	1	81	7	1	.989

CHAMPIONSHIP SERIES RECORD

RECORDS: Shares career record for most doubles—7. ... Shares single-game record for most runs—4 (October 14, 1996). ... Holds N.L. single-series record for most runs—8 (1996). ... Shares N.L. single-series record for most consecutive hits—5 (1996). ... Holds single-series records for most doubles—5 (1996); and most long hits—7 (1996). ... Shares single-series record for most total bases—24 (1996).
NOTES: Named N.L. Championship Series Most Valuable Player (1996).

Year	Team (League)	Pos.	G	AB	R	H	2B	3B	HR	RBI	Avg.	BB	SO	SB	PO	A	E	Avg.
1992—Atlanta (N.L.)		C	1	1	0	0	0	0	0	0	.000	0	0	0	2	0	0	1.000
1995—Atlanta (N.L.)		C	3	14	2	5	1	0	1	3	.357	0	1	0	28	2	0	1.000
1996—Atlanta (N.L.)		C	7	24	8	13	5	0	2	6	.542	4	1	1	48	3	0	1.000
1997—Atlanta (N.L.)		C-PH	5	17	0	1	1	0	0	2	.059	1	7	0	40	3	0	1.000
1998—Atlanta (N.L.)		C-PH	6	20	2	6	0	0	1	1	.300	0	7	0	43	2	1	.978
Championship series totals (5 years)			22	76	12	25	7	0	4	12	.329	5	16	1	161	10	1	.994

WORLD SERIES RECORD

NOTES: Member of World Series championship team (1995).

Year	Team (League)	Pos.	G	AB	R	H	2B	3B	HR	RBI	Avg.	BB	SO	SB	PO	A	E	Avg.
1992—Atlanta (N.L.)							Did not play.											
1995—Atlanta (N.L.)		C-PH	6	17	1	3	2	0	1	3	.176	1	1	0	32	4	0	1.000
1996—Atlanta (N.L.)		C	6	21	3	4	0	0	0	1	.190	3	4	0	41	4	0	1.000
World Series totals (2 years)			12	38	4	7	2	0	1	4	.184	4	5	0	73	8	0	1.000

ALL-STAR GAME RECORD

RECORDS: Hit home run in first at-bat (July 8, 1997).

Year	League	Pos.	AB	R	H	2B	3B	HR	RBI	Avg.	BB	SO	SB	PO	A	E	Avg.
1997—National		C	1	1	1	0	0	0	1	1	1.000	0	0	0	4	1	0	1.000
1998—National		C	1	0	0	0	0	0	0	0	.000	0	1	0	3	0	0	1.000
All-Star Game totals (2 years)			2	1	1	0	0	0	1	1	.500	0	1	0	7	1	0	1.000

LOPEZ, LUIS   IF   BREWERS

PERSONAL: Born September 4, 1970, in Cidra, Puerto Rico. ... 5-11/166. ... Bats both, throws right. ... Full name: Luis Manuel Lopez.
HIGH SCHOOL: San Jose (Caguas, Puerto Rico).
TRANSACTIONS/CAREER NOTES: Signed as non-drafted free agent by San Diego Padres organization (September 9, 1987). ... On Las Vegas disabled list (July 3-14, 1994). ... Granted free agency (October 15, 1994). ... Re-signed by Padres (April 20, 1995). ... On disabled list (April 24, 1995-entire season). ... On San Diego disabled list (March 29-April 18 and July 31-September 1, 1996); included rehabilitation assignments to Las Vegas (March 30-April 18 and August 17-September 1). ... Traded by Padres to Houston Astros for P Sean Runyan (March 15, 1997). ... Traded by Astros to New York Mets for IF Tim Bogar (March 31, 1997). ... Traded by Mets to Milwaukee Brewers for P Bill Pulshiper (January 21, 2000).
STATISTICAL NOTES: Led South Atlantic League shortstops with 703 total chances and 78 double plays in 1989. ... Led Pacific Coast League shortstops with 30 errors in 1992. ... Tied for Pacific Coast League lead with 13 sacrifice hits in 1993. ... Career major league grand slams: 1.

Year	Team (League)	Pos.	G	AB	R	H	2B	3B	HR	RBI	Avg.	BB	SO	SB	PO	A	E	Avg.
1988—Spokane (N.W.)		SS	70	312	50	95	13	1	0	35	.304	18	59	14	*118	217	*47	.877
1989—Char., S.C. (SAL)		SS	127	460	50	102	15	1	1	29	.222	17	85	12	*256	*373	*74	.895
1990—Riverside (Calif.)		SS	14	46	5	17	3	1	1	4	.370	3	3	4	18	38	6	.903
1991—Wichita (Texas)		2B-SS	125	452	43	121	17	1	1	41	.268	18	70	6	274	339	26	.959
1992—Las Vegas (PCL)		SS-OF	120	395	44	92	8	8	1	31	.233	19	65	6	200	358	†30	.949
1993—Las Vegas (PCL)		SS-2B-DH	131	491	52	150	36	6	6	58	.305	27	62	8	230	380	29	.955
—San Diego (N.L.)		2B	17	43	1	5	1	0	0	1	.116	0	8	0	23	34	1	.983
1994—Las Vegas (PCL)		2B	12	49	2	10	2	2	0	6	.204	1	5	0	28	43	2	.973
—San Diego (N.L.)		SS-2B-3B	77	235	29	65	16	1	2	20	.277	15	39	3	101	174	14	.952
1995—San Diego (N.L.)							Did not play.											
1996—Las Vegas (PCL)		2B-SS	18	68	4	14	3	0	1	12	.206	2	15	0	39	43	2	.976
—San Diego (N.L.)		SS-2B-3B	63	139	10	25	3	0	2	11	.180	9	35	0	57	100	4	.975
1997—Norfolk (I.L.)		SS-2B-DH	48	203	32	67	12	1	4	19	.330	9	29	2	79	123	14	.935
—New York (N.L.)		SS-2B-3B	78	178	19	48	12	1	1	19	.270	12	42	2	79	156	9	.963
1998—New York (N.L.)		2B-SS-3B-OF	117	266	37	67	13	2	2	22	.252	20	60	2	123	144	11	.960
1999—New York (N.L.)		SS-2B-3B	68	104	11	22	4	0	2	13	.212	12	33	1	34	68	4	.962
Major League totals (6 years)			420	965	107	232	49	4	9	86	.240	68	217	8	417	676	43	.962

Year Team (League)	Pos.	G	AB	R	H	2B	3B	HR	RBI	Avg.	BB	SO	SB	PO	A	E	Avg.
1996— San Diego (N.L.)	PR	1	0	0	0	0	0	0	0	...	0	0	0	...	...	...	...
1999— New York (N.L.)..........							Did not play.										

CHAMPIONSHIP SERIES RECORD

Year Team (League)	Pos.	G	AB	R	H	2B	3B	HR	RBI	Avg.	BB	SO	SB	PO	A	E	Avg.
1999— New York (N.L.)							Did not play.										

LOPEZ, MENDY — IF

PERSONAL: Born October 15, 1974, in Santo Domingo, Dominican Republic. ... 6-2/190. ... Bats right, throws right. ... Full name: Mendy Aude Lopez.

HIGH SCHOOL: Liceo Los Trinitanos (Santo Domingo, Dominican Republic).

TRANSACTIONS/CAREER NOTES: Signed as non-drafted free agent by Kansas City Royals organization (February 26, 1992). ... On Omaha disabled list (May 28-July 7, 1999). ... Released by Royals (December 13, 1999).

STATISTICAL NOTES: Led Gulf Coast League shortstops with .971 fielding percentage, 80 putouts, 154 assists, 241 total chances and 39 double plays in 1994. ... Tied for Texas League lead with 28 double plays by third baseman in 1996.

Year Team (League)	Pos.	G	AB	R	H	2B	3B	HR	RBI	Avg.	BB	SO	SB	PO	A	E	Avg.
1992— Dom. Royals (DSL)	SS	49	145	22	40	1	0	1	23	.276	22	15	7	81	155	26	.901
1993— Dom. Royals (DSL)	IF	28	98	15	27	5	2	0	20	.276	11	5	2	52	75	15	.894
1994— GC Royals (GCL)	SS-3B-2B	59	*235	56	85	*19	3	5	*50	.362	22	27	10	†84	†195	12	†.959
1995— Wilmington (Caro.).....	3B-SS	130	428	42	116	29	3	2	36	.271	28	73	18	84	335	25	.944
1996— Wichita (Texas)	3B-SS	93	327	47	92	20	5	6	32	.281	26	67	14	80	265	24	.935
1997— Omaha (A.A.)..............	3B	17	52	6	12	2	0	1	6	.231	8	21	0	15	38	6	.898
— Wichita (Texas)	SS	101	357	56	83	16	3	5	42	.232	36	70	7	193	296	20	.961
1998— Omaha (PCL)..............	SS-3B	60	195	18	35	6	1	3	14	.179	18	44	2	71	167	10	.960
— Kansas City (A.L.)	SS-3B	74	206	18	50	10	2	1	15	.243	12	40	5	102	225	15	.956
1999— Omaha (PCL)........SS-2B-3B-DH		61	222	41	69	8	0	12	40	.311	18	41	2	98	171	8	.971
— GC Royals (GCL)	SS-DH	3	5	0	1	1	0	0	2	.200	3	1	0	2	4	0	1.000
— Kansas City (A.L.)	2B-SS	7	20	2	8	0	1	0	3	.400	0	5	0	11	16	0	1.000
Major League totals (2 years)		81	226	20	58	10	3	1	18	.257	12	45	5	113	241	15	.959

LOPEZ, RODRIGO — P — PADRES

PERSONAL: Born December 14, 1975, in Mexico City, Mexico. ... 6-1/180. ... Throws right, bats right. ... Full name: Rodrigo Munoz Lopez.

TRANSACTIONS/CAREER NOTES: Signed by Aguila of Mexican League (1994). ... Contract sold by Aguila to San Diego Padres organization (March 17, 1995). ... Loaned by Padres to Mexico City Red Devils of Mexican League (March 13, 1998). ... Returned to Padres organization (August 19, 1998).

Year League	W	L	Pct.	ERA	G	GS	CG	ShO	Sv.	IP	H	R	ER	BB	SO
1994— Aguila (Mex.).....................	0	0	...	4.97	10	0	0	0	0	12²/₃	15	7	7	3	5
1995— Arizona Padres (Ariz.)■.....	1	1	.500	5.45	11	7	0	0	1	34²/₃	41	29	21	14	33
1996— Idaho Falls (Pio.)	4	4	.500	5.70	15	14	0	0	1	71	76	52	45	34	72
1997— Clinton (Midw.)	6	8	.429	3.18	37	14	2	0	9	121²/₃	103	49	43	42	123
1998— M.C. Red Devils (Mex.)■...	10	6	.625	3.35	26	26	1	0	0	163²/₃	165	73	61	79	95
— Mobile (Sou.)■	3	0	1.000	1.40	4	4	2	1	0	25²/₃	21	11	4	4	20
1999— Mobile (Sou.)	10	8	.556	4.41	28	•28	2	1	0	169¹/₃	187	91	83	58	138

LORETTA, MARK — IF — BREWERS

PERSONAL: Born August 14, 1971, in Santa Monica, Calif. ... 6-0/190. ... Bats right, throws right. ... Full name: Mark David Loretta.

HIGH SCHOOL: St. Francis (La Canada, Calif.).

COLLEGE: Northwestern.

TRANSACTIONS/CAREER NOTES: Selected by Milwaukee Brewers organization in seventh round of free-agent draft (June 3, 1993). ... On New Orleans suspended list (May 17-20, 1996).

STATISTICAL NOTES: Led American Association shortstops with 200 putouts and 591 total chances in 1995.

Year Team (League)	Pos.	G	AB	R	H	2B	3B	HR	RBI	Avg.	BB	SO	SB	PO	A	E	Avg.
1993— Helena (Pio.)	SS	6	28	5	9	1	0	1	8	.321	1	4	0	11	18	0	1.000
— Stockton (Calif.)	SS-3B	53	201	36	73	4	1	4	31	.363	22	17	8	75	173	15	.943
1994— El Paso (Texas).........	SS-P	77	302	50	95	13	6	0	38	.315	27	33	8	125	271	11	.973
— New Orleans (A.A.)	SS-2B	43	138	16	29	7	0	1	14	.210	12	13	2	68	121	11	.945
1995— New Orleans (A.A.)....	SS-3-DH-2	127	479	48	137	22	5	7	79	.286	34	47	8	†204	376	25	.959
— Milwaukee (A.L.)	SS-2B-DH	19	50	13	13	3	0	1	3	.260	4	7	1	18	42	1	.984
1996— New Orleans (A.A.)	SS	19	71	10	18	5	1	0	11	.254	9	8	1	31	60	5	.948
— Milwaukee (A.L.)	2B-3B-SS	73	154	20	43	3	0	1	13	.279	14	15	2	63	116	2	.989
1997— Milwaukee (A.L.) 2-S-1-3-DH		132	418	56	120	17	5	5	47	.287	47	60	5	334	277	15	.976
1998— Milwaukee (N.L.)	1-S-3-2-0	140	434	55	137	29	0	6	54	.316	42	47	9	450	215	6	.991
1999— Milwaukee (N.L.)	S-1-2-3	153	587	93	170	34	5	5	67	.290	52	59	4	625	260	13	.986
American League totals (3 years)		224	622	89	176	23	5	7	63	.283	65	82	8	415	435	18	.979
National League totals (2 years)		293	1021	148	307	63	5	11	121	.301	94	106	13	1075	475	19	.988
Major League totals (5 years)		517	1643	237	483	86	10	18	184	.294	159	188	21	1490	910	37	.985

RECORD AS PITCHER

Year League	W	L	Pct.	ERA	G	GS	CG	ShO	Sv.	IP	H	R	ER	BB	SO
1994— El Paso (Texas)..................	0	0	...	...	1	0	0	0	0	0	1	1	1	1	0

PERSONAL: Born August 11, 1972, in Los Angeles. ... 6-3/200. ... Throws left, bats left. ... Full name: Andrew Jason Lorraine.
HIGH SCHOOL: William S. Hart (Newhall, Calif.).
COLLEGE: Stanford.
TRANSACTIONS/CAREER NOTES: Selected by New York Mets organization in 38th round of free-agent draft (June 4, 1990); did not sign. ... Selected by California Angels organization in fourth round of free-agent draft (June 3, 1993). ... Traded by Angels with OF McKay Christensen, P Bill Simas and P John Snyder to Chicago White Sox for P Jim Abbott and P Tim Fortugno (July 27, 1995). ... Traded by White Sox with OF Charles Poe to Oakland Athletics for OF/DH Danny Tartabull (January 22, 1996). ... Released by A's (October 16, 1997). ... Signed by Seattle Mariners organization (October 17, 1997). ... Granted free agency (October 3, 1998). ... Signed by Chicago Cubs organization (November 13, 1998).
MISCELLANEOUS: Scored a run in only appearance as pinch runner (1999).

Year	League	W	L	Pct.	ERA	G	GS	CG	ShO	Sv.	IP	H	R	ER	BB	SO
1993—	Boise (N.W.)	4	1	.800	1.29	6	6	3	1	0	42	33	6	6	6	39
1994—	Vancouver (PCL)	12	4	.750	3.42	22	22	•4	•2	0	142	156	63	54	34	90
—	California (A.L.)	0	2	.000	10.61	4	3	0	0	0	18 2/3	30	23	22	11	10
1995—	Vancouver (PCL)	6	6	.500	3.96	18	18	4	1	0	97 2/3	105	49	43	30	51
—	Nashville (A.A.)■	4	1	.800	6.00	7	7	0	0	0	39	51	29	26	12	26
—	Chicago (A.L.)	0	0	...	3.38	5	0	0	0	0	8	3	3	3	2	5
1996—	Edmonton (PCL)■	8	10	.444	5.68	30	25	0	0	0	141	181	95	89	46	73
1997—	Edmonton (PCL)	8	6	.571	4.74	23	20	2	2	0	117 2/3	143	72	62	34	75
—	Oakland (A.L.)	3	1	.750	6.37	12	6	0	0	0	29 2/3	45	22	21	15	18
1998—	Tacoma (PCL)■	7	4	.636	4.82	52	4	0	0	2	80 1/3	93	44	43	36	70
—	Seattle (A.L.)	0	0	...	2.45	4	0	0	0	0	3 2/3	3	1	1	4	0
1999—	Iowa (PCL)■	9	8	.529	3.71	22	21	1	0	0	143	149	67	59	34	96
—	Chicago (N.L.)	2	5	.286	5.55	11	11	2	1	0	61 2/3	71	42	38	22	40
A.L. totals (4 years)		3	3	.500	7.05	25	9	0	0	0	60	81	49	47	32	33
N.L. totals (1 year)		2	5	.286	5.55	11	11	2	1	0	61 2/3	71	42	38	22	40
Major League totals (5 years)		5	8	.385	6.29	36	20	2	1	0	121 2/3	152	91	85	54	73

L

PERSONAL: Born July 25, 1965, in Santa Monica, Calif. ... 6-0/185. ... Bats both, throws right. ... Full name: Salvatore Anthony Lovullo. ... Name pronounced leh-VOO-lo.
HIGH SCHOOL: Montclair Prep (Van Nuys, Calif.).
COLLEGE: UCLA (degree in psychology).
TRANSACTIONS/CAREER NOTES: Selected by Kansas City Royals organization in 27th round of free-agent draft (June 2, 1986); did not sign. ... Selected by Detroit Tigers organization in fifth round of free-agent draft (June 2, 1987). ... Traded by Tigers to New York Yankees for P Mark Leiter (March 19, 1991). ... Granted free agency (October 16, 1992). ... Signed by California Angels (November 19, 1992). ... Claimed on waivers by Seattle Mariners (April 1, 1994). ... Granted free agency (October 15, 1994). ... Signed by Cleveland Indians (November 21, 1994). ... Granted free agency (October 16, 1995). ... Signed by Oakland Athletics organization (December 5, 1995). ... Granted free agency (October 15, 1996). ... Signed by Ottawa, Expos organization (December 17, 1996). ... Released by Expos (May 20, 1997). ... Signed by Buffalo, Indians organization (May 20, 1997). ... Granted free agency (October 15, 1997). ... Re-signed by Indians organization (December 19, 1997). ... On Buffalo disabled list (June 25-July 30, 1998). ... Granted free agency (October 15, 1998). ... Signed by Philadelphia Phillies organization (November 5, 1998). ... Granted free agency (October 6, 1999).
HONORS: Named second baseman on THE SPORTING NEWS college All-America team (1987).
STATISTICAL NOTES: Tied for International League lead with 10 intentional bases on balls received in 1989. ... Led International League with .509 slugging percentage in 1992. ... Tied for International League lead with 20 errors by third baseman in 1998. ... Led International League second basemen with 664 total chances, 262 putouts, 390 assists, .982 fielding percentage and 99 double plays in 1999.

							BATTING								FIELDING		
Year	Team (League)	Pos.	G	AB	R	H	2B	3B	HR	RBI	Avg.	BB	SO	SB	PO	A	E	Avg.
1987—	Fayetteville (SAL)	3B-2B	55	191	34	49	13	0	8	32	.257	37	30	6	41	133	22	.888
—	Lakeland (FSL)	3B	18	60	11	16	3	0	1	16	.267	10	8	0	11	30	2	.953
1988—	Glens Falls (East.)	3B-2B	78	270	37	74	17	1	9	50	.274	36	44	2	63	173	21	.918
—	Toledo (I.L.)	2B-3B-SS	57	177	18	41	8	1	5	20	.232	9	24	2	120	149	5	.982
—	Detroit (A.L.)	2B-3B	12	21	2	8	1	1	1	2	.381	1	2	0	12	19	0	1.000
1989—	Toledo (I.L.)	1B-3B-2B-SS	112	409	48	94	23	2	10	52	.230	44	57	2	217	257	20	.960
—	Detroit (A.L.)	1B-3B	29	87	8	10	2	0	1	4	.115	14	20	1	134	24	1	.994
1990—	Toledo (I.L.)	2B-3B-1B	141	486	71	131	*38	1	14	58	.270	61	74	4	280	352	18	.972
1991—	New York (A.L.)■	3B	22	51	0	9	2	0	0	2	.176	5	7	0	14	33	3	.940
—	Columbus (I.L.)	3B-1B-2B-OF	106	395	74	107	24	5	10	75	.271	59	54	4	277	164	16	.965
1992—	Columbus (I.L.)	2B-3B-1B-OF	131	468	69	138	*33	5	19	89	.295	64	65	9	187	206	8	.980
1993—	California (A.L.)■	2-3-S-O-D-1	116	367	42	92	20	0	6	30	.251	36	49	7	208	249	11	.976
1994—	Seattle (A.L.)■	2B-3B-DH	36	72	9	16	5	0	2	7	.222	9	13	1	19	49	1	.986
—	Calgary (PCL)	SS-2B-3B	54	211	43	62	18	1	11	47	.294	34	28	2	85	165	9	.965
1995—	Buffalo (A.A.)■	2-3-1-S-DH	132	474	84	121	20	5	16	61	.255	70	62	3	235	303	18	.968
1996—	Oakland (A.L.)■	1-3-DH-2-S-O	65	82	15	18	4	0	3	9	.220	11	17	1	134	21	1	.994
—	Edmonton (PCL)	1-2-D-3-P-O-S	26	93	18	26	4	0	4	19	.280	18	12	0	112	39	3	.981
1997—	Ottawa (I.L.)■	2B-DH-3B	28	64	6	9	3	0	0	6	.141	6	13	0	31	42	0	1.000
—	Buffalo (A.A.)■	3-2-1-DH-S	97	321	40	73	18	0	12	40	.227	51	64	0	115	203	12	.964
1998—	Buffalo (I.L.)	3B-2B-1B	92	328	66	107	17	4	17	65	.326	54	32	3	114	168	‡23	.925
—	Cleveland (A.L.)	2B-3B	6	19	1	4	1	0	0	1	.211	1	2	0	4	15	1	.950
1999—	Scran./W.B. (I.L.)■	2-1-DH-3	139	519	90	145	36	3	21	106	.279	78	89	3	†288	†398	14	†.980
—	Philadelphia (N.L.)	1B-2B	17	38	3	8	0	0	2	5	.211	3	11	0	36	13	0	1.000
American League totals (7 years)			286	699	77	157	35	1	13	55	.225	77	110	10	525	410	18	.981
National League totals (1 year)			17	38	3	8	0	0	2	5	.211	3	11	0	36	13	0	1.000
Major League totals (8 years)			303	737	80	165	35	1	15	60	.224	80	121	10	561	423	18	.982

RECORD AS PITCHER

Year	Team (League)	W	L	Pct.	ERA	G	GS	CG	ShO	Sv.	IP	H	R	ER	BB	SO
1996—	Edmonton (PCL)	0	0	...	4.50	26	0	0	0	0	4	3	2	2	3	0

LOWE, DEREK   P   RED SOX

PERSONAL: Born June 1, 1973, in Dearborn, Mich. ... 6-6/200. ... Throws right, bats right. ... Full name: Derek Christopher Lowe.
HIGH SCHOOL: Edsel Ford (Dearborn, Mich.).
TRANSACTIONS/CAREER NOTES: Selected by Seattle Mariners organization in eighth round of free-agent draft (June 3, 1991). ... Traded by Mariners with C Jason Varitek to Boston Red Sox for P Heathcliff Slocumb (July 31, 1997).
STATISTICAL NOTES: Led Southern League with seven balks in 1994.

Year	League	W	L	Pct.	ERA	G	GS	CG	ShO	Sv.	IP	H	R	ER	BB	SO
1991—	Arizona Mariners (Ariz.)	5	3	.625	2.41	12	12	0	0	0	71	58	26	19	21	60
1992—	Bellingham (N.W.)	7	3	.700	2.42	14	13	2	•1	0	85 2/3	69	34	23	22	66
1993—	Riverside (Calif.)	12	9	.571	5.26	27	26	3	2	0	154	189	104	90	60	80
1994—	Jacksonville (Sou.)	7	10	.412	4.94	26	26	2	0	0	151 1/3	177	92	83	50	75
1995—	Port City (Sou.)	1	6	.143	6.07	10	10	1	0	0	53 1/3	70	41	36	22	30
—	Arizona Mariners (Ariz.)	1	0	1.000	0.93	2	2	0	0	0	9 2/3	5	1	1	2	11
1996—	Port City (Sou.)	5	3	.625	3.05	10	10	0	0	0	65	56	27	22	17	33
—	Tacoma (PCL)	6	9	.400	4.54	17	16	1	1	0	105	118	64	53	37	54
1997—	Tacoma (PCL)	3	4	.429	3.45	10	9	1	0	0	57 1/3	53	26	22	20	49
—	Seattle (A.L.)	2	4	.333	6.96	12	9	0	0	0	53	59	43	41	20	39
—	Pawtucket (I.L.)■	4	0	1.000	2.37	6	5	0	0	0	30 1/3	23	8	8	11	21
—	Boston (A.L.)	0	2	.000	3.38	8	0	0	0	0	16	15	6	6	3	13
1998—	Boston (A.L.)	3	9	.250	4.02	63	10	0	0	4	123	126	65	55	42	77
1999—	Boston (A.L.)	6	3	.667	2.63	74	0	0	0	15	109 1/3	84	35	32	25	80
Major League totals (3 years)		**11**	**18**	**.379**	**4.00**	**157**	**19**	**0**	**0**	**19**	**301 1/3**	**284**	**149**	**134**	**90**	**209**

DIVISION SERIES RECORD

Year	League	W	L	Pct.	ERA	G	GS	CG	ShO	Sv.	IP	H	R	ER	BB	SO
1998—	Boston (A.L.)	0	0	...	2.08	2	0	0	0	0	4 1/3	3	1	1	2	2
1999—	Boston (A.L.)	1	1	.500	4.32	3	0	0	0	0	8 1/3	6	7	4	1	7
Division series totals (2 years)		**1**	**1**	**.500**	**3.55**	**5**	**0**	**0**	**0**	**0**	**12 2/3**	**9**	**8**	**5**	**3**	**9**

CHAMPIONSHIP SERIES RECORD

Year	League	W	L	Pct.	ERA	G	GS	CG	ShO	Sv.	IP	H	R	ER	BB	SO
1999—	Boston (A.L.)	0	0	...	1.42	3	0	0	0	0	6 1/3	6	3	1	2	7

LOWE, SEAN   P   WHITE SOX

PERSONAL: Born March 29, 1971, in Dallas. ... 6-2/205. ... Throws right, bats right. ... Full name: Jonathan Sean Lowe.
HIGH SCHOOL: Mesquite (Texas).
JUNIOR COLLEGE: McLennan Community College (Texas).
COLLEGE: Arizona State.
TRANSACTIONS/CAREER NOTES: Selected by Cincinnati Reds organization in 43rd round of free-agent draft (June 5, 1989); did not sign. ... Selected by Oakland Athletics organization in 43rd round of free-agent draft (June 4, 1990); did not sign. ... Selected by St. Louis Cardinals organization in first round (15th pick overall) of free-agent draft (June 1, 1992). ... On St. Petersburg disabled list (July 19-August 8, 1994). ... On Arkansas disabled list (May 28-June 4, 1996). ... On Louisville disabled list (April 9-18, 1997). ... Traded by Cardinals to Chicago White Sox for P John Ambrose (February 9, 1999).
STATISTICAL NOTES: Tied for American Association lead with 10 hit batsmen in 1997.

Year	League	W	L	Pct.	ERA	G	GS	CG	ShO	Sv.	IP	H	R	ER	BB	SO
1992—	Hamilton (NY-P)	2	0	1.000	1.61	5	5	0	0	0	28	14	8	5	14	22
1993—	St. Petersburg (FSL)	6	11	.353	4.27	25	25	0	0	0	132 2/3	152	80	63	62	87
1994—	St. Petersburg (FSL)	5	6	.455	3.47	21	21	0	0	0	114	119	51	44	37	92
—	Arkansas (Texas)	2	1	.667	1.40	3	3	0	0	0	19 1/3	13	3	3	8	11
1995—	Arkansas (Texas)	9	8	.529	4.88	24	24	0	0	0	129	143	84	70	64	77
1996—	Louisville (A.A.)	8	9	.471	4.70	25	18	0	0	0	115	127	72	60	51	76
—	Arkansas (Texas)	2	3	.400	6.00	6	6	0	0	0	33	32	24	22	15	25
1997—	Louisville (A.A.)	6	10	.375	4.37	26	23	1	0	1	131 2/3	142	74	64	53	117
—	St. Louis (N.L.)	0	2	.000	9.35	6	4	0	0	0	17 1/3	27	21	18	10	8
1998—	Memphis (PCL)	12	8	.600	3.18	25	21	0	0	0	153	147	57	54	61	114
—	St. Louis (N.L.)	0	3	.000	15.19	4	1	0	0	0	5 1/3	11	9	9	5	2
1999—	Chicago (A.L.)■	4	1	.800	3.67	64	0	0	0	0	95 2/3	90	39	39	46	62
A.L. totals (1 year)		**4**	**1**	**.800**	**3.67**	**64**	**0**	**0**	**0**	**0**	**95 2/3**	**90**	**39**	**39**	**46**	**62**
N.L. totals (2 years)		**0**	**5**	**.000**	**10.72**	**10**	**5**	**0**	**0**	**0**	**22 2/3**	**38**	**30**	**27**	**15**	**10**
Major League totals (3 years)		**4**	**6**	**.400**	**5.02**	**74**	**5**	**0**	**0**	**0**	**118 1/3**	**128**	**69**	**66**	**61**	**72**

LOWELL, MIKE   3B   MARLINS

PERSONAL: Born February 24, 1974, in San Juan, Puerto Rico. ... 6-4/205. ... Bats right, throws right. ... Full name: Michael Averett Lowell.
HIGH SCHOOL: Coral Gables (Fla.).
COLLEGE: Florida International.
TRANSACTIONS/CAREER NOTES: Selected by New York Yankees organization in 20th round of free-agent draft (June 1, 1995). ... Traded by Yankees to Florida Marlins for P Ed Yarnall, P Mark Johnson and P Todd Noel (February 1, 1999). ... On Florida disabled list (March 26-May 29, 1999); included rehabilitation assignments to Calgary (April 8-13 and May 6-29).
STATISTICAL NOTES: Led New York-Pennsylvania League third basemen with 271 total chances in 1995. ... Led South Atlantic League third basemen with .926 fielding percentage, 301 putouts and 421 total chances in 1996. ... Tied for International League lead with 20 errors by third baseman in 1998. ... Career major league grand slams: 1.

Year Team (League)	Pos.	G	AB	R	H	2B	3B	HR	RBI	Avg.	BB	SO	SB	PO	A	E	Avg.
1995—Oneonta (NY-P)	3B	72	281	36	73	18	0	1	27	.260	23	34	3	59	188	24	.911
1996—Greensboro (SAL)	3B-SS	113	433	58	122	33	0	8	64	.282	46	43	10	91	†302	32	.925
—Tampa (FSL)	3B	24	78	8	22	5	0	0	11	.282	3	13	1	22	40	3	.954
1997—Norwich (East.)	3B-SS	78	285	60	98	17	0	15	47	.344	48	30	2	57	133	15	.927
—Columbus (I.L.)	3B-SS	57	210	36	58	13	1	15	45	.276	23	34	2	31	73	5	.954
1998—Columbus (I.L.)	3B-1B-SS	126	510	79	155	34	3	26	99	.304	37	85	4	114	283	‡21	.950
—New York (A.L.)	3B-DH	8	15	1	4	0	0	0	0	.267	0	1	0	2	5	0	1.000
1999—Calgary (PCL)■	3B	24	83	11	26	3	0	2	9	.313	8	19	0	11	51	4	.939
—Florida (N.L.)	3B	97	308	32	78	15	0	12	47	.253	26	69	0	59	143	4	.981
American League totals (1 year)		8	15	1	4	0	0	0	0	.267	0	1	0	2	5	0	1.000
National League totals (1 year)		97	308	32	78	15	0	12	47	.253	26	69	0	59	143	4	.981
Major League totals (2 years)		105	323	33	82	15	0	12	47	.254	26	70	0	61	148	4	.981

LOWERY, TERRELL   OF

PERSONAL: Born October 25, 1970, in Oakland. ... 6-3/195. ... Bats right, throws right. ... Full name: Quenton Terrell Lowery. ... Brother of Josh Lowery, minor league shortstop (1989-90).
HIGH SCHOOL: Oakland Technical.
COLLEGE: Loyola Marymount.
TRANSACTIONS/CAREER NOTES: Selected by Texas Rangers organization in second round of free-agent draft (June 3, 1991). ... On Butte disabled list (June 17-27, 1992). ... On restricted list (June 27, 1992-February 5, 1993). ... On Oklahoma City disabled list (April 6-August 24, 1995). ... Traded by Rangers to New York Mets for OF Damon Buford (January 25, 1996). ... Selected by Chicago Cubs organization from Mets organization in Rule 5 minor league draft (December 9, 1996). ... On Iowa disabled list (September 4, 1998-remainder of season). ... Granted free agency (October 15, 1998). ... Signed by Tampa Bay Devil Rays organization (November 19, 1998). ... Granted free agency (October 10, 1999).
STATISTICAL NOTES: Led Texas League outfielders with 303 total chances in 1994. ... Led American Association with .401 on-base percentage in 1997. ... Career major league grand slams: 1.

Year Team (League)	Pos.	G	AB	R	H	2B	3B	HR	RBI	Avg.	BB	SO	SB	PO	A	E	Avg.
1991—Butte (Pio.)	OF	54	214	38	64	10	7	3	33	.299	29	44	23	92	7	6	.943
1992—								Did not play.									
1993—Charlotte (FSL)	OF	65	257	46	77	7	9	3	36	.300	46	47	14	156	5	4	.976
—Tulsa (Texas)	OF	66	258	29	62	5	1	3	14	.240	28	50	10	152	6	2	.988
1994—Tulsa (Texas)	OF	129	496	89	142	34	8	8	54	.286	59	113	33	*280	16	7	.977
1995—GC Rangers (GCL)	DH-OF	10	34	10	9	3	1	3	7	.265	6	7	1	7	0	0	1.000
—Charlotte (FSL)	OF	11	35	4	9	2	2	0	4	.257	6	6	1	18	0	0	1.000
1996—Norfolk (I.L.)■	OF	62	193	25	45	7	2	4	21	.233	22	44	6	106	4	1	.991
—Binghamton (East.)	OF-DH	62	211	34	58	13	4	7	32	.275	44	44	5	97	3	3	.971
1997—Iowa (A.A.)■	OF-DH	110	386	69	116	28	3	17	71	.301	65	97	9	244	8	3	.988
—Chicago (N.L.)	OF	9	14	2	4	0	0	0	0	.286	3	3	1	7	2	0	1.000
1998—Iowa (PCL)	OF	65	246	41	73	14	1	12	49	.297	27	63	5	155	5	1	.994
—Chicago (N.L.)	OF	24	15	2	3	1	0	0	1	.200	3	7	0	13	0	1	.929
1999—Durham (I.L.)■	OF-DH	71	275	69	92	20	5	15	57	.335	43	62	10	129	3	1	.992
—Tampa Bay (A.L.)	OF-DH	66	185	25	48	15	1	2	17	.259	19	53	0	97	4	3	.971
American League totals (1 year)		66	185	25	48	15	1	2	17	.259	19	53	0	97	4	3	.971
National League totals (2 years)		33	29	4	7	1	0	0	1	.241	6	10	1	20	2	1	.957
Major League totals (3 years)		99	214	29	55	16	1	2	18	.257	25	63	1	117	6	4	.969

LUDWICK, ERIC   P   BREWERS

PERSONAL: Born December 14, 1971, in Whiteman AFB, Mo. ... 6-5/210. ... Throws right, bats right. ... Full name: Eric David Ludwick.
HIGH SCHOOL: El Dorado (Las Vegas).
COLLEGE: California, then UNLV.
TRANSACTIONS/CAREER NOTES: Selected by New York Mets organization in second round of free-agent draft (June 3, 1993). ... Traded by Mets with P Erik Hiljus and OF Yudith Ozorio to St. Louis Cardinals for OF Bernard Gilkey (January 22, 1996). ... Traded by Cardinals with P T.J. Mathews and P Blake Stein to Oakland Athletics for 1B Mark McGwire (July 31, 1997). ... Traded by A's to Florida Marlins for IF Kurt Abbott (December 19, 1997). ... On Florida disabled list (April 9-26, May 3-July 9 and July 20-August 28, 1998); included rehabilitation assignments to Charlotte (June 26-July 9 and August 4-28). ... Selected by Detroit Tigers from Marlins organization in Rule 5 major league draft; then traded by Tigers to Toronto Blue Jays for P Beiker Graterol (December 14, 1998). ... Returned by Blue Jays to Marlins organization (April 16, 1999). ... Granted free agency (October 12, 1999). ... Signed by Milwaukee Brewers organization (December 7, 1999).

Year League	W	L	Pct.	ERA	G	GS	CG	ShO	Sv.	IP	H	R	ER	BB	SO
1993—Pittsfield (NY-P)	4	4	.500	3.18	10	10	1	0	0	51	51	27	18	18	40
1994—St. Lucie (FSL)	7	13	.350	4.55	27	27	3	0	0	150 1/3	162	*102	76	77	77
1995—Binghamton (East.)	12	5	.706	2.95	23	22	3	2	0	143 1/3	108	52	47	68	131
—Norfolk (I.L.)	1	1	.500	5.85	4	3	0	0	0	20	22	15	13	7	9
1996—Louisville (A.A.)■	3	4	.429	2.83	11	11	0	0	0	60 1/3	55	24	19	24	73
—St. Louis (N.L.)	0	1	.000	9.00	6	1	0	0	0	10	11	11	10	3	12
1997—St. Louis (N.L.)	0	1	.000	9.45	5	0	0	0	0	6 2/3	12	7	7	6	7
—Louisville (A.A.)	6	8	.429	2.92	24	11	1	0	4	80	67	31	26	26	85
—Edmonton (PCL)■	1	1	.500	3.32	6	3	0	0	0	19	22	7	7	4	20
—Oakland (A.L.)	1	4	.200	8.25	6	5	0	0	0	24	32	24	22	16	14
1998—Florida (N.L.)■	1	4	.200	7.44	13	6	0	0	0	32 2/3	46	31	27	17	27
—Charlotte (I.L.)	1	3	.250	3.71	8	8	0	0	0	26 2/3	25	17	11	13	26
1999—Toronto (A.L.)■	0	0	...	27.00	1	0	0	0	0	1	3	3	3	2	0
—Calgary (PCL)■	11	6	.647	3.86	48	0	0	0	14	58 1/3	65	33	25	36	61
A.L. totals (2 years)	1	4	.200	9.00	7	5	0	0	0	25	35	27	25	18	14
N.L. totals (3 years)	1	6	.143	8.03	24	7	0	0	0	49 1/3	69	49	44	26	46
Major League totals (4 years)	2	10	.167	8.35	31	12	0	0	0	74 1/3	104	76	69	44	60

LUEBBERS, LARRY   P   REDS

PERSONAL: Born October 11, 1969, in Cincinnati. ... 6-6/210. ... Throws right, bats right. ... Full name: Larry Christopher Luebbers.
HIGH SCHOOL: St. Henry (Erlanger, Ky.).
COLLEGE: Kentucky.
TRANSACTIONS/CAREER NOTES: Selected by Cincinnati Reds organization in eighth round of free-agent draft (June 4, 1990). ... Traded by Reds with P Mike Anderson and C Darron Cox to Chicago Cubs for P Chuck McElroy (December 10, 1993). ... Claimed on waivers by Reds (November 18, 1994). ... Granted free agency (October 15, 1996). ... Signed by Atlanta Braves organization (February 24, 1997). ... Granted free agency (October 15, 1997). ... Signed by St. Louis Cardinals organization (November 24, 1997). ... Granted free agency (October 15, 1998). ... Re-signed by Cardinals organization (November 12, 1998). ... Granted free agency (October 15, 1999). ... Signed by Reds organization (November 16, 1999).

Year	League	W	L	Pct.	ERA	G	GS	CG	ShO	Sv.	IP	H	R	ER	BB	SO
1990—	Billings (Pio.)	5	4	.556	4.48	13	13	1	•1	0	72 1/3	74	46	36	31	48
1991—	Cedar Rapids (Midw.)	8	10	.444	3.12	28	28	3	0	0	184 2/3	177	85	64	64	98
1992—	Cedar Rapids (Midw.)	7	0	1.000	2.62	14	14	1	0	0	82 1/3	71	33	24	33	56
	—Chattanooga (Sou.)	6	5	.545	2.27	14	14	1	0	0	87 1/3	86	34	22	34	56
1993—	Indianapolis (A.A.)	4	7	.364	4.16	15	15	0	0	0	84 1/3	81	45	39	47	51
	—Cincinnati (N.L.)	2	5	.286	4.54	14	14	0	0	0	77 1/3	74	49	39	38	38
1994—	Iowa (A.A.)■	10	12	.455	6.04	27	26	0	0	0	138 2/3	149	100	93	87	90
1995—	Chattanooga (Sou.)■	10	6	.625	4.65	28	21	0	0	0	118	112	71	61	59	87
1996—	Chattanooga (Sou.)	3	5	.375	3.63	11	11	0	0	0	69 1/3	64	32	28	26	38
	—Indianapolis (A.A.)	5	4	.556	3.91	14	11	0	0	0	71 1/3	76	44	31	23	35
1997—	Richmond (I.L.)■	3	*14	.176	5.38	27	26	2	0	0	144	180	101	86	44	91
1998—	Memphis (PCL)■	11	11	.500	4.10	29	29	2	2	0	173 1/3	183	90	79	47	110
1999—	Memphis (PCL)	13	4	.765	4.03	21	19	1	1	0	129 2/3	134	61	58	33	84
	—St. Louis (N.L.)	3	3	.500	5.12	8	8	1	0	0	45 2/3	46	27	26	16	16
Major League totals (2 years)		5	8	.385	4.76	22	22	1	0	0	123	120	76	65	54	54

LUGO, JULIO   SS   ASTROS

PERSONAL: Born November 16, 1975, in Barahona, Dominican Republic. ... 6-1/165. ... Bats right, throws right. ... Full name: Julio Cesar Lugo.
JUNIOR COLLEGE: Connors State College (Okla.).
TRANSACTIONS/CAREER NOTES: Selected by Houston Astros organization in 43rd round of free-agent draft (June 2, 1994). ... On Jackson disabled list (July 21-29, 1999).
STATISTICAL NOTES: Led Florida State League shortstops with 40 errors in 1997.

Year	Team (League)	Pos.	G	AB	R	H	2B	3B	HR	RBI	Avg.	BB	SO	SB	PO	A	E	Avg.
1995—Auburn (NY-P)		2B-SS-OF	59	230	36	67	6	3	1	16	.291	26	31	17	85	116	12	.944
1996—Quad City (Midw.)		SS-2B-3B	101	393	60	116	18	2	10	50	.295	32	75	24	122	289	29	.934
1997—Kissimmee (FSL)		SS-2B-3B	125	505	89	135	22	*14	7	61	.267	46	99	35	186	433	†41	.938
1998—Kissimmee (FSL)		SS	128	509	81	154	20	*14	7	62	.303	49	72	51	181	308	42	.921
1999—Jackson (Texas)		SS-2B-DH	116	445	77	142	24	5	10	42	.319	44	53	25	185	328	29	.946

LUKE, MATT   OF   BREWERS

PERSONAL: Born February 26, 1971, in Long Beach, Calif. ... 6-5/220. ... Bats left, throws left. ... Full name: Matthew Clifford Luke.
HIGH SCHOOL: El Dorado (Calif.).
COLLEGE: California.
TRANSACTIONS/CAREER NOTES: Selected by New York Yankees organization in eighth round of free-agent draft (June 1, 1992). ... On Tampa disabled list (April 22-May 9, 1994). ... On Columbus disabled list (April 5-May 1 and May 12-June 2, 1996). ... On temporarily inactive list (April 3-May 13, 1997). ... Claimed on waivers by Los Angeles Dodgers (September 25, 1997). ... Claimed on waivers by Cleveland Indians (June 8, 1998). ... Traded by Indians to Dodgers for cash (June 19, 1998). ... Granted free agency (December 21, 1998). ... Signed by Anaheim Angels (January 12, 1999). ... On Edmonton disabled list (April 8-June 5, 1999). ... On Anaheim disabled list (June 26-September 3, 1999); included rehabilitation assignment to Lake Elsinore (August 23-September 3, 1999). ... Granted free agency (October 15, 1999). ... Signed by Milwaukee Brewers organization (December 1, 1999).
STATISTICAL NOTES: Led South Atlantic League with 267 total bases in 1993.

Year	Team (League)	Pos.	G	AB	R	H	2B	3B	HR	RBI	Avg.	BB	SO	SB	PO	A	E	Avg.
1992—Oneonta (NY-P)		OF-1B	69	271	30	67	11	*7	2	34	.247	19	32	4	230	16	7	.972
1993—Greensboro (SAL)		OF	135	*549	83	•157	37	5	21	91	.286	47	79	11	218	11	3	*.987
1994—Tampa (FSL)		OF	57	222	52	68	11	2	16	42	.306	28	27	4	100	12	5	.957
	—Alb./Colonie (East.)	OF-1B	63	236	34	67	11	2	8	40	.284	28	50	6	158	8	3	.982
1995—Norwich (East.)		OF	93	365	48	95	17	5	8	53	.260	20	68	5	178	12	4	.979
	—Columbus (I.L.)	OF	23	77	11	23	4	1	3	12	.299	2	12	1	36	1	2	.949
1996—New York (A.L.)		PR	1	0	1	0	0	0	0	0	...	0	0	0	...	...	...	...
	—Columbus (I.L.)	OF-DH-1B	74	264	46	74	14	2	19	70	.280	17	52	1	159	8	2	.988
	—Tampa (FSL)	OF	2	7	1	2	0	0	0	1	.286	1	1	0	3	0	0	1.000
1997—Columbus (I.L.)		OF-1B-DH	87	337	42	77	19	3	8	45	.228	29	64	0	263	23	4	.986
1998—Los Angeles (N.L.)■		OF-1B	102	237	34	56	12	1	12	34	.236	17	60	2	161	19	1	.994
	—Cleveland (A.L.)■	PH	2	2	0	0	0	0	0	0	.000	0	0	0	0	0	0	...
1999—Edmonton (PCL)■		DH-OF	6	21	7	9	2	1	5	15	.429	6	4	0	6	0	0	1.000
	—Anaheim (A.L.)	OF-1B	18	30	4	9	0	0	3	6	.300	2	10	0	28	4	0	1.000
	—Lake Elsinore (Calif.)	OF-DH	13	53	10	18	5	3	0	7	.340	7	14	2	15	2	0	1.000
American League totals (3 years)			21	32	5	9	0	0	3	6	.281	2	10	0	28	4	0	1.000
National League totals (1 year)			102	237	34	56	12	1	12	34	.236	17	60	2	161	19	1	.994
Major League totals (3 years)			123	269	39	65	12	1	15	40	.242	19	70	2	189	23	1	.995

PERSONAL: Born June 4, 1973, in Beverly, Mass. ... 6-2/200. ... Throws right, bats right. ... Full name: David Bruce Lundquist.
HIGH SCHOOL: Carson City (Nev.).
JUNIOR COLLEGE: Cochise County Community College (Ariz.).
TRANSACTIONS/CAREER NOTES: Selected by Chicago White Sox organization in fifth round of free-agent draft (June 3, 1993). ... On Prince William disabled list (April 5-June 5 and June 19, 1996-remainder of season). ... On Charlotte disabled list (July 1, 1999-remainder of season). ... Claimed on waivers by Kansas City Royals (October 15, 1999).

Year	League	W	L	Pct.	ERA	G	GS	CG	ShO	Sv.	IP	H	R	ER	BB	SO
1993—GC White Sox (GCL)		5	3	.625	3.14	11	10	0	0	0	63	70	26	22	15	40
1994—Hickory (SAL)		13	10	.565	3.48	27	27	3	2	0	178 2/3	170	88	69	43	133
1995—South Bend (Midw.)		8	4	.667	3.58	18	18	5	1	0	118	107	54	47	38	60
1996—GC White Sox (GCL)		1	1	.500	2.63	3	3	0	0	0	13 2/3	8	4	4	2	16
— Prince William (Caro.)		0	2	.000	5.67	5	5	0	0	0	27	31	17	17	14	23
1997—Winston-Salem (Caro.)		3	1	.750	6.75	20	6	0	0	0	48	65	41	36	23	39
— Birmingham (Sou.)		0	0	...	8.77	7	0	0	0	0	13 1/3	26	20	13	5	15
1998—Winston-Salem (Caro.)		1	0	1.000	2.53	6	0	0	0	0	10 2/3	9	4	3	3	9
— Birmingham (Sou.)		1	1	.500	3.29	33	0	0	0	10	41	28	15	15	15	41
— Calgary (PCL)		3	0	1.000	3.60	12	0	0	0	2	15	12	6	6	7	12
1999—Chicago (A.L.)		1	1	.500	8.59	17	0	0	0	0	22	28	21	21	12	18
— Charlotte (I.L.)		0	0	...	0.00	3	0	0	0	0	3 2/3	3	0	0	1	4
Major League totals (1 year)		1	1	.500	8.59	17	0	0	0	0	22	28	21	21	12	18

PERSONAL: Born October 17, 1970, in Wilmington, Del. ... 6-4/195. ... Bats left, throws right. ... Full name: John Steven Mabry. ... Name pronounced MAY-bree.
HIGH SCHOOL: Bohemia Manor (Chesapeake City, Md.).
COLLEGE: West Chester (Pa.) University.
TRANSACTIONS/CAREER NOTES: Selected by St. Louis Cardinals organization in sixth round of free-agent draft (June 3, 1991). ... On disabled list (April 22-30 and May 6-18, 1992). ... On disabled list (August 20-September 24, 1997). ... Granted free agency (December 21, 1998). ... Signed by Seattle Mariners (December 30, 1998). ... On disabled list (August 14, 1999-remainder of season).
STATISTICAL NOTES: Led Texas League in grounding into double plays with 17 in 1993. ... Led Texas League outfielders with six double plays in 1993. ... Hit for the cycle (May 18, 1996). ... Had 20-game hitting streak (May 19-June 9, 1997).

Year	Team (League)	Pos.	G	AB	R	H	2B	3B	HR	RBI	Avg.	BB	SO	SB	PO	A	E	Avg.
							BATTING									FIELDING		
1991—Hamilton (NY-P)		OF	49	187	25	58	11	0	1	31	.310	17	18	9	73	*10	5	.943
— Savannah (SAL)		OF	22	86	10	20	6	1	0	8	.233	7	12	1	36	1	1	.974
1992—Springfield (Midw.)		OF	115	438	63	115	13	6	11	57	.263	24	39	2	171	14	6	.969
1993—Arkansas (Texas)		OF	*136	528	68	153	32	2	16	72	.290	27	68	7	262	15	3	*.989
— Louisville (A.A.)		OF	4	7	0	1	0	0	0	1	.143	0	1	0	3	0	0	1.000
1994—Louisville (A.A.)		OF	122	477	76	125	30	1	15	68	.262	32	67	2	237	4	2	.992
— St. Louis (N.L.)		OF	6	23	2	7	3	0	0	3	.304	2	4	0	16	0	0	1.000
1995—St. Louis (N.L.)		1B-OF	129	388	35	119	21	1	5	41	.307	24	45	0	652	58	4	.994
— Louisville (A.A.)		OF	4	12	0	1	0	0	0	0	.083	0	0	0	8	0	1	.889
1996—St. Louis (N.L.)		1B-OF	151	543	63	161	30	2	13	74	.297	37	84	3	1182	76	8	.994
1997—St. Louis (N.L.)		OF-1B-3B	116	388	40	110	19	0	5	36	.284	39	77	0	455	30	1	.998
1998—St. Louis (N.L.)		OF-3B-1B	142	377	41	94	22	0	9	46	.249	30	76	0	206	64	9	.968
1999—Seattle (A.L.)■		OF-3B-1B-DH	87	262	34	64	14	0	9	33	.244	20	60	2	221	50	10	.964
American League totals (1 year)			87	262	34	64	14	0	9	33	.244	20	60	2	221	50	10	.964
National League totals (5 years)			544	1719	181	491	95	3	32	200	.286	132	286	3	2511	228	22	.992
Major League totals (6 years)			631	1981	215	555	109	3	41	233	.280	152	346	5	2732	278	32	.989

DIVISION SERIES RECORD

RECORDS: Shares career record for most triples—1.

Year	Team (League)	Pos.	G	AB	R	H	2B	3B	HR	RBI	Avg.	BB	SO	SB	PO	A	E	Avg.
							BATTING									FIELDING		
1996—St. Louis (N.L.)		1B	3	10	1	3	0	1	0	1	.300	2	1	0	20	1	0	1.000

CHAMPIONSHIP SERIES RECORD

Year	Team (League)	Pos.	G	AB	R	H	2B	3B	HR	RBI	Avg.	BB	SO	SB	PO	A	E	Avg.
							BATTING									FIELDING		
1996—St. Louis (N.L.)		1B-OF	7	23	1	6	0	0	0	0	.261	0	6	0	45	1	0	1.000

PERSONAL: Born April 12, 1964, in Stockton, Calif. ... 6-1/210. ... Bats right, throws right. ... Full name: Michael Andrew Macfarlane.
HIGH SCHOOL: Lincoln (Stockton, Calif.).
COLLEGE: Santa Clara.
TRANSACTIONS/CAREER NOTES: Selected by Kansas City Royals organization in fourth round of free-agent draft (June 3, 1985). ... On disabled list (April 9-July 9, 1986 and July 16-September 14, 1991). ... Granted free agency (October 17, 1994). ... Signed by Boston Red Sox (April 8, 1995). ... Granted free agency (November 6, 1995). ... Signed by Royals (December 16, 1995). ... On disabled list (March 29-April 13 and May 3-23, 1997). ... Granted free agency (October 28, 1997). ... Re-signed by Royals (November 25, 1997). ... Traded by Royals to Oakland Athletics for OF Shane Mack and a player to be named later (April 8, 1998); Royals acquired P Greg Hansell to complete deal (May 10, 1998). ... Granted free agency (October 23, 1998). ... Re-signed by A's (December 16, 1998). ... On disabled list (June 27-July 12, 1999). ... Announced retirement (October 1, 1999). ... Granted free agency (November 10, 1999).
STATISTICAL NOTES: Tied for A.L. lead in being hit by pitch with 15 in 1992. ... Led A.L. in being hit by pitch with 18 in 1994. ... Led A.L. catchers with nine double plays in 1994. ... Led A.L. with 26 passed balls in 1995. ... Career major league grand slams: 4.

L
M

Year	Team (League)	Pos.	G	AB	R	H	2B	3B	HR	RBI	Avg.	BB	SO	SB	PO	A	E	Avg.
1985—	Memphis (Sou.)	C	65	223	29	60	15	4	8	39	.269	11	30	0	295	24	9	.973
1986—	Memphis (Sou.)	DH-OF	40	141	26	34	7	2	12	29	.241	10	26	0	0	0	0	...
1987—	Omaha (A.A.).............	C	87	302	53	79	25	1	13	50	.262	22	50	0	408	37	6	.987
—	Kansas City (A.L.)	C	8	19	0	4	1	0	0	3	.211	2	2	0	29	2	0	1.000
1988—	Kansas City (A.L.)	C	70	211	25	56	15	0	4	26	.265	21	37	0	309	18	2	.994
—	Omaha (A.A.)	C	21	76	8	18	7	2	2	8	.237	4	15	0	85	5	1	.989
1989—	Kansas City (A.L.)	C-DH	69	157	13	35	6	0	2	19	.223	7	27	0	249	17	1	.996
1990—	Kansas City (A.L.)	C-DH	124	400	37	102	24	4	6	58	.255	25	69	1	660	23	6	.991
1991—	Kansas City (A.L.)	C-DH	84	267	34	74	18	2	13	41	.277	17	52	1	391	28	3	.993
1992—	Kansas City (A.L.)	C-DH	129	402	51	94	28	3	17	48	.234	30	89	1	527	43	4	.993
1993—	Kansas City (A.L.)	C	117	388	55	106	27	0	20	67	.273	40	83	2	647	68	11	.985
1994—	Kansas City (A.L.)	C-DH	92	314	53	80	17	3	14	47	.255	35	71	1	498	39	4	.993
1995—	Boston (A.L.)■	C-DH	115	364	45	82	18	1	15	51	.225	38	78	2	618	49	5	.993
1996—	Kansas City (A.L.)■ ...	C-DH	112	379	58	104	24	2	19	54	.274	31	57	3	511	35	4	.993
1997—	Kansas City (A.L.)	C	82	257	34	61	14	2	8	35	.237	24	47	0	439	20	4	.991
1998—	Kansas City (A.L.)	C	3	11	1	1	0	0	0	0	.091	0	2	0	13	3	0	1.000
—	Oakland (A.L.)■	C	78	207	28	52	12	0	7	34	.251	12	34	1	355	20	4	.989
1999—	Oakland (A.L.)	C-DH	81	226	24	55	17	0	4	31	.243	13	52	0	351	43	1	.997
Major League totals (13 years)			1164	3602	458	906	221	17	129	514	.252	295	700	12	5597	408	49	.992

DIVISION SERIES RECORD

Year	Team (League)	Pos.	G	AB	R	H	2B	3B	HR	RBI	Avg.	BB	SO	SB	PO	A	E	Avg.
1995—	Boston (A.L.)..............	C	3	9	0	3	0	0	0	1	.333	0	3	0	18	0	2	.900

MACHADO, ROBERT   C   MARINERS

PERSONAL: Born June 3, 1973, in Caracas, Venezuela. ... 6-1/205. ... Bats right, throws right. ... Full name: Robert Alexis Machado.

TRANSACTIONS/CAREER NOTES: Signed as non-drafted free agent by Chicago White Sox organization (August 10, 1989). ... Released by White Sox (April 8, 1999). ... Signed by Montreal Expos organization (May 21, 1999). ... Granted free agency (October 15, 1999). ... Signed by Seattle Mariners organization (November 17, 1999).

STATISTICAL NOTES: Led Gulf Coast League catchers with 349 total chances in 1991. ... Tied for Southern League lead in double plays by catcher with 10 in 1996. ... Tied for American Association lead in passed balls with nine in 1997.

Year	Team (League)	Pos.	G	AB	R	H	2B	3B	HR	RBI	Avg.	BB	SO	SB	PO	A	E	Avg.
1991—	GC White Sox (GCL) ..	C	38	126	11	31	4	1	0	15	.246	6	21	2	*287	*54	8	.977
1992—	Utica (NY-P)	C	45	161	16	44	13	1	2	20	.273	5	26	1	279	30	12	.963
1993—	South Bend (Midw.) ...	C	75	281	34	86	14	3	2	33	.306	19	59	1	490	66	12	.979
1994—	Prince William (Caro.)	C	93	312	45	81	17	1	11	47	.260	27	68	0	562	66	*16	.975
1995—	Nashville (A.A.)	C	16	49	7	7	3	0	1	5	.143	7	12	0	87	17	3	.972
—	Prince William (Caro.)	C	83	272	37	69	14	0	6	31	.254	40	47	0	548	78	5	.992
1996—	Birmingham (Sou.).....	C-DH	87	309	35	74	16	0	6	28	.239	20	56	1	502	67	5	.991
—	Chicago (A.L.)	C	4	6	1	4	1	0	0	2	.667	0	0	0	6	0	0	1.000
1997—	Nashville (A.A.)	C-DH	84	308	43	83	18	0	8	30	.269	12	61	5	461	49	6	.988
—	Chicago (A.L.)	C	10	15	1	3	0	1	0	2	.200	1	6	0	34	3	0	1.000
1998—	Calgary (PCL)............	C-DH	66	239	31	63	19	0	4	27	.264	20	33	2	409	39	6	.987
—	Chicago (A.L.)	C	34	111	14	23	6	0	3	15	.207	7	22	0	189	17	4	.981
1999—	Charlotte (I.L.).............	C	16	54	4	11	3	0	2	7	.204	4	13	0	111	12	3	.976
—	Ottawa (I.L.)■	C-DH	21	75	6	17	5	0	0	3	.227	0	13	0	141	12	3	.981
—	Montreal (N.L.)..........	C	17	22	3	4	1	0	0	0	.182	2	6	0	33	3	0	1.000
American League totals (3 years)			48	132	16	30	7	1	3	19	.227	8	28	0	229	20	4	.984
National League totals (1 year)			17	22	3	4	1	0	0	0	.182	2	6	0	33	3	0	1.000
Major League totals (4 years)			65	154	19	34	8	1	3	19	.221	10	34	0	262	23	4	.986

MACIAS, JOSE   2B   TIGERS

PERSONAL: Born January 25, 1974, in Panama City, Panama. ... 5-10/175. ... Bats both, throws right. ... Full name: Jose Prade Macias.

HIGH SCHOOL: Instituto Technologico (Panama City, Panama).

TRANSACTIONS/CAREER NOTES: Signed as non-drafted free agent by Montreal Expos organization (February 14, 1992). ... Selected by Detroit Tigers organization from Expos organization in Rule 5 minor league draft (December 9, 1996).

STATISTICAL NOTES: Led Florida State League second basemen with 255 putouts, 349 assists, 611 total chances and .989 fielding percentage in 1997. ... Tied for International League lead with 16 errors by second baseman in 1999.

Year	Team (League)	Pos.	G	AB	R	H	2B	3B	HR	RBI	Avg.	BB	SO	SB	PO	A	E	Avg.
1992—	Dom. Expos (DSL)	OF	61	198	58	58	5	1	2	23	.293	60	11	41	73	41	7	.942
1993—	Dom. Expos (DSL)		64	211	60	66	12	1	4	26	.313	59	26	38	100	44	7	.954
1994—	GC Expos (GCL)	OF-2B-3B	31	104	23	28	8	2	1	6	.269	14	15	4	39	20	4	.937
1995—	Vermont (NY-P)	OF-2B-3B	53	176	24	42	4	2	0	9	.239	19	19	11	93	76	9	.949
1996—	Delmarva (SAL)...........	OF-2B-3B	116	369	64	91	13	4	1	33	.247	56	48	38	179	80	8	.970
1997—	Lakeland (FSL)■	2B-OF	122	424	54	113	18	2	2	52	.267	52	33	10	†255	†349	7	†.989
1998—	Jacksonville (Sou.)......	2B	128	511	82	156	28	10	12	71	.305	52	46	6	246	354	14	*.977
1999—	Toledo (I.L.)...............	2B-OF-SS	112	438	44	107	18	8	2	36	.244	36	60	10	218	351	‡18	.969
—	Detroit (A.L.)	2B	5	4	2	1	0	0	1	2	.250	0	1	0	1	6	0	1.000
Major League totals (1 year)			5	4	2	1	0	0	1	2	.250	0	1	0	1	6	0	1.000

RECORD AS PITCHER

Year	League	W	L	Pct.	ERA	G	GS	CG	ShO	Sv.	IP	H	R	ER	BB	SO
1994—	GC Expos (GCL)	0	0	...	0.00	1	0	0	0	0	1	0	0	0	0	0

PERSONAL: Born April 14, 1966, in San Angelo, Texas. ... 6-0/185. ... Throws right, bats right. ... Full name: Gregory Alan Maddux. ... Brother of Mike Maddux, pitcher with eight major league teams (1986-99).

HIGH SCHOOL: Valley (Las Vegas).

TRANSACTIONS/CAREER NOTES: Selected by Chicago Cubs organization in second round of free-agent draft (June 4, 1984). ... Granted free agency (October 26, 1992). ... Signed by Atlanta Braves (December 9, 1992).

RECORDS: Holds major league career records for most years leading league in putouts by pitcher—7; and most years leading league in chances accepted by pitcher—10. ... Holds major league single-season record for fewest complete games by pitcher for leader—8 (1993). ... Shares major league career records for most years leading league in double plays by pitcher—5; and most years leading league in assists by pitcher—6. ... Shares major league single-season record for fewest complete games for leader—8 (1993). ... Shares major league single-game record for most putouts by pitcher—7 (April 29, 1990). ... Holds N.L. career record for most putouts by pitcher—378. ... Shares N.L. career record for most years leading league in assists by pitcher—5. ... Shares modern N.L. single-season record for most putouts by pitcher—39 (1990, 1991 and 1993).

HONORS: Won N.L. Gold Glove at pitcher (1990-99). ... Named righthanded pitcher on THE SPORTING NEWS N.L. All-Star team (1992-95). ... Named N.L. Cy Young Award winner by Baseball Writers' Association of America (1992-95). ... Named N.L. Pitcher of the Year by THE SPORTING NEWS (1993-95).

STATISTICAL NOTES: Led Appalachian League with eight hit batsmen in 1984. ... Led American Association with 12 hit batsmen in 1986. ... Led N.L. with 14 hit batsmen in 1992. ... Pitched 3-1 one-hit, complete-game victory against Houston (May 28, 1995). ... Pitched 2-0 one-hit, complete-game victory against San Diego (April 27, 1997).

MISCELLANEOUS: Appeared in three games as pinch runner (1988). ... Singled and scored and struck out in two appearances as pinch hitter (1991).

Year League	W	L	Pct.	ERA	G	GS	CG	ShO	Sv.	IP	H	R	ER	BB	SO
1984— Pikeville (Appl.)	6	2	.750	2.63	14	12	2	•2	0	85 2/3	63	35	25	41	62
1985— Peoria (Midw.)	13	9	.591	3.19	27	27	6	0	0	186	176	86	66	52	125
1986— Pittsfield (East.)	4	3	.571	2.73	8	8	4	2	0	62 2/3	49	22	19	15	35
— Iowa (A.A.)	10	1	*.909	3.02	18	18	5	•2	0	128 1/3	127	49	43	30	65
— Chicago (N.L.)	2	4	.333	5.52	6	5	1	0	0	31	44	20	19	11	20
1987— Chicago (N.L.)	6	14	.300	5.61	30	27	1	1	0	155 2/3	181	111	97	74	101
— Iowa (A.A.)	3	0	1.000	0.98	4	4	2	•2	0	27 2/3	17	3	3	12	22
1988— Chicago (N.L.)	18	8	.692	3.18	34	34	9	3	0	249	230	97	88	81	140
1989— Chicago (N.L.)	19	12	.613	2.95	35	35	7	1	0	238 1/3	222	90	78	82	135
1990— Chicago (N.L.)	15	15	.500	3.46	35	•35	8	2	0	237	*242	*116	91	71	144
1991— Chicago (N.L.)	15	11	.577	3.35	37	*37	7	2	0	*263	232	113	98	66	198
1992— Chicago (N.L.)	•20	11	.645	2.18	35	•35	9	4	0	*268	201	68	65	70	199
1993— Atlanta (N.L.)■	20	10	.667	*2.36	36	•36	*8	1	0	*267	228	85	70	52	197
1994— Atlanta (N.L.)	•16	6	.727	*1.56	25	25	*10	•3	0	*202	150	44	35	31	156
1995— Atlanta (N.L.)	*19	2	*.905	*1.63	28	28	*10	•3	0	•209 2/3	147	39	38	23	181
1996— Atlanta (N.L.)	15	11	.577	2.72	35	35	5	1	0	245	225	85	74	28	172
1997— Atlanta (N.L.)	19	4	*.826	2.20	33	33	5	2	0	232 2/3	200	58	57	20	177
1998— Atlanta (N.L.)	18	9	.667	*2.22	34	34	9	*5	0	251	201	75	62	45	204
1999— Atlanta (N.L.)	19	9	.679	3.57	33	33	4	0	0	219 1/3	258	103	87	37	136
Major League totals (14 years)	221	126	.637	2.81	436	432	93	28	0	3068 2/3	2761	1104	959	691	2160

DIVISION SERIES RECORD

RECORDS: Holds career record for most hits allowed—46. ... Shares career records for most wins—4; and complete games—1. ... Holds N.L. career records for most games started—6; innings pitched—44; and runs allowed—14. ... Shares N.L. career records for most earned runs allowed—12; and games pitched—7.

Year League	W	L	Pct.	ERA	G	GS	CG	ShO	Sv.	IP	H	R	ER	BB	SO
1995— Atlanta (N.L.)	1	0	1.000	4.50	2	2	0	0	0	14	19	7	7	2	7
1996— Atlanta (N.L.)	1	0	1.000	0.00	1	1	0	0	0	7	3	2	0	0	7
1997— Atlanta (N.L.)	1	0	1.000	1.00	1	1	1	0	0	9	7	1	1	1	6
1998— Atlanta (N.L.)	1	0	1.000	2.57	1	1	0	0	0	7	7	2	2	0	4
1999— Atlanta (N.L.)	0	1	.000	2.57	2	1	0	0	0	7	10	2	2	5	5
Division series totals (5 years)	4	1	.800	2.45	7	6	1	0	0	44	46	14	12	8	29

CHAMPIONSHIP SERIES RECORD

RECORDS: Holds career records for most runs allowed—42; and sacrifice hits—6. ... Shares single-series record for most earned runs allowed—11 (1989). ... Holds N.L. single-series record for most runs allowed—12 (1989).

NOTES: Scored in only appearance as pinch runner (1989).

Year League	W	L	Pct.	ERA	G	GS	CG	ShO	Sv.	IP	H	R	ER	BB	SO
1989— Chicago (N.L.)	0	1	.000	13.50	2	2	0	0	0	7 1/3	13	12	11	4	5
1993— Atlanta (N.L.)	1	1	.500	4.97	2	2	0	0	0	12 2/3	11	8	7	7	11
1995— Atlanta (N.L.)	1	0	1.000	1.13	1	1	0	0	0	8	7	1	1	2	4
1996— Atlanta (N.L.)	1	1	.500	2.51	2	2	0	0	0	14 1/3	15	9	4	3	10
1997— Atlanta (N.L.)	0	2	.000	1.38	2	2	0	0	0	13	9	7	2	4	16
1998— Atlanta (N.L.)	0	1	.000	3.00	2	1	0	0	1	6	5	2	2	3	4
1999— Atlanta (N.L.)	1	0	1.000	1.93	2	2	0	0	0	14	12	3	3	1	7
Champ. series totals (7 years)	4	6	.400	3.58	13	12	0	0	1	75 1/3	72	42	30	24	57

WORLD SERIES RECORD

NOTES: Member of World Series championship team (1995).

Year League	W	L	Pct.	ERA	G	GS	CG	ShO	Sv.	IP	H	R	ER	BB	SO
1995— Atlanta (N.L.)	1	1	.500	2.25	2	2	1	0	0	16	9	6	4	3	8
1996— Atlanta (N.L.)	1	1	.500	1.72	2	2	0	0	0	15 2/3	14	3	3	1	5
1999— Atlanta (N.L.)	0	1	.000	2.57	1	1	0	0	0	7	5	4	2	3	5
World Series totals (3 years)	2	3	.400	2.09	5	5	1	0	0	38 2/3	28	13	9	7	18

ALL-STAR GAME RECORD

Year League	W	L	Pct.	ERA	GS	CG	ShO	Sv.	IP	H	R	ER	BB	SO
1988— National						Did not play.								
1992— National	0	0	...	6.75	0	0	0	0	1 1/3	1	1	1	0	0

M

Year League	W	L	Pct.	ERA	GS	CG	ShO	Sv.	IP	H	R	ER	BB	SO
1994—National	0	0	...	3.00	1	0	0	0	3	3	1	1	0	2
1995—National					Selected, did not play—injured.									
1996—National					Did not play.									
1997—National	0	0	...	4.50	1	0	0	0	2	2	1	1	0	0
1998—National	0	0	...	0.00	1	0	0	0	2	3	0	0	1	1
All-Star Game totals (4 years)	0	0	...	3.24	3	0	0	0	8 1/3	9	3	3	1	3

MADDUX, MIKE   P

PERSONAL: Born August 27, 1961, in Dayton, Ohio. ... 6-2/185. ... Throws right, bats left. ... Full name: Michael Ausley Maddux. ... Brother of Greg Maddux, pitcher, Atlanta Braves.
HIGH SCHOOL: Rancho (Las Vegas).
COLLEGE: Texas-El Paso.
TRANSACTIONS/CAREER NOTES: Selected by Cincinnati Reds organization in 36th round of free-agent draft (June 5, 1979); did not sign. ... Selected by Philadelphia Phillies organization in fifth round of free-agent draft (June 7, 1982). ... On Philadelphia disabled list (April 21-June 1, 1988); included rehabilitation assignment to Maine (May 13-22). ... Released by Phillies (November 20, 1989). ... Signed by Los Angeles Dodgers (December 21, 1989). ... Granted free agency (October 15, 1990). ... Signed by San Diego Padres (March 30, 1991). ... On disabled list (April 5-26, 1992). ... Traded by Padres to New York Mets for P Roger Mason and P Mike Freitas (December 17, 1992). ... On disabled list (April 27-May 13, 1994). ... Granted free agency (October 18, 1994). ... Signed by Pittsburgh Pirates organization (April 10, 1995). ... Released by Pirates (May 16, 1995). ... Signed by Boston Red Sox (May 30, 1995). ... Granted free agency (November 6, 1995). ... Re-signed by Red Sox (December 15, 1995). ... On Boston disabled list (May 6-August 2, 1996); included rehabilitation assignments to Pawtucket (May 24-25, July 12-16 and July 25-31). ... Granted free agency (November 1, 1996). ... Re-signed by Red Sox (December 7, 1996). ... Released by Red Sox (March 26, 1997). ... Signed by Seattle Mariners organization (April 11, 1997). ... On Seattle disabled list (June 22-July 11, 1997). ... Released by Mariners (July 23, 1997). ... Signed by Padres organization (August 19, 1997). ... Granted free agency (October 15, 1997). ... Signed by Montreal Expos (March 30, 1998). ... On disabled list (April 8-May 1 and June 7-July 9, 1998). ... Granted free agency (September 29, 1998). ... Re-signed by Expos organization (February 2, 1999). ... Released by Expos (April 15, 1999). ... Signed by Dodgers organization (April 25, 1999). ... Granted free agency (October 14, 1999).
MISCELLANEOUS: Appeared in one game as pinch runner with Philadelphia (1988).

Year League	W	L	Pct.	ERA	G	GS	CG	ShO	Sv.	IP	H	R	ER	BB	SO
1982—Bend (N.W.)	3	6	.333	3.99	11	10	3	0	0	65 1/3	68	35	29	26	59
1983—Spartanburg (SAL)	4	6	.400	5.44	13	13	3	0	0	84 1/3	98	62	51	47	85
— Peninsula (Caro.)	8	4	.667	3.62	14	14	6	0	0	99 1/3	92	46	40	35	78
— Reading (East.)	0	0	...	6.00	1	1	0	0	0	3	4	2	2	1	2
1984—Reading (East.)	3	•12	.200	5.04	20	19	4	0	0	116	143	82	65	49	77
— Portland (PCL)	2	4	.333	5.84	8	8	1	0	0	44 2/3	58	32	29	17	22
1985—Portland (PCL)	9	12	.429	5.31	27	26	6	1	0	166	195	106	98	51	96
1986—Portland (PCL)	5	2	.714	2.36	12	12	3	0	0	84	70	26	22	22	65
— Philadelphia (N.L.)	3	7	.300	5.42	16	16	0	0	0	78	88	56	47	34	44
1987—Maine (I.L.)	6	6	.500	4.35	18	16	3	1	0	103 1/3	116	58	50	26	71
— Philadelphia (N.L.)	2	0	1.000	2.65	7	2	0	0	0	17	17	5	5	5	15
1988—Philadelphia (N.L.)	4	3	.571	3.76	25	11	0	0	0	88 2/3	91	41	37	34	59
— Maine (I.L.)	0	2	.000	4.18	5	3	1	0	0	23 2/3	25	18	11	10	18
1989—Philadelphia (N.L.)	1	3	.250	5.15	16	4	2	1	1	43 2/3	52	29	25	14	26
— Scranton/W.B. (I.L.)	7	7	.500	3.66	19	17	3	1	0	123	119	55	50	26	100
1990—Albuquerque (PCL)■	8	5	.615	4.25	20	19	2	0	0	108	122	59	51	32	85
— Los Angeles (N.L.)	0	1	.000	6.53	11	2	0	0	0	20 2/3	24	15	15	4	11
1991—San Diego (N.L.)■	7	2	.778	2.46	64	1	0	0	5	98 2/3	78	30	27	27	57
1992—San Diego (N.L.)	2	2	.500	2.37	50	1	0	0	5	79 2/3	71	25	21	24	60
1993—New York (N.L.)■	3	8	.273	3.60	58	0	0	0	5	75	67	34	30	27	57
1994—New York (N.L.)	2	1	.667	5.11	27	0	0	0	2	44	45	25	25	13	32
1995—Pittsburgh (N.L.)■	1	0	1.000	9.00	8	0	0	0	0	9	14	9	9	3	4
— Boston (A.L.)■	4	1	.800	3.61	36	4	0	0	1	89 2/3	86	40	36	15	65
1996—Boston (A.L.)	3	2	.600	4.48	23	7	0	0	0	64 1/3	76	37	32	27	32
— Pawtucket (I.L.)	2	0	1.000	3.21	3	3	0	0	0	14	13	5	5	2	9
1997—Tacoma (PCL)■	0	0	...	0.00	1	1	0	0	0	5	1	0	0	2	5
— Seattle (A.L.)	1	0	1.000	10.13	6	0	0	0	0	10 2/3	20	12	12	8	7
— Las Vegas (PCL)■	0	2	.000	5.63	3	3	0	0	0	16	23	11	10	9	13
1998—Montreal (N.L.)■	3	4	.429	3.72	51	0	0	0	1	55 2/3	50	24	23	15	33
1999—Montreal (N.L.)	0	0	...	9.00	4	0	0	0	0	5	9	5	5	3	4
— San Bernardino (Calif.)■	0	0	...	3.00	5	0	0	0	2	9	8	4	3	2	10
— Los Angeles (N.L.)	1	1	.500	3.29	49	0	0	0	0	54 2/3	54	21	20	19	41
A.L. totals (3 years)	8	3	.727	4.37	65	11	0	0	1	164 2/3	182	89	80	50	104
N.L. totals (12 years)	29	32	.475	3.88	386	37	2	1	19	669 2/3	660	319	289	222	443
Major League totals (14 years)	37	35	.514	3.98	451	48	2	1	20	834 1/3	842	408	369	272	547

DIVISION SERIES RECORD

Year League	W	L	Pct.	ERA	G	GS	CG	ShO	Sv.	IP	H	R	ER	BB	SO
1995—Boston (A.L.)	0	0	...	0.00	2	0	0	0	0	3	2	0	0	1	1

MADURO, CALVIN   P   ORIOLES

PERSONAL: Born September 5, 1974, in Santa Cruz, Aruba. ... 6-0/188. ... Throws right, bats right. ... Full name: Calvin Gregory Maduro.
HIGH SCHOOL: Tourist Economy School (Santa Cruz, Aruba).
COLLEGE: St. Antonius College.
TRANSACTIONS/CAREER NOTES: Signed as non-drafted free agent by Baltimore Orioles organization (September 9, 1991). ... Traded by Orioles with P Garrett Stephenson to Philadelphia Phillies (September 4, 1996), completing deal in which Phillies traded 3B Todd Zeile and OF Pete Incaviglia to Orioles for two players to be named later (August 29, 1996). ... Released by Phillies (November 19, 1998). ... Signed by Orioles organization (February 5, 1999).
STATISTICAL NOTES: Pitched 5-0 no-hit victory for Bowie against Portland (May 28, 1996, first game).
MISCELLANEOUS: Appeared in one game as pinch runner with Philadelphia (1997).

Year League	W	L	Pct.	ERA	G	GS	CG	ShO	Sv.	IP	H	R	ER	BB	SO
1992— Gulf Coast Orioles (GCL)....	1	4	.200	2.27	13	•12	1	1	0	71⅓	56	29	18	26	66
1993— Bluefield (Appl.)	•9	4	.692	3.96	14	•14	*3	0	0	*91	90	46	40	17	*83
1994— Frederick (Caro.)	9	8	.529	4.25	27	26	0	0	0	152⅓	132	86	72	59	137
1995— Frederick (Caro.)	8	5	.615	2.94	20	20	2	2	0	122⅓	109	43	40	34	120
— Bowie (East.).................	0	6	.000	5.09	7	7	0	0	0	35⅓	39	28	20	27	26
1996— Bowie (East.).................	9	7	.563	3.26	19	19	4	*3	0	124⅓	116	50	45	36	87
— Rochester (I.L.)................	3	5	.375	4.74	8	8	0	0	0	43⅔	49	25	23	18	40
— Philadelphia (N.L.)■....	0	1	.000	3.52	4	2	0	0	0	15⅓	13	6	6	3	11
1997— Philadelphia (N.L.).......	3	7	.300	7.23	15	13	0	0	0	71	83	59	57	41	31
— Scranton/W.B. (I.L.).....	6	4	.600	4.99	13	13	2	0	0	79⅓	71	48	44	57	53
1998— Scranton/W.B. (I.L.).....	12	9	.571	5.98	28	27	4	1	0	177⅔	*211	123	118	68	120
1999— Rochester (I.L.)■...........	11	11	.500	3.99	29	•28	2	1	0	169	179	88	75	60	149
Major League totals (2 years)......	3	8	.273	6.57	19	15	0	0	0	86⅓	96	65	63	44	42

MAGADAN, DAVE   3B/1B   PADRES

PERSONAL: Born September 30, 1962, in Tampa. ... 6-4/215. ... Bats left, throws right. ... Full name: David Joseph Magadan. ... Cousin of Lou Piniella, manager, Seattle Mariners, and outfielder/designated hitter with four major league teams (1964 and 1968-84). ... Name pronounced MAG-uh-dun.

HIGH SCHOOL: Jesuit (Tampa).

COLLEGE: Alabama.

TRANSACTIONS/CAREER NOTES: Selected by Boston Red Sox organization in 12th round of free-agent draft (June 3, 1980); did not sign. ... Selected by New York Mets organization in second round of free-agent draft (June 6, 1983). ... On disabled list (August 7-September 10, 1984; March 29-April 17, 1987; May 5-20, 1988; and August 9, 1992-remainder of season). ... Granted free agency (October 27, 1992). ... Signed by Florida Marlins organization (December 8, 1992). ... Traded by Marlins to Seattle Mariners for OF Henry Cotto and P Jeff Darwin (June 27, 1993). ... Traded by Mariners to Marlins for P Jeff Darwin and cash (November 9, 1993). ... On disabled list (March 29-April 13 and July 21, 1994-remainder of season). ... Granted free agency (October 19, 1994). ... Signed by Houston Astros (April 15, 1995). ... Granted free agency (October 30, 1995). ... Signed by Chicago Cubs (December 26, 1995). ... On Chicago disabled list (March 22-April 16 and April 17-May 31, 1996); included rehabilitation assignment to Daytona (May 17-29). ... Granted free agency (November 18, 1996). ... Signed by Oakland Athletics organization (January 23, 1997). ... Granted free agency (October 27, 1997). ... Re-signed by A's (November 12, 1997). ... On disabled list (May 16, 1998-remainder of season). ... Granted free agency (October 29, 1998). ... Signed by San Diego Padres (December 21, 1998).

HONORS: Named Golden Spikes Award winner by USA Baseball (1983). ... Named designated hitter on THE SPORTING NEWS college All-America team (1983).

STATISTICAL NOTES: Led Carolina League with 10 intentional bases on balls received in 1984. ... Led Texas League third basemen with 87 putouts, 275 assists, 393 total chances and 31 errors in 1985. ... Led International League third basemen with .934 fielding percentage, 283 assists and 31 double plays in 1986. ... Led N.L. first basemen with .998 fielding percentage in 1990.

							BATTING								FIELDING		
Year Team (League)	Pos.	G	AB	R	H	2B	3B	HR	RBI	Avg.	BB	SO	SB	PO	A	E	Avg.
1983— Columbia (SAL).........	1B	64	220	41	74	13	1	3	32	.336	51	29	2	520	37	7	.988
1984— Lynchburg (Caro.).......	1B	112	371	78	130	22	4	0	62	*.350	104	43	2	896	64	16	.984
1985— Jackson (Texas).......	3B-1B	134	466	84	144	22	0	0	76	.309	*106	57	0	†106	†276	†31	.925
1986— Tidewater (I.L.).........	3B-1B	133	473	68	147	33	6	1	64	.311	84	45	2	78	†284	25	†.935
— New York (N.L.)..........	1B	10	18	3	8	0	0	0	3	.444	3	1	0	48	5	0	1.000
1987— New York (N.L.).........	3B-1B	85	192	21	61	13	1	3	24	.318	22	22	0	88	92	4	.978
1988— New York (N.L.).........	1B-3B	112	314	39	87	15	0	1	35	.277	60	39	0	459	99	10	.982
1989— New York (N.L.).........	1B-3B	127	374	47	107	22	3	4	41	.286	49	37	1	587	89	7	.990
1990— New York (N.L.).........	1B-3B	144	451	74	148	28	6	6	72	.328	74	55	2	837	99	3	†.997
1991— New York (N.L.).........	1B	124	418	58	108	23	0	4	51	.258	83	50	1	1035	90	5	.996
1992— New York (N.L.).........	3B-1B	99	321	33	91	9	1	3	28	.283	56	44	1	54	136	11	.945
1993— Florida (N.L.)■.........	3B-1B	66	227	22	65	12	0	4	29	.286	44	30	0	55	122	7	.962
— Seattle (A.L.)■.......	1B-3B-DH	71	228	27	59	11	0	1	21	.259	36	33	2	325	72	5	.988
1994— Florida (N.L.)■.........	3B-1B	74	211	30	58	7	0	1	17	.275	39	25	0	127	78	4	.981
1995— Houston (N.L.)■.........	3B-1B	127	348	44	109	24	0	2	51	.313	71	56	0	121	163	18	.940
1996— Daytona (FSL)■.........	3B-DH	7	20	5	6	1	0	0	3	.300	7	2	0	0	6	1	.857
— Iowa (A.A.)............	3B	3	9	0	2	1	0	0	1	.222	1	2	0	3	3	0	1.000
— Chicago (N.L.)............	3B-1B	78	169	23	43	10	0	3	17	.254	29	29	1	75	67	3	.979
1997— Oakland (A.L.)■.........	3B-1B-DH	128	271	38	82	10	1	4	30	.303	50	40	1	148	65	5	.977
1998— Oakland (A.L.)..........	3B	35	109	12	35	8	0	1	13	.321	13	12	0	48	55	6	.945
1999— San Diego (N.L.)■.....	3B-1B	116	248	20	68	12	1	2	30	.274	45	36	1	209	85	6	.980
American League totals (3 years)		234	608	77	176	29	1	6	64	.289	99	85	3	521	192	16	.978
National League totals (12 years)		1162	3291	414	953	175	12	33	398	.290	575	418	8	3695	1125	78	.984
Major League totals (14 years)		1396	3899	491	1129	204	13	39	462	.290	674	503	11	4216	1317	94	.983

CHAMPIONSHIP SERIES RECORD

							BATTING								FIELDING		
Year Team (League)	Pos.	G	AB	R	H	2B	3B	HR	RBI	Avg.	BB	SO	SB	PO	A	E	Avg.
1988— New York (N.L.).........	PH	3	3	0	0	0	0	0	0	.000	0	2	0	...	...	...	...

MAGEE, WENDELL   OF   PHILLIES

PERSONAL: Born August 3, 1972, in Hattiesburg, Miss. ... 6-0/220. ... Bats right, throws right. ... Full name: Wendell Errol Magee Jr.

HIGH SCHOOL: Hattiesburg (Miss.).

JUNIOR COLLEGE: Pearl River Community College (Miss.).

COLLEGE: Samford.

TRANSACTIONS/CAREER NOTES: Selected by Philadelphia Phillies organization in 12th round of free-agent draft (June 2, 1994).

STATISTICAL NOTES: Led International League outfielders with 320 total chances in 1998. ... Led International League outfielders with 325 total chances in 1999.

M

Year	Team (League)	Pos.	G	AB	R	H	2B	3B	HR	RBI	Avg.	BB	SO	SB	PO	A	E	Avg.
								BATTING								FIELDING		
1994—Batavia (NY-P)		OF	63	229	42	64	12	4	2	35	.279	16	24	10	115	7	6	.953
1995—Clearwater (FSL)		OF	96	388	67	137	24	5	6	46	*.353	33	40	7	166	12	5	.973
—Reading (East.)		OF	39	136	17	40	9	1	3	21	.294	21	17	3	65	4	5	.932
1996—Reading (East.)		OF	71	270	38	79	15	5	6	30	.293	24	40	10	101	8	3	.973
—Scranton/W.B. (I.L.)		OF	44	155	31	44	9	2	10	32	.284	21	31	3	92	2	4	.959
—Philadelphia (N.L.)		OF	38	142	9	29	7	0	2	14	.204	9	33	0	88	2	2	.978
1997—Philadelphia (N.L.)		OF	38	115	7	23	4	0	1	9	.200	9	20	1	95	4	4	.960
—Scranton/W.B. (I.L.)		OF	83	294	39	72	20	1	10	39	.245	30	56	4	167	3	3	.983
1998—Scranton/W.B. (I.L.)		OF	126	507	86	147	30	7	24	72	.290	46	102	7	*302	7	•11	.966
—Philadelphia (N.L.)		OF	20	75	9	22	6	1	1	11	.293	7	11	0	31	1	2	.941
1999—Scranton/W.B. (I.L.)		OF	*142	*566	95	160	34	2	20	79	.283	55	124	10	*310	7	*8	.975
—Philadelphia (N.L.)		OF	12	14	4	5	1	0	2	5	.357	1	4	0	5	0	0	1.000
Major League totals (4 years)			108	346	29	79	18	1	6	39	.228	26	68	1	219	5	8	.966

MAGNANTE, MIKE — P — ATHLETICS

PERSONAL: Born June 17, 1965, in Glendale, Calif. ... 6-1/185. ... Throws left, bats left. ... Full name: Michael Anthony Magnante. ... Name pronounced mag-NAN-tee.

HIGH SCHOOL: John Burroughs (Burbank, Calif.).

COLLEGE: UCLA (bachelor of science degree in applied mathematics).

TRANSACTIONS/CAREER NOTES: Selected by Kansas City Royals organization in 11th round of free-agent draft (June 1, 1988). ... On disabled list (June 17, 1990-remainder of season; July 2-20, 1992; and July 16-31, 1994). ... On Kansas City disabled list (May 19-June 13, 1996); included rehabilitation assignment to Omaha (June 8-13). ... Released by Royals (October 2, 1996). ... Signed by Houston Astros organization (December 19, 1996). ... On disabled list (May 10-25, 1998). ... Granted free agency (October 23, 1998). ... Signed by Anaheim Angels (January 27, 1999). ... Granted free agency (October 28, 1999). ... Signed by Oakland Athletics (November 18, 1999).

RECORDS: Shares major league record for striking out side on nine pitches (August 22, 1997, ninth inning).

Year	League	W	L	Pct.	ERA	G	GS	CG	ShO	Sv.	IP	H	R	ER	BB	SO
1988—Eugene (N.W.)		1	1	.500	0.56	3	3	0	0	0	16	10	6	1	2	26
—Appleton (Midw.)		3	2	.600	3.21	9	8	0	0	0	47 2/3	48	20	17	15	40
—Baseball City (FSL)		1	1	.500	4.13	4	4	1	0	0	24	19	12	11	8	19
1989—Memphis (Sou.)		8	9	.471	3.66	26	26	4	1	0	157 1/3	137	70	64	53	118
1990—Omaha (A.A.)		2	5	.286	4.11	13	13	2	0	0	76 2/3	72	39	35	25	56
1991—Omaha (A.A.)		6	1	.857	3.02	10	10	2	0	0	65 2/3	53	23	22	23	50
—Kansas City (A.L.)		0	1	.000	2.45	38	0	0	0	0	55	55	19	15	23	42
1992—Kansas City (A.L.)		4	9	.308	4.94	44	12	0	0	0	89 1/3	115	53	49	35	31
1993—Omaha (A.A.)		2	6	.250	3.67	33	13	0	0	2	105 1/3	97	46	43	29	74
—Kansas City (A.L.)		1	2	.333	4.08	7	6	0	0	0	35 1/3	37	16	16	11	16
1994—Kansas City (A.L.)		2	3	.400	4.60	36	1	0	0	0	47	55	27	24	16	21
1995—Omaha (A.A.)		5	1	.833	2.84	15	8	0	0	0	57	55	23	18	13	38
—Kansas City (A.L.)		1	1	.500	4.23	28	0	0	0	0	44 2/3	45	23	21	16	28
1996—Kansas City (A.L.)		2	2	.500	5.67	38	0	0	0	0	54	58	38	34	24	32
—Omaha (A.A.)		1	0	1.000	0.00	1	0	0	0	0	3	3	1	0	0	6
1997—New Orleans (A.A.)■		2	3	.400	4.50	17	0	0	0	1	24	31	14	12	5	23
—Houston (N.L.)		3	1	.750	2.27	40	0	0	0	1	47 2/3	39	16	12	11	43
1998—Houston (N.L.)		4	7	.364	4.88	48	0	0	0	2	51 2/3	56	28	28	26	39
1999—Anaheim (A.L.)■		5	2	.714	3.38	53	0	0	0	0	69 1/3	68	30	26	29	44
A.L. totals (7 years)		15	20	.429	4.22	244	19	0	0	0	394 2/3	433	206	185	154	214
N.L. totals (2 years)		7	8	.467	3.62	88	0	0	0	3	99 1/3	95	44	40	37	82
Major League totals (9 years)		22	28	.440	4.10	332	19	0	0	3	494	528	250	225	191	296

DIVISION SERIES RECORD

Year	League	W	L	Pct.	ERA	G	GS	CG	ShO	Sv.	IP	H	R	ER	BB	SO
1997—Houston (N.L.)		0	0	...	4.50	2	0	0	0	0	2	4	3	1	0	2
1998—Houston (N.L.)									Did not play.							

MAHAY, RON — P — ATHLETICS

PERSONAL: Born June 28, 1971, in Crestwood, Ill. ... 6-2/190. ... Throws left, bats left. ... Full name: Ronald Matthew Mahay.

HIGH SCHOOL: Alan B. Shepard (Palos Heights, Ill.).

JUNIOR COLLEGE: South Suburban College (Ill.).

TRANSACTIONS/CAREER NOTES: Selected by Boston Red Sox organization in 18th round of free-agent draft (June 3, 1991). ... On disabled list (May 5, 1992-remainder of season). ... On Lynchburg disabled list (August 6-September 9, 1993). ... On disabled list (August 23-September 1, 1994). ... On Pawtucket temporarily inactive list (April 19-25, 1995). ... On Sarasota disabled list (April 4-25, 1996). ... Claimed on waivers by Oakland Athletics (March 30, 1999).

MISCELLANEOUS: Played outfield (1991-95).

Year	League	W	L	Pct.	ERA	G	GS	CG	ShO	Sv.	IP	H	R	ER	BB	SO
1996—Sarasota (FSL)		2	2	.500	3.82	31	4	0	0	2	70 2/3	61	33	30	35	68
—Trenton (East.)		0	1	.000	29.45	1	1	0	0	0	3 2/3	12	13	12	6	0
1997—Trenton (East.)		3	3	.500	3.10	17	4	0	0	5	40 2/3	29	16	14	13	47
—Pawtucket (I.L.)		1	0	1.000	0.00	2	0	0	0	0	4 2/3	3	0	0	1	6
—Boston (A.L.)		3	0	1.000	2.52	28	0	0	0	0	25	19	7	7	11	22
1998—Pawtucket (I.L.)		3	1	.750	4.17	23	1	0	0	3	41	37	20	19	19	41
—Boston (A.L.)		1	1	.500	3.46	29	0	0	0	1	26	26	16	10	15	14
1999—Oakland (A.L.)■		2	0	1.000	1.86	6	1	0	0	1	19 1/3	8	4	4	3	15
—Vancouver (PCL)		7	2	.778	4.29	32	15	0	0	0	107	116	57	51	45	73
Major League totals (4 years)		6	1	.857	2.69	68	1	0	0	2	70 1/3	53	27	21	29	51

M

RECORD AS POSITION PLAYER

Year	Team (League)	Pos.	G	AB	R	H	2B	3B	HR	RBI	Avg.	BB	SO	SB	PO	A	E	Avg.
1991—	GC Red Sox (GCL)	OF	54	187	30	51	6	5	1	29	.273	33	40	2	97	2	3	.971
1992—	Winter Haven (FSL)	OF	19	63	6	16	2	1	0	4	.254	2	19	0	33	2	1	.972
1993—	Lynchburg (Caro.)	OF-C	73	254	28	54	8	1	5	23	.213	11	63	2	174	7	5	.973
—	New Britain (East.)	OF	8	25	2	3	0	0	1	2	.120	1	6	1	15	1	2	.889
1994—	Sarasota (Fla. St.)	OF	105	367	43	102	18	0	4	46	.278	39	67	3	189	16	4	.981
1995—	Pawtucket (Int'l)	OF	11	44	5	14	4	0	0	3	.318	4	9	1	30	2	0	1.000
—	Trenton (Eastern)	OF	93	310	37	73	12	3	5	28	.235	44	90	5	187	9	6	.970
—	Boston (A.L.)	OF	5	20	3	4	2	0	1	3	.200	1	6	0	9	0	0	1.000
Major league totals (1 year)			5	20	3	4	2	0	1	3	.200	1	6	0	9	0	0	1.000

MAHOMES, PAT   P   METS

PERSONAL: Born August 9, 1970, in Bryan, Texas. ... 6-4/212. ... Throws right, bats right. ... Full name: Patrick Lavon Mahomes. ... Name pronounced muh-HOMES.

HIGH SCHOOL: Lindale (Texas).

TRANSACTIONS/CAREER NOTES: Selected by Minnesota Twins organization in sixth round of free-agent draft (June 1, 1988). ... On disabled list (July 6-23, 1994). ... Traded by Twins to Boston Red Sox for a player to be named later (August 26, 1996); Twins acquired P Brian Looney to complete deal (December 17, 1996). ... Signed by Yokohoma of Japan Central League (1997). ... Signed by New York Mets (December 21, 1998).

MISCELLANEOUS: Appeared in one game as pinch runner (1994). ... Struck out in only appearance as pinch hitter and appeared in one game as pinch runner (1999).

Year	League	W	L	Pct.	ERA	G	GS	CG	ShO	Sv.	IP	H	R	ER	BB	SO
1988—	Elizabethton (Appl.)	6	3	.667	3.69	13	13	3	0	0	78	66	45	32	51	93
1989—	Kenosha (Midw.)	13	7	.650	3.28	25	25	3	1	0	156 1/3	120	66	57	•100	167
1990—	Visalia (Calif.)	11	11	.500	3.30	28	*28	5	1	0	•185 1/3	136	77	68	*118	178
1991—	Orlando (Sou.)	8	5	.615	*1.78	18	17	2	0	0	116	77	30	23	57	136
—	Portland (PCL)	3	5	.375	3.44	9	9	2	0	0	55	50	26	21	36	41
1992—	Minnesota (A.L.)	3	4	.429	5.04	14	13	0	0	0	69 2/3	73	41	39	37	44
—	Portland (PCL)	9	5	.643	3.41	17	16	3	*3	1	111	97	43	42	43	87
1993—	Minnesota (A.L.)	1	5	.167	7.71	12	5	0	0	0	37 1/3	47	34	32	16	23
—	Portland (PCL)	11	4	•.733	*3.03	17	16	3	1	0	115 2/3	89	47	39	54	94
1994—	Minnesota (A.L.)	9	5	.643	4.72	21	21	0	0	0	120	121	68	63	62	53
1995—	Minnesota (A.L.)	4	10	.286	6.37	47	7	0	0	3	94 2/3	100	74	67	47	67
1996—	Minnesota (A.L.)	1	4	.200	7.20	20	5	0	0	0	45	63	38	36	27	30
—	Salt Lake (PCL)	3	1	.750	3.74	22	2	0	0	7	33 2/3	32	14	14	12	41
—	Boston (A.L.)■	2	0	1.000	5.84	11	0	0	0	2	12 1/3	9	8	8	6	6
1997—	Boston (A.L.)	1	0	1.000	8.10	10	0	0	0	0	10	15	10	9	10	5
—	Pawtucket (I.L.)	5	1	.833	2.84	18	1	0	0	7	31 2/3	22	11	10	17	40
—	Yokohama (Jap. Cen.)■	3	4	.429	4.82	11	9	0	0	0	52 1/3	54	30	28	25	42
1998—	Yokohama (Jap. Cen.)	0	4	.000	5.98	10	8	0	0	0	43 2/3	61	30	29	29	24
1999—	Norfolk (I.L.)■	4	1	.800	3.49	6	6	0	0	0	38 2/3	38	17	15	12	24
—	New York (N.L.)■	8	0	1.000	3.68	39	0	0	0	0	63 2/3	44	26	26	37	51
A.L. totals (6 years)		21	28	.429	5.88	135	51	0	0	5	389	428	273	254	205	228
N.L. totals (1 year)		8	0	1.000	3.68	39	0	0	0	0	63 2/3	44	26	26	37	51
Major League totals (7 years)		29	28	.509	5.57	174	51	0	0	5	452 2/3	472	299	280	242	279

DIVISION SERIES RECORD

Year	League	W	L	Pct.	ERA	G	GS	CG	ShO	Sv.	IP	H	R	ER	BB	SO
1999—	New York (N.L.)	0	0	...	5.40	1	0	0	0	0	1 2/3	3	1	1	0	1

CHAMPIONSHIP SERIES RECORD

Year	League	W	L	Pct.	ERA	G	GS	CG	ShO	Sv.	IP	H	R	ER	BB	SO
1999—	New York (N.L.)	0	0	...	1.42	3	0	0	0	0	6 1/3	4	1	1	3	3

MANN, JIM   P   METS

PERSONAL: Born November 17, 1974, in Brockton, Mass. ... 6-3/225. ... Throws right, bats right. ... Full name: James Joseph Mann.

HIGH SCHOOL: Holbrook (Mass.).

JUNIOR COLLEGE: Massasoit Community College (Mass.).

TRANSACTIONS/CAREER NOTES: Selected by Toronto Blue Jays organization in 54th round of free-agent draft (June 3, 1993). ... Selected by New York Mets from Blue Jays organization in Rule 5 major league draft (December 13, 1999).

Year	League	W	L	Pct.	ERA	G	GS	CG	ShO	Sv.	IP	H	R	ER	BB	SO
1994—	Gulf Coast Blue Jays (GCL)	3	2	.600	3.74	11	9	0	0	0	53	54	28	22	26	41
1995—	Medicine Hat (Pio.)	5	4	.556	4.29	14	14	1	•1	0	77 2/3	78	47	37	37	66
1996—	St. Catharines (NY-P)	2	1	.667	3.62	26	0	0	0	17	27 1/3	22	12	11	10	37
1997—	Hagerstown (SAL)	0	1	.000	5.06	19	0	0	0	4	26 2/3	35	18	15	11	30
—	Dunedin (FSL)	1	0	1.000	6.00	12	0	0	0	0	18	27	12	12	6	13
1998—	Dunedin (FSL)	0	2	.000	3.04	51	0	0	0	25	50 1/3	31	19	17	24	59
1999—	Knoxville (Sou.)	1	2	.333	0.93	6	0	0	0	0	9 2/3	6	2	1	1	12
—	Syracuse (I.L.)	6	5	.545	4.64	47	0	0	0	5	66	53	35	34	39	72

MANTEI, MATT   P   DIAMONDBACKS

PERSONAL: Born July 7, 1973, in Tampa. ... 6-1/190. ... Throws right, bats right. ... Full name: Matthew Bruce Mantei. ... Name pronounced MAN-tay.

HIGH SCHOOL: River Valley (Three Oaks, Mich.).

M

TRANSACTIONS/CAREER NOTES: Selected by Seattle Mariners organization in 25th round of free-agent draft (June 3, 1991). ... Selected by Florida Marlins from Mariners organization in Rule 5 major league draft (December 5, 1994). ... On Florida disabled list (April 20-June 18 and July 29-September 1, 1995); included rehabilitation assignments to Portland and Charlotte (May 13-June 18). ... On Florida disabled list (June 19, 1996-remainder of season). ... On Florida disabled list (March 31, 1997-entire season). ... Granted free agency (December 21, 1997). ... Re-signed by Marlins organization (December 21, 1997). ... On Florida disabled list (August 19-September 4, 1998). ... Traded by Marlins to Arizona Diamondbacks for P Vladimir Nunez, P Brad Penny and a player to be named later (July 9, 1999); Marlins acquired OF Abraham Nunez to complete deal (December 13, 1999).

Year — League	W	L	Pct.	ERA	G	GS	CG	ShO	Sv.	IP	H	R	ER	BB	SO
1991— Arizona Mariners (Ariz.)	1	4	.200	6.69	17	5	0	0	0	40 1/3	54	40	30	28	29
1992— Arizona Mariners (Ariz.)	1	1	.500	5.63	3	3	0	0	0	16	18	10	10	5	19
1993— Bellingham (N.W.)	1	1	.500	5.96	26	0	0	0	*12	25 2/3	26	19	17	15	34
1994— Appleton (Midw.)	5	1	.833	2.06	48	0	0	0	26	48	42	14	11	21	70
1995— Portland (East.)■	1	0	1.000	2.38	8	0	0	0	1	11 1/3	10	3	3	5	15
— Charlotte (I.L.)	0	1	.000	2.57	6	0	0	0	0	7	1	3	2	5	10
— Florida (N.L.)	0	1	.000	4.72	12	0	0	0	0	13 1/3	12	8	7	13	15
1996— Florida (N.L.)	1	0	1.000	6.38	14	0	0	0	0	18 1/3	13	13	13	21	25
— Charlotte (I.L.)	0	2	.000	4.70	7	0	0	0	2	7 2/3	6	4	4	7	8
1997— Brevard County (FSL)	0	0	...	6.00	4	0	0	0	0	6	4	4	4	6	11
— Portland (East.)	1	0	1.000	6.75	5	0	0	0	0	4	1	3	3	8	7
1998— Charlotte (I.L.)	1	2	.333	5.51	16	0	0	0	3	16 1/3	11	10	10	18	25
— Florida (N.L.)	3	4	.429	2.96	42	0	0	0	9	54 2/3	38	19	18	23	63
1999— Florida (N.L.)	1	2	.333	2.72	35	0	0	0	10	36 1/3	24	11	11	25	50
— Arizona (N.L.)■	0	1	.000	2.79	30	0	0	0	22	29	20	10	9	19	49
Major League totals (4 years)	**5**	**8**	**.385**	**3.44**	**133**	**0**	**0**	**0**	**41**	**151 2/3**	**107**	**61**	**58**	**101**	**202**

DIVISION SERIES RECORD

Year — League	W	L	Pct.	ERA	G	GS	CG	ShO	Sv.	IP	H	R	ER	BB	SO
1999— Arizona (N.L.)	0	1	.000	4.50	1	0	0	0	0	2	1	1	1	3	1

MANTO, JEFF — 3B

PERSONAL: Born August 23, 1964, in Bristol, Pa. ... 6-3/210. ... Bats right, throws right. ... Full name: Jeffrey Paul Manto.
HIGH SCHOOL: Bristol (Pa.).
COLLEGE: Temple.
TRANSACTIONS/CAREER NOTES: Selected by New York Yankees organization in 35th round of free-agent draft (June 7, 1982); did not sign. ... Selected by California Angels organization in 14th round of free-agent draft (June 3, 1985). ... On disabled list (July 16, 1986-remainder of season). ... Traded by Angels organization with P Colin Charland to Cleveland Indians for P Scott Bailes (January 9, 1990). ... Released by Indians (November 27, 1991). ... Signed by Richmond, Atlanta Braves organization (January 23, 1992). ... On disabled list (May 4-14, 1992). ... Granted free agency (October 15, 1992). ... Signed by Philadelphia Phillies organization (December 16, 1992). ... Granted free agency (October 15, 1993). ... Signed by New York Mets organization (December 16, 1993). ... Traded by Mets to Baltimore Orioles for future considerations (May 19, 1994). ... On Baltimore disabled list (June 26-July 13, 1995); included rehabilitation assignments to Bowie (July 9-10) and Frederick (July 10-13). ... Signed by Yomiuri Giants of Japan Central League (January 25, 1996). ... Released by Giants (April 23, 1996). ... Signed by Boston Red Sox organization (May 7, 1996). ... On Boston disabled list (May 26-June 27, 1996); included rehabilitation assignment to Trenton (June 21-27). ... Traded by Red Sox to Seattle Mariners for IF Arquimedez Pozo (July 23, 1996). ... Released by Mariners (August 29, 1996). ... Claimed on waivers by Red Sox (August 29, 1996). ... Granted free agency (October 8, 1996). ... Signed by Syracuse, Blue Jays organization (February 17, 1997). ... On Syracuse disabled list (May 26-June 2, 1997). ... Traded by Blue Jays to Cleveland Indians for OF Ryan Thompson (June 6, 1997). ... Claimed on waivers by Detroit Tigers (April 24, 1998). ... Released by Tigers (June 12, 1998). ... Signed by Indians organization (June 16, 1998). ... Released by Indians (October 15, 1998). ... Re-signed by Indians organization (January 5, 1999). ... Claimed on waivers by Yankees (July 2, 1999). ... Released by Yankees (August 10, 1999). ... Signed by Indians organization (August 13, 1999). ... Granted free agency (October 15, 1999).
RECORDS: Shares major league record for most consecutive home runs in three games—4 (June 8 [1], 9 [2] and 10 [1], 1995).
HONORS: Named Texas League Most Valuable Player (1988). ... Named International League Most Valuable Player (1994).
STATISTICAL NOTES: Led California League third basemen with 245 assists and 365 total chances in 1987. ... Tied for Texas League lead in errors by third baseman with 32 in 1988. ... Led Texas League in grounding into double plays with 17 in 1988. ... Led Pacific Coast League with .446 on-base percentage in 1990. ... Led Pacific Coast League third basemen with .943 fielding percentage, 265 assists and 22 double plays in 1989. ... Led International League with 12 sacrifice flies in 1992. ... Led International League with .404 on-base percentage, 260 total bases, 31 home runs, 100 RBIs and tied for lead in being hit by pitch with 11 in 1994.

Year — Team (League)	Pos.	G	AB	R	H	2B	3B	HR	RBI	Avg.	BB	SO	SB	PO	A	E	Avg.
1985— Quad Cities (Midw.)	OF-3B	74	233	34	46	5	2	11	34	.197	40	74	3	87	8	3	.969
1986— Quad Cities (Midw.)	3B	73	239	31	59	13	0	8	49	.247	37	70	2	48	114	28	.853
1987— Palm Springs (Calif.)	3B-1B	112	375	61	96	21	4	7	63	.256	102	85	8	93	†246	37	.902
1988— Midland (Texas)	3B-2B-1B	120	408	88	123	23	3	24	101	.301	62	76	7	82	208	‡32	.901
1989— Edmonton (PCL)	3B-1B	127	408	89	113	25	3	23	67	.277	91	81	4	140	†266	21	†.951
1990— Colo. Springs (PCL)■	3B-1B	96	316	73	94	27	1	18	82	.297	78	65	10	340	131	10	.979
— Cleveland (A.L.)	1B-3B	30	76	12	17	5	1	2	14	.224	21	18	0	185	24	2	.991
1991— Cleveland (A.L.)	3B-1B-C-OF	47	128	15	27	7	0	2	13	.211	14	22	2	109	63	8	.956
— Colo. Springs (PCL)	3B-1B-C-SS-OF	43	153	36	49	16	0	6	36	.320	33	24	1	169	53	11	.953
1992— Richmond (I.L.)	3B-2B-1B	127	450	65	131	24	1	13	68	.291	57	63	1	89	245	23	.936
1993— Scranton/W.B. (I.L.)	3B-1B-C	106	388	62	112	30	1	17	88	.289	55	58	4	401	134	8	.985
— Philadelphia (N.L.)	3B-SS	8	18	0	1	0	0	0	0	.056	0	3	0	2	8	0	1.000
1994— Norfolk (I.L.)	3B-DH-1B-2B	37	115	20	30	6	0	4	17	.261	27	28	1	73	46	4	.967
— Rochester (I.L.)■	3B-1B-DH	94	329	61	102	25	2	§27	§83	.310	43	47	2	277	102	15	.962
1995— Baltimore (A.L.)	3B-DH-1B	89	254	31	65	9	0	17	38	.256	24	69	0	68	103	6	.966
— Bowie (East.)	DH	1	4	1	1	0	0	0	0	.250	1	0	0	0	0	0	...
— Frederick (Caro.)	DH-3B	2	8	1	3	0	0	1	3	.375	0	1	0	0	2	0	1.000
1996— Yomiuri (Jap. Cen.)■	...	10	27	1	3	...	...	0	1	.111	...	...	...	...	...	...	...
— Pawtucket (I.L.)	3B-2B	12	45	6	11	5	0	2	6	.244	5	8	1	13	29	2	.955
— Boston (A.L.)	3B-2B-SS-1B	22	48	8	10	3	1	2	6	.208	8	12	0	25	47	4	.947
— Trenton (East.)	3B-DH-2B-SS	6	21	3	6	0	0	0	5	.286	1	5	0	5	5	3	.769
— Seattle (A.L.)■	3B-DH-OF	21	54	7	10	3	0	1	4	.185	9	12	0	8	26	1	.971

Year	Team (League)	Pos.	G	AB	R	H	2B	3B	HR	RBI	Avg.	BB	SO	SB	PO	A	E	Avg.
1997—Syracuse (I.L.)■	DH-3B-OF-1B	40	132	18	27	5	1	3	11	.205	22	30	1	23	19	1	.977
—Buffalo (A.A.)■	3B-DH-1B-OF	54	187	37	60	11	0	20	54	.321	31	43	0	59	54	6	.950
—Cleveland (A.L.)	3B-1B-OF	16	30	3	8	3	0	2	7	.267	1	10	0	35	5	0	1.000
1998—Buffalo (I.L.)■	3B-1B-2B	15	37	8	8	1	0	2	6	.216	2	10	0	49	8	1	.983
—Detroit (A.L.)■	1B-DH-OF	16	30	6	8	2	0	1	3	.267	3	11	1	43	0	1	.977
—Buffalo (I.L.)■	1B-DH-3B	62	209	46	65	11	0	23	63	.311	58	48	4	282	35	2	.994
1999—Buffalo (I.L.)	1B-DH	66	203	47	60	9	0	23	44	.296	66	47	3	417	22	3	.993
—Cleveland (A.L.)	3B-1B	12	25	5	5	0	0	1	2	.200	11	11	0	12	16	0	1.000
—New York (A.L.)■	1B-3B	6	8	0	1	0	0	0	0	.125	2	4	0	14	1	0	1.000
American League totals (7 years)		274	690	95	159	33	2	30	93	.230	95	179	3	548	293	23	.973
National League totals (1 year)		8	18	0	1	0	0	0	0	.056	0	3	0	2	8	0	1.000
Major League totals (8 years)		282	708	95	160	33	2	30	93	.226	95	182	3	550	301	23	.974

MANWARING, KIRT   C

PERSONAL: Born July 15, 1965, in Elmira, N.Y. ... 5-11/198. ... Bats right, throws right. ... Full name: Kirt Dean Manwaring.
HIGH SCHOOL: Horseheads (N.Y.).
COLLEGE: Coastal Carolina (S.C.).
TRANSACTIONS/CAREER NOTES: Selected by Boston Red Sox organization in 12th round of free-agent draft (June 6, 1983); did not sign. ... Selected by San Francisco Giants organization in second round of free-agent draft (June 2, 1986). ... On disabled list (August 31-September 15, 1989 and June 24-July 18, 1990). ... On San Francisco disabled list (May 30-July 11, 1991); included rehabilitation assignments to Phoenix (July 1-8) and San Jose (July 8-11). ... On disabled list (July 22-August 6, 1992). ... On San Francisco disabled list (April 10-May 23, 1996); included rehabilitation assignment to Phoenix (May 18-23). ... Traded by Giants to Houston Astros for C Rick Wilkins and cash (July 27, 1996). ... Granted free agency (October 28, 1996). ... Signed by Colorado Rockies (December 9, 1996). ... Granted free agency (October 28, 1998). ... Re-signed by Rockies (December 17, 1998). ... On Colorado disabled list (May 1-June 3, 1999); included rehabilitation assignment to Colorado Springs (May 28-June 3). ... Granted free agency (November 1, 1999).
HONORS: Won N.L. Gold Glove at catcher (1993).
STATISTICAL NOTES: Led Texas League catchers with 688 total chances and eight double plays in 1987. ... Led N.L. catchers with 12 double plays in 1992 and 10 in 1994.

Year	Team (League)	Pos.	G	AB	R	H	2B	3B	HR	RBI	Avg.	BB	SO	SB	PO	A	E	Avg.
1986—Clinton (Midw.)	C	49	147	18	36	7	1	2	16	.245	14	26	1	243	31	5	.982
1987—Shreveport (Texas)	C	98	307	27	82	13	2	2	22	.267	19	33	1	603	*81	4	.994
—San Francisco (N.L.)	C	6	7	0	1	0	0	0	0	.143	0	1	0	9	1	1	.909
1988—Phoenix (PCL)	C	81	273	29	77	12	2	2	35	.282	14	32	3	411	51	6	.987
—San Francisco (N.L.)	C	40	116	12	29	7	0	1	15	.250	2	21	0	162	24	4	.979
1989—San Francisco (N.L.)	C	85	200	14	42	4	2	0	18	.210	11	28	2	289	32	6	.982
1990—Phoenix (PCL)	C	74	247	20	58	10	2	3	14	.235	24	34	0	352	45	4	*.990
—San Francisco (N.L.)	C	8	13	0	2	0	1	0	1	.154	0	3	0	22	3	0	1.000
1991—San Francisco (N.L.)	C	67	178	16	40	9	0	0	19	.225	9	22	1	315	28	4	.988
—Phoenix (PCL)	C	24	81	8	18	0	0	4	14	.222	8	15	0	100	15	3	.975
—San Jose (Calif.)	C	1	3	1	0	0	0	0	0	.000	1	1	0	16	0	0	1.000
1992—San Francisco (N.L.)	C	109	349	24	85	10	5	4	26	.244	29	42	2	564	68	4	.994
1993—San Francisco (N.L.)	C	130	432	48	119	15	1	5	49	.275	41	76	1	739	70	2	*.998
1994—San Francisco (N.L.)	C	97	316	30	79	17	1	1	29	.250	25	50	1	541	52	4	.993
1995—San Francisco (N.L.)	C	118	379	21	95	15	2	4	36	.251	27	72	1	607	55	7	.990
1996—San Francisco (N.L.)	C	49	145	9	34	6	0	1	14	.234	16	24	0	268	26	2	.993
—Phoenix (PCL)	C	4	11	1	2	0	0	0	1	.182	2	0	0	15	3	0	1.000
—Houston (N.L.)■	C	37	82	5	18	3	0	0	4	.220	3	16	0	171	21	1	.995
1997—Colorado (N.L.)■	C	104	337	22	76	6	4	1	27	.226	30	78	1	488	40	3	.994
1998—Colorado (N.L.)	C	110	291	30	72	12	3	2	26	.247	38	49	1	528	48	7	.988
1999—Colorado (N.L.)	C-DH	48	137	17	41	7	1	2	14	.299	12	23	0	243	21	5	.981
—Colo. Springs (PCL)	C-DH	7	22	3	5	0	0	1	2	.227	1	2	0	32	0	0	1.000
Major League totals (13 years)		1008	2982	248	733	111	20	21	278	.246	243	505	10	4946	489	50	.991

CHAMPIONSHIP SERIES RECORD

Year	Team (League)	Pos.	G	AB	R	H	2B	3B	HR	RBI	Avg.	BB	SO	SB	PO	A	E	Avg.
1989—San Francisco (N.L.)	C-PH	3	2	0	0	0	0	0	0	.000	0	0	0	5	0	0	1.000

WORLD SERIES RECORD

Year	Team (League)	Pos.	G	AB	R	H	2B	3B	HR	RBI	Avg.	BB	SO	SB	PO	A	E	Avg.
1989—San Francisco (N.L.)	C	1	1	1	1	1	0	0	0	1.000	0	0	0	0	0	0	...

MANZANILLO, JOSIAS   P

PERSONAL: Born October 16, 1967, in San Pedro de Macoris, Dominican Republic ... 6-0/190. ... Throws right, bats right. ... Brother of Ravelo Manzanillo, pitcher with Chicago White Sox (1988) and Pittsburgh Pirates (1994-1995). ... Name pronounced hose-EYE-ess MAN-zan-EE-oh..
TRANSACTIONS/CAREER NOTES: Signed as non-drafted free agent by Boston Red Sox organization (January 10, 1983). ... On disabled list (June 8, 1987-remainder of season and April 8, 1988-entire season). ... Granted free agency (March 24, 1992). ... Signed by Omaha, Kansas City Royals organization (April 3, 1992). ... Granted free agency (October 15, 1992). ... Signed by Milwaukee Brewers (November 20, 1992). ... Traded by Brewers to New York Mets for OF Wayne Housie (June 12, 1993). ... On New York disabled list (July 27, 1994-remainder of season). ... Claimed on waivers by New York Yankees (June 5, 1995). ... On New York Yankees disabled list (July 6, 1995-remainder of season). ... Granted free agency (October 16, 1995). ... Signed to play in Taiwan for 1996 season. ... Signed by Seattle Mariners organization (December 21, 1996). ... On Seattle disabled list (April 9-May 6 and May 25-July 1, 1997); included rehabilitation assignments to Memphis (May 1-6) and Tacoma (May 25-July 1). ... Released by Mariners organization (July 17, 1997). ... Signed by New Orleans, Houston Astros

M

organization (July 27, 1997). ... Granted free agency (October 15, 1997). ... Signed by Tampa Bay Devil Rays organization (December 18, 1997). ... Released by Devil Rays (July 1, 1998). ... Signed by Mets organization (July 3, 1998). ... Granted free agency (October 15, 1998). ... Re-signed by Mets organization (December 18, 1998). ... On Norfolk disabled list (June 21, 1999-remainder of season). ... Granted free agency (October 4, 1999).

MISCELLANEOUS: Appeared in one game as pinch runner (1999).

Year — League	W	L	Pct.	ERA	G	GS	CG	ShO	Sv.	IP	H	R	ER	BB	SO
1983— Elmira (NY-P)	1	5	.167	7.98	12	4	0	0	0	38 1/3	52	44	34	20	19
1984— Elmira (NY-P)	2	3	.400	5.26	14	0	0	0	1	25 2/3	27	24	15	26	15
1985— Greensboro (SAL)	1	1	.500	9.75	7	0	0	0	0	12	12	13	13	18	10
— Elmira (NY-P)	2	4	.333	3.86	19	4	0	0	1	39 2/3	36	19	17	36	43
1986— Winter Haven (FSL)	13	5	.722	2.27	23	21	3	2	0	142 2/3	110	51	36	81	102
1987— New Britain (East.)	2	0	1.000	4.50	2	2	0	0	0	10	8	5	5	8	12
1988— New Britain (East.)							Did not play.								
1989— New Britain (East.)	9	10	.474	3.66	26	•26	3	1	0	147 2/3	129	78	60	85	93
1990— New Britain (East.)	4	4	.500	3.41	12	12	2	1	0	74	66	34	28	37	51
— Pawtucket (I.L.)	4	7	.364	5.55	15	15	5	0	0	82 2/3	75	57	51	45	77
1991— Pawtucket (I.L.)	5	5	.500	5.61	20	16	0	0	0	102 2/3	109	69	64	53	65
— New Britain (East.)	2	2	.500	2.90	7	7	0	0	0	49 2/3	37	25	16	28	35
— Boston (A.L.)	0	0	...	18.00	1	0	0	0	0	1	2	2	2	3	1
1992— Omaha (A.A.)■	7	10	.412	4.36	26	21	0	0	0	136 1/3	138	76	66	71	114
— Memphis (Sou.)	0	2	.000	7.36	2	0	0	0	0	7 1/3	6	6	6	6	8
1993— Milwaukee (A.L.)■	1	1	.500	9.53	10	1	0	0	1	17	22	20	18	10	10
— New Orleans (A.A.)	0	1	.000	9.00	1	0	0	0	0	1	1	1	1	0	3
— Norfolk (I.L.)■	1	5	.167	3.11	14	12	2	1	0	84	82	40	29	25	79
— New York (N.L.)	0	0	...	3.00	6	0	0	0	0	12	8	7	4	9	11
1994— Norfolk (I.L.)	0	1	.000	4.38	8	0	0	0	3	12 1/3	12	6	6	6	10
— New York (N.L.)	3	2	.600	2.66	37	0	0	0	2	47 1/3	34	15	14	13	48
1995— New York (N.L.)	1	2	.333	7.88	12	0	0	0	0	16	18	15	14	6	14
— New York (A.L.)■	0	0	...	2.08	11	0	0	0	0	17 1/3	19	4	4	9	11
1996—							Statistics unavailable.								
1997— Seattle (A.L.)■	0	1	.000	5.40	16	0	0	0	0	18 1/3	19	13	11	17	18
— Memphis (Sou.)	0	0	...	3.00	2	0	0	0	0	3	1	1	1	0	6
— Tacoma (PCL)	0	0	...	6.43	11	0	0	0	1	14	16	10	10	8	15
— New Orleans (A.A.)■	0	0	...	4.40	11	0	0	0	0	14 1/3	17	7	7	6	11
1998— Durham (I.L.)■	7	6	.538	4.64	19	14	0	0	1	85 1/3	93	57	44	30	61
— Norfolk (I.L.)■	4	4	.500	3.24	13	12	1	0	1	77 2/3	77	35	28	31	72
1999— New York (N.L.)	0	0	...	5.79	12	0	0	0	0	18 2/3	19	12	12	4	25
A.L. totals (4 years)	1	2	.333	5.87	38	1	0	0	1	53 2/3	62	39	35	39	40
N.L. totals (4 years)	4	4	.500	4.21	67	0	0	0	2	94	79	49	44	32	98
Major League totals (6 years)	5	6	.455	4.81	105	1	0	0	3	147 2/3	141	88	79	71	138

MARQUIS, JASON   P   BRAVES

PERSONAL: Born August 21, 1978, in Manhasset, N.Y. ... 6-1/185. ... Throws right, bats left. ... Full name: Jason Scott Marquis.

HIGH SCHOOL: Tottenville (Staten Island, N.Y.).

TRANSACTIONS/CAREER NOTES: Selected by Atlanta Braves organization as "sandwich" pick between first and second round of free-agent draft (June 4, 1996); pick received as supplemental pick for failure to signed 1995 first-round choice. ... On Greenville disabled list (July 5-31, 1999).

Year — League	W	L	Pct.	ERA	G	GS	CG	ShO	Sv.	IP	H	R	ER	BB	SO
1996— Danville (Appl.)	1	1	.500	4.63	7	4	0	0	0	23 1/3	30	18	12	7	24
1997— Macon (SAL)	•14	10	.583	4.38	28	28	0	0	0	141 2/3	156	78	69	55	121
1998— Danville (Caro.)	2	12	.143	4.87	22	22	1	0	0	114 2/3	120	65	62	41	135
1999— Myrtle Beach (Caro.)	3	0	1.000	0.28	6	6	0	0	0	32	22	2	1	17	41
— Greenville (Sou.)	3	4	.429	4.58	12	12	1	0	0	55	52	33	28	29	35

MARRERO, ELI   C   CARDINALS

PERSONAL: Born November 17, 1973, in Havana, Cuba. ... 6-1/180. ... Bats right, throws right. ... Full name: Elieser Marrero.

HIGH SCHOOL: Coral Gables (Fla.).

TRANSACTIONS/CAREER NOTES: Selected by St. Louis Cardinals organization in third round of free-agent draft (June 3, 1993). ... On St. Louis disabled list (March 22-April 13, 1998).

STATISTICAL NOTES: Led Texas League catchers with 746 total chances in 1996. ... Led American Association catchers with 750 total chances in 1997.

							BATTING								FIELDING		
Year — Team (League)	Pos.	G	AB	R	H	2B	3B	HR	RBI	Avg.	BB	SO	SB	PO	A	E	Avg.
1993— Johnson City (Appl.)	C	18	61	10	22	8	0	2	14	.361	12	9	2	154	18	1	.994
1994— Savannah (SAL)	C	116	421	71	110	16	3	21	79	.261	39	92	5	821	92	•15	.984
1995— St. Petersburg (FSL)	C	107	383	43	81	16	1	10	55	.211	23	55	9	574	52	10	.984
1996— Arkansas (Texas)	C-DH	116	374	65	101	17	3	19	65	.270	32	55	9	*676	67	3	*.996
1997— Louisville (A.A.)	C-DH	112	395	60	108	21	7	20	68	.273	25	53	4	*675	*68	7	.991
— St. Louis (N.L.)	C	17	45	4	11	2	0	2	7	.244	2	13	4	82	12	3	.969
1998— St. Louis (N.L.)	C-1B	83	254	28	62	18	1	4	20	.244	28	42	6	427	31	4	.991
— Memphis (PCL)	C-DH	32	130	22	31	5	0	7	21	.238	13	23	5	195	17	2	.991
1999— St. Louis (N.L.)	C-1B	114	317	32	61	13	1	6	34	.192	18	56	11	537	47	7	.988
Major League totals (3 years)		214	616	64	134	33	2	12	61	.218	48	111	21	1046	90	14	.988

PERSONAL: Born February 14, 1975, in Santo Domingo, Dominican Republic. ... 6-0/170. ... Throws left, bats left. ... Full name: Damaso Sabinon Marte.

TRANSACTIONS/CAREER NOTES: Signed as non-drafted free agent by Seattle Mariners organization (October 28, 1992). ... On disabled list (April 3-17, 1997). ... On Orlando disabled list (April 2-May 3 and September 2, 1998-remainder of season).

Year	League	W	L	Pct.	ERA	G	GS	CG	ShO	Sv.	IP	H	R	ER	BB	SO
1993—Dom. Mariners (DSL)		2	5	.286	6.55	17	15	2	0	0	56 1/3	62	48	41	50	29
1994—Dom. Mariners (DSL)		7	0	1.000	3.86	17	13	0	0	0	65 1/3	53	41	28	48	80
1995—Everett (N.W.)		2	2	.500	2.21	11	11	5	0	0	36 2/3	25	11	9	10	39
1996—Wisconsin (Midw.)		8	6	.571	4.49	26	26	2	1	0	142 1/3	134	82	71	75	115
1997—Lancaster (Calif.)		8	8	.500	4.13	25	25	2	1	0	139 1/3	144	75	64	62	127
1998—Orlando (Sou.)		7	6	.538	5.27	22	20	0	0	0	121 1/3	136	82	71	47	99
1999—Tacoma (PCL)		3	3	.500	5.13	31	11	0	0	0	73 2/3	79	43	42	40	59
—Seattle (A.L.)		0	1	.000	9.35	5	0	0	0	0	8 2/3	16	9	9	6	3
Major League totals (1 year)		0	1	.000	9.35	5	0	0	0	0	8 2/3	16	9	9	6	3

PERSONAL: Born November 24, 1967, in West Covina, Calif. ... 6-2/214. ... Bats left, throws left. ... Full name: Albert Lee Martin. ... Formerly known as Albert Scales-Martin. ... Nephew of Rod Martin, linebacker with Oakland/Los Angeles Raiders (1977-88).

HIGH SCHOOL: Rowland (West Covina, Calif.).

COLLEGE: Southern California.

TRANSACTIONS/CAREER NOTES: Selected by Atlanta Braves organization in eighth round of free-agent draft (June 3, 1985). ... Granted free agency (October 15, 1991). ... Signed by Pittsburgh Pirates organization (November 11, 1991). ... On suspended list (September 17-20, 1993). ... On disabled list (July 11, 1994-remainder of season). ... On Pittsburgh disabled list (May 22-June 24, 1997); included rehabilitation assignment to Carolina (June 21-23).

RECORDS: Shares major league record for fewest double plays by outfielder (150 or more games)—0 (1996). ... Holds modern N.L. single-season record for fewest putouts by outfielder (150 or more games)—217 (1996). ... Holds N.L. single-season record for fewest chances accepted by outfielder (150 or more games)—222 (1996).

STATISTICAL NOTES: Led Gulf Coast League first basemen with 15 errors in 1985. ... Led American Association with .557 slugging percentage in 1992. ... Led American Association outfielders with six double plays in 1992. ... Had 20-game hitting streak (June 20-July 11, 1999). ... Had 15-game hitting streak (August 25-September 11, 1999). ... Career major league grand slams: 1.

								BATTING							FIELDING			
Year	Team (League)	Pos.	G	AB	R	H	2B	3B	HR	RBI	Avg.	BB	SO	SB	PO	A	E	Avg.
1985—GC Braves (GCL)		1B-OF	40	138	16	32	3	0	0	9	.232	19	36	1	246	13	†15	.945
1986—Sumter (SAL)		1B	44	156	23	38	5	0	1	24	.244	23	36	6	299	12	8	.975
—Idaho Falls (Pio.)		OF-1B	63	242	39	80	17	•6	4	44	.331	20	53	11	272	15	8	.973
1987—Sumter (SAL)		OF-1B	117	375	59	95	18	5	12	64	.253	44	69	27	137	7	9	.941
1988—Burlington (Midw.)		OF	123	480	69	134	21	3	7	42	.279	30	88	40	224	4	8	.966
1989—Durham (Caro.)		OF	128	457	*84	124	26	3	9	48	.271	34	107	27	169	7	7	.962
1990—Greenville (Sou.)		OF	133	455	64	110	17	4	11	50	.242	43	102	20	200	8	7	.967
1991—Greenville (Sou.)		OF-1B	86	301	38	73	13	3	7	38	.243	32	84	19	134	7	6	.959
—Richmond (I.L.)		OF	44	151	20	42	11	1	5	18	.278	7	33	11	73	4	2	.975
1992—Buffalo (A.A.)■		OF	125	420	85	128	16	*15	20	59	.305	35	93	20	222	10	8	.967
—Pittsburgh (N.L.)		OF	12	12	1	2	0	1	0	2	.167	0	5	0	6	0	0	1.000
1993—Pittsburgh (N.L.)		OF	143	480	85	135	26	8	18	64	.281	42	122	16	268	6	7	.975
1994—Pittsburgh (N.L.)		OF	82	276	48	79	12	4	9	33	.286	34	56	15	129	8	3	.979
1995—Pittsburgh (N.L.)		OF	124	439	70	124	25	3	13	41	.282	44	92	20	206	8	5	.977
1996—Pittsburgh (N.L.)		OF	155	630	101	189	40	1	18	72	.300	54	116	38	217	5	8	.965
1997—Pittsburgh (N.L.)		OF	113	423	64	123	24	7	13	59	.291	45	83	23	125	8	6	.957
—Carolina (Sou.)		OF	3	9	0	1	0	0	0	0	.111	0	0	0	2	0	0	1.000
1998—Pittsburgh (N.L.)		OF-DH	125	440	57	105	15	2	12	47	.239	32	91	20	192	6	3	.985
1999—Pittsburgh (N.L.)		OF	143	541	97	150	36	8	24	63	.277	49	119	20	196	3	10	.952
Major League totals (8 years)			897	3241	523	907	178	34	107	381	.280	300	684	152	1339	44	42	.971

PERSONAL: Born December 10, 1966, in Santo Domingo, Dominican Republic. ... 5-10/182. ... Bats right, throws right. ... Full name: Norberto Edonal Martin. ... Name pronounced mar-TEEN.

TRANSACTIONS/CAREER NOTES: Signed as non-drafted free agent by Chicago White Sox organization (March 27, 1984). ... On Peninsula disabled list (April 10-May 5, 1986). ... On Appleton disabled list (May 14, 1986-remainder of season). ... On disabled list (April 7, 1989-entire season and May 5-June 9, 1991). ... On Chicago disabled list (April 6-June 5, 1996); included rehabilitation assignment to Nashville (May 14-June 1). ... On disabled list (June 20-July 3 and July 21-August 8, 1997). ... Granted free agency (December 21, 1997). ... Signed by Anaheim Angels (January 9, 1998). ... On disabled list (August 6-21, 1998). ... Granted free agency (December 21, 1998). ... Signed by Toronto Blue Jays organization (March 14, 1999). ... Granted free agency (October 5, 1999). ... Signed by Milwaukee Brewers organization (December 1, 1999).

STATISTICAL NOTES: Led Gulf Coast League shortstops with 37 errors in 1984. ... Led Pacific Coast League second basemen with 681 total chances in 1992. ... Led American Association second basemen with 291 putouts, 438 assists, 18 errors and 747 total chances in 1993. ... Career major league grand slams: 1.

								BATTING							FIELDING			
Year	Team (League)	Pos.	G	AB	R	H	2B	3B	HR	RBI	Avg.	BB	SO	SB	PO	A	E	Avg.
1984—GC White Sox (GCL)		SS-OF	56	205	36	56	8	2	1	30	.273	21	31	18	66	149	†37	.853
1985—Appleton (Midw.)		SS	30	196	15	19	2	0	0	5	.097	9	23	2	39	86	12	.912
—Niagara Falls (NY-P)		SS	60	217	22	55	9	0	1	13	.253	7	41	6	85	173	35	.881
1986—Appleton (Midw.)		SS	9	33	4	10	2	0	0	2	.303	2	5	1	13	16	6	.829
—GC White Sox (GCL)		PR	1	0	0	0	0	0	0	0	...	0	0	0	...	...	...	...

Year	Team (League)	Pos.	G	AB	R	H	2B	3B	HR	RBI	Avg.	BB	SO	SB	PO	A	E	Avg.
								BATTING								FIELDING		
1987—Char., W.Va. (SAL)......		SS-OF-2B	68	250	44	78	14	1	5	35	.312	17	40	14	84	152	25	.904
— Peninsula (Caro.)		2B	41	162	21	42	6	1	1	18	.259	18	19	11	94	108	15	.931
1988—Tampa (FSL).............		2B	101	360	44	93	10	4	2	33	.258	17	49	24	196	268	20	.959
1989—Tampa (FSL)								Did not play.										
1990—Vancouver (PCL)		2B	130	508	77	135	20	4	3	45	.266	27	63	10	283	324	17	.973
1991—Vancouver (PCL)		2B-SS	93	338	39	94	9	0	0	20	.278	21	38	11	196	265	16	.966
1992—Vancouver (PCL)		2B	135	497	72	143	12	7	0	29	.288	29	44	29	266	*395	•20	.971
1993—Nashville (A.A.)		2B-SS	•137	*580	87	*179	21	6	9	74	.309	26	59	31	†292	†442	†18	.976
— Chicago (A.L.)		2B-DH	8	14	3	5	0	0	0	2	.357	1	1	0	13	9	1	.957
1994—Nashville (A.A.)		S-3-2-DH-O	43	172	26	44	8	0	2	12	.256	10	14	4	47	72	10	.922
— Chicago (A.L.)		2-S-3-0-DH	45	131	19	36	7	1	1	16	.275	9	16	4	58	77	2	.985
1995—Chicago (A.L.)		2-0-DH-3-S	72	160	17	43	7	4	2	17	.269	3	25	5	52	67	7	.944
1996—Chicago (A.L.)		SS-DH-2B	70	140	30	49	7	0	1	14	.350	6	17	10	61	79	6	.959
— Nashville (A.A.)		2B-SS-DH-3B	17	68	9	14	3	0	2	8	.206	4	10	1	27	43	2	.972
1997—Chicago (A.L.)		SS-3B-2B-DH	71	213	24	64	7	1	2	27	.300	6	31	1	50	97	5	.967
1998—Anaheim (A.L.)		2-DH-3-0-S	79	195	20	42	2	0	1	13	.215	6	29	3	91	144	4	.983
1999—Syracuse (I.L.)		SS-2B-OF-DH	81	319	45	94	11	2	5	34	.295	12	33	14	124	201	10	.970
— Toronto (A.L.)		2B-SS	9	27	3	6	2	0	0	0	.222	4	4	0	9	29	1	.974
Major League totals (7 years)			354	880	116	245	32	6	7	89	.278	35	123	23	334	502	26	.970

MARTIN, TOM   P   INDIANS

PERSONAL: Born May 21, 1970, in Charleston, S.C. ... 6-1/200. ... Throws left, bats left. ... Full name: Thomas Edgar Martin.
HIGH SCHOOL: Bay (Panama City, Fla.).
TRANSACTIONS/CAREER NOTES: Selected by Baltimore Orioles organization in sixth round of free-agent draft (June 1, 1988). ... Traded by Orioles with 3B Craig Worthington to San Diego Padres for P Jim Lewis and OF Steve Martin (February 17, 1992). ... Selected by Atlanta Braves organization from Padres organization in Rule 5 minor league draft (December 13, 1993). ... Released by Braves (January 25, 1996). ... Signed by Houston Astros organization (February 21, 1996). ... On disabled list (May 30-June 15, 1997). ... Selected by Arizona Diamondbacks in second round (29th pick overall) of expansion draft (November 18, 1997). ... Traded by Diamondbacks with 3B Travis Fryman and cash to Cleveland Indians for 3B Matt Williams (December 1, 1997). ... On Cleveland disabled list (April 30-May 18 and August 31-September 19, 1998); included rehabilitation assignments to Buffalo (May 13-18 and September 3-19). ... On Cleveland disabled list (April 4-August 9, 1999); included rehabilitation assignment to Akron (July 27-August 9).

Year	League	W	L	Pct.	ERA	G	GS	CG	ShO	Sv.	IP	H	R	ER	BB	SO
1989— Bluefield (Appl.)		3	3	.500	4.62	8	8	0	0	0	39	36	28	20	25	31
— Erie (NY-P)		0	5	.000	6.64	7	7	0	0	0	40²/₃	42	39	30	25	44
1990— Wausau (Midw.)..........		2	3	.400	2.47	9	9	0	0	0	40	31	25	11	27	45
1991— Kane County (Midw.).......		4	10	.286	3.64	38	10	0	0	6	99	92	50	40	56	106
1992— High Desert (Calif.)■		0	2	.000	9.37	11	0	0	0	0	16¹/₃	23	19	17	16	10
— Waterloo (Midw.)		2	6	.250	4.25	39	2	0	0	3	55	62	38	26	22	57
1993— Rancho Cuca. (Calif.)		1	4	.200	5.61	47	1	0	0	0	59¹/₃	72	41	37	39	53
1994— Greenville (Sou.)■		5	6	.455	4.62	36	6	0	0	0	74	82	40	38	27	51
1995— Richmond (I.L.)		0	0	...	9.00	7	0	0	0	0	9	10	9	9	10	3
1996— Tucson (PCL)■		0	0	...	0.00	5	0	0	0	0	6	6	0	0	2	1
— Jackson (Texas)		6	2	.750	3.24	57	0	0	0	3	75	71	35	27	42	58
1997— Houston (N.L.)		5	3	.625	2.09	55	0	0	0	2	56	52	13	13	23	36
1998— Cleveland (A.L.)■...........		1	1	.500	12.89	14	0	0	0	0	14²/₃	29	21	21	12	9
— Buffalo (I.L.)		3	1	.750	6.00	41	0	0	0	0	36	46	25	24	13	35
1999— Akron (East.)		0	0	...	1.00	3	3	0	0	0	9	4	1	1	3	9
— Cleveland (A.L.)		0	1	.000	8.68	6	0	0	0	0	9¹/₃	13	9	9	3	8
— Buffalo (I.L.)		1	0	1.000	3.00	5	0	0	0	0	6	5	2	2	1	6
A.L. totals (2 years)		1	2	.333	11.25	20	0	0	0	0	24	42	30	30	15	17
N.L. totals (1 year)		5	3	.625	2.09	55	0	0	0	2	56	52	13	13	23	36
Major League totals (3 years)		6	5	.545	4.84	75	0	0	0	2	80	94	43	43	38	53

DIVISION SERIES RECORD

Year	League	W	L	Pct.	ERA	G	GS	CG	ShO	Sv.	IP	H	R	ER	BB	SO
1997— Houston (N.L.)		0	0	...	0.00	2	0	0	0	0	²/₃	1	1	0	1	0

MARTINEZ, BELVANI   IF   ROCKIES

PERSONAL: Born December 14, 1978, in San Cristobal, Dominican Republic. ... 5-11/172. ... Bats right, throws right.
TRANSACTIONS/CAREER NOTES: Signed as non-drafted free agent by Arizona Diamondbacks organization (November 8, 1995). ... On High Desert disabled list (April 21-May 2, 1999). ... Traded by Diamondbacks to Colorado Rockies for OF Lenny Harris (August 31, 1999).
STATISTICAL NOTES: Led California League in caught stealing with 30 in 1999.

Year	Team (League)	Pos.	G	AB	R	H	2B	3B	HR	RBI	Avg.	BB	SO	SB	PO	A	E	Avg.
								BATTING								FIELDING		
1996—Dom. D'backs (DSL) ..		2B	50	175	27	46	10	0	2	23	.263	14	18	17	70	73	13	.917
1997—Dom. D'backs (DSL) ..			30	134	25	43	11	2	0	11	.321	3	18	7	...	...	...	...
— Lethbridge (Pio.)		2B-SS	25	90	21	31	4	1	6	13	.344	5	13	4	42	61	12	.896
1998—South Bend (Midw.) ...		SS	18	80	11	20	2	0	6	6	.250	3	22	5	20	72	11	.893
— Lethbridge (Pio.)		2B-SS-3B	63	256	56	78	11	3	5	25	.305	12	30	30	104	177	17	.943
1999—High Desert (Calif.).....		2B-3B	109	477	84	159	23	9	8	55	.333	18	69	35	186	274	33	.933

MARTINEZ, DAVE   OF   DEVIL RAYS

PERSONAL: Born September 26, 1964, in Brooklyn, N.Y. ... 5-10/175. ... Bats left, throws left. ... Full name: David Martinez.
HIGH SCHOOL: Lake Howell (Casselberry, Fla.).
JUNIOR COLLEGE: Valencia Community College (Fla.).

M

TRANSACTIONS/CAREER NOTES: Selected by Texas Rangers organization in 40th round of free-agent draft (June 7, 1982); did not sign. ... Selected by Chicago Cubs organization in secondary phase of free-agent draft (January 11, 1983). ... On disabled list (April 27, 1984-remainder of season). ... Traded by Cubs to Montreal Expos for OF Mitch Webster (July 14, 1988). ... On disqualified list (October 4-5, 1991). ... Traded by Expos with P Scott Ruskin and SS Willie Greene to Cincinnati Reds for P John Wetteland and P Bill Risley (December 11, 1991). ... Granted free agency (October 27, 1992). ... Signed by San Francisco Giants (December 9, 1992). ... On San Francisco disabled list (April 30-June 4, 1993); included rehabilitation assignment to Phoenix (June 1-4). ... Granted free agency (October 14, 1994). ... Signed by Chicago White Sox (April 5, 1995). ... Granted free agency (November 3, 1995). ... Re-signed by White Sox (November 14, 1995). ... Granted free agency (October 27, 1997). ... Signed by Tampa Bay Devil Rays (December 4, 1997). ... On disabled list (July 22, 1998-remainder of season).
RECORDS: Shares major league single-game record for most unassisted double plays by first baseman—2 (June 21, 1997).
STATISTICAL NOTES: Career major league grand slams: 2.

Year Team (League)	Pos.	G	AB	R	H	2B	3B	HR	RBI	Avg.	BB	SO	SB	PO	A	E	Avg.
1983— Quad Cities (Midw.)....	OF	44	119	17	29	6	2	0	10	.244	26	30	10	47	8	1	.982
— Geneva (NY-P)...........	OF	64	241	35	63	15	2	5	33	.261	40	52	16	132	6	8	.945
1984— Quad Cities (Midw.)....	OF	12	41	6	9	2	2	0	5	.220	9	13	3	13	2	1	.938
1985— Win.-Salem (Car.).......	OF	115	386	52	132	14	4	5	54	*.342	62	35	38	206	11	7	.969
1986— Iowa (A.A.)...............	OF	83	318	52	92	11	5	5	32	.289	36	34	42	214	7	2	.991
— Chicago (N.L.)...........	OF	53	108	13	15	1	1	1	7	.139	6	22	4	77	2	1	.988
1987— Chicago (N.L.)...........	OF	142	459	70	134	18	8	8	36	.292	57	96	16	283	10	6	.980
1988— Chicago (N.L.)...........	OF	75	256	27	65	10	1	4	34	.254	21	46	7	162	2	5	.970
— Montreal (N.L.)■........	OF	63	191	24	49	3	5	2	12	.257	17	48	16	119	2	1	.992
1989— Montreal (N.L.)...........	OF	126	361	41	99	16	7	3	27	.274	27	57	23	199	7	7	.967
1990— Montreal (N.L.)..........	OF-P	118	391	60	109	13	5	11	39	.279	24	48	13	257	6	3	.989
1991— Montreal (N.L.)...........	OF	124	396	47	117	18	5	7	42	.295	20	54	16	213	10	4	.982
1992— Cincinnati (N.L.)■.......	OF-1B	135	393	47	100	20	5	3	31	.254	42	54	12	382	18	6	.985
1993— San Fran. (N.L.)■......	OF	91	241	28	58	12	1	5	27	.241	27	39	6	131	6	1	.993
— Phoenix (PCL)...........	OF	3	15	4	7	0	0	0	2	.467	1	1	1	5	1	0	1.000
1994— San Francisco (N.L.)....	OF-1B	97	235	23	58	9	3	4	27	.247	21	22	3	256	18	3	.989
1995— Chicago (A.L.)■........OF-1B-DH-P		119	303	49	93	16	4	5	37	.307	32	41	8	392	25	3	.993
1996— Chicago (A.L.).........	OF-1B	146	440	85	140	20	8	10	53	.318	52	52	15	368	16	6	.985
1997— Chicago (A.L.)...........	OF-1B-DH	145	504	78	144	16	6	12	55	.286	55	69	12	485	30	7	.987
1998— Tampa Bay (A.L.)■......	OF-DH-1B	90	309	31	79	11	0	3	20	.256	35	52	8	163	9	1	.994
1999— Tampa Bay (A.L.)........	OF	143	514	79	146	25	5	6	66	.284	60	76	13	253	8	4	.985
American League totals (5 years)		643	2070	322	602	88	23	36	231	.291	234	290	56	1661	88	21	.988
National League totals (9 years)		1024	3031	380	804	120	41	48	282	.265	262	486	116	2079	81	37	.983
Major League totals (14 years)		1667	5101	702	1406	208	64	84	513	.276	496	776	172	3740	169	58	.985

RECORD AS PITCHER

Year League	W	L	Pct.	ERA	G	GS	CG	ShO	Sv.	IP	H	R	ER	BB	SO
1990— Montreal (N.L.).................	0	0	...	54.00	1	0	0	0	0	1/3	2	2	2	2	0
1995— Chicago (A.L.).................	0	0	...	0.00	1	0	0	0	0	1	0	0	0	2	0
Major League totals (2 years)	0	0	...	13.50	2	0	0	0	0	1 1/3	2	2	2	4	0

MARTINEZ, EDDY   SS   ORIOLES

M

PERSONAL: Born October 23, 1977, in San Pedro de Macoris, Dominican Republic. ... 6-2/173. ... Bats right, throws right.
TRANSACTIONS/CAREER NOTES: Signed as non-drafted free agent by Baltimore Orioles organization (December 19, 1994).
STATISTICAL NOTES: Led Appalachian League shortstops with 31 double plays in 1995. ... Led Carolina League shortstops with 611 total chances and 80 double plays in 1999.

Year Team (League)	Pos.	G	AB	R	H	2B	3B	HR	RBI	Avg.	BB	SO	SB	PO	A	E	Avg.
1995— Bluefield (Appl.)	SS	57	185	42	57	11	3	1	35	.308	23	42	5	71	135	22	.904
1996— Frederick (Caro.)	SS	74	244	21	54	4	0	2	25	.221	21	48	13	94	209	19	.941
— Bluefield (Appl.)	SS	37	122	18	27	3	0	1	15	.221	13	29	15	43	80	14	.898
1997— Frederick (Caro.)	SS	54	174	14	42	6	0	1	14	.241	19	43	6	100	112	19	.918
— Bowie (East.)	SS	16	45	3	7	3	0	0	1	.156	6	12	2	17	49	4	.943
— Rochester (I.L.)	SS	12	27	0	2	1	0	0	3	.074	1	8	0	6	25	1	.969
1998— Delmarva (SAL)	SS	113	361	46	95	18	1	2	39	.263	33	66	21	153	319	25	.950
— Bowie (East.)	SS	5	14	1	4	0	0	0	1	.286	1	3	0	5	6	1	.917
1999— Frederick (Caro.)	SS-DH	127	416	68	121	21	1	2	55	.291	52	99	8	*189	386	36	.941

MARTINEZ, EDGAR   DH   MARINERS

PERSONAL: Born January 2, 1963, in New York. ... 5-11/200. ... Bats right, throws right. ... Cousin of Carmelo Martinez, first baseman/outfielder with six major league teams (1983-91).
HIGH SCHOOL: Dorado (Puerto Rico).
COLLEGE: American College (Puerto Rico).
TRANSACTIONS/CAREER NOTES: Signed as non-drafted free agent by Seattle Mariners organization (December 19, 1982). ... On Seattle disabled list (April 4-May 17, June 15-July 21 and August 17, 1993-remainder of season); included rehabilitation assignment to Jacksonville (July 17-21). ... On disabled list (April 16-May 6, 1994 and July 31-August 12, 1996).
RECORDS: Shares A.L. single-game record for most errors by third baseman—4 (May 6, 1990).
HONORS: Named third baseman on THE SPORTING NEWS A.L. All-Star team (1992). ... Named third baseman on THE SPORTING NEWS A.L. Silver Slugger team (1992). ... Named designated hitter on THE SPORTING NEWS A.L. All-Star team (1995 and 1997). ... Named designated hitter on THE SPORTING NEWS A.L. Silver Slugger team (1995 and 1997).
STATISTICAL NOTES: Led Southern League third basemen with 360 total chances and 34 double plays in 1985. ... Led Southern League with 12 sacrifice flies in 1985. ... Led Southern League third basemen with .960 fielding percentage in 1986. ... Led Pacific Coast League third basemen with 389 total chances and 31 double plays in 1987. ... Led A.L. in on-base percentage with .479 in 1995 and .429 in 1998. ... Hit three home runs in one game (July 6, 1996 and May 18, 1999). ... Led A.L. with a .447 on-base percentage in 1999. ... Career major league grand slams: 4.
MISCELLANEOUS: Holds Seattle Mariners franchise all-time records for most doubles (372) and highest batting average (.320).

Year Team (League)	Pos.	G	AB	R	H	2B	3B	HR	RBI	Avg.	BB	SO	SB	PO	A	E	Avg.
1983—Bellingham (N.W.)	3B	32	104	14	18	1	1	0	5	.173	18	24	1	22	58	6	.930
1984—Wausau (Midw.)	3B	126	433	72	131	32	2	15	66	.303	84	57	11	85	246	25	.930
1985—Chattanooga (Sou.)	3B	111	357	43	92	15	5	3	47	.258	71	30	1	*94	*247	19	*.947
—Calgary (PCL)	3B-2B	20	68	8	24	7	1	0	14	.353	12	7	1	15	44	4	.937
1986—Chattanooga (Sou.)	3B-2B	132	451	71	119	29	5	6	74	.264	89	35	2	94	263	15	†.960
1987—Calgary (PCL)	3B	129	438	75	144	31	1	10	66	.329	82	47	3	*91	*278	20	.949
—Seattle (A.L.)	3B-DH	13	43	6	16	5	2	0	5	.372	2	5	0	13	19	0	1.000
1988—Calgary (PCL)	3B-2B	95	331	63	120	19	4	8	64	*.363	66	40	9	48	185	20	.921
—Seattle (A.L.)	3B	14	32	0	9	4	0	0	5	.281	4	7	0	5	8	1	.929
1989—Seattle (A.L.)	3B	65	171	20	41	5	0	2	20	.240	17	26	2	40	72	6	.949
—Calgary (PCL)	3B-2B	32	113	30	39	11	0	3	23	.345	22	13	2	22	56	12	.867
1990—Seattle (A.L.)	3B-DH	144	487	71	147	27	2	11	49	.302	74	62	1	89	259	*27	.928
1991—Seattle (A.L.)	3B-DH	150	544	98	167	35	1	14	52	.307	84	72	0	84	299	15	.962
1992—Seattle (A.L.)	3B-DH-1B	135	528	100	181	•46	3	18	73	*.343	54	61	14	88	211	17	.946
1993—Seattle (A.L.)	DH-3B	42	135	20	32	7	0	4	13	.237	28	19	0	5	11	2	.889
—Jacksonville (Sou.)	DH	4	14	2	5	0	0	1	3	.357	2	0	0	...	...	...	...
1994—Seattle (A.L.)	3B-DH	89	326	47	93	23	1	13	51	.285	53	42	6	44	128	9	.950
1995—Seattle (A.L.)	DH-3B-1B	•145	511	•121	182	•52	0	29	113	*.356	116	87	4	30	4	2	.944
1996—Seattle (A.L.)	DH-1-3-O	139	499	121	163	52	2	26	103	.327	123	84	3	29	1	1	.968
1997—Seattle (A.L.)	DH-1B-3B	155	542	104	179	35	1	28	108	.330	119	86	2	68	4	1	.986
1998—Seattle (A.L.)	DH-1B	154	556	86	179	46	1	29	102	.322	106	96	1	22	6	0	1.000
1999—Seattle (A.L.)	DH-1B	142	502	86	169	35	1	24	86	.337	97	99	7	29	2	0	1.000
Major League totals (13 years)		1387	4876	880	1558	372	14	198	780	.320	877	746	40	546	1024	81	.951

DIVISION SERIES RECORD

RECORDS: Holds single-series record for most hits—12 (1995). ... Shares single-game records for most runs batted in—7; and most home runs—2 (October 7, 1995).

NOTES: Shares postseason single-game record for most RBIs—7 (October 7, 1995).

Year Team (League)	Pos.	G	AB	R	H	2B	3B	HR	RBI	Avg.	BB	SO	SB	PO	A	E	Avg.
1995—Seattle (A.L.)	DH	5	21	6	12	3	0	2	10	.571	6	2	0	...	...	...	...
1997—Seattle (A.L.)	DH	4	16	2	3	0	0	2	3	.188	0	3	0	...	...	...	...
Division series totals (2 years)		9	37	8	15	3	0	4	13	.405	6	5	0	...	...	...	...

CHAMPIONSHIP SERIES RECORD

Year Team (League)	Pos.	G	AB	R	H	2B	3B	HR	RBI	Avg.	BB	SO	SB	PO	A	E	Avg.
1995—Seattle (A.L.)	DH	6	23	0	2	0	0	0	0	.087	2	5	1	...	...	...	...

ALL-STAR GAME RECORD

Year League	Pos.	AB	R	H	2B	3B	HR	RBI	Avg.	BB	SO	SB	PO	A	E	Avg.
1992—American	PH	1	0	0	0	0	0	0	.000	0	0	0	...	...	...	...
1995—American	DH	3	0	0	0	0	0	0	.000	0	1	0	...	...	...	...
1996—American	PH	1	0	0	0	0	0	0	.000	0	0	0	...	...	...	...
1997—American	DH	2	1	2	0	0	1	1	1.000	0	0	0	...	...	...	...
All-Star Game totals (4 years)		7	1	2	0	0	1	1	.286	0	1	0	...	...	...	...

M

MARTINEZ, FELIX   SS   PHILLIES

PERSONAL: Born May 18, 1974, in Nagua, Dominican Republic. ... 6-0/180. ... Bats both, throws right.
HIGH SCHOOL: Solome Urena (Nagua, Dominican Republic).
TRANSACTIONS/CAREER NOTES: Contract purchased by Kansas City Royals organization from Hiroshima Toyo Carp of Japan Central League (March 5, 1993). ... Suspended four games by American League (June 5, 1998) to be served in 1999 season. ... On suspended list (September 1-6, 1999). ... Claimed on waivers by Philadelphia Phillies (October 6, 1999).
STATISTICAL NOTES: Led Texas League shortstops with 643 total chances in 1995.

Year Team (League)	Pos.	G	AB	R	H	2B	3B	HR	RBI	Avg.	BB	SO	SB	PO	A	E	Avg.
1993—GC Royals (GCL)	SS-2B-3B	57	165	23	42	5	1	0	12	.255	17	26	22	79	136	30	.878
1994—Wilmington (Caro.)	SS	117	400	65	107	16	4	2	43	.268	30	91	19	177	329	30	.944
1995—Wichita (Texas)	SS	127	426	53	112	15	3	3	30	.263	31	71	*44	*222	371	*50	.922
1996—Omaha (A.A.)	SS	118	395	54	93	13	3	5	35	.235	44	79	18	177	374	*42	.929
1997—Omaha (A.A.)	SS	112	410	55	104	19	4	2	36	.254	29	86	21	175	312	*36	.931
—Kansas City (A.L.)	SS-DH	16	31	3	7	1	1	0	3	.226	6	8	0	17	22	1	.975
1998—Kansas City (A.L.)	SS-2B	34	85	7	11	1	1	0	5	.129	5	21	3	49	80	6	.956
—Omaha (PCL)	SS-DH-2B	51	164	27	41	8	3	2	16	.250	15	40	6	74	135	14	.937
1999—Wichita (Texas)	SS-2B-3B-DH	87	327	57	88	22	2	4	37	.269	37	43	19	141	274	23	.947
—Omaha (PCL)	SS	8	23	2	7	5	0	0	2	.304	2	6	0	8	18	1	.963
—Kansas City (A.L.)	SS-2B	6	7	1	1	0	0	0	0	.143	0	0	0	1	2	0	1.000
Major League totals (3 years)		56	123	11	19	2	2	0	8	.154	11	29	3	67	104	7	.961

MARTINEZ, MANNY   OF   EXPOS

PERSONAL: Born October 3, 1970, in San Pedro de Macoris, Dominican Republic. ... 6-0/180. ... Bats right, throws right. ... Full name: Manuel DeJesus Martinez.
TRANSACTIONS/CAREER NOTES: Signed as non-drafted free agent by Oakland Athletics organization (March 9, 1988). ... Played in Dominican Summer League (1988-89). ... Granted free agency (October 15, 1994). ... Signed by Chicago Cubs organization (February 13, 1995). ... Granted free agency (October 15, 1995). ... Signed by Seattle Mariners organization (January 29, 1996). ... Claimed on waivers by Philadelphia

Phillies organization (July 11, 1996). ... Granted free agency (October 15, 1996). ... Signed by Pittsburgh Pirates organization (December 19, 1996) ... On Calgary disabled list (April 30-May 8 and June 20-27, 1997). ... Claimed on waivers by Montreal Expos (December 18, 1998). ... On disabled list (July 8-23, 1999).

STATISTICAL NOTES: Tied for Northwest League lead in double plays by outfielder with three in 1990. ... Led American Association outfielders with 302 total chances in 1995.

									BATTING						FIELDING		
Year	Team (League)	Pos.	G	AB	R	H	2B	3B	HR	RBI	Avg.	BB	SO	SB	PO	A	E	Avg.
1990—	S. Oregon (N'west)....	OF-P	66	244	36	60	5	0	2	17	.246	16	59	6	124	9	6	.957
1991—	Modesto (Calif.)	OF	125	502	73	136	32	3	3	55	.271	34	80	26	267	13	8	.972
1992—	Modesto (Calif.)	OF	121	495	70	125	23	1	9	45	.253	39	75	17	232	12	10	.961
1993—	San Bern. (Calif.).......	OF	109	459	88	148	26	3	11	52	.322	41	60	28	222	15	4	.983
	—Tacoma (PCL)	OF	20	59	9	18	2	0	1	6	.305	4	12	2	33	6	0	1.000
1994—	Tacoma (PCL)	OF	*137	*536	76	137	25	5	9	60	.256	28	72	18	*322	11	9	.974
1995—	Iowa (A.A.)■...........	OF	122	397	63	115	17	•8	8	49	.290	20	64	11	*281	16	5	.983
1996—	Tacoma (PCL)■	OF-DH	66	277	54	87	15	1	4	24	.314	23	41	14	181	11	5	.975
	—Seattle (A.L.)............	OF	9	17	3	4	2	1	0	3	.235	3	5	2	12	2	0	1.000
	—Scranton/W.B. (I.L.)■	OF	17	67	8	14	1	1	0	5	.209	4	17	3	40	0	1	.976
	—Philadelphia (N.L.)......	OF	13	36	2	8	0	2	0	0	.222	1	11	2	20	1	1	.955
1997—	Calgary (PCL)■........	OF-DH	109	420	78	139	34	1	16	66	.331	33	80	17	196	7	5	.976
1998—	Nashville (PCL) ..	OF-DH-2B	22	75	12	18	5	0	1	6	.240	7	20	5	31	2	2	.943
	—Pittsburgh (N.L.)	OF-DH	73	180	21	45	11	2	6	24	.250	9	44	0	92	0	1	.989
1999—	Montreal (N.L.)■........	OF	137	331	48	81	12	7	2	26	.245	17	51	19	234	10	8	.968
American League totals (1 year)			9	17	3	4	2	1	0	3	.235	3	5	2	12	2	0	1.000
National League totals (3 years)			223	547	71	134	23	11	8	50	.245	27	106	21	346	11	10	.973
Major League totals (3 years)			232	564	74	138	25	12	8	53	.245	30	111	23	358	13	10	.974

RECORD AS PITCHER

Year	Team (League)	W	L	Pct.	ERA	G	GS	CG	ShO	Sv.	IP	H	R	ER	BB	SO
1990—	S. Oregon (N'west)............	0	0	...	45.00	1	0	0	0	0	1	5	5	5	2	0

MARTINEZ, PEDRO J. P RED SOX

PERSONAL: Born October 25, 1971, in Manoguayabo, Dominican Republic. ... 5-11/170. ... Throws right, bats right. ... Full name: Pedro Jaime Martinez. ... Brother of Ramon J. Martinez, pitcher, Boston Red Sox; and brother of Jesus Martinez, pitcher in Los Angeles Dodgers (1991-97) and Cincinnati Reds (1998) organizations.

COLLEGE: Ohio Dominican College (Dominican Republic).

TRANSACTIONS/CAREER NOTES: Signed as non-drafted free agent by Los Angeles Dodgers organization (June 18, 1988). ... On Albuquerque disabled list (June 20-July 2 and July 13-August 25, 1992). ... Traded by Dodgers to Montreal Expos for 2B Delino DeShields (November 19, 1993). ... On suspended list (April 1-9, 1997). ... Traded by Expos to Boston Red Sox for P Carl Pavano and a player to be named later (November 18, 1997); Expos acquired P Tony Armas Jr. to complete deal (December 18, 1997). ... On disabled list (July 19-August 3, 1999).

HONORS: Named Minor League Player of the Year by THE SPORTING NEWS (1991). ... Named N.L. Pitcher of the Year by THE SPORTING NEWS (1997). ... Named righthanded pitcher on THE SPORTING NEWS N.L. All-Star team (1997). ... Named N.L. Cy Young Award winner by Baseball Writers' Association of America (1997). ... Named righthanded pitcher on THE SPORTING NEWS A.L. All-Star team (1998 and 1999). ... Named A.L. Pitcher of the Year by THE SPORTING NEWS (1999). ... Named A.L. Cy Young Award winner by Baseball Writers' Association of America (1999).

STATISTICAL NOTES: Led N.L. with 11 hit batsmen in 1994. ... Pitched nine perfect innings against San Diego, before being relieved after yielding leadoff double in 10th inning (June 3, 1995). ... Tied for N.L. lead with 16 sacrifice hits in 1996. ... Pitched 2-0 one-hit, complete-game victory against Cincinnati (July 13, 1997). ... Struck out 15 batters in one game (May 7, May 12, August 24 and September 4, 1999). ... Struck out 16 batters in one game (June 4, 1999). ... Struck out 17 batters in one game (September 10, 1999). ... Pitched 3-1 one-hit, complete-game victory against New York Yankees (September 10, 1999).

Year	League	W	L	Pct.	ERA	G	GS	CG	ShO	Sv.	IP	H	R	ER	BB	SO
1988—	Dom. Dodgers (DSL)	5	1	.833	3.10	8	7	1	0	0	49 1/3	45	25	17	16	28
1989—	Dom. Dodgers (DSL)	7	2	.778	2.73	13	7	2	3	1	85 2/3	59	30	26	25	63
1990—	Great Falls (Pio.)	8	3	.727	3.62	14	•14	0	0	0	77	74	39	31	40	82
1991—	Bakersfield (Calif.)	8	0	1.000	2.05	10	10	0	0	0	61 1/3	41	17	14	19	83
	—San Antonio (Texas)..........	7	5	.583	1.76	12	12	4	•3	0	76 2/3	57	21	15	31	74
	—Albuquerque (PCL)	3	3	.500	3.66	6	6	0	0	0	39 1/3	28	17	16	16	35
1992—	Albuquerque (PCL)	7	6	.538	3.81	20	20	3	1	0	125 1/3	104	57	53	57	124
	—Los Angeles (N.L.)	0	1	.000	2.25	2	1	0	0	0	8	6	2	2	1	8
1993—	Albuquerque (PCL)	0	0	...	3.00	1	1	0	0	0	3	1	1	1	1	4
	—Los Angeles (N.L.)	10	5	.667	2.61	65	2	0	0	2	107	76	34	31	57	119
1994—	Montreal (N.L.)■..................	11	5	.688	3.42	24	23	1	1	1	144 2/3	115	58	55	45	142
1995—	Montreal (N.L.)	14	10	.583	3.51	30	30	2	2	0	194 2/3	158	79	76	66	174
1996—	Montreal (N.L.)	13	10	.565	3.70	33	33	4	1	0	216 2/3	189	100	89	70	222
1997—	Montreal (N.L.)	17	8	.680	*1.90	31	31	*13	4	0	241 1/3	158	65	51	67	305
1998—	Boston (A.L.)■....................	19	7	.731	2.89	33	33	3	2	0	233 2/3	188	82	75	67	251
1999—	Boston (A.L.)	*23	4	*.852	*2.07	31	29	5	1	0	213 1/3	160	56	49	37	*313
A.L. totals (2 years)		42	11	.792	2.50	64	62	8	3	0	447	348	138	124	104	564
N.L. totals (6 years)		65	39	.625	3.00	185	120	20	8	3	912 1/3	702	338	304	306	970
Major League totals (8 years)		107	50	.682	2.83	249	182	28	11	3	1359 1/3	1050	476	428	410	1534

DIVISION SERIES RECORD

Year	League	W	L	Pct.	ERA	G	GS	CG	ShO	Sv.	IP	H	R	ER	BB	SO
1998—	Boston (A.L.)	1	0	1.000	3.86	1	1	0	0	0	7	6	3	3	0	8
1999—	Boston (A.L.)	1	0	1.000	0.00	2	1	0	0	0	10	3	0	0	4	11
Division series totals (2 years)		2	0	1.000	1.59	3	2	0	0	0	17	9	3	3	4	19

CHAMPIONSHIP SERIES RECORD

Year	League	W	L	Pct.	ERA	G	GS	CG	ShO	Sv.	IP	H	R	ER	BB	SO
1999—	Boston (A.L.)	1	0	1.000	0.00	1	1	0	0	0	7	2	0	0	2	12

M

NOTES: Named Most Valuable Player (1999).

Year League	W	L	Pct.	ERA	GS	CG	ShO	Sv.	IP	H	R	ER	BB	SO
1996— National	0	0	...	0.00	0	0	0	0	1	2	0	0	0	1
1997— National	0	0	...	0.00	0	0	0	0	1	0	0	0	0	2
1998— American							Did not play.							
1999— American	1	0	1.000	0.00	1	0	0	0	2	0	0	0	0	5
All-Star Game totals (3 years)	1	0	1.000	0.00	1	0	0	0	4	2	0	0	0	8

MARTINEZ, RAMON E.   2B/SS   GIANTS

PERSONAL: Born October 10, 1972, in Philadelphia. ... 6-1/187. ... Bats right, throws right. ... Full name: Ramon E. Martinez.
HIGH SCHOOL: Escuela Superior Catholica (Bayamon, Puerto Rico).
JUNIOR COLLEGE: Vernon (Texas) Regional Junior College.
TRANSACTIONS/CAREER NOTES: Signed as non-drafted free agent by Kansas City Royals organization (January 15, 1994). ... Traded by Royals to San Francisco Giants (December 9, 1996), completing deal in which Giants traded P Jamie Brewington to Royals for a player to be named later (November 26, 1996). ... On Fresno disabled list (June 10-23, 1999). ... On San Francisco disabled list (August 21-September 5, 1999).
STATISTICAL NOTES: Led Texas League with 18 sacrifice hits and nine sacrifice flies in 1995. ... Led Texas League second basemen with .984 fielding percentage in 1995. ... Led American Association with 13 sacrifice hits in 1996.

							BATTING								FIELDING		
Year Team (League)	Pos.	G	AB	R	H	2B	3B	HR	RBI	Avg.	BB	SO	SB	PO	A	E	Avg.
1993— GC Royals (GCL)		37	97	16	23	5	0	0	9	.237	8	6	3	71	108	5	.973
— Wilmington (Caro.)	2B-SS	24	75	8	19	4	0	0	6	.253	11	9	1	52	72	6	.954
1994— Wilmington (Caro.)	2B	90	325	40	87	13	2	2	35	.268	35	25	6	176	249	16	.964
— Rockford (Midw.)	2B	6	18	3	5	0	0	0	3	.278	4	2	1	9	12	1	.955
1995— Wichita (Texas)	2B-SS	103	393	58	108	20	2	3	51	.275	42	50	11	186	311	9	†.982
1996— Omaha (A.A.)	2B	85	320	35	81	12	3	6	41	.253	21	34	3	163	207	12	.969
— Wichita (Texas)	2B	26	93	16	32	4	1	1	8	.344	7	8	4	47	84	6	.956
1997— Shreveport (Texas)■	SS	105	404	72	129	32	4	5	54	.319	40	48	4	167	370	18	.968
— Phoenix (PCL)	2B-SS	18	57	6	16	2	0	1	7	.281	5	9	1	26	44	3	.959
1998— Fresno (PCL)	2B-SS	98	364	58	114	21	2	14	59	.313	38	42	0	209	280	10	.980
— San Francisco (N.L.)	2B	19	19	4	6	1	0	0	0	.316	4	2	0	15	20	0	1.000
1999— San Francisco (N.L.)	2B-SS-3B-DH	61	144	21	38	6	0	5	19	.264	14	17	1	66	102	6	.966
— Fresno (PCL)	SS-DH-3B	29	114	13	37	7	1	2	17	.325	10	17	2	26	72	5	.951
Major League totals (2 years)		80	163	25	44	7	0	5	19	.270	18	19	1	81	122	6	.971

MARTINEZ, RAMON J.   P   RED SOX

PERSONAL: Born March 22, 1968, in Santo Domingo, Dominican Republic. ... 6-4/184. ... Throws right, bats right. ... Full name: Ramon Jaime Martinez. ... Brother of Pedro J. Martinez, pitcher, Boston Red Sox; and brother of Jesus Martinez, pitcher with Los Angeles Dodgers (1991-97) and Cincinnati Reds (1998) organizations.
HIGH SCHOOL: Liceo Secunderia Las Americas (Dominican Republic).
TRANSACTIONS/CAREER NOTES: Signed as non-drafted free agent by Los Angeles Dodgers organization (September 1, 1984). ... On suspended list (July 8-12, 1993). ... Granted free agency (November 1, 1995). ... Re-signed by Dodgers (November 16, 1995). ... On Los Angeles disabled list (April 7-May 14, 1996); included rehabilitation assignments to San Antonio (May 4-9) and Vero Beach (May 9-14). ... On Los Angeles disabled list (June 15-August 20, 1997); included rehabilitation assignment to San Bernardino (July 26-August 20). ... On disabled list (June 19, 1998-remainder of season). ... Granted free agency (November 17, 1998). ... Signed by Boston Red Sox (March 11, 1999). ... On Boston disabled list (April 1-September 2, 1999); included rehabilitation assignments to Lowell (June 21-25), Gulf Coast Red Sox (July 11-August 1), Sarasota (August 2-21) and Pawtucket (August 22-30).
STATISTICAL NOTES: Struck out 18 batters in one game (June 4, 1990). ... Pitched 7-0 no-hit victory against Florida (July 14, 1995).
MISCELLANEOUS: Member of 1984 Dominican Republic Olympic baseball team. ... Appeared in one game as pinch runner (1989). ... Appeared in one game as pinch runner (1992). ... Appeared in one game as pinch hitter and appeared in one game as pinch runner with Los Angeles (1996).

Year League	W	L	Pct.	ERA	G	GS	CG	ShO	Sv.	IP	H	R	ER	BB	SO
1985— Gulf Coast Dodgers (GCL)	4	1	.800	2.59	23	6	0	0	1	59	57	30	17	23	42
1986— Bakersfield (Calif.)	4	8	.333	4.75	20	20	2	1	0	106	119	73	56	63	78
1987— Vero Beach (FSL)	16	5	.762	2.17	25	25	6	1	0	170 1/3	128	45	41	78	148
1988— San Antonio (Texas)	8	4	.667	2.46	14	14	2	1	0	95	79	29	26	34	89
— Albuquerque (PCL)	5	2	.714	2.76	10	10	1	1	0	58 2/3	43	24	18	32	49
— Los Angeles (N.L.)	1	3	.250	3.79	9	6	0	0	0	35 2/3	27	17	15	22	23
1989— Albuquerque (PCL)	10	2	.833	2.79	18	18	2	1	0	113	92	40	35	50	127
— Los Angeles (N.L.)	6	4	.600	3.19	15	15	2	2	0	98 2/3	79	39	35	41	89
1990— Los Angeles (N.L.)	20	6	.769	2.92	33	33	*12	3	0	234 1/3	191	89	76	67	223
1991— Los Angeles (N.L.)	17	13	.567	3.27	33	33	6	4	0	220 1/3	190	89	80	69	150
1992— Los Angeles (N.L.)	8	11	.421	4.00	25	25	1	1	0	150 2/3	141	82	67	69	101
1993— Los Angeles (N.L.)	10	12	.455	3.44	32	32	4	3	0	211 2/3	202	88	81	*104	127
1994— Los Angeles (N.L.)	12	7	.632	3.97	24	24	4	•3	0	170	160	83	75	56	119
1995— Los Angeles (N.L.)	17	7	.708	3.66	30	30	4	2	0	206 1/3	176	95	84	*81	138
1996— San Antonio (Texas)	0	0	...	0.00	1	1	0	0	0	2 2/3	0	0	0	3	1
— Vero Beach (FSL)	1	0	1.000	0.00	1	1	0	0	0	7	5	1	0	0	10
— Los Angeles (N.L.)	15	6	.714	3.42	29	27	2	2	0	168 2/3	153	76	64	86	133
1997— Los Angeles (N.L.)	10	5	.667	3.64	22	22	1	0	0	133 2/3	123	64	54	68	120
— San Bernardino (Calif.)	0	1	.000	1.15	4	4	0	0	0	15 2/3	10	2	2	4	16
1998— Los Angeles (N.L.)	7	3	.700	2.83	15	15	1	0	0	101 2/3	76	41	32	41	91
1999— Lowell (NY-P)■	0	0	...	0.00	1	1	0	0	0	2	0	0	0	0	3
— Gulf Coast Red Sox (GCL)	1	0	1.000	1.38	4	4	0	0	0	13	9	4	2	3	15
— Sarasota (FSL)	1	0	1.000	3.00	3	3	0	0	0	12	11	7	4	7	9
— Pawtucket (I.L.)	0	1	.000	9.00	2	2	0	0	0	9	10	9	9	6	7
— Boston (A.L.)	2	1	.667	3.05	4	4	0	0	0	20 2/3	14	8	7	8	15
A.L. totals (1 year)	2	1	.667	3.05	4	4	0	0	0	20 2/3	14	8	7	8	15
N.L. totals (11 years)	123	77	.615	3.45	267	262	37	20	0	1731 2/3	1518	763	663	704	1314
Major League totals (12 years)	125	78	.616	3.44	271	266	37	20	0	1752 1/3	1532	771	670	712	1329

M

Year	League	W	L	Pct.	ERA	G	GS	CG	ShO	Sv.	IP	H	R	ER	BB	SO
1995— Los Angeles (N.L.)		0	1	.000	14.54	1	1	0	0	0	4⅓	10	7	7	2	3
1996— Los Angeles (N.L.)		0	0	...	1.13	1	1	0	0	0	8	3	1	1	3	6
1999— Boston (A.L.)		0	0		3.18	1	1	0	0	0	5⅔	5	2	2	3	6
Division series totals (3 years)		0	1	.000	5.00	3	3	0	0	0	18	18	10	10	8	15

CHAMPIONSHIP SERIES RECORD

Year	League	W	L	Pct.	ERA	G	GS	CG	ShO	Sv.	IP	H	R	ER	BB	SO
1999— Boston (A.L.)....................		0	1	.000	4.05	1	1	0	0	0	6⅔	6	3	3	3	5

MARTINEZ, SANDY — C

PERSONAL: Born October 3, 1972, in Villa Mella, Dominican Republic. ... 6-2/215. ... Bats left, throws right. ... Full name: Angel Sandy Martinez.

HIGH SCHOOL: Villa Mella (Dominican Republic).

TRANSACTIONS/CAREER NOTES: Signed as non-drafted free agent by Toronto Blue Jays organization (January 10, 1990). ... On disabled list (May 15-June 8, 1993). ... On Toronto disabled list (August 17-September 1, 1996); included rehabilitation assignment to Knoxville (August 26-September 1). ... On Syracuse disabled list (June 14-24, 1997). ... Traded by Blue Jays to Chicago Cubs for a player to be named later (December 11, 1997); Blue Jays acquired P Trevor Schaffer to complete deal (December 19, 1997). ... On suspended list (July 1-3, 1998). ... On Chicago disabled list (May 13-June 10, 1999); included rehabilitation assignment to Iowa (June 5-10). ... Granted free agency (October 15, 1999). ... Signed by Calgary, Florida Marlins organization (December 6, 1999).

RECORDS: Shares major league single-game record for most putouts by catcher (nine-inning game)—20 (May 6, 1998); and most chances accepted by catcher (nine-inning game) since 1900—20 (May 6, 1998).

STATISTICAL NOTES: Led Pioneer League with 24 passed balls in 1992. ... Led Florida State League catchers with 14 errors in 1994.

						BATTING								FIELDING			
Year	Team (League)	Pos.	G	AB	R	H	2B	3B	HR	RBI	Avg.	BB	SO	SB	PO	A	E	Avg.
1990— Dom. Blue Jays (DSL)	C	44	145	21	35	2	0	0	10	.241	18	15	1	...	...	...	
1991— Dunedin (FSL)	C	12	38	3	7	1	0	0	3	.184	7	7	0	82	9	2	.978
— Medicine Hat (Pio.) ...	C	34	98	8	17	1	0	2	16	.173	12	29	0	141	19	3	.982
1992— Dunedin (FSL)	C	4	15	4	3	1	0	2	4	.200	0	3	0	11	2	1	.929
— Medicine Hat (Pio.) ...	C-1B-SS	57	206	27	52	15	0	4	39	.252	14	62	0	275	58	5	.985
1993— Hagerstown (SAL)	C-DH	94	338	41	89	16	1	9	46	.263	19	71	1	493	68	14	.976
1994— Dunedin (FSL)	C-DH-1B	122	450	50	117	14	6	7	52	.260	22	79	1	615	79	†14	.980
1995— Knoxville (Sou.)	C-DH	41	144	14	33	8	1	2	22	.229	6	34	0	219	30	5	.980
— Toronto (A.L.).............	C	62	191	12	46	12	0	2	25	.241	7	45	0	329	28	5	.986
1996— Toronto (A.L.).............	C	76	229	17	52	9	3	3	18	.227	16	58	0	413	33	3	.993
— Knoxville (Sou.).........	C-DH	4	16	2	3	0	0	0	0	.188	0	5	0	17	2	1	.950
1997— Syracuse (I.L.)	C-DH	96	322	28	72	12	1	4	29	.224	27	76	7	588	50	9	.986
— Toronto (A.L.).............	C	3	2	1	0	0	0	0	0	.000	1	1	0	12	2	1	.933
1998— Chicago (N.L.)■........	C	45	87	7	23	9	1	0	7	.264	13	21	1	185	7	3	.985
1999— Chicago (N.L.)...........	C	17	30	1	5	0	0	1	1	.167	0	11	0	45	2	2	.959
— Iowa (PCL)	C	36	125	8	29	6	0	2	18	.232	5	29	1	239	17	1	.996
American League totals (3 years)		141	422	30	98	21	3	5	43	.232	24	104	0	754	63	9	.989
National League totals (2 years)		62	117	8	28	9	1	1	8	.239	13	32	1	230	9	5	.980
Major League totals (5 years)		203	539	38	126	30	4	6	51	.234	37	136	1	984	72	14	.987

DIVISION SERIES RECORD

						BATTING								FIELDING			
Year	Team (League)	Pos.	G	AB	R	H	2B	3B	HR	RBI	Avg.	BB	SO	SB	PO	A	E	Avg.
1998— Chicago (N.L.)	C	1	1	1	1	0	0	0	0	1.000	0	0	0	1	0	0	1.000

MARTINEZ, TINO — 1B — YANKEES

PERSONAL: Born December 7, 1967, in Tampa. ... 6-2/210. ... Bats left, throws right. ... Full name: Constantino Martinez.

HIGH SCHOOL: Tampa Catholic (Tampa).

COLLEGE: Tampa (Fla.).

TRANSACTIONS/CAREER NOTES: Selected by Boston Red Sox organization in third round of free-agent draft (June 3, 1985); did not sign. ... Selected by Seattle Mariners organization in first round (14th pick overall) of free-agent draft (June 1, 1988). ... On disabled list (August 10, 1993-remainder of season). ... Traded by Mariners with P Jeff Nelson and P Jim Mecir to New York Yankees for P Sterling Hitchcock and 3B Russ Davis (December 7, 1995).

HONORS: Named first baseman on THE SPORTING NEWS college All-America team (1988). ... Named Pacific Coast League Most Valuable Player (1991). ... Named first baseman on THE SPORTING NEWS A.L. All-Star team (1997). ... Named first baseman on THE SPORTING NEWS A.L. Silver Slugger team (1997).

STATISTICAL NOTES: Led Eastern League with 13 intentional bases on balls received in 1989. ... Led Eastern League first basemen with 1,348 total chances and 106 double plays in 1989. ... Tied for Pacific Coast League lead with 11 intentional bases on balls received in 1990. ... Led Pacific Coast League first basemen with .991 fielding percentage, 1,051 putouts, 98 assists, 1,159 total chances and 117 double plays in 1990. ... Led Pacific Coast League first basemen with .992 fielding percentage and 122 double plays in 1991. ... Hit three home runs in one game (April 2, 1997). ... Led A.L. with 13 sacrifice flies in 1997. ... Led A.L. first baseman with 1,410 total chances in 1999. ... Career major league grand slams: 7.

MISCELLANEOUS: Member of 1988 U.S. Olympic baseball team.

						BATTING								FIELDING			
Year	Team (League)	Pos.	G	AB	R	H	2B	3B	HR	RBI	Avg.	BB	SO	SB	PO	A	E	Avg.
1989— Williamsport (East.) ...	1B	*137	*509	51	131	29	2	13	64	.257	59	54	7	*1260	*81	7	*.995
1990— Calgary (PCL)............	1B-3B	128	453	83	145	28	1	17	93	.320	74	37	8	†1051	†98	10	†.991
— Seattle (A.L.)	1B	24	68	4	15	4	0	0	5	.221	9	9	0	155	12	0	1.000
1991— Calgary (PCL)............	1B-3B	122	442	94	144	34	5	18	86	.326	82	44	3	1078	106	9	†.992
— Seattle (A.L.)	1B-DH	36	112	11	23	2	0	4	9	.205	11	24	0	249	22	2	.993
1992— Seattle (A.L.)	1B-DH	136	460	53	118	19	2	16	66	.257	42	77	2	678	58	4	.995

M

Year	Team (League)	Pos.	G	AB	R	H	2B	3B	HR	RBI	Avg.	BB	SO	SB	PO	A	E	Avg.
1993—	Seattle (A.L.)	1B-DH	109	408	48	108	25	1	17	60	.265	45	56	0	932	60	3	.997
1994—	Seattle (A.L.)	1B-DH	97	329	42	86	21	0	20	61	.261	29	52	1	705	45	2	.997
1995—	Seattle (A.L.)	1B-DH	141	519	92	152	35	3	31	111	.293	62	91	0	1048	101	8	.993
1996—	New York (A.L.)■	1B-DH	155	595	82	174	28	0	25	117	.292	68	85	2	1238	83	5	*.996
1997—	New York (A.L.)	1B-DH	158	594	96	176	31	2	44	141	.296	75	75	3	1302	105	8	.994
1998—	New York (A.L.)	1B	142	531	92	149	33	1	28	123	.281	61	83	2	1180	93	10	.992
1999—	New York (A.L.)	1B	159	589	95	155	27	2	28	105	.263	69	86	3	1297	*106	7	.995
Major League totals (10 years)			1157	4205	615	1156	225	11	213	798	.275	471	638	13	8784	685	49	.995

DIVISION SERIES RECORD

RECORDS: Shares career record for most doubles—6. ... Shares single-game record for most at-bats—7 (October 4, 1995).

Year	Team (League)	Pos.	G	AB	R	H	2B	3B	HR	RBI	Avg.	BB	SO	SB	PO	A	E	Avg.
1995—	Seattle (A.L.)	1B	5	22	4	9	1	0	1	5	.409	3	4	0	39	5	0	1.000
1996—	New York (A.L.)	1B	4	15	3	4	2	0	0	0	.267	4	1	0	33	3	0	1.000
1997—	New York (A.L.)	1B	5	18	1	4	1	0	1	4	.222	2	4	0	48	6	0	1.000
1998—	New York (A.L.)	1B	3	11	1	3	2	0	0	0	.273	0	2	0	27	1	0	1.000
1999—	New York (A.L.)	1B	3	11	2	2	0	0	0	0	.182	2	2	0	29	1	1	.968
Division series totals (5 years)			20	77	11	22	6	0	2	9	.286	11	13	0	176	16	1	.995

CHAMPIONSHIP SERIES RECORD

RECORDS: Shares A.L. career record for most times hit by pitch—3.

Year	Team (League)	Pos.	G	AB	R	H	2B	3B	HR	RBI	Avg.	BB	SO	SB	PO	A	E	Avg.
1995—	Seattle (A.L.)	1B	6	22	1	3	0	0	0	0	.136	3	7	0	45	5	1	.980
1996—	New York (A.L.)	1B	5	22	3	4	1	0	0	0	.182	0	2	0	49	2	0	1.000
1998—	New York (A.L.)	1B	6	19	1	2	1	0	0	1	.105	6	8	2	47	4	1	.981
1999—	New York (A.L.)	1B	5	19	3	5	1	0	1	3	.263	2	4	0	29	5	0	1.000
Championship series totals (4 years)			22	82	8	14	3	0	1	4	.171	11	21	2	170	16	2	.989

WORLD SERIES RECORD

RECORDS: Shares single-game record for most grand slams—1 (October 17, 1998). ... Shares single-inning record for most runs batted in—4 (October 17, 1998, seventh inning).

NOTES: Member of World Series championship team (1996, 1998 and 1999).

Year	Team (League)	Pos.	G	AB	R	H	2B	3B	HR	RBI	Avg.	BB	SO	SB	PO	A	E	Avg.
1996—	New York (A.L.)	1B-PH	6	11	0	1	0	0	0	0	.091	2	5	0	27	0	0	1.000
1998—	New York (A.L.)	1B	4	13	4	5	0	0	1	4	.385	6	2	0	36	3	0	1.000
1999—	New York (A.L.)	1B	4	15	3	4	0	0	1	5	.267	2	4	0	41	2	0	1.000
World Series totals (3 years)			14	39	7	10	0	0	2	9	.256	10	11	0	104	5	0	1.000

ALL-STAR GAME RECORD

Year	League	Pos.	AB	R	H	2B	3B	HR	RBI	Avg.	BB	SO	SB	PO	A	E	Avg.
1995—	American	PH	1	0	1	0	0	0	0	1.000	0	0	0	...	...	...	...
1997—	American	1B	2	0	0	0	0	0	0	.000	0	0	0	10	0	0	1.000
All-Star Game totals (2 years)			3	0	1	0	0	0	0	.333	0	0	0	10	0	0	1.000

MARTINEZ, WILLIE — P — INDIANS

PERSONAL: Born January 4, 1978, in Barquisimeto, Venezuela. ... 6-2/185. ... Throws right, bats right. ... Full name: William Jose Martinez.
HIGH SCHOOL: Barquisimeto (Venezuela).
TRANSACTIONS/CAREER NOTES: Signed as non-drafted free agent by Cleveland Indians organization (January 16, 1995). ... On Akron disabled list (May 3-17 and July 11-18, 1998). ... On Cleveland disabled list (September 8, 1999-remainder of season).
STATISTICAL NOTES: Tied for Eastern League lead with six errors by pitcher in 1999.

Year	League	W	L	Pct.	ERA	G	GS	CG	ShO	Sv.	IP	H	R	ER	BB	SO
1995—	Burlington (Appl.)	0	7	.000	9.45	11	11	0	0	0	40	64	50	42	25	36
1996—	Watertown (NY-P)	6	5	.545	2.40	14	14	1	1	0	90	79	25	24	21	92
1997—	Kinston (Caro.)	8	2	.800	3.09	23	23	1	0	0	137	125	61	47	42	120
1998—	Akron (East.)	9	7	.563	4.38	26	26	2	1	0	154	169	92	75	44	117
1999—	Akron (East.)	9	8	.529	4.09	24	24	0	0	0	147 1/3	163	83	67	45	91
—	Buffalo (I.L.)■	2	2	.500	6.85	4	4	0	0	0	22 1/3	28	17	17	7	12

MASAOKA, ONAN — P — DODGERS

PERSONAL: Born October 27, 1977, in Hilo, Hawaii. ... 6-0/180. ... Throws left, bats right. ... Full name: Onan Kainoa Satoshi Masaoka.
HIGH SCHOOL: Waiakea (Hilo, Hawaii).
TRANSACTIONS/CAREER NOTES: Selected by Los Angeles Dodgers organization in third round of free-agent draft (June 1, 1995).

Year	League	W	L	Pct.	ERA	G	GS	CG	ShO	Sv.	IP	H	R	ER	BB	SO
1995—	Yakima (N.W.)	2	4	.333	3.65	15	7	0	0	3	49 1/3	28	25	20	47	75
1996—	Savannah (SAL)	2	5	.286	4.29	13	13	0	0	0	65	55	35	31	35	80
1997—	Vero Beach (FSL)	6	8	.429	3.87	28	24	2	1	1	148 2/3	113	72	64	55	132
1998—	San Antonio (Texas)	6	6	.500	5.32	27	20	1	1	1	110	114	79	65	63	94
1999—	Los Angeles (N.L.)	2	4	.333	4.32	54	0	0	0	1	66 2/3	55	33	32	47	61
Major League totals (1 year)		2	4	.333	4.32	54	0	0	0	1	66 2/3	55	33	32	47	61

MATEO, RUBEN   OF   RANGERS

PERSONAL: Born February 10, 1978, in San Cristobal, Dominican Republic. ... 6-0/185. ... Bats right, throws right. ... Full name: Ruben Amaurys Mateo.

TRANSACTIONS/CAREER NOTES: Signed as non-drafted free agent by Texas Rangers organization (October 24, 1994). ... On Tulsa disabled list (April 13-May 13, 1998). ... On Texas disabled list (June 23-July 9 and August 5, 1999-remainder of season); included rehabilitation assignment to Oklahoma (July 6-9).

							BATTING								FIELDING		
Year Team (League)	Pos.	G	AB	R	H	2B	3B	HR	RBI	Avg.	BB	SO	SB	PO	A	E	Avg.
1995—Dom. Rangers (DSL)..	OF	48	176	30	53	9	3	4	42	.301	20	23	1	55	1	1	.982
1996—Char., S.C. (SAL)........	OF-DH	134	496	65	129	30	8	8	58	.260	26	78	30	215	15	7	.970
1997—Charlotte (FSL)..........	OF-DH	99	385	63	121	23	8	12	67	.314	22	55	20	174	10	8	.958
1998—Tulsa (Texas)	OF	107	433	79	134	32	3	18	75	.309	30	56	18	215	11	7	.970
—Charlotte (FSL).......	OF	1	4	0	0	0	0	0	1	.000	0	1	0	2	0	0	1.000
1999—Texas (A.L.)................	OF-DH	32	122	16	29	9	1	5	18	.238	4	28	3	62	3	0	1.000
—Oklahoma (PCL)........	OF-DH	63	253	53	85	12	0	18	62	.336	14	36	6	128	3	5	.963
Major League totals (1 year)		32	122	16	29	9	1	5	18	.238	4	28	3	62	3	0	1.000

MATHENY, MIKE   C   CARDINALS

PERSONAL: Born September 22, 1970, in Reynoldsburg, Ohio. ... 6-3/205. ... Bats right, throws right. ... Full name: Michael Scott Matheny.
HIGH SCHOOL: Reynoldsburg (Ohio).
COLLEGE: Michigan.
TRANSACTIONS/CAREER NOTES: Selected by Toronto Blue Jays organization in 31st round of free-agent draft (June 1, 1988); did not sign. ... Selected by Milwaukee Brewers organization in eighth round of free-agent draft (June 3, 1991). ... On Milwaukee suspended list (June 20-23, 1996). ... On Milwaukee disabled list (June 15-July 12, 1998); included rehabilitation assignment to Beloit (July 11-13). ... Granted free agency (December 21, 1998). ... Signed by Blue Jays (December 23, 1998). ... Released by Blue Jays (November 17, 1999). ... Signed by St. Louis Cardinals (December 15, 1999).
STATISTICAL NOTES: Led California League catchers with 20 double plays in 1992. ... Led Texas League catchers with 18 double plays in 1993. ... Career major league grand slams: 2.

							BATTING								FIELDING		
Year Team (League)	Pos.	G	AB	R	H	2B	3B	HR	RBI	Avg.	BB	SO	SB	PO	A	E	Avg.
1991—Helena (Pio.)	C	64	253	35	72	14	0	2	34	.285	19	52	2	456	68	5	*.991
1992—Stockton (Calif.)	C	106	333	42	73	13	2	6	46	.219	35	81	2	582	114	8	*.989
1993—El Paso (Texas)..........	C	107	339	39	86	21	2	2	28	.254	17	73	1	524	*100	9	.986
1994—Milwaukee (A.L.)	C	28	53	3	12	3	0	1	2	.226	3	13	0	81	8	1	.989
—New Orleans (A.A.).....	C-DH-1B	57	177	20	39	10	1	4	21	.220	16	39	1	345	43	5	.987
1995—New Orleans (A.A.).....	C	6	17	3	6	2	0	3	4	.353	0	5	0	30	4	0	1.000
—Milwaukee (A.L.)	C	80	166	13	41	9	1	0	21	.247	12	28	2	261	18	4	.986
1996—Milwaukee (A.L.)	C-DH	106	313	31	64	15	2	8	46	.204	14	80	3	475	40	8	.985
—New Orleans (A.A.).....	C-DH	20	66	3	15	4	0	1	6	.227	2	17	1	87	6	0	1.000
1997—Milwaukee (A.L.)	C-1B	123	320	29	78	16	1	4	32	.244	17	68	0	697	58	5	.993
1998—Milwaukee (N.L.)	C	108	320	24	76	13	0	6	27	.238	11	63	1	570	45	8	.987
—Beloit (Midw.)............	DH-C	2	8	1	2	1	0	0	2	.250	1	3	0	13	1	0	1.000
1999—Toronto (A.L.)■.........	C	57	163	16	35	6	0	3	17	.215	12	37	0	346	33	2	.995
American League totals (5 years)		394	1015	92	230	49	4	16	118	.227	58	226	5	1860	157	20	.990
National League totals (1 year)		108	320	24	76	13	0	6	27	.238	11	63	1	570	45	8	.987
Major League totals (6 years)		502	1335	116	306	62	4	22	145	.229	69	289	6	2430	202	28	.989

M

MATHEWS, T.J.   P   ATHLETICS

PERSONAL: Born January 19, 1970, in Belleville, Ill. ... 6-1/214. ... Throws right, bats right. ... Full name: Timothy Jay Mathews. ... Son of Nelson Mathews, outfielder with Chicago Cubs (1960-63) and Kansas City Athletics (1964-65).
HIGH SCHOOL: Columbia (Ill.).
COLLEGE: UNLV.
TRANSACTIONS/CAREER NOTES: Selected by St. Louis Cardinals organization in 36th round of free-agent draft (June 1, 1992). ... On Louisville disabled list (May 30-June 6, 1995). ... On suspended list (April 1-7, 1997). ... Traded by Cardinals with P Eric Ludwick and P Blake Stein to Oakland Athletics for 1B Mark McGwire (July 31, 1997). ... On Oakland disabled list (July 1-24, 1999); included rehabilitation assignment to Vancouver (July 21-24).
STATISTICAL NOTES: Pitched 4-0 no-hit victory against Burlington (August 13, 1993).

Year League	W	L	Pct.	ERA	G	GS	CG	ShO	Sv.	IP	H	R	ER	BB	SO
1992—Hamilton (NY-P)................	10	1	*.909	2.18	14	14	1	0	0	86²/₃	70	25	21	30	89
1993—Springfield (Midw.)	12	9	.571	2.71	25	25	5	2	0	159¹/₃	121	59	48	29	144
1994—St. Petersburg (FSL)	5	5	.500	2.44	11	11	1	0	0	66¹/₃	52	22	18	23	62
—Arkansas (Texas)............	5	5	.500	3.15	16	16	1	0	0	97	83	37	34	24	93
1995—Louisville (A.A.).............	9	4	.692	2.70	32	7	0	0	1	66²/₃	60	35	20	27	50
—St. Louis (N.L.).................	1	1	.500	1.52	23	0	0	0	2	29²/₃	21	7	5	11	28
1996—St. Louis (N.L.)................	2	6	.250	3.01	67	0	0	0	6	83²/₃	62	32	28	32	80
1997—St. Louis (N.L.)................	4	4	.500	2.15	40	0	0	0	0	46	41	14	11	18	46
—Oakland (A.L.)■..............	6	2	.750	4.40	24	0	0	0	3	28²/₃	34	18	14	12	24
1998—Oakland (A.L.)................	7	4	.636	4.58	66	0	0	0	1	72²/₃	71	44	37	29	53
1999—Oakland (A.L.)................	9	5	.643	3.81	50	0	0	0	3	59	46	28	25	20	42
—Vancouver (PCL)	0	0	...	9.00	1	1	0	0	0	1	1	1	1	0	0
A.L. totals (3 years)	22	11	.667	4.27	140	0	0	0	7	160¹/₃	151	90	76	61	119
N.L. totals (3 years)	7	11	.389	2.49	130	0	0	0	8	159¹/₃	124	53	44	61	154
Major League totals (5 years)	29	22	.569	3.38	270	0	0	0	15	319²/₃	275	143	120	122	273

DIVISION SERIES RECORD

Year League	W	L	Pct.	ERA	G	GS	CG	ShO	Sv.	IP	H	R	ER	BB	SO
1996— St. Louis (N.L.)..................	1	0	1.000	0.00	1	0	0	0	0	1	1	0	0	0	2

CHAMPIONSHIP SERIES RECORD

Year League	W	L	Pct.	ERA	G	GS	CG	ShO	Sv.	IP	H	R	ER	BB	SO
1996— St. Louis (N.L.)..................	0	0	...	0.00	2	0	0	0	0	2/3	2	0	0	2	2

MATHEWS, TERRY　　　　　　P　　　　　DEVIL RAYS

PERSONAL: Born October 5, 1964, in Alexandria, La. ... 6-2/225. ... Throws right, bats left. ... Full name: Terry Alan Mathews.
HIGH SCHOOL: Menard (Alexandria, La.).
COLLEGE: Northeast Louisiana.
TRANSACTIONS/CAREER NOTES: Selected by Texas Rangers organization in fifth round of free-agent draft (June 2, 1987). ... On Texas disabled list (July 29-September 12, 1992). ... Released by Rangers organization (April 4, 1993). ... Signed by Houston Astros organization (April 4, 1993). ... Granted free agency (October 15, 1993). ... Signed by Florida Marlins organization (November 9, 1993). ... On Florida disabled list (August 19-September 3, 1995); included rehabilitation assignment to Charlotte (August 29-September 1). ... On Florida disabled list (April 2-17, 1996). ... Traded by Marlins to Baltimore Orioles for a player to be named later (August 21, 1996); Marlins acquired C Greg Zaun to complete deal (August 23, 1996). ... On Baltimore disabled list (April 30-May 26 and June 2-17, 1998); included rehabilitation assignment to Bowie (June 7-11) and Rochester (June 12-17). ... Released by Orioles (July 7, 1998). ... Signed by Oakland Athletics organization (July 17, 1998). ... Granted free agency (October 15, 1998). ... Signed by Kansas City Royals organization (January 14, 1999). ... On Kansas City disabled list (July 1-August 10, 1999); included rehabilitation assignments to Gulf Coast Royals (July 29-31), Wichita (August 1-3) and Omaha (August 4-9). ... Released by Royals (August 14, 1999). ... Signed by Tampa Bay Devil Rays organization (January 20, 2000).
MISCELLANEOUS: Grounded into double play in only appearance as pinch hitter with Florida (1995).

Year League	W	L	Pct.	ERA	G	GS	CG	ShO	Sv.	IP	H	R	ER	BB	SO
1987— Gastonia (SAL)..................	3	3	.500	5.59	34	1	0	0	0	48 1/3	53	35	30	32	46
1988— Charlotte (FSL)..................	13	6	.684	2.80	27	26	2	1	0	163 2/3	141	68	51	49	94
1989— Tulsa (Texas)..................	2	5	.286	6.15	10	10	1	0	0	45 1/3	53	40	31	24	32
— Charlotte (FSL)..................	4	2	.667	3.64	10	10	0	0	0	59 1/3	55	28	24	17	30
1990— Tulsa (Texas)..................	5	7	.417	4.27	14	14	4	2	0	86 1/3	88	50	41	36	48
— Oklahoma City (A.A.)..................	2	7	.222	3.69	12	11	1	1	0	70 2/3	81	39	29	15	36
1991— Oklahoma City (A.A.)..................	5	6	.455	3.49	18	13	1	0	1	95 1/3	98	39	37	34	63
— Texas (A.L.)..................	4	0	1.000	3.61	34	2	0	0	1	57 1/3	54	24	23	18	51
1992— Texas (A.L.)..................	2	4	.333	5.95	40	0	0	0	1	42 1/3	48	29	28	31	26
— Oklahoma City (A.A.)..................	1	1	.500	4.32	9	2	0	0	1	16 2/3	17	8	8	7	13
1993— Jackson (Texas)■..................	6	5	.545	3.67	17	17	0	0	0	103	116	55	42	29	74
— Tucson (PCL)..................	5	0	1.000	3.55	16	4	0	0	2	33	40	14	13	11	34
1994— Edmonton (PCL)■..................	4	4	.500	4.29	13	12	3	0	0	84	88	43	40	22	46
— Florida (N.L.)..................	2	1	.667	3.35	24	2	0	0	0	43	45	16	16	9	21
1995— Florida (N.L.)..................	4	4	.500	3.38	57	0	0	0	3	82 2/3	70	32	31	27	72
— Charlotte (I.L.)..................	0	0	...	4.91	2	0	0	0	0	3 2/3	5	2	2	0	5
1996— Florida (N.L.)..................	2	4	.333	4.91	57	0	0	0	4	55	59	33	30	27	49
— Baltimore (A.L.)■..................	2	2	.500	3.38	14	0	0	0	0	18 2/3	20	7	7	7	13
1997— Baltimore (A.L.)..................	4	4	.500	4.41	57	0	0	0	1	63 1/3	63	35	31	36	39
1998— Baltimore (A.L.)..................	0	1	.000	6.20	17	0	0	0	0	20 1/3	26	15	14	8	10
— Bowie (East.)..................	0	0	...	6.00	1	1	0	0	0	3	3	2	2	1	2
— Rochester (I.L.)..................	0	1	.000	3.00	1	1	0	0	0	3	4	1	1	2	4
— Edmonton (PCL)■..................	2	2	.500	4.57	13	8	0	0	1	43 1/3	47	22	22	11	33
1999— Omaha (PCL)■..................	1	0	1.000	1.65	7	0	0	0	0	16 1/3	11	4	3	5	11
— Kansas City (A.L.)..................	2	1	.667	4.38	24	1	0	0	1	39	44	21	19	17	19
— Gulf Coast Royals (GCL)....	0	0	...	0.00	1	1	0	0	0	2	0	0	0	0	2
— Wichita (Texas)..................	0	0	...	4.50	1	0	0	0	0	2	2	1	1	0	2
A.L. totals (6 years)	14	12	.538	4.56	186	3	0	0	3	241	255	131	122	117	158
N.L. totals (3 years)	8	9	.471	3.84	138	2	0	0	7	180 2/3	174	81	77	63	142
Major League totals (8 years)	22	21	.512	4.25	324	5	0	0	10	421 2/3	429	212	199	180	300

DIVISION SERIES RECORD

Year League	W	L	Pct.	ERA	G	GS	CG	ShO	Sv.	IP	H	R	ER	BB	SO
1996— Baltimore (A.L.)..................	0	0	...	0.00	3	0	0	0	0	2 2/3	3	0	0	1	2
1997— Baltimore (A.L.)..................	0	0	...	18.00	1	0	0	0	0	1	2	2	2	0	1
Division series totals (2 years)	0	0	...	4.91	4	0	0	0	0	3 2/3	5	2	2	1	3

CHAMPIONSHIP SERIES RECORD

Year League	W	L	Pct.	ERA	G	GS	CG	ShO	Sv.	IP	H	R	ER	BB	SO
1996— Baltimore (A.L.)..................	0	0	...	0.00	3	0	0	0	0	2 1/3	0	0	0	2	3

MATOS, LUIS　　　　　　OF　　　　　ORIOLES

PERSONAL: Born October 30, 1978, in Bayamon, Puerto Rico. ... 6-0/179. ... Bats left, throws right. ... Full name: Luis D. Matos.
HIGH SCHOOL: Disciple of Christ Academy (Bayamon, Puerto Rico).
TRANSACTIONS/CAREER NOTES: Selected by Baltimore Orioles organization in 10th round of free-agent draft (June 4, 1996).

Year Team (League)	Pos.	G	AB	R	H	2B	3B	HR	RBI	Avg.	BB	SO	SB	PO	A	E	Avg.
1996— GC Orioles (GCL)........	OF	43	130	21	38	2	0	0	13	.292	15	18	12	56	3	1	.983
1997— Delmarva (SAL).........	OF	36	119	10	25	1	2	0	13	.210	9	21	8	66	3	2	.972
— Bluefield (Appl.)........	OF	61	240	37	66	7	3	2	35	.275	20	36	26	125	4	3	.977
1998— Delmarva (SAL)........	OF	133	503	73	137	26	6	7	32	.272	38	90	42	254	12	10	.964
— Bowie (East.).............	OF	5	19	2	5	0	0	1	3	.263	1	1	1	4	1	1	.833
1999— Frederick (Caro.).......	OF-DH	68	273	40	81	15	1	7	41	.297	20	35	27	143	6	2	.987
— Bowie (East.).............	OF	66	283	41	67	11	1	9	36	.237	15	39	14	152	8	3	.982

MATOS, PASCUAL   C   BRAVES

PERSONAL: Born December 23, 1974, in Barahona, Dominican Republic. ... 6-2/160. ... Bats right, throws right. ... Full name: Pascual Cuevas Matos.
HIGH SCHOOL: Colegio Divino Tesoro (Barahona, Dominican Republic).
TRANSACTIONS/CAREER NOTES: Signed as non-drafted free agent by Atlanta Braves organization (March 5, 1992).
STATISTICAL NOTES: Led Pioneer League catchers with three double plays in 1994. ... Led Carolina League catchers with 26 passed balls and tied for league lead with eight double plays in 1997.

								BATTING						FIELDING		
Year Team (League)	Pos.	G	AB	R	H	2B	3B	HR	RBI	Avg.	BB	SO	SB	PO	A	E	Avg.
1992— Dom. Braves (DSL)	C	19	58	6	19	4	1	1	14	.328	6	12	0	105	15	3	.976
— GC Braves (GCL)	C	13	33	3	5	1	0	0	0	.152	10	12	0	97	11	0	1.000
1993— GC Braves (GCL)	C	36	119	12	27	5	1	0	15	.227	3	32	3	259	39	10	.968
1994— Idaho Falls (Pio.)	C	43	157	22	40	7	1	7	29	.255	2	39	7	226	48	13	.955
— Macon (SAL)	C	11	29	1	5	2	0	0	2	.172	0	10	1	48	5	6	.898
1995— Macon (SAL)	C	72	238	23	44	11	1	5	26	.185	11	86	2	498	76	9	.985
1996— Durham (Caro.)	C	67	219	24	49	9	3	6	28	.224	7	70	6	394	54	8	.982
1997— Durham (Caro.)	C	117	430	51	104	18	3	18	50	.242	14	122	4	783	*109	*13	.986
1998— Greenville (Sou.)	C	99	338	40	84	16	1	12	58	.249	14	102	4	690	99	*15	.981
1999— Richmond (I.L.)	C	66	224	17	47	7	0	3	21	.210	6	47	3	456	43	5	.990
— Atlanta (N.L.)	C	6	8	0	1	0	0	0	2	.125	0	1	0	13	1	0	1.000
Major League totals (1 year)		6	8	0	1	0	0	0	2	.125	0	1	0	13	1	0	1.000

MATTHEWS, GARY   OF   PADRES

PERSONAL: Born August 25, 1974, in San Francisco. ... 6-3/200. ... Bats both, throws right. ... Full name: Gary Nathaniel Matthews Jr. ... Son of Gary Matthews, batting coach with Toronto Blue Jays (1997-99), and outfielder with five major league teams (1972-87).
HIGH SCHOOL: Granada Hills (Calif.).
JUNIOR COLLEGE: Mission College (Calif.).
TRANSACTIONS/CAREER NOTES: Selected by San Diego Padres organization in 13th round of free-agent draft (June 3, 1993).

								BATTING						FIELDING		
Year Team (League)	Pos.	G	AB	R	H	2B	3B	HR	RBI	Avg.	BB	SO	SB	PO	A	E	Avg.
1994— Spokane (N.W.)	OF-2B	52	191	23	40	6	1	0	18	.209	19	58	3	96	2	4	.961
1995— Clinton (Midw.)	OF	128	421	57	100	18	4	2	40	.238	68	109	28	245	9	9	.966
1996— Rancho Cuca. (Calif.) .	OF	123	435	65	118	21	11	7	54	.271	60	102	7	218	7	16	.934
1997— Rancho Cuca. (Calif.) .	OF	69	268	66	81	15	4	8	40	.302	49	57	10	110	6	5	.959
— Mobile (Sou.)	OF	28	90	14	22	4	1	2	12	.244	15	29	3	45	3	2	.960
1998— Mobile (Sou.)	OF	72	254	62	78	15	4	7	51	.307	55	50	11	184	8	1	.995
1999— Las Vegas (PCL)	OF	121	422	57	108	22	3	9	52	.256	58	104	17	273	7	7	.976
— San Diego (N.L.)	OF	23	36	4	8	0	0	0	7	.222	9	9	2	22	0	0	1.000
Major League totals (1 year)		23	36	4	8	0	0	0	7	.222	9	9	2	22	0	0	1.000

MATTHEWS, MIKE   P   CARDINALS

M

PERSONAL: Born October 24, 1973, in Fredericksburg, Va. ... 6-2/175. ... Throws left, bats left. ... Full name: Michael Scott Matthews.
HIGH SCHOOL: Woodbridge Senior (Va.).
JUNIOR COLLEGE: Montgomery-Rockville College (Md.).
TRANSACTIONS/CAREER NOTES: Selected by Cleveland Indians organization in second round of free-agent draft (June 1, 1992). ... On Watertown disabled list (June 17-September 12, 1993). ... On disabled list (June 7-28, 1995). ... On Buffalo disabled list (June 8-July 1, 1998). ... Traded by Indians to Boston Red Sox for IF Jose Olmeda (August 4, 1999). ... Traded by Red Sox with C David Menham to St. Louis Cardinals for P Kent Mercker (August 24, 1999).
STATISTICAL NOTES: Tied for Eastern League lead with four balks in 1997.

Year League	W	L	Pct.	ERA	G	GS	CG	ShO	Sv.	IP	H	R	ER	BB	SO
1992— Burlington (Appl.).................	7	0	•1.000	*1.01	10	10	0	0	0	62 1/3	33	13	7	27	55
— Watertown (NY-P)	1	0	1.000	3.27	2	2	2	0	0	11	10	4	4	8	5
1993— Watertown (NY-P)							Did not play.								
1994— Columbus (SAL).................	6	8	.429	3.08	23	23	0	0	0	119 2/3	120	53	41	44	99
1995— Canton/Akron (East.).........	5	8	.385	5.93	15	15	1	0	0	74 1/3	82	62	49	43	37
1996— Canton/Akron (East.).........	9	11	.450	4.66	27	27	3	0	0	162 1/3	178	96	84	74	112
1997— Buffalo (A.A.).................	0	2	.000	7.71	5	5	0	0	0	21	32	19	18	10	17
— Akron (East.).................	6	8	.429	3.82	19	19	3	1	0	113	116	62	48	57	69
1998— Buffalo (I.L.).................	9	6	.600	4.63	24	23	0	0	0	130 1/3	137	79	67	68	86
1999— Buffalo (I.L.).................	1	2	.333	7.59	25	0	0	0	0	21 1/3	23	18	18	18	16
— Akron (East.).................	0	5	.000	8.77	6	6	0	0	0	25 2/3	36	30	25	15	10
— Trenton (East.)■.............	0	0	...	4.63	3	3	0	0	0	11 2/3	11	7	6	9	8
— Arkansas (Texas)■.............	2	0	1.000	0.00	2	2	1	0	0	12	3	0	0	1	10

MAURER, DAVID   P   GIANTS

PERSONAL: Born February 23, 1975, in Minneapolis. ... 6-2/205. ... Throws left, bats right. ... Full name: David Charles Maurer. ... Brother of Mike Maurer, pitcher, Oakland Athletics organization.
HIGH SCHOOL: Apple Valley (Minn.).
COLLEGE: Oklahoma State.
TRANSACTIONS/CAREER NOTES: Selected by San Diego Padres organization in 11th round of free-agent draft (June 3, 1997). ... Selected by San Francisco Giants from Padres organization in Rule 5 major league draft (December 13, 1999).

Year League	W	L	Pct.	ERA	G	GS	CG	ShO	Sv.	IP	H	R	ER	BB	SO
1997— Clinton (Midw.)	0	4	.000	2.88	25	0	0	0	3	34 1/3	24	15	11	15	43
1998— Rancho Cuca. (Calif.)	5	2	.714	2.70	48	0	0	0	5	83 1/3	56	27	25	46	93
1999— Mobile (Sou.).................	4	4	.500	3.63	54	0	0	0	3	72	59	30	29	26	59

PERSONAL: Born July 14, 1968, in Rochester, N.Y. ... 6-4/225. ... Bats left, throws right. ... Full name: Derrick Brant May. ... Son of Dave May, outfielder with five major league teams (1967-78).
HIGH SCHOOL: Newark (Del.).
TRANSACTIONS/CAREER NOTES: Selected by Chicago Cubs organization in first round (ninth pick overall) of free-agent draft (June 2, 1986). ... On Iowa disabled list (April 14-May 27 and June 6-24, 1991). ... Granted free agency (April 7, 1995). ... Signed by New Orleans, Milwaukee Brewers organization (April 12, 1995). ... Traded by Brewers to Houston Astros for a player to be named later (June 21, 1995); Brewers acquired IF Tommy Nevers to complete deal (July 21, 1996). ... On disabled list (June 20-July 5, 1996). ... Granted free agency (December 20, 1996). ... Signed by Philadelphia Phillies organization (January 29, 1997). ... Released by Phillies (August 6, 1997). ... Signed by Montreal Expos organization (March 30, 1998). ... Granted free agency (October 1, 1998). ... Re-signed by Expos organization (January 13, 1999). ... Released by Expos (April 8, 1999). ... Signed to play for Monterrey, Mexican League (April 1999). ... Signed by Baltimore Orioles organization (June 3, 1999). ... Granted free agency (October 12, 1999). ... Re-signed by Orioles organization (November 11, 1999).
STATISTICAL NOTES: Tied for Carolina League lead in double plays by outfielder with four in 1988. ... Career major league grand slams: 2.

Year	Team (League)	Pos.	G	AB	R	H	2B	3B	HR	RBI	Avg.	BB	SO	SB	PO	A	E	Avg.
1986—	Wytheville (Appl.).......	OF	54	178	25	57	6	1	0	23	.320	16	15	17	47	3	5	.909
1987—	Peoria (Midw.)...........	OF	128	439	60	131	19	8	9	52	.298	42	106	5	181	13	8	.960
1988—	Win.-Salem (Car.).......	OF	130	485	76	•148	29	*9	8	65	.305	37	82	13	209	13	10	.957
1989—	Charlotte (Sou.)........	OF	136	491	72	145	26	5	9	70	.295	34	77	19	239	8	•13	.950
1990—	Iowa (A.A.).................	OF-1B	119	459	55	136	27	1	8	69	.296	23	50	5	159	10	8	.955
	—Chicago (N.L.)..........	OF	17	61	8	15	3	0	1	11	.246	2	7	1	34	1	1	.972
1991—	Iowa (A.A.).................	OF	82	310	47	92	18	4	3	49	.297	19	38	7	130	2	5	.964
	—Chicago (N.L.)..........	OF	15	22	4	5	2	0	1	3	.227	2	1	0	11	1	0	1.000
1992—	Iowa (A.A.).................	OF	8	30	6	11	4	1	2	8	.367	3	3	0	11	1	0	1.000
	—Chicago (N.L.)..........	OF	124	351	33	96	11	0	8	45	.274	14	40	5	153	3	5	.969
1993—	Chicago (N.L.)..........	OF	128	465	62	137	25	2	10	77	.295	31	41	10	220	8	7	.970
1994—	Chicago (N.L.)..........	OF	100	345	43	98	19	2	8	51	.284	30	34	3	155	4	1	.994
1995—	Milwaukee (A.L.)■.....	OF	32	113	15	28	3	1	1	9	.248	5	18	0	65	1	2	.971
	—Houston (N.L.)■.......	OF-1B	78	206	29	62	15	1	8	41	.301	19	24	5	74	0	2	.974
1996—	Houston (N.L.).........	OF	109	259	24	65	12	3	5	33	.251	30	33	2	125	5	4	.970
1997—	Philadelphia (N.L.)■ ..	OF	83	149	8	34	5	1	1	13	.228	8	26	4	69	4	3	.961
1998—	Montreal (N.L.)■......	OF-DH	85	180	13	43	8	0	5	15	.239	11	24	0	57	3	1	.984
	—Ottawa (I.L.).........	OF-DH	21	69	16	26	6	0	6	21	.377	13	7	0	23	1	1	.960
1999—	Monterrey (Mex.)■		32	108	19	35	5	0	4	29	.324	28	10	...	...	...	...	...
	—Rochester (I.L.)■......	OF-DH	71	295	39	82	19	3	5	43	.278	22	28	4	116	7	4	.969
	—Baltimore (A.L.).......	DH-OF	26	49	5	13	0	0	4	12	.265	4	6	0	7	1	0	1.000
American League totals (2 years)			58	162	20	41	3	1	5	21	.253	9	24	0	72	2	2	.974
National League totals (9 years)			739	2038	224	555	100	9	47	289	.272	147	230	30	898	29	24	.975
Major League totals (10 years)			797	2200	244	596	103	10	52	310	.271	156	254	30	970	31	26	.975

PERSONAL: Born April 19, 1968, in Loma Linda, Calif. ... 6-1/192. ... Bats left, throws right. ... Full name: Brent Danem Mayne.
HIGH SCHOOL: Costa Mesa (Calif.).
JUNIOR COLLEGE: Orange Coast College (Calif.).
COLLEGE: Cal State Fullerton.
TRANSACTIONS/CAREER NOTES: Selected by Kansas City Royals organization in first round (13th pick overall) of free-agent draft (June 5, 1989). ... On disabled list (July 24, 1989-remainder of season). ... Traded by Royals to New York Mets for OF Al Shirley (December 19, 1995). ... Granted free agency (December 7, 1996). ... Signed by Seattle Mariners organization (January 10, 1997). ... Released by Mariners (March 28, 1997). ... Signed by Oakland Athletics organization (April 8, 1997). ... Granted free agency (October 30, 1997). ... Signed by San Francisco Giants (November 21, 1997). ... Granted free agency (October 28, 1999). ... Signed by Colorado Rockies (December 9, 1999).
STATISTICAL NOTES: Led A.L. catchers with 11 double plays in 1995. ... Career major league grand slams: 2.

Year	Team (League)	Pos.	G	AB	R	H	2B	3B	HR	RBI	Avg.	BB	SO	SB	PO	A	E	Avg.
1989—	Baseball City (FSL).....	C	7	24	5	13	3	1	0	8	.542	0	3	0	31	2	0	1.000
1990—	Memphis (Sou.).........	C	115	412	48	110	16	3	2	61	.267	52	51	5	591	61	11	.983
	—Kansas City (A.L.)......	C	5	13	2	3	0	0	0	1	.231	3	3	0	29	3	1	.970
1991—	Kansas City (A.L.)......	C-DH	85	231	22	58	8	0	3	31	.251	23	42	2	425	38	6	.987
1992—	Kansas City (A.L.)......	C-3B-DH	82	213	16	48	10	0	0	18	.225	11	26	0	281	33	3	.991
1993—	Kansas City (A.L.)......	C-DH	71	205	22	52	9	1	2	22	.254	18	31	3	356	27	2	.995
1994—	Kansas City (A.L.)......	C-DH	46	144	19	37	5	1	2	20	.257	14	27	1	246	14	1	.996
1995—	Kansas City (A.L.)......	C	110	307	23	77	18	1	1	27	.251	25	41	0	540	40	3	.995
1996—	New York (N.L.)■......	C	70	99	9	26	6	0	1	6	.263	12	22	0	85	3	0	1.000
1997—	Edmonton (PCL)■	C	2	3	0	0	0	0	0	0	.000	0	1	0	5	0	0	1.000
	—Oakland (A.L.)........	C	85	256	29	74	12	0	6	22	.289	18	33	1	419	36	2	.996
1998—	San Fran. (N.L.)■......	C	94	275	26	75	15	0	3	32	.273	37	47	2	493	39	5	.991
1999—	San Francisco (N.L.) ..	C	117	322	39	97	32	0	2	39	.301	43	65	2	597	47	3	.995
American League totals (7 years)			484	1369	133	349	62	3	14	141	.255	112	203	7	2296	191	18	.993
National League totals (3 years)			281	696	74	198	53	0	6	77	.284	92	134	4	1175	89	8	.994
Major League totals (10 years)			765	2065	207	547	115	3	20	218	.265	204	337	11	3471	280	26	.993

PERSONAL: Born December 10, 1975, in Flint, Mich. ... 6-1/185. ... Throws right, bats both. ... Full name: Joseph E. Mays.
HIGH SCHOOL: Southeast (Bradenton, Fla.).
JUNIOR COLLEGE: Manatee.

TRANSACTIONS/CAREER NOTES: Selected by Seattle Mariners organization in sixth round of free-agent draft (June 2, 1994). ... Traded by Mariners to Minnesota Twins (October 8, 1997), completing deal in which Twins traded OF Roberto Kelly to Mariners for P Jeromy Palki and a player to be named later (August 20, 1997).

Year League	W	L	Pct.	ERA	G	GS	CG	ShO	Sv.	IP	H	R	ER	BB	SO
1995— Arizona Mariners (Ariz.)	2	3	.400	3.25	10	10	0	0	0	44 1/3	41	24	16	18	44
1996— Everett (N.W.)..................	4	4	.500	3.08	13	10	0	0	0	64 1/3	55	33	22	22	56
1997— Wisconsin (Midw.)............	9	3	.750	2.09	13	13	1	0	0	81 2/3	62	20	19	23	79
— Lancaster (Calif.)..............	7	4	.636	4.86	15	15	1	0	0	96 1/3	108	55	52	34	82
1998— Fort Myers (FSL)■..........	7	2	.778	3.04	16	15	0	0	0	94 2/3	101	45	32	23	83
— New Britain (East.)	5	3	.625	4.99	11	10	0	0	0	57 2/3	63	40	32	21	45
1999— Minnesota (A.L.)	6	11	.353	4.37	49	20	2	1	0	171	179	92	83	67	115
Major League totals (1 year)........	6	11	.353	4.37	49	20	2	1	0	171	179	92	83	67	115

McCRACKEN, QUINTON — OF — DEVIL RAYS

PERSONAL: Born March 16, 1970, in Wilmington, N.C. ... 5-7/173. ... Bats both, throws right. ... Full name: Quinton Antoine McCracken.
HIGH SCHOOL: South Brunswick (Southport, N.C.).
COLLEGE: Duke.
TRANSACTIONS/CAREER NOTES: Selected by Colorado Rockies organization in 25th round of free-agent draft (June 1, 1992). ... Selected by Tampa Bay Devil Rays in first round (fourth pick overall) of expansion draft (November 18, 1997). ... On disabled list (May 25, 1999-remainder of season).
STATISTICAL NOTES: Led California League with 12 sacrifice hits in 1993. ... Led Eastern League in caught stealing with 19 in 1994. ... Had 18-game hitting streak (August 18-September 9, 1998).

							BATTING							FIELDING		
Year Team (League)	Pos.	G	AB	R	H	2B	3B	HR	RBI	Avg.	BB	SO	SB	PO	A	E	Avg.
1992— Bend (N.W.)................	2B-OF	67	232	37	65	13	2	0	27	.280	25	39	18	98	129	17	.930
1993— Central Valley (Calif.)...	OF-2B	127	483	94	141	17	7	2	58	.292	78	90	60	153	75	13	.946
1994— New Haven (East.)......	OF	136	544	94	151	27	4	5	39	.278	48	72	36	273	6	8	.972
1995— New Haven (East.)......	OF-DH	55	221	33	79	11	4	1	26	.357	21	32	26	92	10	3	.971
— Colo. Springs (PCL) ...	OF-DH	61	244	55	88	14	6	3	28	.361	23	30	17	104	5	1	.991
— Colorado (N.L.)	OF	3	1	0	0	0	0	0	0	.000	0	1	0	0	0	0	...
1996— Colorado (N.L.)	OF	124	283	50	82	13	6	3	40	.290	32	62	17	131	3	6	.957
1997— Colorado (N.L.)	OF	147	325	69	95	11	1	3	36	.292	42	62	28	195	5	4	.980
1998— Tampa Bay (A.L.)■......	OF	155	614	77	179	38	7	7	59	.292	41	107	19	343	18	3	.992
1999— Tampa Bay (A.L.)........	OF	40	148	20	37	6	1	1	18	.250	14	23	6	80	1	1	.988
American League totals (2 years)		195	762	97	216	44	8	8	77	.283	55	130	25	423	19	4	.991
National League totals (3 years)		274	609	119	177	24	7	6	76	.291	74	125	45	326	8	10	.971
Major League totals (5 years)		469	1371	216	393	68	15	14	153	.287	129	255	70	749	27	14	.982

McCURRY, JEFF — P

PERSONAL: Born January 21, 1970, in Tokyo, Japan. ... 6-6/220. ... Throws right, bats right. ... Full name: Jeffrey Dee McCurry.
HIGH SCHOOL: St. Thomas (Houston).
JUNIOR COLLEGE: San Jacinto College (Texas).
COLLEGE: Texas Christian.
TRANSACTIONS/CAREER NOTES: Selected by Pittsburgh Pirates organization in 20th round of free-agent draft (June 5, 1989); did not sign. ... Selected by Pirates organization in 14th round of free-agent draft (June 4, 1990). ... On Welland disabled list (June 19-July 12, 1991). ... Claimed on waivers by Detroit Tigers (November 20, 1995). ... Selected by Colorado Rockies organization from Tigers organization in Rule 5 minor league draft (December 9, 1996). ... Granted free agency (November 10, 1997). ... Signed by Pirates organization (December 18, 1997). ... Granted free agency (October 14, 1998). ... Signed by Houston Astros organization (January 21, 1999). ... Granted free agency (October 4, 1999).

Year League	W	L	Pct.	ERA	G	GS	CG	ShO	Sv.	IP	H	R	ER	BB	SO
1991— Gulf Coast Pirates (GCL)	1	0	1.000	2.57	6	1	0	0	0	14	19	10	4	4	8
— Welland (NY-P)............	2	1	.667	0.57	9	0	0	0	0	15 2/3	11	4	1	10	18
1992— Augusta (SAL)..................	2	1	.667	3.30	19	0	0	0	7	30	36	14	11	15	34
— Salem (Caro.)..................	6	2	.750	2.87	30	0	0	0	3	62 2/3	49	22	20	24	52
1993— Salem (Caro.)..................	1	4	.200	3.89	41	0	0	0	22	44	41	21	19	15	32
— Carolina (Sou.)...............	2	1	.667	2.79	23	0	0	0	0	29	24	11	9	14	14
1994— Carolina (Sou.)...............	6	5	.545	3.21	48	2	0	0	11	81 1/3	74	35	29	30	60
1995— Calgary (PCL).................	0	0	...	1.80	3	0	0	0	1	5	3	1	1	2	2
— Pittsburgh (N.L.)............	1	4	.200	5.02	55	0	0	0	1	61	82	38	34	30	27
1996— Toledo (I.L.)■...............	1	4	.200	4.76	39	0	0	0	2	58 2/3	66	37	31	26	56
— Detroit (A.L.)................	0	0	...	24.30	2	0	0	0	0	3 1/3	9	9	9	2	0
1997— Colorado (N.L.)■............	1	4	.200	4.43	33	0	0	0	0	40 2/3	43	22	20	20	19
— Colo. Springs (PCL)	1	1	.500	5.09	16	0	0	0	3	17 2/3	17	12	10	6	13
1998— Nashville (PCL)■............	2	5	.286	4.96	40	0	0	0	23	45 1/3	45	26	25	15	34
— Pittsburgh (N.L.)............	1	3	.250	6.52	16	0	0	0	0	19 1/3	24	14	14	9	11
1999— New Orleans (PCL)■........	0	7	.000	4.15	40	0	0	0	14	43 1/3	48	23	20	14	26
— Houston (N.L.)................	0	1	.000	15.75	5	0	0	0	0	4	11	8	7	2	3
A.L. totals (1 year)	0	0	...	24.30	2	0	0	0	0	3 1/3	9	9	9	2	0
N.L. totals (4 years)	3	12	.200	5.40	109	0	0	0	1	125	160	82	75	61	60
Major League totals (5 years).......	3	12	.200	5.89	111	0	0	0	1	128 1/3	169	91	84	63	60

McDONALD, DONZELL — OF — YANKEES

PERSONAL: Born February 20, 1975, in Long Beach, Calif. ... 5-11/165. ... Bats both, throws right. ... Brother of Darnell McDonald, outfielder, Baltimore Orioles organization.
HIGH SCHOOL: Cherry Creek (Colo.).

M

JUNIOR COLLEGE: Yavapai College (Ariz.).
TRANSACTIONS/CAREER NOTES: Selected by New York Yankees organization in 22nd round of free-agent draft (June 1, 1995). ... On disabled list (July 3-August 6, 1997).
STATISTICAL NOTES: Led New York-Pennsylvania League outfielders with 179 total chances in 1996. ... Led Eastern League in caught stealing with 22 in 1998. ... Led Eastern League outfielders with 328 total chances in 1998.

Year Team (League)	Pos.	G	AB	R	H	2B	3B	HR	RBI	Avg.	BB	SO	SB	PO	A	E	Avg.
													BATTING			FIELDING	
1995— GC Yankees (GCL)......	OF	28	110	23	26	5	1	0	9	.236	16	24	11	44	0	3	.936
1996— Oneonta (NY-P).........	OF	74	282	57	78	8	*10	2	30	.277	43	62	*54	*169	4	6	.966
1997— Tampa (FSL)..............	OF	77	297	69	88	23	8	3	23	.296	48	75	39	173	3	4	.978
1998— Norwich (East.).........	OF	134	495	80	125	20	7	6	36	.253	55	127	35	*312	8	8	.976
— Tampa (FSL)..............	OF	5	18	6	6	1	2	0	2	.333	2	7	2	14	0	0	1.000
1999— Norwich (East.).........	OF-DH	137	533	95	145	19	10	4	33	.272	90	110	54	314	8	9	.973

McDONALD, JASON   OF   RANGERS

PERSONAL: Born March 20, 1972, in Modesto, Calif. ... 5-7/182. ... Bats both, throws right. ... Full name: Jason Adam McDonald.
HIGH SCHOOL: Elk Grove (Calif.) Unified School.
COLLEGE: Houston.
TRANSACTIONS/CAREER NOTES: Selected by Oakland Athletics organization in fourth round of free-agent draft (June 3, 1993). ... On Oakland disabled list (April 19-May 4 and May 24-August 4, 1998); included rehabilitation assignments to Edmonton (April 30-May 4) and Huntsville (July 27-August 4). ... Granted free agency (October 15, 1999). ... Signed by Texas Rangers organization (January 10, 2000).
STATISTICAL NOTES: Led California League shortstops with 43 errors in 1995. ... Tied for Pacific Coast League lead in being hit by pitch with 15 in 1996. ... Led Pacific Coast League second basemen with 254 putouts, 352 assists, 24 errors, 630 total chances and 75 double plays in 1996.

Year Team (League)	Pos.	G	AB	R	H	2B	3B	HR	RBI	Avg.	BB	SO	SB	PO	A	E	Avg.
													BATTING			FIELDING	
1993— S. Oregon (N'west).....	2B	35	112	26	33	5	2	0	8	.295	31	17	22	70	77	7	.955
1994— W. Mich. (Mid.)	2B-OF-SS	116	404	67	96	11	*9	2	31	.238	81	87	52	253	167	21	.952
1995— Modesto (Calif.)	SS-OF-2B	133	493	109	129	25	7	6	50	.262	*110	84	*70	247	246	†50	.908
1996— Edmonton (PCL)	2B-OF-DH	137	479	71	114	7	5	8	46	.238	63	82	33	†302	†352	†25	.963
1997— Edmonton (PCL)	OF-DH	79	276	74	73	14	6	4	30	.264	74	58	31	187	10	5	.975
— Oakland (A.L.)	OF	78	236	47	62	11	4	4	14	.263	36	49	13	151	3	5	.969
1998— Oakland (A.L.)	OF-DH	70	175	25	44	9	0	1	16	.251	27	33	10	122	7	6	.956
— Edmonton (PCL)	OF	12	43	12	10	1	1	2	5	.233	15	11	7	37	3	0	1.000
— Huntsville (Sou.)	OF-DH	7	20	9	6	2	0	2	4	.300	8	6	4	10	1	0	1.000
1999— Oakland (A.L.)	OF-DH-2B	100	187	26	39	2	1	3	8	.209	25	48	6	150	3	1	.994
— Vancouver (PCL)	OF-2B	32	129	27	42	9	1	4	18	.326	19	33	8	79	6	1	.988
Major League totals (3 years)		248	598	98	145	22	5	8	38	.242	88	130	29	423	13	12	.973

McDONALD, JOHN   SS/2B   INDIANS

M

PERSONAL: Born September 24, 1974, in New London, Conn. ... 5-11/175. ... Bats right, throws right. ... Full name: John J. McDonald.
HIGH SCHOOL: East Lyme (Conn.).
JUNIOR COLLEGE: Univ. of Connecticut-Avery Point.
COLLEGE: Providence.
TRANSACTIONS/CAREER NOTES: Selected by Cleveland Indians organization in 12th round of free-agent draft (June 4, 1996).
STATISTICAL NOTES: Led Carolina League shortstops with 647 total chances and 105 double plays in 1997. ... Led Eastern League shortstops with 672 total chances in 1998. .

Year Team (League)	Pos.	G	AB	R	H	2B	3B	HR	RBI	Avg.	BB	SO	SB	PO	A	E	Avg.
													BATTING			FIELDING	
1996— Watertown (NY-P)	SS	75	278	48	75	11	0	2	26	.270	32	49	11	85	228	18	.946
1997— Kinston (Caro.)...........	SS	130	541	77	140	27	3	5	53	.259	51	75	6	*209	*413	25	*.961
1998— Akron (East.)	SS	132	514	68	118	18	2	2	43	.230	43	61	17	*242	407	23	.966
1999— Akron (East.)	SS-2B	55	226	31	67	12	0	1	26	.296	19	26	7	102	153	8	.970
— Buffalo (I.L.)	SS-3B-2B	66	237	30	75	12	1	0	25	.316	11	23	6	87	194	13	.956
— Cleveland (A.L.)..........	2B-SS	18	21	2	7	0	0	0	0	.333	0	3	0	8	21	1	.967
Major League totals (1 year)		18	21	2	7	0	0	0	0	.333	0	3	0	8	21	1	.967

McDOWELL, JACK   P

PERSONAL: Born January 16, 1966, in Van Nuys, Calif. ... 6-5/190. ... Throws right, bats right. ... Full name: Jack Burns McDowell. ... Nickname: Blackjack.
HIGH SCHOOL: Notre Dame (Van Nuys, Calif.).
COLLEGE: Stanford.
TRANSACTIONS/CAREER NOTES: Selected by Boston Red Sox organization in 20th round of free-agent draft (June 4, 1984); did not sign. ... Selected by Chicago White Sox organization in first round (fifth pick overall) of free-agent draft (June 2, 1987). ... On suspended list (August 20-24, 1991). ... Traded by White Sox to New York Yankees for P Keith Heberling and a player to be named later (December 14, 1994); White Sox acquired OF Lyle Mouton to complete deal (April 22, 1995). ... Granted free agency (October 31, 1995). ... Signed by Cleveland Indians (December 14, 1995). ... On disabled list (July 22-August 9, 1996 and May 13, 1997-remainder of season). ... Granted free agency (November 5, 1997). ... Signed by Anaheim Angels (February 27, 1998). ... On Anaheim disabled list (April 27-May 21 and June 1-August 15, 1998); included rehabilitation assignments to Vancouver (July 25-29), Lake Elsinore (July 30-August 9) and Midland (August 10-15). ... On suspended list (August 15-18, 1998). ... Granted free agency (October 23, 1998). ... Re-signed by Angels (December 7, 1998). ... On Anaheim disabled list (March 24-July 23, 1999); included rehabilitation assignments to Edmonton (July 5-14) and Lake Elsinore (July 15-23). ... Released by Angels (August 9, 1999).

HONORS: Named righthanded pitcher on THE SPORTING NEWS A.L. All-Star team (1992-93). ... Named A.L. Pitcher of the Year by THE SPORTING NEWS (1993). ... Named A.L. Cy Young Award winner by Baseball Writers' Association of America (1993).

STATISTICAL NOTES: Pitched 15-1 one-hit, complete-game victory against Milwaukee (July 14, 1991).

Year League	W	L	Pct.	ERA	G	GS	CG	ShO	Sv.	IP	H	R	ER	BB	SO
1987— GC White Sox (GCL)	0	1	.000	2.57	2	1	0	0	0	7	4	3	2	1	12
— Birmingham (Sou.)...........	1	2	.333	7.84	4	4	1	1	0	20²/₃	19	20	18	8	17
— Chicago (A.L.)	3	0	1.000	1.93	4	4	0	0	0	28	16	6	6	6	15
1988— Chicago (A.L.)	5	10	.333	3.97	26	26	1	0	0	158²/₃	147	85	70	68	84
1989— Vancouver (PCL)	5	6	.455	6.13	16	16	1	0	0	86²/₃	97	60	59	50	65
— GC White Sox (GCL)	2	0	1.000	0.75	4	4	0	0	0	24	19	2	2	4	25
1990— Chicago (A.L.)	14	9	.609	3.82	33	33	4	0	0	205	189	93	87	77	165
1991— Chicago (A.L.)	17	10	.630	3.41	35	•35	*15	3	0	253²/₃	212	97	96	82	191
1992— Chicago (A.L.)	20	10	.667	3.18	34	34	*13	1	0	260²/₃	247	95	92	75	178
1993— Chicago (A.L.)	*22	10	.688	3.37	34	34	10	*4	0	256²/₃	261	104	96	69	158
1994— Chicago (A.L.)	10	9	.526	3.73	25	•25	6	2	0	181	186	82	75	42	127
1995— New York (A.L.)■...........	15	10	.600	3.93	30	30	*8	2	0	217²/₃	211	106	95	78	157
1996— Cleveland (A.L.)■............	13	9	.591	5.11	30	30	5	1	0	192	214	119	109	67	141
1997— Cleveland (A.L.)................	3	3	.500	5.09	8	6	0	0	0	40²/₃	44	25	23	18	38
1998— Anaheim (A.L.)■.............	5	3	.625	5.09	14	14	0	0	0	76	96	45	43	19	45
— Vancouver (PCL)	0	0	...	6.00	1	1	0	0	0	3	4	2	2	2	0
— Lake Elsinore (Calif.)	0	1	.000	9.00	1	1	0	0	0	5	7	5	5	0	4
— Midland (Texas).................	0	1	.000	3.86	1	1	0	0	0	7	5	3	3	2	5
1999— Edmonton (PCL)	1	0	1.000	5.73	2	2	0	0	0	11	12	7	7	3	2
— Lake Elsinore (Calif.)	0	1	.000	7.36	1	1	0	0	0	7¹/₃	11	7	6	1	7
— Anaheim (A.L.)	0	4	.000	8.05	4	4	0	0	0	19	31	17	17	5	12
Major League totals (12 years)	**127**	**87**	**.593**	**3.85**	**277**	**275**	**62**	**13**	**0**	**1889**	**1854**	**874**	**809**	**606**	**1311**

DIVISION SERIES RECORD

RECORDS: Holds A.L. career record for most hit batsmen—2.

Year League	W	L	Pct.	ERA	G	GS	CG	ShO	Sv.	IP	H	R	ER	BB	SO
1995— New York (A.L.)................	0	2	.000	9.00	2	1	0	0	0	7	8	7	7	4	6
1996— Cleveland (A.L.)...............	0	0	...	6.35	1	1	0	0	0	5²/₃	6	4	4	1	5
Division series totals (2 years)	**0**	**2**	**.000**	**7.82**	**3**	**2**	**0**	**0**	**0**	**12²/₃**	**14**	**11**	**11**	**5**	**11**

CHAMPIONSHIP SERIES RECORD

RECORDS: Shares single-game record for most hits allowed—13 (October 5, 1993); and earned runs allowed—7 (October 5, 1993).

Year League	W	L	Pct.	ERA	G	GS	CG	ShO	Sv.	IP	H	R	ER	BB	SO
1993— Chicago (A.L.)	0	2	.000	10.00	2	2	0	0	0	9	18	10	10	5	5

ALL-STAR GAME RECORD

Year League	W	L	Pct.	ERA	GS	CG	ShO	Sv.	IP	H	R	ER	BB	SO
1991— American	0	0	...	0.00	0	0	0	0	2	1	0	0	2	0
1992— American	0	0	...	0.00	0	0	0	0	1	0	0	0	0	0
1993— American	1	0	1.000	0.00	0	0	0	0	1	0	0	0	0	0
All-Star Game totals (3 years)	**1**	**0**	**1.000**	**0.00**	**0**	**0**	**0**	**0**	**4**	**1**	**0**	**0**	**2**	**0**

McELROY, CHUCK   P   ORIOLES

PERSONAL: Born October 1, 1967, in Port Arthur, Texas. ... 6-0/205. ... Throws left, bats left. ... Full name: Charles Dwayne McElroy. ... Name pronounced MACK-il-roy.

HIGH SCHOOL: Lincoln (Port Arthur, Texas).

TRANSACTIONS/CAREER NOTES: Selected by Philadelphia Phillies organization in eighth round of free-agent draft (June 2, 1986). ... Traded by Phillies with P Bob Scanlan to Chicago Cubs for P Mitch Williams (April 7, 1991). ... Traded by Cubs to Cincinnati Reds for P Larry Luebbers, P Mike Anderson and C Darron Cox (December 10, 1993). ... On disabled list (June 7-23, 1995). ... On Cincinnati disabled list (March 28-April 28, 1996); included rehabilitation assignment to Indianapolis (April 12-28). ... Traded by Reds to California Angels for P Lee Smith (May 27, 1996). ... On California disabled list (August 11-28, 1996). ... Angels franchise renamed Anaheim Angels for 1997 season. ... Traded by Angels with C Jorge Fabregas to Chicago White Sox for OF Tony Phillips and C Chad Kreuter (May 18, 1997). ... Selected by Arizona Diamondbacks in third round (67th pick overall) of expansion draft (November 18, 1997). ... Traded by Diamondbacks to Colorado Rockies for OF Harvey Pulliam (November 18, 1997). ... Traded by Rockies with OF Darryl Hamilton to New York Mets for OF Brian McRae, P Rigo Beltran and OF Thomas Johnson (July 31, 1999). ... Traded by Mets to Baltimore Orioles for P Jesse Orosco (December 10, 1999).

MISCELLANEOUS: Appeared in one game as pinch runner with Chicago (1997). ... Appeared in one game as outfielder with one putout for Mets (1999).

Year League	W	L	Pct.	ERA	G	GS	CG	ShO	Sv.	IP	H	R	ER	BB	SO
1986— Utica (NY-P)	4	6	.400	2.95	14	14	5	1	0	94²/₃	85	40	31	28	91
1987— Spartanburg (SAL)	14	4	.778	3.11	24	21	5	2	0	130¹/₃	117	51	45	48	115
— Clearwater (FSL)	1	0	1.000	0.00	2	2	0	0	0	7¹/₃	1	1	0	4	7
1988— Reading (East.).................	9	12	.429	4.50	28	26	4	2	0	160	•173	89	*80	70	92
1989— Reading (East.).................	3	1	.750	2.68	32	0	0	0	12	47	39	14	14	14	39
— Scranton/W.B. (I.L.)	1	2	.333	2.93	14	0	0	0	3	15¹/₃	13	6	5	11	12
— Philadelphia (N.L.)............	0	0	...	1.74	11	0	0	0	0	10¹/₃	12	2	2	4	8
1990— Scranton/W.B. (I.L.)	6	8	.429	2.72	57	1	0	0	7	76	62	24	23	34	78
— Philadelphia (N.L.)............	0	1	.000	7.71	16	0	0	0	0	14	24	13	12	10	16
1991— Chicago (N.L.)■..............	6	2	.750	1.95	71	0	0	0	3	101¹/₃	73	33	22	57	92
1992— Chicago (N.L.)..................	4	7	.364	3.55	72	0	0	0	6	83²/₃	73	40	33	51	83
1993— Chicago (N.L.)..................	2	2	.500	4.56	49	0	0	0	0	47¹/₃	51	30	24	25	31
— Iowa (A.A.)	0	1	.000	4.60	9	0	0	0	2	15²/₃	19	10	8	9	13
1994— Cincinnati (N.L.)■............	1	2	.333	2.34	52	0	0	0	5	57²/₃	52	15	15	15	38
1995— Cincinnati (N.L.)...............	3	4	.429	6.02	44	0	0	0	0	40¹/₃	46	29	27	15	27
1996— Indianapolis (A.A.).............	1	1	.500	2.70	5	3	0	0	0	13¹/₃	11	4	4	4	10
— Cincinnati (N.L.)	2	0	1.000	6.57	12	0	0	0	0	12¹/₃	13	10	9	10	13
— California (A.L.)■.............	5	1	.833	2.95	40	0	0	0	0	36²/₃	32	12	12	13	32

Year League	W	L	Pct.	ERA	G	GS	CG	ShO	Sv.	IP	H	R	ER	BB	SO
1997—Anaheim (A.L.)	0	0	...	3.45	13	0	0	0	0	15 2/3	17	7	6	3	18
—Chicago (A.L.)■	1	3	.250	3.94	48	0	0	0	1	59 1/3	56	29	26	19	44
1998—Colorado (N.L.)■	6	4	.600	2.90	78	0	0	0	2	68 1/3	68	23	22	24	61
1999—Colorado (N.L.)	3	1	.750	6.20	41	0	0	0	0	40 2/3	48	29	28	28	37
—New York (N.L.)■	0	0	...	3.38	15	0	0	0	0	12	5	5	8	7	
A.L. totals (2 years)	6	4	.600	3.55	101	0	0	0	1	111 2/3	105	48	44	35	94
N.L. totals (10 years)	27	23	.540	3.66	461	0	0	0	16	489 1/3	472	229	199	247	413
Major League totals (11 years)	33	27	.550	3.64	562	0	0	0	17	601	577	277	243	282	507

DIVISION SERIES RECORD

Year League	W	L	Pct.	ERA	G	GS	CG	ShO	Sv.	IP	H	R	ER	BB	SO
1999—New York (N.L.)							Did not play.								

CHAMPIONSHIP SERIES RECORD

Year League	W	L	Pct.	ERA	G	GS	CG	ShO	Sv.	IP	H	R	ER	BB	SO
1999—New York (N.L.)							Did not play.								

McEWING, JOE — 2B/OF — CARDINALS

PERSONAL: Born October 19, 1972, in Bristol, Pa. ... 5-11/170. ... Bats right, throws right. ... Full name: Joseph Earl McEwing.
HIGH SCHOOL: Bishop Egan (Fairless Hills, Pa.).
JUNIOR COLLEGE: County College of Morris (N.J.).
TRANSACTIONS/CAREER NOTES: Selected by St. Louis Cardinals organization in 28th round of free-agent draft (June 1, 1992).
STATISTICAL NOTES: Led Arizona League outfielders with 94 putouts, 11 assists, four double plays, 106 total chances and .991 fielding percentage in 1992. ... Led South Atlantic League with 15 sacrifice hits in 1993. ... Led Texas League with 5 sacrifice hits in 1996. ... Tied for Pacific Coast League lead with three double plays by outfielder in 1998. ... Had 25-game hitting streak (June 8-July 4, 1999).

Year Team (League)	Pos.	G	AB	R	H	2B	3B	HR	RBI	Avg.	BB	SO	SB	PO	A	E	Avg.
1992—Ariz. Cardinals (Ariz.)	OF-SS	55	211	*55	71	4	2	0	13	.336	24	18	23	†94	†12	1	.991
1993—Savannah (SAL)	OF	138	511	*94	127	35	1	0	43	.249	89	73	22	262	13	5	.982
1994—Madison (Midw.)	OF	90	346	58	112	24	2	4	47	.324	32	53	18	184	6	5	.974
—St. Petersburg (FSL)	OF-2B	50	197	22	49	7	0	1	20	.249	19	32	8	105	23	2	.985
1995—St. Petersburg (FSL)	2B-OF	75	281	33	64	13	0	1	23	.228	25	49	2	139	176	15	.955
—Arkansas (Texas)	OF-2B	42	121	16	30	4	0	2	12	.248	9	13	3	61	12	0	1.000
1996—Arkansas (Texas)	OF-2B	106	216	27	45	7	3	2	14	.208	13	32	2	134	15	2	†.987
1997—Arkansas (Texas)	OF-2B-1B-3B	103	263	33	68	6	3	4	35	.259	19	39	2	134	24	2	.988
1998—Arkansas (Texas)	OF-SS-P	60	223	45	79	21	4	9	46	.354	21	18	4	130	25	1	.994
—Memphis (PCL)	OF-3B-SS-2B	78	329	52	110	30	7	6	46	.334	21	39	11	143	24	3	.982
—St. Louis (N.L.)	2B-OF	10	20	5	4	1	0	0	1	.200	1	3	0	10	10	0	1.000
1999—St. Louis (N.L.)	2-0-3-1-S	152	513	65	141	28	4	9	44	.275	41	87	7	320	246	11	.981
Major League totals (2 years)		162	533	70	145	29	4	9	45	.272	42	90	7	330	256	11	.982

RECORD AS PITCHER

Year League	W	L	Pct.	ERA	G	GS	CG	ShO	Sv.	IP	H	R	ER	BB	SO
1997—Arkansas (Texas)	0	0	...	27.00	1	0	0	0	0	1/3	1	1	1	0	0
1998—Arkansas (Texas)	0	0	...	27.00	1	0	0	0	0	1	3	3	3	1	1

McGEE, WILLIE — OF

PERSONAL: Born November 2, 1958, in San Francisco. ... 6-1/185. ... Bats both, throws right. ... Full name: Willie Dean McGee.
HIGH SCHOOL: Harry Ellis (Richmond, Calif.).
JUNIOR COLLEGE: Diablo Valley College (Calif.).
TRANSACTIONS/CAREER NOTES: Selected by Chicago White Sox organization in seventh round of free-agent draft (June 8, 1976); did not sign. ... Selected by New York Yankees organization in secondary phase of free-agent draft (January 11, 1977). ... On disabled list (May 22-June 7 and July 14-August 7, 1980; and April 24-June 4, 1981). ... Traded by Yankees organization to St. Louis Cardinals organization for P Bob Sykes (October 21, 1981). ... On Louisville disabled list (April 13-23, 1982). ... On St. Louis disabled list (March 30-April 29, 1983); included rehabilitation assignment to Arkansas (April 18-29). ... On St. Louis disabled list (March 3-27, 1986). ... On disabled list (June 7-July 18, 1989); included rehabilitation assignment to Louisville (July 8-18). ... On St. Louis disabled list (July 26-August 14, 1989). ... Traded by Cardinals to Oakland Athletics for OF Felix Jose, 3B Stan Royer and P Daryl Green (August 29, 1990). ... Granted free agency (November 5, 1990). ... Signed by San Francisco Giants (December 3, 1990). ... On San Francisco disabled list (July 12-August 1, 1991); included rehabilitation assignment to Phoenix (July 28-August 1). ... On disabled list (July 10-30, 1993 and June 8, 1994-remainder of season). ... Granted free agency (October 14, 1994). ... Signed by Pawtucket, Boston Red Sox organization (June 6, 1995). ... Granted free agency (November 3, 1995). ... Signed by Cardinals (December 15, 1995). ... Granted free agency (November 13, 1996). ... Re-signed by Cardinals (December 4, 1996). ... On disabled list (July 12-29, 1997). ... Granted free agency (October 29, 1997). ... Re-signed by Cardinals (December 5, 1997). ... Granted free agency (October 23, 1998). ... Re-signed by Cardinals (December 7, 1998). ... Granted free agency (November 5, 1999).
RECORDS: Holds modern N.L. single-season record for highest batting average by switch hitter (100 or more games)—.353 (1985). ... Shares major league single-season record for fewest double plays by outfielder who led league in double plays—3 (1991).
HONORS: Won N.L. Gold Glove as outfielder (1983, 1985-86). ... Named N.L. Player of the Year by THE SPORTING NEWS (1985). ... Named outfielder on THE SPORTING NEWS N.L. All-Star team (1985). ... Named outfielder on THE SPORTING NEWS N.L. Silver Slugger team (1985). ... Named N.L. Most Valuable Player by Baseball Writers' Association of America (1985).
STATISTICAL NOTES: Hit for the cycle (June 23, 1984). ... Led N.L. in grounding into double plays with 24 in 1987. ... Had 22-game hitting streak (July 5-August 1, 1990). ... Tied for N.L. lead in double plays by outfielder with three in 1991. ... Career major league grand slams: 2.

Year Team (League)	Pos.	G	AB	R	H	2B	3B	HR	RBI	Avg.	BB	SO	SB	PO	A	E	Avg.
1977—Oneonta (NY-P)	OF	65	225	31	53	4	3	2	22	.236	13	65	13	103	5	10	.915
1978—Fort Lauderdale (FSL)	OF	124	423	62	106	6	6	0	37	.251	50	78	25	243	12	9	.966
1979—West Haven (East.)	OF	49	115	21	28	3	1	1	8	.243	13	17	7	88	3	3	.968
—Fort Lauderdale (FSL)	OF	46	176	25	56	8	3	1	18	.318	17	34	16	103	3	2	.981
1980—Nashville (Sou.)	OF	78	223	35	63	4	5	1	22	.283	19	39	7	127	6	6	.957

Year	Team (League)	Pos.	G	AB	R	H	2B	3B	HR	RBI	Avg.	BB	SO	SB	PO	A	E	Avg.
1981—Nashville (Sou.).........	OF	100	388	77	125	20	5	7	63	.322	24	46	24	203	10	6	.973
1982—Louisville (A.A.)■......	OF	13	55	11	16	2	2	1	3	.291	2	7	5	40	0	1	.976
—St. Louis (N.L.)..........	OF	123	422	43	125	12	8	4	56	.296	12	58	24	245	3	11	.958
1983—St. Louis (N.L.)..........	OF	147	601	75	172	22	8	5	75	.286	26	98	39	385	7	5	.987
—Arkansas (Texas)........	OF	7	29	5	8	1	1	0	2	.276	4	6	1	7	0	0	1.000
1984—St. Louis (N.L.)..........	OF	145	571	82	166	19	11	6	50	.291	29	80	43	374	10	6	.985
1985—St. Louis (N.L.)..........	OF	152	612	114	*216	26	*18	10	82	*.353	34	86	56	382	11	9	.978
1986—St. Louis (N.L.)..........	OF	124	497	65	127	22	7	7	48	.256	37	82	19	325	9	3	*.991
1987—St. Louis (N.L.)..........	OF-SS	153	620	76	177	37	11	11	105	.285	24	90	16	354	10	7	.981
1988—St. Louis (N.L.)..........	OF	137	562	73	164	24	6	3	50	.292	32	84	41	348	9	9	.975
1989—St. Louis (N.L.)..........	OF	58	199	23	47	10	2	3	17	.236	10	34	8	118	2	3	.976
—Louisville (A.A.).........	OF	8	27	5	11	4	0	0	4	.407	3	4	3	20	1	1	.955
1990—St. Louis (N.L.)..........	OF	125	501	76	168	32	5	3	62	*.335	38	86	28	341	13	*16	.957
—Oakland (A.L.)■.........	OF-DH	29	113	23	31	3	2	0	15	.274	10	18	3	72	1	1	.986
1991—San Fran. (N.L.)■......	OF	131	497	67	155	30	3	4	43	.312	34	74	17	259	6	6	.978
—Phoenix (PCL)............	OF	4	10	4	5	1	0	0	1	.500	3	1	2	10	0	1	.909
1992—San Francisco (N.L.) ..	OF	138	474	56	141	20	2	1	36	.297	29	88	13	231	11	6	.976
1993—San Francisco (N.L.) ..	OF	130	475	53	143	28	1	4	46	.301	38	67	10	224	9	5	.979
1994—San Francisco (N.L.) ..	OF	45	156	19	44	3	0	5	23	.282	15	24	3	80	2	1	.988
1995—Pawtucket (I.L.)■.......	OF-DH	5	21	9	10	0	0	0	2	.476	0	4	2	7	0	1	.875
—Boston (A.L.).............	OF	67	200	32	57	11	3	2	15	.285	9	41	5	101	7	3	.973
1996—St. Louis (N.L.)■	OF-1B	123	309	52	95	15	2	5	41	.307	18	60	5	142	10	5	.968
1997—St. Louis (N.L.)..........	OF-DH	122	300	29	90	19	4	3	38	.300	22	59	8	99	6	2	.981
1998—St. Louis (N.L.)..........	OF-DH-1B	120	269	27	68	10	1	3	34	.253	14	49	7	102	8	7	.940
1999—St. Louis (N.L.)..........	OF-1B	132	271	25	68	7	0	0	20	.251	17	60	7	112	2	3	.974
American League totals (2 years)		96	313	55	88	14	5	2	30	.281	19	59	8	173	8	4	.978
National League totals (17 years)		2105	7336	955	2166	336	89	77	826	.295	429	1179	344	4121	128	104	.976
Major League totals (18 years)		2201	7649	1010	2254	350	94	79	856	.295	448	1238	352	4294	136	108	.976

DIVISION SERIES RECORD

Year	Team (League)	Pos.	G	AB	R	H	2B	3B	HR	RBI	Avg.	BB	SO	SB	PO	A	E	Avg.
1995—Boston (A.L.)..............	OF-PH	2	4	0	1	0	0	0	1	.250	0	2	0	0	0	0	...
1996—St. Louis (N.L.)...........	OF	3	10	1	1	0	0	0	1	.100	1	3	0	9	0	1	.900
Division series totals (2 years)		5	14	1	2	0	0	0	2	.143	1	5	0	9	0	1	.900

CHAMPIONSHIP SERIES RECORD

RECORDS: Shares single-series record for most triples—2 (1982). ... Shares N.L. career records for most triples—3; and most times caught stealing—4. ... Shares N.L. single-series record for most times caught stealing—3 (1985).

Year	Team (League)	Pos.	G	AB	R	H	2B	3B	HR	RBI	Avg.	BB	SO	SB	PO	A	E	Avg.
1982—St. Louis (N.L.)..........	OF	3	13	4	4	0	2	1	5	.308	0	5	0	12	0	1	.923
1985—St. Louis (N.L.)..........	OF	6	26	6	7	1	0	0	3	.269	3	6	2	18	0	0	1.000
1987—St. Louis (N.L.)..........	OF	7	26	2	8	1	1	0	2	.308	0	5	0	16	0	0	1.000
1990—Oakland (A.L.)	OF-PR-DH	3	9	3	2	1	0	0	0	.222	1	2	2	2	0	0	1.000
1996—St. Louis (N.L.)..........	OF-PH	6	15	0	5	0	0	0	0	.333	0	3	0	5	0	1	.833
Championship series totals (5 years)		25	89	15	26	3	3	1	10	.292	4	21	4	53	0	2	.964

WORLD SERIES RECORD

NOTES: Member of World Series championship team (1982).

Year	Team (League)	Pos.	G	AB	R	H	2B	3B	HR	RBI	Avg.	BB	SO	SB	PO	A	E	Avg.
1982—St. Louis (N.L.)..........	OF	6	25	6	6	0	0	2	5	.240	1	3	2	24	0	0	1.000
1985—St. Louis (N.L.)..........	OF	7	27	2	7	2	0	1	2	.259	1	3	1	15	0	0	1.000
1987—St. Louis (N.L.)..........	OF	7	27	2	10	2	0	0	4	.370	0	9	0	21	1	1	.957
1990—Oakland (A.L.)	OF-PH	4	10	1	2	1	0	0	0	.200	0	2	1	5	0	0	1.000
World Series totals (4 years)		24	89	11	25	5	0	3	11	.281	2	17	4	65	1	1	.985

ALL-STAR GAME RECORD

Year	League	Pos.	AB	R	H	2B	3B	HR	RBI	Avg.	BB	SO	SB	PO	A	E	Avg.
1983—National	OF	2	0	1	0	0	0	0	.500	0	0	0	2	0	0	1.000
1985—National	OF	2	0	1	1	0	0	2	.500	0	0	0	1	0	0	1.000
1987—National	OF	4	0	0	0	0	0	0	.000	0	0	0	2	0	0	1.000
1988—National	PR-OF	2	0	0	0	0	0	0	.000	0	0	0	1	0	0	1.000
All-Star Game totals (4 years)		10	0	2	1	0	0	2	.200	0	0	0	6	0	0	1.000

M

McGLINCHY, KEVIN　　　　　P　　　　　BRAVES

PERSONAL: Born June 28, 1977, in Malden, Mass. ... 6-5/220. ... Throws right, bats right. ... Full name: Kevin Michael McGlinchy.
HIGH SCHOOL: Malden (Mass.).
JUNIOR COLLEGE: Central Florida Community College.
TRANSACTIONS/CAREER NOTES: Selected by Atlanta Braves organization in fifth round of free-agent draft (June 1, 1995).

Year	League	W	L	Pct.	ERA	G	GS	CG	ShO	Sv.	IP	H	R	ER	BB	SO
1996—Danville (Appl.).................	3	2	.600	1.13	13	13	0	0	0	72	52	21	9	11	77
—Eugene (N.W.).................	0	0	...	5.40	2	2	0	0	0	6²/₃	7	5	4	1	5
1997—Durham (Caro.)	3	7	.300	4.90	26	26	0	0	0	139²/₃	145	78	76	39	113
1998—Danville (Caro.)	9	8	.529	2.91	22	22	1	0	0	142¹/₃	122	55	46	29	129
—Greenville (Sou.).................	1	1	.500	5.18	6	6	0	0	0	33	35	19	19	15	20
1999—Atlanta (N.L.).....................	7	3	.700	2.82	64	0	0	0	0	70¹/₃	66	25	22	30	67
Major League totals (1 year).........	7	3	.700	2.82	64	0	0	0	0	70¹/₃	66	25	22	30	67

Year League	W	L	Pct.	ERA	G	GS	CG	ShO	Sv.	IP	H	R	ER	BB	SO
1999—Atlanta (N.L.)	0	0	...	0.00	1	0	0	0	0	$1/_3$	0	0	0	0	0

CHAMPIONSHIP SERIES RECORD

Year League	W	L	Pct.	ERA	G	GS	CG	ShO	Sv.	IP	H	R	ER	BB	SO
1999—Atlanta (N.L.)	0	1	.000	18.00	1	0	0	0	0	1	2	2	2	4	1

WORLD SERIES RECORD

Year League	W	L	Pct.	ERA	G	GS	CG	ShO	Sv.	IP	H	R	ER	BB	SO
1999—Atlanta (N.L.)	0	0	...	0.00	1	0	0	0	0	2	2	0	0	1	2

McGRIFF, FRED   1B   DEVIL RAYS

PERSONAL: Born October 31, 1963, in Tampa. ... 6-3/215. ... Bats left, throws left. ... Full name: Frederick Stanley McGriff. ... Cousin of Terry McGriff, catcher with four major league teams (1987-90, 1993 and 1994); and uncle of Charles Johnson, catcher, Baltimore Orioles.
HIGH SCHOOL: Jefferson (Tampa).
TRANSACTIONS/CAREER NOTES: Selected by New York Yankees organization in ninth round of free-agent draft (June 8, 1981). ... Traded by Yankees organization with OF Dave Collins, P Mike Morgan and cash to Toronto Blue Jays for OF/C Tom Dodd and P Dale Murray (December 9, 1982). ... On disabled list (June 5-August 14, 1985). ... Traded by Blue Jays with SS Tony Fernandez to San Diego Padres for OF Joe Carter and 2B Roberto Alomar (December 5, 1990). ... On suspended list (June 23-26, 1992). ... Traded by Padres to Atlanta Braves for OF Melvin Nieves, P Donnie Elliott and OF Vince Moore (July 18, 1993). ... Granted free agency (November 6, 1995). ... Re-signed by Braves (December 2, 1995). ... Traded by Braves to Tampa Bay Devil Rays for a player to be named later or cash (November 18, 1997); Braves received an undisclosed amount of cash to complete deal (April 1, 1998).
RECORDS: Holds major league career record for most major league ballparks, one or more home runs (since 1900)—36. ... Shares major league record for most grand slams in two consecutive games—2 (August 13 and 14, 1991). ... Shares N.L. single-season record for fewest errors by first baseman who led league in errors—12 (1992).
HONORS: Named first baseman on THE SPORTING NEWS A.L. All-Star team (1989). ... Named first baseman on THE SPORTING NEWS A.L. Silver Slugger team (1989). ... Named first baseman on THE SPORTING NEWS N.L. All-Star team (1992-93). ... Named first baseman on THE SPORTING NEWS N.L. Silver Slugger team (1992-93).
STATISTICAL NOTES: Led International League first basemen with .992 fielding percentage, 1,219 putouts, 85 assists, 1,314 total chances and 108 double plays in 1986. ... Tied for International League lead in intentional bases on balls received with eight and in grounding into double plays with 16 in 1986. ... Led A.L. first basemen with 1,592 total chances and 148 double plays in 1989. ... Led N.L. with 26 intentional base on balls received in 1991. ... Led N.L. first basemen with 1,077 total chances in 1994. ... Led N.L. in grounding into double plays with 22 in 1997. ... Led A.L. first basemen with 140 double plays in 1998. ... Career major league grand slams: 5.
MISCELLANEOUS: Holds Tampa Bay Devil Rays all-time records for most runs (148), hits (324), doubles (63), home runs (51), runs batted in (185) and highest career batting average (.296).

Year Team (League)	Pos.	G	AB	R	H	2B	3B	HR	RBI	Avg.	BB	SO	SB	PO	A	E	Avg.
1981—GC Yankees (GCL)	1B	29	81	6	12	2	0	0	9	.148	11	20	0	176	8	7	.963
1982—GC Yankees (GCL)	1B	62	217	38	59	11	1	•9	•41	.272	•48	63	6	514	•56	8	.986
1983—Florence (SAL)■	1B	33	119	26	37	3	1	7	26	.311	20	35	3	250	14	6	.978
—Kinston (Caro.)	1B	94	350	53	85	14	1	21	57	.243	55	112	3	784	57	10	.988
1984—Knoxville (Sou.)	1B	56	189	29	47	13	2	9	25	.249	29	55	0	481	45	10	.981
—Syracuse (I.L.)	1B	70	238	28	56	10	1	13	28	.235	26	89	0	644	45	3	.996
1985—Syracuse (I.L.)	1B	51	176	19	40	8	2	5	20	.227	23	53	0	433	37	5	.989
1986—Syracuse (I.L.)	1B-OF	133	468	69	121	23	4	19	74	.259	83	119	0	†1219	†85	10	†.992
—Toronto (A.L.)	DH-1B	3	5	1	1	0	0	0	0	.200	0	2	0	3	0	0	1.000
1987—Toronto (A.L.)	DH-1B	107	295	58	73	16	0	20	43	.247	60	104	3	108	7	2	.983
1988—Toronto (A.L.)	1B	154	536	100	151	35	4	34	82	.282	79	149	6	1344	93	5	*.997
1989—Toronto (A.L.)	1B-DH	161	551	98	148	27	3	•36	92	.269	119	132	1	1460	115	*17	.989
1990—Toronto (A.L.)	1B-DH	153	557	91	167	21	1	35	88	.300	94	108	5	1246	126	6	.996
1991—San Diego (N.L.)■	1B	153	528	84	147	19	1	31	106	.278	105	135	4	1370	87	14	.990
1992—San Diego (N.L.)	1B	152	531	79	152	30	4	*35	104	.286	96	108	8	1219	108	•12	.991
1993—San Diego (N.L.)	1B	83	302	52	83	11	1	18	46	.275	42	55	4	640	47	12	.983
—Atlanta (N.L.)■	1B	68	255	59	79	18	1	19	55	.310	34	51	1	563	45	5	.992
1994—Atlanta (N.L.)	1B	113	424	81	135	25	1	34	94	.318	50	76	7	*1004	66	7	.994
1995—Atlanta (N.L.)	1B	•144	528	85	148	27	1	27	93	.280	65	99	3	1285	96	5	.996
1996—Atlanta (N.L.)	1B	159	617	81	182	37	1	28	107	.295	68	116	7	1416	124	12	.992
1997—Atlanta (N.L.)	1B	152	564	77	156	25	1	22	97	.277	68	112	5	1191	96	13	.990
1998—Tampa Bay (A.L.)■	1B-DH	151	564	73	160	33	0	19	81	.284	79	118	7	1150	81	6	.995
1999—Tampa Bay (A.L.)	1B-DH	144	529	75	164	30	1	32	104	.310	86	107	1	1037	88	13	.989
American League totals (7 years)		873	3037	496	864	162	9	176	490	.284	517	719	29	6348	510	49	.993
National League totals (7 years)		1024	3749	598	1082	192	11	214	702	.289	528	752	39	8688	669	80	.992
Major League totals (14 years)		1897	6786	1094	1946	354	20	390	1192	.287	1045	1471	68	15036	1179	129	.992

DIVISION SERIES RECORD

RECORDS: Holds N.L. single-game record for most runs batted in—5 (October 7, 1995). ... Shares single-game record for most home runs—2 (October 7, 1995).

Year Team (League)	Pos.	G	AB	R	H	2B	3B	HR	RBI	Avg.	BB	SO	SB	PO	A	E	Avg.
1995—Atlanta (N.L.)	1B	4	18	4	6	0	0	2	6	.333	2	3	0	39	2	0	1.000
1996—Atlanta (N.L.)	1B	3	9	1	3	1	0	1	3	.333	2	1	0	25	3	0	1.000
1997—Atlanta (N.L.)	1B	3	9	4	2	0	0	0	1	.222	3	2	0	27	3	0	1.000
Division series totals (3 years)		10	36	9	11	1	0	3	10	.306	7	6	0	91	8	0	1.000

CHAMPIONSHIP SERIES RECORD

RECORDS: Shares N.L. single-game record for most at-bats—6 (October 14, 1996). ... Shares N.L. single-game record for most runs—4 (October 17, 1996). ... Shares career record for most doubles—7.

Year Team (League)	Pos.	G	AB	R	H	2B	3B	HR	RBI	Avg.	BB	SO	SB	PO	A	E	Avg.
							BATTING								FIELDING		
1989— Toronto (A.L.)..............	1B	5	21	1	3	0	0	0	3	.143	0	4	0	35	2	1	.974
1993— Atlanta (N.L.)..............	1B	6	23	6	10	2	0	1	4	.435	4	7	0	49	4	0	1.000
1995— Atlanta (N.L.)..............	1B	4	16	5	7	4	0	0	0	.438	3	0	0	42	4	0	1.000
1996— Atlanta (N.L.)..............	1B	7	28	6	7	0	1	2	7	.250	3	5	0	55	2	1	.983
1997— Atlanta (N.L.)..............	1B	6	21	0	7	1	0	0	4	.333	2	7	0	41	2	1	.977
Championship series totals (5 years)		28	109	18	34	7	1	3	18	.312	12	23	0	222	14	3	.987

WORLD SERIES RECORD

NOTES: Hit home run in first at-bat (October 21, 1995). ... Member of World Series championship team (1995).

Year Team (League)	Pos.	G	AB	R	H	2B	3B	HR	RBI	Avg.	BB	SO	SB	PO	A	E	Avg.
							BATTING								FIELDING		
1995— Atlanta (N.L.)..............	1B	6	23	5	6	2	0	2	3	.261	3	7	1	68	2	1	.986
1996— Atlanta (N.L.)..............	1B	6	20	4	6	0	0	2	6	.300	6	4	0	62	5	0	1.000
World Series totals (2 years)		12	43	9	12	2	0	4	9	.279	9	11	1	130	7	1	.993

ALL-STAR GAME RECORD

NOTES: Named Most Valuable Player (1994).

Year League	Pos.	AB	R	H	2B	3B	HR	RBI	Avg.	BB	SO	SB	PO	A	E	Avg.
						BATTING								FIELDING		
1992— National	1B	3	0	2	0	0	0	1	.667	0	0	0	7	1	0	1.000
1994— National	PH-1B	1	1	1	0	0	1	2	1.000	0	0	0	0	0	0	...
1995— National	1B	3	0	0	0	0	0	0	.000	0	2	0	5	0	0	1.000
1996— National	1B	2	0	0	0	0	0	0	.000	0	2	0	2	1	0	1.000
All-Star Game totals (4 years)		9	1	3	0	0	1	3	.333	0	4	0	14	2	0	1.000

McGUIRE, RYAN   1B   METS

PERSONAL: Born November 23, 1971, in Bellflower, Calif. ... 6-0/215. ... Bats left, throws left. ... Full name: Ryan Byron McGuire.
HIGH SCHOOL: El Camino Real (Woodland Hills, Calif.).
COLLEGE: UCLA.
TRANSACTIONS/CAREER NOTES: Selected by Boston Red Sox organization in third round of free-agent draft (June 3, 1993). ... Traded by Red Sox with P Rheal Cormier and P Shayne Bennett to Montreal Expos for SS Wil Cordero and P Bryan Eversgerd (January 10, 1996). ... Granted free agency (November 19, 1999). ... Signed by New York Mets organization (December 13, 1999).
STATISTICAL NOTES: Led Carolina League first basemen with 1,312 total chances in 1994.

Year Team (League)	Pos.	G	AB	R	H	2B	3B	HR	RBI	Avg.	BB	SO	SB	PO	A	E	Avg.
							BATTING								FIELDING		
1993— Fort Lauderdale (FSL)	1B	56	213	23	69	12	2	4	38	.324	27	34	2	513	61	5	.991
1994— Lynchburg (Caro.)......	1B	*137	489	70	133	29	0	10	73	.272	79	77	10	*1165	*129	18	.986
1995— Trenton (East.)	1B	109	414	59	138	29	1	7	59	.333	58	51	11	708	55	10	.987
1996— Ottawa (I.L.).■............	1B-DH-OF	134	451	62	116	21	2	12	60	.257	59	80	11	987	73	8	.993
1997— Ottawa (I.L.)	1B	50	184	37	55	11	1	3	15	.299	36	29	5	421	52	2	.996
— Montreal (N.L.)..........	OF-1B-DH	84	199	22	51	15	2	3	17	.256	19	34	1	226	19	3	.988
1998— Montreal (N.L.)..........	1B	130	210	17	39	9	0	1	10	.186	32	50	0	326	26	7	.981
1999— Ottawa (I.L.)..............	1B-OF-DH	53	183	23	46	6	1	4	27	.251	35	37	1	275	15	1	.997
— Montreal (N.L.)..........	1B-OF	88	140	17	31	7	2	2	18	.221	27	33	1	290	38	2	.994
Major League totals (3 years)		302	549	56	121	31	4	6	45	.220	78	122	2	842	83	12	.987

McGWIRE, MARK   1B   CARDINALS

PERSONAL: Born October 1, 1963, in Pomona, Calif. ... 6-5/250. ... Bats right, throws right. ... Full name: Mark David McGwire. ... Brother of Dan McGwire, quarterback with Seattle Seahawks (1991-94) and Miami Dolphins (1995).
HIGH SCHOOL: Damien (Claremont, Calif.).
COLLEGE: Southern California.
TRANSACTIONS/CAREER NOTES: Selected by Montreal Expos organization in eighth round of free-agent draft (June 8, 1981); did not sign. ... Selected by Oakland Athletics organization in first round (10th pick overall) of free-agent draft (June 4, 1984). ... On disabled list (April 11-26, 1989 and August 22-September 11, 1992). ... Granted free agency (October 26, 1992). ... Re-signed by A's (December 24, 1992). ... On disabled list (May 14-September 3, 1993; April 30-June 18 and July 27, 1994-remainder of season). ... On suspended list (September 4-8, 1993). ... On disabled list (July 18-August 2 and August 5-26, 1995). ... On disabled list (March 22-April 23, 1996). ... Traded by A's to St. Louis Cardinals for P T.J. Mathews, P Eric Ludwick and P Blake Stein (July 31, 1997).
RECORDS: Holds major league career record for most home runs by first baseman—507 (1986-99). ... Holds major league single-season records for most home runs—70 (1998); and most home runs by first baseman—69 (1998). ... Holds major league records for most home runs in consecutive games—135 (1998-99); most consecutive games with 50 or more home runs—4 (1996-99); and fewest singles in season (150 or more games)—53 (1991). ... Holds major league rookie-season records for most home runs—49; and extra bases on long hits—183 (1987). ... Shares major league single-season record for most games with three home runs—2 (1998). ... Shares major league single-inning recor for most home runs—2 (September 22, 1996, fifth inning). ... Shares major league records for most home runs in two consecutive games—5 (June 27 [3] and 28 [2], 1987 and June 10 [2] and 11 [3], 1995); and most home runs in one inning—2 (September 22, 1996, fifth inning); most seasons with 50 or more home runs—4; and most home runs in July—16 (1999). ... Shares modern major league record for most runs in two consecutive games—9 (June 27 and 28, 1987). ... Holds N.L. single-season record for most bases on balls—162 (1998). ... Holds N.L. record for most consecutive seasons with 50 or more home runs—2 (1998-99). ... Holds A.L. rookie-season record for highest slugging percentage—.618 (1987).
HONORS: Named College Player of the Year by THE SPORTING NEWS (1984). ... Named first baseman on THE SPORTING NEWS college All-America team (1984). ... Named A.L. Rookie Player of the Year by THE SPORTING NEWS (1987). ... Named A.L. Rookie of the Year by Baseball Writers' Association of America (1987). ... Won A.L. Gold Glove at first base (1990). ... Named first baseman on THE SPORTING NEWS A.L. All-Star team (1992 and 1996). ... Named first baseman on THE SPORTING NEWS A.L. Silver Slugger team (1992 and 1996). ... Named Sportsman of the Year by THE SPORTING NEWS (1997). ... Named first baseman on THE SPORTING NEWS N.L. All-Star team (1998). ... Named first baseman on THE SPORTING NEWS N.L. Silver Slugger team (1998). ... Named co-Sportsman of the Year by THE SPORTING NEWS (1998).

M

STATISTICAL NOTES: Led California League third basemen with 239 assists and 354 total chances in 1985. ... Hit three home runs in one game (June 27, 1987; June 11, 1995; April 14 and May 19, 1998). ... Led A.L. in slugging percentage with .618 in 1987, .585 in 1992 and .730 in 1996. ... Led A.L. first basemen with 1,429 total chances in 1990. ... Led A.L. with .467 on-base percentage in 1996. ... Led major leagues with 58 home runs in 1997. ... Led N.L. with .752 slugging percentage and .470 on-base percentage in 1998. ... Led N.L. first basemen with 1,435 total chances in 1998. ... Led N.L. with 21 intentional bases on balls received in 1999. ... Career major league grand slams: 13.

MISCELLANEOUS: Holds Oakland Athletics franchise all-time records for most home runs (363) and runs batted in (941). ... Member of 1984 U.S. Olympic baseball team.

							BATTING								FIELDING		
Year Team (League)	Pos.	G	AB	R	H	2B	3B	HR	RBI	Avg.	BB	SO	SB	PO	A	E	Avg.
1984— Modesto (Calif.)	1B	16	55	7	11	3	0	1	1	.200	8	21	0	107	6	1	.991
1985— Modesto (Calif.)	3B-1B	138	489	95	134	23	3	•24	•106	.274	96	108	1	105	†240	33	.913
1986— Huntsville (Sou.)	3B	55	195	40	59	15	0	10	53	.303	46	45	3	34	124	16	.908
— Tacoma (PCL)	3B	78	280	42	89	21	5	13	59	.318	42	67	1	53	126	25	.877
— Oakland (A.L.)	3B	18	53	10	10	1	0	3	9	.189	4	18	0	10	20	6	.833
1987— Oakland (A.L.)	1B-3B-OF	151	557	97	161	28	4	*49	118	.289	71	131	1	1176	101	13	.990
1988— Oakland (A.L.)	1B-OF	155	550	87	143	22	1	32	99	.260	76	117	0	1228	88	9	.993
1989— Oakland (A.L.)	1B-DH	143	490	74	113	17	0	33	95	.231	83	94	1	1170	114	6	.995
1990— Oakland (A.L.)	1B-DH	156	523	87	123	16	0	39	108	.235	*110	116	2	*1329	95	5	.997
1991— Oakland (A.L.)	1B	154	483	62	97	22	0	22	75	.201	93	116	2	1191	•101	4	.997
1992— Oakland (A.L.)	1B	139	467	87	125	22	0	42	104	.268	90	105	0	1118	71	6	.995
1993— Oakland (A.L.)	1B	27	84	16	28	6	0	9	24	.333	21	19	0	197	14	0	1.000
1994— Oakland (A.L.)	1B-DH	47	135	26	34	3	0	9	25	.252	37	40	0	307	18	4	.988
1995— Oakland (A.L.)	1B-DH	104	317	75	87	13	0	39	90	.274	88	77	1	775	64	*12	.986
1996— Oakland (A.L.)	1B-DH	130	423	104	132	21	0	*52	113	.312	116	112	0	913	60	10	.990
1997— Oakland (A.L.)	1B	105	366	48	104	24	0	34	81	.284	58	98	1	884	60	6	.994
— St. Louis (N.L.)■	1B	51	174	38	44	3	0	§24	42	.253	43	61	2	438	34	1	.998
1998— St. Louis (N.L.)	1B	155	509	130	152	21	0	*70	147	.299	*162	155	1	1326	97	12	.992
1999— St. Louis (N.L.)	1B	153	521	118	145	21	1	•65	*147	.278	133	141	0	1180	80	13	.990
American League totals (12 years)		1329	4448	773	1157	195	5	363	941	.260	847	1043	8	10298	806	81	.993
National League totals (3 years)		359	1204	286	341	45	1	159	336	.283	338	357	3	2944	211	26	.992
Major League totals (14 years)		1688	5652	1059	1498	240	6	522	1277	.265	1185	1400	11	13242	1017	107	.993

CHAMPIONSHIP SERIES RECORD

							BATTING								FIELDING		
Year Team (League)	Pos.	G	AB	R	H	2B	3B	HR	RBI	Avg.	BB	SO	SB	PO	A	E	Avg.
1988— Oakland (A.L.)	1B	4	15	4	5	0	0	1	3	.333	1	5	0	24	2	0	1.000
1989— Oakland (A.L.)	1B	5	18	3	7	1	0	1	3	.389	1	4	0	46	1	1	.979
1990— Oakland (A.L.)	1B	4	13	2	2	0	0	0	2	.154	3	3	0	40	0	0	1.000
1992— Oakland (A.L.)	1B	6	20	1	3	0	0	1	3	.150	5	4	0	46	2	1	.980
Championship series totals (4 years)		19	66	10	17	1	0	3	11	.258	10	16	0	156	5	2	.988

WORLD SERIES RECORD

NOTES: Member of World Series championship team (1989).

							BATTING								FIELDING		
Year Team (League)	Pos.	G	AB	R	H	2B	3B	HR	RBI	Avg.	BB	SO	SB	PO	A	E	Avg.
1988— Oakland (A.L.)	1B	5	17	1	1	0	0	1	1	.059	3	4	0	40	3	0	1.000
1989— Oakland (A.L.)	1B	4	17	0	5	1	0	0	1	.294	1	3	0	28	2	0	1.000
1990— Oakland (A.L.)	1B	4	14	1	3	0	0	0	0	.214	2	4	0	42	1	2	.956
World Series totals (3 years)		13	48	2	9	1	0	1	2	.188	6	11	0	110	6	2	.983

ALL-STAR GAME RECORD

NOTES: Named to A.L. All-Star team for 1991 game; replaced by Rafael Palmeiro due to injury.

						BATTING							FIELDING		
Year League	Pos.	AB	R	H	2B	3B	HR	RBI	Avg.	BB	SO	SB	PO	A	E	Avg.
1987— American	1B	3	0	0	0	0	0	0	.000	0	0	0	7	0	1	.875
1988— American	1B	2	0	1	0	0	0	0	.500	0	1	0	8	0	0	1.000
1989— American	1B	3	0	1	0	0	0	0	.333	0	0	0	5	0	0	1.000
1990— American	1B	2	0	0	0	0	0	0	.000	0	2	0	7	0	0	1.000
1991— American						Selected, did not play—injured.										
1992— American	1B	3	1	1	0	0	0	2	.333	0	0	0	4	0	0	1.000
1995— American						Selected, did not play—injured.										
1996— American	1B	1	0	1	0	0	0	0	1.000	0	0	0	2	1	0	1.000
1997— American	1B	2	0	0	0	0	0	0	.000	0	2	0	4	0	0	1.000
1998— National	1B	2	1	0	0	0	0	0	.000	1	1	0	6	0	0	1.000
1999— National	1B	2	0	0	0	0	0	0	.000	1	2	0	3	0	0	1.000
All-Star Game totals (9 years)		20	2	4	0	0	0	2	.200	2	8	0	46	1	1	.979

M

McKNIGHT, TONY   P   ASTROS

PERSONAL: Born June 29, 1977, in Texarkana, Ark. ... 6-5/205. ... Throws right, bats right. ... Full name: Tony Mark McKnight.
HIGH SCHOOL: Arkansas (Texarkana, Ark.).
TRANSACTIONS/CAREER NOTES: Selected by Houston Astros organization in first round (22nd pick overall) of free-agent draft (June 1, 1995). ... On disabled list (June 19-July 15, 1996). ... On Jackson disabled list (July 20-August 2, 1999).
STATISTICAL NOTES: Led Texas League pitchers with 18 putouts in 1999.

Year League	W	L	Pct.	ERA	G	GS	CG	ShO	Sv.	IP	H	R	ER	BB	SO
1995— Gulf Coast Astros (GCL).....	1	1	.500	3.86	3	3	0	0	0	11 2/3	14	5	5	2	8
1996— Gulf Coast Astros (GCL).....	2	1	.667	6.23	8	5	0	0	0	21 2/3	28	21	15	7	15
1997— Quad City (Midw.)	4	9	.308	4.68	20	20	0	0	0	115 1/3	116	71	60	55	92
1998— Kissimmee (FSL)	11	13	.458	4.67	28	•28	0	0	0	154 1/3	191	101	80	50	104
1999— Jackson (Texas)	9	9	.500	2.75	24	24	0	0	0	160 1/3	134	60	49	44	118

PERSONAL: Born October 26, 1974, in Kettering, Ohio. ... 6-5/212. ... Throws right, bats right. ... Full name: Marty Lee McLeary.
HIGH SCHOOL: Mansfield (Ohio) Christian.
COLLEGE: Mount Vernon (Ohio) Nazarene.
TRANSACTIONS/CAREER NOTES: Selected by Boston Red Sox organization in 10th round of free-agent draft (June 3, 1997). ... Selected by Montreal Expos from Red Sox organization in Rule 5 major league draft (December 13, 1999).

Year	League	W	L	Pct.	ERA	G	GS	CG	ShO	Sv.	IP	H	R	ER	BB	SO
1997—	Lowell (NY-P)	3	6	.333	3.75	13	13	0	0	0	62 1/3	53	38	26	36	43
1998—	Michigan (Midw.)	5	7	.417	4.16	37	7	0	0	0	88 2/3	99	58	41	35	54
1999—	Sarasota (FSL)	1	0	1.000	12.08	8	0	0	0	0	12 2/3	29	20	17	7	11
—	Augusta (SAL)	5	6	.455	3.12	35	9	0	0	3	80 2/3	73	34	28	25	90

PERSONAL: Born October 4, 1964, in San Diego. ... 5-11/207. ... Bats both, throws right. ... Full name: Mark Tremell McLemore.
HIGH SCHOOL: Morse (San Diego).
TRANSACTIONS/CAREER NOTES: Selected by California Angels organization in ninth round of free-agent draft (June 7, 1982). ... On disabled list (May 15-27, 1985). ... On California disabled list (May 24-August 2, 1988); included rehabilitation assignments to Palm Springs (July 7-21) and Edmonton (July 22-27). ... On California disabled list (May 17-August 17, 1990); included rehabilitation assignments to Edmonton (May 24-June 6) and Palm Springs (August 9-13). ... Traded by Angels to Cleveland Indians (August 17, 1990), completing deal in which Indians traded C Ron Tingley to Angels for a player to be named later (September 6, 1989). ... Released by Indians (December 13, 1990). ... Signed by Tucson, Houston Astros organization (March 6, 1991). ... On Houston disabled list (May 9-June 25, 1991); included rehabilitation assignments to Tucson (May 24-29) and Jackson (June 14-22). ... Released by Astros (June 25, 1991). ... Signed by Baltimore Orioles organization (July 5, 1991). ... Granted free agency (October 15, 1991). ... Re-signed by Orioles organization (February 5, 1992). ... Granted free agency (December 19, 1992). ... Re-signed by Orioles organization (January 6, 1993). ... Granted free agency (October 18, 1994). ... Signed by Texas Rangers (December 13, 1994). ... Granted free agency (December 7, 1996). ... Re-signed by Rangers (December 13, 1996). ... On Texas disabled list (May 15-June 12 and August 19-September 28, 1997); included rehabilitation assignments to Charlotte (June 7-8) and Oklahoma City (June 9-12). ... On disabled list (June 7-22, 1998). ... Granted free agency (October 28, 1999). ... Signed by Seattle Mariners (December 20, 1999).
STATISTICAL NOTES: Led California League second basemen with 400 assists and 84 double plays in 1984. ... Led Pacific Coast League second basemen with 597 total chances and 95 double plays in 1989. ... Led A.L. second basemen with 473 assists and 798 total chances in 1996.

Year	Team (League)	Pos.	G	AB	R	H	2B	3B	HR	RBI	Avg.	BB	SO	SB	PO	A	E	Avg.
1982—	Salem (N.W.)	2B-SS	55	165	42	49	6	2	0	25	.297	39	38	14	81	125	11	.949
1983—	Peoria (Midw.)	2B-SS	95	329	42	79	7	3	0	18	.240	53	64	15	170	250	24	.946
1984—	Redwood (Calif.)	2B-SS	134	482	102	142	8	3	0	45	.295	106	75	59	274	†429	25	.966
1985—	Midland (Texas)	2B-SS	117	458	80	124	17	6	2	46	.271	66	59	31	301	339	19	.971
1986—	Midland (Texas)	2B	63	237	54	75	9	1	1	29	.316	48	18	38	155	194	13	.964
—	Edmonton (PCL)	2B	73	286	41	79	13	1	0	23	.276	39	30	29	173	215	7	.982
—	California (A.L.)	2B	5	4	0	0	0	0	0	0	.000	1	2	0	3	10	0	1.000
1987—	California (A.L.)	2B-SS-DH	138	433	61	102	13	3	3	41	.236	48	72	25	293	363	17	.975
1988—	California (A.L.)	2B-3B-DH	77	233	38	56	11	2	2	16	.240	25	25	13	108	178	6	.979
—	Palm Springs (Calif.)	2B	11	44	9	15	3	1	0	6	.341	11	7	7	18	24	1	.977
—	Edmonton (PCL)	2B	12	45	7	12	3	0	0	6	.267	4	4	7	35	33	1	.986
1989—	Edmonton (PCL)	2B	114	430	60	105	13	2	2	34	.244	49	67	26	*264	323	10	*.983
—	California (A.L.)	2B-DH	32	103	12	25	3	1	0	14	.243	7	19	6	55	88	5	.966
1990—	California (A.L.)	2B	20	48	4	7	2	0	0	2	.146	4	9	1	14	15	0	1.000
—	Edmonton (PCL)	2B-SS	9	39	4	10	2	0	0	3	.256	6	10	0	24	32	4	.933
—	Palm Springs (Calif.)	2B	6	22	3	6	0	0	0	2	.273	3	7	0	20	22	0	1.000
—	Colo. Springs (PCL)■	2B-3B-SS	14	54	11	15	2	0	1	7	.278	11	8	5	23	40	2	.969
—	Cleveland (A.L.)	SS-3B-2B	8	12	2	2	0	0	0	0	.167	0	6	0	23	24	4	.922
1991—	Houston (N.L.)■	2B	21	61	6	9	1	0	0	2	.148	6	13	0	25	54	2	.975
—	Tucson (PCL)	2B	4	14	2	5	1	0	0	0	.357	2	1	0	8	6	0	1.000
—	Jackson (Texas)	2B	7	22	6	5	3	0	1	4	.227	6	3	1	27	24	0	1.000
—	Rochester (I.L.)■	2B	57	228	32	64	11	4	1	28	.281	27	29	12	134	166	5	.984
1992—	Baltimore (A.L.)	2B-DH	101	228	40	56	7	2	0	27	.246	21	26	11	126	186	7	.978
1993—	Baltimore (A.L.)	O-2-3-DH	148	581	81	165	27	5	4	72	.284	64	92	21	335	80	6	.986
1994—	Baltimore (A.L.)	2B-OF-DH	104	343	44	88	11	1	3	29	.257	51	50	20	219	269	9	.982
1995—	Texas (A.L.)■	OF-2B-DH	129	467	73	122	20	5	5	41	.261	59	71	21	248	184	4	.991
1996—	Texas (A.L.)	2B-OF	147	517	84	150	23	4	5	46	.290	87	69	27	313	†473	12	.985
1997—	Texas (A.L.)	2B-OF	89	349	47	91	17	2	1	25	.261	40	54	7	148	254	8	.980
—	Charlotte (FSL)	2B	2	7	1	4	1	0	0	3	.571	2	1	1	3	3	0	1.000
—	Oklahoma City (A.A.)	2B-DH	3	10	0	1	0	0	0	1	.100	1	1	1	2	3	0	1.000
1998—	Texas (A.L.)	2B-DH	126	461	79	114	15	1	5	53	.247	89	64	12	249	332	15	.975
1999—	Texas (A.L.)	2B-OF-DH	144	566	105	155	20	7	6	45	.274	83	79	16	276	433	12	.983
American League totals (13 years)			1268	4345	670	1133	169	33	34	411	.261	579	638	180	2410	2889	105	.981
National League totals (1 year)			21	61	6	9	1	0	0	2	.148	6	13	0	25	54	2	.975
Major League totals (14 years)			1289	4406	676	1142	170	33	34	413	.259	585	651	180	2435	2943	107	.980

DIVISION SERIES RECORD

Year	Team (League)	Pos.	G	AB	R	H	2B	3B	HR	RBI	Avg.	BB	SO	SB	PO	A	E	Avg.
1996—	Texas (A.L.)	2B	4	15	1	2	0	0	0	2	.133	0	4	0	10	16	0	1.000
1998—	Texas (A.L.)	2B	3	10	0	1	1	0	0	0	.100	2	3	0	4	12	0	1.000
1999—	Texas (A.L.)	2B	3	10	0	1	0	0	0	0	.100	1	3	0	2	9	0	1.000
Division series totals (3 years)			10	35	1	4	1	0	0	2	.114	3	10	0	16	37	0	1.000

M

McMICHAEL, GREG   P

PERSONAL: Born December 1, 1966, in Knoxville, Tenn. ... 6-3/215. ... Throws right, bats right. ... Full name: Gregory Winston McMichael.
HIGH SCHOOL: Webb School of Knoxville (Knoxville, Tenn.).
COLLEGE: Tennessee.
TRANSACTIONS/CAREER NOTES: Selected by Cleveland Indians organization in seventh round of free-agent draft (June 1, 1988). ... Released by Indians (April 4, 1991). ... Signed by Atlanta Braves organization (April 16, 1991). ... Traded by Braves to New York Mets for P Paul Byrd and a player to be named later (November 25, 1996); Braves acquired P Andy Zwirchitz to complete deal (May 25, 1997). ... Traded by Mets with P Dave Mlicki to Los Angeles Dodgers for P Hideo Nomo and P Brad Clontz (June 5, 1998). ... Traded by Dodgers with cash to Mets for P Brian Bohanon (July 10, 1998). ... On New York disabled list (March 21-June 11, 1999); included rehabilitation assignments to Binghamton (May 26-June 1) and Norfolk (June 2-11). ... Traded by Mets with P Jason Isringhausen to Oakland Athletics for P Billy Taylor (July 31, 1999). ... Granted free agency (November 3, 1999).

Year League	W	L	Pct.	ERA	G	GS	CG	ShO	Sv.	IP	H	R	ER	BB	SO
1988— Burlington (Appl.)	2	0	1.000	2.57	3	3	1	1	0	21	17	9	6	4	20
—Kinston (Caro.)	4	2	.667	2.68	11	11	2	0	0	77⅓	57	31	23	18	35
1989— Canton/Akron (East.)	11	11	.500	3.49	26	•26	8	•5	0	170	164	81	66	64	101
1990— Canton/Akron (East.)	2	3	.400	3.35	13	4	0	0	0	40⅓	39	17	15	17	19
—Colo. Springs (PCL)	2	3	.400	5.80	12	12	1	1	0	59	72	45	38	30	34
1991— Durham (Caro.)■	5	6	.455	3.62	36	6	0	0	2	79⅔	83	34	32	29	82
1992— Greenville (Sou.)	4	2	.667	1.36	15	4	0	0	1	46⅓	37	14	7	13	53
—Richmond (I.L.)	6	5	.545	4.38	19	13	0	0	2	90⅓	89	52	44	34	86
1993— Atlanta (N.L.)	2	3	.400	2.06	74	0	0	0	19	91⅔	68	22	21	29	89
1994— Atlanta (N.L.)	4	6	.400	3.84	51	0	0	0	21	58⅔	66	29	25	19	47
1995— Atlanta (N.L.)	7	2	.778	2.79	67	0	0	0	2	80⅔	64	27	25	32	74
1996— Atlanta (N.L.)	5	3	.625	3.22	73	0	0	0	2	86⅔	84	37	31	27	78
1997— New York (N.L.)■	7	10	.412	2.98	73	0	0	0	7	87⅔	73	34	29	27	81
1998— New York (N.L.)	5	3	.625	4.02	52	0	0	0	1	53⅔	64	31	24	29	44
—Los Angeles (N.L.)■	0	1	.000	4.40	12	0	0	0	1	14⅓	17	8	7	6	11
1999— Binghamton (East.)■	0	0	...	0.00	2	2	0	0	0	3	2	1	0	1	5
—Norfolk (I.L.)	0	0	...	2.70	3	1	0	0	0	3⅓	4	1	1	3	4
—New York (N.L.)	1	1	.500	4.82	19	0	0	0	0	18⅔	20	10	10	8	18
—Oakland (A.L.)■	0	0	...	5.40	17	0	0	0	0	15	15	9	9	12	3
A.L. totals (1 year)	0	0	...	5.40	17	0	0	0	0	15	15	9	9	12	3
N.L. totals (7 years)	31	29	.517	3.15	421	0	0	0	53	492	456	198	172	177	442
Major League totals (7 years)	31	29	.517	3.21	438	0	0	0	53	507	471	207	181	189	445

DIVISION SERIES RECORD

Year League	W	L	Pct.	ERA	G	GS	CG	ShO	Sv.	IP	H	R	ER	BB	SO
1995— Atlanta (N.L.)	0	0	...	6.75	2	0	0	0	0	1⅓	1	1	1	2	1
1996— Atlanta (N.L.)	0	0	...	6.75	2	0	0	0	0	1⅓	1	1	1	1	3
Division series totals (2 years)	0	0	...	6.75	4	0	0	0	0	2⅔	2	2	2	3	4

CHAMPIONSHIP SERIES RECORD

Year League	W	L	Pct.	ERA	G	GS	CG	ShO	Sv.	IP	H	R	ER	BB	SO
1993— Atlanta (N.L.)	0	1	.000	6.75	4	0	0	0	0	4	7	3	3	2	1
1995— Atlanta (N.L.)	1	0	1.000	0.00	3	0	0	0	1	2⅔	0	0	0	1	2
1996— Atlanta (N.L.)	0	1	.000	9.00	3	0	0	0	0	2	4	2	2	1	3
Champ. series totals (3 years)	1	2	.333	5.19	10	0	0	0	1	8⅔	11	5	5	4	6

WORLD SERIES RECORD

NOTES: Member of World Series championship team (1995).

Year League	W	L	Pct.	ERA	G	GS	CG	ShO	Sv.	IP	H	R	ER	BB	SO
1995— Atlanta (N.L.)	0	0	...	2.70	3	0	0	0	0	3⅓	3	2	1	2	2
1996— Atlanta (N.L.)	0	0	...	27.00	2	0	0	0	0	1	5	3	3	0	1
World Series totals (2 years)	0	0	...	8.31	5	0	0	0	0	4⅓	8	5	4	2	3

McNEAL, AARON   1B   ASTROS

PERSONAL: Born April 28, 1978, in Oakland. ... 6-3/230. ... Bats right, throws right. ... Full name: Aaron G. McNeal.
HIGH SCHOOL: Castro Valley (Calif.).
JUNIOR COLLEGE: Chabot College (Calif.).
TRANSACTIONS/CAREER NOTES: Selected by Houston Astros organization in 27th round of free-agent draft (June 1, 1995).
HONORS: Named Midwest League Most Valuable Player (1999).
STATISTICAL NOTES: Led Gulf Coast League first basemen with 423 total chances in 1996. ... Led Midwest League with 315 total bases in 1999. ... Led Midwest League first basemen with 1,141 total chances in 1999.

						BATTING								FIELDING		
Year Team (League)	Pos.	G	AB	R	H	2B	3B	HR	RBI	Avg.	BB	SO	SB	PO	A	E	Avg.
1996— GC Astros (GCL)	1B	55	200	22	50	10	2	2	31	.250	13	52	0	381	*35	7	.983
1997— Auburn (NY-P)	1B	12	40	5	10	3	0	0	3	.250	4	10	1	88	8	2	.980
—GC Astros (GCL)	1B	46	164	22	48	12	0	3	26	.293	11	28	0	279	16	5	.983
1998— Quad City (Midw.)	1B	112	370	54	105	15	1	14	61	.284	31	112	3	850	69	11	.988
1999— Michigan (Midw.)	1B	133	*536	95	*166	29	3	*38	*131	.310	40	121	7	1013	*111	17	.985

McNICHOL, BRIAN   P   CUBS

PERSONAL: Born May 20, 1974, in Fairfax, Va. ... 6-5/225. ... Throws left, bats left. ... Full name: Brian David McNichol.
HIGH SCHOOL: Garfield (Woodbridge, Va.).
COLLEGE: James Madison.
TRANSACTIONS/CAREER NOTES: Selected by Chicago Cubs organization in second round of free-agent draft (June 1, 1995).

M

Year	League	W	L	Pct.	ERA	G	GS	CG	ShO	Sv.	IP	H	R	ER	BB	SO
1995—	Williamsport (NY-P)	3	1	.750	3.08	9	9	0	0	0	49²/₃	57	28	17	8	35
1996—	Daytona (FSL)	1	2	.333	4.67	8	7	0	0	0	34²/₃	39	24	18	14	22
—	Gulf Coast Cubs (GCL)	0	0		0.00	1	1	0	0	0	3¹/₃	4	2	0	0	2
1997—	Daytona (FSL)	2	2	.500	2.31	6	6	0	0	0	39	32	14	10	10	40
—	Orlando (Sou.)	7	10	.412	5.81	22	22	0	0	0	119¹/₃	153	89	77	42	97
1998—	West Tenn (Sou.)	12	9	.571	3.72	28	26	•4	1	0	179	170	88	74	62	168
—	Iowa (PCL)	0	0		7.71	1	1	0	0	0	7	12	6	6	1	5
1999—	Iowa (PCL)	10	11	.476	5.58	28	•28	2	1	0	161¹/₃	194	108	100	55	120
—	Chicago (N.L.)	0	2	.000	6.75	4	2	0	0	0	10²/₃	15	8	8	7	12
Major League totals (1 year)		0	2	.000	6.75	4	2	0	0	0	10²/₃	15	8	8	7	12

McRAE, BRIAN   OF

PERSONAL: Born August 27, 1967, in Bradenton, Fla. ... 6-0/195. ... Bats both, throws right. ... Full name: Brian Wesley McRae. ... Son of Hal McRae, hitting coach, Philadelphia Phillies; outfielder/designated hitter with Cincinnati Reds (1968 and 1970-72) and Kansas City Royals (1973-87); and manager with Royals (1991-94).

HIGH SCHOOL: Blue Springs (Mo.), then Manatee (Bradenton, Fla.).

COLLEGE: Kansas.

TRANSACTIONS/CAREER NOTES: Selected by Kansas City Royals organization in first round (17th pick overall) of free-agent draft (June 3, 1985). ... Traded by Royals to Chicago Cubs for P Derek Wallace and P Geno Morones (April 5, 1995). ... Traded by Cubs with P Mel Rojas and P Turk Wendell to New York Mets for OF Lance Johnson and two players to be named later (August 8, 1997); Mets traded P Mark Clark (August 11, 1997) and IF Manny Alexander (August 14, 1997) to Cubs to complete deal. ... Traded by Mets with P Rigo Beltran and OF Thomas Johnson to Colorado Rockies for OF Darryl Hamilton and P Chuck McElroy (July 31, 1999). ... Traded by Rockies to Toronto Blue Jays for a player to be named later (August 9, 1999); Rockies acquired P Pat Lynch to complete deal (August 23, 1999). ... Granted free agency (November 3, 1999).

RECORDS: Shares major league single-season record for fewest double plays by outfielder (150 or more games)—0 (1991). ... Shares major league single-game record for most unassisted double plays by outfielder—1 (August 23, 1992). ... Shares N.L. single-season record for fewest assists by outfielder (150 or more games)—2 (1996).

STATISTICAL NOTES: Led Northwest League second basemen with 373 total chances in 1986. ... Tied for Southern League lead in double plays by outfielder with five in 1989. ... Had 22-game hitting streak (July 20-August 13, 1991). ... Led N.L. outfielders with 352 total chances in 1995. ... Career major league grand slams: 5.

							BATTING								FIELDING		
Year	Team (League)	Pos.	G	AB	R	H	2B	3B	HR	RBI	Avg.	BB	SO	SB	PO	A	E	Avg.
1985—	GC Royals (GCL)	2B-SS	60	217	40	58	6	5	0	23	.267	28	34	27	116	142	18	.935
1986—	Eugene (N.W.)	2B	72	306	*66	82	10	3	1	29	.268	41	49	28	146	*214	13	*.965
1987—	Fort Myers (FSL)	2B	131	481	62	121	14	1	1	31	.252	22	70	33	*284	346	18	.972
1988—	Baseball City (FSL)	2B	30	107	18	33	2	0	1	11	.308	9	11	8	70	103	4	.977
—	Memphis (Sou.)	2B	91	288	33	58	13	1	4	15	.201	16	60	13	147	231	18	.955
1989—	Memphis (Sou.)	OF	138	*533	72	121	18	8	5	42	.227	43	65	23	249	11	5	.981
1990—	Memphis (Sou.)	OF	116	470	78	126	24	6	10	64	.268	44	66	21	265	8	7	.975
—	Kansas City (A.L.)	OF	46	168	21	48	8	3	2	23	.286	9	29	4	120	1	0	1.000
1991—	Kansas City (A.L.)	OF	152	629	86	164	28	9	8	64	.261	24	99	20	405	2	3	.993
1992—	Kansas City (A.L.)	OF	149	533	63	119	23	5	4	52	.223	42	88	18	419	8	3	.993
1993—	Kansas City (A.L.)	OF	153	627	78	177	28	9	12	69	.282	37	105	23	394	4	7	.983
1994—	Kansas City (A.L.)	OF-DH	114	436	71	119	22	6	4	40	.273	54	67	28	252	2	3	.988
1995—	Chicago (N.L.)■.......	OF	137	*580	92	167	38	7	12	48	.288	47	92	27	*345	4	3	.991
1996—	Chicago (N.L.)	OF	157	624	111	172	32	5	17	66	.276	73	84	37	345	2	5	.986
1997—	Chicago (N.L.)	OF	108	417	63	100	27	5	6	28	.240	52	62	14	242	3	1	.996
—	New York (N.L.)■......	OF	45	145	23	36	5	2	5	15	.248	13	22	3	65	1	3	.957
1998—	New York (N.L.)	OF	159	552	79	146	36	5	21	79	.264	80	90	20	302	8	4	.987
1999—	New York (N.L.)■........	OF	96	298	35	66	12	1	8	36	.221	39	57	2	152	1	1	.994
—	Colorado (N.L.)■.......	OF	7	23	1	6	2	0	1	1	.261	2	7	0	14	0	0	1.000
—	Toronto (A.L.)■..........	DH-OF	31	82	11	16	3	1	3	11	.195	16	22	0	28	1	0	1.000
American League totals (6 years)			645	2475	330	643	112	33	33	259	.260	182	410	93	1618	18	16	.990
National League totals (5 years)			709	2639	404	693	152	25	70	273	.263	306	414	103	1465	19	17	.989
Major League totals (10 years)			1354	5114	734	1336	264	58	103	532	.261	488	824	196	3083	37	33	.990

MEADOWS, BRIAN   P   PADRES

PERSONAL: Born November 21, 1975, in Montgomery, Ala. ... 6-4/200. ... Throws right, bats right. ... Full name: Matthew Brian Meadows.

HIGH SCHOOL: Charles Henderson (Troy, Ala.).

TRANSACTIONS/CAREER NOTES: Selected by Florida Marlins organization in third round of free-agent draft (June 2, 1994); pick received as compensation for Colorado Rockies signing Type B free-agent SS Walt Weiss. ... On disabled list (July 28-August 13, 1998). ... Traded by Marlins to San Diego Padres for P Dan Miceli (November 15, 1999).

RECORDS: Shares major league single-inning record for most putouts by pitcher—3 (June 2, 1998, second inning).

Year	League	W	L	Pct.	ERA	G	GS	CG	ShO	Sv.	IP	H	R	ER	BB	SO
1994—	Gulf Coast Marlins (GCL) ...	3	0	1.000	1.95	8	7	0	0	0	37	34	9	8	6	33
1995—	Kane County (Midw.)	9	9	.500	4.22	26	26	1	1	0	147	163	90	69	41	103
1996—	Portland (East.)	0	1	.000	4.33	4	4	1	0	0	27	26	15	13	4	13
—	Brevard County (FSL)	8	7	.533	3.58	24	23	3	1	0	146	129	73	58	25	69
1997—	Portland (East.)	9	7	.563	4.61	29	*29	4	0	0	175²/₃	204	99	90	48	115
1998—	Florida (N.L.)	11	13	.458	5.21	31	31	1	0	0	174¹/₃	222	106	101	46	88
1999—	Florida (N.L.)	11	15	.423	5.60	31	31	0	0	0	178¹/₃	214	117	111	57	72
Major League totals (2 years)	22	28	.440	5.41	62	62	1	0	0	352²/₃	436	223	212	103	160

MEARES, PAT   SS   PIRATES

PERSONAL: Born September 6, 1968, in Salina, Kan. ... 6-0/187. ... Bats right, throws right. ... Full name: Patrick James Meares.
HIGH SCHOOL: Sacred Heart (Salina, Kan.).
COLLEGE: Wichita State.
TRANSACTIONS/CAREER NOTES: Selected by Minnesota Twins organization in 15th round of free-agent draft (June 4, 1990). ... On disabled list (June 22-July 7, 1994 and August 11-26, 1997). ... Granted free agency (December 21, 1998). ... Signed by Pittsburgh Pirates (February 20, 1999). ... On Pittsburgh disabled list (April 2-23 and May 12-September 21, 1999); included rehabilitation assignment to Nashville (August 26-September 3).
RECORDS: Holds major league single-season record for fewest assists by shortstop (150 or more games)—344 (1996).

| | | | | | | | BATTING | | | | | | | | | FIELDING | |
Year Team (League)	Pos.	G	AB	R	H	2B	3B	HR	RBI	Avg.	BB	SO	SB	PO	A	E	Avg.
1990— Kenosha (Midw.)	3B-2B	52	197	26	47	10	2	4	22	.239	25	45	2	35	94	16	.890
1991— Visalia (Calif.)	2B-3B-OF	89	360	53	109	21	4	6	44	.303	24	63	15	155	224	26	.936
1992— Orlando (Sou.)	SS	81	300	42	76	19	0	3	23	.253	11	57	5	91	190	35	.889
1993— Portland (PCL)	SS	18	54	6	16	5	0	0	3	.296	3	11	0	28	48	5	.938
— Minnesota (A.L.)	SS	111	346	33	87	14	3	0	33	.251	7	52	4	165	304	19	.961
1994— Minnesota (A.L.)	SS	80	229	29	61	12	1	2	24	.266	14	50	5	133	209	13	.963
1995— Minnesota (A.L.)	SS-OF	116	390	57	105	19	4	12	49	.269	15	68	10	187	317	•18	.966
1996— Minnesota (A.L.)	SS-OF	152	517	66	138	26	7	8	67	.267	17	90	9	257	344	22	.965
1997— Minnesota (A.L.)	SS	134	439	63	121	23	3	10	60	.276	18	86	7	211	415	20	.969
1998— Minnesota (A.L.)	SS	149	543	56	141	26	3	9	70	.260	24	86	7	263	412	24	.966
1999— Pittsburgh (N.L.)■	SS	21	91	15	28	4	0	0	7	.308	9	20	0	26	67	6	.939
— Nashville (PCL)	SS	5	18	3	3	0	0	0	0	.167	1	3	1	2	6	2	.800
American League totals (6 years)		742	2464	304	653	120	21	41	303	.265	95	432	42	1216	2001	116	.965
National League totals (1 year)		21	91	15	28	4	0	0	7	.308	9	20	0	26	67	6	.939
Major League totals (7 years)		763	2555	319	681	124	21	41	310	.267	104	452	42	1242	2068	122	.964

MEARS, CHRIS   P   MARINERS

PERSONAL: Born January 20, 1978, in Ottawa, Ont. ... 6-4/180. ... Throws right, bats right. ... Full name: Christopher Peter Mears.
HIGH SCHOOL: Lord Byng (Vancouver, B.C.).
TRANSACTIONS/CAREER NOTES: Selected by Seattle Mariners organization in fifth round of free agent draft (June 4, 1996). ... On Lancaster disabled list (August 20-29, 1999).

Year League	W	L	Pct.	ERA	G	GS	CG	ShO	Sv.	IP	H	R	ER	BB	SO
1996— Arizona Mariners (Ariz.)	1	2	.333	3.60	6	5	0	0	0	25	23	11	10	5	27
1997— Everett (N.W.)	3	5	.375	5.34	12	12	0	0	0	62 1/3	82	47	37	20	47
1998— Orlando (Sou.)	0	1	.000	9.64	1	1	0	0	0	4 2/3	8	5	5	2	4
— Everett (N.W.)	•9	1	*.900	2.74	15	15	•1	0	0	*98 2/3	86	39	30	33	67
1999— Wisconsin (Midw.)	10	1	*.909	2.43	13	13	2	1	0	89	76	33	24	16	78
— Lancaster (Calif.)	3	6	.333	7.08	10	10	0	0	0	54 2/3	71	44	43	18	45

MECHE, GIL   P   MARINERS

PERSONAL: Born September 8, 1978, in Lafayette, La. ... 6-3/180. ... Throws right, bats right. ... Full name: Gilbert Allen Meche.
HIGH SCHOOL: Acadiana (Lafayette, La.).
TRANSACTIONS/CAREER NOTES: Selected by Seattle Mariners organization in first round (22nd pick overall) of free-agent draft (June 4, 1996).

Year League	W	L	Pct.	ERA	G	GS	CG	ShO	Sv.	IP	H	R	ER	BB	SO
1996— Arizona Mariners (Ariz.)	0	1	.000	6.00	2	0	0	0	0	3	4	2	2	1	4
1997— Everett (N.W.)	3	4	.429	3.98	12	12	1	0	0	74 2/3	75	40	33	24	62
— Wisconsin (Midw.)	0	2	.000	3.00	2	2	0	0	·0	12	12	5	4	4	14
1998— Wisconsin (Midw.)	8	7	.533	3.44	26	0	0	0	0	149	136	77	57	63	168
1999— New Haven (East.)	3	4	.429	3.05	10	10	0	0	0	59	51	24	20	26	56
— Tacoma (PCL)	2	2	.500	3.19	6	6	0	0	0	31	31	12	11	13	24
— Seattle (A.L.)	8	4	.667	4.73	16	15	0	0	0	85 2/3	73	48	45	57	47
Major League totals (1 year)	8	4	.667	4.73	16	15	0	0	0	85 2/3	73	48	45	57	47

MECIR, JIM   P   DEVIL RAYS

PERSONAL: Born May 16, 1970, in Queens, N.Y. ... 6-1/195. ... Throws right, bats both. ... Full name: James Jason Mecir. ... Name pronounced ma-SEER.
HIGH SCHOOL: Smithtown East (St. James, N.Y.).
COLLEGE: Eckerd (Fla.).
TRANSACTIONS/CAREER NOTES: Selected by Seattle Mariners organization in third round of free-agent draft (June 3, 1991). ... On disabled list (June 25-August 25, 1992). ... Traded by Mariners with 1B Tino Martinez and P Jeff Nelson to New York Yankees for P Sterling Hitchcock and 3B Russ Davis (December 7, 1995). ... Traded by Yankees to Boston Red Sox (September 29, 1997), completing deal in which Yankees traded P Tony Armas Jr. and a player to be named later to Red Sox for C Mike Stanley and IF Randy Brown (August 13, 1997). ... Selected by Tampa Bay Devil Rays in second round (36th pick overall) of expansion draft (November 18, 1997). ... On disabled list (May 12, 1999-remainder of season).
STATISTICAL NOTES: Led California League with 15 hit batsmen in 1993.

Year League	W	L	Pct.	ERA	G	GS	CG	ShO	Sv.	IP	H	R	ER	BB	SO
1991— San Bernardino (Calif.)	3	5	.375	4.22	14	12	0	0	1	70 1/3	72	40	33	37	48
1992— San Bernardino (Calif.)	4	5	.444	4.67	14	11	0	0	0	61 2/3	72	40	32	26	53
1993— Riverside (Calif.)	9	11	.450	4.33	26	26	1	0	0	145 1/3	160	89	70	58	85
1994— Jacksonville (Sou.)	6	5	.545	2.69	46	0	0	0	13	80 1/3	73	28	24	35	53

Year	League	W	L	Pct.	ERA	G	GS	CG	ShO	Sv.	IP	H	R	ER	BB	SO
1995—Tacoma (PCL)		1	4	.200	3.10	40	0	0	0	8	69 2/3	63	29	24	28	46
—Seattle (A.L.)		0	0	...	0.00	2	0	0	0	0	4 2/3	5	1	0	2	3
1996—Columbus (I.L.)■		3	3	.500	2.27	33	0	0	0	7	47 2/3	37	14	12	15	52
—New York (A.L.)		1	1	.500	5.13	26	0	0	0	0	40 1/3	42	24	23	23	38
1997—Columbus (I.L.)		1	1	.500	1.00	24	0	0	0	11	27	14	4	3	6	34
—New York (A.L.)		0	4	.000	5.88	25	0	0	0	0	33 2/3	36	23	22	10	25
1998—Tampa Bay (A.L.)■		7	2	.778	3.11	68	0	0	0	0	84	68	30	29	33	77
1999—Tampa Bay (A.L.)		0	1	.000	2.61	17	0	0	0	0	20 2/3	15	7	6	14	15
Major League totals (5 years)		8	8	.500	3.93	138	0	0	0	0	183 1/3	166	85	80	82	158

MEDINA, RAFAEL — P — BRAVES

PERSONAL: Born February 15, 1975, in Panama City, Panama. ... 6-3/200. ... Throws right, bats right. ... Brother of Ricardo Medina, third baseman with Chicago Cubs organization (1989-94).

TRANSACTIONS/CAREER NOTES: Signed as non-drafted free agent by New York Yankees organization (September 6, 1992). ... On disabled list (July 11-22 and August 5-September 30, 1996). ... Traded by Yankees with OF Ruben Rivera and cash to San Diego Padres for rights to P Hideki Irabu, 2B Homer Bush, OF Gordon Amerson and a player to be named later (April 22, 1997); Padres traded OF Vernon Maxwell to Yankees to complete deal (June 9, 1997). ... Traded by Padres with P Steve Hoff and 1B Derrek Lee to Florida Marlins for P Kevin Brown (December 15, 1997). ... On Florida disabled list (April 18-July 17, 1998); included rehabilitation assignment to Charlotte (June 26-July 17). ... Claimed on waivers by Atlanta Braves (December 6, 1999).

Year	League	W	L	Pct.	ERA	G	GS	CG	ShO	Sv.	IP	H	R	ER	BB	SO
1993—Gulf Coast Yankees (GCL)		2	0	1.000	0.66	5	5	0	0	0	27 1/3	16	6	2	12	21
1994—Oneonta (NY-P)		3	7	.300	4.66	14	14	1	0	0	73 1/3	67	54	38	35	59
1995—Greensboro (SAL)		4	4	.500	4.01	19	19	1	0	0	98 2/3	86	48	44	38	108
—Tampa (FSL)		2	2	.500	2.37	6	6	0	0	0	30 1/3	29	12	8	12	25
1996—Norwich (East.)		5	8	.385	3.06	19	19	1	0	0	103	78	48	35	55	112
1997—Rancho Cuca. (Calif.)■		2	0	1.000	2.00	3	3	0	0	0	18	13	4	4	5	14
—Las Vegas (PCL)		4	5	.444	7.56	13	13	0	0	0	66 2/3	90	60	56	39	50
1998—Florida (N.L.)■		2	6	.250	6.01	12	12	0	0	0	67 1/3	76	50	45	52	49
—Charlotte (I.L.)		4	2	.667	3.90	11	9	3	1	0	57 2/3	53	27	25	26	41
1999—Calgary (PCL)		1	2	.333	3.34	25	0	0	0	1	35	29	15	13	21	34
—Florida (N.L.)		1	1	.500	5.79	20	0	0	0	0	23 1/3	20	15	15	20	16
Major League totals (2 years)		3	7	.300	5.96	32	12	0	0	0	90 2/3	96	65	60	72	65

MELUSKEY, MITCH — C — ASTROS

PERSONAL: Born September 18, 1973, in Yakima, Wash. ... 6-0/185. ... Bats both, throws right. ... Full name: Mitchell Wade Meluskey.
HIGH SCHOOL: Eisenhower (Yakima, Wash.).
TRANSACTIONS/CAREER NOTES: Selected by Cleveland Indians organization in 12th round of free-agent draft (June 1, 1992). ... Traded by Indians to Houston Astros for OF Buck McNabb (April 27, 1995). ... On disabled list (April 26, 1999-remainder of season).
STATISTICAL NOTES: Led South Atlantic catchers with nine double plays in 1993. ... Tied for Texas League lead with four intentional bases on balls in 1997. ... Led Pacific Coast League with 10 intentional bases on balls received in 1998.

Year	Team (League)	Pos.	G	AB	R	H	2B	3B	HR	RBI	Avg.	BB	SO	SB	PO	A	E	Avg.
								BATTING							FIELDING			
1992—Burlington (Appl.)		C	43	126	23	29	7	0	3	16	.230	29	36	3	227	29	4	.985
1993—Columbus (SAL)		C	101	342	36	84	18	3	3	47	.246	35	69	1	639	87	7	.990
1995—Kinston (Caro.)		C	8	29	5	7	5	0	0	2	.241	2	9	0	58	6	1	.985
—Kissimmee (FSL)■		C	78	261	23	56	18	1	3	31	.215	27	33	3	443	40	10	.980
1996—Kissimmee (FSL)		C	74	231	29	77	19	0	1	31	.333	29	26	1	315	27	9	.974
—Jackson (Texas)		C	38	134	18	42	11	0	0	21	.313	18	24	0	207	18	5	.978
1997—Jackson (Texas)		C	73	241	49	82	18	0	14	46	.340	31	39	1	356	43	6	.985
—New Orleans (A.A.)		C	51	172	22	43	7	0	3	21	.250	25	38	0	323	26	4	.989
1998—New Orleans (PCL)		C-OF	121	397	76	140	41	0	17	71	.353	85	59	2	702	49	10	.987
—Houston (N.L.)		C	8	8	1	2	1	0	0	0	.250	1	4	0	9	0	0	1.000
1999—Houston (N.L.)		C	10	33	4	7	1	0	1	3	.212	5	6	1	62	6	0	1.000
Major League totals (2 years)			18	41	5	9	2	0	1	3	.220	6	10	1	71	6	0	1.000

MENDOZA, RAMIRO — P — YANKEES

PERSONAL: Born June 15, 1972, in Los Santos, Panama. ... 6-2/155. ... Throws right, bats right.
TRANSACTIONS/CAREER NOTES: Signed as non-drafted free agent by New York Yankees organization (November 13, 1991).

Year	League	W	L	Pct.	ERA	G	GS	CG	ShO	Sv.	IP	H	R	ER	BB	SO
1992—Dominican Yankees (DSL)		10	2	.833	2.13	15	15	5	0	0	109 2/3	93	37	26	28	79
1993—Gulf Coast Yankees (GCL)		4	5	.444	2.79	15	9	0	0	1	67 2/3	59	26	21	7	61
—Greensboro (SAL)		0	1	.000	2.45	2	0	0	0	0	3 2/3	3	1	1	5	3
1994—Tampa (FSL)		12	6	.667	3.01	22	21	1	0	0	134 1/3	133	54	45	35	110
1995—Norwich (East.)		5	6	.455	3.21	19	19	2	1	0	89 2/3	87	39	32	33	68
—Columbus (I.L.)		1	0	1.000	2.57	2	2	0	0	0	14	10	4	4	2	13
1996—Columbus (I.L.)		6	2	.750	2.51	15	15	0	0	0	97	96	30	27	19	61
—New York (A.L.)		4	5	.444	6.79	12	11	0	0	0	53	80	43	40	10	34
1997—Columbus (I.L.)		0	0	...	5.68	1	1	0	0	0	6 1/3	7	6	4	1	4
—New York (A.L.)		8	6	.571	4.24	39	15	0	0	2	133 2/3	157	67	63	28	82
1998—New York (A.L.)		10	2	.833	3.25	41	14	1	1	1	130 1/3	131	50	47	30	56
1999—New York (A.L.)		9	9	.500	4.29	53	6	0	0	3	123 2/3	141	68	59	27	80
Major League totals (4 years)		31	22	.585	4.27	145	46	1	1	6	440 2/3	509	228	209	95	252

M

DIVISION SERIES RECORD

Year League	W	L	Pct.	ERA	G	GS	CG	ShO	Sv.	IP	H	R	ER	BB	SO
1997— New York (A.L.)..................	1	1	.500	2.45	2	0	0	0	0	3 $^2/_3$	3	1	1	0	2
1998— New York (A.L.)..................						Did not play.									
1999— New York (A.L.)..................						Did not play.									

CHAMPIONSHIP SERIES RECORD

Year League	W	L	Pct.	ERA	G	GS	CG	ShO	Sv.	IP	H	R	ER	BB	SO
1998— New York (A.L.)..................	0	0	...	0.00	2	0	0	0	0	4 $^1/_3$	4	0	0	0	1
1999— New York (A.L.)..................	0	0	...	0.00	2	0	0	0	1	2 $^1/_3$	0	0	0	0	2
Champ. series totals (2 years)	0	0	...	0.00	4	0	0	0	1	6 $^2/_3$	4	0	0	0	3

WORLD SERIES RECORD

NOTES: Member of World Series championship team (1998 and 1999).

Year League	W	L	Pct.	ERA	G	GS	CG	ShO	Sv.	IP	H	R	ER	BB	SO
1998— New York (A.L.)..................	1	0	1.000	9.00	1	0	0	0	0	1	2	1	1	0	1
1999— New York (A.L.)..................	0	0	...	10.80	1	0	0	0	0	1 $^2/_3$	3	2	2	1	0
World Series totals (2 years)	1	0	1.000	10.13	2	0	0	0	0	2 $^2/_3$	5	3	3	1	1

MENECHINO, FRANK   IF   ATHLETICS

PERSONAL: Born January 7, 1971, in Staten Island, N.Y. ... 5-9/175. ... Bats right, throws right.
HIGH SCHOOL: Susan E. Wagner (Staten Island, N.Y.).
JUNIOR COLLEGE: Gulf Coast Community College (Fla.).
COLLEGE: Alabama.
TRANSACTIONS/CAREER NOTES: Selected by Chicago White Sox organization in 45th round of free-agent draft (June 3, 1993). ... Selected by Oakland Athletics organization from White Sox organization in Rule 5 minor league draft (December 15, 1997).
STATISTICAL NOTES: Led Carolina League second basemen with 603 total chances in 1995. ... Led Pacific Coast League with seven intentional bases on balls received in 1999.

								BATTING								FIELDING			
Year Team (League)	Pos.	G	AB	R	H	2B	3B	HR	RBI	Avg.	BB	SO	SB	PO	A	E	Avg.
1993— GC White Sox (GCL) ..	2B	17	45	10	11	4	1	1	9	.244	12	4	3	22	25	1	.979
— Hickory (SAL)............	2B	50	178	35	50	6	3	4	19	.281	33	28	11	102	148	6	.977
1994— South Bend (Midw.) ...	2B	106	379	77	113	21	5	5	48	.298	78	70	15	213	254	10	*.979
1995— Prince Will. (Caro.)......	2B	137	476	65	124	31	3	6	58	.261	96	75	6	*293	295	15	.975
1996— Birmingham (Sou.).......	2B	125	415	77	121	25	3	12	62	.292	64	84	7	*273	308	13	.978
1997— Nashville (A.A.).........	2B-3B-OF	37	113	20	26	4	0	4	11	.230	26	31	3	79	86	9	.948
— Birmingham (Sou.).......	2B-3B	90	318	78	95	28	4	12	60	.299	79	77	7	176	237	11	.974
1998— Edmonton (PCL)■......	2B	378	72	105	11	7	10	40	.278	70	75	9	133	192	7	.979
1999— Vancouver (PCL).........	3-S-2-DH	130	501	103	155	31	•9	15	88	.309	73	97	4	152	341	10	.980
— Oakland (A.L.)...........	SS-3B	9	9	0	2	0	0	0	0	.222	0	4	0	4	7	0	1.000
Major League totals (1 year)		9	9	0	2	0	0	0	0	.222	0	4	0	4	7	0	1.000

MERCED, ORLANDO   OF/1B

M

PERSONAL: Born November 2, 1966, in San Juan, Puerto Rico. ... 6-1/195. ... Bats left, throws right. ... Full name: Orlando Luis Merced. ... Name pronounced mer-SED.
HIGH SCHOOL: University Garden (San Juan, Puerto Rico).
TRANSACTIONS/CAREER NOTES: Signed as non-drafted free agent by Pittsburgh Pirates organization (February 22, 1985). ... On Macon disabled list (April 18-28, 1987). ... On Watertown disabled list (June 23, 1987-remainder of season). ... On disabled list (May 1-18, August 1-16 and August 22-September 6, 1996). ... Traded by Pirates with IF Carlos Garcia and P Dan Plesac to Toronto Blue Jays for P Jose Silva, P Jose Pett, IF Brandon Cromer and three players to be named later (November 14, 1996); Pirates acquired P Mike Halperin, IF Abraham Nunez and C/OF Craig Wilson to complete deal (December 11, 1996). ... On disabled list (July 29-September 28, 1997). ... Granted free agency (October 27, 1997). ... Signed by Minnesota Twins organization (January 12, 1998). ... Traded by Twins with P Greg Swindell to Boston Red Sox for P Matt Kinney, P Joe Thomas and P John Barnes (July 31, 1998). ... Released by Red Sox (August 31, 1998). ... Signed by Chicago Cubs (September 5, 1998). ... Granted free agency (October 28, 1998). ... Signed by Montreal Expos organization (January 28, 1999). ... On disabled list (July 1-28, 1999). ... Granted free agency (October 15, 1999).
STATISTICAL NOTES: Led N.L. outfielders in double plays with five in 1993 and five in 1996. ... Career major league grand slams: 2.
MISCELLANEOUS: Batted as switch hitter (1985-92).

								BATTING								FIELDING			
Year Team (League)	Pos.	G	AB	R	H	2B	3B	HR	RBI	Avg.	BB	SO	SB	PO	A	E	Avg.
1985— GC Pirates (GCL) ...	SS-3B-1B	40	136	16	31	6	0	1	13	.228	9	9	3	46	78	28	.816
1986— Macon (SAL).............	OF-3B	65	173	20	34	4	1	2	24	.197	12	38	5	53	15	13	.840
— Watertown (NY-P).......	3B-1B-OF	27	89	12	16	0	1	3	9	.180	14	21	6	49	28	10	.885
1987— Macon (SAL).............	OF	4	4	1	0	0	0	0	0	.000	1	3	0	1	1	0	1.000
— Watertown (NY-P).......	2B	4	12	4	5	0	1	0	3	.417	1	1	1	11	7	2	.900
1988— Augusta (SAL)...........	2B-3B-SS	37	136	19	36	6	3	1	17	.265	7	20	2	35	39	7	.914
— Salem (Caro.)...........3B-2B-OF-SS	80	298	47	87	12	7	7	42	.292	27	64	13	77	183	31	.893
1989— Harrisburg (East.).......	1B-OF-3B	95	341	43	82	16	4	6	48	.240	32	66	13	435	32	10	.979
— Buffalo (A.A.).............	1B-OF-3B	35	129	18	44	5	3	1	16	.341	7	26	0	173	15	3	.984
1990— Buffalo (A.A.).............	1B-3B-OF	101	378	52	99	12	6	9	55	.262	46	63	14	689	83	20	.975
— Pittsburgh (N.L.).........	OF-C	25	24	3	5	1	0	0	0	.208	1	9	0	0	0	0	...
1991— Buffalo (A.A.).............	1B	3	12	1	2	0	0	0	0	.167	1	4	1	29	2	0	1.000
— Pittsburgh (N.L.).........	1B-OF	120	411	83	113	17	2	10	50	.275	64	81	8	916	60	12	.988
1992— Pittsburgh (N.L.)........	1B-OF	134	405	50	100	28	5	6	60	.247	52	63	5	906	75	5	.995
1993— Pittsburgh (N.L.)........	OF-1B	137	447	68	140	26	4	8	70	.313	77	64	3	485	31	10	.981
1994— Pittsburgh (N.L.)........	OF-1B	108	386	48	105	21	3	9	51	.272	42	58	4	508	29	5	.991
1995— Pittsburgh (N.L.)........	OF-1B	132	487	75	146	29	4	15	83	.300	52	74	7	374	23	6	.985
1996— Pittsburgh (N.L.)........	OF-1B	120	453	69	130	24	1	17	80	.287	51	74	8	242	15	3	.988
1997— Toronto (A.L.)■.........	OF-DH-1B	98	368	45	98	23	2	9	40	.266	47	62	7	193	10	3	.985

Year	Team (League)	Pos.	G	AB	R	H	2B	3B	HR	RBI	Avg.	BB	SO	SB	PO	A	E	Avg.
									BATTING							FIELDING		
1998—Minnesota (A.L.)■		1B-OF-DH	63	204	22	59	12	0	5	33	.289	17	29	1	324	23	6	.983
—Boston (A.L.)■		DH-OF	9	9	0	0	0	0	0	2	.000	2	3	0	2	0	0	1.000
—Chicago (N.L.)■		OF	12	10	2	3	0	0	1	5	.300	1	2	0	3	0	0	1.000
1999—Montreal (N.L.)■		OF-1B-DH	93	194	25	52	12	1	8	26	.268	26	27	2	95	4	5	.952
American League totals (2 years)			170	581	67	157	35	2	14	75	.270	66	94	8	519	33	9	.984
National League totals (9 years)			881	2817	423	794	158	20	74	425	.282	366	452	37	3529	237	46	.988
Major League totals (10 years)			1051	3398	490	951	193	22	88	500	.280	432	546	45	4048	270	55	.987

DIVISION SERIES RECORD

Year	Team (League)	Pos.	G	AB	R	H	2B	3B	HR	RBI	Avg.	BB	SO	SB	PO	A	E	Avg.
									BATTING							FIELDING		
1998—Chicago (N.L.)									Did not play.									

CHAMPIONSHIP SERIES RECORD

NOTES: Hit home run in first at-bat (October 12, 1991).

Year	Team (League)	Pos.	G	AB	R	H	2B	3B	HR	RBI	Avg.	BB	SO	SB	PO	A	E	Avg.
									BATTING							FIELDING		
1991—Pittsburgh (N.L.)		1B-PH	3	9	1	2	0	0	1	1	.222	0	1	0	13	0	1	.929
1992—Pittsburgh (N.L.)		1B-PH	4	10	0	1	1	0	0	2	.100	2	4	0	27	2	1	.967
Championship series totals (2 years)			7	19	1	3	1	0	1	3	.158	2	5	0	40	2	2	.955

MERCKER, KENT   P

PERSONAL: Born February 1, 1968, in Dublin, Ohio. ... 6-2/195. ... Throws left, bats left. ... Full name: Kent Franklin Mercker.
HIGH SCHOOL: Dublin (Ohio).
TRANSACTIONS/CAREER NOTES: Selected by Atlanta Braves organization in first round (fifth pick overall) of free-agent draft (June 2, 1986). ... On Richmond disabled list (March 30-May 6, 1990). ... On disabled list (August 9-24, 1991). ... Traded by Braves to Baltimore Orioles for P Joe Borowski and P Rachaad Stewart (December 17, 1995). ... Traded by Orioles to Cleveland Indians for 1B Eddie Murray (July 21, 1996). ... Granted free agency (November 4, 1996). ... Signed by Cincinnati Reds (December 10, 1996). ... On disabled list (August 17-September 2, 1997). ... Granted free agency (October 27, 1997). ... Signed by St. Louis Cardinals (December 16, 1997). ... On disabled list (June 14-July 1, 1998). ... Traded by Cardinals to Boston Red Sox for P Mike Matthews and C David Benham (August 24, 1999). ... On Boston disabled list (September 7-23, 1999). ... Granted free agency (November 8, 1999).
HONORS: Named Carolina League co-Pitcher of the Year (1988).
STATISTICAL NOTES: Pitched six innings, combining with Mark Wohlers (two innings) and Alejandro Pena (one inning) in 1-0 no-hit victory against San Diego (September 11, 1991). ... Pitched 6-0 no-hit victory against Los Angeles (April 8, 1994). ... Career major league grand slams: 1.
MISCELLANEOUS: Had a sacrifice hit and received a base on balls in two games as pinch hitter (1991). ... Appeared in one game as pinch runner (1997). ... Appeared in one game as pinch runner (1998). ... Scored a run in only appearance as pinch runner with Cardinals (1999).

Year	League	W	L	Pct.	ERA	G	GS	CG	ShO	Sv.	IP	H	R	ER	BB	SO
1986—Gulf Coast Braves (GCL)		4	3	.571	2.47	9	8	0	0	0	47 1/3	37	21	13	16	42
1987—Durham (Caro.)		0	1	.000	5.40	3	3	0	0	0	11 2/3	11	8	7	6	14
1988—Durham (Caro.)		11	4	.733	*2.75	19	19	5	0	0	127 2/3	102	44	39	47	159
—Greenville (Sou.)		3	1	.750	3.35	9	9	0	0	0	48 1/3	36	20	18	26	60
1989—Richmond (I.L.)		9	12	.429	3.20	27	•27	4	0	0	168 2/3	107	66	60	*95	*144
—Atlanta (N.L.)		0	0	...	12.46	2	1	0	0	0	4 1/3	8	6	6	6	4
1990—Richmond (I.L.)		5	4	.556	3.55	12	10	0	0	1	58 1/3	60	30	23	27	69
—Atlanta (N.L.)		4	7	.364	3.17	36	0	0	0	7	48 1/3	43	22	17	24	39
1991—Atlanta (N.L.)		5	3	.625	2.58	50	4	0	0	6	73 1/3	56	23	21	35	62
1992—Atlanta (N.L.)		3	2	.600	3.42	53	0	0	0	6	68 1/3	51	27	26	35	49
1993—Atlanta (N.L.)		3	1	.750	2.86	43	6	0	0	0	66	52	24	21	36	59
1994—Atlanta (N.L.)		9	4	.692	3.45	20	17	2	1	0	112 1/3	90	46	43	45	111
1995—Atlanta (N.L.)		7	8	.467	4.15	29	26	0	0	0	143	140	73	66	61	102
1996—Baltimore (A.L.)■		3	6	.333	7.76	14	12	0	0	0	58	73	56	50	35	22
—Buffalo (A.A.)■		0	2	.000	3.94	3	3	0	0	0	16	11	7	7	9	11
—Cleveland (A.L.)■		1	0	1.000	3.09	10	0	0	0	0	11 2/3	10	4	4	3	7
1997—Cincinnati (N.L.)■		8	11	.421	3.92	28	25	0	0	0	144 2/3	135	65	63	62	75
1998—St. Louis (N.L.)■		11	11	.500	5.07	30	29	0	0	0	161 2/3	199	99	91	53	72
1999—St. Louis (N.L.)		6	5	.545	5.12	25	18	0	0	0	103 2/3	125	73	59	51	64
—Boston (A.L.)■		2	0	1.000	3.51	5	5	0	0	0	25 2/3	23	12	10	13	17
A.L. totals (2 years)		6	6	.500	6.04	29	17	0	0	0	95 1/3	106	72	64	51	46
N.L. totals (10 years)		56	52	.519	4.02	316	126	2	1	19	925 2/3	899	458	413	408	637
Major League totals (11 years)		62	58	.517	4.20	345	143	2	1	19	1021	1005	530	477	459	683

DIVISION SERIES RECORD

Year	League	W	L	Pct.	ERA	G	GS	CG	ShO	Sv.	IP	H	R	ER	BB	SO
1995—Atlanta (N.L.)		0	0	...	0.00	1	0	0	0	0	1/3	0	0	0	0	0
1999—Boston (A.L.)		0	0	...	10.80	1	1	0	0	0	1 2/3	3	2	2	3	1
Division series totals (2 years)		0	0	...	9.00	2	1	0	0	0	2	3	2	2	3	1

CHAMPIONSHIP SERIES RECORD

Year	League	W	L	Pct.	ERA	G	GS	CG	ShO	Sv.	IP	H	R	ER	BB	SO
1991—Atlanta (N.L.)		0	1	.000	13.50	1	0	0	0	0	2/3	0	1	1	2	0
1992—Atlanta (N.L.)		0	0	...	0.00	2	0	0	0	0	3	1	0	0	1	1
1993—Atlanta (N.L.)		0	0	...	1.80	5	0	0	0	0	5	3	1	1	2	4
1999—Boston (A.L.)		0	1	.000	4.70	2	2	0	0	0	7 2/3	12	4	4	4	5
Champ. series totals (4 years)		0	2	.000	3.31	10	2	0	0	0	16 1/3	16	6	6	9	10

NOTES: Member of World Series championship team (1995).

WORLD SERIES RECORD

Year	League	W	L	Pct.	ERA	G	GS	CG	ShO	Sv.	IP	H	R	ER	BB	SO
1991—Atlanta (N.L.)		0	0	...	0.00	2	0	0	0	0	1	0	0	0	0	1
1995—Atlanta (N.L.)		0	0	...	4.50	1	0	0	0	0	2	1	1	1	2	2
World Series totals (2 years)		0	0	...	3.00	3	0	0	0	0	3	1	1	1	2	3

M

MERLONI, LOU — IF

PERSONAL: Born April 6, 1971, in Framingham, Mass. ... 5-10/195. ... Bats right, throws right. ... Full name: Louis William Merloni.
HIGH SCHOOL: Framingham (Mass.) South.
COLLEGE: Providence.
TRANSACTIONS/CAREER NOTES: Selected by Boston Red Sox organization in 10th round of free-agent draft (June 3, 1993). ... On Boston disabled list (June 29-September 12, 1998); included rehabilitation assignment to Gulf Coast Red Sox (August 8-20). ... Released by Red Sox (November 22, 1999).

							BATTING								FIELDING		
Year	Team (League)	Pos.	G	AB	R	H	2B	3B	HR	RBI	Avg.	BB	SO	SB	PO	A	E	Avg.
1993— GC Red Sox (GCL)	SS	4	14	4	5	1	0	0	1	.357	1	1	1	7	13	1	.952
— Fort Laud. (FSL)	3B-SS	44	156	14	38	1	1	2	21	.244	13	26	1	40	114	8	.951
1994— Sarasota (FSL)	2B-3B-SS	113	419	59	120	16	2	1	63	.286	36	57	5	196	304	18	.965
1995— Trenton (East.)	2B-3B-SS	93	318	42	88	16	1	1	30	.277	39	50	7	166	222	20	.951
1996— GC Red Sox (GCL)	2B	1	4	1	1	0	0	0	1	.250	0	0	0	3	3	0	1.000
— Trenton (East.) 3B-2B-SS-1B	28	95	11	22	6	1	3	16	.232	9	18	0	39	67	8	.930
— Pawtucket (I.L.)	3B-2B-SS	38	115	19	29	6	0	1	12	.252	10	20	0	39	99	8	.945
1997— Trenton (East.)	3B-2B-SS	69	255	49	79	17	4	5	37	.310	30	43	3	68	130	9	.957
— Pawtucket (I.L.)	2B-3B-SS	49	165	24	49	10	0	5	24	.297	15	20	0	61	122	4	.979
1998— Pawtucket (I.L.)	SS-2B-3B	27	88	17	34	3	1	8	22	.386	16	13	2	27	56	2	.976
— Boston (A.L.)	2B-3B-SS	39	96	10	27	6	0	1	15	.281	7	20	1	52	73	5	.962
— GC Red Sox (GCL)	2B	1	1	0	0	0	0	0	0	.000	0	0	0	0	0	0	...
1999— Boston (A.L.).............S-3-2-D-1-O	43	126	18	32	7	0	1	13	.254	8	16	0	68	88	10	.940
— Pawtucket (I.L.).........S-3-DH-1-2	66	229	45	64	14	1	7	36	.279	30	38	1	79	127	12	.945
Major League totals (2 years)		82	222	28	59	13	0	2	28	.266	15	36	1	120	161	15	.949

DIVISION SERIES RECORD

							BATTING								FIELDING		
Year	Team (League)	Pos.	G	AB	R	H	2B	3B	HR	RBI	Avg.	BB	SO	SB	PO	A	E	Avg.
1999— Boston (A.L.)..............	SS-PH	3	6	1	2	0	0	0	1	.333	1	1	0	3	2	1	.833

CHAMPIONSHIP SERIES RECORD

							BATTING								FIELDING		
Year	Team (League)	Pos.	G	AB	R	H	2B	3B	HR	RBI	Avg.	BB	SO	SB	PO	A	E	Avg.
1999— Boston (A.L.)..............	PH	1	0	0	0	0	0	0	0	...	1	0	0	0	0	0	...

MESA, JOSE — P — MARINERS

PERSONAL: Born May 22, 1966, in Azua, Dominican Republic. ... 6-3/225. ... Throws right, bats right. ... Full name: Jose Ramon Mesa.
HIGH SCHOOL: Santa School (Azua, Dominican Republic).
TRANSACTIONS/CAREER NOTES: Signed as non-drafted free agent by Toronto Blue Jays organization (October 31, 1981). ... On Kinston disabled list (August 27, 1984-remainder of season). ... Traded by Blue Jays to Baltimore Orioles (September 4, 1987), completing deal in which Orioles traded P Mike Flanagan to Blue Jays for P Oswald Peraza and a player to be named later (August 31, 1987). ... On Rochester disabled list (April 18-May 16 and June 30, 1988-remainder of season; May 27, 1989-remainder of season; and August 21-September 5, 1991). ... Traded by Orioles to Cleveland Indians for OF Kyle Washington (July 14, 1992). ... On suspended list (April 5-8, 1993). ... Traded by Indians with IF Shawon Dunston and P Alvin Morman to San Francisco Giants for P Steve Reed and OF Jacob Cruz (July 23, 1998). ... Granted free agency (October 23, 1998). ... Signed by Seattle Mariners (November 13, 1998).
HONORS: Named A.L. Fireman of the Year by THE SPORTING NEWS (1995).
STATISTICAL NOTES: Tied for Carolina League lead with nine hit batsmen in 1985.
MISCELLANEOUS: Appeared in one game as pinch runner for Baltimore (1991).

Year	League	W	L	Pct.	ERA	G	GS	CG	ShO	Sv.	IP	H	R	ER	BB	SO
1982— Gulf Coast Blue Jays (GCL)	6	4	.600	2.70	13	12	6	*3	1	83 1/3	58	34	25	20	40
1983— Florence (SAL)	6	12	.333	5.48	28	27	1	0	0	141 1/3	153	*116	86	93	91
1984— Florence (SAL)	4	3	.571	3.76	7	7	0	0	0	38 1/3	38	24	16	25	35
— Kinston (Caro.)	5	2	.714	3.91	10	9	0	0	0	50 2/3	51	23	22	28	24
1985— Kinston (Caro.)	5	10	.333	6.16	30	20	0	0	1	106 2/3	110	89	73	79	71
1986— Ventura County (Calif.)	10	6	.625	3.86	24	24	2	1	0	142 1/3	141	71	61	58	113
— Knoxville (Sou.)	2	2	.500	4.35	9	8	2	1	0	41 1/3	40	32	20	23	30
1987— Knoxville (Sou.)	10	•13	.435	5.21	35	*35	4	2	0	*193 1/3	*206	*131	*112	104	115
— Baltimore (A.L.)■...............	1	3	.250	6.03	6	5	0	0	0	31 1/3	38	23	21	15	17
1988— Rochester (I.L.)	0	3	.000	8.62	11	2	0	0	0	15 2/3	21	20	15	14	15
1989— Rochester (I.L.)	0	2	.000	5.40	7	1	0	0	0	10	10	6	6	6	3
— Hagerstown (East.)	0	0	...	1.38	3	3	0	0	0	13	9	2	2	4	12
1990— Hagerstown (East.)..............	5	5	.500	3.42	15	15	3	1	0	79	77	35	30	30	72
— Rochester (I.L.)	1	2	.333	2.42	4	4	0	0	0	26	21	11	7	12	23
— Baltimore (A.L.)	3	2	.600	3.86	7	7	0	0	0	46 2/3	37	20	20	27	24
1991— Baltimore (A.L.)	6	11	.353	5.97	23	23	2	1	0	123 2/3	151	86	82	62	64
— Rochester (I.L.)	3	3	.500	3.86	8	8	1	1	0	51 1/3	37	25	22	30	48
1992— Baltimore (A.L.)	3	8	.273	5.19	13	12	0	0	0	67 2/3	77	41	39	27	22
— Cleveland (A.L.)■...............	4	4	.500	4.16	15	15	1	1	0	93	92	45	43	43	40
1993— Cleveland (A.L.)	10	12	.455	4.92	34	33	3	0	0	208 2/3	232	122	114	62	118
1994— Cleveland (A.L.)	7	5	.583	3.82	51	0	0	0	2	73	71	33	31	26	63
1995— Cleveland (A.L.)	3	0	1.000	1.13	62	0	0	0	*46	64	49	9	8	17	58
1996— Cleveland (A.L.)	2	7	.222	3.73	69	0	0	0	39	72 1/3	69	32	30	28	64
1997— Cleveland (A.L.)	4	4	.500	2.40	66	0	0	0	16	82 1/3	83	28	22	28	69
1998— Cleveland (A.L.)	3	4	.429	5.17	44	0	0	0	1	54	61	36	31	20	35
— San Francisco (N.L.)■	5	3	.625	3.52	32	0	0	0	0	30 2/3	30	14	12	18	28
1999— Seattle (A.L.)■	3	6	.333	4.98	68	0	0	0	33	68 2/3	84	42	38	40	42
A.L. totals (11 years)	49	66	.426	4.38	458	95	6	2	137	985 1/3	1044	517	479	395	616
N.L. totals (1 year)	5	3	.625	3.52	32	0	0	0	0	30 2/3	30	14	12	18	28
Major League totals (11 years)	54	69	.439	4.35	490	95	6	2	137	1016	1074	531	491	413	644

DIVISION SERIES RECORD

Year League	W	L	Pct.	ERA	G	GS	CG	ShO	Sv.	IP	H	R	ER	BB	SO
1995— Cleveland (A.L.)..................	0	0	...	0.00	2	0	0	0	0	2	0	0	0	2	0
1996— Cleveland (A.L.)..................	0	1	.000	3.86	2	0	0	0	0	4 2/3	8	2	2	0	7
1997— Cleveland (A.L.)..................	0	0	...	2.70	2	0	0	0	1	3 1/3	5	1	1	1	2
Division series totals (3 years)	0	1	.000	2.70	6	0	0	0	1	10	13	3	3	3	9

CHAMPIONSHIP SERIES RECORD

Year League	W	L	Pct.	ERA	G	GS	CG	ShO	Sv.	IP	H	R	ER	BB	SO
1995— Cleveland (A.L.)..................	0	0	...	2.25	4	0	0	0	1	4	3	1	1	1	1
1997— Cleveland (A.L.)..................	1	0	1.000	3.38	4	0	0	0	2	5 1/3	5	2	2	3	5
Champ. series totals (2 years)	1	0	1.000	2.89	8	0	0	0	3	9 1/3	8	3	3	4	6

WORLD SERIES RECORD

Year League	W	L	Pct.	ERA	G	GS	CG	ShO	Sv.	IP	H	R	ER	BB	SO
1995— Cleveland (A.L.)..................	1	0	1.000	4.50	2	0	0	0	1	4	5	2	2	1	4
1997— Cleveland (A.L.)..................	0	0	...	5.40	5	0	0	0	1	5	10	3	3	1	5
World Series totals (2 years)	1	0	1.000	5.00	7	0	0	0	2	9	15	5	5	2	9

ALL-STAR GAME RECORD

Year League	W	L	Pct.	ERA	GS	CG	ShO	Sv.	IP	H	R	ER	BB	SO
1995— American	0	0	...	0.00	0	0	0	0	1	0	0	0	0	1
1996— American							Did not play.							

MEYERS, CHAD — 2B/OF — CUBS

PERSONAL: Born August 8, 1975, in Omaha, Neb. ... 6-0/190. ... Bats right, throws right. ... Full name: Chad William Meyers.
HIGH SCHOOL: Daniel J. Gross (Omaha, Neb.).
COLLEGE: Creighton.
TRANSACTIONS/CAREER NOTES: Selected by Chicago Cubs organization in fifth round of free-agent draft (June 4, 1996).
STATISTICAL NOTES: Led New York-Pennsylvania League second basemen with 33 double plays in 1996.

Year Team (League)	Pos.	G	AB	R	H	2B	3B	HR	RBI	Avg.	BB	SO	SB	PO	A	E	Avg.
1996— Williamsport (NY-P)	2B-OF	67	230	46	56	9	2	2	26	.243	33	39	27	123	136	12	.956
1997— Rockford (Midw.)	2-O-3-S	125	439	89	132	28	4	4	58	.301	74	72	54	205	266	26	.948
1998— Daytona (FSL)	2B-OF	48	186	39	60	8	3	3	25	.323	33	29	23	97	109	13	.941
— West Tenn (Sou.)	2B	77	293	63	79	14	0	0	26	.270	58	43	37	154	173	23	.934
1999— West Tenn (Sou.)	2B	64	238	45	69	19	2	3	29	.290	26	40	22	106	148	9	.966
— Iowa (PCL)	2B-OF	44	175	39	62	13	2	0	16	.354	29	20	17	104	99	4	.981
— Chicago (N.L.)	2B-OF	43	142	17	33	9	0	0	4	.232	9	27	4	76	69	2	.986
Major League totals (1 year)		43	142	17	33	9	0	0	4	.232	9	27	4	76	69	2	.986

MEYERS, MIKE — P — CUBS

M

PERSONAL: Born October 18, 1977, in London, Ont. ... 6-2/210. ... Throws right, bats right. ... Full name: Michael Gregory Meyers.
HIGH SCHOOL: Annadale (Tillsonburg, Ont.).
JUNIOR COLLEGE: Black Hawk College (Ill.).
TRANSACTIONS/CAREER NOTES: Selected by Chicago Cubs organization in 26th round of free-agent draft (June 3, 1997).

Year League	W	L	Pct.	ERA	G	GS	CG	ShO	Sv.	IP	H	R	ER	BB	SO
1997— Arizona Cubs (Ariz.)	3	1	.750	1.41	12	2	0	0	3	38 1/3	34	15	6	13	45
— Williamsport (NY-P)	0	0	...	0.00	1	1	0	0	0	4	3	0	0	1	2
1998— Rockford (Midw.)	7	5	.583	3.36	17	16	0	0	0	85 2/3	75	37	32	32	86
1999— Daytona (FSL)	10	3	.769	1.93	19	17	2	0	0	107 1/3	68	30	23	40	122
— West Tenn (Sou.)	4	0	1.000	1.09	5	5	0	0	0	33	21	5	4	10	51

MICELI, DAN — P — MARLINS

PERSONAL: Born September 9, 1970, in Newark, N.J. ... 6-0/216. ... Throws right, bats right. ... Full name: Daniel Miceli.
HIGH SCHOOL: Dr. Phillips (Orlando).
TRANSACTIONS/CAREER NOTES: Signed as non-drafted free agent by Kansas City Royals organization (March 7, 1990). ... Traded by Royals with P Jon Lieber to Pittsburgh Pirates for P Stan Belinda (July 31, 1993). ... Traded by Pirates to Detroit Tigers for P Clint Sodowsky (November 1, 1996). ... Traded by Tigers with P Donne Wall and 3B Ryan Balfe to San Diego Padres for P Tim Worrell and OF Trey Beamon (November 19, 1997). ... Traded by Padres to Florida Marlins for P Brian Meadows (November 15, 1999).

Year League	W	L	Pct.	ERA	G	GS	CG	ShO	Sv.	IP	H	R	ER	BB	SO
1990— Gulf Coast Royals (GCL)	3	4	.429	3.91	*27	0	0	0	4	53	45	27	23	29	48
1991— Eugene (N.W.)	0	1	.000	2.14	25	0	0	0	10	33 2/3	18	8	8	18	43
1992— Appleton (Midw.)...............	1	1	.500	1.93	23	0	0	0	9	23 1/3	12	6	5	4	44
— Memphis (Sou.)	3	0	1.000	1.91	32	0	0	0	4	37 2/3	20	10	8	13	46
1993— Memphis (Sou.)................	6	4	.600	4.60	40	0	0	0	7	58 2/3	54	30	30	39	68
— Carolina (Sou.)■..............	0	2	.000	5.11	13	0	0	0	10	12 1/3	11	8	7	4	19
— Pittsburgh (N.L.)	0	0	...	5.06	9	0	0	0	0	5 1/3	6	3	3	3	4
1994— Buffalo (A.A.)..................	1	1	.500	1.88	19	0	0	0	2	24	15	5	5	6	31
— Pittsburgh (N.L.)	2	1	.667	5.93	28	0	0	0	2	27 1/3	28	19	18	11	27
1995— Pittsburgh (N.L.)	4	4	.500	4.66	58	0	0	0	21	58	61	30	30	28	56
1996— Pittsburgh (N.L.)	2	10	.167	5.78	44	9	0	0	1	85 2/3	99	65	55	45	66
— Carolina (Sou.)	1	0	1.000	1.00	3	0	0	0	1	9	4	1	1	1	17
1997— Detroit (A.L.)■	3	2	.600	5.01	71	0	0	0	3	82 2/3	77	49	46	38	79
1998— San Diego (N.L.)■	10	5	.667	3.22	67	0	0	0	0	72 2/3	64	28	26	27	70
1999— San Diego (N.L.)	4	5	.444	4.46	66	0	0	0	2	68 2/3	67	39	34	36	59
A.L. totals (1 year)	3	2	.600	5.01	71	0	0	0	3	82 2/3	77	49	46	38	79
N.L. totals (6 years)	22	25	.468	4.70	272	9	0	0	28	317 2/3	325	184	166	150	282
Major League totals (7 years)	25	27	.481	4.77	343	9	0	0	31	400 1/3	402	233	212	188	361

DIVISION SERIES RECORD

Year League	W	L	Pct.	ERA	G	GS	CG	ShO	Sv.	IP	H	R	ER	BB	SO
1998— San Diego (N.L.)	1	1	.500	2.70	3	0	0	0	0	3 1/3	2	1	1	0	4

CHAMPIONSHIP SERIES RECORD

Year League	W	L	Pct.	ERA	G	GS	CG	ShO	Sv.	IP	H	R	ER	BB	SO
1998— San Diego (N.L.)	0	0	...	13.50	3	0	0	0	0	2/3	4	1	1	0	1

WORLD SERIES RECORD

Year League	W	L	Pct.	ERA	G	GS	CG	ShO	Sv.	IP	H	R	ER	BB	SO
1998— San Diego (N.L.)	0	0	...	0.00	2	0	0	0	0	1 2/3	2	0	0	2	1

MIDDLEBROOK, JASON   P   PADRES

PERSONAL: Born June 26, 1975, in Jackson, Mich. ... 6-3/215. ... Throws right, bats right. ... Full name: Jason Douglas Middlebrook.
HIGH SCHOOL: Grass Lake (Mich.).
COLLEGE: Stanford.
TRANSACTIONS/CAREER NOTES: Selected by New York Mets organization in 18th round of free-agent draft (June 3, 1993); did not sign. ... Selected by San Diego Padres organization in ninth round of free-agent draft (June 4, 1996). ... On Rancho Cucamonga disabled list (April 8-June 25, 1999).

Year League	W	L	Pct.	ERA	G	GS	CG	ShO	Sv.	IP	H	R	ER	BB	SO
1997— Rancho Cuca. (Calif.)	0	2	.000	4.03	6	6	0	0	0	22 1/3	29	15	10	12	18
— Clinton (Midw.)	6	4	.600	3.98	14	14	2	1	0	81 1/3	76	46	36	39	86
1998— Rancho Cuca. (Calif.)	10	12	.455	4.92	28	•28	0	0	0	150	162	99	82	63	132
1999— Arizona Padres (Ariz.)	1	0	1.000	7.20	1	1	0	0	0	5	9	5	4	1	3
— Mobile (Sou.)	4	6	.400	8.06	13	13	0	0	0	63 2/3	78	59	57	30	38

MIENTKIEWICZ, DOUG   1B   TWINS

PERSONAL: Born June 19, 1974, in Toledo, Ohio. ... 6-2/193. ... Bats left, throws right. ... Full name: Douglas Andrew Mientkiewicz. ... Name pronounced mint-KAY-vich.
HIGH SCHOOL: Westminster Christian (Miami).
COLLEGE: Florida State.
TRANSACTIONS/CAREER NOTES: Selected by Minnesota Twin organization in fifth round of free-agent draft (June 1, 1995).
STATISTICAL NOTES: Led Florida State League first basemen with 1,271 total chances and 113 double plays in 1996. ... Led Eastern League first basemen with .995 fielding percentage in 1997.

						BATTING								FIELDING		
Year Team (League)	Pos.	G	AB	R	H	2B	3B	HR	RBI	Avg.	BB	SO	SB	PO	A	E	Avg.
1995— Fort Myers (FSL)	1B	38	110	9	27	6	1	1	15	.245	18	19	2	160	12	1	.994
1996— Fort Myers (FSL)	1B	133	492	69	143	•36	4	5	79	.291	66	47	12	*1183	85	3	*.998
1997— New Britain (East.)	1B-OF	132	467	87	119	28	2	15	61	.255	*98	67	21	989	63	5	†.995
1998— New Britain (East.)	1B-OF	139	502	*96	162	*45	0	16	88	*.323	96	58	11	1171	92	12	.991
— Minnesota (A.L.)	1B	8	25	1	5	1	0	0	2	.200	4	3	1	61	3	0	1.000
1999— Minnesota (A.L.)	1B	118	327	34	75	21	3	2	32	.229	43	51	1	882	50	3	*.997
Major League totals (2 years)		126	352	35	80	22	3	2	34	.227	47	54	2	943	53	3	.997

M

MIESKE, MATT   OF   ASTROS

PERSONAL: Born February 13, 1968, in Midland, Mich. ... 6-0/194. ... Bats right, throws right. ... Full name: Matthew Todd Mieske. ... Name pronounced MEE-skee.
HIGH SCHOOL: Bay City Western (Auburn, Mich.).
COLLEGE: Western Michigan.
TRANSACTIONS/CAREER NOTES: Selected by Oakland Athletics organization in 20th round of free-agent draft (June 5, 1989); did not sign. ... Selected by San Diego Padres organization in 17th round of free-agent draft (June 4, 1990). ... Traded by Padres with P Ricky Bones and SS Jose Valentin to Milwaukee Brewers for 3B Gary Sheffield and P Geoff Kellogg (March 27, 1992). ... On New Orleans disabled list (May 25-June 10 and June 13-July 29, 1993). ... On disabled list (August 9-September 2, 1997). ... Granted free agency (December 21, 1997). ... Signed by Chicago Cubs (December 29, 1997). ... Released by Cubs (December 7, 1998). ... Signed by Seattle Mariners (December 17, 1998). ... Traded by Mariners to Houston Astros for P Kevin Hodges (June 20, 1999).
HONORS: Named Northwest League Most Valuable Player (1990). ... Named California League Most Valuable Player (1991).
STATISTICAL NOTES: Led Northwest League with 155 total bases in 1990. ... Led Northwest League outfielders with 148 total chances in 1990. ... Led California League with 261 total bases and .456 on-base percentage in 1991. ... Career major league grand slams: 3.

						BATTING								FIELDING		
Year Team (League)	Pos.	G	AB	R	H	2B	3B	HR	RBI	Avg.	BB	SO	SB	PO	A	E	Avg.
1990— Spokane (N.W.)	OF	*76	*291	*59	99	20	0	*12	*63	.340	45	43	26	*134	7	7	.953
1991— High Desert (Calif.).....	OF	•133	492	108	*168	*36	6	15	119	*.341	*94	82	39	258	14	*15	.948
1992— Denver (A.A.)■	OF	134	*524	80	140	29	11	19	77	.267	39	90	13	252	*23	*13	.955
1993— New Orleans (A.A.).....	OF	60	219	36	57	14	2	8	22	.260	27	46	6	114	4	2	.983
— Milwaukee (A.L.)	OF	23	58	9	14	0	0	3	7	.241	4	14	0	43	1	3	.936
1994— Milwaukee (A.L.)	OF-DH	84	259	39	67	13	1	10	38	.259	21	62	3	154	7	4	.976
— New Orleans (A.A.)	OF	2	8	2	2	0	0	1	3	.250	1	1	1	2	0	0	1.000
1995— Milwaukee (A.L.)	OF-DH	117	267	42	67	13	1	12	48	.251	27	45	2	177	7	4	.979
1996— Milwaukee (A.L.)	OF	127	374	46	104	24	3	14	64	.278	26	76	1	250	7	1	.996
1997— Milwaukee (A.L.)	OF-DH	84	253	39	63	15	3	5	21	.249	19	50	1	121	6	5	.962
1998— Chicago (N.L.)■	OF	77	97	16	29	7	0	1	12	.299	11	17	0	36	1	1	.974
— Iowa (PCL)	OF-DH	35	106	17	27	5	0	7	19	.255	10	27	0	35	3	2	.950
1999— Seattle (A.L.)■	OF-DH	24	41	11	15	0	0	4	7	.366	2	9	0	25	1	0	1.000
— Houston (N.L.)■	OF	54	109	13	31	5	0	5	22	.284	6	22	0	54	1	0	1.000
American League totals (6 years)		459	1252	186	330	65	8	48	185	.264	99	256	7	770	29	17	.979
National League totals (2 years)		131	206	29	60	12	0	6	34	.291	17	39	0	90	2	1	.989
Major League totals (7 years)		590	1458	215	390	77	8	54	219	.267	116	295	7	860	31	18	.980

					BATTING									FIELDING		
Year	Team (League)	Pos.	G	AB	R	H	2B	3B	HR	RBI	Avg.	BB	SO	SB	PO	A	E	Avg.
1999— Houston (N.L.)	PH-OF	2	4	1	0	0	0	0	0	.000	1	0	0	0	0	0	...

MILLAR, KEVIN — 1B/3B — MARLINS

PERSONAL: Born September 24, 1971, in Los Angeles. ... 6-0/185. ... Bats right, throws right. ... Full name: Kevin Charles Millar. ... Nephew of Wayne Nordhagen, outfielder with four major league teams (1976-83).
HIGH SCHOOL: University (Los Angeles).
JUNIOR COLLEGE: Los Angeles Community College.
TRANSACTIONS/CAREER NOTES: Contract purchased by Florida Marlins organization from St. Paul, Northern League (September 20, 1993). ... Granted free agency (December 21, 1997). ... Re-signed by Marlins (December 21, 1997). ... On Florida disabled list (April 19, 1998-remainder of season); included rehabilitation assignment to Charlotte (June 14-29).
HONORS: Named Eastern League Player of the Year (1997).
STATISTICAL NOTES: Led Midwest League with 240 total bases in 1994. ... Led Florida State League with 10 sacrifice flies in 1995. ... Led Florida State League first basemen with 1,320 total chances in 1995. ... Led Eastern League with 309 total bases and .423 on-base percentage and tied for league lead with seven sacrifice flies in 1997. ... Led Eastern League first basemen with 93 assists and 116 double plays in 1997.

						BATTING									FIELDING		
Year	Team (League)	Pos.	G	AB	R	H	2B	3B	HR	RBI	Avg.	BB	SO	SB	PO	A	E	Avg.
1993— St. Paul (Nor.)	3B-2B	63	227	33	59	11	1	5	30	.260	24	27	2	51	133	18	.911
1994— Kane Co. (Midw.)■	1B	135	477	75	144	35	2	19	93	.302	74	88	3	1010	64	11	.990
1995— Brevard County (FSL).	1B	129	459	53	132	32	2	13	68	.288	70	66	4	*1213	95	12	.991
1996— Portland (East.)	1B-3B	130	472	69	150	32	0	18	86	.318	37	53	6	753	134	15	.983
1997— Portland (East.)	1B-3B	135	511	94	*175	•34	2	32	*131	*.342	66	53	2	1146	†121	17	.987
1998— Florida (N.L.)	3B	2	2	1	1	0	0	0	0	.500	1	0	0	2	3	1	.833
— Charlotte (I.L.)............	3B-1B	14	46	14	15	3	0	4	15	.326	9	7	1	34	19	4	.930
1999— Calgary (PCL).............	OF-3B-1B	36	143	24	43	11	1	7	26	.301	11	19	2	63	9	2	.973
— Florida (N.L.).............	1B-3B-OF	105	351	48	100	17	4	9	67	.285	40	64	1	720	53	4	.995
Major League totals (2 years)		107	353	49	101	17	4	9	67	.286	41	64	1	722	56	5	.994

MILLER, DAMIAN — C — DIAMONDBACKS

PERSONAL: Born October 13, 1969, in La Crosse, Wis. ... 6-2/190. ... Bats right, throws right. ... Full name: Damian Donald Miller.
HIGH SCHOOL: West Salem (Wis.).
COLLEGE: Viterbo (Wis.).
TRANSACTIONS/CAREER NOTES: Selected by Minnesota Twins organization in 20th round of free-agent draft (June 4, 1990). ... Selected by Arizona Diamondbacks in second round (47th pick overall) of expansion draft (November 18, 1997).
RECORDS: Shares major league single-game records for most double plays (nine-inning game)—3 (May 25, 1999); and most double plays started (nine-inning game)—3 (May 25, 1999).
STATISTICAL NOTES: Led Pacific Coast League catchers with .998 fielding percentage in 1995. ... Led Pacific Coast League catchers with 70 assists and 695 total chances in 1996. ... Tied for N.L. lead with 11 passed balls in 1999. ... Career major league grand slams: 2.

						BATTING									FIELDING		
Year	Team (League)	Pos.	G	AB	R	H	2B	3B	HR	RBI	Avg.	BB	SO	SB	PO	A	E	Avg.
1990— Elizabethton (Appl.)....	C	14	45	7	10	1	0	1	6	.222	9	3	1	102	6	2	.982
1991— Kenosha (Midw.)........	C-1B-OF	80	267	28	62	11	1	3	34	.232	24	53	3	357	52	4	.990
1992— Kenosha (Midw.)........	C	115	377	53	110	27	2	5	56	.292	53	66	6	696	89	9	.989
1993— Fort Myers (FSL)........	C	87	325	31	69	12	1	1	26	.212	31	44	6	465	62	8	.985
— Nashville (Sou.)..........	C	4	13	0	3	0	0	0	0	.231	2	4	0	26	3	0	1.000
1994— Nashville (Sou.)..........	C	103	328	36	88	10	0	8	35	.268	35	51	4	628	81	8	.989
1995— Salt Lake (PCL)	C-OF	83	295	39	84	23	1	3	41	.285	15	39	2	395	52	1	†.998
1996— Salt Lake (PCL)	C	104	385	54	110	27	1	7	55	.286	25	58	1	619	†70	6	.991
1997— Salt Lake (PCL)	C-DH	85	314	48	106	19	3	11	82	.338	29	62	6	445	35	6	.988
— Minnesota (A.L.)	C-DH	25	66	5	18	1	0	2	13	.273	2	12	0	85	3	0	1.000
1998— Tucson (PCL)■..........	C	18	63	14	22	7	1	0	11	.349	9	9	0	95	15	3	.973
— Arizona (N.L.).............C-DH-OF-1B	57	168	17	48	14	2	3	14	.286	11	43	1	255	27	4	.986
1999— Arizona (N.L.).............	C	86	296	35	80	19	0	11	47	.270	19	78	0	622	61	6	.991
American League totals (1 year)		25	66	5	18	1	0	2	13	.273	2	12	0	85	3	0	1.000
National League totals (2 years)		143	464	52	128	33	2	14	61	.276	30	121	1	877	88	10	.990
Major League totals (3 years)		168	530	57	146	34	2	16	74	.275	32	133	1	962	91	10	.991

MILLER, JUSTIN — P — ATHLETICS

PERSONAL: Born August 27, 1977, in Torrance, Calif. ... 6-2/195. ... Throws right, bats right. ... Full name: Justin M. Miller.
HIGH SCHOOL: Torrance (Calif.).
JUNIOR COLLEGE: Los Angeles Harbor College.
TRANSACTIONS/CAREER NOTES: Selected by San Francisco Giants organization in 34th round of free-agent draft (June 1, 1995); did not sign. ... Selected by Colorado Rockies organization in fifth round of free-agent draft (June 3, 1997). ... On Salem disabled list (May 5-June 18, 1999). ... Traded by Rockies with cash to Oakland Athletics as part of three-way deal in which Brewers received P Jimmy Haynes from Athletics, Rockies received 3B Jeff Cirillo, P Scott Karl and cash from Brewers and Brewers received P Jamey Wright and C Henry Blanco from Rockies (December 13, 1999).

Year	League	W	L	Pct.	ERA	G	GS	CG	ShO	Sv.	IP	H	R	ER	BB	SO
1997— Portland (N.W.)	4	2	.667	*2.14	14	11	0	0	0	67¹/₃	68	26	16	20	54
1998— Asheville (SAL)..................	13	8	.619	3.69	27	27	3	1	0	163¹/₃	177	89	67	40	142
1999— Salem (Caro.)	1	2	.333	4.14	8	8	0	0	0	37	35	18	17	11	35

MILLER, KURT　　　　　　　P　　　　　　　CUBS

PERSONAL: Born August 24, 1972, in Tucson, Ariz. ... 6-5/225. ... Throws right, bats right. ... Full name: Kurt Everett Miller.
HIGH SCHOOL: Bowie (Texas), then Tulsa (Okla.) Union, then West (Bakersfield, Calif.).
TRANSACTIONS/CAREER NOTES: Selected by Pittsburgh Pirates organization in first round (fifth pick overall) of free-agent draft (June 4, 1990). ... On Augusta disabled list (July 10-August 3, 1991). ... Traded by Pirates with a player to be named later to Texas Rangers for 3B Steve Buechele (August 30, 1991); Rangers acquired P Hector Fajardo to complete deal (September 6, 1991). ... Traded by Rangers with P Robb Nen to Florida Marlins for P Cris Carpenter (July 17, 1993). ... On Florida disabled list (March 31-September 1, 1997); included rehabilitation assignments to Brevard County (April 13-18) and Charlotte (May 27-September 1). ... Traded by Marlins to Chicago Cubs for cash considerations (November 18, 1997). ... On Chicago disabled list (April 12-27 and April 28-May 28, 1999); included rehabilitation assignment to Iowa (May 20-28).
STATISTICAL NOTES: Tied for Texas League lead with four balks in 1992.

Year	League	W	L	Pct.	ERA	G	GS	CG	ShO	Sv.	IP	H	R	ER	BB	SO
1990—	Welland (NY-P)	3	2	.600	3.29	14	12	0	0	0	65 2/3	59	39	24	37	62
1991—	Augusta (SAL)	6	7	.462	2.50	21	21	2	2	0	115 1/3	89	49	32	57	103
1992—	Charlotte (FSL)■	5	4	.556	2.39	12	12	0	0	0	75 1/3	51	23	20	29	58
—	Tulsa (Texas)	7	5	.583	3.68	16	15	0	0	0	88	82	42	36	35	73
1993—	Tulsa (Texas)	6	8	.429	5.06	18	18	0	0	0	96	102	69	54	45	68
—	Edmonton (PCL)■	3	3	.500	4.50	9	9	0	0	0	48	42	24	24	34	19
1994—	Edmonton (PCL)	7	*13	.350	6.88	23	23	0	0	0	125 2/3	164	105	96	64	58
—	Florida (N.L.)	1	3	.250	8.10	4	4	0	0	0	20	26	18	18	7	11
1995—	Charlotte (I.L.)	8	11	.421	4.62	22	22	0	0	0	126 2/3	143	76	65	55	83
1996—	Charlotte (I.L.)	3	5	.375	4.66	12	12	2	0	0	65 2/3	77	39	34	26	38
—	Florida (N.L.)	1	3	.250	6.80	26	5	0	0	0	46 1/3	57	41	35	33	30
1997—	Brevard County (FSL)	0	0	...	1.80	2	2	0	0	0	5	6	1	1	2	7
—	Charlotte (I.L.)	2	1	.667	3.58	21	0	0	0	0	27 2/3	25	12	11	22	31
—	Florida (N.L.)	0	1	.000	9.82	7	0	0	0	0	7 1/3	12	8	8	7	7
1998—	Iowa (PCL)■	14	3	.824	3.81	28	27	2	0	0	167 2/3	153	77	71	77	145
—	Chicago (N.L.)	0	0	...	0.00	3	0	0	0	0	4	3	0	0	0	6
1999—	Chicago (N.L.)	0	0	...	18.00	4	0	0	0	0	3	6	6	6	3	1
—	Iowa (PCL)	1	2	.333	5.09	8	2	0	0	1	17 2/3	17	10	10	8	23
Major League totals (5 years)		2	7	.222	7.48	44	9	0	0	0	80 2/3	104	73	67	50	55

MILLER, TRAVIS　　　　　　　P　　　　　　　TWINS

PERSONAL: Born November 2, 1972, in Dayton, Ohio. ... 6-3/209. ... Throws left, bats right. ... Full name: Travis Eugene Miller.
HIGH SCHOOL: National Trail (New Paris, Ohio).
COLLEGE: Kent.
TRANSACTIONS/CAREER NOTES: Selected by Minnesota Twins organization in supplemental round ("sandwich pick" between first and second round, 34th pick overall) of free-agent draft (June 2, 1994); pick received as compensation for Twins failing to sign 1993 first-round pick C Jason Varitek. ... On Salt Lake disabled list (April 20-May 3, 1998).

Year	League	W	L	Pct.	ERA	G	GS	CG	ShO	Sv.	IP	H	R	ER	BB	SO
1994—	Fort Wayne (Midw.)	4	1	.800	2.60	11	9	1	0	0	55 1/3	52	17	16	12	50
—	Nashville (Sou.)	0	0	...	2.84	1	1	0	0	0	6 1/3	3	3	2	2	4
1995—	New Britain (East.)	7	9	.438	4.37	28	27	1	1	0	162 2/3	*172	93	79	65	151
1996—	Minnesota (A.L.)	1	2	.333	9.23	7	7	0	0	0	26 1/3	45	29	27	9	15
—	Salt Lake (PCL)	8	10	.444	4.83	27	27	1	0	0	160 1/3	187	97	86	57	*143
1997—	Salt Lake (PCL)	10	6	.625	4.73	21	21	0	0	0	125 2/3	140	73	66	57	86
—	Minnesota (A.L.)	1	5	.167	7.63	13	7	0	0	0	48 1/3	64	49	41	23	26
1998—	Salt Lake (PCL)	3	4	.429	4.84	34	2	0	0	9	57 2/3	60	33	31	31	65
—	Minnesota (A.L.)	0	2	.000	3.86	14	0	0	0	0	23 1/3	25	10	10	11	23
1999—	Salt Lake (PCL)	1	2	.333	2.50	16	0	0	0	1	18	16	7	5	6	19
—	Minnesota (A.L.)	2	2	.500	2.72	52	0	0	0	0	49 2/3	55	19	15	16	40
Major League totals (4 years)		4	11	.267	5.67	86	14	0	0	0	147 2/3	189	107	93	59	104

MILLER, TREVER　　　　　　　P　　　　　　　ASTROS

PERSONAL: Born May 29, 1973, in Louisville, Ky. ... 6-4/195. ... Throws left, bats right. ... Full name: Trever Douglas Miller.
HIGH SCHOOL: Trinity (Louisville, Ky.).
TRANSACTIONS/CAREER NOTES: Selected by Detroit Tigers organization in supplemental round ("sandwich pick" between first and second round, 41st pick overall) of free-agent draft (June 3, 1991); pick received as part of compensation for Atlanta Braves signing Type A free-agent C Mike Heath. ... Traded by Tigers with C Brad Ausmus, P Jose Lima, P C.J. Nitkowski and IF Daryle Ward to Houston Astros for OF Brian Hunter, IF Orlando Miller, P Doug Brocail, P Todd Jones and cash (December 10, 1996). ... On disabled list (August 23-September 7, 1998).
STATISTICAL NOTES: Tied for Appalachian League lead with seven home runs allowed in 1991.

Year	League	W	L	Pct.	ERA	G	GS	CG	ShO	Sv.	IP	H	R	ER	BB	SO
1991—	Bristol (Appl.)	2	7	.222	5.67	13	13	0	0	0	54	60	44	34	29	46
1992—	Bristol (Appl.)	3	•8	.273	4.93	12	12	1	0	0	69 1/3	75	45	38	27	64
1993—	Fayetteville (SAL)	8	13	.381	4.19	28	28	2	0	0	161	151	99	75	67	116
1994—	Trenton (East.)	7	•16	.304	4.39	26	26	*6	0	0	174 1/3	*198	95	85	51	73
1995—	Jacksonville (Sou.)	8	2	.800	2.72	31	16	3	2	0	122 1/3	122	46	37	34	77
1996—	Toledo (I.L.)	13	6	.684	4.90	27	27	0	0	0	165 1/3	167	98	90	65	115
—	Detroit (A.L.)	0	4	.000	9.18	5	4	0	0	0	16 2/3	28	17	17	9	8
1997—	New Orleans (A.A.)■	6	7	.462	3.30	29	27	2	0	0	163 2/3	177	71	60	54	99
1998—	Houston (N.L.)	2	0	1.000	3.04	37	1	0	0	1	53 1/3	57	21	18	20	30
1999—	Houston (N.L.)	3	2	.600	5.07	47	0	0	0	1	49 2/3	58	29	28	29	37
A.L. totals (1 year)		0	4	.000	9.18	5	4	0	0	0	16 2/3	28	17	17	9	8
N.L. totals (2 years)		5	2	.714	4.02	84	1	0	0	2	103	115	50	46	49	67
Major League totals (3 years)		5	6	.455	4.74	89	5	0	0	2	119 2/3	143	67	63	58	75

M

Year League	W	L	Pct.	ERA	G	GS	CG	ShO	Sv.	IP	H	R	ER	BB	SO
1998— Houston (N.L.)	0	0	...		1	0	0	0	0		0	0	0	1	0
1999— Houston (N.L.)	0	0	...	0.00	2	0	0	0	0	1 1/3	1	0	0	0	2
Division series totals (2 years)	0	0	...	0.00	3	0	0	0	0	1 1/3	1	0	0	1	2

MILLER, WADE P ASTROS

PERSONAL: Born September 13, 1976, in Reading, Pa. ... 6-2/185. ... Throws right, bats right. ... Full name: Wade T. Miller.
HIGH SCHOOL: Brandywine Heights (Pa.).
COLLEGE: Alvernia College (Pa.).
TRANSACTIONS/CAREER NOTES: Selected by Houston Astros organization in 20th round of free-agent draft (June 4, 1996). ... On disabled list (June 1, 1998-remainder of season).

Year League	W	L	Pct.	ERA	G	GS	CG	ShO	Sv.	IP	H	R	ER	BB	SO
1996— Auburn (NY-P)	1	1	.500	5.00	2	2	0	0	0	9	8	9	5	4	11
— Gulf Coast Astros (GCL) ...	3	4	.429	3.79	11	10	0	0	0	57	49	26	24	12	53
1997— Quad City (Midw.)	5	3	.625	3.36	10	8	2	0	0	59	45	27	22	10	50
— Kissimmee (FSL)	10	2	.833	1.80	14	14	4	1	0	100	79	28	20	14	76
1998— Jackson (Texas)	5	0	1.000	2.32	10	10	0	0	0	62	49	23	16	27	48
1999— New Orleans (PCL)	11	9	.550	4.38	26	26	2	0	0	162 1/3	156	85	79	64	135
— Houston (N.L.)	0	1	.000	9.58	5	1	0	0	0	10 1/3	17	11	11	5	8
Major League totals (1 year)	0	1	.000	9.58	5	1	0	0	0	10 1/3	17	11	11	5	8

MILLS, ALAN P DODGERS

PERSONAL: Born October 18, 1966, in Lakeland, Fla. ... 6-1/195. ... Throws right, bats right. ... Full name: Alan Bernard Mills.
HIGH SCHOOL: Kathleen (Fla.).
JUNIOR COLLEGE: Polk Community College (Fla.).
TRANSACTIONS/CAREER NOTES: Selected by Boston Red Sox organization in first round (13th pick overall) of free-agent draft (January 14, 1986); did not sign. ... Selected by California Angels organization in secondary phase of free-agent draft (June 2, 1986). ... Traded by Angels to New York Yankees (June 22, 1987), completing deal in which Angels traded P Ron Romanick and a player to be named later to Yankees for C Butch Wynegar (December 19, 1986). ... Traded by Yankees to Baltimore Orioles for two players to be named later (February 29, 1992); Yankees acquired P Francisco de la Rosa (February 29, 1992) and P Mark Carper (June 8, 1992) to complete deal. ... On suspended list (June 26-30, 1993). ... On Rochester disabled list (July 4-September 16, 1995). ... On disabled list (March 22-May 12, 1996 and April 10-June 15, 1997). ... On suspended list (May 29-30, 1998). ... Granted free agency (October 23, 1998). ... Signed by Los Angeles Dodgers (December 10, 1998).

Year League	W	L	Pct.	ERA	G	GS	CG	ShO	Sv.	IP	H	R	ER	BB	SO
1986— Salem (N.W.)	6	6	.500	4.63	14	14	1	0	0	83 2/3	77	58	43	60	50
1987— Prince William (Caro.)■	2	11	.154	6.09	35	8	0	0	1	85 2/3	102	75	58	64	53
1988— Prince William (Caro.)	3	8	.273	4.13	42	5	0	0	4	93 2/3	93	56	43	43	59
1989— Prince William (Caro.)	6	1	.857	0.91	26	0	0	0	7	39 2/3	22	5	4	13	44
— Fort Lauderdale (FSL)	1	4	.200	3.77	22	0	0	0	6	31	40	15	13	9	25
1990— New York (A.L.)	1	5	.167	4.10	36	0	0	0	0	41 2/3	48	21	19	33	24
— Columbus (I.L.)	3	3	.500	3.38	17	0	0	0	6	29 1/3	22	11	11	14	30
1991— Columbus (I.L.)	7	5	.583	4.43	38	15	0	0	8	113 2/3	109	65	56	75	77
— New York (A.L.)	1	1	.500	4.41	6	2	0	0	0	16 1/3	16	9	8	8	11
1992— Rochester (I.L.)■	0	1	.000	5.40	3	0	0	0	1	5	6	3	3	2	8
— Baltimore (A.L.)	10	4	.714	2.61	35	3	0	0	2	103 1/3	78	33	30	54	60
1993— Baltimore (A.L.)	5	4	.556	3.23	45	0	0	0	4	100 1/3	80	39	36	51	68
1994— Baltimore (A.L.)	3	3	.500	5.16	47	0	0	0	2	45 1/3	43	26	26	24	44
1995— Baltimore (A.L.)	3	0	1.000	7.43	21	0	0	0	0	23	30	20	19	18	16
— Rochester (I.L.)	0	1	.000	0.00	1	1	0	0	0	2 2/3	2	6	0	5	2
— Gulf Coast Orioles (GCL)	0	0	...	0.00	1	1	0	0	0	2	3	0	0	2	1
1996— Baltimore (A.L.)	3	2	.600	4.28	49	0	0	0	3	54 2/3	40	26	26	35	50
1997— Baltimore (A.L.)	2	3	.400	4.89	39	0	0	0	0	38 2/3	41	23	21	33	32
1998— Baltimore (A.L.)	3	4	.429	3.74	72	0	0	0	2	77	55	32	32	50	57
1999— Los Angeles (N.L.)■	3	4	.429	3.73	68	0	0	0	0	72 1/3	70	33	30	43	49
A.L. totals (9 years)	31	26	.544	3.90	350	5	0	0	13	500 1/3	431	229	217	306	362
N.L. totals (1 year)	3	4	.429	3.73	68	0	0	0	0	72 1/3	70	33	30	43	49
Major League totals (10 years)	34	30	.531	3.88	418	5	0	0	13	572 2/3	501	262	247	349	411

DIVISION SERIES RECORD

Year League	W	L	Pct.	ERA	G	GS	CG	ShO	Sv.	IP	H	R	ER	BB	SO
1997— Baltimore (A.L.)	0	0	...	0.00	1	0	0	0	0	1	1	0	0	0	1

CHAMPIONSHIP SERIES RECORD

Year League	W	L	Pct.	ERA	G	GS	CG	ShO	Sv.	IP	H	R	ER	BB	SO
1996— Baltimore (A.L.)	0	0	...	3.86	3	0	0	0	0	2 1/3	3	1	1	1	3
1997— Baltimore (A.L.)	0	1	.000	2.70	3	0	0	0	0	3 1/3	1	1	1	2	3
Champ. series totals (2 years)	0	1	.000	3.18	6	0	0	0	0	5 2/3	4	2	2	3	6

MILLWOOD, KEVIN P BRAVES

PERSONAL: Born December 24, 1974, in Gastonia, N.C. ... 6-4/220. ... Throws right, bats right. ... Full name: Kevin Austin Millwood.
HIGH SCHOOL: Bessemer City (N.C.).
TRANSACTIONS/CAREER NOTES: Selected by Atlanta Braves organization in 11th round of free-agent draft (June 3, 1993).
STATISTICAL NOTES: Pitched 6-0 one-hit, complete-game victory against Pittsburgh (April 14, 1998).

M

Year League	W	L	Pct.	ERA	G	GS	CG	ShO	Sv.	IP	H	R	ER	BB	SO
1993— Gulf Coast Braves (GCL)	3	3	.500	3.06	12	9	0	0	0	50	36	27	17	28	49
1994— Danville (Appl.).................	3	3	.500	3.72	13	5	0	0	1	46	42	25	19	34	56
— Macon (SAL).................	0	5	.000	5.79	12	4	0	0	1	32 2/3	31	31	21	32	24
1995— Macon (SAL).................	5	6	.455	4.63	29	12	0	0	0	103	86	65	53	57	89
1996— Durham (Caro.).................	6	9	.400	4.28	33	20	1	0	1	149 1/3	138	77	71	58	139
1997— Greenville (Sou.).............	3	5	.375	4.11	11	11	0	0	0	61 1/3	59	37	28	24	61
— Richmond (I.L.).............	7	0	1.000	1.93	9	9	1	0	0	60 2/3	38	13	13	16	46
— Atlanta (N.L.).................	5	3	.625	4.03	12	8	0	0	0	51 1/3	55	26	23	21	42
1998— Atlanta (N.L.).................	17	8	.680	4.08	31	29	3	1	0	174 1/3	175	86	79	56	163
1999— Atlanta (N.L.).................	18	7	.720	2.68	33	33	2	0	0	228	168	80	68	59	205
Major League totals (3 years).......	40	18	.690	3.37	76	70	5	1	0	453 2/3	398	192	170	136	410

DIVISION SERIES RECORD

Year League	W	L	Pct.	ERA	G	GS	CG	ShO	Sv.	IP	H	R	ER	BB	SO
1999— Atlanta (N.L.).....................	1	0	1.000	0.90	2	1	1	0	1	10	1	1	1	0	9

CHAMPIONSHIP SERIES RECORD

Year League	W	L	Pct.	ERA	G	GS	CG	ShO	Sv.	IP	H	R	ER	BB	SO
1999— Atlanta (N.L.).....................	1	0	1.000	3.55	2	2	0	0	0	12 2/3	13	6	5	1	9

WORLD SERIES RECORD

Year League	W	L	Pct.	ERA	G	GS	CG	ShO	Sv.	IP	H	R	ER	BB	SO
1999— Atlanta (N.L.).....................	0	1	.000	18.00	1	1	0	0	0	2	8	5	4	2	2

ALL-STAR GAME RECORD

Year League	W	L	Pct.	ERA	GS	CG	ShO	Sv.	IP	H	R	ER	BB	SO
1999— National...............	0	0	...	0.00	0	0	0	0	1	1	0	0	0	1

MILTON, ERIC — P — TWINS

PERSONAL: Born August 4, 1975, in State College, Pa. ... 6-3/220. ... Throws left, bats left. ... Full name: Eric Robert Milton.
HIGH SCHOOL: Bellefonte (Pa.).
COLLEGE: Maryland.
TRANSACTIONS/CAREER NOTES: Selected by New York Yankees organization in first round (20th pick overall) of free-agent draft (June 2, 1996). ... Traded by Yankees with P Danny Mota, OF Brian Buchanan, SS Cristian Guzman and cash to Minnesota Twins for 2B Chuck Knoblauch (February 6, 1998).
STATISTICAL NOTES: Tied for Eastern League lead with four balks in 1997. ... Pitched 7-0 no-hit victory against Anaheim (September 11, 1999).

Year League	W	L	Pct.	ERA	G	GS	CG	ShO	Sv.	IP	H	R	ER	BB	SO
1997— Tampa (FSL).....................	8	3	.727	3.09	14	14	1	0	0	93 1/3	78	35	32	14	95
— Norwich (East.)	6	3	.667	3.13	14	14	1	0	0	77 2/3	59	29	27	36	67
1998— Minnesota (A.L.)■..............	8	14	.364	5.64	32	32	1	0	0	172 1/3	195	113	108	70	107
1999— Minnesota (A.L.)	7	11	.389	4.49	34	34	5	2	0	206 1/3	190	111	103	63	163
Major League totals (2 years).......	15	25	.375	5.01	66	66	6	2	0	378 2/3	385	224	211	133	270

M

MINOR, DAMON — 1B — GIANTS

PERSONAL: Born January 9, 1975, in Canton, Ohio. ... 6-7/230. ... Bats left, throws left. ... Full name: Damon Reed Minor. ... Brother of Ryan Minor, third baseman, Baltimore Orioles.
HIGH SCHOOL: Hammon (Okla.).
COLLEGE: Oklahoma.
TRANSACTIONS/CAREER NOTES: Selected by San Francisco Giants organization in 12th round of free-agent draft (June 4, 1996).
STATISTICAL NOTES: Tied for Northwest League lead in intentional bases on balls received with four in 1996. ... Led Northwest League first basemen with 693 total chances in 1996. ... Led California League with eight intentional bases in balls received in 1997. ... Led California League first basemen with 127 double plays and 1,371 total chances in 1997. ... Led Texas League first baseman with 1,273 total chances in 1999.

Year Team (League)	Pos.	G	AB	R	H	2B	3B	HR	RBI	Avg.	BB	SO	SB	PO	A	E	Avg.
1996— Bellingham (N.W.)	1B	75	269	44	65	11	1	12	55	.242	47	86	0	*650	38	5	.993
1997— Bakersfield (Calif.)	1B	*140	532	98	154	34	1	31	99	.289	87	143	2	*1261	*88	*22	.984
1998— Shreveport (Texas)	1B	81	289	39	69	11	1	14	52	.239	30	51	1	641	39	8	.988
— San Jose (Calif.)	1B	48	176	26	50	10	1	7	36	.284	28	40	0	413	36	6	.987
1999— Shreveport (Texas)	1B-DH	136	473	76	129	33	4	20	82	.273	80	115	1	*1160	*104	9	*.993

MINOR, RYAN — 3B — ORIOLES

PERSONAL: Born January 5, 1974, in Canton, Ohio. ... 6-7/245. ... Bats right, throws right. ... Full name: Ryan Dale Minor. ... Brother of Damon Minor, first baseman, San Francisco Giants organization.
HIGH SCHOOL: Hammon (Okla.).
COLLEGE: Oklahoma.
TRANSACTIONS/CAREER NOTES: Selected by Baltimore Orioles organization in 15th round of free-agent draft (June 1, 1992); did not sign. ... Selected by Orioles organization in 33rd round of free-agent draft (June 4, 1996).
STATISTICAL NOTES: Led Eastern League third basemen with 27 double plays in 1998.

Year Team (League)	Pos.	G	AB	R	H	2B	3B	HR	RBI	Avg.	BB	SO	SB	PO	A	E	Avg.
1996— Bluefield (Appl.)	3B-SS	25	87	14	22	6	0	4	9	.253	7	32	1	13	45	5	.921
1997— Delmarva (SAL).........	3B-1B-DH	134	488	83	150	42	1	24	97	.307	51	102	7	193	209	34	.922
1998— Bowie (East.).............	3B-DH	138	521	73	130	20	3	17	71	.250	34	*152	2	89	245	*26	.928
— Baltimore (A.L.)	3B-1B-DH	9	14	3	6	1	0	0	1	.429	0	3	0	6	5	1	.917

							BATTING								FIELDING		
Year	Team (League)	Pos.	G	AB	R	H	2B	3B	HR	RBI	Avg.	BB	SO	SB	PO	A	E	Avg.
1999	—Rochester (I.L.).........	3B-1B-DH	101	383	56	98	24	1	21	67	.256	37	119	3	170	148	13	.961
	—Baltimore (A.L.).........	3B-1B	46	124	13	24	7	0	3	10	.194	8	43	1	36	80	5	.959
	Major League totals (2 years)		55	138	16	30	8	0	3	11	.217	8	46	1	42	85	6	.955

CBA REGULAR-SEASON RECORD

TRANSACTIONS/CAREER NOTES: Selected by Philadelphia 76ers in second round (32nd pick overall) of 1996 NBA draft. ... Played in Continental Basketball Association with Oklahoma City Calvary (1996-97).

												AVERAGES		
Season Team	G	Min.	FGM	FGA	Pct.	FTM	FTA	Pct.	Reb.	Ast.	Pts.	RPG	APG	PPG
96-97—Oklahoma City	32	892	124	270	.459	38	50	.760	141	62	304	4.4	1.9	9.5

MINTZ, STEVE   P   ANGELS

PERSONAL: Born November 24, 1968, in Leland, N.C. ... 5-10/195. ... Throws right, bats left. ... Full name: Stephen Wayne Mintz.
HIGH SCHOOL: North Brunswick, N.C.
JUNIOR COLLEGE: Mount Olive (N.C.).
TRANSACTIONS/CAREER NOTES: Selected by Los Angeles Dodgers organization in 17th round of free-agent draft (June 4, 1990). ... Released by Dodgers (March 31, 1993). ... Signed by New Britain, Boston Red Sox organization (April 21, 1993). ... On disabled list (April 30-May 13, 1993). ... Granted free agency (October 15, 1993). ... Signed by Phoenix, San Francisco Giants organization (December 15, 1993). ... Granted free agency (October 15, 1996). ... Signed by Milwaukee Brewers organization (November 6, 1996). ... Released by Brewers (March 7, 1997). ... Signed by Chia-nan, Taiwan League (1997). ... Signed by San Diego Padres organization (May 30, 1997). ... Granted free agency (October 15, 1997). ... Signed by Pittsburgh Pirates organization (January 7, 1998). ... Released by Pirates (August 28, 1998). ... Signed by Anaheim Angels organization (January 25, 1999). ... Granted free agency (October 14, 1999). ... Re-signed by Angels organization (January 24, 2000).
HONORS: Named Pacific Coast League Most Valuable Player (1996).

Year	League	W	L	Pct.	ERA	G	GS	CG	ShO	Sv.	IP	H	R	ER	BB	SO
1990—Yakima (N.W.)	4	3	.571	3.88	12	12	0	0	0	67$\frac{1}{3}$	58	36	29	39	72
1991—Bakersfield (Calif.)..............	6	6	.500	4.30	28	11	0	0	3	92	85	56	44	58	101
1992—Vero Beach (FSL)	3	6	.333	3.13	43	2	0	0	6	77$\frac{2}{3}$	66	29	27	30	66
1993—New Britain (East.)■..........	2	4	.333	2.08	43	1	0	0	7	69$\frac{1}{3}$	52	22	16	30	51
1994—Shreveport (Texas)■..........	10	2	*.833	2.20	30	0	0	0	0	65$\frac{1}{3}$	45	29	16	22	42
—Phoenix (PCL)	0	1	.000	5.50	24	0	0	0	3	36	40	24	22	13	27
1995—Phoenix (PCL)	5	2	.714	2.39	31	0	0	0	7	49	42	16	13	21	36
—San Francisco (N.L.)	1	2	.333	7.45	14	0	0	0	0	19$\frac{1}{3}$	26	16	16	12	7
1996—Phoenix (PCL)	3	5	.375	5.37	*59	0	0	0	*27	57	63	39	34	25	35
1997—Chia-nan (Taiwan)■...........	1	0	1.000	0.73	9	0	0	0	3	12	8	...	...	7	8
—Las Vegas (PCL)■............	5	2	.714	8.05	27	0	0	0	5	34$\frac{2}{3}$	50	31	31	17	28
1998—Nashville (PCL)■.............	4	4	.500	5.45	56	0	0	0	1	72$\frac{2}{3}$	85	48	44	32	45
1999—Erie (East.)■...................	1	1	.500	2.23	26	0	0	0	9	32$\frac{1}{3}$	26	12	8	12	33
—Edmonton (PCL)	4	3	.571	2.35	31	0	0	0	9	30$\frac{2}{3}$	31	11	8	6	17
—Anaheim (A.L.)	0	0	...	3.60	3	0	0	0	0	5	8	2	2	2	2
A.L. totals (1 year)	0	0	...	3.60	3	0	0	0	0	5	8	2	2	2	2
N.L. totals (1 year)	1	2	.333	7.45	14	0	0	0	0	19$\frac{1}{3}$	26	16	16	12	7
Major League totals (2 years)	1	2	.333	6.66	17	0	0	0	0	24$\frac{1}{3}$	34	18	18	14	9

MIRABELLI, DOUG   C   GIANTS

PERSONAL: Born October 18, 1970, in Kingman, Ariz. ... 6-1/218. ... Bats right, throws right. ... Full name: Douglas Anthony Mirabelli.
HIGH SCHOOL: Valley (Las Vegas).
COLLEGE: Wichita State.
TRANSACTIONS/CAREER NOTES: Selected by Detroit Tigers organization in sixth round of free-agent draft (June 5, 1989); did not sign. ... Selected by San Francisco Giants organization in fifth round of free-agent draft (June 1, 1992). ... On Phoenix disabled list (May 16-23, 1995).
STATISTICAL NOTES: Led Texas League with .419 on-base percentage in 1996. ... Led Pacific Coast League catchers with 680 total chances in 1997.

							BATTING								FIELDING		
Year	Team (League)	Pos.	G	AB	R	H	2B	3B	HR	RBI	Avg.	BB	SO	SB	PO	A	E	Avg.
1992—San Jose (Calif.).........	C	53	177	30	41	11	1	0	21	.232	24	18	1	321	38	10	.973
1993—San Jose (Calif.).........	C	113	371	58	100	19	2	1	48	.270	72	55	0	737	99	9	.989
1994—Shreveport (Texas).....	C-1B	85	255	23	56	8	0	4	24	.220	36	48	3	391	51	3	.993
1995—Shreveport (Texas).....	C-1B	40	126	14	38	13	0	0	16	.302	20	14	1	193	21	3	.986
—Phoenix (PCL)	C	23	66	3	11	0	1	0	7	.167	12	10	1	115	17	2	.985
1996—Shreveport (Texas).....	C-DH-1B	115	380	60	112	23	0	21	70	.295	76	49	0	548	56	7	.989
—Phoenix (PCL)	C	14	47	10	14	7	0	0	7	.298	4	7	0	97	10	2	.982
—San Francisco (N.L.) ..	C	9	18	2	4	1	0	0	1	.222	3	4	0	29	2	0	1.000
1997—Phoenix (PCL)	C-DH	100	332	49	88	23	2	8	48	.265	58	69	1	*629	47	4	.994
—San Francisco (N.L.) ..	C	6	7	0	1	0	0	0	0	.143	1	3	0	16	0	0	1.000
1998—Fresno (PCL)	C-DH	85	265	45	69	12	2	13	53	.260	52	55	2	605	50	3	*.995
—San Francisco (N.L.) ..	C	10	17	2	4	2	0	1	4	.235	2	6	0	34	4	1	.974
1999—Fresno (PCL)	C-1B-DH	86	320	63	100	24	1	14	51	.313	48	56	8	619	73	5	.993
—San Francisco (N.L.) ..	C	33	87	10	22	6	0	1	10	.253	9	25	0	156	11	0	1.000
Major League totals (4 years)		58	129	14	31	9	0	2	15	.240	15	38	0	235	17	1	.996

MLICKI, DAVE   P   TIGERS

PERSONAL: Born June 8, 1968, in Cleveland. ... 6-4/205. ... Throws right, bats right. ... Full name: David John Mlicki. ... Brother of Doug Mlicki, minor league pitcher (1992-99). ... Name pronounced muh-LICK-ee.
HIGH SCHOOL: Cheyenne Mountain (Colorado Springs, Colo.).
COLLEGE: Oklahoma State.

TRANSACTIONS/CAREER NOTES: Selected by Seattle Mariners organization in 23rd round of free-agent draft (June 5, 1989); did not sign. ... Selected by Cleveland Indians organization in 17th round of free-agent draft (June 4, 1990). ... On Cleveland disabled list (April 4-August 4, 1993); included rehabilitation assignment to Canton/Akron (July 19-August 4). ... Traded by Indians with P Jerry DiPoto, P Paul Byrd and a player to be named later to New York Mets for OF Jeromy Burnitz and P Joe Roa (November 18, 1994); Mets acquired 2B Jesus Azuaje to complete deal (December 6, 1994). ... Traded by Mets with P Greg McMichael to Los Angeles Dodgers for P Hideo Nomo and P Brad Clontz (June 5, 1998). ... Traded by Dodgers with P Mel Rojas and cash considerations to Detroit Tigers for P Robinson Checo, P Apostol Garcia and P Rick Roberts (April 16, 1999).

STATISTICAL NOTES: Led International League with 26 home runs allowed in 1994.

MISCELLANEOUS: Struck out in only appearance as pinch hitter (1996). ... Appeared in one game as pinch runner (1997).

Year League	W	L	Pct.	ERA	G	GS	CG	ShO	Sv.	IP	H	R	ER	BB	SO
1990— Burlington (Appl.)	3	1	.750	3.50	8	1	0	0	0	18	16	11	7	6	17
— Watertown (NY-P)	3	0	1.000	3.38	7	4	0	0	0	32	33	15	12	11	28
1991— Columbus (SAL)	8	6	.571	4.20	22	19	2	0	0	115²/₃	101	70	54	70	136
1992— Canton/Akron (East.)	11	9	.550	3.60	27	*27	0	0	0	172²/₃	143	77	69	•80	146
— Cleveland (A.L.)	0	2	.000	4.98	4	4	0	0	0	21²/₃	23	14	12	16	16
1993— Canton/Akron (East.)	2	1	.667	0.39	6	6	0	0	0	23	15	2	1	8	21
— Cleveland (A.L.)	0	0	...	3.38	3	3	0	0	0	13¹/₃	11	6	5	6	7
1994— Charlotte (I.L.)	6	10	.375	4.25	28	28	0	0	0	165¹/₃	179	85	78	64	152
1995— New York (N.L.)■	9	7	.563	4.26	29	25	0	0	0	160²/₃	160	82	76	54	123
1996— New York (N.L.)	6	7	.462	3.30	51	2	0	0	1	90	95	46	33	33	83
1997— New York (N.L.)	8	12	.400	4.00	32	32	1	1	0	193²/₃	194	89	86	76	157
1998— New York (N.L.)	1	4	.200	5.68	10	10	1	0	0	57	68	38	36	25	39
— Los Angeles (N.L.)■	7	3	.700	4.05	20	20	2	1	0	124¹/₃	120	64	56	38	78
1999— Los Angeles (N.L.)	0	1	.000	4.91	2	0	0	0	0	7¹/₃	10	4	4	2	1
— Detroit (A.L.)■	14	12	.538	4.60	31	31	2	0	0	191²/₃	209	108	98	70	119
A.L. totals (3 years)	14	14	.500	4.57	38	38	2	0	0	226²/₃	243	128	115	92	142
N.L. totals (5 years)	31	34	.477	4.14	144	89	4	2	1	633	647	323	291	228	481
Major League totals (7 years)	45	48	.484	4.25	182	127	6	2	1	859²/₃	890	451	406	320	623

MOEHLER, BRIAN P TIGERS

PERSONAL: Born December 31, 1971, in Rockingham, N.C. ... 6-3/235. ... Throws right, bats right. ... Full name: Brian Merritt Moehler.
HIGH SCHOOL: Richmond (N.C.) South.
COLLEGE: UNC Greensboro.
TRANSACTIONS/CAREER NOTES: Selected by Detroit Tigers organization in sixth round of free-agent draft (June 3, 1993). ... On disabled list (August 9-22, 1997). ... On suspended list (May 3-13, 1999).

Year League	W	L	Pct.	ERA	G	GS	CG	ShO	Sv.	IP	H	R	ER	BB	SO
1993— Niagara Falls (NY-P)	6	5	.545	3.22	12	11	0	0	0	58²/₃	51	33	21	27	38
1994— Lakeland (FSL)	12	12	.500	3.01	26	25	5	2	0	164²/₃	153	66	55	65	92
1995— Jacksonville (Sou.)	8	10	.444	4.82	28	27	0	0	0	162¹/₃	176	94	87	52	89
1996— Detroit (A.L.)	0	1	.000	4.35	2	2	0	0	0	10¹/₃	11	10	5	8	2
— Jacksonville (Sou.)	15	6	.714	3.48	28	28	1	0	0	173¹/₃	186	80	67	50	120
1997— Detroit (A.L.)	11	12	.478	4.67	31	31	2	1	0	175¹/₃	198	97	91	61	97
1998— Detroit (A.L.)	14	13	.519	3.90	33	33	4	3	0	221¹/₃	220	103	96	56	123
1999— Detroit (A.L.)	10	*16	.385	5.04	32	32	2	2	0	196¹/₃	229	116	110	59	106
Major League totals (4 years)	35	42	.455	4.50	98	98	8	6	0	603¹/₃	658	326	302	184	328

MOELLER, CHAD C TWINS

PERSONAL: Born February 18, 1975, in Upland, Calif. ... 6-3/207. ... Bats right, throws right. ... Full name: Chad Edward Moeller.
HIGH SCHOOL: Upland (Calif.).
COLLEGE: Southern California.
TRANSACTIONS/CAREER NOTES: Selected by New York Yankees organization in 25th round of free-agent draft (June 3, 1993); did not sign. ... Selected by Minnesota Twins organization in seventh round of free-agent draft (June 4, 1996). ... On disabled list (July 12, 1996-remainder of season).

					BATTING								FIELDING		
Year Team (League)	Pos.	G	AB	R	H	2B	3B	HR	RBI	Avg.	BB	SO	SB	PO	A	E	Avg.
---	---	---	---	---	---	---	---	---	---	---	---	---	---	---	---	---	---
1996— Elizabethton (Appl.)	C	17	59	17	21	4	0	4	13	.356	18	9	1	99	16	1	.991
1997— Fort Wayne (Midw.)	C	108	384	58	111	18	3	9	39	.289	48	76	11	824	90	*15	.984
1998— Fort Myers (FSL)	C	66	254	37	83	24	1	6	39	.327	31	37	2	395	36	9	.980
— New Britain (East.)	C	58	187	21	44	10	0	6	23	.235	24	41	2	414	25	6	.987
1999— New Britain (East.)	C	89	250	29	62	11	3	4	24	.248	21	44	0	548	59	10	.984

MOHLER, MIKE P CARDINALS

PERSONAL: Born July 26, 1968, in Dayton, Ohio. ... 6-2/208. ... Throws left, bats right. ... Full name: Michael Ross Mohler.
HIGH SCHOOL: East Ascension (Gonzales, La.).
COLLEGE: Nicholls State (La.).
TRANSACTIONS/CAREER NOTES: Selected by Oakland Athletics organization in 42nd round of free-agent draft (June 5, 1989). ... On Tacoma disabled list (April 7-May 24, 1994). ... Granted free agency (December 21, 1998). ... Signed by St. Louis Cardinals (January 15, 1999).
MISCELLANEOUS: Appeared in two games as pinch runner (1997).

Year League	W	L	Pct.	ERA	G	GS	CG	ShO	Sv.	IP	H	R	ER	BB	SO
1990— Madison (Midw.)	1	1	.500	3.41	42	2	0	0	1	63¹/₃	56	34	24	32	72
1991— Modesto (Calif.)	9	4	.692	2.86	21	20	1	0	0	122²/₃	106	48	39	45	98
— Huntsville (Sou.)	4	2	.667	3.57	8	8	0	0	0	53	55	22	21	20	27
1992— Huntsville (Sou.)	3	8	.273	3.59	44	6	0	0	3	80¹/₃	72	41	32	39	56
1993— Oakland (A.L.)	1	6	.143	5.60	42	9	0	0	0	64¹/₃	57	45	40	44	42

M

Year League	W	L	Pct.	ERA	G	GS	CG	ShO	Sv.	IP	H	R	ER	BB	SO
1994— Modesto (Calif.)	1	1	.500	2.76	7	5	0	0	1	29 1/3	21	9	9	6	29
— Tacoma (PCL)	1	3	.250	3.53	17	11	0	0	0	63 2/3	66	31	25	21	50
— Oakland (A.L.)	0	1	.000	7.71	1	1	0	0	0	2 1/3	2	3	2	2	4
1995— Edmonton (PCL)	2	1	.667	2.60	29	0	0	0	5	45	40	16	13	20	28
— Oakland (A.L.)	1	1	.500	3.04	28	0	0	0	1	23 2/3	16	8	8	18	15
1996— Oakland (A.L.)	6	3	.667	3.67	72	0	0	0	7	81	79	36	33	41	64
1997— Oakland (A.L.)	1	10	.091	5.13	62	10	0	0	1	101 2/3	116	65	58	54	66
1998— Oakland (A.L.)	3	3	.500	5.16	57	0	0	0	0	61	70	38	35	26	42
1999— St. Louis (N.L.)■	1	1	.500	4.38	48	0	0	0	1	49 1/3	47	26	24	23	31
— Memphis (PCL)	2	1	.667	3.07	10	0	0	0	1	14 2/3	16	5	5	5	17
A.L. totals (6 years)	12	24	.333	4.74	262	20	0	0	9	334	340	195	176	185	233
N.L. totals (1 year)	1	1	.500	4.38	48	0	0	0	1	49 1/3	47	26	24	23	31
Major League totals (7 years)	13	25	.342	4.70	310	20	0	0	10	383 1/3	387	221	200	208	264

MOLINA, BENJIE   C   ANGELS

PERSONAL: Born July 20, 1974, in Rio Pedras, Puerto Rico. ... 5-11/207. ... Bats right, throws right. ... Full name: Benjamin Jose Molina.
TRANSACTIONS/CAREER NOTES: Signed as non-drafted free agent by California Angels organization (May 23, 1993). ... Angels franchise renamed Anaheim Angels for 1997 season. ... On Vancouver disabled list (May 13-22, 1998). ... On Edmonton disabled list (June 4-14, 1999).
STATISTICAL NOTES: Led Texas League catchers with 703 total chances and nine double plays in 1996.

								BATTING						FIELDING		
Year Team (League)	Pos.	G	AB	R	H	2B	3B	HR	RBI	Avg.	BB	SO	SB	PO	A	E	Avg.
1993— Ariz. Angels (Ariz.)	C	27	80	9	21	6	2	0	10	.263	10	4	0	47	2	0	1.000
1994— Cedar Rapids (Mid.)	C	48	171	14	48	8	0	3	16	.281	8	12	1	349	40	10	.975
1995— Vancouver (PCL)		2	2	0	0	0	0	0	0	.000	0	1	0	4	0	0	1.000
— Cedar Rapids (Mid.) ..	C	39	133	15	39	9	0	4	17	.293	15	11	1	283	32	7	.978
— Lake Elsinore (Calif.) ..	C	27	96	21	37	7	2	2	12	.385	8	7	0	195	16	1	.995
1996— Midland (Texas).........	C	108	365	45	100	21	2	8	54	.274	25	25	0	*615	*81	7	.990
1997— Lake Elsinore (Calif.) ..	C	36	149	18	42	10	2	4	33	.282	7	9	0	239	36	1	.996
— Midland (Texas).........	C	29	106	18	35	8	0	6	30	.330	10	7	0	74	15	2	.978
1998— Vancouver (PCL)	C	49	184	13	54	9	1	1	22	.293	5	14	1	316	24	5	.986
— Midland (Texas).........	C	41	154	28	55	8	0	9	39	.357	14	7	0	233	21	3	.988
— Anaheim (A.L.)	C	2	1	0	0	0	0	0	0	.000	0	0	0	1	0	0	1.000
1999— Edmonton (PCL)	C-DH	65	241	28	69	16	0	7	41	.286	15	17	1	351	47	3	.993
— Anaheim (A.L.)	C	31	101	8	26	5	0	1	10	.257	6	6	0	192	19	2	.991
Major League totals (2 years)		33	102	8	26	5	0	1	10	.255	6	6	0	193	19	2	.991

MOLINA, GABE   P   ORIOLES

PERSONAL: Born May 3, 1975, in Denver. ... 5-11/207. ... Throws right, bats right. ... Full name: Cruz Gabriel Molina.
HIGH SCHOOL: John F. Kennedy (Denver).
COLLEGE: Arizona State.
TRANSACTIONS/CAREER NOTES: Selected by Baltimore Orioles organization in 21st round of free-agent draft (June 4, 1996).

Year League	W	L	Pct.	ERA	G	GS	CG	ShO	Sv.	IP	H	R	ER	BB	SO
1996— Bluefield (Appl.)	4	0	1.000	3.60	23	0	0	0	7	30	29	12	12	13	33
1997— Delmarva (SAL)................	8	6	.571	2.18	46	0	0	0	7	91	66	24	22	32	119
1998— Bowie (East.)...................	3	2	.600	3.36	47	0	0	0	24	61 2/3	48	24	23	27	75
1999— Rochester (I.L.).................	2	2	.500	3.14	45	0	0	0	18	57 1/3	45	22	20	23	58
— Baltimore (A.L.)..................	1	2	.333	6.65	20	0	0	0	0	23	22	19	17	16	14
Major League totals (1 year)........	1	2	.333	6.65	20	0	0	0	0	23	22	19	17	16	14

MOLINA, JOSE   C   CUBS

PERSONAL: Born June 3, 1975, in Bayamon, Puerto Rico. ... 6-1/215. ... Bats right, throws right. ... Full name: Jose Benjamin Molina.
HIGH SCHOOL: Maestro Ladi (Vega Alta, Puerto Rico).
TRANSACTIONS/CAREER NOTES: Selected by Chicago Cubs organization in 14th round of free-agent draft (June 3, 1993). ... On Iowa disabled list (July 31-August 10, 1999).
STATISTICAL NOTES: Led Southern League catchers with 108 assists and tied for lead with 21 passed balls in 1998.

								BATTING						FIELDING		
Year Team (League)	Pos.	G	AB	R	H	2B	3B	HR	RBI	Avg.	BB	SO	SB	PO	A	E	Avg.
1993— GC Cubs (GCL)	C-1B	33	78	5	17	2	0	0	4	.218	12	12	3	143	27	7	.960
— Daytona (FSL)	C	3	7	0	1	0	0	0	1	.143	2	0	0	13	2	0	1.000
1994— Peoria (Midw.)..........	C	78	253	31	58	13	1	1	33	.229	24	61	4	567	79	13	.980
1995— Daytona (FSL)	C	82	233	27	55	9	1	1	19	.236	29	53	1	501	91	8	.987
1996— Rockford (Midw.)	C	96	305	35	69	10	1	2	27	.226	36	71	2	620	98	11	.985
1997— Daytona (FSL)	C	55	179	17	45	9	1	0	23	.251	14	25	4	341	71	8	.981
— Iowa (A.A.)	C	3	3	0	1	0	0	0	0	.333	1	1	0	1	0	0	1.000
— Orlando (Sou.)	C	37	99	10	17	3	0	1	15	.172	12	28	0	237	28	2	.993
1998— West Tenn (Sou.)	C-1B	109	320	33	71	10	1	2	28	.222	32	74	1	740	†108	8	.991
1999— West Tenn (Sou.)	C	14	35	2	6	3	0	0	5	.171	2	14	0	97	13	2	.982
— Iowa (PCL)	C	74	240	24	63	11	1	4	26	.263	20	54	0	488	44	7	.987
— Chicago (N.L.)	C	10	19	3	5	1	0	0	1	.263	2	4	0	44	5	0	1.000
Major League totals (1 year)		10	19	3	5	1	0	0	1	.263	2	4	0	44	5	0	1.000

M

MONAHAN, SHANE OF MARINERS

PERSONAL: Born August 12, 1974, in Syosset, N.Y. ... 6-0/195. ... Bats left, throws right. ... Full name: Shane Hartland Monahan. ... Son of Hartland Monahan, right winger with six NHL teams (1973-74 through 1980-81); great-grandson of Howie Morenz, Hockey Hall of Fame center with three NHL teams (1923-24 through 1936-37); grandson of Bernie "Boom Boom" Geoffrion, Hall of Fame right winger with Montreal Canadiens and New York Rangers (1950-51 through 1967-68).
HIGH SCHOOL: Wheeler (Marietta, Ga.).
COLLEGE: Clemson.
TRANSACTIONS/CAREER NOTES: Selected by Seattle Mariners organization in second round of free-agent draft (June 1, 1995).
STATISTICAL NOTES: Led California League outfielders with 265 total chances in 1996.

								BATTING							FIELDING		
Year	Team (League)	Pos.	G	AB	R	H	2B	3B	HR	RBI	Avg.	BB	SO	SB	PO	A	E	Avg.
1995— Wisconsin (Midw.)		OF	59	233	34	66	9	6	1	32	.283	11	40	9	100	0	3	.971
1996— Lancaster (Calif.)		OF	132	*584	107	164	31	*12	14	97	.281	30	124	19	*248	10	7	.974
1997— Tacoma (PCL)		OF	21	85	15	25	4	0	2	12	.294	5	21	5	46	3	2	.961
— Memphis (Sou.)		OF	107	401	52	121	24	6	12	76	.302	30	100	14	139	10	3	.980
1998— Tacoma (PCL)		OF	69	277	32	69	8	5	4	33	.249	19	47	6	141	1	1	.993
— Seattle (A.L.)		OF	62	211	17	51	8	1	4	28	.242	8	53	1	117	3	1	.992
1999— Tacoma (PCL)		OF-DH-2B	108	399	51	102	21	2	7	32	.256	19	81	9	205	9	1	.995
— Seattle (A.L.)		OF-DH	16	15	3	2	0	0	0	0	.133	0	6	0	7	0	0	1.000
Major League totals (2 years)			78	226	20	53	8	1	4	28	.235	8	59	1	124	3	1	.992

MONDESI, RAUL OF BLUE JAYS

PERSONAL: Born March 12, 1971, in San Cristobal, Dominican Republic. ... 5-11/215. ... Bats right, throws right. ... Name pronounced MON-de-see.
HIGH SCHOOL: Liceo Manuel Maria Valencia (Dominican Republic).
TRANSACTIONS/CAREER NOTES: Signed as non-drafted free agent by Los Angeles Dodgers organization (June 6, 1988). ... On Bakersfield disabled list (May 8-July 5, 1991). ... On Albuquerque disabled list (May 8-16, 1992). ... On San Antonio disabled list (June 2-16, June 24-August 10 and August 24, 1992-remainder of season). ... Traded by Dodgers with P Pedro Borbon to Toronto Blue Jays for OF Shawn Green and 2B Jorge Nunez (November 8, 1999).
HONORS: Named N.L. Rookie Player of the Year by THE SPORTING NEWS (1994). ... Named N.L. Rookie of the Year by Baseball Writers' Association of America (1994). ... Won N.L. Gold Glove as outfielder (1995 and 1997).
STATISTICAL NOTES: Career major league grand slams: 2.

								BATTING							FIELDING		
Year	Team (League)	Pos.	G	AB	R	H	2B	3B	HR	RBI	Avg.	BB	SO	SB	PO	A	E	Avg.
1990— Great Falls (Pio.)		OF	44	175	35	53	10	4	8	31	.303	11	30	30	65	4	1	.986
1991— Bakersfield (Calif.)		OF	28	106	23	30	7	2	3	13	.283	5	21	9	42	5	3	.940
— San Antonio (Texas) ...		OF	53	213	32	58	11	5	5	26	.272	8	47	8	101	6	4	.964
— Albuquerque (PCL).....		OF	2	9	3	3	0	1	0	0	.333	0	1	1	0	0	1	.000
1992— Albuquerque (PCL).....		OF	35	138	23	43	4	7	4	15	.312	9	35	2	89	8	7	.933
— San Antonio (Texas) ...		OF	18	68	8	18	2	2	2	14	.265	1	24	3	31	6	1	.974
1993— Albuquerque (PCL).....		OF	110	425	65	119	22	7	12	65	.280	18	85	13	211	10	10	.957
— Los Angeles (N.L.)		OF	42	86	13	25	3	1	4	10	.291	4	16	4	55	3	3	.951
1994— Los Angeles (N.L.)		OF	112	434	63	133	27	8	16	56	.306	16	78	11	206	*16	8	.965
1995— Los Angeles (N.L.)		OF	139	536	91	153	23	6	26	88	.285	33	96	27	282	*16	6	.980
1996— Los Angeles (N.L.)		OF	157	634	98	188	40	7	24	88	.297	32	122	14	337	11	*12	.967
1997— Los Angeles (N.L.)		OF	159	616	95	191	42	5	30	87	.310	44	105	32	338	10	4	.989
1998— Los Angeles (N.L.)		OF	148	580	85	162	26	5	30	90	.279	30	112	16	284	6	6	.980
1999— Los Angeles (N.L.)		OF	159	601	98	152	29	5	33	99	.253	71	134	36	315	7	6	.982
Major League totals (7 years)			916	3487	543	1004	190	37	163	518	.288	230	663	140	1817	69	45	.977

DIVISION SERIES RECORD

								BATTING							FIELDING		
Year	Team (League)	Pos.	G	AB	R	H	2B	3B	HR	RBI	Avg.	BB	SO	SB	PO	A	E	Avg.
1995— Los Angeles (N.L.)		OF	3	9	0	2	0	0	0	1	.222	0	2	0	8	0	0	1.000
1996— Los Angeles (N.L.)		OF	3	11	0	2	2	0	0	1	.182	0	4	0	2	0	0	1.000
Division series totals (2 years)			6	20	0	4	2	0	0	2	.200	0	6	0	10	0	0	1.000

ALL-STAR GAME RECORD

						BATTING						FIELDING		
Year	League	Pos.	AB	R	H	2B	3B	HR	RBI	Avg.	BB	SO	SB	PO	A	E	Avg.
1995— National		OF	1	0	0	0	0	0	0	.000	0	0	0	2	0	0	1.000

MONTANE, IVAN P MARINERS

PERSONAL: Born June 3, 1973, in Santurce, Puerto Rico. ... 6-2/195. ... Throws right, bats right. ... Full name: Ivan Carlos Montane.
HIGH SCHOOL: Miam Killian.
JUNIOR COLLEGE: Miami-Dade (South) Community College.
TRANSACTIONS/CAREER NOTES: Selected by Seattle Mariners organization in ninth round of free-agent draft (June 1, 1992). ... On Orlando disabled list (April 6, 1998-remainder of season).
STATISTICAL NOTES: Led Arizona League with 18 wild pitches in 1992.

Year	League	W	L	Pct.	ERA	G	GS	CG	ShO	Sv.	IP	H	R	ER	BB	SO
1992— Arizona Mariners (Ariz.)		1	3	.250	5.67	13	11	0	0	0	46	44	39	29	*44	48
1993— Bellingham (N.W.)..............		5	4	.556	3.93	15	15	1	0	0	73 1/3	55	36	32	37	53
1994— Appleton (Midw.)..............		8	9	.471	3.85	29	26	1	1	0	159	132	79	68	82	155
1995— Riverside (Calif.)..............		5	5	.500	5.63	24	16	0	0	0	92 2/3	101	67	58	71	79
1996— Lancaster (Calif.)................		2	2	.500	3.64	11	0	0	0	0	59 1/3	57	37	24	43	54
— Port City (Sou.)		3	8	.273	5.20	18	18	0	0	0	100 1/3	96	67	58	75	81

Year League	W	L	Pct.	ERA	G	GS	CG	ShO	Sv.	IP	H	R	ER	BB	SO
1997—Memphis (Sou.)	0	8	.000	7.53	22	12	0	0	0	71²/₃	83	70	60	51	63
—Lancaster (Calif.)	1	2	.333	5.29	6	6	0	0	0	32¹/₃	40	25	19	13	34
1998—Orlando (Sou.)	0	0	...	11.57	2	0	0	0	0	2¹/₃	3	3	3	2	0
1999—Wisconsin (Midw.)	0	0	...	0.71	10	0	0	0	3	12²/₃	5	1	1	5	18
—New Haven (East.)	4	2	.667	2.47	41	0	0	0	10	54²/₃	38	16	15	22	70

PERSONAL: Born January 7, 1962, in Wellston, Ohio. ... 5-11/175. ... Throws right, bats right. ... Full name: Jeffrey Thomas Montgomery.
HIGH SCHOOL: Wellston (Ohio).
COLLEGE: Marshall (bachelor of science degree in computer science, 1984).
TRANSACTIONS/CAREER NOTES: Selected by Cincinnati Reds organization in ninth round of free-agent draft (June 6, 1983). ... Traded by Reds to Kansas City Royals for OF Van Snider (February 15, 1988). ... Granted free agency (November 8, 1995). ... Re-signed by Royals (December 15, 1995). ... On Kansas City disabled list (April 18-May 3, 1997); included rehabilitation assignment to Omaha (April 29-May 3). ... Granted free agency (October 28, 1998). ... Re-signed by Royals (December 7, 1998). ... On Kansas City disabled list (July 10-August 10, 1999); included rehabilitation assignments to Wichita (August 1-3) and Omaha (August 4-9). ... Granted free agency (November 10, 1999).
RECORDS: Shares major league record for striking out side on nine pitches (April 29, 1990, eighth inning).
HONORS: Named A.L. Fireman of the Year by THE SPORTING NEWS (1993).
MISCELLANEOUS: Holds Kansas City Royals all-time record for most games pitched (686) and most saves (304).

Year League	W	L	Pct.	ERA	G	GS	CG	ShO	Sv.	IP	H	R	ER	BB	SO
1983—Billings (Pio.)	6	2	.750	2.42	20	0	0	0	5	44²/₃	31	13	12	13	90
1984—Tampa (FSL)	5	3	.625	2.44	31	0	0	0	•14	44¹/₃	29	15	12	30	56
—Vermont (East.)	2	0	1.000	2.13	22	0	0	0	4	25¹/₃	14	7	6	24	20
1985—Vermont (East.)	5	3	.625	2.05	*53	1	0	0	9	101	63	25	23	48	89
1986—Denver (A.A.)	11	7	.611	4.39	30	22	2	2	1	151²/₃	162	88	74	57	78
1987—Nashville (A.A.)	8	5	.615	4.14	24	21	1	0	0	139	132	76	64	51	121
—Cincinnati (N.L.)	2	2	.500	6.52	14	1	0	0	0	19¹/₃	25	15	14	9	13
1988—Omaha (A.A.)■	1	2	.333	1.91	20	0	0	0	13	28¹/₃	15	6	6	11	36
—Kansas City (A.L.)	7	2	.778	3.45	45	0	0	0	1	62²/₃	54	25	24	30	47
1989—Kansas City (A.L.)	7	3	.700	1.37	63	0	0	0	18	92	66	16	14	25	94
1990—Kansas City (A.L.)	6	5	.545	2.39	73	0	0	0	24	94¹/₃	81	36	25	34	94
1991—Kansas City (A.L.)	4	4	.500	2.90	67	0	0	0	33	90	83	32	29	28	77
1992—Kansas City (A.L.)	1	6	.143	2.18	65	0	0	0	39	82²/₃	61	23	20	27	69
1993—Kansas City (A.L.)	7	5	.583	2.27	69	0	0	0	•45	87¹/₃	65	22	22	23	66
1994—Kansas City (A.L.)	2	3	.400	4.03	42	0	0	0	27	44²/₃	48	21	20	15	50
1995—Kansas City (A.L.)	2	3	.400	3.43	54	0	0	0	31	65²/₃	60	27	25	25	49
1996—Kansas City (A.L.)	4	6	.400	4.26	48	0	0	0	24	63¹/₃	59	31	30	19	45
1997—Kansas City (A.L.)	1	4	.200	3.49	55	0	0	0	14	59¹/₃	53	24	23	18	48
—Omaha (A.A.)	0	0	...	0.00	2	0	0	0	0	2	1	0	0	1	2
1998—Kansas City (A.L.)	2	5	.286	4.98	56	0	0	0	36	56	58	35	31	22	54
1999—Kansas City (A.L.)	1	4	.200	6.84	49	0	0	0	12	51¹/₃	72	40	39	21	27
—Wichita (Texas)	0	0	...	9.00	1	0	0	0	0	1	2	1	1	1	1
—Omaha (PCL)	0	0	...	0.00	4	0	0	0	1	5	1	0	0	1	3
A.L. totals (12 years)	44	50	.468	3.20	686	0	0	0	304	849¹/₃	760	332	302	287	720
N.L. totals (1 year)	2	2	.500	6.52	14	1	0	0	0	19¹/₃	25	15	14	9	13
Major League totals (13 years)	46	52	.469	3.27	700	1	0	0	304	868²/₃	785	347	316	296	733

ALL-STAR GAME RECORD

Year League	W	L	Pct.	ERA	GS	CG	ShO	Sv.	IP	H	R	ER	BB	SO
1992—American	0	0	...	27.00	0	0	0	0	²/₃	2	2	2	0	0
1993—American	0	0	...	0.00	0	0	0	0	1	0	0	0	0	1
1996—American							Did not play.							
All-Star Game totals (2 years)	0	0	...	10.80	0	0	0	0	1²/₃	2	2	2	0	1

PERSONAL: Born December 25, 1970, in Westminster, Calif. ... 6-4/200. ... Throws right, bats right. ... Full name: Steven L. Montgomery.
HIGH SCHOOL: Fountain Valley (Calif.).
COLLEGE: Pepperdine.
TRANSACTIONS/CAREER NOTES: Selected by St. Louis Cardinals organization in third round of free-agent draft (June 1, 1992). ... Traded by Cardinals to Oakland Athletics for P Dennis Eckersley (February 13, 1996). ... Claimed on waivers by Cleveland Indians (August 7, 1997). ... Released by Indians (March 30, 1998). ... Signed by Baltimore Orioles organization (April 4, 1998). ... Granted free agency (October 15, 1998). ... Signed by Philadelphia Phillies organization (November 5, 1998). ... On Philadelphia disabled list (August 4-20, 1999); included rehabilitation assignment to Scranton/Wilkes-Barre (August 18-19). ... Traded by Phillies with P Carlton Loewer and P Adam Eaton to San Diego Padres for P Andy Ashby (November 10, 1999).

Year League	W	L	Pct.	ERA	G	GS	CG	ShO	Sv.	IP	H	R	ER	BB	SO
1993—St. Petersburg (FSL)	2	1	.667	2.66	14	5	0	0	3	40²/₃	33	14	12	9	34
—Arkansas (Texas)	3	3	.500	3.94	6	6	0	0	0	32	34	17	14	12	19
1994—Arkansas (Texas)	4	5	.444	3.28	50	9	0	0	2	107	97	43	39	33	73
1995—Arkansas (Texas)	5	2	.714	3.25	*55	0	0	0	*36	61	52	22	22	22	56
1996—Oakland (A.L.)■	1	0	1.000	9.22	8	0	0	0	0	13²/₃	18	14	14	13	8
—Edmonton (PCL)	2	0	1.000	2.89	37	0	0	0	1	56	51	19	18	12	40
1997—Edmonton (PCL)	2	1	.667	5.79	30	0	0	0	3	46²/₃	61	30	30	17	38
—Oakland (A.L.)	0	1	.000	9.95	4	0	0	0	0	6¹/₃	10	7	7	8	1
—Buffalo (A.A.)■	1	2	.333	5.63	7	0	0	0	1	8	12	6	5	3	5
1998—Rochester (I.L.)■	4	6	.400	4.40	51	4	0	0	8	88	79	50	43	24	66
1999—Scranton/W.B. (I.L.)■	0	0	...	6.23	14	0	0	0	7	13	17	9	9	11	13
—Philadelphia (N.L.)	1	5	.167	3.34	53	0	0	0	3	64²/₃	54	25	24	31	55
A.L. totals (2 years)	1	1	.500	9.45	12	0	0	0	0	20	28	21	21	21	9
N.L. totals (1 year)	1	5	.167	3.34	53	0	0	0	3	64²/₃	54	25	24	31	55
Major League totals (3 years)	2	6	.250	4.78	65	0	0	0	3	84²/₃	82	46	45	52	64

M

MOORE, TREY   P   EXPOS

PERSONAL: Born October 2, 1972, in Houston. ... 6-0/190. ... Throws left, bats left. ... Full name: Warren Neal Moore III.
HIGH SCHOOL: Keller (Texas).
COLLEGE: Texas A&M.
TRANSACTIONS/CAREER NOTES: Selected by Seattle Mariners organization in second round of free-agent draft (June 2, 1994). ... Traded by Mariners with C Chris Widger and P Matt Wagner to Montreal Expos for P Alex Pacheco and P Jeff Fassero (October 29, 1996). ... On Montreal disabled list (June 7, 1998-remainder of season); included rehabilitation assignment to Ottawa (July 9-20). ... On disabled list (March 31, 1999-entire season).
MISCELLANEOUS: Struck out in only appearance as pinch hitter with Montreal (1998).

Year League	W	L	Pct.	ERA	G	GS	CG	ShO	Sv.	IP	H	R	ER	BB	SO
1994— Bellingham (N.W.)	5	2	.714	2.63	11	10	1	0	0	61 $^2/_3$	48	18	18	24	73
1995— Riverside (Calif.)	14	6	.700	3.09	24	24	0	0	0	148 $^1/_3$	122	65	51	58	134
1996— Port City (Sou.)	1	6	.143	7.71	11	11	0	0	0	53 $^2/_3$	73	54	46	33	42
— Lancaster (Calif.)	7	5	.583	4.10	15	15	2	0	0	94 $^1/_3$	106	57	43	31	77
1997— Harrisburg (East.)■	11	6	.647	4.15	27	27	2	•2	0	162 $^2/_3$	152	91	75	66	137
1998— Montreal (N.L.)	2	5	.286	5.02	13	11	0	0	0	61	78	37	34	17	35
— Ottawa (I.L.)	1	1	.500	5.54	3	3	0	0	0	13	18	8	8	4	8
1999— Montreal (N.L.)							Did not play.								
Major League totals (1 year)	2	5	.286	5.02	13	11	0	0	0	61	78	37	34	17	35

MORA, MELVIN   OF   METS

PERSONAL: Born February 2, 1972, in Aqua Negar, Venezuela. ... 5-10/180. ... Bats right, throws right.
HIGH SCHOOL: Libertader (Venezuela).
TRANSACTIONS/CAREER NOTES: Signed as non-drafted free agent by Houston Astros organization (March 30, 1991). ... Granted free agency (October 17, 1997). ... Played in Taiwan (1998). ... Signed by New York Mets organization (July 24, 1998). ... Granted free agency (October 16, 1998). ... Re-signed by Mets organization (February 5, 1999).
STATISTICAL NOTES: Tied for Texas League lead in double plays by outfielder with six in 1995.

Year Team (League)	Pos.	G	AB	R	H	2B	3B	HR	RBI	Avg.	BB	SO	SB	PO	A	E	Avg.
1991— Dom. Astros (DSL)	...	58	211	38	63	18	1	0	20	.299	19	22	21	...	...	...	...
1992— GC Astros (GCL)	OF-2B-3B	49	144	28	32	3	0	0	8	.222	18	16	16	71	27	4	.961
1993— Asheville (SAL)	2-0-3-S	108	365	66	104	22	2	2	31	.285	36	46	20	135	114	17	.936
1994— Osceola (FSL)	OF-3B	118	425	57	120	29	4	8	46	.282	37	60	24	198	70	15	.947
1995— Jackson (Texas)	OF-3B-2B	123	467	63	139	32	0	4	45	.298	32	57	22	244	16	6	.977
— Tucson (PCL)	OF	2	5	3	3	0	1	0	1	.600	2	0	1	2	0	0	1.000
1996— Jackson (Texas)	0-2-S-3	70	255	36	73	6	1	5	23	.286	14	23	4	108	56	7	.959
— Tucson (PCL)	3B-OF-2B	62	228	35	64	11	2	3	26	.281	17	27	3	75	70	14	.912
1997— New Orleans (A.A.)	0-3-2-S	119	370	55	95	15	3	2	38	.257	47	52	7	161	80	11	.956
1998— Mercury (Taiwan)■	...		164	34	55	11	2	3	11	335	...	...	...	...	...	...	...
— St. Lucie (FSL)■	2B-SS-OF	17	55	5	15	0	0	0	8	.273	5	9	1	21	43	1	.985
— Norfolk (I.L.)	3B-OF-2B	11	28	5	5	1	0	0	2	.179	5	7	0	8	6	2	.875
1999— Norfolk (I.L.)	S-O-2-3	82	304	55	92	17	2	8	36	.303	41	54	18	126	134	16	.942
— New York (N.L.)	0-2-3-S	66	31	6	5	0	0	0	1	.161	4	7	2	21	7	0	1.000
Major League totals (1 year)		66	31	6	5	0	0	0	1	.161	4	7	2	21	7	0	1.000

DIVISION SERIES RECORD

Year Team (League)	Pos.	G	AB	R	H	2B	3B	HR	RBI	Avg.	BB	SO	SB	PO	A	E	Avg.
1999— New York (N.L.)	OF	3	1	1	0	0	0	0	0	.000	1	0	0	2	1	0	1.000

CHAMPIONSHIP SERIES RECORD

Year Team (League)	Pos.	G	AB	R	H	2B	3B	HR	RBI	Avg.	BB	SO	SB	PO	A	E	Avg.
1999— New York (N.L.)	PH-OF	6	14	3	6	0	0	1	2	.429	2	2	2	7	3	0	1.000

RECORD AS PITCHER

Year League	W	L	Pct.	ERA	G	GS	CG	ShO	Sv.	IP	H	R	ER	BB	SO
1993— Asheville (SAL)	0	0	...	0.00	1	0	0	0	0	$^2/_3$	1	0	0	0	0
1997— New Orleans (A.A.)	0	0	...	0.00	1	0	0	0	0	1	2	1	1	1	0

MORANDINI, MICKEY   2B

PERSONAL: Born April 22, 1966, in Leechburg, Pa. ... 5-11/180. ... Bats left, throws right. ... Full name: Michael Robert Morandini. ... Name pronounced MOR-an-DEEN-ee.
HIGH SCHOOL: Leechburg (Pa.) Area.
COLLEGE: Indiana.
TRANSACTIONS/CAREER NOTES: Selected by Pittsburgh Pirates organization in seventh round of free-agent draft (June 2, 1987); did not sign. ... Selected by Philadelphia Phillies organization in fifth round of free-agent draft (June 1, 1988). ... On disabled list (June 15-30, 1996). ... Traded by Phillies to Chicago Cubs for OF Doug Glanville (December 23, 1997). ... On suspended list (September 23-25, 1999). ... Granted free agency (October 28, 1999).
RECORDS: Holds N.L. single-season record for fewest chances accepted by second baseman (150 games or more)—671 (1998).
STATISTICAL NOTES: Led International League second basemen with 271 putouts, 419 assists and 701 total chances in 1990.
MISCELLANEOUS: Member of 1988 U.S. Olympic baseball team. ... Turned unassisted triple play while playing second base (September 20, 1992, sixth inning); ninth player ever to accomplish feat and first ever by second baseman during regular season.

M

Year	Team (League)	Pos.	G	AB	R	H	2B	3B	HR	RBI	Avg.	BB	SO	SB	PO	A	E	Avg.
1989—Spartanburg (SAL)		SS	63	231	43	78	19	1	1	30	.338	35	45	18	87	198	10	.966
—Clearwater (FSL)		SS	17	63	14	19	4	1	0	4	.302	7	8	3	20	59	2	.975
—Reading (East.)		SS	48	188	39	66	12	1	5	29	.351	23	32	5	73	137	10	.955
1990—Scranton/W.B. (I.L.) ...		2B-SS	139	503	76	131	24	*10	1	31	.260	60	90	16	†271	†419	11	.984
—Philadelphia (N.L.)		2B	25	79	9	19	4	0	1	3	.241	6	19	3	37	61	1	.990
1991—Scranton/W.B. (I.L.) ...		2B	12	46	7	12	4	0	1	9	.261	5	6	2	19	38	1	.983
—Philadelphia (N.L.)		2B	98	325	38	81	11	4	1	20	.249	29	45	13	183	254	6	.986
1992—Philadelphia (N.L.)		2B-SS	127	422	47	112	8	8	3	30	.265	25	64	4	239	336	6	.990
1993—Philadelphia (N.L.)		2B	120	425	57	105	19	9	3	33	.247	34	73	13	208	288	5	.990
1994—Philadelphia (N.L.)		2B	87	274	40	80	16	5	2	26	.292	34	33	10	167	216	6	.985
1995—Philadelphia (N.L.)		2B	127	494	65	140	34	7	6	49	.283	42	80	9	269	336	7	.989
1996—Philadelphia (N.L.)		2B	140	539	64	135	24	6	3	32	.250	49	87	26	286	352	12	.982
1997—Philadelphia (N.L.)		2B-SS	150	553	83	163	40	2	1	39	.295	62	91	16	254	350	6	.990
1998—Chicago (N.L.)■		2B	154	582	93	172	20	4	8	53	.296	72	84	13	267	404	5	*.993
1999—Chicago (N.L.)		2B	144	456	60	110	18	5	4	37	.241	48	61	6	239	319	5	.991
Major League totals (10 years)			1172	4149	556	1117	194	50	32	322	.269	401	637	117	2149	2916	59	.988

DIVISION SERIES RECORD

Year	Team (League)	Pos.	G	AB	R	H	2B	3B	HR	RBI	Avg.	BB	SO	SB	PO	A	E	Avg.
1998—Chicago (N.L.)		2B	3	9	1	2	0	0	0	1	.222	3	2	0	5	3	0	1.000

CHAMPIONSHIP SERIES RECORD

Year	Team (League)	Pos.	G	AB	R	H	2B	3B	HR	RBI	Avg.	BB	SO	SB	PO	A	E	Avg.
1993—Philadelphia (N.L.)		2B-PH	4	16	1	4	0	1	0	2	.250	0	3	1	8	9	1	.944

WORLD SERIES RECORD

Year	Team (League)	Pos.	G	AB	R	H	2B	3B	HR	RBI	Avg.	BB	SO	SB	PO	A	E	Avg.
1993—Philadelphia (N.L.)		PH-2B	3	5	1	1	0	0	0	0	.200	1	2	0	2	0	0	1.000

ALL-STAR GAME RECORD

Year	League	Pos.	AB	R	H	2B	3B	HR	RBI	Avg.	BB	SO	SB	PO	A	E	Avg.
1995—National		2B	1	0	0	0	0	0	0	.000	0	1	0	0	1	0	1.000

MORDECAI, MIKE · IF · EXPOS

PERSONAL: Born December 13, 1967, in Birmingham, Ala. ... 5-10/185. ... Bats right, throws right. ... Full name: Michael Howard Mordecai.
HIGH SCHOOL: Hewitt Trussville (Ala.).
COLLEGE: Southern Alabama.
TRANSACTIONS/CAREER NOTES: Selected by Pittsburgh Pirates organization in 33rd round of free-agent draft (June 2, 1986); did not sign. ... Selected by Atlanta Braves organization in sixth round of free-agent draft (June 5, 1989). ... On disabled list (April 8-29, 1993). ... On Atlanta disabled list (April 19-May 11, 1996); included rehabilitation assignment to Richmond (May 8-11). ... Granted free agency (December 21, 1997). ... Signed by Montreal Expos organization (March 27, 1998). ... On Montreal disabled list (June 24-July 24, 1998); included rehabilitation assignments to Jupiter (July 16-19) and Ottawa (July 19-24).

Year	Team (League)	Pos.	G	AB	R	H	2B	3B	HR	RBI	Avg.	BB	SO	SB	PO	A	E	Avg.
1989—Burlington (Midw.)		SS-3B	65	241	39	61	11	1	1	22	.253	33	43	12	80	163	21	.920
—Greenville (Sou.)		3B-2B	4	8	0	3	0	0	0	1	.375	1	1	0	4	6	0	1.000
1990—Durham (Caro.)		SS	72	271	42	76	11	7	3	36	.280	42	45	10	111	221	29	.920
1991—Durham (Caro.)		SS	109	397	52	104	15	2	4	42	.262	40	58	30	164	302	27	.945
1992—Greenville (Sou.)		SS	65	222	31	58	13	1	4	31	.261	29	31	9	93	204	11	.964
—Richmond (I.L.)	SS-2B-3B		36	118	12	29	3	0	1	6	.246	5	19	0	48	101	10	.937
1993—Richmond (I.L.)	2-S-3-O-C-1		72	205	29	55	8	1	2	14	.268	14	33	10	98	145	9	.964
1994—Richmond (I.L.)	SS-1B-DH-3B		99	382	67	107	25	1	14	57	.280	35	50	14	117	279	22	.947
—Atlanta (N.L.)		SS	4	4	1	1	0	0	1	3	.250	1	0	0	1	4	0	1.000
1995—Atlanta (N.L.)	2-1-3-S-O		69	75	10	21	6	0	3	11	.280	9	16	0	39	31	0	1.000
1996—Atlanta (N.L.)	2B-3B-SS-1B		66	108	12	26	5	0	2	8	.241	9	24	1	33	52	2	.977
—Richmond (I.L.)		SS	3	11	2	2	0	0	1	2	.182	0	3	0	3	13	0	1.000
1997—Atlanta (N.L.)	3-2-S-1-DH-O		81	81	8	14	2	1	0	3	.173	6	16	0	26	17	0	1.000
—Richmond (I.L.)	2B-3B-DH-SS		31	122	23	38	10	0	3	15	.311	9	17	0	29	61	1	.989
1998—Montreal (N.L.)■	SS-2B-3B-1B		73	119	12	24	4	2	3	10	.202	9	20	1	38	82	5	.960
—Jupiter (FSL)		2B-SS	2	8	0	0	0	0	0	0	.000	1	3	0	4	4	0	1.000
—Ottawa (I.L.)		SS-2B	6	22	2	5	2	0	0	1	.227	3	3	0	9	22	1	.969
1999—Montreal (N.L.)	2-S-3-1		109	226	29	53	10	2	5	25	.235	20	31	2	72	156	7	.970
Major League totals (6 years)			382	613	72	139	27	5	14	60	.227	54	107	4	209	342	14	.975

DIVISION SERIES RECORD

Year	Team (League)	Pos.	G	AB	R	H	2B	3B	HR	RBI	Avg.	BB	SO	SB	PO	A	E	Avg.
1995—Atlanta (N.L.)		PH-SS	2	3	1	2	1	0	0	2	.667	0	0	0	1	0	0	1.000
1996—Atlanta (N.L.)									Did not play.									

CHAMPIONSHIP SERIES RECORD

Year	Team (League)	Pos.	G	AB	R	H	2B	3B	HR	RBI	Avg.	BB	SO	SB	PO	A	E	Avg.
1995—Atlanta (N.L.)		PH-SS	2	2	0	0	0	0	0	0	.000	0	1	0	0	0	0	...
1996—Atlanta (N.L.)		3B-PH-2B	4	4	1	1	0	0	0	0	.250	0	1	0	1	1	0	1.000
Championship series totals (2 years)			6	6	1	1	0	0	0	0	.167	0	2	0	1	1	0	1.000

M

WORLD SERIES RECORD

NOTES: Member of World Series championship team (1995).

Year Team (League)	Pos.	G	AB	R	H	2B	3B	HR	RBI	Avg.	BB	SO	SB	PO	A	E	Avg.
1995—Atlanta (N.L.)	SS-DH	3	3	0	1	0	0	0	0	.333	0	1	0	0	6	0	1.000
1996—Atlanta (N.L.)	PH	1	1	0	0	0	0	0	0	.000	0	0	0	...	...	...	...
World Series totals (2 years)		**4**	**4**	**0**	**1**	**0**	**0**	**0**	**0**	**.250**	**0**	**1**	**0**	**0**	**6**	**0**	**1.000**

MORENO, JUAN   P   RANGERS

PERSONAL: Born February 28, 1975, in Maiquetia, Venezuela. ... 6-1/205. ... Throws left, bats left. ... Full name: Juan Carlos Moreno.
TRANSACTIONS/CAREER NOTES: Signed as non-drafted free agent by Oakland Athletics organization (April 14, 1993). ... Missed entire 1997 season due to injury. ... Released by Athletics (February 4, 1997). ... Missed entire 1998 season due to injury. ... Signed by Texas Rangers organization (November 24, 1998).

Year League	W	L	Pct.	ERA	G	GS	CG	ShO	Sv.	IP	H	R	ER	BB	SO
1995—Arizona Athletics (Ariz.)	6	2	.750	1.21	20	0	0	0	0	44 2/3	36	10	6	20	49
1996—West Michigan (Midw.)	4	6	.400	4.37	38	11	0	0	0	107	98	60	52	69	97
1997—								Did not play.							
1998—								Did not play.							
1999—Tulsa (Texas)■	4	3	.571	2.30	42	0	0	0	3	62 2/3	33	20	16	32	83

MORENO, ORBER   P   ROYALS

PERSONAL: Born April 27, 1977, in Caracas, Venezuela. ... 6-2/190. ... Throws right, bats right. ... Full name: Orber Aquiles Moreno.
HIGH SCHOOL: Luisa Caceres (Venezuela).
TRANSACTIONS/CAREER NOTES: Signed as non-drafted free agent by Kansas City Royals organization (November 10, 1993). ... On Kansas City disabled list (June 10, 1999-remainder of season); included rehabilitation assignment to Gulf Coast Royals (July 26-27).

Year League	W	L	Pct.	ERA	G	GS	CG	ShO	Sv.	IP	H	R	ER	BB	SO
1994—Dominican Royals (DSL)	3	3	.500	3.19	16	11	0	0	1	67 2/3	51	33	24	27	44
1995—Gulf Coast Royals (GCL)	1	1	.500	2.45	8	3	0	0	0	22	15	9	6	7	21
1996—Gulf Coast Royals (GCL)	5	1	.833	1.36	12	7	0	0	1	46 1/3	37	15	7	10	50
1997—Lansing (Midw.)	4	8	.333	4.81	27	25	0	0	0	138 1/3	150	83	74	45	128
1998—Wilmington (Caro.)	3	2	.600	0.82	23	0	0	0	7	33	8	3	3	10	50
—Wichita (Texas)	0	1	.000	2.88	24	0	0	0	7	34 1/3	28	13	11	12	40
1999—Omaha (PCL)	3	1	.750	2.10	16	0	0	0	4	25 2/3	17	6	6	4	30
—Kansas City (A.L.)	0	0	...	5.63	7	0	0	0	0	8	4	5	5	6	7
—Gulf Coast Royals (GCL)	0	0	...	0.00	1	1	0	0	0	1	0	0	0	0	1
Major League totals (1 year)	**0**	**0**	**...**	**5.63**	**7**	**0**	**0**	**0**	**0**	**8**	**4**	**5**	**5**	**6**	**7**

MORGAN, MIKE   P   DIAMONDBACKS

M

PERSONAL: Born October 8, 1959, in Tulare, Calif. ... 6-2/220. ... Throws right, bats right. ... Full name: Michael Thomas Morgan.
HIGH SCHOOL: Valley (Las Vegas).
TRANSACTIONS/CAREER NOTES: Selected by Oakland Athletics organization in first round (fourth pick overall) of free-agent draft (June 6, 1978). ... On disabled list (May 14-June 27, 1980). ... Traded by A's organization to New York Yankees for SS Fred Stanley and a player to be named later (November 3, 1980); A's acquired 2B Brian Doyle to complete deal (November 17, 1980). ... On disabled list (April 9-22, 1981). ... Traded by Yankees with OF/1B Dave Collins, 1B Fred McGriff and cash to Toronto Blue Jays for P Dale Murray and OF/C Tom Dodd (December 9, 1982). ... On Toronto disabled list (July 2-August 23, 1983); included rehabilitation assignment to Syracuse (August 1-18). ... Selected by Seattle Mariners from Blue Jays organization in Rule 5 major league draft (December 3, 1984). ... On Seattle disabled list (April 17, 1985-remainder of season); included rehabilitation assignment to Calgary (July 19-22). ... Traded by Mariners to Baltimore Orioles for P Ken Dixon (December 9, 1987). ... On Baltimore disabled list (June 9-July 19, 1988); included rehabilitation assignment to Rochester (June 30-July 17). ... On Baltimore disabled list (August 12, 1988-remainder of season). ... Traded by Orioles to Los Angeles Dodgers for OF Mike Devereaux (March 12, 1989). ... Granted free agency (October 28, 1991). ... Signed by Chicago Cubs (December 3, 1991). ... On disabled list (June 14-29, 1993; May 9-27, June 2-22 and July 28, 1994-remainder of season). ... On Chicago disabled list (April 24-May 25, 1995); included rehabilitation assignment to Orlando (May 15-25). ... Traded by Cubs with 3B/OF Paul Torres and C Francisco Morales to St. Louis Cardinals for 3B Todd Zeile and cash (June 16, 1995). ... On St. Louis disabled list (July 4-24, 1995). ... Granted free agency (November 6, 1995). ... Re-signed by Cardinals (December 7, 1995). ... On St. Louis disabled list (March 22-May 18, 1996); included rehabilitation assignment to St. Petersburg (April 20-May 15). ... Released by Cardinals (August 28, 1996). ... Signed by Cincinnati Reds (September 4, 1996). ... On disabled list (June 8-24, 1997). ... Granted free agency (October 28, 1997). ... Signed by Minnesota Twins (December 16, 1997). ... On Minnesota disabled list (June 27-July 13 and July 15-August 16, 1998). ... Traded by Twins to Cubs for cash and a player to be named later (August 25, 1998); Twins acquired P Scott Downs to complete deal (November 3, 1998). ... Granted free agency (October 30, 1998). ... Signed by Texas Rangers organization (January 26, 1999). ... On disabled list (May 25-June 9, 1999). ... Granted free agency (November 8, 1999). ... Signed by Arizona Diamondbacks organization (January 14, 2000).
RECORDS: Holds major league record for most clubs played and pitched for in career (since 1900)—11.

Year League	W	L	Pct.	ERA	G	GS	CG	ShO	Sv.	IP	H	R	ER	BB	SO
1978—Oakland (A.L.)	0	3	.000	7.50	3	3	1	0	0	12	19	12	10	8	0
—Vancouver (PCL)	5	6	.455	5.58	14	14	5	1	0	92	109	67	57	54	31
1979—Ogden (PCL)	5	5	.500	3.48	13	13	6	0	0	101	93	48	39	49	42
—Oakland (A.L.)	2	10	.167	5.96	13	13	2	0	0	77	102	57	51	50	17
1980—Ogden (PCL)	6	9	.400	5.40	20	20	3	0	0	115	135	79	69	77	46
1981—Nashville (Sou.)■	8	7	.533	4.42	26	26	7	0	0	169	164	97	83	83	100
1982—New York (A.L.)	7	11	.389	4.37	30	23	2	0	0	150 1/3	167	77	73	67	71
1983—Toronto (A.L.)■	0	3	.000	5.16	16	4	0	0	0	45 1/3	48	26	26	21	22
—Syracuse (I.L.)	0	3	.000	5.59	5	4	0	0	1	19 1/3	20	12	12	13	17
1984—Syracuse (I.L.)	13	11	.542	4.07	34	28	10	•4	0	•185 2/3	167	•101	84	•100	105
1985—Seattle (A.L.)■	1	1	.500	12.00	2	2	0	0	0	6	11	8	8	5	2
—Calgary (PCL)	0	0	...	4.50	1	1	0	0	0	2	3	1	1	0	0
1986—Seattle (A.L.)	11	•17	.393	4.53	37	33	9	1	1	216 1/3	243	122	109	86	116
1987—Seattle (A.L.)	12	17	.414	4.65	34	31	8	2	0	207	245	117	107	53	85
1988—Baltimore (A.L.)■	1	6	.143	5.43	22	10	2	0	1	71 1/3	70	45	43	23	29
—Rochester (I.L.)	0	2	.000	4.76	3	3	0	0	0	17	19	10	9	6	7
1989—Los Angeles (N.L.)■	8	11	.421	2.53	40	19	0	0	0	152 2/3	130	51	43	33	72

Year	League	W	L	Pct.	ERA	G	GS	CG	ShO	Sv.	IP	H	R	ER	BB	SO
1990— Los Angeles (N.L.)		11	15	.423	3.75	33	33	6	•4	0	211	216	100	88	60	106
1991— Los Angeles (N.L.)		14	10	.583	2.78	34	33	5	1	1	236 1/3	197	85	73	61	140
1992— Chicago (N.L.)■		16	8	.667	2.55	34	34	6	1	0	240	203	80	68	79	123
1993— Chicago (N.L.)		10	15	.400	4.03	32	32	1	1	0	207 2/3	206	100	93	74	111
1994— Chicago (N.L.)		2	10	.167	6.69	15	15	1	0	0	80 2/3	111	65	60	35	57
1995— Orlando (Sou.)		0	2	.000	7.59	2	2	0	0	0	10 2/3	13	9	9	7	5
— Chicago (N.L.)		2	1	.667	2.19	4	4	0	0	0	24 2/3	19	8	6	9	15
— St. Louis (N.L.)■		5	6	.455	3.88	17	17	1	0	0	106 2/3	114	48	46	25	46
1996— St. Petersburg (FSL)		1	0	1.000	0.00	1	1	0	0	0	5 2/3	4	0	0	1	4
— Louisville (A.A.)		1	3	.250	7.04	4	4	1	0	0	23	29	18	18	11	10
— St. Louis (N.L.)		4	8	.333	5.24	18	18	0	0	0	103	118	63	60	40	55
— Cincinnati (N.L.)■		2	3	.400	2.30	5	5	0	0	0	27 1/3	28	9	7	7	19
1997— Cincinnati (N.L.)		9	12	.429	4.78	31	30	1	0	0	162	165	91	86	49	103
1998— Minnesota (A.L.)■		4	2	.667	3.49	18	17	0	0	0	98	108	41	38	24	50
— Chicago (N.L.)■		0	1	.000	7.15	5	5	0	0	0	22 2/3	30	21	18	15	10
1999— Texas (A.L.)■		13	10	.565	6.24	34	25	1	0	0	140	184	108	97	48	61
A.L. totals (10 years)		51	80	.389	4.94	209	161	25	3	2	1023 1/3	1197	613	562	385	453
N.L. totals (10 years)		83	100	.454	3.70	268	245	21	7	1	1574 2/3	1537	721	648	487	857
Major League totals (19 years)		134	180	.427	4.19	477	406	46	10	3	2598	2734	1334	1210	872	1310

DIVISION SERIES RECORD

Year	League	W	L	Pct.	ERA	G	GS	CG	ShO	Sv.	IP	H	R	ER	BB	SO
1998— Chicago (N.L.)		0	0	...	0.00	2	0	0	0	0	1 1/3	0	0	0	0	1

ALL-STAR GAME RECORD

Year	League	W	L	Pct.	ERA	GS	CG	ShO	Sv.	IP	H	R	ER	BB	SO
1991— National		0	0	...	0.00	0	0	0	0	1	0	0	0	0	1

MORGAN, SCOTT   OF   INDIANS

PERSONAL: Born July 19, 1973, in Westlake, Calif. ... 6-7/230. ... Bats right, throws right. ... Full name: Scott Alexander Morgan.
HIGH SCHOOL: Lompoc (Calif.).
JUNIOR COLLEGE: Allan Hancock College (Calif.).
COLLEGE: Gonzaga.
TRANSACTIONS/CAREER NOTES: Selected by Milwaukee Brewers organization in 45th round of free-agent draft (June 1, 1992); did not sign. ... Selected by Cleveland Indians organization in seventh round of free-agent draft (June 1, 1995). ... On disabled list (July 11, 1996-remainder of season). ... On Akron disabled list (April 21-30 and June 22-29, 1998).
STATISTICAL NOTES: Led Carolina League with .606 slugging percentage in 1997.

Year	Team (League)	Pos.	G	AB	R	H	2B	3B	HR	RBI	Avg.	BB	SO	SB	PO	A	E	Avg.
1995— Watertown (NY-P)		OF	66	244	42	64	18	0	2	33	.262	26	63	6	50	3	3	.946
1996— Columbus (SAL)		OF	87	305	62	95	25	1	22	80	.311	46	70	9	106	6	4	.966
1997— Kinston (Caro.)		OF	95	368	*86	116	32	3	23	67	.315	47	87	4	143	7	2	.987
— Akron (East.)		OF	21	69	11	12	3	0	2	6	.174	8	20	1	37	4	1	.976
1998— Akron (East.)		OF	119	456	95	134	31	4	25	89	.294	56	124	4	201	4	5	.976
1999— Akron (East.)		OF-DH	88	344	72	97	26	2	26	70	.282	38	96	6	170	6	6	.967
— Buffalo (I.L.)		OF-DH	48	171	32	44	9	0	8	31	.257	18	38	2	101	3	3	.972

MORMAN, ALVIN   P

PERSONAL: Born January 6, 1969, in Rockingham, N.C. ... 6-3/210. ... Throws left, bats right.
HIGH SCHOOL: Richmond Senior (Rockingham, N.C.).
COLLEGE: Wingate (N.C.).
TRANSACTIONS/CAREER NOTES: Selected by Houston Astros organization in 39th round of free-agent draft (June 3, 1991). ... On disabled list (August 26, 1993-remainder of season and May 23-June 14, 1995). ... On temporarily inactive list (July 25-August 2, 1994). ... Traded by Astros to Cleveland Indians for P Jose Cabrera (May 9, 1997). ... On Cleveland disabled list (July 28-September 1, 1997). ... On Cleveland disabled list (May 4-19, 1998); included rehabilitation assignment to Buffalo (May 14-19). ... Traded by Indians with P Jose Mesa and IF Shawon Dunston to San Francisco Giants for P Steve Reed and OF Jacob Cruz (July 23, 1998). ... On San Francisco disabled list (August 7-September 1, 1998); included rehabilitation assignment to Fresno (August 18-26). ... Granted free agency (December 21, 1998). ... Signed by Kansas City Royals (December 21, 1998). ... Released by Royals (December 13, 1999).

Year	League	W	L	Pct.	ERA	G	GS	CG	ShO	Sv.	IP	H	R	ER	BB	SO
1991— Gulf Coast Astros (GCL)		1	0	1.000	2.16	11	0	0	0	1	16 2/3	15	7	4	5	24
— Osceola (FSL)		0	0	...	1.50	3	0	0	0	0	6	5	3	1	2	3
1992— Asheville (SAL)		8	0	1.000	1.55	57	0	0	0	15	75 1/3	60	17	13	26	70
1993— Jackson (Texas)		8	2	*.800	2.96	19	19	0	0	0	97 1/3	77	35	32	28	101
1994— Tucson (PCL)		3	7	.300	5.11	58	0	0	0	5	74	84	51	42	26	49
1995— Tucson (PCL)		5	1	.833	3.91	45	0	0	0	3	48 1/3	50	26	21	20	36
1996— Houston (N.L.)		4	1	.800	4.93	53	0	0	0	0	42	43	24	23	24	31
1997— New Orleans (A.A.)		0	1	.000	4.50	8	0	0	0	0	10	11	5	5	2	14
— Cleveland (A.L.)■		0	0	...	5.89	34	0	0	0	2	18 1/3	19	13	12	14	13
— Buffalo (A.A.)		0	0	...	0.00	3	0	0	0	0	3 1/3	2	0	0	0	3
1998— Cleveland (A.L.)		0	1	.000	5.32	31	0	0	0	0	22	25	13	13	11	16
— Buffalo (I.L.)		0	0	...	0.00	2	0	0	0	0	2	3	0	0	0	4
— San Francisco (N.L.)■		1	0	1.000	5.14	9	0	0	0	0	7	8	4	4	3	7
— Fresno (PCL)		2	0	1.000	4.15	4	1	0	0	0	4 1/3	7	2	2	0	3
1999— Omaha (PCL)■		0	0	...	3.14	8	1	0	0	1	14 1/3	8	5	5	1	15
— Kansas City (A.L.)		2	4	.333	4.05	49	0	0	0	1	53 1/3	66	27	24	23	31
A.L. totals (3 years)		2	5	.286	4.71	114	0	0	0	3	93 2/3	110	53	49	48	60
N.L. totals (2 years)		4	2	.667	4.96	62	0	0	0	0	49	51	28	27	27	38
Major League totals (4 years)		6	7	.462	4.79	176	0	0	0	3	142 2/3	161	81	76	75	98

M

DIVISION SERIES RECORD

Year	League	W	L	Pct.	ERA	G	GS	CG	ShO	Sv.	IP	H	R	ER	BB	SO
1997— Cleveland (A.L.).................		0	0	...	...	1	0	0	0	0		0	0	0	1	0

CHAMPIONSHIP SERIES RECORD

Year	League	W	L	Pct.	ERA	G	GS	CG	ShO	Sv.	IP	H	R	ER	BB	SO
1997— Cleveland (A.L.).................		0	0	...	0.00	2	0	0	0	0	1⅓	0	0	0	0	1

WORLD SERIES RECORD

Year	League	W	L	Pct.	ERA	G	GS	CG	ShO	Sv.	IP	H	R	ER	BB	SO
1997— Cleveland (A.L.).................		0	0	...	0.00	2	0	0	0	0	⅓	0	2	0	2	1

MORRIS, HAL 1B REDS

PERSONAL: Born April 9, 1965, in Fort Rucker, Ala. ... 6-2/195. ... Bats left, throws left. ... Full name: William Harold Morris. ... Brother of Bobby Morris, second baseman, Cleveland Indians organization.
HIGH SCHOOL: Munster (Ind.).
COLLEGE: Michigan.
TRANSACTIONS/CAREER NOTES: Selected by New York Yankees organization in eighth round of free-agent draft (June 2, 1986). ... On Albany/Colonie disabled list (August 14, 1986-remainder of season). ... Traded by Yankees with P Rodney Imes to Cincinnati Reds for P Tim Leary and OF Van Snider (December 12, 1989). ... On Cincinnati disabled list (April 16-May 17, 1992); included rehabilitation assignment to Nashville (May 14-17). ... On Cincinnati disabled list (August 5-21, 1992). ... On Cincinnati disabled list (March 27-June 7, 1993); included rehabilitation assignment to Indianapolis (June 4-7). ... On suspended list (August 10, 1993). ... On Cincinnati disabled list (June 18-July 13, 1995); included rehabilitation assignment to Indianapolis (July 7-10). ... Granted free agency (November 2, 1995). ... Re-signed by Reds (December 6, 1995). ... On Cincinnati disabled list (July 2-17, 1996); included rehabilitation assignment to Indianapolis (July 16-17). ... On Cincinnati disabled list (July 31-September 10, 1997). ... Granted free agency (October 29, 1997). ... Signed by Kansas City Royals (December 22, 1997). ... On disabled list (May 8-23, 1998). ... Granted free agency (October 23, 1998). ... Signed by Reds (January 14, 1999). ... On disabled list (August 27-September 24, 1999).
RECORDS: Shares major league single-inning record for most doubles—2 (August 17, 1996, eighth inning).
STATISTICAL NOTES: Had 29-game hitting streak (August 27-September 29, 1996). ... Career major league grand slams: 1.

Year	Team (League)	Pos.	G	AB	R	H	2B	3B	HR	RBI	Avg.	BB	SO	SB	PO	A	E	Avg.
1986— Oneonta (NY-P).........		1B	36	127	26	48	9	2	3	30	.378	18	15	1	317	26	3	.991
— Alb./Colonie (East.)		1B	25	79	7	17	5	0	0	4	.215	4	10	0	203	19	2	.991
1987— Alb./Colonie (East.)		1B-OF	135	*530	65	*173	31	4	5	73	.326	36	43	7	1086	79	17	.986
1988— Columbus (I.L.).........		OF-1B	121	452	41	134	19	4	3	38	.296	36	62	8	543	26	8	.986
— New York (A.L.).........		OF-DH	15	20	1	2	0	0	0	0	.100	0	9	0	7	0	0	1.000
1989— Columbus (I.L.).........		1B-OF	111	417	70	136	24	1	17	66	*.326	28	47	5	636	67	9	.987
— New York (A.L.).........		OF-1B-DH	15	18	2	5	0	0	0	4	.278	1	4	0	12	0	0	1.000
1990— Cincinnati (N.L.)■...		1B-OF	107	309	50	105	22	3	7	36	.340	21	32	9	595	53	4	.994
— Nashville (A.A.).........		OF	16	64	8	22	5	0	1	10	.344	5	10	4	23	1	1	.960
1991— Cincinnati (N.L.).........		1B-OF	136	478	72	152	33	1	14	59	.318	46	61	10	979	100	9	.992
1992— Cincinnati (N.L.).........		1B	115	395	41	107	21	3	6	53	.271	45	53	6	841	86	1	*.999
— Nashville (A.A.).........		1B	2	6	1	1	1	0	0	0	.167	2	1	0	13	3	0	1.000
1993— Indianapolis (A.A.).....		1B	3	13	4	6	0	1	1	5	.462	1	2	0	26	3	0	1.000
— Cincinnati (N.L.).........		1B	101	379	48	120	18	0	7	49	.317	34	51	2	746	75	5	.994
1994— Cincinnati (N.L.)........		1B	112	436	60	146	30	4	10	78	.335	34	62	6	901	80	6	.994
1995— Cincinnati (N.L.)........		1B	101	359	53	100	25	2	11	51	.279	29	58	1	757	72	5	.994
— Indianapolis (A.A.).........		1B	2	5	2	2	0	0	0	1	.400	1	0	0	13	2	0	1.000
1996— Cincinnati (N.L.)........		1B	142	528	82	165	32	4	16	80	.313	50	76	7	1129	91	8	.993
— Indianapolis (A.A.).........		1B	1	4	1	2	1	0	1	1	.500	0	1	0	2	0	0	1.000
1997— Cincinnati (N.L.).........		1B	96	333	42	92	20	1	1	33	.276	23	43	3	672	52	7	.990
1998— Kansas City (A.L.)■...		1B-DH-OF	127	472	50	146	27	2	1	40	.309	32	52	1	396	35	4	.991
1999— Cincinnati (N.L.).........		1B-OF-DH	80	102	10	29	9	0	0	16	.284	10	21	0	110	6	1	.991
American League totals (3 years)			157	510	53	153	27	2	1	44	.300	33	65	1	415	35	4	.991
National League totals (9 years)			990	3319	458	1016	210	18	72	455	.306	292	457	44	6730	615	46	.994
Major League totals (12 years)			1147	3829	511	1169	237	20	73	499	.305	325	522	45	7145	650	50	.994

DIVISION SERIES RECORD

Year	Team (League)	Pos.	G	AB	R	H	2B	3B	HR	RBI	Avg.	BB	SO	SB	PO	A	E	Avg.
1995— Cincinnati (N.L.).........		1B	3	10	5	5	1	0	0	2	.500	3	1	1	22	2	0	1.000

CHAMPIONSHIP SERIES RECORD

Year	Team (League)	Pos.	G	AB	R	H	2B	3B	HR	RBI	Avg.	BB	SO	SB	PO	A	E	Avg.
1990— Cincinnati (N.L.).........		1B-PH	5	12	3	5	1	0	0	1	.417	1	0	0	20	2	0	1.000
1995— Cincinnati (N.L.).........		1B-PH	4	12	0	2	1	0	0	1	.167	1	1	1	27	3	0	1.000
Championship series totals (2 years)			9	24	3	7	2	0	0	2	.292	2	1	1	47	5	0	1.000

NOTES: Member of World Series championship team (1990).

WORLD SERIES RECORD

Year	Team (League)	Pos.	G	AB	R	H	2B	3B	HR	RBI	Avg.	BB	SO	SB	PO	A	E	Avg.
1990— Cincinnati (N.L.).........		1B-DH	4	14	0	1	0	0	0	2	.071	1	1	0	18	1	0	1.000

MORRIS, JIM P DEVIL RAYS

PERSONAL: Born January 19, 1964, in Brownwood, Texas. ... 6-3/215. ... Throws left, bats left. ... Full name: James Samuel Morris Jr.
HIGH SCHOOL: Brownwood (Texas).

M

JUNIOR COLLEGE: Ranger (Texas) College.
TRANSACTIONS/CAREER NOTES: Selected by Milwaukee Brewers organization in first round of secondary phase of free-agent draft (January 11, 1983). ... On disabled list (August 16-29, 1984). ... On temporary inactive list (April 12-May 13, 1985). ... On disabled list (April 11, 1986-entire season). ... Released by Brewers (June 15, 1987). ... Missed entire 1988 season due to injury. ... Signed by Chicago White Sox organization (September 25, 1988). ... Granted free agency (October 22, 1989). ... Out of organized baseball (1990-99). ... Signed by Tampa Bay Devil Rays organization (June 23, 1999). ... On St. Petersburg disabled list (June 25-July 15, 1999).

Year League	W	L	Pct.	ERA	G	GS	CG	ShO	Sv.	IP	H	R	ER	BB	SO
1983— Paintsville (Appl.)	3	6	.333	5.10	13	13	0	0	0	67	58	50	38	42	75
1984— Beloit (Midw.)	8	9	.471	5.05	24	22	1	0	0	112 1/3	107	80	63	79	109
1985— Beloit (Midw.)	0	0	...	0.00	1	0	0	0	1	3	0	0	0	0	4
— Stockton (Calif.)	5	6	.455	6.04	19	13	0	0	0	73	85	63	49	57	43
1986—									Did not play.						
1987— Stockton (Calif.)	1	0	1.000	0.75	4	0	0	0	0	12	6	5	1	12	9
1988—									Did not play.						
1989— Sarasota (FSL)■	0	1	.000	10.13	2	2	0	0	0	2 2/3	3	3	3	2	4
1999— Orlando (Sou.)■	0	1	.000	1.80	3	0	0	0	1	5	6	1	1	1	6
— Durham (I.L.)	3	1	.750	5.48	18	0	0	0	0	23	21	14	14	19	16
— Tampa Bay (A.L.)	0	0	...	5.79	5	0	0	0	0	4 2/3	3	3	3	2	3
Major League totals (1 year)	0	0	...	5.79	5	0	0	0	0	4 2/3	3	3	3	2	3

MORRIS, MATT — P — CARDINALS

PERSONAL: Born August 9, 1974, in Middletown, N.Y. ... 6-5/210. ... Throws right, bats right. ... Full name: Matthew Christian Morris.
HIGH SCHOOL: Valley Central (Montgomery, N.Y.).
COLLEGE: Seton Hall.
TRANSACTIONS/CAREER NOTES: Selected by Milwaukee Brewers organization in 25th round of free-agent draft (June 1, 1992); did not sign. ... Selected by St. Louis Cardinals organization in first round (12th pick overall) of free-agent draft (June 1, 1995). ... On St. Louis disabled list (March 24-April 11 and April 12-July 10, 1998); included rehabilitation assignments to Arkansas (April 6-11) and Memphis (June 21-July 10). ... On disabled list (March 26, 1999-entire season).
HONORS: Named N.L. Rookie Pitcher of the Year by THE SPORTING NEWS (1997).
MISCELLANEOUS: Struck out in only appearance as pinch hitter (1997).

Year League	W	L	Pct.	ERA	G	GS	CG	ShO	Sv.	IP	H	R	ER	BB	SO
1995— New Jersey (NY-P)	2	0	1.000	1.64	2	2	0	0	0	11	12	3	2	3	13
— St. Petersburg (FSL)	3	2	.600	2.38	6	6	1	1	0	34	22	16	9	11	31
1996— Arkansas (Texas)	12	12	.500	3.88	27	27	4	*4	0	167	178	79	72	48	120
— Louisville (A.A.)	0	1	.000	3.38	1	1	0	0	0	8	8	3	3	1	9
1997— St. Louis (N.L.)	12	9	.571	3.19	33	33	3	0	0	217	208	88	77	69	149
1998— Arkansas (Texas)	0	0	...	0.00	1	0	0	0	1	4	4	0	0	0	2
— St. Louis (N.L.)	7	5	.583	2.53	17	17	2	1	0	113 2/3	101	37	32	42	79
— Memphis (PCL)	1	0	1.000	4.50	4	4	0	0	0	14	16	8	7	4	21
1999— St. Louis (N.L.)									Did not play.						
Major League totals (2 years)	19	14	.576	2.97	50	50	5	1	0	330 2/3	309	125	109	111	228

MORRIS, WARREN — 2B — PIRATES

PERSONAL: Born January 11, 1974, in Alexandria, La. ... 5-11/179. ... Bats left, throws right. ... Full name: Warren Randall Morris.
HIGH SCHOOL: Bolton (Alexandria, La.).
TRANSACTIONS/CAREER NOTES: Selected by Texas Rangers organization in fifth round of free-agent draft (June 2, 1996). ... Traded by Rangers with P Todd Van Poppel to Pittsburgh Pirates for P Esteban Loaiza (July 17, 1998).
MISCELLANEOUS: Member of 1996 U.S. Olympic baseball team.

Year Team (League)	Pos.	G	AB	R	H	2B	3B	HR	RBI	Avg.	BB	SO	SB	PO	A	E	Avg.
1997— Charlotte (FSL)	2B-3B	128	494	78	151	27	9	12	75	.306	62	100	16	193	247	18	.961
— Oklahoma City (A.A.)..	2B	8	32	3	7	1	0	1	3	.219	3	5	0	17	31	0	1.000
1998— Tulsa (Texas)	2B	95	390	59	129	22	5	14	73	.331	43	63	12	179	274	17	.964
— Carolina (Sou.)■	2B	44	151	28	50	8	3	5	30	.331	24	34	5	87	100	7	.964
1999— Pittsburgh (N.L.)	2B	147	511	65	147	20	3	15	73	.288	59	88	3	263	403	14	.979
Major League totals (1 year)		147	511	65	147	20	3	15	73	.288	59	88	3	263	403	14	.979

MOSS, DAMIAN — P — BRAVES

PERSONAL: Born November 24, 1976, in Darlinghurst, Australia. ... 6-0/187. ... Throws left, bats right. ... Full name: Damian Joseph Moss.
HIGH SCHOOL: Liverpool Boys (Australia).
TRANSACTIONS/CAREER NOTES: Signed as non-drafted free agent by Atlanta Braves organization (July 1, 1993). ... On disabled list (March 27, 1998-entire season). ... On Atlanta disabled list (April 3-June 1, 1999).
STATISTICAL NOTES: Led Appalachian League with 14 hit batsmen in 1994.

Year League	W	L	Pct.	ERA	G	GS	CG	ShO	Sv.	IP	H	R	ER	BB	SO
1994— Danville (Appl.)	2	5	.286	3.58	12	12	1	1	0	60 1/3	30	28	24	55	77
1995— Macon (SAL)	9	10	.474	3.56	27	27	0	0	0	149 1/3	134	73	59	70	•177
1996— Durham (Caro.)	9	1	*.900	2.25	14	14	0	0	0	84	52	25	21	40	89
— Greenville (Sou.)	2	5	.286	4.97	11	10	0	0	0	58	57	41	32	35	48
1997— Greenville (Sou.)	6	8	.429	5.35	21	19	1	0	0	112 2/3	111	73	67	58	116
1998— Greenville (Sou.)									Did not play.						
1999— Macon (SAL)	0	3	.000	4.32	12	12	0	0	0	41 2/3	33	20	20	15	49
— Greenville (Sou.)	1	3	.250	8.54	7	7	0	0	0	32 2/3	50	33	31	21	22

M

MOTA, GUILLERMO P EXPOS

PERSONAL: Born July 25, 1973, in San Pedro de Macoris, Dominican Republic. ... 6-4/205. ... Throws right, bats right.
HIGH SCHOOL: Jose Joaquin Perez (San Pedro de Macoris, Dominican Republic).
TRANSACTIONS/CAREER NOTES: Signed as non-drafted free agent by New York Mets organization (September 7, 1990). ... Selected by Montreal Expos organization from Mets organization in Rule 5 minor league draft (December 9, 1996).
STATISTICAL NOTES: Led Gulf Coast League third basemen with .943 fielding percentage; tied for lead with 40 putouts and 11 double plays in 1993. ... Led Appalachian League third basemen with 44 putouts, 157 assists, 214 total chances, 12 double plays and .939 fielding percentage in 1994. ... Led South Atlantic League shortstops with 615 total chances and 66 double plays in 1995. ... Hit home run in first major league at-bat (June 9, 1999).
MISCELLANEOUS: Played infield (1991-96).

Year League	W	L	Pct.	ERA	G	GS	CG	ShO	Sv.	IP	H	R	ER	BB	SO
1997—Cape Fear (SAL)■	5	10	.333	4.36	25	23	...	...	0	126	135	65	61	33	112
1998—Jupiter (FSL)	3	2	.600	0.66	20	0	0	0	2	41	18	6	3	6	27
—Harrisburg (East.)	2	0	1.000	1.06	12	0	0	0	4	17	10	2	2	2	19
1999—Ottawa (I.L.)	2	0	1.000	1.89	14	0	0	0	5	19	16	6	4	5	17
—Montreal (N.L.)	2	4	.333	2.93	51	0	0	0	0	55 1/3	54	24	18	25	27
Major League totals (1 year)	2	4	.333	2.93	51	0	0	0	0	55 1/3	54	24	18	25	27

RECORD AS POSITION PLAYER

Year Team (League)	Pos.	G	AB	R	H	2B	3B	HR	RBI	Avg.	BB	SO	SB	PO	A	E	Avg.
1991—Dom. Mets (DSL)	...	32	90	4	22	2	0	0	12	.244	9	19	0	...	...	...	...
1992—Dom. Mets (DSL)	...	70	228	49	68	10	3	6	40	.298	28	40	10	...	...	...	...
1993—GC Mets (GCL)	3B-SS	43	169	23	42	7	2	1	22	.249	7	37	1	‡42	95	8	*.945
1994—St. Lucie (Fla. St.)	3B	1	4	1	0	0	0	0	0	.000	0	0	0	1	5	1	.857
—Kingsport (Appal.)	3B-SS	65	245	40	60	10	2	9	37	.245	20	78	5	†55	†175	16	†.935
1995—Columbia (S. Atl.)	SS-1B	123	400	45	97	24	3	4	45	.243	32	127	8	205	373	40	.935
1996—St. Lucie (Fla. St.)	SS-3B	102	304	34	71	10	3	1	21	.234	34	90	8	127	293	21	.952

MOTA, TONY OF DODGERS

PERSONAL: Born October 31, 1977, in Glendale, Calif. ... 6-1/170. ... Bats both, throws right. ... Full name: Antonio N. Mota. ... Son of Manny Mota, roving minor league instructor, Los Angeles Dodgers and outfielder with four major league teams (1962-82).
HIGH SCHOOL: Miami Springs (Fla.).
TRANSACTIONS/CAREER NOTES: Selected by Los Angeles Dodgers organization in 17th round of free-agent draft (June 1, 1995).
STATISTICAL NOTES: Led California League outfielders with four double plays in 1997.

Year Team (League)	Pos.	G	AB	R	H	2B	3B	HR	RBI	Avg.	BB	SO	SB	PO	A	E	Avg.
1996—Yakima (N.W.)	OF	60	225	29	62	11	3	3	29	.276	13	37	13	59	2	0	1.000
1997—San Bern. (Calif.)	OF	111	420	53	101	14	13	4	49	.240	30	97	11	225	15	4	.984
1998—Vero Beach (FSL)	OF	61	254	45	81	18	5	7	35	.319	18	27	13	118	3	2	.984
—San Antonio (Texas)	OF	59	222	20	54	10	6	2	22	.243	12	36	16	89	5	3	.969
1999—San Antonio (Texas)	OF	98	345	65	112	31	2	15	75	.325	41	56	13	111	8	3	.975

MOUTON, JAMES OF BREWERS

PERSONAL: Born December 29, 1968, in Denver. ... 5-9/175. ... Bats right, throws right. ... Full name: James Raleigh Mouton. ... Name pronounced MOO-tawn.
HIGH SCHOOL: Burbank (Calif.).
COLLEGE: St. Mary's (Calif.).
TRANSACTIONS/CAREER NOTES: Selected by New York Yankees organization in 42nd round of free-agent draft (June 2, 1987); did not sign. ... Selected by Minnesota Twins organization in eighth round of free-agent draft (June 4, 1990); did not sign. ... Selected by Houston Astros organization in seventh round of free-agent draft (June 3, 1991). ... On Houston disabled list (June 12-30, 1995); included rehabilitation assignment to Tucson (June 27-30). ... Traded by Astros to San Diego Padres for P Sean Bergman (January 14, 1998). ... On San Diego disabled list (May 16-June 1, 1998); included rehabilitation assignment to Las Vegas (May 27-June 1). ... Granted free agency (December 21, 1998). ... Signed by Montreal Expos organization (April 5, 1999). ... Granted free agency (October 15, 1999). ... Signed by Milwaukee Brewers organization (December 13, 1999).
HONORS: Named Pacific Coast League Most Valuable Player (1993).
STATISTICAL NOTES: Led New York-Pennsylvania League in caught stealing with 18 in 1991. ... Led New York-Pennsylvania League second basemen with 382 total chances in 1991. ... Led Florida State League second basemen with 623 total chances in 1992. ... Led Pacific Coast League with 286 total bases and tied for lead in caught stealing with 18 in 1993. ... Led Pacific Coast League second basemen with 674 total chances and 75 double plays in 1993. ... Career major league grand slams: 1.

Year Team (League)	Pos.	G	AB	R	H	2B	3B	HR	RBI	Avg.	BB	SO	SB	PO	A	E	Avg.
1991—Auburn (NY-P)	2B	76	288	71	76	15	*10	2	40	.264	55	32	*60	*170	184	*28	.927
1992—Osceola (FSL)	2B	133	507	*110	143	*30	6	11	62	.282	71	78	*51	*288	294	*41	.934
1993—Tucson (PCL)	2B	134	*546	*126	*172	*42	12	16	92	.315	72	82	40	*277	*354	*43	.936
1994—Houston (N.L.)	OF	99	310	43	76	11	0	2	16	.245	27	69	24	163	5	3	.982
—Tucson (PCL)	OF	4	17	2	7	1	0	1	1	.412	2	3	1	7	1	0	1.000
1995—Tucson (PCL)	OF	3	11	1	5	0	0	1	1	.455	0	2	0	1	0	1	.500
—Houston (N.L.)	OF	104	298	42	78	18	2	4	27	.262	25	59	25	136	4	0	1.000
1996—Houston (N.L.)	OF	122	300	40	79	15	1	3	34	.263	38	55	21	158	7	5	.971
—Tucson (PCL)	OF	4	4	1	1	0	0	0	0	.250	1	0	0	2	0	0	1.000
1997—Houston (N.L.)	OF	86	180	24	38	9	1	3	23	.211	18	30	9	86	1	0	1.000
1998—San Diego (N.L.)■	OF-DH	55	63	8	12	2	1	0	7	.190	7	11	4	30	1	1	.969
—Las Vegas (PCL)	OF-DH-2B	50	192	38	68	17	3	4	31	.354	17	31	15	57	2	1	.983
1999—Montreal (N.L.)■	OF-DH	95	122	18	32	5	1	2	13	.262	18	31	6	50	2	1	.981
Major League totals (6 years)		561	1273	175	315	60	6	14	120	.247	133	255	89	623	20	10	.985

PERSONAL: Born May 13, 1969, in Lafayette, La. ... 6-4/230. ... Bats right, throws right. ... Full name: Lyle Joseph Mouton. ... Name pronounced MOO-tawn.
HIGH SCHOOL: St. Thomas More (Lafayette, La.).
COLLEGE: Louisiana State.
TRANSACTIONS/CAREER NOTES: Selected by New York Yankees organization in fifth round of free-agent draft (June 3, 1991). ... Traded by Yankees to Chicago White Sox (April 22, 1995), completing deal in which White Sox traded P Jack McDowell to Yankees for P Keith Heberling and a player to be named later (December 14, 1994). ... On Chicago disabled list (May 11-27, 1997); included rehabilitation assignment to Birmingham (May 25-27). ... Contract sold to Yakult Swallows of Japan Central League (November 21, 1997). ... Contract purchased by Baltimore Orioles organization (July 2, 1998). ... Traded by Orioles to Milwaukee Brewers for OF Todd Dunn (June 1, 1999).

Year Team (League)	Pos.	G	AB	R	H	2B	3B	HR	RBI	Avg.	BB	SO	SB	PO	A	E	Avg.
						BATTING								FIELDING			
1991— Oneonta (NY-P)	OF	70	272	53	84	11	2	7	41	.309	31	38	15	106	5	5	.957
1992— Prince William (Caro.)	OF	50	189	28	50	14	1	6	34	.265	17	42	4	49	5	4	.931
— Albany (East.)	OF	64	214	25	46	12	2	2	27	.215	24	55	1	102	1	0	1.000
1993— Albany (East.)	OF	135	491	74	125	22	3	16	76	.255	50	125	18	189	9	5	.975
1994— Alb./Colonie (East.)	OF-3B	74	274	42	84	23	1	12	42	.307	27	62	7	118	4	2	.984
— Columbus (I.L.)	OF	59	204	26	64	14	5	4	32	.314	14	45	5	99	5	1	.990
1995— Nashville (A.A.)■	OF-DH	71	267	40	79	17	0	8	41	.296	23	58	10	123	8	3	.978
— Chicago (A.L.)	OF-DH	58	179	23	54	16	0	5	27	.302	19	46	1	93	5	1	.990
1996— Chicago (A.L.)	OF-DH	87	214	25	63	8	1	7	39	.294	22	50	3	64	1	2	.970
1997— Chicago (A.L.)	OF-DH	88	242	26	65	9	0	5	23	.269	14	66	4	126	1	4	.969
— Birmingham (Sou.)	OF	3	11	1	2	0	0	1	1	.182	1	4	0	5	0	0	1.000
1998— Yakult (Jap. Cen.)■	OF	30	97	7	21	8	0	3	12	.216	9	27	0	...	...	...	...
— Rochester (I.L.)■	OF-DH	37	137	23	44	9	2	7	32	.321	13	31	1	56	1	1	.983
— Baltimore (A.L.)	OF-DH	18	39	5	12	2	0	2	7	.308	4	8	0	19	1	0	1.000
1999— Rochester (I.L.)	OF-DH	44	162	25	36	9	1	4	17	.222	13	31	3	63	1	4	.941
— Louisville (I.L.)■	OF-DH-1B	83	305	64	109	34	2	19	77	.357	27	67	19	181	7	2	.989
— Milwaukee (N.L.)	OF	14	17	2	3	1	0	1	3	.176	2	3	0	1	0	0	1.000
American League totals (4 years)		251	674	79	194	35	1	19	96	.288	59	170	8	302	8	7	.978
National League totals (1 year)		14	17	2	3	1	0	1	3	.176	2	3	0	1	0	0	1.000
Major League totals (5 years)		265	691	81	197	36	1	20	99	.285	61	173	8	303	8	7	.978

PERSONAL: Born November 18, 1962, in Sellersville, Pa. ... 6-0/170. ... Throws left, bats left. ... Son-in-law of Digger Phelps, ESPN college basketball analyst, and Notre Dame basketball coach (1971-72 through 1990-91).
HIGH SCHOOL: Souderton (Pa.) Area.
COLLEGE: St. Joseph's (Pa.).
TRANSACTIONS/CAREER NOTES: Selected by Chicago Cubs organization in sixth round of free-agent draft (June 4, 1984). ... Traded by Cubs with OF Rafael Palmeiro and P Drew Hall to Texas Rangers for P Mitch Williams, P Paul Kilgus, P Steve Wilson, IF Curtis Wilkerson, IF Luis Benitez and OF Pablo Delgado (December 5, 1988). ... On Texas disabled list (May 31-September 1, 1989); included rehabilitation assignments to Gulf Coast Rangers (August 5-14) and Tulsa (August 15-24). ... Released by Rangers (November 13, 1990). ... Signed by Louisville, St. Louis Cardinals organization (January 9, 1991). ... Released by Cardinals (October 14, 1991). ... Signed by Cubs organization (January 8, 1992). ... Released by Cubs (March 30, 1992). ... Signed by Toledo, Detroit Tigers organization (May 24, 1992). ... Granted free agency (December 8, 1992). ... Signed by Baltimore Orioles organization (December 14, 1992). ... Granted free agency (November 1, 1995). ... Signed by Boston Red Sox (January 2, 1996). ... Traded by Red Sox to Seattle Mariners for OF Darren Bragg (July 30, 1996). ... Granted free agency (October 29, 1996). ... Re-signed by Mariners (November 20, 1996). ... On Seattle disabled list (March 23-April 29, 1997); included rehabilitation assignment to Tacoma (April 24-29).
HONORS: Named lefthanded pitcher on THE SPORTING NEWS A.L. All-Star team (1999).
STATISTICAL NOTES: Led American Association with 16 home runs allowed in 1991. ... Led A.L. with .813 winning percentage in 1996. ... Led A.L. pitchers with 47 assists and nine double plays in 1999.

Year League	W	L	Pct.	ERA	G	GS	CG	ShO	Sv.	IP	H	R	ER	BB	SO
1984— Geneva (NY-P)	•9	3	.750	1.89	14	14	5	2	0	*104 2/3	59	27	22	31	*120
1985— Win.-Salem (Car.)	8	2	.800	2.30	12	12	6	2	0	94	82	36	24	22	94
— Pittsfield (East.)	7	6	.538	3.72	15	15	3	0	0	96 2/3	99	49	40	32	51
1986— Pittsfield (East.)	3	1	.750	0.88	6	6	0	0	0	41	27	10	4	16	42
— Iowa (A.A.)	3	2	.600	2.55	6	6	2	0	0	42 1/3	25	14	12	11	25
— Chicago (N.L.)	7	4	.636	5.05	16	16	1	1	0	87 1/3	107	52	49	42	45
1987— Chicago (N.L.)	12	15	.444	5.10	35	33	1	0	0	201	210	127	*114	97	147
1988— Chicago (N.L.)	9	15	.375	3.48	34	30	3	1	0	202	212	84	78	55	121
1989— Texas (A.L.)■	4	9	.308	4.86	15	15	1	0	0	76	84	51	41	33	44
— Gulf Coast Rangers (GCL)	1	0	1.000	1.64	3	3	0	0	0	11	8	4	2	1	18
— Tulsa (Texas)	1	1	.500	5.11	2	2	1	1	0	12 1/3	16	8	7	3	9
1990— Texas (A.L.)	2	6	.250	4.66	33	10	1	0	0	102 1/3	115	59	53	39	58
1991— St. Louis (N.L.)■	0	5	.000	5.74	8	7	0	0	0	31 1/3	38	21	20	16	20
— Louisville (A.A.)	5	10	.333	3.80	20	20	1	0	0	125 2/3	125	64	53	43	69
1992— Toledo (I.L.)■	10	8	.556	2.86	21	20	5	0	0	138 2/3	128	48	44	37	80
1993— Rochester (I.L.)■	6	0	1.000	1.67	8	8	1	1	0	54	42	13	10	13	41
— Baltimore (A.L.)	12	9	.571	3.43	25	25	3	1	0	152	154	63	58	38	90
1994— Baltimore (A.L.)	5	7	.417	4.77	23	23	0	0	0	149	158	81	79	38	87
1995— Baltimore (A.L.)	8	6	.571	5.21	27	18	0	0	0	115 2/3	117	70	67	30	65
1996— Boston (A.L.)■	7	1	.875	4.50	23	10	0	0	0	90	111	50	45	27	50
— Seattle (A.L.)■	6	2	§.750	3.31	11	11	0	0	0	70 2/3	66	36	26	19	29
1997— Tacoma (PCL)	1	0	1.000	0.00	1	1	0	0	0	5	1	0	0	0	6
— Seattle (A.L.)	17	5	.773	3.86	30	30	2	0	0	188 2/3	187	82	81	43	113
1998— Seattle (A.L.)	15	9	.625	3.53	34	34	4	3	0	234 1/3	234	99	92	42	158
1999— Seattle (A.L.)	14	8	.636	3.87	32	32	4	0	0	228	235	108	98	48	137
A.L. totals (9 years)	90	62	.592	4.09	253	208	15	4	0	1406 2/3	1461	699	640	357	831
N.L. totals (4 years)	28	39	.418	4.50	93	86	5	2	0	521 2/3	567	284	261	210	333
Major League totals (13 years)	118	101	.539	4.21	346	294	20	6	0	1928 1/3	2028	983	901	567	1164

M

DIVISION SERIES RECORD

Year	League	W	L	Pct.	ERA	G	GS	CG	ShO	Sv.	IP	H	R	ER	BB	SO
1997—	Seattle (A.L.)	0	1	.000	5.79	1	1	0	0	0	4²/₃	5	3	3	1	2

MUELLER, BILL   3B   GIANTS

PERSONAL: Born March 17, 1971, in Maryland Heights, Mo. ... 5-10/180. ... Bats both, throws right. ... Full name: William Richard Mueller. ... Name pronounced MILL-er.

HIGH SCHOOL: DeSmet (Creve Coeur, Mo.).

COLLEGE: Southwest Missouri State.

TRANSACTIONS/CAREER NOTES: Selected by San Francisco Giants organization in 15th round of free-agent draft (June 3, 1993). ... On disabled list (July 1-16, 1997). ... On San Francisco disabled list (April 6-May 17, 1999); included rehabilitation assignment to Fresno (May 11-17).

STATISTICAL NOTES: Led California League with .435 on-base percentage in 1994. ... Led Pacific Coast League third basemen with 25 double plays in 1996. ... Had 17-game hitting streak (April 24-May 14, 1998). ... Career major league grand slams: 2.

								BATTING							FIELDING		
Year	Team (League)	Pos.	G	AB	R	H	2B	3B	HR	RBI	Avg.	BB	SO	SB	PO	A	E	Avg.
1993—	Everett (N.W.)	2B	58	200	31	60	8	2	1	24	.300	42	17	13	86	143	8	.966
1994—	San Jose (Calif.)	3B-2B-SS	120	431	79	130	20	•9	5	72	.302	*103	47	4	83	276	29	.925
1995—	Shreveport (Texas)	3B-2B	88	330	56	102	16	2	1	39	.309	53	36	6	52	169	5	.978
	— Phoenix (PCL)	3B-2B	41	172	23	51	13	6	2	19	.297	19	31	0	26	85	7	.941
1996—	Phoenix (PCL)	3-S-2-DH	106	440	73	133	14	6	4	36	.302	44	40	2	92	250	11	.969
	— San Francisco (N.L.)	3B-2B	55	200	31	66	15	1	0	19	.330	24	26	0	51	99	6	.962
1997—	San Francisco (N.L.)	3B	128	390	51	114	26	3	7	44	.292	48	71	4	85	218	14	.956
1998—	San Francisco (N.L.)	3B-2B	145	534	93	157	27	0	9	59	.294	79	83	3	99	287	19	.953
1999—	San Francisco (N.L.)	3B-2B	116	414	61	120	24	0	2	36	.290	65	52	4	83	195	12	.959
	— Fresno (PCL)	3B	3	12	3	5	0	1	0	6	.417	0	0	0	2	10	3	.800
Major League totals (4 years)			444	1538	236	457	92	4	18	158	.297	216	232	11	318	799	51	.956

DIVISION SERIES RECORD

								BATTING							FIELDING		
Year	Team (League)	Pos.	G	AB	R	H	2B	3B	HR	RBI	Avg.	BB	SO	SB	PO	A	E	Avg.
1997—	San Francisco (N.L.)	3B	3	12	1	3	0	0	1	1	.250	0	0	0	2	9	0	1.000

MULHOLLAND, TERRY   P   BRAVES

PERSONAL: Born March 9, 1963, in Uniontown, Pa. ... 6-3/220. ... Throws left, bats right. ... Full name: Terence John Mulholland.

HIGH SCHOOL: Laurel Highlands (Uniontown, Pa.).

COLLEGE: Marietta College (Ohio).

TRANSACTIONS/CAREER NOTES: Selected by San Francisco Giants organization in first round (24th pick overall) of free-agent draft (June 4, 1984); pick received as compensation for Detroit Tigers signing free-agent IF Darrell Evans. ... On San Francisco disabled list (August 1, 1988-remainder of season). ... Traded by Giants with P Dennis Cook and 3B Charlie Hayes to Philadelphia Phillies for P Steve Bedrosian and a player to be named later (June 18, 1989); Giants organization acquired IF Rick Parker to complete deal (August 7, 1989). ... On Philadelphia disabled list (June 12-28, 1990); included rehabilitation assignment to Scranton/Wilkes-Barre (June 23-24). ... Traded by Phillies with a player to be named later to New York Yankees for P Bobby Munoz, 2B Kevin Jordan and P Ryan Karp (February 9, 1994); Yankees acquired P Jeff Patterson to complete deal (November 8, 1994). ... Granted free agency (October 17, 1994). ... Signed by Giants (April 8, 1995). ... On San Francisco disabled list (June 6-July 4, 1995); included rehabilitation assignment to Phoenix (June 23-July 4). ... Granted free agency (November 3, 1995). ... Signed by Reading, Phillies organization (February 17, 1996). ... Traded by Phillies to Seattle Mariners for IF Desi Relaford (July 31, 1996). ... Granted free agency (October 28, 1996). ... Signed by Chicago Cubs (December 10, 1996). ... Claimed on waivers by Giants (August 8, 1997). ... Granted free agency (October 27, 1997). ... Signed by Cubs (February 2, 1998). ... Granted free agency (October 28, 1998). ... Re-signed by Cubs (November 6, 1998). ... Traded by Cubs with IF Jose Hernandez to Atlanta Braves for P Micah Bowie, P Ruben Quevado and a minor league player to be named later (July 31, 1999); Cubs acquired P Joey Nation to complete deal (August 24, 1999).

STATISTICAL NOTES: Pitched 6-0 no-hit victory for Philadelphia against San Francisco (August 15, 1990).

MISCELLANEOUS: Appeared in one game as pinch runner (1991). ... Appeared in one game as pinch runner with San Francisco (1995).

Year	League	W	L	Pct.	ERA	G	GS	CG	ShO	Sv.	IP	H	R	ER	BB	SO
1984—	Everett (N.W.)	1	0	1.000	0.00	3	3	0	0	0	19	10	2	0	4	15
	— Fresno (Calif.)	5	2	.714	2.95	9	9	0	0	0	42²/₃	32	17	14	36	39
1985—	Shreveport (Texas)	9	8	.529	2.90	26	26	8	*3	0	176²/₃	166	79	57	87	122
1986—	Phoenix (PCL)	8	5	.615	4.46	17	17	3	0	0	111	112	60	55	56	77
	— San Francisco (N.L.)	1	7	.125	4.94	15	10	0	0	0	54²/₃	51	33	30	35	27
1987—	Phoenix (PCL)	7	12	.368	5.07	37	*29	3	1	1	172¹/₃	200	*124	•97	90	94
1988—	Phoenix (PCL)	7	3	.700	3.58	19	14	3	2	0	100²/₃	116	45	40	44	57
	— San Francisco (N.L.)	2	1	.667	3.72	9	6	2	1	0	46	50	20	19	7	18
1989—	San Francisco (N.L.)	0	0	...	4.09	5	1	0	0	0	11	15	5	5	4	6
	— Phoenix (PCL)	4	5	.444	2.99	13	10	3	0	0	78¹/₃	67	30	26	26	61
	— Philadelphia (N.L.)■	4	7	.364	5.00	20	17	2	1	0	104¹/₃	122	61	58	32	60
1990—	Philadelphia (N.L.)	9	10	.474	3.34	33	26	6	1	0	180²/₃	172	78	67	42	75
	— Scranton/W.B. (I.L.)	0	1	.000	3.00	1	1	0	0	0	6	9	4	2	2	2
1991—	Philadelphia (N.L.)	16	13	.552	3.61	34	34	8	3	0	232	231	100	93	49	142
1992—	Philadelphia (N.L.)	13	11	.542	3.81	32	32	*12	2	0	229	227	101	97	46	125
1993—	Philadelphia (N.L.)	12	9	.571	3.25	29	28	7	2	0	191	177	80	69	40	116
1994—	New York (A.L.)■	6	7	.462	6.49	24	19	2	0	0	120²/₃	150	94	87	37	72
1995—	San Francisco (N.L.)■	5	13	.278	5.80	29	24	2	0	0	149	190	112	96	38	65
	— Phoenix (PCL)	0	0	...	2.25	1	1	0	0	0	4	4	3	1	1	4
1996—	Philadelphia (N.L.)■	8	7	.533	4.66	21	21	0	0	0	133¹/₃	157	74	69	21	52
	— Seattle (A.L.)■	5	4	.556	4.67	12	12	0	0	0	69¹/₃	75	38	36	28	34
1997—	Chicago (N.L.)■	6	12	.333	4.07	25	25	1	0	0	157	162	79	71	45	74

Year League	W	L	Pct.	ERA	G	GS	CG	ShO	Sv.	IP	H	R	ER	BB	SO
— San Francisco (N.L.)■	0	1	.000	5.16	15	2	0	0	0	29 2/3	28	21	17	6	25
1998—Chicago (N.L.)	6	5	.545	2.89	70	6	0	0	3	112	100	49	36	39	72
1999—Chicago (N.L.)	6	6	.500	5.15	26	16	0	0	0	110	137	71	63	32	44
— Atlanta (N.L.)■..............	4	2	.667	2.98	16	8	0	0	1	60 1/3	64	24	20	13	39
A.L. totals (2 years)	11	11	.500	5.83	36	31	2	0	0	190	225	132	123	65	106
N.L. totals (12 years)	92	104	.469	4.05	379	256	43	10	4	1800	1883	908	810	449	940
Major League totals (13 years).....	103	115	.472	4.22	415	287	45	10	4	1990	2108	1040	933	514	1046

DIVISION SERIES RECORD

Year League	W	L	Pct.	ERA	G	GS	CG	ShO	Sv.	IP	H	R	ER	BB	SO
1998—Chicago (N.L.)	0	1	.000	11.57	2	0	0	0	0	2 1/3	2	3	3	2	2
1999—Atlanta (N.L.)	0	0	...	27.00	2	0	0	0	0	2/3	3	2	2	0	0
Division series totals (2 years)	0	1	.000	15.00	4	0	0	0	0	3	5	5	5	2	2

CHAMPIONSHIP SERIES RECORD

Year League	W	L	Pct.	ERA	G	GS	CG	ShO	Sv.	IP	H	R	ER	BB	SO
1993—Philadelphia (N.L.).............	0	1	.000	7.20	1	1	0	0	0	5	9	5	4	1	2
1999—Atlanta (N.L.)	0	0	...	0.00	2	0	0	0	0	2 2/3	1	0	0	1	2
Champ. series totals (2 years)	0	1	.000	4.70	3	1	0	0	0	7 2/3	10	5	4	2	4

WORLD SERIES RECORD

Year League	W	L	Pct.	ERA	G	GS	CG	ShO	Sv.	IP	H	R	ER	BB	SO
1993—Philadelphia (N.L.).............	1	0	1.000	6.75	2	2	0	0	0	10 2/3	14	8	8	3	5
1999—Atlanta (N.L.)	0	0	...	7.36	2	0	0	0	0	3 2/3	5	3	3	1	3
World Series totals (2 years)	1	0	1.000	6.91	4	2	0	0	0	14 1/3	19	11	11	4	8

ALL-STAR GAME RECORD

Year League	W	L	Pct.	ERA	GS	CG	ShO	Sv.	IP	H	R	ER	BB	SO
1993—National	0	0	...	4.50	1	0	0	0	2	1	1	1	2	0

MUNOZ, MIKE — P — RANGERS

PERSONAL: Born July 12, 1965, in Baldwin Park, Calif. ... 6-2/198. ... Throws left, bats left. ... Full name: Michael Anthony Munoz.
HIGH SCHOOL: Bishop Amat (La Puente, Calif.).
COLLEGE: Cal Poly Pomona.
TRANSACTIONS/CAREER NOTES: Selected by Los Angeles Dodgers organization in third round of free-agent draft (June 2, 1986). ... Traded by Dodgers to Detroit Tigers for P Mike Wilkins (September 30, 1990). ... Granted free agency (May 12, 1993). ... Signed by Colorado Springs, Colorado Rockies organization (May 14, 1993). ... On Colorado disabled list (July 27-August 15, 1996); included rehabilitation assignment to Colorado Springs (August 10-15). ... Granted free agency (October 27, 1997). ... Re-signed by Rockies (January 27, 1998). ... Granted free agency (October 26, 1998). ... Signed by Texas Rangers organization (January 12, 1999). ... Granted free agency (November 1, 1999). ... Re-signed by Rangers (December 7, 1999).

Year League	W	L	Pct.	ERA	G	GS	CG	ShO	Sv.	IP	H	R	ER	BB	SO
1986—Great Falls (Pio.)	4	4	.500	3.21	14	14	2	2	0	81 1/3	85	44	29	38	49
1987—Bakersfield (Calif.)	8	7	.533	3.74	52	12	2	0	9	118	125	68	49	43	80
1988—San Antonio (Texas)	7	2	.778	1.00	56	0	0	0	14	71 2/3	63	18	8	24	71
1989—Albuquerque (PCL)	6	4	.600	3.08	60	0	0	0	6	79	72	32	27	40	81
— Los Angeles (N.L.)	0	0	...	16.88	3	0	0	0	0	2 2/3	5	5	5	2	3
1990—Los Angeles (N.L.)	0	1	.000	3.18	8	0	0	0	0	5 2/3	6	2	2	3	2
— Albuquerque (PCL)	4	1	.800	4.25	49	0	0	0	6	59 1/3	65	33	28	19	40
1991—Toledo (I.L.)■.....................	2	3	.400	3.83	38	1	0	0	8	54	44	30	23	35	38
— Detroit (A.L.)	0	0	...	9.64	6	0	0	0	0	9 1/3	14	10	10	5	3
1992—Detroit (A.L.)	1	2	.333	3.00	65	0	0	0	2	48	44	16	16	25	23
1993—Detroit (A.L.)	0	1	.000	6.00	8	0	0	0	0	3	4	2	2	6	1
— Colo. Springs (PCL)■	1	2	.333	1.67	40	0	0	0	3	37 2/3	46	10	7	9	30
— Colorado (N.L.)	2	1	.667	4.50	21	0	0	0	0	18	21	12	9	9	16
1994—Colorado (N.L.)	4	2	.667	3.74	57	0	0	0	1	45 2/3	37	22	19	31	32
1995—Colorado (N.L.)	2	4	.333	7.42	64	0	0	0	2	43 2/3	54	38	36	27	37
1996—Colorado (N.L.)	2	2	.500	6.65	54	0	0	0	0	44 2/3	55	33	33	16	45
— Colo. Springs (PCL)	1	1	.500	2.03	10	0	0	0	3	13 1/3	8	3	3	6	13
1997—Colorado (N.L.)	3	3	.500	4.53	64	0	0	0	2	45 2/3	52	25	23	13	26
1998—Colorado (N.L.)	2	2	.500	5.66	40	0	0	0	3	41 1/3	53	32	26	16	24
1999—Texas (A.L.)■....................	2	1	.667	3.93	56	0	0	0	1	52 2/3	54	24	23	18	27
A.L. totals (4 years)	3	4	.429	4.06	135	0	0	0	3	113	114	52	51	54	54
N.L. totals (8 years)	15	15	.500	5.57	311	0	0	0	8	247 1/3	283	169	153	117	185
Major League totals (11 years).....	18	19	.486	5.10	446	0	0	0	11	360 1/3	397	221	204	171	239

DIVISION SERIES RECORD

Year League	W	L	Pct.	ERA	G	GS	CG	ShO	Sv.	IP	H	R	ER	BB	SO
1995—Colorado (N.L.)	0	1	.000	13.50	4	0	0	0	0	1 1/3	4	2	2	1	1
1999—Texas (A.L.)							Did not play.								

MUNRO, PETER — P — BLUE JAYS

PERSONAL: Born June 14, 1975, in Flushing, N.Y. ... 6-2/210. ... Throws right, bats right. ... Full name: Peter Daniel Munro.
HIGH SCHOOL: Benjamin Cardozo (Bayside, N.Y.).
JUNIOR COLLEGE: Okaloosa-Walton Community College (Fla.).
TRANSACTIONS/CAREER NOTES: Signed as non-drafted free agent by Boston Red Sox organization (May 25, 1994). ... On Pawtucket disabled list (May 24-June 8, 1998). ... Traded by Red Sox with P Jay Yennaco to Toronto Blue Jays for 1B/DH Mike Stanley (July 30, 1998).

M

Year League	W	L	Pct.	ERA	G	GS	CG	ShO	Sv.	IP	H	R	ER	BB	SO
1995— Utica (NY-P)	5	4	.556	2.60	14	14	0	0	0	90	79	38	26	33	74
1996— Sarasota (FSL)	11	6	.647	3.60	27	25	2	•2	1	155	153	76	62	62	115
1997— Trenton (East.)	7	10	.412	4.95	22	22	1	0	0	116 1/3	113	76	64	47	109
1998— Pawtucket (I.L.)................	5	4	.556	4.05	18	17	0	0	0	106 2/3	111	49	48	35	75
— Syracuse (I.L.)■	2	5	.286	7.46	8	8	0	0	0	44 2/3	58	42	37	23	42
1999— Toronto (A.L.)...................	0	2	.000	6.02	31	2	0	0	0	55 1/3	70	38	37	23	38
— Syracuse (I.L.)...................	6	1	.857	3.10	18	11	0	0	0	69 2/3	70	29	24	33	68
Major League totals (1 year)........	0	2	.000	6.02	31	2	0	0	0	55 1/3	70	38	37	23	38

MUNSON, ERIC — C/1B — TIGERS

PERSONAL: Born October 3, 1977, in San Diego, Calif. ... 6-3/220. ... Bats left, throws right.
HIGH SCHOOL: Mount Carmel (San Diego).
COLLEGE: Southern California.
TRANSACTIONS/CAREER NOTES: Selected by Atlanta Braves organization in second round of free-agent draft (June 4, 1996); did not sign. ... Selected by Detroit Tigers organization in first round (third pick overall) of free-agent draft (June 2, 1999).

							BATTING						FIELDING		
Year Team (League)	Pos.	G	AB	R	H	2B	3B	HR	RBI	Avg.	BB	SO	SB	PO	A	E	Avg.
1999— Lakeland (FSL)	DH	2	6	0	2	0	0	0	1	.333	1	1	0	0	0	0	...
— W. Mich. (Mid.)	1B-C	67	252	42	67	16	1	14	44	.266	37	47	3	319	29	3	.991

MURRAY, CALVIN — OF — GIANTS

PERSONAL: Born July 30, 1971, in Dallas. ... 5-11/190. ... Bats right, throws right. ... Full name: Calvin Duane Murray.
HIGH SCHOOL: Warren Travis White (Dallas).
COLLEGE: Texas.
TRANSACTIONS/CAREER NOTES: Selected by San Francisco Giants organization in first round (seventh pick overall) of free-agent draft (June 1, 1992).
HONORS: Named Pacific Coast League Most Valuable Player (1999).
STATISTICAL NOTES: Led Pacific Coast League with 297 total bases in 1999.
MISCELLANEOUS: Member of 1992 U.S. Olympic Baseball team.

							BATTING						FIELDING		
Year Team (League)	Pos.	G	AB	R	H	2B	3B	HR	RBI	Avg.	BB	SO	SB	PO	A	E	Avg.
1993— San Jose (Calif.).........	OF	85	345	61	97	24	1	9	42	.281	40	63	42	203	9	2	.991
— Shreveport (Texas).....	OF	37	138	15	26	6	0	0	6	.188	14	29	12	79	2	2	.976
— Phoenix (PCL)...........	OF	5	19	4	6	1	0	1	0	.316	2	5	1	13	0	2	.867
1994— Shreveport (Texas).....	OF	480	480	67	111	19	5	2	35	.231	47	81	33	268	5	3	.989
1995— Phoenix (PCL)...........	OF	13	50	8	9	1	0	4	10	.180	4	6	2	19	2	0	1.000
— Shreveport (Texas).....	OF	110	441	77	104	17	3	2	29	.236	59	70	26	286	9	2	.993
1996— Shreveport (Texas).....	OF	50	169	32	44	7	0	7	24	.260	25	33	6	89	4	3	.969
— Phoenix (PCL)...........	OF	83	311	50	76	16	6	3	28	.244	43	60	12	207	3	2	.991
1997— Shreveport (Texas).....	OF	122	419	83	114	25	3	10	56	.272	66	73	*52	214	9	5	.978
1998— Fresno (PCL)	OF	33	90	16	21	3	1	3	5	.233	12	18	3	27	1	0	1.000
— Shreveport (Texas).....	OF	88	337	63	104	22	5	8	39	.309	58	45	34	198	3	7	.966
1999— Fresno (PCL)	OF-DH	130	*548	*122	*183	31	7	23	73	.334	49	88	*42	284	8	6	.980
— San Francisco (N.L.) ..	OF	15	19	1	5	2	0	0	5	.263	2	4	1	6	0	0	1.000
Major League totals (1 year)		15	19	1	5	2	0	0	5	.263	2	4	1	6	0	0	1.000

MURRAY, DAN — P — ROYALS

PERSONAL: Born November 21, 1973, in Los Alamitos, Calif. ... 6-1/195. ... Throws right, bats right. ... Full name: Daniel Saffle Murray.
HIGH SCHOOL: Pacifica (Garden Grove, Calif.).
COLLEGE: San Diego State.
TRANSACTIONS/CAREER NOTES: Selected by New York Mets organization in 10th round of free-agent draft (June 1, 1995). ... Traded by Mets to Kansas City Royals for P Glendon Rusch (September 14, 1999).

Year League	W	L	Pct.	ERA	G	GS	CG	ShO	Sv.	IP	H	R	ER	BB	SO
1995— Pittsfield (NY-P)	0	6	.000	1.97	22	0	0	0	6	32	24	17	7	16	34
1996— St. Lucie (FSL)	7	5	.583	4.25	33	13	0	0	0	101 2/3	114	60	48	53	56
1997— St. Lucie (FSL)	12	10	.545	3.45	30	24	4	•2	0	156 1/3	150	75	60	55	91
1998— Binghamton (East.)	11	6	.647	3.18	27	27	1	1	0	164 1/3	153	64	58	54	159
1999— Norfolk (I.L.)	12	10	.545	4.97	29	27	3	1	0	145	149	91	80	70	96
— New York (N.L.).................	0	0	...	13.50	1	0	0	0	0	2	4	3	3	2	1
— Kansas City (A.L.)■	0	0	...	6.48	4	0	0	0	0	8 1/3	9	8	6	4	8
A.L. totals (1 year)	0	0	...	6.48	4	0	0	0	0	8 1/3	9	8	6	4	8
N.L. totals (1 year)	0	0	...	13.50	1	0	0	0	0	2	4	3	3	2	1
Major League totals (1 year)........	0	0	...	7.84	5	0	0	0	0	10 1/3	13	11	9	6	9

MURRAY, HEATH — P — REDS

PERSONAL: Born April 19, 1973, in Troy, Ohio. ... 6-4/215. ... Throws left, bats left. ... Full name: Heath Robertson Murray.
HIGH SCHOOL: Troy (Ohio).
COLLEGE: Michigan.

M

TRANSACTIONS/CAREER NOTES: Selected by San Diego Padres organization in third round of free-agent draft (June 2, 1994). ... On San Diego disabled list (June 23-July 10, 1997). ... On San Diego disabled list (September 19, 1998-remainder of season). ... Claimed on waivers by Cincinnati Reds (October 6, 1999).
STATISTICAL NOTES: Tied for Pacific Coast League lead with four double plays by pitcher in 1999.

Year League	W	L	Pct.	ERA	G	GS	CG	ShO	Sv.	IP	H	R	ER	BB	SO
1994—Spokane (N.W.)	5	6	.455	2.90	15	15	•2	•1	0	*99 1/3	101	46	32	18	78
1995—Rancho Cuca. (Calif.)	9	4	.692	3.12	14	14	4	•2	0	92 1/3	80	37	32	38	81
—Memphis (Sou.)	5	4	.556	3.38	14	14	0	0	0	77 1/3	83	36	29	42	71
1996—Memphis (Sou.)	13	9	.591	3.21	27	27	1	1	0	174	154	83	62	60	156
1997—Las Vegas (PCL)	6	8	.429	5.45	19	19	2	1	0	109	142	72	66	41	99
—San Diego (N.L.)	1	2	.333	6.75	17	3	0	0	0	33 1/3	50	25	25	21	16
1998—Las Vegas (PCL)	9	11	.450	4.99	27	27	3	0	0	162 1/3	191	103	90	62	121
1999—Las Vegas (PCL)	5	4	.556	4.26	15	15	1	1	0	82 1/3	99	45	39	32	65
—San Diego (N.L.)	0	4	.000	5.76	22	8	0	0	0	50	60	33	32	26	25
Major League totals (2 years)	1	6	.143	6.16	39	11	0	0	0	83 1/3	110	58	57	47	41

MUSSINA, MIKE — P — ORIOLES

PERSONAL: Born December 8, 1968, in Williamsport, Pa. ... 6-2/183. ... Throws right, bats both. ... Full name: Michael Cole Mussina. ... Name pronounced myoo-SEEN-uh.
HIGH SCHOOL: Montoursville (Pa.).
COLLEGE: Stanford (degree in economics, 1990).
TRANSACTIONS/CAREER NOTES: Selected by Baltimore Orioles organization in 11th round of free-agent draft (June 2, 1987); did not sign. ... Selected by Orioles organization in first round (20th pick overall) of free-agent draft (June 4, 1990). ... On Rochester disabled list (May 5-12, 1991). ... On Baltimore disabled list (July 22-August 20, 1993); included rehabilitation assignment to Bowie (August 9-20). ... On disabled list (April 17-May 3 and May 15-June 6, 1998).
HONORS: Named International League Most Valuable Pitcher (1991). ... Named righthanded pitcher on THE SPORTING NEWS A.L. All-Star team (1995). ... Won A.L. Gold Glove at pitcher (1996-99).
STATISTICAL NOTES: Pitched 8-0 one-hit, complete-game victory against Texas (July 17, 1992). ... Pitched 3-0 one-hit, complete-game victory against Cleveland (May 30, 1997).

Year League	W	L	Pct.	ERA	G	GS	CG	ShO	Sv.	IP	H	R	ER	BB	SO
1990—Hagerstown (East.)	3	0	1.000	1.49	7	7	2	1	0	42 1/3	34	10	7	7	40
—Rochester (I.L.)	0	0	...	1.35	2	2	0	0	0	13 1/3	8	2	2	4	15
1991—Rochester (I.L.)	10	4	.714	2.87	19	19	3	1	0	122 1/3	108	42	39	31	107
—Baltimore (A.L.)	4	5	.444	2.87	12	12	2	0	0	87 2/3	77	31	28	21	52
1992—Baltimore (A.L.)	18	5	*.783	2.54	32	32	8	4	0	241	212	70	68	48	130
1993—Baltimore (A.L.)	14	6	.700	4.46	25	25	3	2	0	167 2/3	163	84	83	44	117
—Bowie (East.)	1	0	1.000	2.25	2	2	0	0	0	8	5	2	2	1	10
1994—Baltimore (A.L.)	16	5	.762	3.06	24	24	3	0	0	176 1/3	163	63	60	42	99
1995—Baltimore (A.L.)	*19	9	.679	3.29	32	32	7	*4	0	221 2/3	187	86	81	50	158
1996—Baltimore (A.L.)	19	11	.633	4.81	36	*36	4	1	0	243 1/3	264	137	130	69	204
1997—Baltimore (A.L.)	15	8	.652	3.20	33	33	4	1	0	224 2/3	197	87	80	54	218
1998—Baltimore (A.L.)	13	10	.565	3.49	29	29	4	2	0	206 1/3	189	85	80	41	175
1999—Baltimore (A.L.)	18	7	.720	3.50	31	31	4	0	0	203 1/3	207	88	79	52	172
Major League totals (9 years)	136	66	.673	3.50	254	254	39	14	0	1772	1659	731	689	421	1325

DIVISION SERIES RECORD

Year League	W	L	Pct.	ERA	G	GS	CG	ShO	Sv.	IP	H	R	ER	BB	SO
1996—Baltimore (A.L.)	0	0	...	4.50	1	1	0	0	0	6	7	4	3	2	6
1997—Baltimore (A.L.)	2	0	1.000	1.93	2	2	0	0	0	14	7	3	3	3	16
Division series totals (2 years)	2	0	1.000	2.70	3	3	0	0	0	20	14	7	6	5	22

CHAMPIONSHIP SERIES RECORD

Year League	W	L	Pct.	ERA	G	GS	CG	ShO	Sv.	IP	H	R	ER	BB	SO
1996—Baltimore (A.L.)	0	1	.000	5.87	1	1	0	0	0	7 2/3	8	5	5	2	6
1997—Baltimore (A.L.)	0	0	...	0.60	2	2	0	0	0	15	4	1	1	4	25
Champ. series totals (2 years)	0	1	.000	2.38	3	3	0	0	0	22 2/3	12	6	6	6	31

ALL-STAR GAME RECORD

Year League	W	L	Pct.	ERA	GS	CG	ShO	Sv.	IP	H	R	ER	BB	SO
1992—American	0	0	...	0.00	0	0	0	0	1	0	0	0	0	0
1993—American						Did not play.								
1994—American	0	0	...	0.00	0	0	0	0	1	1	0	0	0	1
1997—National						Did not play.								
1999—American	0	0	...	0.00	0	0	0	0	1	1	0	0	1	2
All-Star Game totals (3 years)	0	0	...	0.00	0	0	0	0	3	2	0	0	1	3

MYERS, GREG — C — ORIOLES

PERSONAL: Born April 14, 1966, in Riverside, Calif. ... 6-2/225. ... Bats left, throws right. ... Full name: Gregory Richard Myers.
HIGH SCHOOL: Riverside (Calif.) Polytechnical.
TRANSACTIONS/CAREER NOTES: Selected by Toronto Blue Jays organization in third round of free-agent draft (June 4, 1984). ... On disabled list (June 17, 1988-remainder of season). ... On Toronto disabled list (March 26-June 5, 1989); included rehabilitation assignment to Knoxville (May 17-June 5). ... On Toronto disabled list (May 5-25, 1990); included rehabilitation assignment to Syracuse (May 21-24). ... Traded by Blue Jays with OF Rob Ducey to California Angels for P Mark Eichhorn (July 30, 1992). ... On California disabled list (August 27, 1992-remainder of season). ... On California disabled list (April 24-June 21, 1994); included rehabilitation assignments to Lake Elsinore (May 20-June 6 and June 13-21). ... On disabled list (April 21-May 6, June 1-21 and September 30, 1995-remainder of season). ... Granted free agency (November 3, 1995). ... Signed by Minnesota Twins (December 8, 1995). ... On disabled list (July 14-August 2, 1996). ... On Minnesota disabled list (August 9-24, 1997). ... Traded by Twins to Atlanta Braves for a player to be named later (September 5, 1997); Twins acquired 1B Steve Hacker to complete deal (December 18, 1997). ... Granted free agency (October 28, 1997). ... Signed by San Diego Padres (November 25, 1997). ...

M

On San Diego disabled list (June 4-July 24, 1998); included rehabilitation assignments to Rancho Cucamonga (July 17-19) and Las Vegas (July 21-23). ... On San Diego disabled list (June 29-July 26, 1999); included rehabilitation assignment to Rancho Cucamonga (July 20-26). ... Traded by Padres to Braves for P Doug Dent (July 26, 1999). ... Granted free agency (November 1, 1999). ... Signed by Baltimore Orioles (December 17, 1999).

STATISTICAL NOTES: Led California League catchers with 967 total chances in 1986. ... Led International League catchers with 698 total chances in 1987.

Year Team (League)	Pos.	G	AB	R	H	2B	3B	HR	RBI	Avg.	BB	SO	SB	PO	A	E	Avg.
1984— Medicine Hat (Pio.)	C	38	133	20	42	9	0	2	20	.316	16	6	0	216	24	4	.984
1985— Florence (SAL)	C	134	489	52	109	19	2	5	62	.223	39	54	0	551	61	7	*.989
1986— Ventura (Calif.)	C	124	451	65	133	23	4	20	79	.295	43	46	9	*849	99	19	.980
1987— Syracuse (I.L.)	C	107	342	35	84	19	1	10	47	.246	22	46	3	*637	50	11	.984
— Toronto (A.L.)..............	C	7	9	1	1	0	0	0	0	.111	0	3	0	24	1	0	1.000
1988— Syracuse (I.L.)	C	34	120	18	34	7	1	7	21	.283	8	24	1	63	9	1	.986
1989— Knoxville (Sou.).........	C	29	90	11	30	10	0	5	19	.333	3	16	1	130	12	1	.993
— Toronto (A.L.)..............	C-DH	17	44	0	5	2	0	0	1	.114	2	9	0	46	6	0	1.000
— Syracuse (I.L.).............	C	24	89	8	24	6	0	1	11	.270	4	9	0	60	7	1	.985
1990— Toronto (A.L.)...........	C	87	250	33	59	7	1	5	22	.236	22	33	0	411	30	3	.993
— Syracuse (I.L.).............	C	3	11	0	2	1	0	0	2	.182	1	1	0	14	0	0	1.000
1991— Toronto (A.L.)...........	C	107	309	25	81	22	0	8	36	.262	21	45	0	484	37	11	.979
1992— Toronto (A.L.)	C	22	61	4	14	6	0	1	13	.230	5	5	0	92	13	1	.991
— California (A.L.)■.......	C-DH	8	17	0	4	1	0	0	0	.235	0	6	0	33	3	0	1.000
1993— California (A.L.)	C-DH	108	290	27	74	10	0	7	40	.255	17	47	3	369	44	6	.986
1994— California (A.L.)	C-DH	45	126	10	31	6	0	2	8	.246	10	27	0	194	28	2	.991
— Lake Elsinore (Calif.)..	C-DH	10	32	4	8	2	0	0	5	.250	2	6	0	31	3	0	1.000
1995— California (A.L.)	C-DH	85	273	35	71	12	2	9	38	.260	17	49	0	341	21	4	.989
1996— Minnesota (A.L.)■.....	C	97	329	37	94	22	3	6	47	.286	19	52	0	488	27	8	.985
1997— Minnesota (A.L.)	C-DH	62	165	24	44	11	1	5	28	.267	16	29	0	196	11	3	.986
— Atlanta (N.L.)■..........	C	9	9	0	1	0	0	0	1	.111	1	3	0	11	2	0	1.000
1998— San Diego (N.L.)■.....	C	69	171	19	42	10	0	4	20	.246	17	36	0	276	29	4	.987
— Rancho Cuca. (Calif.) .	C-DH	3	9	1	0	0	0	0	0	.000	2	1	0	8	0	0	1.000
— Las Vegas (PCL)	C	3	9	0	5	0	0	0	1	.556	0	0	0	16	1	0	1.000
1999— San Diego (N.L.)	C	50	128	9	37	4	0	3	15	.289	13	14	0	199	14	3	.986
— Rancho Cuca. (Calif.) .	C-DH	3	3	0	0	0	0	0	0	.000	1	1	0	7	1	0	1.000
— Atlanta (N.L.)■............	C	34	72	10	16	2	0	2	9	.222	13	16	0	166	12	1	.994
American League totals (10 years)		645	1873	196	478	99	7	43	233	.255	129	305	3	2678	221	38	.987
National League totals (3 years)		162	380	38	96	16	0	9	45	.253	44	69	0	652	57	8	.989
Major League totals (12 years)		807	2253	234	574	115	7	52	278	.255	173	374	3	3330	278	46	.987

DIVISION SERIES RECORD

Year Team (League)	Pos.	G	AB	R	H	2B	3B	HR	RBI	Avg.	BB	SO	SB	PO	A	E	Avg.
1998— San Diego (N.L.)	C	1	0	0	0	0	0	0	0	...	0	0	0	0	0	0	...
1999— Atlanta (N.L.)							Did not play.										

CHAMPIONSHIP SERIES RECORD

Year Team (League)	Pos.	G	AB	R	H	2B	3B	HR	RBI	Avg.	BB	SO	SB	PO	A	E	Avg.
1991— Toronto (A.L.)								Did not play.									
1998— San Diego (N.L.)	PH	2	1	1	1	0	0	1	2	1.000	1	0	0	...	...	...	...
1999— Atlanta (N.L.).............	C	2	2	0	0	0	0	0	0	.000	1	1	0	8	0	0	1.000
Championship series totals (2 years)		4	3	1	1	0	0	1	2	.333	2	1	0	8	0	0	1.000

WORLD SERIES RECORD

Year Team (League)	Pos.	G	AB	R	H	2B	3B	HR	RBI	Avg.	BB	SO	SB	PO	A	E	Avg.
1998— San Diego (N.L.)	PH-C	2	4	0	0	0	0	0	0	.000	0	2	0	4	1	0	1.000
1999— Atlanta (N.L.).............	PH-C	4	6	0	2	0	0	0	1	.333	1	0	0	9	...	0	1.000
World Series totals (2 years)		6	10	0	2	0	0	0	1	.200	1	2	0	13	1	0	1.000

M

MYERS, MIKE   P   ROCKIES

PERSONAL: Born June 26, 1969, in Arlington Heights, Ill. ... 6-4/214. ... Throws left, bats left. ... Full name: Michael Stanley Myers.
HIGH SCHOOL: Crystal Lake (Ill.) Central.
COLLEGE: Iowa State.
TRANSACTIONS/CAREER NOTES: Selected by San Francisco Giants organization in fourth round of free-agent draft (June 4, 1990). ... On Clinton disabled list (June 3-September 16, 1991; April 9-June 2 and June 21-July 6, 1992). ... Selected by Florida Marlins from Giants organization in Rule 5 major league draft (December 7, 1992). ... On Edmonton disabled list (April 13-June 7, 1994). ... On Florida disabled list (June 7-August 5, 1994); included rehabilitation assignment to Brevard County (June 23-July 11). ... Traded by Marlins to Detroit Tigers (August 9, 1995), completing deal in which Marlins acquired P Buddy Groom for a player to be named later (August 7, 1995). ... Traded by Tigers with P Rick Greene and SS Santiago Perez to Milwaukee Brewers for P Bryce Florie and a player to be named later (November 20, 1997). ... Traded by Brewers to Colorado Rockies for P Curtis Leskanic (November 17, 1999).
STATISTICAL NOTES: Led Pacific Coast League with 10 hit batsmen in 1993.

Year League	W	L	Pct.	ERA	G	GS	CG	ShO	Sv.	IP	H	R	ER	BB	SO
1990— Everett (N.W.).............	4	5	.444	3.90	15	14	1	0	0	85 1/3	91	43	37	30	73
1991— Clinton (Midw.)	5	3	.625	2.62	11	11	1	0	0	65 1/3	61	23	19	18	59
1992— San Jose (Calif.)..........	5	1	.833	2.30	8	8	0	0	0	54 2/3	43	20	14	17	40
— Clinton (Midw.)	1	2	.333	1.19	7	7	0	0	0	37 2/3	28	11	5	8	32
1993— Edmonton (PCL)■	7	14	.333	5.18	27	27	3	0	0	161 2/3	195	109	93	52	112
1994— Edmonton (PCL)	1	5	.167	5.55	12	11	0	0	0	60	78	42	37	21	55
— Brevard County (FSL).........	0	0	...	0.79	3	2	0	0	0	11 1/3	7	1	1	4	15

Year League	W	L	Pct.	ERA	G	GS	CG	ShO	Sv.	IP	H	R	ER	BB	SO
1995— Charlotte (I.L.)	0	5	.000	5.65	37	0	0	0	0	36⅔	41	25	23	15	24
— Florida (N.L.)	0	0	...	0.00	2	0	0	0	0	2	1	0	0	3	0
— Toledo (I.L.)■	0	0	...	4.32	6	0	0	0	0	8⅓	6	4	4	3	8
— Detroit (A.L.)	1	0	1.000	9.95	11	0	0	0	0	6⅓	10	7	7	4	4
1996— Detroit (A.L.)	1	5	.167	5.01	•83	0	0	0	6	64⅔	70	41	36	34	69
1997— Detroit (A.L.)	0	4	.000	5.70	*88	0	0	0	2	53⅔	58	36	34	25	50
1998— Milwaukee (N.L.)■	2	2	.500	2.70	70	0	0	0	1	50	44	19	15	22	40
1999— Milwaukee (N.L.)	2	1	.667	5.23	71	0	0	0	0	41⅓	46	24	24	13	35
A.L. totals (3 years)	2	9	.182	5.56	182	0	0	0	8	124⅔	138	84	77	63	123
N.L. totals (3 years)	4	3	.571	3.76	143	0	0	0	1	93⅓	91	43	39	38	75
Major League totals (5 years)	6	12	.333	4.79	325	0	0	0	9	218	229	127	116	101	198

MYERS, RANDY   P   PADRES

PERSONAL: Born September 19, 1962, in Vancouver, Wash. ... 6-1/210. ... Throws left, bats left. ... Full name: Randall Kirk Myers.
HIGH SCHOOL: Evergreen (Vancouver, Wash.).
JUNIOR COLLEGE: Clark Community College (Wash.).
TRANSACTIONS/CAREER NOTES: Selected by Cincinnati Reds organization in third round of free-agent draft (January 12, 1982); did not sign. ... Selected by New York Mets organization in secondary phase of free-agent draft (June 7, 1982). ... Traded by Mets with P Kip Gross to Cincinnati Reds for P John Franco and OF Don Brown (December 6, 1989). ... Traded by Reds to San Diego Padres for OF/2B Bip Roberts and a player to be named later (December 8, 1991); Reds acquired OF Craig Pueschner to complete deal (December 9, 1991). ... Granted free agency (October 26, 1992). ... Signed by Chicago Cubs (December 9, 1992). ... Granted free agency (November 3, 1995). ... Signed by Baltimore Orioles (December 14, 1995). ... Granted free agency (October 27, 1997). ... Signed by Toronto Blue Jays (November 26, 1997). ... Traded by Blue Jays to Padres for C Brian Loyd and a player to be named later (August 6, 1998). ... On disabled list (April 3, 1999-entire season).
RECORDS: Shares N.L. single-season record for most saves—53 (1993). ... Shares N.L. single-game record for most consecutive strikeouts by relief pitcher—6 (September 8, 1990).
HONORS: Named Carolina League Pitcher of the Year (1984). ... Named N.L. Fireman of the Year by THE SPORTING NEWS (1993 and 1995).
STATISTICAL NOTES: Tied for Appalachian League lead with three balks in 1982.
MISCELLANEOUS: Had sacrifice hit in only appearance as pinch hitter (1992). ... Grounded into a double play in only appearance as pinch hitter (1993).

Year League	W	L	Pct.	ERA	G	GS	CG	ShO	Sv.	IP	H	R	ER	BB	SO
1982— Kingsport (Appalachian)	6	3	.667	4.12	13	•13	1	0	0	74⅓	68	49	34	69	•86
1983— Columbia (SAL)	14	10	.583	3.63	28	•28	3	0	0	173⅓	146	94	70	108	164
1984— Lynchburg (Caro.)	13	5	.722	*2.06	23	22	•7	1	0	157	123	46	36	61	171
— Jackson (Texas)	2	1	.667	2.06	5	5	1	0	0	35	29	14	8	16	35
1985— Jackson (Texas)	4	8	.333	3.96	19	19	2	1	0	120⅓	99	61	53	69	116
— Tidewater (I.L.)	1	1	.500	1.84	8	7	0	0	0	44	40	13	9	20	25
— New York (N.L.)	0	0	...	0.00	1	0	0	0	0	2	0	0	0	1	2
1986— Tidewater (I.L.)	6	7	.462	2.35	45	0	0	0	12	65	44	19	17	44	79
— New York (N.L.)	0	0	...	4.22	10	0	0	0	0	10⅔	11	5	5	9	13
1987— New York (N.L.)	3	6	.333	3.96	54	0	0	0	6	75	61	36	33	30	92
— Tidewater (I.L.)	0	0	...	4.91	5	0	0	0	3	7⅓	6	4	4	4	13
1988— New York (N.L.)	7	3	.700	1.72	55	0	0	0	26	68	45	15	13	17	69
1989— New York (N.L.)	7	4	.636	2.35	65	0	0	0	24	84⅓	62	23	22	40	88
1990— Cincinnati (N.L.)■	4	6	.400	2.08	66	0	0	0	31	86⅔	59	24	20	38	98
1991— Cincinnati (N.L.)	6	13	.316	3.55	58	12	1	0	6	132	116	61	52	80	108
1992— San Diego (N.L.)■	3	6	.333	4.29	66	0	0	0	38	79⅔	84	38	38	34	66
1993— Chicago (N.L.)■	2	4	.333	3.11	73	0	0	0	*53	75⅓	65	26	26	26	86
1994— Chicago (N.L.)	1	5	.167	3.79	38	0	0	0	21	40⅓	40	18	17	16	32
1995— Chicago (N.L.)	1	2	.333	3.88	57	0	0	0	*38	55⅔	49	25	24	28	59
1996— Baltimore (A.L.)■	4	4	.500	3.53	62	0	0	0	31	58⅔	60	24	23	29	74
1997— Baltimore (A.L.)	2	3	.400	1.51	61	0	0	0	*45	59⅔	47	12	10	22	56
1998— Toronto (A.L.)■	3	4	.429	4.46	41	0	0	0	28	42⅓	44	21	21	19	32
— San Diego (N.L.)■	1	3	.250	6.28	21	0	0	0	0	14⅓	15	10	10	7	9
1999— San Diego (N.L.)							Did not play.								
A.L. totals (3 years)	9	11	.450	3.02	164	0	0	0	104	160⅔	151	57	54	70	162
N.L. totals (12 years)	35	52	.402	3.23	564	12	1	0	243	724	607	281	260	326	722
Major League totals (14 years)	44	63	.411	3.19	728	12	1	0	347	884⅔	758	338	314	396	884

DIVISION SERIES RECORD

Year League	W	L	Pct.	ERA	G	GS	CG	ShO	Sv.	IP	H	R	ER	BB	SO
1996— Baltimore (A.L.)	0	0	...	0.00	3	0	0	0	2	3	0	0	0	0	3
1997— Baltimore (A.L.)	0	0	...	0.00	2	0	0	0	1	2	0	0	0	0	5
1998— San Diego (N.L.)							Did not play.								
Division series totals (2 years)	0	0	...	0.00	5	0	0	0	3	5	0	0	0	0	8

CHAMPIONSHIP SERIES RECORD

RECORDS: Shares N.L. single-series record for most saves—3 (1990).
NOTES: Named N.L. Championship Series co-Most Valuable Player (1990).

Year League	W	L	Pct.	ERA	G	GS	CG	ShO	Sv.	IP	H	R	ER	BB	SO
1988— New York (N.L.)	2	0	1.000	0.00	3	0	0	0	0	4⅔	1	0	0	2	0
1990— Cincinnati (N.L.)	0	0	...	0.00	4	0	0	0	3	5⅔	2	0	0	3	7
1996— Baltimore (A.L.)	0	1	.000	2.25	3	0	0	0	0	4	4	1	1	3	2
1997— Baltimore (A.L.)	0	1	.000	5.06	4	0	0	0	1	5⅓	6	3	3	3	7
1998— San Diego (N.L.)	0	0	...	13.50	4	0	0	0	0	2	3	3	3	2	3
Champ. series totals (5 years)	2	2	.500	2.91	18	0	0	0	4	21⅔	16	7	7	13	19

M

NOTES: Member of World Series championship team (1990).

Year League	W	L	Pct.	ERA	G	GS	CG	ShO	Sv.	IP	H	R	ER	BB	SO
1990— Cincinnati (N.L.)	0	0	...	0.00	3	0	0	0	1	3	2	0	0	0	3
1998— San Diego (N.L.)	0	0	...	9.00	3	0	0	0	0	1	0	1	1	1	2
World Series totals (2 years)	0	0	...	2.25	6	0	0	0	1	4	2	1	1	1	5

ALL-STAR GAME RECORD

Year League	W	L	Pct.	ERA	GS	CG	ShO	Sv.	IP	H	R	ER	BB	SO
1990— National	0	0	...	0.00	0	0	0	0	1	1	0	0	2	0
1994— National	0	0	...	0.00	0	0	0	0	1	1	0	0	0	1
1995— National	0	0	...	0.00	0	0	0	1	1	0	0	0	1	0
1997— National	0	0	...	0.00	0	0	0	0	1	0	0	0	0	2
All-Star Game totals (4 years)	0	0	...	0.00	0	0	0	1	4	2	0	0	3	3

MYERS, RODNEY   P   CUBS

PERSONAL: Born June 26, 1969, in Rockford, Ill. ... 6-1/215. ... Throws right, bats right. ... Full name: Rodney Luther Myers.
HIGH SCHOOL: Rockford (Ill.) East.
COLLEGE: Wisconsin.
TRANSACTIONS/CAREER NOTES: Selected by Kansas City Royals organization in 12th round of free-agent draft (June 4, 1990). ... On disabled list (May 17-June 3 and June 21-September 15, 1994; and June 30-July 21, 1995). ... Selected by Chicago Cubs from Royals organization in Rule 5 major league draft (December 4, 1995). ... On Iowa disabled list (June 7-15, 1998).
MISCELLANEOUS: Doubled in only appearance as pinch hitter (1999).

Year League	W	L	Pct.	ERA	G	GS	CG	ShO	Sv.	IP	H	R	ER	BB	SO
1990— Eugene (N.W.)	0	2	.000	1.19	6	4	0	0	0	22²/₃	19	9	3	13	17
1991— Appleton (Midw.)...............	1	1	.500	2.60	9	4	0	0	0	27²/₃	22	9	8	26	29
1992— Lethbridge (Pio.)..............	5	•8	.385	4.01	15	15	*5	0	0	*103¹/₃	93	57	46	61	76
1993— Rockford (Midw.)...............	7	3	.700	1.79	12	12	5	2	0	85¹/₃	65	22	17	18	65
— Memphis (Sou.)	3	6	.333	5.62	12	12	1	1	0	65²/₃	73	46	41	32	42
1994— Wilmington (Caro.)...........	1	1	.500	4.82	4	0	0	0	1	9¹/₃	9	6	5	1	9
— Memphis (Sou.)	5	1	.833	1.03	42	0	0	0	9	69²/₃	45	20	8	29	53
1995— Omaha (A.A.)...................	4	5	.444	4.10	38	0	0	0	2	48¹/₃	52	26	22	19	38
1996— Chicago (N.L.)■...............	2	1	.667	4.68	45	0	0	0	0	67¹/₃	61	38	35	38	50
1997— Iowa (A.A.)......................	7	8	.467	4.09	24	23	1	0	0	140²/₃	140	76	64	38	79
— Chicago (N.L.)................	0	0	...	6.00	5	1	0	0	0	9	12	6	6	7	6
1998— Iowa (PCL)......................	7	5	.583	3.91	33	13	2	1	11	101¹/₃	84	47	44	45	86
— Chicago (N.L.)................	0	0	...	7.00	12	0	0	0	0	18	26	14	14	6	15
1999— Iowa (PCL)......................	2	4	.333	4.06	20	1	0	0	2	31	29	18	14	11	24
— Chicago (N.L.)................	3	1	.750	4.38	46	0	0	0	0	63²/₃	71	34	31	25	41
Major League totals (4 years)	5	2	.714	4.90	108	1	0	0	0	158	170	92	86	76	112

MYETTE, AARON   P   WHITE SOX

PERSONAL: Born September 26, 1977, in New Westminster, B.C. ... 6-4/195. ... Throws right, bats right. ... Full name: Aaron K. Myette. ... Son of Kenneth Myette, pitcher with Cincinnati Reds organization (1969).
HIGH SCHOOL: Johnston Heights Sectional (Surrey, B.C.).
JUNIOR COLLEGE: Central Arizona College.
TRANSACTIONS/CAREER NOTES: Selected by Chicago White Sox organization in supplemental round ("sandwich pick" between first and second round, 43rd pick overall) of free-agent draft (June 3, 1997); pick received as part of compensation for Florida Marlins signing P Alex Fernandez. ... On Hickory disabled list (April 2-May 2, 1998). ... On Birmingham disabled list (July 25-August 2, 1999).
STATISTICAL NOTES: Led Southern League with 15 hit batsmen in 1999.

Year League	W	L	Pct.	ERA	G	GS	CG	ShO	Sv.	IP	H	R	ER	BB	SO
1997— Bristol (Appl.)...................	4	3	.571	3.61	9	8	1	0	0	47¹/₃	39	28	19	20	50
— Hickory (SAL)...................	3	1	.750	1.14	5	5	0	0	0	31²/₃	19	6	4	11	27
1998— Hickory (SAL)..................	9	4	.692	2.47	17	17	0	0	0	102	84	43	28	30	103
— Win.-Salem (Car.)..............	4	2	.667	2.01	6	6	1	1	0	44²/₃	32	14	10	14	54
1999— Birmingham (Sou.)...........	12	7	.632	3.66	28	•28	0	0	0	164²/₃	138	76	67	77	135
— Chicago (A.L.)	0	2	.000	6.32	4	3	0	0	0	15²/₃	17	11	11	14	11
Major League totals (1 year)........	0	2	.000	6.32	4	3	0	0	0	15²/₃	17	11	11	14	11

NAGY, CHARLES   P   INDIANS

PERSONAL: Born May 5, 1967, in Fairfield, Conn. ... 6-3/200. ... Throws right, bats left. ... Full name: Charles Harrison Nagy. ... Name pronounced NAG-ee.
HIGH SCHOOL: Roger Ludlowe (Fairfield, Conn.).
COLLEGE: Connecticut.
TRANSACTIONS/CAREER NOTES: Selected by Cleveland Indians organization in first round (17th pick overall) of free-agent draft (June 1, 1988); pick received as part of compensation for San Francisco Giants signing Type A free-agent OF Brett Butler. ... On Cleveland disabled list (May 16-October 1, 1993); included rehabilitation assignment to Canton/Akron (June 10-24).
HONORS: Named Carolina League Pitcher of the Year (1989).
STATISTICAL NOTES: Pitched 6-0 one-hit, complete-game victory against Baltimore (August 8, 1992).
MISCELLANEOUS: Member of 1988 U.S. Olympic baseball team. ... Struck out once in two appearances as designated hitter and appeared in one game as pinch runner (1999).

Year League	W	L	Pct.	ERA	G	GS	CG	ShO	Sv.	IP	H	R	ER	BB	SO
1989— Kinston (Caro.)	8	4	.667	1.51	13	13	6	*4	0	95 1/3	69	22	16	24	99
—Canton/Akron (East.)	4	5	.444	3.35	15	14	2	0	0	94	102	44	35	32	65
1990— Canton/Akron (East.)	13	8	.619	2.52	23	23	•9	0	0	175	132	62	49	39	99
—Cleveland (A.L.)	2	4	.333	5.91	9	8	0	0	0	45 2/3	58	31	30	21	26
1991— Cleveland (A.L.)	10	15	.400	4.13	33	33	6	1	0	211 1/3	228	103	97	66	109
1992— Cleveland (A.L.)	17	10	.630	2.96	33	33	10	3	0	252	245	91	83	57	169
1993— Cleveland (A.L.)	2	6	.250	6.29	9	9	1	0	0	48 2/3	66	38	34	13	30
—Canton/Akron (East.)	0	0	...	1.13	2	2	0	0	0	8	8	1	1	2	4
1994— Cleveland (A.L.)	10	8	.556	4.55	23	23	3	0	0	169 1/3	175	76	65	48	108
1995— Cleveland (A.L.)	16	6	.727	4.55	29	29	2	1	0	178	194	95	90	61	139
1996— Cleveland (A.L.)	17	5	.773	3.41	32	32	5	0	0	222	217	89	84	61	167
1997— Cleveland (A.L.)	15	11	.577	4.28	34	34	1	1	0	227	253	115	108	77	149
1998— Cleveland (A.L.)	15	10	.600	5.22	33	33	2	0	0	210 1/3	250	*139	122	66	120
1999— Cleveland (A.L.)	17	11	.607	4.95	33	32	1	0	0	202	238	120	111	59	126
Major League totals (10 years)	121	86	.585	4.20	268	266	31	6	0	1766 1/3	1924	897	824	529	1143

DIVISION SERIES RECORD

RECORDS: Holds career record for most games started—7; runs allowed—25; earned runs allowed—23; and bases on balls allowed—18. ... Holds A.L. record for most innings pitched—40.

Year League	W	L	Pct.	ERA	G	GS	CG	ShO	Sv.	IP	H	R	ER	BB	SO
1995— Cleveland (A.L.)	1	0	1.000	1.29	1	1	0	0	0	7	4	1	1	5	6
1996— Cleveland (A.L.)	0	1	.000	7.15	2	2	0	0	0	11 1/3	15	9	9	5	13
1997— Cleveland (A.L.)	0	1	.000	9.82	1	1	0	0	0	3 2/3	2	5	4	6	1
1998— Cleveland (A.L.)	1	0	1.000	1.13	1	1	0	0	0	8	4	1	1	0	3
1999— Cleveland (A.L.)	1	0	1.000	7.20	2	2	0	0	0	10	11	9	8	2	6
Division series totals (5 years)	3	2	.600	5.18	7	7	0	0	0	40	36	25	23	18	29

CHAMPIONSHIP SERIES RECORD

RECORDS: Shares A.L. single-game record for most consecutive strikeouts—4 (October 13, 1995).

Year League	W	L	Pct.	ERA	G	GS	CG	ShO	Sv.	IP	H	R	ER	BB	SO
1995— Cleveland (A.L.)	0	0	...	1.13	1	1	0	0	0	8	5	2	1	0	6
1997— Cleveland (A.L.)	0	0	...	2.77	2	2	0	0	0	13	17	4	4	5	5
1998— Cleveland (A.L.)	0	1	.000	3.72	2	2	0	0	0	9 2/3	13	7	4	1	6
Champ. series totals (3 years)	0	1	.000	2.64	5	5	0	0	0	30 2/3	35	13	9	6	17

WORLD SERIES RECORD

RECORDS: Shares single-inning record for most consecutive bases on balls allowed—3 (October 21, 1997, third inning).

Year League	W	L	Pct.	ERA	G	GS	CG	ShO	Sv.	IP	H	R	ER	BB	SO
1995— Cleveland (A.L.)	0	0	...	6.43	1	1	0	0	0	7	8	5	5	1	4
1997— Cleveland (A.L.)	0	1	.000	6.43	2	1	0	0	0	7	8	6	5	5	5
World Series totals (2 years)	0	1	.000	6.43	3	2	0	0	0	14	16	11	10	6	9

ALL-STAR GAME RECORD

Year League	W	L	Pct.	ERA	GS	CG	ShO	Sv.	IP	H	R	ER	BB	SO
1992— American	0	0	...	0.00	0	0	0	0	1	0	0	0	0	1
1996— American	0	1	.000	13.50	1	0	0	0	2	4	3	3	0	1
1999— American						Selected, did not play.								
All-Star Game totals (2 years)	0	1	.000	9.00	1	0	0	0	3	4	3	3	0	2

NATHAN, JOE — P — GIANTS

PERSONAL: Born November 22, 1974, in Houston. ... 6-4/195. ... Throws right, bats right. ... Full name: Joseph Michael Nathan.
HIGH SCHOOL: Pine Bush (N.Y.).
COLLEGE: New York-Stony Brook.
TRANSACTIONS/CAREER NOTES: Selected by San Francisco Giants organization in sixth round of free-agent draft (June 1, 1995).
MISCELLANEOUS: Played shortstop (1995).

Year League	W	L	Pct.	ERA	G	GS	CG	ShO	Sv.	IP	H	R	ER	BB	SO
1996—						Did not play—attended New York-Stony Brook.									
1997— Salem-Kaizer (N.W.)	2	1	.667	2.47	18	5	0	0	2	62	53	22	17	26	44
1998— San Jose (Calif.)	8	6	.571	3.32	22	22	0	0	0	122	100	51	45	48	118
—Shreveport (Texas)	1	3	.250	8.80	4	4	0	0	0	15 1/3	20	15	15	9	10
1999— Shreveport (Texas)	0	1	.000	3.12	2	2	0	0	0	8 2/3	5	4	3	7	7
—San Francisco (N.L.)	7	4	.636	4.18	19	14	0	0	1	90 1/3	84	45	42	46	54
—Fresno (PCL)	6	4	.600	4.46	13	13	1	0	0	74 2/3	68	44	37	36	82
Major League totals (1 year)	7	4	.636	4.18	19	14	0	0	1	90 1/3	84	45	42	46	54

RECORD AS POSITION PLAYER

Year Team (League)	Pos.	G	AB	R	H	2B	3B	HR	RBI	Avg.	BB	SO	SB	PO	A	E	Avg.
1995— Bellingham (N'west)	SS	56	177	23	41	7	2	3	20	.232	22	48	3	76	150	26	.897

NAULTY, DAN — P — DODGERS

PERSONAL: Born January 6, 1970, in Los Angeles. ... 6-6/224. ... Throws right, bats right. ... Full name: Daniel Donovan Naulty.
HIGH SCHOOL: Ocean View (Huntington Beach, Calif.).
JUNIOR COLLEGE: Cerritos (Calif.).
COLLEGE: Cal State Fullerton.
TRANSACTIONS/CAREER NOTES: Selected by Minnesota Twins organization in 14th round of free-agent draft (June 1, 1992). ... On disabled list (August 5-September 30, 1996). ... On Minnesota disabled list (May 26-September 1, 1997); included rehabilitation assignments to Gulf

Coast Twins (July 24-26) and Salt Lake (July 28-August 31). ... On Minnesota disabled list (July 12-September 29, 1998). ... Traded by Twins to New York Yankees for 3B Allen Butler (November 16, 1998). ... Traded by Yankees to Los Angeles Dodgers for 1B Nick Leach (December 14, 1999).

Year League	W	L	Pct.	ERA	G	GS	CG	ShO	Sv.	IP	H	R	ER	BB	SO
1992— Kenosha (Midw.)	0	1	.000	5.50	6	2	0	0	0	18	22	12	11	7	14
1993— Fort Myers (FSL)	0	3	.000	5.70	7	6	0	0	0	30	41	22	19	14	20
— Fort Wayne (Midw.)	6	8	.429	3.26	18	18	3	2	0	116	101	45	42	48	96
1994— Fort Myers (FSL)	8	4	.667	2.95	16	15	1	0	0	88 1/3	78	35	29	32	83
— Nashville (Sou.)	0	7	.000	5.89	9	9	0	0	0	47 1/3	48	32	31	22	29
1995— Salt Lake (PCL)	2	6	.250	5.18	42	8	0	0	4	90 1/3	92	55	52	2	76
1996— Minnesota (A.L.)	3	2	.600	3.79	49	0	0	0	4	57	43	26	24	35	56
1997— Minnesota (A.L.)	1	1	.500	5.87	29	0	0	0	1	30 2/3	29	20	20	10	23
— Gulf Coast Twins (GCL)	0	0	...	2.25	2	2	0	0	0	4	2	1	1	3	3
— Salt Lake (PCL)	0	1	.000	11.37	6	0	0	0	0	6 1/3	11	10	8	2	5
1998— Salt Lake (PCL)	1	0	1.000	6.75	5	0	0	0	0	5 1/3	8	4	4	2	5
— Minnesota (A.L.)	0	2	.000	4.94	19	0	0	0	0	23 2/3	25	16	13	10	15
1999— New York (A.L.)■	1	0	1.000	4.38	33	0	0	0	0	49 1/3	40	24	24	22	25
— Columbus (I.L.)	2	1	.667	4.35	7	0	0	0	0	10 1/3	14	6	5	4	5
Major League totals (4 years)	5	5	.500	4.54	130	0	0	0	5	160 2/3	137	86	81	77	119

DIVISION SERIES RECORD

Year League	W	L	Pct.	ERA	G	GS	CG	ShO	Sv.	IP	H	R	ER	BB	SO
1999— New York (A.L.)							Did not play.								

CHAMPIONSHIP SERIES RECORD

Year League	W	L	Pct.	ERA	G	GS	CG	ShO	Sv.	IP	H	R	ER	BB	SO
1999— New York (A.L.)							Did not play.								

WORLD SERIES RECORD

NOTES: Member of World Series championship team (1999).

Year League	W	L	Pct.	ERA	G	GS	CG	ShO	Sv.	IP	H	R	ER	BB	SO
1999— New York (A.L.)							Did not play.								

NAVARRO, JAIME   P   BREWERS

PERSONAL: Born March 27, 1968, in Bayamon, Puerto Rico. ... 6-4/250. ... Throws right, bats right. ... Son of Julio Navarro, major league pitcher with three teams (1962-66 and 1970).
HIGH SCHOOL: Luis Pales Matos (Bayamon, Puerto Rico).
JUNIOR COLLEGE: Miami-Dade Community College-New World Center.
TRANSACTIONS/CAREER NOTES: Selected by Baltimore Orioles organization in second round of free-agent draft (January 14, 1986); did not sign. ... Selected by Orioles organization in secondary phase of free-agent draft (June 2, 1986); did not sign. ... Selected by Milwaukee Brewers organization in third round of free-agent draft (June 2, 1987). ... Granted free agency (April 7, 1995). ... Signed by Chicago Cubs (April 9, 1995). ... Granted free agency (November 1, 1995). ... Re-signed by Cubs (December 8, 1995). ... Granted free agency (November 1, 1996). ... Signed by Chicago White Sox (December 11, 1996). ... Traded by White Sox with P John Snyder to Milwaukee Brewers for P Cal Eldred and SS Jose Valentin (January 12, 2000).
RECORDS: Shares major league record for most errors by pitcher in one inning—3 (August 18, 1996, third inning). ... Shares A.L. single-season record for most sacrifice flies allowed—17 (1993).
STATISTICAL NOTES: Led A.L. with five balks in 1990. ... Tied for A.L. lead with 14 wild pitches in 1997. ... Led A.L. with 18 wild pitches in 1998.

Year League	W	L	Pct.	ERA	G	GS	CG	ShO	Sv.	IP	H	R	ER	BB	SO
1987— Helena (Pio.)	4	3	.571	3.57	13	13	3	0	0	85 2/3	87	37	34	18	95
1988— Stockton (Calif.)	15	5	.750	3.09	26	23	8	2	0	174 2/3	148	70	60	74	151
1989— El Paso (Texas)	5	2	.714	2.47	11	11	1	0	0	76 2/3	61	29	21	35	78
— Denver (A.A.)	1	1	.500	3.60	3	3	1	0	0	20	24	8	8	7	17
— Milwaukee (A.L.)	7	8	.467	3.12	19	17	1	0	0	109 2/3	119	47	38	32	56
1990— Milwaukee (A.L.)	8	7	.533	4.46	32	22	3	0	1	149 1/3	176	83	74	41	75
— Denver (A.A.)	2	3	.400	4.20	6	6	1	0	0	40 2/3	41	27	19	14	28
1991— Milwaukee (A.L.)	15	12	.556	3.92	34	34	10	2	0	234	237	117	102	73	114
1992— Milwaukee (A.L.)	17	11	.607	3.33	34	34	5	3	0	246	224	98	91	64	100
1993— Milwaukee (A.L.)	11	12	.478	5.33	35	34	5	1	0	214 1/3	254	135	*127	73	114
1994— Milwaukee (A.L.)	4	9	.308	6.62	29	10	0	0	0	89 2/3	115	71	66	35	65
1995— Chicago (N.L.)■	14	6	.700	3.28	29	29	1	1	0	200 1/3	194	79	73	56	128
1996— Chicago (N.L.)	15	12	.556	3.92	35	35	4	1	0	*236 2/3	244	116	103	72	158
1997— Chicago (A.L.)■	9	14	.391	5.79	33	33	2	0	0	209 2/3	*267	*155	*135	73	142
1998— Chicago (A.L.)	8	•16	.333	6.36	37	27	1	0	1	172 2/3	223	135	122	77	71
1999— Chicago (A.L.)	8	13	.381	6.09	32	27	0	0	0	159 2/3	206	126	108	71	74
A.L. totals (9 years)	87	102	.460	4.90	285	238	27	6	2	1585	1821	967	863	539	811
N.L. totals (2 years)	29	18	.617	3.62	64	64	5	2	0	437	438	195	176	128	286
Major League totals (11 years)	116	120	.492	4.62	349	302	32	8	2	2022	2259	1162	1039	667	1097

NEAGLE, DENNY   P   REDS

PERSONAL: Born September 13, 1968, in Gambrills, Md. ... 6-3/225. ... Throws left, bats left. ... Full name: Dennis Edward Neagle Jr. ... Name pronounced NAY-ghul.
HIGH SCHOOL: Arundel (Gambrills, Md.).
COLLEGE: Minnesota.
TRANSACTIONS/CAREER NOTES: Selected by Minnesota Twins organization in third round of free-agent draft (June 5, 1989). ... On Portland disabled list (April 5-23, 1991). ... On Minnesota disabled list (July 28-August 12, 1991). ... Traded by Twins with OF Midre Cummings to Pittsburgh Pirates for P John Smiley (March 17, 1992). ... Traded by Pirates to Atlanta Braves for 1B Ron Wright and a player to be named later (August 28, 1996); Pirates acquired P Jason Schmidt to complete deal (August 30, 1996). ... Traded by Braves with OF Michael Tucker

and P Rob Bell to Cincinnati Reds for 2B Bret Boone and P Mike Remlinger (November 10, 1998). ... On Cincinnati disabled list (March 24-April 21 and May 24-July 29, 1999); included rehabilitation assignment to Indianapolis (April 8-21 and July 23-29).

HONORS: Named lefthanded pitcher on THE SPORTING NEWS N.L. All-Star team (1997).

STATISTICAL NOTES: Tied for N.L. lead with 16 sacrifice hits in 1996. ... Career major league grand slams: 1.

MISCELLANEOUS: Appeared in one game as pinch runner (1992). ... Appeared in one game as pinch runner (1995). ... Doubled and had a sacrifice hit in three appearances as pinch hitter with Pittsburgh (1996).

Year League	W	L	Pct.	ERA	G	GS	CG	ShO	Sv.	IP	H	R	ER	BB	SO
1989— Elizabethton (Appl.)	1	2	.333	4.50	6	3	0	0	1	22	20	11	11	8	32
— Kenosha (Midw.)	2	1	.667	1.65	6	6	1	1	0	43²/₃	25	9	8	16	40
1990— Visalia (Calif.)	8	0	1.000	1.43	10	10	0	0	0	63	39	13	10	16	92
— Orlando (Sou.)	12	3	.800	2.45	17	17	4	1	0	121¹/₃	94	40	33	31	94
1991— Portland (PCL)	9	4	.692	3.27	19	17	1	1	0	104²/₃	101	41	38	32	94
— Minnesota (A.L.)	0	1	.000	4.05	7	3	0	0	0	20	28	9	9	7	14
1992— Pittsburgh (N.L.)■	4	6	.400	4.48	55	6	0	0	2	86¹/₃	81	46	43	43	77
1993— Pittsburgh (N.L.)	3	5	.375	5.31	50	7	0	0	1	81¹/₃	82	49	48	37	73
— Buffalo (A.A.)	0	0	...	0.00	3	0	0	0	0	3¹/₃	3	0	0	2	6
1994— Pittsburgh (N.L.)	9	10	.474	5.12	24	24	2	0	0	137	135	80	78	49	122
1995— Pittsburgh (N.L.)	13	8	.619	3.43	31	•31	5	1	0	•209²/₃	*221	91	80	45	150
1996— Pittsburgh (N.L.)	14	6	.700	3.05	27	27	1	0	0	182²/₃	186	67	62	34	131
— Atlanta (N.L.)■	2	3	.400	5.59	6	6	1	0	0	38²/₃	40	26	24	14	18
1997— Atlanta (N.L.)	*20	5	.800	2.97	34	34	4	4	0	233¹/₃	204	87	77	49	172
1998— Atlanta (N.L.)	16	11	.593	3.55	32	31	5	2	0	210¹/₃	196	91	83	60	165
1999— Indianapolis (I.L.)■	2	0	1.000	4.67	3	3	0	0	0	17¹/₃	11	9	9	2	9
— Cincinnati (N.L.)	9	5	.643	4.27	20	19	0	0	0	111²/₃	95	54	53	40	76
A.L. totals (1 year)	0	1	.000	4.05	7	3	0	0	0	20	28	9	9	7	14
N.L. totals (8 years)	90	59	.604	3.82	279	185	18	7	3	1291	1240	591	548	371	984
Major League totals (9 years)	90	60	.600	3.82	286	188	18	7	3	1311	1268	600	557	378	998

DIVISION SERIES RECORD

Year League	W	L	Pct.	ERA	G	GS	CG	ShO	Sv.	IP	H	R	ER	BB	SO
1998— Atlanta (N.L.)				Did not play.											

CHAMPIONSHIP SERIES RECORD

Year League	W	L	Pct.	ERA	G	GS	CG	ShO	Sv.	IP	H	R	ER	BB	SO
1992— Pittsburgh (N.L.)	0	0	...	27.00	2	0	0	0	0	1²/₃	4	5	5	3	0
1996— Atlanta (N.L.)	0	0	...	2.35	2	1	0	0	0	7²/₃	2	2	2	3	8
1997— Atlanta (N.L.)	1	0	1.000	0.00	2	1	1	1	0	12	5	0	0	1	9
1998— Atlanta (N.L.)	0	0	...	3.52	2	1	0	0	0	7²/₃	8	3	3	2	9
Champ. series totals (4 years)	1	0	1.000	3.10	8	3	1	1	0	29	19	10	10	9	26

WORLD SERIES RECORD

Year League	W	L	Pct.	ERA	G	GS	CG	ShO	Sv.	IP	H	R	ER	BB	SO
1996— Atlanta (N.L.)	0	0	...	3.00	2	1	0	0	0	6	5	3	2	4	3

ALL-STAR GAME RECORD

Year League	W	L	Pct.	ERA	GS	CG	ShO	Sv.	IP	H	R	ER	BB	SO
1995— National	0	0	...	0.00	0	0	0	0	1	1	0	0	0	1
1997— National				Did not play.										

NEGRETTE, RICHARD   P   ORIOLES

PERSONAL: Born March 6, 1976, in Maracaibo, Venezuela. ... 6-2/173. ... Throws right, bats right. ... Full name: Richard Alexander Negrette.

TRANSACTIONS/CAREER NOTES: Signed as non-drafted free agent by Cleveland Indians organization (July 2, 1993). ... On Akron disabled list (April 22-May 3 and July 8-26, 1999). ... Traded by Indians to Chicago Cubs for C/3B Tyler Houston (August 31, 1999). ... Traded by Cubs to Baltimore Orioles for SS Augie Ojeda (December 13, 1999).

Year League	W	L	Pct.	ERA	G	GS	CG	ShO	Sv.	IP	H	R	ER	BB	SO
1994— Dom. Indians (DSL)	3	5	.375	2.87	13	12	0	0	0	75¹/₃	56	40	24	32	52
1995— Watertown (NY-P)	3	3	.500	5.52	18	5	0	0	3	45²/₃	42	30	28	23	35
1996— Kinston (Caro.)	0	1	.000	23.14	1	1	0	0	0	2¹/₃	9	7	6	4	0
— Burlington (Appl.)	2	6	.250	5.16	14	13	0	0	0	59¹/₃	57	50	34	36	52
1997— Columbus (SAL)	2	1	.667	4.46	16	0	0	0	1	36¹/₃	24	23	18	16	21
— Watertown (NY-P)	2	3	.400	3.66	17	0	0	0	1	39¹/₃	25	17	16	29	30
1998— Columbus (SAL)	1	3	.250	5.09	21	0	0	0	2	40²/₃	39	24	23	22	35
— Kinston (Caro.)	3	5	.375	2.88	28	0	0	0	0	50	32	22	16	27	41
1999— Akron (East.)	1	3	.250	6.13	33	0	0	0	1	47	49	35	32	47	34
— West Tenn (Sou.)■	1	0	1.000	5.40	3	0	0	0	0	3¹/₃	3	2	2	2	2

NELSON, JEFF   P   YANKEES

PERSONAL: Born November 17, 1966, in Baltimore. ... 6-8/225. ... Throws right, bats right. ... Full name: Jeffrey Allan Nelson. ... Nephew of Cole Nelson, who played in the Washington Senators organization.

HIGH SCHOOL: Catonsville (Md.).

JUNIOR COLLEGE: Catonsville (Md.) Community College.

TRANSACTIONS/CAREER NOTES: Selected by Los Angeles Dodgers organization in 22nd round of free-agent draft (June 4, 1984). ... On Great Falls disabled list (April 10-June 4, 1986). ... Selected by Calgary, Seattle Mariners organization from Dodgers organization in Rule 5 minor league draft (December 9, 1986). ... On disabled list (July 16, 1989-remainder of season). ... Traded by Mariners with 1B Tino Martinez and P Jim Mecir to New York Yankees for P Sterling Hitchcock and 3B Russ Davis (December 7, 1995). ... On suspended list (September 3-5, 1996). ... On suspended list (May 28-29, 1998). ... On New York disabled list (June 26-September 4, 1998); included rehabilitation assignment to Tampa (August 31-September 4). ... On New York disabled list (May 3-20 and June 3-August 11, 1999); included rehabilitation assignments to Gulf Coast Yankees (August 2-4 and August 9-10) and Tampa (August 5-8).

MISCELLANEOUS: Appeared in one game as outfielder with no chances for Seattle (1993).

Year	League	W	L	Pct.	ERA	G	GS	CG	ShO	Sv.	IP	H	R	ER	BB	SO
1984—	Great Falls (Pio.)	0	0	...	54.00	1	0	0	0	0	$^2/_3$	3	4	4	3	1
—	Gulf Coast Dodgers (GCL)..	0	0	...	1.35	9	0	0	0	0	$13^1/_3$	6	3	2	6	7
1985—	Gulf Coast Dodgers (GCL)..	0	5	.000	5.51	14	7	0	0	0	$47^1/_3$	72	50	29	32	31
1986—	Great Falls (Pio.)	0	0	...	13.50	3	0	0	0	0	2	5	3	3	3	1
—	Bakersfield (Calif.)	0	7	.000	6.69	24	11	0	0	0	$71^1/_3$	79	83	53	84	37
1987—	Salinas (Calif.)■	3	7	.300	5.74	17	16	1	0	0	80	80	61	51	71	43
1988—	San Bernardino (Calif.)	8	9	.471	5.54	27	27	1	1	0	$149^1/_3$	163	115	92	91	94
1989—	Williamsport (East.)	7	5	.583	3.31	15	15	2	0	0	$92^1/_3$	72	41	34	53	61
1990—	Williamsport (East.)	1	4	.200	6.44	10	10	0	0	0	$43^1/_3$	65	35	31	18	14
—	Peninsula (Caro.)	2	2	.500	3.15	18	7	1	1	6	60	47	21	21	25	49
1991—	Jacksonville (Sou.)	4	0	1.000	1.27	21	0	0	0	12	$28^1/_3$	23	5	4	9	34
—	Calgary (PCL)	3	4	.429	3.90	28	0	0	0	21	$32^1/_3$	39	19	14	15	26
1992—	Calgary (PCL)	1	0	1.000	0.00	2	0	0	0	0	$3^2/_3$	0	0	0	1	0
—	Seattle (A.L.)	1	7	.125	3.44	66	0	0	0	6	81	71	34	31	44	46
1993—	Calgary (PCL)	1	0	1.000	1.17	5	0	0	0	1	$7^2/_3$	6	1	1	2	6
—	Seattle (A.L.)	5	3	.625	4.35	71	0	0	0	1	60	57	30	29	34	61
1994—	Seattle (A.L.)	0	0	...	2.76	28	0	0	0	0	$42^1/_3$	35	18	13	20	44
—	Calgary (PCL)	1	4	.200	2.84	18	0	0	0	8	$25^1/_3$	21	9	8	7	30
1995—	Seattle (A.L.)	7	3	.700	2.17	62	0	0	0	2	$78^2/_3$	58	21	19	27	96
1996—	New York (A.L.)■	4	4	.500	4.36	73	0	0	0	2	$74^1/_3$	75	38	36	36	91
1997—	New York (A.L.)	3	7	.300	2.86	77	0	0	0	2	$78^2/_3$	53	32	25	37	81
1998—	New York (A.L.)	5	3	.625	3.79	45	0	0	0	3	$40^1/_3$	44	18	17	22	35
—	Tampa (FSL)	0	0	...	0.00	2	1	0	0	0	2	1	1	0	1	4
1999—	New York (A.L.)	2	1	.667	4.15	39	0	0	0	1	$30^1/_3$	27	14	14	22	35
—	Gulf Coast Yankees (GCL)..	0	0	...	0.00	2	2	0	0	0	2	1	0	0	1	3
—	Tampa (FSL)	0	0	...	0.00	3	3	0	0	0	3	1	0	0	2	5
Major League totals (8 years)		**27**	**28**	**.491**	**3.41**	**461**	**0**	**0**	**0**	**17**	**$485^2/_3$**	**420**	**205**	**184**	**242**	**489**

DIVISION SERIES RECORD

RECORDS: Shares career record for most games by pitcher—14.

Year	League	W	L	Pct.	ERA	G	GS	CG	ShO	Sv.	IP	H	R	ER	BB	SO
1995—	Seattle (A.L.)	0	1	.000	3.18	3	0	0	0	0	$5^2/_3$	7	2	2	3	7
1996—	New York (A.L.)	1	0	1.000	0.00	2	0	0	0	0	$3^2/_3$	2	0	0	3	5
1997—	New York (A.L.)	0	0	...	0.00	4	0	0	0	0	4	4	0	0	2	0
1998—	New York (A.L.)	0	0	...	0.00	2	0	0	0	0	$2^2/_3$	2	0	0	1	2
1999—	New York (A.L.)	0	0	...	0.00	3	0	0	0	0	$1^2/_3$	1	0	0	1	3
Division series totals (5 years)		**1**	**1**	**.500**	**1.02**	**14**	**0**	**0**	**0**	**0**	**$17^2/_3$**	**16**	**2**	**2**	**10**	**17**

CHAMPIONSHIP SERIES RECORD

Year	League	W	L	Pct.	ERA	G	GS	CG	ShO	Sv.	IP	H	R	ER	BB	SO
1995—	Seattle (A.L.)	0	0	...	0.00	3	0	0	0	0	3	3	0	0	5	3
1996—	New York (A.L.)	0	1	.000	11.57	2	0	0	0	0	$2^1/_3$	5	3	3	0	2
1998—	New York (A.L.)	0	1	.000	20.25	3	0	0	0	0	$1^1/_3$	3	3	3	1	3
1999—	New York (A.L.)	0	0	...	0.00	2	0	0	0	0	$^2/_3$	0	0	0	0	0
Champ. series totals (4 years)		**0**	**2**	**.000**	**7.36**	**10**	**0**	**0**	**0**	**0**	**$7^1/_3$**	**11**	**6**	**6**	**6**	**8**

WORLD SERIES RECORD

NOTES: Member of World Series championship team (1996, 1998 and 1999).

Year	League	W	L	Pct.	ERA	G	GS	CG	ShO	Sv.	IP	H	R	ER	BB	SO
1996—	New York (A.L.)	0	0	...	0.00	3	0	0	0	0	$4^1/_3$	1	0	0	1	5
1998—	New York (A.L.)	0	0	...	0.00	3	0	0	0	0	$2^1/_3$	2	1	0	1	4
1999—	New York (A.L.)	0	0	...	0.00	4	0	0	0	0	$2^2/_3$	2	0	0	1	3
World Series totals (3 years)		**0**	**0**	**...**	**0.00**	**10**	**0**	**0**	**0**	**0**	**$9^1/_3$**	**5**	**1**	**0**	**3**	**12**

N

NEN, ROBB   P   GIANTS

PERSONAL: Born November 28, 1969, in San Pedro, Calif. ... 6-5/215. ... Throws right, bats right. ... Full name: Robert Allen Nen. ... Son of Dick Nen, first baseman with three major league teams (1963, 1965-68 and 1970).

HIGH SCHOOL: Los Alamitos (Calif.).

TRANSACTIONS/CAREER NOTES: Selected by Texas Rangers organization in 32nd round of free-agent draft (June 2, 1987). ... On Charlotte disabled list (April 6-26 and May 6-24, 1990). ... On disabled list (April 23-June 10, June 28-July 8 and July 11-September 3, 1991; and May 7-September 9, 1992). ... On Texas disabled list (June 12-July 17, 1993); included rehabilitation assignment to Oklahoma City (June 21-July 17). ... Traded by Rangers with P Kurt Miller to Florida Marlins for P Cris Carpenter (July 17, 1993). ... Traded by Marlins to San Francisco Giants for P Mike Villano, P Joe Fontenot and P Mick Pageler (November 18, 1997).

MISCELLANEOUS: Holds Florida Marlins all-time record for most games pitched (269) and most saves (108).

Year	League	W	L	Pct.	ERA	G	GS	CG	ShO	Sv.	IP	H	R	ER	BB	SO
1987—	Gulf Coast Rangers (GCL)..	0	0	...	7.71	2	0	0	0	0	$2^1/_3$	4	2	2	3	4
1988—	Gastonia (SAL)	0	5	.000	7.45	14	10	0	0	0	$48^1/_3$	69	57	40	45	36
—	Butte (Pio.)	4	5	.444	8.75	14	13	0	0	0	$48^1/_3$	65	55	47	45	30
1989—	Gastonia (SAL)	7	4	.636	2.41	24	24	1	1	0	$138^1/_3$	96	47	37	76	146
1990—	Charlotte (FSL)	1	4	.200	3.69	11	11	1	0	0	$53^2/_3$	44	28	22	36	38
—	Tulsa (Texas)	0	5	.000	5.06	7	7	0	0	0	$26^2/_3$	23	20	15	21	21
1991—	Tulsa (Texas)	0	2	.000	5.79	6	6	0	0	0	28	24	21	18	20	23
1992—	Tulsa (Texas)	1	1	.500	2.16	4	4	1	0	0	25	21	7	6	2	20
1993—	Texas (A.L.)	1	1	.500	6.35	9	3	0	0	0	$22^2/_3$	28	17	16	26	12
—	Oklahoma City (A.A.)	0	2	.000	6.67	6	5	0	0	0	$28^1/_3$	45	22	21	18	12
—	Florida (N.L.)■	1	0	1.000	7.02	15	1	0	0	0	$33^1/_3$	35	28	26	20	27
1994—	Florida (N.L.)	5	5	.500	2.95	44	0	0	0	15	58	46	20	19	17	60
1995—	Florida (N.L.)	0	7	.000	3.29	62	0	0	0	23	$65^2/_3$	62	26	24	23	68
1996—	Florida (N.L.)	5	1	.833	1.95	75	0	0	0	35	83	67	21	18	21	92
1997—	Florida (N.L.)	9	3	.750	3.89	73	0	0	0	35	74	72	35	32	40	81

Year	League	W	L	Pct.	ERA	G	GS	CG	ShO	Sv.	IP	H	R	ER	BB	SO
1998— San Francisco (N.L.)■		7	7	.500	1.52	78	0	0	0	40	88²/₃	59	21	15	25	110
1999— San Francisco (N.L.)		3	8	.273	3.98	72	0	0	0	37	72¹/₃	79	36	32	27	77
A.L. totals (1 year)		1	1	.500	6.35	9	3	0	0	0	22²/₃	28	17	16	26	12
N.L. totals (7 years)		30	31	.492	3.15	419	1	0	0	185	475	420	187	166	173	515
Major League totals (7 years)		31	32	.492	3.29	428	4	0	0	185	497²/₃	448	204	182	199	527

DIVISION SERIES RECORD

Year	League	W	L	Pct.	ERA	G	GS	CG	ShO	Sv.	IP	H	R	ER	BB	SO
1997— Florida (N.L.)		1	0	1.000	0.00	2	0	0	0	0	2	1	1	0	2	2

CHAMPIONSHIP SERIES RECORD

Year	League	W	L	Pct.	ERA	G	GS	CG	ShO	Sv.	IP	H	R	ER	BB	SO
1997— Florida (N.L.)		0	0	...	0.00	2	0	0	0	2	2	0	0	0	0	0

NOTES: Member of World Series championship team (1997).

WORLD SERIES RECORD

Year	League	W	L	Pct.	ERA	G	GS	CG	ShO	Sv.	IP	H	R	ER	BB	SO
1997— Florida (N.L.)		0	0	...	7.71	4	0	0	0	2	4²/₃	8	5	4	2	7

ALL-STAR GAME RECORD

Year	League	W	L	Pct.	ERA	GS	CG	ShO	Sv.	IP	H	R	ER	BB	SO
1998— National		0	0	...	9.00	0	0	0	0	1	3	3	1	0	0
1999— National						Selected, did not play—injured.									

NEVIN, PHIL   3B/C   PADRES

PERSONAL: Born January 19, 1971, in Fullerton, Calif. ... 6-2/231. ... Bats right, throws right. ... Full name: Phillip Joseph Nevin.
HIGH SCHOOL: El Dorado (Placentia, Calif.).
COLLEGE: Cal State Fullerton.
TRANSACTIONS/CAREER NOTES: Selected by Los Angeles Dodgers organization in third round of free-agent draft (June 5, 1989); did not sign. ... Selected by Houston Astros organization in first round (first pick overall) of free-agent draft (June 1, 1992). ... On Tucson disabled list (July 12-30, 1995). ... Traded by Astros to Detroit Tigers (August 15, 1995), completing deal in which Astros acquired P Mike Henneman for a player to be named later (August 10, 1995). ... On Detroit disabled list (March 21-April 16, 1997); included rehabilitation assignment to Lakeland (April 8-16). ... Traded by Tigers with C Matt Walbeck to Anaheim Angels for P Nick Skuse (November 20, 1997). ... On suspended list (June 12-15, 1998). ... Traded by Angels with P Keith Volkman to San Diego Padres for INF Andy Sheets and OF Gus Kennedy (March 29, 1999). ... On San Diego disabled list (April 1-16, 1999); included rehabilitaion assignment to Las Vegas (April 12-15).
HONORS: Named Golden Spikes Award winner by USA Baseball (1992). ... Named third baseman on THE SPORTING NEWS college All-America team (1992). ... Named Most Outstanding Player of College World Series (1992).
STATISTICAL NOTES: Led Pacific Coast League third basemen with .891 fielding percentage in 1993. ... Led Pacific Coast League in grounding into double plays with 21 in 1994. ... Led Pacific Coast League third basemen with 31 errors and 32 double plays in 1994. ... Led A.L. catchers with 20 passed balls in 1998.
MISCELLANEOUS: Member of 1992 U.S. Olympic baseball team.

							BATTING							FIELDING			
Year	Team (League)	Pos.	G	AB	R	H	2B	3B	HR	RBI	Avg.	BB	SO	SB	PO	A	E	Avg.
1993— Tucson (PCL)	3B-OF	123	448	67	128	21	3	10	93	.286	52	99	8	68	187	29	†.898
1994— Tucson (PCL)	3B-OF	118	445	67	117	20	1	12	79	.263	55	101	3	73	240	†32	.907
1995— Tucson (PCL)	3B-DH	62	223	31	65	16	0	7	41	.291	27	39	2	39	128	14	.923
— Houston (N.L.)	3B	18	60	4	7	1	0	0	1	.117	7	13	1	10	32	3	.933
— Toledo (I.L.)■...........	OF-DH	7	23	3	7	2	0	1	3	.304	1	5	0	2	0	0	1.000
— Detroit (A.L.)	OF-DH	29	96	9	21	3	1	2	12	.219	11	27	0	50	2	2	.963
1996— Jacksonville (Sou.).....C-DH-3-O-1		98	344	77	101	18	1	24	69	.294	60	83	6	384	76	11	.977
— Detroit (A.L.)	3B-OF-C-DH	38	120	15	35	5	0	8	19	.292	8	39	1	45	51	5	.950
1997— Lakeland (FSL)	DH-1B-3B	3	9	3	5	1	0	1	4	.556	3	2	0	9	4	1	.929
— Toledo (I.L.).............	1B-DH-3B	5	19	1	3	0	0	1	3	.158	2	9	1	19	4	0	1.000
— Detroit (A.L.)	O-DH-3-1-C	93	251	32	59	16	1	9	35	.235	25	68	0	94	18	2	.982
1998— Anaheim (A.L.)■.........	C-DH-1B	75	237	27	54	8	1	8	27	.228	17	67	0	402	32	5	.989
1999— Las Vegas (PCL)■	C-1B-3B	3	10	2	2	0	0	2	2	.200	1	0	0	12	4	0	1.000
— San Diego (N.L.)	3-C-O-1-DH	128	383	52	103	27	0	24	85	.269	51	82	1	276	154	5	.989
American League totals (4 years)		235	704	83	169	32	3	27	93	.240	61	201	1	591	103	14	.980
National League totals (2 years)		146	443	56	110	28	0	24	86	.248	58	95	2	286	186	8	.983
Major League totals (5 years)		381	1147	139	279	60	3	51	179	.243	119	296	3	877	289	22	.981

NEWHAN, DAVID   2B   PADRES

PERSONAL: Born September 7, 1973, in Fullerton, Calif. ... 5-10/180. ... Bats left, throws right. ... Full name: David Matthew Newhan.
HIGH SCHOOL: Esperanza (Calif.).
COLLEGE: Pepperdine.
TRANSACTIONS/CAREER NOTES: Selected by Oakland Athletics organization in 17th round of free-agent draft (June 1, 1995). ... Traded by Athletics with P Don Wengert to San Diego Padres for P Doug Bochtler and SS Jorge Velandia (December 15, 1997).

							BATTING							FIELDING			
Year	Team (League)	Pos.	G	AB	R	H	2B	3B	HR	RBI	Avg.	BB	SO	SB	PO	A	E	Avg.
1995— S. Oregon (N'west).....	OF	42	145	25	39	8	1	6	21	.269	29	30	10	50	4	2	.964
1996— Modesto (Calif.)	OF	117	455	96	137	27	3	25	75	.301	62	106	17	128	5	5	.964
— W. Mich. (Mid.)	OF	25	96	9	21	5	0	3	8	.219	13	26	3	37	3	1	.976
1997— Visalia (Calif.)	2B	67	241	52	67	15	2	7	48	.278	44	58	9	123	157	10	.966
— Huntsville (Sou.)	2B	57	212	40	67	13	2	5	35	.316	28	59	5	96	129	16	.934
1998— Mobile (Sou.)■.........	2B-3B-SS	121	491	89	128	26	3	12	45	.261	68	110	27	228	314	14	.975
1999— Las Vegas (PCL)	2B-SS	98	374	49	107	25	1	14	49	.286	30	84	22	164	235	20	.952
— San Diego (N.L.)	2B-3B-1B	32	43	7	6	1	0	2	6	.140	1	11	2	28	36	2	.970
Major League totals (1 year)		32	43	7	6	1	0	2	6	.140	1	11	2	28	36	2	.970

N

PERSONAL: Born October 2, 1969, in La Habra, Calif. ... 6-6/240. ... Throws left, bats left. ... Full name: Alan Spencer Newman.
HIGH SCHOOL: La Habra (Calif.).
COLLEGE: Cal State Fullerton.
TRANSACTIONS/CAREER NOTES: Selected by San Diego Padres organization in 26th round of free-agent draft (June 2, 1987); did not sign. ... Selected by Minnesota Twins organization in second round of free-agent draft (June 1, 1988). ... On disabled list (April 16-26 and August 5-September 6, 1992). ... Traded by Twins with IF Tom Houk to Cincinnati Reds for 3B Gary Scott (June 30, 1993). ... Selected by Chicago Cubs organization from Reds organization in Rule 5 minor league draft (December 13, 1993). ... Released by Cubs organization (April 1, 1994). ... Signed by Alexandria Aces, Texas-Louisiana League (May 10, 1995). ... Contract sold by Alexandria to San Diego Padres organization (September 27, 1994). ... Released by Padres organization (April 1, 1995). ... Signed by Alexandria (May 1995). ... Contract sold by Alexandria to Chicago White Sox organization (January 14, 1997). ... Granted free agency (October 17, 1997). ... Signed by San Diego Padres organization (November 12, 1997). ... Granted free agency (October 15, 1998). ... Signed by Tampa Bay Devil Rays organization (November 19, 1998). ... Released by Devil Rays (December 13, 1999). ... Signed by Cleveland Indians organization (January 26, 2000).
STATISTICAL NOTES: Led Appalachian League with 17 wild pitches in 1988.

Year League	W	L	Pct.	ERA	G	GS	CG	ShO	Sv.	IP	H	R	ER	BB	SO
1988—Elizabethton (Appl.)	2	•8	.200	8.13	13	12	2	0	0	55 1/3	57	62	50	56	51
1989—Kenosha (Midw.)	3	9	.250	2.84	18	18	1	0	0	88 2/3	65	41	28	74	82
1990—Kenosha (Midw.)	10	4	.714	*1.64	22	22	5	1	0	154	95	41	28	78	158
—Visalia (Calif.)	3	1	.750	2.23	5	5	0	0	0	36 1/3	29	15	9	22	42
1991—Visalia (Calif.)	6	5	.545	3.51	15	15	0	0	0	92 1/3	86	49	36	49	79
—Orlando (Sou.)	5	4	.556	2.69	11	11	2	0	0	67	53	28	20	30	53
1992—Orlando (Sou.)	4	8	.333	4.15	18	18	2	1	0	102	94	54	47	67	86
1993—Nashville (Sou.)	1	6	.143	6.03	14	11	1	0	0	65 2/3	75	52	44	40	35
—Indianapolis (A.A.)■	1	3	.250	8.55	8	3	0	0	0	20	24	23	19	27	15
1994—Alexandria (Texas-La.)■	9	2	.818	2.83	20	21	6	•3	0	143	127	58	45	76	128
1995—Alexandria (Texas-La.)	10	8	.556	5.19	23	21	5	2	0	137	141	87	79	74	*129
1996—Alexandria (Texas-La.)	6	6	.500	4.56	35	11	0	0	2	118 1/3	136	70	60	43	82
1997—Birmingham (Sou.)■	7	3	.700	2.49	44	0	0	0	10	72 1/3	55	34	20	40	64
1998—Las Vegas (PCL)■	3	3	.500	3.30	63	0	0	0	7	76 1/3	58	29	28	50	76
1999—Durham (I.L.)■	10	0	*1.000	2.24	50	0	0	0	0	80 1/3	59	24	20	20	76
—Tampa Bay (A.L.)	2	2	.500	6.89	18	0	0	0	0	15 2/3	22	12	12	9	20
Major League totals (1 year)	2	2	.500	6.89	18	0	0	0	0	15 2/3	22	12	12	9	20

PERSONAL: Born March 29, 1976, in Vancouver, B.C. ... 5-10/190. ... Bats both, throws right. ... Full name: Kevin R. Nicholson.
HIGH SCHOOL: Queen Elizabeth (Surrey, B.C.).
COLLEGE: Stetson.
TRANSACTIONS/CAREER NOTES: Selected by San Diego Padres organization in first round (27th pick overall) of free-agent draft (June 3, 1997).
STATISTICAL NOTES: Led Southern League shortstops with 621 total chances in 1999. ... Tied for Southern League shortstops lead with 75 double plays in 1999.

Year Team (League)	Pos.	G	AB	R	H	2B	3B	HR	RBI	Avg.	BB	SO	SB	PO	A	E	Avg.
1997—Ariz. Padres (Ariz.)	SS	7	34	7	9	1	0	2	8	.265	2	5	0	11	25	3	.923
—Rancho Cuca. (Calif.)	SS	17	65	7	21	5	0	1	9	.323	4	15	2	21	28	6	.891
1998—Mobile (Sou.)	SS	132	488	64	105	27	3	5	52	.215	47	114	9	201	363	*38	.937
1999—Mobile (Sou.)	SS	127	489	84	141	38	3	13	81	.288	46	92	16	187	*402	32	.948

N

PERSONAL: Born October 2, 1974, in Sonoma, Calif. ... 6-4/210. ... Throws right, bats right. ... Full name: Douglas A. Nickle.
HIGH SCHOOL: Sonoma Valley (Sonoma, Calif.).
COLLEGE: California.
TRANSACTIONS/CAREER NOTES: Selected by Anaheim Angels organization in 13th round of free-agent draft (June 3, 1997). ... Traded by Angels to Philadelphia Phillies (September 10, 1998), completing deal in which Phillies traded OF Gregg Jefferies for a player to be named later (August 26, 1998).

Year League	W	L	Pct.	ERA	G	GS	CG	ShO	Sv.	IP	H	R	ER	BB	SO
1997—Boise (N.W.)	0	1	.000	6.41	17	2	0	0	0	19 2/3	27	17	14	8	22
1998—Cedar Rapids (Midw.)	8	4	.667	3.78	20	7	1	1	0	69	66	30	29	20	59
—Lake Elsinore (Calif.)	3	4	.429	4.48	11	10	1	0	0	66 1/3	68	40	33	25	69
1999—Clearwater (FSL)■	2	4	.333	2.29	*60	0	0	0	28	70 2/3	60	25	18	23	70

PERSONAL: Born June 16, 1975, in Guacara, Venezuela. ... 6-1/180. ... Bats right, throws right. ... Full name: Jose Miguel Pinto Nieves. ... Brother of Juan Nieves, outfielder, Toronto Blue Jays. ... Name pronounced nee-A-vez.
HIGH SCHOOL: Enrique Delgado Palacios (Carabobo).
TRANSACTIONS/CAREER NOTES: Signed as non-drafted free agent by Milwaukee Brewers organization (June 10, 1992). ... Released by Brewers organization (October 19, 1993). ... Signed by Chicago Cubs organization (June 30, 1994). ... On disabled list (May 29-June 12, 1997).

Year Team (League)	Pos.	G	AB	R	H	2B	3B	HR	RBI	Avg.	BB	SO	SB	PO	A	E	Avg.
1992—Dom. Brewers (DSL)	IF	8	15	2	5	0	0	1	3	.333	4	4	0	9	13	5	.815
1993—Dom. Brewers (DSL)	IF	54	144	21	29	4	3	2	14	.201	22	25	6	43	78	19	.864
1994—Dom. Cubs (DSL)■	2B	37	137	21	39	6	1	4	24	.285	13	23	5	50	76	9	.933
1995—Williamsport (NY-P)	SS-2B	69	276	46	59	13	1	4	44	.214	21	39	11	85	193	33	.894

Year	Team (League)	Pos.	G	AB	R	H	2B	3B	HR	RBI	Avg.	BB	SO	SB	PO	A	E	Avg.
1996—	Rockford (Midw.)	SS-2B-3B	113	396	55	96	20	4	5	57	.242	33	59	17	156	318	37	.928
1997—	Daytona (FSL)	SS-2B	85	331	51	91	20	1	4	42	.275	17	55	16	151	218	27	.932
1998—	West Tenn (Sou.)	SS-2B	82	314	42	91	27	5	8	39	.290	18	55	17	130	211	24	.934
—Iowa (PCL)		SS	19	75	7	19	4	0	0	4	.253	2	11	1	35	61	4	.960
—Chicago (N.L.)		SS	2	1	0	0	0	0	0	0	.000	0	0	0	0	0	0	...
1999—Iowa (PCL)		SS-2B	104	392	55	105	25	3	11	59	.268	24	65	11	122	315	19	.958
—Chicago (N.L.)		SS	54	181	16	45	9	1	2	18	.249	8	25	0	67	162	16	.935
Major League totals (2 years)			56	182	16	45	9	1	2	18	.247	8	25	0	67	162	16	.935

NILSSON, DAVID — C

PERSONAL: Born December 14, 1969, in Brisbane, Queensland, Australia. ... 6-3/240. ... Bats left, throws right. ... Full name: David Wayne Nilsson.

HIGH SCHOOL: Kedron (Brisbane, Australia).

TRANSACTIONS/CAREER NOTES: Signed as non-drafted free agent by Milwaukee Brewers organization (February 9, 1987). ... On disabled list (April 30-May 26, 1990). ... On Denver disabled list (August 13, 1991-remainder of season). ... On Milwaukee disabled list (July 6-24, 1992); included rehabilitation assignment to Denver (July 16-24). ... On Milwaukee disabled list (March 27-April 14, 1993); included rehabilitation assignment to El Paso (April 5-14). ... On Milwaukee disabled list (May 18-June 22, 1993); included rehabilitation assignment to New Orleans (May 26-June 13). ... On Milwaukee disabled list (April 16-June 24, 1995); included rehabilitation assignments to Beloit (June 10-14), El Paso (June 14-21) and New Orleans (June 21-24). ... On Milwaukee disabled list (April 4-May 8, 1996); included rehabilitation assignment to New Orleans (May 2-8). ... On Milwaukee disabled list (March 17-May 13, 1998); included rehabilitation assignment to Beloit (May 3-6) and El Paso (May 8-13). ... On disabled list (August 30-September 26, 1999). ... Granted free agency (October 28, 1999). ... Signed to play for Chunichi Dragons of Japan Central League (January 17, 2000).

RECORDS: Shares major league record for most home runs in one inning—2 (May 17, 1996, sixth inning).

STATISTICAL NOTES: Career major league grand slams: 2.

Year	Team (League)	Pos.	G	AB	R	H	2B	3B	HR	RBI	Avg.	BB	SO	SB	PO	A	E	Avg.
1987—	Helena (Pio.)	C	55	188	36	74	13	0	1	21	.394	5	7	0	329	28	7	.981
1988—	Beloit (Midw.)	C-1B	95	332	28	74	15	2	4	41	.223	25	49	2	526	64	6	.990
1989—	Stockton (Calif.)	C-2B	125	472	59	115	16	6	5	56	.244	50	76	2	703	66	13	.983
1990—	Stockton (Calif.)	C-1B-3B	107	359	70	104	22	3	7	47	.290	43	36	6	600	86	12	.983
1991—	El Paso (Texas)	C-3B	65	249	52	104	24	3	5	57	.418	27	14	4	348	46	8	.980
—Denver (A.A.)		C-1B-3B	28	95	10	22	8	0	1	14	.232	17	16	1	146	16	2	.988
1992—	Denver (A.A.)	C-1B-3B	66	240	38	76	16	7	3	39	.317	23	19	10	350	51	6	.985
—Milwaukee (A.L.)		C-1B-DH	51	164	15	38	8	0	4	25	.232	17	18	2	231	16	2	.992
1993—	El Paso (Texas)	C	5	17	5	8	1	0	1	7	.471	2	4	1	31	9	0	1.000
—Milwaukee (A.L.)		C-DH-1B	100	296	35	76	10	2	7	40	.257	37	36	3	457	33	9	.982
—New Orleans (A.A.)		C	17	61	9	21	6	0	1	9	.344	5	6	0	55	7	1	.984
1994—	Milwaukee (A.L.)	C-DH-1B	109	397	51	109	28	3	12	69	.275	34	61	1	315	15	2	.994
1995—	Beloit (Midw.)	DH	3	11	2	6	3	0	1	7	.545	2	0	0	...	...	...	...
—El Paso (Texas)		OF	5	15	1	7	1	0	1	4	.467	0	1	1	4	0	0	1.000
—New Orleans (A.A.)		DH-OF	3	9	1	4	0	0	1	4	.444	2	0	0	2	0	0	1.000
—Milwaukee (A.L.)		OF-DH-1B-C	81	263	41	73	12	1	12	53	.278	24	41	2	117	7	2	.984
1996—	New Orleans (A.A.)	DH-1B	7	26	3	7	1	0	1	2	.269	4	3	0	25	3	0	1.000
—Milwaukee (A.L.)		OF-DH-1B	123	453	81	150	33	2	17	84	.331	57	68	2	252	19	7	.975
1997—	Milwaukee (A.L.)	1B-DH-OF	156	554	71	154	33	0	20	81	.278	65	88	2	641	39	6	.991
1998—	Beloit (Midw.)	1B-DH	4	12	3	5	3	0	1	7	.417	2	0	0	23	1	0	1.000
—El Paso (Texas)		C	5	17	4	5	3	0	0	5	.294	2	0	1	32	7	1	.975
—Milwaukee (N.L.)		1B-OF-C	102	309	39	83	14	1	12	56	.269	33	48	2	436	24	9	.981
1999—	Milwaukee (N.L.)	C-DH	115	343	56	106	19	1	21	62	.309	53	64	1	531	44	5	.991
American League totals (6 years)			620	2127	294	600	124	8	72	352	.282	234	312	12	2013	129	28	.987
National League totals (2 years)			217	652	95	189	33	2	33	118	.290	86	112	3	967	68	14	.987
Major League totals (8 years)			837	2779	389	789	157	10	105	470	.284	320	424	15	2980	197	42	.987

ALL-STAR GAME RECORD

Year	League	Pos.	AB	R	H	2B	3B	HR	RBI	Avg.	BB	SO	SB	PO	A	E	Avg.
1999—	National	C	1	0	0	0	0	0	0	.000	0	1	0	3	0	0	1.000

NINA, ELVIN — P — ANGELS

PERSONAL: Born November 25, 1975, in San Cristobal, Dominican Republic. ... 6-0/185. ... Throws right, bats right. ... Full name: Elvin Alexis Nina.

HIGH SCHOOL: Elizabeth (N.J.).

COLLEGE: Oklahoma State.

TRANSACTIONS/CAREER NOTES: Selected by Oakland Athletics organization in 17th round of free-agent draft (June 3, 1997). ... Traded by Athletics with OF Jeff DaVanon and OF Nathan Haynes to Anaheim Angels for P Omar Olivares and 2B Randy Velarde (July 29, 1999). ... On Erie disabled list (August 24, 1999-remainder of season).

Year	League	W	L	Pct.	ERA	G	GS	CG	ShO	Sv.	IP	H	R	ER	BB	SO
1997—	S. Oregon (N'west)	1	3	.250	5.23	18	2	0	0	1	31	36	24	18	18	26
1998—	Visalia (Calif.)	8	8	.500	4.49	30	21	1	1	0	130 1/3	135	77	65	62	131
—Edmonton (PCL)		0	0	...	0.00	1	0	0	0	0	1/3	1	0	0	2	0
1999—	Modesto (Calif.)	5	2	.714	2.09	17	12	0	0	0	73 1/3	59	31	17	41	74
—Midland (Texas)		3	2	.600	4.80	7	4	0	0	0	30	36	21	16	18	18
—Erie (East.)■		3	0	1.000	4.07	4	4	0	0	0	24 1/3	20	12	11	15	19

N

PERSONAL: Born March 9, 1973, in Suffern, N.Y. ... 6-3/205. ... Throws left, bats left. ... Full name: Christopher John Nitkowski.
HIGH SCHOOL: Don Bosco (N.J.).
COLLEGE: St. John's.
TRANSACTIONS/CAREER NOTES: Selected by Cincinnati Reds organization in first round (ninth pick overall) of free-agent draft (June 2, 1994). ... Traded by Reds with P David Tuttle and a player to be named later to Detroit Tigers for P David Wells (July 31, 1995); Tigers acquired IF Mark Lewis to complete deal (November 16, 1995). ... On Detroit disabled list (August 11-29, 1996). ... Traded by Tigers with C Brad Ausmus, P Jose Lima, P Trever Miller and IF Daryle Ward to Houston Astros for OF Brian Hunter, IF Orlando Miller, P Doug Brocail, P Todd Jones and cash (December 10, 1996). ... Traded by Astros with C Brad Ausmus to Tigers for C Paul Bako, P Dean Crow, P Mark Persails, P Brian Powell and 3B Carlos Villalobos (January 14, 1999). ... On suspended list (May 28-30, 1999).
RECORDS: Shares major league record for most hit batsmen in one inning—3 (August 3, 1998, eighth inning).
STATISTICAL NOTES: Tied for A.L. lead with three balks in 1999.
MISCELLANEOUS: Struck out in only appearance as pinch hitter and appeared in one game as pinch runner (1999).

Year League	W	L	Pct.	ERA	G	GS	CG	ShO	Sv.	IP	H	R	ER	BB	SO
1994—Chattanooga (Sou.)	6	3	.667	3.50	14	14	0	0	0	$74\frac{2}{3}$	61	30	29	40	60
1995—Chattanooga (Sou.)	4	2	.667	2.50	8	8	0	0	0	$50\frac{1}{3}$	39	20	14	20	52
—Indianapolis (A.A.)	0	2	.000	5.20	6	6	0	0	0	$27\frac{2}{3}$	28	16	16	10	21
—Cincinnati (N.L.)	1	3	.250	6.12	9	7	0	0	0	$32\frac{1}{3}$	41	25	22	15	18
—Detroit (A.L.)■	1	4	.200	7.09	11	11	0	0	0	$39\frac{1}{3}$	53	32	31	20	13
1996—Toledo (I.L.)	4	6	.400	4.46	19	19	1	0	0	111	104	60	55	53	103
—Detroit (A.L.)	2	3	.400	8.08	11	8	0	0	0	$45\frac{2}{3}$	62	44	41	38	36
1997—New Orleans (A.A.)■	8	10	.444	3.98	28	28	1	0	0	$174\frac{1}{3}$	183	82	77	56	*141
1998—Houston (N.L.)	3	3	.500	3.77	43	0	0	0	3	$59\frac{2}{3}$	49	27	25	23	44
—New Orleans (PCL)	0	1	.000	6.00	5	3	0	0	1	15	22	12	10	7	18
1999—Detroit (A.L.)■	4	5	.444	4.30	68	7	0	0	0	$81\frac{2}{3}$	63	44	39	45	66
A.L. totals (3 years)	7	12	.368	5.99	90	26	0	0	0	$166\frac{2}{3}$	178	120	111	103	115
N.L. totals (2 years)	4	6	.400	4.60	52	7	0	0	3	92	90	52	47	38	62
Major League totals (4 years)	11	18	.379	5.50	142	33	0	0	3	$258\frac{2}{3}$	268	172	158	141	177

NIXON, OTIS OF

PERSONAL: Born January 9, 1959, in Evergreen, N.C. ... 6-2/180. ... Bats both, throws right. ... Full name: Otis Junior Nixon. ... Brother of Donell Nixon, outfielder with three major league teams (1987-90).
HIGH SCHOOL: Columbus (N.C.).
JUNIOR COLLEGE: Louisburg (N.C.) College.
TRANSACTIONS/CAREER NOTES: Selected by Cincinnati Reds organization in 21st round of free-agent draft (June 6, 1978); did not sign. ... Selected by California Angels organization in secondary phase of free-agent draft (January 9, 1979); did not sign. ... Selected by New York Yankees organization in secondary phase of free-agent draft (June 5, 1979). ... Traded by Yankees with P George Frazier and a player to be named later to Cleveland Indians for 3B Toby Harrah and a player to be named later (February 5, 1984); Yankees organization acquired P Rick Browne and Indians organization acquired P Guy Elston to complete deal (February 8, 1984). ... Granted free agency (October 15, 1987). ... Signed by Indianapolis, Montreal Expos organization (March 5, 1988). ... Traded by Expos with 3B Boi Rodriguez to Atlanta Braves for C Jimmy Kremers and a player to be named later (April 1, 1991); Expos acquired P Keith Morrison to complete deal (June 3, 1991). ... On suspended list (August 13-16, 1991). ... On disqualified list (September 16, 1991-April 24, 1992). ... Granted free agency (November 11, 1991). ... Re-signed by Braves (December 12, 1991). ... Granted free agency (October 25, 1993). ... Signed by Boston Red Sox (December 7, 1993). ... Traded by Red Sox with 3B Luis Ortiz to Texas Rangers for DH/OF Jose Canseco (December 9, 1994). ... Granted free agency (November 3, 1995). ... Signed by Toronto Blue Jays (December 7, 1995). ... On disabled list (June 11-26, 1996). ... Traded by Blue Jays to Los Angeles Dodgers for C Bobby Cripps (August 12, 1997). ... Granted free agency (October 27, 1997). ... Signed by Minnesota Twins (December 11, 1997). ... On disabled list (April 29-May 30, 1998). ... Granted free agency (October 27, 1998). ... Signed by Braves (December 1, 1998). ... On disabled list (July 29-September 1, 1999). ... Granted free agency (October 28, 1999).
RECORDS: Shares modern major league single-game record for most stolen bases—6 (June 16, 1991).
STATISTICAL NOTES: Led Appalachian League third basemen with .945 fielding percentage, 52 putouts, 120 assists, 182 total chances and 12 double plays in 1979. ... Led International League in caught stealing with 29 in 1983. ... Led International League outfielders with .992 fielding percentage, 363 putouts and 371 total chances in 1983. ... Had 20-game hitting streak (July 11-31, 1991). ... Led A.L. in caught stealing with 21 in 1995.

Year Team (League)	Pos.	G	AB	R	H	2B	3B	HR	RBI	Avg.	BB	SO	SB	PO	A	E	Avg.
1979—Paintsville (Appl.)	3B-SS	63	203	58	58	10	3	1	25	.286	*57	40	5	†54	†122	11	†.941
1980—Greensboro (SAL)	3B-SS	136	493	*124	137	12	5	3	48	.278	*113	88	*67	164	308	36	.929
1981—Nashville (Sou.)	SS	127	407	89	102	9	2	0	20	.251	*110	101	71	198	348	*56	.907
1982—Nashville (Sou.)	SS-2B	72	283	47	80	3	2	0	20	.283	59	56	61	126	211	23	.936
—Columbus (I.L.)	2B-SS	59	207	43	58	4	0	0	14	.280	49	41	46	104	169	14	.951
1983—Columbus (I.L.)	OF-2B	138	*557	*129	*162	11	6	0	41	.291	96	83	*94	†385	24	4	†.990
—New York (A.L.)	OF	13	14	2	2	0	0	0	0	.143	1	5	2	14	1	1	.938
1984—Cleveland (A.L.)■	OF	49	91	16	14	0	0	0	1	.154	8	11	12	81	3	0	1.000
—Maine (I.L.)	OF	72	253	42	70	5	1	0	22	.277	44	45	39	206	7	1	.995
1985—Cleveland (A.L.)	OF-DH	104	162	34	38	4	0	3	9	.235	8	27	20	129	5	4	.971
1986—Cleveland (A.L.)	OF-DH	105	95	33	25	4	1	0	8	.263	13	12	23	90	3	3	.969
1987—Cleveland (A.L.)	OF-DH	19	17	2	1	0	0	0	1	.059	3	4	2	21	0	0	1.000
—Buffalo (A.A.)	OF	59	249	51	71	13	4	2	23	.285	34	30	36	170	3	3	.983
1988—Indianapolis (A.A.)■	OF	67	235	52	67	6	3	0	19	.285	43	28	40	130	1	1	.992
—Montreal (N.L.)	OF	90	271	47	66	8	2	0	15	.244	28	42	46	176	2	1	.994
1989—Montreal (N.L.)	OF	126	258	41	56	7	2	0	21	.217	33	36	37	160	2	2	.988
1990—Montreal (N.L.)	OF-SS	119	231	46	58	6	2	1	20	.251	28	33	50	149	6	1	.994
1991—Atlanta (N.L.)■	OF	124	401	81	119	10	1	0	26	.297	47	40	72	218	6	3	.987
1992—Atlanta (N.L.)	OF	120	456	79	134	14	2	2	22	.294	39	54	41	333	6	3	.990
1993—Atlanta (N.L.)	OF	134	461	77	124	12	3	1	24	.269	61	63	47	308	4	3	.990
1994—Boston (A.L.)■	OF	103	398	60	109	15	1	0	25	.274	55	65	42	254	4	3	.989
1995—Texas (A.L.)■	OF	139	589	87	174	21	2	0	45	.295	58	85	50	357	4	4	.989

N

						BATTING								FIELDING		
Year Team (League)	Pos.	G	AB	R	H	2B	3B	HR	RBI	Avg.	BB	SO	SB	PO	A	E	Avg.
1996— Toronto (A.L.)■.........	OF	125	496	87	142	15	1	1	29	.286	71	68	54	342	5	2	.994
1997— Toronto (A.L.)...........	OF-DH	103	401	54	105	12	1	1	26	.262	52	54	47	254	1	1	.996
— Los Angeles (N.L.)■..	OF	42	175	30	48	6	2	1	18	.274	13	24	12	97	1	1	.990
1998— Minnesota (A.L.)■.....	OF	110	448	71	133	6	6	1	20	.297	44	56	37	278	4	3	.989
1999— Atlanta (N.L.)■.........	OF	84	151	31	31	2	1	0	8	.205	23	15	26	52	0	1	.981
American League totals (10 years)		870	2711	446	743	77	12	6	164	.274	313	387	289	1820	30	21	.989
National League totals (8 years)		839	2404	432	636	65	15	5	154	.265	272	307	331	1493	27	15	.990
Major League totals (17 years)		1709	5115	878	1379	142	27	11	318	.270	585	694	620	3313	57	36	.989

DIVISION SERIES RECORD

						BATTING								FIELDING		
Year Team (League)	Pos.	G	AB	R	H	2B	3B	HR	RBI	Avg.	BB	SO	SB	PO	A	E	Avg.
1999— Atlanta (N.L.).............	PR-OF	1	1	1	1	0	0	0	0	1.000	0	0	1	0	0	0	...

CHAMPIONSHIP SERIES RECORD

RECORDS: Shares N.L. single-game record for most hits—4 (October 10, 1992).

						BATTING								FIELDING		
Year Team (League)	Pos.	G	AB	R	H	2B	3B	HR	RBI	Avg.	BB	SO	SB	PO	A	E	Avg.
1992— Atlanta (N.L.).............	OF	7	28	5	8	2	0	0	2	.286	4	4	3	16	0	0	1.000
1993— Atlanta (N.L.).............	OF	6	23	3	8	2	0	0	4	.348	5	6	0	13	0	0	1.000
1999— Atlanta (N.L.).............	PR	2	0	1	0	0	0	0	0	...	0	0	2	0	0	0	...
Championship series totals (3 years)		15	51	9	16	4	0	0	6	.314	9	10	5	29	0	0	1.000

WORLD SERIES RECORD

						BATTING								FIELDING		
Year Team (League)	Pos.	G	AB	R	H	2B	3B	HR	RBI	Avg.	BB	SO	SB	PO	A	E	Avg.
1992— Atlanta (N.L.).............	OF	6	27	3	8	1	0	0	1	.296	1	3	5	18	0	0	1.000
1999— Atlanta (N.L.).............	OF-PR	2	2	0	1	0	0	0	0	.500	0	0	0	0	0	0	...
World Series totals (2 years)		8	29	3	9	1	0	0	1	.310	1	3	5	18	0	0	1.000

NIXON, TROT — OF — RED SOX

PERSONAL: Born April 11, 1974, in Durham, N.C. ... 6-2/200. ... Bats left, throws left. ... Full name: Christopher Trotman Nixon.
HIGH SCHOOL: New Hanover (Wilmington, N.C.).
TRANSACTIONS/CAREER NOTES: Selected by Boston Red Sox organization in first round (seventh pick overall) of free-agent draft (June 3, 1993). ... On disabled list (July 12, 1994-remainder of season).
STATISTICAL NOTES: Tied for Eastern League lead with four double plays by outfielders in 1996. ... Tied for International League lead with 11 errors and three double plays by outfielder in 1998. ... Hit three home runs in one game (July 24, 1999).

						BATTING								FIELDING		
Year Team (League)	Pos.	G	AB	R	H	2B	3B	HR	RBI	Avg.	BB	SO	SB	PO	A	E	Avg.
1994— Lynchburg (Caro.)......	OF	71	264	33	65	12	0	12	43	.246	44	53	10	143	8	4	.974
1995— Sarasota (FSL)..........	OF	73	264	43	80	11	4	5	39	.303	45	46	7	140	4	2	.986
— Trenton (East.)...........	OF	25	94	9	15	3	1	2	8	.160	7	20	2	66	2	0	1.000
1996— Trenton (East.)..........	OF-DH	123	438	55	110	11	4	11	63	.251	50	65	7	224	*14	5	.979
— Boston (A.L.).............	OF	2	2	2	1	0	0	0	0	.500	0	1	1	3	0	0	1.000
1997— Pawtucket (I.L.).........	OF	130	475	80	116	18	3	20	61	.244	63	86	11	268	10	4	.986
1998— Pawtucket (I.L.).........	OF-DH-1B	135	509	97	158	26	4	23	74	.310	76	81	26	231	11	‡11	.957
— Boston (A.L.).............	OF-DH	13	37	3	7	1	0	0	0	.259	1	3	0	16	0	1	1.000
1999— Boston (A.L.).............	OF	124	381	67	103	22	5	15	52	.270	53	75	3	209	3	7	.968
Major League totals (3 years)		139	412	72	112	24	5	15	52	.272	54	79	4	228	3	7	.971

DIVISION SERIES RECORD

						BATTING								FIELDING		
Year Team (League)	Pos.	G	AB	R	H	2B	3B	HR	RBI	Avg.	BB	SO	SB	PO	A	E	Avg.
1998— Boston (A.L.).............	OF	2	3	0	1	0	0	0	0	.333	1	0	0	3	0	0	1.000
1999— Boston (A.L.).............	OF	5	14	5	3	3	0	0	6	.214	4	5	0	3	0	0	1.000
Division series totals (2 years)		7	17	5	4	3	0	0	6	.235	5	5	0	6	0	0	1.000

CHAMPIONSHIP SERIES RECORD

						BATTING								FIELDING		
Year Team (League)	Pos.	G	AB	R	H	2B	3B	HR	RBI	Avg.	BB	SO	SB	PO	A	E	Avg.
1999— Boston (A.L.).............	OF	4	14	2	4	2	0	0	0	.286	1	5	0	7	0	0	1.000

N

NOEL, TODD — P — YANKEES

PERSONAL: Born September 28, 1978, in Abbeville, La. ... 6-4/185. ... Throws right, bats right. ... Full name: Todd Anthony Noel.
HIGH SCHOOL: North Vermillion (Maurice, La.).
TRANSACTIONS/CAREER NOTES: Selected by Chicago Cubs organization in first round (17th pick overall) of free-agent draft (June 4, 1996). ... Traded by Cubs with P Justin Speier and 3B Kevin Orie to Florida Marlins for P Steve Hoff and P Felix Heredia (June 31, 1998). ... Traded by Marlins with P Ed Yarnall and P Mark Johnson to New York Yankees for 3B Mike Lowell (February 1, 1999). ... On Tampa disabled list (April 22-May 1 and July 6-August 26, 1999).

Year Team (League)	W	L	Pct.	ERA	G	GS	CG	ShO	Sv.	IP	H	R	ER	BB	SO
1996— Gulf Coast Cubs (GCL).......	0	0	...	6.75	3	0	0	0	0	4	4	4	3	2	4
1997— Arizona Cubs (Ariz.)	5	1	.833	1.98	12	11	0	0	1	59	39	27	13	30	63
1998— Rockford (Midw.)	6	6	.500	4.03	16	16	1	0	0	89 1/3	83	45	40	37	70
— Kane County (Midw.)■.......	2	2	.500	5.30	7	5	0	0	0	37 1/3	45	25	22	17	26
1999— Tampa (FSL)■....................	3	7	.300	4.34	17	17	0	0	0	93 1/3	101	56	45	33	80

PERSONAL: Born August 31, 1968, in Osaka, Japan. ... 6-2/230. ... Throws right, bats right.
HIGH SCHOOL: Seijyo Kogyo (Japan).
TRANSACTIONS/CAREER NOTES: Selected by Kintetsu Buffaloes in first round of 1989 Japanese free-agent draft. ... Signed as free agent by Los Angeles Dodgers organization (February 8, 1995). ... On Albuquerque temporarily inactive list (April 3-27, 1995). ... Traded to Dodgers with P Brad Clontz to New York Mets for P Dave Mlicki and P Greg McMichael (June 4, 1998). ... Released by Mets (March 26, 1999). ... Signed by Chicago Cubs organization (April 1, 1999). ... Released by Cubs (April 22, 1999). ... Signed by Milwaukee Brewers (April 29, 1999). ... Claimed on waivers by Philadelphia Phillies (October 28, 1999). ... Granted free agency (October 29, 1999). ... Signed by Detroit Tigers (January 21, 2000).
HONORS: Named N.L. Rookie Pitcher of the Year by THE SPORTING NEWS (1995). ... Named N.L. Rookie of the Year by Baseball Writers' Association of America (1995).
STATISTICAL NOTES: Struck out 16 batters in one game (June 14, 1995). ... Pitched 3-0 one-hit, complete-game victory against San Francisco (August 5, 1995). ... Led N.L. with 19 wild pitches and five balks in 1995. ... Led N.L. with five balks in 1995 and four in 1997. ... Struck out 17 batters in one game (April 13, 1996). ... Pitched 9-0 no-hit victory against Colorado (September 17, 1996).
MISCELLANEOUS: Member of 1988 Japanese Olympic baseball team. ... Appeared in one game as pinch runner (1999).

Year	League	W	L	Pct.	ERA	G	GS	CG	ShO	Sv.	IP	H	R	ER	BB	SO
1990—	Kintetsu (Jap. Pac.)	*18	8	.692	*2.91	29	27	21	2	0	235	167	...	76	*109	*287
1991—	Kintetsu (Jap. Pac.)	*17	11	.607	3.05	31	29	22	*4	1	242⅓	183	...	82	*128	*287
1992—	Kintetsu (Jap. Pac.)	*18	8	.692	2.66	30	29	17	*5	0	216⅔	150	...	64	*117	*228
1993—	Kintetsu (Jap. Pac.)	*17	12	.586	3.70	32	32	14	2	0	243⅓	*201	...	100	*148	*276
1994—	Kintetsu (Jap. Pac.)	8	7	.533	3.63	17	17	6	0	0	114	...	...	46	86	126
1995—	Bakersfield (Calif.)■	0	1	.000	3.38	1	1	0	0	0	5⅓	6	2	2	1	6
—	Los Angeles (N.L.)	13	6	.684	2.54	28	28	4	•3	0	191⅓	124	63	54	78	*236
1996—	Los Angeles (N.L.)	16	11	.593	3.19	33	33	3	2	0	228⅓	180	93	81	85	234
1997—	Los Angeles (N.L.)	14	12	.538	4.25	33	33	1	0	0	207½	193	104	98	92	233
1998—	Los Angeles (N.L.)	2	7	.222	5.05	12	12	2	0	0	67⅔	57	39	38	38	73
—	New York (N.L.)■	4	5	.444	4.82	17	16	1	0	0	89⅔	73	49	48	56	94
1999—	Iowa (PCL)■	1	1	.500	3.71	3	3	0	0	0	17	12	7	7	12	18
—	Huntsville (Sou.)■	1	0	1.000	0.00	1	1	0	0	0	7	5	0	0	1	7
—	Milwaukee (N.L.)	12	8	.600	4.54	28	28	0	0	0	176⅓	173	96	89	78	161
Major League totals (5 years)		**61**	**49**	**.555**	**3.82**	**151**	**150**	**11**	**5**	**0**	**960⅔**	**800**	**444**	**408**	**427**	**1031**

DIVISION SERIES RECORD

RECORDS: Shares N.L. career record for most earned runs allowed—10.

Year	League	W	L	Pct.	ERA	G	GS	CG	ShO	Sv.	IP	H	R	ER	BB	SO
1995—	Los Angeles (N.L.)	0	1	.000	9.00	1	1	0	0	0	5	7	5	5	2	6
1996—	Los Angeles (N.L.)	0	1	.000	12.27	1	1	0	0	0	3⅔	5	5	5	5	3
Division series totals (2 years)		**0**	**2**	**.000**	**10.38**	**2**	**2**	**0**	**0**	**0**	**8⅔**	**12**	**10**	**10**	**7**	**9**

ALL-STAR GAME RECORD

Year	League	W	L	Pct.	ERA	GS	CG	ShO	Sv.	IP	H	R	ER	BB	SO
1995—	National	0	0	...	0.00	1	0	0	0	2	1	0	0	0	3

PERSONAL: Born December 6, 1977, in Austin, Texas. ... 6-3/185. ... Throws left, bats both. ... Full name: Benjamin Owen Norris.
HIGH SCHOOL: Westwood (Austin, Texas).
TRANSACTIONS/CAREER NOTES: Selected by Arizona Diamondbacks organization in 13th round of free-agent draft (June 4, 1996).

Year	League	W	L	Pct.	ERA	G	GS	CG	ShO	Sv.	IP	H	R	ER	BB	SO
1996—	Ariz. D'backs (Ariz.)	2	2	.500	4.60	8	7	0	0	0	31⅓	33	21	16	4	37
—	Lethbridge (Pio.)	0	0	...	6.35	3	3	0	0	0	11⅓	14	9	8	5	12
1997—	South Bend (Midw.)	1	8	.111	4.03	14	13	0	0	0	60⅓	69	44	27	31	40
—	Lethbridge (Pio.)	7	3	.700	4.86	14	14	0	0	0	83⅓	93	61	45	23	54
1998—	South Bend (Midw.)	1	5	.167	3.32	15	15	0	0	0	89½	98	44	33	27	53
—	High Desert (Calif.)	2	2	.500	5.53	9	6	0	0	1	40⅔	48	27	25	18	17
1999—	High Desert (Calif.)	2	2	.500	4.43	8	8	0	0	0	40⅔	39	27	20	24	45
—	El Paso (Texas)	10	6	.625	4.16	20	20	0	0	0	119	132	61	55	53	87

N

PERSONAL: Born July 6, 1972, in San Leandro, Calif. ... 6-1/205. ... Bats both, throws right. ... Full name: Gregory Blakemoor Norton.
HIGH SCHOOL: Bishop O'Dowd (Oakland).
COLLEGE: Oklahoma.
TRANSACTIONS/CAREER NOTES: Selected by San Francisco Giants organization in seventh round of free-agent draft (June 4, 1990); did not sign. ... Selected by Chicago White Sox organization in second round of free-agent draft (June 3, 1993).
STATISTICAL NOTES: Led Midwest League third basemen with 387 total chances in 1994. ... Led American Association with .534 slugging percentage in 1997. ... Led American Association third basemen with 29 errors in 1997. ... Tied for A.L. third baseman lead with 25 errors in 1999.

Year	Team (League)	Pos.	G	AB	R	H	2B	3B	HR	RBI	Avg.	BB	SO	SB	PO	A	E	Avg.
1993—	GC White Sox (GCL)	3B	3	9	1	2	0	0	0	2	.222	1	1	0	1	7	0	1.000
—	Hickory (SAL)	3B-SS	71	254	36	62	12	2	4	36	.244	41	44	0	57	161	17	.928
1994—	South Bend (Midw.)	3B	127	477	73	137	22	2	6	64	.287	62	71	5	92	*265	30	.922
1995—	Birmingham (Sou.)	3B	133	469	65	162	23	2	6	60	.345	64	90	19	102	277	25	*.938
1996—	Birmingham (Sou.)	SS	76	287	40	81	14	3	8	44	.282	33	55	5	104	214	17	.949
—	Nashville (A.A.)	SS-DH-3B	43	164	28	47	14	2	7	26	.287	17	42	2	43	95	13	.914
—	Chicago (A.L.)	SS-3B-DH	11	23	4	5	0	0	2	3	.217	4	6	0	8	5	2	.867

Year	Team (League)	Pos.	G	AB	R	H	2B	3B	HR	RBI	Avg.	BB	SO	SB	PO	A	E	Avg.
1997—	Nashville (A.A.)	3-S-2-DH	114	414	82	114	27	1	26	76	.275	57	101	3	83	247	†38	.897
—	Chicago (A.L.)	3B-DH	18	34	5	9	2	2	0	1	.265	2	8	0	4	15	3	.864
1998—	Chicago (A.L.)	1-3-DH-2	105	299	38	71	17	2	9	36	.237	26	77	3	654	42	6	.991
1999—	Chicago (A.L.)	3B-1B-DH	132	436	62	111	26	0	16	50	.255	69	93	4	160	204	‡27	.931
Major League totals (4 years)			266	792	109	196	45	4	27	90	.247	101	184	7	826	266	38	.966

NORTON, PHIL — P — CUBS

PERSONAL: Born February 1, 1976, in Texarkana, Texas. ... 6-1/190. ... Throws left, bats both. ... Full name: Phillip Douglas Norton.
HIGH SCHOOL: Pleasant Grove (Texarkana, Texas).
JUNIOR COLLEGE: Texarkana (Texas) College.
TRANSACTIONS/CAREER NOTES: Selected by Chicago Cubs organization in 10th round of free-agent draft (June 4, 1996).

Year	League	W	L	Pct.	ERA	G	GS	CG	ShO	Sv.	IP	H	R	ER	BB	SO
1996—	Gulf Coast Cubs (GCL)	0	0	...	0.00	1	0	0	0	0	3	1	0	0	0	6
—	Williamsport (NY-P)	7	4	.636	2.54	15	13	2	1	0	85	68	33	24	33	77
1997—	Rockford (Midw.)	9	3	.750	3.22	18	18	3	0	0	109	92	51	39	44	114
—	Daytona (FSL)	3	2	.600	2.34	7	6	3	0	0	42⅓	40	11	11	12	44
—	Orlando (Sou.)	1	0	1.000	2.57	2	1	0	0	0	7	8	2	2	2	7
1998—	Daytona (FSL)	4	3	.571	3.27	10	10	0	0	0	66	57	30	24	26	54
—	West Tenn (Sou.)	6	6	.500	3.52	19	19	1	1	0	120⅓	118	60	47	50	119
1999—	West Tenn (Sou.)	7	4	.636	2.39	14	13	0	0	0	86⅔	72	32	23	42	81
—	Iowa (PCL)	5	6	.455	6.67	14	14	0	0	0	79⅔	98	63	59	33	61

NUNEZ, ABRAHAM — SS — PIRATES

PERSONAL: Born March 16, 1976, in Santo Domingo, Dominican Republic. ... 5-11/185. ... Bats both, throws right. ... Full name: Abraham Orlando Nunez Adames.
HIGH SCHOOL: Emmanuel (Santo Domingo, Dominican Republic).
TRANSACTIONS/CAREER NOTES: Signed as non-drafted free agent by Toronto Blue Jays organization (May 5, 1994). ... Traded by Blue Jays with P Mike Halperin and C/OF Craig Wilson to Pittsburgh Pirates (December 11, 1996), completing deal in which Blue Jays traded P Jose Silva, P Jose Pett, IF Brandon Cromer and three players to be named later to Pirates for OF/1B Orlando Merced, IF Carlos Garcia, and P Dan Plesac (November 14, 1996).
STATISTICAL NOTES: Tied for New York-Pennsylvania League lead in caught stealing with 14 in 1996. ... Led New York-Pennsylvania League shortstops in fielding with .953 in 1996.

Year	Team (League)	Pos.	G	AB	R	H	2B	3B	HR	RBI	Avg.	BB	SO	SB	PO	A	E	Avg.
1994—	Dom. Blue Jays (DSL)	2B	59	188	31	47	5	0	0	15	.250	42	37	22	155	27	12	.938
1995—	Dom. Blue Jays (DSL)	2B	54	186	49	56	10	3	4	25	.301	30	27	24	80	97	7	.962
1996—	St. Catharines (NY-P)	SS-2B	75	*297	43	83	6	4	3	26	.279	31	43	37	136	239	15	•.962
1997—	Lynchburg (Caro.)■..	SS	78	304	45	79	9	4	3	32	.260	23	47	29	100	219	15	.955
—	Carolina (Sou.)	SS	47	198	31	65	6	1	1	14	.328	20	28	10	76	129	11	.949
—	Pittsburgh (N.L.)	SS-2B	19	40	3	9	2	2	0	6	.225	3	10	1	14	37	0	1.000
1998—	Nashville (PCL)	SS	94	366	50	91	12	3	3	32	.249	39	73	16	155	274	21	.953
—	Lynchburg (Caro.)	SS-2B	5	18	2	4	1	0	0	2	.222	3	1	1	6	18	1	.960
—	Pittsburgh (N.L.)	SS	24	52	6	10	2	0	1	2	.192	12	14	4	33	60	7	.930
1999—	Pittsburgh (N.L.)	SS-2B	90	259	25	57	8	0	0	17	.220	28	54	9	113	214	14	.959
—	Nashville (PCL)	SS	15	58	12	18	0	0	0	3	.310	5	8	1	23	43	2	.971
Major League totals (3 years)			133	351	34	76	12	2	1	25	.217	43	78	14	160	311	21	.957

NUNEZ, JORGE — 2B/SS — DODGERS

PERSONAL: Born March 1, 1978, in Villa Mella, Dominican Republic. ... 5-10/158. ... Bats right, throws right. ... Full name: Jorge Marte Nunez.
TRANSACTIONS/CAREER NOTES: Signed as non-drafted free agent by Toronto Blue Jays organization (April 17, 1995). ... Traded by Blue Jays with OF Shawn Green to Los Angeles Dodgers for OF Raul Mondesi and P Pedro Borbon (November 8, 1999).
STATISTICAL NOTES: Led Pioneer League shortstops with 35 errors in 1998.

Year	Team (League)	Pos.	G	AB	R	H	2B	3B	HR	RBI	Avg.	BB	SO	SB	PO	A	E	Avg.
1995—	Dom. Blue Jays (DSL)	SS	13	15	1	2	0	0	1	4	.133	1	5	0	0	1	0	1.000
1996—	Dom. Blue Jays (DSL)	IF	69	258	51	76	10	2	7	40	.295	19	36	19	69	182	38	.869
1997—	Dom. Blue Jays (DSL)	1B-2B	71	262	46	66	5	5	4	33	.252	29	48	*44	...	...	...	...
1998—	Medicine Hat (Pio.)....	SS-2B-3B	74	*317	74	101	9	*11	6	52	.319	28	45	31	121	215	38	.898
—	Hagerstown (SAL)......	3B	4	16	0	4	0	0	0	1	.250	0	1	1	2	3	1	.833
1999—	Hagerstown (SAL)	2B-SS-3B	133	564	*116	151	28	•11	14	61	.268	40	103	51	247	387	32	.952

NUNEZ, VLADIMIR — P — MARLINS

PERSONAL: Born March 15, 1975, in Havana, Cuba. ... 6-4/224. ... Throws right, bats right.
TRANSACTIONS/CAREER NOTES: Signed as non-drafted free agent by Arizona Diamondbacks organization (February 1, 1996). ... On Tucson disabled list (April 7-24, 1998). ... Traded by Diamondbacks with P Brad Penny and a player to be named later to Florida Marlins for P Matt Mantei (July 9, 1999); Marlins acquired OF Abraham Nunez to complete deal (December 13, 1999).
STATISTICAL NOTES: Led California League with 36 home runs allowed in 1997.

Year League	W	L	Pct.	ERA	G	GS	CG	ShO	Sv.	IP	H	R	ER	BB	SO
1996— Visalia (Calif.)	1	6	.143	5.43	12	10	0	0	0	53	64	45	32	17	37
— Lethbridge (Pio.)	*10	0	*1.000	*2.22	14	13	0	0	0	85	78	25	21	10	*93
1997— High Desert (Calif.)............	8	5	.615	5.17	28	28	1	1	0	158 1/3	169	102	91	40	142
1998— Tucson (PCL)	4	4	.500	4.91	31	13	1	0	2	95 1/3	103	58	52	37	78
— Arizona (N.L.)	0	0	...	10.13	4	0	0	0	0	5 1/3	7	6	6	2	2
1999— Tucson (PCL)	1	0	1.000	6.75	3	0	0	0	0	2 2/3	5	2	2	0	3
— Arizona (N.L.)...................	3	2	.600	2.91	27	0	0	0	1	34	29	15	11	20	28
— Florida (N.L.)■........	4	8	.333	4.58	17	12	0	0	0	74 2/3	66	48	38	34	58
Major League totals (2 years)	**7**	**10**	**.412**	**4.34**	**48**	**12**	**0**	**0**	**1**	**114**	**102**	**69**	**55**	**56**	**88**

NUNNALLY, JON — OF — METS

PERSONAL: Born November 9, 1971, in Danville, Va. ... 5-10/190. ... Bats left, throws right. ... Full name: Jonathan Keith Nunnally.
HIGH SCHOOL: Hargrave Military Institute (Chatham, Va.).
JUNIOR COLLEGE: Miami-Dade (South) Community College.
TRANSACTIONS/CAREER NOTES: Selected by Baltimore Orioles organization in 39th round of free-agent draft (June 4, 1990); did not sign. ... Selected by Cleveland Indians organization in third round of free-agent draft (June 1, 1992). ... Selected by Kansas City Royals from Indians organization in Rule 5 major league draft (December 5, 1994). ... Traded by Royals with IF/OF Chris Stynes to Cincinnati Reds for P Hector Carrasco and P Scott Service (July 15, 1997). ... Traded by Reds to Boston Red Sox for P Pat Flury (March 25, 1999). ... Traded by Red Sox to New York Mets for OF Jermaine Allensworth (November 12, 1999).
STATISTICAL NOTES: Tied for American Association lead with eight bases on balls received in 1996. ... Tied for American Association lead with five double plays by outfielder in 1996. ... Career major league grand slams: 1.
MISCELLANEOUS: Hit home run in first major league at-bat (April 29, 1995).

								BATTING							FIELDING		
Year Team (League)	Pos.	G	AB	R	H	2B	3B	HR	RBI	Avg.	BB	SO	SB	PO	A	E	Avg.
1992— Watertown (NY-P)	OF	69	246	39	59	10	4	5	43	.240	32	55	12	146	2	8	.949
1993— Columbus (SAL).........	2B-OF	125	438	81	110	15	2	15	56	.251	63	108	17	226	202	25	.945
1994— Kinston (Caro.).........	OF	132	483	70	129	29	2	22	74	.267	64	125	23	263	*14	9	.969
1995— Kansas City (A.L.)■...	OF-DH	119	303	51	74	15	6	14	42	.244	51	86	6	197	5	6	.971
1996— Kansas City (A.L.) ...	OF-DH	35	90	16	19	5	1	5	17	.211	13	25	0	61	0	2	.968
— Omaha (A.A.)	OF-DH	103	345	76	97	21	4	25	77	.281	47	100	10	182	12	4	.980
1997— Omaha (A.A.)	OF	68	230	35	64	11	1	15	33	.278	39	67	8	173	8	7	.963
— Kansas City (A.L.) ...	OF	13	29	8	7	0	1	1	4	.241	5	7	0	12	0	0	1.000
— Cincinnati (N.L.)■...	OF	65	201	38	64	12	3	13	35	.318	26	51	7	120	3	2	.984
1998— Cincinnati (N.L.)	OF	74	174	29	36	9	0	7	20	.207	34	38	3	126	5	6	.956
— Indianapolis (I.L.)	OF	79	290	53	73	18	2	11	53	.252	47	71	7	146	8	8	.951
1999— Pawtucket (I.L.)■......	OF-DH	133	494	90	132	24	3	23	76	.267	85	103	26	271	12	5	.983
— Boston (A.L.)..............	DH-OF	10	14	4	4	1	0	0	1	.286	0	6	0	0	0	0	...
American League totals (4 years)		177	436	79	104	21	8	20	64	.239	69	124	6	270	5	8	.972
National League totals (2 years)		139	375	67	100	21	3	20	55	.267	60	89	10	246	8	8	.969
Major League totals (5 years)		316	811	146	204	42	11	40	119	.252	129	213	16	516	13	16	.971

NUNNARI, TALMADGE — 1B — EXPOS

PERSONAL: Born April 9, 1975, in Pensacola, Fla. ... 6-1/200. ... Bats left, throws left. ... Full name: Talmadge R. Nunnari.
HIGH SCHOOL: Booker T. Washington (Pensacola, Fla.).
COLLEGE: Jacksonville.
TRANSACTIONS/CAREER NOTES: Selected by Montreal Expos organization in ninth round of free-agent draft (June 3, 1997).

								BATTING							FIELDING		
Year Team (League)	Pos.	G	AB	R	H	2B	3B	HR	RBI	Avg.	BB	SO	SB	PO	A	E	Avg.
1997— Vermont (NY-P)..........	1B	62	236	30	75	11	3	4	32	.318	31	37	6	507	35	6	.989
— Cape Fear (SAL)	1B	9	35	8	13	1	1	1	6	.371	1	5	2	73	7	0	1.000
1998— Cape Fear (SAL)	1B-OF	79	299	51	88	18	0	2	51	.294	42	44	4	656	59	7	.990
— Jupiter (FSL)	1B	56	201	18	59	14	0	2	34	.294	30	39	1	491	50	4	.993
1999— Jupiter (FSL)	1B-DH-OF	71	261	41	93	17	1	5	44	.356	27	36	10	391	25	6	.986
— Harrisburg (East.).......	1B-OF-DH	63	239	45	79	17	1	6	29	.331	39	46	7	372	21	4	.990

O'BRIEN, CHARLIE — C

PERSONAL: Born May 1, 1961, in Tulsa, Okla. ... 6-2/205. ... Bats right, throws right. ... Full name: Charles Hugh O'Brien. ... Brother of John O'Brien, first baseman in St. Louis Cardinals organization (1991-93).
HIGH SCHOOL: Bishop Kelley (Tulsa, Okla.).
JUNIOR COLLEGE: McLennan Community College (Texas).
COLLEGE: Wichita State.
TRANSACTIONS/CAREER NOTES: Selected by Texas Rangers organization in 14th round of free-agent draft (June 6, 1978); did not sign. ... Selected by Seattle Mariners organization in 21st round of free-agent draft (June 8, 1981); did not sign. ... Selected by Oakland Athletics organization in fifth round of free-agent draft (June 7, 1982). ... On disabled list (July 31, 1983-remainder of season). ... On Albany/Colonie disabled list (April 13-May 15, 1984). ... Traded by A's with IF Steve Kiefer, P Mike Fulmer and P Pete Kendrick to Milwaukee Brewers for P Moose Haas (March 30, 1986). ... Traded by Brewers with a player to be named later to New York Mets for two players to be named later (August 30, 1990); Brewers acquired P Julio Machado and P Kevin Brown (September 7, 1990) and Mets acquired P Kevin Carmody (September 11, 1990) to complete deal. ... Granted free agency (October 29, 1993). ... Signed by Atlanta Braves (November 26, 1993). ... Granted free agency (October 30, 1995). ... Signed by Toronto Blue Jays (December 14, 1995). ... Granted free agency (October 27, 1997). ... Signed by Chicago White Sox (December 10, 1997). ... On Chicago disabled list (July 19-30, 1998). ... Traded by White Sox to Anaheim Angels for P Jason Stockstill and P Brian Tokarse (July 30, 1998). ... On Anaheim disabled list (July 30-September 1 and September 18, 1998-remainder of season); included rehabilitation assignment to Midland (August 25-31). ... On disabled list (June 3-July 23, 1999). ... Released by Angels (August 6, 1999).
STATISTICAL NOTES: Career major league grand slams: 1.

Year Team (League)	Pos.	G	AB	R	H	2B	3B	HR	RBI	Avg.	BB	SO	SB	PO	A	E	Avg.
1982—Medford (N.W.)	C	17	60	11	17	3	0	3	14	.283	10	10	0	116	18	4	.971
—Modesto (Calif.)	C	41	140	23	42	6	0	3	32	.300	20	19	7	239	44	5	.983
1983—Alb./Colo. (East.)	C-1B	92	285	50	83	12	1	14	56	.291	52	39	3	478	82	11	.981
1984—Modesto (Calif.)	C	9	32	8	9	2	0	1	5	.281	2	4	1	41	8	0	1.000
—Tacoma (PCL)	C-OF	69	195	33	44	11	0	9	22	.226	28	31	0	260	39	0	1.000
1985—Huntsville (Sou.)	C	33	115	20	24	5	0	7	16	.209	16	20	0	182	29	5	.977
—Oakland (A.L.)	C	16	11	3	3	1	0	0	1	.273	3	3	0	23	0	1	.958
—Modesto (Calif.)	C	9	27	5	8	4	1	1	2	.296	2	5	0	33	8	1	.976
—Tacoma (PCL)	C	18	57	5	9	4	0	0	7	.158	6	17	0	110	9	3	.975
1986—Vancouver (PCL)■	C	6	17	1	2	0	0	0	1	.118	4	4	0	22	3	2	.926
—El Paso (Texas)	C-OF-1B	92	336	72	109	20	3	15	75	.324	50	30	0	437	43	4	.992
1987—Denver (A.A.)	C	80	266	37	75	12	1	8	35	.282	41	33	5	415	53	6	.987
—Milwaukee (A.L.)	C	10	35	2	7	3	1	0	0	.200	4	4	0	78	11	0	1.000
1988—Denver (A.A.)	C	48	153	16	43	5	0	4	25	.281	19	19	1	243	44	3	.990
—Milwaukee (A.L.)	C	40	118	12	26	6	0	2	9	.220	5	16	0	210	20	2	.991
1989—Milwaukee (A.L.)	C	62	188	22	44	10	0	6	35	.234	21	11	0	314	36	5	.986
1990—Milwaukee (A.L.)	C	46	145	11	27	7	2	0	11	.186	11	26	0	217	24	2	.992
—New York (N.L.)■	C	28	68	6	11	3	0	0	9	.162	10	8	0	191	21	3	.986
1991—New York (N.L.)	C	69	168	16	31	6	0	2	14	.185	17	25	0	396	37	4	.991
1992—New York (N.L.)	C	68	156	15	33	12	0	2	13	.212	16	18	0	287	44	7	.979
1993—New York (N.L.)	C	67	188	15	48	11	0	4	23	.255	14	14	1	325	39	5	.986
1994—Atlanta (N.L.)■	C	51	152	24	37	11	0	8	28	.243	15	24	0	308	26	3	.991
1995—Atlanta (N.L.)	C	67	198	18	45	7	0	9	23	.227	29	40	0	446	23	4	.992
1996—Toronto (A.L.)■	C	109	324	33	77	17	0	13	44	.238	29	68	0	613	37	3	.995
1997—Toronto (A.L.)	C	69	225	22	49	15	1	4	27	.218	22	45	0	543	41	3	.995
1998—Chicago (A.L.)■	C	57	164	12	43	9	0	4	18	.262	9	31	0	305	22	4	.988
—Midland (Texas)■	C	5	17	1	2	0	0	0	2	.118	2	4	1	33	0	0	1.000
—Anaheim (A.L.)	C	5	11	1	2	0	0	0	0	.182	1	2	0	20	2	0	1.000
1999—Anaheim (A.L.)	C	27	62	3	6	0	0	1	4	.097	1	12	0	140	11	1	.993
American League totals (9 years)		441	1283	121	284	68	4	30	149	.221	106	218	0	2463	204	21	.992
National League totals (6 years)		350	930	94	205	50	0	25	110	.220	101	129	1	1953	190	26	.988
Major League totals (14 years)		791	2213	215	489	118	4	55	259	.221	207	347	1	4416	394	47	.990

DIVISION SERIES RECORD

Year Team (League)	Pos.	G	AB	R	H	2B	3B	HR	RBI	Avg.	BB	SO	SB	PO	A	E	Avg.
1995—Atlanta (N.L.)	C	2	5	0	1	0	0	0	0	.200	1	1	0	8	1	0	1.000

CHAMPIONSHIP SERIES RECORD

Year Team (League)	Pos.	G	AB	R	H	2B	3B	HR	RBI	Avg.	BB	SO	SB	PO	A	E	Avg.
1995—Atlanta (N.L.)	C-PH	2	5	1	2	0	0	1	3	.400	0	1	0	3	1	0	1.000

WORLD SERIES RECORD

NOTES: Member of World Series championship team (1995).

Year Team (League)	Pos.	G	AB	R	H	2B	3B	HR	RBI	Avg.	BB	SO	SB	PO	A	E	Avg.
1995—Atlanta (N.L.)	C	2	3	0	0	0	0	0	0	.000	0	0	0	7	2	0	1.000

OCHOA, ALEX   OF   REDS

PERSONAL: Born March 29, 1972, in Miami Lakes, Fla. ... 6-0/195. ... Bats right, throws right.
HIGH SCHOOL: Hialeah (Fla.) Miami Lakes.
TRANSACTIONS/CAREER NOTES: Selected by Baltimore Orioles organization in third round of free-agent draft (June 3, 1991). ... Traded by Orioles with OF Damon Buford to New York Mets for 3B/OF Bobby Bonilla and a player to be named later (July 28, 1995); Orioles acquired P Jimmy Williams to complete deal (August 17, 1995). ... Traded by Mets to Minnesota Twins for OF Rich Becker (December 12, 1997). ... Traded by Twins to Milwaukee Brewers for a player to be named later (December 14, 1998); Twins acquired OF Darrell Nicholas to complete deal (December 15, 1998). ... Traded by Brewers to Cincinnati Reds for OF/1B Mark Sweeney and a player to be named later (January 14, 2000).
STATISTICAL NOTES: Led Carolina League in grounding into double plays with 15 in 1993. ... Led Eastern League with 12 sacrifice flies in 1994. ... Tied for Eastern League lead in double plays by outfielder with five in 1994. ... Led International League outfielders with 249 putouts and 266 total chances in 1995. ... Hit for the cycle (July 3, 1996). ... Tied for International League lead in double plays by outfielder with three in 1996.

Year Team (League)	Pos.	G	AB	R	H	2B	3B	HR	RBI	Avg.	BB	SO	SB	PO	A	E	Avg.
1991—GC Orioles (GCL)	OF	53	179	26	55	8	3	1	30	.307	16	14	11	45	3	2	.960
1992—Kane County (Midw.)	OF	133	499	65	147	22	7	1	59	.295	58	55	31	225	•17	•12	.953
1993—Frederick (Caro.)	OF	137	532	84	147	29	5	13	90	.276	46	67	34	169	13	11	.943
1994—Bowie (East.)	OF	134	519	77	156	25	2	14	82	.301	49	67	28	237	*22	6	.977
1995—Rochester (I.L.)	OF	91	336	41	92	18	2	8	46	.274	26	50	17	183	9	5	.975
—Norfolk (I.L.)■	OF-DH	34	123	17	38	6	2	2	15	.309	14	12	7	§66	1	2	.971
—New York (N.L.)	OF	11	37	7	11	1	0	0	0	.297	2	10	1	20	1	0	1.000
1996—Norfolk (I.L.)	OF-DH	67	233	45	79	12	4	8	39	.339	32	22	5	110	9	5	.960
—New York (N.L.)	OF	82	282	37	83	19	3	4	33	.294	17	30	4	135	8	5	.966
1997—New York (N.L.)	OF-DH	113	238	31	58	14	1	3	22	.244	18	32	3	104	7	2	.982
1998—Minnesota (A.L.)■	OF-DH	94	249	35	64	14	2	2	25	.257	10	35	6	117	8	4	.969
1999—Milwaukee (N.L.)■	OF-DH	119	277	47	83	16	3	8	40	.300	45	43	6	133	5	3	.979
American League totals (1 year)		94	249	35	64	14	2	2	25	.257	10	35	6	117	8	4	.969
National League totals (4 years)		325	834	122	235	50	7	15	95	.282	82	115	14	392	21	10	.976
Major League totals (5 years)		419	1083	157	299	64	9	17	120	.276	92	150	20	509	29	14	.975

PERSONAL: Born January 4, 1977, in Cincinnati. ... 6-2/190. ... Throws left, bats left. ... Full name: Brian Michael O'Connor.
HIGH SCHOOL: Reading (Ohio).
TRANSACTIONS/CAREER NOTES: Selected by Pittsburgh Pirates organization in 11th round of free-agent draft (June 1, 1995).
STATISTICAL NOTES: Led Eastern League with 21 wild pitches in 1999.

Year League	W	L	Pct.	ERA	G	GS	CG	ShO	Sv.	IP	H	R	ER	BB	SO
1995— Gulf Coast Pirates (GCL)	2	2	.500	1.88	14	5	0	0	1	43	33	22	9	13	43
1996— Augusta (SAL)	0	1	.000	3.06	19	0	0	0	1	35⅓	33	13	12	8	37
— Erie (NY-P)	4	*10	.286	5.85	15	•15	0	0	0	67⅔	75	*60	44	47	60
1997— Augusta (SAL)	2	7	.222	4.41	25	14	0	0	0	85⅔	90	54	42	39	91
— Lynchburg (Caro.)	2	1	.667	3.46	11	0	0	0	2	13	11	5	5	6	14
1998— Lynchburg (Caro.)	6	2	.750	2.60	14	14	1	0	0	86⅔	86	34	25	22	84
— Carolina (Sou.)	2	4	.333	8.25	14	13	0	0	0	64⅓	86	65	59	53	41
1999— Altoona (East.)	7	11	.389	4.70	28	27	1	0	0	153⅓	152	98	80	*92	106

PERSONAL: Born November 8, 1968, in San Pedro de Macoris, Dominican Republic. ... 6-0/190. ... Bats both, throws right. ... Full name: Jose Antonio Dono Offerman.
HIGH SCHOOL: Colegio Biblico Cristiano (Dominican Republic).
TRANSACTIONS/CAREER NOTES: Signed as non-drafted free agent by Los Angeles Dodgers organization (July 24, 1986). ... Traded by Dodgers to Kansas City Royals for P Billy Brewer (December 17, 1995). ... On Kansas City disabled list (April 6-29, July 10-22 and August 14-September 6, 1997). ... Granted free agency (October 23, 1998). ... Signed by Boston Red Sox (November 16, 1998).
RECORDS: Holds A.L. single-season record for most consecutive games batted safely by switch hitter—27 (1998).
HONORS: Named Minor League Player of the Year by The Sporting News (1990). ... Named Pacific Coast League Player of the Year (1990).
STATISTICAL NOTES: Tied for Pioneer League lead in caught stealing with 10 in 1988. ... Tied for Pacific Coast League lead in caught stealing with 18 in 1990. ... Led Pacific Coast League shortstops with 36 errors in 1990. ... Hit home run in first major league at-bat (August 19, 1990). ... Led N.L. with 25 sacrifice hits in 1993. ... Had 27-game hitting streak (July 11-August 7, 1998). ... Career major league grand slams: 1.

							BATTING							FIELDING		
Year Team (League)	Pos.	G	AB	R	H	2B	3B	HR	RBI	Avg.	BB	SO	SB	PO	A	E	Avg.
1987—						Dominican Summer League statistics unavailable.										
1988— Great Falls (Pio.)	SS	60	251	75	83	11	5	2	28	.331	38	42	*57	82	143	18	*.926
1989— Bakersfield (Calif.)	SS	62	245	53	75	9	4	2	22	.306	35	48	37	94	179	30	.901
— San Antonio (Tex.)	SS	68	278	47	80	6	3	2	22	.288	40	39	32	106	168	20	.932
1990— Albuquerque (PCL)....	SS-2B	117	454	104	148	16	11	0	56	.326	71	81	*60	174	361	†36	.937
— Los Angeles (N.L.)	SS	29	58	7	9	0	0	1	7	.155	4	14	1	30	40	4	.946
1991— Albuquerque (PCL).....	SS	79	289	58	86	8	4	0	29	.298	47	58	32	126	241	17	.956
— Los Angeles (N.L.)	SS	52	113	10	22	2	0	0	3	.195	25	32	3	50	121	10	.945
1992— Los Angeles (N.L.)	SS	149	534	67	139	20	8	1	30	.260	57	75	23	208	398	*42	.935
1993— Los Angeles (N.L.)	SS	158	590	77	159	21	6	1	62	.269	71	75	30	250	454	*37	.950
1994— Los Angeles (N.L.)	SS	72	243	27	51	8	4	1	25	.210	38	38	2	123	195	11	.967
— Albuquerque (PCL).....	SS	56	224	43	74	7	5	1	31	.330	37	48	9	91	196	13	.957
1995— Los Angeles (N.L.)	SS	119	429	69	123	14	6	4	33	.287	69	67	2	165	312	*35	.932
1996— Kansas City (A.L.)■ ...1B-2B-SS-OF	151	561	85	170	33	8	5	47	.303	74	98	24	920	234	16	.986
1997— Kansas City (A.L.)	2B-DH	106	424	59	126	23	6	2	39	.297	41	64	9	201	254	9	.981
1998— Kansas City (A.L.)	2B-DH	158	607	102	191	28	*13	7	66	.315	89	96	45	277	440	19	.974
1999— Boston (A.L.)■	2B-DH-1B	149	586	107	172	37	*11	8	69	.294	96	79	18	285	321	14	.977
American League totals (4 years)		564	2178	353	659	121	38	22	221	.303	300	337	96	1683	1249	58	.981
National League totals (6 years)		579	1967	257	503	65	24	8	160	.256	264	324	61	826	1520	139	.944
Major League totals (10 years)		1143	4145	610	1162	186	62	30	381	.280	564	661	157	2509	2769	197	.964

DIVISION SERIES RECORD

							BATTING							FIELDING		
Year Team (League)	Pos.	G	AB	R	H	2B	3B	HR	RBI	Avg.	BB	SO	SB	PO	A	E	Avg.
1995— Los Angeles (N.L.)	PR	1	0	0	0	0	0	0	0	...	0	0	0	...	...	...	...
1999— Boston (A.L.)..............	2B	5	18	4	7	1	0	1	6	.389	7	0	0	11	9	0	1.000
Division series totals (2 years)		6	18	4	7	1	0	1	6	.389	7	0	0	11	9	0	1.000

CHAMPIONSHIP SERIES RECORD

RECORDS: Shares single-game record for most at-bats (nine-inning game)—6 (October 16, 1999).

							BATTING							FIELDING		
Year Team (League)	Pos.	G	AB	R	H	2B	3B	HR	RBI	Avg.	BB	SO	SB	PO	A	E	Avg.
1999— Boston (A.L.)..............	2B	5	24	4	11	0	1	0	2	.458	1	3	1	16	6	2	.917

ALL-STAR GAME RECORD

						BATTING							FIELDING		
Year League	Pos.	AB	R	H	2B	3B	HR	RBI	Avg.	BB	SO	SB	PO	A	E	Avg.
1995— National	SS	0	0	0	0	0	0	0	...	0	0	0	0	0	0	...
1999— American	2B	1	0	0	0	0	0	0	.000	0	0	0	3	0	1	.750
All-Star Game totals (2 years)		1	0	0	0	0	0	0	.000	0	0	0	3	0	1	.750

PERSONAL: Born November 9, 1970, in Lake Charles, La. ... 6-2/220. ... Throws right, bats left. ... Full name: Chad Wayne Ogea. ... Name pronounced OH-jay.
HIGH SCHOOL: St. Louis (Lake Charles, La.).
COLLEGE: Louisiana State.

O

TRANSACTIONS/CAREER NOTES: Selected by Cleveland Indians organization in third round of free-agent draft (June 3, 1991). ... On Cleveland disabled list (April 28-May 28, 1996); included rehabilitation assignment to Buffalo (May 15-June 8). ... On Cleveland disabled list (June 24-September 1, 1997). ... On Cleveland disabled list (March 22-April 21, May 20-July 13 and July 30-September 1, 1998); included rehabilitation assignments to Buffalo (June 20-July 11, April 11-20 and August 22-27). ... Traded by Indians to Philadelphia Phillies for P Jerry Spradlin (November 13, 1998). ... Granted free agency (October 6, 1999). ... Signed by Detroit Tigers organization (November 23, 1999). ... Selected by Tampa Bay Devil Rays from Tigers organization in Rule 5 major league draft (December 13, 1999).

STATISTICAL NOTES: Led International League with 26 home runs allowed in 1993.

Year League	W	L	Pct.	ERA	G	GS	CG	ShO	Sv.	IP	H	R	ER	BB	SO
1992—Kinston (Caro.)	13	3	.813	3.49	21	21	•5	•2	0	139 1/3	135	61	54	29	123
— Canton/Akron (East.)	6	1	.857	2.20	7	7	1	1	0	49	38	12	12	12	40
1993—Charlotte (I.L.)	•13	8	.619	3.82	29	•29	0	0	0	181 1/3	169	91	77	54	135
1994—Charlotte (I.L.)	9	10	.474	3.85	24	23	6	0	1	163 2/3	146	80	70	34	113
— Cleveland (A.L.)	0	1	.000	6.06	4	1	0	0	0	16 1/3	21	11	11	10	11
1995—Buffalo (A.A.)	0	1	.000	4.58	4	4	0	0	0	17 2/3	16	12	9	8	11
— Cleveland (A.L.)	8	3	.727	3.05	20	14	1	0	0	106 1/3	95	38	36	29	57
1996—Cleveland (A.L.)	10	6	.625	4.79	29	21	1	1	0	146 2/3	151	82	78	42	101
— Buffalo (A.A.)	0	1	.000	5.26	5	5	0	0	0	25 2/3	27	15	15	6	20
1997—Cleveland (A.L.)	8	9	.471	4.99	21	21	1	0	0	126 1/3	139	79	70	47	80
— Buffalo (A.A.)	1	1	.500	4.29	4	4	0	0	0	21	24	10	10	6	11
1998—Buffalo (I.L.)	2	1	.667	3.61	9	9	1	0	0	42 1/3	42	19	17	5	34
— Cleveland (A.L.)	5	4	.556	5.61	19	9	0	0	0	69	74	44	43	25	43
1999—Philadelphia (N.L.)■	6	12	.333	5.63	36	28	0	0	0	168	192	110	105	61	77
A.L. totals (5 years)	31	23	.574	4.61	93	66	3	1	0	464 2/3	480	254	238	153	292
N.L. totals (1 year)	6	12	.333	5.63	36	28	0	0	0	168	192	110	105	61	77
Major League totals (6 years)	37	35	.514	4.88	129	94	3	1	0	632 2/3	672	364	343	214	369

DIVISION SERIES RECORD

Year League	W	L	Pct.	ERA	G	GS	CG	ShO	Sv.	IP	H	R	ER	BB	SO
1996—Cleveland (A.L.)	0	0	...	0.00	1	0	0	0	0	1/3	0	0	0	2	0
1997—Cleveland (A.L.)	0	0	...	1.69	1	0	0	0	0	5 1/3	2	1	1	0	1
1998—Cleveland (A.L.)						Did not play.									
Division series totals (2 years)	0	0	...	1.59	2	0	0	0	0	5 2/3	2	1	1	2	1

CHAMPIONSHIP SERIES RECORD

Year League	W	L	Pct.	ERA	G	GS	CG	ShO	Sv.	IP	H	R	ER	BB	SO
1995—Cleveland (A.L.)	0	0	...	0.00	1	0	0	0	0	2/3	1	0	0	0	2
1997—Cleveland (A.L.)	0	2	.000	3.21	2	2	0	0	0	14	12	5	5	5	7
1998—Cleveland (A.L.)	0	1	.000	8.10	2	1	0	0	0	6 2/3	9	6	6	5	4
Champ. series totals (3 years)	0	3	.000	4.64	5	3	0	0	0	21 1/3	22	11	11	10	13

WORLD SERIES RECORD

Year League	W	L	Pct.	ERA	G	GS	CG	ShO	Sv.	IP	H	R	ER	BB	SO
1997—Cleveland (A.L.)	2	0	1.000	1.54	2	2	0	0	0	11 2/3	11	2	2	3	5

OHKA, TOMO   P   RED SOX

PERSONAL: Born March 18, 1976, in Kyoto, Japan. ... 6-1/179. ... Throws right, bats right. Full name: Tomokazu Ohka.

HIGH SCHOOL: Kyoto Siesio (Kyoto, Japan).

TRANSACTIONS/CAREER NOTES: Contract purchased by Boston Red Sox from Yokohama Bay Stars of Japan Central League (November 20, 1998).

Year League	W	L	Pct.	ERA	G	GS	CG	ShO	Sv.	IP	H	R	ER	BB	SO
1994—Yokohama (Jap. Cen.)	1	1	.500	4.18	15	2	0	0	0	28	29	13	13	18	18
1995—Yokohama (Jap. Cen.)	0	0	...	1.93	3	1	0	0	0	9 1/3	3	2	2	13	6
1996—Yokohama (Jap. Cen.)	0	1	.000	9.50	14	1	0	0	0	18	27	19	19	14	11
1997—						Japan minor league statistics unavailable.									
1998—Yokohama (Jap. Cen.)	0	0	...	9.00	2	0	0	0	0	2	2	2	2	2	1
1999—Trenton (East.)■	8	0	1.000	3.00	12	12	0	0	0	72	63	26	24	25	53
— Pawtucket (I.L.)	7	0	1.000	1.58	12	12	1	1	0	68 1/3	60	17	12	11	63
— Boston (A.L.)	1	2	.333	6.23	8	2	0	0	0	13	21	12	9	6	8
Major League totals (1 year)	1	2	.333	6.23	8	2	0	0	0	13	21	12	9	6	8

OJALA, KIRT   P

PERSONAL: Born December 24, 1968, in Kalamazoo, Mich. ... 6-2/215. ... Throws left, bats left. ... Full name: Kirt Stanley Ojala. ... Name pronounced O-juh-luh.

HIGH SCHOOL: Portage (Mich.) Central.

COLLEGE: Michigan.

TRANSACTIONS/CAREER NOTES: Selected by New York Yankees organization in fourth round of free-agent draft (June 4, 1990). ... On disabled list (April 9-23, 1992). ... Selected by Oakland Athletics from Yankees organization in Rule 5 major league draft (December 7, 1992). ... Returned to Yankees organization (March 27, 1993). ... Granted free agency (April 5, 1996). ... Signed by Indianapolis, Cincinnati Reds organization (April 11, 1996). ... Claimed on waivers by Florida Marlins organization (March 27, 1997). ... Granted free agency (October 15, 1997). ... Signed by Arizona Diamondbacks (November 26, 1997). ... Claimed on waivers by Marlins (February 20, 1998). ... On Calgary disabled list (August 18, 1999-remainder of season). ... Granted free agency (October 4, 1999).

RECORDS: Shares major league single-inning record for most strikeouts—4 (September 16, 1998, fourth inning).

Year League	W	L	Pct.	ERA	G	GS	CG	ShO	Sv.	IP	H	R	ER	BB	SO
1990—Oneonta (NY-P)	7	2	.778	2.16	14	14	1	0	0	79	75	28	19	43	87
1991—Prince William (Caro.)	8	7	.533	2.53	25	23	1	0	0	156 2/3	120	52	44	61	112
1992—Albany/Colonie (East.)	12	8	.600	3.62	24	23	2	1	0	151 2/3	130	71	61	•80	116
1993—Columbus (I.L.)	8	9	.471	5.50	31	20	0	0	0	126	145	85	77	71	83
— Albany/Colonie (East.)	1	0	1.000	0.00	1	1	0	0	0	6 1/3	5	0	0	2	6

Year League	W	L	Pct.	ERA	G	GS	CG	ShO	Sv.	IP	H	R	ER	BB	SO
1994— Columbus (I.L.)	11	7	.611	3.83	25	23	1	1	0	148	157	78	63	46	81
1995— Columbus (I.L.)	8	7	.533	3.95	32	20	0	0	1	145 2/3	138	74	64	54	107
1996— Indianapolis (A.A.)■	7	7	.500	3.77	22	21	3	0	0	133 2/3	143	67	56	31	92
1997— Charlotte (I.L.)■	8	7	.533	3.50	25	24	0	0	0	149	148	74	58	55	119
— Florida (N.L.)	1	2	.333	3.14	7	5	0	0	0	28 2/3	28	10	10	18	19
1998— Florida (N.L.)	2	7	.222	4.25	41	13	1	0	0	125	128	71	59	59	75
1999— Florida (N.L.)	0	1	.000	14.34	8	1	0	0	0	10 2/3	21	17	17	6	5
— Calgary (PCL)	3	8	.273	7.21	16	14	1	0	0	78 2/3	110	70	63	44	54
Major League totals (3 years)	3	10	.231	4.71	56	19	1	0	0	164 1/3	177	98	86	83	99

O'LEARY, TROY   OF   RED SOX

PERSONAL: Born August 4, 1969, in Compton, Calif. ... 6-0/200. ... Bats left, throws left. ... Full name: Troy Franklin O'Leary.
HIGH SCHOOL: Cypress (Calif.).
JUNIOR COLLEGE: Chaffey College (Calif.).
TRANSACTIONS/CAREER NOTES: Selected by Milwaukee Brewers organization in 13th round of free-agent draft (June 2, 1987). ... Claimed on waivers by Boston Red Sox (April 14, 1995).
HONORS: Named Texas League Most Valuable Player (1992).
STATISTICAL NOTES: Led Pioneer League with 144 total bases in 1989. ... Led Texas League with 227 total bases and .399 on-base percentage in 1992. ... Led Texas League outfielders with 242 total chances in 1992. ... Had 15-game hitting streak (July 30-August 14, 1999). ... Career major league grand slams: 2.

									BATTING						FIELDING		
Year Team (League)	Pos.	G	AB	R	H	2B	3B	HR	RBI	Avg.	BB	SO	SB	PO	A	E	Avg.
1987— Helena (Pio.)	OF	3	5	0	2	0	0	0	1	.400	0	0	0	0	0	0	...
1988— Helena (Pio.)	OF	67	203	40	70	11	1	0	27	.345	30	32	10	64	4	3	.958
1989— Beloit (Midw.)	OF	42	115	7	21	4	0	0	8	.183	15	20	1	55	1	1	.982
— Helena (Pio.)	OF	•68	263	54	*89	16	3	11	*56	.338	28	43	9	92	6	3	.970
1990— Beloit (Midw.)	OF	118	436	73	130	29	1	6	62	.298	41	90	12	184	14	8	.961
— Stockton (Calif.)	OF	2	6	1	3	1	0	0	0	.500	2	1	0	3	0	1	.750
1991— Stockton (Calif.)	OF	126	418	63	110	20	4	5	46	.263	73	96	4	163	4	3	.982
1992— El Paso (Texas)	OF	*135	*506	*92	*169	27	8	5	79	*.334	59	87	28	*220	11	*11	.955
1993— New Orleans (A.A.)	OF-1B	111	388	65	106	32	1	7	59	.273	43	61	6	189	8	6	.970
— Milwaukee (A.L.)	OF	19	41	3	12	3	0	0	3	.293	5	9	0	32	1	0	1.000
1994— New Orleans (A.A.)	OF-DH-1B	63	225	44	74	18	5	8	43	.329	32	37	10	99	10	2	.982
— Milwaukee (A.L.)	OF-DH	27	66	9	18	1	1	2	7	.273	5	12	1	37	2	0	1.000
1995— Boston (A.L.)■	OF-DH	112	399	60	123	31	6	10	49	.308	29	64	5	196	6	5	.976
1996— Boston (A.L.)	OF	149	497	68	129	28	5	15	81	.260	47	80	3	227	8	7	.971
1997— Boston (A.L.)	OF-DH	146	499	65	154	32	4	15	80	.309	39	70	0	267	6	8	.979
1998— Boston (A.L.)	OF	156	611	95	165	36	8	23	83	.270	36	108	2	303	9	3	.990
1999— Boston (A.L.)	OF	157	596	84	167	36	4	28	103	.280	56	91	1	296	9	2	.993
Major League totals (7 years)		766	2709	384	768	167	28	93	406	.283	217	434	12	1358	43	23	.984

DIVISION SERIES RECORD

RECORDS: Shares single-game record for most home runs—2; grand slams—1; and runs batted in—7 (October 11, 1999). ... Shares single-inning record for most runs batted in—4 (October 11, 1999, third inning).

									BATTING						FIELDING		
Year Team (League)	Pos.	G	AB	R	H	2B	3B	HR	RBI	Avg.	BB	SO	SB	PO	A	E	Avg.
1998— Boston (A.L.)	OF	4	16	0	1	0	0	0	0	.063	1	4	0	8	0	0	1.000
1999— Boston (A.L.)	OF	5	20	4	4	0	0	2	7	.200	2	3	0	7	0	0	1.000
Division series totals (2 years)		9	36	4	5	0	0	2	7	.139	3	7	0	15	0	0	1.000

CHAMPIONSHIP SERIES RECORD

									BATTING						FIELDING		
Year Team (League)	Pos.	G	AB	R	H	2B	3B	HR	RBI	Avg.	BB	SO	SB	PO	A	E	Avg.
1999— Boston (A.L.)		5	20	2	7	3	0	0	1	.350	2	5	0	7	0	0	1.000

OLERUD, JOHN   1B   MARINERS

PERSONAL: Born August 5, 1968, in Seattle. ... 6-5/220. ... Bats left, throws left. ... Full name: John Garrett Olerud. ... Son of John E. Olerud, minor league catcher (1965-70). ... Name pronounced OH-luh-rude.
HIGH SCHOOL: Interlake (Bellevue, Wash.).
COLLEGE: Washington State.
TRANSACTIONS/CAREER NOTES: Selected by New York Mets organization in 27th round of free-agent draft (June 2, 1986); did not sign. ... Selected by Toronto Blue Jays organization in third round of free-agent draft (June 5, 1989). ... Traded by Blue Jays with cash to Mets for P Robert Person (December 20, 1996). ... Granted free agency (October 27, 1997). ... Re-signed by Mets (November 24, 1997). ... Granted free agency (October 28, 1999). ... Signed by Seattle Mariners (December 15, 1999).
RECORDS: Shares A.L. single-season records for most intentional bases on balls received—33 (1993); and most intentional bases on balls received by lefthanded hitter—33 (1993). ... Shares N.L. single-season record for most consecutive times reached base safely—15 (September 16 [1], 18 [5], 20 [4], 22 [1], 1998; 6 singles, 1 double, 2 home runs, 6 bases on balls).
STATISTICAL NOTES: Tied for A.L. lead with 10 sacrifice flies in 1991. ... Had 26-game hitting streak (May 26-June 22, 1993). ... Led A.L. with 33 intentional bases on balls received and .473 on-base percentage in 1993. ... Hit for the cycle (September 11, 1997). ... Had 23-game hitting streak (July 19-August 9, 1998). ... Career major league grand slams: 5.

									BATTING						FIELDING		
Year Team (League)	Pos.	G	AB	R	H	2B	3B	HR	RBI	Avg.	BB	SO	SB	PO	A	E	Avg.
1989— Toronto (A.L.)	1B-DH	6	8	2	3	0	0	0	0	.375	0	1	0	19	2	0	1.000
1990— Toronto (A.L.)	DH-1B	111	358	43	95	15	1	14	48	.265	57	75	0	133	10	2	.986
1991— Toronto (A.L.)	1B-DH	139	454	64	116	30	1	17	68	.256	68	84	0	1120	78	5	.996
1992— Toronto (A.L.)	1B-DH	138	458	68	130	28	0	16	66	.284	70	61	1	1057	81	7	.994

Year	Team (League)	Pos.	G	AB	R	H	2B	3B	HR	RBI	Avg.	BB	SO	SB	PO	A	E	Avg.
1993—	Toronto (A.L.)............	1B-DH	158	551	109	200	*54	2	24	107	*.363	114	65	0	1160	84	7	.992
1994—	Toronto (A.L.)............	1B-DH	108	384	47	114	29	2	12	67	.297	61	53	1	824	68	6	.993
1995—	Toronto (A.L.)............	1B	135	492	72	143	32	0	8	54	.291	84	54	0	1099	89	4	.997
1996—	Toronto (A.L.)............	1B-DH	125	398	59	109	25	0	18	61	.274	60	37	1	781	56	2	.998
1997—	New York (N.L.)■	1B	154	524	90	154	34	1	22	102	.294	85	67	0	1292	120	7	.995
1998—	New York (N.L.).........	1B	160	557	91	197	36	4	22	93	.354	96	73	2	1258	116	5	.996
1999—	New York (N.L.).........	1B	•162	581	107	173	39	0	19	96	.298	125	66	3	1344	105	9	.994
American League totals (8 years)			920	3103	464	910	213	6	109	471	.293	514	430	3	6193	481	36	.995
National League totals (3 years)			476	1662	288	524	109	5	63	291	.315	306	206	5	3894	341	21	.995
Major League totals (11 years)			1396	4765	752	1434	322	11	172	762	.301	820	636	8	10087	822	57	.995

DIVISION SERIES RECORD

Year	Team (League)	Pos.	G	AB	R	H	2B	3B	HR	RBI	Avg.	BB	SO	SB	PO	A	E	Avg.
1999—	New York (N.L.).........	1B	4	16	3	7	0	0	1	6	.438	3	2	0	31	4	0	1.000

CHAMPIONSHIP SERIES RECORD

Year	Team (League)	Pos.	G	AB	R	H	2B	3B	HR	RBI	Avg.	BB	SO	SB	PO	A	E	Avg.
1991—	Toronto (A.L.)............	1B	5	19	1	3	0	0	0	3	.158	3	1	0	40	3	0	1.000
1992—	Toronto (A.L.)............	1B	6	23	4	8	2	0	1	4	.348	2	5	0	51	1	0	1.000
1993—	Toronto (A.L.).........	1B	6	23	5	8	1	0	0	3	.348	4	1	0	48	9	1	.983
1999—	New York (N.L.).........	1B	6	27	4	8	0	0	2	6	.296	2	3	0	59	4	2	.969
Championship series totals (4 years)			23	92	14	27	3	0	3	16	.293	11	10	0	198	17	3	.986

WORLD SERIES RECORD

NOTES: Member of World Series championship team (1992 and 1993).

Year	Team (League)	Pos.	G	AB	R	H	2B	3B	HR	RBI	Avg.	BB	SO	SB	PO	A	E	Avg.
1992—	Toronto (A.L.)............	1B	4	13	2	4	0	0	0	0	.308	0	4	0	25	3	0	1.000
1993—	Toronto (A.L.)............	1B	5	17	5	4	1	0	1	2	.235	4	1	0	36	0	0	1.000
World Series totals (2 years)			9	30	7	8	1	0	1	2	.267	4	5	0	61	3	0	1.000

ALL-STAR GAME RECORD

Year	League	Pos.	AB	R	H	2B	3B	HR	RBI	Avg.	BB	SO	SB	PO	A	E	Avg.
1993—	American	1B	2	0	0	0	0	0	0	.000	0	0	0	4	0	0	1.000

OLIVARES, OMAR   P   ATHLETICS

PERSONAL: Born July 6, 1967, in Mayaguez, Puerto Rico. ... 6-0/205. ... Throws right, bats right. ... Full name: Omar Palqu Olivares. ... Son of Ed Olivares, outfielder with St. Louis Cardinals (1960-61).

HIGH SCHOOL: Hostos (Mayaguez, Puerto Rico).

TRANSACTIONS/CAREER NOTES: Signed as non-drafted free agent by San Diego Padres organization (September 15, 1986). ... Traded by Padres to St. Louis Cardinals for OF Alex Cole and P Steve Peters (February 27, 1990). ... On St. Louis disabled list (May 27-June 13, 1992 and June 4-20, 1993). ... Granted free agency (April 7, 1995). ... Signed by Colorado Rockies (April 9, 1995). ... Claimed on waivers by Philadelphia Phillies (July 11, 1995). ... Granted free agency (October 16, 1995). ... Signed by Detroit Tigers (December 20, 1995). ... On Detroit disabled list (April 16-May 30, 1996); included rehabilitation assignment to Toledo (May 24-30). ... Traded by Tigers with P Felipe Lira to Seattle Mariners for P Scott Sanders, P Dean Crow and 3B Carlos Villalobos (July 18, 1997). ... Granted free agency (October 30, 1997). ... Signed by Anaheim Angels (December 11, 1997). ... Traded by Angels with 2B Randy Velarde to Oakland Athletics for P Elvin Nina, OF Jeff DaVanon and OF Nathan Hayes (July 29, 1999). ... Granted free agency (October 29, 1999). ... Re-signed by A's (January 8, 2000).

RECORDS: Shares major league single-season record for fewest double plays by pitcher who led league in double plays—4 (1992). ... Shares A.L. single-game record for most hit batsmen (nine innings)—4 (June 13, 1999).

STATISTICAL NOTES: Tied for Texas League lead with 10 hit batsmen in 1989.

MISCELLANEOUS: Appeared in one game as pinch runner and singled and scored in three games as pinch hitter (1992). ... Appeared in one game as pinch runner and made an out in one game as pinch hitter (1993). ... Made an out in only appearance as pinch hitter with St. Louis (1994). ... Appeared in one game as pinch runner with Colorado (1995). ... Hit two-run home run in only appearance as pinch hitter with Philadelphia (1995). ... Appeared in three games as pinch runner with Detroit (1997). ... Struck out in only appearance as pinch hitter and scored one run in two games as pinch runner (1998).

Year	League	W	L	Pct.	ERA	G	GS	CG	ShO	Sv.	IP	H	R	ER	BB	SO
1987—	Charleston, S.C. (SAL)	4	14	.222	4.60	31	24	5	0	0	170 1/3	182	107	87	57	86
1988—	Charleston, S.C. (SAL)	13	6	.684	2.23	24	24	*10	3	0	185 1/3	166	63	46	43	94
—	Riverside (Calif.)................	3	0	1.000	1.16	4	3	1	0	0	23 1/3	18	9	3	9	16
1989—	Wichita (Texas)................	12	11	.522	3.39	26	26	6	1	0	*185 2/3	175	87	70	61	79
1990—	Louisville (A.A.)■■............	10	11	.476	2.82	23	23	5	2	0	159 1/3	127	58	50	59	88
—	St. Louis (N.L.).................	1	1	.500	2.92	9	6	0	0	0	49 1/3	45	17	16	17	20
1991—	Louisville (A.A.)................	1	2	.333	3.47	6	6	0	0	0	36 1/3	39	15	14	16	27
1992—	St. Louis (N.L.).................	9	9	.500	3.84	32	30	1	0	0	197	189	84	84	63	124
1993—	St. Louis (N.L.).................	5	3	.625	4.17	58	9	0	0	1	118 2/3	134	60	55	54	63
1994—	Louisville (A.A.)................	2	1	.667	4.37	9	9	0	0	0	47 1/3	47	24	23	16	38
—	St. Louis (N.L.).................	3	4	.429	5.74	14	12	1	0	1	73 2/3	84	53	47	37	26
1995—	Colo. Springs (PCL)■	0	1	.000	5.40	3	2	0	0	0	11 2/3	14	7	7	2	6
—	Colorado (N.L.).................	1	3	.250	7.39	11	6	0	0	0	31 2/3	44	28	26	21	15
—	Philadelphia (N.L.)■	0	1	.000	5.40	5	0	0	0	0	10	11	6	6	2	7
—	Scranton/W.B. (I.L.)	0	3	.000	4.87	7	7	0	0	0	44 1/3	49	25	24	20	28
1996—	Detroit (A.L.)■	7	11	.389	4.89	25	25	4	0	0	160	169	90	87	75	81
—	Toledo (I.L.).....................	1	0	1.000	8.44	1	1	0	0	0	5 1/3	4	5	5	3	5
1997—	Detroit (A.L.)	5	6	.455	4.70	19	19	3	2	0	115	110	68	60	53	74
—	Seattle (A.L.)■	1	4	.200	5.49	13	12	0	0	0	62 1/3	81	41	38	28	29

Year	League	W	L	Pct.	ERA	G	GS	CG	ShO	Sv.	IP	H	R	ER	BB	SO
1998— Anaheim (A.L.)■		9	9	.500	4.03	37	26	1	0	0	183	189	92	82	91	112
1999— Anaheim (A.L.)		8	9	.471	4.05	20	20	3	0	0	131	135	62	59	49	49
— Oakland (A.L.)■		7	2	.778	4.34	12	12	1	0	0	74²/₃	82	43	36	32	36
A.L. totals (4 years)		37	41	.474	4.49	126	114	12	2	0	726	766	396	362	328	381
N.L. totals (5 years)		19	21	.475	4.38	129	63	2	0	2	480¹/₃	507	248	234	194	255
Major League totals (9 years)		56	62	.475	4.45	255	177	14	2	2	1206¹/₃	1273	644	596	522	636

OLIVER, DARREN   P   RANGERS

PERSONAL: Born October 6, 1970, in Kansas City, Mo. ... 6-2/210. ... Throws left, bats right. ... Full name: Darren Christopher Oliver. ... Son of Bob Oliver, first baseman/outfielder with five major league teams (1965 and 1969-75).

HIGH SCHOOL: Rio Linda (Calif.) Senior.

TRANSACTIONS/CAREER NOTES: Selected by Texas Rangers organization in third round of free-agent draft (June 1, 1988). ... On Gulf Coast Rangers disabled list (April 6-August 9, 1990). ... On disabled list (May 1, 1991-remainder of season). ... On Tulsa disabled list (July 1, 1992-remainder of season). ... On disabled list (June 27, 1995-remainder of season). ... On Texas disabled list (June 11-26, 1998); included rehabilitation assignment to Oklahoma City (June 21-26). ... Traded by Rangers with 3B Fernando Tatis and a player to be named later to St. Louis Cardinals for P Todd Stottlemyre and SS Royce Clayton (July 31, 1998); Cardinals acquired OF Mark Little to complete deal (August 9, 1998). ... Granted free agency (October 28, 1999). ... Signed by Rangers (January 12, 2000).

MISCELLANEOUS: Made an out in only appearance as pinch hitter with St. Louis (1998). ... Had one sacrifice hit and struck out once in five appearances as pinch hitter (1999).

Year	League	W	L	Pct.	ERA	G	GS	CG	ShO	Sv.	IP	H	R	ER	BB	SO
1988— Gulf Coast Rangers (GCL)		5	1	.833	2.15	12	9	0	0	0	54¹/₃	39	16	13	18	59
1989— Gastonia (SAL)		8	7	.533	3.16	24	23	2	1	0	122¹/₃	86	54	43	82	108
1990— Gulf Coast Rangers (GCL)		0	0	...	0.00	3	3	0	0	0	6	1	1	0	1	7
— Gastonia (SAL)		0	0	...	13.50	1	1	0	0	0	2	1	3	3	4	2
1991— Charlotte (FSL)		0	1	.000	4.50	2	2	0	0	0	8	6	4	4	3	12
1992— Charlotte (FSL)		1	0	1.000	0.72	8	2	1	1	2	25	11	2	2	10	33
— Tulsa (Texas)		0	1	.000	3.14	3	3	0	0	0	14¹/₃	15	9	5	4	14
1993— Tulsa (Texas)		7	5	.583	1.96	46	0	0	0	6	73¹/₃	51	18	16	41	77
— Texas (A.L.)		0	0	...	2.70	2	0	0	0	0	3¹/₃	2	1	1	1	4
1994— Texas (A.L.)		4	0	1.000	3.42	43	0	0	0	2	50	40	24	19	35	50
— Oklahoma City (A.A.)		0	0	...	0.00	6	0	0	0	1	7¹/₃	1	0	0	3	6
1995— Texas (A.L.)		4	2	.667	4.22	17	7	0	0	0	49	47	25	23	32	39
1996— Charlotte (FSL)		0	1	.000	3.00	2	1	0	0	0	12	8	4	4	3	9
— Texas (A.L.)		14	6	.700	4.66	30	30	1	1	0	173²/₃	190	97	90	76	112
1997— Texas (A.L.)		13	12	.520	4.20	32	32	3	1	0	201¹/₃	213	111	94	82	104
1998— Texas (A.L.)		6	7	.462	6.53	19	19	2	0	0	103¹/₃	140	84	75	43	58
— Oklahoma (PCL)		0	0	...	0.00	1	1	0	0	0	5	2	0	0	1	1
— St. Louis (N.L.)■		4	4	.500	4.26	10	10	0	0	0	57	64	31	27	23	29
1999— St. Louis (N.L.)		9	9	.500	4.26	30	30	2	1	0	196¹/₃	197	96	93	74	119
A.L. totals (6 years)		41	27	.603	4.68	143	88	6	2	2	580²/₃	632	342	302	269	367
N.L. totals (2 years)		13	13	.500	4.26	40	40	2	1	0	253¹/₃	261	127	120	97	148
Major League totals (7 years)		54	40	.574	4.55	183	128	8	3	2	834	893	469	422	366	515

DIVISION SERIES RECORD

Year	League	W	L	Pct.	ERA	G	GS	CG	ShO	Sv.	IP	H	R	ER	BB	SO
1996— Texas (A.L.)		0	1	.000	3.38	1	1	0	0	0	8	6	3	3	2	3

OLIVER, JOE   C   MARINERS

PERSONAL: Born July 24, 1965, in Memphis. ... 6-3/220. ... Bats right, throws right. ... Full name: Joseph Melton Oliver.

HIGH SCHOOL: Boone (Orlando).

TRANSACTIONS/CAREER NOTES: Selected by Cincinnati Reds organization in second round of free-agent draft (June 6, 1983); pick received as compensation for New York Yankees signing Type A free-agent P Bob Shirley. ... On disabled list (April 23-May 6, 1986 and April 12, 1994-remainder of season). ... Released by Reds (November 3, 1994). ... Signed by New Orleans, Milwaukee Brewers organization (March 24, 1995). ... On Milwaukee disabled list (July 14-August 15, 1995); included rehabilitation assignment to New Orleans (August 10-15). ... Granted free agency (October 31, 1995). ... Signed by Reds (February 26, 1996). ... Granted free agency (November 18, 1996). ... Re-signed by Reds organization (February 8, 1997). ... Granted free agency (October 30, 1997). ... Signed by Detroit Tigers organization (December 22, 1997). ... Released by Tigers (July 16, 1998). ... Signed by Seattle Mariners (July 24, 1998). ... Granted free agency (October 27, 1998). ... Signed by Tampa Bay Devil Rays organization (February 3, 1999). ... On Durham disabled list (June 13-24, 1999). ... Traded by Devil Rays with C Humberto Cota to Pittsburgh Pirates for OF Jose Guillen and P Jeff Sparks (July 23, 1999). ... Granted free agency (November 5, 1999). ... Signed by Mariners organization (January 19, 2000).

STATISTICAL NOTES: Led Pioneer League catchers with .989 fielding percentage, 425 putouts, 38 assists and 468 total chances in 1983. ... Led Midwest League catchers with 855 total chances and 30 passed balls in 1984. ... Led Florida State League catchers with 84 assists and 33 passed balls in 1985. ... Led American Association catchers with 13 errors in 1989. ... Tied for N.L. lead with 16 passed balls in 1990. ... Led N.L. catchers with 925 putouts and 997 total chances in 1992. ... Career major league grand slams: 4.

Year	Team (League)	Pos.	G	AB	R	H	2B	3B	HR	RBI	Avg.	BB	SO	SB	PO	A	E	Avg.
1983— Billings (Pio.)		C-1B	56	186	21	40	4	0	4	28	.215	15	47	1	†426	†39	5	†.989
1984— Cedar Rapids (Midw.)		C	102	335	34	73	11	0	3	29	.218	17	83	2	*757	85	13	.985
1985— Tampa (FSL)		C-1B	112	386	38	104	23	2	7	62	.269	32	75	1	615	†94	16	.978
1986— Vermont (East.)		C	84	282	32	78	18	1	6	41	.277	21	47	2	383	62	14	.969
1987— Vermont (East.)		C-1B	66	236	31	72	13	2	10	60	.305	17	30	0	247	35	10	.966
1988— Nashville (A.A.)		C	73	220	19	45	7	2	4	24	.205	18	39	0	413	37	7	.985
— Chattanooga (Sou.)		C	28	105	9	26	6	0	3	12	.248	5	19	0	176	15	0	1.000
1989— Nashville (A.A.)		C-1B	71	233	22	68	13	0	6	31	.292	13	35	0	388	37	†13	.970
— Cincinnati (N.L.)		C	49	151	13	41	8	0	3	23	.272	6	28	0	260	21	4	.986
1990— Cincinnati (N.L.)		C	121	364	34	84	23	0	8	52	.231	37	75	1	686	59	6	*.992
1991— Cincinnati (N.L.)		C	94	269	21	58	11	0	11	41	.216	18	53	0	496	40	11	.980
1992— Cincinnati (N.L.)		C-1B	143	485	42	131	25	1	10	57	.270	35	75	2	†926	64	8	.992
1993— Cincinnati (N.L.)		C-1B-OF	139	482	40	115	28	0	14	75	.239	27	91	0	825	70	7	.992
1994— Cincinnati (N.L.)		C	6	19	1	4	0	0	1	5	.211	2	3	0	48	2	1	.980
1995— Milwaukee (A.L.)■		C-DH-1B	97	337	43	92	20	0	12	51	.273	27	66	2	414	40	8	.983
— New Orleans (A.A.)		C-DH	4	13	0	1	1	0	0	0	.077	0	3	0	14	7	0	1.000

Year	Team (League)	Pos.	G	AB	R	H	2B	3B	HR	RBI	Avg.	BB	SO	SB	PO	A	E	Avg.
								BATTING								FIELDING		
1996—	Cincinnati (N.L.)■.....	C-1B-OF	106	289	31	70	12	1	11	46	.242	28	54	2	583	45	5	.992
1997—	Indianapolis (A.A.).......	C	2	9	1	3	0	0	1	1	.333	0	1	0	21	4	0	1.000
	— Cincinnati (N.L.).......	C-1B	111	349	28	90	13	0	14	43	.258	25	58	1	681	55	7	.991
1998—	Detroit (A.L.)■.....	C-1B-DH	50	155	8	35	8	0	4	22	.226	7	33	0	261	17	5	.982
	— Seattle (A.L.)■.....	C	29	85	12	19	3	0	2	10	.224	10	15	1	174	9	3	.984
1999—	Durham (I.L.)■.....	C-DH-3B	57	219	27	66	18	1	7	43	.301	7	50	1	399	27	7	.984
	— Pittsburgh (N.L.)■.....	C	45	134	10	27	8	0	1	13	.201	10	33	2	285	12	2	.993
American League totals (2 years)			176	577	63	146	31	0	18	83	.253	44	114	3	849	66	16	.983
National League totals (9 years)			814	2542	220	620	128	2	73	355	.244	188	470	8	4790	368	51	.990
Major League totals (11 years)			990	3119	283	766	159	2	91	438	.246	232	584	11	5639	434	67	.989

CHAMPIONSHIP SERIES RECORD

Year	Team (League)	Pos.	G	AB	R	H	2B	3B	HR	RBI	Avg.	BB	SO	SB	PO	A	E	Avg.
								BATTING								FIELDING		
1990—	Cincinnati (N.L.)	C	5	14	1	2	0	0	0	0	.143	0	2	0	27	1	0	1.000

WORLD SERIES RECORD

NOTES: Member of World Series championship team (1990).

Year	Team (League)	Pos.	G	AB	R	H	2B	3B	HR	RBI	Avg.	BB	SO	SB	PO	A	E	Avg.
								BATTING								FIELDING		
1990—	Cincinnati (N.L.)	C	4	18	2	6	3	0	0	2	.333	0	1	0	27	1	3	.903

OLSON, GREGG   P   DODGERS

PERSONAL: Born October 11, 1966, in Omaha, Neb. ... 6-4/210. ... Throws right, bats right. ... Full name: Gregg William Olson.

HIGH SCHOOL: Northwest (Omaha, Neb.).

COLLEGE: Auburn.

TRANSACTIONS/CAREER NOTES: Selected by Baltimore Orioles organization in first round (fourth pick overall) of free-agent draft (June 1, 1988). ... On disabled list (August 9-September 20, 1993). ... Granted free agency (December 20, 1993). ... Signed by Atlanta Braves (February 8, 1994). ... On Atlanta disabled list (March 26-May 30, 1994); included rehabilitation assignment to Richmond (May 14-30). ... Granted free agency (December 23, 1994). ... Signed by Cleveland Indians organization (March 24, 1995). ... On Buffalo disabled list (April 6-14, 1995). ... Contract sold by Buffalo to Kansas City Royals (July 24, 1995). ... Granted free agency (November 1, 1995). ... Signed by St. Louis Cardinals organization (January 23, 1996). ... Released by Cardinals organization (March 26, 1996). ... Signed by Cincinnati Reds organization (March 26, 1996). ... Traded by Reds to Detroit Tigers for IF Yuri Sanchez (April 26, 1996). ... Traded by Tigers to Houston Astros for two players to be named later (August 27, 1996); Tigers acquired P Kevin Gallaher and IF Pedro Santana to complete deal (August 27, 1996). ... Granted free agency (October 28, 1996). ... Signed by Minnesota Twins organization (December 20, 1996). ... Released by Twins (May 16, 1997). ... Signed by Royals organization (May 25, 1997). ... Granted free agency (October 28, 1997). ... Signed by Arizona Diamondbacks organization (January 31, 1998). ... On disabled list (June 23-July 8, 1999). ... Granted free agency (October 28, 1999). ... Signed by Los Angeles Dodgers (January 5, 2000).

HONORS: Named righthanded pitcher on THE SPORTING NEWS college All-America team (1988). ... Named A.L. Rookie of the Year by Baseball Writers' Association of America (1989).

STATISTICAL NOTES: Pitched one inning, combining with starter Bob Milacki (six innings), Mike Flanagan (one inning) and Mark Williamson (one inning) in 2-0 no-hit victory against Oakland (July 13, 1991).

MISCELLANEOUS: Holds Baltimore Orioles all-time record for most saves (160). ... Holds Arizona Diamondbacks all-time records for most games pitched (125) and most saves (44). ... Struck out in only plate appearance (1993).

Year	League	W	L	Pct.	ERA	G	GS	CG	ShO	Sv.	IP	H	R	ER	BB	SO
1988—	Hagerstown (Caro.)	1	0	1.000	2.00	8	0	0	0	4	9	5	2	2	2	9
	— Charlotte (Sou.)	0	1	.000	5.87	8	0	0	0	1	15 1/3	24	13	10	6	22
	— Baltimore (A.L.)	1	1	.500	3.27	10	0	0	0	0	11	10	4	4	10	9
1989—	Baltimore (A.L.)	5	2	.714	1.69	64	0	0	0	27	85	57	17	16	46	90
1990—	Baltimore (A.L.)	6	5	.545	2.42	64	0	0	0	37	74 1/3	57	20	20	31	74
1991—	Baltimore (A.L.)	4	6	.400	3.18	72	0	0	0	31	73 2/3	74	28	26	29	72
1992—	Baltimore (A.L.)	1	5	.167	2.05	60	0	0	0	36	61 1/3	46	14	14	24	58
1993—	Baltimore (A.L.)	0	2	.000	1.60	50	0	0	0	29	45	37	9	8	18	44
1994—	Richmond (I.L.)■	0	0	...	1.59	8	2	0	0	2	11 1/3	8	3	2	8	13
	— Atlanta (N.L.)	0	2	.000	9.20	16	0	0	0	1	14 2/3	19	15	15	13	10
1995—	Buffalo (A.A.)■	1	0	1.000	2.49	18	0	0	0	13	21 2/3	16	6	6	9	25
	— Cleveland (A.L.)	0	0	...	13.50	3	0	0	0	0	2 2/3	5	4	4	2	0
	— Omaha (A.A.)■	0	0	...	0.00	1	0	0	0	0	1	0	0	0	1	1
	— Kansas City (A.L.)	3	3	.500	3.26	20	0	0	0	0	30 1/3	23	11	11	17	21
1996—	Indianapolis (A.A.)■	0	0	...	4.26	7	0	0	0	4	6 1/3	6	4	3	6	4
	— Detroit (A.L.)■	3	0	1.000	5.02	43	0	0	0	8	43	43	25	24	28	29
	— Houston (N.L.)■	1	0	1.000	4.82	9	0	0	0	0	9 1/3	12	5	5	7	8
1997—	Minnesota (A.L.)■	0	0	...	18.36	11	0	0	0	0	8 1/3	19	17	17	11	6
	— Omaha (A.A.)■	3	1	.750	3.31	9	5	0	0	0	35 1/3	30	13	13	10	20
	— Kansas City (A.L.)	4	3	.571	3.02	34	0	0	0	1	41 2/3	39	18	14	17	28
1998—	Arizona (N.L.)	3	4	.429	3.01	64	0	0	0	30	68 2/3	56	25	23	25	55
1999—	Arizona (N.L.)	9	4	.692	3.71	61	0	0	0	14	60 2/3	54	28	25	25	45
A.L. totals (9 years)		27	27	.500	2.99	431	0	0	0	172	476 1/3	410	167	158	233	431
N.L. totals (4 years)		13	10	.565	3.99	150	0	0	0	45	153 1/3	141	73	68	70	118
Major League totals (12 years)		40	37	.519	3.23	581	0	0	0	217	629 2/3	551	240	226	303	549

DIVISION SERIES RECORD

Year	League	W	L	Pct.	ERA	G	GS	CG	ShO	Sv.	IP	H	R	ER	BB	SO
1999—	Arizona (N.L.)	0	0	...	0.00	0	0	0	0	0	1/3	0	1	0	1	0

ALL-STAR GAME RECORD

Year	League	W	L	Pct.	ERA	GS	CG	ShO	Sv.	IP	H	R	ER	BB	SO
1990—	American							Did not play.							

0

PERSONAL: Born February 25, 1963, in Columbus, Ohio. ... 6-4/215. ... Bats left, throws left. ... Full name: Paul Andrew O'Neill. ... Son of Charles O'Neill, minor league pitcher (1945-48).

HIGH SCHOOL: Brookhaven (Columbus, Ohio).

COLLEGE: Otterbein College (Ohio).

TRANSACTIONS/CAREER NOTES: Selected by Cincinnati Reds organization in fourth round of free-agent draft (June 8, 1981). ... On Denver disabled list (May 10-July 16, 1986). ... On Cincinnati disabled list (July 21-September 1, 1989); included rehabilitation assignment to Nashville (August 27-September 1). ... Traded by Reds with 1B Joe DeBerry to New York Yankees for OF Roberto Kelly (November 3, 1992). ... On disabled list (May 7-23, 1995). ... On suspended list (September 6-8, 1996).

STATISTICAL NOTES: Led American Association outfielders with 19 assists and eight double plays in 1985. ... Hit three home runs in one game (August 31, 1995). ... Had 17-game hitting streak (May 24-June 10, 1998). ... Tied for A.L. lead in grounding into double plays with 22 in 1998. ... Led A.L. outfielders with six double plays in 1998. ... Career major league grand slams: 4.

Year	Team (League)	Pos.	G	AB	R	H	2B	3B	HR	RBI	Avg.	BB	SO	SB	PO	A	E	Avg.
1981—	Billings (Pio.)	OF	66	241	37	76	7	2	3	29	.315	21	35	6	87	4	5	.948
1982—	Cedar Rap. (Midw.)	OF	116	386	50	105	19	2	8	71	.272	21	79	12	137	7	8	.947
1983—	Tampa (FSL)	OF-1B	121	413	62	115	23	7	8	51	.278	56	70	20	218	14	10	.959
—	Waterbury (East.)	OF	14	43	6	12	0	0	0	6	.279	6	8	2	26	0	0	1.000
1984—	Vermont (East.)	OF	134	475	70	126	31	5	16	76	.265	52	72	29	246	5	7	.973
1985—	Denver (A.A.)	OF-1B	*137	*509	63	*155	*32	3	7	74	.305	28	73	5	248	†20	7	.975
—	Cincinnati (N.L.)	OF	5	12	1	4	1	0	0	1	.333	0	2	0	3	1	0	1.000
1986—	Cincinnati (N.L.)	PH	3	2	0	0	0	0	0	0	.000	1	1	0	...	...	...	...
—	Denver (A.A.)	OF	55	193	20	49	9	2	5	27	.254	9	28	1	98	7	4	.963
1987—	Cincinnati (N.L.)	OF-1B-P	84	160	24	41	14	1	7	28	.256	18	29	2	90	2	4	.958
—	Nashville (A.A.)	OF	11	37	12	11	0	0	3	6	.297	5	5	1	19	1	0	1.000
1988—	Cincinnati (N.L.)	OF-1B	145	485	58	122	25	3	16	73	.252	38	65	8	410	13	6	.986
1989—	Cincinnati (N.L.)	OF	117	428	49	118	24	2	15	74	.276	46	64	20	223	7	4	.983
—	Nashville (A.A.)	OF	4	12	1	4	0	0	0	0	.333	3	1	1	7	1	0	1.000
1990—	Cincinnati (N.L.)	OF	145	503	59	136	28	0	16	78	.270	53	103	13	271	12	2	.993
1991—	Cincinnati (N.L.)	OF	152	532	71	136	36	0	28	91	.256	73	107	12	301	13	2	.994
1992—	Cincinnati (N.L.)	OF	148	496	59	122	19	1	14	66	.246	77	85	6	291	12	1	*.997
1993—	New York (A.L.)■	OF-DH	141	498	71	155	34	1	20	75	.311	44	69	2	230	7	2	.992
1994—	New York (A.L.)	OF-DH	103	368	68	132	25	1	21	83	*.359	72	56	5	203	7	1	.995
1995—	New York (A.L.)	OF-DH	127	460	82	138	30	4	22	96	.300	71	76	1	220	3	3	.987
1996—	New York (A.L.)	OF-DH-1B	150	546	89	165	35	1	19	91	.302	102	76	0	293	7	0	•1.000
1997—	New York (A.L.)	OF-DH-1B	149	553	89	179	42	0	21	117	.324	75	92	10	293	7	5	.984
1998—	New York (A.L.)	OF-DH	152	602	95	191	40	2	24	116	.317	57	103	15	293	11	4	.987
1999—	New York (A.L.)	OF	153	597	70	170	39	4	19	110	.285	66	89	11	291	10	8	.974
American League totals (7 years)			975	3624	564	1130	245	13	146	688	.312	487	561	44	1823	52	23	.988
National League totals (8 years)			799	2618	321	679	147	7	96	411	.259	306	456	61	1589	60	19	.989
Major League totals (15 years)			1774	6242	885	1809	392	20	242	1099	.290	793	1017	105	3412	112	42	.988

DIVISION SERIES RECORD

RECORDS: Shares career record for most extra-base hits—10; and total bases—44.

Year	Team (League)	Pos.	G	AB	R	H	2B	3B	HR	RBI	Avg.	BB	SO	SB	PO	A	E	Avg.
1995—	New York (A.L.)	OF-PH	5	18	5	6	0	0	3	6	.333	5	5	0	13	0	0	1.000
1996—	New York (A.L.)	OF	4	15	0	2	0	0	0	0	.133	0	2	0	13	0	0	1.000
1997—	New York (A.L.)	OF	5	19	5	8	2	0	2	7	.421	3	0	0	9	0	0	1.000
1998—	New York (A.L.)	OF	3	11	1	4	2	0	1	1	.364	1	1	0	2	0	0	1.000
1999—	New York (A.L.)	OF	2	8	2	2	0	0	0	0	.250	1	1	0	4	0	0	1.000
Division series totals (5 years)			19	71	13	22	4	0	6	14	.310	10	9	0	41	0	0	1.000

CHAMPIONSHIP SERIES RECORD

Year	Team (League)	Pos.	G	AB	R	H	2B	3B	HR	RBI	Avg.	BB	SO	SB	PO	A	E	Avg.
1990—	Cincinnati (N.L.)	OF	5	17	1	8	3	0	1	4	.471	1	1	1	9	2	0	1.000
1996—	New York (A.L.)	OF	4	11	1	3	0	0	1	2	.273	3	2	0	9	1	0	1.000
1998—	New York (A.L.)	OF	6	26	6	7	2	0	1	3	.280	3	4	2	10	0	0	1.000
1999—	New York (A.L.)	OF	5	21	2	6	0	0	1	1	.286	1	5	0	18	0	0	1.000
Championship series totals (4 years)			20	74	10	24	5	0	3	10	.324	8	12	3	46	3	0	1.000

WORLD SERIES RECORD

NOTES: Member of World Series championship team (1990, 1996, 1998 and 1999).

Year	Team (League)	Pos.	G	AB	R	H	2B	3B	HR	RBI	Avg.	BB	SO	SB	PO	A	E	Avg.
1990—	Cincinnati (N.L.)	OF	4	12	2	1	0	0	0	1	.083	5	2	1	11	0	0	1.000
1996—	New York (A.L.)	OF-PH	5	12	1	2	2	0	0	0	.167	3	2	0	12	0	0	1.000
1998—	New York (A.L.)	OF	4	19	3	4	1	0	0	0	.211	1	2	0	8	0	1	.889
1999—	New York (A.L.)	OF	4	15	0	3	0	0	0	4	.200	2	2	0	8	0	0	1.000
World Series totals (4 years)			17	58	6	10	3	0	0	5	.172	11	8	1	39	0	1	.975

ALL-STAR GAME RECORD

Year	League	Pos.	AB	R	H	2B	3B	HR	RBI	Avg.	BB	SO	SB	PO	A	E	Avg.
1991—	National	OF	2	0	0	0	0	0	0	.000	0	1	0	0	0	0	...
1994—	American	PH	1	0	0	0	0	0	0	.000	0	0	0	...	...	...	...
1995—	American	OF	1	0	0	0	0	0	0	.000	0	0	0	0	0	0	...
1997—	American	OF	2	0	0	0	0	0	0	.000	0	1	0	1	0	0	1.000
1998—	American	OF	2	0	0	0	0	0	0	.000	0	0	0	0	1	0	1.000
All-Star Game totals (5 years)			8	0	0	0	0	0	0	.000	0	2	0	1	1	0	1.000

RECORD AS PITCHER

Year League	W	L	Pct.	ERA	G	GS	CG	ShO	Sv.	IP	H	R	ER	BB	SO
1987— Cincinnati (N.L.)	0	0	...	13.50	1	0	0	0	0	2	2	3	3	4	2
Major League totals (1 year)	0	0	...	13.50	1	0	0	0	0	2	2	3	3	4	2

OQUIST, MIKE   P   TIGERS

PERSONAL: Born May 30, 1968, in La Junta, Colo. ... 6-2/189. ... Throws right, bats right. ... Full name: Michael Lee Oquist. ... Name pronounced OH-kwist.
HIGH SCHOOL: La Junta (Colo.).
COLLEGE: Arkansas.
TRANSACTIONS/CAREER NOTES: Selected by Baltimore Orioles organization in 13th round of free-agent draft (June 5, 1989). ... Granted free agency (October 16, 1995). ... Signed by Las Vegas, San Diego Padres organization (December 21, 1995). ... On Las Vegas disabled list (April 4-11, 1996). ... Granted free agency (October 15, 1996). ... Signed by Oakland Athletics organization (November 19, 1996). ... On Oakland disabled list (July 14-August 20, 1997); included rehabilitation assignment to Modesto (August 12-20). ... Granted free agency (December 21, 1998). ... Re-signed by A's organization (January 8, 1999). ... Granted free agency (October 12, 1999). ... Signed by Detroit Tigers organization (November 29, 1999).
MISCELLANEOUS: Appeared in two games as pinch runner with Oakland (1997).

Year League	W	L	Pct.	ERA	G	GS	CG	ShO	Sv.	IP	H	R	ER	BB	SO
1989— Erie (NY-P)	7	4	.636	3.59	15	15	1	1	0	97 2/3	86	43	39	25	109
1990— Frederick (Caro.)	9	8	.529	2.81	25	25	3	1	0	166 1/3	134	64	52	48	*170
1991— Hagerstown (East.)	10	9	.526	4.06	27	26	1	0	0	166 1/3	168	82	75	62	136
1992— Rochester (I.L.)	10	12	.455	4.11	26	24	5	0	0	153 1/3	164	80	70	45	111
1993— Rochester (I.L.)	9	8	.529	3.50	28	21	2	1	0	149 1/3	144	62	58	41	128
— Baltimore (A.L.)	0	0	...	3.86	5	0	0	0	0	11 2/3	12	5	5	4	8
1994— Rochester (I.L.)	3	2	.600	3.73	13	8	0	0	3	50 2/3	54	23	21	15	36
— Baltimore (A.L.)	3	3	.500	6.17	15	9	0	0	0	58 1/3	75	41	40	30	39
1995— Baltimore (A.L.)	2	1	.667	4.17	27	0	0	0	0	54	51	27	25	41	27
— Rochester (I.L.)	0	0	...	5.25	7	0	0	0	0	12	17	8	7	5	11
1996— Las Vegas (PCL)■	9	4	.692	2.89	27	20	2	0	1	140 1/3	136	55	45	44	110
— San Diego (N.L.)	0	0	...	2.35	8	0	0	0	0	7 2/3	6	2	2	4	4
1997— Edmonton (PCL)■	6	1	.857	3.25	9	9	1	0	0	52 2/3	57	23	19	16	37
— Oakland (A.L.)	4	6	.400	5.02	19	17	1	0	0	107 2/3	111	62	60	43	72
— Modesto (Calif.)	0	0	...	4.91	2	2	0	0	0	3 2/3	5	2	2	1	5
1998— Oakland (A.L.)	7	11	.389	6.22	31	29	0	0	0	175	210	125	121	57	112
1999— Vancouver (PCL)	1	0	1.000	0.00	1	1	0	0	0	6	2	0	0	1	2
— Oakland (A.L.)	9	10	.474	5.37	28	24	0	0	0	140 2/3	158	86	84	64	89
A.L. totals (6 years)	25	31	.446	5.51	125	79	1	0	0	547 1/3	617	346	335	239	347
N.L. totals (1 year)	0	0	...	2.35	8	0	0	0	0	7 2/3	6	2	2	4	4
Major League totals (7 years)	25	31	.446	5.46	133	79	1	0	0	555	623	348	337	243	351

ORDAZ, LUIS   SS   DIAMONDBACKS

PERSONAL: Born August 12, 1975, in Maracaibo, Venezuela. ... 5-11/170. ... Bats right, throws right. ... Full name: Luis Javier Ordaz.
HIGH SCHOOL: Santa Maria Gorette (Maracaibo, Venezuela).
TRANSACTIONS/CAREER NOTES: Signed as non-drafted free agent by Cincinnati Reds organization (January 27, 1993). ... Traded by Reds to St. Louis Cardinals as part of three-team deal in which Reds sent P Mike Remlinger to Kansas City Royals, Cardinals sent OF Andre King to Reds and Royals sent OF Miguel Mejia to Cardinals (December 4, 1995). ... On Memphis disabled list (April 7-16, 1998). ... Traded by Cardinals to Arizona Diamondbacks for OF Dante Powell (December 15, 1999).
STATISTICAL NOTES: Led Appalachian League shortstops with 277 total chances and 24 errors and tied for lead with 173 assists in 1994. ... Led Texas League in grounding into double plays with 19 in 1997.

							BATTING							FIELDING		
Year Team (League)	Pos.	G	AB	R	H	2B	3B	HR	RBI	Avg.	BB	SO	SB	PO	A	E	Avg.
1993— Princeton (Appl.)	3B-SS-2B	57	217	28	65	9	7	2	39	.300	7	32	3	58	117	13	.931
1994— Char., W.Va. (SAL)	SS	9	31	3	7	0	0	0	0	.226	1	4	1	16	18	7	.829
— Princeton (Appl.)	SS-2B	60	211	33	52	12	3	0	12	.246	10	27	7	81	‡173	†24	.914
1995— Char., W.Va. (SAL)	SS	112	359	43	83	14	7	2	42	.231	13	47	12	164	290	22	.954
1996— St. Pete. (FSL)■	SS	126	423	46	115	13	3	3	49	.272	30	53	10	228	317	21	.963
1997— Arkansas (Texas)	SS-DH	115	390	44	112	20	6	4	58	.287	22	39	11	149	327	33	.935
— St. Louis (N.L.)	SS	12	22	3	6	1	0	0	1	.273	1	2	3	9	17	1	.963
1998— Memphis (PCL)	SS-2B	59	214	29	62	9	2	6	35	.290	16	20	3	104	174	14	.952
— St. Louis (N.L.)	SS-3B-2B	57	153	9	31	5	0	0	8	.203	12	18	2	70	157	13	.946
1999— St. Louis (N.L.)	SS-2B-3B	10	9	3	1	0	0	0	2	.111	1	2	1	4	8	3	.800
— Memphis (PCL)	SS	107	362	31	103	25	4	1	45	.285	24	40	3	150	346	23	.956
Major League totals (3 years)		79	184	15	38	6	0	0	11	.207	14	22	6	83	182	17	.940

ORDONEZ, MAGGLIO   OF   WHITE SOX

PERSONAL: Born January 28, 1974, in Caracas, Venezuela. ... 6-0/200. ... Bats right, throws right.
TRANSACTIONS/CAREER NOTES: Signed as non-drafted free agent by Chicago White Sox organization (May 18, 1991).
HONORS: Named American Association Most Valuable Player (1997).
STATISTICAL NOTES: Led American Association with nine sacrifice flies and tied for league lead with 249 total bases in 1997. ... Career major league grand slams: 2.

							BATTING							FIELDING		
Year Team (League)	Pos.	G	AB	R	H	2B	3B	HR	RBI	Avg.	BB	SO	SB	PO	A	E	Avg.
1992— GC White Sox (GCL)	OF	38	111	17	20	10	2	1	14	.180	13	26	6	26	2	0	1.000
1993— Hickory (SAL)	OF	84	273	32	59	14	4	3	20	.216	26	66	5	131	10	6	.959

O

Year	Team (League)	Pos.	G	AB	R	H	2B	3B	HR	RBI	Avg.	BB	SO	SB	PO	A	E	Avg.
											BATTING					FIELDING		
1994—	Hickory (SAL)	OF	132	490	86	144	24	5	11	69	.294	45	57	16	275	16	6	.980
1995—	Prince Will. (Caro.)	OF	131	487	61	116	24	2	12	65	.238	41	71	11	256	5	6	.978
1996—	Birmingham (Sou.)	OF	130	479	66	126	41	0	18	67	.263	39	74	9	231	12	6	.976
1997—	Nashville (A.A.)	OF-DH	135	523	65	*172	29	3	14	90	*.329	32	61	14	278	8	5	.983
—Chicago (A.L.)		OF	21	69	12	22	6	0	4	11	.319	2	8	1	43	1	0	1.000
1998—	Chicago (A.L.)	OF	145	535	70	151	25	2	14	65	.282	28	53	9	323	10	5	.985
1999—	Chicago (A.L.)	OF-DH	157	624	100	188	34	3	30	117	.301	47	64	13	331	12	3	.991
Major League totals (3 years)			323	1228	182	361	65	5	48	193	.294	77	125	23	697	23	8	.989

ALL-STAR GAME RECORD

Year	League	Pos.	AB	R	H	2B	3B	HR	RBI	Avg.	BB	SO	SB	PO	A	E	Avg.
							BATTING								FIELDING		
1999—	American	OF	1	0	0	0	0	0	0	.000	0	0	0	0	0	0	...

ORDONEZ, REY — SS — METS

PERSONAL: Born November 11, 1972, in Havana, Cuba. ... 5-9/159. ... Bats right, throws right. ... Full name: Reynaldo Ordonez.
HIGH SCHOOL: Espa (Havana, Cuba).
COLLEGE: Fajardo College (Havana, Cuba).
TRANSACTIONS/CAREER NOTES: Played with St. Paul Saints of Northern League (1993). ... Acquired by New York Mets organization in lottery of Cuban defectors (October 29, 1993). ... Signed by Mets organization (February 8, 1994). ... On disabled list (June 2-July 11, 1997).
RECORDS: Holds major league career record for most consecutive errorless games by shortstop—100 (June 14-October 4, 1999). ... Holds N.L. career record for most consecutive chances accepted without an error by shortstop—412 (June 13-October 4, 1999). ... Holds N.L. single-season records for highest fielding average by shortstop (150 or more games)—.994 (1999); fewest errors by shortstop (150 or more games)—4 (1999); most consecutive errorless games by shortstop—100 (June 14-October 4, 1999); and most consecutive chances accepted without an error by shortstop—412 (June 13-October 4, 1999).
HONORS: Won N.L. Gold Glove at shortstop (1997-99).
STATISTICAL NOTES: Led International League shortstops in total chances with 645 in 1995. ... Led N.L. shortstops with 705 total chances and 102 double plays in 1996. ... Career major league grand slams: 1.

Year	Team (League)	Pos.	G	AB	R	H	2B	3B	HR	RBI	Avg.	BB	SO	SB	PO	A	E	Avg.
								BATTING								FIELDING		
1993—	St. Paul (Nor.)	SS-2B	15	60	10	17	4	0	0	7	.283	3	9	3	18	48	2	.971
1994—	St. Lucie (FSL)■	SS	79	314	47	97	21	2	2	40	.309	14	28	11	141	291	15	.966
—Binghamton (East.)		SS	48	191	22	50	10	2	1	20	.262	4	18	4	57	139	8	.961
1995—	Norfolk (I.L.)	SS	125	439	49	94	21	4	2	50	.214	27	50	11	188	*436	21	.967
1996—	New York (N.L.)	SS	151	502	51	129	12	4	1	30	.257	22	53	1	228	450	27	.962
1997—	New York (N.L.)	SS	120	356	35	77	5	3	1	33	.216	18	36	11	171	355	9	*.983
1998—	New York (N.L.)	SS	153	505	46	124	20	2	1	42	.246	23	60	3	265	401	17	.975
1999—	New York (N.L.)	SS	154	520	49	134	24	2	1	60	.258	49	59	8	220	416	4	*.994
Major League totals (4 years)			578	1883	181	464	61	11	4	165	.246	112	208	23	884	1622	57	.978

DIVISION SERIES RECORD

Year	Team (League)	Pos.	G	AB	R	H	2B	3B	HR	RBI	Avg.	BB	SO	SB	PO	A	E	Avg.
							BATTING								FIELDING		
1999—	New York (N.L.)	SS	4	14	1	4	1	0	0	2	.286	0	5	1	7	9	0	1.000

CHAMPIONSHIP SERIES RECORD

Year	Team (League)	Pos.	G	AB	R	H	2B	3B	HR	RBI	Avg.	BB	SO	SB	PO	A	E	Avg.
							BATTING								FIELDING		
1999—	New York (N.L.)	SS	6	24	0	1	0	0	0	0	.042	0	2	0	7	24	0	1.000

ORIE, KEVIN — 3B — DODGERS

PERSONAL: Born September 1, 1972, in West Chester, Pa. ... 6-4/215. ... Bats right, throws right. ... Full name: Kevin Leonard Orie.
HIGH SCHOOL: Upper St. Clair (Pa.).
COLLEGE: Indiana.
TRANSACTIONS/CAREER NOTES: Selected by Chicago Cubs organization in supplemental round ("sandwich pick" between first and second round, 29th pick overall) of free-agent draft (June 3, 1993); pick received as part of compensation for Atlanta Braves signing Type A free-agent P Greg Maddux. ... On disabled list (May 3, 1994-remainder of season). ... On Iowa disabled list (July 27-August 19, 1996). ... On Chicago disabled list (April 30-May 30, 1997); included rehabilitation assignments to Orlando (May 16-20) and Iowa (May 20-30). ... Traded by Cubs with P Todd Noel and P Justin Speier to Florida Marlins for P Felix Heredia and P Steve Hoff (July 31, 1998). ... On Florida disabled list (May 23-June 8 and July 1-September 6, 1999); included rehabilitation assignments to Calgary (July 28-August 3 and August 17-September 6). ... Traded by Marlins to Los Angeles Dodgers for a player to be named later (November 12, 1999).

Year	Team (League)	Pos.	G	AB	R	H	2B	3B	HR	RBI	Avg.	BB	SO	SB	PO	A	E	Avg.
								BATTING								FIELDING		
1993—	Peoria (Midw.)	SS-OF	65	238	28	64	17	1	7	45	.269	21	51	3	77	149	12	.950
1994—	Daytona (FSL)	DH	6	17	4	7	3	1	1	5	.412	8	4	0	...	...	...	...
1995—	Daytona (FSL)	3B	119	409	54	100	17	4	9	51	.244	42	71	5	80	204	26	.916
1996—	Orlando (Sou.)	3B-DH	82	296	42	93	25	0	8	58	.314	48	52	2	60	144	14	.936
—Iowa (A.A.)		3B	14	48	5	10	1	0	2	6	.208	6	10	0	11	26	1	.974
1997—	Chicago (N.L.)	3B-SS	114	364	40	100	23	5	8	44	.275	39	57	2	91	213	9	.971
—Orlando (Sou.)		DH	3	13	3	5	2	0	2	6	.385	2	1	0	...	...	...	...
—Iowa (A.A.)		3B-DH	9	32	7	12	4	0	1	8	.375	5	5	0	2	13	1	.938
1998—	Chicago (N.L.)	3B	64	204	24	37	14	0	2	21	.181	18	35	1	39	101	5	.966
—Iowa (PCL)		3B	24	92	27	34	8	0	9	24	.370	12	15	1	7	41	2	.960
—Florida (N.L.)■		3B	48	175	23	46	8	1	6	17	.263	14	24	1	49	106	10	.939
1999—	Florida (N.L.)	3B-1B	77	240	26	61	16	0	6	29	.254	22	43	1	52	120	7	.961
—Calgary (PCL)		3B-DH	23	72	10	23	9	0	3	8	.319	13	7	0	12	30	6	.875
Major League totals (3 years)			303	983	113	244	61	6	22	111	.248	93	159	5	231	540	31	.961

OROSCO, JESSE   P   METS

PERSONAL: Born April 21, 1957, in Santa Barbara, Calif. ... 6-2/205. ... Throws left, bats right. ... Name pronounced oh-ROSS-koh.
HIGH SCHOOL: Santa Barbara (Calif.).
COLLEGE: Santa Barbara (Calif.) City College.
TRANSACTIONS/CAREER NOTES: Selected by St. Louis Cardinals organization in seventh round of free-agent draft (January 11, 1977); did not sign. ... Selected by Minnesota Twins organization in second round of free-agent draft (January 10, 1978). ... Traded by Twins to New York Mets (February 7, 1979), completing deal in which Twins traded P Greg Field and a player to be named later to Mets for P Jerry Koosman (December 8, 1978). ... Traded by Mets as part of an eight-player, three-team deal in which Mets sent Orosco to Oakland Athletics (December 11, 1987); A's then traded Orosco, SS Alfredo Griffin and P Jay Howell to Los Angeles Dodgers for P Bob Welch, P Matt Young and P Jack Savage; A's then traded Savage, P Wally Whitehurst and P Kevin Tapani to Mets. ... Granted free agency (November 4, 1988). ... Signed by Cleveland Indians (December 3, 1988). ... Traded by Indians to Milwaukee Brewers for a player to be named later (December 6, 1991); deal settled in cash. ... Granted free agency (November 5, 1992). ... Re-signed by Brewers (December 4, 1992). ... Granted free agency (October 15, 1994). ... Signed by Baltimore Orioles (April 9, 1995). ... Granted free agency (October 27, 1996). ... Re-signed by Orioles (November 15, 1996). ... Traded by Orioles to Mets for P Chuck McElroy (December 10, 1999).
RECORDS: Holds major league career records for most games pitched—1,090; and most games as relief pitcher—1,086.
MISCELLANEOUS: Appeared in one game as outfielder with one putout (1986). ... Struck out in only plate appearance (1993).

Year League	W	L	Pct.	ERA	G	GS	CG	ShO	Sv.	IP	H	R	ER	BB	SO
1978— Elizabethton (Appl.)	4	4	.500	1.13	20	0	0	0	6	40	29	7	5	20	48
1979— Tidewater (I.L.)■	4	4	.500	3.89	16	15	1	0	0	81	82	45	35	43	55
— New York (N.L.)	1	2	.333	4.89	18	2	0	0	0	35	33	20	19	22	22
1980— Jackson (Texas)	4	4	.500	3.68	37	1	0	0	3	71	52	36	29	62	85
1981— Tidewater (I.L.)	9	5	.643	3.31	46	10	0	0	8	87	80	39	32	32	81
— New York (N.L.)	0	1	.000	1.59	8	0	0	0	1	17	13	4	3	6	18
1982— New York (N.L.)	4	10	.286	2.72	54	2	0	0	4	109 1/3	92	37	33	40	89
1983— New York (N.L.)	13	7	.650	1.47	62	0	0	0	17	110	76	27	18	38	84
1984— New York (N.L.)	10	6	.625	2.59	60	0	0	0	31	87	58	29	25	34	85
1985— New York (N.L.)	8	6	.571	2.73	54	0	0	0	17	79	66	26	24	34	68
1986— New York (N.L.)	8	6	.571	2.33	58	0	0	0	21	81	64	23	21	35	62
1987— New York (N.L.)	3	9	.250	4.44	58	0	0	0	16	77	78	41	38	31	78
1988— Los Angeles (N.L.)■	3	2	.600	2.72	55	0	0	0	9	53	41	18	16	30	43
1989— Cleveland (A.L.)■	3	4	.429	2.08	69	0	0	0	3	78	54	20	18	26	79
1990— Cleveland (A.L.)	5	4	.556	3.90	55	0	0	0	2	64 2/3	58	35	28	38	55
1991— Cleveland (A.L.)	2	0	1.000	3.74	47	0	0	0	0	45 2/3	52	20	19	15	36
1992— Milwaukee (A.L.)■	3	1	.750	3.23	59	0	0	0	1	39	33	15	14	13	40
1993— Milwaukee (A.L.)	3	5	.375	3.18	57	0	0	0	8	56 2/3	47	25	20	17	67
1994— Milwaukee (A.L.)	3	1	.750	5.08	40	0	0	0	0	39	32	26	22	26	36
1995— Baltimore (A.L.)■	2	4	.333	3.26	*65	0	0	0	3	49 2/3	28	19	18	27	58
1996— Baltimore (A.L.)	3	1	.750	3.40	66	0	0	0	0	55 2/3	42	22	21	28	52
1997— Baltimore (A.L.)	6	3	.667	2.32	71	0	0	0	0	50 1/3	29	13	13	30	46
1998— Baltimore (A.L.)	4	1	.800	3.18	69	0	0	0	7	56 2/3	46	20	20	28	50
1999— Baltimore (A.L.)	0	2	.000	5.34	65	0	0	0	1	32	28	21	19	20	35
A.L. totals (11 years)	34	26	.567	3.36	663	0	0	0	25	567 1/3	449	236	212	268	554
N.L. totals (9 years)	50	49	.505	2.73	427	4	0	0	116	648 1/3	521	225	197	270	549
Major League totals (20 years)	84	75	.528	3.03	1090	4	0	0	141	1215 2/3	970	461	409	538	1103

DIVISION SERIES RECORD

Year League	W	L	Pct.	ERA	G	GS	CG	ShO	Sv.	IP	H	R	ER	BB	SO
1996— Baltimore (A.L.)	0	1	.000	36.00	4	0	0	0	0	1	2	4	4	3	2
1997— Baltimore (A.L.)	0	0	...	0.00	2	0	0	0	0	1 1/3	1	0	0	0	1
Division series totals (2 years)	0	1	.000	15.43	6	0	0	0	0	2 1/3	3	4	4	3	3

CHAMPIONSHIP SERIES RECORD

RECORDS: Holds single-series record for most games won—3 (1986).

Year League	W	L	Pct.	ERA	G	GS	CG	ShO	Sv.	IP	H	R	ER	BB	SO
1986— New York (N.L.)	3	0	1.000	3.38	4	0	0	0	0	8	5	3	3	2	10
1988— Los Angeles (N.L.)	0	0	...	7.71	4	0	0	0	0	2 1/3	4	2	2	3	0
1996— Baltimore (A.L.)	0	0	...	4.50	4	0	0	0	0	2	2	1	1	2	2
1997— Baltimore (A.L.)	0	0	...	0.00	2	0	0	0	0	1 1/3	0	0	0	1	1
Champ. series totals (4 years)	3	0	1.000	3.95	14	0	0	0	0	13 2/3	11	6	6	8	13

WORLD SERIES RECORD

NOTES: Member of World Series championship team (1986 and 1988).

Year League	W	L	Pct.	ERA	G	GS	CG	ShO	Sv.	IP	H	R	ER	BB	SO
1986— New York (N.L.)	0	0	...	0.00	4	0	0	0	2	5 2/3	2	0	0	0	6
1988— Los Angeles (N.L.)							Did not play.								

ALL-STAR GAME RECORD

Year League	W	L	Pct.	ERA	GS	CG	ShO	Sv.	IP	H	R	ER	BB	SO
1983— National	0	0	...	0.00	0	0	0	0	1/3	0	0	0	0	1
1984— National							Did not play.							

ORTIZ, DAVID   1B   TWINS

PERSONAL: Born November 18, 1975, in Santo Domingo, Dominican Republic. ... 6-4/237. ... Bats left, throws left. ... Full name: David Americo Ortiz.
HIGH SCHOOL: Estudia Espallat (Dominican Republic).
TRANSACTIONS/CAREER NOTES: Signed as non-drafted free agent by Seattle Mariners organization (November 28, 1992). ... Traded by Mariners to Minnesota Twins (September 13, 1996), completing deal in which Twins traded 3B Dave Hollins to Mariners for a player to be named later (August 29, 1996). ... On Minnesota disabled list (May 10-July 9, 1998); included rehabilitation assignment to Salt Lake (June 25-July 9).
STATISTICAL NOTES: Led Arizona League first basemen with 393 total chances in 1994.

Year	Team (League)	Pos.	G	AB	R	H	2B	3B	HR	RBI	Avg.	BB	SO	SB	PO	A	E	Avg.
1994—	Ariz. Mariners (Ariz.) ..	1B	53	167	14	41	10	1	2	20	.246	14	46	1	*372	15	6	.985
1995—	Ariz. Mariners (Ariz.) ..	1B	48	184	30	61	18	4	4	37	.332	23	52	2	436	*27	5	*.989
1996—	Wisconsin (Midw.)	1B-DH-3B	129	485	89	156	34	2	18	93	.322	52	108	3	1126	80	13	.989
1997—	Fort Myers (FSL)■	1B-DH	61	239	45	79	15	0	13	58	.331	22	53	2	524	44	9	.984
—New Britain (East.)		DH-1B	69	258	40	83	22	2	14	56	.322	21	78	2	268	16	3	.990
—Salt Lake (PCL)		1B-DH	10	42	5	9	1	0	4	10	.214	2	11	0	71	2	0	1.000
—Minnesota (A.L.)		1B-DH	15	49	10	16	3	0	1	6	.327	2	19	0	84	10	1	.989
1998—	Minnesota (A.L.)	1B-DH	86	278	47	77	20	0	9	46	.277	39	72	1	503	46	6	.989
—Salt Lake (PCL)		1B-DH	11	37	5	9	3	0	2	6	.243	3	9	0	76	10	3	.966
1999—	Minnesota (A.L.)	1B-DH	130	476	85	150	35	3	30	*110	.315	79	105	2	896	77	•20	.980
—Minnesota (A.L.)		DH-1B	10	20	1	0	0	0	0	0	.000	5	12	0	7	0	0	1.000
Major League totals (3 years)			111	347	58	93	23	0	10	52	.268	46	103	1	594	56	7	.989

ORTIZ, JOSE SS/2B ATHLETICS

PERSONAL: Born June 13, 1977, in Santo Domingo, Dominican Republic. ... 5-9/177. ... Bats right, throws right. ... Full name: Jose Daniel Ortiz.

TRANSACTIONS/CAREER NOTES: Signed as non-drafted free agent by Oakland Athletics organization (November 8, 1994). ... On disabled list (May 10-June 30, 1998). ... On Vancouver disabled list (June 15-25, 1999).

STATISTICAL NOTES: Led Arizona League with .530 slugging percentage in 1996. ... Led Arizona League shortstops with 279 total chances and 42 double plays in 1996. ... Led California League shortstops with 53 errors and 80 double plays in 1997.

Year	Team (League)	Pos.	G	AB	R	H	2B	3B	HR	RBI	Avg.	BB	SO	SB	PO	A	E	Avg.
1995—	Dom. Athletics (DSL) .	SS	61	217	45	65	12	2	9	41	.300	32	22	14	182	38	17	.928
1996—	Ariz. Athletics (Ariz.) ..	SS	52	200	*43	66	12	8	4	25	.330	20	34	16	*93	*165	21	.925
—Modesto (Calif.)		2B	1	4	0	1	0	0	0	0	.250	0	1	0	2	5	0	1.000
1997—	Modesto (Calif.)	SS-2B	128	497	92	122	25	7	16	58	.245	60	107	22	186	373	†53	.913
1998—	Huntsville (Sou.)	2B-SS-OF	94	354	70	98	24	2	6	55	.277	48	63	22	159	274	27	.941
1999—	Vancouver (PCL)	SS-2B	107	377	66	107	29	2	9	45	.284	29	50	13	179	295	28	.944

ORTIZ, RAMON P ANGELS

PERSONAL: Born May 23, 1976, in Cotui, Dominican Republic. ... 6-0/175. ... Throws right, bats right. ... Full name: Ramon Diogenes Ortiz.

HIGH SCHOOL: 8th Intermedian (Dominican Republic).

TRANSACTIONS/CAREER NOTES: Signed as non-drafted free agent by California Angels organization (June 20, 1995). ... Angels franchise renamed Anaheim Angels for 1997 season. ... On disabled list (May 9, 1998-remainder of season).

STATISTICAL NOTES: Pitched 12-0 no-hit victory against Quad City (August 7, 1997).

Year	League	W	L	Pct.	ERA	G	GS	CG	ShO	Sv.	IP	H	R	ER	BB	SO
1996—	Boise (N.W.)	1	1	.500	3.66	3	3	0	0	0	19 2/3	21	10	8	6	18
1997—	Cedar Rapids (Midw.)	11	10	.524	3.58	27	•27	*8	*4	0	181	156	78	72	53	*225
1998—	Midland (Texas)..................	2	1	.667	5.55	7	7	0	0	0	47	50	31	29	16	53
1999—	Erie (East.)	9	4	.692	2.82	15	15	2	2	0	102	88	38	32	40	86
—Edmonton (PCL)		5	3	.625	4.05	9	9	0	0	0	53 1/3	46	26	24	19	64
—Anaheim (A.L.)		2	3	.400	6.52	9	9	0	0	0	48 1/3	50	35	35	25	44
Major League totals (1 year)........		2	3	.400	6.52	9	9	0	0	0	48 1/3	50	35	35	25	44

ORTIZ, RUSS P GIANTS

PERSONAL: Born June 5, 1974, in Encino, Calif. ... 6-1/210. ... Throws right, bats right. ... Full name: Russell Reid Ortiz.

HIGH SCHOOL: Montclair Prep (Van Nuys, Calif.).

COLLEGE: Oklahoma.

TRANSACTIONS/CAREER NOTES: Selected by San Francisco Giants organization in fourth round of free-agent draft (June 1, 1995).

RECORDS: Shares N.L. single-inning record for most consecutive home runs allowed—3 (August 10, 1998, fifth inning).

Year	League	W	L	Pct.	ERA	G	GS	CG	ShO	Sv.	IP	H	R	ER	BB	SO
1995—	Bellingham (N.W.)	2	1	1.000	0.52	25	0	0	0	11	34 1/3	19	4	2	13	55
—San Jose (Calif.)		0	1	.000	1.50	5	0	0	0	0	6	4	1	1	2	7
1996—	San Jose (Calif.).................	0	0	...	0.25	34	0	0	0	23	36 2/3	16	2	1	20	63
—Shreveport (Texas)...........		1	2	.333	4.05	26	0	0	0	13	26 2/3	22	14	12	21	29
1997—	Shreveport (Texas).........	2	3	.400	4.13	12	12	0	0	0	56 2/3	52	28	26	37	50
—Phoenix (PCL)		4	3	.571	5.51	14	14	0	0	0	85	96	57	52	34	70
1998—	San Francisco (N.L.)	4	4	.500	4.99	22	13	0	0	0	88 1/3	90	51	49	46	75
—Fresno (PCL)		3	1	.750	1.60	10	10	0	0	0	50 2/3	35	10	9	22	59
1999—	San Francisco (N.L.)	18	9	.667	3.81	33	33	3	0	0	207 2/3	189	109	88	*125	164
Major League totals (2 years).......		22	13	.629	4.17	55	46	3	0	0	296	279	160	137	171	239

OSBORNE, DONOVAN P

PERSONAL: Born June 21, 1969, in Roseville, Calif. ... 6-2/195. ... Throws left, bats left. ... Full name: Donovan Alan Osborne.

HIGH SCHOOL: Carson City (Nev.).

COLLEGE: UNLV.

TRANSACTIONS/CAREER NOTES: Selected by Montreal Expos organization in ninth round of free-agent draft (June 2, 1987); did not sign. ... Selected by St. Louis Cardinals organization in first round (13th pick overall) of free-agent draft (June 4, 1990). ... On St. Louis disabled list (April 2, 1994-entire season). ... On St. Louis disabled list (May 15-July 14, 1995); included rehabilitation assignments to Arkansas and Louisville (June 28-July 14). ... On St. Louis disabled list (March 25-April 17, 1996); included rehabilitation assignments to St. Petersburg

0

(April 7-12) and Louisville (April 12-17). ... On St. Louis disabled list (May 3-July 29, 1997). ... On St. Louis disabled list (March 22-April 16 and May 8-August 8, 1998); included rehabilitation assignments to Arkansas (April 6-10, April 12-16 and July 17-August 1) and Memphis (April 11). ... On disabled list (May 7, 1999-remainder of season). ... Granted free agency (November 3, 1999).
HONORS: Named lefthanded pitcher on THE SPORTING NEWS college All-America team (1989).
STATISTICAL NOTES: Career major league grand slams: 1.
MISCELLANEOUS: Appeared in three games as pinch runner (1993).

Year	League	W	L	Pct.	ERA	G	GS	CG	ShO	Sv.	IP	H	R	ER	BB	SO
1990—	Hamilton (NY-P)	0	2	.000	3.60	4	4	0	0	0	20	21	8	8	5	14
—	Savannah (SAL)	2	2	.500	2.61	6	6	1	0	0	41 1/3	40	20	12	7	28
1991—	Arkansas (Texas)	8	12	.400	3.63	26	26	3	0	0	166	178	82	67	43	130
1992—	St. Louis (N.L.)	11	9	.550	3.77	34	29	0	0	0	179	193	91	75	38	104
1993—	St. Louis (N.L.)	10	7	.588	3.76	26	26	1	0	0	155 2/3	153	73	65	47	83
1994—	St. Louis (N.L.)								Did not play.							
1995—	St. Louis (N.L.)	4	6	.400	3.81	19	19	0	0	0	113 1/3	112	58	48	34	82
—	Arkansas (Texas)	0	1	.000	2.45	2	2	0	0	0	11	12	4	3	2	6
—	Louisville (A.A.)	0	1	.000	3.86	1	1	0	0	0	7	8	3	3	0	3
1996—	St. Petersburg (FSL)	1	0	1.000	0.00	1	1	0	0	0	6	2	0	0	0	2
—	Louisville (A.A.)	1	0	1.000	2.57	1	1	0	0	0	7	6	2	2	2	3
—	St. Louis (N.L.)	13	9	.591	3.53	30	30	2	1	0	198 2/3	191	87	78	57	134
1997—	St. Louis (N.L.)	3	7	.300	4.93	14	14	0	0	0	80 1/3	84	46	44	23	51
—	Louisville (A.A.)	0	1	.000	4.72	3	3	0	0	0	13 1/3	13	7	7	5	13
1998—	Arkansas (Texas)	2	0	1.000	4.26	5	5	0	0	0	19	16	9	9	3	21
—	Memphis (PCL)	0	0		6.23	1	1	0	0	0	4 1/3	5	4	3	0	6
—	St. Louis (N.L.)	5	4	.556	4.09	14	14	1	1	0	83 2/3	84	42	38	22	60
1999—	St. Louis (N.L.)	1	3	.250	5.52	6	6	0	0	0	29 1/3	34	18	18	10	21
Major League totals (7 years)		47	45	.511	3.92	143	138	4	2	0	840	851	415	366	231	535

DIVISION SERIES RECORD

Year	League	W	L	Pct.	ERA	G	GS	CG	ShO	Sv.	IP	H	R	ER	BB	SO
1996—	St. Louis (N.L.)	0	0	...	9.00	1	1	0	0	0	4	7	4	4	0	5

CHAMPIONSHIP SERIES RECORD

Year	League	W	L	Pct.	ERA	G	GS	CG	ShO	Sv.	IP	H	R	ER	BB	SO
1996—	St. Louis (N.L.)	1	1	.500	9.39	2	2	0	0	0	7 2/3	12	8	8	4	6

OSIK, KEITH — C — PIRATES

PERSONAL: Born October 22, 1968, in Port Jefferson, N.Y. ... 6-0/192. ... Bats right, throws right. ... Full name: Keith Richard Osik. ... Name pronounced OH-sik.
HIGH SCHOOL: Shoreham (N.Y.)-Wading River.
COLLEGE: Louisiana State.
TRANSACTIONS/CAREER NOTES: Selected by Texas Rangers organization in 47th round of free-agent draft (June 2, 1987); did not sign. ... Selected by Pittsburgh Pirates organization in 24th round of free-agent draft (June 4, 1990). ... On Pittsburgh disabled list (July 16-August 13, 1996); included rehabilitation assignment to Erie (August 10-13). ... On Pittsburgh disabled list (July 21-August 13, 1999); included rehabilitation assignment to Nashville (August 9-13).

							BATTING							FIELDING		
Year	Team (League)	Pos.	G	AB	R	H	2B	3B	HR	RBI	Avg.	BB	SO	SB	PO	A	E	Avg.
1990—	Welland (NY-P)	3-C-1-2-S	29	97	13	27	4	0	1	20	.278	11	12	2	59	29	2	.978
1991—	Salem (Caro.)	C-3B-2B	87	300	31	81	12	1	6	35	.270	38	48	2	307	85	12	.970
—	Carolina (Sou.)	C-3B	17	43	9	13	3	1	0	5	.302	5	5	0	84	13	2	.980
1992—	Carolina (Sou.)	3B-C-2B-P	129	425	41	110	17	1	5	45	.259	52	69	2	222	195	19	.956
1993—	Carolina (Sou.)	C-3B-DH	103	371	47	104	21	2	10	47	.280	30	46	0	662	69	6	.992
1994—	Buffalo (A.A.)	C-O-1-D-P-2	83	260	27	55	16	0	5	33	.212	28	41	0	403	50	8	.983
1995—	Calgary (PCL)	C-1B-OF-3B	90	301	40	101	25	1	10	59	.336	21	42	2	458	35	4	.992
1996—	Pittsburgh (N.L.)	C-3B-OF	48	140	18	41	14	1	1	14	.293	14	22	1	237	25	6	.978
—	Erie (NY-P)	C	3	10	1	3	1	0	0	2	.300	1	2	0	19	2	0	1.000
1997—	Pittsburgh (N.L.)	C-2B-1B-3B	49	105	10	27	9	1	0	7	.257	9	21	0	163	14	2	.989
1998—	Pittsburgh (N.L.)	C-3B	39	98	8	21	4	0	0	7	.214	13	16	1	152	30	1	.995
1999—	Pittsburgh (N.L.)	C-P	66	167	12	31	3	1	2	13	.186	11	30	0	289	22	1	.997
—	Nashville (PCL)	C-OF	4	11	0	1	0	0	0	0	.091	0	1	0	24	3	0	1.000
Major League totals (4 years)			202	510	48	120	30	3	3	41	.235	47	89	2	841	91	10	.989

RECORD AS PITCHER

Year	League	W	L	Pct.	ERA	G	GS	CG	ShO	Sv.	IP	H	R	ER	BB	SO
1992—	Carolina (Sou.)	0	0	...	0.00	2	0	0	0	0	2 2/3	2	0	0	0	3
1994—	Buffalo (A.A.)	0	1	.000	13.50	1	0	0	0	0	2/3	2	1	1	0	1
1995—	Calgary (PCL)	0	0	...	4.50	2	0	0	0	0	2	1	1	1	1	3
1999—	Pittsburgh (N.L.)	0	0	...	36.00	1	0	0	0	0	1	2	4	4	2	1

OSTING, JIMMY — P — BRAVES

PERSONAL: Born April 7, 1977, in Louisville, Ky. ... 6-5/180. ... Throws left, bats right. ... Full name: James Michael Osting.
HIGH SCHOOL: Trinity (Louisville, Ky.).
TRANSACTIONS/CAREER NOTES: Selected by Atlanta Braves in fourth round of free-agent draft (June 1, 1995). ... On disabled list (April 2, 1998-remainder of season).

Year	League	W	L	Pct.	ERA	G	GS	CG	ShO	Sv.	IP	H	R	ER	BB	SO
1995—	Danville (Appl.)	2	7	.222	7.15	11	10	0	0	0	39	46	34	31	25	43
1996—	Eugene (N.W.)	2	1	.667	2.59	5	5	0	0	0	24 1/3	14	11	7	13	35
1997—	Macon (SAL)	2	3	.400	3.28	15	15	0	0	0	57 2/3	54	28	21	29	62
1998—									Did not play.							
1999—	Macon (SAL)	*14	4	.778	2.88	27	22	0	0	2	147	130	52	47	30	131

O

OSUNA, ANTONIO   P   DODGERS

PERSONAL: Born April 12, 1973, in Sinaloa, Mexico. ... 5-11/206. ... Throws right, bats right. ... Full name: Antonio Pedro Osuna.
HIGH SCHOOL: Secondaria Federal (Mexico).
TRANSACTIONS/CAREER NOTES: Signed as non-drafted free agent by Los Angeles Dodgers organization (June 12, 1991). ... On suspended list (April 8-July 17, 1993). ... On San Antonio disabled list (April 8-June 6, 1994). ... On Los Angeles disabled list (May 19-June 16, 1995); included rehabilitation assignment to San Bernardino (June 6-16). ... On disabled list (September 9, 1998-remainder of season). ... On Los Angeles disabled list (March 25-April 16, April 18-May 3 and May 19, 1999-remainder of season); included rehabilitation assignments to San Bernardino (April 10-16, April 25-May 3, July 7-15 and September 1-29).

Year League	W	L	Pct.	ERA	G	GS	CG	ShO	Sv.	IP	H	R	ER	BB	SO
1991— Gulf Coast Dodgers (GCL)..	0	0	...	0.82	8	0	0	0	4	11	8	5	1	0	13
— Yakima (N.W.)	0	0	...	3.20	13	0	0	0	5	25 1/3	18	10	9	8	39
1992— Mexico City Tigers (Mex.)..	13	7	.650	4.05	28	26	3	1	0	166 2/3	181	80	75	74	129
1993— Bakersfield (Calif.)	0	2	.000	4.91	14	2	0	0	2	18 1/3	19	10	10	5	20
1994— San Antonio (Texas).........	1	2	.333	0.98	35	0	0	0	19	46	19	6	5	18	53
— Albuquerque (PCL).............	0	0	...	0.00	6	0	0	0	4	6	5	1	0	1	8
1995— Los Angeles (N.L.).............	2	4	.333	4.43	39	0	0	0	0	44 2/3	39	22	22	20	46
— San Bernardino (Calif.).......	0	0	...	1.29	5	0	0	0	0	7	3	1	1	5	11
— Albuquerque (PCL).............	0	1	.000	4.42	19	0	0	0	11	18 1/3	15	9	9	9	19
1996— Albuquerque (PCL).............	0	0	...	0.00	1	0	0	0	0	1	2	0	0	0	1
— Los Angeles (N.L.).............	9	6	.600	3.00	73	0	0	0	4	84	65	33	28	32	85
1997— Albuquerque (PCL).............	1	1	.500	1.93	13	0	0	0	6	14	9	3	3	4	26
— Los Angeles (N.L.).............	3	4	.429	2.19	48	0	0	0	0	61 2/3	46	15	15	19	68
1998— Los Angeles (N.L.).............	7	1	.875	3.06	54	0	0	0	6	64 2/3	50	26	22	32	72
1999— San Bernardino (Calif.).......	0	0	...	2.33	13	4	0	0	0	19 1/3	19	6	5	6	27
— Los Angeles (N.L.).............	0	0	...	7.71	5	0	0	0	0	4 2/3	4	5	4	3	5
Major League totals (5 years)......	**21**	**15**	**.583**	**3.15**	**219**	**0**	**0**	**0**	**10**	**259 2/3**	**204**	**101**	**91**	**106**	**276**

DIVISION SERIES RECORD

Year League	W	L	Pct.	ERA	G	GS	CG	ShO	Sv.	IP	H	R	ER	BB	SO
1995— Los Angeles (N.L.)	0	1	.000	2.70	3	0	0	0	0	3 1/3	3	1	1	1	3
1996— Los Angeles (N.L.)	0	1	.000	4.50	2	0	0	0	0	2	3	1	1	1	4
Division series totals (2 years)	**0**	**2**	**.000**	**3.38**	**5**	**0**	**0**	**0**	**0**	**5 1/3**	**6**	**2**	**2**	**2**	**7**

OTANEZ, WILLIS   3B/1B   BLUE JAYS

PERSONAL: Born April 19, 1973, in Vega Baja, Puerto Rico. ... 6-1/215. ... Bats right, throws right. ... Full name: Willis A. Otanez.
HIGH SCHOOL: Liceo Miguel Angel Garcia (Cotui, Dominican Republic).
TRANSACTIONS/CAREER NOTES: Signed as non-drafted free agent by Los Angeles Dodgers organization (February 10, 1990). ... On disabled list (August 3-September 10, 1993). ... Traded by Dodgers with 2B Miguel Cairo to Seattle Mariners for 3B Mike Blowers (November 29, 1995). ... Claimed on waivers by Baltimore Orioles (February 12, 1996). ... On Rochester disabled list (May 15-July 24, 1997). ... Granted free agency (December 21, 1997). ... Re-signed by Orioles (January 8, 1998). ... On Baltimore disabled list (August 28, 1998-remainder of season). ... Claimed on waivers by Toronto Blue Jays (May 28, 1999). ... On Toronto disabled list (August 13-September 3, 1999).
STATISTICAL NOTES: Led Eastern League second basemen with 106 putouts in 1996. ... Led International League third basemen with .968 fielding percentage and 91 putouts in 1998.

Year Team (League)	Pos.	G	AB	R	H	2B	3B	HR	RBI	Avg.	BB	SO	SB	PO	A	E	Avg.
1990— Dom. Dodgers (DSL) .	...	70	267	44	84	18	0	1	46	.315	51	24	4	...	...	...	...
1991— Great Falls (Pio.)	SS-3B	58	222	38	64	9	2	6	39	.288	19	34	3	64	124	22	.895
1992— Vero Beach (FSL)	SS-3B	117	390	27	86	18	0	3	27	.221	24	60	2	160	305	33	.934
1993— Bakersfield (Calif.)	3B-SS-2B	95	325	34	85	11	2	10	39	.262	29	63	1	76	211	25	.920
1994— Vero Beach (FSL)	3B	131	476	77	132	27	1	19	72	.277	53	98	4	*109	302	23	.947
1995— Vero Beach (FSL)	3B-DH	92	354	39	92	24	0	10	53	.260	28	59	1	59	186	20	.925
— San Antonio (Texas) ...	3B	27	100	8	24	4	1	1	7	.240	6	25	0	18	48	3	.957
1996— Bowie (East.)■...........	3B-DH-SS	138	506	60	134	27	2	24	75	.265	45	97	3	†106	279	24	.941
1997— Rochester (I.L.)	3B-1B	49	168	20	35	9	0	5	25	.208	15	35	0	67	68	12	.918
— Bowie (East.)	DH-3B	19	78	13	26	9	0	3	13	.333	9	19	0	1	20	1	.955
— GC Orioles (GCL)........	DH	8	25	5	8	2	0	2	3	.320	2	4	0	...	...	...	...
1998— Rochester (I.L.)...........3B-1B-DH-DH-OF		124	481	87	137	24	2	27	100	.285	41	104	1	†122	240	12	†.968
— Baltimore (A.L.)..........	OF	3	5	0	1	0	0	0	0	.200	0	2	0	1	0	0	1.000
1999— Baltimore (A.L.)..........	3B-1B-DH	29	80	7	17	3	0	2	11	.213	6	16	0	22	28	4	.926
— Toronto (A.L.)■.........	3B-1B-DH	42	127	21	32	8	0	5	13	.252	9	30	0	105	32	2	.986
Major League totals (2 years)		**74**	**212**	**28**	**50**	**11**	**0**	**7**	**24**	**.236**	**15**	**48**	**0**	**128**	**60**	**6**	**.969**

OWENS, ERIC   OF   PADRES

PERSONAL: Born February 3, 1971, in Danville, Va. ... 6-0/198. ... Bats right, throws right. ... Full name: Eric Blake Owens.
HIGH SCHOOL: Tunstall (Dry Fork, Va.).
COLLEGE: Ferrum (Va.).
TRANSACTIONS/CAREER NOTES: Selected by Cincinnati Reds organization in fourth round of free-agent draft (June 1, 1992). ... On Indianapolis disabled list (August 20-September 11, 1995). ... Traded by Reds to Florida Marlins for a player to be named later (March 21, 1998); Reds acquired P Jesus Martinez to complete deal (March 26, 1998). ... Contract sold by Marlins to Milwaukee Brewers (March 25, 1998). ... Granted free agency (October 15, 1998). ... Signed by San Diego Padres organization (December 10, 1998).
HONORS: Named American Association Most Valuable Player (1995).
STATISTICAL NOTES: Led Pioneer League shortstops with 28 errors in 1992. ... Tied for American Association lead in errors by second baseman with 17 in 1997. ... Had 18-game hitting streak (June 17-July 6, 1999).

O

Year	Team (League)	Pos.	G	AB	R	H	2B	3B	HR	RBI	Avg.	BB	SO	SB	PO	A	E	Avg.
1992—	Billings (Pio.)	SS-3B	67	239	41	72	10	3	3	26	.301	23	22	15	82	164	†29	.895
1993—	Win.-Salem (Car.)......	SS	122	487	74	132	25	4	10	63	.271	53	69	21	*215	347	34	.943
1994—	Chattanooga (Sou.)....	3B-2B	134	523	73	133	17	3	3	36	.254	54	86	38	151	266	40	.912
1995—	Indianapolis (A.A.)......	2B	108	427	*86	134	24	•8	12	63	.314	52	61	*33	219	274	*17	.967
—	Cincinnati (N.L.)	3B	2	2	0	2	0	0	0	1	1.000	0	0	0	0	0	0	...
1996—	Indianapolis (A.A.)...SS-3B-2B-OF		33	128	24	41	8	2	4	14	.320	11	16	6	44	64	6	.947
—	Cincinnati (N.L.)	OF-2B-3B	88	205	26	41	6	0	0	9	.200	23	38	16	76	14	2	.978
1997—	Indianapolis (A.A.)......	OF-2B	27	57	8	15	0	0	0	3	.263	4	11	3	15	0	1	.938
—	Indianapolis (A.A.)......	2-S-O-3	104	391	56	112	15	4	11	44	.286	42	55	23	184	241	‡27	.940
1998—	Milwaukee (N.L.)■.....	OF-2B	34	40	5	5	2	0	1	4	.125	2	6	0	14	2	1	.941
—	Louisville (I.L.)	OF-3B-DH	77	254	48	85	11	4	5	40	.335	34	30	21	85	57	8	.947
1999—	San Diego (N.L.)■.....	O-1-3-2	149	440	55	117	22	3	9	61	.266	38	50	33	278	12	4	.986
Major League totals (5 years)			300	744	94	180	30	3	10	78	.242	67	105	52	383	28	8	.981

OZUNA, PABLO — SS — MARLINS

PERSONAL: Born August 25, 1978, in Santo Domingo, Dominican Republic. ... 6-0/160. ... Bats right, throws right. ... Full name: Pablo Jose Ozuna.

TRANSACTIONS/CAREER NOTES: Signed as non-drafted free agent by St. Louis Cardinals orgnaization (April 8, 1996). ... Traded by Cardinals with P Braden Looper and P Armando Almanza to Florida Marlins for SS Edgar Renteria (December 14, 1998).

HONORS: Named Midwest League Most Valuable Player (1998).

STATISTICAL NOTES: Tied for Appalachian League lead in sacrifice hits with six in 1997. ... Led Midwest League with 26 caught stealing and tied for lead in double plays by a shortstop with 80 in 1998. ... Tied for Midwest League lead with 80 double plays by shortstop in 1998.

Year	Team (League)	Pos.	G	AB	R	H	2B	3B	HR	RBI	Avg.	BB	SO	SB	PO	A	E	Avg.
1996—	Dom. Cardinals (DSL)	SS	74	295	57	107	12	4	6	60	.363	23	19	19	126	219	32	.915
1997—	Johnson City (Appl.) ..	SS	56	232	40	75	13	1	5	24	.323	10	24	23	80	139	25	.898
1998—	Peoria (Midw.)............	SS	133	538	*122	*192	27	10	9	62	*.357	29	56	62	195	*395	45	.929
1999—	Portland (East.)■......	SS	117	502	62	141	25	7	7	46	.281	13	50	31	179	309	28	.946

PADILLA, VICENTE — P — DIAMONDBACKS

PERSONAL: Born September 27, 1977, in Chinandoga, Nicaragua. ... 6-2/200. ... Throws right, bats right.

HIGH SCHOOL: Ruben Dario (Nicaragua).

TRANSACTIONS/CAREER NOTES: Signed as non-drafted free agent by Arizona Diamondbacks organization (August 31, 1998).

Year	League	W	L	Pct.	ERA	G	GS	CG	ShO	Sv.	IP	H	R	ER	BB	SO
1999—	High Desert (Calif.)............	4	1	.800	3.73	9	9	0	0	0	50 2/3	50	27	21	17	55
—	Tucson (PCL)	7	4	.636	3.75	18	14	0	0	0	93 2/3	107	47	39	24	58
—	Arizona (N.L.)	0	1	.000	16.88	5	0	0	0	0	2 2/3	7	5	5	3	0
Major League totals (1 year)........		0	1	.000	16.88	5	0	0	0	0	2 2/3	7	5	5	3	0

PAINTER, LANCE — P — BLUE JAYS

PERSONAL: Born July 21, 1967, in Bedford, England. ... 6-1/200. ... Throws left, bats left. ... Full name: Lance Telford Painter.

HIGH SCHOOL: Nicolet (Glendale, Wis.).

COLLEGE: Wisconsin.

TRANSACTIONS/CAREER NOTES: Selected by San Diego Padres organization in 25th round of free-agent draft (June 4, 1990). ... Selected by Colorado Rockies in second round (34th pick overall) of expansion draft (November 17, 1992). ... On disabled list (April 17-May 6, 1995). ... On disabled list (August 6, 1996-remainder of season). ... Claimed on waivers by St. Louis Cardinals (December 2, 1996). ... On disabled list (April 5-May 12 and May 20-June 20, 1997); included rehabilitation assignment to Louisville (May 1-12). ... On St. Louis disabled list (June 13-29, 1999); included rehabilitation assignment to Arkansas (June 28-29). ... Traded by Cardinals with C Alberto Castillo and P Matt DeWitt to Toronto Blue Jays for P Pat Hentgen and P Paul Spoljaric (November 11, 1999).

STATISTICAL NOTES: Led Texas League with 10 hit batsmen in 1992.

MISCELLANEOUS: Received base on balls in only appearance as pinch hitter with Colorado (1995). ... Struck out twice in two appearances as pinch hitter (1996).

Year	League	W	L	Pct.	ERA	G	GS	CG	ShO	Sv.	IP	H	R	ER	BB	SO
1990—	Spokane (N.W.)	7	3	.700	1.51	23	1	0	0	3	71 2/3	45	18	12	15	104
1991—	Waterloo (Midw.)	14	8	.636	2.30	28	28	7	*4	0	200	162	64	51	57	201
1992—	Wichita (Texas)	10	5	*.667	3.53	27	•27	1	1	0	163 1/3	189	74	64	55	137
1993—	Colorado Springs (PCL)■ ..	9	7	.563	4.30	23	22	•4	1	0	138	165	90	66	44	91
—	Colorado (N.L.)	2	2	.500	6.00	10	6	1	0	0	39	52	26	26	9	16
1994—	Colorado Springs (PCL)	4	3	.571	4.79	13	13	1	0	0	71 1/3	83	42	38	28	59
—	Colorado (N.L.)	4	6	.400	6.11	15	14	0	0	0	73 2/3	91	51	50	26	41
1995—	Colorado (N.L.)	3	0	1.000	4.37	33	1	0	0	1	45 1/3	55	23	22	10	36
—	Colorado Springs (PCL)	0	3	.000	5.96	11	4	0	0	0	25 2/3	32	20	17	11	12
1996—	Colorado (N.L.)	4	2	.667	5.86	34	1	0	0	0	50 2/3	56	37	33	25	48
1997—	St. Louis (N.L.)■	1	1	.500	4.76	14	0	0	0	0	17	13	9	9	8	11
—	Louisville (A.A.)................	1	0	1.000	5.23	18	2	0	0	0	20 2/3	18	14	12	4	22
1998—	St. Louis (N.L.)..................	4	0	1.000	3.99	65	0	0	0	1	47 1/3	42	24	21	28	39
1999—	St. Louis (N.L.)..................	4	5	.444	4.83	56	4	0	0	1	63 1/3	63	37	34	25	56
—	Arkansas (Texas)...............	0	0	...	0.00	1	1	0	0	0	2	1	0	0	0	4
Major League totals (7 years)		22	16	.579	5.22	227	26	1	0	3	336 1/3	372	207	195	131	247

DIVISION SERIES RECORD

NOTES: Struck out in only appearance as pinch hitter (1995).

Year	League	W	L	Pct.	ERA	G	GS	CG	ShO	Sv.	IP	H	R	ER	BB	SO
1995—	Colorado (N.L.)	0	0	...	5.40	1	1	0	0	0	5	5	3	3	2	4

O
P

PERSONAL: Born January 19, 1969, in Hoboken, N.J. ... 5-11/175. ... Bats left, throws left. ... Cousin of Rafael Palmeiro, first baseman, Texas Rangers. ... Name pronounced pal-MAIR-oh.
HIGH SCHOOL: Southridge (Miami).
JUNIOR COLLEGE: Miami-Dade (South) Community College.
COLLEGE: Miami (Fla.).
TRANSACTIONS/CAREER NOTES: Selected by California Angels organization in 33rd round of free-agent draft (June 3, 1991). ... On disabled list (September 1-26, 1994). ... Angels franchise renamed Anaheim Angels for 1997 season. ... On disabled list (August 23-September 7, 1997).
STATISTICAL NOTES: Tied for Northwest League lead in double plays by outfielder with two in 1991. ... Led Texas League with 18 sacrifice hits in 1993. ... Led Texas League outfielders with 328 total chances in 1993. ... Led Pacific Coast League in caught stealing with 16 in 1994. ... Led Pacific Coast League with 11 sacrifice hits in 1995.

								BATTING								FIELDING		
Year	Team (League)	Pos.	G	AB	R	H	2B	3B	HR	RBI	Avg.	BB	SO	SB	PO	A	E	Avg.
1991— Boise (N.W.)		OF	70	277	56	77	11	2	1	24	.278	33	22	8	130	8	2	*.986
1992— Quad City (Midw.)		OF	127	451	83	143	22	4	0	41	*.317	56	41	31	211	9	6	.973
1993— Midland (Texas)		OF	131	*535	85	163	19	5	0	64	.305	42	35	18	*307	12	9	.973
1994— Vancouver (PCL)		OF	117	458	79	150	28	4	1	47	.328	58	46	21	254	6	1	.996
1995— Vancouver (PCL)		OF-DH	107	398	66	122	21	4	0	47	.307	41	34	16	192	4	1	*.995
— California (A.L.)		OF-DH	15	20	3	7	0	0	0	1	.350	1	1	0	7	0	0	1.000
1996— Vancouver (PCL)		OF	62	245	40	75	13	4	0	33	.306	30	19	7	113	4	5	.959
— California (A.L.)		OF-DH	50	87	6	25	6	1	0	6	.287	8	13	0	33	0	0	1.000
1997— Anaheim (A.L.)		OF-DH	74	134	19	29	2	2	0	8	.216	17	11	2	78	1	2	.975
1998— Vancouver (PCL)		OF	43	140	21	42	13	3	1	29	.300	16	10	3	70	4	0	1.000
— Anaheim (A.L.)		OF-DH	75	165	28	53	7	2	0	21	.321	20	11	5	92	0	1	1.000
1999— Anaheim (A.L.)		OF-DH	109	317	46	88	12	1	1	23	.278	39	30	5	154	6	1	.994
Major League totals (5 years)			323	723	102	202	27	6	1	59	.279	85	66	12	364	7	3	.992

PERSONAL: Born September 24, 1964, in Havana, Cuba. ... 6-0/190. ... Bats left, throws left. ... Full name: Rafael Corrales Palmeiro. ... Cousin of Orlando Palmeiro, outfielder, Anaheim Angels. ... Name pronounced pal-MAIR-oh.
HIGH SCHOOL: Jackson (Miami).
COLLEGE: Mississippi State (degree in commercial art).
TRANSACTIONS/CAREER NOTES: Selected by New York Mets organization in eighth round of free-agent draft (June 7, 1982); did not sign. ... Selected by Chicago Cubs organization in first round (22nd pick overall) of free-agent draft (June 3, 1985); pick received as compensation for San Diego Padres signing Type A free-agent P Tim Stoddard. ... Traded by Cubs with P Jamie Moyer and P Drew Hall to Texas Rangers for P Mitch Williams, P Paul Kilgus, P Steve Wilson, IF Curtis Wilkerson, IF Luis Benitez and OF Pablo Delgado (December 5, 1988). ... Granted free agency (October 25, 1993). ... Signed by Baltimore Orioles (December 12, 1993). ... Granted free agency (October 23, 1998). ... Signed by Rangers (December 4, 1998).
RECORDS: Shares A.L. career record for most major league ballparks, one or more home runs (since 1900)—24. ... Shares A.L. record for most seasons leading league in assists by first baseman—6.
HONORS: Named outfielder on THE SPORTING NEWS college All-America team (1985). ... Named Eastern League Most Valuable Player (1986). ... Won A.L. Gold Glove at first base (1997-99). ... Named first baseman on THE SPORTING NEWS A.L. All-Star team (1998 and 1999). ... Named first baseman on THE SPORTING NEWS A.L. Silver Slugger team (1998). ... Named Major League Player of the Year by THE SPORTING NEWS (1999). ... Named designated hitter on THE SPORTING NEWS A.L. Silver Slugger team (1999).
STATISTICAL NOTES: Led Eastern League with 225 total bases, 13 sacrifice flies and 13 intentional bases on balls received in 1986. ... Had 20-game hitting streak (July 18-August 11, 1988). ... Led A.L. first basemen in total chances with 1,540 in 1993 and 1,510 in 1996. ... Led A.L. first basemen in double plays with 133 in 1993 and 157 in 1996. ... Led A.L. first basemen with 1,568 total chances in 1998. ... Had 24-game hitting streak (April 23-May 22, 1994). ... Career major league grand slams: 8.

								BATTING								FIELDING		
Year	Team (League)	Pos.	G	AB	R	H	2B	3B	HR	RBI	Avg.	BB	SO	SB	PO	A	E	Avg.
1985— Peoria (Midw.)		OF	73	279	34	83	22	4	5	51	.297	31	34	9	113	7	1	.992
1986— Pittsfield (East.)		OF	•140	509	66	*156	29	2	12	*95	.306	54	32	15	248	9	3	*.988
— Chicago (N.L.)		OF	22	73	9	18	4	0	3	12	.247	4	6	1	34	2	4	.900
1987— Iowa (A.A.)		OF-1B	57	214	36	64	14	3	11	41	.299	22	22	4	150	13	2	.988
— Chicago (N.L.)		OF-1B	84	221	32	61	15	1	14	30	.276	20	26	2	176	9	1	.995
1988— Chicago (N.L.)		OF-1B	152	580	75	178	41	5	8	53	.307	38	34	12	322	11	5	.985
1989— Texas (A.L.)■		1B-DH	156	559	76	154	23	4	8	64	.275	63	48	4	*1167	*119	12	.991
1990— Texas (A.L.)		1B-DH	154	598	72	*191	35	6	14	89	.319	40	59	3	1215	91	7	.995
1991— Texas (A.L.)		1B-DH	159	631	115	203	*49	3	26	88	.322	68	72	4	1305	96	*12	.992
1992— Texas (A.L.)		1B-DH	159	608	84	163	27	4	22	85	.268	72	83	2	1251	*143	7	.995
1993— Texas (A.L.)		1B	160	597	*124	176	40	2	37	105	.295	73	85	22	*1388	*147	5	.997
1994— Baltimore (A.L.)■		1B	111	436	82	139	32	0	23	76	.319	54	63	7	959	66	4	.996
1995— Baltimore (A.L.)		1B	143	554	89	172	30	2	39	104	.310	62	65	3	1181	*119	4	.997
1996— Baltimore (A.L.)		1B-DH	162	626	110	181	40	2	39	142	.289	95	96	8	*1383	*119	8	.995
1997— Baltimore (A.L.)		1B-DH	158	614	95	156	24	2	38	110	.254	67	109	5	1305	112	10	.993
1998— Baltimore (A.L.)		1B-DH	162	619	98	183	36	1	43	121	.296	79	91	11	*1435	*124	9	.994
1999— Texas (A.L.)■		DH-1B	158	565	96	183	30	1	47	148	.324	97	69	2	261	13	1	.996
American League totals (11 years)			1682	6407	1041	1901	366	27	336	1132	.297	770	840	71	12850	1149	79	.994
National League totals (3 years)			258	874	116	257	60	6	25	95	.294	62	66	15	532	22	10	.982
Major League totals (14 years)			1940	7281	1157	2158	426	33	361	1227	.296	832	906	86	13382	1171	89	.994

DIVISION SERIES RECORD

								BATTING								FIELDING		
Year	Team (League)	Pos.	G	AB	R	H	2B	3B	HR	RBI	Avg.	BB	SO	SB	PO	A	E	Avg.
1996— Baltimore (A.L.)		1B	4	17	4	3	1	0	1	2	.176	1	6	0	35	1	1	.973
1997— Baltimore (A.L.)		1B	4	12	2	3	2	0	0	0	.250	0	2	0	27	2	0	1.000
1999— Texas (A.L.)		DH	3	11	0	3	0	0	0	0	.273	1	1	0	0	0	0	...
Division series totals (3 years)			11	40	6	9	3	0	1	2	.225	2	9	0	62	3	1	.985

P

NOTES: Hit home run in first at-bat (October 9, 1996).

							BATTING								FIELDING		
Year	Team (League)	Pos.	G	AB	R	H	2B	3B	HR	RBI	Avg.	BB	SO	SB	PO	A	E	Avg.
1996—	Baltimore (A.L.)..........	1B	5	17	4	4	0	0	2	4	.235	4	4	0	44	3	0	1.000
1997—	Baltimore (A.L.)..........	1B	6	25	3	7	2	0	1	2	.280	0	10	0	55	2	0	1.000
Championship series totals (2 years)			**11**	**42**	**7**	**11**	**2**	**0**	**3**	**6**	**.262**	**4**	**14**	**0**	**99**	**5**	**0**	**1.000**

ALL-STAR GAME RECORD

						BATTING								FIELDING		
Year	League	Pos.	AB	R	H	2B	3B	HR	RBI	Avg.	BB	SO	SB	PO	A	E	Avg.
1988—	National.....................	PH-OF	0	0	0	0	0	0	0	...	1	0	0	1	0	0	1.000
1991—	American.................	1B	0	0	0	0	0	0	0	...	1	0	0	2	0	0	1.000
1998—	American.................	1B	2	1	2	0	0	0	1	1.000	0	0	0	2	0	0	1.000
1999—	American.................	DH	2	0	1	0	0	0	1	.500	0	0	0	0	0	0	...
All-Star Game totals (4 years)			**4**	**1**	**3**	**0**	**0**	**0**	**2**	**.750**	**2**	**0**	**0**	**5**	**0**	**0**	**1.000**

PALMER, DEAN　　　　3B　　　　TIGERS

PERSONAL: Born December 27, 1968, in Tallahassee, Fla. ... 6-1/210. ... Bats right, throws right. ... Full name: Dean William Palmer.
HIGH SCHOOL: Florida (Tallahassee, Fla.).
TRANSACTIONS/CAREER NOTES: Selected by Texas Rangers organization in third round of free-agent draft (June 2, 1986). ... On disabled list (July 19, 1988-remainder of season; April 28-May 13, 1994; and June 4-September 22, 1995). ... Traded by Rangers to Kansas City Royals for OF Tom Goodwin (July 25, 1997). ... Granted free agency (October 27, 1997). ... Re-signed by Royals (December 15, 1997). ... Granted free agency (October 23, 1998). ... Signed by Detroit Tigers (November 13, 1998).
RECORDS: Shares major league single-season record for fewest assists by third baseman (150 or more games)—221 (1996). ... Holds A.L. single-season record for fewest chances accepted by third baseman (150 or more games)—326 (1996). ... Shares A.L. single-season record for fewest double plays by third baseman (150 or more games)—17 (1996).
HONORS: Named third baseman on The Sporting News A.L. Silver Slugger team (1998 and 1999). ... Named third baseman on The Sporting News A.L. All-Star team (1999).
STATISTICAL NOTES: Led Texas League third basemen with 30 errors in 1989. ... Led A.L. third basemen with 29 errors in 1993. ... Career major league grand slams: 7.

							BATTING								FIELDING		
Year	Team (League)	Pos.	G	AB	R	H	2B	3B	HR	RBI	Avg.	BB	SO	SB	PO	A	E	Avg.
1986—	GC Rangers (GCL)......	3B	50	163	19	34	7	1	0	12	.209	22	34	6	25	75	13	.885
1987—	Gastonia (SAL).........	3B	128	484	51	104	16	0	9	54	.215	36	126	5	58	209	*59	.819
1988—	Charlotte (FSL)..........	3B	74	305	38	81	12	1	4	35	.266	15	69	0	49	144	28	.873
1989—	Tulsa (Texas).............	3B-SS	133	498	82	125	32	5	*25	90	.251	41	*152	15	85	213	†31	.906
	—Texas (A.L.)................3B-DH-SS-OF		16	19	0	2	0	0	1	.105	0	12	0	3	4	2	.778
1990—	Tulsa (Texas).............	3B	7	24	4	7	0	1	3	9	.292	4	10	0	9	6	3	.833
	—Oklahoma City (A.A.).....	3B-1B	88	316	33	69	17	4	12	39	.218	20	106	1	206	110	21	.938
1991—	Oklahoma City (A.A.)..	3B-OF	60	234	45	70	11	2	*22	59	.299	20	61	4	49	105	11	.933
	—Texas (A.L.)............... 3B-OF-DH		81	268	38	50	9	2	15	37	.187	32	98	0	69	75	9	.941
1992—	Texas (A.L.)...............	3B	152	541	74	124	25	0	26	72	.229	62	*154	10	124	254	22	.945
1993—	Texas (A.L.)...............	3B-SS	148	519	88	127	31	2	33	96	.245	53	154	11	86	258	†29	.922
1994—	Texas (A.L.)...............	3B	93	342	50	84	14	2	19	59	.246	26	89	3	50	179	*22	.912
1995—	Texas (A.L.)...............	3B	36	119	30	40	6	0	9	24	.336	21	21	1	19	72	5	.948
1996—	Texas (A.L.)...............	3B-DH	154	582	98	163	26	2	38	107	.280	59	145	2	105	221	16	.953
1997—	Texas (A.L.)...............	3B	94	355	47	87	21	0	14	55	.245	26	84	1	72	162	10	.959
	—Kansas City (A.L.)■...	3B-DH	49	187	23	52	10	1	9	31	.278	15	50	1	27	82	9	.924
1998—	Kansas City (A.L.)......	3B-DH	152	572	84	159	27	2	34	119	.278	48	134	8	69	187	22	.921
1999—	Detroit (A.L.)■..........	3B-DH	150	560	92	147	25	2	38	100	.263	57	153	3	89	240	19	.945
Major League totals (10 years)			**1125**	**4064**	**624**	**1035**	**196**	**13**	**235**	**701**	**.255**	**399**	**1094**	**40**	**713**	**1734**	**165**	**.937**

DIVISION SERIES RECORD

							BATTING								FIELDING		
Year	Team (League)	Pos.	G	AB	R	H	2B	3B	HR	RBI	Avg.	BB	SO	SB	PO	A	E	Avg.
1996—	Texas (A.L.)	3B	4	19	3	4	1	0	1	2	.211	0	5	0	3	10	1	.929

ALL-STAR GAME RECORD

						BATTING								FIELDING		
Year	League	Pos.	AB	R	H	2B	3B	HR	RBI	Avg.	BB	SO	SB	PO	A	E	Avg.
1998—	American...................	PH	1	0	0	0	0	0	0	.000	0	0	0	...	...	...	...

PANIAGUA, JOSE　　　　P　　　　MARINERS

PERSONAL: Born August 20, 1973, in San Jose de Ocoa, Dominican Republic. ... 6-2/185. ... Throws right, bats right. ... Full name: Jose Luis Sanchez Paniagua.
HIGH SCHOOL: Liceo Nuestra Senora del Altagracia (Santo Domingo, Dominican Republic).
TRANSACTIONS/CAREER NOTES: Signed as non-drafted free agent by Montreal Expos organization (September 17, 1990). ... On Montreal disabled list (May 25-June 11, 1996). ... On Ottawa disabled list (July 16-August 2, 1996). ... Selected by Tampa Bay Devil Rays in second round (50th pick overall) of expansion draft (November 18, 1997). ... Claimed on waivers by Seattle Mariners (March 26, 1998). ... On suspended list (August 10-16, 1999).

Year	League	W	L	Pct.	ERA	G	GS	CG	ShO	Sv.	IP	H	R	ER	BB	SO
1992—	Dom. Expos (DSL)...........	3	7	.300	4.15	13	13	3	1	0	73 2/3	69	50	34	46	60
1993—	Gulf Coast Expos (GCL)	3	0	1.000	0.67	4	4	1	0	0	27	13	2	2	5	25
1994—	West Palm Beach (FSL)	9	9	.500	3.64	26	26	1	0	0	141	131	82	57	54	110
1995—	Harrisburg (East.)...............	7	•12	.368	5.34	25	25	2	1	0	126 1/3	140	84	75	62	89

P

Year	League	W	L	Pct.	ERA	G	GS	CG	ShO	Sv.	IP	H	R	ER	BB	SO
1996—	Ottawa (I.L.)	9	5	.643	3.18	15	14	2	1	0	85	72	39	30	23	61
—	Montreal (N.L.)	2	4	.333	3.53	13	11	0	0	0	51	55	24	20	23	27
—	Harrisburg (East.)	3	0	1.000	0.00	3	3	0	0	0	18	12	1	0	2	16
1997—	West Palm Beach (FSL)	1	0	1.000	0.00	2	2	0	0	0	10	5	0	0	2	11
—	Ottawa (I.L.)	8	10	.444	4.64	22	22	1	0	0	137 2/3	164	79	71	44	87
—	Montreal (N.L.)	1	2	.333	12.00	9	3	0	0	0	18	29	24	24	16	8
1998—	Tacoma (PCL)■	3	1	.750	2.77	44	0	0	0	5	68 1/3	66	25	21	22	61
—	Seattle (A.L.)	2	0	1.000	2.05	18	0	0	0	1	22	15	5	5	5	16
1999—	Seattle (A.L.)	6	11	.353	4.06	59	0	0	0	3	77 2/3	75	37	35	52	74
A.L. totals (2 years)		8	11	.421	3.61	77	0	0	0	4	99 2/3	90	42	40	57	90
N.L. totals (2 years)		3	6	.333	5.74	22	14	0	0	0	69	84	48	44	39	35
Major League totals (4 years)		11	17	.393	4.48	99	14	0	0	4	168 2/3	174	90	84	96	125

PAQUETTE, CRAIG — 3B/OF — CARDINALS

PERSONAL: Born March 28, 1969, in Long Beach, Calif. ... 6-0/190. ... Bats right, throws right. ... Full name: Craig Howard Paquette.
HIGH SCHOOL: Ranchos Alamitos (Garden Grove, Calif.).
JUNIOR COLLEGE: Golden West College (Calif.).
TRANSACTIONS/CAREER NOTES: Selected by Minnesota Twins organization in 36th round of free-agent draft (June 2, 1987); did not sign. ... Selected by Oakland Athletics organization in eighth round of free-agent draft (June 5, 1989). ... On Modesto disabled list (April 10-May 5, 1991). ... On Huntsville disabled list (June 1-11, 1991). ... On Tacoma disabled list (July 18, 1994-remainder of season). ... Released by A's (March 26, 1996). ... Signed by Kansas City Royals organization (April 3, 1996). ... Granted free agency (October 15, 1997). ... Signed by New York Mets organization (December 23, 1997). ... On New York disabled list (May 7, 1998-remainder of season). ... Granted free agency (October 15, 1998). ... Re-signed by Mets organization (December 18, 1998). ... On Norfolk disabled list (April 22-May 1, 1999). ... Traded by Mets to St. Louis Cardinals for IF/OF Shawon Dunston (July 31, 1999).
STATISTICAL NOTES: Tied for Northwest League lead with 163 total bases in 1989. ... Led Northwest League third basemen with .936 fielding percentage and 12 double plays in 1989. ... Led Southern League third basemen with 349 total chances in 1992. ... Career major league grand slams: 2.

							BATTING								FIELDING		
Year	Team (League)	Pos.	G	AB	R	H	2B	3B	HR	RBI	Avg.	BB	SO	SB	PO	A	E	Avg.
1989—	S. Oregon (N'west)	3B-SS-2B	71	277	53	93	*22	3	14	56	.336	30	46	9	61	155	15	†.935
1990—	Modesto (Calif.)	3B	130	495	65	118	23	4	15	59	.238	47	123	8	*88	218	26	*.922
1991—	Huntsville (Sou.)	3B-1B	102	378	50	99	18	1	8	60	.262	28	87	0	51	132	16	.920
1992—	Huntsville (Sou.)	3B	115	450	59	116	25	4	17	71	.258	29	118	13	69	*248	*32	.908
—	Tacoma (PCL)	3B	17	66	10	18	7	0	2	11	.273	2	16	3	14	33	3	.940
1993—	Tacoma (PCL)	3B-SS-2B	50	183	29	49	8	0	8	29	.268	14	54	3	32	116	15	.908
—	Oakland (A.L.)	3B-DH-OF	105	393	35	86	20	4	12	46	.219	14	108	4	82	165	13	.950
1994—	Tacoma (PCL)	3B	65	245	39	70	12	3	17	48	.286	14	48	3	40	166	14	.936
—	Oakland (A.L.)	3B	14	49	0	7	2	0	0	0	.143	0	14	1	14	22	0	1.000
1995—	Oakland (A.L.)	3-0-S-1	105	283	42	64	13	1	13	49	.226	12	88	5	72	92	8	.953
1996—	Omaha (A.A.) 3-0-1-S	DH-3B-1B-OF	18	63	9	21	3	0	4	13	.333	8	14	1	24	9	3	.917
—	Kansas City (A.L.)	3-0-1-S-DH	118	429	61	111	15	1	22	67	.259	23	101	5	261	102	14	.963
1997—	Kansas City (A.L.)	3B-OF	77	252	26	58	15	1	8	33	.230	10	57	2	51	130	12	.938
—	Omaha (A.A.)	3B-DH	23	91	9	28	6	0	3	20	.308	6	26	0	12	29	2	.953
1998—	Norfolk (I.L.)■	3B-SS-OF	15	61	11	17	1	1	3	14	.279	1	13	2	9	39	4	.923
—	New York (N.L.)	3B-1B-OF	7	19	3	5	2	0	0	0	.263	0	6	1	5	2	0	1.000
1999—	Norfolk (I.L.) 3B-OF-1B-SS		70	283	40	77	20	3	15	54	.272	10	47	3	168	82	8	.969
—	St. Louis (N.L.)■ OF-3B-2B-1B		48	157	21	45	6	0	10	37	.287	6	38	1	75	42	3	.975
American League totals (5 years)			419	1406	164	326	65	7	55	195	.232	59	368	17	480	511	47	.955
National League totals (2 years)			55	176	24	50	8	0	10	37	.284	6	44	2	80	44	3	.976
Major League totals (7 years)			474	1582	188	376	73	7	65	232	.238	65	412	19	560	555	50	.957

PARK, CHAN HO — P — DODGERS

PERSONAL: Born June 30, 1973, in Kong Ju City, Korea. ... 6-2/204. ... Throws right, bats right. ... Full name: Chan Ho Park.
HIGH SCHOOL: Kong Ju (Kong Ju City, Korea).
COLLEGE: Hanyang University (Seoul, Korea).
TRANSACTIONS/CAREER NOTES: Signed as non-drafted free agent by Los Angeles Dodgers organization (January 14, 1994). ... On Albuquerque disabled list (July 16-29, 1995). ... On suspended list (June 8-17, 1999).
RECORDS: Shares major league single-season record for most grand slams allowed—4 (1999).

Year	League	W	L	Pct.	ERA	G	GS	CG	ShO	Sv.	IP	H	R	ER	BB	SO
1994—	Los Angeles (N.L.)	0	0	...	11.25	2	0	0	0	0	4	5	5	5	5	6
—	San Antonio (Texas)	5	7	.417	3.55	20	20	0	0	0	101 1/3	91	52	40	57	100
1995—	Albuquerque (PCL)	6	7	.462	4.91	23	22	0	0	0	110	93	64	60	76	101
—	Los Angeles (N.L.)	0	0	...	4.50	2	1	0	0	0	4	2	2	2	2	7
1996—	Los Angeles (N.L.)	5	5	.500	3.64	48	10	0	0	0	108 2/3	82	48	44	71	119
1997—	Los Angeles (N.L.)	14	8	.636	3.38	32	29	2	0	0	192	149	80	72	70	166
1998—	Los Angeles (N.L.)	15	9	.625	3.71	34	34	2	0	0	220 2/3	199	101	91	97	191
1999—	Los Angeles (N.L.)	13	11	.542	5.23	33	33	0	0	0	194 1/3	208	120	113	100	174
Major League totals (6 years)		47	33	.588	4.07	151	107	4	0	0	723 2/3	645	356	327	345	663

P   PARQUE, JIM — P — WHITE SOX

PERSONAL: Born February 8, 1976, in Norwalk, Calif. ... 5-11/165. ... Throws left, bats left. ... Full name: Jim Vo Parque.
HIGH SCHOOL: Crescenta Valley (Calif.).
COLLEGE: UCLA.

TRANSACTIONS/CAREER NOTES: Selected by Chicago White Sox organization in second round of free-agent draft (June 3, 1997).
STATISTICAL NOTES: Tied for A.L. lead with three balks in 1998.
MISCELLANEOUS: Member of 1996 U.S. Olympic baseball team.

Year	League	W	L	Pct.	ERA	G	GS	CG	ShO	Sv.	IP	H	R	ER	BB	SO
1997—	Win.-Salem (Car.)...............	7	2	.778	2.77	11	11	0	0	0	61²/₃	29	19	19	23	76
—	Nashville (PCL)	1	0	1.000	4.22	2	2	0	0	0	10²/₃	9	5	5	9	5
1998—	Calgary (PCL)	2	3	.400	3.94	8	8	0	0	0	48	49	26	21	25	31
—	Chicago (A.L.)	7	5	.583	5.10	21	21	0	0	0	113	135	72	64	49	77
1999—	Chicago (A.L.)	9	15	.375	5.13	31	30	1	0	0	173²/₃	210	111	99	79	111
Major League totals (2 years).......		**16**	**20**	**.444**	**5.12**	**52**	**51**	**1**	**0**	**0**	**286²/₃**	**345**	**183**	**163**	**128**	**188**

PARRIS, STEVE — P — REDS

PERSONAL: Born December 17, 1967, in Joliet, Ill. ... 6-0/195. ... Throws right, bats right. ... Full name: Steven Michael Parris.
HIGH SCHOOL: Joliet (Ill.) West.
COLLEGE: College of St. Francis (Ill.).
TRANSACTIONS/CAREER NOTES: Selected by Philadelphia Phillies organization in fifth round of free-agent draft (June 5, 1989). ... Claimed on waivers by Los Angeles Dodgers (April 19, 1993). ... Claimed on waivers by Seattle Mariners (April 26, 1993). ... On Jacksonville disabled list (May 12-June 23 and July 17-31, 1993). ... Released by Mariners (July 31, 1993). ... Signed by Salem, Pittsburgh Pirates organization (June 24, 1994). ... On Pittsburgh disabled list (March 6-July 11 and August 18-September 10, 1996); included rehabilitation assignments to Augusta (June 12-13) and Carolina (June 13-July 11). ... Released by Pirates (March 13, 1997). ... Signed by Cincinnati Reds organization (May 6, 1997). ... Granted free agency (October 15, 1997). ... Re-signed by Reds organization (October 27, 1997). ... On Cincinnati disabled list (July 31-September 1, 1999); included rehabilitation assignment to Indianapolis (August 22-30).
STATISTICAL NOTES: Tied for N.L. lead in double plays by a pitcher with six in 1999.

Year	League	W	L	Pct.	ERA	G	GS	CG	ShO	Sv.	IP	H	R	ER	BB	SO
1989—	Batavia (NY-P)..................	3	5	.375	3.91	13	10	1	0	0	66²/₃	69	38	29	20	46
1990—	Batavia (NY-P)..................	7	1	*.875	2.64	14	14	0	0	0	81²/₃	70	34	24	22	50
1991—	Clearwater (FSL)	7	5	.583	3.39	43	6	0	0	1	93	101	43	35	25	59
1992—	Reading (East.).................	5	7	.417	4.64	18	14	0	0	0	85¹/₃	94	55	44	21	60
—	Scranton/W.B. (I.L.)	3	3	.500	4.03	11	6	0	0	1	51¹/₃	57	25	23	17	29
1993—	Scranton/W.B. (I.L.)	0	0	...	12.71	3	0	0	0	0	5²/₃	9	9	8	3	4
—	Jacksonville (Sou.)■.........	0	1	.000	5.93	7	1	0	0	0	13²/₃	15	9	9	6	5
1994—	Salem (Caro.)■	3	3	.500	3.63	17	7	0	0	0	57	58	24	23	21	48
1995—	Carolina (Sou.)	9	1	.900	2.51	14	14	2	2	0	89²/₃	61	25	25	16	86
—	Pittsburgh (N.L.)	6	6	.500	5.38	15	15	1	1	0	82	89	49	49	33	61
1996—	Augusta (SAL)...................	0	0	...	0.00	1	1	0	0	0	5	1	0	0	1	6
—	Carolina (Sou.)	2	0	1.000	3.04	5	5	0	0	0	26²/₃	24	11	9	6	22
—	Pittsburgh (N.L.)	0	3	.000	7.18	8	4	0	0	0	26¹/₃	35	22	21	11	27
1997—	Chattanooga (Sou.)■	6	2	.750	4.13	14	14	0	0	0	80²/₃	78	44	37	29	68
—	Indianapolis (A.A.)	2	3	.400	3.57	5	5	1	1	0	35¹/₃	26	15	14	11	27
1998—	Indianapolis (I.L.).............	6	1	.857	3.84	13	13	1	1	0	84¹/₃	74	38	36	26	102
—	Cincinnati (N.L.)	6	5	.545	3.73	18	16	1	1	0	99	89	44	41	32	77
1999—	Indianapolis (I.L.)..............	0	2	.000	4.04	6	6	0	0	0	35²/₃	39	16	16	9	31
—	Cincinnati (N.L.)	11	4	.733	3.50	22	21	2	1	0	128²/₃	124	59	50	52	86
Major League totals (4 years).......		**23**	**18**	**.561**	**4.31**	**63**	**56**	**4**	**3**	**0**	**336**	**337**	**174**	**161**	**128**	**251**

PATRICK, BRONSWELL — P — MARLINS

PERSONAL: Born September 16, 1970, in Pitt County, N.C. ... 6-1/220. ... Throws right, bats right. ... Full name: Bronswell Dante Patrick.
HIGH SCHOOL: D.H. Conley (Winterville, N.C.).
TRANSACTIONS/CAREER NOTES: Selected by Oakland Athletics in 23rd round of free-agent draft (June 1, 1988). ... Granted free agency (October 17, 1994). ... Signed by Houston Astros organization (January 18, 1995). ... Granted free agency (October 15, 1996). ... Re-signed by Astros organization (November 22, 1996). ... Granted free agency (October 17, 1997). ... Signed by Milwaukee Brewers organization (November 5, 1997). ... Granted free agency (October 15, 1998). ... Signed by San Francisco Giants organization (December 4, 1998). ... Granted free agency (October 15, 1999). ... Signed by Florida Marlins organization (December 22, 1999).
STATISTICAL NOTES: Tied for Arizona League lead in home runs allowed with seven in 1988. ... Led Southern League with 20 home runs allowed in 1992. ... Led Pacific Coast League with 33 home runs allowed in 1999.

Year	League	W	L	Pct.	ERA	G	GS	CG	ShO	Sv.	IP	H	R	ER	BB	SO
1988—	Arizona Athletics (Ariz.)......	8	3	.727	2.99	14	*13	2	0	0	*96¹/₃	*99	37	32	16	64
1989—	Madison (Midw.)...............	2	5	.286	3.64	12	10	0	0	0	54¹/₃	62	29	22	14	32
1990—	Modesto (Calif.)	3	7	.300	5.18	14	14	0	0	0	74²/₃	92	58	43	32	37
—	Madison (Midw.)...............	3	7	.300	3.60	13	12	3	0	0	80	88	44	32	19	40
1991—	Modesto (Calif.)	12	12	.500	3.24	28	26	3	1	0	169²/₃	158	77	61	60	95
1992—	Huntsville (Sou.)	•13	7	.650	3.76	29	29	3	0	0	179¹/₃	*187	84	75	46	98
1993—	Tacoma (PCL)	3	8	.273	7.05	35	13	1	0	1	104²/₃	156	87	82	42	56
1994—	Huntsville (Sou.)	2	0	1.000	2.93	7	3	0	0	1	27²/₃	31	11	9	10	16
—	Tacoma (PCL)	1	1	.500	4.75	30	0	0	0	2	47¹/₃	50	31	25	20	38
1995—	Tucson (PCL)■	5	1	.833	4.19	43	4	0	0	1	81²/₃	91	42	38	21	62
1996—	Tucson (PCL)■	7	3	.700	3.51	33	15	0	0	1	118	137	59	46	33	82
1997—	New Orleans (A.A.)............	6	5	.545	3.22	30	12	1	1	0	100²/₃	108	45	36	30	88
1998—	Louisville (I.L.)■................	3	1	.750	4.30	6	6	0	0	0	37²/₃	43	21	18	9	28
—	Milwaukee (N.L.)...............	4	1	.800	4.69	32	3	0	0	0	78²/₃	83	43	41	29	49
1999—	Fresno (PCL)■	14	11	.560	4.88	28	•28	1	0	0	164	194	116	89	42	142
—	San Francisco (N.L.)	1	0	1.000	10.13	6	0	0	0	1	5¹/₃	9	7	6	3	6
Major League totals (2 years).......		**5**	**1**	**.833**	**5.04**	**38**	**3**	**0**	**0**	**1**	**84**	**92**	**50**	**47**	**32**	**55**

P

PATTERSON, DANNY P TIGERS

PERSONAL: Born February 17, 1971, in San Gabriel, Calif. ... 6-0/225. ... Throws right, bats right. ... Full name: Danny Shane Patterson.
HIGH SCHOOL: San Gabriel (Calif.).
JUNIOR COLLEGE: Cerritos College (Calif.).
TRANSACTIONS/CAREER NOTES: Selected by Texas Rangers organization in 47th round of free-agent draft (June 5, 1989). ... On Texas disabled list (May 22-June 14, 1997); included rehabilitation assignment to Tulsa (June 9-14). ... On Texas disabled list (March 22-April 17, 1998); included rehabilitation assignments to Tulsa (April 7-12) and Oklahoma (April 13-17). ... Traded by Rangers with OF Juan Gonzalez and C Gregg Zaun to Detroit Tigers for P Justin Thompson, P Francisco Cordero, OF Gabe Kapler, C Bill Haselman, 2B Frank Catalanotto and P Alan Webb (November 2, 1999).

Year League	W	L	Pct.	ERA	G	GS	CG	ShO	Sv.	IP	H	R	ER	BB	SO
1990— Butte (Pio.)	0	3	.000	6.35	13	3	0	0	1	28 1/3	36	23	20	14	18
1991— Gulf Coast Rangers (GCL)..	5	3	.625	3.24	11	9	0	0	0	50	43	21	18	12	46
1992— Gastonia (SAL)	4	6	.400	3.59	23	21	3	1	0	105 1/3	106	47	42	33	84
1993— Charlotte (FSL)	5	6	.455	2.51	47	0	0	0	7	68	55	22	19	28	41
1994— Tulsa (Texas)	1	4	.200	1.64	30	1	0	0	6	44	35	13	8	17	33
— Charlotte (FSL)	1	0	1.000	4.61	7	0	0	0	0	13 2/3	13	7	7	5	9
1995— Tulsa (Texas)	2	2	.500	6.19	26	0	0	0	5	36 1/3	45	27	25	13	24
— Oklahoma City (A.A.)	1	0	1.000	1.65	14	0	0	0	2	27 1/3	23	8	5	9	9
1996— Oklahoma City (A.A.)	6	2	.750	1.68	44	0	0	0	10	80 1/3	79	22	15	15	53
— Texas (A.L.)	0	0	...	0.00	7	0	0	0	0	8 2/3	10	4	0	3	5
1997— Texas (A.L.)	10	6	.625	3.42	54	0	0	0	1	71	70	29	27	23	69
— Tulsa (Texas)	0	0	...	4.50	2	2	0	0	0	2	5	4	1	0	0
1998— Texas (A.L.)	0	0	...	4.50	2	1	0	0	0	4	3	2	2	0	4
— Oklahoma (PCL)	0	0	...	4.50	1	0	0	0	0	2	4	1	1	1	2
— Texas (A.L.)	2	5	.286	4.45	56	0	0	0	2	60 2/3	64	31	30	19	33
1999— Texas (A.L.)	2	0	1.000	5.67	53	0	0	0	0	60 1/3	77	38	38	19	43
— Oklahoma (PCL)	1	0	1.000	0.00	2	0	0	0	0	3	1	0	0	1	4
Major League totals (4 years)	14	11	.560	4.26	170	0	0	0	3	200 2/3	221	102	95	64	150

DIVISION SERIES RECORD

Year League	W	L	Pct.	ERA	G	GS	CG	ShO	Sv.	IP	H	R	ER	BB	SO
1996— Texas (A.L.)	0	0	...	0.00	1	0	0	0	0	1/3	1	0	0	0	0
1999— Texas (A.L.)	0	0	...	0.00	1	0	0	0	0	1	1	0	0	0	0
Division series totals (2 years)	0	0	...	0.00	2	0	0	0	0	1 1/3	2	0	0	0	0

PAUL, JOSH C WHITE SOX

PERSONAL: Born May 19, 1975, in Evanston, III. ... 6-1/185. ... Bats right, throws right. ... Full name: Joshua William Paul.
HIGH SCHOOL: Buffalo Grove (III.).
COLLEGE: Vanderbilt.
TRANSACTIONS/CAREER NOTES: Selected by Chicago White Sox organization in second round of free-agent draft (June 4, 1996). ... On Birmingham disabled list (April 13-July 13, 1997; and July 9-27, 1999).
STATISTICAL NOTES: Led Carolina League catchers with 939 total chances in 1998.

Year Team (League)	Pos.	G	AB	R	H	2B	3B	HR	RBI	Avg.	BB	SO	SB	PO	A	E	Avg.
1996— Hickory (SAL)	C	59	226	41	74	16	0	8	37	.327	21	53	13	197	29	2	.991
1997— Birmingham (Sou.)	C	34	115	18	34	5	0	1	16	.296	12	25	6	221	17	3	.988
— GC White Sox (GCL)	C	5	14	3	6	0	1	0	0	.429	1	3	1	21	6	3	.900
1998— Win.-Salem (Car.)	C	123	444	66	113	20	7	11	63	.255	38	91	20	*818	*118	3	*.997
1999— Birmingham (Sou.)	C-DH	93	319	47	89	19	3	4	42	.279	29	68	6	526	66	5	*.992
— Chicago (A.L.)	C	6	18	2	4	1	0	0	1	.222	0	4	0	40	2	0	1.000
Major League totals (1 year)		6	18	2	4	1	0	0	1	.222	0	4	0	40	2	0	1.000

PAVANO, CARL P EXPOS

PERSONAL: Born January 8, 1976, in New Britain, Conn. ... 6-5/230. ... Throws right, bats right. ... Full name: Carl Anthony Pavano.
HIGH SCHOOL: Southington (Conn.).
TRANSACTIONS/CAREER NOTES: Selected by Boston Red Sox organization in 13th round of free-agent draft (June 2, 1994). ... Traded by Red Sox with a player to be named later to Montreal Expos for P Pedro J. Martinez (November 18, 1997); Expos acquired P Tony Armas Jr. to complete deal (December 18, 1997). ... On Montreal disabled list (July 12-September 11, 1999); included rehabilitation assignments to Ottawa (July 29-30 and September 6-7).
HONORS: Named Eastern League Pitcher of the Year (1996).

Year League	W	L	Pct.	ERA	G	GS	CG	ShO	Sv.	IP	H	R	ER	BB	SO
1994— Gulf Coast Red Sox (GCL)..	4	3	.571	1.84	9	7	0	0	0	44	31	14	9	7	47
1995— Michigan (Midw.)	6	6	.500	3.45	22	22	1	0	0	141	118	63	54	52	138
1996— Trenton (East.)	*16	5	.762	2.63	27	26	•6	2	0	185	154	66	54	47	146
1997— Pawtucket (I.L.)	11	6	.647	3.12	23	23	3	0	0	161 2/3	148	62	56	34	147
1998— Jupiter (FSL)■	0	0	...	6.60	4	4	0	0	0	15	20	11	11	3	14
— Ottawa (I.L.)	1	0	1.000	2.41	3	3	0	0	0	18 2/3	12	5	5	7	14
— Montreal (N.L.)	6	9	.400	4.21	24	23	0	0	0	134 2/3	130	70	63	43	83
1999— Montreal (N.L.)	6	8	.429	5.63	19	18	1	1	0	104	117	66	65	35	70
— Ottawa (I.L.)	0	1	.000	9.00	2	2	0	0	0	5	7	5	5	0	3
Major League totals (2 years)	12	17	.414	4.83	43	41	1	1	0	238 2/3	247	136	128	78	153

P

PAYTON, JAY — OF — METS

PERSONAL: Born November 22, 1972, in Zanesville, Ohio. ... 5-10/185. ... Bats right, throws right. ... Full name: Jayson Lee Payton.
HIGH SCHOOL: Zanesville (Ohio).
COLLEGE: Georgia Tech.
TRANSACTIONS/CAREER NOTES: Selected by New York Mets organization in supplemental round ("sandwich pick" between first and second round, 29th pick overall) of free-agent draft (June 2, 1994); pick received as part of compensation for Baltimore Orioles signing Type A free-agent P Sid Fernandez. ... On Norfolk disabled list (April 29-July 3, 1996). ... On St. Lucie temporarily inactive list (July 11-16, 1996). ... On disabled list (April 3, 1997-entire season). ... On Norfolk disabled list (May 27-June 15 and June 24-July 20, 1998). ... On New York disabled list (March 21-June 8, 1999); included rehabilitation assignment to St. Lucie (May 30-June 8). ... On Norfolk disabled list (July 10-August 19, 1999).

Year	Team (League)	Pos.	G	AB	R	H	2B	3B	HR	RBI	Avg.	BB	SO	SB	PO	A	E	Avg.
1994—	Pittsfield (NY-P)	OF	58	219	47	80	16	2	3	37	.365	23	18	10	124	8	5	.964
	— Binghamton (East.)	OF	8	25	3	7	1	0	0	1	.280	2	3	1	11	0	1	.917
1995—	Binghamton (East.)	OF	85	357	59	123	20	3	14	54	.345	29	32	16	230	7	3	.988
	— Norfolk (I.L.)	OF	50	196	33	47	11	4	4	30	.240	11	22	11	106	3	2	.982
1996—	GC Mets (GCL)	DH	3	13	3	5	1	0	1	2	.385	0	1	1	...	...	...	...
	— Norfolk (Int'l)	OF	55	153	30	47	6	3	6	26	.307	11	26	10	7	1	0	1.000
	— St. Lucie (FSL)	DH	9	26	4	8	2	0	0	1	.308	4	5	2	...	...	...	...
1997—								Did not play.										
1998—	Norfolk (I.L.)	OF-1B-DH	82	322	45	84	14	4	8	30	.261	26	50	12	315	20	7	.980
	— St. Lucie (FSL)	OF	3	7	0	1	0	0	0	0	.143	3	1	0	8	0	0	1.000
	— New York (N.L.).........	OF	15	22	2	7	1	0	0	0	.318	1	4	0	6	1	0	1.000
1999—	St. Lucie (FSL)	OF	7	26	3	9	1	1	0	3	.346	4	5	0	20	1	1	.955
	— Norfolk (I.L.)	OF-DH	38	144	27	56	13	2	8	35	.389	12	13	2	59	3	1	.984
	— New York (N.L.).........	OF	13	8	1	2	1	0	0	1	.250	0	2	1	3	0	0	1.000
Major League totals (2 years)			28	30	3	9	2	0	0	1	.300	1	6	1	9	1	0	1.000

PENA, ALEX — P — PIRATES

PERSONAL: Born September 9, 1977, in Santo Domingo, Dominican Republic. ... 6-2/205. ... Throws right, bats right. ... Full name: Alex J. Pena.
TRANSACTIONS/CAREER NOTES: Signed as non-drafted free agent by Pittsburgh Pirates organization (January 7, 1994).
MISCELLANEOUS: Played outfield (1995-98).

Year	League	W	L	Pct.	ERA	G	GS	CG	ShO	Sv.	IP	H	R	ER	BB	SO
1998—	Augusta (SAL)..................	0	0	...	18.00	1	0	0	0	0	1	2	2	2	3	1
1999—	Hickory (SAL)..................	0	4	.000	6.60	22	7	0	0	0	46 $^1/_3$	68	42	34	31	37
	— Altoona (East.)	1	0	1.000	3.86	9	0	0	0	0	21	22	12	9	9	20

RECORD AS POSITION PLAYER

Year	Team (League)	Pos.	G	AB	R	H	2B	3B	HR	RBI	Avg.	BB	SO	SB	PO	A	E	Avg.
1995—	GC Pirates (GCL)........	OF-3B	48	172	15	41	7	3	1	20	.238	6	26	3	88	8	3	.970
1996—	Augusta (S. Atl.)........	OF	52	167	9	27	4	2	0	12	.162	7	51	2	75	10	5	.944
	— Erie (N.Y.-Penn).........	OF	74	281	31	75	10	3	4	33	.267	14	52	10	131	15	6	.961
1997—	Augusta (S. Atl.)........	OF	111	356	34	87	12	2	5	40	.244	18	81	11	176	11	10	.949
1998—	Lynchburg (Caro.)......	OF	5	16	1	1	1	0	0	0	.063	0	8	0	8	1	0	1.000
	— Augusta (S. Atl.)........	OF	90	292	47	74	15	1	5	26	.253	24	69	7	153	5	5	.969

PENA, ANGEL — C — DODGERS

PERSONAL: Born February 16, 1975, in San Pedro de Macoris, Dominican Republic. ... 5-10/228. ... Bats right, throws right. ... Full name: Angel Maria Pena.
HIGH SCHOOL: Escuela Puerto Rico (San Pedro de Macoris, Dominican Republic).
TRANSACTIONS/CAREER NOTES: Signed as non-drafted free agent by Los Angeles Dodgers organization (July 24, 1992). ... Missed entire 1994 season due to injury. ... On San Bernardino disabled list (July 26-September 17, 1997). ... On Albuquerque disabled list (August 24, 1999-remainder of season).
STATISTICAL NOTES: Led California League catchers with 31 passed balls in 1997. ... Led Texas League catchers with 781 putouts, 81 assists, 14 errors and 876 total chances in 1998.

Year	Team (League)	Pos.	G	AB	R	H	2B	3B	HR	RBI	Avg.	BB	SO	SB	PO	A	E	Avg.
1993—	Dom. Dodgers (DSL) .	C	50	168	27	47	3	2	1	24	.280	10	41	6	197	57	15	.944
1994—	....								Did not play.										
1995—	Great Falls (Pio.)	C	49	138	24	40	11	1	4	15	.290	21	32	2	297	42	7	.980
1996—	Savannah (SAL)	C	36	127	13	26	4	0	6	16	.205	7	37	1	238	39	6	.979
	— Dom. Dodgers (DSL) .	C	23	78	30	37	9	1	8	40	.474	24	12	1	86	11	1	.990
1997—	San Bern. (Calif.)........	C	86	322	53	89	22	4	16	64	.276	32	84	3	661	83	10	.987
1998—	San Antonio (Texas) ...	C-OF	126	483	81	162	32	2	22	105	.335	48	80	9	†781	†81	†14	.984
	— Los Angeles (N.L.)......	C	6	13	1	3	0	0	0	0	.231	0	6	0	26	2	0	1.000
1999—	Albuquerque (PCL).....	C-DH	34	127	15	37	10	1	1	24	.291	10	24	3	200	28	3	.987
	— Los Angeles (N.L.)......	C	43	120	14	25	6	0	4	21	.208	12	24	0	233	26	3	.989
Major League totals (2 years)			49	133	15	28	6	0	4	21	.211	12	30	0	259	28	3	.990

PENA, JESUS — P — WHITE SOX

PERSONAL: Born March 8, 1975, in Santo Domingo, Dominican Republic. ... 6-0/170. ... Throws left, bats left.
HIGH SCHOOL: Liceo Nocturno (Santo Domingo, Dominican Republic).

P

TRANSACTIONS/CAREER NOTES: Signed as non-drafted free agent by Pittsburgh Pirates organization (January 19, 1993). ... On suspended list (June 29-September 11, 1994). ... Selected by Chicago White Sox organization from Pirates organization in Rule 5 minor league draft (December 9, 1996).

Year League	W	L	Pct.	ERA	G	GS	CG	ShO	Sv.	IP	H	R	ER	BB	SO
1993— Dom. Pirates (DSL)...........	6	3	.667	2.37	18	10	0	0	2	68 1/3	48	27	18	51	79
1994—					Did not play—suspended.										
1995— Erie (NY-P)...................	0	3	.000	12.66	3	3	0	0	0	10 2/3	18	16	15	7	5
— Gulf Coast Pirates (GCL)	0	0	...	2.57	7	6	0	0	0	35	20	11	10	19	36
1996— Erie (NY-P)...................	2	5	.286	4.79	21	3	0	0	0	35 2/3	32	24	19	24	34
1997— Hickory (SAL)■...............	5	3	.625	2.22	43	0	0	0	8	65	55	24	16	19	57
1998— Win.-Salem (Car.)..............	3	4	.429	3.13	23	0	0	0	7	31 2/3	20	11	11	12	37
— Birmingham (Sou.)..............	0	2	.000	3.86	22	0	0	0	2	23 1/3	20	12	10	10	28
1999— Birmingham (Sou.)..............	3	2	.600	2.36	40	0	0	0	5	45 2/3	31	12	12	18	49
— Chicago (A.L.).................	0	0	...	5.31	26	0	0	0	0	20 1/3	21	15	12	23	20
Major League totals (1 year)........	**0**	**0**	**...**	**5.31**	**26**	**0**	**0**	**0**	**0**	**20 1/3**	**21**	**15**	**12**	**23**	**20**

PENA, JUAN — P — RED SOX

PERSONAL: Born June 27, 1977, in Santo Domingo, Dominican Republic. ... 6-5/215. ... Throws right, bats right. ... Full name: Juan Francisco Pena.
HIGH SCHOOL: Miami High.
JUNIOR COLLEGE: Miami-Dade (Wolfson) Community College.
TRANSACTIONS/CAREER NOTES: Selected by Boston Red Sox organization in 27th round of free-agent draft (June 1, 1995). ... On disabled list (April 9-24 and June 17-27, 1998). ... On Boston disabled list (May 20-June 6 and June 11-July 22, 1999); included rehabilitation assignments to Pawtucket (May 30-June 6), Gulf Coast Red Sox (July 8-11) and Sarasota (July 12-22). ... On Pawtucket disabled list (July 31-August 9 and August 12, 1999-remainder of season).
STATISTICAL NOTES: Pitched 5-0 no-hit victory for Pawtucket against Durham (July 22, 1998).

Year League	W	L	Pct.	ERA	G	GS	CG	ShO	Sv.	IP	H	R	ER	BB	SO
1995— Gulf Coast Red Sox (GCL)..	3	2	.600	1.95	13	4	2	1	1	55 1/3	41	17	12	6	47
— Sarasota (FSL)	1	1	.500	4.91	2	2	0	0	0	7 1/3	8	4	4	3	5
1996— Michigan (Midw.)	12	10	.545	2.97	26	26	4	0	0	*187 2/3	149	70	62	34	156
1997— Sarasota (FSL)	4	6	.400	2.96	13	13	3	0	0	91 1/3	67	39	30	23	88
— Trenton (East.)	5	6	.455	4.73	16	14	0	0	0	97	98	56	51	31	79
1998— Pawtucket (I.L.)...............	8	10	.444	4.38	24	23	1	1	0	139 2/3	141	73	68	51	*146
1999— Pawtucket (I.L.)...............	4	2	.667	4.13	10	10	0	0	0	48	44	28	22	13	61
— Boston (A.L.)..................	2	0	1.000	0.69	2	2	0	0	0	13	9	1	1	3	15
— Gulf Coast Red Sox (GCL)..	0	0	...	0.00	1	1	0	0	0	2	0	0	0	0	4
— Sarasota (FSL)	0	1	.000	7.11	2	2	0	0	0	6 1/3	12	6	5	0	5
Major League totals (1 year)........	**2**	**0**	**1.000**	**0.69**	**2**	**2**	**0**	**0**	**0**	**13**	**9**	**1**	**1**	**3**	**15**

PENA, WILY — OF — YANKEES

PERSONAL: Born January 23, 1982, in LaGuna Salada, Dominican Republic. ... 6-3/200. ... Bats right, throws right. ... Full name: Wily Mo Pena.
TRANSACTIONS/CAREER NOTES: Signed by New York Mets organization (1998); contract nullified by Baseball Commissioner's Office. ... Declared a free agent (March 7, 1999). ... Signed by New York Yankees organization (April 1, 1999).

						BATTING							FIELDING		
Year Team (League)	Pos.	G	AB	R	H	2B	3B	HR	RBI	Avg.	BB	SO	SB	PO	A	E	Avg.
1999— GC Yankees (GCL)......	OF	45	166	21	41	10	1	7	26	.247	12	54	3	35	1	2	.947

PENNY, BRAD — P — MARLINS

PERSONAL: Born May 24, 1978, in Blackwell, Okla. ... 6-4/200. ... Throws right, bats right. ... Full name: Bradley Wayne Penny.
HIGH SCHOOL: Broken Arrow (Okla.).
TRANSACTIONS/CAREER NOTES: Selected by Arizona Diamondbacks organization in fifth round of free-agent draft (June 4, 1996). ... On El Paso disabled list (April 20-30, 1999). ... Traded by Diamondbacks with P Vladimir Nunez and a player to be named later to Florida Marlins for P Matt Mantei (July 9, 1999); Marlins acquired OF Abraham Nunez to complete deal (December 13, 1999).
HONORS: Named California League Most Valuable Player and Pitcher of the Year (1998).

Year League	W	L	Pct.	ERA	G	GS	CG	ShO	Sv.	IP	H	R	ER	BB	SO
1996— Ariz. D'backs (Ariz.)............	2	2	.500	2.36	11	8	0	0	0	49 2/3	36	18	13	14	52
1997— South Bend (Midw.)	10	5	.667	2.73	25	25	0	0	0	118 2/3	91	44	36	43	116
1998— High Desert (Calif.)............	*14	5	.737	2.96	28	*28	1	0	0	164	138	65	54	35	*207
1999— El Paso (Texas)................	2	7	.222	4.80	17	17	0	0	0	90	109	56	48	25	100
— Portland (East.)■..............	1	0	1.000	3.90	6	6	0	0	0	32 1/3	28	15	14	14	35

PEOPLES, DANNY — 1B — INDIANS

PERSONAL: Born January 20, 1975, in Round Rock, Texas. ... 6-1/225. ... Bats right, throws right. ... Full name: Daniel Laurence Peoples.
HIGH SCHOOL: Round Rock (Texas).
COLLEGE: Texas.
TRANSACTIONS/CAREER NOTES: Selected by Cleveland Indians organization in first round (28th pick overall) of free-agent draft (June 4, 1996). ... On disabled list (July 31, 1996-remainder of season). ... On disabled list (April 10-24, June 3-10, June 15-31 and August 21, 1998-remainder of season).

P

						BATTING							FIELDING		
Year Team (League)	Pos.	G	AB	R	H	2B	3B	HR	RBI	Avg.	BB	SO	SB	PO	A	E	Avg.
1996— Watertown (NY-P)	DH	35	117	20	28	7	0	3	26	.239	28	36	3	...	...	...	...
1997— Kinston (Caro.)..........	OF	121	409	82	102	21	1	*34	84	.249	84	145	8	86	2	4	.957
1998— Akron (East.)	OF	60	222	30	62	19	0	8	32	.279	29	61	1	71	2	2	.973
1999— Akron (East.)	1B-DH	127	494	75	124	23	3	21	78	.251	55	142	2	775	81	14	.984

PERCIVAL, TROY   P   ANGELS

PERSONAL: Born August 9, 1969, in Fontana, Calif. ... 6-3/238. ... Throws right, bats right. ... Full name: Troy Eugene Percival. ... Name pronounced PER-sih-vol.
HIGH SCHOOL: Moreno Valley (Calif.).
COLLEGE: UC Riverside.
TRANSACTIONS/CAREER NOTES: Selected by California Angels organization in sixth round of free-agent draft (June 5, 1990). ... On Palm Springs disabled list (June 3-July 2, 1992). ... On disabled list (May 28, 1993-remainder of season). ... Angels franchise renamed Anaheim Angels for 1997 season. ... On disabled list (April 7-May 16, 1997); included rehabilitation assignment to Lake Elsinore (May 13-16).
MISCELLANEOUS: Played catcher (1990). ... Struck out in only appearance as pinch hitter (1996). ... Holds Anaheim Angels franchise all-time record for most saves (139).

Year	League	W	L	Pct.	ERA	G	GS	CG	ShO	Sv.	IP	H	R	ER	BB	SO
1991—	Boise (N.W.)	2	0	1.000	1.41	28	0	0	0	*12	38 1/3	23	7	6	18	63
1992—	Palm Springs (Calif.)	1	1	.500	5.06	11	0	0	0	2	10 2/3	6	7	6	8	16
—	Midland (Texas)	3	0	1.000	2.37	20	0	0	0	5	19	18	5	5	11	21
1993—	Vancouver (PCL)	0	1	.000	6.27	18	0	0	0	4	18 2/3	24	14	13	13	19
1994—	Vancouver (PCL)	2	6	.250	4.13	49	0	0	0	15	61	63	31	28	29	73
1995—	California (A.L.)	3	2	.600	1.95	62	0	0	0	3	74	37	19	16	26	94
1996—	California (A.L.)	0	2	.000	2.31	62	0	0	0	36	74	38	20	19	31	100
1997—	Anaheim (A.L.)	5	5	.500	3.46	55	0	0	0	27	52	40	20	20	22	72
—	Lake Elsinore (Calif.)	0	0	...	0.00	2	1	0	0	0	2	1	0	0	0	3
1998—	Anaheim (A.L.)	2	7	.222	3.64	67	0	0	0	42	66 2/3	45	31	27	37	87
1999—	Anaheim (A.L.)	4	6	.400	3.79	60	0	0	0	31	57	38	24	24	22	58
Major League totals (5 years)		14	22	.389	2.95	306	0	0	0	139	323 2/3	198	114	106	138	411

ALL-STAR GAME RECORD

Year	League	W	L	Pct.	ERA	GS	CG	ShO	Sv.	IP	H	R	ER	BB	SO
1996—	American	0	0	...	0.00	0	0	0	0	1	1	0	0	0	1
1998—	American	0	0	...	0.00	0	0	0	0	1	1	0	0	0	2
1999—	American							Selected, did not play.							
All-Star Game totals (2 years)		0	0	...	0.00	0	0	0	0	2	2	0	0	0	3

RECORD AS POSITION PLAYER

								BATTING								FIELDING			
Year	Team (League)	Pos.	G	AB	R	H	2B	3B	HR	RBI	Avg.	BB	SO	SB	PO	A	E	Avg.
1990—	Boise (Northwest)	C	29	79	12	16	0	0	0	5	.203	19	25	0	215	25	5	.980

PEREZ, CARLOS   P   DODGERS

PERSONAL: Born January 14, 1971, in Nigua, Dominican Republic. ... 6-3/210. ... Throws left, bats left. ... Full name: Carlos Gross Perez. ... Brother of Melido Perez, pitcher with Chicago White Sox (1988-91) and New York Yankees (1992-96); brother of Pascual Perez, pitcher with four major league teams (1980-85 and 1987-92); brother of Vladimir Perez, minor league pitcher (1986-94); brother of Reuben Dario Perez, minor league pitcher (1988-94); and brother of Valerio Perez, minor league pitcher (1983-84).
TRANSACTIONS/CAREER NOTES: Signed as non-drafted free agent by Montreal Expos organization (January 7, 1988). ... On disabled list (April 9-24 and May 18-July 7, 1992). ... On suspended list (July 7-October 22, 1992). ... On disabled list (March 31, 1996-entire season). ... Traded by Expos with SS Mark Grudzielanek and OF Hiram Bocachica to Los Angeles Dodgers for 2B Wilton Guerrero, P Ted Lilly, OF Peter Bergeron and 1B Jonathan Tucker (July 31, 1998). ... On disabled list (September 7, 1999-remainder of season).

Year	League	W	L	Pct.	ERA	G	GS	CG	ShO	Sv.	IP	H	R	ER	BB	SO
1989—	Dominican Expos (DSL)	3	3	.500	3.07	16	4	0	0	2	44	25	21	15	32	45
1990—	Gulf Coast Expos (GCL)	3	1	.750	2.52	13	2	0	0	2	35 2/3	24	14	10	15	38
1991—	Sumter (SAL)	2	2	.500	2.44	16	12	0	0	0	73 2/3	57	29	20	32	69
1992—	Rockford (Midw.)	0	1	.000	5.79	7	1	0	0	1	9 1/3	12	7	6	5	8
1993—	Burlington (Midw.)	1	0	1.000	3.24	12	1	0	0	0	16 2/3	13	6	6	9	21
—	San Bernardino (Calif.)	8	7	.533	3.44	20	18	0	0	0	131	120	57	50	44	98
1994—	Harrisburg (East.)	7	2	.778	1.94	12	11	2	2	1	79	55	27	17	18	69
—	Ottawa (I.L.)	7	5	.583	3.33	17	17	3	0	0	119	130	50	44	41	82
1995—	Montreal (N.L.)	10	8	.556	3.69	28	23	2	1	0	141 1/3	142	61	58	28	106
1996—	Montreal (N.L.)							Did not play.								
1997—	Montreal (N.L.)	12	13	.480	3.88	33	32	8	*5	0	206 2/3	206	109	89	48	110
1998—	Montreal (N.L.)	7	10	.412	3.75	23	23	3	0	0	163 1/3	177	79	68	33	82
—	Gulf Coast Expos (GCL)	1	0	1.000	0.00	1	0	0	0	0	5	5	2	0	1	2
—	Los Angeles (N.L.)■	4	4	.500	3.24	11	11	4	2	0	77 2/3	67	30	28	30	46
1999—	Los Angeles (N.L.)	2	10	.167	7.43	17	16	0	0	0	89 2/3	116	77	74	39	40
—	Albuquerque (PCL)	3	3	.500	5.92	6	6	2	0	0	38	46	28	25	10	14
Major League totals (4 years)		35	45	.438	4.20	112	105	17	8	0	678 2/3	708	356	317	178	384

ALL-STAR GAME RECORD

Year	League	W	L	Pct.	ERA	GS	CG	ShO	Sv.	IP	H	R	ER	BB	SO
1995—	National	0	0	...	0.00	0	0	0	0	1/3	1	0	0	1	0

PEREZ, EDDIE   C   BRAVES

PERSONAL: Born May 4, 1968, in Cuidad Ojeda, Venezuela. ... 6-1/185. ... Bats right, throws right. ... Full name: Eduardo Rafael Perez.
HIGH SCHOOL: Doctor Raul Cuenca (Cuidad Ojeda, Venezuela).
TRANSACTIONS/CAREER NOTES: Signed as non-drafted free agent by Atlanta Braves organization (September 27, 1986). ... On disabled list (August 30-September 14, 1996).
STATISTICAL NOTES: Led South Atlantic League catchers with 13 double plays in 1989. ... Tied for International League lead in errors by catcher with 11 in 1994. ... Led International League catchers with 539 putouts, 69 assists and 615 total chances in 1995. ... Tied for International League lead with seven double plays in 1995.

P

Year Team (League)	Pos.	G	AB	R	H	2B	3B	HR	RBI	Avg.	BB	SO	SB	PO	A	E	Avg.
1987— GC Braves (GCL)	C	31	89	8	18	1	0	1	5	.202	8	14	0	161	31	4	.980
1988— Burlington (Midw.)	C-1B	64	186	14	43	8	0	4	19	.231	10	33	1	245	42	11	.963
1989— Sumter (SAL)	C-1B	114	401	39	93	21	0	5	44	.232	44	68	2	760	96	16	.982
1990— Sumter (SAL)	C-1B	41	123	11	22	7	1	3	17	.179	14	18	0	315	32	3	.991
— Durham (Caro.)	C-1B	31	93	9	22	1	0	3	10	.237	1	12	0	197	17	3	.986
1991— Durham (Caro.)	C-1B	92	277	38	75	10	1	9	41	.271	17	33	0	497	55	8	.986
— Greenville (Sou.)	1B	1	4	0	1	0	0	0	0	.250	0	1	0	9	0	0	1.000
1992— Greenville (Sou.)	C-1B	91	275	28	63	16	0	6	41	.229	24	41	3	631	64	14	.980
1993— Greenville (Sou.)	1B-C	28	84	15	28	6	0	6	17	.333	2	8	1	146	19	3	.982
1994— Richmond (I.L.)	C-1B	113	388	37	101	16	2	9	49	.260	18	47	1	718	80	‡12	.985
1995— Richmond (I.L.)	C-DH-1B	92	324	31	86	19	0	5	40	.265	12	58	1	†540	†69	7	.989
— Atlanta (N.L.)	C	7	13	1	4	1	0	1	4	.308	0	2	0	34	2	0	1.000
1996— Atlanta (N.L.)	C-1B	68	156	19	40	9	1	4	17	.256	8	19	0	281	22	3	.990
1997— Atlanta (N.L.)	C-1B	73	191	20	41	5	0	6	18	.215	10	35	0	417	24	5	.989
1998— Atlanta (N.L.)	C-1B-DH	61	149	18	50	12	0	6	32	.336	15	28	1	290	29	2	.994
1999— Atlanta (N.L.)	C-1B	104	309	30	77	17	0	7	30	.249	17	40	0	620	48	5	.993
Major League totals (5 years)		313	818	88	212	44	1	24	101	.259	50	124	1	1642	125	15	.992

DIVISION SERIES RECORD

RECORDS: Shares career record for most grand slams—1 (October 3, 1998). ... Shares single-inning record for most runs batted in—4 (October 3, 1998, eighth inning).

Year Team (League)	Pos.	G	AB	R	H	2B	3B	HR	RBI	Avg.	BB	SO	SB	PO	A	E	Avg.
1995— Atlanta (N.L.)								Did not play.									
1996— Atlanta (N.L.)	C	1	3	0	1	0	0	0	0	.333	0	0	0	10	0	0	1.000
1997— Atlanta (N.L.)	C	1	3	0	0	0	0	0	0	.000	0	1	0	6	0	0	1.000
1998— Atlanta (N.L.)	C	1	5	1	1	0	0	1	4	.200	0	2	0	6	0	0	1.000
1999— Atlanta (N.L.)	C	4	16	1	4	0	0	0	3	.250	0	3	0	35	1	0	1.000
Division series totals (4 years)		7	27	2	6	0	0	1	7	.222	0	6	0	57	1	0	1.000

CHAMPIONSHIP SERIES RECORD

NOTES: Named N.L. Championship Series Most Valuable Player (1999).

Year Team (League)	Pos.	G	AB	R	H	2B	3B	HR	RBI	Avg.	BB	SO	SB	PO	A	E	Avg.
1995— Atlanta (N.L.)								Did not play.									
1996— Atlanta (N.L.)	C-1B	4	1	0	0	0	0	0	0	.000	1	0	0	7	0	0	1.000
1997— Atlanta (N.L.)	C	2	3	0	0	0	0	0	0	.000	0	0	0	14	0	0	1.000
1998— Atlanta (N.L.)	C	3	4	0	3	0	0	0	0	.750	0	0	0	6	0	0	1.000
1999— Atlanta (N.L.)	C	6	20	2	10	2	0	2	5	.500	1	3	0	42	2	0	1.000
Championship series totals (4 years)		15	28	2	13	2	0	2	5	.464	2	3	0	69	2	0	1.000

WORLD SERIES RECORD

NOTES: Member of World Series championship team (1995).

Year Team (League)	Pos.	G	AB	R	H	2B	3B	HR	RBI	Avg.	BB	SO	SB	PO	A	E	Avg.
1995— Atlanta (N.L.)								Did not play.									
1996— Atlanta (N.L.)	C	2	1	0	0	0	0	0	0	.000	0	0	0	2	0	0	1.000
1999— Atlanta (N.L.)	C	3	8	0	1	0	0	0	0	.125	1	3	0	23	2	0	1.000
World Series totals (2 years)		5	9	0	1	0	0	0	0	.111	1	3	0	25	2	0	1.000

PEREZ, EDUARDO   1B/3B

PERSONAL: Born September 11, 1969, in Cincinnati. ... 6-4/215. ... Bats right, throws right. ... Full name: Eduardo Antanacio Perez. ... Son of Tony Perez, special assistant to general manager, Florida Marlins; major league infielder with four teams (1964-86) and manager, Cincinnati Reds (1993); and brother of Victor Perez, minor league outfielder/first baseman (1990).

HIGH SCHOOL: Robinson (Santurce, Puerto Rico).

COLLEGE: Florida State.

TRANSACTIONS/CAREER NOTES: Selected by California Angels organization in first round (17th pick overall) of free-agent draft (June 3, 1991). ... On Palm Springs disabled list (May 9-19, 1992). ... On Vancouver disabled list (June 26-July 7, 1994). ... Traded by Angels to Cincinnati Reds for P Will Pennyfeather (April 5, 1996). ... Released by Reds (December 14, 1998). ... Signed by St. Louis Cardinals organization (February 16, 1999). ... Granted free agency (October 15, 1999).

STATISTICAL NOTES: Career major league grand slams: 1.

Year Team (League)	Pos.	G	AB	R	H	2B	3B	HR	RBI	Avg.	BB	SO	SB	PO	A	E	Avg.
1991— Boise (N.W.)	OF-1B	46	160	35	46	13	0	1	22	.288	19	39	12	87	6	3	.969
1992— Palm Springs (Calif.)	3B-SS-OF	54	204	37	64	8	4	3	35	.314	23	33	14	30	90	16	.882
— Midland (Texas)	3B-OF-1B	62	235	27	54	8	1	3	23	.230	22	49	19	53	97	13	.920
1993— Vancouver (PCL)	3B-1B-OF	96	363	66	111	23	6	12	70	.306	28	83	21	98	174	23	.922
— California (A.L.)	3B-DH	52	180	16	45	6	2	4	30	.250	9	39	5	24	101	5	.962
1994— California (A.L.)	1B	38	129	10	27	7	0	5	16	.209	12	29	3	305	15	1	.997
— Vancouver (PCL)	3B-DH	61	219	37	65	14	3	7	38	.297	34	53	9	35	116	12	.926
— Arizona Angels (Ariz.)	3B	1	3	0	0	0	0	0	0	.000	1	1	0	0	3	0	1.000
1995— Vancouver (PCL)	3B-DH-1B	69	246	39	80	12	7	6	37	.325	25	34	6	94	90	6	.968
— California (A.L.)	3B-DH	29	71	9	12	4	1	1	7	.169	12	9	0	16	37	7	.883
1996— Indianapolis (A.A.)■	3B-1B-DH	122	451	84	132	29	5	21	84	.293	51	69	11	110	125	21	.939
— Cincinnati (N.L.)	1B-3B	18	36	8	8	0	0	3	5	.222	5	9	0	59	11	0	1.000
1997— Cincinnati (N.L.)	1-0-3-DH	106	297	44	75	18	0	16	52	.253	29	76	5	506	49	2	.996
1998— Cincinnati (N.L.)	1B-3B-OF	84	172	20	41	4	0	4	30	.238	21	45	0	291	47	5	.985

Year	Team (League)	Pos.	G	AB	R	H	2B	3B	HR	RBI	Avg.	BB	SO	SB	PO	A	E	Avg.
1999—Memphis (PCL)■	1B-3B-DH	119	416	67	133	31	0	18	82	.320	45	92	7	715	95	9	.989
—St. Louis (N.L.)	OF-1B	21	32	6	11	2	0	1	9	.344	7	6	0	29	3	1	.970
American League totals (3 years)		119	380	35	84	17	3	10	53	.221	33	77	8	345	153	13	.975
National League totals (4 years)		229	537	78	135	24	0	24	96	.251	62	136	5	885	110	8	.992
Major League totals (7 years)		348	917	113	219	41	3	34	149	.239	95	213	13	1230	263	21	.986

PEREZ, NEIFI   SS   ROCKIES

PERSONAL: Born June 2, 1975, in Villa Mella, Dominican Republic. ... 6-0/175. ... Bats both, throws right. ... Full name: Neifi Neftali Diaz Perez.
TRANSACTIONS/CAREER NOTES: Signed as non-drafted free agent by Colorado Rockies organization (November 9, 1992).
RECORDS: Holds N.L. single-season record for most at-bats with no intentional bases on balls—690 (1999).
STATISTICAL NOTES: Led California League shortstops with 650 total chances and 86 double plays in 1994. ... Tied for Eastern League lead in double plays by shortstop with 80 in 1995. ... Led Pacific Coast League shortstops with 678 total chances and 91 double plays in 1996. ... Hit for the cycle (July 25, 1998). ... Had 15-game hitting streak (July 27-August 11, 1998). ... Led N.L. with 22 sacrifice hits in 1998. ... Led N.L. shortstops with 272 putouts, 516 assists, 808 total chances and 127 double plays in 1998. ... Career major league grand slams: 1. ... Led N.L. shortstops with 755 total chances and 124 double plays in 1999.
MISCELLANEOUS: Holds Colorado Rockies all-time record for most triples (30).

Year	Team (League)	Pos.	G	AB	R	H	2B	3B	HR	RBI	Avg.	BB	SO	SB	PO	A	E	Avg.
1993—Bend (N.W.)	SS-2B	75	296	35	77	11	4	3	32	.260	19	43	19	127	244	25	.937
1994—Central Valley (Calif.)	SS	•134	506	64	121	16	7	1	35	.239	32	79	9	*223	388	*39	.940
1995—Colo. Springs (PCL)	SS	11	36	4	10	4	0	0	2	.278	0	5	1	16	28	3	.936
—New Haven (East.)	SS	116	427	59	108	28	3	5	43	.253	24	52	5	175	358	18	*.967
1996—Colo. Springs (PCL)	SS	133	*570	77	180	28	12	7	72	.316	21	48	16	*244	*409	*25	.963
—Colorado (N.L.)	SS-2B	17	45	4	7	2	0	0	3	.156	0	8	2	21	28	2	.961
1997—Colo. Springs (PCL)	SS	68	303	68	110	24	3	8	46	.363	17	27	8	119	198	8	.975
—Colorado (N.L.)	SS-2B-3B	83	313	46	91	13	10	5	31	.291	21	43	4	185	287	9	.981
1998—Colorado (N.L.)	SS-C	•162	647	80	177	25	9	9	59	.274	38	70	5	†272	†516	20	.975
1999—Colorado (N.L.)	SS	157	*690	108	193	27	•11	12	70	.280	28	54	13	*260	*481	14	.981
Major League totals (4 years)		419	1695	238	468	67	30	26	163	.276	87	175	24	738	1312	45	.979

PEREZ, ODALIS   P   BRAVES

PERSONAL: Born June 7, 1978, in Las Matas de Farfan, Dominican Republic. ... 6-0/150. ... Throws left, bats left. ... Full name: Odalis Amadol Perez.
HIGH SCHOOL: Damian Davis Ortiz (Las Matas de Farfan, Dominican Republic).
TRANSACTIONS/CAREER NOTES: Signed as non-drafted free agent by Atlanta Braves organization (July 2, 1994). ... On disabled list (July 23, 1999-remainder of season).

Year	League	W	L	Pct.	ERA	G	GS	CG	ShO	Sv.	IP	H	R	ER	BB	SO
1995—Gulf Coast Braves (GCL)		3	5	.375	2.22	12	12	1	1	0	65	48	22	16	18	62
1996—Eugene (N.W.)		2	1	.667	3.80	10	6	0	0	0	23²/₃	26	16	10	11	38
1997—Macon (SAL)		4	5	.444	1.65	36	0	0	0	5	87¹/₃	67	31	16	27	100
1998—Greenville (Sou.)		6	5	.545	4.02	23	21	0	0	0	132	127	67	59	53	143
—Richmond (I.L.)		1	2	.333	2.96	13	0	0	0	3	24¹/₃	26	10	8	7	22
—Atlanta (N.L.)		0	1	.000	4.22	10	0	0	0	0	10²/₃	10	5	5	4	5
1999—Atlanta (N.L.)		4	6	.400	6.00	18	17	0	0	0	93	100	65	62	53	82
Major League totals (2 years)		4	7	.364	5.82	28	17	0	0	0	103²/₃	110	70	67	57	87

DIVISION SERIES RECORD

Year	League	W	L	Pct.	ERA	G	GS	CG	ShO	Sv.	IP	H	R	ER	BB	SO
1998—Atlanta (N.L.)		1	0	1.000	0.00	1	0	0	0	0	²/₃	0	0	0	0	1

CHAMPIONSHIP SERIES RECORD

Year	League	W	L	Pct.	ERA	G	GS	CG	ShO	Sv.	IP	H	R	ER	BB	SO
1998—Atlanta (N.L.)		0	0	...	54.00	2	0	0	0	0	¹/₃	5	2	2	3	0

PEREZ, SANTIAGO   SS   BREWERS

PERSONAL: Born December 30, 1975, in Santo Domingo, Dominican Republic. ... 6-2/150. ... Bats both, throws right. ... Full name: Santiago Alberto Perez.
HIGH SCHOOL: Liceo Victor Estrella Luz (Santo Domingo, Dominican Republic).
TRANSACTIONS/CAREER NOTES: Signed as non-drafted free agent by Detroit Tigers organization (March 10, 1993). ... Traded by Tigers with P Mike Myers and P Rick Greene to Milwaukee Brewers for P Bryce Florie and a player to be named later (November 20, 1997). ... On Louisville disabled list (August 1-14 and August 19-31, 1999).
STATISTICAL NOTES: Led International League shortstops with 29 errors in 1999.

Year	Team (League)	Pos.	G	AB	R	H	2B	3B	HR	RBI	Avg.	BB	SO	SB	PO	A	E	Avg.
1993—Dom. Tigers (DSL)	IF-OF	58	171	28	45	6	2	0	17	.263	20	22	17	59	47	16	.869
1994—Dom. Tigers (DSL)	SS	60	227	54	78	7	9	2	47	.344	32	43	20	106	183	39	.881
1995—Fayetteville (SAL)	SS	130	425	54	101	15	1	4	44	.238	30	98	10	176	327	46	.916
1996—Lakeland (FSL)	SS	122	418	33	105	18	2	1	27	.251	16	88	6	192	310	41	.924
1997—Lakeland (FSL)	SS	111	445	66	122	20	12	4	46	.274	20	98	21	148	322	34	.933
1998—El Paso (Texas)■	SS	107	454	73	139	20	*13	11	64	.306	28	70	21	186	310	*36	.932
—Louisville (I.L.)	SS-2B	36	133	18	36	4	3	3	14	.271	6	31	6	67	91	6	.963
1999—Louisville (I.L.)	SS-2B-DH	108	407	57	107	23	8	7	38	.263	31	94	21	150	281	†30	.935

P

– 445 –

PEREZ, YORKIS   P

PERSONAL: Born September 30, 1967, in Bajos de Haina, Dominican Republic. ... 6-0/180. ... Throws left, bats both. ... Full name: Yorkis Miguel Perez.

TRANSACTIONS/CAREER NOTES: Signed as non-drafted free agent by Minnesota Twins organization (February 23, 1983). ... Traded by Twins with P Neal Heaton, P Al Cardwood and C Jeff Reed to Montreal Expos for P Jeff Reardon and C Tom Nieto (February 3, 1987). ... Granted free agency (October 15, 1990). ... Signed by Atlanta Braves organization (February 1, 1991). ... Traded by Braves with P Turk Wendell to Chicago Cubs for P Mike Bielecki and C Damon Berryhill (September 29, 1991). ... Released by Cubs (December 11, 1991). ... Signed by Yomiuri Giants of Japan Central League (1992). ... Released by Yomiuri (August 17, 1992). ... Signed as free agent by Seattle Mariners organization (August 19, 1992). ... Released by Mariners organization (January 11, 1993). ... Signed by Montreal Expos organization (February 15, 1993). ... Granted free agency (October 15, 1993). ... Signed by Florida Marlins organization (December 15, 1993). ... On Florida disabled list (June 10-30, 1994); included rehabilitation assignment to Portland (June 25-30). ... Traded by Marlins to Braves for P Martin Sanchez (December 13, 1996). ... Claimed on waivers by New York Mets (March 31, 1997). ... On New York disabled list (April 5-June 5, 1997); included rehabilitation assignment to Norfolk (May 15-June 5). ... Granted free agency (October 15, 1997). ... Signed by Philadelphia Phillies organization (January 23, 1998). ... On Scranton/Wilkes-Barre disabled list (April 9-16, 1998). ... On Philadelphia disabled list (May 25-June 17, 1998); included rehabilitation assignments to Reading (June 14) and Scranton/Wilkes-Barre (June 16). ... On disabled list (July 2, 1999-remainder of season). ... Granted free agency (October 6, 1999).

Year League	W	L	Pct.	ERA	G	GS	CG	ShO	Sv.	IP	H	R	ER	BB	SO
1983— Elizabethton (Appl.)	0	1	.000	20.25	3	1	0	0	0	4	5	9	9	9	6
1984— Elizabethton (Appl.)	0	0	...	0.00	1	0	0	0	0	1⅓	1	0	0	1	1
1985— Santiago (DSL)	6	8	.429	3.17	21	16	7	2	1	122	104	58	43	63	69
1986— Kenosha (Midw.)	4	11	.267	5.15	31	18	3	0	0	131	120	81	75	88	144
1987— West Palm Beach (FSL)■ ..	6	2	.750	2.34	15	15	3	0	0	100	78	36	26	46	111
— Jacksonville (Sou.)	2	7	.222	4.05	12	10	1	1	1	60	61	34	27	30	60
1988— Jacksonville (Sou.)	8	12	.400	5.82	27	25	2	1	0	130	142	96	84	94	105
1989— West Palm Beach (FSL)	7	6	.538	2.76	18	12	0	0	1	94⅔	62	34	29	54	85
— Jacksonville (Sou.)	4	3	.571	3.60	20	0	0	0	0	35	25	16	14	34	50
1990— Jacksonville (Sou.)	2	2	.500	6.00	28	2	0	0	1	42	36	34	28	34	39
— Indianapolis (A.A.)	1	1	.500	2.31	9	0	0	0	0	11⅔	8	5	3	6	8
1991— Richmond (I.L.)■	•12	3	•.800	3.79	36	10	0	0	1	107	99	47	45	53	102
— Chicago (N.L.)■	1	0	1.000	2.08	3	0	0	0	0	4⅓	2	1	1	2	3
1992— Yomiuri (Jap. Cen.)■	0	1	.000	7.11	3	0	0	0	0	6⅓	8	6	5	3	6
1993— Harrisburg (East.)■	4	2	.667	3.45	34	0	0	0	3	44⅓	49	26	17	20	58
— Ottawa (I.L.)	0	1	.000	3.60	20	0	0	0	5	20	14	12	8	7	17
1994— Florida (N.L.)■	3	0	1.000	3.54	44	0	0	0	0	40⅔	33	18	16	14	41
— Portland (East.)	0	0	...	0.00	2	0	0	0	0	2	1	0	0	0	2
1995— Florida (N.L.)	2	6	.250	5.21	69	0	0	0	1	46⅔	35	29	27	28	47
1996— Florida (N.L.)	3	4	.429	5.29	64	0	0	0	0	47⅓	51	28	28	31	47
— Charlotte (I.L.)	3	0	1.000	4.22	9	0	0	0	0	10⅔	6	5	5	3	13
1997— New York (N.L.)■	0	1	.000	8.31	9	0	0	0	0	8⅔	15	8	8	4	7
— Norfolk (I.L.)	1	0	1.000	3.48	17	0	0	0	3	20⅔	22	9	8	7	24
— Binghamton (East.)	2	1	.667	0.66	12	3	0	0	0	27⅓	15	4	2	12	39
1998— Scranton/W.B. (I.L.)■	0	0	...	0.00	4	1	0	0	0	4⅓	2	1	0	1	3
— Philadelphia (N.L.)	0	2	.000	3.81	57	0	0	0	0	52	40	23	22	25	42
— Reading (East.)	0	0	...	0.00	1	1	0	0	0	1	0	0	0	0	1
1999— Philadelphia (N.L.)	3	1	.750	3.94	35	0	0	0	0	32	29	15	14	15	26
Major League totals (7 years)	**12**	**14**	**.462**	**4.50**	**281**	**0**	**0**	**0**	**1**	**232**	**205**	**122**	**116**	**119**	**213**

PERISHO, MATT   P   RANGERS

PERSONAL: Born June 8, 1975, in Burlington, Iowa. ... 6-0/205. ... Throws left, bats left. ... Full name: Matthew Alan Perisho.

HIGH SCHOOL: McClintock (Tempe, Ariz.).

TRANSACTIONS/CAREER NOTES: Selected by California Angels organization in third round of free-agent draft (June 3, 1993). ... Angels franchise renamed Anaheim Angels for 1997 season. ... Traded by Angels to Texas Rangers for IF Mike Bell (October 31, 1997). ... On Oklahoma disabled list (June 29-July 25, 1998).

Year League	W	L	Pct.	ERA	G	GS	CG	ShO	Sv.	IP	H	R	ER	BB	SO
1993— Arizona Angels (Ariz.)	7	3	.700	3.66	11	11	1	1	0	64	58	32	26	23	65
1994— Cedar Rapids (Midw.)	12	9	.571	4.33	27	27	0	0	0	147⅔	165	90	71	88	107
1995— Lake Elsinore (Calif.)	8	9	.471	6.32	24	22	0	0	0	115⅓	137	91	81	60	68
1996— Lake Elsinore (Calif.)	7	5	.583	4.20	21	18	1	1	0	128⅔	131	72	60	58	97
— Midland (Texas)	3	2	.600	3.21	8	8	0	0	0	53⅓	48	22	19	20	50
1997— Midland (Texas)	5	2	.714	2.96	10	10	3	•1	0	73	60	26	24	26	62
— Anaheim (A.L.)	0	2	.000	6.00	11	8	0	0	0	45	59	34	30	28	35
— Vancouver (PCL)	4	4	.500	5.33	9	9	1	0	0	52⅓	68	42	31	29	47
1998— Tulsa (Texas)■	0	0	...	6.00	1	1	0	0	0	3	3	2	2	3	1
— Oklahoma (PCL)	8	5	.615	3.89	15	15	1	0	0	90⅓	91	41	39	42	60
— Texas (A.L.)	0	2	.000	27.00	2	2	0	0	0	5	15	17	15	8	2
1999— Oklahoma (PCL)	•15	7	.682	4.61	27	27	2	0	0	156⅓	160	86	80	•78	150
— Texas (A.L.)	0	0	...	2.61	4	1	0	0	0	10⅓	8	3	3	2	17
Major League totals (3 years)	**0**	**4**	**.000**	**7.16**	**17**	**11**	**0**	**0**	**0**	**60⅓**	**82**	**54**	**48**	**38**	**54**

PERKINS, DAN   P   TWINS

PERSONAL: Born March 15, 1975, in Miami. ... 6-2/193. ... Throws right, bats right. ... Full name: Daniel Lee Perkins.

HIGH SCHOOL: Westminster Christian (Miami).

TRANSACTIONS/CAREER NOTES: Selected by Minnesota Twins organization in second round of free-agent draft (June 3, 1993).

Year League	W	L	Pct.	ERA	G	GS	CG	ShO	Sv.	IP	H	R	ER	BB	SO
1993— Elizabethton (Appl.)	3	3	.500	5.00	10	10	0	0	0	45	46	33	25	25	30
1994— Fort Wayne (Midw.)	1	8	.111	6.22	12	12	0	0	0	50⅔	61	38	35	22	34
— Elizabethton (Appl.)	0	2	.000	3.67	10	9	1	0	0	54	51	31	22	14	34

Year	League	W	L	Pct.	ERA	G	GS	CG	ShO	Sv.	IP	H	R	ER	BB	SO
1995— Fort Wayne (Midw.)............		7	12	.368	5.49	29	22	0	0	0	121 1/3	133	86	74	69	82
1996— Fort Myers (FSL).............		13	7	.650	2.96	39	13	3	1	2	136 2/3	125	52	45	37	111
1997— New Britain (East.)		7	10	.412	4.91	24	24	2	0	0	144 2/3	158	94	79	53	114
1998— New Britain (East.)		13	5	.722	3.98	20	19	1	1	0	117 2/3	140	64	52	31	79
— Salt Lake (PCL)		5	0	1.000	4.82	7	7	1	0	0	46 2/3	48	30	25	20	33
1999— Minnesota (A.L.).............		1	7	.125	6.54	29	12	0	0	0	86 2/3	117	69	63	43	44
— Salt Lake (PCL)		0	0	...	4.26	3	2	0	0	0	12 2/3	11	6	6	4	7
Major League totals (1 year)........		1	7	.125	6.54	29	12	0	0	0	86 2/3	117	69	63	43	44

PERRY, HERBERT   1B   DEVIL RAYS

PERSONAL: Born September 15, 1969, in Mayo, Fla. ... 6-2/220. ... Bats right, throws right. ... Full name: Herbert Edward Perry Jr. ... Brother of Chan Perry, outfielder, Cleveland Indians organization.
HIGH SCHOOL: Lafayette (Mayo, Fla.).
COLLEGE: Florida.
TRANSACTIONS/CAREER NOTES: Selected by Cleveland Indians organization in second round of free-agent draft (June 3, 1991). ... On disabled list (June 18-July 13, 1991 and July 23, 1993-remainder of season). ... On Buffalo disabled list (June 7-27, 1996). ... On Cleveland disabled list (September 11, 1996-remainder of season; and March 26, 1997-enitre season). ... Selected by Tampa Bay Devil Rays in third round (68th pick overall) of expansion draft (November 18, 1997). ... On Tampa Bay disabled list (March 25, 1998-entire season); included rehabilitation assignments to Durham (June 1-7), Gulf Coast Devil Rays (August 17-25) and St. Petersburg (August 27-28). ... On Tampa Bay disabled list (July 22-September 1, 1999); included rehabilitation assignment to Durham (August 25-31).
STATISTICAL NOTES: Led Eastern League in being hit by pitch with 15 in 1993.

							BATTING							FIELDING		
Year	Team (League)	Pos.	G	AB	R	H	2B	3B	HR	RBI	Avg.	BB	SO	SB	PO	A	E	Avg.
1991— Watertown (NY-P)		DH	14	52	3	11	2	0	0	5	.212	8	7	0	...	...	...	...
1992— Kinston (Caro.).........	1B-OF-3B	121	449	74	125	16	1	19	77	.278	46	89	12	297	39	5	.985
1993— Canton/Akron (East.)..1B-3B-DH-OF	89	327	52	88	21	1	9	55	.269	37	47	7	378	86	10	.979
1994— Charlotte (I.L.).........	1-3-DH-O	102	376	67	123	20	4	13	70	.327	41	55	9	747	55	6	.993
— Cleveland (A.L.).........	1B-3B	4	9	1	1	0	0	0	1	.111	3	1	0	25	5	1	.968
1995— Buffalo (A.A.).............	1B-DH	49	180	27	57	14	1	2	17	.317	15	18	1	419	44	3	.994
— Cleveland (A.L.).........	1B-3B	52	162	23	51	13	1	3	23	.315	13	28	1	391	30	0	1.000
1996— Buffalo (A.A.)............1B-3B-DH-OF	40	151	21	51	7	1	5	30	.338	7	19	4	217	24	4	.984
— Cleveland (A.L.).........	1B-3B	7	12	1	1	1	0	0	0	.083	1	2	1	29	2	0	1.000
1997—									Did not play.								
1998— Durham (I.L.)■.........	1B-DH	5	17	1	5	4	0	0	1	.294	0	2	0	19	2	0	1.000
— GC Devil Rays (GCL)..	DH-3B	8	26	1	3	0	0	0	1	.115	3	5	0	1	8	1	.900
— St. Petersburg (FSL) ..	3B	2	8	1	1	0	0	0	0	.125	2	2	0	2	5	1	.875
1999— Durham (I.L.).........	DH-1B-3B	27	103	21	32	8	0	5	20	.311	6	21	0	56	12	2	.971
— Tampa Bay (A.L.)......3B-1B-OF-DH	66	209	29	53	10	1	6	32	.254	16	42	0	113	79	5	.975
Major League totals (4 years)		129	392	54	106	24	2	9	56	.270	33	73	2	558	116	6	.991

DIVISION SERIES RECORD

							BATTING							FIELDING		
Year	Team (League)	Pos.	G	AB	R	H	2B	3B	HR	RBI	Avg.	BB	SO	SB	PO	A	E	Avg.
1995— Cleveland (A.L.).........	PH	1	1	0	0	0	0	0	0	.000	0	0	0	...	...	...	...

CHAMPIONSHIP SERIES RECORD

							BATTING							FIELDING		
Year	Team (League)	Pos.	G	AB	R	H	2B	3B	HR	RBI	Avg.	BB	SO	SB	PO	A	E	Avg.
1995— Cleveland (A.L.).........	1B	3	8	0	0	0	0	0	0	.000	1	3	0	30	0	0	1.000

WORLD SERIES RECORD

							BATTING							FIELDING		
Year	Team (League)	Pos.	G	AB	R	H	2B	3B	HR	RBI	Avg.	BB	SO	SB	PO	A	E	Avg.
1995— Cleveland (A.L.).........	1B	3	5	0	0	0	0	0	0	.000	0	2	0	13	2	0	1.000

PERSON, ROBERT   P   PHILLIES

PERSONAL: Born October 6, 1969, in St. Louis. ... 6-0/194. ... Throws right, bats right. ... Full name: Robert Alan Person.
HIGH SCHOOL: University City (Mo.).
JUNIOR COLLEGE: Seminole (Okla.) Junior College.
TRANSACTIONS/CAREER NOTES: Selected by Cleveland Indians organization in 25th round of free-agent draft (June 5, 1989). ... Loaned by Indians organization to Bend, independent (June 12-25, 1991). ... Traded by Indians to Chicago White Sox for P Grady Hall (June 27, 1991). ... On disabled list (April 10-May 13, 1992). ... Selected by Florida Marlins in second round (47th pick overall) of expansion draft (November 17, 1992). ... Granted free agency (December 19, 1992). ... Re-signed by Marlins organization (January 8, 1993). ... Traded by Marlins to New York Mets for P Steve Long (March 30, 1994). ... Traded by Mets to Toronto Blue Jays for 1B John Olerud and cash (December 20, 1996). ... On Toronto disabled list (May 8-26 and September 9-28, 1997). ... On Syracuse disabled list (April 19-27, 1998). ... On Toronto disabled list (March 25-April 12, 1999); included rehabilitation assignment to Dunedin (April 9-10). ... Traded by Blue Jays to Philadelphia Phillies for P Paul Spoljaric (May 5, 1999).
MISCELLANEOUS: Appeared in two games as pinch runner with New York (1996).

Year	League	W	L	Pct.	ERA	G	GS	CG	ShO	Sv.	IP	H	R	ER	BB	SO
1989— Burlington (Appl.)...............		0	1	.000	3.18	10	5	0	0	1	34	23	13	12	17	19
1990— Watertown (NY-P)		1	0	1.000	1.10	5	2	0	0	0	16 1/3	8	2	2	7	19
— Kinston (Caro.).................		1	0	1.000	2.70	4	3	0	0	0	16 2/3	17	6	5	9	7
— Gulf Coast Indians (GCL) ...		0	2	.000	7.36	24	0	0	0	2	7 1/3	10	7	6	4	8
1991— Kinston (Caro.)...................		3	5	.375	4.67	11	11	0	0	0	52	56	37	27	42	45
— Bend (N.W.)■.................		1	1	.500	3.60	2	2	0	0	0	10	6	6	4	5	6
— South Bend (Midw.)■........		4	3	.571	3.30	13	13	0	0	0	76 1/3	50	35	28	56	66
1992— Sarasota (FSL)		5	7	.417	3.59	19	18	1	0	0	105 1/3	90	48	42	62	85

Year League	W	L	Pct.	ERA	G	GS	CG	ShO	Sv.	IP	H	R	ER	BB	SO
1993— High Desert (Calif.)■	12	10	.545	4.69	28	26	4	0	0	169	184	*115	88	48	107
1994— Binghamton (East.)■	9	6	.600	3.45	31	23	3	2	0	159	124	68	61	68	130
1995— Binghamton (East.)	5	4	.556	3.11	26	7	1	0	7	66 2/3	74	30	23	25	65
— Norfolk (I.L.)	2	1	.667	4.50	5	4	0	0	0	32	30	17	16	13	33
— New York (N.L.)	1	0	1.000	0.75	3	1	0	0	0	12	5	1	1	2	10
1996— New York (N.L.)	4	5	.444	4.52	27	13	0	0	0	89 2/3	86	50	45	35	76
— Norfolk (I.L.)	5	0	1.000	3.35	8	8	0	0	0	43	33	16	16	21	32
1997— Toronto (A.L.)■	5	10	.333	5.61	23	22	0	0	0	128 1/3	125	86	80	60	99
— Syracuse (I.L.)	1	0	1.000	0.00	1	1	0	0	0	7	4	1	0	2	5
1998— Toronto (A.L.)	3	1	.750	7.04	27	0	0	0	6	38 1/3	45	31	30	22	31
— Syracuse (I.L.)	3	3	.500	2.29	20	6	1	0	6	59	38	17	15	29	55
1999— Dunedin (FSL)	0	0	...	3.00	1	1	0	0	0	3	4	1	1	1	3
— Toronto (A.L.)	0	2	.000	9.82	11	0	0	0	2	11	9	12	12	15	12
— Philadelphia (N.L.)■	10	5	.667	4.27	31	22	0	0	0	137	130	72	65	70	127
A.L. totals (3 years)	8	13	.381	6.18	61	22	0	0	8	177 2/3	179	129	122	97	142
N.L. totals (3 years)	15	10	.600	4.19	61	36	0	0	0	238 2/3	221	123	111	107	213
Major League totals (5 years)......	23	23	.500	5.04	122	58	0	0	8	416 1/3	400	252	233	204	355

PETERS, CHRIS   P   PIRATES

PERSONAL: Born January 28, 1972, in Fort Thomas, Ky. ... 6-1/170. ... Throws left, bats left. ... Full name: Christopher Michael Peters.
HIGH SCHOOL: Peters Township (McMurray, Pa.).
COLLEGE: Indiana.
TRANSACTIONS/CAREER NOTES: Selected by Pittsburgh Pirates organization in 37th round of free-agent draft (June 3, 1993). ... On Pittsburgh disabled list (May 24-August 21, 1999); included rehabilitation assignments to Nashville (June 8-18, June 28-July 16 and July 30-August 21).

Year League	W	L	Pct.	ERA	G	GS	CG	ShO	Sv.	IP	H	R	ER	BB	SO
1993— Welland (NY-P)	1	0	1.000	4.55	16	0	0	0	0	27 2/3	33	16	14	20	25
1994— Augusta (SAL)	4	5	.444	4.30	54	0	0	0	4	60 2/3	51	34	29	33	83
— Salem (Caro.)	1	0	1.000	13.50	3	0	0	0	0	3 1/3	5	5	5	1	2
1995— Lynchburg (Caro.)	11	5	.688	2.43	24	24	3	*3	0	144 2/3	126	57	39	35	132
— Carolina (Sou.)	2	0	1.000	1.29	2	2	0	0	0	14	9	2	2	2	7
1996— Carolina (Sou.)	7	3	.700	2.64	14	14	0	0	0	92	73	37	27	34	69
— Calgary (PCL)	1	1	.500	0.98	4	4	0	0	0	27 2/3	18	3	3	8	16
— Pittsburgh (N.L.)	2	4	.333	5.63	16	10	0	0	0	64	72	43	40	25	28
1997— Calgary (PCL)	2	4	.333	4.38	14	9	0	0	1	51 1/3	52	32	25	30	55
— Pittsburgh (N.L.)	2	2	.500	4.58	31	1	0	0	0	37 1/3	38	23	19	21	17
1998— Pittsburgh (N.L.)	8	10	.444	3.47	39	21	1	0	1	148	142	63	57	55	103
1999— Pittsburgh (N.L.)	5	4	.556	6.59	19	11	0	0	0	71	98	59	52	27	46
— Nashville (PCL)	3	1	.750	2.19	11	9	0	0	1	49 1/3	54	18	12	15	34
Major League totals (4 years)......	17	20	.459	4.72	105	43	1	0	1	320 1/3	350	188	168	128	194

PETERSEN, CHRIS   IF

PERSONAL: Born November 6, 1970, in Boston. ... 5-11/180. ... Bats right, throws right. ... Full name: Christopher Ronald Petersen.
HIGH SCHOOL: Southington (Conn.).
COLLEGE: Georgia Southern.
TRANSACTIONS/CAREER NOTES: Selected by Chicago Cubs organization in ninth round of free-agent draft (June 1, 1992). ... Granted free agency (October 15, 1998). ... Signed by Colorado Rockies organization (November 7, 1998). ... Granted free agency (October 15, 1999).
STATISTICAL NOTES: Led New York-Pennsylvania League shortstops with .960 fielding percentage in 1992. ... Led Florida State League with 16 sacrfice hits in 1993. ... Led Florida State League shortstops with 105 double plays in 1993. ... Led Southern League with 16 sacrifice hits in 1994. ... Led American Association shortstops with .973 fielding percentage and in double plays with 84 in 1997. ... Led Pacific Coast League shortstops with .985 fielding percentage in 1998. ... Led Pacific Coast League shortstops with 94 double plays in 1999.

Year Team (League)	Pos.	G	AB	R	H	2B	3B	HR	RBI	Avg.	BB	SO	SB	PO	A	E	Avg.
1992— Geneva (NY-P)	SS-2B	71	244	36	55	8	0	1	23	.225	32	69	11	119	224	16	†.955
1993— Daytona (FSL)	SS	130	473	66	101	10	0	0	28	.214	56	105	19	*253	*450	24	.967
1994— Orlando (Sou.)	SS	117	376	34	85	12	3	1	26	.226	37	89	8	197	370	20	.964
1995— Orlando (Sou.)	SS	125	382	48	81	10	3	4	36	.212	45	97	7	*212	357	21	.964
1996— Orlando (Sou.)	SS-2B	47	152	21	45	3	4	2	12	.296	18	31	3	91	121	13	.942
— Iowa (A.A.)	SS-2B-3B	63	194	12	48	6	3	2	23	.247	12	46	1	108	163	5	.982
1997— Iowa (A.A.)	SS-3B	119	391	49	94	16	2	3	33	.240	32	89	1	168	345	14	†.973
1998— Iowa (PCL)	SS-2B	118	389	54	91	16	2	8	41	.234	21	100	2	167	354	10	†.981
1999— Colo. Springs (PCL)■	SS-DH	107	370	56	96	21	1	6	34	.259	29	85	4	*196	340	22	*.961
— Colorado (N.L.)	2B-SS	7	13	1	2	0	0	0	2	.154	2	3	0	12	16	1	.966
Major League totals (1 year)		7	13	1	2	0	0	0	2	.154	2	3	0	12	16	1	.966

Table header spanning: BATTING covers AB through Avg.; FIELDING covers PO through Avg.

PETERSON, KYLE   P   BREWERS

P

PERSONAL: Born April 9, 1976, in Elkhorn, Neb. ... 6-3/215. ... Throws right, bats left. ... Full name: Kyle J. Peterson.
HIGH SCHOOL: Creighton Prep (Omaha, Neb.).
COLLEGE: Stanford.
TRANSACTIONS/CAREER NOTES: Selected by Milwaukee Brewers organization in first round (13th pick overall) of free-agent draft (June 3, 1997).

Year	League	W	L	Pct.	ERA	G	GS	CG	ShO	Sv.	IP	H	R	ER	BB	SO
1997— Ogden (Pio.)		0	0	...	0.87	3	3	0	0	0	10 1/3	5	2	1	4	11
1998— Stockton (Calif.)		4	7	.364	3.55	17	17	0	0	0	96 1/3	99	54	38	33	109
— El Paso (Texas)		3	2	.600	4.40	7	7	1	0	0	43	41	24	21	16	33
— Louisville (I.L.)		1	0	1.000	7.94	1	1	0	0	0	5 2/3	8	5	5	2	4
1999— Louisville (I.L.)		7	6	.538	3.55	18	18	1	1	0	109	90	52	43	42	95
— Milwaukee (N.L.)		4	7	.364	4.56	17	12	0	0	0	77	87	46	39	25	34
Major League totals (1 year)		4	7	.364	4.56	17	12	0	0	0	77	87	46	39	25	34

PETKOVSEK, MARK — P — ANGELS

PERSONAL: Born November 18, 1965, in Beaumont, Texas. ... 6-0/198. ... Throws right, bats right. ... Full name: Mark Joseph Petkovsek. ... Name pronounced PET-kie-zeck.
HIGH SCHOOL: Kelly (Beaumont, Texas).
COLLEGE: Texas.
TRANSACTIONS/CAREER NOTES: Selected by Texas Rangers organization in supplemental round ("sandwich pick" between first and second round, 29th pick overall) of free-agent draft (June 2, 1987); pick received as compensation for New York Yankees signing Type A free-agent OF Gary Ward. ... Granted free agency (October 16, 1991). ... Signed by Pittsburgh Pirates organization (January 22, 1992). ... Granted free agency (October 15, 1992). ... Re-signed by Pirates organization (November 9, 1992). ... On Buffalo disabled list (July 4-23, 1993). ... Granted free agency (October 12, 1993). ... Signed by Tucson, Houston Astros organization (March 4, 1994). ... On disabled list (July 20-August 12, 1994). ... Granted free agency (October 15, 1994). ... Signed by St. Louis Cardinals organization (November 18, 1994). ... On Louisville suspended list (May 12-17, 1995). ... On St. Louis disabled list (March 22-April 19, 1996); included rehabilitation assignments to St. Petersburg (April 5-12) and Louisville (April 12-19). ... On suspended list (September 9-12, 1997). ... Traded by Cardinals to Anaheim Angels for a player to be named later or cash (December 14, 1998); Cardinals acquired C Matt Garrick to complete deal (December 14, 1998).
STATISTICAL NOTES: Pitched 5-0 no-hit victory against Colorado Springs (May 16, 1994).

Year	League	W	L	Pct.	ERA	G	GS	CG	ShO	Sv.	IP	H	R	ER	BB	SO
1987— Gulf Coast Rangers (GCL)..		0	0	...	3.18	3	1	0	0	0	5 2/3	4	2	2	2	7
— Charlotte (FSL)		3	4	.429	4.02	11	10	0	0	0	56	67	36	25	17	23
1988— Charlotte (FSL)		10	11	.476	2.97	28	28	7	•5	0	175 2/3	156	71	58	42	95
1989— Tulsa (Texas)		8	5	.615	3.47	21	21	1	0	0	140	144	63	54	35	66
— Oklahoma City (A.A.)		0	4	.000	7.34	6	6	0	0	0	30 2/3	39	27	25	18	8
1990— Oklahoma City (A.A.)		7	*14	.333	5.25	28	28	2	1	0	151	*187	*103	88	42	81
1991— Oklahoma City (A.A.)		9	8	.529	4.93	25	24	3	1	0	149 2/3	162	89	82	38	67
— Texas (A.L.)		0	1	.000	14.46	4	1	0	0	0	9 1/3	21	16	15	4	6
1992— Buffalo (A.A.)■		8	8	.500	3.53	32	22	1	0	1	150 1/3	150	76	59	44	49
1993— Buffalo (A.A.)		3	4	.429	4.33	14	11	1	0	0	70 2/3	74	38	34	16	27
— Pittsburgh (N.L.)		3	0	1.000	6.96	26	0	0	0	0	32 1/3	43	25	25	9	14
1994— Tucson (PCL)■		10	7	.588	4.62	25	23	1	1	0	138 1/3	176	87	71	40	69
1995— Louisville (A.A.)■		4	1	.800	2.32	8	8	2	1	0	54 1/3	38	16	14	8	30
— St. Louis (N.L.)		6	6	.500	4.00	26	21	1	1	0	137 1/3	136	71	61	35	71
1996— St. Petersburg (FSL)		0	0	...	4.50	3	0	0	0	0	6	6	3	3	0	5
— Louisville (A.A.)		0	1	.000	9.00	2	1	0	0	0	5	5	4	3	1	4
— St. Louis (N.L.)		11	2	.846	3.55	48	6	0	0	0	88 2/3	83	37	35	35	45
1997— St. Louis (N.L.)		4	7	.364	5.06	55	2	0	0	2	96	109	61	54	31	51
1998— St. Louis (N.L.)		7	4	.636	4.77	48	10	0	0	0	105 2/3	131	63	56	36	55
1999— Anaheim (A.L.)■		10	4	.714	3.47	64	0	0	0	1	83	85	37	32	21	43
A.L. totals (2 years)		10	5	.667	4.58	68	1	0	0	1	92 1/3	106	53	47	25	49
N.L. totals (5 years)		31	19	.620	4.52	203	39	1	1	2	460	502	257	231	146	236
Major League totals (7 years)		41	24	.631	4.53	271	40	1	1	3	552 1/3	608	310	278	171	285

DIVISION SERIES RECORD

Year	League	W	L	Pct.	ERA	G	GS	CG	ShO	Sv.	IP	H	R	ER	BB	SO
1996— St. Louis (N.L.)		0	0	...	0.00	1	0	0	0	0	2	0	0	0	0	1

CHAMPIONSHIP SERIES RECORD

RECORDS: Shares single-series record for most games pitched—6 (1996).

Year	League	W	L	Pct.	ERA	G	GS	CG	ShO	Sv.	IP	H	R	ER	BB	SO
1996— St. Louis (N.L.)		0	1	.000	7.36	6	0	0	0	0	7 1/3	11	6	6	4	7

PETRICK, BEN — C — ROCKIES

PERSONAL: Born April 7, 1977, in Hillsboro, Ore. ... 6-0/199. ... Bats right, throws right. ... Full name: Benjamin Wayne Petrick.
HIGH SCHOOL: Glencoe (Hillsboro, Ore.).
TRANSACTIONS/CAREER NOTES: Selected by Colorado Rockies organization in second round of free-agent draft (June 3, 1995). ... On Carolina disabled list (April 26-May 6, 1999).
STATISTICAL NOTES: Led Pacific Coast League catchers with 14 passed balls in 1999.

Year	Team (League)	Pos.	G	AB	R	H	2B	3B	HR	RBI	Avg.	BB	SO	SB	PO	A	E	Avg.
						BATTING										FIELDING		
1996— Asheville (SAL)	C-DH	122	446	74	105	24	2	14	52	.235	75	98	19	766	95	12	.986
1997— Salem (Caro.)	C-DH	121	412	68	102	23	3	15	56	.248	62	100	30	754	91	10	.988
1998— New Haven (East.)	C-DH-OF	106	349	52	83	21	3	18	50	.238	56	89	7	536	43	5	.991
1999— Carolina (Sou.)	C-DH	20	68	18	21	5	1	4	22	.309	9	15	3	113	10	1	.992
— Colo. Springs (PCL)	C-DH-OF	84	282	56	88	16	5	19	64	.312	44	58	9	411	32	9	.980
— Colorado (N.L.)	C	19	62	13	20	3	0	4	12	.323	10	13	1	100	7	2	.982
Major League totals (1 year)		19	62	13	20	3	0	4	12	.323	10	13	1	100	7	2	.982

PETTITTE, ANDY — P — YANKEES

P

PERSONAL: Born June 15, 1972, in Baton Rouge, La. ... 6-5/225. ... Throws left, bats left. ... Full name: Andrew Eugene Pettitte.
HIGH SCHOOL: Deer Park (Texas).
JUNIOR COLLEGE: San Jacinto (North) College (Texas).

TRANSACTIONS/CAREER NOTES: Selected by New York Yankees organization in 22nd round of free-agent draft (June 4, 1990); did not sign. ... Signed as non-drafted free agent by Yankees organization (May 25, 1991). ... On Albany temporarily inactive list (June 5-10, 1994). ... On New York Yankees disabled list (March 26-April 17, 1999); included rehabilitation assignment to Tampa (April 12).

HONORS: Named lefthanded pitcher on THE SPORTING NEWS A.L. All-Star team (1996).

Year League	W	L	Pct.	ERA	G	GS	CG	ShO	Sv.	IP	H	R	ER	BB	SO
1991— Gulf Coast Yankees (GCL) ..	4	1	.800	0.98	6	6	0	0	0	36 2/3	16	6	4	8	51
— Oneonta (NY-P)	2	2	.500	2.18	6	6	1	0	0	33	33	18	8	16	32
1992— Greensboro (SAL)	10	4	.714	2.20	27	27	2	1	0	168	141	53	41	55	130
1993— Prince William (Caro.)	11	9	.550	3.04	26	26	2	1	0	159 2/3	146	68	54	47	129
— Albany (SAL)	1	0	1.000	3.60	1	1	0	0	0	5	5	4	2	2	6
1994— Albany/Colonie (East.)	7	2	.778	2.71	11	11	0	0	0	73	60	32	22	18	50
— Columbus (I.L.)	7	2	.778	2.98	16	16	3	0	0	96 2/3	101	40	32	21	61
1995— Columbus (I.L.)	0	0	...	0.00	2	2	0	0	0	11 2/3	7	0	0	0	8
— New York (A.L.)	12	9	.571	4.17	31	26	3	0	0	175	183	86	81	63	114
1996— New York (A.L.)	*21	8	.724	3.87	35	34	2	0	0	221	229	105	95	72	162
1997— New York (A.L.)	18	7	.720	2.88	35	•35	4	1	0	240 1/3	233	86	77	65	166
1998— New York (A.L.)	16	11	.593	4.24	33	32	5	0	0	216 1/3	226	110	102	87	146
1999— Tampa (FSL)	1	0	1.000	0.00	1	1	0	0	0	5	4	0	0	2	8
— New York (A.L.)	14	11	.560	4.70	31	31	0	0	0	191 2/3	216	105	100	89	121
Major League totals (5 years)	81	46	.638	3.92	165	158	14	1	0	1044 1/3	1087	492	455	376	709

DIVISION SERIES RECORD

RECORDS: Holds A.L. career record for most hits allowed—38.

Year League	W	L	Pct.	ERA	G	GS	CG	ShO	Sv.	IP	H	R	ER	BB	SO
1995— New York (A.L.)	0	0	...	5.14	1	1	0	0	0	7	9	4	4	3	0
1996— New York (A.L.)	0	0	...	5.68	1	1	0	0	0	6 1/3	4	4	4	6	3
1997— New York (A.L.)	0	2	.000	8.49	2	2	0	0	0	11 2/3	15	11	11	1	5
1998— New York (A.L.)	1	0	1.000	1.29	1	1	0	0	0	7	3	1	1	0	8
1999— New York (A.L.)	1	0	1.000	1.23	1	1	0	0	0	7 1/3	7	1	1	0	5
Division series totals (5 years)	2	2	.500	4.81	6	6	0	0	0	39 1/3	38	21	21	10	21

CHAMPIONSHIP SERIES RECORD

Year League	W	L	Pct.	ERA	G	GS	CG	ShO	Sv.	IP	H	R	ER	BB	SO
1996— New York (A.L.)	1	0	1.000	3.60	2	2	0	0	0	15	10	6	6	5	7
1998— New York (A.L.)	0	1	.000	11.57	1	1	0	0	0	4 2/3	8	6	6	3	1
1999— New York (A.L.)	1	0	1.000	2.45	1	1	0	0	0	7 1/3	8	2	2	1	5
Champ. series totals (3 years)	2	1	.667	4.67	4	4	0	0	0	27	26	14	14	9	13

WORLD SERIES RECORD

RECORDS: Shares single-game record for most earned runs allowed—7 (October 20, 1996).
NOTES: Member of World Series championship team (1996, 1998 and 1999).

Year League	W	L	Pct.	ERA	G	GS	CG	ShO	Sv.	IP	H	R	ER	BB	SO
1996— New York (A.L.)	1	1	.500	5.91	2	2	0	0	0	10 2/3	11	7	7	4	5
1998— New York (A.L.)	1	0	1.000	0.00	1	1	0	0	0	7 1/3	5	0	0	3	4
1999— New York (A.L.)	0	0	...	12.27	1	1	0	0	0	3 2/3	10	5	5	1	1
World Series totals (3 years)	2	1	.667	4.98	4	4	0	0	0	21 2/3	26	12	12	8	10

ALL-STAR GAME RECORD

Year League	W	L	Pct.	ERA	GS	CG	ShO	Sv.	IP	H	R	ER	BB	SO
1996— American				Did not play.										

PHELPS, JOSH   C   BLUE JAYS

PERSONAL: Born May 12, 1978, in Anchorage, Alaska. ... 6-3/220. ... Bats right, throws right. ... Full name: Joshua L. Phelps.
HIGH SCHOOL: Lakeland (Rathdrum, Idaho).
TRANSACTIONS/CAREER NOTES: Selected by Toronto Blue Jays organization in 10th round of free-agent draft (June 4, 1996).
STATISTICAL NOTES: Tied for South Atlantic League with seven double plays by catcher in 1997. ... Led South Atlantic League catchers with 19 errors in 1998. ... Led Florida State League with a .562 slugging percentage in 1999.

Year Team (League)	Pos.	G	AB	R	H	2B	3B	HR	RBI	Avg.	BB	SO	SB	PO	A	E	Avg.
1996— Medicine Hat (Pio.)	C-OF	59	191	26	46	3	0	5	29	.241	27	65	5	214	24	9	.964
1997— Hagerstown (SAL)	C	68	233	26	49	9	1	7	24	.210	15	72	3	519	56	21	.965
1998— Hagerstown (SAL)	C-3B-OF	117	385	48	102	24	1	8	44	.265	40	80	2	688	62	†19	.975
1999— Dunedin (FSL)	DH-C	110	406	72	133	27	4	20	88	.328	28	104	6	161	13	1	.994

PHILLIPS, J.R.   1B

PERSONAL: Born April 29, 1970, in West Covina, Calif. ... 6-1/185. ... Bats left, throws left. ... Full name: Charles Gene Phillips.
HIGH SCHOOL: Bishop Amat (La Puente, Calif.).
TRANSACTIONS/CAREER NOTES: Selected by California Angels organization in fourth round of free-agent draft (June 1, 1988). ... Claimed on waivers by San Francisco Giants (December 17, 1992). ... On Phoenix disabled list (August 14, 1994-remainder of season). ... Traded by Giants to Philadelphia Phillies for a player to be named later or cash (May 2, 1996); Phillies sent Giants an undisclosed amount of cash to complete deal (June 14, 1996). ... Granted free agency (October 10, 1996). ... Signed by Houston Astros organization (March 14, 1997). ... Granted free agency (October 15, 1997). ... Re-signed by Astros (November 26, 1997). ... Granted free agency (October 15, 1998). ... Signed by Colorado Rockies organization (December 18, 1998). ... Released by Rockies (November 29, 1999).
STATISTICAL NOTES: Led Northwest League first basemen with 641 putouts, 42 assists and 691 total chances in 1990. ... Led California League first basemen with 1,166 putouts, 1,272 total chances and 117 double plays in 1991. ... Led Texas League first basemen with 1,222 putouts, 100 assists, 17 errors, 1,339 total chances and 106 double plays in 1992. ... Led Pacific Coast League first basemen with 1,135 putouts, 93 assists, 28 errors and 1,256 total chances in 1993. ... Led Pacific Coast League first baseman with 114 assists, 1,118 total chances and 131 double plays in 1999.

P

Year	Team (League)	Pos.	G	AB	R	H	2B	3B	HR	RBI	Avg.	BB	SO	SB	PO	A	E	Avg.
1988—Bend (N.W.)		OF-1B	56	210	24	40	8	0	4	23	.190	21	70	3	197	9	3	.986
1989—Quad City (Midw.)		1B-OF	125	442	41	85	29	1	8	50	.192	49	146	3	954	46	20	.980
1990—Palm Springs (Calif.)		1B	46	162	14	32	4	1	1	15	.198	10	58	3	436	26	16	.967
—Boise (N.W.)		1B-OF	70	237	30	46	6	0	10	34	.194	19	78	1	†642	†42	8	.988
1991—Palm Springs (Calif.)		1B-P	130	471	64	117	22	2	20	70	.248	57	*144	15	†1166	94	12	.991
1992—Midland (Texas)		1B-OF	127	497	58	118	32	4	14	77	.237	32	*165	5	†1223	†100	†17	.987
1993—Phoenix (PCL)■		1B-OF	134	506	80	133	35	2	*27	94	.263	53	127	7	†1138	†93	†29	.977
—San Francisco (N.L.)		1B	11	16	1	5	1	1	1	4	.313	0	5	0	32	2	1	.971
1994—Phoenix (PCL)		1B-DH	95	360	69	108	28	5	27	79	.300	45	96	4	782	78	6	.993
—San Francisco (N.L.)		1B	15	38	1	5	0	0	1	3	.132	1	13	1	79	10	1	.989
1995—San Francisco (N.L.)		1B-OF	92	231	27	45	9	0	9	28	.195	19	69	1	536	37	4	.993
1996—San Francisco (N.L.)		1B	15	25	3	5	0	0	2	5	.200	1	13	0	49	2	1	.981
—Philadelphia (N.L.)■		OF-1B	35	79	9	12	5	0	5	10	.152	10	38	0	113	4	2	.983
—Scranton/W.B. (I.L.)		OF-1B-DH	53	200	33	57	14	2	13	42	.285	19	53	2	112	6	5	.959
1997—New Orleans (A.A.)■		OF-1B-DH	104	411	59	119	28	0	21	71	.290	39	112	0	411	36	7	.985
—Houston (N.L.)		1B-OF	13	15	2	2	0	0	1	4	.133	0	7	0	9	0	0	1.000
1998—New Orleans (PCL)		1B-OF	56	225	51	68	18	0	21	60	.302	21	65	1	381	24	4	.990
—Houston (N.L.)		1B-OF	36	58	4	11	0	0	2	9	.190	7	22	0	72	6	3	.963
1999—Colo. Spr. (PCL)■		1B-P-DH-OF	124	479	87	149	22	0	*41	100	.311	54	143	4	993	†114	11	.990
—Colorado (N.L.)		OF-1B	25	39	5	9	4	0	2	4	.231	0	13	0	14	3	1	.944
Major League totals (7 years)			242	501	52	94	19	1	23	67	.188	38	180	2	904	64	13	.987

RECORD AS PITCHER

Year	League	W	L	Pct.	ERA	G	GS	CG	ShO	Sv.	IP	H	R	ER	BB	SO
1991—Palm Springs (Calif.)		0	0	...	4.50	2	0	0	0	0	2	3	1	1	2	3
1999—Colo. Springs (PCL)		0	0	...	0.00	2	0	0	0	0	3⅓	2	0	0	0	1

PHILLIPS, JASON   P

PERSONAL: Born March 22, 1974, in Williamsport, Pa. ... 6-6/225. ... Throws right, bats right. ... Full name: Jason Charles Phillips.
HIGH SCHOOL: Hughesville (Pa.).
TRANSACTIONS/CAREER NOTES: Selected by Pittsburgh Pirates organization in 14th round of free-agent draft (June 1, 1992). ... On Nashville disabled list (May 26, 1999-remainder of season). ... Granted free agency (October 15, 1999).

Year	League	W	L	Pct.	ERA	G	GS	CG	ShO	Sv.	IP	H	R	ER	BB	SO
1992—Gulf Coast Pirates (GCL)		1	2	.333	8.47	4	4	0	0	0	17	21	21	16	13	10
1993—Welland (NY-P)		4	6	.400	3.53	14	14	0	0	0	71⅓	60	44	28	36	66
1994—Augusta (SAL)		6	12	.333	6.73	23	1	0	0	0	108⅓	118	97	81	88	108
—Welland (NY-P)		4	6	.400	3.53	14	14	0	0	0	71⅓	60	44	28	36	66
1995—Augusta (SAL)		4	3	.571	3.60	30	6	0	0	0	80	76	46	32	53	65
1996—Augusta (SAL)		5	4	.556	2.41	14	14	1	1	0	89⅔	79	35	24	29	75
—Lynchburg (Caro.)		5	6	.455	4.52	13	13	1	1	0	73⅔	82	47	37	35	63
1997—Lynchburg (Caro.)		11	6	.647	3.76	23	23	2	1	0	138⅔	129	66	58	35	140
—Carolina (Sou.)		1	2	.333	2.32	4	4	2	1	0	31	21	8	8	9	22
1998—Carolina (Sou.)		7	•13	.350	4.71	25	25	1	1	0	151	161	89	79	52	114
—Nashville (PCL)		2	0	1.000	2.59	5	5	0	0	0	31⅓	38	10	9	12	21
1999—Nashville (PCL)		0	0	...	15.00	1	1	0	0	0	3	6	6	5	5	5
—Pittsburgh (N.L.)		0	0	...	11.57	6	0	0	0	0	7	11	9	9	6	7
Major League totals (1 year)		0	0	...	11.57	6	0	0	0	0	7	11	9	9	6	7

PHILLIPS, TONY   OF

PERSONAL: Born April 25, 1959, in Atlanta. ... 5-10/175. ... Bats both, throws right. ... Full name: Keith Anthony Phillips.
HIGH SCHOOL: Roswell (Ga.).
JUNIOR COLLEGE: New Mexico Military Institute.
TRANSACTIONS/CAREER NOTES: Selected by Seattle Mariners organization in 16th round of free-agent draft (June 7, 1977); did not sign. ... Selected by Montreal Expos organization in secondary phase of free-agent draft (January 10, 1978). ... On West Palm Beach temporarily inactive list (April 11-May 4, 1978). ... Traded by Expos organization with cash to San Diego Padres for 1B Willie Montanez (August 31, 1980). ... Traded by Padres organization with P Eric Mustad and IF Kevin Bell to Oakland Athletics organization for P Bob Lacey and P Roy Moretti (March 27, 1981). ... On Oakland disabled list (March 26-August 22, 1985); included rehabilitation assignments to Tacoma (July 30-August 5 and August 7-20). ... On disabled list (August 14-October 3, 1986). ... On Oakland disabled list (July 12-August 28, 1987); included rehabilitation assignment to Tacoma (August 20-28). ... Released by A's (December 21, 1987). ... Re-signed by A's (March 9, 1988). ... On Oakland disabled list (May 18-July 8, 1988); included rehabilitation assignment to Tacoma (June 16-July 4). ... Granted free agency (November 13, 1989). ... Signed by Detroit Tigers (December 5, 1989). ... Traded by Tigers to California Angels for OF Chad Curtis (April 12, 1995). ... On suspended list (August 8-10, 1995). ... Granted free agency (October 31, 1995). ... Signed by Chicago White Sox (January 20, 1996). ... On suspended list (April 30-May 3, 1997). ... Traded by White Sox with C Chad Kreuter to Angels for P Chuck McElroy and C Jorge Fabregas (May 18, 1997). ... On Anaheim suspended list (August 17-20, 1997). ... Released by Angels (April 1, 1998). ... Signed by Toronto Blue Jays (July 1, 1998). ... Traded by Blue Jays to New York Mets for P Leo Estrella (July 31, 1998). ... Granted free agency (October 28, 1998). ... Signed by Athletics (December 14, 1998). ... On disabled list (August 16, 1999-remainder of season). ... Granted free agency (November 2, 1999).
RECORDS: Shares major league single-game record for most assists by second baseman (nine-inning game)—12 (July 6, 1986).
STATISTICAL NOTES: Led Southern League shortstops with 42 errors in 1980. ... Led Eastern League in being hit by pitch with 10 in 1981. ... Hit for the cycle (May 16, 1986). ... Led A.L. third basemen with 19 errors in 1995. ... Career major league grand slams: 1.

Year	Team (League)	Pos.	G	AB	R	H	2B	3B	HR	RBI	Avg.	BB	SO	SB	PO	A	E	Avg.
1978—W.P. Beach (FSL)		3B-SS-2B	32	54	8	9	0	0	0	3	.167	9	7	2	13	33	5	.902
—Jamestown (NY-P)		SS-2B-3B	52	152	24	29	5	2	1	17	.191	27	24	3	73	146	16	.932
1979—W.P. Beach (FSL)		2B-SS	60	203	30	47	5	1	0	18	.232	36	26	7	120	156	21	.929
—Memphis (Sou.)		SS-2B	52	156	31	44	4	2	3	11	.282	19	13	3	68	134	18	.918
1980—Memphis (Sou.)		SS-2B	136	502	100	125	18	4	5	41	.249	*98	89	50	226	408	†42	.938

P

Year	Team (League)	Pos.	G	AB	R	H	2B	3B	HR	RBI	Avg.	BB	SO	SB	PO	A	E	Avg.
1981—	West Haven (East.)■..	SS	131	461	79	114	25	3	9	64	.247	67	69	40	200	391	*33	.947
—	Tacoma (PCL)	2B-SS	4	11	1	4	1	0	0	2	.364	0	0	0	8	10	0	1.000
1982—	Tacoma (PCL)	SS	86	300	76	89	18	5	4	47	.297	73	63	29	138	236	30	.926
—	Oakland (A.L.)	SS	40	81	11	17	2	2	0	8	.210	12	26	2	46	95	7	.953
1983—	Oakland (A.L.)	S-2-3-DH	148	412	54	102	12	3	4	35	.248	48	70	16	218	383	30	.952
1984—	Oakland (A.L.)	SS-2B-OF	154	451	62	120	24	3	4	37	.266	42	86	10	255	391	28	.958
1985—	Tacoma (PCL)	3B-2B	20	69	9	9	1	0	0	5	.130	8	28	3	15	36	4	.927
—	Oakland (A.L.)	3B-2B	42	161	23	45	12	2	4	17	.280	13	34	3	54	103	3	.981
1986—	Oakland (A.L.)	2-3-0-DH-S	118	441	76	113	14	5	5	52	.256	76	82	15	191	326	13	.975
1987—	Oakland (A.L.) 2-3-S-O-DH	111	379	48	91	20	0	10	46	.240	57	76	7	179	299	14	.972
—	Tacoma (PCL)	2B-3B	7	26	5	9	2	1	1	6	.346	4	3	1	8	10	0	1.000
1988—	Tacoma (PCL) SS-OF-2B-3B	16	59	10	16	0	0	2	8	.271	12	13	0	25	27	2	.963
—	Oakland (A.L.) 3-0-2-S-1-D	79	212	32	43	8	4	2	17	.203	36	50	0	84	80	10	.943
1989—	Oakland (A.L.)	2-3-S-O-1	143	451	48	118	15	6	4	47	.262	58	66	3	184	321	15	.971
1990—	Detroit (A.L.)■...........3-2-S-O-DH	152	573	97	144	23	5	8	55	.251	99	85	19	180	368	23	.960
1991—	Detroit (A.L.) O-3-2-DH-S	146	564	87	160	28	4	17	72	.284	79	95	10	269	237	8	.984
1992—	Detroit (A.L.) O-2-DH-3-S	159	606	*114	167	32	3	10	64	.276	114	93	12	301	195	11	.978
1993—	Detroit (A.L.)	O-2-DH-3	151	566	113	177	27	0	7	57	.313	*132	102	16	321	165	13	.974
1994—	Detroit (A.L.)	OF-2B-DH	114	438	91	123	19	3	19	61	.281	95	105	13	254	42	6	.980
1995—	California (A.L.)■.......	3B-OF-DH	139	525	119	137	21	1	27	61	.261	113	135	13	166	179	†20	.945
1996—	Chicago (A.L.)■.......	OF-2B-1B	153	581	119	161	29	3	12	63	.277	*125	132	13	351	18	7	.981
1997—	Chicago (A.L.)	OF-3B	36	129	23	40	6	0	2	9	.310	29	29	4	74	15	3	.967
—	Anaheim (A.L.)■.......	2-0-DH-3	105	405	73	107	28	2	6	48	.264	73	89	9	137	103	8	.968
1998—	Syracuse (I.L.)	OF-2B	10	32	7	8	1	0	1	4	.250	15	10	2	17	3	1	.952
—	Toronto (A.L.)	OF	13	48	9	17	5	0	1	7	.354	9	6	0	24	0	1	.960
—	New York (N.L.)■	OF	52	188	25	42	11	0	3	14	.223	38	44	1	86	2	3	.967
1999—	Oakland (A.L.) 2-0-3-DH-S	106	406	76	99	24	4	15	49	.244	71	94	11	181	168	13	.964
American League totals (18 years)			2109	7429	1275	1981	349	50	157	805	.267	1281	1455	176	3469	3488	233	.968
National League totals (1 year)			52	188	25	42	11	0	3	14	.223	38	44	1	86	2	3	.967
Major League totals (18 years)			2161	7617	1300	2023	360	50	160	819	.266	1319	1499	177	3555	3490	236	.968

CHAMPIONSHIP SERIES RECORD

Year	Team (League)	Pos.	G	AB	R	H	2B	3B	HR	RBI	Avg.	BB	SO	SB	PO	A	E	Avg.
1988—	Oakland (A.L.)	OF-2B	2	7	0	2	1	0	0	0	.286	1	3	0	10	0	0	1.000
1989—	Oakland (A.L.)	2B-3B	5	18	1	3	1	0	0	1	.167	2	4	2	4	14	0	1.000
Championship series totals (2 years)			7	25	1	5	2	0	0	1	.200	3	7	2	14	14	0	1.000

WORLD SERIES RECORD

NOTES: Member of World Series championship team (1989).

Year	Team (League)	Pos.	G	AB	R	H	2B	3B	HR	RBI	Avg.	BB	SO	SB	PO	A	E	Avg.
1988—	Oakland (A.L.)	OF-2B	2	4	1	1	0	0	0	0	.250	1	2	2	3	5	0	1.000
1989—	Oakland (A.L.)	2B-3B-OF	4	17	2	4	1	0	1	3	.235	0	3	0	8	15	0	1.000
World Series totals (2 years)			6	21	3	5	1	0	1	3	.238	1	5	2	11	20	0	1.000

PIATT, ADAM   3B   ATHLETICS

PERSONAL: Born February 8, 1976, in Chicago. ... 6-2/195. ... Bats right, throws right. ... Full name: Adam David Piatt.
HIGH SCHOOL: Bishop Verot (Fort Myers, Fla.).
COLLEGE: Mississippi State.
TRANSACTIONS/CAREER NOTES: Selected by Oakland Athletics organization in eighth round of free-agent draft (June 3, 1997).
HONORS: Named Texas League Most Valuable Player (1999).
STATISTICAL NOTES: Led California League third basemen with 32 errors in 1998. ... Led Texas League with 335 total bases, .451 on-base percentage, .704 slugging percentage and 10 intentional bases on balls received in 1999.

Year	Team (League)	Pos.	G	AB	R	H	2B	3B	HR	RBI	Avg.	BB	SO	SB	PO	A	E	Avg.
1997—	S. Oregon (N'west).....	3B-1B	57	216	63	63	9	1	13	35	.292	35	58	19	26	107	21	.864
1998—	Modesto (Calif.)	3B-2B	133	500	91	144	•40	3	20	*107	.288	80	99	20	64	200	†32	.892
1999—	Midland (Texas).........	3B-SS-DH	129	476	*128	164	48	3	*39	*135	.345	•93	101	7	91	253	31	.917
—	Vancouver (PCL)	3B-SS	6	18	1	4	1	0	0	3	.222	6	2	0	6	16	2	.917

PIAZZA, MIKE   C   METS

PERSONAL: Born September 4, 1968, in Norristown, Pa. ... 6-3/215. ... Bats right, throws right. ... Full name: Michael Joseph Piazza. ... Name pronounced pee-AH-za.
HIGH SCHOOL: Phoenixville (Pa.) Area.
JUNIOR COLLEGE: Miami-Dade (North) Community College.
TRANSACTIONS/CAREER NOTES: Selected by Los Angeles Dodgers organization in 62nd round of free-agent draft (June 1, 1988). ... On disabled list (May 11-June 4, 1995). ... Traded by Dodgers with 3B Todd Zeile to Florida Marlins for OF Gary Sheffield, 3B Bobby Bonilla, C Charles Johnson, OF Jim Eisenreich and P Manuel Barrios (May 15, 1998). ... Traded by Marlins to New York Mets for OF Preston Wilson, P Ed Yarnall and P Geoff Goetz (May 22, 1998). ... On disabled list (April 10-25, 1999).
RECORDS: Shares major league record for most grand slams in two consecutive games—2 (August 9 and 10, 1998). ... Shares major league single-month record for most grand slams—3 (April 1998). ... Holds single-season record for highest batting average by a catcher (100 or more games)—.362 (1997).

HONORS: Named N.L. Rookie Player of the Year by THE SPORTING NEWS (1993). ... Named catcher on THE SPORTING NEWS N.L. All-Star team (1993-99). ... Named catcher on THE SPORTING NEWS N.L. Silver Slugger team (1993-99). ... Named N.L. Rookie of the Year by Baseball Writers' Association of America (1993).

STATISTICAL NOTES: Led California League with .540 slugging percentage and in grounding into double plays with 19 in 1991. ... Led N.L. catchers with 98 assists and tied for lead with 11 errors in 1993. ... Led N.L. catchers in total chances with 866 in 1995 and 1,055 in 1996. ... Led N.L. catchers in passed balls with 12 in 1995 and 12 in 1996. ... Hit three home runs in one game (June 29, 1996). ... Led N.L. catchers in total chances with 1,135 in 1997. ... Led N.L. catchers with 83 assists in 1998. ... Had 24-game hitting streak (May 25-June 22, 1999). ... Led N.L. in grounding into double plays with 27 in 1999. ... Led N.L. catchers in total chances with 1,011 in 1999. ... Career major league grand slams: 9.

| | | | | | | | BATTING | | | | | | | | FIELDING | | |
Year	Team (League)	Pos.	G	AB	R	H	2B	3B	HR	RBI	Avg.	BB	SO	SB	PO	A	E	Avg.
1989—	Salem (N.W.)	C	57	198	22	53	11	0	8	25	.268	13	51	0	230	21	6	.977
1990—	Vero Beach (FSL)	C-1B	88	272	27	68	20	0	6	45	.250	11	68	0	428	38	16	.967
1991—	Bakersfield (Calif.)	C-1B	117	448	71	124	27	2	29	80	.277	47	83	0	723	69	15	.981
1992—	San Antonio (Texas)	C	31	114	18	43	11	0	7	21	.377	13	18	0	189	22	4	.981
—	Albuquerque (PCL)	C-1B	94	358	54	122	22	5	16	69	.341	37	57	1	550	50	9	.985
—	Los Angeles (N.L.)	C	21	69	5	16	3	0	1	7	.232	4	12	0	94	7	1	.990
1993—	Los Angeles (N.L.)	C-1B	149	547	81	174	24	2	35	112	.318	46	86	3	901	†98	‡11	.989
1994—	Los Angeles (N.L.)	C	107	405	64	129	18	0	24	92	.319	33	65	1	640	38	*10	.985
1995—	Los Angeles (N.L.)	C	112	434	82	150	17	0	32	93	.346	39	80	1	*805	52	9	.990
1996—	Los Angeles (N.L.)	C	148	547	87	184	16	0	36	105	.336	81	93	0	*1055	70	9	.992
—	National (N.L.)	C	...	3	1	2	1	0	1	2	.667	0	1	0	4	0	0	1.000
1997—	Los Angeles (N.L.)	C-DH	152	556	104	201	32	1	40	124	.362	69	77	5	*1045	74	*16	.986
1998—	Los Angeles (N.L.)	C	37	149	20	42	5	0	9	30	.282	11	27	0	277	25	2	.993
—	Florida (N.L.)■	C	5	18	1	5	0	1	0	5	.278	0	0	0	27	3	1	.968
—	New York (N.L.)■	C-DH	109	394	67	137	33	0	23	76	.348	47	53	1	680	‡57	8	.989
1999—	New York (N.L.)	C-DH	141	534	100	162	25	0	40	124	.303	51	70	2	*953	47	11	.989
Major League totals (8 years)			981	3656	612	1202	174	4	241	770	.329	381	564	13	6481	471	78	.989

DIVISION SERIES RECORD

| | | | | | | | BATTING | | | | | | | | FIELDING | | |
Year	Team (League)	Pos.	G	AB	R	H	2B	3B	HR	RBI	Avg.	BB	SO	SB	PO	A	E	Avg.
1995—	Los Angeles (N.L.)	C	3	14	1	3	1	0	1	1	.214	0	2	0	31	0	0	1.000
1996—	Los Angeles (N.L.)	C	3	10	1	3	0	0	0	2	.300	1	2	0	25	4	0	1.000
1999—	New York (N.L.)	C	2	9	0	2	0	0	0	0	.222	0	4	0	13	0	0	1.000
Division series totals (3 years)			8	33	2	8	1	0	1	3	.242	1	8	0	69	4	0	1.000

CHAMPIONSHIP SERIES RECORD

| | | | | | | | BATTING | | | | | | | | FIELDING | | |
Year	Team (League)	Pos.	G	AB	R	H	2B	3B	HR	RBI	Avg.	BB	SO	SB	PO	A	E	Avg.
1999—	New York (N.L.)	C	6	24	1	4	0	0	1	4	.167	1	6	0	44	3	3	.940

NOTES: Named Most Valuable Player (1996).

ALL-STAR GAME RECORD

| | | | | | | BATTING | | | | | | | | FIELDING | | |
Year	League	Pos.	AB	R	H	2B	3B	HR	RBI	Avg.	BB	SO	SB	PO	A	E	Avg.
1993—	National	C	1	0	0	0	0	0	0	.000	0	1	0	3	0	0	1.000
1994—	National	C	4	0	1	0	0	0	1	.250	0	0	0	6	0	0	1.000
1995—	National	C	3	1	1	0	0	1	1	.333	0	0	0	6	1	0	1.000
1996—	National	C	3	1	2	1	0	1	2	.667	0	1	0	6	1	0	1.000
1997—	National	C	1	0	0	0	0	0	0	.000	1	0	0	2	0	0	1.000
1998—	National	C	3	0	1	0	0	0	0	.333	0	0	0	2	0	0	1.000
1999—	National	C	2	0	1	0	0	0	0	.500	0	1	0	6	0	0	1.000
All-Star Game totals (7 years)			17	2	6	1	0	2	4	.353	1	3	0	31	2	0	1.000

PICKERING, CALVIN   1B   ORIOLES

PERSONAL: Born September 29, 1976, in St. Thomas, Virgin Islands. ... 6-5/278. ... Bats left, throws left. ... Full name: Calvin E. Pickering.
HIGH SCHOOL: King (Tampa).
TRANSACTIONS/CAREER NOTES: Selected by Baltimore Orioles organization in 35th round of free-agent draft (June 3, 1995).
HONORS: Named Eastern League Most Valuable Player (1998).
STATISTICAL NOTES: Led Appalachian League with 135 totals bases, .675 slugging pecentage and four intentional bases on balls received in 1996. ... Led Eastern League with 276 total bases, .434 on-base percentage, .566 slugging percentage, 16 intentional bases on balls received and grounding into double plays with 20 in 1998. ... Led Eastern League first basemen with 20 errors in 1998.

| | | | | | | | BATTING | | | | | | | | FIELDING | | |
Year	Team (League)	Pos.	G	AB	R	H	2B	3B	HR	RBI	Avg.	BB	SO	SB	PO	A	E	Avg.
1995—	GC Orioles (GCL)	1B-DH	15	60	8	30	10	0	1	22	.500	2	6	0	86	6	3	.968
1996—	Bluefield (Appl.)	1B-DH	60	200	45	65	14	0	*18	*66	.325	28	64	8	396	26	9	.979
1997—	Delmarva (SAL)	1B-DH	122	444	88	138	31	1	25	79	.311	53	139	6	940	70	*27	.974
1998—	Bowie (East.)	1B-OF-DH	139	488	93	151	28	2	*31	*114	.309	*98	119	4	1068	60	†22	.981
—	Baltimore (A.L.)	1B-DH	9	21	4	5	0	0	2	3	.238	3	4	1	31	0	1	.969
1999—	Rochester (I.L.)	1B-DH-OF	103	372	63	106	20	0	16	63	.285	60	99	1	822	45	13	.985
—	Baltimore (A.L.)	1B-DH	23	40	4	5	1	0	1	5	.125	11	16	0	46	2	2	.960
Major League totals (2 years)			32	61	8	10	1	0	3	8	.164	14	20	1	77	2	3	.963

PIERZYNSKI, A.J.   C   TWINS

P

PERSONAL: Born December 30, 1976, in Bridgehampton, N.Y. ... 6-3/220. ... Bats left, throws right. ... Full name: Anthony John Pierzynski.
HIGH SCHOOL: Dr. Phillips (Orlando).

TRANSACTIONS/CAREER NOTES: Selected by Minnesota Twins organization in third round of free-agent draft (June 2, 1994). ... On Salt Lake disabled list (August 24, 1999-remainder of season).

STATISTICAL NOTES: Tied for Appalachian League lead in errors by catcher with 12 in 1995. ... Led Appalachian League catchers with 71 assists in 1995. ... Tied for Midwest League lead with 20 errors by catcher in 1996.

								BATTING								FIELDING		
Year Team (League)	Pos.	G	AB	R	H	2B	3B	HR	RBI	Avg.	BB	SO	SB	PO	A	E	Avg.
1994—GC Twins (GCL)	C-DH	43	152	21	44	8	1	1	19	.289	12	19	0	198	28	8	.966
1995—Fort Wayne (Midw.)	C	22	84	10	26	5	1	2	14	.310	2	10	0	119	34	10	.939
—Elizabethton (Appl.)	C-1B	56	205	29	68	13	1	7	45	.332	14	23	0	376	†72	‡12	.974
1996—Fort Wayne (Midw.)	C-DH-OF	114	431	48	118	30	3	7	70	.274	22	53	0	658	80	†21	.972
1997—Fort Myers (FSL)	C-DH-1B	118	412	49	115	23	1	9	64	.279	16	59	2	677	78	10	.987
1998—New Britain (East.)	C-DH	59	212	30	63	11	0	3	17	.297	10	25	0	409	37	2	.996
—Salt Lake (PCL)	C	59	208	29	53	7	2	7	30	.255	9	24	3	366	30	7	.983
—Minnesota (A.L.)	C	7	10	1	3	0	0	0	1	.300	1	2	0	33	2	0	1.000
1999—Salt Lake (PCL)	C-DH	67	228	29	59	10	0	1	25	.259	16	29	0	376	45	7	.984
—Minnesota (A.L.)	C	9	22	3	6	2	0	0	3	.273	1	4	0	35	2	0	1.000
Major League totals (2 years)		16	32	4	9	2	0	0	4	.281	2	6	0	68	4	0	1.000

PISCIOTTA, MARC   P

PERSONAL: Born August 7, 1970, in Edison, N.J. ... 6-5/225. ... Throws right, bats right. ... Full name: Marc George Pisciotta. ... Name pronounced pih-SHO-tuh.

HIGH SCHOOL: George Walton Comprehensive (Marietta, Ga.).

COLLEGE: Georgia Tech.

TRANSACTIONS/CAREER NOTES: Selected by Pittsburgh Pirates organization in 19th round of free-agent draft (June 3, 1991). ... On disabled list (May 22-June 19, 1992). ... Selected by Colorado Rockies from Pirates organization in Rule 5 major league draft (December 13, 1993). ... Returned to Pirates organization (March 28, 1994). ... Claimed on waivers by Chicago Cubs (November 20, 1996). ... Released by Cubs (March 30, 1999). ... Signed by Atlanta Braves organization (April 2, 1999). ... Traded by Braves to Kansas City Royals for IF Jose Cepeda (June 18, 1999). ... On Omaha disabled list (July 30-August 29, 1999). ... Granted free agency (October 4, 1999).

Year League	W	L	Pct.	ERA	G	GS	CG	ShO	Sv.	IP	H	R	ER	BB	SO
1991—Welland (NY-P)	1	1	.500	0.26	24	0	0	0	8	34	16	4	1	20	47
1992—Augusta (SAL)	4	5	.444	4.54	20	12	1	0	1	79 1/3	91	51	40	43	54
1993—Augusta (SAL)	5	2	.714	2.68	34	0	0	0	12	43 2/3	31	18	13	17	49
—Salem (Caro.)	0	0	...	2.95	20	0	0	0	12	18 1/3	23	13	6	13	13
1994—Salem (Caro.)	1	4	.200	1.53	31	0	0	0	19	29 1/3	24	14	5	13	23
—Carolina (Sou.)	3	4	.429	5.61	26	0	0	0	5	25 2/3	32	21	16	15	21
1995—Carolina (Sou.)	6	4	.600	4.15	56	0	0	0	9	69 1/3	60	37	32	45	57
1996—Calgary (PCL)	2	7	.222	4.11	57	0	0	0	1	65 2/3	71	38	30	46	46
1997—Iowa (A.A.)■	6	2	.750	2.36	42	0	0	0	22	45 2/3	29	12	12	23	48
—Chicago (N.L.)	3	1	.750	3.18	24	0	0	0	0	28 1/3	20	10	10	16	21
1998—Chicago (N.L.)	1	2	.333	4.09	43	0	0	0	0	44	44	21	20	32	31
—Iowa (PCL)	3	5	.375	6.46	28	0	0	0	8	30 2/3	34	24	22	16	29
1999—Richmond (I.L.)■	3	2	.600	6.06	23	0	0	0	0	35 2/3	34	25	24	17	27
—Kansas City (A.L.)■	0	2	.000	8.64	8	0	0	0	0	8 1/3	9	8	8	10	3
—Omaha (PCL)	0	1	.000	11.20	10	0	0	0	0	13 2/3	18	18	17	11	8
A.L. totals (1 year)	0	2	.000	8.64	8	0	0	0	0	8 1/3	9	8	8	10	3
N.L. totals (2 years)	4	3	.571	3.73	67	0	0	0	0	72 1/3	64	31	30	48	52
Major League totals (3 years)	4	5	.444	4.24	75	0	0	0	0	80 2/3	73	39	38	58	55

PITTSLEY, JIM   P

PERSONAL: Born April 3, 1974, in DuBois, Pa. ... 6-7/230. ... Throws right, bats right. ... Full name: James Michael Pittsley.

HIGH SCHOOL: DuBois (Pa.).

TRANSACTIONS/CAREER NOTES: Selected by Kansas City Royals organization in first round (17th pick overall) of free-agent draft (June 1, 1992); pick received as part of compensation for San Diego Padres signing Type A free-agent IF Kurt Stillwell. ... On disabled list (May 29-June 6 and July 29-September 13, 1993). ... On Kansas City disabled list (August 17, 1995-remainder of season). ... On Kansas City disabled list (March 30-July 6, 1996); included rehabilitation assignments to Wilmington (June 6-14), Wichita (June 14-28) and Omaha (June 28-July 5). ... On suspended list (June 12-14, 1998). ... Claimed on waivers by Milwaukee Brewers (May 21, 1999). ... Granted free agency (October 15, 1999).

Year League	W	L	Pct.	ERA	G	GS	CG	ShO	Sv.	IP	H	R	ER	BB	SO
1992—Gulf Coast Royals (GCL)	4	1	.800	3.32	9	9	0	0	0	43 1/3	27	16	16	15	47
—Baseball City (FSL)	0	0	...	0.00	1	1	0	0	0	3	2	0	0	1	4
1993—Rockford (Midw.)	5	5	.500	4.26	15	15	2	1	0	80 1/3	76	43	38	32	87
1994—Wilmington (Caro.)	11	5	.688	3.17	27	27	1	1	0	161 2/3	154	73	57	42	*171
1995—Omaha (A.A.)	4	1	.800	3.21	8	8	0	0	0	47 2/3	38	20	17	16	39
—Kansas City (A.L.)	0	0	...	13.50	1	1	0	0	0	3 1/3	7	5	5	1	0
1996—Wilmington (Caro.)	0	1	.000	11.00	2	2	0	0	0	9	13	12	11	5	10
—Wichita (Texas)	3	0	1.000	0.41	3	3	0	0	0	22	9	1	1	5	7
—Omaha (A.A.)	7	1	.875	3.97	13	13	0	0	0	70 1/3	74	34	31	39	53
1997—Omaha (A.A.)	1	2	.333	4.42	7	7	0	0	0	38 2/3	36	21	19	20	30
—Kansas City (A.L.)	5	8	.385	5.46	21	21	0	0	0	112	120	72	68	54	52
1998—Kansas City (A.L.)	1	1	.500	6.59	39	2	0	0	0	68 1/3	88	56	50	37	44
1999—Kansas City (A.L.)	1	2	.333	6.94	5	5	0	0	0	23 1/3	33	22	18	15	7
—Milwaukee (N.L.)■	0	0	...	4.82	15	0	0	0	0	18 2/3	20	12	10	10	13
—Louisville (I.L.)	2	4	.333	8.77	8	8	0	0	0	39	55	42	38	16	26
A.L. totals (4 years)	7	11	.389	6.13	66	29	0	0	0	207	248	155	141	107	103
N.L. totals (1 year)	0	0	...	4.82	15	0	0	0	0	18 2/3	20	12	10	10	13
Major League totals (4 years)	7	12	.368	6.02	81	29	0	0	0	225 2/3	268	167	151	117	116

P

PERSONAL: Born February 4, 1962, in Gary, Ind. ... 6-5/217. ... Throws left, bats left. ... Full name: Daniel Thomas Plesac. ... Name pronounced PLEE-sack.

HIGH SCHOOL: Crown Point (Ind.).

COLLEGE: North Carolina State.

TRANSACTIONS/CAREER NOTES: Selected by St. Louis Cardinals organization in second round of free-agent draft (June 3, 1980); did not sign. ... Selected by Milwaukee Brewers organization in first round (26th pick overall) of free-agent draft (June 6, 1983). ... Granted free agency (October 27, 1992). ... Signed by Chicago Cubs (December 8, 1992). ... Granted free agency (October 25, 1994). ... Signed by Pittsburgh Pirates (November 9, 1994). ... Traded by Pirates with OF Orlando Merced and IF Carlos Garcia to Toronto Blue Jays for P Jose Silva, P Jose Pett, IF Brandon Cromer and three players to be named later (November 14, 1996); Pirates acquired P Mike Halperin, IF Abraham Nunez and C/OF Craig Wilson to complete deal (December 11, 1996). ... Traded by Blue Jays to Arizona Diamondbacks for SS Tony Batista and P John Frascatore (June 12, 1999).

STATISTICAL NOTES: Led Appalachian League pitchers with three balks in 1983.

MISCELLANEOUS: Holds Milwaukee Brewers all-time records for lowest earned run average (3.21), most games pitched (365) and most saves (133).

Year League	W	L	Pct.	ERA	G	GS	CG	ShO	Sv.	IP	H	R	ER	BB	SO
1983—Paintsville (Appl.)	*9	1	.900	3.50	14	•14	2	0	0	82 1/3	76	44	32	57	*85
1984—Stockton (Calif.)	6	6	.500	3.32	16	16	2	0	0	108 1/3	106	51	40	50	101
—El Paso (Texas)	2	2	.500	3.46	7	7	0	0	0	39	43	19	15	16	24
1985—El Paso (Texas)	12	5	.706	4.97	25	24	2	0	0	150 1/3	171	91	83	68	128
1986—Milwaukee (A.L.)	10	7	.588	2.97	51	0	0	0	14	91	81	34	30	29	75
1987—Milwaukee (A.L.)	5	6	.455	2.61	57	0	0	0	23	79 1/3	63	30	23	23	89
1988—Milwaukee (A.L.)	1	2	.333	2.41	50	0	0	0	30	52 1/3	46	14	14	12	52
1989—Milwaukee (A.L.)	3	4	.429	2.35	52	0	0	0	33	61 1/3	47	16	16	17	52
1990—Milwaukee (A.L.)	3	7	.300	4.43	66	0	0	0	24	69	67	36	34	31	65
1991—Milwaukee (A.L.)	2	7	.222	4.29	45	10	0	0	8	92 1/3	92	49	44	39	61
1992—Milwaukee (A.L.)	5	4	.556	2.96	44	4	0	0	1	79	64	28	26	35	54
1993—Chicago (N.L.)■	2	1	.667	4.74	57	0	0	0	0	62 2/3	74	37	33	21	47
1994—Chicago (N.L.)	2	3	.400	4.61	54	0	0	0	1	54 2/3	61	30	28	13	53
1995—Pittsburgh (N.L.)■	4	4	.500	3.58	58	0	0	0	3	60 1/3	53	26	24	27	57
1996—Pittsburgh (N.L.)	6	5	.545	4.09	73	0	0	0	11	70 1/3	67	35	32	24	76
1997—Toronto (A.L.)■	2	4	.333	3.58	73	0	0	0	1	50 1/3	47	22	20	19	61
1998—Toronto (A.L.)	4	3	.571	3.78	78	0	0	0	4	50	41	23	21	16	55
1999—Toronto (A.L.)	0	3	.000	8.34	30	0	0	0	1	22 2/3	28	21	21	9	26
—Arizona (N.L.)■	2	1	.667	3.32	34	0	0	0	1	21 2/3	22	9	8	8	27
A.L. totals (10 years)	35	47	.427	3.46	546	14	0	0	138	647 1/3	576	273	249	230	590
N.L. totals (5 years)	16	14	.533	4.17	276	0	0	0	16	269 2/3	277	137	125	93	260
Major League totals (14 years)	51	61	.455	3.67	822	14	0	0	154	917	853	410	374	323	850

DIVISION SERIES RECORD

Year League	W	L	Pct.	ERA	G	GS	CG	ShO	Sv.	IP	H	R	ER	BB	SO
1999—Arizona (N.L.)	0	0	...	54.00	1	0	0	0	0	1/3	3	2	2	0	0

ALL-STAR GAME RECORD

Year League	W	L	Pct.	ERA	GS	CG	ShO	Sv.	IP	H	R	ER	BB	SO
1987—American	0	0	...	0.00	0	0	0	0	1	0	0	0	0	1
1988—American	0	0	...	0.00	0	0	0	0	1/3	0	0	0	0	1
1989—American	0	0	...		0	0	0	0	1	1	0	0	0	0
All-Star Game totals (3 years)	0	0	...	0.00	0	0	0	0	1 1/3	1	0	0	0	2

PERSONAL: Born September 3, 1963, in Wilmington, Calif. ... 6-6/224. ... Throws right, bats right. ... Full name: Eric Vaughn Plunk.

HIGH SCHOOL: Bellflower (Calif.).

COLLEGE: Cal State Dominguez Hills.

TRANSACTIONS/CAREER NOTES: Selected by New York Yankees organization in fourth round of free-agent draft (June 8, 1981). ... On disabled list (August 11-26, 1983). ... Traded by Yankees with OF Stan Javier, P Jay Howell, P Jose Rijo and P Tim Birtsas to Oakland Athletics for OF Rickey Henderson, P Bert Bradley and cash (December 5, 1984). ... On disabled list (July 2-17, 1988). ... Traded by A's with P Greg Cadaret and OF Luis Polonia to New York Yankees for OF Rickey Henderson (June 21, 1989). ... Released by Yankees (November 20, 1991). ... Signed by Syracuse, Toronto Blue Jays organization (December 12, 1991). ... Released by Syracuse, Blue Jays organization (March 27, 1992). ... Signed by Canton/Akron, Cleveland Indians organization (April 9, 1992). ... Granted free agency (October 27, 1992). ... Re-signed by Indians (November 12, 1992). ... Granted free agency (October 29, 1996). ... Re-signed by Indians (December 10, 1996). ... Traded by Indians to Milwaukee Brewers for P Doug Jones (July 23, 1998). ... Granted free agency (November 4, 1999).

STATISTICAL NOTES: Tied for Florida State League lead with seven balks in 1984. ... Led A.L. with six balks in 1986.

Year League	W	L	Pct.	ERA	G	GS	CG	ShO	Sv.	IP	H	R	ER	BB	SO
1981—Gulf Coast Yankees (GCL)	3	4	.429	3.83	11	11	1	0	0	54	56	29	23	20	47
1982—Paintsville (Appl.)	6	3	.667	4.64	12	8	4	0	0	64	63	35	33	30	59
1983—Fort Lauderdale (FSL)	8	10	.444	2.74	20	20	5	•4	0	125	115	55	38	63	109
1984—Fort Lauderdale (FSL)	12	12	.500	2.86	28	28	7	1	0	176 1/3	153	85	56	*123	*152
1985—Huntsville (Sou.)■	8	2	.800	3.40	13	13	2	1	0	79 1/3	61	36	30	56	68
—Tacoma (PCL)	0	5	.000	5.77	11	10	0	0	0	53	51	41	34	50	43
1986—Tacoma (PCL)	2	3	.400	4.68	6	6	0	0	0	32 2/3	25	18	17	33	31
—Oakland (A.L.)	4	7	.364	5.31	26	15	0	0	0	120 1/3	91	75	71	102	98
1987—Oakland (A.L.)	4	6	.400	4.74	32	11	0	0	2	95	91	53	50	62	90
—Tacoma (PCL)	1	1	.500	1.56	24	0	0	0	9	34 2/3	21	8	6	17	56
1988—Oakland (A.L.)	7	2	.778	3.00	49	0	0	0	5	78	62	27	26	39	79
1989—Oakland (A.L.)	1	1	.500	2.20	23	0	0	0	1	28 2/3	17	7	7	12	24
—New York (A.L.)■	7	5	.583	3.69	27	7	0	0	0	75 2/3	65	36	31	52	61
1990—New York (A.L.)	6	3	.667	2.72	47	0	0	0	0	72 2/3	58	27	22	43	67

P

Year League	W	L	Pct.	ERA	G	GS	CG	ShO	Sv.	IP	H	R	ER	BB	SO
1991— New York (A.L.)	2	5	.286	4.76	43	8	0	0	0	111 2/3	128	69	59	62	103
1992— Canton/Akron (East.)■	1	2	.333	1.72	9	0	0	0	0	15 2/3	11	4	3	5	19
— Cleveland (A.L.)	9	6	.600	3.64	58	0	0	0	4	71 2/3	61	31	29	38	50
1993— Cleveland (A.L.)	4	5	.444	2.79	70	0	0	0	15	71	61	29	22	30	77
1994— Cleveland (A.L.)	7	2	.778	2.54	41	0	0	0	3	71	61	25	20	37	73
1995— Cleveland (A.L.)	6	2	.750	2.67	56	0	0	0	2	64	48	19	19	27	71
1996— Cleveland (A.L.)	3	2	.600	2.43	56	0	0	0	2	77 2/3	56	21	21	34	85
1997— Cleveland (A.L.)	4	5	.444	4.66	55	0	0	0	0	65 2/3	62	37	34	36	66
1998— Cleveland (A.L.)	3	1	.750	4.83	37	0	0	0	0	41	44	23	22	15	38
— Milwaukee (N.L.)■	1	2	.333	3.69	26	0	0	0	1	31 2/3	33	14	13	15	36
1999— Milwaukee (N.L.)	4	4	.500	5.02	68	0	0	0	0	75 1/3	71	44	42	43	63
A.L. totals (13 years)	67	52	.563	3.73	620	41	0	0	34	1044	905	479	433	589	982
N.L. totals (2 years)	5	6	.455	4.63	94	0	0	0	1	107	104	58	55	58	99
Major League totals (14 years)	72	58	.554	3.82	714	41	0	0	35	1151	1009	537	488	647	1081

DIVISION SERIES RECORD

Year League	W	L	Pct.	ERA	G	GS	CG	ShO	Sv.	IP	H	R	ER	BB	SO
1995— Cleveland (A.L.)	0	0	...	0.00	1	0	0	0	0	1 1/3	1	0	0	1	1
1996— Cleveland (A.L.)	0	1	.000	6.75	3	0	0	0	0	4	1	3	3	3	6
1997— Cleveland (A.L.)	0	1	.000	13.50	1	0	0	0	0	1 1/3	4	4	2	0	1
Division series totals (3 years)	0	2	.000	6.75	5	0	0	0	0	6 2/3	6	7	5	4	8

CHAMPIONSHIP SERIES RECORD

Year League	W	L	Pct.	ERA	G	GS	CG	ShO	Sv.	IP	H	R	ER	BB	SO
1988— Oakland (A.L.)	0	0	...	0.00	1	0	0	0	0	1/3	1	0	0	0	1
1995— Cleveland (A.L.)	0	0	...	9.00	3	0	0	0	0	2	1	2	2	3	2
1997— Cleveland (A.L.)	1	0	1.000	0.00	1	0	0	0	0	2/3	1	0	0	0	0
Champ. series totals (3 years)	1	0	1.000	6.00	5	0	0	0	0	3	3	2	2	3	3

WORLD SERIES RECORD

Year League	W	L	Pct.	ERA	G	GS	CG	ShO	Sv.	IP	H	R	ER	BB	SO
1988— Oakland (A.L.)	0	0	...	0.00	2	0	0	0	0	1 2/3	0	0	0	0	3
1995— Cleveland (A.L.)								Did not play.							
1997— Cleveland (A.L.)	0	1	.000	9.00	3	0	0	0	0	3	3	4	3	4	3
World Series totals (2 years)	0	1	.000	5.79	5	0	0	0	0	4 2/3	3	4	3	4	6

POLANCO, PLACIDO — 2B/SS — CARDINALS

PERSONAL: Born October 10, 1975, in Santo Domingo, Dominican Republic. ... 5-10/168. ... Bats right, throws right. ... Full name: Placido Enrique Polanco.
HIGH SCHOOL: Santo Claro (Santo Domingo, Dominican Republic).
JUNIOR COLLEGE: Miami-Dade (Wolfson) Community College.
TRANSACTIONS/CAREER NOTES: Selected by St. Louis Cardinals in 19th round of free-agent draft (June 3, 1994).
STATISTICAL NOTES: Led Florida State League in grounding into double plays with 31 in 1996. ... Tied for Texas League lead in double plays by second baseman with 110 in 1997.

							BATTING							FIELDING			
Year Team (League)	Pos.	G	AB	R	H	2B	3B	HR	RBI	Avg.	BB	SO	SB	PO	A	E	Avg.
1994— Ariz. Cardinals (Ariz.) .	SS-2B	32	127	17	27	4	0	1	10	.213	7	15	4	47	89	10	.932
1995— Peoria (Midw.)	SS-2B	103	361	43	96	7	4	2	41	.266	18	30	7	114	285	21	.950
1996— St. Petersburg (FSL) ..	2B	*137	540	65	*157	29	5	0	51	.291	24	34	4	198	*383	4	*.993
1997— Arkansas (Texas)	2B	129	508	71	148	16	3	2	51	.291	29	51	19	240	*425	14	*.979
1998— Memphis (PCL)	2B-SS	70	246	36	69	19	1	1	21	.280	16	15	6	113	193	5	.984
— St. Louis (N.L.)	SS-2B	45	114	10	29	3	2	1	11	.254	5	9	2	72	102	7	.961
1999— St. Louis (N.L.)	2B-3B-SS	88	220	24	61	9	3	1	19	.277	15	24	1	123	150	8	.972
— Memphis (PCL)	2B-SS-3B	29	120	18	33	4	1	0	10	.275	3	11	2	43	84	2	.984
Major League totals (2 years)		133	334	34	90	12	5	2	30	.269	20	33	3	195	252	15	.968

POLITTE, CLIFF — P — PHILLIES

PERSONAL: Born February 27, 1974, in St. Louis. ... 5-11/185. ... Throws right, bats right. ... Full name: Cliff Anthony Politte. ... Son of Clifford Edward Politte, pitcher in St. Louis Cardinals organization (1959-65). ... Name pronounced po-LEET.
HIGH SCHOOL: Vianney (Kirkwood, Mo.).
JUNIOR COLLEGE: Jefferson College (Mo.).
TRANSACTIONS/CAREER NOTES: Selected by St. Louis Cardinals organization in 54th round of free agent draft (June 1, 1995). ... Traded by Cardinals with OF Ron Gant and P Jeff Brantley to Philadelphia Phillies for P Ricky Bottalico and P Garrett Stephenson (November 19, 1998).
HONORS: Named Carolina League Pitcher of the Year (1997).

Year League	W	L	Pct.	ERA	G	GS	CG	ShO	Sv.	IP	H	R	ER	BB	SO
1996— Peoria (Midw.)	14	6	.700	2.59	25	25	0	0	0	149 2/3	108	50	43	47	151
1997— Prince William (Caro.)	11	1	*.917	*2.24	19	19	0	0	0	120 1/3	89	37	30	31	118
— Arkansas (Texas)	4	1	.800	2.15	6	6	0	0	0	37 2/3	35	15	9	9	26
1998— St. Louis (N.L.)	2	3	.400	6.32	8	8	0	0	0	37	45	32	26	18	22
— Memphis (PCL)	1	4	.200	7.64	10	10	0	0	0	50 2/3	71	46	43	24	42
— Arkansas (Texas)	5	3	.625	2.96	10	10	1	1	0	67	56	25	22	16	61
1999— Reading (East.)■	9	8	.529	3.63	37	13	1	0	5	109	112	45	44	33	97
— Philadelphia (N.L.)	1	0	1.000	7.13	13	0	0	0	0	17 2/3	19	14	14	15	15
Major League totals (2 years)	3	3	.500	6.59	21	8	0	0	0	54 2/3	64	46	40	33	37

P

PERSONAL: Born October 27, 1964, in Santiago City, Dominican Republic. ... 5-8/150. ... Bats left, throws left. ... Full name: Luis Andrew Almonte Polonia. ... Name pronounced po-LONE-yuh.

HIGH SCHOOL: San Francisco (Santiago City, Dominican Republic).

TRANSACTIONS/CAREER NOTES: Signed as non-drafted free agent by Oakland Athletics organization (January 3, 1984). ... Traded by A's with P Greg Cadaret and P Eric Plunk to New York Yankees for OF Rickey Henderson (June 21, 1989). ... Traded by Yankees to California Angels for OF Claudell Washington and P Rich Monteleone (April 28, 1990). ... On suspended list (September 30-October 3, 1992). ... Granted free agency (October 27, 1993). ... Signed by Yankees (December 20, 1993). ... Traded by Yankees to Atlanta Braves for OF Troy Hughes (August 11, 1995). ... Granted free agency (November 2, 1995). ... Signed by Seattle Mariners organization (February 1, 1996). ... Released by Mariners (March 26, 1996). ... Signed by Baltimore Orioles organization (April 19, 1996). ... Released by Orioles (August 12, 1996). ... Signed by Braves (August 17, 1996). ... Granted free agency (November 18, 1996). ... Signed by Tampa Bay Devil Rays organization (March 11, 1997). ... Loaned by Devil Rays to Mexico City Tigres (March 20, 1997-entire season; and April 18, 1998-entire season). ... Granted free agency (October 15, 1998). ... Signed by Detroit Tigers organization (December 18, 1998). ... Granted free agency (November 4, 1999). ... Re-signed by Tigers (November 9, 1999).

STATISTICAL NOTES: Led Midwest League in caught stealing with 24 in 1984. ... Led Pacific Coast League in caught stealing with 21 in 1986. ... Led A.L. in caught stealing with 23 in 1991 and 21 in 1992 and tied for lead with 24 in 1993. ... Had 16-game hitting streak (May 31-June 21, 1999). ... Career major league grand slams: 1.

MISCELLANEOUS: Batted as switch-hitter (1984-86 and Tacoma, 1987-88).

Year	Team (League)	Pos.	G	AB	R	H	2B	3B	HR	RBI	Avg.	BB	SO	SB	PO	A	E	Avg.
1984—	Madison (Midw.)	OF	135	*528	103	*162	21	10	8	64	.307	57	95	55	202	9	10	.955
1985—	Huntsville (Sou.)	OF	130	515	82	149	15	*18	2	36	.289	58	53	39	236	13	12	.954
1986—	Tacoma (PCL)	OF	134	*549	98	*165	20	4	3	63	.301	52	65	36	*318	8	10	.970
1987—	Tacoma (PCL)	OF	14	56	18	18	1	2	0	8	.321	14	6	4	28	1	1	.967
—	Oakland (A.L.)	OF-DH	125	435	78	125	16	10	4	49	.287	32	64	29	235	2	5	.979
1988—	Tacoma (PCL)	OF	65	254	58	85	13	5	2	27	.335	29	28	31	129	7	7	.951
—	Oakland (A.L.)	OF-DH	84	288	51	84	11	4	2	27	.292	21	40	24	155	3	2	.988
1989—	Oakland (A.L.)	OF-DH	59	206	31	59	6	4	1	17	.286	9	15	13	126	3	2	.985
—	New York (A.L.)■	OF-DH	66	227	39	71	11	2	2	29	.313	16	29	9	105	6	2	.982
1990—	New York (A.L.)	DH	11	22	2	7	0	0	0	3	.318	0	1	1	...	...	...	...
—	California (A.L.)■	OF-DH	109	381	50	128	7	9	2	32	.336	25	42	20	142	3	3	.980
1991—	California (A.L.)	OF-DH	150	604	92	179	28	8	2	50	.296	52	74	48	246	9	5	.981
1992—	California (A.L.)	OF-DH	149	577	83	165	17	4	0	35	.286	45	64	51	192	8	4	.980
1993—	California (A.L.)	OF-DH	152	576	75	156	17	6	1	32	.271	48	53	55	286	12	5	.983
1994—	New York (A.L.)■	OF-DH	95	350	62	109	21	6	1	36	.311	37	36	20	155	9	4	.976
1995—	New York (A.L.)	OF	67	238	37	62	9	3	2	15	.261	25	29	10	132	5	0	1.000
—	Atlanta (N.L.)	OF	28	53	6	14	7	0	0	2	.264	3	9	3	9	0	0	1.000
1996—	Rochester (I.L.)■	OF-DH	13	50	9	12	2	0	0	3	.240	7	8	5	18	0	1	1.000
—	Baltimore (A.L.)	OF-DH	58	175	25	42	4	1	2	14	.240	10	20	8	56	1	1	.983
—	Atlanta (A.L.)	OF	22	31	3	13	0	0	0	2	.419	1	3	1	4	0	1	.800
1997—	M.C. Tigres (Mex.)■	OF	110	408	105	154	29	5	7	59	.377	75	33	*48	...	...	...	...
1998—	M.C. Tigres (Mex.)	...	86	357	82	136	15	*14	9	63	.381	52	31	36	...	...	...	...
1999—	Toledo (I.L.)■	OF-DH	42	161	20	52	7	1	3	22	.323	10	28	13	64	2	1	.985
—	Detroit (A.L.)	DH-OF	87	333	46	108	21	8	10	32	.324	16	32	17	68	4	1	.986
American League totals (11 years)			1212	4412	671	1295	168	65	29	371	.294	336	499	305	1898	65	34	.983
National League totals (2 years)			50	84	9	27	7	0	0	4	.321	4	12	4	13	0	1	.929
Major League totals (11 years)			1262	4496	680	1322	175	65	29	375	.294	340	511	309	1911	65	35	.983

DIVISION SERIES RECORD

Year	Team (League)	Pos.	G	AB	R	H	2B	3B	HR	RBI	Avg.	BB	SO	SB	PO	A	E	Avg.
1995—	Atlanta (N.L.)	PH	3	3	0	1	0	0	0	2	.333	0	1	1	...	...	...	...
1996—	Atlanta (N.L.)	PH	2	2	0	0	0	0	0	0	.000	0	1	0	...	...	...	...
Division series totals (2 years)			5	5	0	1	0	0	0	2	.200	0	2	1	...	...	...	...

CHAMPIONSHIP SERIES RECORD

Year	Team (League)	Pos.	G	AB	R	H	2B	3B	HR	RBI	Avg.	BB	SO	SB	PO	A	E	Avg.
1988—	Oakland (A.L.)	PR-OF-PH	3	5	0	2	0	0	0	0	.400	1	2	0	2	0	0	1.000
1995—	Atlanta (N.L.)	OF-PR-PH	3	2	0	1	0	0	0	1	.500	0	0	0	0	0	0	...
1996—	Atlanta (N.L.)	PH	3	3	0	0	0	0	0	0	.000	0	0	0	...	...	...	...
Championship series totals (3 years)			9	10	0	3	0	0	0	1	.300	1	2	0	2	0	0	1.000

WORLD SERIES RECORD

NOTES: Member of World Series championship team (1995).

Year	Team (League)	Pos.	G	AB	R	H	2B	3B	HR	RBI	Avg.	BB	SO	SB	PO	A	E	Avg.
1988—	Oakland (A.L.)	PH-OF	3	9	1	1	0	0	0	0	.111	0	2	0	2	0	0	1.000
1995—	Atlanta (N.L.)	PH-OF	4	14	3	4	1	0	1	4	.286	1	3	1	3	0	0	1.000
1996—	Atlanta (N.L.)	PH	6	5	0	0	0	0	0	0	.000	1	3	0	...	...	...	...
World Series totals (3 years)			13	28	4	5	1	0	1	4	.179	2	8	1	5	0	0	1.000

P

PERSONAL: Born November 2, 1976, in Noord, Aruba. ... 6-1/225. ... Throws right, bats right. ... Full name: Sidney Alton Ponson.

COLLEGE: Maria (Aruba).

TRANSACTIONS/CAREER NOTES: Signed as non-drafted free agent by Baltimore Orioles organization (August 17, 1993). ... On Bowie disabled list (June 13-July 15, 1997).

Year League	W	L	Pct.	ERA	G	GS	CG	ShO	Sv.	IP	H	R	ER	BB	SO
1994— Gulf Coast Orioles (GCL)....	4	3	.571	2.96	12	10	1	0	0	73	68	30	24	17	53
1995— Bluefield (Appl.)	6	3	.667	4.17	13	13	0	0	0	77²/₃	79	44	36	16	56
1996— Frederick (Caro.)	7	6	.538	3.45	18	16	3	0	0	107	98	56	41	28	110
1997— Bowie (East.)....................	2	7	.222	5.42	13	13	1	1	0	74²/₃	7	51	45	32	56
— Gulf Coast Orioles (GCL)....	1	0	1.000	0.00	1	0	0	0	0	2	0	0	0	0	1
1998— Rochester (I.L.)	1	0	1.000	0.00	1	1	0	0	0	5	4	0	0	1	3
— Baltimore (A.L.)................	8	9	.471	5.27	31	20	0	0	1	135	157	82	79	42	85
1999— Baltimore (A.L.)................	12	12	.500	4.71	32	32	6	0	0	210	227	118	110	80	112
Major League totals (2 years)......	**20**	**21**	**.488**	**4.93**	**63**	**52**	**6**	**0**	**1**	**345**	**384**	**200**	**189**	**122**	**197**

POOLE, JIM   P   TIGERS

PERSONAL: Born April 28, 1966, in Rochester, N.Y. ... 6-2/195. ... Throws left, bats left. ... Full name: James Richard Poole.
HIGH SCHOOL: LaSalle (Philadelphia).
COLLEGE: Georgia Tech.
TRANSACTIONS/CAREER NOTES: Selected by Los Angeles Dodgers organization in 34th round of free-agent draft (June 2, 1987); did not sign. ... Selected by Dodgers organization in ninth round of free-agent draft (June 1, 1988). ... Traded by Dodgers with cash to Texas Rangers for P Steve Allen and P David Lynch (December 30, 1990). ... Claimed on waivers by Baltimore Orioles (May 31, 1991). ... On Baltimore disabled list (April 3-June 23, 1992); included rehabilitation assignments to Hagerstown (May 25-June 12) and Rochester (June 12-23). ... Granted free agency (December 23, 1994). ... Signed by Buffalo, Cleveland Indians organization (March 18, 1995). ... Traded by Indians with a player to be named later or cash to San Francisco Giants for 1B/OF Mark Carreon (July 9, 1996). ... Released by Giants (July 15, 1998). ... Signed by Indians organization (July 22, 1998). ... Granted free agency (October 30, 1998). ... Signed by Philadelphia Phillies (December 17, 1998). ... Released by Phillies (August 23, 1999). ... Signed by Indians organization (August 26, 1999). ... Granted free agency (October 4, 1999). ... Signed by Detroit Tigers organization (December 20, 1999).

Year League	W	L	Pct.	ERA	G	GS	CG	ShO	Sv.	IP	H	R	ER	BB	SO
1988— Vero Beach (FSL)	1	1	.500	3.77	10	0	0	0	0	14¹/₃	13	7	6	9	12
1989— Vero Beach (FSL)	11	4	.733	1.61	*60	0	0	0	19	78¹/₃	57	16	14	24	93
— Bakersfield (Calif.)	0	0	...	0.00	1	0	0	0	0	1²/₃	2	1	0	0	1
1990— San Antonio (Texas).........	6	7	.462	2.40	54	0	0	0	16	63²/₃	55	31	17	27	77
— Los Angeles (N.L.)............	0	0	...	4.22	16	0	0	0	0	10²/₃	7	5	5	8	6
1991— Oklahoma City (A.A.)■......	0	0	...	0.00	10	0	0	0	3	12¹/₃	4	0	0	1	14
— Texas (A.L.)...................	0	0	...	4.50	5	0	0	0	1	6	10	4	3	3	4
— Rochester (I.L.)■..............	3	2	.600	2.79	27	0	0	0	9	29	29	11	9	9	25
— Baltimore (A.L.)................	3	2	.600	2.00	24	0	0	0	3	36	19	10	8	9	34
1992— Hagerstown (East.)...........	0	1	.000	2.77	7	3	0	0	0	13	14	4	4	1	4
— Rochester (I.L.)................	1	6	.143	5.31	32	0	0	0	10	42¹/₃	40	26	25	18	30
— Baltimore (A.L.)................	0	0	...	0.00	6	0	0	0	0	3¹/₃	3	3	0	1	3
1993— Baltimore (A.L.)................	2	1	.667	2.15	55	0	0	0	2	50¹/₃	30	18	12	21	29
1994— Baltimore (A.L.)................	1	0	1.000	6.64	38	0	0	0	0	20¹/₃	32	15	15	11	18
1995— Buffalo (A.A.)■	0	0	...	27.00	1	1	0	0	0	2²/₃	7	8	8	2	0
— Cleveland (A.L.)...............	3	3	.500	3.75	42	0	0	0	0	50¹/₃	40	22	21	17	41
1996— Cleveland (A.L.)...............	4	0	1.000	3.04	32	0	0	0	0	26²/₃	29	15	9	14	19
— San Francisco (N.L.)■........	2	1	.667	2.66	35	0	0	0	0	23²/₃	15	7	7	13	19
1997— San Francisco (N.L.)	3	1	.750	7.11	63	0	0	0	0	49¹/₃	73	44	39	25	26
1998— San Francisco (N.L.)	1	3	.250	5.29	26	0	0	0	0	32¹/₃	38	20	19	9	16
— Buffalo (I.L.)■.................	1	0	1.000	0.87	13	0	0	0	0	10¹/₃	6	3	1	2	16
— Cleveland (A.L.)...............	0	0	...	5.14	12	0	0	0	0	7	9	4	4	3	11
1999— Philadelphia (N.L.)■	1	1	.500	4.33	51	0	0	0	1	35¹/₃	48	20	17	15	22
— Akron (East.)■................	0	0	...	0.00	2	0	0	0	0	2²/₃	0	0	0	0	4
— Cleveland (A.L.)................	1	0	1.000	18.00	3	0	0	0	0	1	2	2	2	3	0
A.L. totals (8 years)	**14**	**6**	**.700**	**3.31**	**217**	**0**	**0**	**0**	**3**	**201**	**174**	**93**	**74**	**82**	**159**
N.L. totals (5 years)	**7**	**6**	**.538**	**5.17**	**191**	**0**	**0**	**0**	**1**	**151¹/₃**	**181**	**96**	**87**	**70**	**89**
Major League totals (10 years).....	**21**	**12**	**.636**	**4.11**	**408**	**0**	**0**	**0**	**4**	**352¹/₃**	**355**	**189**	**161**	**152**	**248**

DIVISION SERIES RECORD

Year League	W	L	Pct.	ERA	G	GS	CG	ShO	Sv.	IP	H	R	ER	BB	SO
1995— Cleveland (A.L.)................	0	0	...	5.40	1	0	0	0	0	1²/₃	2	1	1	1	2
1998— Cleveland (A.L.)................	0	0	...	0.00	2	0	0	0	0	2	1	0	0	1	2
Division series totals (2 years).....	**0**	**0**	**...**	**2.45**	**3**	**0**	**0**	**0**	**0**	**3²/₃**	**3**	**1**	**1**	**2**	**4**

CHAMPIONSHIP SERIES RECORD

Year League	W	L	Pct.	ERA	G	GS	CG	ShO	Sv.	IP	H	R	ER	BB	SO
1995— Cleveland (A.L.)................	0	0	...	0.00	1	0	0	0	0	1	0	0	0	0	2
1998— Cleveland (A.L.)................	0	0	...	0.00	4	0	0	0	0	1¹/₃	0	0	0	1	2
Champ. series totals (2 years)	**0**	**0**	**...**	**0.00**	**5**	**0**	**0**	**0**	**0**	**2¹/₃**	**0**	**0**	**0**	**1**	**4**

WORLD SERIES RECORD

Year League	W	L	Pct.	ERA	G	GS	CG	ShO	Sv.	IP	H	R	ER	BB	SO
1995— Cleveland (A.L.)................	0	1	.000	3.86	2	0	0	0	0	2¹/₃	1	1	1	0	1

PORTER, BO   OF   ATHLETICS

PERSONAL: Born July 5, 1972, in Newark, N.J. ... 6-2/195. ... Bats right, throws right. ... Full name: Marquis Donnell Porter.
HIGH SCHOOL: Quequahic (Newark, N.J.).
COLLEGE: Iowa (degree in communication studies).
TRANSACTIONS/CAREER NOTES: Selected by Chicago Cubs organization in 40th round of free-agent draft (June 3, 1993). ... Selected by Oakland A's from Cubs organization in Rule 5 major league draft (December 13, 1999).
STATISTICAL NOTES: Led Midwest League outfielders with seven double plays in 1996. ... Tied for Pacific Coast League lead in caught stealing with 17 in 1999.

Year Team (League)	Pos.	G	AB	R	H	2B	3B	HR	RBI	Avg.	BB	SO	SB	PO	A	E	Avg.
1994— Peoria (Midw.)...........	OF	66	221	40	60	11	2	6	29	.271	27	59	6	128	3	3	.978
1995— Daytona (FSL)	OF	113	336	54	73	12	2	3	19	.217	32	104	22	183	10	4	.980
1996— Daytona (FSL)	OF	20	63	9	11	4	1	0	6	.175	6	24	5	44	3	4	.922
— Rockford (Midw.)	OF	105	378	83	91	22	3	7	44	.241	72	107	30	172	8	3	.984
1997— Daytona (FSL)	OF-2B	122	440	87	135	20	6	17	65	.307	61	115	23	237	10	4	.984
— Orlando (Sou.)	OF	8	31	4	8	1	0	1	3	.258	0	11	0	13	2	1	.938
1998— West Tenn (Sou.)	OF	125	464	91	134	26	*11	10	68	.289	82	117	*50	258	10	3	.989
— Iowa (PCL)	OF	4	11	2	4	1	0	0	3	.364	4	4	1	6	0	0	1.000
1999— Iowa (PCL)	OF-DH	111	414	86	121	24	2	27	64	.292	65	121	15	223	5	0	*1.000
— Chicago (N.L.)	OF	24	26	2	5	1	0	0	0	.192	2	13	0	16	0	1	.941
Major League totals (1 year)		24	26	2	5	1	0	0	0	.192	2	13	0	16	0	1	.941

PORTUGAL, MARK   P   REDS

PERSONAL: Born October 30, 1962, in Los Angeles. ... 6-0/208. ... Throws right, bats right. ... Full name: Mark Steven Portugal.
HIGH SCHOOL: Norwalk (Calif.).
TRANSACTIONS/CAREER NOTES: Signed as non-drafted free agent by Minnesota Twins organization (October 23, 1980). ... On Toledo disabled list (July 22-August 2, 1985). ... On Minnesota disabled list (August 7-28, 1988). ... Traded by Twins to Houston Astros for a player to be named later (December 4, 1988); Twins organization acquired P Todd McClure to complete deal (December 7, 1988). ... On disabled list (July 18-August 13, 1991). ... On disabled list (June 13-July 4 and July 10-September 23, 1992). ... Granted free agency (October 25, 1993). ... Signed by San Francisco Giants (November 21, 1993). ... On disabled list (June 17-July 3 and August 6, 1994-remainder of season). ... Traded by Giants with OF Darren Lewis and P Dave Burba to Cincinnati Reds for OF Deion Sanders, P John Roper, P Ricky Pickett, P Scott Service and IF Dave McCarty (July 21, 1995). ... On disabled list (August 28-September 15, 1996). ... Granted free agency (November 18, 1996). ... Signed by Philadelphia Phillies (December 12, 1996). ... On disabled list (March 24-April 20 and May 4, 1997-remainder of season; and April 3-May 14, 1998). ... Granted free agency (October 28, 1998). ... Signed by Boston Red Sox (December 11, 1998). ... Released by Red Sox (September 27, 1999). ... Signed by Reds organization (January 20, 2000).
HONORS: Named pitcher on THE SPORTING NEWS N.L. Silver Slugger team (1994).
STATISTICAL NOTES: Led Appalachian League with 12 wild pitches, 11 home runs allowed and tied for lead with five hit batsmen in 1981. ... Tied for N.L. lead in games started by pitcher with 31 in 1995.
MISCELLANEOUS: Appeared in one game as pinch runner (1991). ... Had one sacrifice hit in only appearance as pinch hitter (1996).

Year League	W	L	Pct.	ERA	G	GS	CG	ShO	Sv.	IP	H	R	ER	BB	SO
1981— Elizabethton (Appl.)...........	7	1	.875	3.71	14	13	2	0	1	85	65	41	35	39	65
1982— Wisconsin Rapids (Midw.) .	9	8	.529	4.01	36	15	4	1	2	119	110	62	53	62	95
1983— Visalia (Calif.)	10	5	.667	4.18	24	23	2	0	0	131 1/3	142	77	61	84	132
1984— Orlando (Sou.)	14	7	.667	2.98	27	27	10	3	0	196	171	80	65	113	110
1985— Toledo (I.L.).....................	8	5	.615	3.78	19	19	5	1	0	128 2/3	129	60	54	60	89
— Minnesota (A.L.)	1	3	.250	5.55	6	4	0	0	0	24 1/3	24	16	15	14	12
1986— Toledo (I.L.).....................	5	1	.833	2.60	6	6	3	1	0	45	34	15	13	23	30
— Minnesota (A.L.)	6	10	.375	4.31	27	15	3	0	1	112 2/3	112	56	54	50	67
1987— Minnesota (A.L.)	1	3	.250	7.77	13	7	0	0	0	44	58	40	38	24	28
— Portland (PCL)	1	10	.091	6.00	17	16	2	0	0	102	108	75	68	50	69
1988— Portland (PCL)	2	0	1.000	1.37	3	3	1	1	0	19 2/3	15	3	3	8	9
— Minnesota (A.L.)	3	3	.500	4.53	26	0	0	0	3	57 2/3	60	30	29	17	31
1989— Tucson (PCL)■	7	5	.583	3.78	17	17	5	0	0	116 2/3	107	55	49	32	90
— Houston (N.L.)	7	1	.875	2.75	20	15	2	1	0	108	91	34	33	37	86
1990— Houston (N.L.)	11	10	.524	3.62	32	32	1	0	0	196 2/3	187	90	79	67	136
1991— Houston (N.L.)	10	12	.455	4.49	32	27	1	0	1	168 1/3	163	91	84	59	120
1992— Houston (N.L.)	6	3	.667	2.66	18	16	1	1	0	101 1/3	76	32	30	41	62
1993— Houston (N.L.)	18	4	*.818	2.77	33	33	1	1	0	208	194	75	64	77	131
1994— San Francisco (N.L.)■ ...	10	8	.556	3.93	21	21	1	0	0	137 1/3	135	68	60	45	87
1995— San Francisco (N.L.)	5	5	.500	4.15	17	§17	1	0	0	104	106	56	48	34	63
— Cincinnati (N.L.)■	6	5	.545	3.82	14	§14	0	0	0	77 2/3	79	35	33	22	33
1996— Cincinnati (N.L.)	8	9	.471	3.98	27	26	1	1	0	156	146	77	69	42	93
1997— Philadelphia (N.L.)■	0	2	.000	4.61	3	3	0	0	0	13 2/3	17	8	7	5	2
1998— Philadelphia (N.L.)...........	10	5	.667	4.44	26	26	3	0	0	166 1/3	186	88	82	32	104
1999— Boston (A.L.)■	7	12	.368	5.51	31	27	1	0	0	150 1/3	179	100	92	41	79
A.L. totals (5 years)	18	31	.367	5.28	103	53	4	0	4	389	433	242	228	146	217
N.L. totals (10 years)	91	64	.587	3.69	243	230	12	4	1	1437 1/3	1380	654	589	461	917
Major League totals (15 years)	109	95	.534	4.03	346	283	16	4	5	1826 1/3	1813	896	817	607	1134

CHAMPIONSHIP SERIES RECORD

Year League	W	L	Pct.	ERA	G	GS	CG	ShO	Sv.	IP	H	R	ER	BB	SO
1995— Cincinnati (N.L.)	0	1	.000	36.00	1	0	0	0	0	1	3	4	4	1	0

PORZIO, MIKE   P   ROCKIES

PERSONAL: Born August 20, 1972, in Waterbury, Conn. ... 6-3/210. ... Throws left, bats left. ... Full name: Lawrence Michael Porzio.
HIGH SCHOOL: Fairfield Prep (Fairfield, Conn.).
COLLEGE: Villanova.
TRANSACTIONS/CAREER NOTES: Signed as non-drafted free agent by Chicago Cubs organization (June 30, 1993). ... Released by Cubs organization (July 19, 1994). ... Signed by Boston Red Sox organization (February 20, 1995). ... Released by Red Sox organization (April 1, 1995). ... Signed by Moblie, Texas-Louisiana League (May 1995). ... Signed by Ogden, Pioneer League (July 26, 1995). ... Signed by Tennessee, Big South League (June 1996). ... Signed by Baltimore Orioles organization (March 2, 1997). ... Released by Orioles organization (March 25, 1997). ... Signed by Sioux City, Northern League (May 1997). ... Signed by Atlanta Braves organization (March 8, 1998). ... Traded by Braves with P David Cortes and a player to be named later to Colorado Rockies for 1B Greg Colbrunn (July 30, 1998); Rockies acquired P Anthony Briggs to complete deal (September 9, 1998). ... On Colorado Springs disabled list (June 6-25, 1999).

Year League	W	L	Pct.	ERA	G	GS	CG	ShO	Sv.	IP	H	R	ER	BB	SO
1993— Gulf Coast Cubs (GCL)	1	3	.250	3.83	10	8	0	0	0	42 1/3	42	26	18	30	30
1994— Gulf Coast Cubs (GCL)	0	3	.000	5.93	7	0	0	0	1	13 2/3	19	10	9	6	5
1995— Mobile (Texas)■	0	3	.000	5.46	16	2	0	0	0	28	32	19	17	13	15
—Ogden (Pio.)■	4	3	.571	6.38	8	8	2	0	0	48	66	39	34	15	26
1996— Tennessee (BSL)■	7	4	.636	3.64	15	15	3	0	0	99	94	55	40	30	54
1997— Sioux City (North)■	2	2	.500	4.28	27	5	1	1	0	61	75	32	29	27	63
1998— Danville (Caro.)■	3	2	.600	2.51	26	11	1	0	2	97	74	34	27	30	95
—Salem (Caro.)■	2	3	.400	2.76	7	7	0	0	0	42 1/3	40	20	13	12	46
1999— Colo. Springs (PCL)	5	1	.833	3.38	35	0	0	0	0	42 2/3	44	16	16	30	33
—Colorado (N.L.)	0	0	...	8.59	16	0	0	0	0	14 2/3	21	14	14	10	10
Major League totals (1 year)	0	0	...	8.59	16	0	0	0	0	14 2/3	21	14	14	10	10

POSADA, JORGE — C — YANKEES

PERSONAL: Born August 17, 1971, in Santurce, Puerto Rico. ... 6-2/205. ... Bats both, throws right. ... Full name: Jorge Rafael Posada Jr. ... Name pronounced HOR-hay po-SOD-a.

HIGH SCHOOL: Colegio Alejandrino (Puerto Rico).

TRANSACTIONS/CAREER NOTES: Selected by New York Yankees organization in 24th round of free-agent draft (June 4, 1990). ... On disabled list (July 26-September 4, 1994). ... On Columbus disabled list (May 3-12, 1995).

STATISTICAL NOTES: Led New York-Pennsylvania League second basemen with 42 double plays in 1991. ... Led Carolina League with 38 passed balls in 1993. ... Tied for Carolina League lead in intentional bases on balls received with four in 1993. ... Tied for International League lead in errors by catcher with 11 in 1994. ... Tied for International League lead in double plays by catcher with seven in 1995. ... Led International League with 14 passed balls in 1995. ... Switch-hit home runs in one game twice (August 23, 1998; and July 10, 1999).

Year Team (League)	Pos.	G	AB	R	H	2B	3B	HR	RBI	Avg.	BB	SO	SB	PO	A	E	Avg.
1991— Oneonta (NY-P)	2B-C	71	217	34	51	5	5	4	33	.235	51	51	6	172	205	21	.947
1992— Greensboro (SAL)	C-3B	101	339	60	94	22	4	12	58	.277	58	87	11	263	39	11	.965
1993— Prince William (Caro.)	C-3B	118	410	71	106	27	2	17	61	.259	67	90	17	677	98	15	.981
—Albany (East.)	C	7	25	3	7	0	0	0	0	.280	2	7	0	39	7	2	.958
1994— Columbus (I.L.)	C-OF	92	313	46	75	13	3	11	48	.240	32	81	5	425	39	‡11	.977
1995— Columbus (I.L.)	C-DH	108	368	60	94	32	5	8	51	.255	54	101	4	500	58	4	*.993
—New York (A.L.)	C	1	0	0	0	0	0	0	0	...	0	0	0	1	0	0	1.000
1996— Columbus (I.L.)	C-DH-OF	106	354	76	96	22	6	11	62	.271	*79	86	3	598	51	10	.985
—New York (A.L.)	C-DH	8	14	1	1	0	0	0	0	.071	1	6	0	17	2	0	1.000
1997— New York (A.L.)	C	60	188	29	47	12	0	6	25	.250	30	33	1	367	23	3	.992
1998— New York (A.L.)	C-DH-1B	111	358	56	96	23	0	17	63	.268	47	92	0	594	47	4	.994
1999— New York (A.L.)	C-DH-1B	112	379	50	93	19	2	12	57	.245	53	91	1	709	47	5	.993
Major League totals (5 years)		292	939	136	237	54	2	35	145	.252	131	222	2	1688	119	12	.993

DIVISION SERIES RECORD

Year Team (League)	Pos.	G	AB	R	H	2B	3B	HR	RBI	Avg.	BB	SO	SB	PO	A	E	Avg.
1995— New York (A.L.)	PR	1	0	1	0	0	0	0	0	...	0	0	0	...	...	...	...
1997— New York (A.L.)	C-PH	2	2	0	0	0	0	0	0	.000	0	1	0	1	1	0	1.000
1998— New York (A.L.)	C	1	2	1	0	0	0	0	0	.000	1	2	0	11	1	0	1.000
1999— New York (A.L.)	C	1	4	0	1	1	0	0	0	.250	0	0	0	5	0	0	1.000
Division series totals (4 years)		5	8	2	1	1	0	0	0	.125	1	3	0	17	2	0	1.000

CHAMPIONSHIP SERIES RECORD

Year Team (League)	Pos.	G	AB	R	H	2B	3B	HR	RBI	Avg.	BB	SO	SB	PO	A	E	Avg.
1998— New York (A.L.)	C-PH	5	11	1	2	0	0	1	2	.182	4	2	0	35	1	0	1.000
1999— New York (A.L.)	C	3	10	1	1	0	0	1	2	.100	1	2	0	20	1	1	.955
Championship series totals (2 years)		8	21	2	3	0	0	2	4	.143	5	4	0	55	2	1	.983

WORLD SERIES RECORD

NOTES: Member of World Series championship team (1998 and 1999).

Year Team (League)	Pos.	G	AB	R	H	2B	3B	HR	RBI	Avg.	BB	SO	SB	PO	A	E	Avg.
1998— New York (A.L.)	C-PH	4	9	2	3	0	0	1	2	.333	2	2	0	20	0	0	1.000
1999— New York (A.L.)	C	2	8	0	2	1	0	0	1	.250	0	3	0	17	1	0	1.000
World Series totals (2 years)		6	17	2	5	1	0	1	3	.294	2	5	0	37	1	0	1.000

POSE, SCOTT — OF — ROYALS

PERSONAL: Born February 11, 1967, in Davenport, Iowa. ... 5-11/190. ... Bats left, throws right. ... Full name: Scott Vernon Pose.

HIGH SCHOOL: Dowling (West Des Moines, Iowa).

COLLEGE: Arkansas.

TRANSACTIONS/CAREER NOTES: Selected by Cincinnati Reds organization in 34th round of free-agent draft (June 5, 1989). ... Selected by Florida Marlins from Reds organization in Rule 5 major league draft (December 7, 1992). ... Granted free agency (March 23, 1994). ... Signed by New Orleans, Milwaukee Brewers organization (April 5, 1994). ... Contract sold by Brewers organization to Los Angeles Dodgers organization (February 9, 1995). ... Released by Dodgers organization (April 17, 1995). ... Signed by Salt Lake, Minnesota Twins organization (June 1, 1995). ... Granted free agency (October 16, 1995). ... Signed by Cleveland Indians organization (December 6, 1995). ... Traded by Indians to Toronto Blue Jays for IF Joe Lis (March 13, 1996). ... Granted free agency (October 15, 1996). ... Signed by New York Yankees organization (November 27, 1996). ... Granted free agency (October 15, 1997). ... Re-signed by Yankees organizaiton (December 18, 1997). ... Granted free agency (October 15, 1998). ... Signed by Kansas City Royals organization (December 17, 1998).

STATISTICAL NOTES: Tied for Pioneer League lead with three intentional bases on balls received in 1989. ... Led South Atlantic League with eight intentional bases on balls received and .435 on-base percentage in 1990. ... Led Southern League in on-base percentage with .414 and

P

in caught stealing with 27 in 1992. ... Led International League in caught stealing with 16 in 1996. ... Led International League outfielders with .990 fielding percentage in 1996.

								BATTING								FIELDING		
Year	Team (League)	Pos.	G	AB	R	H	2B	3B	HR	RBI	Avg.	BB	SO	SB	PO	A	E	Avg.
1989—Billings (Pio.)		OF-2B	60	210	52	74	7	2	0	25	.352	*54	31	26	94	19	7	.942
1990—Char., W.Va. (SAL)......		OF	135	480	*106	143	13	5	0	46	.298	*114	56	49	210	*17	3	*.987
1991—Chattanooga (Sou.)		OF	117	402	61	110	8	5	1	31	.274	69	50	17	215	9	1	*.996
— Nashville (A.A.)		OF	15	52	7	10	0	0	0	3	.192	2	9	3	23	0	1	.958
1992—Chattanooga (Sou.)		OF	136	•526	*87	*180	22	8	2	45	*.342	63	66	21	216	10	1	*.996
1993—Florida (N.L.)■............		OF	15	41	0	8	2	0	0	3	.195	2	4	0	14	0	0	1.000
— Edmonton (PCL)		OF	109	398	61	113	8	6	0	27	.284	42	36	19	192	4	6	.970
1994—New Orleans (A.A.)■..		OF-P-2B	124	429	60	121	13	7	0	52	.282	47	52	20	196	9	1	.995
1995—Albuquerque (PCL)■..		OF-DH	7	16	5	3	1	0	0	1	.188	2	0	2	2	0	0	1.000
— Salt Lake (PCL)■		OF-DH-P	70	219	46	66	10	1	0	20	.301	31	28	15	92	8	2	.980
1996—Syracuse (I.L.)■		OF-P-1B	113	419	71	114	11	6	0	39	.272	58	71	30	195	9	2	†.990
1997—Columbus (I.L.)■......		OF-DH	57	227	50	70	10	7	2	32	.308	32	29	13	113	6	1	.992
— New York (A.L.)........		OF-DH	54	87	19	19	2	1	0	5	.218	9	11	3	44	2	0	1.000
1998—Columbus (I.L.)		OF-DH	133	489	78	145	23	10	3	46	.297	53	72	*47	158	11	3	.983
1999—Kansas City (A.L.)■ ..		OF-DH	86	137	27	39	3	0	0	12	.285	21	22	6	29	3	1	.970
American League totals (2 years)			140	224	46	58	5	1	0	17	.259	30	33	9	73	5	1	.987
National League totals (1 year)			15	41	0	8	2	0	0	3	.195	2	4	0	14	0	0	1.000
Major League totals (3 years)			155	265	46	66	7	1	0	20	.249	32	37	9	87	5	1	.989

DIVISION SERIES RECORD

								BATTING								FIELDING		
Year	Team (League)	Pos.	G	AB	R	H	2B	3B	HR	RBI	Avg.	BB	SO	SB	PO	A	E	Avg.
1997—New York (A.L.).........		PR	1	0	0	0	0	0	0	0	...	0	0	0	0	0	0	...

RECORD AS PITCHER

Year	League	W	L	Pct.	ERA	G	GS	CG	ShO	Sv.	IP	H	R	ER	BB	SO
1994— New Orleans (A.A.)		0	0	...	0.00	2	0	0	0	0	2	3	0	0	2	2
1995— Salt Lake (PCL)		0	0	...	0.00	1	0	0	0	0	1	0	0	0	1	0
1996— Syracuse (I.L.)...................		0	0	...	13.50	2	0	0	0	0	2	4	3	3	2	3

POTE, LOU — P — ANGELS

PERSONAL: Born August 27, 1971, in Evergreen Park, Ill. ... 6-3/208. ... Throws right, bats right. ... Full name: Louis William Pote.
HIGH SCHOOL: De La Salle Institute (Chicago).
COLLEGE: Kishwaukee College (Ill.).
TRANSACTIONS/CAREER NOTES: Selected by San Francisco Giants organization in 29th round of free-agent draft (June 4, 1990). ... On Shreveport disabled list (April 8-July 31, 1994). ... Traded by Giants to Montreal Expos for P Luis Aquino (July 24, 1995). ... Released by Expos (March 28, 1997). ... Signed by St. Louis Cardinals organization (August 7, 1997). ... Granted free agency (October 17, 1997). ... Signed by Anaheim Angels organization (December 15, 1997).

Year	League	W	L	Pct.	ERA	G	GS	CG	ShO	Sv.	IP	H	R	ER	BB	SO
1991— Arizona Giants (Ariz.)		2	3	.400	2.55	8	8	0	0	0	42 1/3	38	23	12	19	41
— Everett (N.W.)		2	0	1.000	2.51	5	4	0	0	0	28 2/3	24	8	8	7	26
1992— Shreveport (Texas)		4	2	.667	0.96	20	3	0	0	0	37 2/3	20	7	4	15	26
— San Jose (Calif.)................		0	1	.000	4.66	4	3	0	0	0	9 2/3	11	5	5	7	8
1993— Shreveport (Texas)		8	7	.533	4.07	19	19	0	0	0	108 1/3	111	53	49	45	81
1994— Arizona Giants (Ariz.)		1	0	1.000	0.00	4	4	0	0	0	19 2/3	9	0	0	6	30
— Shreveport (Texas)		2	2	.500	2.83	5	5	0	0	0	28 2/3	31	11	9	7	15
1995— Shreveport (Texas)		2	2	.500	5.33	28	0	0	0	3	50 2/3	63	41	30	26	30
— Harrisburg (East.)■.........		0	1	.000	5.40	9	4	0	0	0	28 1/3	32	17	17	7	24
1996— Harrisburg (East.).............		1	7	.125	5.07	25	18	0	0	1	104 2/3	114	66	59	48	61
1997— Arkansas (Texas)■............		0	0	...	1.54	7	3	0	0	0	23 1/3	15	10	4	8	21
1998— Midland (Texas)■.............		8	10	.444	5.31	32	19	6	1	0	154 1/3	194	110	91	54	117
1999— Edmonton (PCL)		7	9	.438	4.50	24	23	3	0	0	150	171	80	75	41	118
— Anaheim (A.L.)		1	1	.500	2.15	20	0	0	0	3	29 1/3	23	9	7	12	20
Major League totals (1 year)........		1	1	.500	2.15	20	0	0	0	3	29 1/3	23	9	7	12	20

POWELL, BRIAN — P — ASTROS

PERSONAL: Born October 10, 1973, in Bainbridge, Ga. ... 6-2/205. ... Throws right, bats right. ... Full name: William Brian Powell.
HIGH SCHOOL: Bainbridge (Ga.).
COLLEGE: Georgia.
TRANSACTIONS/CAREER NOTES: Selected by Detroit Tigers organization in second round of free-agent draft (June 1, 1995). ... Traded by Tigers with C Paul Bako, P Dean Crow, P Mark Persails and 3B Carlos Villalobos to Houston Astros for C Brad Ausmus and P C.J. Nitkowski (January 14, 1999). ... On New Orleans disabled list (May 25, 1999-remainder of season).

Year	League	W	L	Pct.	ERA	G	GS	CG	ShO	Sv.	IP	H	R	ER	BB	SO
1995— Jamestown (NY-P)		2	1	.667	3.08	5	5	0	0	0	26 1/3	19	12	9	8	15
— Fayetteville (SAL)		4	0	1.000	1.61	5	5	0	0	0	28	15	5	5	11	37
1996— Lakeland (FSL)		8	13	.381	4.90	29	27	*5	0	0	*174 1/3	*195	106	*95	47	84
1997— Lakeland (FSL)		13	9	.591	2.50	27	27	*8	2	0	*183 1/3	153	70	51	35	122
1998— Jacksonville (Sou.)...........		10	2	*.833	3.07	14	14	2	1	0	93 2/3	84	37	32	24	51
— Toledo (I.L.).....................		0	0	...	0.00	1	1	0	0	0	7	5	0	0	0	7
— Detroit (A.L.)...................		3	8	.273	6.35	18	16	0	0	0	83 2/3	101	67	59	36	46
1999— New Orleans (PCL)■.........		4	4	.500	6.19	9	9	0	0	0	48	54	39	33	21	36
Major League totals (1 year)........		3	8	.273	6.35	18	16	0	0	0	83 2/3	101	67	59	36	46

P

POWELL, DANTE   OF   CARDINALS

PERSONAL: Born August 25, 1973, in Long Beach, Calif. ... 6-2/185. ... Bats right, throws right. ... Full name: LeJon Dante Powell.
HIGH SCHOOL: Millikan (Long Beach, Calif.).
COLLEGE: Cal State Fullerton.
TRANSACTIONS/CAREER NOTES: Selected by Toronto Blue Jays in supplemental round ("sandwich pick" between first and second round, 42nd pick overall) of free-agent draft (June 3, 1991); did not sign. ... Selected by San Francisco Giants organization in first round (22nd pick overall) of free-agent draft (June 2, 1994). ... Traded by Giants to Arizona Diamondbacks for P Alan Embree (November 10, 1998). ... On Tucson disabled list (May 25-June 26, 1999). ... Traded by Diamondbacks to St. Louis Cardinals for SS Luis Ordaz (December 15, 1999).
STATISTICAL NOTES: Led Texas League with 23 caught stealing in 1996. ... Led Texas League outfielders with 347 total chances in 1996. ... Led Pacific Coast League outfielders with 293 total chances in 1998.

Year	Team (League)	Pos.	G	AB	R	H	2B	3B	HR	RBI	Avg.	BB	SO	SB	PO	A	E	Avg.
								BATTING								FIELDING		
1994—Everett (N.W.)	OF	41	165	31	51	15	1	5	25	.309	19	47	27	88	3	2	.978
—San Jose (Calif.)	OF	1	4	0	2	0	0	0	0	.500	0	1	0	1	0	0	1.000
1995—San Jose (Calif.)	OF	135	505	74	125	23	8	10	70	.248	46	131	43	*308	*18	11	.967
1996—Shreveport (Texas)	OF-DH	135	508	*92	142	27	2	21	78	.280	72	92	*43	*331	8	8	.977
—Phoenix (PCL)	OF	2	8	0	2	0	1	0	0	.250	2	3	0	4	0	0	1.000
1997—Phoenix (PCL)	OF	108	452	91	109	24	4	11	42	.241	52	105	34	*266	7	4	.986
—San Francisco (N.L.)	OF	27	39	8	12	1	0	1	3	.308	4	11	1	27	0	0	1.000
1998—Fresno (PCL)	OF	134	448	83	103	17	3	14	52	.230	71	138	41	*284	2	7	.976
—San Francisco (N.L.)	OF	8	4	2	2	0	0	1	1	.500	3	0	0	2	0	0	1.000
1999—Arizona (N.L.)■	OF	22	25	4	4	3	0	0	1	.160	2	6	2	13	0	1	.929
—Tucson (PCL)	OF-DH	51	187	29	62	14	2	7	30	.332	14	38	22	94	5	5	.952
Major League totals (3 years)		57	68	14	18	4	0	2	5	.265	9	17	3	42	0	1	.977

DIVISION SERIES RECORD

Year	Team (League)	Pos.	G	AB	R	H	2B	3B	HR	RBI	Avg.	BB	SO	SB	PO	A	E	Avg.
								BATTING								FIELDING		
1997—San Francisco (N.L.)	OF	1	0	0	0	0	0	0	0	...	0	0	0	0	0	0	...

POWELL, JAY   P   ASTROS

PERSONAL: Born January 9, 1972, in Meridian, Miss. ... 6-4/225. ... Throws right, bats right. ... Full name: James Willard Powell Jr. ... Brother-in-law of Bud Brown, defensive back with Miami Dolphins (1984-88).
HIGH SCHOOL: West Lauderdale (Collinsville, Miss.).
COLLEGE: Mississippi State.
TRANSACTIONS/CAREER NOTES: Selected by San Diego Padres organization in 11th round of free-agent draft (June 4, 1990); did not sign. ... Selected by Baltimore Orioles organization in first round (19th pick overall) of free-agent draft (June 3, 1993). ... On disabled list (April 7-26, 1994). ... Traded by Orioles to Florida Marlins for IF Bret Barberie (December 6, 1994). ... On Florida disabled list (April 20-May 10, 1996); included rehabilitation assignment to Brevard County (May 8-10). ... Traded by Marlins with C Scott Makarewicz to Houston Astros for C Ramon Castro (July 6, 1998).
MISCELLANEOUS: Struck out in only appearance as pinch hitter with Florida (1996).

Year	League	W	L	Pct.	ERA	G	GS	CG	ShO	Sv.	IP	H	R	ER	BB	SO
1993—Albany (SAL)	0	2	.000	4.55	6	6	0	0	0	27 2/3	29	19	14	13	29
1994—Frederick (Caro.)	7	7	.500	4.96	26	20	0	0	1	123 1/3	132	79	68	54	87
1995—Portland (East.)■	5	4	.556	1.87	50	0	0	0	*24	53	42	12	11	15	53
—Florida (N.L.)	0	0	...	1.08	9	0	0	0	0	8 1/3	7	2	1	6	4
1996—Florida (N.L.)	4	3	.571	4.54	67	0	0	0	2	71 1/3	71	41	36	36	52
—Brevard County (FSL)	0	0	...	0.00	1	1	0	0	0	2	0	0	0	0	4
1997—Florida (N.L.)	7	2	.778	3.28	74	0	0	0	2	79 2/3	71	35	29	30	65
1998—Florida (N.L.)	4	4	.500	4.21	33	0	0	0	3	36 1/3	36	19	17	22	24
—Houston (N.L.)■	3	3	.500	2.38	29	0	0	0	4	34	22	9	9	15	38
1999—Houston (N.L.)	5	4	.556	4.32	67	0	0	0	4	75	82	38	36	40	77
Major League totals (5 years)	23	16	.590	3.78	279	0	0	0	15	304 2/3	289	144	128	149	260

DIVISION SERIES RECORD

Year	League	W	L	Pct.	ERA	G	GS	CG	ShO	Sv.	IP	H	R	ER	BB	SO
1997—Florida (N.L.)								Did not play.								
1998—Houston (N.L.)	0	0	...	11.57	3	0	0	0	0	2 1/3	2	3	3	3	3
1999—Houston (N.L.)	0	1	.000	6.00	3	0	0	0	0	3	3	2	2	1	3
Division series totals (2 years)	0	1	.000	8.44	6	0	0	0	0	5 1/3	5	5	5	4	6

CHAMPIONSHIP SERIES RECORD

Year	League	W	L	Pct.	ERA	G	GS	CG	ShO	Sv.	IP	H	R	ER	BB	SO
1997—Florida (N.L.)	0	0	...	0.00	1	0	0	0	0	2/3	0	0	0	0	1

WORLD SERIES RECORD

NOTES: Member of World Series championship team (1997).

Year	League	W	L	Pct.	ERA	G	GS	CG	ShO	Sv.	IP	H	R	ER	BB	SO
1997—Florida (N.L.)	1	0	1.000	7.36	4	0	0	0	0	3 2/3	5	3	3	4	2

P

POWELL, JEREMY   P   EXPOS

PERSONAL: Born June 18, 1976, in La Miranda, Calif. ... 6-5/230. ... Throws right, bats right. ... Full name: Jeremy Robert Powell.
HIGH SCHOOL: Highlands (North Highlands, Calif.).
TRANSACTIONS/CAREER NOTES: Selected by Montreal Expos organization in fourth round of free-agent draft (June 2, 1994).

Year League	W	L	Pct.	ERA	G	GS	CG	ShO	Sv.	IP	H	R	ER	BB	SO
1994— Gulf Coast Expos (GCL)	2	2	.500	2.93	9	9	1	0	0	43	37	16	14	14	36
1995— Albany (SAL)	1	0	1.000	1.59	1	1	0	0	0	5²/₃	4	1	1	1	6
— Vermont (NY-P)	5	5	.500	4.34	15	•15	0	0	0	87	88	48	42	34	47
1996— Delmarva (SAL)	12	9	.571	3.03	27	27	1	0	0	157²/₃	127	68	53	66	109
1997— West Palm Beach (FSL)	9	10	.474	3.02	26	26	1	0	0	155	162	75	52	62	121
1998— Harrisburg (East.)..............	9	7	.563	3.01	22	22	1	0	0	131²/₃	115	54	44	37	77
— Montreal (N.L.)...............	1	5	.167	7.92	7	6	0	0	0	25	27	25	22	11	14
1999— Ottawa (I.L.)	3	5	.375	2.97	16	16	0	0	0	91	85	37	30	37	72
— Montreal (N.L.)..............	4	8	.333	4.73	17	17	0	0	0	97	113	60	51	44	44
Major League totals (2 years)	5	13	.278	5.39	24	23	0	0	0	122	140	85	73	55	58

PRATT, TODD — C — METS

PERSONAL: Born February 9, 1967, in Bellevue, Neb. ... 6-3/230. ... Bats right, throws right. ... Full name: Todd Alan Pratt.
HIGH SCHOOL: Hilltop (Chula Vista, Calif.).
TRANSACTIONS/CAREER NOTES: Selected by Boston Red Sox organization in sixth round of free-agent draft (June 3, 1985). ... Selected by Cleveland Indians organization from Red Sox organization in Rule 5 minor league draft (December 7, 1987). ... Returned to Red Sox organization (March 28, 1988). ... Granted free agency (October 15, 1991). ... Signed by Baltimore Orioles organization (November 13, 1991). ... Selected by Philadelphia Phillies from Orioles organization in Rule 5 major league draft (December 9, 1991). ... On Philadelphia disabled list (April 28-May 27, 1993); included rehabilitation assignment to Scranton/Wilkes-Barre (May 23-27). ... Granted free agency (December 23, 1994). ... Signed by Iowa, Chicago Cubs organization (April 8, 1995). ... Granted free agency (October 16, 1995). ... Signed by Seattle Mariners organization (January 25, 1996). ... Released by Mariners (March 27, 1996). ... Signed by New York Mets organization (December 23, 1996). ... On New York disabled list (May 7-June 23, 1998); included rehabilitation assignments to St. Lucie (June 14-18), Gulf Coast Mets (June 19-21) and Norfolk (June 22-23).
STATISTICAL NOTES: Led South Atlantic League catchers with 660 putouts and nine double plays and tied for lead with 13 errors in 1986. ... Led Eastern League catchers with 11 errors in 1989.

							BATTING								FIELDING			
Year Team (League)	Pos.	G	AB	R	H	2B	3B	HR	RBI	Avg.	BB	SO	SB	PO	A	E	Avg.
1985— Elmira (NY-P)	C	39	119	7	16	1	1	0	5	.134	10	27	0	254	29	6	.979
1986— Greensboro (SAL)	C-1B	107	348	63	84	16	0	12	56	.241	75	114	0	†826	55	‡15	.983
1987— Winter Haven (FSL)	C-1B-OF	118	407	57	105	22	0	12	65	.258	70	94	0	672	64	15	.980
1988— New Britain (East.)	C-1B	124	395	41	89	15	2	8	49	.225	41	110	1	540	46	15	.975
1989— New Britain (East.)	C-1B	109	338	30	77	17	1	2	35	.228	44	66	1	435	42	†11	.977
1990— New Britain (East.)	C-1B	70	195	15	45	14	1	2	22	.231	18	56	0	166	15	4	.978
1991— Pawtucket (I.L.).........	C-1B	68	219	68	64	16	0	11	41	.292	23	42	0	236	21	4	.985
1992— Reading (East.)	C	41	132	20	44	6	1	6	26	.333	24	28	2	90	6	3	.970
— Scranton/W.B. (I.L.) ...	C-1B	41	125	20	40	9	1	7	28	.320	30	14	1	152	16	4	.977
— Philadelphia (N.L.)......	C	16	46	6	13	1	0	2	10	.283	4	12	0	65	4	2	.972
1993— Philadelphia (N.L.)......	C	33	87	8	25	6	0	5	13	.287	5	19	0	169	7	2	.989
— Scranton/W.B. (I.L.) ...	C	3	9	1	2	1	0	0	1	.222	3	1	0	11	0	0	1.000
1994— Philadelphia (N.L.)......	C	28	102	10	20	6	1	2	9	.196	12	29	0	172	8	0	1.000
1995— Iowa (A.A.)■............	C-1B-DH	23	58	3	19	1	0	0	5	.328	4	17	0	82	8	2	.978
— Chicago (N.L.)	C	25	60	3	8	2	0	0	4	.133	6	21	0	149	9	3	.981
1996—							Out of organized baseball.											
1997— Norfolk (I.L.)■..........	C-DH	59	206	42	62	8	3	9	34	.301	26	48	1	317	24	4	.988
— New York (N.L.)...........	C	39	106	12	30	6	2	2	19	.283	13	32	0	186	22	2	.990
1998— Norfolk (I.L.) DH-C-OF-1B		35	118	16	42	6	0	7	30	.356	15	19	2	115	8	2	.984
— New York (N.L.)...........	C-1B	41	69	9	19	9	1	2	18	.275	2	20	0	78	4	2	.976
— St. Lucie (FSL)	C-1B-OF	5	20	2	9	1	0	1	3	.450	1	5	1	40	6	0	1.000
— GC Mets (GCL)	C-OF	2	4	1	1	0	0	0	0	.250	4	1	0	7	2	0	1.000
1999— New York (N.L.).........	C-1B-OF	71	140	18	41	4	0	3	21	.293	15	32	2	263	13	1	.996
Major League totals (7 years)		253	610	66	156	34	2	16	94	.256	57	165	2	1082	67	12	.990

DIVISION SERIES RECORD

							BATTING								FIELDING			
Year Team (League)	Pos.	G	AB	R	H	2B	3B	HR	RBI	Avg.	BB	SO	SB	PO	A	E	Avg.
1999— New York (N.L.)..........	PH-C	3	8	2	1	0	0	1	1	.125	2	1	0	11	1	0	1.000

CHAMPIONSHIP SERIES RECORD

							BATTING								FIELDING			
Year Team (League)	Pos.	G	AB	R	H	2B	3B	HR	RBI	Avg.	BB	SO	SB	PO	A	E	Avg.
1993— Philadelphia (N.L.)......	C	1	1	0	0	0	0	0	0	.000	0	1	0	1	0	0	1.000
1999— New York (N.L.)..........	PH-C	4	2	0	1	0	0	0	3	.500	1	1	0	6	0	0	1.000
Championship series totals (2 years)		5	3	0	1	0	0	0	3	.333	1	2	0	7	0	0	1.000

WORLD SERIES RECORD

							BATTING								FIELDING			
Year Team (League)	Pos.	G	AB	R	H	2B	3B	HR	RBI	Avg.	BB	SO	SB	PO	A	E	Avg.
1993— Philadelphia (N.L.)								Did not play.										

PRIETO, ARIEL — P — ATHLETICS

PERSONAL: Born October 22, 1969, in Havana, Cuba. ... 6-2/247. ... Throws right, bats right.
COLLEGE: Fajardo University (Isle of Pines, Cuba).
TRANSACTIONS/CAREER NOTES: Selected by Oakland Athletics organization in first round (fifth pick overall) of free-agent draft (June 1, 1995). ... On disabled list (August 19-September 3, 1995). ... On Oakland disabled list (May 19-July 28, 1996); included rehabilitation assignments to Modesto (July 1-11) and Edmonton (July 11-28). ... On Oakland disabled list (July 13-August 8 and August 23, 1997-remainder of season); included rehabilitation assignment to Edmonton (August 8-17). ... On Edmonton disabled list (July 29-September 10, 1998). ... On disabled list (March 26, 1999-remainder of season).

P

Year League	W	L	Pct.	ERA	G	GS	CG	ShO	Sv.	IP	H	R	ER	BB	SO
1995—Oakland (A.L.)	2	6	.250	4.97	14	9	1	0	0	58	57	35	32	32	37
1996—Oakland (A.L.)	6	7	.462	4.15	21	21	2	0	0	125 2/3	130	66	58	54	75
—Modesto (Calif.)	0	0	...	3.00	2	1	0	0	1	9	9	4	3	2	8
—Edmonton (PCL)	3	0	1.000	0.57	3	3	0	0	0	15 2/3	11	1	1	6	18
1997—Oakland (A.L.)	6	8	.429	5.04	22	22	0	0	0	125	155	84	70	70	90
—Edmonton (PCL)	0	0	...	1.50	2	2	0	0	0	6	4	1	1	1	7
1998—Edmonton (PCL)	5	1	.833	2.56	10	10	1	0	0	52 2/3	47	20	15	12	50
—Oakland (A.L.)	0	1	.000	11.88	2	2	0	0	0	8 1/3	17	11	11	5	8
1999—Oakland (A.L.)									Did not play.						
Major League totals (4 years).......	14	22	.389	4.85	59	54	3	0	0	317	359	196	171	161	210

PRINCE, TOM   C   PHILLIES

PERSONAL: Born August 13, 1964, in Kankakee, Ill. ... 5-11/206. ... Bats right, throws right. ... Full name: Thomas Albert Prince.
HIGH SCHOOL: Bradley-Bourbonnais (Bradley, Ill.).
JUNIOR COLLEGE: Kankakee (Ill.) Community College.
TRANSACTIONS/CAREER NOTES: Selected by Atlanta Braves organization in eighth round of free-agent draft (January 11, 1983); did not sign. ... Selected by Braves organization in secondary phase of free-agent draft (June 6, 1983); did not sign. ... Selected by Pittsburgh Pirates organization in secondary phase of free-agent draft (January 17, 1984). ... On Pittsburgh disabled list (August 13-September 1, 1991); included rehabilitation assignment to Buffalo (August 28-September 1). ... Granted free agency (October 15, 1993). ... Signed by Albuquerque, Los Angeles Dodgers organization (November 12, 1993). ... On Albuquerque disabled list (April 30-May 7, 1994). ... Released by Dodgers (December 5, 1994). ... Re-signed by Dodgers organization (January 5, 1995). ... On Los Angeles disabled list (June 4-July 10, 1995); included rehabilitation assignment to Albuquerque (June 26-July 10). ... Granted free agency (October 15, 1995). ... Re-signed by Dodgers organization (November 1, 1995). ... Granted free agency (October 22, 1998). ... Signed by Philadelphia Phillies (December 18, 1998). ... On Philadelphia disabled list (March 23-September 3, 1999); included rehabilitation assignments to Gulf Coast Phillies (July 21-28), Clearwater (July 29-August 9) and Scranton (August 10-29).
STATISTICAL NOTES: Led South Atlantic League catchers with 930 total chances, 10 double plays and 27 passed balls in 1985. ... Led Carolina League catchers with 954 total chances and 15 passed balls in 1986. ... Led Eastern League catchers with 721 total chances and nine double plays in 1987. ... Led American Association catchers with 12 double plays in 1992. ... Led Pacific Coast League catchers with 677 total chances and nine double plays in 1994.

							BATTING							FIELDING		
Year Team (League)	Pos.	G	AB	R	H	2B	3B	HR	RBI	Avg.	BB	SO	SB	PO	A	E	Avg.
1984—Watertown (NY-P)	C-3B	23	69	6	14	3	0	2	13	.203	9	13	0	155	26	2	.989
—GC Pirates (GCL)........	C-1B	18	48	4	11	0	0	1	6	.229	8	10	1	75	16	4	.958
1985—Macon (SAL)	C	124	360	60	75	20	1	10	42	.208	96	92	13	*810	*101	*19	.980
1986—Prince William (Caro.)	C	121	395	59	100	34	1	10	47	.253	50	74	4	*821	•113	20	.979
1987—Harrisburg (East.).......	C	113	365	41	112	23	2	6	54	.307	51	46	6	*622	*88	•11	.985
—Pittsburgh (N.L.)	C	4	9	1	2	1	0	1	2	.222	0	2	0	14	3	0	1.000
1988—Buffalo (A.A.).............	C	86	304	35	79	16	0	14	42	.260	23	53	3	456	51	*12	.977
—Pittsburgh (N.L.)	C	29	74	3	13	2	0	0	6	.176	4	15	0	108	8	2	.983
1989—Buffalo (A.A.).............	C	65	183	21	37	8	1	6	33	.202	22	30	2	312	22	5	.985
—Pittsburgh (N.L.)	C	21	52	1	7	4	0	0	5	.135	6	12	1	85	11	4	.960
1990—Buffalo (A.A.).............	C-1B	4	10	1	1	0	0	0	0	.100	1	2	0	16	1	0	1.000
—Buffalo (A.A.).............	C-1B	94	284	38	64	13	0	7	37	.225	39	46	4	461	62	8	.985
1991—Pittsburgh (N.L.)	C-1B	26	34	4	9	3	0	1	2	.265	7	3	0	53	9	1	.984
—Buffalo (A.A.).............	C	80	221	29	46	8	3	6	32	.208	37	31	3	379	61	5	.989
1992—Pittsburgh (N.L.)	C-3B	27	44	1	4	2	0	0	5	.091	6	9	1	76	8	2	.977
—Buffalo (A.A.).............	C-OF	75	244	34	64	17	0	9	35	.262	20	35	3	307	50	8	.978
1993—Pittsburgh (N.L.)	C	66	179	14	35	14	0	2	24	.196	13	38	1	271	31	5	.984
1994—Albuquerque (PCL)■...	C-DH	103	330	61	94	31	2	20	54	.285	51	67	2	593	*75	9	.987
—Los Angeles (N.L.)	C	3	6	2	2	0	0	0	1	.333	1	3	0	11	1	0	1.000
1995—Los Angeles (N.L.)	C	18	40	3	8	2	1	1	4	.200	4	10	0	71	8	1	.988
—Albuquerque (PCL).....	C-DH	61	192	30	61	15	0	7	36	.318	27	41	0	310	34	4	.989
1996—Albuquerque (PCL)....C-DH-3B-OF	32	95	24	39	5	1	7	22	.411	15	14	0	88	20	1	.991
—Los Angeles (N.L.)	C	40	64	6	19	6	0	1	11	.297	6	15	0	161	11	1	.994
1997—Los Angeles (N.L.)	C	47	100	17	22	5	0	3	14	.220	5	15	0	221	25	1	.996
1998—Los Angeles (N.L.)	C	37	81	7	15	5	1	0	5	.185	7	24	0	175	16	0	1.000
1999—GC Phillies (GCL)■....	C-DH	7	21	3	5	3	0	0	3	.238	4	0	0	19	6	0	1.000
—Clearwater (FSL)........	C	9	33	5	12	0	0	2	9	.364	3	3	1	47	4	1	.981
—Scranton/W.B. (I.L.) ...	C-DH	7	22	2	2	0	0	1	1	.091	3	5	1	31	2	0	1.000
—Philadelphia (N.L.)......	C	4	6	1	1	0	0	0	0	.167	1	1	0	13	1	0	1.000
Major League totals (13 years)		326	699	61	138	44	2	9	79	.197	61	149	3	1275	133	17	.988

PRITCHETT, CHRIS   1B

PERSONAL: Born January 31, 1970, in Merced, Calif. ... 6-4/212. ... Bats left, throws right. ... Full name: Christopher Davis Pritchett.
HIGH SCHOOL: Central Catholic (Modesto, Calif.).
COLLEGE: UCLA.
TRANSACTIONS/CAREER NOTES: Selected by California Angels organization in second round of free-agent draft (June 3, 1991). ... Angels franchise renamed Anaheim Angels for 1997 season. ... On Anaheim disabled list (March 30-April 16, 1998). ... Granted free agency (October 15, 1999).
STATISTICAL NOTES: Tied for Midwest League lead with six intentional bases on balls received in 1992. ... Led Texas League first basemen with 1,075 putouts, 19 errors and 1,182 total chances in 1993. ... Led Texas League with .421 on-base percentage in 1994. ... Led Texas League first basemen with 100 double plays in 1994. ... Tied for Pacific Coast League lead with 11 intentional bases on balls received in 1996. ... Led Pacific Coast League first baseman with 1,107 putouts, 98 assists, 1,211 total chances, .995 fielding percentage and 107 double plays in 1996.

P

Year	Team (League)	Pos.	G	AB	R	H	2B	3B	HR	RBI	Avg.	BB	SO	SB	PO	A	E	Avg.
							BATTING									FIELDING		
1991—	Boise (N.W.)	1B	70	255	41	68	10	3	9	50	.267	47	41	1	636	26	5	*.993
1992—	Quad City (Midw.)	1B	128	448	79	130	19	1	13	72	.290	71	88	9	*1059	84	13	*.989
1993—	Midland (Texas)	1B-2B	127	464	61	143	30	6	2	66	.308	61	72	3	†1076	92	†19	.984
1994—	Midland (Texas)	1B-OF-3B	127	460	86	142	25	4	6	91	.309	*92	87	5	1028	94	13	.989
1995—	Vancouver (PCL)	1B-OF	123	434	66	120	27	4	8	53	.276	56	79	2	999	92	12	.989
1996—	Vancouver (PCL)	1B-OF	130	485	78	143	39	1	16	73	.295	71	96	5	†1116	†98	6	†.995
—	California (A.L.)	1B	5	13	1	2	0	0	0	1	.154	0	3	0	29	1	0	1.000
1997—	Vancouver (PCL)	1B-DH-OF	109	383	60	107	30	3	7	47	.279	42	72	5	621	51	7	.990
1998—	Vancouver (PCL)	1B-DH	104	374	42	97	21	1	7	41	.259	37	72	2	739	55	10	.988
—	Anaheim (A.L.)	1B	31	80	12	23	2	1	2	8	.288	4	16	2	190	20	1	.995
1999—	Edmonton (PCL)	1B-DH-OF	96	348	60	97	15	1	12	45	.279	47	70	1	717	64	9	.989
—	Anaheim (A.L.)	1B-DH	20	45	3	7	1	0	1	2	.156	2	9	1	96	8	1	.990
Major League totals (3 years)			56	138	16	32	3	1	3	11	.232	6	28	3	315	29	2	.994

PULSIPHER, BILL   P   METS

PERSONAL: Born October 9, 1973, in Fort Benning, Ga. ... 6-3/200. ... Throws left, bats left. ... Full name: William Thomas Pulsipher.

HIGH SCHOOL: Fairfax (Va.).

TRANSACTIONS/CAREER NOTES: Selected by New York Mets organization in second round of free-agent draft (June 3, 1991). ... On disabled list (March 22, 1996-entire season). ... On New York disabled list (March 24-May 3, 1997); included rehabilitation assignment to Norfolk (April 4-May 3). ... On Norfolk disabled list (June 30-July 30, 1997). ... Traded by Mets to Milwaukee Brewers for 3B Mike Kinkade (July 31, 1998). ... On Milwaukee disabled list (April 19-July 3, 1999); included rehabilitation assignment to Louisville (June 1-30). ... Traded by Brewers to Mets for IF Luis Lopez (January 21, 2000).

STATISTICAL NOTES: Tied for Eastern League lead with four balks in 1994.

MISCELLANEOUS: Appeared in one game as pinch runner with Mets (1998).

Year	League	W	L	Pct.	ERA	G	GS	CG	ShO	Sv.	IP	H	R	ER	BB	SO
1992—	Pittsfield (NY-P)	6	3	.667	2.84	14	14	0	0	0	95	88	40	30	56	83
1993—	Capital City (SAL)	2	3	.400	2.08	6	6	1	0	0	43 1/3	34	17	10	12	29
—	St. Lucie (FSL)	7	3	.700	2.24	13	13	3	1	0	96 1/3	63	27	24	39	102
1994—	Binghamton (East.)	14	9	.609	3.22	28	28	5	1	0	*201	179	90	72	89	171
1995—	Norfolk (I.L.)	6	4	.600	3.14	13	13	•4	2	0	91 2/3	84	36	32	33	63
—	New York (N.L.)	5	7	.417	3.98	17	17	2	0	0	126 2/3	122	58	56	45	81
1996—	New York (N.L.)							Did not play.								
1997—	Norfolk (I.L.)	0	5	.000	7.81	8	5	0	0	0	27 2/3	23	29	24	38	18
—	St. Lucie (FSL)	1	4	.200	5.89	12	7	0	0	0	36 2/3	29	27	24	35	35
—	Binghamton (East.)	0	0	...	1.42	10	0	0	0	0	12 2/3	11	3	2	7	12
—	Gulf Coast Mets (GCL)	0	0	...	1.80	2	2	0	0	0	5	3	1	1	1	4
1998—	Norfolk (I.L.)	7	5	.583	3.96	14	14	1	0	0	86 1/3	91	50	38	41	58
—	New York (N.L.)	0	0	...	6.91	15	1	0	0	0	14 1/3	23	11	11	5	13
—	Milwaukee (N.L.)■	3	4	.429	4.66	11	10	0	0	0	58	63	30	30	26	38
1999—	Milwaukee (N.L.)	5	6	.455	5.98	19	16	0	0	0	87 1/3	100	65	58	36	42
—	Louisville (I.L.)	0	2	.000	4.28	6	6	0	0	0	27 1/3	22	14	13	19	21
Major League totals (3 years)		13	17	.433	4.87	62	44	2	0	0	286 1/3	308	164	155	112	174

QUANTRILL, PAUL   P   BLUE JAYS

PERSONAL: Born November 3, 1968, in London, Ont. ... 6-1/190. ... Throws right, bats left. ... Full name: Paul John Quantrill.

HIGH SCHOOL: Okemos (Mich.).

COLLEGE: Wisconsin.

TRANSACTIONS/CAREER NOTES: Selected by Los Angeles Dodgers organization in 26th round of free-agent draft (June 2, 1986); did not sign. ... Selected by Boston Red Sox organization in sixth round of free-agent draft (June 5, 1989). ... Traded by Red Sox with OF Billy Hatcher to Philadelphia Phillies for OF Wes Chamberlain and P Mike Sullivan (May 31, 1994). ... Traded by Phillies to Toronto Blue Jays for 3B Howard Battle and P Ricardo Jordan (December 6, 1995). ... On Toronto disabled list (March 27-June 15, 1999); included rehabilitation assignments to Dunedin (June 4-10) and Syracuse (June 11-13).

Year	League	W	L	Pct.	ERA	G	GS	CG	ShO	Sv.	IP	H	R	ER	BB	SO
1989—	GC Red Sox (GCL)	0	0	...	0.00	2	0	0	0	2	5	2	0	0	0	5
—	Elmira (NY-P)	5	4	.556	3.43	20	7	•5	0	2	76	90	37	29	12	57
1990—	Winter Haven (FSL)	2	5	.286	4.14	7	7	1	0	0	45 2/3	46	24	21	6	14
—	New Britain (East.)	7	11	.389	3.53	22	22	1	1	0	132 2/3	148	65	52	23	53
1991—	New Britain (East.)	2	1	.667	2.06	5	5	1	0	0	35	32	14	8	8	18
—	Pawtucket (I.L.)	10	7	.588	4.45	25	23	•6	2	0	155 2/3	169	81	77	30	75
1992—	Pawtucket (I.L.)	6	8	.429	4.46	19	18	4	1	0	119	143	63	59	20	56
—	Boston (A.L.)	2	3	.400	2.19	27	0	0	0	0	49 1/3	55	18	12	15	24
1993—	Boston (A.L.)	6	12	.333	3.91	49	14	1	1	1	138	151	73	60	44	66
1994—	Boston (A.L.)	1	1	.500	3.52	17	0	0	0	0	23	25	10	9	5	15
—	Philadelphia (N.L.)■	2	2	.500	6.00	18	1	0	0	1	30	39	21	20	10	13
—	Scranton/W.B. (I.L.)	3	3	.500	3.47	8	8	1	1	0	57	55	25	22	6	36
1995—	Philadelphia (N.L.)	11	12	.478	4.67	33	29	0	0	0	179 1/3	212	102	93	44	103
1996—	Toronto (A.L.)■	5	14	.263	5.43	38	20	0	0	0	134 1/3	172	90	81	51	86
1997—	Toronto (A.L.)	6	7	.462	1.94	77	0	0	0	5	88	103	25	19	17	56
1998—	Toronto (A.L.)	3	4	.429	2.59	82	0	0	0	7	80	88	26	23	22	59
1999—	Dunedin (FSL)	0	1	.000	4.50	5	4	0	0	0	6	5	3	3	1	2
—	Syracuse (I.L.)	0	0	...	0.00	2	0	0	0	0	2	1	0	0	0	1
—	Toronto (A.L.)	3	2	.600	3.33	41	0	0	0	0	48 2/3	53	19	18	17	28
A.L. totals (7 years)		26	43	.377	3.56	331	34	1	1	14	561 1/3	647	261	222	171	334
N.L. totals (2 years)		13	14	.481	4.86	51	30	0	0	1	209 1/3	251	123	113	54	116
Major League totals (8 years)		39	57	.406	3.91	382	64	1	1	15	770 2/3	898	384	335	225	450

QUEVEDO, RUBEN — P — CUBS

PERSONAL: Born January 5, 1979, in Valencia, Venezuela. ... 6-1/230. ... Throws right, bats right. ... Full name: Ruben Eduardo Quevedo.
HIGH SCHOOL: Don Bosco (Valencia, Venezuela).
TRANSACTIONS/CAREER NOTES: Signed as non-drafted free agent by Atlanta Braves organization (September 6, 1995). ... Traded by Braves with P Micah Bowie and a player to be named later to Chicago Cubs for P Terry Mulholland and SS Jose Hernandez (July 31, 1999); Cubs acquired P Joey Nation to complete deal (August 24, 1999).

Year	W	L	Pct.	ERA	G	GS	CG	ShO	Sv.	IP	H	R	ER	BB	SO
1996—Gulf Coast Braves (GCL)	2	6	.250	2.17	10	10	0	0	0	58	50	19	14	9	49
1997—Danville (Appl.)..................	1	5	.167	3.56	13	11	0	0	0	68 1/3	46	37	27	27	78
1998—Macon (SAL)	11	3	.786	3.13	25	15	1	0	0	112	114	50	39	31	117
—Danville (Caro.)	0	2	.000	3.58	6	6	0	0	0	32 2/3	28	22	13	13	35
1999—Richmond (I.L.)	6	5	.545	5.37	21	21	0	0	0	105 2/3	112	65	63	34	98
—Iowa (PCL)■.....................	3	1	.750	3.45	7	7	1	1	0	44 1/3	34	18	17	21	50

QUINN, MARK — OF — ROYALS

PERSONAL: Born May 21, 1974, in La Miranda, Calif. ... 6-1/195. ... Bats right, throws right. ... Full name: Mark David Quinn.
HIGH SCHOOL: Clements (Sugar Land, Texas).
COLLEGE: Rice.
TRANSACTIONS/CAREER NOTES: Selected by Kansas City Royals organization in 11th round of free-agent draft (June 1, 1995).
RECORDS: Shares major league record for most home runs, first game in major leagues—2 (September 14, 1999, second game).

Year Team (League)	Pos.	G	AB	R	H	2B	3B	HR	RBI	Avg.	BB	SO	SB	PO	A	E	Avg.
1995—Spokane (N.W.)	3B	44	162	28	46	12	2	6	36	.284	15	28	0	8	33	8	.837
1996—Lansing (Midw.)	OF	113	437	63	132	23	3	9	71	.302	43	54	14	143	15	7	.958
1997—Wilmington (Caro.).....	OF	87	299	51	92	22	3	16	71	.308	42	47	3	75	7	6	.932
—Wichita (Texas)	OF	26	96	26	36	13	0	2	19	.375	15	19	1	35	0	1	.972
1998—Wichita (Texas)	OF	100	372	82	130	26	6	16	84	*.349	43	54	4	157	11	8	.955
1999—Omaha (PCL).............	OF-DH	107	428	67	154	27	0	25	84	*.360	28	69	7	216	13	4	.983
—Kansas City (A.L.)	OF-DH	17	60	11	20	4	1	6	18	.333	4	11	1	25	2	1	.964
Major League totals (1 year)		17	60	11	20	4	1	6	18	.333	4	11	1	25	2	1	.964

RADINSKY, SCOTT — P — CARDINALS

PERSONAL: Born March 3, 1968, in Glendale, Calif. ... 6-3/215. ... Throws left, bats left. ... Full name: Scott David Radinsky.
HIGH SCHOOL: Simi Valley (Calif.).
TRANSACTIONS/CAREER NOTES: Selected by Chicago White Sox organization in third round of free-agent draft (June 2, 1986). ... On Chicago disabled list (March 2, 1994-entire season). ... On Chicago disabled list (July 17-August 15, 1995); included rehabilitation assignment to South Bend (August 1-15). ... Granted free agency (December 21, 1995). ... Signed by Los Angeles Dodgers organization (January 16, 1996). ... On Los Angeles disabled list (March 28-April 12, 1996); included rehabilitation assignment to San Bernardino (April 4-12). ... Granted free agency (October 23, 1998). ... Signed by St. Louis Cardinals (November 23, 1998). ... On disabled list (July 27, 1999-remainder of season).

Year League	W	L	Pct.	ERA	G	GS	CG	ShO	Sv.	IP	H	R	ER	BB	SO
1986—GC White Sox (GCL)	1	0	1.000	3.38	7	7	0	0	0	26 2/3	24	20	10	17	18
1987—Peninsula (Caro.)	1	7	.125	5.77	12	8	0	0	0	39	43	30	25	32	37
—GC White Sox (GCL)	3	3	.500	2.31	11	10	0	0	0	58 1/3	43	23	15	39	41
1988—GC White Sox (GCL)	0	0	...	5.40	5	0	0	0	0	3 1/3	2	2	2	4	7
1989—South Bend (Midw.)	7	5	.583	1.75	53	0	0	0	31	61 2/3	39	21	12	19	83
1990—Chicago (A.L.)	6	1	.857	4.82	62	0	0	0	4	52 1/3	47	29	28	36	46
1991—Chicago (A.L.)	5	5	.500	2.02	67	0	0	0	8	71 1/3	53	18	16	23	49
1992—Chicago (A.L.)	3	7	.300	2.73	68	0	0	0	15	59 1/3	54	21	18	34	48
1993—Chicago (A.L.)	8	2	.800	4.28	73	0	0	0	4	54 2/3	61	33	26	19	44
1994—Chicago (A.L.)							Did not play.								
1995—Chicago (A.L.)	2	1	.667	5.45	46	0	0	0	1	38	46	23	23	17	14
—South Bend (Midw.)	0	0	...	0.00	6	0	0	0	2	9 2/3	5	0	0	0	11
1996—San Bernardino (Calif.)■....	0	0	...	2.08	3	0	0	0	0	4 1/3	2	1	1	2	4
—Los Angeles (N.L.)	5	1	.833	2.41	56	0	0	0	1	52 1/3	52	19	14	17	48
1997—Los Angeles (N.L.)	5	1	.833	2.89	75	0	0	0	3	62 1/3	54	22	20	21	44
1998—Los Angeles (N.L.)	6	6	.500	2.63	62	0	0	0	13	61 2/3	63	21	18	20	45
1999—St. Louis (N.L.)■	2	1	.667	4.88	43	0	0	0	3	27 2/3	27	16	15	18	17
A.L. totals (5 years)	24	16	.600	3.62	316	0	0	0	32	275 2/3	261	124	111	129	201
N.L. totals (4 years)	18	9	.667	2.96	236	0	0	0	20	204	196	78	67	76	154
Major League totals (9 years)	42	25	.627	3.34	552	0	0	0	52	479 2/3	457	202	178	205	355

DIVISION SERIES RECORD

Year League	W	L	Pct.	ERA	G	GS	CG	ShO	Sv.	IP	H	R	ER	BB	SO
1996—Los Angeles (N.L.)	0	0	...	0.00	2	0	0	0	0	1 1/3	0	0	0	1	2

CHAMPIONSHIP SERIES RECORD

Year League	W	L	Pct.	ERA	G	GS	CG	ShO	Sv.	IP	H	R	ER	BB	SO
1993—Chicago (A.L.)	0	0	...	10.80	4	0	0	0	0	1 2/3	3	4	2	1	1

RADKE, BRAD — P — TWINS

PERSONAL: Born October 27, 1972, in Eau Claire, Wis. ... 6-2/188. ... Throws right, bats right. ... Full name: Brad William Radke.
HIGH SCHOOL: Jesuit (Tampa).
TRANSACTIONS/CAREER NOTES: Selected by Minnesota Twins organization in eighth round of free-agent draft (June 3, 1991).
STATISTICAL NOTES: Led A.L. in home runs allowed with 32 in 1995 and 40 in 1996. ... Led A.L. pitchers with 1.000 fielding percentage in 1999.

Year	League	W	L	Pct.	ERA	G	GS	CG	ShO	Sv.	IP	H	R	ER	BB	SO
1991— Gulf Coast Twins (GCL)		3	4	.429	3.08	10	9	1	0	1	49²/₃	41	21	17	14	46
1992— Kenosha (Midw.)		10	10	.500	2.93	26	25	4	1	0	165²/₃	149	70	54	47	127
1993— Fort Myers (FSL)		3	5	.375	3.82	14	14	0	0	0	92	85	42	39	21	69
— Nashville (Sou.)		2	6	.250	4.62	13	13	1	0	0	76	81	42	39	16	76
1994— Nashville (Sou.)		12	9	.571	2.66	29	*28	5	1	0	186¹/₃	167	66	55	34	123
1995— Minnesota (A.L.)		11	14	.440	5.32	29	28	2	1	0	181	195	112	107	47	75
1996— Minnesota (A.L.)		11	16	.407	4.46	35	35	3	0	0	232	231	125	115	57	148
1997— Minnesota (A.L.)		20	10	.667	3.87	35	•35	4	1	0	239²/₃	238	114	103	48	174
1998— Minnesota (A.L.)		12	14	.462	4.30	32	32	5	1	0	213²/₃	238	109	102	43	146
1999— Minnesota (A.L.)		12	14	.462	3.75	33	33	4	0	0	218²/₃	239	97	91	44	121
Major League totals (5 years)		66	68	.493	4.30	164	163	18	3	0	1085	1141	557	518	239	664

ALL-STAR GAME RECORD

Year	League	W	L	Pct.	ERA	GS	CG	ShO	Sv.	IP	H	R	ER	BB	SO
1998— American		0	0	...	9.00	0	0	0	0	1	2	1	1	1	1

RADLOSKY, ROB — P — TWINS

PERSONAL: Born January 7, 1974, in West Palm Beach, Fla. ... 6-2/205. ... Throws right, bats right. ... Full name: Robert Vincent Radlosky.
HIGH SCHOOL: West Haven (Conn.).
JUNIOR COLLEGE: County College of Morris (N.J.).
COLLEGE: Central Florida.
TRANSACTIONS/CAREER NOTES: Selected by Minnesota Twins organization in 22nd round of free-agent draft (June 3, 1993). ... On Fort Myers disabled list (April 3-May 1, 1997). ... On Salt Lake disabled list (August 1-19, 1999).

Year	League	W	L	Pct.	ERA	G	GS	CG	ShO	Sv.	IP	H	R	ER	BB	SO
1994— Gulf Coast Twins (GCL)		3	4	.429	3.36	11	11	0	0	0	56¹/₃	54	28	21	19	52
1995— Fort Wayne (Midw.)		11	8	.579	4.03	30	18	1	0	0	120²/₃	111	64	54	55	102
1996— Fort Myers (FSL)		4	6	.400	5.45	28	16	1	1	1	104	116	70	63	46	80
1997— Fort Myers (FSL)		9	5	.643	2.59	23	22	3	1	0	128¹/₃	87	42	37	37	109
1998— New Britain (East.)		10	3	.769	4.02	27	19	0	0	0	132	127	61	59	38	117
1999— Salt Lake (PCL)		8	4	.667	3.91	22	20	1	0	0	101¹/₃	98	49	44	38	68
— Minnesota (A.L.)		0	1	.000	12.46	7	0	0	0	0	8²/₃	15	12	12	4	3
Major League totals (1 year)		0	1	.000	12.46	7	0	0	0	0	8²/₃	15	12	12	4	3

RAIN, STEVE — P — CUBS

PERSONAL: Born June 2, 1975, in Los Angeles. ... 6-6/260. ... Throws right, bats right. ... Full name: Steven Nicholas Rain.
HIGH SCHOOL: Walnut (Calif.).
TRANSACTIONS/CAREER NOTES: Selected by Chicago Cubs organization in 11th round of free-agent draft (June 3, 1993). ... On Iowa disabled list (June 24-July 6, 1998).

Year	League	W	L	Pct.	ERA	G	GS	CG	ShO	Sv.	IP	H	R	ER	BB	SO
1993— Gulf Coast Cubs (GCL)		1	3	.250	3.89	10	6	0	0	0	37	37	20	16	17	29
1994— Huntington (Appl.)		3	3	.500	2.65	14	10	1	1	0	68	55	26	20	19	55
1995— Rockford (Midw.)		5	2	.714	1.21	53	0	0	0	23	59¹/₃	38	12	8	23	66
1996— Orlando (Sou.)		1	0	1.000	2.56	35	0	0	0	10	38²/₃	32	15	11	12	48
— Iowa (A.A.)		2	1	.667	3.12	26	0	0	0	10	26	17	9	9	8	23
1997— Iowa (A.A.)		7	1	.875	5.89	40	0	0	0	1	44¹/₃	51	30	29	34	50
— Orlando (Sou.)		1	2	.333	3.07	14	0	0	0	4	14²/₃	16	7	5	8	11
1998— Iowa (PCL)		4	6	.400	6.68	29	14	1	0	0	103²/₃	118	82	77	64	83
1999— West Tenn (Sou.)		3	1	.750	1.59	40	0	0	0	24	45¹/₃	32	9	8	16	55
— Chicago (N.L.)		0	1	.000	9.20	16	0	0	0	0	14²/₃	28	17	15	7	12
— Iowa (PCL)		0	1	.000	2.00	8	0	0	0	2	9	7	2	2	4	9
Major League totals (1 year)		0	1	.000	9.20	16	0	0	0	0	14²/₃	28	17	15	7	12

RAINES, TIM — OF

PERSONAL: Born September 16, 1959, in Sanford, Fla. ... 5-8/186. ... Bats both, throws right. ... Full name: Timothy Raines. ... Father of Tim Raines Jr., outfielder, Baltimore Orioles organization; and brother of Ned Raines, minor league outfielder (1978-80).
HIGH SCHOOL: Seminole (Sanford, Fla.).
TRANSACTIONS/CAREER NOTES: Selected by Montreal Expos organization in fifth round of free-agent draft (June 7, 1977). ... On disabled list (May 23-June 5, 1978). ... Granted free agency (November 12, 1986). ... Re-signed by Expos (May 2, 1987). ... On disabled list (June 24-July 9, 1988 and June 25-July 10, 1990). ... Traded by Expos with P Jeff Carter and a player to be named later to Chicago White Sox for OF Ivan Calderon and P Barry Jones (December 23, 1990); White Sox acquired P Mario Brito to complete deal (February 15, 1991). ... On Chicago disabled list (April 10-May 22, 1993; included rehabilitation assignment to Nashville (May 19-22). ... Granted free agency (November 1, 1993). ... Re-signed by White Sox (December 22, 1993). ... Traded by White Sox to New York Yankees for a player to be named later (December 28, 1995); White Sox acquired 3B Blaise Kozeniewski to complete deal (February 6, 1996). ... On New York disabled list (March 21-April 16 and May 22-August 11, 1996; included rehabilitation assignments to Tampa (April 12-13 and July 25-August 2), Columbus (April 13-16 and June 23-24), Gulf Coast Yankees (June 22-23) and Norwich (August 2-10). ... On New York disabled list (March 27-April 11 and July 2-August 12, 1997; included rehabilitation assignment to Tampa (April 7-10, July 24-27, and August 5-7), Gulf Coast Yankees (July 24), Norwich (July 26-27) and Columbus (August 8-11). ... Granted free agency (October 29, 1997). ... Re-signed by Yankees (December 19, 1997). ... Granted free agency (October 26, 1998). ... Signed by Oakland Athletics (January 25, 1999). ... On disabled list (July 19, 1999-remainder of season). ... Granted free agency (November 5, 1999).
RECORDS: Holds major league career record for highest stolen-base percentage (300 or more attempts)—.847. ... Holds major league single-season record for most intentional bases on balls received by switch hitter—26 (1987). ... Holds A.L. career record for most consecutive stolen bases without being caught stealing—40 (July 23, 1993 through August 4, 1995). ... Holds N.L. career record for highest stolen-base percentage (300 or more attempts)—.857. ... Shares A.L. single-game record for most consecutive times reached base safely—7 (April 20, 1994, 12 innings).

HONORS: Named Minor League Player of the Year by THE SPORTING NEWS (1980). ... Named N.L. Rookie Player of the Year by THE SPORTING NEWS (1981). ... Named outfielder on THE SPORTING NEWS N.L. All-Star team (1983 and 1986). ... Won THE SPORTING NEWS Gold Shoe Award (1984). ... Named outfielder on THE SPORTING NEWS N.L. Silver Slugger team (1986).

STATISTICAL NOTES: Led N.L. outfielders with 21 assists in 1983. ... Led N.L. with .413 on-base percentage in 1986. ... Hit for the cycle (August 16, 1987). ... Switch-hit home runs in one game (July 16, 1988 and August 31, 1993). ... Hit three home runs in one game (April 18, 1994). ... Career major league grand slams: 6.

MISCELLANEOUS: Holds Montreal Expos all-time records for most runs (934), most triples (81), highest career batting average (.301) and most stolen bases (634).

Year	Team (League)	Pos.	G	AB	R	H	2B	3B	HR	RBI	Avg.	BB	SO	SB	PO	A	E	Avg.
							BATTING								FIELDING			
1977—	GC Expos (GCL)	2B-3B-OF	49	161	28	45	6	2	0	21	.280	27	16	29	79	72	13	.921
1978—	W.P. Beach (FSL)	2B-SS	100	359	67	103	10	0	0	23	.287	64	44	57	219	273	24	.953
1979—	Memphis (Sou.)	2B	•145	552	*104	160	25	10	5	50	.290	90	51	59	*341	*413	*23	.970
—	Montreal (N.L.)	PR	6	0	3	0	0	0	0	0	...	0	0	2	...	...	...	...
1980—	Denver (A.A.)	2B	108	429	105	152	23	•11	6	64	*.354	61	42	*77	226	338	16	.972
—	Montreal (N.L.)	2B-OF	15	20	5	1	0	0	0	0	.050	6	3	5	15	16	0	1.000
1981—	Montreal (N.L.)	OF-2B	88	313	61	95	13	7	5	37	.304	45	31	*71	162	8	4	.977
1982—	Montreal (N.L.)	OF-2B	156	647	90	179	32	8	4	43	.277	75	83	*78	293	126	8	.981
1983—	Montreal (N.L.)	OF-2B	156	615	*133	183	32	8	11	71	.298	97	70	*90	314	†23	4	.988
1984—	Montreal (N.L.)	OF-2B	160	622	106	192	•38	9	8	60	.309	87	69	*75	420	8	6	.986
1985—	Montreal (N.L.)	OF	150	575	115	184	30	13	11	41	.320	81	60	70	284	8	2	.993
1986—	Montreal (N.L.)	OF	151	580	91	194	35	10	9	62	*.334	78	60	70	270	13	6	.979
1987—	Montreal (N.L.)	OF	139	530	*123	175	34	8	18	68	.330	90	52	50	297	9	4	.987
1988—	Montreal (N.L.)	OF	109	429	66	116	19	7	12	48	.270	53	44	33	235	5	3	.988
1989—	Montreal (N.L.)	OF	145	517	76	148	29	6	9	60	.286	93	48	41	253	7	1	.996
1990—	Montreal (N.L.)	OF	130	457	65	131	11	5	9	62	.287	70	43	49	239	3	6	.976
1991—	Chicago (A.L.)■	OF-DH	155	609	102	163	20	6	5	50	.268	83	68	51	273	12	3	.990
1992—	Chicago (A.L.)	OF-DH	144	551	102	162	22	9	7	54	.294	81	48	45	312	12	2	.994
1993—	Chicago (A.L.)	OF	115	415	75	127	16	4	16	54	.306	64	35	21	200	5	0	*1.000
—	Nashville (A.A.)	OF	3	11	3	5	1	0	0	2	.455	2	0	2	3	0	0	1.000
1994—	Chicago (A.L.)	OF	101	384	80	102	15	5	10	52	.266	61	43	13	204	3	4	.981
1995—	Chicago (A.L.)	OF-DH	133	502	81	143	25	4	12	67	.285	70	52	13	193	7	4	.980
1996—	Tampa (FSL)■	OF-DH	9	36	9	13	2	0	2	11	.361	8	3	0	10	2	0	1.000
—	Columbus (I.L.)	DH-OF	4	12	3	3	1	0	0	0	.250	1	3	1	2	0	0	1.000
—	New York (A.L.)	OF-DH	59	201	45	57	10	0	9	33	.284	34	29	10	79	3	1	.988
—	GC Yankees (GCL)	DH	1	5	2	3	2	0	0	3	.600	1	0	0	0	0	0	...
—	Norwich (East.)	OF-DH	8	27	8	5	1	0	1	1	.185	9	2	2	4	0	0	1.000
1997—	Tampa (FSL)	OF	11	35	8	12	0	0	2	5	.343	11	1	1	13	1	0	1.000
—	New York (A.L.)	OF-DH	74	271	56	87	20	2	4	38	.321	41	34	8	79	1	1	.988
—	GC Yankees (GCL)	OF	1	4	0	1	0	0	0	2	.250	1	1	0	2	0	0	1.000
—	Norwich (East.)	OF	2	7	0	2	1	0	0	2	.286	0	2	0	2	0	0	1.000
—	Columbus (I.L.)	OF	4	13	1	2	0	0	0	0	.154	3	2	0	4	0	0	1.000
1998—	New York (A.L.)	DH-OF	109	321	53	93	13	1	5	47	.290	55	49	8	61	3	1	.985
1999—	Oakland (A.L.)	OF-DH	58	135	20	29	5	0	4	17	.215	26	17	4	61	0	0	1.000
American League totals (9 years)			948	3389	614	963	146	31	72	412	.284	515	375	173	1462	46	16	.990
National League totals (12 years)			1405	5305	934	1598	273	81	96	552	.301	775	563	634	2782	226	44	.986
Major League totals (21 years)			2353	8694	1548	2561	419	112	168	964	.295	1290	938	807	4244	272	60	.987

DIVISION SERIES RECORD

Year	Team (League)	Pos.	G	AB	R	H	2B	3B	HR	RBI	Avg.	BB	SO	SB	PO	A	E	Avg.
							BATTING								FIELDING			
1996—	New York (A.L.)	OF	4	16	3	4	0	0	0	0	.250	3	1	0	5	0	0	1.000
1997—	New York (A.L.)	DH-OF	5	19	4	4	0	0	1	3	.211	3	1	2	7	0	0	1.000
1998—	New York (A.L.)	PH-DH	2	4	1	1	1	0	0	0	.250	1	1	0	...	...	...	...
Division series totals (3 years)			11	39	8	9	1	0	1	3	.231	7	3	2	12	0	0	1.000

CHAMPIONSHIP SERIES RECORD

RECORDS: Holds single-series record for most singles—10 (1993). ... Shares A.L. single-series record for most hits—12 (1993).

Year	Team (League)	Pos.	G	AB	R	H	2B	3B	HR	RBI	Avg.	BB	SO	SB	PO	A	E	Avg.
							BATTING								FIELDING			
1981—	Montreal (N.L.)	OF	5	21	1	5	2	0	0	1	.238	0	3	0	9	0	0	1.000
1993—	Chicago (A.L.)	OF	6	27	5	12	2	0	1	1	.444	2	2	1	12	2	0	1.000
1996—	New York (A.L.)	OF	5	15	2	4	1	0	0	0	.267	1	1	0	5	0	0	1.000
1998—	New York (A.L.)	DH-OF	3	10	0	1	0	0	0	1	.100	2	5	0	1	0	0	1.000
Championship series totals (4 years)			19	73	8	22	5	0	1	3	.301	5	11	1	27	2	0	1.000

WORLD SERIES RECORD

NOTES: Member of World Series championship team (1996 and 1998).

Year	Team (League)	Pos.	G	AB	R	H	2B	3B	HR	RBI	Avg.	BB	SO	SB	PO	A	E	Avg.
							BATTING								FIELDING			
1996—	New York (A.L.)	OF	4	14	2	3	0	0	0	0	.214	2	1	0	5	0	1	.833
1998—	New York (A.L.)								Did not play.									

ALL-STAR GAME RECORD

NOTES: Named Most Valuable Player (1987).

Year	League	Pos.	AB	R	H	2B	3B	HR	RBI	Avg.	BB	SO	SB	PO	A	E	Avg.
						BATTING								FIELDING			
1981—	National	PR-OF	0	0	0	0	0	0	0	...	0	0	0	1	0	0	1.000
1982—	National	OF	1	0	0	0	0	0	0	.000	1	1	1	0	0	0	...
1983—	National	OF	3	0	0	0	0	0	0	.000	0	1	1	2	0	0	1.000
1984—	National	OF	1	0	0	0	0	0	0	.000	0	1	0	4	0	0	1.000
1985—	National	PH-OF	0	1	0	0	0	0	0	...	1	0	0	0	0	0	...
1986—	National	PH-OF	2	0	0	0	0	0	0	.000	0	1	0	1	0	0	1.000
1987—	National	OF	3	0	3	0	1	0	2	1.000	0	0	1	1	0	0	1.000
All-Star Game totals (7 years)			10	1	3	0	1	0	2	.300	2	4	3	9	0	0	1.000

RAKERS, JASON   P   ROYALS

PERSONAL: Born June 29, 1973, in Pittsburgh. ... 6-2/200. ... Throws right, bats right. ... Full name: Jason Paul Rakers.
HIGH SCHOOL: Shaler Area (Pittsburgh).
COLLEGE: Pittsburgh, then New Mexico State.
TRANSACTIONS/CAREER NOTES: Selected by Cleveland Indians organization in 25th round of free-agent draft (June 1, 1995). ... On disabled list (April 4-June 23, 1996). ... On Buffalo disabled list (July 8-17, 1999). ... On Cleveland disabled list (August 31, 1999-remainder of season). ... Claimed on waivers by Kansas City Royals (November 17, 1999).
STATISTICAL NOTES: Pitched 8-0 no-hit for Kinston victory against Durham (June 4, 1997, first game).

Year League	W	L	Pct.	ERA	G	GS	CG	ShO	Sv.	IP	H	R	ER	BB	SO
1995— Watertown (NY-P)	4	3	.571	3.00	14	14	1	•1	0	75	72	27	25	24	73
1996— Columbus (SAL)	5	4	.556	3.61	14	14	1	1	0	77⅓	84	37	31	17	64
1997— Kinston (Caro.)	8	5	.615	3.07	17	17	2	2	0	102⅔	93	41	35	18	105
— Buffalo (A.A.)	1	0	1.000	0.00	1	1	0	0	0	7	5	0	0	1	3
— Akron (East.)	1	4	.200	4.39	7	7	1	1	0	41	36	21	20	11	31
1998— Akron (East.)	3	1	.750	2.59	5	5	0	0	0	31⅓	35	10	9	7	27
— Cleveland (A.L.)	0	0	...	9.00	1	0	0	0	0	1	0	1	1	3	0
— Buffalo (I.L.)	8	6	.571	4.57	21	21	1	0	0	126	134	70	64	38	89
1999— Buffalo (I.L.)	7	8	.467	4.92	23	20	1	0	0	131⅔	151	83	72	31	85
— Cleveland (A.L.)	0	0	...	4.50	1	0	0	0	0	2	2	1	1	1	0
Major League totals (2 years)	0	0	...	6.00	2	0	0	0	0	3	2	2	2	4	0

RAMIREZ, ALEX   OF   INDIANS

PERSONAL: Born October 3, 1974, in Caracas, Venezuela. ... 5-11/176. ... Bats right, throws right. ... Full name: Alexander Ramon Ramirez.
TRANSACTIONS/CAREER NOTES: Signed as non-drafted free agent by Cleveland Indians organization (July 1, 1991). ... On Buffalo disabled list (May 21-June 4, 1998).
STATISTICAL NOTES: Led Appalachian League outfielders with three double plays in 1993.

Year Team (League)	Pos.	G	AB	R	H	2B	3B	HR	RBI	Avg.	BB	SO	SB	PO	A	E	Avg.
1992— Dom. Indians (DSL)	OF	69	272	28	79	13	3	8	48	.290	13	34	17	136	9	8	.948
1993— Kinston (Caro.)	OF	3	12	0	2	0	0	0	1	.167	0	5	0	3	0	1	.750
— Burlington (Appl.)	OF	64	252	44	68	14	4	13	58	.270	13	52	13	85	8	7	.930
1994— Columbus (SAL)	OF	125	458	64	115	23	3	18	57	.251	26	100	7	168	6	9	.951
1995— Bakersfield (Calif.)	OF	98	406	56	131	25	2	10	52	.323	18	76	13	150	9	10	.941
— Canton/Akron (East.)	OF	33	133	15	33	3	4	1	11	.248	5	24	3	72	5	2	.975
1996— Canton/Akron (East.)	OF	131	513	79	*169	28	*12	14	85	.329	16	74	18	209	4	5	.977
1997— Buffalo (A.A.)	OF-DH	119	416	59	119	19	*8	11	44	.286	24	95	10	167	8	*10	.946
1998— Buffalo (I.L.)	OF-DH	121	521	94	156	21	8	34	103	.299	16	101	6	224	7	9	.963
— Cleveland (A.L.)	OF	3	8	1	1	0	0	0	0	.125	0	3	0	5	0	1	.833
1999— Buffalo (I.L.)	OF-DH	75	305	50	93	20	2	12	50	.305	17	52	5	167	6	4	.977
— Cleveland (A.L.)	OF-DH	48	97	11	29	6	1	3	18	.299	3	26	1	22	1	2	.920
Major League totals (2 years)		51	105	12	30	6	1	3	18	.286	3	29	1	27	1	3	.903

RAMIREZ, ARAMIS   3B   PIRATES

PERSONAL: Born June 25, 1978, in Santo Domingo, Dominican Republic. ... 6-1/219. ... Bats right, throws right. ... Full name: Aramis Nin Ramirez.
TRANSACTIONS/CAREER NOTES: Signed as non-drafted free agent by Pittsburgh Pirates organization (November 7, 1994). ... On suspended list (July 24-29, 1998). ... On Pittsburgh disabled list (August 10-September 4, 1998); included rehabilitation assignment to Nashville (August 27).
HONORS: Named Carolina League Most Valuable Player (1997).
STATISTICAL NOTES: Led Carolina League third basemen with 379 total chances in 1997.

Year Team (League)	Pos.	G	AB	R	H	2B	3B	HR	RBI	Avg.	BB	SO	SB	PO	A	E	Avg.
1995— Dom. Pirates (DSL)	3B	64	214	41	63	13	0	11	54	.294	42	26	2	65	82	19	.886
1996— Erie (NY-P)	3B	61	223	37	68	14	4	9	42	.305	31	41	0	39	107	17	.896
— Augusta (SAL)	3B	6	20	3	4	1	0	1	2	.200	1	7	0	3	7	2	.833
1997— Lynchburg (Caro.)	3B-DH	137	482	85	134	24	2	29	*114	.278	80	103	5	75	*265	*39	.897
1998— Nashville (PCL)	3B-SS	47	168	19	46	10	0	5	18	.274	24	28	0	33	77	8	.932
— Pittsburgh (N.L.)	3B	72	251	23	59	9	1	6	24	.235	18	72	0	29	114	9	.941
1999— Nashville (PCL)	3B-DH	131	460	92	151	35	1	21	74	.328	73	56	5	70	250	*42	.884
— Pittsburgh (N.L.)	3B	18	56	2	10	2	1	0	7	.179	6	9	0	11	29	3	.930
Major League totals (2 years)		90	307	25	69	11	2	6	31	.225	24	81	0	40	143	12	.938

RAMIREZ, HECTOR   P

PERSONAL: Born December 15, 1971, in El Seybo, Dominican Republic. ... 6-3/218. ... Throws right, bats right. ... Full name: Hector Bienvenido Ramirez.
HIGH SCHOOL: Liceo Local (El Seybo, Dominican Republic).
TRANSACTIONS/CAREER NOTES: Signed as non-drafted free agent by New York Mets organization (August 22, 1988). ... Traded by Mets to Baltimore Orioles for IF Manny Alexander and IF Scott McLain (March 22, 1997). ... Claimed on waivers by New York Yankees (January 20, 1998). ... Claimed on waivers by Orioles (January 30, 1998). ... Traded by Orioles to Florida Marlins for a player to be named later and cash (February 4, 1998). ... Granted free agency (October 15, 1998). ... Signed by Milwaukee Brewers organization (November 20, 1998). ... Granted free agency (December 21, 1999).
STATISTICAL NOTES: Tied for Florida State League lead with eight balks in 1994.

Year	League	W	L	Pct.	ERA	G	GS	CG	ShO	Sv.	IP	H	R	ER	BB	SO
1989—Gulf Coast Mets (GCL)		0	5	.000	4.50	15	5	0	0	0	42	35	29	21	24	14
1990—Gulf Coast Mets (GCL)		3	5	.375	4.26	11	8	1	0	0	50⅔	54	34	24	21	43
1991—Kingsport (Appalachian).....		8	2	.800	2.65	14	13	0	0	0	85	83	39	25	28	64
1992—Columbia (SAL).................		5	4	.556	3.61	17	17	1	0	0	94⅔	93	50	38	33	53
1993—Gulf Coast Mets (GCL)		1	0	1.000	0.00	1	1	0	0	0	7	5	1	0	1	6
— Capital City (SAL)		4	6	.400	5.34	14	14	0	0	0	64	86	51	38	23	42
1994—St. Lucie (FSL)		11	12	.478	3.43	27	27	•6	1	0	*194	*202	86	74	50	110
1995—Binghamton (East.)		4	•12	.250	4.60	20	20	2	0	0	123⅓	127	69	63	48	63
1996—Binghamton (East.)		1	5	.167	5.14	38	0	0	0	6	56	51	34	32	23	49
—Norfolk (I.L.)		1	0	1.000	3.38	3	1	0	0	0	10⅔	13	7	4	3	8
1997—Rochester (I.L.)■		8	7	.533	4.91	39	9	0	0	3	102⅔	114	65	56	38	50
1998—Charlotte (I.L.)■...............		3	3	.500	6.75	55	0	0	0	3	86⅔	106	68	65	30	50
1999—Louisville (I.L.)■		3	3	.500	3.80	58	0	0	0	9	94⅔	91	45	40	33	55
—Milwaukee (N.L.)		1	2	.333	3.43	15	0	0	0	0	21	19	8	8	11	9
Major League totals (1 year)........		**1**	**2**	**.333**	**3.43**	**15**	**0**	**0**	**0**	**0**	**21**	**19**	**8**	**8**	**11**	**9**

RAMIREZ, JULIO   OF   MARLINS

PERSONAL: Born August 10, 1977, in San Juan de la Maguana, Dominican Republic. ... 5-11/170. ... Bats right, throws right. ... Full name: Julio Caesar Ramirez.

HIGH SCHOOL: Escuela Otilia Pelaez (Santo Domingo, Dominican Republic).

TRANSACTIONS/CAREER NOTES: Signed as non-drafted free agent by Florida Marlins organization (December 6, 1993).

STATISTICAL NOTES: Led Florida State League outfielders with 390 total chances in 1998. ... Led Eastern League outfielders with 351 total chances in 1999.

												BATTING				FIELDING		
Year	Team (League)	Pos.	G	AB	R	H	2B	3B	HR	RBI	Avg.	BB	SO	SB	PO	A	E	Avg.
1994—Dom. Marlins (DSL)		OF	67	274	54	75	18	0	7	32	.274	28	41	29	136	11	10	.936
1995—GC Marlins (GCL)		OF	48	204	35	58	9	4	2	13	.284	13	42	17	109	7	2	.983
1996—Brevard County (FSL).		OF	17	61	11	15	0	1	0	2	.246	4	18	2	12	2	1	.933
— GC Marlins (GCL)		OF	43	174	35	50	5	4	0	16	.287	15	34	26	95	2	2	.980
1997—Kane County (Midw.)..		OF	99	376	70	96	18	7	14	53	.255	37	122	41	179	8	4	.979
1998—Brevard County (FSL).		OF	135	*559	90	156	20	12	13	58	.279	45	147	71	*365	•17	8	.979
1999—Portland (East.)		OF	138	*568	87	148	30	10	13	64	.261	39	150	*64	*326	14	•11	.969
—Florida (N.L.)		OF	15	21	3	3	1	0	0	2	.143	1	6	0	19	0	1	.950
Major League totals (1 year)			**15**	**21**	**3**	**3**	**1**	**0**	**0**	**2**	**.143**	**1**	**6**	**0**	**19**	**0**	**1**	**.950**

RAMIREZ, MANNY   OF   INDIANS

PERSONAL: Born May 30, 1972, in Santo Domingo, Dominican Republic. ... 6-0/205. ... Bats right, throws right. ... Full name: Manuel Aristides Ramirez.

HIGH SCHOOL: George Washington (New York).

TRANSACTIONS/CAREER NOTES: Selected by Cleveland Indians organization in first round (13th pick overall) of free-agent draft (June 3, 1991). ... On disabled list (July 10, 1992-remainder of season). ... On suspended list (June 8-11, 1999).

RECORDS: Shares major league record for most consecutive home runs—4 (September 15 [3], 16 [1], 1998); most home runs in two consecutive games—5 (September 15 [3], 16 [2], 1998); and most home runs in three consecutive games—6 (September 15 [3], 16 [2], 17 [1], 1998).

HONORS: Named Appalachian League Most Valuable Player (1991). ... Named outfielder on THE SPORTING NEWS A.L. All-Star team (1995 and 1999). ... Named outfielder on THE SPORTING NEWS A.L. Silver Slugger team (1995 and 1999).

STATISTICAL NOTES: Led Appalachian League with 146 total bases and .679 slugging percentage in 1991. ... Hit three home runs in one game (September 15, 1998 and August 25, 1999). ... Led A.L. with a .663 slugging percentage in 1999. ... Career major league grand slams: 10.

												BATTING				FIELDING		
Year	Team (League)	Pos.	G	AB	R	H	2B	3B	HR	RBI	Avg.	BB	SO	SB	PO	A	E	Avg.
1991—Burlington (Appl.).......		OF	59	215	44	70	11	4	*19	*63	.326	34	41	7	83	2	3	.966
1992—Kinston (Caro.)...........		OF	81	291	52	81	18	4	13	63	.278	45	74	1	128	3	6	.956
1993—Canton/Akron (East.)..		OF	89	344	67	117	32	0	17	79	*.340	45	68	2	142	4	5	.967
—Charlotte (I.L.)............		OF	40	145	38	46	12	0	14	36	.317	27	35	1	70	3	3	.961
—Cleveland (A.L.).........		DH-OF	22	53	5	9	1	0	2	5	.170	2	8	0	3	0	0	1.000
1994—Cleveland (A.L.).........		OF-DH	91	290	51	78	22	0	17	60	.269	42	72	4	150	7	1	.994
1995—Cleveland (A.L.).........		OF-DH	137	484	85	149	26	1	31	107	.308	75	112	6	220	3	5	.978
1996—Cleveland (A.L.).........		OF-DH	152	550	94	170	45	3	33	112	.309	85	104	8	272	*19	9	.970
1997—Cleveland (A.L.).........		OF-DH	150	561	99	184	40	0	26	88	.328	79	115	2	259	10	7	.975
1998—Cleveland (A.L.).........		OF-DH	150	571	108	168	35	2	45	145	.294	76	121	5	291	10	7	.977
1999—Cleveland (A.L.).........		OF-DH	147	522	131	174	34	3	44	*165	.333	96	131	2	267	7	7	.975
Major League totals (7 years)			**849**	**3031**	**573**	**932**	**203**	**9**	**198**	**682**	**.307**	**455**	**663**	**27**	**1462**	**56**	**36**	**.977**

DIVISION SERIES RECORD

RECORDS: Holds career record for most at-bats—81. ... Shares career records for most games—21; doubles—6; and extra-base hits—10. ... Shares single-game record for most home runs—2 (October 2, 1998).

												BATTING				FIELDING		
Year	Team (League)	Pos.	G	AB	R	H	2B	3B	HR	RBI	Avg.	BB	SO	SB	PO	A	E	Avg.
1995—Cleveland (A.L.).........		OF	3	12	1	0	0	0	0	0	.000	1	2	0	3	0	0	1.000
1996—Cleveland (A.L.).........		OF	4	16	4	6	2	0	2	2	.375	1	4	0	8	2	0	1.000
1997—Cleveland (A.L.).........		OF	5	21	2	3	1	0	0	3	.143	0	3	0	3	0	1	.750
1998—Cleveland (A.L.).........		OF	4	14	2	5	2	0	2	3	.357	1	4	0	4	0	0	1.000
1999—Cleveland (A.L.).........		OF	5	18	5	1	1	0	0	1	.056	4	8	0	8	1	0	1.000
Division series totals (5 years)			**21**	**81**	**14**	**15**	**6**	**0**	**4**	**9**	**.185**	**7**	**21**	**0**	**26**	**3**	**1**	**.967**

CHAMPIONSHIP SERIES RECORD

						BATTING								FIELDING		
Year	Team (League)	Pos.	G	AB	R	H	2B	3B	HR	RBI	Avg.	BB	SO	SB	PO	A	E	Avg.
1995—Cleveland (A.L.).........	OF	6	21	2	6	0	0	2	2	.286	2	5	0	9	0	0	1.000
1997—Cleveland (A.L.).........	OF	6	21	3	6	1	0	2	3	.286	5	5	0	14	0	1	.933
1998—Cleveland (A.L.).........	OF	6	21	2	7	1	0	2	4	.333	4	9	0	12	0	0	1.000
Championship series totals (3 years)		18	63	7	19	2	0	6	9	.302	11	19	0	35	0	1	.972

WORLD SERIES RECORD

						BATTING								FIELDING		
Year	Team (League)	Pos.	G	AB	R	H	2B	3B	HR	RBI	Avg.	BB	SO	SB	PO	A	E	Avg.
1995—Cleveland (A.L.).........	OF	6	18	2	4	0	0	1	2	.222	4	5	1	8	0	0	1.000
1997—Cleveland (A.L.).........	OF	7	26	3	4	0	0	2	6	.154	6	5	0	16	1	1	.944
World Series totals (2 years)		13	44	5	8	0	0	3	8	.182	10	10	1	24	1	1	.962

ALL-STAR GAME RECORD

					BATTING								FIELDING		
Year	League	Pos.	AB	R	H	2B	3B	HR	RBI	Avg.	BB	SO	SB	PO	A	E	Avg.
1995—American	PH-OF	0	0	0	0	0	0	0		2	0	0	2	0	0	1.000
1998—American	OF	1	0	0	0	0	0	1	.000	0	0	0	0	0	0	...
1999—American	OF	1	1	0	0	0	0	0	.000	1	1	0	0	0	0	...
All-Star Game totals (3 years)		2	1	0	0	0	0	1	.000	3	1	0	2	0	0	1.000

RAMIREZ, ROBERTO   P

PERSONAL: Born August 17, 1972, in El Laurel, Veracruz, Mexico ... 5-11/170. ... Throws left, bats left. ... Full name: Roberto Sanchez Ramirez.

HIGH SCHOOL: Cetis 145 Technical (Veracruz, Mexico).

TRANSACTIONS/CAREER NOTES: Signed as non-drafted free agent by Mexico City Reds of Mexican League (1989). ... Contract sold by Mexico City to Pittsburgh Pirates organization (January 8, 1990). ... On Augusta disabled list (April 9-May 8, 1992). ... Loaned by Pirates organization to Mexico City Red Devils of Mexican League (May 8, 1992-remainder of season; February 18, 1993-entire season; May 6-August 29, 1994; and April 15, 1995-entire season). ... Granted free agency (October 16, 1995). ... Signed by Mexico City Red Devils, Mexican League (1996). ... Signed by San Diego Padres organization (April 23, 1998). ... Granted free agency (October 15, 1998). ... Signed by Colorado Rockies (October 29, 1998). ... Contract sold by Rockies to Hanshin Tigers of Japan Central League (November 29, 1999).

Year	League	W	L	Pct.	ERA	G	GS	CG	ShO	Sv.	IP	H	R	ER	BB	SO
1989—Mexico City Reds (Mex.)....	0	0	...	4.91	2	1	0	0	0	3²/₃	4	2	2	2	2
1990—Gulf Coast Pirates (GCL)■.	2	1	.667	0.53	11	3	0	0	0	33²/₃	20	4	2	18	27
1991—Welland (NY-P)..................	2	6	.250	4.12	16	12	0	0	1	74¹/₃	66	43	34	35	71
1992—M.C. Red Devils (Mex.)■...	3	9	.250	5.98	19	13	6	0	0	81¹/₃	102	61	54	47	57
1993—M.C. Red Devils (Mex.)......	14	5	.737	3.40	25	24	8	4	0	156¹/₃	136	65	59	65	100
1994—Carolina (Sou.)■...............	0	1	.000	5.27	6	6	0	0	0	27¹/₃	38	19	16	8	21
—M.C. Red Devils (Mex.)■...	12	2	.857	2.68	16	16	7	4	0	111	103	39	33	32	82
1995—M.C. Red Devils (Mex.)......	13	3	.813	2.56	20	20	8	3	0	137¹/₃	125	50	39	35	70
1996—M.C. Red Devils (Mex.)......	14	9	.609	2.84	28	*28	8	1	0	*190¹/₃	179	70	60	76	132
1997—M.C. Red Devils (Mex.)......	12	4	.750	3.76	24	24	1	0	0	150²/₃	157	71	63	64	82
1998—M.C. Red Devils (Mex.)......	5	0	1.000	3.06	6	6	0	0	0	35¹/₃	33	12	12	6	23
—Las Vegas (PCL)■..............	1	1	.500	2.43	26	1	0	0	2	29²/₃	23	14	8	10	33
—San Diego (N.L.)	1	0	1.000	6.14	21	0	0	0	0	14²/₃	12	13	10	12	17
1999—Colorado (N.L.)■	1	5	.167	8.26	32	4	0	0	1	40¹/₃	68	42	37	22	32
—Colorado Springs (PCL).....	3	2	.600	3.50	10	10	0	0	0	61²/₃	64	26	24	17	55
Major League totals (2 years)......	2	5	.286	7.69	53	4	0	0	1	55	80	55	47	34	49

RAMSAY, ROBERT   P   MARINERS

PERSONAL: Born December 3, 1973, in Vancouver, Wash. ... 6-5/220. ... Throws left, bats left. ... Full name: Robert Arthur Ramsay.

HIGH SCHOOL: Mountain View (Vancouver, Wash.).

COLLEGE: Washington State.

TRANSACTIONS/CAREER NOTES: Selected by Boston Red Sox organization in seventh round of free-agent draft (June 2, 1996). ... Traded by Red Sox to Seattle Mariners for OF Butch Huskey (July 26, 1999).

Year	League	W	L	Pct.	ERA	G	GS	CG	ShO	Sv.	IP	H	R	ER	BB	SO
1996—Gulf Coast Red Sox (GCL)..	0	1	.000	4.91	2	0	0	0	0	3²/₃	5	2	2	3	5
—Sarasota (FSL)	2	2	.500	6.09	12	7	0	0	0	34	42	23	23	27	32
1997—Sarasota (FSL)	9	9	.500	4.78	23	22	1	0	0	135²/₃	134	90	72	63	115
1998—Trenton (East.)	12	6	.667	3.49	27	27	1	1	0	162²/₃	137	67	63	50	166
1999—Pawtucket (I.L.).................	6	6	.500	5.35	20	20	0	0	0	114¹/₃	114	81	68	36	79
—Seattle (A.L.)■	0	2	.000	6.38	6	3	0	0	0	18¹/₃	23	13	13	9	11
—Tacoma (PCL)	4	1	.800	1.08	5	5	0	0	0	33¹/₃	20	6	4	14	37
Major League totals (1 year)........	0	2	.000	6.38	6	3	0	0	0	18¹/₃	23	13	13	9	11

RANDA, JOE   3B   ROYALS

PERSONAL: Born December 18, 1969, in Milwaukee. ... 5-11/190. ... Bats right, throws right. ... Full name: Joseph Gregory Randa.

HIGH SCHOOL: Kettle-Moraine (Wales, Wis.).

JUNIOR COLLEGE: Indian River Community College (Fla.).

COLLEGE: Tennessee.

TRANSACTIONS/CAREER NOTES: Selected by California Angels organization in 30th round of free-agent draft (June 5, 1989); did not sign. ... Selected by Kansas City Royals organization in 11th round of free-agent draft (June 3, 1991). ... On Kansas City disabled list (May 5-27, 1996); included rehabilitation assignment to Omaha (May 23-27). ... Traded by Royals with P Jeff Granger, P Jeff Martin and P Jeff Wallace to

Pittsburgh Pirates for SS Jay Bell and 1B Jeff King (December 13, 1996). ... On Pittsburgh disabled list (June 28-July 27, 1997); included rehabilitation assignment to Calgary (July 25-27). ... Selected by Arizona Diamondbacks in third round (57th pick overall) of expansion draft (November 18, 1997). ... Traded by Diamondbacks with P Matt Drews and 3B Gabe Alvarez to Detroit Tigers for 3B Travis Fryman (November 18, 1997). ... Traded by Tigers to New York Mets for P Willie Blair (December 4, 1998). ... Traded by Mets to Royals for OF Juan LeBron (December 10, 1998).

RECORDS: Holds major league single-season record for fewest putouts by third baseman for leader—119 (1999).

HONORS: Named Northwest League Most Valuable Player (1991).

STATISTICAL NOTES: Led Northwest League with 150 total bases and .438 on-base percentage in 1991. ... Led Northwest League third basemen with 182 total chances and 12 double plays in 1991. ... Led Southern League with 10 sacrifice flies in 1993. ... Led American Association third basemen with 433 total chances and 28 double plays in 1994. ... Had 18-game hitting streak (July 1-21, 1999). ... Led A.L. third baseman with 455 total chances and 28 double plays in 1999.

Year	Team (League)	Pos.	G	AB	R	H	2B	3B	HR	RBI	Avg.	BB	SO	SB	PO	A	E	Avg.
1991—	Eugene (N.W.)	3B	72	275	53	*93	20	2	11	59	.338	46	29	6	*57	*111	14	*.923
1992—	Appleton (Midw.)	3B	72	266	55	80	13	0	5	43	.301	34	37	6	53	137	12	.941
—	Baseball City (FSL)	3B-SS	51	189	22	52	7	0	1	12	.275	12	21	4	43	105	6	.961
1993—	Memphis (Sou.)	3B	131	505	74	149	31	5	11	72	.295	39	64	8	*97	309	25	.942
1994—	Omaha (A.A.)	3B	127	455	65	125	27	2	10	51	.275	30	49	5	*85	*324	*24	.945
1995—	Omaha (A.A.)	3B	64	233	33	64	10	2	8	33	.275	22	33	2	42	96	6	.958
—	Kansas City (A.L.)	3B-2B-DH	34	70	6	12	2	0	1	5	.171	6	17	0	15	44	3	.952
1996—	Kansas City (A.L.)	3-2-1-DH	110	337	36	102	24	1	6	47	.303	26	47	13	80	160	10	.960
—	Omaha (A.A.)	3B	3	9	1	1	0	1	0	0	.111	1	1	0	1	10	0	1.000
1997—	Pittsburgh (N.L.)■	3B-2B	126	443	58	134	27	9	7	60	.302	41	64	4	91	288	21	.948
—	Calgary (PCL)	3B	3	11	4	4	1	0	1	4	.364	3	4	0	2	7	1	.900
1998—	Detroit (A.L.)■	3-2-DH-1	138	460	56	117	21	2	9	50	.254	41	70	8	102	252	7	.981
1999—	Kansas City (A.L.)■	3B	156	628	92	197	36	8	16	84	.314	50	80	5	*119	*314	22	.952
American League totals (4 years)			438	1495	190	428	83	11	32	186	.286	123	214	26	316	770	42	.963
National League totals (1 year)			126	443	58	134	27	9	7	60	.302	41	64	4	91	288	21	.948
Major League totals (5 years)			564	1938	248	562	110	20	39	246	.290	164	278	30	407	1058	63	.959

RANDALL, SCOTT   P   TWINS

PERSONAL: Born October 29, 1975, in Fullerton, Calif. ... 6-3/190. ... Throws right, bats right. ... Full name: Scott Phillip Randall.
HIGH SCHOOL: Dos Pueblos (Goleta, Calif.).
JUNIOR COLLEGE: Santa Barbara (Calif.) City.
COLLEGE: UC Santa Barbara.
TRANSACTIONS/CAREER NOTES: Selected by Colorado Rockies organization in 11th round of free-agent draft (June 1, 1995). ... Traded by Rockies to Minnesota Twins for OF Chris Latham (December 7, 1999).

Year	League	W	L	Pct.	ERA	G	GS	CG	ShO	Sv.	IP	H	R	ER	BB	SO
1995—	Portland (N.W.)	7	3	.700	*1.99	15	•15	1	0	0	95	76	35	21	28	78
1996—	Asheville (SAL)	14	4	.778	2.74	24	24	1	1	0	154 1/3	121	53	47	50	136
1997—	Salem (Caro.)	9	10	.474	3.84	27	26	2	1	0	176	167	93	75	66	128
1998—	New Haven (East.)	10	•14	.417	3.83	29	•29	*7	2	0	*202	*210	•102	86	62	135
1999—	Colorado Springs (PCL)	1	4	.200	7.93	9	9	0	0	0	42	62	41	37	22	25
—	Carolina (Sou.)	5	8	.385	3.43	16	16	3	1	0	99 2/3	101	52	38	34	102

RANDOLPH, STEVE   P   DIAMONDBACKS

PERSONAL: Born May 1, 1974, in Okinawa, Japan. ... 6-3/185. ... Throws left, bats left. ... Full name: Stephen LaCharles Randolph.
HIGH SCHOOL: James Bowie (Simms, Texas).
JUNIOR COLLEGE: Galveston (Texas) College.
COLLEGE: Texas.
TRANSACTIONS/CAREER NOTES: Selected by New York Yankees organization in 18th round of free-agent draft (June 1, 1995). ... Selected by Arizona Diamondbacks from Yankees organization in Rule 5 major league draft (December 15, 1997). ... On Tucson disabled list (June 1-July 25, 1999).

Year	League	W	L	Pct.	ERA	G	GS	CG	ShO	Sv.	IP	H	R	ER	BB	SO
1995—	Tampa (FSL)	4	0	1.000	2.22	8	3	0	0	0	24 1/3	11	7	6	16	34
—	Oneonta (NY-P)	0	3	.000	7.48	6	6	0	0	0	21 2/3	19	22	18	23	31
1996—	Greensboro (SAL)	4	7	.364	3.77	32	17	0	0	0	100 1/3	64	46	42	96	111
1997—	Tampa (FSL)	4	7	.364	3.87	34	13	1	0	1	95 1/3	74	55	41	63	108
1998—	High Desert (Calif.)■	4	4	.500	3.59	17	17	0	0	0	85 1/3	71	44	34	42	104
—	Tucson (PCL)	1	3	.250	3.18	17	1	0	0	0	22 2/3	16	11	8	19	23
1999—	El Paso (Texas)	2	2	.500	2.64	8	8	0	0	0	44 1/3	39	14	13	23	38
—	Tucson (PCL)	0	7	.000	6.91	11	10	1	0	0	41 2/3	47	37	32	32	26
—	Ariz. D'backs (Ariz.)	0	0	...	4.50	2	2	0	0	0	6	5	3	3	2	7

RAPP, PAT   P

PERSONAL: Born July 13, 1967, in Jennings, La. ... 6-3/215. ... Throws right, bats right. ... Full name: Patrick Leland Rapp.
HIGH SCHOOL: Sulphur (La.).
JUNIOR COLLEGE: Hinds Community College (Miss.).
COLLEGE: Southern Mississippi.
TRANSACTIONS/CAREER NOTES: Selected by San Francisco Giants organization in 15th round of free-agent draft (June 5, 1989). ... Selected by Florida Marlins in first round (10th pick overall) of expansion draft (November 17, 1992). ... Traded by Marlins to Giants for P Brandon Leese and P Bobby Rector (July 18, 1997). ... On San Francisco disabled list (July 20-August 5, 1997). ... Granted free agency (December 21, 1997). ... Signed by Kansas City Royals organization (January 22, 1998). ... Granted free agency (December 21, 1998). ... Signed by Boston Red Sox (January 11, 1999). ... Granted free agency (November 2, 1999).

STATISTICAL NOTES: Pitched 17-0 one-hit, complete-game victory against Colorado (September 17, 1995).

MISCELLANEOUS: Appeared in one game as pinch runner (1994). ... Holds Florida Marlins all-time records for most wins (37), strikeouts (384) and innings pitched (665.2).

Year League	W	L	Pct.	ERA	G	GS	CG	ShO	Sv.	IP	H	R	ER	BB	SO
1989— Pocatello (Pio.).................	4	6	.400	5.30	16	12	1	0	0	73	90	54	43	29	40
1990— Clinton (Midw.)	14	10	.583	2.64	27	26	4	0	0	167 1/3	132	60	49	79	132
1991— San Jose (Calif.)...............	7	5	.583	2.50	16	15	1	0	0	90	88	41	25	37	73
— Shreveport (Texas)...........	6	2	.750	2.69	10	10	1	1	0	60 1/3	52	23	18	22	46
1992— Phoenix (PCL)	7	8	.467	3.05	39	12	2	1	3	121	115	54	41	40	79
— San Francisco (N.L.)	0	2	.000	7.20	3	2	0	0	0	10	8	8	8	6	3
1993— Edmonton (PCL)■	8	3	.727	3.43	17	17	•4	1	0	107 2/3	89	45	41	34	93
— Florida (N.L.)...................	4	6	.400	4.02	16	16	1	0	0	94	101	49	42	39	57
1994— Florida (N.L.)...................	7	8	.467	3.85	24	23	2	1	0	133 1/3	132	67	57	69	75
1995— Charlotte (I.L.).................	0	1	.000	6.00	1	1	0	0	0	6	6	4	4	1	5
— Florida (N.L.)...................	14	7	.667	3.44	28	28	3	2	0	167 1/3	158	72	64	76	102
1996— Florida (N.L.)...................	8	•16	.333	5.10	30	29	0	0	0	162 1/3	184	95	92	91	86
— Charlotte (I.L.).................	1	1	.500	8.18	2	2	0	0	0	11	18	12	10	4	9
1997— Florida (N.L.)...................	4	6	.400	4.47	19	19	1	1	0	108 2/3	121	59	54	51	64
— San Francisco (N.L.)■	1	2	.333	6.00	8	6	0	0	0	33	37	24	22	21	28
— Phoenix (PCL)	2	0	1.000	3.60	3	3	0	0	0	15	16	6	6	9	6
1998— Kansas City (A.L.)■	12	13	.480	5.30	32	32	1	1	0	188 1/3	208	117	111	107	132
1999— Boston (A.L.)■.................	6	7	.462	4.12	37	26	0	0	0	146 1/3	147	78	67	69	90
A.L. totals (2 years)	18	20	.474	4.79	69	58	1	1	0	334 2/3	355	195	178	176	222
N.L. totals (6 years)	38	47	.447	4.31	128	123	7	4	0	708 2/3	741	374	339	353	415
Major League totals (8 years)	56	67	.455	4.46	197	181	8	5	0	1043 1/3	1096	569	517	529	637

DIVISION SERIES RECORD

Year League	W	L	Pct.	ERA	G	GS	CG	ShO	Sv.	IP	H	R	ER	BB	SO
1999— Boston (A.L.).....................				Did not play.											

CHAMPIONSHIP SERIES RECORD

Year League	W	L	Pct.	ERA	G	GS	CG	ShO	Sv.	IP	H	R	ER	BB	SO
1999— Boston (A.L.).....................	0	0	...	0.00	1	0	0	0	0	1	0	0	0	1	0

RATH, GARY — P

PERSONAL: Born January 10, 1973, in Gulfport, Miss. ... 6-2/186. ... Throws left, bats left. ... Full name: Gary Alfred Rath Jr.
HIGH SCHOOL: Long Beach (Miss.).
COLLEGE: Mississippi State.
TRANSACTIONS/CAREER NOTES: Selected by Los Angeles Dodgers organization in second round of free-agent draft (June 2, 1994). ... Granted free agency (November 30, 1998). ... Signed by Minnesota Twins organization (December 18, 1998). ... On Salt Lake disabled list (July 2-9, 1999). ... Granted free agency (October 7, 1999).

Year League	W	L	Pct.	ERA	G	GS	CG	ShO	Sv.	IP	H	R	ER	BB	SO
1994— Vero Beach (FSL)	5	6	.455	2.73	13	11	0	0	0	62 2/3	55	26	19	23	50
1995— Albuquerque (PCL).............	3	5	.375	5.08	8	8	0	0	0	39	46	31	22	20	23
— San Antonio (Texas)..........	•13	3	*.813	*2.77	18	16	3	1	0	117	96	42	36	48	81
1996— Albuquerque (PCL).............	10	11	.476	4.19	30	•30	1	1	0	180 1/3	177	97	84	*89	125
1997— Albuquerque (PCL).............	7	11	.389	6.05	24	24	0	0	0	132 1/3	177	107	89	49	100
1998— Albuquerque (PCL).............	9	7	.563	4.52	28	24	1	0	1	157 1/3	184	91	79	52	119
— Los Angeles (N.L.)	0	0	...	10.80	3	0	0	0	0	3 1/3	3	4	4	2	4
1999— Salt Lake (PCL)■	3	8	.273	5.62	20	18	1	0	0	99 1/3	129	76	62	27	67
— Minnesota (A.L.)	0	1	.000	11.57	5	1	0	0	0	4 2/3	6	6	6	5	1
A.L. totals (1 year)	0	1	.000	11.57	5	1	0	0	0	4 2/3	6	6	6	5	1
N.L. totals (1 year)	0	0	...	10.80	3	0	0	0	0	3 1/3	3	4	4	2	4
Major League totals (2 years)	0	1	.000	11.25	8	1	0	0	0	8	9	10	10	7	5

RAY, KEN — P — GIANTS

PERSONAL: Born November 27, 1974, in Atlanta. ... 6-2/200. ... Throws right, bats right. ... Full name: Kenneth Alan Ray.
HIGH SCHOOL: Roswell (Ga.).
TRANSACTIONS/CAREER NOTES: Selected by Kansas City Royals organization in 18th round of free-agent draft (June 3, 1993). ... On disabled list (April 7-23, 1996). ... Traded by Royals to San Francisco Giants (January 7, 2000), completing deal in which Giants traded P Jerry Spradlin to Royals for a player to be named later (December 13, 1999).

Year League	W	L	Pct.	ERA	G	GS	CG	ShO	Sv.	IP	H	R	ER	BB	SO
1993— Gulf Coast Royals (GCL)	2	3	.400	2.28	13	7	0	0	0	47 1/3	44	21	12	17	45
1994— Rockford (Midw.)	10	4	.714	1.82	27	18	0	0	3	128 2/3	94	34	26	56	128
1995— Wichita (Texas)	4	5	.444	5.97	14	14	0	0	0	75 1/3	83	55	50	46	53
— Wilmington (Caro.).............	6	4	.600	2.69	13	13	1	0	0	77	74	32	23	22	63
1996— Wichita (Texas)	4	12	.250	6.12	22	22	1	0	0	120 2/3	151	94	82	57	79
1997— Omaha (A.A.)	5	12	.294	6.37	25	21	2	0	0	113	131	86	80	63	96
1998— Wichita (Texas)	10	5	.667	5.20	24	21	0	0	0	117 2/3	149	79	68	47	71
1999— Wichita (Texas)	0	0	...	5.06	14	0	0	0	7	21 1/3	23	12	12	10	18
— Omaha (PCL)...................	1	0	1.000	5.19	27	0	0	0	8	43 1/3	41	27	25	12	36
— Kansas City (A.L.)	1	0	1.000	8.74	13	0	0	0	0	11 1/3	23	12	11	6	0
Major League totals (1 year)	1	0	1.000	8.74	13	0	0	0	0	11 1/3	23	12	11	6	0

REBOULET, JEFF   IF   ROYALS

PERSONAL: Born April 30, 1964, in Dayton, Ohio. ... 6-0/175. ... Bats right, throws right. ... Full name: Jeffrey Allen Reboulet. ... Brother of Jim Reboulet, former second baseman in St. Louis Cardinals and Pittsburgh Pirates organizations. ... Name pronounced REB-uh-lay.
HIGH SCHOOL: Alter (Kettering, Ohio).
COLLEGE: Louisiana State.
TRANSACTIONS/CAREER NOTES: Selected by Houston Astros organization in 26th round of free-agent draft (June 3, 1985); did not sign. ... Selected by Minnesota Twins organization in 10th round of free-agent draft (June 2, 1986). ... Granted free agency (October 4, 1996). ... Signed by Baltimore Orioles organization (January 30, 1997). ... Traded by Orioles to Kansas City Royals for a player to be named later (December 12, 1999).
STATISTICAL NOTES: Led Southern League shortstops with 602 total chances in 1988. ... Led Pacific Coast League with 17 sacrifice hits in 1991. ... Led Pacific Coast League shortstops with 649 total chances and 99 double plays in 1991.

Year Team (League)	Pos.	G	AB	R	H	2B	3B	HR	RBI	Avg.	BB	SO	SB	PO	A	E	Avg.
1986—Visalia (Calif.)	SS	72	254	54	73	13	1	0	29	.287	54	33	14	118	188	20	.939
1987—Orlando (Sou.)	SS-2B-3B	129	422	52	108	15	1	1	35	.256	58	56	9	220	370	26	.958
1988—Orlando (Sou.)	SS	125	439	57	112	24	2	4	41	.255	53	55	18	*225	347	30	.950
—Portland (PCL)	2B-SS	4	12	0	1	0	0	0	1	.083	3	2	0	8	13	1	.955
1989—Portland (PCL)	SS-2B-3B-OF	26	65	9	16	1	0	0	3	.246	12	11	2	38	62	7	.935
—Orlando (Sou.)	SS-2B-OF	81	291	43	63	5	1	0	26	.216	49	33	11	129	228	22	.942
1990—Orlando (Sou.)	2-3-S-O-1	97	287	43	66	12	2	2	28	.230	57	37	10	131	230	12	.968
1991—Portland (PCL)	SS	134	391	50	97	27	3	3	46	.248	57	52	5	*202	415	*32	.951
1992—Portland (PCL)	SS	48	161	21	46	11	1	2	21	.286	35	18	3	72	141	7	.968
—Minnesota (A.L.)	S-3-2-O-DH	73	137	15	26	7	1	1	16	.190	23	26	3	71	163	5	.979
1993—Minnesota (A.L.)	S-3-2-O-DH	109	240	33	62	8	0	1	15	.258	35	37	5	122	215	6	.983
1994—Minnesota (A.L.)	S-2-1-3-O-DH	74	189	28	49	11	1	3	23	.259	18	23	0	150	131	7	.976
1995—Minnesota (A.L.)	S-3-1-2-C	87	216	39	63	11	0	4	23	.292	27	34	1	164	160	4	.988
1996—Minnesota (A.L.)	S-3-2-1-O-D	107	234	40	52	9	0	0	23	.222	25	34	4	138	114	2	.992
1997—Baltimore (A.L.)■	2B-SS-3B-OF	99	228	26	54	9	0	4	27	.237	23	44	3	106	163	7	.975
1998—Baltimore (A.L.)	2B-SS-3B	79	126	20	31	6	0	1	8	.246	19	34	0	51	120	6	.966
1999—Baltimore (A.L.)	3B-2B-SS	99	154	25	25	4	0	0	4	.162	33	29	1	79	152	2	.991
Major League totals (8 years)		727	1524	206	362	65	2	14	139	.238	203	261	17	881	1218	39	.982

DIVISION SERIES RECORD

Year Team (League)	Pos.	G	AB	R	H	2B	3B	HR	RBI	Avg.	BB	SO	SB	PO	A	E	Avg.
1997—Baltimore (A.L.)	2B	2	5	1	1	0	0	1	1	.200	0	2	0	2	3	0	1.000

CHAMPIONSHIP SERIES RECORD

Year Team (League)	Pos.	G	AB	R	H	2B	3B	HR	RBI	Avg.	BB	SO	SB	PO	A	E	Avg.
1997—Baltimore (A.L.)	SS-PR	1	2	1	0	0	0	0	0	.000	0	1	0	0	0	0	...

REDMAN, MARK   P   TWINS

PERSONAL: Born January 5, 1974, in San Diego. ... 6-5/220. ... Throws left, bats left. ... Full name: Mark Allen Redman.
HIGH SCHOOL: Escondido (Calif.).
COLLEGE: The Master's College (Calif.), then Oklahoma.
TRANSACTIONS/CAREER NOTES: Selected by Detroit Tigers organization in 41st round of free-agent draft (June 1, 1992); did not sign. ... Selected by Minnesota Twins organization in first round (13th pick overall) of free-agent draft (June 1, 1995). ... On Salt Lake disabled list (August 1-8, 1998). ... On Minnesota disabled list (July 25-August 10, 1999).

Year League	W	L	Pct.	ERA	G	GS	CG	ShO	Sv.	IP	H	R	ER	BB	SO
1995—Fort Myers (FSL)	2	1	.667	2.76	8	5	0	0	0	32²/₃	28	13	10	13	26
1996—Fort Myers (FSL)	3	4	.429	1.85	13	13	0	0	0	82²/₃	63	24	17	34	75
—New Britain (East.)	7	7	.500	3.81	16	16	3	0	0	106¹/₃	101	51	45	50	96
—Salt Lake (PCL)	0	0	...	9.00	1	1	0	0	0	4	7	4	4	2	4
1997—Salt Lake (PCL)	8	*15	.348	6.31	29	28	0	0	1	158¹/₃	204	*123	111	80	125
1998—New Britain (East.)	4	2	.667	1.52	8	8	0	0	0	47¹/₃	40	11	8	17	51
—Salt Lake (PCL)	6	7	.462	5.53	19	18	0	0	0	99¹/₃	111	75	61	41	88
1999—Salt Lake (PCL)	9	9	.500	5.05	24	24	1	0	0	133²/₃	141	87	75	51	114
—Minnesota (A.L.)	1	0	1.000	8.53	5	1	0	0	0	12²/₃	17	13	12	7	11
Major League totals (1 year)	1	0	1.000	8.53	5	1	0	0	0	12²/₃	17	13	12	7	11

REDMAN, TIKE   OF   PIRATES

PERSONAL: Born March 10, 1977, in Tuscaloosa, Ala. ... 5-11/166. ... Bats left, throws left. ... Full name: Julian Jawann Redman.
HIGH SCHOOL: Tuscaloosa (Ala.) Academy.
TRANSACTIONS/CAREER NOTES: Selected by Pittsburgh Pirates organization in fifth round of free-agent draft (June 4, 1996).

Year Team (League)	Pos.	G	AB	R	H	2B	3B	HR	RBI	Avg.	BB	SO	SB	PO	A	E	Avg.
1996—GC Pirates (GCL)	OF	26	104	20	31	4	1	1	16	.298	12	12	15	43	2	1	.978
—Erie (NY-P)	OF	43	170	31	50	4	6	2	21	.294	17	30	7	79	1	7	.920
1997—Lynchburg (Caro.)	OF-1B	125	415	55	104	18	5	4	45	.251	45	82	21	227	8	6	.975
1998—Lynchburg (Caro.)	OF	131	525	70	135	26	10	6	46	.257	32	73	36	263	7	8	.971
1999—Altoona (East.)	OF	136	532	84	143	20	*12	3	60	.269	52	52	29	301	12	9	.972

PERSONAL: Born May 5, 1971, in Seattle. ... 6-1/185. ... Bats right, throws right. ... Full name: Michael Patrick Redmond.
HIGH SCHOOL: Gonzaga Prep (Spokane, Wash.).
COLLEGE: Gonzaga.
TRANSACTIONS/CAREER NOTES: Signed as a non-drafted free agent by Florida Marlins organization (August 18, 1992). ... On Florida disabled list (August 24-September 8, 1998).
STATISTICAL NOTES: Led Eastern League catchers with 95 assists in 1995. ... Led Eastern League catchers with 906 total chances in 1996.

								BATTING								FIELDING		
Year	Team (League)	Pos.	G	AB	R	H	2B	3B	HR	RBI	Avg.	BB	SO	SB	PO	A	E	Avg.
1993—Kane County (Midw.)..		C	43	100	10	20	2	0	0	10	.200	6	17	2	213	26	1	.996
1994—Kane County (Midw.)..		C	92	306	39	83	10	0	1	24	.271	26	31	3	638	78	6	.992
—Brevard County (FSL).		C	12	42	4	11	4	0	0	2	.262	3	4	0	60	10	0	1.000
1995—Portland (East.).........		C-3B	105	333	37	85	11	1	3	39	.255	22	27	2	657	•95	6	.992
1996—Portland (East.).........		C	120	394	43	113	22	0	4	44	.287	26	45	3	*814	88	4	*.996
1997—Charlotte (I.L.)...........		C	22	61	8	13	5	1	1	2	.213	1	10	0	119	13	2	.985
—GC Marlins (GCL)......		DH	16	55	7	19	3	0	0	5	.345	9	5	2	...	...	...	...
—Brevard County (FSL).		1B	5	17	2	0	0	0	0	0	.000	2	2	0	8	0	0	1.000
1998—Portland (East.).........		C	8	28	7	9	4	0	1	7	.321	2	2	0	53	6	1	.983
—Charlotte (I.L.)...........		C	18	58	4	14	2	0	2	7	.241	0	3	0	101	20	0	1.000
—Florida (N.L.).............		C	37	118	10	39	9	0	2	12	.331	5	16	0	216	25	2	.992
1999—Florida (N.L.).............		C	84	242	22	73	9	0	1	27	.302	26	34	0	444	45	4	.992
Major League totals (2 years)			121	360	32	112	18	0	3	39	.311	31	50	0	660	70	6	.992

PERSONAL: Born November 12, 1962, in Joliet, Ill. ... 6-2/200. ... Bats left, throws right. ... Full name: Jeffrey Scott Reed. ... Brother of Curtis Reed, minor league outfielder (1977-84).
HIGH SCHOOL: West (Joliet, Ill.).
TRANSACTIONS/CAREER NOTES: Selected by Minnesota Twins organization in first round (12th pick overall) of free-agent draft (June 3, 1980). ... Traded by Twins with P Neal Heaton, P Al Cardwood and P Yorkis Perez to Montreal Expos for P Jeff Reardon and C Tom Nieto (February 3, 1987). ... On Montreal disabled list (April 20-May 25, 1987); included rehabilitation assignment to Indianapolis (May 19-25). ... Traded by Expos with OF Herm Winningham and P Randy St. Claire to Cincinnati Reds for OF Tracy Jones and P Pat Pacillo (July 13, 1988). ... On disabled list (July 1-19, 1991). ... On Cincinnati disabled list (April 26-September 1, 1992); included rehabilitation assignment to Nashville (August 17-September 1). ... Granted free agency (October 27, 1992). ... Signed by San Francisco Giants organization (January 15, 1993). ... On San Francisco disabled list (June 30-August 3, 1993); included rehabilitation assignment to San Jose (July 21-22 and July 30-August 3). ... Granted free agency (November 3, 1995). ... Signed by Colorado Rockies (December 18, 1995). ... Granted free agency (October 27, 1997). ... Re-signed by Rockies (November 18, 1997). ... Released by Rockies (July 2, 1999). ... Signed by Chicago Cubs (July 8, 1999).
RECORDS: Holds modern N.L. single-inning record for most errors by catcher—3 (July 28, 1987, seventh inning).
STATISTICAL NOTES: Led California League catchers with 758 total chances and tied for lead with nine double plays in 1982. ... Led Southern League catchers with 714 total chances and 12 double plays in 1983. ... Led International League catchers with 720 total chances in 1985. ... Career major league grand slams: 2.

								BATTING								FIELDING		
Year	Team (League)	Pos.	G	AB	R	H	2B	3B	HR	RBI	Avg.	BB	SO	SB	PO	A	E	Avg.
1980—Elizabethton (Appl.)....		C	65	225	39	64	15	1	1	20	.284	51	23	2	269	*41	9	.972
1981—Wisconsin (Mid.)........		C	106	312	63	73	12	1	4	34	.234	86	36	4	547	*93	7	.989
—Orlando (Sou.)		C	3	4	0	1	0	0	0	0	.250	1	0	0	4	1	0	1.000
1982—Visalia (Calif.)............		C	125	395	69	130	19	2	5	54	.329	78	32	1	*642	•106	10	.987
1983—Orlando (Sou.)		C	118	379	52	100	16	5	6	45	.264	76	40	2	*618	*88	8	*.989
—Toledo (I.L.)...............		C	14	41	5	7	1	1	0	3	.171	5	9	0	77	6	1	.988
1984—Minnesota (A.L.)		C	18	21	3	3	3	0	0	1	.143	2	6	0	41	2	1	.977
—Toledo (I.L.)...............		C	94	301	30	80	16	3	3	35	.266	37	35	1	546	43	5	*.992
1985—Toledo (I.L.)...............		C	122	404	53	100	15	3	5	36	.248	59	49	1	*627	*81	12	.983
—Minnesota (A.L.)		C	7	10	2	2	0	0	0	0	.200	0	3	0	9	3	0	1.000
1986—Minnesota (A.L.)		C	68	165	13	39	6	1	2	9	.236	16	19	1	332	19	2	.994
—Toledo (I.L.)...............		C	25	71	10	22	5	3	1	14	.310	17	9	0	108	22	2	.985
1987—Montreal (N.L.)■.......		C	75	207	15	44	11	0	1	21	.213	12	20	0	357	36	12	.970
—Indianapolis (A.A.)......		C	5	17	0	3	0	0	0	0	.176	1	2	0	27	2	0	1.000
1988—Montreal (N.L.)........		C	43	123	10	27	3	2	0	9	.220	13	22	1	197	20	1	.995
—Indianapolis (A.A.)......		C	8	22	1	7	3	0	0	1	.318	2	2	0	30	11	0	1.000
—Cincinnati (N.L.)■......		C	49	142	10	33	6	0	1	7	.232	15	19	0	271	18	2	.993
1989—Cincinnati (N.L.)........		C	102	287	16	64	11	0	3	23	.223	34	46	0	504	50	7	.988
1990—Cincinnati (N.L.)		C	72	175	12	44	8	1	3	16	.251	24	26	0	358	26	5	.987
1991—Cincinnati (N.L.)		C	91	270	20	72	15	2	3	31	.267	23	38	0	527	29	5	.991
1992—Nashville (A.A.)		C	14	25	1	6	1	0	1	2	.240	2	7	0	47	4	0	1.000
—Cincinnati (N.L.)		C	15	25	2	4	0	0	0	2	.160	1	4	0	29	2	0	1.000
1993—San Fran. (N.L.)■........		C	66	119	10	31	3	0	6	12	.261	16	22	0	180	14	0	1.000
—San Jose (Calif.)........		C	4	10	2	5	1	0	0	2	.500	1	0	0	19	2	0	1.000
1994—San Francisco (N.L.) ..		C	50	103	11	18	3	0	1	7	.175	11	21	0	138	9	1	.993
1995—San Francisco (N.L.) ..		C	66	113	12	30	2	0	0	9	.265	20	17	0	175	21	1	.995
1996—Colorado (N.L.)■........		C	116	341	34	97	20	1	8	37	.284	43	65	2	546	51	11	.982
1997—Colorado (N.L.)		C	90	256	43	76	10	0	17	47	.297	35	55	2	428	37	6	.987
1998—Colorado (N.L.)		C	113	259	43	75	17	1	9	39	.290	37	57	0	452	27	7	.986
1999—Colorado (N.L.)		C-DH	46	106	11	27	5	0	2	11	.255	17	24	0	160	15	3	.983
—Chicago (N.L.)■........		C-3B	57	150	18	39	11	2	1	17	.260	28	34	1	282	17	4	.987
American League totals (3 years)			93	196	18	44	9	1	2	10	.224	18	28	1	382	24	3	.993
National League totals (13 years)			1051	2676	267	681	125	9	55	288	.254	329	470	6	4604	372	65	.987
Major League totals (16 years)			1144	2872	285	725	134	10	57	298	.252	347	498	7	4986	396	68	.988

Year	Team (League)	Pos.	G	AB	R	H	2B	3B	HR	RBI	Avg.	BB	SO	SB	PO	A	E	Avg.
								BATTING									FIELDING	
1990— Cincinnati (N.L.)		C	4	7	0	0	0	0	0	0	.000	2	0	0	24	1	0	1.000

WORLD SERIES RECORD

NOTES: Member of World Series championship team (1990).

Year	Team (League)	Pos.	G	AB	R	H	2B	3B	HR	RBI	Avg.	BB	SO	SB	PO	A	E	Avg.
								BATTING									FIELDING	
1990— Cincinnati (N.L.)								Did not play.										

REED, RICK — P — METS

PERSONAL: Born August 16, 1965, in Huntington, W.Va. ... 6-1/195. ... Throws right, bats right. ... Full name: Richard Allen Reed.
HIGH SCHOOL: Huntington (W.Va.).
COLLEGE: Marshall.
TRANSACTIONS/CAREER NOTES: Selected by Pittsburgh Pirates organization in 26th round of free-agent draft (June 2, 1986). ... On Buffalo disabled list (May 2-13, 1991). ... Granted free agency (April 3, 1992). ... Signed by Kansas City Royals organization (April 4, 1992). ... Granted free agency (August 5, 1993). ... Signed by Texas Rangers organization (August 11, 1993). ... Claimed on waivers by Cincinnati Reds (May 13, 1994). ... On Indianapolis disabled list (May 29-June 9, 1995). ... Granted free agency (October 16, 1995). ... Signed by New York Mets organization (November 7, 1995). ... On New York disabled list (April 12-May 3 and August 9-September 4, 1999); included rehabilitation assignments to Norfolk (August 27-31) and Binghamton (September 1-4).
HONORS: Named American Association Most Valuable Pitcher (1991).
MISCELLANEOUS: Appeared in one game as outfielder with no chances (1999).

Year League	W	L	Pct.	ERA	G	GS	CG	ShO	Sv.	IP	H	R	ER	BB	SO
1986— Gulf Coast Pirates (GCL)	0	2	.000	3.75	8	3	0	0	0	24	20	12	10	6	15
— Macon (SAL)	0	0	...	2.84	1	1	0	0	0	6 1/3	5	3	2	2	1
1987— Macon (SAL)	8	4	.667	2.50	46	0	0	0	7	93 2/3	80	38	26	29	92
1988— Salem (Caro.)	6	2	.750	2.74	15	8	4	1	0	72 1/3	56	28	22	17	73
— Harrisburg (East.)..............	1	0	1.000	1.13	2	2	0	0	0	16	11	2	2	2	17
— Buffalo (A.A.)..................	5	2	.714	1.64	10	9	3	2	0	77	62	15	14	12	50
— Pittsburgh (N.L.)	1	0	1.000	3.00	2	2	0	0	0	12	10	4	4	2	6
1989— Buffalo (A.A.)■	9	8	.529	3.72	20	20	3	0	0	125 2/3	130	58	52	28	75
— Pittsburgh (N.L.)	1	4	.200	5.60	15	7	0	0	0	54 2/3	62	35	34	11	34
1990— Buffalo (A.A.)	7	4	.636	3.46	15	15	2	2	0	91	82	37	35	21	63
— Pittsburgh (N.L.)	2	3	.400	4.36	13	8	1	1	1	53 2/3	62	32	26	12	27
1991— Buffalo (A.A.)	*14	4	*.778	*2.15	25	25	•5	2	0	167 2/3	151	45	40	26	102
— Pittsburgh (N.L.)	0	0	...	10.38	1	1	0	0	0	4 1/3	8	6	5	1	2
1992— Omaha (A.A.)■	5	4	.556	4.35	11	10	3	0	1	62	67	33	30	12	35
— Kansas City (A.L.)	3	7	.300	3.68	19	18	1	1	0	100 1/3	105	47	41	20	49
1993— Omaha (A.A.)	11	4	.733	3.09	19	19	3	*2	0	128 1/3	116	48	44	14	58
— Kansas City (A.L.)	0	0	...	9.82	1	0	0	0	0	3 2/3	6	4	4	1	3
— Oklahoma City (A.A.)■........	1	3	.250	4.19	5	5	1	0	0	34 1/3	43	20	16	2	21
— Texas (A.L.)	1	0	1.000	2.25	2	0	0	0	0	4	6	1	1	1	2
1994— Oklahoma City (A.A.)	1	1	.500	3.86	2	2	0	0	0	11 2/3	10	5	5	0	8
— Texas (A.L.)	1	1	.500	5.94	4	3	0	0	0	16 2/3	17	13	11	7	12
— Indianapolis (A.A.)■	9	5	.643	4.68	21	21	3	1	0	140 1/3	162	80	73	19	79
1995— Indianapolis (A.A.)...........	11	4	.733	3.33	22	21	3	1	0	135	127	60	50	26	92
— Cincinnati (N.L.)	0	0	...	5.82	4	3	0	0	0	17	18	12	11	3	10
1996— Norfolk (I.L.)■	8	10	.444	3.16	28	28	1	0	0	182	164	72	64	33	128
1997— New York (N.L.)...............	13	9	.591	2.89	33	31	2	0	0	208 1/3	186	76	67	31	113
1998— New York (N.L.)...............	16	11	.593	3.48	31	31	2	1	0	212 1/3	208	84	82	29	153
1999— New York (N.L.)...............	11	5	.688	4.58	26	26	1	1	0	149 1/3	163	77	76	47	104
— Norfolk (I.L.)	0	1	.000	27.00	1	1	0	0	0	3	10	9	9	2	2
— Binghamton (East.)	0	0	...	1.80	1	1	0	0	0	5	1	1	1	1	5
A.L. totals (3 years)	5	8	.385	4.11	26	21	1	1	0	124 2/3	134	65	57	29	66
N.L. totals (8 years)	44	32	.579	3.86	125	109	6	3	1	711 2/3	717	326	305	136	449
Major League totals (11 years).....	49	40	.551	3.90	151	130	7	4	1	836 1/3	851	391	362	165	515

DIVISION SERIES RECORD

Year League	W	L	Pct.	ERA	G	GS	CG	ShO	Sv.	IP	H	R	ER	BB	SO
1999— New York (N.L.).................	1	0	1.000	3.00	1	1	0	0	0	6	4	2	2	3	2

CHAMPIONSHIP SERIES RECORD

Year League	W	L	Pct.	ERA	G	GS	CG	ShO	Sv.	IP	H	R	ER	BB	SO
1999— New York (N.L.).................	0	0	...	2.57	1	1	0	0	0	7	3	2	2	0	5

ALL-STAR GAME RECORD

Year League	W	L	Pct.	ERA	GS	CG	ShO	Sv.	IP	H	R	ER	BB	SO
1998— National							Did not play.							

REED, STEVE — P — INDIANS

PERSONAL: Born March 11, 1966, in Los Angeles. ... 6-2/212. ... Throws right, bats right. ... Full name: Steven Vincent Reed.
HIGH SCHOOL: Chatsworth (Calif.).
COLLEGE: Lewis-Clark State College (Idaho).
TRANSACTIONS/CAREER NOTES: Signed as non-drafted free agent by San Francisco Giants organization (June 24, 1988). ... On disabled list (July 17-August 13, 1990). ... Selected by Colorado Rockies in third round (60th pick overall) of expansion draft (November 17, 1992). ... Granted free agency (December 21, 1997). ... Signed by Giants (December 24, 1997). ... Traded by Giants with OF Jacob Cruz to Cleveland Indians for P Jose Mesa, IF Shawon Dunston and P Alvin Morman (July 23, 1998).

MISCELLANEOUS: Holds Colorado Rockies all-time record for lowest earned-run average (3.68).

Year League	W	L	Pct.	ERA	G	GS	CG	ShO	Sv.	IP	H	R	ER	BB	SO
1988—Pocatello (Pio.)..................	4	1	.800	2.54	31	0	0	0	*13	46	42	20	13	8	49
1989—Clinton (Midw.)	5	3	.625	1.05	60	0	0	0	26	94 2/3	54	16	11	38	104
—San Jose (Calif.).................	0	0	...	0.00	2	0	0	0	0	2	0	0	0	1	3
1990—Shreveport (Texas)............	3	1	.750	1.64	45	1	0	0	8	60 1/3	53	20	11	20	59
1991—Shreveport (Texas)............	2	0	1.000	0.83	15	0	0	0	7	21 2/3	17	2	2	3	26
—Phoenix (PCL).................	2	3	.400	4.31	41	0	0	0	6	56 1/3	62	33	27	12	46
1992—Shreveport (Texas)............	1	0	1.000	0.62	27	0	0	0	23	29	18	3	2	0	33
—Phoenix (PCL).................	0	1	.000	3.48	29	0	0	0	20	31	27	13	12	10	30
—San Francisco (N.L.)	1	0	1.000	2.30	18	0	0	0	0	15 2/3	13	5	4	3	11
1993—Colorado (N.L.)■..............	9	5	.643	4.48	64	0	0	0	3	84 1/3	80	47	42	30	51
—Colorado Springs (PCL)	0	0	...	0.00	11	0	0	0	7	12 1/3	8	1	0	3	10
1994—Colorado (N.L.)	3	2	.600	3.94	*61	0	0	0	3	64	79	33	28	26	51
1995—Colorado (N.L.)	5	2	.714	2.14	71	0	0	0	3	84	61	24	20	21	79
1996—Colorado (N.L.)	4	3	.571	3.96	70	0	0	0	0	75	66	38	33	19	51
1997—Colorado (N.L.)	4	6	.400	4.04	63	0	0	0	6	62 1/3	49	28	28	27	43
1998—San Francisco (N.L.)■	2	1	.667	1.48	50	0	0	0	1	54 2/3	30	10	9	19	50
—Cleveland (A.L.)■............	2	2	.500	6.66	20	0	0	0	0	25 2/3	26	19	19	8	23
1999—Cleveland (A.L.)	3	2	.600	4.23	63	0	0	0	0	61 2/3	69	33	29	20	44
A.L. totals (2 years)	5	4	.556	4.95	83	0	0	0	0	87 1/3	95	52	48	28	67
N.L. totals (7 years)	28	19	.596	3.35	397	0	0	0	16	440	378	185	164	145	336
Major League totals (8 years)	33	23	.589	3.62	480	0	0	0	16	527 1/3	473	237	212	173	403

DIVISION SERIES RECORD

Year League	W	L	Pct.	ERA	G	GS	CG	ShO	Sv.	IP	H	R	ER	BB	SO
1995—Colorado (N.L.)	0	0	...	0.00	3	0	0	0	0	2 2/3	2	0	0	1	3
1998—Cleveland (A.L.)	1	0	1.000	40.50	2	0	0	0	0	2/3	1	3	3	1	1
1999—Cleveland (A.L.)	0	0	...	30.86	2	0	0	0	0	2 1/3	9	8	8	1	1
Division series totals (3 years)	1	0	1.000	17.47	7	0	0	0	0	5 2/3	12	11	11	3	5

CHAMPIONSHIP SERIES RECORD

Year League	W	L	Pct.	ERA	G	GS	CG	ShO	Sv.	IP	H	R	ER	BB	SO
1998—Cleveland (A.L.).............	0	0	...	0.00	3	0	0	0	0	1 2/3	0	0	0	1	0

REESE, POKEY — 2B — REDS

PERSONAL: Born June 10, 1973, in Columbia, S.C. ... 5-11/180. ... Bats right, throws right. ... Full name: Calvin Reese Jr.
HIGH SCHOOL: Lower Richland (Hopkins, S.C.).
TRANSACTIONS/CAREER NOTES: Selected by Cincinnati Reds organization in first round (20th pick overall) of free-agent draft (June 3, 1991). ... On disabled list (June 23-July 25, 1995; September 17, 1996-remainder of season; and July 31, 1998-remainder of season).
RECORDS: Shares N.L. record for most errors by shortstop in opening game of season (nine-inning game) since 1900—4 (March 31, 1998).
HONORS: Won N.L. Gold Glove at second base (1999).

Year Team (League)	Pos.	G	AB	R	H	2B	3B	HR	RBI	Avg.	BB	SO	SB	PO	A	E	Avg.
1991—Princeton (Appl.)........	SS	62	231	30	55	8	3	3	27	.238	23	44	10	93	146	*31	.885
1992—Char., W.Va. (SAL)......	SS	106	380	50	102	19	3	6	53	.268	24	75	19	181	287	34	.932
1993—Chattanooga (Sou.)....	SS	102	345	35	73	17	4	3	37	.212	23	77	8	181	300	25	.951
1994—Chattanooga (Sou.)....	SS	134	484	77	130	23	4	12	49	.269	43	75	21	*221	362	38	.939
1995—Indianapolis (A.A.)......	SS	89	343	51	82	21	1	10	46	.239	36	81	8	131	258	27	.935
1996—Indianapolis (A.A.)......	SS-3B	79	280	26	65	16	0	1	23	.232	21	46	5	131	239	22	.944
1997—Cincinnati (N.L.)	SS-2B-3B	128	397	48	87	15	0	4	26	.219	31	82	25	182	284	15	.969
—Indianapolis (A.A.)......	SS-2B	17	72	12	17	2	0	4	11	.236	9	12	4	43	42	3	.966
1998—Cincinnati (N.L.)	3B-2B	59	133	20	34	2	2	1	16	.256	14	28	3	50	78	8	.941
1999—Cincinnati (N.L.)	2B-SS	149	585	85	167	37	5	10	52	.285	35	81	38	340	425	7	.991
Major League totals (3 years)		336	1115	153	288	54	7	15	94	.258	80	191	66	572	787	30	.978

REICHERT, DAN — P — ROYALS

PERSONAL: Born July 12, 1976, in Monterey, Calif. ... 6-3/175. ... Throws right, bats right. ... Full name: Daniel Robert Reichert.
HIGH SCHOOL: Turlock (Calif.).
COLLEGE: Pacific.
TRANSACTIONS/CAREER NOTES: Selected by Kansas City Royals organization in first round (seventh pick overall) of free-agent draft (June 3, 1997). ... On Kansas City disabled list (August 25, 1999-remainder of season).

Year League	W	L	Pct.	ERA	G	GS	CG	ShO	Sv.	IP	H	R	ER	BB	SO
1997—Spokane (N.W.)	3	4	.429	2.84	9	9	0	0	0	38	40	25	12	16	39
1998—Wichita (Texas)	1	4	.200	9.75	8	8	0	0	0	36	52	40	39	29	24
—Lansing (Midw.)	1	1	.500	3.28	13	6	0	0	0	35 2/3	25	16	13	20	35
—Wilmington (Caro.).............	2	0	1.000	3.21	2	2	0	0	0	14	13	5	5	4	10
—Omaha (PCL)....................	1	1	.500	4.67	3	3	0	0	0	17 1/3	14	10	9	2	11
1999—Omaha (PCL)....................	9	2	.818	3.71	17	17	1	0	0	111 2/3	92	51	46	50	123
—Kansas City (A.L.)	2	2	.500	9.08	8	8	0	0	0	36 2/3	48	38	37	32	20
Major League totals (1 year).........	2	2	.500	9.08	8	8	0	0	0	36 2/3	48	38	37	32	20

REITSMA, CHRIS — P — DEVIL RAYS

PERSONAL: Born December 31, 1977, in Minneapolis. ... 6-5/214. ... Throws right, bats right. ... Full name: Christopher Michael Reitsma.
HIGH SCHOOL: Calgary (Alta.) Christian.

TRANSACTIONS/CAREER NOTES: Selected by Boston Red Sox organization as "sandwich pick" between first and second round of free-agent draft (June 4, 1996); pick received as compensation for Toronto Blue Jays signing P Erik Hanson. ... On disabled list (June 5-September 8, 1997). ... On Sarasota disabled list (April 8-May 3, 1999). ... Selected by Tampa Bay Devil Rays from Red Sox organization in Rule 5 major league draft (December 13, 1999).

Year League	W	L	Pct.	ERA	G	GS	CG	ShO	Sv.	IP	H	R	ER	BB	SO
1996— Gulf Coast Red Sox (GCL)..	3	1	.750	1.35	7	6	0	0	0	$26^2/_3$	24	7	4	1	32
1997— Michigan (Midw.)	4	1	.800	2.90	9	9	0	0	0	$49^2/_3$	57	23	16	13	41
1998— Sarasota (FSL)	0	0	...	2.84	8	8	0	0	0	$12^2/_3$	12	6	4	5	9
1999— Sarasota (FSL)	4	10	.286	5.61	19	19	0	0	0	$96^1/_3$	116	71	60	31	79

REKAR, BRYAN   P   DEVIL RAYS

R

PERSONAL: Born June 3, 1972, in Oak Lawn, Ill. ... 6-3/210. ... Throws right, bats right. ... Full name: Bryan Robert Rekar. ... Cousin of Pete Bercich, linebacker, Minnesota Vikings; and nephew of Bob Bercich, defensive back with Dallas Cowboys (1960 and 1961).
HIGH SCHOOL: Providence Catholic (New Lenox, Ill.).
COLLEGE: Bradley.
TRANSACTIONS/CAREER NOTES: Selected by Colorado Rockies organization in second round of free-agent draft (June 3, 1993). ... Selected by Tampa Bay Devil Rays in second round (38th pick overall) of expansion draft (November 18, 1997). ... On Tampa Bay disabled list (March 19-July 6, 1998); included rehabilitation assignments to St. Petersburg (May 16-25 and June 25-July 4) and Durham (May 26-June 1 and July 4-6).

Year League	W	L	Pct.	ERA	G	GS	CG	ShO	Sv.	IP	H	R	ER	BB	SO
1993— Bend (N.W.)......................	3	5	.375	4.08	13	13	1	0	0	75	81	36	34	18	59
1994— Central Valley (Calif.)..........	6	6	.500	3.48	22	19	0	0	0	$111^1/_3$	120	52	43	31	91
1995— New Haven (East.)..............	6	3	.667	2.13	12	12	1	1	0	$80^1/_3$	65	28	19	16	80
— Colorado Springs (PCL)	4	2	.667	1.49	7	7	2	1	0	$48^1/_3$	29	10	8	13	39
— Colorado (N.L.)	4	6	.400	4.98	15	14	1	0	0	85	95	51	47	24	60
1996— Colorado Springs (PCL)	8	8	.500	4.46	19	19	0	0	0	123	138	68	61	36	75
— Colorado (N.L.)	2	4	.333	8.95	14	11	0	0	0	$58^1/_3$	87	61	58	26	25
1997— Colorado Springs (PCL)	10	9	.526	5.46	28	25	0	0	0	145	169	96	88	39	116
— Colorado (N.L.)	1	0	1.000	5.79	2	2	0	0	0	$9^1/_3$	11	7	6	6	4
1998— St. Petersburg (FSL)■	0	0	...	0.69	4	4	0	0	0	13	6	2	1	2	15
— Durham (I.L.)	0	1	.000	3.27	3	3	0	0	0	11	10	4	4	2	9
— Tampa Bay (A.L.)................	2	8	.200	4.98	16	15	1	0	0	$86^2/_3$	95	56	48	21	55
1999— Durham (I.L.)	4	1	.800	3.86	6	5	0	0	0	35	29	15	15	8	26
— Tampa Bay (A.L.)................	6	6	.500	5.80	27	12	0	0	0	$94^2/_3$	121	68	61	41	55
A.L. totals (2 years)	8	14	.364	5.41	43	27	1	0	0	$181^1/_3$	216	124	109	62	110
N.L. totals (3 years)	7	10	.412	6.54	31	27	1	0	0	$152^2/_3$	193	119	111	56	89
Major League totals (5 years).......	15	24	.385	5.93	74	54	2	0	0	334	409	243	220	118	199

RELAFORD, DESI   SS   PHILLIES

PERSONAL: Born September 16, 1973, in Valdosta, Ga. ... 5-9/174. ... Bats both, throws right. ... Full name: Desmond Lamont Relaford.
HIGH SCHOOL: Sandalwood (Jacksonville).
TRANSACTIONS/CAREER NOTES: Selected by Seattle Mariners organization in fourth round of free-agent draft (June 3, 1991). ... Traded by Mariners to Philadelphia Phillies for P Terry Mulholland (July 31, 1996). ... On Philadelphia disabled list (June 17-September 13, 1999); included rehabilitation assignment to Clearwater (September 4-13).
STATISTICAL NOTES: Led California League shortstops with 601 total chances in 1992. ... Led Southern League shortstops with 35 errors in 1993. ... Led International League shortstops with 587 total chances and 81 double plays in 1997.

							BATTING							FIELDING		
Year Team (League)	Pos.	G	AB	R	H	2B	3B	HR	RBI	Avg.	BB	SO	SB	PO	A	E	Avg.
1991— Ariz. Mariners (Ariz.)..	SS-2B	46	163	36	44	7	3	0	18	.270	22	24	17	58	126	24	.885
1992— Peninsula (Caro.)	SS	130	445	53	96	18	1	3	34	.216	39	88	27	167	*382	*52	.913
1993— Jacksonville (Sou.).....	SS-2B-3B	133	472	49	115	16	4	8	47	.244	50	103	16	157	386	†38	.935
1994— Jacksonville (Sou.)......	SS	37	143	24	29	7	3	3	11	.203	22	28	10	71	119	4	.979
— Riverside (Calif.)........	SS	99	374	95	116	27	5	5	59	.310	78	78	27	125	296	36	.921
1995— Port City (Sou.)	SS-2B-DH	90	352	51	101	11	2	7	27	.287	41	58	25	134	276	31	.930
— Tacoma (PCL)	2B-SS	30	113	20	27	5	1	2	7	.239	13	24	6	52	93	6	.960
1996— Tacoma (PCL)	2B-SS-DH	93	317	27	65	12	0	4	32	.205	23	58	10	174	306	20	.960
— Scran./W.B. (I.L.)■ ...	SS	21	85	12	20	4	1	1	11	.235	8	19	7	25	65	6	.938
— Philadelphia (N.L.).......	SS-2B	15	40	2	7	2	0	0	1	.175	3	9	1	21	26	2	.959
1997— Scranton/W.B. (I.L.) ...	SS	131	517	82	138	34	4	9	53	.267	43	77	29	180	*373	34	.942
— Philadelphia (N.L.)......	SS	15	38	3	7	1	2	0	6	.184	5	6	3	12	31	1	.977
1998— Philadelphia (N.L.)......	SS	142	494	45	121	25	3	5	41	.245	33	87	9	189	380	24	.960
1999— Philadelphia (N.L.)......	SS	65	211	31	51	11	2	1	26	.242	19	34	4	97	182	14	.952
— Clearwater (FSL)	SS	2	7	1	2	0	0	0	1	.286	1	1	0	3	1	1	.800
Major League totals (4 years)		237	783	81	186	39	7	6	74	.238	60	136	17	319	619	41	.958

REMLINGER, MIKE   P   BRAVES

PERSONAL: Born March 23, 1966, in Middletown, N.Y. ... 6-1/210. ... Throws left, bats left. ... Full name: Michael John Remlinger. ... Name pronounced REM-lynn-jer.
HIGH SCHOOL: Carver (Plymouth, Mass.).
COLLEGE: Dartmouth.
TRANSACTIONS/CAREER NOTES: Selected by San Francisco Giants organization in first round (16th pick overall) of free-agent draft (June 2, 1987). ... On disabled list (April 30, 1988-remainder of season). ... Traded by Giants with OF Kevin Mitchell to Seattle Mariners for P Bill Swift, P Mike Jackson and P Dave Burba (December 11, 1991). ... On Jacksonville disabled list (July 30, 1992-remainder of season). ... Granted free agency (October 15, 1993). ... Signed by New York Mets organization (November 22, 1993). ... Traded by Mets to Cincinnati Reds for OF Cobi Cradle (May 11, 1995). ... Granted free agency (October 6, 1995). ... Re-signed by Reds (October 22, 1995). ... Traded by Reds to Kansas City Royals as part of a three-team deal in which Reds sent SS Luis Ordaz to St. Louis Cardinals for OF Andre King. Royals then sent OF Miguel Mejia to Cardinals to complete deal (December 4, 1995). ... Claimed on waivers by Reds (April 4, 1996). ... Traded by Reds with 2B Bret Boone to Atlanta Braves for P Denny Neagle, OF Michael Tucker and P Rob Bell (November 10, 1998). ... On disabled list (April 3-18, 1999).

RECORDS: Shares major league record for pitching shutout in first major league game (June 15, 1991).
STATISTICAL NOTES: Led American Association with 18 wild pitches in 1996. ... Led N.L. with 12 wild pitches in 1997.
MISCELLANEOUS: Appeared in two games as pinch runner (1997).

Year	League	W	L	Pct.	ERA	G	GS	CG	ShO	Sv.	IP	H	R	ER	BB	SO
1987—	Everett (N.W.)...................	0	0	...	3.60	2	1	0	0	0	5	1	2	2	5	11
—	Clinton (Midw.)	2	1	.667	3.30	6	5	0	0	0	30	21	12	11	14	43
—	Shreveport (Texas)...........	4	2	.667	2.36	6	6	0	0	0	34⅓	14	11	9	22	51
1988—	Shreveport (Texas)...........	1	0	1.000	0.69	3	3	0	0	0	13	7	4	1	4	18
1989—	Shreveport (Texas)...........	4	6	.400	2.98	16	16	0	0	0	90⅔	68	43	30	73	92
—	Phoenix (PCL)..................	1	6	.143	9.21	11	10	0	0	0	43	51	47	44	52	28
1990—	Shreveport (Texas)...........	9	11	.450	3.90	25	25	2	1	0	147⅔	149	82	64	72	75
1991—	Phoenix (PCL)..................	5	5	.500	6.38	19	19	1	1	0	108⅔	134	86	77	59	68
—	San Francisco (N.L.)	2	1	.667	4.37	8	6	1	1	0	35	36	17	17	20	19
1992—	Calgary (PCL)■.................	1	7	.125	6.65	21	11	0	0	0	70⅓	97	65	52	48	24
—	Jacksonville (Sou.)............	1	1	.500	3.46	5	5	0	0	0	26	25	15	10	11	21
1993—	Calgary (PCL)	4	3	.571	5.53	19	18	0	0	0	84⅔	100	57	52	52	51
—	Jacksonville (Sou.)............	1	3	.250	6.58	7	7	0	0	0	39⅔	40	30	29	19	23
1994—	Norfolk (I.L.)■.................	2	4	.333	3.14	12	9	0	0	0	63	57	29	22	25	45
—	New York (N.L.)..............	1	5	.167	4.61	10	9	0	0	0	54⅔	55	30	28	35	33
1995—	New York (N.L.)...............	0	1	.000	6.35	5	0	0	0	0	5⅔	7	5	4	2	6
—	Cincinnati (N.L.)■.............	0	0	...	9.00	2	0	0	0	0	1	2	1	1	3	1
—	Indianapolis (A.A.).............	5	3	.625	4.05	41	1	0	0	0	46⅔	40	24	21	32	58
1996—	Indianapolis (A.A.).............	4	3	.571	2.52	28	13	0	0	0	89⅓	64	29	25	44	97
—	Cincinnati (N.L.)..............	0	1	.000	5.60	19	4	0	0	0	27⅓	24	17	17	19	19
1997—	Cincinnati (N.L.)..............	8	8	.500	4.14	69	12	2	0	2	124	100	61	57	60	145
1998—	Cincinnati (N.L.)..............	8	15	.348	4.82	35	28	1	1	0	164⅓	164	96	88	87	144
1999—	Atlanta (N.L.)■.................	10	1	.909	2.37	73	0	0	0	1	83⅔	66	24	22	35	81
Major League totals (7 years)		**29**	**32**	**.475**	**4.25**	**221**	**59**	**4**	**2**	**3**	**495⅔**	**454**	**251**	**234**	**261**	**448**

DIVISION SERIES RECORD

Year	League	W	L	Pct.	ERA	G	GS	CG	ShO	Sv.	IP	H	R	ER	BB	SO
1999—	Atlanta (N.L.).....................	0	0	...	9.82	2	0	0	0	0	3⅔	4	4	4	3	4

CHAMPIONSHIP SERIES RECORD

Year	League	W	L	Pct.	ERA	G	GS	CG	ShO	Sv.	IP	H	R	ER	BB	SO
1999—	Atlanta (N.L.).....................	0	1	.000	3.18	5	0	0	0	0	5⅔	3	2	2	3	4

WORLD SERIES RECORD

Year	League	W	L	Pct.	ERA	G	GS	CG	ShO	Sv.	IP	H	R	ER	BB	SO
1999—	Atlanta (N.L.).....................	0	1	.000	9.00	2	0	0	0	0	1	1	1	1	1	0

RENTERIA, EDGAR   SS   CARDINALS

PERSONAL: Born August 7, 1975, in Barranquilla, Colombia. ... 6-1/180. ... Bats right, throws right. ... Full name: Edgar Enrique Renteria. ... Brother of Edinson Renteria, infielder with Houston Astros and Florida Marlins organizations (1985-94).
HIGH SCHOOL: Instituto Los Alpes (Barranquilla, Colombia).
TRANSACTIONS/CAREER NOTES: Signed as non-drafted free agent by Florida Marlins organization (February 14, 1992). ... On Florida disabled list (June 24-July 11, 1996); included rehabilitation assignment to Charlotte (July 3-11). ... On disabled list (August 25-September 9, 1998). ... Traded by Marlins to St. Louis Cardinals for P Braden Looper, P Armando Almanza and SS Pablo Ozuna (December 14, 1998).
STATISTICAL NOTES: Had 22-game hitting streak (July 25-August 16, 1996). ... Led N.L. with 19 sacrifice hits in 1997. ... Led N.L. in caught stealing with 22 in 1998.

Year	Team (League)	Pos.	G	AB	R	H	2B	3B	HR	RBI	Avg.	BB	SO	SB	PO	A	E	Avg.
1992—	GC Marlins (GCL).......	SS	43	163	25	47	8	1	0	9	.288	8	29	10	56	152	*24	.897
1993—	Kane County (Midw.)..	SS	116	384	40	78	8	0	1	35	.203	35	94	7	•173	306	34	.934
1994—	Brevard County (FSL).	SS	128	439	46	111	15	1	0	36	.253	35	56	6	167	372	23	.959
1995—	Portland (East.).........	SS	135	508	70	147	15	7	7	46	.289	32	85	30	179	379	33	.944
1996—	Charlotte (I.L.)...........	SS	35	132	17	37	8	0	2	16	.280	9	17	10	48	114	7	.959
—	Florida (N.L.).............	SS	106	431	68	133	18	3	5	31	.309	33	68	16	163	344	11	.979
1997—	Florida (N.L.).............	SS	154	617	90	171	21	3	4	52	.277	45	108	32	*242	415	17	.975
1998—	Florida (N.L.).............	SS	133	517	79	146	18	2	3	31	.282	48	78	41	194	372	20	.966
1999—	St. Louis (N.L.)■	SS	154	585	92	161	36	2	11	63	.275	53	82	37	219	393	26	.959
Major League totals (4 years)			547	2150	329	611	93	10	23	177	.284	179	336	126	818	1524	74	.969

DIVISION SERIES RECORD

Year	Team (League)	Pos.	G	AB	R	H	2B	3B	HR	RBI	Avg.	BB	SO	SB	PO	A	E	Avg.
1997—	Florida (N.L.).............	SS	3	13	1	2	0	0	0	1	.154	2	4	0	9	11	2	.909

CHAMPIONSHIP SERIES RECORD

Year	Team (League)	Pos.	G	AB	R	H	2B	3B	HR	RBI	Avg.	BB	SO	SB	PO	A	E	Avg.
1997—	Florida (N.L.).............	SS	6	22	4	5	1	0	0	0	.227	3	6	1	14	15	0	1.000

WORLD SERIES RECORD

RECORDS: Holds record for most strikeouts in one inning—2 (October 23, 1997, sixth inning).
NOTES: Member of World Series championship team (1997).

Year	Team (League)	Pos.	G	AB	R	H	2B	3B	HR	RBI	Avg.	BB	SO	SB	PO	A	E	Avg.
1997—	Florida (N.L.).............	SS	7	31	3	9	2	0	0	3	.290	3	5	0	12	26	1	.974

ALL-STAR GAME RECORD

Year	League	Pos.	AB	R	H	2B	3B	HR	RBI	Avg.	BB	SO	SB	PO	A	E	Avg.
1998—	National.....................	SS	1	1	0	0	0	0	0	.000	0	0	0	0	3	0	1.000

REYES, AL   P   ORIOLES

PERSONAL: Born April 10, 1971, in San Cristobal, Dominican Republic. ... 6-1/208. ... Throws right, bats right. ... Full name: Rafael Alberto Reyes.
HIGH SCHOOL: Francisco del Rosario Sanche (Santo Domingo, Dominican Republic).
TRANSACTIONS/CAREER NOTES: Signed as non-drafted free agent by Montreal Expos organization (February 17, 1988). ... On disabled list (May 23, 1991-remainder of season). ... Selected by Milwaukee Brewers from Expos organization in Rule 5 major league draft (December 5, 1994). ... On disabled list (July 19, 1995-remainder of season). ... On New Orleans disabled list (April 4-August 2, 1996). ... On Milwaukee disabled list (July 25-September 8, 1998); included rehabilitation assignment to Louisville (September 1-8). ... Traded by Brewers to Baltimore Orioles (July 21, 1999), completing deal in which Orioles traded P Rocky Coppinger to Brewers for a player to be named later (July 16, 1999).

Year League	W	L	Pct.	ERA	G	GS	CG	ShO	Sv.	IP	H	R	ER	BB	SO
1989— Dom. Expos (DSL)	3	4	.429	2.79	12	10	1	0	0	71	68	36	22	33	49
1990— West Palm Beach (FSL)	5	4	.556	4.74	16	10	0	0	1	57	58	32	30	32	47
1991— Rockford (Midw.)	0	1	.000	5.56	3	3	0	0	0	11 1/3	14	8	7	2	10
1992— Albany (SAL)	0	2	.000	3.95	27	0	0	0	4	27 1/3	24	14	12	13	29
1993— Burlington (Midw.)	7	6	.538	2.68	53	0	0	0	11	74	52	33	22	26	80
1994— Harrisburg (East.)	2	2	.500	3.25	60	0	0	0	*35	69 1/3	68	26	25	13	60
1995— Milwaukee (A.L.)■	1	1	.500	2.43	27	0	0	0	1	33 1/3	19	9	9	18	29
1996— Beloit (Midw.)	1	0	1.000	1.83	13	0	0	0	0	19 2/3	17	7	4	6	22
— Milwaukee (A.L.)	1	0	1.000	7.94	5	0	0	0	0	5 2/3	8	5	5	2	2
1997— Tucson (PCL)	2	4	.333	5.02	38	0	0	0	7	57 1/3	52	39	32	34	70
— Milwaukee (A.L.)	1	2	.333	5.46	19	0	0	0	1	29 2/3	32	19	18	9	28
1998— Milwaukee (N.L.)	5	1	.833	3.95	50	0	0	0	0	57	55	26	25	31	58
— Louisville (I.L.)	0	1	.000	8.31	3	2	0	0	0	4 1/3	5	5	4	2	5
1999— Louisville (I.L.)	0	2	.000	8.38	6	0	0	0	0	9 2/3	12	9	9	7	8
— Milwaukee (N.L.)	2	0	1.000	4.25	26	0	0	0	0	36	27	17	17	25	39
— Baltimore (A.L.)■	2	3	.400	4.85	27	0	0	0	0	29 2/3	23	16	16	16	28
A.L. totals (4 years)	5	6	.455	4.39	78	0	0	0	2	98 1/3	82	49	48	45	87
N.L. totals (2 years)	7	1	.875	4.06	76	0	0	0	0	93	82	43	42	56	97
Major League totals (5 years)	12	7	.632	4.23	154	0	0	0	2	191 1/3	164	92	90	101	184

REYES, CARLOS   P   PHILLIES

PERSONAL: Born April 4, 1969, in Miami. ... 6-0/190. ... Throws right, bats both. ... Full name: Carlos Alberto Reyes.
HIGH SCHOOL: Tampa Catholic.
JUNIOR COLLEGE: Brevard Community College (Fla.).
COLLEGE: Florida Southern.
TRANSACTIONS/CAREER NOTES: Signed as non-drafted free agent by Atlanta Braves organization (June 21, 1991). ... Selected by Oakland Athletics from Braves organization in Rule 5 major league draft (December 13, 1993). ... On Oakland disabled list (July 18-August 4, 1994); included rehabilitation assignment to Modesto (July 25-30). ... Granted free agency (December 20, 1996). ... Signed by New York Yankees organization (February 6, 1997). ... Released by Yankees (April 9, 1997). ... Signed by Athletics (April 10, 1997). ... On Oakland disabled list (August 21-September 12, 1997); included rehabilitation assignment to Edmonton (September 3-12). ... Granted free agency (October 15, 1997). ... Signed by San Diego Padres (November 7, 1997). ... Traded by Padres with P Dario Veras and C Mandy Romero to Boston Red Sox for C Jim Leyritz and OF Ethan Faggett (June 21, 1998). ... Released by Red Sox (December 14, 1998). ... Signed by Padres organization (February 4, 1999). ... Claimed on waivers by Philadelphia Phillies (October 6, 1999).

Year League	W	L	Pct.	ERA	G	GS	CG	ShO	Sv.	IP	H	R	ER	BB	SO
1991— Gulf Coast Braves (GCL)	3	2	.600	1.77	20	0	0	0	5	45 2/3	44	15	9	9	37
1992— Macon (SAL)	2	3	.400	2.10	23	0	0	0	2	60	57	16	14	11	57
— Durham (Caro.)	2	1	.667	2.43	21	0	0	0	5	40 2/3	31	11	11	10	33
1993— Greenville (Sou.)	8	1	.889	2.06	33	2	0	0	2	70	64	22	16	24	57
— Richmond (I.L.)	1	0	1.000	3.77	18	1	0	0	1	28 2/3	30	12	12	11	30
1994— Oakland (A.L.)■	0	3	.000	4.15	27	9	0	0	1	78	71	38	36	44	57
— Modesto (Calif.)	0	0	...	0.00	3	3	0	0	0	5	2	0	0	0	3
1995— Oakland (A.L.)	4	6	.400	5.09	40	1	0	0	1	69	71	43	39	28	48
1996— Oakland (A.L.)	7	10	.412	4.78	46	10	0	0	0	122 1/3	134	71	65	61	78
1997— Columbus (I.L.)■	0	0	...	18.00	1	1	0	0	0	2	5	4	4	0	2
— Edmonton (PCL)■	2	0	1.000	3.48	5	4	1	0	0	31	30	14	12	3	23
— Oakland (A.L.)	3	4	.429	5.82	37	6	0	0	0	77 1/3	101	52	50	25	43
1998— Las Vegas (PCL)■	0	0	...	0.00	1	0	0	0	0	1 2/3	1	0	0	0	2
— San Diego (N.L.)■	2	2	.500	3.58	22	0	0	0	1	27 2/3	23	11	11	6	24
— Boston (A.L.)■	1	1	.500	3.52	24	0	0	0	0	38 1/3	35	15	15	14	23
1999— San Diego (N.L.)■	2	4	.333	3.72	65	0	0	0	1	77 1/3	76	38	32	24	57
A.L. totals (5 years)	15	24	.385	4.79	174	26	0	0	1	385	412	219	205	172	249
N.L. totals (2 years)	4	6	.400	3.69	87	0	0	0	2	105	99	49	43	30	81
Major League totals (6 years)	19	30	.388	4.56	261	26	0	0	3	490	511	268	248	202	330

REYES, DENNYS   P   REDS

PERSONAL: Born April 19, 1977, in Higuera de Zaragoza, Mexico. ... 6-3/246. ... Throws left, bats left.
HIGH SCHOOL: Ignacio Zaragoza (Higuera de Zaragoza, Mexico).
TRANSACTIONS/CAREER NOTES: Signed as non-drafted free agent by Los Angeles Dodgers organization (July 5, 1993). ... Traded by Dodgers with 1B/3B Paul Konerko to Cincinnati Reds for P Jeff Shaw (July 4, 1998).

Year League	W	L	Pct.	ERA	G	GS	CG	ShO	Sv.	IP	H	R	ER	BB	SO
1994— Vero Beach (FSL)	2	4	.333	6.70	9	9	0	0	0	41 2/3	58	37	31	18	25
— Great Falls (Pio.)	7	1	.875	3.78	14	9	0	0	0	66 2/3	71	37	28	25	70
1995— Vero Beach (FSL)	1	0	1.000	1.80	3	2	0	0	0	10	8	2	2	6	9
— M.C. Red Devils (Mex.)■ ...	5	5	.500	6.60	17	15	1	0	0	58 2/3	76	49	43	41	44
1996— San Bernardino (Calif.)■ ...	11	12	.478	4.17	29	•28	0	0	0	166	166	106	77	77	176

Year League	W	L	Pct.	ERA	G	GS	CG	ShO	Sv.	IP	H	R	ER	BB	SO
1997—San Antonio (Texas)	8	1	.889	3.02	12	12	1	0	0	80 1/3	79	33	27	28	66
—Albuquerque (PCL)............	6	3	.667	5.65	10	10	1	0	0	57 1/3	70	40	36	33	45
—Los Angeles (N.L.)	2	3	.400	3.83	14	5	0	0	0	47	51	21	20	18	36
1998—Albuquerque (PCL)............	1	4	.200	1.44	7	7	1	1	0	43 2/3	31	13	7	18	58
—Los Angeles (N.L.)	0	4	.000	4.71	11	3	0	0	0	28 2/3	27	17	15	20	33
—Indianapolis (I.L.)■.............	2	0	1.000	3.00	4	4	0	0	0	24	20	10	8	14	27
—Cincinnati (N.L.)	3	1	.750	4.42	8	7	0	0	0	38 2/3	35	19	19	27	44
1999—Cincinnati (N.L.)	2	2	.500	3.79	65	1	0	0	2	61 2/3	53	30	26	39	72
Major League totals (3 years)......	7	10	.412	4.09	98	16	0	0	2	176	166	87	80	104	185

REYNOLDS, SHANE   P   ASTROS

R

PERSONAL: Born March 26, 1968, in Bastrop, La. ... 6-3/210. ... Throws right, bats right. ... Full name: Richard Shane Reynolds.
HIGH SCHOOL: Ouachita Christian (Monroe, La.).
JUNIOR COLLEGE: Faulkner State Junior College (Ala.).
COLLEGE: Texas.
TRANSACTIONS/CAREER NOTES: Selected by Houston Astros organization in third round of free-agent draft (June 5, 1989). ... On Houston disabled list (June 10-July 14, 1997); included rehabilitation assignment to New Orleans (July 10-14).
STATISTICAL NOTES: Led N.L. with 17 sacrifice hits in 1999. ... Led N.L. pitchers with a 1.000 fielding percentage in 1999.
MISCELLANEOUS: Appeared in one game as pinch runner (1995).

Year League	W	L	Pct.	ERA	G	GS	CG	ShO	Sv.	IP	H	R	ER	BB	SO
1989—Auburn (NY-P)...................	3	2	.600	2.31	6	6	1	0	0	35	36	16	9	14	23
—Asheville (SAL).................	5	3	.625	3.68	8	8	2	1	0	51 1/3	53	25	21	21	33
1990—Columbus (Sou.)................	9	10	.474	4.81	29	27	2	1	0	155 1/3	•181	104	83	70	92
1991—Jackson (Texas)...............	8	9	.471	4.47	27	•27	2	0	0	151	165	93	75	62	116
1992—Tucson (PCL)	9	8	.529	3.68	25	22	2	0	1	142	156	73	58	34	106
—Houston (N.L.)	1	3	.250	7.11	8	5	0	0	0	25 1/3	42	22	20	6	10
1993—Tucson (PCL)	10	6	.625	3.62	25	20	2	0	1	139 1/3	147	74	56	21	106
—Houston (N.L.)	0	0	...	0.82	5	1	0	0	0	11	11	4	1	6	10
1994—Houston (N.L.)	8	5	.615	3.05	33	14	1	1	0	124	128	46	42	21	110
1995—Houston (N.L.)	10	11	.476	3.47	30	30	3	2	0	189 1/3	196	87	73	37	175
1996—Houston (N.L.)	16	10	.615	3.65	35	35	4	1	0	239	227	103	97	44	204
1997—Houston (N.L.)	9	10	.474	4.23	30	30	2	0	0	181	189	92	85	47	152
—New Orleans (A.A.)............	1	0	1.000	0.00	1	1	0	0	0	5	3	0	0	1	6
1998—Houston (N.L.)	19	8	.704	3.51	35	•35	3	1	0	233 1/3	257	99	91	53	209
1999—Houston (N.L.)	16	14	.533	3.85	35	•35	4	2	0	231 2/3	250	108	99	37	197
Major League totals (8 years)......	79	61	.564	3.70	211	185	17	7	0	1234 2/3	1300	561	508	251	1067

DIVISION SERIES RECORD

Year League	W	L	Pct.	ERA	G	GS	CG	ShO	Sv.	IP	H	R	ER	BB	SO
1997—Houston (N.L.)	0	1	.000	3.00	1	1	0	0	0	6	5	2	2	1	5
1998—Houston (N.L.)	0	0	...	2.57	1	1	0	0	0	7	4	2	2	1	5
1999—Houston (N.L.)	1	1	.500	4.09	2	2	0	0	0	11	16	5	5	3	5
Division series totals (3 years)	1	2	.333	3.38	4	4	0	0	0	24	25	9	9	5	15

REYNOSO, ARMANDO   P   DIAMONDBACKS

PERSONAL: Born May 1, 1966, in San Luis Potosi, Mexico. ... 6-0/204. ... Throws right, bats right. ... Full name: Martin Armando Gutierrez Reynoso. ... Name pronounced ray-NO-so.
HIGH SCHOOL: Escuela Secandaria Mita del Estado (Jalisco, Mexico).
TRANSACTIONS/CAREER NOTES: Signed as free agent by Saltillo of Mexican League (1988). ... Contract sold by Saltillo to Atlanta Braves organization (August 15, 1990). ... Selected by Colorado Rockies in third round (58th pick overall) of expansion draft (November 17, 1992). ... On disabled list (May 21, 1994-remainder of season). ... On Colorado disabled list (April 17-June 18, 1995); included rehabilitation assignments to Colorado Springs (May 9-20 and June 8-14). ... Traded by Rockies to New York Mets for P Jerry Dipoto (November 27, 1996). ... On New York disabled list (March 24-April 15 and July 17, 1997-remainder of season); included rehabilitation assignment to St. Lucie (April 5-15). ... On New York disabled list (March 24-July 24, 1998); included rehabilitation assignments to St. Lucie (June 18-July 3) and Norfolk (July 12-17). ... Granted free agency (October 26, 1998). ... Signed by Arizona Diamondbacks (December 2, 1998).
STATISTICAL NOTES: Led International League with six balks in 1991 and five in 1992. ... Tied for International League lead with 10 hit batsmen in 1991.
MISCELLANEOUS: Appeared in one game as pinch runner with Colorado (1993).

Year League	W	L	Pct.	ERA	G	GS	CG	ShO	Sv.	IP	H	R	ER	BB	SO
1988—Saltillo (Mex.)....................	11	11	.500	4.30	32	29	10	2	2	180	176	98	86	85	92
1989—Saltillo (Mex.)....................	13	9	.591	3.48	27	25	7	2	0	160 1/3	155	78	62	64	107
1990—Saltillo (Mex.)....................	*20	3	.870	2.60	27	•27	12	5	0	200 2/3	174	61	58	73	*170
—Richmond (I.L.)■.................	3	1	.750	2.25	4	3	0	0	0	24	26	7	6	7	15
1991—Richmond (I.L.).................	10	6	.625	*2.61	22	19	3	•3	0	131	117	44	38	39	97
—Atlanta (N.L.)....................	2	1	.667	6.17	6	5	0	0	0	23 1/3	26	18	16	10	10
1992—Richmond (I.L.).................	12	9	.571	2.66	28	27	4	1	0	169 1/3	156	65	50	52	108
—Atlanta (N.L.)....................	1	0	1.000	4.70	3	1	0	0	1	7 2/3	11	4	4	2	2
1993—Colo. Springs (PCL)■	2	1	.667	3.22	4	4	0	0	0	22 1/3	19	10	8	8	22
—Colorado (N.L.).................	12	11	.522	4.00	30	30	4	0	0	189	206	101	84	63	117
1994—Colorado (N.L.).................	3	4	.429	4.82	9	9	1	0	0	52 1/3	54	30	28	22	25
1995—Colorado Springs (PCL)	2	1	.667	1.57	5	5	0	0	0	23	14	4	4	6	17
—Colorado (N.L.).................	7	7	.500	5.32	20	18	0	0	0	93	116	61	55	36	40
1996—Colorado (N.L.).................	8	9	.471	4.96	30	30	0	0	0	168 2/3	195	97	93	49	88
1997—St. Lucie (FSL)■.................	1	1	.500	2.70	2	2	0	0	0	10	9	3	3	1	6
—New York (N.L.).................	6	3	.667	4.53	16	16	1	1	0	91 1/3	95	47	46	29	47

Year League	W	L	Pct.	ERA	G	GS	CG	ShO	Sv.	IP	H	R	ER	BB	SO
1998—St. Lucie (FSL)	0	1	.000	3.75	4	4	0	0	0	12	14	6	5	1	6
—Norfolk (I.L.)	0	2	.000	10.61	2	2	0	0	0	9⅓	14	11	11	4	8
—New York (N.L.)	7	3	.700	3.82	11	11	0	0	0	68⅓	64	31	29	32	40
1999—Arizona (N.L.)■	10	6	.625	4.37	31	27	0	0	0	167	178	90	81	67	79
Major League totals (9 years)	56	44	.560	4.56	156	147	6	1	1	860⅔	945	479	436	310	448

DIVISION SERIES RECORD

Year League	W	L	Pct.	ERA	G	GS	CG	ShO	Sv.	IP	H	R	ER	BB	SO
1995—Colorado (N.L.)	0	0	...	0.00	1	0	0	0	0	1	2	0	0	0	0
1999—Arizona (N.L.)									Did not play.						

R

RHODES, ARTHUR — P — MARINERS

PERSONAL: Born October 24, 1969, in Waco, Texas. ... 6-2/205. ... Throws left, bats left. ... Full name: Arthur Lee Rhodes Jr. ... Brother of Ricky Rhodes, pitcher with New York Yankees organization (1988-92).
HIGH SCHOOL: LaVega (Waco, Texas).
TRANSACTIONS/CAREER NOTES: Selected by Baltimore Orioles organization in second round of free-agent draft (June 1, 1988). ... On Hagerstown disabled list (May 13-June 5, 1991). ... On Baltimore disabled list (May 16-August 2, 1993); included rehabilitation assignment to Rochester (July 4-August 2). ... On Baltimore disabled list (May 2-20, 1994); included rehabilitation assignment to Frederick (May 16-20). ... On Baltimore disabled list (August 25, 1995-remainder of season). ... On disabled list (July 14-August 2 and August 6-September 27, 1996). ... On Baltimore disabled list (July 5-August 17, 1998); included rehabilitation assignment to Rochester (August 15-17). ... Granted free agency (November 1, 1999). ... Signed by Seattle Mariners (December 21, 1999).
HONORS: Named Eastern League Pitcher of the Year (1991).
MISCELLANEOUS: Appeared in one game as pinch runner (1997).

Year League	W	L	Pct.	ERA	G	GS	CG	ShO	Sv.	IP	H	R	ER	BB	SO
1988—Bluefield (Appl.)	3	4	.429	3.31	11	7	0	0	0	35⅓	29	17	13	15	44
1989—Erie (NY-P)	2	0	1.000	1.16	5	5	1	0	0	31	13	7	4	10	45
—Frederick (Caro.)	2	2	.500	5.18	7	6	0	0	0	24⅓	19	16	14	19	28
1990—Frederick (Caro.)	4	6	.400	2.12	13	13	3	0	0	80⅔	62	25	19	21	103
—Hagerstown (East.)	3	4	.429	3.73	12	12	0	0	0	72⅓	62	32	30	39	60
1991—Hagerstown (East.)	7	4	.636	2.70	19	19	2	2	0	106⅔	73	37	32	47	115
—Baltimore (A.L.)	0	3	.000	8.00	8	8	0	0	0	36	47	35	32	23	23
1992—Rochester (I.L.)	6	6	.500	3.72	17	17	1	0	0	101⅔	84	48	42	46	115
—Baltimore (A.L.)	7	5	.583	3.63	15	15	2	1	0	94⅓	87	39	38	38	77
1993—Baltimore (A.L.)	5	6	.455	6.51	17	17	0	0	0	85⅔	91	62	62	49	49
—Rochester (I.L.)	1	1	.500	4.05	6	6	0	0	0	26⅔	26	12	12	15	33
1994—Baltimore (A.L.)	3	5	.375	5.81	10	10	3	2	0	52⅔	51	34	34	30	47
—Frederick (Caro.)	0	0	...	0.00	1	1	0	0	0	5	3	0	0	0	7
—Rochester (I.L.)	7	5	.583	2.79	15	15	3	0	0	90⅓	70	41	28	34	86
1995—Rochester (I.L.)	2	1	.667	2.70	4	4	1	0	0	30	27	12	9	8	33
—Baltimore (A.L.)	2	5	.286	6.21	19	9	0	0	0	75⅓	68	53	52	48	77
1996—Baltimore (A.L.)	9	1	.900	4.08	28	2	0	0	1	53	48	28	24	23	62
1997—Baltimore (A.L.)	10	3	.769	3.02	53	0	0	0	1	95⅓	75	32	32	26	102
1998—Baltimore (A.L.)	4	4	.500	3.51	45	0	0	0	4	77	65	30	30	34	83
—Rochester (I.L.)	0	0	...	4.50	1	1	0	0	0	2	3	1	1	1	1
1999—Baltimore (A.L.)	3	4	.429	5.43	43	0	0	0	3	53	43	37	32	45	59
Major League totals (9 years)	43	36	.544	4.86	238	61	5	3	9	622⅓	575	350	336	316	579

DIVISION SERIES RECORD

Year League	W	L	Pct.	ERA	G	GS	CG	ShO	Sv.	IP	H	R	ER	BB	SO
1996—Baltimore (A.L.)	0	0	...	9.00	2	0	0	0	0	1	1	1	1	1	1
1997—Baltimore (A.L.)	0	0	...	0.00	1	0	0	0	0	2⅓	0	0	0	0	4
Division series totals (2 years)	0	0	...	2.70	3	0	0	0	0	3⅓	1	1	1	1	5

CHAMPIONSHIP SERIES RECORD

Year League	W	L	Pct.	ERA	G	GS	CG	ShO	Sv.	IP	H	R	ER	BB	SO
1996—Baltimore (A.L.)	0	0	...	0.00	3	0	0	0	0	2	2	0	0	0	2
1997—Baltimore (A.L.)	0	0	...	0.00	2	0	0	0	0	2⅓	2	0	0	3	2
Champ. series totals (2 years)	0	0	...	0.00	5	0	0	0	0	4⅓	4	0	0	3	4

RICHARD, CHRIS — 1B — CARDINALS

PERSONAL: Born June 7, 1974, in San Diego. ... 6-2/185. ... Bats left, throws left. ... Full name: Christopher Robert Richard.
HIGH SCHOOL: University City (San Diego).
JUNIOR COLLEGE: San Diego City College and San Diego Mesa College.
COLLEGE: Oklahoma State.
TRANSACTIONS/CAREER NOTES: Selected by St. Louis Cardinals organization in 19th round of free-agent draft (June 1, 1995). ... On Arkansas disabled list (April 2-June 16, 1998 and July 31-August 11, 1998). ... On Prince William disabled list (June 28-July 16, 1998).
STATISTICAL NOTES: Led Texas League first baseman with 119 double plays in 1999.

						BATTING								FIELDING		
Year Team (League)	Pos.	G	AB	R	H	2B	3B	HR	RBI	Avg.	BB	SO	SB	PO	A	E	Avg.
1995—New Jersey (NY-P)	1B	75	284	36	80	14	3	3	43	.282	47	31	6	620	43	11	.984
1996—St. Petersburg (FSL)	1B-OF	129	460	65	130	28	6	14	82	.283	57	50	7	1138	58	7	.994
1997—Arkansas (Texas)	1B-OF	113	390	62	105	24	3	11	58	.269	60	59	6	924	68	10	.990
1998—Prince Will. (Caro.)	DH	8	30	5	8	2	0	0	1	.267	1	5	1	0	0	0	...
—Arkansas (Texas)	1B	28	89	7	18	5	1	2	17	.202	9	10	0	202	8	3	.986
1999—Arkansas (Texas)	1B-OF	133	442	78	130	26	3	29	94	.294	43	75	7	1079	68	13	.989
—Memphis (PCL)	1B	4	17	3	7	2	0	1	4	.412	1	2	0	34	5	0	1.000

RICKETTS, CHAD — P — DODGERS

PERSONAL: Born February 12, 1975, in Waterloo, Ont. ... 6-5/225. ... Throws right, bats right. ... Full name: Robert Chad Ricketts.
HIGH SCHOOL: East Lake (Tarpon Springs, Fla.).
JUNIOR COLLEGE: Polk Community College (Fla.).
TRANSACTIONS/CAREER NOTES: Selected by Chicago Cubs organization in ninth round of free-agent draft (June 1, 1995). ... Traded by Cubs with P Terry Adams and a player to be named later to Los Angeles Dodgers for P Ismael Valdes and 2B Eric Young (December 12, 1999); Dodgers acquired P Brian Stephenson to complete deal (December 16, 1999).

Year League	W	L	Pct.	ERA	G	GS	CG	ShO	Sv.	IP	H	R	ER	BB	SO
1995— Gulf Coast Cubs (GCL)	1	0	1.000	0.00	2	2	0	0	0	9	1	1	0	1	5
— Williamsport (NY-P)	4	5	.444	4.19	12	12	0	0	0	$68^2/_3$	89	46	32	16	37
1996— Rockford (Midw.)	3	8	.273	5.03	37	9	0	0	4	$87^2/_3$	89	60	49	29	70
1997— Rockford (Midw.)	4	0	1.000	2.48	16	0	0	0	3	29	19	9	8	11	32
— Daytona (FSL)	3	1	.750	0.44	20	0	0	0	8	$20^1/_3$	13	4	1	6	18
— Orlando (Sou.)	0	0	...	18.00	2	0	0	0	2	2	7	4	4	2	3
1998— Daytona (FSL)	2	1	.667	1.84	47	0	0	0	19	49	41	15	10	11	59
— West Tenn (Sou.)	0	2	.000	3.52	13	0	0	0	6	$15^1/_3$	19	7	6	4	13
1999— West Tenn (Sou.)	6	4	.600	3.09	57	0	0	0	8	67	55	25	23	21	80

RIEDLING, JOHN — P — REDS

PERSONAL: Born August 29, 1975, in Fort Lauderdale. ... 5-11/190. ... Throws right, bats right. ... Full name: John Richard Riedling.
HIGH SCHOOL: Ely (Pompano Beach, Fla.).
TRANSACTIONS/CAREER NOTES: Selected by Cincinnati Reds organization in 22nd round of free-agent draft (June 2, 1994). ... Released by Reds (December 14, 1998). ... Re-signed by Reds organization (January 5, 1999).

Year League	W	L	Pct.	ERA	G	GS	CG	ShO	Sv.	IP	H	R	ER	BB	SO
1994— Billings (Pio.)	4	1	.800	5.48	15	15	0	0	0	$44^1/_3$	62	36	27	28	27
1995— Billings (Pio.)	2	2	.500	7.04	13	7	0	0	1	$38^1/_3$	51	38	30	21	28
1996— Charleston, W.Va. (SAL)	6	10	.375	3.99	26	26	0	0	0	140	135	85	62	66	90
1997— Burlington (Midw.)	4	6	.400	5.26	35	16	0	0	0	$102^2/_3$	101	70	60	47	104
1998— Chattanooga (Sou.)	3	10	.231	5.00	24	20	0	0	0	$102^2/_3$	112	70	57	60	86
1999— Chattanooga (Sou.)	9	5	.643	3.43	40	0	0	0	5	42	41	23	16	20	38
— Indianapolis (I.L.)	1	0	1.000	1.54	24	0	0	0	1	35	19	9	6	18	26

RIGBY, BRAD — P — ROYALS

PERSONAL: Born May 14, 1973, in Milwaukee. ... 6-6/215. ... Throws right, bats right. ... Full name: Bradley Kenneth Rigby.
HIGH SCHOOL: Lake Brantley (Altamonte Springs, Fla.).
COLLEGE: Georgia Tech.
TRANSACTIONS/CAREER NOTES: Selected by Oakland Athletics organization in second round of free-agent draft (June 2, 1994). ... On Oakland disabled list (August 8-23, 1997; and March 26-April 10, 1998). ... On Edmonton disabled list (July 4-September 10, 1998). ... Traded by Athletics with P Blake Stein and P Jeff D'Amico to Kansas City Royals for P Kevin Appier (July 31, 1999).

Year League	W	L	Pct.	ERA	G	GS	CG	ShO	Sv.	IP	H	R	ER	BB	SO
1994— Modesto (Calif.)	2	1	.667	3.80	11	1	0	0	2	$23^2/_3$	20	10	10	10	28
1995— Modesto (Calif.)	11	4	.733	3.84	31	23	0	0	2	$154^2/_3$	135	79	66	48	145
1996— Huntsville (Sou.)	9	12	.429	3.95	26	26	3	0	0	$159^1/_3$	161	89	70	59	127
1997— Edmonton (PCL)	8	4	.667	4.37	15	15	0	0	0	$82^1/_3$	95	49	40	26	49
— Oakland (A.L.)	1	7	.125	4.87	14	14	0	0	0	$77^2/_3$	92	44	42	22	34
1998— Edmonton (PCL)	5	6	.455	5.94	13	13	0	0	0	$69^2/_3$	86	52	46	17	34
1999— Oakland (A.L.)	3	4	.429	4.33	29	0	0	0	0	$62^1/_3$	69	31	30	26	26
— Vancouver (PCL)	0	1	.000	1.93	1	1	0	0	0	$4^2/_3$	6	3	1	2	6
— Kansas City (A.L.)■	1	2	.333	7.17	20	0	0	0	0	$21^1/_3$	33	20	17	5	10
Major League totals (2 years)	5	13	.278	4.96	63	14	0	0	0	$161^1/_3$	194	95	89	53	70

RILEY, MATT — P — ORIOLES

PERSONAL: Born August 2, 1979, in Antioch, Calif. ... 6-1/201. ... Throws left, bats left. ... Full name: Matthew P. Riley.
HIGH SCHOOL: Linerty Union (Oakley, Calif.).
JUNIOR COLLEGE: Sacramento City College.
TRANSACTIONS/CAREER NOTES: Selected by Baltimore Orioles organization in third round of free-agent draft (June 3, 1997). ... On Bowie disabled list (June 30-July 8, 1999).

Year League	W	L	Pct.	ERA	G	GS	CG	ShO	Sv.	IP	H	R	ER	BB	SO
1998— Delmarva (SAL)	5	4	.556	1.19	16	14	0	0	0	83	42	19	11	44	136
1999— Frederick (Caro.)	3	2	.600	2.61	8	8	0	0	0	$51^2/_3$	34	19	15	14	58
— Bowie (East.)	10	6	.625	3.22	20	20	3	0	0	$125^2/_3$	113	53	45	42	131
— Baltimore (A.L.)	0	0	...	7.36	3	3	0	0	0	11	17	9	9	13	6
Major League totals (1 year)	0	0	...	7.36	3	3	0	0	0	11	17	9	9	13	6

RILEY, MICHAEL — P — GIANTS

PERSONAL: Born January 2, 1975, in Milford, Del. ... 6-2/165. ... Throws left, bats left. ... Full name: Michael Eugene Riley.
HIGH SCHOOL: Seaford (Del.).
COLLEGE: West Virginia.
TRANSACTIONS/CAREER NOTES: Selected by San Francisco Giants organization in 16th round of free-agent draft (June 4, 1996).

R

Year League	W	L	Pct.	ERA	G	GS	CG	ShO	Sv.	IP	H	R	ER	BB	SO
1996—Bellingham (N.W.)	1	3	.250	4.17	17	3	0	0	0	36 2/3	38	26	17	29	38
1997—Bakersfield (Calif.)	1	2	.333	8.41	8	4	0	0	0	20 1/3	25	20	19	8	17
—Salem-Kaizer (N.W.)	•9	2	.818	3.46	15	15	•1	0	0	88 1/3	76	39	34	28	*96
1998—Bakersfield (Calif.)	6	12	.333	4.50	40	15	2	0	2	128	130	73	64	58	110
1999—Shreveport (Texas)	8	3	.727	2.11	30	13	1	1	1	111	80	35	26	53	107

RINCON, RICKY — P — INDIANS

PERSONAL: Born April 13, 1970, in Veracruz, Mexico ... 5-10/187. ... Throws left, bats left. ... Full name: Ricardo Rincon Espinoza.

TRANSACTIONS/CAREER NOTES: Signed as non-drafted free agent by Pittsburgh Pirates organization (March 30, 1997). ... On Pittsburgh disabled list (March 22-April 14, 1998); included rehabilitation assignments to Carolina (April 6) and Nashville (April 11-April 14). ... Traded by Pirates to Cleveland Indians for OF Brian Giles (November 18, 1998). ... On Cleveland disabled list (April 12-May 14, 1999); included rehabilitation assignment to Akron (May 11-14).

Year League	W	L	Pct.	ERA	G	GS	CG	ShO	Sv.	IP	H	R	ER	BB	SO
1990—Union Laguna (Mex.)	3	0	1.000	3.78	19	4	0	0	0	47 2/3	53	22	20	32	29
1991—Union Laguna (Mex.)	2	8	.200	6.54	32	9	0	0	1	74 1/3	99	60	54	48	66
1992—Union Laguna (Mex.)	6	5	.545	3.91	49	9	0	0	4	89 2/3	87	45	39	46	91
1993—Torreon (Mex.)■	7	3	.700	3.17	57	4	0	0	8	82 1/3	80	33	29	36	81
1994—M.C. Red Devils (Mex.)■	2	4	.333	3.21	20	9	0	0	1	53 1/3	57	23	19	20	38
1995—M.C. Red Devils (Mex.)	6	6	.500	5.16	27	11	0	0	3	75	86	45	43	41	41
1996—M.C. Red Devils (Mex.)	5	3	.625	2.97	50	0	0	0	10	78 2/3	58	28	26	27	60
1997—Pittsburgh (N.L.)■	4	8	.333	3.45	62	0	0	0	4	60	51	26	23	24	71
1998—Carolina (Sou.)	0	0	...	6.00	2	0	0	0	0	3	5	2	2	2	1
—Nashville (PCL)	0	0	...	0.00	1	0	0	0	0	1	0	0	0	0	1
—Pittsburgh (N.L.)	0	2	.000	2.91	60	0	0	0	14	65	50	31	21	29	64
1999—Cleveland (A.L.)■	2	3	.400	4.43	59	0	0	0	0	44 2/3	41	22	22	24	30
—Akron (East.)	0	0	...	5.40	2	2	0	0	0	1 2/3	2	1	1	0	2
A.L. totals (1 year)	2	3	.400	4.43	59	0	0	0	0	44 2/3	41	22	22	24	30
N.L. totals (2 years)	4	10	.286	3.17	122	0	0	0	18	125	101	57	44	53	135
Major League totals (3 years)	6	13	.316	3.50	181	0	0	0	18	169 2/3	142	79	66	77	165

DIVISION SERIES RECORD

Year League	W	L	Pct.	ERA	G	GS	CG	ShO	Sv.	IP	H	R	ER	BB	SO
1999—Cleveland (A.L.)	0	0	...	40.50	1	0	0	0	0	2/3	2	3	3	1	1

RIOS, ARMANDO — OF — GIANTS

PERSONAL: Born September 13, 1971, in Santurce, Puerto Rico. ... 5-9/185. ... Bats left, throws left.

HIGH SCHOOL: Villa Fontana (Carolina, Puerto Rico).

COLLEGE: UNC Charlotte, then Louisiana State.

TRANSACTIONS/CAREER NOTES: Signed as non-drafted free agent by San Francisco Giants organization (January 6, 1994). ... On disabled list (May 15-29, 1996). ... On San Francisco disabled list (June 22-September 2, 1999); included rehabilitation assignment to Fresno (July 23-30 and August 12-31).

STATISTICAL NOTES: Career major league grand slams: 1.

Year Team (League)	Pos.	G	AB	R	H	2B	3B	HR	RBI	Avg.	BB	SO	SB	PO	A	E	Avg.
1994—Clinton (Midw.)	OF	119	407	67	120	23	4	8	60	.295	59	69	16	216	17	12	.951
1995—San Jose (Calif.)	OF	128	488	76	143	34	3	8	75	.293	74	75	51	220	16	9	.963
1996—Shreveport (Texas)	OF	92	329	62	93	22	2	12	49	.283	44	42	9	165	*15	7	.963
1997—Shreveport (Texas)	OF-DH	127	461	86	133	30	6	14	79	.289	63	85	17	191	*17	6	.972
1998—Fresno (PCL)	OF-DH-1B	125	445	85	134	23	1	26	103	.301	55	73	17	226	14	7	.972
—San Francisco (N.L.)	OF	12	7	3	4	0	0	2	3	.571	3	2	0	5	0	0	1.000
1999—Fresno (PCL)	OF-DH-1B	31	109	24	30	3	0	4	21	.275	11	22	3	28	1	0	1.000
—San Francisco (N.L.)	OF	72	150	32	49	9	0	7	29	.327	24	35	7	84	5	2	.978
Major League totals (2 years)		84	157	35	53	9	0	9	32	.338	27	37	7	89	5	2	.979

RIPKEN, CAL — 3B — ORIOLES

PERSONAL: Born August 24, 1960, in Havre de Grace, Md. ... 6-4/220. ... Bats right, throws right. ... Full name: Calvin Edwin Ripken Jr. ... Son of Cal Ripken Sr., minor league catcher (1957-62 and 1964), manager with Baltimore Orioles (1987-88) and coach, Orioles (1976-86 and 1989-92); and brother of Bill Ripken, infielder with four major league teams (1987-98).

HIGH SCHOOL: Aberdeen (Md.).

TRANSACTIONS/CAREER NOTES: Selected by Baltimore Orioles organization in second round of free-agent draft (June 6, 1978). ... On disabled list (April 18-May 13 and August 1-September 1, 1999).

RECORDS: Holds major league career records for most consecutive games played—2,632 (May 30, 1982-September 19, 1998); most years leading league in games played—9; most consecutive years played all club's games—15 (1983-97); most years played all club's games—15 (1983-97); most home runs by shortstop—345; most years leading league in games by shortstop—12; most consecutive games by shortstop—2,216; and most years leading league in double plays by shortstop—8. ... Holds major league single-season records for most at-bats without a triple—646 (1989); highest fielding percentage by shortstop (150 or more games)—.996 (1990); fewest errors by shortstop (150 or more games)—3 (1990); most consecutive errorless games by shortstop—95 (April 14 through July 27, 1990); and most consecutive chances accepted by shortstop without an error—431 (April 14-July 28, 1990, first game). ... Holds A.L. career records for most double plays by shortstop—1,565; most years leading league in putouts by shortstop—6; most consecutive years played 150 or more games—12 (1982-93); and most years with 600 or more at-bats—13. ... Holds A.L. single-season record for most assists by shortstop—583 (1984). ... Shares A.L. career records for most years leading league in assists by shortstop—7; and most years with 150 or more games played—14.

HONORS: Named A.L. Rookie Player of the Year by THE SPORTING NEWS (1982). ... Named A.L. Rookie of the Year by Baseball Writers' Association of America (1982). ... Named Major League Player of the Year by THE SPORTING NEWS (1983 and 1991). ... Named A.L. Player of the Year by THE SPORTING NEWS (1983 and 1991). ... Named shortstop on THE SPORTING NEWS A.L. All-Star team (1983-85, 1989, 1991 and 1993-95). ... Named shortstop on THE SPORTING NEWS A.L. Silver Slugger team (1983-86, 1989, 1991 and 1993-94). ... Named A.L. Most Valuable Player by Baseball Writers' Association of America (1983 and 1991). ... Won A.L. Gold Glove at shortstop (1991-92). ... Named Sportsman of the Year by THE SPORTING NEWS (1995).

STATISTICAL NOTES: Tied for Appalachian League lead in double plays by shortstop with 31 in 1978. ... Led Southern League third basemen with .933 fielding percentage, 119 putouts, 268 assists, 415 total chances and 34 double plays in 1980. ... Tied for Southern League lead with nine sacrifice flies in 1980. ... Led A.L. shortstops with 831 total chances in 1983, 906 in 1984, 815 in 1989, 806 in 1991 and 738 in 1993. ... Led A.L. shortstops with 113 double plays in 1983, 122 in 1984, 123 in 1985, 119 in 1989, 114 in 1991, 119 in 1992, 72 in 1994 and 100 in 1995. ... Hit for the cycle (May 6, 1984). ... Tied for A.L. lead with 15 game-winning RBIs in 1986. ... Tied for A.L. lead with 10 sacrifice flies in 1988. ... Led A.L. with 368 total bases in 1991. ... Hit three home runs in one game (May 28, 1996). ... Led A.L. in grounding into double plays with 28 in 1996. ... Collected six hits in one game (June 13, 1999). ... Career major league grand slams: 8.
MISCELLANEOUS: Holds Baltimore Orioles all-time records for most hits (2,991), runs (1,561), doubles (571), home runs (402) and runs batted in (1,571).

Year	Team (League)	Pos.	G	AB	R	H	2B	3B	HR	RBI	Avg.	BB	SO	SB	PO	A	E	Avg.
1978—	Bluefield (Appl.)	SS	63	239	27	63	7	1	0	24	.264	24	46	1	*92	204	*33	.900
1979—	Miami (FSL)	3B-SS-2B	105	393	51	119	*28	1	5	54	.303	31	64	4	149	260	30	.932
—	Charlotte (Sou.)	3B	17	61	6	11	0	1	3	8	.180	3	13	1	13	26	3	.929
1980—	Charlotte (Sou.)	3B-SS	•144	522	91	144	28	5	25	78	.276	77	81	4	†151	†341	35	†.934
1981—	Rochester (I.L.)	3B-SS	114	437	74	126	31	4	23	75	.288	66	85	0	128	320	21	.955
—	Baltimore (A.L.)	SS-3B	23	39	1	5	0	0	0	0	.128	1	8	0	13	30	3	.935
1982—	Baltimore (A.L.)	SS-3B	160	598	90	158	32	5	28	93	.264	46	95	3	221	440	19	.972
1983—	Baltimore (A.L.)	SS	•162	*663	*121	*211	*47	2	27	102	.318	58	97	0	272	*534	25	.970
1984—	Baltimore (A.L.)	SS	•162	641	103	195	37	7	27	86	.304	71	89	2	*297	*583	26	.971
1985—	Baltimore (A.L.)	SS	161	642	116	181	32	5	26	110	.282	67	68	2	*286	474	26	.967
1986—	Baltimore (A.L.)	SS	162	627	98	177	35	1	25	81	.282	70	60	4	240	*482	13	.982
1987—	Baltimore (A.L.)	SS	*162	624	97	157	28	3	27	98	.252	81	77	3	240	*480	20	.973
1988—	Baltimore (A.L.)	SS	161	575	87	152	25	1	23	81	.264	102	69	2	*284	480	21	.973
1989—	Baltimore (A.L.)	SS	•162	646	80	166	30	0	21	93	.257	57	72	3	*276	*531	8	.990
1990—	Baltimore (A.L.)	SS	161	600	78	150	28	4	21	84	.250	82	66	3	242	435	3	*.996
1991—	Baltimore (A.L.)	SS	•162	650	99	210	46	5	34	114	.323	53	46	6	*267	*528	11	*.986
1992—	Baltimore (A.L.)	SS	*162	637	73	160	29	1	14	72	.251	64	50	4	*287	445	12	.984
1993—	Baltimore (A.L.)	SS	*162	*641	87	165	26	3	24	90	.257	65	58	1	226	*495	17	.977
1994—	Baltimore (A.L.)	SS	112	444	71	140	19	3	13	75	.315	32	41	1	132	321	7	*.985
1995—	Baltimore (A.L.)	SS	144	550	71	144	33	2	17	88	.262	52	59	0	206	409	7	*.989
1996—	Baltimore (A.L.)	SS-3B	*163	640	94	178	40	1	26	102	.278	59	78	1	233	483	14	.981
1997—	Baltimore (A.L.)	3B-SS	•162	615	79	166	30	0	17	84	.270	56	73	1	100	313	22	.949
1998—	Baltimore (A.L.)	3B	161	601	65	163	27	1	14	61	.271	51	68	0	101	265	8	*.979
1999—	Baltimore (A.L.)	3B	86	332	51	113	27	0	18	57	.340	13	31	0	36	142	13	.932
Major League totals (19 years)			2790	10765	1561	2991	571	44	402	1571	.278	1080	1205	36	3959	7870	275	.977

DIVISION SERIES RECORD

RECORDS: Holds career record for highest batting average (20 or more at-bats)—.441.

Year	Team (League)	Pos.	G	AB	R	H	2B	3B	HR	RBI	Avg.	BB	SO	SB	PO	A	E	Avg.
1996—	Baltimore (A.L.)	SS	4	18	2	8	3	0	0	2	.444	0	3	0	7	15	0	1.000
1997—	Baltimore (A.L.)	3B	4	16	1	7	2	0	0	1	.438	2	2	0	4	4	0	1.000
Division series totals (2 years)			8	34	3	15	5	0	0	3	.441	2	5	0	11	19	0	1.000

CHAMPIONSHIP SERIES RECORD

Year	Team (League)	Pos.	G	AB	R	H	2B	3B	HR	RBI	Avg.	BB	SO	SB	PO	A	E	Avg.
1983—	Baltimore (A.L.)	SS	4	15	5	6	2	0	0	1	.400	2	3	0	7	11	0	1.000
1996—	Baltimore (A.L.)	SS	5	20	1	5	1	0	0	0	.250	1	4	0	4	14	1	.947
1997—	Baltimore (A.L.)	3B	6	23	3	8	2	0	1	3	.348	4	6	0	1	14	0	1.000
Championship series totals (3 years)			15	58	9	19	5	0	1	4	.328	7	13	0	12	39	1	.981

WORLD SERIES RECORD

NOTES: Member of World Series championship team (1983).

Year	Team (League)	Pos.	G	AB	R	H	2B	3B	HR	RBI	Avg.	BB	SO	SB	PO	A	E	Avg.
1983—	Baltimore (A.L.)	SS	5	18	2	3	0	0	0	1	.167	3	4	0	6	14	0	1.000

ALL-STAR GAME RECORD

RECORDS: Shares single-game record for most at-bats (nine-inning game)—5 (July 12, 1994).
NOTES: Named Most Valuable Player (1991).

Year	League	Pos.	AB	R	H	2B	3B	HR	RBI	Avg.	BB	SO	SB	PO	A	E	Avg.
1983—	American	SS	0	0	0	0	0	0	0	...	1	0	0	1	0	0	1.000
1984—	American	SS	3	0	0	0	0	0	0	.000	0	0	0	0	0	0	...
1985—	American	SS	3	0	1	0	0	0	0	.333	0	0	0	2	1	0	1.000
1986—	American	SS	4	0	0	0	0	0	0	.000	0	0	0	0	1	0	1.000
1987—	American	SS	2	0	1	0	0	0	0	.500	0	0	0	5	0	0	1.000
1988—	American	SS	3	0	0	0	0	0	0	.000	1	0	0	1	4	0	1.000
1989—	American	SS	3	0	1	1	0	0	0	.333	0	0	0	0	0	0	...
1990—	American	SS	2	0	0	0	0	0	0	.000	0	0	0	1	1	0	1.000
1991—	American	SS	3	1	2	0	0	1	3	.667	0	0	0	2	1	0	1.000
1992—	American	SS	3	0	1	0	0	0	1	.333	0	0	0	1	1	0	1.000
1993—	American	SS	3	0	0	0	0	0	0	.000	0	1	0	1	2	0	1.000
1994—	American	SS	5	0	1	1	0	0	0	.200	0	2	0	1	2	0	1.000
1995—	American	SS	3	0	2	0	0	0	0	.667	0	0	0	2	1	0	1.000
1996—	American	SS	3	0	0	0	0	0	0	.000	0	0	0	1	1	0	1.000
1997—	American	3B	2	0	1	0	0	0	0	.500	0	0	0	0	4	0	1.000
1998—	American	3B	4	1	1	1	0	0	2	.250	0	0	0	1	1	0	1.000
1999—	American	3B	1	1	1	0	0	0	1	1.000	0	0	0	0	0	0	...
All-Star Game totals (17 years)			47	3	12	3	0	1	7	.255	2	3	0	14	25	0	1.000

RISKE, DAVE · P · INDIANS

PERSONAL: Born October 23, 1976, in Renton, Wash. ... 6-2/175. ... Throws right, bats right. ... Full name: David R. Riske.
HIGH SCHOOL: Lindbergh (Renton, Wash.).
JUNIOR COLLEGE: Green River (Wash.) Community College.
TRANSACTIONS/CAREER NOTES: Selected by Cleveland Indians organization in 56th round of free-agent draft (June 4, 1996).

Year League	W	L	Pct.	ERA	G	GS	CG	ShO	Sv.	IP	H	R	ER	BB	SO
1997— Kinston (Caro.)	4	4	.500	2.25	39	0	0	0	2	72	58	22	18	33	90
1998— Kinston (Caro.)	1	1	.500	2.33	53	0	0	0	*33	54	48	15	14	15	67
— Akron (East.)	0	0	...	0.00	2	0	0	0	1	3	1	0	0	1	5
1999— Akron (East.)	0	0	...	1.90	23	0	0	0	12	23²/₃	5	6	5	13	33
— Buffalo (I.L.)	3	0	1.000	0.65	23	0	0	0	6	27²/₃	14	3	2	7	22
— Cleveland (A.L.)	1	1	.500	8.36	12	0	0	0	0	14	20	15	13	6	16
Major League totals (1 year)	1	1	.500	8.36	12	0	0	0	0	14	20	15	13	6	16

RITCHIE, TODD · P · PIRATES

PERSONAL: Born November 7, 1971, in Portsmouth, Va. ... 6-3/222. ... Throws right, bats right. ... Full name: Todd Everett Ritchie.
HIGH SCHOOL: Duncanville (Texas).
TRANSACTIONS/CAREER NOTES: Selected by Minnesota Twins organization in first round (12th pick overall) of free-agent draft (June 4, 1990). ... On disabled list (August 19, 1991-remainder of season; June 24-July 9, 1993; and April 28, 1994-remainder of season). ... Released by Twins (October 3, 1998). ... Signed by Pittsburgh Pirates organization (December 22, 1998). ... On disabled list (August 21-September 6, 1999).
MISCELLANEOUS: Grounded out in only appearance as pinch hitter (1999).

Year League	W	L	Pct.	ERA	G	GS	CG	ShO	Sv.	IP	H	R	ER	BB	SO
1990— Elizabethton (Appl.)	5	2	.714	1.94	11	11	1	0	0	65	45	22	14	24	49
1991— Kenosha (Midw.)	7	6	.538	3.55	21	21	0	0	0	116²/₃	113	53	46	50	101
1992— Visalia (Calif.)	11	9	.550	5.06	28	•28	3	1	0	172²/₃	193	113	97	65	129
1993— Nashville (Sou.)	3	2	.600	3.66	12	10	0	0	0	46²/₃	46	21	19	15	41
1994— Nashville (Sou.)	0	2	.000	4.24	4	4	0	0	0	17	24	10	8	7	9
1995— New Britain (East.)	4	9	.308	5.73	24	21	0	0	0	113	135	78	72	54	60
1996— New Britain (East.)	3	7	.300	5.44	29	10	0	0	4	82²/₃	101	55	50	30	53
— Salt Lake (PCL)	0	4	.000	5.47	16	0	0	0	0	24²/₃	27	15	15	11	19
1997— Minnesota (A.L.)	2	3	.400	4.58	42	0	0	0	0	74²/₃	87	41	38	28	44
1998— Minnesota (A.L.)	0	0	...	5.63	15	0	0	0	0	24	30	17	15	9	21
— Salt Lake (PCL)	1	3	.250	4.15	36	0	0	0	4	60²/₃	55	38	28	31	62
1999— Nashville (PCL)■	0	0	...	1.80	1	1	0	0	0	5	6	1	1	1	2
— Pittsburgh (N.L.)	15	9	.625	3.50	28	26	2	0	0	172¹/₃	169	79	67	54	107
A.L. totals (2 years)	2	3	.400	4.83	57	0	0	0	0	98²/₃	117	58	53	37	65
N.L. totals (1 year)	15	9	.625	3.50	28	26	2	0	0	172¹/₃	169	79	67	54	107
Major League totals (3 years)	17	12	.586	3.99	85	26	2	0	0	271	286	137	120	91	172

RIVAS, LUIS · SS · TWINS

PERSONAL: Born August 30, 1979, in La Guaria, Venezuela. ... 5-10/175. ... Bats right, throws right. ... Full name: Luis Wilfredo Rivas.
HIGH SCHOOL: Riceniado Le Guaria (La Guaria, Venezuela).
TRANSACTIONS/CAREER NOTES: Signed as non-drafted free agent by Minnesota Twins organization (October 9, 1995).
STATISTICAL NOTES: Led Gulf Coast League shortstops with 40 double plays in 1996. ... Led Midwest League shortstops with 621 total chances and 92 double plays in 1997. ... Led Florida State League shortstops with 632 total chances and 78 double plays in 1998. ... Led Eastern League shortstops with 37 errors in 1999.

Year Team (League)	Pos.	G	AB	R	H	2B	3B	HR	RBI	Avg.	BB	SO	SB	PO	A	E	Avg.
1996— GC Twins (GCL)	SS	53	201	29	52	12	1	1	13	.259	18	37	•35	68	181	21	.922
1997— Fort Wayne (Midw.)	SS	121	419	61	100	20	6	1	30	.239	33	90	28	169	*394	*58	.907
1998— Fort Myers (FSL)	SS	126	463	58	130	21	5	4	51	.281	14	75	34	162	*415	*55	.913
1999— New Britain (East.)	SS-2B	132	527	78	134	30	7	7	49	.254	41	92	31	164	392	†39	.934

RIVERA, LUIS · P · BRAVES

PERSONAL: Born June 21, 1978, in Chihuahua, Mexico. ... 6-3/163. ... Throws right, bats right. ... Full name: Luis Gutierrez Rivera.
HIGH SCHOOL: Sistema Preparatoria Abierta (Telucha, Mexico).
TRANSACTIONS/CAREER NOTES: Signed as non-drafted free agent by Atlanta Braves organization (February 18, 1995). ... On Myrtle Beach disabled list (April 18-May 14, 1999)

Year League	W	L	Pct.	ERA	G	GS	CG	ShO	Sv.	IP	H	R	ER	BB	SO
1996— Gulf Coast Braves (GCL)	1	1	.500	2.59	8	6	0	0	0	24¹/₃	18	9	7	7	26
1997— Danville (Appl.)	3	1	.750	2.41	9	9	0	0	0	41	28	15	11	17	57
— Macon (SAL)	2	0	1.000	1.29	4	4	0	0	0	21	13	4	3	7	22
1998— Macon (SAL)	5	5	.500	3.98	20	20	0	0	0	92²/₃	78	53	41	41	118
1999— Myrtle Beach (Caro.)	0	2	.000	3.11	25	13	0	0	0	66²/₃	45	25	23	23	81

RIVERA, MARIANO · P · YANKEES

PERSONAL: Born November 29, 1969, in Panama City, Panama. ... 6-2/170. ... Throws right, bats right. ... Cousin of Ruben Rivera, outfielder, San Diego Padres.

TRANSACTIONS/CAREER NOTES: Signed as non-drafted free agent by New York Yankees organization (February 17, 1990). ... On disabled list (April 10-May 19, July 11-28 and August 12-September 8, 1992). ... On Albany/Colonie disabled list (April 9-June 28, 1993). ... On Greensboro disabled list (September 6, 1993-remainder of season). ... On Tampa disabled list (April 23-May 9, 1994). ... On Columbus disabled list (August 4-14, 1994). ... On disabled list (April 6-24, 1998).

HONORS: Named A.L. Fireman of the Year by THE SPORTING NEWS (1997 and 1999).

STATISTICAL NOTES: Pitched seven-inning, 3-0 no-hit victory against Gulf Coast Pirates (August 31, 1990). ... Pitched five-inning, 3-0 no-hit victory for Columbus against Rochester (June 26, 1995).

Year League	W	L	Pct.	ERA	G	GS	CG	ShO	Sv.	IP	H	R	ER	BB	SO
1990— Gulf Coast Yankees (GCL) ..	5	1	.833	*0.17	22	1	1	1	1	52	17	3	1	7	58
1991— Greensboro (SAL)	4	9	.308	2.75	29	15	1	0	0	114²/₃	103	48	35	36	123
1992— Fort Lauderdale (FSL)	5	3	.625	2.28	10	10	3	1	0	59¹/₃	40	17	15	5	42
1993— Greensboro (SAL)	1	0	1.000	2.06	10	10	0	0	0	39¹/₃	31	12	9	15	32
— Gulf Coast Yankees (GCL) ..	0	1	.000	2.25	2	2	0	0	0	4	2	1	1	1	6
1994— Tampa (FSL)	3	0	1.000	2.21	7	7	0	0	0	36²/₃	34	12	9	12	27
— Albany/Colonie (East.)	3	0	1.000	2.27	9	9	0	0	0	63¹/₃	58	20	16	8	39
— Columbus (I.L.)	4	2	.667	5.81	6	6	1	0	0	31	34	22	20	10	23
1995— Columbus (I.L.)	2	2	.500	2.10	7	7	1	1	0	30	25	10	7	3	30
— New York (A.L.)	5	3	.625	5.51	19	10	0	0	0	67	71	43	41	30	51
1996— New York (A.L.)	8	3	.727	2.09	61	0	0	0	5	107²/₃	73	25	25	34	130
1997— New York (A.L.)	6	4	.600	1.88	66	0	0	0	43	71²/₃	65	17	15	20	68
1998— New York (A.L.)	3	0	1.000	1.91	54	0	0	0	36	61¹/₃	48	13	13	17	36
1999— New York (A.L.)	4	3	.571	1.83	66	0	0	0	*45	69	43	15	14	18	52
Major League totals (5 years)	**26**	**13**	**.667**	**2.58**	**266**	**10**	**0**	**0**	**129**	**376²/₃**	**300**	**113**	**108**	**119**	**337**

RECORDS: Holds career record for most saves—5.

DIVISION SERIES RECORD

Year League	W	L	Pct.	ERA	G	GS	CG	ShO	Sv.	IP	H	R	ER	BB	SO
1995— New York (A.L.)	1	0	1.000	0.00	3	0	0	0	0	5¹/₃	3	0	0	1	8
1996— New York (A.L.)	0	0	...	0.00	2	0	0	0	0	4²/₃	0	0	0	1	1
1997— New York (A.L.)	0	0	...	4.50	2	0	0	0	1	2	2	1	1	0	1
1998— New York (A.L.)	0	0	...	0.00	3	0	0	0	2	3¹/₃	1	0	0	1	2
1999— New York (A.L.)	0	0	...	0.00	2	0	0	0	2	3	1	0	0	0	3
Division series totals (5 years)	**1**	**0**	**1.000**	**0.49**	**12**	**0**	**0**	**0**	**5**	**18¹/₃**	**7**	**1**	**1**	**3**	**15**

CHAMPIONSHIP SERIES RECORD

Year League	W	L	Pct.	ERA	G	GS	CG	ShO	Sv.	IP	H	R	ER	BB	SO
1996— New York (A.L.)	1	0	1.000	0.00	2	0	0	0	0	4	6	0	0	1	5
1998— New York (A.L.)	0	0	...	0.00	4	0	0	0	1	5²/₃	0	0	0	1	5
1999— New York (A.L.)	1	0	1.000	0.00	3	0	0	0	2	4²/₃	5	0	0	0	3
Champ. series totals (3 years)	**2**	**0**	**1.000**	**0.00**	**9**	**0**	**0**	**0**	**3**	**14¹/₃**	**11**	**0**	**0**	**2**	**13**

NOTES: Named Most Valuable Player (1999). ... Member of World Series championship team (1996, 1998 and 1999).

WORLD SERIES RECORD

Year League	W	L	Pct.	ERA	G	GS	CG	ShO	Sv.	IP	H	R	ER	BB	SO
1996— New York (A.L.)	0	0	...	1.59	4	0	0	0	0	5²/₃	4	1	1	3	4
1998— New York (A.L.)	0	0	...	0.00	3	0	0	0	3	4¹/₃	5	0	0	0	4
1999— New York (A.L.)	1	0	1.000	0.00	3	0	0	0	2	4²/₃	3	0	0	1	3
World Series totals (3 years)	**1**	**0**	**1.000**	**0.61**	**10**	**0**	**0**	**0**	**5**	**14²/₃**	**12**	**1**	**1**	**4**	**11**

ALL-STAR GAME RECORD

Year League	W	L	Pct.	ERA	GS	CG	ShO	Sv.	IP	H	R	ER	BB	SO
1997— American	0	0	...	0.00	0	0	0	1	1	0	0	0	0	1
1999— American					Selected, did not play—injured.									

RIVERA, ROBERTO   P

PERSONAL: Born January 1, 1969, in Bayamon, Puerto Rico. ... 6-0/200. ... Throws left, bats left. ... Full name: Roberto Diaz Rivera.

HIGH SCHOOL: Dr. Augustin Stahl (Bayamon, Puerto Rico).

TRANSACTIONS/CAREER NOTES: Signed as non-drafted free agent by Cleveland Indians organization (January 24, 1988). ... On disabled list (May 22-June 23, 1992). ... Released by Indians organization (October 18, 1993). ... Signed by Chicago Cubs organization (December 10, 1993). ... On Iowa disabled list (July 3-17, 1996). ... Granted free agency (October 15, 1996). ... Missed entire 1997 season due to injury. ... Signed by Houston Astros organization (December 29, 1997). ... Granted free agency (October 16, 1998). ... Signed by San Diego Padres organization (November 23, 1998). ... On Las Vegas disabled list (July 2-August 16, 1999). ... Granted free agency (October 15, 1999).

Year League	W	L	Pct.	ERA	G	GS	CG	ShO	Sv.	IP	H	R	ER	BB	SO
1988— Gulf Coast Indians (GCL) ...	6	5	.545	3.25	14	12	1	1	0	69¹/₃	64	32	25	21	38
1989— Burlington (Appl.)	3	4	.429	3.51	18	2	1	0	2	51¹/₃	44	24	20	16	42
1990— Watertown (NY-P)	4	4	.500	3.60	14	13	2	1	0	85	85	43	34	10	63
1991— Columbus (SAL)	7	1	.875	1.65	30	1	0	0	3	49	48	15	9	12	36
— Kinston (Caro.)	1	0	1.000	4.35	10	0	0	0	0	10¹/₃	10	6	5	2	9
1992— Kinston (Caro.)	3	5	.375	3.25	24	8	4	1	1	88²/₃	83	35	32	11	56
1993— Canton/Akron (East.)	0	1	.000	5.02	8	0	0	0	0	14¹/₃	22	8	8	3	6
— Kinston (Caro.)	2	3	.400	6.17	19	1	0	0	0	35	44	26	24	4	32
1994— Peoria (Midw.)■..............	3	1	.750	2.33	14	0	0	0	0	19¹/₃	27	6	5	3	13
— Orlando (Sou.)	3	2	.600	2.76	34	0	0	0	4	45²/₃	45	14	14	11	31
1995— Orlando (Sou.)	6	2	.750	2.38	49	0	0	0	6	68	50	18	18	11	34
— Chicago (N.L.)	0	0	...	5.40	7	0	0	0	0	5	8	3	3	2	2
1996— Iowa (A.A.)	1	0	1.000	2.70	35	0	0	0	2	33¹/₃	26	10	10	8	18
— Orlando (Sou.)	1	2	.333	6.35	9	0	0	0	1	17	20	13	12	8	14
1997—					Did not play.										
1998— New Orleans (PCL)■..........	5	4	.556	2.45	54	0	0	0	5	62¹/₃	59	22	17	15	38
1999— San Diego (N.L.)■	1	2	.333	3.86	12	0	0	0	0	7	6	4	3	3	3
— Las Vegas (PCL)	1	2	.333	10.16	20	3	0	0	0	33²/₃	61	39	38	14	25
Major League totals (2 years)	**1**	**2**	**.333**	**4.50**	**19**	**0**	**0**	**0**	**0**	**12**	**14**	**7**	**6**	**5**	**5**

PERSONAL: Born November 14, 1973, in La Chorrera, Panama ... 6-3/200. ... Bats right, throws right. ... Full name: Ruben Moreno Rivera. ... Cousin of Mariano Rivera, pitcher, New York Yankees.

TRANSACTIONS/CAREER NOTES: Signed as non-drafted free agent by New York Yankees organization (November 21, 1990). ... On New York disabled list (March 27-May 30, 1997). ... Traded by Yankees with P Rafael Medina and $3 million to San Diego Padres for the rights to P Hideki Irabu, 2B Homer Bush, OF Gordon Amerson and a player to be named later (April 22, 1997); Yankees acquired OF Vernon Maxwell to complete deal (June 9, 1997). ... On San Diego disabled list (May 30-August 13, 1997); included rehabilitation assignments to Rancho Cucamonga (May 30-July 22) and Las Vegas (July 23-August 4).

HONORS: Named New York-Pennsylvania League Most Valuable Player (1993). ... Named South Atlantic League Most Valuable Player (1994).

STATISTICAL NOTES: Led New York-Pennsylvania League outfielders with three double plays in 1993. ... Led South Atlantic League with .573 slugging percentage in 1994. ... Career major league grand slams: 1.

R

Year	Team (League)	Pos.	G	AB	R	H	2B	3B	HR	RBI	Avg.	BB	SO	SB	PO	A	E	Avg.
1991—	Dom. Yankees (DSL)..		51	170	27	34	3	2	2	16	.200	23	37	14	...	...	...	...
1992—	GC Yankees (GCL)......	OF	53	194	37	53	10	3	1	20	.273	42	49	21	67	10	4	.951
1993—	Oneonta (NY-P).........	OF	55	199	45	55	7	6	13	47	.276	32	66	12	111	9	3	.976
1994—	Greensboro (SAL)......	OF	105	400	83	115	24	3	•28	81	.288	47	125	36	217	14	5	.979
—	Tampa (FSL)...............	OF	34	134	18	35	4	3	5	20	.261	8	38	12	76	6	2	.976
1995—	Norwich (East.).........	OF	71	256	49	75	16	8	9	39	.293	37	77	16	176	7	3	.984
—	Columbus (I.L.).........	OF	48	174	37	47	8	2	15	35	.270	26	62	8	113	6	3	.975
—	New York (A.L.).........	OF	5	1	0	0	0	0	0	0	.000	0	1	0	2	0	0	1.000
1996—	Columbus (I.L.).........	OF	101	362	59	85	20	4	10	46	.235	40	96	15	239	6	7	.972
—	New York (A.L.).........	OF	46	88	17	25	6	1	2	16	.284	13	26	6	77	2	0	1.000
1997—	Rancho Cuca. (Cal.)■	DH	6	23	6	4	1	0	1	3	.174	3	9	1	...	...	...	...
—	Las Vegas (PCL).........	DH-1B	12	48	6	12	5	1	1	6	.250	1	20	1	1	0	0	1.000
—	San Diego (N.L.).........	OF	17	20	2	5	1	0	0	1	.250	2	9	2	13	0	0	1.000
1998—	Las Vegas (PCL).........	OF	30	104	9	15	3	0	3	11	.144	11	42	4	53	2	0	1.000
—	San Diego (N.L.).........	OF	95	172	31	36	7	2	6	29	.209	28	52	5	104	3	3	.973
1999—	San Diego (N.L.).........	OF	147	411	65	80	16	1	23	48	.195	55	143	18	312	8	8	.976
American League totals (2 years)			51	89	17	25	6	1	2	16	.281	13	27	6	79	2	0	1.000
National League totals (3 years)			259	603	98	121	24	3	29	78	.201	85	204	25	429	11	11	.976
Major League totals (5 years)			310	692	115	146	30	4	31	94	.211	98	231	31	508	13	11	.979

DIVISION SERIES RECORD

Year	Team (League)	Pos.	G	AB	R	H	2B	3B	HR	RBI	Avg.	BB	SO	SB	PO	A	E	Avg.
1996—	New York (A.L.)..........	OF-PH	2	1	0	0	0	0	0	0	.000	0	1	0	0	0	0	...
1998—	San Diego (N.L.)	OF	3	6	0	0	0	0	0	0	.000	0	3	0	3	0	0	1.000
Division series totals (2 years)			5	7	0	0	0	0	0	0	.000	0	4	0	3	0	0	1.000

CHAMPIONSHIP SERIES RECORD

Year	Team (League)	Pos.	G	AB	R	H	2B	3B	HR	RBI	Avg.	BB	SO	SB	PO	A	E	Avg.
1996—	New York (A..L.).........								Did not play.									
1998—	San Diego (N.L.)	OF-PH	6	13	1	3	2	0	0	0	.231	0	7	1	8	1	0	1.000

WORLD SERIES RECORD

NOTES: Member of World Series championship team (1996); inactive due to injury.

Year	Team (League)	Pos.	G	AB	R	H	2B	3B	HR	RBI	Avg.	BB	SO	SB	PO	A	E	Avg.
1996—	New York (A.L.)								Did not play.									
1998—	San Diego (N.L.)	PH-OF-PR	3	5	1	4	2	0	0	1	.800	0	0	0	3	0	0	1.000

PERSONAL: Born May 24, 1971, in Clifton Heights, Pa. ... 6-2/220. ... Throws left, bats right. ... Full name: Todd Michael Rizzo.

HIGH SCHOOL: Garnet Valley (Concordville, Pa.).

JUNIOR COLLEGE: Delaware County Community College (Pa.).

TRANSACTIONS/CAREER NOTES: Signed as non-drafted free agent by Los Angeles Dodgers organization (May 6, 1992). ... Released by Dodgers organization (June 13, 1993). ... Signed by San Antonio, Texas-Louisiana League (1994). ... Released by San Antonio (1994). ... Signed by Tyler, Texas-Louisiana League (1994). ... Signed by Chicago White Sox organization (March 4, 1995). ... Granted free agency (October 4, 1999). ... Signed by Minnesota Twins organization (December 20, 1999).

Year	League	W	L	Pct.	ERA	G	GS	CG	ShO	Sv.	IP	H	R	ER	BB	SO
1992—	Gulf Coast Dodgers (GCL)..	0	1	.000	3.86	3	1	0	0	0	7	4	4	3	8	7
—	Yakima (N.W.)..................	2	0	1.000	4.50	15	0	0	0	0	26	21	13	13	24	26
1993—	....							Out of organized baseball.								
1994—	San Antonio (Texas-La.)■..	0	2	.000	7.53	17	0	0	0	1	28²/₃	30	32	24	41	20
—	Tyler (Texas-La.)■.............	0	0	...	8.35	14	1	0	0	0	18¹/₃	24	23	17	21	13
1995—	Prince William (Caro.)■.....	3	5	.375	2.78	36	0	0	0	1	68	68	30	21	39	59
1996—	Birmingham (Sou.)...........	4	4	.500	2.75	46	0	0	0	1	68²/₃	61	28	21	40	48
1997—	Nashville (A.A.)	4	5	.444	3.57	54	0	0	0	6	70²/₃	63	39	28	33	60
1998—	Calgary (PCL)...................	7	3	.700	6.75	50	0	0	0	4	72	102	62	54	39	58
—	Chicago (A.L.)	0	0	...	13.50	9	0	0	0	0	6²/₃	12	12	10	6	3
1999—	Charlotte (I.L.)...................	4	5	.444	4.06	53	0	0	0	8	71	68	37	32	31	46
—	Chicago (A.L.)	0	2	.000	6.75	3	0	0	0	0	1¹/₃	4	2	1	3	2
Major League totals (2 years).......		0	2	.000	12.38	12	0	0	0	0	8	16	14	11	9	5

ROBERTS, DAVE　　　　　OF　　　　　INDIANS

PERSONAL: Born May 31, 1972, in Okinawa, Japan. ... 5-10/175. ... Bats left, throws left. ... Full name: David Ray Roberts.
HIGH SCHOOL: Rancho Buena Vista (Oceanside, Calif.).
COLLEGE: UCLA (degree in history).
TRANSACTIONS/CAREER NOTES: Selected by Detroit Tigers organization in 28th round of free-agent draft (June 2, 1994). ... Loaned to Oakland Athletics organization (March 30-August 30, 1996). ... Traded by Tigers with P Tim Worrell to Cleveland Indians for OF Geronimo Berroa (June 24, 1998). ... On Akron disabled list (August 10-18, 1998).
STATISTICAL NOTES: Career major league grand slams: 1.

| | | | | | | | BATTING | | | | | | | | FIELDING | | |
Year Team (League)	Pos.	G	AB	R	H	2B	3B	HR	RBI	Avg.	BB	SO	SB	PO	A	E	Avg.
1994— Jamestown (NY-P)	OF	54	178	33	52	7	2	0	12	.292	29	27	12	2	0	0	1.000
1995— Lakeland (FSL)		92	357	67	108	10	5	3	30	.303	39	43	30	61	3	1	.985
1996— Visalia (Calif.)■.........	OF	126	482	*112	131	24	7	5	37	.272	98	105	*65	201	8	5	.977
— Jacksonville (Sou.).....	OF	3	9	0	2	0	0	0	0	.222	1	0	0	5	0	0	1.000
1997— Jacksonville (Sou.).....	OF	105	415	76	123	24	2	4	41	.296	45	62	23	82	1	4	.954
1998— Jacksonville (Sou.).....	OF	69	279	71	91	14	5	5	42	.326	53	59	21	105	1	0	1.000
— Akron (East.)■..........	OF	56	227	49	82	10	5	7	33	.361	35	30	28	124	4	1	.992
— Buffalo (I.L.)..............	OF	5	15	2	2	0	0	0	2	.133	0	3	2	12	1	0	1.000
1999— Buffalo (I.L.)..............	OF-DH	89	350	65	95	17	*10	0	38	.271	43	52	39	247	4	1	.996
— Cleveland (A.L.).........	OF	41	143	26	34	4	0	2	12	.238	9	16	11	87	0	0	1.000
Major League totals (1 year)		41	143	26	34	4	0	2	12	.238	9	16	11	87	0	0	1.000

DIVISION SERIES RECORD

| | | | | | | | BATTING | | | | | | | | FIELDING | | |
Year Team (League)	Pos.	G	AB	R	H	2B	3B	HR	RBI	Avg.	BB	SO	SB	PO	A	E	Avg.
1999— Cleveland (A.L.)..........	PH-OF	2	3	0	0	0	0	0	0	.000	0	2	0	3	0	0	1.000

ROBERTS, GRANT　　　　　P　　　　　METS

PERSONAL: Born September 13, 1977, in El Cajon, Calif. ... 6-3/205. ... Throws right, bats right. ... Full name: Grant William Roberts.
HIGH SCHOOL: Grossmont (La Mesa, Calif.).
TRANSACTIONS/CAREER NOTES: Selected by New York Mets organization in 11th round of free-agent draft (June 1, 1995).

Year League	W	L	Pct.	ERA	G	GS	CG	ShO	Sv.	IP	H	R	ER	BB	SO
1995— Gulf Coast Mets (GCL)	2	1	.667	2.15	11	3	0	0	0	29 1/3	19	13	7	14	24
1996— Kingsport (Appalachian).....	*9	1	*.900	2.10	13	13	2	*2	0	68 2/3	43	18	16	37	*92
1997— Columbia (SAL).................	11	3	*.786	2.36	22	22	2	1	0	129 2/3	98	37	34	44	122
1998— St. Lucie (FSL).................	4	5	.444	4.23	17	17	0	0	0	72 1/3	72	37	34	37	70
1999— Binghamton (East.)	7	6	.538	4.87	23	23	0	0	0	131 1/3	135	81	71	49	94
— Norfolk (I.L.)	2	1	.667	4.50	5	5	0	0	0	28	32	15	14	11	30

ROBERTS, WILLIS　　　　　P　　　　　TIGERS

PERSONAL: Born June 19, 1975, in San Cristobal, Dominican Republic. ... 6-3/175. ... Throws right, bats right. ... Full name: Willis Augusto Roberts.
TRANSACTIONS/CAREER NOTES: Signed as non-drafted free agent by Detroit Tigers organization (February 18, 1992). ... On disabled list (July 14-August 1 and August 1-September 13, 1994). ... On Toledo disabled list (May 3-20, 1999).

Year League	W	L	Pct.	ERA	G	GS	CG	ShO	Sv.	IP	H	R	ER	BB	SO
1992— Dominican Tigers (DSL).....	0	6	.000	8.23	12	7	1	0	0	35	43	49	32	46	17
1993— Bristol (Appl.)....................	2	3	.400	1.38	10	2	0	0	1	26	24	16	4	11	23
1994— Bristol (Appl.)....................	1	2	.333	3.92	4	4	0	0	0	20 2/3	9	9	9	8	17
1995— Fayetteville (SAL)	6	3	.667	2.70	17	15	0	0	0	80	72	33	24	40	52
1996— Lakeland (FSL)	9	7	.563	2.89	23	22	2	0	0	149 1/3	133	60	48	69	105
1997— Jacksonville (Sou.)...........	6	*15	.286	6.28	26	26	2	0	0	149	181	*120	*104	64	86
1998— Jacksonville (Sou.)...........	3	1	.750	2.19	12	2	0	0	0	24 2/3	21	10	6	10	15
— Toledo (I.L.).....................	3	3	.500	4.61	39	0	0	0	2	54 2/3	63	33	28	28	40
1999— Toledo (I.L.)	5	8	.385	6.26	31	12	2	0	0	92	112	68	64	59	52
— Detroit (A.L.)	0	0	...	13.50	1	0	0	0	0	1 1/3	3	4	2	0	0
Major League totals (1 year)........	0	0	...	13.50	1	0	0	0	0	1 1/3	3	4	2	0	0

ROBERTSON, JEROMIE　　　　　P　　　　　ASTROS

PERSONAL: Born March 30, 1977, in San Jose, Calif. ... 6-1/190. ... Throws left, bats left. ... Full name: Jeromie Paul Robertson.
HIGH SCHOOL: Exeter (Calif.) Union.
TRANSACTIONS/CAREER NOTES: Selected by Houston Astros organization in 24th round of free-agent draft (June 1, 1995).
STATISTICAL NOTES: Tied for Florida State League lead in balks with six in 1998. ... Led Texas League pitchers with nine errors, 58 total chances and seven balks in 1999.

Year League	W	L	Pct.	ERA	G	GS	CG	ShO	Sv.	IP	H	R	ER	BB	SO
1996— Gulf Coast Astros (GCL).....	5	3	.625	1.72	13	•13	1	1	0	78 1/3	51	20	15	15	*98
— Kissimmee (FSL)................	0	0	...	2.57	1	1	0	0	0	7	4	4	2	1	2
1997— Quad City (Midw.)	11	8	.579	4.07	26	25	2	1	1	146	151	86	66	56	135
1998— Kissimmee (FSL).................	10	10	.500	3.70	28	28	2	0	0	*175	185	83	72	53	131
1999— Jackson (Texas)	*15	7	.682	3.06	28	•28	1	0	0	*191	184	81	65	45	133

R

ROBINSON, KERRY — OF — MARINERS

PERSONAL: Born October 3, 1973, in St. Louis. ... 6-0/175. ... Bats left, throws left. ... Full name: Kerry Keith Robinson. ... Son of Rogers Robinson, outfielder with St. Louis Cardinals organization (1957-69).
HIGH SCHOOL: Hazelwood East (St. Louis).
COLLEGE: Southeast Missouri State.
TRANSACTIONS/CAREER NOTES: Selected by St. Louis Cardinals organization in 34th round of free-agent draft (June 1, 1995). ... Selected by Tampa Bay Devil Rays in second round (44th pick overall) of expansion draft (November 18, 1997). ... Claimed on waivers by Seattle Mariners (November 19, 1998). ... Traded by Mariners to Cincinnati Reds for P Todd Williams (July 22, 1999).
STATISTICAL NOTES: Led Midwest League in caught stealing with 27 in 1996. ... Led Texas League in caught stealing with 23 in 1997.

							BATTING								FIELDING		
Year Team (League)	Pos.	G	AB	R	H	2B	3B	HR	RBI	Avg.	BB	SO	SB	PO	A	E	Avg.
1995— Johnson City (Appl.) ..	OF	60	250	44	74	12	8	1	26	.296	16	30	14	86	5	6	.938
1996— Peoria (Midw.)............	OF	123	440	98	158	17	4	2	47	.359	51	51	•50	168	7	7	.962
1997— Arkansas (Texas)........	OF	135	*523	80	168	16	3	2	62	.321	54	64	40	193	6	7	.966
— Louisville (A.A.)........	OF	2	9	0	1	0	0	0	0	.111	0	1	0	3	0	0	1.000
1998— Orlando (Sou.)■........	OF	72	309	45	83	7	5	2	26	.269	27	28	28	135	5	0	1.000
— Durham (I.L.)............	OF	58	242	28	73	7	4	1	28	.302	23	30	18	146	3	2	.987
— Tampa Bay (A.L.)........	OF	2	3	0	0	0	0	0	0	.000	0	1	0	4	0	0	1.000
1999— Tacoma (PCL)■........	OF-DH	79	335	53	108	16	•9	0	34	.322	14	44	30	141	6	4	.974
— Indianapolis (I.L.)■....	OF	34	129	24	34	3	2	1	14	.264	4	12	14	83	3	2	.977
— Cincinnati (N.L.)........	OF	9	1	4	0	0	0	0	0	.000	0	1	0	0	0	0	...
American League totals (1 year)		2	3	0	0	0	0	0	0	.000	0	1	0	4	0	0	1.000
National League totals (1 year)		9	1	4	0	0	0	0	0	.000	0	1	0	0	0	0	...
Major League totals (2 years)		11	4	4	0	0	0	0	0	.000	0	2	0	4	0	0	1.000

ROCKER, JOHN — P — BRAVES

PERSONAL: Born October 17, 1974, in Statesboro, Ga. ... 6-4/225. ... Throws left, bats right. ... Full name: John Loy Rocker.
HIGH SCHOOL: First Presbyterian Day School (Macon, Ga.).
COLLEGE: Mercer (Ga.).
TRANSACTIONS/CAREER NOTES: Selected by Atlanta Braves organization in 18th round of free-agent draft (June 3, 1993).
STATISTICAL NOTES: Pitched 2-0 no-hit victory against Charleston, S.C. (June 9, 1996). ... Led Southern League in wild pitches with 17 in 1997.

Year League	W	L	Pct.	ERA	G	GS	CG	ShO	Sv.	IP	H	R	ER	BB	SO
1994— Danville (Appl.)...................	1	5	.167	3.53	12	12	1	0	0	63 2/3	50	36	25	38	72
1995— Eugene (N.W.)..................	1	5	.167	5.16	12	12	0	0	0	59 1/3	45	40	34	36	74
— Macon (SAL)....................	4	4	.500	4.50	16	16	0	0	0	86	86	50	43	52	61
1996— Macon (SAL)...................	5	3	.625	3.89	20	19	2	2	0	106 1/3	85	60	46	63	107
— Durham (Caro.)...............	4	3	.571	3.39	9	9	0	0	0	58 1/3	63	24	22	25	43
1997— Durham (Caro.)..............	1	1	.500	4.33	11	1	0	0	0	35 1/3	33	21	17	22	39
— Greenville (Sou.)............	5	6	.455	4.86	22	18	0	0	0	113	119	69	61	61	96
1998— Richmond (I.L.).............	1	1	.500	1.42	9	0	0	0	1	19	13	4	3	10	22
— Atlanta (N.L.)...............	1	3	.250	2.13	47	0	0	0	2	38	22	10	9	22	42
1999— Atlanta (N.L.)..............	4	5	.444	2.49	74	0	0	0	38	72 1/3	47	24	20	37	104
Major League totals (2 years).......	5	8	.385	2.37	121	0	0	0	40	110 1/3	69	34	29	59	146

DIVISION SERIES RECORD

Year League	W	L	Pct.	ERA	G	GS	CG	ShO	Sv.	IP	H	R	ER	BB	SO
1998— Atlanta (N.L.)...................	0	0	...	0.00	2	0	0	0	0	1 1/3	1	0	0	0	2
1999— Atlanta (N.L.)..................	1	0	1.000	0.00	2	0	0	0	1	3 1/3	0	0	0	2	5
Division series totals (2 years)	1	0	1.000	0.00	4	0	0	0	1	4 2/3	1	0	0	2	7

CHAMPIONSHIP SERIES RECORD

RECORDS: Shares single-series record for most games pitched—6 (1998 and 1999).

Year League	W	L	Pct.	ERA	G	GS	CG	ShO	Sv.	IP	H	R	ER	BB	SO
1998— Atlanta (N.L.)...................	1	0	1.000	0.00	6	0	0	0	0	4 2/3	3	0	0	1	5
1999— Atlanta (N.L.)..................	0	0	...	0.00	6	0	0	0	2	6 2/3	3	2	0	2	9
Champ. series totals (2 years)	1	0	1.000	0.00	12	0	0	0	2	11 1/3	6	2	0	3	14

WORLD SERIES RECORD

Year League	W	L	Pct.	ERA	G	GS	CG	ShO	Sv.	IP	H	R	ER	BB	SO
1999— Atlanta (N.L.)....................	0	0	...	0.00	2	0	0	0	0	3	2	0	0	2	4

RODRIGUEZ, ALEX — SS — MARINERS

PERSONAL: Born July 27, 1975, in New York. ... 6-3/195. ... Bats right, throws right. ... Full name: Alexander Emmanuel Rodriguez.
HIGH SCHOOL: Westminster Christian (Miami).
TRANSACTIONS/CAREER NOTES: Selected by Seattle Mariners organization in first round (first pick overall) of free-agent draft (June 3, 1993). ... On Seattle disabled list (April 22-May 7, 1996); included rehabilitation assignment to Tacoma (May 5-7). ... On disabled list (June 12-27, 1997; and April 7-May 14, 1999).
RECORDS: Hold A.L. single-season record for most home runs by shortstop—42 (1998).
HONORS: Named Major League Player of the Year by THE SPORTING NEWS (1996). ... Named shortstop on THE SPORTING NEWS A.L. All-Star team (1996 and 1998). ... Named shortstop on THE SPORTING NEWS A.L. Silver Slugger team (1996, 1998 and 1999).
STATISTICAL NOTES: Had 20-game hitting streak (August 16-September 4, 1996). ... Led A.L. with 379 total bases in 1996. ... Hit for the cycle (June 5, 1997). ... Led A.L. shortstops with 731 total chances in 1998. ... Led A.L. in grounding into double plays with 31 in 1999. ... Career major league grand slams: 6.

Year	Team (League)	Pos.	G	AB	R	H	2B	3B	HR	RBI	Avg.	BB	SO	SB	PO	A	E	Avg.
1994—	Appleton (Midw.)........	SS-DH	65	248	49	79	17	6	14	55	.319	24	44	16	86	185	19	.934
	—Jacksonville (Sou.).....	SS	17	59	7	17	4	1	1	8	.288	10	13	2	17	63	3	.964
	—Seattle (A.L.)	SS	17	54	4	11	0	0	0	2	.204	3	20	3	20	45	6	.915
	—Calgary (PCL)	SS	32	119	22	37	7	4	6	21	.311	8	25	2	45	104	3	.980
1995—	Tacoma (PCL)	SS-DH	54	214	37	77	12	3	15	45	.360	18	44	2	90	157	10	.961
	—Seattle (A.L.)	SS-DH	48	142	15	33	6	2	5	19	.232	6	42	4	56	106	8	.953
1996—	Seattle (A.L.)	SS	146	601	*141	215	*54	1	36	123	*.358	59	104	15	238	404	15	.977
	—Tacoma (PCL)	SS	2	5	0	1	0	0	0	0	.200	2	1	0	1	4	1	.833
1997—	Seattle (A.L.)	SS-DH	141	587	100	176	40	3	23	84	.300	41	99	29	209	394	*24	.962
1998—	Seattle (A.L.)	SS-DH	161	*686	123	*213	35	5	42	124	.310	45	121	46	268	445	18	.975
1999—	Seattle (A.L.)	SS	129	502	110	143	25	0	42	111	.285	56	109	21	213	382	14	.977
Major League totals (6 years)			642	2572	493	791	160	11	148	463	.308	210	495	118	1004	1776	85	.970

DIVISION SERIES RECORD

Year	Team (League)	Pos.	G	AB	R	H	2B	3B	HR	RBI	Avg.	BB	SO	SB	PO	A	E	Avg.
1995—	Seattle (A.L.)	SS-PR	1	1	1	0	0	0	0	0	.000	0	0	0	0	0	0	...
1997—	Seattle (A.L.)	SS	4	16	1	5	1	0	1	1	.313	0	5	0	5	10	0	1.000
Division series totals (2 years)			5	17	2	5	1	0	1	1	.294	0	5	0	5	10	0	1.000

CHAMPIONSHIP SERIES RECORD

Year	Team (League)	Pos.	G	AB	R	H	2B	3B	HR	RBI	Avg.	BB	SO	SB	PO	A	E	Avg.
1995—	Seattle (A.L.)	PH	1	1	0	0	0	0	0	0	.000	0	1	0	...	...	...	...

ALL-STAR GAME RECORD

Year	League	Pos.	AB	R	H	2B	3B	HR	RBI	Avg.	BB	SO	SB	PO	A	E	Avg.
1996—	American	SS	1	0	0	0	0	0	0	.000	0	0	0	0	0	0	...
1997—	American	SS	3	0	1	0	0	0	0	.333	0	2	0	0	1	0	1.000
1998—	American	SS	3	2	2	0	0	1	1	.667	0	1	0	1	2	0	1.000
All-Star Game totals (3 years)			7	2	3	0	0	1	1	.429	0	3	0	1	3	0	1.000

RODRIGUEZ, FELIX — P — GIANTS

R

PERSONAL: Born December 5, 1972, in Monte Cristi, Dominican Republic. ... 6-1/190. ... Throws right, bats right. ... Full name: Felix Antonio Rodriguez.

HIGH SCHOOL: Liceo Bijiador (Monte Cristi, Dominican Republic).

TRANSACTIONS/CAREER NOTES: Signed as non-drafted free agent by Los Angeles Dodgers organization (October 17, 1989). ... On disabled list (August 11, 1992-remainder of season). ... On Albuquerque disabled list (July 5-18, 1995). ... On disabled list (April 20-May 2 and May 12-27, 1996). ... Claimed on waivers by Cincinnati Reds (December 18, 1996). ... Traded by Reds to Arizona Diamondbacks for a player to be named later (November 11, 1997); Reds acquired P Scott Winchester to complete deal (November 18, 1997). ... On Arizona disabled list (June 21-July 30, 1998); included rehabilitation assignments to Arizona League Diamondbacks (July 20-27) and Tucson (July 28-30). ... Traded by Diamondbacks to San Francisco Giants for future considerations (December 8, 1998); Diamondbacks acquired P Troy Brohawn and OF Chris Van Rossum to complete deal (December 21, 1998).

STATISTICAL NOTES: Pitched 11-0 no-hit victory against Sarasota (August 28, 1993).

MISCELLANEOUS: Played catcher (1990-92).

Year	League	W	L	Pct.	ERA	G	GS	CG	ShO	Sv.	IP	H	R	ER	BB	SO
1993—	Vero Beach (FSL)	8	8	.500	3.75	32	20	2	1	0	132	109	71	55	71	80
1994—	San Antonio (Texas)	6	8	.429	4.03	26	26	0	0	0	136 1/3	106	70	61	*88	126
1995—	Albuquerque (PCL).............	3	2	.600	4.24	14	11	0	0	0	51	52	29	24	26	46
	—Los Angeles (N.L.)............	1	1	.500	2.53	11	0	0	0	0	10 2/3	11	3	3	5	5
1996—	Albuquerque (PCL).............	3	9	.250	5.53	27	19	0	0	0	107 1/3	111	70	66	60	65
1997—	Indianapolis (A.A.)■	3	3	.500	1.01	23	0	0	0	1	26 2/3	22	10	3	16	26
	—Cincinnati (N.L.)	0	0	...	4.30	26	1	0	0	0	46	48	23	22	28	34
1998—	Arizona (N.L.)■.................	0	2	.000	6.14	43	0	0	0	5	44	44	31	30	29	36
	—Ariz. D'backs (Ariz.)...........	0	0	...	4.15	3	2	0	0	0	4 1/3	3	4	2	2	5
	—Tucson (PCL)	0	0	...	9.00	1	0	0	0	0	1	1	1	1	2	0
1999—	San Francisco (N.L.)■	2	3	.400	3.80	47	0	0	0	0	66 1/3	67	32	28	29	55
Major League totals (4 years)		3	6	.333	4.47	127	1	0	0	5	167	170	89	83	91	130

RECORD AS POSITION PLAYER

Year	Team (League)	Pos.	G	AB	R	H	2B	3B	HR	RBI	Avg.	BB	SO	SB	PO	A	E	Avg.
1990—	Dom. Dodgers (DSL) .	...	63	241	23	55	10	0	2	33	.228	15	52	4	...	...	...	...
1991—	GC Dodgers (GCL)	C	45	139	15	37	8	1	2	21	.266	6	32	1	161	18	5	.973
1992—	Great Falls (Pio.)	C-OF	32	110	20	32	8	0	2	20	.291	1	16	2	221	33	2	.992

RODRIGUEZ, FRANKIE — P — MARINERS

PERSONAL: Born December 11, 1972, in Brooklyn, N.Y. ... 6-0/210. ... Throws right, bats right. ... Full name: Francisco Rodriguez.

HIGH SCHOOL: Eastern District (Brooklyn, N.Y.).

JUNIOR COLLEGE: Howard College (Texas).

TRANSACTIONS/CAREER NOTES: Selected by Boston Red Sox in second round of free-agent draft (June 4, 1990); pick received as compensation for Atlanta Braves signing of Type B free-agent 1B Nick Esasky. ... Traded by Red Sox with a player to be named later to Minnesota Twins for P Rick Aguilera (July 6, 1995); Twins acquired OF J.J. Johnson to complete deal (October 11, 1995). ... Claimed on waivers by Seattle Mariners (May 26, 1999). ... On suspended list (August 17-25, 1999).

STATISTICAL NOTES: Pitched 2-1 no-hit victory for Salt Lake against Iowa (May 8, 1999; first game).

MISCELLANEOUS: Played shortstop (1991). ... Scored one run in two appearances as pinch hitter (1999).

Year League	W	L	Pct.	ERA	G	GS	CG	ShO	Sv.	IP	H	R	ER	BB	SO
1992— Lynchburg (Caro.)	12	7	.632	3.09	25	25	1	0	0	148 2/3	125	56	51	65	129
1993— New Britain (East.)	7	11	.389	3.74	28	26	•4	1	0	170 2/3	147	79	71	78	151
1994— Pawtucket (I.L.)	8	13	.381	3.92	28	28	*8	1	0	*186	182	95	81	60	*160
1995— Boston (A.L.)	0	2	.000	10.57	9	2	0	0	0	15 1/3	21	19	18	10	14
— Pawtucket (I.L.)	1	1	.500	4.00	13	2	0	0	2	27	19	12	12	8	18
— Minnesota (A.L.)■	5	6	.455	5.38	16	16	0	0	0	90 1/3	93	64	54	47	45
1996— Minnesota (A.L.)	13	14	.481	5.05	38	33	3	0	2	206 2/3	218	129	116	78	110
1997— Minnesota (A.L.)	3	6	.333	4.62	43	15	0	0	0	142 1/3	147	82	73	60	65
1998— Minnesota (A.L.)	4	6	.400	6.56	20	11	0	0	0	70	88	58	51	30	62
— Salt Lake (PCL)	5	7	.417	4.67	16	16	2	1	0	96 1/3	97	53	50	35	79
1999— Salt Lake (PCL)	3	4	.429	6.70	9	9	1	0	0	43	40	34	32	14	33
— Seattle (A.L.)■	2	4	.333	5.65	28	5	0	0	3	73 1/3	94	47	46	30	47
Major League totals (5 years)	27	38	.415	5.39	154	82	3	0	5	598	661	399	358	255	343

RECORD AS POSITION PLAYER

Year Team (League)	Pos.	G	AB	R	H	2B	3B	HR	RBI	Avg.	BB	SO	SB	PO	A	E	Avg.
1991— GC Red Sox (GCL)	SS	3	14	3	7	0	1	0	3	.500	0	1	0	9	10	1	.950
— Elmira (N.Y.-Penn)	SS	67	255	36	69	5	3	6	31	.271	13	38	3	95	209	24	.927

RODRIGUEZ, GUILLERMO   C   GIANTS

PERSONAL: Born May 15, 1978, in Barquisimeto, Venezuela. ... 5-11/190. ... Bats right, throws right. ... Full name: Guillermo Segundo Rodriguez.

TRANSACTIONS/CAREER NOTES: Signed as non-drafted free agent by San Francisco Giants organization (November 17, 1995).

Year Team (League)	Pos.	G	AB	R	H	2B	3B	HR	RBI	Avg.	BB	SO	SB	PO	A	E	Avg.
1996— Bellingham (N.W.)	OF	3	4	1	0	0	0	0	0	.000	0	1	0	1	0	0	1.000
1997— Salem-Kaizer (N.W.)	C-1B	11	39	3	9	3	0	0	3	.231	5	12	0	82	10	1	.989
— San Jose (Calif.)	1B-C	13	27	2	4	3	1	0	2	.148	0	9	0	61	7	0	1.000
1998— Salem-Kaizer (N.W.)	C	1	4	0	1	0	0	0	0	.250	0	1	0	8	0	0	1.000
— San Jose (Calif.)	C	32	101	16	33	3	0	5	26	.327	13	19	9	0	0	0	1.000
1999— Bakersfield (Calif.)	C-1B	41	93	10	27	5	0	1	11	.290	3	18	4	159	21	6	.968
— Salem-Kaizer (N.W.)	C	33	114	16	29	5	0	6	34	.254	9	28	1	248	26	5	.982

RODRIGUEZ, HENRY   OF   CUBS

PERSONAL: Born November 8, 1967, in Santo Domingo, Dominican Republic. ... 6-2/225. ... Bats left, throws left. ... Full name: Henry Anderson Lorenzo Rodriguez.

HIGH SCHOOL: Liceo Republica de Paraguay.

TRANSACTIONS/CAREER NOTES: Signed as non-drafted free agent by Los Angeles Dodgers organization (July 14, 1985). ... Traded by Dodgers with IF Jeff Treadway to Montreal Expos for OF Roberto Kelly and P Joey Eischen (May 23, 1995). ... On Montreal disabled list (June 2-September 1, 1995); included rehabilitation assignment to Ottawa (August 7-16). ... On suspended list (August 16-19, 1996). ... Traded by Expos to Chicago Cubs for P Miguel Batista (December 12, 1997). ... On disabled list (August 24-September 8, 1998). ... Granted free agency (October 23, 1998). ... Re-signed by Cubs (December 2, 1998).

RECORDS: Holds N.L. single-season record for most strikeouts by lefthander—160 (1996).

HONORS: Named Texas League Most Valuable Player (1990).

STATISTICAL NOTES: Tied for Gulf Coast League lead with seven intentional bases on balls received in 1987. ... Led Texas League with 14 sacrifice flies in 1990. ... Tied for Pacific Coast League lead with 10 sacrifice flies in 1992. ... Had 15-game hitting streak (July 31-August 14, 1999). ... Career major league grand slams: 4.

Year Team (League)	Pos.	G	AB	R	H	2B	3B	HR	RBI	Avg.	BB	SO	SB	PO	A	E	Avg.
1987— GC Dodgers (GCL)	1B-SS	49	148	23	49	7	3	0	15	*.331	16	15	3	309	23	6	.982
1988— Dom. Dodgers (DSL)	...	19	21	9	8	2	0	0	10	.381	10	6	4	...	...	...	...
— Salem (N.W.)	1B	72	291	47	84	14	4	2	39	.289	21	42	14	585	*38	7	.989
1989— Vero Beach (FSL)	1B-OF	126	433	53	123	*33	1	10	73	.284	48	58	7	1072	66	12	.990
— Bakersfield (Calif.)	1B	3	9	2	2	0	0	1	2	.222	0	3	0	8	0	0	1.000
1990— San Antonio (Texas)	OF	129	495	82	144	22	9	*28	*109	.291	61	66	5	223	5	10	.958
1991— Albuquerque (PCL)	OF-1B	121	446	61	121	22	5	10	67	.271	25	62	4	234	12	5	.980
1992— Albuquerque (PCL)	1B-OF	94	365	59	111	21	5	14	72	.304	31	57	1	484	41	10	.981
1993— Albuquerque (PCL)	1B-OF	46	179	26	53	13	5	4	30	.296	14	37	1	277	18	5	.983
— Los Angeles (N.L.)	OF-1B	76	176	20	39	10	0	8	23	.222	11	39	1	127	9	1	.993
1994— Los Angeles (N.L.)	OF-1B	104	306	33	82	14	2	8	49	.268	17	58	0	198	9	2	.990
1995— Los Angeles (N.L.)	OF-1B	21	80	6	21	4	1	1	10	.263	5	17	0	37	0	0	1.000
— Montreal (N.L.)■	1B-OF	24	58	7	12	0	0	1	5	.207	6	11	0	88	7	1	.990
— Ottawa (I.L.)	DH	4	15	0	3	1	0	0	2	.200	1	4	0	...	...	...	...
1996— Montreal (N.L.)	OF-1B	145	532	81	147	42	1	36	103	.276	37	*160	2	528	33	11	.981
1997— Montreal (N.L.)	OF-1B	132	476	55	116	28	3	26	83	.244	42	149	3	220	6	3	.987
1998— Chicago (N.L.)■	OF-DH	128	415	56	104	21	1	31	85	.251	54	113	1	215	7	1	.996
1999— Chicago (N.L.)	OF-DH	130	447	72	136	29	0	26	87	.304	56	113	2	222	7	6	.974
Major League totals (8 years)		813	2636	341	689	155	8	140	459	.261	236	690	9	1703	86	28	.985

DIVISION SERIES RECORD

Year Team (League)	Pos.	G	AB	R	H	2B	3B	HR	RBI	Avg.	BB	SO	SB	PO	A	E	Avg.
1998— Chicago (N.L.)	OF-PH	3	7	0	1	1	0	0	0	.143	1	2	0	5	1	0	1.000

ALL-STAR GAME RECORD

Year League	Pos.	AB	R	H	2B	3B	HR	RBI	Avg.	BB	SO	SB	PO	A	E	Avg.
1996— National	PH	1	0	1	0	0	0	1	1.000	0	0	0	...	...	...	...

RODRIGUEZ, IVAN   C   RANGERS

PERSONAL: Born November 30, 1971, in Vega Baja, Puerto Rico. ... 5-9/205. ... Bats right, throws right.
HIGH SCHOOL: Lina Padron Rivera (Vega Baja, Puerto Rico).
TRANSACTIONS/CAREER NOTES: Signed as non-drafted free agent by Texas Rangers organization (July 27, 1988). ... On disabled list (June 6-27, 1992).
RECORDS: Holds A.L. single-season record for most home runs by catcher—35 (1999).
HONORS: Won A.L. Gold Glove at catcher (1992-99). ... Named catcher on THE SPORTING NEWS A.L. All-Star team (1994-99). ... Named catcher on THE SPORTING NEWS A.L. Silver Slugger team (1994-99). ... Named A.L. Most Valuable Player by Baseball Writers' Association of America (1999).
STATISTICAL NOTES: Led South Atlantic League catchers with 34 double plays in 1989. ... Led Florida State League catchers with 842 total chances in 1990. ... Led A.L. catchers with 941 total chances and 11 double plays in 1996. ... Hit three home runs in one game (September 11, 1997). ... Led A.L. catchers with 942 total chances in 1998. ... Had 20-game hitting streak (May 8-June 1, 1999). ... Led A.L. in grounding into double plays with 31 in 1999. ... Career major league grand slams: 1.

Year Team (League)	Pos.	G	AB	R	H	2B	3B	HR	RBI	Avg.	BB	SO	SB	PO	A	E	Avg.
1989—Gastonia (SAL)	C	112	386	38	92	22	1	7	42	.238	21	58	2	691	*96	11	.986
1990—Charlotte (FSL)	C	109	408	48	117	17	7	2	55	.287	12	50	1	*727	101	14	.983
1991—Tulsa (Texas)	C	50	175	16	48	7	2	3	28	.274	6	27	1	210	33	3	.988
—Texas (A.L.)	C	88	280	24	74	16	0	3	27	.264	5	42	0	517	62	10	.983
1992—Texas (A.L.)	C-DH	123	420	39	109	16	1	8	37	.260	24	73	0	763	85	*15	.983
1993—Texas (A.L.)	C-DH	137	473	56	129	28	4	10	66	.273	29	70	8	801	76	8	.991
1994—Texas (A.L.)	C	99	363	56	108	19	1	16	57	.298	31	42	6	600	44	5	.992
1995—Texas (A.L.)	C-DH	130	492	56	149	32	2	12	67	.303	16	48	0	707	*67	8	.990
1996—Texas (A.L.)	C-DH	153	639	116	192	47	3	19	86	.300	38	55	5	*850	*81	•10	.989
1997—Texas (A.L.)	C-DH	150	597	98	187	34	4	20	77	.313	38	89	7	821	*75	7	.992
1998—Texas (A.L.)	C-DH	145	579	88	186	40	4	21	91	.321	32	88	9	*864	*72	6	.994
1999—Texas (A.L.)	C-DH	144	600	116	199	29	1	35	113	.332	24	64	25	850	83	7	.993
Major League totals (9 years)		1169	4443	649	1333	261	20	144	621	.300	237	571	60	6773	645	76	.990

DIVISION SERIES RECORD

Year Team (League)	Pos.	G	AB	R	H	2B	3B	HR	RBI	Avg.	BB	SO	SB	PO	A	E	Avg.
1996—Texas (A.L.)	C	4	16	1	6	1	0	0	2	.375	2	3	0	21	3	0	1.000
1998—Texas (A.L.)	C	3	10	0	1	0	0	0	1	.100	0	5	0	27	3	0	1.000
1999—Texas (A.L.)	C	3	12	0	3	1	0	0	0	.250	0	2	1	21	0	0	1.000
Division series totals (3 years)		10	38	1	10	2	0	0	3	.263	2	10	1	69	6	0	1.000

ALL-STAR GAME RECORD

RECORDS: Shares single-game record for most at-bats (nine-inning game)—5 (July 12, 1994).

Year League	Pos.	AB	R	H	2B	3B	HR	RBI	Avg.	BB	SO	SB	PO	A	E	Avg.
1992—American	C	2	0	0	0	0	0	0	.000	0	1	0	4	0	0	1.000
1993—American	C	2	1	1	1	0	0	0	.500	0	0	0	3	0	0	1.000
1994—American	C	5	1	2	0	0	0	0	.400	0	1	0	5	0	0	1.000
1995—American	C	3	0	0	0	0	0	0	.000	0	1	0	6	1	0	1.000
1996—American	C	2	0	0	0	0	0	0	.000	0	1	0	6	2	0	1.000
1997—American	C	2	0	0	0	0	0	0	.000	0	0	0	3	1	0	1.000
1998—American	C	4	1	3	0	0	0	1	.750	0	1	0	5	0	0	1.000
1999—American	C	2	0	0	0	0	0	0	.000	0	1	0	10	1	0	1.000
All-Star Game totals (8 years)		22	3	6	1	0	0	1	.273	0	5	1	42	5	0	1.000

RODRIGUEZ, LIU   2B/SS   WHITE SOX

PERSONAL: Born November 5, 1976, in Caracas, Venezuela. ... 5-9/170. ... Bats both, throws right. ... Full name: Liubiemithz Rodriguez.
HIGH SCHOOL: Simon Rodriguez (Caracas, Venezuela).
TRANSACTIONS/CAREER NOTES: Signed as non-drafted free agent by Chicago White Sox organization (January 25, 1995). ... On Birmingham disabled list (April 11-18, 1999).
STATISTICAL NOTES: Led South Atlantic League second basemen with .989 fielding percentage in 1997. ... Led Carolina League second basemen with .986 fielding percentage in 1998.

Year Team (League)	Pos.	G	AB	R	H	2B	3B	HR	RBI	Avg.	BB	SO	SB	PO	A	E	Avg.
1995—GC White Sox (GCL)	2B	36	119	18	27	6	1	1	11	.227	23	19	4	63	102	5	.971
1996—Hickory (SAL)	2B-SS	122	430	57	107	18	0	0	30	.249	60	77	15	213	329	26	.954
1997—Hickory (SAL)	2B-SS	129	450	72	130	21	6	1	62	.289	65	56	12	225	336	6	†.989
1998—Win.-Salem (Car.)	2B-SS-1B	112	420	62	117	27	3	2	43	.279	45	40	15	201	266	8	†.983
1999—Birmingham (Sou.)	2-S-1-3-OF	64	244	42	71	11	1	3	37	.291	22	35	5	120	149	9	.968
—Chicago (A.L.)	2B-SS-DH-3B	39	93	8	22	2	2	1	12	.237	12	11	0	45	67	3	.974
Major League totals (1 year)		39	93	8	22	2	2	1	12	.237	12	11	0	45	67	3	.974

RODRIGUEZ, NERIO   P   BLUE JAYS

PERSONAL: Born March 22, 1973, in Bani, Dominican Republic. ... 6-1/205. ... Throws right, bats right.
TRANSACTIONS/CAREER NOTES: Signed as non-drafted free agent by Chicago White Sox organization (February 2, 1990). ... Selected by Baltimore Orioles organization from White Sox organization in Rule 5 minor league draft (December 5, 1994). ... On Frederick disabled list (April 5-August 11, 1996). ... On Baltimore disabled list (May 26-June 30, 1998); included rehabilitation assignment to Bowie (June 24-30). ... Traded by Orioles with OF Shannon Carter to Toronto Blue Jays for P Juan Guzman (July 31, 1998).
STATISTICAL NOTES: Led Gulf Coast League catchers with 312 total chances in 1992.

MISCELLANEOUS: Played catcher (1990-95).

Year	League	W	L	Pct.	ERA	G	GS	CG	ShO	Sv.	IP	H	R	ER	BB	SO
1995—	High Desert (Calif.)............	0	0	...	1.80	7	0	0	0	0	10	8	2	2	7	10
1996—	Frederick (Caro.)	8	7	.533	2.26	24	17	1	0	2	111 1/3	83	42	28	40	114
—	Baltimore (A.L.).................	0	1	.000	4.32	8	1	0	0	0	16 2/3	18	11	8	7	12
—	Rochester (I.L.).................	1	0	1.000	1.80	2	2	0	0	0	15	10	3	3	2	6
1997—	Rochester (I.L.).................	11	10	.524	3.90	27	27	1	1	0	168 1/3	124	82	73	62	*160
—	Baltimore (A.L.).................	2	1	.667	4.91	6	2	0	0	0	22	21	15	12	8	11
1998—	Rochester (I.L.).................	1	4	.200	5.47	5	5	0	0	0	24 2/3	24	16	15	10	19
—	Baltimore (A.L.).................	1	3	.250	8.05	6	4	0	0	0	19	25	17	17	9	8
—	Bowie (East.)...................	0	1	.000	4.50	2	2	0	0	0	4	6	2	2	0	7
—	Toronto (A.L.)■.................	1	0	1.000	9.72	7	0	0	0	0	8 1/3	10	9	9	8	3
1999—	Syracuse (I.L.).................	10	8	.556	4.54	27	27	1	1	0	162 2/3	161	84	82	53	137
—	Toronto (A.L.).................	0	1	.000	13.50	2	0	0	0	0	2	3	3	2	2	
Major League totals (4 years)......		4	6	.400	6.49	29	7	0	0	0	68	76	55	49	34	36

RECORD AS POSITION PLAYER

					BATTING								FIELDING			
Year	Team (League)	Pos.	G	AB	R	H	2B	3B	HR	RBI	Avg.	BB	SO	SB	PO	A	E	Avg.
1991—	GC Whi. Sox (GCL)	C	26	89	4	20	1	0	0	8	.225	2	24	3	153	23	5	.972
1992—	GC Whi. Sox (GCL)	C	41	122	18	33	8	1	2	13	.270	10	31	1	*257	43	*12	.962
1993—	Hickory (S. Atl.)	C	82	262	31	54	9	2	4	32	.206	27	70	4	476	45	13	.976
1994—	South Bend (Mid.)....	C	18	59	4	13	4	0	0	8	.220	2	14	0	95	19	0	1.000
—	Prince Will. (Car.)......	C	6	19	2	4	1	1	0	1	.211	1	9	0	34	6	0	1.000
1995—	Bowie (Eastern)■......	C	3	4	0	0	0	0	0	0	.000	2	2	0	13	1	0	1.000
—	High Desert (Calif.).....	C	58	144	20	34	7	0	4	12	.236	18	50	5	325	34	8	.978

RODRIGUEZ, RICH   P   METS

PERSONAL: Born March 1, 1963, in Downey, Calif. ... 6-0/205. ... Throws left, bats left. ... Full name: Richard Anthony Rodriguez.
HIGH SCHOOL: Mountain View (El Monte, Calif.).
COLLEGE: Tennessee.
TRANSACTIONS/CAREER NOTES: Selected by Kansas City Royals organization in 17th round of free-agent draft (June 8, 1981); did not sign. ... Selected by New York Mets organization in ninth round of free-agent draft (June 4, 1984). ... Traded by Mets to San Diego Padres for 1B Brad Pounders and 1B Bill Stevenson (January 13, 1989). ... Traded by Padres with 3B Gary Sheffield to Florida Marlins for P Trevor Hoffman, P Jose Martinez and P Andres Berumen (June 24, 1993). ... Released by Marlins (March 29, 1994). ... Signed by St. Louis Cardinals (April 1, 1994). ... On disabled list (April 27, 1995-remainder of season). ... Released by Cardinals (November 20, 1995). ... Signed by Cincinnati Reds organization (January 2, 1996). ... Released by Reds (March 24, 1996). ... Signed by Kansas City Royals organization (April 9, 1996). ... On disabled list (May 18-29, 1996). ... Granted free agency (October 15, 1996). ... Signed by San Francisco Giants organization (November 25, 1996). ... Granted free agency (October 30, 1997). ... Re-signed by Giants (December 7, 1997). ... Granted free agency (October 28, 1999). ... Signed by Mets (January 21, 2000).
MISCELLANEOUS: Appeared in one game as pinch runner (1991). ... Had sacrifice hit in only appearance as pinch hitter (1992).

Year	League	W	L	Pct.	ERA	G	GS	CG	ShO	Sv.	IP	H	R	ER	BB	SO
1984—	Little Falls (NY-P)	2	1	.667	2.80	25	1	0	0	0	35 1/3	28	21	11	36	27
1985—	Columbia (SAL)	6	3	.667	4.03	49	3	0	0	6	80 1/3	89	41	36	36	71
1986—	Lynchburg (Caro.)	2	1	.667	3.57	36	0	0	0	3	45 1/3	37	20	18	19	38
—	Jackson (Texas)	3	4	.429	9.00	13	5	1	0	0	33	51	35	33	15	15
1987—	Lynchburg (Caro.)	3	1	.750	2.78	*69	0	0	0	5	68	69	23	21	26	59
1988—	Jackson (Texas)	2	7	.222	2.87	47	1	0	0	6	78 1/3	66	35	25	42	68
1989—	Wichita (Texas)■	8	3	.727	3.63	54	0	0	0	8	74 1/3	74	30	30	37	40
1990—	Las Vegas (PCL)	3	4	.429	3.51	27	2	0	0	8	59	50	24	23	22	46
—	San Diego (N.L.)	1	1	.500	2.83	32	0	0	0	1	47 2/3	52	17	15	16	22
1991—	San Diego (N.L.)	3	1	.750	3.26	64	1	0	0	0	80	66	31	29	44	40
1992—	San Diego (N.L.)	6	3	.667	2.37	61	1	0	0	0	91	77	28	24	29	64
1993—	San Diego (N.L.)	2	3	.400	3.30	34	0	0	0	2	30	34	15	11	9	22
—	Florida (N.L.)■.................	0	1	.000	4.11	36	0	0	0	1	46	39	23	21	24	21
1994—	St. Louis (N.L.)■..............	3	5	.375	4.03	56	0	0	0	0	60 1/3	62	30	27	26	43
1995—	St. Louis (N.L.)................	0	0	...	0.00	1	0	0	0	0	1 2/3	0	0	0	0	0
1996—	Omaha (A.A.)■.................	2	3	.400	3.99	47	0	0	0	3	70	75	40	31	20	68
1997—	San Francisco (N.L.)■........	4	3	.571	3.17	71	0	0	0	1	65 1/3	65	24	23	21	32
1998—	San Francisco (N.L.)	4	0	1.000	3.70	68	0	0	0	2	65 2/3	69	28	27	20	44
1999—	San Francisco (N.L.)	3	0	1.000	5.24	62	0	0	0	0	56 2/3	60	33	33	28	44
Major League totals (9 years).......		26	17	.605	3.47	485	2	0	0	7	544 1/3	524	229	210	217	332

DIVISION SERIES RECORD

Year	League	W	L	Pct.	ERA	G	GS	CG	ShO	Sv.	IP	H	R	ER	BB	SO
1997—	San Francisco (N.L.)	0	0	...	0.00	2	0	0	0	0	1	1	0	0	0	0

RODRIGUEZ, WILFREDO   P   ASTROS

PERSONAL: Born March 20, 1979, in Ciudad Bolivar, Venezuela. ... 6-3/180. ... Throws left, bats left. ... Full name: Wilfredo Jose Rodriguez.
TRANSACTIONS/CAREER NOTES: Signed as non-drafted free agent by Houston Astros organization (July 25, 1995).
STATISTICAL NOTES: Led Midwest League with nine balks in 1998.

Year	League	W	L	Pct.	ERA	G	GS	CG	ShO	Sv.	IP	H	R	ER	BB	SO
1996—	Dom. Astros (DSL)............	1	2	.333	2.97	18	0	0	0	0	33 1/3	28	17	11	21	29
1997—	Gulf Coast Astros (GCL).....	•8	2	.800	3.04	12	12	1	1	0	68	54	30	23	32	71
1998—	Quad City (Midw.)	11	5	.688	3.05	28	27	1	0	0	165	122	70	56	62	170
1999—	Kissimmee (FSL)...............	*15	7	.682	2.88	25	24	0	0	0	153 1/3	108	55	49	62	*148

PERSONAL: Born November 10, 1964, in Savannah, Ga. ... 6-1/205. ... Throws left, bats left. ... Full name: Kenneth Scott Rogers.

HIGH SCHOOL: Plant City (Fla.).

TRANSACTIONS/CAREER NOTES: Selected by Texas Rangers organization in 39th round of free-agent draft (June 7, 1982). ... On Tulsa disabled list (April 12-30, 1986). ... Granted free agency (October 31, 1995). ... Signed by New York Yankees (December 30, 1995). ... Traded by Yankees with IF Mariano Duncan and P Kevin Henthorne to San Diego Padres for OF Greg Vaughn, P Kerry Taylor and P Chris Clark (July 4, 1997); trade later voided because Vaughn failed physical (July 6). ... Traded by Yankees with cash to Oakland Athletics for a player to be named later (November 7, 1997); Yankees acquired 3B Scott Brosius to complete deal (November 18, 1997). ... Traded by Athletics to New York Mets for OF Terrance Long and P Leo Vasquez (July 23, 1999). ... Granted free agency (October 29, 1999). ... Signed by Rangers (December 29, 1999).

STATISTICAL NOTES: Tied for A.L. lead with five balks in 1993. ... Pitched 4-0 perfect game against California (July 28, 1994).

Year League	W	L	Pct.	ERA	G	GS	CG	ShO	Sv.	IP	H	R	ER	BB	SO
1982—Gulf Coast Rangers (GCL)..	0	0	...	0.00	2	0	0	0	0	3	0	0	0	0	4
1983—Gulf Coast Rangers (GCL)..	4	1	.800	2.36	15	6	0	0	1	53 1/3	40	21	14	20	36
1984—Burlington (Midw.)	4	7	.364	3.98	39	4	1	0	3	92 2/3	87	52	41	33	93
1985—Daytona Beach (FSL)........	0	1	.000	7.20	6	0	0	0	0	10	12	9	8	11	9
—Burlington (Midw.)	2	5	.286	2.84	33	4	2	1	4	95	67	34	30	62	96
1986—Tulsa (Texas)	0	3	.000	9.91	10	4	0	0	0	26 1/3	39	30	29	18	23
—Salem (Caro.)	2	7	.222	6.27	12	12	0	0	0	66	75	54	46	26	46
1987—Charlotte (FSL).................	0	3	.000	4.76	5	3	0	0	0	17	17	13	9	8	14
—Tulsa (Texas)	1	5	.167	5.35	28	6	0	0	2	69	80	51	41	35	59
1988—Tulsa (Texas)	4	6	.400	4.00	13	13	2	0	0	83 1/3	73	43	37	34	76
—Charlotte (FSL)................	2	0	1.000	1.27	8	6	0	0	1	35 1/3	22	8	5	11	26
1989—Texas (A.L.)	3	4	.429	2.93	73	0	0	0	2	73 2/3	60	28	24	42	63
1990—Texas (A.L.)	10	6	.625	3.13	69	3	0	0	15	97 2/3	93	40	34	42	74
1991—Texas (A.L.)	10	10	.500	5.42	63	9	0	0	5	109 2/3	121	80	66	61	73
1992—Texas (A.L.)	3	6	.333	3.09	*81	0	0	0	6	78 2/3	80	32	27	26	70
1993—Texas (A.L.)	16	10	.615	4.10	35	33	5	0	0	208 1/3	210	108	95	71	140
1994—Texas (A.L.)	11	8	.579	4.46	24	24	6	2	0	167 1/3	169	93	83	52	120
1995—Texas (A.L.)	17	7	.708	3.38	31	31	3	1	0	208	192	87	78	76	140
1996—New York (A.L.)■...........	12	8	.600	4.68	30	30	2	1	0	179	179	97	93	83	92
1997—New York (A.L.)	6	7	.462	5.65	31	22	1	0	0	145	161	100	91	62	78
1998—Oakland (A.L.)■...............	16	8	.667	3.17	34	34	7	1	0	238 2/3	215	96	84	67	138
1999—Oakland (A.L.)	5	3	.625	4.30	19	19	3	0	0	119 1/3	135	66	57	41	68
—New York (N.L.)■	5	1	.833	4.03	12	12	2	1	0	76	71	35	34	28	58
A.L. totals (11 years)	109	77	.586	4.05	490	205	27	5	28	1625 1/3	1615	827	732	623	1056
N.L. totals (1 year)......................	5	1	.833	4.03	12	12	2	1	0	76	71	35	34	28	58
Major League totals (11 years).....	114	78	.594	4.05	502	217	29	6	28	1701 1/3	1686	862	766	651	1114

DIVISION SERIES RECORD

Year League	W	L	Pct.	ERA	G	GS	CG	ShO	Sv.	IP	H	R	ER	BB	SO
1996— New York (A.L.).................	0	0	...	9.00	2	1	0	0	0	2	5	2	2	2	1
1999— New York (N.L.).................	0	1	.000	8.31	1	1	0	0	0	4 1/3	5	4	4	2	6
Division series totals (2 years)	0	1	.000	8.53	3	2	0	0	0	6 1/3	10	6	6	4	7

CHAMPIONSHIP SERIES RECORD

Year League	W	L	Pct.	ERA	G	GS	CG	ShO	Sv.	IP	H	R	ER	BB	SO
1996— New York (A.L.).................	0	0	...	12.00	1	1	0	0	0	3	5	4	4	2	3
1999— New York (N.L.).................	0	2	.000	5.87	3	1	0	0	0	7 2/3	11	5	5	7	2
Champ. series totals (2 years)	0	2	.000	7.59	4	2	0	0	0	10 2/3	16	9	9	9	5

WORLD SERIES RECORD

NOTES: Member of World Series championship team (1996).

Year League	W	L	Pct.	ERA	G	GS	CG	ShO	Sv.	IP	H	R	ER	BB	SO
1996— New York (A.L.).................	0	0	...	22.50	1	1	0	0	0	2	5	5	5	2	0

ALL-STAR GAME RECORD

Year League	W	L	Pct.	ERA	GS	CG	ShO	Sv.	IP	H	R	ER	BB	SO
1995— American	0	0	...	9.00	0	0	0	0	1	1	1	1	0	2

ROJAS, MEL   P

PERSONAL: Born December 10, 1966, in Haina, Dominican Republic. ... 5-11/212. ... Throws right, bats right. ... Full name: Melaquides Rojas. ... Nephew of Felipe Alou, manager, Montreal Expos, and outfielder/first baseman with six major league teams (1958-74); nephew of Matty Alou, outfielder with six major league teams (1960-74); nephew of Jesus Alou, outfielder with four major league teams (1963-75 and 1978-79); brother of Francisco Rojas, minor league outfielder (1978 and 1979); and cousin of Moises Alou, outfielder, Houston Astros. ... Name pronounced RO-hoss.

HIGH SCHOOL: Liceo Manresa (Santo Domingo, Dominican Republic).

TRANSACTIONS/CAREER NOTES: Signed as non-drafted free agent by Montreal Expos organization (November 7, 1985). ... On Rockford disabled list (May 7-June 14, 1988). ... On West Palm Beach disabled list (August 8, 1988-remainder of season). ... On Indianapolis disabled list (June 26-July 5, 1991). ... On disabled list (July 4-19, 1993). ... Granted free agency (December 7, 1996). ... Signed by Chicago Cubs (December 11, 1996). ... Traded by Cubs with OF Brian McRae and P Turk Wendell to Mets for OF Lance Johnson and two players to be named later (August 8, 1997); Cubs acquired P Mark Clark (August 11, 1997) and IF Manny Alexander (August 14, 1997) to complete deal. ... Traded by Mets to Los Angeles Dodgers for 3B/OF Bobby Bonilla (November 11, 1998). ... Traded by Dodgers with P Dave Mlicki to Detroit Tigers for P Robinson Checo, P Apostol Garcia, P Rick Roberts and cash considerations (April 16, 1999). ... Released by Tigers (May 12, 1999). ... Signed by Expos organization (May 17, 1999). ... Released by Expos (July 3, 1999).

RECORDS: Shares major league record for striking out side on nine pitches (May 11, 1994, ninth inning).

Year League	W	L	Pct.	ERA	G	GS	CG	ShO	Sv.	IP	H	R	ER	BB	SO
1986— Gulf Coast Expos (GCL)	4	5	.444	4.88	13	12	1	0	0	55 1/3	63	39	30	37	34
1987— Burlington (Midw.)	8	9	.471	3.80	25	25	4	1	0	158 2/3	146	84	67	67	100
1988— Rockford (Midw.)	6	4	.600	2.45	12	12	0	0	0	73 1/3	52	30	20	29	72
—West Palm Beach (FSL)	1	0	1.000	3.60	2	2	0	0	0	5	4	2	2	1	4
1989— Jacksonville (Sou.).............	10	7	.588	2.49	34	12	1	1	5	112	62	39	31	57	104
1990— Indianapolis (A.A.).............	2	4	.333	3.13	17	17	0	0	0	97 2/3	84	42	34	47	64
—Montreal (N.L.)...............	3	1	.750	3.60	23	0	0	0	1	40	34	17	16	24	26
1991— Montreal (N.L.)...............	3	3	.500	3.75	37	0	0	0	6	48	42	21	20	13	37
—Indianapolis (A.A.).............	4	2	.667	4.10	14	10	0	0	1	52 2/3	50	29	24	14	55
1992— Indianapolis (A.A.).............	2	1	.667	5.40	4	0	0	0	0	8 1/3	10	5	5	3	7
—Montreal (N.L.)...............	7	1	.875	1.43	68	0	0	0	10	100 2/3	71	17	16	34	70
1993— Montreal (N.L.)...............	5	8	.385	2.95	66	0	0	0	10	88 1/3	80	39	29	30	48
1994— Montreal (N.L.)...............	3	2	.600	3.32	58	0	0	0	16	84	71	35	31	21	84
1995— Montreal (N.L.)...............	1	4	.200	4.12	59	0	0	0	30	67 2/3	69	32	31	29	61
1996— Montreal (N.L.)■...............	7	4	.636	3.22	74	0	0	0	36	81	56	30	29	28	92
1997— Chicago (N.L.)■	0	4	.000	4.42	54	0	0	0	13	59	54	30	29	30	61
—New York (N.L.)■	0	2	.000	5.13	23	0	0	0	2	26 1/3	24	17	15	6	32
1998— New York (N.L.)..............	5	2	.714	6.05	50	0	0	0	2	58	68	39	39	30	41
1999— Los Angeles (N.L.)■	0	0	...	12.60	5	0	0	0	0	5	5	7	7	3	3
—Detroit (A.L.)■...................	0	0	...	22.74	5	0	0	0	0	6 1/3	12	16	16	4	6
—Ottawa (I.L.)■....................	0	1	.000	5.14	12	0	0	0	2	21	25	13	12	12	16
—Montreal (N.L.).................	0	0	...	16.88	3	0	0	0	0	2 2/3	5	5	5	2	1
A.L. totals (1 year)	0	0	...	22.74	5	0	0	0	0	6 1/3	12	16	16	4	6
N.L. totals (10 years)	34	31	.523	3.64	520	0	0	0	126	660 2/3	579	289	267	250	556
Major League totals (10 years)	34	31	.523	3.82	525	0	0	0	126	667	591	305	283	254	562

ROLEN, SCOTT   3B   PHILLIES

PERSONAL: Born April 4, 1975, in Jasper, Ind. ... 6-4/226. ... Bats right, throws right. ... Full name: Scott Bruce Rolen.
HIGH SCHOOL: Jasper (Ind.).
TRANSACTIONS/CAREER NOTES: Selected by Philadelphia Phillies organization in second round of free-agent draft (June 3, 1993).
RECORDS: Shares major league single-game record for most strikeouts (nine-inning game)—5 (August 23, 1999).
HONORS: Named N.L. Rookie Player of the Year by THE SPORTING NEWS (1997). ... Named N.L. Rookie of the Year by Baseball Writers' Association of America (1997). ... Won N.L. Gold Glove at third base (1998).
STATISTICAL NOTES: Led South Atlantic League third basemen with 457 total chances and 36 double plays in 1994. ... Led N.L. third basemen in total chances with 459 in 1997 and 468 in 1998. ... Career major league grand slams: 1.

						BATTING								FIELDING		
Year Team (League)	Pos.	G	AB	R	H	2B	3B	HR	RBI	Avg.	BB	SO	SB	PO	A	E	Avg.
1993— Martinsville (Appl.).....	3B	25	80	8	25	5	0	0	12	.313	10	15	3	23	57	10	.889
1994— Spartanburg (SAL)	3B	138	513	83	151	34	5	14	72	.294	55	90	6	96	323	38	.917
1995— Clearwater (FSL)	3B	66	238	45	69	13	2	10	39	.290	37	46	4	43	135	20	.899
—Reading (East.)...........	3B	20	76	16	22	3	0	3	15	.289	7	14	1	10	47	4	.934
1996— Reading (East.)...........	3B	61	230	44	83	22	2	9	42	.361	34	32	8	41	125	9	.949
—Scranton/W.B. (I.L.) ...	3B	45	168	23	46	17	0	2	19	.274	28	28	4	32	88	6	.952
—Philadelphia (N.L.)......	3B	37	130	10	33	7	0	4	18	.254	13	27	0	29	54	4	.954
1997— Philadelphia (N.L.)......	3B	156	561	93	159	35	3	21	92	.283	76	138	16	*144	291	24	.948
1998— Philadelphia (N.L.)......	3B	160	601	120	174	45	4	31	110	.290	93	141	14	*135	319	14	.970
1999— Philadelphia (N.L.)......	3B	112	421	74	113	28	1	26	77	.268	67	114	12	111	227	14	.960
Major League totals (4 years)		465	1713	297	479	115	8	82	297	.280	249	420	42	419	891	56	.959

ROLISON, NATE   1B   MARLINS

PERSONAL: Born March 27, 1977, in Hattiesburg, Miss. ... 6-5/240. ... Bats left, throws right. ... Full name: Nathan M. Rolison.
HIGH SCHOOL: Petal (Miss.).
TRANSACTIONS/CAREER NOTES: Selected by Florida Marlins organization in second round of free-agent draft (June 1, 1995).
STATISTICAL NOTES: Led Midwest League first basemen with 1,254 total chances and 114 double plays in 1996. ... Led Florida State first basemen with 89 double plays in 1997.

						BATTING								FIELDING		
Year Team (League)	Pos.	G	AB	R	H	2B	3B	HR	RBI	Avg.	BB	SO	SB	PO	A	E	Avg.
1995— GC Marlins (GCL)	1B	37	134	22	37	10	2	1	19	.276	15	34	0	283	20	5	.984
1996— Kane County (Midw.)..	1B	131	474	63	115	28	1	14	75	.243	66	170	3	*1161	•80	13	.990
1997— Brevard County (FSL).	1B	122	473	59	121	22	0	16	65	.256	38	*143	3	1036	69	17	.985
1998— Portland (East.)	1B	131	484	80	134	35	2	16	83	.277	64	150	5	1081	85	13	.989
1999— Portland (East.)	1B-DH	124	438	71	131	20	1	17	69	.299	68	112	0	920	69	13	.987

ROLLINS, JIMMY   SS   PHILLIES

PERSONAL: Born November 27, 1978, in Oakland. ... 5-8/154. ... Bats both, throws right. ... Full name: James Calvin Rollins. ... Cousin of Tony Tarasco, outfielder with six major league teams (1988-99).
HIGH SCHOOL: Encinal (Alameda, Calif.).
TRANSACTIONS/CAREER NOTES: Selected by Philadelphia Phillies organization in second round of free-agent draft (June 4, 1996).
STATISTICAL NOTES: Led South Atlantic League shortstops wth 648 total chances in 1997.

						BATTING								FIELDING		
Year Team (League)	Pos.	G	AB	R	H	2B	3B	HR	RBI	Avg.	BB	SO	SB	PO	A	E	Avg.
1996— Martinsville (Appl.).....	SS	49	172	22	41	3	1	1	16	.238	28	20	11	66	126	20	.906
1997— Piedmont (SAL).........	SS	139	560	94	151	22	8	6	59	.270	52	80	46	*201	*421	26	*.960
1998— Clearwater (FSL)	SS	119	495	72	121	18	9	6	35	.244	41	62	23	192	380	29	*.952
1999— Reading (East.)..........	SS	133	532	81	145	21	8	11	56	.273	51	47	24	211	*392	22	.965
—Scranton/W.B. (I.L.) ...	SS	4	13	0	1	1	0	0	0	.077	1	1	1	9	15	1	.960

ROLLS, DAMIAN — 3B — DEVIL RAYS

PERSONAL: Born September 15, 1977, in Manhattan, Kan. ... 6-2/205. ... Bats right, throws right. ... Full name: Damian M. Rolls.
HIGH SCHOOL: F.L Schlagle (Kansas City, Kan.).
TRANSACTIONS/CAREER NOTES: Selected by Los Angeles Dodgers organization in first round (23rd pick overall) of free-agent draft (June 4, 1996). ... Selected by Kansas City Royals from Dodgers organization in Rule 5 major league draft (December 13, 1999). ... Traded by Royals to Tampa Bay Devil Rays for a player to be named later and cash (December 13, 1999).
STATISTICAL NOTES: Led Northwest League third basemen with 215 total chances in 1996. ... Led South Atlantic League third basemen with 388 total chances in 1997.

Year	Team (League)	Pos.	G	AB	R	H	2B	3B	HR	RBI	Avg.	BB	SO	SB	PO	A	E	Avg.
1996—	Yakima (N.W.)	3B	66	257	31	68	11	1	4	27	.265	7	46	8	*58	*134	•23	.893
1997—	Savannah (SAL)	3B	130	475	57	100	17	5	5	47	.211	38	83	11	*111	*246	31	.920
1998—	Vero Beach (FSL)	3B	73	266	28	65	9	0	0	30	.244	23	43	13	65	187	13	.951
	— San Antonio (Texas) ...	3B	50	160	18	35	6	0	1	9	.219	6	28	2	38	124	9	.947
1999—	Vero Beach (FSL)	3B-2B	127	474	68	141	26	2	9	54	.297	36	66	24	91	213	25	.924

ROMANO, MIKE — P

PERSONAL: Born March 3, 1972, in New Orleans. ... 6-2/195. ... Throws right, bats right. ... Full name: Michael Desport Romano.
COLLEGE: Tulane.
TRANSACTIONS/CAREER NOTES: Selected by Toronto Blue Jays organization in third round of free-agent draft (June 3, 1993); choice received from New York Yankees as part of compensation for signing Type A free agent P Jimmy Key. ... Granted free agency (October 15, 1999).

Year	League	W	L	Pct.	ERA	G	GS	CG	ShO	Sv.	IP	H	R	ER	BB	SO
1993—	Medicine Hat (Pio.) ..	4	1	.800	2.63	9	8	0	0	0	41	34	20	12	11	28
1994—	Hagerstown (East.)...	10	2	.833	3.07	18	18	2	0	0	108 1/3	91	47	37	40	90
1995—	Dunedin (FSL)	11	7	.611	4.13	28	26	1	1	0	150 1/3	141	79	69	75	102
1996—	Knoxville (Sou.)...........	9	9	.500	4.98	34	21	0	0	1	130	148	98	72	72	92
1997—	Syracuse (I.L.)............	2	4	.333	4.25	40	12	0	0	0	108	100	56	51	74	83
1998—	Syracuse (I.L.)............	8	6	.571	4.14	27	13	1	0	1	117 1/3	131	66	54	53	69
1999—	Syracuse (I.L.)............	12	8	.600	4.13	29	•28	2	0	0	174 1/3	160	90	80	84	104
	— Toronto (A.L.)....................	0	0	...	11.81	3	0	0	0	0	5 1/3	8	8	7	5	3
Major League totals (1 year)........		**0**	**0**	**...**	**11.81**	**3**	**0**	**0**	**0**	**0**	**5 1/3**	**8**	**8**	**7**	**5**	**3**

ROMERO, J.C. — P — TWINS

PERSONAL: Born June 4, 1976, in Rio Piedras, Puerto Rico. ... 5-11/195. ... Throws left, bats both. ... Full name: Juan C. Romero.
HIGH SCHOOL: Berwing (San Juan, Puerto Rico).
COLLEGE: Mobile.
TRANSACTIONS/CAREER NOTES: Selected by Minnesota Twins organization in 21st round of free-agent draft (June 3, 1997).

Year	League	W	L	Pct.	ERA	G	GS	CG	ShO	Sv.	IP	H	R	ER	BB	SO
1997—	Elizabethton (Appl.)............	3	2	.600	4.88	18	0	0	0	3	24	27	16	13	7	29
	— Fort Myers (FSL)	1	1	.500	4.38	7	1	0	0	0	12 1/3	11	6	6	4	9
1998—	New Britain (East.)	6	3	.667	2.19	51	1	0	0	2	78	48	28	19	43	79
1999—	New Britain (East.)	4	4	.500	3.40	36	1	0	0	7	53	51	25	20	34	53
	— Salt Lake (PCL)	4	1	.800	3.20	15	0	0	0	1	19 2/3	18	11	7	14	20
	— Minnesota (A.L.)	0	0	...	3.72	5	0	0	0	0	9 2/3	13	4	4	0	4
Major League totals (1 year)........		**0**	**0**	**...**	**3.72**	**5**	**0**	**0**	**0**	**0**	**9 2/3**	**13**	**4**	**4**	**0**	**4**

ROQUE, RAFAEL — P — BREWERS

PERSONAL: Born October 27, 1973, in Cotui, Dominican Republic. ... 6-4/189. ... Throws left, bats left. ... Full name: Rafael Antonio Roque.
TRANSACTIONS/CAREER NOTES: Signed as non-drafted free agent by New York Mets organization (March 15, 1991). ... Granted free agency (October 17, 1997). ... Signed by Milwaukee Brewers organization (October 31, 1997).

Year	League	W	L	Pct.	ERA	G	GS	CG	ShO	Sv.	IP	H	R	ER	BB	SO
1991—	Dom. Mets (DSL)	1	0	1.000	5.40	4	0	0	0	1	5	4	6	3	9	1
1992—	Gulf Coast Mets (GCL)	3	1	.750	2.14	20	0	0	0	8	33 2/3	28	13	8	16	33
1993—	Kingsport (Appalachian).....	1	3	.250	6.15	14	7	0	0	0	45 1/3	58	44	31	26	36
1994—	St. Lucie (FSL)	0	0	...	0.00	2	0	0	0	0	3	1	0	0	3	2
	— Columbia (SAL)	6	3	.667	2.40	15	15	0	0	0	86 1/3	73	26	23	30	74
1995—	St. Lucie (FSL)	6	9	.400	3.56	24	24	2	1	0	136 2/3	114	65	54	72	81
1996—	Binghamton (East.)	0	4	.000	7.27	13	13	0	0	0	60 2/3	71	57	49	39	46
	— St. Lucie (FSL)	6	4	.600	2.12	14	12	1	0	0	76 1/3	57	22	18	39	59
1997—	Binghamton (East.)	1	1	.500	6.84	16	0	0	0	0	26 1/3	35	26	20	17	23
	— St. Lucie (FSL)	2	10	.167	4.29	17	13	1	0	0	77 2/3	81	42	37	25	54
1998—	El Paso (Texas)■	5	6	.455	4.40	16	16	1	0	0	94	113	56	46	35	70
	— Louisville (I.L.)	5	2	.714	3.62	9	8	0	0	0	49 2/3	42	21	20	19	43
	— Milwaukee (N.L.)	4	2	.667	4.88	9	9	0	0	0	48	42	28	26	24	34
1999—	Milwaukee (N.L.)	1	6	.143	5.34	43	9	0	0	1	84 1/3	96	52	50	42	66
	— Louisville (I.L.)	1	0	1.000	0.00	2	2	0	0	0	10	4	0	0	3	3
Major League totals (2 years).......		**5**	**8**	**.385**	**5.17**	**52**	**18**	**0**	**0**	**1**	**132 1/3**	**138**	**80**	**76**	**66**	**100**

ROSADO, JOSE P ROYALS

PERSONAL: Born November 9, 1974, in Jersey City, N.J. ... 6-0/185. ... Throws left, bats left. ... Full name: Jose Antonio Rosado.
HIGH SCHOOL: Jose S. Alegria (Dorado, Puerto Rico).
JUNIOR COLLEGE: Galveston College (Texas).
TRANSACTIONS/CAREER NOTES: Selected by Kansas City Royals organization in 12th round of free-agent draft (June 2, 1994).
MISCELLANEOUS: Appeared in one game as pinch runner (1997).

Year League	W	L	Pct.	ERA	G	GS	CG	ShO	Sv.	IP	H	R	ER	BB	SO
1994— Gulf Coast Royals (GCL)	6	2	.750	*1.25	14	12	0	0	0	64²/₃	45	14	9	7	56
1995— Wilmington (Caro.)..........	10	7	.588	3.13	25	25	0	0	0	138	128	53	48	30	117
1996— Wichita (Texas)	2	0	1.000	0.00	2	2	0	0	0	13	10	0	0	1	12
— Omaha (A.A.)...................	8	3	.727	3.17	15	15	1	0	0	96²/₃	80	38	34	38	82
— Kansas City (A.L.)	8	6	.571	3.21	16	16	2	1	0	106²/₃	101	39	38	26	64
1997— Kansas City (A.L.)	9	12	.429	4.69	33	33	2	0	0	203¹/₃	208	117	106	73	129
1998— Kansas City (A.L.)	8	11	.421	4.69	38	25	2	1	1	174²/₃	180	106	91	57	135
1999— Kansas City (A.L.)	10	14	.417	3.85	33	33	5	0	0	208	197	103	89	72	141
Major League totals (4 years)......	35	43	.449	4.21	120	107	11	2	1	692²/₃	686	365	324	228	469

ALL-STAR GAME RECORD

Year League	W	L	Pct.	ERA	GS	CG	ShO	Sv.	IP	H	R	ER	BB	SO
1997— American	1	0	1.000	9.00	0	0	0	0	1	2	1	1	1	1
1999— American	0	0	...	0.00	0	0	0	0	1	1	0	0	0	1
All-Star Game totals (2 years)	1	0	1.000	4.50	0	0	0	0	2	3	1	1	1	2

ROSE, BRIAN P RED SOX

PERSONAL: Born February 13, 1976, in New Bedford, Mass. ... 6-3/215. ... Throws right, bats right. ... Full name: Brian Leonard Rose.
HIGH SCHOOL: Dartmouth (North Dartmouth, Mass.).
TRANSACTIONS/CAREER NOTES: Selected by Boston Red Sox organization in third round of free-agent draft (June 2, 1994). ... On Boston disabled list (May 13, 1998-remainder of season); included rehabilitation assignment to Pawtucket (June 13-July 10).
HONORS: Named International League Most Valuable Pitcher (1997).

Year League	W	L	Pct.	ERA	G	GS	CG	ShO	Sv.	IP	H	R	ER	BB	SO
1995— Michigan (Midw.)	8	5	.615	3.44	21	20	2	0	0	136	127	63	52	31	105
1996— Trenton (East.)	12	7	.632	4.01	27	27	4	2	0	163²/₃	157	82	73	45	115
1997— Pawtucket (I.L.)	*17	5	.773	*3.02	27	26	3	0	0	*190²/₃	188	74	64	46	116
— Boston (A.L.)...................	0	0	...	12.00	1	1	0	0	0	3	5	4	4	2	3
1998— Boston (A.L.)...................	1	4	.200	6.93	8	8	0	0	0	37²/₃	43	32	29	14	18
— Pawtucket (I.L.)..................	0	3	.000	7.64	6	6	0	0	0	17²/₃	24	19	15	4	17
1999— Pawtucket (I.L.)	2	1	.667	2.89	7	7	0	0	0	28	28	10	9	8	30
— Boston (A.L.)...................	7	6	.538	4.87	22	18	0	0	0	98	112	59	53	29	51
Major League totals (3 years)......	8	10	.444	5.58	31	27	0	0	0	138²/₃	160	95	86	45	72

DIVISION SERIES RECORD

Year League	W	L	Pct.	ERA	G	GS	CG	ShO	Sv.	IP	H	R	ER	BB	SO
1999— Boston (A.L.)				Did not play.											

CHAMPIONSHIP SERIES RECORD

Year League	W	L	Pct.	ERA	G	GS	CG	ShO	Sv.	IP	H	R	ER	BB	SO
1999— Boston (A.L.)				Did not play.											

ROSKOS, JOHN 1B/OF PADRES

PERSONAL: Born November 19, 1974, in Victorville, Calif. ... 5-11/195. ... Bats right, throws right. ... Full name: John Edward Roskos.
HIGH SCHOOL: Cibola (Albuquerque, N.M.).
TRANSACTIONS/CAREER NOTES: Selected by Florida Marlins organization in second round of free-agent draft (June 3, 1993). ... On Elmira disabled list (August 9-September 19, 1994). ... On Kane County disabled list (August 28-September 7, 1995). ... Granted free agency (December 21, 1997). ... Re-signed by Marlins organization (December 21, 1997). ... Granted free agency (October 5, 1999). ... Signed by San Diego Paders organization (November 22, 1999).

Year Team (League)	Pos.	G	AB	R	H	2B	3B	HR	RBI	Avg.	BB	SO	SB	PO	A	E	Avg.
1993— GC Marlins (GCL)	C	11	40	6	7	1	0	1	3	.175	5	11	1	18	2	2	.909
1994— Elmira (NY-P)	C	39	136	11	38	7	0	4	23	.279	27	37	0	143	13	4	.975
1995— Kane County (Midw.)..	C	114	418	74	124	36	3	12	88	.297	42	86	2	431	47	7	.986
1996— Portland (East.)	1B-C	121	396	53	109	26	3	9	58	.275	67	102	3	719	50	10	.987
1997— Portland (East.)	C-1B	123	451	66	139	31	1	24	84	.308	50	81	4	630	37	8	.988
1998— Charlotte (I.L.)	1B-OF	115	416	54	118	23	1	10	62	.284	43	84	0	647	38	4	.994
— Florida (N.L.)	1B	10	10	1	1	0	0	0	0	.100	0	5	0	1	0	0	1.000
1999— Calgary (PCL)............O-1-DH-C-3		134	506	85	162	*44	0	24	90	.320	52	112	2	374	22	6	.985
— Florida (N.L.)	C	13	12	0	2	2	0	0	1	.167	1	7	0	5	0	0	1.000
Major League totals (2 years)		23	22	1	3	2	0	0	1	.136	1	12	0	6	0	0	1.000

RUETER, KIRK P GIANTS

PERSONAL: Born December 1, 1970, in Centralia, Ill. ... 6-3/205. ... Throws left, bats left. ... Full name: Kirk Wesley Rueter. ... Name pronounced REE-ter.
HIGH SCHOOL: Nashville (Ill.) Community.
COLLEGE: Murray State.

TRANSACTIONS/CAREER NOTES: Selected by Montreal Expos organization in 19th round of free-agent draft (June 3, 1991). ... On Montreal disabled list (May 10-26, 1996); included rehabilitation assignment to Ottawa (May 20-24). ... Traded by Expos with P Tim Scott to San Francisco Giants for P Mark Leiter (July 30, 1996).

HONORS: Named N.L. Rookie Pitcher of the Year by THE SPORTING NEWS (1993).

STATISTICAL NOTES: Pitched 1-0 one-hit, complete-game victory for Montreal against San Francisco (August 27, 1995).

MISCELLANEOUS: Caught stealing in only appearance as pinch runner (1998).

Year	League	W	L	Pct.	ERA	G	GS	CG	ShO	Sv.	IP	H	R	ER	BB	SO
1991—	Gulf Coast Expos (GCL)	1	1	.500	0.95	5	4	0	0	0	19	16	5	2	4	19
—	Sumter (SAL)	3	1	.750	1.33	8	5	0	0	0	40 2/3	32	8	6	10	27
1992—	Rockford (Midw.)	11	9	.550	2.58	26	26	6	•2	0	174 1/3	150	68	50	36	153
1993—	Harrisburg (East.)..............	5	0	1.000	1.36	9	8	1	1	0	59 2/3	47	10	9	7	36
—	Ottawa (I.L.)	4	2	.667	2.70	7	7	1	0	0	43 1/3	46	20	13	3	27
—	Montreal (N.L.)................	8	0	1.000	2.73	14	14	1	0	0	85 2/3	85	33	26	18	31
1994—	Montreal (N.L.)................	7	3	.700	5.17	20	20	0	0	0	92 1/3	106	60	53	23	50
—	Ottawa (I.L.)	0	0	...	4.50	1	1	0	0	0	2	1	1	1	0	1
1995—	Montreal (N.L.)................	5	3	.625	3.23	9	9	1	1	0	47 1/3	38	17	17	9	28
—	Ottawa (I.L.)	9	7	.563	3.06	20	20	3	1	0	120 2/3	120	50	41	25	67
1996—	Ottawa (I.L.)	1	2	.333	4.20	3	3	1	0	0	15	21	7	7	3	3
—	Montreal (N.L.)................	5	6	.455	4.58	16	16	0	0	0	78 2/3	91	44	40	22	30
—	San Francisco (N.L.)■	1	2	.333	1.93	4	3	0	0	0	23 1/3	18	6	5	5	16
—	Phoenix (PCL)	1	2	.333	3.51	5	5	0	0	0	25 2/3	25	12	10	12	15
1997—	San Francisco (N.L.)	13	6	.684	3.45	32	32	0	0	0	190 2/3	194	83	73	51	115
1998—	San Francisco (N.L.)	16	9	.640	4.36	33	33	1	0	0	187 1/3	193	100	91	57	102
1999—	San Francisco (N.L.)	15	10	.600	5.41	33	33	1	0	0	184 2/3	219	118	111	55	94
Major League totals (7 years)		**70**	**39**	**.642**	**4.21**	**161**	**160**	**4**	**1**	**0**	**890 1/3**	**944**	**461**	**416**	**240**	**466**

DIVISION SERIES RECORD

Year	League	W	L	Pct.	ERA	G	GS	CG	ShO	Sv.	IP	H	R	ER	BB	SO
1997—	San Francisco (N.L.)	0	0	...	1.29	1	1	0	0	0	7	4	1	1	3	5

RUNYAN, SEAN   P   TIGERS

PERSONAL: Born June 21, 1974, in Fort Smith, Ark. ... 6-3/210. ... Throws left, bats left. ... Full name: Sean David Runyan.

HIGH SCHOOL: Urbandale (Iowa).

TRANSACTIONS/CAREER NOTES: Selected by Houston Astros organization in fifth round of free-agent draft (June 1, 1992). ... Traded by Astros to San Diego Padres for IF Luis Lopez (March 15, 1997). ... Selected by Detroit Tigers from Padres organization in Rule 5 major league draft (December 15, 1997). ... On Detroit disabled list (May 7, 1999-remainder of season); included rehabilitation assignment to Toldeo (June 4-July 1).

RECORDS: Holds major league rookie-season record for most games pitched—88 (1998).

Year	League	W	L	Pct.	ERA	G	GS	CG	ShO	Sv.	IP	H	R	ER	BB	SO
1992—	Gulf Coast Astros (GCL).....	3	3	.500	3.20	10	10	0	0	0	45	54	19	16	16	30
1993—	Gulf Coast Astros (GCL).....	4	3	.571	2.98	12	12	0	0	0	66 1/3	66	35	22	24	52
1994—	Auburn (NY-P)..................	7	5	.583	3.49	14	14	2	1	0	95 1/3	90	49	37	19	66
1995—	Quad City (Midw.)	4	6	.400	3.66	22	11	0	0	0	76 1/3	67	37	31	29	65
1996—	Quad City (Midw.)	9	4	.692	3.88	29	17	0	0	0	132 1/3	128	61	57	30	104
1997—	Mobile (Sou.)	5	2	.714	2.34	40	1	0	0	1	61 2/3	54	25	16	28	52
1998—	Detroit (A.L.)■	1	4	.200	3.58	*88	0	0	0	1	50 1/3	47	23	20	28	39
1999—	Detroit (A.L.)	0	1	.000	3.38	12	0	0	0	0	10 2/3	9	4	4	3	6
—	Toledo (I.L.)	0	0	...	3.48	10	0	0	0	0	10 1/3	7	4	4	6	7
Major League totals (2 years)		**1**	**5**	**.167**	**3.54**	**100**	**0**	**0**	**0**	**1**	**61**	**56**	**27**	**24**	**31**	**45**

RUPE, RYAN   P   DEVIL RAYS

PERSONAL: Born March 31, 1975, in Houston. ... 6-5/230. ... Throws right, bats right. ... Full name: Ryan Kittman Rupe.

HIGH SCHOOL: Northbrook (Houston).

COLLEGE: Texas A&M.

TRANSACTIONS/CAREER NOTES: Selected by New York Mets organization in 19th round of free-agent draft (June 3, 1993); did not sign. ... Selected by Kansas City Royals organization in 36th round of free-agent draft (June 4, 1996); did not sign. ... Selected by Tampa Bay Devil Rays organization in sixth round of free-agent draft (June 2, 1998).

Year	League	W	L	Pct.	ERA	G	GS	CG	ShO	Sv.	IP	H	R	ER	BB	SO
1998—	Hudson Valley (NY-P)........	1	0	1.000	0.68	3	3	0	0	0	13 1/3	8	1	1	2	18
—	Charleston, S.C. (SAL)	6	1	.857	2.40	10	10	0	0	0	56 1/3	33	18	15	9	62
1999—	Orlando (Sou.)	2	2	.500	2.73	5	5	0	0	0	26 1/3	18	13	8	6	22
—	Tampa Bay (A.L.)..............	8	9	.471	4.55	24	24	0	0	0	142 1/3	136	81	72	57	97
Major League totals (1 year)		**8**	**9**	**.471**	**4.55**	**24**	**24**	**0**	**0**	**0**	**142 1/3**	**136**	**81**	**72**	**57**	**97**

RUSCH, GLENDON   P   METS

PERSONAL: Born November 7, 1974, in Seattle. ... 6-1/200. ... Throws left, bats left. ... Full name: Glendon James Rusch.

HIGH SCHOOL: Shorecrest (Seattle).

TRANSACTIONS/CAREER NOTES: Selected by Kansas City Royals organization in 17th round of free-agent draft (June 3, 1993). ... On Kansas City disabled list (June 16-July 1, 1997); included rehabilitation assignment to Omaha (June 26-July 1). ... On Kansas City disabled list (August 9-September 4, 1998); included rehabilitation assignment to Omaha (August 24-September 4). ... On Omaha disabled list (May 31-July 1, 1999). ... Traded by Royals to New York Mets for P Dan Murray (September 14, 1999).

STATISTICAL NOTES: Pitched 9-0 no-hit victory against Kane County (August 7, 1994).

Year	League	W	L	Pct.	ERA	G	GS	CG	ShO	Sv.	IP	H	R	ER	BB	SO
1993—	Gulf Coast Royals (GCL)	4	2	.667	1.60	11	10	0	0	0	62	43	14	11	11	48
—	Rockford (Midw.)	0	1	.000	3.38	2	2	0	0	0	8	10	6	3	7	8
1994—	Rockford (Midw.)	8	5	.615	4.66	28	17	1	1	1	114	111	61	59	34	122
1995—	Wilmington (Caro.)	*14	6	.700	*1.74	26	26	1	1	0	165⅔	110	41	32	34	147
1996—	Omaha (A.A.)	11	9	.550	3.98	28	28	1	0	0	169⅔	177	88	75	40	117
1997—	Kansas City (A.L.)	6	9	.400	5.50	30	27	1	0	0	170⅓	206	111	104	52	116
—	Omaha (A.A.)	0	1	.000	4.50	1	1	0	0	0	6	7	3	3	1	2
1998—	Kansas City (A.L.)	6	15	.286	5.88	29	24	1	1	1	154⅔	191	104	101	50	94
—	Omaha (PCL)	1	1	.500	7.98	3	3	0	0	0	14⅔	20	18	13	6	14
1999—	Omaha (PCL)	4	7	.364	4.42	20	20	1	0	0	114	143	68	56	33	102
—	Gulf Coast Royals (GCL)	0	0	...	1.50	2	2	0	0	0	6	3	1	1	3	9
—	Kansas City (A.L.)	0	1	.000	15.75	3	0	0	0	0	4	7	7	7	3	4
—	New York (N.L.)■	0	0	...	0.00	1	0	0	0	0	1	1	0	0	0	0
A.L. totals (3 years)		12	25	.324	5.80	62	51	2	1	1	329	404	222	212	105	214
N.L. totals (1 year)		0	0	...	0.00	1	0	0	0	0	1	1	0	0	0	0
Major League totals (3 years)		12	25	.324	5.78	63	51	2	1	1	330	405	222	212	105	214

R

RYAN, B.J.   P   ORIOLES

PERSONAL: Born December 28, 1975, in Bossier City, La. ... 6-6/230. ... Throws left, bats left. ... Full name: Robert Victor Ryan Jr.
HIGH SCHOOL: Airline (Bossier City, La.).
COLLEGE: Southwestern Louisiana.
TRANSACTIONS/CAREER NOTES: Selected by Cincinnati Reds organization in 17th round of free-agent draft (June 2, 1998). ... Traded by Reds with P Jacobo Sequea to Baltimore Orioles for P Juan Guzman (July 31, 1999).

Year	League	W	L	Pct.	ERA	G	GS	CG	ShO	Sv.	IP	H	R	ER	BB	SO
1998—	Billings (Pio.)	2	1	.667	1.93	14	0	0	0	4	18⅔	15	4	4	5	25
—	Charleston, W.Va. (SAL)	0	0	...	2.08	3	0	0	0	2	4⅓	1	1	1	1	5
—	Chattanooga (Sou.)	1	0	1.000	2.20	16	0	0	0	4	16⅓	13	4	4	6	21
1999—	Chattanooga (Sou.)	2	1	.667	2.59	35	0	0	0	6	41⅔	33	13	12	17	46
—	Indianapolis (I.L.)	1	0	1.000	4.00	11	0	0	0	0	9	9	4	4	3	12
—	Cincinnati (N.L.)	0	0	...	4.50	1	0	0	0	0	2	4	1	1	1	1
—	Rochester (I.L.)■	0	0	...	2.51	11	0	0	0	1	14⅓	8	4	4	4	20
—	Baltimore (A.L.)	1	0	1.000	2.95	13	0	0	0	0	18⅓	9	6	6	12	28
A.L. totals (1 year)		1	0	1.000	2.95	13	0	0	0	0	18⅓	9	6	6	12	28
N.L. totals (1 year)		0	0	...	4.50	1	0	0	0	0	2	4	1	1	1	1
Major League totals (1 year)		1	0	1.000	3.10	14	0	0	0	0	20⅓	13	7	7	13	29

RYAN, JASON   P   TWINS

PERSONAL: Born January 23, 1976, in Long Branch, N.J. ... 6-3/195. ... Throws right, bats both. ... Full name: Jason Paul Ryan. ... Son of Tim Ryan, pitcher with Los Angeles Dodgers and Atlanta Braves organizations; brother of Sean Ryan, minor league infielder with Philadelphia Phillies organization (1990-93); and nephew of Ed Madjeski, catcher with three major league teams (1932-34 and 1937).
HIGH SCHOOL: Immaculata (Somerville, N.J.).
TRANSACTIONS/CAREER NOTES: Selected by Chicago Cubs organization in ninth round of free-agent draft (June 2, 1994). ... Traded by Cubs with P Kyle Lohse to Minnesota Twins for P Rick Aguilera and P Scott Downs (May 21, 1999).

Year	League	W	L	Pct.	ERA	G	GS	CG	ShO	Sv.	IP	H	R	ER	BB	SO
1994—	Gulf Coast Cubs (GCL)	1	2	.333	4.09	7	7	0	0	0	33	32	19	15	4	30
—	Huntington (Appl.)	2	0	1.000	0.35	4	4	1	1	0	26	7	1	1	8	32
—	Orlando (Sou.)	2	0	1.000	2.45	2	2	0	0	0	11	6	3	3	6	12
1995—	Daytona (FSL)	11	5	.688	3.48	26	26	0	0	0	134⅔	128	61	52	54	98
1996—	Orlando (Sou.)	2	5	.286	5.71	7	7	0	0	0	34⅔	39	30	22	24	25
—	Daytona (FSL)	1	8	.111	5.24	17	10	0	0	1	67	72	42	39	33	49
1997—	Daytona (FSL)	9	8	.529	4.44	27	27	5	0	0	170⅓	168	105	84	55	140
1998—	West Tenn (Sou.)	3	•13	.188	4.88	30	25	2	0	0	147⅔	172	97	80	57	121
1999—	West Tenn (Sou.)	5	0	1.000	1.41	8	7	0	0	0	44⅔	29	12	7	15	53
—	New Britain (East.)■	2	4	.333	4.80	8	8	0	0	0	50⅔	48	29	27	24	42
—	Salt Lake (PCL)	4	4	.500	5.13	9	9	0	0	0	54⅓	57	36	31	24	34
—	Minnesota (A.L.)	1	4	.200	4.87	8	8	1	0	0	40⅔	46	23	22	17	15
Major League totals (1 year)		1	4	.200	4.87	8	8	1	0	0	40⅔	46	23	22	17	15

RYAN, KEN   P

PERSONAL: Born October 24, 1968, in Pawtucket, R.I. ... 6-3/230. ... Throws right, bats right. ... Full name: Kenneth Frederick Ryan Jr.
HIGH SCHOOL: Seekonk (Mass.).
TRANSACTIONS/CAREER NOTES: Signed as non-drafted free agent by Boston Red Sox organization (June 16, 1986). ... Traded by Red Sox with OF Lee Tinsley and OF Glenn Murray to Philadelphia Phillies for P Heathcliff Slocumb, P Larry Wimberly and OF Rick Holifield (January 29, 1996). ... On Philadelphia disabled list (March 25-May 9 and June 13-September 1, 1997); included rehabilitation assignment to Reading (May 6-9). ... On Philadelphia disabled list (March 17-July 31, 1998); included rehabilitation assignments to Clearwater (July 5-14) and Scranton/Wilkes-Barre (July 17-30). ... Granted free agency (December 21, 1998). ... Re-signed by Phillies (December 21, 1998). ... Released by Phillies (August 22, 1999). ... Signed by Pittsburgh Pirates organization (August 26, 1999). ... Granted free agency (October 15, 1999).

Year	League	W	L	Pct.	ERA	G	GS	CG	ShO	Sv.	IP	H	R	ER	BB	SO
1986—	Elmira (NY-P)	2	2	.500	5.82	13	1	0	0	0	21⅔	20	14	14	21	22
1987—	Greensboro (SAL)	3	12	.200	5.49	28	19	2	0	0	121⅓	139	88	74	63	75
1988—	Lynchburg (Caro.)	2	7	.222	6.18	19	14	0	0	0	71⅓	79	51	49	45	49
1989—	Winter Haven (FSL)	8	8	.500	3.15	24	22	3	0	0	137	114	58	48	81	78
1990—	Lynchburg (Caro.)	6	•14	.300	5.13	28	•28	3	1	0	161⅓	182	104	92	82	109

Year	League	W	L	Pct.	ERA	G	GS	CG	ShO	Sv.	IP	H	R	ER	BB	SO
1991—	Winter Haven (FSL)...........	1	3	.250	2.05	21	1	0	0	1	52 2/3	40	15	12	19	53
—	New Britain (East.).............	1	2	.333	1.73	14	0	0	0	1	26	23	7	5	12	26
—	Pawtucket (I.L.).................	1	0	1.000	4.91	9	0	0	0	1	18 1/3	15	11	10	11	14
1992—	New Britain (East.).............	1	4	.200	1.95	44	0	0	0	22	50 2/3	44	17	11	24	51
—	Pawtucket (I.L.).................	2	0	1.000	2.08	9	0	0	0	7	8 2/3	6	2	2	4	6
—	Boston (A.L.)....................	0	0	...	6.43	7	0	0	0	1	7	4	5	5	5	5
1993—	Boston (A.L.)....................	7	2	.778	3.60	47	0	0	0	1	50	43	23	20	29	49
—	Pawtucket (I.L.).................	0	2	.000	2.49	18	0	0	0	8	25 1/3	18	9	7	17	22
1994—	Sarasota (FSL)	0	0	...	3.68	8	0	0	0	1	7 1/3	6	3	3	2	11
—	Boston (A.L.)....................	2	3	.400	2.44	42	0	0	0	13	48	46	14	13	17	32
1995—	Boston (A.L.)....................	0	4	.000	4.96	28	0	0	0	7	32 2/3	34	20	18	24	34
—	Trenton (East.)	0	2	.000	5.82	11	0	0	0	2	17	23	13	11	5	16
—	Pawtucket (I.L.).................	0	1	.000	6.30	9	0	0	0	0	10	12	7	7	4	6
1996—	Philadelphia (N.L.)■	3	5	.375	2.43	62	0	0	0	8	89	71	32	24	45	70
1997—	Reading (East.)..................	0	0	...	0.00	2	2	0	0	0	2	1	0	0	1	0
—	Philadelphia (N.L.)..............	1	0	1.000	9.58	22	0	0	0	0	20 2/3	31	23	22	13	10
—	Scranton/W.B. (I.L.)	1	0	1.000	4.50	3	0	0	0	1	4	5	2	2	3	3
1998—	Clearwater (FSL)	0	0	...	3.00	4	4	0	0	0	9	5	3	3	3	10
—	Scranton/W.B. (I.L.)	1	0	1.000	0.00	6	0	0	0	1	8	7	0	0	3	9
—	Philadelphia (N.L.)..............	0	0	...	4.37	17	1	0	0	0	22 2/3	21	12	11	20	16
1999—	Philadelphia (N.L.).............	1	2	.333	6.32	15	0	0	0	0	15 2/3	16	11	11	11	9
—	Scranton/W.B. (I.L.)	2	2	.500	5.66	31	0	0	0	6	41 1/3	54	30	26	19	33
—	Nashville (PCL)■	1	1	.500	3.86	6	0	0	0	0	7	7	3	3	8	9
A.L. totals (4 years)		9	9	.500	3.66	124	0	0	0	22	137 2/3	127	62	56	75	120
N.L. totals (4 years)		5	7	.417	4.14	116	1	0	0	8	148	139	78	68	89	105
Major League totals (8 years).......		14	16	.467	3.91	240	1	0	0	30	285 2/3	266	140	124	164	225

RYAN, ROB OF DIAMONDBACKS

PERSONAL: Born June 24, 1973, in Havre, Mont. ... 5-11/190. ... Bats left, throws left. ... Full name: Robert James Ryan.
HIGH SCHOOL: Shadle Park (Spokane, Wash.).
COLLEGE: Washington State.
TRANSACTIONS/CAREER NOTES: Selected by Arizona Diamondbacks organization in 36th round of free-agent draft (June 4, 1996).

Year	Team (League)	Pos.	G	AB	R	H	2B	3B	HR	RBI	Avg.	BB	SO	SB	PO	A	E	Avg.
							BATTING								FIELDING			
1996—	Lethbridge (Pio.)	OF	59	211	55	64	8	1	4	37	.303	43	33	23	107	3	4	.965
1997—	South Bend (Midw.) ...	OF	121	421	71	132	35	5	8	73	.314	89	58	12	188	11	7	.966
1998—	Tucson (PCL)	OF	116	394	71	125	18	2	17	66	.317	63	61	9	224	3	4	.983
1999—	Tucson (PCL)	OF-DH	117	414	72	120	30	5	19	88	.290	56	70	4	182	6	6	.969
—	Arizona (N.L.).............	OF	20	29	4	7	1	0	2	5	.241	1	8	0	7	0	0	1.000
Major League totals (1 year)			20	29	4	7	1	0	2	5	.241	1	8	0	7	0	0	1.000

SABEL, ERIK P DIAMONDBACKS

PERSONAL: Born October 14, 1974, in West Lafayette, Ind. ... 6-2/185. ... Throws right, bats right. ... Full name: Erik Douglas Sabel.
HIGH SCHOOL: Harrison (West Lafayette, Ind.).
COLLEGE: Tennessee Tech.
TRANSACTIONS/CAREER NOTES: Selected by Arizona Diamondbacks organization in 42nd round of free-agent draft (June 4, 1996). ... Loaned to Texas Rangers organization (June 3-September 14, 1998). ... On Tucson disabled list (May 26-June 15, 1999).

Year	League	W	L	Pct.	ERA	G	GS	CG	ShO	Sv.	IP	H	R	ER	BB	SO
1996—	Lethbridge (Pio.)	1	4	.200	2.79	20	3	0	0	1	42	43	23	13	7	41
1997—	High Desert (Calif.).............	11	11	.500	5.32	31	22	0	0	1	143 2/3	174	101	85	40	86
1998—	High Desert (Calif.).............	0	1	.000	3.18	14	0	0	0	4	22 2/3	25	8	8	4	18
—	Tucson (PCL)	1	0	1.000	8.71	7	0	0	0	0	10 1/3	17	10	10	5	7
—	Tulsa (Texas)■	7	0	1.000	3.20	24	2	0	0	2	56 1/3	46	24	20	13	33
1999—	El Paso (Texas)■	0	1	.000	6.30	8	1	0	0	1	10	16	9	7	4	7
—	Tucson (PCL)	5	2	.714	3.34	22	9	0	0	2	72 2/3	79	36	27	24	38
—	Arizona (N.L.)...................	0	0	...	6.52	7	0	0	0	0	9 2/3	12	7	7	6	6
Major League totals (1 year)........		0	0	...	6.52	7	0	0	0	0	9 2/3	12	7	7	6	6

SABERHAGEN, BRET P RED SOX

PERSONAL: Born April 11, 1964, in Chicago Heights, Ill. ... 6-1/200. ... Throws right, bats right. ... Full name: Bret William Saberhagen. ... Name pronounced SAY-ber-HAY-gun.
HIGH SCHOOL: Cleveland (Reseda, Calif.).
TRANSACTIONS/CAREER NOTES: Selected by Kansas City Royals organization in 19th round of free-agent draft (June 7, 1982). ... On disabled list (August 10-September 1, 1986; July 16-September 10, 1990; and June 15-July 13, 1991). ... Traded by Royals with IF Bill Pecota to New York Mets for OF Kevin McReynolds, IF Gregg Jefferies and 2B Keith Miller (December 11, 1991). ... On disabled list (May 16-July 18 and August 2-September 7, 1992 and August 3, 1993-remainder of season). ... On suspended list (April 3-8, 1994). ... Traded by Mets with a player to be named later to Colorado Rockies for P Juan Acevedo and P Arnold Gooch (July 31, 1995); Rockies acquired P David Swanson to complete deal (August 4, 1995). ... On disabled list (March 22, 1996-entire season). ... Granted free agency (October 29, 1996). ... Signed by Boston Red Sox organization (December 9, 1996). ... On Boston disabled list (March 31-August 22, 1997); included rehabilitation assignments to Lowell (July 27-August 1), Trenton (August 1-12) and Pawtucket (August 12-22). ... Granted free agency (October 31, 1997). ... Re-signed by Red Sox (November 17, 1997). ... On Boston disabled list (May 7-June 1, June 8-23 and August 18-September 10, 1999); included rehabilitation assignment to Trenton (May 27-June 1).

HONORS: Named A.L. Pitcher of the Year by THE SPORTING NEWS (1985 and 1989). ... Named righthanded pitcher on THE SPORTING NEWS A.L. All-Star team (1985 and 1989). ... Named A.L. Cy Young Award winner by Baseball Writers' Association of America (1985 and 1989). ... Named A.L. Comeback Player of the Year by THE SPORTING NEWS (1987 and 1998). ... Won A.L. Gold Glove at pitcher (1989).

STATISTICAL NOTES: Pitched 7-0 no-hit victory against Chicago (August 26, 1991).

MISCELLANEOUS: Appeared in one game as pinch runner (1984). ... Appeared in three games as pinch runner (1989).

Year	League	W	L	Pct.	ERA	G	GS	CG	ShO	Sv.	IP	H	R	ER	BB	SO
1983—	Fort Myers (FSL)	10	5	.667	2.30	16	16	3	1	0	109 2/3	98	34	28	19	82
—	Jacksonville (Sou.)	6	2	.750	2.91	11	11	2	1	0	77 1/3	66	31	25	29	48
1984—	Kansas City (A.L.)	10	11	.476	3.48	38	18	2	1	1	157 2/3	138	71	61	36	73
1985—	Kansas City (A.L.)	20	6	.769	2.87	32	32	10	1	0	235 1/3	211	79	75	38	158
1986—	Kansas City (A.L.)	7	12	.368	4.15	30	25	4	2	0	156	165	77	72	29	112
1987—	Kansas City (A.L.)	18	10	.643	3.36	33	33	15	4	0	257	246	99	96	53	163
1988—	Kansas City (A.L.)	14	16	.467	3.80	35	35	9	0	0	260 2/3	*271	122	110	59	171
1989—	Kansas City (A.L.)	*23	6	.793	*2.16	35	35	*12	4	0	*262 1/3	209	74	63	43	193
1990—	Kansas City (A.L.)	5	9	.357	3.27	20	20	5	0	0	135	146	52	49	28	87
1991—	Kansas City (A.L.)	13	8	.619	3.07	28	28	7	2	0	196 1/3	165	76	67	45	136
1992—	New York (N.L.)■	3	5	.375	3.50	17	15	1	1	0	97 2/3	84	39	38	27	81
1993—	New York (N.L.)	7	7	.500	3.29	19	19	4	1	0	139 1/3	131	55	51	17	93
1994—	New York (N.L.)	14	4	.778	2.74	24	24	4	0	0	177 1/3	169	58	54	13	143
1995—	New York (N.L.)	5	5	.500	3.35	16	16	3	0	0	110	105	45	41	20	71
—	Colorado (N.L.)■	2	1	.667	6.28	9	9	0	0	0	43	60	33	30	13	29
1996—	Colorado (N.L.)							Did not play.								
1997—	Lowell (NY-P)■	0	0	...	0.00	1	1	0	0	0	3	1	0	0	0	2
—	Trenton (East.)	0	0	...	0.00	2	2	0	0	0	8	2	0	0	1	9
—	Pawtucket (I.L.)	0	1	.000	3.27	2	2	0	0	0	11	11	4	4	1	9
—	Boston (A.L.)	0	1	.000	6.58	6	6	0	0	0	26	30	20	19	10	14
1998—	Boston (A.L.)	15	8	.652	3.96	31	31	0	0	0	175	181	82	77	29	100
1999—	Boston (A.L.)	10	6	.625	2.95	22	22	0	0	0	119	122	43	39	11	81
—	Trenton (East.)	1	0	1.000	0.00	1	1	0	0	0	6	2	0	0	0	5
A.L. totals (11 years)		135	93	.592	3.31	311	285	64	14	1	1980 1/3	1884	795	728	381	1288
N.L. totals (4 years)		31	22	.585	3.39	85	83	12	2	0	567 1/3	549	230	214	90	417
Major League totals (15 years)		166	115	.591	3.33	396	368	76	16	1	2547 2/3	2433	1025	942	471	1705

DIVISION SERIES RECORD

Year	League	W	L	Pct.	ERA	G	GS	CG	ShO	Sv.	IP	H	R	ER	BB	SO
1995—	Colorado (N.L.)	0	1	.000	11.25	1	1	0	0	0	4	7	6	5	1	3
1998—	Boston (A.L.)	0	1	.000	3.86	1	1	0	0	0	7	4	3	3	1	7
1999—	Boston (A.L.)	0	1	.000	27.00	2	2	0	0	0	3 2/3	9	11	11	4	2
Division series totals (3 years)		0	3	.000	11.66	4	4	0	0	0	14 2/3	20	20	19	6	12

CHAMPIONSHIP SERIES RECORD

Year	League	W	L	Pct.	ERA	G	GS	CG	ShO	Sv.	IP	H	R	ER	BB	SO
1984—	Kansas City (A.L.)	0	0	...	2.25	1	1	0	0	0	8	6	3	2	1	5
1985—	Kansas City (A.L.)	0	0	...	6.14	2	2	0	0	0	7 1/3	12	5	5	2	6
1999—	Boston (A.L.)	0	1	.000	1.50	1	1	0	0	0	6	5	3	1	1	5
Champ. series totals (3 years)		0	1	.000	3.38	4	4	0	0	0	21 1/3	23	11	8	4	16

WORLD SERIES RECORD

NOTES: Named Most Valuable Player (1985). ... Member of World Series championship team (1985).

Year	League	W	L	Pct.	ERA	G	GS	CG	ShO	Sv.	IP	H	R	ER	BB	SO
1985—	Kansas City (A.L.)	2	0	1.000	0.50	2	2	1	0	0	18	11	1	1	1	10

ALL-STAR GAME RECORD

Year	League	W	L	Pct.	ERA	GS	CG	ShO	Sv.	IP	H	R	ER	BB	SO
1987—	American	0	0	...	0.00	1	0	0	0	3	1	0	0	0	0
1990—	American	1	0	1.000	0.00	0	0	0	0	2	0	0	0	0	1
1994—	National							Did not play.							
All-Star Game totals (2 years)		1	0	1.000	0.00	1	0	0	0	5	1	0	0	0	1

SADLER, DONNIE — IF — RED SOX

PERSONAL: Born June 17, 1975, in Gohlson, Texas. ... 5-6/175. ... Bats right, throws right. ... Full name: Donnie Lamont Sadler.

HIGH SCHOOL: Valley Mills (Texas).

TRANSACTIONS/CAREER NOTES: Selected by Boston Red Sox organization in 10th round of free-agent draft (June 2, 1994). ... On Pawtucket disabled list (May 4-June 4 and June 23-30, 1998). ... On Pawtucket disabled list (June 25-July 18, 1999).

STATISTICAL NOTES: Tied for International League lead in errors by second baseman with 12 in 1997. ... Tied for International League lead in caught stealing with 14 in 1997.

Year	Team (League)	Pos.	G	AB	R	H	2B	3B	HR	RBI	Avg.	BB	SO	SB	PO	A	E	Avg.
1994—	GC Red Sox (GCL)	SS-3B-2B	53	206	52	56	8	6	1	16	.272	23	27	32	80	151	18	.928
—	Fort Myers (GCL)	SS	53	206	52	56	8	6	1	16	.272	23	27	32	...	...	...	...
1995—	Michigan (Midw.)	SS	118	438	*103	124	25	8	9	55	.283	79	85	41	168	307	28	.944
1996—	Trenton (East.)	SS-OF	115	454	68	121	20	8	6	46	.267	38	75	34	185	237	27	.940
1997—	Pawtucket (I.L.)	2B-SS-OF	125	481	74	102	18	2	11	36	.212	57	121	20	252	354	‡15	.976
1998—	Boston (A.L.)	2B-DH-SS	58	124	21	28	4	4	3	15	.226	6	28	4	81	101	5	.973
—	Pawtucket (I.L.)	2B-SS	36	131	25	29	5	1	2	10	.221	26	23	11	73	104	4	.978
1999—	Boston (A.L.)	S-2-3-O-DH	49	107	18	30	5	1	0	4	.280	5	20	2	46	52	9	.916
—	Pawtucket (I.L.)	SS-DH	43	172	23	50	12	4	1	17	.291	16	36	4	73	96	10	.944
—	GC Red Sox (GCL)	SS	4	13	2	5	2	0	0	1	.385	2	1	0	7	12	1	.950
Major League totals (2 years)			107	231	39	58	9	5	3	19	.251	11	48	6	127	153	14	.952

DIVISION SERIES RECORD

							BATTING									FIELDING		
Year	Team (League)	Pos.	G	AB	R	H	2B	3B	HR	RBI	Avg.	BB	SO	SB	PO	A	E	Avg.
1998—	Boston (A.L.).............	2B-PR	3	0	0	0	0	0	0	0	...	0	0	0	1	1	0	1.000
1999—	Boston (A.L.).............PH-3B-PR-DH		2	2	1	1	1	0	0	0	.500	0	1	0	1	1	0	1.000
Division series totals (2 years)			5	2	1	1	1	0	0	0	.500	0	1	0	2	2	0	1.000

CHAMPIONSHIP SERIES RECORD

							BATTING									FIELDING		
Year	Team (League)	Pos.	G	AB	R	H	2B	3B	HR	RBI	Avg.	BB	SO	SB	PO	A	E	Avg.
1999—	Boston (A.L.).............	PR-OF-DH	2	0	0	0	0	0	0	0	...	0	0	0	0	0	0	...

SAENZ, OLMEDO — 3B/1B — ATHLETICS

PERSONAL: Born October 8, 1970, in Chitre Herrera, Panama. ... 6-0/185. ... Bats right, throws right. ... Full name: Olmedo Sanchez Saenz. ... Name pronounced SIGNS.

TRANSACTIONS/CAREER NOTES: Signed as non-drafted free agent by Chicago White Sox organization (May 11, 1990). ... Granted free agency (October 15, 1997). ... Re-signed by White Sox organization (January 25, 1998). ... Granted free agency (October 15, 1998). ... Signed by Oakland Athletics (November 13, 1998). ... On Oakland disabled list (July 26-August 16, 1999); included rehabilitation assignment to Vancouver (August 13-16).

STATISTICAL NOTES: Led American Association third basemen with 395 total chances in 1995. ... Tied for American Association lead in being hit by pitch with 13 in 1996. ... Led American Association third basemen with 363 total chances and 24 double plays in 1996. ... Led Pacific Coast League in being hit by pitch with 22 in 1998.

							BATTING									FIELDING		
Year	Team (League)	Pos.	G	AB	R	H	2B	3B	HR	RBI	Avg.	BB	SO	SB	PO	A	E	Avg.
1991—	South Bend (Midw.) ...	3B	56	192	23	47	10	1	2	22	.245	21	48	5	29	68	12	.890
—	Sarasota (FSL)	3B	5	19	1	2	0	1	0	2	.105	2	0	0	5	11	3	.842
1992—	South Bend (Midw.) ...	3B-1B	132	493	66	121	26	4	7	59	.245	36	52	16	113	294	48	.895
1993—	South Bend (Midw.) ...	3B	13	50	3	18	4	1	0	7	.360	7	7	1	11	31	4	.913
—	Sarasota (FSL)	3B	33	121	13	31	9	4	0	27	.256	9	18	3	15	55	5	.933
—	Birmingham (Sou.).....	3B	49	173	30	60	17	2	6	29	.347	20	21	2	38	87	14	.899
1994—	Nashville (A.A.)	3B-DH	107	383	48	100	27	2	12	59	.261	30	57	3	76	167	22	.917
—	Chicago (A.L.)	3B	5	14	2	2	0	1	0	0	.143	0	5	0	3	5	0	1.000
1995—	Nashville (A.A.)	3B	111	415	60	126	26	1	13	74	.304	45	60	0	*82	*289	*24	*.939
1996—	Nashville (A.A.)	3B-DH	134	476	86	124	29	1	18	63	.261	53	80	4	*97	244	22	.939
1997—	GC White Sox (GCL) ..	DH	2	1	0	1	1	0	0	0	1.000	0	0	0	0	0	0	...
1998—	Calgary (PCL)	3B-DH	124	466	89	146	29	0	29	102	.313	45	49	3	75	235	21	.937
1999—	Oakland (A.L.)■	3B-1B-DH	97	255	41	70	18	0	11	41	.275	22	47	1	180	91	8	.971
—	Vancouver (PCL)	3B	2	5	1	3	1	0	0	2	.600	0	0	0	1	0	0	1.000
Major League totals (2 years)			102	269	43	72	18	1	11	41	.268	22	52	1	183	96	8	.972

SALMON, TIM — OF — ANGELS

PERSONAL: Born August 24, 1968, in Long Beach, Calif. ... 6-3/221. ... Bats right, throws right. ... Full name: Timothy James Salmon. ... Brother of Mike Salmon, safety with San Francisco 49ers (1997). ... Name pronounced SA-mon.

HIGH SCHOOL: Greenway (Phoenix).

COLLEGE: Grand Canyon (Ariz.).

TRANSACTIONS/CAREER NOTES: Selected by Atlanta Braves organization in 18th round of free-agent draft (June 2, 1986); did not sign. ... Selected by California Angels organization in third round of free-agent draft (June 5, 1989). ... On disabled list (May 12-23 and May 27-August 7, 1990, and July 18-August 3, 1994). ... Angels franchise renamed Anaheim Angels for 1997 season. ... On disabled list (April 23-May 9, 1998). ... On Anaheim disabled list (May 4-July 17, 1999); included rehabilitation assignment to Lake Elsinore (July 16-17).

RECORDS: Shares major league record for fewest double plays by outfielder (150 or more games)—0 (1996). ... Shares A.L. record for most hits in three consecutive games—13 (May 10 [4], May 11 [4] and 13 [5], 1994).

HONORS: Named Minor League Player of the Year by THE SPORTING NEWS (1992). ... Named Pacific Coast League Most Valuable Player (1992). ... Named A.L. Rookie Player of the Year by THE SPORTING NEWS (1993). ... Named A.L. Rookie of the Year by Baseball Writers' Association of America (1993). ... Named outfielder on THE SPORTING NEWS A.L. All-Star team (1995 and 1997). ... Named outfielder on THE SPORTING NEWS Silver Slugger team (1995).

STATISTICAL NOTES: Led Pacific Coast League with 275 total bases, .672 slugging percentage and .469 on-base percentage in 1992. ... Led A.L. outfielders with four double plays in 1994. ... Tied for A.L. lead in double plays by outfielder with five in 1997. ... Career major league grand slams: 4.

							BATTING									FIELDING		
Year	Team (League)	Pos.	G	AB	R	H	2B	3B	HR	RBI	Avg.	BB	SO	SB	PO	A	E	Avg.
1989—	Bend (N.W.)................	OF	55	196	37	48	6	5	6	31	.245	33	60	2	84	7	4	.958
1990—	Palm Springs (Calif.)..	OF	36	118	19	34	6	0	2	21	.288	21	44	11	63	3	1	.985
—	Midland (Texas)..........	OF	27	97	17	26	3	1	3	16	.268	18	38	1	51	6	3	.950
1991—	Midland (Texas).........	OF	131	465	100	114	26	4	23	94	.245	*89	*166	12	265	16	10	.966
1992—	Edmonton (PCL)	OF	118	409	•101	142	38	4	*29	*105	.347	91	103	9	231	14	3	.988
—	California (A.L.)	OF	23	79	8	14	1	0	2	6	.177	11	23	1	40	1	2	.953
1993—	California (A.L.)	OF-DH	142	515	93	146	35	1	31	95	.283	82	135	5	335	12	7	.980
1994—	California (A.L.)	OF	100	373	67	107	18	2	23	70	.287	54	102	1	219	9	8	.966
1995—	California (A.L.)	OF-DH	143	537	111	177	34	3	34	105	.330	91	111	5	320	7	4	.988
1996—	California (A.L.)	OF-DH	156	581	90	166	27	4	30	98	.286	93	125	4	299	13	8	.975
1997—	Anaheim (A.L.)	OF-DH	157	582	95	172	28	1	33	129	.296	95	142	9	352	15	11	.971
1998—	Anaheim (A.L.)	DH-OF	136	463	84	139	28	1	26	88	.300	90	100	0	46	1	2	.959
1999—	Anaheim (A.L.)	OF-DH	98	353	60	94	24	2	17	69	.266	63	82	4	204	7	4	.981
—	Lake Elsinore (Calif.)..	DH	1	5	0	3	2	0	0	2	.600	0	1	0	0	0	0	...
Major League totals (8 years)			955	3483	608	1015	195	14	196	660	.291	579	820	29	1815	65	46	.976

SAMPSON, BENJ — P — TWINS

PERSONAL: Born April 27, 1975, in Des Moines, Iowa. ... 6-2/210. ... Throws left, bats left. ... Full name: Benjamin Damon Sampson.
HIGH SCHOOL: Ankeny (Iowa).
TRANSACTIONS/CAREER NOTES: Selected by Minnesota Twins organization in sixth round of free-agent draft (June 3, 1993). ... On disabled list (May 14-23, 1997).

Year League	W	L	Pct.	ERA	G	GS	CG	ShO	Sv.	IP	H	R	ER	BB	SO
1993— Elizabethton (Appl.)	4	1	.800	1.91	11	6	0	0	1	42 1/3	33	12	9	15	34
1994— Fort Wayne (Midw.)	6	9	.400	3.80	25	25	0	0	0	139 2/3	149	72	59	60	111
1995— Fort Myers (FSL)	11	9	.550	3.49	28	27	3	2	0	160	148	71	62	52	95
1996— Fort Myers (FSL)	7	1	.875	3.47	11	11	2	0	0	70	55	28	27	26	65
— New Britain (East.)	5	7	.417	5.73	16	16	1	0	0	75 1/3	108	54	48	25	51
1997— New Britain (East.)	10	6	.625	4.19	25	20	0	0	0	118	112	56	55	49	92
1998— Salt Lake (PCL)	10	7	.588	5.14	28	28	0	0	0	161	198	99	92	52	132
— Minnesota (A.L.)	1	0	1.000	1.56	5	2	0	0	0	17 1/3	10	3	3	6	16
1999— Minnesota (A.L.)	3	2	.600	8.11	30	4	0	0	0	71	107	65	64	34	56
— Salt Lake (PCL)	1	1	.500	8.04	3	3	0	0	0	15 2/3	25	16	14	1	7
Major League totals (2 years)	4	2	.667	6.83	35	6	0	0	0	88 1/3	117	68	67	40	72

SANCHEZ, ALEX — OF — DEVIL RAYS

PERSONAL: Born August 26, 1976, in Havana, Cuba. ... 5-10/180. ... Bats left, throws left. ... Full name: Alexis Sanchez.
JUNIOR COLLEGE: Miami-Dade (Wolfson) Community College.
TRANSACTIONS/CAREER NOTES: Selected by Tampa Bay Devil Rays organization in fifth round of free-agent draft (June 4, 1996).
STATISTICAL NOTES: Led Gulf Coast League with 12 caught stealing in 1996. ... Led South Atlantic League outfielders with 296 total chances in 1997. ... Led South Atlantic League in caught stealing with 40 in 1997. ... Led Florida State League in caught stealing with 33 and sacrifice flies with 12 in 1998. ... Led Southern League in caught stealing with 27 and sacrifice hits with 10 in 1999.

							BATTING							FIELDING		
Year Team (League)	Pos.	G	AB	R	H	2B	3B	HR	RBI	Avg.	BB	SO	SB	PO	A	E	Avg.
1996— GC Devil Rays (GCL)	OF	56	227	36	64	7	6	1	22	.282	10	35	20	91	1	3	.968
1997— Char., S.C. (SAL)	OF	131	537	73	155	15	6	0	34	.289	37	72	*92	279	6	•11	.963
1998— St. Petersburg (FSL)	OF	128	545	77	*180	17	9	1	50	.330	31	70	66	330	5	•12	.965
1999— Orlando (Sou.)	OF	121	500	68	127	12	4	2	29	.254	26	88	48	314	8	*14	.958
— Durham (I.L.)	OF	3	10	2	2	1	0	0	0	.200	1	0	0	8	0	0	1.000

SANCHEZ, JESUS — P — MARLINS

PERSONAL: Born October 11, 1974, in Nizao Bani, Dominican Republic. ... 5-10/155. ... Throws left, bats left. ... Full name: Jesus P. Sanchez.
TRANSACTIONS/CAREER NOTES: Signed as non-drafted free agent by New York Mets organization (June 7, 1992). ... On disabled list (April 4-May 28, 1996). ... Traded by Mets with P A.J. Burnett and OF Robert Stratton to Florida Marlins for P Al Leiter and 2B Ralph Milliard (February 6, 1998).
STATISTICAL NOTES: Led Dominican Summer League in home runs allowed with 14 in 1992.
MISCELLANEOUS: Appeared in two games as pinch runner (1998). ... Appeared in one game as pinch runner (1999).

Year League	W	L	Pct.	ERA	G	GS	CG	ShO	Sv.	IP	H	R	ER	BB	SO
1992— Dom. Mets (DSL)	5	5	.500	4.19	15	15	1	0	0	81 2/3	86	52	38	38	72
1993— Dom. Mets (DSL)	7	3	.700	2.40	16	13	2	•2	0	82 1/3	63	30	22	36	94
1994— Kingsport (Appalachian)	7	4	.636	1.96	13	12	•3	0	0	87 1/3	61	27	19	27	71
1995— Capital City (SAL)	9	7	.563	3.13	27	4	0	0	0	169 2/3	154	76	59	58	•177
1996— St. Lucie (FSL)	9	3	.750	1.96	16	16	2	1	0	92	53	22	20	24	81
1997— Binghamton (East.)	*13	10	.565	4.30	26	26	3	0	0	165 1/3	146	87	79	61	*176
1998— Florida (N.L.)■	7	9	.438	4.47	35	29	0	0	0	173	178	98	86	91	137
1999— Florida (N.L.)	5	7	.417	6.01	59	10	0	0	0	76 1/3	84	53	51	60	62
— Calgary (PCL)	0	0	...	5.79	4	1	0	0	1	9 1/3	8	6	6	5	14
Major League totals (2 years)	12	16	.429	4.95	94	39	0	0	0	249 1/3	262	151	137	151	199

SANCHEZ, REY — SS/2B — ROYALS

PERSONAL: Born October 5, 1967, in Rio Piedras, Puerto Rico. ... 5-9/175. ... Bats right, throws right. ... Full name: Rey Francisco Guadalupe Sanchez.
HIGH SCHOOL: Live Oak (Morgan Hill, Calif.).
TRANSACTIONS/CAREER NOTES: Selected by Texas Rangers organization in 13th round of free-agent draft (June 2, 1986). ... Traded by Rangers to Chicago Cubs for IF Bryan House (January 3, 1990). ... On disabled list (April 6, 1990-entire season). ... On Chicago disabled list (May 6-21, 1992); included rehabilitation assignment to Iowa (May 13-21). ... On disabled list (July 24-August 9, 1995). ... On Chicago disabled list (June 5-July 20 and August 11-September 1, 1996); included rehabilitation assignment to Iowa (July 16-20). ... Traded by Cubs to New York Yankees for P Frisco Parotte (August 16, 1997). ... Granted free agency (November 3, 1997). ... Signed by San Francisco Giants (January 22, 1998). ... Granted free agency (November 5, 1998). ... Signed by Kansas City Royals (December 11, 1998). ... Granted free agency (October 29, 1999). ... Re-signed by Royals (December 7, 1999).
STATISTICAL NOTES: Led Gulf Coast League shortstops with .932 fielding percentage in 1986. ... Led American Association shortstops with 104 double plays in 1989. ... Led American Association shortstops with 596 total chances and 81 double plays in 1992.

							BATTING							FIELDING		
Year Team (League)	Pos.	G	AB	R	H	2B	3B	HR	RBI	Avg.	BB	SO	SB	PO	A	E	Avg.
1986— GC Rangers (GCL)	SS-2B	52	169	27	49	3	1	0	23	.290	41	18	10	69	158	15	†.938
1987— Gastonia (SAL)	SS	50	160	19	35	1	2	1	10	.219	22	17	6	88	162	18	.933
— Butte (Pio.)	SS	49	189	36	69	10	6	0	25	.365	21	12	22	84	162	12	.953
1988— Charlotte (FSL)	SS	128	418	60	128	6	5	0	38	.306	35	24	29	226	*415	35	.948
1989— Oklahoma City (A.A.)	SS	134	464	38	104	10	4	1	39	.224	21	50	4	*237	*418	29	*.958

Year	Team (League)	Pos.	G	AB	R	H	2B	3B	HR	RBI	Avg.	BB	SO	SB	PO	A	E	Avg.
1990—	Iowa (A.A.)■..............										Did not play.							
1991—	Iowa (A.A.)..........	SS	126	417	60	121	16	5	2	46	.290	37	27	13	204	*375	17	*.971
	— Chicago (N.L.)..........	SS-2B	13	23	1	6	0	0	0	2	.261	4	3	0	11	25	0	1.000
1992—	Chicago (N.L.)..........	SS-2B	74	255	24	64	14	3	1	19	.251	10	17	2	148	202	9	.975
	— Iowa (A.A.)..........	SS-2B	20	76	12	26	3	0	0	3	.342	4	1	6	31	77	5	.956
1993—	Chicago (N.L.)..........	SS	105	344	35	97	11	2	0	28	.282	15	22	1	158	316	15	.969
1994—	Chicago (N.L.)..........	2B-SS-3B	96	291	26	83	13	1	0	24	.285	20	29	2	152	278	9	.979
1995—	Chicago (N.L.)..........	2B-SS	114	428	57	119	22	2	3	27	.278	14	48	6	195	351	7	.987
1996—	Chicago (N.L.)..........	SS	95	289	28	61	9	0	1	12	.211	22	42	7	151	307	11	.977
	— Iowa (A.A.)..............	SS	3	12	2	2	0	0	0	1	.167	1	2	2	4	10	1	.933
1997—	Chicago (N.L.)..........	SS-2B-3B	97	205	14	51	9	0	1	12	.249	11	26	4	100	157	6	.977
	— New York (A.L.)■......	2B-SS	38	138	21	43	12	0	1	15	.312	5	21	0	66	110	4	.978
1998—	San Fran. (N.L.)■......	SS-2B	109	316	44	90	14	2	2	30	.285	16	47	0	142	261	8	.981
1999—	Kansas City (A.L.)■...	SS	134	479	66	141	18	6	2	56	.294	22	48	11	242	452	13	.982
	American League totals (2 years)		172	617	87	184	30	6	3	71	.298	27	69	11	308	562	17	.981
	National League totals (8 years)		703	2151	229	571	92	10	8	154	.265	112	234	22	1057	1897	65	.978
	Major League totals (9 years)		875	2768	316	755	122	16	11	225	.273	139	303	33	1365	2459	82	.979

DIVISION SERIES RECORD

Year	Team (League)	Pos.	G	AB	R	H	2B	3B	HR	RBI	Avg.	BB	SO	SB	PO	A	E	Avg.
1997—	New York (A.L.)..........	2B	5	15	1	3	1	0	0	1	.200	0	2	0	15	14	0	1.000

SANDBERG, JARED   3B   DEVIL RAYS   S

PERSONAL: Born March 2, 1978, in Olympia, Wash. ... 6-3/185. ... Bats right, throws right. ... Full name: Jared L. Sandberg. ... Nephew of Ryne Sandberg, second baseman with Philadelphia Phillies (1981) and Chicago Cubs (1982-94 and 1996-97).
HIGH SCHOOL: Capital (Olympia, Wash.).
TRANSACTIONS/CAREER NOTES: Selected by Tampa Bay Devil Rays organization in 16th round of free-agent draft (June 4, 1996).
HONORS: Named Appalachian League Player of the Year (1997).
STATISTICAL NOTES: Led Appalachian League with 157 total bases amd five intentional bases on balls received in 1997. ... Led New York-Pennsylvania League with 133 total bases in 1998. ... Led New York-Pennsylvania League third basemen with 234 total chances and 15 double plays in 1998. ... Led Florida State League third basemen with 423 total chances in 1999. ... Tied for Florida State League lead with 25 double plays by third basemen in 1999.

Year	Team (League)	Pos.	G	AB	R	H	2B	3B	HR	RBI	Avg.	BB	SO	SB	PO	A	E	Avg.
1996—	GC Devil Rays (GCL)..	2B	22	77	6	13	2	1	0	7	.169	9	26	1	30	63	3	.969
1997—	St. Petersburg (FSL)..	2B	2	3	1	1	0	0	0	2	.333	2	2	0	4	5	0	1.000
	— Princeton (Appl.)..........	2B-3B	•67	*268	61	81	15	5	17	*68	.302	42	94	12	84	158	13	.949
1998—	Char., S.C. (SAL)..........	3B	56	191	31	35	11	0	3	15	.183	27	76	4	43	•94	22	.862
	— Hudson Valley (NY-P)..	3B	73	271	49	78	15	2	•12	54	.288	42	76	13	*55	*159	20	.915
1999—	St. Petersburg (FSL)..	3B	136	504	73	139	24	1	22	96	.276	51	133	8	*102	*284	*37	.913

SANDERS, ANTHONY   OF   BLUE JAYS

PERSONAL: Born March 2, 1974, in Tucson, Ariz. ... 6-2/205. ... Bats right, throws right. ... Full name: Anthony Marcus Sanders.
HIGH SCHOOL: Santa Rita (Tucson, Ariz.).
TRANSACTIONS/CAREER NOTES: Selected by Toronto Blue Jays organization in seventh round of free-agent draft (June 1, 1992). ... On Syracuse disabled list (July 22, 1998-remainder of season).

Year	Team (League)	Pos.	G	AB	R	H	2B	3B	HR	RBI	Avg.	BB	SO	SB	PO	A	E	Avg.
1993—	Medicine Hat (Pio.)....	OF	63	225	44	59	9	3	4	33	.262	20	49	6	88	8	2	.980
1994—	St. Catharines (NY-P.)..	OF	74	258	36	66	17	3	6	45	.256	27	53	8	120	9	3	.977
1995—	Hagerstown (SAL)......	OF	133	512	72	119	28	1	8	48	.232	52	103	26	274	15	3	.990
1996—	Dunedin (FSL)..........	OF	102	417	75	108	25	0	17	50	.259	34	93	16	209	8	4	.982
	— Knoxville (Sou.)..........	OF	38	133	16	36	8	0	1	18	.271	7	33	1	66	1	3	.957
1997—	Dunedin (FSL)..........	OF	1	5	0	1	1	0	0	1	.200	1	1	0	1	0	0	1.000
	— Knoxville (Sou.)..........	OF-DH	111	429	68	114	20	4	26	69	.266	44	121	20	224	7	4	.983
1998—	Syracuse (I.L.)..........	OF	60	209	23	40	9	2	4	19	.191	20	65	5	145	6	1	.993
	— Knoxville (Sou.)..........	OF	6	25	9	10	2	0	4	9	.400	2	6	0	15	3	0	1.000
1999—	Syracuse (I.L.)..........	OF-DH	124	496	71	121	22	5	18	59	.244	46	111	18	279	•17	6	.980
	— Toronto (A.L.)..........	DH-OF	3	7	1	2	1	0	0	2	.286	0	2	0	1	0	0	1.000
	Major League totals (1 year)		3	7	1	2	1	0	0	2	.286	0	2	0	1	0	0	1.000

SANDERS, REGGIE   OF   BRAVES

PERSONAL: Born December 1, 1967, in Florence, S.C. ... 6-1/185. ... Bats right, throws right. ... Full name: Reginald Laverne Sanders.
HIGH SCHOOL: Wilson (Florence, S.C.).
COLLEGE: Spartanburg (S.C.) Methodist.
TRANSACTIONS/CAREER NOTES: Selected by Cincinnati Reds organization in seventh round of free-agent draft (June 2, 1987). ... On disabled list (July 11-September 15, 1988 and July 15-September 5, 1989). ... On Chattanooga disabled list (June 30-July 26, 1991). ... On Cincinnati disabled list (August 24-September 20, 1991; and May 13-29 and July 17-August 2, 1992). ... On suspended list (June 3-9, 1994). ... On Cincinnati disabled list (April 20-May 22, May 31-June 15 and September 17, 1996-remainder of season); included rehabilitation assignment to Indianapolis (May 17-22). ... On Cincinnati disabled list (April 19-May 6 and May 24-July 23, 1997); included rehabilitation assignments to Chattanooga (May 3-5) and Indianapolis (July 15-22). ... Traded by Reds with SS Damian Jackson and P Josh Harris to San Diego

Padres for OF Greg Vaughn and OF/1B Mark Sweeney (February 2, 1999). ... On disabled list (June 3-18, 1999). ... Traded by Padres with 2B Quilvio Veras and 1B Wally Joyner to Atlanta Braves for OF/1B Ryan Klesko, 2B Bret Boone and P Jason Shiell (December 22, 1999).
HONORS: Named Midwest League Most Valuable Player (1990). ... Named outfielder on THE SPORTING NEWS N.L. All-Star team (1995).
STATISTICAL NOTES: Hit three home runs in one game (August 15, 1995).

Year	Team (League)	Pos.	G	AB	R	H	2B	3B	HR	RBI	Avg.	BB	SO	SB	PO	A	E	Avg.
1988—	Billings (Pio.)	SS	17	64	11	15	1	1	0	3	.234	6	4	10	18	33	3	.944
1989—	Greensboro (SAL)	SS	81	315	53	91	18	5	9	53	.289	29	63	21	125	169	42	.875
1990—	Cedar Rap. (Midw.)	OF	127	466	89	133	21	4	17	63	.285	59	97	40	241	10	10	.962
1991—	Chattanooga (Sou.)	OF	86	302	50	95	15	•8	8	49	.315	41	67	15	158	2	3	.982
	—Cincinnati (N.L.)	OF	9	40	6	8	0	0	1	3	.200	0	9	1	22	0	0	1.000
1992—	Cincinnati (N.L.)	OF	116	385	62	104	26	6	12	36	.270	48	98	16	262	11	6	.978
1993—	Cincinnati (N.L.)	OF	138	496	90	136	16	4	20	83	.274	51	118	27	312	3	8	.975
1994—	Cincinnati (N.L.)	OF	107	400	66	105	20	8	17	62	.263	41	*114	21	218	12	6	.975
1995—	Cincinnati (N.L.)	OF	133	484	91	148	36	6	28	99	.306	69	122	36	268	12	5	.982
1996—	Cincinnati (N.L.)	OF	81	287	49	72	17	1	14	33	.251	44	86	24	160	7	2	.988
	—Indianapolis (A.A.)......	OF-DH	4	12	3	5	2	0	0	1	.417	1	4	0	4	1	0	1.000
1997—	Cincinnati (N.L.)	OF	86	312	52	79	19	2	19	56	.253	42	93	13	183	4	5	.974
	—Chattanooga (Sou.)	OF	3	11	3	6	1	1	1	3	.545	1	2	0	11	0	0	1.000
	—Indianapolis (A.A.)......	OF	5	19	1	4	0	0	0	1	.211	1	6	0	6	0	2	.750
1998—	Cincinnati (N.L.)	OF	135	481	83	129	18	6	14	59	.268	51	137	20	263	4	6	.978
1999—	San Diego (N.L.)■...	OF-DH	133	478	92	136	24	7	26	72	.285	65	108	36	233	4	6	.975
Major League totals (9 years)			938	3363	591	917	176	40	151	503	.273	411	885	194	1921	57	44	.978

DIVISION SERIES RECORD

Year	Team (League)	Pos.	G	AB	R	H	2B	3B	HR	RBI	Avg.	BB	SO	SB	PO	A	E	Avg.
1995—	Cincinnati (N.L.)	OF	3	13	3	2	1	0	1	2	.154	1	9	2	7	0	1	.875

CHAMPIONSHIP SERIES RECORD

Year	Team (League)	Pos.	G	AB	R	H	2B	3B	HR	RBI	Avg.	BB	SO	SB	PO	A	E	Avg.
1995—	Cincinnati (N.L.)	OF	4	16	0	2	0	0	0	0	.125	2	10	0	7	0	1	.875

ALL-STAR GAME RECORD

Year	League	Pos.	AB	R	H	2B	3B	HR	RBI	Avg.	BB	SO	SB	PO	A	E	Avg.
1995—	National	OF	1	0	0	0	0	0	0	.000	0	1	0	0	0	0	...

SANDERS, SCOTT   P

PERSONAL: Born March 25, 1969, in Hannibal, Mo. ... 6-4/220. ... Throws right, bats right. ... Full name: Scott Gerald Sanders.
HIGH SCHOOL: Thibodaux (La.).
COLLEGE: Nicholls State (La.).
TRANSACTIONS/CAREER NOTES: Selected by San Diego Padres organization in supplemental round ("sandwich pick" between first and second round, 32nd pick overall) of free-agent draft (June 4, 1990); pick received as part of compensation for Kansas City Royals signing Type A free-agent P Mark Davis. ... On disabled list (May 1-17, 1994). ... On San Diego disabled list (July 18, 1995-remainder of season); included rehabilitation assignment to Las Vegas (August 28-September 1). ... Traded by Padres to Seattle Mariners for P Sterling Hitchcock (December 6, 1996). ... Traded by Mariners with P Dean Crow and 3B Carlos Villalobos to Detroit Tigers for P Omar Olivares and P Felipe Lira (July 18, 1997). ... Traded by Tigers to Padres for a player to be named later (May 6, 1998). ... On Las Vegas disabled list (June 21-July 1, 1998). ... Released by Padres (November 17, 1998). ... Signed by Chicago Cubs (December 2, 1998). ... Granted free agency (December 21, 1999).
STATISTICAL NOTES: Tied for N.L. lead with 10 wild pitches in 1994. ... Pitched 4-0 one-hit, complete-game victory for Detroit against Texas (September 9, 1997).
MISCELLANEOUS: Appeared in one game as pinch runner for Detroit (1997).

Year	League	W	L	Pct.	ERA	G	GS	CG	ShO	Sv.	IP	H	R	ER	BB	SO
1990—	Waterloo (Midw.)	2	2	.500	4.86	7	7	0	0	0	37	43	21	20	21	29
	—Spokane (N.W.)	2	1	.667	0.95	3	3	0	0	0	19	12	3	2	5	21
1991—	Waterloo (Midw.)	3	0	1.000	0.68	4	4	0	0	0	26 1/3	17	2	2	6	18
	—High Desert (Calif.)	9	6	.600	3.66	21	21	4	2	0	132 2/3	114	72	54	72	93
1992—	Wichita (Texas)	7	5	.583	3.49	14	14	0	0	0	87 2/3	85	35	34	37	95
	—Las Vegas (PCL)	3	6	.333	5.50	14	12	1	1	0	72	97	49	44	31	51
1993—	Las Vegas (PCL)	5	10	.333	4.96	24	24	•4	0	0	152 1/3	170	101	84	62	*161
	—San Diego (N.L.)	3	3	.500	4.13	9	9	0	0	0	52 1/3	54	32	24	23	37
1994—	San Diego (N.L.)	4	8	.333	4.78	23	20	0	0	1	111	103	63	59	48	109
1995—	San Diego (N.L.)	5	5	.500	4.30	17	15	1	0	0	90	79	46	43	31	88
	—Las Vegas (PCL)	0	0	...	0.00	1	1	0	0	0	3	3	0	0	1	2
1996—	San Diego (N.L.)	9	5	.643	3.38	46	16	0	0	0	144	117	58	54	48	157
1997—	Seattle (A.L.)■	3	6	.333	6.47	33	6	0	0	2	65 1/3	73	48	47	38	62
	—Detroit (A.L.)■	3	8	.273	5.33	14	14	1	1	0	74 1/3	79	44	44	24	58
1998—	Detroit (A.L.)	0	2	.000	17.69	3	2	0	0	0	9 2/3	24	19	19	6	6
	—Las Vegas (PCL)■	1	2	.333	3.44	15	3	0	0	3	36 1/3	34	14	14	12	43
	—San Diego (N.L.)	3	1	.750	4.11	23	6	0	0	0	30 2/3	33	20	14	5	26
1999—	Chicago (N.L.)■	4	7	.364	5.52	67	6	0	0	2	104 1/3	112	69	64	53	89
A.L. totals (2 years)		6	16	.273	6.63	50	22	1	1	2	149 1/3	176	111	110	68	126
N.L. totals (6 years)		28	29	.491	4.36	185	66	1	0	3	532 1/3	498	288	258	208	506
Major League totals (7 years)		34	45	.430	4.86	235	88	2	1	5	681 2/3	674	399	368	276	632

DIVISION SERIES RECORD

Year	League	W	L	Pct.	ERA	G	GS	CG	ShO	Sv.	IP	H	R	ER	BB	SO
1996—	San Diego (N.L.)	0	0	...	8.31	1	1	0	0	0	4 1/3	3	4	4	4	4

SANFORD, CHANCE   2B

PERSONAL: Born June 2, 1972, in Houston. ... 5-10/175. ... Bats left, throws right. ... Full name: Chance Steven Sanford.
HIGH SCHOOL: Stratford (Houston).
JUNIOR COLLEGE: San Jacinto (North) College (Texas).
TRANSACTIONS/CAREER NOTES: Selected by Pittsburgh Pirates organization in 27th round of free-agent draft (June 1, 1992). ... On Nashville disabled list (June 22-September 8, 1998). ... Released by Pirates (October 15, 1998). ... Signed by Los Angeles Dodgers organization (January 20, 1999). ... On Albuquerque disabled list (May 4-27, 1999). ... Granted free agency (October 15, 1999).
STATISTICAL NOTES: Led Carolina League second baseman with 34 errors in 1994.

Year	Team (League)	Pos.	G	AB	R	H	2B	3B	HR	RBI	Avg.	BB	SO	SB	PO	A	E	Avg.
1992—	Welland (NY-P)	2B-SS	59	214	36	61	11	3	5	21	.285	35	39	13	70	165	15	.940
	— Augusta (SAL)	2B	14	46	3	5	1	0	0	2	.109	3	10	0	24	34	2	.967
1993—	Salem (Caro.)	2B	115	428	54	109	21	5	10	37	.255	33	80	11	172	284	34	.931
1994—	Salem (Caro.)	2B-OF	127	474	81	130	32	6	19	78	.274	56	95	12	209	318	•34	.939
1995—	Carolina (Sou.)	DH-PH-PR	16	36	6	10	3	1	3	10	.278	5	7	3	...	...	...	...
	— Brad. Pirates (GCL)	2B	6	19	2	4	0	0	1	1	.211	2	2	0	8	9	1	.944
	— Lynchburg (Caro.)	2B	16	66	8	22	4	0	3	14	.333	7	13	1	34	39	3	.961
1996—	Carolina (Sou.)	2B	131	470	62	115	16	13	4	56	.245	72	106	11	213	336	•22	.961
1997—	Carolina (Sou.)	2B-3B	44	149	30	39	10	2	9	36	.262	20	39	3	58	123	8	.958
	— Calgary (PCL)	3B-2B-SS	89	325	58	95	27	9	6	60	.292	39	82	9	74	189	16	.943
1998—	Nashville (PCL)	2B-3B-SS-OF	27	81	17	21	7	1	4	21	.259	16	12	0	29	41	3	.959
	— Pittsburgh (N.L.)	3B-2B-SS	14	28	3	4	1	1	0	3	.143	1	6	0	5	6	2	.846
1999—	Albuquerque (PCL)■	.3B-OF-2B-DH	77	227	37	56	14	1	8	29	.247	31	55	6	57	118	11	.941
	— Los Angeles (N.L.)	2B	5	8	1	2	0	0	0	2	.250	0	1	0	1	1	0	1.000
Major League totals (2 years)			19	36	4	6	1	1	0	5	.167	1	7	0	6	7	2	.867

SANTANA, JOHAN   P   TWINS

PERSONAL: Born March 13, 1979, in Tovar, Venezuela. ... 6-0/155. ... Throws left, bats left. ... Full name: Johan Alexander Santana.
TRANSACTIONS/CAREER NOTES: Signed as non-drafted free agent by Houston Astros organization (July 2, 1995). ... Selected by Florida Marlins from Astros organization in Rule 5 major league draft (December 13, 1999). ... Traded by Marlins with cash to Minnesota Twins for P Jared Camp (December 13, 1999).
STATISTICAL NOTES: Led New York-Pennsylvania League with 10 hit batsmen in 1998.

Year	League	W	L	Pct.	ERA	G	GS	CG	ShO	Sv.	IP	H	R	ER	BB	SO
1996—	Dom. Astros (DSL)	4	3	.571	2.70	23	1	0	0	3	40	26	16	12	22	51
1997—	GC Astros (GCL)	0	4	.000	7.93	9	5	1	0	0	36 1/3	49	36	32	18	25
	— Auburn (NY-P)	0	0	...	2.25	1	1	0	0	0	4	1	1	1	6	5
1998—	Quad City (Midw.)	0	1	.000	9.45	2	1	0	0	0	6 2/3	14	7	7	3	6
	— Auburn (NY-P)	7	5	.583	4.36	15	15	1	•1	0	86 2/3	81	52	42	21	88
1999—	Michigan (Midw.)	8	8	.500	4.66	27	26	1	0	0	160 1/3	162	94	83	55	150

SANTANA, JULIO   P

PERSONAL: Born January 20, 1974, in San Pedro de Macoris, Dominican Republic. ... 6-0/225. ... Throws right, bats right. ... Full name: Julio Franklin Santana. ... Nephew of Rico Carty, outfielder with seven major league teams (1963-79).
HIGH SCHOOL: Divina Providence (Dominican Republic).
TRANSACTIONS/CAREER NOTES: Signed as non-drafted free agent by Texas Rangers organization (February 18, 1990). ... On Texas disabled list (July 15-August 10, 1997). ... Claimed on waivers by Tampa Bay Devil Rays (April 27, 1998). ... On Tampa Bay disabled list (May 3-24, 1999). ... Traded by Devil Rays to Boston Red Sox for a player to be named later and cash (July 21, 1999); Devil Rays acquired P Will Silverthorn to complete deal (July 30, 1999). ... On Boston disabled list (July 22, 1999-remainder of season). ... Granted free agency (December 21, 1999).

Year	League	W	L	Pct.	ERA	G	GS	CG	ShO	Sv.	IP	H	R	ER	BB	SO
1992—	San Pedro (DSL)	0	1	.000	3.24	17	1	0	0	0	8 1/3	8	5	3	7	5
1993—	Gulf Coast Rangers (GCL)	4	1	.800	1.38	*26	0	0	0	7	39	31	9	6	7	50
1994—	Charleston, W.Va. (SAL)	6	7	.462	2.46	16	16	0	0	0	91 1/3	65	38	25	44	103
	— Tulsa (Texas)	7	2	.778	2.90	11	11	2	0	0	71 1/3	50	26	23	41	45
1995—	Oklahoma City (A.A.)	0	2	.000	39.00	2	2	0	0	0	3	9	14	13	7	6
	— Charlotte (FSL)	0	3	.000	3.73	5	5	1	0	0	31 1/3	32	16	13	16	27
	— Tulsa (Texas)	6	4	.600	3.23	15	15	3	0	0	103	91	40	37	52	71
1996—	Oklahoma City (A.A.)	11	12	.478	4.02	29	29	4	1	0	185 2/3	171	102	83	66	113
1997—	Texas (A.L.)	4	6	.400	6.75	30	14	0	0	0	104	141	86	78	49	64
	— Oklahoma City (A.A.)	0	0	...	15.00	1	1	0	0	0	3	9	6	5	2	1
1998—	Texas (A.L.)	0	0	...	8.44	3	0	0	0	0	5 1/3	7	5	5	4	1
	— Tampa Bay (A.L.)■	5	6	.455	4.23	32	19	1	0	0	140 1/3	144	72	66	58	60
1999—	Tampa Bay (A.L.)	1	4	.200	7.32	22	5	0	0	0	55 1/3	66	49	45	32	34
Major League totals (3 years)		10	16	.385	5.72	87	38	1	0	0	305	358	212	194	143	159

RECORD AS POSITION PLAYER

Year	Team (League)	Pos.	G	AB	R	H	2B	3B	HR	RBI	Avg.	BB	SO	SB	PO	A	E	Avg.
1990—	San Pedro (DSL)	...	11	34	4	7	0	0	1	3	.206	5	7	0	...	...	...	...
1991—	San Pedro (DSL)	...	55	161	27	42	7	0	2	12	.261	27	37	5	...	...	...	...
1992—	San Pedro (DSL)	OF-IF	17	48	7	11	2	0	2	2	.229	11	8	0	50	2	4	.929

SANTANA, MARINO — P

PERSONAL: Born May 10, 1972, in San Jose de los Llanos, Dominican Republic. ... 6-1/190. ... Throws right, bats right.
TRANSACTIONS/CAREER NOTES: Signed as non-drafted free agent by Seattle Mariners organization (April 28, 1990). ... Granted free agency (October 15, 1996). ... Signed by Detroit Tigers organization (November 26, 1996). ... Traded by Tigers to Boston Red Sox for cash (December 10, 1998). ... On Pawtucket disabled list (May 6-13 and June 1-13, 1999). ... On Boston disabled list (July 27, 1999-remainder of season). ... Released by Red Sox (November 18, 1999).

Year League	W	L	Pct.	ERA	G	GS	CG	ShO	Sv.	IP	H	R	ER	BB	SO
1990—Dom. Mariners (DSL)........	3	2	.600	2.94	12	5	0	0	5	49	47	20	16	14	25
1991—Dom. Mariners (DSL)........	4	4	.500	3.87	14	14	2	...	0	86	92	47	37	40	39
1992—Dom. Mariners (DSL)........	6	9	.400	2.38	18	16	4	0	0	106	109	59	28	37	91
1993—Bellingham (N'west)..........	0	1	.000	5.82	15	0	0	0	0	21 $2/3$	27	19	14	22	24
1994—Bellingham (N'west)..........	6	3	.667	3.15	15	15	1	0	0	80	68	35	28	26	88
1995—Wisconsin (Midw.).............	8	3	.727	1.77	15	15	2	1	0	96 $2/3$	57	26	19	25	110
—Riverside (Calif.)................	3	5	.375	6.19	9	9	0	0	0	48	44	44	33	25	57
1996—Lancaster (Calif.)............	8	15	.348	5.03	28	•28	1	0	0	157 $1/3$	164	105	88	57	167
1997—Jacksonville (Sou.)■.........	4	1	.800	3.28	39	0	0	0	1	74	55	28	27	43	98
1998—Toledo (I.L.)....................	6	3	.667	2.90	44	0	0	0	7	68 $1/3$	44	30	22	34	94
—Detroit (A.L.)....................	0	0	...	3.68	7	0	0	0	0	7 $1/3$	9	3	3	8	10
1999—Pawtucket (I.L.)■.............	2	3	.400	2.95	25	0	0	0	1	39 $2/3$	28	15	13	17	45
—Boston (A.L.)....................	0	0	...	15.75	3	0	0	0	0	4	8	7	7	3	4
Major League totals (2 years).......	0	0	...	7.94	10	0	0	0	0	11 $1/3$	17	10	10	11	14

S

SANTANA, PEDRO — 2B — TIGERS

PERSONAL: Born September 21, 1976, in San Pedro de Macoris, Dominican Republic ... 5-11/160. ... Bats right, throws right. ... Full name: Pedro C. Santana.
HIGH SCHOOL: Gaston F. Delinge (San Pedro de Macoris, Dominican Republic).
TRANSACTIONS/CAREER NOTES: Signed as non-drafted free agent by Houston Astros organization (July 2, 1994). ... Traded by Astros with P Kevin Gallaher to Detroit Tigers (August 27, 1996); completing deal in which Tigers traded P Gregg Olson to Astros for two players to be named later (August 26, 1996).

									BATTING					FIELDING		
Year Team (League)	Pos.	G	AB	R	H	2B	3B	HR	RBI	Avg.	BB	SO	SB	PO	A	E	Avg.
1995—Dom. Astros (DSL)....	2B	52	184	39	53	6	1	2	14	.288	31	29	34	110	126	17	.933
1996—GC Astros (GCL) SS-2B-3B-OF	56	207	40	56	6	5	1	20	.271	21	44	33	84	142	14	.942
1997—W. Mich. (Mid.)■......	2B-SS	74	287	36	75	10	6	3	28	.261	14	55	20	120	205	32	.910
1998—W. Mich. (Mid.)	2B	118	438	79	115	21	7	4	45	.263	28	93	64	205	309	*22	.959
1999—Jacksonville (Sou.).....	2B	120	512	89	143	35	6	5	49	.279	34	98	34	277	338	*20	.969

SANTANGELO, F.P. — OF/IF — DODGERS

PERSONAL: Born October 24, 1967, in Livonia, Mich. ... 5-10/190. ... Bats both, throws right. ... Full name: Frank Paul Santangelo.
HIGH SCHOOL: Valley (Sacramento).
JUNIOR COLLEGE: Sacramento City College.
COLLEGE: Miami (Fla.).
TRANSACTIONS/CAREER NOTES: Selected by Montreal Expos organization in 20th round of free-agent draft (June 5, 1989). ... On disabled list (April 21-May 2, 1994). ... On Montreal disabled list (July 16-31, 1998); included rehabilitation assignment to Ottawa (July 28-31). ... Granted free agency (December 21, 1998). ... Signed by San Francisco Giants (December 23, 1998). ... Granted free agency (December 21, 1999). ... Signed by Los Angeles Dodgers (January 7, 2000).
STATISTICAL NOTES: Led Eastern League with 13 sacrifice hits in 1991. ... Switch-hit home runs in one game (June 7, 1997).

									BATTING					FIELDING		
Year Team (League)	Pos.	G	AB	R	H	2B	3B	HR	RBI	Avg.	BB	SO	SB	PO	A	E	Avg.
1989—Jamestown (NY-P)	2B	2	6	0	3	1	0	0	0	.500	1	0	1	5	5	2	.833
—W.P. Beach (FSL).......	SS-2B-OF	57	173	18	37	4	0	0	14	.214	23	12	3	32	67	8	.925
1990—W.P. Beach (FSL).......	S-O-2-3	116	394	63	109	19	2	0	38	.277	51	49	22	151	202	22	.941
1991—Harrisburg (East.).......	2-O-S-3	132	462	78	113	12	7	5	42	.245	74	45	21	234	253	16	.968
1992—Indianapolis (A.A.).......	O-2-S-3	137	462	83	123	25	0	5	34	.266	62	58	12	291	119	4	.990
1993—Ottawa (I.L.)...............	O-S-3-2	131	453	86	124	21	2	4	45	.274	59	52	18	246	186	14	.969
1994—Ottawa (I.L.)...............	O-2-S-3	119	413	62	104	28	1	5	41	.252	59	64	7	235	140	12	.969
1995—Ottawa (I.L.)...............	3-2-O-S-C	95	267	37	68	15	3	2	25	.255	32	22	7	89	185	10	.965
—Montreal (N.L.)............	OF-2B	35	98	11	29	5	1	1	9	.296	12	9	1	47	0	1	.979
1996—Montreal (N.L.)............	O-3-2-S	152	393	54	109	20	5	7	56	.277	49	61	5	251	45	6	.980
1997—Montreal (N.L.)............	O-3-2-S	130	350	56	87	19	5	5	31	.249	50	73	8	175	56	3	.987
1998—Montreal (N.L.)............	OF-2B-3B	122	383	53	82	18	0	4	23	.214	44	72	7	211	77	5	.983
—Ottawa (I.L.)	DH-OF	2	8	1	2	0	0	0	1	.250	0	3	0	2	0	0	1.000
1999—San Fran. (N.L.)■.......	O-2-3-S	113	254	49	66	17	3	3	26	.260	53	54	12	144	25	1	.994
Major League totals (5 years)		552	1478	223	373	79	14	20	145	.252	208	269	33	828	203	16	.985

SANTIAGO, BENITO — C

PERSONAL: Born March 9, 1965, in Ponce, Puerto Rico. ... 6-1/195. ... Bats right, throws right. ... Full name: Benito Rivera Santiago. ... Name pronounced SAHN-tee-AH-go.
HIGH SCHOOL: John F. Kennedy (Ponce, Puerto Rico).
TRANSACTIONS/CAREER NOTES: Signed as non-drafted free agent by San Diego Padres organization (September 1, 1982). ... On disabled list (June 21-July 2, 1985). ... On San Diego disabled list (June 15-August 10, 1990); included rehabilitation assignment to Las Vegas (August 2-9). ... On San Diego disabled list (May 31-July 11, 1992); included rehabilitation assignment to Las Vegas (July 7-11). ... Granted free agency

(October 26, 1992). ... Signed by Florida Marlins (December 16, 1992). ... On suspended list (May 5-9, 1994). ... Granted free agency (October 20, 1994). ... Signed by Cincinnati Reds (April 17, 1995). ... On disabled list (May 8-July 4, 1995). ... Granted free agency (October 31, 1995). ... Signed by Philadelphia Phillies (January 30, 1996). ... Granted free agency (November 18, 1996). ... Signed by Toronto Blue Jays (December 9, 1996). ... On disabled list (April 14-29, 1997). ... On Toronto disabled list (March 18-September 3, 1998); included rehabilitation assignments to Dunedin (August 15-26) and Syracuse (August 28-September 3). ... Granted free agency (October 23, 1998). ... Signed by Chicago Cubs (December 10, 1998). ... Granted free agency (October 29, 1999).

RECORDS: Holds major league rookie-season record for most consecutive games batted safely—34 (August 25-October 2, 1987). ... Shares major league single-season record for fewest passed balls (100 or more games)—0 (1992). ... Shares major league record for most consecutive home runs—4 (September 14 [1] and 15 [3], 1996).

HONORS: Named N.L. Rookie Player of the Year by THE SPORTING NEWS (1987). ... Named catcher on THE SPORTING NEWS N.L. All-Star team (1987, 1989 and 1991). ... Named catcher on THE SPORTING NEWS N.L. Silver Slugger team (1987-88 and 1990-91). ... Named N.L. Rookie of the Year by Baseball Writers' Association of America (1987). ... Won N.L. Gold Glove at catcher (1988-90).

STATISTICAL NOTES: Led Florida State League catchers with 26 passed balls and 12 double plays in 1983. ... Led Texas League catchers with 78 assists and 16 passed balls in 1985. ... Led Pacific Coast League catchers with 655 total chances in 1986. ... Had 34-game hitting streak (August 25-October 2, 1987). ... Led N.L. with 22 passed balls in 1987, 14 in 1989 and 23 in 1993. ... Led N.L. in grounding into double plays with 21 in 1991. ... Tied for N.L. lead in double plays by catcher with 11 in 1988 and 14 in 1991. ... Led N.L. catchers with 100 assists and 14 errors in 1991. ... Led N.L. catchers with .996 fielding percentage in 1995. ... Hit three home runs in one game (September 15, 1996). ... Career major league grand slams: 6.

Year Team (League)	Pos.	G	AB	R	H	2B	3B	HR	RBI	Avg.	BB	SO	SB	PO	A	E	Avg.
1983—Miami (FSL)	C	122	429	34	106	25	3	5	56	.247	11	79	3	471	*69	*21	.963
1984—Reno (Calif.)	C	114	416	64	116	20	6	16	83	.279	36	75	5	692	96	25	.969
1985—Beaumont (Texas)	C-1B-3B	101	372	55	111	16	6	5	52	.298	16	59	12	525	†78	15	.976
1986—Las Vegas (PCL)	C	117	437	55	125	26	3	17	71	.286	17	81	19	*563	71	*21	.968
—San Diego (N.L.)	C	17	62	10	18	2	0	3	6	.290	2	12	0	80	7	5	.946
1987—San Diego (N.L.)	C	146	546	64	164	33	2	18	79	.300	16	112	21	817	80	*22	.976
1988—San Diego (N.L.)	C	139	492	49	122	22	2	10	46	.248	24	82	15	725	*75	*12	.985
1989—San Diego (N.L.)	C	129	462	50	109	16	3	16	62	.236	26	89	11	685	81	*20	.975
1990—San Diego (N.L.)	C	100	344	42	93	8	5	11	53	.270	27	55	5	538	51	12	.980
—Las Vegas (PCL)	C	6	20	5	6	2	0	1	8	.300	3	1	0	25	5	0	1.000
1991—San Diego (N.L.)	C-OF	152	580	60	155	22	3	17	87	.267	23	114	8	830	†100	†14	.985
1992—San Diego (N.L.)	C	106	386	37	97	21	0	10	42	.251	21	52	2	584	53	*12	.982
—Las Vegas (PCL)	C	4	13	3	4	0	0	1	2	.308	1	1	0	13	2	0	1.000
1993—Florida (N.L.)■	C-OF	139	469	49	108	19	6	13	50	.230	37	88	10	740	64	11	.987
1994—Florida (N.L.)	C	101	337	35	92	14	2	11	41	.273	25	57	1	511	*66	5	.991
1995—Cincinnati (N.L.)■	C-1B	81	266	40	76	20	0	11	44	.286	24	48	2	480	35	2	†.996
1996—Philadelphia (N.L.)■ ..	C-1B	136	481	71	127	21	2	30	85	.264	49	104	2	834	67	11	.988
1997—Toronto (A.L.)■	C-DH	97	341	31	83	10	0	13	42	.243	17	80	1	621	40	2	.997
1998—Dunedin (FSL)	DH-C	11	37	4	6	1	0	1	5	.162	3	9	3	19	6	0	1.000
—Syracuse (I.L.)	C-DH	5	22	0	5	2	0	0	2	.227	1	3	0	19	1	0	1.000
—Toronto (A.L.)	C	15	29	3	9	5	0	0	4	.310	1	6	0	45	2	0	1.000
1999—Chicago (N.L.)■	C-1B	109	350	28	87	18	3	7	36	.249	32	71	1	562	43	6	.990
American League totals (2 years)		112	370	34	92	15	0	13	46	.249	18	86	1	666	42	2	.997
National League totals (12 years)		1355	4775	535	1248	216	28	157	631	.261	306	884	78	7386	722	132	.984
Major League totals (14 years)		1467	5145	569	1340	231	28	170	677	.260	324	970	79	8052	764	134	.985

DIVISION SERIES RECORD

NOTES: Hit home run in first at-bat (October 3, 1995).

Year Team (League)	Pos.	G	AB	R	H	2B	3B	HR	RBI	Avg.	BB	SO	SB	PO	A	E	Avg.
1995—Cincinnati (N.L.)	C	3	9	2	3	0	0	1	3	.333	3	3	0	20	0	0	1.000

CHAMPIONSHIP SERIES RECORD

Year Team (League)	Pos.	G	AB	R	H	2B	3B	HR	RBI	Avg.	BB	SO	SB	PO	A	E	Avg.
1995—Cincinnati (N.L.)	C	4	13	0	3	0	0	0	0	.231	2	3	0	23	1	0	1.000

ALL-STAR GAME RECORD

Year League	Pos.	AB	R	H	2B	3B	HR	RBI	Avg.	BB	SO	SB	PO	A	E	Avg.
1989—National	C	1	0	0	0	0	0	0	.000	0	1	0	0	0	1	.000
1990—National		Selected, did not play—injured.														
1991—National	C	3	0	0	0	0	0	0	.000	0	1	0	4	0	0	1.000
1992—National	C	1	0	0	0	0	0	0	.000	0	1	0	3	0	0	1.000
All-Star Game totals (3 years)		5	0	0	0	0	0	0	.000	0	3	0	7	0	1	.875

SANTIAGO, JOSE   P   ROYALS

PERSONAL: Born November 5, 1974, in Fajardo, Puerto Rico. ... 6-3/215. ... Throws right, bats right. ... Full name: Jose Rafael Santiago.
HIGH SCHOOL: Carlos Escobar Lopez (Loiza, Puerto Rico).
TRANSACTIONS/CAREER NOTES: Selected by Kansas City Royals organization in 70th round of free agent draft (June 3, 1994). ... On Kansas City disabled list (June 26-July 9, 1997). ... On Kansas City disabled list (June 20-September 13, 1999); included rehabilitation assignments to Gulf Coast Royals (July 3-9), Wichita (July 10-11 and August 30-September 5) and Omaha (July 18-19 and September 6-12).

Year League	W	L	Pct.	ERA	G	GS	CG	ShO	Sv.	IP	H	R	ER	BB	SO
1994—Gulf Coast Royals (GCL)	1	0	1.000	2.37	10	1	0	0	2	19	17	7	5	7	10
1995—Spokane (N'west)	2	4	.333	3.14	22	0	0	0	1	48²/₃	60	26	17	20	32
1996—Lansing (Midw.)	7	6	.538	3.74	54	0	0	0	19	77	78	34	32	21	55
1997—Wilmington (Caro.)	1	1	.500	4.91	4	0	0	0	2	3²/₃	3	3	2	1	1
—Lansing (Midw.)	1	0	1.000	2.08	9	0	0	0	1	13	10	6	3	6	8
—Kansas City (A.L.)	0	0	...	1.93	4	0	0	0	0	4²/₃	7	2	1	2	1
—Wichita (Texas)	2	1	.667	4.00	22	0	0	0	3	27	32	13	12	8	12

Year League	W	L	Pct.	ERA	G	GS	CG	ShO	Sv.	IP	H	R	ER	BB	SO
1998— Wichita (Texas)	3	4	.429	3.61	52	0	0	0	22	72 1/3	79	36	29	27	31
— Kansas City (A.L.)	0	0	...	9.00	2	0	0	0	0	2	4	2	2	0	2
— Omaha (PCL)	0	0	...	7.04	4	0	0	0	1	7 2/3	10	9	6	5	4
1999— Kansas City (A.L.)	3	4	.429	3.42	34	0	0	0	2	47 1/3	46	23	18	14	15
— Gulf Coast Royals (GCL)	0	0	...	1.80	3	3	0	0	0	5	1	1	1	0	4
— Wichita (Texas)	0	1	.000	2.00	4	2	0	0	0	9	8	2	2	0	4
— Omaha (PCL)	0	0	...	0.00	1	0	0	0	0	1 2/3	3	0	0	0	0
Major League totals (3 years)	3	4	.429	3.50	40	0	0	0	2	54	57	27	21	16	18

SANTOS, VICTOR — P — TIGERS

PERSONAL: Born October 2, 1976, in San Pedro de Macoris, Dominican Republic. ... 6-3/175. ... Throws right, bats right. ... Full name: Victor Irving Santos.
HIGH SCHOOL: Passaic (N.J.).
TRANSACTIONS/CAREER NOTES: Signed as non-drafted free agent by Detroit Tigers organization (June 11, 1995).
STATISTICAL NOTES: Led Southern League pitchers with seven errors in 1999.

Year League	W	L	Pct.	ERA	G	GS	CG	ShO	Sv.	IP	H	R	ER	BB	SO
1995— Dominican Tigers (DSL)	7	5	.583	3.72	15	12	3	2	0	77 1/3	88	46	32	18	75
1996— Lakeland (FSL)	2	2	.500	2.22	5	4	0	0	0	28 1/3	19	11	7	9	25
— Gulf Coast Tigers (GCL)	3	2	.600	1.98	9	9	0	0	0	50	44	12	11	13	39
1997— Lakeland (FSL)	10	5	.667	3.23	26	26	4	•2	0	145	136	74	52	59	108
1998— Lakeland (FSL)	5	2	.714	2.51	16	15	0	0	1	100 1/3	88	38	28	24	74
— Toledo (I.L.)	1	2	.333	11.05	5	3	0	0	0	14 2/3	24	22	18	10	12
— Jacksonville (Sou.)	4	2	.667	4.17	6	6	0	0	0	36 2/3	40	20	17	15	37
1999— Jacksonville (Sou.)	12	6	.667	3.49	28	•28	2	1	0	173	150	86	67	58	*146

SASAKI, KAZUHIRO — P — MARINERS

PERSONAL: Born February 22, 1968, in Sendai City, Japan. ... 6-4/208. ... Throws right, bats right.
COLLEGE: Tohoku Fukushi University (Sendai City, Japan).
TRANSACTIONS/CAREER NOTES: Signed as non-drafted free agent by Seattle Mariners (December 18, 1999).

Year League	W	L	Pct.	ERA	G	GS	CG	ShO	Sv.	IP	H	R	ER	BB	SO
1990— Yokohama (Jap. Cen.)	2	4	.333	5.85	16	...	...	...	2	47 2/3	49	31	31	30	44
1991— Yokohama (Jap. Cen.)	6	9	.400	2.00	58	...	...	...	17	117	72	33	26	55	137
1992— Yokohama (Jap. Cen.)	12	6	.667	2.46	53	...	...	...	21	87 2/3	47	32	24	40	135
1993— Yokohama (Jap. Cen.)	3	6	.333	3.27	38	...	...	...	20	55	35	24	20	23	84
1994— Yokohama (Jap. Cen.)	3	1	.750	2.15	31	...	...	...	10	46	27	11	11	15	59
1995— Yokohama (Jap. Cen.)	7	2	.778	1.75	47	...	...	...	32	56 2/3	30	12	11	17	78
1996— Yokohama (Jap. Cen.)	4	3	.571	2.90	39	...	...	...	25	49 2/3	37	17	16	17	80
1997— Yokohama (Jap. Cen.)	3	0	1.000	0.90	49	...	...	...	38	60	25	6	6	18	99
1998— Yokohama (Jap. Cen.)	1	1	.500	0.64	51	...	...	...	45	56	32	7	4	14	78
1999— Yokohama (Jap. Cen.)	1	1	.500	1.93	23	...	...	...	19	23 1/3	19	5	5	16	34

SASSER, ROB — 3B — TIGERS

PERSONAL: Born March 9, 1975, in Philadelphia. ... 6-3/205. ... Bats right, throws right. ... Full name: Robert Dofell Sasser.
HIGH SCHOOL: Oakland High.
TRANSACTIONS/CAREER NOTES: Selected by Atlanta Braves organization in 10th round of free-agent draft (June 10, 1993). ... Selected by California Angels organization from Braves organization in Rule 5 minor league draft (December 9, 1996). ... Anaheim Angels for 1997 season. ... Traded by Angels to Texas Rangers (October 31, 1997), completing deal in which Rangers traded P Ken Hill to Angels for C Jim Leyritz and a player to be named later (July 29, 1997). ... On Tulsa disabled list (April 6-May 2, 1998). ... Claimed on waivers by Detroit Tigers (April 15, 1999).
STATISTICAL NOTES: Led South Atlantic League third basemen with 45 errors in 1996. ... Led Midwest League third basemen with 435 total chances in 1997. ... Led Texas League third basemen with 229 assists and 321 total chances in 1998. ... Tied for Texas League lead in errors by third basemen with 26 in 1998. ... Led Southern League third baseman with 27 double plays in 1999.

Year Team (League)	Pos.	G	AB	R	H	2B	3B	HR	RBI	Avg.	BB	SO	SB	PO	A	E	Avg.
1993— GC Braves (GCL)	3B	33	113	19	27	4	0	0	7	.239	6	25	2	15	61	10	.884
1994— Idaho Falls (Pio.)	3B-SS	58	219	32	50	9	6	2	26	.228	19	58	13	35	122	20	.887
1995— Danville (Appl.)	3B	12	47	8	15	2	1	0	7	.319	4	7	5	7	16	4	.852
— Eugene (N'west)	SS-3B	57	216	40	58	9	1	9	32	.269	23	51	14	77	111	31	.858
1996— Macon (SAL)	3-1-S-2	135	465	64	122	35	3	8	64	.262	65	108	38	247	262	†51	.909
1997— Cedar Rap. (Midw.)	3B-SS	134	497	103	135	26	5	17	77	.272	69	92	37	104	303	28	.936
1998— Tulsa (Texas)■	3B-2B	111	417	57	117	25	2	8	62	.281	60	98	18	68	†233	‡26	.920
— Charlotte (FSL)	3B	4	13	1	4	2	0	0	3	.308	3	5	1	2	9	0	1.000
— Texas (A.L.)	PH	1	1	0	0	0	0	0	0	.000	0	0	0	...	...	...	...
1999— Tulsa (Texas)	OF-DH	5	19	3	5	2	0	0	0	.263	1	2	0	7	0	0	1.000
— Jacksonville (Sou.)■	3B-DH	117	424	60	120	38	1	7	61	.283	57	101	9	82	*276	*35	.911
Major League totals (1 year)		1	1	0	0	0	0	0	0	.000	0	0	0	0	0	0	...

SATURRIA, LUIS — OF — CARDINALS

PERSONAL: Born July 21, 1976, in San Pedro de Macoris, Dominican Republic. ... 6-2/165. ... Bats right, throws right. ... Full name: Luis Arturo Saturria.
TRANSACTIONS/CAREER NOTES: Signed as non-drafted free agent by St. Louis Cardinals organization (March 5, 1994). ... Selected by Toronto Blue Jays from Cardinals organization in Rule 5 major league draft (December 15, 1997). ... Returned to Cardinals organization (March 20, 1998).

S

STATISTICAL NOTES: Tied for Carolina League lead with three double plays by outfielder in 1998.

Year Team (League)	Pos.	G	AB	R	H	2B	3B	HR	RBI	Avg.	BB	SO	SB	PO	A	E	Avg.
1994—Dom. Cardinals (DSL)	OF	61	227	29	63	2	6	1	23	.278	25	49	16	118	13	8	.942
1995—Dom. Cardinals (DSL)	OF	66	245	48	78	16	7	2	33	.318	34	26	12	126	14	22	.864
1996—Johnson City (Appl.)..	OF	57	227	43	58	7	1	5	40	.256	24	61	12	68	5	3	.961
1997—Peoria (Midw.)...........	OF	122	445	81	122	19	5	11	51	.274	44	95	23	196	*24	9	.961
1998—Prince Will. (Caro.).....	OF	129	462	70	136	25	9	12	73	.294	28	104	26	235	11	*15	.943
1999—Arkansas (Texas)........	OF	•139	484	66	118	30	4	16	61	.244	35	134	16	255	13	9	.968

SAUERBECK, SCOTT   P   PIRATES

PERSONAL: Born November 9, 1971, in Cincinnati. ... 6-3/197. ... Throws left, bats right. ... Full name: Scott William Sauerbeck.
HIGH SCHOOL: Northwest (Cincinnati).
COLLEGE: Miami of Ohio.
TRANSACTIONS/CAREER NOTES: Selected by New York Mets organization in 23rd round of free-agent draft (June 2, 1994). ... Selected by Pittsburgh Pirates from Mets organization in Rule 5 major league draft (December 14, 1998).

Year League	W	L	Pct.	ERA	G	GS	CG	ShO	Sv.	IP	H	R	ER	BB	SO
1994—Pittsfield (NY-P)	3	1	.750	2.05	21	0	0	0	1	48 1/3	39	16	11	19	39
1995—St. Lucie (FSL)	0	1	.000	2.03	20	1	0	0	0	26 2/3	26	10	6	14	25
—Capital City (SAL)	5	4	.556	3.27	19	0	0	0	2	33	28	14	12	14	33
1996—St. Lucie (FSL)	6	6	.500	2.27	17	16	2	2	0	99 1/3	101	37	25	27	62
—Binghamton (East.)	3	3	.500	3.47	8	8	2	0	0	46 2/3	48	24	18	12	30
1997—Binghamton (East.)	8	9	.471	4.93	27	20	2	0	0	131 1/3	144	89	72	50	88
—Norfolk (I.L.)	1	0	1.000	3.60	1	1	0	0	0	5	3	2	2	4	4
1998—Norfolk (I.L.)	7	13	.350	3.93	27	27	2	0	0	160 1/3	178	82	70	69	119
1999—Pittsburgh (N.L.)■	4	1	.800	2.00	65	0	0	0	2	67 2/3	53	19	15	38	55
Major League totals (1 year)........	4	1	.800	2.00	65	0	0	0	2	67 2/3	53	19	15	38	55

SAUNDERS, TONY   P   DEVIL RAYS

PERSONAL: Born April 29, 1974, in Baltimore. ... 6-2/205. ... Throws left, bats left. ... Full name: Anthony Scott Saunders.
HIGH SCHOOL: Glen Burnie (Md.).
TRANSACTIONS/CAREER NOTES: Signed as non-drafted free agent by Florida Marlins organization (June 9, 1992). ... On Florida disabled list (May 19-July 10, 1997). ... Selected by Tampa Bay Devil Rays in first round (first pick overall) of expansion draft (November 18, 1997). ... On Tampa Bay disabled list (May 28, 1999-remainder of season).
STATISTICAL NOTES: Pitched 3-1 one-hit, complete-game victory against Houston (May 28, 1995).

Year League	W	L	Pct.	ERA	G	GS	CG	ShO	Sv.	IP	H	R	ER	BB	SO
1992—Gulf Coast Marlins (GCL) ...	4	1	.800	1.18	24	0	0	0	7	45 2/3	29	10	6	13	37
1993—Kane County (Midw.).........	6	1	.857	2.27	23	10	2	0	1	83 1/3	72	23	21	32	87
1994—Brevard County (FSL)........	5	5	.500	3.15	10	10	1	0	0	60	54	24	21	9	46
1995—Brevard County (FSL)........	6	5	.545	3.04	13	13	0	0	0	71	60	29	24	15	54
1996—Portland (East.)	13	4	.765	2.63	26	26	2	0	0	167 2/3	121	51	49	62	*156
1997—Florida (N.L.)	4	6	.400	4.61	22	21	0	0	0	111 1/3	99	62	57	64	102
—Portland (East.)	0	0	...	9.00	1	1	0	0	0	2	3	2	2	1	3
—Charlotte (I.L.)	1	0	1.000	2.77	3	3	0	0	0	13	9	4	4	6	9
1998—Tampa Bay (A.L.)■............	6	15	.286	4.12	31	31	2	0	0	192 1/3	191	95	88	*111	172
1999—Tampa Bay (A.L.)...............	3	3	.500	6.43	9	9	0	0	0	42	53	39	30	29	30
—Durham (I.L.)	0	0	...	2.57	1	1	0	0	0	7	8	3	2	2	7
A.L. totals (2 years)	9	18	.333	4.53	40	40	2	0	0	234 1/3	244	134	118	140	202
N.L. totals (1 year)........................	4	6	.400	4.61	22	21	0	0	0	111 1/3	99	62	57	64	102
Major League totals (3 years)	13	24	.351	4.56	62	61	2	0	0	345 2/3	343	196	175	204	304

DIVISION SERIES RECORD

Year League	W	L	Pct.	ERA	G	GS	CG	ShO	Sv.	IP	H	R	ER	BB	SO
1997—Florida (N.L.)							Did not play.								

CHAMPIONSHIP SERIES RECORD

Year League	W	L	Pct.	ERA	G	GS	CG	ShO	Sv.	IP	H	R	ER	BB	SO
1997—Florida (N.L.)	0	0	...	3.38	1	1	0	0	0	5 1/3	4	2	2	3	3

WORLD SERIES RECORD

NOTES: Member of World Series championship team (1997).

Year League	W	L	Pct.	ERA	G	GS	CG	ShO	Sv.	IP	H	R	ER	BB	SO
1997—Florida (N.L.)	0	1	.000	27.00	1	1	0	0	0	2	7	6	6	3	2

SCARSONE, STEVE   IF

PERSONAL: Born April 11, 1966, in Anaheim. ... 6-2/192. ... Bats right, throws right. ... Full name: Steven Wayne Scarsone. ... Name pronounced scar-SONE-ee.
HIGH SCHOOL: Canyon (Anaheim).
COLLEGE: Santa Ana (Calif.) College.
TRANSACTIONS/CAREER NOTES: Selected by Philadelphia Phillies organization in second round of free-agent draft (January 14, 1986). ... Traded by Phillies to Baltimore Orioles for SS Juan Bell (August 11, 1992). ... Traded by Orioles to San Francisco Giants for OF Mark Leonard (March 20, 1993). ... On San Francisco disabled list (March 31-June 1, 1993). ... On Phoenix disabled list (June 22-29, 1993). ... Granted free agency (October 4, 1996). ... Signed by St. Louis Cardinals organization (January 13, 1997). ... Released by Cardinals (May 14, 1997). ... Signed by San Diego Padres organization (May 20, 1997). ... Granted free agency (October 15, 1997). ... Signed by Anaheim Angels organization (December 5, 1997). ... Granted free agency (October 15, 1998). ... Signed by Kansas City Royals organization (January 25, 1999). ... Released by Royals (September 11, 1999).

STATISTICAL NOTES: Led Northwest League second basemen with 147 putouts, 29 errors and 45 double plays in 1986. ... Led International League second basemen with 20 errors in 1991. ... Led International League second basemen with 304 assists, 26 errors and 77 double plays in 1992.

Year Team (League)	Pos.	G	AB	R	H	2B	3B	HR	RBI	Avg.	BB	SO	SB	PO	A	E	Avg.
1986— Bend (N'west)	2B-SS	65	219	42	48	10	•4	4	21	.219	30	51	11	†149	188	†30	.918
1987— Char., W.Va. (SAL)	SS-2B-3B	95	259	35	56	11	1	1	17	.216	31	64	8	127	212	25	.931
1988— Clearwater (FSL)	SS-3B-2B	125	456	51	120	21	4	8	46	.263	18	93	14	179	326	33	.939
1989— Reading (East.)	2B-SS	75	240	30	43	5	0	4	22	.179	15	67	2	171	200	11	.971
1990— Clearwater (FSL)	2B	59	211	20	58	9	5	3	23	.275	19	57	3	116	147	13	.953
— Reading (East.)	2B-SS	74	245	26	65	12	1	3	23	.265	14	63	0	141	206	8	.977
1991— Reading (East.)	2B	15	49	6	15	0	0	3	3	.306	4	15	2	43	54	3	.970
— Scranton/W.B. (I.L.)	2B-SS	111	405	52	111	20	6	6	38	.274	19	81	10	222	343	†21	.964
1992— Scranton/W.B. (I.L.)	2B	89	325	43	89	23	4	11	48	.274	24	74	10	174	†253	†19	.957
— Philadelphia (N.L.)	2B	7	13	1	2	0	0	0	0	.154	1	6	0	3	3	0	1.000
— Rochester (I.L.)■	2B-3B	23	82	13	21	3	0	1	12	.256	6	12	3	36	†57	†7	.930
— Baltimore (A.L.)	2B-3B-SS	11	17	2	3	0	0	0	0	.176	1	6	0	6	8	2	.875
1993— Phoenix (PCL)■	2B-3B-SS-1B	19	70	13	18	1	2	3	9	.257	8	21	2	36	48	3	.966
— San Francisco (N.L.)	2B-3B-1B	44	103	16	26	9	0	2	15	.252	4	32	0	53	44	1	.990
1994— San Francisco (N.L.)	2B-3B-1B-SS	52	103	21	28	8	0	2	13	.272	10	20	0	66	80	2	.986
1995— San Francisco (N.L.)	3B-2B-1B	80	233	33	62	10	3	11	29	.266	18	82	3	135	113	11	.958
1996— San Francisco (N.L.)	2-3-1-S	105	283	28	62	12	1	5	23	.219	25	91	2	167	177	11	.969
1997— Louisville (A.A.)■	2B-3B	10	26	5	4	0	0	1	3	.154	7	10	0	13	20	1	.971
— St. Louis (N.L.)	2B-OF-3B	5	10	0	1	0	0	0	0	.100	2	5	1	4	2	0	1.000
— Las Vegas (PCL)■	2-3-S-1-DH-O	82	251	37	58	13	1	11	35	.231	38	78	2	126	209	13	.963
1998— Vancouver (PCL)■	2-3-DH-1-O	115	407	50	110	24	4	20	55	.270	34	112	4	151	236	20	.951
1999— Kansas City (A.L.)■	S-1-2-3-DH	46	68	2	14	5	0	0	6	.206	9	24	1	101	49	3	.980
— Omaha (PCL)	SS-2B-DH-OF	18	58	9	10	1	0	5	7	.172	7	21	1	33	32	0	1.000
American League totals (2 years)		57	85	4	17	5	0	0	6	.200	10	30	1	107	57	5	.970
National League totals (6 years)		293	745	99	181	39	4	20	80	.243	60	236	6	428	419	25	.971
Major League totals (7 years)		350	830	103	198	44	4	20	86	.239	70	266	7	535	476	30	.971

SCHEFFER, AARON — P — MARINERS

PERSONAL: Born October 15, 1975, in Ypsilanti, Mich. ... 6-2/185. ... Throws right, bats left. ... Full name: Aaron Alvin Marcus Scheffer.
HIGH SCHOOL: John Glenn (Westland, Mich.).
TRANSACTIONS/CAREER NOTES: Signed as non-drafted free agent by Seattle Mariners organization (August 2, 1993).

Year League	W	L	Pct.	ERA	G	GS	CG	ShO	Sv.	IP	H	R	ER	BB	SO
1994— Bellingham (N'west)	0	0	...	6.00	2	0	0	0	0	3	4	4	2	3	5
— Arizona Mariners (Ariz.)	2	2	.500	1.95	24	0	0	0	6	32 1/3	18	11	7	10	26
1995— Wisconsin (Midw.)	0	1	.000	6.59	9	0	0	0	0	13 2/3	17	14	10	5	8
— Everett (N'west)	2	5	.286	3.74	24	0	0	0	1	43 1/3	44	23	18	16	38
1996— Wisconsin (Midw.)	8	1	.889	3.72	45	1	0	0	14	67 2/3	55	35	28	34	89
1997— Lancaster (Calif.)	11	3	.786	5.44	37	3	0	0	0	92 2/3	93	58	56	42	103
1998— Lancaster (Calif.)	2	2	.500	3.14	25	0	0	0	10	43	46	19	15	12	65
— Orlando (Sou.)	1	0	1.000	2.20	19	0	0	0	5	32 2/3	23	8	8	13	33
1999— New Haven (East.)	2	0	1.000	3.71	10	0	0	0	0	17	19	9	7	8	24
— Tacoma (PCL)	2	3	.400	2.87	35	1	0	0	9	59 2/3	47	25	19	23	62
— Seattle (A.L.)	0	0	...	1.93	4	0	0	0	0	4 2/3	6	5	1	3	4
Major League totals (1 year)	0	0	...	1.93	4	0	0	0	0	4 2/3	6	5	1	3	4

SCHILLING, CURT — P — PHILLIES

PERSONAL: Born November 14, 1966, in Anchorage, Alaska. ... 6-4/231. ... Throws right, bats right. ... Full name: Curtis Montague Schilling.
HIGH SCHOOL: Shadow Mountain (Phoenix).
JUNIOR COLLEGE: Yavapai College (Ariz.).
TRANSACTIONS/CAREER NOTES: Selected by Boston Red Sox organization in second round of free-agent draft (January 14, 1986). ... Traded by Red Sox with OF Brady Anderson to Baltimore Orioles for P Mike Boddicker (July 29, 1988). ... Traded by Orioles with P Pete Harnisch and OF Steve Finley to Houston Astros for 1B Glenn Davis (January 10, 1991). ... Traded by Astros to Philadelphia Phillies for P Jason Grimsley (April 2, 1992). ... On Philadelphia disabled list (May 17-July 25, 1994); included rehabilitation assignments to Scranton/Wilkes-Barre (July 10-15) and Reading (July 15-20). ... On disabled list (July 19, 1995-remainder of season). ... On Philadelphia disabled list (March 23-May 14, 1996); included rehabilitation assignments to Clearwater (April 23-May 3) and Scranton/Wilkes-Barre (May 3-14). ... On disabled list (August 8-September 3, 1999).
RECORDS: Shares major league single-season record for fewest complete games for leader—8 (1996). ... Holds N.L. single-season record for most strikeouts by righthander—319 (1997).
STATISTICAL NOTES: Tied for International League lead with six balks in 1989. ... Pitched 2-1 one-hit, complete-game victory against New York (September 9, 1992). ... Struck out 15 batters in one game (July 21, 1997 and April 5, 1998). ... Struck out 16 batters in one game (September 1, 1997).
MISCELLANEOUS: Struck out once in two appearances as pinch hitter with Philadelphia (1996).

Year League	W	L	Pct.	ERA	G	GS	CG	ShO	Sv.	IP	H	R	ER	BB	SO
1986— Elmira (NY-P)	7	3	.700	2.59	16	15	2	1	0	93 2/3	92	34	27	30	75
1987— Greensboro (SAL)	8	*15	.348	3.82	29	28	7	3	0	184	179	96	78	65	*189
1988— New Britain (East.)	8	5	.615	2.97	21	17	4	1	0	106	91	44	35	40	62
— Charlotte (Sou.)■	5	2	.714	3.18	7	7	2	1	0	45 1/3	36	19	16	23	32
— Baltimore (A.L.)	0	3	.000	9.82	4	4	0	0	0	14 2/3	22	19	16	10	4
1989— Rochester (I.L.)	•13	1	.542	3.21	27	•27	•9	•3	0	*185 1/3	176	76	66	59	109
— Baltimore (A.L.)	0	1	.000	6.23	5	1	0	0	0	8 2/3	10	6	6	3	4
1990— Rochester (I.L.)	4	4	.500	3.92	15	14	1	0	0	87 1/3	95	46	38	25	83
— Baltimore (A.L.)	1	2	.333	2.54	35	0	0	0	3	46	38	13	13	19	32

S

Year League	W	L	Pct.	ERA	G	GS	CG	ShO	Sv.	IP	H	R	ER	BB	SO
1991— Houston (N.L.)■	3	5	.375	3.81	56	0	0	0	8	75²/₃	79	35	32	39	71
— Tucson (PCL)	0	1	1.000	3.42	13	0	0	0	3	23²/₃	16	9	9	12	21
1992— Philadelphia (N.L.)■	14	11	.560	2.35	42	26	10	4	2	226¹/₃	165	67	59	59	147
1993— Philadelphia (N.L.)	16	7	.696	4.02	34	34	7	2	0	235¹/₃	234	114	105	57	186
1994— Philadelphia (N.L.)	2	8	.200	4.48	13	13	1	0	0	82¹/₃	87	42	41	28	58
— Scranton/W.B. (I.L.)	0	0	...	1.80	2	2	0	0	0	10	6	2	2	5	6
— Reading (East.)	0	0	...	0.00	1	1	0	0	0	4	6	0	0	1	4
1995— Philadelphia (N.L.)	7	5	.583	3.57	17	17	1	0	0	116	96	52	46	26	114
1996— Clearwater (FSL)	2	0	1.000	1.29	2	2	0	0	0	14	9	2	2	1	17
— Scranton/W.B. (I.L.)	1	0	1.000	1.38	2	2	0	0	0	13	9	2	2	5	10
— Philadelphia (N.L.)	9	10	.474	3.19	26	26	*8	2	0	183¹/₃	149	69	65	50	182
1997— Philadelphia (N.L.)	17	11	.607	2.97	35	*35	7	2	0	254¹/₃	208	96	84	58	*319
1998— Philadelphia (N.L.)	15	14	.517	3.25	35	*35	*15	2	0	*268²/₃	236	101	97	61	*300
1999— Philadelphia (N.L.)	15	6	.714	3.54	24	24	8	1	0	180¹/₃	159	74	71	44	152
A.L. totals (3 years)	1	6	.143	4.54	44	5	0	0	3	69¹/₃	70	38	35	32	42
N.L. totals (9 years)	98	77	.560	3.33	282	210	57	13	10	1622¹/₃	1413	650	600	422	1529
Major League totals (12 years)	99	83	.544	3.38	326	215	57	13	13	1691²/₃	1483	688	635	454	1571

CHAMPIONSHIP SERIES RECORD

RECORDS: Holds single-game records for most consecutive strikeouts—5; and most consecutive strikeouts from start of the game—5 (October 6, 1993).
NOTES: Named N.L. Championship Series Most Valuable Player (1993).

Year League	W	L	Pct.	ERA	G	GS	CG	ShO	Sv.	IP	H	R	ER	BB	SO
1993— Philadelphia (N.L.)	0	0	...	1.69	2	2	1	0	0	16	11	4	3	5	19

WORLD SERIES RECORD

Year League	W	L	Pct.	ERA	G	GS	CG	ShO	Sv.	IP	H	R	ER	BB	SO
1993— Philadelphia (N.L.)	1	1	.500	3.52	2	2	1	1	0	15¹/₃	13	7	6	5	9

ALL-STAR GAME RECORD

Year League	W	L	Pct.	ERA	GS	CG	ShO	Sv.	IP	H	R	ER	BB	SO
1997— National	0	0	...	0.00	0	0	0	0	2	2	0	0	0	3
1998— National							Did not play.							
1999— National	0	1	.000	9.00	1	0	0	0	2	3	2	2	1	3
All-Star Game totals (2 years)	0	1	.000	4.50	1	0	0	0	4	5	2	2	1	6

SCHMIDT, JASON   P   PIRATES

PERSONAL: Born January 29, 1973, in Lewiston, Idaho. ... 6-5/213. ... Throws right, bats right. ... Full name: Jason David Schmidt.
HIGH SCHOOL: Kelso (Wash.).
TRANSACTIONS/CAREER NOTES: Selected by Atlanta Braves organization in eighth round of free-agent draft (June 3, 1991). ... On Atlanta disabled list (July 15-August 30, 1996); included rehabilitation assignment to Greenville (August 11-30). ... Traded by Braves to Pittsburgh Pirates (August 30, 1996), completing deal in which Pirates traded P Denny Neagle to Braves for a player to be named later (August 28, 1996).
RECORDS: Shares N.L. single-inning record for most consecutive home runs allowed—3 (August 22, 1999, first inning).
STATISTICAL NOTES: Led N.L. with 15 wild pitches in 1998. ... Tied for N.L. lead with four balks in 1999.
MISCELLANEOUS: Received base on balls in only appearance as pinch hitter with Atlanta (1995).

Year League	W	L	Pct.	ERA	G	GS	CG	ShO	Sv.	IP	H	R	ER	BB	SO
1991— Gulf Coast Braves (GCL)	3	4	.429	2.38	11	11	0	0	0	45¹/₃	32	21	12	23	44
1992— Pulaski (Appl.)	3	4	.429	4.01	11	11	0	0	0	58¹/₃	38	36	26	31	56
— Macon (SAL)	0	3	.000	4.01	7	7	0	0	0	24²/₃	31	18	11	19	33
1993— Durham (Caro.)	7	11	.389	4.94	22	22	0	0	0	116²/₃	128	69	64	47	110
1994— Greenville (Sou.)	8	7	.533	3.65	24	24	1	0	0	140²/₃	135	64	57	54	131
1995— Atlanta (N.L.)	2	2	.500	5.76	9	2	0	0	0	25	27	17	16	18	19
— Richmond (I.L.)	8	6	.571	*2.25	19	19	0	0	0	116	97	40	29	48	95
1996— Atlanta (N.L.)	3	4	.429	6.75	13	11	0	0	0	58²/₃	69	48	44	32	48
— Richmond (I.L.)	3	0	1.000	2.56	7	7	0	0	0	45²/₃	36	17	13	19	41
— Greenville (Sou.)	0	0	...	9.00	1	1	0	0	0	2	4	2	2	0	2
— Pittsburgh (N.L.)■	2	2	.500	4.06	6	6	1	0	0	37²/₃	39	19	17	21	26
1997— Pittsburgh (N.L.)	10	9	.526	4.60	32	32	2	0	0	187²/₃	193	106	96	76	136
1998— Pittsburgh (N.L.)	11	14	.440	4.07	33	33	0	0	0	214¹/₃	228	106	97	71	158
1999— Pittsburgh (N.L.)	13	11	.542	4.19	33	33	2	0	0	212²/₃	219	110	99	85	148
Major League totals (5 years)	41	42	.494	4.51	126	117	5	0	0	736	775	406	369	303	535

SCHNEIDER, BRIAN   C   EXPOS

PERSONAL: Born November 26, 1976, in Jacksonville, Fla. ... 6-1/200. ... Bats left, throws right. ... Full name: Brian Duncan Schneider.
HIGH SCHOOL: Northampton (Pa.).
TRANSACTIONS/CAREER NOTES: Selected by Montreal Expos organization in fifth round of free-agent draft (June 1, 1995).
STATISTICAL NOTES: Led Eastern League catchers with 91 assists in 1999.

Year Team (League)	Pos.	G	AB	R	H	2B	3B	HR	RBI	Avg.	BB	SO	SB	PO	A	E	Avg.
1995— GC Expos (GCL)	C	30	97	7	22	3	0	0	4	.227	14	23	2	138	26	3	.982
1996— GC Expos (GCL)	C	52	144	26	44	5	2	0	23	.306	24	15	2	214	26	3	.988
— Delmarva (SAL)	C	5	9	0	3	0	0	0	1	.333	1	1	0	20	3	0	1.000
1997— Cape Fear (SAL)	C	113	381	46	96	20	1	4	49	.252	53	45	3	724	99	10	.988
1998— Cape Fear (SAL)	C	38	134	33	40	7	2	7	30	.299	16	9	6	261	32	6	.980
— Jupiter (FSL)	C	82	302	32	82	12	1	3	30	.272	22	38	4	483	81	11	.981
1999— Harrisburg (East.)	C-DH-1B	121	421	48	111	19	1	17	66	.264	32	56	2	622	†92	6	.992

SCHOENEWEIS, SCOTT　　　　　P　　　　　ANGELS

PERSONAL: Born October 2, 1973, in Long Branch, N.J. ... 6-0/186. ... Throws left, bats left. ... Full name: Scott David Schoeneweis.
HIGH SCHOOL: Lenape (Medford, N.J.).
COLLEGE: Duke.
TRANSACTIONS/CAREER NOTES: Selected by California Angels organization in third round of free-agent draft (June 4, 1996). ... Angels franchise renamed Anaheim Angels for 1997 season.

Year　League	W	L	Pct.	ERA	G	GS	CG	ShO	Sv.	IP	H	R	ER	BB	SO
1996—Lake Elsinore (Calif.)	8	3	.727	3.94	14	12	0	0	0	93 2/3	86	47	41	27	83
1997—Midland (Texas)................	7	5	.583	5.96	20	20	3	0	0	113 1/3	145	84	75	39	84
1998—Vancouver (PCL)	11	8	.579	4.50	27	27	2	0	0	180	188	102	90	59	133
1999—Anaheim (A.L.)	1	1	.500	5.49	31	0	0	0	0	39 1/3	47	27	24	14	22
—Edmonton (PCL)	2	4	.333	7.64	9	7	0	0	0	35 1/3	58	35	30	12	29
Major League totals (1 year)........	1	1	.500	5.49	31	0	0	0	0	39 1/3	47	27	24	14	22

SCHOUREK, PETE　　　　　P　　　　　PIRATES

PERSONAL: Born May 10, 1969, in Austin, Texas. ... 6-5/220. ... Throws left, bats left. ... Full name: Peter Alan Schourek. ... Name pronounced SHUR-ek.
HIGH SCHOOL: George C. Marshall (Falls Church, Va.).
TRANSACTIONS/CAREER NOTES: Selected by New York Mets organization in second round of free-agent draft (June 2, 1987). ... On disabled list (June 17, 1988-entire season). ... Claimed on waivers by Cincinnati Reds (April 7, 1994). ... On disabled list (June 1-22 and July 2, 1996-remainder of season). ... On disabled list (June 14-July 18 and July 31-September 2, 1997). ... Released by Reds (October 10, 1997). ... Signed by Houston Astros organization (January 9, 1998). ... On New Orleans disabled list (April 7-24, 1998). ... Traded by Astros to Boston Red Sox for cash (August 6, 1998). ... Granted free agency (October 23, 1998). ... Signed by Pittsburgh Pirates (December 18, 1998). ... On disabled list (August 17-September 1, 1999).
HONORS: Named lefthanded pitcher on The Sporting News N.L. All-Star team (1995).
STATISTICAL NOTES: Pitched 9-0 one-hit, complete-game victory for New York against Montreal (September 10, 1991).
MISCELLANEOUS: Appeared in one game as pinch runner with New York (1992). ... Struck out in only appearance as pinch hitter (1996). ... Appeared in one game as pinch runner (1997).

Year　League	W	L	Pct.	ERA	G	GS	CG	ShO	Sv.	IP	H	R	ER	BB	SO
1987—Kingsport (Appalachian).....	4	5	.444	3.68	12	12	2	0	0	78 1/3	70	37	32	34	57
1988—								Did not play.							
1989—Columbia (SAL)................	5	9	.357	2.85	27	19	5	1	1	136	120	66	43	66	131
—St. Lucie (FSL)................	0	0	...	2.25	2	1	0	0	0	4	3	1	1	2	4
1990—St. Lucie (FSL)................	4	1	.800	0.97	5	5	2	2	0	37	29	4	4	8	28
—Tidewater (I.L.)................	1	0	1.000	2.57	2	2	1	1	0	14	9	4	4	5	14
—Jackson (Texas)	11	4	.733	3.04	19	19	1	0	0	124 1/3	109	53	42	39	94
1991—Tidewater (I.L.)................	1	1	.500	2.52	4	4	0	0	0	25	18	7	7	10	17
—New York (N.L.)................	5	4	.556	4.27	35	8	1	1	2	86 1/3	82	49	41	43	67
1992—Tidewater (I.L.)................	2	5	.286	2.73	8	8	2	1	0	52 2/3	46	20	16	23	42
—New York (N.L.)................	6	8	.429	3.64	22	21	0	0	0	136	137	60	55	44	60
1993—New York (N.L.)................	5	12	.294	5.96	41	18	0	0	0	128 1/3	168	90	85	45	72
1994—Cincinnati (N.L.)■............	7	2	.778	4.09	22	10	0	0	0	81 1/3	90	39	37	29	69
1995—Cincinnati (N.L.)	18	7	.720	3.22	29	29	2	0	0	190 1/3	158	72	68	45	160
1996—Cincinnati (N.L.)	4	5	.444	6.01	12	12	0	0	0	67 1/3	79	48	45	24	54
1997—Cincinnati (N.L.)	5	8	.385	5.42	18	17	0	0	0	84 2/3	78	59	51	38	59
1998—Kissimmee (FSL)■............	0	0	...	1.08	2	1	0	0	0	8 1/3	8	1	1	4	9
—Houston (N.L.)................	7	6	.538	4.50	15	15	0	0	0	80	82	43	40	36	59
—Boston (A.L.)■................	1	3	.250	4.30	10	8	0	0	0	44	45	21	21	14	36
1999—Pittsburgh (N.L.)■............	4	7	.364	5.34	30	17	0	0	0	113	128	75	67	49	94
A.L. totals (1 year)	1	3	.250	4.30	10	8	0	0	0	44	45	21	21	14	36
N.L. totals (9 years)	61	59	.508	4.55	224	147	3	1	2	967 1/3	1002	535	489	353	694
Major League totals (9 years)	62	62	.500	4.54	234	155	3	1	2	1011 1/3	1047	556	510	367	730

DIVISION SERIES RECORD

Year　League	W	L	Pct.	ERA	G	GS	CG	ShO	Sv.	IP	H	R	ER	BB	SO
1995—Cincinnati (N.L.)	1	0	1.000	2.57	1	1	0	0	0	7	5	2	2	3	5
1998—Boston (A.L.)................	0	0	...	0.00	1	1	0	0	0	5 1/3	2	0	0	4	1
Division series totals (2 years)	1	0	1.000	1.46	2	2	0	0	0	12 1/3	7	2	2	7	6

CHAMPIONSHIP SERIES RECORD

Year　League	W	L	Pct.	ERA	G	GS	CG	ShO	Sv.	IP	H	R	ER	BB	SO
1995—Cincinnati (N.L.)	0	1	.000	1.26	2	2	0	0	0	14 1/3	14	2	2	3	13

SCHRENK, STEVE　　　　　P　　　　　PHILLIES

PERSONAL: Born November 20, 1968, in Great Lakes, Ill. ... 6-3/215. ... Throws right, bats right. ... Full name: Steven Wayne Schrenk.
HIGH SCHOOL: North Marion (Aurora, Ore.).
TRANSACTIONS/CAREER NOTES: Selected by Chicago White Sox organization in fourth round of free-agent draft (June 2, 1987). ... On disabled list (April 11-September 3, 1991). ... On Nashville disabled list (April 21, 1995-remainder of season). ... On disabled list (April 4-25 and July 30-September 6, 1996). ... Granted free agency (October 15, 1996). ... Signed by Rochester, Baltimore Orioles organization (Janaury 14, 1997). ... Granted free agency (October 15, 1997). ... Signed by St. Louis Cardinals organization (November 25, 1997). ... Released by Cardinals (April 3, 1998). ... Signed by Boston Red Sox organization (May 22, 1998). ... Granted free agency (October 15, 1998). ... Signed by Philadelphia Phillies organization (November 5, 1998).

Year	League	W	L	Pct.	ERA	G	GS	CG	ShO	Sv.	IP	H	R	ER	BB	SO
1987—	GC White Sox (GCL)	1	2	.333	0.95	8	6	1	1	0	28 1/3	23	10	3	12	19
1988—	South Bend (Midw.)	3	7	.300	5.00	21	18	1	0	0	90	95	63	50	37	58
1989—	South Bend (Midw.)	5	2	.714	4.33	16	16	1	1	0	79	71	44	38	44	49
1990—	South Bend (Midw.)	7	6	.538	2.95	20	14	2	1	0	103 2/3	79	44	34	25	92
1991—	GC White Sox (GCL)	1	3	.250	2.92	11	7	0	0	0	37	30	20	12	6	39
1992—	Sarasota (FSL)	15	2	.882	2.05	25	22	4	2	1	154	130	48	35	40	113
—	Birmingham (Sou.)............	1	1	.500	3.65	2	2	0	0	0	12 1/3	13	5	5	11	9
1993—	Birmingham (Sou.)...........	5	1	.833	1.17	8	8	2	1	0	61 2/3	31	11	8	7	51
—	Nashville (A.A.)	6	8	.429	3.90	21	20	0	0	0	122 1/3	117	61	53	47	78
1994—	Nashville (A.A.)	14	6	.700	3.48	29	28	2	1	0	178 2/3	175	82	69	69	134
1995—	GC White Sox (GCL)	0	1	.000	0.00	2	2	0	0	0	7	5	2	0	0	6
1996—	Nashville (A.A.)	4	10	.286	4.42	16	15	1	0	0	95 2/3	93	54	47	29	58
1997—	Rochester (I.L.)	4	7	.364	4.66	25	24	1	0	0	125 2/3	127	73	65	36	99
1998—	Pawtucket (I.L.)■..............	8	3	.727	2.82	34	0	0	0	1	60 2/3	60	27	19	23	45
1999—	Scranton/W.B. (I.L.)■	3	1	.750	2.93	32	0	0	0	2	43	38	17	14	21	34
—	Philadelphia (N.L.)	1	3	.250	4.29	32	2	0	0	1	50 1/3	41	24	24	14	36
Major League totals (1 year)........		1	3	.250	4.29	32	2	0	0	1	50 1/3	41	24	24	14	36

SEANEZ, RUDY · P · BRAVES

PERSONAL: Born October 20, 1968, in Brawley, Calif. ... 5-10/190. ... Throws right, bats right. ... Full name: Rudy Caballero Seanez. ... Name pronounced see-AHN-yez.
HIGH SCHOOL: Brawley (Calif.) Union.
TRANSACTIONS/CAREER NOTES: Selected by Cleveland Indians organization in fourth round of free-agent draft (June 10, 1986). ... On disabled list (May 4-July 11 and August 9-29, 1987). ... On Cleveland disabled list (April 1-16 and July 30-September 2, 1991); included rehabilitation assignment to Colorado Springs (August 14-September 2). ... Traded by Indians to Los Angeles Dodgers for P Dennis Cook and P Mike Christopher (December 10, 1991). ... On disabled list (March 29, 1992-entire season). ... Traded by Dodgers to Colorado Rockies for 2B Jody Reed (November 17, 1992). ... On Colorado disabled list (April 4-July 16, 1993); included rehabilitation assignments to Central Valley (June 16-July 4) and Colorado Springs (July 4-15). ... Granted free agency (July 16, 1993). ... Signed by San Diego Padres organization (July 22, 1993). ... Released by Padres (November 18, 1993). ... Signed by Dodgers organization (January 12, 1994). ... On Los Angeles disabled list (May 28-June 16, 1995); included rehabilitation assignment to San Bernardino (June 9-16). ... Granted free agency (October 15, 1996). ... Signed by New York Mets organization (January 15, 1997). ... Traded by Mets to Kansas City Royals for future considerations (May 30, 1997). ... Granted free agency (October 15, 1997). ... Signed by Atlanta Braves organization (December 9, 1997). ... On disabled list (August 21, 1999-remainder of season). ... Granted free agency (November 2, 1999). ... Re-signed by Braves (December 19, 1999).
STATISTICAL NOTES: Pitched 4-0 no-hit victory against Pulaski (August 2, 1986).

Year	League	W	L	Pct.	ERA	G	GS	CG	ShO	Sv.	IP	H	R	ER	BB	SO
1986—	Burlington (Appl.)...............	5	2	.714	3.20	13	12	1	1	0	76	59	37	27	32	56
1987—	Waterloo (Midw.)	0	4	.000	6.75	10	10	0	0	0	34 2/3	35	29	26	23	23
1988—	Waterloo (Midw.)	6	6	.500	4.69	22	22	1	1	0	113 1/3	98	69	59	68	93
1989—	Kinston (Caro.).................	8	10	.444	4.14	25	25	1	0	0	113	94	66	52	*111	149
—	Colorado Springs (PCL)	0	0	...	0.00	1	0	0	0	0	1	1	0	0	0	0
—	Cleveland (A.L.)..............	0	0	...	3.60	5	0	0	0	0	5	1	2	2	4	7
1990—	Canton/Akron (East.).........	1	0	1.000	2.16	15	0	0	0	5	16 2/3	9	4	4	12	27
—	Cleveland (A.L.)..............	2	1	.667	5.60	24	0	0	0	0	27 1/3	22	17	17	25	24
—	Colorado Springs (PCL)	1	4	.200	6.75	12	0	0	0	1	12	15	10	9	10	7
1991—	Colorado Springs (PCL)	0	0	...	7.27	16	0	0	0	0	17 1/3	17	14	14	22	19
—	Canton/Akron (East.)	4	2	.667	2.58	25	0	0	0	7	38 1/3	17	12	11	30	73
—	Cleveland (A.L.).............	0	0	...	16.20	5	0	0	0	0	5	10	12	9	7	7
1992—	Los Angeles (N.L.)■							Did not play.								
1993—	Central Valley (Calif.)■	0	2	.000	9.72	5	1	0	0	0	8 1/3	9	9	9	11	7
—	Colorado Springs (PCL)	0	0	...	9.00	3	0	0	0	0	3	3	3	3	1	5
—	Las Vegas (PCL)■	0	1	.000	6.41	14	0	0	0	0	19 2/3	24	15	14	11	14
—	San Diego (N.L.)	0	0	...	13.50	3	0	0	0	0	3 1/3	8	6	5	2	1
1994—	Albuquerque (PCL)■	2	1	.667	5.32	20	0	0	0	9	22	28	14	13	13	26
—	Los Angeles (N.L.)	1	1	.500	2.66	17	0	0	0	0	23 2/3	24	7	7	9	18
1995—	Los Angeles (N.L.)	1	3	.250	6.75	37	0	0	0	3	34 2/3	39	27	26	18	29
—	San Bernardino (Calif.).......	2	0	1.000	0.00	4	0	0	0	1	6	2	0	0	3	5
1996—	Albuquerque (PCL)............	0	2	.000	6.52	21	0	0	0	6	19 1/3	27	18	14	11	20
1997—	Norfolk (I.L.)■	1	0	1.000	4.05	9	0	0	0	0	13 1/3	12	8	6	11	17
—	Omaha (A.A.)■	2	5	.286	6.51	28	3	0	0	0	47	53	42	34	25	46
1998—	Richmond (I.L.)■..............	2	0	1.000	1.29	16	0	0	0	7	21	13	9	3	7	33
—	Atlanta (N.L.).................	4	1	.800	2.75	34	0	0	0	2	36	25	13	11	16	50
1999—	Atlanta (N.L.).................	6	1	.857	3.35	56	0	0	0	3	53 2/3	47	21	20	21	41
A.L. totals (3 years)		2	1	.667	6.75	34	0	0	0	0	37 1/3	33	31	28	36	38
N.L. totals (5 years)		12	6	.667	4.10	147	0	0	0	8	151 1/3	143	74	69	66	139
Major League totals (8 years)		14	7	.667	4.63	181	0	0	0	8	188 2/3	176	105	97	102	177

DIVISION SERIES RECORD

Year	League	W	L	Pct.	ERA	G	GS	CG	ShO	Sv.	IP	H	R	ER	BB	SO
1998—	Atlanta (N.L.).....................	0	0	...	0.00	1	0	0	0	0	1	0	0	0	0	0

CHAMPIONSHIP SERIES RECORD

Year	League	W	L	Pct.	ERA	G	GS	CG	ShO	Sv.	IP	H	R	ER	BB	SO
1998—	Atlanta (N.L.).....................	0	0	...	6.00	4	0	0	0	0	3	2	2	2	1	4

SECODA, JASON · P · WHITE SOX

PERSONAL: Born September 2, 1974, in Garden Grove, Calif. ... 6-1/195. ... Throws right, bats right. ... Full name: Jason A. Secoda.
HIGH SCHOOL: Valencia (Placentia, Calif.).
COLLEGE: California State-Los Angeles.
TRANSACTIONS/CAREER NOTES: Selected by Chicago White Sox organization in ninth round of free-agent draft (June 1, 1995).

Year	League	W	L	Pct.	ERA	G	GS	CG	ShO	Sv.	IP	H	R	ER	BB	SO
1995— Bristol (Appl.)		2	8	.200	5.35	13	12	0	0	0	65²/₃	78	57	39	33	63
1996— South Bend (Midw.)		6	12	.333	3.97	31	21	0	0	1	133²/₃	132	84	59	75	94
1997— Win.-Salem (Car.)		7	4	.636	4.14	29	15	1	0	2	119²/₃	118	67	55	57	85
1998— Win.-Salem (Car.)		2	0	1.000	1.59	6	0	0	0	0	11¹/₃	8	2	2	2	8
— Birmingham (Sou.)		2	3	.400	6.34	39	0	0	0	1	65¹/₃	78	50	46	39	45
1999— Birmingham (Sou.)		8	7	.533	3.44	22	17	1	1	0	115	100	49	44	39	94
— Charlotte (I.L.)		2	5	.286	5.28	7	7	3	0	0	44¹/₃	54	35	26	10	33

SEFCIK, KEVIN — OF/IF — PHILLIES

PERSONAL: Born February 10, 1971, in Oak Lawn, Ill. ... 5-10/182. ... Bats right, throws right. ... Full name: Kevin John Sefcik.
HIGH SCHOOL: Victor Andrews (Tinley Park, Ill.).
COLLEGE: St. Xavier (Ill.).
TRANSACTIONS/CAREER NOTES: Selected by Philadelphia Phillies organization in 33rd round of free-agent draft (June 3, 1993).
STATISTICAL NOTES: Led New York-Pennsylvania League second basemen with 212 assists and 359 total chances in 1993.

Year	Team (League)	Pos.	G	AB	R	H	2B	3B	HR	RBI	Avg.	BB	SO	SB	PO	A	E	Avg.
1993— Batavia (NY-P)		2B-3B	74	281	49	84	24	4	2	28	.299	27	22	20	136	†216	16	.957
1994— Clearwater (FSL)		3B-2B	130	516	83	147	29	8	2	46	.285	49	43	30	91	293	21	.948
1995— Scranton/W.B. (I.L.)		2B	7	26	5	9	6	1	0	6	.346	3	1	0	13	16	0	1.000
— Reading (East.)		SS-3B-DH	128	508	68	138	18	4	4	46	.272	38	48	14	166	349	18	.966
— Philadelphia (N.L.)		3B	5	4	1	0	0	0	0	0	.000	0	2	0	0	1	0	1.000
1996— Philadelphia (N.L.)		SS-3B-2B	44	116	10	33	5	3	0	9	.284	9	16	3	30	83	7	.942
— Scranton/W.B. (I.L.)		SS-2B-3B	45	180	34	60	7	5	0	19	.333	15	20	11	63	143	10	.954
1997— Philadelphia (N.L.)		2B-SS-3B	61	119	11	32	3	0	2	6	.269	4	9	1	39	62	4	.962
— Scranton/W.B. (I.L.)		2B-3B-OF	29	123	19	41	11	2	1	7	.333	9	11	5	51	56	6	.947
1998— Philadelphia (N.L.)		O-3-DH-2	104	169	27	53	7	2	3	20	.314	25	32	4	89	1	2	.978
1999— Philadelphia (N.L.)		OF-2B	111	209	28	58	15	3	1	11	.278	29	24	9	93	18	2	.982
Major League totals (5 years)			325	617	77	176	30	8	6	46	.285	67	83	17	251	165	15	.965

SEGUI, DAVID — 1B/DH — BLUE JAYS

PERSONAL: Born July 19, 1966, in Kansas City, Kan. ... 6-1/202. ... Bats both, throws left. ... Full name: David Vincent Segui. ... Son of Diego Segui, pitcher with five major league teams (1962-75 and 1977); and brother of Dan Segui, minor league infielder (1987-90). ... Name pronounced seh-GHEE.
HIGH SCHOOL: Bishop Ward (Kansas City, Kan.).
JUNIOR COLLEGE: Kansas City Kansas Community College.
COLLEGE: Louisiana Tech.
TRANSACTIONS/CAREER NOTES: Selected by Baltimore Orioles organization in 18th round of free-agent draft (June 2, 1987). ... On Rochester disabled list (April 19-26, 1991). ... On suspended list (August 16-19, 1993). ... Traded by Orioles to New York Mets for SS Kevin Baez and P Tom Wegmann (March 27, 1994). ... On disabled list (June 20-July 5, 1994). ... Traded by Mets to Montreal Expos for P Reid Cornelius (June 8, 1995). ... On disabled list (July 4-August 16, 1996). ... On disabled list (June 4-21, 1997). ... On suspended list (July 26, 1997). ... Granted free agency (October 28, 1997). ... Signed by Seattle Mariners (December 12, 1997). ... Traded by Mariners to Toronto Blue Jays for P Tom Davey and P Steve Sinclair (July 28, 1999). ... On suspended list (July 30-31, 1999). ... On Toronto disabled list (August 8-September 2, 1999). ... Granted free agency (October 29, 1999). ... Re-signed by Blue Jays (December 19, 1999).
STATISTICAL NOTES: Led N.L. first basemen with .996 fielding percentage in 1994. ... Switch-hit home runs in one game (April 1, 1998). ... Led A.L. first basemen with .999 fielding percentage in 1998. ... Had 15-game hitting streak (May 10-29, 1999). ... Career major league grand slams: 4.

Year	Team (League)	Pos.	G	AB	R	H	2B	3B	HR	RBI	Avg.	BB	SO	SB	PO	A	E	Avg.
1988— Hagerstown (Caro.)		1B-OF	60	190	35	51	12	4	3	31	.268	22	23	0	342	25	9	.976
1989— Frederick (Caro.)		1B	83	284	43	90	19	0	10	50	.317	41	32	2	707	47	4	.995
— Hagerstown (East.)		1B	44	173	22	56	14	1	1	27	.324	16	16	0	381	30	1	.998
1990— Rochester (I.L.)		1B-OF	86	307	55	103	28	0	2	51	.336	45	28	5	704	62	3	.996
— Baltimore (A.L.)		1B-DH	40	123	14	30	7	0	2	15	.244	11	15	0	283	26	3	.990
1991— Rochester (I.L.)		1B-OF	28	96	9	26	2	0	1	10	.271	15	6	1	165	15	0	1.000
— Baltimore (A.L.)		OF-1B-DH	86	212	15	59	7	0	2	22	.278	12	19	1	264	23	3	.990
1992— Baltimore (A.L.)		1B-OF	115	189	21	44	9	0	1	17	.233	20	23	1	406	35	1	.998
1993— Baltimore (A.L.)		1B-DH	146	450	54	123	27	0	10	60	.273	58	53	2	1152	98	5	.996
1994— New York (N.L.)■			92	336	46	81	17	1	10	43	.241	33	43	0	695	52	5	†.993
1995— New York (N.L.)		OF-1B	33	73	9	24	3	1	2	11	.329	12	9	1	56	5	0	1.000
— Montreal (N.L.)■		1B-OF	97	383	59	117	22	3	10	57	.305	28	38	1	840	70	3	.997
1996— Montreal (N.L.)		1B	115	416	69	119	30	1	11	58	.286	60	54	4	944	90	7	.993
1997— Montreal (N.L.)		1B	125	459	75	141	22	3	21	68	.307	57	66	1	1035	88	6	.995
1998— Seattle (A.L.)■		1B-OF	143	522	79	159	36	1	19	84	.305	49	80	3	1045	116	1	†.999
1999— Seattle (A.L.)		1B	90	345	43	101	22	3	9	39	.293	32	43	1	700	61	3	.996
— Toronto (A.L.)■		DH-1B	31	95	14	30	5	0	5	13	.316	8	17	0	19	2	1	.955
American League totals (6 years)			651	1936	240	546	113	4	48	250	.282	190	250	8	3869	361	17	.996
National League totals (4 years)			462	1667	258	482	94	9	54	237	.289	190	210	7	3570	305	21	.995
Major League totals (10 years)			1113	3603	498	1028	207	13	102	487	.285	380	460	15	7439	666	38	.995

SEGUIGNOL, FERNANDO — 1B/OF — EXPOS

PERSONAL: Born January 19, 1975, in Bocas del Toro, Panama. ... 6-5/230. ... Bats both, throws right. ... Full name: Fernando Alfredo Seguignol.
HIGH SCHOOL: Almirante de Bocas del Toro (Bocas del Toro, Panama).

TRANSACTIONS/CAREER NOTES: Signed as non-drafted free agent by New York Yankees organization (January 29, 1993). ... Traded by Yankees with and cash to Montreal Expos for P John Wetteland (April 5, 1995). ... On Harrisburg disabled list (June 24-July 17, 1998). ... On Montreal disabled list (July 11-September 7, 1999); included rehabilitation assignment to Ottawa (August 9-September 7).
STATISTICAL NOTES: Led Florida State League with 14 sacrifice flies in 1997. ... Tied for Florida State League lead in assists by first basemen with 91 in 1997.

Year Team (League)	Pos.	G	AB	R	H	2B	3B	HR	RBI	Avg.	BB	SO	SB	PO	A	E	Avg.
						BATTING								FIELDING			
1993—GC Yankees (GCL)....	OF-1B	45	161	16	35	3	3	2	20	.217	9	37	2	86	8	2	.979
1994—Oneonta (NY-P)........	OF	73	266	36	77	14	*9	2	32	.289	16	61	4	77	3	4	.952
1995—Albany (SAL)■..........	OF	121	457	59	95	22	2	12	66	.208	28	141	12	205	7	8	.964
1996—Delmarva (SAL).........	OF	118	410	59	98	14	5	8	55	.239	48	126	12	173	4	4	.978
1997—W.P. Beach (FSL)......	1B-OF	124	456	70	116	27	5	18	83	.254	30	129	5	967	‡91	15	.986
1998—Harrisburg (East.).....	1B-OF	80	281	54	81	13	0	25	69	.288	29	77	6	503	50	9	.984
— Ottawa (I.L.)............	OF-1B	32	109	16	28	8	0	6	16	.257	12	43	0	44	2	1	.979
— Montreal (N.L.).........	OF-1B	16	42	6	11	4	0	2	3	.262	3	15	0	65	5	0	1.000
1999—Ottawa (I.L.)..........	1B-DH-OF	87	312	54	89	17	3	23	74	.285	40	96	3	397	40	10	.978
— Montreal (N.L.).........	1B-OF	35	105	14	27	9	0	5	10	.257	5	33	0	183	11	2	.990
Major League totals (2 years)		51	147	20	38	13	0	7	13	.259	8	48	0	248	16	2	.992

SEKANY, JASON P RED SOX

PERSONAL: Born July 20, 1975, in Walnut Creek, Calif. ... 6-4/214. ... Throws right, bats right.
HIGH SCHOOL: Granada (Livermore, Calif.).
JUNIOR COLLEGE: Modesto (Calif.) Junior College.
COLLEGE: Virginia.
TRANSACTIONS/CAREER NOTES: Selected by Boston Red Sox organization in second round of free-agent draft (June 4, 1996).

Year League	W	L	Pct.	ERA	G	GS	CG	ShO	Sv.	IP	H	R	ER	BB	SO
1996—GC Red Sox (GCL).....	0	0	...	2.31	5	2	0	0	1	$11^{2}/_{3}$	14	3	3	3	16
1997—Michigan (Midw.)......	5	6	.455	4.08	16	16	3	0	0	106	92	55	48	41	103
— Sarasota (FSL)........	4	4	.500	5.57	10	9	0	0	0	$64^{2}/_{3}$	56	43	40	41	32
1998—Trenton (East.)........	10	10	.500	5.21	28	28	1	0	0	$148^{2}/_{3}$	151	101	86	57	113
1999—Trenton (East.)........	14	4	.778	3.35	27	22	3	2	0	$161^{1}/_{3}$	143	65	60	64	116
— Pawtucket (I.L.)........	0	1	.000	4.76	1	1	0	0	0	$5^{2}/_{3}$	7	4	3	4	1

SELE, AARON P MARINERS

PERSONAL: Born June 25, 1970, in Golden Valley, Minn. ... 6-5/215. ... Throws right, bats right. ... Full name: Aaron Helmer Sele. ... Name pronounced SEE-lee.
HIGH SCHOOL: North Kitsap (Poulsbo, Wash.).
COLLEGE: Washington State.
TRANSACTIONS/CAREER NOTES: Selected by Minnesota Twins organization in 37th round of free-agent draft (June 1, 1988); did not sign. ... Selected by Boston Red Sox organization in first round (23rd pick overall) of free-agent draft (June 3, 1991). ... On Boston disabled list (May 24, 1995-remainder of season); included rehabilitation assignments to Trenton (June 19-22), Sarasota (July 10-21 and August 7-16) and Pawtucket (August 16-23). ... On Boston disabled list (August 14-September 1, 1996); included rehabilitation assignment to Pawtucket (August 26-27). ... Traded by Red Sox with P Mark Brandenburg and C Bill Haselman to Texas Rangers for C Jim Leyritz and OF Damon Buford (November 6, 1997). ... Granted free agency (November 5, 1999). ... Signed by Seattle Mariners (January 10, 2000).
HONORS: Named A.L. Rookie Pitcher of the Year by THE SPORTING NEWS (1993). ... Named International League Most Valuable Pitcher (1993).
STATISTICAL NOTES: Led Carolina League with 14 hit batsmen in 1992. ... Tied for A.L. lead with nine hit batsmen in 1994.

Year League	W	L	Pct.	ERA	G	GS	CG	ShO	Sv.	IP	H	R	ER	BB	SO
1991—Winter Haven (FSL)..........	3	6	.333	4.96	13	11	4	0	1	69	65	42	38	32	51
1992—Lynchburg (Caro.).............	13	5	.722	2.91	20	19	2	1	0	127	104	51	41	46	112
— New Britain (East.).............	2	1	.667	6.27	7	6	1	0	0	33	43	29	23	15	29
1993—Pawtucket (I.L.)........	8	2	.800	2.19	14	14	2	1	0	$94^{1}/_{3}$	74	30	23	23	87
— Boston (A.L.).....................	7	2	.778	2.74	18	18	0	0	0	$111^{2}/_{3}$	100	42	34	48	93
1994—Boston (A.L.).....................	8	7	.533	3.83	22	22	2	0	0	$143^{1}/_{3}$	140	68	61	60	105
1995—Boston (A.L.).....................	3	1	.750	3.06	6	6	0	0	0	$32^{1}/_{3}$	32	14	11	14	21
— Trenton (East.)	0	1	.000	3.38	2	2	0	0	0	8	8	3	3	2	9
— Sarasota (FSL).................	0	0	...	0.00	2	2	0	0	0	7	6	0	0	1	8
— Pawtucket (I.L.)	0	0	...	9.00	2	2	0	0	0	5	9	5	5	2	1
1996—Boston (A.L.).....................	7	11	.389	5.32	29	29	1	0	0	$157^{1}/_{3}$	192	110	93	67	137
— Pawtucket (I.L.)	0	0	...	6.00	1	1	0	0	0	3	3	2	2	1	4
1997—Boston (A.L.).....................	13	12	.520	5.38	33	33	1	0	0	$177^{1}/_{3}$	196	115	106	80	122
1998—Texas (A.L.)■.....................	19	11	.633	4.23	33	33	3	2	0	$212^{2}/_{3}$	239	116	100	84	167
1999—Texas (A.L.).....................	18	9	.667	4.79	33	33	2	2	0	205	244	115	109	70	186
Major League totals (7 years)......	75	53	.586	4.45	174	174	9	4	0	$1039^{2}/_{3}$	1143	580	514	423	831

DIVISION SERIES RECORD

Year League	W	L	Pct.	ERA	G	GS	CG	ShO	Sv.	IP	H	R	ER	BB	SO
1998—Texas (A.L.)	0	1	.000	6.00	1	1	0	0	0	6	8	4	4	1	4
1999—Texas (A.L.)	0	1	.000	5.40	1	1	0	0	0	5	6	4	3	5	3
Division series totals (2 years)	0	2	.000	5.73	2	2	0	0	0	11	14	8	7	6	7

ALL-STAR GAME RECORD

Year League	W	L	Pct.	ERA	GS	CG	ShO	Sv.	IP	H	R	ER	BB	SO
1998—American						Did not play.								

SERAFINI, DANIEL — P — PADRES

PERSONAL: Born January 25, 1974, in San Francisco. ... 6-3/210. ... Throws left, bats right. ... Full name: Daniel Joseph Serafini.
HIGH SCHOOL: Serra (San Mateo, Calif.).
TRANSACTIONS/CAREER NOTES: Selected by Minnesota Twins organization in first round (26th pick overall) of free-agent draft (June 1, 1992). ... On Salt Lake disabled list (May 11-31, 1996). ... Traded by Twins to Chicago Cubs for cash (March 31, 1999). ... Traded by Cubs to San Diego Padres for OF Brandon Pernell (December 22, 1999).

Year	League	W	L	Pct.	ERA	G	GS	CG	ShO	Sv.	IP	H	R	ER	BB	SO
1992—	Gulf Coast Twins (GCL)	1	0	1.000	3.64	8	6	0	0	0	29²/₃	27	16	12	15	33
1993—	Fort Wayne (Midw.)	10	8	.556	3.65	27	27	1	1	0	140²/₃	117	72	57	83	147
1994—	Fort Myers (FSL)	9	9	.500	4.61	23	23	2	1	0	136²/₃	149	84	70	57	130
1995—	New Britain (East.)	12	9	.571	3.38	27	27	1	1	0	162²/₃	155	74	61	72	123
—	Salt Lake (PCL)	0	0	...	6.75	1	0	0	0	1	4	4	3	3	1	4
1996—	Salt Lake (PCL)	7	7	.500	5.58	25	23	1	0	0	130²/₃	164	84	81	58	109
—	Minnesota (A.L.)	0	1	.000	10.38	1	1	0	0	0	4¹/₃	7	5	5	2	1
1997—	Salt Lake (PCL)	9	7	.563	4.97	28	24	2	0	0	152	166	87	84	55	118
—	Minnesota (A.L.)	2	1	.667	3.42	6	4	1	0	0	26¹/₃	27	11	10	11	15
1998—	Salt Lake (PCL)	2	4	.333	3.71	9	8	0	0	0	53¹/₃	56	29	22	21	39
—	Minnesota (A.L.)	7	4	.636	6.48	28	9	0	0	0	75	95	58	54	29	46
1999—	Chicago (N.L.)■	3	2	.600	6.93	42	4	0	0	1	62¹/₃	86	51	48	32	17
—	Iowa (PCL)	0	0	...	2.77	2	2	0	0	0	13	12	6	4	5	11
A.L. totals (3 years)		9	6	.600	5.88	35	14	1	0	0	105²/₃	129	74	69	42	62
N.L. totals (1 year)		3	2	.600	6.93	42	4	0	0	1	62¹/₃	86	51	48	32	17
Major League totals (4 years)		12	8	.600	6.27	77	18	1	0	1	168	215	125	117	74	79

SERRANO, WASCAR — P — PADRES

PERSONAL: Born June 2, 1978, in Santo Domingo, Dominican Republic. ... 6-2/178. ... Throws right, bats right.
HIGH SCHOOL: Las Carreres (Dominican Republic).
TRANSACTIONS/CAREER NOTES: Signed as non-drafted free agent by San Diego Padres organization (May 31, 1995).

Year	League	W	L	Pct.	ERA	G	GS	CG	ShO	Sv.	IP	H	R	ER	BB	SO
1995—	Dom. Padres (DSL)	3	3	.500	3.11	12	7	0	0	0	46¹/₃	63	24	16	15	23
1996—	Dom. Padres (DSL)	3	7	.300	7.88	22	2	0	0	1	53²/₃	77	58	47	24	44
1997—	Idaho Falls (Pio.)	0	1	.000	11.88	2	2	0	0	0	8¹/₃	13	12	11	4	13
—	Arizona Padres (Ariz.)	•6	3	.667	3.18	12	11	0	0	1	70²/₃	60	43	25	22	75
—	Clinton (Midw.)	0	1	.000	6.00	1	1	1	0	0	6	6	5	4	2	2
1998—	Clinton (Midw.)	9	7	.563	3.22	26	26	0	0	0	156²/₃	150	74	56	54	143
1999—	Rancho Cuca. (Calif.)	9	8	.524	3.33	21	21	1	1	0	132¹/₃	110	58	49	43	129
—	Mobile (Sou.)	2	3	.400	5.53	7	7	0	0	0	42¹/₃	48	27	26	17	29

SERVAIS, SCOTT — C — ROCKIES

PERSONAL: Born June 4, 1967, in La Crosse, Wis. ... 6-2/210. ... Bats right, throws right. ... Full name: Scott Daniel Servais. ... Name pronounced SER-viss.
HIGH SCHOOL: Westby (Wis.).
COLLEGE: Creighton.
TRANSACTIONS/CAREER NOTES: Selected by New York Mets organization in second round of free-agent draft (June 3, 1985); did not sign. ... Selected by Houston Astros organization in third round of free-agent draft (June 1, 1988). ... On Tucson disabled list (June 29-July 1, 1991). ... On Houston disabled list (August 4-September 7, 1991). ... Traded by Astros with OF Luis Gonzalez to Chicago Cubs for C Rick Wilkins (June 28, 1995). ... On Chicago disabled list (July 10-August 3, 1995). ... Granted free agency (October 23, 1998). ... Signed by San Francisco Giants (January 17, 1999). ... On San Francisco disabled list (June 17-July 9, 1999); included rehabilitation assignment to Fresno (July 4-9). ... Granted free agency (October 29, 1999). ... Signed by Colorado Rockies organization (December 17, 1999).
STATISTICAL NOTES: Tied for Pacific Coast League lead in double plays by catcher with nine in 1990. ... Led N.L. catchers with 12 errors in 1995.
MISCELLANEOUS: Member of 1988 U.S. Olympic baseball team.

Year	Team (League)	Pos.	G	AB	R	H	2B	3B	HR	RBI	Avg.	BB	SO	SB	PO	A	E	Avg.
1989—	Osceola (FSL)	C-1B	46	153	16	41	9	0	2	23	.268	16	35	0	168	24	4	.980
—	Columbus (Sou.)	C	63	199	20	47	5	0	1	22	.236	19	42	0	330	45	3	.992
1990—	Tucson (PCL)	C	89	303	37	66	11	3	5	37	.218	18	61	0	453	63	9	.983
1991—	Tucson (PCL)	C	60	219	34	71	12	0	2	37	.324	13	19	0	350	33	6	.985
—	Houston (N.L.)	C	16	37	0	6	3	0	0	6	.162	4	8	0	77	4	1	.988
1992—	Houston (N.L.)	C	77	205	12	49	9	0	0	15	.239	11	25	0	386	27	2	.995
1993—	Houston (N.L.)	C	85	258	24	63	11	0	11	32	.244	22	45	0	493	40	2	.996
1994—	Houston (N.L.)	C	78	251	27	49	15	1	9	41	.195	10	44	0	481	29	2	.996
1995—	Houston (N.L.)	C	28	89	7	20	10	0	1	12	.225	9	15	0	198	17	5	.977
—	Chicago (N.L.)■	C	52	175	31	50	12	0	12	35	.286	23	37	2	328	33	§7	.981
1996—	Chicago (N.L.)	C-1B	129	445	42	118	20	0	11	63	.265	30	75	0	798	73	11	.988
1997—	Chicago (N.L.)	C-DH-1B	122	385	36	100	21	0	6	45	.260	24	56	0	736	73	8	.990
1998—	Chicago (N.L.)	C-1B	113	325	35	72	15	1	7	36	.222	26	51	1	654	48	4	.994
1999—	San Fran. (N.L.)■	C-1B	69	198	21	54	10	0	5	21	.273	13	31	0	363	23	3	.992
—	Fresno (PCL)	C	3	11	3	3	1	1	0	2	.273	0	1	0	23	1	0	1.000
Major League totals (9 years)			769	2368	235	581	126	2	62	306	.245	172	387	3	4514	367	45	.991

DIVISION SERIES RECORD

Year	Team (League)	Pos.	G	AB	R	H	2B	3B	HR	RBI	Avg.	BB	SO	SB	PO	A	E	Avg.
1998—	Chicago (N.L.)	C	1	3	0	2	0	0	0	0	.667	0	0	0	6	1	0	1.000

PERSONAL: Born February 26, 1967, in Cincinnati. ... 6-6/240. ... Throws right, bats right. ... Full name: David Scott Service.
HIGH SCHOOL: Aiken (Cincinnati).
TRANSACTIONS/CAREER NOTES: Signed as non-drafted free agent by Philadelphia Phillies organization (August 24, 1985). ... Granted free agency (October 11, 1990). ... Signed by Montreal Expos organization (November 15, 1990). ... Contract sold by Expos to Chunichi of Japan Central League (July 19, 1991). ... Signed by Expos organization (January 10, 1992). ... Granted free agency (June 8, 1992). ... Signed by Nashville, Cincinnati Reds organization (June 9, 1992). ... On Indianapolis disabled list (May 15-22, 1993). ... Claimed on waivers by Colorado Rockies (June 28, 1993). ... Claimed on waivers by Reds (July 7, 1993). ... On Indianapolis disabled list (April 17-24, 1994). ... Released by Reds (November 17, 1994). ... Re-signed by Reds organization (February 24, 1995). ... Traded by Reds with OF Deion Sanders, P John Roper, P Ricky Pickett and IF Dave McCarty to San Francisco Giants for OF Darren Lewis, P Mark Portugal and P Dave Burba (July 21, 1995). ... Released by Giants (March 26, 1996). ... Signed by Reds organization (April 2, 1996). ... Claimed on waivers by Oakland Athletics (March 27, 1997). ... Claimed on waivers by Reds (April 4, 1997). ... Traded by Reds with P Hector Carrasco to Kansas City Royals for OF Jon Nunnally and IF/OF Chris Stynes (July 15, 1997). ... On suspended list (June 15-16, 1998). ... Released by Royals (December 17, 1999). ... Signed by Oakland Athletics (December 30, 1999).
STATISTICAL NOTES: Led American Association with .800 winning percentage in 1992. ... Led American Association with 24 saves in 1997.
MISCELLANEOUS: Made an out in only appearance as pinch hitter with Cincinnati (1993).

Year	League	W	L	Pct.	ERA	G	GS	CG	ShO	Sv.	IP	H	R	ER	BB	SO
1986—	Spartanburg (SAL)	1	6	.143	5.83	14	9	1	0	0	58 2/3	68	44	38	34	49
	Utica (NY-P)	5	4	.556	2.67	10	10	2	0	0	70 2/3	65	30	21	18	43
	Clearwater (FSL)	1	2	.333	3.20	4	4	1	1	0	25 1/3	20	10	9	15	19
1987—	Reading (East.)	0	3	.000	7.78	5	4	0	0	0	19 2/3	22	19	17	16	12
	Clearwater (FSL)	13	4	.765	2.48	21	21	5	2	0	137 2/3	127	46	38	32	73
1988—	Reading (East.)	3	4	.429	2.86	10	9	1	1	0	56 2/3	52	25	18	22	39
	Maine (I.L.)	8	8	.500	3.67	19	18	1	0	0	110 1/3	109	51	45	31	87
	Philadelphia (N.L.)	0	0	...	1.69	5	0	0	0	0	5 1/3	7	1	1	1	6
1989—	Scranton/W.B. (I.L.)	3	1	.750	2.16	23	0	0	0	6	33 1/3	27	8	8	23	23
	Reading (East.)	6	6	.500	3.26	23	10	1	1	1	85 2/3	71	36	31	23	82
1990—	Scranton/W.B. (I.L.)	5	4	.556	4.76	45	9	0	0	2	96 1/3	96	56	51	44	94
1991—	Indianapolis (A.A.)■	6	7	.462	2.97	18	17	3	1	0	121 1/3	83	42	40	39	91
	Chunichi (Jap. Cen.)■	0	0	...	9.00	1	...	...	...	0	1	...	...	1	0	0
1992—	Indianapolis (A.A.)■	2	0	1.000	0.74	13	0	0	0	0	24 1/3	12	3	2	9	25
	Montreal (N.L.)	0	0	...	14.14	5	0	0	0	0	7	15	11	11	5	11
	Nashville (A.A.)■	6	2	§.750	2.29	39	2	0	0	4	70 2/3	54	22	18	35	87
1993—	Indianapolis (A.A.)	4	2	.667	4.45	21	1	0	0	0	30 1/3	25	16	15	17	28
	Colorado (N.L.)■	0	0	...	9.64	3	0	0	0	0	4 2/3	8	5	5	1	3
	Cincinnati (N.L.)■	2	2	.500	3.70	26	0	0	0	2	41 1/3	36	19	17	15	40
1994—	Indianapolis (A.A.)	5	5	.500	2.31	40	0	0	0	13	58 1/3	35	16	15	27	67
	Cincinnati (N.L.)	1	2	.333	7.36	6	0	0	0	0	7 1/3	8	9	6	3	5
1995—	Indianapolis (A.A.)	4	1	.800	2.18	36	0	0	0	18	41 1/3	33	13	10	15	48
	San Francisco (N.L.)■	3	1	.750	3.19	28	0	0	0	0	31	18	11	11	20	30
1996—	Indianapolis (A.A.)■	1	4	.200	3.00	35	1	0	0	15	48	34	18	16	10	58
	Cincinnati (N.L.)	1	0	1.000	3.94	34	1	0	0	0	48	51	21	21	18	46
1997—	Cincinnati (N.L.)	0	0	...	11.81	4	0	0	0	0	5 1/3	11	7	7	1	3
	Indianapolis (A.A.)	3	2	.600	3.71	33	0	0	0	15	34	30	15	14	12	53
	Omaha (A.A.)■	0	0	...	0.00	16	0	0	0	§9	14 2/3	9	0	0	4	16
	Kansas City (A.L.)	0	3	.000	4.76	12	0	0	0	0	17	17	9	9	5	19
1998—	Kansas City (A.L.)	6	4	.600	3.48	73	0	0	0	4	82 2/3	70	35	32	34	95
1999—	Kansas City (A.L.)	5	5	.500	6.09	68	0	0	0	8	75 1/3	87	51	51	42	68
A.L. totals (3 years)		11	12	.478	4.73	153	0	0	0	12	175	174	95	92	81	182
N.L. totals (7 years)		7	5	.583	4.74	111	1	0	0	2	150	154	84	79	64	144
Major League totals (9 years)		18	17	.514	4.74	264	1	0	0	14	325	328	179	171	145	326

PERSONAL: Born December 29, 1974, in Portland. ... 6-7/206. ... Bats right, throws right. ... Full name: Richmond Lockwood Sexson. ... Name pronounced SECKS-un.
HIGH SCHOOL: Prairie (Brush Prairie, Wash.).
TRANSACTIONS/CAREER NOTES: Selected by Cleveland Indians organization in 24th round of free-agent draft (June 2, 1993).
STATISTICAL NOTES: Led Carolina League with 251 total bases in 1995. ... Led Carolina League first basemen with 1,226 total chances and 109 double plays in 1995. ... Led American Association first basemen with 1,003 total chances and 105 double plays in 1997. ... Career major league grand slams: 2.

Year	Team (League)	Pos.	G	AB	R	H	2B	3B	HR	RBI	Avg.	BB	SO	SB	PO	A	E	Avg.
1993—	Burlington (Appl.)	1B	40	97	11	18	3	0	1	5	.186	18	21	1	309	15	4	.988
1994—	Columbus (SAL)	1B	130	488	88	133	25	2	14	77	.273	37	87	7	933	*63	10	*.990
1995—	Kinston (Caro.)	1B	131	494	80	*151	*34	0	22	*85	.306	43	115	4	*1135	*79	12	.990
1996—	Canton/Akron (East.)	1B	133	518	85	143	33	3	16	76	.276	39	118	2	892	76	11	.989
1997—	Buffalo (A.A.)	1B-DH	115	434	57	113	20	2	*31	88	.260	27	87	5	*922	*77	4	*.996
	Cleveland (A.L.)	1B-DH	5	11	1	3	0	0	0	0	.273	0	2	0	11	1	0	1.000
1998—	Buffalo (I.L.)	OF-1B-DH	89	344	58	102	20	1	21	74	.297	50	68	1	270	29	3	.990
	Cleveland (A.L.)	1B-OF-DH	49	174	28	54	14	1	11	35	.310	6	42	1	325	38	6	.984
1999—	Cleveland (A.L.)	1B-OF-DH	134	479	72	122	17	7	31	116	.255	34	117	3	583	54	7	.989
Major League totals (3 years)			188	664	101	179	31	8	42	151	.270	40	161	4	919	93	13	.987

DIVISION SERIES RECORD

Year	Team (League)	Pos.	G	AB	R	H	2B	3B	HR	RBI	Avg.	BB	SO	SB	PO	A	E	Avg.
1998—	Cleveland (A.L.)	1B	3	2	0	0	0	0	0	0	.000	2	1	0	12	1	0	1.000
1999—	Cleveland (A.L.)	PH-1B-OF	3	6	1	1	0	0	0	1	.167	1	3	0	1	0	0	1.000
Division series totals (2 years)			6	8	1	1	0	0	0	1	.125	3	4	0	13	1	0	1.000

						BATTING								FIELDING		
Year	Team (League)	Pos.	G	AB	R	H	2B	3B	HR	RBI	Avg.	BB	SO	SB	PO	A	E	Avg.
1998— Cleveland (A.L.).........	1B	3	6	0	0	0	0	0	0	.000	0	3	0	20	3	0	1.000

SEXTON, CHRIS — IF/OF — REDS

PERSONAL: Born August 3, 1971, in Cincinnati. ... 5-11/178. ... Bats right, throws right. ... Full name: Christopher Philip Sexton.
HIGH SCHOOL: St. Xavier (Cincinnati).
COLLEGE: Miami of Ohio (degree in business).
TRANSACTIONS/CAREER NOTES: Selected by Cinciannti Reds organization in 10th round of free-agent draft (June 3, 1993). ... Traded by Reds to Colorado Rockies for P Marcus Moore (April 10, 1995). ... Granted free agency (October 15, 1999). ... Signed by Reds organization (November 3, 1999).
STATISTICAL NOTES: Led South Atlantic League with .412 on-base percentage in 1994. ... Led South Atlantic League shortstops with 71 double plays in 1994. ... Led Carolina League with 84 runs and 97 bases on balls received in 1995. ... Led Carolina League shortstops with .966 fielding percentage, 201 putouts, 423 assists, 646 total chances and 73 double plays in 1995.

						BATTING								FIELDING		
Year	Team (League)	Pos.	G	AB	R	H	2B	3B	HR	RBI	Avg.	BB	SO	SB	PO	A	E	Avg.
1993— Billings (Pio.) SS-3B-2B-OF	72	273	*63	91	14	4	4	46	.333	35	27	13	94	174	23	.921
1994— Char., S.C. (SAL)........ SS-OF	133	467	82	140	21	4	5	59	.300	91	67	18	189	326	36	.935
1995— Win.-Salem (Car.)....... SS	4	15	3	6	0	0	1	5	.400	4	0	0	6	17	0	1.000
— Salem (Caro.)■.......... SS	123	461	§81	123	16	6	4	32	.267	§93	55	14	§195	§406	22	§.965
— New Haven (East.)...... SS	1	3	0	0	0	0	0	0	.000	0	0	0	0	3	0	1.000
1996— New Haven (East.)...... SS-OF	127	444	50	96	12	2	0	28	.216	71	68	8	190	294	23	.955
1997— Nashville (East.)........ SS-OF	98	360	65	107	22	4	1	38	.297	62	37	8	178	200	14	.964
— Colo. Springs (PCL) ... SS	33	112	18	30	3	1	1	8	.268	16	21	1	57	87	5	.966
1998— Colo. Springs (PCL) ... S-2-3-O	132	462	88	131	22	6	2	43	.284	72	67	7	219	352	25	.958
1999— Colo. Springs (PCL) ...S-3-O-2-DH	60	171	23	58	9	0	0	17	.339	28	22	5	82	90	5	.972
— Colorado (N.L.) OF-2B-SS	35	59	9	14	0	1	1	7	.237	11	10	4	34	26	2	.968
Major League totals (1 year)	35	59	9	14	0	1	1	7	.237	11	10	4	34	26	2	.968

SHAVE, JON — IF — RANGERS

PERSONAL: Born November 4, 1967, in Waycross, Ga. ... 6-0/185. ... Bats right, throws right. ... Full name: Jonathan Taylor Shave.
HIGH SCHOOL: Fernandina Beach (Fla.).
COLLEGE: Mississippi State.
TRANSACTIONS/CAREER NOTES: Selected by California Angels organization in ninth round of free-agent draft (June 2, 1986); did not sign. ... Selected by Toronto Blue Jays organization in 56th round of free-agent draft (June 5, 1989); did not sign. ... Selected by Texas Rangers organization in fifth round of free-agent draft (June 4, 1990). ... On Texas disabled list (March 25-April 19, 1994). ... On disabled list (April 6-June 1 and June 3-July 22, 1995). ... Granted free agency (October 15, 1996). ... Signed by Minnesota Twins organization (November 6, 1996). ... Granted free agency (October 15, 1997). ... Re-signed by Twins (November 9, 1997). ... Claimed on waivers by Rangers (November 19, 1998). ... Released by Rangers (October 28, 1999). ... Re-signed by Rangers organization (January 6, 2000).
STATISTICAL NOTES: Led Texas League second basemen with 233 putouts, 19 errors, 530 total chances and 63 double plays in 1992. ... Tied for American Association lead with 12 sacrifice hits in 1994.

						BATTING								FIELDING		
Year	Team (League)	Pos.	G	AB	R	H	2B	3B	HR	RBI	Avg.	BB	SO	SB	PO	A	E	Avg.
1990— Butte (Pio.)................. SS	64	250	41	88	9	3	2	42	.352	25	27	21	112	159	22	.925
1991— Gastonia (SAL)........... SS-2B	55	213	29	62	11	0	2	24	.291	20	26	11	103	152	23	.917
— Charlotte (FSL).......... SS-2B	56	189	17	43	4	1	1	20	.228	18	31	7	93	120	15	.934
1992— Tulsa (Texas)............ 2B-SS	118	453	57	130	23	5	2	36	.287	37	59	6	†251	314	†21	.964
1993— Oklahoma City (A.A.).. 2B-SS	100	399	58	105	17	3	4	41	.263	20	60	4	190	277	13	.973
— Texas (A.L.)............ SS-2B	17	47	3	15	2	0	0	7	.319	0	8	1	22	37	3	.952
1994— Oklahoma City (A.A.)..2B-SS-3B-OF	95	332	29	73	15	2	1	31	.220	14	61	6	177	258	20	.956
1995— Oklahoma City (A.A.).. 2B-DH	32	83	10	17	1	0	0	5	.205	7	28	1	43	64	4	.964
1996— Oklahoma City (A.A.).. 2-3-S-DH	116	414	54	110	20	2	7	41	.266	41	97	8	158	283	22	.952
1997— Salt Lake (PCL)■.........S-3-D-2-O-1	103	395	75	130	27	3	7	60	.329	39	62	6	191	192	15	.962
1998— Salt Lake (PCL) 2-3-O-S-DH-1	137	317	63	107	20	1	4	41	.338	34	46	8	149	183	15	.957
— Minnesota (A.L.) 3B-DH-1B-SS	19	40	7	10	3	0	1	5	.250	3	10	1	7	20	0	1.000
1999— Texas (A.L.)■............S-1-3-DH-2	43	73	10	21	4	0	0	9	.288	5	17	1	72	63	5	.964
Major League totals (3 years)	79	160	20	46	9	0	1	21	.288	8	35	3	101	120	8	.965

SHAW, JEFF — P — DODGERS

PERSONAL: Born July 7, 1966, in Washington Court House, Ohio. ... 6-2/200. ... Throws right, bats right. ... Full name: Jeffrey Lee Shaw.
HIGH SCHOOL: Washington (Washington Court House, Ohio).
JUNIOR COLLEGE: Cuyahoga Community College-Western Campus (Ohio).
COLLEGE: Rio Grande (Ohio) College.
TRANSACTIONS/CAREER NOTES: Selected by Cleveland Indians organization in first round (first pick overall) of free-agent draft (January 14, 1986). ... Granted free agency (October 16, 1992). ... Signed by Omaha, Kansas City Royals organization (November 9, 1992). ... Traded by Royals with C Tim Spehr to Montreal Expos for P Mark Gardner and P Doug Piatt (December 9, 1992). ... Granted free agency (February 17, 1995). ... Re-signed by Expos organization (April 9, 1995). ... Traded by Expos to Chicago White Sox for P Jose DeLeon (August 28, 1995). ... Granted free agency (December 21, 1995). ... Signed by Cincinnati Reds organization (January 2, 1996). ... Traded by Reds to Los Angeles Dodgers for 1B/3B Paul Konerko and P Dennis Reyes (July 4, 1998).
HONORS: Named N.L. Fireman of the Year by THE SPORTING NEWS (1997).
STATISTICAL NOTES: Led Eastern League with 14 hit batsmen in 1989. ... Tied for Pacific Coast League lead with 10 hit batsmen in 1992.

Year League	W	L	Pct.	ERA	G	GS	CG	ShO	Sv.	IP	H	R	ER	BB	SO
1986— Batavia (NY-P)	8	4	.667	2.44	14	12	3	1	0	88 2/3	79	32	24	35	71
1987— Waterloo (Midw.)	11	11	.500	3.52	28	*28	6	*4	0	184 1/3	192	89	72	56	117
1988— Williamsport (East.)	5	*19	.208	3.63	27	•27	6	1	0	163 2/3	•173	*94	66	75	61
1989— Canton/Akron (East.)	7	10	.412	3.62	30	22	6	3	0	154 1/3	134	84	62	67	95
1990— Colo. Springs (PCL)	10	3	.769	4.29	17	16	4	0	0	98 2/3	98	54	47	52	55
— Cleveland (A.L.)	3	4	.429	6.66	12	9	0	0	0	48 2/3	73	38	36	20	25
1991— Colo. Springs (PCL)	6	3	.667	4.64	12	12	1	0	0	75 2/3	77	47	39	25	55
— Cleveland (A.L.)	0	5	.000	3.36	29	1	0	0	1	72 1/3	72	34	27	27	31
1992— Colo. Springs (PCL)	10	5	.667	4.76	25	24	1	0	0	155	174	88	82	45	84
— Cleveland (A.L.)	0	1	.000	8.22	2	1	0	0	0	7 2/3	7	7	7	4	3
1993— Ottawa (I.L.)■	0	0	...	0.00	2	1	0	0	0	4	5	0	0	2	1
— Montreal (N.L.)	2	7	.222	4.14	55	8	0	0	0	95 2/3	91	47	44	32	50
1994— Montreal (N.L.)	5	2	.714	3.88	46	0	0	0	1	67 1/3	67	32	29	15	47
1995— Montreal (N.L.)	1	6	.143	4.62	50	0	0	0	3	62 1/3	58	35	32	26	45
— Chicago (A.L.)■	0	0	...	6.52	9	0	0	0	0	9 2/3	12	7	7	1	6
1996— Cincinnati (N.L.)■■	8	6	.571	2.49	78	0	0	0	4	104 2/3	99	34	29	29	69
1997— Cincinnati (N.L.)	4	2	.667	2.38	78	0	0	0	*42	94 2/3	79	26	25	12	74
1998— Cincinnati (N.L.)	2	4	.333	1.81	39	0	0	0	23	49 2/3	40	11	10	12	29
— Los Angeles (N.L.)■	1	4	.200	2.55	34	0	0	0	25	35 1/3	35	11	10	7	26
1999— Los Angeles (N.L.)	2	4	.333	2.78	64	0	0	0	34	68	64	25	21	15	43
A.L. totals (4 years)	3	10	.231	5.01	52	11	0	0	1	138 1/3	164	86	77	52	65
N.L. totals (7 years)	25	35	.417	3.12	444	8	0	0	132	577 2/3	533	221	200	148	383
Major League totals (10 years)	28	45	.384	3.48	496	19	0	0	133	716	697	307	277	200	448

ALL-STAR GAME RECORD

Year League	W	L	Pct.	ERA	GS	CG	ShO	Sv.	IP	H	R	ER	BB	SO
1998— National	0	0	...	9.00	0	0	0	0	1	3	1	1	0	0

SHEETS, ANDY — 2B/SS

PERSONAL: Born November 19, 1971, in Baton Rouge, La. ... 6-2/180. ... Bats right, throws right. ... Full name: Andrew Mark Sheets.
HIGH SCHOOL: St. Amant (La.).
COLLEGE: Tulane, then Louisiana State.
TRANSACTIONS/CAREER NOTES: Selected by Seattle Mariners organization in fourth round of free-agent draft (June 1, 1992). ... Selected by Tampa Bay Devil Rays in first round (24th pick overall) of expansion draft (November 18, 1997). ... Traded by Devil Rays with P Brian Boehringer to San Diego Padres for C John Flaherty (November 18, 1997). ... Traded by Padres with OF Gus Kennedy to Anaheim Angels for C Phil Nevin and P Keith Volkman (March 29, 1999). ... Granted free agency (December 21, 1999).
STATISTICAL NOTES: Led Pacific Coast League shortstops with .973 fielding percentage in 1997. ... Career major league grand slams: 1.

						BATTING								FIELDING		
Year Team (League)	Pos.	G	AB	R	H	2B	3B	HR	RBI	Avg.	BB	SO	SB	PO	A	E	Avg.
1993— Riverside (Calif.)	SS	52	176	23	34	9	1	1	12	.193	17	51	2	80	159	17	.934
— Appleton (Midw.)	SS-2B-OF	69	259	32	68	10	4	1	25	.263	20	59	7	98	194	11	.964
1994— Riverside (Calif.)	SS	31	100	17	27	5	1	2	10	.270	16	22	6	39	95	14	.905
— Jacksonville (Sou.)	SS	70	232	26	51	12	0	0	17	.220	20	54	3	105	205	17	.948
— Calgary (PCL)	SS	26	93	22	32	8	1	2	16	.344	11	20	1	32	80	2	.982
1995— Tacoma (PCL)	SS	132	437	57	128	29	9	2	47	.293	32	83	8	157	382	27	.952
1996— Tacoma (PCL)	SS-2B-3B	62	232	44	83	16	5	5	33	.358	25	56	6	95	176	14	.951
— Seattle (A.L.)	3B-2B-SS	47	110	18	21	8	0	0	9	.191	10	41	2	40	77	5	.959
1997— Tacoma (PCL)	SS-2B-3B	113	401	57	104	23	0	14	53	.259	46	97	7	174	314	13	.974
— Seattle (A.L.)	3B-SS-2B	32	89	18	22	3	0	4	9	.247	7	34	2	14	62	8	.905
1998— San Diego (N.L.)■	SS-3B-2B-1B	88	194	31	47	5	3	7	29	.242	21	62	7	96	145	9	.964
1999— Anaheim (A.L.)■	SS-2B-3B	87	244	22	48	10	0	3	29	.197	14	59	1	113	182	12	.961
— Edmonton (PCL)	SS-2B	12	45	6	13	1	1	0	4	.289	2	11	0	13	34	1	.979
American League totals (3 years)		166	443	58	91	21	0	7	47	.205	31	134	5	167	321	25	.951
National League totals (1 year)		88	194	31	47	5	3	7	29	.242	21	62	7	96	145	9	.964
Major League totals (4 years)		254	637	89	138	26	3	14	76	.217	52	196	12	263	466	34	.955

DIVISION SERIES RECORD

						BATTING								FIELDING		
Year Team (League)	Pos.	G	AB	R	H	2B	3B	HR	RBI	Avg.	BB	SO	SB	PO	A	E	Avg.
1997— Seattle (A.L.)	3B	2	3	0	1	0	0	0	0	.333	0	2	0	0	0	0	...
1998— San Diego (N.L.)	PR-2B	2	0	0	0	0	0	0	0	...	0	0	0	0	0	0	...
Division series totals (2 years)		4	3	0	1	0	0	0	0	.333	0	2	0	0	0	0	...

CHAMPIONSHIP SERIES RECORD

						BATTING								FIELDING		
Year Team (League)	Pos.	G	AB	R	H	2B	3B	HR	RBI	Avg.	BB	SO	SB	PO	A	E	Avg.
1998— San Diego (N.L.)	SS-PH	3	3	0	0	0	0	0	0	.000	0	1	0	0	2	0	1.000

WORLD SERIES RECORD

						BATTING								FIELDING		
Year Team (League)	Pos.	G	AB	R	H	2B	3B	HR	RBI	Avg.	BB	SO	SB	PO	A	E	Avg.
1998— San Diego (N.L.)	SS	2	2	0	0	0	0	0	0	.000	1	0	0	0	2	0	1.000

SHEFFIELD, GARY — OF — DODGERS

PERSONAL: Born November 18, 1968, in Tampa. ... 5-11/205. ... Bats right, throws right. ... Full name: Gary Antonian Sheffield. ... Nephew of Dwight Gooden, pitcher, Houston Astros.
HIGH SCHOOL: Hillsborough (Tampa).

TRANSACTIONS/CAREER NOTES: Selected by Milwaukee Brewers organization in first round (sixth pick overall) of free-agent draft (June 2, 1986). ... On Milwaukee disabled list (July 14-September 9, 1989). ... On suspended list (August 31-September 3, 1990). ... On disabled list (June 15-July 3 and July 25, 1991-remainder of season). ... Traded by Brewers with P Geoff Kellogg to San Diego Padres for P Ricky Bones, SS Jose Valentin and OF Matt Mieske (March 27, 1992). ... Traded by Padres with P Rich Rodriguez to Florida Marlins for P Trevor Hoffman, P Jose Martinez and P Andres Berumen (June 24, 1993). ... On Florida suspended list (July 9-12, 1993). ... On Florida disabled list (May 10-25 and May 28-June 12, 1994); included rehabilitation assignment to Portland (June 10-12). ... On disabled list (June 11-September 1, 1995; and May 14-29, 1997). ... Traded by Marlins with 3B Bobby Bonilla, C Charles Johnson, OF Jim Eisenreich and P Manuel Barrios to Los Angeles Dodgers for C Mike Piazza and 3B Todd Zeile (May 15, 1998). ... On suspended list (August 4-6, 1998).

RECORDS: Shares major league record for fewest double plays by outfielder (150 or more games)—0 (1996). ... Shares major league single-inning record for most home runs—2 (July 13, 1997, fourth inning).

HONORS: Named Minor League co-Player of the Year by THE SPORTING NEWS (1988). ... Named Major League Player of the Year by THE SPORTING NEWS (1992). ... Named N.L. Comeback Player of the Year by THE SPORTING NEWS (1992). ... Named third baseman on THE SPORTING NEWS N.L. All-Star team (1992). ... Named third baseman on THE SPORTING NEWS N.L. Silver Slugger team (1992). ... Named outfielder on THE SPORTING NEWS N.L. All-Star team (1996). ... Named outfielder on THE SPORTING NEWS N.L. Silver Slugger team (1996).

STATISTICAL NOTES: Led Pioneer League shortstops with 34 double plays in 1986. ... Led California League shortstops with 77 double plays in 1987. ... Led N.L. with 323 total bases in 1992. ... Led N.L. with .465 on-base percentage in 1996. ... Career major league grand slams: 6.

MISCELLANEOUS: Holds Florida Marlins all-time records for most home runs (122) and runs (365).

Year	Team (League)	Pos.	G	AB	R	H	2B	3B	HR	RBI	Avg.	BB	SO	SB	PO	A	E	Avg.
1986—Helena (Pio.)		SS	57	222	53	81	12	2	15	*71	.365	20	14	14	97	149	24	.911
1987—Stockton (Calif.)		SS	129	469	84	130	23	3	17	*103	.277	81	49	25	235	345	39	.937
1988—El Paso (Texas)		SS-3B-OF	77	296	70	93	19	3	19	65	.314	35	41	5	130	206	23	.936
—Denver (A.A.)		3B-SS	57	212	42	73	9	5	9	54	.344	21	22	8	54	97	8	.950
—Milwaukee (A.L.)		SS	24	80	12	19	1	0	4	12	.238	7	7	3	39	48	3	.967
1989—Milwaukee (A.L.)		SS-3B-DH	95	368	34	91	18	0	5	32	.247	27	33	10	100	238	16	.955
—Denver (A.A.)		SS	7	29	3	4	1	1	0	0	.138	2	0	0	2	6	0	1.000
1990—Milwaukee (A.L.)		3B	125	487	67	143	30	1	10	67	.294	44	41	25	98	254	25	.934
1991—Milwaukee (A.L.)		3B-DH	50	175	25	34	12	2	2	22	.194	19	15	5	29	65	8	.922
1992—San Diego (N.L.)■		3B	146	557	87	184	34	3	33	100	*.330	48	40	5	99	299	16	.961
1993—San Diego (N.L.)		3B	68	258	34	76	12	2	10	36	.295	18	30	5	41	102	15	.905
—Florida (N.L.)■		3B	72	236	33	69	8	3	10	37	.292	29	34	12	38	123	19	.894
1994—Florida (N.L.)		OF	87	322	61	89	16	1	27	78	.276	51	50	12	154	7	5	.970
—Portland (East.)		OF	2	7	1	2	1	0	0	0	.286	1	3	0	3	0	0	1.000
1995—Florida (N.L.)		OF	63	213	46	69	8	0	16	46	.324	55	45	19	109	5	7	.942
1996—Florida (N.L.)		OF	161	519	118	163	33	1	42	120	.314	142	66	16	238	8	6	.976
1997—Florida (N.L.)		OF-DH	135	444	86	111	22	1	21	71	.250	121	79	11	226	14	5	.980
1998—Florida (N.L.)		OF	40	136	21	37	11	1	6	28	.272	26	16	4	68	3	1	.986
—Los Angeles (N.L.)■		OF	90	301	52	95	16	1	16	57	.316	69	30	18	149	6	1	.994
1999—Los Angeles (N.L.)		OF-DH	152	549	103	165	20	0	34	101	.301	101	64	11	235	7	7	.972
American League totals (4 years)			294	1110	138	287	61	3	21	133	.259	97	96	43	266	605	52	.944
National League totals (8 years)			1014	3535	641	1058	180	13	215	674	.299	660	454	113	1357	574	82	.959
Major League totals (12 years)			1308	4645	779	1345	241	16	236	807	.290	757	550	156	1623	1179	134	.954

DIVISION SERIES RECORD

Year	Team (League)	Pos.	G	AB	R	H	2B	3B	HR	RBI	Avg.	BB	SO	SB	PO	A	E	Avg.
1997—Florida (N.L.)		OF	3	9	3	5	1	0	1	1	.556	5	0	1	6	0	0	1.000

CHAMPIONSHIP SERIES RECORD

Year	Team (League)	Pos.	G	AB	R	H	2B	3B	HR	RBI	Avg.	BB	SO	SB	PO	A	E	Avg.
1997—Florida (N.L.)		OF	6	17	6	4	0	0	1	1	.235	7	3	0	5	2	0	1.000

WORLD SERIES RECORD

NOTES: Member of World Series championship team (1997).

Year	Team (League)	Pos.	G	AB	R	H	2B	3B	HR	RBI	Avg.	BB	SO	SB	PO	A	E	Avg.
1997—Florida (N.L.)		OF	7	24	4	7	1	0	1	5	.292	8	5	0	16	0	1	.941

ALL-STAR GAME RECORD

Year	League	Pos.	AB	R	H	2B	3B	HR	RBI	Avg.	BB	SO	SB	PO	A	E	Avg.
1992—National		3B	2	0	0	0	0	0	0	.000	0	0	0	0	0	0	...
1993—National		3B	3	1	2	0	0	1	2	.667	0	0	0	0	2	0	1.000
1996—National		OF	1	0	0	0	0	0	0	.000	0	0	0	2	0	0	1.000
1998—National		PH	1	0	0	0	0	0	0	.000	0	0	0	0	0	0	...
1999—National		PH-DH	1	0	0	0	0	0	0	.000	0	0	0	0	0	0	...
All-Star Game totals (5 years)			8	1	2	0	0	1	2	.250	0	0	0	2	2	0	1.000

SHELDON, SCOTT   IF   RANGERS

PERSONAL: Born November 20, 1968, in Hammond, Ind. ... 6-3/215. ... Bats right, throws right. ... Full name: Scott Patrick Sheldon.

HIGH SCHOOL: Clear Lake (Houston).

COLLEGE: Houston.

TRANSACTIONS/CAREER NOTES: Selected by Oakland Athletics organization in eighth round of free-agent draft (June 3, 1991). ... Granted free agency (October 17, 1997). ... Signed by Texas Rangers organization (November 20, 1997).

Year	Team (League)	Pos.	G	AB	R	H	2B	3B	HR	RBI	Avg.	BB	SO	SB	PO	A	E	Avg.
1991—S. Oregon (N'west)		2B-3B-SS-1B	65	229	34	58	10	3	0	24	.253	23	44	9	122	124	14	.946
1992—Madison (Midw.)		SS-1B	74	275	41	76	16	0	6	24	.276	32	78	5	107	217	25	.928
1993—Madison (Midw.)		3B-SS	131	428	67	91	22	1	8	67	.213	49	121	8	90	275	26	.934
1994—Huntsville (Sou.)		3-O-S-2-1	91	268	31	62	10	1	0	28	.231	28	69	7	69	185	11	.958

Year	Team (League)	Pos.	G	AB	R	H	2B	3B	HR	RBI	Avg.	BB	SO	SB	PO	A	E	Avg.
1995—Huntsville (Sou.)		2B-SS-1B-3B	66	235	25	51	10	2	4	15	.217	23	60	5	203	188	12	.970
—Edmonton (PCL)		3B-SS-1B-2B	45	128	21	33	7	1	4	12	.258	15	15	4	44	89	5	.964
1996—Edmonton (PCL)		S-1-2-3-O	98	350	61	105	27	3	10	60	.300	43	83	5	259	230	14	.972
1997—Edmonton (PCL)		SS-2B	118	422	89	133	39	6	19	77	.315	59	104	5	139	313	11	.976
—Oakland (A.L.)		SS-2B-3B	13	24	2	6	0	0	1	2	.250	1	6	0	16	18	2	.944
1998—Oklahoma (PCL)■		SS-OF	131	493	74	126	31	4	29	96	.256	62	143	2	163	397	24	.959
—Texas (A.L.)		3B-SS-DH-1B	7	16	0	2	0	0	0	1	.125	1	6	0	8	11	1	.950
1999—Oklahoma (PCL)		2-S-1-3-C-O	122	453	94	141	35	3	28	97	.311	56	112	12	254	325	9	.985
—Texas (A.L.)		3B	2	2	0	0	0	0	0	0	.000	0	0	0	2	3	0	1.000
Major League totals (3 years)			22	42	2	8	0	0	1	3	.190	2	12	0	26	32	3	.951

SHIELDS, SCOT   P   ANGELS

PERSONAL: Born July 22, 1975, in Fort Lauderdale, Fla. ... 6-1/175. ... Throws right, bats right. ... Full name: Robert Scot Shields.
HIGH SCHOOL: Fort Lauderdale (Fla.).
COLLEGE: Lincoln Memorial University (Tenn.).
TRANSACTIONS/CAREER NOTES: Selected by Anaheim Angels organization in 38th round of free-agent draft (June 3, 1997).

Year	League	W	L	Pct.	ERA	G	GS	CG	ShO	Sv.	IP	H	R	ER	BB	SO
1997—Boise (N'west)	7	2	.778	2.94	30	0	0	0	2	52	45	20	17	24	61
1998—Cedar Rapids (Midw.)	6	5	.545	3.65	58	0	0	0	7	74	62	33	30	29	81
1999—Lake Elsinore (Calif.)	10	3	.769	2.52	24	9	2	1	1	107 1/3	91	37	30	39	113
—Erie (East.)	4	4	.500	2.89	10	10	1	1	0	74 2/3	57	26	24	26	81

SHOEMAKER, STEVE   P   ROCKIES

PERSONAL: Born February 3, 1973, in Phoenixville, Pa. ... 6-1/214. ... Throws right, bats left. ... Full name: Stephen Patrick Shoemaker.
HIGH SCHOOL: Phoenixville (Pa.).
COLLEGE: Alabama.
TRANSACTIONS/CAREER NOTES: Selected by New York Yankees organization in fourth round of free-agent draft (June 3, 1994). ... Traded by Yankees to Colorado Rockies (December 6, 1995), completing deal in which Rockies traded C Joe Girardi to Yankees for P Mike DeJean and a player to be named later (November 30, 1995). ... On Colorado Springs disabled list (May 3-June 29, 1999).

Year	League	W	L	Pct.	ERA	G	GS	CG	ShO	Sv.	IP	H	R	ER	BB	SO
1994—Oneonta (NY-P)	3	5	.375	4.30	12	12	0	0	0	58 2/3	62	32	28	28	46
1995—Greensboro (SAL)	4	4	.500	3.11	17	17	0	0	0	81	62	33	28	52	82
—Tampa (FSL)	0	1	.000	1.08	3	2	0	0	0	16 2/3	9	5	2	13	12
1996—Salem (Caro.)■	2	7	.222	4.69	25	13	0	0	1	86 1/3	63	49	45	63	105
1997—Salem (Caro.)	3	3	.500	2.77	9	9	1	0	0	52	31	21	16	25	76
—Nashville (East.)	6	4	.600	3.02	14	14	1	0	0	95 1/3	64	36	32	53	111
—Colo. Springs (PCL)	1	1	.500	8.41	5	4	0	0	0	20 1/3	23	19	19	17	27
1998—Colo. Springs (PCL)	2	7	.222	9.05	15	12	0	0	0	62 2/3	80	68	63	63	56
—New Haven (East.)	3	5	.375	4.89	15	15	0	0	0	84 2/3	69	60	46	63	85
1999—Colo. Springs (PCL)	4	6	.400	6.00	16	16	2	0	0	81	100	59	54	47	46

SHUEY, PAUL   P   INDIANS

PERSONAL: Born September 16, 1970, in Lima, Ohio. ... 6-3/215. ... Throws right, bats right. ... Full name: Paul Kenneth Shuey. ... Name pronounced SHOO-ee.
HIGH SCHOOL: Millbrook (Raleigh, N.C.).
COLLEGE: North Carolina.
TRANSACTIONS/CAREER NOTES: Selected by Cleveland Indians organization in first round (second pick overall) of free-agent draft (June 1, 1992). ... On Cleveland disabled list (June 27-July 21, 1994); included rehabilitation assignment to Charlotte (July 5-21). ... On Cleveland disabled list (May 4-22, 1995). ... On Buffalo disabled list (June 2-July 10, 1995). ... On Cleveland disabled list (April 25-May 18, June 19-July 4 and July 11-August 1, 1997); included rehabilitation assignment to Buffalo (May 5-10) and Akron (May 1-18). ... On Cleveland disabled list (April 11-June 15, 1998); included rehabilitation assignments to Akron (April 24) and Buffalo (May 23-June 14). ... On Cleveland disabled list (April 26-May 11, 1999); included rehabilitation assignment to Buffalo (May 9-11).
RECORDS: Shares major single-inning league record for most strikeouts—4 (May 14, 1994, ninth inning).

Year	League	W	L	Pct.	ERA	G	GS	CG	ShO	Sv.	IP	H	R	ER	BB	SO
1992—Columbus (SAL)	5	5	.500	3.35	14	14	0	0	0	78	62	35	29	47	73
1993—Canton/Akron (East.)	4	8	.333	7.30	27	7	0	0	0	61 2/3	76	50	50	36	41
—Kinston (Caro.)	1	0	1.000	4.84	15	0	0	0	0	22 1/3	29	12	12	8	27
1994—Kinston (Caro.)	1	0	1.000	3.75	13	0	0	0	8	12	10	5	5	3	16
—Cleveland (A.L.)	0	1	.000	8.49	14	0	0	0	5	11 2/3	14	11	11	12	16
—Charlotte (I.L.)	2	1	.667	1.93	20	0	0	0	10	23 1/3	15	9	5	10	25
1995—Cleveland (A.L.)	0	2	.000	4.26	7	0	0	0	0	6 1/3	5	4	3	5	5
—Buffalo (A.A.)	1	2	.333	2.63	25	0	0	0	11	27 1/3	21	9	8	7	27
1996—Buffalo (A.A.)	3	2	.600	0.81	19	0	0	0	4	33 1/3	14	4	3	9	57
—Cleveland (A.L.)	5	2	.714	2.85	42	0	0	0	4	53 2/3	45	19	17	26	44
1997—Cleveland (A.L.)	4	2	.667	6.20	40	0	0	0	2	45	52	31	31	28	46
—Buffalo (A.A.)	0	0	...	3.60	2	0	0	0	0	5	4	2	2	4	6
—Akron (East.)	0	0	...	3.38	3	0	0	0	0	8	10	3	3	0	9
1998—Cleveland (A.L.)	5	4	.556	3.00	43	0	0	0	2	51	44	19	17	25	58
—Akron (East.)	0	0	...	54.00	1	0	0	0	0	1/3	3	2	2	1	0
—Buffalo (I.L.)	0	0	...	2.51	11	0	0	0	2	14 1/3	11	4	4	6	22
1999—Cleveland (A.L.)	8	5	.615	3.53	72	0	0	0	6	81 2/3	68	37	32	40	103
—Buffalo (I.L.)	0	0	...	0.00	1	0	0	0	0	1	0	0	0	1	1
Major League totals (6 years)	22	16	.579	4.01	218	0	0	0	19	249 1/3	228	121	111	136	272

DIVISION SERIES RECORD

Year League	W	L	Pct.	ERA	G	GS	CG	ShO	Sv.	IP	H	R	ER	BB	SO
1996— Cleveland (A.L.)	0	0	...	9.00	3	0	0	0	0	2	5	2	2	2	2
1998— Cleveland (A.L.)	0	0	...	0.00	3	0	0	0	0	3	3	0	0	1	4
1999— Cleveland (A.L.)	1	1	.500	11.25	3	0	0	0	0	4	4	5	5	4	5
Division series totals (3 years)	1	1	.500	7.00	9	0	0	0	0	9	12	7	7	7	11

CHAMPIONSHIP SERIES RECORD

Year League	W	L	Pct.	ERA	G	GS	CG	ShO	Sv.	IP	H	R	ER	BB	SO
1998— Cleveland (A.L.)	0	0	...	0.00	5	0	0	0	0	6 1/3	4	0	0	9	7

SHUMAKER, ANTHONY　　　P　　　PHILLIES

PERSONAL: Born May 14, 1973, in Tucson, Ariz. ... 6-5/219. ... Throws left, bats left. ... Full name: Anthony Warren Shumaker.
HIGH SCHOOL: Kokomo (Ind.).
COLLEGE: Cardinal Stritch (Wis.).
TRANSACTIONS/CAREER NOTES: Selected by Philadelphia Phillies organization in 23rd round of free-agent draft (June 1, 1995).

Year League	W	L	Pct.	ERA	G	GS	CG	ShO	Sv.	IP	H	R	ER	BB	SO
1995— Martinsville (Appl.)	1	3	.250	4.50	6	4	0	0	0	28	31	16	14	8	26
— Batavia (NY-P)	2	2	.500	1.62	9	4	1	1	0	39	38	10	7	4	31
1996— Piedmont (SAL)	3	0	1.000	1.38	20	0	0	0	4	32 2/3	16	7	5	10	51
— Clearwater (FSL)	5	3	.625	5.10	31	0	0	0	3	30	39	17	17	12	24
1997— Clearwater (FSL)	5	4	.556	2.13	61	0	0	0	9	72	64	22	17	17	77
1998— Reading (East.)	7	10	.412	3.35	38	21	1	1	2	166 2/3	152	75	62	44	129
1999— Reading (East.)	4	3	.571	1.78	10	10	1	0	0	60 2/3	48	17	12	17	60
— Scranton/W.B. (I.L.)	3	5	.375	5.72	14	14	1	0	0	89 2/3	119	60	57	32	49
— Philadelphia (N.L.)	0	3	.000	5.96	8	4	0	0	0	22 2/3	23	17	15	14	17
Major League totals (1 year)	0	3	.000	5.96	8	4	0	0	0	22 2/3	23	17	15	14	17

SHUMPERT, TERRY　　　2B　　　ROCKIES

PERSONAL: Born August 16, 1966, in Paducah, Ky. ... 6-2/195. ... Bats right, throws right. ... Full name: Terrance Darnell Shumpert.
HIGH SCHOOL: Paducah (Ky.) Tilghman.
COLLEGE: Kentucky.
TRANSACTIONS/CAREER NOTES: Selected by Kansas City Royals organization in second round of free-agent draft (June 2, 1987). ... On disabled list (July 19-August 13, 1989). ... On Kansas City disabled list (June 3-September 10, 1990); included rehabilitation assignment to Omaha (August 7-25). ... On Kansas City disabled list (August 7-September 7, 1992). ... Traded by Royals to Boston Red Sox for a player to be named later (December 13, 1994). ... Granted free agency (October 6, 1995). ... Signed by Iowa, Chicago Cubs organization (March 12, 1996). ... On Chicago disabled list (August 19-September 3, 1996). ... Granted free agency (October 15, 1996). ... Signed by San Diego Padres (November 4, 1996). ... On San Diego disabled list (May 27-August 5, 1997). ... Released by Padres (August 5, 1997). ... Signed by Colorado Rockies organization (August 13, 1997). ... Granted free agency (October 15, 1998). ... Re-signed by Rockies organization (December 18, 1998). ... On Colorado Springs disabled list (May 13-23, 1999). ... Granted free agency (October 29, 1999). ... Re-signed by Rockies (December 15, 1999).
STATISTICAL NOTES: Led American Association with 21 sacrifice hits in 1993. ... Career major league grand slams: 1.

Year Team (League)	Pos.	G	AB	R	H	2B	3B	HR	RBI	Avg.	BB	SO	SB	PO	A	E	Avg.
1987— Eugene (N'west)	2B	48	186	38	54	16	1	4	22	.290	27	41	16	81	107	11	.945
1988— Appleton (Midw.)	2B-OF	114	422	64	102	*37	2	7	38	.242	56	90	36	235	266	20	.962
1989— Omaha (A.A.)	2B	113	355	54	88	29	2	4	22	.248	25	63	23	218	295	*22	.959
1990— Omaha (A.A.)	2B	39	153	24	39	6	4	2	12	.255	14	28	18	72	95	7	.960
— Kansas City (A.L.)	2B-DH	32	91	7	25	6	1	0	8	.275	2	17	3	56	74	3	.977
1991— Kansas City (A.L.)	2B	144	369	45	80	16	4	5	34	.217	30	75	17	249	368	16	.975
1992— Kansas City (A.L.)	2B-DH-SS	36	94	6	14	5	1	1	11	.149	3	17	2	50	77	4	.969
— Omaha (A.A.)	2B-SS	56	210	23	42	12	0	1	14	.200	13	33	3	113	154	9	.967
1993— Omaha (A.A.)	2B	111	413	70	124	29	1	14	59	.300	41	62	*36	190	303	14	.972
— Kansas City (A.L.)	2B	8	10	0	1	0	0	0	0	.100	2	2	1	11	11	0	1.000
1994— Kansas City (A.L.)	2B-3B-DH-SS	64	183	28	44	6	2	8	24	.240	13	39	18	70	129	8	.961
1995— Boston (A.L.)■	2B-3B-SS-DH	21	47	6	11	3	0	0	3	.234	4	13	3	21	35	2	.966
— Pawtucket (I.L.)	3B-2B-DH-OF	37	133	17	36	7	0	2	11	.271	14	27	10	29	69	11	.899
1996— Iowa (A.A.)-1-S	2-3-DH-1-S	72	246	45	68	13	4	5	32	.276	24	44	13	119	165	7	.976
— Chicago (N.L.)	3B-2B-SS	27	31	5	7	1	0	2	6	.226	2	11	0	11	9	1	.952
1997— Las Vegas (PCL)■	3B-2B-SS-DH	32	109	18	31	8	1	1	16	.284	9	20	3	37	58	4	.960
— San Diego (N.L.)	2B-OF-3B	13	33	4	9	3	0	1	6	.273	3	4	0	23	17	2	.952
— New Haven (East.)■	2B	5	17	2	4	0	0	1	1	.235	2	2	0	8	17	0	1.000
— Colo. Springs (PCL)	SS-2B-3B-OF	10	37	8	11	3	0	1	2	.297	2	7	0	8	20	5	.848
1998— Colo. Springs (PCL)	2-O-3-DH-S	97	376	66	115	29	8	12	50	.306	35	59	11	141	133	4	.986
— Colorado (N.L.)	2B	23	26	3	6	1	0	1	2	.231	2	8	0	2	14	0	1.000
1999— Colo. Springs (PCL)	3B-2B-SS-OF	29	79	15	30	8	1	6	17	.380	4	9	3	23	36	5	.922
— Colorado (N.L.)	2B-OF-3B-SS	92	262	58	91	26	3	10	37	.347	31	41	14	129	165	5	.983
American League totals (6 years)		305	794	92	175	36	8	14	80	.220	54	163	44	457	694	33	.972
National League totals (4 years)		155	352	70	113	31	3	14	51	.321	38	64	14	165	205	8	.979
Major League totals (10 years)		460	1146	162	288	67	11	28	131	.251	92	227	58	622	899	41	.974

SIKORSKI, BRIAN　　　P　　　RANGERS

PERSONAL: Born July 27, 1974, in Detroit. ... 6-1/190. ... Throws right, bats right. ... Full name: Brian Patrick Sikorski.
HIGH SCHOOL: Roseville (Mich.).
COLLEGE: Western Michigan.
TRANSACTIONS/CAREER NOTES: Selected by Houston Astros organization in fourth round of free-agent draft (June 1, 1995). ... Claimed on waivers by Texas Rangers (November 9, 1999).
STATISTICAL NOTES: Led Midwest League with 12 balks in 1996.

Year	League	W	L	Pct.	ERA	G	GS	CG	ShO	Sv.	IP	H	R	ER	BB	SO
1995—Auburn (NY-P)		1	2	.333	2.10	23	0	0	0	12	34⅓	22	8	8	14	35
— Quad City (Midw.)		1	0	1.000	0.00	2	0	0	0	0	3	1	1	0	0	4
1996—Quad City (Midw.)		11	8	.579	3.13	26	25	1	0	0	166⅔	140	79	58	70	150
1997—Kissimmee (FSL)		8	2	.800	3.06	11	11	0	0	0	67⅔	64	29	23	16	46
— Jackson (Texas)		5	5	.500	4.63	17	17	0	0	0	93⅓	91	55	48	31	74
1998—Jackson (Texas)		6	4	.600	4.07	15	15	0	0	0	97⅓	83	50	44	44	80
— New Orleans (PCL)		5	8	.385	5.79	15	14	1	0	0	84	86	57	54	32	64
1999—New Orleans (PCL)		7	10	.412	4.95	28	27	2	1	0	158⅓	169	92	87	58	122

SILVA, JOSE — P — PIRATES

PERSONAL: Born December 19, 1973, in Tijuana, Mexico. ... 6-5/235. ... Throws right, bats right. ... Full name: Jose Leonel Silva.

HIGH SCHOOL: Hilltop (Chula Vista, Calif.).

TRANSACTIONS/CAREER NOTES: Selected by Toronto Blue Jays organization in sixth round of free-agent draft (June 3, 1991). ... On disabled list (April 6-August 17, 1995). ... On Knoxville disabled list (April 4-June 5, 1996). ... Traded by Blue Jays with IF Jose Pett, IF Brandon Cromer and three players to be named later to Pittsburgh Pirates for OF Orlando Merced, IF Carlos Garcia and P Dan Plesac (November 14, 1996); Pirates acquired P Mike Halperin, IF Abraham Nunez and C/OF Craig Wilson to complete deal (December 11, 1996). ... On Calgary disabled list (April 29-June 2, 1997). ... On Pittsburgh disabled list (June 17-September 10, 1998); included rehabilitation assignment to Nashville (August 25-September 6). ... On Pittsburgh disabled list (March 26-April 23, 1999); included rehabilitation assignment to Nashville (April 14-23).

Year	League	W	L	Pct.	ERA	G	GS	CG	ShO	Sv.	IP	H	R	ER	BB	SO
1992—GC Blue Jays (GCL)		6	4	.600	2.28	12	•12	0	0	0	59⅓	42	23	15	18	78
1993—Hagerstown (SAL)		12	5	.706	2.52	24	24	0	0	0	142⅔	103	50	40	62	161
1994—Dunedin (FSL)		0	2	.000	3.77	8	7	0	0	0	43	41	32	18	24	41
— Knoxville (Sou.)		4	8	.333	4.14	16	16	1	1	0	91⅓	89	47	42	31	71
1995—Knoxville (Sou.)		0	0	...	9.00	3	0	0	0	0	2	3	2	2	6	2
1996—Knoxville (Sou.)		2	3	.400	4.91	22	6	0	0	0	44	45	27	24	22	26
— Toronto (A.L.)		0	0	...	13.50	2	0	0	0	0	2	5	3	3	0	0
1997—Calgary (PCL)■		5	1	.833	3.41	17	11	0	0	0	66	74	27	25	22	54
— Pittsburgh (N.L.)		2	1	.667	5.94	11	4	0	0	0	36⅓	52	26	24	16	30
1998—Pittsburgh (N.L.)		6	7	.462	4.40	18	18	1	0	0	100⅓	104	55	49	30	64
— Nashville (PCL)		0	0	...	4.82	3	3	0	0	0	9⅓	10	5	5	4	6
1999—Nashville (PCL)		2	0	1.000	1.50	2	2	0	0	0	12	14	4	2	4	10
— Pittsburgh (N.L.)		2	8	.200	5.73	34	12	0	0	0	97⅓	108	70	62	39	77
A.L. totals (1 year)		0	0	...	13.50	2	0	0	0	0	2	5	3	3	0	0
N.L. totals (3 years)		10	16	.385	5.19	63	34	1	0	4	234	264	151	135	85	171
Major League totals (4 years)		10	16	.385	5.26	65	34	1	0	4	236	269	154	138	85	171

SILVESTRI, DAVE — IF — ANGELS

PERSONAL: Born September 29, 1967, in St. Louis. ... 6-0/196. ... Bats right, throws right. ... Full name: David Joseph Silvestri.

HIGH SCHOOL: Parkway Central (Chesterfield, Mo.).

COLLEGE: Missouri.

TRANSACTIONS/CAREER NOTES: Selected by Houston Astros in second round of free-agent draft (June 1, 1988); pick received as compensation for New York Yankees signing Type B free-agent OF Jose Cruz. ... Traded by Astros with a player to be named later to Yankees for IF Orlando Miller (March 13, 1990); Yankees acquired P Daven Bond to complete deal (June 11, 1990). ... On New York disabled list (May 13-30, 1995). ... Traded by Yankees to Montreal Expos for OF Tyrone Horne (July 16, 1995). ... Claimed on waivers by Seattle Mariners (November 15, 1996). ... Claimed on waivers by Texas Rangers (March 27, 1997). ... Granted free agency (October 8, 1997). ... Signed by Tampa Bay Devil Rays organization (January 27, 1998). ... Granted free agency (October 16, 1998). ... Re-signed by Devil Rays organization (November 25, 1998). ... Released by Devil Rays (April 9, 1999). ... Signed by Anaheim Angels organization (April 19, 1999).

STATISTICAL NOTES: Led Florida State League shortstops with 221 putouts, 473 assists, 726 total chances and 93 double plays in 1989. ... Led Carolina League shortstops with 622 total chances and 96 double plays in 1990. ... Led Eastern League shortstops with 84 double plays in 1991.

MISCELLANEOUS: Member of 1988 U.S. Olympic baseball team.

Year	Team (League)	Pos.	G	AB	R	H	2B	3B	HR	RBI	Avg.	BB	SO	SB	PO	A	E	Avg.
1989—Osceola (FSL)		SS-1B	129	437	67	111	20	1	2	50	.254	68	72	28	†238	†475	32	.957
1990—Prince Will. (Caro.)■		SS	131	465	74	120	30	7	5	56	.258	77	90	37	218	*382	22	*.965
— Alb./Colonie (East.)		SS	2	7	0	2	0	0	0	2	.286	0	1	0	3	5	1	.889
1991—Alb./Colonie (East.)		SS	*140	512	*97	134	31	8	19	83	.262	83	126	20	218	*362	•32	.948
1992—Columbus (I.L.)		SS	118	420	83	117	25	5	13	73	.279	58	110	19	*195	265	11	*.977
— New York (A.L.)		SS	7	13	3	4	0	2	0	1	.308	0	3	0	4	12	2	.889
1993—Columbus (I.L.)		SS-3B-OF	120	428	76	115	26	4	20	65	.269	68	127	6	183	299	16	.968
— New York (A.L.)		SS-3B	7	21	4	6	1	0	1	4	.286	5	3	0	9	20	3	.906
1994—Columbus (I.L.)		2-S-3-0-D-1	114	394	72	99	19	2	25	83	.251	*83	129	18	174	235	19	.956
— New York (A.L.)		2B-3B-SS	12	18	3	2	0	1	1	2	.111	4	9	0	14	16	1	.968
1995—New York (A.L.)		2B-DH-1B-SS	17	21	4	2	0	0	1	4	.095	4	9	0	28	13	0	1.000
— Montreal (N.L.)■		S-3-1-2-0	39	72	12	19	6	0	2	7	.264	9	27	2	34	36	1	.986
1996—Montreal (N.L.)		3-S-0-1-2	86	162	16	33	4	0	1	17	.204	34	41	2	23	92	10	.920
1997—Okla. City (A.A.)■		3-1-D-2-S-0	124	467	54	112	25	3	17	68	.240	55	104	4	215	263	22	.956
— Texas (A.L.)		3B-SS	2	4	0	0	0	0	0	0	.000	0	1	0	0	2	0	1.000
1998—Durham (I.L.)■		2-3-S-1-0	129	480	74	133	31	2	8	56	.277	61	73	12	223	325	13	.977
— Tampa Bay (A.L.)		3B-DH-2B-SS	8	14	0	1	0	0	0	0	.071	0	2	0	5	9	1	.933
1999—Durham (I.L.)		2B	1	3	0	0	0	0	0	0	.000	0	0	0	0	3	0	1.000
— Edmonton (PCL)■		2B-3B-SS-DH	79	318	55	101	18	0	6	42	.318	22	43	4	99	145	7	.972
— Anaheim (A.L.)		2B-SS-OF	3	11	0	1	1	0	0	1	.091	0	1	0	3	6	1	.900
American League totals (7 years)			56	102	14	16	2	3	3	12	.157	13	28	0	63	78	8	.946
National League totals (2 years)			125	234	28	52	10	0	3	24	.222	43	68	4	57	128	11	.944
Major League totals (8 years)			181	336	42	68	12	3	6	36	.202	56	96	4	120	206	19	.945

SIMAS, BILL — P — WHITE SOX

PERSONAL: Born November 28, 1971, in Hanford, Calif. ... 6-3/235. ... Throws right, bats left. ... Full name: William Anthony Simas Jr.
HIGH SCHOOL: St. Joseph (Calif.).
COLLEGE: Fresno (Calif.) City College.
TRANSACTIONS/CAREER NOTES: Selected by California Angels organization in sixth round of free-agent draft (June 1, 1992). ... Traded by Angels with P Andrew Lorraine, P John Snyder and OF McKay Christensen to Chicago White Sox for P Jim Abbott and P Tim Fortugno (July 27, 1995). ... On disabled list (July 23-August 5 and August 17, 1997-remainder of season).

Year	League	W	L	Pct.	ERA	G	GS	CG	ShO	Sv.	IP	H	R	ER	BB	SO
1992—	Boise (N'west)	6	5	.545	3.95	14	12	0	0	1	70²/₃	82	44	31	29	39
1993—	Cedar Rapids (Midw.)	5	8	.385	4.95	35	6	0	0	6	80	93	60	44	36	62
1994—	Lake Elsinore (Calif.)	5	2	.714	2.11	37	0	0	0	13	47	44	17	11	10	34
—	Midland (Texas)	2	0	1.000	0.59	13	0	0	0	6	15¹/₃	5	1	1	2	12
1995—	Vancouver (PCL)	6	3	.667	3.55	30	0	0	0	6	38	44	19	15	14	44
—	Nashville (A.A.)■	1	1	.500	3.86	7	0	0	0	0	11²/₃	12	5	5	3	12
—	Chicago (A.L.)	1	1	.500	2.57	14	0	0	0	0	14	15	5	4	10	16
1996—	Chicago (A.L.)	2	8	.200	4.58	64	0	0	0	2	72²/₃	75	39	37	39	65
1997—	Chicago (A.L.)	3	1	.750	4.14	40	0	0	0	1	41¹/₃	46	23	19	24	38
1998—	Calgary (PCL)	1	0	1.000	0.00	5	0	0	0	1	9	3	1	0	2	11
—	Chicago (A.L.)	4	3	.571	3.57	60	0	0	0	18	70²/₃	54	29	28	22	56
1999—	Chicago (A.L.)	6	3	.667	3.75	70	0	0	0	2	72	73	36	30	32	41
Major League totals (5 years)		16	16	.500	3.92	248	0	0	0	23	270²/₃	263	132	118	127	216

SIMMONS, BRIAN — OF — WHITE SOX

PERSONAL: Born September 4, 1973, in Lebanon, Pa. ... 6-2/190. ... Bats both, throws right. ... Full name: Brian Lee Simmons.
HIGH SCHOOL: Peters Township (McMurray, Pa.).
COLLEGE: Michigan.
TRANSACTIONS/CAREER NOTES: Selected by Baltimore Orioles organization in 35th round of free-agent draft (June 1, 1992); did not sign. ... Selected by Chicago White Sox organization in second round of free-agent draft (June 1, 1995). ... On South Bend disabled list (April 5-17, 1996). ... On Calgary disabled list (June 22-August 10, 1998); included rehabilitation assignment to Arizona White Sox (August 1-8). ... On Chicago disabled list (March 26-April 29, 1999); included rehabilitation assignment to Charlotte (April 8-27).
STATISTICAL NOTES: Led Southern League outfielders with 334 total chances in 1997. ... Switch-hit home runs in one game (September 26, 1998).

Year	Team (League)	Pos.	G	AB	R	H	2B	3B	HR	RBI	Avg.	BB	SO	SB	PO	A	E	Avg.
1995—	Sarasota (GCL)	OF	5	17	5	3	1	0	1	5	.176	6	1	0	13	1	0	1.000
—	Hickory (SAL)	OF	41	163	13	31	6	1	2	11	.190	19	44	4	77	2	1	.988
1996—	South Bend (Midw.)	OF-DH	92	356	73	106	29	6	17	58	.298	48	69	14	204	10	7	.968
—	Prince Will. (Caro.)	OF	33	131	17	26	4	3	4	14	.198	9	39	2	70	2	2	.973
1997—	Birmingham (Sou.)	OF	138	546	108	143	28	*12	15	72	.262	*88	124	15	*322	7	5	.985
1998—	Calgary (PCL)	OF-DH	94	355	72	103	21	4	13	51	.290	41	82	10	197	6	7	.967
—	Ariz. Whi. Sox (Ariz.)	OF-DH	5	12	1	2	0	0	0	0	.167	1	1	0	3	0	0	1.000
—	Chicago (A.L.)	OF	5	19	4	7	0	0	2	6	.368	0	2	0	13	0	0	1.000
1999—	Chicago (A.L.)	OF-DH	54	126	14	29	3	3	4	17	.230	9	30	4	79	2	2	.976
—	Charlotte (I.L.)	OF	78	285	53	77	14	0	10	44	.270	37	60	8	171	6	5	.973
Major League totals (2 years)			59	145	18	36	3	3	6	23	.248	9	32	4	92	2	2	.979

SIMMS, MIKE — OF — RANGERS

PERSONAL: Born January 12, 1967, in Whittier, Calif. ... 6-4/230. ... Bats right, throws right. ... Full name: Michael Howard Simms.
HIGH SCHOOL: Esperanza (Calif.).
TRANSACTIONS/CAREER NOTES: Selected by Houston Astros organization in sixth round of free-agent draft (June 3, 1985). ... On disabled list (May 11-28, 1989). ... On Tucson disabled list (July 31-August 16, 1992). ... Granted free agency (March 30, 1993). ... Signed by San Diego Padres organization (April 7, 1993). ... Granted free agency (October 15, 1993). ... Signed by Pittsburgh Pirates (December 15, 1993). ... Released by Pirates (April 28, 1994). ... Signed by Astros organization (May 2, 1994). ... Granted free agency (October 15, 1994). ... Re-signed by Astros organization (November 18, 1994). ... Granted free agency (October 15, 1996). ... Signed by Texas Rangers organization (December 19, 1996). ... Granted free agency (October 27, 1997). ... Re-signed by Rangers organization (December 17, 1997). ... On Texas disabled list (March 25-September 7, 1999); included rehabilitation assignments to Charlotte (April 15-16 and August 26-September 7) and Oklahoma (April 17-27 and May 18-June 7).
STATISTICAL NOTES: Led South Atlantic League with 264 total bases in 1987. ... Led South Atlantic League first basemen with 1,089 putouts, 19 errors and 1,158 total chances in 1987. ... Led Pacific Coast League first basemen with 19 errors in 1990. ... Career major league grand slams: 1.

Year	Team (League)	Pos.	G	AB	R	H	2B	3B	HR	RBI	Avg.	BB	SO	SB	PO	A	E	Avg.
1985—	GC Astros (GCL)	1B	21	70	10	19	2	1	3	18	.271	6	26	0	186	7	5	.975
1986—	GC Astros (GCL)	1B	54	181	33	47	14	1	4	37	.260	22	48	2	433	28	7	.985
1987—	Asheville (SAL)	1B-3B	133	469	93	128	19	0	*39	100	.273	73	*167	7	†1089	52	†19	.984
1988—	Osceola (FSL)	1B	123	428	63	104	19	1	16	73	.243	76	130	9	1143	41	22	.982
1989—	Columbus (Sou.)	1B	109	378	64	97	21	3	20	81	.257	66	110	12	938	44	10	.990
1990—	Tucson (PCL)	1B-3B-OF	124	421	75	115	34	5	13	72	.273	74	*135	3	1013	75	†19	.983
—	Houston (N.L.)	1B	12	13	3	4	1	0	1	2	.308	0	4	0	20	1	0	1.000
1991—	Tucson (PCL)	OF-1B	85	297	53	73	20	2	15	59	.246	36	94	2	325	25	8	.978
—	Houston (N.L.)	OF	49	123	18	25	5	0	3	16	.203	18	38	1	44	4	6	.889
1992—	Tucson (PCL)	OF-1B	126	404	73	114	22	6	11	75	.282	61	107	7	476	29	11	.979
—	Houston (N.L.)	OF-1B	15	24	1	6	1	0	1	3	.250	2	9	0	10	2	0	1.000
1993—	Las Vegas (PCL)■	1-O-DH-3-P	129	414	74	111	25	2	24	80	.268	67	114	1	774	46	13	.984

Year	Team (League)	Pos.	G	AB	R	H	2B	3B	HR	RBI	Avg.	BB	SO	SB	PO	A	E	Avg.
1994—	Buffalo (A.A.)■	OF-DH	18	55	10	13	5	0	4	8	.236	4	13	0	26	0	0	1.000
	—Tucson (PCL)■	1-O-3-DH	100	373	76	107	34	6	20	85	.287	51	79	9	555	32	9	.985
	—Houston (N.L.)	OF	6	12	1	1	1	0	0	0	.083	0	5	1	6	0	1	.857
1995—	Houston (N.L.)	1B-DH	50	121	14	31	4	0	9	24	.256	13	28	1	221	17	1	.996
	—Tucson (PCL)	1B-OF-DH	85	319	56	94	26	8	13	66	.295	35	65	10	424	30	8	.983
1996—	Tucson (PCL)	1B	17	64	11	19	3	0	7	19	.297	9	17	0	138	9	5	.967
	—Houston (N.L.)	OF-1B	49	68	6	12	2	1	1	8	.176	4	16	1	24	1	0	1.000
1997—	Okla. City (A.A.)■	OF-DH	10	39	7	15	4	0	3	8	.385	6	8	0	17	1	0	1.000
	—Texas (A.L.)	DH-OF-1B	59	111	13	28	8	0	5	22	.252	8	27	0	36	1	2	.949
1998—	Texas (A.L.)	OF-DH-1B	86	186	36	55	11	0	16	46	.296	24	47	0	118	8	2	.984
1999—	Charlotte (FSL)	DH	12	41	7	9	1	0	2	9	.220	8	3	0	0	0	0	...
	—Oklahoma (PCL)	DH-OF-1B	22	73	7	20	1	0	2	16	.274	16	25	0	35	2	1	.974
	—Texas (A.L.)	DH-1B-OF	4	2	0	1	0	0	0	0	.500	0	1	0	1	0	0	1.000
American League totals (3 years)			149	299	49	84	19	0	21	68	.281	32	75	0	154	10	4	.976
National League totals (6 years)			181	361	43	79	14	1	15	53	.219	37	100	4	325	25	8	.978
Major League totals (9 years)			330	660	92	163	33	1	36	121	.247	69	175	4	479	35	12	.977

DIVISION SERIES RECORD

Year	Team (League)	Pos.	G	AB	R	H	2B	3B	HR	RBI	Avg.	BB	SO	SB	PO	A	E	Avg.
1998—	Texas (A.L.)	DH	2	5	0	1	0	0	0	0	.200	0	2	0	...	...	...	...

RECORD AS PITCHER

Year	League	W	L	Pct.	ERA	G	GS	CG	ShO	Sv.	IP	H	R	ER	BB	SO
1993—	Las Vegas (PCL)	0	0	...	0.00	1	0	0	0	0	2/3	1	0	0	0	0

S

SIMON, RANDALL — 1B — BRAVES

PERSONAL: Born May 26, 1975, in Willemstad, Curacao. ... 6-0/180. ... Bats left, throws left. ... Full name: Randall Carlito Simon.
HIGH SCHOOL: Juan Pablo Duarte Tech (Willemstad, Curacao).
TRANSACTIONS/CAREER NOTES: Signed as non-drafted free agent by Atlanta Braves organization (July 17, 1992).
STATISTICAL NOTES: Led International League in grounding into double plays with 18 in 1997 and 22 in 1998.

Year	Team (League)	Pos.	G	AB	R	H	2B	3B	HR	RBI	Avg.	BB	SO	SB	PO	A	E	Avg.
1993—	Danville (Appl.)	1B	61	232	28	59	17	1	3	31	.254	10	34	1	463	37	10	.980
1994—	Macon (SAL)	1B	106	358	48	105	23	1	10	54	.293	6	56	7	582	49	9	.986
1995—	Durham (Caro.)	1B	122	420	56	111	18	1	18	79	.264	36	63	6	864	51	10	.989
1996—	Greenville (Sou.)	1B-OF	134	498	74	139	26	2	18	77	.279	37	61	4	723	55	16	.980
1997—	Richmond (I.L.)	1B-DH	133	519	62	160	*45	1	14	*102	.308	17	76	1	*1063	72	•14	.988
	—Atlanta (N.L.)	1B	13	14	2	6	1	0	0	1	.429	1	2	0	16	2	0	1.000
1998—	Richmond (I.L.)	1B-DH	126	484	52	124	20	1	13	70	.256	24	62	4	981	51	*11	.989
	—Atlanta (N.L.)	1B	7	16	2	3	0	0	0	4	.188	0	1	0	36	1	0	1.000
1999—	Atlanta (N.L.)	1B	90	218	26	69	16	0	5	25	.317	17	25	2	462	27	3	.994
	—Richmond (I.L.)	1B-DH	15	59	7	16	4	0	1	8	.271	3	10	0	115	14	0	1.000
Major League totals (3 years)			110	248	30	78	17	0	5	30	.315	18	28	2	514	30	3	.995

DIVISION SERIES RECORD

Year	Team (League)	Pos.	G	AB	R	H	2B	3B	HR	RBI	Avg.	BB	SO	SB	PO	A	E	Avg.
1999—	Atlanta (N.L.)								Did not play.									

CHAMPIONSHIP SERIES RECORD

Year	Team (League)	Pos.	G	AB	R	H	2B	3B	HR	RBI	Avg.	BB	SO	SB	PO	A	E	Avg.
1999—	Atlanta (N.L.)								Did not play.									

WORLD SERIES RECORD

Year	Team (League)	Pos.	G	AB	R	H	2B	3B	HR	RBI	Avg.	BB	SO	SB	PO	A	E	Avg.
1999—	Atlanta (N.L.)								Did not play.									

SINCLAIR, STEVE — P — MARINERS

PERSONAL: Born August 2, 1971, in Victoria, B.C. ... 6-2/190. ... Throws left, bats left. ... Full name: Steven Scott Sinclair.
HIGH SCHOOL: Oak Bay (Victoria, B.C.).
COLLEGE: Kwantlen (Vancouver, B.C.).
TRANSACTIONS/CAREER NOTES: Selected by Toronto Blue Jays organization in 28th round of free-agent draft (June 3, 1991). ... On Syracuse disabled list (May 21-June 2, 1999). ... Traded by Blue Jays with P Tom Davey to Seattle Mariners for 1B David Segui (July 28, 1999).

Year	League	W	L	Pct.	ERA	G	GS	CG	ShO	Sv.	IP	H	R	ER	BB	SO
1991—	Medicine Hat (Pio.)	0	1	.000	6.75	12	0	0	0	0	14 2/3	17	15	11	11	14
1992—	GC Blue Jays (GCL)	1	2	.333	2.74	5	4	0	0	0	23	23	10	7	5	18
	—Medicine Hat (Pio.)	2	3	.400	4.60	9	7	0	0	0	43	54	25	22	12	28
1993—	Medicine Hat (Pio.)	5	2	.714	3.33	15	12	0	0	0	78 1/3	87	41	29	16	45
1994—	Hagerstown (SAL)	9	2	.818	3.77	38	1	0	0	3	105	127	53	44	25	75
1995—	Dunedin (FSL)	5	3	.625	2.59	46	0	0	0	2	73	69	26	21	17	52
1996—	Dunedin (FSL)	0	1	.000	3.38	3	0	0	0	0	2 2/3	4	2	1	0	1
1997—	Dunedin (FSL)	2	5	.286	2.90	43	0	0	0	3	68 1/3	63	36	22	26	66
	—Syracuse (I.L.)	0	0	...	6.00	6	0	0	0	0	9	11	6	6	3	9

Year	League	W	L	Pct.	ERA	G	GS	CG	ShO	Sv.	IP	H	R	ER	BB	SO
1998—	Syracuse (I.L.)....................	3	1	.750	2.17	43	1	0	0	3	49²/₃	37	15	12	23	45
	— Toronto (A.L.)....................	0	2	.000	3.60	24	0	0	0	0	15	13	7	6	5	8
1999—	Syracuse (I.L.)....................	2	2	.500	2.06	34	0	0	0	18	39¹/₃	24	11	9	12	31
	— Toronto (A.L.)....................	0	0	...	12.71	3	0	0	0	0	5²/₃	7	8	8	4	3
	— Seattle (A.L.)■	0	1	.000	3.95	18	0	0	0	0	13²/₃	15	8	6	10	15
	— Tacoma (PCL)	1	0	1.000	4.50	2	0	0	0	0	2	2	1	1	1	1
Major League totals (2 years).......		0	3	.000	5.24	45	0	0	0	0	34¹/₃	35	23	20	19	26

SINGLETON, CHRIS — OF — WHITE SOX

PERSONAL: Born August 15, 1972, in Mesa, Ariz. ... 6-2/195. ... Bats left, throws left. ... Full name: Christopher Verdell Singleton.
HIGH SCHOOL: Pinole (Calif.) Valley.
COLLEGE: Nevada.
TRANSACTIONS/CAREER NOTES: Selected by San Francisco Giants organization in second round of free-agent draft (June 3, 1993). ... Traded by Giants with P Alberto Castillo to New York Yankees for 3B Charlie Hayes and cash (November 11, 1997). ... Traded by Yankees to Chicago White Sox for a player to be named later (December 8, 1998); Yankees acquired P Rich Pratt to complete deal (January 10, 1999).
STATISTICAL NOTES: Led Texas League with nine sacrifice flies in 1997. ... Led Texas League outfielders with 271 total chances and tied for league lead with four double plays in 1997. ... Tied for Texas League lead with four intentional bases on balls in 1997. ... Hit for the cycle (July 6, 1999).

Year Team (League)	Pos.	G	AB	R	H	2B	3B	HR	RBI	Avg.	BB	SO	SB	PO	A	E	Avg.
1993— Everett (N'west).........	OF	58	219	39	58	14	4	3	18	.265	18	46	14	106	6	3	.974
1994— San Jose (Calif.).........	OF	113	425	51	106	17	5	2	49	.249	27	62	19	248	10	13	.952
1995— San Jose (Calif.).........	OF	94	405	55	112	13	5	2	31	.277	17	49	33	142	6	7	.955
1996— Shreveport (Texas).....	OF	129	500	68	149	31	9	5	72	.298	24	58	27	262	10	4	.986
— Phoenix (PCL)	OF	9	32	3	4	0	0	0	0	.125	1	2	0	18	1	0	1.000
1997— Shreveport (Texas).....	OF	126	464	85	147	26	10	9	61	.317	22	50	27	*253	11	7	.974
1998— Columbus (I.L.)■	OF	121	413	55	105	17	10	6	45	.254	27	78	9	251	10	7	.974
1999— Chicago (A.L.)■	OF-DH	133	496	72	149	31	6	17	72	.300	22	45	20	376	9	4	.990
Major League totals (1 year)		133	496	72	149	31	6	17	72	.300	22	45	20	376	9	4	.990

SIROTKA, MIKE — P — WHITE SOX

PERSONAL: Born May 13, 1971, in Chicago. ... 6-1/200. ... Throws left, bats left. ... Full name: Michael Robert Sirotka.
HIGH SCHOOL: Westfield (Houston).
COLLEGE: Louisiana State.
TRANSACTIONS/CAREER NOTES: Selected by Chicago White Sox organization in 15th round of free-agent draft (June 3, 1993). ... On Hickory disabled list (July 1-28, 1993). ... On South Bend temporarily inactive list (August 27-October 4, 1993).
RECORDS: Shares major league single-inning record for most errors by pitcher—3 (April 9, 1999, fifth inning).

Year	League	W	L	Pct.	ERA	G	GS	CG	ShO	Sv.	IP	H	R	ER	BB	SO
1993—	GC White Sox (GCL)	0	0	...	0.00	3	0	0	0	0	5	4	1	0	2	8
	— South Bend (Midw.)	0	1	.000	6.10	7	1	0	0	0	10¹/₃	12	8	7	6	12
1994—	South Bend (Midw.)	12	9	.571	3.07	27	27	8	2	0	196²/₃	183	99	67	56	173
1995—	Birmingham (Sou.).............	7	6	.538	3.20	16	16	1	0	0	101¹/₃	95	42	36	22	79
	— Chicago (A.L.)	1	2	.333	4.19	6	6	0	0	0	34¹/₃	39	16	16	17	19
	— Nashville (A.A.)	1	5	.167	2.83	8	8	0	0	0	54	51	21	17	13	34
1996—	Nashville (A.A.)	7	5	.583	3.60	15	15	1	1	0	90	90	44	36	24	58
	— Chicago (A.L.)	1	2	.333	7.18	15	4	0	0	0	26¹/₃	34	27	21	12	11
1997—	Nashville (A.A.)	7	5	.583	3.28	19	19	1	0	0	112¹/₃	115	49	41	22	92
	— Chicago (A.L.)	3	0	1.000	2.25	7	4	0	0	0	32	36	9	8	5	24
1998—	Chicago (A.L.)	14	15	.483	5.06	33	33	5	0	0	211²/₃	255	137	119	47	128
1999—	Chicago (A.L.)	11	13	.458	4.00	32	32	3	1	0	209	236	108	93	57	125
Major League totals (5 years).......		30	32	.484	4.51	93	79	8	1	0	513¹/₃	600	297	257	138	307

SLOCUMB, HEATHCLIFF — P — CARDINALS

PERSONAL: Born June 7, 1966, in Jamaica, N.Y. ... 6-3/220. ... Throws right, bats right.
HIGH SCHOOL: John Bowne (Flushing, N.Y.).
TRANSACTIONS/CAREER NOTES: Signed as non-drafted free agent by New York Mets organization (July 10, 1984). ... Selected by Chicago Cubs organization from Mets organization in Rule 5 minor league draft (December 9, 1986). ... Traded by Cubs to Cleveland Indians for SS Jose Hernandez (June 1, 1993). ... Traded by Indians to Philadelphia Phillies for OF Ruben Amaro (November 2, 1993). ... Traded by Phillies with P Larry Wimberly and OF Rick Holifield to Boston Red Sox for P Ken Ryan, OF Lee Tinsley and OF Glenn Murray (January 29, 1996). ... Traded by Red Sox to Seattle Mariners for C Jason Varitek and P Derek Lowe (July 31, 1997). ... Granted free agency (October 23, 1998). ... Signed by Baltimore Orioles (January 15, 1999). ... Released by Orioles (April 30, 1999). ... Signed by St. Louis Cardinals organization (May 15, 1999). ... On St. Louis disabled list (June 23-July 16, 1999). ... Granted free agency (November 8, 1999). ... Re-signed by Cardinals (November 23, 1999).
STATISTICAL NOTES: Led Carolina League with 19 wild pitches in 1988.

Year	League	W	L	Pct.	ERA	G	GS	CG	ShO	Sv.	IP	H	R	ER	BB	SO
1984—	Kingsport (Appalachian).....	0	0	...	0.00	1	0	0	0	0	¹/₃	0	1	0	1	0
	— Little Falls (NY-P)	0	0	...	11.00	4	1	0	0	0	9	8	11	11	16	10
1985—	Kingsport (Appalachian).....	3	2	.600	3.78	11	9	1	0	0	52¹/₃	47	32	22	31	29
1986—	Little Falls (NY-P)	3	1	.750	1.65	25	0	0	0	1	43²/₃	24	17	8	36	41
1987—	Win.-Salem (Car.)■...........	1	2	.333	6.26	9	4	0	0	0	27¹/₃	26	25	19	26	27
	— Peoria (Midw.)..................	10	4	.714	2.60	16	16	3	1	0	103²/₃	97	44	30	42	81
1988—	Win.-Salem (Car.)	6	6	.500	4.96	25	19	2	1	1	119²/₃	122	75	66	90	78
1989—	Peoria (Midw.)	5	3	.625	1.78	49	0	0	0	22	55²/₃	31	16	11	33	52

Year	League	W	L	Pct.	ERA	G	GS	CG	ShO	Sv.	IP	H	R	ER	BB	SO
1990—	Charlotte (Sou.)	3	1	.750	2.15	43	0	0	0	12	50 1/3	50	20	12	32	37
—Iowa (A.A.)		3	2	.600	2.00	20	0	0	0	1	27	16	10	6	18	21
1991—	Chicago (N.L.)	2	1	.667	3.45	52	0	0	0	1	62 2/3	53	29	24	30	34
—Iowa (A.A.)		1	0	1.000	4.05	12	0	0	0	1	13 1/3	10	8	6	6	9
1992—	Chicago (N.L.)	0	3	.000	6.50	30	0	0	0	1	36	52	27	26	21	27
—Iowa (A.A.)		1	3	.250	2.59	36	1	0	0	7	41 2/3	36	13	12	16	47
1993—	Iowa (A.A.)	1	0	1.000	1.50	10	0	0	0	7	12	7	2	2	8	10
—Chicago (N.L.)		1	0	1.000	3.38	10	0	0	0	0	10 2/3	7	5	4	4	4
—Cleveland (A.L.)■		3	1	.750	4.28	20	0	0	0	0	27 1/3	28	14	13	16	18
—Charlotte (I.L.)		3	2	.600	3.56	23	0	0	0	1	30 1/3	25	14	12	11	25
1994—	Philadelphia (N.L.)■	5	1	.833	2.86	52	0	0	0	0	72 1/3	75	32	23	28	58
1995—	Philadelphia (N.L.)	5	6	.455	2.89	61	0	0	0	32	65 1/3	64	26	21	35	63
1996—	Boston (A.L.)■	5	5	.500	3.02	75	0	0	0	31	83 1/3	68	31	28	55	88
1997—	Boston (A.L.)	0	5	.000	5.79	49	0	0	0	17	46 2/3	58	32	30	34	36
—Seattle (A.L.)■		0	4	.000	4.13	27	0	0	0	10	28 1/3	26	13	13	15	28
1998—	Seattle (A.L.)	2	5	.286	5.32	57	0	0	0	3	67 2/3	72	40	40	44	51
1999—	Baltimore (A.L.)■	0	0	...	12.46	10	0	0	0	0	8 2/3	15	12	12	9	12
—Memphis (PCL)■		0	0	...	4.50	2	0	0	0	0	2	3	1	1	0	2
—St. Louis (N.L.)		3	2	.600	2.36	40	0	0	0	2	53 1/3	49	16	14	30	48
A.L. totals (5 years)		10	20	.333	4.67	238	0	0	0	61	262	267	142	136	173	233
N.L. totals (6 years)		16	13	.552	3.36	245	0	0	0	36	300 1/3	300	135	112	148	234
Major League totals (9 years)		26	33	.441	3.97	483	0	0	0	97	562 1/3	567	277	248	321	467

DIVISION SERIES RECORD

Year	League	W	L	Pct.	ERA	G	GS	CG	ShO	Sv.	IP	H	R	ER	BB	SO
1997—	Seattle (A.L.)	0	0	...	4.50	2	0	0	0	0	2	3	1	1	1	0

ALL-STAR GAME RECORD

Year	League	W	L	Pct.	ERA	GS	CG	ShO	Sv.	IP	H	R	ER	BB	SO
1995—	National	1	0	1.000	0.00	0	0	0	0	1	1	0	0	0	2

SLUSARSKI, JOE P ASTROS

PERSONAL: Born December 19, 1966, in Indianapolis. ... 6-4/195. ... Throws right, bats right. ... Full name: Joseph Andrew Slusarski.
HIGH SCHOOL: Griffin (Springfield, Ill.).
JUNIOR COLLEGE: Lincoln Land Community College (Ill.).
COLLEGE: New Orleans.
TRANSACTIONS/CAREER NOTES: Selected by Seattle Mariners organization in sixth round of free-agent draft (June 2, 1987); did not sign. ... Selected by Oakland Athletics organization in second round of free-agent draft (June 1, 1988). ... On Huntsville disabled list (May 18-25, 1990). ... On Tacoma disabled list (August 2-11, 1992 and July 22-August 11, 1993). ... Released by Athletics (May 11, 1994). ... Signed by Reading, Philadelphia Phillies organization (June 3, 1994). ... Granted free agency (October 15, 1994). ... Signed by Cleveland Indians organization (January 20, 1995). ... Released by Indians (April 24, 1995). ... Re-signed by New Orleans, Brewers organization (May 19, 1995). ... Granted free agency (October 16, 1995). ... Signed by California Angels organization (February 26, 1996). ... Released by Angels (April 4, 1996). ... Signed by Brewers organization (May 12, 1996). ... Signed by Sinon, Taiwan (1997). ... Signed by Houston Astros organization (May 4, 1998). ... Granted free agency (October 16, 1998). ... Re-signed by Astros organization (December 17, 1998). ... On Houston disabled list (July 9-24, 1999). ... Granted free agency (October 20, 1999). ... Re-signed by Astros organization (January 3, 2000).
STATISTICAL NOTES: Led California League with 15 home runs allowed in 1989.
MISCELLANEOUS: Member of 1988 U.S. Olympic baseball team.

Year	League	W	L	Pct.	ERA	G	GS	CG	ShO	Sv.	IP	H	R	ER	BB	SO
1989—	Modesto (Calif.)	•13	10	.565	3.18	27	27	4	1	0	184	155	78	65	50	160
1990—	Huntsville (Sou.)	6	8	.429	4.47	17	17	2	0	0	108 2/3	114	65	54	35	75
—Tacoma (PCL)		4	2	.667	3.40	9	9	0	0	0	55 2/3	54	24	21	22	37
1991—	Oakland (A.L.)	5	7	.417	5.27	20	19	1	0	0	109 1/3	121	69	64	52	60
—Tacoma (PCL)		4	2	.667	2.72	7	7	0	0	0	46 1/3	42	20	14	10	25
1992—	Oakland (A.L.)	5	5	.500	5.45	15	14	0	0	0	76	85	52	46	27	38
—Tacoma (PCL)		2	4	.333	3.77	11	10	0	0	0	57 1/3	67	30	24	18	26
1993—	Tacoma (PCL)	7	5	.583	4.76	24	21	1	1	0	113 1/3	133	67	60	40	61
—Oakland (A.L.)		0	0	...	5.19	2	1	0	0	0	8 2/3	9	5	5	11	1
1994—	Tacoma (PCL)	2	3	.400	6.03	7	7	0	0	0	37 1/3	45	28	25	11	24
—Reading (East.)■		1	2	.333	4.63	5	4	0	0	0	23 1/3	25	15	12	5	17
—Scranton/W.B. (I.L.)		2	3	.400	7.82	10	4	0	0	0	38	50	36	33	10	29
1995—	Buffalo (A.A.)■	1	1	.500	6.32	4	2	0	0	0	15 2/3	18	12	11	4	9
—New Orleans (A.A.)■		1	1	.500	1.12	33	0	0	0	11	48 1/3	37	10	6	11	30
—Milwaukee (A.L.)		1	1	.500	5.40	12	0	0	0	0	15	21	11	9	6	6
1996—	New Orleans (A.A.)	2	4	.333	4.95	40	0	0	0	1	60	70	38	33	24	36
1997—	Sinon (Taiwan)■	2	4	.333	4.94	25	...	...	...	2	71	76	...	...	24	31
1998—	Jackson (Texas)■	2	2	.500	6.33	9	2	0	0	0	21 1/3	22	17	15	2	13
—New Orleans (PCL)		1	4	.200	5.11	31	0	0	0	2	49 1/3	53	31	28	9	32
1999—	New Orleans (PCL)	1	4	.200	3.64	40	2	0	0	1	64 1/3	71	31	26	13	40
—Houston (N.L.)		0	0	...	0.00	3	0	0	0	0	3 2/3	1	0	0	3	3
A.L. totals (4 years)		11	13	.458	5.34	49	34	1	0	0	209	236	137	124	96	105
N.L. totals (1 year)		0	0	...	0.00	3	0	0	0	0	3 2/3	1	0	0	3	3
Major League totals (5 years)		11	13	.458	5.25	52	34	1	0	0	212 2/3	237	137	124	99	108

SMART, J.D. P EXPOS

PERSONAL: Born November 12, 1973, in San Saba, Texas. ... 6-2/180. ... Throws right, bats right. ... Full name: Jon David Smart.
HIGH SCHOOL: Westlake (Austin, Texas).
COLLEGE: Texas.

TRANSACTIONS/CAREER NOTES: Selected by Montreal Expos organization in fourth round of free-agent draft (June 1, 1995). ... On Ottawa disabled list (August 16, 1999-remainder of season).

Year League	W	L	Pct.	ERA	G	GS	CG	ShO	Sv.	IP	H	R	ER	BB	SO
1995— Gulf Coast Expos (GCL)	2	0	1.000	1.69	2	2	0	0	0	10 2/3	10	2	2	1	6
— Vermont (NY-P)................	0	1	.000	2.28	5	5	0	0	0	27 2/3	29	9	7	7	21
1996— Delmarva (SAL).................	9	8	.529	3.39	25	25	3	2	0	156 2/3	155	75	59	31	109
1997— W.P. Beach (FSL)............	5	4	.556	3.26	17	13	1	0	1	102	105	45	37	21	65
— Harrisburg (East.)............	6	3	.667	3.69	12	12	0	0	0	70 2/3	75	34	29	24	43
1998— Cape Fear (SAL)	3	0	1.000	2.45	3	1	0	0	0	11	7	3	3	0	12
— Harrisburg (East.)............	3	5	.375	2.45	14	11	2	0	1	77	67	23	21	18	47
— Ottawa (I.L.)....................	2	3	.400	4.89	6	6	0	0	0	35	34	22	19	11	16
1999— Montreal (N.L.)................	0	1	.000	5.02	29	0	0	0	0	52	56	30	29	17	21
— Ottawa (I.L.)....................	0	1	.000	2.61	6	4	0	0	0	20 2/3	22	7	6	6	9
Major League totals (1 year)........	0	1	.000	5.02	29	0	0	0	0	52	56	30	29	17	21

SMITH, CHUCK   P   RANGERS

PERSONAL: Born October 21, 1969, in Memphis, Tenn. ... 6-1/185. ... Throws right, bats right. ... Full name: Charles Edward Smith.
HIGH SCHOOL: John Adams (Cleveland).
JUNIOR COLLEGE: Central Arizona College.
COLLEGE: Indiana State.
TRANSACTIONS/CAREER NOTES: Signed as non-drafted free agent by Houston Astros organization (June 17, 1991). ... Selected by Chicago White Sox organization from Astros organization in Rule 5 minor league draft (December 6, 1994). ... Granted free agency (October 17, 1997). ... Signed by Sioux Falls, Northern League (May 1998). ... Contract purchased by Colorado Rockies organization from Sioux Falls (December 15, 1998). ... Released by Rockies (April 2, 1999). ... Signed by Texas Rangers organization (April 9, 1999). ... On Oklahoma disabled list (July 22-August 5, 1999).

Year League	W	L	Pct.	ERA	G	GS	CG	ShO	Sv.	IP	H	R	ER	BB	SO
1991— Gulf Coast Astros (GCL).....	4	3	.571	3.49	15	7	2	0	0	59 1/3	56	36	23	37	64
1992— Asheville (SAL).................	9	9	.500	5.18	28	20	1	0	1	132	120	93	76	78	117
1993— Quad City (Midw.)	7	5	.583	4.64	22	17	2	0	0	110 2/3	109	73	57	52	103
1994— Jackson (Texas)	0	0	...	4.50	2	0	0	0	0	6	6	6	3	5	7
— Osceola (FSL)...................	4	4	.500	3.72	35	2	0	0	0	84 2/3	73	41	35	49	60
1995— South Bend (Midw.)■.......	10	10	.500	2.69	26	25	4	•2	0	167	128	70	50	61	*145
1996— Prince William (Caro.).......	6	6	.500	4.01	20	20	2	1	0	123 1/3	125	65	55	49	99
— Birmingham (Sou.)............	2	1	.667	2.64	7	3	0	0	1	30 2/3	25	11	9	15	30
— Nashville (A.A.)	0	0	...	27.00	1	0	0	0	0	2/3	2	2	2	1	1
1997— Birmingham (Sou.)............	2	2	.500	3.16	25	0	0	0	0	62 2/3	63	35	22	27	57
— Nashville (A.A.)	0	3	.000	8.81	20	1	0	0	0	31 2/3	39	33	31	23	29
1998— Sioux Falls (Nor.)■..........	5	3	.625	2.62	8	8	2	•1	0	55	44	18	16	21	70
1999— Oklahoma (PCL)■............	5	4	.556	2.96	32	4	2	0	4	85	73	31	28	28	76

SMITH, DAN   P

PERSONAL: Born September 15, 1975, in Flemington, N.J. ... 6-3/210. ... Throws right, bats right. ... Full name: Daniel Charles Smith Jr.
HIGH SCHOOL: Girard (Kan.).
TRANSACTIONS/CAREER NOTES: Selected by Texas Rangers organization in seventh round of free-agent draft (June 3, 1993). ... On Charlotte disabled list (June 12-July 7, 1995). ... Claimed on waivers by Montreal Expos (December 14, 1998). ... Granted free agency (December 21, 1999).

Year League	W	L	Pct.	ERA	G	GS	CG	ShO	Sv.	IP	H	R	ER	BB	SO
1993— GC Rangers (GCL).............	3	2	.600	2.87	12	10	1	0	0	53 1/3	50	19	17	8	27
1994— Charlotte (FSL).................	0	0	...	0.00	2	0	0	0	0	3 2/3	2	0	0	2	3
— Charleston, S.C. (SAL).......	7	10	.412	4.92	27	27	4	0	0	157 1/3	171	*111	86	55	86
1995— GC Rangers (GCL).............	0	3	.000	4.26	4	3	0	0	0	19	19	9	9	5	12
— Charlotte (FSL).................	5	1	.833	2.95	9	9	1	1	0	58	53	23	19	16	34
1996— Charlotte (FSL).................	3	7	.300	5.07	18	18	1	0	0	87	100	61	49	38	55
1997— Charlotte (FSL).................	8	10	.444	4.43	26	25	2	0	0	160 2/3	169	93	79	66	113
1998— Tulsa (Texas)	13	9	.591	5.81	26	25	1	0	0	153 1/3	162	101	99	58	105
— Oklahoma (PCL)	0	0	...	6.00	1	1	0	0	0	6	6	4	4	1	3
1999— Ottawa (I.L.)■■...............	5	4	.556	3.68	11	11	0	0	0	71	61	31	29	27	59
— Montreal (N.L.).................	4	9	.308	6.02	20	17	0	0	0	89 2/3	104	64	60	39	72
Major League totals (1 year)........	4	9	.308	6.02	20	17	0	0	0	89 2/3	104	64	60	39	72

SMITH, ROBERT   3B/SS   DEVIL RAYS

PERSONAL: Born May 10, 1974, in Oakland. ... 6-3/190. ... Bats right, throws right. ... Full name: Robert Eugene Smith.
HIGH SCHOOL: Fremont (Oakland).
TRANSACTIONS/CAREER NOTES: Selected by Atlanta Braves organization in 11th round of free-agent draft (June 1, 1992). ... Selected by Tampa Bay Devil Rays in first round (12th pick overall) of expansion draft (November 18, 1997). ... On disabled list (May 13-28, 1998).
STATISTICAL NOTES: Tied for Carolina League lead in grounding into double plays with 19 in 1994. ... Led Carolina League third basemen with 388 total chances and 27 double plays in 1994.

Year Team (League)	Pos.	G	AB	R	H	2B	3B	HR	RBI	Avg.	BB	SO	SB	PO	A	E	Avg.
1992— GC Braves (GCL)	3B	57	217	31	51	9	1	3	28	.235	17	55	5	37	115	15	.910
1993— Macon (SAL).............	3B	108	384	53	94	16	7	4	38	.245	23	81	12	65	167	30	.885
1994— Durham (Caro.)	3B	127	478	49	127	27	2	12	71	.266	41	112	18	104	253	31	*.920
1995— Greenville (Sou.)	3B	127	444	75	116	27	3	14	58	.261	40	109	12	*120	265	26	.937
1996— Richmond (I.L.).........	3B-SS-DH	124	445	49	114	27	0	8	58	.256	32	114	15	116	228	24	.935
1997— Richmond (I.L.).........	SS-DH	100	357	47	88	10	2	12	47	.246	44	109	6	161	297	*23	.952
1998— Tampa Bay (A.L.)■.....	3-DH-S-2	117	370	44	102	15	3	11	55	.276	34	110	5	89	203	13	.957

Year Team (League)	Pos.	G	AB	R	H	2B	3B	HR	RBI	Avg.	BB	SO	SB	PO	A	E	Avg.
						BATTING								FIELDING			
1999—Tampa Bay (A.L.)........	3B-2B	68	199	18	36	4	1	3	19	.181	16	64	4	48	132	11	.942
—Durham (I.L.)........	3B-SS	57	225	52	75	15	3	14	47	.333	27	61	13	46	126	10	.945
Major League totals (2 years)		185	569	62	138	19	4	14	74	.243	50	174	9	137	335	24	.952

SMOLTZ, JOHN — P — BRAVES

PERSONAL: Born May 15, 1967, in Warren, Mich. ... 6-3/220. ... Throws right, bats right. ... Full name: John Andrew Smoltz.

HIGH SCHOOL: Waverly (Lansing, Mich.).

TRANSACTIONS/CAREER NOTES: Selected by Detroit Tigers organization in 22nd round of free-agent draft (June 3, 1985). ... Traded by Tigers to Atlanta Braves for P Doyle Alexander (August 12, 1987). ... On suspended list (June 20-29, 1994). ... Granted free agency (October 31, 1996). ... Re-signed by Braves (November 20, 1996). ... On Atlanta disabled list (March 29-April 15, and May 24-June 20, 1998); included rehabilitation assignments to Greenville (April 2-10 and June 10-14) and Macon (April 10-14 and June 14-16). ... On Atlanta disabled list (May 17-June 1 and July 5-24, 1999); included rehabilitation assignment to Greenville (July 15-18).

RECORDS: Shares major league record for most home runs allowed in one inning—4 (June 19, 1994, first inning).

HONORS: Named N.L. Pitcher of the Year by THE SPORTING NEWS (1996). ... Named righthanded pitcher on THE SPORTING NEWS N.L. All-Star team (1996). ... Named N.L. Cy Young Award winner by Baseball Writers' Association of America (1996). ... Named pitcher on THE SPORTING NEWS N.L. Silver Slugger team (1997).

STATISTICAL NOTES: Tied for Florida State League lead with six balks in 1986. ... Led N.L. with 14 wild pitches in 1990, 20 in 1991 and 17 in 1992. ... Struck out 15 batters in one game (May 24, 1992). ... Pitched 3-0 one-hit, complete-game victory against Cincinnati (May 28, 1995).

MISCELLANEOUS: Appeared in three games as pinch runner and struck out in only appearance in pinch hitter (1989). ... Appeared in four games as pinch runner (1990). ... Appeared in two games as pinch runner (1991). ... Struck out in only appearance as pinch hitter (1992). ... Appeared in one game as pinch runner (1997).

Year League	W	L	Pct.	ERA	G	GS	CG	ShO	Sv.	IP	H	R	ER	BB	SO
1986—Lakeland (FSL).................	7	8	.467	3.56	17	14	2	1	0	96	86	44	38	31	47
1987—Glens Falls (East.)............	4	10	.286	5.68	21	21	0	0	0	130	131	89	82	81	86
—Richmond (I.L.)■............	0	1	.000	6.19	3	3	0	0	0	16	17	11	11	11	5
1988—Richmond (I.L.)...............	10	5	.667	2.79	20	20	3	0	0	135 1/3	118	49	42	37	115
—Atlanta (N.L.)...............	2	7	.222	5.48	12	12	0	0	0	64	74	40	39	33	37
1989—Atlanta (N.L.)...............	12	11	.522	2.94	29	29	5	0	0	208	160	79	68	72	168
1990—Atlanta (N.L.)...............	14	11	.560	3.85	34	34	6	2	0	231 1/3	206	109	99	*90	170
1991—Atlanta (N.L.)...............	14	13	.519	3.80	36	36	5	0	0	229 2/3	206	101	97	77	148
1992—Atlanta (N.L.)...............	15	12	.556	2.85	35	•35	9	3	0	246 2/3	206	90	78	80	*215
1993—Atlanta (N.L.)...............	15	11	.577	3.62	35	35	3	1	0	243 2/3	208	104	98	100	208
1994—Atlanta (N.L.)...............	6	10	.375	4.14	21	21	1	0	0	134 2/3	120	69	62	48	113
1995—Atlanta (N.L.)...............	12	7	.632	3.18	29	29	2	1	0	192 2/3	166	76	68	72	193
1996—Atlanta (N.L.)...............	*24	8	*.750	2.94	35	35	6	2	0	*253 2/3	199	93	83	55	*276
1997—Atlanta (N.L.)...............	15	12	.556	3.02	35	•35	7	2	0	*256	*234	97	86	63	241
1998—Greenville (Sou.).............	0	1	.000	2.57	3	3	0	0	0	14	11	4	4	3	16
—Macon (SAL).................	0	0	...	3.60	2	2	0	0	0	10	7	4	4	1	14
—Atlanta (N.L.)...............	17	3	*.850	2.90	26	26	2	2	0	167 2/3	145	58	54	44	173
1999—Atlanta (N.L.)...............	11	8	.579	3.19	29	29	1	1	0	186 1/3	168	70	66	40	156
—Greenville (Sou.).............	0	0	...	4.50	2	1	0	0	0	4	5	2	2	1	7
Major League totals (13 years).....	157	113	.581	3.35	356	356	47	14	0	2414 1/3	2092	986	898	774	2098

DIVISION SERIES RECORD

RECORDS: Holds N.L. single-game record for most strikeouts—11 (October 3, 1997). ... Holds N.L. career record for most strikeouts—33. ... Shares career record for most wins—4. ... Shares N.L. career record for most earned runs allowed—12.

Year League	W	L	Pct.	ERA	G	GS	CG	ShO	Sv.	IP	H	R	ER	BB	SO
1995—Atlanta (N.L.)...............	0	0	...	7.94	1	1	0	0	0	5 2/3	5	5	5	1	6
1996—Atlanta (N.L.)...............	1	0	1.000	1.00	1	1	0	0	0	9	4	1	1	2	7
1997—Atlanta (N.L.)...............	1	0	1.000	1.00	1	1	0	0	0	9	3	1	1	1	11
1998—Atlanta (N.L.)...............	1	0	1.000	1.17	1	1	0	0	0	7 2/3	5	1	1	0	6
1999—Atlanta (N.L.)...............	1	0	1.000	5.14	1	1	0	0	0	7	6	4	4	3	3
Division series totals (5 years)	4	0	1.000	2.82	5	5	1	0	0	38 1/3	23	12	12	7	33

CHAMPIONSHIP SERIES RECORD

RECORDS: Holds career record for most innings pitched—92 1/3; most strikeouts—88; and most bases on balls allowed—34. ... Shares career records for most games started—13; and hits allowed—81. ... Holds N.L. career record for most wins—6; and home runs allowed—8.

NOTES: Named Most Valuable Player (1992).

Year League	W	L	Pct.	ERA	G	GS	CG	ShO	Sv.	IP	H	R	ER	BB	SO
1991—Atlanta (N.L.)...............	2	0	1.000	1.76	2	2	1	1	0	15 1/3	14	3	3	3	15
1992—Atlanta (N.L.)...............	2	0	1.000	2.66	3	3	0	0	0	20 1/3	14	7	6	10	19
1993—Atlanta (N.L.)...............	0	1	.000	0.00	1	1	0	0	0	6 1/3	8	2	0	5	10
1995—Atlanta (N.L.)...............	0	0	...	2.57	1	1	0	0	0	7	7	2	2	2	7
1996—Atlanta (N.L.)...............	2	0	1.000	1.20	2	2	0	0	0	15	12	2	2	3	12
1997—Atlanta (N.L.)...............	0	1	.000	7.50	1	1	0	0	0	6	5	5	5	5	9
1998—Atlanta (N.L.)...............	0	0	...	3.95	2	2	0	0	0	13 2/3	13	6	6	6	13
1999—Atlanta (N.L.)...............	0	0	...	6.23	3	1	0	0	1	8 2/3	8	6	6	0	8
Champ. series totals (8 years)	6	2	.750	2.92	15	13	1	1	1	92 1/3	81	33	30	34	88

WORLD SERIES RECORD

NOTES: Appeared in one game as pinch runner (1992). ... Member of World Series championship team (1995).

Year League	W	L	Pct.	ERA	G	GS	CG	ShO	Sv.	IP	H	R	ER	BB	SO
1991—Atlanta (N.L.)...............	0	0	...	1.26	2	2	0	0	0	14 1/3	13	2	2	1	11
1992—Atlanta (N.L.)...............	1	0	1.000	2.70	2	2	0	0	0	13 1/3	13	5	4	7	12
1995—Atlanta (N.L.)...............	0	0	...	15.43	1	1	0	0	0	2 1/3	6	4	4	2	4
1996—Atlanta (N.L.)...............	1	1	.500	0.64	2	2	0	0	0	14	6	2	1	8	14
1999—Atlanta (N.L.)...............	0	1	.000	3.86	1	1	0	0	0	7	6	3	3	3	11
World Series totals (5 years)	2	2	.500	2.47	8	8	0	0	0	51	44	16	14	21	52

S

RECORDS: Shares single-game record for most wild pitches—2 (July 13, 1993). ... Shares single-inning record for most wild pitches—2 (July 13, 1993, sixth inning).

Year League	W	L	Pct.	ERA	GS	CG	ShO	Sv.	IP	H	R	ER	BB	SO
1989— National	0	1	.000	9.00	0	0	0	0	1	2	1	1	0	0
1992— National	0	0	...	0.00	0	0	0	0	1/3	1	0	0	0	0
1993— National	0	0	...	0.00	0	0	0	0	1/3	0	0	0	1	0
1996— National	1	0	1.000	0.00	1	0	0	0	2	2	0	0	0	1
All-Star Game totals (4 years)	1	1	.500	2.45	1	0	0	0	3 2/3	5	1	1	1	1

SNEED, JOHN — P — BLUE JAYS

PERSONAL: Born June 30, 1976, in Houston. ... 6-6/250. ... Throws right, bats left. ... Full name: John Andrew Sneed.
HIGH SCHOOL: Westfield (Houston).
COLLEGE: Texas A&M.
TRANSACTIONS/CAREER NOTES: Selected by Toronto Blue Jays organization in 22nd round of free-agent draft (June 3, 1997).

Year League	W	L	Pct.	ERA	G	GS	CG	ShO	Sv.	IP	H	R	ER	BB	SO
1997— Medicine Hat (Pio.)	6	1	*.857	*1.29	15	10	2	0	0	69 2/3	42	19	10	20	79
1998— Hagerstown (SAL)	*16	2	*.889	2.56	27	27	2	1	0	161 2/3	123	59	46	58	210
1999— Dunedin (FSL)	11	2	*.846	3.45	21	20	0	0	0	125 1/3	107	53	48	36	143
— Knoxville (Sou.)	3	1	.750	5.08	6	6	0	0	0	28 1/3	33	17	16	21	28

SNOW, J.T. — 1B — GIANTS

PERSONAL: Born February 26, 1968, in Long Beach, Calif. ... 6-2/205. ... Bats left, throws left. ... Full name: Jack Thomas Snow Jr. ... Son of Jack Snow, wide receiver with Los Angeles Rams (1965-75).
HIGH SCHOOL: Los Alamitos (Calif.).
COLLEGE: Arizona.
TRANSACTIONS/CAREER NOTES: Selected by New York Yankees organization in fifth round of free-agent draft (June 5, 1989). ... Traded by Yankees with P Jerry Nielsen and P Russ Springer to California Angels for P Jim Abbott (December 6, 1992). ... Traded by Angels to San Francisco Giants for P Allen Watson and P Fausto Macey (November 27, 1996).
HONORS: Named International League Most Valuable Player (1992). ... Won A.L. Gold Glove at first base (1995-96). ... Won N.L. Gold Glove at first base (1997-99).
STATISTICAL NOTES: Led New York-Pennsylvania League first basemen with 649 total chances in 1989. ... Led Carolina League in grounding into double plays with 20 in 1990. ... Led Carolina League first basemen with 1,298 total chances and 120 double plays in 1990. ... Tied for Eastern League lead with 10 sacrifice flies in 1991. ... Led Eastern League first basemen with 1,200 total chances in 1991. ... Led International League with 11 intentional bases on balls received in 1992. ... Led International League first basemen with .995 fielding percentage, 1,097 putouts, 93 assists, 1,196 total chances and 107 double plays in 1992. ... Switch-hit home runs in one game (June 9, 1996). ... Career major league grand slams: 5.

Year Team (League)	Pos.	G	AB	R	H	2B	3B	HR	RBI	Avg.	BB	SO	SB	PO	A	E	Avg.
1989— Oneonta (NY-P)	1B	73	274	41	80	18	2	8	51	.292	29	35	4	*590	53	6	*.991
1990— Prince Will. (Caro.)	1B	*138	520	57	133	25	1	8	72	.256	46	65	2	*1208	*78	12	.991
1991— Alb./Colonie (East.)	1B	132	477	78	133	33	3	13	76	.279	67	78	5	*1102	90	8	.993
1992— Columbus (I.L.)	1B-OF	135	492	81	154	26	4	15	78	•.313	70	65	3	†1103	†93	8	†.993
— New York (A.L.)	1B-DH	7	14	1	2	1	0	0	2	.143	5	5	0	43	2	0	1.000
1993— California (A.L.)■	1B	129	419	60	101	18	2	16	57	.241	55	88	3	1010	81	6	.995
— Vancouver (PCL)	1B	23	94	19	32	9	1	5	24	.340	10	13	0	200	13	2	.991
1994— Vancouver (PCL)	1B-DH	53	189	35	56	13	2	8	43	.296	22	32	1	413	42	1	.998
— California (A.L.)	1B	61	223	22	49	4	0	8	30	.220	19	48	0	489	37	2	.996
1995— California (A.L.)	1B	143	544	80	157	22	1	24	102	.289	52	91	2	1161	57	4	.997
1996— California (A.L.)	1B	155	575	69	148	20	1	17	67	.257	56	96	1	1274	103	10	.993
1997— San Fran. (N.L.)■	1B	157	531	81	149	36	1	28	104	.281	96	124	6	1308	108	7	.995
1998— San Francisco (N.L.)	1B	138	435	65	108	29	1	15	79	.248	58	84	1	1040	94	1	*.999
1999— San Francisco (N.L.)	1B	161	570	93	156	25	2	24	98	.274	86	121	0	1221	122	6	.996
American League totals (5 years)		495	1775	232	457	65	4	65	258	.257	187	328	6	3977	280	22	.995
National League totals (3 years)		456	1536	239	413	90	4	67	281	.269	240	329	7	3569	324	14	.996
Major League totals (8 years)		951	3311	471	870	155	8	132	539	.263	427	657	13	7546	604	36	.996

DIVISION SERIES RECORD

Year Team (League)	Pos.	G	AB	R	H	2B	3B	HR	RBI	Avg.	BB	SO	SB	PO	A	E	Avg.
1997— San Francisco (N.L.)	1B	3	6	0	1	0	0	0	0	.167	1	1	0	12	0	0	1.000

SNYDER, JOHN — P — BREWERS

PERSONAL: Born August 16, 1974, in Southfield, Mich. ... 6-3/200. ... Throws right, bats right. ... Full name: John Michael Snyder.
HIGH SCHOOL: Westlake (Westlake Village, Calif.).
TRANSACTIONS/CAREER NOTES: Selected by California Angels organization in 13th round of free-agent draft (June 1, 1992). ... Traded by Angels with P Andrew Lorraine, P Bill Simas and OF McKay Christensen to Chicago White Sox for P Jim Abbott and P Tim Fortugno (July 27, 1995). ... On disabled list (July 21, 1996-remainder of season). ... On disabled list (April 3-May 4, 1997). ... Traded by White Sox with P Jaime Navarro to Milwaukee Brewers for P Cal Eldred and SS Jose Valentin (January 12, 2000).

Year League	W	L	Pct.	ERA	G	GS	CG	ShO	Sv.	IP	H	R	ER	BB	SO
1992— Arizona Angels (Ariz.)	2	4	.333	3.27	15	0	0	0	3	44	40	27	16	16	38
1993— Cedar Rapids (Midw.)	5	6	.455	5.91	21	16	1	1	0	99	125	88	65	59	79
1994— Lake Elsinore (Calif.)	10	11	.476	4.47	26	26	2	0	0	159	181	101	79	56	108
1995— Midland (Texas)	8	9	.471	5.74	21	21	0	0	0	133 1/3	158	93	85	48	81
— Birmingham (Sou.)■	1	0	1.000	6.64	5	4	0	0	0	20 1/3	24	16	15	6	13
1996— Birmingham (Sou.)	3	5	.375	4.83	9	9	0	0	0	54	59	35	29	16	58
— GC White Sox (GCL)	1	0	1.000	1.65	4	4	0	0	0	16 1/3	5	3	3	4	23

Year League	W	L	Pct.	ERA	G	GS	CG	ShO	Sv.	IP	H	R	ER	BB	SO
1997— Birmingham (Sou.)............	7	8	.467	4.64	20	20	2	1	0	114 1/3	130	76	59	43	90
1998— Calgary (PCL)...................	7	3	.700	4.36	15	15	1	0	0	97	112	49	47	34	63
— Chicago (A.L.)....................	7	2	.778	4.80	15	14	1	0	0	86 1/3	96	49	46	23	52
1999— Chicago (A.L.).................	9	12	.429	6.68	25	25	1	0	0	129 1/3	167	103	96	49	67
— Charlotte (I.L.)..................	3	0	1.000	4.24	3	3	0	0	0	17	17	9	8	5	9
Major League totals (2 years)......	16	14	.533	5.93	40	39	2	0	0	215 2/3	263	152	142	72	119

SODOWSKY, CLINT   P

PERSONAL: Born July 13, 1972, in Ponca City, Okla. ... 6-4/200. ... Throws right, bats left. ... Full name: Clint Rea Sodowsky.
HIGH SCHOOL: Ponca City (Okla.).
JUNIOR COLLEGE: Connors State (Okla.).
TRANSACTIONS/CAREER NOTES: Selected by Detroit Tigers organization in ninth round of free-agent draft (June 3, 1991). ... On disabled list (August 29-September 13, 1994). ... On Jacksonville suspended list (May 15-16, 1995). ... Traded by Tigers to Pittsburgh Pirates for P Dan Miceli (November 1, 1996). ... On Pittsburgh disabled list (August 26-September 10, 1997). ... Selected by Arizona Diamondbacks in second round (35th pick overall) of expansion draft (November 18, 1997). ... Traded by Diamondbacks to St. Louis Cardinals for P John Frascatore (March 30, 1999). ... On Memphis disabled list (July 29-September 1, 1999). ... On St. Louis disabled list (September 1, 1999-remainder of season); included rehabilitation assignment to Memphis (September 1-7). ... Granted free agency (October 15, 1999).
MISCELLANEOUS: Appeared in one game as pinch runner with Arizona (1998).

Year League	W	L	Pct.	ERA	G	GS	CG	ShO	Sv.	IP	H	R	ER	BB	SO
1991— Bristol (Appl.).....................	0	5	.000	3.76	14	8	0	0	0	55	49	34	23	34	44
1992— Bristol (Appl.)....................	2	2	.500	3.54	15	6	0	0	0	56	46	35	22	29	48
1993— Fayetteville (SAL)	14	10	.583	5.09	27	27	1	0	0	155 2/3	177	101	88	51	80
1994— Lakeland (FSL)	6	3	.667	3.83	19	18	1	1	0	110 1/3	111	58	47	34	73
1995— Jacksonville (Sou.).............	5	5	.500	2.55	19	19	5	•3	0	123 2/3	102	46	35	50	77
— Toledo (I.L.).....................	5	1	.833	2.85	9	9	1	0	0	60	47	21	19	30	32
— Detroit (A.L.)...................	2	2	.500	5.01	6	6	0	0	0	23 1/3	24	15	13	18	14
1996— Detroit (A.L.)....................	1	3	.250	11.84	7	7	0	0	0	24 1/3	40	34	32	20	9
— Toledo (I.L.).....................	6	8	.429	3.94	19	19	1	0	0	118 2/3	128	67	52	51	59
1997— Calgary (PCL)■.................	0	1	.000	6.59	8	0	0	0	1	13 2/3	19	10	10	6	9
— Pittsburgh (N.L.)...............	2	2	.500	3.63	45	0	0	0	0	52	49	22	21	34	51
1998— Arizona (N.L.)■................	3	6	.333	5.68	45	6	0	0	0	77 2/3	86	56	49	39	42
— Tucson (PCL)	0	1	.000	3.86	2	2	0	0	0	9 1/3	11	4	4	3	7
1999— Memphis (PCL)■...............	4	5	.444	4.82	19	13	2	1	3	80 1/3	85	55	43	32	52
— St. Louis (N.L.)..................	0	1	.000	15.63	3	1	0	0	0	6 1/3	15	11	11	6	2
A.L. totals (2 years)	3	5	.375	8.50	13	13	0	0	0	47 2/3	64	49	45	38	23
N.L. totals (3 years)	5	9	.357	5.36	93	7	0	0	0	136	150	89	81	79	95
Major League totals (5 years).......	8	14	.364	6.17	106	20	0	0	0	183 2/3	214	138	126	117	118

SOJO, LUIS   IF   PIRATES

PERSONAL: Born January 3, 1966, in Barquisimeto, Venezuela. ... 5-11/175. ... Bats right, throws right. ... Name pronounced SO-ho.
TRANSACTIONS/CAREER NOTES: Signed as non-drafted free agent by Toronto Blue Jays organization (January 3, 1986). ... Traded by Blue Jays with OF Junior Felix and a player to be named later to California Angels for OF Devon White, P Willie Fraser and a player to be named later (December 2, 1990); Blue Jays acquired P Marcus Moore and Angels acquired C Ken Rivers to complete deal (December 4, 1990). ... Traded by Angels to Blue Jays for 3B Kelly Gruber and cash (December 8, 1992). ... On Toronto disabled list (May 10-30, 1993). ... Granted free agency (October 15, 1993). ... Signed by Seattle Mariners organization (January 10, 1994). ... On Seattle disabled list (June 7-23, 1995); included rehabilitation assignment to Tacoma (June 19-23). ... Claimed on waivers by New York Yankees (August 22, 1996). ... Granted free agency (December 20, 1996). ... Re-signed by Yankees (January 9, 1997). ... On disabled list (August 15, 1997-remainder of season). ... Granted free agency (October 31, 1997). ... Re-signed by Yankees (November 12, 1997). ... On New York disabled list (March 22-April 27, 1998); included rehabilitation assignments to Tampa (April 17-20) and Columbus (April 20-27). ... Granted free agency (November 10, 1999). ... Signed by Pittsburgh Pirates organization (January 19, 2000).
STATISTICAL NOTES: Led International League shortstops with .957 fielding percentage in 1989. ... Led International League with nine sacrifice flies in 1990. ... Led A.L. with 19 sacrifice hits in 1991. ... Career major league grand slams: 1.

Year Team (League)	Pos.	G	AB	R	H	2B	3B	HR	RBI	Avg.	BB	SO	SB	PO	A	E	Avg.
1986—					Dominican Summer League statistics unavailable.												
1987— Myrtle Beach (SAL) SS-2B-3B-OF		72	223	23	47	5	4	2	15	.211	17	18	5	104	123	14	.942
1988— Myrtle Beach (SAL)	SS	135	*536	83	*155	22	5	5	56	.289	35	35	14	191	407	28	.955
1989— Syracuse (I.L.)............	SS-2B	121	482	54	133	20	5	3	54	.276	21	42	9	170	348	23	†.957
1990— Syracuse (I.L.)............	2B-SS	75	297	39	88	12	3	6	25	.296	14	23	10	138	212	10	.972
— Toronto (A.L.)............	2-S-O-3-DH	33	80	14	18	3	0	1	9	.225	5	5	1	34	31	5	.929
1991— California (A.L.)....2-S-3-O-DH		113	364	38	94	14	1	3	20	.258	14	26	4	233	335	11	.981
1992— Edmonton (PCL)	3B-2B-SS	37	145	22	43	9	1	1	24	.297	9	17	4	32	106	4	.972
— California (A.L.)......	2B-3B-SS	106	368	37	100	12	3	7	43	.272	14	24	7	196	293	9	.982
1993— Toronto (A.L.)■........	SS-2B-3B	19	47	5	8	2	0	0	6	.170	4	2	0	24	35	2	.967
— Syracuse (I.L.)........	2-O-D-3-S-1	43	142	17	31	7	2	1	12	.218	8	12	2	46	60	4	.964
1994— Calgary (PCL)■........	SS-2B-DH	24	102	19	33	9	3	1	18	.324	10	7	5	36	81	2	.983
— Seattle (A.L.)...........2B-SS-DH-3B		63	213	32	59	9	2	6	22	.277	8	25	2	97	186	7	.976
1995— Seattle (A.L.)............	SS-2B-OF	102	339	50	98	18	2	7	39	.289	23	19	4	141	221	9	.976
— Tacoma (PCL)	2B-DH-SS	4	17	1	3	0	0	1	1	.176	0	2	0	4	9	0	1.000
1996— Seattle (A.L.)............	3B-2B-SS	77	247	20	52	8	1	1	16	.211	10	13	2	97	158	8	.970
— New York (A.L.)■......	2B-SS-3B	18	40	3	11	2	0	0	5	.275	1	4	0	16	37	0	1.000
1997— New York (A.L.)........2B-SS-3B-1B		77	215	27	66	6	1	2	25	.307	16	14	3	131	153	5	.983
1998— Tampa (FSL).............		3	9	1	2	0	0	0	2	.222	2	0	0	4	8	1	.923
— Columbus (I.L.)	SS-DH-2B	6	23	1	5	2	0	0	2	.217	1	1	1	9	16	1	.962
— New York (A.L.)........S-1-2-3-DH		54	147	16	34	3	1	0	14	.231	4	15	1	146	74	3	.987
1999— New York (A.L.)........3-2-S-1-DH		49	127	20	32	6	0	2	16	.252	4	17	1	65	72	2	.986
Major League totals (10 years)		711	2187	262	572	83	11	29	215	.262	103	164	25	1180	1595	61	.978

RECORDS: Shares single-game record for most at-bats—7 (October 4, 1995).

Year Team (League)	Pos.	G	AB	R	H	2B	3B	HR	RBI	Avg.	BB	SO	SB	PO	A	E	Avg.
1995— Seattle (A.L.)	SS	5	20	0	5	0	0	0	3	.250	0	3	0	9	15	1	.960
1996— New York (A.L.)	2B	2	0	0	0	0	0	0	0	...	0	0	0	1	1	0	1.000
1998— New York (A.L.)						Did not play.											
1999— New York (A.L.)						Did not play.											
Division series totals (3 years)		7	20	0	5	0	0	0	3	.250	0	3	0	10	16	1	.963

CHAMPIONSHIP SERIES RECORD

Year Team (League)	Pos.	G	AB	R	H	2B	3B	HR	RBI	Avg.	BB	SO	SB	PO	A	E	Avg.
1995— Seattle (A.L.)	SS	6	20	0	5	2	0	0	1	.250	0	2	0	9	18	1	.964
1996— New York (A.L.)	2B	3	5	0	1	0	0	0	0	.200	0	1	0	4	4	0	1.000
1998— New York (A.L.)	1B	1	0	0	0	0	0	0	0	...	0	0	0	1	1	0	1.000
1999— New York (A.L.)	PH-2B	2	1	0	0	0	0	0	0	.000	0	0	0	1	1	0	1.000
Championship series totals (4 years)		12	26	0	6	2	0	0	1	.231	0	3	0	15	24	1	.975

WORLD SERIES RECORD

NOTES: Member of World Series championship team (1996, 1998 and 1999).

Year Team (League)	Pos.	G	AB	R	H	2B	3B	HR	RBI	Avg.	BB	SO	SB	PO	A	E	Avg.
1996— New York (A.L.)	PH-2B	5	5	0	3	1	0	0	1	.600	0	0	0	5	2	0	1.000
1998— New York (A.L.)						Did not play.											
1999— New York (A.L.)	2B	1	0	0	0	0	0	0	0	...	0	0	0	1	1	0	1.000
World Series totals (2 years)		6	5	0	3	1	0	0	1	.600	0	0	0	6	3	0	1.000

S

SORIANO, ALFONSO　　SS　　YANKEES

PERSONAL: Born January 7, 1978, in San Pedro de Macoris, Dominican Republic. ... 6-1/160. ... Bats right, throws right.
HIGH SCHOOL: Eugenio Mariade Osto (Dominican Republic).
TRANSACTIONS/CAREER NOTES: Signed by Hiroshima Toyo Carp of Japan Central League (November 1994). ... Played in Toyo Carp organization (1995-97). ... Retired from Japan Central League and declared free agent by Major League Baseball (1998). ... Signed by New York Yankees (September 29, 1998). ... On Norwich disabled list (July 15-August 15, 1999).

Year Team (League)	Pos.	G	AB	R	H	2B	3B	HR	RBI	Avg.	BB	SO	SB	PO	A	E	Avg.
1995—					Japan minor league statistics unavailable.												
1996—					Japan minor league statistics unavailable.												
1997— Hiroshima (Jap. Cen.)	OF	9	17	2	2	0	0	0	0	.118	2	4	0	...	...	...	...
1998—					Out of organized baseball.												
1999— Norwich (East.)■	SS-DH	89	361	57	110	20	3	15	68	.305	32	67	24	160	243	27	.937
— GC Yankees (GCL)	SS-DH	5	19	7	5	2	0	1	5	.263	1	3	0	2	11	1	.929
— Columbus (I.L.)	SS-3B-2B	20	82	8	15	5	1	2	11	.183	5	18	1	19	44	3	.955
— New York (A.L.)	DH-SS	9	8	2	1	0	0	1	1	.125	0	3	0	0	1	1	.500
Major League totals (1 year)		9	8	2	1	0	0	1	1	.125	0	3	0	0	1	1	.500

SORRENTO, PAUL　　1B/OF

PERSONAL: Born November 17, 1965, in Somerville, Mass. ... 6-2/220. ... Bats left, throws right. ... Full name: Paul Anthony Sorrento.
HIGH SCHOOL: St. John's Preparatory (Danvers, Mass.).
COLLEGE: Florida State.
TRANSACTIONS/CAREER NOTES: Selected by California Angels organization in fourth round of free-agent draft (June 2, 1986). ... Traded by Angels with P Mike Cook and P Rob Wassenaar to Minnesota Twins for P Bert Blyleven and P Kevin Trudeau (November 3, 1988). ... Traded by Twins to Cleveland Indians for P Oscar Munoz and P Curt Leskanic (March 28, 1992). ... Granted free agency (December 21, 1995). ... Signed by Seattle Mariners (January 3, 1996). ... Granted free agency (October 27, 1997). ... Signed by Tampa Bay Devil Rays (December 8, 1997). ... On disabled list (April 8-23, 1999). ... Granted free agency (November 1, 1999).
STATISTICAL NOTES: Led Southern League first basemen with 103 double plays in 1989. ... Led Pacific Coast League first basemen with 14 errors in 1991. ... Career major league grand slams: 9.

Year Team (League)	Pos.	G	AB	R	H	2B	3B	HR	RBI	Avg.	BB	SO	SB	PO	A	E	Avg.
1986— Quad Cities (Midw.)	OF	53	177	33	63	11	2	6	34	.356	24	40	0	83	7	1	.989
— Palm Springs (Calif.)	OF	16	62	5	15	3	0	1	7	.242	4	15	0	16	1	1	.944
1987— Palm Springs (Calif.)	OF	114	370	66	83	14	2	8	45	.224	78	95	1	123	10	4	.971
1988— Palm Springs (Calif.)	1B-OF	133	465	91	133	30	6	14	99	.286	110	101	3	719	55	18	.977
1989— Orlando (Sou.)■	1B	140	509	81	130	*35	2	27	*112	.255	84	119	1	1070	41	*24	.979
— Minnesota (A.L.)	1B-DH	14	21	2	5	0	0	0	1	.238	5	4	0	13	0	0	1.000
1990— Portland (PCL)	1B-OF	102	354	59	107	27	1	19	72	.302	64	95	3	695	52	13	.983
— Minnesota (A.L.)	DH-1B	41	121	11	25	4	1	5	13	.207	12	31	1	118	7	1	.992
1991— Portland (PCL)	1B-OF	113	409	59	126	30	2	13	79	.308	62	65	1	933	58	†14	.986
— Minnesota (A.L.)	1B-DH	26	47	6	12	2	0	4	13	.255	4	11	0	70	7	0	1.000
1992— Cleveland (A.L.)■	1B-DH	140	458	52	123	24	1	18	60	.269	51	89	0	996	78	8	.993
1993— Cleveland (A.L.)	1B-DH	148	463	75	119	26	1	18	65	.257	58	121	3	1015	86	6	.995
1994— Cleveland (A.L.)	1B-DH	95	322	43	90	14	0	14	62	.280	34	68	0	798	59	4	.995
1995— Cleveland (A.L.)	1B-DH	104	323	50	76	14	0	25	79	.235	51	71	1	816	58	7	.992
1996— Seattle (A.L.)■	1B	143	471	67	136	32	1	23	93	.289	57	103	0	957	81	11	.990
1997— Seattle (A.L.)	1B-DH	146	457	68	123	19	0	31	80	.269	51	112	0	929	86	4	.996
1998— Tampa Bay (A.L.)■	DH-1B-OF	137	435	40	98	27	0	17	57	.225	54	133	2	249	24	0	1.000
1999— Tampa Bay (A.L.)	OF-1B-DH	99	294	40	69	14	1	11	42	.235	49	101	1	290	11	5	.984
Major League totals (11 years)		1093	3412	454	876	176	5	166	565	.257	426	844	8	6251	497	46	.993

DIVISION SERIES RECORD

						BATTING								FIELDING		
Year	Team (League)	Pos.	G	AB	R	H	2B	3B	HR	RBI	Avg.	BB	SO	SB	PO	A	E	Avg.
1995—Cleveland (A.L.).........	1B	3	10	2	3	0	0	0	1	.300	2	3	0	27	5	2	.941
1997—Seattle (A.L.)............	1B-PH	4	10	2	3	1	0	1	1	.300	2	3	0	27	4	1	.969
Division series totals (2 years)		7	20	4	6	1	0	1	2	.300	4	6	0	54	9	3	.955

CHAMPIONSHIP SERIES RECORD

						BATTING								FIELDING		
Year	Team (League)	Pos.	G	AB	R	H	2B	3B	HR	RBI	Avg.	BB	SO	SB	PO	A	E	Avg.
1991—Minnesota (A.L.)	PH	1	1	0	0	0	0	0	0	.000	0	1	0	...	...	...	...
1995—Cleveland (A.L.).........	1B	4	13	2	2	1	0	0	0	.154	2	3	0	34	1	2	.946
Championship series totals (2 years)		5	14	2	2	1	0	0	0	.143	2	4	0	34	1	2	.946

WORLD SERIES RECORD

NOTES: Member of World Series championship team (1991).

						BATTING								FIELDING		
Year	Team (League)	Pos.	G	AB	R	H	2B	3B	HR	RBI	Avg.	BB	SO	SB	PO	A	E	Avg.
1991—Minnesota (A.L.)	PH-1B	3	2	0	0	0	0	0	0	.000	1	2	0	1	1	0	1.000
1995—Cleveland (A.L.).........	1B-PH	6	11	0	2	1	0	0	0	.182	0	4	0	19	2	1	.955
World Series totals (2 years)		9	13	0	2	1	0	0	0	.154	1	6	0	20	3	1	.958

SOSA, JUAN — IF — ROCKIES

S

PERSONAL: Born August 19, 1975, in San Francisco de Macoris, Dominican Republic. ... 6-1/175. ... Bats right, throws right. ... Full name: Juan Luis Sosa.

HIGH SCHOOL: Renacimento (Dominican Republic).

TRANSACTIONS/CAREER NOTES: Signed as non-drafted free agent by Los Angeles Dodgers organization (July 24, 1993). ... Selected by Colorado Rockies organization from Dodgers in Rule 5 minor league draft (December 15, 1997).

STATISTICAL NOTES: Led Carolina League shortstops with 555 total chances in 1998. ... Led Southern League shortstops with 191 putouts and .958 fielding percentage in 1999.

						BATTING								FIELDING		
Year	Team (League)	Pos.	G	AB	R	H	2B	3B	HR	RBI	Avg.	BB	SO	SB	PO	A	E	Avg.
1993—Dom. Dodgers (DSL) .	IF	63	237	51	66	7	4	0	39	.278	45	52	8	209	28	16	.937
1994—Dom. Dodgers (DSL) .	2B	59	224	55	65	11	3	6	60	.290	44	27	13	141	168	17	.948
1995—Vero Beach (FSL)	2B-SS	8	27	2	6	1	1	1	6	.222	0	4	0	10	21	1	.969
— Yakima (N'west)	2B-3B-SS	61	217	26	51	10	4	3	16	.235	15	39	4	93	174	16	.943
1996—Savannah (SAL)	2-S-3-O	112	370	58	94	21	2	7	38	.254	30	64	14	139	261	22	.948
1997—Vero Beach (FSL)	SS-2B-3B	92	250	32	55	5	2	5	29	.220	14	39	20	130	193	19	.944
1998—Salem (Caro.)■........	SS	133	529	88	147	20	*12	8	47	.278	43	83	*64	*196	328	31	.944
1999—Carolina (Sou.)...........	SS-OF	125	490	70	135	22	5	7	42	.276	31	65	38	†202	361	24	†.959
— Colo. Springs (PCL)	OF-SS	6	28	3	11	1	1	1	5	.393	0	1	1	15	8	1	.958
— Colorado (N.L.)	OF-SS	11	9	3	2	0	0	0	0	.222	2	2	0	6	3	1	.900
Major League totals (1 year)		11	9	3	2	0	0	0	0	.222	2	2	0	6	3	1	.900

SOSA, SAMMY — OF — CUBS

PERSONAL: Born November 12, 1968, in San Pedro de Macoris, Dominican Repubic. ... 6-0/220. ... Bats right, throws right. ... Full name: Samuel Sosa.

TRANSACTIONS/CAREER NOTES: Signed as non-drafted free agent by Texas Rangers organization (July 30, 1985). ... Traded by Rangers with SS Scott Fletcher and P Wilson Alvarez to Chicago White Sox for OF Harold Baines and IF Fred Manrique (July 29, 1989). ... Traded by White Sox with P Ken Patterson to Chicago Cubs for OF George Bell (March 30, 1992). ... On Chicago disabled list (June 13-July 27, and August 7-September 16, 1992); included rehabilitation assignment to Iowa (July 21-27). ... On disabled list (August 21, 1996-remainder of season).

RECORDS: Holds major league single-season records for most home runs by outfielder—66 (1998); most major league ballparks, one or more home runs—18 (1998); and most at-bats without a triple—643 (1998). ... Holds major league single-month record for most home runs—20 (June 1998). ... Shares major league record for most grand slams in two consecutive games—2 (July 27 and 28, 1998). ... Shares major league single-season record for most times hitting two or more home runs in a game—11 (1998). ... Shares major league single-inning record for most home runs—2 (May 16, 1996, seventh inning). ... Shares N.L. records for most seasons with 50 or more home runs—2; and most consecutive seasons with 50 or more home runs—2 (1998-99).

HONORS: Named outfielder on THE SPORTING NEWS N.L. All-Star team (1995, 1998 and 1999). ... Named outfielder on THE SPORTING NEWS N.L. Silver Slugger team (1995, 1998 and 1999). ... Named co-Sportsman of the Year by THE SPORTING NEWS (1998). ... Named Major League Player of the Year by THE SPORTING NEWS (1998). ... Named N.L. Most Valuable Player by Baseball Writers' Association of America (1998).

STATISTICAL NOTES: Led Gulf Coast League with 96 total bases in 1986. ... Tied for South Atlantic League lead in double plays by outfielder with four in 1987. ... Collected six hits in one game (July 2, 1993). ... Tied for N.L. lead in double plays by outfielder with four in 1995. ... Hit three home runs in one game (June 5, 1996 and June 15, 1999). ... Led N.L. with 416 total bases in 1998. ... Had 18-game hitting streak (May 26-June 15, 1999). ... Led N.L. with 397 total bases in 1999. ... Career major league grand slams: 3.

						BATTING								FIELDING		
Year	Team (League)	Pos.	G	AB	R	H	2B	3B	HR	RBI	Avg.	BB	SO	SB	PO	A	E	Avg.
1986—GC Rangers (GCL)......	OF	61	229	38	63	*19	1	4	28	.275	22	51	11	92	9	•6	.944
1987—Gastonia (SAL)..........	OF	129	519	73	145	27	4	11	59	.279	21	123	22	183	12	17	.920
1988—Charlotte (FSL)..........	OF	131	507	70	116	13	*12	9	51	.229	35	106	42	227	11	7	.971
1989—Tulsa (Texas)	OF	66	273	45	81	15	4	7	31	.297	15	52	16	110	7	4	.967
— Texas (A.L.)	OF-DH	25	84	8	20	3	0	1	3	.238	0	20	0	33	1	2	.944
— Oklahoma City (A.A.)..	OF	10	39	2	4	2	0	0	3	.103	2	8	4	22	0	2	.917
— Vancouver (PCL)	OF	13	49	7	18	3	0	1	5	.367	0	20	0	43	1	0	1.000
— Chicago (A.L.)■..........	OF	33	99	19	27	5	0	3	10	.273	11	27	7	61	1	2	.969
1990—Chicago (A.L.)	OF	153	532	72	124	26	10	15	70	.233	33	150	32	315	14	*13	.962
1991—Chicago (A.L.)	OF-DH	116	316	39	64	10	1	10	33	.203	14	98	13	214	6	6	.973
— Vancouver (PCL)	OF	32	116	19	31	7	2	3	19	.267	17	32	9	95	2	3	.970

- 535 -

- 535 -

Year Team (League)	Pos.	G	AB	R	H	2B	3B	HR	RBI	Avg.	BB	SO	SB	PO	A	E	Avg.
1992—Chicago (N.L.)■	OF	67	262	41	68	7	2	8	25	.260	19	63	15	145	4	6	.961
—Iowa (A.A.)	OF	5	19	3	6	2	0	0	1	.316	1	2	5	14	0	0	1.000
1993—Chicago (N.L.)	OF	159	598	92	156	25	5	33	93	.261	38	135	36	344	17	9	.976
1994—Chicago (N.L.)	OF	105	426	59	128	17	6	25	70	.300	25	92	22	248	5	7	.973
1995—Chicago (N.L.)	OF	•144	564	89	151	17	3	36	119	.268	58	134	34	320	13	*13	.962
1996—Chicago (N.L.)	OF	124	498	84	136	21	2	40	100	.273	34	134	18	253	15	10	.964
1997—Chicago (N.L.)	OF	•162	642	90	161	31	4	36	119	.251	45	*174	22	325	16	8	.977
1998—Chicago (N.L.)	OF	159	643	*134	198	20	0	66	*158	.308	73	*171	18	334	14	9	.975
1999—Chicago (N.L.)	OF	•162	625	114	180	24	2	63	141	.288	78	*171	7	399	8	9	.978
American League totals (3 years)		327	1031	138	235	44	11	29	116	.228	58	295	52	623	22	23	.966
National League totals (8 years)		1082	4258	703	1178	162	24	307	825	.277	370	1074	172	2368	92	71	.972
Major League totals (11 years)		1409	5289	841	1413	206	35	336	941	.267	428	1369	224	2991	114	94	.971

DIVISION SERIES RECORD

Year Team (League)	Pos.	G	AB	R	H	2B	3B	HR	RBI	Avg.	BB	SO	SB	PO	A	E	Avg.
1998—Chicago (N.L.)	OF	3	11	0	2	1	0	0	0	.182	1	4	0	5	0	0	1.000

ALL-STAR GAME RECORD

NOTES: Named to All-Star team for 1998 game; replaced by Bret Boone due to injury.

Year League	Pos.	AB	R	H	2B	3B	HR	RBI	Avg.	BB	SO	SB	PO	A	E	Avg.
1995—National	OF	1	0	0	0	0	0	0	.000	0	0	0	2	0	0	1.000
1998—National							Selected, did not play—injured.									
1999—National	OF	3	0	0	0	0	0	0	.000	0	2	0	1	0	0	1.000
All-Star Game totals (2 years)		4	0	0	0	0	0	0	.000	0	2	0	3	0	0	1.000

S

SPARKS, JEFF   P   DEVIL RAYS

PERSONAL: Born April 4, 1972, in Houston. ... 6-3/220. ... Throws right, bats right. ... Full name: James Jeffrey Sparks.
HIGH SCHOOL: Waller (Texas).
COLLEGE: St. Mary's (Texas).
TRANSACTIONS/CAREER NOTES: Selected by Cincinnati Reds organization in 24th round of free-agent draft (June 1, 1995). ... Released by Reds (July 25, 1997). ... Signed by Winnipeg, Northern League (August 1997). ... Signed by Colorado Rockies organization (February 18, 1998). ... Released by Rockies (April 4, 1998). ... Signed by Winnipeg (May 1998). ... Signed by Pittsburgh Pirates organization (January 6, 1999). ... Traded by Pirates with OF Jose Guillen to Tampa Bay Devil Rays for C Joe Oliver and C Humberto Cota (July 23, 1999).

Year League	W	L	Pct.	ERA	G	GS	CG	ShO	Sv.	IP	H	R	ER	BB	SO
1995—Princeton (Appl.)	2	0	1.000	3.23	16	2	0	0	2	39	32	19	14	27	49
1996—Charleston, W.Va. (SAL)	2	7	.222	4.74	46	3	0	0	0	89 1/3	79	51	47	46	94
—Chattanooga (Sou.)	0	0	...	4.50	3	0	0	0	0	2	5	1	1	1	2
1997—Burlington (Midw.)	2	5	.286	5.72	22	9	0	0	0	61 1/3	61	49	39	39	72
—Winnipeg (Nor.)■	1	1	.500	4.15	7	0	0	0	0	13	11	8	6	10	20
1998—Winnipeg (Nor.)	2	1	.667	3.12	38	0	0	0	17	49	30	21	17	42	85
1999—Nashville (PCL)■	5	3	.625	3.83	34	0	0	0	0	49 1/3	37	25	21	23	69
—Durham (I.L.)■	3	0	1.000	3.38	18	0	0	0	0	24	16	11	9	14	31
—Tampa Bay (A.L.)	0	0	...	5.40	8	0	0	0	1	10	6	6	6	12	17
Major League totals (1 year)	0	0	...	5.40	8	0	0	0	1	10	6	6	6	12	17

SPARKS, STEVE   P   ANGELS

PERSONAL: Born July 2, 1965, in Tulsa, Okla. ... 6-0/180. ... Throws right, bats right. ... Full name: Steven William Sparks.
HIGH SCHOOL: Holland Hall (Tulsa, Okla.).
COLLEGE: Sam Houston State.
TRANSACTIONS/CAREER NOTES: Selected by Milwaukee Brewers organization in fifth round of free-agent draft (June 2, 1987). ... On disabled list (March 24, 1997-entire season). ... Granted free agency (October 15, 1997). ... Signed by Anaheim Angels (February 23, 1998). ... On Cedar Rapids disabled list (April 9-19, 1998).
RECORDS: Shares major league single-inning record for most hit batsmen—3 (May 22, 1999, third inning). ... Shares A.L. single-game record for most hit batsmen (nine innings)—4 (May 22, 1999).
MISCELLANEOUS: Appeared in one game as pinch runner (1999).

Year League	W	L	Pct.	ERA	G	GS	CG	ShO	Sv.	IP	H	R	ER	BB	SO
1987—Helena (Pio.)	6	3	.667	4.68	10	9	2	0	0	57 2/3	68	44	30	20	47
1988—Beloit (Midw.)	9	13	.409	3.79	25	24	5	1	0	164	162	80	69	51	96
1989—Stockton (Calif.)	•13	5	.722	2.41	23	22	3	2	0	164	125	55	44	53	126
1990—Stockton (Calif.)	10	7	.588	3.69	19	19	5	1	0	129 1/3	136	63	53	31	77
—El Paso (Texas)	1	2	.333	6.53	7	6	1	0	0	30 1/3	43	24	22	15	17
1991—Stockton (Calif.)	9	10	.474	3.06	24	24	•8	2	0	179 2/3	160	70	61	98	139
—El Paso (Texas)	1	2	.333	9.53	4	4	0	0	0	17	30	22	18	9	10
1992—El Paso (Texas)	9	8	.529	5.37	28	22	3	0	1	140 1/3	159	99	84	50	79
1993—New Orleans (A.A.)	9	13	.409	3.84	29	•28	*7	1	0	*180 1/3	174	89	77	*80	104
1994—New Orleans (A.A.)	10	12	.455	4.46	28	27	5	1	0	*183 2/3	183	101	91	68	105
1995—Milwaukee (A.L.)	9	11	.450	4.63	33	27	3	0	0	202	210	111	104	86	96
1996—Milwaukee (A.L.)	4	7	.364	6.60	20	13	1	0	0	88 2/3	103	66	65	52	21
—New Orleans (A.A.)	2	6	.250	4.99	11	10	3	1	0	57 2/3	64	43	32	35	27
1997—Milwaukee (A.L.)							Did not play.								
1998—Midland (Texas)■	0	4	.000	7.08	7	7	0	0	0	40 2/3	49	38	32	15	34
—Vancouver (PCL)	0	4	.000	2.89	4	4	2	0	0	28	23	11	9	6	19
—Anaheim (A.L.)	9	4	.692	4.34	22	20	0	0	0	128 2/3	130	66	62	58	90
1999—Anaheim (A.L.)	5	11	.313	5.42	28	26	0	0	0	147 2/3	165	101	89	82	73
Major League totals (4 years)	27	33	.450	5.08	103	86	4	0	0	567	608	344	320	278	280

SPEHR, TIM　　　　　　　C

PERSONAL: Born July 2, 1966, in Excelsior Springs, Mo. ... 6-2/200. ... Bats right, throws right. ... Full name: Timothy Joseph Spehr. ... Name pronounced SPEAR.
HIGH SCHOOL: Richfield (Waco, Texas).
JUNIOR COLLEGE: McLennan College (Texas).
COLLEGE: Arizona State.
TRANSACTIONS/CAREER NOTES: Selected by Kansas City Royals organization in fifth round of free-agent draft (June 1, 1988). ... On disabled list (June 25-July 27, 1988). ... On Baseball City disabled list (April 7-May 21, 1989). ... Traded by Royals with P Jeff Shaw to Montreal Expos for P Mark Gardner and P Doug Piatt (December 9, 1992). ... On disabled list (July 31, 1995-remainder of season and August 18-September 6, 1996). ... Granted free agency (October 21, 1996). ... Signed by Pawtucket, Boston Red Sox organization (March 6, 1997). ... Traded by Red Sox to Royals for cash (March 26, 1997). ... Released by Royals (May 27, 1997). ... Signed by Atlanta Braves (June 10, 1997). ... Granted free agency (December 21, 1997). ... Signed by New York Mets organization (January 8, 1998). ... On New York disabled list (May 5-August 28, 1998); included rehabilitation assignment to St. Lucie (August 12-27). ... Traded by Mets to Royals for cash (August 31, 1998). ... Granted free agency (November 2, 1999).
STATISTICAL NOTES: Led American Association catchers with 730 total chances and 14 double plays in 1990. ... Tied for American Association lead in being hit by pitch with 11 in 1992. ... Career major league grand slams: 2.

							BATTING								FIELDING		
Year　Team (League)	Pos.	G	AB	R	H	2B	3B	HR	RBI	Avg.	BB	SO	SB	PO	A	E	Avg.
1988—Appleton (Midw.)........	C	31	110	15	29	3	0	5	22	.264	10	28	3	146	14	7	.958
1989—Baseball City (FSL).....	C	18	64	8	16	5	0	1	7	.250	5	17	1	63	7	1	.986
—Memphis (Sou.)	C	61	216	22	42	9	0	8	23	.194	16	59	1	274	36	5	.984
1990—Omaha (A.A.)..............	C	102	307	42	69	10	2	6	34	.225	41	88	5	*658	67	5	*.993
1991—Omaha (A.A.)..............	C	72	215	27	59	14	2	6	26	.274	25	48	3	402	53	8	.983
—Kansas City (A.L.)	C	37	74	7	14	5	0	3	14	.189	9	18	1	190	19	3	.986
1992—Omaha (A.A.)..............	C	109	336	48	85	22	0	15	42	.253	61	89	4	577	65	7	.989
1993—Montreal (N.L.)■........	C	53	87	14	20	6	0	2	10	.230	6	20	2	166	22	9	.954
—Ottawa (I.L.)	C	46	141	15	28	6	1	4	13	.199	14	35	2	248	24	6	.978
1994—Montreal (N.L.).........	C-OF	52	36	8	9	3	1	0	5	.250	4	11	2	104	6	0	1.000
1995—Montreal (N.L.).........	C	41	35	4	9	5	0	1	3	.257	6	7	0	92	12	1	.990
1996—Montreal (N.L.).........	C-OF	63	44	4	4	1	0	1	3	.091	3	15	1	121	7	2	.985
1997—Kansas City (A.L.)■...	C	17	35	3	6	0	0	1	2	.171	2	12	0	78	7	0	1.000
—Richmond (I.L.)■......	C	36	120	13	23	5	0	3	14	.192	12	37	0	262	36	5	.983
—Atlanta (N.L.)	C	8	14	2	3	1	0	1	4	.214	0	4	1	32	4	2	.947
1998—New York (N.L.)■	C-1B	21	51	3	7	1	0	0	3	.137	7	16	1	120	10	0	1.000
—St. Lucie (FSL)	C-DH	14	38	7	7	2	0	1	6	.184	9	16	0	42	3	1	.978
—Norfolk (I.L.)	PH	1	1	0	1	0	0	0	0	1.000	0	0	0	...	...	...	...
—Kansas City (A.L.)■ ...	C	11	25	5	6	2	0	1	2	.240	8	3	0	62	2	0	1.000
1999—Kansas City (A.L.)	C	60	155	26	32	7	0	9	26	.206	22	47	1	274	11	3	.990
American League totals (4 years)		125	289	41	58	14	0	14	44	.201	41	80	2	604	39	6	.991
National League totals (6 years)		238	267	35	52	17	1	5	28	.195	26	73	7	635	61	14	.980
Major League totals (8 years)		363	556	76	110	31	1	19	72	.198	67	153	9	1239	100	20	.985

SPEIER, JUSTIN　　　　　　P　　　　　　INDIANS

PERSONAL: Born November 6, 1973, in Walnut Creek, Calif. ... 6-4/205. ... Throws right, bats right. ... Full name: Justin James Speier. ... Son of Chris Speier, infielder with five major league teams (1971-89).
HIGH SCHOOL: Brophy College Prep (Phoenix).
COLLEGE: San Francisco, then Nicholls State.
TRANSACTIONS/CAREER NOTES: Selected by Chicago Cubs organization in 55th round of free-agent draft (June 1, 1995). ... Traded by Cubs with 3B Kevin Orie and P Todd Noel to Florida Marlins for P Felix Heredia and P Steve Hoff (July 31, 1998). ... Traded by Marlins to Atlanta Braves for a player to be named (April 1, 1999); Marlins acquired P Matthew Targac to complete deal (June 11, 1999). ... Claimed on waivers by Cleveland Indians (November 23, 1999).

Year　League	W	L	Pct.	ERA	G	GS	CG	ShO	Sv.	IP	H	R	ER	BB	SO
1995—Williamsport (NY-P)	2	1	.667	1.49	30	0	0	0	12	36 1/3	27	6	6	4	39
1996—Daytona (FSL)	2	4	.333	3.76	33	0	0	0	13	38 1/3	32	19	16	19	34
—Orlando (Sou.)	4	1	.800	2.05	24	0	0	0	6	26 1/3	23	7	6	5	14
1997—Orlando (Sou.)	6	5	.545	4.48	50	0	0	0	6	78 1/3	77	46	39	23	63
—Iowa (A.A.)	2	0	1.000	0.00	8	0	0	0	1	12 1/3	5	0	0	1	9
1998—Iowa (PCL)	3	3	.500	5.05	45	0	0	0	12	51 2/3	52	31	29	19	49
—Chicago (N.L.)	0	0	...	13.50	1	0	0	0	0	1 1/3	2	2	2	1	2
—Florida (N.L.)■	0	3	.000	8.38	18	0	0	0	0	19 1/3	25	18	18	12	15
1999—Richmond (I.L.)■...........	2	4	.333	5.62	27	0	0	0	3	41 2/3	51	28	26	22	39
—Atlanta (N.L.)	0	0	...	5.65	19	0	0	0	0	28 2/3	28	18	18	13	22
Major League totals (2 years)	0	3	.000	6.93	38	0	0	0	0	49 1/3	55	38	38	26	39

SPENCER, SEAN　　　　　　P　　　　　　MARINERS

PERSONAL: Born May 29, 1975, in Seattle. ... 5-11/185. ... Throws left, bats left. ... Full name: Sean James Spencer.
HIGH SCHOOL: South Kitsap (Port Orchard, Wash.).
COLLEGE: Washington.
TRANSACTIONS/CAREER NOTES: Selected by Seattle Mariners organization in 40th round of free-agent draft (June 4, 1996). ... On disabled list (June 1996-entire season).

Year　League	W	L	Pct.	ERA	G	GS	CG	ShO	Sv.	IP	H	R	ER	BB	SO
1997—Lancaster (Calif.).................	2	3	.400	1.64	39	0	0	0	18	60 1/3	41	12	11	15	72
1998—Orlando (Sou.)	2	1	.667	2.95	37	0	0	0	*18	42 2/3	33	18	14	18	43
—Tacoma (PCL)	2	0	1.000	4.85	9	0	0	0	1	13	10	7	7	7	16
1999—Tacoma (PCL)	2	1	.667	3.47	44	0	0	0	7	49 1/3	41	21	19	23	53
—Seattle (A.L.)	0	0	...	21.60	2	0	0	0	0	1 2/3	5	4	4	3	2
Major League totals (1 year)	0	0	...	21.60	2	0	0	0	0	1 2/3	5	4	4	3	2

PERSONAL: Born February 20, 1972, in Key West, Fla. ... 5-11/210. ... Bats right, throws right. ... Full name: Michael Shane Spencer.
HIGH SCHOOL: Granite Hills (El Cajon, Calif.).
TRANSACTIONS/CAREER NOTES: Selected by New York Yankees organization in 28th round of free-agent draft (June 4, 1990). ... On disabled list (April 10-May 9, 1994). ... On New York disabled list (July 3-27, 1999); included rehabilitation assignment to Columbus (July 21-27).
RECORDS: Shares major league single-month record for most grand slams—3 (September 1998).
HONORS: Named Florida State League Most Valuable Player (1995).
STATISTICAL NOTES: Led Florida State League with 235 total bases in 1995. ... Career major league grand slams: 3.

| | | | | | | | BATTING | | | | | | | | FIELDING | | |
Year Team (League)	Pos.	G	AB	R	H	2B	3B	HR	RBI	Avg.	BB	SO	SB	PO	A	E	Avg.
1990— GC Yankees (GCL)	OF	42	147	20	27	4	0	0	7	.184	20	23	11	79	3	3	.965
1991— GC Yankees (GCL)	OF	44	160	25	49	7	0	0	30	.306	14	19	9	64	6	3	.959
—Oneonta (NY-P)	OF	18	53	10	13	2	1	0	3	.245	10	9	2	11	0	1	.917
1992— Greensboro (SAL)	OF-P	83	258	43	74	10	2	3	27	.287	33	37	8	135	6	0	1.000
1993— Greensboro (SAL)	OF-P	122	431	89	116	35	2	12	80	.269	52	62	14	138	10	5	.967
1994— Tampa (FSL)	OF	90	334	44	97	22	3	8	53	.290	30	53	5	90	10	4	.962
1995— Tampa (FSL)	OF	•134	500	87	*150	31	3	16	*88	.300	61	60	14	166	6	6	.966
1996— Norwich (East.)	OF-1B-3B	126	450	70	114	19	0	29	89	.253	68	99	4	218	24	3	.988
—Columbus (I.L.)	OF	9	31	7	11	4	0	3	6	.355	5	5	0	25	1	1	.963
1997— Columbus (I.L.)	OF-DH-3B	125	452	78	109	34	4	30	86	.241	71	105	0	189	7	4	.980
1998— New York (A.L.)	OF-DH-1B	27	67	18	25	6	0	10	27	.373	5	12	0	29	2	0	1.000
—Columbus (I.L.)	OF-DH-1B	87	342	66	110	29	1	18	67	.322	41	59	1	225	11	5	.979
1999— New York (A.L.)	OF-DH	71	205	25	48	8	0	8	20	.234	18	51	0	108	5	0	1.000
—Columbus (I.L.)	OF-DH	14	50	17	18	2	0	2	10	.360	9	8	0	23	0	1	.958
Major League totals (2 years)		98	272	43	73	14	0	18	47	.268	23	63	0	137	7	0	1.000

DIVISION SERIES RECORD

| | | | | | | | BATTING | | | | | | | | FIELDING | | |
Year Team (League)	Pos.	G	AB	R	H	2B	3B	HR	RBI	Avg.	BB	SO	SB	PO	A	E	Avg.
1998— New York (A.L.)	OF	2	6	3	3	0	0	2	4	.500	0	1	0	1	0	0	1.000
1999— New York (A.L.)									Did not play.								

CHAMPIONSHIP SERIES RECORD

| | | | | | | | BATTING | | | | | | | | FIELDING | | |
Year Team (League)	Pos.	G	AB	R	H	2B	3B	HR	RBI	Avg.	BB	SO	SB	PO	A	E	Avg.
1998— New York (A.L.)	OF	3	10	1	1	0	0	0	0	.100	1	3	0	7	1	0	1.000
1999— New York (A.L.)	OF	3	9	1	1	0	0	0	0	.111	1	6	0	5	0	0	1.000
Championship series totals (2 years)		6	19	2	2	0	0	0	0	.105	2	9	0	12	1	0	1.000

WORLD SERIES RECORD

NOTES: Member of World Series championship team (1998 and 1999).

| | | | | | | | BATTING | | | | | | | | FIELDING | | |
Year Team (League)	Pos.	G	AB	R	H	2B	3B	HR	RBI	Avg.	BB	SO	SB	PO	A	E	Avg.
1998— New York (A.L.)	OF	1	3	1	1	1	0	0	0	.333	0	2	0	2	1	0	1.000
1999— New York (A.L.)									Did not play.								

RECORD AS PITCHER

Year League	W	L	Pct.	ERA	G	GS	CG	ShO	Sv.	IP	H	R	ER	BB	SO
1992— Greensboro (SAL)	0	0	...	0.00	1	0	0	0	0	1	2	0	0	1	1
1993— Greensboro (SAL)	0	0	...	4.50	2	0	0	0	0	4	5	2	2	2	5

PERSONAL: Born August 7, 1969, in Vancouver, B.C. ... 6-4/205. ... Throws right, bats right. ... Full name: Stanley Roger Spencer.
HIGH SCHOOL: Columbia River (Vancouver, B.C.).
COLLEGE: Stanford.
TRANSACTIONS/CAREER NOTES: Selected by Boston Red Sox organization in 26th round of free-agent draft (June 2, 1987); did not sign. ... Selected by Montreal Expos organization in supplemental round ("sandwich pick" between first and second round, 35th pick overall) of free-agent draft (June 4, 1990); pick received as part of compensation for Los Angeles Dodgers signing Type A free-agent OF Hubie Brooks. ... On disabled list (July 2, 1990-entire season and July 18, 1991-remainder of season). ... On Harrisburg disabled list (April 9, 1992-entire season). ... Selected by Florida Marlins from Expos organization in Rule 5 major league draft (December 7, 1992). ... On disabled list (April 8-June 24, 1993). ... On Portland disabled list (July 9-16, 1994). ... Granted free agency (October 11, 1995). ... Signed by San Diego Padres organization (February 7, 1997). ... On Rancho Cucamonga disabled list (May 9-22, 1997). ... Granted free agency (October 15, 1997). ... Re-signed by Padres organization (December 29, 1997). ... On Las Vegas disabled list (May 16-June 1, 1998; and May 27-July 5, 1999). ... Granted free agency (October 12, 1999). ... Re-signed by Padres organization (November 22, 1999).
HONORS: Named righthanded pitcher on THE SPORTING NEWS college All-America team (1990).
STATISTICAL NOTES: Tied for Eastern League lead with three balks in 1991.

Year League	W	L	Pct.	ERA	G	GS	CG	ShO	Sv.	IP	H	R	ER	BB	SO
1990— W.P. Beach (FSL)						Did not play.									
1991— Harrisburg (East.)	6	1	.857	4.40	17	17	1	0	0	92	90	52	45	30	66
1992— Harrisburg (East.)						Did not play.									
1993— High Desert (Calif.)■	4	4	.500	4.09	13	13	0	0	0	$61\frac{2}{3}$	67	33	28	18	38
1994— Brevard County (FSL)	1	0	1.000	3.15	6	5	0	0	0	20	20	9	7	6	22
—Portland (East.)	9	4	.692	3.48	20	20	1	0	0	124	113	52	48	30	96
1995— Charlotte (I.L.)	1	4	.200	7.84	9	9	0	0	0	$41\frac{1}{3}$	61	37	36	24	19
—Portland (East.)	1	4	.200	7.38	8	8	0	0	0	39	57	39	32	19	32
1996—						Out of organized baseball.									
1997— Rancho Cuca. (Calif.)■	3	1	.750	3.35	7	7	0	0	0	$40\frac{1}{3}$	37	18	15	5	46
—Las Vegas (PCL)	3	2	.600	3.75	8	8	0	0	0	48	48	23	20	18	47

Year	League	W	L	Pct.	ERA	G	GS	CG	ShO	Sv.	IP	H	R	ER	BB	SO
1998—Las Vegas (PCL)		12	6	.667	3.93	22	22	0	0	0	137⅓	120	67	60	42	136
—San Diego (N.L.)		1	0	1.000	4.70	6	5	0	0	0	30⅔	29	16	16	4	31
1999—San Diego (N.L.)		0	7	.000	9.16	9	8	0	0	0	38⅓	56	44	39	11	36
—Las Vegas (PCL)		5	4	.556	5.47	12	10	0	0	0	54⅓	69	35	33	15	50
Major League totals (2 years)		1	7	.125	7.17	15	13	0	0	0	69	85	60	55	15	67

SPIERS, BILL — IF — ASTROS

S

PERSONAL: Born June 5, 1966, in Orangeburg, S.C. ... 6-2/190. ... Bats left, throws right. ... Full name: William James Spiers III. ... Name pronounced SPY-ers.

HIGH SCHOOL: Wade Hampton Academy (Orangeburg, S.C.).

COLLEGE: Clemson.

TRANSACTIONS/CAREER NOTES: Selected by Milwaukee Brewers organization in first round (13th pick overall) of free-agent draft (June 2, 1987). ... On Milwaukee disabled list (April 6-May 15, 1990); included rehabilitation assignment to Denver (April 27-May 14). ... On Milwaukee disabled list (April 5-September 2, 1992); included rehabilitation assignments to Beloit (May 6-15 and August 20-September 2). ... Granted free agency (December 20, 1993). ... Re-signed by Brewers (December 21, 1993). ... Claimed on waivers by New York Mets (October 25, 1994). ... On New York disabled list (May 15-June 5 and June 26-July 16, 1995); included rehabilitation assignment to Norfolk (May 22-June 5). ... Granted free agency (November 3, 1995). ... Signed by Houston Astros organization (January 10, 1996). ... Granted free agency (November 14, 1996). ... Re-signed by Astros (December 2, 1996). ... Granted free agency (November 3, 1997). ... Re-signed by Astros (November 25, 1997).

HONORS: Named shortstop on THE SPORTING NEWS college All-America team (1987).

STATISTICAL NOTES: Career major league grand slams: 2.

Year	Team (League)	Pos.	G	AB	R	H	2B	3B	HR	RBI	Avg.	BB	SO	SB	PO	A	E	Avg.
1987—Helena (Pio.)		SS	6	22	4	9	1	0	0	3	.409	3	3	2	8	6	6	.700
—Beloit (Midw.)		SS	64	258	43	77	10	1	3	26	.298	15	38	11	111	160	20	.931
1988—Stockton (Calif.)		SS	84	353	68	95	17	3	5	52	.269	42	41	27	140	240	19	.952
—El Paso (Texas)		SS	47	168	22	47	5	2	3	21	.280	15	20	4	73	141	13	.943
1989—Milwaukee (A.L.)	S-3-2-DH-1		114	345	44	88	9	3	4	33	.255	21	63	10	164	295	21	.956
—Denver (A.A.)		SS	14	47	9	17	2	1	2	8	.362	5	6	1	32	33	2	.970
1990—Denver (A.A.)		SS	11	38	6	12	0	0	1	7	.316	10	8	1	22	23	2	.957
—Milwaukee (A.L.)		SS	112	363	44	88	15	3	2	36	.242	16	46	11	159	326	12	.976
1991—Milwaukee (A.L.)	SS-DH-OF	133	414	71	117	13	6	8	54	.283	34	55	14	201	345	17	.970
1992—Beloit (Midw.)		SS	16	55	9	13	3	0	0	7	.236	7	7	4	12	28	3	.930
—Milwaukee (A.L.)	SS-2B-DH-3B	12	16	2	5	2	0	0	2	.313	1	4	1	6	6	0	1.000
1993—Milwaukee (A.L.)	2-O-S-DH	113	340	43	81	8	4	2	36	.238	29	51	9	213	231	13	.972
1994—Milwaukee (A.L.)	3-S-DH-O-1	73	214	27	54	10	1	0	17	.252	19	42	7	70	129	8	.961
1995—New York (N.L.)■	3B-2B	63	72	5	15	2	1	0	11	.208	12	15	0	13	30	7	.860
—Norfolk (I.L.)	2B-3B	12	41	4	9	2	0	0	4	.220	8	6	0	23	29	4	.929
1996—Houston (N.L.)■	3-2-S-1-O	122	218	27	55	10	1	6	26	.252	20	34	7	44	108	5	.968
1997—Houston (N.L.)	3-S-1-2	132	291	51	93	27	4	4	48	.320	61	42	10	104	200	18	.944
1998—Houston (N.L.)	3-2-1-S	123	384	66	105	27	4	4	43	.273	45	62	11	101	184	9	.969
1999—Houston (N.L.)	3-O-S-2-1	127	393	56	113	18	5	4	39	.288	47	45	10	110	176	9	.969
American League totals (6 years)			557	1692	231	433	57	17	16	178	.256	120	261	52	813	1332	71	.968
National League totals (5 years)			567	1358	205	381	84	15	18	167	.281	185	198	38	372	698	48	.957
Major League totals (11 years)			1124	3050	436	814	141	32	34	345	.267	305	459	90	1185	2030	119	.964

DIVISION SERIES RECORD

RECORDS: Shares N.L. career record for most doubles—3.

Year	Team (League)	Pos.	G	AB	R	H	2B	3B	HR	RBI	Avg.	BB	SO	SB	PO	A	E	Avg.
1997—Houston (N.L.)		3B	3	11	1	0	0	0	0	0	.000	1	2	0	1	3	0	1.000
1998—Houston (N.L.)		3B-PH	4	14	2	4	3	0	0	1	.286	1	3	0	1	5	0	1.000
1999—Houston (N.L.)		OF-PH	4	11	0	3	0	0	0	1	.273	0	1	1	3	0	1	.750
Division series totals (3 years)			11	36	3	7	3	0	0	2	.194	2	6	1	5	8	1	.929

SPIEZIO, SCOTT — IF — ANGELS

PERSONAL: Born September 21, 1972, in Joliet, Ill. ... 6-2/222. ... Bats both, throws right. ... Full name: Scott Edward Spiezio. ... Son of Ed Spiezio, third baseman with St. Louis Cardinals (1964-68), San Diego Padres (1969-72) and Chicago White Sox (1972).

HIGH SCHOOL: Morris (Ill.).

COLLEGE: Illinois.

TRANSACTIONS/CAREER NOTES: Selected by Oakland Athletics organization in sixth round of free-agent draft (June 3, 1993). ... On Oakland disabled list (June 8-25, 1997); included rehabilitation assignment to Southern Oregon (June 23-25). ... On Oakland disabled list (June 15-July 31, 1998); included rehabilitation assignment to Edmonton (July 26-31). ... Granted free agency (December 21, 1999). ... Signed by Anaheim Angels (January 7, 2000).

STATISTICAL NOTES: Led California League third basemen with .948 fielding percentage in 1994. ... Led Southern League with 14 sacrifice flies in 1995. ... Led Southern League third basemen with 291 assists, 29 errors, 424 total chances and 34 double plays in 1995. ... Led Pacific Coast League third basemen with 91 putouts, 302 assists, 405 total chances and .970 fielding percentage in 1996. ... Led A.L. second basemen with .990 fielding percentage in 1997. ... Had 18-game hitting streak (May 21-June 9, 1998). ... Career major league grand slams: 3.

Year	Team (League)	Pos.	G	AB	R	H	2B	3B	HR	RBI	Avg.	BB	SO	SB	PO	A	E	Avg.
1993—S. Oregon (N'west)		3B-1B	31	125	32	41	10	2	3	19	.328	16	18	0	76	40	9	.928
—Modesto (Calif.)		3B-1B	32	110	12	28	9	1	1	13	.255	23	19	1	42	51	5	.949
1994—Modesto (Calif.)		3B-1B-SS	127	453	84	127	32	5	14	68	.280	88	72	5	66	281	18	†.951
1995—Huntsville (Sou.)		3B-1B-2B	141	528	78	149	33	8	13	86	.282	67	78	10	122	†295	†29	.935
1996—Edmonton (PCL)	3B-1B-DH	*140	523	87	137	30	4	20	91	.262	56	66	6	†174	†304	15	†.970
—Oakland (A.L.)		3B-DH	9	29	6	9	2	0	2	8	.310	4	4	0	6	5	2	.846

Year	Team (League)	Pos.	G	AB	R	H	2B	3B	HR	RBI	Avg.	BB	SO	SB	PO	A	E	Avg.
1997—Oakland (A.L.)		2B-3B	147	538	58	131	28	4	14	65	.243	44	75	9	280	415	7	†.990
—S. Oregon (N'west)		DH-2B	2	9	1	5	0	0	0	2	.556	2	1	0	3	4	1	.875
1998—Oakland (A.L.)		2B-DH	114	406	54	105	19	1	9	50	.259	44	56	1	198	316	13	.975
—Edmonton (PCL)		2B-DH	5	13	3	3	1	0	1	4	.231	3	2	0	5	3	1	.889
1999—Oakland (A.L.)		2B-3B-1B-DH	89	247	31	60	24	0	8	33	.243	29	36	0	124	163	7	.976
—Vancouver (PCL)		2B-DH-3B	28	105	27	41	7	1	6	27	.390	15	16	0	50	73	4	.969
Major League totals (4 years)			359	1220	149	305	73	5	33	156	.250	121	171	10	608	899	29	.981

SPIVEY, JUNIOR — 2B/SS — DIAMONDBACKS

PERSONAL: Born January 28, 1975, in Oklahoma City. ... 6-0/185. ... Bats right, throws right. ... Full name: Ernest Lee Spivey Jr.
HIGH SCHOOL: Douglass (Oklahoma City).
JUNIOR COLLEGE: Cowley County Community College (Kan.).
TRANSACTIONS/CAREER NOTES: Selected by Arizona Diamondbacks organization in 26th round of free-agent draft (June 4, 1996). ... Loaned by Diamondbacks to Tulsa, Texas Rangers organization (July 18-August 29, 1998). ... On El Paso disabled list (April 8-May 15 and July 4-August 19, 1999). ... On Arizona disabled list (August 19, 1999-remainder of season).
STATISTICAL NOTES: Led California League second basemen with 653 total chances in 1997. ... Tied for California League lead with 20 errors by second baseman in 1998.

Year	Team (League)	Pos.	G	AB	R	H	2B	3B	HR	RBI	Avg.	BB	SO	SB	PO	A	E	Avg.
1996—Ariz. D'backs (Ariz.)		2B-SS-3B	20	69	13	23	0	0	0	3	.333	12	16	11	35	61	3	.970
—Lethbridge (Pio.)		2B-SS	31	107	30	36	3	4	2	25	.336	23	24	8	63	70	10	.930
1997—High Desert (Calif.)		2B	136	491	88	134	24	6	6	53	.273	69	115	14	226	*394	*33	.949
1998—High Desert (Calif.)		2B-3B-SS	79	285	64	80	14	5	5	35	.281	64	61	34	147	224	‡20	.949
—Tulsa (Texas)■		2B	34	119	26	37	10	1	3	16	.311	28	25	8	62	84	3	.980
1999—El Paso (Texas)■		2B-SS	44	164	40	48	10	4	3	19	.293	36	27	14	115	119	9	.963

SPOLJARIC, PAUL — P — CARDINALS

PERSONAL: Born September 24, 1970, in Kelowna, B.C. ... 6-3/210. ... Throws left, bats right. ... Full name: Paul Nikola Spoljaric. ... Name pronounced spole-JAIR-ick.
HIGH SCHOOL: Springvalley Secondary (Kelowna, B.C.).
COLLEGE: Douglas College (B.C.).
TRANSACTIONS/CAREER NOTES: Signed as non-drafted free agent by Toronto Blue Jays organization (August 26, 1989). ... On Toronto disabled list (July 25-August 18, 1996); included rehabilitation assignment to St. Catharines (August 10-18). ... On Toronto disabled list (March 23-April 18, 1997); included rehabilitation assignment to Dunedin (April 4-17). ... Traded by Blue Jays with P Mike Timlin to Seattle Mariners for OF Jose Cruz Jr. (July 31, 1997). ... Traded by Mariners to Philadelphia Phillies for P Mark Leiter (November 9, 1998). ... Traded by Phillies to Blue Jays for P Robert Person (May 5, 1999). ... On suspended list (September 2-5, 1999). ... Traded by Blue Jays with P Pat Hentgen to St. Louis Cardinals for P Lance Painter, C Alberto Castillo and P Matt DeWitt (November 11, 1999).
HONORS: Named South Atlantic League Most Outstanding Pitcher (1992).
STATISTICAL NOTES: Tied for A.L. lead with three balks in 1997.

Year	League	W	L	Pct.	ERA	G	GS	CG	ShO	Sv.	IP	H	R	ER	BB	SO
1990—Medicine Hat (Pio.)		3	7	.300	4.34	15	13	0	0	1	66 1/3	57	43	32	35	62
1991—St. Catharines (NY-P)		0	2	.000	4.82	4	4	0	0	0	18 2/3	21	14	10	9	21
1992—Myrtle Beach (SAL)		10	8	.556	2.82	26	26	1	0	0	162 1/3	111	68	51	58	161
1993—Dunedin (FSL)		3	0	1.000	1.38	4	4	0	0	0	26	16	5	4	12	29
—Knoxville (Sou.)		4	1	.800	2.28	7	7	0	0	0	43 1/3	30	12	11	22	51
—Syracuse (I.L.)		8	7	.533	5.29	18	18	1	1	0	95 1/3	97	63	56	52	88
1994—Toronto (A.L.)		0	1	.000	38.57	2	1	0	0	0	2 1/3	5	10	10	9	2
—Syracuse (I.L.)		1	5	.167	5.70	8	8	0	0	0	47 1/3	47	37	30	28	38
—Knoxville (Sou.)		6	5	.545	3.62	17	16	0	0	0	102	88	50	41	48	79
1995—Syracuse (I.L.)		2	10	.167	4.93	43	9	0	0	10	87 2/3	69	51	48	54	108
1996—Syracuse (I.L.)		3	0	1.000	3.27	17	0	0	0	4	22	20	9	8	6	24
—Toronto (A.L.)		2	2	.500	3.08	28	0	0	0	1	38	30	17	13	19	38
—St. Catharines (NY-P)		0	0	...	0.00	2	2	0	0	0	5	3	0	0	0	7
1997—Dunedin (FSL)		0	0	...	1.69	4	3	0	0	0	10 2/3	10	3	2	2	10
—Toronto (A.L.)		0	3	.000	3.19	37	0	0	0	3	48	37	17	17	21	43
—Seattle (A.L.)■		0	0	...	4.76	20	0	0	0	0	22 1/3	24	13	12	15	27
1998—Seattle (A.L.)		4	6	.400	6.48	53	6	0	0	0	83 1/3	85	67	60	55	89
1999—Philadelphia (N.L.)■		0	3	.000	15.09	5	3	0	0	0	11 1/3	23	24	19	7	10
—Toronto (A.L.)		2	2	.500	4.65	37	2	0	0	0	62	62	41	32	32	63
A.L. totals (5 years)		8	14	.364	5.06	177	9	0	0	4	256 1/3	243	165	144	151	262
N.L. totals (1 year)		0	3	.000	15.09	5	3	0	0	0	11 1/3	23	24	19	7	10
Major League totals (5 years)		8	17	.320	5.48	182	12	0	0	4	267 2/3	266	189	163	158	272

DIVISION SERIES RECORD

Year	League	W	L	Pct.	ERA	G	GS	CG	ShO	Sv.	IP	H	R	ER	BB	SO
1997—Seattle (A.L.)		0	0	...	0.00	2	0	0	0	0	1 2/3	4	0	0	0	1

SPRADLIN, JERRY — P — ROYALS

PERSONAL: Born June 14, 1967, in Fullerton, Calif. ... 6-7/245. ... Throws right, bats both. ... Full name: Jerry Carl Spradlin.
HIGH SCHOOL: Katella (Anaheim).
COLLEGE: Fullerton (Calif.) College.

TRANSACTIONS/CAREER NOTES: Selected by Cincinnati Reds organization in 19th round of free-agent draft (June 1, 1988). ... Claimed on waivers by Florida Marlins (August 4, 1994). ... Granted free agency (October 16, 1995). ... Signed by Indianapolis, Reds orgnization (February 11, 1996). ... On Indianapolis disabled list (May 24-June 1, 1996). ... Released by Reds (October 30, 1996). ... Signed by Philadelphia Phillies (December 9, 1996). ... Traded by Phillies to Cleveland Indians for P Chad Ogea (November 13, 1998). ... Traded by Indians to San Francisco Giants for OF Dan McKinley and a player to be named later (April 23, 1999); Indians acquired P Josh Santos to complete deal (June 27, 1999). ... Traded by Giants to Kansas City Royals for a player to be named later (December 13, 1999); Giants acquired P Ken Ray to complete deal (January 7, 2000).

HONORS: Named Southern League co-Most Valuable Pitcher (1992).

Year	League	W	L	Pct.	ERA	G	GS	CG	ShO	Sv.	IP	H	R	ER	BB	SO
1988—	Billings (Pio.)	4	1	.800	3.21	17	5	0	0	0	47$^{2}/_{3}$	45	25	17	14	23
1989—	Greensboro (SAL)	7	2	.778	2.76	42	1	0	0	2	94$^{2}/_{3}$	88	35	29	23	56
1990—	Cedar Rapids (Midw.)	0	1	.000	3.00	5	0	0	0	0	12	13	8	4	5	6
	—Charleston, W.Va. (SAL)	3	4	.429	2.54	43	1	1	0	17	74$^{1}/_{3}$	74	23	21	17	39
1991—	Chattanooga (Sou.)	7	3	.700	3.09	48	1	0	0	4	96	95	38	33	32	73
1992—	Chattanooga (Sou.)	3	3	.500	1.38	59	0	0	0	*34	65$^{1}/_{3}$	52	11	10	13	35
	—Cedar Rapids (Midw.)	1	0	1.000	7.71	1	0	0	0	0	2$^{1}/_{3}$	5	2	2	0	4
1993—	Indianapolis (A.A.)	3	2	.600	3.49	34	0	0	0	1	56$^{2}/_{3}$	58	24	22	12	46
	—Cincinnati (N.L.)	2	1	.667	3.49	37	0	0	0	2	49	44	20	19	9	24
1994—	Indianapolis (A.A.)	3	3	.500	3.68	28	5	0	0	3	73$^{1}/_{3}$	87	36	30	16	49
	—Cincinnati (N.L.)	0	0	...	10.13	6	0	0	0	0	8	12	11	9	2	4
	—Edmonton (PCL)■	1	0	1.000	2.53	6	0	0	0	1	10$^{2}/_{3}$	12	3	3	4	3
1995—	Charlotte (I.L.)	3	3	.500	3.03	41	0	0	0	1	59$^{1}/_{3}$	59	26	20	15	38
1996—	Indianapolis (A.A.)■	6	8	.429	3.33	49	8	0	0	15	100	94	49	37	23	79
	—Cincinnati (N.L.)	0	0	...	0.00	1	0	0	0	0	$^{1}/_{3}$	0	0	0	0	0
1997—	Philadelphia (N.L.)■	4	8	.333	4.74	76	0	0	0	1	81$^{2}/_{3}$	86	45	43	27	67
1998—	Philadelphia (N.L.)	4	4	.500	3.53	69	0	0	0	1	81$^{2}/_{3}$	63	34	32	20	76
1999—	Cleveland (A.L.)■	0	0	...	18.00	4	0	0	0	0	3	6	6	6	3	2
	—San Francisco (N.L.)■	3	1	.750	4.19	59	0	0	0	0	58	59	31	27	29	52
A.L. totals (1 year)		0	0	...	18.00	4	0	0	0	0	3	6	6	6	3	2
N.L. totals (5 years)		9	6	.600	3.97	172	0	0	0	3	197	178	96	87	60	156
Major League totals (5 years)		9	6	.600	4.18	176	0	0	0	3	200	184	102	93	63	158

SPRAGUE, ED — 3B

PERSONAL: Born July 25, 1967, in Castro Valley, Calif. ... 6-2/205. ... Bats right, throws right. ... Full name: Edward Nelson Sprague Jr. ... Son of Ed Sprague, pitcher with four major league teams (1968-69 and 1971-76); and husband of Kristen Babb, Olympic gold-medal synchronized swimmer (1992). ... Name pronounced SPRAYGH.

HIGH SCHOOL: St. Mary's (Stockton, Calif.).

COLLEGE: Stanford.

TRANSACTIONS/CAREER NOTES: Selected by Boston Red Sox organization in 26th round of free-agent draft (June 3, 1985); did not sign. ... Selected by Toronto Blue Jays organization in first round (25th pick overall) of free-agent draft (June 1, 1988). ... On suspended list (August 8-10, 1993). ... On disabled list (September 4-28, 1997). ... Traded by Blue Jays to Oakland Athletics for P Scott Rivette (July 31, 1998). ... Granted free agency (October 27, 1998). ... Signed by Pittsburgh Pirates (December 16, 1998). ... On disabled list (September 20, 1999-remainder of season). ... Granted free agency (October 29, 1999).

STATISTICAL NOTES: Led International League third basemen with 31 errors and 364 total chances and tied for lead with 240 assists in 1990. ... Led A.L. in grounding into double plays with 23 in 1993. ... Led A.L. third basemen with 98 putouts in 1994 and 133 in 1995. ... Led A.L. in being hit by pitch with 15 in 1995. ... Led N.L. in being hit by pitch with 17 in 1999. ... Career major league grand slams: 4.

MISCELLANEOUS: Member of 1988 U.S. Olympic baseball team.

							BATTING									FIELDING			
Year	Team (League)	Pos.	G	AB	R	H	2B	3B	HR	RBI	Avg.	BB	SO	SB	PO	A	E	Avg.
1989—	Dunedin (FSL)	3B	52	192	21	42	9	2	7	23	.219	16	40	1	33	86	14	.895
	—Syracuse (I.L.)	3B	86	288	23	60	14	1	5	33	.208	18	73	0	51	149	*25	.889
1990—	Syracuse (I.L.)	3B-1B-C	142	*519	60	124	23	5	20	75	.239	31	100	4	171	‡246	†35	.923
1991—	Syracuse (I.L.)	C-3B	23	88	24	32	8	0	5	25	.364	10	21	2	111	17	6	.955
	—Toronto (A.L.)	3B-1B-C-DH	61	160	17	44	7	0	4	20	.275	19	43	0	167	72	14	.945
1992—	Syracuse (I.L.)	C-1B-3B	100	369	49	102	18	2	16	50	.276	44	73	0	438	44	12	.976
	—Toronto (A.L.)	C-1B-DH-3B	22	47	6	11	2	0	1	7	.234	3	7	0	82	5	1	.989
1993—	Toronto (A.L.)	3B	150	546	50	142	31	1	12	73	.260	32	85	1	*127	232	17	.955
1994—	Toronto (A.L.)	3B	109	405	38	97	19	1	11	44	.240	23	95	1	†111	147	14	.950
1995—	Toronto (A.L.)	3B-1B-DH	144	521	77	127	27	2	18	74	.244	58	96	0	†167	234	17	.959
1996—	Toronto (A.L.)	3B-DH	159	591	88	146	35	2	36	101	.247	60	146	0	108	218	15	.956
1997—	Toronto (A.L.)	3B-DH	138	504	63	115	29	4	14	48	.228	51	102	0	106	202	18	.945
1998—	Toronto (A.L.)	3B	105	382	49	91	20	0	17	51	.238	24	73	0	87	157	20	.924
	—Oakland (A.L.)■	3B-1B	27	87	8	13	5	0	3	7	.149	2	17	1	24	37	6	.910
1999—	Pittsburgh (N.L.)■	3B	137	490	71	131	27	2	22	81	.267	50	93	3	79	254	•29	.920
American League totals (8 years)			915	3243	396	786	175	10	116	425	.242	272	664	3	985	1304	122	.949
National League totals (1 year)			137	490	71	131	27	2	22	81	.267	50	93	3	79	254	29	.920
Major League totals (9 years)			1052	3733	467	917	202	12	138	506	.246	322	757	6	1064	1558	151	.946

CHAMPIONSHIP SERIES RECORD

							BATTING									FIELDING			
Year	Team (League)	Pos.	G	AB	R	H	2B	3B	HR	RBI	Avg.	BB	SO	SB	PO	A	E	Avg.
1991—	Toronto (A.L.)						Did not play.											
1992—	Toronto (A.L.)	PH	2	2	0	1	0	0	0	0	.500	0	1	0	...	...	...	...
1993—	Toronto (A.L.)	3B	6	21	0	6	0	1	0	4	.286	2	4	0	5	9	0	1.000
Championship series totals (2 years)			8	23	0	7	0	1	0	4	.304	2	5	0	5	9	0	1.000

WORLD SERIES RECORD

NOTES: Hit home run in first at-bat (October 18, 1992). ... Member of World Series championship team (1992 and 1993).

Year	Team (League)	Pos.	G	AB	R	H	2B	3B	HR	RBI	Avg.	BB	SO	SB	PO	A	E	Avg.
1992— Toronto (A.L.).............		PH-1B	3	2	1	1	0	0	1	2	.500	1	0	0	0	0	0	...
1993— Toronto (A.L.).............		3B-PH-1B	5	15	0	1	0	0	0	2	.067	1	6	0	4	9	2	.867
World Series totals (2 years)			8	17	1	2	0	0	1	4	.118	2	6	0	4	9	2	.867

ALL-STAR GAME RECORD

Year	League	Pos.	AB	R	H	2B	3B	HR	RBI	Avg.	BB	SO	SB	PO	A	E	Avg.
1999— National......................		3B	1	0	0	0	0	0	0	.000	0	0	0	0	0	0	...

SPRINGER, DENNIS — P

PERSONAL: Born February 12, 1965, in Fresno, Calif. ... 5-10/185. ... Throws right, bats right. ... Full name: Dennis LeRoy Springer.
HIGH SCHOOL: Washington (Fresno, Calif.).
JUNIOR COLLEGE: Kings River Community College (Calif.).
COLLEGE: Fresno State.
TRANSACTIONS/CAREER NOTES: Selected by Los Angeles Dodgers organization in 21st round of free-agent draft (June 2, 1987). ... On San Antonio disabled list (April 19-27, 1992). ... On disabled list (August 24-September 6, 1993). ... Granted free agency (October 15, 1993). ... Signed by Philadelphia Phillies organization (May 19, 1994). ... Granted free agency (December 21, 1995). ... Signed by California Angels organization (January 5, 1996). ... Angels franchise renamed Anaheim Angels for 1997 season. ... Selected by Tampa Bay Devil Rays in first round (26th pick overall) of expansion draft (November 18, 1997). ... Released by Devil Rays (November 3, 1998). ... Signed by Florida Marlins organization (January 29, 1999). ... Granted free agency (October 6, 1999).

Year	League	W	L	Pct.	ERA	G	GS	CG	ShO	Sv.	IP	H	R	ER	BB	SO
1987— Great Falls (Pio.)		4	3	.571	2.88	23	5	1	0	6	65 2/3	70	38	21	16	54
1988— Bakersfield (Calif.)..............		13	7	.650	3.27	32	20	6	•4	2	154	135	75	56	62	108
1989— San Antonio (Texas)..........		6	8	.429	3.15	19	19	4	1	0	140	128	58	49	46	89
— Albuquerque (PCL)............		4	1	.800	4.83	8	7	0	0	0	41	58	28	22	14	18
1990— San Antonio (Texas)..........		8	6	.571	3.31	24	24	3	0	0	*163 1/3	147	76	60	73	77
1991— San Antonio (Texas)..........		10	10	.500	4.43	30	24	2	0	0	164 2/3	153	96	81	91	*138
1992— San Antonio (Texas)..........		6	7	.462	4.35	18	18	4	0	0	122	114	61	59	49	73
— Albuquerque (PCL)............		2	7	.222	5.66	11	11	1	0	0	62	70	45	39	22	36
1993— Albuquerque (PCL)............		3	8	.273	5.99	35	18	0	0	0	130 2/3	173	104	87	39	69
1994— Reading (East.)■		5	8	.385	3.40	24	19	2	0	2	135	125	74	51	44	118
1995— Scranton/W.B. (I.L.)		10	11	.476	4.68	30	23	4	0	0	171	163	*101	89	47	115
— Philadelphia (N.L.)............		0	3	.000	4.84	4	4	0	0	0	22 1/3	21	15	12	9	15
1996— California (A.L.)■		5	6	.455	5.51	20	15	2	1	0	94 2/3	91	65	58	43	64
— Vancouver (PCL)		10	3	.769	2.72	16	12	6	0	0	109 1/3	89	35	33	36	78
1997— Anaheim (A.L.)..................		9	9	.500	5.18	32	28	3	1	0	194 2/3	199	118	112	73	75
— Vancouver (PCL)		1	1	.500	3.00	2	2	2	0	0	15	12	6	5	6	7
1998— Tampa Bay (A.L.)■............		3	11	.214	5.45	29	17	1	0	0	115 2/3	120	77	70	60	46
— Durham (I.L.)		2	3	.400	2.87	5	5	0	0	0	37 2/3	34	13	12	15	23
1999— Florida (N.L.)■		6	16	.273	4.86	38	29	3	2	1	196 1/3	231	121	106	64	83
A.L. totals (3 years)		17	26	.395	5.33	81	60	6	2	0	405	410	260	240	176	185
N.L. totals (2 years)		6	19	.240	4.86	42	33	3	2	1	218 2/3	252	136	118	73	98
Major League totals (5 years).......		23	45	.338	5.17	123	93	9	4	1	623 2/3	662	396	358	249	283

SPRINGER, RUSS — P — DIAMONDBACKS

PERSONAL: Born November 7, 1968, in Alexandria, La. ... 6-4/220. ... Throws right, bats right. ... Full name: Russell Paul Springer.
HIGH SCHOOL: Grant (Dry Prong, La.).
COLLEGE: Louisiana State.
TRANSACTIONS/CAREER NOTES: Selected by New York Yankees organization in seventh round of free-agent draft (June 5, 1989). ... Traded by Yankees with 1B J.T. Snow and P Jerry Nielsen to California Angels for P Jim Abbott (December 6, 1992). ... On California disabled list (August 2, 1993-remainder of season). ... Traded by Angels to Philadelphia Phillies (August 15, 1995), completing deal in which Phillies traded OF Dave Gallagher to Angels for 2B Kevin Flora and a player to be named later (August 9, 1995). ... Released by Phillies (December 20, 1996). ... Signed by Houston Astros organization (December 30, 1996). ... On Houston disabled list (June 17-July 10, 1997); included rehabilitation assignment to Jackson (July 8-10). ... Selected by Arizona Diamondbacks in third round (61st pick overall) of expansion draft (November 18, 1997). ... Traded by Diamondbacks to Atlanta Braves for P Alan Embree (June 23, 1998). ... On Atlanta disabled list (August 6-21, 1998). ... On Atlanta disabled list (April 3-May 17, 1999); included rehabilitation assignment to Richmond (April 20-May 16). ... Granted free agency (November 2, 1999). ... Signed by Diamondbacks (December 3, 1999).

Year	League	W	L	Pct.	ERA	G	GS	CG	ShO	Sv.	IP	H	R	ER	BB	SO
1989— GC Yankees (GCL).............		3	0	1.000	1.50	6	6	0	0	0	24	14	8	4	10	34
1990— GC Yankees (GCL).............		0	2	.000	1.20	4	4	0	0	0	15	10	6	2	4	17
— Greensboro (SAL)		2	3	.400	3.67	10	10	0	0	0	56 1/3	51	33	23	31	51
1991— Fort Lauderdale (FSL)		5	9	.357	3.49	25	25	2	0	0	152 1/3	118	68	59	62	139
— Albany/Colonie (East.)........		1	0	1.000	1.80	2	2	0	0	0	15	9	4	3	6	16
1992— Columbus (I.L.)		8	5	.615	2.69	20	20	1	0	0	123 2/3	89	46	37	54	95
— New York (A.L.)		0	0	...	6.19	14	0	0	0	0	16	18	11	11	10	12
1993— Vancouver (PCL)■		5	4	.556	4.27	11	9	1	0	0	59	58	37	28	33	40
— California (A.L.)		1	6	.143	7.20	14	9	1	0	0	60	73	48	48	32	31
1994— Vancouver (PCL)		7	4	.636	3.04	12	12	•4	0	0	83	77	35	28	19	58
— California (A.L.)		2	2	.500	5.52	18	5	0	0	2	45 2/3	53	28	28	14	28
1995— Vancouver (PCL)		2	0	1.000	3.44	6	6	0	0	0	34	24	16	13	23	23
— California (A.L.)		1	2	.333	6.10	19	6	0	0	1	51 2/3	60	37	35	25	38
— Philadelphia (N.L.)■		0	0	...	3.71	14	0	0	0	0	26 2/3	22	11	11	10	32
1996— Philadelphia (N.L.)..............		3	10	.231	4.66	51	7	0	0	0	96 2/3	106	60	50	38	94
1997— Houston (N.L.)■		3	3	.500	4.23	54	0	0	0	3	55 1/3	48	28	26	27	74
— Jackson (Texas)		0	0	...	9.00	1	0	0	0	0	1	2	1	1	0	2

Year	League	W	L	Pct.	ERA	G	GS	CG	ShO	Sv.	IP	H	R	ER	BB	SO
1998—Arizona (N.L.)■.....................		4	3	.571	4.13	26	0	0	0	0	32²/₃	29	16	15	14	37
—Atlanta (N.L.)■........................		1	1	.500	4.05	22	0	0	0	0	20	22	10	9	16	19
1999—Richmond (I.L.).................		1	0	1.000	1.17	11	0	0	0	0	15¹/₃	9	2	2	1	13
—Atlanta (N.L.)......................		2	1	.667	3.42	49	0	0	0	1	47¹/₃	31	20	18	22	49
A.L. totals (4 years)		4	10	.286	6.33	65	20	1	0	3	173¹/₃	204	124	122	81	109
N.L. totals (5 years)		13	18	.419	4.17	216	7	0	0	4	278²/₃	258	145	129	127	305
Major League totals (8 years)		17	28	.378	5.00	281	27	1	0	7	452	462	269	251	208	414

DIVISION SERIES RECORD

Year	League	W	L	Pct.	ERA	G	GS	CG	ShO	Sv.	IP	H	R	ER	BB	SO
1997—Houston (N.L.)		0	0	...	5.40	2	0	0	0	0	1²/₃	2	1	1	1	3
1998—Atlanta (N.L.).......................									Did not play.							
1999—Atlanta (N.L.)■.....................		0	0	...	0.00	1	0	0	0	0	1	2	0	0	1	1
Division series totals (2 years)		0	0	...	3.38	3	0	0	0	0	2²/₃	4	1	1	2	4

CHAMPIONSHIP SERIES RECORD

Year	League	W	L	Pct.	ERA	G	GS	CG	ShO	Sv.	IP	H	R	ER	BB	SO
1998—Atlanta (N.L.).......................									Did not play.							
1999—Atlanta (N.L.).......................		1	0	1.000	0.00	2	0	0	0	0	2	0	0	0	1	1

WORLD SERIES RECORD

Year	League	W	L	Pct.	ERA	G	GS	CG	ShO	Sv.	IP	H	R	ER	BB	SO
1999—Atlanta (N.L.).......................		0	0	...	0.00	2	0	0	0	0	2¹/₃	1	0	0	0	1

STAIRS, MATT — OF — ATHLETICS

S

PERSONAL: Born February 27, 1968, in Saint John, N.B. ... 5-9/217. ... Bats left, throws right. ... Full name: Matthew Wade Stairs.
HIGH SCHOOL: Fredericton (N.B.).
TRANSACTIONS/CAREER NOTES: Signed as non-drafted free agent by Montreal Expos organization (January 17, 1989). ... On disabled list (May 16-23, 1991). ... On Ottawa disabled list (May 7-18, 1993). ... Contract sold by Expos to Chunichi Dragons of Japan Central League (June 8, 1993). ... Signed by Expos organization (December 15, 1993). ... Traded by Expos with P Pete Young to Boston Red Sox for cash (February 18, 1994). ... Granted free agency (October 14, 1995). ... Signed by Oakland Athletics organization (December 1, 1995).
HONORS: Named Eastern League Most Valuable Player (1991).
STATISTICAL NOTES: Led Eastern League with .509 slugging percentage, 257 total bases and tied for lead with eight intentional bases on balls received in 1991. ... Career major league grand slams: 6.
MISCELLANEOUS: Member of 1988 Canadian Olympic baseball team.

								BATTING								FIELDING		
Year	Team (League)	Pos.	G	AB	R	H	2B	3B	HR	RBI	Avg.	BB	SO	SB	PO	A	E	Avg.
1989—W.P. Beach (FSL)........	3B-SS-2B	36	111	12	21	3	1	1	9	.189	9	18	0	21	66	4	.956
—Jamestown (NY-P)...	2B-3B	14	43	8	11	1	0	1	5	.256	3	5	1	15	35	6	.893
—Rockford (Midw.)...	3B	44	141	20	40	9	2	2	14	.284	15	29	5	30	62	7	.929
1990—W.P. Beach (FSL)........	3B-2B	55	183	30	62	9	3	3	30	.339	41	19	15	40	112	17	.899
—Jacksonville (Sou.).....3B-OF-2B-SS		79	280	26	71	17	0	3	34	.254	22	43	5	76	107	22	.893
1991—Harrisburg (East.)........	2B-3B-OF	129	505	87	*168	30	•10	13	78	*.333	66	47	23	193	314	22	.958
1992—Indianapolis (A.A.)........	OF	110	401	57	107	23	4	11	56	.267	49	61	11	188	11	3	.985
—Montreal (N.L.)............	OF	13	30	2	5	2	0	0	5	.167	7	7	0	14	0	1	.933
1993—Ottawa (I.L.)............	OF	34	125	18	35	4	2	3	20	.280	11	15	4	49	4	0	1.000
—Montreal (N.L.)............	OF	6	8	1	3	1	0	0	2	.375	0	1	0	1	0	0	1.000
—Chunichi (Jap. Cen.)■	N	60	132	10	33	6	0	6	23	.250	7	34	1	...	...	...	...
1994—New Britain (East.)■..	OF-DH-1B	93	317	44	98	25	2	9	61	.309	53	38	10	106	12	3	.975
1995—Pawtucket (I.L.)............	OF-DH	75	271	40	77	17	0	13	56	.284	29	41	3	79	13	0	1.000
—Boston (A.L.)............	OF-DH	39	88	8	23	7	1	1	17	.261	4	14	0	19	2	2	.913
1996—Oakland (A.L.)■........	OF-DH-1B	61	137	21	38	5	1	10	23	.277	19	23	1	65	11	1	.987
—Edmonton (PCL)	DH-OF-1B	51	180	35	62	16	1	8	41	.344	21	34	0	49	2	3	.944
1997—Oakland (A.L.)............	OF-DH-1B	133	352	62	105	19	0	27	73	.298	50	60	3	142	9	4	.974
1998—Oakland (A.L.)............	DH-OF-1B	149	523	88	154	33	1	26	106	.294	59	93	8	67	11	0	1.000
1999—Oakland (A.L.)............	OF-DH-1B	146	531	94	137	26	3	38	102	.258	89	124	2	247	13	5	.981
American League totals (5 years)		528	1631	273	457	90	6	102	321	.280	221	314	14	540	46	12	.980
National League totals (2 years)		19	38	3	8	3	0	0	7	.211	7	8	0	15	0	1	.938
Major League totals (7 years)		547	1669	276	465	93	6	102	328	.279	228	322	14	555	46	13	.979

DIVISION SERIES RECORD

								BATTING								FIELDING		
Year	Team (League)	Pos.	G	AB	R	H	2B	3B	HR	RBI	Avg.	BB	SO	SB	PO	A	E	Avg.
1995—Boston (A.L.)............	PH	1	1	0	0	0	0	0	0	.000	0	1	0	...	...	...	...

STANLEY, MIKE — 1B/DH — RED SOX

PERSONAL: Born June 25, 1963, in Fort Lauderdale, Fla. ... 6-0/205. ... Bats right, throws right. ... Full name: Michael Robert Stanley.
HIGH SCHOOL: St. Thomas Aquinas (Fort Lauderdale, Fla.).
COLLEGE: Florida.
TRANSACTIONS/CAREER NOTES: Selected by Texas Rangers organization in 16th round of free-agent draft (June 3, 1985). ... On disabled list (July 24-August 14, 1988 and August 18-September 2, 1989). ... Granted free agency (November 15, 1990). ... Re-signed by Rangers organization (February 4, 1991). ... Granted free agency (October 14, 1991). ... Signed by Columbus, New York Yankees (January 21, 1992). ... On disabled list (May 14-29, 1994). ... Granted free agency (November 1, 1995). ... Signed by Boston Red Sox (December 14, 1995). ... Traded by Red Sox with IF Randy Brown to Yankees for P Tony Armas Jr. and a player to be named later (August 13, 1997); Red Sox acquired P Jim Mecir to complete deal (September 29, 1997). ... Granted free agency (October 27, 1997). ... Signed by Toronto Blue Jays (December 8, 1997). ... Traded by Blue Jays to Red Sox for P Peter Munro and P Jay Yennaco (July 30, 1998).
HONORS: Named catcher on THE SPORTING NEWS A.L. All-Star team (1993). ... Named catcher on THE SPORTING NEWS A.L. Silver Slugger team (1993).
STATISTICAL NOTES: Hit three home runs in one game (August 10, 1995, first game). ... Led A.L. catchers with 18 passed balls in 1996. ... Career major league grand slams: 8.

Year	Team (League)	Pos.	G	AB	R	H	2B	3B	HR	RBI	Avg.	BB	SO	SB	PO	A	E	Avg.
1985—	Salem (Caro.)	1B-C	4	9	2	5	0	0	0	3	.556	1	1	0	19	1	1	.952
	— Burlington (Midw.)	C-1B-OF	13	42	8	13	2	0	1	6	.310	6	5	0	45	2	0	1.000
	— Tulsa (Texas)	C-1B-OF-2B	46	165	24	51	10	0	3	17	.309	24	18	6	289	18	6	.981
1986—	Tulsa (Texas)	C-1B-3B	67	235	41	69	16	2	6	35	.294	34	26	5	379	45	2	.995
	— Texas (A.L.)	3B-C-DH-OF	15	30	4	10	3	0	1	1	.333	3	7	1	14	8	1	.957
	— Oklahoma City (A.A.)	C-3B-1B	56	202	37	74	13	3	5	49	.366	44	42	1	206	55	9	.967
1987—	Oklahoma City (A.A.)	C-1B	46	182	43	61	8	3	13	54	.335	29	36	2	277	32	2	.994
	— Texas (A.L.)	C-1B-DH-OF	78	216	34	59	8	1	6	37	.273	31	48	3	389	26	7	.983
1988—	Texas (A.L.)	C-DH-1B-3B	94	249	21	57	8	0	3	27	.229	37	62	0	342	17	4	.989
1989—	Texas (A.L.)	C-DH-1B-3B	67	122	9	30	3	1	1	11	.246	12	29	1	117	8	3	.977
1990—	Texas (A.L.)	C-DH-3B-1B	103	189	21	47	8	1	2	19	.249	30	25	1	261	25	4	.986
1991—	Texas (A.L.)	C-1-3-DH-O	95	181	25	45	13	1	3	25	.249	34	44	0	288	20	6	.981
1992—	New York (A.L.)■	C-DH-1B	68	173	24	43	7	0	8	27	.249	33	45	0	287	30	6	.981
1993—	New York (A.L.)	C-DH	130	423	70	129	17	1	26	84	.305	57	85	1	652	46	3	*.996
1994—	New York (A.L.)	C-1B-DH	82	290	54	87	20	0	17	57	.300	39	56	0	442	35	5	.990
1995—	New York (A.L.)	C-DH	118	399	63	107	29	1	18	83	.268	57	106	1	651	35	5	.993
1996—	Boston (A.L.)■	C-DH	121	397	73	107	20	1	24	69	.270	69	62	2	654	19	•10	.985
1997—	Boston (A.L.)	DH-1B-C	97	260	45	78	17	0	13	53	.300	39	50	0	284	21	2	.993
	— New York (A.L.)■	DH-1B	28	87	16	25	8	0	3	12	.287	15	22	0	71	3	0	1.000
1998—	Toronto (A.L.)■	DH-1B-OF	98	341	49	82	13	0	22	47	.240	56	86	2	172	12	1	.995
	— Boston (A.L.)	DH-1B	47	156	25	45	12	0	7	32	.288	26	43	1	108	6	0	1.000
1999—	Boston (A.L.)	1B-DH	136	427	59	120	22	0	19	72	.281	70	94	0	830	60	11	.988
Major League totals (14 years)			1377	3940	592	1071	208	7	173	656	.272	608	864	13	5562	371	68	.989

DIVISION SERIES RECORD

RECORDS: Shares single-game records for most at-bats (nine-inning game)—6; and hits—5 (October 10, 1999). ... Shares single-inning record for most at-bats—2 (October 10, 1999, second inning).

Year	Team (League)	Pos.	G	AB	R	H	2B	3B	HR	RBI	Avg.	BB	SO	SB	PO	A	E	Avg.
1995—	New York (A.L.)	C	4	16	2	5	0	0	1	3	.313	2	1	0	30	0	1	.968
1997—	New York (A.L.)	PH-DH	2	4	1	3	1	0	0	1	.750	0	1	0	...	...	...	...
1998—	Boston (A.L.)	DH	4	15	1	4	0	0	0	0	.267	2	5	0	...	...	...	...
1999—	Boston (A.L.)	1B	5	20	4	10	2	1	0	2	.500	2	3	0	38	6	0	1.000
Division series totals (4 years)			15	55	8	22	3	1	1	6	.400	6	10	0	68	6	1	.987

CHAMPIONSHIP SERIES RECORD

Year	Team (League)	Pos.	G	AB	R	H	2B	3B	HR	RBI	Avg.	BB	SO	SB	PO	A	E	Avg.
1999—	Boston (A.L.)	1B	5	18	1	4	0	0	0	1	.222	2	4	0	35	2	1	.974

ALL-STAR GAME RECORD

Year	League	Pos.	AB	R	H	2B	3B	HR	RBI	Avg.	BB	SO	SB	PO	A	E	Avg.
1995—	American	C	1	0	0	0	0	0	0	.000	0	0	0	3	0	0	1.000

STANTON, MIKE   P   YANKEES

PERSONAL: Born June 2, 1967, in Houston. ... 6-1/215. ... Throws left, bats left. ... Full name: William Michael Stanton.

HIGH SCHOOL: Midland (Texas).

JUNIOR COLLEGE: Alvin (Texas) Community College.

TRANSACTIONS/CAREER NOTES: Selected by Atlanta Braves organization in 13th round of free-agent draft (June 2, 1987). ... On Atlanta disabled list (April 27, 1990-remainder of season); included rehabilitation assignments to Greenville (May 31-June 5 and August 21-29). ... Granted free agency (December 23, 1994). ... Re-signed by Braves (April 12, 1995). ... Traded by Braves with a player to be named later to Boston Red Sox for two players to be named later (July 31, 1995); Red Sox acquired P Matt Murray and Braves acquired OF Marc Lewis and P Mike Jacobs to complete deal (August 31, 1995). ... Traded by Red Sox to Texas Rangers for P Mark Brandenburg and P Kerry Lacy (July 31, 1996). ... Granted free agency (October 27, 1996). ... Signed by New York Yankees (December 11, 1996). ... On suspended list (July 3-10, 1998). ... Granted free agency (November 5, 1999). ... Re-signed by Yankees (December 1, 1999).

Year	League	W	L	Pct.	ERA	G	GS	CG	ShO	Sv.	IP	H	R	ER	BB	SO
1987—	Pulaski (Appl.)	4	8	.333	3.24	15	13	3	2	0	83 1/3	64	37	30	42	82
1988—	Burlington (Midw.)	11	5	.688	3.62	30	23	1	1	0	154	154	86	62	69	160
	— Durham (Caro.)	1	0	1.000	1.46	2	2	1	1	0	12 1/3	14	3	2	5	14
1989—	Greenville (Sou.)	4	1	.800	1.58	47	0	0	0	19	51 1/3	32	10	9	31	58
	— Richmond (I.L.)	2	0	1.000	0.00	13	0	0	0	8	20	6	0	0	13	20
	— Atlanta (N.L.)	0	1	.000	1.50	20	0	0	0	7	24	17	4	4	8	27
1990—	Atlanta (N.L.)	0	3	.000	18.00	7	0	0	0	2	7	16	16	14	4	7
	— Greenville (Sou.)	0	1	.000	1.59	4	0	0	0	0	5 2/3	7	1	1	3	4
1991—	Atlanta (N.L.)	5	5	.500	2.88	74	0	0	0	7	78	62	27	25	21	54
1992—	Atlanta (N.L.)	5	4	.556	4.10	65	0	0	0	8	63 2/3	59	32	29	20	44
1993—	Atlanta (N.L.)	4	6	.400	4.67	63	0	0	0	27	52	51	35	27	29	43
1994—	Atlanta (N.L.)	3	1	.750	3.55	49	0	0	0	3	45 2/3	41	18	18	26	35
1995—	Atlanta (N.L.)	1	1	.500	5.59	26	0	0	0	1	19 1/3	31	14	12	6	13
	— Boston (A.L.)■	1	0	1.000	3.00	22	0	0	0	0	21	17	9	7	8	10
1996—	Boston (A.L.)	4	3	.571	3.83	59	0	0	0	1	56 1/3	58	24	24	23	46
	— Texas (A.L.)■	0	1	.000	3.22	22	0	0	0	0	22 1/3	20	8	8	4	14
1997—	New York (A.L.)■	6	1	.857	2.57	64	0	0	0	3	66 2/3	50	19	19	34	70
1998—	New York (A.L.)	4	1	.800	5.47	67	0	0	0	6	79	71	51	48	26	69
1999—	New York (A.L.)	2	2	.500	4.33	73	1	0	0	0	62 1/3	71	30	30	18	59
A.L. totals (5 years)		17	8	.680	3.98	307	1	0	0	10	307 2/3	287	141	136	113	268
N.L. totals (7 years)		18	21	.462	4.01	304	0	0	0	55	289 2/3	277	146	129	114	223
Major League totals (11 years)		35	29	.547	3.99	611	1	0	0	65	597 1/3	564	287	265	227	491

DIVISION SERIES RECORD

Year	League	W	L	Pct.	ERA	G	GS	CG	ShO	Sv.	IP	H	R	ER	BB	SO
1995—	Boston (A.L.)	0	0	...	0.00	1	0	0	0	0	2 1/3	1	0	0	0	4
1996—	Texas (A.L.)	0	1	.000	2.70	3	0	0	0	0	3 1/3	2	2	1	3	3
1997—	New York (A.L.)	0	0	...	0.00	3	0	0	0	0	1	1	0	0	1	3
1998—	New York (A.L.)							Did not play.								
1999—	New York (A.L.)							Did not play.								
Division series totals (3 years)		0	1	.000	1.35	7	0	0	0	0	6 2/3	4	2	1	4	10

CHAMPIONSHIP SERIES RECORD

Year	League	W	L	Pct.	ERA	G	GS	CG	ShO	Sv.	IP	H	R	ER	BB	SO
1991—	Atlanta (N.L.)	0	0	...	2.45	3	0	0	0	0	3 2/3	4	1	1	3	3
1992—	Atlanta (N.L.)	0	0	...	0.00	5	0	0	0	0	4 1/3	2	1	0	2	5
1993—	Atlanta (N.L.)	0	0	...	0.00	1	0	0	0	0	1	1	0	0	1	0
1998—	New York (A.L.)	0	0	...	0.00	3	0	0	0	0	3 2/3	2	0	0	2	4
1999—	New York (A.L.)	0	0	...	0.00	3	0	0	0	0	1/3	1	0	0	1	0
Champ. series totals (5 years)		0	0	...	0.69	15	0	0	0	0	13	10	2	1	9	12

WORLD SERIES RECORD

NOTES: Member of World Series championship team (1998 and 1999).

Year	League	W	L	Pct.	ERA	G	GS	CG	ShO	Sv.	IP	H	R	ER	BB	SO
1991—	Atlanta (N.L.)	1	0	1.000	0.00	5	0	0	0	0	7 1/3	5	0	0	2	7
1992—	Atlanta (N.L.)	0	0	...	0.00	4	0	0	0	1	5	3	0	0	2	1
1998—	New York (A.L.)	0	0	...	27.00	1	0	0	0	0	2/3	3	2	2	0	1
1999—	New York (A.L.)	0	0	...	0.00	1	0	0	0	0	1/3	0	0	0	0	1
World Series totals (4 years)		1	0	1.000	1.35	11	0	0	0	1	13 1/3	11	2	2	4	10

STARK, DENNIS   P   MARINERS

PERSONAL: Born October 27, 1974, in Hicksville, Ohio. ... 6-2/210. ... Throws right, bats right.
HIGH SCHOOL: Edgerton (Ohio).
COLLEGE: Toledo.
TRANSACTIONS/CAREER NOTES: Selected by Seattle Mariners organization in fourth round of free-agent draft (June 4, 1996). ... On Lancaster disabled list (April 26, 1998-remainder of season); included rehabilitation assignment to Arizona Mariners (July 30-August 11).

Year	League	W	L	Pct.	ERA	G	GS	CG	ShO	Sv.	IP	H	R	ER	BB	SO
1996—	Everett (N'west)	1	3	.250	4.45	12	4	0	0	0	30 1/3	25	19	15	17	49
1997—	Wisconsin (Midw.)	6	3	.667	1.97	16	15	1	0	0	91 1/3	52	27	20	33	105
—	Lancaster (East.)	1	1	.500	3.24	3	3	0	0	0	16 2/3	13	7	6	10	17
1998—	Lancaster (Calif.)	1	2	.333	4.29	5	5	0	0	0	21	18	12	10	17	21
—	Arizona Mariners (Ariz.)	0	0	...	2.16	3	1	0	0	0	8 1/3	9	2	2	2	13
1999—	New Haven (East.)	9	11	.450	4.40	26	26	2	1	0	147 1/3	151	82	72	62	103
—	Seattle (A.L.)	0	0	...	9.95	5	0	0	0	0	6 1/3	10	8	7	4	4
Major League totals (1 year)		0	0	...	9.95	5	0	0	0	0	6 1/3	10	8	7	4	4

STECHSCHULTE, GENE   P   CARDINALS

PERSONAL: Born August 12, 1973, in Lima, Ohio. ... 6-5/210. ... Throws right, bats right. ... Full name: Gene Urban Stechschulte.
HIGH SCHOOL: Kalida (Ohio).
COLLEGE: Ashland (Ohio).
TRANSACTIONS/CAREER NOTES: Signed as non-drafted free agent by St. Louis Cardinals organization (June 13, 1996). ... On Arkansas disabled list (July 31-September 1, 1999).
STATISTICAL NOTES: Led Midwest League pitchers with 51 games finished in 1998.

Year	League	W	L	Pct.	ERA	G	GS	CG	ShO	Sv.	IP	H	R	ER	BB	SO
1996—	New Jersey (NY-P)	1	2	.333	3.27	20	1	0	0	0	33	41	17	12	16	27
1997—	New Jersey (NY-P)	1	1	.500	3.22	30	0	0	0	1	36 1/3	45	16	13	16	28
1998—	Peoria (Midw.)	4	8	.333	2.59	57	0	0	0	*33	66	58	26	19	21	70
1999—	Arkansas (Texas)	2	6	.250	3.40	39	0	0	0	19	42 1/3	41	26	16	20	41
—	Memphis (PCL)	0	0	...	7.71	2	0	0	0	0	2 1/3	2	2	2	5	2

STEIN, BLAKE   P   ROYALS

PERSONAL: Born August 3, 1973, in McComb, Miss. ... 6-7/240. ... Throws right, bats right. ... Full name: William Blake Stein.
HIGH SCHOOL: Covington (La.).
COLLEGE: Spring Hill College (Ala.).
TRANSACTIONS/CAREER NOTES: Selected by St. Louis Cardinals organization in sixth round of free-agent draft (June 2, 1994). ... Traded by Cardinals with P T.J. Mathews and P Eric Ludwick to Oakland Athletics for 1B Mark McGwire (July 31, 1997). ... Traded by Athletics with P Jeff D'Amico and P Brad Rigby to Kansas City Royals for P Kevin Appier (July 31, 1999).
RECORDS: Shares major league single-inning record for most strikeouts—4 (July 27, 1998, fourth inning).

Year	League	W	L	Pct.	ERA	G	GS	CG	ShO	Sv.	IP	H	R	ER	BB	SO
1994—	Johnson City (Appl.)	4	1	.800	2.87	13	13	1	0	0	59 2/3	44	21	19	24	69
1995—	Peoria (Midw.)	10	6	.625	3.80	27	•27	1	0	0	139 2/3	122	69	59	61	133
1996—	St. Petersburg (FSL)	•16	5	.762	*2.15	28	27	2	1	1	172	122	48	41	54	*159
1997—	Arkansas (Texas)	8	7	.533	4.24	22	22	1	0	0	133 2/3	128	67	63	49	114
—	Huntsville (Sou.)■	3	2	.600	5.71	7	7	0	0	0	34 2/3	36	24	22	20	25
1998—	Edmonton (PCL)	3	1	.750	3.47	5	4	0	0	0	23 1/3	22	13	9	11	31
—	Oakland (A.L.)	5	9	.357	6.37	24	20	1	1	0	117 1/3	117	92	83	71	89
1999—	Vancouver (PCL)	4	2	.667	4.10	19	19	0	0	0	109 2/3	94	54	50	43	111
—	Oakland (A.L.)	0	0	...	16.88	1	1	0	0	0	2 2/3	6	5	5	6	4
—	Kansas City (A.L.)■	1	2	.333	4.09	12	11	0	0	0	70 1/3	59	33	32	41	43
Major League totals (2 years)		6	11	.353	5.67	37	32	1	1	0	190 1/3	182	130	120	118	136

S

PERSONAL: Born March 2, 1962, in New Ulm, Minn. ... 6-1/212. ... Bats right, throws right. ... Full name: Terry Lee Steinbach. ... Brother of Tom Steinbach, minor league outfielder (1983).

HIGH SCHOOL: New Ulm (Minn.).

COLLEGE: Minnesota.

TRANSACTIONS/CAREER NOTES: Selected by Cleveland Indians organization in 16th round of free-agent draft (June 3, 1980); did not sign. ... Selected by Oakland Athletics organization in ninth round of free-agent draft (June 6, 1983). ... On disabled list (May 6-June 1, 1988; July 3-28, 1990; and April 10-25, 1992). ... Granted free agency (October 26, 1992). ... Re-signed by A's (December 14, 1992). ... On disabled list (August 16, 1993-remainder of season and August 13-29, 1995). ... Granted free agency (November 17, 1996). ... Signed by Minnesota Twins (December 5, 1996). ... Granted free agency (October 29, 1998). ... Re-signed by Twins organization (January 4, 1999). ... On Minnesota disabled list (May 13-28 and June 1-20, 1999). ... Granted free agency (November 4, 1999). ... Announced retirement (November 16, 1999).

HONORS: Named Southern League Most Valuable Player (1986).

STATISTICAL NOTES: Led Northwest League third basemen with 122 assists and tied for lead with 17 errors in 1983. ... Led Midwest League third basemen with 31 double plays in 1984. ... Led Southern League with 22 passed balls in 1986. ... Hit home run in first major league at-bat (September 12, 1986). ... Led A.L. catchers with 15 errors in 1991. ... Led A.L. catchers with .998 fielding percentage in 1994. ... Career major league grand slams: 8.

								BATTING						FIELDING		
Year Team (League)	Pos.	G	AB	R	H	2B	3B	HR	RBI	Avg.	BB	SO	SB	PO	A	E	Avg.
1983— Medford (N'west)	3B-OF-1B	62	219	42	69	16	0	6	38	.315	28	22	8	105	†124	‡21	.916
1984— Madison (Midw.)	3B-1B-P	135	474	57	140	24	6	11	79	.295	49	59	5	107	257	27	.931
1985— Huntsville (Sou.)	C-3-1-OF-P	128	456	64	124	31	3	9	72	.272	45	36	4	187	43	6	.975
1986— Huntsville (Sou.)	C-1B-3B	138	505	113	164	33	2	24	*132	.325	94	74	10	620	73	14	.980
— Oakland (A.L.)	C	6	15	3	5	0	0	2	4	.333	1	0	0	21	4	1	.962
1987— Oakland (A.L.)	C-3B-DH-1B	122	391	66	111	16	3	16	56	.284	32	66	1	642	44	10	.986
1988— Oakland (A.L.)	C-3-1-DH-O	104	351	42	93	19	1	9	51	.265	33	47	3	536	58	9	.985
1989— Oakland (A.L.)	C-O-1-DH-3	130	454	37	124	13	1	7	42	.273	30	66	1	612	47	11	.984
1990— Oakland (A.L.)	C-DH-1B	114	379	32	95	15	2	9	57	.251	19	66	0	401	31	5	.989
1991— Oakland (A.L.)	C-1B-DH	129	456	50	125	31	1	6	67	.274	22	70	2	639	53	†15	.979
1992— Oakland (A.L.)	C-1B-DH	128	438	48	122	20	1	12	53	.279	45	58	2	598	72	10	.985
1993— Oakland (A.L.)	C-1B-DH	104	389	47	111	19	1	10	43	.285	25	65	3	524	47	7	.988
1994— Oakland (A.L.)	C-DH-1B	103	369	51	105	21	2	11	57	.285	26	62	2	597	59	1	†.998
1995— Oakland (A.L.)	C-1B	114	406	43	113	26	1	15	65	.278	25	74	1	686	57	6	.992
1996— Oakland (A.L.)	C-DH-1B	145	514	79	140	25	1	35	100	.272	49	115	0	732	46	7	.991
1997— Minnesota (A.L.)■	C-1B-DH	122	447	60	111	27	1	12	54	.248	35	106	6	657	51	6	.992
1998— Minnesota (A.L.)	C-DH	124	422	45	102	25	2	14	54	.242	38	89	0	665	52	7	.990
1999— Minnesota (A.L.)	C-DH	101	338	35	96	16	4	4	42	.284	38	54	2	539	30	5	.991
Major League totals (14 years)		1546	5369	638	1453	273	21	162	745	.271	418	938	23	7849	651	100	.988

CHAMPIONSHIP SERIES RECORD

								BATTING						FIELDING		
Year Team (League)	Pos.	G	AB	R	H	2B	3B	HR	RBI	Avg.	BB	SO	SB	PO	A	E	Avg.
1988— Oakland (A.L.)	C	2	4	0	1	0	0	0	0	.250	2	0	0	12	0	0	1.000
1989— Oakland (A.L.)	C-DH	4	15	0	3	0	0	0	1	.200	1	5	0	17	0	0	1.000
1990— Oakland (A.L.)	C	3	11	2	5	0	0	0	1	.455	1	2	0	11	0	0	1.000
1992— Oakland (A.L.)	C	6	24	1	7	0	0	1	5	.292	2	7	0	30	7	0	1.000
Championship series totals (4 years)		15	54	3	16	0	0	1	7	.296	6	14	0	70	7	0	1.000

WORLD SERIES RECORD

NOTES: Member of World Series championship team (1989).

								BATTING						FIELDING		
Year Team (League)	Pos.	G	AB	R	H	2B	3B	HR	RBI	Avg.	BB	SO	SB	PO	A	E	Avg.
1988— Oakland (A.L.)	C-DH	3	11	0	4	1	0	0	0	.364	0	2	0	11	3	0	1.000
1989— Oakland (A.L.)	C	4	16	3	4	0	1	1	7	.250	2	1	0	27	2	0	1.000
1990— Oakland (A.L.)	C	3	8	0	1	0	0	0	0	.125	0	1	0	8	1	0	1.000
World Series totals (3 years)		10	35	3	9	1	1	1	7	.257	2	4	0	46	6	0	1.000

ALL-STAR GAME RECORD

NOTES: Named Most Valuable Player (1988). ... Hit home run in first at-bat (July 12, 1988).

					BATTING								FIELDING		
Year League	Pos.	AB	R	H	2B	3B	HR	RBI	Avg.	BB	SO	SB	PO	A	E	Avg.
1988— American	C	1	1	1	0	0	1	2	1.000	0	0	0	3	1	1	.800
1989— American	C	3	0	1	0	0	0	0	.333	0	0	0	6	1	0	1.000
1993— American	C	2	0	1	1	0	0	1	.500	0	1	0	6	0	0	1.000
All-Star Game totals (3 years)		6	1	3	1	0	1	3	.500	0	1	0	15	2	1	.944

RECORD AS PITCHER

Year League	W	L	Pct.	ERA	G	GS	CG	ShO	Sv.	IP	H	R	ER	BB	SO
1984— Madison (Midw.)	0	0	...	9.00	2	0	0	0	0	3	2	4	3	4	0
1985— Huntsville (Sou.)	0	0	...	0.00	1	0	0	0	0	1	0	0	0	0	0

STENSON, DERNELL   1B   RED SOX

PERSONAL: Born June 17, 1978, in La Grange, Ga. ... 6-1/232. ... Bats left, throws left. ... Full name: Dernell Renauld Stenson.

HIGH SCHOOL: La Grange (Ga.).

TRANSACTIONS/CAREER NOTES: Selected by Boston Red Sox organization in third round of free-agent draft (June 2, 1996). ... On Pawtucket disabled list (June 24-July 15, 1999).

Year	Team (League)	Pos.	G	AB	R	H	2B	3B	HR	RBI	Avg.	BB	SO	SB	PO	A	E	Avg.
1996—GC Red Sox (GCL)		OF	32	97	16	21	3	1	2	15	.216	16	26	4	30	2	0	1.000
1997—Michigan (Midw.)		OF	131	471	79	137	35	2	15	80	.291	72	105	6	145	11	14	.918
1998—Trenton (East.)		OF	138	505	90	130	21	1	24	71	.257	84	135	5	218	*15	6	.975
1999—Pawtucket (I.L.).........		1B-DH	121	440	64	119	28	2	18	82	.270	55	119	2	919	56	*34	.966
— GC Red Sox (GCL)		DH-1B	6	23	2	5	0	0	2	7	.217	3	5	0	16	2	1	.947

STENTZ, BRENT P TWINS

PERSONAL: Born July 24, 1975, in New Port Richey, Fla. ... 6-5/225. ... Throws right, bats right. ... Full name: Brent Daniel Stentz.
HIGH SCHOOL: Brooksville (Hernando, Fla.).
JUNIOR COLLEGE: Pasco-Hernando Community College (Fla.).
TRANSACTIONS/CAREER NOTES: Selected by Detroit Tigers organization in 33rd round of free-agent draft (June 2, 1994). ... Traded by Tigers to Minnesota Twins for C Matt Walbeck (December 11, 1996).
HONORS: Named Eastern League Pitcher of the Year (1998).

Year	League	W	L	Pct.	ERA	G	GS	CG	ShO	Sv.	IP	H	R	ER	BB	SO
1995—Gulf Coast Tigers (GCL)		2	1	.667	2.36	•24	0	0	0	*16	26²/₃	21	7	7	12	28
—Lakeland (FSL)		0	0	...	0.00	2	0	0	0	0	2	0	0	0	0	4
1996—Fayetteville (SAL)		7	8	.467	3.49	45	8	0	0	2	98	91	51	38	27	92
1997—Fort Myers (FSL)■............		7	2	.778	2.47	49	1	0	0	17	69¹/₃	53	20	19	24	70
1998—New Britain (East.)		1	2	.333	1.98	57	0	0	0	*43	59	44	13	13	28	65
1999—Salt Lake (PCL)		0	3	.000	11.22	23	0	0	0	3	25²/₃	43	34	32	21	23
—New Britain (East.)		0	1	.000	3.73	32	0	0	0	9	31¹/₃	23	13	13	12	44

STEPHENSON, GARRETT P CARDINALS

PERSONAL: Born January 2, 1972, in Takoma Park, Md. ... 6-5/208. ... Throws right, bats right. ... Full name: Garrett Charles Stephenson.
HIGH SCHOOL: Boonsboro (Md.).
JUNIOR COLLEGE: Ricks College (Idaho).
COLLEGE: Idaho State.
TRANSACTIONS/CAREER NOTES: Selected by Baltimore Orioles organization in 18th round of free-agent draft (June 1, 1992). ... Traded by Orioles with P Calvin Maduro to Philadelphia Phillies (September 4, 1996), completing deal in which Phillies traded 3B Todd Zeile and OF Pete Incaviglia to Orioles for two players to be named later (August 29, 1996). ... On Philadelphia disabled list (June 5-22 and August 18-September 2, 1997). ... On Scranton/Wilkes-Barre disabled list (July 8-August 3, 1998). ... Traded by Phillies with P Ricky Bottalico to St. Louis Cardinals for OF Ron Gant, P Jeff Brantley and P Cliff Politte (November 19, 1998). ... On Memphis disabled list (April 8-June 13, 1999).
STATISTICAL NOTES: Led Eastern League with 23 home runs allowed and 18 hit batsmen in 1995.

Year	League	W	L	Pct.	ERA	G	GS	CG	ShO	Sv.	IP	H	R	ER	BB	SO
1992—Bluefield (Appl.)		3	1	.750	4.73	12	3	0	0	0	32¹/₃	35	22	17	7	30
1993—Albany (SAL)		16	7	.696	2.84	30	24	3	•2	1	171¹/₃	142	65	54	44	147
1994—Frederick (Caro.)		7	5	.583	4.02	18	17	1	0	0	107¹/₃	91	62	48	36	133
—Bowie (East.)		3	2	.600	5.15	7	7	1	1	0	36²/₃	47	22	21	11	32
1995—Bowie (East.)		7	10	.412	3.64	29	*29	1	0	0	175¹/₃	154	87	71	47	139
1996—Rochester (I.L.)		7	6	.538	4.81	23	21	3	1	0	121²/₃	123	66	65	44	86
—Baltimore (A.L.)		0	1	.000	12.79	3	0	0	0	0	6¹/₃	13	9	9	3	3
1997—Scranton/W.B. (I.L.)■		3	1	.750	5.90	7	3	0	0	0	29	27	19	19	12	27
—Philadelphia (N.L.)............		8	6	.571	3.15	20	18	2	0	0	117	104	45	41	38	81
1998—Philadelphia (N.L.)............		0	2	.000	9.00	6	6	0	0	0	23	31	24	23	19	17
—Scranton/W.B. (I.L.)		1	8	.111	5.25	13	11	2	0	0	73²/₃	81	49	43	16	48
1999—Arkansas (Texas)■............		0	0	...	3.38	1	1	0	0	0	5¹/₃	8	3	2	1	2
—Memphis (PCL)		1	1	.500	3.16	4	4	0	0	0	25²/₃	22	9	9	7	19
—St. Louis (N.L.)................		6	3	.667	4.22	18	12	0	0	0	85¹/₃	90	43	40	29	59
A.L. totals (1 year)		0	1	.000	12.79	3	0	0	0	0	6¹/₃	13	9	9	3	3
N.L. totals (3 years)		14	11	.560	4.15	44	36	2	0	0	225¹/₃	225	112	104	86	157
Major League totals (4 years)		14	12	.538	4.39	47	36	2	0	0	231²/₃	238	121	113	89	160

STEVENS, DAVE P

PERSONAL: Born March 4, 1970, in Fullerton, Calif. ... 6-3/195. ... Throws right, bats right. ... Full name: David James Stevens.
HIGH SCHOOL: La Habra (Calif.).
COLLEGE: Fullerton (Calif.) College.
TRANSACTIONS/CAREER NOTES: Selected by Chicago Cubs organization in 20th round of free-agent draft (June 5, 1989). ... On disabled list (June 17-July 4, 1991). ... On Iowa disabled list (April 8-May 20, 1993). ... Traded by Cubs with C Matt Walbeck to Minnesota Twins for P Willie Banks (November 24, 1993). ... On disabled list (May 30-June 21 and July 21-August 9, 1996). ... Claimed on waivers by Cubs organization (July 31, 1997). ... Released by Cubs (December 3, 1998). ... Signed by Cleveland Indians organization (January 26, 1999). ... Released by Indians (June 10, 1999). ... Signed by Seattle Mariners organization (July 1, 1999). ... Released by Mariners (July 30, 1999).
MISCELLANEOUS: Appeared in one game as pinch runner with Chicago (1998).

Year	League	W	L	Pct.	ERA	G	GS	CG	ShO	Sv.	IP	H	R	ER	BB	SO
1990—Huntington (Appl.)		2	4	.333	4.61	13	11	0	0	0	56²/₃	48	44	29	47	55
1991—Geneva (NY-P)...................		2	3	.400	2.85	9	9	1	0	0	47¹/₃	49	20	15	14	44
1992—Charlotte (Sou.)................		9	13	.409	3.91	26	26	2	0	0	149²/₃	147	79	65	53	89
1993—Iowa (A.A.)		4	0	1.000	4.19	24	0	0	0	4	34¹/₃	24	16	16	14	29
—Orlando (Sou.)		6	1	.857	4.22	11	11	1	1	0	70¹/₃	69	36	33	35	49
1994—Salt Lake (PCL)■		6	2	.750	1.67	23	0	0	0	3	43	41	13	8	16	30
—Minnesota (A.L.)		5	2	.714	6.80	24	0	0	0	0	45	55	35	34	23	24
1995—Minnesota (A.L.)		5	4	.556	5.07	56	0	0	0	10	65²/₃	74	40	37	32	47
1996—Minnesota (A.L.)		3	3	.500	4.66	49	0	0	0	11	58	58	31	30	25	29

S

Year	League	W	L	Pct.	ERA	G	GS	CG	ShO	Sv.	IP	H	R	ER	BB	SO
1997—Salt Lake (PCL)		9	3	.750	4.30	16	14	1	0	0	90	93	52	43	31	71
—Minnesota (A.L.)		1	3	.250	9.00	6	6	0	0	0	23	44	23	23	17	16
—Iowa (A.A.)■		1	1	.500	4.70	6	0	0	0	1	7²/₃	8	4	4	5	8
—Chicago (N.L.)		0	2	.000	9.64	10	0	0	0	0	9¹/₃	13	11	10	9	13
1998—Iowa (PCL)		4	1	.800	3.08	26	0	0	0	2	49²/₃	41	19	17	16	39
—Chicago (N.L.)		1	2	.333	4.74	31	0	0	0	0	38	42	20	20	17	31
1999—Buffalo (I.L.)■		1	0	1.000	1.52	20	0	0	0	12	23²/₃	12	4	4	14	28
—Cleveland (A.L.)■		0	0	...	10.00	5	0	0	0	0	9	10	10	10	8	6
—Tacoma (PCL)■		1	1	.500	12.60	7	0	0	0	0	10	14	14	14	6	8
A.L. totals (5 years)		14	12	.538	6.01	140	6	0	0	21	200²/₃	238	139	134	105	122
N.L. totals (2 years)		1	4	.200	5.70	41	0	0	0	0	47¹/₃	55	31	30	26	44
Major League totals (6 years)		15	16	.484	5.95	181	6	0	0	21	248	293	170	164	131	166

STEVENS, LEE — 1B — RANGERS

PERSONAL: Born July 10, 1967, in Kansas City, Mo. ... 6-4/235. ... Bats left, throws left. ... Full name: DeWain Lee Stevens.
HIGH SCHOOL: Lawrence (Kan.).
TRANSACTIONS/CAREER NOTES: Selected by California Angels organization in first round (22nd pick overall) of free-agent draft (June 2, 1986). ... Traded by Angels to Montreal Expos for P Jeff Tuss (January 15, 1993); Tuss announced his retirement and Angels acquired P Keith Morrison to complete deal (January 21, 1993). ... Released by Expos (March 30, 1993). ... Signed by Toronto Blue Jays organization (April 8, 1993). ... Granted free agency (October 15, 1993). ... Signed by Vancouver, Angels organization (October 25, 1993). ... Contract sold by Angels to Kintetsu of Japan Pacific League (November 16, 1993). ... Signed by Texas Rangers organization (April 3, 1996). ... On Texas disabled list (August 4-September 1, 1996); included rehabilitation assignment to Oklahoma City (August 13-September 1, 1996). ... On Texas disabled list (August 8-September 1, 1998); included rehabilitation assignment to Oklahoma (August 25-September 1).
HONORS: Named American Association Most Valuable Player (1996).
STATISTICAL NOTES: Led California League first basemen with .986 fielding percentage, 1,028 putouts and 66 assists in 1987. ... Led Texas League outfielders with 12 errors in 1988. ... Tied for Pacific Coast League lead with 11 intentional bases on balls received in 1990. ... Led American Association with 277 total bases, .643 slugging percentage and .404 on-base percentage in 1996. ... Tied for American Association lead with eight intentional bases on balls received in 1996. ... Hit three home runs in one game (April 13, 1998). ... Career major league grand slams: 2.

							BATTING								FIELDING		
Year	Team (League)	Pos.	G	AB	R	H	2B	3B	HR	RBI	Avg.	BB	SO	SB	PO	A	E	Avg.
1986—Salem (N'west)		OF-1B	72	267	45	75	18	2	6	47	.281	45	49	13	231	18	5	.980
1987—Palm Springs (Calif.)		1B-OF	140	532	82	130	29	2	19	97	.244	61	117	1	†1031	†68	18	†.984
1988—Midland (Texas)		OF-1B	116	414	79	123	26	2	23	76	.297	58	108	0	217	16	†14	.943
1989—Edmonton (PCL)		1B-OF	127	446	72	110	29	9	14	74	.247	61	115	5	635	40	7	.990
1990—Edmonton (PCL)		OF-1B	90	338	57	99	31	2	16	66	.293	55	83	1	284	10	6	.980
—California (A.L.)		1B	67	248	28	53	10	0	7	32	.214	22	75	1	597	36	4	.994
1991—Edmonton (PCL)		OF-1B	123	481	75	151	29	3	19	96	.314	37	79	3	519	33	7	.987
—California (A.L.)		OF-1B	18	58	8	17	7	0	0	9	.293	6	12	1	100	6	1	.991
1992—California (A.L.)		1B-DH	106	312	25	69	19	0	7	37	.221	29	64	1	764	49	4	.995
1993—Syracuse (I.L.)■		OF-1B	116	401	61	106	30	1	14	66	.264	39	85	2	201	12	3	.986
1994—Kintetsu (Jap. Pac.)■		OF	93	302	44	87	21	0	20	66	.288	28	100	0	...	...	...	...
1995—Kintetsu (Jap. Pac.)		OF	129	476	54	117	29	1	23	70	.246	46	129	0	...	...	...	...
1996—Okla. City (A.A.)■		DH-1B-OF	117	431	84	140	*37	2	*32	94	.325	58	90	3	348	24	3	.992
—Texas (A.L.)		1B-OF	27	78	6	18	2	3	3	12	.231	6	22	0	157	14	1	.994
1997—Texas (A.L.)		1B-DH-OF	137	426	58	128	24	2	21	74	.300	23	83	1	486	33	3	.994
1998—Texas (A.L.)		DH-1B-OF	120	344	52	91	17	4	20	59	.265	31	93	0	220	15	1	.996
—Oklahoma (PCL)		DH-1B	3	12	2	4	0	0	1	1	.333	0	2	0	12	1	0	1.000
1999—Texas (A.L.)		1B-DH	146	517	76	146	31	1	24	81	.282	52	132	2	1228	60	8	.994
Major League totals (7 years)			621	1983	253	522	110	10	82	304	.263	169	481	6	3552	213	22	.994

DIVISION SERIES RECORD

							BATTING								FIELDING		
Year	Team (League)	Pos.	G	AB	R	H	2B	3B	HR	RBI	Avg.	BB	SO	SB	PO	A	E	Avg.
1998—Texas (A.L.)		DH	1	3	0	0	0	0	0	0	.000	0	1	0	...	...	...	...
1999—Texas (A.L.)		1B	3	9	0	1	1	0	0	0	.111	1	2	0	25	2	0	1.000
Division series totals (2 years)			4	12	0	1	1	0	0	0	.083	1	3	0	25	2	0	1.000

STEWART, PAUL — P — BREWERS

PERSONAL: Born October 21, 1978, in Alexandria, Va. ... 6-5/200. ... Throws right, bats right. ... Full name: Paul Allan Stewart.
HIGH SCHOOL: Garner (N.C.).
TRANSACTIONS/CAREER NOTES: Selected by Milwaukee Brewers organization in sixth round of free-agent draft (June 4, 1996).
STATISTICAL NOTES: Led Pioneer League pitchers with 13 home runs allowed in 1997. ... Led Midwest League pitchers with 22 home runs allowed in 1998.

Year	League	W	L	Pct.	ERA	G	GS	CG	ShO	Sv.	IP	H	R	ER	BB	SO
1996—Ogden (Pio.)		1	4	.200	7.83	12	9	0	0	0	43²/₃	47	49	38	26	39
1997—Ogden (Pio.)		5	6	.455	5.31	15	•15	1	1	0	81¹/₃	88	59	48	30	82
1998—Beloit (Midw.)		8	10	.444	4.90	26	25	1	0	0	143¹/₃	164	99	78	45	114
1999—Stockton (Calif.)		10	11	.476	3.96	27	25	•5	1	0	170¹/₃	171	90	75	61	117

STEWART, SHANNON — OF — BLUE JAYS

PERSONAL: Born February 25, 1974, in Cincinnati. ... 6-1/205. ... Bats right, throws right. ... Full name: Shannon Harold Stewart.
HIGH SCHOOL: Southridge Senior (Miami).

TRANSACTIONS/CAREER NOTES: Selected by Toronto Blue Jays organization in first round (19th pick overall) of free-agent draft (June 1, 1992); pick received as part of compensation for Los Angeles Dodgers signing Type A free-agent P Tom Candiotti. ... On disabled list (June 13, 1994-remainder of season). ... On Syracuse disabled list (May 13-31, 1996).
STATISTICAL NOTES: Led International League outfielders with 286 total chances in 1996. ... Had 16-game hitting streak (June 15-30, 1999). ... Had 26-game hitting streak (August 1-29, 1999). ... Tied for A.L. lead in caught stealing with 14 in 1999.

												BATTING				FIELDING		
Year Team (League)	Pos.	G	AB	R	H	2B	3B	HR	RBI	Avg.	BB	SO	SB	PO	A	E	Avg.
1992—GC Blue Jays (GCL)....	OF	50	172	44	40	1	0	1	11	.233	24	27	*32	81	1	1	.988
1993—St. Cath. (NY-P)....	OF	75	*301	•53	84	15	2	3	29	.279	33	43	25	81	0	0	1.000
1994—Hagerstown (SAL)......	OF	56	225	39	73	10	5	4	25	.324	23	39	15	92	4	1	.990
1995—Knoxville (Sou.)..........	OF-DH	138	498	89	143	24	6	5	55	.287	*89	61	42	283	6	6	.980
— Toronto (A.L.).............	OF	12	38	2	8	0	0	0	1	.211	5	5	2	20	1	1	.955
1996—Syracuse (I.L.)...........	OF	112	420	77	125	26	8	6	42	.298	54	61	*35	*274	7	5	.983
— Toronto (A.L.).............	OF	7	17	2	3	1	0	0	2	.176	1	4	1	4	0	1	.800
1997—Toronto (A.L.)............	OF-DH	44	168	25	48	13	7	0	22	.286	19	24	10	97	1	2	.980
—Syracuse (I.L.)............	OF	58	208	41	72	13	1	5	24	.346	36	26	9	115	1	2	.983
1998—Toronto (A.L.)............	OF	144	516	90	144	29	3	12	55	.279	67	77	51	295	4	6	.980
1999—Toronto (A.L.)............	OF-DH	145	608	102	185	28	2	11	67	.304	59	83	37	257	4	5	.981
Major League totals (5 years)		352	1347	221	388	71	12	23	147	.288	151	193	101	673	10	15	.979

STINNETT, KELLY   C   DIAMONDBACKS

S

PERSONAL: Born February 4, 1970, in Lawton, Okla. ... 5-11/195. ... Bats right, throws right. ... Full name: Kelly Lee Stinnett. ... Name pronounced stih-NET.
HIGH SCHOOL: Lawton (Okla.).
JUNIOR COLLEGE: Seminole (Okla.) Junior College.
TRANSACTIONS/CAREER NOTES: Selected by Cleveland Indians organization in 11th round of free-agent draft (June 5, 1989). ... Selected by New York Mets from Indians organization in Rule 5 major league draft (December 13, 1993). ... Traded by Mets to Milwaukee Brewers for P Cory Lidle (January 17, 1996). ... On Milwaukee disabled list (July 27-September 2, 1997). ... Selected by Arizona Diamondbacks in third round (65th pick overall) of expansion draft (November 18, 1997).
STATISTICAL NOTES: Led New York-Pennsylvania League catchers with 18 errors in 1990. ... Led South Atlantic League catchers with 27 errors in 1991. ... Tied for American Association lead in being hit by pitch with 13 in 1996. ... Led American Association catchers with 10 errors and tied for lead with nine double plays in 1996.

												BATTING				FIELDING		
Year Team (League)	Pos.	G	AB	R	H	2B	3B	HR	RBI	Avg.	BB	SO	SB	PO	A	E	Avg.
1990—Watertown (NY-P)......	C-1B	60	192	29	46	10	2	2	21	.240	40	43	3	348	48	†18	.957
1991—Columbus (SAL).........	C-1B	102	384	49	101	15	1	14	74	.263	26	70	4	685	100	†28	.966
1992—Canton/Akron (East.)..	C	91	296	37	84	10	0	6	32	.284	16	43	7	560	57	*13	.979
1993—Charlotte (I.L.)...........	C	98	288	42	79	10	3	6	33	.274	17	52	0	495	48	8	.985
1994—New York (N.L.)■	C	47	150	20	38	6	2	2	14	.253	11	28	2	211	20	5	.979
1995—New York (N.L.).........	C	77	196	23	43	8	1	4	18	.219	29	65	2	380	22	7	.983
1996—Milwaukee (A.L.)■	C-DH	14	26	1	2	0	0	0	0	.077	2	11	0	46	2	2	.960
—New Orleans (A.A.).........	C-DH-3B	95	334	63	96	21	1	27	70	.287	31	83	3	485	52	†11	.980
1997—Tucson (PCL)	C-DH-1B	64	209	50	67	15	3	10	43	.321	42	46	1	256	34	2	.993
—Milwaukee (A.L.)	C-DH	30	36	2	9	4	0	0	3	.250	3	9	0	81	5	1	.989
1998—Arizona (N.L.)■..........	C-DH	92	274	35	71	14	1	11	34	.259	35	74	0	458	37	8	.984
1999—Arizona (N.L.)............	C	88	284	36	66	13	0	14	38	.232	24	83	2	549	37	6	.990
American League totals (2 years)		44	62	3	11	4	0	0	3	.177	5	20	0	127	7	3	.978
National League totals (4 years)		304	904	114	218	41	4	31	104	.241	99	250	6	1598	116	26	.985
Major League totals (6 years)		348	966	117	229	45	4	31	107	.237	104	270	6	1725	123	29	.985

DIVISION SERIES RECORD

												BATTING				FIELDING		
Year Team (League)	Pos.	G	AB	R	H	2B	3B	HR	RBI	Avg.	BB	SO	SB	PO	A	E	Avg.
1999—Arizona (N.L.)............	C	4	14	1	2	1	0	0	0	.143	1	4	0	29	2	0	1.000

STOCKER, KEVIN   SS   DEVIL RAYS

PERSONAL: Born February 13, 1970, in Spokane, Wash. ... 6-1/175. ... Bats both, throws right. ... Full name: Kevin Douglas Stocker.
HIGH SCHOOL: Central Valley (Veradale, Wash.).
COLLEGE: Washington.
TRANSACTIONS/CAREER NOTES: Selected by Philadelphia Phillies organization in second round of free-agent draft (June 3, 1991). ... On Philadelphia disabled list (April 28-June 1, 1994); included rehabilitation assignment to Scranton/Wilkes-Barre (May 28-June 1). ... Traded by Phillies to Tampa Bay Devil Rays for OF Bob Abreu (November 18, 1997). ... On disabled list (August 30, 1998-remainder of season). ... On Tampa Bay disabled list (July 22, 1999-remainder of season); included rehabilitation assignment to St. Petersburg (August 25-31).

												BATTING				FIELDING		
Year Team (League)	Pos.	G	AB	R	H	2B	3B	HR	RBI	Avg.	BB	SO	SB	PO	A	E	Avg.
1991—Spartanburg (SAL)	SS	70	250	26	55	11	1	0	20	.220	31	37	15	83	176	18	.935
1992—Clearwater (FSL)	SS	63	244	43	69	13	4	1	33	.283	27	31	15	102	220	16	.953
—Reading (East.)............	SS	62	240	31	60	9	2	1	13	.250	22	30	17	100	172	14	.951
1993—Scranton/W.B. (I.L.).....	SS-DH	83	313	54	73	14	1	3	17	.233	29	56	17	122	248	15	.961
—Philadelphia (N.L.)......	SS	70	259	46	84	12	3	2	31	.324	30	43	5	118	202	14	.958
1994—Philadelphia (N.L.)......	SS	82	271	38	74	11	2	2	28	.273	44	41	2	118	253	16	.959
—Scranton/W.B. (I.L.) ...	SS	4	13	1	4	1	0	0	2	.308	1	0	0	5	11	0	1.000
1995—Philadelphia (N.L.)......	SS	125	412	42	90	14	3	1	32	.218	43	75	6	147	383	17	.969
1996—Philadelphia (N.L.)......	SS	119	394	46	100	22	6	5	41	.254	43	89	6	165	352	13	.975
—Scranton/W.B. (I.L.) ...	SS	12	44	5	10	3	0	2	6	.227	0	4	1	17	39	1	.982
1997—Philadelphia (N.L.)......	SS	149	504	51	134	23	5	4	40	.266	51	91	11	190	376	11	.981

Year Team (League)	Pos.	G	AB	R	H	2B	3B	HR	RBI	Avg.	BB	SO	SB	PO	A	E	Avg.
1998—Tampa Bay (A.L.)■....	SS	112	336	37	70	11	3	6	25	.208	27	80	5	186	335	11	.979
1999—Tampa Bay (A.L.)........	SS	79	254	39	76	11	2	1	27	.299	24	41	9	137	216	16	.957
— St. Petersburg (FSL) ..	SS	3	11	2	1	0	0	0	0	.091	1	2	0	5	10	0	1.000
American League totals (2 years)		191	590	76	146	22	5	7	52	.247	51	121	14	323	551	27	.970
National League totals (5 years)		545	1840	223	482	82	19	14	172	.262	211	339	30	738	1566	71	.970
Major League totals (7 years)		736	2430	299	628	104	24	21	224	.258	262	460	44	1061	2117	98	.970

CHAMPIONSHIP SERIES RECORD

Year Team (League)	Pos.	G	AB	R	H	2B	3B	HR	RBI	Avg.	BB	SO	SB	PO	A	E	Avg.
1993— Philadelphia (N.L.)......	SS	6	22	0	4	1	0	0	1	.182	2	5	0	10	13	1	.958

WORLD SERIES RECORD

Year Team (League)	Pos.	G	AB	R	H	2B	3B	HR	RBI	Avg.	BB	SO	SB	PO	A	E	Avg.
1993— Philadelphia (N.L.)......	SS	6	19	1	4	1	0	0	1	.211	5	5	0	8	13	0	1.000

STOTTLEMYRE, TODD   P   DIAMONDBACKS

PERSONAL: Born May 20, 1965, in Yakima, Wash. ... 6-3/200. ... Throws right, bats left. ... Full name: Todd Vernon Stottlemyre. ... Son of Mel Stottlemyre Sr., pitching coach, New York Yankees; pitcher with New York Yankees (1964-74) and pitching coach for New York Mets (1984-93); and brother of Mel Stottlemyre Jr., pitcher with Kansas City Royals (1990).

HIGH SCHOOL: A.C. Davis (Yakima, Wash.).

JUNIOR COLLEGE: Yakima (Wash.) Valley College.

COLLEGE: UNLV.

TRANSACTIONS/CAREER NOTES: Selected by New York Yankees organization in fifth round of free-agent draft (June 6, 1983); did not sign. ... Selected by St. Louis Cardinals organization in secondary phase of free-agent draft (January 9, 1985); did not sign. ... Selected by Toronto Blue Jays organization in secondary phase of free-agent draft (June 3, 1985). ... On disabled list (June 20-July 13, 1992). ... On suspended list (September 23-28, 1992). ... On disabled list (May 23-June 13, 1993). ... Granted free agency (October 18, 1994). ... Signed by Oakland Athletics (April 11, 1995). ... Traded by A's to St. Louis Cardinals for P Bret Wagner, P Jay Witasick and P Carl Dale (January 9, 1996). ... Traded by Cardinals with SS Royce Clayton to Texas Rangers for P Darren Oliver, 3B Fernando Tatis and a player to be named later (July 31, 1998); Cardinals acquired OF Mark Little to complete deal (August 9, 1998). ... Granted free agency (October 22, 1998). ... Signed by Arizona Diamondbacks (December 2, 1998). ... On Arizona disabled list (May 18-August 19, 1999); included rehabilitation assignment to Arizona League Diamondbacks (August 3-15).

STATISTICAL NOTES: Pitched 9-0 one-hit, complete-game victory against Chicago (August 26, 1992). ... Struck out 15 batters in one game (June 16, 1995).

MISCELLANEOUS: Struck out in only appearance as pinch hitter (1997).

Year League	W	L	Pct.	ERA	G	GS	CG	ShO	Sv.	IP	H	R	ER	BB	SO
1986—Ventura County (Calif.).......	9	4	.692	2.43	17	17	2	0	0	103 2/3	76	39	28	36	104
— Knoxville (Sou.)............	8	7	.533	4.18	18	18	1	0	0	99	93	56	46	49	81
1987—Syracuse (I.L.).................	11	•13	.458	4.44	34	*34	1	0	0	186 2/3	189	•103	*92	*87	143
1988—Toronto (A.L.)..................	4	8	.333	5.69	28	16	0	0	0	98	109	70	62	46	67
— Syracuse (I.L.)............	5	0	1.000	2.05	7	7	1	0	0	48 1/3	36	12	11	8	51
1989—Toronto (A.L.)..................	7	7	.500	3.88	27	18	0	0	0	127 2/3	137	56	55	44	63
— Syracuse (I.L.)............	3	2	.600	3.23	10	9	2	0	0	55 2/3	46	23	20	15	45
1990—Toronto (A.L.)..................	13	17	.433	4.34	33	33	4	0	0	203	214	101	98	69	115
1991—Toronto (A.L.)..................	15	8	.652	3.78	34	34	1	0	0	219	194	97	92	75	116
1992—Toronto (A.L.)..................	12	11	.522	4.50	28	27	6	2	0	174	175	99	87	63	98
1993—Toronto (A.L.)..................	11	12	.478	4.84	30	28	1	1	0	176 2/3	204	107	95	69	98
1994—Toronto (A.L.)..................	7	7	.500	4.22	26	19	3	1	1	140 2/3	149	67	66	48	105
1995—Oakland (A.L.)■.................	14	7	.667	4.55	31	31	2	0	0	209 2/3	228	117	106	80	205
1996—St. Louis (N.L.)■..............	14	11	.560	3.87	34	33	5	2	0	223 1/3	191	100	96	93	194
1997—St. Louis (N.L.)...............	12	9	.571	3.88	28	28	0	0	0	181	155	86	78	65	160
1998—St. Louis (N.L.)...............	9	9	.500	3.51	23	23	3	0	0	161 1/3	146	74	63	51	147
— Texas (A.L.)■.............	5	4	.556	4.33	10	10	0	0	0	60 1/3	68	33	29	30	57
1999—Arizona (N.L.)■...............	6	3	.667	4.09	17	17	0	0	0	101 3/4	106	51	46	40	74
— Ariz. D'backs (Ariz.)...........	2	0	1.000	0.53	3	3	1	0	0	17	11	1	1	1	25
A.L. totals (9 years)	88	81	.521	4.41	247	216	17	4	1	1409	1478	747	690	524	924
N.L. totals (4 years)	41	32	.562	3.82	102	101	8	2	0	667	598	311	283	249	575
Major League totals (12 years)	129	113	.533	4.22	349	317	25	6	1	2076	2076	1058	973	773	1499

DIVISION SERIES RECORD

Year League	W	L	Pct.	ERA	G	GS	CG	ShO	Sv.	IP	H	R	ER	BB	SO
1996—St. Louis (N.L.)...............	1	0	1.000	1.35	1	1	0	0	0	6 2/3	5	1	1	2	7
1998—Texas (A.L.)...................	0	1	.000	2.25	1	1	0	0	0	8	6	2	2	4	8
1999—Arizona (N.L.)...............	1	0	1.000	1.35	1	1	0	0	0	6 2/3	4	1	1	5	6
Division series totals (3 years)	2	1	.667	1.69	3	3	1	0	0	21 1/3	15	4	4	11	21

CHAMPIONSHIP SERIES RECORD

RECORDS: Shares single-series record for most earned runs allowed—11 (1996). ... Shares single-game record for most earned runs allowed—7 (October 14, 1996). ... Shares record for most hits allowed in one inning—6 (October 14, 1996, first inning).

Year League	W	L	Pct.	ERA	G	GS	CG	ShO	Sv.	IP	H	R	ER	BB	SO
1989—Toronto (A.L.).................	0	1	.000	7.20	1	1	0	0	0	5	7	4	4	2	3
1991—Toronto (A.L.).................	0	1	.000	9.82	1	1	0	0	0	3 2/3	7	4	4	1	3
1992—Toronto (A.L.).................	0	0		2.45	1	0	0	0	0	3 2/3	3	1	1	0	1
1993—Toronto (A.L.).................	0	1	.000	7.50	1	1	0	0	0	6	6	5	5	4	4
1996—St. Louis (N.L.)...............	1	1	.500	12.38	3	2	0	0	0	8	15	11	11	3	11
Champ. series totals (5 years)	1	4	.200	8.54	7	5	0	0	0	26 1/3	38	25	25	10	22

RECORDS: Shares records for most bases on balls allowed in one inning—4 (October 20, 1993, first inning); and most consecutive bases on balls allowed in one inning—3 (October 20, 1993, first inning).

NOTES: Member of World Series championship team (1992 and 1993).

Year	League	W	L	Pct.	ERA	G	GS	CG	ShO	Sv.	IP	H	R	ER	BB	SO
1992— Toronto (A.L.)		0	0	...	0.00	4	0	0	0	0	3²/₃	4	0	0	0	4
1993— Toronto (A.L.)		0	0	...	27.00	1	1	0	0	0	2	3	6	6	4	1
World Series totals (2 years)		0	0	...	9.53	5	1	0	0	0	5²/₃	7	6	6	4	5

STOWERS, CHRISTOPHER — OF — EXPOS

PERSONAL: Born August 18, 1974, in Marietta, Ga. ... 6-3/195. ... Bats left, throws left. ... Full name: Christopher James Stowers.

HIGH SCHOOL: Walton (Marietta, Ga.).

COLLEGE: Georgia.

TRANSACTIONS/CAREER NOTES: Selected by Montreal Expos organization in 17th round of free-agent draft (June 4, 1996). ... On Ottawa disabled list (July 29-August 5, 1999).

STATISTICAL NOTES: Led New York-Pennsylvania League with six intentional bases on balls received in 1996.

Year	Team (League)	Pos.	G	AB	R	H	2B	3B	HR	RBI	Avg.	BB	SO	SB	PO	A	E	Avg.
1996—	Vermont (NY-P)	OF	72	282	*58	*90	21	9	7	44	.319	21	37	16	112	9	3	.976
1997—	Harrisburg (East.)	OF	19	59	9	17	4	2	0	5	.288	5	11	3	37	2	3	.929
	—W.P. Beach (FSL)	OF	111	414	56	113	15	5	4	30	.273	30	77	19	223	7	6	.975
1998—	Harrisburg (East.)	OF	134	510	86	137	31	5	17	66	.269	42	109	24	243	10	4	.984
1999—	Ottawa (I.L.)	OF-DH	118	431	60	102	17	4	5	37	.237	39	92	28	284	11	2	.993
	—Montreal (N.L.)	OF	4	2	0	0	0	0	0	0	.000	0	0	0	1	0	0	1.000
Major League totals (1 year)			4	2	0	0	0	0	0	0	.000	0	0	0	1	0	0	1.000

STRAWBERRY, DARRYL — OF — YANKEES

PERSONAL: Born March 12, 1962, in Los Angeles. ... 6-6/215. ... Bats left, throws left. ... Full name: Darryl Eugene Strawberry. ... Brother of Michael Strawberry, minor league outfielder (1980-81).

HIGH SCHOOL: Crenshaw (Los Angeles).

TRANSACTIONS/CAREER NOTES: Selected by New York Mets organization in first round (first pick overall) of free-agent draft (June 3, 1980). ... On disabled list (May 12-June 28, 1985). ... Granted free agency (November 5, 1990). ... Signed by Los Angeles Dodgers (November 8, 1990). ... On disabled list (June 18-July 3, 1991; May 14-July 6 and July 21-September 1, 1992). ... On Los Angeles disabled list (May 13-June 5, 1993); included rehabilitation assignment to Albuquerque (May 28-June 5). ... On Los Angeles disabled list (June 17, 1993-remainder of season and April 4-May 26, 1994). ... Released by Dodgers (May 26, 1994). ... Signed by San Francisco Giants organization (June 19, 1994). ... Released by Giants (February 8, 1995). ... Signed by New York Yankees organization (June 19, 1995). ... On Columbus disabled list (June 22-July 4, 1995). ... Granted free agency (November 30, 1995). ... Signed by St. Paul of Northern League (May 3, 1996). ... Contract purchased by Yankees organization (July 4, 1996). ... On New York disabled list (April 7-August 15, 1997); included rehabilitation assignments to Norwich (May 19), Columbus (June 9-13 and August 8-15) and Tampa (August 4-7). ... Granted free agency (October 30, 1997). ... Re-signed by Yankees (January 8, 1998). ... On suspended list (May 20-21 and May 24, 1998). ... Granted free agency (December 21, 1998). ... Re-signed by Yankees organization (April 5, 1999). ... On suspended list (April 14-August 11, 1999).

RECORDS: Shares major league single-season record for most grand slams as a pinch hitter—2 (1998). ... Shares major league single-game record for most strikeouts (nine-inning game)—5 (May 1, 1991).

HONORS: Named Texas League Most Valuable Player (1982). ... Named N.L. Rookie Player of the Year by THE SPORTING NEWS (1983). ... Named N.L. Rookie of the Year by Baseball Writers' Association of America (1983). ... Named outfielder on THE SPORTING NEWS N.L. All-Star team (1988 and 1990). ... Named outfielder on THE SPORTING NEWS N.L. Silver Slugger team (1988 and 1990).

STATISTICAL NOTES: Led Texas League in slugging percentage with .602 and in caught stealing with 22 in 1982. ... Hit three home runs in one game (August 5, 1985 and August 6, 1996). ... Led N.L. with .545 slugging percentage in 1988. ... Led Gulf Coast League with five intentional bases on balls received in 1995. ... Career major league grand slams: 8.

MISCELLANEOUS: Holds New York Mets all-time records for most runs (662), home runs (252) and runs batted in (733).

Year	Team (League)	Pos.	G	AB	R	H	2B	3B	HR	RBI	Avg.	BB	SO	SB	PO	A	E	Avg.
1980—	Kingsport (Appal.)	OF	44	157	27	42	5	2	5	20	.268	20	39	5	55	4	3	.952
1981—	Lynchburg (Caro.)	OF	123	420	84	107	22	6	13	78	.255	82	105	31	173	8	13	.933
1982—	Jackson (Texas)	OF	129	435	93	123	19	9	*34	97	.283	*100	145	45	211	8	9	.961
1983—	Tidewater (I.L.)	OF	16	57	12	19	4	1	3	13	.333	14	18	7	22	0	4	.846
	—New York (N.L.)	OF	122	420	63	108	15	7	26	74	.257	47	128	19	232	8	4	.984
1984—	New York (N.L.)	OF	147	522	75	131	27	4	26	97	.251	75	131	27	276	11	6	.980
1985—	New York (N.L.)	OF	111	393	78	109	15	4	29	79	.277	73	96	26	211	5	2	.991
1986—	New York (N.L.)	OF	136	475	76	123	27	5	27	93	.259	72	141	28	226	10	6	.975
1987—	New York (N.L.)	OF	154	532	108	151	32	5	39	104	.284	97	122	36	272	6	8	.972
1988—	New York (N.L.)	OF	153	543	101	146	27	3	*39	101	.269	85	127	29	297	4	9	.971
1989—	New York (N.L.)	OF	134	476	69	107	26	1	29	77	.225	61	105	11	272	4	8	.972
1990—	New York (N.L.)	OF	152	542	92	150	18	1	37	108	.277	70	110	15	268	10	3	.989
1991—	Los Angeles (N.L.)■ ..	OF	139	505	86	134	22	4	28	99	.265	75	125	10	209	11	5	.978
1992—	Los Angeles (N.L.)	OF	43	156	20	37	8	0	5	25	.237	19	34	3	67	2	1	.986
1993—	Los Angeles (N.L.)	OF	32	100	12	14	2	0	5	12	.140	16	19	1	37	1	4	.905
	—Albuquerque (PCL).....	OF	5	19	3	6	2	0	1	2	.316	2	5	1	7	0	0	1.000
1994—	Phoenix (PCL)■..........	OF-DH	3	10	3	3	0	0	2	3	.300	0	4	0	4	0	0	1.000
	—San Francisco (N.L.) ...	OF	29	92	13	22	3	1	4	17	.239	19	22	0	61	1	2	.969
1995—	GC Yankees (GCL)■..	OF-DH	7	20	3	5	2	0	0	4	.250	9	5	2	3	1	0	1.000
	—Tampa (FSL)	DH	2	9	1	2	1	0	1	2	.222	1	2	0	...	...	...	...
	—Columbus (I.L.)	DH-OF	22	83	20	25	3	1	7	29	.301	15	17	1	9	0	0	1.000
	—New York (A.L.)	DH-OF	32	87	15	24	4	1	3	13	.276	10	22	0	18	2	2	.909

Year	Team (League)	Pos.	G	AB	R	H	2B	3B	HR	RBI	Avg.	BB	SO	SB	PO	A	E	Avg.
1996—	St. Paul (Nor.)■	OF	29	108	31	47	7	0	18	39	.435	22	16	4	...	...	...	...
—	Columbus (I.L.)■	DH	2	8	3	3	0	0	3	5	.375	0	3	0	...	...	...	...
—	New York (A.L.)	OF-DH	63	202	35	53	13	0	11	36	.262	31	55	6	45	1	0	1.000
1997—	New York (A.L.)	DH-OF	11	29	1	3	1	0	0	2	.103	3	9	0	5	0	0	1.000
—	Norwich (East.)	OF	1	2	0	0	0	0	0	0	.000	0	1	0	0	0	0	...
—	Columbus (I.L.)	DH	11	38	8	11	3	0	6	19	.289	8	10	0	...	...	...	...
—	Tampa (FSL)	DH	4	16	2	7	1	0	0	4	.438	1	3	0	...	...	...	...
1998—	New York (A.L.)	DH-OF	101	295	44	73	11	2	24	57	.247	46	90	8	19	0	2	.905
1999—	Columbus (I.L.)	DH-OF	21	73	12	21	5	1	4	15	.288	11	13	1	14	0	0	1.000
—	New York (A.L.)	DH	24	49	10	16	5	0	3	6	.327	17	16	2	0	0	0	...
American League totals (5 years)			231	662	105	169	34	3	41	114	.255	107	192	16	87	3	4	.957
National League totals (12 years)			1352	4756	793	1232	222	35	294	886	.259	709	1160	205	2428	73	58	.977
Major League totals (17 years)			1583	5418	898	1401	256	38	335	1000	.259	816	1352	221	2515	76	62	.977

DIVISION SERIES RECORD

RECORDS: Shares A.L. career record for most games by pinch hitter—3.

Year	Team (League)	Pos.	G	AB	R	H	2B	3B	HR	RBI	Avg.	BB	SO	SB	PO	A	E	Avg.
1995—	New York (A.L.)	PH	2	2	0	0	0	0	0	0	.000	0	1	0	...	...	...	...
1996—	New York (A.L.)	DH	2	5	0	0	0	0	0	0	.000	0	2	0	...	...	...	...
1999—	New York (A.L.)	DH	2	6	2	2	0	0	1	3	.333	1	0	0	0	0	0	...
Division series totals (3 years)			6	13	2	2	0	0	1	3	.154	1	3	0	0	0	0	...

CHAMPIONSHIP SERIES RECORD

RECORDS: Shares single-series record for most strikeouts—12 (1986).

Year	Team (League)	Pos.	G	AB	R	H	2B	3B	HR	RBI	Avg.	BB	SO	SB	PO	A	E	Avg.
1986—	New York (N.L.)	OF	6	22	4	5	1	0	2	5	.227	3	12	1	9	0	0	1.000
1988—	New York (N.L.)	OF	7	30	5	9	2	0	1	6	.300	2	5	0	11	0	0	1.000
1996—	New York (A.L.)	OF-PH	4	12	4	5	0	0	3	5	.417	2	2	0	5	0	0	1.000
1999—	New York (A.L.)	DH-PH	3	6	1	2	0	0	1	1	.333	1	2	0	0	0	0	...
Championship series totals (4 years)			20	70	14	21	3	0	7	17	.300	8	21	1	25	0	0	1.000

WORLD SERIES RECORD

NOTES: Member of World Series championship team (1986, 1996 and 1999). ... Member of World Series championship team (1998); inactive due to illness.

Year	Team (League)	Pos.	G	AB	R	H	2B	3B	HR	RBI	Avg.	BB	SO	SB	PO	A	E	Avg.
1986—	New York (N.L.)	OF	7	24	4	5	1	0	1	1	.208	4	6	3	19	0	0	1.000
1996—	New York (A.L.)	OF	5	16	0	3	0	0	0	1	.188	5	6	0	11	0	0	1.000
1999—	New York (A.L.)	PH-DH	2	3	0	1	0	0	0	0	.333	1	2	0	0	0	0	...
World Series totals (3 years)			14	43	4	9	1	0	1	2	.209	10	14	3	30	0	0	1.000

ALL-STAR GAME RECORD

Year	League	Pos.	AB	R	H	2B	3B	HR	RBI	Avg.	BB	SO	SB	PO	A	E	Avg.
1984—	National	OF	2	0	1	0	0	0	0	.500	0	1	0	0	0	0	...
1985—	National	OF	1	2	1	0	0	0	0	1.000	1	0	1	3	0	0	1.000
1986—	National	OF	2	0	1	0	0	0	0	.500	0	1	0	1	0	0	1.000
1987—	National	OF	2	0	0	0	0	0	0	.000	0	0	0	0	0	0	...
1988—	National	OF	4	0	1	0	0	0	0	.250	0	1	0	4	0	0	1.000
1989—	National						Selected, did not play—injured.										
1990—	National	OF	1	0	0	0	0	0	0	.000	0	1	0	3	1	1	.800
1991—	National						Selected, did not play—injured.										
All-Star Game totals (6 years)			12	2	4	0	0	0	0	.333	1	4	1	11	1	1	.923

STRICKLAND, SCOTT   P   EXPOS

PERSONAL: Born April 26, 1976, in Houston. ... 5-11/180. ... Throws right, bats right. ... Full name: Scott M. Strickland.
HIGH SCHOOL: Klein Oak (Spring, Texas).
COLLEGE: New Mexico.
TRANSACTIONS/CAREER NOTES: Selected by Montreal Expos organization in 10th round of free-agent draft (June 3, 1997).

Year	League	W	L	Pct.	ERA	G	GS	CG	ShO	Sv.	IP	H	R	ER	BB	SO
1997—	Cape Fear (SAL)	0	1	.000	6.35	3	1	0	0	1	5 2/3	8	7	4	1	8
—	Vermont (NY-P)	5	2	.714	3.82	15	9	1	0	0	61 1/3	56	27	26	20	69
1998—	Cape Fear (SAL)	0	3	.000	4.46	15	2	0	0	0	36 1/3	36	19	18	12	53
—	Jupiter (FSL)	4	3	.571	3.39	22	11	0	0	2	69	64	28	26	20	51
1999—	Jupiter (FSL)	1	1	.500	3.51	12	1	0	0	2	25 2/3	21	11	10	4	33
—	Harrisburg (East.)	1	1	.500	2.48	14	1	0	0	0	29	25	8	8	10	36
—	Ottawa (I.L.)	3	0	1.000	1.63	19	0	0	0	5	27 2/3	23	5	5	11	34
—	Montreal (N.L.)	0	1	.000	4.50	17	0	0	0	0	18	15	10	9	11	23
Major League totals (1 year)		0	1	.000	4.50	17	0	0	0	0	18	15	10	9	11	23

STULL, EVERETT   P   BRAVES

PERSONAL: Born August 24, 1971, in Fort Riley, Kan. ... 6-3/200. ... Throws right, bats right. ... Full name: Everett James Stull.
HIGH SCHOOL: Redan (Stone Mountain, Ga.).
COLLEGE: Tennessee State.
TRANSACTIONS/CAREER NOTES: Selected by Montreal Expos organization in third round of free-agent draft (June 1, 1992). ... Traded by Expos to Baltimore Orioles (October 31, 1997), completing deal in which Orioles traded P Mike Johnson to Expos for a player to be named

later (July 31, 1997). ... On Baltimore disabled list (March 19-July 27, 1998); included rehabilitation assignment to Rochester (June 13-July 27). ... Granted free agency (October 15, 1998). ... Signed by Atlanta Braves organization (January 20, 1999).

STATISTICAL NOTES: Led New York-Pennsylvania League with 18 wild pitches in 1992.

Year League	W	L	Pct.	ERA	G	GS	CG	ShO	Sv.	IP	H	R	ER	BB	SO
1992—Jamestown (NY-P)	3	5	.375	5.40	14	14	0	0	0	63 1/3	52	49	38	*61	64
1993—Burlington (Midw.)	4	9	.308	3.83	15	15	0	0	0	82 1/3	68	44	35	59	85
1994—W.P. Beach (FSL)	10	10	.500	3.31	27	26	3	1	0	147	116	60	54	78	165
1995—Harrisburg (East.)	3	•12	.200	5.54	24	24	0	0	0	126 2/3	114	88	78	79	132
1996—Harrisburg (East.)	6	3	.667	3.15	14	14	0	0	0	80	64	31	28	52	81
—Ottawa (I.L.)	2	6	.250	6.33	13	13	1	0	0	69 2/3	87	57	49	39	69
1997—Ottawa (I.L.)	8	10	.444	5.82	27	27	1	0	0	159 1/3	166	110	*103	86	130
—Montreal (N.L.)	0	1	.000	16.20	3	0	0	0	0	3 1/3	7	7	6	4	2
1998—Rochester (I.L.)■	1	4	.200	8.86	21	7	0	0	0	42 2/3	49	44	42	45	39
1999—Richmond (I.L.)■	8	8	.500	4.47	30	22	0	0	0	139	124	75	69	73	126
—Atlanta (N.L.)	0	0	...	13.50	1	0	0	0	0	2/3	2	3	1	2	0
Major League totals (2 years)	0	1	.000	15.75	4	0	0	0	0	4	9	10	7	6	2

STURTZE, TANYON   P   WHITE SOX

PERSONAL: Born October 12, 1970, in Worcester, Mass. ... 6-5/205. ... Throws right, bats right. ... Full name: Tanyon James Sturtze. ... Name pronounced STURTS.
HIGH SCHOOL: St. Peter-Marian (Worcester, Mass.).
JUNIOR COLLEGE: Quinsigamond Community College (Mass.).
TRANSACTIONS/CAREER NOTES: Selected by Oakland Athletics organization in 23rd round of free-agent draft (June 4, 1990). ... On Huntsville disabled list (April 7-16, 1994). ... Selected by Chicago Cubs from A's organization in Rule 5 major league draft (December 5, 1994). ... Granted free agency (October 15, 1996). ... Signed by Texas Rangers (November 20, 1996). ... Released by Rangers (March 6, 1998). ... Re-signed by Rangers organization (March 11, 1998). ... Granted free agency (October 15, 1998). ... Signed by Chicago White Sox organization (November 23, 1998).

STATISTICAL NOTES: Pitched 5-0 no-hit victory against Chattanooga (June 13, 1993).

Year League	W	L	Pct.	ERA	G	GS	CG	ShO	Sv.	IP	H	R	ER	BB	SO
1990—Arizona Athletics (Ariz.)	2	5	.286	5.44	12	10	0	0	0	48	55	41	29	27	30
1991—Madison (Midw.)	10	5	.667	3.09	27	27	0	0	0	163	136	77	56	58	88
1992—Modesto (Calif.)	7	11	.389	3.75	25	25	1	0	0	151	143	72	63	78	126
1993—Huntsville (Sou.)	5	12	.294	4.78	28	•28	1	1	0	165 2/3	169	102	*88	85	112
1994—Huntsville (Sou.)	6	3	.667	3.22	17	17	1	0	0	103 1/3	100	40	37	39	63
—Tacoma (PCL)	4	5	.444	4.04	11	9	0	0	0	64 2/3	73	36	29	34	28
1995—Chicago (N.L.)■	0	0	...	9.00	2	0	0	0	0	2	2	2	2	1	0
—Iowa (A.A.)	4	7	.364	6.80	23	17	1	1	0	86	108	66	65	42	48
1996—Iowa (A.A.)	6	4	.600	4.85	51	1	0	0	4	72 1/3	80	42	39	33	51
—Chicago (N.L.)	1	0	1.000	9.00	6	0	0	0	0	11	16	11	11	5	7
1997—Oklahoma City (A.A.)■	8	6	.571	5.10	25	19	1	0	0	114 2/3	133	76	65	47	79
—Texas (A.L.)	1	1	.500	8.27	9	5	0	0	0	32 2/3	45	30	30	18	18
1998—Gulf Coast Rangers (GCL)	0	1	.000	7.71	3	3	0	0	0	7	12	7	6	4	10
—Charlotte (FSL)	0	1	.000	6.00	1	0	0	0	0	3	2	3	2	1	3
—Tulsa (Texas)	1	0	1.000	5.40	1	1	0	0	0	1 2/3	2	1	1	2	1
—Oklahoma (PCL)	3	1	.750	3.34	13	3	0	0	0	35	33	13	13	18	31
1999—Charlotte (I.L.)■	9	4	.692	4.05	33	14	2	1	3	104 1/3	83	53	47	41	107
—Chicago (A.L.)	0	0	...	0.00	1	1	0	0	0	6	4	0	0	2	2
A.L. totals (2 years)	1	1	.500	6.98	10	6	0	0	0	38 2/3	49	30	30	20	20
N.L. totals (2 years)	1	0	1.000	9.00	8	0	0	0	0	13	18	13	13	6	7
Major League totals (4 years)	2	1	.667	7.49	18	6	0	0	0	51 2/3	67	43	43	26	27

STYNES, CHRIS   IF   REDS

PERSONAL: Born January 19, 1973, in Queens, N.Y. ... 5-10/185. ... Bats right, throws right. ... Full name: Christopher Desmond Stynes.
HIGH SCHOOL: Boca Raton (Fla.).
TRANSACTIONS/CAREER NOTES: Selected by Toronto Blue Jays in third round of free-agent draft (June 3, 1991). ... Traded by Blue Jays with P David Sinnes and IF Tony Medrano to Kansas City Royals for P David Cone (April 6, 1995). ... Traded by Royals with OF Jon Nunnally to Cincinnati Reds for P Hector Carrasco and P Scott Service (July 15, 1997).
STATISTICAL NOTES: Tied for Florida State League lead in double plays by third basemen with 22 in 1993. ... Led Southern League with 237 total bases in 1994.

Year Team (League)	Pos.	G	AB	R	H	2B	3B	HR	RBI	Avg.	BB	SO	SB	PO	A	E	Avg.
1991—GC Blue Jays (GCL)	3B	57	219	29	67	15	1	4	39	.306	9	39	10	42	*138	8	*.957
1992—Myrtle Beach (SAL)	3B	127	489	67	139	36	0	7	46	.284	16	43	28	86	208	26	.919
1993—Dunedin (FSL)	3B	123	496	72	151	28	5	7	48	.304	25	40	19	83	234	21	*.938
1994—Knoxville (Sou.)	2B	136	*545	79	*173	32	4	8	79	.317	23	36	28	247	•366	20	.968
1995—Omaha (A.A.)■	2B-3B	83	306	51	84	12	5	9	42	.275	27	24	4	144	204	13	.964
—Kansas City (A.L.)	2B-DH	22	35	7	6	1	0	0	2	.171	4	3	0	21	35	1	.982
1996—Omaha (A.A.)	OF-3B-2B-DH	72	284	50	101	22	2	10	40	.356	18	17	7	98	77	9	.951
—Kansas City (A.L.)	OF-2B-DH-3B	36	92	8	27	6	0	0	6	.293	2	5	5	38	8	3	.939
1997—Omaha (A.A.)	2B-OF-DH-3B	82	332	53	88	18	1	8	44	.265	19	25	3	101	80	10	.948
—Indianapolis (A.A.)■	2B	21	86	14	31	8	0	1	17	.360	2	5	4	47	61	2	.982
—Cincinnati (N.L.)	OF-2B-3B	49	198	31	69	7	1	6	28	.348	11	13	11	87	33	2	.984
1998—Cincinnati (N.L.)	O-3-2-S	123	347	52	88	10	1	6	27	.254	32	36	15	148	54	2	.990
1999—Cincinnati (N.L.)	2B-3B-OF	73	113	18	27	1	0	2	14	.239	12	13	5	50	71	6	.953
American League totals (2 years)		58	127	15	33	7	0	0	8	.260	6	8	5	59	43	4	.962
National League totals (3 years)		245	658	101	184	18	2	14	69	.280	55	62	31	285	158	10	.978
Major League totals (5 years)		303	785	116	217	25	2	14	77	.276	61	70	36	344	201	14	.975

PERSONAL: Born March 13, 1971, in Carrollton, Ala. ... 6-3/210. ... Throws right, bats right. ... Full name: William Scott Sullivan.
HIGH SCHOOL: Pickens Academy (Carrollton, Ala.).
COLLEGE: Auburn.
TRANSACTIONS/CAREER NOTES: Selected by Cincinnati Reds organization in second round of free-agent draft (June 3, 1993). ... On Indianapolis disabled list (August 21, 1995-remainder of season).

Year League	W	L	Pct.	ERA	G	GS	CG	ShO	Sv.	IP	H	R	ER	BB	SO
1993— Billings (Pio.)	5	0	1.000	1.67	18	7	2	2	3	54	33	13	10	25	79
1994— Chattanooga (Sou.)	11	7	.611	3.41	34	13	2	0	7	121 $^1/_3$	101	60	46	40	111
1995— Indianapolis (A.A.)	4	3	.571	3.53	44	0	0	0	1	58 $^2/_3$	51	31	23	24	54
— Cincinnati (N.L.)	0	0	...	4.91	3	0	0	0	0	3 $^2/_3$	4	2	2	2	2
1996— Indianapolis (A.A.)	5	2	.714	2.73	53	3	0	0	1	108 $^2/_3$	95	38	33	37	77
— Cincinnati (N.L.)	0	0	...	2.25	7	0	0	0	0	8	7	2	2	5	3
1997— Cincinnati (N.L.)	5	3	.625	3.24	59	0	0	0	1	97 $^1/_3$	79	36	35	30	96
— Indianapolis (A.A.)	3	1	.750	1.30	19	0	0	0	2	27 $^2/_3$	16	4	4	4	23
1998— Cincinnati (N.L.)	5	5	.500	5.21	67	0	0	0	1	102	98	62	59	36	86
1999— Cincinnati (N.L.)	5	4	.556	3.01	79	0	0	0	3	113 $^2/_3$	88	41	38	47	78
Major League totals (5 years)	15	12	.556	3.77	215	0	0	0	5	324 $^2/_3$	276	143	136	120	265

S

PERSONAL: Born January 2, 1975, in Oklahoma City. ... 6-2/210. ... Throws right, bats right. ... Full name: Jeffrey Scot Suppan.
HIGH SCHOOL: Crespi (Encino, Calif.).
TRANSACTIONS/CAREER NOTES: Selected by Boston Red Sox organization in second round of free-agent draft (June 3, 1993). ... On Trenton disabled list (April 9-29, 1995). ... On Boston disabled list (August 25, 1996-remainder of season). ... Selected by Arizona Diamondbacks in first round (third pick overall) of expansion draft (November 18, 1997). ... Contract purchased by Kansas City Royals from Diamondbacks (September 3, 1998).

Year League	W	L	Pct.	ERA	G	GS	CG	ShO	Sv.	IP	H	R	ER	BB	SO
1993— GC Red Sox (GCL)	4	3	.571	2.18	10	9	2	1	0	57 $^2/_3$	52	20	14	16	64
1994— Sarasota (FSL)	•13	7	.650	3.26	27	27	4	2	0	174	153	74	63	50	*173
1995— Trenton (East.)	6	2	.750	2.36	15	15	1	1	0	99	86	35	26	26	88
— Boston (A.L.)	1	2	.333	5.96	8	3	0	0	0	22 $^2/_3$	29	15	15	5	19
— Pawtucket (I.L.)	2	3	.400	5.32	7	7	0	0	0	45 $^2/_3$	50	29	27	9	32
1996— Boston (A.L.)	1	1	.500	7.54	8	4	0	0	0	22 $^2/_3$	29	19	19	13	13
— Pawtucket (I.L.)	10	6	.625	3.22	22	22	7	1	0	145 $^1/_3$	130	66	52	25	142
1997— Pawtucket (I.L.)	5	1	.833	3.71	9	9	2	1	0	60 $^2/_3$	51	26	25	15	40
— Boston (A.L.)	7	3	.700	5.69	23	22	0	0	0	112 $^1/_3$	140	75	71	36	67
1998— Arizona (N.L.)■	1	7	.125	6.68	13	13	1	0	0	66	82	55	49	21	39
— Tucson (PCL)	4	3	.571	3.63	13	12	0	0	0	67	75	29	27	17	62
— Kansas City (A.L.)■	0	0	...	0.71	4	1	0	0	0	12 $^2/_3$	9	1	1	1	12
1999— Kansas City (A.L.)	10	12	.455	4.53	32	32	4	1	0	208 $^2/_3$	222	113	105	62	103
A.L. totals (5 years)	19	18	.514	5.01	75	62	4	1	0	379	429	223	211	117	214
N.L. totals (1 year)	1	7	.125	6.68	13	13	1	0	0	66	82	55	49	21	39
Major League totals (5 years)	20	25	.444	5.26	88	75	5	1	0	445	511	278	260	138	253

PERSONAL: Born August 4, 1964, in Bronx, N.Y. ... 6-1/200. ... Bats left, throws right. ... Full name: William James Surhoff. ... Son of Dick Surhoff, forward with New York Knicks and Milwaukee Hawks of National Basketball Association (1952-53 and 1953-54); and brother of Rich Surhoff, pitcher with Philadelphia Phillies and Texas Rangers (1985).
HIGH SCHOOL: Rye (N.Y.).
COLLEGE: North Carolina.
TRANSACTIONS/CAREER NOTES: Selected by New York Yankees organization in fifth round of free-agent draft (June 7, 1982); did not sign. ... Selected by Milwaukee Brewers organization in first round (first pick overall) of free-agent draft (June 3, 1985). ... On suspended list (August 23-25, 1990). ... On Milwaukee disabled list (March 25-April 16, April 20-May 23 and July 7, 1994-remainder of season); included rehabilitation assignments to El Paso (April 12-16) and New Orleans (May 17-23). ... Granted free agency (October 20, 1994). ... Re-signed by New Orleans, Brewers organization (April 7, 1995). ... Granted free agency (November 6, 1995). ... Signed by Baltimore Orioles (December 20, 1995). ... On disabled list (May 18-June 2, 1996). ... Granted free agency (October 26, 1998). ... Re-signed by Orioles (December 7, 1998).
RECORDS: Shares major league single-inning record for most doubles—2 (September 14, 1999, fifth inning).
HONORS: Named College Player of the Year by THE SPORTING NEWS (1985). ... Named catcher on THE SPORTING NEWS college All-America team (1985).
STATISTICAL NOTES: Tied for Pacific Coast League lead in double plays by catcher with 10 in 1986. ... Led A.L. catchers with 68 assists in 1991. ... Had 15-game hitting streak (May 9-25, 1999). ... Had 21-game hitting streak (May 29-June 20, 1999). ... Led A.L. outfielders with 1.000 fielding percentage in 1999. ... Career major league grand slams: 5.
MISCELLANEOUS: Member of 1984 U.S. Olympic baseball team.

Year Team (League)	Pos.	G	AB	R	H	2B	3B	HR	RBI	Avg.	BB	SO	SB	PO	A	E	Avg.
1985— Beloit (Midw.)	C	76	289	39	96	13	4	7	58	.332	22	35	10	475	44	3	.994
1986— Vancouver (PCL)	C	116	458	71	141	19	3	5	59	.308	29	30	21	539	70	7	*.989
1987— Milwaukee (A.L.)	C-3B-DH-1B	115	395	50	118	22	3	7	68	.299	36	30	11	648	56	11	.985
1988— Milwaukee (A.L.)	C-3-1-S-O	139	493	47	121	21	0	5	38	.245	31	49	21	530	94	8	.988
1989— Milwaukee (A.L.)	C-DH-3B	126	436	42	108	17	4	5	55	.248	25	29	14	530	58	10	.983
1990— Milwaukee (A.L.)	C-3B	135	474	55	131	21	4	6	59	.276	41	37	18	619	62	12	.983
1991— Milwaukee (A.L.)	C-DH-3-O-2	143	505	57	146	19	4	5	68	.289	26	33	5	665	†71	4	.995
1992— Milwaukee (A.L.)	C-1-DH-O-3	139	480	63	121	19	1	4	62	.252	46	41	14	699	74	6	.992
1993— Milwaukee (A.L.)	3-0-1-C-D	148	552	66	151	38	3	7	79	.274	36	47	12	175	220	18	.956

Year	Team (League)	Pos.	G	AB	R	H	2B	3B	HR	RBI	Avg.	BB	SO	SB	PO	A	E	Avg.
							BATTING									FIELDING		
1994—El Paso (Texas)...........	OF	3	12	2	3	1	0	0	0	.250	0	2	0	3	0	0	1.000
—Milwaukee (A.L.)........3-C-1-O-DH		40	134	20	35	11	2	5	22	.261	16	14	0	121	29	4	.974
—New Orleans (A.A.)......3B-OF-C-1B		5	19	3	6	2	0	0	1	.316	1	2	0	21	3	0	1.000
1995—Milwaukee (A.L.)........OF-1B-C-DH		117	415	72	133	26	3	13	73	.320	37	43	7	530	44	5	.991
1996—Baltimore (A.L.)■......	3-O-DH-1	143	537	74	157	27	6	21	82	.292	47	79	0	137	178	15	.955
1997—Baltimore (A.L.).........	O-DH-1-3	147	528	80	150	30	4	18	88	.284	49	60	1	268	16	2	.993
1998—Baltimore (A.L.).........	OF-1B	162	573	79	160	34	1	22	92	.279	49	81	9	256	12	3	.989
1999—Baltimore (A.L.).........	OF-DH-3B	*162	*673	104	207	38	1	28	107	.308	43	78	5	283	21	0	†1.000
Major League totals (13 years)		1716	6195	809	1738	323	36	146	893	.281	482	621	117	5481	935	98	.985

DIVISION SERIES RECORD

RECORDS: Shares single-game record for most home runs—2 (October 1, 1996).

Year	Team (League)	Pos.	G	AB	R	H	2B	3B	HR	RBI	Avg.	BB	SO	SB	PO	A	E	Avg.
							BATTING									FIELDING		
1996—Baltimore (A.L.).........	OF-PH	4	13	3	5	0	0	3	5	.385	0	1	0	6	0	0	1.000
1997—Baltimore (A.L.).........	OF-PH	3	11	0	3	1	0	0	2	.273	0	2	0	1	1	0	1.000
Division series totals (2 years)		7	24	3	8	1	0	3	7	.333	0	3	0	7	1	0	1.000

CHAMPIONSHIP SERIES RECORD

Year	Team (League)	Pos.	G	AB	R	H	2B	3B	HR	RBI	Avg.	BB	SO	SB	PO	A	E	Avg.
							BATTING									FIELDING		
1996—Baltimore (A.L.)..........	OF-PH	5	15	0	4	0	0	0	2	.267	1	2	0	11	1	0	1.000
1997—Baltimore (A.L.)..........	OF-1B	6	25	1	5	2	0	0	1	.200	2	2	0	13	0	0	1.000
Championship series totals (2 years)		11	40	1	9	2	0	0	3	.225	3	4	0	24	1	0	1.000

ALL-STAR GAME RECORD

Year	League	Pos.	AB	R	H	2B	3B	HR	RBI	Avg.	BB	SO	SB	PO	A	E	Avg.
							BATTING								FIELDING		
1999—American....................	OF	2	0	0	0	0	0	0	.000	0	0	0	0	0	0	...

SUTTON, LARRY   1B/OF   CARDINALS

PERSONAL: Born May 14, 1970, in West Covina, Calif. ... 6-0/185. ... Bats left, throws left. ... Full name: Larry James Sutton.

HIGH SCHOOL: Mater Dei (Santa Ana, Calif.).

COLLEGE: Illinois.

TRANSACTIONS/CAREER NOTES: Selected by Kansas City organization in 21st round of free-agent draft (June 1, 1992). ... On Kansas City disabled list (June 6-July 27, 1999); included rehabilitation assignments to Gulf Coast Royals (July 5-15) and Omaha (July 16-25). ... Granted free agency (October 18, 1999). ... Signed by St. Louis Cardinals organization (December 8, 1999).

HONORS: Named Northwest League Most Valuable Player (1992). ... Named Carolina League Most Valuable Player (1994).

STATISTICAL NOTES: Led Northwest League with 142 total bases in 1992. ... Led Midwest League first basemen with 92 double plays in 1993. ... Led Carolina League with .542 slugging percentage, 10 intentional bases on balls received and nine sacrifice flies in 1994. ... Led Texas League first basemen with .989 fielding percentage in 1996. ... Career major league grand slams: 1.

Year	Team (League)	Pos.	G	AB	R	H	2B	3B	HR	RBI	Avg.	BB	SO	SB	PO	A	E	Avg.
							BATTING									FIELDING		
1992—Eugene (N'west)........	1B	70	238	45	74	17	3	*15	*58	.311	48	33	3	517	29	14	.975
—Appleton (Midw.)........	DH	1	2	1	0	0	0	0	0	.000	2	1	0	...	...	...	...
1993—Rockford (Midw.)........	1B	113	361	67	97	24	1	7	50	.269	*95	65	3	911	76	11	.989
1994—Wilmington (Caro.).....	1B	129	480	91	147	33	1	26	94	.306	*81	71	2	1086	71	12	*.990
1995—Wichita (Texas)	1B	53	197	31	53	11	1	5	32	.269	26	33	1	452	25	7	.986
1996—Wichita (Texas)	1B-OF-DH	125	463	84	137	22	2	22	84	.296	77	66	4	1105	76	13	†.989
1997—Omaha (A.A.).............	1B-DH	106	380	61	114	27	1	19	72	.300	61	57	0	839	54	5	.994
—Kansas City (A.L.) ..	1B-DH-OF	27	69	9	20	2	0	2	8	.290	5	12	0	92	8	0	1.000
1998—Kansas City (A.L.)	OF-1B-DH	111	310	29	76	14	2	5	42	.245	29	46	3	179	7	2	.989
1999—Kansas City (A.L.)	1B-DH-OF	43	102	14	23	6	0	2	15	.225	13	17	1	215	13	3	.987
—GC Royals (GCL) ..	1B-DH-OF	9	31	7	8	2	0	1	6	.258	7	6	0	43	0	1	.977
—Omaha (PCL)	1B-OF	39	148	28	41	8	1	3	12	.277	27	24	4	247	21	4	.985
Major League totals (3 years)		181	481	52	119	22	2	9	65	.247	47	75	4	486	28	5	.990

SUZUKI, MAC   P   ROYALS

PERSONAL: Born May 31, 1975, in Kobe, Japan. ... 6-3/205. ... Throws right, bats right. ... Full name: Makoto Suzuki.

HIGH SCHOOL: Takigawa Daini (Kobe, Japan).

TRANSACTIONS/CAREER NOTES: Played with Salinas, independent (August 30, 1992). ... Signed by San Bernardino, independent (April 9, 1993). ... Contract purchased by Seattle Mariners organization from San Bernardino (September 5, 1993). ... On disabled list (April 19-June 15 and July 10, 1994-remainder of season). ... On Riverside temporarily inactive list (April 22-August 3, 1995). ... On Riverside disabled list (August 3-18, 1995). ... On Port City disabled list (May 8-17, 1996). ... Traded by Mariners with a player to be named later to New York Mets for P Allen Watson and cash (June 18, 1999); Mets acquired P Justin Dunning to complete deal (September 14, 1999). ... Claimed on waivers by Kansas City Royals (June 22, 1999).

Year	League	W	L	Pct.	ERA	G	GS	CG	ShO	Sv.	IP	H	R	ER	BB	SO
1992—Salinas (Calif.)	0	0	...	0.00	1	0	0	0	0	1	0	0	0	0	1
1993—San Bernardino (Calif.)■....	4	4	.500	3.68	48	1	0	0	12	$80^{2}/_{3}$	59	37	33	56	87
1994—Jacksonville (Sou.)■.........	1	0	1.000	2.84	8	0	0	0	1	$12^{2}/_{3}$	15	4	4	6	10
1995—Riverside (Calif.)	0	1	.000	4.70	6	0	0	0	0	$7^{2}/_{3}$	10	4	4	6	6
—Arizona Mariners (Ariz.)	1	0	1.000	6.75	4	3	0	0	0	4	5	4	3	0	3
1996—Tacoma (PCL)	0	3	.000	7.25	13	2	0	0	0	$22^{1}/_{3}$	31	19	18	12	14
—Port City (Sou.)	3	6	.333	4.72	16	16	0	0	0	$74^{1}/_{3}$	69	41	39	32	66
—Seattle (A.L.)	0	0	...	20.25	1	0	0	0	0	$1^{1}/_{3}$	2	3	3	2	1

Year League	W	L	Pct.	ERA	G	GS	CG	ShO	Sv.	IP	H	R	ER	BB	SO
1997—Tacoma (PCL)	4	9	.308	5.94	32	10	0	0	0	83⅓	79	60	55	64	63
1998—Tacoma (PCL)	9	10	.474	4.37	28	21	2	1	0	131⅔	130	70	64	70	117
—Seattle (A.L.)	1	2	.333	7.18	6	5	0	0	0	26⅓	34	23	21	15	19
1999—Seattle (A.L.)	0	2	.000	9.43	16	4	0	0	0	42	47	47	44	34	32
—Kansas City (A.L.)■	2	3	.400	5.16	22	9	0	0	0	68	77	45	39	30	36
Major League totals (3 years)	3	7	.300	7.00	45	18	0	0	0	137⅔	160	118	107	81	88

SVEUM, DALE — IF — PIRATES

PERSONAL: Born November 23, 1963, in Richmond, Calif. ... 6-2/212. ... Bats both, throws right. ... Full name: Dale Curtis Sveum. ... Cousin of John Olerud, first baseman, Seattle Mariners. ... Name pronounced SWAIM.

HIGH SCHOOL: Pinole Valley (Calif.).

TRANSACTIONS/CAREER NOTES: Selected by Milwaukee Brewers organization in first round (25th pick overall) of free-agent draft (June 7, 1982). ... On Milwaukee disabled list (July 23-August 9, 1986). ... On Milwaukee disabled list (March 19, 1989-entire season); included rehabilitation assignments to Beloit (June 30-July 5) and Stockton (July 6-18). ... Traded by Brewers to Philadelphia Phillies for P Bruce Ruffin (December 11, 1991). ... On disabled list (April 9-24, 1992). ... Traded by Phillies to Chicago White Sox for P Keith Shepherd (August 10, 1992). ... Granted free agency (October 26, 1992). ... Signed by Oakland Athletics organization (January 21, 1993). ... Released by A's (June 17, 1993). ... Signed by Calgary, Seattle Mariners organization (June 24, 1993). ... On Calgary disabled list (August 3-13 and August 18, 1993-remainder of season; and June 14-21, 1994). ... Granted free agency (October 7, 1994). ... Signed by Pittsburgh Pirates organization (November 10, 1994). ... Granted free agency (October 16, 1995). ... Re-signed by Pirates organization (February 2, 1996). ... On Calgary disabled list (May 17-June 18, 1996). ... Granted free agency (October 28, 1997). ... Signed by New York Yankees (November 25, 1997). ... Released by Yankees (August 3, 1998). ... Signed by Arizona Diamondbacks organization (February 18, 1999). ... Released by Diamondbacks (May 9, 1999). ... Signed by Pittsburgh Pirates organization (May 17, 1999). ... Granted free agency (November 5, 1999). ... Re-signed by Pirates organization (December 10, 1999).

STATISTICAL NOTES: Led California League third basemen with 261 assists in 1983. ... Led Texas League with 256 total bases in 1984. ... Led Texas League third basemen with 111 putouts and 30 errors in 1984. ... Led American League third basemen with 26 errors in 1986. ... Hit three home runs in one game (July 17, 1987). ... Switch-hit home runs in one game three times (July 17, 1987; June 12, 1988; and August 18, 1999). ... Led American League shortstops with 27 errors in 1988. ... Led Pacific Coast League third basemen with 20 double plays in 1995.

							BATTING								FIELDING		
Year Team (League)	Pos.	G	AB	R	H	2B	3B	HR	RBI	Avg.	BB	SO	SB	PO	A	E	Avg.
1982—Pikeville (Appl.)	SS-3B	58	223	29	52	13	1	2	21	.233	20	50	6	84	158	36	.871
1983—Stockton (Calif.)	3B-SS	135	533	70	139	26	5	5	70	.261	29	73	15	105	†281	40	.906
1984—El Paso (Texas)	3B-SS	131	523	92	*172	*41	8	9	84	.329	43	72	6	†113	259	30	.925
1985—Vancouver (PCL)	3B-SS	122	415	42	98	17	3	6	48	.236	48	79	4	81	200	26	.915
1986—Vancouver (PCL)	3B	28	105	16	31	3	2	1	23	.295	13	22	0	22	54	4	.950
—Milwaukee (A.L.)	3B-SS-2B	91	317	35	78	13	2	7	35	.246	32	63	4	92	179	†30	.900
1987—Milwaukee (A.L.)	SS-2B	153	535	86	135	27	3	25	95	.252	40	133	2	242	396	23	.965
1988—Milwaukee (A.L.)	SS-2B-DH	129	467	41	113	14	4	9	51	.242	21	122	1	209	375	†27	.956
1989—Beloit (Midw.)	DH	6	15	0	2	1	0	0	2	.133	5	6	0	...	...	...	...
—Stockton (Calif.)	DH	11	43	5	8	0	0	1	5	.186	6	14	0	...	...	...	...
1990—Milwaukee (A.L.)	3B-2B-1B-SS	48	117	15	23	7	0	1	12	.197	12	30	0	59	63	6	.953
—Denver (A.A.)	3B-SS-1B-2B	57	218	25	63	17	2	2	26	.289	20	49	1	134	102	12	.952
1991—Milwaukee (A.L.)	SS-3B-DH-2B	90	266	33	64	19	1	4	43	.241	32	78	2	85	189	10	.965
1992—Philadelphia (N.L.)■	SS-3B-1B	54	135	13	24	4	0	2	16	.178	16	39	0	78	100	8	.957
—Chicago (A.L.)	SS-3B-1B	40	114	15	25	9	0	2	12	.219	12	29	1	43	98	8	.946
1993—Tacoma (PCL)■	2B-1B-SS	12	43	10	15	1	0	2	6	.349	6	7	2	29	21	0	1.000
—Oakland (A.L.)	1-3-2-DH-O-S	30	79	12	14	2	1	2	6	.177	16	21	0	128	17	3	.980
—Calgary (PCL)	3B-1B	33	120	31	36	11	1	6	26	.300	24	32	0	62	29	3	.968
1994—Calgary (PCL)	3-DH-1-O	102	393	71	111	21	3	22	78	.282	49	98	1	100	185	30	.905
—Seattle (A.L.)	DH-3B	10	27	3	5	0	0	1	2	.185	2	10	0	2	8	1	.909
1995—Calgary (PCL)■	3-1-DH-P-S	118	408	71	116	34	1	12	70	.284	48	78	2	356	240	16	.974
1996—Calgary (PCL)	3-1-2-DH	101	343	62	103	28	2	23	84	.300	33	71	2	226	161	8	.980
—Pittsburgh (N.L.)	3B	12	34	9	12	5	0	1	5	.353	6	6	0	4	17	2	.913
1997—Pittsburgh (N.L.)	3-S-1-2	126	306	30	80	20	1	12	47	.261	27	81	0	154	142	8	.974
1998—New York (A.L.)■	1B-3B-DH	30	58	6	9	0	0		3	.155	4	16	0	112	15	4	.969
1999—Tucson (PCL)■	3B-DH-1B	20	67	3	14	1	0	1	4	.209	3	23	0	37	24	5	.924
—Nashville (PCL)■	S-2-1-3-DH	42	125	25	43	14	1	3	25	.344	18	30	1	61	86	8	.948
—Pittsburgh (N.L.)	3-1-S-2-O	49	71	7	15	5	1	3	13	.211	7	28	0	29	24	1	.981
American League totals (9 years)		621	1980	246	466	91	11	51	259	.235	171	502	10	972	1340	112	.954
National League totals (4 years)		241	546	59	131	34	2	18	81	.240	56	154	0	265	283	19	.966
Major League totals (12 years)		862	2526	305	597	125	13	69	340	.236	227	656	10	1237	1623	131	.956

RECORD AS PITCHER

Year League	W	L	Pct.	ERA	G	GS	CG	ShO	Sv.	IP	H	R	ER	BB	SO
1995—Calgary (PCL)	0	0	...	0.00	2	0	0	0	0	2	1	0	0	0	2

SWEENEY, MARK — OF/1B — BREWERS

PERSONAL: Born October 26, 1969, in Framingham, Mass. ... 6-1/195. ... Bats left, throws left. ... Full name: Mark Patrick Sweeney.

HIGH SCHOOL: Holliston (Mass.).

COLLEGE: Maine.

TRANSACTIONS/CAREER NOTES: Selected by Los Angeles Dodgers organization in 39th round of free-agent draft (June 4, 1990); did not sign. ... Selected by California Angels organization in ninth round of free-agent draft (June 3, 1991). ... Traded by Angels organization with a player to be named later to St. Louis Cardinals for P John Habyan (July 8, 1995); Cardinals acquired IF Rod Correia to complete deal (January 31, 1996). ... Traded by Cardinals with P Danny Jackson and P Rich Batchelor to San Diego Padres for P Fernando Valenzuela, 3B Scott Livingstone and OF Phil Plantier (June 13, 1997). ... Traded by Padres with OF Greg Vaughn to Cincinnati Reds for OF Reggie Sanders, SS Damian Jackson and P Josh Harris (February 2, 1999). ... Traded by Reds with a player to be named later to Milwaukee Brewers for OF Alex Ochoa (January 14, 2000).

Year	Team (League)	Pos.	G	AB	R	H	2B	3B	HR	RBI	Avg.	BB	SO	SB	PO	A	E	Avg.
									BATTING							FIELDING		
1991—Boise (N'west)............	OF		70	234	45	66	10	3	4	34	.282	*51	42	9	81	2	4	.954
1992—Quad City (Midw.)	OF		120	424	65	115	20	5	14	76	.271	47	85	15	205	5	4	.981
1993—Palm Springs (Calif.)..	OF-1B-DH		66	245	41	87	18	3	3	47	.355	42	29	9	145	2	7	.955
—Midland (Texas).........	OF		51	188	41	67	13	2	9	32	.356	27	22	1	85	3	1	.989
1994—Vancouver (PCL)	DH-1B-DH		103	344	59	98	12	3	8	49	.285	59	50	3	330	12	2	.994
—Midland (Texas).........	OF-1B-DH		14	50	13	15	3	0	3	18	.300	10	10	1	66	5	2	.973
1995—Vancouver (PCL)	OF-DH-1B		69	226	48	78	14	2	7	59	.345	43	33	3	102	2	2	.981
—Louisville (A.A.)■......	1B		22	76	15	28	8	0	2	22	.368	14	8	2	176	19	2	.990
—St. Louis (N.L.)........	1B-OF		37	77	5	21	2	0	2	13	.273	10	15	1	153	11	2	.988
1996—St. Louis (N.L.).........	OF-1B		98	170	32	45	9	0	3	22	.265	33	29	3	126	3	3	.977
1997—St. Louis (N.L.).........	OF-1B		44	61	5	13	3	0	0	4	.213	9	14	0	31	1	0	1.000
—San Diego (N.L.)■	OF-1B		71	103	11	33	4	0	2	19	.320	11	18	2	41	3	2	.957
1998—San Diego (N.L.).........	OF-1B-DH		122	192	17	45	8	3	2	15	.234	26	37	1	165	5	1	.994
1999—Cincinnati (N.L.)■.......	1B-OF		37	31	6	11	3	0	2	7	.355	4	9	0	3	0	0	1.000
—Indianapolis (I.L.)......	OF-DH-1B		86	311	66	100	17	1	12	51	.322	59	40	3	257	9	5	.982
Major League totals (5 years)			409	634	76	168	29	3	11	80	.265	93	122	7	519	23	8	.985

DIVISION SERIES RECORD

Year	Team (League)	Pos.	G	AB	R	H	2B	3B	HR	RBI	Avg.	BB	SO	SB	PO	A	E	Avg.
									BATTING							FIELDING		
1996—St. Louis (N.L.)...........	PH		1	1	0	1	0	0	0	0	1.000	0	0	0	...	...	...	...
1998—San Diego (N.L.)	PH		2	1	0	0	0	0	0	0	.000	1	0	0	...	...	...	...
Division series totals (2 years)			3	2	0	1	0	0	0	0	.500	1	0	0	0	0	0	...

CHAMPIONSHIP SERIES RECORD

Year	Team (League)	Pos.	G	AB	R	H	2B	3B	HR	RBI	Avg.	BB	SO	SB	PO	A	E	Avg.
									BATTING							FIELDING		
1996—St. Louis (N.L.)..........	PH-OF		5	4	1	0	0	0	0	0	.000	0	2	0	2	0	0	1.000
1998—San Diego (N.L.)	PH		3	2	1	0	0	0	0	0	.000	1	1	0	0	0	0	...
Championship series totals (2 years)			8	6	2	0	0	0	0	0	.000	1	3	0	2	0	0	1.000

WORLD SERIES RECORD

Year	Team (League)	Pos.	G	AB	R	H	2B	3B	HR	RBI	Avg.	BB	SO	SB	PO	A	E	Avg.
									BATTING							FIELDING		
1998—San Diego (N.L.)	PH		3	3	0	2	0	0	0	1	.667	0	0	0	...	...	...	...

SWEENEY, MIKE   1B   ROYALS

PERSONAL: Born July 22, 1973, in Orange, Calif. ... 6-2/215. ... Bats right, throws right. ... Full name: Michael John Sweeney.
HIGH SCHOOL: Ontario (Calif.).
TRANSACTIONS/CAREER NOTES: Selected by Kansas City Royals organization in 10th round of free-agent draft (June 3, 1991). ... On disabled list (May 24-July 5, 1994).
RECORDS: Shares A.L. single-season record for most consecutive games with one or more runs batted in—13 (June 23-July 4, 1999).
STATISTICAL NOTES: Led Carolina League with .548 slugging percentage in 1995. ... Tied for A.L. lead in double plays by catcher with 13 in 1997. ... Had 16-game hitting streak (June 22-July 7, 1999). ... Had 25-game hitting streak (July 18-August 13, 1999). ... Career major league grand slams: 1.

Year	Team (League)	Pos.	G	AB	R	H	2B	3B	HR	RBI	Avg.	BB	SO	SB	PO	A	E	Avg.
									BATTING							FIELDING		
1991—GC Royals (GCL)	C-1B		38	102	8	22	3	0	1	11	.216	11	9	1	124	16	4	.972
1992—Eugene (N'west)	C		59	199	17	44	12	1	4	28	.221	13	54	3	367	42	14	.967
1993—Eugene (N'west)	C		53	175	32	42	10	2	6	29	.240	30	41	1	364	46	7	.983
1994—Rockford (Midw.)	C		86	276	47	83	20	3	10	52	.301	55	43	0	453	54	6	.988
1995—Wilmington (Caro.).......	C-DH-3B		99	332	61	103	23	1	18	53	*.310	60	39	6	575	45	7	.989
—Kansas City (A.L.).......	C		4	4	1	1	0	0	0	0	.250	0	0	0	7	0	1	.875
1996—Wichita (Texas)	DH-C		66	235	45	75	18	1	14	51	.319	32	29	3	201	13	1	.995
—Omaha (A.A.)..............	C-DH		25	101	14	26	9	0	3	16	.257	6	13	0	167	8	0	1.000
—Kansas City (A.L.)	C-DH		50	165	23	46	10	0	4	24	.279	18	21	1	158	7	1	.994
1997—Kansas City (A.L.)	C-DH		84	240	30	58	8	0	7	31	.242	17	33	3	425	31	3	.993
—Omaha (A.A.).............	C-DH		40	144	22	34	8	1	10	29	.236	18	20	0	229	15	1	.996
1998—Kansas City (A.L.)	C		92	282	32	73	18	0	8	35	.259	24	38	2	517	33	•9	.984
1999—Kansas City (A.L.)	1B-DH-C		150	575	101	185	44	2	22	102	.322	54	48	6	588	43	12	.981
Major League totals (5 years)			380	1266	187	363	80	2	41	192	.287	113	140	12	1695	114	26	.986

SWINDELL, GREG   P   DIAMONDBACKS

PERSONAL: Born January 2, 1965, in Fort Worth, Texas. ... 6-3/230. ... Throws left, bats right. ... Full name: Forest Gregory Swindell. ... Name pronounced swin-DELL.
HIGH SCHOOL: Sharpstown (Houston).
COLLEGE: Texas.
TRANSACTIONS/CAREER NOTES: Selected by Cleveland Indians organization in first round (second pick overall) of free-agent draft (June 2, 1986). ... On disabled list (June 30, 1987-remainder of season and July 26-August 30, 1989). ... Traded by Indians to Cincinnati Reds for P Jack Armstrong, P Scott Scudder and P Joe Turek (November 15, 1991). ... On disabled list (August 23-September 7, 1992). ... Granted free agency (October 26, 1992). ... Signed by Houston Astros (December 4, 1992). ... On disabled list (July 6-26, 1993). ... On Houston disabled list (April 20-May 22, 1996). ... Released by Astros (June 3, 1996). ... Signed by Indians (June 15, 1996). ... On Cleveland disabled list (July 4-21, 1996). ... Granted free agency (October 3, 1996). ... Signed by Minnesota Twins organization (December 18, 1996). ... Traded by Twins with 1B Orlando Merced to Boston Red Sox for P Matt Kinney, P Joe Thomas and P John Barnes (July 31, 1998). ... Granted free agency (October 27, 1998). ... Signed by Arizona Diamondbacks (November 13, 1998). ... On disabled list (June 13-28, 1999).
HONORS: Named lefthanded pitcher on THE SPORTING NEWS college All-America team (1985-86).
STATISTICAL NOTES: Struck out 15 batters in one game (May 10, 1987).
MISCELLANEOUS: Struck out in only appearance as pinch hitter (1995).

Year League	W	L	Pct.	ERA	G	GS	CG	ShO	Sv.	IP	H	R	ER	BB	SO
1986— Waterloo (Midw.)	2	1	.667	1.00	3	3	0	0	0	18	12	2	2	3	25
— Cleveland (A.L.)	5	2	.714	4.23	9	9	1	0	0	61 2/3	57	35	29	15	46
1987— Cleveland (A.L.)	3	8	.273	5.10	16	15	4	1	0	102 1/3	112	62	58	37	97
1988— Cleveland (A.L.)	18	14	.563	3.20	33	33	12	4	0	242	234	97	86	45	180
1989— Cleveland (A.L.)	13	6	.684	3.37	28	28	5	2	0	184 1/3	170	71	69	51	129
1990— Cleveland (A.L.)	12	9	.571	4.40	34	34	3	0	0	214 2/3	245	110	105	47	135
1991— Cleveland (A.L.)	9	16	.360	3.48	33	33	7	0	0	238	241	112	92	31	169
1992— Cincinnati (N.L.)■	12	8	.600	2.70	31	30	5	3	0	213 2/3	210	72	64	41	138
1993— Houston (N.L.)■	12	13	.480	4.16	31	30	1	1	0	190 1/3	215	98	88	40	124
1994— Houston (N.L.)	8	9	.471	4.37	24	24	1	1	0	148 1/3	175	80	72	26	74
1995— Houston (N.L.)	10	9	.526	4.47	33	26	1	1	0	153	180	86	76	39	96
1996— Houston (N.L.)	0	3	.000	7.83	8	4	0	0	0	23	35	25	20	11	15
— Cleveland (A.L.)■	1	1	.500	6.59	13	2	0	0	0	28 2/3	31	21	21	8	21
1997— Minnesota (A.L.)■	7	4	.636	3.58	65	1	0	0	1	115 2/3	102	46	46	25	75
1998— Boston (A.L.)■	2	3	.400	3.38	29	0	0	0	0	24	25	13	9	13	18
1999— Arizona (N.L.)■	4	0	1.000	2.51	63	0	0	0	1	64 2/3	54	19	18	21	51
A.L. totals (9 years)	70	63	.526	3.83	260	155	32	7	1	1211 1/3	1217	567	515	272	870
N.L. totals (6 years)	46	42	.523	3.84	190	114	8	5	1	793	869	380	338	178	498
Major League totals (14 years)	116	105	.525	3.83	450	269	40	12	2	2004 1/3	2086	947	853	450	1368

DIVISION SERIES RECORD

Year League	W	L	Pct.	ERA	G	GS	CG	ShO	Sv.	IP	H	R	ER	BB	SO
1998— Boston (A.L.)	0	0	...	0.00	1	0	0	0	0	1 1/3	0	0	0	1	1
1999— Arizona (N.L.)	0	0	...	0.00	3	0	0	0	0	3 1/3	1	0	0	3	1
Division series totals (2 years)	0	0	...	0.00	4	0	0	0	0	4 2/3	1	0	0	4	2

ALL-STAR GAME RECORD

Year League	W	L	Pct.	ERA	GS	CG	ShO	Sv.	IP	H	R	ER	BB	SO
1989— American	0	0	...	0.00	0	0	0	0	1 2/3	2	0	0	0	3

TAM, JEFF   P   ATHLETICS

S
T

PERSONAL: Born August 19, 1970, in Fullerton, Calif. ... 6-1/202. ... Throws right, bats right. ... Full name: Jeffery Eugene Tam.
HIGH SCHOOL: Eau Gaille (Melbourne, Fla.).
COLLEGE: Florida State.
TRANSACTIONS/CAREER NOTES: Signed as a non-drafted free agent by New York Mets organization (June 27, 1993). ... On New York disabled list (March 21-May 16, 1999); included rehabilitation assignment to St. Lucie (May 2-16). ... Claimed on waivers by Cleveland Indians (June 18, 1999). ... On Buffalo disabled list (July 23-August 1, 1999). ... Claimed on waivers by Mets (August 11, 1999). ... Granted free agency (October 15, 1999). ... Signed by Oakland Athletics organization (November 23, 1999).

Year League	W	L	Pct.	ERA	G	GS	CG	ShO	Sv.	IP	H	R	ER	BB	SO
1993— Pittsfield (NY-P)	3	3	.500	3.35	21	1	0	0	0	40 1/3	50	21	15	7	31
1994— Columbia (SAL)	1	1	.500	1.29	26	0	0	0	18	28	23	14	4	6	22
— St. Lucie (FSL)	0	0	...	0.00	24	0	0	0	16	26 2/3	13	0	0	6	15
— Binghamton (East.)	0	0	...	8.10	4	0	0	0	0	6 2/3	9	6	6	5	7
1995— Binghamton (East.)	0	2	.000	4.50	14	0	0	0	3	18	20	11	9	4	9
— Gulf Coast Mets (GCL)	0	0	...	3.00	2	1	0	0	0	3	2	1	1	1	2
1996— Binghamton (East.)	6	2	.750	2.44	49	0	0	0	2	62 2/3	51	19	17	16	48
1997— Norfolk (I.L.)	7	5	.583	4.67	40	11	0	0	6	111 2/3	137	72	58	14	67
1998— Norfolk (I.L.)	3	3	.500	1.83	45	0	0	0	11	64	42	14	13	6	54
— New York (N.L.)	1	1	.500	6.28	15	0	0	0	0	14 1/3	13	10	10	4	8
1999— St. Lucie (FSL)	0	0	...	3.38	2	0	0	0	0	2 2/3	4	1	1	0	3
— Norfolk (I.L.)	0	1	.000	3.10	16	0	0	0	3	20 1/3	24	7	7	3	10
— Buffalo (I.L.)■	2	2	.500	2.08	16	0	0	0	0	26	23	9	6	8	13
— Cleveland (A.L.)	0	0	...	81.00	1	0	0	0	0	1/3	2	3	3	1	0
— New York (N.L.)■	0	0	...	3.18	9	0	0	0	0	11 1/3	6	4	4	3	8
A.L. totals (1 year)	0	0	...	81.00	1	0	0	0	0	1/3	2	3	3	1	0
N.L. totals (2 years)	1	1	.500	4.91	24	0	0	0	0	25 2/3	19	14	14	7	16
Major League totals (2 years)	1	1	.500	5.88	25	0	0	0	0	26	21	17	17	8	16

TAPANI, KEVIN   P   CUBS

PERSONAL: Born February 18, 1964, in Des Moines, Iowa. ... 6-1/190. ... Throws right, bats right. ... Full name: Kevin Ray Tapani. ... Name pronounced TAP-uh-nee.
HIGH SCHOOL: Escanaba (Mich.).
COLLEGE: Central Michigan (degree in finance, 1987).
TRANSACTIONS/CAREER NOTES: Selected by Chicago Cubs organization in ninth round of free-agent draft (June 3, 1985); did not sign. ... Selected by Oakland Athletics organization in second round of free-agent draft (June 2, 1986). ... Traded by A's as part of an eight-player, three-team deal in which New York Mets traded P Jesse Orosco to A's (December 11, 1987); A's traded Orosco, SS Alfredo Griffin and P Jay Howell to Los Angeles Dodgers for P Bob Welch, P Matt Young and P Jack Savage. A's then traded Savage, P Wally Whitehurst and Tapani to Mets. ... Traded by Mets with P Tim Drummond to Minnesota Twins (August 1, 1989); as partial completion of deal in which Twins traded P Frank Viola to Mets for P Rick Aguilera, P David West and three players to be named later (July 31, 1989); Twins acquired P Jack Savage to complete deal (October 16, 1989). ... On disabled list (August 17-September 10, 1990). ... Traded by Twins with P Mark Guthrie to Los Angeles Dodgers for 1B/3B Ron Coomer, P Greg Hansell, P Jose Parra and a player to be named later (July 31, 1995); Twins acquired OF Chris Latham to complete deal (October 30, 1995). ... Granted free agency (December 21, 1995). ... Signed by Chicago White Sox (February 3, 1996). ... Granted free agency (October 29, 1996). ... Signed by Cubs (December 16, 1996). ... On Chicago disabled list (March 27-July 23, 1997); included rehabilitation assignments to Rockford (June 25-26 and July 12-13), Orlando (July 1-7), Daytona (July 7-8) and Iowa (July 18-19). ... On disabled list (April 13-May 1 and August 26-September 25, 1999).
STATISTICAL NOTES: Pitched 5-0 one-hit, complete-game victory for Chicago against Cincinnati (September 16, 1997). ... Career major league grand slams: 1.

Year League	W	L	Pct.	ERA	G	GS	CG	ShO	Sv.	IP	H	R	ER	BB	SO
1986— Medford (N'west)	1	0	1.000	0.00	2	2	0	0	0	8 1/3	6	3	0	3	9
— Modesto (Calif.)	6	1	.857	2.48	11	11	1	0	0	69	74	26	19	22	44
— Huntsville (Sou.)	1	0	1.000	6.00	1	1	0	0	0	6	8	4	4	1	2
— Tacoma (PCL)	0	1	.000	15.43	1	1	0	0	0	2 1/3	5	6	4	1	1
1987— Modesto (Calif.)	10	7	.588	3.76	24	24	6	1	0	148 1/3	122	74	62	60	121
1988— St. Lucie (FSL)■	1	0	1.000	1.42	3	3	0	0	0	19	17	5	3	4	11
— Jackson (Texas)	5	1	.833	2.74	24	5	0	0	3	62 1/3	46	23	19	19	35
1989— Tidewater (I.L.)	7	5	.583	3.47	17	17	2	1	0	109	113	49	42	25	63
— New York (N.L.)	0	0	...	3.68	3	0	0	0	0	7 1/3	5	3	3	4	2
— Portland (PCL)■	4	2	.667	2.20	6	6	1	0	0	41	38	15	10	12	30
— Minnesota (A.L.)	2	2	.500	3.86	5	5	0	0	0	32 2/3	34	15	14	8	21
1990— Minnesota (A.L.)	12	8	.600	4.07	28	28	1	1	0	159 1/3	164	75	72	29	101
1991— Minnesota (A.L.)	16	9	.640	2.99	34	34	4	1	0	244	225	84	81	40	135
1992— Minnesota (A.L.)	16	11	.593	3.97	34	34	4	1	0	220	226	103	97	48	138
1993— Minnesota (A.L.)	12	15	.444	4.43	36	35	3	1	0	225 2/3	243	123	111	57	150
1994— Minnesota (A.L.)	11	7	.611	4.62	24	24	4	1	0	156	181	86	80	39	91
1995— Minnesota (A.L.)	6	11	.353	4.92	20	20	3	1	0	133 2/3	155	79	73	34	88
— Los Angeles (N.L.)■	4	2	.667	5.05	13	11	0	0	0	57	72	37	32	14	43
1996— Chicago (A.L.)■	13	10	.565	4.59	34	34	1	0	0	225 1/3	236	123	115	76	150
1997— Rockford (Midw.)■	1	0	1.000	0.82	2	2	0	0	0	11	5	1	1	0	7
— Orlando (Sou.)	0	0	...	4.50	1	1	0	0	0	4	3	2	2	2	2
— Daytona (FSL)	0	0	...	3.86	1	1	0	0	0	4 2/3	5	2	2	2	4
— Iowa (A.A.)	0	1	.000	4.00	1	1	1	0	0	9	5	4	4	1	4
— Chicago (N.L.)	9	3	.750	3.39	13	13	1	1	0	85	77	33	32	23	55
1998— Chicago (N.L.)	19	9	.679	4.85	35	34	2	2	0	219	244	120	118	62	136
1999— Chicago (N.L.)	6	12	.333	4.83	23	23	1	0	0	136	151	81	73	33	73
A.L. totals (8 years)	88	73	.547	4.14	215	214	20	6	0	1396 2/3	1464	688	643	331	874
N.L. totals (5 years)	38	26	.594	4.60	87	81	4	3	0	504 1/3	549	274	258	136	309
Major League totals (11 years)	126	99	.560	4.27	302	295	24	9	0	1901	2013	962	901	467	1183

DIVISION SERIES RECORD

Year League	W	L	Pct.	ERA	G	GS	CG	ShO	Sv.	IP	H	R	ER	BB	SO
1995— Los Angeles (N.L.)	0	0	...	81.00	2	0	0	0	0	1/3	0	3	3	4	1
1998— Chicago (N.L.)	0	0	...	1.00	1	1	0	0	0	9	5	1	1	3	6
Division series totals (2 years)	0	0	...	3.86	3	1	0	0	0	9 1/3	5	4	4	7	7

CHAMPIONSHIP SERIES RECORD

Year League	W	L	Pct.	ERA	G	GS	CG	ShO	Sv.	IP	H	R	ER	BB	SO
1991— Minnesota (A.L.)	0	1	.000	7.84	2	2	0	0	0	10 1/3	16	9	9	3	9

WORLD SERIES RECORD

NOTES: Member of World Series championship team (1991).

Year League	W	L	Pct.	ERA	G	GS	CG	ShO	Sv.	IP	H	R	ER	BB	SO
1991— Minnesota (A.L.)	1	1	.500	4.50	2	2	0	0	0	12	13	6	6	2	7

TARASCO, TONY   OF

PERSONAL: Born December 9, 1970, in New York. ... 6-1/205. ... Bats left, throws right. ... Full name: Anthony Giacinto Tarasco.
HIGH SCHOOL: Santa Monica (Calif.).
TRANSACTIONS/CAREER NOTES: Selected by Atlanta Braves organization in 15th round of free-agent draft (June 1, 1988). ... On disabled list (August 4-September 12, 1991). ... Traded by Braves with OF Roberto Kelly and P Esteban Yan to Montreal Expos for OF Marquis Grissom (April 6, 1995). ... Traded by Expos to Baltimore Orioles for OF Sherman Obando (March 13, 1996). ... On Rochester disabled list (June 16-August 25, 1996). ... On Baltimore disabled list (August 25-September 13, 1996); included rehabilitation assignments to Frederick (August 25-September 8) and Rochester (September 9-13). ... Claimed on waivers by Cincinnati Reds (March 24, 1998). ... On Indianapolis disabled list (April 26-May 29, 1998). ... Released by Reds (November 10, 1998). ... Signed by Kansas City Royals organization (January 25, 1999). ... Released by Royals (March 18, 1999). ... Signed by New York Yankees organization (March 26, 1999). ... Granted free agency (October 4, 1999).
STATISTICAL NOTES: Career major league grand slams: 1.

							BATTING							FIELDING		
Year Team (League)	Pos.	G	AB	R	H	2B	3B	HR	RBI	Avg.	BB	SO	SB	PO	A	E	Avg.
1988— Idaho Falls (Pio.)	OF	7	10	1	0	0	0	0	1	.000	5	2	1	2	0	1	.667
— GC Braves (GCL)	OF	21	64	10	15	6	1	0	4	.234	7	7	3	25	1	1	.963
1989— Pulaski (Appl.)	OF	49	156	22	53	8	2	2	22	.340	21	20	7	45	4	3	.942
1990— Sumter (SAL)	OF	107	355	42	94	13	3	3	37	.265	37	57	9	173	14	9	.954
1991— Durham (Caro.)	OF	78	248	31	62	8	2	12	38	.250	21	64	11	119	6	3	.977
1992— Greenville (Sou.)	OF-2B	133	489	73	140	22	2	15	54	.286	27	84	33	209	17	5	.978
1993— Richmond (I.L.)	OF	93	370	73	122	15	7	15	53	.330	36	54	19	143	8	2	.987
— Atlanta (N.L.)	OF	24	35	6	8	2	0	0	2	.229	0	5	0	11	0	0	1.000
1994— Atlanta (N.L.)	OF	87	132	16	36	6	0	5	19	.273	9	17	5	42	1	0	1.000
1995— Montreal (N.L.)■	OF	126	438	64	109	18	4	14	40	.249	51	78	24	230	7	5	.979
1996— Baltimore (A.L.)■	OF-DH	31	84	14	20	3	0	1	9	.238	7	15	5	50	1	0	1.000
— Rochester (I.L.)	DH-OF	29	103	18	27	6	0	2	9	.262	11	20	4	4	0	0	1.000
— Frederick (Caro.)	DH	9	35	6	8	3	0	1	5	.229	4	4	0	0	0	0	...
— GC Orioles (GCL)	DH	3	8	2	3	1	0	0	3	.375	2	1	0	0	0	0	...
1997— Baltimore (A.L.)	OF-DH	100	166	26	34	8	1	7	26	.205	25	33	2	104	4	1	.991
— Rochester (I.L.)	OF	10	35	4	7	0	0	2	6	.200	7	7	0	19	1	0	1.000
1998— Indianapolis (I.L.)■	OF-DH	90	319	53	100	19	1	16	45	.313	43	46	3	101	3	0	1.000
— Cincinnati (N.L.)	OF	15	24	5	5	2	0	1	4	.208	3	5	0	10	0	0	1.000
1999— Columbus (I.L.)■	OF-DH	95	346	72	102	23	0	19	61	.295	49	39	9	204	1	2	.990
— New York (A.L.)	OF-DH	14	31	5	5	2	0	0	3	.161	3	5	1	11	0	0	1.000
American League totals (3 years)		145	281	45	59	13	1	8	38	.210	35	53	8	165	5	1	.994
National League totals (4 years)		252	629	91	158	28	4	20	65	.251	63	105	29	293	8	5	.984
Major League totals (7 years)		397	910	136	217	41	5	28	103	.238	98	158	37	458	13	6	.987

Year Team (League)	Pos.	G	AB	R	H	2B	3B	HR	RBI	Avg.	BB	SO	SB	PO	A	E	Avg.
								BATTING							FIELDING		
1996— Baltimore (A.L.)								Did not play.									

CHAMPIONSHIP SERIES RECORD

Year Team (League)	Pos.	G	AB	R	H	2B	3B	HR	RBI	Avg.	BB	SO	SB	PO	A	E	Avg.
								BATTING							FIELDING		
1993— Atlanta (N.L.).............	OF-PR	2	1	0	0	0	0	0	0	.000	0	1	0	0	0	0	...
1996— Baltimore (A.L.)...........	OF	2	1	0	0	0	0	0	0	.000	0	1	0	2	0	0	1.000
Championship series totals (2 years)		4	2	0	0	0	0	0	0	.000	0	2	0	2	0	0	1.000

TATIS, FERNANDO — 3B — CARDINALS

PERSONAL: Born January 1, 1975, in San Pedro de Macoris, Dominican Republic. ... 5-10/175. ... Bats right, throws right.

TRANSACTIONS/CAREER NOTES: Signed as non-drafted free agent by Texas Rangers organization (August 25, 1992). ... Traded by Rangers with P Darren Oliver and a player to be named later to St. Louis Cardinals for P Todd Stottlemyre and SS Royce Clayton (July 31, 1998); Cardinals acquired OF Mark Little to complete deal (August 9, 1998).

RECORDS: Holds major league single-inning records for most grand slams—2; and most runs batted in—8 (April 23, 1999, third inning). ... Shares major league single-game record for most grand slams—2 (April 23, 1999). ... Shares major league single-inning record for most home runs—2 (April 23, 1999, third inning).

STATISTICAL NOTES: Tied for Gulf Coast League lead in intentional bases on balls received with four in 1994. ... Led Gulf Coast League third basemen with 165 assists and 227 total chances in 1994. ... Tied for Texas League lead with four intentional bases on balls in 1997. ... Career major league grand slams: 3.

Year Team (League)	Pos.	G	AB	R	H	2B	3B	HR	RBI	Avg.	BB	SO	SB	PO	A	E	Avg.
								BATTING							FIELDING		
1993— Dom. Rangers (DSL)..	IF	59	198	22	54	5	1	4	34	.273	27	12	7	135	37	11	.940
1994— GC Rangers (GCL)......	3B-2B	•60	212	34	70	10	2	6	32	.330	25	33	21	47	†168	17	.927
1995— Char., S.C. (SAL)........	3B	131	499	74	•151	*43	4	15	84	.303	45	94	22	*98	235	37	.900
1996— Charlotte (FSL)..........	3B	85	325	46	93	25	4	12	53	.286	30	48	9	53	148	24	.893
— Oklahoma City (A.A.)..	3B	2	4	0	2	1	0	0	0	.500	0	1	0	0	1	0	1.000
1997— Tulsa (Texas)	3B-DH	102	382	73	120	26	1	24	61	.314	46	72	17	53	193	21	.921
— Texas (A.L.)	3B	60	223	29	57	9	0	8	29	.256	14	42	3	45	90	7	.951
1998— Texas (A.L.)	3B	95	330	41	89	17	2	3	32	.270	12	66	6	74	184	15	.945
— St. Louis (N.L.)■	3B-SS	55	202	28	58	16	2	8	26	.287	24	57	7	36	123	12	.930
1999— St. Louis (N.L.)..........	3B	149	537	104	160	31	2	34	107	.298	82	128	21	101	267	16	.958
American League totals (2 years)		155	553	70	146	26	2	11	61	.264	26	108	9	119	274	22	.947
National League totals (2 years)		204	739	132	218	47	4	42	133	.295	106	185	28	137	390	28	.950
Major League totals (3 years)		359	1292	202	364	73	6	53	194	.282	132	293	37	256	664	50	.948

TATIS, RAMON — P — TIGERS

PERSONAL: Born February 5, 1973, in Guayubin, Dominican Republic. ... 6-3/205. ... Throws left, bats left. ... Full name: Ramon Francisco Tatis.

HIGH SCHOOL: Los Limones (Guayubin, Dominican Republic).

TRANSACTIONS/CAREER NOTES: Signed as non-drafted free agent by New York Mets organization (September 6, 1990). ... Selected by Chicago Cubs from Mets organization in Rule 5 major league draft (December 9, 1996). ... Selected by Tampa Bay Devil Rays in second round (42nd pick overall) of expansion draft (November 18, 1997). ... On Durham disabled list (June 29-July 10, 1998). ... On Tampa Bay disabled list (August 26-September 8, 1998). ... Claimed on waivers by Detroit Tigers (November 24, 1999).

STATISTICAL NOTES: Led International League with nine balks in 1999.

Year League	W	L	Pct.	ERA	G	GS	CG	ShO	Sv.	IP	H	R	ER	BB	SO
1991— Dom. Mets (DSL)	2	6	.250	4.26	12	12	0	0	0	57	59	41	27	34	43
1992— Gulf Coast Mets (GCL)	1	3	.250	8.50	11	5	0	0	0	36	56	40	34	15	25
1993— Kingsport (Appalachian).....	0	2	.000	6.12	13	3	0	0	1	42²/₃	51	42	29	23	25
1994— Kingsport (Appalachian)	1	3	.250	3.32	13	4	0	0	0	40²/₃	35	25	15	31	36
1995— Columbia (SAL).................	2	3	.400	5.63	16	2	0	0	0	32	34	27	20	14	27
— Pittsfield (NY-P)	4	5	.444	3.63	13	13	1	•1	0	79¹/₃	88	40	32	27	69
1996— St. Lucie (FSL).................	4	2	.667	3.39	46	1	0	0	6	74¹/₃	71	35	28	38	46
1997— Chicago (N.L.)■...............	1	1	.500	5.34	56	0	0	0	0	55²/₃	66	36	33	29	33
1998— Durham (I.L.)■................	1	3	.250	3.67	19	9	0	0	2	61¹/₃	66	29	25	24	44
— Tampa Bay (A.L.)................	0	0	...	13.89	22	0	0	0	0	11²/₃	23	19	18	16	5
1999— Durham (I.L.)	12	8	.600	5.50	28	•28	0	0	0	155¹/₃	178	100	95	74	97
A.L. totals (1 year)	0	0	...	13.89	22	0	0	0	0	11²/₃	23	19	18	16	5
N.L. totals (1 year)	1	1	.500	5.34	56	0	0	0	0	55²/₃	66	36	33	29	33
Major League totals (2 years)	1	1	.500	6.82	78	0	0	0	0	67¹/₃	89	55	51	45	38

TAUBENSEE, EDDIE — C — REDS

PERSONAL: Born October 31, 1968, in Beeville, Texas. ... 6-3/230. ... Bats left, throws right. ... Full name: Edward Kenneth Taubensee. ... Name pronounced TAW-ben-see.

HIGH SCHOOL: Lake Howell (Casselberry, Fla.).

TRANSACTIONS/CAREER NOTES: Selected by Cincinnati Reds organization in sixth round of free-agent draft (June 2, 1986). ... Selected by Oakland Athletics from Reds organization in Rule 5 major league draft (December 3, 1990). ... Claimed on waivers by Cleveland Indians (April 4, 1991). ... Traded by Indians with P Willie Blair to Houston Astros for OF Kenny Lofton and IF Dave Rohde (December 10, 1991). ... Traded by Astros to Reds for P Ross Powell and P Marty Lister (April 19, 1994).

STATISTICAL NOTES: Led Pioneer League with 19 passed balls in 1987. ... Tied for South Atlantic League lead in double plays by catcher with seven in 1988. ... Had 16-game hitting streak (May 22-June 13, 1999). ... Career major league grand slams: 1.

Year Team (League)	Pos.	G	AB	R	H	2B	3B	HR	RBI	Avg.	BB	SO	SB	PO	A	E	Avg.
1986—GC Reds (GCL)	C-1B	35	107	8	21	3	0	1	11	.196	11	33	0	208	27	8	.967
1987—Billings (Pio.)	C	55	162	24	43	7	0	5	28	.265	25	47	2	344	29	6	.984
1988—Greensboro (SAL)	C	103	330	36	85	16	1	10	41	.258	44	93	8	640	70	15	.979
—Chattanooga (Sou.)	C	5	12	2	2	0	0	1	1	.167	3	4	0	17	5	1	.957
1989—Cedar Rap. (Midw.)	C	59	196	25	39	5	0	8	22	.199	25	55	4	400	9	1	.998
—Chattanooga (Sou.)	C	45	127	11	24	2	0	3	13	.189	11	28	0	213	31	6	.976
1990—Cedar Rap. (Midw.)	C	122	417	57	108	21	1	16	62	.259	51	98	11	795	94	16	.982
1991—Cleveland (A.L.)■	C	26	66	5	16	2	1	0	8	.242	5	16	0	89	6	2	.979
—Colo. Springs (PCL)	C	91	287	53	89	23	3	13	39	.310	31	61	0	412	47	12	.975
1992—Houston (N.L.)■	C	104	297	23	66	15	0	5	28	.222	31	78	2	557	66	5	.992
—Tucson (PCL)	C	20	74	13	25	8	1	1	10	.338	8	17	0	127	10	4	.972
1993—Houston (N.L.)	C	94	288	26	72	11	1	9	42	.250	21	44	1	551	41	5	.992
1994—Houston (N.L.)	C	5	10	0	1	0	0	0	0	.100	0	3	0	19	2	0	1.000
—Cincinnati (N.L.)■	C	61	177	29	52	8	2	8	21	.294	15	28	2	362	17	4	.990
1995—Cincinnati (N.L.)	C-1B	80	218	32	62	14	2	9	44	.284	22	52	2	338	22	6	.984
1996—Cincinnati (N.L.)	C	108	327	46	95	20	0	12	48	.291	26	64	3	538	42	11	.981
1997—Cincinnati (N.L.)	C-OF-1B-DH	108	254	26	68	18	0	10	34	.268	22	66	0	408	26	5	.989
1998—Cincinnati (N.L.)	C	130	431	61	120	27	0	11	72	.278	52	93	1	776	44	10	.988
1999—Cincinnati (N.L.)	C	126	424	58	132	22	2	21	87	.311	30	67	0	733	48	9	.989
American League totals (1 year)		26	66	5	16	2	1	0	8	.242	5	16	0	89	6	2	.979
National League totals (8 years)		816	2426	301	668	135	7	85	376	.275	219	495	11	4282	308	55	.988
Major League totals (9 years)		842	2492	306	684	137	8	85	384	.274	224	511	11	4371	314	57	.988

CHAMPIONSHIP SERIES RECORD

Year Team (League)	Pos.	G	AB	R	H	2B	3B	HR	RBI	Avg.	BB	SO	SB	PO	A	E	Avg.
1995—Cincinnati (N.L.)	PH-C	2	2	0	1	0	0	0	0	.500	0	0	0	0	0	0	...

TAVAREZ, JULIAN   P   ROCKIES

PERSONAL: Born May 22, 1973, in Santiago, Dominican Republic. ... 6-2/190. ... Throws right, bats left.

HIGH SCHOOL: Santiago (Dominican Republic) Public School.

TRANSACTIONS/CAREER NOTES: Signed as non-drafted free agent by Cleveland Indians organization (March 16, 1990). ... On Cleveland suspended list (June 18-21, 1996). ... Traded by Indians with IF Jeff Kent, IF Jose Vizcaino and a player to be named later to San Francisco Giants for 3B Matt Williams and a player to be named later (November 13, 1996); Indians traded P Joe Roa to Giants for OF Trenidad Hubbard to complete deal (December 16, 1996). ... On San Francisco disabled list (July 13-August 7, 1998); included rehabilitation assignment to Fresno (August 5-7). ... On suspended list (September 14-16, 1998). ... On San Francisco disabled list (May 1-June 1, 1999); included rehabilitation assignment to Fresno (May 25-June 1). ... Claimed on waivers by Colorado Rockies (November 16, 1999).

HONORS: Named A.L. Rookie Pitcher of the Year by THE SPORTING NEWS (1995).

STATISTICAL NOTES: Led Appalachian League with 10 hit batsmen in 1993.

Year League	W	L	Pct.	ERA	G	GS	CG	ShO	Sv.	IP	H	R	ER	BB	SO
1990—Dom. Indians (DSL)	5	5	.500	3.29	14	12	3	0	0	82	85	53	30	48	33
1991—Dom. Indians (DSL)	8	2	.800	2.67	19	18	1	0	0	121 1/3	95	41	36	28	75
1992—Burlington (Appl.)	6	3	.667	2.68	14	*14	2	•2	0	87 1/3	86	41	26	12	69
1993—Kinston (Caro.)	11	5	.688	2.42	18	18	2	0	0	119	102	48	32	28	107
—Canton/Akron (East.)	2	1	.667	0.95	3	2	1	1	0	19	14	2	2	1	11
—Cleveland (A.L.)	2	2	.500	6.57	8	7	0	0	0	37	53	29	27	13	19
1994—Charlotte (I.L.)	•15	6	.714	3.48	26	26	2	2	0	176	167	79	68	43	102
—Cleveland (A.L.)	0	1	.000	21.60	1	1	0	0	0	1 2/3	6	8	4	1	0
1995—Cleveland (A.L.)	10	2	.833	2.44	57	0	0	0	0	85	76	36	23	21	68
1996—Cleveland (A.L.)	4	7	.364	5.36	51	4	0	0	0	80 2/3	101	49	48	22	46
—Buffalo (A.A.)	1	0	1.000	1.29	2	2	0	0	0	14	10	2	2	3	10
1997—San Francisco (N.L.)■	6	4	.600	3.87	*89	0	0	0	0	88 1/3	91	43	38	34	38
1998—San Francisco (N.L.)	5	3	.625	3.80	60	0	0	0	1	85 1/3	96	41	36	36	52
—Fresno (PCL)	0	0	...	19.29	1	0	0	0	0	2 1/3	6	5	5	0	1
1999—San Francisco (N.L.)	2	0	1.000	5.93	47	0	0	0	0	54 2/3	65	38	36	25	33
—Fresno (PCL)	0	0	...	2.25	4	0	0	0	0	8	3	2	2	3	9
—San Jose (Calif.)	0	0	...	0.00	1	1	0	0	0	4	1	0	0	1	3
A.L. totals (4 years)	16	12	.571	4.49	117	12	0	0	0	204 1/3	236	122	102	57	133
N.L. totals (3 years)	13	7	.650	4.34	196	0	0	0	1	228 1/3	252	122	110	95	123
Major League totals (7 years)	29	19	.604	4.41	313	12	0	0	1	432 2/3	488	244	212	152	256

DIVISION SERIES RECORD

Year League	W	L	Pct.	ERA	G	GS	CG	ShO	Sv.	IP	H	R	ER	BB	SO
1995—Cleveland (A.L.)	0	0	...	6.75	3	0	0	0	0	2 2/3	5	2	2	0	3
1996—Cleveland (A.L.)	0	0	...	0.00	2	0	0	0	0	1 1/3	1	0	0	2	1
1997—San Francisco (N.L.)	0	1	.000	4.50	3	0	0	0	0	4	4	2	2	2	0
Division series totals (3 years)	0	1	.000	4.50	8	0	0	0	0	8	10	4	4	4	4

CHAMPIONSHIP SERIES RECORD

Year League	W	L	Pct.	ERA	G	GS	CG	ShO	Sv.	IP	H	R	ER	BB	SO
1995—Cleveland (A.L.)	0	1	.000	2.70	4	0	0	0	0	3 1/3	3	1	1	1	2

WORLD SERIES RECORD

Year League	W	L	Pct.	ERA	G	GS	CG	ShO	Sv.	IP	H	R	ER	BB	SO
1995—Cleveland (A.L.)	0	0	...	0.00	4	0	0	0	0	4 1/3	3	0	0	2	1

PERSONAL: Born October 16, 1961, in Monticello, Fla. ... 6-8/235. ... Throws right, bats right. ... Full name: William Howell Taylor.
HIGH SCHOOL: Central (Thomasville, Ga.).
COLLEGE: Abraham Baldwin Agricultural College (Ga.).
TRANSACTIONS/CAREER NOTES: Selected by Texas Rangers organization in second round of free-agent draft (January 8, 1980). ... Loaned by Rangers organization to Wausau, Seattle Mariners organization (April 5-June 23, 1982). ... Granted free agency (October 22, 1988). ... Signed by Las Vegas, San Diego Padres organization (March 30, 1989). ... Granted free agency (October 22, 1989). ... Signed by Atlanta Braves organization (August 16, 1990). ... Selected by Toronto Blue Jays from Braves organization in Rule 5 major league draft (December 7, 1992). ... Returned to Braves organization (April 3, 1993). ... Granted free agency (October 15, 1993). ... Signed by Oakland Athletics organization (December 13, 1993). ... On disabled list (July 27, 1994-remainder of season; April 12, 1995-entire season; and August 15-September 13, 1996). ... Traded by Athletics to New York Mets for P Jason Isringhausen and P Greg McMichael (July 31, 1999). ... Granted free agency (December 21, 1999). ... Signed by Colorado Rockies (January 24, 2000).

Year — League	W	L	Pct.	ERA	G	GS	CG	ShO	Sv.	IP	H	R	ER	BB	SO
1980— Asheville (SAL)	0	2	.000	10.93	6	2	0	0	0	14	24	24	17	9	12
— GC Rangers (GCL)	0	0	...	2.31	14	2	0	0	0	35	36	14	9	16	22
1981— Asheville (SAL)	1	7	.125	4.64	14	12	1	0	0	64	76	43	33	35	44
— GC Rangers (GCL)	4	2	.667	2.72	12	11	0	0	0	53	42	23	16	29	35
1982— Wausau (Midw.)■	2	5	.286	5.03	19	1	0	0	2	39 1/3	36	27	22	27	34
— Burlington (Midw.)■	5	4	.556	3.72	18	8	2	0	1	72 2/3	64	37	30	36	61
1983— Salem (Caro.)	1	1	.500	6.26	7	7	1	0	0	41 2/3	30	34	29	42	42
— Tulsa (Texas)	5	8	.385	6.87	21	12	0	0	0	76	86	65	58	51	75
1984— Tulsa (Texas)	5	3	.625	3.83	42	2	0	0	7	80	65	38	34	51	80
1985— Tulsa (Texas)	3	9	.250	3.47	20	17	2	0	0	103 2/3	84	55	40	48	87
1986— Tulsa (Texas)	3	7	.300	3.95	11	11	2	1	0	68 1/3	65	40	30	37	64
— Oklahoma City (A.A.)	5	5	.500	4.60	16	16	1	0	0	101 2/3	94	56	52	57	68
1987— Oklahoma City (A.A.)	*12	9	.571	5.61	28	•28	0	0	0	168 1/3	198	122	105	91	100
1988— Oklahoma City (A.A.)	4	8	.333	5.49	20	12	1	1	1	82	98	55	50	35	42
1989— Las Vegas (PCL)■	7	4	.636	5.13	47	0	0	0	1	79	93	48	45	27	71
1990— Durham (Caro.)■	0	0	...	3.24	5	0	0	0	0	8 1/3	8	3	3	1	10
— Richmond (I.L.)	0	0	...	0.00	2	0	0	0	0	2 1/3	4	0	0	0	0
1991— Greenville (Sou.)	6	2	.750	1.51	•59	0	0	0	22	77 1/3	49	16	13	15	65
1992— Richmond (I.L.)	2	3	.400	2.28	47	0	0	0	12	79	72	27	20	27	82
1993— Richmond (I.L.)	2	4	.333	1.98	59	0	0	0	*26	68 1/3	56	19	15	26	81
1994— Oakland (A.L.)■	1	3	.250	3.50	41	0	0	0	1	46 1/3	38	24	18	18	48
1995— Oakland (A.L.)									Did not play.						
1996— Edmonton (PCL)	0	0	...	0.79	7	0	0	0	4	11 1/3	10	1	1	3	13
— Oakland (A.L.)	6	3	.667	4.33	55	0	0	0	17	60 1/3	52	30	29	25	67
1997— Oakland (A.L.)	3	4	.429	3.82	72	0	0	0	23	73	70	32	31	36	66
1998— Oakland (A.L.)	4	9	.308	3.58	70	0	0	0	33	73	71	37	29	22	58
1999— Oakland (A.L.)	1	5	.167	3.98	43	0	0	0	26	43	48	23	19	14	38
— New York (N.L.)■	0	1	.000	8.10	18	0	0	0	0	13 1/3	20	12	12	9	14
A.L. totals (5 years)	15	24	.385	3.84	281	0	0	0	100	295 2/3	279	146	126	115	277
N.L. totals (1 year)	0	1	.000	8.10	18	0	0	0	0	13 1/3	20	12	12	9	14
Major League totals (5 years)	15	25	.375	4.02	299	0	0	0	100	309	299	158	138	124	291

DIVISION SERIES RECORD

Year League	W	L	Pct.	ERA	G	GS	CG	ShO	Sv.	IP	H	R	ER	BB	SO
1999— New York (N.L.)								Did not play.							

CHAMPIONSHIP SERIES RECORD

Year League	W	L	Pct.	ERA	G	GS	CG	ShO	Sv.	IP	H	R	ER	BB	SO
1999— New York (N.L.)								Did not play.							

PERSONAL: Born January 12, 1977, in Newberry, S.C. ... 6-1/178. ... Bats left, throws right. ... Full name: Reginald Tremain Taylor.
HIGH SCHOOL: Newberry (S.C.).
TRANSACTIONS/CAREER NOTES: Selected by Philadelphia Phillies organization in first round (14th pick overall) of free-agent draft (June 1, 1995). ... On disabled list (July 23, 1998-remainder of season).
STATISTICAL NOTES: Led South Atlantic League outfielders with 308 total chances in 1996. ... Led Florida State League outfielders with 354 total chances in 1997. ... Led Eastern League in caught stealing with 22 in 1999.

Year — Team (League)	Pos.	G	AB	R	H	2B	3B	HR	RBI	Avg.	BB	SO	SB	PO	A	E	Avg.
1995— Martinsville (Appl.)	OF	64	239	36	53	4	6	2	32	.222	23	58	18	116	9	8	.940
1996— Piedmont (S.A.L.)	OF	128	499	68	131	20	6	0	31	.263	29	136	36	287	9	*12	.961
1997— Clearwater (FSL)	OF	134	545	73	133	18	6	12	47	.244	30	130	40	324	*19	11	.969
1998— Reading (East.)	OF	79	337	49	92	14	6	5	22	.273	12	73	22	164	6	10	.944
1999— Reading (East.)	OF	127	526	75	140	17	10	15	61	.266	18	79	38	295	9	9	.971

PERSONAL: Born May 25, 1976, in Bani, Dominican Republic. ... 5-9/188. ... Bats right, throws right. ... Full name: Miguel Odalis Martinez Tejada.
TRANSACTIONS/CAREER NOTES: Signed as non-drafted free agent by Oakland Athletics organization (July 17, 1993). ... On suspended list (July 4-7, 1996). ... On disabled list (July 20-August 10, 1996). ... On Oakland disabled list (March 22-May 20, 1998); included rehabilitation assignments to Edmonton (May 11-12) and Huntsville (May 12-20).
STATISTICAL NOTES: Led California League shortstops with 44 errors in 1996. ... Led Southern League shortstops with 688 total chances and 97 double plays in 1997. ... Hit three home runs in one game (June 11, 1999).

Year	Team (League)	Pos.	G	AB	R	H	2B	3B	HR	RBI	Avg.	BB	SO	SB	PO	A	E	Avg.
									BATTING						FIELDING			
1993—	....						Dominican League statistics unavailable.											
1994—	Dom. Athletics (DSL) .	2B	74	218	51	64	9	1	18	62	.294	37	36	13	76	126	16	.927
1995—	S. Oregon (N'west).....	SS	74	269	45	66	15	5	8	44	.245	41	54	19	*129	*214	26	.930
1996—	Modesto (Calif.)	SS-DH-3B	114	458	97	128	12	5	20	72	.279	51	93	27	194	358	†45	.925
1997—	Huntsville (Sou.)	SS	128	502	85	138	20	3	22	97	.275	50	99	15	*229	*423	*36	.948
	—Oakland (A.L.)...........	SS	26	99	10	20	3	2	2	10	.202	2	22	2	54	69	4	.969
1998—	Edmonton (PCL)	SS	1	3	0	0	0	0	0	0	.000	1	1	0	0	5	0	1.000
	—Huntsville (Sou.)........	SS-DH	15	52	9	17	6	0	2	7	.327	4	8	1	18	41	5	.922
	—Oakland (A.L.)...........	SS	105	365	53	85	20	1	11	45	.233	28	86	5	173	327	26	.951
1999—	Oakland (A.L.)...........	SS	159	593	93	149	33	4	21	84	.251	57	94	8	*292	471	21	.973
	Major League totals (3 years)		290	1057	156	254	56	7	34	139	.240	87	202	15	519	867	51	.965

TEJERA, MICHAEL   P   MARLINS

PERSONAL: Born October 18, 1976, in Havana, Cuba. ... 5-9/175. ... Throws left, bats left.
HIGH SCHOOL: Southwest (Miami).
TRANSACTIONS/CAREER NOTES: Selected by Florida Marlins organization in sixth round of free-agent draft (June 1, 1995).
HONORS: Named Eastern League Pitcher of the Year (1999).

Year	League	W	L	Pct.	ERA	G	GS	CG	ShO	Sv.	IP	H	R	ER	BB	SO
1995—	Gulf Coast Marlins (GCL) ...	3	1	.750	2.65	11	3	0	0	2	34	28	13	10	16	28
1996—	Gulf Coast Marlins (GCL) ...	1	0	1.000	3.60	2	0	0	0	0	5	6	2	2	0	2
1997—	Utica (NY-P)	3	3	.500	3.76	12	12	0	0	0	69 1/3	65	36	29	11	67
1998—	Kane County (Midw.).........	6	1	.857	2.77	10	10	0	0	0	55 1/3	44	20	17	13	47
	—Portland (East.)	9	5	.643	4.11	18	18	2	2	0	107 1/3	113	55	49	36	97
1999—	Portland (East.)	13	4	.765	2.62	25	25	0	0	0	154 2/3	137	55	45	45	152
	—Calgary (PCL).....................	0	2	.000	12.00	2	2	0	0	0	9	19	14	12	4	5
	—Florida (N.L.).....................	0	0	...	11.37	3	1	0	0	0	6 1/3	10	8	8	5	7
	Major League totals (1 year)........	0	0	...	11.37	3	1	0	0	0	6 1/3	10	8	8	5	7

TELEMACO, AMAURY   P   PHILLIES

PERSONAL: Born January 19, 1974, in Higuey, Dominican Republic. ... 6-3/222. ... Throws right, bats right. ... Full name: Amaury Regalado Telemaco. ... Name pronounced AH-mer-ee tel-ah-MAH-ko.
HIGH SCHOOL: Cristo Rey (La Romana, Dominican Republic).
TRANSACTIONS/CAREER NOTES: Signed as non-drafted free agent by Chicago Cubs organization (May 23, 1991). ... On temporarily inactive list (July 17, 1993-remainder of season). ... On Orlando disabled list (August 23-September 8, 1994). ... On Chicago disabled list (August 20-September 4, 1996); included rehabilitation assignment to Iowa (September 2-4). ... Claimed on waivers by Arizona Diamondbacks (May 15, 1998). ... On Arizona disabled list (March 26-May 8, 1999); included rehabilitation assignment to Tucson (April 8-May 7). ... Claimed on waivers by Philadelphia Phillies (June 8, 1999).

Year	League	W	L	Pct.	ERA	G	GS	CG	ShO	Sv.	IP	H	R	ER	BB	SO
1991—	Puerta Plata (DSL)	3	3	.500	3.55	15	13	0	0	0	66	81	43	26	32	43
1992—	Huntington (Appl.)	3	5	.375	4.01	12	12	2	0	0	76 1/3	71	45	34	17	*93
	—Peoria (Midw.)...................	0	1	.000	7.94	2	1	0	0	0	5 2/3	9	5	5	5	5
1993—	Peoria (Midw.)...................	8	11	.421	3.45	23	23	3	0	0	143 2/3	129	69	55	54	133
1994—	Daytona (FSL)	7	3	.700	3.40	11	11	2	0	0	76 2/3	62	35	29	23	59
	—Orlando (Sou.)	3	5	.375	3.45	12	12	2	0	0	62 2/3	56	29	24	20	49
1995—	Orlando (Sou.)...................	8	8	.500	3.29	22	22	3	1	0	147 2/3	112	60	54	42	151
1996—	Iowa (A.A.).......................	3	1	.750	3.06	8	8	1	0	0	50	38	19	17	18	42
	—Chicago (N.L.).................	5	7	.417	5.46	25	17	0	0	0	97 1/3	108	67	59	31	64
1997—	Iowa (A.A.).......................	5	9	.357	4.51	18	18	3	•2	0	113 2/3	121	70	57	38	75
	—Chicago (N.L.).................	0	3	.000	6.16	10	5	0	0	0	38	47	26	26	11	29
	—Orlando (Sou.).................	1	0	1.000	2.25	1	1	0	0	0	8	9	2	2	2	6
1998—	Chicago (N.L.).................	1	1	.500	3.90	14	0	0	0	0	27 2/3	23	12	12	13	18
	—Arizona (N.L.)■■...............	6	9	.400	3.94	27	18	0	0	0	121	127	63	53	33	60
1999—	Tucson (PCL)...................	0	3	.000	5.09	13	12	0	0	0	17 2/3	21	11	10	6	17
	—Arizona (N.L.)■...............	1	0	1.000	7.50	5	0	0	0	0	6	7	5	5	6	2
	—Philadelphia (N.L.)■	3	0	1.000	5.55	44	0	0	0	0	47	45	29	29	20	41
	Major League totals (4 years).......	16	20	.444	4.91	125	40	0	0	0	337	357	202	184	114	214

TELFORD, ANTHONY   P   EXPOS

PERSONAL: Born March 6, 1966, in San Jose, Calif. ... 6-0/195. ... Throws right, bats right. ... Full name: Anthony Charles Telford.
HIGH SCHOOL: Silver Creek (Calif.).
COLLEGE: San Jose State.
TRANSACTIONS/CAREER NOTES: Selected by Baltimore Orioles organization in third round of free-agent draft (June 2, 1987). ... On disabled list (April 20, 1988-remainder of season). ... On Frederick disabled list (April 7-18, 1989). ... On Erie disabled list (June 16-30, 1989). ... Granted free agency (October 15, 1993). ... Signed by Atlanta Braves organization (November 23, 1993). ... Granted free agency (October 15, 1994). ... Signed by Edmonton, Oakland Athletics organization (January 20, 1995). ... Released by Edmonton (May 16, 1995). ... Signed by Cleveland Indians organization (June 15, 1995). ... Granted free agency (October 15, 1995). ... Signed by Montreal Expos organization (February 22, 1996). ... Granted free agency (October 15, 1996). ... Re-signed by Montreal Expos organization (December 18, 1996).

Year	League	W	L	Pct.	ERA	G	GS	CG	ShO	Sv.	IP	H	R	ER	BB	SO
1987—	Newark (NY-P)	1	0	1.000	1.02	6	2	0	0	0	17 2/3	16	2	2	3	27
	—Hagerstown (Caro.)...........	1	0	1.000	1.59	2	2	0	0	0	11 1/3	9	2	2	5	10
	—Rochester (I.L.)	0	0	...	0.00	1	0	0	0	0	2	0	0	0	3	3
1988—	Hagerstown (Caro.)...........	1	0	1.000	0.00	1	1	0	0	0	7	3	0	0	0	10
1989—	Frederick (Caro.)	2	1	.667	4.21	9	5	0	0	1	25 2/3	25	15	12	12	19

Year	League	W	L	Pct.	ERA	G	GS	CG	ShO	Sv.	IP	H	R	ER	BB	SO
1990—	Frederick (Caro.)	4	2	.667	1.68	8	8	1	0	0	53²/₃	35	15	10	11	49
—	Hagerstown (East.)	10	2	.833	1.97	14	13	3	1	0	96	80	26	21	25	73
—	Baltimore (A.L.)	3	3	.500	4.95	8	8	0	0	0	36¹/₃	43	22	20	19	20
1991—	Rochester (I.L.)	•12	9	.571	3.95	27	25	3	0	0	157¹/₃	166	82	69	48	115
—	Baltimore (A.L.)	0	0	...	4.05	9	1	0	0	0	26²/₃	27	12	12	6	24
1992—	Rochester (I.L.)	12	7	.632	4.18	27	26	3	0	0	*181	*183	89	84	64	129
1993—	Rochester (I.L.)	7	7	.500	4.27	38	6	0	0	2	90²/₃	98	51	43	33	66
—	Baltimore (A.L.)	0	0	...	9.82	3	0	0	0	0	7¹/₃	11	8	8	1	6
1994—	Richmond (I.L.)■	10	6	.625	4.23	38	20	3	1	0	142²/₃	148	82	67	41	111
1995—	Edmonton (PCL)■	3	2	.600	7.18	8	6	0	0	0	36¹/₃	47	32	29	16	17
—	Canton/Akron (East.)■.......	2	0	1.000	0.82	2	2	0	0	0	11	6	2	1	4	4
—	Buffalo (A.A.)	4	1	.800	3.46	16	2	0	0	0	39	35	15	15	10	24
1996—	Ottawa (I.L.)■	7	2	.778	4.11	30	15	1	1	0	118¹/₃	128	62	54	34	69
1997—	Montreal (N.L.)	4	6	.400	3.24	65	0	0	0	1	89	77	34	32	33	61
1998—	Montreal (N.L.)	3	6	.333	3.86	77	0	0	0	1	91	85	45	39	36	59
1999—	Montreal (N.L.)	5	4	.556	3.94	79	0	0	0	2	96	112	52	42	38	69
A.L. totals (3 years)		3	3	.500	5.12	20	9	0	0	0	70¹/₃	81	42	40	26	50
N.L. totals (3 years)		12	16	.429	3.68	221	0	0	0	4	276	274	131	113	107	189
Major League totals (6 years).......		15	19	.441	3.98	241	9	0	0	4	346¹/₃	355	173	153	133	239

TESSMER, JAY — P — YANKEES

PERSONAL: Born December 26, 1971, in Meadville, Pa. ... 6-3/190. ... Throws right, bats right. ... Full name: Jay Weldon Tessmer.
HIGH SCHOOL: Cochranton (Pa.).
COLLEGE: Miami (Fla.).
TRANSACTIONS/CAREER NOTES: Selected by New York Yankees organization in 19th round of free-agent draft (June 1, 1995).
HONORS: Name Florida State League Most Valuable Player (1996).

Year	League	W	L	Pct.	ERA	G	GS	CG	ShO	Sv.	IP	H	R	ER	BB	SO
1995—	Oneonta (NY-P)	2	0	1.000	0.95	34	0	0	0	20	38	27	8	4	12	52
1996—	Tampa (FSL)	12	4	.750	1.48	*68	0	0	0	*35	97¹/₃	68	18	16	19	104
1997—	Norwich (East.)	3	6	.333	5.31	55	0	0	0	17	62²/₃	78	41	37	24	51
1998—	Norwich (East.)	3	4	.429	1.09	45	0	0	0	29	49²/₃	50	8	6	13	57
—	Columbus (I.L.)	1	1	.500	0.49	12	0	0	0	5	18¹/₃	8	2	1	1	14
—	New York (A.L.)	1	0	1.000	3.12	7	0	0	0	0	8²/₃	4	3	3	4	6
1999—	Columbus (I.L.)	3	3	.500	3.34	51	0	0	0	*28	56²/₃	52	22	21	12	42
—	New York (A.L.)	0	0	...	14.85	6	0	0	0	0	6²/₃	16	11	11	4	3
Major League totals (2 years).......		1	0	1.000	8.22	13	0	0	0	0	15¹/₃	20	14	14	8	9

THOMAS, FRANK — DH/1B — WHITE SOX

PERSONAL: Born May 27, 1968, in Columbus, Ga. ... 6-5/270. ... Bats right, throws right. ... Full name: Frank Edward Thomas.
HIGH SCHOOL: Columbus (Ga.).
COLLEGE: Auburn.
TRANSACTIONS/CAREER NOTES: Selected by Chicago White Sox organization in first round (seventh pick overall) of free-agent draft (June 5, 1989). ... On disabled list (July 11-30, 1996; and June 7-22, 1997).
RECORDS: Shares A.L. single-season record for most intentional bases on balls received by righthanded batter—29 (1995).
HONORS: Named first baseman on THE SPORTING NEWS college All-America team (1989). ... Named designated hitter on THE SPORTING NEWS A.L. All-Star team (1991). ... Named designated hitter on THE SPORTING NEWS A.L. Silver Slugger team (1991). ... Named Major League Player of the Year by THE SPORTING NEWS (1993). ... Named first baseman on THE SPORTING NEWS A.L. All-Star team (1993-94). ... Named first baseman on THE SPORTING NEWS A.L. Silver Slugger team (1993-94). ... Named A.L. Most Valuable Player by Baseball Writers' Association of America (1993-94).
STATISTICAL NOTES: Led Southern League with .581 slugging percentage and .487 on-base percentage in 1990. ... Led A.L. with .453 on-base percentage in 1991, .439 in 1992, .487 in 1994 and .456 in 1997. ... Led A.L. first basemen with 1,533 total chances in 1992. ... Led A.L. with .729 slugging percentage in 1994. ... Led A.L. with 12 sacrifice flies in 1995. ... Led A.L. with 29 intentional bases on balls received in 1995 and 26 in 1996. ... Hit three home runs in one game (September 15, 1996). ... Had 21-game hitting streak (May 24-June 15, 1999). ... Career major league grand slams: 5.
MISCELLANEOUS: Holds Chicago White Sox all-time record for most home runs (301).

							BATTING							FIELDING		
Year	Team (League)	Pos.	G	AB	R	H	2B	3B	HR	RBI	Avg.	BB	SO	SB	PO	A	E	Avg.
1989—	GC White Sox (GCL) ..	1B	17	52	8	19	5	0	1	11	.365	10	24	4	130	8	2	.986
—| Sarasota (FSL)	1B	55	188	27	52	9	1	4	30	.277	31	33	0	420	31	7	.985
1990—	Birmingham (Sou.).....	1B	109	353	85	114	27	5	18	71	.323	*112	74	7	954	77	14	.987
—| Chicago (A.L.)	1B-DH	60	191	39	63	11	3	7	31	.330	44	54	0	428	26	5	.989
1991—	Chicago (A.L.)	DH-1B	158	559	104	178	31	2	32	109	.318	*138	112	1	459	27	2	.996
1992—	Chicago (A.L.)	1B-DH	160	573	108	185	•46	2	24	115	.323	•122	88	6	*1428	92	13	.992
1993—	Chicago (A.L.)	1B-DH	153	549	106	174	36	0	41	128	.317	112	54	4	1222	83	15	.989
1994—	Chicago (A.L.)	1B-DH	113	399	*106	141	34	1	38	101	.353	*109	61	2	735	45	7	.991
1995—	Chicago (A.L.)	1B-DH	•145	493	102	152	27	0	40	111	.308	*136	74	3	738	34	7	.991
1996—	Chicago (A.L.)	1B	141	527	110	184	26	0	40	134	.349	109	70	1	1098	85	9	.992
1997—	Chicago (A.L.)	1B-DH	146	530	110	184	35	0	35	125	*.347	109	69	1	739	49	11	.986
1998—	Chicago (A.L.)	DH-1B	160	585	109	155	35	2	29	109	.265	110	93	7	116	6	2	.984
1999—	Chicago (A.L.)	DH-1B	135	486	74	148	36	0	15	77	.305	87	66	3	385	18	4	.990
Major League totals (10 years)			1371	4892	968	1564	317	10	301	1040	.320	1076	741	28	7348	465	75	.990

CHAMPIONSHIP SERIES RECORD

RECORDS: Holds single-series record for most bases on balls received—10 (1993). ... Shares single-game record for most bases on balls received—4 (October 5, 1993).

Year	Team (League)	Pos.	G	AB	R	H	2B	3B	HR	RBI	Avg.	BB	SO	SB	PO	A	E	Avg.
1993—Chicago (A.L.)	1B-DH	6	17	2	6	0	0	1	3	.353	10	5	0	24	3	0	1.000

ALL-STAR GAME RECORD

Year	League	Pos.	AB	R	H	2B	3B	HR	RBI	Avg.	BB	SO	SB	PO	A	E	Avg.
1993—American	PH-DH	1	0	1	0	0	0	0	1.000	0	0	0	...	...	...	...
1994—American	1B	2	1	2	0	0	0	1	1.000	1	0	0	6	0	0	1.000
1995—American	1B	2	1	1	0	0	1	2	.500	0	0	0	5	1	0	1.000
1996—American						Selected, did not play—injured.										
1997—American						Selected, did not play—injured.										
All-Star Game totals (3 years)		5	2	4	0	0	1	3	.800	1	0	0	11	1	0	1.000

THOME, JIM　　　　1B　　　　INDIANS

PERSONAL: Born August 27, 1970, in Peoria, Ill. ... 6-4/220. ... Bats left, throws right. ... Full name: James Howard Thome. ... Name pronounced TOE-me.

HIGH SCHOOL: Limestone (Bartonville, Ill.).

JUNIOR COLLEGE: Illinois Central College.

TRANSACTIONS/CAREER NOTES: Selected by Cleveland Indians organization in 13th round of free-agent draft (June 5, 1989). ... On Cleveland disabled list (March 28-May 18, 1992); included rehabilitation assignment to Canton/Akron (May 9-18). ... On Cleveland disabled list (May 20-June 15, 1992); included rehabilitation assignment to Canton/Akron (June 1-15). ... On disabled list (August 8-September 16, 1998).

RECORDS: Shares major league single-season record for most strikeouts by lefthander—171 (1999).

HONORS: Named International League Most Valuable Player (1993). ... Named third baseman on THE SPORTING NEWS A.L. All-Star team (1995 and 1996). ... Named third baseman on THE SPORTING NEWS A.L. Silver Slugger team (1996).

STATISTICAL NOTES: Led International League with .441 on-base percentage in 1993. ... Hit three home runs in one game (July 22, 1994). ... Had 16-game hitting streak (May 25-June 10, 1998). ... Career major league grand slams: 5.

Year	Team (League)	Pos.	G	AB	R	H	2B	3B	HR	RBI	Avg.	BB	SO	SB	PO	A	E	Avg.
1989—GC Indians (GCL)	SS-3B	55	186	22	44	5	3	0	22	.237	21	33	6	65	144	21	.909
1990—Burlington (Appl.).......	3B	34	118	31	44	7	1	12	34	.373	27	18	6	28	79	11	.907
—Kinston (Caro.).......	3B	33	117	19	36	4	1	4	16	.308	24	26	4	10	66	8	.905
1991—Canton/Akron (East.)..	3B	84	294	47	99	20	2	5	45	.337	44	58	8	41	167	17	.924
—Colo. Springs (PCL) ...	3B	41	151	20	43	7	3	2	28	.285	12	29	0	28	84	6	.949
—Cleveland (A.L.).........	3B	27	98	7	25	4	2	1	9	.255	5	16	1	12	60	8	.900
1992—Colo. Springs (PCL) ...	3B	12	48	11	15	4	1	2	14	.313	6	16	0	9	20	8	.784
—Cleveland (A.L.).........	3B	40	117	8	24	3	1	2	12	.205	10	34	2	21	61	11	.882
—Canton/Akron (East.)..	3B	30	107	16	36	9	2	1	14	.336	24	30	0	11	35	4	.920
1993—Charlotte (I.L.)...........	3B-DH	115	410	85	136	21	4	25	*102	*.332	76	94	1	67	226	15	.951
—Cleveland (A.L.).........	3B	47	154	28	41	11	0	7	22	.266	29	36	2	29	86	6	.950
1994—Cleveland (A.L.).........	3B	98	321	58	86	20	1	20	52	.268	46	84	3	62	173	15	.940
1995—Cleveland (A.L.).........	3B-DH	137	452	92	142	29	3	25	73	.314	97	113	4	75	214	16	.948
1996—Cleveland (A.L.).........	3B-DH	151	505	122	157	28	5	38	116	.311	123	141	2	86	262	17	.953
1997—Cleveland (A.L.).........	1B	147	496	104	142	25	0	40	102	.286	*120	146	1	1233	95	10	.993
1998—Cleveland (A.L.).........	1B-DH	123	440	89	129	34	2	30	85	.293	89	141	1	998	85	10	.991
1999—Cleveland (A.L.).........	1B-DH	146	494	101	137	27	2	33	108	.277	*127	*171	0	930	83	6	.994
Major League totals (9 years)		916	3077	609	883	181	16	196	579	.287	646	882	16	3446	1119	99	.979

DIVISION SERIES RECORD

RECORDS: Holds career records for most home runs—7; and most strikeouts—26. ... Shares single-game records for most home runs—2 (October 11, 1999); and most grand slams—1 (October 7, 1999). ... Shares single-inning record for most runs batted in—4 (October 7, 1999, fourth inning).

Year	Team (League)	Pos.	G	AB	R	H	2B	3B	HR	RBI	Avg.	BB	SO	SB	PO	A	E	Avg.
1995—Cleveland (A.L.)..........	3B	3	13	1	2	0	0	1	3	.154	1	6	0	6	6	0	1.000
1996—Cleveland (A.L.)..........	3B	4	10	1	3	0	0	0	0	.300	1	5	0	1	1	0	1.000
1997—Cleveland (A.L.)..........	1B	4	15	1	3	0	0	0	1	.200	0	5	0	44	3	0	1.000
1998—Cleveland (A.L.)..........	1B-DH	4	15	2	2	0	0	2	2	.133	3	5	0	26	1	0	1.000
1999—Cleveland (A.L.)..........	1B	5	17	7	6	0	0	4	10	.353	4	5	0	29	7	0	1.000
Division series totals (4 years)		20	70	12	16	0	0	7	16	.229	9	26	0	106	18	0	1.000

CHAMPIONSHIP SERIES RECORD

RECORDS: Shares single-game record for most grand slams—1 (October 13, 1998). ... Shares single-inning record for most runs batted in—4 (October 13, 1998, fifth inning). ... Shares A.L. single series record for most home runs—4 (1998).

Year	Team (League)	Pos.	G	AB	R	H	2B	3B	HR	RBI	Avg.	BB	SO	SB	PO	A	E	Avg.
1995—Cleveland (A.L.)..........	3B	5	15	2	4	0	0	2	5	.267	2	3	0	1	5	1	.857
1997—Cleveland (A.L.)..........	1B-PH	6	14	3	1	0	0	0	0	.071	5	4	0	35	2	0	1.000
1998—Cleveland (A.L.)..........	DH-1B	6	23	4	7	0	0	4	8	.304	1	8	0	45	4	0	1.000
Championship series totals (3 years)		17	52	9	12	0	0	6	13	.231	8	15	0	81	11	1	.989

WORLD SERIES RECORD

Year	Team (League)	Pos.	G	AB	R	H	2B	3B	HR	RBI	Avg.	BB	SO	SB	PO	A	E	Avg.
1995—Cleveland (A.L.)..........	3B-PH	6	19	1	4	1	0	1	2	.211	2	5	0	3	5	1	.889
1997—Cleveland (A.L.)..........	1B	7	28	8	8	0	1	2	4	.286	5	7	0	57	5	1	.984
World Series totals (2 years)		13	47	9	12	1	1	3	6	.255	7	12	0	60	10	2	.972

Year	League	Pos.		BATTING											FIELDING			
			AB	R	H	2B	3B	HR	RBI	Avg.	BB	SO	SB	PO	A	E	Avg.
1997—American		PH-DH	1	0	0	0	0	0	0	.000	0	0	0	...	...	...	...
1998—American		1B	2	1	0	0	0	0	0	.000	2	1	0	4	0	0	1.000
1999—American		1B	2	1	1	0	0	0	1	.500	1	0	0	4	0	0	1.000
All-Star Game totals (3 years)			5	2	1	0	0	0	1	.200	3	1	0	8	0	0	1.000

THOMPSON, ANDY — OF — BLUE JAYS

PERSONAL: Born October 8, 1975, in Oconomowoc, Wis. ... 6-3/215. ... Bats right, throws right. ... Full name: Andrew John Thompson.
HIGH SCHOOL: Sun Prairie (Wis.).
TRANSACTIONS/CAREER NOTES: Selected by Toronto Blue Jays organization in 23rd round of free-agent draft (June 2, 1994).

Year	Team (League)	Pos.	G	AB	R	H	2B	3B	HR	RBI	Avg.	BB	SO	SB	PO	A	E	Avg.
1995—Hagerstown (SAL)		3B	124	461	48	110	19	2	6	57	.239	29	108	2	86	200	*43	.869
1996—Dunedin (FSL)		3B	129	425	64	120	26	5	11	50	.282	60	108	16	75	259	*47	.877
1997—Knoxville (Sou.)		3B	124	448	75	128	25	3	15	71	.286	63	76	0	72	202	31	.898
1998—Knoxville (Sou.)		OF-3B	125	481	74	137	33	2	14	88	.285	54	69	8	138	75	26	.891
1999—Knoxville (Sou.)		OF	67	254	56	62	16	3	15	53	.244	34	55	7	108	3	4	.965
—Syracuse (I.L.)		OF	62	229	42	67	17	2	16	42	.293	21	45	5	89	4	0	1.000

THOMPSON, JUSTIN — P — RANGERS

PERSONAL: Born March 8, 1973, in San Antonio. ... 6-4/215. ... Throws left, bats left. ... Full name: Justin Willard Thompson.
HIGH SCHOOL: Klein Oak (Spring, Texas).
TRANSACTIONS/CAREER NOTES: Selected by Detroit Tigers organization in supplemental round ("sandwich pick" between first and second round, 32nd pick overall) of free-agent draft (June 3, 1991); pick received as part of compensation for Minnesota Twins signing Type A free-agent P Jack Morris. ... On Trenton disabled list (April 8, 1994-entire season). ... On Detroit disabled list (June 3-August 17, 1996); included rehabilitation assignments to Fayetteville (July 19-23), Visalia (July 23-26) and Toledo (July 26-August 11). ... On disabled list (July 6-21, 1997). ... On disabled list (August 16, 1999-remainder of season). ... Traded by Tigers with P Francisco Cordero, OF Gabe Kapler, C Bill Haselman, 2B Frank Catalanotto and P Alan Webb to Texas Rangers for OF Juan Gonzalez, P Danny Patterson and C Gregg Zaun (November 2, 1999).

Year	League	W	L	Pct.	ERA	G	GS	CG	ShO	Sv.	IP	H	R	ER	BB	SO
1991—Bristol (Appl.)		2	5	.286	3.60	10	10	0	0	0	50	45	29	20	24	60
1992—Fayetteville (SAL)		4	4	.500	2.18	20	19	0	0	0	95	79	32	23	40	88
1993—Lakeland (FSL)		4	4	.500	3.56	11	11	0	0	0	55²/₃	65	25	22	16	46
—London (East.)		3	6	.333	4.09	14	14	1	0	0	83²/₃	96	51	38	37	72
1994—Trenton (East.)								Did not play.								
1995—Lakeland (FSL)		2	1	.667	4.88	6	6	0	0	0	24	30	13	13	8	20
—Jacksonville (Sou.)		6	7	.462	3.73	18	18	3	0	0	123	110	55	51	38	98
1996—Toledo (I.L.)		6	3	.667	3.42	13	13	3	1	0	84¹/₃	74	36	32	26	69
—Detroit (A.L.)		1	6	.143	4.58	11	11	0	0	0	59	62	35	30	31	44
—Fayetteville (SAL)		0	0	...	3.00	1	1	0	0	0	3	1	1	1	0	5
—Visalia (Calif.)		0	0	...	0.00	1	1	0	0	0	3	2	0	0	2	7
1997—Detroit (A.L.)		15	11	.577	3.02	32	32	4	0	0	223¹/₃	188	82	75	66	151
1998—Detroit (A.L.)		11	15	.423	4.05	34	34	5	0	0	222	227	114	100	79	149
1999—Detroit (A.L.)		9	11	.450	5.11	24	24	0	0	0	142²/₃	152	85	81	59	83
Major League totals (4 years)		36	43	.456	3.98	101	101	9	0	0	647	629	316	286	235	427

Year	League	W	L	Pct.	ERA	GS	CG	ShO	Sv.	IP	H	R	ER	BB	SO
1997—American		0	0	...	0.00	0	0	0	0	1	0	0	0	0	1

THOMPSON, MARK — P — CARDINALS

PERSONAL: Born April 7, 1971, in Russellville, Ky. ... 6-2/212. ... Throws right, bats right. ... Full name: Mark Radford Thompson.
HIGH SCHOOL: Logan County (Russellville, Ky.).
COLLEGE: Kentucky.
TRANSACTIONS/CAREER NOTES: Selected by Colorado Rockies organization in second round of free-agent draft (June 1, 1992). ... On Colorado Springs disabled list (June 30-September 7, 1993; August 9-18 and August 27-September 5, 1994). ... On Colorado disabled list (May 8, 1997-remainder of season); included rehabilitation assignments to Asheville (June 29-July 15) and Colorado Springs (July 15-July 20). ... On Colorado disabled list (May 7, 1998-remainder of season); included rehabilitation assignments to Arizona League Rockies (August 14), Salem (August 19-29) and Colorado Springs (September 3). ... Granted free agency (October 20, 1998). ... Signed by Cincinnati Reds organization (December 15, 1998). ... On Indianapolis disabled list (May 7-June 15, 1999). ... Released by Reds (July 17, 1999). ... Signed by St. Louis Cardinals organization (July 18, 1999).
RECORDS: Shares N.L. single-inning record for most consecutive home runs allowed—3 (June 30, 1996, third inning).

Year	League	W	L	Pct.	ERA	G	GS	CG	ShO	Sv.	IP	H	R	ER	BB	SO
1992—Bend (N'west)		8	4	.667	1.95	16	•16	*4	0	0	*106¹/₃	81	32	23	31	*102
1993—Central Valley (Calif.)		3	2	.600	2.20	11	11	0	0	0	69²/₃	46	19	17	18	72
—Colo. Springs (PCL)		3	0	1.000	2.70	4	4	2	0	0	33¹/₃	31	13	10	11	22
1994—Colo. Springs (PCL)		8	9	.471	4.49	23	23	•4	1	0	140¹/₃	169	83	70	57	82
—Colorado (N.L.)		1	1	.500	9.00	2	2	0	0	0	9	16	9	9	8	5
1995—Colorado (N.L.)		2	3	.400	6.53	21	5	0	0	0	51	73	42	37	22	30
—Colo. Springs (PCL)		5	3	.625	6.10	11	10	0	0	0	62	73	43	42	25	38
1996—Colorado (N.L.)		9	11	.450	5.30	34	28	3	1	0	169²/₃	189	109	100	74	99
1997—Colorado (N.L.)		3	3	.500	7.89	6	6	0	0	0	29²/₃	40	27	26	13	9
—Asheville (SAL)		0	2	.000	2.70	4	4	0	0	0	13¹/₃	11	5	4	5	9
—Colo. Springs (PCL)		0	0	...	12.00	1	1	0	0	0	3	6	4	4	1	1

Year League	W	L	Pct.	ERA	G	GS	CG	ShO	Sv.	IP	H	R	ER	BB	SO
1998— Colorado (N.L.)	1	2	.333	7.71	6	6	0	0	0	23 1/3	36	22	20	12	14
— Arizona Rockies (Ariz.)........	0	0	...	0.00	1	1	0	0	0	3	1	0	0	0	2
— Salem (Caro.)	0	0	...	3.95	3	3	0	0	0	13 2/3	17	7	6	3	10
— Colo. Springs (PCL)	0	1	.000	18.90	1	1	0	0	0	3 1/3	10	7	7	1	1
1999— Indianapolis (I.L.)■..........	2	6	.250	5.13	11	10	0	0	0	54 1/3	50	31	31	29	28
— Memphis (PCL)■..............	4	2	.667	2.94	9	8	0	0	0	52	50	22	17	20	27
— St. Louis (N.L.)	1	3	.250	2.76	5	5	0	0	0	29 1/3	26	12	9	17	22
Major League totals (6 years)	17	23	.425	5.80	74	52	3	1	0	312	380	221	201	146	179

DIVISION SERIES RECORD

Year League	W	L	Pct.	ERA	G	GS	CG	ShO	Sv.	IP	H	R	ER	BB	SO
1995— Colorado (N.L.)	0	0	...	0.00	1	0	0	0	1	1	0	0	0	0	0

THOMPSON, RYAN — OF

PERSONAL: Born November 4, 1967, in Chestertown, Md. ... 6-3/215. ... Bats right, throws right. ... Full name: Ryan Orlando Thompson.
HIGH SCHOOL: Kent County (Rock Hall, Md.).
TRANSACTIONS/CAREER NOTES: Selected by Toronto Blue Jays organization in 13th round of free-agent draft (June 2, 1987). ... On disabled list (May 29-June 7, 1991). ... On Syracuse disabled list (May 4-11 and July 20-27, 1992). ... Traded by Blue Jays to New York Mets (September 1, 1992); completing deal in which Mets traded P David Cone to Blue Jays for IF Jeff Kent and a player to be named later (August 27, 1992). ... On New York disabled list (April 18-May 30 and July 18-August 18, 1995); included rehabilitation assignments to Norfolk (May 13-30) and Binghamton (August 16-18). ... Traded by Mets with P Reid Cornelius to Cleveland Indians for P Mark Clark (March 30, 1996). ... Granted free agency (December 20, 1996). ... Signed by Kansas City Royals organization (January 16, 1997). ... Released by Royals (March 26, 1997). ... Signed by Indians organization (April 21, 1997). ... Traded by Indians to Blue Jays for IF Jeff Manto (June 6, 1997). ... Granted free agency (October 15, 1997). ... Signed to play for Fukuoka Dalei Hawks of Japan Pacific League (1998). ... Signed by Houston Astros organization (January 21, 1999). ... On New Orleans disabled list (August 5-13, 1999). ... Granted free agency (October 20, 1999).
STATISTICAL NOTES: Led American Association outfielders with 334 total chances in 1996. ... Career major league grand slams: 1.

Year Team (League)	Pos.	G	AB	R	H	2B	3B	HR	RBI	Avg.	BB	SO	SB	PO	A	E	Avg.
1987— Medicine Hat (Pio.)	OF	40	110	13	27	3	1	1	9	.245	6	34	1	56	2	4	.935
1988— St. Catharines (NY-P) .	OF	23	57	13	10	4	0	0	2	.175	24	21	2	29	1	4	.882
— Dunedin (FSL)	OF	17	29	2	4	0	0	1	2	.138	2	12	0	11	0	0	1.000
1989— St. Catharines (NY-P) .	OF	74	278	39	76	14	1	6	36	.273	16	60	9	111	•11	5	.961
1990— Dunedin (FSL)	OF	117	438	56	101	15	5	6	37	.231	20	100	18	237	7	7	.972
1991— Knoxville (Sou.)..........	OF	114	403	48	97	14	3	8	40	.241	26	88	17	222	5	4	.983
1992— Syracuse (I.L.)..........	OF	112	429	74	121	20	7	14	46	.282	43	114	10	270	8	4	.986
— New York (N.L.)■	OF	30	108	15	24	7	1	3	10	.222	8	24	2	77	2	1	.988
1993— New York (N.L.)..........	OF	80	288	34	72	19	2	11	26	.250	19	81	2	228	4	3	.987
— Norfolk (I.L.)	OF	60	224	39	58	11	2	12	34	.259	24	81	6	138	4	4	.973
1994— New York (N.L.)..........	OF	98	334	29	75	14	1	18	59	.225	28	94	1	274	5	3	.989
1995— Norfolk (I.L.)	OF-DH	15	53	7	18	3	0	2	11	.340	4	15	4	15	2	0	1.000
— New York (N.L.)..........	OF	75	267	39	67	13	0	7	31	.251	19	77	3	193	4	3	.985
— Binghamton (East.)	OF	2	8	2	4	0	0	1	4	.500	1	2	0	2	0	0	1.000
1996— Buffalo (A.A.)■	OF-DH	•138	*540	79	140	26	4	21	83	.259	21	119	12	*317	8	*9	.973
— Cleveland (A.L.)..........	OF	8	22	2	7	0	0	1	5	.318	1	6	0	5	0	0	1.000
1997— Buffalo (A.A.)..........	OF-DH	24	66	10	16	0	0	1	6	.242	5	16	2	20	1	1	.955
— Syracuse (I.L.)■	OF-DH	83	330	37	95	23	1	16	58	.288	21	59	4	117	4	1	.992
1998— Fukuoka (Jap. Pac.)■.		26	107	10	29	7	0	2	16	.271	12	32	1	...	...	...	...
1999— New Orleans (PCL)■..	OF-DH	112	404	60	125	23	2	16	58	.309	37	78	4	209	12	6	.965
— Houston (N.L.)	OF	12	20	2	4	1	0	1	5	.200	2	7	0	3	1	1	.800
American League totals (1 year)		8	22	2	7	0	0	1	5	.318	1	6	0	5	0	0	1.000
National League totals (5 years)		295	1017	119	242	54	4	40	131	.238	76	283	8	775	16	11	.986
Major League totals (6 years)		303	1039	121	249	54	4	41	136	.240	77	289	8	780	16	11	.986

THOMPSON, TRAVIS — P — ROCKIES

PERSONAL: Born January 10, 1975, in Milwaukee. ... 6-3/189. ... Throws right, bats right. ... Full name: Travis M. Thompson.
HIGH SCHOOL: Pulaski (Milwaukee).
JUNIOR COLLEGE: Madison (Wis.) Area Technical.
TRANSACTIONS/CAREER NOTES: Selected by Colorado Rockies organization in 12th round of free-agent draft (June 4, 1996).

Year League	W	L	Pct.	ERA	G	GS	CG	ShO	Sv.	IP	H	R	ER	BB	SO
1996— Arizona Rockies (Ariz.)	4	1	.800	3.30	9	3	0	0	0	30	34	12	11	5	25
— Portland (N'west)	0	2	.000	5.94	9	0	0	0	0	16 2/3	21	11	11	6	8
1997— Portland (N'west)	5	5	.500	4.50	18	11	0	0	0	74	88	51	37	16	51
1998— Asheville (SAL)...................	6	7	.462	3.24	26	24	0	0	0	147 1/3	155	71	53	36	113
1999— Salem (Caro.)	3	3	.500	1.74	56	0	0	0	*27	62	54	19	12	24	53

THOMSON, JOHN — P — ROCKIES

PERSONAL: Born October 1, 1973, in Vicksburg, Miss. ... 6-3/187. ... Throws right, bats right. ... Full name: John Carl Thomson.
HIGH SCHOOL: Sulphur (La.).
JUNIOR COLLEGE: Blinn College (Texas).
COLLEGE: McNeese State.
TRANSACTIONS/CAREER NOTES: Selected by Colorado Rockies organization in seventh round of free-agent draft (June 3, 1993). ... On Colorado disabled list (June 16-July 26, 1998); included rehabilitation assignment to Asheville (July 16-22). ... On Colorado Springs disabled list (May 19-July 19, 1999); included rehabilitation assignment to Salem (July 17-19).
STATISTICAL NOTES: Tied for Arizona League lead with 14 wild pitches in 1993.

Year	League	W	L	Pct.	ERA	G	GS	CG	ShO	Sv.	IP	H	R	ER	BB	SO
1993— Arizona Rockies (Ariz.)		3	5	.375	4.62	11	11	0	0	0	50 2/3	43	40	26	31	36
1994— Asheville (SAL)		6	6	.500	2.85	19	15	1	1	0	88 1/3	70	34	28	33	79
— Central Valley (Calif.)		3	1	.750	3.28	9	8	0	0	0	49 1/3	43	20	18	18	41
1995— New Haven (East.)		7	8	.467	4.18	26	24	0	0	0	131 1/3	132	69	61	56	82
1996— New Haven (East.)		9	4	.692	2.86	16	16	1	0	0	97 2/3	82	35	31	27	86
— Colo. Springs (PCL)		4	7	.364	5.04	11	11	0	0	0	69 2/3	76	45	39	26	62
1997— Colo. Springs (PCL)		4	2	.667	3.43	7	7	0	0	0	42	36	18	16	14	49
— Colorado (N.L.)		7	9	.438	4.71	27	27	2	1	0	166 1/3	193	94	87	51	106
1998— Colorado (N.L.)		8	11	.421	4.81	26	26	2	0	0	161	174	86	86	49	106
— Asheville (SAL)		1	0	1.000	0.00	2	2	0	0	0	9	5	1	0	1	12
1999— Colorado (N.L.)		1	10	.091	8.04	14	13	1	0	0	62 2/3	85	62	56	36	34
— Colo. Springs (PCL)		0	2	.000	9.45	5	5	1	0	0	20	36	25	21	8	19
— Salem (Caro.)		0	1	.000	9.00	1	1	0	0	0	2	4	2	2	0	1
Major League totals (3 years)		16	30	.348	5.28	67	66	5	1	0	390	452	242	229	136	246

THURMAN, MIKE — P — EXPOS

PERSONAL: Born July 22, 1973, in Corvallis, Ore. ... 6-5/210. ... Throws right, bats right. ... Full name: Michael Richard Thurman.
HIGH SCHOOL: Philomath (Ore.).
COLLEGE: Oregon State.
TRANSACTIONS/CAREER NOTES: Selected by Montreal Expos organization in supplemental round ("sandwich pick" between first and second round, 31st pick overall) of free-agent draft (June 2, 1994); pick received as compensation for Cleveland Indians signing Type A free-agent P Dennis Martinez. ... On Harrisburg disabled list (June 17-July 5, 1997).

Year	League	W	L	Pct.	ERA	G	GS	CG	ShO	Sv.	IP	H	R	ER	BB	SO
1994— Vermont (NY-P)		0	1	.000	5.40	2	2	0	0	0	6 2/3	6	4	4	2	3
1995— Albany (SAL)		3	8	.273	5.47	22	22	2	0	0	110 1/3	133	79	67	32	77
1996— West Palm Beach (FSL)		6	8	.429	3.33	19	19	0	0	0	113 2/3	122	53	42	23	68
— Harrisburg (East.)		3	1	.750	5.11	4	4	1	0	0	24 2/3	25	14	14	5	14
1997— Harrisburg (East.)		9	6	.600	3.81	20	20	1	0	0	115 2/3	102	54	49	30	85
— Ottawa (I.L.)		1	3	.250	5.49	4	4	0	0	0	19 2/3	17	13	12	9	15
— Montreal (N.L.)		1	0	1.000	5.40	5	2	0	0	0	11 2/3	8	9	7	4	8
1998— Ottawa (I.L.)		7	7	.500	3.41	19	19	0	0	0	105 2/3	107	50	40	49	76
— Montreal (N.L.)		4	5	.444	4.70	14	13	0	0	0	67	60	38	35	26	32
1999— Montreal (N.L.)		7	11	.389	4.05	29	27	0	0	0	146 2/3	140	84	66	52	85
Major League totals (3 years)		12	16	.429	4.31	48	42	0	0	0	225 1/3	208	131	108	82	125

TIMLIN, MIKE — P — ORIOLES

PERSONAL: Born March 10, 1966, in Midland, Texas. ... 6-4/210. ... Throws right, bats right. ... Full name: Michael August Timlin.
HIGH SCHOOL: Midland (Texas).
COLLEGE: Southwestern University (Texas).
TRANSACTIONS/CAREER NOTES: Selected by Toronto Blue Jays organization in fifth round of free-agent draft (June 2, 1987). ... On disabled list (April 4-May 2, 1989 and August 2-17, 1991). ... On Toronto disabled list (March 27-June 12, 1992); included rehabilitation assignments to Dunedin (April 11-15 and May 24-June 5) and Syracuse (June 5-12). ... On disabled list (May 25-June 9, 1994). ... On Toronto disabled list (June 22-August 18, 1995); included rehabilitation assignment to Syracuse (July 31-August 18). ... Traded by Blue Jays with P Paul Spoljaric to Seattle Mariners for OF Jose Cruz Jr. (July 31, 1997). ... Granted free agency (October 22, 1998). ... Signed by Baltimore Orioles (November 16, 1998).
STATISTICAL NOTES: Led South Atlantic League with 19 hit batsmen in 1988.

Year	League	W	L	Pct.	ERA	G	GS	CG	ShO	Sv.	IP	H	R	ER	BB	SO
1987— Medicine Hat (Pio.)		4	8	.333	5.14	13	12	2	0	0	75 1/3	79	50	43	26	66
1988— Myrtle Beach (SAL)		10	6	.625	2.86	35	26	0	0	0	151	119	68	48	77	106
1989— Dunedin (FSL)		5	8	.385	3.25	33	7	1	0	7	88 2/3	90	44	32	36	64
1990— Dunedin (FSL)		7	2	.778	1.43	42	0	0	0	22	50 1/3	36	11	8	16	46
— Knoxville (Sou.)		1	2	.333	1.73	17	0	0	0	8	26	20	6	5	7	21
1991— Toronto (A.L.)		11	6	.647	3.16	63	3	0	0	3	108 1/3	94	43	38	50	85
1992— Dunedin (FSL)		0	0	...	0.90	6	1	0	0	1	10	9	2	1	2	7
— Syracuse (I.L.)		0	1	.000	8.74	7	1	0	0	3	11 1/3	15	11	11	5	7
— Toronto (A.L.)		0	2	.000	4.12	26	0	0	0	1	43 2/3	45	23	20	20	35
1993— Toronto (A.L.)		4	2	.667	4.69	54	0	0	0	1	55 2/3	63	32	29	27	49
— Dunedin (FSL)		0	0	...	1.00	4	0	0	0	0	9	4	1	1	0	8
1994— Toronto (A.L.)		0	1	.000	5.18	34	0	0	0	2	40	41	25	23	20	38
1995— Toronto (A.L.)		4	3	.571	2.14	31	0	0	0	5	42	38	13	10	17	36
— Syracuse (I.L.)		1	1	.500	1.04	8	0	0	0	0	17 1/3	13	6	2	4	13
1996— Toronto (A.L.)		1	6	.143	3.65	59	0	0	0	31	56 2/3	47	25	23	18	52
1997— Toronto (A.L.)		3	2	.600	2.87	38	0	0	0	9	47	41	17	15	15	36
— Seattle (A.L.)■		3	2	.600	3.86	26	0	0	0	1	25 2/3	28	13	11	5	9
1998— Seattle (A.L.)		3	3	.500	2.95	70	0	0	0	19	79 1/3	78	26	26	16	60
1999— Baltimore (A.L.)■		3	9	.250	3.57	62	0	0	0	27	63	51	30	25	23	50
Major League totals (9 years)		32	36	.471	3.53	463	3	0	0	99	561 1/3	526	247	220	211	450

DIVISION SERIES RECORD

Year	League	W	L	Pct.	ERA	G	GS	CG	ShO	Sv.	IP	H	R	ER	BB	SO
1997— Seattle (A.L.)		0	0	...	54.00	1	0	0	0	0	2/3	3	4	4	1	1

CHAMPIONSHIP SERIES RECORD

Year	League	W	L	Pct.	ERA	G	GS	CG	ShO	Sv.	IP	H	R	ER	BB	SO
1991— Toronto (A.L.)		0	1	.000	3.18	4	0	0	0	0	5 2/3	5	4	2	2	5
1992— Toronto (A.L.)		0	0	...	6.75	2	0	0	0	0	1 1/3	4	1	1	0	1
1993— Toronto (A.L.)		0	0	...	3.86	1	0	0	0	0	2 1/3	3	1	1	0	2
Champ. series totals (3 years)		0	1	.000	3.86	7	0	0	0	0	9 1/3	12	6	4	2	8

NOTES: Member of World Series championship team (1992 and 1993).

Year	League	W	L	Pct.	ERA	G	GS	CG	ShO	Sv.	IP	H	R	ER	BB	SO
1992—	Toronto (A.L.).................	0	0	...	0.00	2	0	0	0	1	1 1/3	0	0	0	0	0
1993—	Toronto (A.L.).................	0	0	...	0.00	2	0	0	0	0	2 1/3	2	0	0	0	4
World Series totals (2 years)		0	0	...	0.00	4	0	0	0	1	3 2/3	2	0	0	0	4

TIMMONS, OZZIE — OF

PERSONAL: Born September 18, 1970, in Tampa. ... 6-2/220. ... Bats right, throws right. ... Full name: Osborne Llewellyn Timmons.
HIGH SCHOOL: Brandon (Fla.).
COLLEGE: University of Tampa.
TRANSACTIONS/CAREER NOTES: Selected by Chicago White Sox organization in 44th round of free-agent draft (June 1, 1988); did not sign. ... Selected by Chicago Cubs organization in fifth round of free-agent draft (June 3, 1991). ... On disabled list (August 9, 1993-remainder of season). ... Traded by Cubs with P Jayson Peterson to Cincinnati Reds for P Curt Lyons (March 31, 1997). ... Granted free agency (October 15, 1998). ... Signed by Seattle Mariners organization (March 12, 1999). ... Granted free agency (October 11, 1999).

Year	Team (League)	Pos.	G	AB	R	H	2B	3B	HR	RBI	Avg.	BB	SO	SB	PO	A	E	Avg.
1991—	Geneva (NY-P)...........	OF	73	294	35	65	10	1	•12	47	.221	18	39	4	118	3	4	.968
1992—	Win.-Salem (Car.).......	OF	86	305	64	86	18	0	18	56	.282	58	46	11	90	7	1	.990
	—Charlotte (Sou.)..........	OF	36	122	13	26	7	0	3	13	.213	12	26	2	41	3	1	.978
1993—	Orlando (Sou.)..........	OF	107	359	65	102	22	2	18	58	.284	62	80	5	169	14	6	.968
1994—	Iowa (A.A.)	OF-DH	126	440	63	116	30	2	22	66	.264	36	93	0	228	14	6	.976
1995—	Chicago (N.L.)	OF	77	171	30	45	10	1	8	28	.263	13	32	3	63	1	2	.970
1996—	Chicago (N.L.)	OF	65	140	18	28	4	0	7	16	.200	15	30	1	65	1	1	.985
	—Iowa (A.A.)	OF-DH	59	213	32	53	7	0	17	40	.249	28	42	1	98	1	3	.971
1997—	Cincinnati (N.L.)■......	OF	6	9	1	3	1	0	0	0	.333	0	1	0	0	0	1	.000
	—Indianapolis (A.A.).......	OF-DH	125	407	46	103	14	1	14	55	.253	60	100	1	172	3	3	.983
1998—	Indianapolis (I.L.).......	OF-DH-3B	117	327	46	86	21	3	12	36	.263	29	65	2	134	5	2	.986
1999—	Tacoma (PCL)■	OF-DH	82	297	56	81	22	0	21	66	.273	53	81	0	106	3	3	.973
	—Seattle (A.L.)	OF-DH-1B	26	44	4	5	2	0	1	3	.114	4	12	0	13	0	0	1.000
American League totals (1 year)			26	44	4	5	2	0	1	3	.114	4	12	0	13	0	0	1.000
National League totals (3 years)			148	320	49	76	15	1	15	44	.238	28	63	4	128	2	4	.970
Major League totals (4 years)			174	364	53	81	17	1	16	47	.223	32	75	4	141	2	4	.973

TOCA, JORGE — 1B — METS

PERSONAL: Born January 7, 1975, in Villaclara, Cuba. ... 6-3/220. ... Bats right, throws right. ... Full name: Jorge Luis Toca.
TRANSACTIONS/CAREER NOTES: Signed as non-drafted free agent by New York Mets organization (September 7, 1998).
MISCELLANEOUS: Member of Cuban National Team (1994-95).

Year	Team (League)	Pos.	G	AB	R	H	2B	3B	HR	RBI	Avg.	BB	SO	SB	PO	A	E	Avg.
1999—	Binghamton (East.) OF-1B-DH-3B		75	279	60	86	15	1	20	67	.308	32	43	5	251	22	5	.982
	—Norfolk (I.L.)	1B-DH-OF	49	176	25	59	12	1	5	29	.335	6	23	0	351	42	5	.987
	—New York (N.L.)..........	1B	4	3	0	1	0	0	0	0	.333	0	2	0	2	0	0	1.000
Major League totals (1 year)			4	3	0	1	0	0	0	0	.333	0	2	0	2	0	0	1.000

TOMKO, BRETT — P — REDS

PERSONAL: Born April 7, 1973, in San Diego. ... 6-4/216. ... Throws right, bats right. ... Full name: Brett Daniel Tomko.
HIGH SCHOOL: El Dorado (Placentia, Calif.).
JUNIOR COLLEGE: Mt. San Antonio College (Calif.).
COLLEGE: Florida Southern.
TRANSACTIONS/CAREER NOTES: Selected by Cincinnati Reds organization in second round of free-agent draft (June 1, 1995).
RECORDS: Shares N.L. single-inning record for most consecutive home runs allowed—3 (April 28, 1999, first inning).
MISCELLANEOUS: Appeared in two games as pinch runner (1997). ... Appeared in one game as pinch runner and struck out in only appearance as pinch hitter (1998).

Year	League	W	L	Pct.	ERA	G	GS	CG	ShO	Sv.	IP	H	R	ER	BB	SO
1995—	Charleston, W.Va. (SAL).....	4	2	.667	1.84	9	7	0	0	0	49	41	12	10	9	46
1996—	Chattanooga (Sou.)	11	7	.611	3.88	27	27	0	0	0	157 2/3	131	73	68	54	164
1997—	Indianapolis (A.A.)..........	6	3	.667	2.95	10	10	0	0	0	61	53	21	20	9	60
	—Cincinnati (N.L.)	11	7	.611	3.43	22	19	0	0	0	126	106	50	48	47	95
1998—	Cincinnati (N.L.)	13	12	.520	4.44	34	34	1	0	0	210 2/3	198	111	104	64	162
1999—	Cincinnati (N.L.)	5	7	.417	4.92	33	26	1	0	0	172	175	103	94	60	132
	—Indianapolis (I.L.)	2	0	1.000	4.97	2	2	0	0	0	12 2/3	15	7	7	1	9
Major League totals (3 years)		29	26	.527	4.35	89	79	2	0	0	508 2/3	479	264	246	171	389

TOMLINSON, GOEF — OF — ROYALS

PERSONAL: Born August 19, 1976, in St. Elizabeth, Jamaica. ... 6-1/190. ... Bats left, throws left. ... Full name: Goefrey Maurise Tomlinson.
HIGH SCHOOL: Everman (Texas).
COLLEGE: Houston.
TRANSACTIONS/CAREER NOTES: Selected by Kansas City Royals organization in fourth round of free-agent draft (June 3, 1997).
STATISTICAL NOTES: Led Northwest League with .440 on-base-percentage in 1997.

Year — Team (League)	Pos.	G	AB	R	H	2B	3B	HR	RBI	Avg.	BB	SO	SB	PO	A	E	Avg.
1997— Spokane (N'west).......	OF	58	210	49	71	16	0	4	28	*.338	32	20	19	99	6	3	.972
1998— Lansing (Midw.).........	OF	68	274	55	78	16	7	7	39	.285	39	34	21	143	2	3	.980
—Wilmington (Caro.)......	OF	38	136	15	38	8	1	0	16	.279	14	26	2	63	0	3	.955
1999— Wichita (Texas)	OF	128	479	100	134	31	4	4	46	.280	72	82	24	*313	2	5	.984

TORREALBA, YORVIT — C — GIANTS

PERSONAL: Born July 19, 1978, in Caracas, Venezuela. ... 5-11/180. ... Bats right, throws right. ... Full name: Yorvit Adolfo Torrealba.
TRANSACTIONS/CAREER NOTES: Signed as non-drafted free agent by San Francisco Giants organization (September 14, 1994).
STATISTICAL NOTES: Led California League catchers with 10 double plays in 1997.

Year — Team (League)	Pos.	G	AB	R	H	2B	3B	HR	RBI	Avg.	BB	SO	SB	PO	A	E	Avg.
1995— Bellingham (N'west)...	C	26	71	2	11	3	0	0	8	.155	2	14	0	152	26	5	.973
1996— San Jose (Calif.)	C	2	5	0	0	0	0	0	0	.000	1	1	0	16	1	0	1.000
—Burlington (Midw.)	C	1	4	0	0	0	0	0	0	.000	0	1	0	7	1	0	1.000
—Bellingham (N'west)...	C	48	150	23	40	4	0	1	10	.267	9	27	4	290	33	2	.994
1997— Bakersfield (Calif.)......	C	119	446	52	122	15	3	4	40	.274	31	58	4	779	*119	6	.993
1998— Shreveport (Texas).....	C	59	196	18	46	7	0	0	13	.235	18	30	0	397	70	2	.996
—San Jose (Calif.)........	C	21	70	10	20	2	0	0	10	.286	1	6	2	171	16	2	.989
—Fresno (PCL)	C	4	11	1	2	1	0	0	1	.182	1	4	0	22	0	0	1.000
1999— Shreveport (Texas).....	C-DH	65	217	25	53	10	1	4	19	.244	9	34	0	299	43	2	.994
—Fresno (PCL)	C	17	63	9	16	2	0	2	10	.254	4	11	0	155	12	2	.988
—San Jose (Calif.)........	C	19	73	10	23	3	0	2	14	.315	6	15	0	176	16	5	.975

TRACHSEL, STEVE — P — DEVIL RAYS

PERSONAL: Born October 31, 1970, in Oxnard, Calif. ... 6-4/205. ... Throws right, bats right. ... Full name: Stephen Christopher Trachsel. ... Name pronounced TRACK-sul.
HIGH SCHOOL: Troy (Fullerton, Calif.).
JUNIOR COLLEGE: Fullerton (Calif.) College.
COLLEGE: Long Beach State.
TRANSACTIONS/CAREER NOTES: Selected by Chicago Cubs organization in eighth round of free-agent draft (June 3, 1991). ... On Chicago disabled list (July 20-August 4, 1994). ... Granted free agency (October 29, 1999). ... Signed by Tampa Bay Devil Rays (January 13, 2000).
HONORS: Named N.L. Rookie Pitcher of the Year by THE SPORTING NEWS (1994).
STATISTICAL NOTES: Pitched 4-2 no-hit victory for Winston-Salem against Peninsula (July 12, 1991, second game). ... Pitched 6-0 one-hit, complete-game victory against Houston (May 13, 1996). ... Led N.L. with 32 home runs allowed in 1997.

Year — League	W	L	Pct.	ERA	G	GS	CG	ShO	Sv.	IP	H	R	ER	BB	SO
1991— Geneva (NY-P)..................	1	0	1.000	1.26	2	2	0	0	0	14 1/3	10	2	2	6	7
—Win.-Salem (Car.)..............	4	4	.500	3.67	12	12	1	0	0	73 2/3	70	38	30	19	69
1992— Charlotte (Sou.)...............	•13	8	.619	3.06	29	•29	5	2	0	*191	180	76	65	35	135
1993— Iowa (A.A.)	13	6	.684	3.96	27	26	1	1	0	170 2/3	170	78	75	45	135
—Chicago (N.L.)	0	2	.000	4.58	3	3	0	0	0	19 2/3	16	10	10	3	14
1994— Chicago (N.L.)	9	7	.563	3.21	22	22	1	0	0	146	133	57	52	54	108
—Iowa (A.A.)	0	2	.000	10.00	2	2	0	0	0	9	11	10	10	7	8
1995— Chicago (N.L.)	7	13	.350	5.15	30	29	2	0	0	160 2/3	174	104	92	76	117
1996— Orlando (Sou.)	0	1	.000	2.77	2	2	0	0	0	13	11	6	4	0	12
—Chicago (N.L.)	13	9	.591	3.03	31	31	3	2	0	205	181	82	69	62	132
1997— Chicago (N.L.)	8	12	.400	4.51	34	34	0	0	0	201 1/3	225	110	101	69	160
1998— Chicago (N.L.)	15	8	.652	4.46	33	33	1	0	0	208	204	107	103	84	149
1999— Chicago (N.L.)	8	*18	.308	5.56	34	34	4	0	0	205 2/3	226	133	127	64	149
Major League totals (8 years)	60	69	.465	4.35	187	186	11	2	0	1146 1/3	1159	603	554	412	829

ALL-STAR GAME RECORD

Year — League	W	L	Pct.	ERA	GS	CG	ShO	Sv.	IP	H	R	ER	BB	SO
1996— National..................	0	0	...	0.00	0	0	0	0	1	0	0	0	0	3

TRAMMELL, BUBBA — OF — DEVIL RAYS

PERSONAL: Born November 6, 1971, in Knoxville, Tenn. ... 6-2/220. ... Bats right, throws right. ... Full name: Thomas Bubba Trammell.
HIGH SCHOOL: Knoxville (Tenn.) Central.
JUNIOR COLLEGE: Cleveland (Tenn.) State Community College.
COLLEGE: Tennessee.
TRANSACTIONS/CAREER NOTES: Selected by Detroit Tigers organization in 11th round of free-agent draft (June 2, 1994). ... Selected by Tampa Bay Devil Rays in first round (22nd pick overall) of expansion draft (November 18, 1997). ... On Durham disabled list (May 17-25, 1999).

Year — Team (League)	Pos.	G	AB	R	H	2B	3B	HR	RBI	Avg.	BB	SO	SB	PO	A	E	Avg.
1994— Jamestown (NY-P)	OF	65	235	37	70	18	6	5	41	.298	23	32	9	77	3	5	.941
1995— Lakeland (FSL)	OF	122	454	61	129	32	6	16	72	.284	48	80	13	176	7	5	.973
1996— Jacksonville (Sou.)......	OF	83	311	63	102	23	2	27	75	.328	32	61	3	100	6	5	.955
—Toledo (I.L.).............	OF	51	180	32	53	14	1	6	24	.294	22	44	5	72	5	1	.987
1997— Detroit (A.L.)	OF-DH	44	123	14	28	5	0	4	13	.228	15	35	3	52	1	0	1.000
—Toledo (I.L.).............	OF-DH	90	319	56	80	15	1	28	75	.251	38	91	2	103	3	3	.972
1998— Tampa Bay (A.L.)■...	OF-DH	59	199	28	57	18	1	12	35	.286	16	45	0	50	3	0	1.000
—Durham (I.L.)............	OF	57	217	46	63	12	0	16	48	.290	38	42	6	110	5	2	.983
1999— Durham (I.L.)	OF-DH-3B	47	186	25	50	12	0	7	31	.269	15	36	0	65	8	3	.961
—Tampa Bay (A.L.)........	OF-DH	82	283	49	82	19	0	14	39	.290	43	37	0	142	2	1	.993
Major League totals (3 years)		185	605	91	167	42	1	30	87	.276	74	117	3	244	6	0	.996

TREMIE, CHRIS — C — MARLINS

PERSONAL: Born October 17, 1969, in Houston. ... 6-0/200. ... Bats right, throws right. ... Full name: Christopher James Tremie.
HIGH SCHOOL: South Houston.
COLLEGE: Houston.
TRANSACTIONS/CAREER NOTES: Selected by Houston Astros organization in 41st round of free-agent draft (June 1, 1988); did not sign. ... Selected by Chicago White Sox organization in 39th round of free-agent draft (June 1, 1992). ... On disabled list (July 22, 1992-remainder of season). ... Selected by Philadelphia Phillies organization from White Sox organization in Rule 5 minor league draft (December 9, 1996). ... Traded by Phillies to Texas Rangers for future considerations (March 29, 1998). ... Granted free agency (October 15, 1998). ... Signed by Pittsburgh Pirates organization (December 22, 1998). ... On Nashville disabled list (August 26-September 7, 1999). ... Granted free agency (October 4, 1999). ... Signed by Florida Marlins organization (November 2, 1999).
STATISTICAL NOTES: Led Southern League catchers with 13 double plays in 1994.

Year Team (League)	Pos.	G	AB	R	H	2B	3B	HR	RBI	Avg.	BB	SO	SB	PO	A	E	Avg.
1992— Utica (NY-P)	C	6	16	1	1	0	0	0	0	.063	0	5	0	37	5	1	.977
1993— Hickory (SAL).............	C	49	155	7	29	6	1	1	17	.187	9	26	0	343	44	4	.990
— GC White Sox (GCL) ..	C	2	4	0	0	0	0	0	0	.000	0	0	0	11	0	0	1.000
— Sarasota (FSL)	C	14	37	2	6	1	0	0	5	.162	2	4	0	71	13	0	1.000
1994— Birmingham (Sou.).....	C	92	302	32	68	13	0	2	29	.225	17	44	4	561	70	6	.991
1995— Nashville (A.A.)	C	67	190	13	38	4	0	2	16	.200	13	37	0	394	30	1	.998
— Chicago (A.L.)	C-DH	10	24	0	4	0	0	0	0	.167	1	2	0	39	2	1	.976
1996— Nashville (A.A.)	C	70	215	17	47	10	1	0	26	.219	18	48	2	433	*52	2	.996
1997— Reading (East.)■......	C	97	295	20	60	11	1	2	31	.203	36	61	0	650	84	4	.995
1998— Oklahoma (PCL)■......	C	78	247	35	55	10	0	0	12	.223	24	47	1	498	45	3	.995
— Texas (A.L.)	DH	2	3	2	1	1	0	0	0	.333	1	1	0	...	...	...	...
1999— Nashville (PCL)■......	C-3B	47	121	20	30	7	0	3	16	.248	14	29	4	292	31	4	.988
— Pittsburgh (N.L.)	C	9	14	1	1	0	0	0	1	.071	2	4	0	29	2	0	1.000
American League totals (2 years)		12	27	2	5	1	0	0	0	.185	2	3	0	39	2	1	.976
National League totals (1 year)		9	14	1	1	0	0	0	1	.071	2	4	0	29	2	0	1.000
Major League totals (3 years)		21	41	3	6	1	0	0	1	.146	4	7	0	68	4	1	.986

TROMBLEY, MIKE — P — ORIOLES

PERSONAL: Born April 14, 1967, in Springfield, Mass. ... 6-2/210. ... Throws right, bats right. ... Full name: Michael Scott Trombley.
HIGH SCHOOL: Minnechaug Regional (Wilbraham, Mass.).
COLLEGE: Duke.
TRANSACTIONS/CAREER NOTES: Selected by Minnesota Twins organization in 14th round of free-agent draft (June 5, 1989). ... Granted free agency (October 29, 1999). ... Signed by Baltimore Orioles (November 17, 1999).
STATISTICAL NOTES: Pitched 3-0 no-hit victory against Knoxville (August 8, 1991). ... Led Pacific Coast League with 18 home runs allowed in 1992.

Year League	W	L	Pct.	ERA	G	GS	CG	ShO	Sv.	IP	H	R	ER	BB	SO
1989— Kenosha (Midw.)	5	1	.833	3.12	12	3	0	0	2	49	45	23	17	13	41
— Visalia (Calif.)	2	2	.500	2.14	6	6	2	1	0	42	31	12	10	11	36
1990— Visalia (Calif.)	14	6	.700	3.43	27	25	3	1	0	176	163	79	67	50	164
1991— Orlando (Sou.)	12	7	.632	2.54	27	27	7	2	0	*191	153	65	54	57	*175
1992— Portland (PCL)	10	8	.556	3.65	25	25	2	0	0	165	149	70	67	58	*138
— Minnesota (A.L.)	3	2	.600	3.30	10	7	0	0	0	46 1/3	43	20	17	17	38
1993— Minnesota (A.L.)	6	6	.500	4.88	44	10	0	0	2	114 1/3	131	72	62	41	85
1994— Minnesota (A.L.)	2	0	1.000	6.33	24	0	0	0	0	48 1/3	56	36	34	18	32
— Salt Lake (PCL)	4	4	.500	5.04	11	10	0	0	0	60 2/3	75	37	34	20	63
1995— Salt Lake (PCL)	5	3	.625	3.62	12	12	0	0	0	69 2/3	71	32	28	26	59
— Minnesota (A.L.)	4	8	.333	5.62	20	18	0	0	0	97 2/3	107	68	61	42	68
1996— Salt Lake (PCL)	2	2	.500	2.45	24	0	0	0	10	36 2/3	24	12	10	10	38
— Minnesota (A.L.)	5	1	.833	3.01	43	0	0	0	6	68 2/3	61	24	23	25	57
1997— Minnesota (A.L.)	2	3	.400	4.37	67	0	0	0	1	82 1/3	77	43	40	31	74
1998— Minnesota (A.L.)	6	5	.545	3.63	77	1	0	0	1	96 2/3	90	41	39	41	89
1999— Minnesota (A.L.)	2	8	.200	4.33	75	0	0	0	24	87 1/3	93	42	42	28	82
Major League totals (8 years).......	30	33	.476	4.46	360	36	0	0	34	641 2/3	658	346	318	243	525

TRUBY, CHRIS — 3B — ASTROS

PERSONAL: Born December 9, 1973, in Palm Springs, Calif. ... 6-2/190. ... Bats right, throws right. ... Full name: Christopher John Truby.
HIGH SCHOOL: Damien (Hawaii).
TRANSACTIONS/CAREER NOTES: Signed as non-drafted free agent by Houston Astros organization (August 25, 1992). ... On Jackson disabled list (April 26-May 11, 1999).
STATISTICAL NOTES: Led Gulf Coast League third basemen with 21 errors in 1993. ... Led New York-Pennsylvania League with 114 total bases and eight sacrifice flies in 1994. ... Led Midwest League third basemen with 279 assists and 26 double plays in 1995. ... Led Texas League with 12 sacrifice flies in 1999. ... Led Texas League third baseman with 93 putouts, 35 double plays and a .950 fielding percentage in 1999.

Year Team (League)	Pos.	G	AB	R	H	2B	3B	HR	RBI	Avg.	BB	SO	SB	PO	A	E	Avg.
1993— GC Astros (GCL)	3B-SS	57	215	30	49	10	2	1	24	.228	22	30	16	42	158	†26	.885
— Osceola (FSL)............	3B	3	13	0	0	0	0	0	0	.000	0	2	0	3	9	2	.857
1994— Quad City (Midw.)	3B-1B	36	111	12	24	4	1	2	19	.216	3	29	1	54	29	6	.933
— Auburn (NY-P)...........	3B	73	282	*56	*91	17	6	7	*61	.323	23	48	20	48	153	•27	.882
1995— Quad City (Midw.)	3B-OF	118	400	68	93	23	4	9	64	.233	41	66	27	73	†279	38	.903
1996— Quad City (Midw.)	1B-3B	109	362	45	91	15	3	8	37	.251	28	74	6	545	128	17	.975

Year	Team (League)	Pos.	G	AB	R	H	2B	3B	HR	RBI	Avg.	BB	SO	SB	PO	A	E	Avg.
1997—Quad City (Midw.)		3B	68	268	34	75	14	1	7	46	.280	22	32	13	39	149	15	.926
— Kissimmee (FSL)........	3B-1B-SS-2B	57	199	23	49	11	0	2	29	.246	8	40	8	52	122	16	.916
1998—Kissimmee (FSL)		3B	52	212	36	66	16	1	14	478	.311	19	30	6	45	130	9	.951
— Jackson (Texas)	3B-1B	80	308	46	89	20	5	16	63	.289	20	50	8	94	161	15	.944
— New Orleans (PCL).....	3B	5	17	6	7	1	1	1	1	.412	1	3	1	4	7	1	.917
1999—Jackson (Texas)	3B-SS	124	465	78	131	21	3	28	87	.282	36	88	20	†95	275	20	†.949

TUCCI, PETER   OF   PADRES

PERSONAL: Born October 8, 1975, in Norwalk, Conn. ... 6-2/205. ... Bats right, throws right. ... Full name: Peter Joseph Tucci.
HIGH SCHOOL: Norwalk (Conn.).
COLLEGE: Providence.
TRANSACTIONS/CAREER NOTES: Selected by Toronto Blue Jays organization in supplemental round ("sandwich pick" between first and second round, 31st pick overall) of free-agent draft (June 4, 1996). ... Traded by Blue Jays organization with P Woody Williams and P Carlos Almanzar to San Diego Padres for P Joey Hamilton (December 13, 1998). ... On Mobile disabled list (July 7-August 3 and August 13, 1999-remainder of season).
STATISTICAL NOTES: Led Florida State League with .624 slugging percentage in 1998.

Year	Team (League)	Pos.	G	AB	R	H	2B	3B	HR	RBI	Avg.	BB	SO	SB	PO	A	E	Avg.
1996—St. Catharines (NY-P).		OF	54	205	28	52	8	7	7	33	.254	23	58	5	90	3	0	*1.000
1997—Hagerstown (SAL)......		OF	127	466	60	123	28	5	10	75	.264	35	95	9	147	11	1	.994
1998—Dunedin (FSL)...........		OF	92	356	72	117	30	3	23	76	.329	29	97	8	139	9	7	.955
— Knoxville (Sou.)..........		OF	38	141	25	41	7	4	7	36	.291	13	29	3	64	2	3	.957
1999—Mobile (Sou.)■	OF-DH-1B	83	312	45	78	15	0	11	35	.250	26	83	11	163	2	5	.971

TUCKER, MICHAEL   OF   REDS

PERSONAL: Born June 25, 1971, in South Boston, Va. ... 6-2/185. ... Bats left, throws right. ... Full name: Michael Anthony Tucker.
HIGH SCHOOL: Bluestone (Skipwith, Va.).
COLLEGE: Longwood (Va.).
TRANSACTIONS/CAREER NOTES: Selected by Kansas City Royals organization in first round (10th pick overall) of free-agent draft (June 1, 1992). ... On Kansas City disabled list (June 4-21 and August 28, 1996-remainder of season); included rehabilitation assignment to Wichita (June 15-21). ... Traded by Royals with IF Keith Lockhart to Atlanta Braves for OF Jermaine Dye and P Jamie Walker (March 27, 1997). ... Traded by Braves with P Denny Neagle and P Rob Bell to Cincinnati Reds for 2B Bret Boone and P Mike Remlinger (November 10, 1998).

Year	Team (League)	Pos.	G	AB	R	H	2B	3B	HR	RBI	Avg.	BB	SO	SB	PO	A	E	Avg.
1993—Wilmington (Caro.).....		2B	61	239	42	73	14	2	6	44	.305	34	49	12	120	157	10	.965
— Memphis (Sou.)		2B	72	244	38	68	7	4	9	35	.279	42	51	12	153	176	13	.962
1994—Omaha (A.A.).............		OF	132	485	75	134	16	7	21	77	.276	69	111	11	196	11	•7	.967
1995—Kansas City (A.L.)	OF-DH	62	177	23	46	10	0	4	17	.260	18	51	2	67	3	1	.986
— Omaha (A.A.).............		OF	71	275	37	84	18	4	4	28	.305	24	39	11	133	11	2	.986
1996—Kansas City (A.L.)	OF-1B-DH	108	339	55	88	18	4	12	53	.260	40	69	10	235	8	2	.992
— Wichita (Texas)	OF-1B	6	20	4	9	1	3	0	7	.450	5	4	0	17	1	0	1.000
1997—Atlanta (N.L.)■..........		OF	138	499	80	141	25	7	14	56	.283	44	116	12	237	6	5	.980
1998—Atlanta (N.L.).............		OF	130	414	54	101	27	3	13	46	.244	49	112	8	194	5	1	.995
1999—Cincinnati (N.L.)■		OF	133	296	55	75	8	5	11	44	.253	37	81	11	182	8	2	.990
American League totals (2 years)			170	516	78	134	28	4	16	70	.260	58	120	12	302	11	3	.991
National League totals (3 years)			401	1209	189	317	60	15	38	146	.262	130	309	31	613	19	8	.988
Major League totals (5 years)			571	1725	267	451	88	19	54	216	.261	188	429	43	915	30	11	.988

DIVISION SERIES RECORD

Year	Team (League)	Pos.	G	AB	R	H	2B	3B	HR	RBI	Avg.	BB	SO	SB	PO	A	E	Avg.
1997—Atlanta (N.L.).............		OF	2	6	0	1	0	0	0	1	.167	0	1	0	3	0	0	1.000
1998—Atlanta (N.L.).............		OF	3	8	1	2	0	0	1	2	.250	3	0	1	6	0	0	1.000
Division series totals (2 years)			5	14	1	3	0	0	1	3	.214	3	1	1	9	0	0	1.000

CHAMPIONSHIP SERIES RECORD

Year	Team (League)	Pos.	G	AB	R	H	2B	3B	HR	RBI	Avg.	BB	SO	SB	PO	A	E	Avg.
1997—Atlanta (N.L.).............	OF-PH	5	10	1	1	0	0	1	1	.100	3	4	0	5	1	0	1.000
1998—Atlanta (N.L.).............	OF-PH	6	13	1	5	1	0	1	5	.385	2	5	0	7	0	0	1.000
Championship series totals (2 years)		11	23	2	6	1	0	2	6	.261	5	9	0	12	1	0	1.000

TURNBOW, DERRICK   P   ANGELS

PERSONAL: Born January 25, 1978, in Union City, Tenn. ... 6-3/180. ... Throws right, bats right. ... Full name: Thomas Derrick Turnbow.
HIGH SCHOOL: Franklin (Tenn.).
TRANSACTIONS/CAREER NOTES: Selected by Philadelphia Phillies organization in fifth round of free-agent draft (June 3, 1997). ... Selected by Anaheim Angels from Phillies organization in Rule 5 major league draft (December 13, 1999).

Year	League	W	L	Pct.	ERA	G	GS	CG	ShO	Sv.	IP	H	R	ER	BB	SO
1997—Martinsville (Appl.).......		1	3	.250	7.40	7	7	0	0	0	24 1/3	34	29	20	16	7
1998—Martinsville (Appl.).......		2	6	.250	5.01	13	13	1	0	0	70	66	44	39	26	45
1999—Piedmont (SAL).................		12	8	.600	3.35	26	26	•4	1	0	161	130	67	60	53	149

TURNER, CHRIS   C

PERSONAL: Born March 23, 1969, in Bowling Green, Ky. ... 6-3/200. ... Bats right, throws right. ... Full name: Christopher Wan Turner.

HIGH SCHOOL: Warren Central (Bowling Green, Ky.).

COLLEGE: Western Kentucky (degree in psychology, 1991).

TRANSACTIONS/CAREER NOTES: Selected by California Angels organization in seventh round of free-agent draft (June 3, 1991). ... Angels franchise renamed Anaheim Angels for 1997 season. ... On Anaheim disabled list (March 31-July 4, 1997); included rehabilitation assignment to Lake Elsinore (July 2-4). ... Granted free agency (October 10, 1997). ... Signed by Minnesota Twins organization (December 5, 1997). ... On Salt Lake suspended list (April 7-17, 1998). ... Released by Twins (April 20, 1998) ... Signed by Kansas City Royals organization (April 20, 1998). ... Granted free agency (October 15, 1998). ... Signed by Cleveland Indians organization (January 5, 1999). ... Granted free agency (October 4, 1999).

STATISTICAL NOTES: Led Northwest League catchers with .997 fielding percentage in 1991. ... Led Pacific Coast League with 17 passed balls in 1993.

Year	Team (League)	Pos.	G	AB	R	H	2B	3B	HR	RBI	Avg.	BB	SO	SB	PO	A	E	Avg.
								BATTING								FIELDING		
1991—Boise (N'west)	C-OF	52	163	26	37	5	0	2	29	.227	32	32	10	360	39	2	†.995
1992—Quad City (Midw.)	C-1B	109	330	66	83	18	1	9	53	.252	85	65	8	727	98	9	.989
1993—Vancouver (PCL)	C-1B-DH	90	283	50	78	12	1	4	57	.276	49	44	6	524	56	6	.990
—California (A.L.)	C	25	75	9	21	5	0	1	13	.280	9	16	1	116	14	1	.992
1994—California (A.L.)	C	58	149	23	36	7	1	1	12	.242	10	29	3	268	29	1	.997
—Vancouver (PCL)	DH-C	3	10	1	2	1	0	0	1	.200	0	2	0	10	1	1	.917
1995—Vancouver (PCL)	C-3-DH-1-O	80	282	44	75	20	2	3	48	.266	34	54	3	345	49	6	.985
—California (A.L.)	C	5	10	0	1	0	0	0	1	.100	0	3	0	17	2	0	1.000
1996—Vancouver (PCL)	C-DH-O-3-1	113	390	51	100	19	1	2	47	.256	61	85	1	396	57	8	.983
—California (A.L.)	C-OF	4	3	1	1	0	0	0	1	.333	1	0	0	3	2	0	1.000
1997—Lake Elsinore (Calif.)	C	3	12	0	1	0	1	0	1	.083	0	3	0	25	1	1	.963
—Vancouver (PCL)	1B-C-DH-OF	37	135	26	50	10	0	4	22	.370	14	22	0	291	15	5	.984
—Anaheim (A.L.)	C-1B-DH-OF	13	23	4	6	1	1	1	2	.261	5	8	0	34	2	0	1.000
1998—Kansas City (A.L.)■	C	4	9	0	0	0	0	0	0	.000	0	4	0	16	0	0	1.000
—Omaha (PCL)	C-DH-OF-3B	66	196	31	60	14	1	1	16	.306	38	36	6	328	19	3	.991
1999—Buffalo (I.L.)■	C-1B	69	231	36	63	9	0	9	33	.273	34	45	2	424	43	6	.987
—Cleveland (A.L.)	C	12	21	3	4	0	0	0	0	.190	1	8	1	50	3	2	.964
Major League totals (7 years)		121	290	40	69	13	2	3	29	.238	26	68	5	504	52	4	.993

UNROE, TIM   1B/3B

PERSONAL: Born October 7, 1970, in Round Lake, Ill. ... 6-3/220. ... Bats right, throws right. ... Full name: Timothy Brian Unroe.

HIGH SCHOOL: Round Lake (Ill.).

JUNIOR COLLEGE: College of Lake County (Ill.).

COLLEGE: Lewis University (Ill.).

TRANSACTIONS/CAREER NOTES: Selected by Milwaukee Brewers organization in 28th round of free-agent draft (June 1, 1992). ... Released by Brewers (September 2, 1997). ... Signed by Chicago Cubs organization (January 7, 1998). ... On West Tenn disabled list (June 26-July 15, 1998). ... Released by Cubs (July 15, 1998). ... Signed by Anaheim Angels organization (October 27, 1998). ... Released by Angels (July 22, 1999). ... Signed by Kansas City Royals organization (September 2, 1999). ... Granted free agency (October 15, 1999).

HONORS: Named Texas League Player of the Year (1994).

STATISTICAL NOTES: Led Pioneer League third basemen with 62 putouts, 155 assists, 16 double plays and 236 total chances in 1992. ... Led California League third basemen with .936 fielding percentage, 78 putouts, 244 assists and 344 total chances in 1993. ... Led Texas League with 242 total bases and nine sacrifice flies in 1994. ... Career major league grand slams: 1.

Year	Team (League)	Pos.	G	AB	R	H	2B	3B	HR	RBI	Avg.	BB	SO	SB	PO	A	E	Avg.
								BATTING								FIELDING		
1992—Helena (Pio.)	3B-OF	74	266	61	74	13	2	*16	58	.278	47	91	3	†70	†155	20	.918
1993—Stockton (Calif.)	3B-OF	108	382	57	96	21	6	12	63	.251	36	96	9	†81	†244	23	†.934
1994—El Paso (Texas)	3B-1B-OF	126	474	*97	*147	36	7	15	*103	.310	42	107	14	383	203	19	.969
1995—New Orleans (A.A.)	3-1-DH-O	102	371	43	97	21	2	6	45	.261	18	94	4	373	160	12	.978
—Milwaukee (A.L.)	1B	2	4	0	1	0	0	0	0	.250	0	0	0	11	0	0	1.000
1996—New Orleans (A.A.)	3-1-S-DH-O	109	404	72	109	26	4	25	67	.270	36	121	8	175	231	25	.942
—Milwaukee (A.L.)	1B-3B-DH-OF	14	16	5	3	0	0	0	0	.188	4	5	0	41	10	1	.981
1997—Tucson (PCL)	3-0-2-DH-S	63	234	45	68	17	1	9	46	.291	9	62	3	65	92	7	.957
—Milwaukee (A.L.)	1B-3B-OF-2B	32	16	3	4	1	0	2	5	.250	2	9	2	59	9	2	.971
1998—Iowa (PCL)■	3B-1B-OF-2B	39	104	9	18	5	0	1	9	.173	10	30	1	37	53	1	.989
—West Tenn (Sou.)	3B-2B	16	54	6	13	6	0	0	9	.241	8	20	0	17	32	7	.875
1999—Anaheim (A.L.)■	OF-DH-3B-2B	27	54	5	13	2	0	1	6	.241	4	16	0	14	3	0	1.000
—Edmonton (PCL)	OF-3B	10	44	10	17	5	1	5	18	.386	5	9	0	17	4	1	.955
—Omaha (PCL)■	DH-OF	5	22	4	5	0	0	1	2	.227	0	5	0	3	0	0	1.000
Major League totals (4 years)		75	90	13	21	3	0	3	11	.233	10	30	2	125	22	3	.980

URBINA, UGUETH   P   EXPOS

PERSONAL: Born February 15, 1974, in Caracas, Venezuela. ... 6-0/205. ... Throws right, bats right. ... Full name: Ugueth Urtain Urbina. ... Name pronounced OO-get.

HIGH SCHOOL: Liceo Peres Bonalde de Miranda (Miranda, Venezuela).

TRANSACTIONS/CAREER NOTES: Signed as non-drafted free agent by Montreal Expos organization (July 2, 1990). ... On disabled list (April 8-17, 1994). ... On temporarily inactive list (May 9-June 6, 1994). ... On Ottawa disabled list (August 10-September 14, 1995).

HONORS: Named N.L. Fireman of the Year by THE SPORTING NEWS (1999).

Year	League	W	L	Pct.	ERA	G	GS	CG	ShO	Sv.	IP	H	R	ER	BB	SO
1991— Gulf Coast Expos (GCL)		3	3	.500	2.29	10	10	3	•1	0	63	58	24	16	10	51
1992— Albany (SAL)		7	•13	.350	3.22	24	24	5	2	0	142 1/3	111	68	51	54	100
1993— Burlington (Midw.)		2	3	.400	4.50	10	8	0	0	0	46	41	31	23	22	30
— Harrisburg (East.)...............		4	5	.444	3.99	11	11	3	1	0	70	66	32	31	32	45
1994— Harrisburg (East.)...............		9	3	.750	3.28	21	21	0	0	0	120 2/3	95	49	44	43	86
1995— West Palm Beach (FSL)		1	0	1.000	0.00	2	2	0	0	0	9	4	0	0	1	11
— Ottawa (I.L.)....................		6	2	.750	3.04	13	11	2	1	0	68	46	26	23	26	55
— Montreal (N.L.)..................		2	2	.500	6.17	7	4	0	0	0	23 1/3	26	17	16	14	15
1996— West Palm Beach (FSL)		1	1	.500	1.29	3	3	0	0	0	14	13	3	2	3	21
— Ottawa (I.L.)....................		2	0	1.000	2.66	5	5	0	0	0	23 2/3	17	9	7	6	28
— Montreal (N.L.)..................		10	5	.667	3.71	33	17	0	0	0	114	102	54	47	44	108
1997— Montreal (N.L.)..................		5	8	.385	3.78	63	0	0	0	27	64 1/3	52	29	27	29	84
1998— Montreal (N.L.)..................		6	3	.667	1.30	64	0	0	0	34	69 1/3	37	11	10	33	94
1999— Montreal (N.L.)..................		6	6	.500	3.69	71	0	0	0	*41	75 2/3	59	35	31	36	100
Major League totals (5 years).......		**29**	**24**	**.547**	**3.40**	**238**	**21**	**0**	**0**	**102**	**346 2/3**	**276**	**146**	**131**	**156**	**401**

ALL-STAR GAME RECORD

Year	League	W	L	Pct.	ERA	GS	CG	ShO	Sv.	IP	H	R	ER	BB	SO
1998— National		0	1	.000	27.00	0	0	0	0	1	3	3	3	1	2

VALDES, ISMAEL — P — CUBS

PERSONAL: Born August 21, 1973, in Victoria, Mexico. ... 6-3/215. ... Throws right, bats right.
HIGH SCHOOL: CBTIS #119 (Victoria, Mexico).
TRANSACTIONS/CAREER NOTES: Signed as non-drafted free agent by Los Angeles Dodgers (June 14, 1991). ... Loaned by Dodgers organization to Mexico City Tigers of Mexican League (April 21-June 26, 1992; and March 17-August 19, 1993). ... On disabled list (July 6-28, 1997). ... On Los Angeles disabled list (July 26-September 1, 1998); included rehabilitation assignments to Vero Beach (August 22) and San Bernardino (August 27). ... Traded by Dodgers with 2B Eric Young to Chicago Cubs for P Terry Adams, P Chad Ricketts and a player to be named later (December 12, 1999); Dodgers acquired P Brian Stephenson to complete deal (December 16, 1999).
STATISTICAL NOTES: Led N.L. with five balks in 1996. ... Pitched 2-0 one-hit, complete-game victory against Pittsburgh (June 27, 1998).

Year	League	W	L	Pct.	ERA	G	GS	CG	ShO	Sv.	IP	H	R	ER	BB	SO
1991— GC Dodgers (GCL)		2	2	.500	2.32	10	10	0	0	0	50 1/3	44	15	13	13	44
1992— M.C. Tigers (Mex.)■		0	0	...	19.64	5	0	0	0	0	3 2/3	15	9	8	1	2
— La Vega (DSL)■................		3	0	1.000	1.42	6	0	0	0	0	38	27	9	6	17	34
1993— M.C. Tigers (Mex.)■		16	7	.696	3.94	26	25	11	1	0	173 2/3	192	87	76	55	113
— San Antonio (Texas)■.........		1	0	1.000	1.38	3	2	0	0	0	13	12	2	2	0	11
1994— San Antonio (Texas)..........		2	3	.400	3.38	8	8	0	0	0	53 1/3	54	22	20	9	55
— Albuquerque (PCL).............		4	1	.800	3.40	8	8	0	0	0	45	44	21	17	13	39
— Los Angeles (N.L.).............		3	1	.750	3.18	21	1	0	0	0	28 1/3	21	10	10	10	28
1995— Los Angeles (N.L.).............		13	11	.542	3.05	33	27	6	2	1	197 2/3	168	76	67	51	150
1996— Los Angeles (N.L.).............		15	7	.682	3.32	33	33	0	0	0	225	219	94	83	54	173
1997— Los Angeles (N.L.).............		10	11	.476	2.65	30	30	0	0	0	196 2/3	171	68	58	47	140
1998— Los Angeles (N.L.).............		11	10	.524	3.98	27	27	2	2	0	174	171	82	77	66	122
— Vero Beach (FSL)		0	0	...	0.00	1	1	0	0	0	3	2	0	0	1	3
— San Bernardino (Calif.).......		1	0	1.000	2.84	1	1	0	0	0	6 1/3	7	2	2	1	4
1999— Los Angeles (N.L.).............		9	14	.391	3.98	32	32	2	1	0	203 1/3	213	97	90	58	143
Major League totals (6 years).......		**61**	**54**	**.530**	**3.38**	**176**	**150**	**10**	**5**	**1**	**1025**	**963**	**427**	**385**	**286**	**756**

DIVISION SERIES RECORD

Year	League	W	L	Pct.	ERA	G	GS	CG	ShO	Sv.	IP	H	R	ER	BB	SO
1995— Los Angeles (N.L.)		0	0	...	0.00	1	1	0	0	0	7	3	2	0	1	6
1996— Los Angeles (N.L.)		0	1	.000	4.26	1	1	0	0	0	6 1/3	5	3	3	0	5
Division series totals (2 years)		**0**	**1**	**.000**	**2.03**	**2**	**2**	**0**	**0**	**0**	**13 1/3**	**8**	**5**	**3**	**1**	**11**

VALDEZ, MARIO — 1B/OF — TWINS

PERSONAL: Born November 19, 1974, in Obregon, Mexico ... 6-2/190. ... Bats left, throws right. ... Full name: Mario A. Valdez.
HIGH SCHOOL: Miami Senior.
JUNIOR COLLEGE: Miami-Dade (North) Community College.
TRANSACTIONS/CAREER NOTES: Selected by Chicago White Sox organization in 48th round of free-agent draft (June 3, 1993). ... On Charlotte disabled list (June 18-26 and July 25-August 1, 1999). ... Claimed on waivers by Minnesota Twins (September 29, 1999).
STATISTICAL NOTES: Led Pacific Coast League first basemen with 14 errors in 1998.

Year	Team (League)	Pos.	G	AB	R	H	2B	3B	HR	RBI	Avg.	BB	SO	SB	PO	A	E	Avg.
1994— GC White Sox (GCL) ..		1B-OF	53	157	20	37	11	2	2	25	.236	30	28	0	351	28	8	.979
1995— Hickory (SAL).............		1B	130	441	65	120	30	5	11	56	.272	67	107	9	1040	67	12	.989
1996— South Bend (Midw.) ...		1B	61	202	46	76	19	0	10	43	.376	36	42	2	438	41	8	.984
— Birmingham (Sou.).....		1B-OF	50	168	22	46	10	2	3	28	.274	32	34	0	284	26	2	.994
1997— Nashville (A.A.).............		1B-DH	81	282	44	79	20	1	15	61	.280	43	77	1	616	44	6	.991
— Chicago (A.L.)		1B-DH-3B	54	115	11	28	7	0	1	13	.243	17	39	1	256	12	0	1.000
1998— Calgary (PCL)		1B-DH-OF	123	448	86	148	32	0	20	81	.330	60	102	1	1003	75	†15	.986
1999— Charlotte (I.L.).............		1B-OF-DH	121	402	78	110	17	2	26	76	.274	76	91	1	762	54	7	.991
Major League totals (1 year)			54	115	11	28	7	0	1	13	.243	17	39	1	256	12	0	1.000

VALENTIN, JAVIER — C — TWINS

PERSONAL: Born September 19, 1975, in Manati, Puerto Rico. ... 5-10/192. ... Bats both, throws right. ... Full name: Jose Javier Valentin. ... Brother of Jose Valentin, shortstop, Chicago White Sox. ... Name pronounced VAL-un-TEEN.

U V

HIGH SCHOOL: Fernando Callejo (Manati, Puerto Rico).

TRANSACTIONS/CAREER NOTES: Selected by Minnesota Twins organization in third round of free-agent draft (June 3, 1993).

STATISTICAL NOTES: Led Appalachian League catchers with 48 assists and 348 total chances in 1994. ... Led Midwest League catchers with 730 putouts, 108 assists, 861 total chances, 23 errors and 11 double plays in 1995.

| | | | | | | | | BATTING | | | | | | | | FIELDING | | |
Year Team (League)	Pos.	G	AB	R	H	2B	3B	HR	RBI	Avg.	BB	SO	SB	PO	A	E	Avg.
1993— GC Twins (GCL)..........	C-DH-3B	32	103	18	27	6	1	1	19	.262	14	19	0	120	23	5	.966
— Elizabethton (Appl.)....	C	9	24	3	5	1	0	0	3	.208	4	2	0	81	3	2	.977
1994— Elizabethton (Appl.)....	C-3B	54	210	23	44	5	0	9	27	.210	15	44	0	288	†50	12	.966
1995— Fort Wayne (Midw.)....	C-3B	112	383	59	124	26	5	19	65	.324	47	75	0	†736	†122	†23	.974
1996— Fort Myers (FSL)........	C-DH-3B	87	338	34	89	26	1	7	54	.263	32	65	1	360	71	4	.991
— New Britain (East.)	C-3B-DH	48	165	22	39	8	0	3	14	.236	16	35	0	188	36	5	.978
1997— New Britain (East.)	C-DH-3B	102	370	41	90	17	0	8	50	.243	30	61	2	516	65	6	.990
— Minnesota (A.L.)	C	4	7	1	2	0	0	0	0	.286	0	3	0	11	2	0	1.000
1998— Minnesota (A.L.)	C-DH	55	162	11	32	7	1	3	18	.198	11	30	0	281	17	5	.983
1999— Minnesota (A.L.)	C	78	218	22	54	12	1	5	28	.248	22	39	0	387	27	1	.998
Major League totals (3 years)		137	387	34	88	19	2	8	46	.227	33	72	0	679	46	6	.992

VALENTIN, JOHN   3B   RED SOX

PERSONAL: Born February 18, 1967, in Mineola, N.Y. ... 6-0/185. ... Bats right, throws right. ... Full name: John William Valentin. ... Name pronounced VAL-en-tin.

HIGH SCHOOL: St. Anthony (Jersey City, N.J.).

COLLEGE: Seton Hall.

TRANSACTIONS/CAREER NOTES: Selected by Boston Red Sox organization in fifth round of free-agent draft (June 1, 1988). ... On Boston disabled list (April 1-20, 1993); included rehabilitation assignment to Pawtucket (April 16-20). ... On Boston disabled list (May 4-June 6, 1994); included rehabilitation assignment to Pawtucket (May 31-June 6). ... On disabled list (August 3-18, 1996; and June 26-July 11 and August 31-September 23, 1999).

HONORS: Named shortstop on THE SPORTING NEWS A.L. Silver Slugger team (1995).

STATISTICAL NOTES: Led New York-Pennsylvania League shortstops with .949 fielding percentage in 1988. ... Hit three home runs in one game (June 2, 1995). ... Led A.L. shortstops with 659 total chances in 1995. ... Hit for the cycle (June 6, 1996). ... Led A.L. third basemen with 121 putouts in 1998. ... Career major league grand slams: 4.

MISCELLANEOUS: Turned unassisted triple play while playing shortstop (July 8, 1994, sixth inning); 10th player ever to accomplish feat.

| | | | | | | | | BATTING | | | | | | | | FIELDING | | |
Year Team (League)	Pos.	G	AB	R	H	2B	3B	HR	RBI	Avg.	BB	SO	SB	PO	A	E	Avg.
1988— Elmira (NY-P)	SS-3B	60	207	18	45	5	1	2	16	.217	36	35	5	96	175	14	†.951
1989— Winter Haven (FSL)....	SS-3B	55	215	27	58	13	1	3	18	.270	13	29	4	99	177	12	.958
— Lynchburg (Caro.).......	SS	75	264	47	65	7	2	8	34	.246	41	40	5	105	220	16	.953
1990— New Britain (East.)	SS	94	312	20	68	18	1	2	31	.218	25	46	1	139	266	21	.951
1991— New Britain (East.)	SS	23	81	8	16	3	0	0	5	.198	9	14	1	50	65	3	.975
— Pawtucket (I.L.)...........	SS	100	329	52	87	22	4	9	49	.264	60	42	0	184	300	25	.951
1992— Pawtucket (I.L.)..........	SS	97	331	47	86	18	1	9	29	.260	48	50	1	148	*358	20	.962
— Boston (A.L.)..............	SS	58	185	21	51	13	0	5	25	.276	20	17	1	79	182	10	.963
1993— Pawtucket (I.L.)..........	SS	2	9	3	3	0	0	1	1	.333	0	1	0	8	9	0	1.000
— Boston (A.L.)..............	SS	144	468	50	130	40	3	11	66	.278	49	77	3	238	432	20	.971
1994— Boston (A.L.)..............	SS-DH	84	301	53	95	26	2	9	49	.316	42	38	3	134	242	8	.979
— Pawtucket (I.L.)..........	SS	5	18	2	6	0	0	1	2	.333	3	4	0	7	16	3	.885
1995— Boston (A.L.)..............	SS	135	520	108	155	37	2	27	102	.298	81	67	20	227	*414	•18	.973
1996— Boston (A.L.).............	SS-3B-DH	131	527	84	156	29	3	13	59	.296	63	59	9	202	357	17	.970
1997— Boston (A.L.)..............	2B-3B	143	575	95	176	*47	5	18	77	.306	58	66	7	239	380	22	.966
1998— Boston (A.L.)..............	3B-2B	153	588	113	145	44	1	23	73	.247	77	82	4	†121	292	15	.965
1999— Boston (A.L.)..............	3B-DH	113	449	58	114	27	1	12	70	.254	40	68	0	84	208	14	.954
Major League totals (8 years)		961	3613	582	1022	263	17	118	521	.283	430	474	47	1324	2507	124	.969

DIVISION SERIES RECORD

RECORDS: Shares single-game records for most home runs—2; and most runs batted in—7 (October 10, 1999).

| | | | | | | | | BATTING | | | | | | | | FIELDING | | |
Year Team (League)	Pos.	G	AB	R	H	2B	3B	HR	RBI	Avg.	BB	SO	SB	PO	A	E	Avg.
1995— Boston (A.L.)..............	SS	3	12	1	3	1	0	1	2	.250	3	1	0	5	5	1	.909
1998— Boston (A.L.)..............	3B	4	15	5	7	1	0	0	0	.467	3	1	0	5	10	0	1.000
1999— Boston (A.L.)..............	3B	5	22	6	7	2	0	3	12	.318	0	4	0	5	11	2	.889
Division series totals (3 years)		12	49	12	17	4	0	4	14	.347	6	6	0	15	26	3	.932

CHAMPIONSHIP SERIES RECORD

RECORDS: Shares single-game record for most at-bats (nine-inning game)—6 (October 16, 1999).

| | | | | | | | | BATTING | | | | | | | | FIELDING | | |
Year Team (League)	Pos.	G	AB	R	H	2B	3B	HR	RBI	Avg.	BB	SO	SB	PO	A	E	Avg.
1999— Boston (A.L.)..............	3B	5	23	3	8	2	0	1	5	.348	2	4	0	4	7	0	1.000

VALENTIN, JOSE   SS   WHITE SOX

PERSONAL: Born October 12, 1969, in Manati, Puerto Rico. ... 5-10/173. ... Bats left, throws right. ... Full name: Jose Antonio Valentin. ... Brother of Javier Valentin, catcher, Minnesota Twins. ... Name pronounced VAL-un-TEEN.

HIGH SCHOOL: Fernando Callejo (Manati, Puerto Rico).

TRANSACTIONS/CAREER NOTES: Signed as non-drafted free agent by San Diego Padres organization (October 12, 1986). ... On disabled list (April 16-May 1 and May 18-July 11, 1990). ... Traded by Padres with P Ricky Bones and OF Matt Mieske to Milwaukee Brewers for 3B Gary Sheffield and P Geoff Kellogg (March 27, 1992). ... On Milwaukee disabled list (April 14-May 5, 1997); included rehabilitation assignment to

Beloit (May 3-5). ... On Milwaukee disabled list (April 13-June 16, 1999); included rehabilitation assignment to Louisville (June 9-16). ... Traded by Brewers with P Cal Eldred to Chicago White Sox for P Jaime Navarro and P John Snyder (January 12, 2000).

STATISTICAL NOTES: Led Texas League shortstops with 658 total chances in 1991. ... Led American Association shortstops with 639 total chances and 70 double plays in 1992. ... Led American Association shortstops with 211 putouts and 80 double plays in 1993. ... Led A.L. shortstops with 20 errors in 1994. ... Hit three home runs in one game (April 3, 1998). ... Switch-hit home runs in one game (July 1, 1999). ... Career major league grand slams: 3.

							BATTING							FIELDING		
Year Team (League)	Pos.	G	AB	R	H	2B	3B	HR	RBI	Avg.	BB	SO	SB	PO	A	E	Avg.
1987—Spokane (N'west)	SS	70	244	52	61	8	2	2	24	.250	35	38	8	101	175	26	.914
1988—Char., S.C. (SAL)	SS	133	444	56	103	20	1	6	44	.232	45	83	11	204	412	60	.911
1989—Riverside (Calif.)	SS	114	381	40	74	10	5	10	41	.194	37	93	8	*227	333	*46	.924
—Wichita (Texas)	SS-3B	18	49	8	12	1	0	2	5	.245	5	12	1	26	45	8	.899
1990—Wichita (Texas)	SS	11	36	4	10	2	0	0	2	.278	5	7	2	14	33	2	.959
1991—Wichita (Texas)	SS	129	447	73	112	22	5	17	68	.251	55	115	8	176	*442	40	.939
1992—Denver (A.A.)■	SS	*139	492	78	118	19	11	3	45	.240	53	99	9	*187	*414	*38	.941
—Milwaukee (A.L.)	SS-2B	4	3	1	0	0	0	0	1	.000	0	0	0	1	1	1	.667
1993—New Orleans (A.A.)	SS-1B	122	389	56	96	22	5	9	53	.247	47	87	9	†212	351	29	.951
—Milwaukee (A.L.)	SS	19	53	10	13	1	2	1	7	.245	7	16	1	20	51	6	.922
1994—Milwaukee (A.L.)	SS-2B-DH-3B	97	285	47	68	19	0	11	46	.239	38	75	12	151	336	†20	.961
1995—Milwaukee (A.L.)	SS-DH-3B	112	338	62	74	23	3	11	49	.219	37	83	16	164	335	15	.971
1996—Milwaukee (A.L.)	SS	154	552	90	143	33	7	24	95	.259	66	145	17	243	460	*37	.950
1997—Milwaukee (A.L.)	SS-DH	136	494	58	125	23	1	17	58	.253	39	109	19	208	383	20	.967
—Beloit (Midw.)	SS	2	6	3	3	1	0	0	1	.500	2	1	0	1	8	0	1.000
1998—Milwaukee (A.L.)	SS-DH	151	428	65	96	24	0	16	49	.224	63	105	10	173	370	21	.963
1999—Milwaukee (N.L.)	SS	89	256	45	58	9	5	10	38	.227	48	52	3	113	214	22	.937
—Louisville (I.L.)	SS	6	20	6	5	0	0	3	3	.250	4	3	0	7	17	0	1.000
American League totals (6 years)		522	1725	268	423	99	13	64	256	.245	187	428	65	787	1566	99	.960
National League totals (2 years)		240	684	110	154	33	5	26	87	.225	111	157	13	286	584	43	.953
Major League totals (8 years)		762	2409	378	577	132	18	90	343	.240	298	585	78	1073	2150	142	.958

VANDER WAL, JOHN OF PADRES

PERSONAL: Born April 29, 1966, in Grand Rapids, Mich. ... 6-2/197. ... Bats left, throws left. ... Full name: John Henry Vander Wal.
HIGH SCHOOL: Hudsonville (Mich.).
COLLEGE: Western Michigan.
TRANSACTIONS/CAREER NOTES: Selected by Houston Astros organization in eighth round of free-agent draft (June 4, 1984); did not sign. ... Selected by Montreal Expos organization in third round of free-agent draft (June 2, 1987). ... Contract purchased by Colorado Rockies with OF Ronnie Hall from Expos (March 31, 1994). ... Traded by Rockies to San Diego Padres for a player to be named later (August 31, 1998). ... Granted free agency (October 26, 1998). ... Re-signed by Padres (November 13, 1998).
RECORDS: Holds major league single-season record for most hits by pinch hitter—28 (1995).

							BATTING							FIELDING		
Year Team (League)	Pos.	G	AB	R	H	2B	3B	HR	RBI	Avg.	BB	SO	SB	PO	A	E	Avg.
1987—Jamestown (NY-P)	OF	18	69	24	33	12	3	3	15	.478	3	14	3	20	0	0	1.000
—W.P. Beach (FSL)	OF	50	189	29	54	11	2	2	22	.286	30	25	8	103	1	3	.972
1988—W.P. Beach (FSL)	OF	62	231	50	64	15	2	10	33	.277	32	40	11	109	3	1	.991
—Jacksonville (Sou.)	OF	58	208	22	54	14	0	3	14	.260	17	49	3	99	0	0	1.000
1989—Jacksonville (Sou.)	OF	71	217	30	55	9	2	6	24	.253	22	51	2	72	3	1	.987
1990—Indianapolis (A.A.)	OF	51	135	16	40	6	0	2	14	.296	13	28	0	48	4	2	.963
—Jacksonville (Sou.)	OF	77	277	45	84	25	3	8	40	.303	39	46	6	106	4	1	.991
1991—Indianapolis (A.A.)	OF	133	478	84	140	36	8	15	71	.293	79	118	8	197	7	1	*.995
—Montreal (N.L.)	OF	21	61	4	13	4	1	1	8	.213	1	18	0	29	0	0	1.000
1992—Montreal (N.L.)	OF-1B	105	213	21	51	8	2	4	20	.239	24	36	3	122	6	2	.985
1993—Montreal (N.L.)	1B-OF	106	215	34	50	7	4	5	30	.233	27	30	6	271	14	4	.986
1994—Colorado (N.L.)■	1B-OF	91	110	12	27	3	1	5	15	.245	16	31	2	106	3	0	1.000
1995—Colorado (N.L.)	1B-OF	105	101	15	35	8	1	5	21	.347	16	23	1	51	4	2	.965
1996—Colorado (N.L.)	OF-1B	104	151	20	38	6	2	5	31	.252	19	38	2	72	2	1	.987
1997—Colorado (N.L.)	OF-1B-DH	76	92	7	16	2	0	1	11	.174	10	33	1	38	0	1	.974
—Colo. Springs (PCL)	1B-OF-DH	25	103	29	42	12	1	3	19	.408	11	28	1	158	10	4	.977
1998—Colorado (N.L.)	OF-DH-1B	89	104	18	30	10	1	5	20	.288	16	29	0	29	3	0	1.000
—San Diego (N.L.)■	OF-1B	20	25	3	6	3	0	0	0	.240	6	5	0	21	2	0	1.000
1999—San Diego (N.L.)	OF-1B-DH	132	246	26	67	18	0	6	41	.272	37	59	2	227	10	1	.996
Major League totals (9 years)		849	1318	160	333	69	12	37	197	.253	172	302	17	966	44	11	.989

DIVISION SERIES RECORD

RECORDS: Holds career record for most games by pinch hitter—7. ... Shares career record for most triples—1.

							BATTING							FIELDING		
Year Team (League)	Pos.	G	AB	R	H	2B	3B	HR	RBI	Avg.	BB	SO	SB	PO	A	E	Avg.
1995—Colorado (N.L.)	PH	4	4	0	0	0	0	0	0	.000	0	2	0	...	...	...	...
1998—San Diego (N.L.)	PH	3	3	1	1	0	1	0	2	.333	0	1	0	...	...	...	...
Division series totals (2 years)		7	7	1	1	0	1	0	2	.143	0	3	0	0	0	0	...

CHAMPIONSHIP SERIES RECORD

							BATTING							FIELDING		
Year Team (League)	Pos.	G	AB	R	H	2B	3B	HR	RBI	Avg.	BB	SO	SB	PO	A	E	Avg.
1998—San Diego (N.L.)	OF-PH	3	7	1	3	0	0	1	2	.429	0	2	0	5	1	0	1.000

WORLD SERIES RECORD

							BATTING							FIELDING		
Year Team (League)	Pos.	G	AB	R	H	2B	3B	HR	RBI	Avg.	BB	SO	SB	PO	A	E	Avg.
1998—San Diego (N.L.)	OF-PH	4	5	0	2	1	0	0	0	.400	0	2	0	1	0	0	1.000

VARGAS, MARTIN   P   INDIANS

PERSONAL: Born February 22, 1978, in San Pedro de Macoris, Dominican Republic. ... 6-0/155. ... Throws right, bats right.
TRANSACTIONS/CAREER NOTES: Signed as non-drafted free agent by Cleveland Indians organization (July 5, 1995).

Year	League	W	L	Pct.	ERA	G	GS	CG	ShO	Sv.	IP	H	R	ER	BB	SO
1997—Dom. Indians (DSL)	....	3	5	.375	2.45	14	14	0	0	0	69²/₃	52	33	19	39	43
1998—Burlington (Appl.)	....	3	7	.300	4.76	13	13	1	0	0	73²/₃	78	49	39	35	64
—Columbus (SAL)	....	1	4	.200	10.01	7	7	0	0	0	29²/₃	42	36	33	24	25
1999—Columbus (SAL)	....	6	3	.667	4.95	15	12	0	0	0	67¹/₃	80	46	37	20	51
—Kinston (Caro.)	....	6	1	.857	2.76	20	0	0	0	2	42¹/₃	31	16	13	20	44

RECORD AS POSITION PLAYER

Year	Team (League)	Pos.	G	AB	R	H	2B	3B	HR	RBI	Avg.	BB	SO	SB	PO	A	E	Avg.
1996—Dom. Indians (DSL)		...	39	103	7	23	6	1	0	12	.223	12	25	1	...	...	...	...

VARITEK, JASON   C   RED SOX

PERSONAL: Born April 11, 1972, in Rochester, Minn. ... 6-2/220. ... Bats right, throws right. ... Full name: Jason A. Varitek.
HIGH SCHOOL: Lake Brantley (Longwood, Fla.).
COLLEGE: Georgia Tech.
TRANSACTIONS/CAREER NOTES: Selected by Minnesota Twins organization first round (21st pick overall) of free-agent draft (June 3, 1993); did not sign. ... Selected by Seattle Mariners organization in first round (14th pick overall) of free-agent draft (June 2, 1994). ... Traded by Mariners with P Derek Lowe to Boston Red Sox for P Heathcliff Slocumb (July 31, 1997).
STATISTICAL NOTES: Tied for Southern League lead in double plays by catcher with 10 in 1996. ... Led Southern League catchers with .993 fielding percentage and tied for lead with 10 double plays in 1996. ... Led A.L. catchers with 1,049 total chances and 25 passed balls in 1999.

Year	Team (League)	Pos.	G	AB	R	H	2B	3B	HR	RBI	Avg.	BB	SO	SB	PO	A	E	Avg.
1995—Port City (Sou.)	....	C	104	352	42	79	14	3	10	44	.224	61	126	0	589	59	8	.988
1996—Port City (Sou.)	.........C-DH-3B-OF	134	503	63	132	34	1	12	67	.262	66	93	7	663	79	5	*.993
1997—Tacoma (PCL)	......	C-DH	87	307	54	78	13	0	15	48	.254	34	71	0	613	49	3	*.995
—Pawtucket (I.L.)■......		C	20	66	6	13	5	0	1	5	.197	8	12	0	123	10	1	.993
—Boston (A.L.)	....	C	1	1	0	1	0	0	0	0	1.000	0	0	0	1	0	0	1.000
1998—Boston (A.L.)	....	C-DH	86	221	31	56	13	0	7	33	.253	17	45	2	367	32	5	.988
1999—Boston (A.L.)	....	C-DH	144	483	70	130	39	2	20	76	.269	46	85	1	*972	66	*11	.990
Major League totals (3 years)			231	705	101	187	52	2	27	109	.265	63	130	3	1340	98	16	.989

DIVISION SERIES RECORD

RECORDS: Holds single-game record for most runs scored—5 (October 10, 1999). ... Shares career and single-series record for most consecutive hits—5 (October 9-10, 1999).

Year	Team (League)	Pos.	G	AB	R	H	2B	3B	HR	RBI	Avg.	BB	SO	SB	PO	A	E	Avg.
1998—Boston (A.L.)	....	C	1	4	0	1	0	0	0	1	.250	0	1	0	5	0	0	1.000
1999—Boston (A.L.)	....	C	5	21	7	5	3	0	1	3	.238	0	4	0	40	0	0	1.000
Division series totals (2 years)			6	25	7	6	3	0	1	4	.240	0	5	0	45	0	0	1.000

CHAMPIONSHIP SERIES RECORD

Year	Team (League)	Pos.	G	AB	R	H	2B	3B	HR	RBI	Avg.	BB	SO	SB	PO	A	E	Avg.
1999—Boston (A.L.)	....	C	5	20	1	4	1	1	1	1	.200	1	4	0	44	1	1	.978

VASQUEZ, LEO   P   ATHLETICS

V

PERSONAL: Born July 1, 1973, in LaRomana, Dominican Republic. ... 6-4/193. ... Throws left, bats left. ... Full name: Leoner Vasquez.
HIGH SCHOOL: Mercedes Laura (LaRomana, Dominican Republic).
TRANSACTIONS/CAREER NOTES: Signed by Aberdeen, Prairie League (May 1996). ... Contract sold by Aberdeen to New York Mets organization (September 13, 1996). ... On Binghamton disabled list (April 24-May 13, 1999). ... Traded by Mets with OF Terrence Long to Oakland Athletics for P Kenny Rogers (July 23, 1999). ... On Vancouver disabled list (September 11, 1999-remainder of season).

Year	League	W	L	Pct.	ERA	G	GS	CG	ShO	Sv.	IP	H	R	ER	BB	SO
1996—Aberdeen (Prairie)	....	11	2	.846	2.23	19	16	2	2	0	105	79	39	26	39	106
1997—Capital City (SAL)■	....	4	5	.444	5.14	22	8	0	0	1	56	63	37	32	22	49
—Binghamton (East.)	....	0	1	.000	10.13	1	1	0	0	0	5¹/₃	7	6	6	2	2
1998—St. Lucie (FSL)	....	3	2	.600	2.22	24	6	0	0	4	69	44	20	17	24	46
—Binghamton (East.)	....	1	1	.500	4.60	14	2	0	0	1	29¹/₃	28	16	15	25	28
1999—Binghamton (East.)	....	1	2	.333	3.83	27	0	0	0	1	42¹/₃	39	18	18	28	43
—Midland (Texas)■	....	3	1	.750	3.09	13	0	0	0	1	23¹/₃	18	11	8	13	24
—Vancouver (PCL)	....	0	0	...	5.40	1	0	0	0	0	1²/₃	2	1	1	2	0

VAUGHN, GREG   OF   DEVIL RAYS

PERSONAL: Born July 3, 1965, in Sacramento. ... 6-0/202. ... Bats right, throws right. ... Full name: Gregory Lamont Vaughn. ... Cousin of Mo Vaughn, first baseman, Anaheim Angels; and cousin of Jerry Royster, infielder with five major league teams (1973-88).
HIGH SCHOOL: John F. Kennedy (Sacramento).
JUNIOR COLLEGE: Sacramento City College.
COLLEGE: Miami (Fla.).
TRANSACTIONS/CAREER NOTES: Selected by St. Louis Cardinals organization in fifth round of free-agent draft (January 17, 1984); did not sign. ... Selected by Milwaukee Brewers organization in secondary phase of free-agent draft (June 4, 1984); did not sign. ... Selected by

Pittsburgh Pirates organization in secondary phase of free-agent draft (January 9, 1985); did not sign. ... Selected by California Angels organization in secondary phase of free-agent draft (June 3, 1985); did not sign. ... Selected by Brewers organization in secondary phase of free-agent draft (June 2, 1986). ... On disabled list (May 26-June 10, 1990). ... On Milwaukee disabled list (April 8-27, 1994); included rehabilitation assignment to Beloit (April 25-27). ... Traded by Brewers with a player to be named later to San Diego Padres for P Bryce Florie, P Ron Villone and OF Marc Newfield (July 31, 1996); Padres acquired OF Gerald Parent to complete deal (September 16, 1996). ... Granted free agency (October 28, 1996). ... Re-signed by Padres (December 19, 1996). ... Traded by Padres with P Kerry Taylor and P Chris Clark to New York Yankees for P Kenny Rogers, IF Mariano Duncan and P Kevin Henthorne (July 4, 1997); trade later voided because Vaughn failed physical (July 6, 1997). ... Traded by Padres with OF/1B Mark Sweeney to Cincinnati Reds for OF Reggie Sanders, SS Damian Jackson and P Josh Harris (February 2, 1999). ... Granted free agency (October 29, 1999). ... Signed by Tampa Bay Devil Rays (December 13, 1999).

HONORS: Named Midwest League co-Most Valuable Player (1987). ... Named American Association Most Valuable Player (1989). ... Named N.L. Comeback Player of the Year by THE SPORTING NEWS (1998). ... Named outfielder on THE SPORTING NEWS N.L. All-Star team (1998). ... Named outfielder on THE SPORTING NEWS N.L. Silver Slugger team (1998).

STATISTICAL NOTES: Led Midwest League with 292 total bases in 1987. ... Led Texas League with 279 total bases in 1988. ... Led American Association with .548 slugging percentage in 1989. ... Hit three home runs in one game (September 7, 1999). ... Career major league grand slams: 4.

							BATTING							FIELDING		
Year Team (League)	Pos.	G	AB	R	H	2B	3B	HR	RBI	Avg.	BB	SO	SB	PO	A	E	Avg.
1986—Helena (Pio.)	OF	66	258	64	75	13	2	16	54	.291	30	69	23	99	5	3	.972
1987—Beloit (Midw.)............	OF	139	492	*120	150	31	6	*33	105	.305	102	115	36	247	11	10	.963
1988—El Paso (Texas)..........	OF	131	505	*104	152	*39	2	*28	*105	.301	63	120	22	216	12	7	.970
1989—Denver (A.A.).............	OF	110	387	74	107	17	5	*26	*92	.276	62	94	20	140	4	3	.980
—Milwaukee (A.L.)	OF-DH	38	113	18	30	3	0	5	23	.265	13	23	4	32	1	2	.943
1990—Milwaukee (A.L.)	OF-DH	120	382	51	84	26	2	17	61	.220	33	91	7	195	8	7	.967
1991—Milwaukee (A.L.)	OF-DH	145	542	81	132	24	5	27	98	.244	62	125	2	315	5	2	.994
1992—Milwaukee (A.L.)	OF-DH	141	501	77	114	18	2	23	78	.228	60	123	15	288	6	3	.990
1993—Milwaukee (A.L.)	OF-DH	154	569	97	152	28	2	30	97	.267	89	118	10	214	1	3	.986
1994—Milwaukee (A.L.)	OF-DH	95	370	59	94	24	1	19	55	.254	51	93	9	162	5	3	.982
—Beloit (Midw.)............	DH	2	6	1	1	0	0	0	0	.167	4	1	0	...	...	...	...
1995—Milwaukee (A.L.)	DH	108	392	67	88	19	1	17	59	.224	55	89	10	...	...	...	...
1996—Milwaukee (A.L.)	OF-DH	102	375	78	105	16	0	31	95	.280	58	99	5	192	5	4	.980
—San Diego (N.L.)■........	OF	43	141	20	29	3	1	10	22	.206	24	31	4	74	2	2	.974
1997—San Diego (N.L.)	OF-DH	120	361	60	78	10	0	18	57	.216	56	110	7	153	7	1	.994
1998—San Diego (N.L.)	OF-DH	158	573	112	156	28	4	50	119	.272	79	121	11	270	5	2	.993
1999—Cincinnati (N.L.)■........	OF-DH	153	550	104	135	20	2	45	118	.245	85	137	15	264	8	4	.986
American League totals (8 years)		903	3244	528	799	158	13	169	566	.246	421	761	62	1398	31	24	.983
National League totals (4 years)		474	1625	296	398	61	7	123	316	.245	244	399	37	761	22	9	.989
Major League totals (11 years)		1377	4869	824	1197	219	20	292	882	.246	665	1160	99	2159	53	33	.985

DIVISION SERIES RECORD

							BATTING							FIELDING		
Year Team (League)	Pos.	G	AB	R	H	2B	3B	HR	RBI	Avg.	BB	SO	SB	PO	A	E	Avg.
1996—San Diego (N.L.)	PH	3	3	0	0	0	0	0	0	.000	0	1	0	...	...	...	...
1998—San Diego (N.L.)	OF	4	15	2	5	1	0	1	1	.333	0	4	0	2	0	0	1.000
Division series totals (2 years)		7	18	2	5	1	0	1	1	.278	0	5	0	2	0	0	1.000

CHAMPIONSHIP SERIES RECORD

							BATTING							FIELDING		
Year Team (League)	Pos.	G	AB	R	H	2B	3B	HR	RBI	Avg.	BB	SO	SB	PO	A	E	Avg.
1998—San Diego (N.L.)	OF-PH	3	8	1	2	0	0	0	0	.250	1	1	0	2	0	0	1.000

WORLD SERIES RECORD

							BATTING							FIELDING		
Year Team (League)	Pos.	G	AB	R	H	2B	3B	HR	RBI	Avg.	BB	SO	SB	PO	A	E	Avg.
1998—San Diego (N.L.)	OF-DH	4	15	3	2	0	0	2	4	.133	1	2	0	4	0	1	.800

ALL-STAR GAME RECORD

					BATTING							FIELDING		
Year League	Pos.	AB	R	H	2B	3B	HR	RBI	Avg.	BB	SO	SB	PO	A	E	Avg.
1993— American	OF	1	1	1	0	0	0	0	1.000	0	0	0	0	0	0	...
1996— American...................							Did not play.									
1998— National	OF	1	0	1	0	0	0	2	1.000	0	0	0	0	0	0	...
All-Star Game totals (2 years)		2	1	2	0	0	0	2	1.000	0	0	0	0	0	0	...

VAUGHN, MO   1B   ANGELS

PERSONAL: Born December 15, 1967, in Norwalk, Conn. ... 6-1/268. ... Bats left, throws right. ... Full name: Maurice Samuel Vaughn. ... Cousin of Greg Vaughn, outfielder, Tampa Bay Devil Rays.

HIGH SCHOOL: Trinity Pawling Prep (Pawling, N.Y.).

COLLEGE: Seton Hall.

TRANSACTIONS/CAREER NOTES: Selected by Boston Red Sox organization in first round (23rd pick overall) of free-agent draft (June 9, 1989). ... On disabled list (June 17-July 10, 1997). ... Granted free agency (October 23, 1998). ... Signed by Anaheim Angels (December 11, 1998). ... On disabled list (April 7-22, 1998).

RECORDS: Shares A.L. record for most seasons leading league in errors by first baseman—5.

HONORS: Named first baseman on THE SPORTING NEWS A.L. All-Star team (1995). ... Named first baseman on THE SPORTING NEWS A.L. Silver Slugger team (1995). ... Named A.L. Most Valuable Player by Baseball Writers' Association of America (1995).

STATISTICAL NOTES: Led A.L. with 20 intentional bases on balls received in 1994. ... Led A.L. first basemen with 103 double plays in 1994. ... Led A.L. first basemen with 1,368 total chances and 128 double plays in 1995. ... Hit three home runs in one game (September 24, 1996 and May 30, 1997). ... Had 16-game hitting streak (September 13-27, 1998). ... Career major league grand slams: 8.

Year Team (League)	Pos.	G	AB	R	H	2B	3B	HR	RBI	Avg.	BB	SO	SB	PO	A	E	Avg.
							BATTING								FIELDING		
1989— New Britain (East.)	1B	73	245	28	68	15	0	8	38	.278	25	47	1	541	45	•10	.983
1990— Pawtucket (I.L.)..........	1B	108	386	62	114	26	1	22	72	.295	44	87	3	828	60	11	.988
1991— Pawtucket (I.L.)..........	1B	69	234	35	64	10	0	14	50	.274	60	44	2	432	24	3	.993
— Boston (A.L.)..............	1B-DH	74	219	21	57	12	0	4	32	.260	26	43	2	378	26	6	.985
1992— Boston (A.L.)..............	1B-DH	113	355	42	83	16	2	13	57	.234	47	67	3	741	57	*15	.982
— Pawtucket (I.L.)..........	1B	39	149	15	42	6	0	6	28	.282	18	35	1	368	15	8	.980
1993— Boston (A.L.)..............	1B-DH	152	539	86	160	34	1	29	101	.297	79	130	4	1110	70	*16	.987
1994— Boston (A.L.)..............	1B-DH	111	394	65	122	25	1	26	82	.310	57	112	4	880	57	•10	.989
1995— Boston (A.L.)..............	1B-DH	140	550	98	165	28	3	39	•126	.300	68	*150	11	*1262	95	11	.992
1996— Boston (A.L.)..............	1B-DH	161	635	118	207	29	1	44	143	.326	95	154	2	1207	74	*15	.988
1997— Boston (A.L.)..............	1B-DH	141	527	91	166	24	0	35	96	.315	86	154	2	1088	75	*14	.988
1998— Boston (A.L.)..............	1B-DH	154	609	107	205	31	2	40	115	.337	61	144	0	1176	90	12	.991
1999— Anaheim (A.L.)■.......	1B-DH	139	524	63	147	20	0	33	108	.281	54	127	0	584	35	3	.995
Major League totals (9 years)		1186	4355	691	1313	220	10	263	860	.301	573	1081	28	8431	580	102	.989

DIVISION SERIES RECORD

RECORDS: Shares single-game records for most home runs—2 (September 29, 1998); and most runs batted in—7 (September 29, 1998).
NOTES: Shares postseason single-game record for most runs batted in—7 (September 29, 1998).

Year Team (League)	Pos.	G	AB	R	H	2B	3B	HR	RBI	Avg.	BB	SO	SB	PO	A	E	Avg.
							BATTING								FIELDING		
1995— Boston (A.L.)..............	1B	3	14	0	0	0	0	0	0	.000	1	7	0	27	2	0	1.000
1998— Boston (A.L.)..............	1B	4	17	3	7	2	0	2	7	.412	1	5	0	30	4	0	1.000
Division series totals (2 years)		7	31	3	7	2	0	2	7	.226	2	12	0	57	6	0	1.000

ALL-STAR GAME RECORD

NOTES: Named to A.L. All-Star team for 1998 game; replaced by Rafael Palmeiro due to injury.

Year League	Pos.	AB	R	H	2B	3B	HR	RBI	Avg.	BB	SO	SB	PO	A	E	Avg.
						BATTING								FIELDING		
1995— American....................	1B	2	0	0	0	0	0	0	.000	0	2	0	4	0	0	1.000
1998— American....................						Selected, did not play—injured.										

VAZQUEZ, JAVIER   P   EXPOS

PERSONAL: Born July 25, 1976, in Ponce, Puerto Rico. ... 6-2/195. ... Throws right, bats right. ... Full name: Javier Carlos Vazquez.
HIGH SCHOOL: Colegio de Ponce (Ponce, Puerto Rico).
TRANSACTIONS/CAREER NOTES: Selected by Montreal Expos organization in fifth round of free-agent draft (June 2, 1994). ... On suspended list (July 23-27, 1998).
STATISTICAL NOTES: Pitched 3-0 one-hit, complete-game victory against Los Angeles (September 14, 1999).

Year League	W	L	Pct.	ERA	G	GS	CG	ShO	Sv.	IP	H	R	ER	BB	SO
1994— Gulf Coast Expos (GCL)	5	2	.714	2.53	15	11	1	1	0	67 2/3	37	25	19	15	56
1995— Albany (SAL)	6	6	.500	5.08	21	21	1	0	0	102 2/3	109	67	58	47	87
1996— Delmarva (SAL).................	14	3	*.824	2.68	27	27	1	0	0	164 1/3	138	64	49	57	173
1997— Harrisburg (East.)..............	4	0	1.000	1.07	6	6	1	0	0	42	15	5	5	12	47
— West Palm Beach (FSL)	6	3	.667	2.16	19	19	1	0	0	112 2/3	98	40	27	28	100
1998— Montreal (N.L.)..................	5	15	.250	6.06	33	32	0	0	0	172 1/3	196	121	116	68	139
1999— Montreal (N.L.)..................	9	8	.529	5.00	26	26	3	1	0	154 2/3	154	98	86	52	113
— Ottawa (I.L.)	4	2	.667	4.85	7	7	0	0	0	42 2/3	45	24	23	16	46
Major League totals (2 years).......	14	23	.378	5.56	59	58	3	1	0	327	350	219	202	120	252

VELANDIA, JORGE   IF   ATHLETICS

PERSONAL: Born January 12, 1975, in Caracas, Venezuela. ... 5-9/185. ... Bats right, throws right. ... Full name: Jorge Macias Velandia.
TRANSACTIONS/CAREER NOTES: Signed as non-drafted free agent by Detroit Tigers organization (January 15, 1992). ... Traded by Tigers with 3B Scott Livingstone to San Diego Padres for P Gene Harris (May 11, 1994). ... Traded by Padres with P Doug Bochtler to Oakland Athletics for P Don Wengert and IF David Newhan (November 26, 1997). ... On disabled list (August 7, 1999-remainder of season).
STATISTICAL NOTES: Led Pacific Coast League shortstop with 648 total chances and 93 double plays in 1998.

Year Team (League)	Pos.	G	AB	R	H	2B	3B	HR	RBI	Avg.	BB	SO	SB	PO	A	E	Avg.
							BATTING									FIELDING		
1992— Bristol (Appl.)..............	SS-2B	45	119	20	24	6	1	0	9	.202	15	16	3	54	88	12	.922
1993— Niagara Falls (NY-P) ...	SS	72	212	30	41	11	0	1	22	.193	19	48	22	82	186	24	.918
— Fayetteville (SAL)	SS-2B-3B	37	106	15	17	4	0	0	11	.160	13	21	5	47	94	9	.940
1994— Lakeland (FSL)	SS-2B-3B	22	60	8	14	4	0	0	3	.233	6	14	0	40	56	4	.960
— Springfield (Mid.)■...	SS-2B	98	290	42	71	14	0	4	36	.245	21	46	5	118	303	26	.942
1995— Memphis (Sou.)	SS	63	186	23	38	10	2	4	17	.204	14	37	0	88	152	12	.952
— Las Vegas (PCL)	SS	66	206	25	54	12	3	0	25	.262	13	37	0	97	190	*31	.903
1996— Memphis (Sou.)	SS	122	392	42	94	19	0	9	48	.240	31	65	3	173	368	33	.943
1997— Las Vegas (PCL)	SS	114	405	46	110	15	2	3	35	.272	29	62	13	170	*347	21	.961
— San Diego (N.L.)	SS-2B-3B	14	29	0	3	2	0	0	0	.103	1	7	0	11	23	3	.919
1998— Oakland (A.L.)■.......	SS-2B	8	4	0	1	0	0	0	0	.250	0	1	0	4	10	1	.933
— Edmonton (PCL)	SS-DH	128	488	64	140	35	1	6	57	.287	37	52	8	203	*428	17	.974
1999— Oakland (A.L.) 2B-SS-3B-DH	63	48	4	9	1	0	0	2	.188	2	13	2	46	79	3	.977
American League totals (2 years)		71	52	4	10	1	0	0	2	.192	2	14	2	50	89	4	.972
National League totals (1 year)		14	29	0	3	2	0	0	0	.103	1	7	0	11	23	3	.919
Major League totals (3 years)		85	81	4	13	3	0	0	2	.160	3	21	2	61	112	7	.961

V

VELARDE, RANDY   2B   ATHLETICS

PERSONAL: Born November 24, 1962, in Midland, Texas. ... 6-0/200. ... Bats right, throws right. ... Full name: Randy Lee Velarde. ... Name pronounced vel-ARE-dee.
HIGH SCHOOL: Robert E. Lee (Midland, Texas).
COLLEGE: Lubbock (Texas) Christian College.
TRANSACTIONS/CAREER NOTES: Selected by Chicago White Sox organization in 19th round of free-agent draft (June 3, 1985). ... Traded by White Sox with P Pete Filson to New York Yankees for P Scott Nielsen and IF Mike Soper (January 5, 1987). ... On New York disabled list (August 9-29, 1989). ... On New York disabled list (June 6-July 30, 1993); included rehabilitation assignment to Albany/Colonie (July 24-30). ... Granted free agency (December 23, 1994). ... Re-signed by Oneonta, Yankees organization (April 12, 1995). ... Granted free agency (November 2, 1995). ... Signed by California Angels (November 21, 1995). ... Angels franchise renamed Anaheim Angels for 1997 season. ... On disabled list (March 23-September 1 and September 2, 1997-remainder of season). ... On Anaheim disabled list (March 19-May 13 and May 16-August 3, 1998); included rehabilitation assignments to Lake Elsinore (May 7-13) and Vancouver (July 29-August 3). ... Granted free agency (October 23, 1998). ... Re-signed by Angels (December 7, 1998). ... Traded by Angels with P Omar Olivares to Oakland Athletics for P Elvin Nina, OF Jeff DaVanon and OF Nathan Hayes (July 29, 1999).
STATISTICAL NOTES: Led Midwest League shortstops with 52 errors in 1986. ... Had 21-game hitting streak (June 9-July 4, 1996). ... Led A.L. second baseman with 805 total chances in 1999. ... Career major league grand slams: 1.

							BATTING								FIELDING		
Year	Team (League)	Pos.	G	AB	R	H	2B	3B	HR	RBI	Avg.	BB	SO	SB	PO	A	E	Avg.
1985—Niagara Falls (NY-P)	...OF-SS-2B-3B		67	218	28	48	7	3	1	16	.220	35	72	8	124	117	15	.941
1986—Appleton (Midw.)	SS-3B-OF		124	417	55	105	31	4	11	50	.252	58	96	13	205	300	†54	.903
—Buffalo (A.A.)	SS		9	20	2	4	1	0	0	2	.200	2	4	1	9	28	3	.925
1987—Alb./Colonie (East.)■.	SS-OF		71	263	40	83	20	2	7	32	.316	25	47	8	128	254	17	.957
—Columbus (I.L.)	SS		49	185	21	59	10	6	5	33	.319	15	36	8	100	164	16	.943
—New York (A.L.)	SS		8	22	1	4	0	0	0	1	.182	0	6	0	8	20	2	.933
1988—Columbus (I.L.)	SS-2B-3B		78	293	39	79	23	4	5	37	.270	25	71	7	123	271	25	.940
—New York (A.L.)	2B-SS-3B		48	115	18	20	6	0	5	12	.174	8	24	1	72	98	8	.955
1989—Columbus (I.L.)	SS-3B		103	387	59	103	26	3	11	53	.266	38	105	3	150	295	22	.953
—New York (A.L.)	3B-SS		33	100	12	34	4	2	2	11	.340	7	14	0	26	61	4	.956
1990—New York (A.L.)	3-S-O-2-DH		95	229	21	48	6	2	5	19	.210	20	53	0	70	159	12	.950
1991—New York (A.L.)	3B-SS-OF		80	184	19	45	11	1	1	15	.245	18	43	3	64	148	15	.934
1992—New York (A.L.)	S-3-O-2		121	412	57	112	24	1	7	46	.272	38	78	7	179	257	15	.967
1993—New York (A.L.)	...OF-SS-3B-DH		85	226	28	68	13	2	7	24	.301	18	39	2	102	92	9	.956
—Alb./Colonie (East.)	SS-OF-DH		5	17	2	4	0	0	1	2	.235	2	2	0	6	12	2	.900
1994—New York (A.L.)	SS-3B-OF-2B		77	280	47	78	16	1	9	34	.279	22	61	4	92	188	19	.936
1995—New York (A.L.)	2-S-O-3		111	367	60	102	19	1	7	46	.278	55	64	5	168	258	10	.977
1996—California (A.L.)■.	2B-3B-SS		136	530	82	151	27	3	14	54	.285	70	118	7	255	306	16	.972
1997—Anaheim (A.L.)	PR		1	0	0	0	0	0	0	0	...	0	0	0	...	...	...	...
1998—Lake Elsinore (Calif.)	2B		5	20	6	11	2	1	1	7	.550	2	0	1	10	18	1	.966
—Anaheim (A.L.)	2B		51	188	29	49	13	1	4	26	.261	34	42	7	88	132	4	.982
—Vancouver (PCL)	2B-DH		4	16	0	4	2	0	0	2	.250	1	4	1	3	7	0	1.000
1999—Anaheim (A.L.)	2B		95	376	57	115	15	4	9	48	.306	43	56	13	191	§307	7	.986
—Oakland (A.L.)■	2B		61	255	48	85	10	3	7	28	.333	27	42	11	107	§186	7	.977
Major League totals (13 years)			1002	3284	479	911	164	21	77	364	.277	360	640	60	1422	2212	128	.966

DIVISION SERIES RECORD

							BATTING								FIELDING		
Year	Team (League)	Pos.	G	AB	R	H	2B	3B	HR	RBI	Avg.	BB	SO	SB	PO	A	E	Avg.
1995—New York (A.L.)	2B-3B-OF		5	17	3	3	0	0	0	1	.176	6	4	0	15	11	1	.963

VENAFRO, MIKE   P   RANGERS

PERSONAL: Born August 2, 1973, in Takoma Park, Md. ... 5-10/180. ... Throws left, bats left. ... Full name: Michael R. Venafro.
HIGH SCHOOL: Paul VI (Fairfax, Va.).
TRANSACTIONS/CAREER NOTES: Selected by Texas Rangers organization in 29th round of free-agent draft (June 1, 1995).

Year	League	W	L	Pct.	ERA	G	GS	CG	ShO	Sv.	IP	H	R	ER	BB	SO
1995—Hudson Valley (NY-P)		9	1	.900	2.13	32	0	0	0	2	$50^{2/3}$	37	13	12	21	32
1996—Charleston, S.C. (SAL)		1	3	.250	3.51	50	0	0	0	19	59	57	27	23	21	62
1997—Charlotte (FSL)		4	2	.667	3.43	35	0	0	0	10	$44^{2/3}$	51	17	17	21	35
—Tulsa (Texas)		0	1	.000	3.45	11	0	0	0	1	$15^{2/3}$	13	12	6	12	13
1998—Tulsa (Texas)		3	4	.429	3.10	46	0	0	0	14	$52^{1/3}$	42	21	18	26	45
—Oklahoma (PCL)		0	0	...	6.35	13	0	0	0	0	17	19	12	12	10	15
1999—Oklahoma (PCL)		0	0	...	5.40	6	0	0	0	1	$11^{2/3}$	16	7	7	0	7
—Texas (A.L.)		3	2	.600	3.29	65	0	0	0	0	$68^{1/3}$	63	29	25	22	37
Major League totals (1 year)		3	2	.600	3.29	65	0	0	0	0	$68^{1/3}$	63	29	25	22	37

DIVISION SERIES RECORD

Year	League	W	L	Pct.	ERA	G	GS	CG	ShO	Sv.	IP	H	R	ER	BB	SO
1999—Texas (A.L.)		0	0	...	0.00	2	0	0	0	0	1	2	2	0	1	0

VENTURA, ROBIN   3B   METS

PERSONAL: Born July 14, 1967, in Santa Maria, Calif. ... 6-1/198. ... Bats left, throws right. ... Full name: Robin Mark Ventura.
HIGH SCHOOL: Righetti (Santa Maria, Calif.).
COLLEGE: Oklahoma State.
TRANSACTIONS/CAREER NOTES: Selected by Chicago White Sox organization in first round (10th pick overall) of free-agent draft (June 1, 1988). ... On suspended list (August 23-25, 1993). ... On disabled list (March 31-July 24, 1997); included rehabilitation assignments to Nashville (July 13-17) and Birmingham (July 18-22). ... Granted free agency (October 23, 1998). ... Signed by New York Mets (December 1, 1998).

RECORDS: Holds A.L. single-season record for fewest chances accepted by third baseman for leader—372 (1996). ... Shares major league single-season record for highest fielding average by third baseman (150 or more games)—.980 (1999). ... Shares major league single-game record for most grand slams—2 (September 4, 1995).

HONORS: Named College Player of the Year by THE SPORTING NEWS (1987-88). ... Named third baseman on THE SPORTING NEWS college All-America team (1987-88). ... Named Golden Spikes Award winner by USA Baseball (1988). ... Won A.L. Gold Glove at third base (1991-93, 1996 and 1998). ... Won N.L. Gold Glove at third base (1999).

STATISTICAL NOTES: Led Southern League with 12 intentional bases on balls received in 1989. ... Led Southern League third basemen with .930 fielding percentage and tied for lead with 21 double plays in 1989. ... Led A.L. third basemen with 18 errors in 1991. ... Led A.L. third basemen in putouts with 134 in 1991, 141 in 1992 and 133 in 1996. ... Led A.L. third basemen in total chances with 536 in 1992, 404 in 1993 and 382 in 1996. ... Led A.L. third basemen with 372 assists and tied for lead in double plays with 29 in 1992. ... Led A.L. third basemen in double plays with 22 in 1994 and 34 in 1996 and tied for lead with 29 in 1992. ... Led A.L. with 15 intentional bases on balls in 1998. ... Led A.L. third basemen with 447 total chances and 38 double plays in 1998. ... Led N.L. third basemen with 320 assists, 452 total chances and .980 fielding percentage in 1999. ... Career major league grand slams: 13.

MISCELLANEOUS: Member of 1988 U.S. Olympic baseball team.

						BATTING									FIELDING		
Year Team (League)	Pos.	G	AB	R	H	2B	3B	HR	RBI	Avg.	BB	SO	SB	PO	A	E	Avg.
1989—Birmingham (Sou.)....	3B-1B-2B	129	454	75	126	25	2	3	67	.278	93	51	9	108	249	27	†.930
—Chicago (A.L.)...........	3B	16	45	5	8	3	0	0	7	.178	8	6	0	17	33	2	.962
1990—Chicago (A.L.)...........	3B-1B	150	493	48	123	17	1	5	54	.249	55	53	1	116	268	25	.939
1991—Chicago (A.L.)...........	3B-1B	157	606	92	172	25	1	23	100	.284	80	67	2	†225	291	†18	.966
1992—Chicago (A.L.)...........	3B-1B	157	592	85	167	38	1	16	93	.282	93	71	2	†141	†375	23	.957
1993—Chicago (A.L.)...........	3B-1B	157	554	85	145	27	1	22	94	.262	105	82	1	119	278	14	.966
1994—Chicago (A.L.)...........	3B-1B-SS	109	401	57	113	15	1	18	78	.282	61	69	3	89	180	20	.931
1995—Chicago (A.L.)...........	3B-1B-DH	135	492	79	145	22	0	26	93	.295	75	98	4	201	216	19	.956
1996—Chicago (A.L.)...........	3B-1B	158	586	96	168	31	2	34	105	.287	78	81	1	†189	247	11	.975
1997—Nashville (A.A.)........	3B-DH	5	15	3	6	1	0	2	5	.400	2	1	0	1	12	0	1.000
—Birmingham (Sou.).....	3B	4	17	3	5	1	0	1	2	.294	1	1	0	2	3	2	.714
—Chicago (A.L.)...........	3B	54	183	27	48	10	1	6	26	.262	34	21	0	53	99	7	.956
1998—Chicago (A.L.) ■......	3B	161	590	84	155	31	4	21	91	.263	79	111	1	102	*330	15	.966
1999—New York (N.L.)■......	3B-1B	161	588	88	177	38	0	32	120	.301	74	109	1	124	†320	9	†.980
American League totals (10 years)		1254	4542	658	1244	219	12	171	741	.274	668	659	15	1252	2317	154	.959
National League totals (1 year)		161	588	88	177	38	0	32	120	.301	74	109	1	124	320	9	.980
Major League totals (11 years)		1415	5130	746	1421	257	12	203	861	.277	742	768	16	1376	2637	163	.961

DIVISION SERIES RECORD

						BATTING									FIELDING		
Year Team (League)	Pos.	G	AB	R	H	2B	3B	HR	RBI	Avg.	BB	SO	SB	PO	A	E	Avg.
1999—New York (N.L.)..........	3B	4	14	1	3	2	0	0	1	.214	4	2	0	3	8	0	1.000

CHAMPIONSHIP SERIES RECORD

						BATTING									FIELDING		
Year Team (League)	Pos.	G	AB	R	H	2B	3B	HR	RBI	Avg.	BB	SO	SB	PO	A	E	Avg.
1993—Chicago (A.L.)	3B-1B	6	20	2	4	0	0	1	5	.200	6	6	0	9	6	1	.938
1999—New York (N.L.)...........	3B	6	25	2	3	1	0	0	1	.120	2	5	0	5	16	0	1.000
Championship series totals (2 years)		12	45	4	7	1	0	1	6	.156	8	11	0	14	22	1	.973

ALL-STAR GAME RECORD

					BATTING								FIELDING		
Year League	Pos.	AB	R	H	2B	3B	HR	RBI	Avg.	BB	SO	SB	PO	A	E	Avg.
1992—American..................	3B	2	1	2	1	0	0	1	1.000	0	0	0	1	1	0	1.000

VERAS, QUILVIO — 2B — BRAVES

PERSONAL: Born April 3, 1971, in Santo Domingo, Dominican Republic. ... 5-10/183. ... Bats both, throws right. ... Full name: Quilvio Alberto Perez Veras.

HIGH SCHOOL: Victor E. Liz (Santo Domingo, Dominican Republic).

TRANSACTIONS/CAREER NOTES: Signed as non-drafted free agent by New York Mets organization (November 22, 1989). ... On suspended list (July 31-August 2, 1994). ... On disabled list (August 7-15, 1994). ... Traded by Mets to Florida Marlins for OF Carl Everett (November 29, 1994). ... On Florida disabled list (May 10-June 21, 1996); included rehabilitation assignment to Charlotte (June 13-21). ... Traded by Marlins to San Diego Padres for P Dustin Hermanson (November 21, 1996). ... On disabled list (August 8-23). ... Traded by Padres with 1B Wally Joyner and OF Reggie Sanders to Atlanta Braves for OF/1B Ryan Klesko, 2B Bret Boone and P Jason Shiell (December 22, 1999).

STATISTICAL NOTES: Tied for Appalachian League lead in double plays by second baseman with 30 in 1991. ... Led Appalachian League second basemen with 282 total chances in 1991. ... Led South Atlantic League in on-base percentage with .441 and in caught stealing with 35 in 1992. ... Led Eastern League in on-base percentage .430 and in caught stealing with 19 in 1993. ... Led Eastern League second basemen with 669 total chances in 1993. ... Led International League in caught stealing with 18 in 1994. ... Led International League second basemen with 589 total chances and 84 double plays in 1994. ... Led N.L. in caught stealing with 21 in 1995. ... Career major league grand slams: 1.

						BATTING									FIELDING		
Year Team (League)	Pos.	G	AB	R	H	2B	3B	HR	RBI	Avg.	BB	SO	SB	PO	A	E	Avg.
1990—GC Mets (GCL)..........	2B	30	98	26	29	3	3	1	5	.296	19	16	16	45	76	3	.976
—Kingsport (Appal.)......	2B	24	94	21	36	6	0	1	14	.383	13	14	9	55	79	8	.944
1991—Kingsport (Appal.)......	2B	64	226	*54	76	11	4	1	16	.336	36	28	38	*113	*161	8	.972
—Pittsfield (NY-P)......	2B-SS	5	15	3	4	0	1	0	2	.267	5	1	2	16	16	1	.970
1992—Columbia (SAL).........	2B	117	414	97	132	24	10	2	40	*.319	84	52	*66	208	313	20	.963
1993—Binghamton (East.) ...	2B	128	444	87	136	19	7	2	51	.306	*91	62	52	*274	*372	23	.966
1994—Norfolk (I.L.).............	2B-DH	123	457	71	114	22	4	0	43	.249	59	56	40	*267	*308	*14	.976
1995—Florida (N.L.)■..........	2B-OF	124	440	86	115	20	7	5	32	.261	80	68	*56	299	315	9	.986
1996—Florida (N.L.)	2B	73	253	40	64	8	1	4	14	.253	51	42	8	174	191	5	.986
—Charlotte (I.L.)........	2B-DH	28	104	22	34	5	2	2	8	.327	13	14	8	44	66	3	.973
1997—San Diego (N.L.)■	2B	145	539	74	143	23	1	3	45	.265	72	84	33	276	407	11	.984
1998—San Diego (N.L.)	2B	138	517	79	138	24	2	6	45	.267	84	78	24	258	405	9	.987
1999—San Diego (N.L.)	2B	132	475	95	133	25	2	6	41	.280	65	88	30	271	334	12	.981
Major League totals (5 years)		612	2224	374	593	100	13	24	177	.267	352	360	151	1278	1652	46	.985

Year Team (League)	Pos.	G	AB	R	H	2B	3B	HR	RBI	Avg.	BB	SO	SB	PO	A	E	Avg.
1998—San Diego (N.L.)	2B	4	15	1	2	0	0	0	0	.133	1	6	0	8	12	0	1.000

CHAMPIONSHIP SERIES RECORD

Year Team (League)	Pos.	G	AB	R	H	2B	3B	HR	RBI	Avg.	BB	SO	SB	PO	A	E	Avg.
1998—San Diego (N.L.)	2B	6	24	2	6	1	0	0	2	.250	5	7	0	7	13	0	1.000

WORLD SERIES RECORD

Year Team (League)	Pos.	G	AB	R	H	2B	3B	HR	RBI	Avg.	BB	SO	SB	PO	A	E	Avg.
1998—San Diego (N.L.)	2B	4	15	3	3	2	0	0	1	.200	3	4	0	9	16	0	1.000

VERAS, WILTON   3B   RED SOX

PERSONAL: Born January 19, 1978, in Monte Cristi, Dominican Republic. ... 6-2/198. ... Bats right, throws right. ... Full name: Wilton Andres Veras.
HIGH SCHOOL: Monte Cristi (Dominican Republic).
TRANSACTIONS/CAREER NOTES: Signed as non-drafted free agent by Boston Red Sox organization (February 9, 1995).
STATISTICAL NOTES: Led New York-Pennsylvania League in grounding into double plays with nine in 1996. ... Led Midwest League third basemen with 29 double plays in 1997. ... Led Midwest League in grounding into double plays with 19 in 1997. ... Led Eastern League third basemen with 377 total chances in 1998. ... Led Eastern League in grounding into double plays with 23 in 1999. ... Led Eastern League third basemen with 27 double plays in 1999.

Year Team (League)	Pos.	G	AB	R	H	2B	3B	HR	RBI	Avg.	BB	SO	SB	PO	A	E	Avg.
1995—GC Red Sox (GCL)	1B-3B	31	91	7	24	1	0	0	5	.264	7	9	1	80	2	1	.988
1996—Lowell (NY-P)	3B	67	250	22	60	15	0	0	19	.240	13	29	2	*57	106	12	.931
1997—Michigan (Midw.)	3B	131	489	51	141	21	3	8	68	.288	31	51	3	99	220	19	*.944
1998—Trenton (East.)	3B	126	470	70	137	27	4	16	67	.291	15	66	5	*100	*259	18	*.952
1999—Trenton (East.)	3B-DH	116	474	65	133	23	2	11	75	.281	23	55	7	83	*245	19	.945
—Boston (A.L.)	3B	36	119	14	34	5	1	2	13	.286	5	14	0	23	56	6	.929
Major League totals (1 year)		36	119	14	34	5	1	2	13	.286	5	14	0	23	56	6	.929

DIVISION SERIES RECORD

Year Team (League)	Pos.	G	AB	R	H	2B	3B	HR	RBI	Avg.	BB	SO	SB	PO	A	E	Avg.
1999—Boston (A.L.)								Did not play.									

CHAMPIONSHIP SERIES RECORD

Year Team (League)	Pos.	G	AB	R	H	2B	3B	HR	RBI	Avg.	BB	SO	SB	PO	A	E	Avg.
1999—Boston (A.L.)								Did not play.									

VERES, DAVE   P   CARDINALS

PERSONAL: Born October 19, 1966, in Montgomery, Ala. ... 6-2/220. ... Throws right, bats right. ... Full name: David Scott Veres. ... Name pronounced VEERZ.
HIGH SCHOOL: Gresham (Ore.).
JUNIOR COLLEGE: Mount Hood Community College (Ore.).
TRANSACTIONS/CAREER NOTES: Selected by Oakland Athletics organization in fourth round of free-agent draft (January 14, 1986). ... Traded by A's to Los Angeles Dodgers for P Kevin Campbell (January 15, 1991). ... Loaned by Dodgers organization to Mexico City Tigers of Mexican League (April 3-May 15, 1992). ... Released by Dodgers (May 15, 1992). ... Signed by Houston Astros organization (May 28, 1992). ... Traded by Astros with C Raul Chavez to Montreal Expos for 3B Sean Berry (December 20, 1995). ... On disabled list (August 21-September 17, 1997). ... Traded by Expos with a player to be named later to Colorado Rockies for OF Terry Jones and a player to be named later (December 10, 1997). ... Traded by Rockies with P Darryl Kile and P Luther Hackman to St, Louis Cardinals for P Jose Jimenez, P Manny Aybar, P Rick Croushore and SS Brent Butler (November 16, 1999).
STATISTICAL NOTES: Tied for California League lead with 29 wild pitches in 1987. ... Led Southern League with 16 wild pitches in 1989.
MISCELLANEOUS: Made an out in only appearance as pinch hitter (1998).

Year League	W	L	Pct.	ERA	G	GS	CG	ShO	Sv.	IP	H	R	ER	BB	SO
1986—Medford (N'west)	5	2	.714	3.26	15	•15	0	0	0	77 1/3	58	38	28	57	60
1987—Modesto (Calif.)	8	9	.471	4.79	26	26	2	0	0	148 1/3	124	90	79	108	124
1988—Modesto (Calif.)	4	11	.267	3.31	19	19	3	0	0	125	100	61	46	78	91
—Huntsville (Sou.)	3	4	.429	4.15	8	8	0	0	0	39	50	20	18	15	17
1989—Huntsville (Sou.)	8	11	.421	4.86	29	28	2	1	0	159 1/3	160	93	86	83	105
1990—Tacoma (PCL)	11	8	.579	4.69	32	23	2	0	1	151 2/3	136	90	79	88	88
1991—Albuquerque (PCL)■	7	6	.538	4.47	57	3	0	0	5	100 2/3	89	52	50	52	81
1992—M.C. Tigers (Mex.)■	1	5	.167	8.10	14	1	0	0	1	23 1/3	29	21	21	12	12
—Tucson (PCL)■	2	3	.400	5.30	29	1	0	0	0	52 2/3	60	36	31	17	46
1993—Tucson (PCL)	6	10	.375	4.90	43	15	1	0	5	130 1/3	156	88	71	32	122
1994—Tucson (PCL)	1	1	.500	1.88	16	0	0	0	1	24	17	8	5	10	19
—Houston (N.L.)	3	3	.500	2.41	32	0	0	0	1	41	39	13	11	7	28
1995—Houston (N.L.)	5	1	.833	2.26	72	0	0	0	1	103 1/3	89	29	26	30	94
1996—Montreal (N.L.)■	6	3	.667	4.17	68	0	0	0	4	77 2/3	85	39	36	32	81
1997—Montreal (N.L.)	2	3	.400	3.48	53	0	0	0	1	62	68	28	24	27	47
1998—Colorado (N.L.)■	3	1	.750	2.83	63	0	0	0	8	76 1/3	67	26	24	27	74
1999—Colorado (N.L.)	4	8	.333	5.14	73	0	0	0	31	77	88	46	44	37	71
Major League totals (6 years)	23	19	.548	3.40	361	0	0	0	46	437 1/3	436	181	165	160	395

VIDRO, JOSE — 2B — EXPOS

PERSONAL: Born August 27, 1974, in Mayaguez, Puerto Rico. ... 5-11/190. ... Bats both, throws right. ... Full name: Jose Angel Cetty Vidro.
HIGH SCHOOL: Blanco Morales (Sabana Grande, Puerto Rico).
TRANSACTIONS/CAREER NOTES: Selected by Montreal Expos organization in sixth round of free agent draft (June 1, 1992). ... On disabled list (June 1-15 and July 26, 1993-remainder of season).
STATISTICAL NOTES: Career major league grand slams: 1.

								BATTING							FIELDING		
Year Team (League)	Pos.	G	AB	R	H	2B	3B	HR	RBI	Avg.	BB	SO	SB	PO	A	E	Avg.
1992— GC Expos (GCL)	2B	54	200	29	66	6	2	4	31	.330	16	31	10	114	107	4	*.982
1993— Burlington (Midw.)	2B	76	287	39	69	19	0	2	34	.240	28	54	3	107	153	7	.974
1994— W.P. Beach (FSL).......	2B	125	465	57	124	30	2	4	49	.267	51	56	8	204	328	20	.964
1995— W.P. Beach (FSL).......	IF	44	163	20	53	15	2	3	24	.325	8	21	0	101	110	4	.981
— Harrisburg (East.)......	IF	64	246	33	64	16	2	4	38	.260	20	37	7	97	162	9	.966
1996— Harrisburg (East.)......	IF	126	452	57	117	25	3	18	82	.259	29	71	3	135	271	15	.964
1997— Ottawa (I.L.)	3B-2B-DH	73	279	40	90	17	0	13	47	.323	22	40	2	70	161	8	.967
— Montreal (N.L.)...........	3B-DH-2B	67	169	19	42	12	1	2	17	.249	11	20	1	25	59	4	.955
1998— Montreal (N.L.)..........	2B-3B	83	205	24	45	12	0	0	18	.220	27	33	2	81	126	6	.972
— Ottawa (I.L.)	2B-3B-DH	63	235	35	68	14	2	2	32	.289	24	25	5	91	124	6	.973
1999— Montreal (N.L.)..........	2-1-0-3	140	494	67	150	45	2	12	59	.304	29	51	0	270	296	11	.981
Major League totals (3 years)		290	868	110	237	69	3	14	94	.273	67	104	3	376	481	21	.976

VILLAFUERTE, BRANDON — P — TIGERS

PERSONAL: Born December 17, 1975, in Hilo, Hawaii. ... 5-11/165. ... Throws right, bats right. ... Full name: Brandon Paul Villafuerte.
HIGH SCHOOL: Live Oak (Morgan Hill, Calif.).
JUNIOR COLLEGE: West Valley College (Calif.).
TRANSACTIONS/CAREER NOTES: Selected by New York Mets organization 66th round of free-agent draft (June 2, 1994). ... Traded by Mets with a player to be named later to Florida Marlins for OF Robert Stratton (March 20,1998); Marlins acquired 2B Cesar Crespo to complete deal (September 14, 1998). ... Traded by Marlins to Detroit Tigers for P Mike Drumright (July 31, 1999).

Year League	W	L	Pct.	ERA	G	GS	CG	ShO	Sv.	IP	H	R	ER	BB	SO
1995— Little Falls (NY-P)	5	1	.833	5.63	20	0	0	0	0	32	28	21	20	26	42
1996— Pittsfield (NY-P)	8	3	.727	3.02	18	7	1	0	1	62 2/3	53	21	21	27	59
1997— Capital City (SAL).............	3	1	.750	2.38	47	3	0	0	7	75 2/3	58	23	20	33	88
1998— Brevard County (FSL)■......	1	0	1.000	0.93	3	0	0	0	0	9 2/3	7	3	1	1	6
— Portland (East.)	0	2	.000	4.97	30	0	0	0	1	54 1/3	68	35	30	33	52
— Charlotte (I.L.)	1	0	1.000	6.35	10	0	0	0	0	11 1/3	15	8	8	8	9
1999— Portland (East.)	6	8	.429	3.50	22	12	0	0	0	100 1/3	97	45	39	40	85
— Jacksonville (Sou.)■.........	0	2	.000	1.88	15	0	0	0	5	24	17	6	5	12	20

VILLEGAS, ISMAEL — P — BRAVES

PERSONAL: Born August 12, 1976, in Rio Piedras, Puerto Rico. ... 6-1/188. ... Throws right, bats right.
HIGH SCHOOL: Magarita Janer Palacios (Guaynabo, Puerto Rico).
TRANSACTIONS/CAREER NOTES: Selected by Chicago Cubs in fifth round of free-agent draft (June 1, 1995). ... Traded by Cubs to Atlanta Braves for C Tyler Houston (July 27, 1996).

Year League	W	L	Pct.	ERA	G	GS	CG	ShO	Sv.	IP	H	R	ER	BB	SO
1995— Gulf Coast Cubs (GCL).......	3	2	.600	2.40	11	10	0	0	0	41 1/3	33	17	11	11	26
1996— Rockford (Midw.)	2	5	.286	5.13	10	10	1	0	0	47 1/3	63	40	27	25	30
— Williamsport (NY-P)	0	0	...	2.57	2	2	0	0	0	7	7	3	2	4	5
— Danville (Appl.)■	0	0	...	3.00	1	0	0	0	0	3	2	1	1	1	4
— Macon (SAL)	3	7	.300	5.00	12	12	2	1	0	72	80	46	40	19	60
1997— Durham (Caro.)	2	5	.286	5.07	30	1	0	0	1	55	60	33	31	32	44
1998— Greenville (Sou.)	7	6	.538	5.28	40	17	1	0	3	124 1/3	134	78	73	71	120
1999— Richmond (I.L.)................	6	7	.462	4.40	44	2	0	0	1	92	93	51	45	39	61

VILLONE, RON — P — REDS

PERSONAL: Born January 16, 1970, in Englewood, N.J. ... 6-3/237. ... Throws left, bats left. ... Full name: Ronald Thomas Villone Jr.
HIGH SCHOOL: South Bergenfield (Bergenfield, N.J.).
COLLEGE: Massachusetts.
TRANSACTIONS/CAREER NOTES: Selected by Seattle Mariners in first round (14th pick overall) of free-agent draft (June 1, 1992). ... On disabled list (April 19-26, 1994). ... Traded by Mariners with OF Marc Newfield to San Diego Padres for P Andy Benes and a player to be named later (July 31, 1995); Mariners acquired P Greg Keagle to complete deal (September 16, 1995). ... Traded by Padres with P Bryce Florie and OF Marc Newfield to Milwaukee Brewers for OF Greg Vaughn and a player to be named later (July 31, 1996); Padres acquired OF Gerald Parent to complete deal (September 16, 1996). ... Traded by Brewers with P Ben McDonald and P Mike Fetters to Cleveland Indians for OF Marquis Grissom and P Jeff Juden (December 8, 1997). ... On Cleveland disabled list (August 15-September 1, 1998); included rehabilitation assignment to Buffalo (August 22-September 1). ... Released by Indians (April 2, 1999). ... Signed by Cincinnati Reds organization (April 5, 1999).
STATISTICAL NOTES: Tied for N.L. lead in errors by a pitcher with six in 1999.
MISCELLANEOUS: Member of 1992 U.S. Olympic baseball team.

Year League	W	L	Pct.	ERA	G	GS	CG	ShO	Sv.	IP	H	R	ER	BB	SO
1993— Riverside (Calif.)................	7	4	.636	4.21	16	16	0	0	0	83 1/3	74	47	39	62	82
— Jacksonville (Sou.)............	3	4	.429	4.38	11	11	0	0	0	63 2/3	49	34	31	41	66
1994— Jacksonville (Sou.)............	6	7	.462	3.86	41	5	0	0	8	79 1/3	56	37	34	68	94

Year	League	W	L	Pct.	ERA	G	GS	CG	ShO	Sv.	IP	H	R	ER	BB	SO
1995— Seattle (A.L.)		0	2	.000	7.91	19	0	0	0	0	19 1/3	20	19	17	23	26
— Tacoma (PCL)		1	0	1.000	0.61	22	0	0	0	13	29 2/3	9	6	2	19	43
— San Diego (N.L.)■		2	1	.667	4.21	19	0	0	0	1	25 2/3	24	12	12	11	37
1996— Las Vegas (PCL)		2	1	.667	1.64	23	0	0	0	3	22	13	5	4	9	29
— San Diego (N.L.)		1	1	.500	2.95	21	0	0	0	0	18 1/3	17	6	6	7	19
— Milwaukee (A.L.)■		0	0	...	3.28	23	0	0	0	2	24 2/3	14	9	9	18	19
1997— Milwaukee (A.L.)		1	0	1.000	3.42	50	0	0	0	0	52 2/3	54	23	20	36	40
1998— Buffalo (I.L.)■		2	2	.500	2.01	23	0	0	0	7	22 1/3	20	11	5	11	28
— Cleveland (A.L.)		0	0	...	6.00	25	0	0	0	0	27	30	18	18	22	15
1999— Indianapolis (I.L.)■		2	0	1.000	1.42	18	0	0	0	1	19	9	3	3	13	23
— Cincinnati (N.L.)		9	7	.563	4.23	29	22	0	0	2	142 2/3	114	70	67	73	97
A.L. totals (4 years)		1	2	.333	4.66	117	0	0	0	2	123 2/3	118	69	64	99	100
N.L. totals (3 years)		12	9	.571	4.10	69	22	0	0	3	186 2/3	155	88	85	91	153
Major League totals (5 years)		13	11	.542	4.32	186	22	0	0	5	310 1/3	273	157	149	190	253

VINA, FERNANDO — 2B — CARDINALS

PERSONAL: Born April 16, 1969, in Sacramento. ... 5-9/170. ... Bats left, throws right. ... Name pronounced VEEN-ya.
HIGH SCHOOL: Valley (Sacramento).
JUNIOR COLLEGE: Cosumnes River College (Calif.), then Sacramento City College.
COLLEGE: Arizona State.
TRANSACTIONS/CAREER NOTES: Selected by New York Yankees organization in 51st round of free-agent draft (June 1, 1988); did not sign. ... Selected by New York Mets organization in ninth round of free-agent draft (June 4, 1990). ... Selected by Seattle Mariners from Mets organization in Rule 5 major league draft (December 7, 1992). ... Returned to Mets organization (June 15, 1993). ... On New York disabled list (May 22-June 6, 1994). ... On Norfolk disabled list (August 30-September 6, 1994). ... Traded by Mets to Milwaukee Brewers (December 22, 1994), completing deal in which Brewers traded P Doug Henry for two players to be named later (November 30, 1994); Brewers acquired C Javier Gonzalez as partial completion of deal (December 6, 1994). ... On Milwaukee disabled list (April 20-July 17, 1997); included rehabilitation assignments to Stockton (July 9-11) and Tucson (July 12-17). ... On suspended list (May 11-13 and May 25-27, 1999). ... On Milwaukee disabled list (May 10-25 and June 4, 1999-remainder of season); included rehabilitation assignment to Beloit (August 6-8). ... Traded by Brewers to St. Louis Cardinals for P Juan Acevedo and two players to be named later (December 20, 1999).
STATISTICAL NOTES: Tied for South Atlantic League lead in caught stealing with 22 in 1991. ... Led South Atlantic League second basemen with 600 total chances and 61 double plays in 1991. ... Led Florida State League second basemen with 85 double plays in 1992. ... Led N.L. in being hit by pitch with 12 in 1994. ... Led A.L. second basemen with 116 double plays in 1996. ... Led N.L. second basemen with 884 total chances and 135 double plays in 1998. ... Career major league grand slams: 1.

Year	Team (League)	Pos.	G	AB	R	H	2B	3B	HR	RBI	Avg.	BB	SO	SB	PO	A	E	Avg.
1991— Columbia (SAL)		2B	129	498	77	135	23	6	6	50	.271	46	27	42	194	*385	21	*.965
1992— St. Lucie (FSL)		2B	111	421	61	124	15	5	1	42	.295	32	26	36	219	*360	17	.971
— Tidewater (I.L.)		2B	11	30	3	6	0	0	0	2	.200	0	2	0	16	28	1	.978
1993— Seattle (A.L.)■	2B-SS-DH	24	45	5	10	2	0	0	2	.222	4	3	6	28	40	0	1.000
— Norfolk (I.L.)■	SS-2B-DH-OF	73	287	24	66	6	4	4	27	.230	7	17	16	146	232	14	.964
1994— New York (N.L.)	2B-SS-SS-OF	79	124	20	31	6	0	0	6	.250	12	11	3	46	59	4	.963
— Norfolk (I.L.)	SS-2B	6	17	2	3	0	0	0	1	.176	1	1	1	9	11	1	.952
1995— Milwaukee (A.L.)■	2B-SS-3B	113	288	46	74	7	7	3	29	.257	22	28	6	194	245	8	.982
1996— Milwaukee (A.L.)		2B	140	554	94	157	19	10	7	46	.283	38	35	16	*333	412	*16	.979
1997— Milwaukee (A.L.)	2B-DH	79	324	37	89	12	2	4	28	.275	12	23	8	149	227	7	.982
— Stockton (Calif.)		2B	3	9	2	4	0	1	0	3	.444	0	0	0	2	7	0	1.000
— Tucson (PCL)		2B	6	19	3	9	3	0	1	5	.474	3	1	0	8	16	2	.923
1998— Milwaukee (N.L.)		2B	159	637	101	198	39	7	7	45	.311	54	46	22	404	468	12	.986
1999— Milwaukee (N.L.)		2B	37	154	17	41	7	0	1	16	.266	14	6	5	84	104	1	.995
— Beloit (Midw.)	DH-2B	2	10	1	2	1	0	0	0	.200	0	2	0	0	2	2	.500
American League totals (4 years)			356	1211	182	330	40	19	14	105	.273	76	89	36	704	924	31	.981
National League totals (3 years)			275	915	138	270	52	7	8	67	.295	80	63	30	534	631	17	.986
Major League totals (7 years)			631	2126	320	600	92	26	22	172	.282	156	152	66	1238	1555	48	.983

ALL-STAR GAME RECORD

Year	League	Pos.	AB	R	H	2B	3B	HR	RBI	Avg.	BB	SO	SB	PO	A	E	Avg.
1998— National	2B	1	0	1	0	0	0	0	1.000	1	0	0	1	1	1	.667

VITIELLO, JOE — 1B/3B — PADRES

PERSONAL: Born April 11, 1970, in Cambridge, Mass. ... 6-3/230. ... Bats right, throws right. ... Full name: Joseph David Vitiello. ... Name pronounced VIT-ee-ELL-oh.
HIGH SCHOOL: Stoneham (Mass.).
COLLEGE: Alabama.
TRANSACTIONS/CAREER NOTES: Selected by New York Yankees organization in 31st round of free-agent draft (June 1, 1988); did not sign. ... Selected by Kansas City Royals organization in first round (seventh pick overall) of free-agent draft (June 3, 1991). ... On disabled list (April 12-23, 1992; June 2-11, 1993; and May 23-June 16, 1994). ... On disabled list (June 17-July 28 and August 13, 1997-remainder of season); included rehabilitation assignment to Omaha (July 15-28). ... On Kansas City disabled list (April 8-May 18, 1998); included rehabilitation assignment to Omaha (April 21-May 9). ... On Omaha disabled list (August 4-12, 1998). ... Granted free agency (October 15, 1998). ... Re-signed by Royals organization (December 17, 1998). ... Granted free agency (October 8, 1999). ... Signed by San Diego Padres organization (November 22, 1999).
STATISTICAL NOTES: Led American Association with .440 on-base percentage in 1994.

Year	Team (League)	Pos.	G	AB	R	H	2B	3B	HR	RBI	Avg.	BB	SO	SB	PO	A	E	Avg.
1991— Eugene (N'west)	OF-1B	19	64	16	21	2	0	6	21	.328	11	18	1	49	4	1	.981
— Memphis (Sou.)	OF-1B	36	128	15	28	4	1	0	18	.219	23	36	0	77	4	1	.988

V

Year	Team (League)	Pos.	G	AB	R	H	2B	3B	HR	RBI	Avg.	BB	SO	SB	PO	A	E	Avg.
1992—Baseball City (FSL)....	1B	115	400	52	113	16	1	8	65	.283	46	101	0	879	44	13	.986
1993—Memphis (Sou.)........	1B	117	413	62	119	25	2	15	66	.288	57	95	2	830	53	•17	.981
1994—Omaha (A.A.)...........	1B-DH	98	352	46	121	28	3	10	61	*.344	56	63	3	605	46	8	.988
1995—Kansas City (A.L.).....	DH-1B	53	130	13	33	4	0	7	21	.254	8	25	0	51	3	1	.982
—Omaha (A.A.)..............	DH-1B-OF	59	229	33	64	14	2	12	42	.279	12	50	0	225	21	4	.984
1996—Kansas City (A.L.)....	DH-1B-OF	85	257	29	62	15	1	8	40	.241	38	69	2	40	5	0	1.000
—Omaha (A.A.)..............	1B	36	132	26	37	7	0	9	31	.280	16	32	1	281	20	3	.990
1997—Kansas City (A.L.)....	OF-DH-1B	51	130	11	31	6	0	5	18	.238	14	37	0	56	0	1	.982
—Omaha (A.A.)..............	DH-OF	13	42	5	9	1	0	3	9	.214	5	16	0	1	0	0	1.000
1998—Kansas City (A.L.)....	DH	3	7	0	1	0	0	0	0	.143	1	2	0	...	...	...	...
—Omaha (PCL).............	1B-DH-3B	103	376	44	107	20	2	18	71	.285	39	68	0	738	56	8	.990
1999—Omaha (PCL).............	DH-1B	122	447	70	142	33	0	28	98	.318	66	84	3	289	21	6	.981
—Kansas City (A.L.).....	1B-DH	13	41	4	6	1	0	1	4	.146	2	9	0	65	7	0	1.000
Major League totals (5 years)		205	565	57	133	26	1	21	83	.235	63	142	2	212	15	2	.991

VIZCAINO, JOSE — SS — DODGERS

PERSONAL: Born March 26, 1968, in San Cristoban, Dominican Republic. ... 6-1/180. ... Bats both, throws right. ... Full name: Jose Luis Pimental Vizcaino. ... Name pronounced VIS-ky-EE-no.

HIGH SCHOOL: Americo Tolentino (Palenque de San Cristobal, Dominican Republic).

TRANSACTIONS/CAREER NOTES: Signed as non-drafted free agent by Los Angeles Dodgers organization (February 18, 1986). ... Traded by Dodgers to Chicago Cubs for IF Greg Smith (December 14, 1990). ... On disabled list (April 20-May 6 and August 26-September 16, 1992). ... Traded by Cubs to New York Mets for P Anthony Young and P Ottis Smith (March 30, 1994). ... Traded by Mets with IF Jeff Kent to Cleveland Indians for 2B Carlos Baerga and IF Alvaro Espinoza (July 29, 1996). ... Traded by Indians with IF Jeff Kent, P Julian Tavarez and a player to be named later to San Francisco Giants for 3B Matt Williams and a player to be named later (November 13, 1996); Indians traded P Joe Roa to Giants for OF Trenidad Hubbard to complete deal (December 16, 1996). ... Granted free agency (October 29, 1997). ... Signed by Dodgers (December 8, 1997). ... On disabled list (June 22-September 9, 1998; and May 19-June 4, 1999).

STATISTICAL NOTES: Led Gulf Coast League shortstops with 23 double plays in 1987. ... Led Pacific Coast League shortstops with 611 total chances and 82 double plays in 1989. ... Tied for N.L. lead in fielding percentage by shortstop with .984 and assists by shortstop with 411 in 1995.

Year	Team (League)	Pos.	G	AB	R	H	2B	3B	HR	RBI	Avg.	BB	SO	SB	PO	A	E	Avg.
1987—GC Dodgers (GCL).....	SS-1B	49	150	26	38	5	1	0	12	.253	22	24	8	73	107	13	.933
1988—Bakersfield (Calif.)......	SS	122	433	77	126	11	4	0	38	.291	50	54	13	185	340	30	.946
1989—Albuquerque (PCL).....	SS	129	434	60	123	10	4	1	44	.283	33	41	16	*191	*390	*30	.951
—Los Angeles (N.L.).....	SS	7	10	2	2	0	0	0	0	.200	0	1	0	6	9	2	.882
1990—Albuquerque (PCL).....	2B-SS	81	276	46	77	10	2	2	38	.279	30	33	13	141	229	14	.964
—Los Angeles (N.L.).....	SS-2B	37	51	3	14	1	1	0	2	.275	4	8	1	23	27	2	.962
1991—Chicago (N.L.)■........	3B-SS-2B	93	145	7	38	5	0	0	10	.262	5	18	2	49	118	7	.960
1992—Chicago (N.L.).........	SS-3B-2B	86	285	25	64	10	4	1	17	.225	14	35	3	93	195	9	.970
1993—Chicago (N.L.).........	SS-3B-2B	151	551	74	158	19	4	4	54	.287	46	71	12	217	410	17	.974
1994—New York (N.L.)■........	SS	103	410	47	105	13	3	3	33	.256	33	62	1	136	291	13	.970
1995—New York (N.L.)........	SS-2B	135	509	66	146	21	5	3	56	.287	35	76	8	189	‡411	10	‡.984
1996—New York (N.L.)........	2B	96	363	47	110	12	6	1	32	.303	28	58	9	179	259	6	.986
—Cleveland (A.L.)■......	2B-SS-DH	48	179	23	51	5	2	0	13	.285	7	24	6	82	135	4	.982
1997—San Fran. (N.L.)■......	SS-2B	151	568	77	151	19	7	5	50	.266	48	87	8	206	450	16	.976
1998—Los Angeles (N.L.)■....	SS	67	237	30	62	9	0	3	29	.262	17	35	7	89	172	4	.985
1999—Los Angeles (N.L.)	SS-2B-3B-OF	94	266	27	67	9	0	1	29	.252	20	23	2	98	192	7	.976
American League totals (1 year)		48	179	23	51	5	2	0	13	.285	7	24	6	82	135	4	.982
National League totals (11 years)		1020	3395	405	917	118	30	21	312	.270	250	474	53	1285	2534	93	.976
Major League totals (11 years)		1068	3574	428	968	123	32	21	325	.271	257	498	59	1367	2669	97	.977

DIVISION SERIES RECORD

Year	Team (League)	Pos.	G	AB	R	H	2B	3B	HR	RBI	Avg.	BB	SO	SB	PO	A	E	Avg.
1996—Cleveland (A.L.).........	2B	3	12	1	4	2	0	0	1	.333	1	1	0	4	3	1	.875
1997—San Francisco (N.L.) ..	SS	3	11	1	2	1	0	0	0	.182	0	5	0	3	10	0	1.000
Division series totals (2 years)		6	23	2	6	3	0	0	1	.261	1	6	0	7	13	1	.952

V

VIZCAINO, LUIS — P — ATHLETICS

PERSONAL: Born June 1, 1977, in Bani, Dominican Republic. ... 5-11/169. ... Throws right, bats right. ... Full name: Luis Viczaino Arias.

TRANSACTIONS/CAREER NOTES: Signed as non-drafted free agent by Oakland Athletics organization (December 9, 1994).

Year	League	W	L	Pct.	ERA	G	GS	CG	ShO	Sv.	IP	H	R	ER	BB	SO
1995—Dom. Athletics (DSL)...	10	2	.833	2.27	16	15	5	1	0	*115	93	41	29	29	89
1996—Arizona Athletics (Ariz.)......	6	3	.667	4.07	15	10	0	0	1	$59\frac{2}{3}$	58	36	27	24	52
1997—S. Oregon (N'west)......	1	6	.143	7.93	22	5	0	0	0	$47\frac{2}{3}$	62	51	42	27	42
—Modesto (Calif.)..........	0	3	.000	13.19	7	0	0	0	0	$14\frac{1}{3}$	24	24	21	13	15
1998—Modesto (Calif.)	6	3	.667	2.74	23	16	0	0	0	102	72	39	31	43	108
—Huntsville (Sou.)	3	2	.600	4.66	7	7	0	0	0	$38\frac{2}{3}$	43	27	20	22	26
1999—Midland (Texas).........	8	7	.533	5.85	25	19	0	0	0	$104\frac{2}{3}$	120	74	68	48	88
—Vancouver (PCL)	0	1	.000	1.38	7	0	0	0	0	13	13	4	2	6	7
—Oakland (A.L.)	0	0	...	5.40	1	0	0	0	0	$3\frac{1}{3}$	3	2	2	3	2
Major League totals (1 year)........	0	0		5.40	1	0	0	0	0	$3\frac{1}{3}$	3	2	2	3	2

PERSONAL: Born April 24, 1967, in Caracas, Venezuela. ... 5-9/175. ... Bats both, throws right. ... Full name: Omar Enrique Vizquel. ... Name pronounced vis-KEL.

HIGH SCHOOL: Francisco Espejo (Caracas, Venezuela).

TRANSACTIONS/CAREER NOTES: Signed as non-drafted free agent by Seattle Mariners organization (April 1, 1984). ... On Seattle disabled list (April 7-May 13, 1990); included rehabilitation assignments to Calgary (May 3-7) and San Bernardino (May 8-12). ... On Seattle disabled list (April 13-May 11, 1992); included rehabilitation assignment to Calgary (May 5-11). ... Traded by Mariners to Cleveland Indians for SS Felix Fermin, 1B Reggie Jefferson and cash (December 20, 1993). ... On Cleveland disabled list (April 23-June 13, 1994); included rehabilitation assignment to Charlotte (June 6-13). ... On suspended list (September 17-18, 1998).

RECORDS: Shares major league career record for highest fielding percentage by shortstop (1,000 or more games)—.981.

HONORS: Won A.L. Gold Glove at shortstop (1993-99).

STATISTICAL NOTES: Led Midwest League shortstops with .969 fielding percentage in 1986. ... Tied for A.L. lead in double plays by shortstop with 108 in 1993. ... Led A.L. with 16 sacrifice hits in 1997 and with 17 in 1999. ... Career major league grand slams: 3.

MISCELLANEOUS: Batted righthanded only (1984-88).

Year	Team (League)	Pos.	G	AB	R	H	2B	3B	HR	RBI	Avg.	BB	SO	SB	PO	A	E	Avg.
1984—	Butte (Pio.)	SS-2B	15	45	7	14	2	0	0	4	.311	3	8	2	13	29	5	.894
1985—	Bellingham (N'west)	SS-2B	50	187	24	42	9	0	5	17	.225	12	27	4	85	175	19	.932
1986—	Wausau (Midw.)	SS-2B	105	352	60	75	13	2	4	28	.213	64	56	19	153	328	16	†.968
1987—	Salinas (Calif.)	SS-2B	114	407	61	107	12	8	0	38	.263	57	55	25	81	295	25	.938
1988—	Vermont (East.)	SS	103	374	54	95	18	2	2	35	.254	42	44	30	173	268	19	*.959
—	Calgary (PCL)	SS	33	107	10	24	2	3	1	12	.224	5	14	2	43	92	6	.957
1989—	Calgary (PCL)	SS	7	28	3	6	2	0	0	3	.214	3	4	0	15	14	0	1.000
—	Seattle (A.L.)	SS	143	387	45	85	7	3	1	20	.220	28	40	1	208	388	18	.971
1990—	Calgary (PCL)	SS	48	150	18	35	6	2	0	8	.233	13	10	4	70	142	6	.972
—	San Bern. (Calif.)	SS	6	28	5	7	0	0	0	3	.250	3	1	1	11	21	3	.914
—	Seattle (A.L.)	SS	81	255	19	63	3	2	2	18	.247	18	22	4	103	239	7	.980
1991—	Seattle (A.L.)	SS-2B	142	426	42	98	16	4	1	41	.230	45	37	7	224	422	13	.980
1992—	Seattle (A.L.)	SS	136	483	49	142	20	4	0	21	.294	32	38	15	223	403	7	*.989
—	Calgary (PCL)	SS	6	22	0	6	1	0	0	2	.273	1	3	0	14	21	1	.972
1993—	Seattle (A.L.)	SS-DH	158	560	68	143	14	2	2	31	.255	50	71	12	245	475	15	.980
1994—	Cleveland (A.L.)■	SS	69	286	39	78	10	1	1	33	.273	23	23	13	113	204	6	.981
—	Charlotte (I.L.)	SS	7	26	3	7	1	0	0	1	.269	2	1	1	11	18	1	.967
1995—	Cleveland (A.L.)	SS	136	542	87	144	28	0	6	56	.266	59	59	29	210	405	9	.986
1996—	Cleveland (A.L.)	SS	151	542	98	161	36	1	9	64	.297	56	42	35	226	447	20	.971
1997—	Cleveland (A.L.)	SS	153	565	89	158	23	6	5	49	.280	57	58	43	245	428	10	.985
1998—	Cleveland (A.L.)	SS	151	576	86	166	30	6	2	50	.288	62	64	37	*273	442	5	*.993
1999—	Cleveland (A.L.)	SS-OF	144	574	112	191	36	4	5	66	.333	65	50	42	221	396	15	.976
Major League totals (11 years)			1464	5196	734	1429	223	33	34	449	.275	495	504	238	2291	4249	125	.981

DIVISION SERIES RECORD

RECORDS: Holds career records for most hits—23; and most stolen bases—9. ... Shares career record for most games—21.

Year	Team (League)	Pos.	G	AB	R	H	2B	3B	HR	RBI	Avg.	BB	SO	SB	PO	A	E	Avg.
1995—	Cleveland (A.L.)	SS	3	12	2	2	1	0	0	4	.167	2	2	1	4	11	0	1.000
1996—	Cleveland (A.L.)	SS	4	14	4	6	1	0	0	2	.429	3	4	4	6	10	0	1.000
1997—	Cleveland (A.L.)	SS	5	18	3	9	0	0	0	1	.500	2	1	4	12	14	0	1.000
1998—	Cleveland (A.L.)	SS	4	15	1	1	0	0	0	0	.067	1	0	0	4	16	0	1.000
1999—	Cleveland (A.L.)	SS	5	21	3	5	1	1	0	3	.238	2	3	0	7	9	0	1.000
Division series totals (5 years)			21	80	13	23	3	1	0	10	.288	10	10	9	33	60	0	1.000

CHAMPIONSHIP SERIES RECORD

Year	Team (League)	Pos.	G	AB	R	H	2B	3B	HR	RBI	Avg.	BB	SO	SB	PO	A	E	Avg.
1995—	Cleveland (A.L.)	SS	6	23	2	2	1	0	0	2	.087	5	2	3	9	21	0	1.000
1997—	Cleveland (A.L.)	SS	6	25	1	1	0	0	0	0	.040	2	10	0	16	15	0	1.000
1998—	Cleveland (A.L.)	SS	6	25	2	11	0	1	0	0	.440	1	3	4	11	26	1	.974
Championship series totals (3 years)			18	73	5	14	1	1	0	2	.192	8	15	7	36	62	1	.990

WORLD SERIES RECORD

RECORDS: Shares single-inning record for most stolen bases—2 (October 26, 1997).

Year	Team (League)	Pos.	G	AB	R	H	2B	3B	HR	RBI	Avg.	BB	SO	SB	PO	A	E	Avg.
1995—	Cleveland (A.L.)	SS	6	23	3	4	0	1	0	1	.174	3	5	1	12	22	0	1.000
1997—	Cleveland (A.L.)	SS	7	30	5	7	2	0	0	1	.233	3	5	5	12	17	0	1.000
World Series totals (2 years)			13	53	8	11	2	1	0	2	.208	6	10	6	24	39	0	1.000

ALL-STAR GAME RECORD

Year	League	Pos.	AB	R	H	2B	3B	HR	RBI	Avg.	BB	SO	SB	PO	A	E	Avg.
1998—	American	SS	2	0	1	0	0	0	0	.500	0	0	0	1	1	0	1.000
1999—	American	SS	1	0	0	0	0	0	0	.000	0	0	0	1	4	0	1.000
All-Star Game totals (2 years)			3	0	1	0	0	0	0	.333	0	0	0	2	5	0	1.000

V

VOSBERG, ED   P   DIAMONDBACKS

PERSONAL: Born September 28, 1961, in Tucson, Ariz. ... 6-1/210. ... Throws left, bats left. ... Full name: Edward John Vosberg. ... Nephew of Don Vosberg, defensive end with New York Giants (1941).

HIGH SCHOOL: Salpointe (Tucson, Ariz.).

COLLEGE: Arizona.

TRANSACTIONS/CAREER NOTES: Selected by St. Louis Cardinals organization in third round of free-agent draft (June 5, 1979); did not sign. ... Selected by Toronto Blue Jays organization in 11th round of free-agent draft (June 7, 1982); did not sign. ... Selected by San Diego Padres organization in third round of free-agent draft (June 6, 1983). ... Traded by Padres to Houston Astros for C Dan Walters (December 13, 1988). ... Traded by Astros to Los Angeles Dodgers (August 1, 1989), completing deal in which Dodgers traded OF Javier Ortiz to Astros organization for a player to be named later (July 22, 1989). ... Granted free agency (October 15, 1989). ... Signed by Phoenix, San Francisco Giants organization (March 13, 1990). ... Granted free agency (October 15, 1990). ... Signed by California Angels organization (December 4, 1990). ... Released by Angels (May 11, 1991). ... Signed by Calgary, Seattle Mariners organization (May 20, 1991). ... Released by Mariners (July 10, 1991). ... Pitched in Italy (1992). ... Signed by Iowa, Chicago Cubs organization (March 17, 1993). ... Granted free agency (October 15, 1993). ... Signed by Oakland Athletics organization (December 3, 1993). ... Granted free agency (October 15, 1994). ... Re-signed by A's organization (November 11, 1994). ... Selected by Los Angeles Dodgers from A's organization in Rule 5 major league draft (December 5, 1994). ... Granted free agency (April 24, 1995). ... Signed by Texas Rangers organization (April 26, 1995). ... Traded by Rangers to Florida Marlins for P Rick Helling (August 12, 1997). ... Traded by Marlins to Padres for P Chris Clark (November 20, 1997). ... On disabled list (March 25, 1998-entire season). ... On San Diego disabled list (March 30-April 24, 1999); included rehabilitation assignment to Las Vegas (April 8-24). ... Released by Padres (June 5, 1999). ... Signed by Arizona Diamondbacks organization (June 10, 1999).

STATISTICAL NOTES: Led Pacific Coast League with 11 balks in 1987.

Year	League	W	L	Pct.	ERA	G	GS	CG	ShO	Sv.	IP	H	R	ER	BB	SO
1983—	Reno (Calif.)	6	6	.500	3.87	15	15	3	0	0	97²/₃	111	61	42	39	70
	Beaumont (Texas)	1	0	1.000	0.00	1	1	1	1	0	7	2	0	0	2	1
1984—	Beaumont (Texas)	13	•11	.542	3.43	27	•27	5	2	0	183²/₃	196	87	70	74	100
1985—	Beaumont (Texas)	9	11	.450	3.91	27	•27	2	1	0	175	178	92	76	69	124
1986—	Las Vegas (PCL)	7	8	.467	4.72	25	24	2	1	0	129²/₃	136	80	68	64	93
	San Diego (N.L.)	0	1	.000	6.59	5	3	0	0	0	13²/₃	17	11	10	9	8
1987—	Las Vegas (PCL)	9	8	.529	3.92	34	24	3	0	0	167³/₄	154	88	73	97	98
1988—	Las Vegas (PCL)	11	7	.611	4.15	45	11	1	0	2	128	137	67	59	56	75
1989—	Tucson (PCL)■	4	7	.364	6.78	23	14	0	0	1	87²/₃	122	70	66	49	68
	Albuquerque (PCL)■	2	1	.667	2.70	12	0	0	0	0	20	17	8	6	5	18
1990—	Phoenix (PCL)■	1	3	.250	2.65	24	0	0	0	3	34	36	14	10	16	28
	San Francisco (N.L.)	1	1	.500	5.55	18	0	0	0	0	24¹/₃	21	16	15	12	12
1991—	Edmonton (PCL)■	0	1	.000	6.28	12	0	0	0	0	14¹/₃	19	10	10	5	14
	Calgary (PCL)■	0	2	.000	7.23	16	0	0	0	2	23²/₃	38	26	19	12	15
1992—								Italian statistics unavailable.								
1993—	Iowa (A.A.)■	5	1	.833	3.57	52	0	0	0	3	63	67	32	25	22	64
1994—	Tacoma (PCL)■	4	2	.667	3.35	26	1	0	0	3	53²/₃	39	21	20	19	54
	Oakland (A.L.)	0	2	.000	3.95	16	0	0	0	0	13²/₃	16	7	6	5	12
1995—	Oklahoma City (A.A.)■	1	0	1.000	0.00	1	0	0	0	0	1²/₃	1	0	0	1	2
	Texas (A.L.)	5	5	.500	3.00	44	0	0	0	4	36	32	15	12	16	36
1996—	Texas (A.L.)	1	1	.500	3.27	52	0	0	0	8	44	51	17	16	21	32
1997—	Texas (A.L.)	1	2	.333	4.61	42	0	0	0	0	41	44	23	21	15	29
	Florida (N.L.)	1	1	.500	3.75	17	0	0	0	1	12	15	7	5	6	8
1998—	San Diego (N.L.)■								Did not play.							
1999—	Las Vegas (PCL)	0	0	...	1.08	8	0	0	0	1	8¹/₃	3	1	1	4	12
	San Diego (N.L.)	0	0	...	9.72	15	0	0	0	0	8¹/₃	16	11	9	3	6
	Tucson (PCL)■	1	0	1.000	0.78	26	0	0	0	7	34²/₃	26	5	3	8	30
	Arizona (N.L.)	0	1	.000	3.38	4	0	0	0	0	2²/₃	6	1	1	0	2
A.L. totals (4 years)		7	10	.412	3.68	154	0	0	0	12	134²/₃	143	62	55	57	109
N.L. totals (4 years)		2	4	.333	5.90	59	3	0	0	1	61	75	46	40	30	36
Major League totals (7 years)		9	14	.391	4.37	213	3	0	0	13	195²/₃	218	108	95	87	145

DIVISION SERIES RECORD

Year	League	W	L	Pct.	ERA	G	GS	CG	ShO	Sv.	IP	H	R	ER	BB	SO
1996—	Texas (A.L.)	0	0	...	...	1	0	0	0	0	1	0	0	0	0	0

CHAMPIONSHIP SERIES RECORD

Year	League	W	L	Pct.	ERA	G	GS	CG	ShO	Sv.	IP	H	R	ER	BB	SO
1997—	Florida (N.L.)	0	0	...	0.00	2	0	0	0	0	2²/₃	2	0	0	1	3

WORLD SERIES RECORD

NOTES: Member of World Series championship team (1997).

Year	League	W	L	Pct.	ERA	G	GS	CG	ShO	Sv.	IP	H	R	ER	BB	SO
1997—	Florida (N.L.)	0	0	...	6.00	2	0	0	0	0	3	3	2	2	3	2

WAGNER, BILLY — P — ASTROS

PERSONAL: Born July 25, 1971, in Tannersville, Va. ... 5-11/180. ... Throws left, bats left. ... Full name: William Edward Wagner.
HIGH SCHOOL: Tazewell (Va.).
COLLEGE: Ferrum (Va.).
TRANSACTIONS/CAREER NOTES: Selected by Houston Astros organization in first round (12th pick overall) of free-agent draft (June 3, 1993). ... On Houston disabled list (August 23-September 7, 1996). ... On Houston disabled list (July 16-August 7, 1998); included rehabilitation assignment to Jackson (August 1-7).

Year	League	W	L	Pct.	ERA	G	GS	CG	ShO	Sv.	IP	H	R	ER	BB	SO
1993—	Auburn (NY-P)	1	3	.250	4.08	7	7	0	0	0	28²/₃	25	19	13	25	31
1994—	Quad City (Midw.)	8	9	.471	3.29	26	26	2	0	0	153	99	71	56	*91	*204
1995—	Jackson (Texas)	2	2	.500	2.57	12	12	0	0	0	70	49	25	20	36	77
	Tucson (PCL)	5	3	.625	3.18	13	13	0	0	0	76¹/₃	70	28	27	32	80
	Houston (N.L.)	0	0	...	0.00	1	0	0	0	0	¹/₃	0	0	0	0	0
1996—	Tucson (PCL)	6	2	.750	3.28	12	12	1	1	0	74	62	32	27	33	86
	Houston (N.L.)	2	2	.500	2.44	37	0	0	0	9	51²/₃	28	16	14	30	67
1997—	Houston (N.L.)	7	8	.467	2.85	62	0	0	0	23	66¹/₃	49	23	21	30	106
1998—	Houston (N.L.)	4	3	.571	2.70	58	0	0	0	30	60	46	19	18	25	97
	Jackson (Texas)	0	0	...	0.00	3	1	0	0	0	3	1	0	0	0	7
1999—	Houston (N.L.)	4	1	.800	1.57	66	0	0	0	39	74²/₃	35	14	13	23	124
Major League totals (5 years)		17	14	.548	2.35	224	0	0	0	101	253	158	72	66	108	394

V
W

DIVISION SERIES RECORD

Year League	W	L	Pct.	ERA	G	GS	CG	ShO	Sv.	IP	H	R	ER	BB	SO
1997—Houston (N.L.)	0	0	...	18.00	1	0	0	0	0	1	3	2	2	0	2
1998—Houston (N.L.)	1	0	1.000	18.00	1	0	0	0	0	1	4	2	2	0	1
1999—Houston (N.L.)	0	0	...	0.00	1	0	0	0	0	1	0	0	0	0	1
Division series totals (3 years)	1	0	1.000	12.00	3	0	0	0	0	3	7	4	4	0	4

ALL-STAR GAME RECORD

Year League	W	L	Pct.	ERA	GS	CG	ShO	Sv.	IP	H	R	ER	BB	SO
1999—National	0	0	...	0.00	0	0	0	0	2/3	0	0	0	0	2

WAGNER, PAUL   P   METS

PERSONAL: Born November 14, 1967, in Milwaukee. ... 6-1/210. ... Throws right, bats right. ... Full name: Paul Allen Wagner.
HIGH SCHOOL: Washington (Germantown, Wis.).
COLLEGE: Illinois State.
TRANSACTIONS/CAREER NOTES: Selected by Pittsburgh Pirates organization in 12th round of free-agent draft (June 5, 1989). ... On disabled list (August 3-19, 1993 and July 3-21, 1995). ... On Pittsburgh disabled list (June 7-July 2 and July 20, 1996-remainder of season); included rehabilitation assignment to Gulf Coast Pirates (June 24-28). ... On Pittsburgh disabled list (March 31-May 28, 1997); included rehabilitation assignment to Carolina (May 9-28). ... Released by Pirates (August 26, 1997). ... Signed by Milwaukee Brewers (September 2, 1997). ... On Milwaukee disabled list (May 18-June 2 and June 22-July 23, 1998); included rehabilitation assignments to Beloit (May 28-June 1) and Louisville (July 9-23). ... Released by Brewers (July 26, 1998). ... Signed by Atlanta Braves organization (August 5, 1998). ... Released by Braves (September 1, 1998). ... Signed by Cleveland Indians organization (February 3, 1999). ... Granted free agency (October 4, 1999). ... Signed by New York Mets organization (January 17, 2000).
STATISTICAL NOTES: Pitched 4-0 one-hit, complete-game victory against Colorado (August 29, 1995).
MISCELLANEOUS: Made an out in only appearance as pinch hitter (1995). ... Walked in only appearance as pinch hitter with Pittsburgh (1996).

Year League	W	L	Pct.	ERA	G	GS	CG	ShO	Sv.	IP	H	R	ER	BB	SO
1989—Welland (NY-P)	4	5	.444	4.47	13	10	0	0	0	50 1/3	54	34	25	15	30
1990—Augusta (SAL)	7	7	.500	2.75	35	1	0	0	4	72	71	30	22	30	71
—Salem (Caro.)	0	1	.000	5.00	11	4	0	0	2	36	39	22	20	17	28
1991—Salem (Caro.)	11	6	.647	3.12	25	25	5	•2	0	158 2/3	124	70	55	60	113
1992—Carolina (Sou.)	6	6	.500	3.03	19	19	2	1	0	121 2/3	104	52	41	47	101
—Pittsburgh (N.L.)	2	0	1.000	0.69	6	1	0	0	0	13	9	1	1	5	5
—Buffalo (A.A.)	3	3	.500	5.49	8	8	0	0	0	39 1/3	51	27	24	14	19
1993—Pittsburgh (N.L.)	8	8	.500	4.27	44	17	1	1	2	141 1/3	143	72	67	42	114
1994—Pittsburgh (N.L.)	7	8	.467	4.59	29	17	1	0	0	119 2/3	136	69	61	50	86
1995—Pittsburgh (N.L.)	5	*16	.238	4.80	33	25	3	1	1	165	174	96	88	72	120
1996—Pittsburgh (N.L.)	4	8	.333	5.40	16	15	1	0	0	81 2/3	86	49	49	39	81
—Gulf Coast Pirates (GCL)	0	0	...	0.00	1	1	0	0	0	3	2	0	0	0	4
1997—Carolina (Sou.)	0	1	.000	10.13	12	3	0	0	0	16	25	20	18	16	20
—Pittsburgh (N.L.)	0	0	...	3.94	14	0	0	0	0	16	17	7	7	13	9
—Milwaukee (A.L.)■	1	0	1.000	9.00	2	0	0	0	0	2	3	2	2	0	0
1998—Milwaukee (A.L.)	1	5	.167	7.11	13	9	0	0	0	55 2/3	67	49	44	31	37
—Beloit (Midw.)	0	1	.000	7.20	1	1	0	0	0	5	7	4	4	0	3
—Louisville (I.L.)	1	0	1.000	8.76	3	3	0	0	0	12 1/3	17	12	12	5	6
—Richmond (I.L.)■	1	0	1.000	1.98	8	0	0	0	0	13 2/3	11	4	3	3	9
1999—Buffalo (I.L.)■	8	4	.667	3.82	23	23	0	0	0	129 2/3	123	67	55	55	95
—Cleveland (A.L.)	1	0	1.000	4.15	3	0	0	0	0	4 1/3	5	4	2	3	4
A.L. totals (2 years)	2	0	1.000	5.68	5	0	0	0	0	6 1/3	8	6	4	3	0
N.L. totals (7 years)	27	45	.375	4.82	155	84	6	2	3	592 1/3	632	343	317	252	452
Major League totals (8 years)	29	45	.392	4.83	160	84	6	2	3	598 2/3	640	349	321	255	452

WAINHOUSE, DAVE   P   CARDINALS

PERSONAL: Born November 7, 1967, in Toronto. ... 6-2/196. ... Throws right, bats left. ... Full name: David Paul Wainhouse.
HIGH SCHOOL: Mercer Island (Wash.).
COLLEGE: Washington State.
TRANSACTIONS/CAREER NOTES: Selected by Montreal Expos organization in first round (19th pick overall) of free-agent draft (June 1, 1988). ... On Harrisburg disabled list (April 25-May 3, 1991). ... On disabled list (August 13-September 8, 1992). ... Traded by Expos with P Kevin Foster to Seattle Mariners for IF Frank Bolick and a player to be named later (November 20, 1992); Expos acquired C Miah Bradbury to complete deal (December 8, 1992). ... On Calgary disabled list (April 23-August 3, 1993). ... Released by Mariners (March 29, 1994). ... Signed by Syracuse, Toronto Blue Jays organization (December 20, 1994). ... Released by Syracuse (June 5, 1995). ... Signed by Florida Marlins organization (June 8, 1995). ... Granted free agency (October 16, 1995). ... Signed by Carolina, Pittsburgh Pirates organization (January 28, 1996). ... Granted free agency (October 15, 1997). ... Signed by Colorado Rockies organization (November 14, 1997). ... Granted free agency (October 12, 1999). ... Signed by St. Louis Cardinals organization (January 19, 2000).
MISCELLANEOUS: Member of 1988 Canadian Olympic baseball team.

Year League	W	L	Pct.	ERA	G	GS	CG	ShO	Sv.	IP	H	R	ER	BB	SO
1989—West Palm Beach (FSL)	1	5	.167	4.07	13	13	0	0	0	66 1/3	75	35	30	19	26
1990—West Palm Beach (FSL)	6	3	.667	2.11	12	12	2	1	0	76 2/3	68	28	18	34	58
—Jacksonville (Sou.)	7	7	.500	4.33	17	16	2	0	0	95 2/3	97	59	46	47	59
1991—Harrisburg (East.)	2	2	.500	2.60	33	0	0	0	11	52	49	17	15	17	46
—Indianapolis (A.A.)	2	0	1.000	4.08	14	0	0	0	1	28 2/3	28	14	13	15	13
—Montreal (N.L.)	0	1	.000	6.75	2	0	0	0	0	2 2/3	2	2	2	4	1
1992—Indianapolis (A.A.)	5	4	.556	4.11	44	0	0	0	21	46	48	22	21	24	37
1993—Seattle (A.L.)■	0	0	...	27.00	3	0	0	0	0	2 1/3	7	7	7	5	2
—Calgary (PCL)	0	1	.000	4.02	13	0	0	0	0	15 2/3	10	7	7	7	7
1994—						Out of organized baseball.									
1995—Syracuse (I.L.)■	3	2	.600	3.70	26	0	0	0	5	24 1/3	29	13	10	11	18
—Portland (East.)■	2	1	.667	7.20	17	0	0	0	0	25	39	22	20	8	16
—Charlotte (I.L.)	0	0	...	9.82	4	0	0	0	0	3 2/3	6	6	4	4	2
1996—Carolina (Sou.)■	5	3	.625	3.16	46	0	0	0	25	51 1/3	43	22	18	31	34
—Pittsburgh (N.L.)	1	0	1.000	5.70	17	0	0	0	0	23 2/3	22	16	15	10	16
1997—Pittsburgh (N.L.)	0	1	.000	8.04	25	0	0	0	0	28	34	28	25	17	21

W

Year League	W	L	Pct.	ERA	G	GS	CG	ShO	Sv.	IP	H	R	ER	BB	SO
—Calgary (PCL)	2	0	1.000	5.92	25	0	0	0	1	38	46	25	25	13	24
1998—Colorado Springs (PCL)■	2	3	.400	3.60	38	0	0	0	4	50	47	25	20	23	44
—Colorado (N.L.)	1	0	1.000	4.91	10	0	0	0	0	11	15	6	6	5	3
1999—Colorado Springs (PCL)	1	3	.250	3.19	38	0	0	0	*22	42 1/3	42	19	15	7	42
—Colorado (N.L.)	0	0	...	6.91	19	0	0	0	0	28 2/3	37	22	22	16	18
A.L. totals (1 year)	0	0	...	27.00	3	0	0	0	0	2 1/3	7	7	7	5	2
N.L. totals (5 years)	2	2	.500	6.70	73	0	0	0	0	94	110	74	70	52	59
Major League totals (6 years)	2	2	.500	7.19	76	0	0	0	0	96 1/3	117	81	77	57	61

WAKEFIELD, TIM   P   RED SOX

PERSONAL: Born August 2, 1966, in Melbourne, Fla. ... 6-2/210. ... Throws right, bats right. ... Full name: Timothy Stephen Wakefield.
HIGH SCHOOL: Eau Gallie (Melbourne, Fla.).
COLLEGE: Florida Tech.
TRANSACTIONS/CAREER NOTES: Selected by Pittsburgh Pirates organization in eighth round of free-agent draft (June 1, 1988). ... Released by Pirates (April 20, 1995). ... Signed by Boston Red Sox organization (April 26, 1995). ... On disabled list (April 15-May 6, 1997).
RECORDS: Shares major league single-inning record for most strikeouts—4 (August 10, 1999, ninth inning).
HONORS: Named N.L. Rookie Pitcher of the Year by THE SPORTING NEWS (1992). ... Named A.L. Comeback Player of the Year by THE SPORTING NEWS (1995).
STATISTICAL NOTES: Led Carolina League with 24 home runs allowed in 1990. ... Led American Association with 27 home runs allowed and 23 hit batsmen in 1994. ... Led A.L. with 16 hit batsmen in 1997.
MISCELLANEOUS: Played infield (1988-89). ... Appeared in one game as pinch runner with Pittsburgh (1992). ... Had a sacrifice hit in only appearance as pinch hitter (1998).

Year League	W	L	Pct.	ERA	G	GS	CG	ShO	Sv.	IP	H	R	ER	BB	SO
1989—Welland (NY-P)	1	1	.500	3.40	36	1	0	0	2	39 2/3	30	17	15	21	42
1990—Salem (Caro.)	10	•14	.417	4.73	28	•28	2	0	0	*190 1/3	*187	109	*100	*85	127
1991—Carolina (Sou.)	15	8	.652	2.90	26	25	•8	1	0	183	155	68	59	51	120
—Buffalo (A.A.)	0	1	.000	11.57	1	1	0	0	0	4 2/3	8	6	6	1	4
1992—Buffalo (A.A.)	10	3	.769	3.06	20	20	*6	1	0	135 1/3	122	52	46	51	71
—Pittsburgh (N.L.)	8	1	.889	2.15	13	13	4	1	0	92	76	26	22	35	51
1993—Pittsburgh (N.L.)	6	11	.353	5.61	24	20	3	2	0	128 1/3	145	83	80	75	59
—Carolina (Sou.)	3	5	.375	6.99	9	9	1	0	0	56 2/3	68	48	44	22	36
1994—Buffalo (A.A.)	5	*15	.250	5.84	30	•29	4	1	0	175 2/3	*197	*127	*114	*98	83
1995—Pawtucket (I.L.)■	2	1	.667	2.52	4	4	0	0	0	25	23	10	7	9	14
—Boston (A.L.)	16	8	.667	2.95	27	27	6	1	0	195 1/3	163	76	64	68	119
1996—Boston (A.L.)	14	13	.519	5.14	32	32	6	0	0	211 2/3	238	*151	121	90	140
1997—Boston (A.L.)	12	•15	.444	4.25	35	29	4	2	0	201 1/3	193	109	95	87	151
1998—Boston (A.L.)	17	8	.680	4.58	36	33	2	0	0	216	211	123	110	79	146
1999—Boston (A.L.)	6	11	.353	5.08	49	17	0	0	15	140	146	93	79	72	104
A.L. totals (5 years)	65	55	.542	4.38	179	138	18	3	15	964 1/3	951	552	469	396	660
N.L. totals (2 years)	14	12	.538	4.17	37	33	7	3	0	220 1/3	221	109	102	110	110
Major League totals (7 years)	79	67	.541	4.34	216	171	25	6	15	1184 2/3	1172	661	571	506	770

DIVISION SERIES RECORD

Year League	W	L	Pct.	ERA	G	GS	CG	ShO	Sv.	IP	H	R	ER	BB	SO
1995—Boston (A.L.)	0	1	.000	11.81	1	1	0	0	0	5 1/3	5	7	7	5	4
1998—Boston (A.L.)	0	1	.000	33.75	1	1	0	0	0	1 1/3	3	5	5	2	1
1999—Boston (A.L.)	0	0	...	13.50	2	0	0	0	0	2	3	3	3	4	4
Division series totals (3 years)	0	2	.000	15.58	4	2	0	0	0	8 2/3	11	15	15	11	9

CHAMPIONSHIP SERIES RECORD

RECORDS: Shares single-series record for most complete games—2 (1992). ... Shares N.L. career record for most complete games—2.

Year League	W	L	Pct.	ERA	G	GS	CG	ShO	Sv.	IP	H	R	ER	BB	SO
1992—Pittsburgh (N.L.)	2	0	1.000	3.00	2	2	2	0	0	18	14	6	6	5	7
1999—Boston (A.L.)							Did not play.								

RECORD AS POSITION PLAYER

Year Team (League)	Pos.	G	AB	R	H	2B	3B	HR	RBI	Avg.	BB	SO	SB	PO	A	E	Avg.
1988—Watertown (NYP)	1B	54	159	24	30	6	2	3	20	.189	25	57	3	377	25	8	.980
1989—Augusta (S. Atl.)	3B-1B	11	34	5	8	2	1	0	5	.235	1	14	1	27	6	3	.917
—Welland (NYP)	3B-2B-1B	36	63	7	13	4	0	1	3	.206	3	21	1	26	31	8	.877

WAKELAND, CHRIS   OF   TIGERS

W

PERSONAL: Born June 15, 1974, in Huntington Beach, Calif. ... 6-0/185. ... Bats left, throws left. ... Full name: Christopher Robert Wakeland.
HIGH SCHOOL: St. Helens (Ore.).
COLLEGE: Oregon State.
TRANSACTIONS/CAREER NOTES: Selected by Detroit Tigers organization in 15th round of free-agent draft (June 4, 1996). ... On Jacksonville disabled list (June 6-August 26, 1999).

Year Team (League)	Pos.	G	AB	R	H	2B	3B	HR	RBI	Avg.	BB	SO	SB	PO	A	E	Avg.
1996—Jamestown (NY-P)	OF	70	220	38	68	14	5	10	49	.309	43	83	8	79	9	2	.978
1997—W. Mich. (Mid.)	OF	111	414	64	118	38	2	7	75	.285	43	120	20	169	7	5	.972
1998—Lakeland (FSL)	OF	131	487	82	147	26	5	18	89	.302	66	111	19	194	•17	9	.959
1999—Jacksonville (Sou.)	OF	55	212	42	68	16	3	13	36	.321	35	53	6	97	4	6	.944
—GC Tigers (GCL)	OF	4	14	2	1	0	0	0	1	.071	0	4	0	6	0	0	1.000
—Lakeland (FSL)	OF	4	17	3	7	1	0	0	7	.412	0	0	1	4	0	0	1.000

WALBECK, MATT — C — ANGELS

PERSONAL: Born October 2, 1969, in Sacramento. ... 5-11/188. ... Bats both, throws right. ... Full name: Matthew Lovick Walbeck.
HIGH SCHOOL: Sacramento High.
TRANSACTIONS/CAREER NOTES: Selected by Chicago Cubs organization in eighth round of free-agent draft (June 2, 1987). ... On Winston-Salem disabled list (April 12-July 11, 1990). ... On Charleston, W.Va. disabled list (September 5, 1992-remainder of season). ... Traded by Cubs with P Dave Stevens to Minnesota Twins for P Willie Banks (November 24, 1993). ... On Minnesota disabled list (March 31-June 17, 1996); included rehabilitation assignments to Fort Myers (May 31-June 11) and New Britain (June 12-17). ... Traded by Twins to Detroit Tigers for P Brent Stentz (December 11, 1996). ... On Detroit disabled list (April 19-July 9, 1997); included rehabilitation assignments to Lakeland (June 12-15) and Toledo (June 16-July 9). ... Traded by Tigers with 3B Phil Nevin to Anaheim Angels for P Nick Skuse (November 20, 1997).
STATISTICAL NOTES: Tied for Carolina League lead with 10 sacrifice flies in 1991. ... Led American Association catchers with 561 total chances and tied for lead with nine double plays in 1993. ... Career major league grand slams: 2.
MISCELLANEOUS: Batted righthanded only (1987-89).

Year	Team (League)	Pos.	G	AB	R	H	2B	3B	HR	RBI	Avg.	BB	SO	SB	PO	A	E	Avg.
1987—	Wytheville (Appl.)	C	51	169	24	53	9	3	1	28	.314	22	39	0	293	22	1	*.997
1988—	Char., W.Va. (SAL)	C	104	312	28	68	9	0	2	24	.218	30	44	7	549	68	14	.978
1989—	Peoria (Midw.)	C	94	341	38	86	19	0	4	47	.252	20	47	5	605	72	11	.984
1990—	Peoria (Midw.)	C	25	66	2	15	1	0	0	5	.227	5	7	1	137	16	2	.987
1991—	Win.-Salem (Car.)	C	91	260	25	70	11	0	3	41	.269	20	23	3	473	64	12	.978
1992—	Charlotte (Sou.)	C-1B	105	385	48	116	22	1	7	42	.301	33	56	0	552	80	10	.984
1993—	Chicago (N.L.)	C	11	30	2	6	2	0	1	6	.200	1	6	0	49	2	0	1.000
—	Iowa (A.A.)	C	87	331	31	93	18	2	6	43	.281	18	47	1	496	*64	1	*.998
1994—	Minnesota (A.L.)■	C-DH	97	338	31	69	12	0	5	35	.204	17	37	1	496	45	4	.993
1995—	Minnesota (A.L.)	C	115	393	40	101	18	1	1	44	.257	25	71	3	604	35	6	.991
1996—	Fort Myers (FSL)	C-DH	9	33	4	9	1	1	0	9	.273	4	2	0	46	6	0	1.000
—	New Britain (East.)	DH-C	7	24	1	5	0	0	0	0	.208	1	1	0	11	2	0	1.000
—	Minnesota (A.L.)	C	63	215	25	48	10	0	2	24	.223	9	34	3	326	19	2	.994
1997—	Detroit (A.L.)■	C	47	137	18	38	3	0	3	10	.277	12	19	3	240	15	3	.988
—	Lakeland (FSL)	C-DH	4	10	4	5	1	0	0	3	.500	4	1	0	14	0	1	.933
—	Toledo (I.L.)	C-DH	17	59	6	18	2	1	1	8	.305	4	15	0	55	9	3	.955
1998—	Anaheim (A.L.)■	C-DH	108	338	41	87	15	2	6	46	.257	30	68	1	682	46	7	.990
1999—	Anaheim (A.L.)	C-DH	107	288	26	69	8	1	3	22	.240	26	46	2	407	46	5	.989
American League totals (6 years)			537	1709	181	412	66	4	20	181	.241	119	275	13	2755	206	27	.991
National League totals (1 year)			11	30	2	6	2	0	1	6	.200	1	6	0	49	2	0	1.000
Major League totals (7 years)			548	1739	183	418	68	4	21	187	.240	120	281	13	2804	208	27	.991

WALKER, JAMIE — P — ROYALS

PERSONAL: Born July 1, 1971, in McMinnville, Tenn. ... 6-2/190. ... Throws left, bats left. ... Full name: Jamie Ross Walker.
HIGH SCHOOL: Warren County (McMinnville, Tenn.).
COLLEGE: Austin Peay.
TRANSACTIONS/CAREER NOTES: Selected by Houston Astros organization in 10th round of free-agent draft (June 1, 1992). ... Selected by Atlanta Braves organization from Astros organization in Rule 5 major league draft (December 9, 1996). ... Traded by Braves with OF Jermaine Dye to Kansas City Royals for OF Michael Tucker and IF Keith Lockhart (March 27, 1997). ... On Kansas City disabled list (June 5-24, 1997); included rehabilitation assignment to Wichita (June 11-24). ... On Kansas City disabled list (June 1, 1998-remainder of season). ... Granted free agency (December 21, 1998). ... Re-signed by Royals organization (December 21, 1998). ... On Omaha disabled list (April 8-May 17 and May 25-August 27, 1999).

Year	League	W	L	Pct.	ERA	G	GS	CG	ShO	Sv.	IP	H	R	ER	BB	SO
1992—	Auburn (NY-P)	4	6	.400	3.13	15	14	0	0	0	83 1/3	75	35	29	21	67
1993—	Quad City (Midw.)	3	11	.214	5.13	25	24	1	1	0	131 2/3	140	92	75	48	121
1994—	Quad City (Midw.)	8	10	.444	4.18	32	18	0	0	1	125	133	80	58	42	104
1995—	Jackson (Texas)	4	2	.667	4.50	50	0	0	0	2	58	59	29	29	24	38
1996—	Jackson (Texas)	5	1	.833	2.50	45	7	0	0	2	101	94	34	28	35	79
1997—	Kansas City (A.L.)■	3	3	.500	5.44	50	0	0	0	0	43	46	28	26	20	24
—	Wichita (Texas)	0	1	.000	9.45	5	0	0	0	0	6 2/3	6	8	7	5	6
1998—	Omaha (PCL)	5	1	.833	2.70	7	7	0	0	0	46 2/3	57	15	14	11	21
—	Kansas City (A.L.)	0	1	.000	9.87	6	2	0	0	0	17 1/3	30	20	19	3	15
1999—	Omaha (PCL)	0	1	.000	4.67	4	0	0	0	0	17 1/3	22	12	9	4	11
—	Gulf Coast Royals (GCL)	1	0	1.000	3.38	2	2	0	0	0	8	10	3	3	0	9
Major League totals (2 years)		3	4	.429	6.71	56	2	0	0	0	60 1/3	76	48	45	23	39

WALKER, KEVIN — P — PADRES

PERSONAL: Born September 20, 1976, in Grand Prairie, Texas. ... 6-4/190. ... Throws left, bats left. ... Full name: Kevin Michael Walker.
HIGH SCHOOL: Grand Prairie (Texas).
TRANSACTIONS/CAREER NOTES: Selected by San Diego Padres organization in sixth round of free-agent draft (June 1, 1995). ... On Mobile disabled list (April 8-24, 1999). ... On Rancho Cucamonga disabled list (June 19-July 30, 1999).

Year	League	W	L	Pct.	ERA	G	GS	CG	ShO	Sv.	IP	H	R	ER	BB	SO
1995—	Arizona Padres (Ariz.)	5	5	.500	3.01	13	12	0	0	0	71 2/3	74	34	24	12	69
1996—	Idaho Falls (Pio.)	1	0	1.000	3.00	1	1	0	0	0	6	4	3	2	2	4
—	Clinton (Midw.)	4	6	.400	4.74	13	13	0	0	0	76	80	46	40	33	43
1997—	Clinton (Midw.)	6	10	.375	4.88	19	19	3	1	0	110 2/3	133	80	60	37	80
1998—	Clinton (Midw.)	2	0	1.000	1.23	2	2	0	0	0	14 2/3	11	2	2	7	10
—	Rancho Cuca. (Calif.)	11	7	.611	4.15	22	22	0	0	0	121 1/3	122	62	56	48	94
1999—	Rancho Cuca. (Calif.)	1	1	.500	3.46	27	1	0	0	4	39	35	19	15	19	35

PERSONAL: Born December 1, 1966, in Maple Ridge, B.C. ... 6-3/237. ... Bats left, throws right. ... Full name: Larry Kenneth Robert Walker.

HIGH SCHOOL: Maple Ridge (B.C.) Senior Secondary School.

TRANSACTIONS/CAREER NOTES: Signed as non-drafted free agent by Montreal Expos organization (November 14, 1984). ... On disabled list (April 4, 1988-entire season; June 28-July 13, 1991; and May 26-June 10, 1993). ... Granted free agency (October 24, 1994). ... Signed by Colorado Rockies (April 8, 1995). ... On Colorado disabled list (June 10-August 15, 1996; included rehabilitation assignments to Salem (August 6-9) and Colorado Springs (August 9-15). ... On disabled list (June 18-July 3, 1998; and March 29-April 14, 1999).

RECORDS: Shares major league record for most extra-base hits in two consecutive games (May 21-22, 1996; 2 doubles, 3 triples and 1 home run). ... Holds N.L. single-season records for most consecutive long hits—6 (May 21-22, 1996; 2 doubles, 3 triples and 1 home run); and highest slugging average by a lefthander (100 or more games)—.720 (1997).

HONORS: Named outfielder on THE SPORTING NEWS N.L. All-Star team (1992, 1997 and 1999). ... Won N.L. Gold Glove as outfielder (1992-93 and 1997-99). ... Named outfielder on THE SPORTING NEWS N.L. Silver Slugger team (1992, 1997 and 1999). ... Named N.L. Most Valuable Player by Baseball Writers' Association of America (1997).

STATISTICAL NOTES: Hit three home runs in one game (April 5, 1997 and April 28, 1999). ... Led N.L. with 409 total bases in 1997. ... Led N.L. with .452 on-base percentage in 1997. ... Led N.L. in slugging percentage with .720 in 1997. ... Led N.L. outfielders in double plays with four in 1997. ... Had 20-game hitting streak (May 4-25, 1998). ... Had 21-game hitting streak (April 25-May 21, 1999). ... Had 18-game hitting streak (June 14-July 3, 1999). ... Led N.L. with a .710 slugging percentage and a .458 on-base percentage in 1999. ... Career major league grand slams: 3.

MISCELLANEOUS: Holds Colorado Rockies all-time record for highest career batting average (.344).

Year Team (League)	Pos.	G	AB	R	H	2B	3B	HR	RBI	Avg.	BB	SO	SB	PO	A	E	Avg.
1985—Utica (NY-P)	1B-3B	62	215	24	48	8	2	2	26	.223	18	57	12	354	62	8	.981
1986—Burlington (Midw.)	OF-3B	95	332	67	96	12	6	29	74	.289	46	112	16	106	51	10	.940
—W.P. Beach (FSL)	OF	38	113	20	32	7	5	4	16	.283	26	32	2	44	5	0	1.000
1987—Jacksonville (Sou.)	OF	128	474	91	136	25	7	26	83	.287	67	120	24	263	9	9	.968
1988—Montreal (N.L.)							Did not play.										
1989—Indianapolis (A.A.)	OF	114	385	68	104	18	2	12	59	.270	50	87	36	241	*18	*11	.959
—Montreal (N.L.)	OF	20	47	4	8	0	0	0	4	.170	5	13	1	19	2	0	1.000
1990—Montreal (N.L.)	OF	133	419	59	101	18	3	19	51	.241	49	112	21	249	12	4	.985
1991—Montreal (N.L.)	OF-1B	137	487	59	141	30	2	16	64	.290	42	102	14	536	36	6	.990
1992—Montreal (N.L.)	OF	143	528	85	159	31	4	23	93	.301	41	97	18	269	16	2	.993
1993—Montreal (N.L.)	OF-1B	138	490	85	130	24	5	22	86	.265	80	76	29	316	16	6	.982
1994—Montreal (N.L.)	OF-1B	103	395	76	127	44	2	19	86	.322	47	74	15	423	29	9	.980
1995—Colorado (N.L.)■	OF	131	494	96	151	31	5	36	101	.306	49	72	16	225	13	3	.988
1996—Colorado (N.L.)	OF	83	272	58	75	18	4	18	58	.276	20	58	18	153	4	1	.994
—Salem (Caro.)	DH	2	8	3	4	3	0	1	1	.500	0	1	0	...	...	...	...
—Colo. Springs (PCL)	OF	3	11	2	4	0	0	2	8	.364	1	4	0	6	2	0	1.000
1997—Colorado (N.L.)	OF-1B-DH	153	568	143	208	46	4	*49	130	.366	78	90	33	254	14	2	.993
1998—Colorado (N.L.)	O-DH-2-3	130	454	113	165	46	3	23	67	*.363	64	61	14	236	8	4	.984
1999—Colorado (N.L.)	OF-DH	127	438	108	166	26	4	37	115	*.379	57	52	11	204	13	4	.982
Major League totals (11 years)		1298	4592	886	1431	314	36	262	855	.312	532	807	190	2884	163	41	.987

DIVISION SERIES RECORD

Year Team (League)	Pos.	G	AB	R	H	2B	3B	HR	RBI	Avg.	BB	SO	SB	PO	A	E	Avg.
1995—Colorado (N.L.)	OF	4	14	3	3	0	0	1	3	.214	3	4	1	3	0	0	1.000

ALL-STAR GAME RECORD

Year League	Pos.	AB	R	H	2B	3B	HR	RBI	Avg.	BB	SO	SB	PO	A	E	Avg.
1992—National	PH	1	0	1	0	0	0	0	1.000	0	0	0	...	...	...	...
1997—National	OF	1	0	0	0	0	0	0	.000	1	0	0	0	0	0	...
1998—National	OF	1	1	0	0	0	0	0	.000	0	1	0	2	0	0	1.000
1999—National	OF	2	0	0	0	0	0	0	.000	1	0	0	1	0	0	1.000
All-Star Game totals (4 years)		5	1	1	0	0	0	0	.200	2	1	0	3	0	0	1.000

PERSONAL: Born May 25, 1973, in Bakersfield, Calif. ... 6-0/181. ... Bats left, throws right. ... Full name: Todd Arthur Walker.

HIGH SCHOOL: Airline (Bossier City, La.).

COLLEGE: Louisiana State.

TRANSACTIONS/CAREER NOTES: Selected by Texas Rangers organization in 51st round of free-agent draft (June 3, 1991); did not sign. ... Selected by Minnesota Twins organization in first round (eighth pick overall) of free-agent draft (June 2, 1994).

HONORS: Named Most Outstanding Player of College World Series (1993).

STATISTICAL NOTES: Led Pacific Coast League with 330 total bases and .599 slugging percentage and tied for lead in intentional bases on balls received with 11 in 1996.

Year Team (League)	Pos.	G	AB	R	H	2B	3B	HR	RBI	Avg.	BB	SO	SB	PO	A	E	Avg.
1994—Fort Myers (FSL)	2B	46	171	29	52	5	2	10	34	.304	32	15	6	98	112	9	.959
1995—New Britain (East.)	2B-3B	137	513	83	149	27	3	21	85	.290	63	101	23	215	355	27	.955
1996—Salt Lake (PCL)	3B-2B-DH	135	551	94	*187	*41	9	*28	*111	.339	57	91	13	129	276	19	.955
—Minnesota (A.L.)	3B-2B-DH	25	82	8	21	6	0	0	6	.256	4	13	2	16	39	2	.965
1997—Minnesota (A.L.)	3B-2B-DH	52	156	15	37	7	1	3	16	.237	11	30	1	35	86	4	.968
—Salt Lake (PCL)	3B-DH	83	322	69	111	20	1	11	53	.345	46	49	5	44	174	*24	.901
1998—Minnesota (A.L.)	2B-DH	143	528	85	167	41	3	12	62	.316	47	65	19	219	363	13	.978
1999—Minnesota (A.L.)	2B-DH	143	531	62	148	37	4	6	46	.279	52	83	18	168	270	7	.984
Major League totals (4 years)		363	1297	170	373	91	8	21	130	.288	114	191	46	438	758	26	.979

PERSONAL: Born July 11, 1967, in Potosi, Mo. ... 6-1/205. ... Throws right, bats right. ... Full name: Donnell Lee Wall. ... Name pronounced DON-ee.

HIGH SCHOOL: Festus (Mo.).

JUNIOR COLLEGE: Jefferson College (Mo.), then St. Louis Community College at Meramec.

COLLEGE: Southwestern Louisiana.

TRANSACTIONS/CAREER NOTES: Selected by Houston Astros organization in 18th round of free-agent draft (June 5, 1989). ... On disabled list (May 27-June 16, 1994). ... Claimed on waivers by Cincinnati Reds (October 7, 1997). ... Traded by Reds with C Paul Bako to Detroit Tigers for OF Melvin Nieves (November 11, 1997). ... Traded by Tigers with P Dan Miceli and 3B Ryan Balfe to San Diego Padres for P Tim Worrell and OF Trey Beamon (November 19, 1997).

HONORS: Named Pacific Coast League Most Valuable Player (1995).

STATISTICAL NOTES: Led South Atlantic League with 18 home runs allowed in 1990.

Year League	W	L	Pct.	ERA	G	GS	CG	ShO	Sv.	IP	H	R	ER	BB	SO
1989— Auburn (NY-P)	7	0	*1.000	1.79	12	8	3	1	1	65 1/3	45	17	13	12	69
1990— Asheville (SAL)	6	8	.429	5.18	28	22	1	0	1	132	149	87	76	47	111
1991— Burlington (Midw.)	7	5	.583	2.03	16	16	3	1	0	106 2/3	73	30	24	21	102
— Osceola (FSL)	6	3	.667	2.09	12	12	4	2	0	77 1/3	55	22	18	11	62
1992— Osceola (FSL)	3	1	.750	2.63	7	7	0	0	0	41	37	13	12	8	30
— Jackson (Texas)	9	6	.600	3.54	18	18	2	0	0	114 1/3	114	51	45	26	99
1993— Tucson (PCL)	6	4	.600	3.83	25	22	0	0	0	131 2/3	147	73	56	25	89
1994— Tucson (PCL)	11	8	.579	4.43	26	24	2	2	0	148 1/3	171	87	73	35	84
1995— Tucson (PCL)	*17	6	.739	*3.30	28	•28	0	0	0	*177 1/3	190	72	65	32	*119
— Houston (N.L.)	3	1	.750	5.55	6	5	0	0	0	24 1/3	33	19	15	5	16
1996— Tucson (PCL)	3	3	.500	4.13	8	8	0	0	0	52 1/3	67	30	24	6	36
— Houston (N.L.)	9	8	.529	4.56	26	23	2	1	0	150	170	84	76	34	99
1997— New Orleans (A.A.)	8	7	.533	3.85	17	17	1	0	0	110	109	49	47	24	84
— Houston (N.L.)	2	5	.286	6.26	8	8	0	0	0	41 2/3	53	31	29	16	25
1998— Las Vegas (PCL)■	2	0	1.000	4.80	3	3	0	0	0	15	11	8	8	8	12
— San Diego (N.L.)	5	4	.556	2.43	46	1	0	0	1	70 1/3	50	20	19	32	56
1999— San Diego (N.L.)	7	4	.636	3.07	55	0	0	0	0	70 1/3	58	31	24	23	53
Major League totals (5 years)	26	22	.542	4.11	141	37	2	1	1	356 2/3	364	185	163	110	249

DIVISION SERIES RECORD

Year League	W	L	Pct.	ERA	G	GS	CG	ShO	Sv.	IP	H	R	ER	BB	SO
1998— San Diego (N.L.)	0	0	...	9.00	1	0	0	0	0	1	2	1	1	0	2

CHAMPIONSHIP SERIES RECORD

Year League	W	L	Pct.	ERA	G	GS	CG	ShO	Sv.	IP	H	R	ER	BB	SO
1998— San Diego (N.L.)	0	0	...	3.00	3	0	0	0	1	3	3	2	1	4	4

WORLD SERIES RECORD

Year League	W	L	Pct.	ERA	G	GS	CG	ShO	Sv.	IP	H	R	ER	BB	SO
1998— San Diego (N.L.)	0	1	.000	6.75	2	0	0	0	0	2 2/3	3	2	2	3	1

PERSONAL: Born September 1, 1971, in Van Nuys, Calif. ... 6-3/215. ... Throws right, bats right. ... Full name: Derek Robert Wallace.

HIGH SCHOOL: Chatsworth (Calif.).

COLLEGE: Pepperdine.

TRANSACTIONS/CAREER NOTES: Selected by Pittsburgh Pirates organization in 36th round of free-agent draft (June 5, 1989); did not sign. ... Selected by Chicago Cubs organization in first round (11th pick overall) of free-agent draft (June 1, 1992). ... Traded by Cubs with P Geno Morones to Kansas City Royals for OF Brian McRae (April 5, 1995). ... Traded by Royals with a player to be named later to New York Mets for P Jason Jacome and P Allen McDill (July 21, 1995); Mets acquired P John Carter to complete deal (November 16, 1995). ... On New York disabled list (March 27, 1997-entire season); included rehabilitation assignments to Gulf Coast Mets (July 22-August 17), St. Lucie (August 18-August 31) and Norfolk (September 1). ... Traded by Mets to Kansas City Royals for P Jeremy Jackson (August 13, 1999).

RECORDS: Shares major league record for most strikeouts in one inning—4 (September 13, 1996, ninth inning).

STATISTICAL NOTES: Led Florida State League with 11 balks in 1993.

Year League	W	L	Pct.	ERA	G	GS	CG	ShO	Sv.	IP	H	R	ER	BB	SO
1992— Peoria (Midw.)	0	1	.000	4.91	2	0	0	0	0	3 2/3	3	2	2	1	2
1993— Daytona (FSL)	5	6	.455	4.20	14	12	0	0	1	79 1/3	85	50	37	23	34
— Iowa (A.A.)	0	0	...	11.25	1	1	0	0	0	4	8	5	5	1	2
— Orlando (Sou.)	5	7	.417	5.03	15	15	2	0	0	96 2/3	105	59	54	28	69
1994— Orlando (Sou.)	2	9	.182	5.74	33	12	1	0	8	89 1/3	95	61	57	31	49
— Iowa (A.A.)	0	1	.000	4.15	5	0	0	0	1	4 1/3	4	4	2	4	3
1995— Wichita (Texas)■	4	3	.571	4.40	26	0	0	0	6	43	51	23	21	13	24
— Binghamton (East.)■	0	1	.000	5.28	15	0	0	0	2	15 1/3	11	9	9	9	8
1996— Norfolk (I.L.)	5	2	.714	1.72	49	0	0	0	26	57 2/3	37	20	11	17	52
— New York (N.L.)	2	3	.400	4.01	19	0	0	0	3	24 2/3	29	12	11	14	15
1997— Gulf Coast Mets (GCL)	0	1	.000	3.38	8	5	0	0	0	8	6	3	3	1	9
— St. Lucie (FSL)	0	0	...	6.43	5	0	0	0	0	7	7	6	5	2	8
— Norfolk (I.L.)	0	1	.000	9.00	1	0	0	0	0	1	2	2	1	1	0
1998— Norfolk (I.L.)	5	2	.714	3.88	54	0	0	0	16	60 1/3	58	31	26	27	50
1999— Norfolk (I.L.)	2	5	.286	3.60	36	0	0	0	7	55	53	24	22	25	38
— Kansas City (A.L.)■	0	1	.000	3.24	8	0	0	0	0	8 1/3	7	4	3	5	5
A.L. totals (1 year)	0	1	.000	3.24	8	0	0	0	0	8 1/3	7	4	3	5	5
N.L. totals (1 year)	2	3	.400	4.01	19	0	0	0	3	24 2/3	29	12	11	14	15
Major League totals (2 years)	2	4	.333	3.82	27	0	0	0	3	33	36	16	14	19	20

W

WALLACE, JEFF   P   PIRATES

PERSONAL: Born April 12, 1976, in Wheeling, W.Va. ... 6-2/238. ... Throws left, bats left. ... Full name: Jeffrey Allen Wallace.
HIGH SCHOOL: Minerva (Ohio).
TRANSACTIONS/CAREER NOTES: Selected by Kansas City Royals organization in 25th round of free-agent draft (June 1, 1995). ... Traded by Royals with P Jeff Granger, P Jeff Martin and 3B Joe Randa to Pittsburgh Pirates for SS Jay Bell and 1B Jeff King (December 13, 1996). ... On disabled list (March 22, 1998-entire season). ... On Pittsburgh disabled list (July 3-August 19, 1999); included rehabilitation assignment to Nashville (July 20-August 18).

Year	League	W	L	Pct.	ERA	G	GS	CG	ShO	Sv.	IP	H	R	ER	BB	SO
1995—	Sarasota Royals (GCL)	5	3	.625	1.22	12	7	0	0	1	44 1/3	28	20	6	15	51
1996—	Lansing (Midw.)	4	9	.308	5.30	30	21	0	0	0	122 1/3	140	79	72	66	84
1997—	Lynchburg (Caro.)■	5	0	1.000	1.65	9	0	0	0	1	16 1/3	9	3	3	10	13
—	Carolina (Sou.)	4	8	.333	5.40	38	0	0	0	3	43 1/3	43	37	26	36	39
—	Pittsburgh (N.L.)	0	0	...	0.75	11	0	0	0	0	12	8	2	1	8	14
1998—	Pittsburgh (N.L.)							Did not play.								
1999—	Nashville (PCL)	2	2	.500	8.79	15	0	0	0	3	14 1/3	18	15	14	8	14
—	Pittsburgh (N.L.)	1	0	1.000	3.69	41	0	0	0	0	39	26	17	16	38	41
Major League totals (2 years)		**1**	**0**	**1.000**	**3.00**	**52**	**0**	**0**	**0**	**0**	**51**	**34**	**19**	**17**	**46**	**55**

WARD, BRYAN   P

PERSONAL: Born January 25, 1972, in Bristol, Pa. ... 6-2/210. ... Throws left, bats left. ... Full name: Bryan Matthew Ward.
HIGH SCHOOL: Rancoccas Valley Regional (Mount Holly, N.J.).
JUNIOR COLLEGE: County College of Morris (N.J.).
COLLEGE: South Carolina-Aiken.
TRANSACTIONS/CAREER NOTES: Selected by Florida Marlins organization in 20th round of free-agent draft (June 3, 1993). ... On Portland disabled list (April 23-May 1, 1997). ... Claimed on waivers by Chicago White Sox (October 14, 1997). ... Granted free agency (October 4, 1999).

Year	League	W	L	Pct.	ERA	G	GS	CG	ShO	Sv.	IP	H	R	ER	BB	SO
1993—	Elmira (NY-P)	2	5	.286	4.99	14	11	0	0	0	61 1/3	82	41	34	26	63
1994—	Kane County (Midw.)	3	4	.429	3.40	47	0	0	0	11	55 2/3	46	27	21	21	62
1995—	Brevard County (FSL)	5	1	.833	2.88	11	11	0	0	0	72	68	27	23	17	65
—	Portland (East.)	7	3	.700	4.50	20	11	1	1	2	72	70	42	36	31	71
1996—	Portland (East.)	9	9	.500	4.91	28	25	2	0	0	146 2/3	170	97	80	32	124
1997—	Portland (East.)	6	3	.667	3.91	12	12	0	0	0	76	71	39	33	19	69
—	Charlotte (I.L.)	2	9	.182	6.93	15	14	2	0	0	75 1/3	102	62	58	30	48
1998—	Birmingham (Sou.)■	2	3	.400	2.36	29	0	0	0	12	42	33	19	11	25	41
—	Chicago (A.L.)	1	2	.333	3.33	28	0	0	0	1	27	30	13	10	7	17
1999—	Chicago (A.L.)	0	1	.000	7.55	40	0	0	0	0	39 1/3	63	36	33	11	35
—	Charlotte (I.L.)	2	0	1.000	3.52	14	0	0	0	1	15 1/3	15	7	6	3	15
Major League totals (2 years)		**1**	**3**	**.250**	**5.83**	**68**	**0**	**0**	**0**	**1**	**66 1/3**	**93**	**49**	**43**	**18**	**52**

WARD, DARYLE   1B/OF   ASTROS

PERSONAL: Born June 27, 1975, in Lynwood, Calif. ... 6-2/230. ... Bats left, throws left. ... Full name: Daryle Lamar Ward. ... Son of Gary Ward, outfielder with four major league teams (1979-90); and hitting coach, Charlotte Knights of International League.
HIGH SCHOOL: Brethren Christian (Riverside, Calif.).
JUNIOR COLLEGE: Rancho Santiago College (Calif.).
TRANSACTIONS/CAREER NOTES: Selected by Detroit Tigers organization in 15th round of free-agent draft (June 2, 1994). ... Traded by Tigers with C Brad Ausmus, P Jose Lima, P C.J. Nitkowski and P Trever Miller to Houston Astros for OF Brian Hunter, IF Orlando Miller, P Doug Brocail, P Todd Jones and cash (December 10, 1996).
STATISTICAL NOTES: Tied for Texas League lead with four intentional bases on balls in 1997.

							BATTING							FIELDING		
Year	Team (League)	Pos.	G	AB	R	H	2B	3B	HR	RBI	Avg.	BB	SO	SB	PO	A	E	Avg.
1994—	Bristol (Appl.)	1B	48	161	17	43	6	0	5	30	.267	19	33	5	308	23	11	.968
1995—	Fayetteville (SAL)	1B	137	524	75	149	32	6	14	106	.284	46	111	1	1009	77	14	.987
1996—	Lakeland (FSL)	1B-DH	128	464	65	135	29	4	10	68	.291	57	77	1	1058	83	8	.993
—	Toledo (I.L.)	1B	6	23	1	4	0	0	0	1	.174	0	3	0	42	5	1	.979
1997—	Jackson (Texas)■	1B-DH	114	422	72	139	25	0	19	90	.329	46	68	4	951	76	12	.988
—	New Orleans (A.A.)	1B-DH	14	48	4	18	1	0	2	8	.375	7	7	0	75	6	2	.976
1998—	New Orleans (PCL)	OF-1B-DH	116	463	78	141	31	6	23	96	.305	41	78	2	482	48	13	.976
—	Houston (N.L.)	PH	4	3	1	1	0	0	0	0	.333	1	2	0	...	...	...	...
1999—	New Orleans (PCL)	1B-OF	61	241	56	85	15	1	28	65	.353	23	43	1	528	35	5	.991
—	Houston (N.L.)	OF-1B-DH	64	150	11	41	6	0	8	30	.273	9	31	0	69	3	2	.973
Major League totals (2 years)			**68**	**153**	**12**	**42**	**6**	**0**	**8**	**30**	**.275**	**10**	**33**	**0**	**69**	**3**	**2**	**.973**

DIVISION SERIES RECORD

							BATTING							FIELDING		
Year	Team (League)	Pos.	G	AB	R	H	2B	3B	HR	RBI	Avg.	BB	SO	SB	PO	A	E	Avg.
1999—	Houston (N.L.)	OF-PH	3	7	1	1	0	0	1	1	.143	0	2	0	3	0	1	.750

WARD, TURNER   OF

PERSONAL: Born April 11, 1965, in Orlando. ... 6-2/204. ... Bats both, throws right. ... Full name: Turner Max Ward.
HIGH SCHOOL: Satsuma (Ala.).
JUNIOR COLLEGE: Faulkner State Community College (Ala.).

W

COLLEGE: South Alabama.

TRANSACTIONS/CAREER NOTES: Selected by New York Yankees organization in 18th round of free-agent draft (June 2, 1986). ... Traded by Yankees with C Joel Skinner to Cleveland Indians for OF Mel Hall (March 19, 1989). ... On Gulf Coast Indians disabled list (April 7-July 24, 1989). ... Traded by Indians with P Tom Candiotti to Toronto Blue Jays for P Denis Boucher, OF Glenallen Hill, OF Mark Whiten and a player to be named later (June 27, 1991); Indians acquired cash to complete deal (October 15, 1991). ... On Toronto disabled list (August 2-September 1, 1993); included rehabilitation assignment to Knoxville (August 21-September 1). ... Claimed on waivers by Milwaukee Brewers (November 24, 1993). ... On Milwaukee disabled list (June 7-22, July 2-19 and July 24, 1995-remainder of season); included rehabilitation assignments to Beloit (July 17-19) and New Orleans (August 10-17 and August 31-September 5). ... On Milwaukee disabled list (May 25-September 1, 1996). ... Released by Brewers (November 1, 1996). ... Signed by Pittsburgh Pirates organization (April 22, 1997). ... On disabled list (August 5-20, 1998). ... On Pittsburgh disabled list (June 9-August 11, 1999); included rehabilitation assignments to Altoona (June 23-24) and Nashville (June 25-August 1 and August 2-9). ... Released by Pirates (August 11, 1999). ... Signed by Arizona Diamondbacks organization (August 18, 1999). ... On Arizona disabled list (August 31-September 15, 1999). ... Granted free agency (November 1, 1999).

STATISTICAL NOTES: Led Pacific Coast League outfielders with 292 putouts and 308 total chances in 1990.

Year Team (League)	Pos.	G	AB	R	H	2B	3B	HR	RBI	Avg.	BB	SO	SB	PO	A	E	Avg.
1986— Oneonta (NY-P)	OF-1B-3B	63	221	42	62	4	1	1	19	.281	31	39	6	97	6	5	.954
1987— Fort Lauderdale (FSL)	OF-3B	130	493	83	145	15	2	7	55	.294	64	83	25	332	11	8	.977
1988— Columbus (I.L.)	OF	134	490	55	123	24	1	7	50	.251	48	100	28	223	5	1	*.996
1989— GC Indians (GCL)■	DH	4	15	2	3	0	0	0	1	.200	2	2	1	...	...	...	...
— Canton/Akron (East.)	OF	30	93	19	28	5	1	0	3	.301	15	16	1	2	0	0	1.000
1990— Colo. Springs (PCL)	OF-2B	133	495	89	148	24	9	6	65	.299	72	70	22	†292	7	9	.971
— Cleveland (A.L.)	OF-DH	14	46	10	16	2	1	1	10	.348	3	8	3	20	2	1	.957
1991— Cleveland (A.L.)	OF	40	100	11	23	7	0	0	5	.230	10	16	0	65	1	0	1.000
— Colo. Springs (PCL)	OF	14	51	5	10	1	1	1	3	.196	6	9	2	30	0	1	.968
— Toronto (A.L.)■	OF	8	13	1	4	0	0	0	2	.308	1	2	0	5	0	0	1.000
— Syracuse (I.L.)	OF	59	218	40	72	11	3	7	32	.330	47	22	9	136	5	0	1.000
1992— Toronto (A.L.)	OF	18	29	7	10	3	0	1	3	.345	4	4	0	18	1	0	1.000
— Syracuse (I.L.)	OF	81	280	41	67	10	2	10	29	.239	44	43	7	143	3	5	.967
1993— Toronto (A.L.)	OF-1B	72	167	20	32	4	2	4	28	.192	23	26	3	97	2	1	.990
— Knoxville (Sou.)	OF	7	23	6	6	2	0	0	2	.261	7	3	3	20	0	0	1.000
1994— Milwaukee (A.L.)■	OF-3B	102	367	55	85	15	2	9	45	.232	52	68	6	260	9	4	.985
1995— Milwaukee (A.L.)	OF-DH	44	129	19	34	3	1	4	16	.264	14	21	6	81	5	1	.989
— Beloit (Midw.)	OF	2	5	0	0	0	0	0	0	.000	3	1	0	1	0	0	1.000
— New Orleans (A.A.)	OF-DH	11	33	3	8	1	1	1	3	.242	4	10	0	9	0	1	.900
1996— Milwaukee (A.L.)	OF-DH	43	67	7	12	2	1	2	10	.179	13	17	3	54	1	0	1.000
— New Orleans (A.A.)	DH	9	23	4	8	1	0	1	1	.348	7	4	0	...	...	...	...
1997— Calgary (PCL)■	OF-DH-1B	59	209	44	71	18	3	9	44	.340	24	26	7	87	6	3	.969
— Pittsburgh (N.L.)	OF	71	167	33	59	16	1	7	33	.353	18	17	4	71	2	0	1.000
1998— Pittsburgh (N.L.)	OF-DH	123	282	33	74	13	3	9	46	.262	27	40	5	163	7	3	.983
1999— Pittsburgh (N.L.)	OF	49	91	2	19	2	0	0	8	.209	13	9	2	41	1	2	.955
— Altoona (East.)	DH	1	3	1	0	0	0	0	0	.000	2	2	0	0	0	0	...
— Nashville (PCL)	OF-DH	35	89	15	26	3	1	2	17	.292	16	14	3	17	1	2	.900
— Tucson (PCL)■	OF	12	40	9	15	2	0	2	8	.375	7	4	4	18	1	2	.905
— Arizona (N.L.)	OF	10	23	6	8	1	0	2	7	.348	2	6	0	11	0	0	1.000
American League totals (7 years)		341	918	130	216	36	7	21	119	.235	120	162	21	600	21	7	.989
National League totals (3 years)		253	563	74	160	32	4	18	94	.284	60	72	11	286	10	5	.983
Major League totals (10 years)		594	1481	204	376	68	11	39	213	.254	180	234	32	886	31	12	.987

DIVISION SERIES RECORD

Year Team (League)	Pos.	G	AB	R	H	2B	3B	HR	RBI	Avg.	BB	SO	SB	PO	A	E	Avg.
1999— Arizona (N.L.)	PH	3	2	2	1	0	0	1	3	.500	1	0	0	0	0	0	...

WASDIN, JOHN   P   RED SOX

PERSONAL: Born August 5, 1972, in Fort Belvoir, Va. ... 6-2/195. ... Throws right, bats right. ... Full name: John Truman Wasdin.

HIGH SCHOOL: Amos P. Godby (Tallahassee, Fla.).

COLLEGE: Florida State.

TRANSACTIONS/CAREER NOTES: Selected by New York Yankees organization in 41st round of free-agent draft (June 4, 1990); did not sign. ... Selected by Oakland Athletics organization in first round (25th pick overall) of free-agent draft (June 3, 1993). ... Traded by A's with cash to Boston Red Sox for OF Jose Canseco (January 27, 1997). ... On Boston disabled list (July 18-August 5, 1999); included rehabilitation assignment to Gulf Coast Red Sox (July 30-31).

STATISTICAL NOTES: Led Pacific Coast League with 26 home runs allowed in 1995.

Year League	W	L	Pct.	ERA	G	GS	CG	ShO	Sv.	IP	H	R	ER	BB	SO
1993— Arizona Athletics (Ariz.)	0	0	...	3.00	1	1	0	0	0	3	3	1	1	0	1
— Madison (Midw.)	2	3	.400	1.86	9	9	0	0	0	48 1/3	32	11	10	9	40
— Modesto (Calif.)	0	3	.000	3.86	3	3	0	0	0	16 1/3	17	9	7	4	11
1994— Modesto (Calif.)	3	1	.750	1.69	6	4	0	0	0	26 2/3	17	6	5	5	30
— Huntsville (Sou.)	12	3	.800	3.43	21	21	0	0	0	141 2/3	126	61	54	29	108
1995— Edmonton (PCL)	12	8	.600	5.52	29	•28	2	1	0	174 1/3	193	117	107	38	111
— Oakland (A.L.)	1	1	.500	4.67	5	2	0	0	0	17 1/3	14	9	9	3	6
1996— Edmonton (PCL)	2	1	.667	4.14	9	9	0	0	0	50	52	23	23	17	30
— Oakland (A.L.)	8	7	.533	5.96	25	21	1	0	0	131 1/3	145	96	87	50	75
1997— Boston (A.L.)■	4	6	.400	4.40	53	7	0	0	0	124 2/3	121	68	61	38	84
1998— Boston (A.L.)	6	4	.600	5.25	47	8	0	0	0	96	111	57	56	27	59
— Pawtucket (I.L.)	1	0	1.000	3.00	4	2	0	0	0	12	11	6	4	5	10
1999— Pawtucket (I.L.)	1	1	.500	2.12	5	5	0	0	0	29 2/3	19	9	7	7	28
— Boston (A.L.)	8	3	.727	4.12	45	6	0	0	2	74 1/3	66	38	34	18	52
— GC Red Sox (GCL)	0	0	...	0.00	1	1	0	0	0	2	1	0	0	0	4
Major League totals (5 years)	27	21	.563	5.01	175	38	1	0	2	443 2/3	457	268	247	136	281

Year League	W	L	Pct.	ERA	G	GS	CG	ShO	Sv.	IP	H	R	ER	BB	SO
1998—Boston (A.L.)	0	0	...	10.80	1	0	0	0	0	1 2/3	2	2	2	1	2
1999—Boston (A.L.)	0	0	...	27.00	2	0	0	0	0	1 2/3	2	5	5	4	1
Division series totals (2 years)	0	0	...	18.90	3	0	0	0	0	3 1/3	4	7	7	5	3

CHAMPIONSHIP SERIES RECORD

Year League	W	L	Pct.	ERA	G	GS	CG	ShO	Sv.	IP	H	R	ER	BB	SO
1999—Boston (A.L.)							Did not play.								

WASHBURN, JARROD   P   ANGELS

PERSONAL: Born August 13, 1974, in La Crosse, Wis. ... 6-1/198. ... Throws left, bats left. ... Full name: Jarrod Michael Washburn.
HIGH SCHOOL: Webster (Wis.).
COLLEGE: Wisconsin-Oshkosh.
TRANSACTIONS/CAREER NOTES: Selected by California Angels organization in second round of free-agent draft (June 1, 1995). ... On Edmonton disabled list (April 26-June 17, 1999).

Year League	W	L	Pct.	ERA	G	GS	CG	ShO	Sv.	IP	H	R	ER	BB	SO
1995—Cedar Rapids (Midw.)	0	1	.000	3.44	3	3	0	0	0	18 1/3	17	7	7	7	20
— Boise (N'west)	3	2	.600	3.33	8	8	0	0	0	46	35	17	17	14	54
1996—Lake Elsinore (Calif.)	6	3	.667	3.30	14	14	3	0	0	92 2/3	79	38	34	33	93
— Midland (Texas)	5	6	.455	4.40	13	13	1	0	0	88	77	44	43	25	58
— Vancouver (PCL)	0	2	.000	10.80	2	2	0	0	0	8 1/3	12	16	10	...	12
1997—Midland (Texas)	15	•12	.556	4.80	29	*29	29	•1	0	*189 1/3	*211	*115	*101	65	*146
— Vancouver (PCL)	0	0	...	3.60	1	1	0	0	0	5	4	2	2	2	6
1998—Vancouver (PCL)	4	5	.444	4.32	14	14	2	0	0	91 2/3	91	44	44	43	66
— Anaheim (A.L.)	6	3	.667	4.62	15	11	0	0	0	74	70	40	38	27	48
— Midland (Texas)	0	1	.000	6.23	1	1	0	0	0	8 2/3	13	8	6	2	8
1999—Edmonton (PCL)	1	5	.167	4.73	11	11	1	0	0	59	50	31	31	17	55
— Anaheim (A.L.)	4	5	.444	5.25	16	10	0	0	0	61 2/3	61	36	36	26	39
Major League totals (2 years)	10	8	.556	4.91	31	21	0	0	0	135 2/3	131	76	74	53	87

WASHINGTON, RICO   3B/C   PIRATES

PERSONAL: Born May 30, 1978, in Milledgeville, Ga. ... 5-10/179. ... Bats left, throws right. ... Full name: Enrico Alicene Washington.
HIGH SCHOOL: Jones County (Gray, Ga.).
TRANSACTIONS/CAREER NOTES: Selected by Pittsburgh Pirates organization in 10th round of free-agent draft (June 3, 1997).
STATISTICAL NOTES: Led South Atlantic League with seven intentional bases on balls received in 1999.

							BATTING						FIELDING		
Year Team (League)	Pos.	G	AB	R	H	2B	3B	HR	RBI	Avg.	BB	SO	SB	PO	A	E	Avg.
1997—GC Pirates (GCL)	3B-2B-SS	28	98	12	24	6	0	1	11	.245	4	13	1	21	46	17	.798
1998—Erie (NY-P)	3B-2B	51	197	31	65	14	2	6	31	.330	17	33	1	24	104	8	.941
— Augusta (SAL)	3B-2B-SS	12	50	12	15	2	1	2	12	.300	7	9	2	4	14	0	1.000
1999—Hickory (SAL)	C-3B	76	287	70	102	15	1	13	50	.355	48	45	5	471	46	9	.983
— Lynchburg (Caro.)	3B-2B-C	57	205	31	58	7	0	7	32	.283	30	45	4	132	109	10	.960

WATKINS, PAT   OF   REDS

PERSONAL: Born September 2, 1972, in Raleigh, N.C. ... 6-2/195. ... Bats right, throws right. ... Full name: William Patrick Watkins.
HIGH SCHOOL: Garner (N.C.).
COLLEGE: East Carolina.
TRANSACTIONS/CAREER NOTES: Selected by Cincinnati Reds organization in supplemental round ("sandwich pick" between first and second round, 32nd pick overall) of free-agent draft (June 3, 1993); pick recieved as part of compensation for Houston Astros signing Type A free-agent P Greg Swindell. ... Traded by Reds to Florida Marlins for P Pedro Minaya (January 6, 1999). ... Traded by Marlins to Colorado Rockies for a player to be named (March 29, 1999); Marlins acquired P Keith Gordon to complete deal (July 16, 1999). ... Granted free agency (October 15, 1999). ... Signed by Reds organization (November 3, 1999).
STATISTICAL NOTES: Led Carolina League with 267 total bases in 1994. ... Tied for Carolina League lead in double plays by outfielder with four in 1994. ... Tied for International League lead in double plays by outfielder with three in 1998.

							BATTING						FIELDING		
Year Team (League)	Pos.	G	AB	R	H	2B	3B	HR	RBI	Avg.	BB	SO	SB	PO	A	E	Avg.
1993—Billings (Pio.)	OF	66	235	46	63	10	3	6	30	.268	22	44	15	123	5	2	.985
1994—Win.-Salem (Car.)	OF	132	*524	*107	*152	24	5	27	83	.290	62	84	31	262	13	7	.975
1995—Win.-Salem (Car.)	OF	27	107	14	22	3	1	4	13	.206	10	24	1	51	5	1	.982
— Chattanooga (Sou.)	OF	105	358	57	104	26	2	12	57	.291	33	53	5	185	8	8	.960
1996—Chattanooga (Sou.)	OF	127	492	63	136	31	2	8	59	.276	30	64	15	220	*21	4	.984
1997—Chattanooga (Sou.)	OF-DH	46	177	35	62	15	1	7	30	.350	15	16	9	78	3	0	1.000
— Indianapolis (A.A.)	OF	84	325	46	91	14	7	9	35	.280	24	55	13	170	5	2	.989
— Cincinnati (N.L.)	OF	17	29	2	6	2	0	0	0	.207	0	5	1	12	1	0	1.000
1998—Cincinnati (N.L.)	OF	83	147	11	39	8	1	2	15	.265	8	26	1	98	1	3	.971
— Indianapolis (I.L.)	OF	44	188	37	71	12	1	3	24	.378	15	26	8	98	5	2	.981
1999—Colorado (N.L.)■	OF	16	19	2	1	0	0	0	0	.053	2	5	0	10	0	0	1.000
— Colo. Springs (PCL)	OF-2B	12	30	4	10	1	0	0	2	.333	2	6	0	14	0	0	1.000
— Carolina (Sou.) OF-2B-DH-SS	88	312	38	93	27	1	3	40	.298	24	49	6	133	36	7	.960
Major League totals (3 years)		116	195	15	46	10	1	2	15	.236	10	36	2	120	2	3	.976

W

PERSONAL: Born November 18, 1970, in New York. ... 6-1/212. ... Throws left, bats left. ... Full name: Allen Kenneth Watson.
HIGH SCHOOL: Christ the King (Queens, N.Y.).
COLLEGE: New York State Institute of Technology.
TRANSACTIONS/CAREER NOTES: Selected by St. Louis Cardinals organization in first round (21st pick overall) of free-agent draft (June 3, 1991); pick received as part of compensation for Toronto Blue Jays signing Type A free-agent P Ken Dayley. ... On Savannah disabled list (August 19, 1991-remainder of season). ... On suspended list (June 25-July 3, 1994). ... On St. Louis disabled list (June 7-July 8, 1995); included rehabilitation assignments to Arkansas (June 21-26) and Louisville (June 26-July 8). ... Traded by Cardinals with P Rich DeLucia and P Doug Creek to San Francisco Giants for SS Royce Clayton and a player to be named later (December 14, 1995); Cardinals acquired 2B Chris Wimmer to complete deal (January 16, 1996). ... On San Francisco disabled list (July 2-25, 1996); included rehabilitation assignment to San Jose (July 15-25). ... Traded by Giants with P Fausto Macey to Anaheim Angels for 1B J.T. Snow (November 27, 1996). ... On Anaheim disabled list (May 24-July 13, 1998); included rehabilitation assignments to Midland (June 16), Lake Elsinore (June 21) and Vancouver (June 26). ... Granted free agency (December 21, 1998). ... Signed by New York Mets (January 19, 1999). ... Traded by Mets with cash to Seattle Mariners for P Mac Suzuki and a player to be named later (June 18, 1999); Mets acquired P Justin Dunning to complete deal (September 14, 1999). ... Released by Mariners (June 28, 1999). ... Signed by New York Yankees organization (July 3, 1999). ... Granted free agency (November 5, 1999). ... Re-signed by Yankees (December 7, 1999).
STATISTICAL NOTES: Led A.L. with 37 home runs allowed in 1997.
MISCELLANEOUS: Singled in three games as pinch hitter with San Francisco (1996).

Year	League	W	L	Pct.	ERA	G	GS	CG	ShO	Sv.	IP	H	R	ER	BB	SO
1991—	Hamilton (NY-P)	1	1	.500	2.52	8	8	0	0	0	39 1/3	22	15	11	17	46
—	Savannah (SAL)	1	1	.500	3.95	3	3	0	0	0	13 2/3	16	7	6	8	12
1992—	St. Petersburg (FSL)	5	4	.556	1.91	14	14	2	0	0	89 2/3	81	31	19	18	80
—	Arkansas (Texas)	8	5	.615	2.15	14	14	3	1	0	96 1/3	77	24	23	23	93
—	Louisville (A.A.)	1	0	1.000	1.46	2	2	0	0	0	12 1/3	8	4	2	5	9
1993—	Louisville (A.A.)	5	4	.556	2.91	17	17	2	0	0	120 2/3	101	46	39	31	86
—	St. Louis (N.L.)	6	7	.462	4.60	16	15	0	0	0	86	90	53	44	28	49
1994—	St. Louis (N.L.)	6	5	.545	5.52	22	22	0	0	0	115 2/3	130	73	71	53	74
1995—	St. Louis (N.L.)	7	9	.438	4.96	21	19	0	0	0	114 1/3	126	68	63	41	49
—	Louisville (A.A.)	2	2	.500	2.63	4	4	1	1	0	24	20	10	7	6	19
—	Arkansas (Texas)	1	0	1.000	0.00	1	1	0	0	0	5	4	1	0	0	7
1996—	San Francisco (N.L.)■	8	12	.400	4.61	29	29	2	0	0	185 2/3	189	105	95	69	128
—	San Jose (Calif.)	0	0	...	1.42	2	2	0	0	0	6 1/3	7	1	1	0	12
1997—	Anaheim (A.L.)■	12	12	.500	4.93	35	34	0	0	0	199	220	121	109	73	141
1998—	Anaheim (A.L.)	6	7	.462	6.04	28	14	1	0	0	92 1/3	122	67	62	34	64
—	Midland (Texas)	0	0	...	2.25	1	1	0	0	0	4	6	2	1	1	3
—	Lake Elsinore (Calif.)	1	0	1.000	0.00	1	1	0	0	0	5	3	0	0	1	6
—	Vancouver (PCL)	0	1	.000	4.50	1	1	0	0	0	6	6	3	3	2	8
1999—	New York (N.L.)■	2	2	.500	4.08	14	4	0	0	1	39 2/3	36	18	18	22	32
—	Seattle (A.L.)■	0	1	.000	12.00	3	0	0	0	0	3	6	9	4	3	2
—	Columbus (I.L.)■	0	0	...	6.14	2	2	0	0	0	7 1/3	7	5	5	2	5
—	New York (A.L.)	4	0	1.000	2.10	21	0	0	0	0	34 1/3	30	8	8	10	30
A.L. totals (3 years)		**22**	**20**	**.524**	**5.01**	**87**	**48**	**1**	**0**	**0**	**328 2/3**	**378**	**205**	**183**	**120**	**237**
N.L. totals (5 years)		**29**	**35**	**.453**	**4.84**	**102**	**89**	**2**	**0**	**1**	**541 1/3**	**571**	**317**	**291**	**213**	**332**
Major League totals (7 years)		**51**	**55**	**.481**	**4.90**	**189**	**137**	**3**	**0**	**1**	**870**	**949**	**522**	**474**	**333**	**569**

DIVISION SERIES RECORD

Year	League	W	L	Pct.	ERA	G	GS	CG	ShO	Sv.	IP	H	R	ER	BB	SO
1999—	New York (A.L.)							Did not play.								

CHAMPIONSHIP SERIES RECORD

Year	League	W	L	Pct.	ERA	G	GS	CG	ShO	Sv.	IP	H	R	ER	BB	SO
1999—	New York (A.L.)	0	0	...	0.00	3	0	0	0	0	1	2	0	0	2	1

WORLD SERIES RECORD

NOTES: Member of World Series championship team (1999).

Year	League	W	L	Pct.	ERA	G	GS	CG	ShO	Sv.	IP	H	R	ER	BB	SO
1999—	New York (A.L.)							Did not play.								

W

PERSONAL: Born September 25, 1969, in Lawrenceburg, Tenn. ... 6-3/230. ... Throws right, bats right. ... Full name: John David Weathers.
HIGH SCHOOL: Loretto (Tenn.).
JUNIOR COLLEGE: Motlow State Community College (Tenn.).
TRANSACTIONS/CAREER NOTES: Selected by Toronto Blue Jays organization in third round of free-agent draft (June 1, 1988). ... On Syracuse disabled list (May 11-July 31, 1992). ... Selected by Florida Marlins in second round (29th pick overall) of expansion draft (November 17, 1992). ... On Florida disabled list (June 26-July 13, 1995); included rehabilitation assignments to Brevard County (July 4-10) and Charlotte (July 11-13). ... Traded by Marlins to New York Yankees for P Mark Hutton (July 31, 1996). ... Traded by Yankees to Cleveland Indians for OF Chad Curtis (June 9, 1997). ... Claimed on waivers by Cincinnati Reds (December 20, 1997). ... Claimed on waivers by Milwaukee Brewers (June 24, 1998). ... Granted free agency (October 29, 1999). ... Re-signed by Brewers (December 2, 1999).
MISCELLANEOUS: Appeared in two games as pinch runner (1994). ... Appeared in one game as pinch runner with Florida (1996). ... Struck out in only appearance as pinch hitter.

Year	League	W	L	Pct.	ERA	G	GS	CG	ShO	Sv.	IP	H	R	ER	BB	SO
1988—	St. Catharines (NY-P)	4	4	.500	3.02	15	12	0	0	0	62 2/3	58	30	21	26	36
1989—	Myrtle Beach (SAL)	11	•13	.458	3.86	31	*31	2	0	0	172 2/3	163	99	74	86	111
1990—	Dunedin (FSL)	10	7	.588	3.70	27	•27	2	0	0	158	158	82	65	59	96
1991—	Knoxville (Sou.)	10	7	.588	2.45	24	22	5	2	0	139 1/3	121	51	38	49	114
—	Toronto (A.L.)	1	0	1.000	4.91	15	0	0	0	0	14 2/3	15	9	8	17	13

Year League	W	L	Pct.	ERA	G	GS	CG	ShO	Sv.	IP	H	R	ER	BB	SO
1992—Syracuse (I.L.)	1	4	.200	4.66	12	10	0	0	0	48 1/3	48	29	25	21	30
— Toronto (A.L.)	0	0	...	8.10	2	0	0	0	0	3 1/3	5	3	3	2	3
1993—Edmonton (PCL)■	11	4	•.733	3.83	22	22	3	1	0	141	150	77	60	47	117
— Florida (N.L.)	2	3	.400	5.12	14	6	0	0	0	45 2/3	57	26	26	13	34
1994—Florida (N.L.)	8	12	.400	5.27	24	24	0	0	0	135	166	87	79	59	72
1995—Florida (N.L.)	4	5	.444	5.98	28	15	0	0	0	90 1/3	104	68	60	52	60
— Brevard County (FSL)	0	0	...	0.00	1	1	0	0	0	4	4	0	0	1	3
— Charlotte (I.L.)	0	1	.000	9.00	1	1	0	0	0	5	10	5	5	5	0
1996—Florida (N.L.)	2	2	.500	4.54	31	8	0	0	0	71 1/3	85	41	36	28	40
— Charlotte (I.L.)	0	0	...	7.71	1	1	0	0	0	2 1/3	5	2	2	3	0
— New York (A.L.)■	0	2	.000	9.35	11	4	0	0	0	17 1/3	23	19	18	14	13
— Columbus (I.L.)	0	2	.000	5.40	3	3	0	0	0	16 2/3	20	13	10	5	7
1997—New York (A.L.)	0	1	.000	10.00	10	0	0	0	0	9	15	10	10	7	4
— Columbus (I.L.)	2	2	.500	3.19	5	5	1	0	0	36 2/3	35	18	13	7	35
— Buffalo (A.A.)■	4	3	.571	3.15	11	11	2	1	0	68 2/3	71	37	24	17	51
— Cleveland (A.L.)	1	2	.333	7.56	9	1	0	0	0	16 2/3	23	14	14	8	14
1998—Cincinnati (N.L.)■	2	4	.333	6.21	16	9	0	0	0	62 1/3	86	47	43	27	51
— Milwaukee (N.L.)■	4	1	.800	3.21	28	0	0	0	0	47 2/3	44	22	17	14	43
1999—Milwaukee (N.L.)	7	4	.636	4.65	63	0	0	0	2	93	102	49	48	38	74
A.L. totals (4 years)	2	5	.286	7.82	47	5	0	0	0	61	81	55	53	48	47
N.L. totals (6 years)	29	31	.483	5.10	204	62	0	0	2	545 1/3	644	340	309	231	374
Major League totals (9 years)	31	36	.463	5.37	251	67	0	0	2	606 1/3	725	395	362	279	421

DIVISION SERIES RECORD

Year League	W	L	Pct.	ERA	G	GS	CG	ShO	Sv.	IP	H	R	ER	BB	SO
1996— New York (A.L.)	1	0	1.000	0.00	2	0	0	0	0	5	1	0	0	0	5

CHAMPIONSHIP SERIES RECORD

Year League	W	L	Pct.	ERA	G	GS	CG	ShO	Sv.	IP	H	R	ER	BB	SO
1996— New York (A.L.)	1	0	1.000	0.00	2	0	0	0	0	3	3	0	0	0	0

WORLD SERIES RECORD

NOTES: Member of World Series championship team (1996).

Year League	W	L	Pct.	ERA	G	GS	CG	ShO	Sv.	IP	H	R	ER	BB	SO
1996— New York (A.L.)	0	0	...	3.00	3	0	0	0	0	3	2	1	1	4	3

WEAVER, ERIC   P

PERSONAL: Born August 4, 1973, in Springfield, Ill. ... 6-5/230. ... Throws right, bats right. ... Full name: James Eric Weaver.
HIGH SCHOOL: Illiopolis (Ill.).
TRANSACTIONS/CAREER NOTES: Signed as non-drafted free agent by Los Angeles Dodgers organization (July 22, 1991). ... On disabled list (May 1-August 31, 1994). ... Traded by Dodgers to Seattle Mariners for P Scott Proutty (October 12, 1998). ... On Seattle disabled list (May 15, 1999-remainder of season); included rehabilitation assignment to Tacoma (July 23-August 13 and August 26-September 7). ... Granted free agency (October 8, 1999).
STATISTICAL NOTES: Pitched 2-1 no-hit victory against Fort Lauderdale (July 17, 1992, first game).

Year League	W	L	Pct.	ERA	G	GS	CG	ShO	Sv.	IP	H	R	ER	BB	SO
1992—Vero Beach (FSL)	4	11	.267	4.12	19	18	1	0	0	89 2/3	73	52	41	57	73
1993—Bakersfield (Calif.)	6	11	.353	4.28	28	•27	0	0	0	157 2/3	135	89	75	*118	110
1994—Vero Beach (FSL)	1	3	.250	6.75	7	7	0	0	0	24	28	20	18	9	22
1995—San Antonio (Texas)	8	11	.421	4.07	27	26	1	0	0	141 2/3	147	83	64	72	105
1996—San Antonio (Texas)	10	5	.667	3.30	18	18	1	1	0	122 2/3	106	51	45	44	69
— Albuquerque (PCL)	1	4	.200	5.40	13	8	0	0	0	46 2/3	63	39	28	22	38
1997—San Antonio (Texas)	7	2	.778	3.61	13	13	2	•1	0	84 2/3	80	43	34	38	60
— Albuquerque (PCL)	0	3	.000	6.42	21	8	0	0	0	68 2/3	101	53	49	38	54
1998—Albuquerque (PCL)	2	5	.286	5.55	46	0	0	0	3	61 2/3	65	41	38	32	63
— Los Angeles (N.L.)	2	0	1.000	0.93	7	0	0	0	0	9 2/3	5	1	1	6	5
1999—Seattle (A.L.)■	0	1	.000	10.61	8	0	0	0	0	9 1/3	14	12	11	8	14
— Tacoma (PCL)	1	2	.333	3.86	16	3	0	0	1	25 2/3	22	11	11	7	22
A.L. totals (1 year)	0	1	.000	10.61	8	0	0	0	0	9 1/3	14	12	11	8	14
N.L. totals (1 year)	2	0	1.000	0.93	7	0	0	0	0	9 2/3	5	1	1	6	5
Major League totals (2 years)	2	1	.667	5.68	15	0	0	0	0	19	19	13	12	14	19

WEAVER, JEFF   P   TIGERS

W

PERSONAL: Born August 22, 1976, in Northridge, Calif. ... 6-5/200. ... Throws right, bats right. ... Full name: Jeffery C. Weaver. ... Cousin of Jed Weaver, tight end, Philadelphia Eagles.
HIGH SCHOOL: Simi Valley (Calif.).
COLLEGE: Fresno State.
TRANSACTIONS/CAREER NOTES: Selected by Detroit Tigers organization in first round (14th pick overall) of free-agent draft (June 2, 1998).
STATISTICAL NOTES: Led A.L. pitchers with 17 hit batsmen in 1999.
MISCELLANEOUS: Member of 1996 U.S. Olympic baseball team. ... Appeared in one game as pinch runner (1999).

Year League	W	L	Pct.	ERA	G	GS	CG	ShO	Sv.	IP	H	R	ER	BB	SO
1998—Jamestown (NY-P)	1	0	1.000	1.50	3	3	0	0	0	12	6	4	2	1	12
— West Michigan (Midw.)	1	0	1.000	1.38	2	2	0	0	0	13	8	3	2	0	21
1999—Detroit (A.L.)	9	12	.429	5.55	30	29	0	0	0	163 2/3	176	104	101	56	114
— Jacksonville (Sou.)	0	0	...	3.00	1	1	0	0	0	6	5	2	2	0	6
Major League totals (1 year)	9	12	.429	5.55	30	29	0	0	0	163 2/3	176	104	101	56	114

PERSONAL: Born November 17, 1969, in Port Arthur, Texas. ... 6-4/180. ... Throws right, bats right. ... Full name: Benjamin Edward Weber.
HIGH SCHOOL: Port Neches-Groves (Port Neches, Texas).
COLLEGE: Houston.
TRANSACTIONS/CAREER NOTES: Selected by Toronto Blue Jays organization in 20th round of free-agent draft (June 3, 1991). ... Released by Blue Jays (March 24, 1996). ... Signed by Salinas, Western League (May 1996). ... Signed by Taipei, Taiwan League (1997). ... Signed by San Francisco Giants organization (October 30, 1998).

Year	League	W	L	Pct.	ERA	G	GS	CG	ShO	Sv.	IP	H	R	ER	BB	SO
1991	St. Catharines (NY-P)	6	3	.667	3.24	16	14	1	0	0	97 1/3	•105	43	35	24	60
1992	Myrtle Beach (SAL)	4	7	.364	1.64	41	1	0	0	6	98 2/3	83	27	18	29	65
1993	Dunedin (FSL)	8	3	.727	2.92	55	0	0	0	12	83 1/3	87	36	27	25	45
1994	Dunedin (FSL)	3	2	.600	2.73	18	0	0	0	3	26 1/3	25	8	8	5	19
	Knoxville (Sou.)	4	3	.571	3.76	25	10	0	0	0	95 2/3	103	49	40	16	55
1995	Syracuse (I.L.)	4	5	.444	5.40	25	15	0	0	1	91 2/3	111	62	55	27	38
	Knoxville (Sou.)	4	1	.800	3.91	12	1	0	0	0	25 1/3	26	12	11	6	16
1996	Salinas (West.)■	•12	6	.667	3.47	22	22	2	...	0	148	138	68	57	42	102
1997	Taipei (Taiwan)■	7	3	.700	5.18	40	...	...	...	5	99	85	...	...	33	78
1998	Taipei (Taiwan)■	12	7	.632	3.56	56	...	...	...	7	144	150	...	...	52	122
1999	Fresno (PCL)■	2	4	.333	3.34	51	0	0	0	8	86 1/3	78	34	32	28	67

PERSONAL: Born February 10, 1965, in New Orleans. ... 5-9/200. ... Bats right, throws right. ... Full name: Leonard Irell Webster.
HIGH SCHOOL: Lutcher (La.).
COLLEGE: Grambling State.
TRANSACTIONS/CAREER NOTES: Selected by Minnesota Twins organization in 16th round of free-agent draft (June 7, 1982); did not sign. ... Selected by Twins organization in 21st round of free-agent draft (June 3, 1985). ... Traded by Twins to Montreal Expos for a player to be named later (March 14, 1994). ... Granted free agency (December 23, 1994). ... Signed by Philadelphia Phillies organization (April 7, 1995). ... Claimed on waivers by Expos (March 29, 1996). ... Granted free agency (October 16, 1996). ... Signed by Baltimore Orioles organization (December 18, 1996). ... Granted free agency (October 30, 1997). ... Re-signed by Orioles (November 24, 1997). ... On Baltimore disabled list (May 13-July 16, 1999); included rehabilitation assignment to Rochester (June 22-July 8). ... Released by Orioles (July 21, 1999). ... Signed by Boston Red Sox (July 28, 1999). ... Released by Red Sox (August 20, 1999).
HONORS: Named Midwest League Most Valuable Player (1988).

Year	Team (League)	Pos.	G	AB	R	H	2B	3B	HR	RBI	Avg.	BB	SO	SB	PO	A	E	Avg.
1986	Kenosha (Midw.)	C	22	65	2	10	2	0	0	8	.154	10	12	0	87	9	0	1.000
	Elizabethton (Appl.)	C	48	152	29	35	4	0	3	14	.230	22	21	1	88	11	3	.971
1987	Kenosha (Midw.)	C	52	140	17	35	7	0	3	17	.250	17	20	2	228	29	5	.981
1988	Kenosha (Midw.)	C	129	465	82	134	23	2	11	87	.288	71	47	3	606	96	14	.980
1989	Visalia (Calif.)	C	63	231	36	62	7	0	5	39	.268	27	27	2	352	57	4	.990
	Orlando (Sou.)	C	59	191	29	45	7	0	2	17	.236	44	20	2	293	46	4	.988
	Minnesota (A.L.)	C	14	20	3	6	2	0	0	1	.300	3	2	0	32	0	0	1.000
1990	Orlando (Sou.)	C	126	455	69	119	31	0	8	71	.262	68	57	0	629	70	9	.987
	Minnesota (A.L.)	C	2	6	1	2	1	0	0	0	.333	1	1	0	9	0	0	1.000
1991	Portland (PCL)	C	87	325	43	82	18	0	7	34	.252	24	32	1	477	65	6	*.989
	Minnesota (A.L.)	C	18	34	7	10	1	0	3	8	.294	6	10	0	61	10	1	.986
1992	Minnesota (A.L.)	C-DH	53	118	10	33	10	1	1	13	.280	9	11	0	190	11	1	.995
1993	Minnesota (A.L.)	C-DH	49	106	14	21	2	0	1	8	.198	11	8	1	177	13	0	1.000
1994	Montreal (N.L.)■	C	57	143	13	39	10	0	5	23	.273	16	24	0	237	19	1	.996
1995	Philadelphia (N.L.)■ ...	C	49	150	18	40	9	0	4	14	.267	16	27	0	274	18	3	.990
1996	Montreal (N.L.)■	C	78	174	18	40	10	0	2	17	.230	25	21	0	390	25	1	.998
1997	Baltimore (A.L.)■	C-DH	98	259	29	66	8	1	7	37	.255	22	46	0	532	36	3	.995
1998	Baltimore (A.L.)	C-DH	108	309	37	88	16	0	10	46	.285	15	38	0	528	39	4	.993
1999	Baltimore (A.L.)	C-DH	16	36	1	6	1	0	0	3	.167	8	5	0	67	6	1	.986
	Rochester (I.L.)	C-DH	13	43	8	13	5	0	3	9	.302	4	8	0	49	4	0	1.000
	Boston (A.L.)	C	6	14	0	0	0	0	1	.000	2	2	0	25	3	0	1.000
American League totals (8 years)			364	902	102	232	41	2	22	117	.257	77	123	1	1621	118	10	.994
National League totals (3 years)			184	467	49	119	29	0	11	54	.255	57	72	0	901	62	5	.995
Major League totals (11 years)			548	1369	151	351	70	2	33	171	.256	134	195	1	2522	180	15	.994

DIVISION SERIES RECORD

| | | | | | | | | | BATTING | | | | | | | FIELDING | | |
Year	Team (League)	Pos.	G	AB	R	H	2B	3B	HR	RBI	Avg.	BB	SO	SB	PO	A	E	Avg.
1997	Baltimore (A.L.)	C	3	6	1	1	0	0	0	1	.167	1	0	0	20	0	0	1.000

CHAMPIONSHIP SERIES RECORD

| | | | | | | | | | BATTING | | | | | | | FIELDING | | |
Year	Team (League)	Pos.	G	AB	R	H	2B	3B	HR	RBI	Avg.	BB	SO	SB	PO	A	E	Avg.
1997	Baltimore (A.L.)	C-PH	4	9	0	2	0	0	0	0	.222	0	1	0	14	0	2	.875

PERSONAL: Born June 29, 1967, in Pittsburgh. ... 6-3/206. ... Bats right, throws right. ... Full name: John Paul Wehner. ... Name pronounced WAY-ner.
HIGH SCHOOL: Carrick (Pittsburgh).
COLLEGE: Indiana.

W

TRANSACTIONS/CAREER NOTES: Selected by Pittsburgh Pirates organization in seventh round of free-agent draft (June 1, 1988). ... On Pittsburgh disabled list (August 29-October 7, 1991 and July 20, 1994-remainder of season). ... Claimed on waivers by Los Angeles Dodgers (October 15, 1996). ... Released by Dodgers (March 17, 1997). ... Signed by Florida Marlins organization (March 21, 1997). ... On Florida disabled list (June 26-September 1, 1997). ... Released by Marlins (November 20, 1997). ... Re-signed by Marlins organization (March 4, 1998). ... Granted free agency (September 29, 1998). ... Signed by Pittsburgh Pirates organization (June 9, 1999). ... Granted free agency (October 12. 1999). ... Re-signed by Pirates organization (January 18, 2000).

STATISTICAL NOTES: Led New York-Pennsylvania League third basemen with 219 total chances and 14 double plays in 1988. ... Led Carolina League third basemen with 403 total chances and tied for lead with 24 double plays in 1989. ... Led Eastern League third basemen with 476 total chances and 40 double plays in 1990.

| | | | | | | | BATTING | | | | | | | | FIELDING | | |
Year	Team (League)	Pos.	G	AB	R	H	2B	3B	HR	RBI	Avg.	BB	SO	SB	PO	A	E	Avg.
1988—	Watertown (NY-P)	3B	70	265	41	73	6	0	3	31	.275	21	39	18	*65	137	17	.922
1989—	Salem (Caro.)	3B	*137	*515	69	*155	32	6	14	73	.301	42	81	21	*89	*278	36	.911
1990—	Harrisburg (East.)	3B	•138	*511	71	147	27	1	4	62	.288	40	51	24	*109	*317	*50	.895
1991—	Carolina (Sou.)	3B-1B	61	234	30	62	5	1	3	21	.265	24	32	17	182	134	10	.969
	— Buffalo (A.A.)	3B	31	112	18	34	9	2	1	15	.304	14	12	6	30	69	8	.925
	— Pittsburgh (N.L.)	3B	37	106	15	36	7	0	0	7	.340	7	17	3	23	65	6	.936
1992—	Buffalo (A.A.)	2B-1B-3B	60	223	37	60	13	2	7	27	.269	29	30	10	226	122	7	.980
	— Pittsburgh (N.L.)	3B-1B-2B	55	123	11	22	6	0	0	4	.179	12	22	3	96	64	4	.976
1993—	Pittsburgh (N.L.)	OF-3B-2B	29	35	3	5	0	0	0	0	.143	6	10	0	17	8	0	1.000
	— Buffalo (A.A.)	3B-2B-OF	89	330	61	83	22	2	7	34	.252	40	53	17	133	256	17	.958
1994—	Buffalo (A.A.)	OF-3B-2B	88	330	52	100	19	3	7	44	.303	32	36	21	131	113	11	.957
	— Pittsburgh (N.L.)	3B	2	4	1	1	1	0	0	3	.250	0	1	0	0	2	0	1.000
1995—	Calgary (PCL)	3B-2B-OF	40	158	30	52	12	2	4	24	.329	12	16	8	36	98	12	.918
	— Pittsburgh (N.L.)	OF-3B-C-SS	52	107	13	33	0	3	0	5	.308	10	17	3	35	29	0	1.000
1996—	Pittsburgh (N.L.)	OF-3B-2B-C	86	139	19	36	9	1	2	13	.259	8	22	1	60	43	2	.981
1997—	Charlotte (I.L.)■	3B-OF-1B-2B	31	93	16	26	5	0	3	11	.280	6	18	3	32	33	2	.970
	— Florida (N.L.)	OF-3B	44	36	8	10	2	0	0	2	.278	2	5	1	14	3	0	1.000
1998—	Charlotte (I.L.)	OF-DH-P	30	83	12	27	1	0	3	15	.325	4	16	5	29	3	2	.941
	— Florida (N.L.)	OF-3B	53	88	10	20	2	0	0	5	.227	7	12	1	27	12	0	1.000
1999—	Altoona (East.)■	3B-OF	4	12	2	2	0	0	0	2	.167	0	0	1	2	5	1	.875
	— Nashville (PCL)	SS-OF-2B	17	58	14	25	3	0	8	15	.431	3	6	0	22	37	3	.952
	— Pittsburgh (N.L.)	OF-3B-SS-2B	39	65	6	12	2	0	1	4	.185	7	12	1	28	4	1	.970
Major League totals (9 years)			397	703	86	175	29	4	3	43	.249	59	118	13	300	230	13	.976

DIVISION SERIES RECORD

| | | | | | | | BATTING | | | | | | | | FIELDING | | |
Year	Team (League)	Pos.	G	AB	R	H	2B	3B	HR	RBI	Avg.	BB	SO	SB	PO	A	E	Avg.
1997—	Florida (N.L.)	PR-OF	1	0	0	0	0	0	0	0	...	0	0	0	0	0	0	...

CHAMPIONSHIP SERIES RECORD

| | | | | | | | BATTING | | | | | | | | FIELDING | | |
Year	Team (League)	Pos.	G	AB	R	H	2B	3B	HR	RBI	Avg.	BB	SO	SB	PO	A	E	Avg.
1992—	Pittsburgh (N.L.)	PH	2	2	0	0	0	0	0	0	.000	0	2	0	...	...	...	...

RECORD AS PITCHER

Year	League	W	L	Pct.	ERA	G	GS	CG	ShO	Sv.	IP	H	R	ER	BB	SO
1998—	Charlotte (I.L.)	0	0	...	0.00	1	0	0	0	0	1	0	0	0	1	0

WEISS, WALT　　　　　SS　　　　　BRAVES

PERSONAL: Born November 28, 1963, in Tuxedo, N.Y. ... 6-0/168. ... Bats both, throws right. ... Full name: Walter William Weiss Jr.
HIGH SCHOOL: Suffern (N.Y.).
COLLEGE: North Carolina.
TRANSACTIONS/CAREER NOTES: Selected by Baltimore Orioles organization in 10th round of free-agent draft (June 7, 1982); did not sign. ... Selected by Oakland Athletics organization in first round (11th pick overall) of free-agent draft (June 3, 1985). ... On Oakland disabled list (May 18-July 31, 1989); included rehabilitation assignments to Tacoma (July 18-25) and Modesto (July 26-31). ... On disabled list (August 23-September 7, 1990; April 15-30 and June 7, 1991-remainder of season). ... On Oakland disabled list (March 30-June 3, 1992); included rehabilitation assignment to Tacoma (May 26-June 3). ... Traded by A's to Florida Marlins for C Eric Helfand and a player to be named later (November 17, 1992); A's acquired P Scott Baker to complete deal (November 20, 1992). ... Granted free agency (October 25, 1993). ... Signed by Colorado Rockies (January 7, 1994). ... Granted free agency (November 3, 1995). ... Re-signed by Rockies (December 6, 1995). ... On disabled list (July 22-August 8, 1997). ... Granted free agency (October 27, 1997). ... Signed by Atlanta Braves (November 17, 1997). ... On disabled list (June 7-July 1, 1999).
HONORS: Named A.L. Rookie Player of the Year by THE SPORTING NEWS (1988). ... Named A.L. Rookie of the Year by Baseball Writers' Association of America (1988).
STATISTICAL NOTES: Led N.L. shortstops with 99 double plays in 1995. ... Career major league grand slams: 1.

| | | | | | | | BATTING | | | | | | | | FIELDING | | |
Year	Team (League)	Pos.	G	AB	R	H	2B	3B	HR	RBI	Avg.	BB	SO	SB	PO	A	E	Avg.
1985—	Pocatello (Pio.)	SS	40	158	19	49	9	3	0	21	.310	12	18	6	51	126	11	.941
	— Modesto (Calif.)	SS	30	122	17	24	4	1	0	7	.197	12	20	3	36	97	7	.950
1986—	Madison (Midw.)	SS	84	322	50	97	15	5	2	54	.301	33	66	12	143	251	20	.952
	— Huntsville (Sou.)	SS	46	160	19	40	2	1	0	13	.250	11	39	5	72	142	11	.951
1987—	Huntsville (Sou.)	SS	91	337	43	96	16	2	1	32	.285	47	67	23	152	259	17	.960
	— Oakland (A.L.)	SS-DH	16	26	3	12	4	0	0	1	.462	2	2	1	8	30	1	.974
	— Tacoma (PCL)	SS	46	179	35	47	4	3	0	17	.263	28	31	8	76	140	11	.952
1988—	Oakland (A.L.)	SS	147	452	44	113	17	3	3	39	.250	35	56	4	254	431	15	.979
1989—	Oakland (A.L.)	SS	84	236	30	55	11	0	3	21	.233	21	39	6	106	195	15	.953
	— Tacoma (PCL)	SS	2	9	1	1	0	0	1	.111	0	0	0	0	3	1	.750
	— Modesto (Calif.)	SS	5	8	1	3	0	0	0	1	.375	4	1	0	6	9	0	1.000
1990—	Oakland (A.L.)	SS	138	445	50	118	17	1	2	35	.265	46	53	9	194	373	12	.979
1991—	Oakland (A.L.)	SS	40	133	15	30	6	1	0	13	.226	12	14	6	64	99	5	.970

Year Team (League)	Pos.	G	AB	R	H	2B	3B	HR	RBI	Avg.	BB	SO	SB	PO	A	E	Avg.
1992— Tacoma (PCL)	SS	4	13	2	3	1	0	0	3	.231	2	1	0	8	14	1	.957
—Oakland (A.L.)	SS	103	316	36	67	5	2	0	21	.212	43	39	6	144	270	19	.956
1993— Florida (N.L.)■	SS	158	500	50	133	14	2	1	39	.266	79	73	7	229	406	15	.977
1994— Colorado (N.L.)■	SS	110	423	58	106	11	4	1	32	.251	56	58	12	157	318	13	.973
1995— Colorado (N.L.)	SS	137	427	65	111	17	3	1	25	.260	98	57	15	201	406	16	.974
1996— Colorado (N.L.)	SS	155	517	89	146	20	2	8	48	.282	80	78	10	220	450	*30	.957
1997— Colorado (N.L.)	SS	121	393	52	106	23	5	4	38	.270	66	56	5	191	372	10	.983
1998— Atlanta (N.L.)■	SS	96	347	64	97	18	2	0	27	.280	59	53	7	97	257	12	.967
1999— Atlanta (N.L.)	SS	110	279	38	63	13	4	2	29	.226	35	48	7	108	203	12	.963
American League totals (6 years)		528	1608	178	395	60	7	8	130	.246	159	203	32	770	1398	67	.970
National League totals (7 years)		887	2886	416	762	116	22	17	238	.264	473	423	63	1203	2412	108	.971
Major League totals (13 years)		1415	4494	594	1157	176	29	25	368	.257	632	626	95	1973	3810	175	.971

DIVISION SERIES RECORD

Year Team (League)	Pos.	G	AB	R	H	2B	3B	HR	RBI	Avg.	BB	SO	SB	PO	A	E	Avg.
1995— Colorado (N.L.)	SS	4	12	1	2	0	0	0	0	.167	3	3	1	6	12	0	1.000
1998— Atlanta (N.L.)	SS	3	13	2	2	0	0	0	0	.154	1	3	0	6	3	0	1.000
1999— Atlanta (N.L.)	SS-PH	3	6	1	1	0	0	0	0	.167	0	2	0	0	5	0	1.000
Division series totals (3 years)		10	31	4	5	0	0	0	0	.161	4	8	1	12	20	0	1.000

CHAMPIONSHIP SERIES RECORD

Year Team (League)	Pos.	G	AB	R	H	2B	3B	HR	RBI	Avg.	BB	SO	SB	PO	A	E	Avg.
1988— Oakland (A.L.)	SS	4	15	2	5	2	0	0	2	.333	0	4	0	7	10	0	1.000
1989— Oakland (A.L.)	SS-PR	4	9	2	1	1	0	0	0	.111	1	1	1	5	9	0	1.000
1990— Oakland (A.L.)	SS	2	7	2	0	0	0	0	0	.000	2	2	0	2	7	1	.900
1992— Oakland (A.L.)	SS	3	6	1	1	0	0	0	0	.167	2	1	2	5	6	0	1.000
1998— Atlanta (N.L.)	SS	4	15	0	3	0	0	0	1	.200	2	5	1	4	11	0	1.000
1999— Atlanta (N.L.)	SS	6	21	2	6	2	0	0	1	.286	2	4	2	9	14	1	.958
Championship series totals (6 years)		23	73	9	16	5	0	0	4	.219	9	17	6	32	57	2	.978

WORLD SERIES RECORD

NOTES: Member of World Series championship team (1989).

Year Team (League)	Pos.	G	AB	R	H	2B	3B	HR	RBI	Avg.	BB	SO	SB	PO	A	E	Avg.
1988— Oakland (A.L.)	SS	5	16	1	1	0	0	0	0	.063	0	1	0	5	11	1	.941
1989— Oakland (A.L.)	SS	4	15	3	2	0	0	1	1	.133	2	2	0	7	8	0	1.000
1999— Atlanta (N.L.)	SS	3	9	1	2	0	0	0	0	.222	0	1	0	6	5	0	1.000
World Series totals (3 years)		12	40	5	5	0	0	1	1	.125	2	4	0	18	24	1	.977

ALL-STAR GAME RECORD

Year League	Pos.	AB	R	H	2B	3B	HR	RBI	Avg.	BB	SO	SB	PO	A	E	Avg.
1998— National	SS	3	1	2	0	0	0	1	.667	0	0	0	2	2	0	1.000

WELLS, BOB — P — TWINS

PERSONAL: Born November 1, 1966, in Yakima, Wash. ... 6-0/200. ... Throws right, bats right. ... Full name: Robert Lee Wells.
HIGH SCHOOL: Eisenhower (Yakima, Wash.).
JUNIOR COLLEGE: Spokane Falls Community College (Wash.).
TRANSACTIONS/CAREER NOTES: Signed as non-drafted free agent by Philadelphia Phillies organization (August 18, 1988). ... On Reading disabled list (July 21, 1991-remainder of season). ... On Scranton/Wilkes-Barre disabled list (April 9-28, 1992). ... On Reading disabled list (June 9, 1992-remainder of season and April 8-June 13, 1993). ... Claimed on waivers by Seattle Mariners (June 30, 1994). ... On Seattle disabled list (April 16-May 19, 1998; included rehabilitation assignment to Wisconsin (May 12-19). ... Released by Mariners (November 19, 1998). ... Signed by Minnesota Twins organization (January 19, 1999).

Year League	W	L	Pct.	ERA	G	GS	CG	ShO	Sv.	IP	H	R	ER	BB	SO
1989— Martinsville (Appl.)	0	0	...	4.50	4	0	0	0	0	6	8	5	3	2	3
1990— Spartanburg (SAL)	5	8	.385	2.87	20	19	2	0	0	113	94	47	36	40	73
—Clearwater (FSL)	0	2	.000	4.91	6	1	0	0	1	14²/₃	17	9	8	6	11
1991— Clearwater (FSL)	7	2	.778	3.11	24	9	1	0	0	75¹/₃	63	27	26	19	66
—Reading (East.)	1	0	1.000	3.60	1	1	0	0	0	5	4	2	2	1	3
1992— Clearwater (FSL)	1	0	1.000	3.86	9	0	0	0	5	9¹/₃	10	4	4	3	9
—Reading (East.)	0	1	.000	1.17	3	3	0	0	0	15¹/₃	12	2	2	5	11
1993— Clearwater (FSL)	1	0	1.000	0.98	12	1	0	0	2	27²/₃	23	5	3	6	24
—Scranton/W.B. (I.L.)	1	1	.500	2.79	11	0	0	0	0	19¹/₃	19	7	6	5	8
1994— Clearwater (FSL)	1	3	.250	2.79	14	0	0	0	4	19¹/₃	18	6	6	3	19
—Philadelphia (N.L.)	1	0	1.000	1.80	6	0	0	0	0	5	4	1	1	3	4
—Scranton/W.B. (I.L.)	0	2	.000	2.45	11	0	0	0	0	14²/₃	18	6	4	6	13
—Calgary (PCL)■	3	2	.600	6.54	6	6	0	0	0	31²/₃	43	27	23	9	17
—Seattle (A.L.)	1	0	1.000	2.25	1	0	0	0	0	4	4	1	1	1	3
1995— Seattle (A.L.)	4	3	.571	5.75	30	4	0	0	0	76²/₃	88	51	49	39	38
1996— Seattle (A.L.)	12	7	.632	5.30	36	16	1	1	0	130²/₃	141	78	77	46	94
1997— Seattle (A.L.)	2	0	1.000	5.75	46	1	0	0	2	67¹/₃	88	49	43	18	51
1998— Seattle (A.L.)	2	2	.500	6.10	30	0	0	0	0	51²/₃	54	38	35	16	29
—Wisconsin (Midw.)	0	1	.000	3.00	1	1	0	0	0	3	4	2	1	0	2
1999— Minnesota (A.L.)■	8	3	.727	3.81	•76	0	0	0	1	87¹/₃	79	41	37	28	44
A.L. totals (6 years)	29	15	.659	5.21	219	21	1	1	3	417²/₃	454	258	242	148	259
N.L. totals (1 year)	1	0	1.000	1.80	6	0	0	0	0	5	4	1	1	3	3
Major League totals (6 years)	30	15	.667	5.17	225	21	1	1	3	422²/₃	458	259	243	151	262

W

DIVISION SERIES RECORD

Year	League	W	L	Pct.	ERA	G	GS	CG	ShO	Sv.	IP	H	R	ER	BB	SO
1995—	Seattle (A.L.)	0	0	...	9.00	1	0	0	0	0	1	2	1	1	1	0
1997—	Seattle (A.L.)	0	0	...	0.00	1	0	0	0	0	1 1/3	1	0	0	0	1
Division series totals (2 years)		0	0	...	3.86	2	0	0	0	0	2 1/3	3	1	1	1	1

CHAMPIONSHIP SERIES RECORD

Year	League	W	L	Pct.	ERA	G	GS	CG	ShO	Sv.	IP	H	R	ER	BB	SO
1995—	Seattle (A.L.)	0	0	...	3.00	1	0	0	0	0	3	2	1	1	2	2

WELLS, DAVID   P   BLUE JAYS

PERSONAL: Born May 20, 1963, in Torrance, Calif. ... 6-4/235. ... Throws left, bats left. ... Full name: David Lee Wells.

HIGH SCHOOL: Point Loma (San Diego).

TRANSACTIONS/CAREER NOTES: Selected by Toronto Blue Jays organization in second round of free-agent draft (June 7, 1982). ... On Knoxville disabled list (June 28, 1984-remainder of season). ... On disabled list (April 10, 1985-entire season). ... On Knoxville disabled list (July 7-August 20, 1986). ... Released by Blue Jays (March 30, 1993). ... Signed by Detroit Tigers (April 3, 1993). ... On disabled list (August 1-20, 1993). ... Granted free agency (October 28, 1993). ... Re-signed by Tigers (December 13, 1993). ... On Detroit disabled list (April 19-June 6, 1994); included rehabilitation assignment to Lakeland (May 27-June 6). ... Traded by Tigers to Cincinnati Reds for P C.J. Nitkowski, P David Tuttle and a player to be named later (July 31, 1995); Tigers acquired IF Mark Lewis to complete deal (November 16, 1995). ... Traded by Reds to Baltimore Orioles for OF Curtis Goodwin and OF Trovin Valdez (December 26, 1995). ... Granted free agency (October 29, 1996). ... Signed by New York Yankees (December 24, 1996). ... Traded by Yankees with P Graeme Lloyd and 2B Homer Bush to Blue Jays for P Roger Clemens (February 18, 1999).

RECORDS: Holds A.L. single-season records for most consecutive batsmen retired—38 (May 12 [last 10], 17 [all 27] and 23 [first], 1998); fewest innings pitched by leader—231.2 (1999); and fewest complete games for leader—7 (1999).

HONORS: Named lefthanded pitcher on THE SPORTING NEWS A.L. All-Star team (1998).

STATISTICAL NOTES: Struck out 16 batters in one game (July 30, 1997). ... Pitched 4-0 perfect game against Minnesota (May 17, 1998).

Year	League	W	L	Pct.	ERA	G	GS	CG	ShO	Sv.	IP	H	R	ER	BB	SO
1982—	Medicine Hat (Pio.)	4	3	.571	5.18	12	12	1	0	0	64 1/3	71	42	37	32	53
1983—	Kinston (Caro.)	6	5	.545	3.73	25	25	5	0	0	157	141	81	65	71	115
1984—	Kinston (Caro.)	1	6	.143	4.71	7	7	0	0	0	42	51	29	22	19	44
	— Knoxville (Sou.)	3	2	.600	2.59	8	8	3	1	0	59	58	22	17	17	34
1985—	Syracuse (I.L.)							Did not play.								
1986—	Florence (SAL)	0	0	...	3.55	4	1	0	0	0	12 2/3	7	6	5	9	14
	— Ventura (Calif.)	2	1	.667	1.89	5	2	0	0	0	19	13	5	4	4	26
	— Knoxville (Sou.)	1	3	.250	4.05	10	7	1	0	0	40	42	24	18	18	32
	— Syracuse (I.L.)	0	1	.000	9.82	3	0	0	0	0	3 2/3	6	4	4	1	2
1987—	Syracuse (I.L.)	4	6	.400	3.87	43	12	0	0	6	109 1/3	102	49	47	32	106
	— Toronto (A.L.)	4	3	.571	3.99	18	2	0	0	1	29 1/3	37	14	13	12	32
1988—	Toronto (A.L.)	3	5	.375	4.62	41	0	0	0	4	64 1/3	65	36	33	31	56
	— Syracuse (I.L.)	0	0	...	0.00	6	0	0	0	0	5 2/3	7	1	0	2	8
1989—	Toronto (A.L.)	7	4	.636	2.40	54	0	0	0	2	86 1/3	66	25	23	28	78
1990—	Toronto (A.L.)	11	6	.647	3.14	43	25	0	0	3	189	165	72	66	45	115
1991—	Toronto (A.L.)	15	10	.600	3.72	40	28	2	0	1	198 1/3	188	88	82	49	106
1992—	Toronto (A.L.)	7	9	.438	5.40	41	14	0	0	2	120	138	84	72	36	62
1993—	Detroit (A.L.)■	11	9	.550	4.19	32	30	0	0	0	187	183	93	87	42	139
1994—	Lakeland (FSL)	0	0	...	0.00	2	2	0	0	0	6	5	1	0	0	3
	— Detroit (A.L.)	5	7	.417	3.96	16	16	5	1	0	111 1/3	113	54	49	24	71
1995—	Detroit (A.L.)	10	3	.769	3.04	18	18	3	0	0	130 1/3	120	54	44	37	83
	— Cincinnati (N.L.)■	6	5	.545	3.59	11	11	3	0	0	72 2/3	74	34	29	16	50
1996—	Baltimore (A.L.)■	11	14	.440	5.14	34	34	3	0	0	224 1/3	247	132	128	51	130
1997—	New York (A.L.)■	16	10	.615	4.21	32	32	5	2	0	218	239	109	102	45	156
1998—	New York (A.L.)	18	4	*.818	3.49	30	30	8	*5	0	214 1/3	195	86	83	29	163
1999—	New York (A.L.)■	17	10	.630	4.82	34	34	*7	1	0	*231 2/3	*246	132	124	62	169
A.L. totals (13 years)		135	94	.590	4.07	433	263	33	9	13	2004 1/3	2002	979	906	491	1360
N.L. totals (1 year)		6	5	.545	3.59	11	11	3	0	0	72 2/3	74	34	29	16	50
Major League totals (13 years)		141	99	.588	4.05	444	274	36	9	13	2077	2076	1013	935	507	1410

DIVISION SERIES RECORD

RECORDS: Shares career record for most wins—4. ... Shares A.L. career record for most wins—3.

Year	League	W	L	Pct.	ERA	G	GS	CG	ShO	Sv.	IP	H	R	ER	BB	SO
1995—	Cincinnati (N.L.)	1	0	1.000	0.00	1	1	0	0	0	6 1/3	6	1	0	1	8
1996—	Baltimore (A.L.)	1	0	1.000	4.61	2	2	0	0	0	13 2/3	15	7	7	5	6
1997—	New York (A.L.)	1	0	1.000	1.00	1	1	1	0	0	9	5	1	1	0	1
1998—	New York (A.L.)	1	0	1.000	0.00	1	1	0	0	0	8	5	0	0	1	9
Division series totals (4 years)		4	0	1.000	1.95	5	5	1	0	0	37	31	9	8	7	24

CHAMPIONSHIP SERIES RECORD

NOTES: Named A.L. Championship Series Most Valuable Player (1998).

Year	League	W	L	Pct.	ERA	G	GS	CG	ShO	Sv.	IP	H	R	ER	BB	SO
1989—	Toronto (A.L.)	0	0	...	0.00	1	0	0	0	0	1	0	1	0	2	1
1991—	Toronto (A.L.)	0	0	...	2.35	4	0	0	0	0	7 2/3	6	2	2	2	9
1992—	Toronto (A.L.)							Did not play.								
1995—	Cincinnati (N.L.)	0	1	.000	4.50	1	1	0	0	0	6	8	3	3	2	3
1996—	Baltimore (A.L.)	1	0	1.000	4.05	1	1	0	0	0	6 2/3	8	3	3	3	6
1998—	New York (A.L.)	2	0	1.000	2.87	2	2	0	0	0	15 2/3	12	5	5	2	18
Champ. series totals (5 years)		3	1	.750	3.16	9	4	0	0	0	37	34	14	13	11	37

W

NOTES: Member of World Series championship team (1992 and 1998).

Year League	W	L	Pct.	ERA	G	GS	CG	ShO	Sv.	IP	H	R	ER	BB	SO
1992— Toronto (A.L.)	0	0	...	0.00	4	0	0	0	0	4 1/3	1	0	0	2	3
1998— New York (A.L.)	1	0	1.000	6.43	1	1	0	0	0	7	7	5	5	2	4
World Series totals (2 years)	1	0	1.000	3.97	5	1	0	0	0	11 1/3	8	5	5	4	7

ALL-STAR GAME RECORD

Year League	W	L	Pct.	ERA	GS	CG	ShO	Sv.	IP	H	R	ER	BB	SO
1995— American	0	0	...	0.00	0	0	0	0	1/3	0	0	0	0	1
1998— American	0	0	...	0.00	1	0	...	...	2	0	0	0	1	1
All-Star Game totals (2 years)	0	0	...	0.00	1	0	0	0	2 1/3	0	0	0	1	2

WELLS, KIP   P   WHITE SOX

PERSONAL: Born April 21, 1977, in Houston. ... 6-3/196. ... Throws right, bats right. ... Full name: Robert Kip Wells.
HIGH SCHOOL: Elkins (Fort Bend, Texas).
COLLEGE: Baylor.
TRANSACTIONS/CAREER NOTES: Selected by Milwaukee Brewers organization in 58th round of free-agent draft (June 1, 1995); did not sign. ... Selected by Chicago White Sox organization in first round (16th pick overall) of free-agent draft (June 2, 1998).

Year League	W	L	Pct.	ERA	G	GS	CG	ShO	Sv.	IP	H	R	ER	BB	SO
1999— Win.-Salem (Car.)	5	6	.455	3.57	14	14	0	0	0	85 2/3	78	39	34	34	95
— Birmingham (Sou.)	8	2	.800	2.94	11	11	0	0	0	70 1/3	49	24	23	31	44
— Chicago (A.L.)	4	1	.800	4.04	7	7	0	0	0	35 2/3	33	17	16	15	29
Major League totals (1 year)	4	1	.800	4.04	7	7	0	0	0	35 2/3	33	17	16	15	29

WELLS, VERNON   OF   BLUE JAYS

PERSONAL: Born December 8, 1978, in Shreveport, La. ... 6-1/210. ... Bats right, throws right. ... Full name: Vernon Wells III.
HIGH SCHOOL: Bowie (Arlington, Texas).
TRANSACTIONS/CAREER NOTES: Selected by Toronto Blue Jays organization in first round (fifth pick overall) of free-agent draft (June 3, 1997).
HONORS: Named Florida State League Most Valuable Player (1999).

Year Team (League)	Pos.	G	AB	R	H	2B	3B	HR	RBI	Avg.	BB	SO	SB	PO	A	E	Avg.
1997— St. Catharines (NY-P)	OF	66	264	52	81	20	1	10	31	.307	30	44	8	135	6	7	.953
1998— Hagerstown (SAL)	OF	134	509	86	145	35	2	11	65	.285	49	84	13	243	6	5	.980
1999— Dunedin (FSL)	OF-DH	70	265	43	91	16	2	11	43	.343	26	34	13	130	3	1	.993
— Knoxville (Sou.)	OF	26	106	18	36	6	2	3	17	.340	12	15	6	56	4	0	1.000
— Syracuse (I.L.)	OF	33	129	20	40	8	1	4	21	.310	10	22	5	79	2	2	.976
— Toronto (A.L.)	OF	25	88	8	23	5	0	1	8	.261	4	18	1	50	4	0	1.000
Major League totals (1 year)		25	88	8	23	5	0	1	8	.261	4	18	1	50	4	0	1.000

WENDELL, TURK   P   METS

PERSONAL: Born May 19, 1967, in Pittsfield, Mass. ... 6-2/205. ... Throws right, bats left. ... Full name: Steven John Wendell.
HIGH SCHOOL: Wahconah Regional (Dalton, Mass.).
COLLEGE: Quinnipiac College (Conn.).
TRANSACTIONS/CAREER NOTES: Selected by Atlanta Braves organization in fifth round of free-agent draft (June 1, 1988). ... Traded by Braves with P Yorkis Perez to Chicago Cubs for P Mike Bielecki and C Damon Berryhill (September 29, 1991). ... On disabled list (May 4, 1992-remainder of season). ... On Chicago disabled list (April 16-May 27, 1995); included rehabilitation assignments to Daytona (May 5-15) and Orlando (May 15-27). ... Traded by Cubs with OF Brian McRae and P Mel Rojas to New York Mets for OF Lance Johnson and two players to be named later (August 8, 1997); Cubs acquired P Mark Clark (August 11, 1997) and IF Manny Alexander (August 14, 1997) to complete deal.

Year League	W	L	Pct.	ERA	G	GS	CG	ShO	Sv.	IP	H	R	ER	BB	SO
1988— Pulaski (Appl.)	3	•8	.273	3.83	14	14	•6	1	0	*101	85	50	43	30	87
1989— Burlington (Midw.)	9	11	.450	2.21	22	22	•9	*5	0	159	127	63	39	41	153
— Greenville (Sou.)	0	0	...	9.82	1	1	0	0	0	3 2/3	7	5	4	1	3
— Durham (Caro.)	2	0	1.000	1.13	3	3	1	0	0	24	13	4	3	6	27
1990— Durham (Caro.)	1	3	.250	1.86	6	5	1	0	0	38 2/3	24	10	8	15	26
— Greenville (Sou.)	4	9	.308	5.74	36	13	1	1	2	91	105	70	58	48	85
1991— Greenville (Sou.)	11	3	*.786	2.56	25	20	1	1	0	147 2/3	130	47	42	51	122
— Richmond (I.L.)	0	2	.000	3.43	3	3	1	0	0	21	20	9	8	16	18
1992— Iowa (A.A.)■	2	0	1.000	1.44	4	4	0	0	0	25	17	7	4	15	12
1993— Iowa (A.A.)	10	8	.556	4.60	25	25	3	0	0	148 2/3	148	88	76	47	110
— Chicago (N.L.)	1	2	.333	4.37	7	4	0	0	0	22 2/3	24	13	11	8	15
1994— Iowa (A.A.)	11	6	.647	2.95	23	23	6	•3	0	168	141	58	55	28	118
— Chicago (N.L.)	0	1	.000	11.93	6	2	0	0	0	14 1/3	22	20	19	10	9
1995— Daytona (FSL)	0	0	...	1.17	4	2	0	0	0	7 2/3	5	2	1	1	8
— Orlando (Sou.)	1	0	1.000	3.86	5	0	0	0	1	7	6	3	3	4	7
— Chicago (N.L.)	3	1	.750	4.92	43	0	0	0	0	60 1/3	71	35	33	24	50
1996— Chicago (N.L.)	4	5	.444	2.84	70	0	0	0	18	79 1/3	58	26	25	44	75
1997— Chicago (N.L.)	3	5	.375	4.20	52	0	0	0	4	60	53	32	28	39	54
— New York (N.L.)■	0	0	...	4.96	13	0	0	0	1	16 1/3	15	10	9	14	10
1998— New York (N.L.)	5	1	.833	2.93	66	0	0	0	4	76 2/3	62	25	25	33	58
1999— New York (N.L.)	5	4	.556	3.05	80	0	0	0	3	85 2/3	80	31	29	37	77
Major League totals (7 years)	21	19	.525	3.88	337	6	0	0	30	415 1/3	385	192	179	209	348

W

Year	League	W	L	Pct.	ERA	G	GS	CG	ShO	Sv.	IP	H	R	ER	BB	SO
1999—	New York (N.L.)	1	0	1.000	0.00	2	0	0	0	0	2	0	0	0	2	0

CHAMPIONSHIP SERIES RECORD

Year	League	W	L	Pct.	ERA	G	GS	CG	ShO	Sv.	IP	H	R	ER	BB	SO
1999—	New York (N.L.)	1	0	1.000	4.76	5	0	0	0	0	5 2/3	2	3	3	4	5

WENGERT, DON · P · ASTROS

PERSONAL: Born November 6, 1969, in Sioux City, Iowa. ... 6-2/212. ... Throws right, bats right. ... Full name: Donald Paul Wengert. ... Brother of Bill Wengert, pitcher with Los Angeles Dodgers, San Diego Padres and Boston Red Sox organizations (1988-95).

HIGH SCHOOL: Heelan Catholic (Sioux City, Iowa).

COLLEGE: Iowa State.

TRANSACTIONS/CAREER NOTES: Selected by Cincinnati Reds organization in 60th round of free-agent draft (June 1, 1988); did not sign. ... Selected by Oakland Athletics organization in fourth round of free-agent draft (June 1, 1992). ... On Oakland disabled list (July 30-August 18, 1995); included rehabilitation assignment to Edmonton (August 7-18). ... On disabled list (July 24-August 8, 1996). ... Traded by A's with IF David Newhan to San Diego Padres for P Doug Bochtler and IF Jorge Velandia (November 26, 1997). ... Traded by Padres to Chicago Cubs for P Ben VanRyn (May 5, 1998). ... Granted free agency (November 25, 1998). ... Signed by Kansas City Royals organization (December 21, 1998). ... Released by Royals (July 15, 1999). ... Signed by New York Yankees organization (July 27, 1999). ... Released by Yankees (August 27, 1999). ... Signed by Atlanta Braves organization (August 30, 1999). ... Granted free agency (October 15, 1999). ... Signed by Houston Astros organization (January 5, 2000).

MISCELLANEOUS: Appeared in two games as pinch runner and had a sacrifice hit in only appearance as pinch hitter with Chicago (1998).

Year	League	W	L	Pct.	ERA	G	GS	CG	ShO	Sv.	IP	H	R	ER	BB	SO
1992—	Southern Oregon (N'west)	2	0	1.000	1.46	6	5	1	0	0	37	32	6	6	7	29
—	Madison (Midw.)	3	4	.429	3.38	7	7	0	0	0	40	42	20	15	17	29
1993—	Madison (Midw.)	6	5	.545	3.32	13	13	2	0	0	78 2/3	79	30	29	18	46
—	Modesto (Calif.)	3	6	.333	4.73	12	12	0	0	0	70 1/3	75	42	37	29	43
1994—	Modesto (Calif.)	4	1	.800	2.95	10	7	0	0	0	42 2/3	40	15	14	11	52
—	Huntsville (Sou.)	6	4	.600	3.26	17	17	1	0	0	99 1/3	86	43	36	33	92
1995—	Oakland (A.L.)	1	1	.500	3.34	19	0	0	0	0	29 2/3	30	14	11	12	16
—	Edmonton (PCL)	1	1	.500	7.38	16	6	0	0	1	39	55	32	32	16	20
1996—	Oakland (A.L.)	7	11	.389	5.58	36	25	1	1	0	161 1/3	200	102	100	60	75
1997—	Oakland (A.L.)	5	11	.313	6.04	49	12	1	0	2	134	177	96	90	41	68
1998—	San Diego (N.L.)■	0	0	...	5.93	10	0	0	0	1	13 2/3	21	9	9	5	5
—	Chicago (N.L.)■	1	5	.167	5.07	21	6	0	0	0	49 2/3	55	29	28	23	41
—	Iowa (PCL)	3	1	.750	4.58	9	9	1	0	0	53	58	30	27	14	48
1999—	Kansas City (A.L.)■	0	1	.000	9.25	11	1	0	0	0	24 1/3	41	26	25	5	10
—	Omaha (PCL)	4	0	1.000	4.17	16	2	0	0	1	41	41	20	19	9	24
—	Columbus (I.L.)■	0	1	.000	7.63	6	2	0	0	0	15 1/3	25	13	13	3	5
—	Richmond (I.L.)■	0	0	...	4.50	1	1	0	0	0	6	7	3	3	0	3
A.L. totals (4 years)		13	24	.351	5.82	115	38	2	1	2	349 1/3	448	238	226	118	169
N.L. totals (1 year)		1	5	.167	5.26	31	6	0	0	1	63 1/3	76	38	37	28	46
Major League totals (5 years)		14	29	.326	5.74	146	44	2	1	3	412 2/3	524	276	263	146	215

WESTBROOK, JAKE · P · YANKEES

PERSONAL: Born September 29, 1977, in Athens, Ga. ... 6-3/200. ... Throws right, bats right. ... Full name: Jacob C. Westbrook.

HIGH SCHOOL: Madison County (Danielsville, Ga.).

TRANSACTIONS/CAREER NOTES: Selected by Colorado Rockies organization in first round (21st pick overall) of free-agent draft (June 4, 1996). ... Traded by Rockies with P John Nicholson and OF Mark Hamlin to Montreal Expos for 2B Mike Lansing (December 16, 1997). ... Traded by Expos with two players to be named later to New York Yankees for P Hideki Irabu (December 22, 1999).

STATISTICAL NOTES: Led Eastern League pitchers with 19 putouts, 40 assists, 61 total chances and six double plays in 1999.

Year	League	W	L	Pct.	ERA	G	GS	CG	ShO	Sv.	IP	H	R	ER	BB	SO
1996—	Arizona Rockies (Ariz.)	4	2	.667	2.87	11	11	0	0	0	62 2/3	66	33	20	14	57
—	Portland (N'west)	1	1	.500	2.55	4	4	0	0	0	24 2/3	22	8	7	5	19
1997—	Asheville (SAL)	*14	11	.560	4.82	28	27	3	2	0	170	176	93	91	55	92
1998—	Jupiter (FSL)■	11	6	.647	3.26	27	27	2	0	0	171	169	70	62	60	79
1999—	Harrisburg (East.)	11	5	.688	3.92	27	27	2	2	0	174 2/3	180	88	76	63	90

WETTELAND, JOHN · P · RANGERS

PERSONAL: Born August 21, 1966, in San Mateo, Calif. ... 6-2/215. ... Throws right, bats right. ... Full name: John Karl Wetteland.

HIGH SCHOOL: Cardinal Newman (Santa Rosa, Calif.).

COLLEGE: College of San Mateo (Calif.).

TRANSACTIONS/CAREER NOTES: Selected by New York Mets organization in 12th round of free-agent draft (June 4, 1984); did not sign. ... Selected by Los Angeles Dodgers organization in secondary phase of free-agent draft (January 9, 1985). ... Selected by Detroit Tigers from Dodgers organization in Rule 5 major league draft (December 7, 1987). ... Returned to Dodgers organization (March 29, 1988). ... On Albuquerque disabled list (May 1-8 and June 3-29, 1991). ... Traded by Dodgers with P Tim Belcher to Cincinnati Reds for OF Eric Davis and P Kip Gross (November 25, 1991). ... Traded by Reds with P Bill Risley to Montreal Expos for OF Dave Martinez, P Scott Ruskin and SS Willie Greene (December 11, 1991). ... On Montreal disabled list (March 23-April 23, 1993); included rehabilitation assignment to West Palm Beach (April 18-23). ... On disabled list (April 18-May 4, 1994). ... Traded by Expos to New York Yankees for OF Fernando Seguignol and cash (April 5, 1995). ... On disabled list (August 13-September 6, 1996). ... Granted free agency (November 5, 1996). ... Signed by Texas Rangers (December 17, 1996).

HONORS: Named A.L. Fireman of the Year by THE SPORTING NEWS (1996).

STATISTICAL NOTES: Tied for Florida State League lead with 11 home runs allowed and 17 wild pitches in 1987. ... Led Texas League with 22 wild pitches in 1988.

W

Year League	W	L	Pct.	ERA	G	GS	CG	ShO	Sv.	IP	H	R	ER	BB	SO
1985— Great Falls (Pio.)	1	1	.500	3.92	11	2	0	0	0	20²/₃	17	10	9	15	23
1986— Bakersfield (Calif.)	0	7	.000	5.78	15	12	4	0	0	67	71	50	43	46	38
— Great Falls (Pio.)	4	3	.571	5.45	12	12	1	0	0	69¹/₃	70	51	42	40	59
1987— Vero Beach (FSL)	12	7	.632	3.13	27	27	7	2	0	175²/₃	150	81	61	92	144
1988— San Antonio (Texas)	10	8	.556	3.88	25	25	3	1	0	162¹/₃	141	74	70	•77	140
1989— Albuquerque (PCL)	5	3	.625	3.65	10	10	1	0	0	69	61	28	28	20	73
— Los Angeles (N.L.)	5	8	.385	3.77	31	12	0	0	1	102²/₃	81	46	43	34	96
1990— Los Angeles (N.L.)	2	4	.333	4.81	22	5	0	0	0	43	44	28	23	17	36
— Albuquerque (PCL)	2	2	.500	5.59	8	5	1	0	0	29	27	19	18	13	26
1991— Albuquerque (PCL)	4	3	.571	2.79	41	4	0	0	20	61¹/₃	48	22	19	26	55
— Los Angeles (N.L.)	1	0	1.000	0.00	6	0	0	0	0	9	5	2	0	3	9
1992— Montreal (N.L.)■	4	4	.500	2.92	67	0	0	0	37	83¹/₃	64	27	27	36	99
1993— West Palm Beach (FSL)	0	0	...	0.00	2	2	0	0	0	3	0	0	0	0	6
— Montreal (N.L.)	9	3	.750	1.37	70	0	0	0	43	85¹/₃	58	17	13	28	113
1994— Montreal (N.L.)	4	6	.400	2.83	52	0	0	0	25	63²/₃	46	22	20	21	68
1995— New York (A.L.)■	1	5	.167	2.93	60	0	0	0	31	61¹/₃	40	22	20	14	66
1996— New York (A.L.)	2	3	.400	2.83	62	0	0	0	*43	63²/₃	54	23	20	21	69
1997— Texas (A.L.)■	7	2	.778	1.94	61	0	0	0	31	65	43	18	14	21	63
1998— Texas (A.L.)	3	1	.750	2.03	63	0	0	0	42	62	47	17	14	14	72
1999— Texas (A.L.)	4	4	.500	3.68	62	0	0	0	43	66	67	30	27	19	60
A.L. totals (5 years)	17	15	.531	2.69	308	0	0	0	190	318	251	110	95	89	330
N.L. totals (6 years)	25	25	.500	2.93	248	17	0	0	106	387	298	142	126	139	421
Major League totals (11 years)	42	40	.512	2.82	556	17	0	0	296	705	549	252	221	228	751

DIVISION SERIES RECORD

Year League	W	L	Pct.	ERA	G	GS	CG	ShO	Sv.	IP	H	R	ER	BB	SO
1995— New York (A.L.)	0	1	.000	14.54	3	0	0	0	0	4¹/₃	8	7	7	2	5
1996— New York (A.L.)	0	0	...	0.00	3	0	0	0	2	4	2	0	0	5	4
1998— Texas (A.L.)	0	0	...	0.00	1	0	0	0	0	1	0	0	0	1	1
1999— Texas (A.L.)	0	0	...	0.00	1	0	0	0	0	1	0	0	0	0	1
Division series totals (4 years)	0	1	.000	6.10	8	0	0	0	2	10¹/₃	10	7	7	8	11

CHAMPIONSHIP SERIES RECORD

Year League	W	L	Pct.	ERA	G	GS	CG	ShO	Sv.	IP	H	R	ER	BB	SO
1996— New York (A.L.)	0	0	...	4.50	4	0	0	0	1	4	2	2	2	1	5

WORLD SERIES RECORD

RECORDS: Holds single-series record for most saves—4 (1996).
NOTES: Named Most Valuable Player (1996). ... Member of World Series championship team (1996).

Year League	W	L	Pct.	ERA	G	GS	CG	ShO	Sv.	IP	H	R	ER	BB	SO
1996— New York (A.L.)	0	0	...	2.08	5	0	0	0	4	4¹/₃	4	1	1	1	6

ALL-STAR GAME RECORD

Year League	W	L	Pct.	ERA	GS	CG	ShO	Sv.	IP	H	R	ER	BB	SO
1996— American					Did not play.									
1998— American	0	0	...	0.00	0	0	0	0	1	0	0	0	0	1
1999— American	0	0	...	0.00	0	0	0	1	1	1	0	0	0	1
All-Star Game totals (2 years)	0	0	...	0.00	0	0	0	1	2	1	0	0	0	2

WHEELER, DAN   P   DEVIL RAYS

PERSONAL: Born December 10, 1977, in Providence, R.I. ... 6-3/222. ... Throws right, bats right. ... Full name: Daniel M. Wheeler.
HIGH SCHOOL: Pilgrim (Warwick, R.I.).
JUNIOR COLLEGE: Central Arizona College.
TRANSACTIONS/CAREER NOTES: Selected by Tampa Bay Devil Rays organization in 34th round of free-agent draft (June 4, 1996).

Year League	W	L	Pct.	ERA	G	GS	CG	ShO	Sv.	IP	H	R	ER	BB	SO
1997— Hudson Valley (NY-P)	6	7	.462	3.00	15	15	0	0	0	84	75	38	28	17	81
1998— Charleston, S.C. (SAL)	12	14	.462	4.43	29	29	3	1	0	181	206	96	89	29	136
1999— Orlando (Sou.)	3	0	1.000	3.26	9	9	0	0	0	58	56	27	21	8	53
— Durham (I.L.)	7	5	.583	4.92	14	14	2	1	0	82¹/₃	103	59	45	25	58
— Tampa Bay (A.L.)	0	4	.000	5.87	6	6	0	0	0	30²/₃	35	20	20	13	32
Major League totals (1 year)	0	4	.000	5.87	6	6	0	0	0	30²/₃	35	20	20	13	32

WHISENANT, MATT   P   PADRES

PERSONAL: Born June 8, 1971, in Los Angeles. ... 6-3/215. ... Throws left, bats right. ... Full name: Matthew Michael Whisenant.
HIGH SCHOOL: La Canada (Calif.).
JUNIOR COLLEGE: Glendale (Ariz.) Community College.
TRANSACTIONS/CAREER NOTES: Selected by Philadelphia Phillies organization in 18th round of free-agent draft (June 5, 1989). ... Traded by Phillies with P Joel Adamson to Florida Marlins for P Danny Jackson (November 17, 1992). ... On disabled list (July 13, 1993-remainder of season). ... On Florida disabled list (March 28-July 4, 1997); included rehabilitation assignments to Brevard County (April 18-21) and Charlotte (May 5-July 4). ... Traded by Marlins to Kansas City Royals for C Matt Treanor (July 29, 1997). ... Released by Royals (August 14, 1999). ... Signed by San Diego Padres (August 20, 1999).
STATISTICAL NOTES: Led International League with 30 wild pitches in 1996.
MISCELLANEOUS: Appeared in one game as pinch runner with Kansas City (1997).

Year League	W	L	Pct.	ERA	G	GS	CG	ShO	Sv.	IP	H	R	ER	BB	SO
1990— Princeton (Appl.)	0	0	...	11.40	9	2	0	0	0	15	16	27	19	20	25
1991— Batavia (NY-P)	2	1	.667	2.45	11	10	0	0	0	47²/₃	31	19	13	42	55
1992— Spartanburg (SAL)	11	7	.611	3.23	27	27	2	0	0	150²/₃	117	69	54	85	151
1993— Kane County (Midw.)■	2	6	.250	4.69	15	15	0	0	0	71	68	45	37	56	74

W

Year League	W	L	Pct.	ERA	G	GS	CG	ShO	Sv.	IP	H	R	ER	BB	SO
1994— Brevard County (FSL)........	6	9	.400	3.38	28	26	5	1	0	160	125	71	60	82	103
1995— Portland (East.).................	10	6	.625	3.50	23	22	2	0	0	128²/₃	106	57	50	65	107
— Portland (East.).................	10	6	.625	3.50	23	22	2	0	0	128²/₃	103	57	50	65	107
1996— Charlotte (I.L.).................	8	10	.444	6.92	28	22	1	0	0	121	149	107	93	101	97
1997— Brevard County (FSL)........	0	0	...	8.10	2	1	0	0	0	3¹/₃	3	3	3	3	4
— Charlotte (I.L.).................	2	1	.667	7.20	16	0	0	0	0	15	16	12	12	12	19
— Florida (N.L.).................	0	0	...	16.88	4	0	0	0	0	2²/₃	4	6	5	6	4
— Kansas City (A.L.)■	1	0	1.000	2.84	24	0	0	0	0	19	15	7	6	12	16
1998— Kansas City (A.L.)	2	1	.667	4.90	70	0	0	0	2	60²/₃	61	37	33	33	45
1999— Kansas City (A.L.)	4	4	.500	6.35	48	0	0	0	1	39²/₃	40	28	28	26	27
— San Diego (N.L.)■	0	1	.000	3.68	19	0	0	0	0	14²/₃	10	6	6	10	10
A.L. totals (3 years)	7	5	.583	5.05	142	0	0	0	3	119¹/₃	116	72	67	71	88
N.L. totals (2 years)	0	1	.000	5.71	23	0	0	0	0	17¹/₃	14	12	11	16	14
Major League totals (3 years)	7	6	.538	5.14	165	0	0	0	3	136²/₃	130	84	78	87	102

WHITE, DEVON — OF — DODGERS

PERSONAL: Born December 29, 1962, in Kingston, Jamaica. ... 6-2/190. ... Bats both, throws right. ... Full name: Devon Markes White. ... Name pronounced de-VON.

HIGH SCHOOL: Park West (New York).

TRANSACTIONS/CAREER NOTES: Selected by California Angels organization in sixth round of free-agent draft (June 8, 1981). ... On suspended list (June 11-12 and July 19, 1982-remainder of season). ... On Edmonton disabled list (May 12-22, 1986). ... On disabled list (May 7-June 10, 1988). ... Traded by Angels with P Willie Fraser and a player to be named later to Toronto Blue Jays for OF Junior Felix, IF Luis Sojo and a player to be named later (December 2, 1990); Blue Jays acquired P Marcus Moore and Angels acquired C Ken Rivers to complete deal (December 4, 1990). ... Granted free agency (November 1, 1995). ... Signed by Florida Marlins (November 21, 1995). ... On disabled list (April 25-May 30 and June 8-July 28, 1997). ... Traded by Marlins to Arizona Diamondbacks for P Jesus Martinez (November 18, 1997). ... Granted free agency (October 23, 1998). ... Signed by Los Angeles Dodgers (November 9, 1998).

RECORDS: Shares major league record for most stolen bases in one inning—3 (September 9, 1989, sixth inning).

HONORS: Won A.L. Gold Glove as outfielder (1988-89 and 1991-95).

STATISTICAL NOTES: Led Midwest League outfielders with 286 total chances in 1983. ... Led California League outfielders with 351 total chances in 1984. ... Led Pacific Coast League outfielders with 339 total chances in 1986. ... Switch-hit home runs in one game three times (June 23, 1987; June 29, 1990; and June 1, 1992). ... Led A.L. outfielders with 449 total chances in 1987, 448 in 1991 and 458 in 1992. ... Career major league grand slams: 8.

								BATTING						FIELDING		
Year Team (League)	Pos.	G	AB	R	H	2B	3B	HR	RBI	Avg.	BB	SO	SB	PO	A	E	Avg.
1981— Idaho Falls (Pio.)........	OF-3B-1B	30	106	10	19	2	0	0	10	.179	12	34	4	33	10	3	.935
1982— Danville (Midw.)........	OF	57	186	21	40	6	1	1	11	.215	11	41	11	89	3	8	.920
1983— Peoria (Midw.)...........	OF	117	430	69	109	17	6	13	66	.253	36	124	32	267	8	11	.962
— Nashua (East.)........	OF	17	70	11	18	7	2	0	2	.257	7	22	5	37	0	3	.925
1984— Redwood (Calif.)........	OF	138	520	101	147	25	5	7	55	.283	56	118	36	*322	16	13	.963
1985— Midland (Texas)........	OF	70	260	52	77	10	4	4	35	.296	35	46	38	176	10	4	.979
— Edmonton (PCL)........	OF	66	277	53	70	16	5	4	39	.253	24	77	21	205	6	2	.991
— California (A.L.)........	OF	21	7	7	1	0	0	0	0	.143	1	3	3	10	1	0	1.000
1986— Edmonton (PCL).......	OF	112	461	84	134	25	10	14	60	.291	31	90	*42	317	•16	6	.982
— California (A.L.).......	OF	29	51	8	12	1	1	1	3	.235	6	8	6	49	0	2	.961
1987— California (A.L.).......	OF	159	639	103	168	33	5	24	87	.263	39	135	32	*424	16	9	.980
1988— California (A.L.).......	OF	122	455	76	118	22	2	11	51	.259	23	84	17	364	7	9	.976
1989— California (A.L.).......	OF-DH	156	636	86	156	18	13	12	56	.245	31	129	44	430	10	5	.989
1990— California (A.L.).......	OF	125	443	57	96	17	3	11	44	.217	44	116	21	302	11	9	.972
— Edmonton (PCL)	OF	14	55	9	20	4	4	0	6	.364	7	12	4	31	1	3	.914
1991— Toronto (A.L.)■........	OF	156	642	110	181	40	10	17	60	.282	55	135	33	*439	8	1	*.998
1992— Toronto (A.L.)........	OF-DH	153	641	98	159	26	7	17	60	.248	47	133	37	*443	6	7	.985
1993— Toronto (A.L.)........	OF	146	598	116	163	42	6	15	52	.273	57	127	34	399	6	3	.993
1994— Toronto (A.L.)........	OF	100	403	67	109	24	6	13	49	.270	21	80	11	268	3	6	.978
1995— Toronto (A.L.)........	OF	101	427	61	121	23	5	10	53	.283	29	97	11	261	7	3	.989
1996— Florida (N.L.)■........	OF	146	552	77	151	37	6	17	84	.274	38	99	22	296	5	4	.987
1997— Florida (N.L.)........	OF	74	265	37	65	13	1	6	34	.245	32	65	13	152	4	2	.987
1998— Arizona (N.L.)■........	OF	146	563	84	157	32	1	22	85	.279	42	102	22	371	3	5	.987
1999— Los Angeles (N.L.)■ ..	OF-DH	134	474	60	127	20	2	14	68	.268	39	88	19	273	3	4	.986
American League totals (11 years)		1268	4942	789	1284	246	58	131	515	.260	353	1047	249	3389	77	54	.985
National League totals (4 years)		500	1854	258	500	102	10	59	271	.270	151	354	76	1092	15	15	.987
Major League totals (15 years)		1768	6796	1047	1784	348	68	190	786	.263	504	1401	325	4481	92	69	.985

DIVISION SERIES RECORD

								BATTING						FIELDING		
Year Team (League)	Pos.	G	AB	R	H	2B	3B	HR	RBI	Avg.	BB	SO	SB	PO	A	E	Avg.
1997— Florida (N.L.)	OF	3	11	1	2	0	0	1	4	.182	2	3	0	3	0	0	1.000

CHAMPIONSHIP SERIES RECORD

RECORDS: Holds A.L. career record for highest batting average (50 or more at-bats)—.392. ... Holds single-series record for most times caught stealing—4 (1992). ... Shares A.L. single-series record for most hits—12 (1993). ... Shares A.L. single-game record for most at-bats—6 (October 11, 1992, 11 innings).

								BATTING						FIELDING		
Year Team (League)	Pos.	G	AB	R	H	2B	3B	HR	RBI	Avg.	BB	SO	SB	PO	A	E	Avg.
1986— California (A.L.)	OF-PR	4	2	2	1	0	0	0	0	.500	0	1	0	3	0	0	1.000
1991— Toronto (A.L.)	OF	5	22	5	8	1	0	0	0	.364	2	3	3	16	0	0	1.000
1992— Toronto (A.L.)	OF	6	23	2	8	2	0	0	2	.348	5	6	0	16	0	1	.941
1993— Toronto (A.L.)	OF	6	27	3	12	1	1	1	2	.444	1	5	0	15	0	0	1.000
1997— Florida (N.L.)	OF	6	21	4	4	1	0	0	1	.190	2	7	1	16	0	0	1.000
Championship series totals (5 years)		27	95	16	33	5	1	1	5	.347	10	22	4	66	0	1	.985

W

RECORDS: Shares record for most consecutive strikeouts in one series—5 (October 21 [1] and 22 [4], 1997).
NOTES: Member of World Series championship team (1992, 1993 and 1997).

Year Team (League)	Pos.	G	AB	R	H	2B	3B	HR	RBI	Avg.	BB	SO	SB	PO	A	E	Avg.
1992— Toronto (A.L.).............	OF	6	26	2	6	1	0	0	2	.231	0	6	1	22	0	0	1.000
1993— Toronto (A.L.).............	OF	6	24	8	7	3	2	1	7	.292	4	7	1	16	0	0	1.000
1997— Florida (N.L.).............	OF	7	33	0	8	3	1	0	2	.242	3	10	1	16	0	0	1.000
World Series totals (3 years)		19	83	10	21	7	3	1	11	.253	7	23	3	54	0	0	1.000

ALL-STAR GAME RECORD

Year League	Pos.	AB	R	H	2B	3B	HR	RBI	Avg.	BB	SO	SB	PO	A	E	Avg.
1989— American..................	OF	1	0	0	0	0	0	0	.000	0	0	0	0	0	0	...
1993— American..................	OF	2	1	1	1	0	0	1	.500	0	0	1	1	0	0	1.000
1998— National..................	OF	3	1	3	0	1	0	0	1.000	0	0	0	0	0	0	...
All-Star Game totals (3 years)		6	2	4	1	1	0	1	.667	0	0	1	1	0	0	1.000

WHITE, GABE   P   REDS

PERSONAL: Born November 20, 1971, in Sebring, Fla. ... 6-2/200. ... Throws left, bats left. ... Full name: Gabriel Allen White.
HIGH SCHOOL: Sebring (Fla.).
TRANSACTIONS/CAREER NOTES: Selected by Montreal Expos organization in supplemental round ("sandwich pick" between first and second round, 28th pick overall) of free-agent draft (June 4, 1990); pick received as part of compensation for California Angels signing Type A free-agent P Mark Langston. ... On Harrisburg disabled list (July 2-27, 1993). ... On Ottawa disabled list (April 7-May 6, 1994). ... Traded by Expos to Cincinnati Reds for 2B Jhonny Carvajal (December 15, 1995). ... On disabled list (September 17, 1996-remainder of season).
RECORDS: Shares N.L. record for most consecutive home runs allowed in one inning—3 (July 7, 1995, second inning).

Year League	W	L	Pct.	ERA	G	GS	CG	ShO	Sv.	IP	H	R	ER	BB	SO
1990— Gulf Coast Expos (GCL)	4	2	.667	3.14	11	11	1	0	0	57 1/3	50	21	20	12	41
1991— Sumter (SAL)	6	9	.400	3.26	24	24	5	0	0	149	127	73	54	53	140
1992— Rockford (Midw.)	14	8	.636	2.84	27	27	7	0	0	187	148	73	59	61	*176
1993— Harrisburg (East.)........	7	2	.778	2.16	16	16	2	1	0	100	80	30	24	28	80
— Ottawa (I.L.)..................	2	1	.667	3.12	6	6	1	1	0	40 1/3	38	15	14	6	28
1994— West Palm Beach (FSL)	1	0	1.000	1.50	1	1	0	0	0	6	2	2	1	1	4
— Ottawa (I.L.)..................	8	3	.727	5.05	14	14	0	0	0	73	77	49	41	28	63
— Montreal (N.L.).................	1	1	.500	6.08	7	5	0	0	1	23 2/3	24	16	16	11	17
1995— Ottawa (I.L.)..................	2	3	.400	3.90	12	12	0	0	0	62 1/3	58	31	27	17	37
— Montreal (N.L.).................	1	2	.333	7.01	19	1	0	0	0	25 2/3	26	21	20	9	25
1996— Indianapolis (A.A.)■	6	3	.667	2.77	11	11	0	0	0	68 1/3	69	25	21	9	51
1997— Indianapolis (A.A.)	7	4	.636	2.82	20	19	0	0	0	118	119	46	37	18	62
— Cincinnati (N.L.)	2	2	.500	4.39	12	6	0	0	1	41	39	20	20	8	25
1998— Cincinnati (N.L.)	5	5	.500	4.01	69	3	0	0	9	98 2/3	86	46	44	27	83
1999— Cincinnati (N.L.)	1	2	.333	4.43	50	0	0	0	0	61	68	31	30	14	61
Major League totals (5 years)	10	12	.455	4.68	157	15	0	0	11	250	243	134	130	69	211

WHITE, RICK   P   DEVIL RAYS

PERSONAL: Born December 23, 1968, in Springfield, Ohio. ... 6-4/215. ... Throws right, bats right. ... Full name: Richard Allen White.
HIGH SCHOOL: Kenton Ridge (Springfield, Ohio).
JUNIOR COLLEGE: Paducah (Ky.) Community College.
TRANSACTIONS/CAREER NOTES: Selected by Pittsburgh Pirates organization in 15th round of free-agent draft (June 4, 1990). ... On Carolina disabled list (May 15-July 6, 1993). ... On Buffalo disabled list (August 28-September 4, 1993). ... On Pittsburgh disabled list (April 14-May 17, 1995); included rehabilitation assignment to Gulf Coast Pirates (April 26-May 17). ... Granted free agency (December 21, 1995). ... Re-signed by Pirates organization (December 21, 1995). ... On Calgary disabled list (April 4-August 7, 1996). ... On Carolina disabled list (August 7-23, 1996). ... Granted free agency (October 15, 1996). ... Signed by Tampa Bay Devil Rays organization (February 4, 1997). ... Loaned by Devil Rays to Chicago Cubs organization (April 3-September 11, 1997).

Year League	W	L	Pct.	ERA	G	GS	CG	ShO	Sv.	IP	H	R	ER	BB	SO
1990— Gulf Coast Pirates (GCL)	3	1	.750	0.76	7	6	0	0	0	35 2/3	26	11	3	4	27
— Welland (NY-P).................	1	4	.200	3.26	9	5	1	0	0	38 2/3	39	19	14	14	43
1991— Augusta (SAL)..................	4	4	.500	3.00	34	0	0	0	6	63	68	26	21	18	52
— Salem (Caro.)..................	2	3	.400	4.66	13	5	1	0	1	46 1/3	41	27	24	9	36
1992— Salem (Caro.)..................	7	9	.438	3.80	18	18	•5	0	0	120 2/3	116	58	51	24	70
— Carolina (Sou.)	1	7	.125	4.21	10	10	1	0	0	57 2/3	59	32	27	18	45
1993— Carolina (Sou.)	4	3	.571	3.50	12	12	1	0	0	69 1/3	59	29	27	12	52
— Buffalo (A.A.).................	0	3	.000	3.54	7	3	0	0	0	28	25	13	11	8	16
1994— Pittsburgh (N.L.)	4	5	.444	3.82	43	5	0	0	6	75 1/3	79	35	32	17	38
1995— Pittsburgh (N.L.)	2	3	.400	4.75	15	9	0	0	0	55	66	33	29	18	29
— Calgary (PCL)	6	4	.600	4.20	14	11	1	0	0	79 1/3	97	40	37	10	56
1996— Carolina (Sou.)	0	1	.000	11.37	2	1	0	0	0	6 1/3	9	8	8	1	7
— Gulf Coast Pirates (GCL)	0	0	...	2.25	3	3	0	0	0	12	8	4	3	3	8
1997— Orlando (Sou.)■.............	5	7	.417	4.71	39	8	0	0	12	86	93	55	45	22	65
1998— Durham (I.L.)■.............	4	2	.667	4.22	9	9	1	0	0	53 1/3	63	29	25	11	31
— Tampa Bay (A.L.).............	2	6	.250	3.80	38	3	0	0	0	68 2/3	66	32	29	23	39
1999— Tampa Bay (A.L.)..............	5	3	.625	4.08	63	1	0	0	0	108	132	56	49	38	81
A.L. totals (2 years)	7	9	.438	3.97	101	4	0	0	0	176 2/3	198	88	78	61	120
N.L. totals (2 years)	6	8	.429	4.21	58	14	0	0	6	130 1/3	145	68	61	35	67
Major League totals (4 years)	13	17	.433	4.07	159	18	0	0	6	307	343	156	139	96	187

W

PERSONAL: Born February 23, 1972, in Milledgeville, Ga. ... 6-0/210. ... Bats right, throws right. ... Full name: Rondell Bernard White.
HIGH SCHOOL: Jones County (Gray, Ga.).
TRANSACTIONS/CAREER NOTES: Selected by Montreal Expos organization in first round (24th pick overall) of free-agent draft (June 4, 1990); pick received as part of compensation for California Angels signing Type A free-agent P Mark Langston. ... On Montreal disabled list (April 28-July 16, 1996); included rehabilitation assignments to West Palm Beach (July 5-10), Gulf Coast Expos (July 5-10) and Harrisburg (July 10-16). ... On disabled list (July 21, 1998-remainder of season; and June 14-29 and July 2-17, 1999).
STATISTICAL NOTES: Led Gulf Coast League with 96 total bases in 1990. ... Hit for the cycle (June 11, 1995, 13 innings). ... Collected six hits in one game (June 11, 1995). ... Led N.L. outfielders in total chances with 385 in 1997. ... Career major league grand slams: 2.

								BATTING						FIELDING		
Year Team (League)	Pos.	G	AB	R	H	2B	3B	HR	RBI	Avg.	BB	SO	SB	PO	A	E	Avg.
1990— GC Expos (GCL)	OF	57	221	33	66	7	4	5	34	.299	17	33	10	71	1	2	.973
1991— Sumter (SAL)	OF	123	465	80	122	23	6	13	68	.262	57	109	50	215	6	3	*.987
1992— W.P. Beach (FSL)........	OF	111	450	80	142	10	*12	4	41	.316	46	78	42	187	2	3	.984
—Harrisburg (East.)........	OF	21	89	22	27	7	1	2	7	.303	6	14	6	29	1	2	.938
1993— Harrisburg (East.)........	OF	90	372	72	122	16	10	12	52	.328	22	72	21	179	4	1	.995
—Ottawa (I.L.)	OF-DH	37	150	28	57	8	2	7	32	.380	12	20	10	79	0	1	.988
—Montreal (N.L.)........	OF	23	73	9	19	3	1	2	15	.260	7	16	1	33	0	0	1.000
1994— Montreal (N.L.)........	OF	40	97	16	27	10	1	2	13	.278	9	18	1	34	1	2	.946
—Ottawa (I.L.)	OF	42	169	23	46	7	0	7	18	.272	15	17	9	91	4	2	.979
1995— Montreal (N.L.)........	OF	130	474	87	140	33	4	13	57	.295	41	87	25	270	5	4	.986
1996— Montreal (N.L.)........	OF	88	334	35	98	19	4	6	41	.293	22	53	14	185	5	2	.990
—W.P. Beach (FSL)........	DH-OF	3	10	0	2	1	0	0	2	.200	0	4	0	2	0	0	1.000
—GC Expos (GCL)	OF	3	12	3	3	0	0	2	4	.250	0	1	1	4	0	0	1.000
—Harrisburg (East.)........	OF	5	20	5	7	1	0	3	6	.350	1	1	1	12	0	0	1.000
1997— Montreal (N.L.)........	OF	151	592	84	160	29	5	28	82	.270	31	111	16	*376	6	3	*.992
1998— Montreal (N.L.)........	OF-DH	97	357	54	107	21	2	17	58	.300	30	57	16	261	7	1	.996
1999— Montreal (N.L.)........	OF	138	539	83	168	26	6	22	64	.312	32	85	10	286	7	11	.964
Major League totals (7 years)		667	2466	368	719	141	23	90	330	.292	172	427	83	1445	31	23	.985

PERSONAL: Born November 25, 1966, in Pensacola, Fla. ... 6-3/235. ... Bats both, throws right. ... Full name: Mark Anthony Whiten. ... Name pronounced WHITT-en.
HIGH SCHOOL: Pensacola (Fla.).
JUNIOR COLLEGE: Pensacola (Fla.) Junior College.
TRANSACTIONS/CAREER NOTES: Selected by Toronto Blue Jays organization in fifth round of free-agent draft (January 14, 1986). ... On Toronto suspended list (May 23-25, 1991). ... Traded by Blue Jays with P Denis Boucher, OF Glenallen Hill and a player to be named later to Cleveland Indians for P Tom Candiotti and OF Turner Ward (June 27, 1991); Indians acquired cash to complete deal (October 15, 1991). ... Traded by Indians to St. Louis Cardinals for P Mark Clark and SS Juan Andujar (March 31, 1993). ... On St. Louis disabled list (April 18-May 5, 1994); included rehabilitation assignment to Louisville (May 2-5). ... Traded by Cardinals with P Rheal Cormier to Boston Red Sox for 3B Scott Cooper, P Cory Bailey and a player to be named later (April 8, 1995). ... On Boston disabled list (May 22-June 9, 1995); included rehabilitation assignment to Pawtucket (June 2-9). ... Traded by Red Sox to Philadelphia Phillies for 1B Dave Hollins (July 24, 1995). ... Released by Phillies (June 17, 1996). ... Signed by Atlanta Braves (June 24, 1996). ... Traded by Braves to Seattle Mariners for P Roger Blanco (August 14, 1996). ... Granted free agency (December 7, 1996). ... Signed by New York Yankees (January 9, 1997). ... Released by Yankees (August 15, 1997). ... Signed by Indians (May 6, 1998). ... Granted free agency (October 30, 1998). ... Re-signed by Indians (December 8, 1998). ... On Cleveland disabled list (March 30-June 23, 1999); included rehabilitation assignment to Buffalo (June 2-21). ... On Buffalo disabled list (August 2-9 and August 13-20, 1999). ... Granted free agency (October 15, 1999).
RECORDS: Shares major league single-game records for most home runs—4 (September 7, 1993, second game); and most runs batted in—12 (September 7, 1993, second game). ... Shares major league record for most runs batted in during doubleheader—13 (September 7, 1993). ... Shares N.L. record for most runs batted in during two consecutive games—13 (September 7, 1993, first and second games).
STATISTICAL NOTES: Tied for Pioneer League lead in being hit by pitch with six in 1986. ... Led South Atlantic League outfielders with 322 total chances and tied for lead with four double plays in 1987. ... Led South Atlantic League in being hit by pitch with 16 and tied for lead in intentional bases on balls received with 10 in 1987. ... Led Southern League in being hit by pitch with 11 in 1989. ... Hit four home runs in one game (September 7, 1993, second game). ... Switch-hit home runs in one game (September 14, 1993). ... Career major league grand slams: 4.
MISCELLANEOUS: Batted righthanded only (1988-89).

								BATTING						FIELDING		
Year Team (League)	Pos.	G	AB	R	H	2B	3B	HR	RBI	Avg.	BB	SO	SB	PO	A	E	Avg.
1986— Medicine Hat (Pio.)	OF	•70	270	53	81	16	3	10	44	.300	29	56	22	111	9	*10	.923
1987— Myrtle Beach (SAL)	OF	*139	494	90	125	22	5	15	64	.253	76	149	49	*292	*18	12	.963
1988— Dunedin (FSL)	OF	99	385	61	97	8	5	7	37	.252	41	69	17	200	*21	9	.961
—Knoxville (Sou.)..........	OF	28	108	20	28	3	1	2	9	.259	12	20	6	62	3	4	.942
1989— Knoxville (Sou.)..........	OF	129	423	75	109	13	6	12	47	.258	60	114	11	223	17	8	.968
1990— Syracuse (I.L.)	OF	104	390	65	113	19	4	14	48	.290	37	72	14	158	14	6	.966
—Toronto (A.L.)............	OF-DH	33	88	12	24	1	1	2	7	.273	7	14	2	60	3	0	1.000
1991— Toronto (A.L.)............	OF	46	149	12	33	4	3	2	19	.221	11	35	0	90	2	0	1.000
—Cleveland (A.L.)■.......	OF-DH	70	258	34	66	14	4	7	26	.256	19	50	4	166	11	7	.962
1992— Cleveland (A.L.)	OF-DH	148	508	73	129	19	4	9	43	.254	72	102	16	321	14	7	.980
1993— St. Louis (N.L.)■	OF	152	562	81	142	13	4	25	99	.253	58	110	15	329	9	10	.971
1994— St. Louis (N.L.)........	OF	92	334	57	98	18	2	14	53	.293	37	75	10	234	9	9	.964
—Louisville (A.A.)..........	OF	3	10	2	3	1	0	1	3	.300	1	1	0	3	0	0	1.000
1995— Boston (A.L.)■..........	OF-DH	32	108	13	20	3	0	1	10	.185	8	23	1	52	4	0	1.000
—Pawtucket (I.L.)..........	OF-DH	28	102	19	29	3	1	4	13	.284	19	30	4	43	4	3	.940
—Philadelphia (N.L.)■ ..	OF	60	212	38	57	10	1	11	37	.269	31	63	7	105	4	4	.965
1996— Philadelphia (N.L.)......	OF	60	182	33	43	8	0	7	21	.236	33	62	13	97	6	6	.945
—Atlanta (N.L.)■	OF	36	90	12	23	5	1	3	17	.256	16	25	2	41	1	3	.933
—Seattle (A.L.)■..........	OF	40	140	31	42	7	0	12	33	.300	21	40	2	90	4	3	.969

W

Year Team (League)	Pos.	G	AB	R	H	2B	3B	HR	RBI	Avg.	BB	SO	SB	PO	A	E	Avg.
						BATTING									FIELDING		
1997— New York (A.L.)■......	OF-DH	69	215	34	57	11	0	5	24	.265	30	47	4	102	2	5	.954
1998— Cleveland (A.L.)■......	OF-DH-P	88	226	31	64	14	0	6	29	.283	29	60	2	124	7	4	.970
1999— Buffalo (I.L.)	OF-DH	48	175	32	49	10	0	6	19	.280	22	38	3	88	4	1	.989
— Cleveland (A.L.)	OF	8	25	2	4	1	0	1	4	.160	3	4	0	11	1	0	1.000
American League totals (8 years)		534	1717	242	439	74	12	45	195	.256	200	375	31	1016	48	26	.976
National League totals (4 years)		400	1380	221	363	54	8	60	227	.263	175	335	47	806	29	32	.963
Major League totals (10 years)		934	3097	463	802	128	20	105	422	.259	375	710	78	1822	77	58	.970

DIVISION SERIES RECORD

Year Team (League)	Pos.	G	AB	R	H	2B	3B	HR	RBI	Avg.	BB	SO	SB	PO	A	E	Avg.
						BATTING									FIELDING		
1998— Cleveland (A.L.)						Did not play.											

CHAMPIONSHIP SERIES RECORD

Year Team (League)	Pos.	G	AB	R	H	2B	3B	HR	RBI	Avg.	BB	SO	SB	PO	A	E	Avg.
						BATTING									FIELDING		
1998— Cleveland (A.L.).........	OF	2	7	2	2	1	0	1	1	.286	1	3	0	3	0	0	1.000

RECORD AS PITCHER

Year League	W	L	Pct.	ERA	G	GS	CG	ShO	Sv.	IP	H	R	ER	BB	SO
1998— Cleveland (A.L.)................	0	0	...	9.00	1	0	0	0	0	1	1	1	1	2	3

WHITESIDE, MATT   P   PADRES

PERSONAL: Born August 8, 1967, in Charleston, Mo. ... 6-0/205. ... Throws right, bats right. ... Full name: Matthew Christopher Whiteside.
HIGH SCHOOL: Charleston (Mo.).
COLLEGE: Arkansas State (degree in physical education).
TRANSACTIONS/CAREER NOTES: Selected by Texas Rangers organization in 25th round of free-agent draft (June 4, 1990). ... On disabled list (May 9-25, 1995). ... Granted free agency (October 30, 1996). ... Re-signed by Rangers (November 22, 1996). ... Released by Rangers (March 23, 1998). ... Signed by Philadelphia Phillies (March 27, 1998). ... Granted free agency (October 15, 1998). ... Signed by San Diego Padres organization (November 23, 1998). ... Granted free agency (October 8, 1999). ... Re-signed by Padres (October 25, 1999).
STATISTICAL NOTES: Tied for American Association lead with three balks in 1996.

Year League	W	L	Pct.	ERA	G	GS	CG	ShO	Sv.	IP	H	R	ER	BB	SO
1990— Butte (Pio.)........................	4	4	.500	3.45	18	5	0	0	2	57 1/3	57	33	22	25	45
1991— Gastonia (SAL)	3	1	.750	2.15	48	0	0	0	29	62 2/3	44	19	15	21	71
1992— Tulsa (Texas)	0	1	.000	2.41	33	0	0	0	21	33 2/3	31	9	9	3	30
— Oklahoma City (A.A.)...........	1	0	1.000	0.79	12	0	0	0	8	11 1/3	7	1	1	3	13
— Texas (A.L.)	1	1	.500	1.93	20	0	0	0	4	28	26	8	6	11	13
1993— Texas (A.L.)	2	1	.667	4.32	60	0	0	0	1	73	78	37	35	23	39
— Oklahoma City (A.A.)...........	2	1	.667	5.56	8	0	0	0	1	11 1/3	17	7	7	8	10
1994— Texas (A.L.)	2	2	.500	5.02	47	0	0	0	1	61	68	40	34	28	37
1995— Texas (A.L.)	5	4	.556	4.08	40	0	0	0	3	53	48	24	24	19	46
1996— Texas (A.L.)	0	1	.000	6.68	14	0	0	0	0	32 1/3	43	24	24	11	15
— Oklahoma City (A.A.)...........	9	6	.600	3.45	36	7	0	0	4	94	95	41	36	24	52
1997— Oklahoma City (A.A.)........	1	1	.500	3.54	10	1	0	0	1	28	30	14	11	13	11
— Texas (A.L.)	4	1	.800	5.08	42	1	0	0	0	72 2/3	85	45	41	26	44
1998— Philadelphia (N.L.)■	1	1	.500	8.50	10	0	0	0	0	18	27	18	17	5	14
— Scranton/W.B. (I.L.)	1	4	.200	6.48	30	1	0	0	5	33 1/3	47	24	24	7	21
1999— Las Vegas (PCL)■	9	5	.643	5.12	47	3	1	1	7	89 2/3	99	59	51	29	88
— San Diego (N.L.)	1	0	1.000	13.91	10	0	0	0	0	11	19	17	17	5	9
A.L. totals (6 years)	14	10	.583	4.61	223	1	0	0	9	320	348	178	164	118	194
N.L. totals (2 years)	2	1	.667	10.55	20	0	0	0	0	29	46	35	34	10	23
Major League totals (8 years).......	16	11	.593	5.11	243	1	0	0	9	349	394	213	198	128	217

WICKMAN, BOB   P   BREWERS

PERSONAL: Born February 6, 1969, in Green Bay, Wis. ... 6-1/227. ... Throws right, bats right. ... Full name: Robert Joe Wickman.
HIGH SCHOOL: Oconto Falls (Wis.).
COLLEGE: Wisconsin-Whitewater.
TRANSACTIONS/CAREER NOTES: Selected by Chicago White Sox organization in second round of free-agent draft (June 4, 1990). ... Traded by White Sox with P Melido Perez and P Domingo Jean to New York Yankees for 2B Steve Sax and cash (January 10, 1992). ... Traded by Yankees with OF Gerald Williams to Milwaukee Brewers for P Graeme Lloyd and OF Pat Listach (August 23, 1996).

Year League	W	L	Pct.	ERA	G	GS	CG	ShO	Sv.	IP	H	R	ER	BB	SO
1990— GC White Sox (GCL)	2	0	1.000	2.45	2	2	0	0	0	11	7	4	3	1	15
— Sarasota (FSL)	0	1	.000	1.98	2	2	0	0	0	13 2/3	17	7	3	4	8
— South Bend (Midw.)	7	2	.778	1.38	9	9	3	0	0	65 1/3	50	16	10	16	50
1991— Sarasota (FSL)	5	1	.833	2.05	7	7	1	1	0	44	43	16	10	11	32
— Birmingham (Sou.)............	6	10	.375	3.56	20	20	4	1	0	131 1/3	127	68	52	50	81
1992— Columbus (I.L.)■	12	5	.706	2.92	23	23	2	1	0	157	131	61	51	55	108
— New York (A.L.)	6	1	.857	4.11	8	8	0	0	0	50 1/3	51	25	23	20	21
1993— New York (A.L.)	14	4	.778	4.63	41	19	1	1	4	140	156	82	72	69	70
1994— New York (A.L.)	5	4	.556	3.09	*53	0	0	0	6	70	54	26	24	27	56
1995— New York (A.L.)	2	4	.333	4.05	63	1	0	0	1	80	77	38	36	33	51
1996— New York (A.L.)	4	1	.800	4.67	58	0	0	0	0	79	94	41	41	34	61
— Milwaukee (A.L.)■	3	0	1.000	3.24	12	0	0	0	0	16 2/3	12	9	6	10	14
1997— Milwaukee (A.L.)	7	6	.538	2.73	74	0	0	0	1	95 2/3	89	32	29	41	78
1998— Milwaukee (N.L.)	6	9	.400	3.72	72	0	0	0	25	82 1/3	79	38	34	39	71
1999— Milwaukee (N.L.)	3	8	.273	3.39	71	0	0	0	37	74 1/3	75	31	28	38	60
A.L. totals (6 years)	41	20	.672	3.91	309	28	1	1	12	531 2/3	533	253	231	234	351
N.L. totals (2 years)	9	17	.346	3.56	143	0	0	0	62	156 2/3	154	69	62	77	131
Major League totals (8 years).......	50	37	.575	3.83	452	28	1	1	74	688 1/3	687	322	293	311	482

W

DIVISION SERIES RECORD

Year	League	W	L	Pct.	ERA	G	GS	CG	ShO	Sv.	IP	H	R	ER	BB	SO
1995—New York (A.L.)		0	0	...	0.00	3	0	0	0	0	3	5	0	0	0	3

WIDGER, CHRIS   C   EXPOS

PERSONAL: Born May 21, 1971, in Wilmington, Del. ... 6-2/215. ... Bats right, throws right. ... Full name: Christopher Jon Widger. ... Nephew of Mike Widger, linebacker with Montreal Alouettes and Ottawa Rough Riders of Canadian Football League (1970-78).
HIGH SCHOOL: Pennsville (N.J.).
COLLEGE: George Mason.
TRANSACTIONS/CAREER NOTES: Selected by Seattle Mariners organization in third round of free-agent draft (June 1, 1992). ... On disabled list (June 6-16, 1993). ... Traded by Mariners with P Trey Moore and P Matt Wagner to Montreal Expos for P Jeff Fassero and P Alex Pacheco (October 29, 1996).
STATISTICAL NOTES: Led N.L. catchers with 14 passed balls and tied for lead with 12 double plays in 1998. ... Career major league grand slams: 1.

							BATTING							FIELDING		
Year	Team (League)	Pos.	G	AB	R	H	2B	3B	HR	RBI	Avg.	BB	SO	SB	PO	A	E	Avg.
1992—Bellingham (N'west)		C	51	166	28	43	7	2	5	30	.259	22	36	8	266	39	4	*.987
1993—Riverside (Calif.)		C-OF	97	360	44	95	28	2	9	58	.264	19	64	5	472	63	14	.974
1994—Jacksonville (Sou.)		C-OF-1B	116	388	58	101	15	3	16	59	.260	39	69	8	564	73	13	.980
1995—Tacoma (PCL)		C-DH-OF	50	174	29	48	11	1	9	21	.276	9	29	0	189	22	4	.981
—Seattle (A.L.)		C-OF-DH	23	45	2	9	0	0	1	2	.200	3	11	0	64	1	0	1.000
1996—Tacoma (PCL)		C-DH	97	352	42	107	20	2	13	48	.304	27	62	7	622	41	8	.988
—Seattle (A.L.)		C	8	11	1	2	0	0	0	0	.182	0	5	0	18	1	2	.905
1997—Montreal (N.L.)■		C	91	278	30	65	20	3	7	37	.234	22	59	2	516	40	11	.981
1998—Montreal (N.L.)		C	124	417	36	97	18	1	15	53	.233	29	85	6	752	64	14	.983
1999—Montreal (N.L.)		C	124	383	42	101	24	1	14	56	.264	28	86	1	662	54	6	.992
American League totals (2 years)			31	56	3	11	0	0	1	2	.196	3	16	0	82	2	2	.977
National League totals (3 years)			340	1078	108	263	62	5	36	146	.244	79	230	9	1930	158	31	.985
Major League totals (5 years)			371	1134	111	274	62	5	37	148	.242	82	246	9	2012	160	33	.985

DIVISION SERIES RECORD

							BATTING							FIELDING		
Year	Team (League)	Pos.	G	AB	R	H	2B	3B	HR	RBI	Avg.	BB	SO	SB	PO	A	E	Avg.
1995—Seattle (A.L.)		C	2	3	0	0	0	0	0	0	.000	0	3	0	14	0	0	1.000

CHAMPIONSHIP SERIES RECORD

							BATTING							FIELDING		
Year	Team (League)	Pos.	G	AB	R	H	2B	3B	HR	RBI	Avg.	BB	SO	SB	PO	A	E	Avg.
1995—Seattle (A.L.)		C	3	1	0	0	0	0	0	0	.000	0	1	0	7	0	0	1.000

WILCOX, LUKE   OF

PERSONAL: Born November 15, 1973, in Lansing, Mich. ... 6-4/225. ... Bats left, throws right. ... Full name: Christopher Luke Wilcox.
HIGH SCHOOL: St. John's (Mich.).
COLLEGE: Western Michigan.
TRANSACTIONS/CAREER NOTES: Selected by New York Yankees organization in third round of free-agent draft (June 1, 1995). ... On Norwich disabled list (April 6-June 3, 1997). ... Selected by Tampa Bay Devil Rays in third round (66th pick overall) of expansion draft (November 18, 1997). ... Released by Devil Rays (January 13, 2000).

							BATTING							FIELDING		
Year	Team (League)	Pos.	G	AB	R	H	2B	3B	HR	RBI	Avg.	BB	SO	SB	PO	A	E	Avg.
1995—Oneonta (NY-P)		OF	59	223	25	73	16	7	1	28	.327	20	28	9	84	6	5	.947
1996—Tampa (FSL)		OF	119	470	72	133	32	5	11	76	.283	40	71	14	209	10	3	.986
1997—Norwich (East.)		OF	74	300	45	83	13	1	6	34	.277	18	36	13	141	6	3	.980
—Tampa (FSL)		OF	12	40	7	12	4	0	0	4	.300	7	6	1	10	0	0	1.000
1998—Orlando (Sou.)■		OF	88	331	57	95	23	3	17	69	.287	39	54	2	141	10	2	.987
—Durham (I.L.)		OF	43	151	17	34	11	0	2	17	.225	16	27	0	98	4	0	1.000
1999—Orlando (Sou.)		OF-DH	90	333	60	90	24	1	20	64	.270	35	54	3	132	5	4	.972
—Durham (I.L.)		OF-DH	39	134	32	44	12	5	9	34	.328	22	18	1	46	1	2	.959

WILKINS, MARC   P   PIRATES

W

PERSONAL: Born October 21, 1970, in Mansfield, Ohio ... 5-11/212. ... Throws right, bats right. ... Full name: Marc Allen Wilkins.
HIGH SCHOOL: Ontario (Ohio).
COLLEGE: Toledo.
TRANSACTIONS/CAREER NOTES: Selected by Pittsburgh Pirates organization in 47th round of free-agent draft (June 1, 1992). ... On Pittsburgh disabled list (April 26-May 11 and May 23, 1998-remainder of season); included rehabilitation assignments to Carolina (May 8-10) and Nashville (August 7-September 6). ... On Pittsburgh disabled list (March 26-May 1, 1999); included rehabilitation assignments to Altoona (April 16-25) and Nashville (April 26-May 1).
STATISTICAL NOTES: Led Carolina League with 22 hit batsmen in 1994.

Year	League	W	L	Pct.	ERA	G	GS	CG	ShO	Sv.	IP	H	R	ER	BB	SO
1992—Welland (NY-P)		4	2	.667	7.29	28	1	0	0	1	42	49	36	34	24	42
1993—Augusta (SAL)		5	6	.455	4.21	48	5	0	0	1	77	83	52	36	31	73
1994—Salem (Caro.)		8	5	.615	3.70	28	•28	0	0	0	151	155	84	62	45	90
1995—Carolina (Sou.)		5	3	.625	3.99	37	12	0	0	0	99 1/3	91	47	44	44	80
1996—Carolina (Sou.)		2	3	.400	4.01	11	3	0	0	0	24 2/3	19	12	11	11	19
—Pittsburgh (N.L.)		4	3	.571	3.84	47	2	0	0	1	75	75	36	32	36	62

Year League	W	L	Pct.	ERA	G	GS	CG	ShO	Sv.	IP	H	R	ER	BB	SO
1997— Pittsburgh (N.L.)	9	5	.643	3.69	70	0	0	0	2	75 2/3	65	33	31	33	47
1998— Pittsburgh (N.L.)	0	0	...	3.52	16	0	0	0	0	15 1/3	13	6	6	9	17
— Carolina (Sou.)	0	0	...	4.50	2	0	0	0	0	2	1	1	1	0	4
— Nashville (PCL)	1	0	1.000	10.38	5	0	0	0	0	4 1/3	3	5	5	3	4
1999— Altoona (East.)	0	1	.000	1.50	4	0	0	0	0	6	4	2	1	4	5
— Nashville (PCL)	1	1	.500	0.79	8	0	0	0	3	11 1/3	9	3	1	3	8
— Pittsburgh (N.L.)	2	3	.400	4.24	46	0	0	0	0	51	49	28	24	26	44
Major League totals (4 years)	15	11	.577	3.86	179	2	0	0	3	217	202	103	93	104	170

WILKINS, RICK   C

PERSONAL: Born June 4, 1967, in Jacksonville. ... 6-2/215. ... Bats left, throws right. ... Full name: Richard David Wilkins.
HIGH SCHOOL: The Bolles School (Jacksonville).
JUNIOR COLLEGE: Florida Community College-Jacksonville.
COLLEGE: Furman.
TRANSACTIONS/CAREER NOTES: Selected by Chicago Cubs organization in 23rd round of free-agent draft (June 2, 1986). ... On Chicago disabled list (June 2-28, 1995). ... Traded by Cubs to Houston Astros for OF Luis Gonzalez and C Scott Servais (June 28, 1995). ... On Houston disabled list (July 2-September 5, 1995); included rehabilitation assignments to Jackson (August 28-September 1) and Tucson (September 1-5). ... Traded by Astros with cash to San Francisco Giants for C Kirt Manwaring (July 27, 1996). ... Released by Giants (August 1, 1997). ... Signed by Seattle Mariners organization (August 15, 1997). ... On Seattle disabled list (August 15-September 1, 1997); included rehabilitation assignment to Tacoma (August 15-September 1). ... Granted free agency (October 16, 1997). ... Re-signed by Mariners (December 15, 1997). ... Traded by Mariners to New York Mets for P Lindsay Gulin (May 12, 1998). ... On Norfolk disabled list (July 20-August 30, 1998). ... Granted free agency (October 15, 1998). ... Signed by Los Angeles Dodgers organization (March 3, 1999). ... Granted free agency (October 4, 1999).
STATISTICAL NOTES: Led Appalachian League with eight intentional bases on balls received in 1987. ... Led Appalachian League catchers with .989 fielding percentage, 483 putouts and 540 total chances and tied for lead with six double plays in 1987. ... Led Midwest League catchers with 984 total chances in 1988. ... Led Carolina League catchers with 860 total chances and tied for lead with eight double plays in 1989. ... Led Southern League catchers with 857 total chances, 11 double plays and 15 passed balls in 1990. ... Tied for N.L. lead with 10 sacrifice flies in 1996. ... Career major league grand slams: 2.

								BATTING						FIELDING		
Year Team (League)	Pos.	G	AB	R	H	2B	3B	HR	RBI	Avg.	BB	SO	SB	PO	A	E	Avg.
1987— Geneva (NY-P)	C-1B	75	243	35	61	8	2	8	43	.251	58	40	7	†503	51	7	†.988
1988— Peoria (Midw.)	C	137	490	54	119	30	1	8	63	.243	67	110	4	*864	*101	*19	.981
1989— Win.-Salem (Car.)	C	132	445	61	111	24	1	12	54	.249	50	87	6	*764	*78	*18	.979
1990— Charlotte (Sou.)	C	127	449	48	102	18	1	17	71	.227	43	95	4	*740	*103	14	.984
1991— Iowa (A.A.)	C-OF	38	107	12	29	3	1	5	14	.271	11	17	1	204	24	3	.987
— Chicago (N.L.)	C	86	203	21	45	9	0	6	22	.222	19	56	3	373	42	3	.993
1992— Chicago (N.L.)	C	83	244	20	66	9	1	8	22	.270	28	53	0	408	47	3	.993
— Iowa (A.A.)	C	47	155	20	43	11	2	5	28	.277	19	42	0	177	18	2	.990
1993— Chicago (N.L.)	C	136	446	78	135	23	1	30	73	.303	50	99	2	717	89	3	.996
1994— Chicago (N.L.)	C-1B	100	313	44	71	25	2	7	39	.227	40	86	4	550	51	4	.993
1995— Chicago (N.L.)	C-1B	50	162	24	31	2	0	6	14	.191	36	51	0	294	31	4	.988
— Houston (N.L.)	C	15	40	6	10	1	0	1	5	.250	10	10	0	87	4	0	1.000
— Jackson (Texas)	C	4	11	0	0	0	0	0	0	.000	3	2	0	23	1	0	1.000
— Tucson (PCL)	C	4	12	0	4	0	0	0	4	.333	2	0	0	27	4	0	1.000
1996— Houston (N.L.)	C	84	254	34	54	8	2	6	23	.213	46	81	0	550	39	6	.990
— San Fran. (N.L.)■	C-1B	52	157	19	46	10	0	8	36	.293	21	40	0	240	34	2	.993
1997— San Francisco (N.L.) ..	C	66	190	18	37	5	0	6	23	.195	17	65	0	326	37	5	.986
— Tacoma (PCL)■	C-DH-1B	17	68	16	23	8	0	1	14	.338	8	12	0	82	4	1	.989
— Seattle (A.L.)	C-DH	5	12	2	3	1	0	1	4	.250	1	2	0	9	1	0	1.000
1998— Seattle (A.L.)	C-1B-DH	19	41	5	8	1	1	1	4	.195	4	14	0	70	4	0	1.000
— New York (N.L.)■	C	5	15	3	2	0	0	0	1	.133	2	2	0	21	1	1	.957
— Norfolk (I.L.)	C-DH-1B	45	158	17	41	13	1	1	20	.259	14	37	1	231	15	3	.988
1999— Los Angeles (N.L.)■ ...	C	3	4	0	0	0	0	0	0	.000	0	2	0	1	0	0	1.000
— Albuquerque (PCL).....	C-1B-DH	92	300	39	76	8	1	8	33	.253	29	87	1	546	49	9	.985
American League totals (2 years)		24	53	7	11	2	1	2	8	.208	5	16	0	79	5	0	1.000
National League totals (9 years)		680	2028	267	497	92	6	78	258	.245	269	545	9	3567	375	31	.992
Major League totals (9 years)		704	2081	274	508	94	7	80	266	.244	274	561	9	3646	380	31	.992

DIVISION SERIES RECORD

								BATTING						FIELDING		
Year Team (League)	Pos.	G	AB	R	H	2B	3B	HR	RBI	Avg.	BB	SO	SB	PO	A	E	Avg.
1997— Seattle (A.L.)	C-PH	1	1	0	0	0	0	0	0	.000	1	0	0	2	0	0	1.000

W   WILLIAMS, BERNIE   OF   YANKEES

PERSONAL: Born September 13, 1968, in San Juan, Puerto Rico. ... 6-2/205. ... Bats both, throws right. ... Full name: Bernabe Figueroa Williams.
HIGH SCHOOL: Escuela Libre de Musica (San Juan, Puerto Rico).
COLLEGE: Puerto Rico.
TRANSACTIONS/CAREER NOTES: Signed as non-drafted free agent by New York Yankees organization (September 13, 1985). ... On disabled list (July 15, 1988-remainder of season and May 13-June 7, 1993). ... On disabled list (May 11-May 26, 1996; June 16-July 2 and July 15-August 1, 1997). ... On New York disabled list (June 11-July 18, 1998); included rehabilitation assignments to Tampa (July 6-7) and Norwich (July 14-16). ... Granted free agency (October 26, 1998). ... Re-signed by Yankees (November 25, 1998).
RECORDS: Shares major league single-game record for most strikeouts (nine-inning game)—5 (August 21, 1991). ... Shares major league single-inning record for most doubles—2 (June 22, 1994, seventh inning). ... Shares modern major league record for most long hits in one inning—2 (June 22, 1994, seventh inning).
HONORS: Won A.L. Gold Glove as outfielder (1997-99).

STATISTICAL NOTES: Led Gulf Coast League outfielders with 123 total chances in 1986. ... Tied for Gulf Coast League lead in caught stealing with 12 in 1986. ... Led Eastern League in caught stealing with 18 in 1990. ... Led Eastern League outfielders with 307 total chances and tied for lead with four double plays in 1990. ... Had 21-game hitting streak (August 1-23, 1993). ... Switch-hit home runs in one game four times (June 6, 1994; September 12, 1996; September 4, 1998; and May 4, 1999). ... Led A.L. outfielders with 441 total chances in 1995. ... Had 16-game hitting streak (July 31-August 14, 1998). ... Had 17-game hitting streak (June 8-July 6, 1999). ... Tied for A.L. lead with 17 intentional bases on balls received in 1999. ... Career major league grand slams: 7.

MISCELLANEOUS: Batted righthanded only (1986-88).

							BATTING									FIELDING		
Year Team (League)	Pos.	G	AB	R	H	2B	3B	HR	RBI	Avg.	BB	SO	SB	PO	A	E	Avg.
1986— GC Yankees (GCL)......	OF	61	230	*45	62	5	3	2	25	.270	39	40	33	*117	3	3	.976
1987— Fort Laud. (FSL)........	OF	25	71	11	11	3	0	0	4	.155	18	22	9	49	1	0	1.000
— Oneonta (NY-P).........	OF	25	93	13	32	4	0	0	15	.344	10	14	9	40	0	2	.952
1988— Prince Will. (Caro.).....	OF	92	337	72	113	16	7	7	45	*.335	65	65	29	186	8	5	.975
1989— Columbus (I.L.).........	OF	50	162	21	35	8	1	2	16	.216	25	38	11	112	2	1	.991
— Alb./Colonie (East.)	OF	91	314	63	79	11	8	11	42	.252	60	72	26	180	5	5	.974
1990— Alb./Colonie (East.)	OF	134	466	*91	131	28	5	8	54	.281	*98	97	*39	*288	15	4	.987
1991— Columbus (I.L.).........	OF	78	306	52	90	14	6	8	37	.294	38	43	9	164	2	1	.994
— New York (A.L.).........	OF	85	320	43	76	19	4	3	34	.238	48	57	10	230	3	5	.979
1992— New York (A.L.).........	OF	62	261	39	73	14	2	5	26	.280	29	36	7	187	5	1	.995
— Columbus (I.L.).........	OF	95	363	68	111	23	•9	8	50	.306	52	61	20	205	2	2	.990
1993— New York (A.L.).........	OF	139	567	67	152	31	4	12	68	.268	53	106	9	366	5	4	.989
1994— New York (A.L.).........	OF	108	408	80	118	29	1	12	57	.289	61	54	16	277	7	3	.990
1995— New York (A.L.).........	OF	144	563	93	173	29	9	18	82	.307	75	98	8	*432	1	•8	.982
1996— New York (A.L.).........	OF-DH	143	551	108	168	26	7	29	102	.305	82	72	17	334	10	5	.986
1997— New York (A.L.).........	OF	129	509	107	167	35	6	21	100	.328	73	80	15	270	2	2	.993
1998— New York (A.L.).........	OF-DH	128	499	101	169	30	5	26	97	*.339	74	81	15	298	4	3	.990
— Tampa (FSL)..............	OF	1	2	0	1	1	0	0	0	.500	1	0	0	2	0	0	1.000
— Norwich (East.)	OF	3	11	6	6	2	0	2	5	.545	2	1	0	5	0	0	1.000
1999— New York (A.L.).........	OF-DH	158	591	116	202	28	6	25	115	.342	100	95	9	381	9	5	.987
Major League totals (9 years)		1096	4269	754	1298	241	44	151	681	.304	595	679	106	2775	46	36	.987

DIVISION SERIES RECORD

RECORDS: Holds career records for most runs—18; and runs batted in—17. ... Holds A.L. career record for most bases on balls—15. ... Shares career record for most extra-base hits—10; and most total bases—44. ... Shares single-game record for most home runs—2 (October 6, 1995 and October 5, 1996).

							BATTING									FIELDING		
Year Team (League)	Pos.	G	AB	R	H	2B	3B	HR	RBI	Avg.	BB	SO	SB	PO	A	E	Avg.
1995— New York (A.L.)..........	OF	5	21	8	9	2	0	2	5	.429	7	3	1	13	0	0	1.000
1996— New York (A.L.)..........	OF	4	15	5	7	0	0	3	5	.467	2	1	1	10	0	0	1.000
1997— New York (A.L.)..........	OF	5	17	3	2	1	0	0	1	.118	4	3	0	7	0	0	1.000
1998— New York (A.L.)..........	OF	3	11	0	0	0	0	0	0	.000	1	4	0	8	0	0	1.000
1999— New York (A.L.)..........	OF	3	11	2	4	1	0	1	6	.364	1	2	0	15	0	0	1.000
Division series totals (5 years)		20	75	18	22	4	0	6	17	.293	15	13	2	53	0	0	1.000

CHAMPIONSHIP SERIES RECORD

NOTES: Named Most Valuable Player (1996).

							BATTING									FIELDING		
Year Team (League)	Pos.	G	AB	R	H	2B	3B	HR	RBI	Avg.	BB	SO	SB	PO	A	E	Avg.
1996— New York (A.L.)..........	OF	5	19	6	9	3	0	2	6	.474	6	4	1	20	0	0	1.000
1998— New York (A.L.)..........	OF	6	21	4	8	1	0	0	5	.381	7	4	1	14	0	0	1.000
1999— New York (A.L.)..........	OF	5	20	3	5	1	0	1	2	.250	2	5	1	13	1	0	1.000
Championship series totals (3 years)		16	60	13	22	5	0	3	13	.367	15	13	3	47	1	0	1.000

WORLD SERIES RECORD

NOTES: Member of World Series championship team (1996, 1998 and 1999).

							BATTING									FIELDING		
Year Team (League)	Pos.	G	AB	R	H	2B	3B	HR	RBI	Avg.	BB	SO	SB	PO	A	E	Avg.
1996— New York (A.L.)..........	OF	6	24	3	4	0	0	1	4	.167	4	6	1	15	0	0	1.000
1998— New York (A.L.)..........	OF	4	16	2	1	0	0	1	3	.063	3	5	0	6	0	0	1.000
1999— New York (A.L.)..........	OF	4	13	2	3	0	0	0	0	.231	4	2	1	2	0	0	1.000
World Series totals (3 years)		14	53	7	8	0	0	2	7	.151	11	13	2	23	0	0	1.000

ALL-STAR GAME RECORD

NOTES: Named to All-Star team for 1998 game; replaced by Manny Ramirez due to injury.

						BATTING								FIELDING		
Year League	Pos.	AB	R	H	2B	3B	HR	RBI	Avg.	BB	SO	SB	PO	A	E	Avg.
1997— American..................	OF	0	1	0	0	0	0	0	...	1	0	1	1	0	0	1.000
1998— American..................							Selected, did not play—injured.									
1999— American..................	OF	1	0	0	0	0	0	0	.000	0	1	0	0	0	0	...
All-Star Game totals (2 years)		1	1	0	0	0	0	0	.000	1	1	1	1	0	0	1.000

WILLIAMS, BRIAN   P   CUBS

PERSONAL: Born February 15, 1969, in Lancaster, S.C. ... 6-2/225. ... Throws right, bats right. ... Full name: Brian O'Neal Williams.
HIGH SCHOOL: Lewisville (Fort Lawn, S.C.).
COLLEGE: South Carolina.
TRANSACTIONS/CAREER NOTES: Selected by Pittsburgh Pirates organization in third round of free-agent draft (June 2, 1987); did not sign. ... Selected by Houston Astros organization in supplemental round ("sandwich pick" between first and second round, 31st pick overall) of free-agent draft (June 4, 1990); pick received as part of compensation for San Francisco Giants signing Type A free-agent OF Kevin Bass. ... On Tucson disabled list (May 25-June 1, 1992). ... On Houston disabled list (August 5-20, 1993); included rehabilitation assignment to Tucson (August 15-20). ... On Houston disabled list (August 1-September 19, 1994). ... Traded by Astros with 3B Ken Caminiti, OF Steve Finley, SS

W

Andujar Cedeno, 1B Robert Petagine and a player to be named later to San Diego Padres for OF Phil Plantier, OF Derek Bell, P Pedro Martinez, P Doug Brocail, IF Craig Shipley and SS Ricky Gutierrez (December 28, 1994); Padres acquired P Sean Fesh to complete deal (May 1, 1995). ... Granted free agency (December 21, 1995). ... Signed by Detroit Tigers (January 10, 1996). ... Released by Tigers following 1996 season. ... Signed by Baltimore Orioles organization (January 21, 1997). ... Released by Orioles (December 11, 1997). ... Signed by Astros organization (January 21, 1999). ... Granted free agency (October 29, 1999). ... Signed by Chicago Cubs (January 7, 2000).

MISCELLANEOUS: Appeared in four games as pinch runner with Houston (1992).

Year	League	W	L	Pct.	ERA	G	GS	CG	ShO	Sv.	IP	H	R	ER	BB	SO
1990—	Auburn (NY-P)	0	0	...	4.05	3	3	0	0	0	6²/₃	6	5	3	6	7
1991—	Osceola (FSL)	6	4	.600	2.91	15	15	0	0	0	89²/₃	72	41	29	40	67
—	Jackson (Texas)	2	1	.667	4.20	3	3	0	0	0	15	17	8	7	7	15
—	Tucson (PCL)	0	1	.000	4.93	7	7	0	0	0	38¹/₃	39	25	21	22	29
—	Houston (N.L.)	0	1	.000	3.75	2	2	0	0	0	12	11	5	5	4	4
1992—	Tucson (PCL)	6	1	.857	4.50	12	12	0	0	0	70	78	37	35	26	58
—	Houston (N.L.)	7	6	.538	3.92	16	16	0	0	0	96¹/₃	92	44	42	42	54
1993—	Houston (N.L.)	4	4	.500	4.83	42	5	0	0	3	82	76	48	44	38	56
—	Tucson (PCL)	1	0	1.000	0.00	2	0	0	0	0	3	1	0	0	0	3
1994—	Houston (N.L.)	6	5	.545	5.74	20	13	0	0	0	78¹/₃	112	64	50	41	49
—	Tucson (PCL)	2	0	1.000	2.21	3	3	0	0	0	20¹/₃	22	6	5	9	17
1995—	San Diego (N.L.)■	3	10	.231	6.00	44	6	0	0	0	72	79	54	48	38	75
1996—	Detroit (A.L.)■	3	10	.231	6.77	40	17	2	1	2	121	145	107	91	85	72
—	Toledo (I.L.)	1	2	.333	5.49	3	3	1	0	0	19²/₃	22	13	12	9	21
1997—	Rochester (I.L.)■	4	3	.571	3.89	22	9	0	0	8	69¹/₃	68	33	30	23	78
—	Baltimore (A.L.)	0	0	...	3.00	13	0	0	0	0	24	20	8	8	18	14
1999—	Houston (N.L.)■	2	1	.667	4.41	50	0	0	0	0	67¹/₃	69	35	33	35	53
A.L. totals (2 years)		3	10	.231	6.14	53	17	2	1	2	145	165	115	99	103	86
N.L. totals (6 years)		22	27	.449	4.90	174	42	0	0	3	408	439	250	222	198	291
Major League totals (8 years)		25	37	.403	5.22	227	59	2	1	5	553	604	365	321	301	377

WILLIAMS, GERALD   OF   DEVIL RAYS

PERSONAL: Born August 10, 1966, in New Orleans. ... 6-2/187. ... Bats right, throws right. ... Full name: Gerald Floyd Williams.
HIGH SCHOOL: East St. John (Reserve, La.).
COLLEGE: Grambling State.
TRANSACTIONS/CAREER NOTES: Selected by New York Yankees organization in 14th round of free-agent draft (June 2, 1987). ... Traded by Yankees with P Bob Wickman to Milwaukee Brewers for P Graeme Lloyd and OF Pat Listach (August 23, 1996). ... Traded by Brewers to Atlanta Braves for P Chad Fox (December 11, 1997). ... Granted free agency (November 3, 1999). ... Signed by Tampa Bay Devil Rays (December 19, 1999).
STATISTICAL NOTES: Led Carolina League outfielders with 307 total chances in 1989. ... Led International League outfielders with 354 total chances in 1992. ... Tied for International League lead in double plays by outfielder with five in 1992. ... Collected six hits in one game (May 1, 1996). ... Had 15-game hitting streak (July 23-August 13, 1999). ... Career major league grand slams: 3.

							BATTING								FIELDING		
Year	Team (League)	Pos.	G	AB	R	H	2B	3B	HR	RBI	Avg.	BB	SO	SB	PO	A	E	Avg.
1987—	Oneonta (NY-P)	OF	29	115	26	42	6	2	2	29	.365	16	18	6	68	3	3	.959
1988—	Prince Will. (Caro.)	OF	54	159	20	29	3	0	2	18	.182	15	47	6	71	2	3	.961
—	Fort Laud. (FSL)	OF	63	212	21	40	7	2	2	17	.189	16	56	4	163	2	6	.965
1989—	Prince Will. (Caro.)	OF	134	454	63	104	19	6	13	69	.229	51	120	15	*292	7	8	.974
1990—	Fort Laud. (FSL)	OF	50	204	25	59	4	5	7	43	.289	16	52	19	115	1	3	.975
—	Alb./Colonie (East.)	OF	96	324	54	81	17	2	13	58	.250	35	74	18	210	6	7	.969
1991—	Alb./Colonie (East.)	OF	45	175	28	50	15	0	5	32	.286	18	26	18	109	4	3	.974
—	Columbus (I.L.)	OF	61	198	20	51	8	3	2	27	.258	16	39	9	124	1	3	.977
1992—	Columbus (I.L.)	OF	*142	547	92	*156	31	6	16	86	.285	38	98	36	*332	*14	8	.977
—	New York (A.L.)	OF	15	27	7	8	2	0	3	6	.296	0	3	2	20	1	2	.913
1993—	Columbus (I.L.)	OF	87	336	53	95	19	6	8	38	.283	20	66	29	191	6	3	.985
—	New York (A.L.)	OF-DH	42	67	11	10	2	3	0	6	.149	1	14	2	41	2	2	.956
1994—	New York (A.L.)	OF-DH	57	86	19	25	8	0	4	13	.291	4	17	1	43	2	2	.957
1995—	New York (A.L.)	OF-DH	100	182	33	45	18	2	6	28	.247	22	34	4	138	6	1	.993
1996—	New York (A.L.)	OF-DH	99	233	37	63	15	4	5	30	.270	15	39	7	132	1	3	.978
—	Milwaukee (A.L.)■	OF	26	92	6	19	4	0	0	4	.207	4	18	3	75	3	1	.987
1997—	Milwaukee (A.L.)	OF-DH	155	566	73	143	32	2	10	41	.253	19	90	23	357	11	3	.992
1998—	Atlanta (N.L.)■	OF	129	266	46	81	19	2	10	44	.305	17	48	11	158	2	5	.970
1999—	Atlanta (N.L.)	OF	143	422	76	116	24	1	17	68	.275	33	67	19	188	9	3	.985
American League totals (6 years)			494	1253	186	313	81	11	28	128	.250	65	215	42	806	26	14	.983
National League totals (2 years)			272	688	122	197	43	3	27	112	.286	50	115	30	346	11	8	.978
Major League totals (8 years)			766	1941	308	510	124	14	55	240	.263	115	330	72	1152	37	22	.982

DIVISION SERIES RECORD

							BATTING								FIELDING		
Year	Team (League)	Pos.	G	AB	R	H	2B	3B	HR	RBI	Avg.	BB	SO	SB	PO	A	E	Avg.
1995—	New York (A.L.)	OF-PR	5	5	1	0	0	0	0	0	.000	2	3	0	7	1	0	1.000
1998—	Atlanta (N.L.)	OF	2	2	1	1	0	0	0	1	.500	0	1	0	2	0	0	1.000
1999—	Atlanta (N.L.)	OF	4	18	2	7	1	0	0	3	.389	0	3	1	4	0	0	1.000
Division series totals (3 years)			11	25	4	8	1	0	0	4	.320	2	7	1	13	1	0	1.000

CHAMPIONSHIP SERIES RECORD

RECORDS: Shares single-game record for most strikeouts—4 (October 10, 1998).

							BATTING								FIELDING		
Year	Team (League)	Pos.	G	AB	R	H	2B	3B	HR	RBI	Avg.	BB	SO	SB	PO	A	E	Avg.
1998—	Atlanta (N.L.)	PH-OF	5	13	0	2	0	0	0	0	.154	1	6	1	3	0	0	1.000
1999—	Atlanta (N.L.)	OF	6	28	4	5	2	0	0	1	.179	2	2	3	12	0	1	.923
Championship series totals (2 years)			11	41	4	7	2	0	0	1	.171	3	8	4	15	0	1	.938

W

WORLD SERIES RECORD

				BATTING												FIELDING		
Year	Team (League)	Pos.	G	AB	R	H	2B	3B	HR	RBI	Avg.	BB	SO	SB	PO	A	E	Avg.
1999—Atlanta (N.L.)		OF	4	17	2	3	0	1	0	0	.176	0	4	0	6	0	0	1.000

WILLIAMS, JEFF   P   DODGERS

PERSONAL: Born June 6, 1972, in Canberra, Australia. ... 6-0/185. ... Throws left, bats right. ... Full name: Jeffrey F. Williams.

COLLEGE: Hawker (Canberra, Australia), then Southeastern Louisiana.

TRANSACTIONS/CAREER NOTES: Signed as non-drafted free agent by Los Angeles Dodgers organization (July 3, 1996).

Year	League	W	L	Pct.	ERA	G	GS	CG	ShO	Sv.	IP	H	R	ER	BB	SO
1997—San Bernardino (Calif.)		10	4	.714	3.10	18	18	0	0	0	116	101	52	40	34	72
—San Antonio (Texas)		2	1	.667	5.81	5	5	0	0	0	26 1/3	30	17	17	7	14
1998—San Antonio (Texas)		3	0	1.000	2.59	7	7	0	0	0	41 2/3	43	19	12	13	35
—Albuquerque (PCL)		8	8	.500	4.98	21	21	0	0	0	121	160	87	67	49	93
1999—Albuquerque (PCL)		9	7	.563	5.01	42	14	1	1	4	125 2/3	151	77	70	47	86
—Los Angeles (N.L.)		2	0	1.000	4.08	5	3	0	0	0	17 2/3	12	10	8	9	7
Major League totals (1 year)		2	0	1.000	4.08	5	3	0	0	0	17 2/3	12	10	8	9	7

WILLIAMS, MATT   3B   DIAMONDBACKS

PERSONAL: Born November 28, 1965, in Bishop, Calif. ... 6-2/210. ... Bats right, throws right. ... Full name: Matthew Derrick Williams. ... Grandson of Bartholomew (Bart) Griffith, outfielder/first baseman with Brooklyn Dodgers and Washington Senators (1922-24).

HIGH SCHOOL: Carson (Nev.).

COLLEGE: UNLV.

TRANSACTIONS/CAREER NOTES: Selected by New York Mets organization in 27th round of free-agent draft (June 6, 1983); did not sign. ... Selected by San Francisco Giants organization in first round (third pick overall) of free-agent draft (June 2, 1986). ... On disabled list (June 28-July 14, 1993). ... On San Francisco disabled list (June 4-August 19, 1995); included rehabilitation assignments to San Jose (July 24-25 and August 13-19). ... On disabled list (August 5, 1996-remainder of season). ... Traded by Giants with a player to be named later to Cleveland Indians for IF Jeff Kent, IF Jose Vizcaino, P Julian Tavarez and a player to be named later (November 13, 1996); Giants traded OF Trenidad Hubbard to Indians for P Joe Roa to complete deal (December 16, 1996). ... Traded by Indians to Arizona Diamondbacks for 3B Travis Fryman, P Tom Martin and cash (December 1, 1997). ... On Arizona disabled list (July 18-August 3, 1998); included rehabilitation assignment to Tucson (July 31-August 3).

RECORDS: Shares major league record for most home runs in two consecutive games—5 (April 25 [3] and 26 [2], 1997).

HONORS: Named shortstop on THE SPORTING NEWS college All-America team (1986). ... Named third baseman on THE SPORTING NEWS N.L. All-Star team (1990 and 1993-94). ... Named third baseman on THE SPORTING NEWS N.L. Silver Slugger team (1990 and 1993-94). ... Won N.L. Gold Glove at third base (1991 and 1993-94). ... Named third baseman on THE SPORTING NEWS A.L. All-Star team (1997). ... Won A.L. Gold Glove at third base (1997). ... Named third baseman on THE SPORTING NEWS A.L. Silver Slugger team (1997).

STATISTICAL NOTES: Led N.L. third basemen with 33 double plays in 1990 and 1992 and 34 in 1993. ... Tied for N.L. lead in total chances by third baseman with 465 in 1990. ... Led N.L. third basemen with 131 putouts in 1991. ... Led N.L. third basemen with 326 total chances in 1994. ... Hit three home runs in one game (April 25, 1997). ... Had 24-game hitting streak (August 13-September 8, 1997). ... Had 19-game hitting streak (May 26-June 18, 1999). ... Career major league grand slams: 9.

MISCELLANEOUS: Holds Arizona Diamondbacks all-time records for most hits (326), doubles (63) and runs batted in (213).

				BATTING											FIELDING		
Year	Team (League)	Pos.	G	AB	R	H	2B	3B	HR	RBI	Avg.	BB	SO	SB	PO	A	E	Avg.
1986—Everett (N'west)		SS	4	17	3	4	0	1	1	10	.235	1	4	0	5	10	2	.882
—Clinton (Midw.)		SS	68	250	32	60	14	3	7	29	.240	23	62	3	89	150	10	.960
1987—Phoenix (PCL)		3B-2B-SS	56	211	36	61	15	2	6	37	.289	19	53	6	53	136	14	.931
—San Francisco (N.L.)		SS-3B	84	245	28	46	9	2	8	21	.188	16	68	4	110	234	9	.975
1988—Phoenix (PCL)		3B-SS-2B-OF	82	306	45	83	19	1	12	51	.271	13	56	6	56	173	13	.946
—San Francisco (N.L.)		3B-SS	52	156	17	32	6	1	8	19	.205	8	41	0	48	108	7	.957
1989—San Francisco (N.L.)		3B-SS	84	292	31	59	18	1	18	50	.202	14	72	1	90	168	10	.963
—Phoenix (PCL)		3B-SS-OF	76	284	61	91	20	2	26	61	.320	32	51	9	57	197	11	.958
1990—San Francisco (N.L.)		3B	159	617	87	171	27	2	33	*122	.277	33	138	7	*140	306	19	.959
1991—San Francisco (N.L.)		3B-SS	157	589	72	158	24	5	34	98	.268	33	128	5	†134	295	16	.964
1992—San Francisco (N.L.)		3B	146	529	58	120	13	5	20	66	.227	39	109	7	105	289	*23	.945
1993—San Francisco (N.L.)		3B	145	579	105	170	33	4	38	110	.294	27	80	1	117	266	12	.970
1994—San Francisco (N.L.)		3B	112	445	74	119	16	3	*43	96	.267	33	87	1	79	*235	12	.963
1995—San Francisco (N.L.)		3B	76	283	53	95	17	1	23	65	.336	30	58	2	49	178	10	.958
—San Jose (Calif.)		3B	4	11	2	2	0	0	1	2	.182	0	3	0	0	4	0	1.000
1996—San Francisco (N.L.)		3B-1B-SS	105	404	69	122	16	1	22	85	.302	39	91	1	164	191	14	.962
1997—Cleveland (A.L.)■		3B	151	596	86	157	32	3	32	105	.263	34	108	12	89	301	12	.970
1998—Arizona (N.L.)■		3B	135	510	72	136	26	1	20	71	.267	43	102	5	99	282	11	.972
—Tucson (PCL)		3B	2	5	0	1	0	0	0	0	.200	0	0	0	0	1	0	1.000
1999—Arizona (N.L.)		3B	154	627	98	190	37	2	35	142	.303	41	93	2	123	299	10	.977
American League totals (1 year)			151	596	86	157	32	3	32	105	.263	34	108	12	89	301	12	.970
National League totals (12 years)			1409	5276	764	1418	242	28	302	945	.269	356	1067	36	1258	2851	153	.964
Major League totals (13 years)			1560	5872	850	1575	274	31	334	1050	.268	390	1175	48	1347	3152	165	.965

DIVISION SERIES RECORD

				BATTING											FIELDING		
Year	Team (League)	Pos.	G	AB	R	H	2B	3B	HR	RBI	Avg.	BB	SO	SB	PO	A	E	Avg.
1997—Cleveland (A.L.)		3B	5	17	4	4	1	0	1	3	.235	3	3	0	2	10	0	1.000
1999—Arizona (N.L.)		3B	4	16	3	6	1	0	0	0	.375	0	1	0	3	9	0	1.000
Division series totals (2 years)			9	33	7	10	2	0	1	3	.303	3	4	0	5	19	0	1.000

CHAMPIONSHIP SERIES RECORD

RECORDS: Holds N.L. single-series record for most runs batted in—9 (1989).

W

Year Team (League)	Pos.	G	AB	R	H	2B	3B	HR	RBI	Avg.	BB	SO	SB	PO	A	E	Avg.
								BATTING							FIELDING		
1987— San Francisco (N.L.) ..							Did not play.										
1989— San Francisco (N.L.) ..	3B-SS	5	20	2	6	1	0	2	9	.300	0	2	0	5	12	0	1.000
1997—Cleveland (A.L.).........	3B	6	23	1	5	1	0	0	2	.217	3	7	1	6	18	2	.923
Championship series totals (2 years)		**11**	**43**	**3**	**11**	**2**	**0**	**2**	**11**	**.256**	**3**	**9**	**1**	**11**	**30**	**2**	**.953**

WORLD SERIES RECORD

Year Team (League)	Pos.	G	AB	R	H	2B	3B	HR	RBI	Avg.	BB	SO	SB	PO	A	E	Avg.
								BATTING							FIELDING		
1989— San Francisco (N.L.) ..	SS-3B	4	16	1	2	0	0	1	1	.125	0	6	0	4	12	0	1.000
1997—Cleveland (A.L.).........	3B	7	26	8	10	1	0	1	3	.385	7	6	0	5	9	0	1.000
World Series totals (2 years)		**11**	**42**	**9**	**12**	**1**	**0**	**2**	**4**	**.286**	**7**	**12**	**0**	**9**	**21**	**0**	**1.000**

ALL-STAR GAME RECORD

NOTES: Named to N.L. All-Star team for 1996 game; replaced by Ken Caminiti due to injury.

Year League	Pos.	AB	R	H	2B	3B	HR	RBI	Avg.	BB	SO	SB	PO	A	E	Avg.
							BATTING							FIELDING		
1990— National.....................	PH	1	0	0	0	0	0	0	.000	0	1	0	...	...	...	...
1994— National.....................	3B	3	0	0	0	0	0	0	.000	0	2	0	0	1	1	.500
1995— National.....................						Selected, did not play—injured.										
1996— National.....................						Selected, did not play—injured.										
1999— National.....................	3B	3	0	1	0	0	0	0	.333	0	1	0	1	0	1	.500
All-Star Game totals (3 years)		**7**	**0**	**1**	**0**	**0**	**0**	**0**	**.143**	**0**	**4**	**0**	**1**	**1**	**2**	**.500**

WILLIAMS, MATT   P   BREWERS

PERSONAL: Born April 12, 1971, in Virginia Beach, Va. ... 6-0/175. ... Throws left, bats both. ... Full name: Matthew Taylor Williams.
HIGH SCHOOL: Floyd Kellam (Virginia Beach, Va.).
COLLEGE: Virginia Commonwealth.
TRANSACTIONS/CAREER NOTES: Selected by Cleveland Indians organization in fourth round of free-agent draft (June 1, 1992). ... Loaned to High Desert (July 21-August 15, 1994). ... Loaned to Bakersfield (April 5-May 13, 1995). ... Traded by Indians to Houston Astros for C Scooter Tucker (May 15, 1995). ... Released by Astros (March 28, 1996). ... Signed by Pittsburgh Pirates organization (April 20, 1996). ... Granted free agency (October 15, 1996). ... Signed by Tampa Bay Devil Rays organization (December 18, 1996). ... Selected by New York Yankees from Devil Rays organization in Rule 5 major league draft (December 15, 1997). ... Selected by Milwaukee Brewers from Yankees organization in Rule 5 major league draft (December 13, 1999).

Year League	W	L	Pct.	ERA	G	GS	CG	ShO	Sv.	IP	H	R	ER	BB	SO
1992—Watertown (NY-P)	1	0	1.000	1.65	6	6	0	0	0	32 2/3	22	15	6	9	29
1993—Kinston (Caro.)	12	•12	.500	3.17	27	27	2	1	0	153 1/3	125	65	54	*100	134
1994—Kinston (Caro.)	4	6	.400	6.09	15	15	1	0	0	81 1/3	86	63	55	33	67
—Canton/Akron (East.)	0	3	.000	7.61	5	4	0	0	1	23 2/3	30	22	20	14	9
—High Desert (Calif.)■.........	1	4	.200	13.00	5	5	0	0	0	18	33	29	26	13	10
1995—Bakersfield (Calif.)■...........	2	0	1.000	2.36	7	7	0	0	0	34 1/3	34	9	9	14	30
—Kissimmee (FSL)■..............	4	6	.400	4.63	19	18	2	0	0	101	115	60	52	44	71
1996—Lynchburg (Caro.)■............	0	0	...	5.23	23	0	0	0	0	41 1/3	40	27	24	28	45
1997—St. Petersburg (FSL)■........	9	5	.643	2.97	43	0	0	0	1	63 2/3	57	26	21	24	50
1998—Norwich (East.)	8	11	.421	4.60	31	28	2	0	0	160 1/3	186	93	82	66	112
1999—Norwich (East.)	1	1	.500	2.40	22	0	0	0	0	30	22	9	8	18	44
—Columbus (I.L.)	0	2	.000	3.86	13	1	0	0	0	21	15	9	9	11	22

WILLIAMS, MIKE   P   PIRATES

PERSONAL: Born July 29, 1968, in Radford, Va. ... 6-2/204. ... Throws right, bats right. ... Full name: Michael Darren Williams.
HIGH SCHOOL: Giles (Pearisburg, Va.).
COLLEGE: Virginia Tech.
TRANSACTIONS/CAREER NOTES: Selected by Philadelphia Phillies organization in 14th round of free-agent draft (June 4, 1990). ... On suspended list (September 26, 1996-remainder of season). ... Granted free agency (December 20, 1996). ... Signed by Boston Red Sox organization (February 15, 1997). ... Released by Red Sox (March 14, 1997). ... Signed by Kansas City Royals organization (April 30, 1997). ... On suspended list (May 16-18, 1997). ... Granted free agency (October 15, 1997). ... Signed by Pittsburgh Pirates organization (December 18, 1997). ... On disabled list (June 24-July 9, 1999).
STATISTICAL NOTES: Led N.L. with 16 wild pitches in 1996.
MISCELLANEOUS: Appeared in one game as pinch runner (1996).

Year League	W	L	Pct.	ERA	G	GS	CG	ShO	Sv.	IP	H	R	ER	BB	SO
1990—Batavia (NY-P)	2	3	.400	2.30	27	0	0	0	11	47	39	17	12	13	42
1991—Clearwater (FSL)	7	3	.700	1.74	14	14	2	1	0	93 1/3	65	23	18	14	76
—Reading (East.)	7	5	.583	3.69	16	15	2	1	0	102 1/3	93	44	42	36	51
1992—Reading (East.)	1	2	.333	5.17	3	3	0	0	0	15 2/3	17	10	9	7	12
—Scranton/W.B. (I.L.)	9	1	*.900	2.43	16	16	3	1	0	92 2/3	84	26	25	30	59
—Philadelphia (N.L.)	1	1	.500	5.34	5	5	1	0	0	28 2/3	29	20	17	7	5
1993—Scranton/W.B. (I.L.)	9	2	*.818	2.87	14	13	1	1	0	97 1/3	93	34	31	16	53
—Philadelphia (N.L.)	1	3	.250	5.29	17	4	0	0	0	51	50	32	30	22	33
1994—Philadelphia (N.L.)	2	4	.333	5.01	12	8	0	0	0	50 1/3	61	31	28	20	29
—Scranton/W.B. (I.L.)	2	7	.222	5.79	14	14	1	0	0	84	91	55	54	36	53
1995—Philadelphia (N.L.)	3	3	.500	3.29	33	8	0	0	0	87 2/3	78	37	32	29	57
—Scranton/W.B. (I.L.)	0	1	.000	4.66	3	3	1	0	0	9 2/3	8	5	5	2	8
1996—Philadelphia (N.L.)	6	14	.300	5.44	32	29	0	0	0	167	188	107	101	67	103
1997—Omaha (A.A.)■	3	6	.333	4.22	20	11	1	0	5	79	71	41	37	38	68
—Kansas City (A.L.)	0	2	.000	6.43	10	0	0	0	1	14	20	11	10	8	10
1998—Pittsburgh (N.L.)■	4	2	.667	1.94	37	0	0	0	0	51	39	12	11	16	59
—Nashville (PCL)	0	2	.000	5.59	16	4	0	0	1	37	36	25	23	14	34
1999—Pittsburgh (N.L.)	3	4	.429	5.09	58	0	0	0	23	58 1/3	63	36	33	37	76
A.L. totals (1 year)	**0**	**2**	**.000**	**6.43**	**10**	**0**	**0**	**0**	**1**	**14**	**20**	**11**	**10**	**8**	**10**
N.L. totals (7 years)	**20**	**31**	**.392**	**4.59**	**194**	**55**	**1**	**0**	**23**	**494**	**508**	**275**	**252**	**198**	**362**
Major League totals (8 years)	**20**	**33**	**.377**	**4.64**	**204**	**55**	**1**	**0**	**24**	**508**	**528**	**286**	**262**	**206**	**372**

W

PERSONAL: Born May 5, 1966, in Laurens, S.C. ... 6-1/180. ... Bats both, throws right. ... Full name: Reginald Bernard Williams.
HIGH SCHOOL: Laurens (S.C.) District 55.
COLLEGE: South Carolina-Aiken.
TRANSACTIONS/CAREER NOTES: Selected by San Francisco Giants organization in 25th round of free-agent draft (June 1, 1988). ... Released by Giants organization (June 20, 1989). ... Signed by Boise, Northwest League (July 20, 1989). ... Signed by California Angels organization (February 15, 1990). ... On Quad City disabled list (April 12-May 22, 1991). ... Traded by Angels to Los Angeles Dodgers for P Mike James (October 26, 1993). ... Released by Dodgers (October 13, 1994). ... Re-signed by Dodgers (April 11, 1995). ... Granted free agency (October 16, 1995). ... Re-signed by Dodgers (January 1, 1996). ... On disabled list (July 27-September 20, 1996). ... Granted free agency (October 15, 1996). ... Signed to play for Monterrey, Mexican League (1997). ... Contract purchased by Anaheim Angels organization from Monterrey (August 19, 1997). ... On Anaheim disabled list (March 29-April 22, 1999). ... On Edmonton disabled list (August 23-31, 1999). ... Released by Angels (August 31, 1999).
STATISTICAL NOTES: Led Northwest League with 10 caught stealing in 1988. ... Led Pacific Coast League outfielders with 324 total chances in 1992 and 303 in 1993. ... Tied for Pacific Coast League lead in double plays by outfielder with four in 1993.

Year	Team (League)	Pos.	G	AB	R	H	2B	3B	HR	RBI	Avg.	BB	SO	SB	PO	A	E	Avg.
1988—Everett (N'west).........		OF	60	223	52	56	8	1	3	29	.251	47	43	36	131	1	4	.971
1989—Clinton (Midw.).......		OF	68	236	38	46	9	2	3	18	.195	29	66	14	146	7	3	.981
—Boise (N'west)■........		OF	42	153	33	41	5	1	3	14	.268	24	29	18	64	3	2	.971
1990—Quad City (Midw.)■...		OF	58	189	50	46	11	2	3	12	.243	39	60	24	110	6	1	.991
1991—Midland (Texas).........		OF	83	319	77	99	12	3	1	30	.310	62	67	21	187	9	7	.966
—Palm Springs (Calif.)...		OF	14	44	10	13	1	0	1	2	.295	21	15	6	33	1	1	.971
1992—Edmonton (PCL)........		OF	139	519	96	141	26	9	3	64	.272	88	110	44	*313	8	3	.991
—California (A.L.).......		OF-DH	14	26	5	6	1	1	0	2	.231	1	10	0	26	0	0	1.000
1993—Vancouver (PCL)........		OF	130	481	92	132	17	6	2	53	.274	*88	99	*50	*293	6	4	.987
1994—Albuquerque (PCL)■..		OF-DH	104	288	55	90	15	8	4	42	.313	33	62	21	137	6	4	.973
1995—Los Angeles (N.L.).....		OF	15	11	2	1	0	0	0	1	.091	2	3	0	6	0	0	1.000
—Albuquerque (PCL).....		OF-DH	66	234	44	73	15	5	6	29	.312	30	46	6	141	10	0	1.000
1996—Albuquerque (PCL)....		OF	92	352	60	101	25	2	6	42	.287	37	72	17	197	10	4	.981
1997—Monterrey (Mex.)■...		OF	59	218	23	56	13	2	1	20	.257	29	37	10	...	...	...	...
—Vancouver (PCL)■....		OF-2B-DH	12	40	10	10	3	0	2	5	.250	6	13	3	27	5	0	1.000
1998—Vancouver (PCL)		OF-DH-2B	100	373	58	105	25	5	5	39	.282	53	98	13	221	13	2	.992
—Anaheim (A.L.)..........		OF-DH	29	36	7	13	1	0	1	5	.361	7	11	3	25	0	0	1.000
1999—Anaheim (A.L.)..........		OF-DH	30	63	8	14	1	2	1	6	.222	5	21	2	34	3	1	.974
—Edmonton (PCL)		O-DH-1-2-3	35	137	25	43	9	1	6	31	.314	16	29	3	55	5	2	.968
American League totals (3 years)			73	125	20	33	3	3	2	13	.264	13	42	5	85	3	1	.989
National League totals (1 year)			15	11	2	1	0	0	0	1	.091	2	3	0	6	0	0	1.000
Major League totals (4 years)			88	136	22	34	3	3	2	14	.250	15	45	5	91	3	1	.989

PERSONAL: Born February 13, 1971, in Syracuse, N.Y. ... 6-3/210. ... Throws right, bats right. ... Full name: Todd Michael Williams.
HIGH SCHOOL: Minoa (East Syracuse N.Y.).
JUNIOR COLLEGE: Onondaga Community College (N.Y.).
TRANSACTIONS/CAREER NOTES: Selected by Los Angeles Dodgers organization in 54th round of free-agent draft (June 4, 1990). ... On disabled list (April 7-16, 1994). ... Traded by Dodgers to Oakland Athletics for P Matt McDonald (September 8, 1995). ... Released by A's (January 16, 1997). ... Signed by Cincinnati Reds organization (February 3, 1997). ... Traded by Reds to Seattle Mariners for OF Kerry Robinson (July 22, 1999).

Year League	W	L	Pct.	ERA	G	GS	CG	ShO	Sv.	IP	H	R	ER	BB	SO
1991—Great Falls (Pio.)	5	2	.714	2.72	28	0	0	0	8	53	50	26	16	24	59
1992—Bakersfield (Calif.)..............	0	0	...	2.30	13	0	0	0	9	$15\frac{2}{3}$	11	4	4	7	11
—San Antonio (Texas)..........	7	4	.636	3.27	39	0	0	0	13	44	47	17	16	23	35
1993—Albuquerque (PCL)..........	5	5	.500	4.99	*65	0	0	0	*21	$70\frac{1}{3}$	87	44	39	31	56
1994—Albuquerque (PCL)..........	4	2	.667	3.11	59	0	0	0	13	$72\frac{1}{3}$	78	29	25	17	30
1995—Los Angeles (N.L.)	2	2	.500	5.12	16	0	0	0	0	$19\frac{1}{3}$	19	11	11	7	8
—Albuquerque (PCL).............	4	1	.800	3.38	25	0	0	0	0	$45\frac{1}{3}$	59	21	17	15	23
1996—Edmonton (PCL)■............	5	3	.625	5.50	35	10	0	0	0	$91\frac{2}{3}$	125	71	56	37	33
1997—Chattanooga (Sou.)■.........	3	3	.500	2.10	48	0	0	0	*31	$55\frac{2}{3}$	38	16	13	25	45
—Indianapolis (A.A.)............	2	0	1.000	2.13	12	0	0	0	2	$12\frac{2}{3}$	11	4	3	6	11
1998—Indianapolis (I.L.)............	0	3	.000	2.31	53	0	0	0	*26	$58\frac{1}{3}$	54	19	15	24	35
—Cincinnati (N.L.)...............	0	1	.000	7.71	6	0	0	0	0	$9\frac{1}{3}$	15	8	8	6	4
1999—Indianapolis (I.L.).............	1	3	.250	5.10	38	0	0	0	24	$42\frac{1}{3}$	38	24	24	13	35
—Tacoma (PCL)■..............	0	0	...	0.00	1	0	0	0	1	$1\frac{2}{3}$	1	0	0	0	0
—Seattle (A.L.).....................	0	0	...	4.66	13	0	0	0	0	$9\frac{2}{3}$	11	5	5	7	7
A.L. totals (1 year)	0	0	...	4.66	13	0	0	0	0	$9\frac{2}{3}$	11	5	5	7	7
N.L. totals (2 years)	2	3	.400	5.97	22	0	0	0	0	$28\frac{2}{3}$	34	19	19	13	12
Major League totals (3 years)	2	3	.400	5.63	35	0	0	0	0	$38\frac{1}{3}$	45	24	24	20	19

W

PERSONAL: Born August 19, 1966, in Houston. ... 6-0/195. ... Throws right, bats right. ... Full name: Gregory Scott Williams.
HIGH SCHOOL: Cypress-Fairbanks (Houston).
COLLEGE: Houston.
TRANSACTIONS/CAREER NOTES: Selected by Toronto Blue Jays organization in 28th round of free-agent draft (June 1, 1988). ... On disabled list (April 9-May 17, 1992). ... On Toronto disabled list (July 17, 1995-remainder of season); included rehabilitation assignment to Syracuse (August 15-25). ... On Toronto disabled list (March 22-May 31 and June 11-July 26, 1996); included rehabilitation assignments to Dunedin

(May 2-10), Syracuse (May 10-28 and July 13-20) and St. Catharines (July 20-26). ... Traded by Blue Jays with P Carlos Almanzar and OF Peter Tucci to San Diego Padres for P Joey Hamilton (December 13, 1998).
MISCELLANEOUS: Appeared in one game as pinch runner (1999).

Year League	W	L	Pct.	ERA	G	GS	CG	ShO	Sv.	IP	H	R	ER	BB	SO
1988— St. Catharines (NY-P)	8	2	.800	1.54	12	12	2	0	0	76	48	22	13	21	58
— Knoxville (Sou.)	2	2	.500	3.81	6	4	0	0	0	28 1/3	27	13	12	12	25
1989— Dunedin (FSL)	3	5	.375	2.32	20	9	0	0	3	81 1/3	63	26	21	27	60
— Knoxville (Sou.)	3	5	.375	3.55	14	12	2	•2	1	71	61	32	28	33	51
1990— Knoxville (Sou.)	7	9	.438	3.14	42	12	0	0	5	126	111	55	44	39	74
— Syracuse (I.L.)	0	1	.000	10.00	3	0	0	0	0	9	15	10	10	4	8
1991— Knoxville (Sou.)	3	2	.600	3.59	18	1	0	0	3	42 2/3	42	18	17	14	37
— Syracuse (I.L.)	3	4	.429	4.12	31	0	0	0	6	54 2/3	52	27	25	27	37
1992— Syracuse (I.L.)	6	8	.429	3.13	25	16	1	0	1	120 2/3	115	46	42	41	81
1993— Syracuse (I.L.)	1	1	.500	2.20	12	0	0	0	3	16 1/3	15	5	4	5	16
— Toronto (A.L.)	3	1	.750	4.38	30	0	0	0	0	37	40	18	18	22	24
— Dunedin (FSL)	0	0	...	0.00	2	0	0	0	0	4	0	0	0	2	2
1994— Toronto (A.L.)	1	3	.250	3.64	38	0	0	0	0	59 1/3	44	24	24	33	56
— Syracuse (I.L.)	0	0	...	0.00	1	0	0	0	1	1 2/3	0	0	0	0	1
1995— Toronto (A.L.)	1	2	.333	3.69	23	3	0	0	0	53 2/3	44	23	22	28	41
— Syracuse (I.L.)	0	0	...	3.52	5	1	0	0	1	7 2/3	5	3	3	5	13
1996— Dunedin (FSL)	0	2	.000	8.22	2	2	0	0	0	7 2/3	9	7	7	2	11
— Syracuse (I.L.)	3	1	.750	1.41	7	7	1	1	0	32	22	5	5	7	33
— Toronto (A.L.)	4	5	.444	4.73	12	10	1	0	0	59	64	33	31	21	43
— St. Catharines (NY-P)	0	0	...	3.68	2	2	0	0	0	7 1/3	7	3	3	4	12
1997— Toronto (A.L.)	9	14	.391	4.35	31	31	0	0	0	194 1/3	201	98	94	66	124
1998— Toronto (A.L.)	10	9	.526	4.46	32	32	1	1	0	209 2/3	196	112	104	81	151
1999— San Diego (N.L.) ■	12	12	.500	4.41	33	33	0	0	0	208 1/3	213	106	102	73	137
A.L. totals (6 years)	28	34	.452	4.30	166	76	2	1	0	613 1/3	589	308	293	251	439
N.L. totals (1 year)	12	12	.500	4.41	33	33	0	0	0	208 1/3	213	106	102	73	137
Major League totals (7 years)	40	46	.465	4.33	199	109	2	1	0	821 2/3	802	414	395	324	576

WILLIAMSON, SCOTT — P — REDS

PERSONAL: Born February 17, 1976, in Fort Polk, La. ... 6-0/185. ... Throws right, bats right. ... Full name: Scott Ryan Williamson.
HIGH SCHOOL: Friendswood (Texas).
COLLEGE: Tulane, then Oklahoma State.
TRANSACTIONS/CAREER NOTES: Selected by Cincinnati Reds organization in ninth round of free-agent draft (June 3, 1997).
RECORDS: Shares N.L. single-game record for most consecutive strikeouts by relief pitcher—6 (May 27, 1999).
HONORS: Named N.L. Rookie Pitcher of the Year by The Sporting News (1999). ... Named N.L. Rookie of the Year by Baseball Writers' Association of America (1999).
STATISTICAL NOTES: Tied for Pioneer League lead in shutouts with one and in wild pitches with 12 in 1997.

Year League	W	L	Pct.	ERA	G	GS	CG	ShO	Sv.	IP	H	R	ER	BB	SO
1997— Billings (Pio.)	•8	2	.800	1.78	13	13	2	•1	0	86	66	25	17	23	*101
1998— Chattanooga (Sou.)	4	5	.444	3.78	18	18	0	0	0	100	85	49	42	46	105
— Indianapolis (I.L.)	0	0	...	3.48	5	5	0	0	0	20 2/3	20	9	8	9	17
1999— Cincinnati (N.L.)	12	7	.632	2.41	62	0	0	0	19	93 1/3	54	29	25	43	107
Major League totals (1 year)	12	7	.632	2.41	62	0	0	0	19	93 1/3	54	29	25	43	107

ALL-STAR GAME RECORD

Year League	W	L	Pct.	ERA	GS	CG	ShO	Sv.	IP	H	R	ER	BB	SO
1999— National							Selected—did not play.							

WILSON, CRAIG — IF — WHITE SOX

PERSONAL: Born September 3, 1970, in Chicago. ... 6-0/185. ... Bats right, throws right. ... Full name: Craig Franklin Wilson.
HIGH SCHOOL: Leyden (Franklin Park, Ill.).
COLLEGE: Kansas State.
TRANSACTIONS/CAREER NOTES: Selected by San Francisco Giants in 13th round of free-agent draft (June 3, 1991); did not sign. ... Selected by Chicago White Sox in 13th round of free-agent draft (June 1, 1992).

Year Team (League)	Pos.	G	AB	R	H	2B	3B	HR	RBI	Avg.	BB	SO	SB	PO	A	E	Avg.
1993— South Bend (Midw.) ...	SS	132	455	56	118	27	2	5	59	.259	49	50	4	166	388	21	.963
1994— Prince William (Caro.)	SS	131	496	70	131	36	4	4	66	.264	58	44	1	187	388	11	.981
1995— Birmingham (Sou.).....	SS	132	471	56	136	19	1	4	46	.289	43	44	2	193	389	34	.945
1996— Nashville (A.A.)	SS	44	123	13	22	4	1	1	6	.179	10	5	0	43	97	10	.933
— Birmingham (Sou.).....	SS	58	202	36	57	9	0	3	26	.282	40	28	1	67	148	19	.919
1997— Nashville (A.A.)	SS	137	453	71	123	20	2	6	42	.272	48	31	4	189	398	20	.967
1998— Calgary (PCL)	2-S-3-1-0	120	432	67	132	21	1	14	69	.306	37	41	4	279	248	9	.983
— Chicago (A.L.)	SS-2B-3B	13	47	14	22	5	0	3	10	.468	3	6	1	20	27	0	1.000
1999— Chicago (A.L.) 3-S-2-DH-1		98	252	28	60	8	1	4	26	.238	23	22	1	86	155	7	.972
Major League totals (2 years)		111	299	42	82	13	1	7	36	.274	26	28	2	106	182	7	.976

WILSON, DAN — C — MARINERS

PERSONAL: Born March 25, 1969, in Arlington Heights, Ill. ... 6-3/202. ... Bats right, throws right. ... Full name: Daniel Allen Wilson.
HIGH SCHOOL: Barrington (Ill.).
COLLEGE: Minnesota.

W

TRANSACTIONS/CAREER NOTES: Selected by New York Mets organization in 26th round of free-agent draft (June 2, 1987); did not sign. ... Selected by Cincinnati Reds organization in first round (seventh pick overall) of free-agent draft (June 4, 1990). ... Traded by Reds with P Bobby Ayala to Seattle Mariners for P Erik Hanson and 2B Bret Boone (November 2, 1993). ... On disabled list (July 21-September 1, 1998).

RECORDS: Shares major league single-game record for most putouts by catcher (nine-inning game)—20 (August 8, 1997); most putouts by catcher (extra-inning game)—21 (March 31, 1996, 12 innings); and most chances accepted by catcher (nine-inning game) since 1900—20 (August 8, 1997). ... Shares A.L. single-game record for most putouts by catcher (extra-inning game)—21 (March 31, 1996, 12 innings).

STATISTICAL NOTES: Led American Association catchers with 810 total chances in 1992. ... Led A.L. catchers with 952 total chances in 1995 and 1,129 in 1996. ... Hit three home runs in one game (April 11, 1996). ... Tied for A.L. lead in double plays by catcher with 13 in 1997. ... Career major league grand slams: 2.

Year Team (League)	Pos.	G	AB	R	H	2B	3B	HR	RBI	Avg.	BB	SO	SB	PO	A	E	Avg.
1990— Char., W.Va. (SAL)......	C	32	113	16	28	9	1	2	17	.248	13	17	0	190	24	1	.995
1991— Char., W.Va. (SAL)......	C	52	197	25	62	11	1	3	29	.315	25	21	1	355	41	3	.992
— Chattanooga (Sou.)	C	81	292	32	75	19	2	2	38	.257	21	39	2	486	49	4	.993
1992— Nashville (A.A.)......	C	106	366	27	92	16	1	4	34	.251	31	58	1	*733	*69	*8	.990
— Cincinnati (N.L.).........	C	12	25	2	9	1	0	0	3	.360	3	8	0	42	4	0	1.000
1993— Cincinnati (N.L.).........	C	36	76	6	17	3	0	0	8	.224	9	16	0	146	9	1	.994
— Indianapolis (A.A.)........	C	51	191	18	50	11	1	1	17	.262	19	31	1	314	24	2	.994
1994— Seattle (A.L.)■..........	C	91	282	24	61	14	2	3	27	.216	10	57	1	602	45	*9	.986
1995— Seattle (A.L.).............	C	119	399	40	111	22	3	9	51	.278	33	63	2	*895	52	5	.995
1996— Seattle (A.L.).............	C	138	491	51	140	24	0	18	83	.285	32	88	1	834	58	4	.996
1997— Seattle (A.L.).............	C	146	508	66	137	31	1	15	74	.270	39	72	7	*1051	72	6	.995
1998— Seattle (A.L.).............	C	96	325	39	82	17	1	9	44	.252	24	56	2	677	35	4	.994
1999— Seattle (A.L.).............	C-1B	123	414	46	110	23	2	7	38	.266	29	83	5	753	48	4	.995
American League totals (6 years)		713	2419	266	641	131	9	61	317	.265	167	419	18	4812	310	32	.994
National League totals (2 years)		48	101	8	26	4	0	0	11	.257	12	24	0	188	13	1	.995
Major League totals (8 years)		761	2520	274	667	135	9	61	328	.265	179	443	18	5000	323	33	.994

DIVISION SERIES RECORD

Year Team (League)	Pos.	G	AB	R	H	2B	3B	HR	RBI	Avg.	BB	SO	SB	PO	A	E	Avg.
1995— Seattle (A.L.)	C	5	17	0	2	0	0	1	.118	2	6	0	34	1	0	1.000
1997— Seattle (A.L.)	C	4	13	0	0	0	0	0	0	.000	0	9	0	29	1	0	1.000
Division series totals (2 years)		9	30	0	2	0	0	0	1	.067	2	15	0	63	2	0	1.000

CHAMPIONSHIP SERIES RECORD

Year Team (League)	Pos.	G	AB	R	H	2B	3B	HR	RBI	Avg.	BB	SO	SB	PO	A	E	Avg.
1995— Seattle (A.L.)	C	6	16	0	0	0	0	0	0	.000	0	4	0	35	3	1	.974

ALL-STAR GAME RECORD

Year League	Pos.	AB	R	H	2B	3B	HR	RBI	Avg.	BB	SO	SB	PO	A	E	Avg.
1996— American	PH	1	0	0	0	0	0	0	.000	0	0	0	...	...	...	...

WILSON, ENRIQUE   IF   INDIANS

PERSONAL: Born July 27, 1975, in Santo Domingo, Dominican Republic. ... 5-11/160. ... Bats both, throws right. ... Full name: Enrique Martes Wilson.

HIGH SCHOOL: Liceo Ramon Amelio Jiminez (Santo Domingo, Dominican Republic).

TRANSACTIONS/CAREER NOTES: Signed as non-drafted free agent by Minnesota Twins organization (April 15, 1992). ... Traded by Twins to Cleveland Indians (February 21, 1994), completing deal in which Twins acquired P Shawn Bryant for a player to be named later (February 21, 1994). ... On Cleveland disabled list (April 4-June 15, 1998); included rehabilitation assignment to Buffalo (June 2-15).

STATISTICAL NOTES: Led South Atlantic League shortstops with 625 total chances and 66 double plays in 1994. ... Led Carolina League with 10 sacrifice flies in 1995. ... Led Eastern League shortstops with 74 double plays in 1996. ... Career major league grand slams: 1.

Year Team (League)	Pos.	G	AB	R	H	2B	3B	HR	RBI	Avg.	BB	SO	SB	PO	A	E	Avg.
1992— GC Twins (GCL).........	SS	13	44	12	15	1	0	0	8	.341	4	4	3	9	26	4	.897
1993— Elizabethton (Appl.).....	SS-3B	58	197	42	57	8	4	13	50	.289	14	18	5	50	139	19	.909
1994— Columbus (SAL)■.....	SS	133	512	82	143	28	12	10	72	.279	44	34	21	*185	*407	33	.947
1995— Kinston (Caro.)...........	SS-2B	117	464	55	124	24	•7	6	52	.267	25	38	18	181	375	21	.964
1996— Canton/Akron (East.)..	SS-2B	117	484	70	147	17	5	5	50	.304	31	46	23	179	344	28	.949
— Buffalo (A.A.)...............	3B-SS	8	1	4	1	0	0	0	.500	1	1	0	1	2	1	.750
1997— Buffalo (A.A.).............	SS-2B-3B	118	451	78	138	20	3	11	39	.306	42	41	9	218	332	20	.965
— Cleveland (A.L.).........	SS-2B	5	15	2	5	0	0	1	.333	0	2	0	7	13	1	.952
1998— Cleveland (A.L.).........	2B-SS-3B	32	90	13	29	6	0	2	12	.322	4	8	2	43	76	2	.983
— Buffalo (I.L.)...............	2B-SS	56	221	40	62	13	0	4	23	.281	19	21	8	108	141	6	.976
1999— Cleveland (A.L.).........	3-S-2-DH	113	332	41	87	22	1	2	24	.262	25	41	5	77	163	8	.968
Major League totals (3 years)		150	437	56	121	28	1	4	37	.277	29	51	7	127	252	11	.972

DIVISION SERIES RECORD

Year Team (League)	Pos.	G	AB	R	H	2B	3B	HR	RBI	Avg.	BB	SO	SB	PO	A	E	Avg.
1998— Cleveland (A.L.)..........	2B	1	2	0	0	0	0	0	0	.000	0	0	0	2	2	0	1.000
1999— Cleveland (A.L.)..........	2B-PH	3	2	0	0	0	0	0	0	.000	0	0	0	3	0	0	1.000
Division series totals (2 years)		4	4	0	0	0	0	0	0	.000	0	0	0	5	2	0	1.000

CHAMPIONSHIP SERIES RECORD

Year Team (League)	Pos.	G	AB	R	H	2B	3B	HR	RBI	Avg.	BB	SO	SB	PO	A	E	Avg.
1998— Cleveland (A.L.)..........	PR-2B	5	14	2	3	0	0	0	1	.214	1	3	0	5	19	1	.960

W

PERSONAL: Born March 28, 1973, in Orlando. ... 6-5/235. ... Throws right, bats right. ... Full name: Paul Anthony Wilson.
HIGH SCHOOL: William R. Boone (Orlando).
COLLEGE: Florida State.
TRANSACTIONS/CAREER NOTES: Selected by New York Mets organization in first round (first pick overall) of free-agent draft (June 2, 1994). ... On New York disabled list (June 5-July 15, 1996); included rehabilitation assignments to St. Lucie (June 28-July 10) and Binghamton (July 10-15). ... On New York disabled list (March 27, 1997-entire season); included rehabilitation assignments to Gulf Coast Mets (August 2-23) and St. Lucie (August 28-September 8). ... On New York disabled list (March 13-August 4, 1998); included rehabilitation assignment to St. Lucie (July 9-August 1). ... On Norfolk disabled list (April 8, 1999-entire season).
STATISTICAL NOTES: Named Eastern League Pitcher of the Year (1995).

Year	League	W	L	Pct.	ERA	G	GS	CG	ShO	Sv.	IP	H	R	ER	BB	SO
1994—	Gulf Coast Mets (GCL)	0	2	.000	3.00	3	3	0	0	0	12	8	4	4	4	13
	—St. Lucie (FSL)	0	5	.000	5.06	8	8	0	0	0	37 1/3	32	23	21	17	37
1995—	Binghamton (East.)	6	3	.667	*2.17	16	16	4	1	0	120 1/3	89	34	29	24	127
	—Norfolk (I.L.)	5	3	.625	2.85	10	10	*4	2	0	66 1/3	59	25	21	20	67
1996—	New York (N.L.)	5	12	.294	5.38	26	26	1	0	0	149	157	102	89	71	109
	—St. Lucie (FSL)	0	1	.000	3.38	2	2	0	0	0	8	6	5	3	4	5
	—Binghamton (East.)	0	1	.000	7.20	1	1	0	0	0	5	6	4	4	5	5
1997—	Gulf Coast Mets (GCL)	1	0	1.000	1.45	4	3	0	0	1	18 2/3	14	7	3	4	18
	—St. Lucie (FSL)	0	0	...	2.57	1	1	0	0	0	7	6	2	2	0	6
1998—	St. Lucie (FSL)	0	1	.000	6.38	5	5	0	0	0	18 1/3	23	13	13	4	16
	—Norfolk (I.L.)	4	1	.800	4.42	7	7	0	0	0	38 2/3	42	19	19	9	30
1999—	Norfolk (I.L.)								Did not play.							
Major League totals (1 year)		5	12	.294	5.38	26	26	1	0	0	149	157	102	89	71	109

PERSONAL: Born July 19, 1974, in Bamberg, S.C. ... 6-2/193. ... Bats right, throws right. ... Full name: Preston James David Wilson. ... Son of Mookie Wilson, first base/outfield coach, New York Mets; and outfielder with Mets (1980-89) and Toronto Blue Jays (1989-91).
HIGH SCHOOL: Bamberg Erhardt (Bamberg, S.C.).
TRANSACTIONS/CAREER NOTES: Selected by New York Mets organization in first round (ninth pick overall) of free-agent draft (June 1, 1992). ... On disabled list (April 4-29, May 21-July 13 and July 29-September 8, 1996). ... On Norfolk disabled list (April 20-May 2, 1998). ... Traded by Mets with P Ed Yarnall and P Geoff Goetz to Florida Marlins for C Mike Piazza (May 22, 1998).
HONORS: Named N.L. Rookie Player of the Year by THE SPORTING NEWS (1999).
STATISTICAL NOTES: Led Appalachian League third basemen with 197 total chances in 1993. ... Career major league grand slams: 1.

Year	Team (League)	Pos.	G	AB	R	H	2B	3B	HR	RBI	Avg.	BB	SO	SB	PO	A	E	Avg.
1993—	Kingsport (Appal.)	3B	66	259	44	60	10	0	*16	48	.232	24	75	6	*45	*127	*25	.873
	—Pittsfield (NY-P)	3B	8	29	6	16	5	1	1	12	.552	2	7	1	5	9	6	.700
1994—	Capital City (SAL)	3B	131	474	55	108	17	4	14	58	.228	20	135	10	78	281	47	.884
1995—	Capital City (SAL)	OF	111	442	70	119	26	5	20	61	.269	19	114	20	189	10	8	.961
1996—	St. Lucie (FSL)	OF	23	85	6	15	3	0	1	7	.176	8	21	1	39	4	2	.956
1997—	St. Lucie (FSL)	OF-DH	63	245	32	60	12	1	11	48	.245	8	66	3	104	5	3	.973
	—Binghamton (East.)	OF-DH-3B	70	259	37	74	12	1	19	47	.286	21	71	7	116	3	6	.952
1998—	Norfolk (I.L.)	OF	18	73	9	18	5	1	1	9	.247	2	22	1	44	2	2	.958
	—New York (N.L.)	OF	8	20	3	6	2	0	0	2	.300	2	8	1	10	0	1	.909
	—Charlotte (I.L.■)	OF-DH	94	356	71	99	25	3	25	77	.278	34	121	14	180	8	4	.979
	—Florida (N.L.)	OF	14	31	4	2	0	0	1	1	.065	4	13	0	13	0	0	1.000
1999—	Florida (N.L.)	OF	149	482	67	135	21	4	26	71	.280	46	156	11	320	10	9	.973
Major League totals (2 years)			171	533	74	143	23	4	27	74	.268	52	177	12	343	10	10	.972

PERSONAL: Born March 17, 1973, in Mesa, Ariz. ... 5-11/190. ... Bats right, throws right. ... Full name: Vance Allen Wilson.
HIGH SCHOOL: Red Mountain (Mesa, Ariz.).
JUNIOR COLLEGE: Mesa (Ariz.) Community College.
TRANSACTIONS/CAREER NOTES: Selected by New York Mets organization in 44th round of free-agent draft (June 3, 1993). ... On Norfolk disabled list (May 2-July 18, 1998). ... On New York disabled list (September 8, 1998-remainder of season). ... On Norfolk disabled list (May 13-August 28, 1999). ... On New York disabled list (August 28, 1999-remainder of season).

W

Year	Team (League)	Pos.	G	AB	R	H	2B	3B	HR	RBI	Avg.	BB	SO	SB	PO	A	E	Avg.
1994—	Pittsfield (NY-P)	C	44	166	22	51	12	0	2	20	.307	5	27	4	190	25	5	.977
1995—	Columbia (SAL)	C	91	324	34	81	11	0	6	32	.250	19	45	4	605	99	*14	.981
1996—	St. Lucie (FSL)	C	93	311	29	76	14	2	6	44	.244	31	41	2	502	87	8	.987
1997—	Binghamton (East.)	C	92	322	46	89	17	0	15	40	.276	20	46	2	604	69	11	.984
1998—	Norfolk (I.L.)	C	46	154	18	40	3	0	4	16	.260	9	29	0	348	29	4	.990
	—GC Mets (GCL)	C	10	28	5	10	5	0	2	9	.357	0	0	0	35	9	2	.957
	—St. Lucie (FSL)	C	4	16	0	1	0	0	0	0	.063	0	5	0	19	3	0	1.000
1999—	Norfolk (I.L.)	C	15	53	10	14	3	0	3	5	.264	4	8	1	95	11	1	.991
	—New York (N.L.)	C	1	0	0	0	0	0	0	0	...	0	0	0	0	0	0	...
Major League totals (1 year)			1	0	0	0	0	0	0	0	...	0	0	0	0	0	0	...

PERSONAL: Born April 20, 1973, in Midland, Mich. ... 6-2/210. ... Throws right, bats right. ... Full name: Scott J. Winchester.
HIGH SCHOOL: H.H. Dow (Midland, Mich.).

COLLEGE: Clemson.
TRANSACTIONS/CAREER NOTES: Selected by Cleveland Indians organization in 14th round of free-agent draft (June 1, 1995). ... Traded by Indians with P Jim Crowell, P Danny Graves and IF Damian Jackson to Cincinnati Reds for P John Smiley and IF Jeff Branson (July 31, 1997). ... Selected by Arizona Diamondbacks in second round (33rd pick overall) of expansion draft (November 18, 1997). ... Traded by Diamondbacks to Reds (November 18, 1997), completing deal in which Reds traded P Felix Rodriguez to Diamondbacks for a player to be named later (November 11, 1997). ... On Indianapolis disabled list (August 18-September 8, 1998). ... On Cincinnati disabled list (March 24, 1999-entire season); included rehabilitation assignment to Rockford (August 8-September 6).

Year League	W	L	Pct.	ERA	G	GS	CG	ShO	Sv.	IP	H	R	ER	BB	SO
1995—Watertown (NY-P)	3	1	.750	2.83	23	0	0	0	11	$28\frac{2}{3}$	24	10	9	6	27
1996—Columbus (SAL)	7	3	.700	3.23	52	0	0	0	26	$61\frac{1}{3}$	50	27	22	16	60
—Columbus (SAL)	7	3	.700	3.23	52	0	0	0	26	$61\frac{1}{3}$	50	27	22	16	60
1997—Kinston (Caro.)	2	1	.667	1.47	34	0	0	0	29	$36\frac{2}{3}$	21	6	6	11	45
—Akron (East.)	0	0	...	3.86	6	0	0	0	1	7	8	3	3	2	8
—Chattanooga (Sou.)■	2	1	.667	1.69	9	0	0	0	3	$10\frac{2}{3}$	9	4	2	3	3
—Indianapolis (A.A.)	0	0	...	0.00	4	0	0	0	0	$5\frac{2}{3}$	2	0	0	2	2
—Cincinnati (N.L.)	0	0	...	6.00	5	0	0	0	0	6	9	5	4	2	3
1998—Indianapolis (I.L.)	3	2	.600	6.67	6	5	0	0	0	$29\frac{2}{3}$	39	23	22	8	12
—Cincinnati (N.L.)	3	6	.333	5.81	16	16	1	0	0	79	101	56	51	27	40
1999—Rockford (Midw.)	1	1	.500	2.79	6	6	0	0	0	$19\frac{1}{3}$	19	7	6	3	11
Major League totals (2 years)	3	6	.333	5.82	21	16	1	0	0	85	110	61	55	29	43

WINKELSAS, JOE — P — BRAVES

PERSONAL: Born September 13, 1973, in Buffalo. ... 6-3/188. ... Throws right, bats right. ... Full name: Joseph Winkelsas.
HIGH SCHOOL: Bishop Timon (Buffalo).
JUNIOR COLLEGE: South Carolina-Salkehatchie.
COLLEGE: Elon College (N.C.).
TRANSACTIONS/CAREER NOTES: Signed as non-drafted free agent by Atlanta Braves organization (June 7, 1996).

Year League	W	L	Pct.	ERA	G	GS	CG	ShO	Sv.	IP	H	R	ER	BB	SO
1996—Danville (Appl.)	1	1	.500	7.15	8	0	0	0	2	$11\frac{1}{3}$	11	10	9	4	9
1997—Macon (SAL)	3	2	.600	2.01	38	0	0	0	5	$62\frac{2}{3}$	44	17	14	13	45
—Durham (Caro.)	1	4	.200	7.11	13	0	0	0	1	19	24	18	15	11	17
1998—Danville (Caro.)	6	9	.400	2.22	50	0	0	0	22	69	66	26	17	24	53
—Greenville (Sou.)	0	0	...	4.15	4	0	0	0	0	$4\frac{1}{3}$	3	2	2	4	3
1999—Greenville (Sou.)	4	4	.500	3.75	55	0	0	0	12	$62\frac{1}{3}$	71	32	26	30	38
—Atlanta (N.L.)	0	0	...	54.00	1	0	0	0	0	$\frac{1}{3}$	4	2	2	1	0
Major League totals (1 year)	0	0	...	54.00	1	0	0	0	0	$\frac{1}{3}$	4	2	2	1	0

WINN, RANDY — OF — DEVIL RAYS

PERSONAL: Born June 9, 1974, in Los Angeles. ... 6-2/175. ... Bats both, throws right. ... Full name: Dwight Randolph Winn.
HIGH SCHOOL: San Ramon Valley (Danville, Calif.).
COLLEGE: Santa Clara.
TRANSACTIONS/CAREER NOTES: Selected by Florida Marlins organization in third round of free-agent draft (June 1, 1995). ... On disabled list (August 22-September 11, 1995). ... Selected by Tampa Bay Devil Rays in third round (58th pick overall) of expansion draft (November 18, 1997).
STATISTICAL NOTES: Led Eastern League in caught stealing with 20 in 1997. ... Career major league grand slams: 1.
MISCELLANEOUS: Holds Tampa Bay Devil Rays record for most triples (13).

Year Team (League)	Pos.	G	AB	R	H	2B	3B	HR	RBI	Avg.	BB	SO	SB	PO	A	E	Avg.
1995—Elmira (NY-P)	OF	51	213	38	67	7	4	0	22	.315	15	31	19	103	1	5	.954
1996—Kane County (Midw.)	OF	130	514	90	139	16	3	0	35	.270	47	115	30	260	2	8	.970
1997—Brevard County (FSL)	OF	36	143	26	45	8	2	0	15	.315	16	28	16	95	0	0	1.000
—Portland (East.)	OF	96	384	66	112	15	6	8	36	.292	42	92	35	182	6	4	.979
1998—Durham (I.L.)	OF	29	123	25	35	5	2	1	16	.285	15	24	10	55	1	2	.966
—Tampa Bay (A.L.)	OF-DH	109	338	51	94	9	9	1	17	.278	29	69	26	192	7	4	.980
1999—Tampa Bay (A.L.)	OF	79	303	44	81	16	4	2	24	.267	17	63	9	180	4	1	.995
—Durham (I.L.)	OF	46	207	38	73	20	3	3	30	.353	16	27	9	113	2	4	.966
Major League totals (2 years)		188	641	95	175	25	13	3	41	.273	46	132	35	372	11	5	.987

WISE, DeWAYNE — OF — BLUE JAYS

PERSONAL: Born February 24, 1978, in Columbia, S.C. ... 6-1/180. ... Bats left, throws left. ... Full name: Larry DeWayne Wise.
HIGH SCHOOL: Chapin (S.C.).
TRANSACTIONS/CAREER NOTES: Selected by Cincinnati Reds organization in fifth round of free-agent draft (June 3, 1997). ... Selected by Toronto Blue Jays from Reds organization in Rule 5 major league draft (December 13, 1999).
STATISTICAL NOTES: Led Pioneer League outfielders with 140 total chances in 1997. ... Led Midwest League with nine sacrifice flies in 1998. ... Led Midwest League with 14 sacrifice flies in 1999.

Year Team (League)	Pos.	G	AB	R	H	2B	3B	HR	RBI	Avg.	BB	SO	SB	PO	A	E	Avg.
1997—Billings (Pio.)	OF	62	268	53	84	13	*9	7	41	.313	9	47	18	•118	9	*13	.907
1998—Burlington (Midw.)	OF	127	496	61	111	15	9	2	44	.224	41	111	27	233	8	7	.972
1999—Rockford (Midw.)	OF	131	502	70	127	20	13	11	81	.253	42	81	35	294	16	8	.975

W

PERSONAL: Born November 18, 1975, in Montclair, Calif. ... 6-4/190. ... Throws right, bats right. ... Full name: Matthew John Wise.
HIGH SCHOOL: Bonita (Calif.).
COLLEGE: Cal State Fullerton.
TRANSACTIONS/CAREER NOTES: Selected by Anaheim Angels organization in sixth round of free-agent draft (June 3, 1997). ... On Erie disabled list (July 9, 1999-remainder of season).

Year League	W	L	Pct.	ERA	G	GS	CG	ShO	Sv.	IP	H	R	ER	BB	SO
1997— Boise (N'west)	•9	1	*.900	3.25	15	15	0	0	0	83	82	37	30	34	86
1998— Midland (Texas)	9	10	.474	5.42	27	27	3	•1	0	167 2/3	195	111	101	48	131
1999— Erie (East.)	8	5	.615	3.77	16	16	3	0	0	98	102	48	41	24	72

PERSONAL: Born August 28, 1972, in Baltimore. ... 6-4/235. ... Throws right, bats right. ... Full name: Gerald Alphonse Witasick.
HIGH SCHOOL: C. Milton Wright (Bel Air, Md.).
JUNIOR COLLEGE: Brevard Community College (Fla.).
COLLEGE: Maryland-Baltimore County.
TRANSACTIONS/CAREER NOTES: Selected by St. Louis Cardinals organization in second round of free-agent draft (June 3, 1993). ... On disabled list (July 17, 1995-remainder of season). ... Traded by Cardinals with OF Allen Battle, P Bret Wagner and P Carl Dale to Oakland Athletics for P Todd Stottlemyre (January 9, 1996). ... On Oakland disabled list (March 31-June 14, 1997); included rehabilitation assignment to Modesto (June 11-14). ... Traded by Athletics to Kansas City Royals for a player to be named later and cash (March 30, 1999); Athletics acquired P Scott Chiasson to complete deal (June 10, 1999).

Year League	W	L	Pct.	ERA	G	GS	CG	ShO	Sv.	IP	H	R	ER	BB	SO
1993— Johnson City (Appl.)	4	3	.571	4.12	12	12	0	0	0	67 2/3	65	42	31	19	74
— Savannah (SAL)	1	0	1.000	4.50	1	1	0	0	0	6	7	3	3	2	8
1994— Madison (Midw.)	10	4	.714	2.32	18	18	2	0	0	112 1/3	74	36	29	42	141
1995— St. Petersburg (FSL)	7	7	.500	2.74	18	18	1	1	0	105	80	39	32	36	109
— Arkansas (Texas)	2	4	.333	6.88	7	7	0	0	0	34	46	29	26	16	26
1996— Huntsville (Sou.)■	0	3	.000	2.30	25	6	0	0	4	66 2/3	47	21	17	26	63
— Oakland (A.L.)	1	1	.500	6.23	12	0	0	0	0	13	12	9	9	5	12
— Edmonton (PCL)	0	0	...	4.15	6	0	0	0	2	8 2/3	9	4	4	6	9
1997— Modesto (Calif.)	0	1	.000	4.15	9	2	0	0	1	17 1/3	16	9	8	5	29
— Edmonton (PCL)	3	2	.600	4.28	13	1	0	0	0	27 1/3	25	13	13	15	17
— Oakland (A.L.)	0	0	...	5.73	8	0	0	0	0	11	14	7	7	6	8
1998— Edmonton (PCL)	11	7	.611	3.87	27	26	2	1	0	149	126	74	64	49	155
— Oakland (A.L.)	1	3	.250	6.33	7	3	0	0	0	27	36	24	19	15	29
1999— Kansas City (A.L.)■	9	12	.429	5.57	32	28	1	1	0	158 1/3	191	108	98	83	102
Major League totals (4 years)	11	16	.407	5.72	59	31	1	1	0	209 1/3	253	148	133	109	151

PERSONAL: Born May 11, 1964, in Arlington, Va. ... 6-2/205. ... Throws right, bats right. ... Full name: Robert Andrew Witt.
HIGH SCHOOL: Canton (Mass.).
COLLEGE: Oklahoma.
TRANSACTIONS/CAREER NOTES: Selected by Cincinnati Reds organization in seventh round of free-agent draft (June 7, 1982); did not sign. ... Selected by Texas Rangers organization in first round (third pick overall) of free-agent draft (June 3, 1985). ... On Texas disabled list (May 21-June 20, 1987); included rehabilitation assignments to Oklahoma City (June 7-12) and Tulsa (June 13). ... On Texas disabled list (May 27-July 31, 1991); included rehabilitation assignment to Oklahoma City (July 22-29). ... Traded by Rangers with OF Ruben Sierra, P Jeff Russell and cash to Oakland Athletics for OF Jose Canseco (August 31, 1992). ... Granted free agency (October 26, 1994). ... Signed by Florida Marlins (April 9, 1995). ... Traded by Marlins to Rangers for two players to be named later (August 8, 1995); Marlins acquired P Wilson Heredia (August 11, 1995) and OF Scott Podsednik (October 2, 1995) to complete deal. ... Granted free agency (November 3, 1995). ... Re-signed by Rangers (December 24, 1995). ... Granted free agency (October 27, 1997). ... Re-signed by Rangers (January 19, 1998). ... Traded by Rangers to St. Louis Cardinals for a player to be named later or cash (June 23, 1998). ... Granted free agency (October 29, 1998). ... Signed by Tampa Bay Devil Rays organization (January 20, 1999). ... Granted free agency (November 5, 1999). ... Signed by Cleveland Indians organization (January 19, 2000).
RECORDS: Shares major league record for most strikeouts in one inning—4 (August 2, 1987, second inning).
HONORS: Named righthanded pitcher on THE SPORTING NEWS college All-America team (1985).
STATISTICAL NOTES: Led A.L. with 22 wild pitches in 1986 and tied for lead with 16 in 1988. ... Pitched 4-0 one-hit, complete-game victory against Kansas City (June 23, 1994).
MISCELLANEOUS: Member of 1984 U.S. Olympic baseball team. ... Struck out in only appearance as pinch hitter with Texas (1987). ... Appeared in two games as pinch runner (1990). ... Appeared in one game as pinch runner (1994). ... Appeared in two games as pinch runner with Florida (1995). ... Made an out in only appearance as pinch hitter with Texas (1998). ... Shares Tampa Bay Devil Rays all-time record for most shutouts (2).

Year League	W	L	Pct.	ERA	G	GS	CG	ShO	Sv.	IP	H	R	ER	BB	SO
1985— Tulsa (Texas)	0	6	.000	6.43	11	8	0	0	0	35	26	26	25	44	39
1986— Texas (A.L.)	11	9	.550	5.48	31	31	0	0	0	157 2/3	130	104	96	*143	174
1987— Texas (A.L.)	8	10	.444	4.91	26	25	1	0	0	143	114	82	78	*140	160
— Oklahoma City (A.A.)	1	0	1.000	9.00	1	1	0	0	0	5	5	5	5	3	2
— Tulsa (Texas)	0	1	.000	5.40	1	1	0	0	0	5	5	9	3	6	2
1988— Texas (A.L.)	8	10	.444	3.92	22	22	13	2	0	174 1/3	134	83	76	101	148
— Oklahoma City (A.A.)	4	6	.400	4.34	11	11	3	0	0	76 2/3	69	42	37	47	70
1989— Texas (A.L.)	12	13	.480	5.14	31	31	5	1	0	194 1/3	182	123	•111	*114	166
1990— Texas (A.L.)	17	10	.630	3.36	33	32	7	1	0	222	197	98	83	110	221
1991— Texas (A.L.)	3	7	.300	6.09	17	16	1	1	0	88 2/3	84	66	60	74	82
— Oklahoma City (A.A.)	1	1	.500	1.13	2	2	0	0	0	8	3	1	1	8	12
1992— Texas (A.L.)	9	13	.409	4.46	25	25	0	0	0	161 1/3	152	87	80	95	100
— Oakland (A.L.)■	1	1	.500	3.41	6	6	0	0	0	31 2/3	31	12	12	19	25
1993— Oakland (A.L.)	14	13	.519	4.21	35	33	5	1	0	220	226	112	103	91	131

W

Year League	W	L	Pct.	ERA	G	GS	CG	ShO	Sv.	IP	H	R	ER	BB	SO
1994—Oakland (A.L.)	8	10	.444	5.04	24	24	5	3	0	135²/₃	151	88	76	70	111
1995—Florida (N.L.)■	2	7	.222	3.90	19	19	1	0	0	110²/₃	104	52	48	47	95
—Texas (A.L.)■	3	4	.429	4.55	10	10	1	0	0	61¹/₃	81	35	31	21	46
1996—Texas (A.L.)	16	12	.571	5.41	33	32	2	0	0	199²/₃	235	129	120	96	157
1997—Texas (A.L.)	12	12	.500	4.82	34	32	3	0	0	209	245	118	112	74	121
1998—Texas (A.L.)	5	4	.556	7.66	14	13	0	0	0	69¹/₃	95	62	59	33	30
—St. Louis (N.L.)■	2	5	.286	4.94	17	5	0	0	0	47¹/₃	55	32	26	20	28
1999—Tampa Bay (A.L.)■	7	15	.318	5.84	32	32	3	2	0	180¹/₃	213	130	117	96	123
A.L. totals (14 years)	134	143	.484	4.86	373	364	46	11	0	2248¹/₃	2270	1329	1214	1277	1795
N.L. totals (2 years)	4	12	.250	4.22	36	24	1	0	0	158	159	84	74	67	123
Major League totals (14 years)	138	155	.471	4.82	409	388	47	11	0	2406¹/₃	2429	1413	1288	1344	1918

DIVISION SERIES RECORD

Year League	W	L	Pct.	ERA	G	GS	CG	ShO	Sv.	IP	H	R	ER	BB	SO
1996—Texas (A.L.)	0	0	...	8.10	1	1	0	0	0	3¹/₃	4	3	3	2	3

CHAMPIONSHIP SERIES RECORD

Year League	W	L	Pct.	ERA	G	GS	CG	ShO	Sv.	IP	H	R	ER	BB	SO
1992—Oakland (A.L.)	0	0	...	18.00	1	0	0	0	0	1	2	2	2	1	1

WITT, KEVIN — 1B/OF — BLUE JAYS

PERSONAL: Born January 5, 1976, in High Point, N.C. ... 6-4/210. ... Bats left, throws right. ... Full name: Kevin Joseph Witt.
HIGH SCHOOL: Bishop Kenny (Jacksonville, Fla.).
TRANSACTIONS/CAREER NOTES: Selected by Toronto Blue Jays organization in first round (28th pick overall) of free-agent draft (June 2, 1994).
STATISTICAL NOTES: Tied for Southern League lead with seven intentional bases on balls in 1997. ... Led International League first basemen with .996 fielding percentage and 105 double plays in 1998.

Year Team (League)	Pos.	G	AB	R	H	2B	3B	HR	RBI	Avg.	BB	SO	SB	PO	A	E	Avg.
1994—Medicine Hat (Pio.)	SS	60	243	37	62	10	4	7	36	.255	15	52	4	*99	167	25	.914
1995—Hagerstown (SAL)	SS	119	479	58	111	35	1	14	50	.232	28	148	1	203	338	46	.919
1996—Dunedin (FSL)	SS	124	446	63	121	18	6	13	70	.271	39	96	9	161	369	48	.917
1997—Knoxville (Sou.)	1-3-DH-O-S	127	501	76	145	27	4	•30	91	.289	44	109	1	553	118	15	.978
1998—Syracuse (I.L.)	1B-OF-DH	126	455	71	124	20	3	23	67	.273	53	124	3	973	68	4	†.996
—Toronto (A.L.)	1B	5	7	0	1	0	0	0	0	.143	0	3	0	5	1	0	1.000
1999—Syracuse (I.L.)	1B-OF-DH	114	421	72	117	24	3	24	71	.278	64	109	0	579	55	4	.994
—Toronto (A.L.)	DH	15	34	3	7	1	0	1	5	.206	2	9	0	0	0	0	...
Major League totals (2 years)		20	41	3	8	1	0	1	5	.195	2	12	0	5	1	0	1.000

WOHLERS, MARK — P

PERSONAL: Born January 23, 1970, in Holyoke, Mass. ... 6-4/207. ... Throws right, bats right. ... Full name: Mark Edward Wohlers.
HIGH SCHOOL: Holyoke (Mass.).
TRANSACTIONS/CAREER NOTES: Selected by Atlanta Braves organization in eighth round of free-agent draft (June 1, 1988). ... On Atlanta disabled list (May 3-24 and August 21, 1998-remainder of season); included rehabilitation assignments to Greenville (May 23) and Richmond (August 25-September 8). ... Traded by Braves with cash to Cincinnati Reds for P John Hudek (April 16, 1999). ... On Cincinnati disabled list (April 17, 1999-remainder of season); included rehabilitation assignments to Indianapolis (May 2-3), Rockford (June 17-21) and Chattanooga (June 22-July 1). ... Granted free agency (November 5, 1999).
RECORDS: Shares major league single-inning record for most strikeouts—4 (June 7, 1995, ninth inning).
HONORS: Named Southern League Outstanding Pitcher (1991).
STATISTICAL NOTES: Pitched two innings, combining with starter Kent Mercker (six innings) and Alejandro Pena (one inning) in 1-0 no-hit victory for Atlanta against San Diego (September 11, 1991). ... Led International League with 17 wild pitches in 1998.

Year League	W	L	Pct.	ERA	G	GS	CG	ShO	Sv.	IP	H	R	ER	BB	SO
1988—Pulaski (Appl.)	5	3	.625	3.32	13	9	1	0	0	59²/₃	47	37	22	50	49
1989—Sumter (SAL)	2	7	.222	6.49	14	14	0	0	0	68	74	55	49	59	51
—Pulaski (Appl.)	1	1	.500	5.48	14	8	0	0	0	46	48	36	28	28	50
1990—Greenville (Sou.)	0	1	.000	4.02	14	0	0	0	6	15²/₃	14	7	7	14	20
—Sumter (SAL)	5	4	.556	1.88	37	2	0	0	5	52²/₃	27	13	11	20	85
1991—Greenville (Sou.)	0	0	...	0.57	28	0	0	0	21	31¹/₃	9	4	2	13	44
—Richmond (I.L.)	1	0	1.000	1.03	23	0	0	0	11	26¹/₃	23	4	3	12	22
—Atlanta (N.L.)	3	1	.750	3.20	17	0	0	0	2	19²/₃	17	7	7	13	13
1992—Richmond (I.L.)	0	2	.000	3.93	27	2	0	0	9	34¹/₃	32	16	15	17	33
—Atlanta (N.L.)	1	2	.333	2.55	32	0	0	0	4	35¹/₃	28	11	10	14	17
1993—Richmond (I.L.)	1	3	.250	1.84	25	0	0	0	4	29¹/₃	21	7	6	11	39
—Atlanta (N.L.)	6	2	.750	4.50	46	0	0	0	4	48	37	25	24	22	45
1994—Atlanta (N.L.)	7	2	.778	4.59	51	0	0	0	1	51	51	35	26	33	58
1995—Atlanta (N.L.)	7	3	.700	2.09	65	0	0	0	25	64²/₃	51	16	15	24	90
1996—Atlanta (N.L.)	2	4	.333	3.03	77	0	0	0	39	77¹/₃	71	30	26	21	100
1997—Atlanta (N.L.)	5	7	.417	3.50	71	0	0	0	33	69¹/₃	57	29	27	38	92
1998—Atlanta (N.L.)	0	1	.000	10.18	27	0	0	0	8	20¹/₃	18	23	23	33	22
—Greenville (Sou.)	0	0	...	0.00	1	1	0	0	0	1	1	1	0	1	1
—Richmond (I.L.)	0	3	.000	20.43	16	0	0	0	0	12¹/₃	21	28	28	36	16
1999—Atlanta (N.L.)	0	0	...	27.00	2	0	0	0	0	²/₃	1	2	2	6	0
—Indianapolis (I.L.)■	0	0	...	108.00	1	0	0	0	0	¹/₃	1	4	4	5	1
—Rockford (Midw.)	0	0	...	4.50	2	0	0	0	0	2	1	1	1	2	4
—Chattanooga (Sou.)	0	0	...	16.20	2	0	0	0	0	1²/₃	1	3	3	3	3
Major League totals (10 years)	31	22	.585	3.73	388	0	0	0	112	386¹/₃	331	178	160	204	437

W

DIVISION SERIES RECORD

RECORDS: Shares career record for most saves—5. ... Shares N.L. career record for most games pitched—7.

Year League	W	L	Pct.	ERA	G	GS	CG	ShO	Sv.	IP	H	R	ER	BB	SO
1995—Atlanta (N.L.)	0	1	.000	6.75	3	0	0	0	2	2²/₃	6	2	2	2	4
1996—Atlanta (N.L.)	0	0	...	0.00	3	0	0	0	3	3¹/₃	1	0	0	0	4
1997—Atlanta (N.L.)	0	0	...	0.00	1	0	0	0	0	1	1	0	0	0	1
Division series totals (3 years)	0	1	.000	2.57	7	0	0	0	5	7	8	2	2	2	9

CHAMPIONSHIP SERIES RECORD

RECORDS: Holds N.L. career records for most games pitched—18; and most games as relief pitcher—18.

Year League	W	L	Pct.	ERA	G	GS	CG	ShO	Sv.	IP	H	R	ER	BB	SO
1991—Atlanta (N.L.)	0	0	...	0.00	3	0	0	0	0	1²/₃	3	0	0	1	1
1992—Atlanta (N.L.)	0	0	...	0.00	3	0	0	0	0	3	2	0	0	1	2
1993—Atlanta (N.L.)	0	1	.000	3.38	4	0	0	0	0	5¹/₃	2	2	2	3	10
1995—Atlanta (N.L.)	1	0	1.000	1.80	4	0	0	0	0	5	2	1	1	0	8
1996—Atlanta (N.L.)	0	0	...	0.00	3	0	0	0	2	3	0	0	0	0	4
1997—Atlanta (N.L.)	0	0	...	0.00	1	0	0	0	0	1	0	0	0	1	1
Champ. series totals (6 years)	1	1	.500	1.42	18	0	0	0	2	19	9	3	3	6	26

WORLD SERIES RECORD

NOTES: Member of World Series championship team (1995).

Year League	W	L	Pct.	ERA	G	GS	CG	ShO	Sv.	IP	H	R	ER	BB	SO
1991—Atlanta (N.L.)	0	0	...	0.00	3	0	0	0	0	1²/₃	2	0	0	2	1
1992—Atlanta (N.L.)	0	0	...	0.00	2	0	0	0	0	²/₃	0	0	0	1	0
1995—Atlanta (N.L.)	0	0	...	1.80	4	0	0	0	0	5	4	1	1	3	3
1996—Atlanta (N.L.)	0	0	...	6.23	4	0	0	0	0	4¹/₃	7	3	3	3	4
World Series totals (4 years)	0	0	...	3.09	13	0	0	0	0	11²/₃	13	4	4	9	8

ALL-STAR GAME RECORD

Year League	W	L	Pct.	ERA	GS	CG	ShO	Sv.	IP	H	R	ER	BB	SO
1996—National	0	0	...	0.00	0	0	0	0	²/₃	1	0	0	0	0

WOLCOTT, BOB   P

PERSONAL: Born September 8, 1973, in Huntington Beach, Calif. ... 6-0/190. ... Throws right, bats right. ... Full name: Robert William Wolcott.
HIGH SCHOOL: North Medford (Ore.).
TRANSACTIONS/CAREER NOTES: Selected by Seattle Mariners organization in second round of free-agent draft (June 1, 1992). ... Selected by Arizona Diamondbacks in second round (53rd pick overall) of expansion draft (November 18, 1997). ... Traded by Diamondbacks to Boston Red Sox for a player to be named later (November 11, 1998); Diamondbacks acquired P Bart Miadich to complete deal (December 14, 1998). ... Released by Red Sox (November 18, 1999).

Year League	W	L	Pct.	ERA	G	GS	CG	ShO	Sv.	IP	H	R	ER	BB	SO
1992—Bellingham (N'west)	0	1	.000	6.85	9	7	0	0	0	22¹/₃	25	18	17	19	17
1993—Bellingham (N'west)	8	4	.667	2.64	15	15	1	0	0	95¹/₃	70	31	28	26	79
1994—Riverside (Calif.)	14	8	.636	2.84	26	26	•5	1	0	*180²/₃	173	75	57	50	142
—Calgary (PCL)	0	1	.000	3.00	1	1	0	0	0	6	6	2	2	3	5
1995—Port City (Sou.)	7	3	.700	2.20	12	12	2	1	0	86	60	26	21	13	53
—Tacoma (PCL)	6	3	.667	4.08	13	13	2	1	0	79¹/₃	94	49	36	16	43
—Seattle (A.L.)	3	2	.600	4.42	7	6	0	0	0	36²/₃	43	18	18	14	19
1996—Seattle (A.L.)	7	10	.412	5.73	30	28	1	0	0	149¹/₃	179	101	95	54	78
—Lancaster (Calif.)	0	1	.000	10.50	1	1	0	0	0	6	9	7	7	0	6
—Tacoma (PCL)	0	2	.000	7.30	3	3	0	0	0	12¹/₃	17	13	10	3	16
1997—Seattle (A.L.)	5	6	.455	6.03	19	18	0	0	0	100	129	71	67	29	58
—Tacoma (PCL)	1	3	.250	5.11	7	7	0	0	0	37	40	23	21	7	29
1998—Tucson (PCL)■	8	6	.571	5.18	23	21	2	1	0	128²/₃	156	79	74	26	100
—Arizona (N.L.)	1	3	.250	7.09	6	6	0	0	0	33	32	27	26	13	21
1999—Pawtucket (I.L.)■	6	13	.316	3.59	26	16	2	0	2	125¹/₃	131	67	50	28	69
—Boston (A.L.)	0	0	...	8.10	4	0	0	0	0	6²/₃	8	6	6	3	2
A.L. totals (4 years)	15	18	.455	5.72	60	52	1	0	0	292²/₃	359	196	186	100	157
N.L. totals (1 year)	1	3	.250	7.09	6	6	0	0	0	33	32	27	26	13	21
Major League totals (5 years)	16	21	.432	5.86	66	58	1	0	0	325²/₃	391	223	212	113	178

CHAMPIONSHIP SERIES RECORD

Year League	W	L	Pct.	ERA	G	GS	CG	ShO	Sv.	IP	H	R	ER	BB	SO
1995—Seattle (A.L.)	1	0	1.000	2.57	1	1	0	0	0	7	8	2	2	5	2

WOLF, RANDY   P   PHILLIES

PERSONAL: Born August 22, 1976, in Canoga Park, Calif. ... 6-0/194. ... Throws left, bats left. ... Full name: Randall C. Wolf.
HIGH SCHOOL: El Camino Real (Los Angeles).
COLLEGE: Pepperdine.
TRANSACTIONS/CAREER NOTES: Selected by Los Angeles Dodgers organization in 25th round of free-agent draft (June 2, 1994); did not sign. ... Selected by Philadelphia Phillies organization in second round of free-agent draft (June 3, 1997).

Year League	W	L	Pct.	ERA	G	GS	CG	ShO	Sv.	IP	H	R	ER	BB	SO
1997—Batavia (NY-P)	4	0	1.000	1.58	7	7	0	0	0	40	29	8	7	8	53
1998—Reading (East.)	2	0	1.000	1.44	4	4	0	0	0	25	15	4	4	4	33
—Scranton/W.B. (I.L.)	9	7	.563	4.62	24	23	1	0	0	148	167	88	76	48	118
1999—Scranton/W.B. (I.L.)	4	5	.444	3.61	12	12	0	0	0	77¹/₃	73	36	31	29	72
—Philadelphia (N.L.)	6	9	.400	5.55	22	21	0	0	0	121²/₃	126	78	75	67	116
Major League totals (1 year)	6	9	.400	5.55	22	21	0	0	0	121²/₃	126	78	75	67	116

W

WOMACK, TONY   2B   DIAMONDBACKS

PERSONAL: Born September 25, 1969, in Danville, Va. ... 5-9/159. ... Bats left, throws right. ... Full name: Anthony Darrell Womack.
HIGH SCHOOL: Gretna (Va.).
COLLEGE: Guilford (N.C.), degree in sports management; then UNC Greensboro (did not play), master's degree in sports management.
TRANSACTIONS/CAREER NOTES: Selected by Pittsburgh Pirates organization in seventh round of free-agent draft (June 3, 1991). ... On disabled list (April 17-26 and August 28, 1992-remainder of season). ... Traded by Pirates to Arizona Diamondbacks for OF Paul Weichard and a player to be named later (February 26, 1999); Pirates acquired P Jason Boyd to complete deal (August 25, 1999). ... On Arizona disabled list (March 26-April 12, 1999); included rehabilitation assignment to Tucson (April 8-12).
STATISTICAL NOTES: Tied for American Association lead with 12 sacrifice hits in 1994. ... Led Pacific Coast League with 14 sacrifice hits in 1996. ... Led N.L. second basemen with 20 errors in 1997. ... Had 16-game hitting streak (July 3-22, 1998). ... Career major league grand slams: 1.
MISCELLANEOUS: Holds Arizona Diamondbacks all-time record for most stolen bases (72).

						BATTING								FIELDING		
Year Team (League)	Pos.	G	AB	R	H	2B	3B	HR	RBI	Avg.	BB	SO	SB	PO	A	E	Avg.
1991— Welland (NY-P)	SS-2B	45	166	30	46	3	0	1	8	.277	17	39	26	78	109	16	.921
1992— Augusta (SAL)	SS-2B	102	380	62	93	8	3	0	18	.245	41	59	50	186	291	40	.923
1993— Salem (Caro.)	SS	72	304	41	91	11	3	2	18	.299	13	34	28	130	223	28	.927
— Carolina (Sou.)	SS	60	247	41	75	7	2	0	23	.304	17	34	21	102	169	11	.961
— Pittsburgh (N.L.)	SS	15	24	5	2	0	0	0	0	.083	3	3	2	11	22	1	.971
1994— Buffalo (A.A.)	SS-2B	106	421	40	93	9	2	0	18	.221	19	76	41	211	283	22	.957
— Pittsburgh (N.L.)	2B-SS	5	12	4	4	0	0	0	1	.333	2	3	0	3	6	2	.818
1995— Calgary (PCL)	2B-SS	30	107	12	30	3	1	0	6	.280	12	11	7	37	94	5	.963
— Carolina (Sou.)	SS-2B	82	332	52	85	9	4	1	19	.256	19	36	27	126	241	18	.953
1996— Calgary (PCL)	S-2-O-DH	131	506	75	151	19	11	1	47	.298	31	79	37	258	335	24	.961
— Pittsburgh (N.L.)	OF-2B	17	30	11	10	3	1	0	7	.333	6	1	2	11	8	2	.905
1997— Pittsburgh (N.L.)	2B-SS	155	641	85	178	26	9	6	50	.278	43	109	*60	335	430	†20	.975
1998— Pittsburgh (N.L.)	2B-OF-SS	159	655	85	185	26	7	3	45	.282	38	94	*58	309	451	17	.978
1999— Tucson (PCL)■	OF	4	16	1	4	1	0	1	3	.250	2	3	0	8	1	0	1.000
— Arizona (N.L.)	OF-2B-SS	144	614	111	170	25	10	4	41	.277	52	68	*72	293	85	5	.987
Major League totals (6 years)		495	1976	301	549	80	27	13	144	.278	144	278	194	962	1002	47	.977

DIVISION SERIES RECORD

						BATTING								FIELDING		
Year Team (League)	Pos.	G	AB	R	H	2B	3B	HR	RBI	Avg.	BB	SO	SB	PO	A	E	Avg.
1999— Arizona (N.L.)	OF-SS	4	18	2	2	0	1	0	0	.111	0	6	0	5	5	2	.833

ALL-STAR GAME RECORD

					BATTING								FIELDING		
Year League	Pos.	AB	R	H	2B	3B	HR	RBI	Avg.	BB	SO	SB	PO	A	E	Avg.
1997— National	2B	1	0	0	0	0	0	0	.000	0	0	0	1	0	0	1.000

WOOD, JASON   IF   PIRATES

PERSONAL: Born December 16, 1969, in San Bernadino, Calif. ... 6-1/170. ... Bats right, throws right. ... Full name: Jason William Wood.
HIGH SCHOOL: McLane (Fresno, Calif.).
TRANSACTIONS/CAREER NOTES: Selected by Oakland Athletics organzation in 11th round of free-agent draft (June 3, 1991). ... Traded by Athletics to Detroit Tigers (June 23, 1998), completing trade in which Tigers traded IF Bip Roberts to A's for a player to be named later (July 18, 1998). ... On Detroit disabled list (March 29-May 11, 1999); included rehabilitation assignment to Lakeland (May 4-11). ... Granted free agency (October 15, 1999). ... Signed by Pittsburgh Pirates organization (December 7, 1999).

						BATTING								FIELDING		
Year Team (League)	Pos.	G	AB	R	H	2B	3B	HR	RBI	Avg.	BB	SO	SB	PO	A	E	Avg.
1991— S. Oregon (N'west)	SS-2B	44	142	30	44	3	4	3	23	.310	28	30	5	64	117	14	.928
1992— Modesto (Calif.)	SS	128	454	66	105	28	3	6	49	.231	40	106	5	203	360	37	.938
1993— Huntsville (Sou.)	SS	103	370	44	85	21	2	3	36	.230	33	97	2	161	227	32	.924
1994— Huntsville (Sou.)	SS	134	468	54	128	29	2	6	84	.274	46	83	3	190	371	25	.957
1995— Edmonton (PCL)	3B-2B-SS	127	421	49	99	20	5	2	50	.235	29	72	1	173	331	26	.951
1996— Huntsville (Sou.)	3B-1B-SS	133	491	77	128	21	1	20	84	.261	72	87	2	337	292	20	.969
— Edmonton (PCL)	1B	3	12	0	0	0	0	0	0	.000	5	6	0	39	1	1	.976
1997— Edmonton (PCL)	3B-SS	130	505	83	162	35	7	19	87	.321	45	74	2	103	264	17	.956
1998— Oakland (A.L.)	SS-3B	3	1	1	0	0	0	0	0	.000	0	1	0	1	3	0	1.000
— Edmonton (PCL)	3B-2B-OF-SS	80	307	52	86	20	0	18	73	.280	37	71	1	91	175	10	.964
— Detroit (A.L.)■	1B-DH-SS	10	23	5	8	2	0	1	1	.348	3	4	0	38	2	0	1.000
— Toledo (I.L.)	3B-1B-SS	46	169	24	47	9	0	7	29	.278	16	30	0	99	66	5	.971
1999— Lakeland (FSL)	SS-1B-2B-3B	5	17	0	4	0	0	0	1	.235	4	2	0	14	8	2	.917
— Detroit (A.L.)	3-S-1-DH-2	27	44	5	7	1	0	1	8	.159	2	13	0	42	13	4	.932
— Toledo (I.L.)	3-1-S-C-2-O	48	185	34	53	11	0	6	24	.286	22	43	0	100	83	4	.979
Major League totals (2 years)		40	68	11	15	3	0	2	9	.221	5	18	0	81	18	4	.961

WOOD, KERRY   P   CUBS

PERSONAL: Born June 16, 1977, in Irving, Texas. ... 6-5/230. ... Throws right, bats right. ... Full name: Kerry Lee Wood.
HIGH SCHOOL: Grand Prairie (Texas).
TRANSACTIONS/CAREER NOTES: Selected by Chicago Cubs organization in first round (fourth pick overall) of free-agent draft (June 1, 1995). ... On disabled list (May 24-June 19, 1996). ... On disabled list (March 31, 1999-entire season).
RECORDS: Shares major league single-game record for most strikeouts (nine-inning game)—20 (May 6, 1998). ... Holds N.L. record for most strikeouts in consecutive games—33 (May 6 [20] and 11 [13], 1998).

W

HONORS: Named N.L. Rookie Pitcher of the Year by THE SPORTING NEWS (1998). ... Named N.L. Rookie of the Year by Baseball Writers' Association of America (1998).

STATISTICAL NOTES: Led Florida State League with 14 hit batsmen and seven balks in 1996. ... Pitched 2-0 one-hit, complete-game victory against Houston (May 6, 1998). ... Struck out 20 batters in one game (May 6, 1998). ... Struck out 16 batters in one game (August 26, 1998).

Year	League	W	L	Pct.	ERA	G	GS	CG	ShO	Sv.	IP	H	R	ER	BB	SO
1995—	Fort Myers (FSL)	0	0	...	0.00	1	1	0	0	0	3	0	0	0	1	2
—	Williamsport (NY-P)	0	0	...	10.38	2	2	0	0	0	4 1/3	5	8	5	5	5
1996—	Daytona (FSL)	10	2	•.833	2.91	22	22	0	0	0	114 1/3	72	51	37	70	136
1997—	Orlando (Sou.)	6	7	.462	4.50	19	19	0	0	0	94	58	49	47	79	106
—	Iowa (A.A.)	4	2	.667	4.21	10	10	0	0	0	57 2/3	35	35	30	52	80
1998—	Iowa (PCL)	1	0	1.000	0.00	1	1	0	0	0	5	1	0	0	2	11
—	Chicago (N.L.)	13	6	.684	3.40	26	26	1	1	0	166 2/3	117	69	63	85	233
1999—	Chicago (N.L.)								Did not play.							
Major League totals (1 year)		13	6	.684	3.40	26	26	1	1	0	166 2/3	117	69	63	85	233

DIVISION SERIES RECORD

Year	League	W	L	Pct.	ERA	G	GS	CG	ShO	Sv.	IP	H	R	ER	BB	SO
1998—	Chicago (N.L.)	0	1	.000	1.80	1	1	0	0	0	5	3	1	1	4	5

WOODALL, BRAD — P

PERSONAL: Born June 25, 1969, in Atlanta. ... 6-0/181. ... Throws left, bats both. ... Full name: David Bradley Woodall.

HIGH SCHOOL: Spring Valley (Columbia, S.C.).

COLLEGE: North Carolina.

TRANSACTIONS/CAREER NOTES: Signed as non-drafted free agent by Atlanta Braves (June 10, 1991). ... On Greenville disabled list (April 8-May 3, 1993). ... On Richmond disabled list (July 8-August 18, 1995). ... Granted free agency (October 17, 1997). ... Signed by Milwaukee Brewers organization (December 19, 1997). ... Claimed on waivers by Chicago Cubs (March 31, 1999). ... On Iowa disabled list (July 5-August 10 and August 28, 1999-remainder of season). ... Granted free agency (October 15, 1999).

HONORS: Named International League Pitcher of the Year (1994).

MISCELLANEOUS: Scored one run in four appearances as pinch runner and had an RBI single, scored a run and struck out in two games as pinch hitter with Milwaukee (1998).

Year	League	W	L	Pct.	ERA	G	GS	CG	ShO	Sv.	IP	H	R	ER	BB	SO
1991—	Idaho Falls (Pio.)	4	1	.800	1.37	28	0	0	0	11	39 1/3	29	9	6	19	57
—	Durham (Caro.)	0	0	...	2.45	4	0	0	0	0	7 1/3	4	3	2	4	14
1992—	Durham (Caro.)	1	2	.333	2.13	24	0	0	0	4	42 1/3	30	11	10	11	51
—	Greenville (Sou.)	3	4	.429	3.20	21	1	0	0	1	39 1/3	26	15	14	17	45
1993—	Durham (Caro.)	3	1	.750	3.00	6	5	1	1	0	30	21	10	10	6	27
—	Idaho Falls (Pio.)	2	4	.333	3.38	8	7	1	0	0	53 1/3	43	24	20	24	38
—	Richmond (I.L.)	5	3	.625	4.21	10	9	0	0	0	57 2/3	59	32	27	16	45
1994—	Richmond (I.L.)	•15	6	.714	*2.38	27	27	4	*3	0	185 2/3	159	62	49	49	137
—	Atlanta (N.L.)	0	1	.000	4.50	1	1	0	0	0	6	5	3	3	2	2
1995—	Atlanta (N.L.)	1	1	.500	6.10	9	0	0	0	0	10 1/3	13	10	7	8	5
—	Richmond (I.L.)	4	4	.500	5.10	13	11	0	0	0	65 1/3	70	39	37	17	44
1996—	Richmond (I.L.)	9	7	.563	3.38	21	21	5	1	0	133 1/3	124	59	50	36	74
—	Atlanta (N.L.)	2	2	.500	7.32	8	3	0	0	0	19 2/3	28	19	16	4	20
1997—	Richmond (I.L.)	8	11	.421	5.51	26	26	1	0	0	148 2/3	177	100	91	52	117
1998—	Louisville (I.L.)■	1	1	.500	3.90	5	5	0	0	0	30	32	19	13	15	27
—	Milwaukee (N.L.)	7	9	.438	4.96	31	20	0	0	0	138	145	81	76	47	85
1999—	Chicago (N.L.)■	0	1	.000	5.63	6	3	0	0	0	16	17	12	10	6	7
—	Iowa (PCL)	2	2	.500	6.84	15	9	0	0	1	52 2/3	67	40	40	23	41
Major League totals (5 years)		10	14	.417	5.31	55	27	0	0	0	190	208	125	112	67	119

WOODARD, STEVE — P — BREWERS

PERSONAL: Born May 15, 1975, in Hartselle, Ala. ... 6-4/217. ... Throws right, bats left. ... Full name: Steve Larry Woodard Jr.

HIGH SCHOOL: Hartselle (Ala.).

TRANSACTIONS/CAREER NOTES: Selected by Milwaukee Brewers organization in fifth round of free-agent draft (June 2, 1994). ... On disabled list (August 14-September 11, 1999).

RECORDS: Shares A.L. record for most strikeouts in first major league game—12 (July 28, 1997).

HONORS: Named Texas League Pitcher of the Year (1997).

Year	League	W	L	Pct.	ERA	G	GS	CG	ShO	Sv.	IP	H	R	ER	BB	SO
1994—	Stockton (Calif.)	8	0	1.000	2.40	15	12	2	0	0	82 2/3	68	29	22	13	85
—	Arizona Brewers (Ariz.)	•8	0	1.000	2.40	15	12	2	0	0	82 2/3	68	29	22	13	85
1995—	Beloit (Midw.)	7	4	.636	4.54	21	21	0	0	0	115	113	68	58	31	94
1996—	Stockton (Calif.)	12	9	.571	4.02	28	•28	0	0	0	*181 1/3	201	89	81	33	142
1997—	El Paso (Texas)	14	3	.824	3.17	19	19	*6	•1	0	136 1/3	136	56	48	25	97
—	Tucson (PCL)	1	0	1.000	0.00	1	1	0	0	0	7	3	0	0	1	6
—	Milwaukee (A.L.)	3	3	.500	5.15	7	7	0	0	0	36 2/3	39	25	21	6	32
1998—	Milwaukee (N.L.)	10	12	.455	4.18	34	26	0	0	0	165 2/3	170	83	77	33	135
1999—	Milwaukee (N.L.)	11	8	.579	4.52	31	29	2	0	0	185	219	101	93	36	119
A.L. totals (1 year)		3	3	.500	5.15	7	7	0	0	0	36 2/3	39	25	21	6	32
N.L. totals (2 years)		21	20	.512	4.36	65	55	2	0	0	350 2/3	389	184	170	69	254
Major League totals (3 years)		24	23	.511	4.44	72	62	2	0	0	387 1/3	428	209	191	75	286

WOODWARD, CHRIS — SS — BLUE JAYS

PERSONAL: Born June 27, 1976, in Covina, Calif. ... 6-0/173. ... Bats right, throws right. ... Full name: Christopher Michael Woodward.

HIGH SCHOOL: Northview (Covina, Calif.).

W

JUNIOR COLLEGE: Mount San Antonio (Walnut, Calif.).
TRANSACTIONS/CAREER NOTES: Selected by Toronto Blue Jays organization in 54th round of free-agent draft (June 2, 1994). ... On Syracuse disabled list (May 2-17 and May 21-June 6, 1999).
STATISTICAL NOTES: Led Pioneer League shortstops with 338 total chances in 1995.

Year Team (League)	Pos.	G	AB	R	H	2B	3B	HR	RBI	Avg.	BB	SO	SB	PO	A	E	Avg.
1995—Medicine Hat (Pio.)	SS	72	241	44	56	8	0	3	21	.232	33	41	9	*106	*202	*30	.911
1996—Hagerstown (SAL)......	SS	123	424	41	95	24	2	1	48	.224	43	70	11	*214	366	30	.951
1997—Dunedin (FSL).........	SS	91	314	38	92	13	4	1	38	.293	52	52	4	145	267	12	.972
1998—Knoxville (Sou.).........	SS	73	253	36	62	12	0	3	27	.245	26	47	3	145	220	11	.971
—Syracuse (I.L.)...........	SS	25	85	9	17	6	0	2	6	.200	7	20	1	29	69	4	.961
1999—Syracuse (I.L.).......	SS-2B	75	281	46	82	20	3	1	20	.292	38	49	4	114	200	11	.966
—Toronto (A.L.)............	SS-3B	14	26	1	6	1	0	0	2	.231	2	6	0	8	26	2	.944
Major League totals (1 year)		14	26	1	6	1	0	0	2	.231	2	6	0	8	26	2	.944

WOOLF, JASON   SS   CARDINALS

PERSONAL: Born June 6, 1977, in Miami. ... 6-1/170. ... Bats both, throws right. ... Full name: Jason D. Woolf.
HIGH SCHOOL: American (Hialeah, Fla.).
TRANSACTIONS/CAREER NOTES: Selected by St. Louis Cardinals organization in second round of free-agent draft (June 1, 1995); choice received as part of compensation for Philadelphia Phillies signing Type A free-agent 1B-OF Gregg Jefferies. ... On disabled list (April 10-22 and April 29-June 21, 1998). ... On Arkansas disabled list (April 8-19, May 24-June 14 and July 14-23, 1999).

Year Team (League)	Pos.	G	AB	R	H	2B	3B	HR	RBI	Avg.	BB	SO	SB	PO	A	E	Avg.
1995—Johnson City (Appl.) ..	SS	31	111	16	31	7	1	0	14	.279	8	21	6	49	62	26	.810
1996—Peoria (Midw.)...........	SS	108	362	68	93	12	8	1	27	.257	57	87	28	128	295	*39	.916
1997—Prince William (Caro.)	SS	70	251	59	62	11	3	6	18	.247	55	75	26	99	207	20	.939
1998—Arkansas (Texas)	SS	76	294	63	78	22	5	4	16	.265	34	84	28	116	235	20	.946
1999—Arkansas (Texas)........	SS-OF-DH	86	320	46	87	18	4	8	15	.272	28	86	11	138	209	20	.946

WORRELL, TIM   P

PERSONAL: Born July 5, 1967, in Pasadena, Calif. ... 6-4/215. ... Throws right, bats right. ... Full name: Timothy Howard Worrell. ... Brother of Todd Worrell, pitcher with St. Louis Cardinals (1985-92) and Los Angeles Dodgers (1993-97). ... Name pronounced wor-RELL.
HIGH SCHOOL: Maranatha (Sierra Madre, Calif.).
COLLEGE: Biola (Calif.).
TRANSACTIONS/CAREER NOTES: Selected by San Diego Padres organization in 20th round of free-agent draft (June 5, 1989). ... On disabled list (April 19, 1994-remainder of season). ... On San Diego disabled list (April 24-September 1, 1995); included rehabilitation assignments to Rancho Cucamonga (May 3-17 and August 1-10) and Las Vegas (May 17-June 1 and August 10-30). ... Traded by Padres with OF Trey Beamon to Detroit Tigers for P Dan Miceli, P Donne Wall and 3B Ryan Balfe (November 19, 1997). ... Traded by Tigers with OF David Roberts to Cleveland Indians for OF Geronimo Berroa (June 24, 1998). ... Traded by Indians to Oakland Athletics for a player to be named later (July 12, 1998); Indians acquired SS Adam Robinson to complete deal (July 27, 1998). ... On Oakland disabled list (July 20-August 8, 1999); included rehabilitation assignment to Modesto (August 5-8). ... Granted free agency (October 29, 1999).
STATISTICAL NOTES: Pitched 2-0 no-hit victory for Las Vegas against Phoenix (September 5, 1992).

Year League	W	L	Pct.	ERA	G	GS	CG	ShO	Sv.	IP	H	R	ER	BB	SO
1989—								Did not play.							
1990—Charleston, S.C. (SAL)	5	8	.385	4.64	20	19	3	0	0	110²/₃	120	65	57	28	68
1991—Waterloo (Midw.)	8	4	.667	3.34	14	14	3	2	0	86¹/₃	70	36	32	33	83
—High Desert (Calif.).............	5	2	.714	4.24	11	11	2	0	0	63²/₃	65	32	30	33	70
1992—Wichita (Texas)	8	6	.571	2.86	19	19	1	1	0	125²/₃	115	46	40	32	109
—Las Vegas (PCL)	4	2	.667	4.26	10	10	1	1	0	63¹/₃	61	32	30	19	32
1993—Las Vegas (PCL)	5	6	.455	5.48	15	14	2	0	0	87	102	61	53	26	89
—San Diego (N.L.)	2	7	.222	4.92	21	16	0	0	0	100²/₃	104	63	55	43	52
1994—San Diego (N.L.)	0	1	.000	3.68	3	3	0	0	0	14²/₃	9	7	6	5	14
1995—Rancho Cuca. (Calif.)	0	2	.000	5.16	9	3	0	0	1	22²/₃	25	17	13	6	17
—Las Vegas (PCL)	0	2	.000	6.00	10	3	0	0	0	24	27	21	16	17	18
—San Diego (N.L.)	1	0	1.000	4.72	9	0	0	0	0	13¹/₃	16	7	7	6	13
1996—San Diego (N.L.)	9	7	.563	3.05	50	11	0	0	1	121	109	45	41	39	99
1997—San Diego (N.L.)	4	8	.333	5.16	60	10	0	0	3	106¹/₃	116	67	61	50	81
1998—Detroit (A.L.)■	2	6	.250	5.98	15	9	0	0	0	61²/₃	66	42	41	19	47
—Cleveland (A.L.)■	0	0	...	5.06	3	0	0	0	0	5¹/₃	6	3	3	2	2
—Oakland (A.L.)■	0	1	.000	4.00	25	0	0	0	0	36	34	17	16	8	33
1999—Oakland (A.L.)	2	2	.500	4.15	53	0	0	0	0	69¹/₃	69	38	32	34	62
—Modesto (Calif.)	0	0	...	0.00	1	1	0	0	0	2	0	0	0	0	5
A.L. totals (2 years)	4	9	.308	4.80	96	9	0	0	0	172¹/₃	175	100	92	63	144
N.L. totals (5 years)	16	23	.410	4.30	143	40	0	0	4	356	354	189	170	143	259
Major League totals (7 years)	20	32	.385	4.46	239	49	0	0	4	528¹/₃	529	289	262	206	403

DIVISION SERIES RECORD

Year League	W	L	Pct.	ERA	G	GS	CG	ShO	Sv.	IP	H	R	ER	BB	SO
1996—San Diego (N.L.)	0	0	...	2.45	2	0	0	0	0	3²/₃	4	1	1	1	2

WRIGHT, JAMEY   P   BREWERS

PERSONAL: Born December 24, 1974, in Oklahoma City. ... 6-5/221. ... Throws right, bats right. ... Full name: Jamey Alan Wright.
HIGH SCHOOL: Westmoore (Oklahoma City).
TRANSACTIONS/CAREER NOTES: Selected by Colorado Rockies organization in first round (28th pick overall) of free-agent draft (June 3, 1993). ... On Colorado disabled list (May 15-June 8, 1997); included rehabilitation assignment to Salem (June 1-8). ... Traded by Rockies with

W

C Henry Blanco to Milwaukee Brewers as part of three-way deal in which Rockies received 3B Jeff Cirillo, P Scott Karl and cash from Brewers, Oakland Athletics received P Justin Miller and cash from Rockies and Brewers received P Jimmy Haynes to Athletics (December 13, 1999).

Year League	W	L	Pct.	ERA	G	GS	CG	ShO	Sv.	IP	H	R	ER	BB	SO
1993— Arizona Rockies (Ariz.)	1	3	.250	4.00	8	8	8	0	0	36	35	19	16	9	26
1994— Asheville (SAL)	7	•14	.333	5.97	28	27	2	0	0	143¹⁄₃	*188	107	*95	59	103
1995— Salem (Caro.)	10	8	.556	2.47	26	26	2	1	0	*171	160	74	47	72	95
— New Haven (East.)	0	1	.000	9.00	1	1	1	0	0	3	6	6	3	3	0
1996— New Haven (East.)	5	1	.833	0.81	7	7	1	1	0	44²⁄₃	27	7	4	12	54
— Colo. Springs (PCL)	4	2	.667	2.72	9	9	0	0	0	59²⁄₃	53	20	18	22	40
— Colorado (N.L.)	4	4	.500	4.93	16	15	0	0	0	91¹⁄₃	105	60	50	41	45
1997— Colorado (N.L.)	8	12	.400	6.25	26	26	1	0	0	149²⁄₃	198	113	104	71	59
— Salem (Caro.)	0	1	.000	9.00	1	1	0	0	0	1	1	1	1	1	1
— Colo. Springs (PCL)	1	0	1.000	1.64	2	2	0	0	0	11	9	3	2	5	11
1998— Colorado (N.L.)	9	14	.391	5.67	34	34	1	0	0	206¹⁄₃	235	143	130	95	86
1999— Colorado (N.L.)	4	3	.571	4.87	16	16	0	0	0	94¹⁄₃	110	52	51	54	49
— Colo. Springs (PCL)	5	7	.417	6.46	17	16	2	0	0	100¹⁄₃	133	87	72	38	75
Major League totals (4 years)	25	33	.431	5.57	92	91	2	0	0	541²⁄₃	648	368	335	261	239

WRIGHT, JARET   P   INDIANS

PERSONAL: Born December 29, 1975, in Anaheim, Calif. ... 6-2/230. ... Throws right, bats right. ... Full name: Jaret Samuel Wright. ... Son of Clyde Wright, pitcher with California Angels (1966-73), Milwaukee Brewers (1974) and Texas Rangers (1975).
HIGH SCHOOL: Katella (Anaheim, Calif.).
TRANSACTIONS/CAREER NOTES: Selected by Cleveland Indians organization in first round (10th pick overall) of free-agent draft (June 2, 1994). ... On disabled list (June 19-September 23, 1996). ... On suspended list (May 10-16, 1999). ... On disabled list (July 19-August 3 and August 9-September 10, 1999) including rehabilitation assignments to Buffalo (September 2) and Akron (September 6).

Year League	W	L	Pct.	ERA	G	GS	CG	ShO	Sv.	IP	H	R	ER	BB	SO
1994— Burlington (Appl.)	0	1	.000	5.40	4	4	0	0	0	13¹⁄₃	13	10	8	9	16
1995— Columbus (SAL)	5	6	.455	3.00	24	24	0	0	0	129	93	55	43	79	113
1996— Kinston (Caro.)	7	4	.636	2.50	19	19	0	0	0	101	65	32	28	55	109
1997— Cleveland (A.L.)	8	3	.727	4.38	16	16	0	0	0	90¹⁄₃	81	45	44	35	63
— Buffalo (A.A.)	4	1	.800	1.80	7	7	1	1	0	45	30	16	9	19	47
— Akron (East.)	3	3	.500	3.67	8	8	1	0	0	54	43	26	22	23	59
1998— Cleveland (A.L.)	12	10	.545	4.72	32	32	1	1	0	192²⁄₃	207	109	101	87	140
1999— Cleveland (A.L.)	8	10	.444	6.06	26	26	0	0	0	133²⁄₃	144	99	90	77	91
— Buffalo (I.L.)	0	0	...	0.00	1	1	0	0	0	3	0	0	0	0	4
— Akron (East.)	1	0	1.000	0.00	1	1	0	0	0	5	3	0	0	1	6
Major League totals (3 years)	28	23	.549	5.08	74	74	1	1	0	416²⁄₃	432	253	235	199	294

DIVISION SERIES RECORD

Year League	W	L	Pct.	ERA	G	GS	CG	ShO	Sv.	IP	H	R	ER	BB	SO
1997— Cleveland (A.L.)	2	0	1.000	3.97	2	2	0	0	0	11¹⁄₃	11	6	5	7	10
1998— Cleveland (A.L.)	0	1	.000	12.46	1	1	0	0	0	4¹⁄₃	7	6	6	2	6
1999— Cleveland (A.L.)	0	1	.000	22.50	1	0	0	0	0	2	4	5	5	1	1
Division series totals (3 years)	2	2	.500	8.15	4	3	0	0	0	17²⁄₃	22	17	16	10	17

CHAMPIONSHIP SERIES RECORD

RECORDS: Shares single-game record for most home runs allowed—3 (October 12, 1997).

Year League	W	L	Pct.	ERA	G	GS	CG	ShO	Sv.	IP	H	R	ER	BB	SO
1997— Cleveland (A.L.)	0	0	...	15.00	1	1	0	0	0	3	6	5	5	2	3
1998— Cleveland (A.L.)	0	1	.000	8.10	2	1	0	0	0	6²⁄₃	7	6	6	8	4
Champ. series totals (2 years)	0	1	.000	10.24	3	2	0	0	0	9²⁄₃	13	11	11	10	7

WORLD SERIES RECORD

Year League	W	L	Pct.	ERA	G	GS	CG	ShO	Sv.	IP	H	R	ER	BB	SO
1997— Cleveland (A.L.)	1	0	1.000	2.92	2	2	0	0	0	12¹⁄₃	7	4	4	10	12

WRIGHT, RON   1B   REDS

W

PERSONAL: Born January 21, 1976, in Delta, Utah. ... 6-1/230. ... Bats right, throws right. ... Full name: Ronald Wade Wright.
HIGH SCHOOL: Kamiakin (Kennewick, Wash.).
TRANSACTIONS/CAREER NOTES: Selected by Atlanta Braves organization in seventh round of free-agent draft (June 2, 1994). ... Traded by Braves with OF Corey Pointer and a player to be named later to Pittsburgh Pirates for P Denny Neagle (August 28, 1996); Pirates acquired P Jason Schmidt to complete deal (August 30, 1996). ... On Calgary disabled list (July 24-September 2, 1997). ... On Nashville disabled list (April 29-September 8, 1998); included rehabilitation assignment to Gulf Coast Pirates (August 3-6). ... On Altoona disabled list (April 26-May 3 and May 23, 1999-remainder of season). ... Claimed on waivers by Cincinnati Reds (October 14, 1999).
STATISTICAL NOTES: Led South Atlantic League first baseman with 1,152 total chances in 1995.

Year Team (League)	Pos.	G	AB	R	H	2B	3B	HR	RBI	Avg.	BB	SO	SB	PO	A	E	Avg.
1994— GCt Braves (GCL)	1B	45	169	10	29	9	0	1	16	.172	10	21	1	382	31	6	.986
1995— Macon (SAL)	1B	135	537	93	143	23	1	•32	104	.266	62	118	2	1035	*99	18	.984
1996— Durham (Caro.)	1B	66	240	47	66	15	2	20	62	.275	37	71	1	494	34	7	.987
— Greenville (Sou.)	1B-DH	63	232	39	59	11	1	16	52	.254	38	73	1	434	45	6	.988
— Carolina (Sou.)■	1B	4	14	1	2	0	0	0	0	.143	2	7	0	32	0	2	.941
1997— Calgary (PCL)	1B-DH	91	336	50	102	31	0	16	63	.304	24	81	0	610	44	3	.995
1998— Nashville (PCL)	1B-DH	17	56	6	12	3	0	0	9	.214	9	18	0	125	11	2	.986
— GC Pirates (GCL)	DH-1B	3	10	4	6	0	0	2	5	.600	2	0	0	11	0	0	1.000
1999— Altoona (East.)	DH-1B	24	80	2	17	6	0	0	4	.213	9	27	0	94	12	1	.991

PERSONAL: Born June 22, 1974, in Campina Del Seibo, Dominican Republic. ... 6-4/230. ... Throws right, bats right. ... Full name: Esteban Luis Yan.

HIGH SCHOOL: Escuela Hicayagua (Dominican Republic).

TRANSACTIONS/CAREER NOTES: Signed as non-drafted free agent by Atlanta Braves organization (November 21, 1990). ... Traded by Braves with OF Roberto Kelly and OF Tony Tarasco to Montreal Expos for OF Marquis Grissom (April 6, 1995). ... Contract sold by Expos organization to Baltimore Orioles organization (April 6, 1996). ... Selected by Tampa Bay Devil Rays in first round (18th pick overall) of expansion draft (November 18, 1997). ... On Tampa Bay disabled list (June 17-July 15, 1999); included rehabilitation assignment to St. Petersburg (July 10-15).

STATISTICAL NOTES: Led South Atlantic League with six balks in 1994.

Year League	W	L	Pct.	ERA	G	GS	CG	ShO	Sv.	IP	H	R	ER	BB	SO
1991—San Pedro (DSL)	4	1	.800	3.63	18	11	0	0	0	72	61	36	29	26	34
1992—San Pedro (DSL)	12	3	.800	1.32	16	16	7	4	0	115²/₃	85	37	17	23	86
1993—Danville (Appl.)	4	7	.364	3.03	14	.14	0	0	0	71¹/₃	73	46	24	24	50
1994—Macon (SAL)	11	12	.478	3.27	28	•28	4	•3	0	170²/₃	155	85	62	34	121
1995—W.P. Beach (FSL)■	6	8	.429	3.07	24	21	1	0	1	137²/₃	139	63	47	33	89
1996—Bowie (East.)■	0	2	.000	5.63	9	1	0	0	0	16	18	12	10	8	15
— Rochester (I.L.)	5	4	.556	4.27	22	10	0	0	1	71²/₃	75	37	34	18	61
— Baltimore (A.L.)	0	0	...	5.79	4	0	0	0	0	9¹/₃	13	7	6	3	7
1997—Rochester (I.L.)	11	5	.688	3.10	34	12	0	0	2	119	107	54	41	37	131
— Baltimore (A.L.)	0	1	.000	15.83	3	2	0	0	0	9²/₃	20	18	17	7	4
1998—Tampa Bay (A.L.)■	5	4	.556	3.86	64	0	0	0	1	88²/₃	78	41	38	41	77
1999—Tampa Bay (A.L.)	3	4	.429	5.90	50	1	0	0	0	61	77	41	40	32	46
— St. Petersburg (FSL)	0	0	...	0.00	2	2	0	0	0	4	3	1	0	1	0
Major League totals (4 years)	8	9	.471	5.39	121	3	0	0	1	168²/₃	188	107	101	83	134

PERSONAL: Born December 4, 1975, in Lima, Pa. ... 6-3/234. ... Throws left, bats left. ... Full name: Harvey Edward Yarnall.

HIGH SCHOOL: St. Thomas Aquinas (Fort Lauderdale, Fla.).

COLLEGE: Louisiana State.

TRANSACTIONS/CAREER NOTES: Selected by New York Mets organization in third round of free-agent draft (June 4, 1996). ... Traded by Mets with OF Preston Wilson and P Geoff Goetz to Florida Marlins for C Mike Piazza (May 22, 1998). ... Traded by Marlins with P Mark Johnson and P Todd Noel to New York Yankees for 3B Mike Lowell (February 1, 1999).

HONORS: Named International League Most Valuable Pitcher (1999).

Year League	W	L	Pct.	ERA	G	GS	CG	ShO	Sv.	IP	H	R	ER	BB	SO
1998—Binghamton (East.)	7	0	1.000	0.39	7	7	0	0	0	46²/₃	20	5	2	17	52
— Portland (East.)■	2	0	1.000	2.93	2	2	0	0	0	15¹/₃	9	5	5	4	15
— Charlotte (I.L.)	4	5	.444	6.20	15	13	2	0	0	69²/₃	79	60	48	39	47
1999—Columbus (I.L.)■	13	4	.765	•3.47	23	23	1	1	0	145¹/₃	136	61	56	57	146
— New York (A.L.)	1	0	1.000	3.71	5	2	0	0	0	17	17	8	7	10	13
Major League totals (1 year)	1	0	1.000	3.71	5	2	0	0	0	17	17	8	7	10	13

PERSONAL: Born April 20, 1965, in Osaka, Japan. ... 6-2/210. ... Throws right, bats right.

HIGH SCHOOL: Minoshima (Japan).

TRANSACTIONS/CAREER NOTES: Played for Kintetsu Buffaloes of Japan Pacific League (1985-94). ... Played for Yakult Swallows of Japan Central League (1995-97). ... Signed as non-drafted free agent by New York Mets (January 13, 1998). ... Traded by Mets to Colorado Rockies for P Bobby M. Jones and P Lariel Gonzalez (January 14, 2000).

Year League	W	L	Pct.	ERA	G	GS	CG	ShO	Sv.	IP	H	R	ER	BB	SO
1985—Kintetsu (Jap. Pac.)	0	1	.000	21.00	2	...	...	...	0	3	...	...	7	3	1
1986—Kintetsu (Jap. Pac.)	0	0	...	23.14	2	...	...	...	0	2¹/₃	...	...	6	2	2
1987—Kintetsu (Jap. Pac.)	2	1	.667	4.75	13	...	...	...	0	36	...	...	19	12	23
1988—Kintetsu (Jap. Pac.)	10	2	.833	2.69	50	...	...	...	24	80¹/₃	...	...	24	44	44
1989—Kintetsu (Jap. Pac.)	5	5	.500	2.99	47	...	...	...	20	84¹/₃	...	...	28	37	44
1990—Kintetsu (Jap. Pac.)	8	9	.471	3.39	45	...	...	...	15	74¹/₃	...	...	28	30	55
1991—Kintetsu (Jap. Pac.)	2	1	.667	3.42	21	...	...	...	2	26¹/₃	...	...	10	6	13
1992—Kintetsu (Jap. Pac.)	1	0	1.000	2.31	9	...	...	...	0	11²/₃	...	...	3	2	4
1993—Kintetsu (Jap. Pac.)	5	5	.500	2.67	22	...	...	...	0	104²/₃	...	...	31	25	66
1994—Kintetsu (Jap. Pac.)	7	7	.500	5.47	21	...	...	...	0	97	...	...	59	37	42
1995—Yakult (Jap. Cen.)■	10	7	.588	3.12	25	...	...	...	0	147¹/₃	...	...	51	39	91
1996—Yakult (Jap. Cen.)	10	7	.588	3.24	25	9	...	...	0	180¹/₃	...	...	65	47	145
1997—Yakult (Jap. Cen.)	13	6	.684	2.99	28	26	6	2	0	174¹/₃	149	61	58	48	104
1998—New York (N.L.)■	6	8	.429	3.93	29	29	1	0	0	171²/₃	166	79	75	53	117
1999—New York (N.L.)	12	8	.600	4.40	31	29	1	0	0	174	168	86	85	58	105
Major League totals (2 years)	18	16	.529	4.17	60	58	2	0	0	345²/₃	334	165	160	111	222

DIVISION SERIES RECORD

Year League	W	L	Pct.	ERA	G	GS	CG	ShO	Sv.	IP	H	R	ER	BB	SO
1999—New York (N.L.)	0	0	...	6.75	1	1	0	0	0	5¹/₃	6	4	4	0	3

CHAMPIONSHIP SERIES RECORD

Year League	W	L	Pct.	ERA	G	GS	CG	ShO	Sv.	IP	H	R	ER	BB	SO
1999—New York (N.L.)	0	1	.000	4.70	2	2	0	0	0	7²/₃	9	4	4	3	4

Y

PERSONAL: Born November 3, 1971, in Smyrna, Texas. ... 6-4/210. ... Throws left, bats right. ... Full name: Daniel Bracey Young Jr.
HIGH SCHOOL: Cannon County (Woodbury, Tenn.).
JUNIOR COLLEGE: Aquinas College (Tenn.).
TRANSACTIONS/CAREER NOTES: Selected by Houston Astros organization in 83rd round of free-agent draft (June 4, 1990). ... Released by Astros (April 1, 1994). ... Signed by Pittsburgh Pirates organization (April 3, 1994). ... Selected by Chicago Cubs organization from Pirates organization in Rule 5 minor league draft (December 15, 1997). ... On West Tenn disabled list (April 8-May 6 and May 13-22, 1999).

Year — League	W	L	Pct.	ERA	G	GS	CG	ShO	Sv.	IP	H	R	ER	BB	SO
1991—Gulf Coast Astros (GCL).....	1	4	.200	7.99	13	7	0	0	0	32 2/3	32	33	29	39	41
1992—Asheville (SAL)................	3	10	.231	4.28	20	20	0	0	0	94 2/3	106	65	45	70	64
1993—Asheville (SAL)................	5	14	.263	6.12	32	24	2	1	0	142 2/3	174	*114	*97	95	101
1994—Augusta (SAL)■..............	2	5	.286	3.38	21	9	0	0	0	66 2/3	58	32	25	33	73
—Salem (Caro.)..................	2	0	1.000	7.71	10	0	0	0	0	18 2/3	32	17	16	9	12
1995—Lynchburg (Caro.)..........	2	4	.333	7.40	24	2	0	0	0	41 1/3	52	37	34	27	34
—Augusta (SAL)................	1	0	1.000	2.51	6	2	0	0	0	14 1/3	9	6	4	16	11
1996—Augusta (SAL)................	0	4	.000	5.88	22	1	0	0	2	33 2/3	36	33	22	29	36
1997—Lynchburg (Caro.)..........	0	0	...	5.92	15	0	0	0	0	24 1/3	27	17	16	14	22
—Augusta (SAL)................	0	2	.000	9.82	3	2	0	0	0	7 1/3	16	15	8	2	5
1998—Daytona (FSL)■.............	1	1	.500	5.19	7	0	0	0	0	8 2/3	9	5	5	8	6
—West Tenn (Sou.)............	0	2	.000	3.67	23	1	0	0	0	27	22	13	11	15	20
—Iowa (PCL)	0	0	...	0.00	2	0	0	0	0	2	1	0	0	1	1
1999—West Tenn (Sou.)	3	5	.375	3.28	27	8	0	0	0	60 1/3	48	25	22	38	67

PERSONAL: Born October 11, 1973, in Vicksburg, Miss. ... 6-2/235. ... Bats both, throws right. ... Full name: Dmitri Dell Young. ... Name pronounced duh-MEE-tree.
HIGH SCHOOL: Rio Mesa (Oxnard, Calif.).
TRANSACTIONS/CAREER NOTES: Selected by St. Louis Cardinals organization in first round (fourth pick overall) of free-agent draft (June 3, 1991). ... On disabled list (June 2-9, 1994). ... On Arkansas suspended list (August 1-11 and August 17-27, 1995). ... On Louisville disabled list (July 14-24, 1996). ... On St. Louis disabled list (May 11-29, 1997); included rehabilitation assignment to Louisville (May 25-29). ... Traded by Cardinals to Cincinnati Reds for P Jeff Brantley (November 10, 1997). ... Selected by Tampa Bay Devil Rays in first round (16th pick overall) of expansion draft (November 18, 1997). ... Traded by Devil Rays to Reds (November 18, 1997), completing deal in which Reds traded OF Mike Kelly to Devil Rays for a player to be named later (November 11, 1997).
STATISTICAL NOTES: Led Texas League with 14 intentional bases on balls received in 1994. ... Led Texas League first basemen with 15 errors in 1994. ... Tied for American Association lead with eight bases on balls received in 1996. ... Led American Association first basemen with 1,182 total chances and 102 double plays in 1996.

Year — Team (League)	Pos.	G	AB	R	H	2B	3B	HR	RBI	Avg.	BB	SO	SB	PO	A	E	Avg.
1991—Johnson City (Appl.) ..	3B	37	129	22	33	10	0	2	22	.256	21	28	2	19	49	5	.932
1992—Springfield (Midw.)	3B	135	493	74	153	*36	6	14	72	.310	51	44	14	66	239	42	.879
1993—St. Petersburg (FSL) ..	3B-1B	69	270	31	85	13	3	5	43	.315	24	28	3	260	90	10	.972
—Arkansas (Texas)........	1B-3B	45	166	13	41	11	2	3	21	.247	9	29	4	348	29	7	.982
1994—Arkansas (Texas)........	OF-1B	125	453	53	123	33	2	8	54	.272	36	60	0	485	44	†16	.971
1995—Arkansas (Texas)........	OF-DH	97	367	54	107	18	6	10	62	.292	30	46	2	116	5	9	.931
—Louisville (A.A.)..........	OF	2	7	3	2	0	0	0	0	.286	1	1	0	3	0	1	.750
1996—Louisville (A.A.)..........	1B	122	459	*90	153	31	8	15	64	*.333	34	67	16	*1091	83	8	.993
—St. Louis (N.L.)..........	1B	16	29	3	7	0	0	0	2	.241	4	5	0	39	1	1	.976
1997—St. Louis (N.L.)..........	1B-OF-DH	110	333	38	86	14	3	5	34	.258	38	63	6	641	47	13	.981
—Louisville (A.A.)..........	OF-1B	24	84	10	23	7	0	4	14	.274	13	15	1	64	2	1	.985
1998—Cincinnati (N.L.)■......	OF-1B	144	536	81	166	48	1	14	83	.310	47	94	2	458	25	12	.976
1999—Cincinnati (N.L.)	OF-1B-DH	127	373	63	112	30	2	14	56	.300	30	71	3	216	5	4	.982
Major League totals (4 years)		397	1271	185	371	92	6	33	175	.292	119	233	11	1354	78	30	.979

DIVISION SERIES RECORD

Year Team (League)	Pos.	G	AB	R	H	2B	3B	HR	RBI	Avg.	BB	SO	SB	PO	A	E	Avg.
1996—St. Louis (N.L.)..........					Did not play.												

CHAMPIONSHIP SERIES RECORD

Year Team (League)	Pos.	G	AB	R	H	2B	3B	HR	RBI	Avg.	BB	SO	SB	PO	A	E	Avg.
1996—St. Louis (N.L.)..........	PH-1B	4	7	1	2	0	1	0	2	.286	0	2	0	11	1	0	1.000

PERSONAL: Born May 18, 1967, in New Brunswick, N.J. ... 5-8/175. ... Bats right, throws right. ... Full name: Eric Orlando Young.
HIGH SCHOOL: New Brunswick (N.J.).
COLLEGE: Rutgers.
TRANSACTIONS/CAREER NOTES: Selected by Los Angeles Dodgers organization in 43rd round of free-agent draft (June 5, 1989). ... Selected by Colorado Rockies in first round (11th pick overall) of expansion draft (November 17, 1992). ... On Colorado disabled list (March 22-April 22, 1996); included rehabilitation assignments to New Haven (April 5-10), Salem (April 10-13) and Colorado Springs (April 13-22). ... Traded by Rockies to Dodgers for P Pedro Astacio (August 19, 1997). ... On Los Angeles disabled list (July 13-31, 1998). ... On Los Angeles disabled list (July 24-August 13, 1999); included rehabilitation assignment to San Bernardino (August 8-13). ... Traded by Dodgers with P Ismael Valdes to Chicago Cubs for P Terry Adams, P Chad Ricketts and a player to be named later (December 12, 1999); Dodgers acquired P Brian Stephenson to complete deal (December 16, 1999).
RECORDS: Shares major league record for most stolen bases in one inning—3 (June 30, 1996, third inning).

Y

HONORS: Named second baseman on THE SPORTING NEWS N.L. All-Star team (1996). ... Named second baseman on THE SPORTING NEWS N.L. Silver Slugger team (1996).
STATISTICAL NOTES: Led Florida State League second basemen with 24 errors in 1990. ... Led Texas League in caught stealing with 26 in 1991. ... Led Texas League second basemen with .974 fielding percentage in 1991. ... Tied for N.L. lead in errors by second baseman with 11 in 1995. ... Hit three home runs in one game (May 10, 1996). ... Led N.L. in caught stealing with 19 in 1996. ... Led N.L. second basemen with 109 double plays in 1996 and 111 in 1997. ... Led N.L. in caught stealing with 22 in 1999.
MISCELLANEOUS: Holds Colorado Rockies all-time record for most stolen bases (180).

Year	Team (League)	Pos.	G	AB	R	H	2B	3B	HR	RBI	Avg.	BB	SO	SB	PO	A	E	Avg.
1989	GC Dodgers (GCL)	2B	56	197	53	65	11	5	2	22	.330	33	16	*41	104	128	*15	.939
1990	Vero Beach (FSL)	2B-OF	127	460	*101	132	23	7	2	50	.287	69	35	*76	156	218	†25	.937
1991	San Antonio (Texas) ...	2B-OF	127	461	82	129	17	4	3	35	.280	67	36	*70	206	282	13	†.974
	— Albuquerque (PCL).....	2B	1	5	0	2	0	0	0	0	.400	0	0	0	1	2	0	1.000
1992	Albuquerque (PCL)	2B	94	350	61	118	16	5	3	49	.337	33	18	28	210	287	*20	.961
	— Los Angeles (N.L.)	2B	49	132	9	34	1	0	1	11	.258	8	9	6	85	114	9	.957
1993	Colorado (N.L.)■	2B-OF	144	490	82	132	16	8	3	42	.269	63	41	42	254	230	18	.964
1994	Colorado (N.L.)	OF-2B	90	228	37	62	13	1	7	30	.272	38	17	18	97	4	2	.981
1995	Colorado (N.L.)	2B-OF	120	366	68	116	21	•9	6	36	.317	49	29	35	180	230	11	.974
1996	New Haven (East.)	2B	3	15	0	1	0	0	0	0	.067	0	3	0	9	5	0	1.000
	— Salem (Caro.)	2B	3	10	2	3	3	0	0	0	.300	3	1	2	8	6	2	.875
	— Colo. Springs (PCL) ...	2B	7	23	4	6	1	1	0	3	.261	5	1	0	15	18	3	.917
	— Colorado (N.L.)	2B	141	568	113	184	23	4	8	74	.324	47	31	*53	340	431	12	.985
1997	Colorado (N.L.)	2B	118	468	78	132	29	6	6	45	.282	57	37	32	258	414	15	.978
	— Los Angeles (N.L.)■ ..	2B	37	154	28	42	4	2	2	16	.273	14	17	13	60	79	3	.979
1998	Los Angeles (N.L.)	2B-DH	117	452	78	129	24	1	8	43	.285	45	32	42	225	304	13	.976
1999	Los Angeles (N.L.)	2B	119	456	73	128	24	2	2	41	.281	63	26	51	216	321	9	.984
	— San Bern. (Calif.)	2B	3	12	0	3	0	0	0	0	.250	0	2	0	3	7	2	.833
Major League totals (8 years)			935	3314	566	959	155	33	43	338	.289	384	239	292	1715	2127	92	.977

DIVISION SERIES RECORD

Year	Team (League)	Pos.	G	AB	R	H	2B	3B	HR	RBI	Avg.	BB	SO	SB	PO	A	E	Avg.
1995	Colorado (N.L.)	2B	4	16	3	7	1	0	1	2	.438	2	2	1	8	13	3	.875

ALL-STAR GAME RECORD

Year	League	Pos.	AB	R	H	2B	3B	HR	RBI	Avg.	BB	SO	SB	PO	A	E	Avg.
1996	National	PR-2B	1	0	0	0	0	0	0	.000	0	0	0	2	1	0	1.000

YOUNG, ERNIE — OF — CARDINALS

PERSONAL: Born July 8, 1969, in Chicago. ... 6-1/234. ... Bats right, throws right. ... Full name: Ernest Wesley Young.
HIGH SCHOOL: Mendel Catholic (Chicago).
COLLEGE: Lewis University (Ill.).
TRANSACTIONS/CAREER NOTES: Selected by Oakland Athletics organization in 10th round of free-agent draft (June 4, 1990). ... On disabled list (July 11, 1992-remainder of season). ... Traded by A's to Kansas City Royals for cash (March 17, 1998). ... On Kansas City disabled list (May 22-June 15, 1998); included rehabilitation assignment to Omaha (June 5-15). ... Granted free agency (October 15, 1998). ... Signed by Arizona Diamondbacks organization (December 17, 1998). ... Released by Diamondbacks (November 22, 1999). ... Signed by St. Louis Cardinals organization (January 19, 2000).
STATISTICAL NOTES: Led California League with .635 slugging percentage in 1993.

Year	Team (League)	Pos.	G	AB	R	H	2B	3B	HR	RBI	Avg.	BB	SO	SB	PO	A	E	Avg.
1990	S. Oregon (N'west.)....	OF	50	168	34	47	6	2	6	23	.280	29	53	4	62	5	2	.971
1991	Madison (Midw.)	OF	114	362	75	92	19	2	15	71	.254	58	115	20	204	9	7	.968
1992	Modesto (Calif.)	OF	74	253	55	63	12	4	11	33	.249	47	74	11	126	11	6	.958
1993	Modesto (Calif.)	OF	85	301	83	92	18	6	23	71	.306	72	92	23	178	8	3	.984
	— Huntsville (Sou.)	OF-DH	45	120	26	25	5	0	5	15	.208	24	36	8	97	8	4	.963
1994	Huntsville (Sou.)	OF-DH	72	257	45	89	19	4	14	55	.346	37	45	5	98	13	2	.982
	— Oakland (A.L.)	OF-DH	11	30	2	2	1	0	0	3	.067	1	8	0	22	1	1	.958
	— Tacoma (PCL)	OF-DH	29	102	19	29	4	0	6	16	.284	13	27	0	53	2	2	.965
1995	Edmonton (PCL)	OF-DH	95	347	70	96	21	4	15	72	.277	49	73	2	194	7	6	.971
	— Oakland (A.L.)	OF	26	50	9	10	3	0	2	5	.200	8	12	0	35	0	2	.946
1996	Oakland (A.L.)	OF	141	462	72	112	19	4	19	64	.242	52	118	7	353	8	1	.997
1997	Oakland (A.L.)	OF	71	175	22	39	7	0	5	15	.223	19	57	1	135	4	4	.972
	— Edmonton (PCL)	OF-DH	54	195	39	63	10	0	9	45	.323	37	46	5	100	5	1	.991
1998	Kansas City (A.L.)■ ...	OF	25	53	2	10	3	0	1	3	.189	2	9	2	43	2	0	1.000
	— Omaha (PCL)	OF-DH	79	297	58	97	13	1	22	55	.327	29	68	6	174	10	2	.989
1999	Arizona (N.L.)■	OF	6	11	1	2	0	0	0	0	.182	3	2	0	10	1	0	1.000
	— Tucson (PCL)	OF-DH	126	453	78	133	25	1	30	95	.294	57	129	4	142	11	2	.987
American League totals (5 years)			274	770	107	173	33	4	27	90	.225	82	204	10	588	15	8	.987
National League totals (1 year)			6	11	1	2	0	0	0	0	.182	3	2	0	10	1	0	1.000
Major League totals (6 years)			280	781	108	175	33	4	27	90	.224	85	206	10	598	16	8	.987

YOUNG, KEVIN — 1B — PIRATES

Y

PERSONAL: Born June 16, 1969, in Alpena, Mich. ... 6-3/222. ... Bats right, throws right. ... Full name: Kevin Stacey Young.
HIGH SCHOOL: Washington (Kansas City, Kan.).
JUNIOR COLLEGE: Kansas City Kansas Community College.
COLLEGE: Southern Mississippi.

TRANSACTIONS/CAREER NOTES: Selected by Pittsburgh Pirates organization in seventh round of free-agent draft (June 4, 1990). ... On Pittsburgh disabled list (July 24-August 8, 1995). ... Released by Pirates (March 26, 1996). ... Signed by Kansas City Royals organization (April 1, 1996). ... Released by Royals (December 5, 1996). ... Signed by Pirates (March 31, 1997).

STATISTICAL NOTES: Tied for Southern League lead in errors by third baseman with 26 in 1991. ... Tied for American Association lead in being hit by pitch with 11 in 1992. ... Led American Association third basemen with 300 assists, 32 errors, 436 total chances and 41 double plays in 1992. ... Led N.L. first basemen with .998 fielding percentage in 1993. ... Had 15-game hitting streak (April 23-May 8, 1999). ... Led N.L. first basemen with 1,533 total chances in 1999. ... Career major league grand slams: 2.

							BATTING								FIELDING		
Year	Team (League)	Pos.	G	AB	R	H	2B	3B	HR	RBI	Avg.	BB	SO	SB	PO	A	E	Avg.
1990— Welland (NY-P)		SS	72	238	46	58	16	2	5	30	.244	31	36	10	*79	118	26	.883
1991— Salem (Caro.)		3B	56	201	38	63	12	4	6	28	.313	20	34	3	54	93	12	.925
— Carolina (Sou.)		3B-1B	75	263	36	90	19	6	3	33	.342	15	38	9	157	116	‡28	.907
— Buffalo (A.A.)		3B-1B	4	9	1	2	1	0	0	2	.222	0	0	1	6	6	2	.857
1992— Buffalo (A.A.)		3B-1B	137	490	*91	154	29	6	8	65	.314	67	67	18	129	†313	†32	.932
— Pittsburgh (N.L.)		3B-1B	10	7	2	4	0	0	0	4	.571	2	0	1	3	1	1	.800
1993— Pittsburgh (N.L.)		1B-3B	141	449	38	106	24	3	6	47	.236	36	82	2	1122	112	3	†.998
1994— Pittsburgh (N.L.)		1B-3B-OF	59	122	15	25	7	2	1	11	.205	8	34	0	179	45	3	.987
— Buffalo (A.A.)		3B-1B	60	228	26	63	14	5	5	27	.276	15	45	6	59	162	4	.982
1995— Calgary (PCL)		3B-1B-DH	45	163	24	58	23	1	8	34	.356	15	21	6	144	85	12	.950
— Pittsburgh (N.L.)		3B-1B	56	181	13	42	9	0	6	22	.232	8	53	1	58	110	12	.933
1996— Omaha (A.A.)■		1B-3B-DH	50	186	29	57	11	1	13	46	.306	12	41	3	280	45	5	.985
— Kansas City (A.L.)		1B-OF-3B-DH	55	132	20	32	6	0	8	23	.242	11	32	3	199	19	1	.995
1997— Pittsburgh (N.L.)■		1B-3B-OF	97	333	59	100	18	3	18	74	.300	16	89	11	644	66	5	.993
1998— Pittsburgh (N.L.)		1B	159	592	88	160	40	2	27	108	.270	44	127	15	*1334	80	8	.994
1999— Pittsburgh (N.L.)		1B	156	584	103	174	41	6	26	106	.298	75	124	22	*1413	97	*23	.985
American League totals (1 year)			55	132	20	32	6	0	8	23	.242	11	32	3	199	19	1	.995
National League totals (7 years)			678	2268	318	611	139	16	84	372	.269	189	509	52	4753	511	55	.990
Major League totals (8 years)			733	2400	338	643	145	16	92	395	.268	200	541	55	4952	530	56	.990

YOUNG, MIKE　　　　2B/SS　　　　BLUE JAYS

PERSONAL: Born October 19, 1976, in Covina, Calif. ... 6-1/175. ... Bats right, throws right. ... Full name: Michael B. Young.
HIGH SCHOOL: Bishop Amat (La Puente, Calif.).
COLLEGE: UC Santa Barbara.
TRANSACTIONS/CAREER NOTES: Selected by Toronto Blue Jays organization in fifth round of free-agent draft (June 3, 1997).
STATISTICAL NOTES: Led South Atlantic League second basemen with .978 fielding percentage in 1998.

							BATTING								FIELDING		
Year	Team (League)	Pos.	G	AB	R	H	2B	3B	HR	RBI	Avg.	BB	SO	SB	PO	A	E	Avg.
1997— St. Catharines (NY-P)		SS-2B	74	276	49	85	18	3	9	48	.308	33	59	9	115	199	18	.946
1998— Hagerstown (SAL)		2B-SS-OF	*140	522	86	147	33	5	16	87	.282	55	96	16	216	341	13	†.977
1999— Dunedin (FSL)		2B-SS	129	495	86	155	•36	3	5	83	.313	61	78	30	163	375	22	.961

YOUNG, TIM　　　　P　　　　RED SOX

PERSONAL: Born October 15, 1973, in Gulfport, Miss. ... 5-9/170. ... Throws left, bats left. ... Full name: Timothy R. Young.
HIGH SCHOOL: Liberty County (Bristol, Fla.).
JUNIOR COLLEGE: Chipola Junior College (Fla.).
COLLEGE: Alabama.
TRANSACTIONS/CAREER NOTES: Selected by Montreal Expos organization in 19th round of free-agent draft (June 4, 1996). ... Granted free agency (December 21, 1998). ... Signed by Boston Red Sox organization (February 3, 1999). ... On Pawtucket disabled list (April 8-June 5, 1999).

Year	League	W	L	Pct.	ERA	G	GS	CG	ShO	Sv.	IP	H	R	ER	BB	SO
1996— Vermont (NY-P)		1	0	1.000	0.31	27	0	0	0	18	29 1/3	14	1	1	4	46
1997— Cape Fear (SAL)		1	1	.500	1.50	45	0	0	0	18	54	33	12	9	15	66
— West Palm Beach (FSL)		0	0	...	0.57	11	0	0	0	5	15 2/3	8	1	1	4	13
— Harrisburg (East.)		0	0	...	0.00	1	0	0	0	0	2	1	0	0	0	3
1998— Harrisburg (East.)		3	3	.500	3.79	26	0	0	0	3	35 2/3	28	17	15	10	52
— Ottawa (I.L.)		1	1	.500	2.03	20	0	0	0	2	26 2/3	26	14	6	12	34
— Montreal (N.L.)		0	0	...	6.00	10	0	0	0	0	6	6	4	4	4	7
1999— Trenton (East.)■		4	4	.500	4.37	31	0	0	0	2	45 1/3	38	26	22	26	52
Major League totals (1 year)		0	0	...	6.00	10	0	0	0	0	6	6	4	4	4	7

ZAUN, GREGG　　　　C　　　　TIGERS

PERSONAL: Born April 14, 1971, in Glendale, Calif. ... 5-10/190. ... Bats both, throws right. ... Full name: Gregory Owen Zaun. ... Nephew of Rick Dempsey, manager, Norfolk Tides and catcher with six major league teams (1969-92).
HIGH SCHOOL: St. Francis (La Canada, Calif.).
TRANSACTIONS/CAREER NOTES: Selected by Baltimore Orioles organization in 17th round of free-agent draft (June 5, 1989). ... On Bowie disabled list (June 17-July 15, 1993). ... Traded by Orioles to Florida Marlins (August 23, 1996), completing deal in which Marlins traded P Terry Mathews to Orioles for a player to be named later (August 21, 1996). ... Traded by Marlins to Texas Rangers for a player to be named later or cash (November 23, 1998); Marlins received cash to complete deal (April 15, 1999). ... Traded by Rangers with OF Juan Gonzalez and P Danny Patterson to Detroit Tigers for P Justin Thompson, P Francisco Cordero, OF Gabe Kapler, C Bill Haselman, 2B Frank Catalanotto and P Alan Webb (November 2, 1999).
STATISTICAL NOTES: Led Appalachian League catchers with 460 putouts and 501 total chances in 1990. ... Led Midwest League catchers with 796 total chances in 1991. ... Led Carolina League catchers with 746 putouts, 91 assists, 18 errors, 855 total chances and 10 double plays in 1992. ... Led International League catchers with 841 total chances and 11 double plays in 1994. ... Tied for N.L. lead with 12 double plays by catcher in 1998.

								BATTING								FIELDING		
Year	Team (League)	Pos.	G	AB	R	H	2B	3B	HR	RBI	Avg.	BB	SO	SB	PO	A	E	Avg.
1990—	Wausau (Midw.)	C	37	100	3	13	0	1	1	7	.130	7	17	0	270	26	3	.990
	—Bluefield (Appl.)	C-3B-SS-P	61	184	29	55	5	2	2	21	.299	23	15	5	†462	34	10	.980
1991—	Kane County (Midw.)..	C	113	409	67	112	17	5	4	51	.274	50	41	4	*697	83	16	.980
1992—	Frederick (Caro.)	C-2B	108	383	54	96	18	6	6	52	.251	42	45	3	†746	†91	†18	.979
1993—	Bowie (East.)..............	C-DH-2-3-P	79	258	25	79	10	0	3	38	.306	27	26	4	423	51	10	.979
	—Rochester (I.L.)..........	C	21	78	10	20	4	2	1	11	.256	6	11	0	141	18	4	.975
1994—	Rochester (I.L.)..........	C	123	388	61	92	16	4	7	43	.237	56	72	4	*750	82	9	*.989
1995—	Rochester (I.L.)..........	C-DH	42	140	26	41	13	1	6	18	.293	14	21	0	243	18	3	.989
	—Baltimore (A.L.)..........	C	40	104	18	27	5	0	3	14	.260	16	14	1	216	13	3	.987
1996—	Baltimore (A.L.)..........	C	50	108	14	25	8	1	1	13	.231	11	15	0	215	10	3	.987
	—Rochester (I.L.)..........	C-DH	14	47	11	15	2	0	0	4	.319	11	6	0	52	3	2	.965
	—Florida (N.L.)■..........	C	10	31	4	9	1	0	1	2	.290	3	5	1	60	6	0	1.000
1997—	Florida (N.L.)..........	C-1B	58	143	21	43	10	2	2	20	.301	26	18	1	329	25	8	.978
1998—	Florida (N.L.)..........	C-2B	106	298	19	56	12	2	5	29	.188	35	52	5	531	49	8	.986
1999—	Texas (A.L.)■..........	C-DH	43	93	12	23	2	1	1	12	.247	10	7	1	165	15	3	.984
American League totals (3 years)			133	305	46	75	15	2	5	39	.246	37	36	2	596	38	9	.986
National League totals (3 years)			174	472	44	108	23	4	8	51	.229	64	75	7	920	80	16	.984
Major League totals (5 years)			307	777	90	183	38	6	13	90	.236	101	111	9	1516	118	25	.985

DIVISION SERIES RECORD

								BATTING								FIELDING		
Year	Team (League)	Pos.	G	AB	R	H	2B	3B	HR	RBI	Avg.	BB	SO	SB	PO	A	E	Avg.
1997—	Florida (N.L.)							Did not play.										

CHAMPIONSHIP SERIES RECORD

								BATTING								FIELDING		
Year	Team (League)	Pos.	G	AB	R	H	2B	3B	HR	RBI	Avg.	BB	SO	SB	PO	A	E	Avg.
1997—	Florida (N.L.)	C	1	0	0	0	0	0	0	0	...	0	0	0	2	0	0	1.000

WORLD SERIES RECORD

NOTES: Member of World Series championship team (1997).

								BATTING								FIELDING		
Year	Team (League)	Pos.	G	AB	R	H	2B	3B	HR	RBI	Avg.	BB	SO	SB	PO	A	E	Avg.
1997—	Florida (N.L.)	PH-C-PR	2	2	0	0	0	0	0	0	.000	0	0	0	3	0	0	1.000

RECORD AS PITCHER

Year	League	W	L	Pct.	ERA	G	GS	CG	ShO	Sv.	IP	H	R	ER	BB	SO
1990—	Bluefield (Appl.)	0	0	...	0.00	1	0	0	0	0	1	1	0	0	1	1
1993—	Bowie (East.)	0	0	...	0.00	1	0	0	0	0	2⅓	1	0	0	0	0

ZEILE, TODD — 3B — METS

PERSONAL: Born September 9, 1965, in Van Nuys, Calif. ... 6-1/200. ... Bats right, throws right. ... Full name: Todd Edward Zeile. ... Husband of Julianne McNamara, Olympic gold-medal gymnast (1984). ... Name pronounced ZEEL.

HIGH SCHOOL: Hart (Newhall, Calif.).

COLLEGE: UCLA.

TRANSACTIONS/CAREER NOTES: Selected by Kansas City Royals organization in 30th round of free-agent draft (June 6, 1983); did not sign. ... Selected by St. Louis Cardinals organization in supplemental round ("sandwich pick" between second and third round 55th pick overall) of free-agent draft (June 2, 1986); pick received as compensation for New York Yankees signing Type C free-agent IF Ivan DeJesus. ... On St. Louis disabled list (April 23-May 9, 1995); included rehabilitation assignment to Louisville (May 6-9). ... Traded by Cardinals with cash to Chicago Cubs for P Mike Morgan, 3B/OF Paul Torres and C Francisco Morales (June 16, 1995). ... Granted free agency (December 21, 1995). ... Signed by Philadelphia Phillies (December 22, 1995). ... Traded by Phillies with OF Pete Incaviglia to Baltimore Orioles for two players to be named later (August 29, 1996); Phillies acquired P Calvin Maduro and P Garrett Stephenson to complete deal (September 4, 1996). ... Granted free agency (October 27, 1996). ... Signed by Los Angeles Dodgers (December 8, 1996). ... Traded by Dodgers with C Mike Piazza to Florida Marlins for OF Gary Sheffield, 3B Bobby Bonilla, C Charles Johnson, OF Jim Eisenreich and P Manuel Barrios (May 15, 1998). ... Traded by Marlins to Texas Rangers for 3B Jose Santo and P Dan DeYoung (July 31, 1999). ... Granted free agency (October 29, 1999). ... Signed by New York Mets (December 11, 1999).

RECORDS: Holds N.L. single-season record for fewest putouts by third baseman (150 or more games)—83 (1993). ... Shares A.L. single-game record for most errors by first baseman—4 (August 7, 1996).

HONORS: Named Midwest League co-Most Valuable Player (1987).

STATISTICAL NOTES: Led New York-Penn League with six sacrifice flies in 1986. ... Tied for New York-Penn League lead in double plays by catcher with seven in 1986. ... Led Texas League catchers with 687 putouts and 761 total chances in 1988. ... Led American Association catchers with .992 fielding percentage and 17 passed balls in 1989. ... Had 17-game hitting streak (June 21-July 10, 1999). ... Tied for A.L. third baseman lead with 25 errors in 1999. ... Career major league grand slams: 8.

								BATTING								FIELDING		
Year	Team (League)	Pos.	G	AB	R	H	2B	3B	HR	RBI	Avg.	BB	SO	SB	PO	A	E	Avg.
1986—	Erie (NY-P)	C	70	248	40	64	14	1	14	*63	.258	37	52	5	407	*66	8	.983
1987—	Springfield (Midw.)	C-3B	130	487	94	142	24	4	25	*106	.292	70	85	1	867	79	14	.985
1988—	Arkansas (Texas)	C-OF-1B	129	430	95	117	33	2	19	75	.272	83	64	6	†697	66	10	.987
1989—	Louisville (A.A.)	C-3B-1B	118	453	71	131	26	3	19	85	.289	45	78	0	583	71	6	†.991
	—St. Louis (N.L.)	C	28	82	7	21	3	1	1	8	.256	9	14	0	125	10	4	.971
1990—	St. Louis (N.L.)	C-3B-1B-OF	144	495	62	121	25	3	15	57	.244	67	77	2	648	106	15	.980
1991—	St. Louis (N.L.)	3B	155	565	76	158	36	3	11	81	.280	62	94	17	124	290	*25	.943
1992—	St. Louis (N.L.)	3B	126	439	51	113	18	4	7	48	.257	68	70	7	81	235	13	.960
	—Louisville (A.A.)..........	3B	21	74	11	23	4	1	5	13	.311	9	13	0	15	41	5	.918
1993—	St. Louis (N.L.)..........	3B	157	571	82	158	36	1	17	103	.277	70	76	5	83	310	33	.923
1994—	St. Louis (N.L.)..........	3B	113	415	62	111	25	1	19	75	.267	52	56	1	66	224	12	.960

Year Team (League)	Pos.	G	AB	R	H	2B	3B	HR	RBI	Avg.	BB	SO	SB	PO	A	E	Avg.
						BATTING									FIELDING		
1995—Louisville (A.A.).........	1B	2	8	0	1	0	0	0	0	.125	0	2	0	11	1	1	.923
—St. Louis (N.L.)............	1B	34	127	16	37	6	0	5	22	.291	18	23	1	310	30	7	.980
—Chicago (N.L.)■.......	3B-OF-1B	79	299	34	68	16	0	9	30	.227	16	53	0	52	134	12	.939
1996—Philadelphia (N.L.)■..	3B-1B	134	500	61	134	24	0	20	80	.268	67	88	1	295	195	14	.972
—Baltimore (A.L.)■......	3B	29	117	17	28	8	0	5	19	.239	15	16	0	24	56	3	.964
1997—Los Angeles (N.L.)■..	3B	160	575	89	154	17	0	31	90	.268	85	112	8	105	248	*26	.931
1998—Los Angeles (N.L.)....	3B-1B	40	158	22	40	6	1	7	27	.253	10	24	1	27	53	6	.930
—Florida (N.L.)■..........	3B	66	234	37	68	12	1	6	39	.291	31	34	2	43	122	5	.971
—Texas (A.L.)■...........	3B	52	180	26	47	14	1	6	28	.261	28	32	1	38	91	12	.915
1999—Texas (A.L.)	3B-DH-1B	156	587	80	172	41	1	24	98	.293	56	94	1	105	294	‡25	.941
American League totals (3 years)		237	884	123	247	63	2	35	145	.279	99	142	2	167	441	40	.938
National League totals (10 years)		1236	4460	599	1183	224	15	148	660	.265	555	721	45	1959	1957	172	.958
Major League totals (11 years)		1473	5344	722	1430	287	17	183	805	.268	654	863	47	2126	2398	212	.955

DIVISION SERIES RECORD

Year Team (League)	Pos.	G	AB	R	H	2B	3B	HR	RBI	Avg.	BB	SO	SB	PO	A	E	Avg.
						BATTING									FIELDING		
1996—Baltimore (A.L.).........	3B	4	19	2	5	1	0	0	0	.263	2	5	0	4	9	2	.867
1998—Texas (A.L.)	3B	3	9	0	3	0	0	0	0	.333	0	2	0	0	4	0	1.000
1999—Texas (A.L.)	3B	3	10	0	1	0	0	0	0	.100	2	1	0	1	4	2	.714
Division series totals (3 years)		10	38	2	9	1	0	0	0	.237	4	8	0	5	17	4	.846

CHAMPIONSHIP SERIES RECORD

Year Team (League)	Pos.	G	AB	R	H	2B	3B	HR	RBI	Avg.	BB	SO	SB	PO	A	E	Avg.
						BATTING									FIELDING		
1996—Baltimore (A.L.).........	3B	5	22	3	8	17	0	0	3	.364	5	2	1	3	7	1	.909

ZIMMERMAN, JEFF   P   RANGERS

PERSONAL: Born August 9, 1972, in Kelowna, B.C. ... 6-1/200. ... Throws right, bats right. ... Full name: Jeffery Ross Zimmerman.
HIGH SCHOOL: John G. Diefenbaker (Vancouver).
COLLEGE: Texas Christian, then Simon Fraser (B.C.).
TRANSACTIONS/CAREER NOTES: Signed by Winnipeg, Northern League (May 1997). ... Signed as non-drafted free agent by Texas Rangers organization (January 6, 1998).

Year League	W	L	Pct.	ERA	G	GS	CG	ShO	Sv.	IP	H	R	ER	BB	SO
1997—Winnipeg (Nor.).................	9	2	.818	2.82	18	16	3	0	0	118	94	49	37	35	140
1998—Charlotte (FSL)■...............	2	1	.667	1.26	10	0	0	0	0	14 1/3	10	2	2	1	14
—Tulsa (Texas).............	3	1	.750	1.29	41	0	0	0	9	63	38	16	9	20	67
1999—Oklahoma (PCL).................	1	0	1.000	0.00	2	0	0	0	1	3 2/3	0	0	0	0	2
—Texas (A.L.)...............	9	3	.750	2.36	65	0	0	0	3	87 2/3	50	24	23	23	67
Major League totals (1 year)........	9	3	.750	2.36	65	0	0	0	3	87 2/3	50	24	23	23	67

DIVISION SERIES RECORD

Year League	W	L	Pct.	ERA	G	GS	CG	ShO	Sv.	IP	H	R	ER	BB	SO
1999—Texas (A.L.)......................	0	0	...	0.00	1	0	0	0	0	1	1	0	0	0	1

ZIMMERMAN, JORDAN   P   MARINERS

PERSONAL: Born April 28, 1975, in Kelowna, B.C. ... 6-0/200. ... Throws left, bats right. ... Full name: Jordan William Zimmerman.
HIGH SCHOOL: Brenham (Texas).
JUNIOR COLLEGE: Blinn College (Texas).
TRANSACTIONS/CAREER NOTES: Selected by Seattle Mariners organization in 32nd round of free-agent draft (June 2, 1994). ... On disabled list (July 7, 1995-remainder of season). ... On disabled list (June 18, 1996-remainder of season). ... On Lancaster disabled list (April 2-August 12, 1998). ... On Seattle disabled list (July 5-August 8, 1999); included rehabilitation assignment to Tacoma (July 18-23) and Everett (July 24-August 8).

Year League	W	L	Pct.	ERA	G	GS	CG	ShO	Sv.	IP	H	R	ER	BB	SO
1995—					Did not play.										
1996—					Did not play.										
1997—Everett (N'west).................	2	3	.400	4.15	11	9	0	0	0	39	37	27	18	23	54
—Wisconsin (Midw.)........	0	1	.000	5.82	3	3	0	0	0	17	18	11	11	10	18
1998—Arizona Mariners (Ariz.).....	0	1	.000	3.00	5	3	0	0	0	12	14	6	4	7	11
—Lancaster (Calif.)■........	0	1	.000	4.86	3	3	0	0	0	16 2/3	21	9	9	8	8
1999—New Haven (East.)...........	1	4	.200	1.08	22	0	0	0	2	33 1/3	26	8	4	19	33
—Seattle (A.L.)..............	0	0	...	7.88	12	0	0	0	0	8	14	8	7	4	3
—Tacoma (PCL)	0	0	...	5.14	9	0	0	0	0	7	13	4	4	4	4
—Everett (N'west)...........	0	0	...	27.00	1	0	0	0	0	2/3	3	2	2	0	1
Major League totals (1 year)........	0	0	...	7.88	12	0	0	0	0	8	14	8	7	4	3

ZOSKY, EDDIE   SS   PIRATES

PERSONAL: Born February 10, 1968, in Whittier, Calif. ... 6-0/180. ... Bats right, throws right. ... Full name: Edward James Zosky. ... Name pronounced ZAH-skee.
HIGH SCHOOL: St. Paul (Sante Fe Springs, Calif.).
COLLEGE: Fresno State.

TRANSACTIONS/CAREER NOTES: Selected by New York Mets organization in fifth round of free-agent draft (June 2, 1986); did not sign. ... Selected by Toronto Blue Jays organization in first round (19th pick overall) of free-agent draft (June 5, 1989). ... On Toronto disabled list (March 26-August 11, 1993); included rehabilitation assignments to Hagerstown (July 26-August 2) and Syracuse (August 2-11). ... On disabled list (June 29-August 10, 1994). ... Traded by Blue Jays to Florida Marlins for a player to be named later (November 18, 1994); Blue Jays acquired P Scott Pace to complete deal (December 14, 1994). ... Granted free agency (October 16, 1995). ... Signed by Rochester, Baltimore Orioles organization (January 24, 1996). ... On Rochester disabled list (July 24-August 19, 1996). ... Granted free agency (October 15, 1996). ... Signed by San Francisco Giants organization (November 25, 1996). ... Granted free agency (October 15, 1997). ... Signed by Milwaukee Brewers organization (December 17, 1997). ... On Louisville disabled list (June 13-20 and July 2-9, 1998). ... Granted free agency (October 15, 1998). ... Re-signed by Brewers organization (December 11, 1998). ... Granted free agency (October 11, 1999). ... Signed by Pittsburgh Pirates organization (January 18, 2000).

HONORS: Named shortstop on The Sporting News college All-America team (1989).

STATISTICAL NOTES: Led Southern League shortstops with 80 double plays in 1990. ... Led International League shortstops with 616 total chances and 88 double plays in 1991.

| | | | | | | BATTING | | | | | | | | | FIELDING | | |
Year Team (League)	Pos.	G	AB	R	H	2B	3B	HR	RBI	Avg.	BB	SO	SB	PO	A	E	Avg.
1989— Knoxville (Sou.)	SS	56	208	21	46	5	3	2	14	.221	10	32	1	94	135	8	.966
1990— Knoxville (Sou.)	SS	115	450	53	122	20	7	3	45	.271	26	72	3	*196	295	31	*.941
1991— Syracuse (I.L.)	SS	119	511	69	135	18	4	6	39	.264	35	82	9	*221	*371	24	*.961
—Toronto (A.L.)	SS	18	27	2	4	1	1	0	2	.148	0	8	0	12	26	0	1.000
1992— Syracuse (I.L.)	SS	96	342	31	79	11	6	4	38	.231	19	53	3	123	249	27	.932
—Toronto (A.L.)	SS	8	7	1	2	0	1	0	1	.286	0	2	0	2	10	1	.923
1993— Hagerstown (SAL)	SS	5	20	2	2	0	0	0	1	.100	2	1	0	10	15	0	1.000
—Syracuse (I.L.)	SS	28	93	9	20	5	0	0	8	.215	1	20	0	48	71	5	.960
1994— Syracuse (I.L.)	2B-SS-DH-3B	85	284	41	75	15	3	7	37	.264	9	46	3	120	212	15	.957
1995— Florida (N.L.)■	SS-2B	6	5	0	1	0	0	0	0	.200	0	0	0	1	2	1	.750
—Charlotte (I.L.)	SS-2B-3B	92	312	27	77	15	2	3	42	.247	7	48	2	161	279	15	.967
1996— Rochester (I.L.)■	SS-2B-3B	95	340	42	87	22	4	3	34	.256	21	40	5	159	257	21	.952
—GC Orioles (GCL)	SS	1	3	1	1	1	0	0	0	.333	1	0	0	3	2	0	1.000
1997— Phoenix (PCL)■	3B-SS-2B	86	241	38	67	10	4	9	45	.278	16	38	3	93	161	11	.958
1998— Louisville (I.L.)■	S-3-2-P-O	90	257	36	63	12	1	8	35	.245	15	47	1	99	211	14	.957
1999— Louisville (I.L.)	3B-SS-2B	116	415	60	122	22	3	12	47	.294	23	68	5	141	278	19	.957
—Milwaukee (N.L.)	3B-2B	8	7	1	1	0	0	0	0	.143	1	2	0	1	4	0	1.000
American League totals (2 years)		26	34	3	6	1	2	0	3	.176	0	10	0	14	36	1	.980
National League totals (2 years)		14	12	1	2	0	0	0	0	.167	1	2	0	2	6	1	.889
Major League totals (4 years)		40	46	4	8	1	2	0	3	.174	1	12	0	16	42	2	.967

RECORD AS PITCHER

Year League	W	L	Pct.	ERA	G	GS	CG	ShO	Sv.	IP	H	R	ER	BB	SO
1998— Louisville (I.L.)	0	0	...	0.00	1	0	0	0	0	$1/3$	1	0	0	0	1

ZULETA, JULIO — 1B — CUBS

PERSONAL: Born March 28, 1975, in Panama City, Panama. ... 6-6/230. ... Bats right, throws right. ... Full name: Julio Ernesto Zuleta.

HIGH SCHOOL: Don Bosco Institute (Panama City, Panama).

COLLEGE: Panama Technological University.

TRANSACTIONS/CAREER NOTES: Signed as non-drafted free agent by Chicago Cubs organization (September 15, 1992).

STATISTICAL NOTES: Led Southern League in being hit by pitch with 20 in 1999.

| | | | | | | BATTING | | | | | | | | | FIELDING | | |
Year Team (League)	Pos.	G	AB	R	H	2B	3B	HR	RBI	Avg.	BB	SO	SB	PO	A	E	Avg.
1993— GC Cubs (GCL)	C-OF	17	53	3	13	0	1	0	6	.245	3	12	0	20	2	3	.880
1994— Huntington (Appl.)	C	6	15	0	1	0	0	0	2	.067	4	4	0	22	7	2	.935
—GC Cubs (GCL)	C	30	100	11	31	1	0	0	8	.310	8	18	5	176	19	2	.990
1995— Williamsport (NY-P)	C	30	75	9	13	3	1	0	6	.173	11	12	0	131	12	5	.966
1996— Williamsport (NY-P)	1B	62	221	35	57	12	2	1	29	.258	19	36	7	338	25	4	.989
1997— Rockford (Midw.)	1B	119	430	59	124	30	5	6	77	.288	35	88	5	828	62	14	.985
1998— Daytona (FSL)	1B	94	366	69	126	25	1	16	86	.344	35	59	6	643	58	13	.982
—West Tenn (Sou.)	1B	40	139	18	41	9	0	2	20	.295	10	30	0	203	18	2	.991
1999— West Tenn (Sou.)	1B	133	482	75	142	37	4	21	97	.295	35	122	4	897	63	9	.991

MAJOR LEAGUE MANAGERS

ALOU, FELIPE — EXPOS

PERSONAL: Born May 12, 1935, in Haina, Dominican Republic. ... 6-1/195. ... Batted right, threw right. ... Full name: Felipe Rojas Alou. ... Father of Moises Alou, outfielder, Houston Astros; brother of Jesus Alou, major league outfielder with four teams (1965-75 and 1978-79); brother of Matty Alou, major league outfielder with six teams (1960-74); and uncle of Mel Rojas, pitcher with five major league teams (1990-99).

COLLEGE: Santo Domingo (Dominican Republic).

TRANSACTIONS/CAREER NOTES: Signed as free agent by New York Giants organization (November 14, 1955). ... Giants franchise moved from New York to San Francisco (1958). ... Traded by Giants with P Billy Hoeft, C Ed Bailey and a player to be named later to Milwaukee Braves for P Bob Hendley, P Bob Shaw and C Del Crandall (December 3, 1963); Braves acquired IF Ernie Bowman to complete deal (January 8, 1964). ... On disabled list (June 24-July 25, 1964). ... Braves franchise moved from Milwaukee to Atlanta (1966). ... Traded by Braves to Oakland Athletics for P Jim Nash (December 3, 1969). ... Traded by A's to New York Yankees for P Rob Gardner and P Ron Klimkowski (April 9, 1971). ... Contract sold by Yankees to Montreal Expos (September 5, 1973). ... Contract sold by Expos to Milwaukee Brewers (December 7, 1973). ... Released by Brewers (April 29, 1974).

HONORS: Named first baseman on THE SPORTING NEWS N.L. All-Star team (1966).

STATISTICAL NOTES: Led N.L. with 355 total bases in 1966. ... Career major league grand slams: 2.

Year — Team (League)	Pos.	G	AB	R	H	2B	3B	HR	RBI	Avg.	BB	SO	SB	PO	A	E	Avg.
1956— Lake Charles (Evan.) ..	OF	5	9	1	2	0	0	0	1	.222	...	...	0	6	1	0	1.000
—Cocoa (FSL)	OF-3B	119	445	111	169	15	6	21	99	*.380	68	40	*48	199	60	23	.918
1957— Minneapolis (A.A.)......	OF	24	57	7	12	2	0	0	3	.211	5	8	1	32	1	1	.971
—Springfield (East.)	OF-3B	106	359	45	110	14	3	12	71	.306	27	29	18	215	26	9	.964
1958— Phoenix (PCL)	OF	55	216	61	69	16	2	13	42	.319	17	24	10	150	3	3	.981
—San Francisco (N.L.) ..	OF	75	182	21	46	9	2	4	16	.253	19	34	4	126	2	2	.985
1959— San Francisco (N.L.) ..	OF	95	247	38	68	13	2	10	33	.275	17	38	5	111	2	3	.974
1960— San Francisco (N.L.) ..	OF	106	322	48	85	17	3	8	44	.264	16	42	10	156	5	7	.958
1961— San Francisco (N.L.) ..	OF	132	415	59	120	19	0	18	52	.289	26	41	11	196	10	2	.990
1962— San Francisco (N.L.) ..	OF	154	561	96	177	30	3	25	98	.316	33	66	10	262	7	8	.971
1963— San Francisco (N.L.) ..	OF	157	565	75	159	31	9	20	82	.281	27	87	11	279	9	4	.986
1964— Milwaukee (N.L.)■......	OF-1B	121	415	60	105	26	3	9	51	.253	30	41	5	329	12	5	.986
1965— Milwaukee (N.L.).......	O-1-3-S	143	555	80	165	29	2	23	78	.297	31	63	8	626	43	6	.991
1966— Atlanta (N.L.).............	1-O-3-S	154	*666	*122	*218	32	6	31	74	.327	24	51	5	935	64	13	.987
1967— Atlanta (N.L.).............	1B-OF	140	574	76	157	26	3	15	43	.274	32	50	6	864	34	9	.990
1968— Atlanta (N.L.).............	OF	160	*662	72	•210	37	5	11	57	.317	48	56	12	379	8	8	.980
1969— Atlanta (N.L.).............	OF	123	476	54	134	13	1	5	32	.282	23	23	4	260	4	3	.989
1970— Oakland (A.L.)■..........	OF-1B	154	575	70	156	25	3	8	55	.271	32	31	10	290	11	7	.977
1971— Oakland (A.L.)	OF	2	8	0	2	1	0	0	0	.250	0	1	0	7	0	0	1.000
—New York (A.L.)■........	OF-1B	131	461	52	133	20	6	8	69	.289	32	24	5	506	23	4	.992
1972— New York (A.L.).........	1B-OF	120	324	33	90	18	1	6	37	.278	22	27	1	669	54	7	.990
1973— New York (A.L.).........	1B-OF	93	280	25	66	12	0	4	27	.236	9	25	0	512	31	7	.987
—Montreal (N.L.)■........	OF-1B	19	48	4	10	1	0	1	4	.208	2	4	0	30	3	0	1.000
1974— Milwaukee (A.L.)■......	OF	3	3	0	0	0	0	0	0	.000	0	2	0	0	0	1	.000
American League totals (5 years)		503	1651	180	447	76	10	26	188	.271	95	110	16	1984	119	26	.988
National League totals (13 years)		1579	5688	805	1654	283	39	180	664	.291	328	596	91	4553	203	70	.985
Major league totals (17 years)		2082	7339	985	2101	359	49	206	852	.286	423	706	107	6537	322	96	.986

CHAMPIONSHIP SERIES RECORD

Year — Team (League)	Pos.	G	AB	R	H	2B	3B	HR	RBI	Avg.	BB	SO	SB	PO	A	E	Avg.
1969— Atlanta (N.L.).............	PH	1	1	0	0	0	0	0	0	.000	0	0	0	...	...	...	...

WORLD SERIES RECORD

Year — Team (League)	Pos.	G	AB	R	H	2B	3B	HR	RBI	Avg.	BB	SO	SB	PO	A	E	Avg.
1962— San Francisco (N.L.) ..	OF	7	26	2	7	1	1	0	1	.269	1	4	0	8	0	1	.889

ALL-STAR GAME RECORD

Year — League	Pos.	AB	R	H	2B	3B	HR	RBI	Avg.	BB	SO	SB	PO	A	E	Avg.
1962— National	OF	0	0	0	0	0	0	1	...	0	0	0	0	0	0	...
1966— National						Did not play.										
1968— National	OF	0	0	0	0	0	0	0	...	0	0	0	0	0	0	...
All-Star Game totals (2 years)		0	0	0	0	0	0	1	...	0	0	0	0	0	0	...

RECORD AS MANAGER

BACKGROUND: Spring training instructor, Montreal Expos (1976). ... Coach, Expos (1979-80, 1984 and October 8, 1991-May 22, 1992).

HONORS: Named Florida State League Manager of the Year (1990). ... Named N.L. Manager of the Year by THE SPORTING NEWS (1994). ... Named N.L. Manager of the Year by Baseball Writers' Association of America (1994).

		REGULAR SEASON				POSTSEASON							
						Playoff		Champ. Series		World Series		All-Star Game	
Year — Team (League)	W	L	Pct.	Pos.		W	L	W	L	W	L	W	L
1977— West Palm Beach (Florida State)	77	55	.583	1st (S)		1	2	—	—	—	—	—	—
1978— Memphis (Southern)................................	71	73	.493	2nd (W)		—	—	—	—	—	—	—	—
1981— Denver (American Association)	76	60	.559	2nd (W)		4	0	—	—	—	—	—	—
1982— Wichita (American Association)................	70	67	.511	2nd (W)		—	—	—	—	—	—	—	—
1983— Wichita (American Association)................	65	71	.478	3rd (W)		—	—	—	—	—	—	—	—
1985— Indianapolis (American Association)	61	81	.430	4th (E)		—	—	—	—	—	—	—	—
1986— West Palm Beach (Florida State)	80	55	.593	1st (S)		3	3	—	—	—	—	—	—

Year Team (League)	REGULAR SEASON				POSTSEASON							
					Playoff		Champ. Series		World Series		All-Star Game	
	W	L	Pct.	Pos.	W	L	W	L	W	L	W	L
1987—West Palm Beach (Florida State)	75	63	.543	2nd (S)	—	—	—	—	—	—	—	—
1988—West Palm Beach (Florida State)	41	27	.603	2nd (E)	—	—	—	—	—	—	—	—
— (Second half)	30	36	.455	3rd (E)	2	2	—	—	—	—	—	—
1989—West Palm Beach (Florida State)	39	31	.557	T2nd (E)	—	—	—	—	—	—	—	—
— (Second half)	35	33	.515	2nd (E)	—	—	—	—	—	—	—	—
1990—West Palm Beach (Florida State)	49	19	.721	1st (E)	—	—	—	—	—	—	—	—
— (Second half)	43	21	.672	1st (E)	3	3	—	—	—	—	—	—
1991—West Palm Beach (Florida State)	33	31	.516	4th (E)	—	—	—	—	—	—	—	—
— (Second half)	39	28	.582	2nd (E)	6	1	—	—	—	—	—	—
1992—Montreal (N.L.)	70	55	.560	2nd (E)	—	—	—	—	—	—	—	—
1993—Montreal (N.L.)	94	68	.580	2nd (E)	—	—	—	—	—	—	—	—
1994—Montreal (N.L.)	74	40	.649		—	—	—	—	—	—	—	—
1995—Montreal (N.L.)	66	78	.458	5th (E)	—	—	—	—	—	—	—	—
1996—Montreal (N.L.)	88	74	.543	2nd (E)	—	—	—	—	—	—	—	—
1997—Montreal (N.L.)	78	84	.481	4th (E)	—	—	—	—	—	—	—	—
1998—Montreal (N.L.)	65	97	.401	4th (E)	—	—	—	—	—	—	—	—
1999—Montreal (N.L.)	68	94	.420	4th (E)	—	—	—	—	—	—	—	—
Major league totals (8 years)	603	590	.505		—	—	—	—	—	—	1	0

NOTES:
1977—Lost to St. Petersburg in semifinals.
1978—Memphis tied one game.
1981—Defeated Omaha in league championship.
1986—Defeated Winter Haven, two games to none, in semifinals; lost to St. Petersburg, three games to one, in league championship.
1988—Defeated Vero Beach, two games to none, in first round; lost to Osceola, two games to none, in semifinals.
1990—Defeated Lakeland, two games to one, in semifinals; lost to Vero Beach, two games to one, in league championship.
1991—Defeated Vero Beach, two games to one, in first round; defeated Lakeland, two games to none, in semifinals; defeated Clearwater, two games to none, in league championship.
1992—Replaced Montreal manager Tom Runnells with club in fourth place and record of 17-20 (May 22).
1994—Montreal was in first place in N.L. East at time of season-ending strike (August 12).

BAKER, DUSTY — GIANTS

PERSONAL: Born June 15, 1949, in Riverside, Calif. ... 6-2/200. ... Batted right, threw right. ... Full name: Johnnie B. Baker Jr.
HIGH SCHOOL: Del Campo (Fair Oaks, Calif.).
COLLEGE: American River College (Calif.).
TRANSACTIONS/CAREER NOTES: Selected by Atlanta Braves organization in 26th round of free-agent draft (June 6, 1967). ... On West Palm Beach restricted list (April 5-June 13, 1968). ... On Atlanta military list (January 24-April 3, 1969 and June 17-July 3, 1972). ... Traded by Braves with 1B/3B Ed Goodson to Los Angeles Dodgers for OF Jimmy Wynn, 2B Lee Lacy, 1B/OF Tom Paciorek and IF Jerry Royster (November 17, 1975). ... Released on waivers by Dodgers (February 10, 1984); San Francisco Giants claim rejected (February 16, 1984). ... Granted free agency (February 21, 1984). ... Signed by Giants (April 1, 1984). ... On restricted list (April 2-11, 1984). ... Traded by Giants to Oakland Athletics for P Ed Puikunas and C Dan Winters (March 24, 1985). ... Granted free agency (November 10, 1986).
RECORDS: Shares major league records for most plate appearances, most at-bats and most times faced pitcher as batsman in one inning—3 (September 20, 1972, second inning); and most stolen bases in one inning—3 (June 27, 1984, third inning).
HONORS: Named outfielder on THE SPORTING NEWS N.L. All-Star team (1980). ... Named outfielder on THE SPORTING NEWS N.L. Silver Slugger team (1980-81). ... Won N.L. Gold Glove as outfielder (1981).
STATISTICAL NOTES: Led N.L. outfielders with 407 total chances in 1973. ... Career major league grand slams: 4.

Year Team (League)	Pos.	G	AB	R	H	2B	3B	HR	RBI	Avg.	BB	SO	SB	PO	A	E	Avg.
1967—Austin (Texas)	OF	9	39	6	9	1	0	0	1	.231	2	7	0	17	0	1	.944
1968—W.Palm Beach (FSL) ..	OF	6	21	2	4	0	0	0	2	.190	1	4	0	6	2	0	1.000
— Greenwood (W. Car.)..	OF	52	199	45	68	11	3	6	39	.342	23	39	6	82	1	3	.965
— Atlanta (N.L.)...............	OF	6	5	0	2	0	0	0	0	.400	0	1	0	0	0	0	...
1969—Shreveport (Texas).....	OF	73	265	40	68	5	1	9	31	.257	36	41	2	135	10	3	.980
— Richmond (Int'l)	OF-3B	25	89	7	22	4	0	0	8	.247	11	22	3	40	9	4	.925
— Atlanta (N.L.)...............	OF	3	7	0	0	0	0	0	0	.000	0	3	0	2	0	0	1.000
1970—Richmond (I.L.).........	OF	118	461	97	150	29	3	11	51	.325	53	45	10	236	10	7	.972
— Atlanta (N.L.)...............	OF	13	24	3	7	0	0	0	4	.292	2	4	0	11	1	3	.800
1971—Richmond (I.L.).........	OF-3B	80	341	62	106	23	2	11	41	.311	25	37	10	136	13	4	.974
— Atlanta (N.L.)...............	OF	29	62	2	14	2	0	0	4	.226	1	14	0	29	1	0	1.000
1972—Atlanta (N.L.).............	OF	127	446	62	143	27	2	17	76	.321	45	68	4	344	8	4	.989
1973—Atlanta (N.L.).............	OF	159	604	101	174	29	4	21	99	.288	67	72	24	*390	10	7	.983
1974—Atlanta (N.L.).............	OF	149	574	80	147	35	0	20	69	.256	71	87	18	359	10	7	.981
1975—Atlanta (N.L.).............	OF	142	494	63	129	18	2	19	72	.261	67	57	12	287	10	3	.990
1976—Los Angeles (N.L.)■..	OF	112	384	36	93	13	0	4	39	.242	31	54	2	254	3	1	.996
1977—Los Angeles (N.L.)	OF	153	533	86	155	26	1	30	86	.291	58	89	2	227	8	3	.987
1978—Los Angeles (N.L.)	OF	149	522	62	137	24	1	11	66	.262	47	66	12	250	13	4	.985
1979—Los Angeles (N.L.)	OF	151	554	86	152	29	1	23	88	.274	56	70	11	289	14	3	.990
1980—Los Angeles (N.L.)	OF	153	579	80	170	26	4	29	97	.294	43	66	12	308	5	3	.991
1981—Los Angeles (N.L.)	OF	103	400	48	128	17	3	9	49	.320	29	43	10	181	8	2	.990
1982—Los Angeles (N.L.)	OF	147	570	80	171	19	1	23	88	.300	56	62	17	226	7	6	.975
1983—Los Angeles (N.L.)	OF	149	531	71	138	25	1	15	73	.260	72	59	7	249	4	5	.981
1984—San Fran. (N.L.)■......	OF	100	243	31	71	7	2	3	32	.292	40	27	4	112	1	3	.974
1985—Oakland (A.L.)■.........	1B-OF-DH	111	343	48	92	15	1	14	52	.268	50	47	2	465	29	5	.990
1986—Oakland (A.L.)	OF-DH-1B	83	242	25	58	8	0	4	19	.240	27	37	0	90	4	0	1.000
American League totals (2 years)		194	585	73	150	23	1	18	71	.256	77	84	2	555	33	5	.992
National League totals (17 years)		1845	6532	891	1831	297	22	224	942	.280	685	842	135	3518	103	54	.985
Major league totals (19 years)		2039	7117	964	1981	320	23	242	1013	.278	762	926	137	4073	136	59	.986

DIVISION SERIES RECORD

Year Team (League)	Pos.	G	AB	R	H	2B	3B	HR	RBI	Avg.	BB	SO	SB	PO	A	E	Avg.
							BATTING									FIELDING	
1981—Los Angeles (N.L.)	OF	5	18	2	3	1	0	0	1	.167	2	0	0	12	0	0	1.000

CHAMPIONSHIP SERIES RECORD

RECORDS: Shares single-game record for most grand slams—1 (October 5, 1977). ... Shares single-inning record for most runs batted in—4 (October 5, 1977, fourth inning). ... Shares N.L. single-game record for most hits—4 (October 7, 1978).
NOTES: Named N.L. Championship Series Most Valuable Player (1977).

Year Team (League)	Pos.	G	AB	R	H	2B	3B	HR	RBI	Avg.	BB	SO	SB	PO	A	E	Avg.
							BATTING									FIELDING	
1977—Los Angeles (N.L.)	OF	4	14	4	5	1	0	2	8	.357	2	3	0	3	0	0	1.000
1978—Los Angeles (N.L.)	OF	4	15	1	7	2	0	0	1	.467	3	0	0	5	0	0	1.000
1981—Los Angeles (N.L.)	OF	5	19	3	6	1	0	0	3	.316	1	0	0	10	0	1	.909
1983—Los Angeles (N.L.)	OF	4	14	4	5	1	0	1	1	.357	2	0	0	9	0	0	1.000
Championship series totals (4 years)		17	62	12	23	5	0	3	13	.371	8	3	0	27	0	1	.964

WORLD SERIES RECORD

NOTES: Member of World Series championship team (1981).

Year Team (League)	Pos.	G	AB	R	H	2B	3B	HR	RBI	Avg.	BB	SO	SB	PO	A	E	Avg.
							BATTING									FIELDING	
1977—Los Angeles (N.L.)	OF	6	24	4	7	0	0	1	5	.292	0	2	0	11	0	1	.917
1978—Los Angeles (N.L.)	OF	6	21	2	5	0	0	1	1	.238	1	3	0	12	0	0	1.000
1981—Los Angeles (N.L.)	OF	6	24	3	4	0	0	0	1	.167	1	6	0	13	0	0	1.000
World Series totals (3 years)		18	69	9	16	0	0	2	7	.232	2	11	0	36	0	1	.973

ALL-STAR GAME RECORD

Year League	Pos.	AB	R	H	2B	3B	HR	RBI	Avg.	BB	SO	SB	PO	A	E	Avg.
						BATTING									FIELDING	
1981—National	OF	2	0	1	0	0	0	0	.500	0	0	0	2	0	0	1.000
1982—National	OF	2	0	0	0	0	0	0	.000	0	0	0	0	0	0	...
All-Star Game totals (2 years)		4	0	1	0	0	0	0	.250	0	0	0	2	0	0	1.000

RECORD AS MANAGER

BACKGROUND: Coach, San Francisco Giants (1988-92). ... Manager, Scottsdale Scorpions, Arizona Fall League (1992, record: 20-22, second place/Northern Division).
HONORS: Named N.L. Manager of the Year by Baseball Writers' Association of America (1993). ... Coach, N.L. All-Star team (1994 and 1997). ... Named N.L. Manager of the Year by THE SPORTING NEWS (1997).

	REGULAR SEASON				POSTSEASON				World		All-Star	
					Playoff		Champ. Series		Series		Game	
Year Team (League)	W	L	Pct.	Pos.	W	L	W	L	W	L	W	L
1993—San Francisco (N.L.)	103	59	.636	2nd (W)	—	—	—	—	—	—	—	—
1994—San Francisco (N.L.)	55	60	.478		—	—	—	—	—	—	—	—
1995—San Francisco (N.L.)	67	77	.465	4th (W)	—	—	—	—	—	—	—	—
1996—San Francisco (N.L.)	68	94	.420	4th (W)	—	—	—	—	—	—	—	—
1997—San Francisco (N.L.)	90	72	.556	1st (W)	0	3	—	—	—	—	—	—
1998—San Francisco (N.L.)	89	74	.546	2nd (W)	—	—	—	—	—	—	—	—
1999—San Francisco (N.L.)	86	76	.531	2nd (W)	—	—	—	—	—	—	—	—
Major league totals (7 years)	558	512	.521		0	3	—	—	—	—	—	—

NOTES:
1994—San Francisco was in second place in N.L. West at time of season-ending strike (August 12).
1997—Lost to Florida in N.L. divisional playoff.

BAYLOR, DON   CUBS

PERSONAL: Born June 28, 1949, in Austin, Texas. ... 6-1/220. ... Batted right, threw right. ... Full name: Donald Edward Baylor. ... Cousin of Pat Ballage, safety with Indianapolis Colts (1986-87).
HIGH SCHOOL: Stephen F. Austin (Austin, Texas).
JUNIOR COLLEGE: Miami-Dade Junior College and Blinn College (Texas).
TRANSACTIONS/CAREER NOTES: Selected by Baltimore Orioles organization in second round of free-agent draft (June 6, 1967). ... Traded by Orioles with P Mike Torrez and P Paul Mitchell to Oakland Athletics for OF Reggie Jackson, P Ken Holtzman and P Bill Van Bommel (April 2, 1976). ... Granted free agency (November 1, 1976). ... Signed by California Angels (November 16, 1976). ... On disabled list (May 11-June 26, 1980). ... Granted free agency (November 10, 1982). ... Signed by New York Yankees (December 1, 1982). ... Traded by Yankees to Boston Red Sox for DH Mike Easler (March 28, 1986). ... Traded by Red Sox to Minnesota Twins for a player to be named later (August 31, 1987); Red Sox acquired P Enrique Rios to complete deal (December 18, 1987). ... Released by Twins (December 21, 1987). ... Signed by A's (February 9, 1988). ... Granted free agency (November 4, 1988).
RECORDS: Holds major league career record for most times hit by pitch—267. ... Shares major league records for most consecutive home runs in two consecutive games—4 (July 1 [1] and 2 [3], 1975, bases on balls included); and most long hits in opening game of season—4 (2 doubles, 1 triple, 1 home run, April 6, 1973). ... Shares major league record for most times caught stealing in one inning—2 (June 15, 1974, ninth inning). ... Shares modern major league single-game record for most at-bats (nine-inning game)—7 (August 25, 1979). ... Holds A.L. single-season record for most times hit by pitch—35 (1986).
HONORS: Named Appalachian League Player of the Year (1967). ... Named Minor League Player of the Year by THE SPORTING NEWS (1970). ... Named A.L. Player of the Year by THE SPORTING NEWS (1979). ... Named A.L. Most Valuable Player by Baseball Writers' Association of America (1979). ... Named designated hitter on THE SPORTING NEWS A.L. All-Star team (1979, 1985-86). ... Named designated hitter on THE SPORTING NEWS A.L. Silver Slugger team (1983 and 1985-86).

STATISTICAL NOTES: Led Appalachian League with 135 total bases and tied for lead in caught stealing with 6 in 1967. ... Led Texas League in being hit by pitch with 13 in 1969. ... Led International League with 296 total bases in 1970. ... Led International League in being hit by pitch with 19 in 1970 and 16 in 1971. ... Led A.L. in being hit by pitch with 13 in 1973, 20 in 1976, 18 in 1978, 23 in 1984, 24 in 1985, 35 in 1986, 28 in 1987 and tied for lead with 13 in 1975. ... Hit three home runs in one game (July 2, 1975). ... Led A.L. with 12 sacrifice flies in 1978. ... Led A.L. with 21 game-winning RBIs in 1982. ... Career major league grand slams: 12.

Year — Team (League)	Pos.	G	AB	R	H	2B	3B	HR	RBI	Avg.	BB	SO	SB	PO	A	E	Avg.
1967— Bluefield (Appal.)........	OF	•67	246	50	*85	10	*8	8	47	*.346	35	52	*26	106	5	5	.957
1968— Stockton (California) ..	OF	68	244	52	90	6	3	7	40	.369	35	65	14	135	3	7	.952
— Elmira (East.)	OF	6	24	4	8	1	1	1	3	.333	3	4	1	10	1	0	1.000
— Rochester (I.L.)	OF	15	46	4	10	2	0	0	4	.217	3	17	1	29	1	4	.882
1969— Miami (FSL)	OF	17	56	13	21	5	4	3	24	.375	7	8	3	30	2	3	.914
— Dall./Ft. Worth (Tex.)..	OF	109	406	71	122	17	•10	11	57	.300	48	77	19	241	7	*13	.950
1970— Rochester (I.L.).........	OF	•140	508	*127	166	*34	*15	22	107	.327	76	99	26	286	5	7	.977
— Baltimore (A.L.)	OF	8	17	4	4	0	0	0	4	.235	2	3	1	15	0	0	1.000
1971— Rochester (I.L.).........	OF	136	492	104	154	•31	10	20	95	.313	79	73	25	210	4	9	.960
— Baltimore (A.L.)	OF	1	2	0	0	0	0	0	1	.000	2	1	0	4	0	0	1.000
1972— Baltimore (A.L.).........	OF-1B	102	320	33	81	13	3	11	38	.253	29	50	24	206	4	5	.977
1973— Baltimore (A.L.).........	OF-1B-DH	118	405	64	116	20	4	11	51	.286	35	48	32	228	10	6	.975
1974— Baltimore (A.L.).........	OF-1B	137	489	66	133	22	1	10	59	.272	43	56	29	260	2	5	.981
1975— Baltimore (A.L.).........	OF-DH-1B	145	524	79	148	21	6	25	76	.282	53	64	32	286	8	5	.983
1976— Oakland (A.L.)■........	OF-1B-DH	157	595	85	147	25	1	15	68	.247	58	72	52	781	45	12	.986
1977— California (A.L.)■......	OF-DH	154	561	87	141	27	0	25	75	.251	62	76	26	280	16	7	.977
1978— California (A.L.)........	DH-OF-1B	158	591	103	151	26	0	34	99	.255	56	71	22	194	9	6	.971
1979— California (A.L.)........	OF-DH-1B	•162	628	*120	186	33	3	36	*139	.296	71	51	22	203	3	5	.976
1980— California (A.L.)........	OF-DH	90	340	39	85	12	2	5	51	.250	24	32	6	119	4	4	.969
1981— California (A.L.)........	DH-1B-OF	103	377	52	90	18	1	17	66	.239	42	51	3	38	1	0	1.000
1982— California (A.L.)........	DH	157	608	80	160	24	1	24	93	.263	57	69	10	...	...	...	...
1983— New York (A.L.)■......	DH-OF-1B	144	534	82	162	33	3	21	85	.303	40	53	17	23	2	1	.962
1984— New York (A.L.)........	DH-OF	134	493	84	129	29	1	27	89	.262	38	68	1	8	0	1	.889
1985— New York (A.L.)........	DH	142	477	70	110	24	1	23	91	.231	52	90	0	...	...	...	...
1986— Boston (A.L.)■.........	DH-1B-OF	160	585	93	139	23	1	31	94	.238	62	111	3	71	4	1	.987
1987— Boston (A.L.)...........	DH	108	339	64	81	8	0	16	57	.239	40	47	5	...	...	...	...
— Minnesota (A.L.)■	DH	20	49	3	14	1	0	0	6	.286	5	12	0	...	...	...	...
1988— Oakland (A.L.)■........	DH	92	264	28	58	7	0	7	34	.220	34	44	0	...	...	...	...
Major league totals (19 years)		2292	8198	1236	2135	366	28	338	1276	.260	805	1069	285	2716	110	58	.980

CHAMPIONSHIP SERIES RECORD

RECORDS: Holds career record for most clubs played with—5. ... Holds single-series record for most runs batted in—10 (1982). ... Shares single-game records for most times reached base safely—5 (October 8, 1986); and most grand slams—1 (October 9, 1982). ... Shares record for most runs batted in in one inning—4 (October 9, 1982, eighth inning). ... Holds A.L. record for most consecutive games with one or more hits—12 (1982 [last three games], 1986-87). ... Shares A.L. single-game record for most runs batted in—5 (October 5, 1982).

Year — Team (League)	Pos.	G	AB	R	H	2B	3B	HR	RBI	Avg.	BB	SO	SB	PO	A	E	Avg.
1973— Baltimore (A.L.).........	OF-PH	4	11	3	3	0	0	0	1	.273	3	5	0	7	0	0	1.000
1974— Baltimore (A.L.).........	OF-DH	4	15	0	4	0	0	0	1	.267	0	2	0	9	0	0	1.000
1979— California (A.L.).........	DH-OF	4	16	2	3	0	0	1	2	.188	1	2	0	4	0	0	1.000
1982— California (A.L.).........	DH	5	17	2	5	1	1	1	10	.294	2	0	0	...	...	...	...
1986— Boston (A.L.)............	DH	7	26	6	9	3	0	1	2	.346	4	5	0	...	...	...	...
1987— Minnesota (A.L.)	PH-DH	2	5	0	2	0	0	0	1	.400	0	0	0	...	...	...	...
1988— Oakland (A.L.)	DH	2	6	0	0	0	0	0	1	.000	1	2	0	...	...	...	...
Championship series totals (7 years)		28	96	13	26	4	1	3	17	.271	11	16	0	20	0	0	1.000

WORLD SERIES RECORD

RECORDS: Shares record for most at-bats in one inning—2 (October 17, 1987, fourth inning).
NOTES: Member of World Series championship team (1987).

Year — Team (League)	Pos.	G	AB	R	H	2B	3B	HR	RBI	Avg.	BB	SO	SB	PO	A	E	Avg.
1986— Boston (A.L.).............	DH-PH	4	11	1	2	1	0	0	1	.182	1	3	0	...	...	...	...
1987— Minnesota (A.L.)	DH-PH	5	13	3	5	0	0	1	3	.385	1	1	0	...	...	...	...
1988— Oakland (A.L.)	PH	1	1	0	0	0	0	0	0	.000	0	1	0	...	...	...	...
World Series totals (3 years)		10	25	4	7	1	0	1	4	.280	2	5	0	...	...	...	...

ALL-STAR GAME RECORD

Year — League	Pos.	AB	R	H	2B	3B	HR	RBI	Avg.	BB	SO	SB	PO	A	E	Avg.
1979— American..................	OF	4	2	2	1	0	0	1	.500	0	0	0	1	0	0	1.000

RECORD AS MANAGER

BACKGROUND: Special assistant to general manager, Milwaukee Brewers (September 5-December 4, 1989). ... Coach, Brewers (December 4, 1989-91). ... Coach, St. Louis Cardinals (1992) ... Hitting coach, Atlanta Braves (1999).
HONORS: Coach, N.L. All-Star team (1994). ... Named N.L. Manager of the Year by THE SPORTING NEWS (1995). ... Named N.L. Manager of the Year by Baseball Writers' Association of America (1995).

	REGULAR SEASON				POSTSEASON					
					Playoff		Champ. Series		World Series		All-Star Game
Year — Team (League)	W	L	Pct.	Pos.	W	L	W	L	W	L	W	L
1993— Colorado (N.L.)	67	95	.414	6th (W)	—	—	—	—	—	—	—	—
1994— Colorado (N.L.)	53	64	.453		—	—	—	—	—	—	—	—
1995— Colorado (N.L.)	77	67	.535	2nd (W)	1	3	—	—	—	—	—	—
1996— Colorado (N.L.)	83	79	.512	3rd (W)	—	—	—	—	—	—	—	—

MAJOR LEAGUE MANAGERS

		REGULAR SEASON				POSTSEASON							
								Champ.		World		All-Star	
						Playoff		Series		Series		Game	
Year Team (League)	W	L	Pct.	Pos.		W	L	W	L	W	L	W	L
1997—Colorado (N.L.)	83	79	.512	3rd (W)		—	—	—	—	—	—	—	—
1998—Colorado (N.L.)	77	85	.475	4th (W)		—	—	—	—	—	—	—	—
Major league totals (6 years)	440	469	.484			1	3	—	—	—	—	—	—

NOTES:
1994—Colorado was in third place in N.L. West at time of season-ending strike (August 12).
1995—Lost to Atlanta in N.L. divisional playoff.

BELL, BUDDY — ROCKIES

PERSONAL: Born August 27, 1951, in Pittsburgh. ... 6-3/200. ... Batted right, threw right. ... Full name: David Gus Bell. ... Father of David Bell, second baseman, Seattle Mariners; father of Mike Bell, minor league infielder (1993-99); and son of Gus Bell, major league outfielder with four teams (1950-64).

HIGH SCHOOL: Moeller (Cincinnati).

COLLEGE: Xavier, then Miami of Ohio.

TRANSACTIONS/CAREER NOTES: Selected by Cleveland Indians organization in 16th round of free-agent draft (June 5, 1969). ... On disabled list (May 27-June 17 and August 8-September 1, 1974). ... Traded by Indians to Texas Rangers for 3B Toby Harrah (December 8, 1978). ... On disabled list (June 9-24, 1980). ... Traded by Rangers to Cincinnati Reds for OF Duane Walker and a player to be named later (July 19, 1985); Rangers acquired P Jeff Russell to complete deal (July 23, 1985). ... On Cincinnati disabled list (March 26-April 10 and April 14-May 11, 1988). ... Traded by Reds to Houston Astros for a player to be named later (June 19, 1988); Reds acquired P Carl Grovom to complete deal (October 20, 1988). ... On Houston disabled list (August 4-19, 1988). ... Released by Astros (December 21, 1988). ... Signed by Rangers (January 9, 1989). ... On disabled list (April 8-28, 1989). ... Announced retirement (June 24, 1989).

HONORS: Won A.L. Gold Glove at third base (1979-84). ... Named third baseman on THE SPORTING NEWS A.L. All-Star team (1981 and 1984). ... Named third baseman on THE SPORTING NEWS A.L. Silver Slugger team (1984).

STATISTICAL NOTES: Led Gulf Coast League second basemen with 26 double plays in 1969. ... Led A.L. third basemen with 144 putouts and 44 double plays in 1973. ... Led A.L. third basemen with 495 total chances in 1978, 361 in 1981, 540 in 1982 and 523 in 1983. ... Tied for A.L. lead in double plays by third basemen with 30 in 1978. ... Had 21-game hitting streak (June 24-July 17, 1980). ... Led A.L. third basemen with 364 assists in 1979 and 281 in 1981. ... Led A.L. third basemen with .981 fielding percentage in 1980 and .976 in 1982. ... Led A.L. with 10 sacrifice flies in 1981. ... Career major league grand slams: 8.

| | | | | | BATTING | | | | | | | | | | FIELDING | | |
Year Team (League)	Pos.	G	AB	R	H	2B	3B	HR	RBI	Avg.	BB	SO	SB	PO	A	E	Avg.
1969—Sarasota (GCL)	2B	51	170	18	39	4	•3	3	24	.229	17	15	3	119	108	7	*.970
1970—Sumter (SAL)	3B-2B-SS	121	442	81	117	19	3	12	75	.265	44	43	9	116	189	27	.919
1971—Wichita (A.A.)	3-2-S-O	129	470	65	136	23	1	11	59	.289	42	51	7	*139	203	16	.955
1972—Cleveland (A.L.)	OF-3B	132	466	49	119	21	1	9	36	.255	34	29	5	284	23	3	.990
1973—Cleveland (A.L.)	3B-OF	156	631	86	169	23	7	14	59	.268	49	47	7	†146	363	22	.959
1974—Cleveland (A.L.)	3B	116	423	51	111	15	1	7	46	.262	35	29	1	112	274	15	.963
1975—Cleveland (A.L.)	3B	153	553	66	150	20	4	10	59	.271	51	72	6	*146	330	25	.950
1976—Cleveland (A.L.)	3B-1B	159	604	75	170	26	2	7	60	.281	44	49	3	109	331	20	.957
1977—Cleveland (A.L.)	3B-OF	129	479	64	140	23	4	11	64	.292	45	63	1	134	253	16	.960
1978—Cleveland (A.L.)	3B	142	556	71	157	27	8	6	62	.282	39	43	1	125	*355	15	.970
1979—Texas (A.L.)■	3B-SS	•162	*670	89	200	42	3	18	101	.299	30	45	5	147	†429	17	.971
1980—Texas (A.L.)	3B-SS	129	490	76	161	24	4	17	83	.329	40	39	3	125	282	8	†.981
1981—Texas (A.L.)	3B-SS	97	360	44	106	16	1	10	64	.294	42	30	3	67	†284	14	.962
1982—Texas (A.L.)	3B-SS	148	537	62	159	27	2	13	67	.296	70	50	5	*131	397	13	†.976
1983—Texas (A.L.)	3B	156	618	75	171	35	3	14	66	.277	50	48	3	123	*383	17	.967
1984—Texas (A.L.)	3B	148	553	88	174	36	5	11	83	.315	63	54	2	129	323	•20	.958
1985—Texas (A.L.)	3B	84	313	33	74	13	3	4	32	.236	33	21	3	70	192	16	.942
—Cincinnati (N.L.)■	3B	67	247	28	54	15	2	6	36	.219	34	27	0	54	105	9	.946
1986—Cincinnati (N.L.)	3B-2B	155	568	89	158	29	3	20	75	.278	73	49	2	105	291	10	.975
1987—Cincinnati (N.L.)	3B	143	522	74	148	19	2	17	70	.284	71	39	4	93	241	7	*.979
1988—Cincinnati (N.L.)	3B-1B	21	54	3	10	0	0	0	3	.185	7	3	0	14	26	2	.952
—Houston (N.L.)■	3B-1B	74	269	24	68	10	1	7	37	.253	19	29	1	74	114	13	.935
1989—Texas (A.L.)■	3B-1B	34	82	4	15	4	0	0	3	.183	7	10	0	10	13	0	1.000
American League totals (15 years)		1945	7335	933	2076	352	48	151	885	.283	632	629	48	1858	4232	221	.965
National League totals (4 years)		460	1660	218	438	73	8	50	221	.264	204	147	7	340	777	41	.965
Major league totals (18 years)		2405	8995	1151	2514	425	56	201	1106	.279	836	776	55	2198	5009	262	.965

ALL-STAR GAME RECORD

| | | | | | BATTING | | | | | | | | FIELDING | | |
Year League	Pos.	AB	R	H	2B	3B	HR	RBI	Avg.	BB	SO	SB	PO	A	E	Avg.
1973—American	PH	1	0	1	0	1	0	0	1.000	0	0	0	...	...	...	...
1980—American	3B	2	0	0	0	0	0	0	.000	0	1	0	0	2	0	1.000
1981—American	3B	1	0	0	0	0	0	1	.000	0	0	0	1	2	0	1.000
1982—American	PH-3B	3	0	0	0	0	0	0	.000	0	2	0	0	1	1	.500
1984—American	3B	1	0	0	0	0	0	0	.000	0	0	0	0	1	0	1.000
All-Star Game totals (5 years)		8	0	1	0	1	0	1	.125	0	3	0	1	6	1	.875

RECORD AS MANAGER

BACKGROUND: Minor league hitting instructor, Cleveland Indians organization (1990). ... Director of minor league instruction, Chicago White Sox organization (1991-93). ... Coach, Indians (1994-95). ... Minor league field coordinator, Cincinnati Reds (September 23, 1998-August 4, 1999). ... Director of player development, Reds (August 5, 1999-remainder of season).

			REGULAR SEASON				POSTSEASON						
						Playoff		Champ. Series		World Series		All-Star Game	
Year Team (League)	W	L	Pct.	Pos.		W	L	W	L	W	L	W	L
1996—Detroit (A.L.)	53	109	.327	5th (E)		—	—	—	—	—	—	—	—
1997—Detroit (A.L.)	79	83	.488	3rd (E)		—	—	—	—	—	—	—	—
1998—Detroit (A.L.)	52	85	.379			—	—	—	—	—	—	—	—
Major league totals (3 years)	184	277	.399			—	—	—	—	—	—	—	—

NOTES:
1998—Replaced as Detroit manager on interim basis by Larry Parrish with club in fifth place (September 1).

BOCHY, BRUCE — PADRES

PERSONAL: Born April 16, 1955, in Landes de Boussac, France. ... 6-4/225. ... Batted right, threw right. ... Full name: Bruce Douglas Bochy. ... Brother of Joe Bochy, catcher in Minnesota Twins organization (1969-72). ... Name pronounced BO-chee.

HIGH SCHOOL: Melbourne (Fla.).

JUNIOR COLLEGE: Brevard Community College (Fla.).

COLLEGE: Florida State.

TRANSACTIONS/CAREER NOTES: Selected by Chicago White Sox organization in eighth round of free-agent draft (January 9, 1975); did not sign. ... Selected by Houston Astros organization in secondary phase of free-agent draft (June 4, 1975). ... Traded by Astros to New York Mets organization for two players to be named later (February 11, 1981); Astros acquired IF Randy Rodgers and C Stan Hough to complete deal (April 3, 1981). ... Released by Mets (January 21, 1983). ... Signed by Las Vegas, San Diego Padres organization (February 23, 1983). ... On disabled list (April 13-May 6, 1987). ... Granted free agency (November 9, 1987).

STATISTICAL NOTES: Tied for Florida State League lead with 12 passed balls in 1977.

							BATTING							FIELDING			
Year Team (League)	Pos.	G	AB	R	H	2B	3B	HR	RBI	Avg.	BB	SO	SB	PO	A	E	Avg.
1975—Covington (Appal.)	C	37	145	31	49	9	0	4	34	.338	11	18	0	231	36	4	.985
1976—Columbus (Sou.)	C	69	230	9	53	6	0	0	16	.230	14	30	0	266	45	6	.981
—Dubuque (Midwest)	C-1B	30	103	9	25	4	0	1	8	.243	12	11	1	165	25	5	.974
1977—Cocoa (FSL)	C	128	430	40	109	18	2	3	35	.253	35	50	0	*492	67	12	.979
1978—Columbus (Sou.)	C	79	261	25	70	10	2	7	34	.268	13	30	0	419	49	7	.985
—Houston (N.L.)	C	54	154	8	41	8	0	3	15	.266	11	35	0	268	35	8	.974
1979—Houston (N.L.)	C	56	129	11	28	4	0	1	6	.217	17	25	0	198	29	7	.970
1980—Houston (N.L.)	C-1B	22	22	0	4	1	0	0	0	.182	0	0	0	19	1	0	1.000
1981—Tidewater (I.L.)■	C	85	269	23	61	11	2	8	38	.227	22	47	0	253	35	3	.990
1982—Tidewater (I.L.)	C	81	251	32	57	11	0	15	52	.227	19	47	2	427	57	5	.990
—New York (N.L.)	C-1B	17	49	4	15	4	0	2	8	.306	4	6	0	92	8	4	.962
1983—Las Vegas (PCL)■	C	42	145	28	44	8	1	11	33	.303	15	25	3	157	21	3	.983
—San Diego (N.L.)	C	23	42	2	9	1	1	0	3	.214	0	9	0	51	5	0	1.000
1984—Las Vegas (PCL)	C	34	121	18	32	7	0	7	22	.264	17	13	0	189	17	2	.990
—San Diego (N.L.)	C	37	92	10	21	5	1	4	15	.228	3	21	0	147	12	2	.988
1985—San Diego (N.L.)	C	48	112	16	30	2	0	6	13	.268	6	30	0	148	11	2	.988
1986—San Diego (N.L.)	C	63	127	16	32	9	0	8	22	.252	14	23	1	202	22	2	.991
1987—San Diego (N.L.)	C	38	75	8	12	3	0	2	11	.160	11	21	0	95	7	4	.962
1988—Las Vegas (PCL)	C	53	147	17	34	5	0	5	13	.231	17	28	0	207	19	3	.987
Major league totals (9 years)		358	802	75	192	37	2	26	93	.239	66	170	1	1220	130	29	.979

CHAMPIONSHIP SERIES RECORD

							BATTING							FIELDING			
Year Team (League)	Pos.	G	AB	R	H	2B	3B	HR	RBI	Avg.	BB	SO	SB	PO	A	E	Avg.
1980—Houston (N.L.)	C	1	1	0	0	0	0	0	0	.000	0	0	0	5	1	0	1.000

WORLD SERIES RECORD

							BATTING							FIELDING			
Year Team (League)	Pos.	G	AB	R	H	2B	3B	HR	RBI	Avg.	BB	SO	SB	PO	A	E	Avg.
1984—San Diego (N.L.)	PH	1	1	0	0	0	0	0	0	1.000	0	0	0	...	...	...	...

RECORD AS MANAGER

BACKGROUND: Player/coach, Las Vegas, San Diego Padres organization (1988). ... Coach, Padres (1993-94).

HONORS: Named N.L. Manager of the Year by THE SPORTING NEWS (1996 and 1998). ... Named N.L. Manager of the Year by Baseball Writers' Association of America (1996).

			REGULAR SEASON				POSTSEASON						
						Playoff		Champ. Series		World Series		All-Star Game	
Year Team (League)	W	L	Pct.	Pos.		W	L	W	L	W	L	W	L
1989—Spokane (Northwest)	41	34	.547	1st (N)		2	1	—	—	—	—	—	—
1990—Riverside (California)	35	36	.493	4th (S)		—	—	—	—	—	—	—	—
—(Second half)	29	42	.408	5th (S)		—	—	—	—	—	—	—	—
1991—High Desert (California)	31	37	.456	3rd (S)		—	—	—	—	—	—	—	—
—(Second half)	42	26	.618	1st (S)		6	2	—	—	—	—	—	—
1992—Wichita (Texas)	39	29	.574	1st (W)		—	—	—	—	—	—	—	—
—(Second half)	31	37	.456	4th (W)		6	1	—	—	—	—	—	—
1995—San Diego (N.L.)	70	74	.486	3rd (W)		—	—	—	—	—	—	—	—
1996—San Diego (N.L.)	91	71	.562	1st (W)		0	3	—	—	—	—	—	—
1997—San Diego (N.L.)	76	86	.469	4th (W)		—	—	—	—	—	—	—	—
1998—San Diego (N.L.)	98	64	.605	1st (W)		3	1	4	2	0	4	—	—
1999—San Diego (N.L.)	74	88	.457	4th (W)		—	—	—	—	—	—	—	—
Major league totals (5 years)	409	383	.516			3	4	4	2	0	4	—	—

NOTES:
1989—Defeated Southern Oregon in league championship.
1991—Defeated Bakersfield, three games to none, in semifinals; defeated Stockton, three games to two, in league championship.
1992—Defeated El Paso, two games to one, in semifinals; defeated Shreveport, four games to none, in league championship.
1996—Lost to St. Louis in N.L. divisional playoff.
1998—Defeated Houston in N.L. divisional playoff; defeated Atlanta in N.L. Championship Series; lost to New York Yankees in World Series.

BOLES, JOHN — MARLINS

PERSONAL: Born August 19, 1948, in Chicago. ... 5-10/165. ... Full name: John Boles Jr.
COLLEGE: Lewis University (degree in sociology), then St. Xavier College.

RECORD AS MANAGER

BACKGROUND: Head coach, St. Xavier College (1973-79). ... Head coach, University of Louisville (1980-81). ... Director of player development, Kansas City Royals (July 26, 1986-1989). ... Minor league coordinator, Montreal Expos (1990). ... Director of player development, Expos (1991). ... Director of player development, Florida Marlins (November 1, 1991-July 28, 1995). ... Vice president of player development, Marlins (July 28, 1995-present).
HONORS: Named Gulf Coast League Manager of the Year (1982).

| | | REGULAR SEASON | | | | POSTSEASON | | | | | | | |
| | | | | | | Playoff | | Champ. Series | | World Series | | All-Star Game | |
Year Team (League)	W	L	Pct.	Pos.	W	L	W	L	W	L	W	L
1981— Gulf Coast White Sox (GCL)	41	23	.641	2nd	—	—	—	—	—	—	—	—
1982— Gulf Coast White Sox (GCL)	40	23	.635	2nd	—	—	—	—	—	—	—	—
1983— Appleton (Midwest)	87	50	.635	1st (N)	5	2	—	—	—	—	—	—
1984— Glens Falls (Eastern)	75	63	.543	2nd	1	3	—	—	—	—	—	—
1985— Buffalo (American Association)	66	76	.465	3rd (E)	—	—	—	—	—	—	—	—
1986— Omaha (American Association)	40	36	.526		—	—	—	—	—	—	—	—
1996— Florida (N.L.)	40	35	.540	3rd (E)	—	—	—	—	—	—	—	—
1999— Florida (N.L.)	64	98	.395	5th (E)	—	—	—	—	—	—	—	—
Major league totals (2 years)	104	133	.438		—	—	—	—	—	—	—	—

NOTES:
1983—Defeated Waterloo, two games to one, in league semifinals; defeated Springfield, three games to one, to win league championship.
1984—Glens Falls tied one game; lost to Waterbury in league semifinals.
1986—Replaced as Omaha manager by Frank Funk (June 25).
1996—Replaced Florida manager Rene Lachemann with club in fourth place and record of 40-47 (July 8).

COX, BOBBY — BRAVES

PERSONAL: Born May 21, 1941, in Tulsa, Okla. ... 6-0/185. ... Batted right, threw right. ... Full name: Robert Joe Cox.
HIGH SCHOOL: Selma (Calif.).
JUNIOR COLLEGE: Reedley Junior College (Calif.).
TRANSACTIONS/CAREER NOTES: Signed by Los Angeles Dodgers organization (1959). ... Selected by Chicago Cubs organization from Dodgers organization in Rule 5 minor league draft (November 30, 1964). ... Acquired by Atlanta Braves organization (1966). ... On Austin disabled list (May 8-18 and May 30-June 9, 1966). ... On disabled list (May 1-June 12, 1967). ... Traded by Braves to New York Yankees for C Bob Tillman and P Dale Roberts (December 7, 1967); Roberts later was transferred to Richmond. ... On disabled list (May 28-June 18, 1970). ... Released by Yankees organization (September 22, 1970). ... Signed by Fort Lauderdale, Yankees organization (July 17, 1971). ... Released as player by Fort Lauderdale (August 28, 1971).
STATISTICAL NOTES: Led Alabama-Florida League shortstops with 71 double plays in 1961. ... Led Pacific Coast League third basemen with .954 fielding percentage in 1965.

| | | | | | | | BATTING | | | | | | | | FIELDING | | |
Year Team (League)	Pos.	G	AB	R	H	2B	3B	HR	RBI	Avg.	BB	SO	SB	PO	A	E	Avg.
1960— Reno (California)	2B	125	440	99	112	20	5	13	75	.255	95	129	28	282	*385	*39	.945
1961— Salem (Northwest)	2B	14	44	3	9	2	0	0	2	.205	0	14	0	25	25	2	.962
— Panama City (Al.-Fla.)	2B	92	335	66	102	27	4	17	73	.304	48	72	17	220	247	8	*.983
1962— Salem (Northwest)	3B-2B	*141	514	83	143	26	7	16	82	.278	63	119	7	174	296	28	.944
1963— Albuquerque (Texas)	3B	17	53	5	15	2	0	2	5	.283	3	12	1	8	27	1	.972
— Great Falls (Pio.)	3B	109	407	103	137	*31	4	19	85	.337	73	84	7	82	211	21	*.933
1964— Albuquerque (Texas)	2B	138	523	98	152	29	13	16	91	.291	52	84	8	*322	*415	*28	.963
1965— Salt Lake (PCL)■	3B-2B	136	473	58	125	32	1	12	55	.264	35	96	1	133	337	22	†.955
1966— Tacoma (PCL)	3B-2B	10	34	2	4	1	0	0	4	.118	6	9	0	23	15	0	1.000
— Austin (Texas)■	2B-3B	92	339	35	77	11	1	7	30	.227	25	55	7	140	216	12	.967
1967— Richmond (I.L.)	3B-1B	99	350	52	104	17	4	14	51	.297	34	73	3	84	136	8	.965
1968— New York (A.L.)■	3B	135	437	33	100	15	1	7	41	.229	41	85	3	98	279	17	.957
1969— New York (A.L.)	3B-2B	85	191	17	41	7	1	2	17	.215	34	41	0	50	147	11	.947
1970— Syracuse (I.L.)	3B-SS-2B	90	251	34	55	15	0	9	30	.219	49	40	0	86	163	13	.950
1971— Fort Laud. (FSL)	2B-P	4	9	1	1	0	0	0	0	.111	1	0	0	4	5	0	1.000
Major league totals (2 years)		220	628	50	141	22	2	9	58	.225	75	126	3	148	426	28	.953

RECORD AS PITCHER

Year Team (League)	W	L	Pct.	ERA	G	GS	CG	ShO	Sv.	IP	H	R	ER	BB	SO
1971— Fort Lauderdale (FSL)	0	1	.000	5.40	3	0	0	0	0	10	15	9	6	5	4

RECORD AS MANAGER

BACKGROUND: Minor league instructor, New York Yankees (October 28, 1970-March 24, 1971). ... Player/manager, Fort Lauderdale, Yankees organization (1971). ... Coach, Yankees (1977).
HONORS: Named Major League Manager of the Year by THE SPORTING NEWS (1985). ... Named A.L. Manager of the Year by Baseball Writers' Association of America (1985). ... Named N.L. Manager of the Year by THE SPORTING NEWS (1991, 1993 and 1999). ... Named N.L. Manager of the Year by the Baseball Writers' Association of America (1991).

Year Team (League)	W	L	Pct.	Pos.	Playoff W	L	Champ. Series W	L	World Series W	L	All-Star Game W	L
1971— Fort Lauderdale (Florida State)	71	70	.504	4th (E)	—	—	—	—	—	—	—	—
1972— West Haven (East.)	84	56	.600	1st (A)	3	0	—	—	—	—	—	—
1973— Syracuse (International)	76	70	.521	3rd (A)	—	—	—	—	—	—	—	—
1974— Syracuse (International)	74	70	.514	2nd (N)	—	—	—	—	—	—	—	—
1975— Syracuse (International)	72	64	.529	3rd	—	—	—	—	—	—	—	—
1976— Syracuse (International)	82	57	.590	2nd	6	1	—	—	—	—	—	—
1978— Atlanta (N.L.)	69	93	.426	6th (W)	—	—	—	—	—	—	—	—
1979— Atlanta (N.L.)	66	94	.413	6th (W)	—	—	—	—	—	—	—	—
1980— Atlanta (N.L.)	81	80	.503	4th (W)	—	—	—	—	—	—	—	—
1981— Atlanta (N.L.)	25	29	.463	4th (W)	—	—	—	—	—	—	—	—
— (Second half)	25	27	.481	5th (W)	—	—	—	—	—	—	—	—
1982— Toronto (A.L.)	78	84	.481	T6th (E)	—	—	—	—	—	—	—	—
1983— Toronto (A.L.)	89	73	.549	4th (E)	—	—	—	—	—	—	—	—
1984— Toronto (A.L.)	89	73	.549	2nd (E)	—	—	—	—	—	—	—	—
1985— Toronto (A.L.)	99	62	.615	1st (E)	—	—	3	4	—	—	—	—
1990— Atlanta (N.L.)	40	57	.412	6th (W)	—	—	—	—	—	—	—	—
1991— Atlanta (N.L.)	94	68	.580	1st (W)	—	—	4	3	3	4	—	—
1992— Atlanta (N.L.)	98	64	.605	1st (W)	—	—	4	3	2	4	0	1
1993— Atlanta (N.L.)	104	58	.642	1st (W)	—	—	2	4	—	—	0	1
1994— Atlanta (N.L.)	68	46	.596		—	—	—	—	—	—	—	—
1995— Atlanta (N.L.)	90	54	.625	1st (E)	3	1	4	0	4	2	—	—
1996— Atlanta (N.L.)	96	66	.593	1st (E)	3	0	4	3	2	4	1	0
1997— Atlanta (N.L.)	101	61	.623	1st (E)	3	0	2	4	—	—	0	1
1998— Atlanta (N.L.)	106	56	.654	1st (E)	3	0	2	4	—	—	—	—
1999— Atlanta (N.L.)	103	59	.636	1st (E)	3	0	4	2	0	4	—	—
American League totals (4 years)	355	292	.549		—	—	3	4	—	—	—	—
National League totals (14 years)	1166	912	.561		15	1	26	23	11	18	1	3
Major league totals (18 years)	1521	1204	.558		15	1	29	27	11	18	1	3

NOTES:
1972—Defeated Three Rivers in playoff.
1976—Defeated Memphis, three games to none, in playoffs; defeated Richmond, three games to one, in league championship.
1985—Lost to Kansas City in A.L. Championship Series.
1990—Replaced Atlanta manager Russ Nixon with club in sixth place and record of 25-40 (June 22).
1991—Defeated Pittsburgh in N.L. Championship Series; lost to Minnesota in World Series.
1992—Defeated Pittsburgh in N.L. Championship Series; lost to Toronto in World Series.
1993—Lost to Philadelphia in N.L. Championship Series.
1994—Atlanta was in second place at time of season-ending strike (August 12).
1995—Defeated Colorado in N.L. divisional playoff; defeated Cincinnati in N.L. Championship Series; defeated Cleveland in World Series.
1996—Defeated Los Angeles in N.L. divisional playoff; defeated St. Louis in N.L. Championship Series; lost to New York Yankees in World Series.
1997—Defeated Houston in N.L. divisional playoff; lost to Florida in N.L. Championship Series.
1998—Defeated Chicago Cubs in N.L. divisional playoff; lost to San Diego in N.L. Championship Series.
1999—Defeated Houston in N.L. divisional playoff; defeated New York Mets in N.L. Championship Series; lost to New York Yankees in World Series.

DIERKER, LARRY — ASTROS

PERSONAL: Born September 22, 1946, in Hollywood, Calif. ... 6-4/205. ... Threw right, batted right. ... Full name: Lawrence Edward Dierker. ... Brother of Richard Dierker, pitcher in Baltimore Orioles organization (1972-75). ... Name pronounced DUR-ker.

COLLEGE: UC Santa Barbara, then Houston.

TRANSACTIONS/CAREER NOTES: Signed as free agent by Houston Astros organization (1964). ... Served in military (June 25, 1967-remainder of season). ... On disabled list (March 21-May 22 and June 16-July 12, 1973). ... Traded by Astros with IF Jerry DaVanon to St. Louis Cardinals for C/OF Joe Ferguson and OF Bobby Detherage (November 23, 1976). ... On disabled list (March 23-May 19 and July 23, 1977-remainder of season). ... Released by Cardinals (March 28, 1978).

STATISTICAL NOTES: Led N.L. with 20 wild pitches in 1968. ... Pitched 6-0 no-hit victory against Montreal (July 9, 1976).

MISCELLANEOUS: Holds Houston Astros franchise all-time records for most innings pitched (2,296) and shutouts (25). ... Television and radio color analyst, Astros (1979-1996).

Year Team (League)	W	L	Pct.	ERA	G	GS	CG	ShO	Sv.	IP	H	R	ER	BB	SO
1964— Cocoa (Cocoa Rookie)	2	3	.400	3.23	9	9	0			39	21	19	14	18	61
— Houston (N.L.)	0	1	.000	2.00	3	1	0	0	0	9	7	4	2	3	5
1965— Houston (N.L.)	7	8	.467	3.49	26	19	1	0	0	147	135	69	57	37	109
1966— Houston (N.L.)	10	8	.556	3.18	29	28	8	2	0	187	173	73	66	45	108
1967— Houston (N.L.)	6	5	.545	3.36	15	15	4	0	0	99	95	44	37	25	68
1968— Houston (N.L.)	12	15	.444	3.31	32	32	10	1	0	234	206	95	86	89	161
1969— Houston (N.L.)	20	13	.606	2.33	39	37	20	4	0	305	240	97	79	72	232
1970— Houston (N.L.)	16	12	.571	3.87	37	36	17	2	1	270	263	124	116	82	191
1971— Houston (N.L.)	12	6	.667	2.72	24	23	6	2	0	159	150	50	48	33	91
1972— Houston (N.L.)	15	8	.652	3.39	31	31	12	5	0	215	209	87	81	51	115
1973— Houston (N.L.)	1	1	.500	4.33	14	3	0	0	0	27	27	14	13	13	18
1974— Houston (N.L.)	11	10	.524	2.89	33	33	7	3	0	224	189	76	72	82	150
1975— Houston (N.L.)	14	16	.467	4.00	34	34	14	2	0	232	225	109	103	91	127
1976— Houston (N.L.)	13	14	.481	3.69	28	28	7	4	0	188	171	85	77	72	112
1977— St. Louis (N.L.)■	2	6	.250	4.62	11	9	0	0	0	39	40	21	20	16	6
Major league totals (14 years)	139	123	.531	3.30	356	329	106	25	1	2335	2130	948	857	711	1493

ALL-STAR GAME RECORD

Year League	W	L	Pct.	ERA	GS	CG	ShO	Sv.	IP	H	R	ER	BB	SO
1969— National	0	0	...	0.00	0	0	0	0	$1/3$	1	0	0	0	0
1971— National				Selected, did not play—injured.										

RECORD AS MANAGER

HONORS: Named N.L. Manager of the Year by Baseball Writers' Association of America (1998).

		REGULAR SEASON				POSTSEASON							
						Playoff		Champ. Series		World Series		All-Star Game	
Year Team (League)	W	L	Pct.	Pos.	W	L	W	L	W	L	W	L	
1997— Houston (N.L.)	84	78	.519	1st (C)	0	3	—	—	—	—	—	—	
1998— Houston (N.L.)	102	60	.630	1st (C)	1	3	—	—	—	—	—	—	
1999— Houston (N.L.)	97	65	.599	1st (C)	1	3	—	—	—	—	—	—	
Major league totals (3 years)	**283**	**203**	**.582**		**2**	**9**	**—**	**—**	**—**	**—**	**—**	**—**	

NOTES:
1997—Lost to Atlanta in N.L. divisional playoff.
1998—Lost to San Diego in N.L. divisional playoff.
1999—Lost to Atlanta in N.L. divisional playoff.

FRANCONA, TERRY — PHILLIES

PERSONAL: Born April 22, 1959, in New Brighton, Pa. ... 6-1/175. ... Batted left, threw left. ... Full name: Terry Jon Francona. ... Son of Tito Francona, outfielder/first baseman with nine major league teams (1956-70).

HIGH SCHOOL: New Brighton (Pa.).

COLLEGE: Arizona.

TRANSACTIONS/CAREER NOTES: Selected by Chicago Cubs organization in second round of free-agent draft (June 7, 1977); did not sign. ... Selected by Montreal Expos organization in first round (22nd pick overall) of free-agent draft (June 3, 1980); pick received as compensation for New York Yankees signing free-agent P Rudy May. ... On disabled list (June 17-September 27, 1982 and June 15-September 5, 1984). ... Released by Expos (April 1, 1986). ... Signed by Chicago Cubs organization (May 2, 1986). ... Granted free agency (October 18, 1986). ... Signed by Cincinnati Reds (March 23, 1987). ... Granted free agency (November 12, 1987). ... Signed by Colorado Springs, Cleveland Indians organization (February 28, 1988). ... Granted free agency (November 4, 1988). ... Signed by Milwaukee Brewers (March 30, 1989). ... Granted free agency (November 13, 1989). ... Re-signed by Brewers (December 12, 1989). ... Released by Brewers (April 27, 1990). ... Signed by Louisville, St. Louis Cardinals organization (May 5, 1990). ... Released by Cardinals organization (April 2, 1991).

HONORS: Named Golden Spikes Award winner by USA Baseball (1980). ... Named College Player of the Year by THE SPORTING NEWS (1980). ... Named outfielder on THE SPORTING NEWS college All-America team (1980).

								BATTING							FIELDING			
Year Team (League)	Pos.	G	AB	R	H	2B	3B	HR	RBI	Avg.	BB	SO	SB	PO	A	E	Avg.
1980— Memphis (Sou.)	OF	60	210	20	63	13	2	1	23	.300	10	20	1	59	4	4	.940
1981— Memphis (Sou.)	OF-1B	41	161	20	56	8	1	0	18	.348	7	18	0	102	7	5	.956
— Denver (A.A.)	OF	93	355	53	125	17	*9	1	58	.352	16	22	7	158	7	3	.982
— Montreal (N.L.)	OF-1B	34	95	11	26	0	1	1	8	.274	5	6	1	41	5	0	1.000
1982— Montreal (N.L.)	OF-1B	46	131	14	42	3	0	0	9	.321	8	11	2	65	0	3	.956
1983— Montreal (N.L.)	OF-1B	120	230	21	59	11	1	3	22	.257	6	20	0	172	10	3	.984
1984— Montreal (N.L.)	1B-OF	58	214	18	74	19	2	1	18	.346	5	12	0	431	50	3	.994
1985— Montreal (N.L.)	1B-OF-3B	107	281	19	75	15	1	2	31	.267	12	12	5	431	40	6	.987
1986— Chicago (N.L.)■	OF-1B	86	124	13	31	3	0	2	8	.250	6	8	0	123	7	0	1.000
— Iowa (A.A.)	1B-OF	17	60	7	15	3	2	0	8	.250	4	5	1	82	3	1	.988
1987— Cincinnati (N.L.)■	1B-OF	102	207	16	47	5	0	3	12	.227	10	12	2	377	45	2	.995
1988— Colo. Spr. (PCL)■	OF-1B	68	235	29	76	15	5	0	32	.323	13	18	0	115	11	3	.977
— Cleveland (A.L.)	DH-1B-OF	62	212	24	66	8	0	1	12	.311	5	18	0	47	5	1	.981
1989— Milwaukee (A.L.)	1-DH-O-P	90	233	26	54	10	1	3	23	.232	8	20	2	339	26	4	.989
1990— Milwaukee (A.L.)	1B	3	4	1	0	0	0	0	0	.000	0	0	0	6	0	0	1.000
— Louisville (A.A.)■	OF-1B-P	86	285	29	75	9	3	6	30	.263	12	23	1	126	7	2	.985
American League totals (3 years)		155	449	51	120	18	1	4	35	.267	13	38	2	392	31	5	.988
National League totals (7 years)		553	1282	112	354	56	5	12	108	.276	52	81	10	1640	157	17	.991
Major league totals (10 years)		708	1731	163	474	74	6	16	143	.274	65	119	12	2032	188	22	.990

DIVISION SERIES RECORD

						BATTING								FIELDING			
Year Team (League)	Pos.	G	AB	R	H	2B	3B	HR	RBI	Avg.	BB	SO	SB	PO	A	E	Avg.
1981— Montreal (N.L.)	OF	5	12	0	4	0	0	0	0	.333	2	2	2	8	0	0	1.000

CHAMPIONSHIP SERIES RECORD

						BATTING								FIELDING			
Year Team (League)	Pos.	G	AB	R	H	2B	3B	HR	RBI	Avg.	BB	SO	SB	PO	A	E	Avg.
1981— Montreal (N.L.)	PH-OF	2	1	0	0	0	0	0	0	.000	0	1	0	0	0	0	...

RECORD AS PITCHER

Year Team (League)	W	L	Pct.	ERA	G	GS	CG	ShO	Sv.	IP	H	R	ER	BB	SO
1989— Milwaukee (A.L.)	0	0	...	0.00	1	0	0	0	0	1	0	0	0	0	1
1990— Louisville (A.A.)	0	0	...	1.17	5	0	0	0	0	7 2/3	4	1	1	2	6

RECORD AS MANAGER

BACKGROUND: Manager, Scottsdale Scorpions, Arizona Fall League (1994, record: 26-25, second place/Northern Division). ... Coach, Detroit Tigers (1996).

HONORS: Named Southern League Manager of the Year (1993).

		REGULAR SEASON				POSTSEASON							
						Playoff		Champ. Series		World Series		All-Star Game	
Year Team (League)	W	L	Pct.	Pos.	W	L	W	L	W	L	W	L	
1992— South Bend (Midwest)	35	33	.515	3rd (N)	—	—	—	—	—	—	—	—	
— (Second half)	38	31	.551	2nd (N)	—	—	—	—	—	—	—	—	
1993— Birmingham (Southern)	35	36	.493	2nd (W)	—	—	—	—	—	—	—	—	
— (Second half)	43	28	.606	1st (W)	6	1	—	—	—	—	—	—	

| | | REGULAR SEASON | | | | POSTSEASON | | | | | | | |
| | | | | | | Playoff | | Champ. Series | | World Series | | All-Star Game | |
Year Team (League)		W	L	Pct.	Pos.	W	L	W	L	W	L	W	L
1994— Birmingham (Southern)		31	38	.449	4th (W)	—	—	—	—	—	—	—	—
— (Second half)		34	36	.486	5th (W)	—	—	—	—	—	—	—	—
1995— Birmingham (Southern)		33	39	.458	4th (W)	—	—	—	—	—	—	—	—
— (Second half)		47	25	.653	2nd (W)	—	—	—	—	—	—	—	—
1997— Philadelphia (N.L.)		68	94	.420	5th (E)	—	—	—	—	—	—	—	—
1998— Philadelphia (N.L.)		75	87	.463	3rd (E)	—	—	—	—	—	—	—	—
1999— Philadelphia (N.L.)		77	85	.475	3rd (E)	—	—	—	—	—	—	—	—
Major league totals (3 years)		220	266	.453		—	—	—	—	—	—	—	—

NOTES:
1992—South Bend tied one game in first half of season.
1993—Defeated Nashville, three games to none, in first round; defeated Knoxville, three games to one, in league championship.

FREGOSI, JIM   BLUE JAYS

PERSONAL: Born April 4, 1942, in San Francisco. ... 6-2/197. ... Batted right, threw right. ... Full name: James Louis Fregosi. ... Father of Jim Fregosi Jr., minor league shortstop (1985-87).

HIGH SCHOOL: Serra (San Mateo, Calif.).

COLLEGE: Menlo College (Calif.).

TRANSACTIONS/CAREER NOTES: Signed by Boston Red Sox organization (September 6, 1959). ... Selected by Los Angeles Angels in A.L. expansion draft (December 14, 1960). ... On disabled list (July 12-August 5, 1961). ... Traded by Angels to New York Mets for P Nolan Ryan, P Don Rose, OF Leroy Stanton and C Francisco Estrada (December 10, 1971). ... Traded by Mets to Texas Rangers for a player to be named later (July 11, 1973); deal settled in cash. ... On disabled list (April 22-May 12, 1977). ... Traded by Rangers to Pittsburgh Pirates for 1B/C Ed Kirkpatrick (June 15, 1977). ... Released by Pirates in order to accept managerial position with California Angels (June 1, 1978).

RECORDS: Shares major league single-game record for most double plays started by shortstop (nine-inning game)—5 (May 1, 1966, first game).

HONORS: Named shortstop on THE SPORTING NEWS A.L. All-Star team (1964 and 1967). ... Won A.L. Gold Glove at shortstop (1967).

STATISTICAL NOTES: Tied for American Association lead in double plays by shortstop with 100 in 1961. ... Led American League with 15 sacrifice hits in 1965. ... Led American League shortstops with 125 double plays in 1966 and tied for lead with 92 in 1968. ... Led American League shortstops with 531 assists and tied for lead with 35 errors in 1966. ... Career major league grand slams: 1.

| | | | | | | | BATTING | | | | | | | | FIELDING | | |
Year Team (League)	Pos.	G	AB	R	H	2B	3B	HR	RBI	Avg.	BB	SO	SB	PO	A	E	Avg.
1960— Alpine (Soph.)	IF-OF	112	404	96	108	17	7	6	58	.267	74	99	4	198	261	39	.922
1961— Dall./Fort W. (A.A.)	SS	150	516	54	131	18	4	6	50	.254	50	70	6	247	*495	*53	.933
— Los Angeles (A.L.)......	SS	11	27	7	6	0	0	0	3	.222	1	4	0	12	22	2	.944
1962— Dall./Fort W. (A.A.)	SS-OF	64	219	25	62	9	3	1	14	.283	32	37	1	94	164	22	.921
— Los Angeles (A.L.)......	SS	58	175	15	51	3	4	3	23	.291	18	27	2	96	150	15	.943
1963— Los Angeles (A.L.)......	SS	154	592	83	170	29	12	9	50	.287	36	104	2	271	446	27	.964
1964— Los Angeles (A.L.)......	SS	147	505	86	140	22	9	18	72	.277	72	87	8	225	421	23	.966
1965— California (A.L.)........	SS	161	602	66	167	19	7	15	64	.277	54	107	13	*312	481	26	.968
1966— California (A.L.)........	SS-1B	162	611	78	154	32	7	13	67	.252	67	89	17	299	†531	†35	.960
1967— California (A.L.)........	SS	151	590	75	171	23	6	9	56	.290	49	77	9	258	435	25	.965
1968— California (A.L.)........	SS	159	614	77	150	21	*13	9	49	.244	60	101	9	273	454	29	.962
1969— California (A.L.)........	SS	161	580	78	151	22	6	12	47	.260	93	86	9	255	465	21	.972
1970— California (A.L.)........	SS-1B	158	601	95	167	33	5	22	82	.278	69	92	0	313	475	20	.975
1971— California (A.L.)........	SS-1B-OF	107	347	31	81	15	1	5	33	.233	39	61	2	241	251	22	.957
1972— New York (N.L.)■......	3B-SS-1B	101	340	31	79	15	4	5	32	.232	38	71	0	91	162	15	.944
1973— New York (N.L.)........	S-3-1-O	45	142	7	29	4	1	0	11	.234	20	25	1	47	70	9	.929
— Texas (A.L.)■............	3B-1B-SS	45	157	25	42	6	2	6	16	.268	12	31	0	98	53	5	.968
1974— Texas (A.L.)	1B-3B	78	230	31	60	5	0	12	34	.261	22	41	0	331	73	5	.988
1975— Texas (A.L.)	1B-DH-3B	77	191	25	50	5	0	7	33	.262	20	39	0	356	35	6	.985
1976— Texas (A.L.)	1B-DH-3B	58	133	17	31	7	0	2	12	.233	23	33	2	183	18	2	.990
1977— Texas (A.L.)	1B-DH	13	28	4	7	1	0	1	5	.250	3	4	0	31	4	0	1.000
— Pittsburgh (N.L.)■......	1B-3B	36	56	10	16	1	1	3	16	.286	13	10	2	99	5	2	.981
1978— Pittsburgh (N.L.)........	3B-1B-2B	20	20	3	4	1	0	0	1	.200	6	8	0	14	4	2	.900
American League totals (16 years)		1700	5983	793	1598	243	72	143	646	.267	638	983	73	3554	4314	263	.968
National League totals (4 years)		202	540	51	128	21	6	8	60	.237	77	114	3	251	241	28	.946
Major league totals (18 years)		1902	6523	844	1726	264	78	151	706	.265	715	1097	76	3805	4555	291	.966

ALL-STAR GAME RECORD

| | | | | | BATTING | | | | | | | | FIELDING | | |
Year League	Pos.	AB	R	H	2B	3B	HR	RBI	Avg.	BB	SO	SB	PO	A	E	Avg.
1964— American	SS	4	1	1	0	0	0	1	.250	0	1	0	4	1	0	1.000
1966— American	SS	2	0	0	0	0	0	0	.000	0	1	0	0	1	0	1.000
1967— American	SS	4	0	1	0	0	0	0	.250	0	2	0	2	3	0	1.000
1968— American	SS	3	0	1	1	0	0	0	.333	0	1	0	1	6	0	1.000
1969— American	SS	1	0	0	0	0	0	0	.000	0	0	0	0	0	0	...
1970— American	PH	1	0	0	0	0	0	0	.000	0	0	0	...	...	...	...
All-Star Game totals (6 years)		15	1	3	1	0	0	1	.200	0	5	0	7	11	0	1.000

RECORD AS MANAGER

BACKGROUND: Special assignment scout and coach, Philadelphia Phillies (1989-90). ... Minor league pitching instructor and special assignment scout, Phillies (beginning of 1991 season-April 23, 1991). ... Special assistant to general manager, San Francisco Giants (1996-98).

HONORS: Named American Association Manager of the Year (1983). ... Named American Association co-Manager of the Year (1985). ... Named Minor League Manager of the Year by THE SPORTING NEWS (1985). ... Coach, A.L. All-Star team (1987). ... Coach, N.L. All-Star team (1993).

| | | REGULAR SEASON | | | POSTSEASON | | | | | |
| | | | | | | Playoff | | Champ. Series | | World Series | | All-Star Game | |
Year Team (League)	W	L	Pct.	Pos.	W	L	W	L	W	L	W	L
1978— California (A.L.)	62	54	.534	T2nd (W)	—	—	—	—	—	—	—	—
1979— California (A.L.)	88	74	.543	1st (W)	—	—	1	3	—	—	—	—
1980— California (A.L.)	65	95	.406	6th (W)	—	—	—	—	—	—	—	—
1981— California (A.L.)	22	25	.468		—	—	—	—	—	—	—	—
1983— Louisville (American Association)	78	57	.578	1st (E)	3	6	—	—	—	—	—	—
1984— Louisville (American Association)	79	76	.510	4th	8	3	—	—	—	—	—	—
1985— Louisville (American Association)	74	68	.521	1st (E)	4	1	—	—	—	—	—	—
1986— Louisville (American Association)	32	34	.485	3rd (E)	—	—	—	—	—	—	—	—
— Chicago (A.L.)	45	51	.469	5th (W)	—	—	—	—	—	—	—	—
1987— Chicago (A.L.)	77	85	.475	5th (W)	—	—	—	—	—	—	—	—
1988— Chicago (A.L.)	71	90	.441	5th (W)	—	—	—	—	—	—	—	—
1991— Philadelphia (N.L.)	74	75	.497	3rd (E)	—	—	—	—	—	—	—	—
1992— Philadelphia (N.L.)	70	92	.432	6th (E)	—	—	—	—	—	—	—	—
1993— Philadelphia (N.L.)	97	65	.599	1st (E)	—	—	4	2	2	4	—	—
1994— Philadelphia (N.L.)	54	61	.470		—	—	—	—	—	—	1	0
1995— Philadelphia (N.L.)	69	75	.479	T2nd (E)	—	—	—	—	—	—	—	—
1999— Toronto (A.L.)	84	78	.515	3rd (E)	—	—	—	—	—	—	—	—
American League totals (8 years)	514	552	.482		—	—	1	3	—	—	—	—
National League totals (5 years)	364	368	.497		—	—	4	2	2	4	1	0
Major league totals (13 years)	878	920	.488		—	—	5	5	2	4	1	0

NOTES:
1978—Replaced California manager Dave Garcia with club in third place and record of 25-21 (June 1).
1979—Lost to Baltimore in A.L. Championship Series.
1981—Replaced as California manager by Gene Mauch with club in fourth place (May 28).
1983—Defeated Oklahoma City, three games to two, in playoff; lost to Denver, four games to none, in championship playoff.
1984—Defeated Indianapolis, four games to two, in playoff; defeated Denver, four games to one, in championship playoff.
1985—Defeated Oklahoma City, four games to one, in championship playoff.
1986—Replaced manager Tony La Russa (26-38) and interim manager Doug Rader (1-1) with club in fifth place and record of 27-39 (June 22).
1991—Replaced Philadelphia manager Nick Leyva with club in sixth place and record of 4-9 (April 23).
1993—Defeated Atlanta in N.L. Championship Series; lost to Toronto in World Series.
1994—Philadelphia was in fourth place in N.L. East at time of season-ending strike (August 12).

GARNER, PHIL — TIGERS

PERSONAL: Born April 30, 1949, in Jefferson City, Tenn. ... 5-10/177. ... Batted right, threw right. ... Full name: Philip Mason Garner.
HIGH SCHOOL: Beardon (Knoxville, Tenn.).
COLLEGE: Tennessee (degree in general business, 1973).
TRANSACTIONS/CAREER NOTES: Selected by Montreal Expos organization in eighth round of free-agent draft (June 4, 1970); did not sign. ... Selected by Oakland Athletics organization in secondary phase of free-agent draft (January 13, 1971). ... Traded by A's with IF Tommy Helms and P Chris Batton to Pittsburgh Pirates for P Doc Medich, P Dave Giusti, P Rick Langford, P Doug Bair, OF Mitchell Page and OF Tony Armas (March 15, 1977). ... On Pittsburgh disabled list (April 2-23, 1981). ... Traded by Pirates to Houston Astros for 2B Johnny Ray and two players to be named later (August 31, 1981); Pirates organization acquired OF Kevin Houston and P Randy Niemann to complete deal (September 9, 1981). ... Granted free agency (November 12, 1986). ... Re-signed by Astros (January 6, 1987). ... Traded by Astros to Los Angeles Dodgers for a player to be named later (June 19, 1987); Astros organization acquired P Jeff Edwards to complete deal (June 26, 1987). ... Granted free agency (November 9, 1987). ... Signed by San Francisco Giants (January 28, 1988). ... On San Francisco disabled list (April 13-September 2, 1988); included rehabilitation assignment to Phoenix (August 5-24). ... Granted free agency (November 3, 1988).
RECORDS: Shares major league record for most grand slams in two consecutive games—2 (September 14-15, 1978).
STATISTICAL NOTES: Led Pacific Coast League third basemen with 104 putouts, 261 assists, 35 errors, 400 total chances and 23 double plays in 1973. ... Led A.L. second basemen with 26 errors in 1975. ... Led A.L. second basemen with 865 total chances in 1976. ... Led N.L. second basemen with 499 assists, 21 errors, 869 total chances and 116 double plays in 1980. ... Career major league grand slams: 3.

| | | | | | | | BATTING | | | | | | | | FIELDING | | | |
Year Team (League)	Pos.	G	AB	R	H	2B	3B	HR	RBI	Avg.	BB	SO	SB	PO	A	E	Avg.
1971— Burlington (Midw.)	3B	116	439	73	122	22	4	11	70	.278	49	73	8	*122	203	29	.918
1972— Birmingham. (Sou.)	3B	71	264	45	74	10	6	12	40	.280	27	43	3	74	116	13	.936
— Iowa (A.A.)	3B	70	247	33	60	18	4	9	22	.243	30	73	7	50	140	10	.950
1973— Tucson (PCL)	3B-2B	138	516	87	149	23	12	14	73	.289	72	90	3	†107	†270	†35	.915
— Oakland (A.L.)	3B	9	5	0	0	0	0	0	0	.000	0	3	0	2	3	0	1.000
1974— Tucson (PCL)	3B-SS	96	388	78	128	29	10	11	51	.330	53	58	8	92	182	15	.948
— Oakland (A.L.)	3B-SS-2B	30	28	4	5	1	0	0	1	.179	1	5	1	11	24	1	.972
1975— Oakland (A.L.)	2B-SS	•160	488	46	120	21	5	6	54	.246	30	65	4	355	427	†26	.968
1976— Oakland (A.L.)	2B	159	555	54	145	29	12	8	74	.261	36	71	35	378	*465	22	.975
1977— Pittsburgh (N.L.)■	3B-2B-SS	153	585	99	152	35	10	17	77	.260	55	65	32	223	351	17	.971
1978— Pittsburgh (N.L.)	3B-2B-SS	154	528	66	138	25	9	10	66	.261	66	71	27	258	389	28	.959
1979— Pittsburgh (N.L.)	3B-2B-SS	150	549	76	161	32	8	11	59	.293	55	74	17	234	396	22	.966
1980— Pittsburgh (N.L.)	2B-SS	151	548	62	142	27	6	5	58	.259	46	53	32	349	†500	†21	.976
1981— Pittsburgh (N.L.)	2B	56	181	22	46	6	2	1	20	.254	21	21	4	121	148	9	.968
— Houston (N.L.)■	2B	31	113	13	27	3	1	0	6	.239	15	11	6	62	102	3	.982
1982— Houston (N.L.)	2B-3B	155	588	65	161	33	8	13	83	.274	40	92	24	285	464	17	.978
1983— Houston (N.L.)	3B	154	567	76	135	24	2	14	79	.238	63	84	18	100	311	24	.945
1984— Houston (N.L.)	3B-2B	128	374	60	104	17	6	4	45	.278	43	63	3	136	251	12	.970
1985— Houston (N.L.)	3B-2B	135	463	65	124	23	10	6	51	.268	34	72	4	101	229	21	.940
1986— Houston (N.L.)	3B-2B	107	313	43	83	14	3	9	41	.265	30	45	12	66	152	23	.905
1987— Houston (N.L.)	SS-2B	43	112	15	25	5	0	3	15	.223	8	20	1	28	55	2	.976
— Los Angeles (N.L.)■..	3B-2B-SS	70	126	14	24	4	0	2	8	.190	20	24	5	37	89	11	.920
1988— San Fran. (N.L.)■	3B	15	13	0	2	0	0	0	1	.154	1	3	0	0	0	0	
— Phoenix (PCL)	2B-3B	17	45	5	12	2	1	1	5	.267	4	4	0	12	22	0	1.000
American League totals (4 years)		358	1076	104	270	51	17	14	129	.251	67	144	40	746	919	49	.971
National League totals (12 years)		1502	5060	676	1324	248	65	95	609	.262	497	698	185	2000	3437	210	.963
Major league totals (16 years)		1860	6136	780	1594	299	82	109	738	.260	564	842	225	2746	4356	259	.965

DIVISION SERIES RECORD

							BATTING									FIELDING		
Year	Team (League)	Pos.	G	AB	R	H	2B	3B	HR	RBI	Avg.	BB	SO	SB	PO	A	E	Avg.
1981— Houston (N.L.)		2B	5	18	1	2	0	0	0	0	.111	3	3	0	6	8	1	.933

CHAMPIONSHIP SERIES RECORD

							BATTING									FIELDING		
Year	Team (League)	Pos.	G	AB	R	H	2B	3B	HR	RBI	Avg.	BB	SO	SB	PO	A	E	Avg.
1975— Oakland (A.L.)		2B	3	5	0	0	0	0	0	0	.000	0	1	0	7	4	1	.917
1979— Pittsburgh (N.L.)		2B-SS	3	12	4	5	0	1	1	1	.417	1	0	0	8	9	0	1.000
1986— Houston (N.L.)		3B	3	9	1	2	1	0	0	2	.222	1	2	0	1	9	0	1.000
Championship series totals (3 years)			9	26	5	7	1	1	1	3	.269	2	3	0	16	22	1	.974

WORLD SERIES RECORD

RECORDS: Shares single-series record for collecting one or more hits in each game (1979).

NOTES: Member of World Series championship team (1979).

							BATTING									FIELDING		
Year	Team (League)	Pos.	G	AB	R	H	2B	3B	HR	RBI	Avg.	BB	SO	SB	PO	A	E	Avg.
1979— Pittsburgh (N.L.)		2B	7	24	4	12	4	0	0	5	.500	3	1	0	21	23	2	.957

ALL-STAR GAME RECORD

					BATTING								FIELDING		
Year	League	Pos.	AB	R	H	2B	3B	HR	RBI	Avg.	BB	SO	SB	PO	A	E	Avg.
1976— American		2B	1	0	0	0	0	0	0	.000	0	1	0	1	1	0	1.000
1980— National		2B	2	1	1	0	0	0	0	.500	1	1	1	1	3	0	1.000
1981— National		2B	0	0	0	0	0	0	0	...	0	0	0	0	0	0	...
All-Star Game totals (3 years)			3	1	1	0	0	0	0	.333	1	2	1	2	4	0	1.000

RECORD AS MANAGER

BACKGROUND: Coach, Houston Astros (1989-91).

		REGULAR SEASON				POSTSEASON					
						Playoff		Champ. Series		World Series		All-Star Game	
Year	Team (League)	W	L	Pct.	Pos.	W	L	W	L	W	L	W	L
1992— Milwaukee (A.L.)		92	70	.568	2nd (E)	—	—	—	—	—	—	—	—
1993— Milwaukee (A.L.)		69	93	.426	7th (E)	—	—	—	—	—	—	—	—
1994— Milwaukee (A.L.)		53	62	.461		—	—	—	—	—	—	—	—
1995— Milwaukee (A.L.)		65	79	.451	4th (C)	—	—	—	—	—	—	—	—
1996— Milwaukee (A.L.)		80	82	.494	3rd (C)	—	—	—	—	—	—	—	—
1997— Milwaukee (A.L.)		78	83	.484	3rd (C)	—	—	—	—	—	—	—	—
1998— Milwaukee (N.L.)		74	88	.457	5th (C)	—	—	—	—	—	—	—	—
1999— Milwaukee (N.L.)		52	60	.464		—	—	—	—	—	—	—	—
American League totals (6 years)		437	469	.482		—	—	—	—	—	—	—	—
National League totals (2 year)		126	148	.460		—	—	—	—	—	—	—	—
Major league totals (8 years)		563	617	.477		—	—	—	—	—	—	—	—

NOTES:

1993—On suspended list (September 24-27).

1994—Milwaukee was in fifth place in A.L. Central at time of season-ending strike (August 12).

1995—On suspended list (July 27-31).

1999—Replaced as manager on interim basis by Joe Lefebvre, with team in fifth place (August 11).

HARGROVE, MIKE   ORIOLES

PERSONAL: Born October 26, 1949, in Perryton, Texas. ... 6-0/195. ... Batted left, threw left. ... Full name: Dudley Michael Hargrove.

HIGH SCHOOL: Perryton (Texas).

COLLEGE: Northwestern State, Okla. (degree in physical education and social sciences).

TRANSACTIONS/CAREER NOTES: Selected by Texas Rangers organization in 25th round of free-agent draft (June 6, 1972). ... Traded by Rangers with 3B Kurt Bevacqua and C Bill Fahey to San Diego Padres for OF Oscar Gamble, C Dave Roberts and cash (October 25, 1978). ... Traded by Padres to Cleveland Indians for OF Paul Dade (June 14, 1979). ... Granted free agency (November 12, 1985).

HONORS: Named Western Carolinas League Player of the Year (1973). ... Named A.L. Rookie Player of the Year by THE SPORTING NEWS (1974). ... Named A.L. Rookie of the Year by Baseball Writers' Association of America (1974).

STATISTICAL NOTES: Led New York-Pennsylvania League first basemen with 58 double plays in 1972. ... Led Western Carolinas League with 247 total bases in 1973. ... Led Western Carolinas League first basemen with 118 double plays in 1973. ... Had 23-game hitting streak (April 16-May 15, 1980). ... Led A.L. first basemen with 1,489 total chances in 1980. ... Led A.L. with .432 on-base percentage in 1981. ... Career major league grand slams: 1.

							BATTING									FIELDING		
Year	Team (League)	Pos.	G	AB	R	H	2B	3B	HR	RBI	Avg.	BB	SO	SB	PO	A	E	Avg.
1972— Geneva (NY-Penn)......		1B	•70	243	38	65	8	0	4	37	.267	52	44	3	*537	•40	10	*.983
1973— Gastonia (W. Car.)		1B	•130	456	88	*160	*35	8	12	82	*.351	68	47	10	*1121	•77	14	.988
1974— Texas (A.L.)		1B-DH-OF	131	415	57	134	18	6	4	66	.323	49	42	0	638	72	9	.987
1975— Texas (A.L.)		OF-1B-DH	145	519	82	157	22	2	11	62	.303	79	66	4	513	45	13	.977
1976— Texas (A.L.)		1B	151	541	80	155	30	1	7	58	.287	*97	64	2	1222	110	*21	.984
1977— Texas (A.L.)		1B	153	525	98	160	28	4	18	69	.305	103	59	2	1393	100	11	.993
1978— Texas (A.L.)		1B-DH	146	494	63	124	24	1	7	40	.251	*107	47	2	1221	*116	*17	.987
1979— San Diego (N.L.)■		1B	52	125	15	24	5	0	0	8	.192	25	15	0	323	17	5	.986
—Cleveland (A.L.)■■.....		OF-1B-DH	100	338	60	110	21	4	10	56	.325	63	40	2	356	16	2	.995
1980— Cleveland (A.L.)..........		1B	160	589	86	179	22	2	11	85	.304	111	36	4	*1391	88	10	.993
1981— Cleveland (A.L.)..........		1B-DH	94	322	43	102	21	0	2	49	.317	60	16	5	766	76	•9	.989
1982— Cleveland (A.L.)..........		1B-DH	160	591	67	160	26	1	4	65	.271	101	58	2	1293	*123	5	.996

Year	Team (League)	Pos.	G	AB	R	H	2B	3B	HR	RBI	Avg.	BB	SO	SB	PO	A	E	Avg.
1983— Cleveland (A.L.)..........		1B-DH	134	469	57	134	21	4	3	57	.286	78	40	0	1098	115	7	.994
1984— Cleveland (A.L.)..........		1B	133	352	44	94	14	2	2	44	.267	53	38	0	790	83	8	.991
1985— Cleveland (A.L.)..........		1B-DH-OF	107	284	31	81	14	1	1	27	.285	39	29	1	599	66	6	.991
American League totals (12 years)			1614	5439	768	1590	261	28	80	678	.292	940	535	24	11280	1010	118	.990
National League totals (1 year)			52	125	15	24	5	0	0	8	.192	25	15	0	323	17	5	.986
Major league totals (12 years)			1666	5564	783	1614	266	28	80	686	.290	965	550	24	11603	1027	123	.990

ALL-STAR GAME RECORD

Year	League	Pos.	AB	R	H	2B	3B	HR	RBI	Avg.	BB	SO	SB	PO	A	E	Avg.
1975— American	PH	1	0	0	0	0	0	0	.000	0	0	0	...	...	...	...	

RECORD AS MANAGER

BACKGROUND: Minor league coach, Cleveland Indians organization (1986). ... Coach, Indians (1990-July 6, 1991).

HONORS: Named Carolina League Manager of the Year (1987). ... Named Pacific Coast League Manager of the Year (1989). ... Named A.L. Manager of the Year by The Sporting News (1995).

		REGULAR SEASON				POSTSEASON						
						Playoff		Champ. Series		World Series		All-Star Game
Year Team (League)	W	L	Pct.	Pos.	W	L	W	L	W	L	W	L
1987— Kinston (Carolina)	33	37	.471	T3rd (S)	—	—	—	—	—	—	—	—
— (Second half)	42	28	.600	1st (S)	3	3	—	—	—	—	—	—
1988— Williamsport (East.)	66	73	.475	6th	—	—	—	—	—	—	—	—
1989— Colorado Springs (Pacific Coast)	44	26	.629	1st (S)	—	—	—	—	—	—	—	—
— (Second half)	34	38	.472	3rd (S)	2	3	—	—	—	—	—	—
1991— Cleveland (A.L.)	32	53	.376	7th (E)	—	—	—	—	—	—	—	—
1992— Cleveland (A.L.)	76	86	.469	T4th (E)	—	—	—	—	—	—	—	—
1993— Cleveland (A.L.)	76	86	.469	6th (E)	—	—	—	—	—	—	—	—
1994— Cleveland (A.L.)	66	47	.584		—	—	—	—	—	—	—	—
1995— Cleveland (A.L.)	100	44	.694	1st (C)	3	0	4	2	2	4	—	—
1996— Cleveland (A.L.)	99	62	.615	1st (C)	1	3	—	—	—	—	0	1
1997— Cleveland (A.L.)	86	75	.534	1st (C)	3	2	4	2	3	4	—	—
1998— Cleveland (A.L.)	89	73	.549	1st (C)	3	1	2	4	—	—	1	0
1999— Cleveland (A.L.)	97	65	.599	1st (C)	2	3	—	—	—	—	—	—
Major league totals (9 years)	721	591	.549		11	9	10	8	5	8	1	1

NOTES:
1987—Defeated Winston-Salem, two games to none, in playoffs; lost to Salem, three games to one, in league championship.
1989—Lost to Albuquerque in playoffs.
1991—Replaced Cleveland manager John McNamara with club in seventh place and record of 25-52 (July 6).
1994—Cleveland was in second place in A.L. Central at time of season-ending strike (August 12).
1995—Defeated Boston in A.L. divisional playoff; defeated Seattle in A.L. Championship Series; lost to Atlanta in World Series.
1996—Lost to Baltimore in A.L. divisional playoff.
1997—Defeated New York in A.L. divisional playoff; defeated Baltimore in A.L. Championship Series; lost to Florida in World Series.
1998—Defeated Boston in A.L. divisional playoff; lost to New York Yankees in A.L. Championship Series.
1999—Lost to Boston in A.L. divisional playoff.

HOWE, ART — ATHLETICS

PERSONAL: Born December 15, 1946, in Pittsburgh. ... 6-1/185. ... Batted right, threw right. ... Full name: Arthur Henry Howe Jr.

HIGH SCHOOL: Shaler (Glenshaw, Pa.).

COLLEGE: Wyoming (bachelor of science degree in business administration, 1969).

TRANSACTIONS/CAREER NOTES: Signed as free agent by Pittsburgh Pirates organization (June, 1971). ... On disabled list (August 17-September 2, 1972 and April 13-May 6, 1973). ... Traded by Pirates to Houston Astros (January 6, 1976), completing deal in which Astros traded 2B Tommy Helms to Pirates for a player to be named later (December 12, 1975). ... On disabled list (May 12-June 19, 1982 and March 27, 1983-entire season). ... Granted free agency (November 7, 1983). ... Signed by St. Louis Cardinals (March 21, 1984). ... Released by Cardinals (April 22, 1985).

STATISTICAL NOTES: Tied for Carolina League lead in putouts by third baseman with 95 in 1971. ... Led International League third basemen with 22 errors and 24 double plays in 1972. ... Had 23-game hitting streak (May 1-24, 1981). ... Career major league grand slams: 1.

Year	Team (League)	Pos.	G	AB	R	H	2B	3B	HR	RBI	Avg.	BB	SO	SB	PO	A	E	Avg.
1971— Salem (Carolina)	3B-SS	114	382	77	133	27	7	12	79	*.348	82	74	11	‡110	221	21	.940
1972— Char., W.Va. (I.L.)	3B-2B-SS	109	365	68	99	21	3	14	53	.271	63	69	8	105	248	†24	.936
1973— Char., W.Va. (I.L.)	3B-2B-SS	119	372	50	85	20	1	8	44	.228	54	70	6	141	229	21	.946
1974— Char., W.Va. (I.L.)	3B	60	207	26	70	17	4	8	36	.338	31	27	4	35	90	9	.933
— Pittsburgh (N.L.)	3B-SS	29	74	10	18	4	1	1	5	.243	9	13	0	11	49	4	.938
1975— Char., W.Va. (I.L.)	3B-2B	11	42	4	15	1	3	0	3	.357	2	4	0	15	23	1	.974
— Pittsburgh (N.L.)	3B-SS	63	146	13	25	9	0	1	10	.171	15	15	1	19	89	7	.939
1976— Memphis (I.L.)■	3B-1B	74	259	50	92	21	3	12	59	.355	34	31	1	93	120	14	.938
— Houston (N.L.)	3B-2B	21	29	0	4	1	0	0	0	.138	6	6	0	17	16	1	.971
1977— Houston (N.L.)	2B-3B-SS	125	413	44	109	23	7	8	58	.264	41	60	0	213	333	8	.986
1978— Houston (N.L.)	2B-3B-1B	119	420	46	123	33	3	7	55	.293	34	41	2	240	302	13	.977
1979— Houston (N.L.)	2B-3B-1B	118	355	32	88	15	2	6	33	.248	36	37	3	188	261	7	.985
1980— Houston (N.L.)	1-3-2-S	110	321	34	91	12	5	10	46	.283	34	29	1	598	86	10	.986
1981— Houston (N.L.)	3B-1B	103	361	43	107	22	4	3	36	.296	41	23	1	67	206	9	.968
1982— Houston (N.L.)	3B-1B	110	365	29	87	15	1	5	38	.238	41	45	2	344	174	7	.987
1983—						Did not play.												
1984— St. Louis (N.L.)■	3-1-2-S	89	139	17	30	5	0	2	12	.216	18	18	0	71	80	3	.981
1985— St. Louis (N.L.)..........	1B-3B	4	3	0	0	0	0	0	0	.000	0	0	0	5	1	0	1.000
Major league totals (11 years)		891	2626	268	682	139	23	43	293	.260	275	287	10	1773	1597	69	.980

MAJOR LEAGUE MANAGERS

DIVISION SERIES RECORD

Year Team (League)	Pos.	G	AB	R	H	2B	3B	HR	RBI	Avg.	BB	SO	SB	PO	A	E	Avg.
1981— Houston (N.L.)	3B	5	17	1	4	0	0	1	1	.235	2	1	0	6	9	0	1.000

CHAMPIONSHIP SERIES RECORD

Year Team (League)	Pos.	G	AB	R	H	2B	3B	HR	RBI	Avg.	BB	SO	SB	PO	A	E	Avg.
1974— Pittsburgh (N.L.)	PH	1	1	0	0	0	0	0	0	.000	0	0	0	...	...	...	
1980— Houston (N.L.)	1B-PH	5	15	0	3	1	1	0	2	.200	2	2	0	29	3	0	1.000
Championship series totals (2 years)		6	16	0	3	1	1	0	2	.188	2	2	0	29	3	0	1.000

RECORD AS MANAGER

BACKGROUND: Coach, Texas Rangers (May 21, 1985-88). ... Scout, Los Angeles Dodgers organization (1994). ... Coach, Colorado Rockies (1995).

| | | REGULAR SEASON | | | | POSTSEASON | | | | | | |
| | | | | | | Playoff | | Champ. Series | | World Series | | All-Star Game |
Year Team (League)	W	L	Pct.	Pos.	W	L	W	L	W	L	W	L
1989— Houston (N.L.)	86	76	.531	3rd (W)	—	—	—	—	—	—	—	—
1990— Houston (N.L.)	75	87	.463	T4th (W)	—	—	—	—	—	—	—	—
1991— Houston (N.L.)	65	97	.401	6th (W)	—	—	—	—	—	—	—	—
1992— Houston (N.L.)	81	81	.500	4th (W)	—	—	—	—	—	—	—	—
1993— Houston (N.L.)	85	77	.525	3rd (W)	—	—	—	—	—	—	—	—
1996— Oakland (A.L.)	78	84	.481	3rd (W)	—	—	—	—	—	—	—	—
1997— Oakland (A.L.)	65	97	.401	4th (W)	—	—	—	—	—	—	—	—
1998— Oakland (A.L.)	74	88	.457	4th (W)	—	—	—	—	—	—	—	—
1999— Oakland (A.L.)	87	75	.537	2nd (W)	—	—	—	—	—	—	—	—
National League totals (5 years)	392	418	.484		—	—	—	—	—	—	—	—
American League totals (4 years)	304	344	.469		—	—	—	—	—	—	—	—
Major league totals (9 years)	696	762	.477		—	—	—	—	—	—	—	—

JOHNSON, DAVEY — DODGERS

PERSONAL: Born January 30, 1943, in Orlando. ... 6-1/182. ... Bats right, throws right. ... Full name: David Allen Johnson.

HIGH SCHOOL: Alamo Heights (San Antonio).

COLLEGE: Texas A&M; then Trinity University, Texas (degree in mathematics); then Johns Hopkins.

TRANSACTIONS/CAREER NOTES: Signed as free agent by Baltimore Orioles organization (June 2, 1962). ... On Rochester disabled list (August 7-September 1, 1965). ... Traded by Orioles with P Pat Dobson, P Roric Harrison and C Johnny Oates to Atlanta Braves for C Earl Williams and IF Taylor Duncan (November 30, 1972). ... Released by Braves (April 11, 1975). ... Signed by Yomiuri Giants of Japan Central League (1975). ... Released by Yomiuri (January 21, 1977). ... Signed by Philadelphia Phillies (February 3, 1977). ... On disabled list (June 15-July 1, 1977). ... Traded by Phillies to Chicago Cubs for P Larry Anderson (August 6, 1978). ... Released by Cubs (October 17, 1978). ... Served as player/manager with Miami of Inter-American League (1979). ... Granted free agency when league folded (June 30, 1979).

RECORDS: Shares major league single-season records for most home runs by second baseman—42 (1973, also had one home run as pinch hitter); fewest triples (150 or more games)—0 (1973); and most grand slams by pinch hitter—2 (1978).

HONORS: Won A.L. Gold Glove at second base (1969-71). ... Named second baseman on THE SPORTING NEWS A.L. All-Star team (1970). ... Named N.L. Comeback Player of the Year by THE SPORTING NEWS (1973). ... Named second baseman on THE SPORTING NEWS N.L. All-Star team (1973).

STATISTICAL NOTES: Led California League shortstops with 63 double plays in 1962. ... Led A.L. second basemen with 19 errors in 1966. ... Tied for A.L. lead in putouts by second baseman with 379 in 1970. ... Tied for A.L. lead with eight sacrifice flies in 1967. ... Led A.L. second basemen with 103 double plays in 1971. ... Led N.L. second basemen with 877 total chances and tied for lead with 106 double plays in 1973. ... Career major league grand slams: 5.

| | | | | | BATTING | | | | | | | | | FIELDING | | | |
Year Team (League)	Pos.	G	AB	R	H	2B	3B	HR	RBI	Avg.	BB	SO	SB	PO	A	E	Avg.
1962— Stockton (California) ..	SS	97	343	58	106	18	•12	10	63	.309	43	61	8	135	307	40	*.917
1963— Elmira (East.)	SS-2B	63	233	47	76	11	6	13	42	.326	29	42	12	115	155	12	.957
— Rochester (I.L.)	2B-OF	63	211	31	52	9	3	6	22	.246	25	39	4	141	138	11	.962
1964— Rochester (I.L.)	2B-SS	•155	590	87	156	29	14	19	73	.264	71	95	7	326	445	39	.952
1965— Baltimore (A.L.)	3B-2B-SS	20	47	5	8	3	0	0	1	.170	5	6	3	11	37	3	.941
— Rochester (I.L.)	SS	52	193	29	58	9	3	4	22	.301	16	34	4	96	161	10	.963
1966— Baltimore (A.L.)	2B-SS	131	501	47	129	20	3	7	56	.257	31	64	3	294	357	†20	.970
1967— Baltimore (A.L.)	2B-3B	148	510	62	126	30	3	10	64	.247	59	82	4	344	351	14	.980
1968— Baltimore (A.L.)	2B-SS	145	504	50	122	24	4	9	56	.242	44	80	7	294	370	15	.978
1969— Baltimore (A.L.)	2B-SS	142	511	52	143	34	1	7	57	.280	57	52	3	358	370	12	.984
1970— Baltimore (A.L.)	2B-SS	149	530	68	149	27	1	10	53	.281	66	68	2	‡382	391	8	.990
1971— Baltimore (A.L.)	2B	142	510	67	144	26	1	18	72	.282	51	55	3	361	367	12	.984
1972— Baltimore (A.L.)	2B	118	376	31	83	22	3	5	32	.221	52	68	1	286	307	6	*.990
1973— Atlanta (N.L.)■..........	2B	157	559	84	151	25	0	43	99	.270	81	93	5	383	464	*30	.966
1974— Atlanta (N.L.)	1B-2B	136	454	56	114	18	0	15	62	.251	75	59	1	789	231	11	.989
1975— Atlanta (N.L.)	PH	1	1	0	1	1	0	0	1	1.000	0	0	0	...	...	...	
— Yomiuri (Jp. Cen.)■....	3B-SS	91	289	29	57	7	0	13	38	.197	32	71	1	85	157	11	.957
1976— Yomiuri (Jp. Cen.)	2B-3B-1B	108	371	48	102	16	2	26	74	.275	55	62	1	226	28	11	.958
1977— Philadelphia (N.L.)■....	1B-2B-3B	78	156	23	50	9	1	8	36	.321	23	20	1	299	31	0	1.000
1978— Philadelphia (N.L.)......	2B-3B-1B	44	89	14	17	2	0	2	14	.191	10	19	0	56	41	6	.942
— Chicago (N.L.)■..........	3B	12	49	5	15	1	1	2	6	.306	5	9	0	4	22	5	.839
1979— Miami (In.-Am.)■	1B	10	25	7	6	2	0	1	2	.240	...	...	0	...	...	...	
American League totals (8 years)		995	3489	382	904	186	16	66	391	.259	365	475	26	2330	2550	90	.982
National League totals (5 years)		428	1308	182	348	56	2	70	218	.266	194	200	7	1531	789	52	.978
Major league totals (13 years)		1423	4797	564	1252	242	18	136	609	.261	559	675	33	3861	3339	142	.981

CHAMPIONSHIP SERIES RECORD

Year	Team (League)	Pos.	G	AB	R	H	2B	3B	HR	RBI	Avg.	BB	SO	SB	PO	A	E	Avg.
						BATTING									FIELDING			
1969— Baltimore (A.L.)..........		2B	3	13	2	3	0	0	0	0	.231	2	1	0	5	11	0	1.000
1970— Baltimore (A.L.)..........		2B	3	11	4	4	0	0	2	4	.364	1	1	0	11	4	0	1.000
1971— Baltimore (A.L.)..........		2B	3	10	2	3	2	0	0	0	.300	3	1	0	5	6	1	.917
1977— Philadelphia (N.L.)......		1B	1	4	0	1	0	0	0	2	.250	0	1	0	8	0	0	1.000
Championship series totals (4 years)			10	38	8	11	2	0	2	6	.289	6	4	0	29	21	1	.980

WORLD SERIES RECORD

NOTES: Member of World Series championship team (1966 and 1970).

Year	Team (League)	Pos.	G	AB	R	H	2B	3B	HR	RBI	Avg.	BB	SO	SB	PO	A	E	Avg.
						BATTING									FIELDING			
1966— Baltimore (A.L.)..........		2B	4	14	1	4	1	0	0	1	.286	0	1	0	12	12	0	1.000
1969— Baltimore (A.L.)..........		2B	5	16	1	1	0	0	0	0	.063	2	1	0	8	15	0	1.000
1970— Baltimore (A.L.)..........		2B	5	16	2	5	2	0	0	2	.313	5	2	0	15	9	0	1.000
1971— Baltimore (A.L.)..........		2B	7	27	1	4	0	0	0	3	.148	0	1	0	18	12	0	1.000
World Series totals (4 years)			21	73	5	14	3	0	0	6	.192	7	5	0	53	48	0	1.000

ALL-STAR GAME RECORD

Year	League	Pos.	AB	R	H	2B	3B	HR	RBI	Avg.	BB	SO	SB	PO	A	E	Avg.
						BATTING								FIELDING				
1968— American		2B	1	0	0	0	0	0	0	.000	0	1	0	1	1	0	1.000
1969— American							Selected, did not play—injured.										
1970— American		2B	5	0	1	0	0	0	0	.200	0	1	0	5	1	0	1.000
1973— National		2B	1	0	0	0	0	0	0	.000	0	0	0	1	1	0	1.000
All-Star Game totals (3 years)			7	0	1	0	0	0	0	.143	0	2	0	7	3	0	1.000

RECORD AS MANAGER

BACKGROUND: Instructor, New York Mets organization (1982). ... Consultant, Cincinnati Reds (December 31, 1992-May 24, 1993).

HONORS: Named A.L. Manager of the Year by The Sporting News (1997). ... Named A.L. Manager of the Year by Baseball Writer's Association of America (1997).

Year	Team (League)	W	L	Pct.	Pos.	Playoff W	Playoff L	Champ. Series W	Champ. Series L	World Series W	World Series L	All-Star Game W	All-Star Game L
			REGULAR SEASON					POSTSEASON					
1979— Miami (Inter-American)...........................	43	17	.717	1st	—	—	—	—	—	—	—	—	
— (Second half)	8	4	.667	1st	—	—	—	—	—	—	—	—	
1981— Jackson (Texas)	39	27	.591	1st (E)	—	—	—	—	—	—	—	—	
— (Second half)	29	39	.426	3rd (E)	5	1	—	—	—	—	—	—	
1983— Tidewater (International)...........................	71	68	.511	4th	6	3	—	—	—	—	—	—	
1984— New York (N.L.)	90	72	.556	2nd (E)	—	—	—	—	—	—	—	—	
1985— New York (N.L.)	98	64	.605	2nd (E)	—	—	—	—	—	—	—	—	
1986— New York (N.L.)	108	54	.667	1st (E)	—	—	4	2	4	3	—	—	
1987— New York (N.L.)	92	70	.568	2nd (E)	—	—	—	—	—	—	1	0	
1988— New York (N.L.)	100	60	.625	1st (E)	—	—	3	4	—	—	—	—	
1989— New York (N.L.)	87	75	.537	2nd (E)	—	—	—	—	—	—	—	—	
1990— New York (N.L.)	20	22	.476		—	—	—	—	—	—	—	—	
1993— Cincinnati (N.L.)	53	65	.449	5th (W)	—	—	—	—	—	—	—	—	
1994— Cincinnati (N.L.)	66	48	.579		—	—	—	—	—	—	—	—	
1995— Cincinnati (N.L.)	85	59	.590	1st (C)	3	0	0	4	—	—	—	—	
1996— Baltimore (A.L.)	88	74	.543	2nd (E)	3	1	1	4	—	—	—	—	
1997— Baltimore (A.L.)	98	64	.605	1st (E)	3	1	2	4	—	—	—	—	
1999— Los Angeles (N.L.)	77	85	.475	3rd (W)	—	—	—	—	—	—	—	—	
National League totals (11 years)......................	876	674	.565		3	0	7	10	4	3	1	0	
American League totals (2 years)......................	186	138	.574		6	2	3	8	—	—	—	—	
Major league totals (13 years)......................	1062	812	.567		9	2	10	18	4	3	1	0	

NOTES:
1979—Inter-American League folded June 30. Miami finished first in both halves of season and was declared league champion.
1981—Defeated Tulsa, two games to one, in playoffs; defeated San Antonio, three games to none, in league championship.
1983—Defeated Columbus, three games to two, in playoffs; defeated Richmond, three games to one, in league championship.
1986—Defeated Houston in N.L. Championship Series; defeated Boston in World Series.
1988—Lost to Los Angeles in N.L. Championship Series.
1990—Replaced as New York manager by Bud Harrelson, with club in fourth place (May 29).
1993—Replaced Cincinnati manager Tony Perez, with club in fifth place and record of 20-24 (May 24).
1994—Cincinnati was in first place in N.L. Central at time of season-ending strike (August 12).
1995—Defeated Los Angeles in N.L. divisional playoff; lost to Atlanta in N.L. Championship Series.
1996—Defeated Cleveland in A.L. divisional playoff; lost to New York in A.L. Championship Series.
1997—Defeated Seattle in A.L. divisional playoff; lost to Cleveland in A.L. Championship Series

KELLY, TOM   TWINS

PERSONAL: Born August 15, 1950, in Graceville, Minn. ... 5-11/185. ... Batted left, threw left. ... Full name: Jay Thomas Kelly.

HIGH SCHOOL: St. Mary's (South Amboy, N.J.).

JUNIOR COLLEGE: Mesa (Ariz.) Community College.

COLLEGE: Monmouth College (N.J.).

TRANSACTIONS/CAREER NOTES: Selected by Seattle Pilots organization in eighth round of free-agent draft (June 7, 1968). ... Seattle franchise moved to Milwaukee and renamed Brewers (1970). ... On temporarily inactive list (April 16-20, April 25-30 and August 21, 1970-remainder of season). ... On military list (August 27, 1970-February 3, 1971). ... Released by Brewers organization (April 6, 1971). ... Signed by Charlotte, Minnesota Twins organization (April 28, 1971). ... Loaned by Twins organization to Rochester, Baltimore Orioles organization (April 5-September 22, 1976). ... On temporarily inactive list (April 15-19, 1977). ... On disabled list (July 25-August 4, 1977). ... Released by Toledo (December 18, 1978). ... Re-signed by Visalia, Twins organization (January 2, 1979). ... Released by Twins organization (December 2, 1980).

STATISTICAL NOTES: Led Pacific Coast League outfielders with six double plays in 1972.

Year	Team (League)	Pos.	G	AB	R	H	2B	3B	HR	RBI	Avg.	BB	SO	SB	PO	A	E	Avg.
1968— Newark (NY-Penn)......		OF	65	218	50	69	11	4	2	10	.317	43	31	*16	*144	*9	3	.981
1969— Clinton (Midwest).......		OF	100	269	47	60	10	2	6	35	.223	82	31	10	158	15	4	.977
1970— Jacksonville (Sou.).....		OF-1B	93	266	33	64	10	1	8	38	.241	41	37	2	204	19	4	.982
1971— Charlotte (Sou.)■.......		1B-OF	100	303	50	89	17	0	6	41	.294	59	52	2	508	38	9	.984
1972— Tacoma (PCL)		OF-1B	132	407	76	114	19	2	10	52	.280	70	95	4	282	19	10	.968
1973— Tacoma (PCL)		OF-1B	114	337	67	87	10	2	17	49	.258	89	64	4	200	20	6	.973
1974— Tacoma (PCL)		OF-1B	115	357	68	110	16	0	18	69	.308	78	41	4	514	41	3	.995
1975— Tacoma (PCL)		OF-1B	62	202	38	51	5	0	9	29	.252	47	36	6	185	12	6	.970
— Minnesota (A.L.)		1B-DH-OF	49	127	11	23	5	0	1	11	.181	15	22	0	360	28	6	.985
1976— Rochester (I.L.)■........		OF-1B	127	405	71	117	19	3	18	70	.289	85	71	2	323	28	4	.989
1977— Tacoma (PCL)■		1B-OF-P	113	363	80	99	12	1	12	64	.273	78	61	11	251	15	6	.978
1978— Toledo (I.L.).............		1B-OF	119	325	47	74	13	0	10	49	.228	*91	61	2	556	46	5	.992
1979— Visalia (California)■...		1B-P	2	0	0	0	0	0	0	0	...	1	0	0	3	4	0	1.000
Major league totals (1 year)			49	127	11	23	5	0	1	11	.181	15	22	0	360	28	6	.985

RECORD AS PITCHER

Year	Team (League)	W	L	Pct.	ERA	G	GS	CG	ShO	Sv.	IP	H	R	ER	BB	SO
1977— Tacoma (PCL)		0	0	...	6.00	1	0	0	0	0	3	2	2	2	3	0
1979— Visalia (California)		1	0	1.000	2.25	1	1	0	0	0	8	5	3	2	7	2
1980— Visalia (California)		0	0	...	0.69	2	1	0	0	0	13	12	1	1	6	2

RECORD AS MANAGER

BACKGROUND: Player/manager, Tacoma, Minnesota Twins organization (June 1977-remainder of season). ... Player/coach, Toledo, Twins organization (1978). ... Coach, Twins (1983-September 11, 1986).

HONORS: Named California League Manager of the Year (1979). ... Named California League co-Manager of the Year (1980). ... Named Southern League Manager of the Year (1981). ... Named A.L. Manager of the Year by THE SPORTING NEWS (1991). ... Named A.L. Manager of the Year by Baseball Writers' Association of America (1991).

		REGULAR SEASON				POSTSEASON							
						Playoff		Champ. Series		World Series		All-Star Game	
Year	Team (League)	W	L	Pct.	Pos.	W	L	W	L	W	L	W	L
1977— Tacoma (Pacific Coast)		28	26	.519	3rd (W)	—	—	—	—	—	—	—	—
1979— Visalia (California)..........................		44	26	.629	1st (S)	—	—	—	—	—	—	—	—
— (Second half)		42	28	.600	2nd (S)	1	2	—	—	—	—	—	—
1980— Visalia (California)..........................		27	43	.386	4th (S)	—	—	—	—	—	—	—	—
— (Second half)		44	26	.629	1st (S)	2	4	—	—	—	—	—	—
1981— Orlando (Southern)..........................		42	27	.609	1st (E)	—	—	—	—	—	—	—	—
— (Second half)		37	36	.507	3rd (E)	6	2	—	—	—	—	—	—
1982— Orlando (Southern)..........................		31	38	.449	5th (E)	—	—	—	—	—	—	—	—
— (Second half)		43	32	.573	2nd (E)	—	—	—	—	—	—	—	—
1986— Minnesota (A.L.)..........................		12	11	.522	6th (W)	—	—	—	—	—	—	—	—
1987— Minnesota (A.L.)..........................		85	77	.525	1st (W)	—	—	4	1	4	3	—	—
1988— Minnesota (A.L.)..........................		91	71	.562	2nd (W)	—	—	—	—	—	—	1	0
1989— Minnesota (A.L.)..........................		80	82	.494	5th (W)	—	—	—	—	—	—	—	—
1990— Minnesota (A.L.)..........................		74	88	.457	7th (W)	—	—	—	—	—	—	—	—
1991— Minnesota (A.L.)..........................		95	67	.586	1st (W)	—	—	4	1	4	3	—	—
1992— Minnesota (A.L.)..........................		90	72	.556	2nd (W)	—	—	—	—	—	—	1	0
1993— Minnesota (A.L.)..........................		71	91	.438	T5th (W)	—	—	—	—	—	—	—	—
1994— Minnesota (A.L.)..........................		53	60	.469	—	—	—	—	—	—	—	—	—
1995— Minnesota (A.L.)..........................		56	88	.389	5th (C)	—	—	—	—	—	—	—	—
1996— Minnesota (A.L.)..........................		78	84	.481	4th (C)	—	—	—	—	—	—	—	—
1997— Minnesota (A.L.)..........................		68	94	.420	4th (C)	—	—	—	—	—	—	—	—
1998— Minnesota (A.L.)..........................		70	92	.432	4th (C)	—	—	—	—	—	—	—	—
1999— Minnesota (A.L.)..........................		63	97	.394	5th (C)	—	—	—	—	—	—	—	—
Major league totals (14 years)..........................		986	1074	.478		—	—	8	2	8	6	2	0

NOTES:
1977—Replaced Tacoma manager Del Wilber with record of 40-49 and became player/manager (June).
1979—Lost to San Jose in semifinals.
1980—Defeated Fresno, two games to one, in semifinals; lost to Stockton, three games to none, in league championship.
1981—Defeated Savannah, three games to one, in semifinals; defeated Nashville, three games to one, in league championship.
1986—Replaced Minnesota manager Ray Miller with club in seventh place and record of 59-80 (September 12).
1987—Defeated Detroit in A.L. Championship Series; defeated St. Louis in World Series.
1991—Defeated Toronto in A.L. Championship Series; defeated Atlanta in World Series.
1994—Minnesota was in fourth place in A.L. Central at time of season-ending strike (August 12).

LA RUSSA, TONY — CARDINALS

PERSONAL: Born October 4, 1944, in Tampa. ... 6-0/185. ... Batted right, threw right. ... Full name: Anthony La Russa Jr.

HIGH SCHOOL: Jefferson (Tampa).

COLLEGE: University of Tampa, then South Florida (degree in industrial management), then Florida State (law degree, 1980).

TRANSACTIONS/CAREER NOTES: Signed by Kansas City Athletics organization (June 6, 1962). ... On disabled list (May 9-September 8, 1964; June 3-July 15, 1965; and April 12-May 6 and July 3-September 5, 1967). ... A's franchise moved from Kansas City to Oakland (October 1967). ... Contract sold by A's to Atlanta Braves (August 14, 1971). ... Traded by Braves to Chicago Cubs for P Tom Phoebus (October 20, 1972). ... Contract sold by Cubs to Pittsburgh Pirates organization (March 23, 1974). ... Released by Pirates organization (April 4, 1975). ... Signed by Chicago White Sox organization (April 7, 1975). ... On disabled list (August 8-18, 1976). ... Contract sold by White Sox to St. Louis Cardinals organization (December 13, 1976). ... Released by Cardinals organization (September 29, 1977).

STATISTICAL NOTES: Led International League in being hit by pitch with 11 in 1972.

Year Team (League)	Pos.	G	AB	R	H	2B	3B	HR	RBI	Avg.	BB	SO	SB	PO	A	E	Avg.
1962— Daytona Beach (FSL)..	SS	64	225	37	58	7	0	1	32	.258	42	47	11	135	173	38	.890
— Binghamton (East.)	SS-2B	12	43	3	8	0	0	0	4	.186	5	9	2	20	27	8	.855
1963— Kansas City (A.L.)	SS-2B	34	44	4	11	1	1	0	1	.250	7	12	0	29	25	2	.964
1964— Lewiston (N'west)	2B-SS	90	329	50	77	22	1	1	25	.234	53	56	10	188	218	18	.958
1965— Birmingham (Sou.)	2B	75	259	24	50	11	2	1	18	.193	26	37	5	202	161	21	.945
1966— Modesto (California) ..	2B	81	316	67	92	20	1	7	54	.291	44	37	18	201	212	20	.954
— Mobile (Southern)	2B	51	170	20	50	9	4	4	26	.294	23	24	4	117	133	10	.962
1967— Birmingham (Sou.)	2B	41	139	12	32	6	1	5	22	.230	10	11	3	88	120	5	.977
1968— Oakland (A.L.)	PH	5	3	0	1	0	0	0	0	.333	0	0	0	...	...	...	...
— Vancouver (PCL)	2B	122	455	55	109	16	8	5	29	.240	52	58	4	249	321	14	*.976
1969— Iowa (A.A.)	2B	67	235	37	72	11	1	4	27	.306	0	1	5	177	222	15	.964
— Oakland (A.L.)	PH	8	8	0	0	0	0	0	0	.000	42	30	0	...	...	...	...
1970— Iowa (A.A.)	2B	22	88	13	22	5	0	2	5	.250	9	14	0	52	59	3	.974
— Oakland (A.L.)	2B	52	106	6	21	4	1	0	6	.198	15	19	0	67	89	5	.969
1971— Iowa (A.A.)	2-3-S-O	28	107	21	31	5	1	2	11	.290	10	11	0	70	85	2	.987
— Oakland (A.L.)	2B-SS-3B	23	8	3	0	0	0	0	0	.000	0	4	0	8	7	2	.882
— Atlanta (N.L.)■..........	2B	9	7	1	2	0	0	0	0	.286	1	1	0	8	6	1	.933
1972— Richmond (I.L.)	2B	122	389	68	120	13	2	10	42	.308	72	41	0	305	289	20	.967
1973— Wichita (A.A.)■...........	2B-1B-3B	106	392	82	123	16	0	5	75	.314	60	46	10	423	213	26	.961
— Chicago (N.L.)	PR	1	0	1	0	0	0	0	0	...	0	0	0	...	...	...	...
1974— Char., W.Va. (I.L.)■.....	2B	139	457	50	119	17	1	8	35	.260	51	50	4	262	*378	17	.974
1975— Denver (A.A.)■	3-0-S-2	118	354	87	99	23	2	7	46	.280	70	46	13	95	91	10	.949
1976— Iowa (A.A.) 3-2-S-1-O-P		107	332	53	86	11	0	4	34	.259	40	43	10	132	160	22	.930
1977— New Orleans (A.A.)■.....	2B-3B	50	128	17	24	2	2	3	6	.188	20	21	0	66	87	7	.956
American League totals (5 years)		122	169	13	33	5	2	0	7	.195	64	65	0	104	121	9	.962
National League totals (2 years)		10	7	2	2	0	0	0	0	.286	1	1	0	8	6	1	.933
Major league totals (6 years)		132	176	15	35	5	2	0	7	.199	65	66	0	112	127	10	.960

RECORD AS PITCHER

Year Team (League)	W	L	Pct.	ERA	G	GS	CG	ShO	Sv.	IP	H	R	ER	BB	SO
1976— Iowa (A.A.)	0	0	...	3.00	3	0	0	0	0	3	3	1	1	0	0

RECORD AS MANAGER

BACKGROUND: Coach, St. Louis Cardinals organization (June 20-September 29, 1977). ... Coach, Chicago White Sox (July 3, 1978-remainder of season).

RECORDS: Shares major league single-season record for most clubs managed—2 (1986).

HONORS: Named Major League Manager of the Year by THE SPORTING NEWS (1983). ... Named A.L. Manager of the Year by Baseball Writers' Association of America (1983, 1988 and 1992). ... Named A.L. Manager of the Year by THE SPORTING NEWS (1988 and 1992).

| | REGULAR SEASON | | | | POSTSEASON | | | | | | |
| | | | | | Playoff | | Champ. Series | | World Series | | All-Star Game | |
Year Team (League)	W	L	Pct.	Pos.	W	L	W	L	W	L	W	L
1978— Knoxville (Southern)	49	21	.700	1st (W)	—	—	—	—	—	—	—	—
— (Second half)	4	4	.500		—	—	—	—	—	—	—	—
1979— Iowa (American Association)	54	52	.509		—	—	—	—	—	—	—	—
— Chicago (A.L.)	27	27	.500	5th (W)	—	—	—	—	—	—	—	—
1980— Chicago (A.L.)	70	90	.438	5th (W)	—	—	—	—	—	—	—	—
1981— Chicago (A.L.)	31	22	.585	3rd (W)	—	—	—	—	—	—	—	—
— (Second half)	23	30	.434	6th (W)	—	—	—	—	—	—	—	—
1982— Chicago (A.L.)	87	75	.537	3rd (W)	—	—	—	—	—	—	—	—
1983— Chicago (A.L.)	99	63	.611	1st (W)	—	—	1	3	—	—	—	—
1984— Chicago (A.L.)	74	88	.457	T5th (W)	—	—	—	—	—	—	—	—
1985— Chicago (A.L.)	85	77	.525	3rd (W)	—	—	—	—	—	—	—	—
1986— Chicago (A.L.)	26	38	.406		—	—	—	—	—	—	—	—
— Oakland (A.L.)	45	34	.570	T3rd (W)	—	—	—	—	—	—	—	—
1987— Oakland (A.L.)	81	81	.500	3rd (W)	—	—	—	—	—	—	—	—
1988— Oakland (A.L.)	104	58	.642	1st (W)	—	—	4	0	1	4	—	—
1989— Oakland (A.L.)	99	63	.611	1st (W)	—	—	4	1	4	0	1	0
1990— Oakland (A.L.)	103	59	.636	1st (W)	—	—	4	0	0	4	1	0
1991— Oakland (A.L.)	84	78	.519	4th (W)	—	—	—	—	—	—	1	0
1992— Oakland (A.L.)	96	66	.593	1st (W)	—	—	2	4	—	—	—	—
1993— Oakland (A.L.)	68	94	.420	7th (W)	—	—	—	—	—	—	—	—
1994— Oakland (A.L.)	51	63	.447		—	—	—	—	—	—	—	—
1995— Oakland (A.L.)	67	77	.465	4th (W)	—	—	—	—	—	—	—	—
1996— St. Louis (N.L.)	88	74	.543	1st (C)	3	0	3	4	—	—	—	—
1997— St. Louis (N.L.)	73	89	.451	4th (C)	—	—	—	—	—	—	—	—
1998— St. Louis (N.L.)	83	79	.512	3rd (C)	—	—	—	—	—	—	—	—
1999— St. Louis (N.L.)	75	86	.466	4th (C)	—	—	—	—	—	—	—	—
American League totals (17 years)	1320	1183	.527		—	—	15	8	5	8	3	0
National League totals (4 years)	319	328	.493		3	0	3	4	—	—	—	—
Major League totals (21 years)	1639	1511	.520		3	0	18	12	5	8	3	0

NOTES:
1978—Became Chicago White Sox coach and replaced as Knoxville manager by Joe Jones, with club in third place (July 3).
1979—Replaced as Iowa manager by Joe Sparks, with club in second place (August 3); replaced Chicago manager Don Kessinger with club in fifth place and record of 46-60 (August 3).
1983—Lost to Baltimore in A.L. Championship Series.
1986—Replaced as White Sox manager by interim manager Doug Rader, with club in sixth place (June 20); replaced Oakland manager Jackie Moore (record of 29-44) and interim manager Jeff Newman (record of 2-8) with club in seventh place and record of 31-52 (July 7).
1988—Defeated Boston in A.L. Championship Series; lost to Los Angeles in World Series.
1989—Defeated Toronto in A.L. Championship Series; defeated San Francisco in World Series.
1990—Defeated Boston in A.L. Championship Series; lost to Cincinnati in World Series.

1992—Lost to Toronto in A.L. Championship Series.
1993—On suspended list (October 1-remainder of season).
1994—Oakland was in second place in A.L. West at time of season-ending strike (August 12).
1996—Defeated San Diego in N.L. divisional playoff; lost to Atlanta in N.L. Championship Series.

LAMONT, GENE — PIRATES

PERSONAL: Born December 25, 1946, in Rockford, Ill. ... 6-1/190. ... Batted both, threw right. ... Full name: Gene William Lamont.
HIGH SCHOOL: Hiawatha (Kirkland, Ill.).
COLLEGE: Northern Illinois, then Western Illinois.
TRANSACTIONS/CAREER NOTES: Selected by Detroit Tigers organization in first round (13th pick overall) of free-agent draft (June 29, 1965). ... On disabled list (May 18-28, 1966). ... On temporarily inactive list (May 20-25, 1967). ... On military list (May 25, 1967-remainder of season). ... On temporarily inactive list (July 15-31, 1972). ... Traded by Tigers to Atlanta Braves organization for C Bob Didier (May 14, 1973). ... Selected by Tigers from Braves organization in Rule 5 major league draft (December 3, 1973). ... Released by Tigers organization (December 20, 1977).
STATISTICAL NOTES: Led Southern League catchers with nine errors in 1969. ... Led Southern League catchers with 730 putouts, 72 assists, 814 total chances, 9 double plays and 15 passed balls in 1972. ... Led American Association catchers with eight double plays in 1976.

														BATTING			FIELDING		
Year	Team (League)	Pos.	G	AB	R	H	2B	3B	HR	RBI	Avg.	BB	SO	SB	PO	A	E	Avg.
1965— Syracuse (I.L.)............		C	5	9	1	1	0	0	1	1	.111	0	6	0	...	...	...	...
— Daytona Beach (FSL)..		C	38	104	9	24	5	1	1	16	.231	13	33	1	222	19	3	.988
1966— States. (W. Caro.)......		C	45	137	14	27	4	2	3	19	.197	21	49	1	283	28	8	.975
— Rocky Mt. (Caro.).......		C	36	102	9	26	4	1	2	9	.255	16	23	0	213	19	5	.979
1967— Rocky Mt. (Caro.).......		C	19	56	4	8	2	0	1	5	.143	8	8	0	107	16	1	.992
1968— Rocky Mt. (Caro.).......	C-OF-3B	101	304	36	76	10	0	4	39	.250	24	60	1	498	72	7	.988
1969— Montgomery (Sou.).....	C-3B	86	268	24	63	15	1	3	29	.235	32	37	0	410	92	†16	.969
1970— Toledo (I.L.)...............	C-3B-OF	74	230	27	61	9	1	4	32	.265	19	46	1	313	59	5	.987
— Detroit (A.L.).............		C	15	44	3	13	3	1	1	4	.295	2	9	0	87	8	0	1.000
1971— Toledo (I.L.)...............		C	63	180	17	41	8	1	5	19	.228	19	29	0	321	43	9	.976
— Detroit (A.L.).............		C	7	15	2	1	0	0	0	1	.067	0	5	0	38	2	2	.952
1972— Montgomery (Sou.)....	C-OF	119	385	47	105	19	1	6	51	.273	64	72	1	†731	†72	12	.985
— Detroit (A.L.)		C	1	0	0	0	0	0	0	0	...	0	0	0	1	0	0	1.000
1973— Richmond (I.L.)■......	C-1B	101	275	29	69	11	1	2	25	.251	41	64	0	411	34	3	.993
1974— Detroit (A.L.)■...........		C	60	92	9	20	4	0	3	8	.217	7	19	0	204	21	6	.974
1975— Detroit (A.L.)		C	4	8	1	3	1	0	1	1	.375	0	2	1	14	3	1	.944
— Evansville (A.A.)		C	49	130	15	40	9	0	3	20	.308	20	20	1	211	23	4	.983
1976— Evansville (A.A.)		C	96	269	23	63	13	0	5	25	.234	36	47	2	467	47	7	.987
1977— Evansville (A.A.)		C	3	5	0	2	1	0	0	0	.400	1	1	0	4	1	0	1.000
Major league totals (5 years)			87	159	15	37	8	1	4	14	.233	9	35	1	344	34	9	.977

RECORD AS MANAGER

BACKGROUND: Coach, Pittsburgh Pirates (1986-91). ... Scout and adviser to the general manager (July 7, 1995-remainder of season). ... Coach, Pirates (1996).
HONORS: Named Southern League Manager of the Year (1982). ... Named A.L. Manager of the Year by the Baseball Writers' Association of America (1993).

						REGULAR SEASON		POSTSEASON							
								Playoff		Champ. Series		World Series		All-Star Game	
Year	Team (League)	W	L	Pct.	Pos.			W	L	W	L	W	L	W	L
1978— Fort Myers (Florida State)........................		38	30	.559	1st (S)			—	—	—	—	—	—	—	—
— (Second half)		33	36	.478	5th (S)			0	1	—	—	—	—	—	—
1979— Fort Myers (Florida State)		38	32	.543	3rd (S)			—	—	—	—	—	—	—	—
— (Second half)		31	37	.456	4th (S)			—	—	—	—	—	—	—	—
1980— Jacksonville (Southern)		31	40	.437	4th (E)			—	—	—	—	—	—	—	—
— (Second half)		32	41	.438	5th (E)			—	—	—	—	—	—	—	—
1981— Jacksonville (Southern)		34	36	.486	4th (E)			—	—	—	—	—	—	—	—
— (Second half)		31	41	.431	4th (E)			—	—	—	—	—	—	—	—
1982— Jacksonville (Southern)		41	31	.569	1st (E)			—	—	—	—	—	—	—	—
— (Second half)		42	30	.583	1st (E)			4	4	—	—	—	—	—	—
1983— Jacksonville (Southern)		36	36	.500	2nd (E)			—	—	—	—	—	—	—	—
— (Second half)		41	32	.562	1st (E)			4	4	—	—	—	—	—	—
1984— Omaha (American Association)		68	86	.442	8th			—	—	—	—	—	—	—	—
1985— Omaha (American Association)		73	69	.514	3rd (W)			—	—	—	—	—	—	—	—
1992— Chicago (A.L.)		86	76	.531	3rd (W)			—	—	—	—	—	—	—	—
1993— Chicago (A.L.)		94	68	.580	1st (W)			—	—	2	4	—	—	—	—
1994— Chicago (A.L.)		67	46	.593				—	—	—	—	—	—	—	—
1995— Chicago (A.L.)		11	20	.355				—	—	—	—	—	—	—	—
1997— Pittsburgh (N.L.)		79	83	.488	2nd (C)			—	—	—	—	—	—	—	—
1998— Pittsburgh (N.L.)		69	93	.426	6th (C)			—	—	—	—	—	—	—	—
1999— Pittsburgh (N.L.)		78	83	.484	3rd (C)			—	—	—	—	—	—	—	—
American League totals (4 years)		258	210	.551				—	—	2	4	—	—	—	—
National League totals (3 years)		226	259	.466				—	—	—	—	—	—	—	—
Major league totals (7 years)		484	469	.508				—	—	2	4	—	—	—	—

NOTES:
1978—Lost to Miami in Southern Division championship.
1981—Jacksonville tied one game.
1982—Defeated Columbus, three games to one, in Eastern Division championship; lost to Nashville, three games to one, in league championship.
1983—Defeated Savannah, three games to one, in Eastern Division championship; lost to Birmingham, three games to one, in league championship.
1993—Lost to Toronto in A.L. Championship Series.
1994—Chicago was in first place in A.L. Central at time of season-ending strike (August 12).
1995—Replaced as White Sox manager by Terry Bevington, with club in fourth place (June 2).

MAJOR LEAGUE MANAGERS

PERSONAL: Born May 3, 1945, in East Providence, R.I. ... 5-9/170. ... Batted right, threw right. ... Full name: David Earl Lopes. ... Name rhymes with ropes.

HIGH SCHOOL: LaSalle Academy (Providence, R.I.).

COLLEGE: Iowa Weslyan, then Washburn (Kan.), degree in education, 1969.

TRANSACTIONS/CAREER NOTES: Selected by San Francisco Giants organization in 28th round of free agent draft (June 6, 1967); did not sign. ... Selected by Los Angeles Dodgers organization in secondary phase of free-agent draft (January 27, 1968). ... On restricted list (April 11-June 13, 1968). ... On temporary inactive list (April 11-27, 1969). ... On military list (July 22, 1969-April 8, 1970). ... On temporary inactive list (June 9-30, 1970). ... On temporary inactive list (April 26-29 and June 8-July 2, 1971). ... On temporary inactive list (June 16-30 and August 28-September 1, 1972). ... On disabled list (March 31-May 3, 1976). ... On disabled list (August 18-September 2,1981). ... Traded by Dodgers to Oakland Athletics for 2B Lance Hudson (February 8, 1982). ... On disabled list (July 7-August 8, 1984). ... Traded by Athletics to Chicago Cubs (August 31, 1984) as partial completion of deal in which Cubs traded P Chuck Rainey and a player to be named later to Athletics for a player to be named later (July 15, 1984); Athletics acquired OF Damon Farmar to complete deal (March 18, 1985). ... Traded by Cubs to Houston Astros for P Frank DiPino (July 21, 1986). ... Granted free agency (November 12, 1986). ... Re~signed by Astros (December 19, 1986). ... On disabled list (April 12-June 19, 1987); included rehabilitation assignment to Tucson (June 9-13, 1987). ... Released by Astros (November 12, 1987).

RECORDS: Shares major league single-inning record for most errors by a second baseman—3 (June 2, 1973, first inning). ... Shares N.L. single-game record for most double plays by a second baseman—5 (May 18, 1975).

HONORS: Named second baseman on The Sporting News National League All-Star Team (1978 and 1979). ... Named second baseman on The Sporting News National League All-Star fielding team (1978).

STATISTICAL NOTES: Led Pacific Coast League second basemen in errors with 18 in 1972. ... Tied for Pacific Coast League lead in errors by outfielders with 10 in 1970. ... Hit three home runs in one game (August 20, 1974).

Year Team (League)	Pos.	G	AB	R	H	2B	3B	HR	RBI	Avg.	BB	SO	SB	PO	A	E	Avg.
1968—Daytona Beach (FSL)..	OF	82	271	39	67	6	6	5	33	.247	24	74	26	109	7	4	.967
1969—Daytona Beach (FSL)....	OF	72	264	53	74	7	4	9	33	.280	49	42	32	138	16	7	.957
1970—Spokane (PCL)..........	OF-2B	100	343	48	90	15	4	6	35	.262	37	65	11	202	19	12	.948
1971—Spokane (PCL)..........	2B	94	353	78	108	9	9	6	36	.306	44	65	37	157	103	11	.959
1972—Albuquerque (PCL)......	2B-OF-SS	104	397	94	126	18	6	11	53	.317	59	64	*48	213	270	21	.958
— Los Angeles (N.L.)	2B	11	42	6	9	4	0	0	1	.214	7	6	4	27	27	2	.964
1973—Los Angeles (N.L.)	2-0-S-3	142	535	77	147	13	5	6	37	.275	62	77	36	323	380	11	.985
1974—Los Angeles (N.L.)	2B	145	530	95	141	26	3	10	35	.266	66	71	59	309	360	*24	.965
1975—Los Angeles (N.L.)	2B-OF-SS	155	618	108	162	24	6	8	41	.262	91	93	*77	360	386	16	.979
1976—Los Angeles (N.L.)	2B-OF	117	427	72	103	17	7	4	20	.241	56	49	*63	254	268	19	.965
1977—Los Angeles (N.L.)	2B	134	502	85	142	19	5	11	53	.283	73	69	47	287	380	14	.979
1978—Los Angeles (N.L.)	2B-OF	151	587	93	163	25	4	17	58	.278	71	70	45	340	424	*20	.974
1979—Los Angeles (N.L.)	2B	153	582	109	154	20	6	28	73	.265	97	88	44	341	*384	14	.981
1980—Los Angeles (N.L.)	2B	141	553	79	139	15	3	10	49	.251	58	71	23	304	416	15	.980
1981—Los Angeles (N.L.)	2B	58	214	35	44	2	0	5	17	.206	22	35	20	129	161	2	.993
1982—Oakland (A.L.)■........	2B-OF	138	450	58	109	19	3	11	42	.242	40	51	28	295	338	15	.977
1983—Oakland (A.L.).........	2B-OF-3B	147	494	64	137	13	4	17	67	.277	51	61	22	267	287	9	.984
1984—Oakland (A.L.)	OF-2B-3B	72	230	32	59	11	1	9	36	.257	31	36	12	99	47	6	.961
— Chicago (N.L.)■........	OF-2B	16	17	5	4	1	0	0	0	.235	6	5	3	6	2	0	1.000
1985—Chicago (N.L.)	OF-3B-2B	99	275	52	78	11	0	11	44	.284	46	37	47	115	6	1	.992
1986—Chicago (N.L.)	3B-OF	59	157	38	47	8	2	6	22	.299	31	16	17	51	54	8	.929
— Houston (N.L.)■........	OF-3B	37	98	11	23	2	1	1	13	.235	12	9	8	45	11	0	1.000.
1987—Houston (N.L.)	OF	47	43	4	10	2	0	1	6	.233	13	8	2	6	0	1	.857
— Tucson (PCL)	DH	4	14	2	9	3	0	0	3	.643				...	...	...	.000
National League totals (14 years)		1465	5180	869	1366	189	42	118	469	.264	711	704	495	2897	3259	147	.977
American League totals (3 years)		347	1174	154	305	43	8	37	145	.260	122	148	62	661	672	30	.978
Major league totals (16 years)		1812	6354	1023	1671	232	50	155	614	.263	833	852	557	3358	3931	177	.977

DIVISION SERIES RECORD

Year Team (League)	Pos.	G	AB	R	H	2B	3B	HR	RBI	Avg.	BB	SO	SB	PO	A	E	Avg.
1981—Los Angeles (N.L.)	2B	5	20	1	4	1	0	0	0	.200	3	7	1	7	12	0	1.000

CHAMPIONSHIP SERIES RECORD

RECORDS: Holds N.L. career record for most stolen bases—9. ... Shares career record for most consecutive games, one or more runs batted in—4. ... Shares N.L. career record for most clubs total Series—3.

Year Team (League)	Pos.	G	AB	R	H	2B	3B	HR	RBI	Avg.	BB	SO	SB	PO	A	E	Avg.
1974—Los Angeles (N.L.)	2B	4	15	4	4	0	1	0	3	.267	3	5	1	9	18	1	.964
1977—Los Angeles (N.L.)	2B	4	17	2	4	0	0	0	3	.235	2	0	0	9	10	1	.950
1978—Los Angeles (N.L.)	2B	4	18	3	7	1	1	2	5	.389	0	1	1	10	10	2	.909
1981—Los Angeles (N.L.)	2B	5	18	0	5	0	0	0	0	.278	1	3	5	13	13	0	1.000
1984—Chicago (N.L.)..........	OF-PH	2	1	0	0	0	0	0	0	.000	0	0	0	0	0	0	.000
1986—Houston (N.L.)	PH	3	2	1	0	0	0	0	0	.000	0	0	0	0	0	0	.000
Championship series totals (6 years)		22	71	10	20	1	2	2	11	.282	9	5	9	41	51	4	.958

WORLD SERIES RECORD

RECORDS: Shares World Series records for most stolen bases, inning—2 (October 15, 1974, first inning); most putouts by second baseman, game—8 (October 16, 1974); most chances accepted by second baseman, game—13 (October 16, 1974); most putouts by second baseman, inning—3 (October 16, 1974, sixth inning and October 21, 1981, fourth inning); most times home run as leadoff batter, start of game—1 (October 17, 1978); most errors by second baseman, game—3 (October 25, 1981); most errors by second baseman, inning—2 (October 25, 1981, fourth inning).

Year Team (League)	Pos.	G	AB	R	H	2B	3B	HR	RBI	Avg.	BB	SO	SB	PO	A	E	Avg.
									BATTING						FIELDING		
1974— Los Angeles (N.L.)	2B	5	18	2	2	0	0	0	0	.111	3	4	2	19	9	0	1.000
1977— Los Angeles (N.L.)	2B	6	24	3	4	0	1	1	2	.167	4	3	2	12	22	0	1.000
1978— Los Angeles (N.L.)	2B	6	26	7	8	0	0	3	7	.308	2	1	3	10	19	1	.967
1981— Los Angeles (N.L.)	2B	6	22	6	5	1	0	0	2	.227	4	3	4	26	14	6	.870
World Series totals (4 years)		23	90	18	19	1	1	3	11	.211	13	11	11	67	64	7	.949

ALL.STAR GAME RECORD

Year Team (League)	Pos.	AB	R	H	2B	3B	HR	RBI	Avg.	BB	SO	SB	PO	A	E	Avg.
									BATTING					FIELDING		
1978— National	PH-2B	1	0	1	0	0	0	1	1.000	0	0	0	0	1	0	1.000
1979— National	2B	3	0	1	0	0	0	0	.333	0	1	0	4	1	0	1.000
1980— National	2B	1	0	0	0	0	0	0	.000	0	0	0	0	2	0	1.000
1981— National	2B	0	0	0	0	0	0	0	.000	1	0	0	1	0	0	1.000
All-Star Game totals (4 years)		5	0	2	0	0	0	1	.400	1	1	0	5	7	0	1.000

MANUEL, CHARLIE — INDIANS

PERSONAL: Born January 4, 1944, in North Fork, W.Va. ... 6-3/200. ... Batted left, threw right. ... Full name: Charles Fuqua Manuel.
HIGH SCHOOL: Parry McCluer (Buena Vista, Va.).
HONORS: Named Most Valuable Player of Japan Pacific League (1979).
STATISTICAL NOTES: Led Midwest League in total bases with 205 in 1967. ... Led Southern League in total bases with 230 and in sacrifice hits with 10 in 1968.

Year Team (League)	Pos.	G	AB	R	H	2B	3B	HR	RBI	Avg.	BB	SO	SB	PO	A	E	Avg.
									BATTING					FIELDING		
1963— Wytheville (Appal.)	OF	58	173	32	62	9	2	7	45	.358	25	21	7	58	6	3	.955
1964— Orlando (FSL)	OF	114	373	43	99	21	7	4	37	.265	43	47	3	155	*15	5	.966
1965— Wilson (Carolina)	OF	61	167	16	34	6	1	0	19	.204	19	27	2	68	5	0	1.000
1966— Orlando (FSL)	OF	61	187	14	42	6	1	1	21	.225	21	26	4	...	...	...	...
— Wilson (Carolina)	OF	118	347	39	80	13	5	6	47	.231	43	53	7	140	13	5	.968
1967— Wisconsin (Midw.)	OF	111	399	*76	125	29	3	15	•70	*.313	56	74	4	178	18	4	.980
1968— Charlotte (Sou.)	OF	138	505	59	143	26	11	13	79	.283	43	89	6	202	8	5	.977
1969— Minnesota (A.L.)	OF	83	164	14	34	6	0	2	24	.207	28	33	1	57	2	2	.967
1970— Evansville (A.A.)	OF-1B	21	70	13	23	5	0	6	26	.329	6	5	0	43	6	4	.925
— Minnesota (A.L.)	OF	56	64	4	12	0	0	1	7	.188	6	17	1	7	0	0	1.000
1971— Portland (PCL)	OF-1B	63	191	47	71	8	5	19	46	.372	31	29	0	112	2	7	.942
— Minnesota (A.L.)	OF	18	16	1	2	1	0	0	1	.125	1	8	0	0	0	0	.000
1972— Minnesota (A.L.)	OF	63	122	6	25	5	0	1	8	.205	4	16	0	39	4	1	.977
1973— Tacoma (PCL)	OF	105	343	47	94	18	3	16	68	.274	42	58	0	...	...	...	...
1974— Albuquerque (PCL)■..	OF	129	432	82	142	23	2	30	102	.329	80	68	3	...	...	...	...
— Los Angeles (N.L.)	PH	4	3	0	1	0	0	0	1	.333	1	0	0	...	...	...	...
1975— Albuquerque (PCL)..	OF	81	243	40	79	17	1	16	64	.325	39	32	0	...	...	...	...
— Los Angeles (N.L.)	PH	15	15	0	2	0	0	0	2	.133	0	3	0	...	...	...	...
1976— Yakult (Jap. Cen.)■..	OF	84	263	...	64	...	...	11	32	.243	...	...	0	...	...	...	...
1977— Yakult (Jap. Cen.)	OF	114	358	70	113	8	0	42	97	.316	...	...	3	...	...	...	...
1978— Yakult (Jap. Cen.)	OF	127	468	85	146	12	2	39	103	.312	...	...	1	...	...	...	...
1979— Kintetsu (Jp. Pac.)■ ..	OF	97	333	69	108	18	0	*37	94	.324	...	...	0	...	...	...	...
1980— Kintetsu (Jap. Pac.)..	OF	118	459	88	149	16	0	*48	*129	.325	...	...	0	...	...	...	...
1981— Yakult (Jap. Cen.)■..	OF	81	246	...	64	...	...	12	36	.260	...	...	0	...	...	...	...
American League totals (4 years)		220	366	25	73	12	0	4	40	.199	39	74	1	...	...	...	...
National League totals (2 years)		19	18	0	3	0	0	0	3	.167	1	3	0	...	...	...	...
Major league totals (6 years)		239	384	25	76	12	0	4	43	.198	40	77	1	...	...	...	...

CHAMPIONSHIP SERIES RECORD

Year Team (League)	Pos.	G	AB	R	H	2B	3B	HR	RBI	Avg.	BB	SO	SB	PO	A	E	Avg.
									BATTING					FIELDING		
1969— Minnesota (A.L.)	PH	1	0	0	0	0	0	0	0	.000	0	0	0	0	0	0	.000
1970— Minnesota (A.L.)	PH	1	1	0	0	0	0	0	0	.000	0	0	0	0	0	0	.000
Championship series totals (2 years)		2	1	0	0	0	0	0	0	.000	0	0	0	0	0	0	.000

RECORD AS MANAGER

BACKGROUND: Scout, MInnesota Twins (1982). ... Hitting instructor, Cleveland Indians (1988-89 and 1994-99).
HONORS: Named International League Manager of the Year (1993).

Year Team (League)	W	L	Pct.	Pos.	Playoff W	Playoff L	Champ. Series W	Champ. Series L	World Series W	World Series L	All-Star Game W	All-Star Game L
	REGULAR SEASON				POSTSEASON							
1983— Wisconsin (Midwest)	71	67	.518	2nd (N)	—	—	—	—	—	—	—	—
1984— Orlando (Southern)	34	35	.493	3rd (E)	—	—	—	—	—	—	—	—
— (Second half)	45	30	.600	2nd (E)	0	1	—	—	—	—	—	—
1985— Orlando (Southern)	29	35	.453	5th (E)	—	—	—	—	—	—	—	—
— (Second half)	43	36	.544	2nd (E)	—	—	—	—	—	—	—	—
1986— Toledo (International)	62	77	.446	6th	—	—	—	—	—	—	—	—
1987— Portland (PCL)	20	49	.290	5th (N)	—	—	—	—	—	—	—	—
— (Second half)	25	47	.347	5th (N)	—	—	—	—	—	—	—	—
1990— Colorado Springs (PCL)	37	34	.521	2nd (S)	—	—	—	—	—	—	—	—
— (Second half)	39	33	.541	3rd (S)	—	—	—	—	—	—	—	—
1991— Colorado Springs (PCL)	30	41	.422	5th (S)	—	—	—	—	—	—	—	—
— (Second half)	42	26	.617	1st (S)	1	3	—	—	—	—	—	—
1992— Colorado Springs (PCL)	36	33	.521	2nd (S)	—	—	—	—	—	—	—	—
— (Second half)	48	24	.666	1st (S)	6	2	—	—	—	—	—	—
1993— Charlotte (International)	86	55	.610	1st (W)	6	4	—	—	—	—	—	—

MAJOR LEAGUE MANAGERS

MANUEL, JERRY — WHITE SOX

PERSONAL: Born December 23, 1953, in Hahira, Ga. ... 5-11/180. ... Batted right, threw right.

HIGH SCHOOL: Cordova (Rancho Cordova, Calif.).

TRANSACTIONS/CAREER NOTES: Selected by Detroit Tigers organization in first round (20th pick overall) of free-agent draft (June 6, 1972). ... On disabled list (August 18-September 1, 1978). ... Traded by Tigers to Montreal Expos organization for C Duffy Dyer (March 14, 1980). ... On disabled list (May 2-July 31, and August 15-September 1, 1981). ... Traded by Expos to San Diego Padres organization for P Kim Seaman (May 22, 1982). ... Traded by Padres to Expos organization for a player to be named later (June 8, 1982); Padres acquired P Mike Griffin to complete deal (August 30, 1982). ... Traded by Expos to Chicago Cubs organization for C Butch Benton (February 4, 1983). ... Granted free agency following 1983 season. ... Signed by Chicago White Sox organization (April 8, 1984). ... Granted free agency following 1985 season. ... Signed by Expos organization for 1986 season. ... On disabled list (June 23-July 17 and July 25-August 4, 1986).

STATISTICAL NOTES: Led Appalachian League shortstops with 303 total chances and 29 double plays in 1972. ... Led American Association second basemen with 688 total chances and 81 double plays in 1974. ... Led American Association second basemen with 758 total chances and 108 double plays in 1975. ... Led American Association second basemen with 234 putouts, 363 assists and 611 total chances in 1979. ... Led American Association shortstops with 612 total chances in 1980.

						BATTING								FIELDING			
Year	Team (League)	Pos.	G	AB	R	H	2B	3B	HR	RBI	Avg.	BB	SO	SB	PO	A	E	Avg.
1972—Bristol (Appal.)		SS	67	233	31	56	8	8	4	29	.240	19	61	11	*112	*176	15	*.950
1973—Lakeland (FSL)		SS	117	433	66	109	17	4	2	28	.252	52	98	20	167	349	29	.947
—Toledo (I.L.)		SS	27	72	8	20	0	0	0	2	.278	3	16	2	44	90	4	.971
1974—Evansville (A.A.)		2B	127	384	44	81	5	5	1	24	.211	35	74	3	*315	356	17	.975
1975—Evansville (A.A.)		2B	*137	501	63	115	10	4	4	43	.230	44	101	5	*348	*394	16	.979
—Detroit (A.L.)		2B	6	18	0	1	0	0	0	0	.056	0	4	0	11	23	2	.944
1976—Detroit (A.L.)		2B-SS	54	43	4	6	1	0	0	2	.140	3	9	1	40	64	8	.929
—Evansville (A.A.)		2B	11	44	6	8	1	0	1	3	.182	2	9	0	25	29	1	.982
1977—Evansville (A.A.)		2B-SS	110	375	52	102	19	7	1	38	.272	45	55	12	198	304	17	.967
1978—Evansville (A.A.)		2B-SS	114	430	65	113	18	5	7	50	.263	50	83	8	264	321	20	.967
1979—Evansville (A.A.)		2B-SS	130	460	71	116	26	3	9	75	.252	67	67	8	†265	†434	22	.969
1980—Denver (A.A.)■		SS	128	491	105	136	23	2	3	61	.277	81	62	11	*233	*357	22	.964
—Montreal (N.L.)		SS	7	6	0	0	0	0	0	0	.000	0	2	0	5	11	1	.941
1981—Montreal (N.L.)		2B-SS	27	55	10	11	5	0	3	10	.200	6	11	0	37	41	1	.987
1982—Wichita (A.A.)■		S-3-2-O	71	263	31	67	22	0	3	37	.255	15	34	2	99	152	11	.958
—San Diego (N.L.)		2B-3B-SS	2	5	0	1	0	1	0	1	.200	1	0	0	1	1	0	1.000
—Hawaii (PCL)		SS	26	92	8	18	3	1	0	7	.196	11	12	2	41	73	1	.991
1983—Iowa (A.A.)■		2-O-S-3	85	279	37	74	14	3	3	33	.265	22	46	6	129	143	9	.968
1984—Denver (A.A.)■		SS-2B-OF	109	335	43	98	14	3	4	40	.293	37	32	7	184	262	18	.961
1985—									Did not play.									
1986—Indianapolis (A.A.)■		3B-2B	22	41	4	16	2	0	1	9	.390	2	5	0	5	7	1	.923
American League totals (2 years)			60	61	4	7	1	0	0	2	.115	3	13	1	51	87	10	.932
National League totals (3 years)			36	66	10	12	5	1	3	11	.182	7	13	0	43	53	2	.980
Major league totals (5 years)			96	127	14	19	6	1	3	13	.150	10	26	1	94	140	12	.951

DIVISION SERIES RECORD

						BATTING								FIELDING			
Year	Team (League)	Pos.	G	AB	R	H	2B	3B	HR	RBI	Avg.	BB	SO	SB	PO	A	E	Avg.
1981—Montreal (N.L.)		2B	5	14	0	1	0	0	0	0	.071	2	5	0	13	19	3	.914

CHAMPIONSHIP SERIES RECORD

						BATTING								FIELDING			
Year	Team (League)	Pos.	G	AB	R	H	2B	3B	HR	RBI	Avg.	BB	SO	SB	PO	A	E	Avg.
1981—Montreal (N.L.)		PR	1	1	0	0	0	0	0	0	.000	0	0	0	...	...	...	...

RECORD AS MANAGER

BACKGROUND: Scout, Chicago White Sox (1985). ... Player/coach, Indianapolis, American Association (1986). ... Roving infield instructor, Montreal Expos organization (1987). ... Minor league field coordinator, Expos (1988-89). ... Coach, Expos (June 3, 1991-1996). ... Coach, Florida Marlins (1997).

HONORS: Named Southern League co-Manager of the Year (1990).

		REGULAR SEASON			POSTSEASON						
						Playoff		Champ. Series		World Series		All-Star Game	
Year	Team (League)	W	L	Pct.	Pos.	W	L	W	L	W	L	W	L
1990—Jacksonville (Southern)	38	33	.535	2nd (E)	—	—	—	—	—	—	—	—
—(Second half)	46	27	.630	1st (E)	1	3	—	—	—	—	—	—
1991—Indianapolis (A.A.)	28	22	.560	—	—	—	—	—	—	—	—	—
1998—Chicago (A.L.)	80	82	.494	2nd (C)	—	—	—	—	—	—	—	—
1999—Chicago (A.L.)	75	86	.466	2nd (C)	—	—	—	—	—	—	—	—
Major league totals (2 years)	155	168	.480		—	—	—	—	—	—	—	—

NOTES:
1990—Lost to Orlando in playoffs.
1991—Replaced as Indianapolis manager by Pat Kelly (June 2).

PERSONAL: Born November 23, 1930, in South Amboy, N.J. ... 5-8/205. ... Batted right, threw right. ... Full name: John Aloysius McKeon. ... Brother of Bill McKeon, minor league catcher (1952-54 and 1956-57); scout, Kansas City Royals (1969-70); scout, San Diego Padres (1981-87); and father-in-law of Greg Booker, pitcher with San Diego Padres and Minnesota Twins (1983-89).

HIGH SCHOOL: St. Mary's (South Amboy, N.J.).

COLLEGE: Holy Cross, then Seton Hall, then Elon (N.C.) College (degree in physical education and science).

TRANSACTIONS/CAREER NOTES: Released by Pittsburgh Pirates organization (September 28, 1954). ... Played 10 games with Fayetteville, five games with Greensboro and was player/manager with Fayetteville for 44 games during 1955 season. ... Player/manager, Missoula, Pioneer League (1956-58).

STATISTICAL NOTES: Led Carolina catchers with 17 double plays in 1953. ... Led Alabama State League catchers with nine double plays in 1949.

							BATTING								FIELDING		
Year Team (League)	Pos.	G	AB	R	H	2B	3B	HR	RBI	Avg.	BB	SO	SB	PO	A	E	Avg.
1949— Greenville (Alabama St.)	C	116	390	54	98	12	1	1	49	.251	41	34	8	*806	65	13	*.985
1950— York (Inter-State)	C	1	3	...	1	...	...	...	...	.333	...	...	...	...	...	...	...
—Gloverton (Can.-Am.) .	C	72	209	18	45	5	0	0	14	.215	19	28	2	281	30	15	.954
1951—						In military service.											
1952— Hutchinson (W.A.)......	C	116	358	42	78	10	1	4	40	.218	69	54	0	756	68	11	.987
1953— Burlington (Caro.)	C	140	474	46	86	19	2	6	52	.181	60	110	3	*836	*82	21	.978
1954— Burlington (Caro.)	C	17	30	1	4	0	0	0	2	.133	1	5	0	60	9	0	1.000
—Hutchinson (W.A.)......	C	46	140	18	29	5	0	1	13	.207	27	31	1	273	33	4	.987
1955— Fay.-Greens. (Caro.) ..	C	59	172	20	29	3	0	1	17	.169	29	28	1	292	20	6	.981
1956— Missoula (Pioneer).....	C-P	113	370	44	63	8	0	0	29	.170	53	62	3	630	78	9	.987
1957— Missoula (Pioneer).....	C-P	102	299	37	65	7	0	4	40	.217	60	44	6	645	55	10	.986
1958— Missoula (Pioneer).....	C-P	108	354	49	93	16	0	8	51	.263	51	55	2	739	64	12	.985
1959— Fox Cities (Three-I)	C	11	20	1	2	0	0	0	1	.100	8	3	0	...	...	...	...

RECORD AS PITCHER

Year Team (League)	W	L	Pct.	ERA	G	GS	CG	ShO	Sv.	IP	H	R	ER	BB	SO
1956— Missoula (Pioneer)............	0	0	...	0.00	8	...	...	...	...	...	...	...	...	...	...
1957— Missoula (Pioneer)............	0	0	...	0.00	6	...	...	...	...	...	...	...	...	...	...
1958— Missoula (Pioneer)............	0	0	...	0.00	2	...	...	...	...	...	...	...	...	...	...

RECORD AS MANAGER

BACKGROUND: Scout, Minnesota Twins (1965-67). ... Coach, Oakland Athletics (April 7-May 22, 1978). ... Scout/assistant to general manager, San Diego Padres (1980). ... Vice-president of baseball operations, Padres (1981-90). ... Senior adviser/player personnel, Cincinnati Reds (January 6, 1993-July 25, 1997).

HONORS: Named N.L. Manager of the Year by Baseball Writers' Association of America (1999).

		REGULAR SEASON			POSTSEASON						
					Playoff		Champ. Series		World Series		All-Star Game
Year Team (League)	W	L	Pct.	Pos.	W	L	W	L	W	L	W L
1955— Fayetteville (Carolina)................	70	67	.511	3rd	—		—		—		—
1956— Missoula (Pioneer)......................	61	71	.462	7th	—		—		—		—
1957— Missoula (Pioneer)......................	26	35	.426	6th	—		—		—		—
— (Second half)	36	29	.554	3rd	—		—		—		—
1958— Missoula (Pioneer)......................	34	29	.540	4th	—		—		—		—
— (Second half)	36	30	.545	3rd	—		—		—		—
1959— Fox Cities (Three-I)	26	39	.400	7th	—		—		—		—
— (Second half)	33	28	.541	4th	—		—		—		—
1960— Wilson (Carolina)	36	34	.514	3rd	—		—		—		—
— (Second half)	37	31	.544	2nd	—		—		—		—
1961— Wilson (Carolina)	41	28	.594	1st	—		—		—		—
— (Second half)	42	28	.600	1st	—		—		—		—
1962— Vancouver (Pacific Coast.)...........	72	79	.477	7th	—		—		—		—
1963— Dallas-Fort Worth (Pacific Coast)	79	79	.500	3rd (S)	—		—		—		—
1964— Atlanta (International)	19	42	.311		—		—		—		—
1968— High Point-Thomasville (Carolina)	69	71	.493	2nd (W)	5	1	—		—		—
1969— Omaha (American Association)	85	55	.607	1st	—		—		—		—
1970— Omaha (American Association)	73	65	.529	1st (E)	5	5	—		—		—
1971— Omaha (American Association)	69	70	.496	3rd (E)	—		—		—		—
1972— Omaha (American Association)	71	69	.507	2nd (E)	—		—		—		—
1973— Kansas City (A.L.)	88	74	.543	2nd (W)	—		—		—		—
1974— Kansas City (A.L.)	77	85	.475	5th (W)	—		—		—		—
1975— Kansas City (A.L.)	50	46	.521		—		—		—		—
1976— Richmond (International)	69	71	.493	4th	—		—		—		—
1977— Oakland (A.L.)	26	27	.491		—		—		—		—
1978— Oakland (A.L.)	45	78	.366	4th (W)	—		—		—		—
1980— Denver (American Association)	62	73	.459	3rd	—		—		—		—
1988— San Diego (N.L.)	67	48	.583	3rd (W)	—		—		—		—
1989— San Diego (N.L.)	89	73	.549	2nd (W)	—		—		—		—
1990— San Diego (N.L.)	37	43	.436		—		—		—		—
1997— Cincinnati (N.L.)	33	30	.524	3rd (C)	—		—		—		—
1998— Cincinnati (N.L.)	77	85	.475	4th (C)	—		—		—		—
1999— Cincinnati (N.L.)	96	67	.588	2nd (C)	—		—		—		—
American League totals (5 years)......................	286	310	.480		—		—		—		—
National League totals (6 years)......................	399	346	.535		—		—		—		—
Major league totals (11 years)..........................	685	656	.511		—		—		—		—

NOTES:
1955—Replaced Fayetteville manager Aaron Robinson (June 11). Replaced as Fayetteville manager by John Sanford (August 6) because of hand injury with team tied for first place (record is for full season).
1964—Replaced as Atlanta manager by Peter Appleton with club in eighth place (June 21).
1968—Defeated Greensboro, one game to none, in quarterfinals; defeated Lynchburg, two games to none in semifinals; defeated Raleigh-Durham, two games to one, in championship.

MAJOR LEAGUE MANAGERS

1970—Defeated Denver, four games to one, in championship; lost to Syracuse, four games to one, in Junior World Series.
1975—Replaced as Kansas City manager by Whitey Herzog, with club in second place (July 24).
1977—Replaced as Oakland manager by Bobby Winkles, with club tied for fifth place (June 10).
1978—Replaced Oakland manager Bobby Winkles, with club in first place and record of 24-15 (May 23).
1988—Replaced San Diego manager Larry Bowa, with club in fifth place and record of 16-30 (May 28).
1990—Replaced as San Diego manager by Greg Riddoch, with club in fourth place (July 11).
1997—Replaced Cincinnati manager Ray Knight, with club in fourth place and record of 43-56 (July 25).

MUSER, TONY   ROYALS

PERSONAL: Born August 1, 1947, in Los Angeles. ... 6-2/190. ... Batted left, threw left. ... Full name: Anthony Joseph Muser.
HIGH SCHOOL: Lakewood (Calif.).
JUNIOR COLLEGE: San Diego Mesa.
TRANSACTIONS/CAREER NOTES: Signed as non-drafted free agent by Boston Red Sox organization (1967). ... On military list (beginning of 1968 season-July 15, 1968). ... Traded by Red Sox with P Vicente Romo to Chicago White Sox for P Danny Murphy and C Duane Josephson (March 30, 1971). ... Traded by White Sox to Baltimore Orioles for P Jesse Jefferson (June 15, 1975). ... Released by Orioles (February 21, 1978). ... Signed by Milwaukee Brewers organization (March 20, 1978). ... Released by Brewers (February 12, 1979). ... Played in Japan (1979).

							BATTING							FIELDING		
Year Team (League)	Pos.	G	AB	R	H	2B	3B	HR	RBI	Avg.	BB	SO	SB	PO	A	E	Avg.
1967—Waterloo (Midw.)	1B	68	251	40	71	15	1	6	42	.283	38	42	3	674	28	11	.985
1968—Greenv. (W. Car.)........	1B-OF	33	114	13	31	7	0	2	12	.272	18	17	1	223	23	2	.992
— Win.-Salem (Car.)...	OF-1B	7	21	1	8	0	0	0	2	.381	1	3	1	13	1	0	1.000
1969—Louisville (I.L.)	1B	120	457	57	129	14	4	7	62	.282	43	53	7	1029	63	15	.986
— Boston (A.L.).............	1B	2	9	0	1	0	0	0	1	.111	1	1	0	17	3	0	1.000
1970—Louisville (I.L.)	1B	114	462	66	130	25	7	5	45	.281	38	49	1	1013	45	9	*.992
1971—Indianapolis (A.A.)■ ..	1B	85	310	36	91	10	3	3	31	.294	35	27	0	720	42	6	.992
— Chicago (A.L.)...........	1B	11	16	2	5	0	1	0	0	.313	1	1	0	23	3	1	.963
1972—Tucson (PCL)	1B	83	318	41	86	17	0	3	40	.270	29	28	3	680	49	12	.984
— Chicago (A.L.)...........	1B-OF	44	61	6	17	2	2	1	9	.279	2	6	1	135	7	2	.986
1973—Chicago (A.L.)	1B-OF	109	309	38	88	14	3	4	30	.285	33	36	8	681	38	6	.992
1974—Chicago (A.L.)	1B	103	206	16	60	5	1	1	18	.291	6	22	1	419	13	1	.998
1975—Chicago (A.L.)	1B	43	111	11	27	3	0	0	6	.243	7	8	2	263	22	2	.993
— Baltimore (A.L.)■......	1B	80	82	11	26	3	0	0	11	.317	8	9	0	213	15	1	.996
1976—Baltimore (A.L.).......	1B-OF	136	326	25	74	7	1	1	30	.227	21	34	1	693	63	7	.991
1977—Baltimore (A.L.).......	1B-OF	120	118	14	27	6	0	0	7	.229	13	16	1	232	20	3	.988
1978—Spokane (PCL)■.......	1B-OF	78	283	48	83	13	0	6	38	.293	33	25	2	572	50	4	.994
— Milwaukee (A.L.)	1B	15	30	0	4	1	1	0	5	.133	3	5	0	79	5	1	.988
1979—Seibu (Jp. Pac.)■......	...	65	168	...	33	...	...	2	10	.196	...	...	...	...	...	...	...
Major league totals (9 years)		663	1268	123	329	41	9	7	117	.259	95	138	14	2755	189	24	.992

RECORD AS MANAGER

BACKGROUND: Coach, Milwaukee Brewers (1985-89). ... Scout, Brewers (1990). ... Coach, Chicago Cubs (1993-July 8, 1997).

		REGULAR SEASON					POSTSEASON					
						Playoff		Champ. Series		World Series		All-Star Game
Year Team (League)	W	L	Pct.	Pos.	W	L	W	L	W	L	W	L
1980—Stockton (California)................................	49	21	.700	1st (N)	—	—	—	—	—	—	—	—
— (Second half)	41	30	.577	1st (N)	3	0	—	—	—	—	—	—
1981—El Paso (Texas)......................................	37	31	.544	2nd (W)	—	—	—	—	—	—	—	—
— (Second half)	28	38	.424	4th (W)	—	—	—	—	—	—	—	—
1982—El Paso (Texas)......................................	42	23	.646	1st (W)	—	—	—	—	—	—	—	—
— (Second half)	34	37	.479	2nd (W)	2	3	—	—	—	—	—	—
1983—El Paso (Texas)......................................	35	33	.515	2nd (W)	—	—	—	—	—	—	—	—
— Vancouver(Pacific Coast).............................	29	41	.414	4th (N)	—	—	—	—	—	—	—	—
1984—Vancouver (Pacific Coast)	32	40	.444	3rd (N)	—	—	—	—	—	—	—	—
— (Second half)	39	31	.557	3rd (N)	—	—	—	—	—	—	—	—
1991—Denver (American Association)	79	65	.549	1st (W)	7	3	—	—	—	—	—	—
1992—Denver (American Association)	73	71	.507	2nd (W)	—	—	—	—	—	—	—	—
1997—Kansas City (A.L.)	31	48	.392	4th (C)	—	—	—	—	—	—	—	—
1998—Kansas City (A.L.)	72	89	.447	3rd (C)	—	—	—	—	—	—	—	—
1999—Kansas City (A.L.)	64	97	.398	4th (C)	—	—	—	—	—	—	—	—
Major league totals (3 years)...........................	167	234	.416		—	—	—	—	—	—	—	—

NOTES:
1980—Defeated Visalia in league championship.
1982—Defeated Midland, two games to one, in playoffs; lost to Tulsa, three games to none, in league championship.
1983—Replaced Vancouver manager Dick Phillips (June 22).
1991—Defeated Buffalo, three games to two, in league championship; defeated Columbus (International League), four games to one, in Class AAA Alliance championship.
1997—Replaced Kansas City manager Bob Boone with club in fourth place and record of 36-46 (July 9).
1998—On suspended list (June 9-17).

OATES, JOHNNY   RANGERS

PERSONAL: Born January 21, 1946, in Sylva, N.C. ... 5-11/185. ... Batted left, threw right. ... Full name: Johnny Lane Oates.
HIGH SCHOOL: Prince George (Va.).
COLLEGE: Virginia Tech (bachelor of science degree in health and physical education).

TRANSACTIONS/CAREER NOTES: Selected by Chicago White Sox organization in second round of free-agent draft (June 1966); did not sign. ... Selected by Baltimore Orioles organization in secondary phase of free-agent draft (January 28, 1967). ... On military list (April 21-August 22, 1970). ... Traded by Orioles with P Pat Dobson, P Roric Harrison and 2B Dave Johnson to Atlanta Braves for C Earl Williams and IF Taylor Duncan (November 30, 1972). ... On disabled list (July 17-September 2, 1973). ... Traded by Braves with 1B Dick Allen to Philadelphia Phillies for C Jim Essian, OF Barry Bonnell and cash (May 7, 1975). ... On disabled list (April 14-June 1, 1976). ... Traded by Phillies with P Quency Hill to Los Angeles Dodgers for IF Ted Sizemore (December 20, 1976). ... Released by Dodgers (March 27, 1980). ... Signed by New York Yankees (April 4, 1980). ... Granted free agency (November 13, 1980). ... Re-signed by Yankees organization (January 23, 1981). ... On Columbus disabled list (August 3-25, 1981). ... Released by Yankees organization (October 27, 1981).

STATISTICAL NOTES: Led International League catchers with 727 total chances in 1971. ... Led N.L. with 15 passed balls in 1974. ... Tied for N.L. lead in double plays by catcher with 10 in 1975.

							BATTING								FIELDING		
Year Team (League)	Pos.	G	AB	R	H	2B	3B	HR	RBI	Avg.	BB	SO	SB	PO	A	E	Avg.
1967—Bluefield (Appal.)........	C	5	12	5	5	1	0	1	4	.417	2	0	0	23	5	0	1.000
— Miami (FSL)	C-OF	48	156	22	45	5	2	3	19	.288	24	13	2	271	37	8	.975
1968— Miami (FSL)	C-OF	70	194	24	51	9	3	0	23	.263	33	14	2	384	42	3	.993
1969— Dall./Ft. Worth (Tex.) ..	C	66	191	24	55	12	2	1	18	.288	20	9	0	253	42	4	.987
1970— Rochester (I.L.)	C	9	16	1	6	1	0	0	4	.375	4	2	0	24	2	0	1.000
— Baltimore (A.L.).........	C	5	18	2	5	0	1	0	2	.278	2	0	0	30	1	2	.939
1971— Rochester (I.L.)	C	114	346	49	96	16	3	7	44	.277	49	31	10	*648	*73	6	.992
1972—Baltimore (A.L.)	C	85	253	20	66	12	1	4	21	.261	28	31	5	391	31	2	*.995
1973— Atlanta (N.L.)■..........	C	93	322	27	80	6	0	4	27	.248	22	31	1	409	57	9	.981
1974— Atlanta (N.L.)	C	100	291	22	65	10	0	1	21	.223	23	24	2	434	55	4	.992
1975— Atlanta (N.L.)..............	C	8	18	0	4	1	0	0	0	.222	1	4	0	21	1	0	1.000
— Philadelphia (N.L.)■ ..	C	90	269	28	77	14	0	1	25	.286	33	29	1	429	44	5	.990
1976— Philadelphia (N.L.).....	C	37	99	10	25	2	0	0	8	.253	8	12	0	155	15	1	.994
1977— Los Angeles (N.L.)■ ..	C	60	156	18	42	4	0	3	11	.269	11	11	1	258	37	4	.987
1978— Los Angeles (N.L.)	C	40	75	5	23	1	0	0	6	.307	5	3	0	77	10	4	.956
1979— Los Angeles (N.L.)	C	26	46	4	6	2	0	0	2	.130	4	1	0	64	13	2	.975
1980— New York (A.L.)■......	C	39	64	6	12	3	0	1	3	.188	2	3	1	99	10	1	.991
1981— New York (A.L.)..........	C	10	26	4	5	1	0	0	0	.192	2	0	0	49	3	2	.963
American League totals (4 years)		139	361	32	88	16	2	5	26	.244	34	34	6	569	45	7	.989
National League totals (7 years)		454	1276	114	322	40	0	9	100	.252	107	115	5	1847	232	29	.986
Major league totals (11 years)		593	1637	146	410	56	2	14	126	.250	141	149	11	2416	277	36	.987

CHAMPIONSHIP SERIES RECORD

							BATTING								FIELDING		
Year Team (League)	Pos.	G	AB	R	H	2B	3B	HR	RBI	Avg.	BB	SO	SB	PO	A	E	Avg.
1976— Philadelphia (N.L.).......	C	1	1	0	0	0	0	0	0	.000	0	0	0	1	0	0	1.000

WORLD SERIES RECORD

							BATTING								FIELDING		
Year Team (League)	Pos.	G	AB	R	H	2B	3B	HR	RBI	Avg.	BB	SO	SB	PO	A	E	Avg.
1977— Los Angeles (N.L.)	C	1	1	0	0	0	0	0	0	.000	0	0	0	1	0	0	1.000
1978— Los Angeles (N.L.)	C	1	1	0	1	0	0	0	0	1.000	1	0	0	3	1	0	1.000
World Series totals (2 years)		2	2	0	1	0	0	0	0	.500	1	0	0	4	1	0	1.000

RECORD AS MANAGER

BACKGROUND: Coach, Columbus, New York Yankees organization (July 30, 1981-remainder of season). ... Coach, Chicago Cubs (1984-87). ... Coach, Baltimore Orioles (1989-May 23, 1991).

HONORS: Named International League Manager of the Year (1988). ... Coach, A.L. All-Star team (1993, 1995 and 1997). ... Named A.L. Manager of the Year by THE SPORTING NEWS (1993 and 1996). ... Named co-A.L. Manager of the Year by Baseball Writers' Association of America (1996).

		REGULAR SEASON				POSTSEASON						
						Playoff		Champ. Series		World Series		All-Star Game
Year Team (League)	W	L	Pct.	Pos.	W	L	W	L	W	L	W	L
1982— Nashville (Southern)	32	38	.457	4th (W)	—	—	—	—	—	—	—	—
— (Second half)	45	29	.608	1st (W)	6	2	—	—	—	—	—	—
1983— Columbus (International)	83	57	.593	1st	2	3	—	—	—	—	—	—
1988— Rochester (International)	77	64	.546	1st (W)	5	5	—	—	—	—	—	—
1991—Baltimore (A.L.)........	54	71	.432	6th (E)	—	—	—	—	—	—	—	—
1992—Baltimore (A.L.)........	89	73	.549	3rd (E)	—	—	—	—	—	—	—	—
1993—Baltimore (A.L.)........	85	77	.525	T3rd (E)	—	—	—	—	—	—	—	—
1994—Baltimore (A.L.)........	63	49	.563	—	—	—	—	—	—	—	—	—
1995— Texas (A.L.)................	74	70	.514	3rd (W)	—	—	—	—	—	—	—	—
1996— Texas (A.L.)................	90	72	.556	1st (W)	1	3	—	—	—	—	—	—
1997— Texas (A.L.)................	77	85	.475	3rd (W)	—	—	—	—	—	—	—	—
1998— Texas (A.L.)................	88	74	.543	1st (W)	0	3	—	—	—	—	—	—
1999— Texas (A.L.)................	95	67	.586	1st (W)	0	3	—	—	—	—	—	—
Major league totals (9 years)...........	715	638	.528		1	9	—	—	—	—	—	—

NOTES:
1982—Defeated Knoxville, three games to one, in playoffs; defeated Jacksonville, three games to one, in league championship.
1983—Lost to Tidewater in playoffs.
1988—Defeated Tidewater, three games to one, in league championship; lost to Indianapolis (American Association), four games to two, in Class AAA-Alliance championship.
1991—Replaced Baltimore manager Frank Robinson with club in seventh place and record of 13-24 (May 23).
1994—Baltimore was in second place in A.L. East at time of season ending strike (August 12).
1996—Lost to New York Yankees in A.L. divisional playoff.
1998—Lost to New York Yankees in A.L. divisional playoff.
1999—Lost to New York Yankees in A.L. divisional playoff.

MAJOR LEAGUE MANAGERS

PERSONAL: Born August 28, 1943, in Tampa. ... 6-2/199. ... Batted right, threw right. ... Full name: Louis Victor Piniella. ... Cousin of Dave Magadan, third baseman/first baseman, San Diego Padres. ... Name pronounced pin-ELL-uh.

HIGH SCHOOL: Jesuit (Tampa).

COLLEGE: Tampa.

TRANSACTIONS/CAREER NOTES: Signed as free agent by Cleveland Indians organization (June 9, 1962). ... Selected by Washington Senators organization from Jacksonville, Indians organization, in Rule 5 major league draft (November 26, 1962). ... On military list (March 9-July 20, 1964). ... Traded by Senators organization to Baltimore Orioles organization (August 4, 1964), completing deal in which Orioles traded P Lester (Buster) Narum to Senators for cash and a player to be named later (March 31, 1964). ... On suspended list (June 27-29, 1965). ... Traded by Orioles organization to Indians organization for C Camilo Carreon (March 10, 1966). ... On temporarily inactive list (May 19-22, 1967). ... On disabled list (May 22-June 6, 1968). ... On temporarily inactive list (June 6-25, 1968). ... Selected by Seattle Pilots in expansion draft (October 15, 1968). ... Traded by Pilots to Kansas City Royals for OF Steve Whitaker and P John Gelnar (April 1, 1969). ... On military list (August 7-22, 1969). ... On disabled list (May 5-June 8, 1971). ... Traded by Royals with P Ken Wright to New York Yankees for P Lindy McDaniel (December 7, 1973). ... On disabled list (June 17-July 6, 1975; August 23-September 7, 1981; and March 30-April 22, 1983). ... Placed on voluntarily retired list (June 17, 1984).

RECORDS: Shares major league record for most assists by outfielder in one inning—2 (May 27, 1974, third inning).

HONORS: Named A.L. Rookie of the Year by Baseball Writers' Association of America (1969).

STATISTICAL NOTES: Led A.L. in grounding into double plays with 25 in 1972. ... Career major league grand slams: 1.

Year	Team (League)	Pos.	G	AB	R	H	2B	3B	HR	RBI	Avg.	BB	SO	SB	PO	A	E	Avg.
1962—	Selma (Ala.-Fla.)	OF	70	278	40	75	10	5	8	44	.270	10	57	4	94	6	9	.917
1963—	Peninsula (Caro.)■	OF	143	548	71	170	29	4	16	77	.310	34	70	8	271	*23	8	.974
1964—	Aberdeen (North.)	OF	20	74	8	20	8	3	0	12	.270	6	9	1	37	1	1	.974
—	Baltimore (A.L.)■	PH	4	1	0	0	0	0	0	0	.000	0	0	0	...	...	...	...
1965—	Elmira (East.)	OF	126	490	64	122	29	6	11	64	.249	22	57	5	176	5	7	.963
1966—	Portland (PCL)■	OF	133	457	47	132	22	3	7	52	.289	20	52	6	177	11	11	.945
1967—	Portland (PCL)	OF	113	396	46	122	20	1	8	56	.308	23	47	2	199	7	6	.972
1968—	Portland (PCL)	OF	88	331	49	105	15	3	13	62	.317	19	31	0	167	6	7	.961
—	Cleveland (A.L.)	OF	6	5	1	0	0	0	0	1	.000	0	0	1	1	0	0	1.000
1969—	Kansas City (A.L.)■	OF	135	493	43	139	21	6	11	68	.282	33	56	2	278	13	7	.977
1970—	Kansas City (A.L.)	OF-1B	144	542	54	163	24	5	11	88	.301	35	42	3	250	6	4	.985
1971—	Kansas City (A.L.)	OF	126	448	43	125	21	5	3	51	.279	21	43	5	201	6	3	.986
1972—	Kansas City (A.L.)	OF	151	574	65	179	*33	4	11	72	.312	34	59	7	275	8	7	.976
1973—	Kansas City (A.L.)	OF-DH	144	513	53	128	28	1	9	69	.250	30	65	5	196	9	3	.986
1974—	New York (A.L.)■	OF-DH-1B	140	518	71	158	26	0	9	70	.305	32	58	1	270	16	3	.990
1975—	New York (A.L.)	OF-DH	74	199	7	39	4	1	0	22	.196	16	22	0	65	5	1	.986
1976—	New York (A.L.)	OF-DH	100	327	36	92	16	6	3	38	.281	18	34	0	199	10	4	.981
1977—	New York (A.L.)	OF-DH-1B	103	339	47	112	19	3	12	45	.330	20	31	2	86	3	2	.978
1978—	New York (A.L.)	OF-DH	130	472	67	148	34	5	6	69	.314	34	36	3	213	4	7	.969
1979—	New York (A.L.)	OF-DH	130	461	49	137	22	2	11	69	.297	17	31	3	204	13	4	.982
1980—	New York (A.L.)	OF-DH	116	321	39	92	18	0	2	27	.287	29	20	0	157	8	5	.971
1981—	New York (A.L.)	OF-DH	60	159	16	44	9	0	5	18	.277	13	9	0	69	2	1	.986
1982—	New York (A.L.)	DH-OF	102	261	33	80	17	1	6	37	.307	18	18	0	68	2	0	1.000
1983—	New York (A.L.)	OF-DH	53	148	19	43	9	1	2	16	.291	11	12	1	67	4	3	.959
1984—	New York (A.L.)	OF-DH	29	86	8	26	4	1	1	6	.302	7	5	0	40	3	0	1.000
Major league totals (18 years)			1747	5867	651	1705	305	41	102	766	.291	368	541	33	2639	112	54	.981

DIVISION SERIES RECORD

Year	Team (League)	Pos.	G	AB	R	H	2B	3B	HR	RBI	Avg.	BB	SO	SB	PO	A	E	Avg.
1981—	New York (A.L.)	DH-PH	4	10	1	2	1	0	1	3	.200	0	0	0	...	...	...	...

CHAMPIONSHIP SERIES RECORD

Year	Team (League)	Pos.	G	AB	R	H	2B	3B	HR	RBI	Avg.	BB	SO	SB	PO	A	E	Avg.
1976—	New York (A.L.)	DH-PH	4	11	1	3	1	0	0	0	.273	0	1	0	...	...	...	...
1977—	New York (A.L.)	OF-DH	5	21	1	7	3	0	0	2	.333	0	1	0	9	1	0	1.000
1978—	New York (A.L.)	OF	4	17	2	4	0	0	0	0	.235	0	3	0	13	0	0	1.000
1980—	New York (A.L.)	OF	2	5	1	1	0	0	1	1	.200	2	1	0	5	0	0	1.000
1981—	New York (A.L.)	PH-DH-OF	3	5	2	3	0	0	1	3	.600	0	0	0	0	0	0	...
Championship series totals (5 years)			18	59	7	18	4	0	2	6	.305	2	6	0	27	1	0	1.000

WORLD SERIES RECORD

RECORDS: Shares single-series record for collecting one or more hits in each game (1978).

NOTES: Member of World Series championship team (1977-1978).

Year	Team (League)	Pos.	G	AB	R	H	2B	3B	HR	RBI	Avg.	BB	SO	SB	PO	A	E	Avg.
1976—	New York (A.L.)	DH-OF-PH	4	9	1	3	1	0	0	0	.333	0	0	0	1	0	0	1.000
1977—	New York (A.L.)	OF	6	22	1	6	0	0	0	3	.273	0	3	0	16	1	1	.944
1978—	New York (A.L.)	OF	6	25	3	7	0	0	0	4	.280	0	0	1	14	1	0	1.000
1981—	New York (A.L.)	OF-PH	6	16	2	7	1	0	0	3	.438	0	1	1	7	0	0	1.000
World Series totals (4 years)			22	72	7	23	2	0	0	10	.319	0	4	2	38	2	1	.976

ALL-STAR GAME RECORD

Year	League	Pos.	AB	R	H	2B	3B	HR	RBI	Avg.	BB	SO	SB	PO	A	E	Avg.
1972—	American	PH	1	0	0	0	0	0	0	.000	0	0	0	...	...	...	...

RECORD AS MANAGER

BACKGROUND: Coach, New York Yankees (June 25, 1984-85). ... Vice-president/general manager, Yankees (beginning of 1988 season-June 22, 1988). ... Special adviser, Yankees (1989).

HONORS: Named A.L. Manager of the Year by Baseball Writers' Association of America (1995).

		REGULAR SEASON				POSTSEASON								
						Playoff		Champ. Series		World Series		All-Star Game		
Year	Team (League)	W	L	Pct.	Pos.	W	L	W	L	W	L	W	L	
1986—	New York (A.L.)	90	72	.556	2nd (E)	—	—	—	—	—	—	—	—	
1987—	New York (A.L.)	89	73	.549	4th (E)	—	—	—	—	—	—	—	—	
1988—	New York (A.L.)	45	48	.484	5th (E)	—	—	—	—	—	—	—	—	
1990—	Cincinnati (N.L.)	91	71	.562	1st (W)	—	—	4	2	4	0	—	—	
1991—	Cincinnati (N.L.)	74	88	.457	5th (W)	—	—	—	—	—	—	0	1	
1992—	Cincinnati (N.L.)	90	72	.556	2nd (W)	—	—	—	—	—	—	—	—	
1993—	Seattle (A.L.)	82	80	.506	4th (W)	—	—	—	—	—	—	—	—	
1994—	Seattle (A.L.)	49	63	.438		—	—	—	—	—	—	—	—	
1995—	Seattle (A.L.)	79	66	.545	1st (W)	3	2	2	4	—	—	—	—	
1996—	Seattle (A.L.)	85	76	.528	2nd (W)	—	—	—	—	—	—	—	—	
1997—	Seattle (A.L.)	90	72	.556	1st (W)	1	3	—	—	—	—	—	—	
1998—	Seattle (A.L.)	76	85	.472	3rd (W)	—	—	—	—	—	—	—	—	
1999—	Seattle (A.L.)	79	83	.488	3rd (W)	—	—	—	—	—	—	—	—	
American League totals (10 years)		764	718	.515		4	5	2	4	—	—	—	—	
National League totals (3 years)		255	231	.525		—	—	4	2	4	0	0	1	
Major league totals (13 years)		1019	949	.518		4	5	6	6	4	0	0	1	

NOTES:
1988—Replaced New York manager Billy Martin, with club in second place and record of 40-28 (June 23).
1990—Defeated Pittsburgh in N.L. Championship Series; defeated Oakland in World Series.
1994—Seattle was in third place in A.L. West at time of season-ending strike (August 12).
1995—Defeated New York in A.L. divisional playoff; lost to Cleveland in A.L. Championship Series.
1997—Lost to Baltimore in A.L. divisional playoff.

ROTHSCHILD, LARRY — DEVIL RAYS

PERSONAL: Born March 12, 1954, in Chicago. ... 6-2/185. ... Threw right, batted right. ... Full name: Lawrence Lee Rothschild.
HIGH SCHOOL: Homewood-Flossmoor (Flossmoor, Ill.).
COLLEGE: Bradley, then Florida State.
TRANSACTIONS/CAREER NOTES: Signed as non-drafted free agent by Cincinnati Reds organization (June 10, 1975). ... Loaned to San Diego Padres organization (May 11, 1978). ... Returned to Reds organization (July 18, 1978). ... Selected by Detroit Tigers from Reds organization in major league draft (December 8, 1980). ... Sold to Las Vegas, Pacific Coast League (February 25, 1983). ... On disabled list (April 10-May 4, 1983). ... Sold to Denver, American Association (December 18, 1983). ... Sold to Iowa, American Association (October 15, 1984).

Year	Team (League)	W	L	Pct.	ERA	G	GS	CG	ShO	Sv.	IP	H	R	ER	BB	SO
1975—	Billings (Pioneer)	0	2	.000	7.88	6	0	0	0	1	8	14	11	7	7	12
	Eugene (Northwest)	3	0	1.000	2.73	21	0	0	0	•6	33	17	11	10	21	36
1976—	Three Rivers (East.)	11	3	*.786	2.05	30	12	10	5	5	123	96	33	28	29	75
1977—	Indianapolis (A.A.)	4	4	.500	4.21	29	14	2	1	1	92	93	51	43	34	43
1978—	Nashville (Southern)	0	0	...	4.50	5	0	0	0	1	12	14	7	6	4	9
	Amarillo (Texas)■	5	5	.500	4.17	12	12	5	1	0	82	83	42	38	21	57
	Indianapolis (A.A.)■	4	0	1.000	2.20	8	6	2	0	0	45	31	15	11	19	38
1979—	Indianapolis (A.A.)	1	6	.143	5.27	33	10	0	0	6	82	85	52	48	56	68
1980—	Indianapolis (A.A.)	8	7	.533	4.22	33	14	1	0	1	113	111	60	53	44	74
1981—	Evansville (A.A.)■	8	5	.615	3.27	56	0	0	0	15	77	62	32	28	29	81
	Detroit (A.L.)	0	0	...	1.50	5	0	0	0	0	6	4	1	1	6	1
1982—	Evansville (A.A.)	6	4	.600	3.65	45	0	0	0	10	69	73	34	28	30	45
	Detroit (A.L.)	0	0	...	13.50	2	0	0	0	0	2⅔	4	4	4	2	0
1983—	Las Vegas (PCL)■	9	2	.818	5.09	38	0	0	0	2	74⅓	88	43	42	34	39
1984—	Denver (Am. Assoc.)■	6	3	.667	4.02	31	9	1	1	2	109⅔	109	58	49	51	71
1985—	Iowa (Am. Assoc.)■	1	5	.167	5.32	40	3	0	0	0	89⅔	101	58	53	34	58
Major league totals (2 years)		0	0	...	5.19	7	0	0	0	0	8⅔	8	5	5	8	1

RECORD AS MANAGER

BACKGROUND: Coach, Cincinnati Reds organization (1986-89). ... Coach, Reds (1990-May 24, 1993). ... Coach, Atlanta Braves organization (1994). ... Coach, Florida Marlins (1995-97).

		REGULAR SEASON				POSTSEASON								
						Playoff		Champ. Series		World Series		All-Star Game		
Year	Team (League)	W	L	Pct.	Pos.	W	L	W	L	W	L	W	L	
1998—	Tampa Bay (A.L.)	63	99	.389	5th (E)	—	—	—	—	—	—	—	—	
1999—	Tampa Bay (A.L.)	69	93	.426	5th (E)	—	—	—	—	—	—	—	—	
Major League totals (2 years)		132	192	.407		—	—	—	—	—	—	—	—	

SCIOSCIA, MIKE — ANGELS

PERSONAL: Born November 27, 1958, in Upper Darby, Pa. ... 6-2/220. ... Batted left, threw right. ... Full name: Michael Lorri Scioscia. ... Name pronounced SO-sha.
HIGH SCHOOL: Springfield (Pa.).
COLLEGE: Penn State.
TRANSACTIONS/CAREER NOTES: Selected by Los Angeles Dodgers organization in first round (19th pick overall) of free-agent draft (June 8, 1976). ... On disabled list (May 19-August 4, 1978; April 10-20, 1980; May 15, 1983-remainder of season; May 6-21, 1984; June 10-July 15, 1986; June 1-16, 1987; and July 5-20, 1991). ... Granted free agency (November 4, 1992). ... Signed by San Diego Padres (February 11, 1993). ... On San Diego disabled list (March 29, 1993-entire season). ... Released by Padres (October 15, 1993). ... Signed by Texas Rangers organization (December 14, 1993). ... Placed on voluntary retired list (August 2, 1994).
HONORS: Named catcher on THE SPORTING NEWS N.L. All-Star team (1990).

STATISTICAL NOTES: Led Midwest League catchers with 20 errors and 12 double plays in 1977. ... Led Pacific Coast League catchers with 19 double plays and 22 passed balls in 1979. ... Tied for Pacific Coast League lead in being hit by pitch with seven in 1979. ... Led N.L. with 11 passed balls in 1981 and 14 in 1992. ... Led N.L. catchers with 1,016 total chances in 1987, 915 in 1989 and 910 in 1990.

							BATTING								FIELDING		
Year Team (League)	Pos.	G	AB	R	H	2B	3B	HR	RBI	Avg.	BB	SO	SB	PO	A	E	Avg.
1976— Bellingham (N.W.)	C	46	151	25	42	6	0	7	26	.278	36	22	2	202	35	14	.944
1977— Clinton (Midw.)	C-1B	121	364	58	92	20	1	7	44	.253	79	25	9	764	95	†22	.975
1978— San Antonio (Texas) ...	C	58	204	29	61	16	0	2	34	.299	31	20	3	214	17	4	.983
1979— Albuquerque (PCL).....	C	143	461	80	155	34	0	3	68	.336	73	33	5	*690	*86	*15	.981
1980— Albuquerque (PCL).....	C	52	160	33	53	11	1	3	33	.331	36	13	3	207	19	5	.978
— Los Angeles (N.L.).....	C	54	134	8	34	5	1	1	8	.254	12	9	1	226	26	2	.992
1981— Los Angeles (N.L.)	C	93	290	27	80	10	0	2	29	.276	36	18	0	493	48	7	.987
1982— Los Angeles (N.L.)	C	129	365	31	80	11	1	5	38	.219	44	31	2	631	57	10	.986
1983— Los Angeles (N.L.)	C	12	35	3	11	3	0	1	7	.314	5	2	0	55	4	0	1.000
1984— Los Angeles (N.L.)	C	114	341	29	93	18	0	5	38	.273	52	26	2	701	64	12	.985
1985— Los Angeles (N.L.)	C	141	429	47	127	26	3	7	53	.296	77	21	3	818	66	•13	.986
1986— Los Angeles (N.L.)	C	122	374	36	94	18	1	5	26	.251	62	23	3	756	64	15	.982
1987— Los Angeles (N.L.)	C	142	461	44	122	26	1	6	38	.265	55	23	7	*925	80	11	.989
1988— Los Angeles (N.L.)	C	130	408	29	105	18	0	3	35	.257	38	31	0	748	63	7	.991
1989— Los Angeles (N.L.)	C	133	408	40	102	16	0	10	44	.250	52	29	0	*822	*82	11	.988
1990— Los Angeles (N.L.)	C	135	435	46	115	25	0	12	66	.264	55	31	4	*842	58	10	.989
1991— Los Angeles (N.L.)	C	119	345	39	91	16	2	8	40	.264	47	32	4	677	51	7	.990
1992— Los Angeles (N.L.)	C	117	348	19	77	6	3	3	24	.221	32	31	3	641	*74	9	.988
1993— San Diego (N.L.)■.....						Did not play.											
1994— Charlotte (FSL)■........	C	1	2	0	1	0	0	0	0	.500	0	0	0	3	1	0	1.000
Major League totals (13 years)		1441	4373	398	1131	198	12	68	446	.259	567	307	29	8335	737	114	.988

DIVISION SERIES RECORD

							BATTING								FIELDING		
Year Team (League)	Pos.	G	AB	R	H	2B	3B	HR	RBI	Avg.	BB	SO	SB	PO	A	E	Avg.
1981— Los Angeles (N.L.)	C	4	13	0	2	0	0	0	1	.154	1	2	0	21	3	0	1.000

CHAMPIONSHIP SERIES RECORD

							BATTING								FIELDING		
Year Team (League)	Pos.	G	AB	R	H	2B	3B	HR	RBI	Avg.	BB	SO	SB	PO	A	E	Avg.
1981— Los Angeles (N.L.)	C	5	15	1	2	0	0	1	1	.133	2	1	0	27	1	0	1.000
1985— Los Angeles (N.L.)	C	6	16	2	4	0	0	0	1	.250	4	0	0	31	4	1	.972
1988— Los Angeles (N.L.)	C	7	22	3	8	1	0	1	2	.364	1	2	0	37	4	0	1.000
Championship series totals (3 years)		18	53	6	14	1	0	2	4	.264	7	3	0	95	9	1	.990

WORLD SERIES RECORD

NOTES: Member of World Series championship teams (1981 and 1988).

							BATTING								FIELDING		
Year Team (League)	Pos.	G	AB	R	H	2B	3B	HR	RBI	Avg.	BB	SO	SB	PO	A	E	Avg.
1981— Los Angeles (N.L.)	C-PH	3	4	1	1	0	0	0	0	.250	1	0	0	7	1	0	1.000
1988— Los Angeles (N.L.)	C	4	14	0	3	0	0	0	1	.214	0	2	0	28	0	1	.966
World Series totals (2 years)		7	18	1	4	0	0	0	1	.222	1	2	0	35	1	1	.973

ALL-STAR GAME RECORD

						BATTING								FIELDING		
Year League	Pos.	AB	R	H	2B	3B	HR	RBI	Avg.	BB	SO	SB	PO	A	E	Avg.
1989— National	C	1	0	0	0	0	0	0	.000	0	0	0	3	0	0	1.000
1990— National	C	2	0	0	0	0	0	0	.000	0	1	0	6	0	0	1.000
All-Star Game totals (2 years)		3	0	0	0	0	0	0	.000	0	1	0	9	0	0	1.000

RECORD AS MANAGER

BACKGROUND: Minor league catching coordinator, Dodgers organization (1995-96). ... Bench coach, Dodgers (1997-98). ... Manager, Peoria Javelinas, Dodgers organization (1997).

	REGULAR SEASON				POSTSEASON						
					Playoff		Champ. Series		World Series		All-Star Game
Year Team (League)	W	L	Pct.	Pos.	W	L	W	L	W	L	W	L
1999— Albuquerque (PCL)	65	74	.468	3rd	—	—	—	—	—	—	—	—

SHOWALTER, BUCK   DIAMONDBACKS

PERSONAL: Born May 23, 1956, in DeFuniak Springs, Fla. ... 5-9/195. ... Batted left, threw left. ... Full name: William Nathaniel Showalter III.
JUNIOR COLLEGE: Chipola Junior College (Fla.).
COLLEGE: Mississippi State.
TRANSACTIONS/CAREER NOTES: Selected by New York Yankees organization in fifth round of free-agent draft (June 7, 1977). ... On disabled list (July 1-11 and July 19-August 4, 1981).
STATISTICAL NOTES: Led Southern League first basemen with 1,281 putouts in 1982.

Year	Team (League)	Pos.	G	AB	R	H	2B	3B	HR	RBI	Avg.	BB	SO	SB	PO	A	E	Avg.
1977—	Fort Lauderdale (FSL)	OF	56	196	32	71	8	1	1	25	.362	36	13	4	96	2	2	.980
1978—	West Haven (East.)	OF	123	429	52	124	13	2	3	46	.289	55	34	19	192	•15	7	.967
1979—	West Haven (East.)	1B-OF	129	469	71	131	7	3	6	51	.279	36	30	8	575	52	7	.989
1980—	Nashville (Sou.)	OF-1B	142	550	84	*178	19	3	1	82	.324	53	23	6	71	2	1	.986
1981—	Columbus (I.L.)	OF	14	37	6	7	1	0	1	3	.189	3	0	0	11	0	1	.917
—	Nashville (Sou.)	OF-1B	90	307	46	81	17	6	0	38	.264	46	16	3	201	14	7	.968
1982—	Nashville (Sou.)	1B-OF	132	517	66	*152	29	3	3	46	.294	61	42	2 †1282		51	13	.990
1983—	Nashville (Sou.)	1B-OF-P	89	297	35	82	13	4	1	37	.276	39	22	1	127	6	2	.985
—	Columbus (I.L.)	1B-P	18	63	9	15	3	0	1	8	.238	7	3	1	139	14	1	.994

RECORD AS PITCHER

Year	Team (League)	W	L	Pct.	ERA	G	GS	CG	ShO	Sv.	IP	H	R	ER	BB	SO
1983—	Nashville (Sou.)	0	0	...	9.00	1	0	0	0	0	1	2	1	1	0	1
—	Columbus (I.L.)	0	0	...	0.00	1	0	0	0	0	2	0	0	0	0	2

RECORD AS MANAGER

BACKGROUND: Minor league coach, New York Yankees organization (1984). ... Coach, Yankees (1990-91). ... Manager/scout, Arizona Diamondbacks (1996-97).

HONORS: Named New York-Pennsylvania League Manager of the Year (1985). ... Named Eastern League Manager of the Year (1989). ... Coach, A.L. All-Star team (1992). ... Named A.L. Manager of the Year by THE SPORTING NEWS (1994). ... Named A.L. Manager of the Year by Baseball Writers' Association of America (1994).

		REGULAR SEASON				POSTSEASON						
						Playoff		Champ. Series		World Series		All-Star Game
Year	Team (League)	W	L	Pct.	Pos.	W	L	W	L	W	L	W	L
1985—	Oneonta (New York-Pennsylvania)	55	23	.705	1st (N)	3	0	—	—	—	—	—	—
1986—	Oneonta (New York-Pennsylvania)	59	18	.766	1st (Y)	0	1	—	—	—	—	—	—
1987—	Fort Lauderdale (Florida State)	85	53	.616	1st (S)	5	1	—	—	—	—	—	—
1988—	Fort Lauderdale (Florida State)	39	29	.574	3rd (E)	—	—	—	—	—	—	—	—
—	(Second half)	30	36	.455	T3rd (E)	—	—	—	—	—	—	—	—
1989—	Albany/Colonie (East.)	92	48	.657	1st	6	2	—	—	—	—	—	—
1992—	New York (A.L.)	76	86	.469	T4th (E)	—	—	—	—	—	—	—	—
1993—	New York (A.L.)	88	74	.543	2nd (E)	—	—	—	—	—	—	—	—
1994—	New York (A.L.)	70	43	.619		—	—	—	—	—	—	—	—
1995—	New York (A.L.)	79	65	.549	2nd (E)	2	3	—	—	—	—	—	—
1998—	Arizona (N.L.)	65	97	.401	5th (W)	—	—	—	—	—	—	—	—
1999—	Arizona (N.L.)	100	62	.617	1st (W)	1	3	—	—	—	—	—	—
American League totals (4 years)		313	268	.539		2	3	—	—	—	—	—	—
National League totals (2 years)		165	159	.509		1	3	—	—	—	—	—	—
Major league totals (6 years)		478	427	.528		3	6	—	—	—	—	—	—

NOTES:
1985—Defeated Geneva in one-game semifinal playoff; defeated Auburn, two games to none, in league championship.
1986—Lost to Newark in playoffs.
1987—Defeated Lakeland, two games to none, in playoffs; defeated Osceola, three games to one, in league championship.
1989—Defeated Reading, three games to one, in playoffs; defeated Harrisburg, three games to one, in league championship.
1994—New York was in first place in A.L. East at time of season-ending strike (August 12).
1995—Lost to Seattle in A.L. divisional playoff. Named Arizona Diamondbacks manager (November 15).
1999—Lost to New York Mets in divisional playoff.

TORRE, JOE — YANKEES

PERSONAL: Born July 18, 1940, in Brooklyn, N.Y. ... 6-1/210. ... Batted right, threw right. ... Full name: Joseph Paul Torre. ... Brother of Frank Torre, first baseman with Milwaukee Braves (1956-60) and Philadelphia Phillies (1962-63). ... Name pronounced TORE-ee.

HIGH SCHOOL: St. Francis Prep (Brooklyn, N.Y.).

TRANSACTIONS/CAREER NOTES: Signed by Jacksonville, Milwaukee Braves organization (August 24, 1959). ... On military list (September 30, 1962-March 26, 1963). ... Braves franchise moved from Milwaukee to Atlanta (1966). ... On disabled list (April 18-May 9, 1968). ... Traded by Braves to St. Louis Cardinals for 1B Orlando Cepeda (March 17, 1969). ... Traded by Cardinals to New York Mets for P Tommy Moore and P Ray Sadecki (October 13, 1974). ... Released as player by Mets (June 18, 1977).

RECORDS: Shares major league single-game record for most times grounded into double play—4 (July 21, 1975).

HONORS: Named catcher on THE SPORTING NEWS N.L. All-Star team (1964-66). ... Won N.L. Gold Glove at catcher (1965). ... Named Major League Player of the Year by THE SPORTING NEWS (1971). ... Named N.L. Player of the Year by THE SPORTING NEWS (1971). ... Named third baseman on THE SPORTING NEWS N.L. All-Star team (1971). ... Named N.L. Most Valuable Player by Baseball Writers' Association of America (1971).

STATISTICAL NOTES: Led N.L. catchers with .995 fielding percentage in 1964 and .996 in 1968. ... Led N.L. in grounding into double plays with 26 in 1964, 22 in 1965, 22 in 1967 and 21 in 1968. ... Led N.L. catchers with 12 double plays in 1967. ... Led N.L. with 352 total bases in 1971. ... Hit for the cycle (June 27, 1973). ... Led N.L. first basemen with 102 assists and 144 double plays in 1974. ... Career major league grand slams: 3.

Year	Team (League)	Pos.	G	AB	R	H	2B	3B	HR	RBI	Avg.	BB	SO	SB	PO	A	E	Avg.
1960—	Eau Claire (North.)	C	117	369	63	127	23	3	16	74	*.344	70	45	7	636	64	9	.987
—	Milwaukee (N.L.)	PH	2	2	0	1	0	0	0	0	.500	0	1	0	...	...	...	...
1961—	Louisville (A.A.)	C	27	111	18	38	8	2	3	24	.342	6	9	0	185	14	2	.990
—	Milwaukee (N.L.)	C	113	406	40	113	21	4	10	42	.278	28	60	3	494	50	10	.982
1962—	Milwaukee (N.L.)	C	80	220	23	62	8	1	5	26	.282	24	24	1	325	39	5	.986
1963—	Milwaukee (N.L.)	C-1B-OF	142	501	57	147	19	4	14	71	.293	42	79	1	919	76	6	.994
1964—	Milwaukee (N.L.)	C-1B	154	601	87	193	36	5	20	109	.321	36	67	4	1081	94	7	†.994
1965—	Milwaukee (N.L.)	C-1B	148	523	68	152	21	1	27	80	.291	61	79	0	1022	73	8	.993
1966—	Atlanta (N.L.)	C-1B	148	546	83	172	20	3	36	101	.315	60	61	0	874	87	12	.988
1967—	Atlanta (N.L.)	C-1B	135	477	67	132	18	1	20	68	.277	75	49	2	785	81	8	.991

Year	Team (League)	Pos.	G	AB	R	H	2B	3B	HR	RBI	Avg.	BB	SO	SB	PO	A	E	Avg.
								BATTING								**FIELDING**		
1968—Atlanta (N.L.)	C-1B	115	424	45	115	11	2	10	55	.271	34	72	1	733	48	2	†.997
1969—St. Louis (N.L.)■	1B-C	159	602	72	174	29	6	18	101	.289	66	85	0	1360	91	7	.995
1970—St. Louis (N.L.)	C-3B-1B	•161	624	89	203	27	9	21	100	.325	70	91	2	651	162	13	.984
1971—St. Louis (N.L.)	3B	161	634	97	*230	34	8	24	*137	*.363	63	70	4	*136	271	•21	.951
1972—St. Louis (N.L.)	3B-1B	149	544	71	157	26	6	11	81	.289	54	74	3	336	198	15	.973
1973—St. Louis (N.L.)	1B-3B	141	519	67	149	17	2	13	69	.287	65	78	2	881	128	12	.988
1974—St. Louis (N.L.)	1B-3B	147	529	59	149	28	1	11	70	.282	69	68	1	1173	†121	14	.989
1975—New York (N.L.)■	3B-1B	114	361	33	89	16	3	6	35	.247	35	55	0	172	157	15	.956
1976—New York (N.L.)	1B-3B	114	310	36	95	10	3	5	31	.306	21	35	1	593	52	7	.989
1977—New York (N.L.)	1B-3B	26	51	2	9	3	0	1	9	.176	2	10	0	83	3	1	.989
Major league totals (18 years)		2209	7874	996	2342	344	59	252	1185	.297	805	1058	25	11618	1731	163	.988

ALL-STAR GAME RECORD

Year	League	Pos.	AB	R	H	2B	3B	HR	RBI	Avg.	BB	SO	SB	PO	A	E	Avg.
						BATTING									**FIELDING**		
1963—National							Did not play.										
1964—National	C	2	0	0	0	0	0	0	.000	0	0	0	5	0	0	1.000
1965—National	C	4	1	1	0	0	1	2	.250	0	0	0	5	1	0	1.000
1966—National	C	3	0	0	0	0	0	0	.000	0	1	0	5	0	0	1.000
1967—National	C	2	0	0	0	0	0	0	.000	0	0	0	4	1	0	1.000
1970—National	PH	1	0	0	0	0	0	0	.000	0	0	0	...	...	...	...
1971—National	3B	3	0	0	0	0	0	0	.000	0	1	0	1	0	0	1.000
1972—National	3B	3	0	0	0	0	0	0	.000	0	1	0	1	2	0	1.000
1973—National	1B-3B	3	0	0	0	0	0	0	.000	0	0	0	5	0	0	1.000
All-Star Game totals (8 years)		21	1	1	0	0	1	2	.048	0	3	0	26	4	0	1.000

RECORD AS MANAGER

BACKGROUND: Player/manager, New York Mets (May 31-June 18, 1977).

HONORS: Named Sportsman of the Year by THE SPORTING NEWS (1996). ... Named co-A.L. Manager of the Year by Baseball Writers' Association of America (1996). ... Named A.L. Manager of the Year by The Sporting News (1998). ... Named A.L. Manager of the Year by Baseball Writers' Association of America (1998).

Year	Team (League)	W	L	Pct.	Pos.	Playoff W	Playoff L	Champ. Series W	Champ. Series L	World Series W	World Series L	All-Star Game W	All-Star Game L
				REGULAR SEASON				**POSTSEASON**					
1977—New York (N.L.)	49	68	.419	6th (E)	—	—	—	—	—	—	—	—	
1978—New York (N.L.)	66	96	.407	6th (E)	—	—	—	—	—	—	—	—	
1979—New York (N.L.)	63	99	.389	6th (E)	—	—	—	—	—	—	—	—	
1980—New York (N.L.)	67	95	.414	5th (E)	—	—	—	—	—	—	—	—	
1981—New York (N.L.)	17	34	.333	5th (E)	—	—	—	—	—	—	—	—	
—(Second half)	24	28	.462	4th (E)	—	—	—	—	—	—	—	—	
1982—Atlanta (N.L.)	89	73	.549	1st (W)	—	—	0	3	—	—	—	—	
1983—Atlanta (N.L.)	88	74	.543	2nd (W)	—	—	—	—	—	—	—	—	
1984—Atlanta (N.L.)	80	82	.494	T2nd (W)	—	—	—	—	—	—	—	—	
1990—St. Louis (N.L.)	24	34	.414	6th (E)	—	—	—	—	—	—	—	—	
1991—St. Louis (N.L.)	84	78	.519	2nd (E)	—	—	—	—	—	—	—	—	
1992—St. Louis (N.L.)	83	79	.512	3rd (E)	—	—	—	—	—	—	—	—	
1993—St. Louis (N.L.)	87	75	.537	3rd (E)	—	—	—	—	—	—	—	—	
1994—St. Louis (N.L.)	53	61	.465		—	—	—	—	—	—	—	—	
1995—St. Louis (N.L.)	20	27	.426	4th (C)	—	—	—	—	—	—	—	—	
1996—New York (N.L.)	92	70	.568	1st (E)	3	1	4	1	4	2	—	—	
1997—New York (A.L.)	96	66	.593	2nd (E)	2	3	—	—	—	—	1	0	
1998—New York (A.L.)	114	48	.704	1st (E)	3	0	4	2	4	0	—	—	
1999—New York (A.L.)	98	64	.605	1st (E)	3	0	4	1	4	0	—	—	
American League totals (4 years)	400	248	.621		11	4	12	4	12	2	1	0	
National League totals (14 years)	894	1003	.471		—	—	0	3	—	—	—	—	
Major league totals (18 years)	1294	1251	.508		11	4	12	7	12	2	1	0	

NOTES:

1977—Replaced New York manager Joe Frazier with club in sixth place and record of 15-30 (May 31); served as player/manager (May 31-June 18, when released as player).

1982—Lost to St. Louis in N.L. Championship Series.

1990—Replaced St. Louis manager Whitey Herzog (33-47) and interim manager Red Schoendienst (13-11) with club in sixth place and record of 46-58 (August 1).

1994—St. Louis was tied for third place in N.L. Central at time of season-ending strike (August 12).

1995—Replaced as Cardinals manager by interim manager Mike Jorgensen, with club in fourth place (June 16).

1996—Defeated Texas in A.L. divisional playoff; defeated Baltimore in A.L. Championship Series; defeated Atlanta in World Series.

1997—Lost to Cleveland in A.L. divisional playoff.

1998—Defeated Texas in A.L. divisional playoff; defeated Cleveland in A.L. Championship Series; defeated San Diego in World Series.

1999—Defeated Texas in A.L. divisional playoff; defeated Boston in A.L. Championship Series; defeated Atlanta in World Series.

VALENTINE, BOBBY — METS

PERSONAL: Born May 13, 1950, in Stamford, Conn. ... 5-10/185. ... Batted right, threw right. ... Full name: Robert John Valentine. ... Son-in-law of Ralph Branca, pitcher with Brooklyn Dodgers (1944-53 and 1956), Detroit Tigers (1953-54), New York Yankees (1955).

HIGH SCHOOL: Rippowan (Stamford, Conn.).

COLLEGE: Arizona State, then Southern California.

TRANSACTIONS/CAREER NOTES: Selected by Los Angeles Dodgers organization in first round (fifth pick overall) of free-agent draft (June 7, 1968). ... Traded by Dodgers with IF Billy Grabarkewitz, OF Frank Robinson, P Bill Singer and P Mike Strahler to California Angels for P Andy Messersmith and 3B Ken McMullen (November 28, 1972). ... On disabled list (May 17, 1973-remainder of season and May 29-June 13,

1974). ... Loaned by Angels to Charleston, Pittsburgh Pirates organization (April 4-June 20, 1975). ... Traded by Angels with a player to be named later to San Diego Padres for P Gary Ross (September 17, 1975); Padres acquired IF Rudy Meoli to complete deal (November 4, 1975). ... Traded by Padres with P Paul Siebert to New York Mets for IF/OF Dave Kingman (June 15, 1977). ... Released by Mets (March 26, 1979). ... Signed by Seattle Mariners (April 10, 1979). ... Granted free agency (November 1, 1979).

HONORS: Named Pacific Coast League Player of the Year (1970).

STATISTICAL NOTES: Led Pioneer League outfielders with 107 putouts and tied for lead with eight assists in 1968. ... Led Pacific Coast League shortstops with 38 errors in 1969. ... Led Pacific Coast League with 324 total bases, with 10 sacrifice flies and in double plays by shortstop with 106 in 1970. ... Led Pacific Coast League shortstops with 217 putouts and 54 errors in 1970.

Year	Team (League)	Pos.	G	AB	R	H	2B	3B	HR	RBI	Avg.	BB	SO	SB	PO	A	E	Avg.
1968—	Ogden (Pioneer)	OF-SS	62	224	*62	63	14	4	6	26	.281	39	27	*20	†111	‡10	6	.953
1969—	Spokane (PCL)	SS-OF	111	402	61	104	19	5	3	35	.259	32	57	34	166	254	†38	.917
	— Los Angeles (N.L.)	PR	5	0	3	0	0	0	0	0	...	0	0	0	...	...	...	...
1970—	Spokane (PCL)	SS-2B	•146	*621	*122	*211	*39	*16	14	80	*.340	47	51	29	†217	474	†54	.928
1971—	Spokane (PCL)	SS	7	30	7	10	2	0	1	2	.333	3	6	3	13	18	3	.912
	— Los Angeles (N.L.)	S-3-2-0	101	281	32	70	10	2	1	25	.249	15	20	5	123	176	16	.949
1972—	Los Angeles (N.L.)	2-3-0-S	119	391	42	107	11	2	3	32	.274	27	33	5	178	245	23	.948
1973—	California (A.L.) ■	SS-OF	32	126	12	38	5	2	1	13	.302	5	9	6	63	75	6	.958
1974—	California (A.L.)	O-S-3-DH	117	371	39	97	10	3	3	39	.261	25	25	8	160	116	17	.942
1975—	Char., W.Va. (I.L.) ■	3B	56	175	27	41	4	0	1	17	.234	30	16	8	44	74	6	.952
	— Salt Lake (PCL) ■	1-0-3-2	46	147	29	45	6	1	0	17	.306	31	15	13	92	14	3	.972
	— California (A.L.)	DH-1-3-0	26	57	5	16	2	0	0	5	.281	4	3	0	27	1	2	.933
	— San Diego (N.L.) ■	OF	7	15	1	2	0	0	1	1	.133	4	0	1	4	0	0	1.000
1976—	Hawaii (PCL)	1-0-3-S	120	395	67	120	23	2	13	89	.304	47	32	9	578	47	4	.994
	— San Diego (N.L.) ■	OF-1B	15	49	3	18	4	0	0	4	.367	6	2	0	55	6	0	1.000
1977—	San Diego (N.L.) ■	...	44	67	5	12	3	0	1	10	.179	7	10	0	...	...	...	...
	— New York (N.L.) ■	...	42	83	8	11	1	0	1	3	.133	6	9	0	...	...	...	...
1978—	New York (N.L.)	2B-3B	69	160	17	43	7	0	1	18	.269	19	18	1	78	109	6	.969
1979—	Seattle (A.L.) ■	S-O-2-3-C-DH	62	98	9	27	6	0	0	7	.276	22	5	1	32	38	2	.972
American League totals (4 years)			237	652	65	178	23	5	4	64	.273	56	42	15	282	230	27	.950
National League totals (7 years)			488	1196	124	286	40	4	10	106	.239	97	111	12	...	...	...	...
Major league totals (10 years)			725	1848	189	464	63	9	14	170	.251	153	153	27	...	...	...	...

RECORD AS MANAGER

BACKGROUND: Scout and minor league instructor, San Diego Padres (1981). ... Minor league instructor, New York Mets (1982). ... Coach, Mets (1983-May 15, 1985). ... Coach, Cincinnati Reds (1993).

		REGULAR SEASON					POSTSEASON						
									Champ.		World		All-Star
						Playoff		Series		Series		Game	
Year	Team (League)	W	L	Pct.	Pos.	W	L	W	L	W	L	W	L
1985—	Texas (A.L.)	53	76	.411	7th (W)	—	—	—	—	—	—	—	—
1986—	Texas (A.L.)	87	75	.537	2nd (W)	—	—	—	—	—	—	—	—
1987—	Texas (A.L.)	75	87	.463	T6th (W)	—	—	—	—	—	—	—	—
1988—	Texas (A.L.)	70	91	.435	6th (W)	—	—	—	—	—	—	—	—
1989—	Texas (A.L.)	83	79	.512	4th (W)	—	—	—	—	—	—	—	—
1990—	Texas (A.L.)	83	79	.512	3rd (W)	—	—	—	—	—	—	—	—
1991—	Texas (A.L.)	85	77	.525	3rd (W)	—	—	—	—	—	—	—	—
1992—	Texas (A.L.)	45	41	.523		—	—	—	—	—	—	—	—
1994—	Norfolk (I.L.)	67	75	.472	4th (W)	—	—	—	—	—	—	—	—
1995—	Chiba Lotte (Jp. Cen.)	69	58	.543	2nd (P)	—	—	—	—	—	—	—	—
1996—	Norfolk (I.L.)	76	57	.571		—	—	—	—	—	—	—	—
	— New York (N.L.)	12	19	.387	4th (E)	—	—	—	—	—	—	—	—
1997—	New York (N.L.)	88	74	.543	3rd (E)	—	—	—	—	—	—	—	—
1998—	New York (N.L.)	88	74	.543	2nd (E)	—	—	—	—	—	—	—	—
1999—	New York (N.L.)	97	66	.595	2nd (E)	3	1	2	4	—	—	—	—
American League totals (8 years)		581	605	.490		—	—	—	—	—	—	—	—
National League totals (4 years)		285	233	.550		3	1	2	4	—	—	—	—
Major league totals (12 years)		866	838	.508		3	1	2	4	—	—	—	—

NOTES:
1985—Replaced Texas manager Doug Rader with club in seventh place and record of 9-23 (May 16).
1992—Replaced as Texas manager by Toby Harrah with club in third place (July 9).
1995—Chiba Lotte tied three games.
1996—Replaced New York manager Dallas Green with club in fourth place and record of 59-72 (August 26).
1999—Defeated Arizona in N.L. divisional playoff; lost to Atlanta in N.L. Championship Series.

WILLIAMS, JIMY — RED SOX

PERSONAL: Born October 4, 1943, in Santa Maria, Calif. ... 5-11/170. ... Batted right, threw right. ... Full name: James Francis Williams.

COLLEGE: Fresno State College (bachelor of science degree in agribusiness).

TRANSACTIONS/CAREER NOTES: Selected by St. Louis Cardinals organization from Toronto, Boston Red Sox organization (November 29, 1965). ... In military service (July 24, 1966-remainder of season). ... Traded by Cardinals with C Pat Corrales to Cincinnati Reds for C John Edwards (February 8, 1968). ... Selected by Montreal Expos in expansion draft (October 14, 1968). ... On disabled list (May 13-30 and June 24-September 2, 1969). ... On suspended list (June 7-16, 1971). ... Sold to New York Mets organization (June 16, 1971). ... On temporary inactive list (August 12-16, 1971). ... On disabled list (May 15-July 17 and July 29-August 20, 1975).

Year	Team (League)	Pos.	G	AB	R	H	2B	3B	HR	RBI	Avg.	BB	SO	SB	PO	A	E	Avg.
1965—	Waterloo (Midw.)	SS	115	435	64	125	19	3	2	31	.287	41	74	10	173	*312	26	*.949
1966—	St. Louis (N.L.)	SS-2B	13	11	1	3	0	0	0	1	.273	1	5	0	2	5	0	1.000

Year	Team (League)	Pos.	G	AB	R	H	2B	3B	HR	RBI	Avg.	BB	SO	SB	PO	A	E	Avg.
						BATTING										FIELDING		
1967—Arkansas (Texas)........	SS	28	101	8	21	1	1	0	8	.208	9	14	0	49	80	2	.985	
—Tulsa (PCL)	SS	61	164	18	37	2	0	1	21	.226	18	33	4	87	156	26	.903	
—St. Louis (N.L.)...........	SS	1	2	0	0	0	0	0	0	.000	0	1	0	6	1	0	1.000	
1968—Indianapolis (PCL)■..	SS-2B	120	403	38	91	19	5	2	34	.226	20	59	5	198	323	27	.951	
1969—Vancouver (PCL)■.....	3B-OF-SS	35	66	7	17	1	1	0	9	.258	4	8	1	17	23	2	.952	
1970—Winnipeg (I.L.)...........	SS-2B-3B	109	361	49	83	15	0	3	18	.230	34	48	5	178	244	30	.934	
1971—Winn.-Tide. (I.L.)■.....	SS-3B-2B	105	327	40	84	7	4	5	31	.257	38	46	7	120	219	22	.939	
1972—								Did not play.										
1973—								Did not play.										
1974—								Did not play.										
1975—El Paso (Texas)..........	DH	6	17	3	2	0	0	0	2	.118	2	2	0	...	...	...	...	
Major league totals (2 years)		14	13	1	3	0	0	0	1	.231	0	0	0	8	6	0	1.000	

RECORD AS MANAGER

BACKGROUND: Coach, Toronto Blue Jays (1980-85). ... Minor league instructor, Atlanta Braves (October 4, 1989-June 25, 1990). ... Coach, Braves (1990-96).

HONORS: Named Pacific Coast League Manager of the Year (1976 and 1979). ... Named A.L. Manager of the Year by THE SPORTING NEWS (1999). ... Named A.L. Manager of the Year by Baseball Writers' Association of America (1999).

			REGULAR SEASON			POSTSEASON							
						Playoff		Champ. Series		World Series		All-Star Game	
Year	Team (League)	W	L	Pct.	Pos.	W	L	W	L	W	L	W	L
1974—Quad Cities (Midwest)		33	26	.559	1st (S)	—	—	—	—	—	—	—	—
—(Second half)		32	32	.500	3rd (S)	1	2	—	—	—	—	—	—
1975—El Paso (Texas)		62	71	.466	3rd (W)	—	—	—	—	—	—	—	—
1976—Salt Lake City (Pacific Coast)....................		90	54	.625	1st (E)	2	3	—	—	—	—	—	—
1977—Salt Lake City (Pacific Coast)....................		74	65	.532	2nd (E)	—	—	—	—	—	—	—	—
1978—Springfield (American Association)		70	66	.515	3rd (E)	—	—	—	—	—	—	—	—
1979—Salt Lake City (Pacific Coast)....................		34	40	.447	4th (S)	—	—	—	—	—	—	—	—
—(Second half)		46	28	.622	1st (S)	5	0	—	—	—	—	—	—
1986—Toronto (A.L.)		86	76	.531	4th (E)	—	—	—	—	—	—	—	—
1987—Toronto (A.L.)		96	66	.593	2nd (E)	—	—	—	—	—	—	—	—
1988—Toronto (A.L.)		87	75	.537	T3rd (E)	—	—	—	—	—	—	—	—
1989—Toronto (A.L.)		12	24	.333		—	—	—	—	—	—	—	—
1997—Boston (A.L.)		78	84	.481	4th (E)	—	—	—	—	—	—	—	—
1998—Boston (A.L.)		92	70	.568	2nd (E)	1	3	—	—	—	—	—	—
1999—Boston (A.L.)		94	68	.580	2nd (E)	3	2	1	4	—	—	—	—
Major league totals (7 years)............................		545	463	.540		4	5	1	4	—	—	—	—

NOTES:
1974—Lost to Danville in playoffs.
1976—Lost to Hawaii in championship playoff.
1979—Defeated Albuquerque, two games to none, in playoff; defeated Hawaii, three games to none, in championship playoff.
1989—Replaced as Toronto manager by Cito Gaston, with club tied for sixth place (May 15).
1998—Lost to Cleveland in A.L. divisional playoff.
1999—Defeated Cleveland in A.L. divisional playoff; lost to New York Yankees in A.L. Championship Series.

THE CLASS OF 2000

FISK, CARLTON   C

PERSONAL: Born December 26, 1947, in Bellows Falls, Vt. ... 6-2/225. ... Bats right, throws right. ... Full name: Carlton Ernest Fisk.
HIGH SCHOOL: Charlestown (N.H.).
COLLEGE: New Hampshire.
TRANSACTIONS/CAREER NOTES: Selected by Baltimore Orioles organization in 36th round of free-agent draft (June 8, 1965); did not sign. ... Selected by Boston Red Sox organization in first round (fourth pick overall) of free-agent draft (January 1967). ... On temporarily inactive list (April 17, 1967); transferred to military list (May 18, 1967-April 19, 1968). ... On temporarily inactive list (August 5-20, 1968). ... On disabled list (March 21-April 26 and June 28, 1974-remainder of season; March 24-June 23, 1975; and April 14-May 21, 1979). ... Granted free agency by arbitrator's ruling (February 12, 1981). ... Signed by Chicago White Sox (March 18, 1981). ... On disabled list (June 13-July 5, 1984). ... Granted free agency (November 12, 1985). ... Re-signed by White Sox (January 8, 1986). ... Granted free agency (January 22, 1988). ... Re-signed by White Sox (February 9, 1988). ... On disabled list (May 11-July 28, 1988 and April 11-June 1, 1989). ... Granted free agency (November 4, 1991). ... Re-signed by White Sox (December 11, 1991). ... On Chicago disabled list (March 28-June 4, 1992); included rehabilitation assignment to South Bend (May 26-27) and Sarasota (May 27-June 4). ... Granted free agency (December 19, 1992). ... Re-signed by White Sox (February 5, 1993). ... Released by White Sox (June 28, 1993).
RECORDS: Holds major league career records for most games by catcher—2,226; and most home runs by catcher—351. ... Holds major league records for longest game with no passed balls—25 innings; most innings played by catcher in game—25 (May 8, finished May 9, 1984, 25 innings). ... Shares major league single-game records for most at-bats—11; and plate appearances—12 (May 8, finished May 9, 1984, 25 innings). ... Shares modern major league record for most long hits in one inning—2 (May 15, 1975, eighth inning, and June 30, 1977, eighth inning). ... Holds A.L. career catching records for most years—24; putouts—11,369; and chances accepted—12,417. ... Holds A.L. single-season record for fewest assists by catcher (150 or more games)--69 (1977). ... Shares A.L. single-season record for fewest passed balls (150 or more games)—4 (1977).
HONORS: Named A.L. Rookie Player of the Year by The Sporting News (1972). ... Named catcher on The Sporting News A.L. All-Star team (1972, 1977, 1983, 1985 and 1990). ... Won A.L. Gold Glove at catcher (1972). ... Named A.L. Rookie of the Year by Baseball Writers' Association of America (1972). ... Named catcher on The Sporting News A.L. Silver Slugger team (1981, 1985 and 1988).
STATISTICAL NOTES: Led International League catchers with 12 double plays in 1971. ... Led A.L. catchers with 933 total chances in 1972, 803 in 1973, 519 in 1981 and 871 in 1985. ... Led A.L. catchers with 17 errors in 1978 and 10 in 1980. ... Led A.L. in being hit by pitch with 13 in 1980. ... Led A.L. catchers with 470 putouts in 1981. ... Led A.L. catchers with 10 double plays in 1981 and 15 in 1987. ... Led A.L. with 11 passed balls in 1983. ... Hit for the cycle (May 16, 1984). ... Career major league grand slams: 6.

Year Team (League)	Pos.	G	AB	R	H	2B	3B	HR	RBI	Avg.	BB	SO	SB	PO	A	E	Avg.
1967— Greenville (W. Car.)....					In military service.												
1968— Waterloo (Midw.)	C	62	195	31	66	11	2	12	34	.338	21	49	2	385	42	8	.982
1969— Pittsfield (East.).......	C	97	309	38	75	18	3	10	41	.243	33	60	2	551	65	*22	.966
— Boston (A.L.)............	C	2	5	0	0	0	0	0	0	.000	0	2	0	2	0	0	1.000
1970— Pawtucket (East.).......	C-OF-1B	93	284	43	65	18	1	12	44	.229	42	66	6	482	50	7	.987
1971— Louisville (I.L.)............	C-OF-3B	94	308	45	81	10	4	10	43	.263	35	61	4	588	51	13	.980
— Boston (A.L.)............	C	14	48	7	15	2	1	2	6	.313	1	10	0	72	6	2	.975
1972— Boston (A.L.)............	C	131	457	74	134	28	•9	22	61	.293	52	83	5	*846	*72	•15	.984
1973— Boston (A.L.)............	C-DH	135	508	65	125	21	0	26	71	.246	37	99	7	*739	50	*14	.983
1974— Boston (A.L.)............	C-DH	52	187	36	56	12	1	11	26	.299	24	23	5	267	26	6	.980
1975— Boston (A.L.)............	C-DH	79	263	47	87	14	4	10	52	.331	27	32	4	347	30	8	.979
1976— Boston (A.L.)............	C-DH	134	487	76	124	17	5	17	58	.255	56	71	12	649	73	12	.984
1977— Boston (A.L.)............	C	152	536	106	169	26	3	26	102	.315	75	85	7	779	69	11	.987
1978— Boston (A.L.)............	C-OF-DH	157	571	94	162	39	5	20	88	.284	71	83	7	734	90	†17	.980
1979— Boston (A.L.)............	DH-C	91	320	49	87	23	2	10	42	.272	10	38	3	155	8	3	.982
1980— Boston (A.L.)..........C-1-O-DH-3		131	478	73	138	25	3	18	62	.289	36	62	11	543	56	†11	.982
1981— Chicago (A.L.)■....C-1B-3B-OF		96	338	44	89	12	0	7	45	.263	38	37	3	†479	46	6	.989
1982— Chicago (A.L.)...........	C	135	476	66	127	17	3	14	65	.267	46	60	17	648	63	5	.993
1983— Chicago (A.L.)...........	C-DH	138	488	85	141	26	4	26	86	.289	46	88	9	*709	46	7	.991
1984— Chicago (A.L.)...........	C-DH	102	359	54	83	20	1	21	43	.231	26	60	6	421	38	6	.987
1985— Chicago (A.L.)...........	C-DH	153	543	85	129	23	1	37	107	.238	52	81	17	*801	60	10	.989
1986— Chicago (A.L.)...........	C-OF-DH	125	457	42	101	11	0	14	63	.221	22	92	2	455	44	8	.984
1987— Chicago (A.L.)...........	C-DH	135	454	68	116	22	1	23	71	.256	39	72	1	597	66	7	.990
1988— Chicago (A.L.)...........	C	76	253	37	70	8	1	19	50	.277	37	40	0	338	36	2	.995
1989— Chicago (A.L.)...........	C-DH	103	375	47	110	25	2	13	68	.293	36	60	1	419	37	3	*.993
1990— Chicago (A.L.)...........	C-DH	137	452	65	129	21	0	18	65	.285	61	73	7	660	63	4	.994
1991— Chicago (A.L.)...........	C-DH-1B	134	460	42	111	25	0	18	74	.241	32	86	1	625	65	6	.991
1992— South Bend (Midw.) ...	C	1	2	1	1	0	0	1	3	.500	1	0	0	4	0	1	.800
— Sarasota (FSL)	C	7	25	3	3	1	0	1	2	.120	3	6	1	31	3	0	1.000
— Chicago (A.L.)	C-DH	62	188	12	43	4	1	3	21	.229	23	38	3	252	26	2	.993
1993— Chicago (A.L.)...........	C	25	53	2	10	0	0	1	4	.189	2	11	0	75	5	0	1.000
Major League totals (24 years)		2499	8756	1276	2356	421	47	376	1330	.269	849	1386	128	11612	1075	165	.987

CHAMPIONSHIP SERIES RECORD

Year Team (League)	Pos.	G	AB	R	H	2B	3B	HR	RBI	Avg.	BB	SO	SB	PO	A	E	Avg.
1975— Boston (A.L.).............	C	3	12	4	5	1	0	0	2	.417	0	2	1	15	0	0	1.000
1983— Chicago (A.L.).............	C	4	17	0	3	1	0	0	0	.176	1	3	0	27	3	0	1.000
Championship series totals (2 years)		7	29	4	8	2	0	0	2	.276	1	5	1	42	3	0	1.000

WORLD SERIES RECORD

RECORDS: Shares single-inning record for most at-bats—2 (October 15, 1975, fourth inning).

Year Team (League)	Pos.	G	AB	R	H	2B	3B	HR	RBI	Avg.	BB	SO	SB	PO	A	E	Avg.
1975— Boston (A.L.).............	C	7	25	5	6	0	0	2	4	.240	7	7	0	37	3	2	.952

Year	League	Pos.	AB	R	H	2B	3B	HR	RBI	Avg.	BB	SO	SB	PO	A	E	Avg.
1972— American		C	2	1	1	0	0	0	0	.500	0	1	0	2	0	0	1.000
1973— American		C	2	0	0	0	0	0	0	.000	0	0	0	3	0	0	1.000
1974— American							Selected, did not play—injured.										
1976— American		C	1	0	0	0	0	0	0	.000	0	0	0	1	0	0	1.000
1977— American		C	2	0	0	0	0	0	0	.000	0	1	0	6	1	0	1.000
1978— American		C	2	0	0	0	0	0	1	.000	0	0	0	4	0	0	1.000
1980— American		C	2	0	0	0	0	0	0	.000	0	2	0	5	0	0	1.000
1981— American		C	3	1	1	0	0	0	0	.333	0	1	0	4	0	0	1.000
1982— American		C	2	0	0	0	0	0	0	.000	0	1	0	2	0	0	1.000
1985— American		C	2	0	0	0	0	0	0	.000	0	0	0	2	0	0	1.000
1991— American		C	2	0	1	0	0	0	0	.500	0	1	0	5	0	0	1.000
All-Star Game totals (10 years)			20	2	3	0	0	0	1	.150	0	7	0	34	1	0	1.000

PEREZ, TONY

PERSONAL: Born May 14, 1942, in Ciego de Avila, Camaguey, Cuba. ... 6-2/210. ... Bats right, throws right. ... Full name: Atanasio Rigal Perez. ... Father of Eduardo Perez, first baseman/third baseman with California Angels (1993-1995), Cincinnati Reds (1996-1998), St. Louis Cardinals (1999); and father of Victor Perez, minor league outfielder/first basemen (1990). ... Name pronounced PER-ez.

HIGH SCHOOL: Vidleta Central (Cuba).

TRANSACTIONS/CAREER NOTES: Signed as free agent by Cincinnati Reds organization (March 12, 1960). ... On disabled list (June 25-July 5, 1960). ... On suspended list (April 13-16, 1962). ... On disabled list (July 30-September 4, 1962). ... On San Diego suspended list (April 11, 1963); transferred to restricted list (April 23-June 25, 1963). ... Traded by Reds with P Will McEnaney to Montreal Expos for P Woodie Fryman and P Dale Murray (December 16, 1976). ... Granted free agency (November 1, 1979). ... Signed by Boston Red Sox (November 16, 1979). ... Released by Red Sox (November 1, 1982). ... Signed by Philadelphia Phillies (January 31, 1983). ... Traded by Phillies to Reds for a player to be named later (December 5, 1983); deal settled in cash. ... Granted free agency (November 8, 1984). ... Re-signed by Reds (April 10, 1985). ... Granted free agency (November 12, 1985). ... Re-signed by Reds (January 20, 1986). ... Placed on voluntarily retired list (October 28, 1986).

RECORDS: Shares modern major league single-game record for most at-bats—7 (June 13, 1975).

HONORS: Named Pacific Coast League Most Valuable Player (1964). ... Named third baseman on The Sporting News N.L. All-Star team (1970). ... Named first baseman on The Sporting News N.L. All-Star team (1973).

STATISTICAL NOTES: Led Carolina League third basemen with 23 double plays in 1962. ... Tied for N.L. lead in double plays by third baseman with 33 in 1968. ... Led N.L. third basemen with 35 double plays in 1969. ... Led N.L. third basemen with 35 errors in 1970. ... Led N.L. third basemen with 304 assists and 435 total chances in 1971. ... Led N.L. first basemen with 1,416 total chances and 131 double plays in 1973. ... Led A.L. in grounding into double plays with 25 in 1980.

Year	Team (League)	Pos.	G	AB	R	H	2B	3B	HR	RBI	Avg.	BB	SO	SB	PO	A	E	Avg.
1960— Geneva (NY-P)		IF-OF	104	384	82	107	21	4	6	43	.279	45	68	11	199	197	31	.927
1961— Geneva (NY-P)		3B	121	460	110	*160	32	7	27	*132	.348	61	86	17	107	*232	*42	.890
1962— Rocky Mount (Caro.)		3B	100	384	72	112	20	8	18	74	.292	68	61	8	88	178	30	.899
1963— San Diego (PCL)		3B	8	29	4	11	3	1	1	5	.379	2	8	1	6	8	1	.933
— Macon (SAL)		3B	69	256	44	79	19	3	11	48	.309	24	52	8	57	100	18	.897
1964— San Diego (PCL)		1B-3B-OF	124	479	96	148	20	8	34	107	.309	45	102	4	816	104	19	.980
— Cincinnati (N.L.)		1B	12	25	1	2	1	0	0	1	.080	3	9	0	51	0	1	.981
1965— Cincinnati (N.L.)		1B	104	281	40	73	14	4	12	47	.260	21	67	0	525	40	6	.989
1966— Cincinnati (N.L.)		1B	99	257	25	68	10	4	4	39	.265	14	44	1	530	23	6	.989
1967— Cincinnati (N.L.)		3B-1B-2B	156	600	78	174	28	7	26	102	.290	33	102	0	249	234	13	.974
1968— Cincinnati (N.L.)		3B	160	625	93	176	25	7	18	92	.282	51	92	3	*151	343	*25	.952
1969— Cincinnati (N.L.)		3B	160	629	103	185	31	2	37	122	.294	63	131	4	136	*342	*32	.937
1970— Cincinnati (N.L.)		3B-1B	158	587	107	186	28	6	40	129	.317	83	134	8	167	292	†35	.929
1971— Cincinnati (N.L.)		3B-1B	158	609	72	164	22	3	25	91	.269	51	120	4	281	†308	20	.967
1972— Cincinnati (N.L.)		1B	136	515	64	146	33	7	21	90	.283	55	121	4	1207	68	9	.993
1973— Cincinnati (N.L.)		1B	151	564	73	177	33	3	27	101	.314	74	117	3	*1318	85	*13	.991
1974— Cincinnati (N.L.)		1B	158	596	81	158	28	2	28	101	.265	61	112	1	1292	75	6	*.996
1975— Cincinnati (N.L.)		1B	137	511	74	144	28	3	20	109	.282	54	101	1	1192	72	9	.993
1976— Cincinnati (N.L.)		1B	139	527	77	137	32	6	19	91	.260	50	88	10	1158	73	5	.996
1977— Montreal (N.L.)■		1B	154	559	71	158	32	6	19	91	.283	63	111	4	1312	100	11	.992
1978— Montreal (N.L.)		1B	148	544	63	158	38	3	14	78	.290	38	104	2	1181	82	11	.991
1979— Montreal (N.L.)		1B	132	489	58	132	29	4	13	73	.270	38	82	2	1114	65	11	.991
1980— Boston (A.L.)■		1B-DH	151	585	73	161	31	3	25	105	.275	41	93	1	1301	87	10	.993
1981— Boston (A.L.)		1B-DH	84	306	35	77	11	3	9	39	.252	27	66	0	519	37	4	.993
1982— Boston (A.L.)		DH-1B	69	196	18	51	14	2	6	31	.260	19	48	0	5	1	1	.857
1983— Philadelphia (N.L.)■		1B	91	253	18	61	11	2	6	43	.241	28	57	1	514	40	1	.998
1984— Cincinnati (N.L.)		1B	71	137	9	33	6	1	2	15	.241	11	21	0	186	12	2	.990
1985— Cincinnati (N.L.)		1B	72	183	25	60	8	0	6	33	.328	22	22	0	340	22	2	.995
1986— Cincinnati (N.L.)		1B	77	200	14	51	12	1	2	29	.255	25	25	0	398	29	7	.984
American League totals (3 years)			304	1087	126	289	56	8	40	175	.266	87	207	1	1825	125	15	.992
National League totals (20 years)			2473	8691	1146	2443	449	71	339	1477	.281	838	1660	48	13302	2315	225	.986
Major League totals (23 years)			2777	9778	1272	2732	505	79	379	1652	.279	925	1867	49	15127	2440	240	.987

CHAMPIONSHIP SERIES RECORD

RECORDS: Shares career record for most consecutive games with one or more runs batted in—4.

Year	Team (League)	Pos.	G	AB	R	H	2B	3B	HR	RBI	Avg.	BB	SO	SB	PO	A	E	Avg.
1970— Cincinnati (N.L.)		3B-1B	3	12	1	4	2	0	1	2	.333	1	1	0	6	6	1	.923
1972— Cincinnati (N.L.)		1B	5	20	0	4	1	0	0	2	.200	0	7	0	45	3	0	1.000
1973— Cincinnati (N.L.)		1B	5	22	1	2	0	0	1	2	.091	0	4	0	47	4	0	1.000
1975— Cincinnati (N.L.)		1B	3	12	3	5	0	0	1	4	.417	1	2	0	27	5	0	1.000
1976— Cincinnati (N.L.)		1B	3	10	1	2	0	0	0	3	.200	1	2	0	27	2	1	.967
1983— Philadelphia (N.L.)		PH	1	1	0	1	0	0	0	0	1.000	0	0	0	...	...	...	...

HALL OF FAME INDUCTEES

| Championship series totals (6 years) | 20 | 77 | 6 | 18 | 3 | 0 | 3 | 13 | .234 | 3 | 16 | 0 | 152 | 20 | 2 | .989 |

WORLD SERIES RECORD

RECORDS: Shares single-series record for collecting one or more hits in each game (1972).

NOTES: Member of World Series championship team (1975).

Year	Team (League)	Pos.	G	AB	R	H	2B	3B	HR	RBI	Avg.	BB	SO	SB	PO	A	E	Avg.
								BATTING								FIELDING		
1970— Cincinnati (N.L.)	3B	5	18	2	1	0	0	0	0	.056	3	4	0	3	13	1	.941
1972— Cincinnati (N.L.)	1B	7	23	3	10	2	0	0	2	.435	4	4	0	73	3	1	.987
1975— Cincinnati (N.L.)	1B	7	28	4	5	0	0	3	7	.179	3	9	1	66	5	1	.986
1976— Cincinnati (N.L.)	1B	4	16	1	5	1	0	0	2	.313	1	2	0	32	4	0	1.000
1983— Philadelphia (N.L.)	PH-1B	4	10	0	2	0	0	0	0	.200	0	2	0	13	1	0	1.000
World Series totals (5 years)		27	95	10	23	3	0	3	11	.242	11	21	1	187	26	3	.986

ALL-STAR GAME RECORD

NOTES: Named Most Valuable Player (1967).

Year	League	Pos.	AB	R	H	2B	3B	HR	RBI	Avg.	BB	SO	SB	PO	A	E	Avg.
						BATTING									FIELDING		
1967— National	3B	2	1	1	0	0	1	1	.500	0	1	0	0	3	0	1.000
1968— National	3B	0	0	0	0	0	0	0	...	0	0	0	0	1	0	1.000
1969— National	3B	1	0	0	0	0	0	0	.000	0	1	0	1	1	0	1.000
1970— National	3B	3	0	0	0	0	0	0	.000	0	2	0	1	1	0	1.000
1974— National	PH	1	0	0	0	0	0	0	.000	0	1	0	...	...	...	...
1975— National	1B	1	0	0	0	0	0	0	.000	0	1	0	1	1	0	1.000
1976— National	1B	0	0	0	0	0	0	0	...	1	0	0	2	0	0	1.000
All-Star Game totals (7 years)		8	1	1	0	0	1	1	.125	1	6	0	5	7	0	1.000

RECORD AS MANAGER

BACKGROUND: First base coach, Cincinnati Reds (1987). ... Hitting coach, Reds (1988-89). ... First base/hitting coach, Reds (1990-92). ... Special assistant to general manager, Florida Marlins (July 19, 1993-present).

Year	Team (League)	W	L	Pct.	Pos.	Playoff W	L	Champ. Series W	L	World Series W	L	All-Star Game W	L
			REGULAR SEASON					POSTSEASON					
1993— Cincinnati (N.L)	20	24	.454		—	—	—	—	—	—	—	—

NOTES:

1993—Replaced as Cincinnati manager by Davey Johnson, with club in fifth place (May 24).

1999 STATISTICAL LEADERS

AMERICAN LEAGUE

BATTING LEADERS

Games
162 B.J. Surhoff, Bal.
161 Albert Belle, Bal.
160 Mike Bordick, Bal.
160 Ken Griffey Jr., Sea.
159 Roberto Alomar, Cle.
159 Miguel Tejada, Oak.
159 Tino Martinez, N.Y.

At-bats
673 B.J. Surhoff, Bal.
663 Carlos Beltran, K.C.
631 Mike Bordick, Bal.
631 Randy Velarde, Ana.-Oak.
628 Joe Randa, K.C.

Runs scored
138 Roberto Alomar, Cle.
134 Derek Jeter, N.Y.
134 Shawn Green, Tor.
131 Manny Ramirez, Cle.
123 Ken Griffey Jr., Sea.

Hits
219 Derek Jeter, N.Y.
207 B.J. Surhoff, Bal.
202 Bernie Williams, N.Y.
200 Randy Velarde, Ana.-Oak.
199 Ivan Rodriguez, Tex.

RBIs
165 Manny Ramirez, Cle.
148 Rafael Palmeiro, Tex.
134 Ken Griffey Jr., Sea.
134 Carlos Delgado, Tor.
128 Juan Gonzalez, Tex.

Total bases
361 Shawn Green, Tor.
356 Rafael Palmeiro, Tex.
349 Ken Griffey Jr., Sea.
346 Manny Ramirez, Cle.
346 Derek Jeter, N.Y.

Doubles
45 Shawn Green, Tor.
44 Jermaine Dye, K.C.
44 Mike Sweeney, K.C.
42 Nomar Garciaparra, Bos.
41 Todd Zeile, Tex.
41 Rusty Greer, Tex.
41 Tony Fernandez, Tor.

Triples
11 Jose Offerman, Bos.
9 Johnny Damon, K.C.
9 Derek Jeter, N.Y.
9 Carlos Febles, K.C.
8 Jermaine Dye, K.C.
8 Joe Randa, K.C.
8 Ray Durham, Chi.
8 Luis Polonia, Det.

Home runs
48 Ken Griffey Jr., Sea.
47 Rafael Palmeiro, Tex.
44 Manny Ramirez, Cle.
44 Carlos Delgado, Tor.
42 Shawn Green, Tor.
42 Alex Rodriguez, Sea.

Walks
127 Jim Thome, Cle.
105 Jason Giambi, Oak.
101 Albert Belle, Bal.
101 John Jaha, Oak.
100 Bernie Williams, N.Y.

On-base percentage
.447 Edgar Martinez, Sea.
.442 Manny Ramirez, Cle.
.438 Derek Jeter, N.Y.
.435 Bernie Williams, N.Y.
.427 Tony Fernandez, Tor.

Slugging percentage
.663 Manny Ramirez, Cle.
.630 Rafael Palmeiro, Tex.
.603 Nomar Garciaparra, Bos.
.601 Juan Gonzalez, Tex.
.588 Shawn Green, Tor.

Stolen bases
44 Brian L. Hunter, Det.-Sea.
42 Omar Vizquel, Cle.
39 Tom Goodwin, Tex.
37 Roberto Alomar, Cle.
37 Shannon Stewart, Tor.

Caught stealing
14 Shannon Stewart, Tor.
14 Mike Caruso, Chi.
12 Juan Encarnacion, Det.
12 Ivan Rodriguez, Tex.
12 Jose Offerman, Bos.

Sacrifice bunts
17 Omar Vizquel, Cle.
14 Darren Lewis, Bos.
14 Deivi Cruz, Det.
12 Roberto Alomar, Cle.
12 Carlos Febles, K.C.

Sacrifice flies
13 Roberto Alomar, Cle.
12 Juan Gonzalez, Tex.
10 Mike Bordick, Bal.
10 John Flaherty, T.B.
10 Paul O'Neill, N.Y.
10 Carlos Beltran, K.C.

Strikeouts
171 Jim Thome, Cle.
153 Dean Palmer, Det.
143 Troy Glaus, Ana.
141 Carlos Delgado, Tor.
135 Jose Canseco, T.B.

Intentional walks
17 Ken Griffey Jr., Sea.
17 Bernie Williams, N.Y.
15 Albert Belle, Bal.
14 Rafael Palmeiro, Tex.
13 Jim Thome, Cle.
13 Frank Thomas, Chi.

PITCHING LEADERS

Wins
23 Pedro Martinez, Bos.
18 Bartolo Colon, Cle
18 Mike Mussina, Bal.
18 Aaron Sele, Tex.
17 Freddy Garcia, Sea.
17 Orlando Hernandez, N.Y.
17 Charles Nagy, Cle.
17 David Wells, Tor.

Losses
16 Brian Moehler, Det.
15 Jim Parque, Chi.
15 Bobby Witt, T.B.
14 Kevin Appier, K.C.-Oak.
14 Jeff Fassero, Sea.-Tex.
14 LaTroy Hawkins, Min.
14 Brad Radke, Min.
14 Jose Rosado, K.C.

Games
76 Buddy Groom, Oak.
76 Bob Wells, Min.
75 Mike Trombley, Min.
74 Graeme Lloyd, Tor.
74 Derek Lowe, Bos.

Games started
35 Rick Helling, Tex.
34 Kevin Appier, K.C.-Oak.
34 Dave Burba, Cle.
34 Scott Erickson, Bal.
34 Pat Hentgen, Tor.
34 Eric Milton, Min.
34 David Wells, Tor.

Games finished
66 Roberto Hernandez, T.B.
65 Mike Jackson, Cle.
63 Mariano Rivera, N.Y.
62 Todd Jones, Det.
60 Jose Mesa, Sea.

Complete games
7 David Wells, Tor.
6 Scott Erickson, Bal.
6 Sidney Ponson, Bal.
5 Pedro Martinez, Bos.
5 Eric Milton, Min.
5 Jose Rosado, K.C.

Innings pitched
231.2 David Wells, Tor.
230.1 Scott Erickson, Bal.
228.0 Jaime Moyer, Sea.
220.0 Dave Burba, Cle.
219.1 Rick Helling, Tex.

Shutouts
3 Scott Erickson, Bal.
2 Eric Milton, Min.
2 Brian Moehler, Det.
2 Aaron Sele, Tex.
2 Bobby Witt, T.B.

Hits allowed
246 David Wells, Tor.
244 Scott Erickson, Bal.
244 Aaron Sele, Tex.
239 Brad Radke, Min.
238 LaTroy Hawkins, Min.
238 Charles Nagy, Cle.

Home runs allowed
41 Rick Helling, Tex.
35 Jeff Fassero, Sea.-Tex.
35 Sidney Ponson, Bal.
34 James Baldwin, Chi.
32 Pat Hentgen, Tor.
32 David Wells, Tor.

Runs allowed
136 LaTroy Hawkins, Min.
135 Jeff Fassero, Sea.-Tex.
132 David Wells, Tor.
131 Kevin Appier, K.C.-Oak.
130 Bobby Witt, T.B.

Earned runs allowed
129 LaTroy Hawkins, Min.
125 Jeff Fassero, Sea.-Tex.
124 David Wells, Tor.
123 Scott Erickson, Bal.
120 Kevin Appier, K.C.-Oak.

Batting average yielded
.205 Pedro Martinez, Bos.
.229 David Cone, N.Y.
.233 Orlando Hernandez, N.Y.
.242 Bartolo Colon, Cle.
.243 Eric Milton, Min.

Walks
99 Scott Erickson, Bal.
96 Dave Burba, Cle.
96 Bobby Witt, T.B.
94 Chuck Finley, Ana.
90 Roger Clemens, N.Y.
90 David Cone, N.Y.
90 Freddy Garcia, Sea.

Strikeouts
313 Pedro Martinez, Bos.
200 Chuck Finley, Ana.
186 Aaron Sele, Tex.
177 David Cone, N.Y.
174 Dave Burba, Cle.

Hit batsmen
17 Jeff Weaver, Det.
14 Rolando Arrojo, T.B.
12 Dave Mlicki, Det.
12 Ryan Rupe, T.B.
12 Aaron Sele, Tex.

Wild pitches
15 Chuck Finley, Ana.
13 Dave Burba, Cle.
13 Tom Candiotti, Oak.-Cle.
12 Freddy Garcia, Sea.
11 James Baldwin, Chi.
11 John Snyder, Chi.
11 Makoto Suzuki, Sea.-K.C.

Saves
45 Mariano Rivera, N.Y.
43 Roberto Hernandez, T.B.
43 John Wetteland, Tex.
39 Mike Jackson, Cle.
33 Jose Mesa, Sea.

BATTING LEADERS

Games
162 Jeff Bagwell, Hou.
162 Andruw Jones, Atl.
162 John Olerud, N.Y.
162 Sammy Sosa, Chi.
161 Mark Grace, Chi.
161 Barry Larkin, Cin.
161 J.T. Snow, S.F.
161 Robin Ventura, N.Y.

At-bats
690 Neifi Perez, Col.
639 Craig Biggio, Hou.
628 Edgardo Alfonzo, N.Y.
628 Doug Glanville, Phi.
627 Matt Williams, Ari.

Runs scored
143 Jeff Bagwell, Hou.
132 Jay Bell, Ari.
123 Craig Biggio, Hou.
123 Edgardo Alfonzo, N.Y.
118 Bobby Abreu, Phi.
118 Mark McGwire, St.L.

Hits
206 Luis Gonzalez, Ari.
204 Doug Glanville, Phi.
198 Jeff Cirillo, Mil.
197 Sean Casey, Cin.
193 Neifi Perez, Col.
193 Vladimir Guerrero, Mon.

RBIs
147 Mark McGwire, St.L.
142 Matt Williams, Ari.
141 Sammy Sosa, Chi.
133 Dante Bichette, Col.
131 Vladimir Guerrero, Mon.

Total bases
397 Sammy Sosa, Chi.
366 Vladimir Guerrero, Mon.
363 Mark McGwire, St.L.
359 Chipper Jones, Atl.
339 Todd Helton, Col.

Doubles
56 Craig Biggio, Hou.
45 Luis Gonzalez, Ari.
45 Jose Vidro, Mon.
44 Mark Grace, Chi.
43 Geoff Jenkins, Mil.

Triples
11 Bobby Abreu, Phi.
11 Neifi Perez, Col.
10 Steve Finley, Ari.
10 Tony Womack, Ari.
9 Mike Cameron, Cin.
9 Mark Kotsay, Fla.

Home runs
65 Mark McGwire, St.L.
63 Sammy Sosa, Chi.
45 Greg Vaughn, Cin.
45 Chipper Jones, Atl.
42 Vladimir Guerrero, Mon.
42 Jeff Bagwell, Hou.

Walks
149 Jeff Bagwell, Hou.
133 Mark McGwire, St.L.
126 Chipper Jones, Atl.
125 John Olerud, N.Y.
109 Bobby Abreu, Phi.

On-base percentage
.458 Larry Walker, Col.
.454 Jeff Bagwell, Hou.
.446 Bobby Abreu, Phi.
.441 Chipper Jones, Atl.
.427 John Olerud, N.Y.

Slugging percentage
.710 Larry Walker, Col.
.697 Mark McGwire, St.L.
.635 Sammy Sosa, Chi.
.633 Chipper Jones, Atl.
.614 Brian S. Giles, Pit.

Stolen bases
72 Tony Womack, Ari.
66 Roger Cedeno, N.Y.
51 Eric Young, L.A.
50 Luis Castillo, Fla.
38 Mike Cameron, Cin.
38 Pokey Reese, Cin.

Caught stealing
22 Eric Young, L.A.
17 Roger Cedeno, N.Y.
17 Luis Castillo, Fla.
17 Quilvio Veras, S.D.
14 Rickey Henderson, N.Y.
14 Craig Biggio, Hou.
14 Marvin Benard, S.F.

Sacrifice bunts
17 Shane Reynolds, Hou.
13 Abraham Nunez, Pit.
13 Greg Maddux, Atl.
13 Jose Lima, Hou.
13 Kevin Brown, L.A.

Sacrifice flies
10 Dante Bichette, Col.
10 Mark Grace, Chi.
9 Jay Bell, Ari.
9 Mark Kotsay, Fla.
9 Edgardo Alfonzo, N.Y.
9 Brian Jordan, Atl.
9 Gary Sheffield, L.A.

Strikeouts
171 Sammy Sosa, Chi.
156 Preston Wilson, Fla.
145 Mike Cameron, Cin.
145 Jose Hernandez, Chi.-Atl.
143 Ruben Rivera, S.D.

Intentional walks
21 Mark McGwire, St.L.
18 Chipper Jones, Atl.
16 Jeff Bagwell, Hou.
14 Vladimir Guerrero, Mon.
13 Sean Casey, Cin.

PITCHING LEADERS

Wins
22 Mike Hampton, Hou.
21 Jose Lima, Hou.
19 Greg Maddux, Atl.
18 Kent Bottenfield, St.L.
18 Kevin Brown, L.A.
18 Kevin Millwood, Atl.
18 Russ Ortiz, S.F.

Losses
18 Steve Trachsel, Chi.
16 Dennis Springer, Fla.
15 Brian Meadows, Fla.
14 Shane Reynolds, Hou.
14 Sterling Hitchcock, S.D.
14 Kris Benson, Pit.
14 Dustin Hermanson, Mon.
14 Ismael Valdes, L.A.
14 Jose Jimenez, St.L.

Games
82 Steve Kline, Mon.
80 Turk Wendell, N.Y.
79 Scott Sullivan, Cin.
79 Anthony Telford, Mon.
77 Armando Benitez, N.Y.

Games started
35 Shane Reynolds, Hou.
35 Tom Glavine, Atl.
35 Jose Lima, Hou.
35 Kevin Brown, L.A.
35 Randy Johnson, Ari.

Games finished
64 Robb Nen, S.F.
63 Dave Veres, Col.
63 Bob Wickman, Mil.
62 Ugueth Urbina, Mon.
61 John Rocker, Atl.

Complete games
12 Randy Johnson, Ari.
8 Curt Schilling, Phi.
7 Pedro Astacio, Col.
5 Kevin Brown, L.A.
4 Shane Reynolds, Hou.
4 Steve Trachsel, Chi.
4 Greg Maddux, Atl.
4 Andy Ashby, S.D.

Innings pitched
271.2 Randy Johnson, Ari.
252.1 Kevin Brown, L.A.
246.1 Jose Lima, Hou.
239.0 Mike Hampton, Hou.
234.0 Tom Glavine, Atl.

Shutouts
3 Andy Ashby, S.D.
2 Randy Johnson, Ari.
2 Mike Hampton, Hou.
2 Shane Reynolds, Hou.
2 Pete Harnisch, Cin.
2 Dennis Springer, Fla.
2 Jose Jimenez, St.L.

Hits allowed
259 Tom Glavine, Atl.
258 Pedro Astacio, Col.
258 Greg Maddux, Atl.
256 Jose Lima, Hou.
250 Shane Reynolds, Hou.

Home runs allowed
38 Pedro Astacio, Col.
36 Chad Ogea, Phi.
34 Andy Benes, Ari.
34 Paul Byrd, Phi.
33 Darryl Kile, Col.
33 Woody Williams, S.D.

Runs allowed
150 Darryl Kile, Col.
146 Brian Bohanon, Col.
140 Pedro Astacio, Col.
133 Steve Trachsel, Chi.
121 Dennis Springer, Fla.
121 Scott Karl, Mil.
121 Shawn Estes, S.F.

Earned runs allowed
140 Darryl Kile, Col.
136 Brian Bohanon, Col.
130 Pedro Astacio, Col.
127 Steve Trachsel, Chi.
113 Chan Ho Park, L.A.

Batting average yielded
.202 Kevin Millwood, Atl.
.208 Randy Johnson, Ari.
.222 Kevin Brown, L.A.
.236 Omar Daal, Ari.
.237 Curt Schilling, Phi.

Walks
125 Russ Ortiz, S.F.
112 Shawn Estes, S.F.
109 Darryl Kile, Col.
101 Mike Hampton, Hou.
100 Chan Ho Park, L.A.

Strikeouts
364 Randy Johnson, Ari.
221 Kevin Brown, L.A.
210 Pedro Astacio, Col.
205 Kevin Millwood, Atl.
197 Shane Reynolds, Hou.

Hit batsmen
17 Paul Byrd, Phi.
14 Chan Ho Park, L.A.
14 Brian Bohanon, Col.
11 Pedro Astacio, Col.
11 Darren Oliver, St.L.
11 Jose Jimenez, St.L.
11 Orel Hershiser, N.Y.

Wild pitches
15 Sterling Hitchcock, S.D.
15 Shawn Estes, S.F.
13 Russ Ortiz, S.F.
13 Darryl Kile, Col.
13 Scott Williamson, Cin.

Saves
41 Ugueth Urbina, Mon.
40 Trevor Hoffman, S.D.
39 Billy Wagner, Hou.
38 John Rocker, Atl.
37 Robb Nen, S.F.
37 Bob Wickman, Mil.

STATISTICAL LEADERS

LEADERS OF THE '90s

STATISTICAL LEADERS

BATTING AVERAGE

(minimum 3,000 at-bats)

1.	Tony Gwynn	344
2.	Mike Piazza	329
3.	Edgar Martinez	322
4.	Frank Thomas	320
5.	Paul Molitor	313
	Larry Walker	313
7.	Kirby Puckett	312
8.	Mark Grace	310
	Kenny Lofton	310
10.	Roberto Alomar	308
11.	Manny Ramirez	307
	Hal Morris	307
13.	Julio Franco	304
	Wade Boggs	304
	Jeff Bagwell	304
	Bernie Williams	304
17.	Dante Bichette	303
	Barry Larkin	303
19.	Barry Bonds	302
	Will Clark	302
	Ken Griffey Jr.	302

GAMES

1.	Rafael Palmeiro	1,526
2.	Craig Biggio	1,515
3.	Mark Grace	1,491
4.	Jay Bell	1,487
5.	Cal Ripken	1,475
6.	Fred McGriff	1,472
7.	Steve Finley	1,457
8.	Todd Zeile	1,445
9.	Barry Bonds	1,434
10.	Roberto Alomar	1,421
11.	Paul O'Neill	1,420
12.	Marquis Grissom	1,409
13.	Ken Griffey Jr.	1,408
14.	Robin Ventura	1,399
15.	John Olerud	1,390

AT-BATS

1.	Rafael Palmeiro	5,848
2.	Craig Biggio	5,823
3.	Cal Ripken	5,710
4.	Mark Grace	5,650
5.	Jay Bell	5,619
6.	Steve Finley	5,571
7.	Marquis Grissom	5,529
8.	Roberto Alomar	5,443
9.	Fred McGriff	5,399
10.	Ken Griffey Jr.	5,377
11.	Todd Zeile	5,262
12.	Dante Bichette	5,231
13.	Matt Williams	5,179
14.	Travis Fryman	5,176
15.	Paul O'Neill	5,155

RUNS

1.	Barry Bonds	1,091
2.	Craig Biggio	1,042
3.	Ken Griffey Jr.	1,002
4.	Frank Thomas	968
5.	Rafael Palmeiro	965
6.	Roberto Alomar	951
7.	Chuck Knoblauch	950
8.	Tony Phillips	946
9.	Rickey Henderson	932
10.	Jeff Bagwell	921
11.	Jay Bell	890
12.	Larry Walker	882
13.	Albert Belle	881
14.	Steve Finley	870
15.	Edgar Martinez	854

HITS

1.	Mark Grace	1,754
2.	Rafael Palmeiro	1,747
3.	Craig Biggio	1,728
4.	Tony Gwynn	1,713
5.	Roberto Alomar	1,678
6.	Ken Griffey Jr.	1,622
7.	Cal Ripken	1,589
8.	Dante Bichette	1,584
9.	Fred McGriff	1,573
10.	Paul Molitor	1,568
11.	Frank Thomas	1,564
12.	Chuck Knoblauch	1,533
13.	Steve Finley	1,532
14.	Marquis Grissom	1,531
15.	Jay Bell	1,529

DOUBLES

1.	Mark Grace	364
2.	Craig Biggio	362
3.	Edgar Martinez	358
4.	Albert Belle	344
5.	Rafael Palmeiro	343
6.	Dante Bichette	330
	Tony Gwynn	330
8.	Paul O'Neill	328
9.	John Olerud	322
10.	Roberto Alomar	321
11.	Thomas, Frank	317
12.	Jeff Bagwell	314
	Larry Walker	314
14.	Jay Bell	309
15.	Cal Ripken	305

TRIPLES

1.	Lance Johnson	113
2.	Steve Finley	83
3.	Delino DeShields	63
4.	Jose Offerman	62
5.	Kenny Lofton	60
6.	Chuck Knoblauch	59
7.	Brady Anderson	58
	Brian McRae	58
9.	Brett Butler	57
10.	Jay Bell	55
11.	Paul Molitor	54
12.	Roberto Alomar	51
	Barry Larkin	51
14.	Mickey Morandini	50
15.	Tony Fernandez	48

HOME RUNS

1.	Mark McGwire	405
2.	Ken Griffey Jr.	382
3.	Barry Bonds	361
4.	Albert Belle	351
5.	Juan Gonzalez	339
6.	Sammy Sosa	332
7.	Rafael Palmeiro	328
8.	Jose Canseco	303
9.	Frank Thomas	301
10.	Fred McGriff	300
	Matt Williams	300
12.	Cecil Fielder	288
13.	Greg Vaughn	287
14.	Jeff Bagwell	263
	Mo Vaughn	263
16.	Larry Walker	262
17.	Jay Buhner	260
18.	Andres Galarraga	255
19.	Joe Carter	245

RUNS BATTED IN

1.	Albert Belle	1,099
2.	Ken Griffey Jr.	1,091
3.	Barry Bonds	1,076
4.	Juan Gonzalez	1,068
	Rafael Palmeiro	1,068
6.	Frank Thomas	1,040
7.	Dante Bichette	979
8.	Fred McGriff	975
9.	Jeff Bagwell	961
10.	Matt Williams	960
11.	Mark McGwire	956
12.	Sammy Sosa	928
13.	Cecil Fielder	924
14.	Paul O'Neill	923
15.	Joe Carter	914

WALKS

1.	Barry Bonds	1,146
2.	Frank Thomas	1,076
3.	Tony Phillips	977
4.	Rickey Henderson	976
5.	Mark McGwire	951
6.	Jeff Bagwell	885
7.	Edgar Martinez	854
8.	John Olerud	820
9.	Fred McGriff	787
10.	Mickey Tettleton	740
11.	Robin Ventura	734
12.	Craig Biggio	730
13.	Brady Anderson	724
14.	Gary Sheffield	723
15.	Chili Davis	716

STRIKEOUTS

1.	Sammy Sosa	1,322
2.	Jose Canseco	1,205
3.	Cecil Fielder	1,172
4.	Jay Buhner	1,145
5.	Ray Lankford	1,141
6.	Greg Vaughn	1,137
7.	Travis Fryman	1,113

8.	Jay Bell	1,095
9.	Fred McGriff	1,085
10.	Dean Palmer	1,082
11.	Mo Vaughn	1,081
12.	Andres Galarraga	1,080
13.	Devon White	1,042
14.	Mark McGwire	1,040
15.	Tony Phillips	1,009

STOLEN BASES

1.	Otis Nixon	478
2.	Rickey Henderson	463
3.	Kenny Lofton	433
4.	Delino DeShields	393
5.	Marquis Grissom	381
6.	Barry Bonds	343
7.	Chuck Knoblauch	335

8.	Craig Biggio	319
9.	Roberto Alomar	311
10.	Lance Johnson	297
11.	Eric Young	292
12.	Vince Coleman	280
13.	Barry Larkin	266
14.	Brady Anderson	257
15.	Tom Goodwin	252

PITCHERS

EARNED RUN AVERAGE
(minimum 1,000 innings pitched)

1.	Greg Maddux	2.58
2.	Jose Rijo	2.74
3.	Pedro J. Martinez	2.83
4.	Roger Clemens	3.02
5.	Randy Johnson	3.14
6.	Tom Glavine	3.21
	David Cone	3.21
8.	Kevin Brown	3.25
9.	Curt Schilling	3.31
10.	John Smoltz	3.32
11.	Dennis Martinez	3.37
12.	Ismael Valdes	3.38
13.	Bret Saberhagen	3.43
14.	Ramon J. Martinez	3.45
15.	Kevin Appier	3.47
16.	Mike Mussina	3.50
	Mike Hampton	3.50
18.	Bill Swift	3.53
19.	Zane Smith	3.55
20.	Jimmy Key	3.62

WINS

1.	Greg Maddux	176
2.	Tom Glavine	164
3.	Roger Clemens	152
4.	Randy Johnson	150
5.	Kevin Brown	143
	John Smoltz	143
7.	David Cone	141
8.	Mike Mussina	136
9.	Chuck Finley	135
10.	Scott Erickson	130
11.	David Wells	127
12.	Andy Benes	125
13.	Kevin Tapani	124
14.	Charles Nagy	121
15.	Kevin Appier	120
16.	John Burkett	119
	Jack McDowell	119

LOSSES

1.	Andy Benes	116
2.	Tim Belcher	115
3.	Bobby Witt	113
4.	Jaime Navarro	112
5.	Tom Candiotti	110
6.	Scott Erickson	108
	Chuck Finley	108
8.	John Burkett	101
	Mike Morgan	101
10.	Terry Mulholland	100
11.	Kevin Brown	98
	Todd Stottlemyre	98
13.	Kevin Tapani	97
14.	Jim Abbott	96
15.	Doug Drabek	95

	Darryl Kile	95
	John Smoltz	95
18.	Kevin Appier	90
19.	Roger Clemens	89
	Bob Tewksbury	89

GAMES

1.	Paul Assenmacher	644
	Mike Jackson	644
3.	Doug Jones	618
4.	Dan Plesac	612
5.	Jesse Orosco	594
6.	Mike Stanton	591
7.	Jeff Montgomery	578
8.	Eric Plunk	557
9.	Rick Aguilera	553
10.	Scott Radinsky	552
11.	Chuck McElroy	551
12.	Randy Myers	543
13.	Rod Beck	540
14.	Dennis Eckersley	530
15.	Mel Rojas	525
	John Wetteland	525

GAMES STARTED

1.	Greg Maddux	331
2.	Tom Glavine	327
3.	Chuck Finley	316
4.	John Smoltz	315
5.	Andy Benes	314
	Kevin Brown	314
7.	John Burkett	308
8.	Scott Erickson	306
9.	Roger Clemens	305
10.	Tim Belcher	302
11.	Randy Johnson	290
	Kevin Tapani	290
13.	David Cone	287
14.	Jaime Navarro	285
15.	Todd Stottlemyre	283

COMPLETE GAMES

1.	Greg Maddux	75
2.	Randy Johnson	65
3.	Jack McDowell	61
4.	Kevin Brown	58
5.	Roger Clemens	57
	Curt Schilling	57
7.	Scott Erickson	47
8.	Chuck Finley	46
9.	John Smoltz	42
10.	Doug Drabek	41
	Terry Mulholland	41
12.	David Cone	40
13.	Mike Mussina	39
14.	Tom Glavine	38
15.	Dennis Martinez	36
	David Wells	36

SHUTOUTS

1.	Randy Johnson	25
2.	Roger Clemens	24
3.	Greg Maddux	23
4.	Ramon J. Martinez	18
5.	Kevin Brown	16
	David Cone	16
	Scott Erickson	16
8.	Doug Drabek	14
	Tom Glavine	14
	Dennis Martinez	14
	Mike Mussina	14
	John Smoltz	14
13.	Chuck Finley	13
	Jack McDowell	13
	Curt Schilling	13

SAVES

1.	John Wetteland	295
2.	Dennis Eckersley	293
3.	Randy Myers	291
4.	Jeff Montgomery	285
5.	Rick Aguilera	282
6.	John Franco	268
7.	Rod Beck	260
8.	Lee Smith	244
9.	Roberto Hernandez	234
10.	Trevor Hoffman	228
11.	Doug Jones	223
12.	Gregg Olson	190
13.	Tom Henke	189
14.	Robb Nen	185
15.	Mike Henneman	156

INNINGS PITCHED

1.	Greg Maddux	2,394.2
2.	Tom Glavine	2,228.0
3.	Kevin Brown	2,211.1
4.	Roger Clemens	2,178.2
5.	Chuck Finley	2,144.0
6.	John Smoltz	2,143.1
7.	Andy Benes	2,069.1
8.	Randy Johnson	2,064.1
9.	David Cone	2,018.0
10.	Scott Erickson	2,014.2
11.	Tim Belcher	1,959.1
12.	John Burkett	1,935.0
13.	Jaime Navarro	1,913.1
14.	David Wells	1,897.0
15.	Kevin Appier	1,868.2

WALKS

1.	Randy Johnson	910
2.	Chuck Finley	888
3.	Bobby Witt	846
4.	David Cone	774

5. Darryl Kile 767
6. Tom Glavine.......................764
7. Roger Clemens 731
8. Tom Gordon......................714
9. Wilson Alvarez 706
10. Tim Belcher 700
11. Andy Benes 698
12. Scott Erickson 697
13. Ken Hill 683
    Todd Stottlemyre 683
15. John Smoltz.....................669

STRIKEOUTS

1. Randy Johnson.............2,538
2. Roger Clemens 2,101
3. David Cone 1,928
4. John Smoltz 1,893
5. Chuck Finley 1,784
6. Greg Maddux 1,764
7. Andy Benes...................1,655
8. Kevin Brown 1,581
9. Curt Schilling 1,561
10. Pedro J. Martinez 1,534

11. Kevin Appier 1,494
12. Tom Glavine 1,465
13. Todd Stottlemyre 1,369
14. Mike Mussina 1,325
15. Bobby Witt 1,270
16. Tom Gordon 1,260
17. Darryl Kile 1,247
18. David Wells....................1,244
19. Juan Guzman 1,240
20. John Burkett 1,233